March 5–8, 2014
Atlanta, Georgia, USA

Association for
Computing Machinery

Advancing Computing as a Science & Profession

SIGCSE'14

Proceedings of the 45th ACM Technical Symposium on

Computer Science Education

Sponsored by:

ACM SIGCSE

Editors:

John Dougherty, Haverford College

Kris Nagel, Georgia Gwinnett College

Adrienne Decker, Rochester Institute of Technology

Kurt Eiselt, University of British Columbia

Association for Computing Machinery

Advancing Computing as a Science & Profession

The Association for Computing Machinery
2 Penn Plaza, Suite 701
New York, New York 10121-0701

Notice to Past Authors of ACM-Published Articles
ACM intends to create a complete electronic archive of all articles and/or other material previously published by ACM. If you have written a work that has been previously published by ACM in any journal or conference proceedings prior to 1978, or any SIG Newsletter at any time, and you do NOT want this work to appear in the ACM Digital Library, please inform permissions@acm.org, stating the title of the work, the author(s), and where and when published.

ISBN: 978-1-4503-2605-6 (Digital)

ISBN: 978-1-4503-3104-3 (Print)

Additional copies may be ordered prepaid from:

ACM Order Department
PO Box 30777
New York, NY 10087-0777, USA

Phone: 1-800-342-6626 (USA and Canada)
+1-212-626-0500 (Global)
Fax: +1-212-944-1318
E-mail: acmhelp@acm.org
Hours of Operation: 8:30 am – 4:30 pm ET

Printed in the USA

Welcome from the SIGCSE Chair

Welcome to the *45th SIGCSE Technical Symposium on Computer Science Education* (*SIGCSE 2014*) - the premiere technical conference for computer science educators. *SIGCSE 2014* is sponsored by the ACM Special Interest Group on Computer Science Education (the SIGCSE organization).

SIGCSE is an organization of about 2600 members interested in computer science education. Many of these members volunteer for SIGCSE's numerous activities and events held throughout the year. The largest such event is SIGCSE 2014. I want to thank the two main volunteers for organizing this conference, Co-Chairs Kris Nagel and J.D. Dougherty. Kris and J.D. have spent countless hours over the past three years in planning this event, and in leading a large committee of over fifty volunteers to help with all aspects of the conference. It is quite a task to prepare an invigorating program, while at the same time dealing with the logistics of housing and feeding around 1300 attendees. On behalf of the SIGCSE Organization, I thank Kris and J.D. for their contributions towards the organization and management of this conference.

The conference is a great chance for you to make new connections and to learn about exciting innovations and new pedagogies related to computer science education. I always find great ideas that I am eager to try out in my courses. This conference is also a chance for us to honor two special people who have made significant contributions to our community. The annual SIGCSE award for Outstanding Contributions to Computer Science Education will be awarded to Robert M. Panoff for his significant contributions to computational science education. The annual SIGCSE award for Lifetime Service will be awarded to Andrea Lawrence for her substantial contributions to broadening participation in computing. Join me in congratulating them with these honors.

2013 was an election year for the SIGCSE Executive Board. This conference is a chance for you to meet us, and to give us feedback on issues you would like the SIGCSE Board to address. Please also let us know if you are interested in being more involved with SIGCSE. The other new board members are Vice Chair Paul Tymann, Secretary Judy Sheard, Treasurer Amber Settle, At-Large Board Members Tiffany Barnes, Sue Fitzgerald, and Alison Clear, and Past Chair Renée McCauley.

Finally, I encourage you to attend the SIGCSE Business meeting on Friday, from 5:15pm to 6:00pm in room Regency VI to meet the SIGCSE Board. At this annual meeting we will discuss the overall structure of the SIGCSE organization and describe projects SIGCSE members are currently working on. We hope this will be a first step in getting you more involved with SIGCSE that may lead to many rewarding years working with colleagues on sharing ideas about computer science education.

Enjoy the conference and find something interesting to take back with you!

Susan H. Rodger
SIGCSE Chair, 2013-2016

Message from the Symposium & Program Chairs

Welcome to the 45th ACM Technical Symposium on Computer Science Education (*i.e.*, SIGCSE 2014). We invite you to explore this collection of papers, posters, workshops and other materials that capture the latest ideas, tools and pedagogy in computer science education. We also encourage you to connect with the people that generate, document and "implement" this body of knowledge, take this experience with you and share.

The theme is "Leveraging Computing to Change Education," and features a number of talks and sessions focused on how the ideas and applications of computing can benefit not only those learning computer science, but learning overall. SIGCSE 2014 is co-located with a new ACM conference on Learning at Scale; it will be interesting to see what ideas and connections emerge between the two conferences, and we urge you to consider attending both.

We are happy to announce the winners of the two annual SIGCSE Awards. Robert M. Panoff, Founder and Executive Director of the Shodor Education Foundation, Inc., will receive the SIGCSE Award for Outstanding Contribution to Computer Science Education, and will provide Thursday morning's keynote address. Andrea W. Lawrence of Spelman College will accept the SIGCSE Award for Lifetime Service to the Computer Science Education Community and speak at our First Timer's Lunch on Thursday. (SIGCSE First Timers will receive lunch for free; more seasoned SIGCSE attendees can purchase a ticket and (a) enjoy a delicious meal and (b) mentor a First Timer).

We are also quite excited about the remaining keynote presentations, which include Hadi Partovi, Founder and CEO of Code.org, and A.J. Brush of Microsoft Research, who will each present on Friday morning and Saturday lunch, respectively.

Symposium statistics are presented in the following table. We thank the authors, reviewers, and Program Committee members involved in the production of this program. The schedule this year has the usual varied selection of events, including the Evening Reception on Thursday and the ACM SIGCSE Student Research Competition on Thursday afternoon. There are also some atypical offerings, such as *Experience-IT*, and of course the co-located Learning at Scale conference. The latest in hardware, software tools, textbooks, educational programs and research are found in the exhibit hall.

Proposal type	*Accepted*	*Received*	*Acceptance Rate*
Paper	108	274	39.4%
Panel	14	23	60.9%
Special Session	12	16	75.0%
Workshop	35	75	49.3 %
Poster	56	122	45.9 %
Birds of a Feather	37	52	71.1 %

SIGCSE 2014 Pre-symposium Events will occur on Wednesday and cover the following topics:

- Process Oriented Guided Inquiry Learning (POGIL)
- Integrating Professional/Ethical Issues into the CS Curriculum
- New Educators Workshop
- SIGCAS Nowadays: What is it? What should it be?
- Git & GitHub Foundations for Educators

Our sincere thanks go out to the people who made this Symposium happen. First, our Symposium Committee: Carl Alphonce, Paul Carter, Stephen Cooper, Tom Cortina, Annemieke Craig, Pam Cutter, Lynn Degler, John Dooley, Mary Anne Egan, Susan Haller, Michael T. Helmick, Cary Laxer, James Maher, Scott McElfresh, Sara Melnick, Larry Merkle, Deepa Muralidhar, Susan Rodger, Marc Rubin, Jaime Spacco, Cheryl Seals, Ann Sobel, Kimberly Voll, Henry Walker and Steven Wolfman. Additional thanks go to our

Associate Program Chairs who provided meta-reviews for papers: Eric Aaron, Ruth E. Anderson, Don Blaheta, Stephen Edwards, Mary Anne Egan, Allison Elliott Tew, Dave Levine, Sam Rebelsky, Ellen Walker, and Steven Wolfman. We also recognize and thank our International Liaison Committee (Reyyan Ayfer, Karen Bradshaw, Alison Clear, Judith Gal-Ezer, Michail Giannakos, Simon Humphreys, Sridhar Iyer, Carsten Kleiner, Claudia Bauzer Madeiros, Yasuto Shirai, Gary K.W. Wong and Ming Zhang) for helping ensure SIGCSE 2014 is welcoming to attendees from around the world. Our appreciation goes out to our student volunteers, there to help us with all of the important details that make the conference run so well. Finally, we want to offer special thanks to John Dooley for his ongoing work "in the background" transitioning to a new system for online conference management.

We wish to thank all our supporters, vendors, exhibitors and in-kind donors whose participation does more than make the Symposium possible; your participation enhances the collaboration and learning experiences all week. A special thank you to the following supporters: Google (Platinum Plus), Microsoft (Platinum), ABET (Gold), GitHub (Silver), Oracle Academy (Silver), Intel (Bronze) and Turingscraft (Bronze). Special thanks to Dorothea Heck and her team at D. Lawrence Planners for coordinating an outstanding exhibition and their creative efforts with conference planning and logistics.

We thank SIGCSE President Susan Rodger and the entire Board for their continuing support and guidance, and acknowledge the SIGCSE Symposium Site Coordinators Bob Beck and Scott Grissom, as well as April Mosqus, Ashley Cozzi and Ann Lane of ACM. Lisa Tolles of Sheridan Communications brought all materials together. Also, SIGCSE 2014 thanks Jenna Bornschein of the Atlanta Convention and Visitors Bureau, as well as Todd Tamer and his team at the Hyatt Regency Atlanta.

Special thanks to our home institutions for providing needed resources: Georgia Gwinnett College, Haverford College, the Rochester Institute of Technology and the University of British Columbia. We hope you enjoy the Symposium and leverage the SIGCSE 2014 Proceedings in your future activities.

Symposium Chairs

John Dougherty
Haverford College

Kris Nagel
Georgia Gwinnett College

Program Chairs

Adrienne Decker
Rochester Institute of Technology

Kurt Eiselt
University of British Columbia

Table of Contents

Special Session

Session Chair: Joseph Hollingsworth *(Indiana University Southeast)*

Paper Session: Focus on K-12 – Growing the Profession and Professional Development

Session Chair: Shaileen Pokress *(Massachusetts Institute of Technology)*

Paper Session: Design – Courses and Curricula

Session Chair: Carl Alphonce *(University at Buffalo)*

Paper Session: Collecting and Analyzing Student Data I

Session Chair: Don Blahcta *(Longwood University)*

Paper Session: Tactile Computing

Session Chair: Robert Lutz *(Georgia Gwinnett College)*

Panel Session
Session Chair: Annemieke Craig *(Deakin University)*

Paper Session: Peer Instruction
Session Chair: Jian Zhang *(Texas Woman's University)*

Paper Session: Software Engineering – Courses
Session Chair: Cam MacDonell *(Grant MacEwan University)*

Paper Session: Web-based Instruction
Session Chair: John Dooley *(Knox College)*

Paper Session: Recruitment and Retention of Underrepresented Groups
Session Chair: Alvaro Monge *(California State University Long Beach)*

Paper Session: Interdisciplinary Courses and Curricula

Session Chair: Eric Aaron *(Vassar College)*

Panel Session

Session Chair: Daniel D. Garcia *(University of California, Berkeley)*

Special Session

Session Chair: Ruth Anderson *(University of Washington)*

Panel Session

Session Chair: Helen H. Hu *(Westminster College)*

Paper Session: Research – Predictors, Creative Thinking, Co-linking Courses

Session Chair: Brian Dorn *(University of Nebraska at Omaha)*

Paper Session: Focus on K-12 – Informal Education, Curriculum, and Robots

Session Chair: Daniela Marghitu *(Auburn University)*

Paper Session: Focus on K-12 – Before Middle School

Session Chair: Valerie Henderson *(Emory University)*

Paper Session: Security Among the Cloud

Session Chair: Elizabeth Hawthorne *(University of Maryland University College)*

Panel Session

Session Chair: Leisa D. Thompson *(NCWIT & University of Virginia)*

Panel Session

Session Chair: Jan Cuny *(National Science Foundation)*

Panel Session

Session Chair: Paul Medlock-Walton *(Massachusetts Institute of Technology)*

Panel Session

Session Chair: Richard Brown *(St. Olaf College)*

Paper Session: Operating Systems and Programming Languages

Session Chair: Ariel Ortiz Ramírez *(Tecnológico de Monterrey, Campus Estado de México)*

Paper Session: Soft Skills – Academic Perspectives

Session Chair: Briana Morrison *(Georgia Institute of Technology)*

Paper Session: What We Say, What They Do

Session Chair: Raghuram Ramanujan *(Davidson College)*

Paper Session: Extending Frameworks

Session Chair: Ellen Walker *(Hiram College)*

Special Session

Session Chair: Nick Parlante *(Stanford University)*

Panel Session
Session Chair: Ursula Wolz *(Riversound Solutions, LLC)*

Special Session
Session Chair: Murali Sitaraman *(Clemson University)*

Special Session
Session Chair: Wanda Dann *(Carnegie Mellon University)*

Paper Session: Tools
Session Chair: Martha Kosa *(Tennessee Technological University)*

Paper Session: Focus on K-12 – Outreach and Computational Thinking
Session Chair: Giti Javidi *(Virginia State University)*

Paper Session: MOOCs
Session Chair: Michelle Craig *(University of Toronto)*

Paper Session: Collecting and Analyzing Student Data II

Session Chair: Ruth Anderson *(University of Washington)*

Special Session

Session Chair: Paul Tymann *(Rochester Institute of Technology)*

Special Session

Session Chair: Owen Astrachan *(Duke University)*

Panel Session

Session Chair: Paul Anderson *(Westminster College)*

Poster Session I

Poster Session II

Birds of a Feather: Flock I

Birds of a Feather: Flock II

Wednesday Workshops

Friday Workshops

Saturday Workshops

Back Matter

Author Index 757

SIGCSE 2014 Symposium Committee

Symposium Chairs
J.D. Dougherty, *Haverford College*
Kris Nagel, *Georgia Gwinnett College*

Program Chairs
Adrienne Decker, *Rochester Institute of Technology*
Kurt Eiselt, *University of British Columbia*

Panels and Special Sessions
Stephen C. Cooper, *Stanford University*

Workshops
Susan Haller, *SUNY Potsdam*
Paul Carter, *University of British Columbia*

Publications
J.D. Dougherty, *Haverford College*

Database Administrators
John Dooley, *Knox College*
Henry Walker, *Grinnell College*

Registration
Lynn Degler, *Rose-Hulman Institute of Technology*
Cary Laxer, *Rose-Hulman Institute of Technology*
Larry Merkle, *Computational Optimization Services*

Posters
Michael T. Helmick, *University of Cincinnati*

Birds of a Feather
Marc Rubin, *Colorado School of Mines*

Student Volunteers and Activities
Pam Cutter, *Kalamazoo College*
Sara Melnick, *Bronx Academy for Software Engineering*
Steven Wolfman, *University of British Columbia*

Treasurer
Scott McElfresh, *Longwood University*

Evaluations
Carl Alphonce, *University at Buffalo*

Kids Camp
Cheryl Seals, *Auburn University*
James Maher, *Colorado School of Mines*

Publicity / Social Media / Website
Jaime Spacco, *Knox College*
Michael T. Helmick, *University of Cincinnati*
Kimberly Voll, *Centre for Digital Media*

Support / Exhibitor Liaison
Susan Rodger, *Duke University*
Tom Cortina, *Carnegie Mellon University*

Pre-Conference Events Liaison
Mary Anne Egan, *Siena College*

K-12 Liaison
Crystal Furman, *Brookwood High School*

Local Arrangements
Deepa Muralidhar, *North Gwinnett High School*

Accessibility
Raghuram Ramanujan, *Davidson College*

Student Research Competition
Ann Sobel, *Miami University (Ohio)*

International Liaison Committee
Annemieke Craig (Chair), *Deakin University, Australia*
Rayyan Ayfer, *Bilkent University, Turkey*
Karen Bradshaw, *Rhodes University, South Africa*
Alison Clear, *Christchurch Polytechnic Institute of Technology, New Zealand*
Judith Gal-Ezer, *The Open University of Israel*
Michail Giannakos, *Norwegian University of Science and Technology*
Simon Humphreys, *Cambridge, United Kingdom*
Sridhar Iyer, *Indian Institute of Technology, India*
Carsten Kleiner, *Hanover, Germany*
Claudia Bauzer Madeiros, *UNICAMP, Brazil*
Yasuto Shirai, *Shizuoka University, Japan*
Gary K. W. Wong, *The Hong Kong Institute of Education*
Ming Zhang, *Peking University, China*

Associate Program Chairs
Eric Aaron, *Vassar College*
Ruth E. Anderson, *University of Washington*
Don Blaheta, *Longwood University*
Stephen Edwards, *Virginia Tech*
Mary Anne Egan, *Siena College*
Dave Levine, *St. Bonaventure University*
Sam Rebelsky, *Grinnell College*
Allison Elliott Tew, *University of Washington Tacoma*
Ellen Walker, *Hiram College*
Steve Wolfman, *University of British Columbia*

SIGCSE 2014 Reviewers

Eric Aaron, *Vassar College*
Safurah Abdul Jalil, *The University of Auckland*
Donald Acton, *University of British Columbia*
Raman Adaikkalavan, *Indiana University South Bend*
Elizabeth Adams, *James Madison University*
Robert Adams, *Grand Valley State University*
Paul Addison, *Ivy Tech Community College*
Rajeev Agrawal, *North Carolina A & T State University*
Shakil Akhtar, *Clayton State University*
Farha Ali, *Lander University*
Carl Alphonce, *University at Buffalo, The State University of New York*
Jamal Alsabbagh, *Grand Valley State University*
Christine Alvarado, *University of California, San Diego*
Ashish Amresh, *Arizona State University*
Ruth Anderson, *University of Washington*
Peter Andreae, *Victoria University of Wellington*
Peter Andrews, *Eastern Illinois University*
Steven K. Andrianoff, *St. Bonaventure University*
Karen Anewalt, *University of Mary Washington*
Fred Annexstein, *University of Cincinnati*
Barbara Anthony, *Southwestern University*
Florence Appel, *Saint Xavier University*
Antonio Araujo, *Faculdade de Engenharia da Universidade do Porto*
Michal Armoni, *Weizmann Institute of Science*
David Arnow, *Brooklyn College*
Mansoor Arshad, *SZABIST*
Owen Astrachan, *Duke University*
Thushari Atapattu, *University of Adelaide*
Isabel Azevedo, *ISEP*
AbdelHameed Badawy, *Arkansas Tech University*
Chunyan Bai, *Roger Williams University*
Laura Baker, *St. Edward's University*
Doug Baldwin, *SUNY Geneseo*
Catherine Bareiss, *Olivet Nazarene University*
Ian Barland, *Radford University*
David Barnes, *University of Kent*
Lewis Barnett, *University of Richmond*
N. Dwight Barnette, *Virginia Tech*
Valerie Barr, *Union College*
Martin Barrett, *East Tennessee State University*
Joao Barros, *Instituto Politecnico de Beja - ESTIG*
Phillip Barry, *University of Minnesota*
Michael Bauer, *University of Hawaii - Leeward Community College*
Robert Beck, *Villanova University*
Andrew Begel, *Microsoft Research*
Wendy Belcher, *Colorado School of Mines*
Scott Bell, *Kansas State University*
Jens Bennedsen, *Aarhus School of Engineering*
Mikael Berndtsson, *School of Humanities and Informatics, University of Skovde*
Bradley Beth, *The University of Texas at Austin*
Ivona Bezakova, *Rochester Institute of Technology*
Marie Bienkowski, *SRI International*
William Birmingham, *Grove City College*
Donald Blaheta, *Longwood University*
Stephen Bloch, *Adelphi University*
Steven Bogaerts, *DePauw University*
Christopher Bohn, *US Air Force*
Esmail Bonakdarian, *Dominican University*
Kristy Boyer, *North Carolina State University*
Evelyn Brannock, *Georgia Gwinnett College*
Bo Brinkman, *Miami University*
Allison Brown, *University of Colorado*
Neil Brown, *University of Kent*
Robert Bryant, *Gonzaga University*
Dennis Brylow, *Marquette University*
Suzanne Buchele, *Southwestern University*
Greg Bucks, *University of Cincinnati*
Kevin Buell, *Arizona State University*
Kevin Buffardi, *Virginia Tech*
David Bunde, *Knox College*
Barry Burd, *Drew University*
Kevin Burger, *Arizona State University*
Richard Burns, *West Chester University*
Vicky Bush, *University of Gloucestershire*
Mary Elaine Califf, *Illinois State University*
Andre Paul Calitz, *Nelson Mandela Metropolitan University*
Johan Calu, *KHBO*
Jennifer Campbell, *University of Toronto*
Daniel Canas, *Wake Forest University*
James Caristi, *Valparaiso University*
Andy Carle, *Marvell Semiconductor, Inc.*
Martin Carlisle, *US Air Force Academy*
Lori Carter, *Point Loma Nazarene University*
Paul Carter, *University of British Columbia*
Steven Case, *University of West Florida*
Lillian N. Cassel, *Villanova University*
Sheila Castaneda, *Clarke University*
Tim Chamillard, *University of Colorado at Colorado Springs*
Craig Champlin, *Colorado School of Mines*
Albert Chan, *Fayetteville State University*
Maiga Chang, *Athabasca University*
Mahesh Chaudhari, *Arizona State University*
Ranjan Chaudhuri, *Eastern Michigan University*

Jimmy Chen, *Salt Lake Community College*
Peng-Wen Chen, *Oriental Institute of Technology*
Robert Chen, *Framingham State University*
Wei Kian Chen, *Champlain College*
Li-hsiang Cheo, *William Paterson University of New Jersey*
Donald Chinn, *University of Washington, Tacoma*
Jayan Kurian Chirayath, *Royal Melbourne Institute of Technology*
Radhouane Chouchane, *Columbus State University*
Vincent Cicirello, *Richard Stockton College*
John Cigas, *Park University*
Liezel Cilliers, *University of Fort Hare*
Dawn Cizmar, *St. Edward's University*
Michael Clancy, *University of California, Berkeley*
Peter Clarke, *Florida International University*
Alison Clear, *Christchurch Polytechnic Institute of Technology*
Joe Clifton, *University of Wisconsin, Platteville*
Osvaldo Clua, *Universidad de Buenos Aires*
Marge Coahran, *Toronto Rehabilitation Institute*
Porter Coggins, *Bemidji State University*
Tim Comber, *Southern Cross University*
Randy Connolly, *Mount Royal University*
Phillip Conrad, *UC Santa Barbara*
Kevin Coogan, *Blackburn College*
Robert Cook, *Georgia Southern University*
Stephen Cooper, *Stanford University*
Jean Coppola, *Pace University*
David Cordes, *University of Alabama*
Jose L. Cordova, *University of Louisiana at Monroe*
Tom Cortina, *Carnegie Mellon University*
Monica Costa, *IPCB*
Mary Courtney, *Pace University*
Thad Crews, *Western Kentucky University*
Mark Crouch, *Angelo State University*
Joyce Blair Crowell, *Belmont University*
Steve Cunningham, *Brown Cunningham Associates*
Edwin P. Curran, *University of Ulster*
Douglas Dankel, *University of Florida*
Lawrence D'Antonio, *Ramapo College of New Jersey*
Vibhuti Dave, *Colorado School of Mines*
Janet Davis, *Grinnell College*
Armando De Giusti, *III-LIDI Facultad de Informatica UNLP*
Susan Dean, *UMUC - Europe*
Adrienne Decker, *Rochester Institute of Technology*
Hannah Mary Dee, *Aberystwyth University*
Katherine Deibel, *University of Washington-Seattle*
Leigh Ann DeLyser, *Carnegie Mellon University*
Stavros Demetriadis, *Aristotle University of Thessaloniki*
Yogesh Deshpande, *University of Western Sydney*
Kamyar Dezhgosha, *University of Illinois at Springfield*
Martin Dick, *RMIT University*
Suzanne W. Dietrich, *Arizona State University*
Wei Ding, *University of Massachusetts-Boston*
Adair Dingle, *Seattle University*
Betsy DiSalvo, *Georgia Institute of Technology*
William Doane, *Science & Technology Policy Institute*
Priscilla Dodds, *Georgia Perimeter College*
Zachary Dodds, *Harvey Mudd College*
Michael Doherty, *University of the Pacific*
Marguerite Doman, *Winthrop University*
Toby Donaldson, *Simon Fraser University*
Brian Dorn, *University of Nebraska at Omaha*
Mohsen Doroodchi, *Cardinal Stritch University*
Peter Drexel, *Plymouth State University*
John Duncan, *Indiana University*
J. Philip East, *University of Northern Iowa*
Jeffrey Edgington, *University of Denver*
Stephen Edwards, *Virginia Tech*
Mary Anne Egan, *Siena College*
Christopher Egert, *Rochester Institute of Technology*
Roger Eggen, *University of North Florida*
Kurt Eiselt, *University of British Columbia*
Joseph Ekstrom, *Brigham Young University*
Ahmed El-Deeb, *Upland Software*
Allison Elliott Tew, *University of Washington Tacoma*
Richard Enbody, *Michigan State University*
Alec Engebretson, *Doane College*
Gerald Engel, *University of Connecticut, Stamford*
Daniel Ernst, *Cray, Inc.*
John Estell, *Ohio Northern University*
Henry Etlinger, *Rochester Institute of Technology/Department of Computer Science*
Barry Fagin, *US Air Force Academy*
Daisy Fan, *Cornell University*
David Farrell, *Glasgow Caledonian University*
Mili Fatma, *Purdue University*
Alan Fekete, *University of Sydney*
Maria Feldgen, *Universidad de Buenos Aires*
Roger Ferguson, *Grand Valley State University*
Francesc J. Ferri, *Universitat de Valencia*
Ronald Finkbine, *Indiana University Southeast*
Sue Fitzgerald, *Metropolitan State University*
Robin Flatland, *Siena College*
Samantha Foley, *University of Wisconsin-La Crosse*
Timothy Fossum, *SUNY College at Potsdam*
Susan Fox, *Macalester College*
Charles Frank, *Northern Kentucky University*

Robert Franks, *Central College*
Bill Freitas, *The Lawrenceville School*
Frank Friedman, *Temple University*
S. Jane Fritz, *St. Joseph's College*
Peter Froehlich, *Johns Hopkins University*
Mohammad Fuad, *Winston-Salem State University*
Angel Garcia-Beltran, *Universidad Politecnica de Madrid*
Charlie Garrod, *Carnegie Mellon University*
Alessio Gaspar, *University of South Florida Polytechnic*
Dick Gayler, *Kennesaw State University*
Rick Gee, *Okanagan College*
Joe Geigel, *Rochester Institute of Technology*
Adrian German, *Indiana University School of Informatics and Computing*
Paul Gestwicki, *Ball State University*
Lila Ghemri, *Texas Southern University*
Michail Giannakos, *Norwegian University of Science and Technology - NTNU*
J. Paul Gibson, *T&M Sud Paris*
Don Goelman, *Villanova University*
Sherri Goings, *Carleton College*
Debra Goldberg, *University of Colorado at Boulder*
Michael Goldweber, *Xavier University*
Mercedes Gomez-Albarran, *Dep. Ingenieria del Software e Inteligencia Artificial*
Kinnis Gosha, *Morehouse College*
Jean Goulet, *Universite de Sherbrooke*
Michael Gousie, *Wheaton College (MA)*
Becky Grasser, *Lakeland Community College*
Scott Grissom, *Grand Valley State University*
Joshua Gross, *Northeastern University*
Paul Gross, *Washington University in St. Louis*
Andrew Grover, *Thiel College*
Joshua Guerin, *University of Tennessee at Martin*
Carlos Guerrero, *University of the Balearic Islands*
Mark Guzdial, *Georgia Institute of Technology*
Steven Hadfield, *US Air Force Academy*
Susan Haller, *SUNY Potsdam*
Ranette Halverson, *Midwestern State University*
John Hamer, *University of Glasgow*
Nadeem Hamid, *Berry College*
Brian Hanks, *BFH Educational Consulting*
Arthur Hanna, *St. Mary's University*
Stuart Hansen, *University of Wisconsin - Parkside*
Brian Harvey, *University of California, Berkeley*
Scott Hawker, *Rochester Institute of Technology*
Orit Hazzan, *Technion –Israel Institute of Technology*
Sarah Heckman, *North Carolina State University*
Cecily Heiner, *Southern Utah University*
James Heliotis, *Rochester Institute of Technology*
Keith Hellman, *Colorado School of Mines*
Michael Helmick, *University of Cincinnati*
David Hemmendinger, *Union College*
Tyson Henry, *California State University, Chico*
Katherine Herbert, *Montclair State University*
Matthew Hertz, *Canisius College*
Jose R. Hilera, *University of Alcala*
Curtis Hill, *Valley City State University*
Rachelle Kristof Hippler, *Bowling Green State University*
William Hochstettler, *Franklin University*
Mark A. Holliday, *Western Carolina University*
William Hooper, *Belmont University*
Charles Hoot, *Oklahoma City University*
Cay Horstmann, *San Jose State University*
Thomas Horton, *Dept. of Computer Science, Univ. of Virginia*
Hoda Hosny, *The American University in Cairo*
Mahmood Hossain, *Fairmont State University*
Shahadat Hossain, *University of Lethbridge*
Dwight House, *Fayetteville State University*
David Hovemeyer, *York College of Pennsylvania*
Brian Howard, *DePauw University*
Trudy Howles, *Rochester Institute of Technology*
Wen-Jung Hsin, *Park University*
Chenglie Hu, *Carroll University*
Helen Hu, *Westminster College*
Josh Hug, *Princeton University*
Meriel Huggard, *Trinity College, Dublin*
Janet Hughes, *University of Dundee*
Chris Hundhausen, *Washington State University*
Dalton Hunkins, *St. Bonaventure University*
Frances Hunt, *Educational Testing Service*
Steven Huss-Lederman, *Beloit College*
Deborah Hwang, *University of Evansville*
Jorge Eduardo Ibarra-Esquer, *Universidad Autonoma de Baja California*
Petri Ihantola, *Aalto University*
Lubomir Ivanov, *Iona College, Computer Science Department*
Sridhar Iyer, *Indian Institute of Technology, Bombay*
Clemente Izurieta, *Montana State University*
Jana Jackova, *Matej Bel University*
Matthew Jadud, *Berea College*
Mark Jaeger, *Baker College*
Giti Javidi, *Virginia State University*
Mike Jipping, *Hope College*
William Joel, *Western Connecticut State University*
David John, *Wake Forest University*
Chris Johnson, *University of Wisconsin, Eau Claire*
Colin Johnson, *University of Kent at Canterbury*
Julie Johnson, *Vanderbilt University*
Anthony Joseph, *Pace University*
Mike Joy, *University of Warwick*
Daniel Joyce, *Villanova University*
Maria Jump, *King's College*

Ilker Kalender, *Bilkent University*
Alan Kaminsky, *Rochester Institute of Technology*
Pankaj Kamthan, *Concordia University*
Debbie Kaneko, *Old Dominion University*
Elizabeth Katz, *Millersville University*
David Kauchak, *Middlebury College*
David G. Kay, *University of California, Irvine*
Jennifer Kay, *Rowan University*
Siddharth Kaza, *Towson University*
Fereydoun Kazemian, *Rochester Institute of Technology*
Petros Kefalas, *University of Sheffield*
Tom Kelliher, *Goucher College*
Andreas Kerren, *Linnaeus University*
David Kerven, *Georgia Gwinnett College*
Arshia Khan, *The College of St. Scholastica*
Jeff Kinne, *Indiana State University*
Nancy Kinnersley, *University of Kansas*
Jim Kiper, *Miami University*
Michael Kirkpatrick, *James Madison University*
David Klappholz, *Stevens Institute of Technology*
Carsten Kleiner, *University of Applied Sciences & Arts Hannover*
Jane Kochanov, *Pennsylvania State University - Capital College*
Sinan Kockara, *University of Central Arkansas*
James Kolasa, *Bluegrass Community and Technical College*
Michael Kölling, *University of Kent at Canterbury*
Yana Kortsarts, *Widener University, Chester*
David Kosbie, *Carnegie Mellon University*
Janet Kourik, *Webster University*
Nicholas Kraft, *The University of Alabama*
Douglas Kranch, *North Central State College*
Joan Krone, *Denison University*
Jan Kruger, *Unisa School for Business Leadership*
Norm Krumpe, *Miami University*
Marja Kuittinen, *University of Joensuu*
Deepak Kumar, *Bryn Mawr College*
Benjamin Kuperman, *Oberlin College*
Stan Kurkovsky, *Central Connecticut State University*
Zachary Kurmas, *Grand Valley State University*
Clif Kussmaul, *Muhlenberg College*
Brian Ladd, *SUNY Potsdam*
Lynn Lambert, *Christopher Newport University*
H. Chad Lane, *University of Southern California*
Matthew Lang, *Moravian College*
Joan Langdon, *Bowie State University*
Yedidyah Langsam, *CIS Department Brooklyn College of CUNY*
Mick Lantis, *Purdue University North Central*
David Largent, *Ball State University*
Brian Larkins, *Coastal Carolina University*
Eric Larson, *Seattle University*
Mary Last, *self-employed*
Robert Law, *Glasgow Caledonian University*
Barry Lawson, *University of Richmond*
Lucas Layman, *Fraunhofer USA*
Alina Lazar, *Youngstown State University*
Cathie LeBlanc, *Plymouth State College*
Arthur Lee, *Claremont McKenna College*
Byong Lee, *Bennett College*
Choong-Soo Lee, *St. Lawrence University*
Cornell Lee, *Minnesota State University*
Cynthia Lee, *Stanford University*
En-Shiun Lee, *University of Waterloo*
Gilliean Lee, *Lander University*
Chi Un Lei, *The University of Hong Kong*
Terry Letsche, *Wartburg College*
David Levine, *St. Bonaventure University*
Anany Levitin, *Villanova University*
Gary Lewandowski, *Xavier University*
John Lewis, *Virginia Tech*
Hai-Ning Liang, *Xi'an Jiaotong-Liverpool University*
Weidong Liao, *Shepherd University*
Panos Linos, *Butler University*
Jigang Liu, *Metropolitan State University*
Peter Liu, *Seneca College*
Yue Liu, *National University of Defense Technology*
William S. Lloyd, *University of West Georgia*
Sergio F. Lopes, *University of Minho*
Pengfei Lu, *CUNY Graduate Center*
Joan Lucas, *The College at Brockport, State University of New York*
Stephanie Ludi, *Rochester Institute of Technology*
Robert Lutz, *Georgia Gwinnett College*
Andrew Luxton-Reilly, *The University of Auckland*
William Lyle, *Murray State University*
Bonnie MacKellar, *St John's University*
Peter Macpherson, *Rogers State University*
Joaquim Madeira, *University of Aveiro*
James Maher, *Colorado School of Mines*
Francesco Maiorana, *University of Catania*
Davad Malan, *Harvard University*
Bill Manaris, *College of Charleston*
Mercedes Marques, *University Jaume I*
Fred Martin, *University of Massachusetts Lowell*
Hélène Martin, *University of Washington*
Kenneth Martin, *University of North Florida*
Manuel Martins Barata, *ISEL - Instituto Superior de Engenharia de Lisboa*
Dave Mason, *Ryerson University*
Julian Mason, *Duke University*
Suzanne Matthews, *United States Military Academy*
Bruce R. Maxim, *University of Michigan-Dearborn*
Bruce Maxwell, *Colby College*
Chris Mayfield, *James Madison University*
Lester McCann, *The University of Arizona*
Renee McCauley, *College of Charleston*
Robert McCloskey, *University of Scranton*

O. William McClung, *Nebraska Wesleyan University*
Jeffrey McConnell, *Canisius College*
Frank McCown, *Harding University*
Sean McCulloch, *Ohio Wesleyan University*
Chris McDonald, *The University of Western Australia*
Monica McGill, *Bradley University*
James McGuffee, *Northern Kentucky University*
Hugh McGuire, *Grand Valley State University*
Michael McMillan, *Pulaski Technical College*
Bonita McVey, *St. Norbert College*
Pedro Medeiros, *Universidade Nova de Lisboa*
Antonio Jose Mendes, *University of Coimbra*
Susan Mengel, *Texas Tech University*
Joseph Mertz, *Carnegie Mellon University*
Jose Carlos Metrolho, *Polytechnic Institute of Castelo Branco*
Timothy Meyer, *Edinboro University of Pennsylvania*
Mark Meysenburg, *Doane College*
Lisa Michaud, *Merrimack College*
Bradley Miller, *Luther College*
Afsaneh Minaie, *Utah Valley University*
Joe Miro, *Universitat de les Illes Balears*
Roland Mittermeir, *University of Klagenfurt*
Selvarajah Mohanarajah, *Edward Waters College*
Nelma Moreira, *University of Porto*
Patricia Morreale, *Kean University*
Briana Morrison, *Southern Polytechnic State University*
Thyago Mota, *Colorado School of Mines*
Srikanth Mudigonda, *Saint Louis University*
Christian Murphy, *University of Pennsylvania*
Laurie Murphy, *Pacific Lutheran University*
Michael Murphy, *Concordia University Texas*
David Musicant, *Carleton College*
Adity Mutsuddi, *University of Cincinnati*
Mario Nakazawa, *Berea College*
Krish Narayanan, *Eastern Michigan University*
Pavol Navrat, *Slovak University of Technology*
Rance Necaise, *Randolph-Macon College*
Tia Newhall, *Swarthmore College*
Lijun Ni, *Georgia Institute of Technology*
Victor Norman, *Calvin College*
Cindy Norris, *Appalachian State University*
Linda Null, *Penn State University*
Amanda Ochsner, *University of Wisconsin-Madison*
Rainer Oechsle, *University of Applied Sciences, Trier*
Chris Okasaki, *USMA*
Edward Okie, *Radford University*
Amos Olagunju, *St. Cloud State University*
Lawrence Osborne, *Lamar University*
Peter-Michael Osera, *University of Pennsylvania*
Peter-Michael Osera, *University of Pennsylvania*
Barbara Owens, *Southwestern University*
Christopher Painter-Wakefield, *Colorado School of Mines*
Jill Pala, *Girls Preparatory School*
Iraklis Paraskakis, *City College, Intern. Faculty of the University of Sheffield*
Young Park, *Bradley University*
David Parker, *Salisbury University*
Jeff Parker, *Harvard Extension*
Rembert Parker, *Anderson University*
James Paterson, *Glasgow Caledonian University*
Elizabeth Patitsas, *University of Toronto*
Brian Patterson, *Oglethorpe University*
Arnold Pears, *Uppsala University*
Charlie Peck, *Earlham College*
Ramanee Peiris, *University of Dundee*
Eileen Peluso, *Lycoming College*
Bin Peng, *Franklin University*
Manuel A. Perez-Quinones, *Virginia Tech*
Teresa Peterman, *Grand Valley State University*
Andrew Petersen, *University of Toronto Mississauga*
Chrisila C. C. Pettey, *Middle Tennessee State University*
Charles Pheatt, *Emporia State University*
Vreda Pieterse, *University of Pretoria*
Nelishia Pillay, *University of KwaZulu-Natal*
Francois Pitt, *University of Toronto*
Paul Piwowarski, *University of Kentucky*
Wayne Pollock, *Hillsborough Community College*
Irene Polycarpou, *UCLan Cyprus*
Elvira Popescu, *University of Craiova*
Lori Postner, *Nassau Community College*
Barbara Price, *Georgia Southern University*
Rhys Price Jones, *Wellesley College*
Roger Priebe, *Texas State University - San Marcos*
Viera Proulx, *Northeastern University*
Sarah Monisha Pulimood, *The College of New Jersey*
Cyndi Rader, *Colorado School of Mines*
John Rager, *Amherst College*
Imad Rahal, *College of Saint Benedict & Saint John's University*
Farzana Rahman, *James Madison University*
Rajendra Raj, *Rochester Institute of Technology*
Lakshmi Ramachandran, *Pearson Knowledge Technologies*
Muthu Ramachandran, *Leeds Metropolitan University*
Raghuram Ramanujan, *Davidson College*
Praveen Rao, *University of Missouri-Kansas City*
Saquib Razak, *Carnegie Mellon University*
Eliseo Reategui, *Universidade Federal do Rio Grande do Sul*
Samuel Rebelsky, *Grinnell College*
Michael Redmond, *La Salle University*

David Reed, *Creighton University*
Donna Reese, *Mississippi State University*
Dan Resler, *Virginia Commonwealth University*
Eugene K. Ressler, *United States Military Academy*
Loren Rhodes, *Juniata College*
Brad Richards, *University of Puget Sound*
Detlef Rick, *Universität Hamburg*
Kelly Rivers, *Carnegie Mellon University*
Suzanne Rivoire, *Sonoma State University*
Steven Robbins, *University of Texas at San Antonio*
Christian Roberson, *Plymouth State University*
Eric Roberts, *Stanford University*
Stefan Robila, *Montclair State University*
Guido Roessling, *Technische Universitaet Darmstadt*
Joel Ross, *University of Puget Sound*
John Ross, *Indiana University Kokomo*
Jerry Roth, *Vanderbilt University*
Krishnendu Roy, *Valdosta State University*
Marc Rubin, *Colorado School of Mines*
Anthony Ruocco, *Roger Williams University*
Paulo Rupino da Cunha, *University of Coimbra*
Ingrid Russell, *University of Hartford*
Adrian Rusu, *Rowan University*
Amalia Rusu, *Fairfield University*
Rebecca Rutherfoord, *Southern Polytechnic State University*
Roberta Evans Sabin, *Loyola College*
Mehran Sahami, *Stanford University*
Samuel Sambasivam, *Azusa Pacific University*
Ian Sanders, *University of South Africa*
Andre Santos, *Lisbon University Institute*
Vijayalakshmi Saravanan, *Ryerson University, Canada & VIT University*
Walter Schilling, *Milwaukee School of Engineering*
Karl Schmitt, *Valparaiso University*
Diane Schwartz, *California State University Northridge*
Michael Scott, *Brunel University*
Otto Seppälä, *Aalto University*
Amber Settle, *DePaul University*
Cliff Shaffer, *Virginia Tech*
Steven Shaffer, *The Pennsylvania State University*
Samir Shah, *Drexel University*
Hossain Shahriar, *Kennesaw State University*
Christine Shannon, *Centre College*
Bonita Sharif, *Youngstown State University*
Ching-Kuang Shene, *Michigan Technological University*
Mark Sherriff, *University of Virginia*
Yasuto Shirai, *Shizuoka University*
Keith Shomper, *Cedarville University*
Scott Sigman, *Drury University*
Gavin Sim, *University of Central Lancashire*
Ambareen Siraj, *Tennessee Tech University*
William Slough, *Eastern Illinois University*
Joslyn Smith, *Florida International University*
Peter Smith, *California State University - Channel Islands*
Robert Snapp, *University of Vermont*
Eric Snow, *SRI International*
Takako Soma, *Illinois College*
Raja Sooriamurthi, *Carnegie Mellon University*
Greg Speegle, *Baylor University*
Carol Spradling, *Northwest Missouri State University*
Nathan Sprague, *James Madison University*
Denbigh Starkey, *Montana State University*
Michael Stein, *Metropolitan State University*
Theresa Steinbach, *DePaul University*
Josh Steinhurst, *Intel Corporation*
Ben Stephenson, *University of Calgary*
Vojislav Stojkovic, *Morgan State University*
Tom Stokke, *University of North Dakota*
Christopher Stone, *Harvey Mudd College*
Jeffrey Stone, *Pennsylvania State University*
Forrest Stonedahl, *Centre College*
Fred Strickland, *South University*
Kristina Striegnitz, *Union College*
Catherine Stringfellow, *Midwestern State University/Associate Professor*
Svetlana Strunjas, *Ebay*
David Stucki, *Otterbein University*
Deborah Sturm, *College of Staten Island CUNY*
Fred Sullivan, *Wilkes University*
Wayne Summers, *Columbus State University*
Valerie Summet, *Emory University*
Weiqing Sun, *University of Toledo*
Ken Surendran, *Southeast Missouri State University*
Paul Talaga, *University of Cincinnati*
Joo Tan, *Kutztown University*
Cara Tang, *Portland Community College*
Stewart Tansley, *Microsoft Research*
Rahman Tashakkori, *Appalachian State University*
Michael Tashbook, *Stony Brook University*
Cynthia Taylor, *Oberlin College*
James Teresco, *The College of Saint Rose*
William Thacker, *Winthrop University*
Mariamma Thomas, *Carnegie Mellon University*
Megan Thomas, *California State University Stanislaus*
Rebecca Thomas, *Bard College*
Stan Thomas, *Wake Forest University*
Jodi Tims, *Baldwin-Wallace University*
Frances P. Trees, *Rutgers University*
Christian Trefftz, *Grand Valley State University*
Deborah Trytten, *University of Oklahoma*
William Turkett, *Wake Forest University*
William Turner, *Wabash College*
Hakan Tuzun, *Hacettepe University*
Paul Tymann, *Rochester Institute of Technology*

Susan D. Urban, *Texas Tech University*
Timothy Urness, *Drake University*
Jaime Urquiza-Fuentes, *Rey Juan Carlos University/Lecturer*
Ian Utting, *University of Kent at Canterbury*
Jan Vahrenhold, *WWU Münster*
Ignatios Vakalis, *California Polytechnic and State University*
David Valentine, *Slippery Rock University*
James Vallino, *Rochester Institute of Technology*
Robert Van Camp, *Marietta College*
Tammy VanDeGrift, *University of Portland*
Brad Vander Zanden, *University of Tennessee*
James Vanderhyde, *Benedictine College*
Yaakov Varol, *University of Nevada Reno*
Jorge Vasconcelos, *National Autonomous University of Mexico*
Troy Vasiga, *University of Waterloo*
Kam Vat, *University of Macau*
Steven Vegdahl, *University of Portland*
Nanette Veilleux, *Simmons College*
J. Angel Velazquez-Iturbide, *Universidad Rey Juan Carlos*
Gabriela Vilanova, *National Patagonia Austral University*
Tamar Vilner, *The Open University of Israel*
Giovanni Vincenti, *University of Baltimore*
Ken Vollmar, *Missouri State University*
David Voorhees, *Le Moyne College*
Rosita Wachenchauzer, *Universidad de Buenos Aires*
Amber Wagner, *University of Alabama*
Sally Wahba, *Clemson University*
Gursimran Walia, *North Dakota State University*
Ellen Walker, *Hiram College*
Xinli Wang, *Michigan Technological University*
Xueyi Wang, *Microsoft*
Karen Ward, *University of Portland*
Stan Warford, *Pepperdine University*
Richard Wasniowski, *California State University Channel Islands*
Thomas Way, *Villanova University*
Amali Weerasinghe, *University of Adelaide*
Duo (Helen) Wei, *Richard Stockton College of NJ*
Scott Weiss, *Mt. St. Mary's University*
Stephen Weiss, *University of North Carolina at Chapel Hill*
Emily Wenk, *Penn State York*
Linda Werner, *University of California, Santa Cruz*
Roger West, *University of Illinois at Springfield*
Elizabeth White, *George Mason University*
Howard Whitston, *University of South Alabama*
Richard Wicentowski, *Swarthmore College*
Linda Wilkens, *Providence College*
Judith Williams, *William Penn University*
Craig Wills, *Worcester Polytechnic Institute*
Linda Wilson, *Texas Lutheran University*
Marty Wolf, *Bemidji State University*
Rosalee Wolfe, *DePaul University*
David Wolff, *Pacific Lutheran University*
Greg Wolffe, *Grand Valley State University*
Steven Wolfman, *University of British Columbia*
Ursula Wolz, *Riversound Solutions, LLC*
Ka Wai Gary Wong, *The Hong Kong Institute of Education*
Wilson Wong, *Bentley University*
Karl Wurst, *Worcester State University*
Stelios Xinogalos, *Department of Applied Informatics, University of Macedonia*
Arthur Yanushka, *Christian Brothers University*
Juang Yih-Ruey, *Jinwen University of Science & Technology*
Duane Yoder, *University of West Georgia*
Chad Yoshikawa, *University of Cincinnati*
Kwok-Bun Yue, *University of Houston-Clear Lake*
Timothy Yuen, *UTSA*
Carol Zander, *University of Washington Bothell*
Mark Zarb, *University of Dundee*
Alan Zaring, *Ohio Wesleyan University*
Jian Zhang, *Texas Womans' University*
Jinghua Zhang, *Winston-Salem State University*
Lynn Ziegler, *College of St. Benedict/St. John's University*
Stephen Zilora, *Rochester Institute of Technology*
Guy Zimmerman, *Bowling Green State University*
Jill Zimmerman, *Goucher College*
Daniel Zingaro, *University of Toronto*
Fani Zlatarova, *Elizabethtown College*
Michael Zmuda, *Miami University*

CALL FOR PARTICIPATION

SIGCSE 2015

Keep Connected – Keep Committed – Keep Computing

The 46th ACM Technical Symposium on Computer Science Education

March 4 – 7, 2015, Kansas City, Missouri, USA

http://www.sigcse2015.sigcse.org

SIGCSE 2015 continues our long tradition of bringing together colleagues from around the world to present papers, panels, posters, special sessions, and workshops, and to discuss computer science education in birds-of-a-feather sessions and informal settings. The SIGCSE Technical Symposium addresses problems common among educators working to develop, implement and/or evaluate computing programs, curricula, and courses. The symposium provides a forum for sharing new ideas for syllabi, laboratories, and other elements of teaching and pedagogy, at all levels of instruction.

Submissions in line with the conference theme, "**Keep Connected – Keep Committed – Keep Computing**," are encouraged. The theme is a call for all of us to make sure that our efforts in this field keep us moving in the right directions. We need to keep connected with each other for the sharing of ideas. We want our students to be connected to each other and to us to help further their educational experience. We need to keep our focus and commitment on the efforts we are pursuing to further computing education. And most importantly we need to keep our students committed to the field so that they will keep computing.

PAPERS

Papers describe an educational research project, classroom experience, teaching technique, curricular initiative, or pedagogical tool. Submitted papers for review will be anonymous. Papers will undergo a blind reviewing process and must not exceed six pages. Accepted papers will need to submit a non-anonymous version for publication in the proceedings after acceptance. Authors will have approximately 25 minutes for their presentations, including questions and answers.

PANELS

Panels present multiple perspectives on a specific topic. To allow each panelist sufficient time to present his or her perspective and still enable audience participation, a panel will normally have at most four panelists, including one moderator. Panel submissions should include a list of the panelists, their affiliations, and a description of the topic, with brief position statements from panelists. Proposals with more than four panelists must provide a statement connecting the extra panelist to the effectiveness of the panel and must convincingly show that each panelist will be able to speak, and the audience able to respond, within the session time. Panel abstracts must not exceed two pages. A panel session is approximately 75 minutes.

SPECIAL SESSIONS

Special sessions are your opportunity to customize and experiment with the SIGCSE conference format. Possible special sessions include a seminar on a new topic, a committee report, or a forum on curriculum issues. More generally, they must be 75 minutes in length, held in standard conference spaces, and justifiably be distinct from the panel, paper, and poster tracks. Within those constraints, the form is yours to design. Special session abstracts must not exceed two pages.

WORKSHOPS

Workshops offer participants opportunities to learn new techniques and technologies designed to foster education, scholarship, and collaborations. A workshop proposal (including abstract) must not exceed two pages. Proposals must specify equipment needs (e.g., participant-supplied laptops, room configurations, and A/V equipment) and any limitation on the number of participants. Workshops are scheduled for a three-hour session and do not conflict with the technical sessions.

BIRDS OF A FEATHER SESSIONS

Birds of a Feather (BOF) sessions provide an environment for colleagues with similar interests to meet for informal discussions. A maximum one-page description (including abstract) is requested to describe the informal discussion topic. A/V equipment will not be provided for these sessions. Approximately 45 minutes are allocated to each BOF topic.

POSTERS

Posters describe computer science education materials or research, particularly works in progress. Proposals (including abstract) are limited to two pages. Poster demonstrations are scheduled to permit one-on-one discussion with conference attendees, typically during session breaks. Prepared handouts are encouraged in order to share your work.

Association for Computing Machinery

Advancing Computing as a Science & Profession

SIGCSE ACM Special Interest Group on Computer Science Education

STUDENT RESEARCH COMPETITION

Research from all areas of computer science is considered for awards in two categories of competition: graduate and undergraduate. All submissions must represent a student's individual research contribution and a student must be an ACM student member to qualify for awards and travel grants. Entry due date is September 29, 2014.

PROCEEDINGS AVAILABILITY

The proceedings will be publicly available from the ACM Digital Library 14 days before the start of the conference. Therefore, the official publication date for the proceedings will be February 18, 2015.

IMPORTANT DUE DATES

Friday, September 5, 2014: *Paper, Panel, Special Session, and Workshop submissions*
Monday, October 27, 2014: *Birds of a Feather and Poster submissions*

PROGRAM COMMITTEE

Symposium Chairs

Adrienne Decker
Rochester Institute of Technology
adrienne.decker@rit.edu

Kurt Eiselt
University of British Columbia
eiselt@cs.ubc.ca

Program Chairs

Carl Alphonce
University at Buffalo
alphonce@buffalo.edu

Jodi Tims
Baldwin Wallace University
jltims@bw.edu

Panels and Special Sessions

Peter DePasquale
The College of New Jersey
depasqua@tcnj.edu

Workshops

Paul Carter
University of British Columbia
pcarter@cs.ubc.ca

Alvaro Monge
California State University, Long Beach
alvaro.monge@csulb.edu

Publications

Jian Zhang
Texas Woman's University
jzhang@mail.twu.edu

Database Administrators

John Dooley
Knox College
jdooley@knox.edu

Henry Walker
Grinnell College
walker@cs.grinnell.edu

Registration

Lynn Degler
Rose-Hulman Institute of Technology
degler@rose-hulman.edu

Cary Laxer
Rose-Hulman Institute of Technology
laxer@rose-hulman.edu

Larry Merkle
Computational Optimization Services
l.merkle@ieee.org

Posters

Michelle Craig
University of Toronto
mcraig@cs.toronto.edu

Birds Of A Feather

Ria Galanos
Thomas Jefferson High School for Science and Technology
ria.galanos@gmail.com

Student Volunteers and Activities

Pam Cutter
Kalamazoo College
Pam.Cutter@kzoo.edu

Sarah Heckman
North Carolina State University
sarah_heckman@ncsu.edu

Webmaster

Matt Jadud
Berea College
matt_jadud@berea.edu

Publicity/Social Media

Briana Morrison
Southern Polytechnic State University
bmorriso@spsu.edu

Treasurer

Paul Tymann
Rochester Institute of Technology
ptt@rit.edu

Evaluations

Steve Cooper
Stanford University
coopers@cs.stanford.edu

Kids' Camp

Cheryl Seals
Auburn University
sealscd@auburn.edu

Valerie Henderson Summet
Emory University
valerie@mathcs.emory.edu

Support/Exhibitor Liaison

Susan Rodger
Duke University
rodger@cs.duke.edu

Pre-Conference Events & Affiliated Events Liaison

Allison Elliott Tew
University of Washington - Tacoma
aetew@u.washington.edu

K-12 Liaison

RJ Dake
Kansas State Department of Education
rjdake@ksde.org

International Liaison

Paul Denny
University of Auckland
paul@cs.auckland.ac.nz

Local Arrangements

Brian Hare
University of Missouri – Kansas City
hareb@umkc.edu

Student Research Competition

Ann Sobel
Miami University (Ohio)
sobelae@miamioh.edu

Association for Computing Machinery
Advancing Computing as a Science & Profession

SIGCSE
ACM Special Interest Group on Computer Science Education

Recipients of the SIGCSE Award for Outstanding Contributions to Computer Science Education

1981 **William F. Atchison**, *University of Maryland*

1982 **Alan Perlis**, *Yale University*

1983 **Karl V. Karlstrom**, *Prentice-Hall*

1985 **Elliot I. Organick**, *University of Utah*

1986 **Donald Knuth**, *Stanford University*

1987 **Niklaus Wirth**, *ETH, Zurich*

1988 **Grace Murray Hopper**, *Rear Admiral, USN, Digital Equipment Corp.*

1989 **Edsger W. Dijkstra**, *The University of Texas at Austin*

1990 **Curriculum '68 Committee**:
William F. Atchison, Samuel D. Conte, John Hamblen, Thomas E. Hull, Thomas A. Keenan, William B. Kehl, Edward J. McClusey, Silvio O. Navarro, Werner Rheinboldt, Earl J. Schweppe, William Viavant, David M. Young, Jr.

1991 **David Gries**, *Cornell University*

1992 **Daniel D. McCracken**, *City College, City University of New York*

1993 **Alan C. Kay**, *Apple Computer*

1994 **Norman E. Gibbs**, *Software Engineering Institute*

1995 **Robert M. Aiken**, *Temple University*

1996 **Nell B. Dale**, *The University of Texas at Austin*

1997 **Andrew Tannenbaum**, *Vrije University*

1998 **William A. Wulf**, *University of Virginia and National Academy of Engineering*

1999 **Peter J. Denning**, *George Mason University*

2000 **Andries Van Dam**, *Brown University*

2001 **Allen B. Tucker**, *Bowdoin College*

2002 **Elliot Soloway**, *University of Michigan*

2003 **Eric Roberts**, *Stanford University*

2004 **Mordechai Ben-Ari**, *Weizmann Institute of Science*

2005 **Kim Bruce**, *Williams College*

2006 **Richard Pattis**, *Carnegie Mellon University*

2007 **Judith Gal-Ezer,** *Open University of Israel* and **John Hughes**, *University of Technology, Sydney*

2008 **Randy Pausch,** *Carnegie Mellon University*

2009 **Elliot B. Koffman,** *Temple University*

2010 **Sally Fincher,** *University of Kent, Canterbury*

2011 **Matthias Felleisen,** *Northeastern University*

2012 **Harold (Hal) Abelson,** *Massachusetts Institute of Technology*

2013 **Michael Kölling**, *University of Kent, Canterbury*

2014 **Robert M. Panoff,** *The Shodor Education Foundation, Inc.*

Recipients of the SIGCSE Lifetime Service Award

1997 **Richard Austing**, *University of Maryland*
1998 **Della Bonnette**, *University of Southwestern Louisiana*
1999 **Robert Aiken**, *Temple University*
2000 **James E. Miller**, *University of Southern Mississippi*
2001 **Lillian N. (Boots) Cassel**, *Villanova University*
2002 **Joe Turner**, *Clemson University and Zayed University*
2003 **Harriet Taylor**, *National Science Foundation and Louisiana State University*
2004 **Bruce Klein**, *Grand Valley State University*
2005 **Andrew McGettrick**, *University of Strathclyde*
2006 **Joyce Currie Little**, *Towson State University*
2007 **John Impagliazzo**, *Hofstra University*
2008 **Dennis Frailey**, *Raytheon Corporation*
2009 **Michael J. Clancy**, *University of California, Berkeley*
2010 **Peter Denning**, *Naval Postgraduate School*
2011 **Gordon Davies**, *Open University*
2012 **Jane Prey**, *Microsoft Research*
2013 **Henry Walker**, *Grinnell College*
2014 **Andrea Lawrence**, *Spelman College*

Computational Thinking for All: The Power and the Peril

Robert M. Panoff
Shodor Education Foundation
National Computational Science Institute
rpanoff@shodor.org

ABSTRACT

Students and faculty alike at all education levels are clearly spending much more of their time interacting with computing and communication tools than with each other. Is this good? Are all uses of computational technology in education helpful, and if not, how does one separate the benefits from the burdens? We will explore how computing enables multiple representations in the sciences, arts, and humanities, giving us the opportunity to be more fully human as we seek new knowledge in service to society. Moving "beyond PowerPointless-ness," we have the opportunity to demonstrate that computing really matters in teaching and learning. Computing "matters" because quantitative reasoning, computational thinking, and multi-scale modeling are the intellectual "heart and soul" of 21st Century science and therefore are the essential skills of the 21st Century workforce. Computing "matters" because we can apply the power of dynamic, visual, and interactive computing to reach a deeper understanding of models across math and science while exploring their role in understanding our world.

Categories and Subject Descriptors

D.2.13 [**Computers and Education**]: Computer and Information Science Education – *Computer science education; Information systems education; Curriculum*

Keywords

Computational Science, Computational Thinking, Visualization, Modeling, Simulation

SIGCSE'14, March 5–8, 2014, Atlanta, Georgia, USA.
ACM 978-1-4503-2605-6/14/03.
http://dx.doi.org/10.1145/2538862.2554795

SIGCSE Plus You Equals Leverage

Andrea W. Lawrence
Spelman College
350 Spelman Lane, Box 362
Atlanta, GA 30314
1-404-270-5875
Lawrence@spelman.edu

ABSTRACT

This paper describes the many possibilities that SIGCSE affords to those who make use of the resources and opportunities the organization and the annual conferences provide.

Categories and Subject Descriptors

A.1 [**General Literature**]:Introductory and Survey.
K.3 [Computing Mileux]: Computers and Education.

General Terms

Human Factors

Keywords

SIGCSE, computing, pedagogy, curriculum, research, networking

1. INTRODUCTION

Archimedes once said "Give me a place to stand, and a level long enough, and I will move the world." [1] Over the years I have worked to move forward teaching, research, students and their endeavors, a computer science department, Spelman College as a producer of students, and the computing discipline.

2. SIGCSE AS A LEVER

SIGCSE and its members provide a multitude of possibilities for computer science professionals. This talk will address some of these possibilities and ways for those participating in the organization and in the annual conferences to explore and profit from these possibilities. The opportunities include learning about computer science history, keeping abreast of changes and developments in curriculum, and learning new pedagogical techniques. In addition there are opportunities to attend workshops, explore opportunities for students, and develop new skills.

The area of the organization and the conferences that is not so easily quantified is the networking opportunities that come from a meeting of those of like mind and purpose who will join to make computer science education as strong as it can possibly be. This talk addresses how SIGCSE has served in all these ways and possibilities for the future.

3. ACKNOWLEDGMENTS

Our thanks to ACM SIGCSE and the members of LACS (Liberal Arts Computer Science)

REFERENCES

[1] Archimedes, 2002. *The Works of Archimedes.* Dover Publications.

SIGCSE'14, March 5–8, 2014, Atlanta, Georgia, USA.
ACM 978-1-4503-2605-6/14/03.
http://dx.doi.org/10.1145/2538862.2554796

Transforming US Education with Computer Science

Hadi Partovih
Code.org
Seattle, WA, USA
hadi_partovi@code.org

ABSTRACT

Code.org first exploded on the CS education scene in Feb 2013 with its first video featuring Mark Zuckerberg and Bill Gates talking about computer science. 10 months later, it launched an Hour of Code campaign that has taken the world by storm. Reaching 10 million students in just 3 days, the Hour of Code became the fastest-spreading service in the history of technology OR education. Code.org founder Hadi Partovi will talk about how he came up with the concepts behind these grassroots campaigns, and how Code.org hopes to harness the reach of the broader CS community to grow computer science education in schools.

Bio

I was born in Iran and lived much of my early childhood under Ayatollah Khomeini's totalitarian regime during a bloody war with Iraq. My family spent most evenings huddled in the dark, holding our ears as Iraqi planes bombed our neighborhood.

When I was 10, my father gave my twin brother and me a Commodore 64 computer to learn how it worked. Computers back then were not easy to use. Instead of buying Kids coding - Hadi someday wants all classrooms to look like thissoftware or games, our dad told us to "learn to write your own." With little else to do, we devoured the available information and taught ourselves BASIC. By the time we came to America a few years later, I was already a proficient programmer and empowered enough to change the course of my own life. I had my first job as a software engineer at the age of 15.

During a technology roundtable 18 months ago, I spoke briefly with President Obama about the importance of CS education and how addressing the shortage of computer Girls Can Code, a programming course already in placescientists could help solve our nation's unemployment problem. Research on the impact of growing CS education shows projected jobs in software outnumbering students 3 to 1. The gap between jobs and students amounts to 1 million jobs over ten years, or over $500 billion in salaries across all industries. These are some of the highest paying jobs in the world, with a 3-4x multiplicative impact on neighborhood jobs. Additionally, basic knowledge about software and the Internet is going to be increasingly critical for all students who want to join the knowledge economy.

The day that Steve Jobs died, I realized that time would run out if I continued thinking of ideas without acting on them. To leverage technology "celebrities" to motivate more people to pursue CS, I launched Code.org with a video starring Bill Gates, Mark Zuckerberg, Jack Dorsey, and others, prefaced by a quote from Steve Jobs that acknowledges my original vision. It attracted 20 million views.

More than 3.5 million students tried the programming example online, and over 12,000 schools asked for our help to add Computer Science courses to their curriculum.

The original vision of Code.org was to bring computer programming into the mainstream dialogue and raise national awareness about this issue. But with thousands of schools asking for our help, I embarked to create a larger organization and started fundraising for its larger vision: to bring CS to every American public school, district by district, city by city, until it becomes a core tenet of US education. (Only 10% of K-12 schools teach CS today.) It will cost $300 million to solve this problem if schools, parents, and students are engaged.

We've struck a chord with millions who want this problem fixed. Anybody can learn the basics. That's the Code.org vision.

SIGCSE'14, March 5–8, 2014, Atlanta, Georgia, USA.
ACM 978-1-4503-2605-6/14/03
http://dx.doi.org/10.1145/2538862.2554793

Lab of Things: A Devices Research and Teaching Platform for Home and Beyond

A.J. Bernheim Brush
Microsoft Research
One Microsoft Way
Redmond, WA 98052
ajbrush@microsoft.com

ABSTRACT

Inspired by the availability of inexpensive connected devices—such as lights, water sensors, security cameras, power meters, and thermostats—we built the Lab of Things (LoT) platform to enable easy interaction with devices for a range of applications, including automation, security, energy management, and elder care. Our goal is to substantially lower the barrier for researchers and students to develop and experiment with new technologies for the home environment. LoT provides a common framework to write applications that use connected devices and includes a set of cloud services that enable remote command/control of devices, monitoring of system health, and data collection. We released the LoT SDK in July 2013 for non-commercial use. I will describe the research studies that motivated the development of Lab of Things, student and research projects developed using Lab of Things and its precursor HomeOS, and our long-term vision of research groups working together to create a test bed of homes around the world that are willing to participate in field studies.

Bio

My research area is Human-Computer Interaction with a focus on Ubiquitous Computing and Computer Supported Cooperative Work. I study and build technology for homes and families. My current focus is home automation as co-leader of the Lab of Things project which was built on HomeOS. I have studied home heating, mobile context-aware applications for activity recognition and location sharing, reducing email overload, interacting with technology beyond the desktop, and annotations for asynchronous collaboration. I am a Senior Member of the ACM and was honored to receive a Borg Early Career Award in 2010. I co-organized the HomeSys 2013 workshop at UbiComp 2013 and am co-general chair of UbiComp 2014. I am also a board member of CRA-W, a group that works to increase the number of women in computing research.

Presently at Microsoft Research, I am a member of the Computational User Experiences (CUE) group. I graduated summa cum laude from Williams College in 1996 with a double major in Computer Science and Mathematics. I received my Ph.D. in Computer Science from the University of Washington in Sept 2002 and I have been at Microsoft Research since 2004.

SIGCSE'14, March 5–8, 2014, Atlanta, Georgia, USA.
ACM 978-1-4503-2605-6/14/03
http://dx.doi.org/10.1145/2538862.2554794

Increasing the Effectiveness of Automated Assessment By Increasing Marking Granularity and Feedback Units

Nickolas Falkner, Rebecca Vivian, David Piper and Katrina Falkner
School of Computer Science
The University of Adelaide
Adelaide, South Australia, Australia, 5005
nickolas.falkner@adelaide.edu.au

ABSTRACT

Computer-based assessment is a useful tool for handling large-scale classes and is extensively used in the automated assessment of student programming assignments in Computer Science. The forms that this assessment takes, however, can vary widely from simple acknowledgement to a detailed analysis of output, structure and code. This study focusses on output analysis of submitted student assignment code and the degree to which changes in automated feedback influence student marks and persistence in submission. Data was collected over a four year period, over 22 courses but we focus on one course for this paper. Assignments were grouped by the number of different units of automated feedback that were delivered per assignment to investigate if students changed their submission behaviour or performance as the possible set of marks, that a student could achieve, changed. We discovered that pre-deadline results improved as the number of feedback units increase and that post-deadline activity was also improved as more feedback units were available.

Categories and Subject Descriptors

K.3.2 [**Computers and Education**]: Computer and Information Science EducationComputer Science Education

General Terms

Human Factors

Keywords

automated assessment, feedback, student performance

1. INTRODUCTION

Automated assessment is used for many different assignment types including quizzes and computer programs. Marking student programs is a substantial source of workload in Computer Science courses and is often carried out automatically. Timely feedback is essential to students and, where an automated marking system is in use, we have the opportunity to provide feedback on a work-in-progress, prior to final submission, if we choose to do so. While this raises the spectre of students attempting to 'hack' their solution to match the testing harness [9], a practice Ben-Ari referred to as *bricolage* [3], this must be balanced against any benefit of providing this early feedback [16]. Automated feedback can feel mechanical, inauthentic and, as noted, can provoke mindless repetitive attempts to second guess the mechanism, but we will focus on how we can make the most beneficial use out of what is a growing necessity.

As we have seen in project-based learning[4], student development is greatly assisted by revision and review to allow steady improvement over time. We have an obvious motivation to provide continuous feedback as students make progress to encourage their development. An automated system can provide students with a measure of their progress towards achieving a 'successful' program by awarding a response, possibly including a grade, which we define as a feedback *unit*. The range of feedback units available to most automated systems is a set of scripted responses with associated mark awards that are awarded based on the comparison and analysis of program output relative to a set of known inputs, syntactic analysis of key structures in the program, limited semantic analysis or graph analysis to determine correspondence to a known algorithm.

The term *grain* is often used in the context of *fine-grained* or *coarse-grained* marking schemes [18, 17]. We focus on the granularity of marks awarded as an issue of assessment reliability and consistency [7, 18] and the extent to which difference in achievement is reflected in a single mark. We would like any marks to reflect sufficient progress and to have the marks awarded reflect that the work being assessed is a sufficient improvement upon a previous piece of work with a lower mark, with any useful associated textual feedback. When used as part of pre-submission feedback, this requirement is even more important. However, the marks apparently available for students may not all actually be available, and corresponding textual feedback may thus not be displayed. A range of 0–100 implies a fine-grained scheme but it is not fine-grained if we only award the marks 0, 50 and 100. As we will explore, we use the term *granularity* in this paper to reflect the *actual* marking granularity that students have achieved after attempting the assignment, which is the only perception of granularity that is truly meaningful to students. A granularity of one would state that the same single mark was awarded to all students, where a granularity of six would indicate that there are six possible marks available, such as $\{0,20,40,60,80,100\}$ or $\{0,1,2,4,7,10\}$. The granularity that we make available to students is a combi-

SIGCSE '14 March 5–8, 2014, Atlanta, Georgia, USA

ACM 978-1-4503-2605-6/14/03 ...$15.00
http://dx.doi.org/10.1145/2538862.2538896.

nation of the granularity we initially define, modified by the feedback units available through an automated marking system. As we will discuss, what appears to be fine-grained can easily become coarse in implementation.

In this paper, we will discuss the effects of granularity and then assess the impact of changes in the number of feedback units on students' submission times and automatically assessed marks. As part of this, we will identify outstanding questions about our theories regarding student interpretation of marking granularity and discuss follow-up work and our conclusions. While a mark, by itself, does not constitute constructive feedback for improvement, it does provide useful feedback to the student on the degree of progress made, even in the absence of additional text. However, in the majority of cases in this study, each mark awarded was also presented with associated textual feedback identifying which tests had been passed, what this meant and, in some cases, possible places to look for improvement.

2. EXISTING WORK

The role of the marking system is to encourage the student to produce a working piece of software as building something that is complete and functional is of great assistance to inspiring and developing student confidence [5]. The advantages of automated assessment for programming tasks are the same as for any computer-based assessment scheme: objective assessment, removal of halo effects, and reduction in manual, error-prone, marking burden [11]. Kay *et al* [13] further identify the benefits of automated marking in efficiently assessing multiple execution paths in computer programs.

A detailed review of existing automated assessment tools within Computer Science is presented in [1], identifying that in Computer Science, automated assessment is used more frequently than manual assessment methods for practical work. Automated assessment is frequently applied to the areas of functionality, program efficiency, and the development of testing skills, with a small number of specialised automated systems developed to explore assessment criteria more typically performed using manual marking, including structural aspects of design and software metric analysis.

Although we may not all agree on a specific numeric grade, the majority of instructors can agree upon whether programs are "very good" or "very bad" [8], supporting the derivation of automated marking scripts that are able to clearly identify both ends of the spectrum. While automated assessment may not by able to assess all criteria of programming assignments to the same degree of quality [1], the additional benefits that automated marking systems provide such as repeatability of assessment, timely feedback and formative reassessment provide alternative pedagogical benefits.

Providing constructive feedback to students improves their ability to correct their mistakes. As observed in [11], multiple choice questions did not show any difference in performance between automated and manual assessment, while programming assignments did benefit from in-progress feedback and the automated assessment of these assignments achieved a better result than having the same work coded in a paper and pencil environment. Students who have the opportunity to resubmit their work, with feedback, also improve outside of the programming structure, where compiler and execution feedback is inherently more objective.

Considerable existing work explores the issue of assessment granularity and impact upon student learning. Fincher *et al* [7] identify that the granularity of the mark awarded is most easily understood and effective when it matches the weight of the assessment item to which it is matched. However, the granularity of the marking scheme applied can have further impact depending on whether it is coarse- or fine-grained. Sadler [18] illustrates the problem of becoming too fine grained in our assessment scheme overall, which reinforces [7], but there is a tension between too much detail and insufficient detail. Where too much granularity distorts the initial intent of the learning objective then we risk losing the coherency of the overall assessment scheme. Sadler notes [18] that increasing the granularity of the marking scheme risks the assignment being seen as a set of atomic challenges, unified administratively rather than semantically, reducing a student's ability to integrate understanding in this area of knowledge. [7] and [18] agree that a clear alignment between objectives and learning activities is essential and that finer granularity may be justified providing that a reasonable correspondence is maintained between mark returned and actual value of the mark.

Sadler [18] explores exemplars as part of a grading scheme, noting that it is rare to find one exemplar that provides all of the desirable learning activities. Automatic marking systems are effectively providing comparison to an exemplar and, hence, may not capture the richness needed for fair and equitable assessment. Naude [14] explores this issue in the development of an automated marking system that exploits graph similarity to avoid simplistic approaches to automated program assessment.

Panadero *et al* [16] explore the distinction between self-assessment scripts and rubrics in the development of self-regulated learning behaviour. Rubrics provide criteria for assessing goals, scales for grading achievement levels and a clear description of different qualitative levels that allows discrimination. Scripts are a step-structured set of questions to organise the task in the sequence an expert might employ and allow us to assess process, as well as, potentially outcome. The issue of granularity, when applied in the context of the prescriptive nature of the script, can potentially lead students to focus on successfully completing the script steps rather than learning the lesson associated with the activity. In the rubric, which is more outcome focussed and less process-locked, we reduce this risk. A marks scheme from an electronic system can potentially function as a rubric but we are aware that students are not guaranteed to read all or any of a rubric and that the perception of even the most helpful rubric could be of a prescriptive statement of teacher intent, rather than a supportive document to encourage participation and achievement of learning outcomes [2]. Rubrics make implicit requirements explicit and clearly allocate marks to the successful attainment of certain goals, facilitating feedback and self-assessment [10]. Clearly, a reliable and correctly constructed electronic marking scheme, even one that is scripted, can meet this requirement and has equal validity to a rubric, which is also rarely customised to the individual student level.

Ihantola *et al* [9] identify that the iterative nature of automated marking, where students are able to resubmit their work multiple times so that they are able to realise improvements upon their mark, can lead to a stress on the summative nature of automated marking and an attempt by students to "hack" their way to a correct solution. Nikula *et al* [15] present a longitudinal study of a first year programming course restructure, where they introduced an automated marking system, the Virtual Learning Environment, which tested their submissions for correctness as well as tracking student performance metrics. Nikula *et al* identify student frustration upon receiving feedback that they were not able to act upon once the deadline had passed. Edwards et al [6] examine the combined effect of a student's starting time for an assignment on their mark, when presented with feedback from the Web-CAT system, which confirmed the overall result that starting earlier is usually correlated with better grades but also identified that average student marks appear to drop 1-2 days before the assignment is due, as measured by the Web-Cat system, and then start to rise again following submission, despite marks penalties preventing students from benefiting from these marks. Where students are allowed to carry out an unrestricted number of submissions, we can either see students using this to best ability or practicing, *bricolage*, where progress is haphazard and accidental, being constructed from the random changes the student puts together, rather than from intent. Karavirta et al [12] studied this as part of an investigation to cluster students based on the way in which they employed the resubmission mechanism for an automatically assessed assignments, noting that it was possible to use semi-random mutation through iteration to solve a problem without necessarily understanding the source of error. Although both ambitious and iterative students made great use of resubmission, [12] noted that only the ambitious had a corresponding improvement in their final examination grade.

As noted in [16] and regularly observed in the classroom, intervention and feedback provided during an assignment have a noticeably different effect from post-hoc feedback once no further improvement is possible, and we use this as motivation to observe what students do when we provide immediate feedback during the assignment process.

3. METHODOLOGY

This is ongoing work on an investigation of student behaviour through the analysis of a data corpus, collected as part of an automated marking system for a school of Computer Science at a mid-scale University. The main corpus spans the years 2007 to 2010, over eight semesters, with over 200,000 recorded (valid) submissions and over 20,000 individual students across 22 courses. The data were collected by an automated marking system that required students to commit their work to an repository and then accept boilerplate text describing University policies, which then resulted in the student's work being sent to the web submission system. Student submissions were automatically marked on submission, with any feedback and marks returned immediately. In 2007, school policy was to operate a 25% cumulative mark cap for each day, or part of day, late but this was not strictly enforced. In 2008, staff conformance to the cumulative mark cap was mandated. However, students could not receive a lower mark than one previously awarded, hence a student who submitted on time for 80% would not be capped at 75% were they to submit a superior version of their code after the due date. The assignments allowed for unlimited resubmission.

The dataset was constructed from the student submission data through automated extraction of the course, student, submission time, automatically assessed mark and on-time or late status, with each record being normalised to provide a stand-alone entry containing the mark received, the mark awarded after any late penalties and whether the work was on time or not and, if so, by how much. This data was then analysed using R-64 statistical software, under R Studio, with coordinating packages written in Ruby. An initial sweep of the data was carried out to produce graphs, using `ggplot2`, to identify key areas of interest and, following this, the investigation was refined to specific courses and the extraction of features in numerical form for statistical analysis.

The observed activity period for each assignment is the 120 hours preceding the established submission deadline and the 120 hours following the submission deadline. The activity in this interval dominates the activity in the surrounding weeks by orders of magnitude. For statistical reasons, we have not carried out any further analysis on the data in the weeks outside of this area. In effect, the number of students active over a week before a deadline in an undergraduate course are, from our observations, so small as to be considered negligible.

Some components of the original data could not be captured in the final dataset due to ambiguous dates or non-standard or external automated marking and these data have been excluded. The original data capture was a by-product of an assessment system and, while individual instructors could determine the marks obtained under non-standard schemes, a decision was made to exclude them at this time, pending more work on the automated harvesting. The total number excluded for non-standard marking schemes is small, less than 0.1% of total submissions. The data from our investigation is noisy and, where smoothing has been used, we have uniformly used LOESS smoothing, with the default parameters, as part of the `ggplot2` package. Numerical data is provided, later in the paper, to identify that interesting facets in the graphs are not due to smoothing errors introduced by the LOESS smoothing.

4. RESULTS

The initial discussions of the granularity identify one immediate question: given that increased granularity increases the complexity of both the assignment and the automated marking systems, what granularity do we choose to provide student benefit without overloading the teaching staff?

4.1 The Impact of Granularity

Analysis of the different granularities across all schemes in use in the study showed that most courses had perceived granularities of 5 or less, with a spike at granularity 11. For the four years under study, over the150 courses that had granularities less than or equal to 5, of a range from 2 to 46. Unsurprisingly, given the complexity of establishing automated marking as the number of handled cases increases, the count of the different awarded marks decreases with the number of items available. The spike at 11 reflects the $0 - 10$ scheme with unit steps or a $0 - 100$ in steps of 10.

4.2 Student Performance

Although we can look at the student performance across the entire school, the range of entry points, the differing assignment types found across courses and the risk of the artificial dominance of larger enrolments in less advanced courses means that such analysis will only give us a very broad indication of trends. What about the performance within a given course, where the content, student body and overall assessment consistency allows us to isolate given treatments? We have identified a major contributor to the data set that has a similar distribution of assessment granularities under automated marking to that found in our initial assessment of school data but is a well-defined course with no major structural changes across the four year period, in second year of a Bachelors degree with a computer science major. This course has been de-identified and will be labelled as "bee3". After consolidation, the summary data for the whole school consists of 27,744 'final' records, showing the last time a student submitted an assignment across 1,917 unique students. bee3 is a significant contributor to school data, with 7,010 of these records (the most for any course) and 971 unique students represented. This course was the major programming course for the degree and a pre-requisite for further study in Computer Science. All students in our cohort are required to take this course, resulting in a representative range of students who had successfully completed first year foundation programming courses. Annual enrolments in bee3 ranged from 210 to 260 students. All assignments were coding activities that were designed to take at most one week to solve and were available to students for at least two weeks prior to deadline. All assignments allowed an unlimited number of resubmissions, including beyond the due date, and were worth between 3-4% of the final mark for the course. Student submission did not significantly vary if the mark was 4% rather than 3%. Each of the assignments consisted of three to six questions with increasing degree of difficulty. The goal for each student was to submit code for each problem in a week's question set. Feedback was provided in addition to marks, at least informing the students of the nature of test being performed, the presented input, the expected output and any variation. In some cases, individual goal statements were also presented to identify when students had met specific stages in a development process or to provide guidance as to how to move forward.

Obviously, a granularity of 2 (binary grading) does not provide a great range of feedback, nor does granularity 3. Although assignments were used with these granularities, these were frequently for early assignments which encouraged behaviour such as handing up files successfully or single lines of output. The point at which the assignments started to provide more detailed feedback was, unsurprisingly, at the point where there were 4 or more possible marks available. Hence, we will focus on student performance and mark achievement for granularities of 4, 5, 6 and 11. Each graph is LOESS smoothed and shows the standard deviation as a grey shadow below each line. As expected, the deviation is higher for the lower groupings, because of the introduction of the artificially high 100% grades introduced by granularity 2 and 3 mark schemes. For each graph, where we state "granularity split at x", this indicates that the solid blue line is for all assignment marking schemes that achieved at least granularity x and the dotted red line represented all assignments that had less than this granularity. Hence, in Figure 1 (granularity split at 4), the solid blue line represents all marking schemes that had a granularity of 4 or up in awarded marks, while the dotted red line represents marking schemes with granularity of 2 or 3. (Obviously, granularity 1 can provide no feedback and anything less than 1 or non-integer is not possible.)

As can be seen from the graphs, students are achieving noticeably greater average marks when the marking granularity increases and, while this effect appears to be temporarily neutralised at the major deadline, they continue to receive higher marks after the deadline. Investigating the mean mark and standard deviation for each hour confirms that the separations of average marks are greater than one standard deviation for periods up to two days prior to the submission deadline. Once we proceed beyond a granularity of 15, while the graphs start to converge before the deadline, we see a clear separation of marks after submission, indicating that average student mark (for late submissions) increases as we increase the granularity of marking, as shown in Figure 5 for granularity split 15. While our late submission penalty scheme would, in theory, reduce the benefit in completing the work as students would not be receiving many, if any, of additionally earned marks, the high granularity schemes are seeing students continuing to work for longer and achieving higher marks.

By aligning the average marks received from automatic marking with the hour of activity, we identify an immediate observation that the peak average mark returned by automated marking occurs well before the submission date, in the range of 48 to 72 hours ahead of the no-penalty sub-

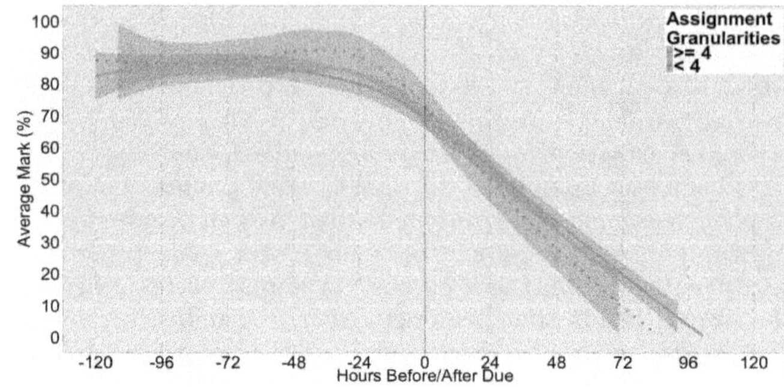

Figure 1: Granularity split at 4

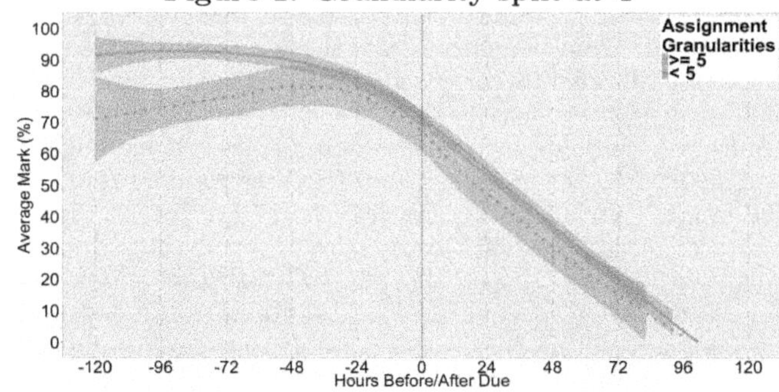

Figure 2: Granularity split at 5

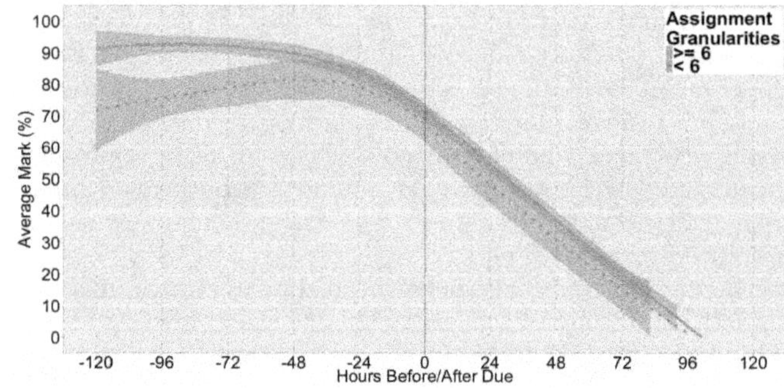

Figure 3: Granularity split at 6

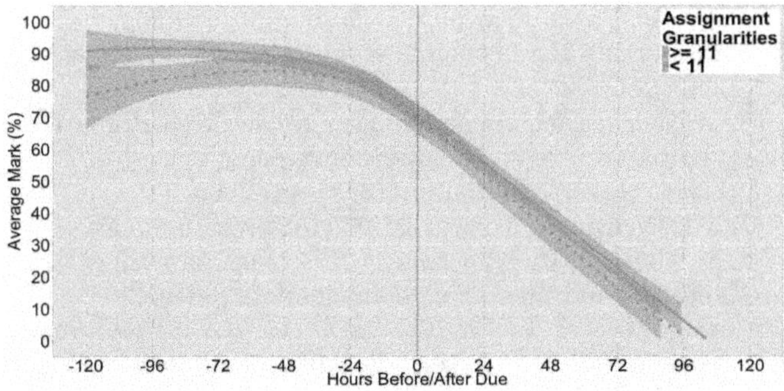

Figure 4: Granularity split at 11

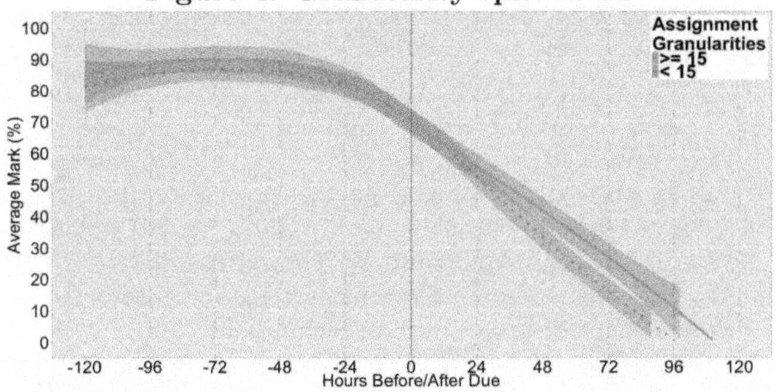

Figure 5: Granularity split at 15

mission date, which is also seen in [6]. While, as has been documented in the literature previously, we expect to see a concentration of activity immediately prior to the due date, assessing the automated mark that is assigned clearly identifies a downwards trend in average mark and, in most cases, the average mark (for an on-time submission) starts to approach the mark that would be received if the work were handed in one day late. Across the school, the marks start a downward trend over the final 48 hours prior to submission, dropping steeply in the four hours prior to submission. This is also the time at which the greatest number of per hour submissions occur, with a very high peak in the final hour. [6] also noted the existence of outliers who continued working after the due date, even at a stage where further work would attract more marks. Our work confirms this effect and, if late penalties are removed, there is a clear climb back towards the highest average mark achieved prior to the submission deadline.

4.3 Numerical analysis

Because of the large number of possible hours available for submission, we have 240 possible submission points and a great deal of noise due to conflating factors such as low granularity scores that introduce binary marking schemes. However, cleaning the data to remove single entries, which would return an invalid standard deviation, we then determined which hours saw an increase in mean mark and which hours saw an increase in mean mark that was beyond one standard deviation. These results for granularity less than 5, 5 and 15 are shown in Table 1. The first two columns compare the mean mark for everything below granularity 5 with granularities of 5 and greater, then 15 and greater, where we note that the column for granularity 5 or greater does subsume the following column but that this has been added to clearly isolate benefit at higher levels of granularity. Columns three and four then determine the mark

Table 1: Percentile increase with granularity

Hour	$\mu_5 > \mu_0$	$\mu_{15} > \mu_0$	$\mu_5 > \mu_0$*	$\mu_{15} > \mu_0$*	n
-109	4	5		5	12
-108	24	11			15
-107	33	14			15
-106	32	6	32		15
-105	4				23
-103	18	18	18	18	12
-102	48	48	48	48	14
-101	49	29	49	29	18
-100	42	37	42	37	14
-99	33	33	33	33	20
-92	100	100	100	100	4
-86	40	37	40	37	9
-85	39	46	39	46	18
-84	14	12			13
-82	30	31	30	31	14
-79	11	16			19
-78	2	2			16
-77	6	13			14
-76	14	22		22	17
-75	7				19
-74	16	16	16	16	18
-61	27	30	27	30	16
-60		9		9	38
-59	26	26	26	26	32
-58	18	5			37
-57	13				50
-56	13	7			44
-55	29	24	29		38
-54	3	9			23
-53	18	18	18	18	18
-52	9	5			25
47	40	50	40	50	7
60	20	18	20	18	4
68	20	20	20	20	4

increase, marked with an asterisk, but require that the difference in mark be greater than the standard deviation in marks. The final column is the total number of students across each hour band. It is immediately apparent that, as identified in the graphs, students are gaining higher marks as we improve granularity and, despite the inherent noise of this data, we are able to clearly identify points before and after a given deadline where students appear to be deriving benefit from the additional effort invested in making the automated marking scheme more granular.

To summarise this data, within this course, using a granularity of 5 increased the automated assessment mark received for 30 of a possible 120 hours, with 15 of these 30 hours showing a mark increase that was one standard deviation above granularity 4 and below. Similarly, using a granularity of 15 led to 28 of the 120 hours before submission having a better average mark than for all of the granularities 14 and down - which includes granularity 5 - with 16 being significantly larger (greater than one standard deviation).

An additional 14 hours in the span 44-88 showed substantially higher marks for 60 students across this period when higher granularity was used but had to be eliminated because we had no comparator in the low granularity data set - the students submitted in an additional 14 hours in the area under study. There were at least 14 additional hours when students submitted work, providing the teacher had provided at least 5 marking intervals. The students undertaking assignments with higher granularity schemes are working over more of the post-deadline period, for longer, well after any on-time benefit of additional granularity has stopped increasing, which we interpret as an overall increase in persistence. This, again, confirms results observed in [6], which clearly shows an increasing average grade after the due date, with a minimum mark granularity of 10 marks.

5. CONCLUSIONS

This study suggests that marking schema and granularity of marks is important to consider when using and designing automated assessment of programming assignments. Our study shows that students perform differently as we vary the granularity that they can perceive. There is, however, a need for additional investigation into the behaviour of the individual student in response to these factors.

Does a more detailed marking scheme indicate the presence of a more methodical and pedagogical approach to assignment formation or material delivery? Again, we have all of the source assignments and the vast majority of teaching materials so, over time, we plan to go through and carry out a quality assessment of the works, to finish the isolation of the marking scheme from the materials to which they are attached. An assignment with 100 possible marks should provide a similarly enumerated set of actual marks but, across four years of assignments, there is only one assignment that has 46 different marks awarded, yet there are many assignments that notionally have 100 marks available and only offer 11 different marks. By concentrating on a single course with a reasonable range of assignment mark granularities, we have started to reduce the potential impact of the teacher in terms of motivation and content delivery outside of the assignments, but there is work to be done on the quality and nature of the assignment.

We need to find reliable, high-quality alternatives to manual marking so that we can handle the increasing number of students with a decreasing, and steadily more over-worked, academic faculty. What is apparent from our analysis is that automated feedback, even when it is confined to marks, does provide some impetus to continue working, even when the marks returned are low - if a student can see that they are making progress then, unsurprisingly, they may strive for longer. There has never really been a question about the value of formative feedback delivered during a project but automated marking scripts have long been seen as a very poor cousin to their manual and face-to-face alternative, being neither personalised nor human! Despite the occasional issues with an overly pedantic comparison or a case that was not foreseen by the lecturer, it appears that students will perform better, earlier, when we take the time to provide a more detailed and granular marking scheme for our automatically marked assignments.

6. REFERENCES

[1] K. M. Ala-Mutka. A survey of automated assessment approaches for programming assignments. *Computer Science Education*, 15(2):83–102, 2005.

[2] H. Andrade and Y. Du. Student perspectives on rubric-referenced assessment. *Practical Assessment Research & Evaluation*, 10(3), Apr. 2005.

[3] M. Ben-Ari. Constructivism in computer science education. In *Proceedings of the twenty-ninth SIGCSE technical symposium on Computer science education*, SIGCSE '98, pages 257–261, New York, NY, USA, 1998. ACM.

[4] P. C. Blumenfeld, E. Soloway, R. W. Marx, J. S. Krajcik, M. Guzdial, and A. Palincsar. Motivating Project-Based Learning: Sustaining the Doing, Supporting the Learning. *Educational Psychologist*, 26(3):369–398, 1991.

[5] C. Douce, D. Livingstone, and J. Orwell. Automatic test-based assessment of programming: A review. *J. Educ. Resour. Comput.*, 5(3), Sept. 2005.

[6] S. H. Edwards, J. Snyder, M. A. Pérez-Quiñones, A. Allevato, D. Kim, and B. Tretola. Comparing effective and ineffective behaviors of student programmers. In *Proceedings of the fifth international workshop on Computing education research workshop*, ICER '09, New York, NY, USA, 2009. ACM.

[7] S. Fincher, M. Petre, and M. Clark, editors. *Computer Science Project Work: Principles and Pragmatics*. Springer, 2001.

[8] S. Fitzgerald, B. Hanks, R. Lister, R. McCauley, and L. Murphy. What are we thinking when we grade programs? In *Proceeding of the 44th ACM technical symposium on Computer science education*, SIGCSE '13, pages 471–476, New York, NY, USA, 2013. ACM.

[9] P. Ihantola, T. Ahoniemi, V. Karavirta, and O. Seppälä. Review of recent systems for automatic assessment of programming assignments. In *Proceedings of the 10th Koli Calling International Conference on Computing Education Research*, Koli Calling '10, pages 86–93, New York, NY, USA, 2010. ACM.

[10] A. Jonsson and G. Svingby. The use of scoring rubrics: Reliability, validity and educational consequences. *Educational Research Review*, 2(2):130 – 144, 2007.

[11] N. Kalogeropoulos, I. Tzigounakis, E. A. Pavlatou, and A. G. Boudouvis. Computer-based assessment of student performance in programing courses. *Computer Applications in Engineering Education*, 2011.

[12] V. Karavirta, A. Korhonen, and L. Malmi. On the use of resubmissions in automatic assessment systems. *Computer Science Education*, 16(3):229–240, 2006.

[13] D. Kay, T. Scott, P. Isaacson, and K. Reek. Automated grading assistance for student programs. In *Proceedings of the 25th SIGCSE technical symposium on Computer science education*, pages 381–382, 1994.

[14] K. A. Naudé, J. H. Greyling, and D. Vogts. Marking student programs using graph similarity. *Comput. Educ.*, 54(2):545–561, Feb. 2010.

[15] U. Nikula, O. Gotel, and J. Kasurinen. A motivation guided holistic rehabilitation of the first programming course. *Trans. Comput. Educ.*, 11(4):24:1–24:38, Nov. 2011.

[16] E. Panadero, J. A. Tapia, and J. A. Huertas. Rubrics and self-assessment scripts effects on self-regulation, learning and self-efficacy in secondary education. *Learning and Individual Differences*, 22(6):806 – 813, 2012.

[17] D. R. Sadler. Interpretations of criteria-based assessment and grading in higher education. *Assessment & Evaluation in Higher Education*, 30(2):175–194, 2005.

[18] D. R. Sadler. Perils in the meticulous specification of goals and assessment criteria. *Assessment in Education: Principles, Policy & Practice*, 14(3):387–392, 2007.

Adaptively Identifying Non-terminating Code When Testing Student Programs

Stephen H. Edwards, Zalia Shams, and Craig Estep
Department of Computer Science, Virginia Tech
114 McBryde Hall (0106)
Blacksburg, VA 24061
edwards@cs.vt.edu, zalia18@vt.edu, craigy@vt.edu

ABSTRACT

Infinite looping problems that keep student programs from terminating may occur in many kinds of programming assignments. While non-terminating code is easier to diagnose interactively, it poses different concerns when software tests are being run automatically in batch. The common strategy of using a timeout to preemptively kill test runs that execute for too long has limitations, however. When one test case gets stuck in an infinite loop, forcible termination prevents any later test cases from running. Worse, when test results are buffered inside a test execution framework, forcible termination may prevent any information from being produced. Further, overly generous timeouts can delay the availability of results, and when tests are executed on a shared server, one non-terminating program can delay results for many people. This paper describes an alternative strategy that uses a fine-grained timeout on the execution of each individual test case in a test suite, and that adaptively adjusts this timeout dynamically based on the termination behavior of test cases completed so far. By avoiding forcible termination of test runs, this approach allows all test cases an opportunity to run and produce results, even when infinite looping behaviors occur. Such fine-grained timeouts also result in faster completion of entire test runs when non-terminating code is present. Experimental results from applying this strategy to 4,214 student-written programs are discussed, along with experiences from live deployment in the classroom where 8,926 non-termination events were detected over the course of one academic year.

Categories and Subject Descriptors

K.3.2 [**Computers and Education**]: Computer and Information Science Education; D.1.5 [**Programming Techniques**]: Object oriented Programming; D.2.5 [**Software Engineering**]: Testing and Debugging—testing tools.

Keywords

Automated assessment, automated grading, software testing, programming assignments, JUnit, infinite loop, timeout.

1. INTRODUCTION

As students learn to program and master basic control constructs, and then to implement their own data structures, one kind of error that recurs is that of non-terminating repetition, or the *infinite loop*. While identifying that a program is "stuck" in a repeating pattern is a skill students must learn, infinite loops pose unique problems when running software tests, particularly if software tests are run unattended. It is often impossible for the testing tool to determine if the unresponsive program is performing some useful computation or if it is executing an infinite loop.

The most common approach to dealing with this situation is simply to use a timer. If a program runs "too long," then it can be preemptively terminated under the presumption that "it should have finished by now." Unfortunately, this common strategy has weaknesses, particularly when software tests are used to automatically assess student assignments for correctness. Timeouts must necessarily be generous to avoid false positives, where a program would have terminated but is somewhat slower than expected. However, when programs do get stuck, longer timeouts imply greater delays in handling them, leading to greater delays in providing feedback to students. When a single server must handle a number of students, for example, even one such nonterminating method can cause a slowdown for all of the students waiting for feedback. Further, forcibly terminating a "stuck" program often limits (or completely eliminates) any software test results, reducing the information that can be learned from a test run.

This paper describes a novel approach to this problem in Java. Adaptive timeout periods are independently enforced on each test case that is executed, dynamically adjusting the allowed execution time based on the observed behavior of the code under test. We also present an empirical evaluation of its application on a data structure implementation assignment that poses multiple opportunities for infinite looping mistakes. Results from the evaluation suggest that this approach restricts the impact of non-terminating behavior to just the test cases that trigger the problem, allowing all other tests to run to completion and allowing us to avoid any forcible termination of the entire test run. Experiences gained from one year of in-class deployment in multiple courses indicate that the approach works well under real-world usage.

2. RELATED WORK

Currently, one problem teachers face is how to deal with occasional student programs that run for a long time, perhaps indefinitely. Non-responsiveness is often found while automatically running software tests on student work. It is often impossible to determine if the unresponsive program is performing useful computation or if it is stuck in an infinite loop.

Several industrial tools have been developed to detect infinite looping in programs. Burnim et al. describe LOOPER [1], a tool for analyzing a running program to find out if there is any infinite loop running inside the program. LOOPER diagnoses loops using a combination of symbolic execution, concrete execution, and theorem proving. It constructs non-termination arguments for infinite loops dependent on both program values and the shape of

SIGCSE'14, March 5–8, 2014, Atlanta, Georgia, USA.

http://dx.doi.org/10.1145/2538862.2538926

heap, and then checks those arguments using an SMT solver. Unfortunately, LOOPER is designed for on-demand analysis of a program once a user has discovered a possible infinite loop, and is not intended for continual monitoring—that is, it diagnoses "stuck" programs, but requires a person to identify when this diagnosis is needed. Further, it is not designed for efficiency, imposing additional run-time overhead of up to 10,000X [1].

Gupta et al. [2] describe TNT, a tool for checking C for non-termination. It uses concolic test generation [3] to deduce constraints on program state values, and then exhaustively searches for control-flow patterns that are provably non-terminating. Its value lies in performing off-line analysis to alert the programmer of the presence of infinite loops. Knowing that a program contains one or more infinite loops does not indicate which tests are safe to run or aid in identifying test cases that have triggered infinite loops, however. TNT has not been adapted to Java and its run-time costs have not been described.

Velroyen et al. [4] have proposed another static approach to find non-terminating inputs for a program. This approach relies heavily on automated, iterative invariant generation, which limits its scalability. Most of the industry tools used for detecting infinite loops either prove termination or non-termination of the program by using static methods or symbolic execution. However, existing educational tools (e.g., automated graders, automated tutoring systems etc.) usually do not use such approaches.

Efopoulos et al. researched a Programming Environment for Novices [5]. They found that the most common logic errors that beginners made are failure to increment a loop counter variable (typically causing an infinite loop) and erroneous incrementing of a loop counter variable (i.e., modifying a counter outside the loop). As a result, it is clear that infinite loops in student code must be anticipated, and automated grading or testing systems must find an efficient way to handle them.

Most automated grading tools use a timeout strategy to preemptively terminate non-terminating code (e.g., potentially containing infinite loops). This strategy imposes a fixed time limit while executing a student's code. Most often, this is an *end-to-end* time limit on an entire test run, which is simplest to implement. If a program's test run exceeds that limit then it is considered as having an infinite loop and its execution is forcibly terminated. Roberts et. al. set up a generous time limit for program execution in their online assessment tool [6]. Similarly, Morris et. al. [7] used a fixed execution duration to decide whether a running program has encountered an infinite loop, as do Web-CAT [10] and ASSYST [11]. Marmoset [8], on the other hand, does use an infinite loop detector that uses a database of program code to detect infinite loop patterns in student code. It also uses stack overflow condition to detect infinite recursion problems—although in most modern languages, infinite recursion is usually identified relatively quickly by a runtime failure and does not typically result in the same problems as non-terminating code. Striewe et. al. developed an automated tutoring system [9] where they use an end-to-end timeout strategy. Although their tutoring system cancels running a solution after the time limit is exceeded, they then use program state analysis to check if the program had entered a duplicate program state and use the outcome of this analysis to generate traces. These traces are intended to help students debug their code.

3. THE PROBLEM

Using a single end-to-end execution timeout strategy is simple, since running a test suite is usually performed as a single action, and using a timer to determine whether to kill the test run is straightforward. The strategy is independent of the programming language in which code (or the test suite) is written. At the same time, however, in the context of automatically executing software tests on student code, a single end-to-end timeout has limitations.

This approach creates two basic problems:

- **Results might not be received from the test run**: If the entire test run itself is terminated due to a timeout, this termination may prevent test results from being reported. At a minimum, none of the test cases following the point where the infinite loop was triggered will even be executed, so they cannot produce results. Worse, however, if output is buffered by the test execution framework, it is possible that no results at all will be available under premature termination.
- **Slowing down the entire process**: In the context of a grading system that serves a large number of students, overly generous timeouts allow programs that do exhibit infinite looping problems to absorb disproportionately larger amounts of computing time, decreasing availability for processing other work.

Addressing these two problems requires a different strategy that does not involve timing (and aborting) the entire test execution process as a single monolithic task.

4. SOLUTION STRATEGY

A desire to avoid aborting the entire test run, coupled with the need for a shorter—and hence, finer grained—time limit, led to investigating a new strategy: applying individual time limits to each separate test case in a test suite, rather than a single end-to-end limit on the entire process. But a single, fixed time limit applied to individual test cases could still result in a fairly long delay in completing an entire test run if nontermination is triggered in a significant proportion of the tests. As a result, we instead focused on employing an *adaptive* time limit, where the time limit is dynamically adjusted for later tests based on results from earlier tests in the same test suite. If a program repeatedly fails to terminate in multiple test cases, the time limit can be actively reduced in order to promote timely completion of the entire test suite. Similarly, if a program is properly terminating but doing so slowly, the time limit can be dynamically increased to reduce the chance of incorrectly terminating later test cases.

This adaptive timeout strategy is realized using a parameterized model that begins with an initial time limit for individual test

```
for every test case do
   diff = current_time - previous_time
   if (diff > limit)
      nontermCount = nontermCount + 1
      if (nontermCount > 1)
         limit =
            max(floor, limit * rampdown)
      end if
   else if (diff > limit * safeZone)
      limit =
         min(ceiling, limit * rampup)
   end if
end for
```

Figure 1: Pseudocode for time limit adjustment. Floor and ceiling form hard bounds; rampdown and safeZone are < 1, while rampup > 1.

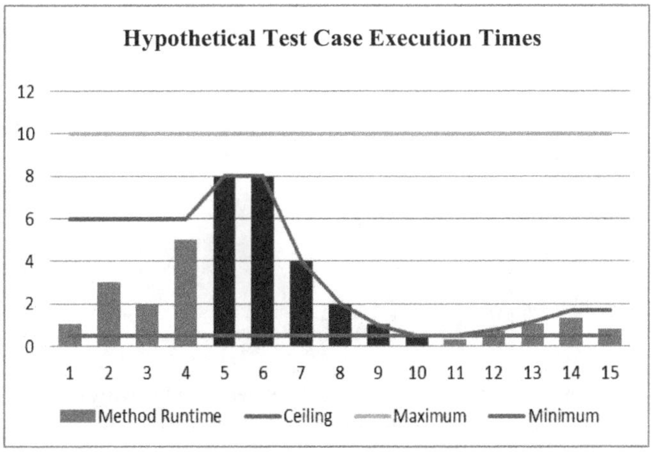

Figure 2: Hypothetical time limit adaptation over time.

cases in each test run. In addition, there is a hard "floor" defining the minimum amount of time allowed for any test case, and a "ceiling" defining the maximum amount of time that will be allowed. These serve as upper and lower bounds for the time limit, as the time limit is adjusted over time during execution of the test suite. Finally, there is a "ramp down" rate indicating how swiftly the time limit should be reduced for repeated non-termination observations, and also a "ramp up" rate indicating how quickly the limit should be increased when slow-but-terminating behavior is observed. Figure 1 shows the basic logic for adjusting the time limit for each test case.

Figure 2 shows a hypothetical illustration of how this adaptive strategy is intended to work. The horizontal axis in Figure 2 represents the individual test cases in a test suite, with the height of each bar indicating the running time of that test case. Flat lines depict the upper ceiling and lower floor allowed for the time limit on these individual test cases. We can also see the initial timeout beginning as a flat limit over the first four test cases, each of which completes successfully within the allowed time. The fourth test case uses a substantial portion of the allowed time, however, and so the limit is dynamically adjusted upward for the next test case. Test case 5 in this hypothetical example exceeds the time limit and is preemptively cut off. This does not terminate the entire test run, however, and later tests still execute.

Our adaptive strategy uses a "one strike free" approach, so that the very first test case does not actually trigger a reduction of the time limit—after all, the Pareto principle suggests that infinite looping is more likely to show up in a small proportion of test cases. Active reductions to the time limit begin with the *second* test case to exceed the limit—test case 6 in Figure 2. The time limit continues to be reduced as long as test cases continue to exceed the limit. Finally in Figure 2, the limit begins to increase again as test cases terminate successfully within the time limit but consume the bulk of the allowed time.

5. IMPLEMENTATION

While the concept of an adaptive time limit applied to each test case is straightforward, implementing the strategy does raise issues. For software written in Java, JUnit is the framework of choice for unit tests written by educators and students. JUnit v.4 in particular provides built-in support for limiting the execution time of individual test cases using a feature called *test rules*. A test rule can be used to adjust the policy used to execute an individual test method in a JUnit 4 test class, where test methods correspond to the individual tests in a suite.

In fact, JUnit 4 provides a built-in test rule called Timeout that allows a programmer to set a fixed timeout that is applied uniformly to all tests in a suite [13]. Using this feature, we implemented our adaptive timeout strategy as a custom JUnit 4 test rule that provides a dynamically varying time limit for each test method in a test class.

Unfortunately, this facility is only available in JUnit 4. The earlier JUnit v.3 API does not support test rules. However, many educators still use JUnit 3 in part because it is simpler for beginning students to understand and use and many textbooks still describe JUnit 3. JUnit 3 relies on method naming conventions and extending a predefined base class, while JUnit 4 instead relies on extensive use of annotations.

To address this problem and to support educators who use JUnit 3, we also wrote a custom JUnit 4 runner that allows JUnit 3 tests to be run without change using the more flexible JUnit 4 infrastructure and test rule support. While supporting every possible JUnit 3 test class within JUnit 4's infrastructure is challenging [12], our approach supports all common uses of JUnit 3 by educators (everything but custom overrides of internal framework execution machinery). This custom test runner also automatically injects the adaptive timing test rule into every JUnit 3 and JUnit 4 test class it processes, so all test methods are executed under the new policy.

One side benefit of this implementation design is that educators who wish to stick with the older JUnit 3 approach can now take advantage of the newer features of JUnit 4 where desired.

While we expect the parameters of the adaptation model to be customizable in different situations, it is also important to pick appropriate "default" values for them. The default initial time limit for each test case is 10 seconds, with a ceiling of 20 seconds and a floor of 0.25 seconds (for comparison, instructors using Web-CAT often use end-to-end time limits of 60 seconds, with nearly all end-to-end limits in the range of 45–120 seconds). Each test case that exceeds its time limit (other than the very first) causes the time limit to be divided in half (ramp-down of 50%). Test cases that take more than 60% of the allowed time cause the time limit to be raised by 40% (ramp-up). These parameters can be set externally without modifying the rule or the tests.

6. EVALUATING THE SOLUTION

To evaluate the practicality of this solution, we applied it to a CS2 assignment from Spring 2011 at Virginia Tech. Students originally completed this assignment using a traditional end-to-end time limit of 60 seconds on the entire test suite's execution time, meaning that non-terminating solutions received little or no feedback on what behaviors they could perform correctly. For our evaluation, we revisited work from this past assignment to re-run the same test suites with an adaptive timeout strategy instead.

This CS2 assignment required students to write two different implementations of a generic queue interface in Java—one using a linked representation and one using an array-based implementation. In addition to basic queue operations, students were also required to implement equals(), hashCode(), clone(), toString(), and iterator(). Since all of these features require loop-based (or recursive) implementations, and students had to provide these features for both the array-based and link-based implementations of their data structure, this assignment appears to pose a more significant opportunity for student solutions to exhibit runaway looping. Further, students were required to implement the remove() operation on the iterator they provided, leading to increased risk of internal data structure corruption and greater possibilities for incomplete or faulty loop logic.

Students were also required to write their own software tests and were graded in part on the statement coverage and decision coverage they achieved. This encourages students to find their own logic problems and fix them before submitting the final version of their work.

In the semester under consideration, 136 students completed the assignment, making a total of 4,214 submissions to the electronic grading system. The average number of submissions per student was 31, with the maximum by any individual being 121 submissions. The instructor provided a suite of 82 reference tests for the assignment, and these tests were run against every student submission using the adaptive timeout strategy, producing a total of 345,456 test cases executed. Again, the adaptive timeout implementation worked as expected, although three of the submissions did produce severe enough errors to crash the Java virtual machine during testing, giving only partial results (e.g., out of memory errors that the test execution framework could not recover from, forcing the test run to be aborted).

As expected, a number of students did run into infinite looping difficulties on this data structure implementation assignment. A total of 195 submissions (4.6%) failed to terminate within the allowed time on at least one reference test case. These submissions were made by 33 students, or 24.3% of the class. At the same time, however, only 6 students (4.4%) made final submissions that still exhibited non-terminating behavior on at least one reference test case. This indicates that on this assignment the majority of students did not experience infinite looping problems on any of their submissions (although they may have during their own testing), and of those that did, the majority were able to fix their problems before completing the assignment.

6.1 Frequency of Non-termination

Examining the submissions that exhibited non-terminating behavior provides some insight into the frequency of infinite looping problems. Figure 3 shows the number of submissions with non-termination problems made by each of the 33 students who experienced these issues, ranked from largest number of submissions to smallest. The distribution roughly approximates a negative exponential distribution. From this, it seems that a significant portion of students who experienced non-termination behaviors on some of their submissions had this issue only on a relatively small number of submissions.

Although the average number of submissions on this assignment across the class was 31, if we normalize the data in Figure 3 by the total number of submissions made by each individual student, we see the relative proportion of submissions with non-termination problems for each student in Figure 4, again in rank order. The shape of the distribution is similar, suggesting that a relatively small proportion of students regularly experienced infinite looping problems on most of their submissions, while the majority of students who saw non-termination issues experienced them on a smaller proportion of their submission attempts. This is consistent with the evidence that most students were able to address their infinite looping problems before completing the assignment.

The reference test suite used in this assignment included 82 test cases. So, for the 195 submissions that exhibiting non-terminating behavior, how many test cases were affected? Figure 5 shows the proportion of the 195 misbehaving submissions that were over the time limit on differing numbers of test cases. Approximately one third of these submissions were over time on exactly one test case (out of 82). 60% of the submissions with non-terminating behavior exceeded the time limit on two or fewer test cases, and 88% timed out on four or fewer test cases. This is good evidence that the majority of student work with infinite looping problems exhibits this behavior in only a few cases, rather than most of the time.

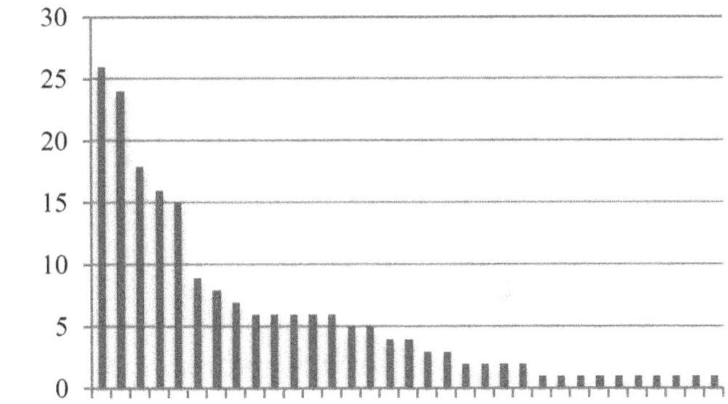

Figure 3: Number of submissions per student with non-termination problems.

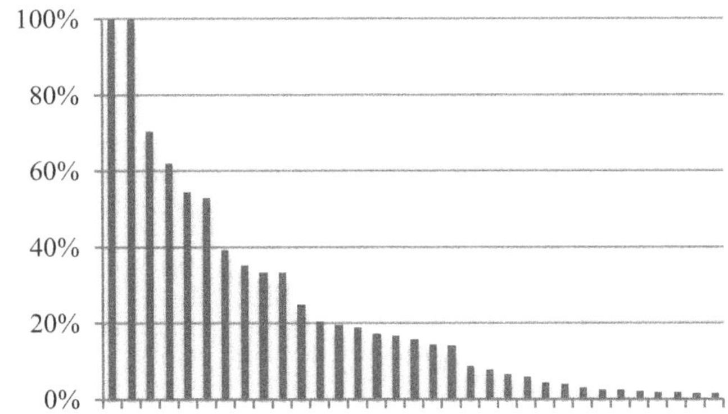

Figure 4: Proportion of submissions per student with non-termination problems.

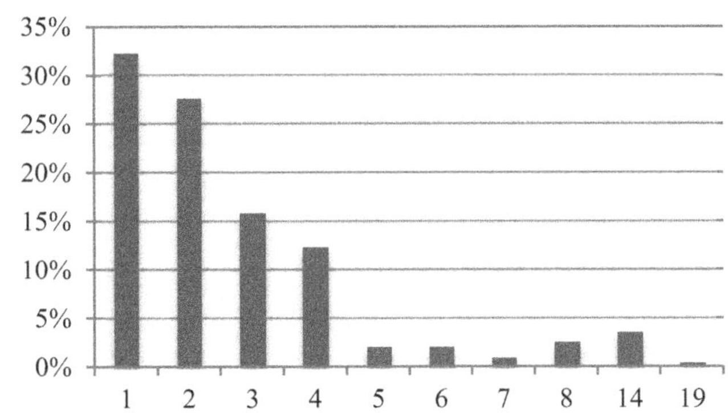

Figure 5: The number of test cases triggering infinite looping behavior in student submissions.

At the same time, however, there were a number of submissions that exceeded the time limit on significantly more test cases—as many as 19. If we used a non-adaptive approach, say, allowing a flat 10-second time limit per test case, those submissions could take over three minutes to process. While submissions with this frequency of over-limit behavior are not the norm, the adaptive approach ensures they do not consume significantly more time than necessary.

Interestingly, the non-termination failures in the array-based queue implementation outnumbered those in the linked implementation by a factor of 5 to 1. The single most common feature that caused infinite looping problems was the task of expanding the capacity of an array-based queue—that is, inserting an item in the queue when the internal array was already full. The second most common feature that caused problems was implementing equals() for the array-based implementation.

6.2 Dynamically Adjusting Timeouts

Of the 195 submissions that did show non-terminating behavior, 60% exceeded the timeout in only one or two of 82 test cases. In all of those situations, the adaptive strategy described here played no real role. The "one strike free" aspect of the strategy means that the timeout will not be adjusted downward the first time a test case exceeds the limit—the adjustment will only be performed when a *second* test case also exceeds the limit. That means the lower limit will only affect submissions that exceed the time limit on at least three test cases.

For the assignment we investigated, 7,273 (2.1%) of the test cases were executed with dynamically lowered timeout limits. Of these, only 248 exceeded the lowered limit. This suggests that although the rampdown factor of 0.5 cut the time limit in half for each successive test method that timed out (after the first), this factor is not necessarily overly aggressive, since relatively few test cases exceeded their dynamically reduced limits.

6.3 Total Execution Time

The principal motivation for using an adaptive strategy was to attempt to keep non-terminating programs from consuming an unduly large amount of execution time, in part because of generous end-to-end timeouts. In the CS2 assignment discussed here, submissions were originally processed using a 60-second end-to-end timeout. All non-terminating submissions used this full amount of time, and produced little or no feedback after being forcibly terminated. Did the adaptive strategy help?

First, consider overall running time. The 4,019 submissions that did not exhibit any infinite looping problems took an average of 0.25 seconds to execute all 82 test cases, although the maximum time was just over 42 seconds (!). Only 12 of those submissions took longer than one second to complete.

Of the 195 submissions with infinite looping behavior, however, the average time was 20.3 seconds. This average time makes sense, since only about one third of the submissions timed out on just a single test case, and all the others would have allowed a full ten seconds for both the first and the second non-terminating events before they began ramping down the time limit. This behavior suggests that the initial timeout setting and the "one strike free" allowance are closely related to the amount of extra time taken. Interestingly, the maximum time for any submission with infinite looping behavior was just over 40 seconds, suggesting that the upper limit was similar in both groups of submissions.

Overall, elapsed test run time indicates that the adaptive strategy kept end-to-end times manageable. All submissions that exhibited infinite looping behaviors completed in less time than when the single end-to-end timeout of 60 seconds was used. Further, the average end-to-end time was approximately twice the initial individual test case timeout, a natural consequence of the number of submissions that exceeded the timeout on only a small number of test cases, as well as the "one strike free" choice.

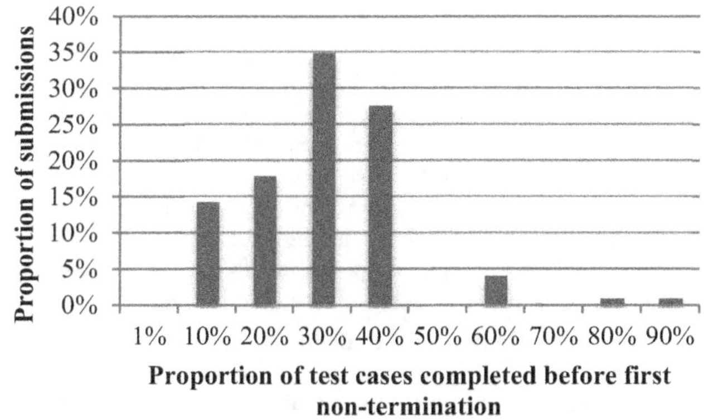

Figure 6: Fraction of test case results available before an infinite loop blocks a test run.

Most importantly, however, if a flat (non-adaptive) timeout were applied at the level of individual test cases, some of the non-terminating submissions would have taken significantly longer. From Figure 5, a small proportion (approximately 10%) of non-terminating submissions exceeded the time limit in six or more test cases—up to a maximum of 19. A non-adaptive limit on test cases would lead to a running time of over one minute for many of these submissions, with a worst-case scenario of over 190 seconds for the submission with the most errors. As a result, although a single end-to-end timeout has disadvantages, it is clear that a non-adaptive timeout applied to individual test cases also has undesirable properties in some circumstances, and that the adaptive strategy addresses these effectively.

6.4 Increased Feedback

Finally, one drawback to forcibly terminating test runs based on an end-to-end timeout is the limitations it places on test results. At most, one can receive results on only the test cases that successfully completed before the program got stuck in an infinite loop. At worst, you may lose all results if they are buffered. In fact, JUnit as used here does cause the worst-case behavior because of test result buffering, leading to the complete loss of all feedback when an end-to-end timeout forces early termination.

Hypothetically, under a different testing framework or with modifications to JUnit's listener structure, it may be possible to still report the results of test cases that complete before the first non-terminating test case. To examine this issue for the CS2 assignment used here, we examined how many test cases were successfully completed before the first non-terminating test case.

Figure 6 summarizes the proportion of the 82 test cases that were completed by the 195 submissions with timeout problems. On average, 34% of the test cases were successfully completed before the first non-terminating test case would block an end-to-end timeout strategy and force termination. That means that no results would be received for at least 66% of the test cases on average.

In comparison, the adaptive timeout strategy presented here lets later test cases run after an earlier test case fails to terminate. The result is that all test cases that do terminate get to run. So test cases where feedback is available include all terminating test cases. For the assignment used in this evaluation, submissions with non-terminating behavior still received full results on an average of 96% of test cases—only 4% of test cases (those that did not terminate) failed to receive results. With the original end-to-end timeout approach, no test results for any of these submissions were available, however—a 100% loss.

6.5 Experiences in the Classroom

As a result of our experimental evaluation, the adaptive timeout rule was deployed on Web-CAT for the Fall 2012 semester for use in the classroom, and employed in all courses that used Web-CAT for grading Java assignments during the 2012-2013 academic year. Experiences with live use by students submitting assignments corroborate the results from the experimental evaluation: students receive more feedback in the face of non-terminating code, and such non-terminating programs do not impose noticeable processing or feedback delays for students.

Based on the experimental evaluation, it appears that non-terminating code is fairly uncommon, and may not pose a serious issue for students. However, the adaptive timeout infrastructure detected and handled 8,926 non-terminating test cases during this period. Of these, 78% occurred in CS1-level courses (perhaps because of the higher volume of students at that level), compared to 22% in CS2 courses. Handling these cases eliminated at least 99.2 hours of cumulative delays in returning feedback to students. While infinite looping problems may be less common in practice, it is clear that smarter techniques for detecting and addressing them are beneficial.

7. CONCLUSION

While infinite loop problems are not the most frequent bugs that students encounter, they come up often enough that all programmers must learn to deal with them. In situations where student programs are automatically tested, a strategy for coping with infinite looping problems is important. The most common approach is to use a timeout, assuming that code that takes too long to complete has problems with proper termination.

However, using a single end-to-end timeout on an entire test suite poses issues, particularly when student work is automatically processed on a shared server. First, forcibly terminating a test run because it takes too long significantly impacts the results produced by that test run, reducing the information available to students and instructors. Second, using a "generous" end-to-end timeout may waste computing time that could be better spent on other tasks—like testing the work of other students.

To address these issues, we developed an adaptive timeout strategy that applies a dynamically variable time limit to each individual test case in a test suite. For programs that show non-terminating behavior, the time limit is automatically adjusted downward as the number of non-terminating tests increase in order to keep the overall running time from growing too large. At the same time, code that is "slow" but does properly terminate is handled by dynamically increasing the time limit on test cases.

Our implementation of this strategy built on useful features of JUnit 4, but also required us to find a practical way of bringing that support to JUnit 3 users. The net result is a custom test runner that allows JUnit 3 tests to be run with all the support provided to JUnit 4 users, and that automatically injects the adaptive timeout test rule into all test suites without requiring any changes to student code or to instructor-written tests.

Applying this strategy to a CS2 data structure implementation assignment provided many opportunities for students to exercise their loop writing skills, and resulted in a wide variety of non-termination behaviors in student work. Examining these student programs indicates that **nearly one quarter of the students** had trouble with non-termination at some point on the assignment, although nearly all of them repaired these problems before finishing. When they did have problems, however, their programs typically exhibited non-termination on only a few test cases. At the same time, the adaptive strategy discussed here ensured that test results could be reported for all terminating tests, and that overall end-to-end time was restricted to a range similar to properly terminating solutions, even when timeouts were violated.

By deploying this solution full-scale on Web-CAT, we saw a large number of non-terminating test cases during the past academic year. Proper handling of these non-termination events led to a measurable reduction in the cumulative amount of feedback waiting time across all students during the academic year. As a result, this strategy appears to be a beneficial advance over simpler end-to-end timeout schemes, so as those used by most automated grading systems. By providing this support in a grading tool, the large existing user base has been able to immediately take advantage of this work. In the future, we plan to do more investigative work to appropriately tune the default settings for the parameters to the adaptive timeout model.

8. REFERENCES

[1] J. Burnim, et al., Looper: Lightweight detection of infinite loops at runtime, in *Proceedings of the 2009 IEEE/ACM International Conference on Automated Software Engineering*, 2009.

[2] A. Gupta, et al., Proving non-termination, in *Proceedings of the 35th Annual ACM SIGPLAN-SIGACT Symposium on Principles of Programming Languages*, San Francisco, California, USA, 2008.

[3] K. Sen, et al., CUTE: A concolic unit testing engine for C, *SIGSOFT Softw. Eng. Notes,* vol. 30, pp. 263-272, 2005.

[4] H. Velroyen and P. Rümmer, *Non-termination Checking for Imperative Programs Tests and Proofs*. vol. 4966, B. Beckert and R. Hähnle, Eds., ed: Springer Berlin / Heidelberg, 2008, pp. 154-170.

[5] V. Efopoulos, et al., WIPE: A programming environment for novices, *SIGCSE Bull.,* vol. 37, pp. 113-117, 2005.

[6] G. H. B. Roberts and J. L. M. Verbyla, An online programming assessment tool, in *Proceedings of the 5th Australasian Conference on Computing Education*, Adelaide, Australia, 2003.

[7] D. S. Morris, Automatic grading of student's programming assignments: An interactive process and suite of programs, in *Frontiers in Education, 2003. FIE 2003 33rd Annual*, 2003, pp. S3F-1-6 vol.3.

[8] J. Spacco, et al., Software repository mining with Marmoset: An automated programming project snapshot and testing system, in *Proceedings of the 2005 International Workshop on Mining Software Repositories*, St. Louis, Missouri, 2005.

[9] M. Striewe and M. Goedicke, Using run time traces in automated programming tutoring, in *Proceedings of the 16th Annual Joint Conference on Innovation and Technology in Computer Science Education*, Darmstadt, Germany, 2011.

[10] S. H. Edwards, Rethinking computer science education from a test-first perspective, in *Companion to the 18th Annual ACM SIGPLAN Conference on Object-oriented Programming, Systems, Languages, and Applications*, Anaheim, CA, USA, 2003.

[11] D. Jackson and M. Usher, Grading student programs using ASSYST, *SIGCSE Bull.,* vol. 29, pp. 335-339, 1997.

[12] S. Sankaran. JUnit 3 & JUnit 4: Oil & water. *Technophilia*. 13 (Feb. 2009).

[13] George, G. Enhancing JUnit with default timeouts and stack traces. *Attivio*. 17 (Mar. 2009).

Can Computers Compare Student Code Solutions as Well as Teachers?

Matheus Gaudencio
Software Practices Laboratory
Universidade Federal de Campina Grande
Zip Code: 58429-900
Campina Grande, PB, Brazil
matheusgr@copin.ufcg.edu.br

Ayla Dantas
Departamento de Ciências Exatas
Universidade Federal da Paraíba – Campus IV
Zip Code: 58297-000
Rio Tinto, PB, Brazil
ayla@dce.ufpb.br

Dalton D. S. Guerrero
Software Practices Laboratory
Universidade Federal de Campina Grande
Zip Code: 58429-900
Campina Grande, PB, Brazil
dalton@dsc.ufcg.edu.br

ABSTRACT

In introductory programming courses it is common to demand from students exercises based on the production of code. However, it is difficult for the teacher to give fast feedback to the students about the main solutions tried, the main errors and the drawbacks and advantages of certain solutions. If we could use automatic code comparison algorithms to build visualisation tools to support the teacher in analysing how each solution provided is similar or different from another, such information would be able to be rapidly obtained. However, can computers compare students code solutions as well as teachers? In this work we present an experiment in which we have requested teachers to compare different code solutions to the same problem. Then we have evaluated the level of agreement among each teacher comparison strategy and some algorithms generally used for plagiarism detection and automatic grading. We found out a maximum rate of 77% of agreement between one of the teachers and the algorithms, but a minimum agreement of 75%. However, for most of the teachers, the maximum agreement rate was over 90% for at least one of the automatic strategies to compare code. We have also detected that the level of agreement among teachers regarding their personal strategies to compare students solutions was between 62% and 95%, which shows that there may be more agreement between a teacher and an algorithm than between a teacher and one of her colleagues regarding their strategies to compare students' solutions. The results also seem to support that comparison of students' codes has significant potential to be automated to help teachers in their work.

Categories and Subject Descriptors

K.3.2 [**Computer Science and Information Science Education**]: Computer science education

SIGCSE'14, March 5–8, 2014, Atlanta, Georgia, USA.

http://dx.doi.org/10.1145/2538862.2538973.

General Terms

Algorithms

Keywords

Programming, CS1, Code Comparison Algorithms

1. INTRODUCTION

Teaching introductory courses of programming is a challenge and a great concern on computer education research. Sahami et. al [7] argue that programming skills are currently a basic and important requirement to understand and work with computer related activities. However, teaching such topic is often a hard task. Not only must a teacher understand what her students think but she also needs to receive and provide good and fast feedback in order to get better results considering the learning process.

According to Chamillard and Joiner [1], tasks that require code production are the most used way that teachers and tutors apply to assess the student knowledge in programming courses. When evaluating students codes we often see different solutions for the same problem. Even the same student can give solutions that are not so similar. Each solution may present distinct positive qualities that, with discussion, can improve programming learning.

Despite the potential diversity of codes, solutions for the same task often can be grouped by similarity of their approaches. For instance, one group of codes may use a 'while' instruction as the repetition control structure while others may have used a 'for' to achieve the same goal. By understanding how student solutions are related, i. e. what their differences and similarities are, as well as how close they are from known solutions, a teacher would be in a much better position to properly discuss the problem in classroom and to give feedback to her students. Nevertheless, the identification of such relations is not trivial and a fast feedback is desirable. Since it is not easy to analyse even one code, the comparison and identification of relations on a small set of codes may impose a prohibitive time cost causing a missed educational opportunity.

In this work we evaluated how automatic strategies and teachers of introductory courses in Python compare different code solutions. We test the hypothesis that **there is a high agreement in the way automatic strategies and teachers compare different code solutions**. If there is a good way to automatically compare code, such information can be used to reduce that burden from the teacher, allowing her to concentrate on using that information to improve students performance. The same result and also the methodology used on this work can be proven of great value to related researches that rely on code comparison.

We tested our hypothesis by asking 11 teachers and executing 7 automatic strategies to compare 40 triples of code. In each triple, one code is chosen to be a reference code. Then, each teacher and automatic strategy must decide which of the other 2 codes is more similar to the reference one. They could also choose both codes as equally similar (or equally different) to the reference code. Then we calculated the agreement of choices made by each teacher to the choices evaluated by each automatic strategy. If a teacher and an automatic strategy always make the same choice for the same triple of code, we have a 100% rate of agreement between them.

We take those automatic strategies from the research on plagiarism detection [6] and automatic grading [5]. Each automatic strategy works by comparing two codes and defining a similarity score (between 0 and 1, where 0=totally different and 1=totally similar). One of such techniques is the Jaccard index of token set [8]. For two codes, the Jaccard index is calculated by the length of common programming language syntax tokens over the size of all tokens in both codes. When comparing two codes with a reference code, the code that has the highest Jaccard index with the reference code is the one more similar to it unless the difference of both calculated Jaccard index is lower than a given threshold. If so, we can say that both codes are equally similar (or different) to the reference code.

There isn't a default threshold to define how each automatic strategy should choose when two codes are equally similar (or different) to a reference code. In our work we also evaluate the impact of different thresholds in the agreement level of each pair of teacher and automatic strategy. We found that three strategies presented a high level of agreement (between 92% and 97%) with 6 teachers.

However, we do not always find this high level of agreement. One of the subjects that was evaluated achieved a maximum of 77% of agreement with all evaluated automatic strategies. The same teacher, could only have at most a 72% rate of agreement with another teacher. We can say that some of the evaluated strategies may be able to mimic how teachers compare codes. Also, this is not applicable to all teachers with the same degree of success. We explain each of those results in the analysis section of this paper.

This paper is organized as follows. We initially discuss current research on plagiarism detection and automatic grading and how they relates to this work. Then we present the methodology used to test our hypothesis and the results of our experiment. After that, we present a discussion about the results obtained. Finally we argue about threats to the validity of this work, and show our conclusions and future work.

2. RELATED WORK

In this work, we use similarity detection algorithms to compare different code solutions to a given introductory programming problem. The use of this technique is not novel and has been explored in automatic grading of programming assignments and in plagiarism detection. While the former focus is on how to provide an automatic grade feedback for students, the latter tries to detect assignments that are very likely to be a copy in a pairwise comparison.

Automatic grading studies like Naudé [5] only show the relation of references solutions to the students codes. So, two solutions that received the same grade can be really different from each other. By identifying how all codes are related, our work allows the teacher to take any student code as a possible reference solution and to visualize how close/far are the other solutions to these ones. Besides, it becomes simpler to discover the most popular solutions.

Our work is closely related to studies in plagiarism detection, as they also focus in pairwise comparisons. However, we have a different purpose. The first studies in plagiarism detection used extracted software metrics from codes to be used on copy detections [2]. Later works focused on similarity detection based on syntax and semantic elements to do the same task. Roy [6] survey evaluated how different techniques of similarity detection act in a synthetic created set of codes. Roy's evaluation and the evaluation of plagiarism related works only focused on seeing how clones are detected and thus only analysed codes that are almost identical.

We try to fill the gap about constructing and detecting code relations among all codes for a given assignment and easily visualising how different or similar are all the solutions provided by students.

3. EVALUATING HOW TEACHERS AND ALGORITHMS COMPARE CODES

Most of the work on similarity detection only focus on how good are such algorithms in the detection of plagiarism or automatic grading. For instance, given two solutions x and y and a similarity score function $\text{Score}(x, y) \rightarrow \{s | s \in [0, 1]\}$, s represents the similarity score (1 meaning identical clones). Plagiarism research only evaluates how good the similarity score works on codes A and B that have $\text{Score}(A, B) \sim 1$. Automatic grading only focus on how effective is the Score function for a given code of reference G. We take another direction by allowing that any code can be seen as a reference solution as this is important when a teacher observes all students solutions and wants to give a class about the main types of solutions provided and how appropriate or not they are.

To identify if algorithms make comparisons between students code solutions as well as teachers, we have evaluated the output of each individual teacher or algorithm to the SIMILAR function. We have defined this function in the following way: Given a triple of codes (C_1, R, C_2), the output of the SIMILAR function should be: -1 if code C_1 is more similar to R than C_2 for this teacher or algorithm; 1 if code C_2 is more similar to R than C_1; and 0 if codes C_1 and C_2 are considered equally similar or different than R by the teacher or algorithm.

Notice that by defining SIMILAR we can be able to do a much more precise comparison among codes than asking for each teacher to evaluate a score function for a pair of codes. It's more consistent, less error prone, and easy to ask which code is more similar of two pairs of code than to ask for a given value between 0 and 1 for each pair of code.

By comparing outputs of the SIMILAR function for the same set of inputs, we can calculate agreement (p_0) among teachers and between a teacher and an algorithm. Agree-

Figure 1: Screenshot of our web application that asks a teacher to compare three codes.

ment is defined as the number of equal outputs evaluated over the number of total outputs. For instance, if there is 100% agreement between a teacher and an algorithm, that means that both SIMILAR functions give the same outputs for the same inputs. This also means that this teacher probably follows a similar strategy to this algorithm to compare students code solutions.

3.1 Evaluation of the Way Teachers Compare Students' Code Solutions

In our evaluation, we initially observed the results provided to the SIMILAR function considering 11 teachers. The teacher had to choose which of two solutions, C_1 and C_2, is more similar to a given reference solution R. Alternatively, the teacher could say she considers both C_1 and C_2 equally similar to R. The teachers evaluation was performed through a web application that presented R at the middle of the page and two codes C_1 and C_2 at each side, as illustrated by the screenshot presented in Figure 1. Below each solution there was a button to allow the teacher to choose which code is more similar to R. If both C_1 and C_2 are equally similar (or different) the user could press the button in the middle. Hotkeys were also made available for the teachers to perform this evaluation.

The solutions code set used for the evaluation was created by taking a known assignment from introductory programming courses (the Fibonacci series problem) and creating a synthetic base of codes using well defined variations used on the research about plagiarism detection by Roy et al. [6]. The statement of our problem was the following:

> Given the Fibonacci series (0, 1, 1, 2, 3, 5, 8, ...), where the value of each term is devised from the sum of the two previous numbers (except the two first terms at indexes 0 and 1). Create a program that receives as input two numbers **A** and **B** (for $2 \leq a < b$) representing indexes and that produces all Fibonacci numbers in the series between (and including) indexes A and B.

We created three base solutions for this assignment. Those three solutions are shown at Figure 2. The first solution used a function to explicitly calculate the fibonacci number. The second solution used a recursive function to achieve the same result and the third solution used only one function instead of two.

Table 1: Description of Codes Variations

var	description
s0a	Base solution
s1a	Used 2 tabs as indentation instead of 1 tab
s2a	One variable name changed
s2b	One variable name changed and function parameters swapped
s2d	A new null arithmetic operation is added
s3a	New parameter added to a function
s3b	One parameter removed from a function (two parameters became a tuple)
s3c	Added a conditional flow (but it is always true) when calling the main function
s3d	Two lines combined in one
s3e	Added a conditional flow inside a block of code
s4b	Swapped two lines
s4d	Using an while op instead of a for

To synthetically construct other solutions that students could possibly provide, we considered Roy et al.'s work on plagiarism research. This work presents a series of variations that occurs on cases of plagiarism. Since we used python code, not all code variations where applicable (for example, changes on value types or type definitions). We used the variations defined on Table 1.

With these 12 defined variations (the base solution being one of them), we created a set of 36 codes considering the three base solutions illustrated by Table 1.

For our experiment, 8 different solutions were randomly chosen as reference codes (the R to be used for the SIMILAR function evaluation). For each reference code, 5 pairs of solutions C_1 and C_2 were also randomly chosen. After this process, each of these pairs represent the C_1 and C_2 values to be used. After this process, we have got 40 triples. The only restriction for creating these triples was that $R \neq C_1 \neq C_2$.

3.2 Evaluation of the Way Automatic Strategies Compare Students' Code Solutions

In order to investigate if automatic strategies (similarity detection algorithms) compare students code solutions like teachers, we have evaluated the results produced for the SIMILAR function considering each algorithm and the same 40 triples of codes that have been submitted for the teachers. The output for this function was obtained using the Score function and defining a threshold Δ for each algorithm that is used to determine when two codes C_1 and C_2 should be considered equally similar/different from a code R. This way, the output of the SIMILAR function for each algorithm was computed in the following way:

$$\begin{cases} 1 & \text{if } \text{Score}(C_1, R) - \text{Score}(C_2, R) > \Delta \\ -1 & \text{if } \text{Score}(C_1, R) - \text{Score}(C_2, R) < -\Delta \\ 0 & \text{if } |\text{Score}(C_1, R) - \text{Score}(C_2, R)| \leq \Delta \end{cases}$$

We don't know beforehand which Δ value is more adequate. Considering a given strategy of comparison, if a teacher considers that a small difference in code is not relevant to create really different solutions, a small Δ value could decrease the agreement between a teacher and an algorithm since the former will have more 0 as outputs for

```
def fib(x):
    f_i = 0
    f_j = 1
    for step in xrange(2, x + 1):
        f_i, f_j = f_j, f_i + f_j
    return f_j

def main(x, y):
    for step in xrange(x, y + 1):
        print fib(step)

input_a = int(raw_input())
input_b = int(raw_input())

main(input_a, input_b)
```

```
def fib(x):
    if x in [1, 2]:
        return 1
    return fib(x - 2) + fib(x - 1)

def main(x, y):
    for step in xrange(x, y + 1):
        print fib(step)

input_a = int(raw_input())
input_b = int(raw_input())

main(input_a, input_b)
```

```
def main(x, y):
    f_i = 0
    f_j = 1

    for step in range(2, y + 1):
        f_i, f_j = f_j, f_i + f_j
        if step >= x:
            print f_j

input_a = int(raw_input())
input_b = int(raw_input())

main(input_a, input_b)
```

Figure 2: Base code solutions.

the SIMILAR function than the automatic strategy. On the other hand, when we increase Δ value, we are increasing the number of 0 outputs for the SIMILAR function of an automatic strategy. So, for each pair of teacher and algorithm there will be an optimum value for Δ that would allow an automatic strategy to best capture how a teacher compares codes and how a teacher decides whether two codes are equally different or similar to another one.

We used 7 well known automatic strategies of similarity detection. All of those strategies are based upon on the syntax tokens extracted from the Abstract Syntax Tree of a Python code. There are other strategies that use the Call Flow Graph and/or semantic properties of code but that were not explored here due to the codes' simplicity that we expect from introductory course assignments.

One of the automatic strategies used was the Jaccard distance, which is calculated by the length of common tokens over the size of all tokens in both codes (Jaccard) [8]. Then we use two similarity strategies that take the token order in consideration when calculating the similarity score: i) the text edition distance (text) [3] and ii) the tree edition distance (Zhang-Shasha) [9]. The latter will try to swap lines of code before comparing how distant tokens are.

We also used 4 well known variations of term frequency (TF) distance algorithms. Each one will create a TF vector for each code and calculate the distance between those vectors using the cosine distance. The four variations define how each TF is created: 1) normal count of terms from codes (TFIDF-NNC using the SMART [4] notation); 2) the augmented count of term frequency that takes in account each frequency according to the max frequency of a document (TFIDF-ANC); 3) the binary count of terms that will set the frequency of a term as 1 if it is present and 0 otherwise (TFIDF-BNC), and; 4) log average of term frequencies TFIDF-LNC.

It is important to know that each human evaluator may possibly try different strategies of code comparisons that may possibly mimic those automatic strategies evaluated. For instance, if one teacher considers only what keywords were used in each code to compare them, we expect a high agreement with a TFIDF-BNC strategy. If only a few tokens of low frequency are important, then a TFIDF-LNC strategy is more relevant to this teacher. If order of elements is the teacher strategy to compare codes, then a high agreement with tree or text edition will exist.

4. RESULTS AND DISCUSSION

To evaluate the level of agreement between the way humans and automatic strategies compare codes, we first evaluated the SIMILAR function with the 40 randomly chosen triples considering each of the 11 teachers that participated in our experiment. Then, for each pair of teacher and automatic strategy we found Δ value that would allow each automatic strategy' SIMILAR function to better capture how teachers compare codes.

We can see the agreement and Δ values between automatic strategies and teachers on Table 2. We found that different pairs of teachers and automatic strategies may present different Δ values but that value is always lower than 0.20. For 6 teachers, the automatic strategy based on Jaccard distance has provided the best agreement. For 3 teachers, the automatic strategy based on Tree edition distance is what matters most.

To understand the presence of different Δ values, we looked how each teacher defines the SIMILAR function. We counted the number of choices where both codes are equally similar/different (output 0) for the 40 evaluated triples of code and present this information in Figure 3. When is frequent for a teacher to choose two codes as equally similar (or different), than greater is the Δ value needed for some automatic strategy to compare codes like that teacher.

Since teachers choose different outputs for the SIMILAR function, there is disagreement between their choices regarding the most similar code among C1 and C2. Table 3 presents the agreement level between each pair of teachers and also the best level of agreement between each teacher and one of the automatic strategies analyzed. While the agreement between teachers ranges from 62% to 95%, the agreement between the evaluated algorithms and teachers is always over 75%.

Overall, our experiment found that teachers don't have a very high level of agreement among them in the first place. Some of them consider a large Δ when defining when two codes are equaly different or similar to a reference code and some are more sensitive regarding what is considered a significant difference. For 6 teachers, we could achieve a level of agreement over 92% regarding an strategy and using an op-

Table 2: Agreement and Δ Values Between Automatic Strategies and Teachers

		A	B	C	D	E	F	G	H	I	J	K
jaccard	p_o	0.97	0.92	0.92	0.87	0.92	0.87	0.75	0.85	0.97	0.92	0.80
	Δ	0.08	0.04	0.04	0.03	0.05	0.17	0.05	0.02	0.17	0.17	0.04
tree	p_o	0.95	0.95	0.90	0.82	0.95	0.82	0.75	0.87	0.95	0.90	0.75
	Δ	0.20	0.06	0.04	0.04	0.06	0.12	0.04	0.07	0.20	0.20	0.04
text	p_o	0.95	0.92	0.90	0.82	0.92	0.82	0.75	0.87	0.95	0.90	0.75
	Δ	0.20	0.06	0.07	0.07	0.06	0.11	0.15	0.04	0.20	0.20	0.04
NNC	p_o	0.87	0.87	0.90	0.82	0.87	0.82	0.77	0.80	0.87	0.85	0.72
	Δ	0.01	0.01	0.01	0.01	0.01	0.01	0.02	0.01	0.04	0.16	0.01
ANC	p_o	0.92	0.85	0.85	0.85	0.87	0.85	0.77	0.80	0.90	0.85	0.80
	Δ	0.08	0.06	0.08	0.07	0.08	0.08	0.07	0.01	0.08	0.08	0.10
BNC	p_o	0.92	0.85	0.85	0.85	0.85	0.85	0.77	0.80	0.90	0.85	0.82
	Δ	0.06	0.06	0.06	0.06	0.06	0.09	0.01	0.06	0.09	0.09	0.09
LNC	p_o	0.92	0.87	0.85	0.82	0.85	0.82	0.77	0.80	0.92	0.87	0.80
	Δ	0.04	0.04	0.10	0.05	0.04	0.08	0.04	0.05	0.09	0.10	0.08

Table 3: Agreement Between Teachers and with the Best Algorithm

	A	B	C	D	E	F	G	H	I	J	K
A	-	0.85	0.85	0.85	0.82	0.80	0.70	0.72	0.95	0.90	0.80
B	0.85	-	0.90	0.78	0.90	0.80	0.68	0.88	0.85	0.88	0.72
C	0.85	0.90	-	0.82	0.90	0.75	0.70	0.88	0.80	0.82	0.75
D	0.85	0.78	0.82	-	0.78	0.78	0.70	0.80	0.80	0.78	0.75
E	0.82	0.90	0.90	0.78	-	0.80	0.72	0.88	0.82	0.85	0.75
F	0.80	0.80	0.75	0.78	0.80	-	0.68	0.75	0.85	0.85	0.72
G	0.70	0.68	0.70	0.70	0.72	0.68	-	0.62	0.65	0.68	0.62
H	0.72	0.88	0.88	0.80	0.88	0.75	0.62	-	0.72	0.75	0.68
I	0.95	0.85	0.82	0.80	0.82	0.85	0.65	0.72	-	0.95	0.80
J	0.90	0.88	0.85	0.78	0.85	0.85	0.68	0.75	0.95	-	0.80
K	0.80	0.72	0.75	0.75	0.75	0.72	0.62	0.68	0.80	0.80	-
Best Alg	0.97	0.95	0.92	0.87	0.95	0.87	0.77	0.87	0.97	0.92	0.82

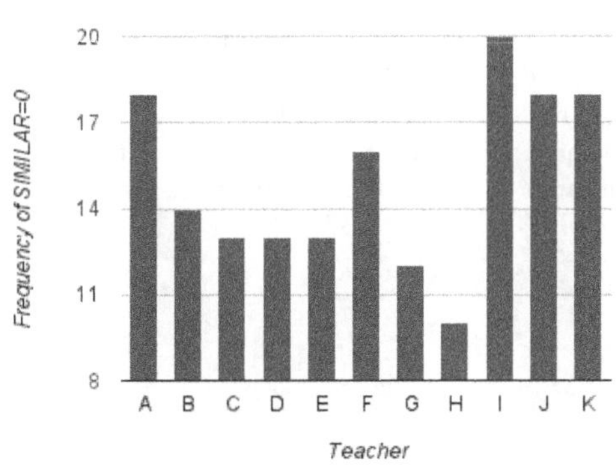

Figure 3: Frequency of choices where SIMILAR=0 for each teacher.

timal Δ. Three strategies proved to be superior for them: i) Jaccard distance; ii) Text edition distance, and; iii) Tree edition distance. For 5 other theachers we found that our evaluated automatic strategies achieved an agreement of 77% - 87%.

Since automatic strategies were able to compare codes almost like some teachers, we created a prototype of a tool that would allow us to visualize in a graph the main kinds of solutions tried. In this graph, the distance between each node represents how similar or different is each kind of solution regarding another one. We also use delta as a threshold to join neighbour nodes which represents how sensitive should be the algorithm regarding small changes. In Figure 4 we can see an example of a graph generated by our prototype using Jaccard distance and $\Delta = 0.05$ to evaluate the 36 codes that we used on our experiment. By clicking in each node, the prototype user would be able to see the different code solutions provided from the groups visualised. The idea of the visualisation tool is to provide default visualisations (with a given algorithm and delta) but also to allow the teacher to choose among different ones and adjust the delta value.

5. THREATS TO VALIDITY

We acknowledge that we only tested such automatic strategies for one assignment. Nevertheless, this assignment is a common exercise used in introductory programming courses.

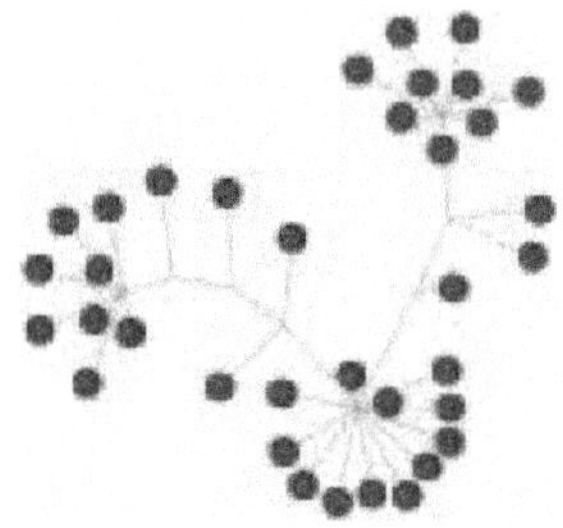

Figure 4: Visualization of codes comparison for Jaccard distance strategy with $\Delta = 0.05$.

We choose an assignment that could explore three different base solutions but would also present variations that impose disadvantages to automatic strategies. Even in this scenario we found a better agreement between automatic strategies and teachers (75% 97%) than among teachers (62% 95%) which indicates that automatic strategies can be used to compare codes.

We acknowledge that there are thousands of teachers of introductory programming courses. However, our small subset allows us to say that there may be some disagreement when they want to decide which and what codes are more similar/different.

Our last threat to validity is the chosen programming language. Python may impose different issues for automatic strategies than when we deal with another language. Nonetheless, we expected that some teachers from introductory courses that use another language could achieve the same success that we had. This is possible because problems exposed for students of introductory courses are simple enough to not be overworked by syntax and semantic details of a programming language.

6. CONCLUSIONS AND FUTURE WORK

This paper describes an experiment to evaluate if automatic strategies can compare students' code solutions like teachers. We used a sound methodology and found out that for the code set used there was agreement in the way teachers and some algorithms generally used for plagiarism detection and automatic grading compare code. Sometimes this agreement is even greater than the agreement between teachers. However, this depends on the algorithm chosen, as it reflects the strategy each teacher uses to make a comparison between her students' codes. Besides, the level of agreement also depends on how sensible should be the algorithm to detect small differences (the Δ chosen), which is also a factor that varies from one teacher to another.

As future work we plan to evaluate future versions of our visualisation tool prototype regarding its use by teachers and different programming exercises. The idea is to explore visualisations of students' solutions using a default algorithm (such as Jaccard) and Δ but also other visualisations obtained by allowing the teachers to adjust these parameters. We also plan to evaluate the impact on the students learning process of allowing them to use such visualisation tool to see their colleagues solutions and easily compare them with the solutions she has provided.

7. ACKNOWLEDGEMENTS

This project was financially supported by Departamento de Polícia Federal (Brazil) through project e-Pol and by CAPES (Brazil).

8. REFERENCES

[1] A. Chamillard and K. A. Braun. Evaluating programming ability in an introductory computer science course. *ACM SIGCSE Bulletin*, 32(1):212–216, 2000.

[2] J. L. Donaldson, A.-M. Lancaster, and P. H. Sposato. A plagiarism detection system. In *ACM SIGCSE Bulletin*, volume 13, pages 21–25. ACM, 1981.

[3] C. D. Manning, P. Raghavan, and H. Schütze. *Introduction to Information Retrieval*. Cambridge University Press, New York, NY, USA, 2008.

[4] C. D. Manning, P. Raghavan, and H. Schütze. *Introduction to information retrieval*, volume 1. Cambridge University Press Cambridge, 2008.

[5] K. A. Naudé. *Assessing program code through static structural similarity*. PhD thesis, Nelson Mandela Metropolitan University, jan 2007.

[6] C. K. Roy. *Detection and analysis of near-miss software clones*. PhD thesis, Kingston, Ont., Canada, Canada, 2009. AAINR65337.

[7] M. Sahami, S. Roach, E. Cuadros-Vargas, and R. LeBlanc. Acm/ieee-cs computer science curriculum 2013: reviewing the ironman report. In *Proceeding of the 44th ACM technical symposium on Computer science education*, pages 13–14. ACM, 2013.

[8] P.-N. Tan, M. Steinbach, and V. Kumar. *Introduction to Data Mining, (First Edition)*. Addison-Wesley Longman Publishing Co., Inc., Boston, MA, USA, 2005.

[9] K. Zhang and D. Shasha. Simple fast algorithms for the editing distance between trees and related problems. *SIAM J. Comput.*, 18(6):1245–1262, Dec. 1989.

An Experience Report on Using Gamification in Technical Higher Education

Alexandru Iosup
Parallel and Distributed Systems Group
Delft University of Technology
Mekelweg 4, 2628CD Delft,
The Netherlands
A.Iosup@tudelft.nl

Dick Epema
Parallel and Distributed Systems Group
Delft University of Technology
Mekelweg 4, 2628CD Delft,
The Netherlands
D.H.J.Epema@tudelft.nl

ABSTRACT

Technical universities, especially in Europe, are facing an important challenge in attracting more diverse groups of students, and in keeping the students they attract motivated and engaged in the curriculum. We describe our experience with gamification, which we loosely define as a teaching technique that uses social gaming elements to deliver higher education. Over the past three years, we have applied gamification to undergraduate and graduate courses in a leading technical university in the Netherlands and in Europe. Ours is one of the first long-running attempts to show that gamification can be used to teach technically challenging courses. The two gamification-based courses, the first-year B.Sc. course Computer Organization and an M.Sc.-level course on the emerging technology of Cloud Computing, have been cumulatively followed by over 450 students and passed by over 75% of them, at the first attempt. We find that gamification is correlated with an increase in the percentage of passing students, and in the participation in voluntary activities and challenging assignments. Gamification seems to also foster interaction in the classroom and trigger students to pay more attention to the design of the course. We also observe very positive student assessments and volunteered testimonials, and a Teacher of the Year award.

Categories and Subject Descriptors

K.3.2 [**Computer and Information Science Education**]: Computer science education; C.0 [**Computer Systems Organization**]: General—*System architectures*; C.1.0 [**Computer Systems Organization**]: Processor Architectures—*General*; H.3.4 [**Information Systems**]: Systems and Software—*Distributed systems*

Keywords

CS Ed research; gamification; experience report

1. INTRODUCTION

SIGCSE'14, March 3–8, 2014, Atlanta, GA, USA.

http://dx.doi.org/10.1145/2538862.2538899.

Technical higher education, in Europe and in many other parts of the world, is at a crossroad. The pace and complexity of technological progress, the economic pressure, and the cultural changes occurring over the past century have increased the need for a well-educated body of technical-university graduates. However, from the 2000s and onwards the number of students who enroll has started to decrease and the percentage of students who finish their studies in time has decreased. In the Netherlands, under 40% of the students enrolled in technical universities in the three-year B.Sc. curriculum finish in less than *four* years. In several European countries, including the Netherlands, the quality of education in sciences, especially mathematics, at pre-university levels has decreased significantly over the past decade[1]. Concurrently, students in South Korea, etc., are pressured into completing their courses not only on time, but also with top grades. In this context, an approach that balances between laxity and strictness is desirable. Towards this end, we present in this work an approach to teach computer science courses in technical universities that is based on gamification, that is, on using social gaming elements in the design of undergraduate or graduate courses.

Gamification may have originated in the early-Communist thought and matured in the Soviet era [15], as a substitute for monetary incentives to perform at work, and saw a re-emergence in the U.S. in the early 1980s [14]. More recently, in the 2000s gamification received various definitions [6, 11], and was used with promising results in various curricular [7, 4] and organizational [8, 15] settings.

However much already applied, for example to engage university students in a limited setting [7], gamification is not easy to apply to a new topic. For example, giving students points may foster competition and incentivize them to study harder, but it may also diminish their intrinsic motivation and (when points are not well balanced) make them feel discriminated against. The vast array of gaming elements available to designers [3], the loose theories of fun [13], and the contradictory evidence regarding the use of gamification in practice, make applying gamification in higher education a challenging task. Thus, we have set to investigate the following main research question *Can gamification be effective in teaching higher-education courses?*

[1]Dijsselbloem Committee (2008) End report to Parliamentary investigation (2007–2008), Dutch Government, Second Chamber Report.

We have applied gamification to the design of two courses in university-level computer science, both taught at `GamificationU`, which is one of the leading universities in the Netherlands and in Europe. Chronologically, the first of these courses is a first-year undergraduate course on Computer Organization that matches the Architecture and Organization (AR) knowledge area in the ACM/IEEE CS2013 curriculum [1]. We have taught a gamification-based version of this course for three consecutive years, since the academic year 2010–2011. The second of the two courses is an M.Sc.-level (graduate) course on Cloud Computing, which we have taught during the academic year 2012-2013. In total, we have educated using gamification over 450 students, of which over 75% have completed the course. Although we agree that gamification cannot solve the intrinsic problems of education units, such as poor course content and inadequate teaching skills, we find that it can lead to better course experience for the students and to better overall course outcomes.

With the two gamified courses, we have followed a variety of *instructional goals*. Our primary goal was to develop curriculum elements related to computer science education in systems at undergraduate and graduate level, especially focusing on parallel and distributed systems courses (PDC). Firstly, we have tried to help our students gain experience with system design. Understanding the relationship between abstract architectures and real-world implementation is difficult to acquire at all ages, but, for first-year students, it can be dispiriting and may be a cause for quitting studies. Secondly, we have attempted to foster learning of topics that are challenging technically, and broad and possibly also deep conceptually. The natural consequence, which we have observed first-hand in the Netherlands for the past decade, is a high failure rate among students. Thirdly, scalability and elasticity are some of the most long-lasting, challenging problems in computer science [12, 2, 10], and we are trying to educate students about them early on (the first-year undergraduate course) or in-depth (the M.Sc.-level course). Fourthly, to make the courses more relevant to emerging computer science topics [5], we have added to the undergraduate course elements of GPU architecture and programming, and, to both courses, elements of or a focus on distributed/cloud computing architecture and programming.

Towards answering the main research question, our contribution is fourfold:

1. We introduce a gamification toolbox for academic-level computer science (Section 2).
2. We design two gamification-based courses, which together cover a variety of desirable instructional goals (Section 3).
3. We approach gamification through an empirical method (Section 4). For three years, we have taught hundred of students who succeeded more than usual. We use passing ratios, participation counts, and results of evaluation surveys to quantify the effectiveness of using gamification in teaching our courses.
4. We summarize the lessons we have learned in applying gamification in academic-level CS education (Section 5). Our lessons are personal, but hopefully educative: we made mistakes, encountered student and organizational resistance, and read eye-opening student testimonials of how gamification has changed the life of our students.

2. COURSE GAMIFICATION TOOLBOX

In this section we analyze gamification as an education technique. We see gamification as using social gaming elements, such as team-work, game thinking, and game mechanics, in non-game environments (here, higher education). The main promise of gamification is that it gives the educator a number of powerful and predictable tools for influencing human motivation and behavior and, when done right, to activate various types of students in pursuing learning activities. The main challenge is to make technically and conceptually challenging courses interesting for classroom of students with various personalities and skill-levels. We describe in the following 4 types of students (Section 2.1) and 7 core tools for course gamification (Section 2.2).

2.1 Player Classes

The astute professor needs to understand and cater to different student skill-levels and personalities. We propose that skill can be assessed dynamically, via tests offered during the operation of the course, and that personality (or motivation) can be understood within the framework of four primary player-motivations defined by Bartle [3]:

1. *Explorers* are players who enjoy understanding the world–the student who is curious. Designing courses for these students is challenging for the educator, as students are interested in both the quality and the quantity of the material.
2. *Achievers* enjoy completing most of the challenges they are presented with. These are our ambitious, high-achieving students, who would strive not only to pass the course, but also to achieve at least a grade of 80%.
3. *Socializers* participate in the game mainly because other players, in particular players like them, also do. Passing the course is interesting for them, if it allows them to continue being part of the same social circle.
4. *Winners* (*Killers* in Bartle's taxonomy) want to complete challenges at the expense of other players. For them, a challenge is good if it can only have one winner (preferably themselves). Many of the top-percentile students could belong to this category. Winners may be self-destructive, in that competitiveness may push them into burn-out, depression, or boredom.

Bartle also finds [3] that any long-running game community needs players from every personality type. In particular, he finds that winners and achievers are classes of players without whom game ecosystems cannot survive. In this model, a classroom without the participation of top students quickly collapses, in both level and attendance.

2.2 Seven Core Tools for Course Gamification

Our current approach for gamification of education units fits within the framework of Zichermann and Cunningham [17]. For them, as for many traditional theorists of computer games, games contain mechanics, dynamics, and aesthetics. *Mechanics* define how games operate as systems, that is, the way they convert specific inputs into specific outputs. *Dynamics* guide how players and the game mechanics interact during the runtime of the game. *Aesthetics* refer to the way the game mechanics and dynamics interact with the game designer's artistry, to produce cultural and emotional outcomes.

We propose that mechanics and dynamics are what a course designer can systematically employ and tune to produce desired student and community behaviors; aesthetics, albeit also important, are less predictable and thus not explicitly investigated in this work.

We identify 7 core tools for gamification. The 3 core mechanics are:

1. *Point systems* are managing the acquisition and expenditure of points, that is, of units of value internal to the game, that quantify student performance. Students may be rewarded with points that count towards the course grade; for example, 1,000 points may translate into the maximum course grade of 100%. Students may also earn points that are not directly linked to the course grade; for example, points that can be spent to propose a topic to be discussed in the next course. Points that *expire*, for example after each major component of the course or after one year, may be used to level the playing field or to prevent inflation.
2. *Levels, access, and power* are ways to incentivize students to play, achieve, and excel, respectively. Levels are typically a direct result of accumulating experience (points). For example, the level of a student may be the final course grade of that student. Access describes what players can see and do inside the game system; access may be granted through level restrictions, continued good behavior, etc. For example, students may get access to additional material, one-hour mentoring sessions with the educator, exta lectures, etc. Power refers to what players are entitled to do, including access to and control of course topics. Power may be achieved through active and continuous participation in the course, acing exams, helping other students, etc.
3. *Leaderboards* are routinely used to compare achievements. Anonymous leaderboards, while not as fun as full-disclosure leaderboards, allow individual students to assess their own ranking. This may be demoralizing if actual ranks are displayed; instead, presenting a long general list of ratings and placing low-ranked players always in the middle may be a better approach.

The 4 core dynamics are:

1. *Badges and other status displays* refer to ways to show achievement. Badges quantify achievement through their challenge and scarcity, but may also be offered to surprise the students. For example, an educator may invent fun badges such as "late but smart" badge for late students who can answer a question when they first enter the class.
2. *Onboarding* is the "act of bringing a novice into the system" [17]. Most modern online games employ the simple technique of starting with "tutorial" game tasks, that is, tasks that every user is guaranteed to be able to solve with relative ease and in a short period of time. Once successful, novice players find it more difficult to leave the system.
3. *Social engagement loops* are designs that make players return to the game. Students that are part of a team have a strong social incentive to be present, if missing out diminishes the chances of the team to perform well. In-class interactions between groups of students are also important.
4. *Unlocking content* is a powerful dynamic tool for controlling the evolution of the course. Students may not be allowed access to a course component, prior to completing the core requirements of another. Top students may be allowed access to supplementary course material, tougher assignments, etc.

Table 1: Course topics and curricular reward, in credits. Each credit (EC) require abouts 28 hours of study.

`BSc-CO`, 6EC (168h)	`MSc-CC`, 5EC (140h)
Digital Logic and Data Representation	Overview of cloud computing
Computer Architecture and Organization	Scheduling and Resource Management
Interfacing and I/O Strategies	Data Centers and Energy Efficiency
Memory Architecture	Multi-tenancy concepts, incl.virtualization
Functional Organization	Cloud programming models
Multiprocessing	Case studies
Performance Enhancements	Guest lecturer
Directions in Computing	

3. DESIGN OF GAMIFIED COURSES

To gain experience with the use of gamification in practice, we have implemented two courses using the toolbox for course gamification introduced in the previous section.

The courses are a first-year undergraduate course on Computer Organization (`BSc-CO`) and a graduate course on Cloud Computing (`MSc-CC`). Table 1 summarizes the main topics for each course. `BSc-CO` covers the topics recommended by the ACM/IEEE CS2013. For the topic "Performance Enhancements", `BSc-CO` students learn about pipelining. In "Directions in Computing", `BSc-CO` includes several basic concepts of parallel and distributed computing, such as Amdahl's Law and synchronization; such approaches have been discussed in a recent SIGCSE panel [5]. We also include here extra lectures on the basics of GPU architectures and programming, and on Cloud computing architecture and programming, which are unlocked for the top 20% of the students and do not count for the course grade. `MSc-CC` is an innovative course in cloud computing, in that it focuses on the architectural (systems-building) perspective, rather than courses that focus on MapReduce [2]. Instead of programming in MapReduce, which is one of the many possible big data programming models, we focus on resource provisioning and allocation. Students can choose to deploy MapReduce-based applications, but the course does not prescribe this.

3.1 Supporting Player Classes

We devise the two courses to accommodate the various types of players described in Section 2.1, as follows. `BSc-CO` proposes to students in-class discussion about concepts, weekly tutorials that bridge the gap between concepts and practice, pair-programming in the laboratory to experiment, and self-study in teams of 6 to create opportunities for social learning. `MSc-CC` uses in-class discussion, reviews of articles and team presentations, and pair-programming in the lab.

The match to player-motivations is straightforward. Explorers have multiple paths to explore. Achievers have sufficient paths of advancement, and several options within each path. Socializers benefit from being part of two teams per course. Winners compete with each other for the most challenging aspects of the lab-work and during in-class discussion. Students can pass the course by following the path(s) that suit their intrinsic motivation.

Table 2: Use of gamification mechanics and dynamics in course design.

	BSc-CO	MSc-CC
Course level	First-year, Bachelors	Masters
Point Systems	Course points, access tokens	
Levels and access	Access to various elements	
Leaderboards	Hall of Fame	
Badges	Various	No
Onboarding	Entry quiz, 5% bonus to final grade	
Social engagement loops	Teams of 2–4 for Lab	
	Teams of 6 for Self-Study	—
Unlocking content	Unlocking Lab bonus assignments	

Table 3: Row B'xy (M'xy) has results for BSc-CO (MSc-CC) in year 20xy. The ⋆ denotes a course without gamification, used as comparison. Percentages without parentheses are relative to In-class participation.

	Participants (Completed)		Bonuses		
Spring,	In-class	Lab	Self-Study	In-class	Lab
B'10⋆	93 (65%)	118 (78%)	—	—	—
B'11	122 (65%)	114 (96%)	—	1.1%	10%
B'12	147 (65%)	130 (95%)	15%	25%	4%
B'13	161 (80%)	118 (97%)	25%	32%	10%
M'13	34 (76%)	26 (92%)	—	88%	59%

3.2 Using the Course Gamification Toolbox

To gamify the two courses, we employ the mechanics and dynamics described in Table 2. We set for both courses a points-scale in which 10,000 points are required for a course grade of 10; this large number decouples the reality of the final course grade (from 1 to 10 at GamificationU) from the abstract in-course denomination. Various access tokens challenge competitive and exploring students. Onboarding offers a small reward to students at the start of the course. Various teams offer the needed social engagement loops. For MSc-CC, where students are more mature, we use peer assessment for the presentation component of the course, after preliminary instruction on evaluation criteria.

The highest rewards require multiple steps of unlocking. The toughest *bonus* lab-assignments may ask from students the prior completion of several other course-components. The top 20% of the students are offered additional course-work, which deepen the course topic "Directions in Computing" via lectures and practical work.

To enable the use of gamification in large-enrollment courses, we use game analytics, here, analyzing the behavior and performance of students while the course is ongoing. We collect meaningful information through end-lecture and in-class quizzes, which we analyze before the next lecture. Game analytics allow us to understand, through the use of traditional data mining techniques, what the students are interested in, how each of them performs, and where individuals and the community need more guidance. In particular, they allow us to repeat in our lectures information that many students have not yet assimilated. Updating the results of individual students also keeps achievers and winners motivated.

4. EMPIRICAL EVALUATION

We summarize in this section the results of a multi-year, empirical evaluation we have conducted via the two gamification-based courses at GamificationU (see Section 1).

4.1 Impact of Gamification on Participation, Completion, and Retry On Failure

We report on data collected over 4 course sessions, characterizing over 450 students. We have managed BSc-CO, the first-year undergraduate course, for 3 Spring sessions that accommodate each 100–150 fresh students and 50–60 students who have failed the course in previous years. MSc-CC, the M.Sc.-level course, was given for the first time in Fall 2012 and attracted an unexpectedly high enrollment of over 50 students (only 36 actively participated). For BSc-CO, we also report on results prior to the introduction of gamification, for the Spring 2010 session (the limit of our access to old-course data); however, other elements of the course, such as the lecturer and the lab-work support team, have also been changed.

We summarize the results observed for our student cohorts in Table 3. These results indicate that:

- As indicated by the in-class completion percentages (column "Participants", "In-class", between parentheses), courses that use gamification achieve good results. The completion percentage, which only counts first-try completions, is encouraging. In 2013, over 75% of the students completed both courses; for previous years, only 65% have completed in their first try. From student surveys and testimonials, we find completion percentages to be correlated with (although perhaps not caused by) increased student satisfaction, which many students agree is due to gamification. The high completion percentage addresses one of the major problems we have set to solve via gamification.
- For BSc-CO, In-class achievement ("Bonuses, In-class") has increased every year, although the number of fresh students has not changed significantly. We attribute this to the social dynamic we have added to the course, where interaction and competition between students motivate them to return to class. This is further supported by the increasing number of students who complete in teams the social track ("Bonuses, Self-Study").
- As indicated by the fraction of students who receive bonuses, the multiple paths of advancement already attract a significant fraction of our students. As new students get to learn course best-practices from the previous, and find class-time useful, we expect that participation will increase. For the first-year undergraduate course, we also conclude that more incentives are needed to attract the students.

We also find that:

- Based on the attendance to extra lectures, to which almost 100% of the students invited show up, we find that top students do like to learn for the sake of learning—they have high attendance even for lectures that do not impact the course grade.
- Mid-term performance characterizes well the top performers in the BSc-CO cohorts. Among the Top-20% at the end of the course, less 15% were not already part of the same top, mid-term. This allows for an early identification of achievers and winners.
- About 10–15% of the students fit the profile of winners or achievers. Less than 5% of the students will try to improve their grade if they have already passed the course in the first try; these correspond to achiever profiles.

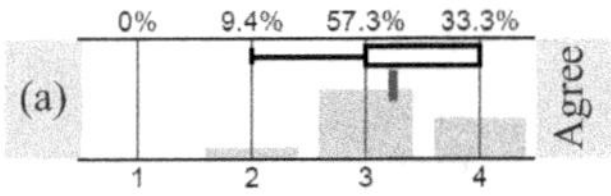

Figure 1: Official survey, BSc-CO: (a) "I have learned much from this course". (N=96) (b) "I found the content of this course interesting". (N=98)

- Unlike previous years, when failing students did not return to take the re-sit exam the same year after failing for the first time, for the gamification-based BSc-CO over 90% of the students who failed tried again the same year; about 65% of them passed at their second attempt.

4.2 Student Satisfaction

We report on three types of student satisfaction evaluations, official surveys, volunteered testimonials, and in-class participation.

Our university runs detailed *official surveys* for every first-year course. Figure 1 depicts a selection of results for two of the most important questions in the survey, related to learning and interest in the course content. On a scale from 1 to 4, where 4 indicates complete approval and 1 complete disapproval (neutral opinion is not allowed), over 96 students (60-75% of the enrollment) have responded. For the two statements, the study indicates approval, with an average of 3.24 (standard deviation 0.61) and 3 (0.85), respectively.

In our own survey, run in-class and anonymized, we have asked students to evaluate various aspects of gamification. Surprisingly to us, more students thought more carefully about the course due to gamification (over 90%) than felt more motivated by gamification (only 50%–75%); in other words, even students who did not care about the particulars of the teaching technique were pushed by gamification to think more carefully about the advancement paths (the course design). We also find that over 90% of the respondents enjoyed the interactive part of the lectures and enjoyed the exercises at the end of the lectures.

We find that *In-class participation is high.* Lectures are often the bane of modern education, especially for large-enrollment classes. Participation in our lectures is voluntary and not rewarded, and videotapes of the lectures (from previous years) are available to students, yet students participate in large numbers to our In-class activity. Anecdotally, we observe 60–70% of our students in the classroom, even late in the course. For the extra lectures, we observe even higher levels of participation (as reported in Section 4.1). Also anecdotally, these are much higher numbers than the numbers regularly observed in the same faculty.

During and at the end of the course, we have received a large number of *Volunteered testimonials*, some via email. A few examples of the enthusiastic response of our students: "I just would like to say that the extra lectures are a great concept to reward the motivated students." "Lectures were nice, different in a good way from other teachers." and "I really like the rewards [during lectures]".

4.3 The Cost of Gamification

For the two courses we have explored in this work, we estimate the cost of gamification in time spent to create the gamification elements and to adapt the course content, which is in our experience:

- One week to consider gamification elements.
- One day per lecture for adaptation.
- Two hours per lecture, for analyzing end-lecture quizzes and adapting the next lecture accordingly.
- Two days after each major exam, to tabulate results.
- One week to compile final course results, using spreadsheet technology.

5. LESSONS LEARNED

We summarize in this section what we have learned as instructors and designers of two gamification-based courses.

5.1 Educator Experience

Gamification can be personally rewarding (see Section 5.2). In addition to rewarding interaction with the students, one of the authors of this article received, after students voted anonymously, a Teacher of the Year award. The reasons for this award include gamification.

Gamification can also be difficult on the instructor, in addition to the time overheads it incurs (see Section 4.3):

- There is a need for computer-assisted management of bonuses, etc., especially for large-enrollment courses.
- Introducing gamification can be difficult. Among the hurdles, we found: explaining a new system to students, conquering organizational inertia to get initial approval, limited university support before the approach became a success, etc.

From a technical perspective, we believe that:

- Offering points through announced tests leads to class rhythm. Unannounced formative tests, both within a lecture and across a course, may offer strong incentives for students to stay focused.
- Performance-related badges are very popular. Although negative badges exist in the world of gaming, for education we recommend that only positive badges should be used.
- Using short end-of-lecture quizzes and continuously asking for student feedback can provide meaningful information for gaming analytics.

5.2 A Testimonial

Among the testimonials, several have shown us that gamification can have an important impact on (student) lives. The following example is from a student who was not able to complete her B.Sc. studies for several years, in part because of failing to pass BSc-CO; she was helped by our alternative paths of advancement: `I want to thank you for showing that even though I'm not that good at written exams, I still can excel at other points in my study. I'd love to have a copy of my badge, as physical reminder of a course that made me eager to learn about things. Even when some of those things will never really have my interest. This course, and the way it was given, learned me a few things about what motivates me, and only for that reason it was totally worth getting up for every lecture.`

6. RELATED WORK

We discuss in this section related work on instructional methodology and on curriculum content.

Methodologically, our work is one of the first to assess gamification in university settings, and the first long-term study of gamification effects in undergraduate and graduate *courses*. In a recent study [7], gamification was used to present orientation information to university students.

Content-wise, ours is one of the first long-term studies on how to mesh advanced PDC topics (GPUs, cloud computing) into first-year undergraduate courses. Our two years of practice could contribute to the debate on this topic [5]. This work also complements previous studies on the use of programming models for advanced distributed systems, in particular MapReduce [9, 16]. In contrast to these studies, which focus on enabling cloud infrastructure for students, ours focuses on diversifying the content paths within the topic of (distributed) computer systems.

7. CONCLUSION AND ONGOING WORK

Responding to an increasing need to find new techniques for teaching academic-level computer science, we have proposed in this work to use gamification to improve student participation and success in technical higher education.

Drawing from various game studies, theory of fun, and education methodology, we have designed a toolbox for course gamification, which adapts to different types of students via a set of mechanisms and dynamics. Using this toolbox, we have designed two gamified courses, one at undergraduate and one at graduate levels. Key features of our design include enabling various paths of advancement, and fostering social interaction inside and outside the classroom. Our empirical evaluation reports on three years of experience with the undergraduate and one year with the graduate courses, during which we have educated over 450 students. We have found that gamification can help in many ways our students, from increasing passing rates and participation, to high student satisfaction and heart-warming testimonials.

We are currently extending this work via additional surveys. We have collected already over 300 new, more in-depth responses, and are currently analyzing them. We are also trying to help others apply the techniques described in this work, for (semi-)independent validation. We also plan to investigate far-reaching questions about gamification: How to enable longitudinal studies of gamification? How to design a prototypical gamification-based course in computer science? Which type of instructional goal gains most from gamification? Which type of student gains most from gamification? Which gamification element is responsible for the largest improvement? etc.

8. ACKNOWLEDGMENTS

We would like to thank our system administrators, teaching assistants, and student assistants for helping with these two courses. This project was partially funded by a TU Delft Talent Grant, by the NWO/STW Veni grant large (11881), by the EU projects PEDCA (FP7 #320013) and EYE (FP7 #619241), and by the COMMIT.

9. REFERENCES

[1] ACM/IEEE-CS Joint Task Force. Computer Science Curricula 2013. Online reports, Strawman and Ironman., Feb 2012/2013.

[2] M. Armbrust et al. A view of cloud computing. *Commun. ACM*, 53(4):50–58, 2010.

[3] R. Bartle. *Designing Virtual Worlds*. New Riders Games, 2003.

[4] R. Brewer, L. Anthony, Q. Brown, G. Irwin, J. Nias, and B. Tate. Using gamification to motivate children to complete empirical studies in lab environments. In *IDC*, pages 388–391, 2013.

[5] R. A. Brown, J. C. Adams, D. P. Bunde, J. Mache, and E. Shoop. Strategies for adding the emerging pdc curriculum recommendations into cs courses. In *SIGCSE*, pages 109–110, 2013.

[6] S. Deterding, D. Dixon, R. Khaled, and L. Nacke. From game design elements to gamefulness: defining "gamification". In *MindTrek*, pages 9–15, 2011.

[7] Z. Fitz-Walter, D. Tjondronegoro, and P. Wyeth. Orientation passport: using gamification to engage university students. In *OZCHI*, pages 122–125, 2011.

[8] D. R. Flatla, C. Gutwin, L. E. Nacke, S. Bateman, and R. L. Mandryk. Calibration games: making calibration tasks enjoyable by adding motivating game elements. In *UIST*, pages 403–412, 2011.

[9] P. Garrity, T. Yates, R. A. Brown, and E. Shoop. Webmapreduce: an accessible and adaptable tool for teaching map-reduce computing. In *SIGCSE*, pages 183–188, 2011.

[10] S. Hull. 20 obstacles to scalability. *ACM Queue*, 11(7):20, 2013.

[11] K. Huotari and J. Hamari. Defining gamification: a service marketing perspective. In *MindTrek*, pages 17–22, 2012.

[12] Jim Gray. Twelve computer science challenges, 1998. ACM A. M. Turing Award Lecture.

[13] R. Koster. *Theory of Fun for Game Design*. Paraglyph Press, kindle edition, 2010.

[14] T. W. Malone. Heuristics for designing enjoyable user interfaces: Lessons from computer games. In *CHI*, pages 63–68, 1982.

[15] M. J. Nelson. Soviet and american precursors to the gamification of work. In *MindTrek*, pages 23–26, 2012.

[16] A. Rabkin, C. Reiss, R. H. Katz, and D. A. Patterson. Using clouds for mapreduce measurement assignments. *TOCE*, 13(1):2, 2013.

[17] G. Zichermann and C. Cunningham. *Gamification by Design: Implementing Game Mechanics in Web and Mobile Apps*. O'Reilly Media, 2011.

How (not) to Introduce Badges to Online Exercises

Lassi Haaranen, Petri Ihantola, Lasse Hakulinen and Ari Korhonen
Department of Computer Science and Engineering
Aalto University, School of Science
Espoo, Finland
firstname.lastname@aalto.fi

ABSTRACT

Achievement badges are increasingly used to enhance educational systems and they have been shown to affect student behavior in different ways. However, details on best practices and effective concepts to implement badges from a non-technical point of view are scarce. We implemented badges to our learning management system, used them on a large course and collected feedback from students. Based on our experiences, we present recommendations to other educators that plan on using badges.

Categories and Subject Descriptors

K.3.2 [**Computers and Education**]: Computer and Information Science Education—*Computer science education*

Keywords

Gamification, Achievement badges, Computer science education

1. INTRODUCTION

Gamification is a fairly new and rapidly growing field defined by Deterding et al. [5] as *"the use of game design elements in non-game contexts."* Motivation behind this is to bring elements which are considered fun and engaging into tasks which might not inherently possess those qualities. Thus, perhaps, improving the user's experience and leading to an enhanced performance, which can be anything from exercises submitted earlier than necessary to increased activity in a forum. Interest in gamification has increased over the past few years and it has even 'earned' its place in the Gartner's Emerging Technologies 2012 Hype Cycle nearing the peak of inflated expectations [9]. Whether it can move in the Hype Cycle past the peak and 'trough of disillusionment' into something that provides considerable value remains to be seen.

A common way to bring game-like elements to educational systems is by adding badges (aka achievements, achievement badges, or trophies). Badges can be defined as optional sub-goals which are not required for completion of the main task [13]. Badges in gamification have their parallels in the real world, for instance, in the form of boy scout badges, which are awarded for acquiring a new set of skills or mastering certain skill levels. Even airline bonus point systems, which aim to encourage customer loyalty, employ game-like mechanics. If these real world achievements and points are considered gamification, then the concept dates further back than the actual name gamification.

Education in the past centuries has already had certain game like elements embedded into the system. Students are awarded points in tests and in different types of assignments. In universities, students complete courses and credit by credit work towards unlocking the last challenge – the final thesis. There are also certain known problems in education, such as procrastination of studying until the deadline and motivational problems in general. Gamification (e.g. badges), at least in the minds of its proponents, could offer some alleviation to these problems.

The purpose of this study is to increase understanding how badges may affect students when introduced to a large course where automatic assessment is already in place. Even though automatic assessment is a valuable tool, especially in large courses, it also might bring some negative side effects. For example, it can promote bad learning habits such as trial-and-error in some exercise types. In addition, we are looking for novel ways to teach some latent learning goals in our courses such as time management. Our research question related to this is:

How will the students react to gamification features such as badges and will it have any positive or negative effect on their behavior? We are especially interested in their attitudes towards badges.

Previous research related to this question is described in Section 2. After that, data collection and the research methods are described in Section 3. The course where badges were introduced had eight rounds of automatically assessed exercises and the badges were used only on the last four rounds. Right after the course we sent a survey to all students to learn their reactions. The survey results and other data we collected are described in Section 4. The results and badges in general will be discussed in Section 5. Finally, in Section 6 we make some recommendations based on our observations described in previous sections.

SIGCSE'14, March 5–8, 2014, Atlanta, GA, USA.

ACM 978-1-4503-2605-6/14/03 ...$15.00.
http://dx.doi.org/10.1145/2538862.2538921.

2. RELATED WORK

Gamification is closely related to toys, playful design and serious games. As illustrated in Figure 1, Deterding et al [5] separate gamification from these other terms by applying two axis: 1) designing something that is complete in itself vs. adding gameful or playful elements to something that already exists and 2) games vs. toys. Caillois [2] makes the distinction between game and play using terms *ludus* which encompasses games (usually with specific rules) and *paidia* which refers to more freeform play. The whole versus parts axis encapsulates the idea whether something implements a whole idea of either paidia or ludus or just parts of it. On the whole side of the spectrum are games and toys which focus completely on their core function.

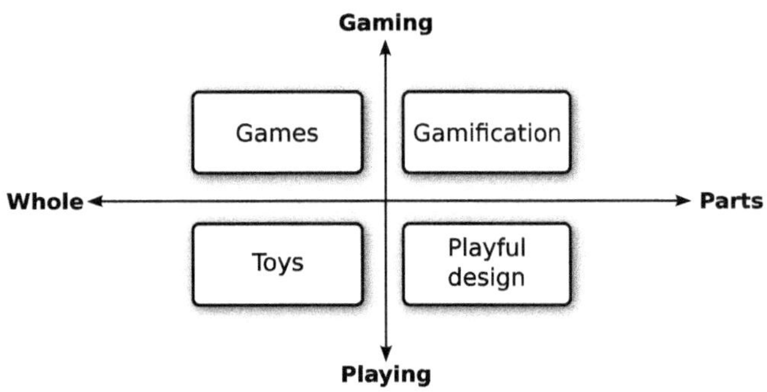

Figure 1: Gaming versus playing and whole versus parts [5]

Gamification has been used in a variety of educational systems. An example of gamification in an educational system, which is open to everyone, is Khan Academy[1]. In Khan Academy, badges are awarded to users, for example, for watching videos and completing exercises. Another free educational service that uses gamification is Duolingo[2]. It aims at teaching a foreign language. Points and levels are used to track the users' progress in learning a language. Points, which are represented by golden coins, are awarded for completing exercises and learning new words.

Clearly there are many kinds of badges. They look different and are rewarded for different reasons. Hamari et al. [8] have presented a method of describing badges. They divide them in three separate parts: signifier, completion logic, and reward. Signifier consists of the visual image and name of the badge. They found three categories for rewards: achievement (meta-)game, in-game, and out-game. The first category of rewards is part of a bigger meta-game (such as the Xbox Live's gamerscore) of collecting badges while the second one is a reward that stays within the game. The last category is external rewards that exist outside the system. An example of rewards in the last category would be to offer better grades on a course for completing badges. Completion logic refers to the conditions that must be satisfied in order for the badge to be awarded.

An empirical study was done in the spring of 2012 on "Data Structures and Algorithms" course in Aalto University [7]. The experiment used a between subject design, where half of the 281 students in the course were given badges which they could earn by doing exercises with certain additional restrictions, such as completing the exercises a full week before deadline or getting exercises completely correct on the first try. Quantitative analysis of the results revealed that student's behavior can be affected, at least in some cases, with badges. An example of affected behavior was submitting correct answers with fewer attempts. However, significant effect on the grades were not observed between the treatment and control groups.

A gamification study done on a course for "Qualification for users of ICT" found qualitative and quantitative differences between control (N=80) and treatment (N=131) groups [6]. 58 students from treatment group opted for the gamified version. Those students had higher scores in initial activity and practical exercises in various modules. However, they found that the treatment group had lower scores on the final examination of the course and the participation, which was also scored. In their setup, students were able to choose whether or not they would participate in the gamified version of the course, which might have had a significant impact on the results. They argue that the gamified version improved the practical competence but at the same time had a negative effect on understanding theoretical concepts. Qualitatively they also found that gamification has a significant emotional and social impact. While some students liked public leaderboards and found them motivating, some students disliked the leaderboards and did not appreciate the competitive element they created.

University of Central Florida's course, "Adventures in Emergent Media", implemented badges for their online course in which part of their grade was determined by how many achievements they got during the course [12]. After the course, they held a survey about the course in general and badges in particular to which 138 students responded. Although, they found the effects of badges to be slightly positive, many students reported frustration because some of the badges were hidden and had to be discovered, which proved to be too difficult in some cases. They also noted a social aspect to badges where half of the students said they were motivated to get a badge if they noticed that one of their friends had achieved it.

Denny conducted a large-scale ($N > 1000$) controlled experiment on a course where they implemented badges to PeerWise platform, which is aimed at students creating and answering questions [4]. They found a positive motivational effect. The treatment group was active during more days and answered more questions. However, badges did not have an effect on the number of questions created. On a survey after the course, the majority of students preferred the system with badges. They did not observe any negative effects, and thus conclude that badges can be useful motivators in educational contexts.

3. METHODOLOGY

This is a follow-up study to the aforementioned study in Aalto University [7]. We implemented badges to a course that is described in Section 3.1. To map out how students perceived badges, we collected and analyzed data from various sources as described in Section 3.2.

3.1 Course description

The data was collected from a 5 ECTS Data Structures and Algorithms course taught at Aalto University in spring

[1]https://www.khanacademy.org/
[2]http://www.duolingo.com/

2013. The course is a bachelor level course with basics of programming as prerequisites. Part of the course were individual online exercises that are assessed and graded automatically. For the CS major students, the online exercises contribute 20 per cent to their final course grade and for the minor students, the online exercises contribute 30 per cent to their final grade.[3] Online exercises were divided into eight rounds with distinct deadlines. Separate rounds did not have any minimum requirements, but only the sum of the total points from all rounds was used to determine the grade. 50 % of the maximum points was required to pass the exercises with grade 1 and 60, 70, 80 and 90 % of total points resulted correspondingly to grades 2, 3, 4 and 5. Thus, students were able to pass the exercises by doing only the first four rounds with full points. There were several exercises on each round and resubmissions were also allowed.

Badges were added as a plugin to A+ learning management system [10] that we used to deliver the online assignments. On the first four exercise rounds, there were no badges at all and students were unaware that they would be revealed after round four. Starting from round five, students could achieve various badges as described in Section 3.1.1. Badges were visible on the side bar when viewing course schedule, exercise page or submissions for an exercise. Only newly achieved badges were shown, or if no new badges were achieved the latest achieved badge was visible. In addition to the view in the sidebar, a summary page to visualize all achieved and available badges was also implemented. These are illustrated in Figure 2.

3.1.1 Completion Logic and Reward for Badges

Badges were awarded in three different categories: learning, time management, and carefulness. Basis for the different categories for the badges were derived from the previous research [7]. All of the badges come in three different levels (bronze, silver, gold) based on an increase in difficulty in completion logic and stricter criteria. Badges did not have any external rewards and they did not affect the course grade in any way. Since the badges could not be shared with friends via social media they did not have social aspect to them[4].

In the learning category, badges were achieved by completing the exercises with 50, 75 or 100 % of the score from the rounds maximum score. A factor that affected the completed score of the round was that submissions which arrived after the deadline suffered a 50 % penalty to the score.

Time management badges encouraged submitting earlier. They were awarded for completing 50 % of the exercise round's score at least a week (gold), three days (silver) or a day (bronze) before the deadline. Learning category badges were somewhat dependent on time management because late submissions were allowed, but penalized 50 %.

Final category of badges was carefulness. These badges were awarded for completing exercises with perfect score and no more than one submission per exercise, meaning that the student needed to submit a perfect answer on the first try. The aim was to encourage the students to submit well thought out answers on the first try and subsequently curb trial-and-error method of solving problems. The levels to achieve bronze, silver or gold were 5, 10 or 15 respectively. The total number of exercises which counted towards this badge was 23.

3.2 Research Method

After the course, a link to an anonymous online survey was sent to all students. A total of 162 students (53 %), out of 306 registered to the course, responded to the survey that contained multiple choice questions and an option for freeform feedback. Results of this survey are presented in Section 4.1. We used data based content analysis on all the textual answers by manually and iteratively grouping them to categories that emerged from the data [11].

In addition to the survey, we also had the students' submissions, submission times, and feedback (including points) that a student got from his or her submission. Moreover, every time a user viewed the badge summary view (on right in Figure 2) was also recorded. 252 students (82 %) passed the online assignments with at least minimum points. The log data dissected in Section 4.2 focuses on these students.

4. RESULTS

4.1 Survey

Numeric questions used a likert scale from 0 (completely disagree) to 4 (strongly agree) with 2 as the neutral option. Translated questions and answers to those are presented in Table 1.

A majority of the students liked the look of the badges and about half of the students were satisfied with the completion logic. Correspondingly, most of the students did not find that the badges disturbed their work. About one third of the students agreed with the statement that badges were motivating, one third disagreed, and one third simply thought they were neither motivating nor demotivating. Still, 52 % of students were in favor of having badges in the next year's course while 20 % were opposed to that.

Altogether 88 students responded with written feedback to the last question of "*Please give additional comments about the badges*". Approximately half of those felt indifferent towards the badges. A quarter of students gave positive feedback while ten assessed them negatively. This was also reflected in the numerical answers where the majority of students did not find achievement badges particularly motivating or demotivating. We analyzed the written feedback and found some common themes in them.

Suggesting improvements

A lot of the responses contained ideas and suggestions for improvement. Seven of the suggestions mentioned an UI glitch, where two exercises in earlier rounds were partially covered by achievement badges on some browsers. In addition to problems with UI, four students did not notice badges or were confused and not certain why they got badges or if it affected course grades in any way, commenting: "*You could never really know when one of them would appear.*"[5]

Badges did not impress

28 of the students reported that they were indifferent towards badges or "*don't see the usefulness of achievement*

[3]The rest of the final grade is determined by other projects and the final examination.

[4]Technically sharing the URL for the summary page was possible. But there was no designed way to share achieved badges.

[5]quoted feedback is translated

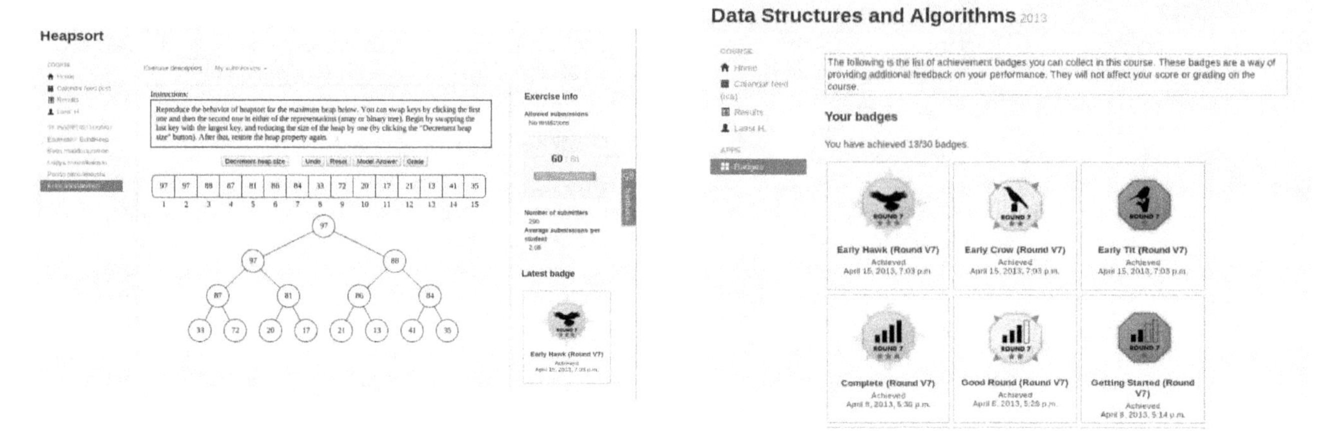

Figure 2: Screenshots of badges in A+. On the left is an exercise view showing latest achieved badge. On the right is the summary view that lists achieved and available badges.

Table 1: Numeric feedback regarding achievement badges (N=162)

Question	0	1	2	3	4
I found the badges motivating	20 %	**24** %	17 %	**24** %	14 %
Badges disturbed my work	**61** %	15 %	15 %	6 %	3 %
Trying to achieve badges had an effect on my behavior	**40** %	21 %	13 %	15 %	11 %
Visual look of the badges was good	3 %	6 %	22 %	**42** %	27 %
I was satisfied with the criteria for awarding badges	3 %	8 %	**42** %	29 %	18 %
I think that badges should be used in A+ for the next year's course as well.	8 %	12 %	28 %	22 %	**30** %

badges". However, seven of those students said that they would have been motivated if badges affected the course results somehow or if they would just get bonus points without the badges. "*They did not really affect my studying at all. It would be more motivating to give bonus points as a reward.*"

Emotions

Three students wrote very negative feedback on the badges. One person noted that they should be taken away and that he "*died internally*" every time he saw them. Nine of the responses described a positive reaction towards the achievements: "*Wonderful idea. Would it be possible to add some funny badges?*"

Social

Even though the system did not have a way of sharing badges with other students, at least some students compared with their friends how many badges they got. Three students mentioned it in the feedback. Particularly one student noted: "*I did not particularly care about achievement badges because I realized they did not have any real meaning, and that's good. I did, however, have some natural instinct to collect more of them than my friend.*"

Affecting behavior

In total, 14 students reported that the implemented badges affected their behavior. Time management was mentioned in five responses, such as: "*[badges] brought immediately feeling of achieving that motivated me to do the online exercises on time and with care.*" Seven responses pertained to carefulness and the number of submissions per exercise. One student told that before badges he "*did not care how many times he had to try an exercise before passing*", but after badges were implemented he "*always tried to get a perfect submission on the first try.*"

Few students noted that the completion logic of the badges was unimaginative and boring. "*Badges that appeared in the middle of the course had a little forced feeling to them ... I would make badges more epic by adding familiar concepts and humor from games*". Completion logic of the badges resembled closely the goals of the online exercises. Carefulness badges had the only completion logic that was not somehow tied to course grading and they were most mentioned when students discussed their changed behavior.

4.2 Log data

Since students only needed to complete 50 % of the total amount of points, some of them do not work on exercises after achieving that limit. This leads to decreasing number of students submitting in each round. In Figure 3, we can see the average score for each round as well as the percentage of students submitting solutions. In the first round, almost all students enrolled in the course submit at least one exercise. In the last round, however, only 75% of students submit something. In addition, the average score in each round is also decreasing, which indicates that students do more exercises in the beginning of the semester than at the end of semester. Some of the fluctuation is caused by the level of difficulty, though. Typically, easier rounds collect more submissions.

The amount of badges achieved for the first four rounds (badges not visible) was calculated with same criteria as the implemented badges for the last four rounds (badges visible). The decreasing number of submissions towards the end of the course, however, hinders our ability to assess the effect of the badges. More submissions in the beginning of the course means also more badges achieved (even though the students did not know about them). In addition, the exercises in the first four rounds were easier than the rest of the exercises. Thus, it was easier to achieve some of the badges as well. Thus, comparing the number of achieved badges in the first four rounds to the last four rounds showed no statistically significant improvements. Despite this, however, some (small portion of) students indeed improved their badge-performance by collecting more badges on the second half of the course.

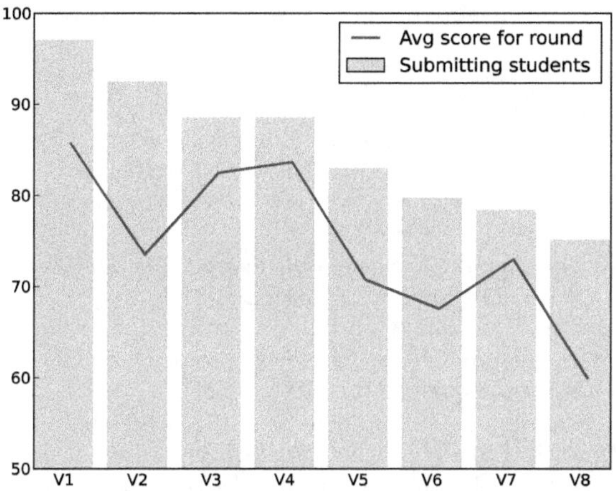

Figure 3: Percentage of enrolled students submitting to exercises and average points for each round.

The students' interest in the badge system was also measured by the number of visits to the summary page where all achieved and available badges were shown. Figure 4 shows the amount of badges earned on the last four rounds and the number of times the summary view was visited. The plotted linear correlation indicates a connection between the amount of badges earned and the number of times information about them was viewed. 23 % of the students that passed the online exercises did not visit the summary page at all, 21 % visited it once and 56 % visited it multiple times. There is also a separate group of students who viewed the summary page a lot more often than others, indicating interest in the badges.

5. DISCUSSION

The numerical feedback suggests that the system did not hinder or annoy the majority of students in a way that would have been detrimental to the learning outcome. Furthermore, we did not observe any negative effects on learning results either. Overall the implemented badges did not have a significant effect on the course results or student behavior because some students stop doing the exercises once they have enough points to pass or have achieved their desired grade[6]. However, the written feedback suggests that students perceive badges in varied ways.

Based on the results from the freeform questions in the survey, there seemed to be two axis where most of the students can be placed: emotional and effect. Students' emotions towards badges ranged from very negative to very positive with majority of reactions being indifferent. The other axis ranges from badges having no effect on behavior to having a positive effect. We did not observe negative effect from badges. Placing students on these two axis would be interesting to study in the future.

[6]This is an effect that we have observed previously on the course as well.

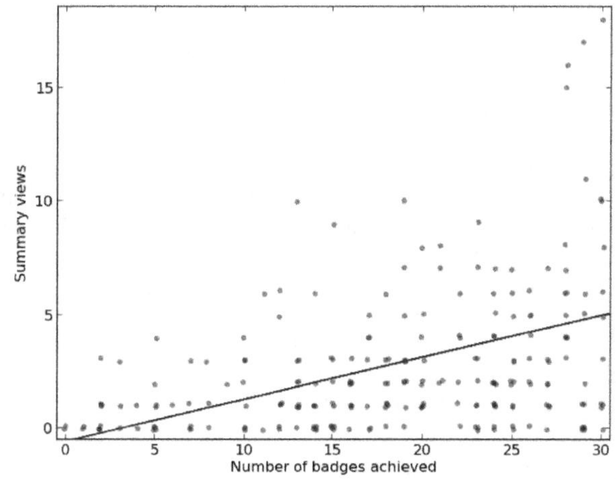

Figure 4: Achieved badges and summary views. A small amount of jitter has been added to separate the datapoints

Gamification is not unanimously viewed as a positive contribution to learning. It poses challenges especially in the area of motivation. While adding points and badges to a core service might sound like an easy way to improve user experience and engagement, it is not as trivial in practise.

Gamification has been criticized for having a negative effect on intrinsic motivation by granting extrinsic rewards which undermine the underlying intrinsic motivation. Meta-analysis on the literature has shown that in educational context giving out external rewards reduces internal motivation [3]. If adding badges discourages those who have a deep motivation to learn for the sake of learning and understanding, then clearly they should be used with caution. However, we did not find any negative effects on learning that could be tied to badges and this was also the case in Denny's experiment [4].

Nicholson has presented a theoretical framework for meaningful gamification [14]. He concluded that meaning is defined differently by each individual so customization is required to achieve better outcomes. Furthermore, meaningful gamification should focus more on the aspects of playing and less on the aspect of scoring. We found this to be true in our case as well. Students experience varied, thus customization would have been beneficial, for example we could have provided an option to turn the badges off. In addition, based on the feedback, adding a social element, for instance a way of sharing badges with friends, would have also improved the system.

Another risk related to intrinsic and extrinsic motivation is that gamification might induce unwanted behavior where gamification becomes more important than the actual core function [1]. When this happens in an educational context, students start to care more about acquiring points and badges than knowledge. An example of this type of behavior is a site called whatbadgenext[7] which scans through your current progress for different badges in Khan Academy and suggests activities that will lead to a new badge with least amount of time and effort.

Moreover, it is possible that by encouraging students to achieve competitive time management badges might have had a negative effect on the carefulness [7]. This has the implication that achieving badges was becoming more important than the actual core service. This type of unwanted behavior can be especially detrimental in an educational context. In our study, none of the badges were competitive in the sense that only certain fraction of students would be able to get them, so this did not lead to negative results.

6. CONCLUSIONS

To find out how students react to gamification implemented with badges, we introduced badges to a large course with automatically assessed exercises in place. We collected and analyzed data from survey and from logs. Based on the observations from our experiment, we make some recommendations to other educators planning to bring badges to their teaching:

- We found that some students have strongly negative emotions towards badges. Therefore, one should make it technically easy to opt out from badges or make them opt in.
- Although we did not plan so, our students shared badges and discussed them. Therefore, one should make badges social in the first place. However, at the same time, it should be kept in mind that some students do not like to compete with peers.
- If there is already an automatic assessment system with points in place, badges telling how many points a student got are of little novelty. Instead, it would be a good idea to make badges something completely orthogonal to the grading policy. In addition, one should encourage latent aspects that are beneficial to learning but not graded. Moreover, badges should be fun (e.g. one could give a Santa badge if an exercise was submitted at Christmas).
- Our badges did not affect grading, but feedback from points and badges can confuse students. Therefore, one should give students clear instructions what else, if anything, is affected by badges.
- One should always make sure that adding badges does not hinder the usability of learning platform where the exercises and other core tasks related to learning are carried out.

Based on our log data, we were able to confirm Denny's [4] observation that there is a positive correlation between the number of badges collected and how often a user views information about badges. In addition, although our survey hinted so, we were not able to find statistically significant results to support the claims that time management badges guide students to submit their work earlier and carefulness badges encourage students to avoid bricolage approach (trial-and-error) in problem solving.

[7] `http://whatbadgenext.appspot.com/`

7. REFERENCES

[1] G. Boulet. Gamification: The Latest Buzzword and the Next Fad. *eLearn*, 2012(12):3, 2012.

[2] R. Caillois. *Man, Play, and Games.* University of Illinois Press, 2001.

[3] E. L. Deci, R. Koestner, and R. M. Ryan. A Meta-Analytic Review of Experiments Examining The Effects of Extrinsic Rewards on Intrinsic Motivation. *Psychological bulletin*, 125(6):627, 1999.

[4] P. Denny. The Effect of Virtual Achievements on Student Engagement. In *Proceedings of the SIGCHI Conference on Human Factors in Computing Systems*, CHI '13, pages 763–772, New York, NY, USA, 2013. ACM.

[5] S. Deterding, D. Dixon, R. Khaled, and L. Nacke. From Game Design Elements to Gamefulness: Defining Gamification. In *Proceedings of the 15th International Academic MindTrek Conference: Envisioning Future Media Environments*, pages 9–15. ACM, 2011.

[6] A. Domínguez, J. Saenz-de Navarrete, L. De-Marcos, L. Fernández-Sanz, C. Pagés, and J.-J. Martínez-Herráiz. Gamifying Learning Experiences: Practical Implications and Outcomes. *Computers & Education*, 63:380–392, 2013.

[7] L. Hakulinen, T. Auvinen, and A. Korhonen. Empirical Study on the Effect of Achievement Badges in TRAKLA2 Online Learning Environment. In *Proceedings of the Conference on Learning and Teaching in Computing and Engineering (LaTiCE)*, 2013.

[8] J. Hamari and V. Eranti. Framework for Designing and Evaluating Game Achievements. *Proc. DiGRA 2011: Think Design Play*, 115:122–134, 2011.

[9] Hung LeHong and Jackie Fenn. Key Trends to Watch in Gartner 2012 Emerging Technologies Hype Cycle, 2012. `http://onforb.es/RnGawX`. Accessed 10.6.2013.

[10] V. Karavirta, P. Ihantola, and T. Koskinen. Service-Oriented Approach to Improve Interoperability of e-Learning Systems. In *Proceedings of the 13th IEEE International Conference on Advanced Learning Technologies*, pages 341–345, 2013.

[11] P. Mayring. Qualitative Content Analysis. *Forum Qualitative Sozialforschung / Forum: Qualitative Social Research*, 1(2), 2000.

[12] R. McDaniel, R. Lindgren, and J. Friskics. Using Badges for Shaping Interactions in Online Learning Environments. In *Professional Communication Conference (IPCC), 2012 IEEE International*, pages 1–4. IEEE, 2012.

[13] M. Montola, T. Nummenmaa, A. Lucero, M. Boberg, and H. Korhonen. Applying Game Achievement Systems to Enhance User Experience in a Photo Sharing Service. In *Proceedings of the 13th International MindTrek Conference: Everyday Life in the Ubiquitous Era*, pages 94–97. ACM, 2009.

[14] S. Nicholson. A User-Centered Theoretical Framework for Meaningful Gamification. *Games Learning Society2012: Madison*, 2012.

Khan Academy Gamifies Computer Science

Briana B. Morrison Betsy DiSalvo
School of Interactive Computing
Georgia Institute of Technology
85 5th Street NW
Atlanta, GA, 30332-0760
bmorrison@gatech.edu, bdisalvo@cc.gatech.edu

ABSTRACT

Gamification is the buzzword for adding gaming elements such as points or badges to learning experiences to make them more engaging and to increase motivation. In this paper we explore how Khan Academy has incorporated gaming elements into its CS learning platform. By mapping the literature on motivational processes to popular games we critically analyze how successful Khan Academy is at gamifying their site.

Categories and Subject Descriptors

K.3.2 [**Computer and Information Science Education**]: Computer Science education

General Terms

Design

Keywords

Khan Academy, motivation, gamification.

1. INTRODUCTION

Within the past year, a number of organizations have publicly begun a more vocal push for additional computer science education within K-12 in the United States. While some organizations (e.g., ACM and CSTA) have been active in this area for years, others (e.g., code.org) are more recent. Many sites on the internet have appeared which allow anyone with a desire to learn to program. Khan Academy, an internet learning site founded in 2006, added computer science to its content in September, 2012. Because Khan Academy has approximately 6 million users a month [13] from around the world who desire to learn specific educational content, it deserves to be critically examined in terms of its learning environment and curriculum.

Khan Academy also has incorporated the notion of gamification into its site by adding gaming elements to the learning environment. This paper critically explores how Khan Academy approaches its computer science curriculum and its use of gaming elements to motivate learners.

In this paper we first provide an overview of Khan Academy, its learning environment, and its computer science curriculum. Then we discuss gamification and how it has been incorporated into Khan Academy. Finally we map motivational processes to gamification and critically analyze Khan Academy's use of gaming elements in relationship to motivation. We conclude with a discussion of how each motivational process could successfully be implemented in an online learning environment.

SIGCSE'14, March 5–8, 2014, Atlanta, Georgia, USA.

ACM 978-1-4503-2605-6/14/03…$15.00.
http://dx.doi.org/10.1145/2538862.2538946

2. DEFINING KHAN ACADEMY

Khan Academy defines itself as "a not-for-profit with the goal of changing education for the better by providing a free world-class education for anyone anywhere."[1] The site has over 4500 mini-lectures that are accessed via online videos. It also contains a web-based self-assessment mechanism which generates problems for students based on their skill level and past performance. Most of the practice exercises are found in the math area of the site, but some do exist for other areas as well.

The site contains a community forum which allows for peer-to-peer tutoring. Parents and teachers can create "classrooms" and have students enroll in the class so the instructor can follow the learner's progress, provide assignments, and offer support.

The philosophy behind Khan Academy is to provide content for almost every subject to create "the world's first free, world-class virtual school where anyone can learn anything."[1] This is in keeping with the recommendations of Bloom's 1984 study on the effectiveness of one-on-one tutoring. Khan Academy attempts to provide "almost" individual tutoring for students at a reasonable cost (free to the student) and allow the solution to scale via the internet. In 2010 Khan introduced badges and points into the environment. Now the site is "full of game mechanics."[1]

2.1 Content

Khan Academy contains lessons in math, science, economics, humanities, and computer programming. The math section covers everything from arithmetic to linear algebra and is where the bulk of the content is located. The science section includes biology, physics, chemistry, organic chemistry, cosmology and astronomy. In addition there are lessons on healthcare and medicine. The site includes a projects and discovery lab section which contains videos showing common science labs such as building a projectile launcher. In the science area is also an entire section on learning how to program in Python. This set of lessons is completely separate from the computer programming section of the site.

Micro- and macroeconomics as well as finance and capital markets and entrepreneurship are covered in the economics and finance section of the site. The humanities section includes world history, art history, and American civics. The computer programming section is discussed in depth in sections 2.2 and 2.3.

In addition to these content areas, there are sections of the site that contain "partner content," content developed outside of Khan Academy. These include crash courses in world history, biology and ecology, health and medicine information developed by the Stanford School of Medicine, and content on physics, natural

[1] https://www.khanacademy.org/about

science, materials, and measurement provided by MIT. There is also a section from the J. Paul Getty Museum.

2.2 Learning Environment

The majority of the Khan Academy learning environment involves watching a video explanation of the topic followed by self-assessments in the form of questions (short answer or multiple choice). However, the Computer Programming learning environment is different, as it involves a built in code editor and execution window (Figure 1).

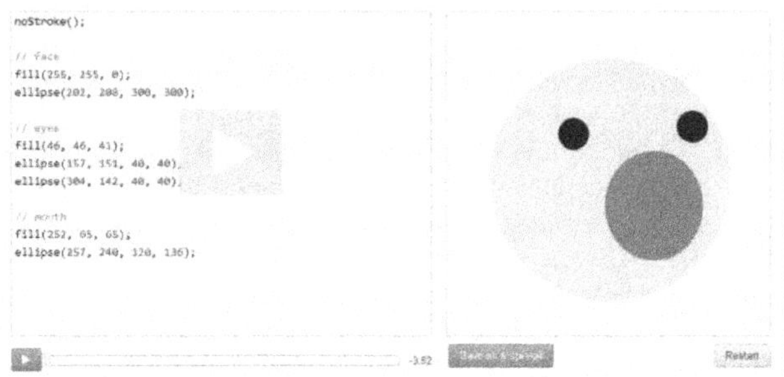

Figure 1. JavaScript Programming Environment

The left frame contains and editor with the Processing.js (a specialized version of JavaScript) code that generates the output in the right frame. At the bottom of the left frame are the controls for the video. The video is a demonstration of how to code the solution for the topic (e.g., the introduction of variables to allow all elements to be offset from a central location). The video contains a developer "talking-through" the development of the code. While the code is being altered, the output on the right changes *immediately* to reflect the new code, much like Bret Victor's environment[2]. At any time the user can pause the video and begin to explore and alter the code, and the changes are immediately reflected in the output frame. Within the editor frame, users may also use the "drag" feature to alter values. When the user clicks on a specific number, a box will appear to allow the user to "drag" the number to a larger or smaller value. This also works with colors, as a color shade box appears to allow the user select a specific color and the associated RGB values are reflected back in the code.

The JavaScript lessons primarily use a drawing and animation context – users create their own pictures and animations using code. Users are encouraged to remix existing programs by creating "spin-offs." Learners are encouraged to take others' programs and modify them to explore the environment and serve as starting point for learning.

Instead of compilation errors, a character appears overlaying the output frame with the explanation of the error, along with a prompt to "show me where" the error occurs in the code (Figure 2). Once the error has been corrected, the appropriate output appears once again.

Each programming lesson begins with code already in the editor frame. The video then shows the learner how to create the new code or alter the existing code to learn a new concept. At any time the user can stop the video, experiment with the code and then restart the video from the beginning or continue where he or she left off. If the user continues the video after changing the code, the code immediately reverts to where it was when the video was stopped, erasing the user's changes.

Interspersed with the lessons are challenge assignments. Challenge assignments are specific assignments (e.g., color the ice cream cone) that allow the learner to practice the material learned in the previous lesson. The code is scaffolded (much of it already exists) and hints are provided to the learner. Each challenge is broken down into several steps where each step is a single line of code to be added or modified.

Figure 2. Error Condition

2.3 CS Curriculum

As mentioned earlier, there are two distinct sets of lessons for CS, one for learning JavaScript and another for learning Python. As of this writing the lessons for Python are more developed, but do not use the new learning environment discussed in the previous section. Instead, the Python lessons are all videos of a computer screen with voice over instructions. The Python lessons begin with an introduction to data types and variables but also cover loops (both for and while), function definitions, function calls, recursion, and insertion sort.

The JavaScript lessons are less developed at this time, but are slowly being introduced. As of this writing, there are 12 categories of lessons: Introduction, Drawing basics, Variables, Animation basics, Manipulating text on the screen, Functions, Logic and if statements, Looping, Arrays, Objects, Becoming a better programmer, and Object-Oriented design. The Introduction lessons give an overview of programming in general, a glimpse into writing programs, and an overview of the learning programming environment within Khan Academy.

The remaining content can be broken down into three categories: (1) beginning programming lessons, (2) drawing and animation lessons, and (3) programming standards. The introductory programming content include lessons on variables and expressions, including arithmetic operations, introduction to functions, Boolean logic and conditional statements, loops, arrays, and even some object based programming.

The next category of lessons teach students how to draw or animate using JavaScript: drawing, simple shapes, coloring, animation, mouse interaction, and displaying text.

The final category of lessons aim to teach some of the less technical, but still important, aspects of programming such as the power of documentation, pseudo-code, commenting, and object oriented design with the purposes of creating more re-usable code. These lessons were added to provide additional techniques "that will help you be more productive and write more beautiful code."[3]

While the current programming lessons in Khan Academy cannot yet be considered equivalent with a full introductory programming course, it is still expanding (based on answers to questions within

[2] http://worrydream.com/#!/InventingOnPrinciple

[3] https://www.khanacademy.org/cs/programming

the discussion forums of Khan Academy). It also represents an environment for the casual learner.

3. GAMIFICATION

The term "gamification" was coined in 2002 by Nick Pelling, a British programmer and inventor who created a series of computer games in the 1980s for BBC Micro, the machine used by most schools in the UK at the time. Gamification is the use of game mechanics in a non-game context [7]. Its purpose within a learning environment is to engage the users within the learning context while allowing them to master the material. The use of gamification has both its supporters and detractors.

The main purpose behind gamification is to enhance the user's motivation [14]. Proponents of gamification suggest that it leverages the user's natural desires to compete and obtain achievements. Gamification allows the users to boost their status within the context while at the same time allowing self-expression. Finally, gamification satisfies the need for closure for many people, by allowing them to "beat" the game indicating completion of the task.

Detractors of gamification suggest that it is exploitive [5] and "pointsification" [6], rather than tied to the essential elements of gaming. They argue that the use of the term gamification is primarily a cheap marketing tool that promises the rich immersive experience of games but leaves the user collecting points for no understandable reason. There are also potential negative impacts of gamification. Nicholson argues that once gamification is used to provide external motivation, the user's internal motivation decreases [18].

Despite the very vocal and often colorful debate around gamification, we found little rigorous academic work that looked at the use of game mechanics in learning environments. This prompted us to critically analyze the gaming elements in Khan Academy, a unique learning environment available to anyone via the Internet with approximately 15 million registered users [13]. Because we do not have access to user data within the Khan Academy site, we cannot definitively state whether or not the added game mechanics are having any effect on users. However for the gaming elements to be successful they must rely on aspects of motivational theory, which we discuss in section 4.

3.1 Gamification in Khan Academy

Khan Academy has implemented several specific gaming elements within its online environment. Each is discussed below.

Knowledge Map – A common element in gaming is to show an overall map or tree structure to guide the user in accomplishing the next task. Khan Academy has its own version of this entitled the "Knowledge Map." A portion of this map can be seen in Figure 3. Each dot on the map represents a mathematical skill (decimals, addition and subtraction, factors and multiples. etc.). Each of these dots can be further broken down into a specific unit. For example, Addition and Subtraction breaks into 1-digit addition, 2-digit addition, 1-digit subtraction, multiple digit subtraction, addition and subtraction word problems and so forth. Each of these topics represents a single skill unit within Khan Academy which can be mastered through video and practice problems. While the Knowledge Map illustrates some of the pre-requisite topics needed for a unit, it does not necessarily act as a map toward completion of a "game" or goal. Various topics can be chosen at random to explore without enforcement of the pre-requisites, which is much different from a traditional game. While only math content is currently represented in the Knowledge Map, we can easily see this expanding to include the CS content or providing a separate Knowledge Map for the computing topics.

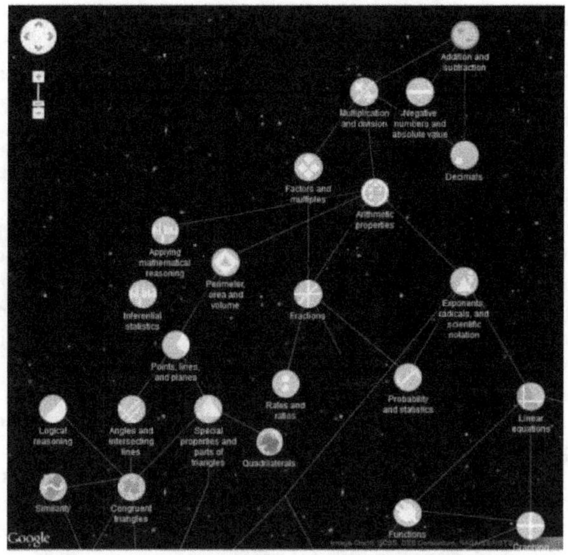

Figure 3. Knowledge Tree in Khan Academy

Badges – One very common element in gamification is the use of badges and points. Khan Academy has both. Khan Academy has 5 different types of badges as well as challenge patches, all of which are listed in Table 1. The badges represent achievement of different levels. Badges appear in the user's profile and may be shared through Facebook.

Table 1. Khan Academy Badges

Badge Name	#	How Earned	CS Specific
Meteorite	35	Mastering a certain number of skills, participating in a discussion forum, or watching a certain amount of video instruction	Yes - 6
Moon	33	Master a specific area or through consistent learning (mastering a number of unique skills, watching videos for a specific number of sequential days)	Yes - 2
Earth	17	Mastering additional skills, correctly answering problems in a row, watching a number of hours of video, forum participation, or by donating money	Yes - 2
Sun	11	Additional mastery of skills, large participation in discussion forums, or vast video watching (10 hours of a single topic).	No
Black Hole	3	Unknown – not given	?
Challenge Patches	35	Proving proficiency in a specific skill	No

Energy Points – Completing activities will allow the user to earn energy points, which are then displayed on their personalized dashboard, along with the number of videos they have completed watching and the badges they have earned. Earning enough energy points will also earn the user specific badges.

Goals – Goals can be ones the system suggests for you (watching any 5 videos or completing 5 skills) or may be defined by the user (custom goals). Custom goals originally have suggestions based on past performance or can be selected by the user. Currently only math topics can be selected as skill goals, but any video from any topic can be added as a goal as well.

Progress Indicators – Khan Academy provides several different indicators for showing progress to the user. It will display information for achieving goals, activity indicators, focus information and skill progression. For accomplishing goals, a bar indicator is used to display how many goals have been accomplished and how many have yet to be attained. Activity information is displayed through a bar graph indicating the amount of activity within Khan Academy each day and how many energy points were earned within a specific time period. Focus progression illustrates in a circle graph the skills and topic areas on which the user has spent their time. The graph displays the amount of time spent in different areas for selected time units (past 24 hours, past week, past month, etc.). There is one circle graph for videos and another for skills.

The final indicator is one of skill progression. All of the skills are listed for the user and each one lists the users' overall progress. The viewer can drill down for each topic unit to see the exact number of attempts and correct and incorrect answers for each subset of practice problems. An example of this progression is given in Figure 4.

Addition and subtraction	Attempts	Correct	Progress
1-digit addition	8	100%	Proficient
2-digit addition	0	-	Needs Practice
1-digit subtraction	0	-	Needs Practice
2 and 3-digit subtraction	0	-	Needs Practice
Addition with carrying	0	-	Needs Practice
Addition and subtraction word problems	0	-	Needs Practice
Subtraction with borrowing	0	-	Needs Practice
4-digit addition with carrying	0	-	Needs Practice
4-digit subtraction with borrowing	0	-	Needs Practice

Figure 4. Progress Indicator

4. MOTIVATIONAL PROCESSES

Some critical motivational processes include goals and self-evaluation, outcome expectations, values, social comparisons, and self-efficacy [20]. Our analysis finds that aspects of gaming align with these motivational processes. In this section we outline these motivational processes and the gaming mechanics that can help facilitate these processes.

4.1 Setting Goals

Setting goals is an important element in learning motivation. It would seem that gamification of learning environments is ultimately about goal setting with all of the badges and stars and points awarded. However, goal setting is not just about gaining more points but a willingness to attempt the goals and self-evaluation on attaining the goals. And the user must be allowed to set their own goals [18].

4.1.1 Specific rather than general

Games that give specific rather than general goals are considered more motivational [3]. An example of this type of specific goal setting is stating exactly how many points are needed to earn a specific badge. Examples of this can be found in many different games (e.g., Hay Day displays exactly how many orders must be filled in order to earn a specific badge). Within Khan Academy, some badges are very explicit in how they can be earned while others are vague or depend on the actions of others in order to be obtained. Several Khan Academy badges have more general goals (any five unique skills, any videos). By allowing general goals it may allow the user to earn the badge more quickly, however it may not serve as motivation to continue down a certain path to master a skill.

4.1.2 Indicate the effort needed

Self-evaluation of the effort needed to attain goals is important in motivation [3]. In game environments, goals that allow the users to estimate the amount of effort needed to attain the next level or badge would be more effective. Most games display this through either the map or progression indicator. Khan Academy shows the skill progression but has no effort indicator. The learner has no way of knowing how much effort is required before completing the next skill level. The learner does not know how many practice set problems are going to be presented or how much time it will take to complete the task.

4.1.3 Proximal, near goals

Short-term goals can enhance motivation and learning better than long term goals [4]. To be motivating, games should offer proximal goals that are easy to understand and can be readily attained. A good example of this can be found in the game Pet Rescue. It readily shows how many levels are required until the next power-up is awarded. Khan Academy's version of short-term goals is to complete another skill level or watch another video, with suggestions based on past performance. These suggestions do not illustrate a specific path or explicitly state the next step in achieving a specific badge or challenge patch. Earning badges cannot be an explicit goal currently within Khan Academy. The idea of "just earning points" can actually reduce motivation. The goal of scoring points is less likely to be relevant to a learner if the activity that the points measure is not first relevant to that learner [18]. In other words, the user must want to learn the material to earn points; simply having the points isn't enough to motivate the user to learn. Having a scoring system that has no deeper connection to the underlying activity than a quantification process provides no way for the user to make a meaningful connection to the activity [18].

4.1.4 Setting difficulty for motivation

If people perceive a goal to be more difficult they will be more willing to expend energy on it than if they perceive it to be easy [20]. So while short-term goals are important, making long-term objectives apparent while noting that time and effort are needed to attain them is also valuable in motivation. In games we can see this type of difficulty introduced when an epic narrative unfolds in the opening sequence that sets the ultimate quest for the player. In contrast, Khan Academy never lays out the difficulty and persistence needed to attain mastery of computer science or any other skill set. Yet, setting this difficulty level is about finding the balance between what is challenging and requires effort and what is so difficult that it overwhelming.

4.1.5 *Focus on process vs. outcome*

Children working on a goal of learning how to solve a problem and then reflecting on their progress toward that goal tend to be more motivated and learn more than children motivated just to achieve an outcome [1]. The use of game elements in learning environments such as Khan Academy is frequently only applied to outcomes and the process of learning is treated as a separate portion of the experience. Game elements can focus on process, rather than outcomes, in a number of ways. For example in Candy Crush Saga, one is not just trying to earn points but is also required to perform special moves (such as setting off double striped candy). This special move is required to pass a level in the game and move on, but this also teaches the process of playing the game and methods for achieving more points. A program like Khan could focus on incorporating gaming elements in novel ways, such as requiring a process oriented task such as design or documentation to be completed before leveling up.

4.2 Outcome Expectation

Outcome expectations are beliefs about what will come from a set of actions and are shaped by our expectations of internal changes, external accomplishments, and models of outcomes we observe. In gaming, outcome expectations could be described by what we expect the experience with a game to provide, both in terms of internal changes and external accomplishments, and the models we have for those changes.

4.2.1 *Internal and external expectations*

Both internal outcome expectations and external outcome expectations provide motivation [3]. For internal motivation, the user should feel pride in their accomplishments. For external motivation, the ability to show that they have beaten the game or passed the level is motivating. Many games frequently include the internal expectation that it is relaxing to play the game or it is considered "fun". External expectations are the ability to demonstrate to others that they are competitive or skilled. Khan allows for the internal expectation of the learner knowing they have completed or mastered the skill but limited external expectation because sharing accomplishments is difficult.

4.2.2 *Models*

People can be more motivated if they have models for what success looks like in any given domain [20]. In gaming models that motivate, behavior may be made apparent through non-player characters who navigate a difficult pathway, or in friends that achieve higher levels or points in a game. In Khan Academy the CS videos are excellent models of how to achieve the programming task at hand, and the young female voice who narrates them may be a model to other young women. However, these aspects of modeling do not tie into the gaming elements of Khan. There is no model for how to achieve points or badges.

4.3 Values

The role of values is important in motivation literature [20]. Values are individuals' beliefs about the importance of acting in certain ways in the world. Motivational theory suggests that if one believes learning, working, or playing are important, then they will act on those values.

4.3.1 *Value on agency leads to motivation*

People who place a value on agency, the ability to exert control over what they can achieve, are more motivated to try and achieve [2, 9]. In games, the agency is exerted in the choice to play and in a feeling that that one can become skilled enough to win. In Khan Academy, one is exhibiting his or her agency by being there and participating in learning. However, the gaming elements offer no agency; you cannot opt out and you cannot make private selected gaming elements of your participation. A user's profile showing their accomplishments is a completely public or private setting, sharing all accomplishments (and user information) or none.

4.3.2 *Values lead to learning and non-learning*

Values can lead to learning because the learner values the outcomes or actions needed to produce said learning [10]. Values can also motivate the student to reject learning, because the outcomes or actions needed to produce learning is in contrast to their own values [15]. Gaming elements offer these non-learners an opportunity to construct face saving tactics when learning is in conflict with values [8]. For example, a student who rejects an identity of being interested in math can still try at math if they state their motivation is earning points or badges. In this way game elements may offer face saving strategies for navigating around cultural values that conflict with learning motivation.

4.4 Social Comparisons

In addition to the social element of values impacting motivation, social comparisons also impact motivation. The plethora of social gaming suggests opportunities for these aspects of gaming to be incorporated into online learning environments to improve motivation. However, it is important to construct correct comparisons and to not overemphasize social comparisons.

4.4.1 *Comparisons with similar people*

Social comparisons encourage self-evaluation, an effective motivational process [19]. However, comparisons with dissimilar people can thwart motivation. If someone is much more advanced it can seem like a daunting task to reach their level of mastery. If someone is far behind, one is not motivated to move forward to keep pace. Players comparing themselves to others, in a game can be very motivating and lead to higher self-efficacy. Many casual social games do this very well by linking into the user's Facebook profile and showing the user's friends on the overall map (e.g., Candy Crush Saga) as well as their friends' scores on individual levels. If the user beats a friend's score on a particular level, they can "share" that information on their timeline. This non-synchronous sharing offers continual similar comparisons. Within Khan Academy there are no social comparisons. The learner is a solitary unit within the environment. While the learner can share accomplishments through their Facebook profile, there is no direct comparison with other users. Another shortcoming of Khan with respect to social comparisons is that user profiles are private by default. All user accomplishments are private and there is no ability to share accomplishments while hiding other user information. Thus, it is nearly impossible to see the activities and accomplishments of others on the site.

4.4.2 *Setting difficult goals*

While competitive elements can seem like easy gaming aspects to incorporate, it is important to temper the desire to construct social comparisons for motivation. Researchers have found that elements that contribute to goals, such as setting difficult goals (see section 4.1.4), leads to greater motivation than social comparisons [20]. Allowing users to self-identify with goals that are meaningful is more likely to produce autonomous, internalized behaviors [18].

5. DISCUSSION

We admire Khan Academy as an informal CS learning environment. There are qualities that make it ideal for novice informal learners that are self-motivated. Drawing users that are self-motivated suggests that Khan Academy is addressing issues of short-term engagement and seeks to use gamification to keep learners engaged and moving forward to more difficult tasks. However, in our analysis Khan has missed critical motivational elements in the application of gamification that might dramatically improve the quality of the gaming elements and increase motivation. Table 2 is a summary of promising approaches that may better address the motivational aspects of the gamification of Khan Academy than their current system.

Specifically, Khan is missing the notion of meaningful gamification, where the user is at the center. Nicholson defines meaningful gamification as the integration of user-centered game design elements into non-game contexts [18]. Using external rewards such as points without matching them to the underlying activities can create a hollow gamification experience and actually create a negative feeling in the user [18]. Instead, meaningful gamification also involves adding elements of pure play to the system instead of just scoring systems. By simply tacking on the gaming elements to the existing system, Khan Academy has missed the opportunity to make the gaming "playful."

Table 2. Learning Examples of Gamification

Motivational Processes	Gamification of Learning Example
Setting goals that are specific rather than general	Clear specification as to what needs to be completed to earn points, badges and complete map/tree.
Indicating effort needed	Allow "level testing" to move through lower level achievements quickly. This will serve as a formative assessment to gauge where participants should start for challenging yet achievable levels
Setting proximal, near goals that are easy to understand and attain are more motivating	Award badges / points upon mastery of individual control structures, topics, etc.
Demonstrating difficulty of long-term goals (if they have self-efficacy)	Initially letting learners know that achieving difficult or long-term goal and will take effort and time, and reinforcing their self-efficacy to achieve these more difficult goals.
Focusing on process vs. outcome	Peer awards for projects that encourage reflection, development of process oriented game elements that match learning goals.
Providing comparisons with similar people	Dashboards showing your progress against others in your class / cohort and the amount of time each spent studying, completing level.

In opposition to Khan Academy, we offer two other CS learning systems as better examples of incorporating gaming elements with motivational elements. Sarah Esper's work with CodeSpells [11, 12] and Michael Lee's work with Gidget [16, 17] represent true games which also teach introductory programming skills.

6. CONCLUSION

Combining gaming with an informal learning environment is very difficult. To create a user-centered meaningful gamification learning environment is even more difficult. While Khan Academy has included gaming elements, we believe they have missed an opportunity to have the desired motivational impact. By changing the implementation of the badges and points system to allow more well-defined goals (both near-term and long-term) and expanding the social aspects of the gaming elements the gamification of the site may provide better and more long term impact on motivation in this informal learning environment.

7. REFERENCES

[1] Anderman, E.M. and Wolters, C.A. 2006. Goals, Values, and Affect: Influences on Student Motivation. (2006).

[2] Bandura, A. 1994. *Self-efficacy*. Wiley Online Library.

[3] Bandura, A. 1986. Social foundations of thought and action. *Englewood Cliffs, NJ.* (1986).

[4] Bandura, A. and Schunk, D.H. 1981. Cultivating competence, self-efficacy, and intrinsic interest through proximal self-motivation. *Journal of personality and social psychology*. 41, 3 (1981), 586.

[5] Bogost, I. 2011. Gamification is bullshit. *Ian Bogost blog*. 8, (2011).

[6] Robertson, M. Can't play, won't play: 2010. *http://hideandseek.net/2010/10/06/cant-play-wont-play/*. Accessed: 2013-09-06.

[7] Deterding, S. et al. 2011. From game design elements to gamefulness: defining gamification. *Proceedings of the 15th International Academic MindTrek Conference: Envisioning Future Media Environments* (2011), 9–15.

[8] DiSalvo, B. et al. Saving face while geeking out: Navigating motivations of non-learners. *Journal of Learning Sciences*. In Press.

[9] Dweck, C.S. 2000. *Self-theories: Their role in motivation, personality, and development*. Psychology Press.

[10] Eccles, J.S. and Wigfield, A. 2002. Motivational beliefs, values, and goals. *Annual review of psychology*. 53, 1 (2002), 109–132.

[11] Esper, S. et al. 2013. CodeSpells: Embodying the Metaphor of Wizardry for Programming. *2013 ITiCSE Conference* (Canterbury, England, 2013), 249–254.

[12] Esper, S. et al. 2013. On the Nature of Fires and How to Spark Them when You'Re Not There. *2013 SIGCSE Conference* (Denver, CO, USA, 2013), 305–310.

[13] High Scalability - High Scalability - Khan Academy Checkbook Scaling to 6 Million Users a Month on GAE: *http://highscalability.com/blog/2013/4/1/khan-academy-checkbook-scaling-to-6-million-users-a-month-on.html*. Accessed: 2013-09-06.

[14] Kapp, K.M. 2012. *The gamification of learning and instruction: game-based methods and strategies for training and education*. Wiley. com.

[15] Kohl, H.R. 1994. *I won't learn from you*. New Press New York.

[16] Lee, M.J. 2013. How Can a Social Debugging Game Effectively Teach Computer Programming Concepts? *2013 ICER Conference* (San Diego, CA, USA, 2013), 181–182.

[17] Lee, M.J. et al. 2013. In-game assessments increase novice programmers' engagement and level completion speed. *2013 ICER Conference* (San Diego, CA, USA, 2013), 153–160.

[18] Nicholson, S. 2012. A user-centered theoretical framework for meaningful gamification. *Proceedings GLS*. 8, (2012).

[19] Schunk, D.H. 1987. Peer models and children's behavioral change. *Review of educational research*. 57, 2 (1987), 149–174.

[20] Schunk, D.H. and Usher, E.L. 2012. Social Cognitive Theory and. *The Oxford Handbook of Human Motivation*. (2012), 13.

Course-Embedded Research in Software Development Courses

Sonal Dekhane and Richard Price
Georgia Gwinnett College
1000 University Center Lane
Lawrenceville, GA
001-678-407-5000
{sdekhane, rprice}@ggc.edu

ABSTRACT

In this paper we describe our initiative to incorporate research, professional practice and methodologies into two undergraduate software engineering courses. As part of the Undergraduate Research Experience (URE) initiative on our campus, we modified two of our core software engineering courses. In our Software Development II (junior level) and Software Development Project (senior level) courses we integrated research projects, corporate visits and research talks to develop a deeper understanding of software engineering research and practice amongst our students.

Categories and Subject Descriptors

K.3.2 [**Computers and Information Science Education**]: Computer science education – *curriculum*

General Terms

Experimentation

Keywords

Software engineering education, undergraduate research experience

1. INTRODUCTION

Georgia Gwinnett College (GGC) is an open access public institution offering a B.S. degree in Information Technology. The Information Technology program has four tracks, Software Development, Systems and Security, Enterprise Systems and Digital Media. GGC is also one of the seven institutions participating in the University System of Georgia's STEM initiative. This initiative was designed in an effort to respond to national and state challenges in STEM education (http://www.usg.edu/educational_access/stem). As part of this initiative GGC has established a four year Undergraduate Research Experience (URE) program to promote the success of STEM students and to promote early and active involvement in systematic investigation and research.

SIGCSE'14, March 5–8, 2014, Atlanta, Georgia, USA.

http://dx.doi.org/10.1145/2538862.2538927

This program encourages faculty to develop course embedded research experiences for students through all four years of their study. The goals of the URE program also align with extensive research indicating use of summer research experience programs to retain students in computing.

ITEC 3870, Software Development II is the second course in a sequence that teaches students to use the software development life cycle including problem definition, systems analysis, requirements gathering, designing systems, development of systems, testing and implementation. Upon completion of this course students will be able to: (1) apply project management concepts to the software development process; (2) effectively measure the software process using various metrics; (3) identify and describe various specialized software systems; (4) describe the differences in developing various specialized software systems; (5) develop a specialized software system of medium complexity using a software development process appropriate for it.

ITEC 4860 Software Development Project is the capstone project course for Information Technology majors. Upon completion of this course students will be able to: (1) apply common software project practice; (2) develop software projects; (3) understand the importance of system documentation; (4) deliver practical software following industry practice.

These two courses focus on Software Development implementation using industry standards and became a natural selection for this research. Students are expected to apply all of their prior coursework to expand their knowledge of software engineering. Independent research has long been a part of these courses and the formalization of this research resulted in significant improvement in student achievement of learning objectives.

In our Software Development II and Software Development Project courses the principles learned in Software Development I course are put into practice. As the students work on a software development project throughout the semester, their software development practice should be well founded in software engineering research. Development decisions should be made based on a thorough understanding of existing problems and requirements, tools, best practices and design principles. Many times students' development decisions are influenced by time constraints and existing proficiency in a set of tools. Students need to be exposed to different aspects of software engineering research and be familiar with current software engineering literature and evolving best practices. To address these needs, we proposed to strengthen our core courses by incorporating research projects, corporate visits and research talks. Through this redesign of courses we aimed to connect classroom material to the real world and motivate students to pursue graduate degrees. The goals of this project were:

1. Improve students' ability to read, summarize and synthesize peer-reviewed literature on software development and engineering with a focus on mobile computing and user experience. Students will develop the following skills:
    a. Read primary literature and extract needed information.
    b. Use the library to obtain in-house materials or request out-of-house materials.
    c. Create a bibliography for specific research area using standard citation formats.
2. Improve students' ability to integrate software engineering research principles in practice. Students will develop the skill to use the information extracted from peer-reviewed literature surveys to make informed decisions about design, tools and techniques to use.
3. Improve students' quantitative reasoning skills. Students will be able to:
    a. Collect and analyze quantitative data from usability testing process.
    b. Graph data and recognize trends.
    c. Summarize findings and recommend changes to the solution as necessary.
4. Improve students' ability to communicate ideas in written and oral form.
5. Increase student understanding of and interest in conducting software engineering research at the undergraduate or graduate level. As a result of this experience, more students will:
    a. Express confidence in their ability to conduct research.
    b. Express interest in participating in undergraduate research opportunities in IT.
    c. Express interest in attending graduate school in computing fields.
    d. More comprehensively answer: "What is software engineering research"?

2. BACKGROUND RESEARCH

Extensive research discusses the importance of undergraduate research in student success and retention in computing. Barker et. al. [1] observe that undergraduate research experiences have a potential of increasing students' likelihood of pursuing graduate degrees and expanding their awareness of their discipline and career opportunities. Zagar et. al. in [8] also discuss the use of literature to help students construct knowledge and solve the problems faced with it. In [5] Holz et.al. provide a road map for creating computing research methodology courses. In [6] Knox et.al. report using undergraduate summer experiences to study emerging technologies and discuss how this can be a meaningful student-faculty collaboration. Many, including Rahal [7] have used this strategy of using undergraduate research to investigate emerging technologies to stay updated. While the importance and benefits of undergraduate research experiences are established, it is also true that intense research programs are beneficial to a small number of students. The working group report by Carter et.al. [3] notes that the research enrichment programs are usually offered to top-performing students, usually outside the formal curriculum and they are usually sponsored. The costs associated with such summer enrichment programs result in these programs being offered to a select few students. By embedding research experiences in core courses we can make these experiences available to many more students. To take advantage of these experiences, students first have to be aware and motivated to apply to participate in such programs. Given our institutional context and student population, we decided that increasing students' awareness about research and opportunities associated with it was important. We decided to implement a strategy where students would be introduced to computing research in small steps through various core courses in their discipline. We hope that this will allow us to impact more students and create a culture of research on our campus.

3. PROJECT DESCRIPTION

In response to the 4 year URE initiative, faculty teaching courses in the Software Development track modified Advanced Programming and Software Development I courses to introduce software engineering research to students. In these courses students underwent a training led by library instructors to search for and obtain appropriate scholarly material to meet research requirements. Further details of this project are described in the paper by Brannock et.al. [2]. To further continue and extend this project, we integrated several activities in our Software Development II and Software Development Project courses. Students were required to participate in these activities and were responsible for deliverables related to these activities.

All students were required to participate in a research project. The research project was closely tied to the semester-long project that students had to work on. To achieve goal 1, students were assigned papers to read. The instructor selected these papers based on their applicability to course goals. To support this reading, students then had to find and read additional scholarly papers on the topic. Students were then required to summarize their findings in a paper written in a scholarly manner with appropriate citations. All of this was done as an individual project. Students then presented their findings to the class. The knowledge base created by these individual projects was then used to assist the students in their semester-long group project. Since the group project was a mobile application development project, the research projects addressed various areas of mobile computing and user experience in Software Development II course. In Software Development Project course the research focused on usability design, planning and testing. Along with the class presentations students also wrote an abstract and created a poster of their group project at the end of the semester. The winning abstract and poster were submitted to and presented at STARS Celebration conference in Atlanta, GA.

To achieve goal 2, all students participated in two corporate visits. These visits gave us an opportunity to connect the classroom content to the real world. Students visited a mobile game development organization to learn about the development process and tools used. The visit consisted of a campus tour, product demonstration and discussions about game development process and tools used, career paths and skills required. The visit ended with students playing the role of testers to test one of the products. Students also visited another larger organization that is a provider of accounting and payroll products and services. At this visit the students had an opportunity to closely interact with user experience experts and to participate in a usability testing experience. This visit was preceded by literature review and class discussions on usability testing. Students were also asked to design a usability test for their class project. During the visit, the user experience team discussed their methodology with the students and gave them a tour of their facilities. The team also demonstrated usability testing to the students and included the students in this demonstration. Once the students had experienced this first-hand they then had the opportunity to conduct usability testing of their term projects (designed and developed as part of course requirement). At the end of their testing they received feedback from the experts. These corporate visits not only helped the students gain deep appreciation of software engineering practice, but it also helped them apply their research in practice.

To meet goals 3 and 4 students conducted usability testing of their finished products in other classes on campus. Students redesigned the usability-testing plan after the corporate visit. They collected responses and data from students in two Chemistry classes. They then analyzed this data and reported their findings as part of the final presentation. Students also presented their group projects to their peers and faculty at our annual Science and Technology Research Showcase.

To meet goal 5 students attended two research talks on campus. The first talk was by ACM Distinguished Speaker, titled "Software Development: More Than Just Programming". This talk focused on current research, practices and standards in software development. The second talk was presented by a graduate student at Purdue University and was titled "HFOSS: Doing Good with Open Source". This talk not only introduced the students to open source software development, but also provided them an opportunity to learn about graduate school experiences and possibilities.

4. DATA COLLECTION AND ANALYSIS

In this pilot program, we used two major types of data collection. Data was collected measuring the students' perceptions of their ability to perform scholarly research and learn about new software engineering techniques. We conducted subjective comparisons of the quality of products created by previous teams with the current student efforts. This pilot program spanned two semesters.

Usability techniques, planning and testing were the focus of the research done by our students. We began our research by providing usability training for our students and then following up with a series of "starter" articles to begin our student research. Once the students had completed their initial reading, they provided an annotated bibliography detailing the information from their article. We reviewed and critiqued these bibliographies providing guidance for the preparation of these documents. Once the students had absorbed this feedback, they were required to find two more related articles and add them to their bibliography. During this time, the students designed and engaged in usability testing for the software projects they were delivering. Finally, students presented their findings to their peers and discussed application of their new knowledge.

Our data is from a limited population and is heavily influenced by the ratio of students. Our junior level students contributed 4/5s of our data.

The data we obtained through our surveys surprised us at first. We had some categories that declined unexpectedly. When we examined this data more closely, we realized changes in data actually showed improved understanding of the complexity of research. Table 2 shows the different areas of declining results.

During the pre-research survey, students showed confidence in their ability to perform these tasks. Interestingly, students who had previously performed research studies in other courses rated their abilities higher than those in their first research study. Figure 1 not only compares the average ratings among pre and post surveys, but it also compares pre and post survey results of

Figure 1: Research Survey Data Part 1

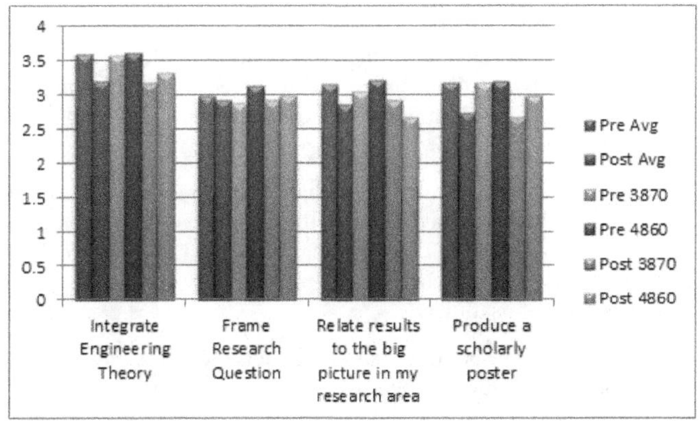

the two different courses. Our more experienced students rated their abilities higher on both the pre and post research surveys. Based on the students second exposure to scholarly research, we saw a significant improvement in the ability of our students to frame a specific research question and relate their research to the greater body of knowledge in their research area.

Student survey data clearly shows the improvement made by our students as this research was applied to their academic careers. Students clearly improved their confidence in performing scholarly research and their ability to present their findings. Data is reflected in Figure 2.

Figure 2: Research Survey Data Part 2

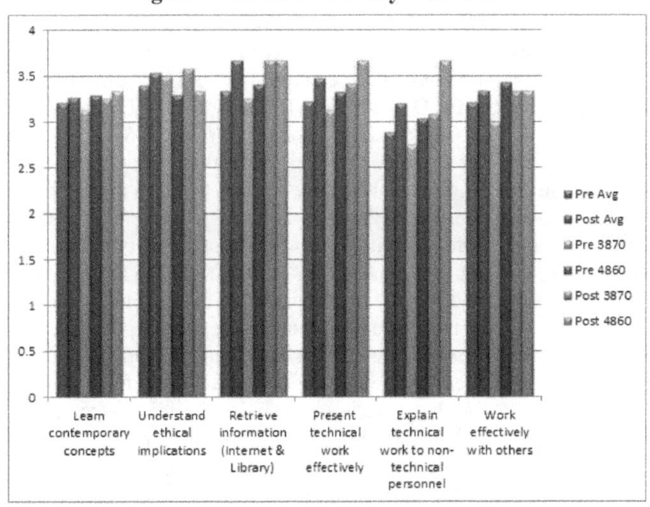

Making the same comparison between courses reveals students at all levels benefited from the research conducted in conjunction with these courses. Significant improvements were made and students gained the confidence to perform and present research.

Usability testing showed only one significant issue in the two products we tested. This flaw was resolved by minor re-design and re-work. When several usability experts evaluated the product, the designed user interface scored highly in all of their tests.

Post research interviews showed a clear understanding of the research area covered by this study by the students. Some students felt overwhelmed with the additional work required to complete this research but most found it an academically rewarding experience. Several of the student comments praised the academic knowledge gained while performing this research and give further insight into the effectiveness of this program. Specific comments include:

"Conducting research allows the student to slow down and take time to research and fully understand a subject. Research papers allow students to break down a subject to small parts to help them fully understand."

"Before this research I cannot say that I had no understanding of usability. Now after having read these articles and conducted some testing of my own I can say that compared to how I feel on the subject at this moment, before I did actually have next to no understanding of usability."

"Usability Testing is important to better meet the customer's needs and expectations of the user interface"

An unexpected benefit of this project was a significant improvement in unrelated code quality. Fewer defects were discovered and performance metrics were well within acceptable limits.

4.1 Faculty Perceptions

Faculty reflection on this project at the end of the year brought forth several benefits and challenges of this project. The transformation of the core software development courses is a recent initiative. Many of our students had no research experience at all. Some of them had attended the library training, while others had not received that opportunity. At the same time majority of them had not created a poster before. As time goes by, we anticipate that students will come in with beginner-level skills on how to find scholarly material, how to write an abstract and create a poster. While in the Advanced Programming and Software Development I the research project is based on scholarly readings, in Software Development II and Software Development Project the focus is on creating a solution/product. We anticipate that in the future, students will smoothly transition from conducting peer-reviewed literature search to applying research results into practice. Faculty members were highly encouraged by student success in submitting an abstract and creating and presenting a poster at a conference. On the flip side many of our students had already made up their mind about finding a job, instead of going to graduate school. They had preconceived notions about software engineering research and practice being completely unrelated. While we were able to change these notions through the research projects and their application to group projects, many students still believed that research experience and graduate school would not be of interest or benefit to them. Some of our students were non-traditional students and believed that they were too old to go to graduate school and hence were not interested in learning about research. Many of the students in the beginning found it hard to understand the connection between research and job. This was the main challenge that faculty faced at the beginning of the semester. As we learn more about students' perceptions we hope to be able to address their concerns proactively and earlier. On a positive note, students were excited about the opportunity to present their work at GGC's annual research showcase and at STARS Celebration conference. Student feedback and challenges faced during this first year have also made us realize that streamlining our efforts is necessary for future course offerings. Logistics require more planning than anticipated.

5. CONCLUSIONS AND FUTURE WORK

Our initiative to transform core courses in the software development track allowed us to introduce the students to undergraduate research and teach them basic research skills. In the two upper level courses students were able to analyze research findings and apply them to their group projects. Students applied research findings to software development projects and created posters to present at a conference. Students rated corporate visits as highly valuable to their learning experience. In order to increase student interest and engagement in research we need to extend these efforts to our lower level classes. By the time students take junior and senior level classes it is a little hard to change their notions. But a culture of research and repeated opportunities to interact with professionals will help us influence students' mindset.

6. ACKNOWLEDGMENTS

The University System of Georgia STEM Initiative II program funded this project.

7. REFERENCES

[1] Barker, L. 2009. Student and Faculty Perceptions of Undergraduate Research Experiences in Computing. Transactions on Computing Education 9(1): 1-28.

[2] Brannock, E., Napier, N., and Nagel, K. 2012. Transforming Programming-Intensive Courses With Course-Embedded Research. In *Proceedings of the 13th Annual Conference On Information Technology Education.* ACM, New York, 203-208.

[3] Carter, J., Bouvier, D., Cardell-Oliver, R., Hamilton, M., Kurkovsky, S., Markham, S., McClung, O, McDermott, R., Riedesel, C., Shi, J. and White, S. 2011. *Motivating All our Students?* ITiCSE 2011 Working Group Report.

[4] Dahlberg, T., Barnes, T., Rorrer, A. and Powell, E. 2008. Improving Retention and Graduate Recruitment Through Immersive Research Experiences For Undergraduates. In *Proceedings of the 39th SIGCSE technical symposium on Computer science education.* ACM, New York, 466-470.

[5] Holz, H., Applin, A., Haberman, B., Joyce, D., Purchase, H and Reed, C. 2011. *Research Methods in Computing: What Are They, And How Should We Teach Them?* ITiCSE Working Group Reports on ITiCSE on Innovation and Technology in Computer Science Education, 96-114.

[6] Knox, D., DePasquale, P. and Pulimood, S. 2006. A Model For Summer Undergraduate Research Experiences in Emerging Technologies. In *Proceedings of the 37th SIGCSE Technical Symposium on Computer Science Education.* ACM, New York, 214-218.

[7] Rahal, I. 2008. Undergraduate Research Experiences in Data Mining. In *Proceedings of the 39th SIGCSE Technical Symposium on Computer Science Education.* ACM, New York, 461-465.

[8] Zagar, M., Bosnic, I and Orlic, M. 2008. Enhancing Software Engineering Education: A Creative Approach. In *Proceedings of the 2008 International Workshop on Software Engineering in East and South Europe.* ACM, New York, 51-58.

Using a Real World Project in a Software Testing Course

Daniel E. Krutz, Samuel A. Malachowsky, and Thomas Reichlmayr
Software Engineering Department
Rochester Institute of Technology
1 Lomb Memorial Drive
Rochester, NY 14623
{dxkvse, samvse, tjrese}@rit.edu

ABSTRACT

Although testing often accounts for 50% of the budget of a typical software project, the subject of software testing is often overlooked in computing curriculum. Students often view testing as a boring and unnecessary task, and education is usually focused on building software, not ensuring its quality. Previous works have focused on either making the subject of testing more exciting for students or on a more potent lecture-based learning process.

At the Department of Software Engineering at the Rochester Institute of Technology, recent efforts have been focused on the project component of our Software Testing course as an area of innovation. Rather than previous methods such as a tightly controlled and repetitive testbed, our students are allowed to choose a real-world, open source project to test throughout the term. With the instructor as both counsel and client, students are expected to deliver a test plan, a final report, and several class-wide presentations.

This project has achieved significant student praise; qualitative and quantitative feedback demonstrates both increased satisfaction and fulfilled curricular requirements. Students enjoy the real-world aspect of the project and the ability to work with relevant applications and technologies. This paper outlines the project details and educational goals.

Categories and Subject Descriptors

K.3.2 [**Computers and Education**]: Computers and Information Science Education- Computer science education; Curriculum

General Terms

Design, Reliability, Verification

Keywords

Software Testing, Software Engineering Education, Software Project

SIGCSE'14, March 3–8, 2014, Atlanta, GA, USA.

1. INTRODUCTION

Software testing is an important aspect of creating reliable software. Defects can have numerous adverse affects on an application, ranging from unhappy customers and users to injury or even death. Projects should place a more significant focus on testing; recent studies have indicated that testing makes up over 50% of the cost of a typical software project [15] and a third of the cost of all software bugs could be eliminated through improved testing [21]. Unfortunately, testing is far too often overlooked in both industry and academia.

Software Engineering education is far too often deficient in this area as well. Although most universities have programs in computing, very few offer courses with a primary focus in software testing [11] [14] [18]. Additionally, the educational mindset of most schools is to teach students how to build software, not break it [13]. Largely due to the difficulty of grading such a component or a lack of course time, testing often comprises only a minor portion of the student's grade in the majority of programming courses [19] [10]. Students often lack enthusiasm about testing; they are usually much more interested in building software than in ensuring its quality [1]. Finally, testing as both a concept and a practice can be very difficult to teach through lectures. Kaner *et al.* [9] stated that "the challenge is to develop group activities that can foster insight—a level of abstract understanding that can apply from situation to situation—rather than emphasizing detailed procedural understanding."

There is a significant amount of research which shows the importance of software testing, with a substantial amount of improvement needing to be done in both academia and industry [15] [12]. Additionally, software testing in our educational institutions needs to have a more practical focus with educators doing a better job readying their students for industry [20] [8].

At the Rochester Institute of Technology (RIT), we have offered an upper division Software Testing course since 1998, with a wide focus including process, tools, and analysis. A project component has always been a significant portion of this course, but it became obvious that improvements needed to be made. We have recently altered this project to more directly address a lack of student enthusiasm regarding testing, the desire for students to work on a real-world project, and the need for students to become better acclimated with contemporary testing technologies.

In this paper, we describe an innovative approach to teaching software testing through a project component. Under the supervision of the instructor, who also plays the role as customer, small student teams first choose a moderately sized open source project. Each team then develops a test plan to be followed for the rest of the project term and proceeds to test the chosen application using this plan. Teams give presentations throughout the term to report their progress. The project culminates with a final presentation and test report.

This updated project component has been included in several class offerings and has had substantial success. Students have stated that it has not only significantly increased their knowledge of software testing as a discipline, but of its value as well. Feedback has shown praise both for the real-world nature of the project and the reinforcement it gave to the need for testing.

The remainder of this paper is organized as follows. Section 2 describes the Software Testing course with its general structure and main components. Section 3 provides an overview of the project. Section 4 discusses a sample student project. Section 5 discusses project results. Section 6 offers student feedback based on the project. Section 7 describes related work. Section 8 discusses future work on the project, and section 9 provides a summary of this work.

2. ABOUT THE COURSE

Primarily comprised of upper division Software Engineering students, the Software Testing course is also offered to other programs including Computer Science, Computer Engineering, Electrical Engineering, and Game Design. The only prerequisite for our testing course is an earlier class which introduces basic concepts of software engineering including teamwork, development processes, and proper documentation. In this prerequisite Introduction to Software Engineering course, students have already been introduced to some aspects of testing, including unit testing, system testing, integration testing, and acceptance testing. In many cases, other non-required courses and a required one-year co-operative internship (co-op) have exposed students to various aspects of testing as well. The Software Engineering department considers the 3-credit Software Testing course to be the primary means of fully exploring software testing and closely related disciplines.

The course has three primary learning outcomes: to instruct students on the importance of software testing, to expose them to various testing-related tools and techniques, and to explain and exercise the decision process and situations in which certain tests should and should not be used. While various tools such as jUnit[1], DJUnit[2], jMock[3], and Selenium[4] are discussed throughout the course, it is their underlying categorization and appropriate use that is emphasized. The studies regarding the importance of testing are expounded both by looking at use cases that illustrate a need for testing and by exploring why testing is often neglected by development teams.

While most students do not become overly enthralled with software testing, we do expend effort to dispel the myth that testing is the bland, monotonous field that many believe it to be. While approximately half of each classroom session is devoted to a lecture, the remaining time is reserved for a relevant hands-on activity or discussion. As an example, each class begins with an interactive "Bug of the Day" (BotD) activity [11] in which students study a real world software bug, its impacts, and the ways it could have been avoided. This activity is designed to highlight common bugs and practical application of course topics to actual examples.

Students are graded on several criteria. Each term there are three exams, several homework assignments, and a project based component. Class size is typically 25-40 students.

3. ABOUT THE PROJECT

The Software Testing course at RIT has always had a significant project component. Previously, the project involved all student groups being assigned the same set of code in which they were expected to find known bugs. The tools and testing techniques they were allowed to use was restricted, and the project was largely viewed as bland and unexciting for the students. They did not enjoy working on the same cookie cutter project, wanted something more realistic, were interested in making a real-world contribution, and wanted something that would look better to potential employers. In order to address these concerns and to meet educational goals, we decided to create a new project for the course.

During the first week of the 15 week term, teams are formed. Students are able to assist in the team creation process by choosing which other students they would like to be partnered with. Team size is targeted to 4-6 students, as this is often the size of groups in industry and has been found to be conducive to student learning in previous research [6] [16].

Once the teams have been formed, their first step is to choose an application to be tested. Students are asked to select medium-sized open source applications for testing. They must be large enough to provide an adequately sized test bed, but not so large as to overwhelm the teams. Applications with roughly 100-200 classes have been found to be appropriate for this project, and students are not limited by programming language, even if the instructor is not familiar with the chosen language. Projects with a high level of documentation are preferred, as this provides a basis for acceptance tests and the documentation itself can also be tested. The final step in the application selection process is to have the program approved by the instructor. This must be done by week 3.

The next major deliverable, due in week 5, is the project test plan. Students are provided with an initial template, but test plans are expected to significantly differ from one another due to the wide variety of applications selected. Groups are encouraged to make the best test plans possible, but are not necessarily held to them during the remainder of the course term. Because of expected but unforeseen hurdles as well as new concepts covered in class, students are allowed to build on to and deviate from this test plan as necessary.

In week 6, each team presents their test plan, along with any results already gathered by the team. This gives the teams an opportunity to receive feedback from their peers, gain valuable public speaking experience, and exposure for their classmates to new testing tools and techniques (which they may use on their own projects). After the presentation, a question and answer session takes place in which students must often defend the choices made for their project. Addi-

[1]http://junit.org/

[2]http://works.dgic.co.jp/djunit/

[3]http://jmock.org/

[4]http://docs.seleniumhq.org/

Table 1: Discovered Defect Types

Week	Deliverable
1	Teams Formed
3	Application Chosen
5	Test Plan
5-15	Plan Execution
6	Plan Presentations
10	Progress Report
15	Final Report & Presentation
15	Postmortem

tionally, students must write a 2-4 page reflection document describing what has and has not gone well so far. A primary objective of this reflection is to allow the students to understand and continue to build upon their strengths while also identifying and remedying areas of improvement. Groups are expected to perform a critical analysis of these findings and propose resolutions for problematic areas.

In week 10 of the term, groups are asked to submit a brief report detailing their progress to that point. This deliverable serves two purposes: it gives the instructor insight with an opportunity to intervene, and it provides a milestone for groups mid-project.

In the final week, students submit their final report, which details not only the findings of their testing, but also the specific tests used and relevant data. Students are also encouraged to state why they chose and carried out particular tests and provide a rationale for the processes and techniques they employed. They are not expected to propose resolutions for the discovered bugs, as this could violate the intent of the exercise and serve to distract the team. Groups are, however, encouraged to identify the steps needed to duplicate the defect, which appropriately represents the similar action needed in industry to resolve defects. Much like in week 6, students again present their findings to the rest of the class, including a 5-10 minute window for questions and answers.

The final project deliverable is a postmortem. In this document, students reflect on what went well, what went poorly, and how they could improve upon each. This critical analysis is also expected to contain possible resolutions for all difficulties encountered along the way.

Grading of all deliverables is done using a rubric. The presentations, for example, are evaluated on how well they prepared, the quality of project information conveyed to the class, and how well they answered project questions. No significant part of the grading is based upon the number of bugs found by a team, as students are encouraged to be more concerned with the processes and techniques they are using rather than the number of defects they discover.

4. SAMPLE PROJECT

As stated in the last section, the primary criteria for selection were size and a restriction to open-source projects. Students selected a wide range of open source applications, including both traditional and mobile applications, applications written for Unix, Windows, and OSX operating systems, and applications written by both small groups and organizations the size of Mozilla. A few of the tested applications included JBrick [5], tuxGuitar [6], Notepad++ [7] and components of Firefox [8].

In the following example, we will discuss an example student testing project which analyzed jBrick, an application designed to assist handicapped students in programming Lego robots. The group was comprised of 6 students, 3 of which had previously indicated that they wished to work together. Because one of the team members had previous experience with jBrick, it was chosen as the test application after a brief team discussion.

The students were able to gather both the source code and a significant amount of documentation from the jBrick project website. Their initial plan was largely devoted to usability and acceptance testing of the project. While these tests would have yield some results, instructor feedback indicated that they should explore a wider variety of applicable tests, keeping in mind the cost/benefit trade-off in their choices.

The team ultimately decided to add unit and mutation testing. They met twice a week for 1-2 hours and stayed in touch via text, Google Docs, and social media. The team regularly met with the instructor who played both the role of teacher and customer for the project. During their final presentation, they indicated that they had performed most of their intended testing on the application, but were unable to perform some of the unit tests due to time constraints and some of the mutation testing due to technical limitations.

The team's testing revealed some compelling results. Since jBrick was intended for both the visually and non-visually impaired, usability testing was performed on the application using representatives of both groups. While some usability issues were identified by visually impaired users, a surprisingly higher number were found by non-impaired users. Additional issues found included negative application performance due to poorly written code and functions which needed repair (revealed in unit testing).

In their postmortem, the team indicated that although they believed their project went well, they felt there was room for significant improvement in both their testing methodologies and their team dynamics. The team expressed that they should have used more automated testing tools to reduce the monotony of some of the tests as well as a wider variety of tests, including fuzz testing. The team also stated that they should have met more as a group and stayed in closer contact with one another throughout the course of the project. Members indicated that lack of communication significantly hindered their team's performance.

5. PROJECT RESULTS

Students have uncovered a wide variety of bugs with varying levels of severity. Table 2 shows some of the types of bugs discovered by 18 groups spanning several course offerings with each group testing a unique project. Instructors should remember that all projects are different and that the types and number of defects students discover will significantly vary. All examined projects are different and a properly developed testing process does not necessarily lead to the discovery of a large number or variety of defects.

[5]http://code.google.com/p/jbrick/
[6]http://sourceforge.net/projects/tuxguitar/
[7]http://notepad-plus-plus.org
[8]http://www.mozilla.org/en-US/firefox/

Table 2: Discovered Defect Types

Type of bug	# Found
Minor, non-functional	153
Incorrect Documentation	287
Poor Usability	113
Incorrect Functionality	49
Crash	35

Table 4: Student Responses

	Yes	No	Total
Did you enjoy the software project?	66	12	85%
Would you recommend this project?	60	18	77%
Resembles a real world project?	60	18	77%
How much did you learn? (0-5)	-	-	4.15

The majority of issues discovered have been relatively minor, such as grammar mistakes, inadequate documentation, and poor usability. In most cases, however, students were able to find significant numbers of more serious issues such as crashes in the application and functionality that was incorrect. In measuring the severity of defects, teams studied the accuracy of results and if requirements were met or failed.

Students were able to find bugs using a wide variety of testing tools and technologies. Table 3 includes a list of those most frequently chosen by the students. The majority of teams chose to conduct unit, acceptance, usability, and compatibility testing. While these tests were certainly good choices, it is likely that teams selected them because they were both relatively easy to implement and students had been exposed to them early in the course.

Table 3: Types of Testing Conducted by Teams

Type of test	# Found
Unit	16
Acceptance	17
Usability	17
Fuzz	10
Accessibility	8
Security	3
Performance	10
Compatibility	18

After completion, most teams chose to submit their bug reports to the application's development team. Several have received messages from the developers thanking them and confirming the existence of the errors they had discovered.

6. STUDENT FEEDBACK

Students have expressed a significant amount of satisfaction in this project and it has contributed to their overall satisfaction with the course. At the conclusion of the term, students are asked to submit an anonymous survey rating several aspects of the course, instructor, and project. Several of these questions and student responses are shown in Table 4. These questions have been posed to students in the last three course offerings, all of which have used this project component. A total of 78 students from these sections have responded to the survey.

These results indicate that the vast majority of students not only enjoyed the project, but would also recommend it to a classmate as well. Additionally, most students felt that it reassembled a project which they were likely to encounter in the real world and were similar to tasks they were asked to complete while on co-op. Finally, students were asked to rate how much they learned from the project on a 0-5 scale, with 0 representing them learning very little and 5 representing the maximum amount of learning. The average student response was a 4.15/5 indicating that, on average, students felt the project to be very educational.

The end of term feedback also allowed students to write some of their thoughts regarding the course project. The following are samples of written feedback that have been received:

> "The Software Testing course helped to drive home the importance of testing at every stage in the software development life cycle. The project component was especially helpful in this area. We were able to see the abundance of errors that existed even in our favorite applications."

> "Testing one of my favorite open source applications helped to keep me interested in the project. Not only was I able to examine the source code of a tool I regularly used, but it made me feel good to know that I was assisting in removing defects from a tool I used on a regular basis, for both myself and other open source users as well. "

> "Testing is a difficult, time consuming and sometimes monotonous process. It is however, very important. I was shocked by all the bugs our team discovered in what I thought to be a heavily tested and defect free application."

> "Like with many aspects of software engineering, software testing is heavily process based. Before this project, I viewed testing as an ad-hoc process that waited until the conclusion of a project. This project has taught me the importance of documentation and process in software testing. Additionally, I've learned that testing should occur at numerous stages in software development."

After taking the course and returning from co-op, students have stated they this course project prepared them very well for projects which they worked on in industry. The project has also helped to increase specific interest in software testing for several students, some of which have subsequently taken full time jobs in the field of software testing. Many students have reported that they were able to gain a co-op or full time job in a field of software testing or a related discipline largely from their experiences with this project.

The enthusiasm students have about the project has also been stated as a major reason why many decide to enroll in the class. One testament to this is the growing enrollment figures for the elective course. The first term in which the new project was offered was in the Fall of 2010. Since this offering, student enrollment figures have progressively increased for the course. The second offering of 2012 saw the maximum number of students allowed for a course, 40, to be reached, leaving numerous students on the waiting list unable to attend. While it is impossible to unequivocally state that the project is the sole reason for the increased student enrollment figures, we believe that these numbers act as yet another testament for student enthusiasm regarding the project. It is possible that the enthusiasm of the class instructors regarding the new project and its inherent variative nature has been a factor in student satisfaction as well. A chart representing student enrollment for the course since 2008 is shown in Figure 1. The line in the chart represents when the project was first offered as part of the course.

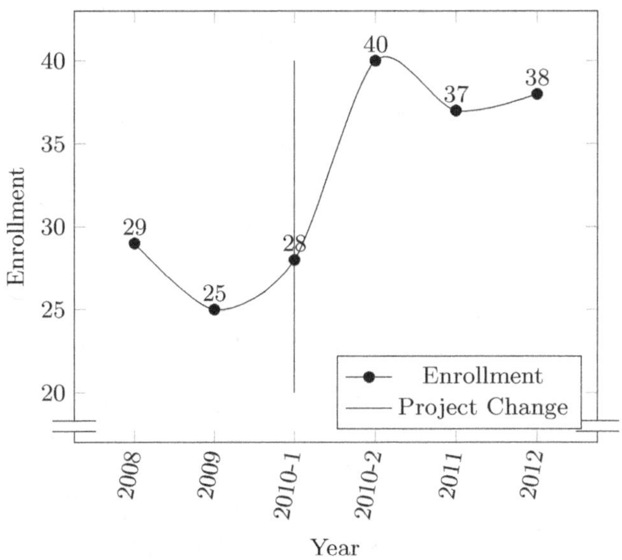

Figure 1: Student Enrollment Change

7. RELATED WORK

There have been numerous works which have stated the need of further emphasis on software testing education [1] [9] [2]. Some the deficiencies in software testing education include the inability to excite students about the topic, lack of relevant projects for students to interact with, and a primary educational focus on building rather than breaking software [13] [7] [1].

In order to assist software testing education, previous works have focused on enhancing the education process either through making it more exciting for students, or through a more educational experience. Gotel *et al.* [5] described the use of an open source web-based system for teaching software testing. This project revolved around having student-created problems which other students were expected to solve. Elbaum *et al.* [3] created a web-based tutorial known as Bug Hunt. The goal of this hands on activity was to teach students software testing at their own pace. Tutorials provided instant feedback to the user and automatically assessed the student's performance.

Preston [17] described the use of real-world projects in Information Technology education. The use of such projects was found to allow students to apply the theoretical knowledge they previously learned and solidify their understanding of the subject matter. Harrison [7] described a method of teaching software testing using viewpoints from both the developer and the software tester. This approach is beneficial since this allows students to see the importance and impact of proper software testing from each perspective. Goldwasser [4] described several fun and innovative methods of including software testing into a curriculum. In one example, students acted in a competitive fashion against a common test set.

8. FUTURE WORK

This project has been utilized in several sections of our Software Testing course and has been very successful, but there are enhancements which may be done to the project and further data which may be collected. One of the main purposes of the project is to allow a significant amount of freedom for each project team while achieving stated educational goals. While project deliverables are defined, each team is allowed to assign their own team roles, select their own projects, and choose the tests to run on the target application. The opportunity to make their own decisions and learn how to self-manage team in a supervised setting has presented some issues. Some of the teams have struggled with the extent of afforded freedom and have requested an extra deliverable and guidance during the term. In future implementations of this project, an extra deliverable will be added in week 10 which will include a written status and brief presentation. Finally, in past iterations some teams have been comprised of as many as 6 students; in the future, groups will be limited to 4-5 students to make meeting scheduling and communication demands more manageable.

This type of real world project is applicable to other educational areas of computing and may be applied to these courses as well. As an example, a software security course could implement a similar project to check for vulnerabilities in open source applications and propose fixes. A software design course could review the design of an application including the positive or negative ramifications of that design. In order to further measure the effectiveness of the project outlined above, we would like to poll seniors who took the Software Testing course regarding the effect of the project had on their subsequent experiences with software testing (i.e. co-op and senior capstone).

9. SUMMARY

Software Engineers need to understand the importance of developing high quality, defect free software. In order to ensure students are prepared for this task, we have developed an innovative software testing project which closely resembles tasks students will face upon graduation.

We have witnessed a significant increase in student enthusiasm in software testing as a subject and a discipline. This is largely due to us allowing students to select contemporary real world projects to test. Students have generally found the project to be very educational and feedback has indicated that it been a significant asset to them in industry. At least two other universities are planning to incorporate a similar project in their Software Testing classes and we encourage others to consider this approach in their courses as well.

10. REFERENCES

[1] N. Clark. Peer testing in software engineering projects. In *Proceedings of the Sixth Australasian Conference on Computing Education - Volume 30*, ACE '04, pages 41–48, Darlinghurst, Australia, Australia, 2004. Australian Computer Society, Inc.

[2] S. H. Edwards. Teaching software testing: automatic grading meets test-first coding. In *Companion of the 18th annual ACM SIGPLAN conference on Object-oriented programming, systems, languages, and applications*, OOPSLA '03, pages 318–319, New York, NY, USA, 2003. ACM.

[3] S. Elbaum, S. Person, J. Dokulil, and M. Jorde. Bug hunt: Making early software testing lessons engaging and affordable. In *Proceedings of the 29th international conference on Software Engineering*, ICSE '07, pages 688–697, Washington, DC, USA, 2007. IEEE Computer Society.

[4] M. H. Goldwasser. A gimmick to integrate software testing throughout the curriculum. *SIGCSE Bull.*, 34(1):271–275, Feb. 2002.

[5] O. Gotel, C. Scharff, and A. Wildenberg. Teaching software quality assurance by encouraging student contributions to an open source web-based system for the assessment of programming assignments. *SIGCSE Bull.*, 40(3):214–218, June 2008.

[6] J. Guo. Group projects in software engineering education. *J. Comput. Sci. Coll.*, 24(4):196–202, Apr. 2009.

[7] N. B. Harrison. Teaching software testing from two viewpoints. *J. Comput. Sci. Coll.*, 26(2):55–62, Dec. 2010.

[8] E. L. Jones and C. L. Chatmon. A perspective on teaching software testing. In *Proceedings of the seventh annual consortium for computing in small colleges central plains conference on The journal of computing in small colleges*, pages 92–100, USA, 2001. Consortium for Computing Sciences in Colleges.

[9] C. Kaner and S. Padmanabhan. Practice and transfer of learning in the teaching of software testing. In *Software Engineering Education Training, 2007. CSEET '07. 20th Conference on*, pages 157–166, 2007.

[10] F. Kazemian and T. Howles. A software testing course for computer science majors. *SIGCSE Bull.*, 37(4):50–53, Dec. 2005.

[11] D. Krutz and M. Lutz. Bug of the day: Reinforcing the importance of testing. In *Frontiers in Education*, 2013.

[12] C. Mao. Towards a question-driven teaching method for software testing course. In *Computer Science and Software Engineering, 2008 International Conference on*, volume 5, pages 645–648, 2008.

[13] A. Meneely and S. Lucidi. Vulnerability of the day: concrete demonstrations for software engineering undergraduates. In *Proceedings of the 2013 International Conference on Software Engineering*, ICSE '13, pages 1154–1157, Piscataway, NJ, USA, 2013. IEEE Press.

[14] G. J. Myers and C. Sandler. *The Art of Software Testing*. John Wiley & Sons, 2004.

[15] L. Osterweil. Strategic directions in software quality. *ACM Comput. Surv.*, 28(4):738–750, Dec. 1996.

[16] D. Petkovic, G. Thompson, and R. Todtenhoefer. Teaching practical software engineering and global software engineering: evaluation and comparison. *SIGCSE Bull.*, 38(3):294–298, June 2006.

[17] J. A. Preston. Utilizing authentic, real-world projects in information technology education. *SIGITE Newsl.*, 2(1):4:1–4:10, Apr. 2005.

[18] T. Shepard, M. Lamb, and D. Kelly. More testing should be taught. *Commun. ACM*, 44(6):103–108, June 2001.

[19] J. Smith, J. Tessler, E. Kramer, and C. Lin. Using peer review to teach software testing. In *Proceedings of the ninth annual international conference on International computing education research*, ICER '12, pages 93–98, New York, NY, USA, 2012. ACM.

[20] J. A. Whittaker. What is software testing? and why is it so hard? *IEEE Softw.*, 17(1):70–79, Jan. 2000.

[21] W. Wong, A. Bertolino, V. Debroy, A. Mathur, J. Offutt, and M. Vouk. Teaching software testing: Experiences, lessons learned and the path forward. In *Software Engineering Education and Training (CSEE T), 2011 24th IEEE-CS Conference on*, pages 530–534, 2011.

Student Projects Are Not Throwaways: Teaching Practical Software Maintenance in a Software Engineering Course

Claudia Szabo
School of Computer Science
The University of Adelaide
Adelaide, Australia
claudia.szabo@adelaide.edu.au

ABSTRACT

Teaching software engineering through group-based project work supported by theory lectures is effective, as recognized by both academia and industry. However, exposing students to practical software maintenance is often overlooked in favor of building software from scratch under the guidance of a lecturer or client. The developed software is usually delivered to the lecturer/client and no maintenance efforts are further required. In contrast, industry projects require fresh graduates to perform maintenance exercises and very rarely to build software from scratch. To address this issue, existing software maintenance assignments usually focus on small codebases of very good quality, in which artificial issues are introduced. In this paper, we propose to enhance a group-based project course with a software maintenance assignment that uses a medium-sized, student-produced codebase with real software bugs. Our analysis shows the effectiveness of our approach and highlights future avenues for improvement.

Categories and Subject Descriptors

K.3.2 [**Computing Milieux**]: Computers and Education-Computer and Information Science Education

Keywords

Computer Science Education, Software Maintenance, Software Engineering

1. INTRODUCTION

Approaches to teaching Software Engineering have recognized the importance of including practical applications of software engineering theory in the curriculum [15]. This is usually achieved by constructing the course around a group-based student project that gives students the opportunity to develop a small to medium size project through all its lifecyle steps, from requirements gathering through to deployment [5]. The projects generally run over the entire duration of the teaching period and have students develop a software from scratch [6] or as an extension to an open source project [15]. Students produce documentation artefacts that accompany the codebase, and by the end of the project become versed in team-based software development and all that it entails. However, as our students move into industry, it is rarely the case that they develop an entire project from scratch, and they will usually focus on maintaining existing codebases by either adding new features or fixing existing issues. Effectively incorporating software maintenance in the curriculum remains an issue as the software maintenance component needs to have a difficulty that is high enough to make it realistic, but small is enough to make it approachable for junior Software Engineering undergraduates [13, 20]. In addition, an appropriate amount of time needs to be dedicated to this activity such that the students can experience all four types of maintenance, namely, corrective (resolving issues), adaptive (adding features), perfective (improving features), and preventive (extracting code for reuse, refactoring), through their various stages [2]. This further increases the required complexity of the maintenance codebase in order for the exercise to be effective.

These issues have prompted educators to create software maintenance courses aimed at senior undergraduate students that have already experienced a team-based project [15, 20]. In these courses, the size of the codebase is fairly large (up to 70,000 lines of code) and students attempt maintenance as a team, rather than through individual effort. This assumes that students have already previously worked in group-based projects and have been exposed to more complicated software architectures than the usual coding assignments. Other approaches include software maintenance components as an individual exercise to complement q the team-based project, but perform a tradeoff in either including small codebases [4, 16, 20] or introducing small bugs in otherwise good quality code [4], thus not providing an accurate view of industry realities [3, 22, 17].

This paper discusses a component of an undergraduate Software Engineering Group Project (SEGP) course that focuses on exposing students to software maintenance. The SEGP course, the first of three undergraduate group-based project courses part of our Software Engineering degree, has students build a medium to large-scale software from scratch in teams of up to five students. Software Engineering theory is taught through the use of lectures and two assignments, which had previously required the writing of a code review report and of an essay detailing the lessons learned during project development. The following two courses only consist

SIGCSE'14, March 5–8, 2014, Atlanta, GA, USA.
Copyright 2014 ACM 978-1-4503-2605-6/14/03 ...$15.00.
http://dx.doi.org/10.1145/2538862.2538965.

of group-based project work taking up one and two semesters respectively. In the last course industry partners act as clients. As the projects generally required students to build software from scratch, we realized that software maintenance was only theoretically introduced in the SEGP course. To aid students in understanding the issues and factors that influence software maintenance beyond the theory taught in lectures, we replaced one of the assignments with a practical maintenance component that involved both adaptive and corrective maintenance on a medium-sized codebase. The students were asked to add a feature to past year's students project, which contained approximately 11,000 Lines of Code (LOC), and was written in a programming language in which the majority of the students were not experts. Furthermore, the codebase had issues that required corrective maintenance. These bugs were not artificially introduced, but were significant issues that the initial team had encountered as part of their project development.[1] Students were given four weeks for this assignment and were required to submit the modified and tested codebase, together with a report detailing their changes and lessons learned.

We analyze student learning outcomes through a quantitative analysis of the students' maintenance reports to determine: a) if students are able to identify crucial factors that influence maintenance and b) what scaffolding or additional resources are required in order to further understanding of these issues. Our contributions are twofold. Firstly, we propose a practical approach to teaching software maintenance using medium-sized, student-produced projects that have issues that are not artificially introduced. Secondly, our analysis shows that students were able to identify factors that influence software maintenance as well as strategies to improve the maintenance effort, but also opens avenues of improvement of teaching methods.

2. RELATED WORK

Software maintenance is defined as the process of making changes to a system after it has been put into operation. The high cost of software maintenance has been recognized since the 1980's [2, 9] and has not changed over the years [8, 19]. As such, educators have recognized the importance of teaching software maintenance as part of a software engineering degree [7, 10, 15]. Teaching software maintenance has proved difficult for two main reasons [10, 15, 20]. Firstly, software maintenance is a lengthy, multiple-stage process focused around understanding the software, generating and integrating the maintenance proposal, and retesting the code [2]. Effective teaching of software maintenance requires extensive component design and significant time allocation within the course. As such, some approaches propose dedicating entire software engineering courses to software maintenance [15, 20], which might be a luxury that some degrees cannot afford [4, 16]. Secondly, for the software maintenance exercise to be practical rather than theoretical, students require a codebase to maintain. This has to be complex enough such that the maintenance is not trivial, but also it must be accessible enough such that the maintenance task can be performed. We discuss related approaches below.

To expose students to the four main types of software maintenance, namely, namely, adaptive, corrective, perfective, and preventive [2], Postema et al. [16] include a software maintenance assignment in a Software Engineering course. The component requires students to maintain a 2,000 LOC codebase that is well-documented and well-tested. The codebase is bug-free but artificial errors are introduced. Students are also provided with a complete system specification and test plan and experience the four types of maintenance by fixing the artificial bug (corrective), adding another class (perfective), extracting code for reuse (preventive) and adding a small GUI component (adaptive). However, the codebase employed was small and of good quality in terms of documentation and testing, and no insight into the student learning outcomes is discussed.

Students are exposed to small codebases in maintenance components in other approaches as well [4, 20]. In [20], students are exposed to a small software program that manages the authors' book lending library and are asked to reengineer scripting commands into code, to remove magic numbers and generally improve the quality of the software. A test harness developed by the lecturers was supplied to the students, who then used it to test their code. [4] proposes a course dedicated exclusively to the use of software maintenance tools and enforces the use of a ticketing system and the fixing of artificial issues introduced by the lecturers. In a staged exercise that finishes with student teams adding new functionality after fixing the artificial bugs, the student teams are closely guided by lecturers. Significantly larger codebases in terms of LOC have been proposed by Wayne State University [15]. In the Advanced Software Engineering course dedicated to senior undergraduates and first year postgraduates, student teams practice software evolution and maintenance following the Software Change (SC) process [18] on open source projects of 6,000 LOC to 68,000 LOC. Teams are closely supervised and assessed during weekly meetings by PhD students, who act as project managers and customers. Assessment analysis shows that students perform equally well regardless of the size of the project and that they find the SC process easy to follow and effective. This approach shows that it is possible to use large codebases for software maintenance exercises, but the study focused on *senior* undergraduate students with prior experience in a group-based software project. In our approach, we expose junior Software Engineering students to a medium-sized codebase of 11,000 LOC in an individual exercise of adaptive and corrective maintenance.

3. APPROACH

The software maintenance component added to the SEGP course was valued at 10% of the final course mark. It required students to add a new feature to a codebase that students found quite large (see Section 4). At approximately 11,000 LOC spread over 45 files, the code was the result of the previous year's student group project. The code was a Java Graphical User Interface (GUI) simulation of a traffic intersection close to the University, complete with cars, one taxi stand, buses and pedestrians. The simulation was implemented in Java as a multi-threaded program that implemented a discrete event simulator with a very large (in the hundreds of thousands) number of events caused by the large number of entities, as shown in Figure 1.

The code was a combination of Java Swing GUI components that followed an MVC pattern and standard Java classes in a fairly complex architecture as shown in Figure 2

[1]The lecturer was aware of the issues having closely supervised the projects the year before.

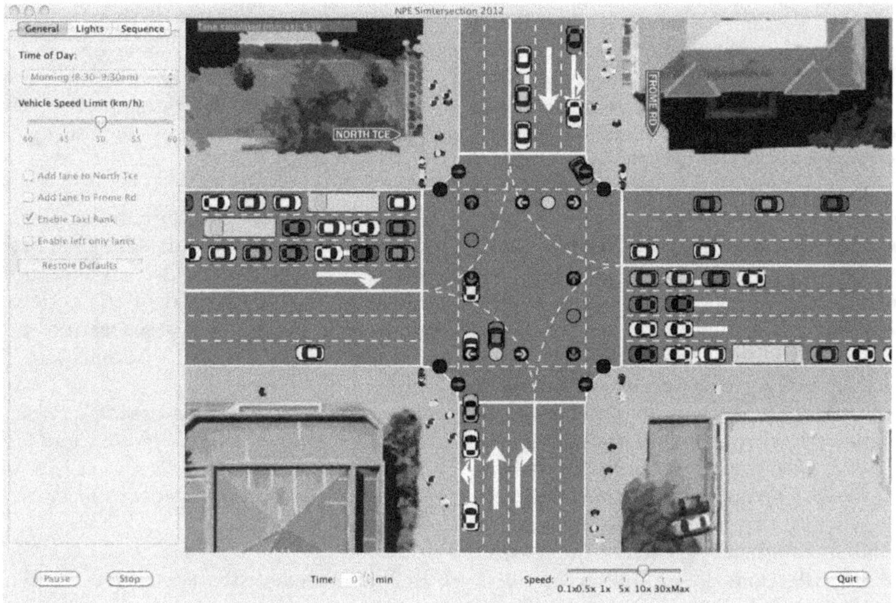

Figure 1: Software Used for Maintenance

(non-GUI components). The use of such a codebase for the

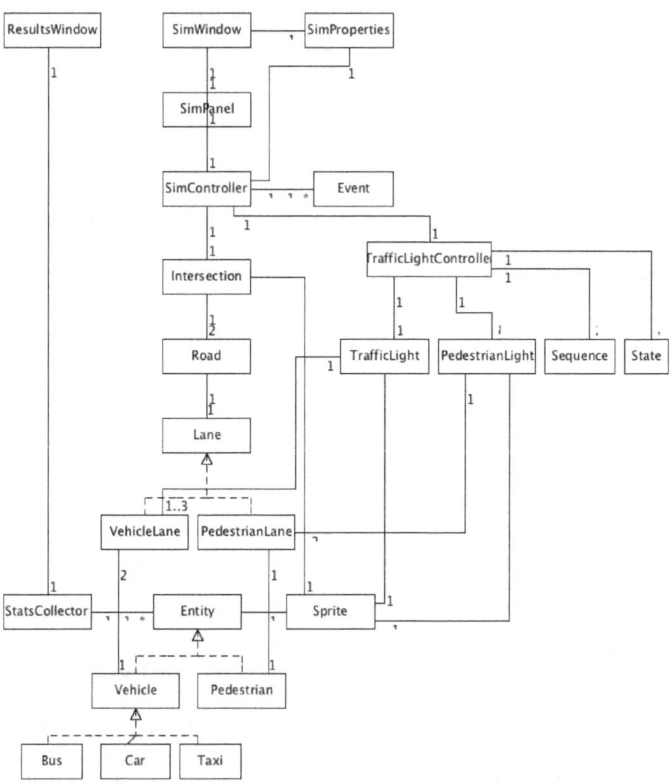

Figure 2: Class Diagram of Maintained Software

maintenance component had two advantages. Firstly, it was not a contrived, textbook example and felt real to the students (see Section 4). Secondly, the lecturer was familiar with the codebase and could accurately estimate the difficulty of the maintenance task. Despite introducing an additional layer of complexity, we believe that the use of an animated simulation in a GUI had the additional benefit of keeping the students engaged with the assignment.

Students were given access to only the codebase, without any documentation other than that present in the code, and were asked to add a feature to it, thus performing *adaptive* maintenance. The feature was the addition of a new taxi stand in another part of the intersection. Taxis would have to stop at the taxi stand, and pick up and drop off passengers. The test harness that came with the code was removed, but students were asked to test that their new feature worked. Unbeknownst to the students, the supplied codebase was buggy in that taxis did stop at the already existing taxi stand but did not pick and drop passengers. This was an issue with the TaxiStand Java class but also with the PedestrianLane class and five other event classes. Thus, to ensure that adaptive maintenance was performed, students would have to perform *corrective* maintenance as well. This buggy version was obtained from the previous years' group SVN repository. As discussed above, the project was familiar to the author as she had supervised its development the year before. Using the project and lecturer notes, the lecturer was able to identify the buggy SVN revision and provide that as a codebase. Besides adding this feature and fixing the existing issues with the code, students had to perform unit and system-wide tests, and reflect on their experience in a report detailing their process, performed changes, testing strategy, and lessons learned.

4. ANALYSIS

We perform an analysis on software maintenance experience reports collected from 14 students and show results of NVivo matrix queries in Table 1 and 2. We focus on students' perception of the four phases of software maintenance [8], as (i) understanding the software, (ii) generating a maintenance proposal, (iii) integrating the maintenance proposal, and (iv) retesting. In *software understanding*, we focus on two main classes of strategies, *as-needed* (or opportunistic), and *sys-*

tematic [12]. Following the *as-needed* strategy, a student will focus only on localized information about the object behavior without context information about how that behavior fits with the rest of the program. Other students might attempt random changes and observe their effects. A student employing the *systematic* strategy will trace the data flow through the entire program to determine its behavior. Studies show that there is a direct correlation between successfully modifying an unknown program or codebase and a systematic strategy [12, 21, 23].

We propose to determine if the practical exercise helps students identify the main factors that influence maintenance, which are defined in the literature as tool support [11, 14], software quality as a direct cause of lack of understanding of software [1, 2, 12, 14], and lack of experience [12]. We defined a coding framework with two main nodes, *maintenance phases* and *maintenance factors* respectively, with sub-nodes as discussed above. Our analysis methodology is the following: for each student report, the researcher goes through and encodes student comments to each of the nodes defined above. If particular reflections do not match the predefined nodes, a new node is created, with a comment and an exemplar. Once all student reports are encoded, the research team analyses the encoding, and discusses and resolves differences if any. We show the results of the queries in Table 1, which collates the number of student comments with respect to each node, as well as the percentage of those comments from the total number of comments recorded. From the 14 reports, a total of 135 student comments were of interest. The student marks were well distributed across the range: 20% of students received marks between 40-50 (out of 100), 35% were in the range 50-70, 28% were in the range 70-80, and the remaining in the range of 80-90.

Table 1: Frequency of Identified Maintenance Phases and Factors

Category	Sub-category	Freq.	Freq. (%)
Phases	1. Understanding of software	8	**14.5%**
(total 55)	As-needed	3	5.45%
	Systematic	5	9.09%
	2. Generating proposal	11	20.00%
	3. Integrating proposal	14	25.45%
	4. Retesting	22	**40.00%**
	Unit testing	10	18.18%
	System testing	8	14.5%
Factors	Software quality	65	81.25%
(total 80)	Tool support	6	7.5%
	Time management	6	7.5%
	Lack of experience	3	3.75%

4.1 Maintenance Stages

Students went through the four phases of software maintenance defined above, focusing on coding and testing.

4.1.1 Software Understanding

Only few students reported on going through an initial stage of understanding the software. Their reports on the importance of tool support to navigate complex code structures suggests nevertheless that there existed an unreported struggle with understanding. A student reports:

I found that a thorough understanding of the code was needed first before anything could be achieved. this includes knowing the purpose of each class in a broad sense, and also knowing the in depth purpose of the classes and methods which needed to be edited. When I first started working on the project I opened the SimWindow.jar file and attempted for half an hour to create a second TaxiRank. This was time wasted, as SimWindow did not need to be edited at all.

Of the reported software understanding stage, 50% of students that discussed this challenge attempted an as-needed strategy towards software understanding whereby random changes were performed in the codebase in order to determine what particular classes were responsible for. A student reports on a systematic approach:

I spent the next few hours reading through the contents of each subfolder contained in the project, and identifying places I would need to make changes. I then went back through those important locations and read through each of those files until I understood how the program worked.

An as-needed strategy proves inefficient and frustrating:

After having tried a brute force method of finding where to add a segment and only looking up how things work when they are immediately needed, I discovered that I very soon had a huge amount of information I was trying to keep track of. This method essentially created a tree that needed to be searched for answers, where each answer required two extra sections to look into. I soon learned despite it seeming like a slower method, it would be much more efficient to learn what everything does first, really get familiar with the system, and then start to add new things.

4.1.2 Integrating Maintenance Proposals

Students report on their integration strategies: when encountering coding standard issues such as hardcoding the taxi rank locations and other attributes, most students attempt to refactor, whereas some, pressed for time, do not:

Hence I opted to just add logic to the code for a second taxi rank, the position of which was also hardcoded. In retrospect, this sheds light on some of the effects that programming under pressure (which came about as a result of poor time management) had on me while working on this assignment.

4.1.3 Testing

A large percentage (40%) of student comments focussed on testing. Of the 14 submissions, 10 performed unit test using JUnit, 8 performed automated system tests, and 4 submissions tested the code by running it and observing the changes. The small number of automated system tests can be attributed to the inherent complexity of the task, as the system has to be significantly modified to output state information to files that can then be compared with expected outputs. A student notes on the difficulty of performing unit tests on object functionality where the context of the object depends on a variety of classes:

I also learned why is recommended to to keep objects independent from each other as much as possible. In the Simtersection code, objects as simple as the TaxiRank could not exist a lone, and were reliant on other objects to exist. [...] This caused many problems with unit testing, and just learning how the TaxiRank works required the knowledge of many other parts of the system.

4.2 Maintenance Factors

Four main factors that influenced the students' exercise in software maintenance were identified in the student reports, namely, tool support, the quality of the software, time management to succeed in the assignment, and students' lack of experience with large codebases. Time management does not figure in the literature as related work does not focus on student work, but, as expected, we have found it to be an important factor, together with the student lack of experience, as shown in Table 1. A student notes:

However, work I had done in Introduction to Software Engineering had only prepared me for single file programs that were for the most part working, where only simple bug testing was required. The addition of multiple files along with adding your own content combined with the huge scope of this system meant that I was dealing with something completely new.

The most prevalent factor identified was *software quality*, which is presented in detail in Table 2.

Table 2: Identified Software Quality Factors that Influence Maintenance (total = 65)

Category	Sub-category	Freq.	Freq. (%)
Design		8	12.33%
Comment quality	Lack of comments	5	7.69%
(total 26)	Good comments	18	27.69%
	Comments used for communication	3	4.61%
Code quality	Naming conventions	5	7.69%
(total 31)	Modularization	10	15.38%
	Hardcoded information	4	6.15%
	Class dependencies	9	13.84%
	Debugging options	3	4.61%

Students noted that Eclipse, together with good quality comments, provided tremendous support in understanding and navigating the complexities of the code:

The functions were documented in such a way that Eclipse was able to get each of the method names and what they did. [...] working with this large software made me realise how useful it can be.

While the presence of comments seemed to help significantly (the comments, together with the source code, were the only documentation available), students nevertheless noted the need and importance of more explicit comments:

[...] comment stating they were 'lanes on the other side of the road'. I found it really difficult to work out what that meant. Does that mean lanes going the opposite direction? If so, which set is which direction? Why do these lanes need to be included?

The use of modularized code helped in managing and understanding the complexity of the software. However, heavy modularization incurred a large number of dependencies between classes and methods, which made testing difficult:

The dependence that each class had on each other decreased the maintainability of the code significantly as it is very difficult to test each class seperately if it is a difficult thing to seperate the classes.

4.3 Discussion

Besides teaching software maintenance in a practical assignment, this course component has also revealed to us an area of software maintenance that we had overlooked in our teaching. Specifically, our lectures covered the types of maintenance and their various stages but touched only very briefly into approaches to understanding complex software implementations. A better coverage of re-engineering and discussions about how to deal with complex software might have made for a gentler introduction to maintaining the proposed codebase. Furthermore, while students had been previously very well exposed to testing approaches and strategies, they had never before performed testing on a such a complex system. This made some students conclude that testing a codebase like this was absolutely impossible, when, in fact, it had been thoroughly done by past year's teams.

Nevertheless, student reports show that software maintenance on medium-sized codebases is possible and that beneficial learning outcomes can be obtained even without dedicating an entire course to software maintenance. Next, the use of student-produced codebases with issues that have not been artificially introduced and without providing documentation artefacts other than the code and its comments, may seem challenging but also has its benefits. Firstly, comments are the most up-to-date documentation available for a program, and it is in comments that the intricate functionality of the software is revealed. Next, this assignment had a compelling GUI that did not need much introduction. Lastly, students identified and reflected on what facilitated or hindered their maintenance exercise and their first exposure to non-textbook codebases seem to have made them more aware of their own practices:

What this code has shown me about my practice as a software engineer is that I need to put more effort into making my code as maintainable as possible. I am relatively happy with how I name my variables and functions to reflect on what it is that they do, and also my commenting within function that tell the reader why I am doing what I am doing in my code. What I am less than happy with is how I comment above functions to describe exactly what it is that they do, as the naming conventions that I choose may make sense to me but someone else may not intuitively grasp what it is I am trying to achieve with a function just with the name of it alone. Also I have a tendency to use the "magic numbers" within my code just because it is easier at the time of coding to do so.

5. CONCLUSION

Teaching software maintenance using practical assignments is challenging because the codebase size and maintenance demands need to be high enough to make the exercise realistic, but also low enough to be achievable by junior software engineering students. In this paper, we propose a software maintenance assignment to complement lectures on software maintenance theory. In contrast to existing work, the assignment uses a student-produced, medium-sized codebase as a maintenance artefact to which students are asked to add a feature. Towards adding the desired feature, the students needed to fix existing issues. No documentation other than that provided in the code (in form of comments) was provided. The 11,000 lines of code software used in our maintenance exercise had been produced by students in previous years. This implied that the quality of the code was *not* textbook-perfect thus allowing for a more realistic feel to the assignment. Student reports show that they did go through the maintenance stages identified in the literature. Students were also able to identify and report on the factors that influence software maintenance, as tool support, software quality, and programmer experience. These factors have also been identified by existing literature when looking at mature programmers. The use of a medium-sized codebase as a maintenance codebase proved beneficial with respect to student learning as the students were able to reflect on their own practices as software engineers, as outlined by the analysis of their reflections. Student reports also highlighted areas that we had overlooked in our teaching, specifically discussions about reverse engineering approaches and about testing in large software systems. In the future, we aim to expand this assignment and its associated teaching to include these aspects. Furthermore, we plan to explore how the cognitive program model of the novice software engineer evolves as the student becomes more familiar with the code through its maintenance.

6. ACKNOWLEDGMENTS

We would like to thank the students of SEGP1A 2012 and 2013 at The University of Adelaide for bearing with us during this non-traditional assignment.

7. REFERENCES

[1] M. A. Austin III and M. Samadzadeh. Software Comprehension/Maintenance: An Introductory Course. In *Proceedings of the International Conference on Systems Engineering*, pages 414–419, 2005.

[2] J. S. Collofello. Teaching Practical Software Maintenance Skills in a Software Engineering Course. In *ACM SIGCSE Bulletin*, volume 21, pages 182–184, 1989.

[3] J. R. Cordy. Comprehending Reality - Practical Barriers to Industrial Adoption of Software Maintenance Automation. In *Proceedings of the 11th International Workshop on Program Comprehension*, pages 196–205, 2003.

[4] R. Dupuis, R. Champagne, A. April, and N. Séguin. Experiments with Adding to the Experience that can be Acquired from Software Courses. In *Proceedings of the International Conference on the Quality of Information and Communications Technology*, pages 1–6, 2010.

[5] M. Gnatz, L. Kof, F. Prilmeier, and T. Seifert. A Practical Approach of Teaching Software Engineering. In *Proceedings of the Conference on Software Engineering Education and Training*, pages 120–127, 2003.

[6] L. Johns-Boast and G. Patch. A Win-Win Situation: Benefits of industry-based group projects. In *Proceedings of Australasian Association for Engineering Education Conference (AaeE 2010)*, 2010.

[7] Joint IEEE CS/ACM Task Force on Computing Curricula. Software Engineering 2004: Curriculum Guidelines for Undergraduate Degree Programs in Software Engineering. http://sites.computer.org/ccse/SE2004Volume.pdf. Last accessed 27th August 2013.

[8] M. Jørgensen. An empirical study of software maintenance tasks. *Journal of Software Maintenance: Research and Practice*, 7(1):27–48, 1995.

[9] M. Lehman. Survey of Software Maintenance Issues. In *Proceedings of the Software Maintenance Workshop*, pages 226–242, 1984.

[10] T. C. Lethbridge, J. Diaz-Herrera, R. J. LeBlanc, and J. B. Thompson. Improving Software Practice Through Education: Challenges and Future Trends. In *Proceedings of the Future of Software Engineering*, pages 12–28, 2007.

[11] B. P. Lientz, E. B. Swanson, and G. E. Tompkins. Characteristics of Application Software Maintenance. *Communications of the ACM*, 21(6):466–471, 1978.

[12] D. C. Littman, J. Pinto, S. Letovsky, and E. Soloway. Mental Models and Software Maintenance. *Journal of Systems and Software*, 7(4):341–355, 1987.

[13] E. Navarro and A. Van Der Hoek. Multi-site Evaluation of SimSE. In *ACM SIGCSE Bulletin*, volume 41, pages 326–330, 2009.

[14] M. Newby. Legacy systems, software maintenance and computing curricula. In *Proceedings of the International Software Education Conference*, pages 96–102, 1994.

[15] M. Petrenko, D. Poshyvattyk, V. Rajlich, and J. Buchta. Teaching Software Evolution in Open Source. *Computer*, 40(11):25–31, 2007.

[16] M. Postema, J. Miller, and M. Dick. Including Practical Software Evolution in Software Engineering Education. In *Proceedings of the Conference on Software Engineering Education and Training*, pages 127–135, 2001.

[17] A. Radermacher and G. Walia. Gaps between industry expectations and the abilities of graduates. In *Proceeding of the 44th ACM Technical Symposium on Computer Science Education*, pages 525–530, 2013.

[18] V. Rajlich and P. Gosavi. Incremental Change in Object-oriented Programming. *Software, IEEE*, 21(4):62–69, 2004.

[19] I. Sommerville. *Software Engineering*. Pearson Higher Ed, 2011.

[20] G. Tremblay, B. Malenfant, A. Salah, and P. Zentilli. Introducing Students to Professional Software Construction: A Software Construction and Maintenance Course and its Maintenance Corpus. In *ACM SIGCSE Bulletin*, volume 39, pages 176–180, 2007.

[21] A. Von Mayrhauser and A. M. Vans. Program Comprehension During Software Maintenance and Evolution. *Computer*, 28(8):44–55, 1995.

[22] A. von Mayrhauser, A. M. Vans, and A. E. Howe. Program understanding behaviour during enhancement of large-scale software. *Journal of Software Maintenance: Research and Practice*, 9(5):299–327, 1997.

[23] N. Wilde and M. C. Scully. Software reconnaissance: Mapping program features to code. *Journal of Software Maintenance: Research and Practice*, 7(1):49–62, 1995.

Syrus: Providing Practice Problems in Discrete Mathematics With Instant Feedback

Diego Zaccai[1] Aditi Tagore[1] Dustin Hoffman[1] Jason Kirschenbaum[1]
Zakariya Bainazarov[1] Harvey M. Friedman[2] Dennis K. Pearl[3]
Bruce W. Weide[1]

[1]Dept. of Computer Science and Engineering [2]Dept. of Mathematics [3]Dept. of Statistics

The Ohio State University
Columbus OH 43210, USA
(zaccai.1, tagore.2, hoffman.373, kirschenbaum.9, bainazarov.2, friedman.8, pearl.1, weide.1)@osu.edu

ABSTRACT

Syrus is courseware designed with the goal of helping students better understand logical sentences involving quantifiers. *Syrus* uses template-guided mutation of "seed" formulas to generate candidate practice problems, and third-party theorem-provers to automatically determine the truth value of each. It provides students with a virtually unlimited supply of unique and relevant practice problems and provides immediate feedback on each problem. Results of an empirical study of its efficacy are reported.

Categories and Subject Descriptors

I.2.6 [**Computing Methodologies**]: Learning—*Induction, Concept learning*; K.3.2 [**Computers and Education**]: Computer and Infomation Science Education—*Computer science education, Self-assessment*

General Terms

Human Factors, Theory

Keywords

Interactive Learning, Mathematical Theories in CS, On-line Education, Discrete Mathematics, Predicate Calculus

1. INTRODUCTION

For nearly every major topic in an elementary science or engineering course, student assignments include many practice problems, all of a similar nature. Evidently instructors believe that, as the saying goes, "practice makes perfect" because it helps students hone their skills in solving problems of a certain kind.

SIGCSE'14, March 5–8, 2014, Atlanta, GA, USA.

http://dx.doi.org/10.1145/2538862.2538929 .

With the advent of on-line courses and many universities' rush toward on-line education, the traditional constructs of education such as classrooms and homework are being challenged. Without the constraint of in-person instruction, classes become bigger and students more remote. In this context, traditional pedagogical tools such as graded homework assignments become either impossible or prohibitively expensive. Can software produce good practice problems? Can it solve them? Can students learn this way?

Syrus seeks to address such questions in one disciplinary area (formal logic, specifically predicate calculus) by adapting existing powerful research software (automated theorem-provers) to generate and solve many practice problems of pedagogical value.

2. EDUCATIONAL GOALS

The key learning outcome targeted by *Syrus* is that students should be able to understand and reason rigorously with logical statements in predicate calculus over various mathematical domains of interest in CS. The approach helps novices develop more expert-like skills through effortful practice [2]. The generic inspiration for building and evaluating such a tool is based on the following observations:

1. Introductory courses in many STEM areas involve students practicing on many homework problems.
2. Typical human grading of such assignments severely limits the number of such problems that can be attempted by students with useful and timely feedback.
3. State-of-the-art tools used by researchers in the field can sometimes solve student problems automatically.
4. Large numbers of problems with similar (pedagogically useful) structure can be generated automatically.

Before we describe *Syrus* and its evaluation, some history is in order. The original idea was that the student is given a sentence in predicate calculus over some rich collection of mathematical domains (integers, reals, sets, strings, etc.), is asked whether it is valid, and is then challenged to *prove* that claim. We discovered there are two basic dimensions to the "space" occupied by any tool that attempts to accomplish this. One is the depth of interaction between the software and the student: how much feedback is provided in real-time as the student works her way through the proof? A tool with deep interaction needs to check proof steps proposed by the student and advise about possible next steps. The other dimension is the domain of discourse: over what mathematical domains are the sentences that constitute the practice problems? A tool should help the student learn to understand sentences over diverse mathematical domains, not simply (for example) statements about a very constrained domain such as integer arithmetic modulo 2.

One might initially prefer deep interaction on problems over multiple rich mathematical domains. Yet it turns out this is impractical at present because of both technological shortcomings in automated theorem-provers and open theoretical issues in formal logic (details of which are beyond the scope of this paper). In short, it is arguably feasible to move significantly along one dimension but not both. We first built a prototype tool supporting deep interaction on proof development for logical sentences over a very limited mathematical domain involving integers with addition of constants and relational operators. Some new theory to support this was developed by one of the authors (Friedman). There were two problems. First, more new theory is required to suitably constrain other interesting mathematical domains to support proof strategies for students and permit deep interaction with the tool. Second, and more urgently, it became evident that students had to improve their reading and understanding of logical sentences with quantifiers. Simply deciding whether a fairly short statement in predicate calculus is valid turns out to be a difficult enough initial task for learners.

So, we next built a second prototype in which that *was* the student's problem: decide whether a given sentence is valid. Now, the sentences are over the much broader and more interesting collection of mathematical domains mentioned above, but with no deep interaction. The student says "true" or "false" for each sentence and the tool reports whether she is correct. The *Syrus* tool described in this paper generates a large number of sentences in predicate calculus over some key mathematical theories of interest in a discrete math course for CS majors; it solves these problems (determines the validity of these sentences) automatically using automated theorem-proving tools, so that the answers are known to the system; it issues these sentences as true/false problems; and it collects data to be used to evaluate the extent to which learning outcomes are achieved (as related to various measures of student engagement with, and success in solving, these practice problems).

Syrus contributes to STEM education by demonstrating the potential for using research tools to create related pedagogical tools and practice problems, as well as the difficulties faced when attempting to do so. The techniques used in *Syrus* suggest that it is likely feasible to adapt research tools for education in areas other than mathematics. The reason for optimism is that problems that challenge novice learners remain basically static even as the capabilities of research tools to solve such problems (automatically) continues to improve.

3. INTERACTING WITH *SYRUS*

Once a student logs in to the *Syrus* system using an email address, she is presented with a random problem, i.e., a mathematical sentence, from the currently enabled problem set. When a problem is displayed, the student is asked whether the mathematical sentence is true. The student must determine this and answer by pressing either the **True** or **False** button below it. Figure 1 shows a sample question.

After selecting an answer, the student gets instant feedback from *Syrus* on whether the answer is correct, and may move to the next problem. Additionally, via the **My Account** button on the left, the website allows the student to track how many problems have been

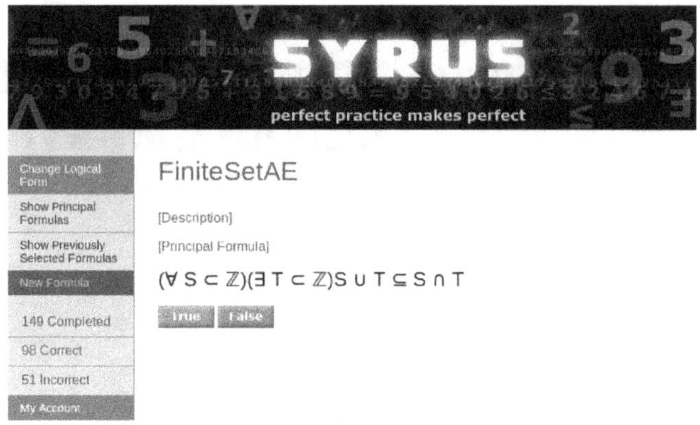

Figure 1: A sample problem in the *Syrus* webpage

completed, how many were answered correctly, and the average time spent on each problem.

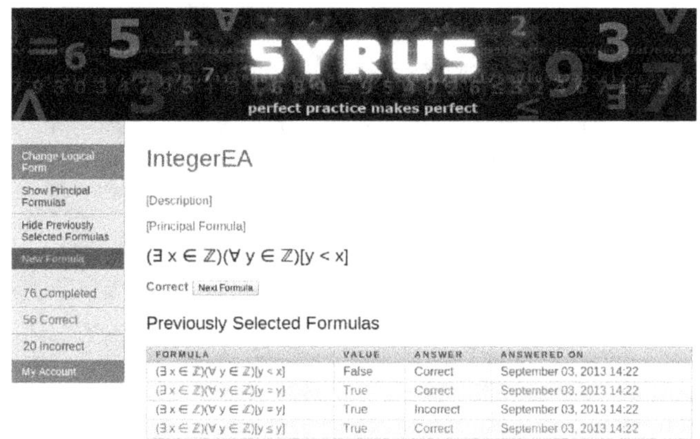

Figure 2: A sample list of previously solved problems in the *Syrus* web page

While working a problem set, a student can review past performance by selecting the **Show Previously Selected Formulas** button. This provides a list of all the problems completed since the start of the current problem set, as well as the selected answer, and whether the response was correct. Figure 2 shows a sample list of previously answered problems.

To view the problems that inspired the currently selected problem set, a student can select the **Show Principal Formulas** button on the left. This provides a listing of the seed formulas from which the current problem set was generated, as shown in Figure 3. Having access to the seed formulas allows a student to ask questions about a group of problems in a class discussion. This is particularly important, since the large number of sentences makes it unlikely that many students will encounter the same problem. Furthermore, since the discussion is based on the seed problem, the techniques discussed in class are likely to remain relevant for all the problems generated from it.

Once a student feels confident in her ability to solve problems of the current form, she can select the **Change Logical Form** button to move toward more complex problems. This button allows the student to increase the difficulty by selecting a problem set within

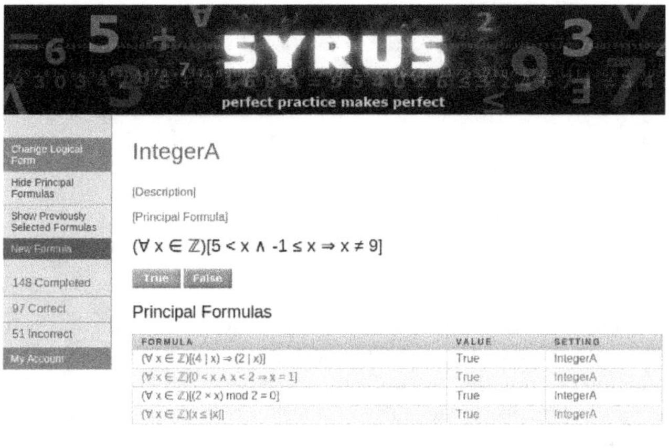

Figure 3: A display of the seed formulas used to generate a problem set

the same class of problems but with a higher number of quantifiers, or to move on to a completely different type of problem.

After deciding to change the logical form, the student is presented with a list that is categorized by mathematical theories with sub-categories represented by the quantifier structure of the formulas. For example, in Figure 1, `FiniteSetAE` shows that the current problem set involves finite sets and that the sentences contain variables that are universally quantified followed by variables that are existentially quantified. Figure 4 shows different problem sets involving integers. (Such details in the user interface are incidentally part of *Syrus* now, but are not essential to the idea).

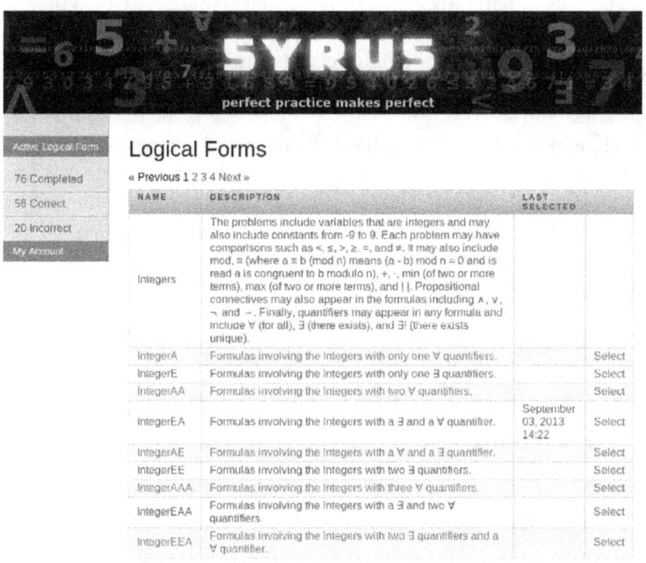

Figure 4: Various problem structures in the *Syrus* webpage

In order to provide a seemingly endless number of problems, *Syrus* has a large number of sentences ranging over different mathematical theories relevant to CS students including integers, reals, sets and strings. The problem sets are first organized by the type of problems. For example, one problem set includes problems about finite sets and their basic operators with a single universal quantifier, while another includes problems dealing with Presburger arithmetic and two alternating quantifiers. Inside each of those problem types, further sub-categories allow students to select an increasing number of quantifiers for each. Sentences (1)-(3) illustrate the different kinds of mathematical theories built into *Syrus*.

Sentence (1) is a sample problem involving integers. *Syrus* allows the comparison of numerical types. It can also handle addition, subtraction, multiplication, modulus, and divisibility of integers. The max function evaluates to the larger of its two integer arguments; the min function is similar. Sentence (1) is false.

$$(\forall x \in \mathbb{Z})(\exists y \in \mathbb{Z})[y = y - \max(7, x)] \tag{1}$$

Sentence (2) is a problem involving real numbers. Real numbers can be added, subtracted, and multiplied. The absolute value function is also available. Sentence (2) is true.

$$(\exists x, y \in \mathbb{R})[|x - y| = |x| + |y|] \tag{2}$$

Sentence (3) involves strings (represented by the Kleene star) over the alphabet of integers. In terms of comparison of strings, only equality and non-equality are allowed. String functions include concatenation, represented by the $\circ$ operator, and length, represented by $| \bullet |$. The reverse function evaluates to the reverse of a string, i.e., its entries in the opposite order. A substring function is also provided. Sentence (3) is an example of a problem involving both string concatenations and their reverse. Sentence (3) is true.

$$(\forall s, t \in \mathbb{Z}^*)[\text{reverse}(s \circ t) = \text{reverse}(t) \circ \text{reverse}(s)] \tag{3}$$

Problems involving finite sets are also available in *Syrus*. These kinds of sentences and the possible operators on sets are described in detail in Section 4.

4. DESIGN

The *Syrus* courseware is delivered to students via the web. Behind the scenes is an integrated tool-chain shown in Figure 5.

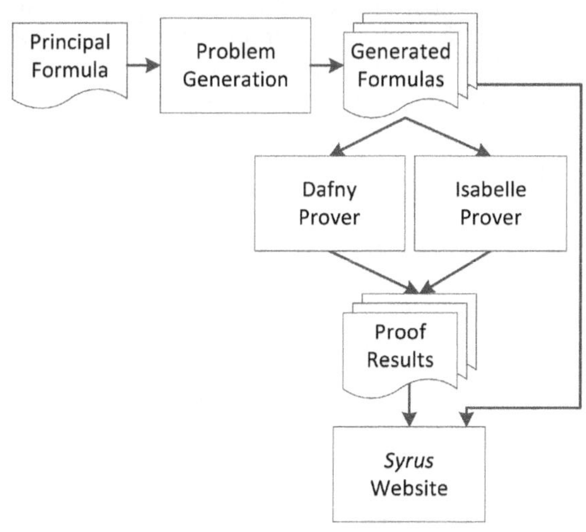

Figure 5: *Syrus* toolchain.

The first component is the problem generation tool. Ideally, every problem presented to a student would be of intellectual and pedagogical value. The easiest way to ensure this would be to present students only with problems carefully designed by an instructor or other expert. However, that process would be prohibitively expensive for a domain as rich as predicate calculus over multiple theories relevant to CS students. We would like thousands of problems in each problem set to ensure that students have the necessary volume of practice problems. There should ideally be a substantially large number of problems in each problem set to allow students to practice without running into the same problem multiple times. To achieve this, a problem generator takes a *principal formula* as input and generates multiple variant problems from it. A principal formula may be taken from a textbook or otherwise created manually by an instructor.

After the creation of a candidate problem set, each of the problems in the set must be answered. Given that a problem set typically contains a large number of problems, we turn to off-the-shelf theorem provers to perform the task of determining the validity of each candidate problem sentence. Thus, the second component consists of third-party theorem provers that are used to automatically determine the correct answer for each generated problem.

The last major piece is the website that serves as an interface for the students. The website takes the problems generated by the first component, along with the results of the automated answering process, and presents them to students. The following subsections describe the design and development of each of these components.

4.1 Problem Generation and Proof

Randomly generating arbitrary mathematical sentences would provide us with a very large problem set, but at the cost of quality. While randomly generated (but syntactically correct) sentences might be proven true or false, their intellectual and pedagogical value would be questionable. Sentences that are either too short-/easy or too long/difficult or just nonsensical semantically are bound to be created by a random process, and the labor-intensive job of filtering uninteresting problems would again fall to an instructor.

As a result, our problem generator uses a hybrid approach. Instructors provide *Syrus* with mathematical sentences that are considered to be interesting for the subject matter being taught, be it because they are important lemmas or because students in previous courses have had difficulties understanding sentences of a similar form. These sentences become principal formulas. The tool-set generates mutations of them using a syntactic approach. For example, students might be expected to understand that a non-empty set of integers contains an integer. This principal formula is sentence (4).

$$(\forall S \subset \mathbb{Z})[\phi \subset S \implies (\exists x \in \mathbb{Z})[x \in S]] \quad (4)$$

Similarly, instructors using the tools have noticed that students have special difficulty reasoning about long chains of operations. We therefore introduced principal formulas that contain two relatively long sequences of operations, requiring students to simplify such chains of operations to determine how the resulting sets are related to one another. An example of such a principal formula is (5).

$$(\forall S, T \subset \mathbb{Z})[(\exists R \subset \mathbb{Z})[((S-T) \cup R) \cap S = (S \cup T) \cap R]] \quad (5)$$

This formula is not true. However, this does not pose a problem because the truth values of the formulas generated from it are determined by theorem provers independently of the principal formula.

New candidate problems are generated by replacing some operators and variables in the principal formula in a manner that preserves its overall structure. The mutation of the sentence allows variables and constants to be interchanged with other variables that have already been bound by a quantifier and are of the same type, as well as constant values. These variations can be limited in various ways, e.g., to a fixed number of occurrences per generated formula, to ensure that the problem set does not deviate too significantly from its seed principal formula.

$$(\exists S \subset \mathbb{Z})[\phi \neq S \iff (\forall x \in \mathbb{Z})[x \notin S]]$$

$$(\exists S \subset \mathbb{Z})[\neg((\exists x \in \mathbb{Z})[x \notin S] \vee \phi \neq S)]$$

$$(\forall S \subset \mathbb{Z})[(\forall x \in \mathbb{Z})[x \in S] \vee \phi \subseteq S]$$

Figure 6: Some of the resulting variations of sentence (4)

Similarly, logical connectives such as $\wedge$, $\vee$, $\implies$ and $\iff$ can be interchanged with one another. When these exchanges occur, the mutation ensures that the operation types do not change (thus the sentences remain syntactically correct). For example, for numeric types the operators $+$, $-$, $*$, $\max$, $\min$ may be interchanged within the formula. Similarly for sets, $\cup$, $\cap$, and $-$ (set difference) may be replaced by one another. Finally, mutations on the quantifiers are also permitted, with $\forall$, $\exists$ and $\exists!$ as possible choices. Some of the variants of the principal formula in sentence (4) are shown in Figure 6.

The Isabelle [7] or Z3 [1] theorem prover is used to check the validity of each candidate problem. We use Isabelle to check the validity of problems involving integers and real numbers, and Z3 to check problems involving sets and strings. When interfacing with Z3, the problems, along with the theories and mathematical definitions used in them, are expressed as assumptions and assertions in the Dafny [5, 3] programming language. Dafny is a programming language for software verification that uses Z3 as its back-end prover. We chose to use Dafny as the front-end to Z3 because it provides an easier route for translating statements about strings and sets than interacting with Z3 directly. Dafny translates these statements into the Boogie [4] intermediate language, which in turn generates verification conditions to be proved by Z3.

When adapting a problem for processing by Isabelle, the formula statement is translated in a manner similar to the Dafny translation previously discussed. The primary difference is the translation target language. Specifically, the Isabelle proof environment is built on a meta-logic framework (called Pure) with object logics (such as first-order logic) layered on top. Pure is a natural deduction system that includes rules for handling quantifiers, propositional connectives (negation, and, or, and implies), as well as unification. An object logic includes the syntax to express formulas in it, as well as the axioms and proof rules/theorems required to reason in it.

Each generated problem is initially represented in an XML format. We have built translation tools for Isabelle and Dafny/Z3 that convert from our XML format into their respective input formats.

4.2 Website

The *Syrus* website is implemented using Ruby on Rails. It serves as the only client-facing component of the courseware (the generation and proof process previously described are performed off-line). In addition to allowing students to view and answer questions, it also tracks statistics on the progress of each student. Problem sets containing sentences and their truth values are loaded into the website in bulk, formatted according to the notation used in the course, and then stored in a database.

The statistics tracked by the website are not only useful to the students, but also to instructors and researchers. For example, the detailed statistics allow us, as researchers, to gather data on the effectiveness of the product. Those same statistics, when viewed in the scope of particular problems, allow the course instructors to determine what types of problems students need additional help on. Also, the more limited information such as success rate and average response time serve to guide the students and motivate them in a similar way to points in a game.

5. IMPACT AND EVALUATION

During the 2010-2011 academic year the *Syrus* software was developed and tested by students taking a discrete mathematics course, which has computer science students as its primary audience. During this period, data collection methods were also tested, and a short assessment of the skills that *Syrus* focused on was created by the course coordinator. This assessment was embedded in the course's final exam to allow for one method of project evaluation.

Complicating the study was the Summer 2012 change of the university calendar from quarters to semesters, and a change of the former math course to a new computer science course. Fortunately, we were able to work around these problems, but further studies would be complicated by the need for new baseline data. *Syrus* is currently being used in some sections of the new computer science foundations course.

In the Winter and Spring 2012 terms, the assessment was embedded in the course's final exam and scored consistently using a rubric designed by the course coordinator. There were two sections in each of these two terms. In Winter, neither section used *Syrus*. In Spring, the instructor of one section strongly suggested that students study using *Syrus* and one did not mention it. This allowed us to judge the effect of *Syrus* (Spring comparison) versus the typical degree of section-to-section differences without *Syrus* (Winter comparison).

The data collected was merged from three sources. The university's Student Information System was queried to get student age, ethnicity, gender, grade in the course, GPA in other Math courses, overall GPA, and Math Placement scores. Secondly, the *Syrus* system itself was queried to get information on the number of questions attempted, correctly answered, incorrectly answered, and skipped, together with the number of seconds taken in each of these activities. Finally, the course professors provided the scores on the embedded final exam question (20 points maximum) for each student in the four sections taking the final.

Section	Students	Used *Syrus*	Embedded Question	Course Grade - Math GPA
WI 1	65	No	15 (13 to 16)	-0.04 (-0.4 to 0.4)
WI 2	57	No	15 (13 to 16)	0.10 (-0.50 to 0.73)
SP 1	51	Yes	16 (12 to 18)	0.05 (-0.40 to 0.70)
SP 2	57	No	15 (11 to 19.25)	-0.17 (-1.20 to 0.45)

Table 1: Comparison of courses using *Syrus* with those that don't. The numerical results are presented with the median on top and the 25th and 75th percentile in parentheses.

Two principal response variables were studied: the grade on the embedded final exam question, and the difference between the student's grade in the course and their GPA in previous Math courses. This second response variable thus measured student performance in the logic course normalized by their expected grade given their performance in previous courses. A general overview of the results is presented in Table 1.

The students in the section asked to use *Syrus* as a study aid had a median score one point higher than the other three sections studied in the embedded final exam question. However the distribution of scores overlapped, and this difference may easily have been explained by random chance. The students in the Spring section that used *Syrus* also did better in the Math course relative to their previous math grades when compared to students in the other sections. Due to some skewness in the distributions, the change in the means was greater than the change in the medians, moving from -0.33 to $+0.11$. This difference was not easily explained by random chance ($p \approx 0.05$).

The fact that only small differences are seen in student learning as a result of using *Syrus* is probably to be expected since its use was not required by the course: even in the section where it was highly recommended for study, no grade was directly given for its use. As a result the median usage was a little under 10 minutes total, though some students did use it more. Only six students used *Syrus* for more than an hour total (spread over multiple sessions). This small group had a median score of 17.5 on the embedded question and had a median of 0.43 on the course grade minus previous math GPA.

The improved grades in the course compared to previous math courses for the section that used *Syrus* was seen across both sexes consistently. For males the median went from -0.51 in the *Syrus* section to -0.76 in the non-*Syrus* section; while for females the median went from -0.31 to -0.59. The improved grades in the discrete logic course compared to previous math courses for the section that used *Syrus* was also seen in both minority and white students. For the white students the median went from -0.51 in the *Syrus* section to -1.02 in the non-*Syrus* section; while for the minority students the median went from -0.46 to -0.60.

A statistical model controlling for gender, minority status, math placement scores and age did not change the significance of the difference between the Spring *Syrus* section and the non-*Syrus* section for the grades-based measure (neither did it change the lack of a significant difference in the scoring of the embedded question).

In the section using *Syrus*, the percent of the total time using *Syrus* that resulted in a correct answer to a *Syrus* question was correlated with both response variables. The rank correlation with the grade-based response was 0.40, while the rank correlation with the embedded question was 0.52. This is to be expected since all three measures gauge the degree to which the students learned core material in the class, but it does reinforce the underlying assumption that success in using *Syrus* is correlated with success in the class and in learning the material at hand.

The *Syrus* project showed some promise in improved outcomes in the discrete mathematics course, when adjusted for expectations based on grades in previous math courses. This result was consistent among different subpopulations. However, no effect of the use of *Syrus* was seen in a question embedded in the final exam that was specifically designed to gauge the knowledge that *Syrus* most directly covered. Further study in an experimental setting with heavy use of *Syrus* would seem to be needed to better understand its value.

6. DISCUSSIONS AND RELATED WORK

The disparity in the number of sentences that are determined either true or false for a given quantifier structure makes it impractical to randomly select a problem from the current logical form. For example, a student might realize that the percentage of true sentences in a setting that is universally quantified is larger that that of the false ones. This would improve the student's odds of getting a correct answer by simply guessing true all the time. To avoid this problem, our website first decides whether it will provide a student with a true or false sentence, and then selects a sentence from the setting that matches the intended answer. This way the distribution of results seen by the student is independent of that of the proving mechanisms and the chances of a student getting a correct answer through guesswork is always 50%.

In terms of related educational software, the works of Suppes, *et al.*[9], at Stanford, and Sieg, *et al.* [8], at CMU, stand out as the best developed and the most closely related to *Syrus*. They are also among the very few such tools to have been evaluated with student subjects.

The CMU group observed [8] that resolution theorem provers gave little help to students in thinking about how to prove something, and hence set out to develop a proof search system based on natural deduction: the CMU Proof Tutor. An important difference from the (original) CMU Proof Tutor, however, is that *Syrus* focuses on quantified formulas over mathematical theories of central importance in CS education. *Syrus* also automatically generates targeted practice problems; it is not clear whether the new Proof Tutor will do that.

The EPGY Theorem Proving Environment is used by gifted students in Stanford's Education Program for Gifted Youth. Its published evaluation [9] involved 170 students doing geometry proofs. This is a sophisticated and rather heavyweight proof environment that can be used across a variety of mathematical domains, with a pedagogical focus on proving interesting results in a variety of underlying mathematical theories (including geometry, linear algebra, multivariate calculus, and differential equations). The tool's purpose is to fill in gaps in student proofs – anything that can be completed by the proof assistant Otter [6] within 4-5 seconds. It attempts to supply automatically the below-the-radar details that normally would not appear in a proof in the mathematical literature, and hence to allow students to prove theorems as would be done in "standard mathematical practice". Besides being far less interactive (being intended for a completely different purpose), *Syrus* differs in several important respects. It provides students with a platform for repeated practice with logic problems that involve underlying mathematics in theories of interest to CS students, so it can focus specifically on student understanding of quantified sentences and reasoning involving them.

7. CONCLUSION

Syrus provides a unique and novel approach to improving access to practice problems while providing instant feedback. The technique of using research tools to solve large numbers of intelligently generated candidate problems is one that could certainly be adapted to other topics in mathematics. Additionally, disciplines outside of mathematics are also candidates for using this method. For example, further research could determine whether software tools used by researchers could be adapted to generate and solve appropriate practice problems for students in an introductory chemistry or physics course. Unfortunately, the jury is still out on how effective such tools might be. Our study of *Syrus* does not establish efficacy but rather promise.

It has become especially clear that the key ideas behind *Syrus* will become increasingly important as higher education struggles with the impact of massive open on-line courses (MOOCs). MOOC students in STEM courses in particular will need to practice solving problems, some of which are of a sort that can be solved automatically with sophisticated research tools used by researchers in the same discipline. They must receive automated and, preferably, instantaneous feedback; having instructors grade homework for such a large number of students remains unfeasible and hiring armies of other human graders could prove expensive. It is likely that all results, positive and negative, regarding the use of technologies such as those developed and evaluated in this project, will prove relevant to the future of on-line education in general and MOOCs in particular.

8. ACKNOWLEDGMENTS

This material is based upon work supported by the National Science Foundation under grants DUE-0942542 and CCF-1162331. Any opinions, findings, conclusions, or recommendations expressed here are those of the authors and do not necessarily reflect the views of the National Science Foundation.

9. REFERENCES

[1] L. M. de Moura and N. Bjørner. Z3: An efficient SMT solver. In *Proc. Tools and Algorithms for the Construction and Analysis of Systems (TACAS)*, pages 337–340. Springer, 2008.

[2] K. A. Ericsson, R. T. Krampe, and C. Tesch-romer. The role of deliberate practice in the acquisition of expert performance. *Psychological Review*, pages 363–406, 1993.

[3] K. R. M. Leino. Specification and verification of object-oriented software. Marktoberdorf International Summer School 2008, lecture notes.

[4] K. R. M. Leino. This is Boogie 2. Manuscript KRML 178, 2008. Available at http://research.microsoft.com/en-us/um/people/leino/papers.html.

[5] K. R. M. Leino. Dafny: An automatic program verifier for functional correctness. In *Proc. Logic for Programming Artificial Intelligence and Reasoning (LPAR)*, pages 348–370. Springer, 2010.

[6] W. McCune. Otter and Mace2. http://www.cs.unm.edu/∼mccune/otter/, Aug. 2012.

[7] T. Nipkow, M. Wenzel, and L. C. Paulson. *Isabelle/HOL: A proof assistant for higher-order logic*. Springer-Verlag, 2002.

[8] W. Sieg and R. Scheines. *Philosophy and the Computer*. Westview Press, 1992.

[9] R. Sommer and G. Nuckols. A proof environment for teaching mathematics. *J. Autom. Reason.*, 32(3):227–258, Apr. 2004.

Teaching Theoretical Computer Science using a Cognitive Apprenticeship Approach

Maria Knobelsdorf
New York University
Computer Science Department
719 Broadway
New York, NY, 10003, USA
(+1) 212 998 3497
maria.knobelsdorf@cs.nyu.edu

Christoph Kreitz
University of Potsdam
Department of Computer Science
August-Bebel Str. 89
D-14482 Potsdam, Germany
(+49) 331 977 3060
kreitz@cs.uni-potsdam.de

Sebastian Böhne
University of Potsdam
Department of Computer Science
August-Bebel Str. 89
D-14482 Potsdam, Germany
(+49) 331 977 3014
boehne@uni-potsdam.de

ABSTRACT

High failure rates in introductory courses on theoretical computer science are a common problem at universities in Germany, Europe, and North America, as students often have difficulties coping with the contents of such courses due to their abstract and theoretical nature. This paper describes modifications to the pedagogy of a theory course held at the University of Potsdam, Germany that are motivated by a cognitive apprenticeship approach and have led to a significant reduction of the course's failure rates. Since our approach is based on the typical infrastructure for teaching introductory computer science courses and does not require additional expenses or special resources, it can be replicated by other institutions. We believe that it is a serious contribution to better support teaching as well as student learning success in this field.

Categories and Subject Descriptors

K.3.2 **[Computer and Information Science Education]**: Computers and Education - Computer and Information Science Education

General Terms

Human Factors

Keywords

Theoretical Computer Science, Theory of Computation, Cognitive Apprenticeship, Pedagogy, High Failure Rates.

SIGCSE'14, March 5–8, 2014, Atlanta, Georgia, USA.

http://dx.doi.org/10.1145/2538862.2538944

1. INTRODUCTION

At German universities, theoretical Computer Science (CS) is considered one of the fundaments of undergraduate CS education. Introductory courses cover the foundations of automata, programming languages, computability, and computational complexity. Introducing idealized mathematical models of the computer and discussing methods for designing and analyzing them, students are supposed to develop the ability of thinking abstractly about computational processes. However, many students have problems understanding and following the course topics and failure rates in final exams are usually very high. This was also the case at the department of CS at the University of Potsdam, Germany. The introduction to theoretical CS is covered by an undergraduate course (briefly "Theory I") that initially had very high failure rates (usually between 30-60%). Teaching assistants who worked weekly with the students reported on their difficulties in coping with the course material, observing a learning edge momentum very early during the course, see [10]. High failure rates in theoretical CS at the University of Potsdam are not a single phenomenon. Failure rates in other undergraduate CS courses tend to be very high as well and dropout rates from the CS major are not much lower than the national average, which is about 40-50% with most students giving up during the first four semesters, see [7].

Reasons for failing a final exam can be very different and change over time. In addition, various factors can have different influence on a student's overall progress and final learning outcome. In the past 30 years, a considerable number of studies investigated possible influencing factors on student success in CS courses like mathematical pre-knowledge, abstract thinking abilities, gender or social aspects, see ([12], p. 224-228) and ([2], p. 30-32). These and further recent studies indicate that there is no silver bullet to explain student success just by specific factors. Instead, the whole teaching and learning process needs to be focused on.

Standing in the tradition of constructivism and student-oriented pedagogy, there is a variety of approaches to improving learning success in courses on theoretical computer science. Chesñevar et al. [3] focused on student engagement for deeper understanding and introduced "the historical context in which the theory of computing emerged as a new discipline" (p. 8). Hämäläinen [6] used problem-based learning and Korte et al. [8] developed a constructionist approach with game-building. In addition, Rodger et al. [11] suggested the visualization tool JFLAP for formal languages and automata theory, which shall enable students to interact more with the introduced theoretical concepts. All approaches succeeded to engage students in more learning activities resulting in lower dropout and failure rates. Since we did not have access to additional resources, we focused on developing new ways to engage students in more learning activities with the resources we had.

During the winter semesters 2011/2012[1] and 2012/2013 we modified the setup of Theory I by consolidating experiences from ad-hoc changes to the courses in the past eight years and taking into account the pedagogical approach of cognitive apprenticeship, a well known approach in education that has already been applied to CS education; see for example [2]. In the literature, however, there is no report that it has been used to improve theoretical CS education at university level. The result of our adjustments to the course was that less than 10% of all students failed the final exam while the remaining students' scores were evenly distributed. Apart from a small amount of additional contact time our approach does not require any extra resources beyond the common infrastructure given at German universities for an introductory CS course. Therefore, our approach can be replicated by other institutions as well. In this paper, we will introduce cognitive apprenticeship and describe the adjustments to the setup of our course and discuss the final assessment that indicates the credibility and impact of our approach.

2. THE THEORY I COURSE

In this section we will introduce the Theory I course, the students who attend it, as well as the traditional pedagogy applied before we introduced our first modifications.

2.1 Course Content and Learning Outcome

The Theory I course focuses on the theory of automata and formal languages. It begins with an investigation of simple automata models and increases the level of complexity until the models reach the capabilities of modern computers. Specifically it covers the following topics:

- Regular languages: finite automata, non-determinism, regular expressions, type 3 grammars, closure properties, and limitations.
- Context free languages and type 2 grammars, pushdown automata, normal forms, parsing algorithms, closure properties, and limitations.
- General and context sensitive languages and grammars, Turing machines, linear-bounded automata, closure properties.

In the course of the lectures, students are supposed to develop specific skills that enable them to work with the models introduced in the course. For this reason, the department of CS of the University of Potsdam defined in 2010 normatively the intended learning outcomes that are described by three fields of specific skills ([9], p. 36-38):

- Domain specific skills, for example: students are able to analyze deterministic and non-deterministic automata and grammars with mathematical methods and to prove their correctness; students know methods for translating between different automata models, grammars, and regular expressions and are able to justify the correctness of these conversions.
- Methods skills, for example: students can employ mathematical proof techniques for the analysis of automata and formal languages; they can transform grammars into normal forms; they are able to prove whether a given formal language is regular (context free) or not.
- Behavioral skills, for example: students are capable of working in small teams when developing solutions for given problems; they are able to give an oral presentation of their solutions and they can write them down in a precise language.

Through the course, students are supposed to develop these skills and the final exam is supposed to assess these.

2.2 The Theory I students

Before entering an undergraduate program at a university in Germany, students are required to finish upper secondary education, which, depending on the school type, takes two or three years (grade 11-13 where students usually are 17-19 years old). With specific mandatory basic and advanced courses, upper secondary schooling can be roughly compared to the first one or two years of attending a college in the US. In consequence, entering a German university students immediately start with their major. The predominant majority of German universities are public and students do not pay tuition. Students are admitted to university in Germany based on their final grades at upper secondary school.

The number of students attending the Theory I course usually varies between 150-300 (which is a rather small number for an introductory course at a German university) and consists of 50-150 students majoring in CS, about 60-100 students majoring in Software-Engineering, 40-80 students majoring in business informatics, 10-25 prospective teachers with one of their majors in CS, and approximately ten students majoring in different fields (like mathematics, linguistics or others). CS and business informatics majors are supposed to attend the course in their first semester and software engineering majors in their third. While at many other German universities, CS majors attend an introductory course in theoretical CS in their third or fourth semester, the CS curriculum at the University of Potsdam places the course at the beginning of undergraduate studies, since many subsequent courses expect students to be familiar with automata theory and Turing machines.

2.3 Traditional Course Setup and Problems

Until we modified the course setup and its pedagogical approach, the course consisted of the following components, which are typical for an introductory CS course of this size in Germany:

- 135 minutes of lectures peer week given by a faculty member who presents the course topics, central concepts, algorithms, and their proofs and illustrates them with examples.
- Weekly homework assignments based on the current lecture topics, which students are expected to solve individually and submit in writing for reviewing and grading by tutors (usually senior students). Handing in homework can but doesn't need to be mandatory.

[1] The German academic system has a winter and a summer semester with teaching periods between mid October and mid February (with a two weeks Christmas break) and between mid April and mid July, respectively.

- 90 minutes student session every other week attended by approx. 25-30 students and chaired by tutors, during which attending students are expected to present their solutions to last weeks' homework assignment. This shall give them an opportunity to check the correctness of their solutions and discuss them with the group.
- One final written exam during the assessment period after the end of the lectures, which in the winter takes place at the end of February, determines the grade students receive for the course.

The pedagogical approach behind these course components assumes that students understand the presented concepts, theorems, and proofs during the lectures and are able to deal with the homework assignments by themselves. There are students who respond positively to this approach. However, our tutors reported that most students remained very passive during the student sessions and did not participate in discussions even when their own solutions contained mistakes. Taking the high failure rate in the finals into account, we concluded that based on the course's pedagogical approach most of our students are not able to build understanding and become well prepared for the finals. This forced us to reconsider all elements of the course and seek for improvement.

3. FIRST COURSE ADJUSTEMENTS

Starting in 2003, we began introducing a variety of modifications to the traditional setup of the course. We converted the bi-weekly student sessions to weekly sessions that focused on student activities instead of the presentation of solutions. We reduced the time for lectures to 90 minutes per week, made homework submissions mandatory, and offered an additional weekly "tutorial". We hoped that these modifications would help reducing the failure rates without reducing the requirements for passing the final exams.

3.1 Tutorial and Exercise Sessions

As described in Sec. 2.3, the goal of the Theory I lecture is to present new topics, central concepts, algorithms, and their proofs and to illustrate them by examples. We noticed that, due to the number of attendees, the lecture lacks interaction between students and the instructor. Also, there was only little time for individual questions and discussions.. Therefore, one of our first changes was to install an additional weekly 90 minutes session that we named *tutorial*. In the tutorial, held by the instructor, students are encouraged to ask questions and discuss issues that were still unclear after lecture and student sessions. The topics discussed in the tutorial are not prepared in advance but suggested by the attending students, as the main objective is not the solution to a problem but the process of producing it.

We also believe that student interaction is much easier to accomplish during student sessions attended by approx. 25 students than during a lecture. Therefore, we also shortened the lecture to 90 minutes and expanded the exercise session to 90 minutes per week. In order to enable the teacher to present the same amount of topics in less time, lecture topics started to be presented on slides that are prepared in advance instead of being written onto the blackboard. In addition, the use of a tablet PC enabled the lecturer to add details and illustrations to the slides during the lecture and thus preserve the advantages of a "blackboard lecture". In order to offer students the possibility to prepare before and after the lecture, the slides were made available at the beginning of the entire course. Furthermore, in 2006/07 and again in 2011/2012 the lectures were recorded on video and made available on the course webpage.

3.2 Weekly Exercises for Student Sessions

In the traditional approach, the student session was focused on discussing students' solutions to homework assignments. However, we were (and still are) convinced that students need to engage more in joint work in order to be better prepared for the actual homework assignments. In order to accomplish this, we began offering additional exercises that were meant to be solved jointly *during* the student session. The tutors responsible for these weekly *exercise* sessions encourage the attending students to participate actively in ongoing discussions and ask questions. To support the latter, we also offered quiz questions. *Quizzes* contain approximately five right-or-wrong statements related to the topics of the previous week's lecture. Answers are discussed in the first 15 minutes of the exercises session. This is supposed to help students to check their understanding and serve as a warm-up and first discussion before working with exercises.

3.3 Homework assignments

Experience with teaching introductory CS courses has shown that it is very important to make homework submissions mandatory. Otherwise students do not work regularly enough to succeed in the final exam. To encourage teamwork and reduce the student's workload homework assignments are to be solved by teams of 2-4 students without support from tutors or instructors and to be submitted for grading in written form. Each submission is checked and commented by the tutors and students receive points for each homework assignment. Students must obtain at least 50% of the possible points to be admitted to final exam.

Since the final exam is a situated activity, students must experience and learn how to deal with this as well, especially when this is their very first university exam. For this reason, we also started to offer a *pre-exam* shortly before the two weeks of Christmas break. The pre-exam has the same form and amount of assignments as the final exam, counts as one submitted homework, but does not count to the course grade. It gives the students an opportunity to practice the assessment situation and explicates what will be expected from them during the finals. The pre-exam is reviewed the same way as the finals and gives students direct feedback about their current effort and achievements.

3.4 Results of first Adjustments

All the adjustments to the course mentioned above were made permanent by the end of 2007. However, the failure rate in the final exams was still varying as table 1 shows.

Table 1: Distribution of student scores (in %) before 2012 (where 1.0 is the highest and 4.0 the lowest score corresponding to A+ and D respectively)

Grade/ Year	1.0	1.3-1.7	2.0-2.3	2.7.- 3.3	3.7- 4.0	failed
2008	4.0%	8.1%	11.4%	36.2%	24.2%	16.1%
2009	4.9%	7.4%	18.9%	24.6%	21.3%	23.0%
2010	18.3%	13.6%	22.5%	28.2%	9.9%	**7.5%**
2011	0%	0%	3.4%	17.6%	19.6%	**59.5%**

At a first glance this variation in grades and failure rates seemed hard to explain, since most parameters of the course were identical in all these years. However, each year a different faculty member was responsible for supervising the tutors and for designing the exercises, homework, and exams. We observed that in the years with low failure rates the problem sets in the exercises, homework, and finals were similar in nature. In 2011, the correspondence between these problem sets was a lot weaker and it seemed that this was one of the reasons why the students were less prepared for what was expected from them in the final exam.

4. DEVELOPING A PEDAGOGY

Given our student-oriented approach in teaching and a strong focus situated cognition theories, we approached the adjustments done in Theory I from a perspective of learning sciences. Here, we found the cognitive apprenticeship approach as the most helpful theory to reflect on our adjustments and improve them.

4.1 Cognitive Apprenticeship

Collins et al. [5] argue that for the longest time in human history the natural form of learning was apprenticeship: a master-students relationship that focuses on practicing contextualized knowledge and skills in authentic situations that provide meaning to the activities involved. Learning was not only a form of "acquiring" knowledge and developing skills to handle it but also a form of enculturation into a certain community. Being set in a specific workplace, tasks and problems arose not from pedagogical concerns but from the demands of the authentic environment ([4], p. 48ff). Of this master-student-relationship Collins et al. describe the following techniques to be essential:

- *Modeling,* where the teacher demonstrates how to do something and makes single steps of a process visible such that students can observe and be than able to imitate it.
- *Scaffolding & Fading* is the framework or certain plan the teacher provides students with in order to carry out specific tasks. Once students are on their own, the scaffolding framework is gradually removed in the process of fading.
- *Coaching* where the teacher guides or supervises students' activities, efforts, and experiences evaluating them, offering encouragement and feedback.

Nowadays, master-student-relationships can be found for example in learning to play an instrument or to do research as well as multiple forms of trades like plumbing or tailoring.

Collins et al. argue that typical forms of academic formal schooling are the opposite of apprenticeship and reflect mostly a view of learning that focuses on knowledge presentation ([5], p. 38-39), ([4], p. 47ff). In a lecture the teacher introduces and demonstrates knowledge as a stand-alone generalized product, which is decontextualized from the situated activities in which it was once developed and in which it is supposed to be used by the students in future. As a consequence, the expertise to create and use the knowledge remains tacit since a specific context is not emphasized. But for the members of the scientific research community who created this knowledge, it is not a decontextualized stand-alone product, but a cognitive tool they use and apply in activities where it is meaningful and relevant to them. Bereiter ([1], p. 295ff) argues that learning in formal schooling is particularly difficult for two reasons. First, there is no sufficient distinction between knowledge as the *material* or item of inquiry and knowledge and skills that are needed to handle this material; second, the latter remains mostly tacit since little attention is paid "to the reasoning and strategies that experts employ when they acquire knowledge or put it to work to solve complex or real-life tasks. [...] To make real differences in students' skill, we need both to understand the nature of expert practice and to devise methods that are appropriate to learning that practice" ([5], p. 38-39).

Collins et al. argue that in contrast to craft, activities that handle "knowledge material" are in part invisible and that therefore it is almost impossible for students to observe and imitate them in the same way as in traditional apprenticeship. Still, students in higher education institutions are supposed to adopt the expertise of a particular scientific community and to be able to work with the domain knowledge introduced in a lecture. As a pedagogical approach that focuses on the gap between process and product Collins et al. suggest *cognitive apprenticeship*, [4], [5]. The idea of this approach is to focus not just on domain knowledge as a decontextualized product but to make the required skills and knowledge more explicit and the thought processes of teachers and students more visible ([5], p. 40). For this reason, they propose to use the key methods of traditional apprenticeship as well as additional methods specific to their approach ([4], p. 50ff): The teacher is supposed to explain and demonstrate knowledge and skills (modeling and articulation), which students can observe and then repeat under the guidance of the teacher (coaching). Different frameworks are proposed to the students that help them to orientate themselves and their learning activities (scaffolding). Since most of the activities are cognitive and not visible, it is important that teachers and students develop the ability to articulate and reflect their activities.

Another important aspect of cognitive apprenticeship is providing the context in which domain knowledge is meaningful. In the workspace of traditional apprenticeship, reasons for specific activities are much better understood than in formal schooling: students "are motivated to work and to learn the subcomponents of the task, because [...] they have seen the expert's model of the finished product, and so the subcomponents of the task make sense. But in school, teachers are working with a curriculum centered around reading, writing, science, math, history, etc. that is, in large part, separated from what students and most adults do in their lives. In cognitive apprenticeship, the challenge is to situate the abstract tasks of the school curriculum in contexts that make sense to students" ([4], p. 50).

4.2 Improving the Adjustments

The Cognitive Apprenticeship approach helped us better understand how our adjustments could support our students in their learning efforts and how we could improve them to create a pedagogical approach for the Theory I course.

4.2.1 Modeling

The Cognitive Apprenticeship approach helped us understand that with a course setup as described in section 2.3 the emphasis lies mostly on presenting theoretical CS domain knowledge (the concepts, definitions, algorithms, etc.) as stand-alone products and does not sufficiently explicate the methods, approaches, and strategies of dealing with this knowledge as well as techniques how to learn them. Since all lecture topics are prepared in advance for a smooth presentation, students experience them as knowledge products without seeing the enormous effort it took to create them. Skills to handle and work with this knowledge that students are supposed to develop in the course are only implicitly demonstrated during the lecture and are not addressed and exposed sufficiently. Therefore, we started to focus on theory practices and demonstrate them more explicitly with regard to *modeling*. While the lecture presents the ready-made "products" of theoretical CS, the tutorial is the natural place in the course where the process of creating them is shown. So, we understood that the tutorial is mostly helpful to students when it serves as a modeling session where students can experience that even a professor has to try different approaches and alternatives before accomplishing a solution.

4.2.2 Scaffolding & Fading

Our main idea was to use the exercise sessions to enable students to solve their homework by themselves and to motivate them to become more actively involved in the exercise and tutorial sessions. Therefore, we redesigned the weekly exercise sessions and assignments entirely with regard to the *scaffolding & fading* method.

We offered specific *preparatory exercises* that are to be solved jointly during the exercise session and serve as preparation for homework. After the exercise sessions we also posted detailed written solutions to the preparatory exercises on the web pages. These solutions demonstrate what a correct solution should look like *in written* form and what is expected from the students when they turn in their homework. Especially for the latter there is not enough time during the exercise session, since possible solutions to the exercises are developed together and only sketched on the blackboard. But students must also learn how to produce a complete and precisely formulated solution using mathematical formalisms.

Redesigning the exercise sessions, the major change was to align the preparatory exercises with the homework with respect to structure and content. This means that in each session the same type and amount of problems is used for the exercises as well as for the homework assignments. This way, it makes sense for students to work with the preparatory exercises, to participate during tutorial and exercises sessions, since all these activities prepare them to do their homework assignments.

In the traditional approach, it was assumed that students gain understanding from attending the lecture. The cognitive apprenticeship approach taught us that cognitive methods and strategies used in theoretical CS needs to be explicated. The alignment between exercises and homework together with the written solutions to the exercises is the *scaffolding* framework for students. However, this framework's objective is to get students more self-reliant in working with the theory of computation. Therefore, in the second part of the course, we gradually removed the strong alignment between preparatory exercises and homework. In addition, we also started reducing detailed information in written solutions.

4.2.3 Coaching

The weekly homework grading as well as the tutors' support during the exercise session is a form of *coaching*. In addition, it corresponds to students' activities during final exam, where students have to formulate a written solution for an assignment, which then will be graded by tutors under supervision of the instructors. In order to understand the expectations, especially with respect to the very strict and formal character of solutions to assignments, students need to train this skill as well and to receive a weekly feedback about their efforts.

4.3 The Final Exam

In the Theory I course, the measure of students' learning success is a student's performance on homework, pre-exam, and final assessment. The points or grade students obtain are supposed to measure the learning outcome see sec. 2.1 and [9]. We are aware that a valid measurement can only be achieved by methods and tools that diagnose the defined competences in ([9], p. 35-38). However, these competences have been defined normatively by the Department of CS and lack a competences model as well as diagnostic methods. Therefore, we rely on assignments that we developed in the past years and that represent typical assignments for a Theory I course.

The course staff recorded student performance on each individual question on the homework assignments as well as performance on each question on the practice and final exam. During the whole course 14 homework exercises (8 before and 6 after the Christmas break) were offered, each with 3 mandatory and one more difficult optional assignment. For each assignment students could score 1-3 points and altogether they needed at least 50% of all points from obligatory assignments in order to attend finals. Most of the assignments have been used in similar form in the past five years and included only minor alterations, like exchanging a concrete language or Turing machine.

The final exam contained 15 simple questions focusing on definitions and methods knowledge and 5 assignments with 3-7 sub-assignments, which are aligned with the homework assignments students are already familiar with. Each sub-assignment in the exam assesses one particular skill without relying on results from previous sub-assignments. In addition, we use typical automata, regular languages or Turing machines with a simple structure and without containing unusual cases. Each of the 15 simple questions has been used for final exams in the last five years. Therefore the requirements of the final exam correspond to the requirements of the last five years.

Table 2: Distribution of student scores in 2012 and 2013

grade	1.0	1.3-1.7	2.0-2.3	2.7.-3.3	3.7-4.0	failed
2012	10.7%	20.5%	30.2%	22.9%	9.8%	**6.3%**
2013	1.9%	8.3%	25.5%	34.4%	20.4%	**9.6%**

Among the 205 students attending the finals during winter semester 2011/2012 only 6% of the students failed to pass. Among the 157 students attending the finals one year later only 9.6% failed to pass, see Table 2. Altogether, all student grades are evenly distributed. This finding strengthens the assertion that the course's final exam assessed student performance in a similar way it did in the previous years. Note that in 2013 there is a reduction in better grade due to slightly increased requirements for receiving a straight 1.0 grade (i.e. A+) in the final exam. These requirements were based on our belief that top students should demonstrate the ability of "thinking out of the box". The design of the final exam made sure that the requirements for passing remained unchanged.

5. CONCLUSION

In this paper we introduced a pedagogical approach for a theory of computation course at the University of Potsdam based on cognitive apprenticeship. Our goal was to make the practices of theoretical CS more visible to the students and therefore easier to adopt. We reinforced modeling by introducing a tutorial session; we scaffold students' activities through a strong alignment between exercises, homework, and the final exam; and we tried to coach students' activities in the exercise sessions and by providing feedback for their homework submissions. At the same time, we kept the requirements for final exams comparable to those of the last 5 years and had a failure rate below 10% two years in a row. Therefore our approach demonstrates that it is possible to enhance students' success and reduce failure rates in a theoretical CS course while keeping the requirements high.

Most students who attended the course during the last two winter semesters appeared regularly during exercise sessions and participated actively during the quiz and working with the exercises. The tutorial was attended by more students than in the years before, when we did not align homework assignments with the exercises. During the tutorial, students asked very precise and concrete questions related to the contents of the lectures and the exercises. They also asked for solutions to the more difficult assignments already submitted. In the years before, students mostly asked questions about the *current* homework assignments, which were difficult to answer without providing solutions to tasks still ahead of them. With the alignment between homework and exercises, students seemed to be more successful in solving homework assignments by themselves once they had attended the exercise sessions, seen a written solution to the exercises, and discussed the more difficult aspects in the tutorial. Altogether, our impression was that our changes helped students to be more focused, to stay motivated, and to keep working on their weekly assignments.

We were not yet able to accomplish all aspects of cognitive apprenticeship. For example, it is important that students articulate their activities and reflect on them ([4], p. 51). Since we cannot change the teacher-learner-ratio and introduce more study sessions, most of students' activities can be only modeled and scaffold. The rest has to happen during their individual studies. We only have little influence on the latter and know that when students manage to find an adequate study group they perform very well. But a lot of students are not able to do this and besides encouraging them to look for a study group, we have not found a method how to support this better. Furthermore, it remains open if and how to situate ([4], p. 52ff) the course topics and abstract tasks of the weekly assignments in contexts that make sense to the students. In its role as a cognitive tool the domain knowledge of theoretical CS will become meaningful for them as they rely on it during their whole professional career. But it remains open how this can be more explicitly highlighted during the course. Altogether, it is important for us to further elaborate on these issues in future.

Since none of our modifications to the course were specific to the University of Potsdam or to the topic of the course we believe that our approach could be also applied in introductory courses to theory of computation at other departments of CS as well as be adapted to other introductory courses in CS in order to contribute to student learning success.

REFERENCES

[1] Bereiter, C. 1997. Situated cognition and how to overcome it. In Situated cognition: Social, semiotic, and psychological perspectives, Kirshner, D. and Whitson, J. A., Eds. NJ: Erlbaum, Hillsdale, 281-300.

[2] Caspersen, M. and Bennedsen, J. 2007. Instructional design of a programming course: a learning theoretic approach. In Proceedings of the third international workshop on Computing education research (ICER '07). ACM, New York, NY, USA, 111-122

[3] Chesñevar, C. I., González, M. P., and Maguitman, A. G. 2004. Didactic strategies for promoting significant learning in formal languages and automata theory. In Proceedings of the 9th annual SIGCSE conference on Innovation and technology in computer science education (ITiCSE '04). ACM, 7-11.

[4] Collins, A. 2006. Cognitive apprenticeship. In *Cambridge Handbook of the Learning Sciences*, Sawyer, R. K., Ed. Cambridge University Press, 47-60.

[5] Collins, A., Brown, J. S., and Holum, A. 1991. Cognitive apprenticeship: Making thinking visible. American Educator, 6(11), 38-46.

[6] Hämäläinen, W. 2004. Problem-based learning of theoretical computer science. In Proceedings of the 34th ASEE/IEEE Frontiers in Education Conference, S1H/1 -S1H/6 Vol. 3.

[7] Heublein, U., Richter, J., Schmelzer, R. and Sommer, D. 2012. Die Entwicklung der Schwund- und Studienabbruch-quoten an den deutschen Hochschulen, HIS: Forum Hochschule 3/2012.

[8] Korte, L., Anderson, S., Pain, H., and Good, J. 2007. Learning by game-building: a novel approach to theoretical computer science education. In Proceedings of the 12th annual SIGCSE conference on Innovation and technology in computer science education (ITiCSE '07). ACM, 53-57.

[9] Modulhandbuch für den Bachelor- und Masterstudiengang Informatik an der Universität Potsdam. 2011. www.uni-potsdam.de/fileadmin/projects/mnfakul/assets/Studium/Modulhandbuch_Informatik.pdf

[10] Robins, A. 2010. Learning edge momentum: A new account of outcomes in CS1. *Computer Science Education*, *20*(1), 37–71.

[11] Rodger, S. H., Bressler, B., Finley, T., and Reading, S. 2006. Turning automata theory into a hands-on course. In Proceedings of the 37th SIGCSE technical symposium on Computer science education (SIGCSE '06). ACM, 379-383.

[12] Ventura, P. R. 2005. Identifying predictors of success for an objects-frst CS1. In: Computer Science Education 15, 3, 223-243.

Learning Relational Algebra by Snapping Blocks

Jason Gorman
Dept of Computer Science
James Madison University
Harrisonburg, Virginia, USA
gorma2jp@dukes.jmu.edu

Sebastian Gsell
Dept of Computer Science
James Madison University
Harrisonburg, Virginia, USA
gsellsl@dukes.jmu.edu

Chris Mayfield
Dept of Computer Science
James Madison University
Harrisonburg, Virginia, USA
mayfiecs@jmu.edu

ABSTRACT

Relational algebra provides a theoretical foundation for how modern database management systems optimize and execute queries. Its main concepts are based on set theory and first order logic, which can be challenging for students to learn due to their abstract nature. This paper presents Bags, a new type of visual programming environment (inspired by Snap!) for the teaching of relational operations and data analysis. Students formulate algebraic queries by snapping together graphical blocks that represent data sets and relational operators, resulting in an interactive visualization of the underlying concepts. The outcomes of this work will not only enhance university-level database courses, but also provide an engaging computational thinking resource for K-12 teachers in content areas outside of science and engineering.

Categories and Subject Descriptors

K.3.2 [**Computer and Information Science Education**]: Computer Science Education

General Terms

Design, Theory

Keywords

Computational thinking, data analysis, query design

1. INTRODUCTION

Over the past decade, Computer Science education researchers have developed drag-and-drop environments for teaching computer programming [8]. Notable examples include Alice (CMU), Scratch (MIT), Greenfoot (Kent), and App Inventor (Google). Although each project has its own emphasis (e.g., object oriented design, interaction with media, simulation and games, mobile development), they all focus on teaching introductory programming concepts. Students learn about instructions, decisions, loops, variables, operators, and so forth by manipulating "blocks" that represent these structures. This approach has a number of pedagogical advantages, including simplifying the programming environment, encouraging self-directed learning, making the execution of programs visual, eliminating syntax error messages, and making data more concrete [5].

In this paper we present Bags,[1] a new type of drag-and-drop environment suitable for teaching relational algebra. In contrast to current tools like Scratch and Alice that allow students to interact with computation, our software will enable students to explore and manipulate data. Students formulate database queries by combining blocks representing relational operations, including selection, projection, inner/outer join, grouping, aggregation, and sorting. As in [10], we are developing an online introduction to fundamental database theory concepts. But our approach allows users to evaluate ad hoc queries in real-time, giving them an interactive visualization of the data as they add or remove individual operations. Students are also able to experiment with different configurations of blocks and observe the corresponding query results.

What we are proposing is very different from graphical query editors, such as the visual designer in Microsoft Access. Students are not writing declarative queries that have a straightforward translation to SQL. In contrast, they are building relational algebra expressions based on set theory and first order logic, which in turn are evaluated sequentially. As in [2], the goal is for students to understand how database management systems apply selections, projections, and joins to answer queries over relational data. Query optimizers use similar algebraic representations to analyze and evaluate query execution plans. In a sense, students play the role of the optimizer while exploring data of their choice.

Bags will not only benefit database courses at the university level, but also have significant impact on K-12 education [1]. Recent efforts have developed new curricula for middle school and high school students to explore computational thinking (see e.g., [6]). Most activities for teaching computational thinking—available in the literature and on the Internet—have been successfully integrated in after-school programs with a science or technology emphasis [9]. This project aims to provide an engaging computational thinking resource for K-12 teachers in other content areas, such as social studies or humanities. For example, students in a geography course may use Bags to explore census or world

SIGCSE'14, March 5–8, 2014, Atlanta, GA, USA.

ACM 978-1-4503-2605-6/14/03 ...$15.00.
http://dx.doi.org/10.1145/2538862.2538961.

[1]The name of our environment makes reference to set theory, i.e., a bag is a multiset. SQL and other database languages are based on bag semantics.

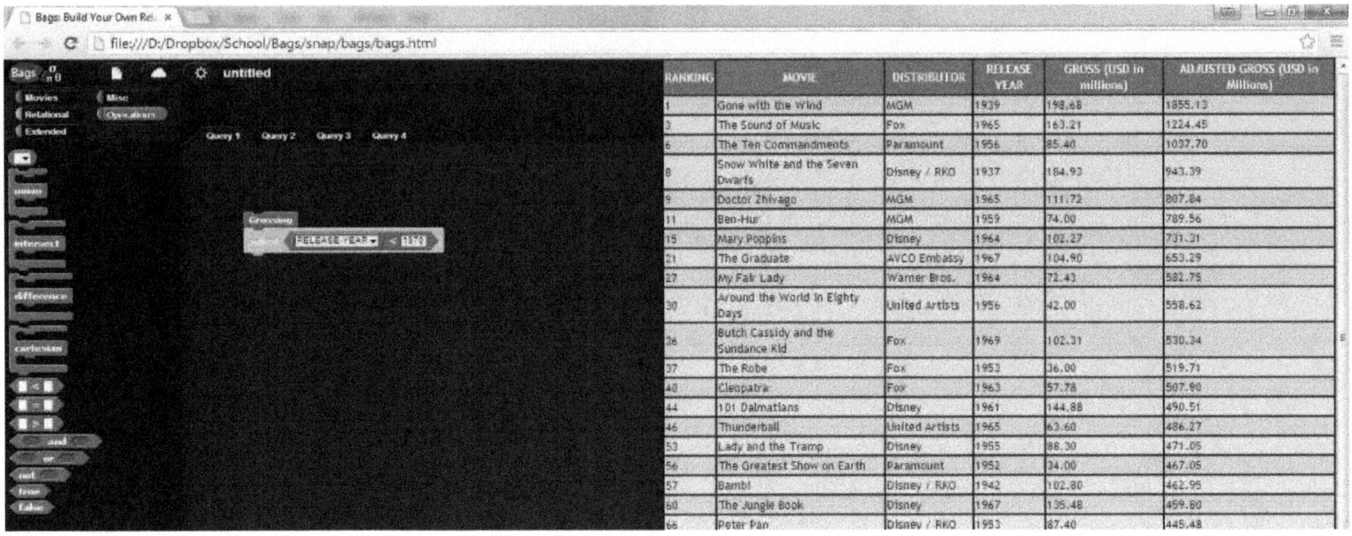

Figure 1: Screenshot of Bags executing a selection query. The data set is based on the top grossing films from IMDb. The query includes a selection predicate returning films with a release date before 1970.

almanac data as part of a research project, while at the same time gaining exposure to relational operations and database query design.

Our initial prototype is based on Snap,[2] a recent web-based environment developed by Jens Mönig at MioSoft Corporation and Brian Harvey at the University of California at Berkeley [4]. Snap is the highly interactive software featured in Berkeley's "The Beauty and Joy of Computing" course, one of the original pilot courses for AP CS Principles [7]. Harvey, Garcia, and others involved with that effort have made extensive resources available, including the Snap source code itself [3]. Although we have extended this code base to create a fundamentally different teaching tool, many of the design decisions, pedagogical features, and educational benefits share a common ancestry with Snap through its underlying JavaScript libraries.

As with Snap and the most recent version of Scratch, Bags is completely web-based and requires no additional software to be installed. The latest version and a number of educational materials are available on our website.[3] This setup not only makes it easier for us to distribute updates and enhancements to the software, but it also makes it more practical to deploy in K-12 schools. If a connection to the Internet is not available, Bags may also be downloaded in advance for offline use.

2. A QUICK TOUR OF BAGS

At a high level, Bags has a very similar layout to Snap and Scratch. Figure 1 shows the software in action. On the left we have several *palettes*, each of which consists of a set of related *blocks*. Each block represents either a data set or a relational, arithmetic, or logical operator. The user drags and drops these blocks onto the *query editor* in the center, and the corresponding *query result* appears on the right.

Suppose a student using Bags would like to look at the "Top Grossing Movies" data set and find out which of those movies were released before 1970. In relational algebra, this query would be represented as follows:

$$\sigma_{\text{Release Year}<1970}(\text{Grossing})$$

In Bags, this query is easy to formulate by using drag-and-drop functionality to create a simple selection query. The procedure of creating this query (as illustrated in Figure 1) includes the following steps:

1. Open the `Movies` data set palette, and drag and drop the `Grossing` data set block onto the query editor.

2. Open the `Relational` palette and drag and drop the `Select` operation block under the `Grossing` data set block, so that it snaps below it.

3. Open the `Operations` palette and drag and drop a "<" predicate block into the open gray circular slot in the `Select` operation block.

4. Drag and drop the *attribute block* (a drop down list that contains the current schema) into the left open slot of the "<" predicate block. Type in 1970 into the right slot of that block.

5. Click the downward arrow on the attribute block, and choose "Release Year" as the column to be evaluated.

6. Finally, click the `Select` operation block itself to execute the query. The resulting data set will appear on the right in an HTML table.

This process helps students break down a query into its component parts. Because the query design is visual, the student can see how everything fits together. It is difficult to make a syntax error because the blocks (and their slots) only snap in appropriate ways. In addition, the user may click on any block in the current query to show the result of the query up to that point. In other words, he or she can visualize the data set both before and after the selection block to understand the effect of that operation.

[2]For simplicity, we will refer to "Snap!" as "Snap" without the exclamation mark throughout the paper.

[3]`http://bags.cs.jmu.edu/`

This example is relatively trivial, but it gives students insight about how relational databases evaluate queries during their first experience with Bags. There are many other blocks available that allow students to create more sophisticated queries. The following list gives a brief summary of each palette.

- Data sets: We have compiled a diverse collection of sample data from IMDb, Wikipedia, UCI ML repository, and other websites. Users may query one of these built-in data sets or create their own from a CSV file.
- Relational: The three basic relational algebra blocks are the σ selection block, the π projection block, and the ρ rename block. There are three join blocks in Bags as well. The first is the natural join, $R \bowtie S$. The second is the theta join, $R \bowtie_\theta S$. The final is the full outer join, $R \overset{\circ}{\bowtie} S$.
- Operations: Bags also supports four set operations including union $R \cup S$, intersection $R \cap S$, difference $R - S$, and finally Cartesian product $R \times S$. The comparison operators $x > y$, $x < y$, and $x = y$ are also included, as well as the logical operations of $\wedge$ and, $\vee$ or, and $\neg$ not. Finally, there are `true` and `false` blocks that can be used in the logical operations.
- Extended: We also have blocks for γ group by, τ order by, δ duplicate elimination, and aggregate functions like `min`, `max`, `count` (and `count*`), `avg`, and `sum`.
- Attribute block: This drop down block does not relate to any one relational algebra or mathematical function. Its purpose is for the user to specify a column from the current schema. When placed near the top of a query, it corresponds to a column of the original data set. But it may also be used later in the query to refer to attributes resulting from relational operations.

Bags is free and open source software, released under the GNU Affero General Public License (AGPL 3.0). At the time of writing, we are evaluating the effectiveness of Bags as an educational tool in introductory courses as well as our upper division database course. We encourage readers to experiment with the environment, take a look at the source code, and provide feedback.

3. EXAMPLE LAB ACTIVITIES

In a classroom setting, instructors can use Bags for a variety of purposes ranging from interactive demonstrations to homework assignments. At a high level, Bags makes it easy for students to learn about relational operations in a hands-on manner. Students can also use Bags to visualize and analyze interesting data sets. This aspect of the environment is particularly applicable at the K-12 level, where the objective would not be to "learn relational algebra" but rather to develop computational thinking skills.

As a natural starting point, we recommend that students explore the built-in data sets. Figure 2 illustrates two simple queries about movies from IMDb. Notice the different elements of the each query. We start with a data set (blue) and apply a relational operation (orange) that includes a greater than operation (purple) which in turn refers back to the schema (blue). The triangle buttons on the right side of the projection block allow the user to specify how many attributes to project from the relation.

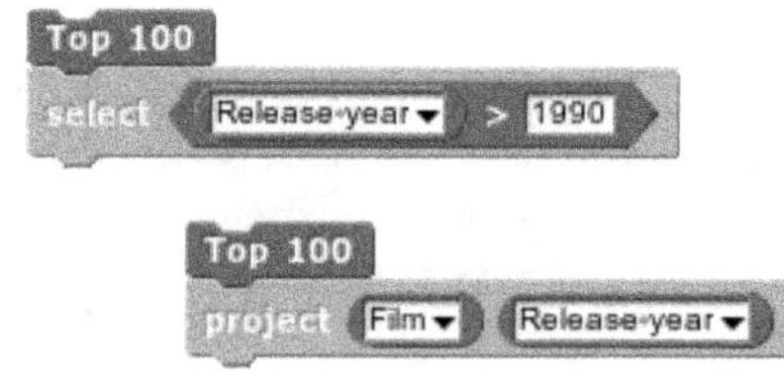

Figure 2: Introducing selection and projection using the Top 100 movies data set.

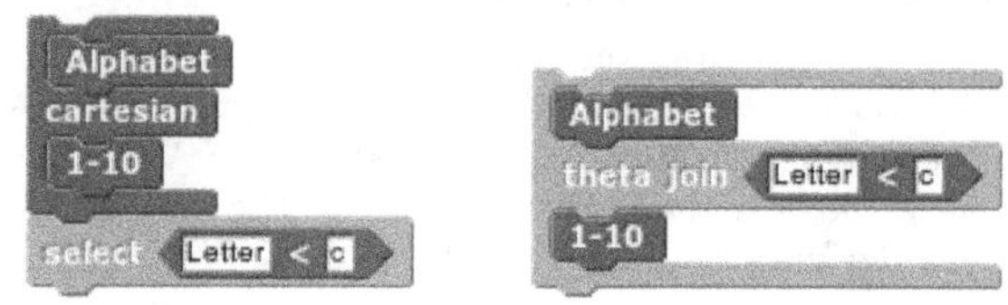

Figure 3: The relationship of Cartesian product and theta join, using the letters A–Z and numbers 1–10.

The types of queries that students should be able to answer on day one include: "What are the top five Disney movies, in terms of adjusted gross income?" "What are the title, author, and year of books from Russia in the top 100 list?" "What are the names and symbols of the periodic elements with an atomic mass of more than 250?" In Bags, the block shapes and colors help students learn what elements are necessary for each type of query. An important concept to emphasize is that each block (or group of blocks snapped together) defines a new relation. Because of this design, students may work on multiple queries at the same time and compare their results interactively by clicking on each one.

It is often possible to design the same query in many different ways. Relational algebra provides the tools for manipulating expressions without changing their mathematical meaning. Query optimizers use *algebraic equivalences* to generate multiple query plans and select one with the minimal cost. Bags allows students to explore these types of equivalences in a visual manner by composing multiple queries and/or dragging blocks within the same query.

For example, students can visualize what it means to join two relations during a lesson with Bags. A join operation is closely related to the Cartesian product. As illustrated in Figure 3, a Cartesian product followed by a selection is essentially a theta join. By building these queries one block at a time, students can think about each step of the query and visualize what the data looks like. Using simple data sets like letters and numbers makes it easier for students to see patterns in the query results.

Consider another example query that joins "US Presidents" with "Top 100 Books" (abbreviated below as P and B). To determine which president was in office when each of the books was published, we use the join condition "P.Start $\leq$ B.Year $\leq$ P.End" (denoted by θ below). Finally, we only wish to display books published after the year 1900:

$$\sigma_{B.Year>1900}(P \bowtie_\theta B)$$

One way to rewrite this query is to "push" the selection operator inside the join as follows:

$$P \bowtie_\theta \sigma_{B.Year>1900}(B)$$

For this exercise, a student may simply rearrange the block order to confirm it produces the same result. The latter query is more efficient in practice, because it's better to filter data before sending it through an expensive join operation.

This section briefly presented some of the tasks that students and instructors might carry out using Bags. Please refer to our website for additional lab activities, homework assignments, and other resources.

4. BAGS ARCHITECTURE

The second contribution of this paper—in addition to introducing the educational tool itself—is a detailed discussion of how we designed and implemented Bags. As discussed previously, Bags makes extensive use of the JavaScript libraries underlying Snap. It is neither a fork nor a plugin of Snap, and demonstrates how Snap can be extended to create new educational environments. By documenting what we have learned in this process, we hope that others will be able to innovate educational tools in additional areas of computer science such as architecture, networking, and graphics.

4.1 Understanding Snap

Snap runs inside a virtual machine named Morphic, which is similar in architecture to how MIT's Scratch was built on top of Squeak.[4] Morphic is "a lively Web-GUI inspired by Squeak" implemented entirely in JavaScript. In order to understand how Snap works, it is necessary to become familiar with each of its main files.

- `Morphic.js` is the foundation of Snap as it creates the virtual machine and the basic objects and functions which are extended through other classes. It is based on HTML5 and supports the creation of "lively" GUI elements inside of a single Canvas object.
- `GUI.js` initializes all of the visual objects in the canvas including the toolbar, palette, scripting area, and the stage; it does not create the blocks in the palette, `Objects.js` will do this.
- `Objects.js` defines the blocks that will reside in the palette and pushes them into the GUI when a different palette is chosen and loaded.
- `Blocks.js` holds the functionality for all of the blocks that the user will create their programs with.
- `BYOB.js` provides Snap's "Build Your Own Block" functionality that allows the user to create their own custom blocks. A block editor is used that can condense a longer string of blocks into a single block.
- `Threads.js` contains the interpreter for Snap. A thread manager is used to schedule execution tasks, and each process is a *morph* that is executed an element on the Canvas object.

Morphs are the basic objects in Snap, and they can be extended into any number of submorphs. A few building block morphs from `Morphic.js` include `Color`, `Point`, `Node`, and `Morph` itself. Figure 4 illustrates the most common morphs visible to the user.

[4]See `http://www.squeak.org/`

Figure 4: Three of Snap's basic blocks.

- `BlockMorph` is the basic form of all morphs in Snap and provides a number of essential functions for all submorphs.
- `CommandBlockMorph` is the rectangle block that snaps together with other CommandBlockMorphs in order to simulate the flow of a program (by executing them in order from top to bottom).
- `HatBlockMorph` is the rectangle block with a curved top that must be at the top of a stack of blocks, usually this provides conditions for the program to execute.
- `ReporterBlockMorph` is the rounded rectangle block that is inserted in open slots in order to provide input, Booleans, mathematical functions, and many other potential uses.
- `InputSlotMorph` is a text input slot that is usually included in ReporterBlockMorphs and some CommandBlockMorphs.

As with any complex software there are many connections and interactions between each of the different files. Figure 5 summarizes the initialization process of both Snap and Bags.

Snap relies on multiple JavaScript files and at least one html file. The html file is the origin for the entire application. It creates a new WorldMorph upon loading the page. The WorldMorph is the backdrop for all of Snap. To create the WorldMorph, the html code utilizes morphic.js. After the WorldMorph is created, the IDE_Morph is created. The IDE_Morph is defined by the `gui.js` file. The gui.js file defines how the program looks and feels. This includes the palette, which holds the blocks; the scripting area, where blocks are combined to form processes; the stage; the sprite utilities (sprites are all of the images or objects in the stage); and the top of the screen including the logo, buttons, etc.

Once the IDE_Morph is created, the next file to be utilized is `objects.js`. Here, the contents of the palette are defined. There are two parts to the palette: (1) the categories (motion, control, looks, sound, etc.) and (2) the contents of each category (which has its own unique set of blocks). To create the blocks, objects.js relies on the block morphs defined in `blocks.js` (see Figure 4). Using these morphs, one can create all of the blocks in Snap. Blocks.js also defines the functions associated with each block.

The remaining files are not to be forgotten or dismissed. They all serve a function, but their function is unrelated to how we extended Snap. The design in Snap is laid out rather well, so in Bags we used a similar approach. The main differences are (1) we created our own html file, `bags.html`, and (2) we designed a change set—a group of files that contain the changes and additions to Snap. The progression of files and creation of objects works essentially the same. We did not fundamentally change how Snap works internally. Figure 6 compares how blocks work in Snap versus Bags.

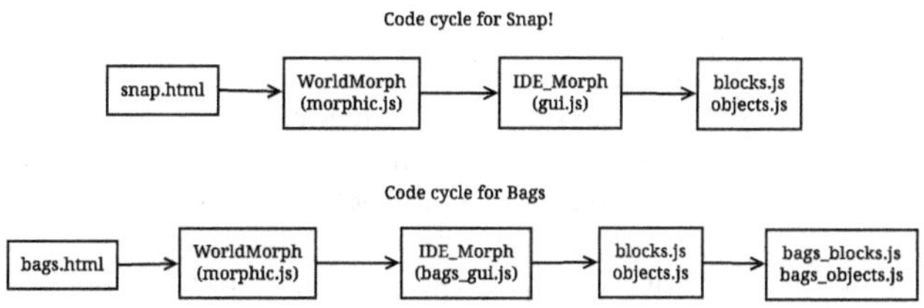

Figure 5: When Snap or Bags is instantiated.

4.2 Extending Snap

In order to extend Snap, the use of "change sets" is recommended instead of modifying the source code directly. Change sets allow one to do minimum code alternation, as well as inheriting new functionality and bug fixes as Snap is updated. To install Bags and apply our change sets, we download the latest version of Snap and extract it to its own folder. Then we add our own code in a nested folder. Our bags.html file loads Snap's JavaScript files first, and then Bags's files second in order to override some of the objects' definitions. As a result, the change sets are automatically applied without the need of patching or maintaining 3rd party code.

The overriding files for Bags include: `bags_blocks.js`, `bags_gui.js`, and `bags_objects.js`. While we did not alter every file in Snap using change sets, it should be possible to modify all of them without causing issues with updated versions of Snap.

- `bags.html` is the application entry point. After including each of Snap's JavaScript files, we include our own (e.g., first `../blocks.js` then `bags_blocks.js`).
- In `bags_blocks.js`, we edited and added new types of slots in SyntaxElementMorph's `labelPart` function. %schema adds a slot for a schema drop-down block to be snapped into. CommandBlockMorph was modified with new variables and functions to accommodate relational algebra computations.
- `bags_datasets.js` initializes example data sets (such as Top Grossing Movies). We adapted ReporterBlockMorph to provide support for attribute blocks. When it is snapped into a block connected to a data set block, it will pull in the columns in the underlying data. This file also includes all of the implementation for each of the relational algebra functions.
- The `bags_gui.js` file contains all of the changes for the GUI itself. Snap utilizes a single canvas which allows it to resize to fit nearly any window. In Bags, we currently use an html <div> to display the data alongside the canvas. There are a number of features in Snap (e.g., cloud storage) that we have not yet implemented, so some visual features had to be removed.
- Finally, `bags_objects.js` changes the categories for the palettes and the their blocks.

As noted in the previous section, the foundation of Snap is the morph objects. It is important to utilize the basic functionality already present in Snap. Any program extending Snap will most likely be able to use the basic functionality because it is particularly robust. Snap carefully defines

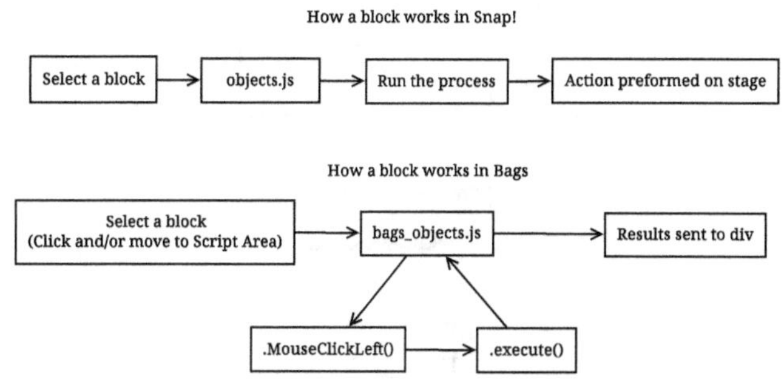

Figure 6: How a block works in Snap and in Bags.

all the interactions that can happen, i.e., how blocks snap together, but separates the behavior from the actual function of each block. This separation allows developers create the blocks they need without needing to rewrite how the program works.

Once again, we did not use custom block morphs is Bags. Instead, we found ways to take the existing morphs and alter them to suit our needs. We used functions and variables to create the desired alterations. For example, to create a data set block we re-purposed the CommandBlockMorph. We had to alter the .snap() function for this morph so that it would not allow two data set blocks to snap together—this would result in nothing meaningful in terms of relational algebra. We use a simple flag to determine whether a block is a data block. After solving the snapping issue, the next step is to assign a data set to a data block. This was accomplished by adding variables to the CommandBlockMorph. The new variables allowed us to assign a data set to a data block and pass the data set to the next block in the process.

Consider for example a user that (1) places a data block onto the scripting area, (2) connects a project block to the bottom of the data block, and finally (3) adds the drop down block to the project block. When the project block is snapped to the data block, the data set in the data block is copied to the project block. This is easily done because both the data block and the project block use the CommandBlockMorph and have the same available variables. In the case of projection, it is necessary to determine the schema that is going to be modified. Figure 7 provides a diagram of how data flows through Bags. For simplicity, we store the data set as two matrices: one is the schema and the other is the data. For each CommandBlockMorph, we added four variables for the data: schema in/out and data in/out.

We also had to introduce other flags in CommandBlockMorph to support joins and set operations. Creating these blocks required the most retooling of Snap. Unlike the other relational operations that act as filters, joins require two inputs. In other words, we need to execute two separate relational algebra functions before we could join them together. We were able to introduce a modified version of the if-else Snap block for this purpose. The top half of the block holds the left input, and the bottom half holds the right. Although the behavior of this block varies drastically from its original purpose, the design of Snap is such that we could reuse most of the code for natural join, theta join, and outer join, as well as the set operations union, difference, intersection, and Cartesian product.

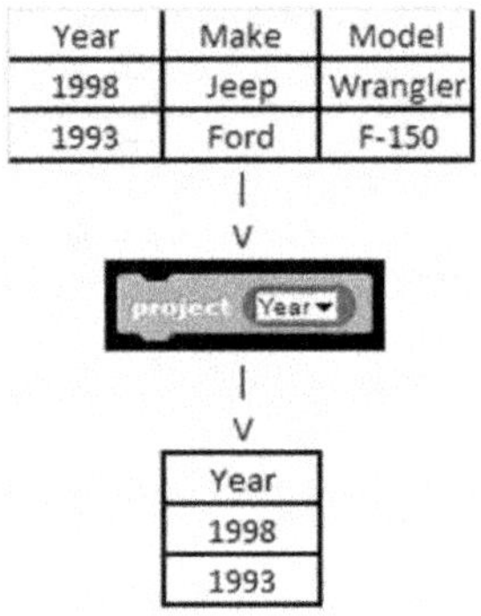

Figure 7: Illustration of a projection. Each block in Bags stores a copy of the relation (and its schema) coming in and going out of the block.

5. DISCUSSION

As previously stated in the above section, we used new functions and variables to accomplish what we needed. The reason we went this route was based on the trouble and problems we ran into when trying to create custom block morphs. The initial development of Bags was started with trying to create at least three custom block morphs. There was a DataMorph for data blocks, a JoinMorph for join blocks, and a DropDownMorph for the dropdown. The original join block was going to be a block that had two snap points on the top of the block. This was chosen because we wanted to create a top-to-bottom visualization of relational algebra (rather than left-to-right as on paper).

Implementing custom blocks in Snap is fairly easy. In an early prototype, we created custom blocks as new morphs. But as we began adding more code, we found that it caused many visual and functional challenges to spring up. Some of these included not being able to move blocks from the palettes to the scripting area, and unintentionally creating multiple instances of the block as the user attempted to release it onto the scripting area. These issues convinced us that using change sets to alter the morphs themselves was necessary to implement our desired functionality.

In addition, the custom block design had two major issues. The first was a technical issue that we were unable to have two blocks simultaneously snapped on top of a join block. Second, if someone attempted to create a long chain of joins, the process would take up a large amount of horizontal space. This design issue was deemed counterproductive, so we eventually found a new way to create the join block using the CommandBlockMorph and the if-else style block. The other morphs had similar technical and design problems that led to similar changes.

We are preparing to conduct educational research in the next stages of the project's development. One main question is whether using an interactive drag-and-drop environment changes students' perception of relational algebra. To evaluate the effectiveness of our approach, we plan to use a pre-post assessment. The pre-survey will determine prior knowledge and attitudes of the students. A control group of students will learn about relational algebra using an online tutorial by Dietrich and Goelman [2]. Another group of students will study relational algebra using the proposed environment. All students will then complete a homework assignment, followed by a post-survey. We will use the assignment to assess their understanding and the post-survey to measure changes in perception.

Bags is a robust and versatile educational tool. Just as the design of Snap allows almost anyone to learn basic computer programming concepts, Bags will open new doors to teaching students how to analyze relational data sets. We are developing a number of activities to accompany Bags and reinforce computational thinking skills at the middle school, high school, and university levels. These types of learning environments are essential for bringing new and diverse students into the computing field.

6. ACKNOWLEDGMENTS

We express gratitude to Jens Mönig and Brian Harvey for answering our many questions about the Snap code base, and for developing such a tremendous resource in the open. We would also like to thank Long Nguyen for his contributions to the initial prototype of Bags. And finally, we appreciate the thoughtful suggestions of the anonymous reviewers of this paper.

7. REFERENCES

[1] V. Barr and C. Stephenson. Bringing Computational Thinking to K-12: What is Involved and What is the Role of the Computer Science Education Community? *ACM Inroads*, 2(1):48–54, 2011.

[2] S. W. Dietrich and D. Goelman. Database Animations for Many Majors: Conference Tutorial. *J. Comput. Sci. Coll.*, 27(4):174–174, Apr. 2012.

[3] B. Harvey, D. D. Garcia, T. Barnes, N. Titterton, D. Armendariz, L. Segars, E. Lemon, S. Morris, and J. Paley. SNAP! (Build Your Own Blocks). In *Proceedings of the 44th ACM Technical Symposium on Computer Science Education*, SIGCSE '13, pages 759–759, 2013.

[4] B. Harvey and J. Mönig. Bringing "No Ceiling" to Scratch: Can One Language Serve Kids and Computer Scientists? In *Constructionism*, Paris, France, 2010.

[5] J. Maloney, M. Resnick, N. Rusk, B. Silverman, and E. Eastmond. The Scratch Programming Language and Environment. *Trans. Comput. Educ.*, 10(4):16:1–16:15, Nov. 2010.

[6] A. Repenning, D. Webb, and A. Ioannidou. Scalable Game Design and the Development of a Checklist for Getting Computational Thinking Into Public Schools. In *Proceedings of the 41st ACM technical symposium on Computer science education*, SIGCSE '10, pages 265–269, New York, NY, USA, 2010. ACM.

[7] L. Snyder, T. Barnes, D. Garcia, J. Paul, and B. Simon. The First Five Computer Science Principles Pilots: Summary and Comparisons. *ACM Inroads*, 3(2):58–60, 2012.

[8] I. Utting, S. Cooper, M. Kölling, J. Maloney, and M. Resnick. Alice, Greenfoot, and Scratch – A Discussion. *Trans. Comput. Educ.*, 10(4):17:1–17:11, Nov. 2010.

[9] U. Wolz, M. Stone, K. Pearson, S. M. Pulimood, and M. Switzer. Computational Thinking and Expository Writing in the Middle School. *Trans. Comput. Educ.*, 11(2):9:1–9:22, July 2011.

[10] F.-J. Yang. A Virtual Tutor for Relational Schema Normalization. *ACM Inroads*, 2(3):38–42, Aug. 2011.

Bringing CS2013 Recommendations for Parallel and Distributed Computing Into Your CS Curriculum

Richard Brown
St. Olaf College
rab@stolaf.edu

Elizabeth Shoop
Macalester College
shoop@macalester.edu

Joel Adams
Calvin College
adams@calvin.edu

Categories and Subject Descriptors
K.3.2 [**Computers and Education**]: Computer and Information Science Education – *Curriculum.*

General Terms
Algorithms, Performance

Keywords
Curriculum, CS curriculum, Parallelism, Distributed computing, Parallelism and Distributed Computing, PDC, Curriculum planning, CS major.

1. SUMMARY
The ACM-IEEE CS2013 curricular recommendations include a dramatic growth in parallel and distributed computing (PDC) topics, in response to the necessary industry shift toward multicore computing, and to emerging technologies such as cloud computing. How can your institution integrate those recommendations into your undergraduate CS curriculum? In this special session, leaders in PDC education will succinctly present their curricular strategies in relation to CS2013 recommendations, while attendees carry out a workshop-style activity to identify opportunities and assemble resources for blending more PDC content into their own local CS curricula.

2. OVERALL OBJECTIVE OF THE SESSION
The proposed CS2013 curriculum recommendations for undergraduate CS majors [1] include a substantial increase in topics related to parallel and distributed computing (PDC) and concurrency, represented not only in the new PD (Parallel and Distributed) and SF (System Fundamentals) knowledge areas, but also in PDC-related learning objectives for Tier-1 knowledge units in seven other knowledge areas. Incorporating so much PDC into existing packed undergraduate CS curricula presents professors with a major challenge. This special session is designed to engage faculty in starting or continuing to make progress on getting these PDC requirements into their institution's CS curricula. The topic is timely because of the newness of CS2013 and the need to prepare CS students for increased use of parallelism and distributed computation in their futures.

The session features a simple activity for attendees, in which participants use a short worksheet to record ideas, strategies, issues, and resources for incorporating CS2013 recommendations involving PDC to their own institutions' undergraduate CS curricula. The worksheet lists facets of curricular change, including courses, curricular structure, curricular resources, challenges, and opportunities. The session leader will prompt attendees to record notes in these categories throughout the session. As a resource, participants will also receive a one-page spreadsheet listing CS2013 knowledge units that include PDC learning objectives. A more extensive spreadsheet detailing those items will be available online, as part of a website of resources.

Between introductory remarks and a final discussion, four educators from various types of institutions will present five-minute "lightning talks", each followed immediately by up to five minutes for questions and answers, in order to stimulate and inform the attendees' curricular reflections, for recording on their individual worksheets.

3. OUTLINE OF THE SESSION
1. Brief introduction (1-2 min), by session leader Dick Brown. Session agenda displayed on a side projector throughout.
2. Parallel and Distributed Computing in CS2013 (10 min), by Mehran Sahami, Stanford, Chair of ACM delegation and of PD knowledge area group in CS2013.
3. Describe resources and begin the worksheet activity (10 min, session leader). Activity worksheet and one-page spreadsheet presented, and other web resources noted. *Respondents begin to make notes on their worksheets, continuing throughout the remainder of the session.*
4. Five-minute lightning talks, each followed by up to five minutes discussion (four speakers, up to 40 min total). Speakers relate their PDC undergraduate curricular work to CS2013, referring to the spreadsheet resource during each lightning talk. Speakers:
    a. Steven Bogaerts, DePauw University -- Teaching parallelism in a Python-based CS1 at a small institution.
    b. Libby Shoop, Macalester College -- CSinParallel, an incremental modular strategy
    c. Apan Qasem, Texas State University/San Marcos -- adding PDC within a six-course subset of the major.
    d. Paul Tymann, Rochester Institute of Technology – PDC in the undergraduate CS curriculum at a research-1 institution.

SIGCSE'14, March 5–8, 2014, Atlanta, Georgia, USA.
ACM 978-1-4503-2605-6/14/03.
http://dx.doi.org/10.1145/2538862.2538996

5. Final discussion (approx. 15 min), moderated by session leader.

This totals approximately 35 min of participant discussion, plus the integrated worksheet activity, during the 75-minute session.

4. EXPECTATIONS

The intended audience is faculty in undergraduate CS major programs. We expect those faculty members to emerge with an awareness of the nature and extent of PDC recommendations within the CS2013 curriculum, with resources such as the spreadsheet for further exploration of PDC topics that appear in CS 2013, with new ideas for incorporating those PDC topics specifically into their own local CS curricula, and with more understanding of the particular challenges and opportunities for increasing the presence of PDC in undergraduate CS major programs. Two types of voluntary feedback will be sought using anonymous online forms: feedback on the session and its materials; and suggestions for additional kinds of curricular resources that could assist faculty in modifying their curricula to use more parallelism and distributed computing.

While we expect faculty who energetically engage in the worksheet activity to get the most out of this special session, others who may prefer simply to observe and listen on their own will also learn about the extent of PDC in CS2013, receive the one-page spreadsheet and online resources for later investigation, and hear ideas and issues about shifting to include more PDC topics in the undergraduate CS curricula.

5. SUITABILITY FOR A SPECIAL SESSION

The proposed 75-minute activity-based session more like a mini-workshop than a paper or panel. On the surface, the series of focused presentations from persons at various kinds of institutions may seem like a modified panel; however, the worksheet activity (intended specifically for imagining, reflecting, and beginning to plan for curricular change at one's own institution) supported by the spreadsheet and other resources is quite unlike a standard panel session.

Although a three-hour curriculum workshop would allow for more planning activities and greater depth, a special session during the SIGCSE regular program has potential to reach a much larger audience for this timely and significant session topic.

6. REFERENCES

[1] ACM/IEEE-CS Joint Task Force, "Computer Science Curricula 2013." [Online]. [Accessed: 11-Dec-2013]: http://ai.stanford.edu/users/sahami/CS2013/.

Toward Curricular Guidelines for Cybersecurity

Andrew McGettrick
Chair, ACM Education Board
+44.(0)141.552.4400
Andrew.McGettrick@cis.strath.ac.uk

Lillian N Cassel (Moderator)
Villanova University
Dept of Computing Sciences
Villanova PA 19085 USA
1 610 519 7341
cassel@acm.org

Melissa Dark
Purdue University
401 N Grant Street
West Lafayette, IN 47907
1 765 494 7661
mdark@tech.purdue.edu

Elizabeth K. Hawthorne
Union County College
1033 Springfield Avenue
Cranford, NJ 07016
1 610 519 7310
hawthorne@ucc.edu

John Impagliazzo (Scribe)
Hofstra University, Emeritus
Hempstead, NY 11549 USA
+1 516 463 6774
John.Impagliazzo@Hofstra.edu

SUMMARY

This session reports on a workshop convened by the ACM Education Board with funding by the US National Science Foundation and invites discussion from the community on the workshop findings. The topic, curricular directions for cybersecurity, is one that resonates in many departments considering how best to prepare graduates to face the challenges of security issues in employment and future research. The session will include presentation of the workshop context and conclusions, but will be open to participant discussion. This will be the first public presentation of the results of the workshop and the first opportunity for significant response.

Categories and Subject Descriptors

K.6.5 Security and Protection (D.4.6, K.4.2), K.3.2 Computer and Information Science Education

Keywords

Curriculum, Cybersecurity

1. OVERALL OBJECTIVE

This session presents the results of an NSF sponsored workshop on curriculum needs related to Cybersecurity. The workshop brought together a core leadership group including experts from industry, government, and academia to consider how computing education could best address the need to build a cybersecurity workforce to meet the needs of industry and government. The purpose of this session is to present the outcomes of this workshop to the computing education community and to generate discussion, both during the session and afterwards, of the issues raised and the approaches recommended.

SIGCSE'14, March 5–8, 2014, Atlanta, Georgia, USA.
ACM 978-1-4503-2605-6/14/03.
http://dx.doi.org/10.1145/2538862.2538990

2. OUTLINE OF THE SESSION

Beth Hawthorne and Melissa Dark represent the participants in the workshop and will describe the nature of the discussions that occurred and present the major points of view that characterized the workshop discussions. Andrew McGettrick, chair of the ACM Education Board, will summarize the ways in which the workshop deliberations impact future Education Board curriculum plans with respect to cybersecurity education Boots Cassel will serve as moderator for the session and will assure that community discussion has ample time and that everyone who wishes to contribute will have a fair share of the available time. John Impagliazzo will serve as scribe to record the comments from the participants and to be sure that an accurate record of the discussion is available to the Education Board.

The major points of the workshop report will form an outline for the session:

- The Core Leadership Group identified the main elements (*i.e.* knowledge areas or sub-disciplines) of cybersecurity and emphasized the important fact that it is a multidisciplinary subject.
- Cybersecurity is currently an immature and ill-defined subject and not a true discipline since it lacks some of the criteria normally applied to disciplines.
- The "mind set" of the cybersecurity professional is an important factor in preventing, detecting, and mitigating security breaches. Developing this way of thinking must be part of recruiting and educating cybersecurity professionals.
- Every citizen and institution has a role to play in cybersecurity; its comparison with public health is worth exploring. Everyone, and in particular all students, should have some form of cybersecurity education.
- There is need for a whole variety of academic degree programs in cybersecurity from the technical aspects through to courses based on psychology, psychiatry, criminal justice, business (*i.e.* policy and economics) and more.
- Technical courses are necessary for producing high-quality graduates who can develop as computing professionals into cybersecurity experts of the future, crucial for protecting vital assets. The scope of cybersecurity education must also

include programs for the computing professional, for operations staff, and to provide for the public good and the needs of society.

- Deeply technical master's courses of various kinds are needed to produce high-quality cybersecurity graduates capable of addressing the most sophisticated technological cybersecurity issues.
- Two-year colleges serve a very important need in cybersecurity education and deserve encouragement to continue their work.
- Institutions of higher education should put effort into drawing the attention of computing students to the challenges of cybersecurity. The Core Leadership Group felt that all computing graduates should have at least one technical course in cybersecurity.
- The attention to security within the various knowledge areas in the CS2013 curriculum is a positive development likely to influence curricular guidance in computing areas such as software engineering, computer engineering, and information technology.
- Credentials, properly vetted by a governing body and carrying the imprimatur of a respected institution, can attract students to cybersecurity and help advance their careers. These credentials need to be challenging for students and to be seen as addressing deep issues in the area.
- Cybersecurity education requires a lot of hands-on activities; experiential, guided learning that is time- and labor-intensive for both students and faculty. It will be expensive, so sources of public and private funding should be sought to help talented students afford their education to the level they desire.
- There is a continuing need for PhD graduates in cybersecurity, and to encourage them to remain in academia to help educate the high-quality cybersecurity graduates of the future.
- Cyber competitions and awards have an important role to play in motivating students toward cybersecurity careers.
- Ensemble is a valuable tool to help develop and disseminate resources and share ideas in support of a community of cybersecurity educators.

Workshop participants also noted the availability and the usefulness of the Ensemble computing education portal and supported its use as a vehicle for sharing educational resources related to security and as a place for discussion of ongoing projects and opportunities. Current funding for the Ensemble project targets support of education in cybersecurity as a special focus.

The workshop report concludes with specific recommendations for Institutions of Higher Education, for general stakeholders such as government and business, and for the National Science Foundation.

3. EXPECTATIONS

The session will present the findings from the workshop, but will include ample time for discussion. In addition to the workshop results, there will be discussion of the place of cybersecurity in the new ACM/IEEE-CS CS2013 curriculum guidelines. The participation of the SIGCSE community is highly desired and will contribute to the fuller understanding of the issues involved in appropriate curricular attention to cybersecurity.

With John Impagliazzo as scribe for the session, input from the community will be carefully recorded and presented to the ACM Education Board as a response to the Workshop Report and as relevant material for consideration in planning ACM activities. A report of the session will be prepared and communicated with the SIGCSE community through Inroads and/or posts to the mailing list, as well as through the Ensemble portal.

4. SUITABILITY FOR A SPECIAL SESSION

SIGCSE Special Sessions were originally designed to provide a forum for connecting SIGCSE participants to results of major NSF initiatives and the relevant activities of the ACM Education Board and other organizations with a commitment to computing education. This session matches that purpose exactly by sharing an important ACM Education Board activity, conducted with funding from NSF. The topic is one of current interest and the involvement of ACM and NSF provides both resources and expertise to address the issue effectively. This opportunity to bring the results to the SIGCSE community is a natural and important component of the effort.

Understanding NSF Funding

Jan Cuny, Jeffrey Forbes & Harriet Taylor
National Science Foundation
Directorate of Computer and Information Science and Engineering
jcuny@nsf.gov, jforbes@nsf.gov, htaylor@nsf.gov

Valerie Barr, Victor Piotrowski, Jane Prey, & Paul Tymann
National Science Foundation
Directorate of Education and Human Resources
vbarr@nsf.gov, vpiotrow@nsf.gov, jprey@nsf.gov, ptymann@nsf.gov

SUMMARY

This session will provide information about the current status of Federal budget as it impacts NSF and the computing community.

Representatives from both Education and Human Resources (EHR) and Computer and Information Science and Engineering (CISE) directorates will provide the most up-to-date information about available funding opportunities.

It is anticipated that the session will include information about the below listed programs plus others. In addition, proposal and review processes as well as strategies for writing competitive proposals will be discussed.

Categories and Subject Descriptors

K.3.2 Computer and Information Science Education

Keywords

Grants, awards, proposals, National Science Foundation, education.

1. OVERALL OBJECTIVE, AUDIENCE, SUITABILITY

NSF supports projects to improve education in science, technology, engineering, and mathematics (STEM) through several programs in its Education and Human Resources (EHR) directorate, as well as in its research directorates, including Computer and Information Science and Engineering (CISE). This forum presents a description of some education-related programs in the EHR and CISE directorates, and enables faculty to interact with the presenters concerning specific project ideas that could be appropriate for the various programs. This type of forum is best suited to a special session to encourage audience interaction and for making connections between faculty and NSF program directors.

SIGCSE'14, March 5–8, 2014, Atlanta, Georgia, USA.
ACM 978-1-4503-2605-6/14/03.
http://dx.doi.org/10.1145/2538862.2538988

2. SESSION OUTLINE

The presenters will describe each of the following programs and encourage questions from the audience. Complete details about the programs can be found on the NSF websites for the Directorate of Education and Human Resources [1] and the Directorate for Computer & Information Science & Engineering (CISE) [2].

2.1 Advanced Technological Education (ATE)

ATE is a program specifically geared for community colleges, or for four-year schools working closely with community colleges. This program focuses on improvement in the "education of science and engineering technicians at the undergraduate and the secondary school levels. [2]" Specific technological fields include computer and information technology, cybersecurity, forensics, and telecommunications.

2.2 IUSE (TUES-STEP-WIDER++) solicitation

The goals of TUES, STEP, and WIDER are enduring, as are the challenges and opportunities institutions are facing as they seek to improve UG STEM education. So NSF remains committed to supporting innovation efforts along these lines and identifying models that can be implemented (adapted/adopted) more widely.

The IUSE solicitation was posted at http://www.nsf.gov/funding/pgm_summ.jsp?pims_id=504976.

2.3 CyberCorps: Scholarships for Service (SFS)

The SFS program seeks to increase the number of qualified students entering information assurance and cybersecurity and to increase the capacity of the US higher education enterprise to produce professionals in these fields. The SFS program has two tracks: (1) the Scholarship Track which provides funding for scholarships to students in information assurance and cybersecurity, and (2) the Capacity Track which provides funding for professional development of information assurance and cybersecurity faculty and for the development of academic programs in these fields.

2.4 Innovative Technology Experiences for Students and Teachers (ITEST)

The ITEST program seeks to encourage K-12 students to develop interest in and to be prepared for careers in STEM and information and communications technology (ICT). ITEST projects must engage K-12 students and may also provide opportunities for teachers. While there are four types of ITEST projects, the two most likely to be of interest are (1) Strategies projects that develop, implement, and evaluate novel interventions for K-12 students, and (2) Research projects that contribute to the knowledge base about which approaches, models, and interventions with K-12 students and teachers are most likely to increase capacity in the STEM and ICT-intensive workforce of the future.

2.5 Research Experiences for Undergraduates Sites (REU Sites)

Research experience is one of the most effective ways of attracting talented undergraduates to, and retaining them in careers in science and engineering, including careers in teaching and research. The REU Sites program aims to provide appropriate and valuable educational experiences for cohorts of 8-10 undergraduate students in the summer through participation in research and professional development activities. REU projects engage students, most of whom are from institutions different than the host institution, in meaningful ways in ongoing research programs or in research projects specifically designed for the REU program. REU projects feature high-quality interaction of students with faculty and/or other research mentors and access to appropriate facilities and professional development opportunities.

2.6 Research Experiences for Teachers in Engineering and Computer Science (RET Sites)

The RET Sites program provides support for the active participation of in-service and pre-service K-12 STEM teachers and community college faculty in ongoing engineering and computer science research. Institutions build bridges with their communities through hosting a cohort of 10-15 teachers for summer research and ongoing community activities during the school year. Encouraging active participation of K-12 educators and community college faculty in research is an excellent way to broaden and increase the capacity of the teacher pool in the U. S. to teach engineering and computer science concepts to their students and to encourage students to pursue engineering and computer science careers.

2.7 STEM-C which includes Computing Education for the 21st Century (CE21)

The CE21 program goals are to build a robust computing research community, a computationally competent 21st century workforce, and a computationally empowered citizenry. The program addresses three interrelated challenges: the significant underproduction of degrees needed for the computing and computing-related workforce, the longstanding underrepresentation of many segments of our population, and the lack of a presence of computing in K-12. CE21 has three tracks: (1) CS10K projects develop the partnershiops and knowledge base necessary to ensure broad access to engaging, rigorous computer science courses in 10,000 high schools taught by 10,000 well-trained teachers; (2) Computing Education Research projects will contribute to the knowledge base for computing education by conducting basic research on the teaching and learning of computational competencies at any level from elementary school through undergraduate study; and (3) Broadeining Participation projects develop and assess novel interventions that contribute to our knowledge base on the effective teaching and learning of computing for students from groups underrepresented in computing.

3. WRITING COMPETITIVE PROPOSALS

NSF programs are quite competitive but there are simple strategies you should be aware of when writing proposals to improve your chances of success. First and foremost, read the Program Solicitation carefully. Your goal is to help reviewers quickly understand *what* you intend to do and that you have given sufficient thought of *how* you intend to do it. Organize the proposal to address the essential components described in the solicitation. Use headings, boldface and bulleted lists to help the reader quickly understand the organization of the proposals. Address each point thoroughly but succinctly. And finally, start well before the submission deadline. Include sufficient lead time to allow colleagues to provide feedback and for your research office to approve the proposal. Specific directions for completing your proposal can be found online [3].

4. REFERENCES

[1] http://nsf.gov/div/index.jsp?org=EHR

[2] http://nsf.gov/dir/index.jsp?org=CISE

[3] http://nsf.gov/funding/preparing/

Engaging Underrepresented Groups in High School Introductory Computing through Computational Remixing with EarSketch

Jason Freeman[1], Brian Magerko[1], Tom McKlin[3], Mike Reilly[2], Justin Permar[1], Cameron Summers[1], and Eric Fruchter[1]

[1] School of Music, Digital Media Program
Georgia Institute of Technology
Atlanta, GA 30332
001-404-385-7257
{jason.freeman, magerko, jpermar, csummers3, efruchter}@gatech.edu

[2]Lanier High School
Gwinnett County Public Schools
Sugar Hill, GA 30518
001-678-765-4040
Michael_Reilly@Gwinnett.k12.ga.us

[3]The Findings Group
1201 Clairmont Road, Suite 305
Decatur, GA 30030
001-404-633-9091
tom@theFindingsGroup.com

ABSTRACT

In this paper, we describe a pilot study of EarSketch, a computational remixing approach to introductory computer science, in a formal academic computing course at the high school level. The EarSketch project provides an integrated curriculum, Python API, digital audio workstation (DAW), audio loop library, and social sharing site. The goal for EarSketch is to broaden participation in computing, particularly by traditionally underrepresented groups, through a thickly authentic learning environment that has personal and industry relevance in both computational and artistic domains. The pilot results show statistically significant gains in computing attitudes across multiple constructs, with particularly strong results for female and minority participants.

Categories and Subject Descriptors

J.5 [**Arts and Humanities**], K.3.2 [**Computer Education**]: Computers and Information Science Education – *computer science education, curriculum.*

Keywords

Remixing; music composition; broadening participation; CS education; computing principles; music production

1. INTRODUCTION

Our research seeks to address the problem of recruitment and retention of underrepresented populations in high school computing courses [1]. STEAM (science, technology, engineering, arts, and math) approaches to computing education have attempted to engage such students by integrating artistic creativity within pedagogical practices [2], [3]. However, we contend such approaches rarely satisfy two criteria crucial for success – *cultural relevance in the artistic domain* and *authentic learning in both computing and the arts.*

The cultural relevance of an artistic domain relates to how central the artistic practice is to the target student culture. If an artistic domain does not effectively engage a large enough portion of the target student population (e.g. square dancing), then its integration into a computational curriculum may have little positive effect or even negative repercussions. We therefore assert that STEAM designers must consider artistic practices that have broad appeal across ethnicities, socio-economic backgrounds, and gender. To further support broad and effective adoption, the integrated artistic practices must have low barriers of entry, enabling personal, creative expression by students with no prior domain-specific experience (i.e. a musical domain must be accessible to students who are not musicians).

The integration of artistic practices into computing pedagogy can also be considered from the perspective of authenticity. The authenticity of a learning experience, according to Lee and Butler [4], is based on how well it focuses on the interrelated authentic learning practices of: a) having personally meaningful learning experiences; b) learning that relates to the world outside of the learning context; c) learning that encourages thinking within a particular discipline (e.g. music composition); and d) allowing for assessment that reflects the learning process. *Thick authenticity*, according to Shaffer and Resnick [5], meets all of these requirements in a single approach / system. We contend that a STEAM approach is most effective when both the technical and artistic elements of the learning experience are thickly authentic. For example, in a computational music context, thick authenticity suggests that students learn to code in an industry-relevant language, use music production paradigms common in the recording industry, and create music in popular, personally relevant styles and genres. Because of music's near-universal appeal and cross-cultural relevance [6], we believe it is a particularly compelling domain for thickly authentic STEAM learning experiences.

In our research, we hypothesize that a thickly authentic music and CS learning environment increases engagement in computer science, particularly among groups traditionally underrepresented in the discipline. We have developed EarSketch for introductory computing courses in high school and especially the new Computer Science Principles course that will be an Advanced Placement course by the 2016-2017 school year.

SIGCSE'14, March 5–8, 2014, Atlanta, Georgia, USA.

ACM 978-1-4503-2605-6/14/03…$15.00.
http://dx.doi.org/10.1145/2538862.2538906

EarSketch focuses on computational music remixing, which is a popular composition form in hip hop music [7]. Music remixing is similar to creating a collage of pictures from magazines. EarSketch attempts to connect to students in a culturally relevant fashion that spans gender, ethnicity, and socioeconomic status. It does so by explicitly connecting the learning environment to popular music production software (Figure 1), by drawing from industry practice in the features it supports, and by visualizing computational output within standard industry paradigms. It also focuses on the level of beats, loops, and effects more than individual notes, enabling students with no background in music theory or composition to begin creating personally relevant music immediately. Unlike more graphically oriented environments such as Scratch, EarSketch builds directly on professional development techniques using an industry-relevant, text-based programming language (Python).

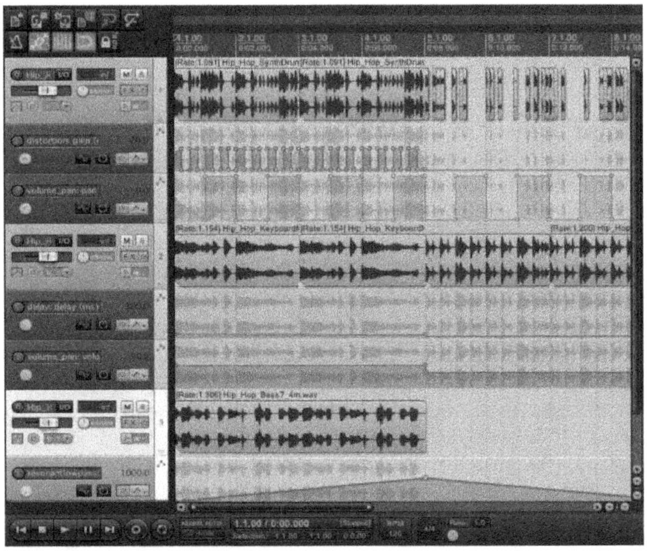

Figure 1: The Reaper digital audio workstation (DAW) music production software integrated into EarSketch.

EarSketch has been iteratively tested in afterschool programs at the 4th and 5th grade level, in individual user tests at Georgia Tech with high school students, and in summer workshops for high school students. The results of our 2012 summer pilot suggested that students' attitudes positively and statistically significantly increased across three constructs at $p<.01$: Computing Confidence, Motivation to Succeed in Computing, and Creativity [8]. Students indicated that they are statistically significantly more likely to see themselves in a computing field in the future as a result of the workshop. To further investigate how EarSketch impacted students' intent to persist in computing, a correlation analysis was conducted whereby the change in responses from Before to Now across our survey constructs were entered into a Pearson's correlation. The results indicated that to the extent that students gained in confidence, belongingness and creativity, their intent to persist in computing increased [8]. Interestingly, growth in creativity was statistically significantly correlated with growth in confidence, motivation and belongingness.

While our preliminary work has shown statistically significant findings, it was done primarily within the context of a week-long summer workshop, which is a very different learning environment from an academic course. To better understand EarSketch's role in this more formal learning environment, we conducted a 10 week pilot EarSketch program in a high school introductory computing course (see Section 3 for details). The larger number of participants in this pilot, as compared to our prior studies, also enabled us to analyze differences in outcomes for female and male and majority and minority participants, helping us to better understand EarSketch's potential to reach traditionally underrepresented populations. The remaining sections of this article summarize work related to this research, present the methods, findings, and results from the high-school pilot study, and discuss the results and future work.

2. RELATED WORK

Although computers are an important part of everyday life, interest in programming remains relatively low for many demographics [1]. Common introductory pedagogy lacks relevance, dating back to a time when computers could only manipulate text in a terminal. Leveraging the ability of computers to render complex audio and visuals to craft media-centric curricula is a promising way of teaching computer science and keeping students engaged in coursework [9].

Several projects have attempted to frame mathematics and computer science education in an artistic or cultural context, focusing mainly on visuals and interactivity. For example, Eglash's Culturally Situated Design Tools allow students to digitally simulate art from various cultures, increasing engagement for students who might typically find mathematics uninviting or feel culturally excluded from the subjects [10]. The eTextiles project blends programmable circuits with fabrics, engaging students' creativity while lowering the technical barriers-to-entry [11]. Both Scratch and Alice teach programming through the creation of interactive media [12], [13], [14]. All of these platforms support a diverse range of projects, giving students the tools to create something that resonates with and captivates them.

Like visual and interactive art, music is an approachable domain with broad appeal, and its production relies on several important concepts in computer science [8]. The MediaComp course at Georgia Tech has successfully engaged women in computing practices through the manipulation of different media forms (images, sound, etc.) with code [15], [16]. Other attempts have been made to reinforce programming concepts through music education in the hopes of appealing to a broad range of students. In a four-year curriculum study on material linking computer science and digital audio, students demonstrated a boost to their perceived aptitude of the science of sound [17]. It was also found that students benefited most from practical projects that they felt were relevant to themselves and to others. Musicomputation, an advanced computer music/science course, also found success in crafting coursework that was relevant to the students' areas of interest, and linking those back to computer science [18]. Other curriculums have focused on other areas of music creation. The Squeak-based curriculum Sound Thinking, for example, has students design and program novel musical instruments [19].

While the above approaches have reported success, it is unclear how authentic the learning experience is in both target domains. For example, the MediaComp course uses audio at a very low level (e.g. writing an algorithm to compute reverb) while Scratch presents a coding environment that is visually oriented rather than using a typical IDE. It is unclear how these approaches in both the artistic domain and technical domain offer thick authenticity (as mentioned in the Introduction), and therefore may not be as effective as approaches that tackle both domains authentically.

3. METHODS

3.1 Pilot Population and Learning Context

EarSketch was piloted with sixty-nine 9th graders (first-year high school students) as a module in the Computing in the Modern World course at Lanier High School. The 10-week pilot took place from January to March 2013. Lanier High School is a public high school in Sugar Hill, Georgia with 1605 students, 44% of whom are on free or reduced lunches (suggesting a diverse range of socioeconomic backgrounds). The 69 students enrolled in the pilot course were 30% female, 7% Hispanic, and 16% African-American.

Computing in the Modern World is the first course in a three course computing pathway in the Career, Technical and Agricultural Education (CTAE) program in Georgia. [20]. Its curriculum includes some programming and computer science principles along with modules on topics such as web design, networking, and hardware. The EarSketch pilot served as the programming module of the course.

Lanier High School teaches Computing in the Modern World within its Center for Design and Technology (CDAT). Ninth graders in CDAT take four courses: 1) science (biology or chemistry), 2) language arts, 3) digital media (Computing in the Modern World), and 4) Physical Education/Health [21]. The CDAT teaching methodology is founded upon a project-based, "flipped classroom" learning model, which resembles a studio-based learning approach that has seen effective application in computer science curricula [22]. Students within CDAT are expected to be hands-on, interdisciplinary and independent; projects are commonly utilized as a means to demonstrate knowledge and comprehension [23].

The pilot teacher, Mike Reilly, created a curriculum derived from the openly accessible EarSketch online curriculum. He taught two separate sections of 30-35 students and installed the EarSketch software in standard PC labs equipped with high fidelity headphones. Mr. Reilly was an experienced software developer and computer science teacher but had little prior experience with music, which aligns with our expectations for the background of most EarSketch teachers.

The students enrolled in the EarSketch pilot did not self-select for a course with EarSketch or even a course in computer science; their interest was in the broader CDAT program at Lanier. Students did not begin the class with strong experience in computers and computing, as evidenced by their responses to an engagement survey (see Evaluation below).

3.2 Curriculum and Teaching Strategies

During the pilot, the teacher focused on 1) maximizing student motivation, 2) interweaving the teaching of programming and music concepts and techniques, 3) encouraging creative application of the acquired knowledge via projects, and 4) benchmarking progress via quizzes. The remainder of this section details each of these four areas of focus.

3.2.1 Motivating Students

The teacher employed a number of complementary strategies to motivate students. The immediate goal of producing personally expressive, creative music motivated students to learn programming. In particular, the course emphasized how programming (as opposed to creating music manually in the DAW) enables students to work more efficiently by automating repetitive tasks, to more rapidly experiment with different musical possibilities and variations, and to create more unique musical structures and sounds to make their music stand out. The teacher also emphasized the importance of programming to the future of the music industry and the opportunities to become industry leaders through developing new tools for making, performing, and distributing music. Finally, he noted the broader applicability of programming skills and the demand for computer scientists and software engineers across many different industries.

These points were reinforced by references to famous musicians, such as Will.I.Am [24], who have discussed the importance of programming expertise to the music industry's future. Near the end of the pilot, Young Guru [25], a professional audio engineer and DJ best known for his collaborations with Jay Z, visited the class (Figure 2) to personally communicate his excitement about programming within the field of music (Young Guru also created much of the audio loop library content for EarSketch.)

Figure 2: A student (sitting) shares his project with Young Guru (standing) at Lanier High School.

3.2.2 Interweaving Programming and Music

Throughout the pilot, the curriculum taught music, music technology, and computing concepts together, always linking new computational concepts to a musical application. Weeks 1 and 2 provided an introduction to fundamental music and music production concepts, including tracks, tempo, instrument pairings, and sound effects; relevant programming concepts included variables, function calls, and core EarSketch API functions for placing sounds and effects on tracks. In addition, the course addressed sharing both music and code, open licensing models in both domains, and sharing practices on the EarSketch social media site. Throughout the course, but especially early on, the teacher played popular music to demonstrate specific concepts.

Week 3 and 4 introduced rhythms and repetitions; relevant programming concepts included strings and iteration. Weeks 5 and 6 focused on the arrangement of musical compositions as a series of musical sections, with students learning to define their own functions to encapsulate and re-use musical sections. In the remainder of the pilot, students reviewed and reinforced previous material, deepened their understanding of computing concepts, API functions, and musical techniques, and developed individual projects that served as final projects for the EarSketch module.

3.2.3 Quizzes and Projects

To ensure that students effectively acquired and internalized the EarSketch curriculum, the teacher created two types of assessments: 1) quizzes, which were not multiple-choice exams but instead asked for answers in the form of handwritten Python code; and 2) projects that demonstrated integration and application of music and programming concepts and techniques, including utilization of the EarSketch API.

The quizzes all asked the students to write Python scripts to make music with stated computational and musical requirements. The requirements incorporated learned programming techniques (such as variables, constants, strings, loops, functions, and lists) and EarSketch API functions (to perform tasks such as placing audio files on the timeline, creating rhythmic beats, and controlling track effects and effect envelopes). Quiz 1, for example, asked the students to write a Python script that creates a minimum of three tracks of varying lengths, uses multiple sound files, and applies volume level adjustments to the tracks. Projects were similar to the quizzes, as they required the development of working code to create music given a set of requirements, but were more open-ended in order to provide students with more opportunities for artistic creativity. Projects typically required students to incorporate a particular set of API functions, computing concepts, and musical structures but left most of the choices about how they should be incorporated into the music up to the student. Projects were completed on the computer rather than written on paper.

Both quizzes and projects were commonly "graded by interview", a technique similar to pedagogical code review processes [22]. The teacher engaged in one-on-one discussions to peruse each student's code and composition. This grading format allowed the teacher to identify errors that an individual student was making, such as incorrect API usage or improper application of iteration, which resulted in personalized curriculum customization in the hope of obtaining improved student comprehension.

4. EVALUATION

Students in the pilot were measured on attitudes changes and content knowledge. A student engagement survey was given to students as a pre/post retrospective at the end of the pilot. The approach asks students to consider how they felt "before" the course and to indicate their perceptions "now" at the end of the course. This format was chosen to diminish response shift bias.

The instrument measures seven psychosocial constructs: 1) computing confidence (e.g. "I can get good grades in computing"); 2) computing enjoyment (e.g. "I feel comfortable working with a computer"); 3) computing importance/perceived usefulness (e.g. "I believe that it is very important for me to learn how to use a computer."); 4) motivation to succeed (e.g. "I like solving computer problems"); 5) identity and belonging in computing (e.g. "I take pride in my computer abilities"); 6) intent to persist in computing (e.g. "I can see myself working in the field of computing"); and 7) creativity in computing (e.g. "I am able to be very expressive and creative while doing computing"). The forty-one question survey, which included negated formulations, was designed to address whether students report increases in these seven pyschosocial constructs as a result of participating in program activities and was based on scales from [26] and [27]. Cronbach's Alpha for each construct ranged from 0.691 to 0.893.

Literature reviews suggest that there is no standard for reporting responses to individual likert-scaled responses; the literature reveals significant *disagreement* among psychostatisticians and others about whether a likert scale is nominal (appropriate for n, % reporting) or ordinal (appropriate for mean, standard deviation). However, psychostatisticians agree that when several likert questions are summed to compute an average construct, then the data may be treated as interval data measuring a latent variable. Parametric statistical tests such as ANOVA or t-test can be applied. Our analysis consisted of a paired samples t-test whereby statistically significant changes from before to now were assessed.

Our content knowledge assessment (CKA) measures students' mastery of pre-defined computing standards. It was administered as a pre/post assessment with ten multiple choice items. It covers typical introductory computing topics in Python such as function definitions, calls, and arguments; iteration and loop indices; and syntax and debugging; as well as EarSketch functionality. Items were classified by difficulty based on student answers to determine if students learned the concept being tested [28].

Overall, the results of the student engagement survey (Table 1) indicate a positive and statistically significant increase in students' attitudes towards computing across all constructs at $p<0.01$. Before the course, female students were statistically significantly lower in confidence ($p=.041$) than male students; likewise, female students rated their identity and belongingness in computing lower than male students ($p=.078$). However, after the course, these gender differences disappeared. Additionally, gains in female motivation to succeed was greater than males ($p=0.045$) suggesting that the course may be particularly effective in increasing female motivations to persist on computing problems.

Table 2 shows that both minority and majority racial/ethnic groups' attitudes toward computing increased statistically significantly in all constructs. While race/ethnicity groups alone didn't show as strong a correlation (i.e. not statistically significant) as gender, after the course minority students showed slightly higher ratings than majority students in four constructs - confidence, perceived usefulness, intentions to persist, and creativity. This could suggest that EarSketch is particularly effective for minority students. Follow up surveys and qualitative studies may give more insight into the long-term impacts of EarSketch on intention to persist in computing.

Students across all gender and racial/ethnic groups rated the course as being good or excellent. Many free-response comments specifically addressed the thickly authentic aspects of the learning environment: one student "got to express my ideas and it was fun and inspiring to see that I could be good at computing;" another liked "learning how music is made and how we can learn and get good at doing things that people in the music industry do now;" and another enjoyed "making my own music tracks that people, including myself, actually liked." Though not statistically significant, female and minority students rated the course higher than their counterparts, again suggesting the possibility that EarSketch is particularly effective among underrepresented groups in computing.

The results of the content knowledge assessment (CKA) indicated statistically significant increases in computing content knowledge from pre to post. On average, students answered 23% of the items correct at the beginning of the course (pre) and 60% correct at the end of the course (post), and they exhibited statistically significant gains in 9 of the 10 CKA items. (There was an error in the formulation of the tenth question that did not exhibit gains.)

Table 1. Constructs by Gender

	Female (n=21)				Male (n=47)			
Construct	Before	Now	t-test	Effect Size	Before	Now	t-test	Effect Size
Computing Confidence	2.58	3.88	<0.01**	1.95^{L}	3.00	3.99	<0.01**	1.26^{L}
Computing Enjoyment	3.74	4.29	<0.01**	0.93^{L}	3.79	4.36	<0.01**	1.05^{L}
Importance/ Perceived Usefulness	3.64	4.39	<0.01**	1.48^{L}	3.89	4.46	<0.01**	0.93^{L}
Motivation to Succeed	2.84	3.82	<0.01**	1.43^{L}	3.09	3.67	<0.01**	0.59^{M}
Identity and Belongingness	2.86	3.75	<0.01**	1.03^{L}	3.29	3.89	<0.01**	0.70^{M}
Intent to Persist	2.93	3.80	<0.01**	0.99^{L}	3.29	3.83	<0.01**	0.61^{M}
Creativity in Computing	3.19	3.86	<0.01**	0.89^{L}	3.33	3.93	<0.01**	0.73^{M}

Scale= 1, Strongly Disagree to 5, Strongly Agree. **p<.01, *p<.05, †p<.10. Negatively worded statements were reverse-coded to assess construct means. Effect size= (s) Small (0.20), (M) Medium (0.50), (L) Large (0.80).

Table 2. Constructs by Race/Ethnicity

	Minority (n=28)				Majority (n=41)			
Construct	Before	Now	t-test	Effect Size	Before	Now	t-test	Effect Size
Computing Confidence	2.95	4.05	<0.01**	1.48^{L}	2.82	3.90	<0.01**	1.41^{L}
Computing Enjoyment	3.75	4.30	<0.01**	1.02^{L}	3.79	4.36	<0.01**	1.03^{L}
Importance/ Perceived Usefulness	3.87	4.46	<0.01**	0.97^{L}	3.78	4.43	<0.01**	1.16^{L}
Motivation to Succeed	3.04	3.72	<0.01**	0.75^{M}	3.02	3.73	<0.01**	0.81^{L}
Identity and Belongingness	3.18	3.80	<0.01**	0.66^{M}	3.14	3.88	<0.01**	0.93^{L}
Intent to Persist	3.16	3.86	<0.01**	0.79^{M}	3.22	3.81	<0.01**	0.67^{M}
Creativity in Computing	3.41	4.02	<0.01**	0.84^{L}	3.21	3.84	<0.01**	0.76^{M}

Scale= 1, Strongly Disagree to 5, Strongly Agree. Assessment: Good=Above 4.0; Attention=Below 4.0; Action=Below 3.5. **p<.01, *p<.05, †p<.10. Negatively worded statements (n) were reverse-coded to assess construct means. Effect size= (s) Small (0.20), (M) Medium (0.50), (L) Large (0.80).

5. DISCUSSION

These evaluation results suggest that EarSketch's thickly authentic music and computing learning environment effectively teaches introductory computing concepts to high school students in a formal academic course and that it substantially improves student attitudes towards computing. Some of the data suggests that EarSketch may be particularly effective for groups that are traditionally underrepresented in computing.

We must temper these encouraging results with a few important caveats. The pilot took place within Lanier's CDAT program, an innovative flipped classroom, studio-based setting that is still unusual within most high schools. The teacher, Mike Reilly, is a project collaborator who invested additional time and energy into customizing the curriculum to best fit his classroom and acquiring music and music technology skills important to the pedagogy. While students did not self-select to participate, they did self-select for the CDAT program, indicating a broader interest in design and technology. The pilot program concluded with a personal visit from a major hip hop figure (Young Guru, as shown in Figure 2) to critique student work and argue for the importance of computation to the music industry. These specific aspects of the pilot cannot, of course, be replicated at scale (though we are creating videos with music industry role models intended to serve similar motivational purposes to Young Guru's visit). We therefore cannot yet assume that the results of this pilot can be replicated at scale either. However, the positive outcomes of this pilot as well as our summer camp pilots (see Section 1) do together suggest EarSketch's effectiveness in multiple learning contexts.

Moving forward, we plan to deploy and evaluate EarSketch on a larger scale, to determine the effectiveness of EarSketch when the unique aspects of the Lanier pilot are absent. To this end, we: a) have made our curriculum and software available online, b) are developing formal teacher training materials and planning teacher training workshops, and c) are collaborating with a metro Atlanta school district to deploy EarSketch at multiple high schools locally. We are also teaching EarSketch as part of a MOOC on Coursera, with approximately 24,000 students enrolled. We are also beginning to create an entirely web-based version of EarSketch to support more straightforward deployment and a more integrated user experience.

We also wish to learn more about why EarSketch has been effective, developing new assessment tools and software enhancements, informed by learning sciences, to better understand the specific aspects of EarSketch that have contributed to particular student engagement and content knowledge outcomes.

6. ACKNOWLEDGMENTS

Thanks to Cockos, Inc., Lanier High School, the Marist School, Georgia Tech's Institute for Computing Education, and our project team (Barbara Ericsson, Ziwen Fan, Tom Jordan, Elise Livingston, Christopher Michaud, Scott McCoid, Casey Feisler, Aneesh Vartakavi, Brad Short, Alex Duncan, Laurie Marion, David Poore, Tom Jenkins, Hera Kan, Neeraj Vaidya, Shannon Yao, Jonathan Streater, Erica Richards, Charles Hancock, Arun Marsten, Juan Carlos Martinez, Anand Mahadevan, Michael Madaio, Mikhail Jacob, Young Guru, and Richard Devine). This work is funded by the National Science Foundation under CNS grant #1138469. EarSketch is available at http://earsketch.gatech.edu.

7. REFERENCES

[1] J. Cuny, "Address to the Computer Science Community," presented at the CE21 PI and Community Meeting, New Orleans, LA, 21-Jan-2011.

[2] J. D. Burge and T. L. Suarez, "Preliminary analysis of factors affecting women and african americans in the computing sciences," in *Proceedings of the 2005 conference on Diversity in computing*, Albuquerque, New Mexico, USA, 2005, pp. 53–56.

[3] Eglash, R. et al, "Culturally Situated Design Tools: Ethnocomputing from Field Site to Classroom," *American Anthropologist*, vol. 108, no. 2, pp. 347–362, 2006.

[4] H.-S. Lee and N. Butler, "Making authentic science accessible to students - International Journal of Science Education," 2003.. [Online]. Available: http://www.informaworld.com/smpp/content~content=a713865046&db=all. [Accessed: 07-Jun-2010].

[5] D. W. Shaffer and M. Resnick, "Thick authenticity: new media and authentic learning," *J Interact Learn Res*, vol. 10, no. 2, pp. 195–215, Dec. 1999.

[6] I. Peretz and R. J. Zatorre, "Brain organization for music processing," 2004.

[7] S. Vaidhyanathan, *Copyrights and copywrongs□: the rise of intellectual property and how it threatens creativity*. New York: New York University Press, 2003.

[8] B. Magerko et al, "Tackling Engagement in Computing with Computational Music Remixing," in *Proceedings of the ACM SIGSCE Technical Symposium on Computer Science Education, Denver, CO, USA, 2013.*

[9] M. Guzdial and E. Soloway, "Teaching the Nintendo generation to program," *Commun Acm*, vol. 45, no. 4, pp. 17–21, Apr. 2002.

[10] R. Eglash, A. Bennett, C. O'donnell, S. Jennings, and M. Cintorino, "Culturally Situated Design Tools: Ethnocomputing from Field Site to Classroom," *Am. Anthr.*, vol. 108, no. 2, pp. 347–362, 2006.

[11] L. Buechley, M. Eisenberg, J. Catchen, and A. Crockett, "The LilyPad Arduino: using computational textiles to investigate engagement, aesthetics, and diversity in computer science education," in *Proceedings of the twenty-sixth annual SIGCHI conference on Human factors in computing systems*, New York, NY, USA, 2008, pp. 423–432.

[12] M. Conway, S. Audia, T. Burnette, D. Cosgrove, and K. Christiansen, "Alice: lessons learned from building a 3D system for novices," in *Proceedings of the SIGCHI conference on Human factors in computing systems*, The Hague, The Netherlands, 2000, pp. 486–493.

[13] C. Kelleher, R. Pausch, and S. Kiesler, "Storytelling alice motivates middle school girls to learn computer programming," in *Proceedings of the SIGCHI conference on Human factors in computing systems*, San Jose, California, USA, 2007, pp. 1455–1464.

[14] M. Resnick, J. Maloney, A. Monroy-Hernández, N. Rusk, E. Eastmond, K. Brennan, A. Millner, E. Rosenbaum, J. Silver, B. Silverman, and others, "Scratch: programming for all," *Commun. Acm*, vol. 52, no. 11, pp. 60–67, 2009.

[15] M. Guzdial, "A media computation course for non-majors," in *ACM SIGCSE Bulletin*, 2003, vol. 35, pp. 104–108.

[16] M. Guzdial, D. Ranum, B. Miller, B. Simon, B. Ericson, S. A. Rebelsky, J. Davis, K. Deepak, and D. Blank, "Variations on a theme: role of media in motivating computing education," in *Proceedings of the 41st ACM technical symposium on Computer science education*, New York, NY, USA, 2010, pp. 66–67.

[17] J. Burg, J. Romney, and E. Schwartz, "Computer science 'big ideas' play well in digital sound and music," in *Proceeding of the 44th ACM technical symposium on Computer science education*, New York, NY, USA, 2013, pp. 663–668.

[18] A. L. Meyers, M. C. Cole, E. Korth, and S. Pluta, "Musicomputation: teaching computer science to teenage musicians," in *Proceeding of the seventh ACM conference on Creativity and cognition*, Berkeley, California, USA, 2009, pp. 29–38.

[19] J. M. Heines, G. R. Greher, and S. A. Ruthmann, "Techniques at the intersection of computing and music," in *Proceedings of the 17th ACM annual conference on Innovation and technology in computer science education*, New York, NY, USA, 2012, pp. 372–372.

[20] "CTAE." [Online]. Available: http://public.doe.k12.ga.us/Curriculum-Instruction-and-Assessment/CTAE/Documents/Career_Pathway_Chart_080612.pdf. [Accessed: 31-Aug-2013].

[21] "CDAT." [Online]. Available: http://cdat.lanierhs.org/. [Accessed: 31-Aug-2013].

[22] C. D. Hundhausen, N. H. Narayanan, and M. E. Crosby, "Exploring studio-based instructional models for computing education," in *Proceedings of the 39th SIGCSE technical symposium on Computer science education*, New York, NY, USA, 2008, pp. 392–396.

[23] D. R. Krathwohl, B. S. Bloom, and B. Masia, *Taxonomy of educational objectives: The classification of educational goals*, vol. 2. New York: David McKay Company, Inc., 1956.

[24] T. Olmstead, "Will.I.Am Says Coders Are Today's Rock Stars," 30-Aug-2012. .

[25] L. Stouffer, "P2P GA Tech Computer Engineering / Lanier High," *People 2 People*, WSB-TV, 11-Mar-2013.

[26] E. Wiebe, L. Williams, K. Yang, and C. Miller, "Computer Science Attitude Survey," *computer*, vol. 14, no. 25, pp. 0–86, 2003.

[27] G. Knezek and R. Christensen, "Validating the Computer Attitude Questionnaire (CAQ)." 1996.

[28] F. Lord, "The Relationship of the Reliability of Multiple Choice Test to the Distribution of Item Difficulties," *Psychometrika*, vol. 18, pp. 181–194, 1952.

Dancing Alice: Exploring Embodied Pedagogical Strategies for Learning Computational Thinking

Shaundra Bryant Daily, Alison E. Leonard*, Sophie Jörg, Sabarish Babu, Kara Gundersen
School of Computing, *Eugene T. Moore School of Education
Clemson University
Clemson, SC 29634
{sdaily, aleona2, sjoerg, sbabu, kgunder}@clemson.edu

ABSTRACT

In this paper, we introduce an embodied pedagogical approach for learning computational concepts, utilizing computational practices, and developing computational perspectives. During a five-week pilot, a group of students spent after-school time learning the basic elements of dance and then using them to program three-dimensional characters that could perform. Throughout the pilot, we found students consistently standing up in front of their computers and using their bodies to think through the actuation of their characters. Preliminary results suggest that designing a virtual-physical dance performance is a motivating and engaging social context in which to introduce students, especially girls, to alternative applications in computing.

Categories and Subject Descriptors

K.3.2 [**Computer and Information Science Education**]: Computer science education; J.5 [**Arts and Humanities**]: Performing arts

General Terms

Design, Human Factors

Keywords

Embodiment, broadening participation, virtual environments

1. INTRODUCTION

The U.S. Department of Labor has predicted an increase in demand for computer system analysts (29%), database administrators (37%), and software engineers (38%) [1]. Even with these increasing demands, there is a severe lack of representation of women in the field. In order to expand opportunities for girls to enter computing, this research program promotes and examines the use of an interactive virtual environment (VE) utilizing a grounded embodied pedagogy as a way of building computational thinking.

SIGCSE'14, March 5–8, 2014, Atlanta, Georgia, USA.

http://dx.doi.org/10.1145/2538862.2538917

2. BACKGROUND

Computational thinking (CT) has received considerable attention recently and has been defined in a variety of ways. Initially coined by Jeanette Wing [2] as "a way of solving problems, designing systems, and understanding human behavior that draws on concepts fundamental to computer science," many others have refined the construct. Cuny et al. [3], for example, define computational thinking as, "the thought processes involved in formulating problems and their solutions so that the solutions are represented in a form that can be effectively carried out by an information-processing agent," while the Computer Science Teachers Association [4] defines computational thinking as, "thinking about data and ideas, and using and combining these resources to solve problems."

In general, there is no agreed-upon definition of CT. In this work, we adopt the view that computational thinking is a set of concepts, practices, and perspectives that draw upon the world of computing, but are applicable in many STEM domains [5], [6]. Computational thinking consists of concepts, practices, and perspectives. Concepts focus on what the student is learning, namely sequences, loops, parallelism, events, conditionals, operators, and data, including aspects of logical reasoning skills. Practices focus on the processes of thinking and learning. Practices include being incremental and iterative, reusing and remixing, abstracting and modularizing, and testing and debugging. Finally, perspectives relate to "evolving understandings of themselves, their relationships to others, and the technological world around them". Perspectives are formed by students seeing computation as something that can be used for self-expression, the social aspects of engaging, equipping and educating others, and seeing a connection between technologies that surround them and their ability to negotiate the world.

2.1 Attracting Girls to Computing

Prior research suggests that situating computing in activities outside of traditional applications can serve to attract girls to and retain girls in computing. For example, storytelling [7], [8], [9], art projects [10], religion [11], fashion [12], and other non-traditional means have been used successfully to increase interest in computing, develop computational thinking, and foster digital fluency with girls in both in and out of school contexts. Most applicable to the current research are the findings from introductory programming languages Scratch and Alice.

In Scratch, for example, students must coordinate timing and interactions between multiple programmable moving objects. These objects manage multiple forms of media including audio recordings, images, and text. By changing pieces of code that snap together similar to physical LEGO™ blocks, students have the ability to create dynamics and interactive animations and games. Center for Women in Information Technology (NCWIT) has called Scratch a "promising practice" for increasing gender diversity in computing; NCWIT cites Scratch's visual appeal and affordance of allowing users to express their own creativity as part of its effectiveness as a learning tool [13]. Similarly, Alice is a 3-dimensional programming interface specifically designed to teach object-oriented programming in an accessible fashion. The environment has a drag-and-drop interface that enables students to program without having to learn the syntax that prevents many students from engaging with computer science. Kelleher et al. [8], [9] found that Storytelling Alice, a version that supports high-level animations, social characters, and scenery for stories, motivated longer programming time and interest in girls than the traditional version of Alice. What we gather across these approaches is that it is possible to address both the social and contextual barriers to interest and participation in computing.

2.2 Grounded Embodied Pedagogy

With the assertion that situating programming in non-traditional contexts can help overcome some of the barriers to girls engaging in computational thinking, we turn our attention to *how* best to scaffold learners in understanding computational concepts and utilizing computational practices. A growing body of research suggests that cognition is grounded and embodied in the sensorimotor system [14], [15]. In other words, the embodiment perspective is a view of cognition that "depends on the kinds of experiences from having a body with a particular and motor capacities that are inseparably linked and that together form the matrix within which memory, emotion, language, and all other aspects of life are meshed" [16].This view of cognition is echoed in the dance education world. For example, as dance scholar Deidre Sklar [17] writes, "[r]ather than underline the fact that thinking can be abstracted and separated from corporeality, I am underlining the fact that thinking depends upon it".

Recent embodied pedagogical approaches have targeted chemistry, mathematics [18], physics [19], geology [20], Chinese characters [21], and computational thinking [22], [23]; they have also seen improvement in concept learning. Fadjo's conceptual framework for grounded embodied pedagogy, called Instructional Embodiment (IE), is most related to the current research approach. In IE, action, perception, and environment are utilized to create a dynamic, interactive teaching and learning scenario. In studies used to refine this framework, learners physically enact and/or mentally simulate the predefined Scratch blocks. His findings suggest that physically embodying the actions leads to greater implementation of the same structures in personal artifacts and that this embodied approach is effective in teaching abstract concepts. An important difference in our proposed approach is that beyond moving in certain trajectories under certain operations, learners perform the actions they are constructing for their characters.

2.3 Learning in Virtual Environments

VE technology has been used successfully in many applications that involve simulation of virtual scenarios based on real-world settings and events for the purpose of learning specialized skills [24], studying human behavior [25], therapy and rehabilitation [26], rapid prototyping [27], and exploration [28]. Researchers have shown that VEs are highly effective for learning complex tasks such as the operation of machinery [29], learning inter-personal conversational protocol [30], leadership and crisis management skills [31], learning the scientific method [32], and solving complex tasks. Transfer of knowledge gained in interactive VEs has also been shown to be applicable directly in real-world situations [33].

Many virtual humans in virtual reality simulations have been developed for training, pedagogy, and education. Interactive virtual humans in virtual reality simulations have been used in diverse collaborative communicative tasks such as patient interview training [34], virtual physiotherapists [35], mission rehearsal exercises in social scenarios [31], and virtual task-oriented companions in inter-personal social settings [36].

3. PILOT STUDY

3.1 Platform

For this pilot, we built a minority female character, named Shannon, who could be used in Carnegie Mellon's Alice, the 3-D interactive graphics programming environment. In building Shannon, an individual piece of geometry had to be modeled for every joint that needed to move. Then, rigging through parenting created a hierarchy to control the limbs. Once this was accomplished, Shannon was textured (i.e., given a visual appearance) and exported to a format that Alice accepts. Once in Alice, we captured left and right arm, left and right leg, and head positions using the native pose command in Alice. As shown in Figure 1, Shannon can be posed to move her limbs in a variety of horizontal, vertical, and diagonal positions.

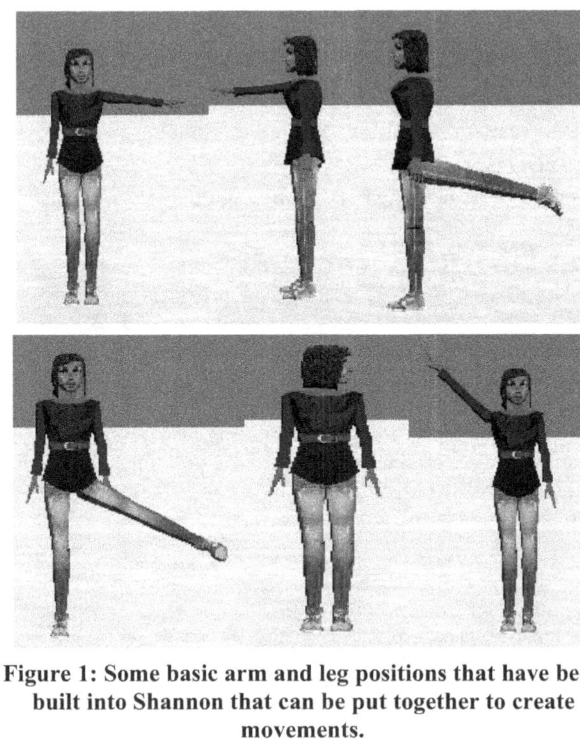

Figure 1: Some basic arm and leg positions that have been built into Shannon that can be put together to create movements.

In order to actuate Shannon, various commands are utilized including Alice's control structures "DoTogether," "DoinOrder," and "Loop". Motion commands can also be used to move within the world (e.g., **Move**) and rotate the limbs about their 3-D axes (e.g., **Turn** and **Roll**). Poses are created and named similar to a procedure, and then assembled to create full dance movements. Arranging these poses to create a dance will be described in more detail in section 3.5.

3.2 Participants

For this pilot, we partnered with a school in the Southeastern United States that serves as an elementary school of choice (4K - 5th grade) with children from the school's surrounding neighborhoods being provided first choice to attend. This school also serves as the home of the countywide gifted center of choice program for highly gifted students (i.e., scoring in the 97-99 percentile on the ITBS or MAP in reading and math) in grades three through eight. The school has a female population of 319 (48%) and a minority population of 28%. Furthermore, 19.6% of the students qualify for free and reduced lunch. Out of this population, our participants were 9 students (eight female and one male) from the fifth and sixth grades. Six were Caucasian and three were African American. One student did not complete the study because of other commitments; therefore, her results will not be included in the remainder of the discussion.

3.3 Methods

Each week, students met with instructors learning basic dance curriculum involving the elements of dance (body, space, time, energy) and dance choreography (theme & variation, repetition, unison, canon, etc.) and Alice programming. We began by recreating a popular line dance, the Cha Cha slide and then moved into creating a different dance based on variations of this initial sequence, and, finally, we created new choreography and replicated it in Alice.

3.4 Measures

3.4.1 Biographical Questionnaire

A written biographical questionnaire was administered to each participant before the study began and after it was over. The questionnaire was designed to provide the researchers with demographic information about the participants as well as information related to their previous experiences with computers and programming, their possible intention to pursue a career in STEM in the future, and their experience with dance.

3.4.2 Participant Observations

Throughout the ten sessions, serving as both researchers and instructors, we collected the data as participant-observers [37] paying attention to both the students and the artifacts they created.

3.4.3 Interviews

Interviews were utilized to gain a more nuanced understanding of student experiences. Interview prompts included: How did you get the idea for your final project? How did you get started? Describe a time when you got stuck. Did anyone else's work influence your own? How did your project change as you created it? Describe how your project works. What are you most proud of? How would you change it?

3.5 Results & Discussion

Although this was a brief pilot with a small number of students, a number of preliminary findings related to the embodied pedagogy, the programming environment, computational thinking, and the performance aspects that can be drawn from the observations and discussions with students.

3.5.1 Biographical Questionnaire

With respect to access to and experience with computing as well as dance, all students have access to a computer or tablet at home, while six of them have their own device on which they play games, participate in social media networks, and complete school work. Five of the students said they did not know what a programming language was. Furthermore, four of the students reported science as their favorite topic, while four reported mathematics as their least favorite topic in school. In the dance/artistic domain, seven reported watching dance at least moderately often and dancing themselves an average of one to four hours per week. Three saw themselves as dancers, and all students viewed themselves as artistic.

3.5.2 Participant Observations & Interviews

Here, we combine the observational data with the interview data as one serves to confirm and elucidate meaning from the other, and vice versa. Throughout the program, we saw that as students are building their characters they are actively moving, either in their chairs or by standing up, to think through the positions as they program the dance of the virtual character. One student said,

Sometimes I'd move to see if I could do it because it looked kind of hard when she did it. I would move my body to do the moves so I could get them into my head and then program them onto her.

Similarly, another student said,

Like, if I were to twirl, I knew I would have to make her do one whole revolution... [This movement helped] because if I show myself that this is how you would do it, then that's how I would program it into the computer to make it work.

Body syntonicity [38] is the idea that understanding an object's objectives, behaviors, and rules of operation can be related to the understanding of a learner's own body. In this pilot, it seems that Shannon served as an object to think with for students. Students were also observed performing with Shannon to see if she was performing as desired, while students who struggled to choreograph created movements for the character and then learned the performance from what they created on screen.

Another observation relates to the students' desire to perform. When the time came to perform, all but one of the students were extremely hesitant to perform; three decided just to stand next to Shannon as she performed. It is important to note that, during the construction process, all of the students were observed standing and performing. This brings up a number of important possible approaches for future implementations, such as providing more preparation time to support their confidence with performing, allowing students simply to demonstrate their character's dance without performing, supporting students in creating a virtual dance to perform alongside professional dancers, or working with students who are already dancers. Although more related to the experience of the curriculum itself (i.e., not crucial for the programming aspects of the approach), we will explore some combination of these options in future iterations.

Within the Alice environment, there were challenges. Some students utilized the "native" Alice methods to create poses not available in our pose database. The motions typically created with these methods are not (typically) humanly possible (e.g., floating in the air and flipping upside down repeatedly). One student specifically included a part in her choreography where Shannon's legs went in one direction and her torso went in another. Although this was a mistake at first, she decided to re-conceptualize her vision for how the dance should look after finding the effect very amusing. Finally, we found that students were "put-off" by the disjointed appearance of the character. One student said her least favorite part of the software was "when the arm would fall off," an effect that would sometimes happen when the native Alice commands were overriding the posing commands created for the character. When asked what should be changed about the program, one student said, "I would figure out how to make the movements smoother." As shown in Figure 2, the necessity of creating a simplified version of a character with a rigid body animation within Alice led to an effect of Shannon looking as though her hips were detached from her body or she was missing knees.

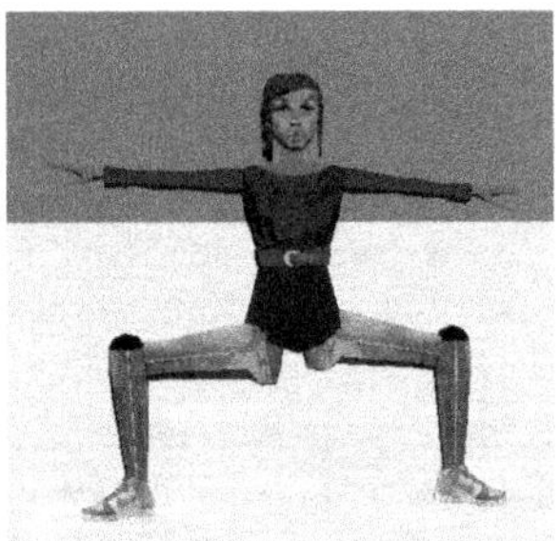

Figure 2: The rigid skinning of the dancer results in a disjointed and unappealing look.

Finally, students immediately wanted to change the characteristics of the dancer to be male, to change her clothes, to change her ethnicity, and to change her body shape, often replicating their own identifying characteristics. One student reported that her least favorite thing about the software program was that, "You can't do any physical changes," while another described the Mii's on the Wii™ gaming console where one gamers change clothing, hair, etc. in order to personalize the character. Similarly, our one male participant consistently expressed a desire to have a male character, going so far in one session as to adopt an authoritative male persona named "Dr. Edward" who insisted that a male character needed to be created for everyone to fully enjoy the program.

While the previous discussion of preliminary findings contributes to the students' experience of the program, we turn our focus here to findings related to the promise of a virtual environment utilizing embodied pedagogical strategies to support the development computational thinking—computational concepts, practice, perspectives. Throughout the different projects created (e.g., Cha Cha slide, Cha Cha slide with variation, and personal choreography), students used *computational concepts*. All projects contained "DoTogether," "DoinOrder," "Loop," and "Wait," commands. Some students described the combination of these blocks as "layering" and talked about putting the commands in order to achieve the desired performance. One student describes her use of these commands in describing her project, saying

I had put in noises [chicken clucking], because I just figured out how to do this...I didn't put it as a 'do together,' I just had it play the sound before it does the move, so now you have to wait a long time before it actually does it's thing... then I had a loop for it to do the woosh [dance move], and then fuete [dance move].

A combination of an arabesque (i.e., movement with one leg back in the air and arms posed in an "L") into a chasse (i.e., moving feet similar to a horse galloping) observed in one project demonstrates the need to utilize these control structures. As shown in **Figure 3**, this position requires the following combination of positions to be executed at the same time using one of Alice's control structures called **DoTogether**: left leg—back horizontal, right arm—front horizontal, left arm—right horizontal, body—right ¼ revolutions. Once the arabesque is complete, the next sequence was to complete the chasse (Figure 4), which involved **DoTogether**: left leg low diagonal—right leg low diagonal (placing legs apart) and **DoTogether**: left leg on ground—right leg on ground (placing legs together).

Figure 3: Dancer developed with Maya and imported into Alice to support the programming of dance moves.

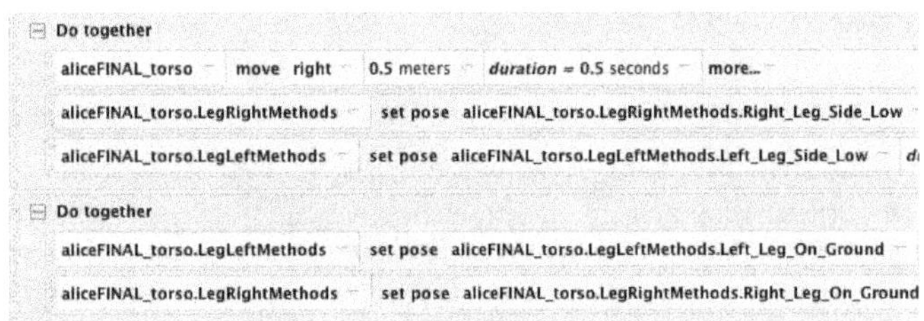

Figure 4: Commands for chasse

One student's interview reveals elements of the problem-solving strategies used in the program. When asked, "What was the hardest part about making your character?" she responded:

Student: There would be times where you would not know exactly what to do and you would have to problem solve. And then, that might take a while, but then you would finally get it in the end.

Interview: Can you talk me through one of those times or one of those problems?

Student: That one time where I had to keep moving computers. I had moved computers, like three times, I think. When I got on that last one...we disabled everything and we went from the top down to the bottom and we figured out what was playing, and everything was working, it was just that something had happened.

Students used the *computational practice* of modularization in that they created scripts for smaller dance moves that they strung together. Testing and debugging practices were also observed;

interestingly, these were typically occurring in parallel with the students standing up to perform the movement themselves and then working to refine the character. In expressing a frustration about the project, one student describes her process of problem solving in saying, "You had to do all the different layers and so . . . you'd take it out of this layer and put it into that layer.... I didn't really like the trial and error." Although, trial and error is a disorganized way of finding the cause of an error, it presents an opportunity to introduce students to a more organized debugging process.

Finally, students' *perspectives* about the purpose of computing showed some initial change. One student, for example, reported that she enjoyed the program because she could use it to "make the character do what I want." This sentiment was echoed by other students who liked being able to manipulate the character to express through dance, and yet another student who expressed feelings of empowerment when she said, "Well, it [the program] was something where, I could.... I wasn't being controlled; I could tell it what to do, and usually, I'm used to being told what to do."

4. CONCLUSIONS & FUTURE WORK

In the development of this environment and curriculum, it has become clear that the juxtaposition of dance and programming is a natural fit. In dance choreography, there exists a similar process of sequencing steps (sequences), repeating steps (looping), and unison (parallelism). In many ways, the practice of computer programming is very much like the compositional process of choreographing a dance, where small pieces are integrated into a larger whole (modularization) and body positions are incorporated and changed slightly to create something new (remixing and reusing).

In addition to the low number of participants involved in the current pilot, a limitation of this work is the lack of quantitative data. In future studies, we will include a computational thinking test which will help us to examine student understanding of computational concepts. This test will also draw upon the work of Griffin et al. [39] and include debug'ems, which are programs intentionally designed with flaws that the learner can fix. In the context of our assessment, rather than providing pseudocode describing the way in which the code should work, the participants will be taught a dance sequence and then asked to replicate it on the screen beginning their process with a virtual character that does not perform the dance sequence properly.

Another focus moving forward will include the move away from the use of Alice, pioneering the design, development, and evaluation of a novel interactive virtual environment and associated curriculum for blending dance and programming as an innovative and embodied way to engage 5th- and 6th-grade girls with computational thinking. This program will build on previous successes of programs such as Alice and Scratch and allow us to fully explore such questions as to what extent does an embodiment-centered curriculum support the development of computational thinking, and how does an embodiment-centered curriculum support interest in computing?

There are two key issues we seek to address in this project: 1) the underproduction of degrees that can support a computationally savvy 21st century workforce [40], and 2) the gap in participation of women in computing [41]. By studying ways to increase engagement of women in computing, we have the opportunity to impact the current lack of diversity in computing fields tremendously.

5. ACKNOWLEDGMENTS

We would like to acknowledge the various graduate and undergraduate summer students who have participated in the development of this program, as well as our partner school.

6. REFERENCES

[1] Buzzetto-More, N., O. Ukoha, and N. Rustagi. 2010. Unlocking the barriers to women and minorities in computer science and information systems studies: results from a multi-methodological study conducted at two minority-serving institutions, *J. Inf. Technol. Educ.* 9 (2010), 115–131.

[2] Wing, J. M. 2006. Computational thinking. *Commun. Acm.* 49.3 (2006), 33–35.

[3] Cuny, J., L. Snyder, and J. M. Wing. 2010. Demystifying computational thinking for non-computer scientists. *Work in Prog.*

[4] Phillips, P. (2007, June 24). *Computational Thinking: A Problem-solving Tool for Every Classroom.* Presented at the National Educational Computing Conference, Atlanta, Georgia.

[5] Resnick, M., B. Silverman, Y. Kafai, J. Maloney, A. Monroy-Hernández, N. Rusk, E. Eastmond, K. Brennan, A. Millner, E. Rosenbaum, and J. Silver. 2009. Scratch. *Commun. Acm.* 52.11 (Nov. 2009), 60.

[6] Brennan, K. and M. Resnick. 2012. New frameworks for studying and assessing the development of computational thinking. In *2012 Annual Meeting of the American Educational Research Association*, Vancouver, Canada, 2012.

[7] Bers, M. U., J. Gonzalez-Heydrich, and D. R. DeMaso. 2001. Identity construction environments: supporting a virtual therapeutic community of pediatric patients undergoing dialysis. In *Proceedings of the SIGCHI Conference on Human Factors in Computing Systems*, Seattle, Washington, United States, March 31 - April 4, 2001, 380–387.

[8] Kelleher, C., R. Pausch, and S. Kiesler. 2007. Storytelling Alice motivates middle school girls to learn computer programming. In *Proceedings of the SIGCHI Conference on Human Factors in Computing Systems*, New York, NY, USA, April 28- May 3, 2007, 1455–1464.

[9] Kelleher, C. and R. Pausch. 2007. Using storytelling to motivate programming," *Commun. Acm.* 50.7 (Jul. 2007), 58–64.

[10] Rusk, N., M. Resnick, R. Berg, and M. Pezalla-Granlund. 2008. New pathways into robotics: strategies for broadening participation. *J. Sci. Educ. Technol.*17.1 (2008), 59–69.

[11] Bers, M. and Claudia, U. 2000. Technological prayers: parents and children exploring values. In *Robots for Kids: Exploring New Technologies for Learning*, A. Druin and J. A. Hendler, Eds. Morgan Kaufmann: San Diego, CA. pp 193-217.

[12] Buechley, L., M. Eisenberg, J. Catchen, and A. Crockett. 2008. The LilyPad Arduino: using computational textiles to investigate engagement, aesthetics, and diversity in computer science education. In *Proceedings of the SIGCHI*

Conference on Human Factors in Computing Systems, New York, NY, USA, April 5-10, 2008, 423–432.

[13] Barker, L. and Cohoon, and J. McGrath. 2008. Snap, create, and share with scratch: an engaging way to introduce computing. University of Colorado, Boulder, Colorado, Case Study 5.

[14] Barsalou, L. W. 2008. Grounded Cognition. *Annu. Rev. Psychol.* 59.1 (2008), 617–645.

[15] Fauconnier, G. and M. Turner. 2008. *The Way We Think: Conceptual Blending and the Mind's Hidden Complexities*. Basic Books.

[16] Thelen, E., G. Schöner, C. Scheier, and L. B. Smith. 2001. The dynamics of embodiment: a field theory of infant perseverative reaching. *Behav. Brain Sci.* 24.1 (2001), 1–34; discussion 34–86.

[17] Sklar, D. 1994. Can Bodylore be brought to its senses? *J. Am. Folk.* 107, 9–22.

[18] Howison, M., D. Trninic, D. Reinholz, and D. Abrahamson. 2011. The mathematical imagery trainer: from embodied interaction to conceptual learning. In *Proceedings of the SIGCHI Conference on Human Factors in Computing Systems*, New York, NY, USA, May 7-12, 2011, 1989–1998.

[19] Kontra, C., S. Goldin-Meadow, and S. L. Beilock. 2012. Embodied learning across the life span. *Top. Cogn. Sci.* 4. 4 (2012), 731–739.

[20] Birchfield, D. and M. Johnson-Glenberg. 2010. A next gen interface for embodied learning. *Int. J. Gaming Comput.-Mediat. Simulations* 2.1 (2010), 49–58.

[21] Lu, M.-T., C.-Y. Wu, C. Fadjo, and J. Black. 2010. Future trends in Chinese character teaching: use of embodiment and technologies in classrooms. *Soc. Inf. Technol. Teach. Educ. Int. Conf. 2010*, 2010.1 (2010), 2485–2492, 20100329.

[22] Fadjo, C. L., M.-T. Lu, and J. B. Black. 2009. Instructional embodiment and video game programming in an after-school program. *World Conf. Educ. Multimed. Hypermedia Telecommun. 2009*, 2009.1 (2009), 4041–4046, 20090622.

[23] Fadjo, C. L., G. H. Jr, R. Harris, and J. B. Black. 2009. Surrogate embodiment, mathematics instruction and video game programming. *World Conf. Educ. Multimed. Hypermedia Telecommun. 2009*, 2009.1 (2009), 2787–2792, 20090622.

[24] Szekély, G., C. Brechbühler, J. Dual, R. Enzler, J. Hug, R. Hutter, N. Ironmonger, M. Kauer, V. Meier, and P. Niederer. 2000. Virtual reality-based simulation of endoscopic surgery. *Presence Teleoperators Virtual Environ.* 9.3 (2000), 310–333.

[25] Babu, S., T. Grechkin, B. Chihak, C. Ziemer, J. Kearney, J. Cremer, and J. Plumert. 2009. A virtual peer for investigating social influences on children's bicycling. In *IEEE Virtual Reality Conference, 2009. 2009*(2009), 91–98.

[26] Whitney, S. L., P. J. Sparto, L. F. Hodges, S. V. Babu, J. M. Furman, and M. S. Redfern. 2006. Responses to a virtual reality grocery store in persons with and without vestibular dysfunction. *Cyberpsychol. Behav.* 9.2 (2006), 152–156.

[27] Smith, S. P., and D. Trenholme. 2009. Rapid prototyping a virtual fire drill environment using computer game technology. *Fire Saf. J.* 44.4 (2009), 559–569.

[28] Brooks Jr., F. P. 1999. What's real about virtual reality? *Comput. Graph. Appl. Ieee* 19.6 (1999), 16–27.

[29] Quarles, J., S. Lampotang, I. Fischler, P. Fishwick, and B. Lok. 2009. Scaffolded learning with mixed reality. *Comput. Graph.* 33.1 (2009), 34–46.

[30] Babu, S., E. Suma, T. Barnes, and L. F. Hodges. 2007. Can immersive virtual humans teach social conversational protocols? In *IEEE Virtual Reality Conference, 2007. VR '07*, 2007, 215–218.

[31] Hill Jr., R. W., J. Gratch, S. Marsella, J. Rickel, W. R. Swartout, and D. R. Traum. 2003. Virtual humans in the mission rehearsal exercise system. *KI* 17.4 (2003), 5.

[32] Nelson, B., D. J. Ketelhut, J. Clarke, C. Bowman, and C. Dede. 2005. Design-based research strategies for developing a scientific inquiry curriculum in a multi-user virtual environment. *Educ. Technol.* 45.1 (2005), 21–27.

[33] Reger, G. M., and G. A. Gahm. 2008. Virtual reality exposure therapy for active duty soldiers. *J. Clin. Psychol.* 64.8 (2008), 940–946.

[34] Johnsen, K., R. Dickerson, A. Raij, C. Harrison, B. Lok, A. Stevens, and D. S. Lind. 2006. Evolving an immersive medical communication skills trainer. *Presence Teleoperators Virtual Environ.* 15.1 (2006), 33–46.

[35] Babu, S., C. Zanbaka, J. Jackson, T. Chung, B. Lok, M. C. Shin, and L. F. Hodges. 2005. Virtual human physiotherapist framework for personalized training and rehabilitation. In *Graphics Interface*, 9–11.

[36] Babu, S. V., E. Suma, L. F. Hodges, and T. Barnes. 2011. Learning cultural conversational protocols with immersive interactive virtual humans. *Int. J. Virtual Real.* 10.4 (2011), 25.

[37] Tedlock, B. 2000. Ethnography and ethnographic representation. In *Handbook of Qualitative Research*, 2nd ed., Denzin, N.K. and Lincoln, Y.S., Eds. Sage, Thousand Oaks, NJ, 455–486.

[38] Papert, S. A. 1993. *Mindstorms: Children, Computers, and Powerful Ideas*, 2nd ed. Basic Books.

[39] Griffin, J., E. Kaplan, and Q. Burke. 2012. Debug'ems and other deconstruction kits for STEM learning. In *IEEE Integrated STEM Education Conference (ISEC), Trenton, NJ*, 1–4.

[40] Cuny, J. 2010. Changing what's happening in HS and introductory college CS: keynote address. *J Comput Sci Coll.* 26.2 (Dec. 2010), 5–6.

[41] Margolis, J. 2008. *Stuck in the Shallow End: Education, Race, and Computing*. The MIT Press.

Underrepresented Middle School Girls: On the Path to Computer Science through Paper Prototyping

Ashley Robinson
Department of Computer Science
Virginia Tech
Blacksburg, VA 24060
arrobin@vt.edu

Manuel A. Pérez-Quiñones
Department of Computer Science
Virginia Tech
Blacksburg, VA 24060
perez@cs.vt.edu

ABSTRACT

The computing profession is lacking representation that mirrors the fabric of society in the United States. Most studies show a low percentage of participation for women and minority groups. In this paper, we present our experiences conducting a week-long Human-Computer Interaction (HCI) workshop with underrepresented middle school girls. Our description is focused on an activity where girls created a paper prototype for a chat application. We present qualitative results showing characteristics of the prototypes built, and discuss the participant responses to a few of the questions in an interview at the end of the week. Our results reveal that paper prototyping can be used as a motivator for a career path in computer science. In spite of the negative stereotypes that the underrepresented females had prior to the intervention, the HCI workshop revealed a user-centric component of computer science that gave participants a positive perception of the discipline.

Categories and Subject Descriptors

H.5.2 [**Information Interfaces and Presentation**]: User Interfaces—*Prototyping*; K.3.2 [**Computers and Education**]: Computer and Information Science Education—*Computer Science Education*

General Terms

Human Factors

Keywords

Human-Computer Interaction, User Interface Design, Prototyping, K-12, Women, Minorities

1. INTRODUCTION

There has been a vast amount of research pertaining to the underrepresentation of women in computer science. According to the National Science Foundation [12], in 2010, 57.2% of the total number of Bachelor's degree recipients were women. In reference to science and engineering Bachelor's degree recipients, women made up 50.3% of the total population in 2010. The relatively equivalent numbers of female and male graduates is nonexistent in computer science Bachelor's degree recipients, with women being severely underrepresented. In 2010, women only made up 18.2% of the total number of computer science Bachelor's degree recipients.

When African American women were factored in, the percentages were even smaller, with African American women making up only 0.14% of female computer science Bachelor's degree recipients. More recent data reported in the Computer Research Association's 2011-2012 annual Taulbee Survey indicates that women were awarded 12.9% of the total number of Computer Science Bachelor's degrees, with African American females making up only 4.5% of the total population of Bachelor's degree recipients [23]. While research about women in computing is vast, the investigation of African American women and other minority ethnic groups in computing is in need of further study.

Human-Computer Interaction (HCI) is a sub-area of computer science [5, 2] that is dedicated to designing, implementing, and evaluating computer systems for human use [9]. HCI is an appropriate gate-way to computing because it tends to be design, application, and user centered. Women are often motivated to pursue computing because of the perception that computing provides them with opportunities to be creative, communicate [18], and address societal concerns [14, 18]. HCI contains several characteristics in which women can relate (e.g. people-oriented, interdisciplinary, collaborative, real-world problems). The ability to design facilitates creativity while the application and user focus of HCI enables women to communicate and help people. This is contrary to a focus on the workings of technology as in computer programming, a known barrier to students persisting in computing [6].

This paper presents the exploration of the use of a HCI workshop to influence the perception of minority middle school females towards computer science. It is anticipated that exposure to HCI will create a more positive perception of computer science. The results presented in this paper are qualitative in nature and provide insights to what underrepresented middle school girls think of computer science.

2. RELATED WORK

When Cohoon et al. [4] surveyed female authorship in ACM-affiliated conferences, results showed that women had

SIGCSE'14, March 5–8, 2014, Atlanta, GA, USA.

http://dx.doi.org/10.1145/2538862.2538951.

Day	Description
1	Introduction Pre-Survey Video about the computing from code.org Discussion about computer science careers
2	HCI and user interface design intro Group UI evaluation on the iPad UI design guideline discussion
3	Abstraction introduction Group iPhone social networking UI prototyping activity
4	iPad POP app tutorial Group prototype and iPad integration Prototype presentations
5	Finish prototype presentations Post Survey Focus Group Interviews

Table 1: HCI workshop activities

a greater proportion of authorship than men in HCI-related conferences. Between 1998 and 2008, the average share of women authors were 28% at CHI, the premiere ACM conference in Human Factors. This number is high considering that women made up 22.6% of people who earned computer science Master's degrees and 17.8% of people who earned computer science PhDs according to the 2011-2012 annual Taulbee Survey [23]. Therefore, women not only are interested in HCI but they are very active in the field. This aligns with notion of women navigating towards the social sciences and other people-oriented disciplines [22]. HCI is also interdisciplinary in nature which relates to the broad set of interest that a majority of women in computing tend to have. This differs from the majority of men who identify with the "geek" computer science stereotype of their lives revolving around computers [11]. It is this notion of catering computers to human use that may be needed to attract and retain women in computing.

There have been several recent interventions conducted for middle school students with a focus on increasing their interest in computer science [10, 21]. Khoja et al. conducted a four-week long, four hour per day, Computer Science camp for middle school girls [10]. Participants learned about a different topic every week which included Introduction to Computer Science, Robotics, Programming, and Hardware. While this study was successful in that it increased student confidence and skills in using the computer, HCI was not incorporated into the workshop materials. Previous research has shown that HCI can positively impact interest and retention in computer science. When Yardi et al. [21] taught HCI to ten students ages 11-13, they found that practicing HCI increased their interest in taking future computer related courses, raised awareness of the role that computer plays in their everyday lives, and influenced their perception of computing. These students designed a digital desktop prototype and evaluated it through user studies and heuristic evaluations. However, the sample size was small with no control for gender or ethnicity.

Researchers in the computer science department at Carnegie Mellon University implemented institutional, cultural, and curricular changes, with an emphasis on HCI that resulted in increased retention rates amongst women. In spite of the curricula changes at Carnegie Mellon University yielding an undergraduate concentration in human-computer interaction [7], the combination of the institutional, cultural, and curricular changes failed to reveal the impact of HCI on female Computer Science retention. Even though this research does not solely credit HCI for increased retention rates, Fisher's [7] work in light of Yardi's [21] shows that HCI has some promise in serving as a gateway to computing for females.

Usability is a largely recognized key concept of HCI [8] that is concerned with the quality of a system for use, often by humans. Usability Engineering is a sub-area of HCI, stemming from the concept of usability, that is concerned with "concepts and techniques for planning, achieving, and verifying objectives for system usability" [15]. Since interaction between users and computers occurs at the user interface, this often involves user interface (UI) design. Therefore, our workshop focused on the specific HCI practice of user interface design, which maintains the HCI principles of designing, implementation, and evaluation of systems for human use, in order to operationalize HCI.

Paper prototyping has been advocated as a valid HCI design technique for at least 20 years [13]. Still today, with the advances on prototyping tools, it is considered an effective prototyping mechanism [16]. For our workshop, we made use of an application available in iOS and Android devices that brings paper prototypes to life. This application, named POP for Prototyping on Paper [19], takes advantage of pen and paper. POP enables the user to transform their paper designs into digital interactive prototypes. POP has a three step work-flow where the user would design their user interface on paper, take pictures of each user interface screen, and finally, link the pictures together and allows the user to "play" the interface. Figure 1 shows several screenshots of the POP app. The frontmost screenshot (bottom left) shows several pictures of paper prototypes. The top-right picture shows a picture with "active regions" highlighted in green. These areas are linked by the user to other pictures and when the prototype is "run" then POP makes the transitions. This gives an illusion of a working app.

3. WORKSHOP

We provided a series of HCI workshops at four different outreach sites, three Boys and Girls Clubs and one YMCA, all located in the South Hampton Roads area of Virginia. Each workshop took place approximately one hour a day for five days. A total of nineteen middle school girls participated in the workshops. The majority of the participants (16 out of 19) were African American, with two being multi-racial and one Asian. These participants were all a part of summer day programs with a non computing-based focus. This provided a unique opportunity to gain access to girls who may not be initially interested in computer science rather than girls who voluntarily sign up for a computing-based activities. Table 1 shows the daily activities of the workshop. This paper reports on the user interface prototyping activity that primarily occurred on the third and fourth day of the workshop.

Participants engaged in a discussion about the definition of a user interface and the overall characteristics of a good user interface. Then the participants worked in groups to evaluate two user interfaces on the iPad. The two user inter-

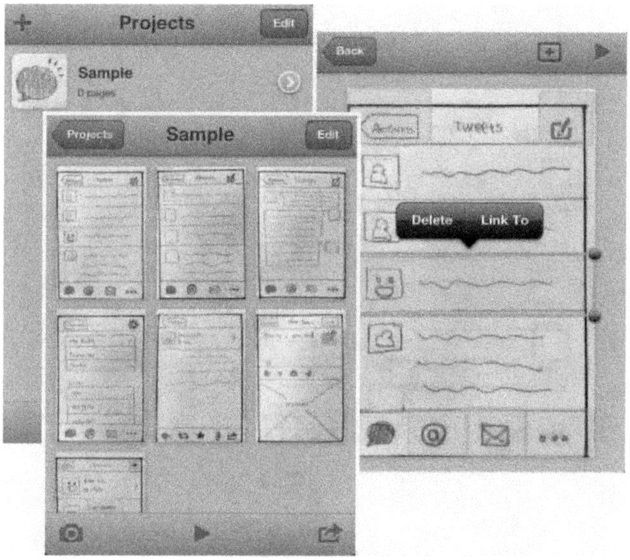

Figure 1: POP app Screenshots [19]

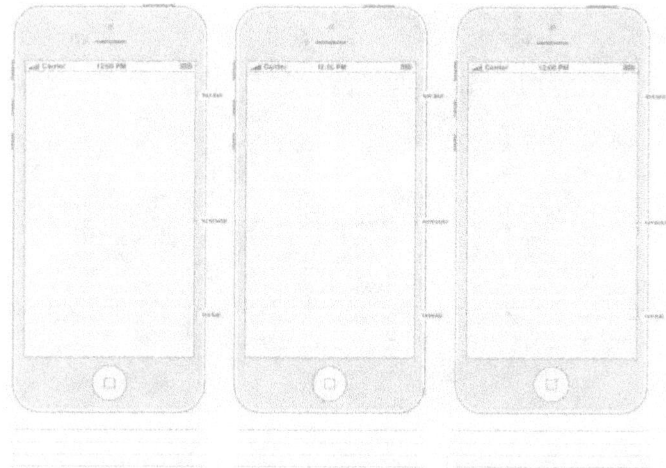

Figure 2: iPhone 5 Template [17]

face belonged to apps that were designed to enable students to record homework assignments. The participants were instructed to use both apps by creating a homework assignment, editing it, and marking it as complete. The groups then shared what the liked/disliked about each user interface. Following the evaluation, participants learned about several user interface design guidelines (learnability, efficiency, memorability, error, and satisfaction) and suggested changes that could be made to their least favorite user interface to make it better. This activity made participants aware of the nature of user interface design in order to prepare them for the prototyping activity.

The prototyping lesson began with a discussion about abstraction in user interface design and prototyping. Participants worked in groups to create a low-fidelity prototype of an iPhone that included text chat, video chat, and/or audio chat features. They were reminded to utilized the user interface design guidelines they learned about the previous day. Participants used paper, pencil, and markers to create a low-fidelity paper prototype of an iPhone app. The paper contained images of multiple iPhones with blanks screens Figure 2 that they used to design their user interfaces. The template contained guides for the navigation bar, keyboard, and tab bar, along with a grid for guidance and accuracy. The next day, participants used the POP app [19] on the iPad to connect the screens of their user interface prototype. Figure 3a shows one of the participants using the POP app to make their user interface interactive. The activity concluded with each group demonstrating their prototypes to the other participants as pictured in Figure 3b.

At the end of the week, we conducted focus group interviews with the participants. The focus group interviews were approximately thirty minutes. Among the questions asked to the participants, in this paper we report on the following questions:

- What do think about the workshop?
- What did you like the most and the least about the workshop?
- What did you think about computer science before the workshop?
- What do you think about computer science after the workshop?
- Do you want a computer science career?

The next section presents our observations from this activity.

4. RESULTS AND DISCUSSION

The demographic of our participants indicated that the participants were diverse in terms of age, grade level, socioeconomic status, and home computer technology access. The ages ranged from ages 11-13 with 42% 11-year olds, 42% 12-year olds, and 26% 13-year olds. The grade level ranged from grades 6th-8th with 47% in 6th grade, 26% in 7th grade, and 26% in 8th grade. Social economic status was evaluated based on participants' free/reduced lunch status as reported by their parent/guardian. The social economic status of the participants were almost evenly distributed with 53% receiving free/reduced lunch in school. The participants all had access to at least one type of computing device at home with 11% having one device, 21% having two devices, 32% having three devices, 26% having four devices, and 11% having five devices. These devices included desktop computers, laptops, tablets, smart phones, video game consoles, and electronic readers.

4.1 Evidence of Ownership

The majority of the participants took the user interface prototyping activity very seriously. The participants were only instructed to create a low-fidelity prototype of an iPhone that included text chat, video chat, and/or audio chat features. Students were encouraged to use abstraction when designing their user interface in order to alleviate the pressure that may be associated with having to draw detailed objects due to the varying drawing abilities of the participants. However, some groups went above and beyond their instructions in an effort to make their apps appear as realistic as possible and displayed signs of taking ownership of their prototypes.

Figure 3: A participant using the POP app (a) and a participant presenting their user interface created in POP (b).

Figure 4: Two examples of varying degrees of abstraction used in prototyping

4.1.1 Personalization

A lot of participants decided to name their apps. These names ranged from unique names such as "Fun Chat App", "U Talk" and "Kids Meet" to names inspired by popular existing apps like "Instaface", "Insta-kik", and "Talk-Time". The app called "Chirp Messaging" even had theme where would-be contacts were called "Chirpers". Some groups demonstrated the integration of some of their personal interests into their app names (e.g. "Musicana") and others used names that represented the functionality of the application in fun way (e.g. "Mingle"). The integration of personal interest indicates that the participants were aware that computer science is capable of going beyond the computer screen, into other disciplines that may also spark their interest. Only two of the participants chose not to give their apps a name.

4.1.2 Attention to Detail

The participants often payed special attention to details when creating their prototypes. All participants, to some degree, followed the template guides that indicated the location of the navigation bar, keyboard, and tab bar. Although participants were encouraged to use abstraction, some used it more than others. Those who chose not to use much abstraction did more work but their prototypes looked more realistic. An example of varying usage of abstraction in two different prototypes are shown in Figure 4.

4.1.3 Consideration of Social Implications

When creating their prototypes, the participants also took social implications into consideration. One group added a button called "background check" to their screen entitled "extra stuff". This indicates the participants in this group thought beyond the immediate tangible aspect of the design process and thought about the safety of the users of their app. Another group created a screen with a button to download their app and rating stars. This is an indicator that this group was a aware of the fact that an app is larger than its creator(s) and it is something that users will evaluate often using the rating stars. Another group wanted to not only make their apps appealing to themselves but they also wanted to make sure that others will have very little trouble using it as well. In-spite of it being an interactive "paper prototype" they specified features and included instructions with their mock-up. These instructions were very detailed step-by-step instructions on how to use their app. They even provide instructions on how to troubleshoot problems and recover from errors. This group took their first time users into consideration when creating their prototype.

4.2 POP App Influence

The participants did not have any technical issues when using the POP app to digitize their paper prototypes. The POP app played an essential role in the prototyping activity. It helped participants to easily identify errors in their paper prototypes when they created active regions and linked their screens. Participants would often navigate their apps on the iPad and realize that additional active regions were necessary or that the app did not perform as expected. This knowledge encouraged students to "debug" their apps to figure out the problem and sometimes literally go back to the drawing board to include any missing components. Participants were introduced to the iterative process of user interface design through POP.

4.3 Perception of Computer Science

On the last day of the workshop, we conducted focus group interviews with the participants. We asked several questions to get an understanding of the participants' perception of computer science.

4.3.1 What did you think about the workshop?

All of the participants stated that they enjoyed the workshop and thought that it was really fun. Participants did not view it as a typical assignment that they would receive in school. One participant stated that "I thought it was fun because we got to create our own apps and do stuff that you don't normally do in a classroom." However, they still viewed it as a learning experience with statements like "I like the workshop because it teaches us how to work with computer science" and "I like the workshop because you got to learn more about computers and what they do and you got to play with iPads." A lot of other participants also indicated that they enjoyed working with the iPads. Participants also liked the ability to hang out with friends during the workshop.

4.3.2 What did you like the most and the least about the workshop?

Participants liked using the iPads and creating their own apps the most. They also enjoyed "taking pictures of stuff" and "putting a program together." One participant said "I like that we actually got to make our own apps and I can download this on my ipad at home and make my own apps and maybe one day [my app] will come true." This indicated that she had intentions to not only work more with prototyping but to go beyond prototyping and make it into a real app. Some participants also indicated that they liked the instructor, who was also a female from an underrepresented population. While several students said there was nothing that they did not like about the workshop, others indicated that they wished that it was longer than a week and that more children participated.

4.3.3 What did you think about computer science before the workshop?

Prior to the workshop, the majority of the participants thought that computer science was "boring", "pretty stupid", "kind of nerdy", and "hard." Other participants "didn't know about it" or "thought that it was about science on a computer." One participant stated that "I thought it was going to be boring and only about science because I am not really a fan of science." Another participant stated that "I thought we were going to do science like, where we learn about matter and animals, but we would do it on the computer. I didn't know it was going to be about computer science." It is clear that some participants had misconceptions about what computer science actually is. There were also concerns about peers not being interested in the workshop. One participant stated, "at first I thought it was going to be really small and intimate, and a lot of my friends wouldn't do it because it sounded boring."

4.3.4 What do you think about computer science after the workshop?

All of the participants thought that computer science was "fun", "pretty cool", "exciting", "interesting", and "very informative" after the workshop. One participant indicated that they "might want to try it out more", while another participant thinks that "it was something that I might take interest in when I'm older." Perceptions of what computer science actually is changed for at least one participant, as indicated by the statement "I think of it as doing programs and getting to know the computer," when compared to statements mention earlier about computer science being about doing science on a computer. References to peers were also indicated in responses to this question where one participant stated "afterward I thought it was fun because my friends were here."

4.3.5 Do you want a computer science career?

The responses to this question varied amongst the participants. The majority of participants who said 'no' enjoyed computer science but had other career interest that they thought they would like better. One participant said "no because I like computer science and I am pretty good at it and I can figure things out, but I am better at art and stuff like that, but if that never worked out, and I tried everything, then I would probably go into the field of computer science." Another participant said 'maybe' for a similar reason when she stated "I really want to pursue my dreams of being on TV and being a news reporter talking about the stars, but if that doesn't work out, I guess I can be in a computer science career." That same participant indicated that she was able to connect computing to her existing career interest when she stated "... but I learned just now that news reporters need to have some knowledge of computer science because science is in our everyday life and so is math and reading." Another participant said maybe because she wanted to be a lawyer but stated that "computer science may be a second career that I may think about". These responses indicate that most of the participants are not completely excluding computer science as a career option even with other career interests.

5. CONCLUSION

In this paper, we have presented our experiences working with middle school girls from underrepresented groups. We conducted a week-long workshop with the goal of encouraging more women to pursue computer science as a career. We use HCI and, in particular, paper prototypes as the motivator for a career path in computer science. The POP application played an essential role in helping the participants understand the user interface design process and enabled them to visualize their designs as realistic applications. Based on the prototypes developed and the comments provided by the girls, it was evident they enjoyed the workshop.

As a result of the workshop, our findings are in agreement with current women in computing literature [3, 1]. The workshop participants thought that computer science was boring [20] and indicated that their peer opinions and existing stereotypes were factors in their initial negative perceptions of the field. The lack of a role model from a similar background [3, 1] may have also influenced their negative perceptions. Once the participants were introduced to computer science through paper prototyping, however, and met a role model from a similar background, the stereotypes were less apparent and their peers became less of an influence. This research demonstrates the promise in using HCI to introduce women from underrepresented ethnic groups to computer science.

6. ACKNOWLEDGEMENTS

We would like to thank Dr. Glenda Scales, Dr. Tonya Smith-Jackson, Dr. Andrea Kavanaugh, and Dr. Scott McCrickard for their thoughtful comments on the preparation of the materials for the workshop. We also would like to thank the Boys & Girls Clubs of Southeast Virginia, the Southside Boys & Girls Club, the YMCA of South Hampton Roads for allowing us to do the workshops in their facilities.

7. REFERENCES

[1] E. Bunderson and M. Christensen. An Analysis of Retention Problems for Female Students in University Computer Science Programs. *Journal of Research on Computing in Education*, 28(1):1–18, 1995.

[2] L. Cassel, A. Clements, G. Davies, and M. Guzdial. Computer science curriculum 2008: An interim revision of CS 2001. Technical Report December, Association for Computing Machinery and IEEE Computer Society, 2008.

[3] J. Cohoon. Just get over it or just get on with it: retaining women in undergraduate computing. *Women and Information Technology: Research on Underrepresentation, J. McGrath Cohoon and William Aspray eds. The MIT Press, Cambridge MA*, pages 205–237, 2006.

[4] J. Cohoon, S. Nigai, and J. Kaye. Gender and computing conference papers. *Communications of the ACM*, 54(8):72–80, 2011.

[5] P. Denning, D. Comer, D. Gries, M. Mulder, A. Tucker, A. Turner, and P. Young. Computing as a discipline. *Communications of the ACM*, 32(1):9–23, 1989.

[6] P. J. Denning. Great principles in computing curricula. *ACM SIGCSE Bulletin*, 36(1):336–341, 2004.

[7] A. Fisher and J. Margolis. Unlocking the clubhouse: the Carnegie Mellon experience. *ACM SIGCSE Bulletin*, 34(2):7, 2002.

[8] G. Guida and G. Lamperti. AMMETH: a methodology for requirements analysis of advanced human-system interfaces. *IEEE Transactions on Systems, Man and Cybernetics, Part A: Systems and Humans*, 30(3):298–321, 2000.

[9] T. Hewett, R. Baecker, S. Card, T. Carey, J. Gasen, M. Mantei, G. Perlman, G. Strong, and W. Verplank. ACM SIGCHI Curricula for Human-Computer Interaction, 1996. Retrieved September 23, 2011 from http://old.sigchi.org/cdg/.

[10] S. Khoja, C. Wainwright, J. Brosing, and J. Barlow. Changing girls' attitudes towards Computer Science. *Journal of Computing Sciences in Colleges*, 28(1):210–216, 2012.

[11] J. Margolis and A. Fisher. *Unlocking the Clubhouse: Women in Computing*, volume 34. MIT Press, 2002.

[12] N. C. f. S. National Science Foundation and E. Statistics. Women, Minorities & Persons With Disabilities in Science & Engineering, 2012. Retrieved September 24, 2012 from http://www.nsf.gov/statistics/wmpd/.

[13] M. Rettig. Prototyping for tiny fingers. *Commun. ACM*, 37(4):21–27, 1994.

[14] S. Rosser. *Teaching the Majority: Breaking the Gender Barrier in Science, Mathematics, and Engineering.* Teachers College Press, Columbia University, New York, NY, 1995.

[15] M. B. Rosson and J. M. Carroll. *Usability Engineering: Scenario-Based Development of Human-Computer Interaction.* Morgan Kaufmann, New York, NY, 2002.

[16] C. Snyder. *Paper Prototyping: The Fast and Easy Way to Design and Refine User Interfaces.* Morgan Kaufmann Publishers Inc., San Francisco, CA, USA, 2003.

[17] M. Stephens. Free Printable iPhone 5 Templates (PDF), 2012. Retrieved September 6, 2013 from http://www.matthewstephens.com/.

[18] H. K. Tillberg and J. M. Cohoon. Attracting Women to the CS Major. *Frontiers: A Journal of Women Studies*, 26(1):126–140, 2005.

[19] WOOMOO. POP prototyping on paper. Retrieved September 6, 2013 from https://popapp.in/.

[20] S. Yardi and A. Bruckman. What is computing? bridging the gap between teenagers' perceptions and graduate students' experiences. *Proceedings of the third international workshop on Computing education research*, pages 39–49, 2007.

[21] S. Yardi, P. Krolikowski, T. Marshall, and A. Bruckman. An HCI approach to computing in the real world. *ACM Journal on Educational Resources in Computing*, 8(3), 2008.

[22] B. Zafar. College major choice and the gender gap. *Federal Reserve Bank of New York Staff Report*, 364, 2009.

[23] S. Zweben. CRA Taulbee Survey, 2013. Retrieved September 24, 2013 from http://cra.org/resources/taulbee/.

Developing a Pre- and Post-Course Concept Inventory to Gauge Operating Systems Learning

Kevin C. Webb
Computer Science Department
Swarthmore College
Swarthmore, PA
kwebb@cs.swarthmore.edu

Cynthia Taylor
Computer Science Department
Oberlin College
Oberlin, OH
ctaylor@oberlin.edu

ABSTRACT

Operating systems courses often present students with multiple approaches to solve a problem, often with differing trade-offs. While students are more than capable of memorizing the details of these competing approaches, they often struggle to recommend a specific approach and analyze its implications. In particular, we find that students exhibit difficultly in interpreting text-based scenario descriptions in a way that allows them to correctly choose between potential solutions when presented with a high-level, conceptual scenario.

In this paper, we describe the development of a pre- and post-course concept inventory, which we utilize to explore students' misconceptions of operating systems and their associated trade-offs. We compare the results of our assessment with in-class peer instruction questions and exam questions to characterize the areas in which students most commonly struggle with operating systems material.

Categories and Subject Descriptors

K.3.2 [**Computer and Information Science Education**]: Computer Science Education

General Terms

Human Factors

Keywords

Concept Inventory, Misconceptions, Operating Systems

1. INTRODUCTION AND BACKGROUND

Students begin courses with intuition and prior knowledge about how to solve tasks. These preconceptions can be leveraged to guide them to a deeper understanding of computer science concepts [5], or it may lead to misconceptions, which if not corrected by the instructor, may persist and hinder their understanding of a subject. In computer science, previous work has shown that students have trouble with even the most basic concepts of programming [4, 18, 22].

SIGCSE'14, March 5–8, 2014, Atlanta, GA, USA.

ACM 978-1-4503-2605-6/14/03 ...$15.00.
http://dx.doi.org/10.1145/2538862.2538886 .

In this work, we present the results of a preliminary pre- and post-course inventory of operating systems concepts, designed to examine both students' preconceptions about the material and the misconceptions they hold after completing an upper-division operating systems course.

Most collegiate courses combine a variety of assessments to gauge student learning, with student evaluation primarily centered around midterm and final exams. Such exams often ask students to perform calculations or provide explanations (that may be memorized) in addition to examining student understanding of the course's key high-level conceptual "take-aways." This assessment diversity has led to the development of concept inventories, which exclusively aim to reveal student understanding of critical high-level concepts.

In physics, the Force Concept Inventory (FCI) [15] revealed a dramatic difference between how students and instructors think about mechanics concepts. It demonstrated that final exams were not sufficient for revealing the persistence of students' basic misconceptions, even after they had completed introductory physics coursework. Subsequent work using the FCI to compare new, interactive pedagogical approaches to traditional lecture techniques has transformed the way introductory physics classes are taught, yielding significant student learning gains [11].

Concept inventories are now widely used in a variety of disciplines [9] to assess the impact of pedagogical methods. In the field of computer science, concept inventories have been created for digital logic [12, 13], algorithms and data structures [8], introductory courses [10, 17], and discrete math [2]. However, most pedagogical literature on the subject of operating systems has focused on designing student projects [3, 6, 14]. While some work has been done identifying overall principles of computer systems [16], there has not yet been any work towards characterizing student misconceptions of operating systems principles.

In this work, we discuss our experiences in developing a concept inventory for operating systems courses. This effort is part of a broader initiative to apply the principles of open source software to the development of concept inventories. We believe that by applying rapid, multi-author development models to the construction of computer science concept inventories, the educational community will benefit from high-quality, dynamic concept assessments that will lead to a significant increase in course coverage. Our assessment is publicly available online [1], and we welcome collaboration from interested parties.

We compare student results on our assessment, given as pre- and post-course multiple choice quizzes, to the results of similar questions from both in-class peer instruction questions and traditional exam questions. Our analysis of data collected from four operating systems courses provides insights into student understand-

Table 1: A brief summary of the courses in which our assessment has been deployed.

Course	Weeks	Students	Methodology	Instructor
A	5	21	Peer Instruction	I_1
B	10	133	Lecture	I_2
C	10	133	Lecture	I_2
D	14	9	Peer Instruction	I_3

ing of the material. In this paper, we specifically examine the lowest-performing assessment questions and discuss what they reveal about student comprehension of operating systems concepts.

2. METHODS

For our inventory, we created questions to be administered before and after collegiate operating systems courses. This section characterizes the courses in which the assessment was administered and describes our question development goals.

2.1 Course Context

To date, our concept inventory has been administered in four courses, at two institutions, by three instructors. We summarize the course summaries in Table 1, referring to the courses as A through D and instructors as I_1, I_2, and I_3. Courses A through C were taught at a public, research-intensive university in the western United States. Approximately 23,000 undergraduate students attend the university, with about 1,200 students majoring in computer science. Course D was taught at a small, private liberal arts college in the midwestern United States. Approximately 2,800 undergraduate students attend this college, with about 60 students majoring in computer science.

Courses A through C are required for majors in the computer science department of the respective institution and are typically taken by students in their junior or senior year. Prerequisites for the course include computer organization, algorithms, and software engineering. Course D is an elective, which was taken exclusively by seniors. Its prerequisites include computer organization, algorithms, and systems programming. Students are expected to be comfortable with programming in C and working in a Unix-like environment prior to enrolling in all courses.

Course A was a five week, intensive summer course, with 21 students enrolled at the time of the final exam. Courses B and C were ten-week quarters, each with 133 students enrolled at the time of the final exam. Course D was a fourteen-week semester long course, with 9 students enrolled at the time of the final exam.

In courses A and D, students were given the pre-test as an in-class assessment prior to the first lecture, and the post-test on the final day of instruction. In courses B and C, the pre and post tests were given as part of an optional discussion section. The pre-test was given in the first discussion section, and the post-test was given as part of a final review section.

Courses B and C were taught by an experienced instructor who has taught the course many times. They were taught in a traditional lecture format. Courses A and D were taught by relatively inexperienced instructors using peer instruction (PI) pedagogy [7]. PI utilizes frequent student discussion to engage students and provide a more interactive learning environment. Students were presented with four to six multiple-choice PI questions per class period. Students responded twice for each question, and we collected data at both points. The first time, students responded individually to the presented questions. Afterwards, they discussed the question in small groups of three or four and then responded again, as a group. Student response data was captured using hand-held "clickers," and we refer to individual and group response data in our results. After the group response phase completed, the instructor guided the class though a class-wide discussion. In this paper, we incorporate the data collected through the peer instruction process to give us more insight into how and why students performed as they did on specific questions in the concept inventory.

Table 2: A brief summary of our assessment's questions.

Question	Concept
1	Timing of system calls and context switching
2	How kernel code is executed
3	Choosing a scheduling algorithm
4	The bounded buffer problem (discussed in 4.3)
5	Segments versus pages in memory management
6	Indirection in file pointers (discussed in 4.1)
7	Polling versus interrupts (discussed in 4.2)
8	Access Control Lists versus Capabilities
9	Multiprocess execution on a single CPU
10	Least recently used eviction (Courses B-D only)

2.2 Goals and Question Development

Operating systems courses typically focus on analyzing design trade-offs and selecting the best solution for a specific set of circumstances. Rather than identifying a single right answer, students in an operating systems course must often choose from among a set of viable answers, each of which is ideal for a specific situation. Unlike exam questions, which may involve students reciting memorized pros and cons for different approaches, we aim for our assessment's questions to force students to examine the *implications* of choosing between opposing trade-offs. Many of our questions present a scenario and ask students to apply the course's principles in choosing the most appropriate option. We feel that this form of question better allows us to assess their understanding of the subject's core concepts.

At the same time, we intend for our inventory to be used as both a pre- and post-test, and thus we would like our questions to be reasonably accessible to students who do not have prior knowledge of the subject. To this end, we minimized our use of specialized vocabulary where possible and defined terms when we felt it might improve the accessibility of a question. By doing this, we hope to capture how students conceptualize important material prior to any formal instruction. To reduce the effects of students randomly guessing, we provide an option of "I am not familiar with this terminology / I don't know" as the final choice (E) for every question.

With these goals in mind, we developed questions based on our past experiences teaching operating systems courses and working with students who had difficulties with the material. We identified areas that students frequently have trouble understanding and developed multiple choice questions with distractor answers based on our experiences with common student misconceptions. We created a ten-question, multiple choice inventory that poses high-level, conceptual questions about key concepts in operating systems. Table 2 outlines the topic of each question.

Our inventory is available online in its entirety [1], and we encourage collaborative development and refinement from additional authors. Moving forward, we intend to rigorously validate our assessment by consulting with other experts in teaching operating systems, interviewing students, and collecting additional data by giving our assessment to more classes of students. Our goal is to construct a validated and widely-adopted operating systems concept inventory in collaboration with the operating systems academic community.

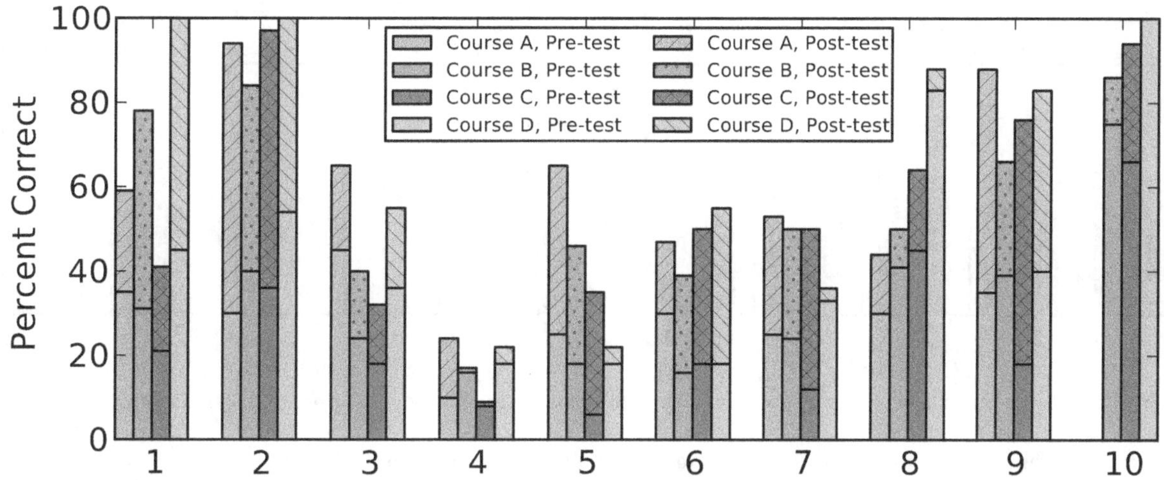

Figure 1: An overview of concept question scores, grouped by question number as identified in Table 2. Each group of bars depicts student performance across the four courses (A–D) in which the inventory was deployed. We focus our analysis of selected results (Section 4) on questions 4, 6, and 7, which showed relatively poor performance.

3. RESULTS OVERVIEW

All courses showed improvement across each question between the pre- and post-test. In courses B, C, and D, students averaged 3.3 correct responses (median of four) on the pre-test, and 5.5 correct responses (median of five) on the post-test. In course A, where students were only given questions 1 through 9, students averaged 2.7 correct responses (median of three) on the pre-test and 5.0 correct responses (median of six) on the post-test.

Figure 1 illustrates the pre-test scores and post-test improvement, grouped by question and class. While variation is to be expected between multiple courses taught by different instructors, there are clear trends across classes, particularly for questions on which students performed poorly. Students uniformly performed the worst on question 4, a fairly straightforward question on the bounded buffer problem. They uniformly did well, even in the pre-test, on question 10, which uses an analogy about bookshelves to discuss the least recently used eviction policy. They also all show a great deal of post-course improvement on question 2, which covers how kernel code is executed, and question 9, on the relative execution rates of processes.

This uniformity in student answers across classes allows us to generalize about the content students struggle with in operating systems courses. They generally have trouble with synchronization, indirection, and I/O, all of which we discuss at length in Section 4. High student performance on the pre-test for question 10 shows that many students already have an intuitive understanding of the concept of least recently used eviction, which can be leveraged when teaching that concept.

Figure 2 depicts the cumulative percentage of responses, across all four courses, that selected "I don't know." or chose the most popular distractor. While every question showed improvement on the post-test, the extent of the improvement varied significantly across questions. Interestingly, students chose a much wider selection of answer choices on the pre-test than the post-test, where their incorrect responses tended to strongly favor one distractor. This implies that even for questions that students did not perform well on, their answer selection was influenced by the material in the course. In other words, while they may not have always selected the correct choice, students narrowed their selections, and when incorrect, they tended to focus on the "most attractive" distractor choice. Furthermore, the sharp decrease in the rate of *E* responses indicates that students felt more confident answering the questions, even if their selections were incorrect.

3.1 Changes to the Concept Inventory

As we continue to refine the inventory, we have modified the content several times, mainly to improve student comprehension of the questions. The most significant change was the addition of question 10, on LRU replacement. This question was given to courses B through D. Additionally, the wording of question 8, on access control lists (ACLs) versus capabilities, was changed after course A. This question originally used the analogy of a theater, where patrons would either be let in by a bouncer checking names on a list (representing ACLs), or a ticket (representing capabilities), along with two additional distractor answers. In course A, 44% of students chose the correct answer of ACLs, but an equal number chose the distractor answer of tickets. We suspected that the analogy to the theater was leading them to choose the wrong answer, so the question was rephrased to use the analogy of a party instead. Question 7, about polling versus interrupts, was also changed after course A, in order to better characterize the device. However, this clarification did not have a discernible effect on students answering this question correctly.

4. SELECTED RESULTS

In this section, we present a selected subset of our OS concept assessment results. We discuss individual questions and examine the questions' core concepts in the context of student responses. Due to space constraints, we cannot cover every question in detail. Instead, we choose to focus on the three of the lowest-performing questions. We feel that these questions best illustrate common student misconceptions and that their analysis provides the most potential to positively affect student learning.

These three questions covered important operating systems topics like indirection (44% answered correctly), I/O (50%), and synchronization (16%). We emphasize these questions because, even after completing an operating systems course, our results indicate that students still harbor misconceptions on these topics. For each question, we present the question along with the cumulative percentage of answer choices annotated by a (pre-test %, post-test %) tuple to indicate how frequently students selected each answer on the pre- and post-test, respectively, from all four courses. We mark

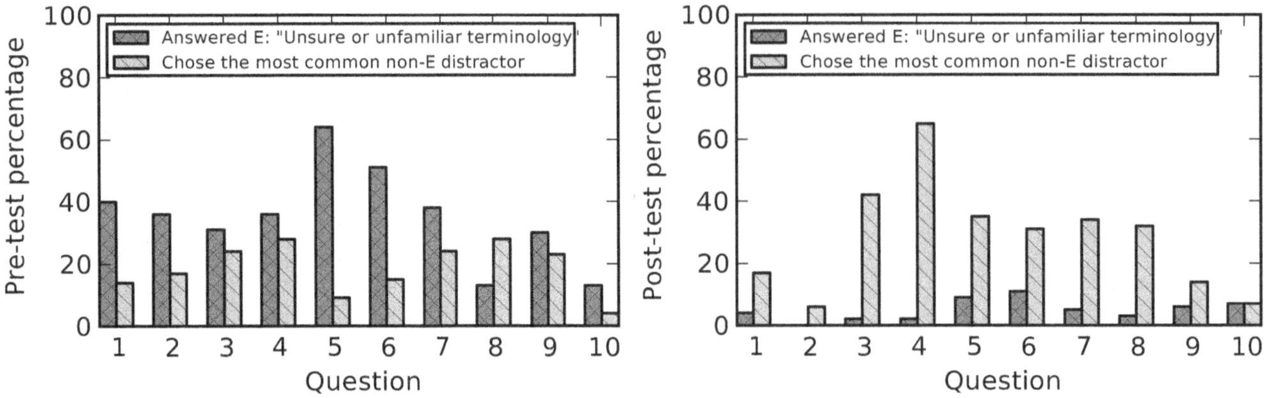

Figure 2: The cumulative percentage of *E* and popular distractor responses, per question, on the pre-test (left) and post-test (right).

the correct answer with italics. All comparisons with exam and clicker questions are taken from course A.

4.1 Indirection: File System Block Map

Suppose we have a file system that uses two forms of pointers to find file data: direct and indirect pointers. We refer to this set of pointers as a "block map." Direct pointers point directly at file data, and indirect pointers point at a separate disk block that contains multiple pointers to file data. Every file in the system uses the same block map structure, with unused pointers directed at null. Eliminating the indirect pointers while supporting the same maximum file size would be...

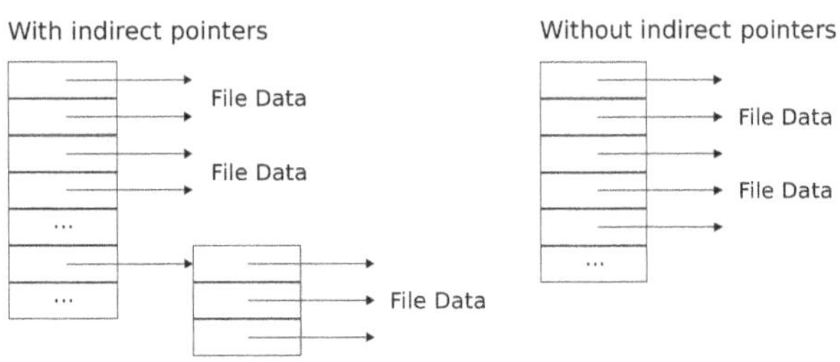

A) (7%, 7%) Beneficial - The new block map would save space storing small files.

B) (8%, 7%) Beneficial - The new block map would save space storing large files.

C) (19%, 44%) *Detrimental - The new block map would waste space storing small files.*

D) (15%, 31%) Detrimental - The new block map would waste space storing large files.

E) (51%, 11%) I am not familiar with this terminology / I don't know.

Concept Question 6: File System Block Map Indirection

Indirection is a recurring concept in many areas of computer science. Students typically face it first in the form of pointers, where indirection often proves to be difficult for novice programmers [19]. In the context of operating systems, indirection is often used to make the metadata associated with storing a variably-sized entity (like a file or process memory) proportional the entity's size.

Question 6 examines this concept of indirection, specifically for storing file metadata (the same concept applies to using multiple levels of page tables to reduce page table sizes). Our pre-test results show that this question had the second-highest rate of *E* answer selections at 51% (the highest was 64% for a segmentation vs. paging question). We suspect that this concept is intimidating to students who have not previously encountered the terminology and constructed a mental model of indirection. In our experience, students are typically much more comfortable with direct pointers, likely because their behavior resembles that of an array, which is a familiar construct.

We presented two in-class peer instruction questions to students on this topic, and the resulting data confirms that students more easily reason about direct pointers. The first question introduced the idea of using only direct pointers to store file metadata. Our data shows that 78% of the class responded correctly to the individual response, and 100% responded correctly after discussing the question with their group. The second PI question asked students to compute the amount of metadata that would be needed to store a particular file when given a block map structure with both direct and indirect pointers. The correct response rate was 44% individually and 39% after the group discussion. This was one of a small minority of questions for the entire course in which the correct response rate *decreased* after group discussion, which indicates that students were uncomfortable with the concept of indirection.

Adding indirect pointers introduces a challenging concept, since systems often use indirection as an optimization as opposed to it being necessary for correctness. We included question 6 on the assessment due to our observation that students often ask why we bother with this added complexity. We believe that the challenge of indirection may stem from the fact that a solution using only direct pointers *seems* to be attractive to students because it would be relatively straightforward.

Final exam results further corroborate this observation with two questions related to the concept of indirection. The first question presented a scenario in which we asked students to determine the numerical properties of a hypothetical page table and then explain (as free-response text) whether or not they would recommend using multiple levels of page tables (indirection) in this scenario. The second question presented a similar hypothetical scenario of a file system block map and eventually asked students how we justify the complexity of using indirect pointers. Unsurprisingly, students performed better on second question, where they were implicitly told that the complexity was useful, as opposed to the former, in which students had to make that decision themselves.

Given these types of responses to exam questions and the results of question 6, indirection is clearly an unintuitive concept. Even after demonstrating indirection for multiple class topics, many students still struggle with indirection misconceptions. We believe that students who are learning these concepts may benefit from instructors initially introducing an abstract form of indirection, perhaps by relating it to C memory pointers, which students are likely to find familiar. Discussing indirection abstractly by mapping it to a more comfortable topic [20] may enable students to construct a mental model of indirection prior to adding the confounding details of memory management or file systems.

4.2 I/O: Polling vs. Interrupts

The core concept for Question 7 is the use of polling vs. interrupts to retrieve data from an I/O device. To force students to consider the device's characteristics without relying on memorization, we invented a new device with no obviously recognizable "type." Ideally, students answering this question would recognize answer *B* as polling and *D* as interrupts. Options *A* and *C* were meant as plausible distractors, despite being impractical for this device.

> Your company has developed a new I/O device, and you've been tasked with writing its driver. The device produces a byte of data at frequent, regular times. The device does not save data after it has been produced. Which of the following options for accessing the device would best suit your driver?
>
> A) (0%, 1%) Have the kernel check the device for new data when it is idle.
>
> B) (23%, 50%) *Have the kernel check the device for new data at set time intervals.*
>
> C) (15%, 10%) Have the kernel check the device for data when applications request it.
>
> D) (24%, 34%) Have the device alert the kernel when it has new data so that the kernel can collect the data as soon as it is available.
>
> E) (38%, 5%) I am not familiar with this terminology / I don't know.

Concept Question 7: Polling vs. Interrupts

Students taking the post-test predominantly chose between *B* and *D*, indicating that they recognized these two options. In another assessment question, 90% of students correctly identified the role of interrupts in transferring execution control to the kernel. We therefore believe that students are comfortable with these terms and their definitions.

However, despite recognizing polling and interrupts, applying them to a scenario remains non-intuitive to students. Having been given an explanation of polling and interrupts in class, we presented the students with a peer instruction question in which we asked whether they would use polling or interrupts for keyboard and disk devices. Like the indirection concept described in section 4.1, this was another of the few PI questions whose correct response rate *dropped* after group discussion (41% individually to 29% after discussion), with most students opting to use polling for disk devices. Such a drop indicates that students found the concept difficult and that many students lacked confidence in their original answer.

We asked a similar free-response question on the final exam regarding the use of polling or interrupts for a disk device. Students performed better on the exam, with 81% correctly identifying interrupts as the correct choice for disks. However, only 62% correctly articulated *why* they made that decision, despite the class having directly discussed this topic after the PI question. Our conclusion is that, like the other common misconceptions we identify in this paper, students most frequently struggle when asked to analyze the trade-offs of a scenario when described primarily using text (as opposed to code).

4.3 Synchronization: Bounded Buffer

Proper use of synchronization and concurrency is a difficult subject for students to understand [21, 23]. To examine this concept, question 4 addresses synchronization using a producer–consumer (bounded buffer) scenario. We chose this scenario because it benefits from applying the less-common approach of using semaphores purely for synchronization, rather than mutual exclusion.

In our experience teaching operating systems, students commonly believe that mutual exclusion is required to solve this problem correctly. The results here show this to be the case, despite lecture slides and peer instruction questions indicating the contrary to students. While not incorrect, enforcing mutual exclusion is inefficient and unnecessary for this scenario.

> Suppose you have a fixed-size queue shared between two processes on a system that has one CPU. One process produces data and puts it into the queue, and the other process reads data from the queue and removes it. For correctness, you want to ensure that the producing process only writes when there is space available, and the consuming process only reads when there is data available. Your solution needs to be as efficient as possible. You should:
>
> A) (4%, 2%) Only let one process access the queue at a time.
>
> B) (17%, 15%) Have the producing process signal to the consuming process when it fills a slot - the consuming process will only consume as many slots as received signals.
>
> C) (14%, 16%) *Have the producing process signal when it fills a slot, and the consuming process signal when it empties a slot.*
>
> D) (29%, 65%) Have the producing process signal when it fills a slot, the consuming process signal when it empties a slot, and let only one of them access the queue at a time.
>
> E) (36%, 2%) I am not familiar with this terminology / I don't know.

Concept Question 4: Bounded Buffer

Initially, students performed well on related peer instruction questions. When shown unsynchronized bounded buffer code and asked why synchronization was required, 81% of students correctly identified (after group discussion) that synchronization is necessary to prevent overflowing or underflowing the buffer rather than to provide mutual exclusion. Likewise, when asked to add semaphores to this unsynchronized example, 81% of students responded correctly, and no students voted for a mutual exclusion distractor. This indicates that students are capable of understanding the basics of using semaphores for synchronization, but they struggle applying this understanding to a less familiar "word problem" scenario that does not involve code.

We compared this to a midterm question, which had a component that required a bounded buffer style synchronization solution and a different component that required a mutex exclusion solution. The question displayed unsynchronized code for two processes: one representing a refinement department, refining raw materials into a product, and another representing a shipping/receiving department, providing the refinement department with raw materials, and then shipping the finished product. Students were asked to identify why the code needed semaphores and to correctly insert them to eliminate any problems they identified. To categorize whether students use synchronization versus mutual exclusion, we count as synchronization any call to wait(a) followed by signal(b) in one process, and wait(b) followed by signal(a) in the other process, regardless of whether the student put the calls in the correct place.

Looking at just the synchronization component of the question, only one student (5% of the class), attempted to solve the problem using both synchronization and mutual exclusion, a solution which would correspond with question 4's *D* choice. Forty-five percent of students used mutual exclusion with no attempt at synchronization, which would correspond to answer *A*, and fifty percent of students made some attempt at synchronization with no additional mutual exclusion, an answer that corresponds to the correct option, *C*.

Of the four students who answered C on the post-test in course A, three of them also used synchronization on the midterm, consistently indicating that they understood using synchronization without mutual exclusion. Of the ten students who answered D, five had used mutexes, and five had used synchronization (including the student who used both). Since very few students chose A in either the pre- or post-test, this could indicate that students simply didn't recognize it as the bounded buffer problem. However, when asked to describe in words why synchronization was needed, almost all of them correctly identified a buffering problem, although none used the phrases "Bounded Buffer" or "Producer–Consumer."

Eighty-six percent of the students could accurately describe why synchronization was needed. One student wrote, "One problem that could occur is that, if T2 tries to unload and there is no product produced from T1, there is nothing to tell T2 to wait if there is nothing available from T1" while describing the problem on the midterm. Despite his accurate description of the bounded buffer problem, he both used mutual exclusion on the midterm and answered D to question 4, indicating that while he conceptually understood the need for synchronization in this scenario, he was unable to connect it to the correct solution.

Despite what we might tell them, most in-class and textbook examples (besides the bounded buffer) *do* use synchronization to enforce mutual exclusion, and many operating systems courses often strongly emphasize identifying critical sections and resolving race conditions with mutual exclusion. Our results indicate that when teaching operating systems, instructors should cautiously emphasize the different uses of synchronization, rather than focusing primarily on mutual exclusion.

5. CONCLUSION

This paper looks at preliminary results of a concept inventory for operating systems material. We use these results to explore areas in which students harbor misconceptions regarding indirection, I/O, and synchronization in an operating systems context. The misconceptions we identified point to student difficulty in analyzing trade-off scenarios and interpreting the implications of competing solutions. Our concept assessment and preliminary results provide valuable insights to help operating systems instructors understand student misconceptions. These results will be expanded as we continue to collect additional student responses, and we encourage other instructors to collaborate in constructing an operating systems concept inventory.

6. ACKNOWLEDGEMENTS

We are indebted to Beth Simon, Leo Porter, Cynthia Lee, and Sat Garcia for providing valuable feedback on earlier drafts of our concept inventory, and to Joe Pasquale for allowing us to adapt his course materials for peer instruction, and all his other help.

7. REFERENCES

[1] `http://git.io/ZRngng`.

[2] V. Almstrum, P. Henderson, V. Harvey, C. Heeren, W. Marion, C. Riedesel, L. Soh, and A. Tew. Concept Inventories in Computer Science for the Topic Discrete Mathematics. *ACM SIGCSE Bulletin*, 38(4):132–145, 2006.

[3] J. Andrus and J. Nieh. Teaching Operating Systems Using Android. In *SIGCSE*, 2012.

[4] P. Bayman and R. Mayer. A diagnosis of beginning programmers' misconceptions of basic programming statements. *Communications of the ACM*, 26(9), 1983.

[5] T.-Y. Chen, G. Lewandowski, R. McCartney, K. Sanders, and B. Simon. Commonsense Computing: using student sorting abilities to improve instruction. In *SIGCSE*, 2007.

[6] W. Christopher, S. Procter, and T. Anderson. The Nachos Instructional Operating System. In *USENIX Winter*, 1993.

[7] C. H. Crouch and E. Mazur. Peer Instruction: Ten Years of Experience and Results. *American Journal of Physics*, 69(9), September 2001.

[8] H. Danielsiek, W. Paul, and J. Vahrenhold. Detecting and Understanding Students' Misconceptions Related to Algorithms and Data Structures. In *SIGCSE*, 2012.

[9] D. Evans, G. Gray, S. Krause, J. Martin, C. Midkiff, B. Notaros, M. Pavelich, et al. Progress on Concept Inventory Assessment Tools. In *IEEE Frontiers in Education*, 2003.

[10] K. Goldman, P. Gross, C. Heeren, G. Herman, L. Kaczmarczyk, M. C. Loui, and C. Zilles. Identifying Important and Difficult Concepts in Introductory Computing Courses using a Delphi Process. In *SIGCSE*, 2008.

[11] R. Hake. Interactive-engagement versus traditional methods: A six-thousand-student survey of mechanics test data for introductory physics courses. *American Journal of Physics*, 66:64, 1998.

[12] G. Herman and J. Handzik. A preliminary pedagogical comparison study using the digital logic concept inventory. In *IEEE Frontiers in Education*, 2010.

[13] G. Herman, M. Loui, and C. Zilles. Creating the Digital Logic Concept Inventory. In *SIGCSE*, 2010.

[14] R. Hess and P. Paulson. Linux Kernel Projects for an Undergraduate Operating Systems Course. In *SIGCSE*, 2010.

[15] D. Hestenes, M. Wells, and G. Swackhamer. Force Concept Inventory. *The Physics Teacher*, 30:144–158, March 1992.

[16] M. Holliday. Teaching computer systems through common principles. In *IEEE Frontiers in Education*, 2011.

[17] L. C. Kaczmarczyk, E. R. Petrick, J. P. East, and G. L. Herman. Identifying Student Misconceptions of Programming. In *SIGCSE*, 2010.

[18] L. Ma, J. Ferguson, M. Roper, and M. Wood. Investigating the Viability of Mental Models Held by Novice Programmers. *ACM SIGCSE Bulletin*, 39(1):499–503, 2007.

[19] I. Milne and G. Rowe. Difficulties in Learning and Teaching Programming - Views of Students and Tutors. *Education and Information Technologies*, 7(1), 2002.

[20] J. D. Novak. Concept Mapping: A Useful Tool for Science Education. *Journal of Research in Science Teaching*, 27(10), 1990.

[21] J. Ousterhout. Why Threads Are A Bad Idea (for most purposes). In *Invited presentation at USENIX ATC*, 1996.

[22] R. Pea. Language-Independent Conceptual "Bugs" in Novice Programming. *Journal of Educational Computing Research*, 2(1):25–36, 1986.

[23] H. Sutter and J. Larus. Software and the Concurrency Revolution. *ACM Queue*, 3(7):54–62, Sept. 2005.

Misconceptions and Concept Inventory Questions for Binary Search Trees and Hash Tables

Kuba Karpierz
University of British Columbia, CS
Vancouver, BC, Canada
mr.karpierz@gmail.com

Steven A. Wolfman
University of British Columbia CS
Vancouver, BC, Canada
wolf@cs.ubc.ca

ABSTRACT

In this paper, we triangulate evidence for five misconceptions concerning binary search trees and hash tables. In addition, we design and validate multiple-choice concept inventory questions to measure the prevalence of four of these misconceptions. We support our conclusions with quantitative analysis of grade data and closed-ended problems, and qualitative analysis of interview data and open-ended problems. Instructors and researchers can inexpensively measure the impact of pedagogical changes on these misconceptions by using these questions in a larger concept inventory.

Categories and Subject Descriptors

K.3.2 [**Computers and Education**]: Computer Science Education

General Terms

Human Factors

Keywords

data structures, misconceptions, concept inventory

1. INTRODUCTION

Concept inventories (CIs)—inspired by the Force Concept Inventory (FCI) [7]—have changed pedagogy across many disciplines [6, pp. 20–43]. CIs are "cheap" but powerful tools for probing student misconceptions and the longitudinal impact of pedagogical changes [5].

In this paper, we present several novel data structures CI questions and the research process that led to their design. We focus on Binary Search Trees (BSTs) and Hash Tables—important data structures course topics [11, 12] that were also identified as important during interviews with faculty at our institution. Critically, we *triangulate* evidence for misconceptions and CI question design from a broad data set using quantitative *and* qualitative methods.

SIGCSE'14, March 5–8, 2014, Atlanta, GA, USA.
Copyright 2014 ACM 978-1-4503-2605-6/14/03 ...$15.00.
http://–enter the whole DOI string from rightsreview form confirmation.

CIs exist for some computing subjects, e.g., digital logic [6] and intro programming [13]. For data structures, researchers have identified misconceptions [4, 9] and developed CI questions targeting misconceptions [3, 10]. Our work contributes both results—new misconceptions and questions—and a thorough account of our approach.

2. METHODS

Our process adapts from Adams and Wieman [1] and Almstrum *et al.* [2]. Focusing on three courses—our data structures course and its pre- and post-requisites—we (1) identified key concepts from instructor interviews and aggregate analysis of course artifacts, (2) identified misconceptions from student interviews and deeper analysis of artifacts, and (3) formulated, piloted, and validated multiple-choice CI questions. Specifically, our data sources include:

Instructor Interviews: interviews with 9 instructors of the three courses, focused on sample exam responses and "when students don't get something important, which an expert *should* get."

Exam Statistics: per-student marks on 200+ exam problems taken by 1000+ students from 15 offerings of the courses and reviewed for common yet difficult problems.

Exam Analysis: open coding—qualitative analysis with iteratively developed codes—of responses to a final exam problem from data structures offerings in Jan–Apr and Jul–Aug 2012 (all 67 exams from one section of the former and all 59 exams from the latter). On the Aug exam, this problem was the third most difficult in our **Exam Statistics.** (The two harder problems' topics are outside this paper's scope.) The problem's format echoed a project given in Jan–Apr but *not* in Jul–Aug [8].

Project Analysis: open coding of reports from the project in **Exam Analysis** (all 68 reports from one section of data structures in Jan–Apr 2011 and all 87 from Jan–Apr 2012).

Think-Aloud Interviews: 25 one-hour student interviews, drawing problems from the data sources above. Students gave informed consent and received $15 for participation. We helped them learn to think aloud with two practice problems but subsequently interjected minimally. We audio-recorded, partially transcribed, and open coded interviews. We ran 4 further interviews using multiple-choice CI questions. These aimed particularly to validate that students select answers for our intended reasons.

We achieved a balanced sample of interview subjects across course level and grades. We classify students by the highest of the three courses in progress or completed as "**CS1xx**" (first-year discrete math), "**CS2xx**" (second-year data structures), and "**CS3xx**" (third-year algorithms). 9 were **CS1xx**, 10 were **CS2xx**, and 10 were **CS3xx**. Subjects covered a wide grade range. The **CS3xx** group earned 4 As, 2 Bs, 2 Cs, and 2 Ds in **CS3xx**. The **CS2xx** and **CS3xx** groups earned 9 As, 4 Bs, and 7 Cs in **CS2xx**. The **CS2xx** and **CS3xx** persistors skew **CS1xx** grades high, but the **CS1xx** group alone earned 3 As, 4 Bs, and 2 Cs. However, 59% of interviewees were women, over-representing the roughly 24% women in our major.

CI Pilot: an optional quiz of draft multiple-choice CI questions given on the last day of the May–Jun 2013 data structures offering. All attending students chose to participate (77 of 98 enrolled, plus one auditor).

3. MISCONCEPTIONS

In this section, we report on three categories of misconceptions. We begin by identifying the misconceptions, work through their elaboration in the data, and conclude with design and initial validation of targeted CI questions.

3.1 Duplicates in BSTs

We found that students struggled with the possibility of duplicates in BSTs—keys already present in the structure—through **Exam Analysis** and explored further with other data sources. Through iterative coding, we identified two recurring misconceptions:

- **SeparateOperation:** The misconception that, when inserting a potentially duplicate key, the BST must perform two separate find operations: one to ensure the key isn't already present, and one to find where to insert it.
- **FullSearch:** The misconception that, when inserting a potentially duplicate key, the BST must inspect *every* key in the tree.

We document both misconceptions but focus on **SeparateOperation**, as only it was prevalent in our **CI Pilot**.

3.1.1 Identifying the Misconceptions

The problem in **Exam Analysis** did not ask about duplicates; nonetheless, 8 student answers exhibited patterns that led us to the duplicate-related misconceptions:

- Four students associate BST performance problems with duplicates, but with little explanation. For example, one reasoned "since we are not inserting any duplicates we see normal $\lg n$ behavior."
- Two students' answers hinted that duplicate checking is an important (i.e., expensive) part of insertion. One wrote that a BST "would run in [worst-case] linear time because it has to check for duplicates on every insert." The other states that "[a BST] should be $O(\lg n)$ time for insertion [as it] must check for duplicates when inserting."
- The final two students clearly articulate **SeparateOperation**. One wrote that "[the BSTs] search for duplicate first (lgn) and insert if not there (lgn)." The other stated that a "BST shows $O(n)$ behavior in [worst-case insertion] because it has to find a duplicate before inserting."

```
When we insert a key into a binary search tree (BST), the key may be
a duplicate: a key that is already present somewhere in the tree.

Imagine a BST implementation that assumes that no duplicate key is
ever inserted and that is used in a way that guarantees this
assumption is correct.  Which of these best describes this
assumption's effect on insertion of new keys?

a. We no longer need to search for duplicates, and the rest of the
   work is very fast (takes a constant number of steps).

b. We still need search for where to add the key, but we no longer
   need to test as we go whether the key is equal to each other key
   we access during the search.

c. We can now do only one rather than two searches in the tree: we
   still search for where to add the key, but we do not search for
   duplicates.

d. There is not enough information to tell.
```

Figure 1: CI question targeting SeparateOperation. This version is from the first interview. We reworded after each interview and the CI Pilot.

Spurred by these hints of duplicate-related misconceptions, we analyzed the richer data in the **Project Analysis**. Again, there was no prompt to explore duplicates, but three reports that did offer insight into duplicate misconceptions. In particular, one report one report carefully detailed **FullSearch**: "when we inserted ... a middle value and alternating smaller and larger values ... 50, 49, 51, 48, 52, ... we were making two singly linked list[s] ...Each insertion would supposedly take half as much time as insertion using an ascending list, but since the ADT would have to check for duplicates in the other branch, it took a longer time." Another showed **FullSearch** in the context of vectors, not BSTs: "This corresponds with a sorted vector: ... random numbers are inserted in linear time due to checking the entire list for many values for duplicates."

Our first 25 **Think-Aloud Interviews** posed no problems aimed at these misconceptions. Yet, two students still exhibited **FullSearch** on this problem about a small BST: "In the worst case, how many nodes would we need to look at to find a key in this tree? Which ones?" One was halfway through data structures, the other finishing its post-requisite. The former said, "[in the worst case, we] need to look for 3 ... That means we need to go through everything else." The latter student said "you would need to look at all of the nodes above the bottom layer to find a specific key", and gave a formula for the search cost: $\approx 1/2 \cdot 2^{\text{depth}}$.

3.1.2 Concept Inventory Question Design

We then designed a multiple-choice CI question targeting **SeparateOperation**, shown in Figure 1.

We put (a)–(c) in order by the number of searches they describe (0, 1, and 2). (a) targets a misconception where students attribute no search cost to insertion operations. Since we found this misconception *only* in **Project Analysis**, we discuss it no further. (b) is the intended correct answer, envisioning removing an "equals" case and the resolution it performs for duplicates. (c) targets **SeparateOperation**.

Answer (d) was only present to camouflage for other questions where it was correct (e.g., see Section 3.2.3). After the first interview, we changed it to "This assumption has no effect." Either way, as indicated below, (d) exposed our early wording of (b) as a weak fit for students with a clear understanding of the problem.

```
When we insert a key into a binary search tree (BST), the key may be
a duplicate: a key that is already present somewhere in the tree.

Imagine a BST implementation that assumes (as a precondition) that
no duplicate key is ever inserted. Which of these best describes
this assumption's effect on insertion of new keys compared to a
normal BST implementation?

a. We no longer search the tree at all.  We just add the key
   directly where it belongs.

b. We search the tree once either way.  We still search for where to
   add the key, but we no longer check for duplicates as we go.

c. We search the tree once rather than twice.  We still search for
   where to add the key, but we no longer search first for
   duplicates.
```

Figure 2: Final revision of CI question targeted at SeparateOperation.

In the **CI Pilot**, 44.9% correctly answered (b), but the bulk of the 24.4% answering (d) may have had a correct model of BST insertion. 24.4% selected (c), suggesting they believe **SeparateOperation**.

We asked this question of three students in **Think-Aloud Interviews**. Two gave correct reasoning. One was concerned about not "search[ing] *through* the tree *at all*" on (a) and that "you wouldn't do two searches, you would just continue on" on (c). The student agreed with (b) and preliminarily circled it, saying "That's true. You can stop when you find it." However, the student switched to (d), concluding "I'm feeling like [the absence of duplicates] really actually doesn't have an effect in a BST..." The other student quickly concluded "you wouldn't really need to search for [a duplicate] anyways because it would be where you're inserting [the new key]" and then selected (d).

The third student illustrated **SeparateOperation** and the need for carefully crafted CI questions. While reading (a) but before reading (c), the student said, "...if there were duplicates, you're going to need an extra step to basically search through the tree to see if the same key exists somewhere else. So that would pretty much double our work." The student's final selection was based on how "vague" or "explicit" the answers were. (a) "[is] a little ambiguous" and "doesn't mention anything about adding a key to the tree". Compared to answer (c), answer (b) has "a very nice way of saying 'but we do not search for duplicates' ... [and] a nice way usually involves being more explicit." Thus, the student selected (b) "despite it having the longest answer".

Given (d)'s appeal to students whose reasoning matches (b) and the accidental lack of parallel structure exploited by the last student, we rephrased to eliminate (d) and normalize the other answers, as shown in Figure 2.

Based on our data, we believe this question effectively targets **SeparateOperation**, and that a substantial minority of our students hold this misconception. We believe **FullSearch** is less prevalent but worth exploring further.

3.2 Conflation of Heaps and BSTs

We explored misconceptions related to BSTs and binary heaps because of previous work suggesting some students believe that a heap is also a BST [3, 10]. We attempted to replicate Danielsiek *et al.*'s results on their multiple-choice CI question targeted at heap/BST misconceptions [3]. We later investigated these misconceptions *unintentionally* in **Think-Aloud Interviews**. Our results do suggest students conflate these data structures, but *not* in response to

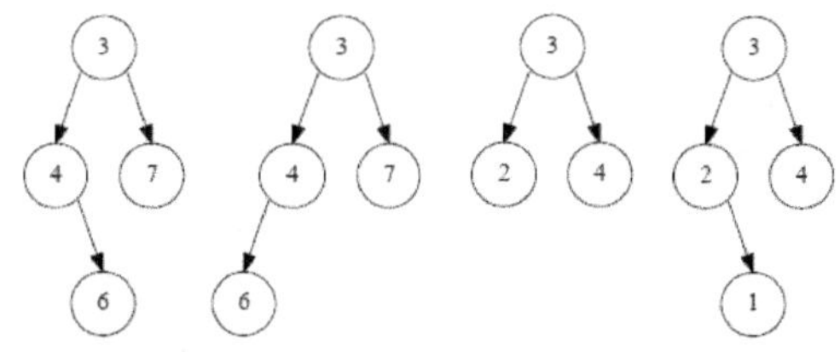

Figure 3: Our rendering of the trees from the heap/BST question [3]. The trees were shown in a column, each prefaced by the options: binary min-heap (only), BST (only), both, or neither.

the initial multiple-choice question. Specifically, we found evidence of the following recurring misconception:

- **DefaultBalanced:** The misconception that, absent concrete information, a BST tends to have a balanced shape, particularly left-complete (binary heap-shaped).

3.2.1 Initial Multiple-Choice Results

We offered the question in Figure 3 on the Apr 2012 data structures final exam. Paul and Vahrenhold highlight two misconceptions the question exposes: (1) overlooking left-completeness, with most respondents indicating that the first tree is a heap, and (2) conflating heaps and BSTs, with 15.6% indicating the third tree is both heap and BST while correctly answering the remaining parts [10].

Consistent with previous work, most students overlooked the left-completeness requirement. Of 67 students, 59.7% indicated that the first tree was a binary heap. Only 34.3% correctly answered that the tree was neither heap nor BST. 17.9% believed this tree was a BST, suggesting they checked the order invariant only between nodes and their immediate children, a misconception identified by Fekete [4]. Although the quantitative results support the presence of both misconceptions, we were unable to gather triangulating evidence and so address them no further here.

Surprisingly, we found little evidence that students conflated BSTs and heaps. Of the 20 students who answered all three other parts correctly, only 5% (one) believed the third tree was both BST and heap. The rest correctly identified it as only a BST. Overall, 92.5% of students selected only a BST, while just 6% believed it was *also* a heap and none believed it was *only* a heap. The vast majority also correctly responded to the second and fourth prompts.

We therefore concluded preliminarily that this heap/BST conflation did not occur in our student population.

3.2.2 BST Think-Alouds

We posed five problems about BSTs—none mentioning heaps—in **Think-Aloud Interviews**. 16 subjects solved at least one of these problems; of these, 11 had completed at least two-thirds of the data structures course.[1] Of these 11, five showed clear evidence of confusing heaps and BSTs. Often, when uncertain about the shape of a BST, they reached for a balanced, left-complete tree—a binary heap-shaped tree—as a sort of "default" shape for a BST, leading us to postulate **DefaultBalanced** as their misconception.

The two most striking examples responded to the prompt: "Draw a binary search tree whose keys printed in post-order

[1]The two other students who had at least started data structures both showed evidence of confusing BSTs and heaps.

Figure 4: A student's heap-shaped guide and final result on the BST post-order traversal problem.

```
What shape is a binary search tree that contains the keys 1, 2, 3,
4, 5, 6, and 7?  (Keys were not necessarily inserted in that order.)

a. Exactly this shape:                          7
                                               6
                                              5
                                             4
                                            3
                                           2
                                          1

b. Exactly this shape:                        4
                                           2     6
                                          1 3   5 7

c. This shape with either 1 or 7 at            *
   the root and the other keys              *     *
   arranged appropriately:                 * *   * *

d. Exactly this shape:                    1
                                           2
                                            3
                                             4
                                              5
                                               6
                                                7

e. There is not enough information to tell.
```

Figure 5: Final version of CI question targeted at DefaultBalanced.

traversal are: 20 15 30 25 75 90 80 65 50". Both sketched empty, heap-shaped trees to get started. Figure 4 shows one student's sketches. The student performed a post-order traversal on this sketch and lined the result up under the given numbers to solve the problem. The other student used the rule that the root is always last to line up keys with nodes. Both noticed that what they had created was not a BST. One gave up, while the other reached a nearly-correct answer by patching a series of problems, such as: "There's four [keys larger than 50], I've only drawn three... So that's a serious problem." One such moment strongly suggests **DefaultBalanced**: "Well, let's just assume we have a properly balanced search tree in search of part marks."

Two others facing BST problems fell back on the heap shape. Asked why a small binary tree was not a BST, one explained "it's not a binary search tree because it's not a complete and full tree." The other simulated a sequence of insertions in decreasing order into a "standard BST", saying "I think the standard [BST] means ... a complete tree. ... [9999] can stay on the bottom for now, but [9998] is going to have to go and complete the tree. ... When we get to the next full complete bottom, there will be some numbers there that won't work; so, we have to rearrange again."

3.2.3 Concept Inventory Question Design

We then designed a multiple-choice CI question targeting **DefaultBalanced**, as shown in Figure 5.

We ordered answers randomly, but ensured that (b) and (c) appeared together and (e) remained last. (e) is correct. (b) and (c) are targeted at **DefaultBalanced**. (d) is targeted at students who do not read the question carefully. After this answer proved very attractive in our **CI Pilot**, we added the parenthetical "... not necessarily ... in that order" but have not yet piloted or validated this phrase. (a) targets students who do not read carefully and hold a misconception noted occasionally in **Think-Aloud Interviews** where students insert keys at the top of the tree rather than the bottom. Due to a lack of triangulating evidence, we do not discuss this misconception further.

In the **CI Pilot**, 42.3% of students chose the correct response. 20.5% chose (d) and so perhaps did not read carefully. However, 35.9% chose (b) or (c)—most choosing (b)—which suggests they believe **DefaultBalanced**.

Think-Aloud Interviews with three students added evidence for **DefaultBalanced** and for the question's validity.

One student did not exhibit the misconception and picked the correct answer for the right reasons. This student began by saying, "Which order were [the keys] inserted? I'm not sure." The student then quickly eliminated each distractor with comments like "We don't know that."

Two students exhibited **DefaultBalanced** and picked the balanced BST distractor because of it. One eliminated the non-BST distractor, saying "I just want to pick [the balanced BST] because it looks the nicest." The student discarded the other distractors with a skeptical "If it's not *technically* balanced, then I guess [the two list-shaped trees] would technically uphold the properties." The other student also selected the balanced BST as a matter of taste, e.g., discarding a distractor with: "I don't like [this list-shaped tree] because that seems like how I would insert keys into a BST back when I didn't know how BSTs worked." The deciding factor was that "[the problem] doesn't exactly tell you the order items inserted. So, I'm going to assume they're looking for the perfect BST that contains said keys."

Our research provides strong evidence that our CI question effectively targets **DefaultBalanced** and that the misconception's prevalence merits broader investigation.

3.3 Hash Table Resizing

As with the duplicate issues, we observed hash table resizing misconceptions in **Exam Analysis** and explored further through other data sources. We found substantial evidence for two misconceptions:

- **NoRehash:** The misconception that, when resizing, the hash table leaves keys at their existing indexes.
- **ResizeInPlace:** The misconception that, when resizing, the table is extended *in place* by appending slots.

3.3.1 Identifying the Misconceptions

In the **Exam Analysis** problem, students analysed a hash table with a simple hash function and probing strategy. They graphed its performance on inserting a contiguous, decreasing sequence of keys. Figure 6 shows a correct diagram with linear (*total* time) regions indicating swift performance (without collisions) and steep jumps indicating resizes.

Two incorrect answers occurred frequently. Figure 7 shows the combined result of these errors: a "scallop-shaped" graph where each point of the scallop shows a transition from rising per-operation insertion cost back to cheap costs after resizing, but does not show an upward jump in total cost of insertions. 22% of students indicated that collisions slowed

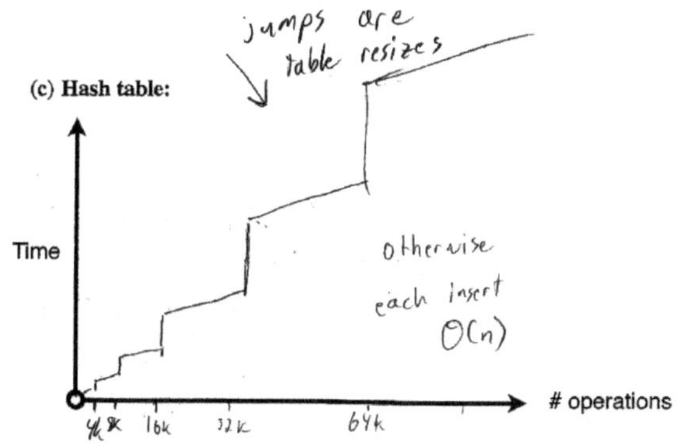

Figure 6: A correct student diagram for the hash table insertion problem.

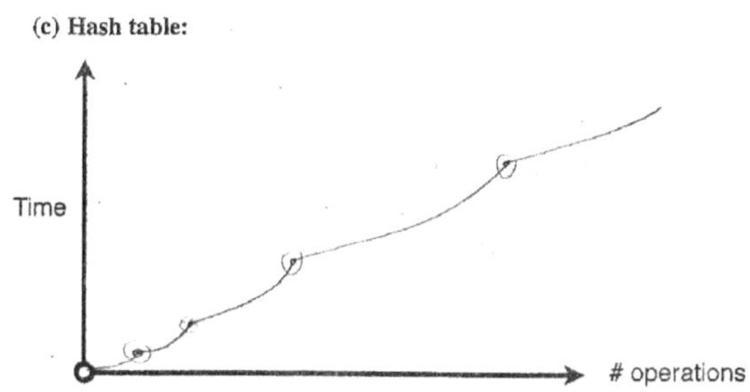

Figure 7: A student's "scallop-shaped" response to the hash table insertion problem.

down the insertion process as the insertion sequence progressed toward resizes. 16% recognized that resizes occurred yet indicated that they had essentially zero cost.

The prompt did not lead many students to explain these features of their answers, but we found evidence that led us to create the **ResizeInPlace** misconception. For example, one student describes the resize as "vector resizing", which does not require individual reinsertion. Another notes that no collisions occur before resizing but writes that then "smaller numbers would have their hash collide with the bigger numbers that was hashed before with a smaller table size."

Isolating the misconception(s) leading to increasingly expensive collision cost proved difficult. Instead, we simply noted common explanations. Two were applications of "book knowledge", statements that are good general guidelines but ignore the details available in the problem: linear probing does a poor job of spreading keys through the hash table, and insertion costs go up with load factor. The last, mentioned in a quote above, led us to the **NoRehash** misconception: the idea that collisions occur between newly inserted keys and keys "... hashed before with a smaller table size."

3.3.2 *Elaborating the Misconceptions*

To learn more, we added a simplified version of this problem late in our **Think-Aloud Interview** process with four students: one just finishing the data structures course and three in its post-requisite. Three of these gave insight into the misconceptions.

One student exhibited **NoRehash** and **ResizeInPlace** in a connected fashion: "When we say the table ... doubles in size, are we literally just like adding an extra bunch of

```
Which of these best describes the process of resizing a hash table to
increase its size?

a. Create a new, separate table larger than the old table, and
   copy the keys from the old table to corresponding slots in the new one.

b. Create a new, separate table larger than the old table, and
   individually re-insert each key from the old table into the new one.

c. Add extra slots at the end of the existing hash table, and
   leave the old keys in place in their existing slots.

d. Add extra slots at the end of the existing hash table, and
   individually re-insert each key from the old table into the new one.
```

Figure 8: Final version of CI question targeted at ResizeInPlace and NoRehash.

elements at the end or are we rehashing everything? ... I'm going to assume that we're not rehashing everything." For this student, rehashing is a way to move keys into a new memory block, not a necessary adjustment. The student later describes keys hashing into locations still occupied by "old" keys that should have been rehashed.

The next student shows evidence of **NoRehash**, seeing allocation as the dominant cost of resizing: "The [delays for resizes] get gradually bigger ... because it needs to take more time to make space for the hash table." Later that student shows evidence of **ResizeInPlace**, saying: "with ... linear probing ... you wouldn't have to rehash, ... it resizes at half full, so it would be like the first half, almost half of it is full and then you would have to move down to the n-over-2 spot."

The last student *may* believe **NoRehash**, emphasizing the cost of copying (rather than rehashing) at resizes: "When the size of the array reaches a certain number ... the performance becomes really ugly because you have to copy all elements [to the new table]."

3.3.3 *Concept Inventory Question Design*

Based on these students' discussion of the problem, we designed a much simplified multiple-choice CI question that asks directly about hash table resizing, as shown in Figure 8.

We chose randomly whether the "create a new" or "add extra slots" answers should go first and, within each group, whether the "copy" or "re-insert" answers should go first. (b) is correct. Together, the answer set targets all possible combinations of **NoRehash**—(a) and (c)—and **ResizeInPlace**—(c) and (d). The answers include phrases from student responses and use line-breaks and consistent wording to draw attention to the differences among answers.

In the **CI Pilot**, 62.8% of students chose the correct response. 33.3% chose (a) or (c), suggesting they believe **NoRehash**. **ResizeInPlace** is rarer in our data, with only 11.5% choosing (c) or (d). The **CI Pilot** version of the question said "...copy the keys from the old table into the new one" in (a). We altered the wording for the final version shown above based on the **Think-Aloud Interviews** described below.

We conducted **Think-Aloud Interviews** with three students over this question, which support both the presence of both **ResizeInPlace** and **NoRehash**.

One student answered correctly with correct reasoning: "[Creating a new table and individually re-inserting] does seem like a better way, cause that way you would keep constant your hashing rule ... and all your collisions will follow your rules that you set."

However, this student did show some evidence of **ResizeInPlace**, e.g., saying of one "add extra slots" answer "that could work," and "[it] seems like a bad way of increasing its size cause [it would cause unpredictable collisions]". The student saw problems with not re-inserting keys and with re-inserting some in place while others remain in the table, but did *not* recognize that resizing an array in place is, in general, infeasible. This suggests some students who believe **ResizeInPlace** *will* be able to eliminate its distractors, which may explain the lower "yield" of students with this misconception in our **CI Pilot**. We do not yet have a more attractive rewording for these students; so, instructors and researchers interested in array resizing misconceptions may want to use this CI question as a conservative estimate of **ResizeInPlace** and develop more tightly targeted items.

Another student showed clear evidence of **ResizeInPlace** and then selected an "add extra slots" distractor. This student drew a diagram of a hash table resizing by adding slots to the end *after* reading the prompt but *before* reading the answers. The student then worked through the answers, eliminating the "re-inserting" ones because "it just seems really cost-heavy to individually re-insert anything," which is consistent with **NoRehash** and selecting the distractor targeted at both misconceptions.

However, the problem version given to this student included a **NoRehash** distractor that said to "copy the contents of the old table into the new one." This wording led the student to worry about copying pointers versus copying the referenced data. We therefore rephrased: first replacing "contents of" with "keys from" and, after the **CI Pilot** and our final interview, to the final version shown above.

That final student clearly displayed **ResizeInPlace** and **NoRehash** and selected the answer targeted at both. Consistent with **NoRehash**, the student eliminated the "re-insert" answers because "[re-inserting] would take forever" and "...if you're just adding extra slots ... [you wouldn't need to] re-insert things." The student had trouble selecting between the "copy the keys" and "leave the old keys in place" distractors but eventually chose the latter. The interviewer made a rare interjection to ask why, and the student gave reasoning consistent with **ResizeInPlace**, saying: "It just didn't really make sense to me to create a new table instead of just increasing the size of the one you already have."

Our quantitative and qualitative data together suggest this CI question is effective in probing **NoRehash** and, perhaps conservatively, probing **ResizeInPlace**. Each is present in a substantial minority of our students.

4. CONCLUSIONS AND FUTURE WORK

We presented important new misconceptions about hash tables and binary search trees. We also created three easily reusable concept inventory questions, and ensured that they assess the intended misconceptions. We demonstrated that students with data structures background harbor these misconceptions, in some cases in much greater numbers than indicated on the exam questions we analyzed.

In future work, we plan to verify the CI questions' applicability at other institutions. Other misconceptions that arose during our study also merit further research, particularly **FullSearch**, for which we lack a satisfactory CI question.

In the long run, with our CI questions and others', we hope to produce a modest-sized inventory that may not cover the breadth of data structures, but—as with the tightly-focused Force Concept Inventory [7]—still provides a valuable thermometer to measure student understanding.

5. ACKNOWLEDGMENTS

Thanks to the many students and faculty at UBC, UW, U Toronto, and elsewhere who participated or supported our studies and advised us on our work. Special thanks to Allison Elliott Tew, Elizabeth Patitsas, and Kimberly Voll. This work was funded by the Carl Wieman Science Education Initiative at the University of British Columbia.

6. REFERENCES

[1] W. K. Adams and C. E. Wieman. Development and validation of instruments to measure learning of expert-like thinking. *Int'l. J. of Science Ed.*, 33(9):1289–1312, 2011.

[2] V. L. Almstrum, P. B. Henderson, V. Harvey, C. Heeren, W. Marion, C. Riedesel, L.-K. Soh, and A. E. Tew. Concept inventories in computer science for the topic discrete mathematics. In *Working Group Reports on Innov. and Tech. in CS Ed.*, pages 132–145, 2006.

[3] H. Danielsiek, W. Paul, and J. Vahrenhold. Detecting and understanding students' misconceptions related to algorithms and data structures. In *Proc. of the Tech. Symp. on CS Ed.*, pages 21–26, 2012.

[4] A. Fekete. Using counter-examples in the data structures course. In *Proc. of the Australasian Conf. on Comp. Ed.*, pages 179–186, 2003.

[5] R. R. Hake. Interactive-engagement versus traditional methods: A six-thousand-student survey of mechanics test data for introductory physics courses. *American Journal of Physics*, 66(1):64–74, 1998.

[6] G. L. Herman. *The development of a digital logic concept inventory.* PhD thesis, UIUC, 2011.

[7] D. Hestenes, M. Wells, and G. Swackhamer. Force concept inventory. *The Physics Teacher*, 30(3):141–158, March 1992.

[8] K. Karpierz, J. Kitching, B. Shillingford, E. Patitsas, and S. A. Wolfman. "Dictionary Wars": an inverted, leaderboard-driven project for learning dictionary data structures. In *Proc. of the Tech. Symp. on CS Ed.*, pages 740–740, 2013.

[9] E. Patitsas, M. Craig, and S. Easterbrook. On the countably many misconceptions about #hashtables. In *Proc. of the Tech. Symp. on CS Ed.*, page 739, 2013.

[10] W. Paul and J. Vahrenhold. Hunting high and low: instruments to detect misconceptions related to algorithms and data structures. In *Proc. of the Tech. Symp. on CS Ed.*, pages 29–34, 2013.

[11] B. Simon, M. Clancy, R. McCartney, B. Morrison, B. Richards, and K. Sanders. Making sense of data structures exams. In *Proc. of the Int'l. Wkshp. on Comp. Ed. Research*, pages 97–106, 2010.

[12] J. Tenenberg and L. Murphy. Knowing what I know: An investigation of undergraduate knowledge and self-knowledge of data structures. *CS Ed.*, 15(4):297–315, 2005.

[13] A. E. Tew and M. Guzdial. Developing a validated assessment of fundamental CS1 concepts. In *Proc. of the Tech. Symp. on CS Ed.*, pages 97–101, 2010.

Neo-Piagetian Theory as a Guide to Curriculum Analysis

Claudia Szabo and Katrina Falkner
School of Computer Science
The University of Adelaide
Adelaide, Australia
{claudia.szabo, katrina.falkner}@adelaide.edu.au

ABSTRACT

The development of a coherent curriculum, encapsulating appropriate topics, learning materials and assessment, is crucial for a successful educational experience. However, designing such a curriculum is a complicated task, with challenges in tracing the development of concepts across multiple courses and ensuring that assessment is at an appropriate level at specific points in the curricula.

In this paper, we introduce a curriculum mapping framework based on Neo-Piagetian theory that assists lecturers in tracing concept development and assessment throughout their courses. This framework supports the identification of *prerequisite concepts*, where students are already assumed to be aware of specific topics, and *assessment leaps*, where students are assessed at a different conceptual level than they have been taught. We illustrate the application of our framework through a case study analysing the syllabus of a sequence of three first year programming courses.

Categories and Subject Descriptors

K.3.2 [**Computing Milieux**]: Computers and Education-Computer and Information Science Education

Keywords

Computer Science Education, Curriculum Mapping

1. INTRODUCTION

In any educational environment, learners are provided with a wealth of information and content knowledge, and formal and informal activities in which to apply and develop their knowledge. The design of a curriculum is a complicated task, involving the selection of appropriate topics, the development of learning objectives, content knowledge, learning activities and formal assessment to ensure that the information and experiences designed for the student present a coherent and structured learning experience.

SIGCSE'14, March 5–8, 2014, Atlanta, GA, USA.
Copyright 2014 ACM 978-1-4503-2605-6/14/03 ...$15.00.
http://dx.doi.org/10.1145/2538862.2538910.

There is considerable work in the area of curriculum design [1, 3], focussed primarily on the development of systematic processes to guide the teacher in identifying their instructional goals and learning objectives, and in developing content and learning activities to support those goals. However, once a course has been developed, it can sometimes be difficult to maintain a deep understanding of the specific course in question, and its relationship with other courses. Further, as courses evolve, and new assessments are introduced to maintain relevance and interest, it can be difficult to retain the coherent focus and structure originally created, and assumptions about the necessary scaffolding and student independent study can be lost.

In this paper, we propose a curriculum analysis methodology based on Neo-Piagetian theory [12] to facilitate lecturers in tracing the development and assessment of concepts throughout their courses. Neo-Piagetian theory describes a model of cognitive development through a series of stages; what separates Neo-Piagetian theory from Piagetian theory [13] is the realisation that stages of cognitive development extend beyond childhood (the Piagetian view) and continue into adulthood as applied in new cognitive contexts. The stages of Neo-Piagetian theory - pre-operational, concrete operational, and formal operational - enable us to model a student's conceptualisation and understanding of a specific task. When applied to the discipline of software development, we are able to make a distinction between concept understanding in relation to specific concrete examples, and the development of an abstract conceptual model.

This distinction is particularly important in computer science, as we know that there are specific difficulties that novice programmers face when moving from concrete stages through to more abstract understanding. Novice programmers tend to approach new problems using known techniques from their previous experiences and attempting to reapply concrete examples they have been exposed to [18]. Further, we know that students struggle in developing their understanding of programming concepts from concrete examples within one language to a more abstract understanding that is independent of language - instead, novice programmers tend to construct problem solving processes around the constraints and specific idiosyncrasies of their first programming language, and must be explicitly scaffolded in the development of an abstract, formal operational model [8].

In our methodology, we analyse syllabi in regard to the learning and assessment activities and the Neo-Piagetian stage at which each activity is targeted. Further, we provide a mapping of the introduction of concepts and the assessment of concepts (at different stages), facilitating the determination of *prerequisite concepts*, which are concepts that are assessed but not taught, and *assessment leaps*, where a concept is taught at one level, e.g., at a concrete operational level, but assessed at another, e.g., at a higher, formal operational level. This permits us to identify the scaffolding assumptions present in the course and observe the progression from teaching to assessment activities. We illustrate our methodology through its application to a first year programming course, enabling us to clearly identify the assumed knowledge of the course, and areas requiring review and refinement in terms of appropriate teaching activities.

2. RELATED WORK

Curriculum design involves a systematic process of identifying learning goals and objectives, core knowledge topics, and subsequently identifying and developing learning activities and assessment activities, both formal and informal, to guide the learner through their educational experience. There are many different approaches to curriculum design, including mastery learning [14], instructional design theory [3] and Kemp's cyclic model of instructional design [6]. What is common in these approaches is the consistent and systematic application of a series of developmental stages. *Curriculum mapping* identifies the process of analysis and understanding of an existing curriculum, either to complement a curriculum design process, or in the subsequent evaluation and analysis of an evolved curriculum. Meinke and Bauer [10] present an early example of curriculum mapping, through the application of topological sorting algorithm to so-called "units of instruction", providing a logical organisation of concepts ordered by prerequisite dependencies. Their approach can be used to support the automatic generation of curriculum pathways designed to support structures based on prerequisite knowledge, and related topics.

More recent work in this area explores the use of concept mapping and visualisation to assist in understanding curriculum. Sekiya *et al.* [15] present an analysis tool that employs LDA and Isomap to map content topics through analysis of the course syllabi. Mima [11] defines a similar tool, although designed to operate at a finer granularity, that uses text processing techniques to construct a map of a course based on course syllabi and technical words. Tungere *et al.* [17] introduce a repository-based system for collecting and completing computer science syllabi, with tools that facilitate lecturers in comparing and interrogating syllabi. Similar tools that support sharing and analysis of curriculum are supported by [5] and [19]. Zucker [20] introduces a curriculum visualisation tool that enables lecturers to explore course dependencies through mapping coarse-grained co-dependencies and prerequisite course information.

Much recent work focusses on a high-level analysis of topics: identifying *which* topics are covered *where* in the curriculum, with the aim of identifying gaps and overlap. The approach that we propose within this paper takes this analysis into a different direction - extending beyond the analysis of topic coverage, to the analysis of assessment level, and the gap between the teaching and assessment of programming. Our basis is the adoption of Neo-Piagetian theories of learning development in the analysis of teaching and assessment activities and their associated assumptions and opportunities for learning development.

Piaget's [13] theories of learning development introduce several, age-related stages that define the behaviours that one would expect to see from a child at different points of intellectual development. The four stages: sensorimotor (ages 0-2), pre-operational (2-7), concrete operational (7-11) and formal operational (11-16), are intended to describe the holistic intellectual state for an individual. Formal operational represents the most developed stage and one that exhibits formal, systematic, and consistent reasoning. Neo-Piagetian theory [12] extends Piagetian theory in several areas, however, the most relevant in this context is the view that the stages of cognitive development extend beyond childhood and continue into adulthood as applied in new cognitive contexts. An important distinction here is that individuals are not viewed to be at a specific stage, but will exhibit stage-related behaviours in a specific activity as they develop a deeper cognitive and metacognitive understanding of that activity. Neo-Piagetian theory can be used as a theoretical framework to describe the intellectual modelling of new activities by individuals, and to assist in understanding what novice and expert mental models look like so that they may be articulated to others.

Lister [9] adopts Neo-Piagetian theory to analyse the cognitive development of novice programmers in terms of their ability to reason about code. In his discussion of predictions of programming ability, Lister hypothesises that discrepancies may be understood by applying Neo-Piagetian reasoning; formal operational behaviours in unrelated areas are not necessarily indicative of a student's ability to rapidly develop in new areas, such as programming. Gluga *et al.* [4] extend this work with their description of an interactive web-based tool designed to assist computer science educators in assessing their assessment activities according to Neo-Piagetian theory. Falkner *et al.* [2] apply Neo-Piagetian theory to the identification of mental models for software development at pre-operational, concrete operational and formal operational stages, facilitating the identification of software development practices and ways of articulating those practices that can be easily understood by novice programmers.

3. MAPPING FRAMEWORK

Our approach to curriculum mapping extends upon Neo-Piagetian theory, where we associate the teaching and assessment activities in a course with the Neo-Piagetian level that students would be exposed to. Our framework proposes a fine-grained analysis of a course, designed to highlight differences in prerequisite knowledge as well as points where we are assessing at a different level to that which we are teaching, enabling us to identify needed scaffolding and changes in course structure.

We propose to answer the following research question:

- For particular concepts, is there a gap between the Neo-Piagetian level at which they are taught and the Neo-Piagetian level at which they are assessed?

Taken further, this analysis allows us to the identify *prerequisite concepts*, where we are assessing a concept that is not taught, and *assessment leaps*, where we are assessing a concept at a different level than we are teaching it. This facilitates the creation of pre-requisite pathways throughout the curriculum, not only in ensuring that specific concepts are taught, but also that they are taught (and perhaps assessed) at an appropriate level.

Table 1: Neo-Piagetian Taxonomy of Teaching and Assessment Activities

Stage Name	Example	Description & Comments
Concrete Operational		
1. Representational Systems	A type is what is written before a variable name	Concrete explanations of specific concepts
2. Single Abstractions - familiar	A type is a classification of various types of data that determines the possible values of the type	General definitions of concepts and their application to problems in a familiar setting
Formal Operational		
1. Single Abstractions - global	Java primitive types are similar to C++. Memory deallocation in Java is done automatically.	General definitions of concepts and their application to problems in a global setting.
2. Abstraction Mapping	Polymorphism, inheritance, and interfaces.	General relations of closely related concepts
3. Abstraction Systems	The JVM garbage collection and operating system memory management.	General relations of two distantly related concepts.
4. Principles	Type systems and programming languages.	Unifying principles.

Our methodology follows the four phases described in Figure 1, namely, *Concept Definition*, *Classification of Teaching Activities*, *Classification of Assessment Activities*, and *Revision and Comparison*. Our approach relies on Neo-Piagetian

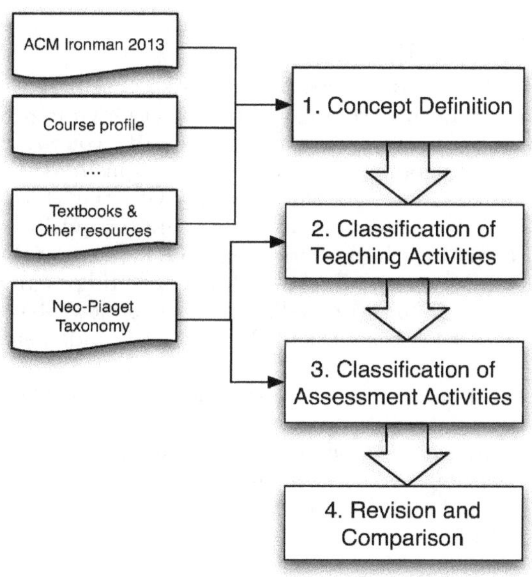

Figure 1: Neo-Piaget Evaluation Methodology

theory using the taxonomy shown in Table 1. We focus on the Concrete Operational and Formal Operational Stages, as they dominate learning at a tertiary level. Our Neo-Piaget taxonomy builds on those proposed by Lister [9] and Knight and Sutton [7] and proposes the introduction of an additional step as shown below.

The *Concrete Operational* stage focuses on concrete definitions of concepts and their applications to familiar settings. It is further divided into two steps, *representational systems* and *single abstractions - familiar.* Students that are at the *representational systems* step can understand concrete explanations of specific concepts. For example, a student in the *representational systems* step would define *memory allocation* as "memory allocation is when you use the keyword `new` to create a variable". Students at the *single abstractions - familiar* step can understand general definitions of concepts and their application in a *familiar* setting, such as a particular programming language or within the framework, system, or codebase in which the learning activities have taken place. For example, a *single abstractions - familiar* step definition for memory allocation using C++ as a teaching language would be "memory allocation dynamically requests memory from the free store, initialises it and returns a pointer to the allocated space". This concept would be differently taught (if at all) if the teaching programming language were Java for example. This leads us to distinguish between *familiar* and *global* steps within the Single Abstractions stage, and introduce the latter as part of the Formal Operational stage. This supports our understanding that transitioning away from a familiar programming language or codebase is a difficult cognitive step for novices.

The *Formal Operational* stage deals with the understanding of higher level abstractions and their relations. It is further divided into four steps, namely, *single abstractions - global*, *abstraction mapping*, *abstraction systems*, and *principles*. In the *single abstractions - global* step, students should understand general definitions of concepts and their applications to problems in a global setting, either in another programming language than the teaching programming language, or outside the previously introduced frameworks or codebases. Following the memory allocation example, a student at this step should be able to understand how memory allocation works in other languages, e.g., from C++ to Java. The *abstraction mapping* step captures understanding of the general relation of two closely related concepts, such as inheritance and multiple inheritance, functions and friend functions in C++ or their Java counterparts. The *abstraction systems* step refers to the understanding of two distantly related concepts. Coming back to the memory allocation example, a student with *abstraction systems* understanding would be able to articulate the relationship between a program stack and memory management in an operating system. The last step, *principles*, contains unifying principles from the entire domain. For a programming language domain, this could be the understanding of type systems and the advantages and disadvantages of dynamic typing versus static typing for example.

Our process of curriculum mapping proposes to analyse courses by classifying the various concepts that are introduced based on the Neo-Piagetian level at which they are taught and assessed. Using this analysis, we can identify prerequisite concepts and assessment leaps, as well as assumptions about scaffolding and independent study that may have been overlooked. Our process can be applied by a single person (called in the following a *mapper*) or by a group to either one or many courses in a stream, e.g., when ensuring that prerequisite concepts have been taught in previous courses at suitable Neo-Piagetian levels. We discuss the four phases of our process in the following section.

3.1 Concept Framework Definition

In this step, a concept framework is established for the courses in question, derived from various sources such as syllabi, textbooks, curriculum development documents, and accreditation descriptions. A concept may be fine-grained such as "memory allocation" or may be coarse-grained, such as "Object Oriented Programming". The degree of granularity implies the granularity of the ensuring analysis process, but also the degree of accuracy in curriculum mapping.

For each of the concepts defined in Phase 1, Phases 2 and 3 are performed iteratively.

3.2 Classification of Teaching Activities

For each teaching activity, e.g., lecture, tutorial, workshop etc., each specific concept is analysed according to the Neo-Piagetian level it is taught at, which is then recorded in a *concept table.* Each entry is annotated with additional information such as the class activity (i.e., lecture number, tutorial number or week), context information and/or examples. For example, in the Object Oriented Programming (OOP) course analysed in Section 4, *Object oriented design* is taught in Tutorial 4, at a *single abstractions - familiar* level. If the concept is taught at many levels, then these levels and their context are recorded. Ideally, for each concept, we would want to observe a progression from teaching at lower cognitive levels in the Neo-Piaget taxonomy to higher levels of abstraction as the course advances.

3.3 Classification of Assessment Activities

Each concept is analysed according to the Neo-Piagetian level(s) at which it is assessed by reviewing all of the summative assessment components of the course (i.e., practical laboratories, quizzes, exams, etc) - specifically, we identify the perceived Neo-Piagetian level at which the student should be in order to perform well in the assessment. This information is then added to the concept table, recording class activity information (i.e. practical number, assignment title, etc). If the concepts are assessed at more than one level, then, as above, these levels and their contexts are recorded. In terms of introductory programming courses, where scaffolding is needed to assist in transitioning from familiar to global understanding [8], we would want to observe that a concept is assessed at the level where it is taught and only afterwards at a higher level. However, the specific context of the course and the degree of independent learning that is expected may require differing expectations. Undertaking this mapping enables us to understand the degree of difference between the level of teaching and assessment that is actually required within a course, providing a valuable mechanism for course analysis.

3.4 Revision and Comparison

In this final phase, the concept table is analysed and reviewed by all course teaching staff, ensuring that concepts have not been incorrectly classified and producing a time-ordered chart of the teaching and assessment activities within the course. This helps establish the classification of each concept according to the following:

- **Prerequisite** - concept is assessed *without* being taught or is assessed *before* being taught
- **Assessment Leap** - concept is taught at a lower Neo-Piagetian level than it is assessed

Concepts that are taught at a higher Neo-Piagetian level than they are assessed are also highlighted but are of lesser interest to this analysis.

Related courses are then analysed in order to complete the analysis of any identified prerequisite concepts; the goal here is to determine whether prerequisite concepts are taught in prerequisite courses, and if so, at which level are they taught and then subsequently assessed. Ideally, the Neo-Piagetian level at which the prerequisite concept is assessed in the current course should be the same or lower that at which it is taught in prior courses, with the future teaching activity in the current course raising the level of abstraction.

4. CASE STUDY

We applied our methodology to a three-course first year programming sequence, comprising of Object Oriented Programming (OOP), which has one prerequisite course, Introduction to Programming, and one post-requisite course, Data Structures and Algorithm Design, with the aims of identifying assumptions about assessment or prerequisite concepts that might have been overlooked in OOP. The syllabus for OOP commences with a review of fundamental programming constructs before proceeding to an overview of programming in C++, object oriented design and fundamental data structures and algorithms. This course is taught using a combination of teaching activities (lectures, workshops, tutorials) and summative assessment activities (practicals, final examination). We focused our initial analysis on OOP as it had a very high failure rate and lecturers observed that students coming into Data Structures and Algorithm Design struggled with fundamental OOP concepts.

4.1 Concept Framework Definition

We derived concepts primarily from the OOP syllabus, and additionally from the Programming Languages stream and Standard Development Framework from the ACM Ironman [16], as well as from learning outcomes of two equivalent Stanford and MIT courses. Lastly, we included concepts from two programming language textbooks.

The resultant concept table contained approximately 50 concepts and detailed the location and context for each teaching and assessment activity, as well as examples. Space constraints prohibit us from showing the completed table here. Instead, we illustrate the relationship between teaching and assessment activities for specific concepts, and their associated levels diagrammatically. Figure 2 illustrates the teaching and assessment of the *memory management* concept, following a scaffolded teaching/assessment pathway, as indicated by the green arrows. In the following figures, teaching activities are shown as lectures (L), tutorials (T), and workshops (W), while assessment components are indicated as practicals (P).

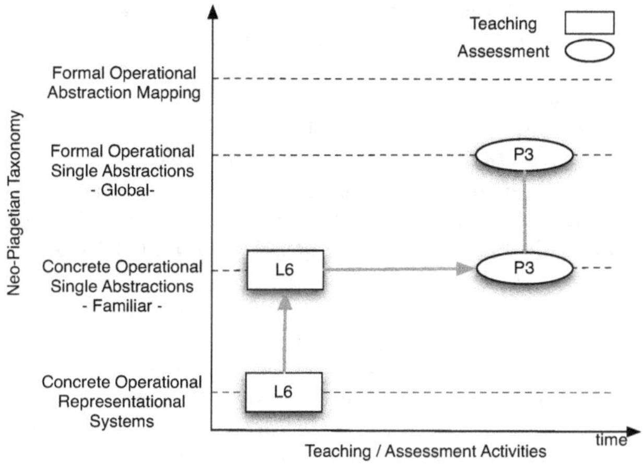

Figure 2: Teaching/Assessment Pathway: Memory Management

In the example in Figure 2, the *memory management* concept is taught at a *representational systems* level in Lecture 6, where it is introduced as "using `new` to create new variables". Then, also in Lecture 6, a discussion about how memory is managed is C++ using pointers follows, at a *single abstractions - familiar* level. Students are then assessed in Practical 3 where they are asked to write functions that allocate and de-allocate memory regions, at a *single abstractions - familiar* level. A subsequent question in the same practical requires students to transition to *single abstractions - global*, when they are asked to perform *string* operations using `char*`, building on the general introduction to pointers provided in Lecture 6.

4.2 Prerequisite Concepts

As shown in Figure 3, we identify prerequisite concepts as those concepts that are assessed without being taught or are assessed before they are taught. The reverse order of teaching/assessment can happen at the same or different Neo-Piagetian levels. For example, within our case study, the concept of *strings* was assessed in two practical sessions prior to any teaching activity. These assessment activities required a *single abstractions - familiar* level of understanding: *write a function that counts the number of letters in a string* and *write a toString method for a structure*, in practicals 0 and 2 respectively. The concept of *strings* is then subsequently taught in Lecture 6, first at a *representational system* level followed by the natural progression to *single abstractions - familiar* level.

In our review of the completed concept table, we analysed the prerequisite course for OOP, Introduction to Programming (taught in Python), and identified that the concept of *strings* is taught at the *single abstractions - familiar* level. This analysis enabled us to determine that the inclusion of the concept "refresher" teaching activity in Lecture 6 was poorly placed, and to be of benefit should be moved prior to any assessment activity.

Within our case study, we identified that *control statements - switch statements* were a prerequisite concept, being assessed at *single abstractions - familiar* in Practical 2. Our continued analysis of the pathway from Introduction to Programming to OOP identified that this prerequisite concept was not previously taught, and accordingly we were then able to identify a needed change. Other examples of identified prerequisite concepts included (broadly): (i) variables & values, (ii) boolean expressions, and (iii) method/functions/parameters.

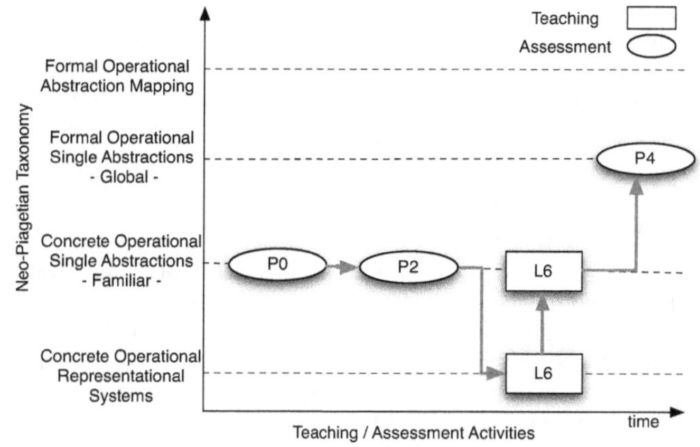

Figure 3: Prerequisite Concepts: String

4.3 Assessment Leaps

Our analysis also permits the identification of assessment leaps as shown in Figure 4 for the concepts of *class definition, methods, and attributes.* Classes are introduced only at a *Representational Systems* level in lecture 9, as: *Classes in C++ are defined as ...; classes represent real objects.* This concept is then assessed at a Single Abstractions - Familiar level when students are asked in Practical 5 to add a `Die` class to a game class hierarchy that is provided to them. Students are then asked to add a `DieRoll` class that would, as the name suggests, roll the die to determine game behaviour. We view this concept as being assessed at a Single Abstractions - Familiar level as students had previously been exposed to the game class hierarchy before, albeit without being introduced to the concept of classes. In contrast, in

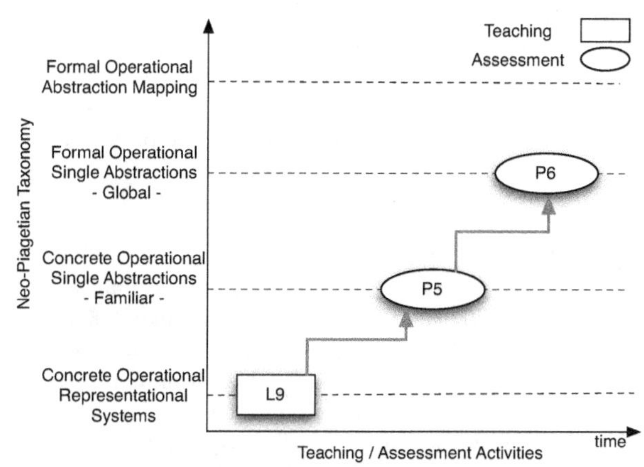

Figure 4: Assessment Leap: Class Definition

Practical 6, the concept of classes is assessed at the Single Abstractions - Global as students are asked to add new classes to QT code. Specifically, students are asked to build custom widgets for a Graphical User Interface. This is their first encounter with QT, the notion of widgets, as well as GUI development, and as such we view this assessment as being at the Single Abstractions - Global level.

4.4 Discussion

Our methodology facilitates the identification of important prerequisite concepts that may be overlooked in initial course design or as the course evolves. Further, it highlights leaps in Neo-Piagetian levels of teaching and assessment, both within and across courses, thus providing a clearer view of specific activities that may need to be revised, expected scaffolding, and assumptions on independent learning. In our case study, we analyse a three course sequence (Introduction to Programming, Object-Oriented Programming and Algorithm Design and Data Structure Analysis) identifying key issues in prerequisite assumptions and gaps in assessment levels. For example, in the third course we had identified that students had previously struggled with practical questions that were classified as *single abstractions - familiar*. Our analysis identified that in the second course (OOP), these same concepts had only been taught at a *representational systems* level and not assessed, leading to a considerable learning gap.

We intend to extend this methodology across our curriculum, continuing to map our prerequisite pathways and assessment leaps. As we progress away from introductory programming, we must contend with differing assumptions and requirements in scaffolding, and also multiple entry pathways complicating our model. In addition, ways to automate our approach will be investigated.

5. CONCLUSIONS

Tracing the development of concepts within and across courses is difficult when various teaching and assessment activities are analysed. We propose a methodology for curriculum analysis that relies on a Neo-Piagetian theory of teaching and assessment activities. For each course, the Neo-Piagetian level at which pre-defined concepts are taught and assessed are recorded. We are then able to identify *prerequisite concepts*, for which a particular Neo-Piagetian level of understanding is required in a course, thus implying that previous courses would require the concept to be taught at a higher or similar Neo-Piagetian level. We further identify *assessment leaps*, in which concepts are only assessed at a higher Neo-Piagetian level than they are taught. Our case study analyses a sequence of three first year programming courses and identifies significant gaps in teaching activities for some core concepts.

6. REFERENCES

[1] W. Dick, L. Carey, and J. Carey. *The Systematic Design of Instruction*. NY: Addison-Wesley, 2001.

[2] K. Falkner, N. Falkner, and R. Vivian. Neo-Piagetian Forms of Reasoning in Software Development Process Construction. In *Proceedings of the First International Conference on Learning and Teaching in Computing and Engineering (LATICE 2013)*, 2013.

[3] R. Gagne and L. Briggs. *Principles of instructional design*. New York: Holt, Rinehart and Winston, 1979.

[4] R. Gluga, J. Kay, R. Lister, and D. Teague. On the reliability of classifying programming tasks using a neo-piagetian theory of cognitive development. In *Proceedings of ICER'12*, pages 31–38, 2012.

[5] Harvard Graduate School of Education. The collaborative curriculum design tool, 2013. http://learnweb.harvard.edu/ccdt/, last accessed August 2013.

[6] J. Kemp, G. Morrison, and S. Ross. *Designing Effective Instruction*. Prentice-Hall, 1996.

[7] C. Knight and R. Sutton. Neo-piagetian theory and research: enhancing pedagogical practice for educators of adults. *London Review of Education*, 2(1):47–60, March 2004.

[8] K.P.Walker and S. Schach. Obstacles to learning a second programming language: An empirical study. *Computer Science Education*, 7:1–20, 1996.

[9] R. Lister. Concrete and other neo-piagetian forms of reasoning in the novice programmer. In *Proceedings of ACE'11*, volume 114, pages 9–18, 2011.

[10] J. Meinke and C. Bauer. Topological sorting as a tool in curriculum planning. In *Proceedings of the sixth SIGCSE technical symposium on Computer science education*, pages 61–66, 1976.

[11] H. Mima. Mima search: a structuring knowledge system towards innovation for engineering education. In *Proceedings of the Association for Computational Linguistics Conference on Interactive Presentation Sessions*, pages 21–24, 2006.

[12] S. Morra, C. Gobbo, Z. Marini, and R. Sheese. *Cognitive Development: Neo-Piagetian Perspectives*. Lawrence Erlbaum Associates, 2008.

[13] J. Piaget and B. Inhelder. *The Psychology of the Child*. Routledge and Kegan Paul, 1969.

[14] R. Reiser and W. Dick. *Instructional Planning: A Guide for Teachers*. Boston, MA: Allyn and Bacon, 2nd edition edition, 1996.

[15] T. Sekiya, Y. Matsuda, and K. Yamaguchi. Analysis of computer science related curriculum on lda and isomap. In *Proceedings of iTiCSE'10*, 2010.

[16] The Joint Task Force on Computing Curricula Association for Computing Machinery IEEE-Computer Society. Computer Science Curricula 2013, Ironman Draft 1.0. Technical report. http://cs2013.org, last accessed 26th August 2013.

[17] M. Tungere, X. Yu, W. Cameron, G. Teng, M. Perez-Quinones, L. Cassel, W. Fan, and E. Fox. Towards a syllabus repository for computer science courses. In *Proceedings of the SIGCSE Technical Symposium on Computer Science Education*, pages 55–59, 2007.

[18] M. Veenman, J. Elshout, and J. Meijer. The generality vs domain-specificity of metacognitive skills in novice learning across domains. *Learning and Instruction*, 7(2):187–209, 1997.

[19] M. Wiske, M. Sick, and S. Wirsig. New technologies to support teaching for understanding. *International Journal of Educational Research*, 35(5):483–501, 2001.

[20] R. Zucker. Vicurrias: a curriculum visualization tool for faculty, advisors, and students. *Journal of Computing Sciences in Colleges*, 25(2):138–145, 2009.

Active Learning During Lecture Using Tablets

Barry L. Kurtz
James B. Fenwick
Rahman Tashakkori
Appalachian State University
Boone, NC 26808
828-262-2370
{blk,jbf,rt}@cs.appstate.edu

Ahmad Esmaili
Stony Brook University
Stony Brook, NY 11794-4400
631-632-1628
esmaili@cs.stonybrook.edu

Stephen R. Tate
University of North Carolina
at Greensboro
Greensboro, NC 27402
336-256-1112
srtate@uncg.edu

ABSTRACT

Closed labs have provided hands-on experience for students under supervised conditions. Microlabs extend this approach into the lecture format with very short hands-on activities in the "middle of the lecture." We have tested this approach using tablets as small as 7 inches; student laptops can also be used. Logical microlabs allow students to solve a conceptual problem in computer science that does not involve any programming. Solutions are entered graphically and submitted for evaluation. Code magnet microlabs allow students to construct a method to solve the same problem programmatically. The code is compiled and, if successful, evaluated by a sequence of unit tests. These are integrated into a Microlab Learning Cycle of exploration (the logical microlab), invention (the instructor guides the students toward an algorithm during lecture), and application (the code magnet microlab). This approach has been evaluated at three universities and proven to be popular with students and educationally effective. This work is supported, in part, by three National Science Foundation grants.

Categories and Subject Descriptors K.3.2 [Computer and Information Science Education] Computer Science Education

Keywords active learning, automated grading, tablets

1. APPROACHES TO ACTIVE LEARNING

A microlab is a 5-10 minute activity that occurs during lecture, students can work individually or in pairs, answers are submitted to an automated grading system, students are given constructive feedback if the submitted solution is not correct, modified solutions can be re-submitted for evaluation. The use of microlabs is based on the Learning Cycle model of instruction.

1.1 The Learning Cycle

The Learning Cycle was developed by Robert Karplus in the 1960s as part of the Science Curriculum Improvement Study [4]. This model of instruction has three phases:

1. Exploration – after a brief introduction to the topic students are asked to explore a particular problem and see whether they can discover a solution. This is guided discovery in the sense that as students work on the problem they receive feedback that guides them towards a correct solution.
2. Invention – once students have experienced trying to solve one or more problems in the target topic, the instructor, supported by the textbook or other learning resources, introduces the topic, as is commonly done in class lectures.
3. Application – Once the students are introduced to the topic both experientially (the exploration phase) and formally (the invention phase) they apply this knowledge to related problems in the domain. For computer science students this often means writing a program or methods in a program that allows the computer to solve problems in the target domain.

1.2 Automated Grading Systems

Ken Bowles at the University of California San Diego introduced the use of automatically-graded programming quizzes to support instruction in UCSD Pascal in the CS1 course in the late 1970s [2]. Kurtz has used this approach at three universities: the University of California Irvine, New Mexico State University [7], and Appalachian State University [6].

WEB-CAT is a grading system developed at Virginia Tech that evaluates student programs on three criteria: a test validity score, a test correctness score, and a code correctness score. [3]

Praktomat [12] is a web-based manager for programming labs; Praktomat automatically compiles, tests and checks the submitted programs; submissions not meeting the quality criteria are rejected.

Our automated grading of code magnet microlabs takes a similar approach to those noted above. We extend this approach to conceptual problems by automatically grading logical microlabs where students have entered a solution to a problem graphically, such as constructing a binary tree with nodes and edges.

1.3 Visual Programming Languages

A visual programming language (VPL) allows users to create programs by manipulating program elements graphically rather than by specifying them textually. Three widely used examples are:

- Alice, a freeware object-oriented educational programming language with an integrated development environment (IDE) that uses a drag and drop environment to create computer animations using 3D models. [1]
- Scratch, created by the MIT Media Lab, is intended to motivate learning in pre-college students through experimenting and creating projects, such as interactive animations, games, etc. [9]
- AppInventor, also from MIT, is a VPL for building mobile applications targeting the Android platform [8].

Our code magnets interface is similar to a visual programming language in using a drag and drop approach to compose program

SIGCSE'14, March 5–8, 2014, Atlanta, Georgia, USA.

http://dx.doi.org/10.1145/2538862.2538907

code for methods but does not attempt to provide the open-ended flexibility of a VPL.

2. THE MICROLAB LEARNING CYCLE

The Microlab Learning Cycle includes exploration (the logical microlab), invention (the instructor guides the students toward an algorithm), and application (the code magnet microlab). In the subsections that follow, we will describe each phase in the context of a problem involving binary trees.

2.1 Exploration – the logical microlab

A logical microlab asks a student to solve a conceptual problem in computer science. The problem does not involve any programming. Solutions are entered graphically and submitted for evaluation. To illustrate this process consider the following microlab where a student is asked to build a binary tree given the preorder and the inorder traversals (see Figure 1).

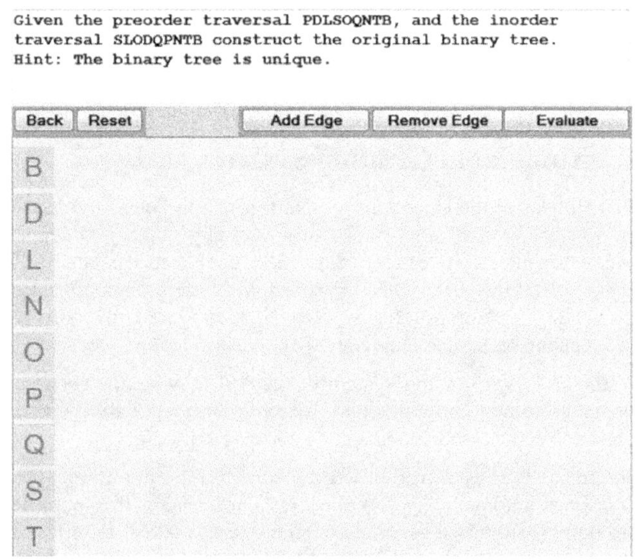

Figure 1: Initial Screen

A solution that is close to correct is shown in Figure 2.

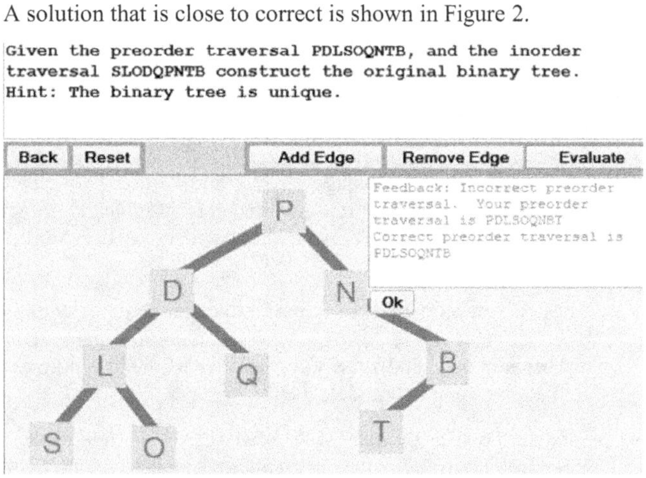

Figure 2: An Incorrect Solution

Notice that the feedback is designed to guide a student to the correct solution. The student can quickly spot that the nodes are mostly correct except for B and T. Adjustment of these nodes leads to the correct solution shown in Figure 3. If students do not find a correct solution in the allotted time, the instructor asks them to stop working on the problem and return their attention to lecture. Some students will not complete the activity in the time allowed, so all attempts are saved by the system allowing students to complete the problem outside of class. We have found that if students are given full credit for solutions submitted by the start of the next lecture period, they are willing to put down unfinished work and engage in lecture again.

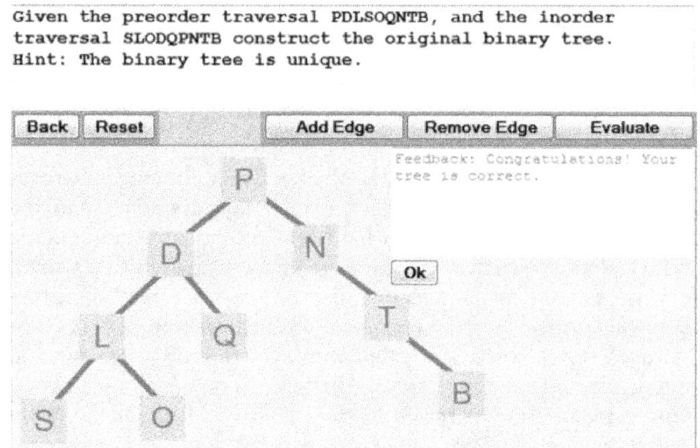

Figure 3: A Correct Solution

2.2 Invention – developing the algorithm

Building on the experiences with the logical microlab, it is the instructor's job to guide students toward an algorithm that will build the binary tree based on the preorder and inorder traversals. An instructor can begin by eliciting observations from the logical microlab activity, such as those below.

- The first node in the preorder traversal is the root of the tree.
- This node divides the inorder traversal into the inorder traversal of the left subtree and the inorder traversal of the right subtree.
- Using the lengths of these two inorder traversals, the left and right preorder traversals can be determined.
- The left and right subtrees can be built recursively.
- One or more base cases are needed to stop the recursion.

Discussion of these observations then leads to a pseudocode algorithm, such as:

- *If the traversals are empty, return null*
- *Create the root using the first node in the preorder traversal*
- *If the traversal has a single node, return the root*
- *Find the preorder and inorder traversals of the left subtree*
- *Use recursion to build the left subtree*
- *Find the preorder and inorder traversals of the right subtree*
- *Use recursion to build the right subtree*
- *Return the root*

2.3 Application – the code magnet microlab

The Head First Java book [10] presents exercises for students using a "code magnets" approach in a static format. We have adapted this approach as a way to allow the student to enter program code for methods using the "drag and drop" approach from logical microlabs to create methods that can be compiled and tested. Figure 4 shows the list of magnets available to create the method that will build a general binary tree (GBT) from the preorder and inorder traversals.

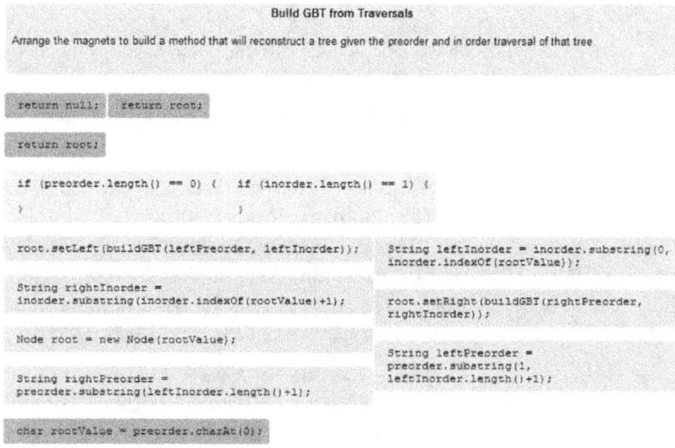

Figure 4: Code Magnets for the buildGBT Method

The student drags and drops these magnets into an initially empty method, shown in Figure 5.

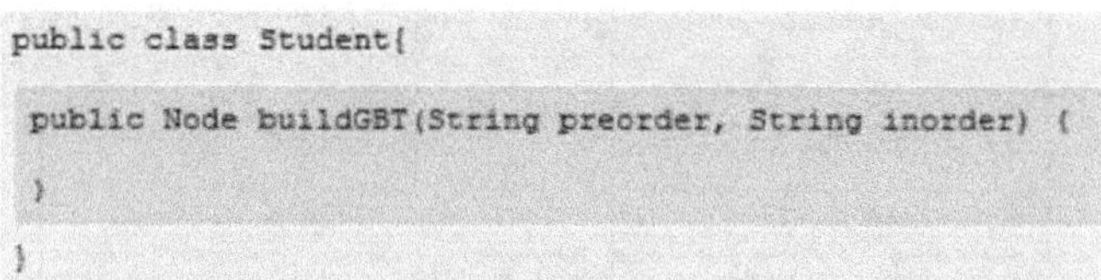

Figure 5: The Empty buildGBT Method

After students place the magnets as desired, they press the Finalize button to compile their code and, if successful, perform unit testing. For the problem shown, the magnets represent actual Java code that is assembled into a program and tested. The feedback for a correct solution for the buildGBT method is shown in Figure 6. In subsequent figures we will show feedback for solutions that do not compile or do not run as intended.

```
Test (0): Passed!

public class Student{

    public Node buildGBT(String preorder, String inorder) {

        if (preorder.length() == 0) {
            return null;
        }

        char rootValue = preorder.charAt(0);
        Node root = new Node(rootValue);

        if (inorder.length() == 1) {
            return root;
        }

        String leftInorder = inorder.substring(0, inorder.indexOf(rootValue));
        String leftPreorder = preorder.substring(1, leftInorder.length()+1);
        root.setLeft(buildGBT(leftPreorder, leftInorder));
        String rightInorder = inorder.substring(inorder.indexOf(rootValue)+1);
        String rightPreorder = preorder.substring(leftInorder.length()+1);
        root.setRight(buildGBT(rightPreorder, rightInorder));
        return root;
    }

}
```

Figure 6: A Correct Solution for buildGBT

Notice that the length of the inorder traversal of the left subtree is used to construct the left preorder traversal. If the student places these code magnets in the incorrect order, there will be a compile error as shown in Figure 7.

```
Compilation Error:
/tmp/magnets/TutorialGuest/Student.java:17: error: cannot find symbol
            String leftPreorder = preorder.substring(1, leftInorder.length()+1);
                                                        ^
  symbol:   variable leftInorder
  location: class Student
1 error
```

Figure 7: A Method with a Compile Error

It is important that the test program includes limiting cases. For the buildGBT method having empty traversals is a limiting case. If the student does not include the magnets for this base case, as shown in Figure 8, the code compiles but produces a runtime error when the unit test with empty traversals is performed.

```
Exception in thread \"main\" java.lang.StringIndexOutOfBoundsException: String index out of range: 0
        at java.lang.String.charAt(String.java:658)
        at Student.buildGBT(Student.java:5)
        at Student.buildGBT(Student.java:17)
        at Student.buildGBT(Student.java:17)
        at Student.buildGBT(Student.java:14)
        at BuildGBTTest.test(BuildGBTTest.java:26)
        at BuildGBTTest.main(BuildGBTTest.java:6)

public class Student{

    public Node buildGBT(String preorder, String inorder) {
        char rootValue = preorder.charAt(0);
        Node root = new Node(rootValue);

        if (inorder.length() == 1) {
            return root;
        }

        String leftInorder = inorder.substring(0, inorder.indexOf(rootValue));
        String leftPreorder = preorder.substring(1, leftInorder.length()+1);
        root.setLeft(buildGBT(leftPreorder, leftInorder));
        String rightInorder = inorder.substring(inorder.indexOf(rootValue)+1);
        String rightPreorder = preorder.substring(leftInorder.length()+1);
        root.setRight(buildGBT(rightPreorder, rightInorder));
        return root;
    }

}
```

Figure 8: A Method with Runtime Errors

In the code magnet lab illustrated above, every given magnet is used to create the correct method. Often it is pedagogically useful to include additional magnets, say one with a < comparison and another with a <= comparison, so that the student must decide which magnet is logically correct. Problems with alternative magnets are more challenging and require more time for students to solve. The instructor can choose whether to include alternative magnets or not. Alternative magnets work well for simple algorithms often found in a CS1 or CS2 course. For complex algorithms, such as the buildGBT, alternative magnets, such as modifying parameters in the substring operation, may appear to be "tricky", slow down the solution process, and not contribute to the main purpose of the microlab (the use of recursion with smaller traversals and including the base cases).

Code magnet labs are not intended to replace programming assignments. Rather they replace explanations of code during lecture with an activity that forces each student to construct the algorithm interactively. Follow up activities can be the basis of programming assignments. For example for the build tree activities described above, students may be asked to write a complete program, including testing, to build a binary tree given the inorder and postorder traversals. Readers interested in trying a variety of logical or code magnet microlabs can visit [11].

We have tested the code magnets approach with students working on tablets, laptops, and desktop computers. Figure 9 shows a student working on a 7" Google Nexus tablet.

Figure 9: Solving a Code Magnet Problem on a 7" Tablet

3. TESTING WITH TABLETS

3.1 Results from Appalachian State

All testing of microlabs in the 2012-2013 academic year was performed on 7" tablets, as seen in Figure 10. We selected the Nexus 7 tablet because it was affordable and could be easily distributed to students at the start of class. It also provided a good test of the lower limits on screen size where students are still able to complete lab activities. Figure 11 shows use of tablets in a large lecture hall.

Figure 10: Students Using Microlabs on the Google Nexus 7

Figure 11: Using Tablets in a Large Lecture Hall

Testing was performed in multiple sections of three courses we call CS1, CS2, and CS3:

- CS1: Introduction to programming using Java and BlueJ
- CS2: Finishes leftover topics in Java (e.g., GUI, file I/O, exceptions, threads), introduces linear data structures (lists, stacks, queues), covers searching and sorting
- CS3: Completes data structures (dictionaries, binary trees, search trees, balanced search trees, heaps, graphs) and introduces advanced algorithms

Code magnets were used at all three levels; logical microlabs were only used in the CS3 course.

Four sections of the CS1 class participated to test code magnet labs taught by three different instructors (sections 101 and 103 had the same instructor). Usage varied with instructor; section 104 used six labs, 101 and 103 used nine labs, and 102 used thirteen labs. As shown in Table 1, the success rate for 647 attempted labs was 89.7% correctly solved by the start of the next class period.

Table 1 – Results for CS1

Topic	# sections	# students	% correct
Arrays: find max	3	57	82.5
Arrays: find average	3	50	98.0
Arrays: index of max	3	53	77.4
Arrays: swap min max	3	39	71.8
ArrayLists:Ins/Remove	2	36	72.2
ArrayList: Add	2	38	97.4
ArrayList: ArithSeries	2	33	84.8
Strings DoubleLetter	4	76	97.4
Strings: DoubleWord	4	73	98.6
Strings: Count Occur.	4	72	98.6
Strings: Palendrome	1	15	73.3
HashMaps: Insert	2	39	97.4
HashMaps: Remove	2	36	97.4
for: sumOddNumbers	1	16	87.5
for: isPerfectSquare	1	14	64.3
TOTAL		**647**	**89.7**

There were two sections of CS2 taught by two different instructors. Each section used the same seven code magnet labs (Table 2). These labs were more challenging than the CS1 labs. The overall success rate was 81.4%. The first lab, a method to check the balance of parentheses in an expression using a stack, caused the most difficulty with a success rate of 56.7%. In general we have found performance improves as students become more familiar with microlabs.

Table 2 – Results for CS2

Lab Description	# students	Overall % Correct
Stacks: Balance Checker	30	56.7
Stacks: Postfix Helper	32	96.9
Stacks: Postfix Evaluation	28	71.4
Big Integer: Add	38	71.1
Big Integer: Digit Multiply	33	90.9
Big Integer: Multiply	32	90.6
Queues: Josephus	33	90.9
TOTAL	**226**	**81.4**

CS3 students used both logical microlabs (30 different labs covering 11 topics) and code magnet microlabs (7 distinct labs). The logical labs were grouped into clusters of 2 to 4 problems of the same type (Table 3). Earlier use of these labs in the previous semester indicated that some students used a "guess and check" strategy where these students rapidly submitted alternative solutions until they stumbled onto the correct solution. By varying the grade based on the number of submissions (100% for 1-5, 90% for 6-10, and 80% for more than 10) we found the average number of submissions dropped dramatically to slightly less than two attempts until a correct solution was found. The average score for the logical microlabs was 95.7% (287.2/300).

Table 3 – Results for Logical Microlabs in CS3

CS3 logical labs	#	Max	Avg
Insert into a BST	2	20	20.0
Build a BST from postorder	3	30	29.6
Build GBT from traversals	3	30	29.6
Hashing - linear probe	2	20	20.0
Hashing - quadratic probe	2	20	19.8
Insert into a heap	4	40	36.5
Delete from a heap	2	20	17.9
Build a heap	4	40	37.1
Heapsort	2	20	16.7
Min Span Tree - Prim	3	30	30.0
Min Span Tree - Kruskal	3	30	30.0
TOTAL	**30**	**300**	**287.2**

Table 4 shows the results for the code magnet microlabs used in CS3. The average of 93.6% (65.5/70) is substantially higher than other graded activities in the course.

Table 4 – Results for Code Magnet Microlabs in CS3

Lab Description	Max	Avg
Linear search - iterative	10	10.0
Linear search - recursive	10	9.8
Binary search - iterative	10	7.3
Binary search - recursive	10	8.8
Insert nodes into a BST	10	9.9
Build BST from Postorder	10	9.9
Build GBT from traversals	10	9.9
TOTAL	**70**	**65.5**

Long term retention was measured by asking similar problems on the course exams. The microlab exam problems required transfer to a new domain, such as "Given the postorder traversal 1 4 7 6 3 13 14 10 8 draw the original binary search tree." These problems were mid-level in difficutly; there were many easier problems (multiple choice, fill in the blank, short answer) and one or two more challenging problems (write the code for a method from scratch). Table 5 summarizes these results. The overall average of 82.6% (72.7/88) is lower than the microlab performance indicated in Tables 3-4; however, students in an exam setting only have one attempt to solve the problem and receive no feedback. We are encouraged because this 82.6% result represented much better performance than other questions on the exam; the averages for the <u>other</u> questions were 69.7% for midterm 1, 72.4% for midterm 2, and 67.2% for the final exam.

Table 5 – Long Term Retention in CS3

Retention on exams	Exam	Max	Avg
Hashing (2), write iterative binary search code	mid 1	15	11.8
Insert BST, Build BST & GBT, insert heap, heapify, heapsort	mid 2	30	22.7
Traversals, heapsort, hash tables, MST, build binary trees	final	43	38.2
TOTAL		**88**	**72.7**

3.2 Appalachian State Focus Groups

Amy Germuth of EvalWorks visited with students in the four CS1 classes, the two CS2 classes, and the CS3 class. She actually observed students using microlabs in two classes (the HashMaps code magnet labs in CS1 and the minimum spanning tree logic microlabs in CS3). Also, she met with each of the instructors. Her evaluation is presented below verbatim.

> ***There is a direct relationship between exposure to Microlabs and how positively students view them.*** Students who had been exposed to the greatest number of Microlabs found them the most useful, liked them the best, and had much fewer complaints about having to log in, the interface, or how much time they took to complete.
>
> ***Students noted multiple positive aspects of Microlabs,*** including that they provide opportunities for practice; are hands-on; provide feedback; engage students in problem-solving; and give the form of coding while allowing students to see the "bigger picture". Students commented that Microlabs "helped me figure out the logic behind the code without having to worry about syntax", "reinforce concepts that we are learning", and "helps you recognize bugs in other people's code". Multiple students suggested that more challenging Microlabs were needed and that instructors should implement a "guessing" penalty so students actually put effort into finding solutions.

3.3 Results from UNCG and Stony Brook

In the Spring 2012 semester 22 students in a data structures class at UNCG completed the logical and the programming microlabs for the binary tree topics. There were no magnet microlabs and no tablets involved in this testing. The results are shown in Table 6. These are comparable with more recent results at other schools. It should be noted the scores for programming microlabs where students had to type in code were lower than the corresponding magnet microlabs used in later testing.

Two groups of students participated in a control group – experimental group study at SUNY Stony Brook. In the Spring 2012 semester the instructor used traditional lecture to teach 26 students how to traverse binary trees, how to build a binary search tree (BST) from a postorder traversal, and how to build a general binary tree (GBT) from the preorder and inorder traversals. These topics were tested using three exam questions. A similar group of 25 students was taught the same topics in the Fall 2012 semester using microlabs; this group was given the same set of exam questions. As seen in Table 7, there was an 8 to 10% gain in performance by the group that used the microlabs. When a t-test was applied to these two groups, the result was statistically significant ($p=0.038$). There was no significant difference in performance between the groups on the remaining test problems.

Table 6: Results at UNCG

UNC Greensboro	% Correct (logical)	% Correct (program)
Traversals	94.1	90.7
BST Insert	89.9	82.1
Build BST	81.2	78.8
Build GBT	79.1	74.5

Table 7 – Results from SUNY Stony Brook

SUNY Stony Brook	traversals	Build BST	Build GBT
Spring 2012	88%	75%	89%
Fall 2012	97%	85%	97%
Gain/Loss	+9%	+10%	+8%

4. CURRENT DEVELOPMENTS

Our microlabs are developed using Google Web Toolkit (GWT) as reported in [5]. Most instructors don't have time to learn GWT to develop new labs from scratch so we are modifying existing labs so instructors can modify content. For example, for the binary tree activities, the instructor can graphically enter the desired tree, either as input (as in traversals) or as the result (as in building a tree from the preorder and inorder traversals). For the logical microlabs dealing with sorting, the instructor can specify the data sets for the sorts. Similar modifications have been made to other logical labs.

Code magnet microlabs are currently implemented for Java. When the instructor designs a code magnet lab there are two levels for each magnet: what appears on the face of the magnet and the code that is generated for compiling and testing. This allows the magnet to appear as psuedocode, such as "Create the root using the first node in the preorder traversal" while the generated code is actual Java code (char rootValue = preorder.charAt(0); Node root = new Node(rootValue);).

We are currently expanding the user interface to allow students to select simple expressions as found in the control of while loops, for loops, and if statements. For example, the code magnet for a for loop will be "for (<<initialization>>; <<termination>>; <<continuation>>) { … }" where each item will be selected from a pull-down menu of possible choices as specified by the problem designer for the given context.

5. CONCLUSIONS

The microlab learning cycle is based on well-established learning theory with three stages of instruction: exploration, invention and application. The logical microlabs are an exploratory activity when the students are asked to solve conceptual problems with a minimum of guidance. Logical microlabs work well on tablets and are the most popular type of microlab. The latest versions can be modified by instructors without having to learn GWT.

During the invention phase the instructor guides students in the development of an algorithm to solve the problem introduced in the logical microlab. Then the application phase focuses on using code magnets to construct, compile and test the algorithm using Java program code.

Testing for the last year has focused on tablets as the delivery mechanism, but laptops and desktops can also be used for delivery. We have used microlabs during lecture but they can also be used during closed labs or outside of class. Students have found microlabs to be valuable review tools when studying for exams. A control group – experimental group model was used at SUNY Stony Brook and there was found to be learning gains of 8-10% with a statistical significance of $p = 0.038$. Similar results are reported at Appalachian State when the success on exam problems based on microlabs was compared with success on other exam problems. We have just received a new NSF grant for the next two years to help disseminate the microlab approach to computer science educators at other universities

6. ACKNOWLEDGMENTS

This work has been supported in part by two active NSF grants: Developing Software and Methodologies for eBook/Browsers to Enhance Learning (DUE1044572) and Transforming Computer Science Education with Microlabs (DUE1122752). Continuing support for the 2013-14 and 2014-15 academic years is provided by Collaborative Research: Innovative Active Learning Using Tablets (DUE 1323178).

7. REFERENCES

[1] Alice Educational Software Website http://www.alice.org/

[2] K. Bowles, A CS1 course based on Stand-Alone Microcomputers, SIGCSE Bulletin, Vol. 9, No. 1, February 1978, 125-127

[3] S. Edwards, M. Perez-Quinones, Web-CAT: automatically grading programming assignments, ITiCSE 2000, ACM Press, page 328

[4] R. Fuller (editor), "A Love of Discovery: Science Education – The Second Career of Robert Karplus", Kluwer Academic/Plenum Publishers, 2002, chapter 4

[5] B. Kurtz, J. Fenwick, and P. Meznar, "Developing Microlabs Using Google Web Toolkit," Proceedings of the 43rd SIGCSE Technical Symposium on Computer Science Education (SIGCSE '12), 2012.

[6] B. Kurtz, J. Fenwick Jr., C. Ellsworth, "The Quiver System," SIGCSE Technical Symposium on Computer Science Education, Norfolk, February 2004.

[7] B. Kurtz, H. Pfeiffer, "Developing Programming Quizzes to Support Instruction in Abstract Data Types", SIGCSE Bulletin, Vol. 21, No. 1, February 1989, pp. 66-70

[8] MIT Center for Mobile Learning, "Welcome to MIT App Inventor." Retrieved Aug 25, 2013 from http://appinventor.mit.edu

[9] Scratch Educational Software Website http://scratch.mit.edu/

[10] K. Sierra, B. Bates, Head First Java, O'Reilly Media; 2nd edition, February 9, 2005

[11] Web Automated Grading System, *http://cs.appstate.edu/wags/guest.*

[12] A. Zeller, Making Students Read and Review Code, ITiCSE 2000, ACM Press, pp. 89-9

Teaching CS 1 with POGIL Activities and Roles

Helen H. Hu
Westminster College
Computer Science Department
Salt Lake City, UT 84105
hhu@westminstercollege.edu

Tricia D. Shepherd
Westminster College
Chemistry Department
Salt Lake City, UT 84105
tshepherd@westminstercollege.edu

ABSTRACT

The computer science community has started to experiment with *process oriented guided inquiry learning*, or POGIL, a learning approach that focuses on concept and process skills development by having students work together in organized teams. By emphasizing the learning process and group discussions, instructors who implement POGIL activities and roles in their classrooms may better address the different needs of their CS 1 students.

After explaining how POGIL activities differ from other group activities, this paper elaborates on the importance of incorporating the learning cycle when developing a POGIL activity, so as to encourage rich group discussions and teamwork. It then describes the role of the instructor in a POGIL activity, and how POGIL roles need to be adapted for programming activities. It presents the results of using six POGIL activities in three CS 1 sections at a comprehensive liberal arts college, where the pass rate for female students increased compared to historical female pass rates for that class. Students who were introduced to recursion through a POGIL activity appear to have learned the material as well and retained the material better than students who learned recursion through a more traditional group activity.

Categories and Subject Descriptors

K.3.2 [**Computers and Education**]: Computer and Information Science Education—*Computer Science Education*

General Terms

Management, Human Factors

Keywords

POGIL, active learning, inquiry based learning, process skills, student-centered learning

SIGCSE'14, March 5–8, 2014, Atlanta, GA, USA.

ACM 978-1-4503-2605-6/14/03 ...$15.00.
http://dx.doi.org/10.1145/2538862.2538954 .

1. INTRODUCTION

One of the challenges of teaching CS 1 classes is that while the focus of the course appears to be programming language syntax and writing correct programs, it is actually as important that students learn computational thinking and debugging skills. In fact, a student who writes an incorrect program and systematically debugs the program may learn more from an assignment than a student who writes a working program on the first try.

Another common feature of many CS 1 classes is the broad range of backgrounds of students taking the course. Some may have learned to program on their own, but could still benefit from a deeper understanding of the computational thinking skills central to a CS 1 course. For others, it may be their first exposure to CS and the only opportunity to capture their interest enough to encourage them to pursue a major. Related to this assortment of programming experience is the goal of attracting more diverse students to the field, including women and underrepresented minorities. The question for a CS 1 instructor is how to best address such a wide variety of needs and students in this context.

Process Oriented Guided Inquiry Learning, or POGIL, is a student-centered learning approach that places as much emphasis on *how* students learn as on *what* students learn. Instead of passively listening to a traditional lecture, students work together in groups on carefully designed activities that guide students through the construction of CS content (the *guided inquiry learning* of POGIL). When students discover concepts for themselves, they remember them better. In addition, this active learning approach emphasizes student development of key process skills, such as critical thinking, problem solving, teamwork, and leadership skills (the *process oriented* focus of POGIL). This research-based pedagogy has been demonstrated to be highly effective in high school and college chemistry classrooms across the country [8].

Detailed comparisons of how POGIL differs from other active learning pedagogies like Peer Instruction and Problem Based Learning are provided in [3, 5], but the three defining features of POGIL are:

1. **Roles in teams**: Students are organized into self-managed learning teams, in which they are assigned specific roles such as Spokesperson and Process Analyst.
2. **Inquiry-based activities**: Students work through guided inquiry-based activities that are designed with the learning process in mind.
3. **Process skills**: The instructor facilitates an environment that promotes the development of process skills.

Recently, several computer science instructors have been implementing these three features in their classrooms. Through the CS POGIL community and at SIGCSE 2013, the authors have met several college and university professors who have incorporated POGIL activities in their CS 1 classes, including instructors from James Madison University and Moravian College. We are also aware of POGIL implementations in high school classes, CS 2, and upper division classes like Software Engineering, Computer Organization, Operating Systems and AI [7]. While some CS instructors have published experience reports about using POGIL in their classrooms, little has been published about its efficacy.

The authors of this paper have used POGIL pedagogy to teach computer programming to science majors five times since 2005. This upper-division science course teaches students how to program, with an emphasis on problem solving and algorithm design. Students also learn how to create dynamic computer simulation models, to interpret models' results, and to use models to develop an understanding of scientific processes. Many of the 24 POGIL activities developed for this science course are available at http://cspogil.org. However, most rely heavily on the science and math pre-requisites for the class and thus are unsuitable for CS 1 classes.

As reported in [5], science students (taught by POGIL in this science course) were more successful than CS 1 students (taught by traditional methods) in completing an identical programming assignment. Of those students who completed the assignment, more of the POGIL-taught students turned in clean and efficient code, while more of the traditionally-taught students turned in working but convoluted programs.

Drawing on the experience of writing and facilitating POGIL to teach programming in a less traditional context, this paper describes the experience of adopting POGIL pedagogy to a CS 1 class. We will address two primary challenges computer science instructors face in implementing POGIL: 1) developing appropriate guided inquiry activities, and 2) facilitating the learning groups and process skill development in the classroom. We will present both our data on the retention of knowledge by CS 1 students continuing on to CS 2, and the pass rates of CS 1 students. Because class sizes are small, the results presented in this paper are not statistically significant, but they do suggest that retention rates and female students' pass rates may be increased by incorporating POGIL activities and roles.

Progress has been made on the first challenge of generating the guided inquiry activities. As part of a NSF funded project, Kussmaul has created an online repository for POGIL activities at http://cspogil.org [6]. The activities described in this paper are available online to instructors who create an account at the repository.

The second challenge of facilitating for POGIL has not previously been addressed in the literature, but appears anecdotally to be a common problem for CS instructors experimenting with POGIL. Traditionally, three to four students work together as a team through a POGIL activity. Group size tends not to be a problem if the activity does not require programming. However in CS 1 classes, programming is central to the course, and most CS 1 POGIL activities require some computer programming. Many instructors report difficulties keeping students engaged in groups of three or more, and at least one has reverted back to groups of two after attempting larger group sizes [10]. This paper describes how a hybrid of POGIL and Pair Programming roles can be used to keep students engaged during programming exercises.

This paper also demonstrates that some difficulties with larger group sizes can be overcome by designing more challenging activities that require the entire group to work together. Instructors can also improve group dynamics by emphasizing each group member's responsibilities (as Facilitator, Spokesperson, Quality Control or Process Analyst) and the benefits of becoming proficient at process skills. The authors believe this extra effort is worthwhile because the larger group sizes encourage more accountability and richer discussions between students, both of which are important features of POGIL. Working in larger groups may also help develop a sense of community among students, which in turn may increase pass rates and retention in the major. This impact may be particularly beneficial to underrepresented student groups, similar to the positive effects of pair programming demonstrated among female students [12]. In addition, the fact that Computer Science students resist working in larger teams suggests that they may have more to learn about process skills than students in other fields.

The next section of this paper describes the process of authoring POGIL activities, followed by a discussion of POGIL classroom implementation and how to improve group dynamics for larger group sizes. The paper then presents results from incorporating POGIL pedagogy in the first author's CS 1 course, concluding with resources for those interested in learning more about POGIL.

2. POGIL ACTIVITIES

POGIL activities are designed to guide students through exploration to construct their own knowledge of computer science concepts. While there is no signature template, all POGIL activities have a series of "Models" that provide students with examples of information from which they can build a deeper understanding. This information is typically not explicitly stated in the Model's text, but rather presented through carefully selected examples from which students can derive concepts when responding to the questions that follow each Model. These questions are designed to guide students through the learning cycle of *exploration, concept invention and application.*

For example, after learning about assignment statements, students would be provided with a Model of code illustrating a series of assignment statements, without explicitly stating that the code segment "swaps" the values of two variables. In the following questions, students would first *explore* what is directly demonstrated in the Model by identifying the values of each variable at the beginning and end of the code segments. *Concept invention* questions would follow, prompting students to discover ideas for themselves before the standard term is introduced (in this example, "swap"). Students would be asked to consider incorrect swap code ($x = y$; $y = x$;) and would *invent* the concept of using an additional variable as a place holder, recognizing this temporary variable as the essential piece of the new knowledge. *Application* questions would require students to *apply* and extend the newly learned concepts in exercises and longer programming problems. (For a more concrete example of a POGIL Model, see [5], which includes one in its entirety, accompanied by detailed commentary.)

POGIL materials differ from many computer science labs because of this guided inquiry design. Students in a typical computer science lab are expected to apply what they have learned in class earlier that week to a series of programming exercises. While the lab exercises may grow progressively more difficult, students are typically only answering application questions, the last step of the learning cycle. For example, after learning about assignment statements, students would simply be asked to come up with the code to swap the value of two variables. At this point, a few students might be able to figure out the answer for themselves, but many will simply implement what is explicitly provided by another student or the professor without realizing the key features that made the solution possible. A POGIL activity is intended to make explicit for a larger number of students the underlying concepts, key features, and experiential process from which the solution to an application is derived.

2.1 Developing POGIL Activities

The authors of this paper first began developing POGIL activities together in 2005 for an introductory programming course for junior and senior science majors that they co-taught at a comprehensive liberal arts college. This course met for two hours at a time, twice a week (for a total of four hours each week) in a classroom with laptops. A new POGIL activity was provided at the start of most class periods, and most POGIL activities concluded with one or more programming exercises to be completed as homework.

The authors continued to refine the POGIL activities each time they taught the course, taking advantage of the pairing of a content expert (the first author) and a POGIL expert (the second author). In the first few iterations, most questions were application questions that resembled a traditional computer lab, but over the years, Models were improved and questions for the full learning cycle were added. Another improvement was leaving only short application questions at the end of each Model, while moving longer programming exercises to the end of the entire lesson. Finally, more higher-level process questions were added to the lessons, explicitly asking students to develop pseudocode. These questions made it possible to remove the more detailed coding instructions from previous versions of the lessons.

In the last year, the first author converted these activities for use in a CS 1 class, by switching programming languages (Python to Java), removing scientific and mathematical applications, and increasing the emphasis on debugging. Other activities were developed with the first author identifying a key computer science concept for the activity, sketching a rough draft of the lesson, and then receiving feedback from the second author on incorporating questions from the full learning cycle. In contrast to the science course, the CS 1 class met weekly for five hours, traditionally allocated as three hours of lecture and two hours of computer lab. The first author retained the two hours of computer lab and separate weekly homework assignments, but substituted POGIL activities for the lecture class time. Most students were able to complete the POGIL activities during class. The POGIL activities were used to help students discover the most important concepts for the week with only a small amount of programming, while the labs and homework assignments required students to apply these concepts to larger programs, which were turned in and graded.

2.2 Evolution of a POGIL Model

In the process of writing and revising introductory programming POGIL activities, the authors have experimented with a variety of Models that progressively shifted from exploring syntax to emphasizing software design. As we began asking questions that required students to reflect more on general features of programming constructs (control structures) and examples of common programming errors, we observed richer and deeper discussions among our groups of four students. It was also equally apparent that the conceptual understanding of the students improved dramatically in terms of their explanations of "what the program should do and why."

One example of this evolution was an activity introducing Python while-loops. In the initial version of this activity, the authors provided a simple example of a while-loop that would successively increment the value of a variable. The Model stated that the "indented code would execute as long as the Boolean expression evaluates as True." Students would explore these features of the while-loop identified in the Model and then jump to an application question requiring code modifications to change the execution. This type of implementation simply encouraged trial and error experimentation rather than concept invention through discussion. In the next iteration of the activity, we introduced a second Model titled "infinite loops" and introduced this feature through demonstration. Again, the Model limited concept development and most students were able to answer the questions with little or no group discussion.

In the latest iteration of the Model, the authors have tried to avoid explicitly stating concepts and replaced easily-answered questions with more complex questions that encourage richer group discussions. The improved questions appear to engage students better and to help them discover the key elements of the while-loop by drawing more on the integration of prior knowledge. Students are guided to recognize the Boolean statement in the condition and how it controls the execution of the loop body. They are led to predict an error that would lead to an infinite loop before the term has been introduced. This initial series of questions directly following the Model leads students to *explore* the programming construct. They are then guided to *construct* knowledge that will lead them to describe how they might use a while-loop to solve a particular problem, identify appropriate test cases for debugging and agree on the development of their pseudocode in groups of four before writing their program as an *application* exercise in teams of two.

3. POGIL IN THE CLASSROOM

Once a POGIL activity has been developed, an instructor must facilitate student learning in the classroom. The authors prefer assigning students to the same groups of four for multiple weeks, rotating roles within the groups with each new lesson. Students are asked to reflect on the process at the end of each lesson, which reminds them regularly of the importance placed on process skills.

While the groups are working through the activities, the instructor is circling the classroom, silently checking that all groups have reached the correct solution on key questions. If a group reaches the incorrect solution, then the instructor

Figure 1: POGIL and Pair Programming Hybrid Setting: All four students at a table worked together through the POGIL activity. Students sitting side-by-side pair programmed whenever programming was required, but merged back to the larger groups after completing the programming.

attempts to redirect the students by asking pointed questions or reminding them of relevant ideas from the Model.

After each Model, or at a minimum at the end of each lesson, the class as a whole should discuss key principles through a variety of "reporting out" techniques. This sometimes leads to a short lecture (3-5 minutes) that pulls the concepts together. Not every question is addressed during this period; instead the instructor targets only key questions. The instructor should also try to avoid lecturing on material the students have already learned in the lesson.

A better summary is to have students turn in a write-up on what was the most important concept they learned in the lesson, or to have students turn in answers to comprehension or analysis questions about the entire lesson. In the authors' classes, only these answers and the reflections on process are graded, not the POGIL activities completed in class. Finally, each lesson is followed by either larger programming problems (in the science class) or a computer lab and homework assignments (in CS 1).

3.1 POGIL Roles

In the co-taught course for science majors where class sizes ranged from six students in the first course offering to 26 students in Spring 2013, the authors have adopted a hybrid of POGIL and pair programming roles. Students are assigned to work side-by-side in pairs at one computer and across the table from another pair (as shown in Figure 1). Each time a POGIL activity requires any computer programming, groups of four would split into pairs. Each pair sits at a single computer, practicing pair programming driver / navigator roles. Once the programming is complete, the pairs would merge and complete the activity as a group of four, returning to their original POGIL roles. As mentioned earlier, the authors further improved on this idea by shifting all substantial programming exercises to the end of the activity, leaving only minor programming questions in the middle of the lesson. This change reduced the likelihood of having the pairs in the group drift apart because one pair programmed faster than the other. The authors also reminded the students to stay together within the larger groups throughout the class period.

Role	Responsibilities
Facilitator	Keeps track of time and makes sure all group members are contributing.
Spokesperson	Serves as the team representative when speaking to the instructor and other teams.
Quality Control	Guides consensus building with group, records answers to questions and provides copies at the end of the activity to all team members and to the instructor.
Process Analyst	Observes group dynamics, reports feedback to group and to instructor.

Table 1: POGIL Roles used in CS 1

The science students worked well together in their larger groups, perhaps because they had been taught how to work in groups in other science classes. The second author's experience as a POGIL facilitator helped her encourage teamwork and reflection, as she reminded groups to merge back together. After each assignment, students wrote insightful reflections about the group dynamics, like this one:

> *"I thought we all provided each other with a very comfortable setting since we all knew roughly the same knowledge of Python. We also communicated between the two computers well and stayed together as a whole while actively discussing the problems and confirming our answers with everyone at the table. I feel like everyone was able to ask any questions that they may have had during the assignment and those who knew the answer were very willing to help explain the answer."*

However in the Fall 2012 CS 1 class (three sections of 16 to 23 students), students did not work as well together in the larger groups, nor did they understand how to reflect on their experience. Most students would report "everything went great", and the first author struggled with how to facilitate better reflection, teamwork and other process skills.

In the Fall 2013 offering of CS 1, the first author improved group dynamics by adopting POGIL roles often used in high school chemistry POGIL activities (described in Table 1) [2, 9]. While the responsibilities of the roles did not actually change significantly from the previous year, the description of the roles now emphasize teamwork and reflection. At the start of each activity, every group is provided with a set of laminated role cards that remind students of their job descriptions (available online [1]). A Model was added to the first POGIL activity of the semester to introduce these POGIL roles [9], and the class discussed in the third week of classes how the process skills emphasized in each role were desirable to employers. Finally, the Process Analysts are now required to report at the end of each activity on evidence of competency for each of their group members, as well as an example of how the group might improve [2].

As with the activities in the co-taught science course, the CS 1 POGIL activities require minimal programming. Most of the Models include typing in a short code segment and a small amount of exploration and/or debugging. (Longer programming exercises are assigned separately for lab or homework.) In groups of three, one student serves as both the

	POGIL Sections		Non-POGIL Section
	$n = 17$	$n = 16$	$n = 11$
Recursion Question	74.7%	75.6%	84.6%
6 Quiz Average	70.2%	70.1%	84.4%

Table 2: All students were given the same recursion question on a CS 1 quiz. Each section's average score on this recursion question was close to that section's average grade across all six quizzes in CS 1.

facilitator and the process analyst, while the spokesperson is the driver when programming. In groups of four, students break into pairs when they reach programming portions of the activity. The spokesperson and process analyst serve as drivers, while the facilitator and quality control serve as navigators. The instructor circles the classroom, reminding students to "come back together" to answer the guided inquiry questions at the end of the programming segments. In just a few class periods, these changes have dramatically improved student self-assessment of group dynamics. Student reflections have included comments such as we should "make sure no one has an answer before asking for help", we need to "wait for everyone to get on the same page before the group starts", and "we were a little disorganized in what our goals were, and there wasn't really a systematic way to make sure everyone communicated."

4. POGIL IN A CS 1 CLASS

After attending her first POGIL regional workshop in 2012, the first author was motivated to develop POGIL activities for her CS 1 class. Six activities were completed in time for the Fall 2012 semester:

- Java Operators (% and /)
- Data Types and Type Casting
- String Class and Methods
- Boolean Expressions
- While Loops
- Recursion

These six activities have since been refined, and seven new activities were developed for 2013. The 13 POGIL activities were used in CS 1 courses at Westminster College and Virginia State University in Fall 2013. They are available online at http://cspogil.org.

In Fall 2012, 58 students in three sections of CS 1 were taught using the original set of POGIL activities and roles. One section (the control) was assigned five POGIL activities in the first half of the semester. The two other sections were assigned six POGIL activities, including a POGIL activity on recursion in the twelfth week of classes. Recursion was selected as the experimental topic because it is relatively independent of the other instructional topics. The control section was taught recursion through a mixture of a traditional, non-POGIL group exercise, a kinesthetic activity and lecture that the first author had used repeatedly in prior course offerings. Otherwise, all three sections were assigned the same labs and homework and were given the same quizzes on the same day. The control section did have stronger students than the other two sections; the average quiz grade over six quizzes for the control section was 84.4,

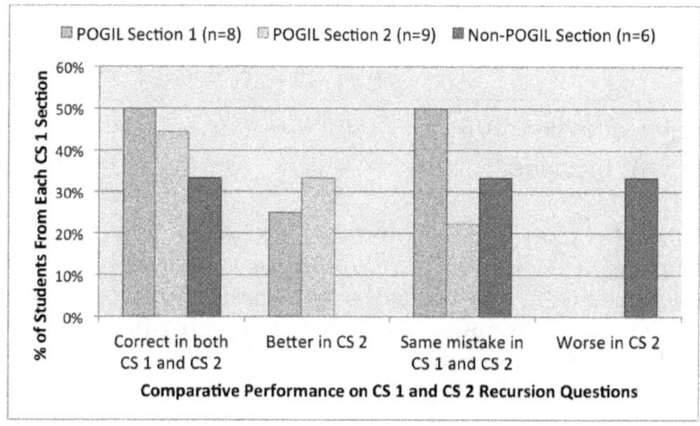

Figure 2: Comparison of students' performance on similar recursion questions on a CS 1 quiz and CS 2 unannounced first-day quiz. While students from all three sections answered both questions correctly or made the same mistake in both the CS 1 and CS 2 quiz, only POGIL students performed better on the CS 2 quiz, and only non-POGIL students performed worse on the CS 2 quiz.

whereas the averages for the other two sections were 70.2 and 70.1.

In the sixteenth week of classes, all three sections took the same quiz and answered the same recursion question. While the students in the control section performed better than the students in the other two sections, all three sections performed slightly better than their own average quiz grade (Table 2). These averages suggest that students learn recursion just as well with POGIL activities as they do with traditional teaching techniques.

Approximately half the CS 1 students from all three sections returned the next semester for CS 2. On the first day, all CS 2 students were given an unannounced quiz, which included a different recursion question of similar difficulty as what was given on the CS 1 quiz (Figure 2). All students' answers from both quizzes were rated based on how well they demonstrated an understanding of recursion (e.g., understood how recursive calls were initiated but did not understand how recursive calls were returned). All students in the POGIL sections performed just as well or better in their CS 2 quiz, whereas some students from the control section performed worse, suggesting that POGIL activities may lead to better retention than traditional methods of teaching. While the student population was too small to result in statistically significant findings, these improvements in retention rates reflect findings in a similarly structured but larger study comparing student retention of Organic Chemistry 1 material [11]. Over 20% of the students from the POGIL section (but none of the students from the lecture section) scored above 90% on an unannounced quiz given on the first day of Organic Chemistry 2. Most lecture students scored under 50%, whereas fewer than a quarter of the POGIL students scored that low.

An examination of pass rates for all three CS 1 sections found a promising trend with respect to female students. The Fall 2012 class in which POGIL was implemented had a higher female pass rate, when compared to historical female students' pass rates in all CS 1 classes taught by the same instructor (Table 3). The male students' pass rate remained

	All CS 1 Students	Female Students	Male Students
Historical: 2003-2010	76.1%	76.5%	75.2%
POGIL Introduced: 2012	77.6%	86.7%	74.4%

Table 3: Comparison of Pass Rates for CS 1. 209 students (68 female, 141 male) were enrolled in the first author's CS 1 classes between 2003-2010. 58 students (15 female, 43 male) were enrolled in her Fall 2013 CS 1 sections.

close to historical rates, suggesting that the class was comparable in difficulty and grading to past offerings, since the male students outnumbered the female students 43 to 15. For a future study, the authors would like to examine CS 1 pass rates across multiple institutions after incorporating POGIL.

5. RESOURCES

Computer science instructors who wish to learn more about POGIL can find computer science activities online at http://cspogil.org. Two excellent guides on how to implement POGIL can be found on the POGIL Project website: the POGIL Instructors Guide [4] and the High School POGIL Initiative Implementation Guide [1]. For computer science instructors who find their students struggling with team work and other process skills, the high school website has several especially useful resources, including role cards that might be laminated and videos on interpersonal effectiveness skills, demonstrating good and poor group dynamics.

One-day workshops are often held in conjunction with CS education conferences like SIGCSE and CSTA, while interdisciplinary regional workshops are held by the POGIL Project throughout the United States and can be found at the http://pogil.org/events.

Finally, a link to the Google Group mailing list for CS POGIL instructors can be found on the http://cspogil.org website (visible only after creating an account and logging in).

6. CONCLUSIONS

As the development of POGIL activities and class implementation strategies continue to evolve in the computer science community, the authors are encouraged by data that seems to correlate with similar educational gains observed in other disciplines. Our experience has convinced us of the importance of continually assessing whether a particular POGIL activity engages students in groups. Classroom experience can be improved through better designed activities and more active facilitation on the part of the instructor. Drawing from best practices of the broader multidisciplinary POGIL network has been helpful in implementing POGIL in CS 1 classes. Preliminary data suggests that incorporating POGIL activities and roles in CS 1 may lead to improved long-term retention of CS material and higher pass rates for female students. The authors speculate that pass rates for other under-represented groups may similarly be increased with POGIL, and this remains a topic for future study.

7. ACKNOWLEDGEMENTS

The authors would like to thank their CMPT 201 and CHEM 370 students for their comments and patience. They are grateful to the reviewers, Florence Appel, Christopher LeCluyse, Sean Raleigh, David Weinstein and Janine Wittwer for their valuable feedback and suggestions on earlier drafts of this paper. Thanks to the National Science Foundation (TUES program) under grant DUE-1044679 that provided opportunities and other support for this work.

8. REFERENCES

[1] High School POGIL Initiative implementation guide. website, 2012.

[2] M. Bartholomew. POGIL reflection and evaluation. Best Practices Presentation at the POGIL Southwest Regional Workshop, July 2013.

[3] T. Eberlein, J. Kampmeier, V. Minderhout, R. Moog, T. Platt, P. Varma-Nelson, and H. White. Pedagogies of engagement in science: A comparison of PBL, POGIL, and PLTL*. *Biochem Mol Biol Educ*, 36(4):262–273, 2008.

[4] D. M. Hanson. *Instructor's Guide to Process-Oriented Guided-Inquiry Learning*. Pacific Crest, 2006.

[5] H. H. Hu and T. D. Shepherd. Using POGIL to help students learn to program. *Trans. Comput. Educ.*, 13(3):13:1–13:23, Aug. 2013.

[6] C. Kussmaul. Process oriented guided inquiry learning (POGIL) for computer science. In *Proceedings of the 43rd ACM technical symposium on Computer Science Education*, SIGCSE '12, pages 373–378, New York, NY, USA, 2012. ACM.

[7] C. Kussmaul, H. Hu, and M. Lang. Using POGIL to help students discover CS concepts and develop process skills (abstract only). In *Proceeding of the 44th ACM technical symposium on Computer science education*, SIGCSE '13, pages 767–767, New York, NY, USA, 2013. ACM.

[8] R. S. Moog and J. N. Spencer, editors. *Process-Oriented Guided Inquiry Learning (POGIL)*. Oxford University Press, 2008.

[9] M. Morehouse. Implementing the PO of POGIL in a high school classroom. Plenary Session at the POGIL Southwest Regional Workshop, July 2013.

[10] L. M. Olivieri. Piloting POGIL in an introductory Python programming course. *J. Comput. Sci. Coll.*, 28(6):194–195, June 2013.

[11] S. M. Ruder and S. S. Hunnicutt. *Process-Oriented Guided Inquiry Learning*, volume 994 of *ACS Symposium Series*, chapter POGIL in Chemistry Courses at a Large Urban University: A Case Study, pages 133–147. American Chemical Society, Washington, D.C., 2008.

[12] L. L. Werner, B. Hanks, and C. McDowell. Pair-programming helps female computer science students. *J. Educ. Resour. Comput.*, 4(1), Mar. 2004.

Effectiveness of a Computational Thinking (CS0) Course on Student Analytical Skills

Michele Van Dyne
Montana Tech of the University of Montana
1300 W. Park St.
Butte, MT 59701
1-406-496-4855
mvandyne@mtech.edu

Jeffrey Braun
Montana Tech of the University of Montana
1300 W. Park St.
Butte, MT 59701
1-406-496-4206
jbraun@mtech.edu

ABSTRACT

In this paper, we describe the content and evaluation of a Computational Thinking (CS0) course developed to improve the analytical problem solving of students participating in the course. The course is targeted to students who are mathematically under-prepared to enter our introductory programming sequence; however, it has recently been included in the University's general education curriculum so that students majoring in any discipline may take the course. Using the Whimbey Analytical Skills Inventory (WASI) students in the CS0 class, along with students in an analogous level engineering class (FESP), were tested at the beginning of the course and again at the end, using different versions of the test. The improvement in scores was statistically significant when measured by both the student t-test and the Cohen d (effect size) for CS0 students but not for the FESP students, providing support that the course does, in fact, increase student analytical problem solving skills. Courses in Computational Thinking have demonstrated success in many schools; however, this research demonstrates its effectiveness in improving analytical skills in majors as well as non-majors.

Categories and Subject Descriptors

K.3.2 [**Computers and Education**]: Computer and Information Science Education

General Terms

Measurement, Performance, Experimentation

Keywords

Computational thinking, problem solving, analytical skills, critical thinking, course effectiveness, CS0

1. INTRODUCTION

The introductory computer science sequence (CS1 and CS2) at Montana Tech does not require any previous programming experience, but it does have a corequisite of at least pre-calculus level math (ACT Math score of 24 – 26). We find that students weak in math skills typically struggle in our CS1 and CS2 courses. To prepare these students for computer science studies, we developed a CS0 level Computational Thinking course. This course primarily covers problem solving and critical thinking skills to assist students in the analytical skills they will need to complete CS1. In initial offerings of our CS0 course, students were those who majored in either computer science or software engineering, but because of its demonstrated success in enhancing analytical and problem solving skills, the University has approved the course as a general education course. Now students majoring in other areas also take the course.

There is a similar course offered to mathematically underprepared students entering traditional engineering programs. This course, FESP 095 (FESP stands for Foundations of Engineering and Science Program), is designed to teach students the skills they will need to complete engineering and science programs.

The computer science education literature shows many different approaches to CS0 courses for both majors and non-majors [2, 3, 7, 10, 13]. Some authors (e.g., Middleton [9]) simply describe their introductory course design and the practical issues in presenting it in order to share their novel teaching techniques. Many researchers try to assess the effectiveness of their CS0 course by examining CS0 student grades and/or retention in CS1 and CS2 courses. Dierbach [3] shows that the group of students taking Towson University's General Computer Science (CS0) course outperformed all other student subgroups in CS1. Rizvi [13] showed Scratch programming based CS0 students performed well in CS1. Huangs [7] assessed Cal Poly's new CS0 course by examining grades in CS1/CS2 and comparing the CS2 retention rates of students who did not take CS0 to those that did.

Other CS0 courses [2, 9, 10] similar to Computational Thinking focus less on computer programming and more on problem solving and critical thinking. Researchers have long recognized the importance of incorporating problem solving into introductory computer science courses [8]. Middleton [9] and Mitchel [10] both describe Problem Solving courses at their institutions and monitor their CS0 students in subsequent courses. Middleton's course uses robots "as the environment for the problem solving because they make errors obvious, better motivating students to finish activities completely". Middleton also concludes that robots are more fun and may improve retention. The Principles of Computation course at Carnegie Mellon "focuses on the principle of computation, and how computer scientists study computation

SIGCSE '14, March 5-8, 2014, Atlanta, GA, USA.

http://dx.doi.org/10.1145/2538862.2538956

through the design and analysis of algorithms, correctness and efficiency, the limits of computation, and several unique applications that build on CS ideas (cryptography, artificial intelligence)" [2]. The assessment for this CS0 course relies on grades and student feedback as mostly non-majors enroll in it and do not move onto CS1.

Other disciplines (e.g., writing, psychology, philosophy) have assessed the effectiveness of their courses by using standardized tests to measure changes in critical thinking and analytical skills. Numerous standardized critical thinking tests exist to assess students [5, 11, 12]. Possin [12] reviews the different critical thinking assessment methods and many of the popular standardized tests, including simple to administer multiple-choice tests. He concludes that objective multiple-choice tests appear to be "fairly accurate for measuring students" acquisition of specific core CT skills".

To measure the effectiveness of a course for improving critical thinking skills, researchers typically give a pre- and post-course test. In the critical thinking literature, the popular way to report the practical significance of the difference from one test to the next within a group is to compute the ratio of the difference in mean scores to the standard deviation [4]. This ratio is often called the *effect size* or Cohen's d. Critical thinking effect sizes for a small subset of writing and psychology courses range from 0.24 of a standard deviation (or 0.24 SD) to 1.47 SD [6, 12, 14]. Hatcher [6] compares three different critical thinking tests and shows the effect sizes for groups varies from 0.57 SD to 0.97 SD depending on which test is administered. Solon [14] infused general critical thinking material into an introductory psychology course and showed significant change (p=0.000004) and an effect size (Cohen's d) = 0.87 versus the control group which was not significant (p=0.49) and effect size (Cohen's d) = 0.10.

2. COURSE CONTENT

2.1 Overview of the Course

Following the lead of Jeannette Wing of Carnegie Mellon University (CMU) [15], we introduced a course called Computational Thinking designed to teach problem solving skills to underprepared students entering the curriculum. Diverging from the CMU approach, but consistent with Middleton's [9] approach, we also incorporated simple robotics in the course offering that includes the lab. Students may take the course as a 2 credit lecture class or a 3 credit lecture and lab class. The course is taught as two hours of lecture and three hours of lab per week. The catalog description is:

> "Computational thinking involves solving problems, designing systems, and to understanding human behavior, by drawing on the concepts fundamental to computer science. It is the study of an effective approach used by people to solve problems. Critical thinking involves the systematic evaluation of information, and is a crucial piece of problem solving. The two are combined in this course to provide the student with a powerful set of tools to understand and solve the kinds of problems they will encounter in their college studies and future careers. The lab incorporates a programming component In this programming lab, students learn to carefully and systematically analyze problems and demonstrate the correctness of their solution by implementing it in program code."

The Computational Thinking course has been through four full offerings, and is in its fifth offering at present. Last year's offering is the first time that the course has been included in Montana Tech's general education curriculum, and its enrollment saw a significant increase.

2.2 Lecture Content

The lecture portion of the course stresses logical and mathematical thinking and problem solving. The topics covered during lecture and reinforced through weekly class assignments include analogies, analysis of trends and patterns, logical reasoning, mathematical word problems, and critical evaluation of information in addition to computer science oriented topics such as algorithm development, data type and structure, abstraction, decomposition, transformations, simulation, iteration, recursion and the introduction of specific algorithms.

The in-class portion of the course is taught very interactively. During each class, students are given about 15 minutes of instruction on a topic then the class as a whole participates in exercises about that topic. An attempt is made to get all students to actively participate. The class is then broken into groups which work on additional exercises. Weekly assignments are given which also reinforce the concepts taught that week.

Material for the course has been drawn from a variety of sources, though much of the computer science oriented topics have been drawn from Backhouse's *Algorithmic Problem Solving* [1], and from pre-publication material from this source available online.

2.3 Lab Content

The lab portion of the CS0 course uses the Lego Mindstorms NXT robotics kits to illustrate concepts taught during lecture. The robotics approach was chosen rather than general programming because of the interactive and visual feedback of results to students. Students in the lab must build their own robots and program them, first using the graphical programming environment provided with the kits, and then moving on to programming them in Java (using LeJos, a Java library for the NXT robots). Lab assignment topics to reinforce the lecture topics include programming as reasoning, programming as math, algorithms, data and variables, decisions, problem solving, functions, iteration, sorting and a final assignment of tying it all together.

As one example of a lab assignment, students are asked to program their robot, which at this point has distance sensing capability, as a "feral robot". The robot is to continually sense objects within a certain distance. If something enters this "unsafe" distance, the robot is to back away, unless the intruder gets even closer, at which point the robot is to attack. The definition of attack behavior is left to the student. This assignment incorporates looping and decision constructs along with the development of the algorithmic logic. The first version of this assignment is done using the graphical programming environment, and a later version is rewritten using Java code.

Students are not required to take the lab, but most do. In the past four offerings, 74% of the students took both the lecture and lab portion of the course.

3. EVALUATION

To test the effectiveness of incorporating the Computational Thinking course into the pre-curriculum, the Whimbey Analytical Skills Inventory (WASI) pre-test and post-test [16] were used in each of the four complete offerings of the course. On the first day of class, the WASI pre-test was administered. It consists of 38 problems that test mathematical and logical thinking in various forms. During the semester, instruction is given which first addresses the types of problems the WASI test covers, and then delves into deeper logical concepts such as algorithm development, using structured logic, invariants, and recursion. Students are not informed they will be taking either the WASI pre-test or post-test; in fact, they are told that the final exam will cover class material, and in fact, the final exam is completely separate from the WASI exams. Furthermore, the WASI tests have no bearing on student grades, and students are informed of this when they take the test. On the last day of classes, the post-WASI was administered. This is a second version of the WASI test, consisting of 37 problems of similar composition, but different content, as the pre-test.

It is possible that any improvement in student performance in the CS0 class could be attributed to some factor outside of the class, such as completion of the first semester of college coursework. To test for this external effect, we also administered the pre- and post-tests to students in the pre-engineering course, FESP 095. Students in the FESP program have a similar background to those that take the CS0 course, in that they are mathematically underprepared to enter into the introductory engineering classes. The FESP 095 course also has similar goals to CS0, that is, to prepare students with the problem solving skills they will need to complete an engineering or science degree. The catalog description of this course is:

> "This course will focus on the skills that are necessary to successfully enter and complete an engineering or science program at Montana Tech. These skills include dimensional analysis, unit conversion, technical writing, and technical drawing. Additional components included in the curriculum are presentation of technical information and applications/problem solving of Intermediate Algebra."

The WASI tests contain questions that are categorized into several categories: verbal reasoning, sequential instructions, analogies, relationship sentences, analysis of trends and patterns, and mathematical word problems. None of these problems requires mathematical skills beyond basic algebra, though most problems require logical or analytical skills and attention to detail.

WASI pre-test and post-tests were included for analysis only if a student took both of the tests. (Not all students are present for the first day of classes, nor do all students attend class, particularly if they are unaware that an exam will be administered.) From the CS0 course, an additional set of pre-test/post-test scores was discarded because one student misunderstood the instructions and answered none of the questions on the pre-test, resulting in a 33 point gain between pre- and post-test scores. Including this data point would have skewed the data favorably, but would have been a misrepresentative sample. Students who enrolled in both the CS0 course and the FESP 095 course and completed the test in both were not included in the data analysis.

It is possible that students who completed both the pre-test and post-test in either the CS0 or the FESP 095 course were more motivated than those who did not complete both tests; that is, these are the students that regularly attended class. By including the same group from each course, we are at least able to measure the effect on those motivated students across different class environments.

4. RESULTS AND DISCUSSION

Over the four completed offerings of the CS0 course, 35 total students enrolled; 22 of these students completed both the pre- and post-tests. In the FESP 095 course, 52 students enrolled; 29 of these students completed both versions of the test. To provide incentive for the FESP 095 students to take the post-test seriously, they were given extra credit if their post-test scores improved. A similar incentive was not offered to CS0 students. There were no students who were enrolled in both classes that completed both tests in both classes.

A student t-test was used to compare pre-test scores in the FESP 095 course and those from the CS0 course to test whether we were testing similar populations. There was a slight difference, but the difference was not significant ($p=0.056$), giving us evidence that we are comparing a similar population of students.

In the FESP 095 course, initial WASI pre-test raw scores ranged from a low of 8 to a high of 31 out of 38 possible, with an average score of 20, while post-test scores ranged from a low of 12 to a high of 30 out of 37 possible, with an average score of 21. Translating this to percentages, the pre-test had a range of 21.1% to 81.6% , and the post-test had a range of 32.4% to 81.1%. The average point improvement over the course of a semester was .93, and the average percentage point improvement was 4%. Distribution of the scores for the pre- and post-tests can be seen in Figures 1 and 2 below.

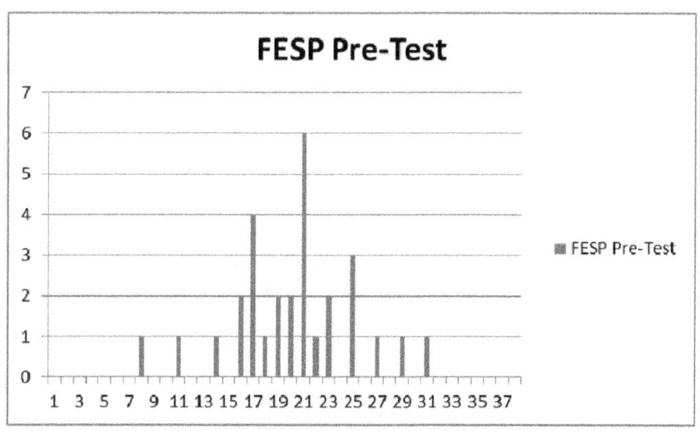

Figure 1. FESP Pre-Test Score Distribution

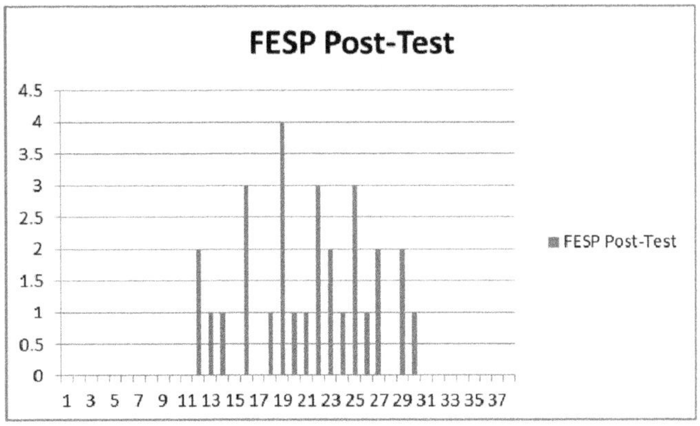

Figure 2. FESP Post-Test Score Distribution

In the CS0 course, initial WASI pre-test raw scores ranged from a low of 12 to a high of 34 out of 38 possible, with an average score of 23, while post-test scores ranged from a low of 19 to a high of 37 out of 37 possible, with an average score of 29. Translating this to percentages, the pre-test had a range of 31.6% to 89.5%, with an average of 60.3%, while the post-test had a range of 51.4% to 100%, with an average of 78.4%. The average point improvement over the course of a semester was 6.09, and the average percentage point improvement was 18.1%. Distribution of the scores for the pre- and post-tests can be seen in Figures 3 and 4 below.

To compare differences between pre- and post-test scores, the student's t-test was used. The percentage correct on both WASI test was used in order to adjust for any differences caused by the number of questions on each test, and thus a difference in raw scores.

In the FESP 095 course, a test of significance between scores using a two-tailed, paired test, since we are not sure of which direction a change would occur, reveals no significant difference between pre- and post-test scores ($p=0.098$). If we assume that change should occur in one direction (positive) and not the other, and using a single-tailed paired test, we get marginal significance ($p=0.05$).

For the CS0 course, assuming the change between test scores should be in the positive direction, and thus using a single-tailed, paired test, a significant difference was found ($p=0.00000014$). If we make the assumption that we don't know the direction of the change, and test for significance using a two-tailed paired test, we still get a significant difference ($p=0.00000028$). This provides evidence that participation in the course had a significant effect in improving analytical skills as tested by the WASI.

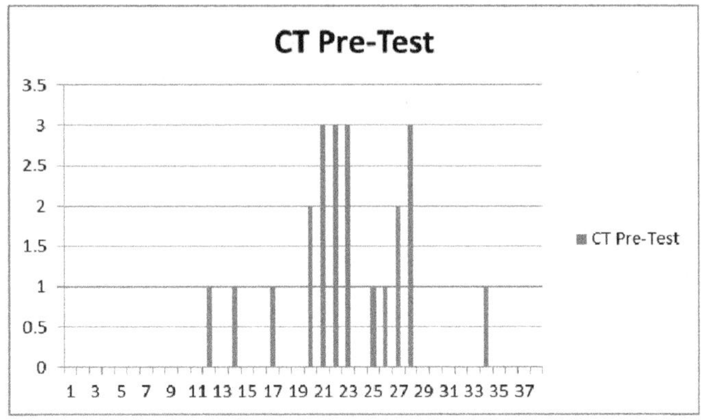

Figure 3. CS0 Pre-Test Score Distribution

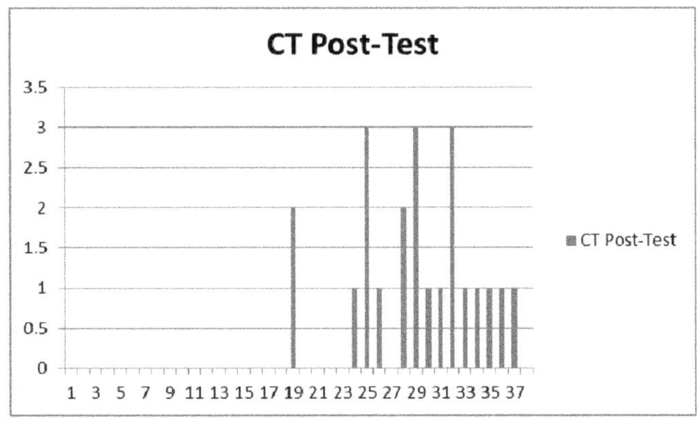

Figure 4. CS0 Post-Test Score Distribution

As discussed previously in this paper, in the critical thinking literature, a common way to report the practical significance of the difference from one test to the next within a group is to compute the ratio of the difference in mean scores to the standard deviation [3], called the *effect size*. For our data, the effect size was calculated to be 1.36 SD for the CS0 course and 0.29 SD for the FESP 095 course. Reported effect sizes on research in the literature ranged from 0.24 SD to 1.47 SD, with researchers expressing satisfaction at effect sizes over 0.5 SD. Our effect size of 1.36 SD lends additional support that participation in the course increased student abilities in analytical skills as measured by the WASI. The FESP 095 control group's effect size of 0.29 SD is within the range (0.23 SD to 0.44 SD) reported for several Critical Thinking courses summarized by Possin[12].

It was previously mentioned that not all students take both the lecture and lab portion of the class; approximately 26% of students take the lecture portion only. Among the students in this study, then, 6 took the lecture portion only, and 16 took both lab and lecture. Although these numbers are getting smaller, we looked at the differences between these two groups. There was no difference at all in pre-test performance between the two groups ($p=0.478$). There is a significant, $p<0.05$, though small difference between the groups, however, in post-test performance ($p=0.037$). That is, those students who also attended lab performed better than those who attended lecture only. Finally, the difference between pre- and post-test performance for those students who only attended lecture was significant ($p=0.0008$), and an even more significant difference was found in the test score of those who attended both lab and lecture (p=0.00004). The effect sizes for these two subgroups are 1.19 SD and 2.97 SD respectively.

5. CONCLUSIONS AND FUTURE WORK

Statistical analysis of our results give promising indications that the CS0, Computational Thinking, course does, in fact, positively and significantly impact the analytical problem solving skills of students that participate. And although the course was initially developed to assist underprepared students who are majoring in computer science and software engineering, particularly since it has been opened as a general education course, we have other majors enrolling in the course. In the data used in this study, 10 of the CS0 students were those declaring a major from our department, while other majors included Health Care Informatics, Electrical Engineering, Chemistry, General Engineering and Petroleum Engineering. This suggests that the result of teaching Computational Thinking improves the analytical ability of students in general, and not just those predisposed to being computer science majors. As a subjective side note, most comments on course evaluations have been very positive. One recent student remark was "I have learned new concepts of problem solving that I feel will be crucial to me later on in life."

We plan on continuing to collect pre- and post-test data on students taking the CS0 class, particularly as our enrollment grows and even more non-majors take the course. We think this course can be an effective recruiting tool in that it introduces all students to the types of problem solving required in computer science. On the other hand, since the impact on increased analytical skills which are not computationally specific has been demonstrated, we would like to see more students encouraged to take a course of this nature to help them in problem-solving in general.

6. REFERENCES

[1] Backhouse, R. 2011, *Algorithmic Problem Solving*, John Wiley & Sons, West Sussex, UK, 2011.

[2] Cortina, T. 2007, An introduction to computer science for non-majors using principles of computation, *ACM SIGCSE Bulletin* 39, 1 (March 2007), 218-222.

[3] Dierbach, C., Taylor, B., Zhou, H. and Zimand, I. 2005, Experiences with a CS0 course targeted for CS1 success, *ACM SIGCSE Bulletin* 37, 1 (March 2005), 317-320.

[4] Ennis, R. H. 2008. Nationwide Testing of Critical Thinking for Higher Education: Vigilance Required, *Teaching Philosophy* 31, 1 (March 2008), 1-26.

[5] Follman, J., Lavely, C., and Berger, N. 1997, Inventory of instruments of critical thinking, *Informal Logic* 18, 2, 261-267.

[6] Hatcher, D. L., 2011, Which test? Whose scores? Comparing standardized critical thinking tests, *New Directions for Institutional Research* 2011, 149, 29-39.

[7] Haungs, M., Clark, C., Clements, J., and Janzen, D. 2012. Improving first-year success and retention through interest-based CS0 courses, *SIGCSE '12 Proceedings of the 43rd ACM technical symposium on Computer Science Education* (Feb. 2012), 589-594.

[8] Hyde, D. C., Gay, B., and Utter, D. 1979. The integration of a Problem Solving Process in the first course, *SIGCSE '79: Proceedings of the tenth SIGCSE technical symposium on Computer science education* (Feb. 1979), 54-59.

[9] Middleton, D. 2012. Trying to teach problem-solving instead of just assigning it: Some Practical Issues. *Journal of Computing Sciences in Colleges* 27, 5 (May, 2012), 60-65.

[10] Mitchell, W. 2001. Another look at CS0, *Journal of Computing Sciences in Colleges* 17, 1 (Oct. 2001), 194-205.

[11] Morante, E. A., Ulesky, A. 1984. Assessment of Reasoning Abilities, *Educational Leadership* 42, 1 (Sept. 1984), 71-74.

[12] Possin, K. 2008. A Field Guide to Critical-Thinking Assessment, *Teaching Philosophy* 31, 3 (Sept. 2008), 201-228.

[13] Rizvi, M., Humpries, T., Major, D., Lauzun, H., and Jones, M. 2011. A new CS0 course for at-risk majors, *24th IEEE-CS Conference on Software Engineering Education and Training* (May 2011), 314-323.

[14] Solon, T. 2007. Generic critical thinking infusion and course content learning in introductory psychology, *Journal of Instructional Psychology* 34, 2 (June 2007), 95-109.

[15] Wing, J. M. 2008. Computational thinking and thinking about computing," *Philosophical Transactions of the Royal Society*, 366 (July 2008) 3717-3725.

[16] Whimbey, A. and Lochhead, J. 1999. *Problem Solving and Comprehension*, 6th ed., Psychology Press, Taylor and Francis Group, New York and London, 1999.

Integrating Big Data into the Computing Curricula

Yasin N. Silva
Arizona State University
ysilva@asu.edu

Suzanne W. Dietrich
Arizona State University
dietrich@asu.edu

Jason M. Reed
Arizona State University
jmreed3@asu.edu

Lisa M. Tsosie
Arizona State University
lmtsosi1@asu.edu

ABSTRACT

An important recent technological development in computer science is the availability of highly distributed and scalable systems to process Big Data, i.e., datasets with high volume, velocity and variety. Given the extensive and effective use of systems incorporating Big Data in many application scenarios, these systems have become a key component in the broad landscape of database systems. This fact creates the need to integrate the study of Big Data Management Systems as part of the computing curricula. This paper presents well-structured guidelines to perform this integration by describing the important types of Big Data systems and demonstrating how each type of system can be integrated into the curriculum. A key contribution of this paper is the description of an array of course resources, e.g., virtual machines, sample projects, and in-class exercises, and how these resources support the learning outcomes and enable a hands-on experience with Big Data technologies.

Categories and Subject Descriptors

K.3.2 [**Computers and Education**]: Computer and Information Science Education

General Terms

Design, Experimentation

Keywords

Databases curricula, big data management systems

1. INTRODUCTION

The development and extensive use of highly distributed and scalable systems to process Big Data is widely considered as one of the recent key technological developments in computer science [14, 10, 18]. These systems, here called Big Data Management Systems (BDMSs), have been successfully used in many application scenarios, e.g., scientific data analysis, social media data mining, recommendation systems, and correlation analysis on web service logs. BDMSs are typically composed of large clusters of commodity machines and are often dynamically scalable, i.e., nodes can be added or removed based on the workload. Examples of such systems are: MapReduce [11], Hadoop [4], HBase [5], and VoltDB [19]. The importance of BDMSs in the current landscape of database systems creates the need to integrate their study as part of the computing curricula, particularly as part of database or data management courses. This paper presents multiple guidelines to perform this integration. The main contributions of the paper are:

- The identification of three important types of BDMSs and the description of their core concepts, taxonomy, sample systems, and guidelines about when to use them.
- Guidelines to integrate each type of BDMS as a course unit and the description of the learning objectives.
- A detailed description of class resources for each unit to enable a hands-on experience with BDMSs. These resources include virtual machines, data generators, sample programs, projects, and in-class exercises.
- Files of all the resources made available to instructors. The goal is to enable instructors to use and extend these resources based on their specific needs.

The rest of the paper is organized as follows. Section 2 describes three important types of BDMSs: MapReduce, NoSQL, and NewSQL. Sections 3, 4, and 5 present the details of how each type of BDMS can be introduced as a learning unit. These sections describe many class resources and how they support the learning outcomes. These resources will be made available in [6]. Section 6 presents a discussion of various facets of integrating the proposed units into the computer science curricula. Section 7 concludes the paper.

2. BIG DATA LEARNING UNITS

While the area of BDMSs is relatively recent (the foundational MapReduce paper [11] was published in 2004), it has quickly developed and there are now dozens of BDMS-related open-source and commercial products. One of the first challenges for computer science educators is to organize these different technologies and products into well-defined learning units to be included into the computing curricula. The authors propose the following units, where each unit corresponds to a core type of BDMS:

SIGCSE'14, March 3–8, 2014, Atlanta, GA, USA.

ACM 978-1-4503-2605-6/14/03 ...$15.00.
http://dx.doi.org/10.1145/2538862.2538877.

- **MapReduce**. It is widely considered to be one of the core programming models for Big Data processing. MapReduce started the wave of BDMS systems. It enables building highly distributed programs that run on failure-tolerant and scalable clusters of commodity machines. Some examples of MapReduce implementations are: Apache Hadoop [4], Google MapReduce [11], and Microsoft's Dryad [13].
- **NoSQL**. This type of BDMS comprises data stores that have been designed to provide higher scalability and availability than conventional relational databases. Many NoSQL systems do not support the SQL query language and implement a simplified transaction and consistency model. Some examples of NoSQL data stores are: Apache Cassandra [3], Google's BigTable [7], MongoDB [2], and Apache HBase [5].
- **NewSQL**. This type of BDMS aims to have the same levels of scalability and availability of NoSQL systems but still maintains the ACID properties (Atomicity, Consistency, Isolation, Durability) and SQL query language of traditional relational databases. Some examples of NewSQL systems are: VoltDB [19], NuoDB [16], Google Spanner [9], and Clustrix [8].

As discussed in Section 6, the proposed units can be integrated into introductory and advanced database and distributed system courses.

In general, the student learning outcomes of these units are that students are able to:

- recognize the key properties, strengths and limitations of each type of BDMS (**LO1**),
- build applications using specific instances of each type of BDMS (**LO2**), and
- understand when to use each type of BDMS (**LO3**).

3. DATA PROCESSING WITH MapReduce

3.1 The MapReduce Framework

MapReduce is an extensively used programming framework for processing large data. MapReduce jobs run on clusters of commodity machines that are dynamically scalable. The MapReduce framework quickly processes massive datasets by splitting them into independent chunks that are processed in parallel. The framework works by dividing the processing task into two main phases: *map* and *reduce*. The framework user is required to provide two functions (*map* and *reduce*) with the following general form:

```
map: (k1,v1) → list(k2,v2)
reduce: (k2,list(v2)) → list(k3,v3)
```

Multiple *map* tasks process independent input chunks in parallel. Each *map* call is given a key-value pair `(k1,v1)` and produces a list of `(k2,v2)` pairs. The output of the *map* calls is transferred to the *reduce* nodes (*shuffle* phase). All the intermediate records with the same intermediate key `(k2)` are sent to the same reducer node. At each *reduce* node, the received intermediate records are sorted and grouped (all the intermediate records with the same key form a single group). Each group is processed in a single *reduce* call.

```
Algorithm WordCount
Map (line_number, line_contents)
   for each word in line_contents
      emit(word, 1)
Reduce (word, values[])
   sum = 0
   for each value in values
      sum = sum + value
   emit(word, sum)
```

Figure 1: MapReduce algorithm of WordCount.

3.2 MapReduce Learning Resources

A popular open-source implementation of the MapReduce framework available to use in support of hands-on in-class exercises and project assignments is Apache Hadoop [4, 20]. Unfortunately, due to the nature of the MapReduce framework, a computer cluster would be needed to directly enable such interaction. Many institutions, however, do not have such clusters available for teaching. Another option is the use of Hadoop's pseudo-distributed mode which allows running MapReduce jobs on a single node where each Hadoop daemon runs on a different Java process. This approach, however, still requires a significant installation and configuration effort. One solution that the authors utilize and contribute as part of the resources in [6] is the development of a virtual machine (VM) with all the required packages already installed and configured. This VM has the following components: (1) Linux as the operating system, (2) Hadoop 1.0.4 using pseudo-distributed mode (this includes the Hadoop MapReduce programming framework and the Hadoop distributed file system - HDFS), (3) the Eclipse development environment and the Hadoop Eclipse plug-in [1], (4) data generators and sample datasets, and (5) source code of multiple sample MapReduce programs.

3.2.1 *Data Generators and Datasets*

The MapReduce programs that will be presented in the next sections make use of two datasets: MobyShakespeare and MStation. MobyShakespeare contains the text of the complete unabridged works of Shakespeare [17]. MStation, a synthetic dataset prepared by the authors, contains meteorological station data. Each line of the MStation dataset contains the following tab-separated attributes: station ID, zip code, latitude, longitude, temperature, precipitation, humidity, year and month. MStation's data generator will be made available to instructors [6].

3.2.2 *MapReduce Program Template*

To facilitate the process of writing MapReduce programs in Hadoop, students could use a provided MapReduce template (MapReduceShell.java). This template imports all the required libraries, provides empty definitions of the Map and Reduce methods, and includes a generic version of the run method, which creates, configures, and runs a generic Hadoop MapReduce job.

One of the first activities the authors suggest after introducing the MapReduce model is to describe the WordCount problem. This is a very illustrative problem where the goal is to count the number of times each word appears in the input dataset (text files). Fig. 1 shows the pseudo-code of the MapReduce WordCount algorithm and Fig. 2 shows the

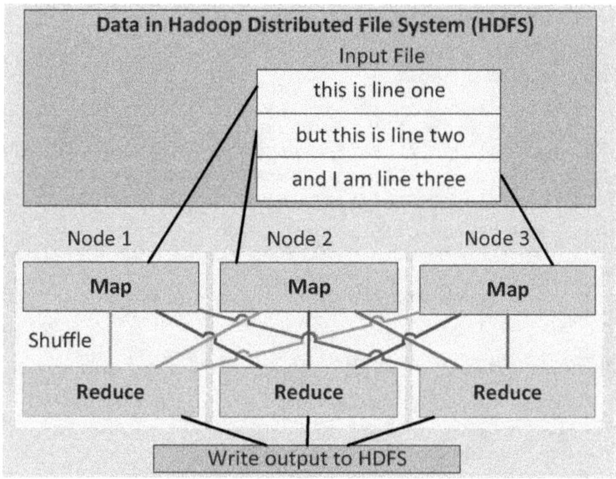

a) Map, shuffle and reduce stages

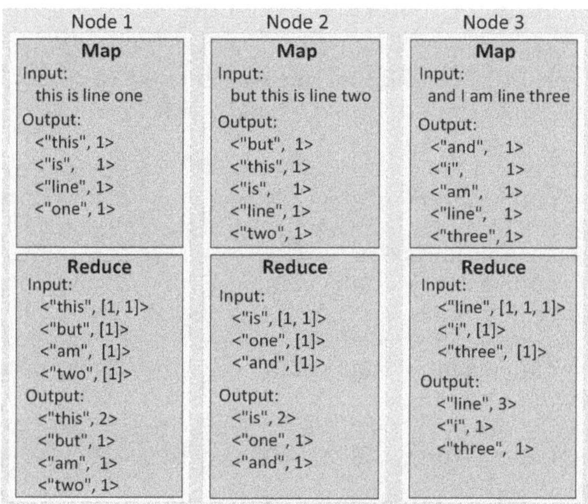

b) Input and output of Map and Reduce tasks

Figure 2: WordCount - MapReduce Processing.

details of how this program is executed on the MapReduce framework. Fig. 2.a provides a high-level representation of how different chunks of the input dataset are processed by different map tasks and the way intermediate data is sent to the reduce tasks in the shuffle stage. This figure also shows that the input and output datasets are stored in the distributed file system. Fig. 2.b shows the distributed processing details in this MapReduce job. Particularly, this figure shows the input and output of each map and reduce task. Since the WordCount code has been built using the template described previously, this is also a good example to show students how to extend the template to solve specific problems using MapReduce. The WordCount example can be run using the MobyShakespeare dataset or any other text input file.

3.2.3 In-class Exercises and Assignments

The MStation dataset provides a basis for additional in-class exercises for illustrating MapReduce programs [6].

- **AverageTempByStation.java**. This program aggregates the data by station ID and outputs the average temperature for each station. The pseudo-code of this MapReduce algorithm is presented in Fig. 3.

```
Algorithm AverageTempByStation

Map (line_number, MStation_line)
   load MStationRecord from MStation_line
   emit(MStationRecord.stationID,
        MStationRecord.temp)

Reduce (stationID, temp_values[])
   sum = 0
   count = 0
   for each value in temp_values
      sum = sum + value
      count = count + 1
   average = sum / count
   emit(stationID, average)
```

Figure 3: MapReduce algorithm of AverageTempByStation.

- **AverageTempByZipCode.java**. This MapReduce program groups the data by zip code and outputs the average temperature at each zip code.
- **SortByStationID.java**. This code sorts the input data by station ID. The output data still contains all the attributes of the input dataset.

Also, the MStation dataset can be used for class assignments and projects to design and implement MapReduce programs, such as: (1) the computation of the total rainfall grouping by zip code and year, (2) the computation of the average rainfall and average temperature, grouping by zip code and year while considering only years greater than 1950, and (3) the identification of the highest 10 temperature readings reporting the temperature, zip code, month and year.

Achieving learning objectives.

The authors have found that the use of diagrams, like the one in Fig. 2, helps students to understand the steps that take place at the various stages of a MapReduce job (learning objective LO1). Also, the use of the described VM provides students with hands-on experience with Hadoop MapReduce (LO2) and reinforces the understanding of the MapReduce features (LO1). The VM enables students to focus on designing and implementing MapReduce programs rather than installation and tedious configuration. Furthermore, the described data generator can be modified by instructors to generate datasets with different sizes or data distribution properties that can be used in additional exercises or projects.

To give students a better understanding of when to use MapReduce, it is important to contrast it with other data processing systems (LO3). For instance, in a database class, MapReduce can be compared with traditional relational databases. It should be highlighted that MapReduce systems do not make older data processing technologies obsolete. Instead, different systems might be more suitable for different tasks. For instance, in the scenario of a retail store, database systems could be the right tool to process selling transactions since these systems provide consistent and durable data processing. On the other hand, a MapReduce system may be the right tool to analyze and get useful insights, e.g., aggregations, trends and correlations, from data that contains selling operations for the last five years.

4. BIG DATA ANALYSIS WITH NoSQL

4.1 NoSQL Data Stores

NoSQL is a broad class of data stores that aims to provide higher scalability and availability compared to conventional relational databases. In many cases, these systems do not adhere to the relational database model, do not support SQL for data manipulation, and implement a simplified transaction/consistency model. Some of the key properties of NoSQL data stores are as follows: (1) they usually have a distributed, fault-tolerant architecture where more machines can be easily added, (2) data is partitioned among different machines, (3) data replication is used for fault tolerance, and (4) NoSQL data stores commonly provide a simplified consistency model, for instance *eventual consistency*: given a sufficiently long period of time in which no changes are made, all the previous updates are expected to eventually propagate through the system.

Several types of NoSQL systems are presented next:

- **Document stores.** Store documents that contain data in some format (XML, JSON, binary, etc.). Examples: MongoDB, Oracle NoSQL Database, CouchDB, and SimpleDB.
- **Key-Value stores.** Store the data in a schema-less way (commonly key-value pairs). Data items could be stored in a data type of a programming language or an object. Examples: Cassandra, Dynamo, Riak, and MemcacheDB.
- **Graph databases.** Stores graph data. For instance: social relations, public transport links, road maps or network topologies. Examples: AllegroGraph, InfiniteGraph, Neo4j, and OrientDB.
- **Tabular data stores.** Stores tabular data with potentially many columns and rows. Examples: HBase, BigTable, and Hypertable.

4.2 NoSQL Learning Resources

Similarly to the case of MapReduce, one of the best ways to introduce NoSQL data stores is to enable students to interact with real NoSQL systems. To accomplish this, it is important to incorporate the use of a specific NoSQL database like Apache HBase [4], which is also included in the provided VM. HBase is an open-source NoSQL distributed database system written in Java and modeled after Google's BigTable [7]. It runs on top of HDFS and provides a fault-tolerant way of storing and processing large amounts of sparse tabular data. HBase provides efficient random reads and writes on top of HDFS, which does not support random writes. HBase has been used by companies like Yahoo! and Facebook [15].

One of the key lessons about NoSQL systems is learning about the different ways in which developers and applications can interact with the database. This can be accomplished with the following in-class activity where students create an HBase table to maintain blog posts and interact with the system using both shell commands and a Java application. First, students use the HBase shell interface to run the *create* and *put* commands to create an HBase table and insert the blog posts data. Next, students use the commands *scan*, *get*, and *delete* to print all the content of the table, get the content of individual records, and delete records, respectively. Fig. 4 shows sample shell commands for this activity. In the second part of this activity students programmatically access the HBase table created in the first part. To this end, students first establish a connection with the blog posts table, and use instances of the *Put*, *Scan*, and *Get* classes to insert additional rows, list all rows, and retrieve the content of single rows, respectively. Fig. 5 shows a fragment of the Java code that performs the described tasks. In addition, complementary resources to incorporate NoSQL using MongoDB [2] are described in [18].

```
Create an HBase table
Create 'blogposts', 'post', 'image'
Adding data to a table
put 'blogposts', 'post1', 'post:title', 'The Title'
put 'blogposts', 'post1', 'post:author', 'The Author'
put 'blogposts', 'post1', 'post:body', 'Body of a post'
put 'blogposts', 'post1', 'image:header', 'image1.jpg'
put 'blogposts', 'post1', 'image:bodyimage', 'image2.jpg'
List all the tables
list
Scan a table (show all the content of a table)
scan 'blogposts'
Show the content of a record (row)
get 'blogposts', 'post1'
Deleting (all the cells of a given row)
deleteall 'blogposts', 'post1'
Drop a table
disable 'blogposts'
drop 'blogposts'
```

Figure 4: Accessing HBase with shell commands.

Achieving learning objectives.

In the authors' experience, the use of a VM with HBase and the described in-class activity have been very important tools to enable students to get a more concrete understanding of the features of a NoSQL system (LO1), and to gain hands-on experience about the different mechanisms to interact with an HBase data store (LO2).

One of the key lessons about NoSQL data stores is when they should be used (LO3). For this, it is important to highlight that NoSQL databases should be considered when there is a need to manage very large amounts of data (currently in the order of terabytes or petabytes), the application scenario does not use a fixed schema, and performance is more important than consistency (the application does not require full ACID guarantees).

It is also important to observe that features and data types supported by NoSQL systems differ, particularly in how the system supports the various levels of consistency (C), availability (A), and network partition tolerance (P). In fact, the CAP theorem states that a system has to pick two of these three properties and that a system cannot have all three simultaneously while maintaining an acceptable latency [12]. For instance, HBase [5] prioritizes consistency and partitioning tolerance (CP), while Cassandra [3] values availability and partitioning tolerance (AP).

NoSQL should also be contrasted against other types of data processing systems (LO3). Traditional relational databases for instance may be the right tool for a banking application where all the data fits in a single server since they

```
//Use HTable object to connect to the blogposts table.
Configuration config = HBaseConfiguration.create();
HTable table = new HTable(config, "blogposts");

//Add a row (post2) to the table
Put p = new Put(Bytes.toBytes("post2"));
p.add(Bytes.toBytes("post"), Bytes.toBytes("title"),
      Bytes.toBytes("Title2"));
p.add(Bytes.toBytes("post"), Bytes.toBytes("author"),
      Bytes.toBytes("Author2"));
table.put(p);

//Retrieve the data of a row using Get
Get g = new Get(Bytes.toBytes("post2"));
Result r = table.get(g);
byte [] valTitle = r.getValue(Bytes.toBytes("post"),
                   Bytes.toBytes("title"));
byte [] valAuthor = r.getValue(Bytes.toBytes("post"),
                   Bytes.toBytes("author"));
System.out.println("GET: " + Bytes.toString(valTitle)+
                   " " + Bytes.toString(valAuthor));

// Retrieve multiple rows using Scan (all titles)
Scan s = new Scan();
s.addColumn(Bytes.toBytes("post"),
            Bytes.toBytes("title"));
ResultScanner scanner = table.getScanner(s);
for (Result rr : scanner)
  System.out.println("Title: " + rr);
```

Figure 5: Accessing HBase table from Java.

provide full ACID guarantees. On the other hand, a NoSQL system like HBase could be the right tool for web-scale messaging or blogging systems since they deal with massive amounts of data and prioritize performance over full consistency. In fact, HBase is used to support the messaging subsystem in Facebook [15]. While MapReduce and NoSQL systems can process massive amounts of data in a highly distributed and scalable fashion, each system may be the best option in different scenarios. Furthermore, it is important to consider the specific features of NoSQL systems. For instance, in the scenario of the messaging system, HBase may be the right tool to run a query that quickly retrieves the messages of a user (random access). In the same scenario, the MapReduce framework could be the best tool to run a job that processes the entire dataset to aggregate the number of messages by sender location.

5. BIG DATA PROCESSING WITH NewSQL

5.1 NewSQL Database Systems

NewSQL is a class of database systems that aims to provide the same levels of scalability and availability of NoSQL systems while still maintaining the ACID guarantees and SQL query language of traditional relational databases. Some of the key properties of NewSQL systems are as follows: (1) they are based on a distributed shared-nothing architecture that can dynamically scale horizontally (adding cluster nodes), (2) they support the relational data model, (3) they provide ACID properties for transactions, and (4) they support SQL as the primary query language.

Several NewSQL systems have been built from scratch to operate on distributed clusters of shared-nothing nodes. Some of these systems, e.g., Google Spanner, NuoDB, and Clustrix, are general purpose databases that support any type of query. Other systems, e.g., VoltDB, are in-memory databases that focus on supporting short-lived and repetitive queries that touch small fractions of the data. Other NewSQL systems are based on optimized storage engines for MySQL, e.g., TokuDB, MemSQL, and Akiban. While applications interact with these systems as if they were standard MySQL databases, they have better scalability properties. There are also some NewSQL systems that are based on middleware components that automatically partition and distribute existing databases, e.g., dbShards and ScaleBase.

```
C1: CREATE TABLE votes(phone_number bigint NOT NULL, state
 varchar(2) NOT NULL, contestant_number integer NOT NULL);
Q1: SELECT contestant_number, count(*) FROM votes
 GROUP BY contestant_number ORDER BY contestant_number;
Q2: SELECT state, COUNT(*) cnt FROM votes GROUP BY state
 order by cnt DESC;
Q3: SELECT contestant_number, state, COUNT(*) FROM votes
 GROUP BY contestant_number, state;
```

Figure 6: VoltDB SQL Queries.

5.2 NewSQL Learning Resources

VoltDB [19] is a well-documented, open-source NewSQL system that can be used to support the introduction of NewSQL technologies with the integration of hands-on activities into the curriculum. VoltDB is an in-memory and ACID-compliant database system that uses a shared nothing architecture. VoltDB is supported on Linux and Mac OS X and provides client libraries for Java, C++, C#, Python, PHP, and Node.js.

The use of a VM is also a great way to enable a hands-on interaction with NewSQL systems like VoltDB. In this case, instructors can use the VM available at VoltDB's web site [19]. Besides the VoltDB software, this VM contains a set of sample applications and tools for application development. The sample applications are particularly useful resources to teach about NewSQL and VoltDB. These applications include: (1) a system that simulates a telephone based voting process, (2) the implementation of a Key-Value store backed by VoltDB, (3) an example that shows memcache-like cache implemented using VoltDB, and (4) an application that shows the use of flexible schema and JSON.

Instructors can use the following in-class activity working with the voting process simulator. Students first analyze and execute the provided scripts that start the database server, create tables, and run a client application that simulates a call center receiving the votes. Fig. 6 shows the SQL (C1) that creates table *votes*. During the execution of the client application, students use a provided web-based interface to monitor in real-time the voting results and the current winner in each state. Next, students use VoltDB Studio to write and run SQL queries. For instance Fig. 6 shows queries prepared by the authors to compute the total number of votes obtained by each contestant (Q1), the total number votes in each state (Q2), and the number of votes for each candidate in each state (Q3). This activity also provides a good opportunity to highlight some of the key properties of this type of NewSQL system, e.g., high transaction throughput (transactions/second) and low latency (time to process a vote).

Achieving learning objectives.

Similarly to the previous units, the use of the VM enables students to get not only hands-on experience with VoltDB

(LO2) but also a better understanding of key features of NewSQL systems (LO1), particularly the support of the relational model and SQL.

It is also important to describe scenarios, beyond the voting system, where NewSQL systems can be the right type of system to use (LO3). While NoSQL and NewSQL systems can handle datasets with massive size and high velocity, NewSQL systems are particularly suitable for applications that require support of the relational model, ACID guarantees, and SQL. For instance, while an HBase (NoSQL) can be the right data store for a web-scale blogging system, a NewSQL system like VoltDB can be the right database to process the rapid stream of stock exchange operations while ensuring transactional consistency.

6. DISCUSSION

The three proposed modules can be integrated into several introductory and advanced computer science courses. For instance, an introduction to MapReduce could be integrated into introductory databases or distributed systems courses. In this case, instructors can incorporate the in-class exercises and activities suggested for the MapReduce module. A high level exposure to NoSQL and NewSQL could also be integrated into an introductory database course through an assignment focused on exploring data management technologies beyond relational databases. The instructor could complement the assignment with an in-class discussion that highlights the key properties of the explored systems and scenarios where they are the right systems to use. A more extensive exposure of the three types of BDMSs can be incorporated in an advanced database class. In this case, instructors could incorporate the different hands-on activities and projects described in this paper. MapReduce could also be integrated into a programming course. This integration should focus on presenting the MapReduce programming model as a simple but effective approach to distribute the execution of a program among multiple computers. The authors have specifically incorporated the three modules into an advanced database course and the MapReduce module into an introductory distributed systems course.

To assess the integration of the three proposed modules and the extent to which the learning objectives were achieved, the authors used an end-of-class survey in the advanced database class. While this was a small class, the results are promising. The score distributions for the three modules were very similar. The average scores are presented next (1: Strongly agree - 5: Strongly disagree). To the question "*I am able to recognize the key properties, strengths and limitations of MapReduce/NoSQL/NewSQL*" (LO1), 50% of students strongly agree and 50% agree. To the question "*I understand when to use MapReduce/NoSQL/NewSQL systems*" (LO3), 67% of students strongly agree and 33% agree. To the question "*I am familiar with Hadoop/HBase/VoltDB and can build applications that interact with these systems*" (LO2), 42% of students strongly agree, 42% agree, and 16% gave lower scores. In the open ended questions, students gave positive comments about the use of hands-on exercises, VMs, and illustrative diagrams, e.g., "*using the VMs really captured my attention when using hands-on exercises and working directly with the systems*", "*the diagrams really helped visualize relationships and comparisons between different technologies*", and "*the hands-on exercises were great*".

7. CONCLUSIONS

Many application scenarios require processing massive datasets in a highly scalable and distributed fashion and different types of BDMSs have been designed to address this challenge. Graduating students gain employment in companies that already use BDMSs or are eager to use them to get better insights from the large datasets they manage. Thus, it is important to integrate the study of these systems as part of the computing curricula. This paper presents a set of guidelines and a wide array of class resources to integrate the study of three core types of BDMSs: MapReduce, NoSQL, and NewSQL. The paper also reports results of integrating the proposed units into a database course.

8. REFERENCES

[1] Hadoop eclipse plug-in. `http://wiki.apache.org/hadoop/EclipsePlugIn`.

[2] 10gen. Mongodb. `http://www.mongodb.org/`.

[3] Apache. Cassandra. `http://cassandra.apache.org/`.

[4] Apache. Hadoop. `http://hadoop.apache.org/`.

[5] Apache. Hbase. `http://hbase.apache.org/`.

[6] ASU. Big data management course resources. `http://www.public.asu.edu/~ynsilva/iBigData`.

[7] F. Chang, J. Dean, S. Ghemawat, W. C. Hsieh, D. A. Wallach, M. Burrows, T. Chandra, A. Fikes, and R. E. Gruber. Bigtable: A distributed storage system for structured data. *ACM Trans. Comput. Syst.*, 26(2):1–26, 2008.

[8] Clustrix. Clustrix. `http://www.clustrix.com/`.

[9] J. C. Corbett, J. Dean, M. Epstein, A. Fikes, C. Frost, J. J. Furman, S. Ghemawat, A. Gubarev, C. Heiser, P. Hochschild, W. Hsieh, S. Kanthak, E. Kogan, H. Li, A. Lloyd, S. Melnik, D. Mwaura, D. Nagle, S. Quinlan, R. Rao, L. Rolig, Y. Saito, M. Szymaniak, C. Taylor, R. Wang, and D. Woodford. Spanner: Google's globally-distributed database. In *USENIX*, 2012.

[10] A. Cron, H. L. Nguyen, and A. Parameswaran. Big data. *XRDS*, 19(1):7–8, Sept. 2012.

[11] J. Dean and S. Ghemawat. Mapreduce: simplified data processing on large clusters. In *OSDI*, 2004.

[12] S. Gilbert and N. Lynch. Brewer's conjecture and the feasibility of consistent, available, partition-tolerant web services. *SIGACT News*, 33(2):51–59, June 2002.

[13] M. Isard, M. Budiu, Y. Yu, A. Birrell, and D. Fetterly. Dryad: distributed data-parallel programs from sequential building blocks. In *EuroSys*, 2007.

[14] D. Kumar. Data science overtakes computer science? *ACM Inroads*, 3(3):18–19, Sept. 2012.

[15] K. Muthukkaruppan. The underlying technology of messages. Retrieved October 28, 2013 from `https://www.facebook.com/note.php?note_id=454991608919`.

[16] NuoDB. Nuodb. `http://www.nuodb.com/`.

[17] M. Project. Moby shakespeare. `http://icon.shef.ac.uk/Moby/`.

[18] A. Sattar, T. Lorenzen, and K. Nallamaddi. Incorporating nosql into a database course. *ACM Inroads*, 4(2):50–53, June 2013.

[19] VoltDB. Voltdb. `https://voltdb.com/`.

[20] T. White. *Hadoop: The Definitive Guide*. O'Reilly Media, 2012.

An Undergraduate Degree in Data Science: Curriculum and a Decade of Implementation Experience

Paul Anderson, James Bowring, Renée McCauley, George Pothering and Christopher Starr
College of Charleston
Charleston, SC
{ andersonpe2 I bowringj I mccauleyr I potheringg I starrc } @ cofc. edu

ABSTRACT

We describe Data Science, a four-year undergraduate program in predictive analytics, machine learning, and data mining implemented at the College of Charleston, Charleston, South Carolina, USA. We present a ten-year status report detailing the program's origins, successes, and challenges. Our experience demonstrates that education and training for big data concepts are possible and practical at the undergraduate level. The development of this program parallels the growing demand for finding utility in data sets and streaming data. The curriculum is a seventy-seven credit-hour program that has been successfully implemented in a liberal arts and sciences institution by the faculties of computer science and mathematics.

Categories and Subject Descriptors

K.3 **Computers & Education]**: Computer and Information Science Education – *computer science education, curriculum*

General Terms

Algorithms, human factors.

Keywords

Informatics, curriculum, cognate, analytics, data mining, machine learning, big data, contextualization, interdisciplinary, data science.

1. INTRODUCTION

By the late 1980s, the exponential growth in accumulated electronic data generated new interest in statistical machine learning to discover value in the data [15,16]. The new discipline of Knowledge Discovery in Databases (KDD) [16] emerged and took root in graduate programs for data-rich areas such as bioinformatics and drug discovery. The ACM Special Interest Group on Knowledge Discovery and Data Mining (SIGKDD) was established in 1998 to support this new field [1].

SIGCSE'14, March 5–8, 2014, Atlanta, Georgia, USA.

DOI string from ACM form confirmation

In 2006, SIGKDD published a two-course curriculum proposal in data mining [11]. In 2011, after 20 years of disciplinary maturation, at least 19 academic programs were available in the US and Canada with a connection to KDD either as a focus or as a supplement to a primary area of study [7]. By August 2013, the number of programs listed had grown to 61 of which only four were clearly undergraduate programs [8] – at the College of Charleston, George Mason, Indiana University and the University of Iowa.

More recently, data science and the related issues surrounding the use and utility of big data formed a cohesive theme for the June 2013 issue of IEEE Computer [13]. Media outlets have also covered stories about big data and emerging programs in higher education [14].

Implementation of the College of Charleston program began in May 2003, when a group of faculty in math, statistics, computer science, and biology believed that it would be possible to create a four-year undergraduate program based on KDD as an emerging discipline. The primary challenge was finding a way to offer the new degree within a liberal arts environment that had fifty-six hours of general education requirements. This paper presents the program development effort, the results of deploying the program, and a review of data collected during the last eight years of deployment.

2. CURRICULAR FOUNDATIONS

2.1 Origin of the Name and Concept

William Agresti, in an August 2003 article [2], coined the term "discovery informatics" to refer to "the study and practice of employing the full spectrum of computing and analytical science and technology to the singular pursuit of discovering new information by identifying and validating patterns in data." He also suggested that "discovery informatics" is a methodology for identifying and validating patterns in data and that belongs alongside artificial intelligence and simulation in the ACM Computing Classification System (CCS). He connected this new methodology to descriptors and topics in the 1998 classification system by identifying descriptors related to information storage and retrieval, AI, document and text processing, pattern recognition, and database management as parent disciplines of discovery informatics. In 2012, the ACM updated the CCS to include a number of related categories such as "data mining" and "web mining" as well as 109 concepts containing the word "data" [4].

The Agresti article appeared while our committee was working on this new undergraduate curriculum. The similarity between what Agresti defined as "discovery informatics" and the curriculum that was already in development inspired us to choose Discovery Informatics (DI) as the original name for the new degree program. Coincidentally, and unbeknownst to us at the time, another term, "data science", was coined in 2001 by William S. Cleveland [5]. His focus was on a multi-disciplinary expansion of the field of data analysis. The two terms competed for relevance during the ensuing decade and by 2010 it was clear the term "data science" was ascendant. Therefore, as a strategy to increase the visibility of our program, we moved to rename the degree as Data Science (DS) in 2012.

2.2 Knowledge Discovery in Datasets

Research related to KDD in the late 1980s had reached such a volume as to be evidence of an emerging discipline. Workshops in KDD were held at AAAI conferences in 1989, 1991 and 1993. Piatetsky-Shapiro and Frawley published a book on KDD in 1991 [16] that encapsulated then current research in the area. ACM's Special Interest Group on Knowledge Discovery in Data (SIGKDD) was formed and has become the primary professional organization for knowledge discovery. It has held an annual conference since 1995 and has published a biannual academic journal, "SIGKDD Explorations," since 1999. Other professional organizations that play a significant role in the advancement of KDD are the Institute of Electrical and Electronics Engineers (IEEE), the Institute for Operations Research and the Management Sciences (INFORMS) and the Society for Industrial and Applied Mathematics (SIAM). An important on-line source for current news in the data mining/knowledge discovery community is KDnuggets, founded by Piateski-Shapiro in 1997. KDnuggets currently lists over 15 journals in data mining and knowledge discovery. It also shows that in 2013 alone there were 82 business-related or research meetings and conferences in these areas.

Initially KDD entered into the academic curriculum in 2001 when Carnegie Mellon University launched the first Ph.D. program named Computational and Statistical Learning [12]. During the process of developing our DS degree, a member of our committee visited CMU to learn more about their program. The CMU graduate program in KDD was seminal, and it influenced the design of our DS undergraduate degree program. Three years after the design of our program, a working group of the SIGKDD published Version 1 of the Data Mining Curriculum [11].

2.3 Computing Curricula

Since 1978, computer science educators have looked to the ACM and the IEEE for guidelines for building undergraduate computer science courses and degrees. The Computer Science volume of Computing Curricula (CC2001) [10] was the most recent set of guidelines available in 2005. CC2001 outlines a set of recommendations for undergraduate degree programs in computer science. It includes a body of knowledge consisting of 132 knowledge units within fourteen core knowledge areas (KAs) of computer science. The KAs are listed in Table 1. For each knowledge unit, it includes multiple learning objectives.

CC2001 was consulted during the development of our DS program. Knowledge units within nine of the fourteen KAs were found to be appropriate to data science. Nearly 200 learning objectives over eight core areas were chosen as fundamental to this new degree. (See Appendix for the KAs and associated learning objectives chosen.) A revision of CC2001 published in 2008 maintained the original fourteen KAs, in which data mining is only an elective course recommendation in the Information Management section.

Table 1: Knowledge areas specified in CC2001 & CC2008.

Algorithms and Complexity	Information Management
Architecture and Organization	Net-Centric Computing
Computational Science	Programming Fundamentals
Discrete Structures	Programming Languages
Graphics and Visual Computing	Operating Systems
Human-Computer Interaction	Social and Professional Issues
Intelligent Systems	Software Engineering

A new curriculum volume, CC2013, was recently published in "draft ironman" form [3]. It maintains much of the content from CC2001 & CC2008. It reorganizes and refactors content between several of the KAs, introducing six additional KAs and renaming others. The new KAs are listed in Table 2. The objectives chosen for the DS degree persist in CC2013. Data mining is elective material.

Table 2: New knowledge areas[1] specified in CC2013.

Networking and Communication
Platform-based Development
Parallel and Distributed Computing
Security and Information Assurance
Software Development Fundamentals
Systems Fundamentals

3. PROGRAM DESIGN

The design of the DS curriculum presented unique problems because of the need to accommodate several disciplines and incorporate multiple learning objectives.

3.1 Interdisciplinary Faculty

DS is an interdisciplinary program that mirrors the interdisciplinary nature of data. Faculty members from mathematics, statistics and computer science, as well as from other disciplines collaborated to design the program. These faculty members routinely use informatics processes and tools in successful research programs such as in bioinformatics and geoinformatics.

3.2 Multidisciplinary Learning Objectives

The design of the curriculum began with the specification of learning objectives. These were derived largely from mathematics, statistics, and computer science. CC2001 proved to be a convenient framework on which to build the program. See Appendix for details.

The DS curriculum balances theory and concepts, tools and current techniques, with elements from a range of contributing disciplines, including computer science, artificial intelligence, mathematics, statistics, data mining, communication, and discussions of social and ethical issues associated with DS. The following outline shows the top two levels of the DS curriculum topic list. See Appendix for details.

1. **Large data sets / streams:** create/design, access, clean, analyze, aggregate, organize, visualize

[1] The CC2001 KA titles "Programming Fundamentals" and "Net-Centric Computing" are not part of CC2013. Their content appears in other KAs.

2. **Database:** design, storage, query, modeling
3. **AI techniques:** genetic algorithms, neural networks, Bayesian networks, intelligent agents, machine learning, pattern matching, heuristic search, knowledge representation and ontologies, natural language processing
4. **Software and Algorithms:** design, programming, testing, algorithms and analysis
5. **Information retrieval:** information theory, data mining, text mining, image mining, indexing, content analysis, linguistic processing, abstracting, search and retrieval, information filtering, query formulation
6. **Mathematics:** logic and counting, discrete structures, statistics, linear algebra, modeling and simulation
7. **Oral and written communication:** effective communication
8. **Social, ethical and legal issues:** privacy and security, property, policy, information validation, professionalism

For each topic in the DS curriculum, one or more learning objectives were specified. CC2001 heavily influenced the specification of learning objectives for the computer science content in the curriculum since, in many cases, appropriate learning objectives already existed. For example, for the Machine Learning topic under AI techniques (above), we incorporated six of the eight learning objectives from the CC2001 knowledge unit "IS8: Machine Learning and Neural Networks" into the DS curriculum.

As noted above, three years after the design of our Data Science program, a working group of the SIGKDD published Version 1 of the Data Mining Curriculum [11]. As with DS program design, the Data Mining Curriculum combines foundational and advanced topics, but with a narrow focus on data mining topics. The model sets prerequisites for entry and success in the Data Mining Curriculum. The DS program design is broader in scope than data mining, and includes topical areas having specific learning objectives. It also includes instruction in areas assumed to be prerequisites in the Data Mining Curriculum, including databases, algorithms, data structures, statistics, and linear algebra.

4. PROGRAM DETAILS

The design and development of the DS program required blending courses from several academic departments and organizing them as cognates to support integration across the liberal arts and sciences environment.

4.1 Multidisciplinary Course Requirements

The program objectives were satisfied by mapping the learning outcomes to undergraduate courses. The result was the use of eleven existing courses and the development of seven new courses. The core requirements are given in Table 3. Courses not previously available and created for the program are in italics. The new courses complete the set of core courses required to deliver the program learning objectives.

Only three of the new courses are unique to the DS program. Four have been incorporated into other degree programs in mathematics and computer science as elective courses and thus enjoy enrollments from two or more student major populations.

Table 3: Fifteen courses in mathematics, computer science, and data science that form the core of the Data Science program.

Core Course Requirements	Semester Credit Hours
Data Science	Total: 9
Introduction to Data Science	3
Dataset Organization & Management	3
Data Science Capstone	3
Computer Science	Total: 19
Computer Programming I	3
Computer Programming II	3
Computer Programming I Lab	1
Data Structures & Algorithms	3
Advanced Algorithms	3
Data Mining	3
Principles of Artificial Intelligence	3
Mathematics	Total: 26
Introductory Calculus	4
Linear Algebra	3
Discrete Structures I	3
Calculus II	4
Statistical Methods I	3
Statistical Methods II	3
Statistical Learning I	3
Statistical Learning II	3

Due to space constraints, only the three courses unique to the DS program are detailed here:

Introduction to Data Science This course has no prerequisites, and it provides an overview of the field. Its primary focus is introducing the field to a wide audience. The course focuses on the algorithms and tools that are required of a data scientist. Topics include: knowledge discovery techniques; tools for the analysis of large data sets; the data science process; inductive data-driven modeling.

Dataset Organization & Management This course covers the principles of big data organization and management. Topics include: relational and entity relationship models; local and distributed storage and access; preparation and management of datasets for analysis; data cleaning, reorganization and security.

Data Science Capstone A project-based capstone course for the application of knowledge discovery and data mining tools and techniques to large data repositories or data streams within the student's cognate area. The capstone experience is designed as an opportunity to synthesize the concepts learned throughout the curriculum to design novel software and algorithms for a domain specific problem related to a student's cognate area.

Details on these and all other required courses are available from the program website: `http://datascience.cofc.edu/`

4.2 Cognates for Contextualization

Initially, faculty in disciplines who had data-intensive research programs identified a set of ten cognates from across the liberal arts and sciences. The DS program requires that students complete one cognate. The number of cognates increased to 14 over the first five years of program implementation. Table 4 lists the cognates available in 2013 for students of the DS program.

Table 4: Cognates that establish a context for study and application of KDD concepts and tools.

Cognates	
Accounting	Geoinformatics
Biomechanics	Molecular Biology
Customer Relationship Mgmt.	Organismal Biology
e-Commerce	Physics and Astronomy
Economics	Psychology
Exercise Physiology	Sociology
Finance	Supply Chain Mgmt.

Each cognate requires between fifteen and twenty-two semester credit hours. The set of courses required for these cognates includes introductory and advanced courses in the cognate's domain discipline.

The purpose of a cognate is to introduce a student to an application domain. Courses in a cognate include coverage of domain terminology and concepts, data acquisition devices, common error types in the domain data and processes, and problems typical of the domain. The capstone course defines a custom project for each student to use KDD in the cognate domain under the direction of the cognate director or a faculty member doing data-driven research in that domain.

4.3 Integration into the Liberal Arts Environment

At the College of Chareslton, degrees in English, philosophy, and history each require 10 courses (thirty semester credit hours), intentionally providing options for students to select courses from other disciplines. The DS program, which requires up to seventy-seven credit hours depending on cognate, leaves little room for free electives.

The difference, however, between DS and the other programs requiring more credit hours than traditional liberal arts degree programs lies in the interdisciplinary nature of KDD. The core courses are equivalent to a liberal arts degree in scope but, additionally, DS exposes students to at least four disciplines (see Tables 3 and 4).

5. EXPERIENCES

The program costs have been marginal. Most significantly, no new faculty were needed because out of the 18 courses in the DS core curriculum, eleven were existing courses and four of the seven new courses also contribute to existing undergraduate majors. All courses in the cognates were existing courses.

The number of enrollments continues to grow, but remains small. Although it was always assumed that the rigorous mathematics and computer science courses together with the requirement of a cognate would keep the total enrollment small (never more than 50 majors in an institution with over 10,000 undergraduates) even this level of interest has not yet been reached. Figure 1 gives enrollment and graduation data per year from 2005 to 2013. No estimates for graduation rates were given in the initial proposal, however the institution's latest six-year graduation rate is 66.1%.

The graduates in 2007 and 2008 were already enrolled as computer science majors when the DS program was launched and were able to incorporate the DS requirements into their programs of study. The decline in majors number of majors in 2008 was disappointing, but the poor state of the U.S. economy at that time may have discouraged students from attempting innovative programs when the prospect of employment for the program's graduates was uncertain. It should be noted that, while there have been years of little or no growth, the overall trend has been positive, so there is reason to be optimistic that the number of majors will continue to increase.

One desired outcome of the program, which is being achieved, is to attract strong students. The average GPA, on a 4 point scale, of students who were matriculated in the DS program in Fall 2013 was 3.34 compared to an institutional average of 2.96 [6].

Another positive outcome is that all cognates have been chosen at least once. The most heavily favored cognates have been molecular biology, geoinformatics, psychology, and e-commerce. Anecdotal evidence from department chairs affiliated with some of the cognate areas indicates a strong interest with the DS program and its majors among new faculty candidates.

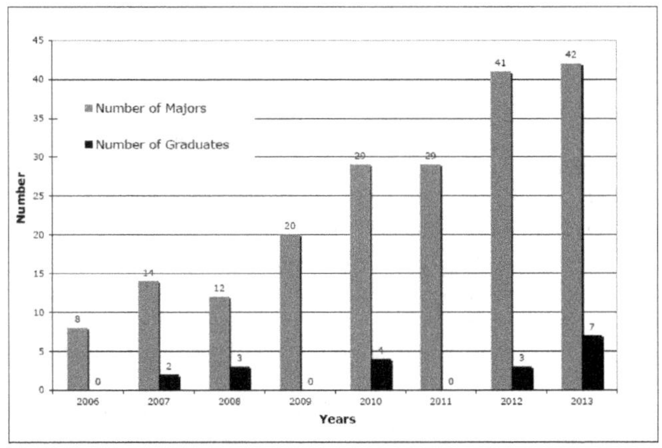

Figure 1: Anticipated enrollments, actual enrollments and number of graduates in the Data Science program.

Of those graduates who have not gone directly to graduate school, all have found career placements in data science, informatics, or computer science positions. Nevertheless, some of the graduates have experienced difficulties during their job search. While this could be attributed to economic conditions, some of the difficulty might be due to a lack of name recognition of the program, which we believe to be resolved with the change to Data Science from Discovery Informatics.

Institutionally, the DS program has been beneficial to the computer science and statistics students. Computer science students now have access to regularly-offered courses in data mining, AI (including machine learning), and advanced algorithms. The mathematics department has created a new statistics track, in part due to the two new upper-level courses in statistical learning required in the DS program.

6. DISCUSSION AND FUTURE PLANS

In 2003, the computer science department at the College of Charleston offered three undergraduate programs: a BS in Computer Science (ABET accredited), a BA in Computer Science, and a BS in Computer Information Systems (CIS). The CIS program is an interdisciplinary program including computer science and business courses. The DS program, launched in 2005, provided a second interdisciplinary computer science program by integrating computer science, mathematics, statistics, and a cognate area. The rigor of this interdisciplinary program attracts high-achieving students.

Several benefits of the DS program development process were:

- The institution has a small and stable faculty. This helped develop professional relationships across disciplines that led to the support of the program and the students who engage in it.
- Faculty drove the program development with the support of administration at all levels, including the institution president. This fostered a heightened level of trust and sense of partnership between the faculty and the administration.
- The new degree attracted new enrollments to existing computer science courses.
- The program generated students capable of being undergraduate research assistants in research labs requiring analytics.

We have learned many lessons and encountered several challenges while implementing our undergraduate program in DS that we believe an institution should consider before starting a similar program:

(1) We believe the lack of a community-supported and established name negatively affected program awareness, which led to lower than expected recruitment numbers. After the community converged on the name Data Science (current name of the program), we believe that name recognition is no longer a problem.

(2) Students with one or two calculus courses prior to collegiate study have more flexibility in their overall schedule. This helps the student navigate through the program since DS requires courses from multiple disciplines.

(3) The interdisciplinary nature of the program leads to advising challenges. We have addressed these by having the director of the DS program advise most majors and minors.

(4) Student retention to graduation could be negatively impacted due to the computational and mathematical rigor of the program. To counteract this, we require a high impact introductory course of all DS majors. This breadth-first introduction to the major engages students in the application of data science. For example, we have the students participate in the online data science competition community (www.kaggle.com). It also helps to build a community or cohort of DS students, making students feel a part of the program early on.

We are working on several initiatives to improve the degree. First, we are revisiting our 14 cognate areas to see if they can or should be simplified or modified. This is an ongoing evaluation that we conduct every few years. We are also examining the curriculum to see if there are ways to increase scheduling flexibility. Finally, we continue to refine the learning objectives for the DS curriculum; this will be necessary until a body of knowledge is derived by the KDD community for undergraduate programs in data science.

Our experience proves that a data science degree program can be successfully mounted at the undergraduate level. To do so requires an interdisciplinary team of computer scientists, mathematicians, and statisticians supported by university administration and domain experts in the specific disciplines. The rigor of this interdisciplinary program attracts high-achieving students, which strengthens all of our programs. DS graduates have been successful in industry positions specific to DS, but also those that typically hire CS graduates. Moreover, graduates have pursued graduate study at the Masters level in Analytics, and others have gone on to graduate study in Computer Science.

7. ACKNOWLEDGEMENTS

Many faculty members contributed their insights and time to the development of this program They are (alphabetical by last name): Paul Buhler, Computer Science; Alex Kasman, Mathematics; Bill Manaris, Computer Science; Norine Noonan, Dean, School of Sciences and Mathematics; Alan Strand, Biology; and James Young, Mathematics. Many other faculty members participated in the program approval and implementation process. Thanks to them all.

REFERENCES

[1] ACM SIGKDD Charter. SIGKDD, June 10, 1998. Accessed September 6, 2013. http://www.acm.org/sigs/bylaws-contents/kdd_bylaws/

[2] Agresti, W.W., Discovery Informatics, *Communications of the ACM*, August 2003, Vol. 46, No. 8, pp 25-28.

[3] CC2013 Ironman. The Joint Task Force on Computing Curricula. ACM, IEEE-Computer Society. Accessed September 5, 2013. http://ai.stanford.edu/users/sahami/CS2013/ironman-draft/cs2013-ironman-v1.0.pdf

[4] CCS2012. Accessed September 6, 2013. http://dl.acm.org/ccs_flat.cfm

[5] Cleveland, W.S., Data Science: An Action Plan for Expanding the Technical Areas of the Field of Statistics, ISI Review, 69, 2001, 21-26.

[6] College of Charleston 2013 Planning and Reference Guide. Accessed September 5. 2013. http://irp.cofc.edu/facts-and-publications/PRFB-Main-Menu.php

[7] Data Mining Education. KDnuggets. http://www.kdnuggets.com/education/usa-canada.html. Accessed January 11, 2011.

[8] Data Mining Education. KDnuggets. http://www.kdnuggets.com/education/usa-canada.html. Accessed August 28, 2013.

[9] Fayyad, U.M., and Uthurusamy, R. editors, Knowledge Discovery in Databases: Papers from the 1994 AAAI Workshop, Seattle, Washington, July 1994. AAAI Press, Technical Report WS-94-03, ISBN 0-929280-73-3, 473 pp.

[10] The IEEE-ACM Joint Task Force on Computing Curricula. Computing Curricula 2001: Computer Science, December 15, 2001.

[11] Intensive Working Group of ACM SIGKDD Curriculum Committee. Data Mining Curriculum: A Proposal (Version 1.0), April 30, 2006. www.sigkdd.org /curriculum.php.

[12] Machine Learning Ph.D. Programs, Machine Learning Department, Carnegie Mellon University, http://www.ml.cmu.edu/prospective_students/phd_programs.html

[13] Michael, M. and Miller, K.W., guest ed. Big Data: New Opportunities and Challenges. IEEE Computer. June 2013.

[14] Miller, C.C., Data Science: The Numbers of Our Lives. *New York Times*. April 11, 2013.

[15] Piatetsky-Shapiro, G. Knowledge discovery in real databases: A report on the IJCAI-89 Workshop. AI Mag. 11, 5 (January 1991, 68-70.

[16] Piateski-Shapiro, G., and Frawley, W., Knowledge Discovery in Databases. MIT Press, Cambridge, MA. 1991.

APPENDIX

Topic List and Learning Objectives[2] for Undergraduate Program in Data Science

1.	**Large data sets / streams - Creation/design/; Access; Clean; Analyze; Aggregate; Organize; Visualization**	
	a.	Information Management, IM4, Relational databases, objectives 1-5
	b.	Graphics and visualization, GV9, Visualization, objectives 1-4
2.	**Database - Design; Storage; Query; Modeling**	
	a.	Information Management, IM 6, Relational database design, objectives 1-7
	b.	Information Management, IM 8, Distributed databases, objectives 1-5
	c.	Information Management, IM 5, Database query languages, objectives 1-5
	d.	Information Management, IM 3, Data modeling, objectives 1-6
3.	**AI techniques - Genetic algorithms; Neural networks; Bayesian networks; Intelligent agents; Machine learning; Pattern matching; Heuristic search; Knowledge representation and ontologies; Natural language processing**	
	a.	Intelligent Systems, IS8. Machine learning and neural networks, objectives 1-8
	b.	Intelligent Systems, IS6. Agents objectives 1-6
	c.	Intelligent Systems, IS2, Search and constraint satisfaction, objectives 1-7
	d.	Intelligent Systems, IS3, Knowledge representation and reasoning, objectives 1-4
	e.	Intelligent Systems, IS5, Advanced knowledge representation and reasoning, objectives 1-6
	f.	Intelligent Systems, IS7, Natural language processing, objectives 1-5
4.	**Software and Algorithms - Design; Programming; Testing; Algorithms and analysis**	
	a.	Programming Fundamentals, PF5, Event-driven programming, objectives 1-3
	b.	Software Engineering, SE9, Component-based computing, objectives 1-5
	c.	Programming Fundamentals, PF2, Algorithms and problem-solving, objectives 1-5
	d.	Programming Fundamentals, PF3, Fundamental data structures, objectives 1-8
	e.	Programming Fundamentals, PF1. Fundamental programming constructs, objectives 1-6
	f.	Algorithms and Complexity, AL1. Basic algorithmic analysis, objectives 1-5
	g.	Algorithms and Complexity, AL2. Algorithmic strategies, objectives 1-8
	h.	Algorithms and Complexity, AL3. Fundamental computing algorithms, objectives 1-7
	i.	Algorithms and Complexity, AL5. Basic computability, objectives 4 & 5
	j.	Algorithms and Complexity, AL6. The complexity classes P and NP, objectives 1-3
	k.	Algorithms and Complexity, AL8, Advanced algorithmic analysis, objectives, 1-4
5.	**Information retrieval - Information theory; Data mining; Text mining; Image mining; Index**	
	a.	Information Management, IM 11, Information storage and retrieval, objectives 1-5
	b.	Information Management, IM 10, Data mining, objectives 1-8
	c.	Information Management, IM 12, Hypertext and hypermedia, objectives 1-5
	d.	Information Management, IM 13, Multimedia information and systems, objectives 1-5
6.	**Mathematics - Logic and counting; Discrete structures; Statistics; Linear Algebra; Modeling and simulation**	
	a.	Discrete Structures, DS2, Basic logic, objectives 1-4
	b.	Discrete Structures, DS4. Basics of counting, objectives
	c.	Discrete Structures, DS1. Functions, relations, and sets, objectives, 1-4
	d.	Discrete Structures, DS3. Proof techniques, objectives 1-4
	e.	Discrete Structures, DS5. Graphs and trees, objectives 1-4
	f.	Discrete Structures, DS5. Discrete probability, objectives 1-4
	g.	Computational Science and Numerical Methods, CN3, Modeling and simulation, objectives 1-4
7.	**Oral & written communication**	
8.	**Social, ethical and legal issues - Privacy and security; Property; Policy; Information validation; Professionalism**	
	a.	Social and Professional Issues, SP7. Privacy and civil liberties, objectives 1-5
	b.	Social and Professional Issues, SP6. Intellectual property, objectives 1-5
	c.	Social and Professional Issues, SP4, Professional and ethical responsibilities, objectives 1-6
	d.	Social and Professional Issues, SP5, Risks and liabilities of computer-based systems, objectives 1-4
	e.	Social and Professional Issues, SP2. Social context of computing, objectives 1-5

[2] All learning outcomes are from CC2001 [10]

CS Principles Goes to Middle School: Learning How to Teach "Big Data"

Philip Sheridan Buffum
Computer Science
North Carolina State Univ.
Raleigh, NC, USA

Allison G. Martinez-Arocho
Computer Science
Meredith College
Raleigh, NC, USA

Megan Hardy Frankosky
Psychology
North Carolina State Univ.
Raleigh, NC, USA

Fernando J. Rodriguez
Computer Science
North Carolina State Univ.
Raleigh, NC, USA

Eric N. Wiebe
STEM Education
North Carolina State Univ.
Raleigh, NC, USA

Kristy Elizabeth Boyer
Computer Science
North Carolina State Univ.
Raleigh, NC, USA

{psbuffum, agmarti5, rmhardy, fjrodri3, wiebe, keboyer}@ncsu.edu

ABSTRACT

Spurred by evidence that students' future studies are highly influenced during middle school, recent efforts have seen a growing emphasis on introducing computer science to middle school learners. This paper reports on the in-progress development of a new middle school curricular module for Big Data, situated as part of a new CS Principles-based middle school curriculum. Big Data is of widespread societal importance and holds increasing implications for the computer science workforce. It also has appeal as a focus for middle school computer science because of its rich interplay with other important computer science principles. This paper examines three key aspects of a Big Data unit for middle school: its alignment with emerging curricular standards; the perspectives of middle school classroom teachers in mathematics, science, and language arts; and student feedback as explored during a middle school pilot study with a small subset of the planned curriculum. The results indicate that a Big Data unit holds great promise as part of a middle school computer science curriculum.

Categories and Subject Descriptors

K.3.2 [**Computers & Education**]: Computer and Information Sciences Education --- *Computer Science Education*

General Terms

Human Factors.

Keywords

Computer science education, middle school, big data

1. INTRODUCTION

Recent years have seen an increased emphasis on introducing computer science to K-12 learners. The motivation for these activities is rooted in an understanding of how students eventually choose and succeed with an undergraduate major: previous positive experience with a subject matter plays a pivotal role [2, 12]. This point has particular significance within the field of computer science; for example, a very small number of US students take the traditional AP CS exam, and there is a troubling participation gap seen in that small body of test-takers [2]. The discrepancy corresponds to similarly disappointing statistics for students who earn bachelor degrees in computer science [29].

In both their stated aspirations and in their development of subject-specific skills, students begin their career trajectory in middle school [14]. Researchers have specifically traced the underproduction and underrepresentation issues in undergraduate computer science departments back to lack of exposure as early as middle school [22, 26]. In the U.S., any middle school computer science intervention must address the challenge that computer science is essentially absent from standard public education curricula. Numerous successful middle school interventions have addressed this challenge through after-school, summer, or enrichment-based activities; for example, these curricula often use various visual programming languages [15] or computer games [25]. Yet important questions remain for a computer science curriculum designed for in-class settings. How can computer science learning objectives be aligned with new curricular standards? How can computer science be successfully delivered by teachers who are trained in other subjects? And finally, how can we build learning activities that are highly engaging and developmentally appropriate for students?

This paper examines these questions in the context of a proposed curricular unit for Big Data, one of the foci of the proposed AP Computer Science Principles course [7]. Although a full formal definition of "Big Data" is still emerging, the phenomenon is often characterized by collection at high *velocity*, storage in a *variety* of structures, and large *volume* [8]. In addition to its widespread societal importance and increasing implications for the computer science workforce, Big Data holds great promise as a focus for middle school computer science because of its rich interplay with other important CS Principles including algorithms, abstraction, and the Internet. As this paper describes, Big Data also represents an area with strong correspondence between CS Principles and emerging US national curricular standards such as the Common Core in Mathematics [5] and the Next Generation Science Standards [17, 18]. In addition to its strong links to other core subjects, the topic of Big Data has great flexibility in

SIGCSE'14, March 5–8, 2014, Atlanta, Georgia, USA.

http://dx.doi.org/10.1145/2538862.2538949

incorporating other highly engaging application domains, including those that are relevant to kids' everyday lives. For instance, an excellent example of Big Data can be seen within social networks and their massive collections of structured and unstructured data.

The work reported here is conducted in the context of the ENGAGE project, a multi-year effort that will see development of a full CS Principles-based middle school curriculum situated within a game-based learning environment. The CS Principles approach may be well suited for the middle school level because the thematic threads of CS Principles Big Ideas can be introduced at a developmentally appropriate level for middle school students and thus provide the basis for more advanced work in high school. We are developing our curriculum in an iterative fashion with pilot studies and focus groups on each set of prototype learning activities. This paper presents the work to date on the Big Data curricular unit, including its alignment with emerging standards, feedback from an interdisciplinary group of teachers, and results from a pilot study with middle school students. While the piloted activity represents only a small subset of the planned curriculum for ENGAGE, results suggest that Big Data holds appeal for achieving computer science learning and for showcasing the relevance of computer science to middle school students.

2. RELATED WORK

Recent years have seen an increase in the number of middle school computing interventions, many of which innovate to teach programming with visual or graphical programming languages. Alice 3D has been used successfully [21], integrating computing within the context of a wide variety of subjects such as math, science, and language arts [20], and to help students understand what their future careers in computing might look like [27]. Scratch programming has also been used extensively [4, 15, 23], including with students with disabilities [1], urban youth [16], or particular underrepresented groups [10]. Other languages such as Logo [15] and more recently Kodu [24] have also been used in middle school interventions. There is also growing momentum for using game design and game programming [25] and robotics [13] as ways to introduce computer science to middle school students. Efforts have also been made to formalize assessment of computational thinking at the middle school level [28].

In complement to this middle school work, the AP Computer Science Principles course is being developed at the high school level and plans to debut as an official, credit-bearing course in the 2016-17 academic year [7]. CS Principles is organized around seven Big Ideas, one of which is Big Data. Students must analyze, interpret, and gain new insight from data sets, both visually and statistically [7]. Relatedly, Berkeley's CS Principles pilot course, "The Beauty and Joy of Computing" has sections on the impact of Big Data and information technology in modern life [11]. Notably, this aspect of social relevance is a motivating factor for women to enter and remain in computer science [9]. Our current work takes inspiration from these CS Principles pilots, in concert with teacher and student focus group feedback, in developing a Big Data curricular unit.

3. BIG DATA CURRICULUM DESIGN

An important focus of our ongoing work is to develop a suite of learning activities that can be adopted within a variety of middle school contexts including standalone computer science courses or as enrichment for subject matter areas including mathematics and science. A vital step toward this goal is aligning the CS Principles-based curriculum with current standards for middle school grade levels. We first analyzed the Common Core State Standards for English and Mathematics, and the Next Generation Science Standards, and then conducted teacher focus groups to gain feedback on this alignment and to help tailor the proposed Big Data curriculum to middle school classrooms.

Table 1. CS Principles Computational Thinking Practices & Common Core Practices for Mathematics

CS Principles Computational Thinking Practices	Common Core Practices for Mathematics
P1: Connecting Computing	MP5: Use appropriate tools strategically
P2: Developing computational artifacts	MP4: Model with Mathematics
P3: Abstracting	MP2: Reason abstractly and quantitatively
P4: Analyzing problems and artifacts	MP1: Make sense of problems and persevere in solving them
P5: Communicating	MP3: Construct viable arguments and critique the reasoning of others MP6: Attend to precision
P6: Collaborating	

3.1 Alignment with Curricular Standards

3.1.1 Common Core State Standards

Beginning in 2009, the Common Core State Standards Initiative created a set of curricular standards intended to align the previously separate curricula of individual states within the U.S. According to its mission statement, these standards, "are designed to be robust and relevant to the real world, reflecting the knowledge and skills that our young people need for success in college and careers" [5]. Common Core for Mathematics laid out a series of high-level practices through which students are expected to find meaning in problems, use abstract and quantitative reasoning, construct arguments, critique the reasoning of others, and model with mathematics. Similarly, the CS Principles curriculum frames seven Big Ideas around the core computational thinking practices of connecting computing, developing computational artifacts, abstracting, analyzing problems and artifacts, communicating, and collaborating [7]. Table 1 highlights some important parallels between the CS Principles Computational Thinking (CT) Practices and the practices for the Common Core in Mathematics.

At a high level, both CS Principles and the Common Core include big ideas on data. While the Common Core standards relating to data do not map directly to the corresponding CS Principles Big Idea, we see the opportunity for a curriculum that serves the goals of both CS Principles and the Common Core in a complementary fashion. Table 2 shows Learning Objectives for CS Principles and selected standards from the Common Core that relate to data.

3.1.2 The Next Generation Science Standards

Similar to the Common Core, the precursor Framework report and Next Generation Science Standards in the U.S. [17, 18] does not explicitly address computer science, but holds promise for the development of complementary curricula. The Framework report states that elements of both computational and mathematical

Table 2. Goals for Data in CS Principles and Common Core

CS Principles Big Idea 3: ***Data and information facilitate the creation of knowledge***
3.1.1 Use computers to process information to gain insight and knowledge
3.1.2 Collaborate when processing information to gain insight and knowledge
3.1.3 Communicate insight and knowledge gained from using computer programs to process information
3.2.1 Use computing to facilitate exploration and the discovery of connections in information
3.2.2 Use large data sets to explore and discover information and knowledge
3.3.1 Analyze the considerations involved in the computational manipulation of information
Common Core Standards that relate to data
Grade 6. SP.A.1 Recognize a statistical question as one that anticipates variability in the data related to the question and accounts for it in the answers
Grade 6. SP.B.4 Display numerical data in plots on a number line, including dot plots, histograms, and box plots
Grade 6. SP.B.5 Summarize numerical data sets in relation to their context
Grade 7. SP.A.1 Understand that statistics can be used to gain information about a population by examining a sample of the population
Grade 7. SP.A.2 Use data from a random sample to draw inferences about a population with an unknown characteristic of interest.
Grade 7. SP.B.4 Use measures of center and measures of variability for numerical data from random samples to draw informal comparative inferences about two populations
Grade 8. SP.A.1 Construct and interpret scatter plots for bivariate measurement data to investigate patterns of association between two quantities
Grade 8. SP.A.4 Understand that patterns of association can also be seen in bivariate categorical data by displaying frequencies and relative frequencies in a two-way table.

thinking are central to K-12 science education, and these are addressed through the discussion of science and engineering practices and crosscutting concepts [18]. These science and engineering practices recognize the importance of identifying student outcomes that go beyond memorizing narrowly focused scientific facts; they provide a broader interpretation of science inquiry that includes computational approaches.

The Next Generation Science Standards stated practices include both analyzing and interpreting data, and using mathematical and computational thinking [17]. The Framework was clear that the eventual Standards documents needed to address how mathematical and computational tools and techniques are deployed in the service of analyzing large data sets: "Such data sets extend the range of students' experiences and help to illuminate this important practice of analyzing and interpreting data" [18]. As this statement illustrates, there is great promise for creating curricula in which the power of computer science is illustrated within the context of widely required subject matter.

3.2 Teacher Focus Groups

With this alignment in hand between the proposed Big Data concepts and standard curricula, the next step was to obtain detailed feedback from experienced middle school teachers to inform the development of specific learning activities. We held a series of in-depth classroom teacher focus groups during the summer of 2013. Three teachers from an urban middle school in Raleigh, North Carolina were recruited to participate for approximately 40 hours each in both group and solo sessions. The teachers were two females and one male, and all three were from minority groups that are underrepresented in computer science. They included one 8th grade math teacher, one 7th grade science teacher, and one 7th grade language arts teacher. Each focus group session lasted between three and four hours and the format varied depending on the topic. Early sessions focused on introducing computer science topics to the teachers. These sessions involved both presentations and guided classroom activities conducted by project team members. Later focus groups were heavily discussion-based, as teachers brainstormed on how to teach computer science principles to middle school students, and drafting classroom activities.

3.2.1 8th Grade Math

The 8th grade math teacher expressed some initial hesitation to the idea of teaching Big Data to middle school students, concerned that its concepts would be out of reach given the students' development level. However, she became much more receptive to the idea after a more thorough discussion and explanation of Big Data. She emphasized the need to introduce topics in "baby steps." She noted that middle school students are still developing the mathematical background to perform statistical computation. A question she raised was, "To what degree and depth do we want them to understand Big Data...and have it support the Common Core?" Another of her primary concerns was, "How do we do it in a way that is not overwhelming to them...and that they say 'Wow, cool. How can I use this in my life today?'" The other two teachers echoed this sentiment, emphasizing that the curriculum should be grounded in human applications to which students can personally relate. As will be described in Section 4, our iterative curriculum development process involves measuring the extent to which students relate to each prototype learning activity.

3.2.2 7th Grade Science

The science teacher provided insight into how to create middle school activities that support what students are learning in their science classes. In particular, she emphasized that we should reinforce the scientific method, which all students in grades six through eight have learned and use in their science classes. She also noted that reading tables and graphs is difficult in general for students, but is an important skill for them to learn. Making inferences or forecasting from data is particularly difficult for middle school students, so she suggested ways to slowly introduce the material over time, and to avoid overly abstract representations. This advice guided the scaffolding included within the first Big Data activity, described in Section 4.

3.2.3 7th Grade Language Arts

The 7th grade language arts teacher quickly saw implications for his classroom. For instance, he uses Wordle[1] to generate "word clouds" from texts before his class reads a book. As a class, they use the most prevalent words to make predictions on the dominant themes that might appear in the book. After the lesson on "What

[1] http://www.wordle.net

is Big Data", the teacher saw this activity as a good opportunity to broaden the discussion in his classroom to include Big Data. Also certified as a social studies teacher, he drew a parallel between a challenge that middle school students might have with programming and one they have in social studies: "sequencing is a difficulty for kids." He noted that middle school students struggle to make the connection from past to present, from present to future, and from self to global community. Our team aims to address some of these challenges with ENGAGE's game-based narrative, designed to give students a strong sense of engagement and personal connection with each problem they solve.

4. PILOT STUDY

Following the conclusion of the focus groups, we conducted a small two-session pilot study with students from an urban middle school in Raleigh, North Carolina. The purpose of the study was to observe students' success at completing a Big Data activity prototype and then to get a sense of their retention and continued interest a week later, as well as have them complete a series of follow-up Big Data learning activities. The first session consisted of a pre-survey, followed by working on the learning activity in collaborative pairs, and then ending with a post-survey. Focus groups held during the second session one week later centered on students' general conceptions surrounding Big Data, as well as their opinions on the various Big Data learning activities.

4.1 Session 1: Big Data Activity

A total of 15 students in 6th and 7th grades participated in the first pilot study session, which was held after school with a total time allotment of 50 minutes including pre-survey and post-survey. Based on experience from prior pilot studies in which students were predominantly male, the after-school coordinator was asked to emphasize recruiting female students. This emphasis succeeded and 13 of the 15 participants were female. The demographic makeup was six white students, four African-American students, one Latino student, one Native American student, one Indian student, one Middle Eastern student, and one multiracial student.

In the pre-survey, students were asked to complete the New General Self Efficacy (NGSE) scale, which aims to explain variance in motivation and performance by measuring students' belief that they can achieve a goal [6]. Scores on the 8-item scale (a 5 point Likert) revealed a high overall level of self-efficacy for the group (M=4.408, SD=0.513). This high overall self-efficacy may reflect a self-selection bias related to the after-school class.

Students also completed Likert scale items scored from 1 (*not at all interested*) to 5 (*very interested*) relating to two application domains: marine life and social networking. Marine life is the application domain for ENGAGE's game-based narrative and an application of Big Data in formal science education. Social networking, on the other hand, is a human application of Big Data that the teacher focus groups indicated would be more relevant to students' everyday lives. On average, students responded to "How interested are you in marine life?" with a 3.1 out of 5 (SD = 1.1), and to "How interested are you in social networks?" with a 3.3 out of 5 (SD = 1.6) While only 2 of the 15 students rated *both* marine life and social networks favorably (4 out of 5, or 5 out of 5), the number of students who rated at least one of these two topics favorably was 12 out of 15, indicating that a Big Data curriculum that includes a variety of topics is much more promising than focusing on just one application domain.

After finishing the online pre-surveys, 37 minutes remained for the Big Data activity prototype. Students were paired at computers equipped with screen capture and video recording for future analysis. In the activity, students progressed through a written narrative in which they took on the role of computer scientists sent to rescue an underwater research station in distress. As part of the adventure, they had to locate a file for a particular fish species within a massive fish database. The activity guides students step-by-step through a *skip list* search algorithm. Figure 1 shows an example subset of the fish database from the learning activity.

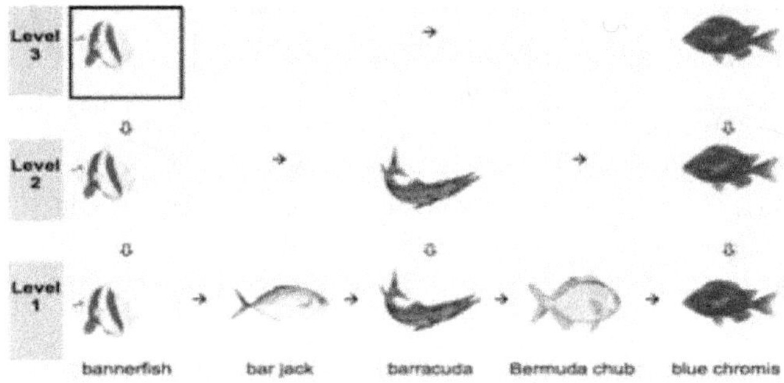

Figure 1. Example visual subset of the fish database

Skip lists, widely used in Big Data applications, provide an excellent context for teaching about data representation and algorithms. While the final curriculum will include many other Big Data learning activities that convey the excitement and conceptual value of Big Data (building upon the success of activities piloted elsewhere [7]), this particular Big Data pilot activity aimed to explore how Big Data applications can provide the framework for addressing other CS Principles Big Ideas, such as computing as a creative activity (Big Idea 1) and algorithms (Big Idea 4). Using a slightly larger subset of the database than the one illustrated in Figure 1, students were tasked with finding the shortest path to various target fish. The activity scaffolded students through each step of the skip list algorithm, using the visual subset of the database. After mastering the searching task manually on that concretely depicted subset, students then used a visual interface (simulating the visual programming language we will use in the ENGAGE game) to arrange pseudo-code blocks into a program that could traverse the entire database to find a desired fish (in this case, Surgeonfish). An ideal algorithmic solution is shown in Figure 2. As described in the next section, this first Big Data activity is designed to occupy one entire classroom session of approximately 50 minutes.

The post-survey included a User Engagement Scale [19] that measured involvement with the activity, focused attention, and the student's desire to repeat a similar activity in the future. Overall, students agreed with the item, "I felt involved with this activity" (3.9 out of 5; SD = 0.9), and generally disagreed with, "I felt discouraged while doing this activity" (1.9 out of 5; SD = 1.0). In contrast to these overall positive ratings, there was one African-

Step 0: Start at **Level 3** Skip List, **Bannerfish**
Step 1: Peek ahead to next fish in current level
Step 2: If the fish you see ahead comes before **<Surgeonfish>**
    Then Move Forward (to that fish)
    And Repeat (return to Step 1)
  Else if the fish you see ahead comes after **<Surgeonfish>**
    Then Move Down (to a lower skip list)
    And Repeat (return to Step 1)
  Else if the fish you see ahead is **<Surgeonfish>**
    Then Move Forward (to that fish)
    And STOP

Figure 2. Target algorithm for students to construct

American female student who responded with a 2 for "I felt involved with the activity", and with a 4 for "I felt discouraged while doing this activity". Among all the students in the study, this student had demonstrated the greatest interest in social networking, with lower stated interest in marine life, possibly explaining her lower feeling of involvement and higher discouragement with the marine life Big Data activity. As will be described in Section 5.2, this student later made contributions during the later focus group that shed light on her experience.

Overall, students rated, "This activity was fun" with 2.8 out of 5 SD = 1.3), lower than hoped. Because the prototype activity is being developed for use within ENGAGE's game-based learning environment, fun is an important emphasis. Upon reflection, we believe that the pace of the learning activity (with several minutes elapsing between achievements on the task) may have hindered a sense of fun, which will be addressed in future iterations. It is important that students frequently feel a sense of achievement, even if the successes represent incremental steps toward the larger goal. Also providing helpful feedback, students did not disagree with "I found this activity to be confusing" (3.2 out of 5; SD = 1.1), indicating room for improvement on the scaffolding. Based on all of the students' feedback, we designed session 2 of the pilot study, which was held one week later.

4.2 Session 2: Focus Groups

Of the original 15 students, 11 returned the next week for the second session, joined by three new students. As with Session 1, all students were in 6th and 7th grades. The demographics for the second session were as follows: 12 female and 2 male; 3 white, 6 African-American, 1 Latino, 1 Native American, 1 Indian, 1 Middle Eastern, and 1 multiracial student. The students were separated into three focus groups of four or five students per group, each facilitated by a member of the research team. Each group spent roughly 15 minutes discussing students' conceptions of computer science and programming, and then 15 minutes on data. A series of follow-up activities to the previous session's Big Data activity were then done in groups, with the new students paired up with students who had attended the previous week. The general purpose of these focus groups was to get student feedback on what works and what needs improvement in our Big Data curriculum. Particular attention was paid to eliciting feedback from students who reported negative opinions on the Big Data activity in session 1.

As predicted, students had a limited understanding of what Big Data might be. They could discuss data on a smaller scale, describing it as information that you can get and store: "anything you want to keep over a long time." They were familiar with examples of data in science, such as weather patterns or plant biology, and some saw the purpose of data being "to do a science project." Although they seemed not to have given much prior thought to other issues related to data, some students got excited thinking about the topic. When asked about data storage, one group of female students interpreted this question in terms of communication and collaboration. Figure 3 shows their conversation.

Facilitator: Where is data stored?
Student 1: On the ground, on a paper, you can put it anywhere.
Student 2: You could put it on the back of a spaghetti can.
Facilitator: Yes you could, but would it be helpful there?
Student 3: You could put [the spaghetti can] in the pantry.
Student 2: Like a community pantry.

Figure 3. Students discuss importance of sharing data

When considered in light of CS Principles Learning Objectives 3.1.2 and 3.1.3 (Table 2), the above dialogue illustrates the potential of data to be socially relevant, a key concern for girls in computer science. Following up on this finding, we also prompted the students to think about data for social networking. Most students had never previously given thought to data outside of science domains, but even students who had been quiet up to this point in the focus group expressed interest in these examples of data in their everyday lives.

After discussing computer science, programming and data, students collaboratively worked on a series of short activities related to the Big Data activity from the session 1. Like that prior activity, these were prototypes of activities being considered for ENGAGE's game-based learning environment. Consequently, they were presented as elements of the game's story, with students told that their feedback would influence the development of the game. In designing these activities, we aimed to improve on the design of the activity from session 1, such as by decreasing the amount of reading required. We also sought to obtain student feedback on Big Data applications that convey the full power and conceptual value of Big Data. Overall, students were noticeably engaged during this session. It included an activity involving cryptography, previously used for engaging middle school students in computer science [3], and a problem in which students solved a mystery by examining clusters of marine data to track a leaked pollutant.

The post-survey revealed that students felt more positively about the activities in this session than they did about the activity from session 1. Students rated these activities highly for "fun" (4.1 out of 5; SD = 0.8) and low for "confusing" (2.1 out of 5; SD = 0.8). Feedback was also more *consistently* positive, including for the African-American female student reporting negative feelings after session 1 (see Section 5.1). During the discussion, she advocated for including social networking features in the ENGAGE game, particularly the ability to chat with other players: "Everyone likes chatting." Similar to the conversation in Figure 3, this student's comments highlight the importance of communication and collaboration, two of the Learning Objectives for CS Principles Big Idea 3 (Table 2). While the improved positivity may be partially explained by repeated exposure to the topic, bringing greater levels of comfort, it also confirms the notion expressed by the classroom teachers in our focus groups: a middle school curriculum can benefit from including activities that are relevant to students' everyday lives.

5. CONCLUSION

A curriculum based on Computer Science Principles holds great promise for middle school, and the CS Principles related to Big Data may be particularly well suited for this age group. We have presented a case for teaching Big Data including its strong alignment with standard U.S. curricula including the Common Core and the Next Generation Science Standards. We have also presented results from classroom teacher focus groups that suggest Big Data can serve to enrich core subject matter including science, mathematics, and language arts. Lastly, we examined the findings of a small pilot study with middle school students that yielded several important lessons for refining the curriculum and learning tasks. First, although we created a learning activity with distinct subtasks, breaking these down even further and providing incremental achievements along the way may increase students' sense of fun and decrease confusion. Second, including a variety of application domains can strategically engage a broader set of learners with the Big Data activities. Finally, focus group feedback indicates that students may intuitively gravitate toward seeing the importance of communication and collaboration, and that these facets may be particularly beneficial to emphasize in Big Data activities for middle school.

To continue creating a successful CS Principles-based Big Data curriculum for middle school, several directions are important to future work. Teacher professional development at the middle school level is key, as computer science and Big Data are new topics for most teachers who might implement the curriculum. Additionally, it is important to develop formal CS Principles-related learning trajectories that map from high school to middle school and eventually to elementary school. Finally, it is hoped that as part of a broader effort to bring CS Principles-based curricula to middle school, this work can substantially increase access to, and interest in, computer science for K-12 learners.

6. ACKNOWLEDGEMENTS

This work is supported in part by the National Science Foundation through Grants CNS-113897 and CNS-1042468. Any opinions, findings, conclusions, or recommendations expressed in this report are those of the participants, and do not necessarily represent the official views, opinions, or policy of the National Science Foundation.

7. REFERENCES

[1] Adams, J.C. 2010. Scratching Middle Schoolers' Creative Itch. *Proceedings of SIGCSE '10* (2010), 356–360.

[2] Arpaci-dusseau, A. et al. 2013. Computer Science Principles□: Analysis of a Proposed Advanced Placement Course. *Proceedings of SIGCSE '13* (2013), 251-256.

[3] Bergner, N. et al. 2012. Cryptography for Middle School Students in an Extracurricular Learning Place. *CSEDU 2012 Proceedings of the 4th International Conference on Computer Supported Education* (2012), 265–270.

[4] Burke, Q. and Kafai, Y.B. 2012. The Writers ' Workshop for Youth Programmers Digital Storytelling with Scratch in Middle School Classrooms. *Proceedings of SIGCSE '12* (2012), 433–438.

[5] CCSSI, Common Core State Standards Initiative: 2012. Retrieved September 05, 2013 from *http://www.corestandards.org/Math*

[6] Chen, G. et al. 2001. Validation of a New General Self-Efficacy Scale. *Organizational Research Methods*. 4, 1 (Jan. 2001), 62–83.

[7] Computer Science: Principles: 2013. Retrieved September 5, 2013 from *http://www.csprinciples.org/*

[8] Crawford, K. 2011. Six Provocations for Big Data. *A Decade in Internet Time: Symposium on the Dynamics of the Internet and Society* (2011), 1–17.

[9] Fisher, A. et al. 1997. Undergraduate Women in Computer Science: Experience, Motivation and Culture. *Computer*. 29, (1997), 106–110.

[10] Franklin, D. et al. 2011. Animal Tlatoque: Attracting Middle School Students to Computing Through Culturally-Relevant Themes. *Proceedings of SIGCSE '11* (2011), 453–458.

[11] Garcia, D.D. et al. 2012. Rediscovering the Passion, Beauty, Joy, and Awe: Making Computing Fun Again, part 5. *Proceedings of SIGCSE '12* (2012), 577–578.

[12] Guzdial, M. et al. 2010. A Statewide Survey on Computing Education Pathways and Influences□: Factors in Broadening Participation in Computing. *Proceedings of the ninth annual international conference on International computing research (ICER '12)* (2012), 143–150.

[13] Larkins, D.B. et al. 2013. Application of the Cognitive Apprenticeship Framework to a Middle School Robotics Camp. *Proceedings of SIGCSE '13* (2013), 89–94.

[14] Lent, R.W. et al. 1994. Toward a Unifying Social Cognitive Theory of Career and Academic Interest, Choice, and Performance. *Journal of Vocational Behavior*. 45, (1994), 79–122.

[15] Lewis, C.M. 2010. How Programming Environment Shapes Perception, Learning and Goals: Logo vs. Scratch. *Proceedings of SIGCSE '10* (2010), 346–350.

[16] Maloney, J. et al. 2008. Programming by Choice□: Urban Youth Learning Programming with Scratch. *Proceedings of SIGCSE '08* (2008), 367–371.

[17] Next Generation Science Standards: 2013. Retrieved September 5, 2013 from *http://www.nextgenscience.org/next-generation-science-standards*

[18] NRC, National Research Council. 2011. *A Framework for K-12 Science Education: Practices, Crosscutting Concepts, and Core Ideas*. The National Academies.

[19] O'Brien, H.L.O. and Toms, E.G. 2010. The Development and Evaluation of a Survey to Measure User Engagement. *Journal of the American Society for Information Science*. 61, (2010), 50–69.

[20] Rodger, S.H. et al. 2009. Engaging Middle School Teachers and Students with Alice in a Diverse Set of Subjects. *Proceedings of SIGCSE '09* (2009), 271–275.

[21] Rodger, S.H. et al. 2010. Enhancing K-12 Education with Alice Programming Adventures. *Proceedings of the fifteenth annual conference on Innovation and technology in computer science education - ITiCSE '10*. (2010), 234.

[22] Shashaani, L. 1994. Gender Differences in Computer Experiences and its Influence on Computer Attitudes. *Journal of Educational Computing Research*. 11, (1994), 347–367.

[23] Sivilotti, P.A.G. and Laugel, S.A. 2008. Scratching the Surface of Advanced Topics in Software Engineering: A Workshop Module for Middle School Students. *Proceedings of SIGCSE '08* (2008), 291–295.

[24] Stolee, K.T. and Fristoe, T. 2011. Expressing computer science concepts through Kodu game lab. *Proceedings of SIGCSE '11* (2011), 99–104.

[25] Webb, D.C. et al. 2012. Toward an Emergent Theory of Broadening Participation in Computer Science Education. *Proceedings of SIGCSE '12* (2012), 173–178.

[26] Webb, H.C. 2011. Injecting Computational Thinking into Career Explorations for Middle School Girls. *2011 IEEE Symposium on Visual Languages and HumanCentric Computing VLHCC*. (2011), 237–238.

[27] Webb, H.C. and Rosson, M.B. 2011. Exploring Careers While Learning Alice 3D: a Summer Camp for Middle School Girls. *Proceedings of SIGCSE '11* (2011), 377–382.

[28] Werner, L. et al. 2012. The Fairy Performance Assessment: Measuring Computational Thinking in Middle School. *Proceedings of SIGCSE '12* (2012), 215-220.

[29] Zweben, B.S. 2013. Computing Degree and Enrollment Trends From the 2011-2012 CRA Taulbee Survey. Computing Research Association.

Lessons Learned and Recommended Strategies for Game Development Components in a Computer Literacy Course

Robert Collier and Jalal Kawash
University of Calgary
2500 University Dr. NW
Calgary, Alberta, Canada
+1 (403) 210 8483
rdcollie@ucalgary.ca, jkawash@ucalgary.ca

ABSTRACT

The challenges that instructors face attempting to motivate novice programming students are amplified when the students are not pursuing degrees or careers in computer science. For the programming module of our course for non-computer science majors we assigned a video game programming deliverable that we expected would engage students and enhance their experiences. After extensive analyses of the survey responses of 245 enrolled students we were surprised to learn that, although the majority believed the game programming experience enhanced their learning overall, another majority reported that the project itself was not enjoyable. Through qualitative analysis we have identified several key areas that seem to have detracted from the overall level of enjoyment, and in this paper we follow this investigation with discussion surrounding how these issues could be remedied in the future. These recommended strategies will bolster student enjoyment and motivation in future offerings and we believe this discussion will prove very useful to other instructors planning to employ game programming components.

Categories and Subject Descriptors

K.3.2 [**Computer and Information Science Education**]: Computer Science Education.

Keywords

Video Game Development, Computer Literacy, Undergraduate.

1. INTRODUCTION

In this paper, we describe our experience with an introductory level course in computer science, targeted at first year undergraduate students who are not currently working towards majors in computer science. Unlike many existing computer literacy courses, the course is designed to promote computational thinking [1, 2, 3] and, thus, programming is a major component.

It has been noted that many software engineering (and, by extension computer science) projects are not sufficiently enjoyable to engage students [4]. It was this original observation that motivated our development of the interactive game project deliverable for the computer programming module. It has also been noted that game design provides "an ideal framework" [5] for students to develop knowledge in topics of computer graphics, artificial intelligence, networking, and high-level programming language skills. Consequently, it was not unreasonable for us to investigate the use of game programming to help our students construct a strong foundation, largely in the absence of any previous programming experience.

Results have also indicated that the creation of games can advance the development of computational thinking [6], representing another potential advantage we considered when designing this module. Some of our previous work reinforced these observations in the context of assembly language programming [7], where it was reported that the vast majority of students preferred interactive video game development to a more traditional assignment. Furthermore, a larger majority of students reported that their learning outcomes are heavily boosted while developing a game [7].

This motivated us to engage students by assigning an interactive game programming project as one of the three major deliverables of the course. At the conclusion of the course we conducted an anonymous survey in which 245 students (representing an average participation level of 55% from three distinct lecture sections) provided feedback about their experiences. The apparent disparity between learning and enjoyment that was indicated by the survey was altogether unexpected. The results of this survey direct attention to several significant issues that can be used to aid designers of undergraduate level curriculums who might be attempting to introduce computer programming to non-majors. In a striking contrast with previous research, a majority of the students that participated in the survey claimed that the experience was not enjoyable, in spite of the fact that a larger majority of students reported that the project was a productive learning experience.

The rest of this document is organized into five sections. A brief description of the interactive game programming component of the course is described in Section 2. Students were asked to provide feedback (in the form of an anonymous survey) on this deliverable, and in Section 3, we discuss the issues and concerns raised by the participants of the survey. Specifically, this section will explore why the majority of students surveyed did not enjoy the game development process. Section 4 will go on to explore how the concerns raised might be addressed in the future, and Section 5 will discuss the surprising result that, despite a majority of participants finding the project unenjoyable, most students surveyed felt that their resultant learning (during the programming module) was considerable. A concluding summary of this research is presented in Section 6.

SIGCSE'14, March 5–8, 2014, Atlanta, Georgia, USA.

ACM 978-1-4503-2605-6/14/03…$15.00.

2. PROGRAMMING COMPONENT

The course is a first year computer literacy course for students not working towards a major in computer science. The bulk of the students belong to the management and social science schools, but students from the natural sciences, communications, and various other disciplines also register for the course on a regular basis, leading to a considerable amount of diversity. The content is delivered in a regular 13-week term through a combination of 150 minute lectures and 100 minute tutorials, with lecture sizes ranging between 100 and 175 students and tutorials capped at 25 students each.

Although the concept topics of this course also include propositional logic, set theory, graph data structures, and database management, this paper is concerned with the programming module. This module runs for two and a half lecture weeks (with the focus on high-level concepts such as object-oriented design and algorithm development) and four overlapping lab weeks (with the focus on hands-on program development).

The nature of the programming deliverable was the development of an interactive game using the Alice programming language [8, 9, 10, 11, 12]. Alice was designed at Carnegie Mellon University as a teaching tool for introducing students to the concept of object-oriented programming [8, 9, 10, 11, 12], and Alice 2.2 was selected because of the greater repository of instructional materials available to students and teachers. With an interactive, 3D development environment, Alice provides students with immediate feedback on the relationship between the program structure and the behaviour of objects in the 3D environment. Students were provided with the specification for the assignment at the same time as the programming module was introduced in the lectures, and they were further supported in their development efforts with interactive labs. Overall, the students had over four weeks for the development of their game.

The requirements for the game were minimal - at least two objects were expected to move through the 3D environment in a nontrivial fashion, accompanied by both random elements and player-controlled movement, ultimately culminating in a win-or-lose scenario. None of these elements is particularly challenging in isolation, but in order to ensure the students would not lose perspective during the development cycle, groups were also required to submit an extensive flowchart. Furthermore, since the ability to work effectively within groups is a crucial skill for software development at any level, students were required to work on their games in groups of (typically) three. Unsurprisingly, this requirement represented the first of several issues raised by the students in the anonymous survey delivered in the final weeks of class, after the programming module had concluded.

3. SURVEY RESULTS

The anonymous survey conducted in class requested that students comment on several distinct items surrounding the interactive game programming project deliverable. The survey polled their sense of individual enjoyment and requested a self-assessment of their learning after completing the deliverable. The survey also assesses their individual enjoyment, learning self-assessment, and performance expectations if the programming deliverable had focused on a topic other than interactive game development. Although the survey had students quantify their level of agreement with each statement, comments were also solicited.

As will be discussed in Section 6, only 29% of the students surveyed claim to have enjoyed working on the interactive game, with 44% of students in disagreement and 27% remaining neutral (Figure 1). Furthermore, although only 17.2% of the students that did enjoy the project characterized their agreement as strong, the number of students that did not enjoy the working on their game and characterized their disagreement as strong was twice as high, at 36.4%. It would not be unreasonable to conclude that those students that did not enjoy working on the game deliverable felt much more strongly about it.

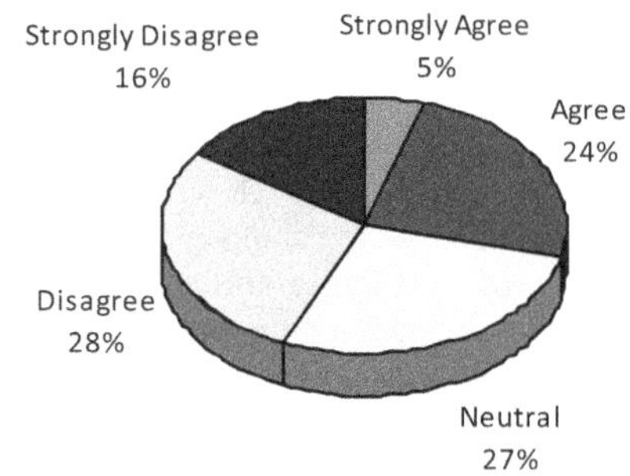

Figure 1. Responses to Survey Item #3 "I enjoyed working on the interactive game..."

The previous result notwithstanding, only 36% of students believed that an alternative project would have been more enjoyable, with 27% of students in disagreement (i.e., 27% of the students surveyed would not have preferred an alternative) and 37% of students remaining neutral (Figure 2). Naturally the survey results from Items #3 and #4 should not be considered independently; it is worth nothing that many students did not enjoy the game development project but did not want an alternative. This is consistent with the comments concerning the relevance of a programming component to this course that will be discussed in Section 4.1.

It should also be noted that 45% of students surveyed felt that they would have performed better had the deliverable not been a game programming project, with 18% in disagreement and 37% remaining neutral (Figure 3). Although several students expressed that they would have preferred the development of an animation project over video game development (again indicating that they believe their performances would have been superior), such a deliverable would hardly support the same diversity of structure that is inherent to game design.

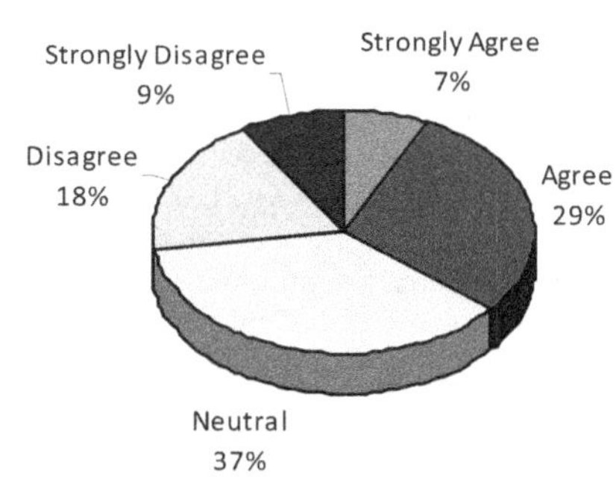

Figure 2. Responses to Survey Item #4. "I could have enjoyed [an alternative] more..."

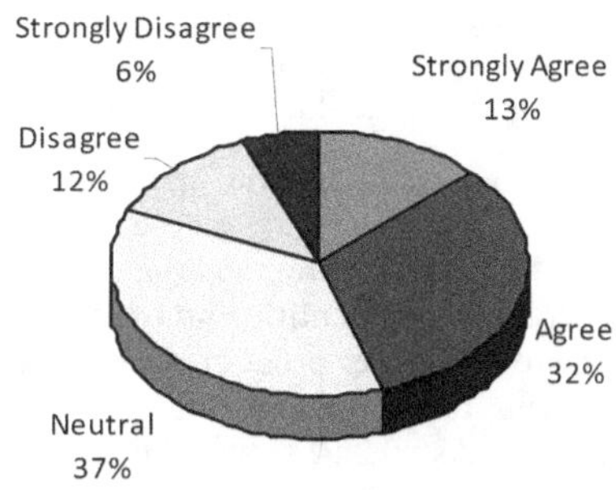

Figure 3. Responses to Survey Item #5. "I could have done better on [an alternative]..."

Although it was only a slight majority (36% vs. 27%, as noted previously) that reported that they would have enjoyed an alternative project more than the game programming deliverable, it is also worth noting that only 22% of the students surveyed felt that they would have learned more from an alternative. Contrarily, 34% reported disagreement, indicated that they feel they would have learned less from an alternative project, with 44% of the students surveyed remaining neural (Figure 4).

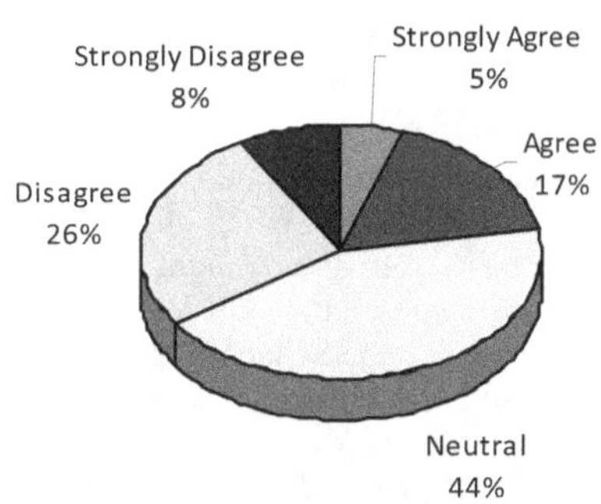

Figure 4. Responses to Survey Item #6. "I could have learned more [from an alternative]..."

Finally, and surprisingly, 60% of the students surveyed felt that their learning was considerable, with only 19% in disagreement and 21% remaining neutral (Figure 5). This was the most polarizing survey item (i.e., yielding the smallest number of students that remained neutral) and the lack of an apparent correlation between student enjoyment and self-assessed learning is somewhat counterintuitive. This topic will be discussed further in Section 6.

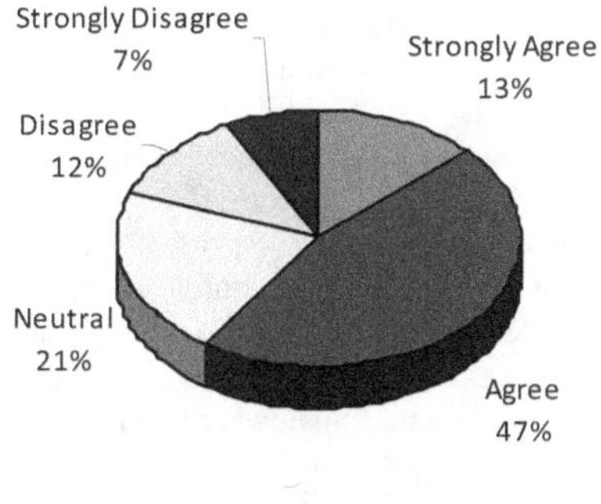

Figure 5. Responses to Survey Item #7 "I think I have learned a lot developing this game..."

The students were asked to explain their choices, and their answers were subjected to a qualitative analysis to investigate recurring issues. The following subsection will explore the three most frequently recurring issues raised by the students surveyed. Specifically, Sections 4.1 through 4.3 will respectively explore student perspectives about (1) the relevance of computer programming (and, specifically, computer game programming) to their own majors, (2) issues and technical difficulties associated with the development language imposed on the students for this deliverable (i.e., Alice 2.2) , and (3) issues associated with working in a group.

3.1 Major Relevance

The results of an informal poll on the first day of classes indicated that the vast majority of the students enrolled in the class were, in fact, majors from the School of Business. Although the Baccalaureate program to which these students were enrolled (at the time this research was conducted) listed the introductory computer science course in question as a required prerequisite, several students surveyed did not believe that elementary programming was a relevant topic, with their enjoyment of the module suffering as a result.

It has been well established (and noted previously in this paper) that game design is an ideal framework for students to develop their knowledge of computer science, since an interactive game incorporates the topics of input/output, branch structures, loop structures, and pseudorandom number generation without any topic feeling incongruous. Nevertheless, students 113 and 151 were not alone in stating explicitly that they were "not interested in programming." Student 120 was somewhat more explicit by stating simply that "I don't see how I will use it in the future," and students 30 and 176 clarified further that "this has no application to my business degree" and "I don't believe working on the interactive game is useful for [a] business degree," respectively. It should be explicitly noted that this attitude was not universal; student 101 stated "I enjoyed the programming aspect of Alice using pseudo-code, and designing flowcharts was highly applicable in real life." Although students were assured that video game development is a serious topic, with project deliverables mirroring software development projects in the real-world, it is our belief that this negative attitude could be further alleviated in future instances of this class by exploring the connections that exist between computer game development and business. This topic will be discussed further in Section 5.1.

Finally, it is worthy of note that some students felt that it was the Alice programming language itself (specifically Alice 2.2) that was not relevant to their individual degree programs. Student 114 stated "I learned a lot in Alice but don't know how it applies to a business degree." In fact, issues with the choice of development language were raised by several of the students surveyed, and these will be explored in the next section.

3.2 Alice Issues

In spite of the fact that Alice has been lauded as "the perfect tool to introduce students to object-oriented programming," [9] informal polls of the lecture sections indicated that Alice was virtually unknown to the students. Student 7 stated explicitly that "[I have] never heard of Alice before this course," and, unfortunately, this perceived obscurity undoubtedly contributed to the recurring perspective that the skills developed for working with Alice would not be useful outside this course.

It should also be noted that since this module represented a first introduction to computer programming for the vast majority of the students, they may have had a below average tolerance for the bugs and glitches that are inherent to the software development cycle. Student 8 stated that "[Alice] was a very unstable program and [had] a lot of bugs" and Student 105 mirrored these concerns "there were often many bugs and technical difficulties in the program." Student 136 stated similarly that "The Alice program made creating the game a bit difficult because of its glitches." Furthermore, student 107 offered a prime example of how the frustration associated with bugs can detract from the enjoyment of the development process when he or she made the statement that "[I] would enjoy it more if Alice was not full of bugs".

In addition to the bugs and glitches encountered by the students surveyed, the limitations of Alice also presented a barrier to the students that, unsurprisingly, detracted from their enjoyment of the process. Failing to recognize that Alice was designed primarily for education purposes, student 9 stated that the "program [is] incapable of making decent game," while student 108 remarked similarly that "Alice doesn't seem very practical." It remains our belief that Alice can be used to construct an appropriate interactive game, and Section 5.2 will discuss some possible approaches for providing additional guidance.

Finally, the absence of resources for the more recently developed versions of Alice (i.e., Alice 2.8 and Alice 3.1) was sufficiently prohibitive to ensure that our deliverables would require students to use Alice 2.2. At least one student (student 153) stated that he or she believed that the class should be using the updated version, but some of the contraindications to this are well established in [18].

3.3 Group Work

The first items in the survey presented to the students were designed to assess the participation of individual students in the group project. In spite of the fact that 94.4% of students stated that they worked on the video game as a member of team, 57.7% of students surveyed claimed to have completed 100% of the game functionality (i.e., the programming deliverable requirement, as opposed to the flowchart requirement). Although this result is surprising and might be cause for concern, it is not altogether implausible given the fact that the average level of student participation across each of the three sections surveyed was approximately 55%. Nevertheless, this indicates a potential depreciator of student enjoyment that should not be solely attributed to the content (i.e., elementary computer programming).

Varying degrees of motivation have been identified as one of the most serious issues associated with group work, with unmotivated students failing to develop sufficient programming experience and, subsequently, experiencing reduced levels of enjoyment. Furthermore, the issue of inequity based motivation (wherein students who typically exhibit satisfactory performance will reduce their own efforts in response to membership in a group with unmotivated students) is strongly indicated by survey results. Student 87 stated, regrettably, that "I ended up doing [the project] all myself and I am so sick of lazy group members that don't want to do anything." Similarly, student 227 stated "It was hard to work with a team for a project like this and I find one person usually ends up doing the bulk of the work," and student 116 stated "There wasn't enough time because the other group members did not participate." It is worth explicitly noting that although students were encouraged to address problems with the division of effort internally, they were also reminded to approach their instructors if they could not satisfactorily resolve their own issues.

Although the concerns raised in the previous paragraph were identified by several participants, these issues cannot be considered unique to computer programming. However, it should be noted that several student identified group work issues that are specific to the task of computer programming. Student 181 stated that it "was difficult to delegate separate components and to divide work evenly" and student 143 stated that "Unless the whole group was together, we couldn't work on the game ... Even when we were together, we were still all huddled around one computer." These concerns can be readily addressed by the well-known practice of pair programming, which is one of several topics that will be introduced in the next section to address the issues that were identified in the survey.

4. RECOMMENDED STRATEGIES

In this section, we entertain possible remedies to the problems that were discussed in the previous section, by discussing the valuation of games and game development, and the skeleton [16] and pair programming techniques [17]. It remains our belief that these topics and techniques could be integrated to address the recurring issues described in Section 4.

4.1 Game Valuation

Game design is used as a teaching tool because it is widely recognized as an engaging approach by which computer programming concepts can be taught. Since computer programming was considered a vital skill for students enrolled in undergraduate programs with the School of Business, engagement alone is sufficient reason to opt for the use of video game design in the computer programming deliverable. However, since the comments of several surveyed students clearly indicate that they consider games to be a pointless endeavor, and since this unfortunate perspective will decrease student motivation, we believe that it is important to convince students that the abstract concepts of game design (i.e., the non-programming components) do indeed have merit and can be applied in their future efforts. For this purpose, we believe that the two significant and distinct fields of gamification and game theory should be introduced to students early in the computer programming module.

Game theory (or decision theory) is the study of mathematical systems that model the behaviour of rational agents, either in co-operation or in conflict [13]. Naturally this field is widely applied to the discipline of economics, where game theory is a major method for modeling competition to facilitate the investigation and exploration of complex strategies. A complete discussion of game theory exceeds the scope of this paper, but it is our position that students would require only the most basic introduction to the topic. It would then suffice to note that while the structures necessary for the development of a video game would impart programming skills, it would not be unreasonable to suggest that the abstraction of decision-making entities in game development can be considered an exercise in preparing students for the task of developing more sophisticated business models.

Another topic that we believe could be introduced to students to restore their motivation would be the field of gamification [14]. The most elementary definition for gamification is the use of game mechanics in applications that are not games. The common areas of application for these principles (to the business domain) include marketing, training, and employee performance - areas that should be of great interest to serious business majors. The field of gamification entails the use of game design principles for the engagement of audiences and these techniques can be used to direct typical human desires for competition, co-operation, status, and achievement. Unsurprisingly, the techniques associated with gamification have been successfully applied to many of the common problems faced in the discipline of marketing, and it is worthy of note that analysts predict that by 2014 "more than 70 percent of Global 2000 organizations will have at least one gamified application" [15].

We maintain and emphasize that it should not be necessary to devote a great deal of time to the introduction of game theory and/or gamification; a brief introduction to these topics will provide students with assurance that the non-programming components of the game design deliverable can be applied to future work in their chosen discipline, alleviating the stigma that video games are nothing but simple toys, lacking inherent value.

4.2 Skeleton Programming

Students eventually learn to accept bugs as a natural part of software development, but it is important that they not become frustrated. Nevertheless, in spite of the availability of several instructors and teaching assistants, many of the surveyed students reported that they encountered too many bugs and glitches when using the Alice programming language. While Alice does indeed have limitations that can be attributed to its express purpose as an educational tool, many of the bugs encountered by the students were the result of their own design flaws. An informal polling of the students following their submission indicated that few groups had designed an overview or flowchart for their game before attempting to begin implementation (in spite of the fact that flowcharting was covered thoroughly in the lectures and required by the project specification). Naturally, for students at this level of experience, this lack of preparation was not advisable and was the source of much frustration. It is our belief that it might be possible to alleviate some of this frustration through the use of skeleton programming [16].

The principle behind skeleton programming is to provide a program composed of high-level structures into which additional code can be inserted. These skeleton programs are designed such that, while resembling pseudo-code (and, consequently, remaining intuitive to non-programmers), the programs can be parsed and tested easily in the development environment. This allows students to pursue development projects from a top-down approach, where a framework can be enhanced incrementally to meet the programming project specifications. Furthermore, this approach could be used to restrict students from attempting to implement a project that is unfeasibly large or complex.

4.3 Pair Programming

A third and frequently recurring issue raised by the surveyed students concerned working in groups. Although group work in general can be fraught with pitfalls, regardless of the discipline, we believe that students at this level might benefit from a brief introduction to the principles of pair programming.

In the practice of pair programming [17], two programmers work together on a single machine. The first programmer, commonly known as the driver, implements the program design directly. The second programmer, commonly known as the navigator, reviews the material implemented by the driver, promptly identifying defects and providing suggestions. The pair of programmers switch roles frequently and can brainstorm as needed. Although many programmers do not initially welcome the idea of pair programming, an experiment conducted at the University of Utah on students at the undergraduate level [17] found that 92% of students were more confident in the deliverables they produced with their partners, and 96% found the experience more enjoyable.

This practice can be readily adapted to groups of three by using two observers and increasing the frequency with which roles are exchanged. We believe that this would address many of the concerns about the division of labour. Instructors wishing to proceed in this manner may also wish to allocate a small amount of lecture or tutorial time to a supervised group programming session, in order to ensure that students understand the merits associated with the technique. It should also be noted that the formation of groups by the instructor (rather than by the students themselves) according to each student's degree of familiarity with programming should also reduce the tension between motivated and unmotivated students.

5. ENJOYMENT AND LEARNING

Considering the widely recognized positive correlation that exists between enjoyment and motivation [4], the most startling result indicated by our investigation was the absence of any significant correlation between the degree to which each student reported his or her enjoyment of the material and the degree to which that assessed his or her learning of the material. With only 28.8% of the students surveyed reported that they enjoyed the video game programming deliverable (with 43.2% reporting that they did not find the experience enjoyable and 28.0% remaining neutral), we did not anticipate that 59.4% of students would self-assess the quality of their learning positively (with only 19.2% of students actually disagreeing that they learned a considerable amount). A plot of student enjoyment versus self-assessed learning (with qualitative survey responses from strong agreement to strong disagreement quantified to integer values one through five, respectively) did not indicate any significant correlation (with a squared Pearson correlation coefficient < 0.3).

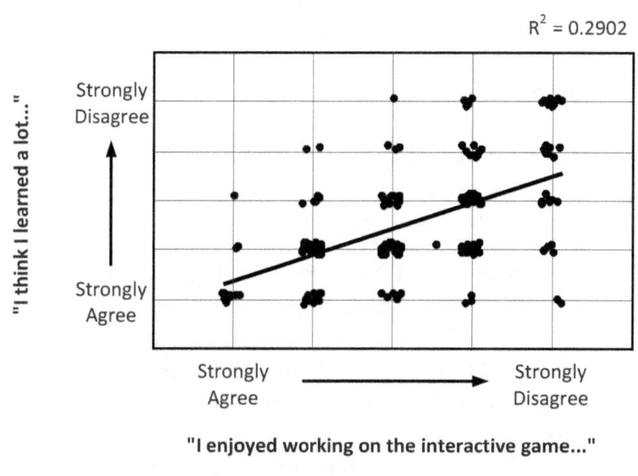

Figure 6. Correlation between enjoyment and learning, with uniformly distributed jitter added to indicate distribution.

This surprising result could be interpreted (optimistically) as an indication that many students were able to recognize the importance and widespread applicability of computer programming and believe that the nature of the game development deliverable, from design through implementation to testing, did contribute to their overall learning may itself hold inherent merit. This further suggests that addressing technical difficulties and the concerns that are typical of group work (through the possible use of the skeleton and pair programming techniques mentioned in sections 5.2 and 5.3) could do much to alleviate student dissatisfaction and improve motivation further.

6. CONCLUDING SUMMARY

Our initial decision to use an interactive game programming deliverable for the programming component of this course was expected to improve student motivation. Although the results of our survey are not contraindicative of this (since many of the students surveyed explicitly noted that they felt that the programming component was neither necessary for, nor relevant to, their own majors), the relatively low level of enjoyment reported was surprising. Thankfully, the comparatively low level of enjoyment was not significantly correlated with the degree to which students assessed their own learning - a substantial number of students reported that they learned a great deal while maintaining that they did not enjoy the project.

Through careful qualitative and quantitative analyses we have explored recurring issues surrounding the relevance of programming to students who are not working towards degrees in computer science, the technical difficulties associated with introductory programming, and the challenge of effectively working in a group to complete a programming project. These concerns are not only relevant to our course specifically; instructors designing or delivering introductory programming courses should consider these issues carefully. As such, we have explored the notion of the valuation of games and game development and the introduction of skeleton and pair programming techniques to directly address student concerns. By integrating these practices into future offerings of the course, we believe that student motivation can be improved considerably, ultimately resulting in a corresponding increase in learning.

7. ACKNOWLEDGMENTS

We thank the students that participated in the survey conducted in the Winter 2013 semester. Without their effort and feedback, this work would not have been possible.

8. REFERENCES

[1] Banerjee, S. and Kawash, J. 2009. Re-thinking computer literacy in post-secondary education. In Proceedings of the 14th Western Canadian Conference on Computing Education (WCCCE '09). ACM, New York, NY, USA, pp. 17-21.

[2] Kawash, J. 2012. Engaging students by intertwining puzzle-based and problem-based learning. In Proceedings of the 13th Annual Conference on Information Technology Education (SIGITE '12). ACM, New York, NY, USA, pp. 227-232.

[3] Kawash, J. 2010. Peeking into Computer Science. Pearson Learning Solutions, New York, NY, USA.

[4] Claypool, K. and Claypool, M. 2005. Teaching software engineering through game design. In Proceedings of the Innovation and Technology in Computer Science Education Conference (ITiCSE '05). ACM, New York, NY, USA, 123-pp. 127.

[5] Schaefer, S. and Warren, J. 2003. Teaching Computer Game Design and Construction. Computer-Aided Design, vol. 36, pp. 1501-1510.

[6] Basawapatna, A., Koh, K. H., and Repenning, A. 2010. Using Scalable Game Design to Teach Computer Science from Middle School to Graduate School. In Proceedings of the 15th Annual Conference on Innovation and Technology in Computer Science Education. ACM, New York, NY, USA, pp. 224-228.

[7] Kawash, J. and Collier, R. 2013. Using Video Game Development to Engage Undergraduate Students of Assembly Language Programming. In Proceedings of the Special Interest Group for Information Technology Education (SIGITE '13). In Press.

[8] Dann, W., Cooper, S., and Pausch, R. 2011. Learning to Program with Alice. 3rd Edition. Prentice Hall.

[9] Alice.org. 2013. Testimonials from Alice users. Retrieved July 7, 2013, from http://www.alice.org/index.php?page=testimonials

[10] Seidman, R. H. 2009. Alice First: 3D Interactive Game Programming. In Proceedings of the 14th Annual ACM SIGCSE Conference on Innovation and Technology in Computer Science Education (ITiCSE '09). ACM, New York, NY, USA, pp. 345.

[11] Daly, T. 2011. Minimizing to Maximize: An Initial Attempt at Teaching Introductory Programming Using Alice. Journal of Computing Sciences in Colleges, vol. 26, iss. 5, pp. 23-30.

[12] Wang, T.-C., Mei, W.-H., Lin, S.-L., Chiu, S.-K., and Lin, J.M.-C. 2009. Teaching Programming Concepts to High School Students with Alice. In Proceedings of the 39th ASEE/IEEE Frontiers in Education Conference (FIE '09). pp. 1-6.

[13] Stahl, S. 1999. A Gentle Introduction to Game Theory. American Mathematical Society.

[14] Werbach, K. and Hunter, D. 2012. For the win. 1st edition. Wharton Digital Press.

[15] Gartner. 2013. Gartner Predicts Over 70 Percent of Global 2000 Organisations Will Have at Least One Gamified Application by 2014. Retrieved July 7, 2013, from http://www.gartner.com/newsroom/id/1844115

[16] WiseGEEK. 2013. What is a Pseudocode? Retrieved July 7, 2013 from http://www.wisegeek.com/what-is-a-pseudocode.htm

[17] Williams, L., Kessler, R., Cunningham, W., and Jeffries, R. 2000. Strengthening the case for pair-programming. IEEE Software, Vol. 17. pp. 19-25.

[18] Alice.org. 2013. Alice 3_1 FAQ. Retrieved July 7, 2013, from http://help.alice.org/w/page/59015092/Alice 3_1 FA

Use and Development of Entertainment Technologies in After School STEM Program

Veronica Cateté
North Carolina State University
890 Oval Drive
Raleigh, North Carolina
vmcatete@ncsu.edu

Kathleen Wassell
North Carolina State University
890 Oval Drive
Raleigh, North Carolina
kmwassel@ncsu.edu

Tiffany Barnes
North Carolina State University
890 Oval Drive
Raleigh, North Carolina
tmbarnes@ncsu.edu

ABSTRACT

This design research paper examines the implementation and curriculum changes of an after school computer science program that promotes computational thinking to middle school students. The program, Students in Programming, Robotics, and Computer Science (SPARCS), can adapt to different presentation environments, such as independent after school sessions or a semester-long apprenticeship program. We trace one implementation of the program through the initial deployment, the development of infrastructure, and a reorganization of content to address student interests. We found that student attrition dropped and the average session enjoyment increased when our sessions integrated consumer technologies such as mobile applications, video games, and the Minecraft computer game. In this paper, we provide readers a framework for running computing outreach activities around similar consumer technologies.

Categories and Subject Descriptors

K.3.2 [**Computers and Education**]: Computer and Information Science Education—*curriculum, computer science education*

General Terms

Measurement; Design

Keywords

CS Education; SPARCS outreach; curriculum; games; mobile applications

1. INTRODUCTION

Prior research has demonstrated that children form opinions and attitudes towards computing at an early age [9], during the middle school years. Preconceptions made during these formative years influence a child's course choices in high school and college, as well as their eventual career goals. The President's Council of Advisors on Science and Technology projects that to maintain the current level of technological progress, the United States needs to increase the number of students who receive undergraduate STEM (Science, Technology, Engineering, and Mathematics) degrees by about 34% annually over current rates[7]. The Council also highlighted the problem of attrition, where, of the students starting post-secondary education in STEM fields in 2003-2004, only 35.1% had attained a STEM degree by 2009. The figures for computer science are especially grim: Of the students who started post-secondary school in computer science, only 24.6% had graduated with a degree in a STEM field. Our area of focus is in recruiting students into the early stages of the STEM pipeline during their middle school years, when they are developing interests and self-perceptions that will shape their future careers. We have created a series of workshop-like classes for middle school students that allow them to have fun exploring areas such as robotics, circuitry, web design, and video game design. When students are excited about the possibilities in computing, we predict they will be more likely to enter into STEM-related degree paths, and more likely to pursue their degrees to completion.

SIGCSE'14, March 5–8, 2014, Atlanta, GA, USA.

http://dx.doi.org/10.1145/2538862.2538952.

2. EXISTING BPC EFFORTS

The National Science Foundation has funded nearly three dozen projects for broadening participation in computing (BPC). The larger projects are alliances like National Center for Women & Technology (NC WIT) and Students & Technology in Academia Research & Service (STARS) Corps[2]. These programs focus on getting more women and minorities enrolled in computing and on retaining the students who are already in computing. NCWIT, A4RC, CAHSI, and AccessComputing are focused on a particular demographic; CAITE, Georgia Computes! and Into The Loop are location based programs for recruiting urban youth; and CDC Computing and EL Alliance are focused on retention of students already in computing majors[1]. STARS is a broader program that incorporates support along each stage of the pipeline, for all underrepresented groups in computing. Our outreach program SPARCS attempts to mirror the example of STARS being both location and population independent.

[1]For a more in depth description of each prject see Chubin 2010

2.1 Resource Programs

Dot-Diva is an organization that supplies promotional items for recruiting women into computer science, however, as a resource hub it does not have feet on the ground directly interacting with its target audience [3]. The National Center for Women in Technology (NC WIT) similarly maintains an extensive library of digital resources to support STEM and computing along all stages of the pipeline. They provide workshops "in-a-box" and roadshow ideas that can be taken to girls all across America.

Recently, NCWIT has implemented a pilot program where high school girls, who have won the NCWIT Aspirations in Computing award, lead a middle school outreach project [5]. These projects are disjoint from each other and often take the form of a summer camp, or one-off events (events that occur only once). In contrast, we have designed our outreach program in a long term fashion, where we work with the same groups of students year-long, with the option of continuing into supported summer camps.

2.2 Outreach Programs

An exemplary outreach program is Georgia Computes!, which has actually taken action to directly interact with students and k-12 teachers. Georgia Computes! works with the YMCA, Girl Scout troops and other existing organizations and schools. By plugging into the existing infrastructure Georgia Computes! has been able to scale their programs state-wide reaching thousands of students[2].

The strategy behind Georgia Computes! is to increase interest in computing at the pre-teen level and to improve the quality of computing education at the high school level [1]. Georgia Computes! trains high school teachers on how to teach engaging AP computing courses. At the pre-teen level students are working with programs like Alice, Lego Mindstorms, and other robotics. Georgia Computes! charges $30 - $285 for most of their workshops and camps, and this is a potential barrier to students from lower-income families.

With SPARCS our goal is to create a 100% free opportunity for students, that introduces them to cool applications in computing. After building interest in computing, we hope to inspire them to take a high school computing course, or even pursue a major and career in STEM or computing. We encourage students in our program to take the new pilot Advanced Placement CS Principles course, a less code-intensive course that operates around seven big ideas of computing that prioritize creativity and impacts on society and innovation over programming alone[8].

3. GOALS & ELEMENTS OF OUR DESIGN

The goal of our research is to build on the theoretical foundations of computer science education by shedding light onto what attracts students to computing, how to retain students from underrepresented groups, and how to successfully evaluate interventions that are attempting to broaden participation in computing (BPC). The STARS Computing Corps (a NSF Funded BPC Alliance) at North Carolina State University created one such intervention in the form of a middle school outreach program called Students in Programming, Robotics, and Computer Science (SPARCS). Through this outreach program, college students in computing majors travel to local middle schools and teach young students about computing.

Since its inception in 2007, the SPARCS program has been replicated in six different middle schools near Raleigh and Charlotte North Carolina. We introduce you to the main locations in section 4. SPARCS has undergone three main phases of implementation which we will discuss in section 5. Each phase of modifications addressed a need for improved sustainability or increased engagement with the content. The design of the SPARCS program was devised in such a way that our participants would "spark" an early interest in computing. With the diverse background of attending students, a potpourri method of introduction occurred where the teachers would cover a wide range of topics over the course of a school year in hopes that at least one of the topics would light a spark of interest for middle school students.

4. SETTINGS

The SPARCS after school program takes place either in a media lab at a local middle school, or if resources are unavailable, we invite the students to a computer lab at one of our participating college campuses. In the following sections we will provide you with an in-depth description of each of our SPARCS locations.

4.1 Centennial Campus Magnet Middle

SPARCS was initiated in October 2007 and is currently in its sixth year of operation at Centennial Campus Magnet Middle School (CCMMS). SPARCS here is sponsored by the Raleigh branch of the STARS Alliance. Students are offered monthly Saturday sessions to introduce them to fun and interesting concepts in Computer Science.

Sessions are held from 10am-3pm and are stand alone workshops so attendance at the previous session is not required. These monthly workshops include hands-on learning activities to introduce the students to computer science concepts and practical applications. Sample workshops include Alice programming, web design, and LEGO Mindstorm robotics.

4.2 North Carolina Math & Science Education Network

In January 2012, SPARCS partnered with UNC Charlotte's branch of the NC Math & Science Education Network (MSEN). SPARCS was offered as a class during the regularly scheduled Saturday Academy that is part of NC MSEN. Students in the UNC Charlotte MSEN program come from schools all across the district and are typically in the top 5% of their class (MSEN requires students to maintain an A/B average). Enrollment in our SPARCS class was limited to female minorities.

Similar to SPARCS at CCMMS, sessions in the MSEN program were offered monthly, the meeting times being 8am - 12pm. We picked out workshops that we thought would be more enjoyable for girls, including iPhone development, digital story books, and web design.

4.3 McPie Family Night

In January of 2012, SPARCS expanded to include schools with greater need. SPARCS at UNC Charlotte approached the McClintock Partners in Education (McPIE) and signed up as an available club during Family Nights at McClintock Middle School. Weekly Tuesday sessions from 5:15-6:30 in-

Table 1: Demographics data from the different SPARCS sites

Program	M	F	Caucasian	Hispanic/ Other	African American	Free/Red. Lunch	Food/Travel provided
Centennial Campus Magnet Middle	74.2	25.8	40	23.3	36.7	37.1	Food
NC Math & Science Education Network	0	100	0	0	100	-	None
McClintock Family Nights	65.4	34.6	12.8	32.5	54.7	80.4	Both
Citizen Schools	77.8	22.2	5	34	61	90	Travel

troduce McPIE students to fun, free, and interesting applications in Computer Science.

Sessions are broken down into three-week themes. Themes are independent from each other; however, within a theme, one session builds upon the previous. Sample themes include game design, android app development, and CS Unplugged activities.

4.4 Citizen Schools

We also offer SPARCS through a 10-week apprenticeship in Citizen Schools. Eastway Middle and Martin Luther King Jr. Middle both host a Citizen School program. Citizen Schools provides the SPARCS team with in-room teacher assistants who are responsible for class conduct and discipline. These programs run after school from 3:30pm to 4:45pm in a regular classroom, with a mobile laptop lab owned by the university when needed. As a part of Citizen Schools, students present what they have learned in a WoW event at the end of the 10 weeks.

In the Citizen Schools implementation, our apprenticeships focus on teaching students fundamental Computer Science concepts through Video Game Design[4]. During the 10-week program, students learn CS concepts such as variables, loops, boolean logic, and conditionals while creating their own unique games designed with Game Maker, a free game design tool. Our newer Citizen Schools implementations now include a Scratch and Lego Mindstorms curriculum.

5. BASE IMPLEMENTATION

Each SPARCS location and implementation is built on the same core computing values: critical thinking, programming, abstraction, creativity, and applications. We begin by encouraging the students to come up with a model for computer scientists, answering questions about what Computer Scientists do, what they need to know, and how they are generally perceived.

Each of our programs encourages students to create digital artifacts that can be taken home, shown to parents, and continually worked on. These artifacts take on many forms including web pages, presentations, games and other tech gadgetry.

6. PHASES

In this section we will discuss the three phases that the SPARCS program has undergone. Phase I is our initial implementation where we were testing to see if students would be interested. In Phase II, after building a following of students, we built infrastructure to support the growing population and gain valuable feedback from students. We conclude with phase III, where we introduced mainstream technologies like mobile apps and games to teach computing.

6.1 Phase I - Start Up

In August of 2007, a group of 4 college undergraduates created a computing club for middle school students. They were fortunate to have a middle school right down the road from their college campus. The college students contacted the school's outreach coordinators and set up a time to come to the school to recruit students. Teachers reminded the middle school students about the upcoming presentation, and 8 children were recruited. The first set of activities designed for these students, described in detail below, were CS Unplugged, Alice, Web design, and Lego Mindstorms. Unfortunately, students did not continually show up to these sessions as students were told the session prior when to come for the next session. By the final session, which is a field trip to the technology museum, only one student was in the program. This phase was a pilot of the SPARCS program and no data were collected.

CS Unplugged Students participate in dynamic and engaging CS Unplugged activities that introduce them to computing concepts without computers. Topics include: binary numbers, programming languages, and algorithms.

Alice Students learn object oriented programming using Alice software by Carnegie Melon. Students work together to complete a tutorial on initial programming tasks. Then students create their own projects or movies in Alice.

Web Design The students are given a tutorial on HTML to design and create their own web page. The lessons are drawn from the W3Schools online modules, and students edit their web pages using a basic plain text editor.

Robotics Students build and program robots using the Lego Mindstorms development kit. They first use guided instructions to learn how to build a robot and how to program it to do simple tasks. Then, the students form teams and build their own designs to compete with other teams if they desire.

6.2 Phase II - Tech Up

By the Fall of 2009, SPARCS coordinators developed a Drupal-based website where parents could register their child and see a calendar of upcoming SPARCS activities. This website also hosted a series of simple feedback surveys on student perception of learning and enjoyment. These surveys also contained brief questions on how much the students knew on a particular topic before and after leaving the session. These surveys were intended to help us create and modify new sessions for the students.

We therefore introduced a full game design workshop where students were better able to meet their personal goals. Instructors also began updating previous sessions and creating a new security workshop.

Game Design Students learn about the basic principles behind the design of video games and implement their first 2D game using GameMaker. The students learn object-oriented programming as they create objects and define their behaviors to various in-game events. The workshop expanded to include Microsoft Kodu game development so students could create 3D games.

Security and Encryption Students are introduced to basic concepts and terms related to cyber-security and encryption protocols. Algorithms such as the Caesar and Vigenère are presented and utilized to solve simple puzzles.

Web Design This curriculum was updated to use new tools. Students are given a tutorial on HTML and CSS to design and create their own webpage. Students also use Tinkerbin and Hackasaurus online tools to modify and edit web pages in real time.

6.3 Phase III - App Up

With the success of the video game design session, we began work on integrating other entertainment technology into the SPARCS sessions. These new sessions encourage student involvement by teaching with tools and games the students are familiar with. An example of this integration was revising our previous Circuitry lesson. Students spent the first part of the session learning about circuitry and logic gates, and then spent the second part of the session applying their learning to building redstone circuitry on Minecraft.net. On the year end post survey, two students stated Circuitry was their favorite of the seven sessions because "it was interesting" and "[because] we did redstone circuitry".

Another entertainment technology students expressed interest in was mobile app development. In Spring 2012, SPARCS added a session on App Inventor for Android, a drag-and-drop mobile application development tool. Feedback for this session was also positive, with students giving it a 4.6/5 rating on the session post-survey. In Spring 2013, the mobile app development session used Microsoft TouchDevelop on Windows Phones, and again had a student enjoyment rating of 4.6/5 on the post-survey.

Circuitry Students use online simulations to learn about the behavior of electrical components and are given an overview of Boolean logic and logic gates. At the end of this session, the students have the option of implementing basic circuits using the Minecraft game.

Mobile App Development Students are introduced to various mobile development platforms and are guided towards implementing their own mobile apps. Depending on the available resources, the apps are developed for iPhone, Android, or Windows phones, the latter using TouchDevelop to implement apps directly on the phone.

7. OUTCOMES & LESSONS LEARNED

The SPARCS program has continually sought to recruit middle school students into the computing field through a series of engaging and educational sessions. As our infrastructure has grown, we have been better able to use student feedback to modify or create sessions to address student interests. As Fig.1 shows, the sessions students enjoyed the most were those that used or developed entertainment technologies. Students were most engaged in sessions that allowed them to create video games, mobile apps, or web pages, or else apply their new knowledge to popular games like Minecraft.

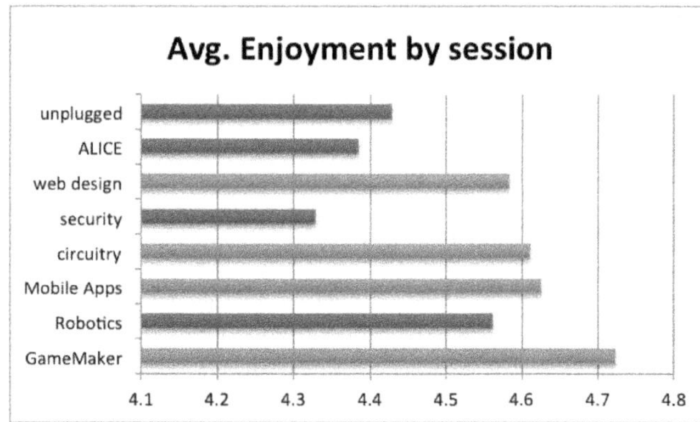

Figure 1: The sessions where students use or create entertainment technology have the highest ratings (scale 1-5, data from 2008-2013).

In the original SPARCS pilot, student attrition had been one of the largest difficulties of the program. In its early years, the program continued to suffer from a high attrition rate, sometimes as much as 60%. To combat this, we introduced a series of email reminders to parents, as well as a survey system to determine if certain sessions were boring or frustrating the students. We discovered that, if students did not enjoy a series of two or more sessions, they would simply give up on the program. With the introduction of the video game design session in 2010, we were able to use entertainment technologies to keep students excited and involved in the program, cutting our attrition rate in half (see Fig.2). One outlying data point was thrown out of aggregate results for the 2011-2012 year.

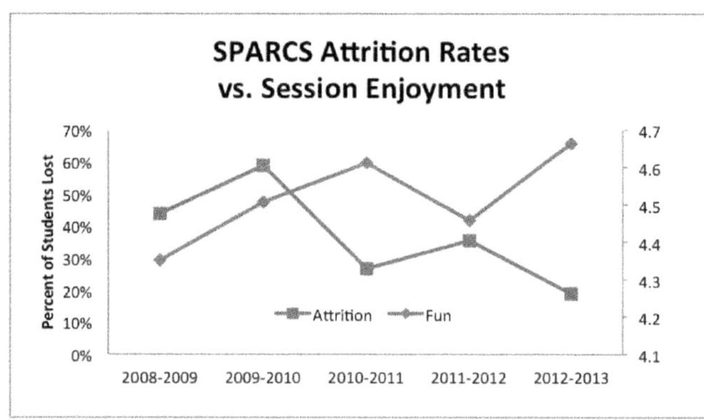

Figure 2: Students were less likely to drop out of the program when they enjoyed the session topics.

In the 2011-2012 school year, our attrition rate spiked again as we had a two month break between semesters. This prolonged break accounted for 29% of student loss; the Fall semester alone had 0% and Spring alone had 10%. We also suspect the average fun had dropped that year as the result of one main instance, the lowest rating of the CSUnplugged session in SPARCS history. We attribute this to the inability to do the outside sorting activity which is listed as the favorite activity each year.

Over the course of the SPARCS program, we have learned the importance of keeping students engaged in the session activities. Our volunteer mentors are college students with no training in disciplining rowdy students, so we built in "gym time" for our weekend sessions. During this time, students and mentors take part in games such as "capture the packet", where "hackers" from each team try to run their "packet" to the other side of the gym without being caught. These gym sessions can be used to reinforce concepts, while helping get rid of excess student energy. Between the gym sessions and entertaining lesson plans, we have been able to avoid having many disciplinary incidents.

We have also learned the necessity of standardizing the data we gather from each session, rather than letting the volunteer who taught the session design the pre- and post-surveys. By standardizing our surveys, we can provide consistent data from year to year, and add sections to test how much knowledge students retained from previous sessions.

8. MOVING FORWARD

We have learned the importance of backup plans during our sessions. When we are unable to load particular software on a school machine or when weather prevents certain activities from taking place, we should be able to adapt ourselves to these situations. As demonstrated through CSUnplugged in 2011, a single activity can make the difference between a good session versus a great session.

Additionally, our upcoming surveys will be standardized to make future data collection more efficient and useful to researchers. We will continue to monitor student feedback so we can offer sessions that get students excited about computing concepts.

We will also be partnering with Project MISO to track student course enrollments up through high school. With Project MISO we will be using a validated instrument called the S-STEM Survey which is intended to measure changes in student confidence and efficacy in STEM subjects, 21st century learning skills, and interest in STEM careers. We will also be conducting follow up surveys from students who have already completed the SPARCS program to check in and see if they continued taking programming and STEM-related courses in high school.

Acknowledgments

The authors would like to thank the members of the STARS Alliance and our community and industry partners who have made SPARCS possible. This research was partially supported by Grant NSF-CNS 0739216. This material is based upon work supported under a National Science Foundation Graduate Research Fellowship 1252376. Any opinions, findings, and conclusions or recommendations expressed in this material are those of the authors and do not necessarily reflect the views of the National Science Foundation.

9. REFERENCES

[1] A. Bruckman, M. Biggers, B. Ericson, T. McKlin, J. Dimond, B. DiSalvo, M. Hewner, L. Ni, and S. Yardi. "georgia computes!": improving the computing education pipeline. *SIGCSE Bull.*, 41(1):86–90, Mar. 2009.

[2] D. E. Chubin and R. Y. Johnson. Telling the stories of the bpc alliances: How one nsf program is changing the face of computing. *American Association for the Advancement of Science*, June 2010.

[3] D. Diva. 2013. dot diva. Retrieved August 28, 2013 From URL: http://www.dotdiva.org.

[4] K. Doran, A. Boyce, S. Finkelstein, and T. Barnes. Outreach for improved student performance: a game design and development curriculum. In *Proceedings of the 17th ACM annual conference on Innovation and technology in computer science education*, ITiCSE '12, pages 209–214, New York, NY, USA, 2012. ACM.

[5] N. C. for Women in Computing. 2013. aspireit 2013 programs. Retrieved August 28, 2013 From URL: https://www.ncwit.org/programs-campaigns/aspirations-computing/aspireit-2013-programs.

[6] S. Kids. 2013. electricity circuits. Retrieved August 28, 2013 From URL: http://www.sciencekids.co.nz/gamesactivities/electricitycircuits.html.

[7] S. Olson and D. G. Riordan. Engage to excel: Producing one million additional college graduates with degrees in science, technology, engineering, and mathematics. report to the president. *Executive Office of the President*, 2012.

[8] C. Principles. 2013. cs principles. Retrieved August 28, 2013 From URL: http://www.csprinciples.org.

[9] S. Yardi and A. Bruckman. What is computing?: bridging the gap between teenagers' perceptions and graduate students' experiences. In *Proceedings of the third international workshop on Computing education research*, ICER '07, pages 39–50, New York, NY, USA, 2007. ACM.

APPENDIX

A. PARTNERS AND RESOURCE WEBSITES

Citizen Schools http://www.citizenschools.org

NC MSEN https://education.uncc.edu/cstem/6-12-stem-student-programs/

STARS Corps http://www.starscomputingcorps.org

Raleigh SPARCS http://go.ncsu.edu/stars_sparcs

Charlotte SPARCS http://www.starscomputingcorps.org/sparcs/

SPARCS Resources https://sites.google.com/a/ncsu.edu/sparcs-resources/

AppInventor http://appinventor.mit.edu

CS Unplugged http://www.csunplugged.org

GameMaker http://www.yoyogames.com

Minecraft Redstones http://www.minecraftwiki.net

Kodu http://www.kodugamelab.com

Lego Mindstorms http://mindstorms.lego.com

TouchDevelop http://www.touchdevelop.com

B. IN DEPTH LOOK AT A LESSON

B.1 Circuits & Digital Logic

This is the sample lesson plan we use for our Circuitry session. In this session students will learn about inner workings of the computer. We explain how circuits work and discuss ways they are used to transmit and store information.

Objectives

- Students will understand logic concepts (e.g. NOT, AND, OR, XOR) and how they interact with each other
- Students will be able to apply this logic to create and debug digital circuits

Connections

This lesson will focus on key concepts in logic and how computers use circuits and logic to preform tasks. This is a more engineering-oriented aspect of computer science, and is a foundation for an overview of computing as a whole.

Materials & Preparation

- Logic Worksheets
- Binary Cards to represent TRUE\FALSE, On\Off
- (optional) Student Minecraft Accounts

B.2 Lesson Breakdown

We start each session with the pre survey. Surveys are available online, and students fill them out as soon as they come to the session. Our website allows students to login, go to the day's session, and complete the survey independently. Students play an online circuitry game while they wait[6]. Once all of the students have arrived and completed their surveys we officially start the day's lesson.

Mini-Lesson 10:30-11:00

We do a quick review with the students asking *what is a circuit?, how do they work?, and what are they used for?*. Students typically mention that circuits are used for "turning on lightbulbs" and are used by computers "to do things". We emphasize the use of circuits in the hardware side of computing; circuits are made of electronic components connected by wires so electricity can flow. The flow of this electricity determines whether a bit is turned on or off. Which transitions us into digital logic, where we discuss truth tables and their applications.

Inputs		Outputs
A	B	AND
False	False	
False	True	
True	False	
True	True	

Table 2: Above is a sample truth table our students work as a class to complete. OR, XOR, and NOT are also completed.

Logic Grouping Games 11:00-11:30

Prep: Create cards with the labels: TRUE, FALSE, AND, OR, NOT (Recommendation: the majority of the cards should be TRUE/FALSE. Label operators and operands in different colors)
Gameplay: Each student is given a card. Shout directive "Make group of NUMBER that equals TRUE/FALSE". Students form groups of that number and have their operators and operands arrive at the given value. Students sit when they find their group. Anyone not in a group is "out". Continue calling directives until there are only a few students left, then restart.
Example Make a group of 5 that equals FALSE, *NOT TRUE OR NOT TRUE.* NOTE: students can get creative with where they would put parentheses, encourage this!

Apply Knowledge 11:30-12:05

Working in pairs students complete a worksheet with basic statements on it, which must be evaluated as TRUE or FALSE. For example, *A triangle has three sides* would be TRUE and *(An octagon has seven sides AND a triangle has three sides) OR 5 is an integer* would also be TRUE. Students lead each other in review when completed.

Break 12:10-1:15

Prep: Find a large open space or gym. Make two students taggers and everyone else runners.
Gameplay: If a tagger tags a runner, the runner becomes a tagger. Taggers can only run if their hands form a complete circuit with other taggers (ie. forming a circular chain). The game area should be small compared to the number of people because the difference in speed; there needs to be limited area over which the runner can run to eventually all the tagger to tag them.

Ex. **2 taggers** must hold each others hands to move. To tag runners, they must separate their hands and therefore cannot move. **3 taggers** may have a ring of 3, or 2 taggers and one tagger stationary in the playing area.

Redstone Logic 1:15-2:40

After lunch students learn how to build circuits in Minecraft using Redstone. We teach students how to make logic gates and use them to lock doors, or turn on different lights. The students work together to solve additional scenarios we've proposed. Once students know the basics we let them onto our personal server where they can work in groups making different logic mechanisms. We provide login ids to students who do not already have one.

Figure 3: Students work together to create a logic circuit for opening a door in Minecraft.

Wrap Up 2:40-3:00

Teams present their work and explain the logic involved. Students then complete a short post survey.

Making Games a "Snap" with Stencyl – A Summer Computing Workshop for K-12 Teachers

Jiangjiang Liu
Department of Computer Science
Lamar University, Beaumont, TX 77706
001 (409) 880-7741
Jane.liu@lamar.edu

Cheng-Hsien Lin
Department of Sociology, Social Work, and Criminal Justice
Lamar University
Beaumont, TX 77706
001 (409) 880-8339
cheng-hsien.lin@lamar.edu

Joshua Wilson, David Hemmenway, Ethan Hasson, Zebulun Barnett, and Yingbo Xu
Department of Computer Science
Lamar University
Beaumont, TX 77706
001 (409) 880-7741
{jlwilson1, dhhemmenway, ephasson, zdbarnett, yxu}@lamar.edu

ABSTRACT
Game design is becoming increasingly popular among K-12 teachers and students. In this paper, we present our experience, findings, and lessons learned from conducting a one-week Stencyl Game Design Summer Computing Workshop for K-12 teachers. Our workshop focused on introducing fundamental computing concepts to K-12 teachers using Stencyl, a drag-and-drop game development environment. During the workshop, the teachers developed curriculum games for the subjects they will teach in the following semesters with the help of our workshop tutors. Our assessment results show that the average score of Stencyl knowledge in the pre-workshop survey was 1.26 out of 5, which was increased to 3.76 in the post-workshop survey and the average score of computing knowledge was improved by 61%.

Categories and Subject Descriptors
K.3.2 [Computers and Education]: Computer and Information Science Education – *computer science education, information systems education, curriculum.*

Keywords
Computer science education, computing education K-12 outreach, K-12 teacher training, computing workshop, summer workshop, summer outreach program.

1. INTRODUCTION
Computer science educators have tried different ways to attract more students to computing fields: computing camps for K-12 students, outreach programs for K-12 teachers, new teaching tools, changes of policy, professional networks, etc. Game design is becoming increasingly popular among K-12 teachers and students. More and more students are interested in developing their own games that would require functionality such as basic graphics, sound, touch-screen inputs, and other sensors. Creating a game requires an understanding of all aspects of programming. Therefore, encouraging game development can potentially inspire students to pursue a career in computer science.

SIGCSE'14, March 5–8, 2014, Atlanta, Georgia, USA.

http://dx.doi.org/10.1145/2538862.2538978

In this paper, we present our experience, findings, and lessons learned from conducting a one-week Stencyl Game Design Summer Computing Workshop for K-12 teachers. The reason Stencyl was chosen for our workshop is that Stencyl is relatively new and it is a video game creation software for Flash, iOS, Windows, and Mac platforms with support for HTML5 and Android in the works for the near future. Stencyl was released in 2011 by Stencyl, LLC. Since its release, many users have been able to easily create their own games with Stencyl because of features such as creating and editing game code in modular pieces through a visual programming language, creating and editing game entities, and the ability to create and edit levels.

K-12 teachers play an important role in preparing students for college and helping them thrive in the 21st-century global workforce. Our workshop focused on introducing fundamental computing concepts to K-12 teachers using Stencyl, a drag-and-drop game development environment. The workshop was designed for K-12 teachers of all subjects at all levels. During the workshop, the participants developed their own curriculum games that they could take back and use in their classrooms to introduce fundamental computing concepts to students. The workshop was assessed by an outside program evaluator for future improvements.

The organization of the rest of this paper is as follows. We briefly review related work in Sec. 2. Next, in Sec. 3, we describe workshop organization including learning objectives, schedules, and lesson plans. Then, in Sec. 4, we discuss various Stencyl curriculum games designed and developed by the participants using the computing concepts learned at the workshop. In Sec. 5, we present assessment results. Finally, we conclude in Sec. 6.

2. RELATED WORK
K-12 teacher outreach programs have been shown to be an effective means of making computer science accessible to those teachers. A survey was conducted by Lamar University on computer science K-12 teacher training programs in 2011 [7].

Carnegie Mellon University offered the CS4HS and CSbots programs which targeted high school computer science teachers [2][6]. Marquette University led the "Computational Thinking for the Sciences" summer workshop for high school science and mathematics teachers starting in 2010 [1][3]. Lamar University offered summer workshops for K-12 teachers in 2013 [8]. Saint Joseph's University became the site at which the Teacher Enrichment in Computer Science course was based [5]. The Georgia Institute of Technology also put in an effort to improve the aging computer science education pipeline currently employed in the state by offering a series of teacher workshops, starting in 2006, to influence CS teaching styles in a positive manner [4]. However, at the time of this writing, to our knowledge, no workshop directed at K-12 teachers based on Stencyl has been attempted.

3. WORKSHOP OVERVIEW

The five-day workshop was divided into morning and afternoon periods. The participants were given pre- and post-session quizzes at the beginning and the end of every morning relevant to the computing topics covered. These pre- and post-session quizzes were designed to assess if the concepts presented were actually absorbed by the participants. Table 1 shows the workshop schedule and the computing concepts covered during the workshop.

The morning period was broken into two sessions, each introducing fundamental computing concepts along with sample games and assignment games used to specifically demonstrate the session's programming topic.

The afternoons were used by the participants to develop their own curriculums that could be taken back and used in their own classrooms. During the afternoon curriculum development period, our tutors would assist the participants as needed. The participants presented their Stencyl curriculum games on the last two days of the workshop.

Table 1: Workshop Schedule & Computing Concepts Covered

	Day				
	Mon.	Tue.	Wed.	Thur.	Fri.
9:00am-9:30am	Opening Session	SA-2 Classes & Variables (Actors & Attributes)	SA-4 Conditional Branching & Boolean	SA-6 Custom Blocks	CG Demo
9:30am-10:30am	Session-0 (SA-0) Stencyl Overview				
10:30am-12:00am	SA-1 Stencyl Introduction	SA-3 Methods (Behaviors & Events)	SA-5 Loops	SA-7 Arrays	Closing Session
1:00pm-3:00pm	Curriculum Games (CG)	CG	CG	CG & Presentation	

3.1 Session-0: Stencyl Overview

In Session 0, participants were taken to the main Stencyl website where they were informed of a few important details: the programming style of Stencyl (drag and drop blocks), that Stencyl is free to use, that users can sell their Stencyl games for a fee, and of Stencyl's large user community where individuals can get help from other users and download additional resources. Then the teachers were shown the Stencyl user interface and a few of the basic windows. For Session 0, no examples or assignments were given since all that were covered was some of the main "selling" points of Stencyl, such as the fact that it is free and anyone, including non-programmers, can use it.

3.2 Session-1: Stencyl Introduction

Session 1 covered all of the windows and features in Stencyl in greater detail. It covered topics such as Actor Types, Backgrounds, and Sounds, as well as StencylForge, where the participants could download additional actors, sounds, backgrounds, etc. that have been created by other Stencyl users. After the participants were introduced to Stencyl's main features, they were shown how to make a simple game from start to finish. This simple game had the participants create a new game scene, add a background image to the scene, place actors in the level, and then give their actors behaviors to make them walk and jump. As with Session 0, Session 1 contained no examples or assignments as we felt this session should be used to better familiarize the participants with Stencyl so that they would be comfortable using and navigating it. This would come in handy since they would be using Stencyl often for the remainder of the week.

3.3 Session-2: Classes & Variables

Session 2 focused on classes and variables. Participants learned how to make a class, encapsulate data, and utilize it to organize data and actions appropriate to that class. They also learned that a variable is just data of a specific type, such as text or numbers. With this knowledge, the participants were able to create their own class with its own set of unique variables. Most of the participants utilized this knowledge by having multiple instances of the same class with different variables in their games as shown in Figure 1. *Sample game*: The sample had the participants place three actors of the same class and then change specific variables in the actor classes such as the names, locations on the screen, and sizes of the actors. *Assignment game*: Session 2's assignment was the same as the sample game in every detail except the participants now had to add another actor by creating a new class with corresponding variables.

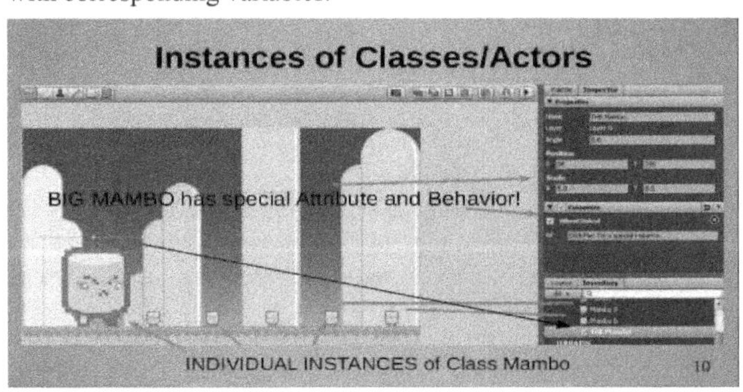

Figure 1. Instances of Classes & Actors Slide.

3.4 Session-3: Methods

In Session 3, methods were the primary focus. The participants were shown that methods were just a sequence of program instructions that could be used to perform a recurring task. The participants were able to quickly assign previously created behaviors to their actors instead of having to completely recode a behavior. This saved participants time and effort and allowed them to easily share behaviors amongst their created actors as shown in Figure 2. *Sample game*: The example had the participants start with a stationary actor in the middle of the screen with an outer space background. Then, the participants created their very own actor method, which would make the actor spin around, and applied it to their actor. *Assignment game*: Session 3's assignment added a new actor by creating a new class to the scene. To practise repetition, the participants were required once again to create a method that would make an actor spin. Then the participants applied this method to both actors of the different classes. This also reinforced the fact that methods could be shared amongst classes.

Figure 2. Method Space Spin Example

3.5 Session-4: Conditional Branching & Boolean

In session 4, the participants learned about Boolean expressions and conditional branching. The participants seemed to quickly understand that Boolean expressions are just expressions that result in a Boolean value which is a data type with only two possible values such as true or false. Participants also seemed to quickly understand that the flow of code execution could be changed due to conditional branching. Now, with the knowledge of Boolean expressions and conditional branching, participants were able to implement more complex methods in their games. *Sample game*: Session 4's example started the participants with an off light bulb with a large green button underneath it that said "on". If the participants tried to click the green "on" button, nothing would happen. Using Boolean expressions and conditional branching, the participants created an "if" statement, causing the light bulb to turn on if the state of the "on" button was true. *Assignment game*: The assignment appeared very similar to the example. However, an "off" button was added. Using an "if...else" statement and Boolean expressions, the participants made the light bulb turn on when the "on" button was pressed and likewise made the light turn off when the "off" button was pressed.

3.6 Session-5: Loops

Session 5 taught the participants about "for" and "while" Loops as shown in Figure 3. Participants learned how loops can be used to repeat a sequence of steps until a certain condition is met. *Sample game*: Session 5's example had a counter that incremented every second. The participants were required to use a loop to make a sound play every three seconds. *Assignment game*: For the assignment, the participants were required to utilize a "for loop" to make a character draw on the screen "n" amount of times, with "n" being a variable set by the participants.

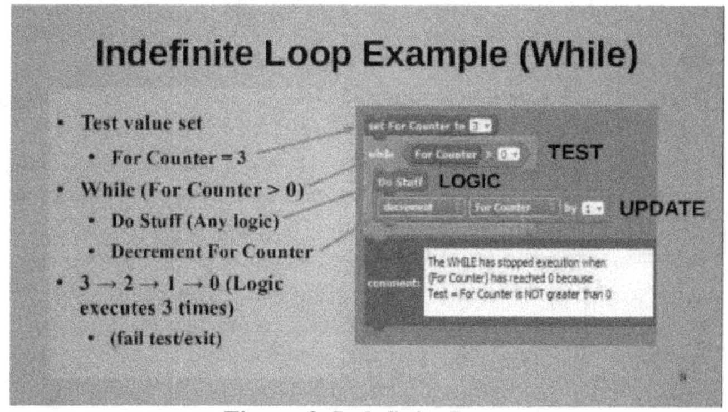

Figure 3. Indefinite Loop

3.7 Session-6: Custom Blocks

Session 6 introduced a powerful feature in Stencyl called Custom Blocks. With Custom Blocks, participants were able to create their own Code Block in Stencyl with functions, incoming parameters, and outgoing return values. *Sample game*: The example for session 6 had the participants create a Custom Block in Stencyl to return a "facing right" value for whether or not a specific actor facing in the "right" direction. This Custom Block used Boolean values and "if" statements to check the returned value. Once the "facing right" value was correct, the participants used another event, along with the custom block they created, to display "TRUE" above the actor if it was facing right and "FALSE" if it was facing left. *Assignment game*: As shown in Figure 4, for the assignment, the participants were required to make "RIGHT" appear above the character when facing right and "LEFT" appear above the character when it was facing left by modifying the custom block they created previously.

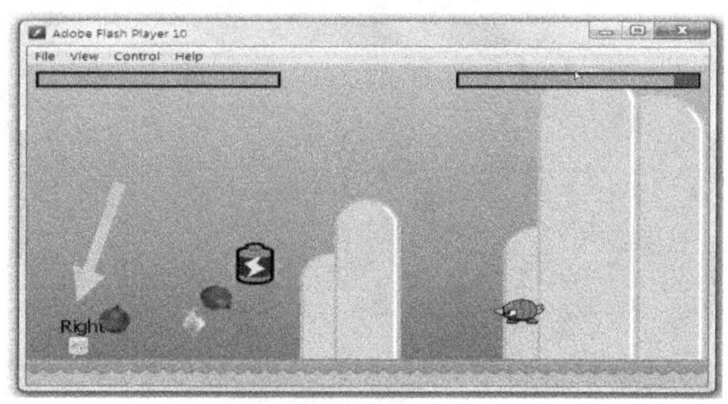

Figure 4. Custom Block Example

3.8 Session-7: Lists

The final session, Session 7, introduced another powerful feature of programming, lists. A list is a data structure used to organize data. Participants seemed to quickly understand that when counting positions in a list, they must start with 0. *Sample game*: For the 7th and last session's example, a character would pick up different colored gems. If a character picked up a red gem, text would appear saying "You picked up a Red gem". However, if the character picked up a blue gem nothing would appear. The participants first added a text element to a list which said, "You picked up a Blue gem". Then the participants modified a drawing even to make the correct text appear when the character picked up a blue gem. *Assignment game*: For the assignment, the participants added another text element to the list which would say whatever the participants wanted. Then they would create a new group for a new colored gem, associate the group with the gem, and then modify another drawing element to display the correct text when the correct gem is picked up.

4. Curriculum Games Developed

During the workshop, participants developed their own curriculum games with the help of our workshop tutors. The workshop tutors were computer science undergraduates and graduate students. The curriculum games may cover any academic subjects including Science, Math, English, and Computing. Stencyl is a flexible enough platform to allow the creation of any of these types of games. With Stencyl, participants utilized various computing concepts such as classes, variables, conditional branching, methods, and lists to achieve their desired results. Next, we show featured curriculum games designed by the workshop participants.

- **Game: Solids, Liquids, and Gases Adventures**

Figures 5&6 show the game layout and Stencyl actors of the game Solids, Liquids, and Gases Adventures. In this 2nd and 3rd grade science example, players are challenged to decipher the difference between different states of matter. The objective is to grab as many objects that are in the chosen state as possible without grabbing objects of the other states. Each "level" of the game is for different states entirely. To create this game, the participant used their knowledge of classes, objects, methods, and variables.

Figure 5. Curriculum game: Solids, Liquids, Gases Adventures

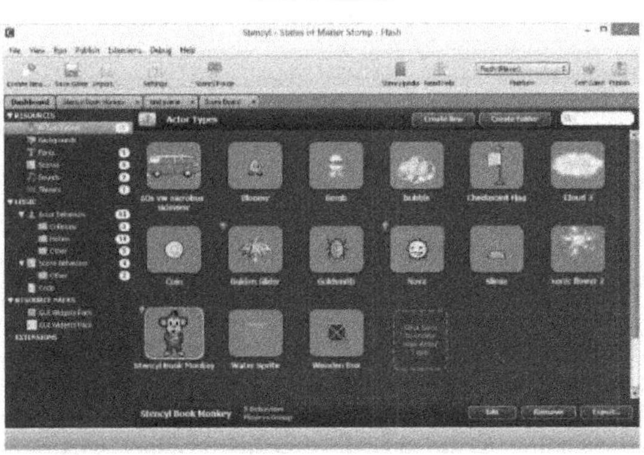

Figure 6. Stencyl Actors of Solids, Liquids, Gases Adventures

- **Game: Order That Number**

Figure 7 shows the game Order That Number. This game is targeted toward 5th grade mathematics students, and the objective of the game is to hit the number block that represents the higher number of the two on-screen. The purpose of this exercise is to teach students place value and counting skills. While this is a simple example, the game is designed to be easily modified to support sequential values on the blocks and even decimal place values. Order That Number incorporates several computing concepts, such as object instances of "blocks", Boolean values, conditional branching, random number generation, and variable storage for the "blocks"' numbers.

Figure 7. Curriculum game: Order That Number

- **Game: Melody Multiplier**

Figure 8 shows the mathematics game Melody Multiplier. It has the player stomp on enemies labeled with numbers that may correspond to an indicated multiple. If players step on an enemy that satisfies the multiple rule, their score increases and vice versa if they step on ones that don't satisfy the rule. Global variables are used to store players' scores and the current stage's goal multiple. Conditional branching helps the game decide whether or not the attacked enemy satisfied the rule and how that affects the aforementioned global score. Special participant-created methods were used to simplify the handling of each enemy's current value, updating the score, and drawing all of this information to the screen in a coherent and convenient manner. Stencyl's Game Attribute System was used to handle the global score variable, and this implementation allows maintenance of the score throughout level progression or scene changes.

Figure 8. Curriculum game: Melody Multiplier

There were many other exceptional projects created during the workshop as well. Next, we briefly discuss those projects. All curriculum projects created by the workshop participants are available at our workshop website. There are several math related games: Alien Numbers Attack, Count Me/On The Farm, Frog Skip, Lame Game, Math Stomp, Poppers, Rounding Run, and What's Up.

English and Grammar is another common subject amongst the workshop participants. In Grammar Down, parts of speech such as verbs, nouns, adjectives, and adverbs are placed in bubbles where the player is supposed to pop the type indicated by the level. Prefix Parade is made with High School English I students in mind. In this vocabulary building game, the player is supposed to hit the required arrow key to choose a correct prefix for the given word.

General computing skills was another game type explored by some participants. The games included Kill the Balloons, Level UP!, and Under the Sea. Kill the Balloons is meant to increase typing speed, assist keyboard layout memorization, and to enjoy this otherwise monotonous activity. Level UP! is a maze game that intends to be used as a tool to teach Stencyl and Computer Science concepts to the students. Under The Sea is another project that is to be used as a platform to teach students about Stencyl and the Computer Science concepts required to make their own games.

5. ASSESSMENT AND FEEDBACK

An outside program evaluator worked with us and designed pre and post-workshop surveys and pre- and post-quizzes with 5-10 open questions for each lecture session. In addition, participants accepted a face-to-face interview to provide some in-depth feedback to the workshop. All surveys and quizzes were distributed to the participants via email using Survey Monkey, a popular survey tool used by many professionals. The details of the assessment results are given below.

There were sixteen females that attended the 2013 Summer Computing Workshop and there were no male participants. The majority of the group was 50 years old or older (mean = 47.25 years old). Eight of them were Africa American, which accounts for 50%, seven were White, and one was Hispanic. 75% of participants have a bachelor's degree, and the others have a master's degree.

There were eleven elementary school teachers which accounted for 68.75% of the participants. 18.75% of participants teach middle school and the other 12.5% of participants were high-school teachers. Their areas of teaching are wide-ranging, from Social Science, Science (Biology/Chemistry), Math, English, Reading/Writing, to computer related subjects. Some participants teach almost all subjects in elementary schools. In addition, most participants have more than nine years teaching experience.

5.1 Computing Background Comparison

As shown in Table 2, there are ten questions to let the participants rank themselves in their conceptual knowledge of General programming. All questions are ranked on a scale from 1 to 5; 1 indicating they felt very uncertain and 5 indicating they felt very comfortable with the concept.

Table 2: Details about Computing Conceptual Questions

1	I understand the normal flow of execution in a program.
2	I understand object oriented programming.
3	I know how to use methods and functions in program design.
4	I know what conditional branching is and how it affects the flow of execution.
5	I can perform variable manipulation and proper type usage.
6	I can use loops in program design.
7	I can use input to allow the user to influence the program as it runs.
8	I can use simple Boolean expressions to affect control flow.
9	I understand how to implement a class and create objects from that class.
10	I can use lists to store a collection of data.

The post-workshop average score of computing knowledge was 3.30, which was a 61% improvement from the pre-workshop average score of only 2.05. Especially, the second, third and eighth questions have showed distinct progress which proved that the participant did absorb the object oriented programming, methods, functions, and Boolean concepts.

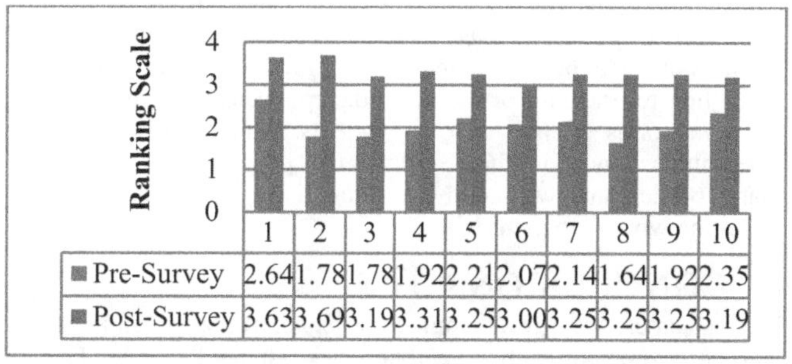

Figure 9. Computer Knowledge Level Comparison.

5.2 Stencyl Knowledge Comparison

As shown in Table 3, there are eight questions which related to Stencyl Knowledge before and after the workshop. All questions are ranked on a scale from 1 to 5; 1 indicating they felt very uncertain and 5 indicating they felt very comfortable with the concept.

Table 3: Stencyl Knowledge Questions

1	I can create and manipulate objects in Stencyl
2	I can use variables in Stencyl
3	I can create and use behaviors/events in Stencyl
4	I can use conditional branching to affect the flow of execution in Stencyl
5	I can utilize loops to repeat blocks in Stencyl
6	I can ask for and store a user's name for later use in an Stencyl program
7	I can create a Boolean expression to make a complex decision in Stencyl
8	I can create and manipulate lists in Stencyl

According to Figure 10, we can see that before the workshop, most of participants have only a little understanding about the Stencyl. The average score of Stencyl Knowledge in pre-workshop survey was 1.26 out of 5 which was increased to 3.76 in the post-workshop Survey.

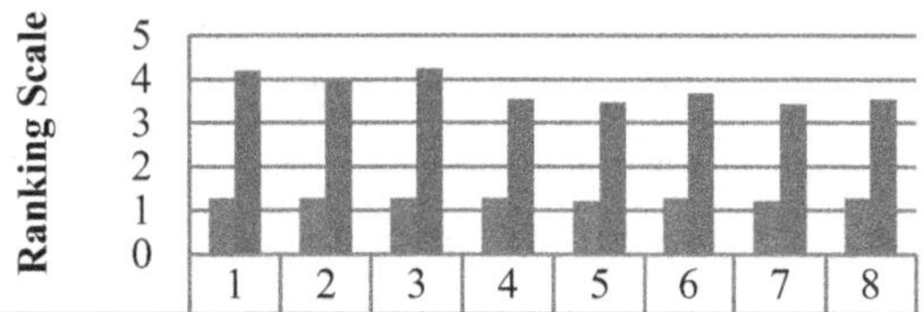

	1	2	3	4	5	6	7	8
Pre-Survey	1.28	1.28	1.28	1.28	1.21	1.28	1.21	1.28
Post-Survey	4.19	3.94	4.25	3.56	3.47	3.69	3.44	3.56

Figure 10. Stencyl Knowledge Level Comparison.

During the face-to-face interviews, participants were given a chance to provide critical feedback about the workshop such as successful strategies and suggestions for improvement. The most highly praised aspect of the workshop by most participants was the tutors in both the normal classroom time and curriculum development time. The workshop tutors are computer science undergraduates and graduate students. Due to the nature of the content and time period allowed, participants would inevitably find themselves unsure of what to do next. The tutors would immediately come to their aid and resolve any confusion they might be experiencing. An unexpected positive aspect that a few participants brought up is the fact that they now have a better understanding of how their students feel when learning something new and difficult. It has been a while since many of the participants had been to school. To find themselves sometimes struggling to grasp all of the new concepts caused them to refresh their memories of their days as students, which allowed them to better understand how their students feel on a regular basis. Also, many participants wished there would have been more time to cover the workshop materials.

6. CONCLUSIONS

In this paper, we present our experience, findings, and lessons learned from conducting a one-week Stencyl Game Design Summer Computing Workshop for K-12 teachers. Our workshop focused on introducing fundamental computing concepts to K-12 teachers using Stencyl, a drag-and-drop game development environment. During the workshop, the teachers developed curriculum games for the subjects they will teach in the following semesters. Our pre- and post-workshop assessment results show that the average score of Stencyl knowledge in the pre-workshop survey was 1.26 out of 5, which increased to 3.76 in the post-workshop survey and the average score of computing knowledge level was improved by 61%. According to the face-to-face interviews, the most highly praised aspect of the workshop was the tutors in both the normal classroom time and curriculum development time and the participants also wished there would have been more time to cover the workshop materials.

7. ACKNOWLEDGMENTS

This project was supported by US National Science Foundation grant #0846053. All opinions reflected in this paper are those of the authors and not necessarily those of NSF.

8. REFERENCES

[1] Ahamed, S. I., Brylow, D., Ge, R., Madiraju, P., Merrill, S. J., Struble, C. A., and Early, J. P. 2010. Computational thinking for the sciences: a three day workshop for high school science teachers. In Proceedings of the 41st ACM Technical Symposium on Computer Science Education (Milwaukee, Wisconsin, USA, March 10 - 13, 2010). SIGCSE '10. ACM, New York, NY, 42-46. DOI= http://doi.acm.org/10.1145/1734263.1734277.

[2] Blum, L. and Cortina, T. J. 2007. CS4HS: an outreach program for high school CS teachers. In Proceedings of the 38th SIGCSE Technical Symposium on Computer Science Education (Covington, Kentucky, USA, March 07 - 11, 2007). SIGCSE '07. ACM, New York, NY, 19-23. DOI= http://doi.acm.org/10.1145/1227310.1227320.

[3] Bort, H. and Brylow, D. 2013. CS4Impact: measuring computational thinking concepts present in CS4HS participant lesson plans. In Proceeding of the 44th ACM technical symposium on Computer science education (SIGCSE '13). ACM, New York, NY, USA, 427-432. DOI=10.1145/2445196.2445323 http://doi.acm.org/10.1145/2445196.2445323

[4] Bruckman, A., Biggers, M., Ericson, B., McKlin, T., Dimond, J., DiSalvo, B., Hewner, M., Ni, L., and Yardi, S. 2009. "Georgia computes!": improving the computing education pipeline. In Proceedings of the 40th ACM Technical Symposium on Computer Science Education (Chattanooga, TN, USA, March 04 - 07, 2009). SIGCSE '09. ACM, New York, NY, 86-90. DOI= http://doi.acm.org/10.1145/1508865.1508899.

[5] Cooper, S., Dann, W., and Harrison, J. 2010. A k-12 college partnership. In Proceedings of the 41st ACM Technical Symposium on Computer Science Education (Milwaukee, Wisconsin, USA, March 10 - 13, 2010). SIGCSE '10. ACM, New York, NY, 320-324. DOI= http://doi.acm.org/10.1145/1734263.1734371.

[6] Lauwers, T., Hamner, E., and Nourbakhsh, I.. 2010. A Strategy for Collaborative Outreach: Lessons from the CSbots Project. In Proceedings of the 41st ACM technical symposium on Computer Science Education (Milwaukee, WI, USA, March 10-13, 2010).SIGCSE '10. ACM, New York, NY, USA, 315-319. DOI= http://doi.acm.org/10.1145/1734263.1734370.

[7] Liu, J., Lin, C., Potter, P., Hasson, E.P., Barnett, Z.D., Singleton, M. 2013. Going mobile with app inventor for android: a one-week computing workshop for K-12 teachers. In Proceeding of the 44th ACM technical symposium on Computer science education (SIGCSE '13). ACM, New York, NY, USA, 433-438. DOI=10.1145/2445196.2445324 http://doi.acm.org/10.1145/2445196.2445324

[8] Liu, J., Lin, C., Hasson, E., and Barnett, Z., and Zhang, P. "A Survey on Computer Science K-12 Outreach: Teacher Training Programs," In Proceedings of the 41st Annual IEEE Frontiers in Education Conference (FIE 2011), pp. T4F-1 – T4F-6, Rapid City, SD, Oct. 12-15, 2011

ACM/IEEE-CS Computer Science Curricula 2013: Implementing the Final Report

Mehran Sahami (moderator)
Stanford University
sahami@cs.stanford.edu

Steve Roach
Exelis, Inc.
roach.steven@gmail.com

Ernesto Cuadros-Vargas
San Pablo Catholic University
ecuadros@ucsp.edu.pe

Elizabeth K. Hawthorne
Union County College
hawthorne@ucc.edu

Amruth Kumar
Ramapo College of New Jersey
amruth@ramapo.edu

Richard LeBlanc
Seattle University
leblanc@seattleu.edu

David Reed
Creighton University
davereed@creighton.edu

Remzi Seker
Embry-Riddle Aeronautical University
sekerr@erau.edu

Categories and Subject Descriptors

K.3.2 [**Computers and Education**]: Computer Science Education; Curriculum

Keywords

Computer Science Curricula 2013, CS2013.

1. SUMMARY

For over 40 years, the ACM and IEEE-Computer Society have sponsored international curricular guidelines for undergraduate programs in computing. The rapid evolution and expansion of the computing field and the growing number of topics in computer science have made regular revision of curricular recommendations necessary. Thus, the Computing Curricula volumes are updated on an approximately 10-year cycle, with the aim of keeping curricula modern and relevant. The latest volume in the series, Computer Science Curricula 2013 (CS2013), is due for release in the Fall of 2013. This panel seeks to inform the SIGCSE community about the final version of the report, provide insight on interpreting the CS2013 guidelines, and give guidance regarding how the guidelines may be implemented at different institutions.

Prior SIGCSE panels on the CS2013 effort [1, 2] resulted in useful feedback on earlier drafts of the report that in turn helped shape the final report. This feedback also included significant interest from the CS education community for guidance on how to implement the recommendations from the final report at a variety of institutions. This panel seeks to address that need. Indeed, the large number of panelists represents a wide array of institutional viewpoints for discussing how the CS2013 guidelines may be adopted in different contexts. We do not expect all panelists to be involved in the brief overview of CS2013 presented at the start of the panel, but having such a breadth of panelists will help to more thoroughly engage the audience in a discussion of how CS2013 can be implemented at a variety of institutions with differing levels of resources.

CS2013 aims to provide advice and guidance to the computing education community throughout the coming decade by redefining the knowledge areas in CS, rethinking the essentials necessary for a CS curriculum, and identifying working exemplars of courses and curricula along these lines. Balancing this topical growth with the need to keep recommendations realistic and implementable in the context of undergraduate education is particularly challenging. As a result, it is important to engage the broader computer science education community in a dialog on the updates encompassed in the CS2013 curricular guidelines and discuss implementing these guidelines within local institutional constraints.

The high-level themes on which the CS2013 effort is based include:

- *The "Big Tent" view of CS* – As CS expands to include more multi-disciplinary work and new programs of the form "Computational X" are developed, it is important to embrace an outward looking view that sees CS as a discipline actively seeking to work with and integrate into other disciplines.
- *Managing the size of the curriculum* – Although the field of computer science has expanded significantly in the past decade, it is simply not feasible to proportionately expand the size of the curriculum. As a result, CS2013 has re-evaluated what are considered essential topics in computing so as to make room for new topics without requiring more instructional hours than the CS2008 guidelines.
- *Actual course and curricular exemplars as opposed to stylized course guidance* – While the previous curricular effort, CC2001, took on the challenge of providing descriptions of stylized courses incorporating the knowledge units defined in that report, it was felt in retrospect that such course guidance did not have much impact on actual course design. CS2013 takes a different approach: identifying examples of actual fielded courses and curricula—from a variety of universities and colleges—to illustrate how topics in the CS body of knowledge may be covered and combined in diverse ways.

SIGCSE'14, March 5–8, 2014, Atlanta, Georgia, USA.
ACM 978-1-4503-2605-6/14/03.
http://dx.doi.org/10.1145/2538862.2538863

- *Institutional needs* Curricula exist in the context of specific institutional needs, goals, and resource constraints. As a result, CS2013 allows for explicit flexibility in curricular structure through a *tiered* set of core topics, where a small set of Tier 1 topics are considered essential for all CS programs, but individual programs have flexibility with regard to their coverage of Tier 2 topics.

The CS2013 final report includes a complete update to the Body of Knowledge in computer science, organized around 18 Knowledge Areas, outlined below:

- Algorithms and Complexity (AL)
- Architecture and Organization (AR)
- Computational Science (CN)
- Discrete Structures (DS)
- Graphics and Visual Computing (GV)
- Human-Computer Interaction (HCI)
- Information Assurance and Security (IAS)
- Information Management (IM)
- Intelligent Systems (IS)
- Networking and Communications (NC)
- Operating Systems (OS)
- Platform-Based Development (PBD)
- Parallel and Distributed Computing (PD)
- Programming Languages (PL)
- Software Development Fundamentals (SDF)
- Software Engineering (SE)
- System Fundamentals (SF)
- Social Issues and Professional Practice (SP)

Two substantial reorganizations in the Body of Knowledge include introductory programming and systems. The area now called Software Development Fundamentals (SDF, previously called Programming Fundamentals) encompasses fundamental software development concepts, including topics in algorithms, design, programming, and software development processes. A new area called Systems Fundamentals (SF) identifies common themes among operating systems, networking, and computer architecture. Additionally, recent developments in the field (such as the ubiquity of parallel computing and a need for better understanding computer security) have given rise to the development of knowledge areas in Parallel and Distributed Computing (PD), Information Assurance and Security (IAS), and Platform-Based Development (PBD).

The goal of this panel is not simply to provide a description of the contents of the CS2013 final report, but to actively engage the community in a discussion of approaches to migrating existing computer science curricula so that they better align with the CS2013 guidelines. Thus, the goals of the panel are to:

- increase awareness of the CS2013 final report and provide the audience with the opportunity to understand the guidelines in more depth,
- highlight changes between CS2013 and previous curricular guidelines (CC2001/CS2008),
- promote discussion of course/curricular exemplars as a means for other programs to adopt the curricular recommendations,
- discuss broad issues related to curricular reinvigoration, including new models for distributing topics across courses while dealing with institutional resource constraints.

Holding this panel at SIGCSE is critical to getting the CS education community more broadly engaged in curricular reform. Indeed, SIGCSE-14 will be the most relevant venue to discuss the CS2013 final report, which will have been published a few months earlier.

2. MEHRAN SAHAMI

Mehran Sahami is co-chair of the CS2013 Steering Committee. He is an Associate Professor and Associate Chair for Education in the Computer Science Department at Stanford University.

3. STEVE ROACH

Steve Roach is co-chair of the CS2013 Steering Committee. He is a Senior Software Engineer at Exelis, Inc. and formerly an Associate Professor of Computer Science at the University of Texas at El Paso.

4. ERNESTO CUADROS-VARGAS

Ernesto Cuadros-Vargas, a member of the CS2013 Steering Committee, is a Professor of Computer Science and Dean of the School of Engineering and Computing at San Pablo Catholic University in Arequipa, Peru.

5. ELIZABETH K. HAWTHORNE

Elizabeth Hawthorne, a member of the CS2013 Steering Committee, is a Senior Professor of Computer Science at Union County College and Chair of the ACM Committee for Computing Education in Community Colleges (CCECC).

6. AMRUTH KUMAR

Amruth Kumar, a member of the CS2013 Steering Committee, is a Professor of Computer Science at Ramapo College of New Jersey.

7. RICHARD LEBLANC

Richard LeBlanc, a member of the CS2013 Steering Committee, is a Professor in and Chair of the Department of Computer Science and Software Engineering at Seattle University

8. DAVID REED

David Reed, a member of the CS2013 Steering Committee, is an Associate Professor and Director of the Computer Science Program at Creighton University.

9. REMZI SEKER

Remzi Seker, a member of the CS2013 Steering Committee, is a Professor of Electrical, Computer, Software & Systems Engineering at Embry-Riddle Aeronautical University.

10. REFERENCES

[1] Sahami, M., Roach, S., Cuadros-Vargas, E., and LeBlanc, R. 2013. ACM/IEEE-CS Computer Science Curriculum 2013: Reviewing the Ironman Report. In *Proc. SIGCSE '13*, 13-14.

[2] Sahami, M., Roach, S., Cuadros-Vargas, E., and Reed, D. 2012. Computing Curricula 2013: Computer Science – Update on the Strawman Report from the ACM/IEEE-CS Task Force. In *Proc. SIGCSE '12*, 3-4.

Diverse Learners, Diverse Courses, Diverse Projects: Learning from Challenges in New Directions

Owen Astrachan
Duke University
ola@cs.duke.edu

R. Brook Osborne
Code.org
brook@code.org

Irene Lee
Santa Fe Institute
lee@santafe.edu

Bradley Beth
University of Texas
bbeth@cs.utexas.edu

Jeff Gray
University of Alabama
gray@cs.ua.edu

Categories and Subject Descriptors

K.3.2 [**Computers and Education**]: Computer and Information Science Education – *computer science education*

General Terms

Management, Human Factors, Standardization.

Keywords

Computer Science Education, K-12 Curriculum, CS Principles, Computational Thinking, Problem Based Learning, Outreach.

1. SUMMARY

Several changes and reforms in teaching computer science have been proposed and championed as part of the CS10K initiative [1-4]. The CS Principles (CSP) project and the overarching CS10K initiative include a public/private partnership offering curricula, curricular frameworks, professional development, online support, and a community of practice to support individual and systemic reforms at scale. In this special session, we hear from those leading large CSP projects and from the teachers participating in these large projects. The session is designed to inform the education community of these efforts and to situate them in the context of understanding how a diversity of approaches to implementing the CSP framework is necessary to succeed with different and diverse student populations, schools, districts, and teachers. Knowledge of these approaches will help those teaching these students as they move from high school to college, bringing related but diverse experiences because of how each student is learning the material that is based on the same curricular framework. This framework is part of the CS Principles project, but the efforts we report on in this session realize the framework at different scales, in different populations, and with different pedagogical approaches.

In this session the PIs on several CS Principles/CS10K initiatives will talk briefly and at a high-level about the projects they are leading, the approaches they are taking to scale their projects, and the curricula, pedagogy, and professional development they are employing to expand and enable teachers and students. Pilot teachers who are part of each of the projects will offer a different, on-the-ground perspective of how each approach is succeeding and the challenges faced from a teacher perspective.

Outlining issues related to equity in the classroom, broadening participation, pedagogical approaches, and supporting diverse learners will be the responsibility of the leadership group from the CS Principles project. They will facilitate the discussion related to these diverse initiatives and call-on or represent pilot teachers from these different projects.

SIGCSE'14, March 5–8, 2014, Atlanta, Georgia, USA.
ACM978-1-4503-2605-6/14/03.
http://dx.doi.org/10.1145/2538862.2538991

2. Overview (Owen Astrachan)

The projects highlighted in this special session are three of many designed to introduce CS Principles at local, regional, state, and national levels. In this overview we will situate these projects and their work in the context of other, related projects to highlight the diversity of approaches that can and should inform related efforts in expanding and transforming computer science education. This session is designed to present these projects in the context of transformational approaches, not simply as exemplars of one facet of the CS10K initiative.

As the PI of the CS Principles project, Owen Astrachan works to help the community of educators working on this and related projects achieve their goals.

3. Project Engage (Bradley Beth)

Project Engage uses the framework from CS Principles to deliver a course rooted in the inquiry-based pedagogies of problem-based-learning. Each of its units (a.k.a. modules) is built around a combination of an authentic problem and project, collaboration, student-centered learning, and engaging multimedia and narratives for information delivery. Teaching and learning are supported via a variety of Problem Based Learning (PBL) scaffolds including rubrics, group contracts, and intermittent checkpoints for feedback.

In addition to a course and professional development for teachers delivering the course, Project Engage includes a research component to understand and evaluate the project's effects on teaching and learning in a variety of contexts.

Classroom observations, multiple surveys, interviews, focus groups, grades, scores, and web analytics address a variety of research questions whose answers we hope will inform both practitioners and academic researchers.

Bradley Beth is the Senior Program Coordinator for Project Engage: Changing the face of computer science through inquiry-based education.

4. CS4Alabama: A Model for Statewide Deployment of CS Principles (Jeff Gray)

The CS4Alabama project is building a professional development program based on in-person training and distance learning collaboration. It provides year-long professional development, rather than the week-long summer institutes that are typical of most AP training programs in other STEM areas. A statewide "Teacher Leader" model is being developed to help new peer cohorts as they establish CS Principles in their schools. Teachers in these cohorts will collaborate together on content and pedagogical learning experiences, fostered by peer leaders and facilitated through A+ College Ready (A+CR), the NMSI partner for Alabama. The pedagogical approach will be centered on inquiry/discovery-based techniques that introduce computer science as a broad set of topics built on the CSP curricular framework and learning objectives. The project not only considers issues of differentiation among students in the CSP classes, but also designs professional development for teachers who have diverse backgrounds and experiences.

Jeff Gray is the PI for the CS4Alabama project.

5. Computing for All (Irene Lee)

In the New Mexico Computer Science for All program the first cohort of teachers have completed their preparations to serve as learning coaches / TAs for the lab portion of a university dual credit (CS 151L) course at their high schools. The first cohort of teachers just started teaching CS to students at their high schools. Preparing this cohort of teachers with different backgrounds, interests, and experience engendered several challenges. These challenges are likely relevant as we face preparing so many high school teachers to become computer science teachers, from those with STEM experience to those for whom computer science is an introduction to STEM.

The dual credit course is designed to attract, prepare and retain diverse groups of students in computer science. The new teachers are successfully attracting and engaging a very diverse group of students (primarily Hispanic and Native American). A primary factor of this success is *relevance* - modeling local issues as complex systems - and through practices within the classroom that promote partnering and collaboration such as peer-instruction, pair programming, and problem based learning (PBL).

Both teachers and students ultimately get to experience being computational scientists - they create computational models of a local issue of importance to themselves and their communities then (after varying degrees of analysis of the model) use those models as experimental test beds to test a proposed solution or mitigation strategy. This experience is both authentic to the learner and prepares the learner with a fundamental understanding of computational thinking.

Irene Lee is the Director of the Learning Lab at Santa Fe Institute. She is the PI of GUTS y Girls, New Mexico Computer Science for All, and Program Director of Project GUTS: Growing Up Thinking Scientifically.

6. Challenges of Piloting at a large scale (Brook Osborne)

Both code.org and the College Board/NSF sponsored CS Principles project work directly with pilot instructors teaching the future AP CS Principles course. In her current and former roles working with teachers in these projects, Brook is deeply connected to the experience of those teaching CSP at a variety of levels. In this session she will represent and discuss the successes and challenges scaling up CSP programs present for both teachers and project leadership.

Brook Osborne is the 9-12 Program Manager at code.org. Previously, she was the Outreach Director and pilot coordinator for CS Principles and the National Director of Outreach in Computer Science at Duke University. She has a plan to change everything.

7. Intended Audience

This special session is designed for all educators, especially those interested in introductory computer science where students move quickly from high school to college, and from one course to the next. The session is intended for educators interested in research- and experience-proven approaches to teaching and learning, including inquiry-based approaches, problem-centric and problem-based learning, and pedagogical approaches rooted in supporting diverse learners.

8. REFERENCES

[1] O. Astrachan, J. Cuny, D. Garcia, L. Snyder, and C. Stephenson, "The CS10K Project and CS Principles," presented at the National Coalition of Women in Technology (NCWIT) Summit on Women in Technology, New York City, 2011.

[2] A. Arpaci-Dusseau, O. Astrachan, D. Barnette, M. Bauer, M. Carrell, R. Dovi, B. Franke, C. Gardner, J. Gray, J. Griffin, R. Kick, A. Kuemmel, R. Morelli, D. Muralidhar, R. B. Osborne, and C. Uche, "Computer Science Principles: Analysis of a Propsed Advanced Placement Course," in *SIGCSE Technical Symposium on Computer Science Education*, Denver, CO, 2013.

[3] J. Goode, G. Chapman, and J. Margolis, "The Exploring Computer Science Program," *ACM Inroads*, vol. 3, pp. 47-52, 2012.

[4] J. Margolis, R. Estrella, J. Goode, J. J. Holme, and K. Nao, *Stuck in the shallow end: Education, race, and computing*: MIT Press, 2008.

Special Session: Engaging Mathematical Reasoning Exercises

Joseph Hollingsworth
Indiana University Southeast
Computer Science
New Albany, IN 47150
1-812-941-2425
jholly@ius.edu

Murali Sitaraman
Clemson University
School of Computing
Clemson, SC 29634
1-864-656-3444
murali@clemson.edu

SUMMARY

At SIGCSE 2013 this special session [1] provided attendees interested in math thinking a place where engaging math reasoning examples and assignments that help connect mathematics and software development could be shared and discussed. The exercises and assignments presented last year were well received by the audience who indicated immediately that they would find ways to incorporate them in classes such as CS1, CS2, data structures and algorithms, discrete math, and software engineering courses. Feedback from our own surveys showed that even as there was much interest in using engaging math reasoning examples, there was also considerable interest in developing new engaging math reasoning assignments for future sessions. Based on these expressions of interest and the general interest of the approximately 100 attendees of last year's special session, we feel compelled to continue the momentum by proposing a second round of this forum for SIGCSE 2014. We have contact information for these potential presenters and we expect to have no difficulty in attracting suitable presenters if the session is accepted.

The remainder of this proposal is nearly identical to last year's proposal except for the example that appears in Section 2. That example is drawn directly from one of the engaging reasoning assignments presented at last year's special session. All exercises are available at [2].

Categories and Subject Descriptors

D.2.4 [**Software Engineering**]: Software/Program Verification – *class invariants, correctness proofs, formal methods, programming by contract.*

F.3.1 [**Logics and Meanings of Programs**]: Specifying and Verifying and Reasoning about Programs – *assertions, invariants, pre- and post-conditions, specification techniques.*

F.4.1 [**Mathematical Logic and Formal Languages**]: Mathematical Logic – *proof theory, set theory, temporal logic.*

Keywords

Correctness proofs; discrete structures; induction; invariants; programming by contract; specification; verification.

SIGCSE'14, March 5–8, 2014, Atlanta, Georgia, USA.
ACM 978-1-4503-2605-6/14/03.
http://dx.doi.org/10.1145/2538862.2538989

1. OVERALL OBJECTIVE

There is near universal agreement in the community that computing students should learn analytical reasoning principles and understand the connections between mathematics and software construction. In the process they realize the importance of the mathematics they learn for software development. Educators need compelling examples and assignments to make such connections, and often they are difficult to come up with, because the environments and background of students at different institutions vary widely. This session aims to provide a forum at SIGCSE where educators can share joys of teaching mathematical reasoning principles throughout the computing curriculum.

2. OUTLINE

The proposed special session will borrow much from the organization of the highly successful, annual "Nifty Assignments" session at SIGCSE. Unlike that session which focuses on programming assignments, the focus of the present session will be on exercises that are engaging essentially because of the mathematical reasoning involved. Also, unlike that session, this session will feature innovative classroom exercises and activities that help highlight the connections between mathematics and software development, not necessarily just major, take-home projects. Ideally, the exercises can be done within one class period and will have corresponding reasoning projects that can be assigned offline to reinforce the concepts considered.

The session will be organized as follows. The proposers will take about 5 minutes to motivate and introduce the special session. Following the introduction, we expect to feature about four engaging exercises over a period of 55 minutes. Each presenter will have 10 minutes to share their reasoning exercises and assignments that help connect mathematics to computing and the engineering of high quality software. The next 15 minutes will be devoted to seeking feedback from session participants on the format of the session, the choice of exercises and assignments presented, the selection process, and any other ways the session could be improved if it were to be considered for a future offering. At this time, feedback from the audience will be gathered using a short anonymous survey asking about quality of the special session as well as their thoughts on future such sessions.

To provide an idea of the kinds of exercises that may be proposed, we provide a summary of one of the exercises presented last year. All four exercises that were presented last year may be accessed at [2]. While those exercises are designed for college courses, exercises may also be targeted towards a high school audience. For example, [3] contains engaging activities on abstraction, analysis, problem solving, and reasoning for a high school *AP CS Principles* class, even before introducing any programming.

Example: It's more fun to be the bad guy

By: Brian C. Dean and Chad Waters, School of Computing, Clemson University

Objectives – Help students realize the intrinsic "funness" of algorithmic problem-solving.

Why It Is Engaging – In security classes, students often study vulnerabilities in software or security mechanisms from a "bad guy" perspective. We incorporate this perspective in algorithm-type classes.

The Exercise – Give students an operation or code fragment containing an algorithm that has some sort of weakness that makes it run inefficiently under some circumstance. Students must examine the code and then submit a working application that generates input for this algorithm. A successful submission will run fast (this is relative to the problem under consideration) and will make the provided algorithm run slow.

One specific exercise: A simplistic hash table of a map component. Given the following hashing function, the student must reverse-engineer the mathematics of the function to create an algorithm that generates inputs so the map component store all these inputs in one single bucket. h(x) = (3x + 17) % table_size.

Topics – performance, algorithm design, algorithm analysis.

Audience – Data structures and algorithms

Difficulty – Medium for the specific example given above. Harder or easier depending on the provided algorithm.

Strengths – One of the strengths of this activity (or related assignments) is that it adds a level of adversarial excitement for students while they are analyzing the algorithm, and then designing their own. Additionally, this is very nice mixture of theory and practice.

Weaknesses – Instructors need to provide an implementation of the algorithm with the weakness and then run each of adversarial inputs through this implementation. However, with some work the grading can be made fully automated.

Dependencies – None.

Variants – Many variations of well-known algorithms are available, from linear search algorithms to the quick-sort algorithm.

3. EXPECTATIONS

The intended audience is the group of SIGCSE educators that have been regularly attending the "Math Thinking" BoFs at recent SIGCSEs as well as the over 100 participants at a SIGCSE 2012 panel [4], and attendees at previous SIGCSE panels [5,6] dating back to 2003. The session will include approximately four engaging mathematical reasoning exercises and assignments with details, slides, and other related material made available at a website for later download. The repository of examples can be hosted at the Math Thinking website [7], for example. The audience will learn how others are injecting excitement in teaching mathematical reasoning in their courses, as well as acquire some specific exercises to expand their repertoire.

4. SUITABILITY FOR SPECIAL SESSION

The strong interest in mathematical reasoning by many SIGCSE attendees is our main justification for this special session. The rationale for the session is indeed similar to that of the present "Nifty Assignments" session. The participants in the session will be chosen by reviewers based on a selection process from several possible submissions. For the session, the proposers of this session will serve as the reviewers. If the session is accepted, the proposers will publicize the session widely and immediately through dedicated mailing lists, internet, and other suitable forums to seek submissions. If the session is continued into the future, past presenters will serve as reviewers.

One possible question is whether the exercises and assignments presented in this session could be presented in the "Nifty Assignments" session itself. A close inspection of the "Nifty Assignments" website information page [8] does not explicitly indicate that "Nifty Assignments" is only for programming assignments; it does however make clear that the emphasis is on nifty programming assignments. The types of mathematical reasoning exercises and assignments we envision would not nominally fit there. Furthermore, this session is at least as concerned with classroom activities in mathematical thinking, as it is with offline assignments.

5. ACKNOWLEDGMENTS

We would like to acknowledge Doug Baldwin and Peter Henderson for their contributions in developing this proposal. We would also like to acknowledge NSF grants DUE-0942542, CCF-1161916, DUE-1022191, and DUE-1022941.

6. REFERENCES

[1] Hollingsworth, J.E., Krone, J., Hallstrom, J.O., Sitaraman, M., and Weide, B.W. 2013. Engaging mathematical reasoning exercises. In *Proceeding of the 44th ACM Technical Symposium on Computer Science Education*. ACM, New York, NY, USA, 459-460. DOI=10.1145/2445196.2445332 http://doi.acm.org.oberon.ius.edu/10.1145/2445196.2445332

[2] Dean, B., Waters, C., Weide, B. W., Hollingsworth, J. E., Krone, J., and Kussmaul, C., "ACM SIGCSE 2013 Special Session: Engaging Mathematical Reasoning Exercises", Web, 6 Sept 2013, http://www.cs.clemson.edu/resolve/teaching/ed_ws/emre/index.html

[3] Sitaraman, M., "A Bit of Computer Science is Good for You No Matter What you Want to Do," Web, January 2010, http://www.cs.clemson.edu/resolve under Tab Talks.

[4] Krone, J., Baldwin, D., Carver, J. C., Hollingsworth, J. E., Kumar, A., and Sitaraman, M., Panel: Teaching Mathematical Reasoning across the Curriculum, *Procs. 43rd ACM SIGCSE Conference*, March 2012.

[5] Baldwin, D., Marion, W., Sitaraman, M., and Heeren, C., Panel: Some Developments in Mathematical Thinking for Computer Science Education Since Computing Curricula 2001, *Procs. 41st ACM SIGCSE Conference*, March 2010.

[6] Marion, W., Bloss, A., Powers, K., Baldwin, D., Panel: How Departments are Responding to the Mathematics Recommendations in CC2001, *Procs. 34th ACM SIGCSE Conference*, February 2003.

[7] Baldwin, D., "Math-thinking-l – Mathematical reasoning in CS curricula", Web, 6 September 2013, http://mail.geneseo.edu/mailman/listinfo/math-thinking-l/.

[8] Parlante, N., "Nifty Assignments Info", Web, 6 September 2013, http://nifty.stanford.edu/info.html.

STEM Teaching as an Additional Profession for Scientists and Engineers: The Case of Computer Science Education

Orit Hazzan
Department of Education in Science and Technology
Technion – Israel Institute of Technology
oritha@tx.technion.ac.il

Noa Ragonis
School of Education - Computer Science Department
Beit Berl College, Israel
Department of Education in Science and Technology
Technion – Israel Institute of Technology
noarag@beitberl.ac.il

ABSTRACT

The conference theme - "Leveraging Computing to Change Education" - focuses on the influence of computing on the way we educate at all levels. In this paper we highlight the conference theme from the perspective of computer science (CS) teacher preparation and describe the *Views* program, launched at the Technion – Israel Institute of Technology, two year ago. *Views* invites Technion graduates back to the Technion to study toward an additional bachelor's degree in the Department of Education in Science and Technology. The degree they earn includes a high school teaching certificate in one of eight tracks: math, physics, biology, chemistry, CS, environmental sciences, electrical engineering, and mechanical engineering. *Views* students receive full study scholarships and are not required to commit to work in the education system after graduation. In the paper, we (a) present the *Views* program; (b) analyze factors that motivate and demotivate CS graduates to enroll in the program; (c) describe the characteristics of students in the program and their contribution to the learning environments and (d) address hopes with respect to the expected future impact of the *Views* program on the education system in Israel in general and on CS education in particular.

Categories and Subject Descriptors

K.3.2 [**Computers and Education**]: Computer and Information Science Education – *Computer science education, Curriculum.*

General Terms

Economics, Human Factors, Standardization.

Keywords

CS teacher preparation, CS education and the job market, CS teachers, CS teaching as a second career, STEM education.

1. INTRODUCTION

Many countries experience difficulties in attracting excellent STEM (science, technology, engineering and mathematics) teachers, especially on the high school level. This shortage is partially explained by the fact that qualified young people, who excel in STEM, prefer to study one of the STEM subjects and work in technology and hi-tech firms as scientists and engineers, rather than join the education system. This phenomenon, in turn, is partially explained by the social norms accepted in these countries.

SIGCSE'14, March 5–8, 2014, Atlanta, Georgia, USA.

http://dx.doi.org/10.1145/2538862.2538879

In response to this shortage, the Technion – Israel Institute of Technology – launched several education initiatives, one of which – the *Views*[1] program – is described and analyzed in this paper from the perspective of CS education. The objective of *Views* is to help alleviate the STEM teachers' shortage in Israel by providing Technion graduates with an additional profession – high school STEM teachers – that they will be able to use if, when and where they choose to switch to education.

As it turns out, many Technion graduates, from all scientific and engineering disciplines, ages and professional backgrounds, find the *Views* program attractive. In this paper, we focus on those Technion graduates who chose to study in the CS education track of *Views* and we address questions such as: What motivates CS graduates to enroll in the program and what demotivates them? What characterizes them? And, how are these characteristics expressed in courses taught in the Technion's CS teacher preparation program? We suggest that the discussion presented in this paper highlights a new perspective on high school CS teacher preparation programs.

We first describe the general background of *Views* and of its CS education track in particular. Then, based on the analysis of data collected from several resources, we describe some observations with respect to students' decisions to choose (or not choose) this track and try to explain them, answer the questions presented above, and propose directions for future research.

2. THE STUDY ENVIRONMENT

2.1 Technion – Israel Institute of Technology

The Technion – Israel Institute of Technology[2] is the major supplier of scientists and engineers to the Israeli industry. Its graduates constitute over 70 percent of the country's founders and managers of hi-tech companies. Due to the ingenuity of Technion alumni, Israel is now home to the largest concentration of technology start-up companies outside of Silicon Valley, and 80 percent of Israeli NASDAQ companies are led by Technion graduates. The Technion recently won, together with Cornell University, a competition to establish an applied sciences graduate school on Roosevelt Island off Manhattan (see The Jacobs Technion-Cornell Innovation Institute - JTCII[3]).

[1] The name of the *Views* program in Hebrew is Mabatim (= Views in English), which is the Hebrew acronym for Engineers/Scientists in Science and Technology Education.

[2] Technion's website: http://www1.technion.ac.il/en

[3] See: http://tech.cornell.edu/experience/jtcii/

2.2 Department of Education in Science and Technology

The Technion's Department of Education in Science and Technology (the department) is one of the Technion's 18 academic units. The department's teaching, research and development activities are varied and focus on learning sciences, educational technologies, and education in a variety of subjects and learning environments. The department offers eight undergraduate study tracks and a comprehensive graduate program. The undergraduate program covers the full range of high school STEM education disciplines and it includes a high school teaching certificate for STEM subjects in one of eight fields: math, physics, biology, chemistry, CS, environmental sciences, electrical engineering, and mechanical engineering.

The department considers its contribution to the Israeli educational system to be not only in preparing prospective high school science and technology teachers, but also in encouraging its graduate students to contribute to Israel's higher education, the hi-tech industry, the Israel Defense Forces, and the third sector.

This is a fertile ground for the *Views* program which reflects the Technion sense of responsibility for improving STEM education in Israel also on the school level. As is described in the continuation of the paper, the *Views* program is one platform that enables the Technion to promote this agenda by training high school STEM teachers with broad world view and vast work experience in a variety of workplaces.

2.3 CS Teacher Preparation

A decrease in the number of students who choose CS undergraduate studies [1, 2, 8, 12] drew attention to CS teacher preparation programs. Surveys indicate the need to (a) update the high school curriculum in parallel to improving teacher preparation programs [5, 11, 13] and (b) to diversify the population of prospective CS teachers [2, 4].

The Technion's CS education track is one of the study tracks offered by the department. It is a high school CS teacher preparation program that illustrates the model, suggested in [6, 7], for the Israeli high school CS curriculum and it includes three main tiers: disciplinary studies, education and pedagogical studies, and pedagogical-disciplinary studies (for more details see [9, 10]).

3. THE VIEWS PROGRAM

As far as we know, the *Views*[4] program proposes a new approach towards the profession of STEM teaching, as is reflected in the following description.

3.1 Program Description and Rationale

Views invites all Technion graduates back to the Technion's Department of Education in Science and Technology, to study toward an additional bachelor's degree in one of the eight study tracks mentioned above.

The rationale guiding the development of *Views* was to offer conditions that would enable Technion graduates to join the program. The Technion approached this challenge in a gradual and proactive manner. First, broad conceptual agreement was solicited among both academic and administrative entities, and later candidates for the program were approached from among Technion graduates (first) and current students (later).

Technion graduates who enroll in the *Views* program receive full study scholarships from the Technion for two years. Since the number of credits required to complete this degree is similar to that required for an MBA, the study program is organized similarly. The students attend classes one full day or two half-days a week for two years, and so they can continue working as scientists/engineers in the industry in parallel to their studies. *Views* students study alongside the Technion's regular undergraduate students, a fact that affects the regular courses studied in the program as is discussed later on in the paper. The framework established for the *Views* program is now open to all Technion undergraduate students who may begin studying in one of the department's disciplinary tracks in parallel to their B.Sc. studies in science and engineering, and join the *Views* program to complete their studies in STEM education after graduating in science or engineering.

Although the students enrolled in the *Views* program receive full study scholarships for two years, they are not required to commit to teaching in the education system. This decision was made for the following reasons: (1) Teaching should not be done only because one made a commitment to do so; (2) the knowledge that *Views* students gain in the program – mainly, learning and teaching processes – is useful also in the hi-tech industry when coping with new knowledge and technological developments. Thus, even if *Views* students decide not to switch to education, they will still use the knowledge they gained in their studies and contribute to Israel's prosperity, but in a different way; (3) the exposure of *Views* students during their studies to schools, to high school students, and to teaching and learning processes will continue to affect them throughout their entire life. Thus, even if they did not originally consider becoming STEM high school teachers, they may consider this option at some future time, either in parallel to their work in the industry or if they ever decide to switch careers to STEM teaching.

3.2 The *Views* Program Participants

Participant recruitment: *Views* is introduced and publicized through the Technion's alumni association mailing list, the Technion newsletter and the department's website. As it turns out, however, the current most popular channel of advertisement is by word of mouth through friends and acquaintances who are already enrolled in the program. Students who are currently studying at the Technion in one of its science and engineering faculties are invited to a meeting we organize each semester to introduce and promote *Views*.

Participants currently enrolled in *Views*: Since *Views* was launched two years ago, 146 Technion graduates enrolled in the program: 60 started the program in its first year, 2012, and have recently completed the two-year program; 90 started the program in its second year, 2013, and have just completed their first year of studies. Current enrollment in the coming Winter semester (2013-2014) is at about 50 graduates and we expect to have about 100 *Views* students each year for the next five to ten years. The department currently has about 300 undergraduate students – half of whom are *Views* students. Sixty percent of *Views* students are males and forty percent are females.

Table 1 presents the distribution of *Views* students among the different study tracks. As can be seen, while the CS Faculty is the

[4] The *Views* program is widely described in Inside Higher Ed (Sep 20, 2012). The number of students studying in *Views*, though, is not updated in the *Inside Higher Ed* paper.

second largest faculty at the Technion (see data in Table 2), only 8% of all *Views* students selected CS education as their STEM education track, and only half of them are CS graduates. This observation led to the questions that we address in this paper.

Table 1. Distribution of *Views* students among the study tracks[5]

Education Track	# of *Views* Students	% of *Views* Students
Mathematics	29	20%
Electrical engineering	26	18%
Biology	22	15%
Mechanical engineering	20	14%
Chemistry	19	13%
Physics	15	10%
Computer Science	12 6 CS graduates, 3 Electrical Engineering graduates, and 3 Industrial Engineering and Management graduates	8%
Environmental Sciences	3	2%
TOTAL	**146**	100%

3.3 The CS Education Track of *Views*

The CS education track of *Views* is open to students and graduates of the Technion's faculties of CS, Industrial Engineering and Management (the Information Systems track only), and Electrical Engineering (the Computer Engineering track only). Students from other faculties are permitted to join this track, under special circumstances, provided they complete required prerequisites, either from the department's designated courses for teachers (for example, Computational Models for CS teachers, Programming Paradigms) or from the courses offered the Faculty of CS.

The program consists of 36 credits as listed below:

- 22 credits of required courses: Introduction to Developmental Psychology, Introduction to Social Psychology, Introduction to Cognitive Psychology, Teaching Methods and Skills, Philosophy of Education, Methods of Teaching CS I and II, School Practicum in CS, Reflective Workshop on Teaching Practicum, and Selected Problems in CS.
- 8 credits of elective courses from the department (e.g., Methods courses of other STEM subjects).
- 6 credits of elective advanced courses from the faculty of CS (seminars, projects, and advanced studies).

4. THE STUDY

The *Views* program is accompanied by a comprehensive formative assessment as is customary with novel programs. This paper presents preliminary observations of the part of that assessment that focuses on the CS education track of *Views*.

4.1 Study Targets and Questions

The study aims to understand the factors influencing Technion CS graduates to explore the option of working as CS teachers as a second career (following or parallel to a career in industry) and to enroll in the *Views* program in preparation for this shift.

[5] These data do not include students who will begin their studies in *Views* in the Winter semester of the 2013-2014 academic year.

The research questions derived from this target were:

- What factors motivate Technion CS graduates to enroll in *Views*?
- What factors demotivate Technion CS graduates from enrolling in *Views*?
- Does the integration of *Views* students into the regular undergraduate study track influence it? If yes – how?

4.2 Population

We collected data from the *Views* students and from Technion alumni who expressed interest in the program. In addition, we analyzed data on the number of students and graduates from the five largest Technion faculties.

4.3 Data-Gathering Tools

Both quantitative and qualitative data were collected:

- Descriptive statistics: Number of current Technion students and graduates;
- Online surveys: Questionnaires enabled us to reach a wide population and to collect data either anonymously or not (according to each respondent's choice). Most of the questions in the questionnaires were open questions since our study just began and we first wished to learn about research participants' perspective before gathering data using closed questions.
- Interviews: In the questionnaires we also asked participants whether they would be willing to be interviewed and we subsequently interviewed three Technion alumni from the CS education track of *Views* and five CS alumni who expressed interest in the program but ultimately did not enroll.

In the online surveys and interviews we asked about the interviewees' background, their perspectives on teaching high school CS as a second career, and their thoughts with respect to factors that motivate CS alumni to enroll in *Views* as opposed to factors that demotivate them.

5. DATA ANALYSES

5.1 The Distribution of *Views* Students

5.1.1 The small number of CS alumni enrolled in Views

To examine the low enrollment in the CS education track of *Views*, we took a broader perspective and looked at the number of students and alumni in the Technion's five largest faculties, of which CS is second in size. For each faculty, we looked at four student groups (Table 2):

- Group A: Students who are currently studying at the faculty;
- Group B: Students who currently study at the Technion and who attended the meetings at which we explained how to start studying towards a second Bachelor's degree in STEM education in order to join *Views* after graduation (Group B is a subset of Group A);
- Group C: Alumni who showed interest in studying in *Views*;
- Group D: Technion graduates who enrolled in *Views* (Group D is a subset of Group C).

Data description: Tables 1 and 2 and some additional data reflect the following facts:

a. Eight CS graduates are enrolled in the *Views* program: six in the CS education track, one in the electrical engineering education track and one in the math education track.

b. As can be seen from the sizes of Groups C and D, between one fourth and one third of alumni who expressed interest in *Views* eventually enrolled in the program;

c. Alumni who enrolled in *Views* did not necessarily select the *Views* track that corresponds to the Technion faculty they graduated from. However, since such cases were relatively few, we did not incorporate them into our analysis as a separate category but rather included them in Group D;

Table 2. Interest in the Views program

Faculty	A: Current students	B: Current students who participated in explanation meetings	C: Alumni who expressed interest after graduation[6]	D: Alumni enrolled in *Views*
Electrical Engineering	1294	24	97	32
Computer Science	1118	26	36	8
Civil & Environmental Engineering	1052	22	36	10
Industrial & Management Eng.	814	22	54	16
Mechanical Engineering	800	23	46	11
Total for above five faculties	**5078**	**117**	**269**	**77**
Total for all 18 Technion faculties	**8571**	**194**	**532**	**146**

d. In most cases, the relative size of the Technion faculty (Group A) corresponds both to the relative number of students who participated in explanation meetings (Group B), to the number of alumni who expressed interest in the program after graduation (Group C), and to the number of graduates studying in the corresponding *Views* track (Group D). This, however, is not the case for the CS and EE (electrical engineering) education tracks. First, the CS education track is the *smallest* track in *Views*, whereas the Faculty of CS is the second biggest after EE in terms of the number of students (1118 students, about one-eighth of the total number of Technion undergraduate students per year and 1294 undergraduate students, respectively). Second, the number of EE alumni in Groups C and D is substantially higher than from any of the other four largest Technion faculties.

Since a relative large number of the CS and EE Technion graduates work in the same hi-tech companies, in many cases in the same working environment and under similar working conditions, several questions arise: Why do the numbers of interested CS Technion students (Group B) and alumni (Group C) decrease when it comes to actual enrollment in the CS education track of *Views* (Group D)? And, why is the situation reversed when it comes to EE graduates? We attempt to answer these questions in the next section.

5.1.2 Engineering versus Science

In this section we focus on the four groups, A-D, of the faculties of CS and EE, which are similar in terms of their number of students and their very high admission criteria. The sizes of these groups raise the question: Why are the sizes of these faculties' respective Groups C and D different, while the sizes of their respective Groups A and B are so similar?

We first speculated that the answer to this question lies in the difference between (computer) science and (electrical) engineering and that the mere, original selection of EE over CS, that is, an engineering profession as opposed to a scientific profession, indicates that EE graduates have an a-priori tendency towards the profession of teaching. This is because engineering professions require skills like teamwork and collaboration with different stakeholders, which are beneficial also in teaching processes. And so we rephrased the questions: Can the differences in the sizes of Groups C-D of CS and EE be explained by the differences between science and engineering? We realized that the answer to this is No, due to three reasons.

First, the sizes of Group B of all five largest faculties are similar; Second, four out of the five largest faculties are engineering faculties while the CS faculty is the only scientific faculty among the top five. However, in terms of Group D, CS is more similar (yet smaller) to the other three engineering faculties than to EE; Third, as it turns out, many CS graduates work as software engineers after graduation, even though they do not have an engineering education.[7]

Therefore, we asked: Since, in practice, both EE and CS graduates work as engineers, is there a difference between these two engineering fields and the kind of work that these graduates do after graduation in the Israeli hi-tech industry? The answer we suggest is based on the following preliminary data we have at this stage.

One of our interviewees, a Technion EE alumnus who graduated from the joint CS/EE track (computer engineering) and is currently enrolled in the CS education track of *Views,* reported having the following work experience: *Management of the development of real-time software in* [names of three companies] *and several start-ups. In the last several years, I focused on product and application development, including hardware, chips, and quality assurance.*

In his interview, we asked this student: How would you explain the low number of CS graduates who have joined *Views*? to which he answered: *In CS, they concentrate on their profession, to develop... In EE, there is more openness. We* [EE engineers] *work with customers, educate and teach a variety of customers. In software there is an API, you define and then you must develop according to that definition, solve problems. In EE there is a need to struggle with service; sometimes an electrical engineer must stay on the customer's site for several days. In other cases, when electrical engineers design an electronic board, it requires a lot of interaction with customers from all over the world. In EE there is more guidance, teaching.*

[6] Numbers for Groups C were retrieved on June 16, 2013 for the preparation of this paper. We counted only those who contacted the department head (the first author of this paper) by email. In addition, many Technion alumni asked questions by contacting the department secretary or calling the department head, but such inquiries were not recorded.

[7] Denning and Riehle [3] claim that "many of our software developers have been raised in a research tradition, not an engineering tradition."

In another interview, it was suggested that EE graduates are promoted to managerial roles quicker than are CS graduates and therefore they gradually lose their flexibility and ability to adjust to new market demands as they approach the age of 30 or 40. Since, as mentioned above, electrical engineers usually gain some teaching experience during their professional development, those who enjoyed that aspect of their job, may consider joining the *Views* program. At the same time, CS graduates tend to stay in software development positions longer, first, enabling them to keep adjusting to new market demands; and second, preventing or at least minimizing their relative exposure to guidance and teaching situations.

To validate this observation, we examined the characterization of the CS alumni who expressed interest in *Views* and analyzed the profile of the 14 (out of 36) Technion CS graduates from Group C who answered our online questionnaire. Indeed, we found that their current work places were:

Hi-tech	9	64%
Traditional industry	2	14%
Education	0	0%
Public sector (not education)	1	7%
Other	2	14%

and their current positions were (they could chose more than one answer):

Research	0	0%
Software development	10	63%
Management	4	25%
Teaching	1	6%
Other	1	6%

Therefore, we speculate that since the actual work of electrical engineers requires listening, teaching, and education skills, the ability to experience processes in which these skills are expressed may help them discern whether or not they are attracted to the field of education; if they are, we believe they will tend to choose programs such as *Views*. At the same time, we suggest, the work of most CS graduates, though it may include such elements, does not expose them to such processes at the same level of intensity. This explanation clearly warrants further investigation.

Additional explanations for the difference in the number of EE and CS graduates in *Views*, that further support the above explanation, were suggested in interviews with CS alumni who expressed interest in *Views* but who did not ultimately enroll. As can be seen, these explanations are all related to differences between the two professions:

a. Salary level: The difference between a teacher's salary, which is fixed regardless of the discipline taught, and salaries in CS is significantly greater than in the case of EE. The low status of the profession of teaching was also mentioned;
b. Intellectual curiosity: The field of CS provides more opportunities for new technological and intellectual development than does the field of EE. Consequently, CS graduates are less attracted to further studies in general and to programs such as *Views* in particular;
c. Kind of work: CS projects tend to be longer-term than do EE projects and so CS employees are more exposed to new developments and academic learning on the job than are their EE counterparts. CS employees may therefore fulfill their desire for learning in other venues than in *Views*;
d. Job security: CS employees are more secure in their jobs than are EE employees. This may be explained by the relative flexibility CS employees exhibit in adjusting to new market demands as mentioned above. Electrical engineers, therefore, tend to be on the lookout for an alternative profession in case it be needed.

5.2 The CS *Views* Students Motivational Factors

In Section 5.1 we explained the low number of CS alumni in the *Views* program and elaborated on some demotivating factors that prevent students from joining the program. Nevertheless, we were also interested in looking into the motivation of those who did enroll in the *Views* program.

We have elicited the following reasons for joining the program from interviews with CS alumni from Group D. These *Views* students said that they:

1. have always dreamt about going back to study in the academia and *Views* was an appropriate opportunity to realize that dream;
2. have dropped out of the race for promotion and now have the time to replenish the soul;
3. are considering a professional alternative with more conventional work hours;
4. wanted to take the opportunity since time has become available between projects;
5. are considering switching to teaching due to a desire to contribute to society and *Views* was deemed the best program for such a career move;
6. are engaged in instruction and thought that *Views* would contribute to their work.

As it turns out, these expectations are fulfilled. Among the different feelings these graduates expressed about their studies, they mentioned that they:

1. very much enjoy returning to academia, studying and connecting to current contents as well as to basic CS contents;
2. enjoy the encounter with younger students, despite conflicts that occasionally arise as to appropriate behavior in academia;
3. are challenged by the hands-on experience in the schools and in the mentorship activities despite the fact that they did not previously consider working in education. They now feel that they could contribute in either a formal or informal framework;
4. are happy and thankful for the opportunity that they have been given.

5.3 The Contribution of the *Views* Program to the Studies in the Department

Though we cannot currently predict the future contribution of *Views* students to the Israeli education system, we can learn about their current contribution to the study atmosphere at the department, in general, and the in courses they attend, in particular.

The increased number (from 150 in 2011 to 300 in 2013) of undergraduate students at the department is immediately reflected in the number of students in each course, which has increased significantly in that same time. Table 3 illustrates this by presenting the number of students enrolled in the two Methods of Teaching CS courses the last three times the courses were offered (every two years).

A reflective analysis of the second author of the paper, who teaches the Methods of Teaching CS courses, indicates that the mere increase in the number of students in the courses has several notable advantages:

- The more students in the class, the more meaningful and interaction-based the teaching may be;
- When group work is facilitated in the class, the size of the class enables its division into sub-groups of a reasonable size to foster a more meaningful learning process;
- The two populations – undergraduate students and Technion alumni – benefit from each other: The more mature students, i.e. the Technion alumni, bring their work experience into the class, while the undergraduate students help the older students relearn and refresh CS contents that they learned (sometimes many) years ago;
- The undergraduate students' self-esteem increases since they realize that they chose a profession that successful Technion CS graduates wish to study as a second career;
- The diversity inherent in this greater cohort of students further enhances the abovementioned phenomena.

Table 3: # of students enrolled in recent Methods of CS courses

Course	2008/9	2010/11	2012/13
Methods of Teaching CS I	5	6	23
Methods of Teaching CS II	4	8	21

6. SUMMARY AND FUTURE RESEARCH

In this paper we presented our preliminary investigations of the *Views* program in general and its CS education track in particular. We learned that: (a) the profession of CS does not expose CS graduates to situations in which they can express teaching skills and therefore, even if they have a tendency towards education, they may not uncover it and consider education as a second career; (b) alumni students appreciate the personal contribution of *Views*; (c) alumni who enroll in *Views* have a significant impact on the department's studies.

In general, from the implementation of the program so far, and from the initial research findings presented here, we see in the program the potential of realizing the meaning of its name, *Views*. The program takes a positive view of the world of teaching, attracts high-quality teaching personnel who hold the future of education close to their heart, and it is evident that the participants in the program have a positive impact on the teacher preparation process.

Our hope is that *Views* will impact CS education on the high-school level as well. Since the accumulated knowledge gained in Israel on CS education in general and on CS teacher preparation in particular is already appreciated worldwide and since Israel is a relatively small country, it may, therefore, serve as a pilot case study for larger countries with respect to CS teaching as a second career.

In the future, we plan to:

- follow up on the integration of *Views* graduates into the education system;
- ask high school CS teachers for their perspective on the issues discussed in the paper;
- collect additional data using closed questionnaires when the number of students increases so as to obtain statistical results;
- expand the research to the perspective of the department's regular undergraduate CS students who studied both with and without *Views* students;
- broaden our research to include all students and all eight tracks offered by the *Views* program.

7. REFERENCES

[1] Carter, L. (2006). Why students with an apparent aptitude for computer science don't choose to major in computer science. *SIGCSE Bull.* 38, 1 (March 2006), 27-31.

[2] Christopher, N., Brown, C., Kölling, M., Crick, T., Jones, S.P., Humphreys, S. and Sentence, S. (2013). Bringing computer science back into schools: Lessons from the UK. *Proceeding of the 44th ACM Technical Symposium on Computer science Education* (SIGCSE '13), 269-274.

[3] Denning, P.J. and Riehle, R.D. (2009). The profession of IT: Is software engineering engineering? *Communications of the ACM*, 52(3), 24-26.

[4] Dennis, A.R., Duffy, T.M. and Cakir, H. (2010). IT programs in high schools: Lessons from the Cisco Networking Academy program. *Commun. ACM* **53**(7), 138-141.

[5] Ericson, B., Armoni, M., Gal-Ezer, J., Seehorn, D., Stephenson, C. and Trees, F. (2008). *Ensuring exemplary teaching in an essential discipline: Addressing the crisis in computer science teacher certification, Final Report of the CSTA Teacher Certification Task Force.* http://www.csta.acm.org/Communications/sub/DocsPresentationFiles/CertificationFinal.pdf

[6] Hazzan, O., Gal-Ezer, J. and Blum, L. (2008). A model for high school Computer Science Education: The four key elements that make it!, Proceedings of *The 39th Technical Symposium on Computer Science Education*, Portland, Oregon, USA, pp. 281-285.

[7] Hazzan, O., Lapidot, T. and Ragonis, N. (2011). *Guide to Teaching Computer Science: An Activity-Based Approach*, Springer.

[8] Marshall, R. (2013). Exclusive: UK faces severe shortfall of computer science teachers. *Publication at v3.co.uk*, 30 Jan 2013 http://www.v3.co.uk/v3-uk/news/2239958/exclusive-uk-faces-severe-shortfall-of-computer-science-teachers

[9] Ragonis, N., Hazzan, O. and Gal-Ezer, J. (2010). A survey of Computer Science teacher preparation programs in Israel tells us: Computer Science deserves a designated high school teacher preparation!, *Proceedings of SIGCSE 2010 - The 41st ACM Technical Symposium on Computer Science Education*, Milwaukee, WI, USA, pp. 401-405.

[10] Ragonis, N., Hazzan, O. and Gal-Ezer, J. (2011). A Study on Attitudes and Emphases in Computer Science Teacher Preparation. *Proceedings of SIGCSE 2011 - The 42st ACM Technical Symposium on Computer Science Education*, Dallas, Texas, USA, pp. 401-405.

[11] Stephenson, C., Gal-Ezer, J., Haberman, B., and Verno, A. (2005). The New Educational Imperative: Improving High School Computer Science Education. *Final Report of the CSTA Curriculum Improvement Task Force.* http://www.csta.acm.org/Communications/sub/DocsPresentationFiles/White_Paper07_06.pdf

[12] Wagstaff, K. (2013). Can we fix computer science education in America? *Time Tec*, 16 July 2013. http://techland.time.com/2012/07/16/can-we-fix-computer-science-education-in-america/

[13] Wilson, C., Sudol, L., Stephenson, C. and Stehlik, M. (2010). *Running on Empty: The Failure to teach K-12 Computer Science in the Digital Age*, ACM and CSTA. http://www.acm.org/runningonempty/

Spreading the Word: Introducing Pre-Service Teachers to Programming in the K-12 Classroom

Scott Bell
Kansas State University
234 Nichols Hall
Manhattan, KS 66506
rsbell@ksu.edu

Tim Frey
Doane College
1014 Boswell Avenue
Crete, NE 68333
timothy.frey@doane.edu

Eugene Vasserman
Kansas State University
234 Nichols Hall
Manhattan, KS 66506
eyv@ksu.edu

ABSTRACT

We present our experiences and outcomes from a programming camp held for sixth through ninth grade students. The instructional team included five pre-service teachers who earned field experience credit for this work, and one in-service teacher. The pre-service teachers were art and music teachers-in-training, providing an opportunity for us to utilize their creative expertise in developing content for the camp. In turn, we helped the teachers explore ways they might incorporate today's user-friendly programming environments (in this case, Scratch) into their curriculum. During each of four week-long sessions, the pre-service teachers gradually took over more teaching responsibilities, modifying and then presenting lessons that incorporate their own music and art expertise into the programming activities.

Student pre-camp and post-camp surveys show that self-efficacy towards programming, enjoyment of programming, and interest in continuing to program increased over the course of the week-long sessions. Meanwhile, the teachers-in-training discovered they are capable of incorporating their subject matter into Scratch-based classroom activities, and teaching this material in a classroom setting. This is an encouraging demonstration of a way to introduce programming to the K-12 teaching community without overloading in-service teachers or requiring additional course work for pre-service teachers.

Categories and Subject Descriptors

K.3 [**Computers and Education**]: General

General Terms

Human Factors

Keywords

K-12, Scratch, Programming, pre-service, outreach, camp

SIGCSE'14, March 5–8, 2014, Atlanta, GA, USA.

ACM 978-1-4503-2605-6/14/03 ...$15.00.
http://dx.doi.org/10.1145/2538862.2538963.

1. INTRODUCTION

A major obstacle in recruiting students into the computing fields is a lack of exposure to relevant topics in K-12 classrooms [4]. This lack of exposure does not result in students having a necessarily negative impression of computing, it simply prevents them from ever developing any sort of informed opinion of the field. By showing pre-service teachers how to incorporate some of these concepts into existing coursework without encountering major obstacles, we can provide a means for the introduction of some computing concepts into the K-12 curriculum. This is an extension of previous work presented in [2].

We know that an introduction to programming through the use of tools such as Scratch can increase students' interest in computing [14, 16], so we focus our efforts on increasing the breadth of delivery and potential usage of these programming tools in K-12 classrooms. Summer camps and after school activities have been shown to be effective at building student interest [7, 8], but they only connect with a self-selected group of students for a brief period of time. What if a large percentage of teachers had experience using such tools, and were able to integrate them into the classroom with *all* of their students on a *regular* basis?

Unfortunately, most teachers have little, if any, training in areas such as programming and little time in which to learn these skills once they enter their professional careers. At our university, for example, only Business and Math Education majors are required to take a single three credit-hour course which covers basic programming constructs using Java. The reason is that teachers from these two concentration areas are those most likely to be assigned to teach programming when they enter the workforce.

Given the current high quality, introductory, software development environments such as Scratch, Kodu, and Alice [6, 9, 11, 12], teachers no longer need to become experts in programming to use basic programming concepts in a variety of contexts. These environments can be utilized as teaching tools, to reinforce or teach other content, instead of being the teaching focus. More importantly, they are very intuitive, reducing the time it takes for teachers and students to become comfortable using them to a few days [5]. With additional time and support, teachers can incorporate more complex material into their classrooms [17].

By having pre-service art and music teachers involved in our programming camp, these future educators are gaining hands-on experience *teaching* with Scratch. They are able to combine this tool with content from the area they plan to teach in when they enter the workforce. In turn, they helped

Figure 1: Progression of geometric figures challenged students to re-use concepts in more creative ways and appealed to the in-service math teacher.

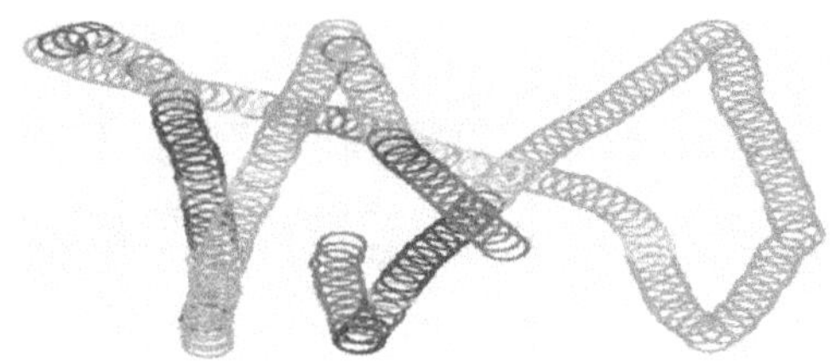

Figure 2: Randomly moving "worm" sprites were the first challenge where we only modeled the program behavior for students.

us refine our content and teaching methods for these activities. Additionally, as part of their pre-service field experience requirements, each pre-service teacher developed lesson plans that utilize programming constructs. These plans can be shared with other teachers who wish to introduce programming concepts into their classroom.

Based on student survey results, the camp achieved positive student outcomes in terms of self-efficacy with respect to programming, enjoyment of programming, and plans to continue programming. Pre-camp surveys show students with relatively neutral to slightly positive opinions about topics such as writing computer programs and self-efficacy as it relates to computer programming. These opinions become decidedly positive after just *four days* of programming.

2. BACKGROUND

The STEM Summer Institute, in its third year, is a summer enrichment program coordinated by the Manhattan-Ogden School District and hosted by Kansas State University's College of Education. During the 4 week camp, nearly 200 sixth through ninth grade students are able to select a different course of study each week, with 12 courses being offered this year. Courses meet for 4 days, with students spending about 3.5 hours in the classroom each day. Sixty nine of these students elected to take the programming course. The institute has two goals: 1) increase student achievement in STEM subjects within the school district by encouraging students to explore these fields through hands on activities, and 2) provide pre-service teachers with STEM teaching experience in a fun, energetic environment.

For secondary education majors at our university, teaching experience is broken into three "blocks." During the first of these blocks, pre-service teachers must participate in a minimum of 30 hours of field experience activities in a secondary education setting. The hours spent working with the camp fulfill this requirement. Many of the students who take the summer section teach 'specials' classes such as music, art, physical education, etc. which have limited opportunities for field experience in regular classrooms. We requested art and music teachers as they would provide content knowledge that could be adapted into the programming lesson plans. As part of the credit, pre-service teachers are responsible for developing lesson plans that fit the context of the course they are assigned to. Additionally, during each successive week of the camp, they take on more of the teaching responsibilities. By the fourth week in our course, the pre-service teachers were responsible for a large percentage of the content being presented. Their lesson plans and teaching activities are reviewed and evaluated by an in-service teacher and an instructor from the College of Education.

Each camp course is led by an in-service teacher selected from the school district based on performance and teaching abilities within a STEM discipline. A team of pre-service teachers (in our case, five) is paired with each in-service teacher to create the instructional team for the course. The pre-service teachers worked in 2 separate shifts, with 2 helping during the first 2 hours and the other 3 helping during the last 2 hours each day (this allowed them to also be enrolled in a Department of Education course running during the same 4 weeks). In several of the courses, this group works with a STEM department on campus to gain access to various resources not readily available to the school district (laboratory space, equipment, personnel, etc.). Since the STEM teachers had limited experience teaching programming, a graduate student from the Computing and Information Sciences department was asked to assist with designing and teaching the programming course this year.

3. INSTRUCTIONAL DESIGN

Previous work has shown that graphical programming environments are a good way to introduce programming to middle-school students [10], and based on our own experiences, we selected Scratch as the development environment for our camp. Due to the abbreviated length of each camp session and to help facilitate learning while reducing frustration, we decided to have students work in pairs [3, 15].

Topics were presented in short lessons with the instructor and students first working together to solve a problem using a new concept and/or commands from the Scratch environment. This was followed by a challenge that required students to apply the new concept to solve some proposed problem. This discretization of the material was very flexible and allowed for an easy transition as the pre-service teachers took over the teaching of individual lessons. It also allowed students to learn the material in steps, repeatedly employing previously used concepts to solve new problems, thus reinforcing those concepts.

Day 1 - Programming Basics and Geometric Shapes

Day one covered the basics of programming such as sequence, selection and iteration in Scratch. After going over basic commands and familiarizing the students with the Scratch environment, we covered four lesson/challenge topics, requiring students to develop algorithms that reproduced various geometric shapes by having a character on the screen (a sprite) "draw" the indicated pattern. Some examples of the patterns used are given in Figure 1. The in-service teacher, who taught middle-school math, appreciated the use of geometric figures (and the need to calculate angles and graphical dimensions) in these challenges.

Day 2 - Algorithm Design and Using Sound

On day two, we began to require students to think more carefully about how they might use the tools, giving less direct instructions for the challenges. We demonstrated the functionality of (but did not show any pieces of the code for) a "worm" type application with a sprite that left randomly shifting trails as it moved around the screen, as shown in Figure 2. We then challenged the students to replicate this behavior. We wanted students to begin developing a habit of thinking about a solution rather than just guessing which blocks should be used. Therefore, student pairs were required to design an algorithm for each challenge on their white board and have it approved before being allowed to program their solution.

The second half of day two focused on using sound in Scratch. We briefly discussed how to use the sounds included with Scratch, and how to import songs and sound files from other sources. Writing music in Scratch has been used successfully in university-level general education courses [13], and the pre-service music teachers were excited about using Scratch as a tool to teach music composition. With their help, we planned a set of lessons incorporating these ideas. We explained reading notes from sheet music and converting them to the numeric values in Scratch, setting tempo, and how to determine the duration of each note. The students then translated one of several melodies from popular contemporary songs using sheet music we provided. The last demonstration of day two involved using broadcast messages (events) to coordinate multiple sprites playing a song in rounds using different instruments.

Day 3 - Broadcast Events, and Variables

Day three started with students writing an application which had sprites talking to one another (using speech bubbles). Students were able to synchronize the order of the conversation using broadcast messages (events).

The final topic we introduced was variables. This was presented using a game in which the user attempted to move one sprite to intercept a ball bouncing around the screen while a computer controlled adversary attempted to catch the user's sprite. Many groups were planning to develop some sort of game for their final project, so this topic was applicable to several pairs of students each week. In most cases, students were able to apply the concepts of incrementing, decrementing and initializing values to their own applications for variables such as score, levels and lives. The remainder of the day was spent starting work on final projects.

Day 4 - Final Project Wrap-up and Presentations

In previous outreach activities, we have had students ask about other languages compared to Scratch (with the insinuation that we were not teaching them "real" programming), so on day four we had a brief discussion and demonstration of other programming languages, comparing constructs they had learned in Scratch with the related code syntax in Java. The remainder of the day was spent finishing projects. We ended the day with students demonstrating their projects.

4. PRE-SERVICE TEACHER PROGRESS

When we first met with the pre-service teachers 10 days prior to the start of camp, they were intimidated by the idea of teaching programming. They had little or no programming experience prior to the Summer Institute, and for some of them, this was the first time they would be evaluated on their teaching methods in the classroom in front of students. The time between this initial meeting and the first day of the institute allowed the pre-service teachers to explore Scratch and get a feeling for the challenges we would be covering during the camp. As was mentioned in Section 2, the institute consisted of four week-long camps, each lasting four days, with the pre-service teachers becoming progressively more involved in the teaching from week to week.

Week 1 - Observing, Helping and Ice Breakers

During the first week, the pre-service teachers were still learning Scratch and observing how we presented the material and interacted with the students. The pre-service teachers had a much better understanding of music than we did, so they helped us teach the musical encoding lessons. During other lessons they primarily helped answer questions when students were working on programming challenges. They also led the group (students and teachers) in ice-breaker activities to help us get to know one another and in "brain breaks" to help refocus the students between lessons.

Week 2 - Lead Enrichment Activity

During week two, in addition to the activities they performed in week one, each pre-service teacher presented an enrichment activity. These activities were about 15 minutes in length and supplemented the material we were covering in one of the existing lessons. For example, one of the activities involved students writing down a sequence of instructions that their partner then had to act out. This allowed us to discuss topics such as what commands were available to the "programmer" and how a command might be interpreted differently by different "actors".

Week 3 - Group Teaching

For week three, the pre-service teachers continued to handle their previous responsibilities and each of the groups (a group of 2 and a group of 3) took over the responsibility for one of the lessons we had been teaching during the previous weeks. This included developing a formal lesson plan, presentation of the material and managing the challenge activities. The pre-service teachers covered the same topics we had covered during previous weeks, but they were free to change the details. Lesson plans were reviewed by the in-service teacher and evaluated by an instructor from the College of Education for pedagogical content and by the CIS graduate student for technical content. The group then took over the teaching of that lesson during the week. This was where the pre-service teachers were able to utilize their education training and specialized background in art or music to improve the presentation and pedagogical approaches we had been using.

Week 4 - Solo Teaching

Finally, during week four, each pre-service teacher developed and taught a separate lesson independently. They were not allowed to repeat a lesson that they had taught during week three. The format and evaluation process were exactly the same as in week three except that the pre-service teachers worked individually on the lesson plans and presentations for this week.

Post-camp Discussions

After the camp concluded, we discussed the outcomes with 4 of the pre-service teachers (3 music and 1 art) to get their impressions and experiences with Scratch and the camp. There were very positive responses:

- Three had shown Scratch to other pre-service teachers as well as relatives and/or friends
- All four felt they were capable of teaching Scratch to their future students
- Two of the music teachers and the art teacher already have ideas of how they can incorporate Scratch into the classroom at various grade levels: *"I think I could apply it to any level, from elementary to high school. Teaching basic notes and rhythms would be easy on Scratch for my younger students and I could have high school students write their own compositions on Scratch."*
- One of the music teachers felt Scratch likely would not fit with the musical concepts they anticipate teaching.

Lesson Plans

As an example of a lesson plan, during week 3, one group took over the square drawing lesson presented on day 1. The plan consisted of:

- Target grade level
- Applicable standards and benchmarks covered
- Lesson goals
- Anticipated learner outcomes
- Vocabulary
- Assessment strategy and criteria
- Classroom set up and resources
- Experience activities
- How students will interact
- Transfer of learning strategy
- A scripted narrative of the lesson

They also developed a work sheet that allowed the students to move step by step through the thought process of building the program plan and had the students start by walking in a square. Students had to then describe these moves on their white boards using only 4 of the Scratch command blocks. If this project is expanded, the set of lesson plans developed in this way would be a valuable resource for other classroom teachers.

5. STUDENT SURVEY RESPONSES

Pre-camp and post-camp surveys were given to each participating student on the first and fourth days each week. The 10 item survey (see Table 1) utilized a 5 point Likert scale, with responses ranging from 1 = strongly disagree to 5 = strongly agree. The statements were designed to evaluate students' self-efficacy as it related to programming, future interest in programming after completion of the camp, and enjoyment of programming. During week 1, we failed to collect the names of students on the survey, so we were not able to use those results when comparing pre-camp and post-camp survey responses using paired data analysis. Additionally, some students missed either the first or last day of camp, leaving us with 52 correlated, completed surveys.

Self-Efficacy Measures		
Statement	**p**	**effect**
I have the ability to earn an A in a computer programming class.	< 0.01	0.4812
I can learn how to write computer programs.	< 0.01	0.5182
I can learn to read code written using a computer programming language.	< 0.01	0.5823
Future Interest Measures		
Statement	**p**	**effect**
I plan to continue writing programs after the Summer Institute is over.	< 0.01	0.5543
I would like to learn more about what computer scientists do.	< 0.05	0.2964
I would take a computer programming class in school if one is available.	0.180	0.1963
I want to learn how to program mobile devices such as phones and tablets.	0.970	-0.0197
Programming Enjoyment Measures		
Statement	**p**	**effect**
I Enjoy Writing Computer Programs.	< 0.01	0.5973
I would enjoy a job that involves writing computer programs.	< 0.05	0.3054
I would enjoy writing computer programs that control robotic parts.	0.65	0.0954

Table 1: Statistical summary of survey items calculated using Wilcoxon signed-rank test (n=52)

5.1 Self-Efficacy

Given that most middle-school-aged students have little or no experience with programming, we expected an increase in self-efficacy in relation to programming after the completion of the camp. We felt that this was an important metric because self-efficacy can be a determining factor in students' selection of career path [1]. The three statements chosen to measure student self-efficacy in programming, along with the measured effect, are shown in Table 1. The results measured for all three items were found to be statistically significant using the Wilcoxon signed-rank test at the 1% level.

The responses were decidedly positive for all three items both before and after the camp, although it is of note that the percentage of students who strongly agreed with each statement increased by at least 50% for all three, and by

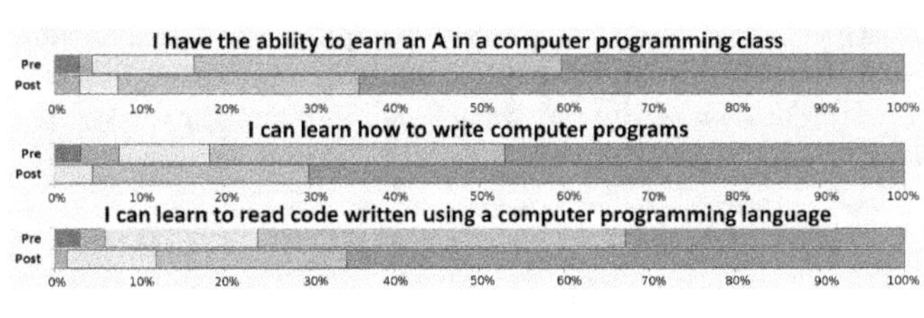

Figure 3: Distribution of responses for statements related to self-efficacy in programming.

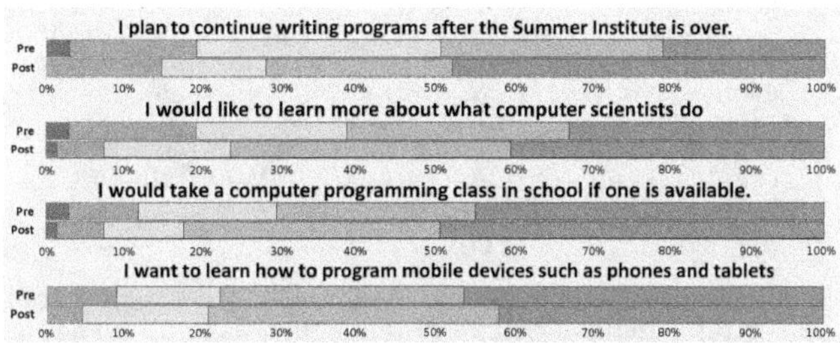

Figure 4: Distribution of responses for statements related to future interest in programming.

100% for 'I can learn to read code written using a computer programming language'. These distributions are shown in Figure 3. Based on these results, the students appear to have come into the camp with moderate beliefs in their ability to program and left with even stronger beliefs in that ability.

5.2 Future Interest in Programming

The survey contained four measures of students' interests in further programming, given in Table 1. The results for these were mixed compared to those for self-efficacy. The change for 'I plan to continue writing programs after the Summer Institute is over' was significant (using the Wilcoxon signed-rank test). This statement also had the greatest percentage increase in students who strongly agreed (120%), as shown in Figure 4. Student excitement about programming increased significantly in just four days.

The other items in this area seemed to suffer from a lack of exposure, with two of them not showing a significant change in value. Interest in mobile device programming and in taking a computer programming class in school both had very small changes that were found to be statistically insignificant. We hypothesize that this is due to the lack of discussion about these topics during the camp. Likewise, we only talked briefly about computer science, and that appears to be reflected in a slight (though significant) positive increase in student curiosity about what computer scientists do.

It is interesting to note that initially only 49% of students stated they had plans to program after the camp ended, but a large percentage *were* interested in learning how to program mobile devices (78%). By the end of the week, the percentage of positive responses for the two items are very similar (72% to 79%, respectively). Student interest in programming increased greatly while interest in mobile programming remained virtually unchanged. This would seem to support the idea that with no exposure to the topic, students don't gain an interest, even if topics seem to be related.

5.3 Programming Enjoyment

There were three items in the survey that measured the students' enjoyment of programming, as shown in Table 1. The first, 'I enjoy writing computer programs' showed the largest measured effect of any statement on the survey. Student response was slightly positive initially on this topic, but by the end of the camp, 85% agreed (Figure 5). While students were not as enthusiastic about a job that involves writing computer programs, this item showed a moderate growth and is reasonable for students that are in middle school. We would hope to see this increase with additional exposure and as the students move closer to graduation. The third statement, "I would enjoy writing computer programs

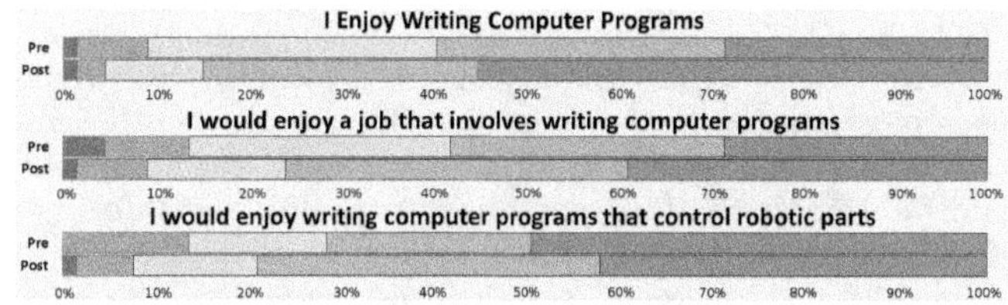

Figure 5: Distribution of responses for statements related to enjoyment of programming

that control robotic parts", performed similar to the previous question about mobile devices. Students showed interest at the start of the camp (72% agreement) and the change by the end of camp was found to be insignificant. As was discussed above, we did not spend time on this topic, so there would be little expected change in this measurement.

6. SUMMARY

This was a positive experience for everyone involved. Pre-camp and post-camp surveys of the students showed significant positive shifts for statements such as "I enjoy writing computer programs," and "I plan to continue writing programs after the summer institute is over," as well as for all statements relating to student self-efficacy. As would be expected, the topics which received little class time had insignificant changes in student attitudes (e.g. mobile device and robotics programming), though they had positive starting responses from students. While not broken out week by week in this paper, the changes we detected occur during every week of the camp. In other words, the pre-service teachers *were* effective in delivering programming content to the students in a way that promoted an increase in student interest in programming while incorporating their context-specific materials into the lessons.

Feedback from pre-service teachers was also collected in the form of reflective discussions, and indicated that they plan to continue exploring the potential of Scratch as a teaching tool. The pre-service teachers discussed ideas for incorporating even more of their topic-specific material into Scratch activities and how these could be applied in their future teaching positions. Some of the comments made by the pre-service teachers after the experience include:

- I've shown Scratch to other K-State students
- I think I'm competent enough and capable enough to use the basics of Scratch in the classroom
- I think I could apply it to any level, from elementary to high school
- Teaching basic notes and rhythms would be easy on Scratch for my younger students
- I could have high school students write their own compositions on Scratch
- I would use Scratch in the classroom, especially in my Art class
- Scratch is far more interesting than the paint program, and it can teach the concept of background, the illusion of object size and distance
- it challenges students creative and higher order thinking skills as well

The STEM Institute format has been received very favorably by faculty within the College of Education, and they have incorporated many of the ideas from this program into their traditional "Block 1" programs taught during spring and fall semesters. Likewise, the Computing and Information Sciences department is now looking at ways to utilize a similar format to expand outreach programs in K-12 classrooms to include pre-service teachers. This was a rewarding and promising step towards empowering new teachers with the ability to introduce programming into the K-12 curriculum and increasing the number of students exposed to computing concepts in K-12 classrooms.

7. LESSONS LEARNED

Looking back, there are a few items we will consider adjusting from this experience:

- The music composition lesson received mixed response. One student found and coded the theme song from Harry Potter while others were not as interested. We will likely limit the length of this lesson, or focus on creative mixing of sounds.
- We will consider offering an advanced course using a different environment for students who took the course this year or who are already familiar with Scratch. This could be challenging for pre-service teachers since few of them have programming experience.
- Final projects were a great part of the camp experience, but some students experienced "writer's block". We should have demonstrated some more advanced applications using Scratch such as simulations and interactive art (some of which are packaged with Scratch).
- It would help for the pre-service teachers to have extra time prior to the institute to work with Scratch. They also felt a tutorial or guide would have helped.
- We incorporated outside activities such as a tour of the campus data center into the camp, but students wanted more time for working on projects so we will consider altering the plans to accommodate this.

8. ACKNOWLEDGEMENTS

The authors thank the Manhattan-Ogden USD 383 school district for sponsoring the Summer Institute. Thanks also to Drs. Eleanor Sayre and Suzanne Dubnicka of K-State for their reviews and input and to Angie Miller of USD 383. This work was funded by United States Department of Defense Education Activity Grant Number HE1254-10-1-0032.

References

[1] A. Bandura, C. Barbaranelli, G. V. Caprara, and C. Pastorelli. Self-efficacy beliefs as shapers of children's aspirations and career trajectories. volume 72, 2001.

[2] S. Bell, T. Frey, A. Miller, and E. Vasserman. Empowering pre-service teachers to utilize programming in the classroom. In *Proceedings of the 2013 Midwest Section Conference of the American Society for Engineering Education*. ASEE, 2013.

[3] G. Braught, L. M. Eby, and T. Wahls. The effects of pair-programming on individual programming skill. In *Proceedings of the 39th SIGCSE technical symposium on Computer science education*, SIGCSE '08, pages 200–204, 2008.

[4] L. Carter. Why students with an apparent aptitude for computer science don't choose to major in computer science. *SIGCSE Bull.*, 38(1):27–31, Mar. 2006.

[5] J. Clark, M. P. Rogers, C. Spradling, and J. Pais. What, no canoes? Lessons Learned While Hosting a Scratch Summer Camp. *J. Comput. Sci. Coll.*, 28(5):204–210, May 2013.

[6] S. Cooper, W. Dann, and R. Pausch. Alice: a 3-d tool for introductory programming concepts. In *Journal of Computing Sciences in Colleges*, volume 15, pages 107–116. Consortium for Computing Sciences in Colleges, 2000.

[7] B. Ericson and T. McKlin. Effective and sustainable computing summer camps. In *Proceedings of the 43rd ACM technical symposium on Computer Science Education*, SIGCSE '12, pages 289–294. ACM, 2012.

[8] D. Franklin, P. Conrad, G. Aldana, and S. Hough. Animal tlatoque: attracting middle school students to computing through culturally-relevant themes. In *Proceedings of the 42nd ACM technical symposium on Computer science education*, SIGCSE '11, pages 453–458, 2011.

[9] C. Kelleher and R. Pausch. Lowering the barriers to programming: A taxonomy of programming environments and languages for novice programmers. *ACM Comput. Surv.*, 37(2):83–137, June 2005.

[10] C. M. Lewis. How programming environment shapes perception, learning and goals: logo vs. scratch. In *Proceedings of the 41st ACM technical symposium on Computer science education*, SIGCSE '10, pages 346–350, 2010.

[11] M. B. MacLaurin. The design of kodu: A tiny visual programming language for children on the xbox 360. *SIGPLAN Not.*, 46(1):241–246, Jan. 2011.

[12] M. Resnick, J. Maloney, A. Monroy-Hernández, N. Rusk, E. Eastmond, K. Brennan, A. Millner, E. Rosenbaum, J. Silver, B. Silverman, and Y. Kafai. Scratch: Programming for all. *Commun. ACM*, 52(11):60–67, Nov. 2009.

[13] A. Ruthmann, J. M. Heines, G. R. Greher, P. Laidler, and C. Saulters, II. Teaching computational thinking through musical live coding in scratch. In *Proceedings of the 41st ACM technical symposium on Computer science education*, SIGCSE '10, pages 351–355. ACM, 2010.

[14] P. A. G. Sivilotti and S. A. Laugel. Scratching the surface of advanced topics in software engineering: a workshop module for middle school students. In *Proceedings of the 39th SIGCSE technical symposium on Computer science education*, SIGCSE '08, pages 291–295, 2008.

[15] L. Williams, E. Wiebe, K. Yang, M. Ferzli, and C. Miller. In support of pair programming in the introductory computer science course. In *Computer Science Education*, volume 12, pages 197–212, 2002.

[16] U. Wolz, M. Stone, K. Pearson, S. M. Pulimood, and M. Switzer. Computational thinking and expository writing in the middle school. *Trans. Comput. Educ.*, 11(2):9:1–9:22, July 2011.

[17] U. Wolz, M. Stone, S. M. Pulimood, and K. Pearson. Computational thinking via interactive journalism in middle school. In *Proceedings of the 41st ACM technical symposium on Computer science education*, SIGCSE '10, pages 239–243, 2010.

Research Experience for Teachers: Data Analysis & Mining, Visualization, and Image Processing

Rahman Tashakkori
Appalachian State University
Computer Science Department
Boone, NC 28608
rt@cs.appstate.edu

R. Mitchell Parry
Appalachian State University
Computer Science Department
Boone, NC 28608
rmp@cs.appstate.edu

Adam Benoit
Lincolnton High School
Lincolnton, NC 28092
abenoit@lincoln.k12.nc.us

Rebecca A. Cooper
West Wilkes High School
Millers Creek, NC 28651
cooperr@wilkes.k12.nc.us

Jessica L. Jenkins
Watauga High School
Boone, NC 28607
jenkinsj@watauga.k12.nc.us

Nicholas T. Westveer
Watauga High School
Boone, NC 28607
westveern@watauga.k12.nc.us

ABSTRACT
Our department received funding from the National Science Foundation to establish a three-year Research Experience for Teachers site in Data Analysis & Mining, Visualization, and Image Processing. The objective is to provide twelve in-service high school teachers and community college faculty to work with faculty mentors and their graduate and undergraduate assistants to conduct research in these fields. During this six-week summer program, participants gain skills that they can utilize to assist their students to solve interdisciplinary problems. In addition, participants design learning modules to teach STEM concepts in their courses. The goal of our program is for teachers to bring knowledge of computer science and its application to their classroom exposing their students to computer science. This paper will share some of the activities of this experience.

Categories and Subject Descriptors
K.3.1 [**Computer Science Education**]: Computer Uses in Education

General Terms
Experimentation

Keywords
Image processing, visualization, data analysis, data mining, high school experience, RET, STEM

1. INTRODUCTION
The NSF supported Research Experiences for Teachers (RET) in Engineering and Computer Science program supports the active involvement of K-12 STEM teachers and community college faculty in engineering and computer science research in order to bring knowledge of engineering, computer science, and technological innovation into their classrooms. The goal is to help build long-term collaborative partnerships between K-12 STEM teachers, community college faculty, and the NSF university research community. This paper reports on the first stage of this process: involving the STEM teachers in computer science research and helping them translate their research experiences into classroom activities. [8]

The active participation of STEM teachers in research activities encourages their students to pursue engineering and computer science careers. This is achieved by building partnerships between the STEM teachers and researchers working together on engineering and computer science research projects. Through these partnerships, the RET in Engineering and Computer Science Program aims to:

- build long-term collaborative relationships between both in service and pre-service K-12 STEM teachers, community college faculty, and the engineering and computer science research community;
- support the active participation of these teachers and future teachers and community college faculty in research and education projects funded by NSF ENG and CISE;
- facilitate professional development of K-12 STEM teachers and community college faculty through strengthened partnerships between institutions of higher education and local school districts; and
- encourage engineering and computer science researchers to build mutually rewarding partnerships with STEM teachers and community college faculty.[8]

2. OUR RET PROGRAM
Our department received funding in the spring of 2013 to establish a three-year RET site in Data Analysis & Mining, Visualization, and Image Processing. Our objective is to provide 12 diverse in-service high school teachers and community college faculty opportunities to work with faculty mentors and their graduate and undergraduate assistants to conduct research in these fields. To facilitate professional development, participants were trained to solve interdisciplinary problems using software tools. In addition, they have hands-on experience in creating learning modules that they can use in their courses.

We continue to assist the participants as they implement research-based activities in their classrooms throughout the academic year. The grant provides funding for participants to create new course modules during the academic year and post them in our online

SIGCSE'14, March 5–8, 2014, Atlanta, Georgia, USA.

http://dx.doi.org/10.1145/2538862.2538967

repository. With the participants' assistance, we are planning the first of our one-day workshops in November 2013 for 15 new teachers and community college faculty. These workshops will occur yearly and provide hands-on experience with several of the sample modules where the participants will learn how to adapt the existing modules for their classrooms and create new ones.

During the summer program, the teachers develop inquiry-based learning materials for integrating their research experiences into their classroom activities during the academic year. The activities are designed to encourage and stimulate students to pursue engineering and computer science careers. The timeline of the six-week summer program is as follows: In the first week, participants receive training with tools and applications and focus on developing project plans. A series of tutorials and hands-on activities are provided to help them establish the necessary background knowledge and learn how to conduct scientific research. During the training all participants work together. Small groups take turns conducting common experiments in which they apply research skills and basic skills in data analysis, data mining, image processing and visualization. As part of the training, participants read related scientific papers and discuss them with faculty and peers. In the second week, participants develop projects in three overlapping areas of research. From the third to fifth week, they carry out their projects under the supervision of their mentors. They also attend weekly seminars by faculty and invited speakers and weekly group meetings to report their progress. In the sixth week, we hold a teaching workshop to prepare them for curriculum development. By the end of the program, participants prepare a written report, an oral presentation, and a plan for curriculum development. The summer program offers a Teachers' Continuing Education Credit through the Mathematics and Science Education Center at Appalachian State.

The main goals and outcomes of this project are the following:

- to provide a group of in-service high school teachers and community college faculty from northwest North Carolina with diverse STEM backgrounds an opportunity to participate in the RET program;
- to improve the participants' ability to solve interdisciplinary problems using data analysis & mining, image processing and visualization and to demonstrate how STEM problems can be solved using these powerful techniques;
- to enable the participants to incorporate the gained research experience and findings into their inquiry-based teaching activities, exposing their students to these techniques, hence motivating students to develop a career interest in these fields;
- to establish a supportive community of peers and faculty that will collaborate after the funding period, hence ensuring sustainability of the activities of the program;
- to disseminate the participants' findings and products with their peers' respective students through the web page of the program as well as local, regional, and national conferences and workshops, hence improving the understanding of computer technology education and their subject matters.

3. OVERVIEW OF THE PROGRAM

Bringing knowledge of engineering, computer science, and technological innovation into K-12 STEM classrooms poses an important but challenging problem [2,5,6,7]. This summer program provides research opportunities to teachers and community college faculty intending for those experiences to manifest in their classrooms during the school year. Among several factors that make transferring the participants' summer experience into their classrooms, we discuss three here:

1) the research experience provided through the RET program may not be directly related to the subjects the participants are teaching;
2) high school teachers in particular have very little flexibility in including the RET activities that are not part of the curriculum;
3) the teachers lack sufficient resources for the implementation of the innovative ideas presented through the RET program.

To address these issues, we expose the participants to some advanced topics during our summer program and assist them in creating related course activities and modules that can be used to teach a topic in their courses. These activities and modules, although stimulating and interesting, are simple and can be implemented in a classroom with limited resources. We present sample classroom modules later in this paper. These modules are designed to teach a concept or subject in a course. Thus, they do not require allocation of additional classroom time and provide the flexibility necessary to include the modules in the classroom. We work with participants to develop activities that are feasible to implement in high school or community college classrooms. More importantly these activities can be sustained with little or no dependence on the university.

The goal of the larger NSF RET initiative is to help build long-term collaborative partnerships between K-12 STEM teachers, community college faculty, and the NSF university research community by involving the participants in engineering and computer science research and helping them translate their research experiences and new knowledge into classroom activities. There are several factors that can help improve the establishment and sustainability of such long-term collaborations:

1) a supportive community of peers;
2) proximity of high schools and community colleges to the sponsoring universities;
3) existing experience with such collaborations;
4) creating a knowledge-based rather than resource-based collaboration; and
5) most importantly, understanding of the limitations on both sides.

To address these issues we hold meetings during the summer program so that the participants and faculty mentors can understand the limitations. The web page of the program and the activities that we hold during the summer create a community of participants, i.e. the RET Community. This community has a common interest in sharing its findings via our web page and the university RET Forum. Also, we schedule occasional visits between faculty mentors and participants during the school year to continue to support and promote the program. Most importantly, the participants continue to contribute by creating and refining modules that can be implemented using the existing resources at the high schools or community colleges.

Data analysis & mining, visualization and image processing provides a good fit for multiple educational disciplines because there is strong evidence that visualization is of interest to all students and can help them learn difficult math and science concepts [3]. Visualization and image processing while being studied in computer science have played a major role in solving interdisciplinary problems in all sciences, engineering, and medicine. These techniques are of interest to students because they can be applied in various disciplines to solve problems where students can visualize the results of their work [9].

4. COURSE MODULES

During our summer RET program participants developed a total of more than 30 course modules [1]. These modules were created with the intention for use in the courses they were teaching. The modules were prepared such that other teachers could use them to enhance the instruction of their similar math and science courses. All modules were prepared to expose students to computer science. Modules are designed for 50-90 minute class periods. The course modules usually have three parts: 1) Teacher's Manual, 2) Lab Activity Manual, 3) Teacher's One-page Power Point slide, and 4) Associated files.

The Teacher's Manual contains information such as: 1) The Subject Area, 2) Computer Science Tools used in the module, 3) Title of the activity, 4) Grade level that can benefit from the experiment, 5) Time required to complete, 6) Recommended group size, 7) Summary, 8) Computer science connection, 9) Keywords, 10) Pre-requisite knowledge, 11) Learning objectives, and 12) Materials list.

The Lab Activity Manual contains information such as: 1) Introduction and Motivation, 2) Materials list, 3) Procedure (Background, Preparation, Lab activity), 4) Data analysis procedure, 5) Graphical analysis, 6) Assessment (Pre-assessment, Results/Conclusions), and 7) References.

The one-page Power Point provides a presentation for teachers to use at the beginning of their class to talk about the module. The associated files are usually contained within zip file with necessary worksheets, data files, and other support material. The following sections describe two teaching modules in more detail.

4.1 Using Kinect to Teach Ratios

In this module students use a Microsoft Kinect sensor to obtain the (*x*, *y*, *z*) coordinates of 20 joint positions (Figure 1) on the skeleton of their own bodies. These coordinates are used to measure the distance between various joints which may represent the length of some bones using the distance formula (1).

$$l = \sqrt{(x_2 - x_1)^2 + (y_2 - y_1)^2 + (z_2 - z_1)^2} \quad (1)$$

where (*x*, *y*, *z*) represent the coordinates of any two joint points on the targeted bone.

An interesting problem students can investigate is finding or confirming some golden ratios for the human body. For example it has long been assumed that the ratio of the distance between the extended human hands to that of their height is one. Students can investigate this to find out whether or not this ratio holds. In addition to the arm span versus height ratio, the project allows students to measure various distances or lengths and find different ratios.

An additional activity on this module was to take snapshots of the Kinect images and analyze them in image processing software. The free software program ImageJ and its Measurement Tool was used to measure the lengths that were investigated using the coordinates that were obtained by the Kinect software. Using an object of known length, a meter stick, the teachers were able to determine the accuracy of the data provided by the Kinect sensors.

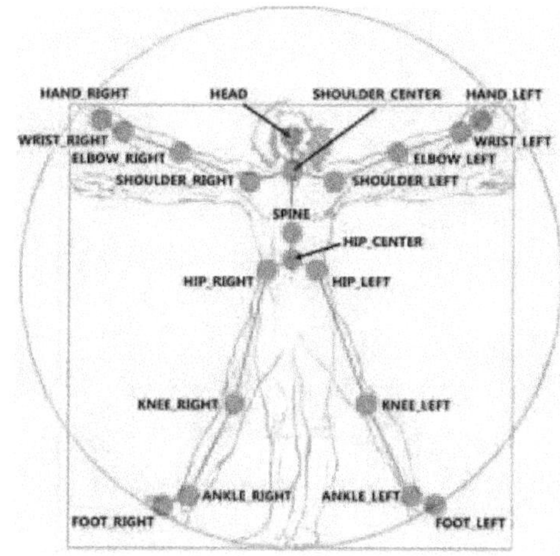

Figure 1: The Kinect Twenty Joint Nodes [10]

4.2 Measuring the areas of unknown shapes

In this experiment, students use a Monte Carlo type approach to measure the area of unknown shapes. Students place these shapes on top of a square or a rectangle of known size that is tightly fitting the shape. Then they count some lentils and drop these lentils as randomly as possible on the combined area (Figure 2).

Figure 2: Teachers conducting the Monte Carlo simulation with lentils

Because the total number of lentils and the area of the square or rectangle underneath the shape are known, the fraction of the lentils that fall on the unknown shape can be a good approximation of the ratio between the area of the unknown shape to the known shape (Figure 3).

$$\frac{\text{Number of dots on unknown shape}}{\text{Number of dots on known shape}} \approx \frac{A_{unknown}}{A_{known}} \quad (2)$$

In the example from Figure 3 this would result in (3).

$$\frac{16}{39} \approx \frac{A_{unknown}}{w \times h} \Longrightarrow A_{unknown} \approx (\frac{16}{39}) \times w \times h \quad (3)$$

Students first experiment with known shapes like a triangle, square, or trapezoid for which they can calculate areas by using the appropriate formulas for these shapes. This provides them an opportunity to improve the accuracy of the approach by 1) increasing the number of lentils, and 2) dropping the lentils on the shapes more uniformly. Students may try various methods to improve the experiment and its accuracy.

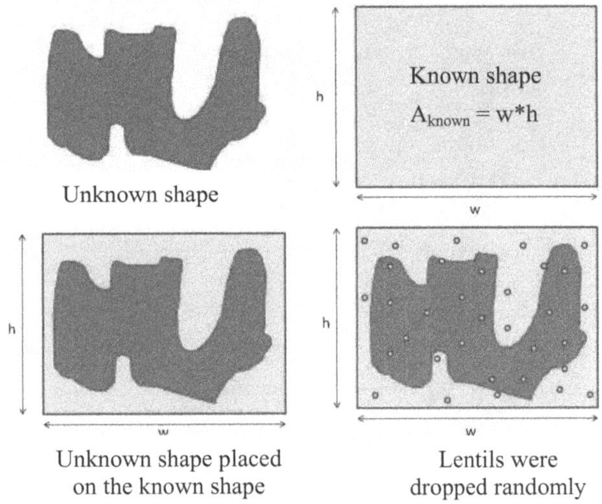

Figure 3: Monte Carlo like process for measuring the area of an unknown shape

Because counting a large number of lentils becomes very tedious, students use a scale to weigh the lentils before dropping them on the shapes. Using this technique, instead of counting, they weigh the lentils that fell on the unknown shape and divide by the total weight of the lentils. Substituting this ratio into (3) also approximates the area of the unknown shape.

Students can take this even further through an approach using Microsoft Excel. To simulate the Monte Carlo type process that was introduced using lentils they use Excel's random number generator, *Rand( )*, to generate random x and y points proportional to the dimensions of the known shape. Then they create a scatter plot of these points and would insert the picture of the two shapes as the background of the plot as shown in Figure 4. Finally, they count the number of dots inside the unknown shape and divide that by the total number of points generated to determine the ratio as they did with lentils. This ratio is used in (3) to estimate the area of unknown shape.

Another approach for solving this problem involves using the ImageJ measurement tool to count the number of pixels within the unknown shape and those contained within the known shape and finding their ratios to estimate the area.

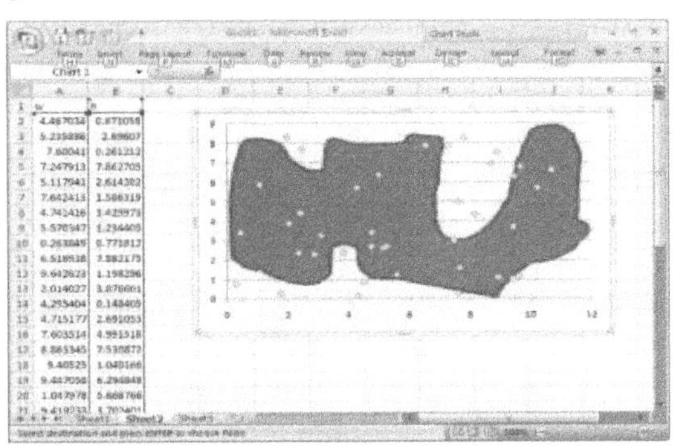

Figure 4: Monte Carlo like process for measuring area of an unknown shape in Excel

5. RESEARCH PROJECTS

In this section, two of the research projects that the RET teachers worked on during the summer of 2013 will be presented. Participating teachers worked in teams of two to conduct their research. They selected their projects from ten options provided by the program directors, or proposed new projects based on interest.

5.1 Plotting 3D Coordinates Using Microsoft Kinect

This project involved two high school teachers from different schools working together to map the Cartesian coordinates in the Kinect's field of view. The project attempted to determine the consistency between the (x, y, z) coordinates as measured by the Kinect sensor and the actual coordinates obtained using a tape measure.

To conduct this research, a Kinect skeleton tracking application was developed based on sample code (Skeleton Basics-WPF) provided on Microsoft's website with the help of graduate assistants in our program. This application allows users to capture and save the (x, y, z) coordinates of the twenty skeleton nodes mapped to joints on the human skeleton.

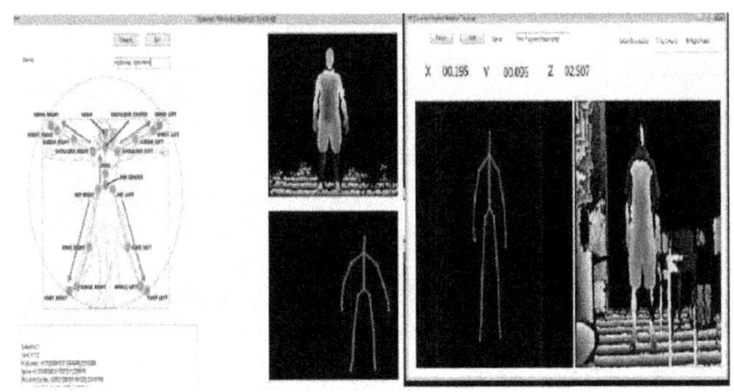

Figure 5 - Left: Original Version. Right: Updated Version

In order to accurately make measurements with the Kinect, the team first determined an effective range in x, y, and z directions. For the Kinect sensor to capture the skeleton, the body must be within view. The Kinect software was used to obtain coordinates on the periphery of the screen, using the left and right hand for the right and left edge of the screen, respectively, at various depths (z-coordinate). The measurement for each hand needed to be within the screen image far enough to correctly recognize it as a hand. These data were used to graph the extent in the x-direction at various depths (gray triangles in Figure 6). These data suggested a much narrower field of view than was plainly visible with the Kinect video. Part of the problem was that the camera is not located at the center of the Kinect, and the skeleton was not centered (in the x-direction) in the original version of the program. A newer version of the Skeleton Basics-WPF was created and the data was collected for the right hand range. With these data the angles were found to be nearly the same on both the right and left side of the field. The angle on the right was 30° and that on the left was 29°, as shown by the orange squares and blue diamonds in Figure 6.

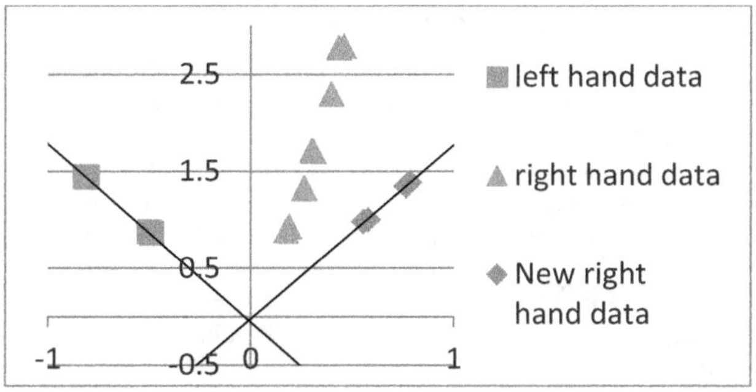

Figure 6 – The X coordinate range at various Z values

Finding the field of view in the *y*-direction presented additional challenges. Interference with the floor caused negative *y*-values, as the team attempted to find the range in *y* at various distances. To improve the estimated field of view in the *y*-direction, image processing was used to find the infrared volumetric field emitted by the Kinect. An infrared camera was placed on the side of the experiment's setup to capture images that were then analyzed to find the viewing angle to be 25° above and below horizontal. This approach was also used to confirm the field of view in the *x*-direction with an angle measure of 30° in both directions.

Once the accuracy of the measurements by the Kinect sensor was improved, the next step was to conduct some volumetric measurements to see how accurate the Kinect sensor would actually measure a known volume. Several boxes were then placed at different distances and experiments were conducted to determine the coordinates of their corners which are used to find the length, width, and height for calculating the volume.

Data collected during this experiment was generated from the eight corner point coordinates of a rectangular prism at various distances, *z*, from the Kinect and at various angles to the right, left, up and down from the center point of the Kinect. Placing the rectangular prism at a distance of $z = 2.0$m centered at $x = 0$ and $y = 0$, the length, width and height were found in 60 repeated trials. Each of these distances was used to calculate the volume of the box, giving 60 values for the volume. The mean for this data was 4766cm^3 with a standard deviation of 888. Of the 60 volume calculations only seven fell outside of three standard deviations.

5.2 A Statistical Analysis of Basketball Comebacks

This project involved two high school teachers from different schools analyzing the chance of a basketball team which is trailing in a game to come back and win in the end. In particular, they focused on the chance of a comeback in National Basketball Association (NBA) games. Data mining and visualization led to an attempt at modeling the empirical data as a function of point differential and time remaining that could potentially be useful in predicting future outcomes. The project was an excellent example of data analysis and data mining in which the team had to collect data, pre-process and clean the data, build a model, and evaluate its performance.

This research began with a focus on basketball, but not necessarily comeback percentage. The original abstract was to analyze free throw techniques and present findings that would enable athletes to adjust a specific part of their free throw routine to produce better results. This had been researched and reported in numerous articles with inconclusive results. Every player shoots differently; every player has a different routine; and many techniques can produce desirable results.

The available play-by-play record [4] for each game provides a wealth of data for analyzing basketball performance. A Perl script was written to extract each of the play-by-play files [4], as well as the time remaining on the clock and current score for each second of each game. MATLAB was used to compile the data and produce visualizations for analysis.

Based on the empirical data, the percentage of teams that came back from a ten point deficit at the beginning of the second, third, and fourth quarter is 31%, 16%, and 12%, respectively. Visualizing the empirical data in Figure 7, there are noticeably unusual features. At first, the dark red regions in Figure 7 (near a 20 point deficit with 2500 seconds remaining) and the extreme peaks in Figure 8 seemed counterintuitive. A large early deficit should typically result in a loss. However, further analysis revealed that the sample size was so small for these early deficits that even one successful comeback created an outlier. These data were removed from further analysis. Figure 7 also illustrates an extensive dark blue region, which can be misleading. The top left area of the chart represents time and point differentials where there was no empirical data, but the dark blue region in the bottom right area of the chart represents a large sample of unsuccessful comeback attempts.

Figure 7. Empirical Data in 2-Dimensions [4]

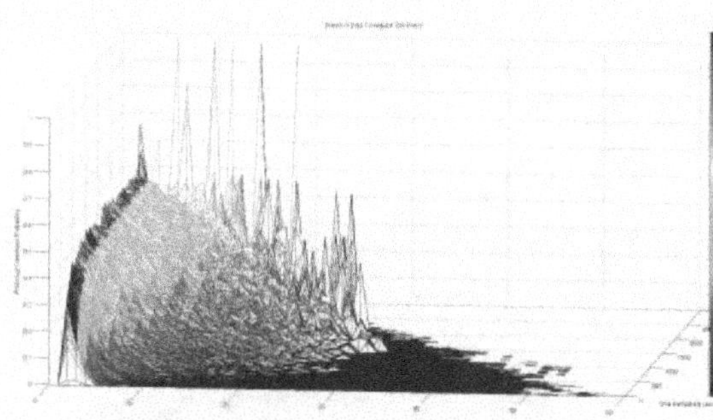

Figure 8. Empirical Data in 3-Dimensions [4]

Looking at the three-dimensional visualization, the teachers thought about a mathematical equation that could model basketball comebacks as a function of time remaining and point differential. They used MATLAB to optimize the parameters for this model, and evaluated it based on how well it matched the empirical data in terms of the root mean square error. Future research teams may propose new models to perform better.

6. SUMMARY AND CONCLUSIONS

The six week summer RET program was able to bring together eleven high-school teachers and one community college faculty member. They conducted research and created course modules that utilized computer science techniques and applications to teach STEM concepts. The program successfully created a strong learning community where faculty mentors and participants shared their experiences. Participants created 33 course modules that were tested and then posted in an online repository [1]. Also, participants conducted six research projects [1], where they applied data analysis, mining, visualization and image processing. The program successfully built a productive community that can expose students in high schools and community colleges within the state to computer science.

The survey conducted by our program evaluator at the end of the program indicates several key points of the success for our RET program. Participants have indicated that they had a challenging but enjoyable experience. Participants reported that their perspective of computer science has widened. The program has helped them identify students who are well-suited to pursue computer science, and the program clarified the connection between computer science and STEM disciplines.

All twelve participants indicated that the program introduced them to new computer science concepts. The high number of course modules indicates a strong connection between this program and the classroom. The quality of the research projects demonstrates the participants' professional development.

By accepting participants in pairs from the same school we initiated collaboration that could continue into the school year. In addition, participants worked in pairs and rotated during the program to foster stronger community and future collaboration. At this early stage we have a strong indication that both RET and non-RET teachers are using the course modules in their classrooms. We just started an online usage form to capture data to potentially report at the conference. We also plan to report on our November workshop for 15 new high school teachers.

7. ACKNOWLEDGMENTS

This RET program is funded by the National Science Foundation through RET 1301089 grant. Our special thanks go to all the participants of the RET Program as well as the graduate and undergraduate assistants Luke Rice, Bahareh Akhtar, Ahmad Ghadiri, Nathan Hernandez, Clint Guin, and Dakota Murray of the Department of Computer Science at Appalachian State University.

8. REFERENCES

[1] Appalachian Research Experience for Teachers, http://www.cs.appstate.edu/ret/

[2] CS4HS, Explorations in Computer Science for High School Educators, A Google Funding Opportunity, www.cs4hs.com.

[3] Camargo Neto, J., Meyer, G.E., & Jones, D.D. (2006). Individual leaf extractions from young canopy images using gustafson-kessel clustering and a genetic algorithm. *Computers and Electronics in Agriculture, 51*, 66-85.

[4] ESPN NBA. (2013, July, 17). [Online]. Available: http://espn.go.com/nba/

[5] Gal-Ezer, J. Shahak, D., Zur, E., Computer Science issues in High School, Proceedings of ITiCSE 09, Paris, France, July 6-9, 2009.

[6] Hambrush, S., Hoffmann, C., Korb, J., Haugan, M., Hosking, A., A Multidisciplinary Approach Toward Computational Thinking for Science majors, Proceedings of SIGCSE 09, Chattanooga, Tennessee, USA, March 3-7, 2009.

[7] Hazzan, O., Gal-Ezer, J., Ragonis, N., Computer Science Teacher Preparation at Your University, ACM Inroads, Vol 1, 1, P 35-39, 2010.

[8] Research Experience for Teachers (RET) in Engineering and Computer Science, NSF 11-509, http://www.nsf.gov/pubs/2011/nsf11509/nsf11509.htm

[9] Tashakkori, R., Encouraging Undergraduate Research: A Digital Image Processing Approach, Journal of Computing Sciences in Colleges (JCSC), Vol. 20, 3, P. 173-180, 2005

[10] Tracking Users with Kinect Skeleton Tracking, Microsoft Inc. http://msdn.microsoft.com/en-us/library/jj131025.aspx

The Design of Sweden's First 5-year Computer Science and Software Engineering Program

Fredrik Heintz
Dept. of Computer and Information Science
Linköping University
fredrik.heintz@liu.se

Inger Erlander Klein
Dept. of Electrical Engineering
Linköping University
inger.klein@liu.se

ABSTRACT

In 2013 Linköping University started the first 5-year engineering program in Computer Science and Software Engineering in Sweden. The goals of the program are to provide a holistic perspective on modern large scale software development, to provide a deep and broad understanding of computer science and computational thinking, and encourage innovation and entrepreneurship. The student response has been very good with more than 600 applicants to the 30 slots, of which more than 130 had this program as their first choice among all programs in Sweden. In this paper we present the goals, the design principles, and the resulting program. The ACM/IEEE CS Curricula has been used to make sure that the program provides a solid foundation in Computer Science. Three pedagogical ideas that we have used are (1) project courses to integrate theory and practice as well as provide experience with the most common form of working in industry; (2) courses that cover multiple programming paradigms and languages as well as multiple software development methodologies so that the students are prepared to take on the continual changes we know will come; and (3) a special course in engineering professionalism with groups of students from the first three years together reflecting on topics related to being a professional engineer. The paper concludes with a discussion about some important aspects such as computational thinking and the relation to the ACM/IEEE CS Curricula.

Categories and Subject Descriptors

K.3.2 [**Computers and Education**]: Computer and Information Science Education

1. INTRODUCTION

We live in a changing world. Our society becomes more and more dependent on computers and software. The pace of change is steadily increasing, with technology as one important driving factor. To manage the pace and the complexity when developing sophisticated large-scale software intensive systems we need software engineers with the appropriate knowledge, skills and attitudes. To meet this challenge Linköping University has developed Sweden's first 5-year Master of Science in Engineering program in Computer Science and Software Engineering (in Swedish Civilingenjör Mjukvaruteknik).

In this paper we describe the vision, goals, and design of the program. Effort has been put in to formulate goals and principles that can be used by other similar programs as well, even though the circumstances and realization may significantly differ. This should also make the presentation more interesting to a larger audience. We then discuss some important aspects such as computational thinking and the relation to the ACM/IEEE CS Curricula, which is also used to compare related programs in Sweden.

One reason for writing this paper is to invite discussion and constructive criticism around the question on how to design a modern computer science and software engineering program for the changing world we live in. We therefore encourage you to contact us if you have questions or comments.

SIGCSE'14, March 5–8, 2014, Atlanta, GA, USA.

http://dx.doi.org/10.1145/2538862.2538925.

2. ENGINEERING EDUCATION IN SWEDEN

2.1 5-year Master of Science in Engineering programs

The Swedish Master of Science in Engineering (Civilingenjör) programs are professional degrees consisting of 5 years of studies. Normally the students are awarded both a Civilingenjör degree, a Bachelor of Science in Engineering degree, and a Master of Science in Engineering degree. There are a number of national requirements these programs must fulfil including engineering skills such as the ability to conceive, design, implement and operate systems, but also other aspects for example communication skills, team work, and aspects regarding social sciences such as the role technology has in society considering both ethical and cultural aspects. The entrance requirement is a high school degree with math level E, physics level B, and chemistry level A. In Austria, Finland, and Greece, as well as previously in Germany, the corresponding degree is called Diploma Engineer. All engineering programs share a common core of problem solving, mathematics and natural sciences.

2.2 Computer Related Programs at Linköping University

Linköping Institute of Technology, which is part of Linköping University, currently has five programs related to computing besides the new program. There are two 5-year Master of Science in Engineering programs, Computer Science and Engineering (Civilingenjör Datateknik) and Information Technology (Civilingenjör Informationsteknologi), one 3-year Bachelor of Science in Engineering program in Computer Engineering (Högskoleingenjör Datateknik), one 3-year Bachelor of Science program called Innovative Programming (Innovativ programmering), and one 2-year Master of

Science program in Computer Science. Here we focus on the 5-year engineering programs. The 5-year engineering program in Computer Science and Engineering covers hardware, software and the interplay, while Information Technology focuses on infrastructure needed to transmitt, structure and present information.

2.3 Related Programs in Sweden

The other institutes of technology in Sweden such as The Royal Institute of Technology (KTH) and Chalmers also have related 5-year Master of Science in Engineering programs. Most of them are closer to computer engineering than to computer science. The programs that are the closest are the 5-year Master of Science in Engineering programs in Computer Science and Engineering at KTH and in Information Technology at Chalmers. Even though the programs have similarities there are important differences. For example, the IT program at Chalmers focuses more on Software Engineering than on Computer Science and mainly learn a single programming language (Java) rather than give a broad foundation of many different languages.

In 2011 a study was conducted that compared 10 of the Swedish 5-year Master of Science in Engineering programs in Computer Science relative to the ACM CS Curricula 2008 [4]. One conclusion from the study is that there is a very wide variate of programs, ranging from hardware oriented to software oriented, from theoretical to more applied, and from general engineering programs to more focused computer science programs. The new Computer Science and Software Engineering program is software oriented, both theoretical and applied, and more focused on computer science than on general engineering even though it has significant computer and electrical engineering content. In Section 5 the new program is compared to these 10 programs.

3. VISION AND GOALS

The vision for the program is to educate the best software engineers in the world. The program should provide the best possible qualification for an exciting, successful and meaningful career in the very broad field of computer science and software engineering. Graduates from the program will take on leading roles in the software industry, be driving forces in the further development of computer science and software engineering, and start new companies based on innovative ideas and an entrepreneurial spirit.

The program should provide the necessary knowledge, skills and attitudes to be able to develop every type of software intensive system, be able to program in every programming language, be able to use every programming methodology, and more importantly be able to choose the appropriate language and methodology for a particular situation. The program should prepare the students for a professional career as software engineers where soft skills such as communication, personal leadership and working together with others in cross-functional teams are essential.

The concrete goals for the program are to:

1. provide a solid foundation in computer science and mathematics;
2. provide an understanding of and experience with computational thinking;
3. provide a holistic understanding of modern software development;
4. provide an understanding of and experience with several different programming languages and paradigms as well as industrial software development methodologies;
5. provide an understanding of and experience with important application areas such as modern large scale distributed and embedded systems, mobile and social applications, data driven decision-making, and AI and robotics;
6. leverage project courses with relevant subject content that integrates and applies theory;
7. encourage entrepreneurship and innovation; and
8. emphasize global challenges, sustainable development and a global world.

By achieving these goals the program will live up to its vision.

4. DESIGN

From the first idea of starting a new program to the first students arrived it has only been 2 years. The real design process started in January 2011 and it has taken approximately 18 months to reach a stable version of the first three years of the program. It has involved a group of teachers from Computer Science, Electrical Engineering and Mathematics as well as student representatives. There were some requirements on the process such as minimizing the number of completely new courses. The main challenges were to select what should be included in the mandatory first three years while making room for project courses; to find a good balance between computer science, computer engineering, electrical engineering, software engineering and mathematics especially considering that this is Master of Science in Engineering program; and to find the right order of the courses so that the prerequisites are satisfied and the courses result in a clear progression through the program. We are very happy with the end result, even though we had to make some compromises.

Many engineering programs take a bottom-up approach to their subject. They start with mathematics and foundational courses the first three years and then study applications and specializations the last two years. A major problem with this approach is that students do not see the full picture until at the very end of their studies. There is clear indications that a significant share of the students that drop out do it because they lack this overview. Another fact is that students develop and mature a lot during their studies. This means that most of them are not able to fully understand and grasp the material the first time. The new program should therefore provide three iterations through the broad and deep areas of Computer Science and Software Engineering. By having three iterations, each basically covering the whole discipline, at different levels of detail, we believe that the students understanding will greatly increase while we also should reduce the number of students dropping out due to a lack of overview.

The first semester is the first iteration which gives a broad overview of the whole field and the whole education. The second iteration is the following 5 semesters which gives a solid foundation in computer science, software engineering and the relevant parts of electrical engineering. It is concluded with a bachelor project where the students clearly demonstrate their knowledge, skills and attitudes developed during the first two iterations. The third iteration is the Master profile the last two years where the students deepen their knowledge in important areas of computer science and software engineering based on interest and aptitude. Linköping University is a large university which means that we can provide a very large selection of advanced courses taught by active researchers based on current research. The third iteration and the whole education program is concluded with a full semester Master's Thesis where the student is required to demonstrate that he or she satisfies all the requirements for a Master of Science in Computer Science and Software Engineering degree.

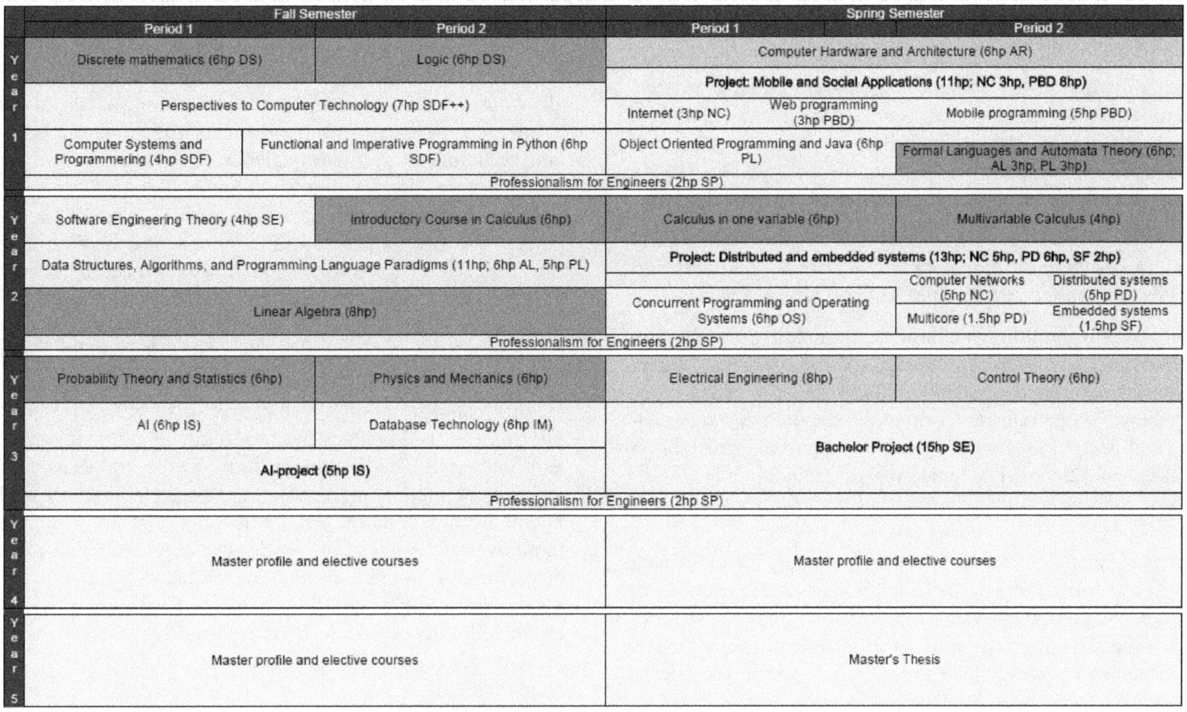

Figure 1: An overview of the program. Light gray boxes are computer science courses and software engineering courses, medium gray boxes are engineering courses, and dark gray boxes are math courses.

Figure 1 gives an overview of the program. Light gray boxes are computer science courses and software engineering courses, medium gray boxes are engineering courses, and dark gray boxes are math courses. Each year is divided into two semesters, one fall semester and one spring semester. Each semester is divided into two periods. Each semester consists of 30 ECTS credits called "hp". Since each semester is 20 weeks, 1.5hp roughly corresponds to one week of work. Courses are normally 6hp and given within a single period. The acronyms in parentheses refer to knowledge areas in the ACM/IEEE Computer Science Curricula 2013 [5]. The subjects mentioned for the two spring project courses describe their content in some more detail. The sum of the credits for the parts is equal to the total amount of credits for the course.

4.1 Design Principles

The design is based on the following general principles:

1. There should be a clear progression through the program, both with regard to the main subjects Computer Science and Software Engineering and with regard to how the work is being done and what is required from the students. The students should be continuously challenged to improve and develop.
2. The first three years should consist of mandatory courses to provide a common foundation while the last two years should provide the students with the largest possible freedom to develop their own interests and specializations.
3. There should normally be three courses in parallel, one of these should be a math or theory course and another should be a programming course. This should stimulate both those who are mainly programming oriented and those that are more math oriented. It also improves the work load balance.
4. Each semester the first two years should focus on a single programming language to provide focus and avoid confusion. The students should learn multiple different programming languages and paradigms with a clear emphasis on the concepts and principles which will allow them to quickly understand and learn any programming language. The set of languages should include at least Python, C/C++ and Java. The set of paradigms should include at least functional, imperative and object oriented programming.
5. Each semester should have a project course characterized by a larger and relatively open-ended assignment that the students should do, either individually or in groups. Projects are very important to integrate and apply theoretical concepts and techniques while developing software systems. A project course may also cover new theory.
6. The project courses should use different software development methodologies to provide experience and understanding of a wide variety of industrial methodologies. At the same time it is very important that the choice of methodology is relevant for the project, otherwise the students will not realize the benefits but rather feel that it is something artificially added. As with programming languages, it is essential to teach the concepts and principles behind the methodologies and to make the students reflect over how the choice of methodology affects the outcome of a project.
7. Mathematics should be an essential and integrated part of the program. It is important to emphasize the strong connections between math and computer science since this provides a foundation for computational thinking. The first year should focus on discrete math and logic which are directly relevant for computer science. The second year should include the continuous math needed mainly for the electrical engineering courses. The third year should include applied math courses, which directly uses the continuous math, where probability

theory and statistics are essential for both computer science and electrical engineering.

8. During the first three years the students should have projects related to the application areas stated in the goals, i.e. mobile and social applications, modern large scale distributed and embedded systems, and AI and data driven decision-making to provide a broad understanding of these important domains.
9. Topics such as testing, usability and security are essential to modern software development and should be a natural part of most software courses, especially the project courses.
10. The program should give a basic understanding of computer architecture, electrical engineering and control theory, which provides the basic understanding of the very interesting interplay between the outside world and computers through sensors and actuators. This is especially important since this is a Master of Science in Engineering program.

4.2 Year 1

The first semester consists of two math courses, discrete math and logic, three computer science courses, perspectives on computer technology, computer systems and programming, and functional and imperative programming in Python, and the engineering professionalism course. The perspectives course provides a broad overview of computer science and related areas. The two programming courses introduces the Unix computer systems used and programming in Python. The functional and imperative programming paradigms are both covered with a special emphasis on solving problems both iteratively and recursively. Recursion, proof by induction and their relations are central concepts. The first programming course also requires the students to try out programming in shell script, Prolog, Haskell and SQL. The purpose is to give a feeling for different languages and different programming styles early on. In the second period, the students do their first project in the perspectives course. The purpose of the project is to do something exciting and to have something to show at the end of the first semester. The projects are quite large, groups of three students each supposed to spend 130 hours on the project, and open-ended. There are projects on programming Lego Mindstorm robots, Nao humanoid robots, web-based map applications using the Google Maps API, programming automated XPilot players, and writing programs to play capture the flag strategy game. The main goal of this project is to make the students realize that they are capable of developing a significant piece of software while at the same time realizing that they have much more to learn. An important side benefit is that the students have something concrete to show at the end of the first semester. Being able to describe to friends and family what they are doing is important both for the students and for recruiting new students to the program.

Last, but not least, the course on Professionalism for Engineers which covers all the first three years. This is an "integrating" course with groups of students from all the first three years. The inspiration to the course comes from a similar course at KTH and is a course with many functions [3]. There are two main purposes of the course. First, to integrate both students from the first three years and the program as a whole. Second, to teach the students about engineering professionalism which is a very important subject that includes soft skills, ethics, personal leadership, and team work. A novel and very exciting improvement to the course, compared to the courses at KTH, is that it uses the dialog seminar method for reflexion and learning from experience [2]. The method is developed by researchers at KTH and Combitech AB, a consultant company with connections to SAAB. Combitech is also involved in developing the course and training the teachers in the methodology. We believe that the reception by the students of the course will be greatly improved by developing the course together with industry that really knows what is essential for being a professional engineer.

After the first semester the students should have a good general understanding of computer science, programming and the formal foundations of discrete math and logic.

The second semester consists of a theory course, a computer engineering course, a programming course and the first large project course. The course on formal languages and automata theory gives an introduction to theoretical computer science and continues the math track. The course on computer hardware and architecture gives an introduction to computer engineering including the basics of digital circuits, the main components of a computer and some assembler programming. The course on Object Oriented Programming and Java adds a new programming paradigm to the imperative and functional paradigms introduced in the first semester. Finally, and maybe most importantly, the project course on Mobile and Social Applications introduces an important application area and more systematic ways of developing software. The focus in this project course is the individual developer designing usable mobile applications with a social component. Special emphasis is placed on considering privacy related issues. The software engineering principles introduced includes design prototyping, unit testing, and code reviews.

4.3 Year 2

The third semester consists of a course on theory of software engineering, a large course on data structures, algorithms and programming paradigms using C++, a course in linear algebra and an introductory course in calculus. This semester concludes the foundational programming courses. The programming paradigm part is especially important for this, as it puts all the programming concepts and languages learned into perspective. It should also show the students that the same concept or principle can be realized in many different ways and that designing a programming language basically means making a set of deliberate choices. After this the students should be competent programmers.

The choice of having the software engineering theory course after the first project course is a deliberate decision. The reason is that we want the students to have experience with software engineering before learning the theory. This way, the students are mentally prepared for the content and have maybe already encountered several of the issues that software engineering handles.

The fourth semester covers single and multi-variable calculus and computer systems. So far, the focus has been on individual computers or devices. This semester the concept of a computer system is studied in great detail and from many different perspectives. The foundation is a computer which can be connected in a network of computers. The concept of an operating system controlling the basic functions of a computer and the concept of a computer network are essential. Starting from this core, extensions to multi-core computers, parallel computers and embedded computers are naturally made. Another important step is to view a set of networked computers as a single distributed system and design and implement programs for these. From a software engineering perspective concepts such as fault tolerance, scalability, security and testing of distributed systems are central.

4.4 Year 3

The third year covers AI and databases which are two very important areas of computer science, probability theory and statistics which are essential for empirical aspects of engineering, and physics and mechanics which provide a basic understanding of the physical world. This knowledge is extended and put to very good use in the electrical engineering and control theory courses where the students learn the fundamentals of electric circuits, signals and systems including measuring, modeling and controlling them. The fifth semester project course is focused on AI and data-driven decision making. The goal is to develop a system with an AI component. The project applies many of the math courses since machine learning and data mining is based on linear algebra and statistics.

The Bachelor Project corresponds to half the work done in the sixth semester. This is a large programming project where students work in teams of 6–8 students for an external customer. The goal of the project is to develop a program or a system for the external customer in the most appropriate way that satisfies the customer's requirements and expectations. This means that the students have to decide which software development methodology is appropriate and then follow it. They also have to deal with issues such as customers changing their minds and coworkers leaving (which is simulated by swapping people between groups). Each student should write a Bachelor thesis based on his or her work.

When all the courses the first three years, including the Bachelor project, are finished the student is awarded a Bachelor of Science in Computer Science and Software Engineering degree. This opens up possibilities to change universities and study somewhere else for the Master's degree. From our experience very few students choose this option, most complete the full five years at the same university.

4.5 Year 4-5

The last two years of the program corresponds to a Master's Program and consists almost exclusively of elective courses. To get a Master's degree a student needs to take 90hp (three semesters worth of) courses on the advanced level including the 30hp Master's Thesis. To guide students there are a number of master profiles consisting of selected courses from which a student has to take at least 36hp of which at least 30hp on the advanced level.

Two new master profiles will be developed for this program: Software Engineering and AI and Data-Driven Decision-Making. There are also existing master profiles from the Computer Science and Computer Engineering program such as Programming and Algorithms (the main computer science profile), Game Programming, Safe and Secure Systems and International Software Engineering (which gives a double degree with Harbin Institute of Technology).

The master profile in Software Engineering deepens and broadens the knowledge and skills of the students in this area. At least two important new courses will be developed. The first, a large scale software engineering course based on an open-source project is essential to give students experience of working on really large software projects together with many other people. Important skills practiced are to take an existing software system and learn to understand it. To be able to take existing legacy code and make solid extensions and improvements is a skill in great demand. Our industry representatives have been very clear that this is an important skill and something that many software engineers are not very good at, since they have mostly developed small programs from scratch. The second course is on software entrepreneurship. The software industry is very exciting and interesting from a commercial perspective. This is probably the industry where the step from an idea to a commercial product is the smallest. A brand new company can easily get global distribution of their products either through the Internet or an app store. The software industry is an extremely expansive and innovative industry where new inventions are made daily and where the right idea at the right time can result in a billion dollar company within a year (such as Instagram).

The master profile in AI and Data-Driven Decision-Making focuses on the very exciting area of artificial intelligence, machine learning, and data-driven decision making which is becoming more important for all types of software. This profile is based on the very strong research in the related areas at Linköping University.

5. DISCUSSION

5.1 Computational Thinking

The general skill of computational thinking is central to the program. This includes recursive decomposition of problems into smaller and more manageable parts; finding and generalizing patterns by for example systematically solving small cases; and using simulation to either approximate solutions or generate and test hypotheses. These problem solving strategies use concepts from both computer science and mathematics and often rely on programming.

An important challenge is to tie the programming and the mathematics courses together. In the programming courses the teachers try to show the connections explicitly, for example by pointing out the relations between inductive proofs and recursive computations and to use functions studied in the math courses as programming examples (the most classical example being the factorial). This shows the benefits of mathematics for programming. Our current challenge is to show the benefits of programming in mathematics. To this end, we are currently exploring how computational thinking can be used in the discrete math course, which is the first math course for these students. As part of this we have conducted a survey to get data about the attitude towards mathematics and programming and the view on the interplay between mathematics and programming. Preliminary data shows that the students have a very positive attitude towards mathematics and an extremely positive attitude towards programming. It also shows that the students realize that there is an important connection between the subjects, but that they do not have the skills to actually combine mathematics and programming yet. To show the students the importance and usefulness of the interplay as well as teach them some basic skills we have extended the normal homework assignments with advice on how to use programming as a tool to explore the mathematical problems as well as to find candidate solutions, which they then need to prove are correct. If our activities are successful, the students should be much better at using mathematics as a tool when programming and programming as a tool when solving mathematical problems.

5.2 The ACM/IEEE CS Curricula

The ACM/IEEE CS Curricula [5] is a very important and impressive document clearly describing the knowledge that every computer scientist should have. Our view is that they have done a very good job in capturing the required content. We have therefore used the curricula as a guide and as a measuring stick for making sure that we cover all the relevant aspects of computer science. In the overview of the program, Figure 1, we have classified the content of each course relative to the ACM CS Curricula 2013. When we look into the details of the knowledge areas we clearly see that we cover most of the content of all the knowledge areas.

As stated earlier, Karlfeldt compares 10 Swedish computer science related Master of Science in Engineering programs relative to the ACM CS Curricula 2008 [4]. Figure 2 shows the computer science content in the new program (blue) for each knowledge area in the curricula compared to the average content in the 10 programs studied by Karlfeldt. It is very important to notice that the data in the figure only shows the obligatory courses during the first three years. This means that the courses studied during the last two years

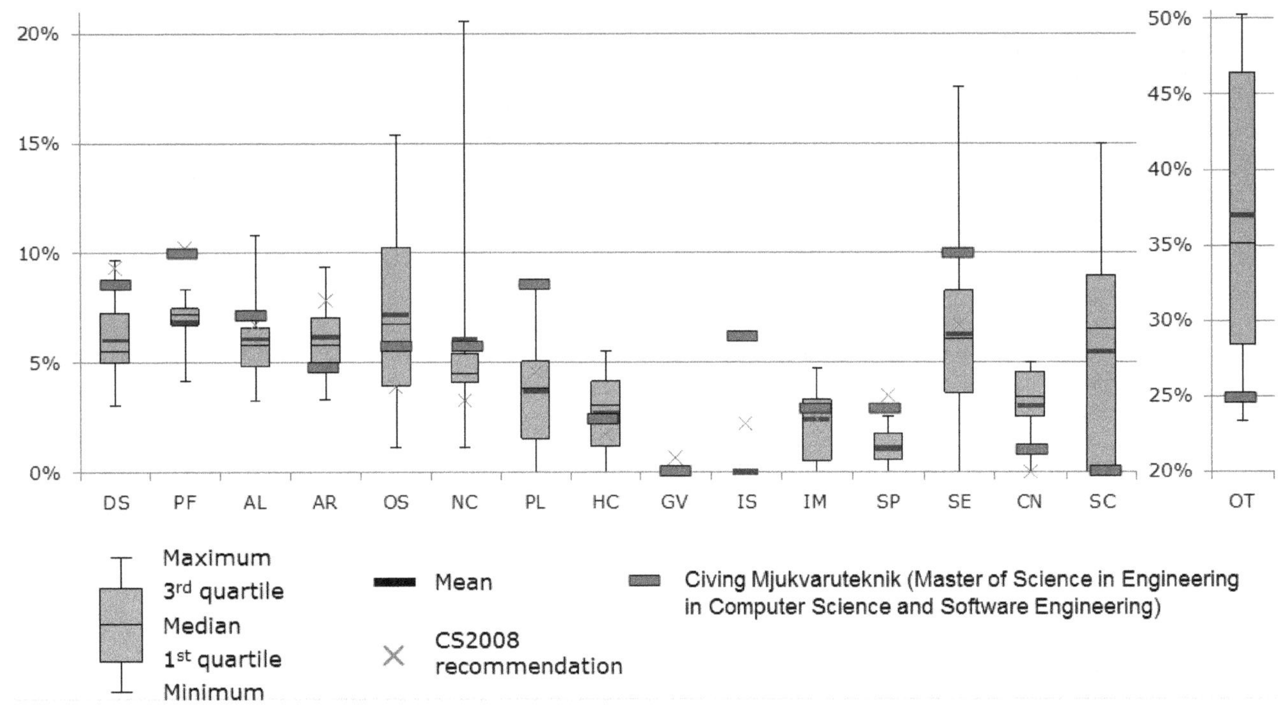

Figure 2: A comparison among Swedish CS related programs based on ACM CS Curricula 2008 based on Figure 1 in [4].

are not shown. Percentages is used instead of actual number of credits due to the different number of obligatory credits.

Two important conclusions can be drawn from Figure 2, first that the new program satisfies the ACM CS Curricula 2008 during the first three years and second that the new program has significantly more computer science content compared to the other programs as it has more than the average share of each knowledge area. There are programs with more content in specific areas, but not the same broad coverage of the whole computer science discipline.

5.3 Engineering Aspects

To be able to specify and verify the goals in a structured and systematic way, all engineering education at Linköping university is based on the CDIO concept (Conceive, Design, Implement, Operate) [1]. This is a concept for developing, executing, evaluating and engineering education including among other things a basic document – the CDIO syllabus – specifying expected knowledge and skills that a student is expected to have. All engineering educations at Linköping university uses a variety of the CDIO syllabus called the LiTH syllabus. The document has four main headlines:

1. Knowledge and reasoning in mathematics, natural sciences and engineering;
2. Personal and professional skills and attributes;
3. Interpersonal skills: teamwork and communication;
4. Conceiving, designing, implementing, and operating systems in the enterprise and social context.

There is a mapping between the LiTH syllabus and the national requirement for a 5-year engineering degree, which means that the national requirements are satisfied if the LiTH syllabus is satisfied.

The syllabus covers technical subjects but also personal, professional and interpersonal skills. These skills are part of the project courses, and is the main focus in the new course Professionalism for Engineers described in section 4.2.

6. CONCLUSIONS

In this paper we have described the vision, goals and design of the first 5-year engineering program in Computer Science and Software Engineering in Sweden. The goals are providing a holistic perspective on modern large scale software development, providing a deep and broad understanding of computer science and computational thinking, and encouraging innovation and entrepreneurship.

Designing a new 5-year program in Computer Science and Software Engineering is an exciting, challenging and very rewarding endeavor. We believe that we have managed to make the appropriate trade-offs when selecting and ordering the content of the program to achieve its goals. The student response has also been very good with more than 600 applicants to the 30 slots, of which more than 130 had this program as their first choice among all programs in Sweden. We are now working hard at making sure that the program really lives up to its vision and provides the best possible software engineering education in the world.

7. REFERENCES

[1] The CDIO initiative, http://www.cdio.org.

[2] B. Goranzon, R. Ennals, and M. Hammeron. *Dialogue, skill and tacit knowledge*. Wiley. com, 2006.

[3] V. Kann. En programsammanhållande kurs med många funktioner (in swedish). In *Proc. 3:e utvecklingskonferensen*, pages 153–156, 2011.

[4] J. Karlfeldt. Den svenska dataingenjören – en jämförande studie av 10 svenska civilingenjörsutbildningar inom det datavetenskapliga området. Master's thesis, KTH, 2012.

[5] M. Sahami, S. Roach, et al. Computer Science Curricula 2013 – Final Report Pre-release Version 0.9, Oct. 2013.

Bringing Business Intelligence to Healthcare Informatics Curriculum: A Preliminary Investigation

Guangzhi Zheng
Southern Polytechnic State University
1100 South Marietta Pkwy
Marietta, GA 30060
1-678-915-5036
jackzheng@spsu.edu

Chi Zhang
Southern Polytechnic State University
1100 South Marietta Pkwy
Marietta, GA 30060
1-678-915-3428
chizhang@spsu.edu

Lei Li
Southern Polytechnic State University
1100 South Marietta Pkwy
Marietta, GA 30060
1-678-915-3915
lli3@spsu.edu

ABSTRACT
Business intelligence (BI) and healthcare analytics are emerging technologies that provide analytical capability to help healthcare industry improve service quality, reduce cost, and manage risks. However, such component on analytical healthcare data processing is largely missed from current healthcare information technology (HIT) or health informatics (HI) curricula. This paper conducts a preliminary analysis on how healthcare business intelligence can be incorporated into a HIT program. A general framework and several exemplar implementation strategies are presented. They can be used to guide the development and improvement of HIT curriculum.

Categories and Subject Descriptors
K.3.2 [**Computers and Education**]: Computer and Information Science Education – *curriculum, information systems education*

Keywords
Business Intelligence, Healthcare Business Intelligence, Health Information Technology, Health Informatics, Curriculum Development

1. INTRODUCTION
The universal need for improved patient care and reduced healthcare costs combined with the 2009 American Recovery and Reinvestment Act (ARRA) has increased the attention on healthcare data management and analysis [14]. Healthcare depends on many sources of data to support the diagnosis, treatment and prevention of disease, illness, injury and other physical and mental impairments in humans, as well as the operation of healthcare service providers and organizations. Healthcare data includes patient information, clinical data, financial data, medical knowledge, and operational data [4].

SIGCSE '14, March 5-8, 2014, Atlanta, GA, USA.

ACM 978-1-4503-2605-6/14/03…$15.00.
http://dx.doi.org/10.1145/2538862.2538935

Healthcare data has some unique features such as multiple sources of data, complexity of different datasets, level of regulation, and the potential impact on a patient's health and life. For example, the data in a hospital or clinic is in various formats and comes from multiple sources including clinical and operational data. As the result, such data is difficult to analyze and often fail to deliver its value to users. Another major challenge to healthcare IT today is the explosive data growth, such as digital imaging and electronic health records in general. This is where business intelligence (BI) systems come in to help manage and integrate data, turn data into in meaningful information, and therefore improve patient care, reduce costs, and optimize business usage and understanding of the data [6]. BI is believed to be the key for enhancing healthcare quality with less cost [6].

Demand for BI applications for healthcare continues to grow as the volume of data and the desire to learn from the data keep growing. The demand for data management and analysis expertise in healthcare is increasing at a rapid rate. "Healthcare as an industry is behind in adopting BI, yet no other industry needs it more", as stated in [6]. However, the lack of industry knowledge and experience slows the implementation and adoption of BI in healthcare settings.

Academic institutions also realize the trend [3][7] and have laid out great visions on developing such programs. But one of the barriers is the limited educational and training resources (e.g., model curriculum and programs) to focus on the use of information for higher level analytical processing. In the already few healthcare information technology or health informatics programs, fewer have specifically cover the BI component.

We believe there is a need to bring education and training on BI concepts, technologies, and processes to HIT curriculum and programs. The question is what should be covered, and how to design the course content in different situations (e.g., is a separate BI course needed or only a couple of BI modules needed?) In this paper, we propose a curriculum framework for delivering BI education in HIT curricula. The paper also discusses different implementation strategies that can potentially serve as a curriculum development reference.

2. BACKGROUND
Business intelligence is a broad term to describe a set of methods, processes, architectures, applications, and technologies that transform raw data into meaningful and useful information to support business operation and growth [1]. It is used to enable more effective strategic, tactical, and operational insights and

decision-making. BI systems combine data gathering, data storage, data integration, and knowledge management with analytical tools to present complex internal and competitive information to planners and decision makers [8]. Traditionally it has evolved from executive information systems and management information systems to specifically focus on data driven decision making [10].

With each new iteration, BI system's capabilities increased as enterprises grew more sophisticated in their computational and analytical needs and as computer hardware and software matured [8]. A complete BI enterprise system is able to cover the full spectrum of a process, including major components include: data management and integration, analysis, presentation, delivery, and applications which involve all components.

The data management and integration component prepares data to be ready for analysis and reports. It corresponds to the lower transactional data processing level of the BI process [9]. The major functions of the component usually include data modeling, storage, collection, integration, and management. Popular technologies and tools used include database, data warehouse, data mart, data model, and ETL (data extraction, transformation, and loading).

The analysis component spans multiple level of data analysis, including simple descriptive and operational queries, specialized multidimensional analysis such as OLAP (online analytical processing, a particular data processing and analysis based on data facts and dimensions), business and statistical analysis, advanced data mining techniques, and even visual analytics [13]. It is the analytics that drives the transformation of data into meaning and relevant information and knowledge, which directly support decision making.

The presentation component is a more recently focused layer which brings sense-making and decision support directly to users. It includes various interaction and visualization techniques that add additional intuition and cognition to decision makers [12]. Common tools include reporting (static and interactive reports), digital dashboards, and more complex analytical visualizations.

The delivery component focuses on user access to data, reports, presentations, and all kinds of analysis and reporting tools. Common delivery approaches include BI web portal, personal office applications such as Excel, mobile applications, etc.

Finally, many common business or industry specific functions require the four components above work together to realize a complete solution. These include common horizontal business functions such as performance management, strategic management, customer relationship management, and also include industry specific businesses and processes such as institutional effectiveness, learning analytics, web analytics, patient care, etc. The goal of healthcare BI is to prepare, analyze, interpret, evaluate and present clinical and operational data to enhance healthcare quality, effectiveness, efficiency and safety.

3. BI EDUCATION IN CURRENT HIT PROGRAMS

We are interested in how higher education institutions have responded to the market demand and what level of healthcare business intelligence is covered in current HIT curricula. For a preliminary investigation, we targeted the 31 institutions in the University System of Georgia (USG). We started with this sample because Atlanta, Georgia had promoted itself as the nation's capital for healthcare information technology [2, 11], and the authors of this study are from a USG member institution. The knowledge of the programs offered in our peer USG institutions will help align our HIT curricula for our own program improvement, and also ensure a smooth transfer from other institutions in USG to our university and vice versa.

In an initial round of investigation, two authors collected data independently by searching and browsing the public information related to HIT programs and curricula published on the institution websites. A general curriculum/program assessment template was used. The assessment items in the template include institution type, HIT program availability, program level, BI course availability, focus, level and coverage.

We then cross-examined the findings and verify the information together for a few schools that showed different results from the individual assessment. The result is further examined by the third author for completeness. The search keywords we used included "health information technology", "health informatics", "business intelligence course", "data mining course", and institution names. For the colleges without any returned search results based on the above keywords, we went directly to their academic webpages about programs or degrees and looked for relevant information.

The result indicates a limited effort in BI-HIT education. Among the 31 USG institutions, eight of them have been found to have health information technology or health informatics curricula and programs but with varied structure and requirements. A good HIT program is expected to include a number of coherent courses focusing on the healthcare domain and cover the major aspects of the domain. For example, the HIT program offered by the Department of IT at Southern Polytechnic State University (SPSU) currently offer four HIT courses at both the graduate and undergraduate levels:

- Foundations of HIT
- Electronic Health Record systems & applications
- Clinical workflow process: analysis & redesign
- Health information security & privacy

Among these eight HIT programs, five of them offer some level of BI or data mining courses, but none currently offers BI in the context of healthcare information (Table 1). Most of the HIT courses focus on an operational or transactional level of data management and processing.

These preliminary findings show that BI is not yet included in the current established HIT curriculum in the institutions in USG. Some institutions have shown a good vision on health informatics and BI. They have recognized that a missing part in health informatics is about using data to facilitate the business of delivering healthcare and enable health practitioners make better decisions about patient care and service [3]. As informatics and BI are getting their due attention in the industry, education and training should also address the gap in the curricula. In the next section, we present a framework to integrate BI content in HIT education. The framework can help guide the integration of BI to the development of HIT curriculum.

Table 1: USG Institutions with HIT programs which also Offer BI Relevant Courses

BI course type	# of institutions
BI in the non-healthcare context	2
Data mining or data warehousing course	2
Healthcare statistics course	1

4. A PROPOSED FRAMEWORK TO DELIVER BI IN HIT CURRICULA AND PROGRAMS

The initial proposed coverage of BI within Healthcare IT is based on the conceptual analysis of general BI systems and processes. The application of BI in healthcare sector is expected to correspond to the full spectrum of business intelligence system (data management, analysis, presentation, and delivery) from both technical and healthcare perspectives (Figure 1). The technical focus emphasizes healthcare BI system development, deployment, and administration. The healthcare focus emphasizes healthcare service provider performance management, healthcare business analysis, and usage of user oriented reporting applications.

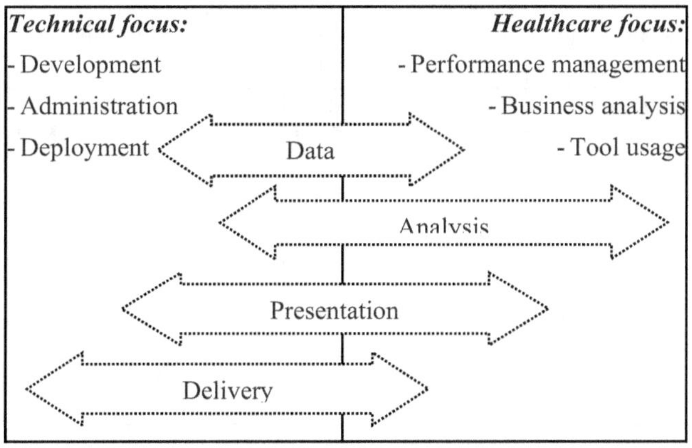

Figure 1: Coverage of BI in an HIT Curriculum

4.1 Data management and Integration

Toward a technical focus, students should know data warehousing technologies and practices with a focus on clinic data warehouse. They should be able to use a data warehouse product to design, implement, and maintain a financial data warehouse or a clinic data warehouse using common data schemas such as star and snowflake.

Data integration is also an important technical skill. Students will learn general data integration approaches as well as hands-on training on using ETL (extract, transform, and load) tools and programming languages to collect and consolidate patient, medical, and financial data from difference sources. To achieve this, students not only need to know the general common data integration systems, but also have hands-on experience with health information exchange systems, such as national health information network (NHIN, or eHealth Exchange) and Health Informatics Service Architecture, and various healthcare data formats and standards such as ICD10 and HL7. The understanding of the data formats and codes used in parsing these files is essential for health information exchange standards.

Toward a business perspective, students need to know the meaning and structure of both general operational data and healthcare domain data from different sources such as health records, clinical data, lab data, insurance data, research, and public health. They should be able to at least describe and specify the multidimensionality of data. A solid understanding of these data and how it is used in real world is a requirement for data modeling, which is a prerequisite for data warehouse design and data integration. A sound knowledge of the data can also help design data queries and reports that make business sense and meet expectations. In addition, the concept of enterprise-wide data governance in healthcare need to be introduced to students on how to manage data, realize value from it, minimize cost and complexity, manage risk, and ensure compliance with regulations and other requirements.

4.2 Analysis

From a technical perspective, students will learn the traditional OLAP (online analytical processing) technologies and how to use commonly used query languages such as MDX (multidimensional expression) to formulate OLAP queries. They also need to learn how to design and maintain OLAP cubes, and configure different analytics program packages to work seamlessly with the data source. All these queries and analysis should be in a healthcare business context. For instance, it is needed to analyze the distribution of disease and health outcomes in relevant population of interest.

From a business point of view, data analysis and business analysis constitute a big portion. An average data analyst should be able to use common business oriented query and analysis software such as Excel to retrieve data from the database, and conduct various levels of analysis. They may not need to know the query language behind the scene but they should know the nature of each kind of query and use typical GUI interface to formulate queries. An analyst should also understand common type of healthcare domain specific calculations and analysis. For example, integration of clinical and business data helps assess the effectiveness and efficiency of clinical interventions or processes.

Analysts are also responsible for designing and specifying key metrics and indicators, and interpreting query results. The clinical analytics results will be applied to various context of quality improvement, such as chronic disease, patient utilization, population health, and public health.

4.3 Presentation and UI

Reporting is essential for assessment and decision making. Healthcare industry needs a variety of reports in enterprise intelligence and medical intelligence to assess patient outcomes and quality of care, understand the potential impacts of many regulatory proposals. The evolving regulations and quality initiatives require the reports on many quality measures, such as Meaningful Use, Physician Quality Reporting System (PQRS), Healthcare Effectiveness Data and Information Set (HEDIS) & Performance Management, Accountable Care Organizations (ACO), Electronic Health Records (EHR) and clinical applications.

From a technical focus, much of the course coverage can be on the development of static and interactive reports, dashboard applications, and information visualizations, among others, in the healthcare context. Report development is a common job role in companies and organizations including healthcare service providers and agencies. Students may have hands-on practice using typical development and programming platform such as Crystal Reports. Another recent hot area is digital dashboard. Students may need to know basic business information visualization techniques (including design of visual properties and elements) and create dashboards using popular software like QlikView.

From a business user perspective, it's important to understand the meaning of common business data visualizations [12], including basic chart types (line chart, pie chart, etc.) and more specific charting and diagrams like bridge chart, perceptual mapping, tree map, etc. They are expected to build non-automated presentations using common office tools like Excel. They should also be clear about the purpose, usage, pros and cons of each type of chart, and correctly choose the chart type to deliver meaning and at the same time correctly interpret the results.

4.4 Delivery

The delivery component is much from a technical aspect. This part follows general BI delivery practices in technology choice (hardware and software) and system administration. Students should know common ways to delivery the application to users and configure devices and applications correctly and securely. Topics include web portal setup, mobile application configuration, mobile device management, user permission management and access control, etc.

4.5 Applications

The technology aspect focuses on the development and implementation of an enterprise data or information systems to cover every component of a BI system and configure them to work together. Such a system can be configured and customized to a number of business functions either healthcare industry specific or not. For example, general performance management and strategic management systems such as a traffic light system and balanced scorecard system [5]. The uniqueness in the healthcare industry is to know healthcare business specific key performance indicators (KPIs), the meaning and definition of the KPIs and how they are measured and used, and what types of decisions are supported. For example, how doctor performance is evaluated, or how hospital utilization is defined and measured.

BI technologies and systems can be applied to a number of healthcare specific processes. For example, the advanced analytics may help suggest treatment options to doctors, based on medical records, patient history, research databases and other sources, and predict whether patients with chronic conditions like diabetes are following doctors' orders based on patient records and claims histories. Systems like these need a complete solution from data collection to results delivery. Many care providers can also use BI system to identify and monitor who is at risk of a hospital admission. Effective prediction of who was going to be hospitalized could reallocate resources to prevent unnecessary hospitalization and put the resources to use for cure rather than care [14].

5. IMPLEMENTATION STRATEGY AND TEACHING RESOURCES

5.1 Implementation Strategy

The curriculum framework describes a theoretic picture of BI education and training in the healthcare domain. However, it is difficult to deliver an HIT or healthcare management degree program that implements every aspects of the framework. The best strategy is to position the program with a focus before deciding how and what courses to offer. There are also a number of factors that impact the choice of strategy – resources and expertise may be two major factors. The availability of data and cases could also limit the course delivery. HIT programs, when considering offering healthcare BI related courses, can use the framework as a guide by (1) picking a focus (technical or healthcare); (2) making it flexible for IT or healthcare programs to customize based on their goals and requirements; and (3) focusing on certain BI modules/phases in the customization process (Table 2).

Table 2. Health BI Course Implementation Strategy

Offering strategies	**Course availability** **(General BI / Healthcare Specific BI)**	**Integration level**	**Coverage depth**
Learning modules	No / No	Include BI modules to HIT courses	Concepts focused
Direct course inclusion	Yes / No	Low. May not be in healthcare context.	Coverage of BI in a general sense
BI course customization	Yes / No	Add healthcare content to BI course	Special sections using clinical data
Specialization	Yes / Yes	Specialized BI course	All components in the BI system and process in healthcare settings
Specialization in-depth	Yes / Yes	Sequence of healthcare BI courses	Technical and management aspects, various healthcare related BI applications

1. If BI-related courses are not available yet, the programs can include specific learning modules of BI in the existing HIT courses. For example, in an EHR course, include one or two modules that focus on data standards and integration technologies.
2. If BI-related courses are already available but not in HIT program, then these courses can be directly included in the curriculum as electives without additional customization.
3. Existing BI courses (or some offering sections of these courses) can be customized to use healthcare context such as healthcare cases and projects. For example, in a data warehousing course, a special section can be offered using clinic data warehouse as a major sample data throughout the course. To provide students with solution-driven project experience, designing a database for a hospital as a term project could also be considered if it is practical.
4. Develop and offer independent healthcare BI courses to cover all the components in the BI system and process in healthcare settings. The course can be flexibly adjusted to have a technical focus or management focus based on the program mission and goals.
5. Develop a more complete curriculum with 2 or more courses that specifically focus on healthcare BI. They may cover technical and management aspects respectively, and include various enterprise and medical intelligence applications.

5.2 Example Healthcare BI course design

In this section, we describe a sample single healthcare BI course with a technical focus. Based on the concepts to be covered in a general BI course and the specifics of healthcare domain, the course objectives of a healthcare BI course can include:

- Discuss concepts and practices of enterprise and medical intelligence and decision support in healthcare settings
- Explain technologies and components of healthcare business intelligence systems
- Describe the structure of clinical data warehouse and the process of data extraction, transformation and loading related to healthcare data
- Model and analyze multidimensional data from various healthcare data sources
- Design reporting solutions utilizing information visualization techniques and digital dashboards for different healthcare stakeholders
- Compare major business intelligence software used in healthcare

The course can have the following learning modules. Some modules may span more than 1 week if needed:

1. BI Introduction
2. Clinical Data Warehouse and Dimensional Modeling
3. Data Integration and ETL
4. OLAP Cube Design
5. OLAP Query – MDX and Client Tools
6. Report Development
7. Healthcare Data Visualization
8. Dashboard
9. Performance Management in Healthcare Service Providers
10. Healthcare BI industry and trend

The above suggested learning outcomes and course topics intend to prepare students for the roles of BI specialist who provide technical support to clinical and operational analysts. Other roles may also benefit from the courses, such as data warehouse administrators, systems analysts and database architects working in different healthcare settings.

5.3 Health-related datasets and resources

The most important resources for healthcare BI courses are Health-related datasets. The datasets ensure students to have a sound context and get familiar with the healthcare data and data sources as well as the entire data analytics process.

Health-related datasets that are available free of charge:

- Health-related data http://www.healthdata.gov/
- Healthcare datasets at the Center of Medicare and Medicaid Services https://data.cms.gov/
- HIMSS analytics http://www.himssanalytics.org/home/index.aspx
- Ambulatory Health Care Data at Centers for Disease Control and Prevention (CDC) http://www.cdc.gov/nchs/ahcd/ahcd_questionnaires.htm
- National health-related data at U.S. Census Bureau http://dataferrett.census.gov/datasets.html
- Web portal for large health data sets at EHDP http://www.ehdp.com/vitalnet/datasets.htm
- The Dartmouth Atlas of Health Care http://www.dartmouthatlas.org/
- NIH Data sets http://www.nlm.nih.gov/hsrinfo/datasites.html
- Agency for Health care Research and Quality http://www.ahrq.gov/research/data/dataresources.html
- World Health Organization Data Sets http://apps.who.int/gho/data/view.main
- World Bank Health Care Data Sets http://data.worldbank.org/country

Understanding the BI software and applications used in healthcare and the emerging BI solution leaders in the industry are important for the course as well. A couple of exemplar BI solutions are:

- Microsoft - business intelligence for healthcare providers http://www.microsoft.com/en-us/bi/default.aspx
- McKesson BI tool specific to healthcare http://www.mckesson.com/en_us/McKesson.com/For%2BHealthcare%2BProviders/Hospitals/Document%2BManagement%2BSystems/Horizon%2BPatient%2BFolder%2BAnalytics.html

6. CONCLUSION

Business intelligence has been a neglected part in many HIT programs yet both the industry and academia have realized its importance. In this paper we described an educational framework for delivering healthcare business intelligence content in HIT curriculum and programs. We are planning to expand our investigation of HIT programs to the regional and national levels, and get more empirical data to validate and improve the framework. The effort will include an HIT program survey (one of the sources is AIS SIG-Health Health IS Programs directory) and an industry survey from practitioner and employer's perspective. Potential respondents include HIT companies, healthcare providers, government agencies, and healthcare service consulting companies. It is our hope that more HIT programs will recognize the importance of the healthcare BI and integrate BI component in their programs, which will better prepare the HIT graduates for the different roles in the healthcare IT industry.

7. REFERENCES

[1] Cardin, L. 2007. *The Forrester Wave: Project Portfolio Management Tools, Q4 2007.*

[2] City will sell itself as health IT capital - Atlanta Business Chronicle: 2010. *http://www.bizjournals.com/atlanta/print-edition/2010/11/26/health.html?page=all*. Accessed: 2013-05-31.

[3] College of Coastal Georgia 2011. Health Informatics: A Simple Definition for a Pile of Information. *College of Coastal Georgia - the Magazine.*

[4] Groves, P. and Kayyli, B. *The "big data" revolution in healthcare*. McKinsey & Company.

[5] Kaplan, R.S. and Norton, D.P. 1996. *The Balanced Scorecard: Translating Strategy into Action*. Harvard Business School Press.

[6] Madsen, L.B. 2012. *Healthcare Business Intelligence: A Guide to Empowering Successful Data Reporting and Analytics*. Wiley.

[7] Martz, B. et al. 2007. Information Systems and Healthcare XIX: Developing an Integrative Health Informatics Graduate Curriculum. *Communications of the Association for Information Systems*. 19, 1 (May. 2007).

[8] Negash, S. 2004. Business intelligence. *Communications of the Association for Information Systems*. 13, 1 (2004), 177–195.

[9] Olszak, C.M. and Ziemba, E. 2007. Approach to building and implementing business intelligence systems. *Interdisciplinary Journal of Information, Knowledge, and Management*. 2, (2007), 134–148.

[10] Power, D.J. 2007. *A Brief History of Decision Support Systems*.

[11] Reiboldt, M. 2011. The Importance of Capital in Building Atlanta as the Center of Healthcare Technology. *Atlanta Journal Constitution: HealthFlock Blog*.

[12] Tegarden, D.P. 1999. Business Information Visualization. *Communications of the AIS*. 1, 4 (1999).

[13] Thomas, J.J. and Cook, K.A. 2006. A visual analytics agenda. *Computer Graphics and Applications, IEEE*. 26, 1 (Feb. 2006), 10 – 13.

[14] Tibken, S. 2013. Numbers, Numbers and More Numbers. *The Wall Street Journal*.

An ACM 2013 Exemplar Course Integrating Fundamentals, Languages, and Software Engineering

Jason O. Hallstrom, Cathy Hochrine, Jacob Sorber, Murali Sitaraman
Clemson University, School of Computing
Clemson, SC, 29634
{ jasonoh, chochri, jsorber, murali }@clemson.edu

ABSTRACT

This paper summarizes our experiences integrating topics in the software development fundamentals (SDF), programming languages (PL), and software engineering (SE) knowledge areas of the ACM 2013 curriculum within a single course. It is novel in combining object-oriented programming and software development practices with fundamental analytical reasoning about software correctness. The aim is to integrate and cover the topics in an effective fashion. The course description in this paper represents an approach we have applied successfully for over 5 years. Students tend to consider this course to be one of the more challenging encountered in the first two years of study. Interestingly, the challenge appears to stem equally from mastering object-oriented programming and design pattern components of the course, as it does from learning to use specifications for analytical reasoning of component correctness.

Categories and Subject Descriptors

K.3.2 [**Computer and Education**]: Computer and Information Science Education – *Computer Science education, Curriculum*

Keywords

ACM curriculum, components, design patterns, formal reasoning, object-oriented programming, software engineering

1. INTRODUCTION

This paper summarizes our experiences in teaching a course that combines multiple knowledge areas within the ACM 2013 curriculum [1]. As the field of computing continues to evolve, such combinations will become ever more necessary to impart requisite skills within a reduced number of required courses for CS majors. We hope that this effort will serve as a case study for other educators in developing courses spanning multiple areas, as well as a specific course outline useful to educators interested in developing courses that combine fundamental and practical aspects of software development.

Beyond introducing students to the basics of software development, the sophomore-level course, CpSc 215 at Clemson, is novel in that it integrates three major themes: object-oriented is novel in that it integrates three major themes: object-oriented programming (in Java), analytical reasoning, and software design patterns. The prerequisite is one semester of imperative programming. The emphasis on object-oriented programming is motivated by the importance of this paradigm in modern software practice. Analytical reasoning along with mathematical thinking and computational thinking, are among topics that have received regular SIGCSE attention (e.g., [2][3]). The emphasis on analytical reasoning is motivated by the supposition that the next generation of software engineers must be able to reason rigorously about the functionality and performance of the software they develop and maintain. Traditional trial-and-error methods of software development alone are insufficient. The emphasis on software design patterns is motivated by the wide adoption of patterns in modern software practice, both as prescriptive and descriptive aids. Together the topics help students learn the essential elements of building the next generation of high-quality software systems.

The course is taught using a "hands-on", collaborative approach [4], motivated by the success of peer instruction and other active learning strategies in mathematics and science. While the students consider the course among the most challenging, feedback suggests that the approach has had a positive impact on students' performance, self-efficacy, perception of computing as a discipline of study [5]. Continuous evolution, interventions, and improvements to the course offerings are documented in [5].

Paper Organization. Section 2 summarizes the ACM 2013 curriculum knowledge areas covered in the course, as well as the major topics addressed. Section 3 presents the key software development foundations, programming languages, and software engineering principles taught in the course. Section 4 shows that student performance across the topic areas is uniformly acceptable. Section 5 presents related work and conclusions.

2. COURSE SUMMARY

2.1 Body of Knowledge Coverage

This section summarizes the topics covered from different knowledge areas prescribed by the ACM 2013 curriculum. Note that only lecture hours are listed below. Of the 42 hours listed, there is some overlap among the hours devoted to knowledge area (KA) topics in software development foundations (SDF), programming languages (PL), and software engineering (SE). The actual coverage of the topics spans about 39 hours. The course covers a few additional background topics (3 hours) and includes a midterm exam (1.5 hours).

2.2 Major Topics/Course Outline

Major topics covered in the lectures, in their approximate order of coverage, include the following.

- **Java Basics:** Introduction, interpreted versus compiled languages
- **Java Basics:** Packages, classpaths, the Java compiler
- **Java Basics:** The Eclipse integrated development environment
- **Java Basics:** Parameter passing, shallow versus deep copying, value versus reference semantics
- **Java Classes:** Fields, methods, accessibility modifiers

SIGCSE'14, March 5–8, 2014, Atlanta, Georgia, USA.

http://dx.doi.org/10.1145/2538862.2538969

- **Java Classes:** Constructors, overloading
- **Java Classes:** Static fields, methods, initializers
- **Design Patterns:** Introduction, historical context
- **Design Patterns:** Singleton, Flyweight
- **Java Libraries:** java.io.*, java.util.*, java.net.*, java.math.*
- **Java Interfaces:** Declaring, implementing, using as types
- **Abstract Data Structures:** Stacks, queues, sets
- **Specification:** Introduction to interface contracts
- **Specification:** Review of basic mathematical types (integers, tuples, strings, sets)
- **Specification:** Formal contract specifications
- **Abstract Data Structures:** Partial maps (dictionaries), linked-lists
- **Analytical Reasoning:** Contract-based testing and tracing
- **Design Patterns:** Decorator
- **Analytical Reasoning:** Assertion-checking wrappers (using Decorator)
- **Java Exceptions:** Concepts, declaring, throwing, catching
- **Java Inheritance:** Concepts, type system integration, polymorphism
- **Design Patterns:** Template Method, Strategy
- **Algorithms as Components:** Parameterized sorting implementations
- **Java Generics:** Concepts, syntax, subclassing issues
- **Design Patterns:** Observer
- **Analytical Reasoning:** Introduction to verification
- **Analytical Reasoning:** Software verification with objects
- **Java Libraries:** javax.swing.*, basic Swing development

2.3 Summary of Closed Labs

The course is a 4-credit course because there is a weekly 2-hour lab session, in addition to lectures. Each principle is reinforced during the laboratory component of the course, where students work in pairs to develop exercise solutions on shared workstations. Full credit is received when students demonstrate their solutions to laboratory assistants.

While each laboratory exercise targets a specific topic, the exercises are designed to integrate the various threads of the course with the objective of creating a unified, coherent view of the course material. In the Decorator pattern exercise, for instance, students are provided with pre- and post-conditions for a new software interface. They are then tasked with developing a decorator class responsible for checking those conditions in *any* implementation of the interface. This not only reinforces Decorator and prior reasoning concepts, but also initiates a discussion on the advantages and disadvantages of "defensive programming" (i.e., pre-condition checking in release code). The Template Method and Strategy exercise requires students to revisit the concept of recasting algorithms as reusable components. In this context, they must define an interface that recasts the fundamental notion of searching as a reusable component. They must then implement this interface using an appropriate search algorithm (e.g., linear search, binary search).

Table 1: Coverage of Knowledge Area Topics

KA	Knowledge Unit	Topics Covered	Hours
SDF	Algorithm Design	Fundamental design concepts and principles	3
SDF	Fundamental Data Structures	Abstract data types and their implementations, references and aliasing, linked lists, strategies for choosing the appropriate data structure	9
SDF	Development Methods	Program correctness, modern programming environments, debugging strategies	6
PL	Object-Oriented Programming	Object-oriented design, definition of classes: fields, methods, and constructors, subclasses, inheritance, and method overriding, dynamic dispatch, definition of method-call, subtyping, object-oriented idioms for encapsulation, using collection classes, iterators, and other common library components	9
PL	Basic Type Systems	Type safety and errors caused by using values inconsistently with their intended types, generic types (parametric polymorphism)	3
SE	Software Design	Design patterns	7.5
SE	Formal Methods	Role of formal specification and analysis techniques in the software development cycle, program assertion languages and analysis approaches (including languages for writing and analyzing pre-and post-conditions), tools in support of formal methods	4.5

This component builds upon students' prior experience recasting sorting as a reusable component; that solution is designed and implemented during class lecture.

We list summaries of closed labs below to show how we manage to weave topics in the three knowledge areas seamlessly. The complete assignments are available at [5].

1. Title: *Hello, World!* Goal: To gain initial experience working with the Java programming language. (SDF)

2. Title: *Card Game, War!* Goal: To introduce Java arrays, classes, and to use Java objects to implement an object-oriented application. (SDF)
3. Title: *War! Peace!* Goal: To use inheritance to extend previously developed classes and applications. (PL)
4. Title: *Linked Lists*. Goal: To introduce interfaces and implementations (along with object references). (SDF and PL)
5. Title: *Echo!* Goal: To introduce Java I/O and networking libraries. (SDF)
6. Title: *Pre-Conditions, Post-Conditions, and Checking Wrappers*. Goal: To reinforce understanding of pre-conditions and post-conditions, and the concept of a wrapper class for runtime checking of those conditions; use of Decorator pattern to implement a checking wrapper. (SE)
7. Title: *The Flyweight Pattern*. Goal: Developing classes that define static methods, fields, and initializers to implement and use a design pattern. (PL, SE)
8. Title: *Formal Specification-Based Unit Testing*: Goal: To implement classes based on understanding of formal interface specifications, and to develop test cases based on those specifications. (SE)
9. Title: *Formal Specification-Based Unit Testing with JUnit*: Goal: To reinforce the goals of #8 by introducing additional mathematical models, and to teach the JUnit testing framework. (SDF, SE)
10. Title: *Checking Un-Wrapped*: Goal: To combine and contrast several of the principles above and reinforce understanding of inheritance, reuse, and checking. (PL)
11. Title: *Sorting and Searching*. Goal: To introduce Java Generics as well as Template and Strategy patterns in the context of a sorting and searching problem. (PL, SE)
12. Title: *Formal Verification*. Goal: To prove the correctness of object-based code using interface specifications and a formal reasoning method. (SE)
13. Title: *Swing!* Goal: To implement a GUI application using Swing, and in the process reinforce understanding of abstract classes, inheritance, and the Template Method pattern. (PL, SE)

The closed labs provide students with a series of hands-on opportunities to apply and reinforce a set of core principles—principles often addressed separately in typical computing courses, but which, when combined, provide a solid foundation for developing high-quality software.

3. SUMMARY OF PRINCIPLES

3.1 Software Development Foundations

Most students in CpSc 215 are new to Java, but not to computer programming. As they learn the basic constructs of a new language and a new programming paradigm (object-oriented programming), the initial lectures and labs also introduce or reinforce techniques and strategies that are fundamental to developing quality software.

For example, in the early labs, students learn language basics and data types, such as linked lists. Students learn to program using an IDE, acquire strategies for debugging their programs (with or without an integrated debugger), and gain experience with standard libraries for I/O and network communication. As the course progresses, students build on these basics and learn principles of programming languages and software engineering.

3.2 Programming Languages

A key challenge for any Computer Science program is to prepare tomorrow's software developers to solve important problems in an ever-growing assortment of computing environments and application domains, using one or more of the many programming languages that are currently available. Understanding the principles behind programming language design, and learning to identify important differences between different languages enables software developers to learn new languages more quickly and produce higher quality software.

In CpSc 215, students learn a new programming language (Java). More importantly, this new language is introduced in order to help students understand the fundamental differences between the procedural languages they have previously been exposed to, and object-oriented programming (OOP) languages. Students are shown how encapsulation can encourage flexibility, how modular software design can make complex programs more manageable, and how inheritance can be used to reuse common code. Students are also introduced to different type systems, calling conventions, approaches to memory management (e.g. garbage collection), error handling, and execution environments (compilation, interpretation, and virtualization). These language topics span the entire course, as evidenced, for example, by the introduction of classes in lab #2, to generics in lab #12.

3.3 Design Patterns (SE)

Over the past two decades, design patterns have had a profound impact on software engineering practice. Their benefits are both prescriptive and descriptive. On the one hand, design patterns codify expert knowledge, providing solution templates for some of the most commonly encountered challenges in object-oriented design. On the other, patterns serve as an extended vocabulary for documenting software. Annotating a system's source base (or UML representations) with the patterns applied in its construction enables new designers to more quickly understand how a system is constructed and why it behaves in particular ways. It is no wonder that patterns play a prominent role in the design of most commercial class libraries. Indeed, based on this trend, many programming languages have been extended to simplify the expression of the most common patterns (e.g., Singleton, Iterator, Observer).

Design patterns are a central component of a well-rounded education in software engineering. The module begins with an introduction to the history of design patterns, beginning with Beck and Cunningham's interface patterns in SmallTalk, through Gamma's early patterns in C++, and finally, the seminal pattern catalog developed by the Gang of Four [7]. This historical overview is followed by a discussion of the benefits of design patterns and the impact that they have had on software engineering practice. Finally, students are introduced to the standard elements of a pattern description.

The course covers a subset of design patterns, motivated by breadth goals as well as their general applicability. The patterns are woven throughout, providing opportunities to showcase the natural integration of design patterns, data abstraction, object-oriented programming, and formal reasoning topics. This is evidenced by noting an earlier lab, such as lab #6, or a later one, such as lab #13. The pattern content tracks the following topical outline.

- **Singleton:** The intent of the Singleton pattern is to ensure that only one instance of a given class is constructed, and to provide global access to the constructed instance. The pattern is introduced in the context of a simple database application involving database access code woven throughout multiple classes. In this context, Singleton provides improved code readability by factoring object construction logic into a single method call. Moreover, efficiency is improved by limiting the number of database connections. This leads to a discussion of Singleton-based connection and thread pooling, which will be leveraged in later systems courses.

- **Decorator:** The intent of the Decorator pattern is to decouple behavioral enhancements from a base object hierarchy and enable those enhancements to be applied without the use of subclassing. The pattern is introduced in a hands-on manner, through the collective, in-class design of an I/O library that mirrors the structure of the standard `java.io.*` classes. The resulting classes decouple buffering and encryption "decorations" from the file and socket streams that use them. This leads to an interesting discussion involving the motivation for interface declarations over class declarations (i.e., concrete-to-abstract dependencies versus concrete-to-concrete dependencies) – a fundamental requirement of Decorator.

- **Template Method:** The intent of the Template Method pattern is to defer a portion of an implementation to an abstract *hook* method – to later be implemented by subclass designers. To cover Template Method, students are first introduced to the concept of a *Sorting Machine*, a class that recasts the concept of sorting as a reusable component. This is, by itself, an interesting topic that reinforces the use of reusable components not only for abstract data types, but also for reusable algorithms. In this context, the sorting class implements a simple insertion sort, implemented over a previously specified `Sequence` implementation. The comparison decision (e.g., increasing, decreasing) is deferred to a hook method, allowing subclass designers to control the sort order.

- **Strategy Method:** The intent of the Strategy pattern is similar to that of Template Method, but defers portions of an implementation to an independent class hierarchy. To motivate the utility of this pattern, the sorting scenario is revisited, and multiple sorting implementations are discussed (e.g., insertion, merge, quick). Accommodating each desired ordering using Template Method results in "subclass explosion"; the class hierarchy quickly becomes unmanageable, with significant redundancy across the hook implementations. To address these deficiencies, the comparison method (or "comparator") is factored into a separate strategy object, passed to the constructor of each sorting class. This leads to an interesting comparison of the two patterns, and a discussion of when each is most suitable.

- **Observer:** The intent of the Observer pattern is to maintain an application-specific notion of consistency between a *subject* object and each of its *observer* objects. This is controlled by the subject class, which maintains a set of references to each subscribed observer. The observers are notified via method call whenever the state of the subject is changed. The pattern is introduced in the context of GUI development using Java Swing. More interesting, perhaps, is that the initial subject implementations rely on previously specified `Set` instances, specified to hold *values*. In this context, the set contains *references*, creating an opportunity to reinforce the distinction between value and reference semantics, as well as the associated tradeoffs between them.

3.4 Specification and Reasoning

A key thread throughout the course is the role of formal specification and mathematical reasoning in high quality software development using components. In the process, students see important connections between the concepts they learn in their discrete structures course and the correctness of computer programs. Specifications discussed in the course include those for stacks, queues, lists, maps, and sorting machines (an object-oriented version of sorting). These specifications use a combination of discrete structures, such as numbers, strings, sets, and functions, to provide mathematical modeling of objects.

A discussion of specifications employed in the course is the topic of [8]. Once suitable discrete structures have been identified for modeling objects, corresponding notations from discrete mathematics are used in formally specifying pre- and post-conditions of operations. To ensure students understand specifications, we employ two methods. The first of these is to have them produce specification-based test points (see closed labs mentioned earlier, and quiz #3 discussed later), whereby students write valid input points (that satisfy pre-conditions) and expected outputs (that satisfy post-conditions); we have also built and used a tool for this purpose, named the Test Case Reasoning Assistant (TCRA) [9]. As another way to ensure students understand specifications, some of the lab assignments, as well as a project, ask students to produce implementations of components, given only their specifications.

A sample Queue specification is given below. In the post-condition of an operation, *#self* denotes the incoming value of an object. Also, <> denotes the empty string, "o" denotes string concatenation, |self| denotes string length.

```
public interface Queue {
  // modeled by: string of object
  // initial value: self = <>

  void clear();
  // post: self = <>

  void enqueue(Object x);
  // preserves: x
  // post: self = #self o <x>

  Object dequeue();
  // pre: self != <>
  // post: #self = <dequeue()> o self
  ...
}
```

Teaching mathematical reasoning in conjunction with specifications helps students see the tangible benefits of using formal specifications. An example piece of code to reverse a 2-element queue is given below, along with expected student answers (also the topic of quiz #4). Some aspects of the methods and proofs are simplified here to a level where the ideas can be communicated to students within one or two class periods.

We use a tabular reasoning method to teach software correctness [10]. In developing verification conditions of correctness, variable values in different states are distinguished by attaching the state number to the variable name (e.g., q0, q1, q2, etc.). The pre-condition of the operation becomes a fact (or given) in state 0, and the post-condition becomes an obligation (that needs to be proved to show correctness) in state 2. When a method is called, in the state before the call, its pre-condition needs to be proved (an obligation), and in the state after the call, the post-condition may be assumed (a fact). The code is correct if all obligations can be proved from the facts.

```
public static void shortQueueReverse (Queue q) {
        // pre: |q| = 2
        // post: q = Reverse(#q)

        Object t;
        t = q.dequeue();
        q.enqueue(t);
}
```

Tabular Reasoning Method

State	Facts	Obligations
0	$\|q0\| = 2$	$\|q0\| \neq 0$

t = q.dequeue();

1	q0 = <t1> o q1	

q.enqueue(t);

2	q2 = q1 o <t1>	q2 = Reverse(q0)

Proofs of obligations:

Proof of $|q0| \neq 0$ in state 0:
true from fact in state 0.

Proof of q2 = Reverse(q0) in state 2:
= q1 o <t1> from fact in state 2
= Reverse(q1) o Reverse(<t1>) because $|q1| = 1$
= Reverse (<t1> o q1)
from string reversal theorem
= Reverse (q0) from fact in state 1.

We have assessed student learning of these ideas extensively using a Reasoning Concept Inventory (RCI). Detailed results from evaluation, along with methods for continuous improvement, including the use of videos [10], are reported in [5].

4. EVALUATION AND RESULTS

4.1 Quizzes

The course principles are all reinforced in the labs, programming assignments, quizzes, and exams. In this section, we focus on quizzes and projects to show how we cover and assess student performance in various knowledge areas. While both quizzes and project assignments cover SDF and PL topics, for SE, the quizzes place more emphasis on formal methods, and assignments place more emphasis on design patterns.

The first quiz requires students to design a simple class that meets a set of specified requirements. The second requires students to apply object-oriented programming principles in order to implement abstract data structures. The third requires students to read and interpret mathematical specifications by selecting input/output test points for a set of methods. Students are also required to develop a JUnit test suite for an abstract data type. The final quiz continues the analytical reasoning path, requiring students to develop the mathematical assertions that must be proven to show that a given code fragment satisfies its specification. For extra credit, students may prove the assertion set to verify the code's correctness.

Table 2, below, summarizes students' quiz performance and the associated knowledge area topics covered for the 2012-13 academic year. Each class had between 25 and 40 students. Together, the data represents the performance of over 200 students. (Though the course has been taught for multiple years, we present the data for the most recent offerings, when the quizzes and assignments have been kept stable.)

In the table, the following abbreviations have been used; they correspond to the body of knowledge coverage in Section 2.1. Under SDF, AD refers to Algorithm Design, FDS refers to Fundamental Data Structures, and DM refers to Development Methods. Under PL, OOP is Object-Oriented Programming, and BTS is Basic Type Systems. Under SE, SD is Software Design (including design patterns), and FM is Formal Methods.

Table 2: Consistent Quiz Averages across Topics

	Instr. A (Fall '12)	Instr. B (Fall '12)	Instr. C (Spr '13)	Instr. B (Spr '13)	Instr. C (Fall '13)	Instr. B (Fall '13)
Q1: SDF(AD), PL(OOP)	79	72	57	78	74	68
Q2: SDF(FDS), PL(OOP)	85	86	72	86	72	85
Q3: SE (FM), specification	82	78	82	82	66	84
Q4: SE (FM), reasoning	59	73	92	81	82	80

Some general observations can be made concerning this data. Students have performed uniformly well across the topics, though three different instructors with varying teaching experience and backgrounds taught the course. For the fourth quiz, the improvement in spring can be attributed to an intervention introduced to improve the teaching of reasoning; details of the intervention are documented elsewhere [5].

4.2 Project Assignments

The programming assignments are designed to provide students with opportunities to design appropriate class hierarchies and combine multiple principles to solve more complex problems. The first course project requires students to develop a basic web crawler. Given a URL as a command-line parameter, the crawler retrieves and stores all embedded images and other documents, and then recursively follows any embedded links, down to a specified maximum depth. First, and most important, students gain experience designing and implementing a small (but interesting) Java application. This reinforces their object-oriented design skills, as well as their ability to effectively apply the Java development tools. More specifically, the project reinforces student understanding of Java interfaces, the Singleton pattern, Java exceptions, and the Java IO library. It also improves their ability to debug Java-based systems.

The second course project also involves topics from multiple knowledge areas. Students must develop a formal interface specification for a linked-list abstraction given a Java interface documented using natural language. Next they must develop an implementation of this interface and develop a robust test suite to validate the correctness of their implementation with respect to their specification. In the process, students gain experience in the following areas: understanding a formal interface specification based on an abstract model, implementing a class based solely on an understanding of its specification, and implementing specification-based unit tests using the JUnit testing framework.

The third project is the most pattern-intensive. Students are required to implement a fully-functional email client using Java Swing, which includes support for a persistent contact database. The suggested architecture is annotated with the required patterns, again underscoring their prescriptive and descriptive benefits. To complete the project, students must understand how Strategy, Decorator, and Observer are used in the Java class libraries, and must be able to implement aspects of Singleton, Strategy, and Observer themselves. This project has been used for many years and continues to be popular with students. It is not uncommon for students to present their work to future employers as evidence of their object-oriented design capabilities.

While all scores are subject to grading variations, there is a notable difference in performance between fall and spring classes on the second assignment. This is perhaps due to a better understanding of specifications (from an intervention). The subsequent decrease for fall 2013 is consistent with decreases across the board; some data is not yet available. Assignment 4 requires students to develop a straight-line interpreter based on the Interpreter Pattern. The near 100% statistic here is somewhat misleading; it became a mandatory assignment only in fall 2013.

We have also collected extensive data on student attitudes using pre- and post-surveys for the course [5]. Space limitations preclude us from detailing attitudinal assessment results, which show a statistically significant positive shift in the perception of students on how to develop high quality software.

5. SUMMARY

It is inevitable that new CS courses that combine multiple topic areas have to be developed because the trend is for institutions to continue to reduce the number of required CS courses for majors, in favor of more electives, as computing evolves as a discipline. This paper details an ACM 2013 curriculum exemplar course that interleaves not only three knowledge areas, but also object-oriented and design pattern practices, with foundations for specification and analytical reasoning. The experimentation with the course over 5 years has shown that the combination is effective in achieving student learning goals.

Table 3: Consistent Project Averages across Topics

	Instr. A (Fall '12)	Instr. B (Fall '12)	Instr. C (Spr '13)	Instr. B (Spr '13)	Instr. C (Fall '13)	Instr. B (Fall '13)
A1: SDF(AD), SDF (DM), PL(OOP)	83	82	89	80	78	63
A2: SDF(FDS), SDF(DM), PL(OOP), SE(FM)	75	82	96	93	87	81
A3: SE(SD), PL(BTS)	82	97	98	94	N/A	N/A
A4*: PL(OOP), PL(BTS), SE(SD)	100	100	100	100	97	100

6. ACKNOWLEDGMENTS

This research was funded in part by the NSF grants CCF-1161916, CNS-0745846, DUE-1022191, and DUE-1022941.

7. REFERENCES

[1] IEEE/ACM Computer Science Curricula 2013, Ironman Draft V1, 2013.

[2] Gries, D., Marion, B., Henderson, P., Schwartz, D., "Panel: How Mathematical Thinking Enhances Computer Science Problem Solving," *Procs. 32nd ACM SIGCSE*, 2001.

[3] Krone, J., Baldwin, D., Carver, J. C., Hollingsworth, J. E., Kumar, A., and Sitaraman, M., "Panel: Teaching Mathematical Reasoning across the Curriculum," *Procs. 43rd ACM SIGCSE Conference*, March 2012.

[4] Sitaraman, M., Hallstrom, J.O., White, J., Drachova-Strang, S., Harton, H., Leonard, D., Krone, J., and Pak, R. "Engaging students in specification and reasoning: 'hands-on' experimentation and evaluation," *ACM SIGCSE ITiCSE*, 2009, 50-54

[5] Drachova, S.V., *Teaching and Assessment of Mathematical Principles for Software Correctness Using a Reasoning Concept Inventory*, Ph.D. Thesis, Clemson University, 2013.

[6] Hallstrom, J. O., www.cs.clemson.edu/~jasonoh/courses/cpsc_215_fall_2012, 2012.

[7] Gamma, E., Helm, R., Johnson, R., Vlissides, J., *Design Patterns: Elements of Reusable Object-Oriented Software*, Addison-Wesley, 1994.

[8] Cook, C.T., Drachova, S., Hallstrom, J.O., Hollingsworth, J., Jacobs, J.P., Krone, J., and Sitaraman, M., "A Systematic Approach to Teaching Abstraction and Mathematical Modeling." *Procs. ACM SIGCSE ITiCSE*, 2012.

[9] Leonard, D.P., Hallstrom, J.O., and Sitaraman, M., "Injecting Rapid Feedback and Collaborative Reasoning in Teaching Specifications," *Procs. 40th ACM SIGCSE*, 2009.

[10] Heym, W. D., *Computer Program Verification: Improvements for Human Reasoning*, Ph.D. Thesis, Ohio State University, 1995.

[11] Hollingsworth, J.H., SIGCSE Workshop 2012 Instructional Video Series. www.cs.clemson.edu/group/resolve/teaching/ed_ws/sigcse2012/.

Measuring Demographics and Performance in Computer Science Education at a Nationwide Scale Using AP CS Data

Barbara Ericson
Georgia Tech
College of Computing
801 Atlantic Drive
Atlanta, Georgia 30033-0280 USA
ericson@cc.gatech.edu

Mark Guzdial
Georgia Tech
School of Interactive Computing
85 5th Drive NW
Atlanta, Georgia 30033-0760 USA
guzdial@cc.gatech.edu

ABSTRACT

We examine the current state of computing education in the United States, in order to be able to identify problems in diversity and performance. Data on computing education are difficult to come by, since computer science courses are not tracked in US public education systems. By using a large and nationwide quantitative data source, we can gain new insights into who is participating in computing education, where the greatest need is, and what factors explain the variance between states. We used data from the Advanced Placement Computer Science A (AP CS A) exam to get a detailed view of the demographics of who is taking the exam across the United States and in each state, and how they are performing on the exam. We use economic and census data to provide explanations for some of the AP CS data. We find that minority group involvement is low in AP CS A, but the variance between states in terms of exam-takers is driven by minority group involvement. We find that wealth in a state influences the number of students taking the AP CS A exam, but indirectly.

Categories and Subject Descriptors

K.3.2 [**Computers and Education**]: Computer and Information Science Education — computer science education

Keywords

Assessment,statewide assessment,education pipeline,education pathways,broadening participation, women, under-represented minorities

1. MEASURING WHERE WE ARE

Most researchers in computing education would say that we are not yet where we want to be. We would like computing education to be more generally available to a diverse range of students. Efforts in the United States [2], England [3], and Denmark [4] are all aiming to increase the accessibility of computer science education across their nations. Before we attempt to *increase* accessibility, we ought to find out what the *current* state is. We need a baseline to help us to identify an increase if it happens. We also need to know where we have a lack of accessibility to computing education, in order to focus efforts to improve.

In the study we describe in this paper, we use the data provided by the College Board about the high school (secondary) school students who took the Advanced Placement Computer Science A exam[1]. The AP CS A exam is given across the United States (and in other countries) to students for possible credit or advanced placement (the ability to skip a course) in computer science when they reach post-secondary (college or university) education. Any student can take the exam. High schools in the United States often offer a course to prepare for the exam. To call a course "AP" (a protected trademark of the College Board), a school must submit their syllabus for the course for audit. Each student's exam is scored out of 5, and a score of 3 or above is considered passing (e.g., recommended for credit or placement). The College Board data includes the number of schools who passed the audit, the number of exam-takers, the number of passing students, and aggregated demographic data. We know of no other similar data set on computer science in the United States, nor any comparable data set in other countries.

Examining the AP CS A results can be useful. Some studies have used the AP CS A data to provide insight into what students get wrong and how problems are related [10, 8]. We can also use it to categorize and explore relationships between the variables that the College Board provides. We can gain new information on who is participating in computing education, where the greatest need for reform is, and what factors explain the variance between states. Other efforts to understand the state of computing education differ from ours in focus, in data sources, or in scope.

Probably the best known effort to measure the state of computing education is the Taulbee Survey[2]. Each year, the Computing Research Association surveys computer science departments in the United States who award the PhD

SIGCSE'14, March 5–8, 2014, Atlanta, GA, USA.

http://dx.doi.org/10.1145/2538862.2538918 .

[1]Accessed at http://research.collegeboard.org/programs/ap/data/archived/2012 in August, 2012.
[2]http://cra.org/resources/taulbee/

degree. Their 2011–2012 report from 127 Computer Science departments says that there were 12,171 bachelors (undergraduate) degrees awarded, with 52,396 students currently enrolled. Only 12.9% of those graduating students were female, 4.5% were Black or African-American, and 6.3% were Hispanic (Mexican American, Other Hispanic, and Puerto Rican). The number of Native Americans is very small, and white or Asian males make up the vast majority. Only surveying PhD-granting institutions could skew our understanding of the entire state of computing education which has led to a new effort to survey all US computing departments [6]. Our study differs from the Taulbee Survey in that our focus is on a high school CS course and in that we are getting all exam-takers' data rather than self-reported department data.

There have been two studies at a statewide level of computing education, one in Massachusetts [1] and one in Georgia [7]. These two studies paint a picture of uneven access to computing education across each state, with relatively low participation by women or members of under-represented groups. Both of these studies reported on post-secondary education, with a particular focus in Massachusetts on community colleges.

There have been other efforts to gather data at the high school level. The University of Chicago effort has used surveys to examine the state of computing education teaching and professional development in the United States [5]. The Computer Science Teachers Association conducts an annual survey of CS teachers[3] as well as targeted surveys and research to understand particular aspects of CS teaching [4]. These studies are mostly focused on the teachers.

The most in-depth study of the student experience of high school computer science is the *Stuck in the Shallow End* study and book [9] which described the state of CS education in three schools in the Los Angeles Unified School District (LAUSD). They found that students who are members of under-represented minority groups did not have access to computer science classes, even in schools with a mostly minority population. A variety of factors (from school overcrowding to uninformed administration choices) combined to prevent the minority students from having access to computer science classes. To our knowledge, the LAUSD study has never been replicated in any other school district. We don't know how the findings generalize. Our study is more quantitative than qualitative, so we can offer less depth and breadth of insight, but we can describe a large set of exam-takers.

Our main source of data is the AP CS A data archives from the College Board. We drew on a few other sources of data to help us interpret the AP CS A data. We gathered population data with demographics from the US Census Bureau[5]. These data are based on the 2010 Census to create estimates for 2012. We drew on economic data from the US Bureau of Economic Analysis[6]. We took the personal income per capita in 2012 to serve as a measure of the wealth of the state, ranging from the District of Columbia ($74, 773.00) to Mississippi ($33, 657.00).

[3]See the series at `http://csta.acm.org/Research/sub/HighSchoolSurveys.html`.

[4]`http://csta.acm.org/Research/sub/CSTAResearch.html`

[5]`http://www.census.gov`

[6]`http://www.bea.gov`

In this paper, we aim to answer three major questions:

- Who takes the AP CS A exam in the United States and what is their performance? We look at the national level, and contrast it with the AP Calculus AB exam data. We then look at all 50 states, and consider especially the participation of under-represented minorities.

- How has participation changed? We choose a sample of six states and look at their details between 2006–2012.

- What variables may be influencing exam-taking?

2. THE NATIONAL PICTURE

Across the United States, 24,782 students took the AP CS A exam in 2012. This was a 14.7% increase from the previous year. The number of schools who passed the audit was 2,103 (averaging 11 students for each school passing the audit). The number of female exam takers was 4,635 (18.7% of all exam takers) which was up from 4,000 the year before. The number of Blacks was 1,014 up from 893 the previous year. The number of Hispanics was 1,919 up from 1,752 the previous year. To determine the number of Hispanics we are combining the College Board categories of Mexican American, Other Hispanic, and Puerto Rican.

However, as a percentage of participation and in terms of success (pass-rates), females and under-represented minority groups did not fare well in 2012. The percentage of exam-takers who were female (18.7%) was lower than the previous year (18.9%) . The overall pass rate was 63.2%. The female pass rate was 56.4%. The Hispanic pass rate was 39.8%. The Black pass rate was 27.3%. In contrast, the white pass rate was 66.4%, and the Asian pass rate was 69.9%.

How many of these findings are due to being an "AP" versus being "CS A"? We contrast the AP CS A exam results for the AP Calculus AB results for 2012. AP Calculus AB is also a STEM (Science, Technology, Engineering, and Mathematics) subject. While much larger, it serves as a benchmark. There were 256,163 AP Calculus AB exam-takers in 2012 (over ten times the number of AP CS A exam-takers).

- On average for each school passing the audit, there were 21 students who took AP Calculus AB, but only 11 for CS A.

- The number of schools that teach Calculus is 11,694 versus 2,103 for AP CS A

- AP CS A actually had a higher pass rate than Calculus – 63% versus 59%

- The pass rates for females and Hispanics are slightly better for AP CS A than Calculus, but very similar: for females 56% (CS) versus 55% (Calculus) and for Hispanics 39.8% (CS) versus 38.4% (Calculus). AP Calculus had a slightly higher Black pass rate than CS, 28.7% (Calculus) versus 27.3% (CS).

- Calculus had a higher percentage of under-represented groups take the exam than CS: for females 48.3% (Calculus) versus 18.7% (CS), for Black students 5.4% versus 4.0%, and for Hispanic students 11.5% versus 7.7%.

Figure 1: Histograms describing (a) the number of schools passing the audit over the population (measured in 10K), (b) number of exam-takers over the population, and (c) percentage of exam-takers who passed.

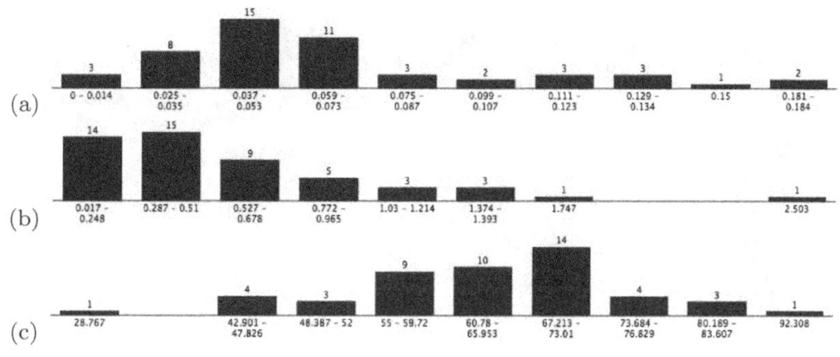

To describe the entire data set, we use histograms with ten bins each (uniformly distributed across the range) for three demographic variables (Figure 1). The range of population is large in the United States (from over 38 million in California, to 576 thousand in Wyoming). The number of schools that passed audit (histogram a), divided by the population (in tens of thousands), has its peak far to the left. The two states in the rightmost bin (Maine and Maryland) have 24 and 108 schools passing audit, respectively. The three states in the leftmost bin (Montana, Mississippi, and North Dakota) have 0, 2, and 1 schools passing audit, respectively. The number of exam-takers over the population (per ten thousand) (histogram b) is even more left-shifted with Maryland far ahead, and Virginia second. The pass rate per state (histogram c) is more normally distributed, with Arkansas in the leftmost bin and Alaska in the rightmost bin. Wyoming and Montana are not represented in this histogram, since the College Board does not report pass rates when a demographic category has fewer than five exam-takers, and Wyoming and Montana had 1 and 3 exam-takers (respectively) in the whole state.

Figure 2 describes three demographic variables associated with under-represented groups in computer science. The percent of female exam-takers per state (histogram d) is fairly uniform, but all are far less than the female share of the population (roughly 50%). The highest percentage is Tennessee with 31% of exam-takers being female. For Black and Hispanic exam-takers, the percentage share in the population varies by state, so we report the *number* of exam takers. The number of Black exam-takers (histogram e) is far left-shifted, with less than 14 Black exam-takers in most (37) states. The three states in the rightmost bin are Maryland, Texas, and Georgia with 144, 142, and 137 Black exam-takers, respectively. (The three states with the largest Black population are Mississippi, Louisiana, and Georgia.) The number of Hispanic exam-takers (histogram f) is similarly left-shifted with fewer than 56 Hispanic exam-takers in 44 states. The state in the rightmost bin is Texas, with California and Florida next, which are the states with the largest Hispanic population. Overall, the United States is 13.1% Black (with a wide range, e.g., 6.6% in California and 31.2% in Georgia). Overall, the United States is 16.9% Hispanic (with another wide range, e.g. 4.1% in Alabama and 38.2% in Texas).

Table 1: 2012 Population and Demographic Data for Sample States

State	Population	% Black	%Hispanic
California	38,041,430	6.6%	38.2%
Georgia	9,919,945	31.2%	9.2%
Indiana	6,537,334	9.4%	6.3%
Maryland	5,884,563	30.0%	8.7%
Massachusetts	6,646,144	7.9%	10.1%
Michigan	9,883,360	14.3%	4.6%

3. A SAMPLE OF STATES OVER TIME

To look at the demographics of exam-takers over time, we chose a sample of six out of the 50 states. We chose Georgia and Massachusetts because both states received NSF funding for statewide alliances to improve computing education in 2006–2007 [7, 1], which gives us the chance to see the impact of an intervention on AP CS A exam-taking data. We chose Michigan and Indiana because of their similarity in population to Georgia and Massachusetts, respectively. We chose California (as the largest state with the most exam-takers) and Maryland (as one of the best-performing AP CS A states), to be a best-case comparison (Table 1)[7].

The graph of exam-taking over time in the six sample states appears in Figure 3. In general, all six lines are on an upward slope which indicates that AP CS A exam-taking has been increasing in these states. We also see a marked difference in Georgia and Massachusetts compared to Indiana and Michigan. Maryland and California are growing even faster. Maryland's results are particularly notable since it's the smallest state in our sample, with a large minority population.

Table 2 summarizes the demographic data for the states. For each of female, Black, and Hispanic groups, we list the number of exam-takers by year, the percentage of students in that category over all exam-takers, and the percentage of those exam-takers who received a 3 or better[8]. In no state in our sample has the percentage of female students taking the exam exceeded 25% in the last six years. Black

[7]All of these data, plus several other states, are available in spreadsheets at `http://coweb.cc.gatech.edu/ice-gt`

[8]Hispanic data combines three categories. If any of those categories received a College Board asterisk, we report the minimum pass rate with an asterisk. At least that many passed, but it could be higher.

Figure 2: Histograms describing (d) the *percent* of female exam-takers, (e) the *number* of Black exam-takers, and (f) the *number* of Hispanic exam-takers.

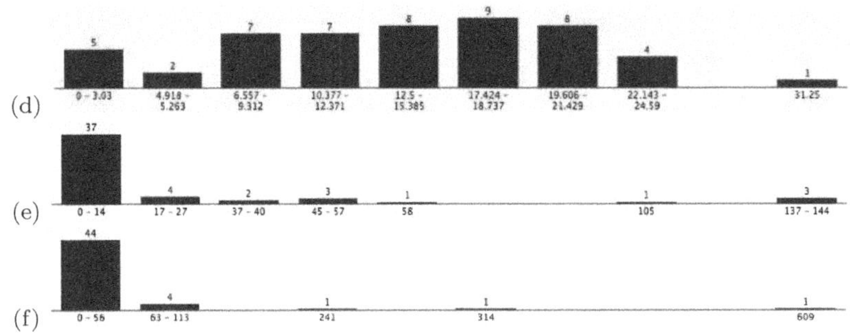

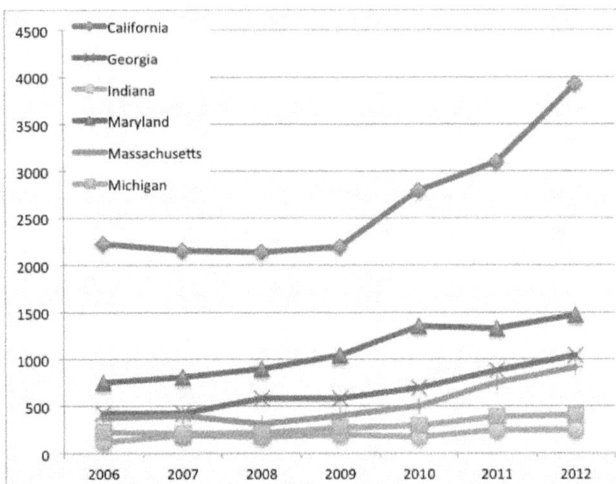

Figure 3: Graph of AP CS A exam-takers over time in sample states.

exam-takers percentage is far less than the Black share of the population in the states. In Michigan and Indiana, which are 14.3% and 9.4% Black respectively, the percentage of Black exam-takers has never exceeded 3%. The percentage of Hispanic students among all exam-takers is closest to the population share in Michigan. The percentage of Hispanic students taking the exam is highest in California (at most, 9.44%), but California's population is 38% Hispanic.

The pass rates vary between states, in part because of few exam-takers in a category. Recall that each asterisk in Table 2 indicates a category where there were less than five exam-takers in the entire state in that demographic group. The number of Black students who earned a passing score in Michigan certainly totals less than 15 over the last six years, and may be zero in Indiana. Georgia and Maryland both do well in terms of number of Black exam-takers (e.g., double-digit percentage Black), but the pass rates are poor – 16% in Georgia and 17.5% in Maryland in 2012. It's useful to compare these results with other states. Washington (Black population 3.9%) had the highest pass rate for Black students at 60%, but that was only 6 of 10 exam-takers. Texas (Black population 12.3%) had the most Black exam-takers pass the exam at 52 (out of 142). Nine states had no Hispanic students take the exam in 2012, even some states with significant Hispanic populations, e.g., Hawaii (9.5%) and Kansas (11%).

4. INFLUENCES ON EXAM-TAKING

We used regression analysis to explore relationships between the variables that influence exam-taking. We looked into two sets of relationships. We looked at wealth and exam-taking, and we looked at the number of exam-takers from under-represented groups in order to look for an explanation for the variance between states.

Socio-economic status influences education outcomes generally [11]. The *Stuck in the Shallow End* study [9] found higher-quality computer science classes in the wealthiest school they studied. However, we know of no previous study looking into a quantitative relationship between wealth and participation in computer science education.

Overall, wealth in a state has an impact on the number of exam-takers, but indirectly. We compared a standard score (*z-score*) for the personal income per capita and population variables (number minus mean, over standard deviation). The total number of exam-takers is not correlated with personal income per capita z-score (Fisher, $p = 0.192$). We constructed a regression analysis using the predictors of the number of schools passing the audit, population z-score, and personal income per capita z-score, with the outcome variable of exam-takers ($R^2 = 0.933$, Table 3). With $p = 0.064$, the per capita personal income z-score is not a significant influence. However, the number of schools passing the audit over the population is positively correlated with the per capita personal income z-score (Fisher, $p < 0.001$). A regression analysis with an outcome variable of the number of schools over the population and an income variable of the per capita personal income z-score explains 23.6% of the variance between states ($R^2 = 0.236$, coefficient 0.021, standard error 0.005, $p < 0.001$).

These results suggest that wealth does not directly drive the number of exam-takers. Personal income per capita predicts the number of schools passing the audit. The number of schools passing the audit strongly influences the number of exam-takers. Wealth creates the opportunity to take AP CS (increases the number of schools passing the audit), and the opportunity combined with a larger population results in more exam-takers.

The total number of exam-takers is positively correlated with the number of female, Black, and Hispanic exam-takers

Table 2: Historical Demographic for Sample States

State	Year	# Female	% Female	% Female Passing	# Black	% Black	% Black Passing	# Hispanic	% Hispanic	% Hispanic Passing
California	2006	452	20.32	51.77	45	2.02	37.78	168	7.55	30.36*
	2007	463	21.52	50.54	37	1.72	27.03	194	9.02	25.26
	2008	441	20.66	55.78	27	1.26	44.44	199	9.32	29.15*
	2009	458	20.88	59.83	30	1.37	40.00	207	9.44	33.82
	2010	582	20.84	61.86	33	1.18	60.61	217	7.77	40.55*
	2011	659	21.25	65.10	29	0.94	51.72	230	7.42	43.91*
	2012	833	21.25	66.39	45	1.15	48.89	314	8.01	43.31
Georgia	2006	93	21.78	22.58	67	15.69	2.99	14	3.28	21.43*
	2007	68	16.11	30.88	40	9.48	22.50	13	3.08	23.08*
	2008	108	18.46	32.41	84	14.36	10.71	22	3.76	31.82*
	2009	110	18.87	46.36	69	11.84	10.14	27	4.63	40.74*
	2010	118	17.05	48.31	68	9.83	23.53	30	4.34	30.00*
	2011	154	17.42	45.45	79	8.94	21.52	54	6.11	38.89
	2012	190	18.32	34.74	137	13.21	16.06	56	5.40	37.50*
Indiana	2006	15	12.50	73.33	1	0.83	*	2	1.67	*
	2007	22	11.64	72.73	3	1.59	*	1	0.53	*
	2008	9	5.06	88.89	3	1.69	*	2	1.12	*
	2009	35	17.59	71.43	2	1.01	*	7	3.52	85.71
	2010	21	11.80	66.67	3	1.69	*	1	0.56	*
	2011	34	13.71	55.88	3	1.21	*	6	2.42	*
	2012	23	9.31	56.52	5	2.02	*	8	3.24	*
Maryland	2006	119	15.82	63.87	67	8.91	34.33	26	3.46	15.38*
	2007	152	18.81	44.08	114	14.11	11.40	27	3.34	29.63*
	2008	138	15.42	51.45	74	8.27	36.49	26	2.91	38.46
	2009	205	19.75	59.51	120	11.56	21.67	34	3.28	38.24*
	2010	305	22.56	52.13	190	14.05	17.89	52	3.85	48.08
	2011	297	22.33	56.90	174	13.08	24.71	62	4.66	43.55*
	2012	276	18.74	58.33	144	9.78	24.31	63	4.28	39.68
Massachusetts	2006	65	17.29	53.85	13	3.46	7.69	10	2.66	30.00*
	2007	54	13.57	53.70	4	1.01	*	9	2.26	*
	2008	41	13.10	78.05	3	0.96	*	15	4.79	26.67*
	2009	73	18.25	58.90	11	2.75	54.55	15	3.75	20.00*
	2010	69	13.72	65.22	13	2.58	23.08	32	4.37	25.00*
	2011	140	18.67	59.29	33	4.40	24.24	32	4.27	40.63*
	2012	179	19.61	49.72	40	4.38	17.50	50	5.48	34.00*
Michigan	2006	37	16.74	67.57	2	0.90	*	4	1.81	*
	2007	32	15.24	65.63	5	2.38	0.00	3	1.43	*
	2008	32	15.02	68.75	2	0.94	*	1	0.47	*
	2009	55	20.45	87.27	6	2.23	33.33	9	3.35	*
	2010	57	19.06	70.18	3	1.00	*	7	2.34	*
	2011	74	19.02	89.19	2	0.51	*	10	2.57	100.00
	2012	61	14.88	83.61	7	1.71	57.14	5	1.22	*

Table 3: Regression coefficients table for outcome variable number of AP CS A exam-takers in 2012 ($R^2 = 0.933$)

Input Variable	Coefficient	Std Err	t	p
# Schools	7.856	1.175	6.688	0.000
PopZScore	372.417	62.064	6.001	0.000
PerCapitaZScore	59.952	31.643	1.895	0.064
constant	151.187	58.092	2.603	0.012

(all three using Fisher, $p < 0.001$). The exam-takers distribution is also positively correlated with female, Black, and Hispanic exam-takers (all Fisher, $p < 0.001$). The number of students who passed is similarly positively correlated with the number of female students who passed, Black students who passed, and Hispanic students who passed. We built a regression model with an outcome variable of the total number of exam-takers with predictor variables of the number of female, Black, and Hispanic exam-takers has an $R^2 = 0.989$ (Table 4). This model suggests that increasing the number of exam-takers among these under-represented groups has a significant impact on the number of exam-takers overall. If you want to increase your state's AP CS exam-taking, focus on the under-represented groups.

Table 4: Regression coefficients table with an outcome variable of number of 2012 AP CS A exam-takers with inputs of number of students from under-represented groups ($R^2 = 0.989$)

Input Variable	Coefficient	Std Err	t	p
# female	5.17	0.17	29.70	0.00
# Black	1.16	0.46	2.50	0.02
# Hispanic	-1.39	0.29	-4.76	0.00
constant	45.98	13.86	3.32	0.00

These results are suggestive but not conclusive. Income is influenced by population in a state, which creates an interaction. The high values of R^2 may suggest additional underlying variables and interactions between these variables, which might be teased out with a more sophisticated multiple linear regression analysis. The mechanisms underlying the regression models described here are still to be explored. A state's wealth may influence the number of schools passing the audit, but we don't know why. For example, is it that wealthier states value computer science more, or do wealthier states have the resources for more elective courses like computer science? It's also unclear why the number of Hispanic exam-takers has a negative coefficient in that last regression model, despite having a positive correlation on its own. Most likely, there are unexplained interactions between the input variables.

5. CONCLUSIONS

The analyses presented in this paper give us a snapshot of the state of computing education in the United States. Overall, this paper describes the current state, against which future progress in US high school computer science education can be measured.

- *Who takes the AP CS A exam?* While the number of AP CS A exam-takers is growing, the majority of exam-takers are still white or Asian males. The participation rate of under-represented groups is less than in AP Calculus AB. The rates of participation among female, Black, and Hispanic students is quite low (compared to share of the population) in most states.

- *The Quality of AP CS A teaching*: As measured by pass rates, AP CS A teachers are doing well. Our pass rates overall are higher than AP Calculus. Students from under-represented groups actually pass the AP CS A exam at a slightly higher rate than in Calculus. Our *yield* (the number of test-takers per school) is low in AP CS, so an easy way to increase the number of exam takers is to increase the number of students per teacher.

- *How to increase the number of AP CS A exam takers*: Our regression model suggests that growth in exam-taking among female, Black, and Hispanic students accounts for much of the variation in the distribution of exam-taking between states. If you want more AP CS A exam takers, the focus should be on the under-represented groups. Wealth also seems to influence AP CS A exam-taking, but indirectly, through the number of schools offering AP CS A classes. Having more access (e.g., more schools offering AP CS A) is the most direct way of growing the number of AP CS A exam-takers – short of increasing the population or increasing the personal wealth in the state.

6. ACKNOWLEDGMENTS

Our thanks to Tom McKlin, Kevin Karplus, Debra Richardson, and our anonymous reviewers who gave us useful advice on this paper. Our work on this paper was funded by NSF grant #1228352. Any opinions, findings, and conclusions or recommendations expressed in this material are those of the authors and do not necessarily reflect the views of the National Science Foundation.

7. REFERENCES

[1] W. R. Adrion, R. Fall, M. Matos, and A. R. Peterfreund. Integrating evaluation into program development: benefits of baselining a NSF-BPC alliance. In *Proceedings of the 41st ACM technical symposium on Computer science education*, SIGCSE '10, pages 27–31, New York, NY, USA, 2010. ACM.

[2] O. Astrachan, A. Briggs, L. Diaz, and R. B. Osborne. CS principles: Development and evolution of a course and a community. In *Proceeding of the 44th ACM technical symposium on Computer science education*, SIGCSE '13, pages 635–636, New York, NY, USA, 2013. ACM.

[3] N. C. C. Brown, M. Kölling, T. Crick, S. Peyton Jones, S. Humphreys, and S. Sentance. Bringing computer science back into schools: lessons from the UK. In *Proceeding of the 44th ACM technical symposium on Computer science education*, SIGCSE '13, pages 269–274, New York, NY, USA, 2013. ACM.

[4] M. E. Caspersen and P. Nowack. Computational thinking and practice: A generic approach to computing in Danish high schools. In A. Carbone and J. Whalley, editors, *The 15th Australasian Computer Education Conference (ACE 2013)*, Adelaide, South Australia, February 2013. Conferences in Research and Practice in Information Technology (CRPIT).

[5] B. Franke, J. Century, M. Lach, C. Wilson, M. Guzdial, G. Chapman, and O. Astrachan. Expanding access to K-12 computer science education: research on the landscape of computer science professional development. In *Proceeding of the 44th ACM technical symposium on Computer science education*, SIGCSE '13, pages 541–542, New York, NY, USA, 2013. ACM.

[6] M. Goldweber. TAURUS: A "Taulbee survey" for the rest of us. *ACM Inroads*, 2(2):38–42, June 2011.

[7] M. Guzdial, B. Ericson, T. McKlin, and S. Engelman. A statewide survey on computing education pathways and influences: factors in broadening participation in computing. In *Proceedings of the Ninth Annual International Conference on Computing Education Research (ICER'12)*, pages 143–150, New York, NY, 2012. ACM.

[8] C. M. Lewis, H. Khayrallah, and A. Tsai. Mining data from the AP CS A exam: patterns, non-patterns, and replication failure. In *Proceedings of the ninth annual international ACM conference on International computing education research*, ICER '13, pages 115–122, New York, NY, USA, 2013. ACM.

[9] J. Margolis, R. Estrella, J. Goode, J. J. Holme, and K. Nao. *Stuck in the Shallow End: Education, Race, and Computing.* MIT Press, Cambridge, MA, 2008.

[10] S. Reges. The mystery of "b := (b = false)". In *Proceedings of the 39th SIGCSE technical symposium on Computer science education*, SIGCSE '08, pages 21–25, New York, NY, USA, 2008. ACM.

[11] S. Tavernise. Education gap grows between rich and poor, studies say. *New York Times*, February 9 2012.

Blackbox: A Large Scale Repository of Novice Programmers' Activity

Neil C. C. Brown, Michael Kölling, Davin McCall and Ian Utting
School of Computing
University of Kent
Canterbury, Kent, UK
{nccb,mik,dm391,iau}@kent.ac.uk

ABSTRACT

Automatically observing and recording the programming behaviour of novices is an established computing education research technique. However, prior studies have been conducted at a single institution on a small or medium scale, without the possibility of data re-use. Now, the widespread availability of always-on Internet access allows for data collection at a much larger, global scale. In this paper we report on the Blackbox project, begun in June 2013. Blackbox is a perpetual data collection project that collects data from worldwide users of the BlueJ IDE – a programming environment designed for novice programmers. Over one hundred thousand users have already opted-in to Blackbox. The collected data is anonymous and is available to other researchers for use in their own studies, thus benefitting the larger research community. In this paper, we describe the data available via Blackbox, show some examples of analyses that can be performed using the collected data, and discuss some of the analysis challenges that lie ahead.

Categories and Subject Descriptors

K.3.2 [**Computer and Information Science Education**]: Computer science education

General Terms

Experimentation

Keywords

Blackbox, BlueJ, data collection, programming education

1. INTRODUCTION

Learning to program is a central challenge of computing education. As programming is performed on a computer, students' programming behaviour can be automatically monitored – an idea decades old [8]. There have been many prior small and medium scale studies monitoring programming behaviour at single institutions (see section 3), but the widespread availability of Internet access means that large-scale cross-institutional studies can be easily run.

The authors develop and maintain BlueJ, a Java IDE designed for beginners. BlueJ has over 1.5 million users each year, and is used widely in the first year course at universities in many different countries. This paper describes the Blackbox data collection project, which draws participants from the worldwide BlueJ user pool and records their interactions with the IDE and the source code that they write. This project provides gigabytes of collected source code, which we are making available to other researchers to benefit the computing education research community. This is not a single completed *study*; rather, it is a perpetual *data collection project* that will continue collecting data and serve as a basis for a potentially wide variety of future studies.

This paper is split into two halves. In the first half, we look at the background of BlueJ and data collection projects (sections 2 and 3), then examine the research issues of the Blackbox project (section 4) and present design decisions and initial outcomes (section 5). In the second half, we show some small examples of the analyses that can be performed with the Blackbox data (section 6), before offering discussion on the challenges in analysing this kind of data (section 7). Our contributions include:

- A discussion of research and analysis issues surrounding projects of this type (sections 4 and 7).
- Initial outcome statistics for the project (section 5).
- Several small analyses, including a replication of previous results (section 6).
- Information for other research groups on how to gain access to this data set for their own research projects.

2. BLUEJ

BlueJ is a programming environment designed to be used by those learning object-oriented programming in Java. It was first released in 1999, and now has a large worldwide user base. In 2012, BlueJ was invoked at least 15 million times, by a total of over 1.8 million users; whenever BlueJ is loaded, it attempts to make a brief one-off connection to a central server (which we term a "phone-home") to report the BlueJ version, Java version, and OS version. This connection will not always be successful; users may temporarily or permanently lack Internet access or have firewalls (on their

SIGCSE'14, March 5–8, 2014, Atlanta, GA, USA.

http://dx.doi.org/10.1145/2538862.2538924.

machine, local network, or whole country) that prevent the connection. Therefore this number only gives a lower bound on the total amount of BlueJ use – but, pertinent to this paper, it gives an accurate reflection of the number of BlueJ users where BlueJ can connect to a remote server.

3. PRIOR WORK

There have been many studies, using many approaches, of students' behaviour in introductory programming classes. Here we will restrict ourselves to discussing those that focused on their interactions with their programming environment, and the resulting program source code.

Thomas et al [9] recorded 4.7 million actions over a six-week period in 2003 from 141 students using an Ada IDE, but these were very low-level events (such as mouse clicks and key presses, captured from the GUI framework) and data-cleaning proved to be a significant problem, although they did also establish the viability of using such data to answer questions formulated after the data was gathered.

In 2005, Ahmadzadeh et al [2] collected much coarser-grained data (including source code) from 192 students in the School of CS & IT at the University of Nottingham, mostly focused on compilation errors encountered by students whilst using the JCreator environment.

Edwards et al [4] collected result-focused data from 1101 students over a five-year period. The data gathered was students' work-in-progress as they submitted their evolving programs for testing by, and feedback from, the Web-CAT tool. They eventually captured 89,879 submissions from two courses using Java and one using C++.

Jadud [6] and Fenwick et al [5] have recently used bespoke extensions to the BlueJ IDE to capture student interactions at an intermediate granularity, capturing Java compiler input and output at every invocation. Jadud captured 42,000 events from 186 students over two years, and Fenwick et al captured 55,000 from 110 students in a single year.

The questions addressed by these studies have ranged from compilation and editing behaviour to time-on-task. In all cases except Thomas et al, the particular research questions to be addressed were part of the design of the data-gathering apparatus, but in many cases the data proved amenable for use in answering other questions which became apparent only after the data had been gathered. Some of the studies have recorded very large numbers of events, some have involved reasonably large numbers of students, but all published cases involved students at a single institution. The Blackbox data differs from these prior studies in several ways, but two are particularly significant: the amount of students involved (and data collected) is larger by several orders of magnitude, and the data is shared with other researchers.

There has also been much work in the analysis of large bodies of program code, e.g. the Mining Software Repositories conference [1], but it is primarily focused on professional or open source repositories at each commit, rather than learners' behaviour at each edit and compilation.

4. RESEARCH ISSUES

The technical challenges of the Blackbox project are fairly straightforward and well understood. The more difficult issues relate to the ethical and research design side of the project; in this section we will explain the pertinent issues.

4.1 Identifiable Data

We wanted to ensure that participants would suffer no negative consequences from participating in the data collection. We could have asked participants demographic information (age, level of experience, etc)[1], but collecting this data places a responsibility on us to safeguard the data, allow individual withdrawal from the study and so on. Managing this for hundreds of thousands of users seemed untenable. Thus we made the decision to keep the data anonymous, as described in the next section.

It is possible for individual researchers to configure Blackbox to identify their own students for the purpose of a study, or to extend the data collected to include identifiable or demographic information – this is discussed in section 4.6.

4.2 Anonymisation

The two main places where identifiable information might be found in the collected data are the local path to the project and the source code.

Paths to BlueJ projects often feature an identifying username, either locally (`C:\Users\john\Documents\proj1`), or on a university network (`\\store\js123\proj2`). To mitigate this, the client transmits only the last directory in the path (above, `proj1` and `proj2`) and a hash of the full path. This allows the same project to be identified across sessions, but stops the identifying paths from being sent to the server.

Anonymising source code is a difficult challenge. Identifying information can appear in comments, string literals, and even names of variables and methods. Strong anonymisation could be achieved by blanking all comments, strings, and by renaming all variables and methods (e.g. by hashing). However, this loses much useful information; the names of methods (e.g. getHeight) can convey information, comments can be useful for analysis and so on. Therefore, Blackbox removes only the comment that occurs before a class header. This is where author names are usually entered, so this should reasonably anonymise the code without losing other useful context. We explain in the information to participants that this level of anonymisation will take place.

4.3 Data Design

One difficulty with the Blackbox project was deciding exactly which data to collect. While many studies collect data with a single analysis in mind, the Blackbox project is intended to support many different researchers for different purposes (much like a census). In an attempt to ensure that the data collected by the Blackbox project was useable by other researchers, we sought to engage interested parties at the SIGCSE 2012 [7] and ICER 2012 [11] conferences to ask for feedback on our design.

The initial design was primarily guided by the features of the BlueJ IDE, and this was then refined based on feedback received during these sessions (e.g. we now collect more fine-grained editing data than initially envisaged). We were keen to pick the right level of granularity for data collection. We believed that collecting data at a very low level (e.g. click-streams, with data on mouse movements and exact keypresses) would be too voluminous and too difficult to analyse. Instead, we work at a higher level, recording line-edits to source code, and IDE actions rather than the mouse/key movements that triggered them.

[1]Although there would have been little motivation for participants to supply this information accurately.

4.4 Data collected

The data collected for the Blackbox project includes the following:

- A persistent unique identifier, which is assigned on opting in and persists across sessions, allowing some longitudinal analyses.
- Start and end times of programming sessions.
- Use of all IDE tools, such as editing, compiling, execution, instantiation of objects, interactive method invocations, runs of unit tests, use of the debugger, use of source repositories, use of the codepad, etc. In all cases, event records include time stamps and relevant details (e.g. method invocations include parameters and return values, compilation events include compilation outcomes/errors, unit test runs include test results).
- Editing behaviour. This is collected at source line level: every time a user edits a line of code and the cursor then leaves that line, an edit event is recorded. Multiple consecutive character edits within the same line are thus collapsed into a single event.
- An optional experiment and participant identifier – see section 4.6.

4.5 Data Caveats

Although the Blackbox data is large scale, there are various notable restrictions in its utility. One obvious restriction is that the data specifically concerns using Java within BlueJ. BlueJ is often taught in an objects-first way, eschewing Java's `main` method. Thus it is a biased subset of the ways in which Java is taught. Another obvious restriction is that we do not know what the user was intending to do (e.g. their current task) or their thought processes at the time; we can only observe the resulting changes to the source code.

The data in Blackbox comes with a persistent unique identifier (a randomly assigned ID for each participant) but no further identifying information. It is possible to track a user longitudinally, but nothing will be known about that user. They may have years of Java experience and be using BlueJ for prototyping, they may be an instructor preparing materials for a lecture, or they may be a beginner who has never programmed before. We believe that the latter is the most prevalent case, but there is no way to confirm this for an individual user from the data. Instead we must rely on heuristics; for example, it may be reasonable to assume that a user who is seen first in September and never again after the following December/January was taking a single-semester Java course. In contrast, a user seen over the course of several years is likely to be an instructor.

The user tracking in BlueJ uses an identifier stored in the client's BlueJ profile. If two people use BlueJ on the same machine with the same profile, they will appear as one user. We believe this case is relatively rare, unlike the reverse: if one person uses BlueJ on multiple machines with different profiles (e.g. a home machine, a laptop and a university machine), they will appear as multiple users. There is no simple way to track this. Instead, they must be viewed as multiple users with gaps in their history. Most users are likely to have some gaps in their data recording history, due to switching machines, or their Internet connection breaking during a BlueJ session and so on. Most gaps can be identified by comparing the state of a project's source code between the end of one session and beginning of the next.

4.6 Local studies and demographics

Blackbox supports local and extended studies in two different ways. The first use case is a researcher who wishes to perform a study only on their home students. For this purpose, an experiment identifier can be generated and added to the configuration information in BlueJ. This identifier can be added by an administrator for a complete installation (e.g. all machines at an institution), or individually by a BlueJ user. Using this identifier, researchers can then identify users from only their own experiment. Experiment identifiers cannot be extracted from the database and are effectively non-guessable, so researchers cannot identify students from other institutions.

The second use case is a researcher who wishes to collect demographic or personal data about their subjects, for example to relate programming behaviour to prior experience, age, gender, etc. For this purpose, a participant identifier can be set in the Blackbox configuration. A researcher could generate participant identifiers and ask students to enter these in their BlueJ preferences. The researcher could then use the same identifiers to collect additional data relating to demographic or personal information.

It is worth emphasising that in this case the researcher is responsible for obtaining ethics approval for that study, obtaining participant consent and safeguarding the data. This extra data is not send to Blackbox, and no personal information is stored on the Blackbox servers at any time.

5. INITIAL OUTCOMES

The Blackbox project went live on 11 June 2013. BlueJ version 3.1.0 was released at that point, and the first time each user loaded it, they were presented with a dialog asking them to opt-in to the Blackbox project. Whether the user opted-in or not, the dialog is never shown again unless they explicitly invoke it via the program options.

5.1 Opt-in Rate and User Numbers

As mentioned previously, when BlueJ loads it "phones home" to a central server. By dividing the total sessions recorded in Blackbox by the number of phone-homes by BlueJ 3.1.0, we can form an opt-in rate for a given time period. After November 2013, the average daily opt-in rate is 42% (min: 37%, max: 48%). Nearly six months after launch we have a total of over 150,000 users participating in the Blackbox project, with over 10,000,000 compilation events. Based on current total BlueJ user numbers, version adoption rates and opt-in rate, we expect that during 2014, the number of users included in the data collection will be over 500,000, with over 100 million compilation events.

5.2 Infrastructure

The Blackbox server and database are supported by two machines running Ubuntu Linux. Each machine has two hyper-threaded 6-core 2.5Ghz Xeon processors with 32GB of RAM and four 2TB drives set up in RAID 5 configuration. The first machine, named *black*, holds a write-only version of the Blackbox database and collects all incoming data. This database is live-mirrored to a second machine, named *white*, where the database copy is read-only. Researchers only have access to the *white* server, ensuring that analysis cannot corrupt the original database. We are very grateful for support by SIGCSE in the form of a SIGCSE Small Grant, which supported part of the cost of these servers.

Error	% of all errors
Unknown variable	16.7
Bracket expected	10.3
Unknown method	10.1
Semicolon expected	10.0
Illegal start of expression	5.0
Unknown class	4.6
Incompatible types	4.0
Method application error	3.5
Private access violation	3.5
Missing return	3.3

Table 1: Top ten most frequent compiler errors from Jadud [6].

Error	% of all errors
Unknown variable	17.7
Semicolon expected	9.5
Unknown method	7.6
Bracket expected	6.5
Unknown class	5.3
Incompatible types	4.5
Illegal start of expression	4.4
Method application error	3.7
Identifier expected	3.6
Not a statement	3.0

Table 2: Top ten most frequent compiler errors from Blackbox, to 2013-12-01 (excl).

6. EXAMPLE ANALYSES

In this section, we will give some small examples of the kinds of analysis that are possible with the Blackbox data. All the results presented in this section are from the Blackbox data set up to 2013-12-01 (exclusive). The source code for these analyses is openly available at: `http://www.cs.kent.ac.uk/~nccb/blackbox/`.

6.1 Error Count Replication

One example of similar prior work is that of Jadud [6]. In his thesis, Jadud gives a table of error frequencies; the top ten are repeated here in table 1

We replicated this analysis, to compare the frequencies in our own larger data set. One complication is that Jadud used the Java compiler's error message to classify the errors. These errors are not guaranteed to be stable across Java compiler versions, and thus we encountered several new messages in our data (e.g. "reached end of file while parsing") that are partial reclassifications of previous errors (e.g. "'}' expected"). This problem notwithstanding[2], our results, given in table 2, were broadly similar to those of Jadud.

Jadud's data had around 70,000 compiler errors to process, collected over two years. Our Blackbox data set, collected over nearly six months to 2013-12-01 (exclusive), has over 5,000,000 compiler errors. More generally, the larger sample sizes available in the Blackbox data will allow us to replicate and verify findings from previous smaller-scale studies.

[2]We hope to address this issue in our future work, by producing stable classifications of errors that are independent of compiler error messages.

```
System.out.println("Ingrese los numeros");
Scanner teclado = new Scanner(System.in);
int numero1 = teclado.nextInt();
int numero2 = teclado.nextInt();
if (numero1 > numero2) {
   // ...
}
if (numero1 < numero2); {
   // ...
}
```

Figure 1: An example of an empty if; note the semicolon on the final if.

6.2 Empty If Statements

When beginners learn Java, they must also learn the syntax. In our personal experience of teaching and delivering workshops, we have found that some beginners learn to put a semicolon at the end of *every* line they write. However, this can lead to a problem with constructs such as if-statements. For example, a student might write:

```
if (x < 5);
{
     x = 5;
}
```

The semicolon at the end of the first line is counted as a single empty statement, which acts as the body of the if-statement. This means that the first line has no effect, and the body (assigning 5 to x) is executed regardless. This error is particularly pernicious, because it is valid Java code and does not cause a compile error, so the user gets no explicit feedback about the problem. It also forms a useful test case, because it can be easily detected through automatic analysis.

We believe it is safe to assume that an if-statement, with no else clause, that has such an empty body is always a mistake by the programmer. The if-statement is redundant if there is no body and no else – and even if there is a side effect (e.g. if (x++ < 5);) then the same effect could be achieved with a normal statement (e.g. x++). We provide a real example from the Blackbox data in figure 1.

Our experience of the error is personal and anecdotal. We have two questions to investigate this error more rigorously:

1. How prevalent is this mistake?
2. How long does it take before the user fixes the mistake?

With the Blackbox data, the method is straightforward. We scan all successful compilations for the first occurrence of this mistake in a source file, then scan forwards in time, to see how many further successful compilations the user makes before this mistake is no longer present in the file.

Searching 1085598 different source files that had been successfully compiled at least once (average: 6.0 times), we found a total of 2647 source files containing these empty if statements. In 1513 cases, these empty ifs were later removed; the number of subsequent successful compilations that were performed before the empty if was removed are shown in figure 2. The results are clearly a power law, and most are immediately fixed, although note that some empty if statements were not fixed before more than 16 compilations. In the case of the other 1134 empty ifs: they were not fixed at all, and some were present for over 20 subsequent successful compilations.

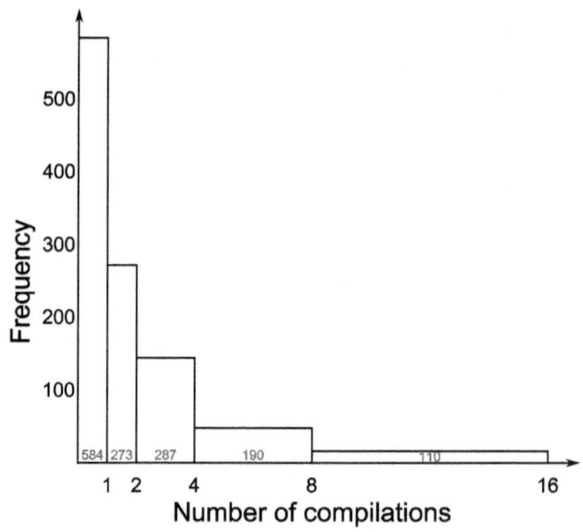

Figure 2: The number of successful compilations before an empty if was removed. For example, 584 empty ifs were removed during the next compilation (i.e. after 1 further successful compilation). A further 69 (not shown here) were removed after more than 16 further successful compilations.

This analysis demonstrates a small example of the sorts of scalable source code analysis that are possible on the Blackbox data set. More in-depth analyses could be performed that look for certain idioms or patterns in students' programs, or the use of certain programming constructs such as inheritance or recursion.

6.3 Tracking User Behaviour

Many students using BlueJ also use the BlueJ 'Objects First' textbook [3] for their course. The textbook is accompanied by a series of starting projects around which the book's exercises are based. By identifying this source code verbatim in the data, we can observe what the Blackbox users do with these projects. For example, the earliest code-writing exercises in the book are reproduced in figure 3, and the starting state of the source code is given in figure 4. We found 1491 users who opened this project and observed their next changes at subsequent successful compilations:

- 48 users changed line D (the wrong line) to use `"blue"` as the parameter, with 1 encountering a compiler error. 24 of these then made the same change to line B (the correct line).
- 503 users changed line B (the correct line) to use `"blue"` as the parameter, with 9 encountering a compiler error. Of these, 450 continued and:
  - 23 changed `"blue"` back to `"yellow"`, with 1 encountering a compiler error.
  - 67 added `"private Circle sun2;"` after line A, with 13 encountering a compiler error.
- 28 users added `"private Circle sun2;"` after line A, with 6 encountering a compiler error.
- 72 users added `"sun.slowMoveVertical(`*N*`);"` after line C, with 18 encountering a compiler error. 34 users chose 250 pixels as the parameter, and 16 users chose 300.

- **Exercise 1.16** In the source code of class `Picture`, find the part that actually draws the picture. Change it so that the sun will be blue rather than yellow.
- **Exercise 1.17** Add a second sun to the picture. To do this, pay attention to the field definitions close to the top of the class. You will find this code:

```
private Square wall;
private Square window;
private Triangle roof;
private Circle sun;
```

  You need to add a line here for the second sun. For example:

```
private Circle sun2;
```

  Then write the appropriate code for creating the second sun.
- **Exercise 1.18** Challenge exercise... Add a sunset to the single-sun version of Picture. That is: make the sun go down slowly. Remember: The circle has a method `slowMoveVertical` that you can use to do this.

Figure 3: The first code-writing exercises from the BlueJ Objects First textbook, fifth edition [3]. The identical exercises appeared in previous editions, labelled 1.13–1.15.

```
public class Picture
{
    private Square wall;
    private Square window;
    private Triangle roof;
    private Circle sun; // A

    public void draw()
    {
        // ... initialise wall, window, roof

        sun = new Circle();
        sun.changeColor("yellow"); // B
        sun.moveHorizontal(180);
        sun.moveVertical(-(10));
        sun.changeSize(60);
        sun.makeVisible(); // C
    }

    public void setBlackAndWhite() { /* ... */ }

    public void setColor()
    {
        if (wall != null)
            wall.changeColor("red");
        window.changeColor("black");
        roof.changeColor("green");
        sun.changeColor("yellow"); // D
    }
}
```

Figure 4: A slightly condensed version of the original source code of the Picture class from the BlueJ Objects First textbook. Comments added to identify truncations and pertinent lines.

These changes were identified by transforming the source code into a canonical form (an abstract syntax tree) to eliminate whitespace differences, and then combining identical versions and ranking them by frequency. This analysis is simple, but gives an idea of some of the chronological traces that can be identified from the source code, and which may be useful, for example, for designing intelligent tutors (or for improving the flow of the BlueJ textbook!). Significant challenges remain in interpreting (and visualising) the results of such an analysis.

7. CONCLUSIONS

Blackbox is a perpetual data collection project. Its novelty lies in its size and in its availability to others. We gather data from hundreds of thousands BlueJ users all around the world into a single dataset, which other researchers can request access to. So far, researchers from eight other institutions have expressed interest and been provided with access to the data, and we welcome more[3]. Interested researchers should contact the authors for more information.

There remain several potential technical challenges in continuing the project. We must ensure that the server can withstand the load of recording all the data sent to it. We may have to manage changes in the data schema in future, should the need for changes arise. However, the project as it stands is ready for other researchers to access the data and start investigating their research questions.

Although researchers will each be investigating different specific questions, they are likely to share some common questions and requirements, both technical and research. Technically, researchers may need similar tools – for example, we have already created a tool that extracts all compilation inputs from the database and stores them in an easily accessible format. We intend to support the community of Blackbox researchers by providing means of communication (initially: a mailing list) and technical support. We hope that, over time, various researchers will create and share analysis and visualisation tools that ease the analysis of the data and allow others to perform investigations more easily. We also hope that joint discussions will serve to generate ideas and generate a common understanding about the potential and the limitations of the data.

There remain many technical challenges in the automated analysis of source code. The scale of the data does not make the analysis impossible, but it does prevent any manual intervention; any analysis must typically be completely automatic. Many research questions will likely also involve chronological analysis of source code, which adds further complexity. Researchers will likely need to look to tools such as source code query languages [10], and/or build new models to analyse source code development over time.

Although the Blackbox project is one of the first educational research projects to operate at such a large scale, it will surely not be the last. Sites such as MOOCs (Udacity, Coursera, etc), Khan Academy, Codecademy, Scratch 2.0 are already operating at a large scale with some or all data already stored server side (rather than having to be sent to a server specifically, as in BlueJ). For these projects, obtaining the source code data and IDE interactions of users will be even easier than the BlueJ project, and can operate at a similar (or even larger) scale. The MOOC sites may also have (and be willing to use) demographic information about their participants. Analysis techniques for source code are likely to be broadly applicable across several of these code bases, but analysis of IDE interactions may be less portable. It is also important to recognise that although large-scale data is useful for investigating some research questions, it is not a panacea. In some cases it is inappropriate and in other cases it will form a useful complement to other techniques, not replace them.

[3]We restrict access to researchers employed at established research institutions and with a record of interest in computer science education, to prevent misuse of the data. If the data were to become publicly accessible, Blackbox would constitute the largest public repository of programming assignment solutions for students.

8. REFERENCES

[1] *MSR '11: Proceedings of the 8th Working Conference on Mining Software Repositories.* ACM, 2011.

[2] M. Ahmadzadeh, D. Elliman, and C. Higgins. An analysis of patterns of debugging among novice computer science students. In *ITiCSE '05*, pages 84–88. ACM, 2005.

[3] D. J. Barnes and M. Kölling. *Objects First with Java: A Practical Introduction using BlueJ.* Prentice Hall / Pearson Education, fifth edition, 2012.

[4] S. H. Edwards, J. Snyder, M. A. Pérez-Quiñones, A. Allevato, D. Kim, and B. Tretola. Comparing effective and ineffective behaviors of student programmers. In *ICER '09*, pages 3–14. ACM, 2009.

[5] J. B. Fenwick, Jr., C. Norris, F. E. Barry, J. Rountree, C. J. Spicer, and S. D. Cheek. Another look at the behaviors of novice programmers. In *SIGCSE '09*, pages 296–300. ACM, 2009.

[6] M. C. Jadud. *An Exploration of Novice Compilation Behaviour in BlueJ.* PhD thesis, Computing Laboratory, University of Kent, January 2007.

[7] M. Kölling and I. Utting. Building an open, large-scale research data repository of initial programming student behaviour. In *SIGCSE '12*, pages 323–324. ACM, 2012.

[8] J. C. Spohrer, E. Soloway, and E. Pope. A goal/plan analysis of buggy pascal programs. *Hum.-Comput. Interact.*, 1(2):163–207, June 1985.

[9] R. Thomas, G. E. Kennedy, S. Draper, R. Mancy, M. Crease, H. Evans, and P. Gray. Generic usage monitoring of programming students. In *ASCILITE '03*, 2003.

[10] R.-G. Urma and A. Mycroft. Programming language evolution via source code query languages. In *PLATEAU '12*, pages 35–38. ACM, 2012.

[11] I. Utting, N. C. C. Brown, M. Kölling, D. McCall, and P. Stevens. Web-scale data gathering with BlueJ. In *ICER '12*, pages 1–4. ACM, 2012.

Using CodeBrowser to Seek Differences between Novice Programmers

Kenny Heinonen, Kasper Hirvikoski, Matti Luukkainen, Arto Vihavainen
University of Helsinki
Department of Computer Science
P.O. Box 68 (Gustaf Hällströmin katu 2b)
Fi-00014 University of Helsinki
{ kennyhei, khirviko, mluukkai, avihavai }@cs.helsinki.fi

ABSTRACT

A large body of systems that gather data on students' programming process exists, and with the increase of massive open online courses in programming, the amount of gathered data is growing even at a higher rate. A common issue for data analysis is the lack of common tools for visualizing source code snapshots. We have created a browser-side snapshot analysis tool called CodeBrowser that provides a clean REST API that anyone can integrate their snapshot data into. In this article, we describe CodeBrowser and as an example, discuss how it has been used to seek differences between novice programmers that have passed (n=10) or failed (n=10) an introductory programming course.

Categories and Subject Descriptors

K.3.2 [**Computer and Information Science Education**]: Computer science education

Keywords

programming education, snapshot analysis, source code analysis, snapshots, visualization

1. INTRODUCTION

Tools and programming environments that assess the work of students have increased in quantity over the last decades. The first automatic assessment systems are from the 1960s, after which many more have been crafted [4, 1, 5]. Initially, the assessment systems were used to ease the load of instructors, but after a while, it became evident that the students' submissions could provide valuable information on their progress, which in turn could be learned from.

A more recent development is the addition of snapshot gathering mechanisms to the environments that students use as they work on assignments. Snapshots typically contain date and source code changes, and are taken whenever a student saves or compiles the program that she is working on. For example, Spacco et al. crafted an assessment system called Marmoset [14] that includes an Eclipse plugin that gathers snapshots as the students work on given assignments.

Similar work has been reported also for other IDEs such as NetBeans [16], and some effort has also been put on independent snapshot-gathering systems that do not rely on any specific IDE, but instead attach into the compilation environment [12].

More than a single snapshot gathering mechanism has been created for the BlueJ project [8], which is often used as an IDE in introductory programming courses. For example, both Jadud [6] and Norris et al. [13] have extended BlueJ in order to gather more information, while more recently, the BlueJ development group announced a large-scale snapshot gathering project [15]. Since summer 2013, the BlueJ "Blackbox" project has been live, and anyone can contribute data to their central snapshot repository.

In large-scale snapshot gathering projects such as the BlueJ initiative as well as massive open online courses related to programming, the amount of participant-generated data is growing at a rapid pace. Often, it no longer makes sense to store and analyze the snapshot data on a specific computer. This is evident especially with teams that have members at multiple locations, many of them needing access to the data and collaboratively crafted notes.

Many of the existing tools for viewing students' programming process, i.e. code snapshots, are either more traditional, desktop-based applications, or have a tight integration with a specific snapshot-gathering mechanism. In addition, although there exists a large body of research related to program animation, see e.g. [11, 7], the systems are often designed for helping the students to visualize their own process and provide additional overhead that is not needed for rapid iteration of snapshots.

In this article, we describe a system called CodeBrowser that has been designed to facilitate collaborative snapshot analysis by providing functionality for annotating and visualizing code snapshots from various sources. The work is partially motivated by our previous work on algorithmic snapshot analysis, where the goal has been to identify novices that have challenges with learning to program. During the work, it has become evident that tools for "looking at the actual data" are both required and scarce, and that the existing ones rarely support collaborative work from multiple locations. Our contributions in this article are (1) a brief review of the existing code snapshot analysis tools, (2)

SIGCSE'14, March 5–8, 2014, Atlanta, GA, USA.

http://dx.doi.org/10.1145/2538862.2538981.

CodeBrowser, a system that provides a convenient lens for analyzing students' snapshots in a collaborative, distributed environment, and (3) the evaluation of CodeBrowser by using it to analyze differences in the programming process of novice programmers (n=20).

This article is organized as follows. In section two, we give a more detailed explanation of CodeBrowser, and in section three, we give a brief overview of related work on snapshot analysis tools with a focus on systems that provide visualization capabilities. In section four, we describe how CodeBrowser has been used to identify differences between novice programmers that either fail or succeed in an introductory programming course, and in Section five, we outline future work and conclude this article.

2. CODEBROWSER

CodeBrowser[1] is a web-based tool for collaborative analysis of source code snapshots. As many of the current snapshot systems store data, often in similar format, but lack the means for visual analysis, CodeBrowser has been purposefully designed as a client-side web application with good integration capability.

2.1 Architecture and Design

CodeBrowser has been built using current web-technologies (HTML5, CSS3 and JavaScript), and structured around Backbone.js[2], a framework that eases building MVC structures and fetching data across REST-APIs. In addition, CodeBrowser utilizes several other frameworks such as jQuery[3], Raphaël.js[4], and the Ace-editor[5]. It is designed to be modular and easily extendable, and has a maintainable structure that is supported by unit tests that support future development.

The backend implementation is abstracted behind a versatile REST-API, see Table 1, which can be implemented with whichever technologies best fit the purpose (data transfer format is JSON). Currently, there exists a starter implementation for integrating your own dataset into CodeBrowser which has been created using Java EE and Spring Framework.

In order to avoid unnecessary file transfers between the client and the server, CodeBrowser utilizes localStorage functionality of HTML5 to cache files on the client when needed.

2.2 Overview

CodeBrowser supports multiple courses, students, and assignments. As the user enters the system, she sees options to either browse courses or students. As the user browses students, she will see the courses that a student has participated in, and the assignments that the student has worked on. When an assignment is selected, the user is shown a page with a snapshot view.

The snapshot view, shown in Figure 1, consists of a timeline, editor, file browser, and tagging functionality. The timeline (top in Figure 1) displays snapshots that have been taken as the student has worked on the specific assignment. Each snapshot is a point in the timeline, and the distance between the points reflects the duration between two subsequent snapshots while the size of the point represents the amount of change i.e. added, modified and deleted lines between them. The timeline is designed to aid navigating the snapshots and identifying interesting points in the solution process of an assignment.

The editor view (main area in Figure 1) can be used to view source code files within a snapshot. It has two modes: single view and split view. The single view displays the contents of a particular file within a snapshot, and the split view provides a second editor that displays the previous version of the same file. The split view makes it easier to compare the files in subsequent snapshots. To provide additional hints to the user, the editor provides diffing in both views: visual feedback of the modified (blue), added (green) and deleted (red) lines makes it easier to spot changes that have occurred between two snapshots.

The file browser (left-hand side in Figure 1) provides access to navigating multiple files within the project, while the area under the file browser contains tags that the users can add as they browse the snapshots. The tags are shared with other users, which makes it easier to share intuitions and opinions, as well as create milestones that could be looked at in the future. Extracting the tags from the backend allows also useful input for data mining tasks.

3. RELATED WORK

A wide range of systems that are either designed to gather snapshots from the students' programming process or to display the process to the user exists. Many of the systems are desktop-based, and focus on e.g. a specific language or a specific IDE. Here, we give a brief overview of work on systems that have been created to analyze students' programming process from snapshots.

One of the earlier snapshot gathering tools that was integrated to an industry standard IDE was Watcher [10], which was created as an Eclipse plugin. Watcher logged the interactions between the user and Eclipse, creating a repository of data that could be mined for analysis of program evaluation. The source code changes were recorded using an XML format, and the analysis and visualization part was done in Excel. The authors of Watcher reported on detecting timewise changes in the programming process, and were able to e.g. analyze and visualize the quantity of events from different input sources including the keyboard and the mouse.

Norris et al. report on the ClockIt toolkit [13], which contains both a data gathering plugin for the BlueJ programming environment as well as a visualization component. The visualization component shows aggregate statistics of the session, showing e.g. the amount of compile errors and successes, displaying sessions when the student has been active, and provides a "play by play" view, where the changes between each snapshot event can be watched through systematically. In addition, a web-interface, which provides functionality for visualizing the BlueJ events on the web is provided.

Retina [12] is a system that records students' programming process both via plugins in Eclipse and BlueJ as well as a modified Java compiler. The snapshots are sent to a centralized repository, which in turn can be accessed by instructors using the Retina Instructor View desktop application. Retina is especially useful in distance education, as the instructors can see the source code that the students

[1]http://codebrowser.io
[2]http://backbonejs.org
[3]http://jquery.com
[4]http://raphaeljs.com
[5]http://ace.c9.io

URI	Description
/courses	Listing of courses
/courses/{id}/exercises	Listing of assignments within a given course
/students	Listing of students
/students/{id}/courses	Listing of courses for a specific student
/students/{id}/courses/{id}/exercises	Listing of assignments that the student has worked on in a specific course
/students/{id}/courses/{id}/exercises/{id}/snapshots	Listing of snapshots for an assignment that the student has worked on in a specific course
/.../snapshots/{id}/files	File details for the given snapshot
/.../snapshots/{id}/files/{id}/content	Retrieving content of a file
/students/{id}/courses/{id}/exercises/{id}/tags	Management of tags for a specific assignment for a given student

Table 1: The REST API that the backend must provide for CodeBrowser. Details for the JSON format are described on the CodeBrowser web-site at http://codebrowser.io

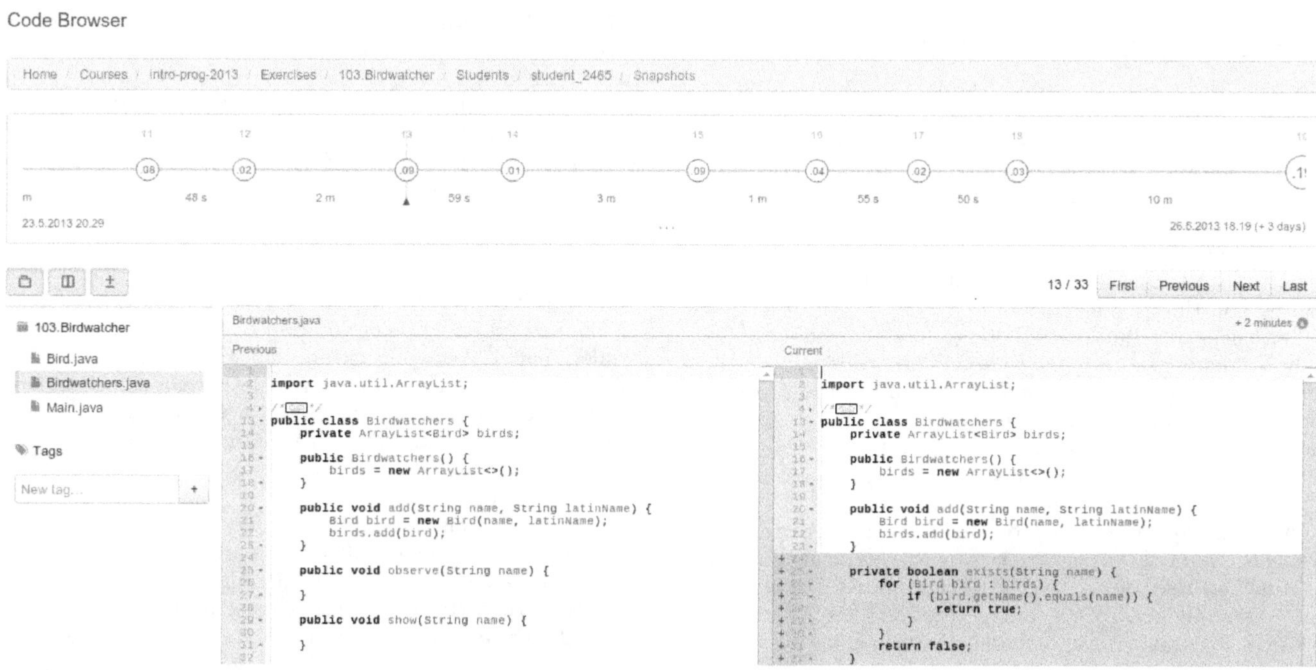

Figure 1: Snapshot view of CodeBrowser. On the top there is a timeline, which visualizes the overall working process, on the left there is the functionality for selecting files within the project as well as adding tags, and in the center is the editor used for observing changes in snapshots.

have been working on through the desktop application, as well as interact with students using a specifically designed IM application.

Blikstein reported on a desktop tool designed to navigate source code changes that have been logged using the NetLogo environment [3]. Currently named LogViewer[6], the desktop application allows users to view students' code changes using a specific XML format, as well as annotate code changes and highlight areas of text that are seen as important.

SCORE [17] is an Eclipse plugin for gathering log data from students' programming process that provides an additional view in Eclipse, which can be used to view the gathered snapshots. The view-mode is intended for the use of both students and researchers, and it has support for annotating and categorizing the performed changes, as well as adding notes on the program process.

Another application that has been designed to allow students a retrospective view on their own programming process is Programming Process Visualizer (PPV) [9]. It is both an editor as well as a timeline navigator, and provides visualization of the overall progress in terms of compilation successes and errors as well as editing, running and viewing the application. In addition, PPV helps students design their work as it provides a notepad into which the students can input subtasks for the current task that they are working on.

One of the few applications that take a system-independent approach to visualizing the students' programming process is SnapViz [2]. SnapViz is a web-based system which can be used to visualize students' working patterns. The users of the system upload data in a tab-separated format through a web-page, and see a report of working patterns of students that were included in the dataset. Typical applications of SnapViz include identifying preferred working times of students as well as moments, when the students' work compiles and possible tests pass.

When comparing CodeBrowser to the previously described

[6]Available at https://code.google.com/p/xml-log-toolkit/

applications, the closest match from the design perspective is perhaps SnapViz, which has been designed as a system-independent approach for providing visualization capabilities leveraging the possibilities of modern web technologies. On the other hand, SnapViz provides a global view on the course, while CodeBrowser focuses on the interactions of single students. The closest match to the timeline view provided by CodeBrowser is perhaps the one provided by PPV. However, PPV is a desktop application, and does not have the collaborative aspect. The split view of CodeBrowser is similar to the LogViewer, however again, CodeBrowser is fully online and allows collaborative source code analysis, which LogViewer does not provide.

4. DIFFERENCES IN NOVICES

In order to evaluate CodeBrowser and its functionality, we asked an instructor to identify working patterns of students who were put into the system. The students selected for the analysis were students who had no previous programming experience. Furthermore, the students were split into two groups; group one had 10 students who had passed the course with high marks (over 90% of the overall score), while group two had 10 students who had failed the course (less than 50% of the overall score).

The gender distributions in both groups were similar; 50% of the students in group one were female, while 60% of the students in group two were female, and all of the students were studying computer science as a minor subject. On average, the students in group one received 91% of the available points from the exam, while the students in group two received 36% of the available points in the exam[7].

The instructor was asked to analyze three assignments from early parts of the course, the same assignments for each student, and to seek e.g. bad working habits. The context that was explained to the instructor was that we needed new eyes for analyzing the students' working process, and would use the data and possible information to improve the course instruction and material. The grade information of the students as well as the motivation to evaluate the system was excluded from the instructor during the early parts of the analysis.

Here, we report aggregated results from the analysis.

4.1 Assignment: Input and Comparison

The first assignment to analyze was a task where the student had to create a program that would ask for two integers and then print the larger of the two. The assignment belongs to the first week of our course, and before the assignment, the students have worked on text I/O, variables, and conditional statements.

Table 2[8] contains specific error types that occurred for at least three of the total 20 participants, and displays the number of participants that had the specific error at least once. When looking at specific error types and problems, only the students in the failing group had indentation errors and random activity in their problem solving process; the random activity was classified as "programming by incident".

[7]In an investigation into the exams, the major difference between the two groups in the exam was that group two had difficulties with questions that required applying the concepts they had learned to new problems.

[8]In the following tables, #SP indicates "Students Pass", and #SF indicates "Students Fail".

Issue	#SP	#SF
Indentation errors	0	4
Syntax errors	2	1
Spelling or output errors	1	2
Programming by incident	0	3
Not printing anything at first	1	4
Using Math.max with wrong parameters	2	1
Bad variable naming	1	2

Table 2: Different errors in the assignment on input and comparison. Label #SP is the group that passed the course, and #SF is the group that failed the course.

Many of the students worked on the solution for a while, and some attempted to build the solution using two if-clauses instead of going for an "if-else". There were students in both groups that first created a single if-condition that worked if the first number was correct, and then copy-pasted the same if-condition to the code for the second time and tested whether it would work, not thinking about the condition. After this, students in both groups were able to reverse the second condition and the program worked correctly.

4.2 Assignment: Leap year

The second assignment to analyze was a task where the student had to create a program that would read in a number and tell whether the number is a leap year. The students received additional information on what it means if a year is a leap year, as well as textual samples on the expected output. This assignment belongs to the later part of the first week of our course.

Table 3 contains error types that occurred during the leap year assignment. The challenging part in the leap year assignment is the condition and modulo, which can be challenging with rusty mathematics background. Three of the students in the failing group were not able to come up with a working solution, and five of them tried at least three different if combinations. There was no difference in the amount of students that attempted to solve the assignment using a single if-clause, and virtually no difference in the amount of students that were able to create the working single if-clause. An interesting notion was that four of the students in the group that contained passing students created additional variables that helped them in solving the assignment; they were able to decompose the problem into smaller subproblems, for which the results were stored in the variables, and that students in both groups had difficulties with the conditions; they were e.g. mixing up OR and AND.

Issue	#SP	#SF
Not able to come up with a solution	0	3
Indentation errors	1	4
Attempts the solution with a single if	5	5
Produces a working single if	3	2
Creates a working if-elseif-else -solution	4	1
Tries at least three different if combinations	0	5
Has challenges with conditions	5	5
Uses additional helper-variable(s)	4	0

Table 3: The number of students that displayed specific issues in the assignment on deciding whether a given year was a leap year or not. Issues that occurred with less than three students were excluded.

In this assignment as well, some programming by incident was observed. A description of one student was written down in the instructor's notes; *"he starts with an if-elseif-else, does not succeed and starts to build a one-liner solution. While iterating through the options, he has several obscure conditions (incl. if(year < 400) { .. }), starts to use a debug print and slowly is able to create a three-level nested if-clause that produces the correct output"*.

4.3 Assignment: Loops and Statistics

The third assignment was about loops and number statistics. The task was to create a program where the user can type in an arbitrary amount of numbers, the reading should stop if the user types in -1. After the user has put in the numbers, the system should print out statistics on the numbers, including the sum, count and average of the numbers as well as the count of even and odd numbers. This assignment belongs to the second week of our course, and the students have just learned about loops and exiting them. The task is given out in five parts, where the first part is just reading in numbers, and the subsequent parts add in statistics features. The students do not yet know about lists, so it is assumed that variables are used to store the data.

Table 4 shows notes from the third assignment. Four of the students in the failing group were having trouble with working in a systematic manner, and although they did construct the program, their process had lots of permutation. Three out of the four students that were programming by permutation also had bad logical mistakes in their code, mostly in the mathematics-related content. As the students were reiterating through the loop construct and learning to use it, many students in both groups were also first having problems with correct indentation. In addition, quite a few students in the first group did not even try to end the input loop initially, and were perhaps simply enjoying to see the endless iterations. When adding an end condition into the loop, many students in the failing group had challenges with coming up with a proper condition that would break out of the loop.

Issue	#SP	#SF
Challenges with ending the loop	1	4
Indentation errors	5	6
Calculating average inside the loop	2	4
Infinite loop	5	2
Input read at a wrong position	6	3
Programming by incident	0	4
Bad logical mistakes	0	3

Table 4: The number of students that displayed specific issues in the assignment on loops and number statistics. Issues that occurred with less than three students were excluded.

One of the students in the failing group did not attempt to solve the assignment at all, and two of them did not complete the full assignment. Here, a few students had difficulties with variable visibility, and were e.g. initially instantiating the sum variable at the beginning of each loop iteration.

One of the students in the failing group worked as follows; *"He starts working well and creates the loop for reading input from the user, but then for some reason creates an additional loop inside the first loop that reads the user input. The inner loop is never terminated, while the student struggles to write a condition that would break out of the outer loop, perhaps not understanding that the program is stuck in the inner loop. It takes a while before he removes the inner loop, after which he struggles with introducing the sum variable; it is first introduced inside the loop. After some time, he succeeds with the sum calculation, after which he has problems with rounding the decimals in the average. Finally, he is able to do it. In the end, he does not finish the part where he would count the even and odd numbers."*.

4.4 Instructor remarks and overall workflow

The overall working process of the instructor was as follows. He had three two-hour sessions with the data set, and during each session, one assignment was analyzed. In each session, the instructor first familiarized himself with the assignment, and then started to skim through the students' working processes using CodeBrowser, drafting notes on paper while doing so. After a while, he started performing a more systematic analysis of the task, going through each of the students' snapshot one-by-one and tagging them in the CodeBrowser as well as making more notes on paper. The notes were further categorized into *global issues* such as whether the student had a controlled programming flow (i.e. she did not "program by incident"), indentation errors, syntax errors, type errors, problems with output and spelling, bad variable naming etc, and *local issues* that were more problem specific. Local issues included possible misunderstandings in the assignment handout as well as the assumed working process related to seeking for an approach.

As an example of a local issue, let us shortly revisit the assignment on loops. Although variable visibility had been covered previously by several assignments, there were still many students that were having difficulties with the assignments. As a variable containing the sum of numbers was needed, many first defined it within the loop and had faulty outputs as the sum was initiated at the end of each iteration. However, once the students recalled the idea variable visibility and moved the sum variable outside the loop, coming up with count, average and the amount of even and odd numbers was almost always straightforward.

5. DISCUSSION AND FUTURE WORK

When we consider that the instructor spent a total of six hours in analyzing how twenty students performed on three assignments, it can be extrapolated that analyzing the programming process of a class with hundreds of students is infeasible without the use of a large team of analysts. A pre-selection of the analyzed students should be performed for example by lecture attendance, final grade, or a background factor such as mathematics. In our case, the students that were investigated were selected based on them having no previous programming performance and the final course grade.

Although we draw no conclusions on the actual analysis due to the small number of students analyzed, it is easy to see that analyzing the assignments would not have been feasible without proper tool support. In the three assignments that were analyzed, the biggest difference was that the students that passed the course were able to solve them all, while some of the students that failed the course had difficulties in finishing the assignments. In the early parts of the course, the students that pasted code into their editors had more indentation errors; however, when a new concept that used indentation was introduced, both groups had students struggling with proper indentation. Based on the current analysis, the main difference between the failing and the passing group was that the failing group had more students who lacked a systematic approach to the problem, were attempting several things at a relatively rapid pace, and had difficulties with understanding and applying conditionals.

In our future work we are looking to further investigate the differences between the novices who pass and the novices who fail, and plan to include more background variables. We acknowledge that attempting to draw a deeper understanding from source code snapshots is hard if not impossible, as parts of the code in the snapshots may be crafted by fellow students or downloaded from the web.

In our current work we are extending CodeBrowser to offer support for the BlueJ large-scale data gathering project, as well as to provide additional program visualizations such as a time-wise file-structure, from which it is easier to see how the students' project has evolved over time. In addition, we are adding the functionality for categorizing the created tags, and identifying the moments when novices who work seemingly randomly start to display a more systematic thought process.

6. ACKNOWLEDGMENTS

We thank Timo Ahlberg, Jonne Airaksinen, Jami Karvanen, Krista Longi, and Riku Niittymäki for their contributions to making CodeBrowser even better.

7. REFERENCES

[1] K. M. Ala-Mutka. A Survey of Automated Assessment Approaches for Programming Assignments. *Computer Science Education*, 15:83–102, June 2005.

[2] E. Balzuweit and J. Spacco. SnapViz: visualizing programming assignment snapshots. In *Proceedings of the 18th ACM conference on Innovation and technology in computer science education*, ITiCSE '13, pages 350–350, New York, NY, USA, 2013. ACM.

[3] P. Blikstein. Using learning analytics to assess students' behavior in open-ended programming tasks. In *Proceedings of the 1st International Conference on Learning Analytics and Knowledge*, LAK '11, pages 110–116, New York, NY, USA, 2011. ACM.

[4] C. Douce, D. Livingstone, and J. Orwell. Automatic test-based assessment of programming: A review. *J. Educ. Resour. Comput.*, 5(3), Sept. 2005.

[5] P. Ihantola, T. Ahoniemi, V. Karavirta, and O. Seppälä. Review of recent systems for automatic assessment of programming assignments. In *Proceedings of the 10th Koli Calling International Conference on Computing Education Research*, Koli Calling '10, pages 86–93, New York, NY, USA, 2010. ACM.

[6] M. C. Jadud. Methods and tools for exploring novice compilation behaviour. In *Proceedings of the second international workshop on Computing education research*, ICER '06, pages 73–84, New York, NY, USA, 2006. ACM.

[7] V. Karavirta, A. Korhonen, L. Malmi, and T. Naps. A comprehensive taxonomy of algorithm animation languages. *J. Vis. Lang. Comput.*, 21(1):1–22, Feb. 2010.

[8] M. Kölling, B. Quig, A. Patterson, and J. Rosenberg. The BlueJ system and its pedagogy. *Computer Science Education*, 13(4):249–268, 2003.

[9] Y. Matsuzawa, K. Okada, and S. Sakai. Programming process visualizer: a proposal of the tool for students to observe their programming process. In *Proceedings of the 18th ACM conference on Innovation and technology in computer science education*, ITiCSE '13, pages 46–51, New York, NY, USA, 2013. ACM.

[10] J. McKeogh and C. Exton. Eclipse plug-in to monitor the programmer behaviour. In *Proceedings of the 2004 OOPSLA workshop on eclipse technology eXchange*, eclipse '04, pages 93–97, New York, NY, USA, 2004. ACM.

[11] A. Moreno, N. Myller, E. Sutinen, and M. Ben-Ari. Visualizing programs with Jeliot 3. In *Proceedings of the working conference on Advanced visual interfaces*, AVI '04, pages 373–376, New York, NY, USA, 2004. ACM.

[12] C. Murphy, G. Kaiser, K. Loveland, and S. Hasan. Retina: helping students and instructors based on observed programming activities. In *Proceedings of the 40th ACM technical symposium on Computer science education*, SIGCSE '09, pages 178–182, New York, NY, USA, 2009. ACM.

[13] C. Norris, F. Barry, J. B. Fenwick Jr., K. Reid, and J. Rountree. ClockIt: collecting quantitative data on how beginning software developers really work. *SIGCSE Bull.*, 40(3):37–41, June 2008.

[14] J. Spacco, J. Strecker, D. Hovemeyer, and W. Pugh. Software repository mining with Marmoset: an automated programming project snapshot and testing system. In *Proceedings of the 2005 international workshop on Mining software repositories*, MSR '05, pages 1–5, New York, NY, USA, 2005. ACM.

[15] I. Utting, N. Brown, M. Kölling, D. McCall, and P. Stevens. Web-scale data gathering with BlueJ. In *Proceedings of the ninth annual international conference on International computing education research*, ICER '12, pages 1–4, New York, NY, USA, 2012. ACM.

[16] A. Vihavainen, T. Vikberg, M. Luukkainen, and M. Pärtel. Scaffolding students' learning using Test My Code. In *Proceedings of the 18th ACM conference on Innovation and technology in computer science education*, ITiCSE '13, pages 117–122, New York, NY, USA, 2013. ACM.

[17] M. R. A. Wittmann, M. Bower, and M. Kavakli-Thorne. Using the SCORE software package to analyse novice computer graphics programming. In *Proceedings of the 16th annual joint conference on Innovation and technology in computer science education*, ITiCSE '11, pages 118–122, New York, NY, USA, 2011. ACM.

Hands-on Introduction to Computer Science at the Freshman Level

Raghuraman Balasubramanian Zachary York Matthew Dorran
Aritra Biswas Timur Girgin Karthikeyan Sankaralingam
University of Wisconsin-Madison
karu@cs.wisc.edu

ABSTRACT

This paper details the creation of a hands-on introduction course that reflects the dramatic growth and diversity in computer science. Our aim was to enable students to get an end-to-end perspective on computer system design by building one. We report on a two-year exercise in using the Arduino platform to build a series of hands-on projects. We have used these projects in two course instances, and have obtained detailed student feedback, which we analyze and present in this paper. The instructions, code and videos developed are available open-source.

1. INTRODUCTION

Computer science as a field has changed dramatically over the past few decades. Today's embedded computing devices, like the Fitbit [5], provide more computing capability than a super-computer from 30 years ago. Such systems embody several computer science principles such as programming, compilation, operating systems, concurrent programming and hardware organization. Computer science education, especially freshman introduction to computer science, typically includes lecture based instructions and simplistic programming assignments and has not evolved much since the 1980s. CS252 from UW-Madison and CS312 [1] from the UT-Austin are representative example of many introductory CS courses. There are a few examples like Stanford's CS1C that make a radical departure. Such a departure may not be amenable to all institutions or undergraduate programs.

Our goal and motivation is to develop a freshman introduction to computer science course which, without major disruption to the existing curriculum, incorporates a hands-on building component. The aim is to develop material in which a team of students design and build a computer or computing system and perform an evaluation of the system. Many studies on teaching computer science have shown that construction and team exercise accelerate learning [7]. Others have shown that the material being "fun" is important [6, 8, 9] and the need for course projects to be challenging but

SIGCSE'14, March 5–8, 2014, Atlanta, GA, USA.

http://dx.doi.org/10.1145/2538862.2538889.

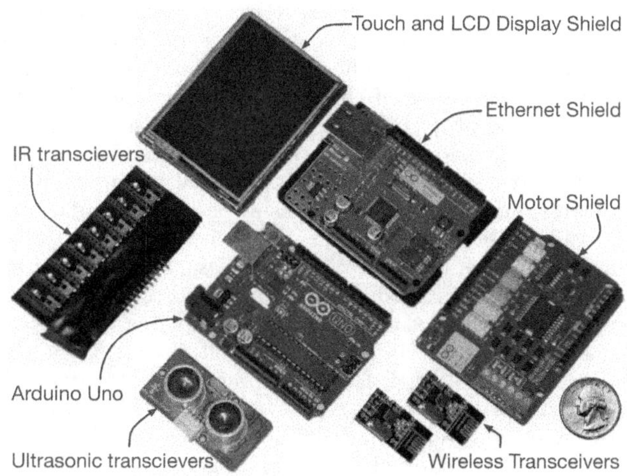

Figure 1: Arduino Uno board and select peripherals.

not daunting. Our other goal is to open source instructional materials to increase availability. We intentionally avoid choosing projects that are specific to a single paradigm, like robotics, by providing hardware and software that can be assembled in a variety of ways to embody a computing platform. This allows students to choose from a diverse array of projects aligning with their natural inclination.

Due to the benefits of Moore's law and constantly reducing costs in the electronics industry, there are many viable platforms to choose from. Specifically, the Arduino [3] platform shown in Figure 1 provides tremendous hardware capability and a simple programming interface based on C language. The Arduino supports a vast array of "shields" or peripherals like ultra-sonic sensors, accelerometers, touch displays and wireless communication hardware that can be connected to the basic platform to build interesting systems. There is a widespread community of hobbyist computing resembling the 80s era of hobbyist PC building that is based on Arduino, which costs only $20. The Arduino platform has wide-spread open source community support, numerous do-it-yourself projects, and is easy to use, making it an excellent gateway to get students excited about computer engineering. The challenge from a curriculum or teaching perspective is to bring all this hardware and software into a cohesive platform for computer science pedagogy. This is particularly complex in a freshman course that is designed to introduce the core ideas of computer science spanning *bits, gates and binary logic* to *programming and computer organization*, The fundamental question is *how to design hands-on projects to enhance the experience of learning the fundamentals of computer science?*

In this paper, we share our experience gained from developing such a course at a public university with a large computer science yearly enrollment of over 2500 students. This paper is a report on the development of this curriculum spanning a pilot version we implemented in Spring 2012, the development of instructional material, assessing the material, and a second version of the course in Spring 2013 based on this new material. In each instance, we also report on detailed survey data and feedback collected from the students.

Summary of implementation The projects were added to an existing freshman introduction to computing course (CS252) which is based on the Patt and Patel [10] book and did not originally include any hands-on building component. In the Spring 2012 offering of the course, the strategy was to get something off the ground. We envisioned a few Arduino-based projects, wrote up a description in a couple of paragraphs, and provided students with hardware. We provided little supplementary instructional materials. One graduate student experienced in using the Arduino platform was available for one hour each week to help students. A 5% bonus credit was offered. We were pleasantly surprised by the outcome. Figure 2 shows the completed projects, which were all functional. All but one team completed the project they had picked. In total, 73 of 191 enrolled students did the projects. Based on their feedback, we then created detailed instruction material with extensive videos, code tutorials, and a week-by-week plan over the Summer and Fall 2012 semesters. The material itself was largely developed by 4 under-graduate students who took the course in Spring 2012. The course was then offered in Spring 2013. We provided the instructional material we developed, extensive daily office hours and support through a Piazza forum. This paper reports on this effort with the goal of providing lessons learned and insights on how others can reuse and enhance our material. We are making all resources publicly available at this URL: `http://www.cs.wisc.edu/vertical/arduino-252`.

Overall our findings are the following :

- Hands-on projects based on Arduino platforms can be effectively built as a 3 or 4 week project.
- The projects help teach and reinforce basic computer science concepts.
- Students feel the projects serve the pedagogical purpose and the experience gives them an enhanced understanding of the subject.
- The projects themselves can each be constructed with hardware costing between $97 and $254 as a one-time expense.

This paper is organized as follows. In Section 2 we describe how the pilot Spring 2012 version was developed, including a detailed explanation of the actual hands-on projects. In Section 3 we describe how we used student feedback to develop instruction material, and what instructional material was developed. In Section 4 we describe how the Spring 2013 version of the course was run based on this instruction material and student feedback. Section 5 addresses potential issues which may arise during the adoption of this material in other institutions. Finally, Section 6 concludes with thoughts on lessons learned.

2. SPRING 2012

We now describe the first instance of the projects offered in a *give it to them and have them build it* mode, covering logistics of implementation, a detailed description of the projects and the outcome and student feedback.

2.1 Mechanics and Implementation

We provided the students choice of five projects and seven weeks to complete them. We provided them some weekly milestones to aim for and a brief progress report was due each Friday. A final demo date was set at the end of seven weeks. Students were informed that "completing" a working demo would be sufficient and no other detailed grading was involved. We provided bonus of 5% course credit awarded for a completed project. We allowed project groups of two to six students, and facilitated some matching of students to projects based on programming experience. A total of seventy three students opted to attempt the extra credit course material. As the projects were optional, no lecture hours were devoted to teaching particular skills to complete the projects.

We provided a simple five minute demo of Arduino platform at the start of the projects. For all projects we provided a description and relevant pointers to Internet resources for the specific "shields" (sensors and actuators - see also Figure 1). We also provided detailed usage notes to get started on the following four topics since they spanned many projects: i) Installing the software and getting a simple blink LED demo to work. ii) Getting two Arduinos to talk to each other through a wireless transceiver. iii) Using Analog ports as Digital Ports. iv) Wiki links on how to use "motor shields" to control the speed and direction of the wheels for the projects with robots.

2.2 Description of Projects

We describe the projects below and in the Appendix list the hardware required and cost per project. All software tools used are free and open source.

Maze Navigating Robots In this project, students built a robot that can auto-navigate in a maze to reach an exit. The robot followed an arbitrarily drawn black path in a bright background using a set of infrared sensors that were positioned roughly orthogonal to the line on the ground. The data generated by the sensors are analyzed by the Arduino processor which in turn controls DC motors to navigate the robot. The students were expected to develop a fully-functional line-tracking robot that could handle any path complexity. We also provided a pointer to a PDF manual of the infrared line follower kit which explained the wiring of the infrared sensors and their communication protocol.

Obstacle Avoiding Robot In this project, the students equipped robots with active range sensors to detect proximity to objects and programmed them to avoid obstacles. Students employed a commonly used method of depth extraction to calculate the distance of objects around the robot by using an ultrasonic sensor. A set of sensors that were positioned around the robot to act as its "eyes". Students wrote code that polled on the value returned by the ultrasonic sensors periodically. They performed calibration to obtain the thresholds to detect proximity. The obstacles were not necessarily stationary — the robot was required to periodically check its surroundings and react dynamically. We provided

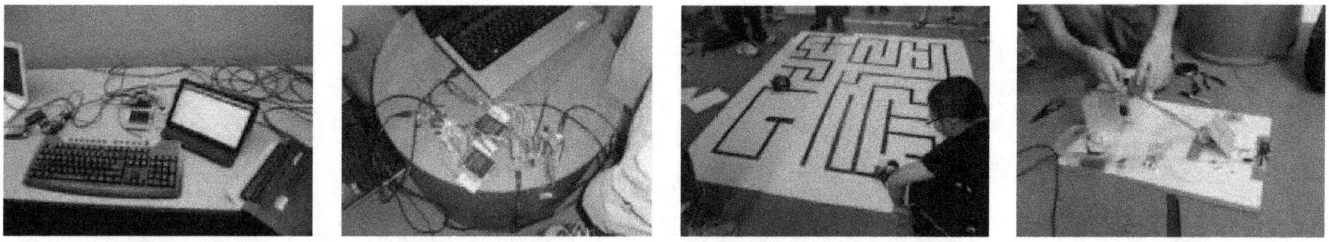

Twitter | Wireless Tic-Tac-Toe | Maze Navigation Robot | Angry Birds

Figure 2: Examples of the four projects students

the following pointers: (i) A Wikipedia link to how an ultrasonic sensor works and (ii) a page describing the ultrasonic range measurement module we used and sample code.

Tic Tac Toe In this project, students created a handheld game console. They were expected to design the game, the input and output interfaces (using a touch screen LCD). They also had to add a wireless module over two devices for a multi-player mode. The students formed three groups (i) the Game Designers - who implemented core game logic. (ii) the user interface team - who coded what was displayed on the screen. (iii) the wireless team - who setup communication between two Arduino boards. We provided links to the following online resources: (i) the hobbyist website [4] which lists instructions on how to use the nRF24L01 wireless transceiver and (ii) the touch screen shield manual [2].

Twitter In this project, the students created a door display that displayed messages of a twitter feed. They used a simple two line LCD (optionally a graphical color LCD) powered by an Arduino combined with an Ethernet shield that allows the Arduino to connect to the Internet. Once connected, students wrote code that used Twitter's APIs to read and write tweets. We provided links to an LCD shield tutorial and a link to the Arduino Ethernet library.

Angry Birds This was the most ambitious project. In this project students used a sensor to determine how far a target was, and hurled an angry bird plush toy at it. We suggested the use of an ultrasound sensor to detect the distance from the target. Students wrote code that used this to calculate the velocity at which the angry bird needed to be launched. We also suggested the use of a servo motor and some kind of spring mechanism and shaft assembly to control the distance to hurl the angry bird. In addition to links on the working of ultrasonic sensors and sample code, we also provided online coding manuals for the servo motor.

2.3 Outcome and Feedback

Outcome Of the 16 teams, all but one team completed their projects before the deadline and successfully demonstrated it on the final demo day. A total of seventy three students finished the projects. The Arduino platform proved to be powerful yet simple. The longest code contained less than 1000 lines. The quality of the projects was quite sophisticated as shown by the photos in Figure 2. In particular, the completion of the Angry Birds projects was impressive, as the students independently improvised the use of rubber-bands to act as springs to control the hurling distance. The grading of the projects was quite straight-forward – we felt all projects were complete and deserved full credit. We elaborate more on enthusiasm and other qualitative comments in the conclusion. Video demos are available on our website: `http://www.cs.wisc.edu/vertical/arduino-252`.

Feedback At the end of the seven week period, students were asked to fill out a survey (anonymously if they chose to) and the feedback was recorded. The top half of Figure 3 shows the response to five basic questions. Overall most students liked the project, but a significant number felt more help was needed and that the project could not be completed as a two person team. We used this feedback to develop instruction materials over the Summer of 2012. The most common responses on what changes the students wanted to see were: i) Better explanation of the Arduino libraries. ii) Detailed and week-by-week instructional materials and milestones. iii) Projects to be given out at the beginning of the semester rather than towards the end of the semester.

Learning In terms of pedagogy and learning, it was quite clear that students learned quite a bit about programming from these projects and felt this was a good introduction to programming and computer science — over 85% answered positively (52.7% say strongly agree) to the question: "Did you learn a lot about computer science from these projects?". Although, we could not keep track of improvements in exams or other homeworks because of the projects, many commented in the survey that they learned a lot about programming. The following are two representative student comments that capture the learning effectiveness: i) *"Arduino opens a wide range of fun projects that you can do, which allow you to/force you to understand how the chip, memory, buses, input.output types, computing, and general computing magic happen. It gets you hooked on learning."* ii) *"Creating our Arduino robot helped me understand more how computers work and function than assembly language did."*

3. INSTRUCTIONAL MATERIAL

The Spring 2012 feedback gave us insights into a few issues in project implementation. We understood that more instructional material was key for the projects to become part of core curriculum. We created a web based directory to house the project instructional materials. Within this web based directory, each project had its own respective page comprising instructional videos, documents on hardware assembly and wiring, pseudo code and basic code structure for each project and a chronologically ordered list of weekly milestones for an eight week plan. This structure provides the students with a user friendly environment to access the materials, which include step-by-step instruction manuals while maintaining the spirit of discovery that is central to these projects.

To expand the options available to the students, we added two more projects. One is a rendition of the famous "Pong" game using the Arduino micro-controller and a "GameBoy"

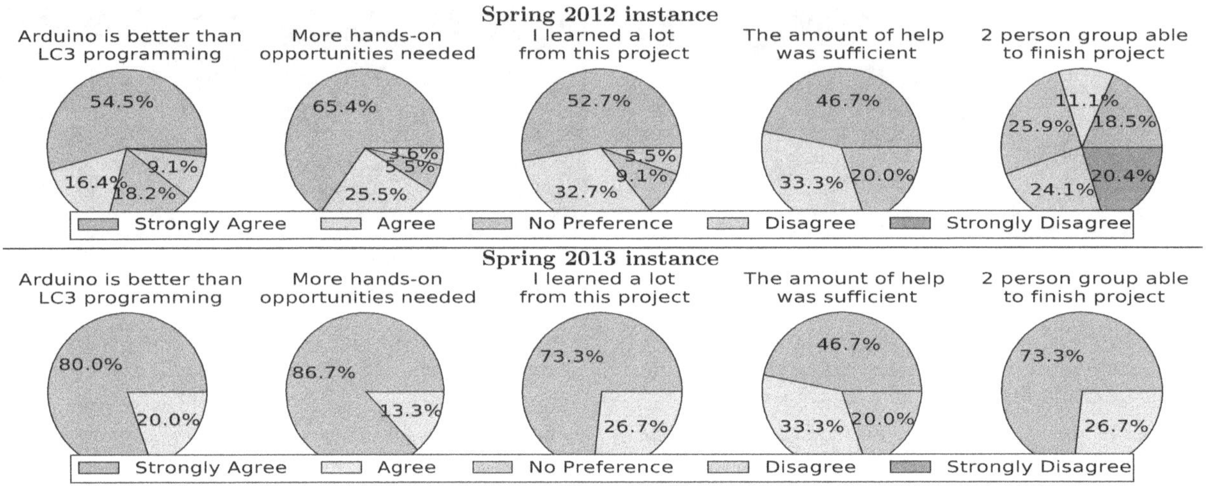

Figure 3: Summary of feedback. LC3 programming refers to the assembly programming originally in CS252.

like accessory that includes a joystick and two selector buttons. The second, was a "Word Scramble" that would give the user a scrambled word on an LCD screen. The user then uses a PS2-based keyboard to enter the unscrambled word. We also provided much more of the mechanical hardware required for the Angry Birds project as part of the instructional development.

Testing We tested the material using two undergraduate students from the Spring 2012 offering. They were requested to follow the step-by-step procedure located in the web directory for each project, just as a real student of the class would do. We monitored and recorded their progress and obtained their feedback at each step. Based on this feedback, we made many presentation changes and improvements.

4. SPRING 2013

We now describe the Spring 2013 offering which was based on the instruction materials created in Summer and Fall 12.

4.1 Mechanics and Implementation

In the Spring of 2013, we offered the students of the CS252 class an opportunity to work with the Arduino microcontroller. Out of 160 students enrolled in the class, more than 60 were interested. But we wanted to test in a more controlled setting with a known TA/student ratio - we randomly selected sixteen for doing the projects. Students were then divided into teams of two to three. Each team had the freedom to choose which of the seven projects they wanted to work on, with some guidance from us based on their skill level. The instructional material housed in the web-page was also made available to the students.

Once the team had chosen the project they wanted to work on, they were given a box containing the necessary material/equipment to accomplish the corresponding project. The goal set for all teams was to finish their assigned project in six weeks or less. In comparison to the Spring 2012 version in which we provided little or no support, we increased the support provided to the Spring 2013 batch. For instance, office hours with multiple (up to 4) TAs were made available every day for 3 hours. A "Frequently Asked Questions" page was also created for each project with answers to questions that students might have while building their project. The Q&A platform "Piazza.com" was also used for students to ask questions about their projects online. A total of 21 questions were asked by the students, and 100% of the questions were answered by the TAs with an average time of 15 minutes. At the end of the given period, the students were required to demonstrate their finished projects.

4.2 Outcome and Feedback

At the end of the given time-frame, all seven projects were correctly completed. Compared to the previous Spring, the final quality of the projects was significantly better, as many groups did more than what was initially expected. For example, the Pong game was implemented with an accelerometer enabling the game to be played by tilting the screen instead of using a joystick. Furthermore, the speed at which the projects were finished was greatly improved, as most teams had completed their project by week 4, and all teams had finished by week 5. It was also observed that teams attended less office hours than the previous year, getting most of the help needed using the online instructional material that was provided to them.

One major concern was to see whether the help provided during Spring 2013 gave better results compared to the implementation of the project in Spring 2012, where guidance was minimal. During the six weeks period of Spring 2013, students' feedback regarding the entire process was obtained on a weekly basis - they were asked to write up a short report each week on the instruction material and critique it. We analyzed this data and used this information to enhance the instructional material.

Overall, the weekly feedbacks we received were positive. However during the first two weeks, we noticed that the main complaints students reported was that the instructional material given to them did not meet their expectations. Students started their projects thinking that all information necessary to finish their project will be given to them. However, we intentionally limited the amount of information we provided – making sure that some browsing and thinking was necessary to understand the given material. Some information was purposely left out to encourage the teams to think by themselves and use their imagination to accomplish their project. By the time they completed their projects, students realized that the instructional material given to them was actually of great help, some teams went further by saying that it was too much help.

We did the same survey as in Spring 2012, and the results are shown in Figure 3. Overall the response was overwhelmingly positive. Except for one question, students answered with a definitely yes or yes. For question-4 about whether there was sufficient help, 20% were neutral, 80% were definitely yes or yes. To one of the most important questions of "Did you feel you learned about programming and computer science from the Arduino projects", 73.3% replied "Definitely yes", and 26.7% replied "Yes".

When asked what they thought of their project and how hard it was for them to build it, one student replied *"Not a lot–for the scope it was intended, I think this was a good project. I think most people with minimal to no prerequisite programming knowledge should be able to accomplish something decent given the code provided, yet there is still room for refinement for more advanced students."* Another student had a valuable comment saying *"I would have liked our project to be a little more complex. This could have been done by providing no skeleton code, allowing students to dig deep into the Arduino reference page."*

Between the comments stating that the projects were too easy, there was too much instructional material, and that all groups but one finished their project early, we can conclude that the provided instructional material is definitely sufficient in helping students complete these hands on projects in the required time frame. It is clear from the surveys and overall time spent completing each project that the result of instructional material is beneficial to the students. From student surveys we can also see that the overall feeling about having these projects as part of the course curriculum is positive. They believe that having a hands on experience similar to one they might have in the real world is an important factor in determining whether or not to pursue Computer Science/Computer Engineering as a major.

5. ADOPTION AT OTHER INSTITUTIONS

Our goal in writing about our experience is to facilitate the adoption of the material we developed in similar courses in other institutions. To that end we now comment on some related issues.

Instructor background and training When we first envisioned the course in Spring 2012, the instructor (the last author on this work) had no experience programming Arduino - neither hardware nor software but was able to ramp up quickly. Coding on the Arduino platform is straightforward to anyone proficient in C/C++ programming. Going through our online tutorials and other Arduino tutorials, one can become proficient with 10 to 20 hours of work. The potentially biggest impediment to implementing certain projects is minor hardware involvement. For example, a few Arduino shields need some soldering - intimidating and unfamiliar to some CS students and CS instructors. This is rare and in our case applied only for the Twitter project - simply avoiding it can eliminate this issue.

Scaling to larger classes We believe these projects can be considered for adoption in large classes in excess of 100 or 200 students. Much of the instructional material is web-based and hands-on input from instructors and TAs are limited. The main issues to consider are cost, physical space, and managing hardware failures - which we comment on briefly. Cost per project ranged from about \$100 to \$250 in 2012 (see Appendix for a breakdown). As the Arduino IDE works across platforms and is free, we left it to the students to use any machine they preferred. For physical space, we feel class room space is sufficient. We over-provisioned our inventory anticipating hardware failures. However failures were extremely rare – two wireless modules failed and a robot kit missed a gear component – and we were able to instantly replace them.

Role of the TAs and TA training In our pilot run, the TA's spent significant time defining the projects. One particular graduate student (the lead author on this paper) was available for consulting on hardware and software issues.

In the second run, the only role of the TAs was to be available for 3 hours per weekday and answer questions on Piazza. These were all under-graduate students who had earlier taken the course. Their training was simple — they were tasked with doing all the projects once and from this learned pretty much all that was involved. The hardware and software components of the Arduino platform are easy to use and learn. In our experience, teaching assistants with basic computer engineering knowledge were able to come up-to-speed with the environment and test run the projects with ease. In this second run, after the first two weeks, there was little to no demand on the TA time - only a total of 21 questions were asked/answered on Piazza.

In summary, if built upon the projects we have already developed, this could be implemented without TA support if need be. It will likely require office hours contact with the instructor, and his/her familiarity with the tools.

Alternatives to Arduino An important question to also consider is alternatives to Arduino, of which quite a few exist. They differ primarily in their software stack, hardware capability, diversity of "shield" and sensors, and cost. Platforms with Arduino-like software environments include mbed, OOPC, RobotC, and TinkerForge. Although they have similar hardware capability and cost, we feel community support and availability of natively supported shields is much less than for Arduino. Platforms with more sophisticated software environments like .NET, Java and Python include ioBridge, Make Controller Kit, Freedom Dev Board, Gadgeteer and Netduino. Finally platforms with full-fledged Linux/GCC include Intel Galileo, UDOO Raspberry Pi, and Beaglebone. The latter two categories introduce more barriers and complexity in interfacing with peripherals (and hence sensors), making system-building harder. In our view, Arduino's simplicity, cost, widespread availability of shields (hardware and software) and vast community support at this time is unmatched and alternatives do not appear compelling to us.

6. CONCLUSION

We have learned many things from the exercise of building these projects, instructional material and getting student feedback. Most importantly, we found that students liked the hands-on learning experience and appreciated this as a great way to get introduced to computer science. Second, we feel that with the materials in-place, and a pipeline of trained TAs providing support, it is quite easy to establish this as a continuous offering without significant recurring capital or human resource investment. As all necessary instructional materials are located in a web based directory, the bandwidth for providing these projects to 40 or more students has already been established. We conclude making a few other observations.

Diversity in technical background A challenge in any introductory course is the diversity in the technical background of the students. Exceptionally talented students sometimes had no computer science background. A few, even at the freshman level, had good understanding of programming. and had modest experience with high level programming languages like Java. Thanks to the the nature of the projects and the capability of the Arduino platform, we were able to create a from-scratch learning environment for students with little exposure and an open-ended structure to challenge students with prior knowledge.

Time spent and enthusiasm We observed that students were extremely enthusiastic about the projects, often spending significantly more time on these than the course homeworks or exam preparation. Some specific anecdotes: i) Two teams wanted to keep the hardware as they wanted to continue modifying and fiddling with them. ii) One team went above and beyond what was required by the Pong game, by adding accelerometers and making the game controller-free and instead simply tilt to play. iii) One team reverse-engineered the PS2 protocol and found a way to add a keyboard to the Twitter project.

Less is more? Compared to the Spring 2012 offering, The Spring 2013 version included a more detailed instruction material. However, we feel that the students learned much more in the Spring 2012 offering. Although it was more time consuming for the students, we think the students learned to learn — with a number of "Aha!" moments while discovering things on their own.

Computer science pedagogy In terms of computer science pedagogy, the projects convey many concepts in a hands-on and principled manner and are more effective than lectures with small homeworks. The students wrote programs and debugged them — getting introduced to a key skill very early on. Many technical concepts like the right hand rule, the fact that the maze can be represented as a graph, the concept of backtracking (and hence stack) are all naturally discovered by students as they implemented the maze project. In handling issues in the ultra-sonic sensor and infra-red sensor the students realize the concept of noisy data, they independently discovered the concept of sampling, averaging and noise correction. Most importantly, when doing the projects, they realize an important principle of system design – not to assume that things will work the first time. Students naturally discover these principles and hence this yields to be more effective than being taught with a contrived or abstract example.

Overall, we feel this exercise in CS252 has provided a project that can be done in a 4 to 6 week time-frame and added to an existing 2 or 3 credit course on introductory computer science. In our experience, it is an effective way to introduce computer science in a hands-on fashion to covey to freshman the excitement and diversity in the field.

7. ACKNOWLEDGMENTS

We thank the anonymous reviewers for comments. Many thanks to Mark Hill and Guri Sohi for facilitating the projects in CS252 in Spring 2013. Thanks to Rebecca Lam and Newsha Ardalani for much support in Spring 2012 in managing the projects. Support for this research was provided by NSF under the following grants: CCF-0845751, CNS-0917213, and CCF-0917238.

8. REFERENCES

[1] "312 introduction to programming, ut-austin, cs, http://www.cs.utexas.edu/undergraduate-program/courses/312-introduction-programming."

[2] "Adafruit, www.adafruit.com."

[3] "Arduino, http://www.arduino.cc/."

[4] "Code for nrf24l01 modules, https://github.com/maniacbug/RF24."

[5] "Fitbit flex teardown, http://www.ifixit.com/Teardown/Fitbit+Flex+Teardown/16050/1."

[6] J. Andrus and J. Nieh, "Teaching operating systems using android," in *SIGCSE '12*, pp. 613–618.

[7] J. Bayzick, B. Askins, S. Kalafut, and M. Spear, "Read, write, play: An educational mobile gaming platform," in *SIGCSE 2013*.

[8] S. Loveland, "Human computer interaction that reaches beyond desktop applications," in *SIGCSE '11*.

[9] R. L. McFall and M. DeJongh, "Increasing engagement and enrollment in breadth-first introductory courses using authentic computing tasks," in *SIGCSE '11*.

[10] S. Patel and Y. Patt, *Introduction to Computing Systems: From Bits & Gates to C & Beyond*. McGraw-Hill Professional.

APPENDIX

Projects budget

1. Obstacle Avoidance - $254.93
   (a) Arduino Uno Starter Pack ($65.00) x1
   (b) Motor Shield ($16.00) x1
   (c) Turtle 2WD Mobile Platform ($41.00) x1
   (d) Ping Ultra Sonic Sensor ($29.99) x3
   (e) Servo Extension Cables ($2.49) x3
   (f) AA Batteries ($1.36) x4
   (g) 9 volt Battery ($2.05) x1
2. Maze Navigating - $139.44
   (a) Arduino Uno Starter Pack ($65.00) x1
   (b) Motor Shield ($16.00) x1
   (c) Turtle 2WD Mobile Platform ($41.00) x1
   (d) Infrared Sensor ($9.95) x1
   (e) AA Batteries ($1.36) x4
   (f) 9 volt Battery ($2.05) x1
3. Tic Tac Toe - $381.40
   (a) Arduino Uno Starter Pack ($65.00) x4
   (b) TFT Touch Shield ($59.00) x2
   (c) NRF24L01 Radio Transceiver ($3.70) x2
4. Pong - $163.36
   (a) Arduino Uno Starter Pack ($65.00) x1
   (b) Liquidware InputShield ($39.36) x1
   (c) TFT Touch Shield ($59.00) x1
5. Twitter - $130.70
   (a) Arduino Uno Starter Pack ($65.00) x1
   (b) Graphic ST7565 Positive LCD (128x64) with RGB backlight + extras ($17.95) x1
   (c) Ethernet Shield ($45.00) x1
   (d) Ethernet Cord ($2.75) x1
6. Word Scramble - $96.65
   (a) Arduino Uno Starter Pack ($65.00) x1
   (b) Graphic ST7565 Positive LCD (128x64) with RGB backlight + extras ($17.95) x1
   (c) PS2 Keyboard ($13.70) x1

Ethnocomputing with Electronic Textiles: Culturally Responsive Open Design to Broaden Participation in Computing in American Indian Youth and Communities

Yasmin B. Kafai, Kristin Searle, Cristóbal Martinez* & Bryan Brayboy*

University of Pennsylvania
Graduate School of Education
Philadelphia, PA
kafai@upenn.edu
searle@gse.upenn.edu

Arizona State University
School of Social Transformation
Tempe, AZ
Christopher.m.martinez@asu.edu,
Bryan.Brayboy@asu.edu

ABSTRACT
There have been many efforts to increase access and participation of indigenous communities in computer science education using ethnocomputing. In this paper, we extend culturally responsive computing by using electronic textiles that leverage traditional crafting and sewing practices to help students learn about engineering and computing as they also engage with local indigenous knowledges. Electronic textiles include sewable microcontrollers that can be connected to sensors and actuators by stitching circuits with conductive thread. We present findings from a junior high Native Arts class and an academically-oriented summer camp in which Native American youth ages 12-15 years created individual and collective e-textile designs using the LilyPad Arduino. In our discussion we address how a culturally responsive open design approach to ethnocomputing with e-textile activities can provide a productive but also challenging context for design agency and cultural connections for American Indian youth, and how these findings can inform the design of a broader range of introductory computational activities for all.

Categories and Subject Descriptors
K.3.0 **[Computers and Education]:** General

General Terms
Human Factors

Keywords
Electronic textiles, education, Indigenous Communities, K-12

1. INTRODUCTION
Though recent observations suggest that computer science is making a comeback [20], participation in computer science and entry into technology-related careers by underrepresented groups continues to be alarmingly low (NSF, 2009). The situation has been particularly dismal for American Indian youth and communities [i]. Efforts in broadening access to and participation of indigenous communities in computer science education over the last two decades have not left any discernible impact. Explanations for this persistent trend point to a combination of factors, such as lack of access to advanced computer science courses and curricula [18], lack of teacher preparation [12], and lack of culturally responsive ways to work with underrepresented groups [10]—all factors which have also impeded the progress of computer science education at large. In order to better understand the critical connection between culture and computing for engaging indigenous students, we focus on approaches that have been developed in ethnocomputing.

Ethnocomputing recognizes local systems of computational knowledge at multiple levels, including data structures, algorithms, tools and theory, and uses [27]. One approach, called culturally responsive computing, has focused on designing tools and environments that help students learn about computation and its cultural relevance [9]. In culturally responsive computing, local practices of ethnocomputing are leveraged to create Situated Design Tools (CSDTs) in which interactive computational models make explicit the deep-seated mathematical and computational principles already present in the cultural practices of particular groups. Eglash and his colleagues have developed a Virtual Bead Loom tool that allows students to virtually create beaded designs following algorithms present in Shoshone-Bannock beadwork that are guided by the principles of recursion and iteration [7]. In a different vein, Lameman and her colleagues [17] developed a game design curriculum for First Nations youth in Canada that taught students the fundamentals of game design while encouraging them to draw upon their own cultural experiences. The goal of culturally responsive computing, with few exceptions that have focused on both computation and cultural knowledge, has been primarily for students to learn about computation.

In this paper, we propose an approach to ethnocomputing that combines the teaching of computation and aspects of local culture [ii]. We do so by introducing electronic textiles (hereafter, e-textiles), which connect crafting practices such as sewing and decorative beading that have a long history in many indigenous communities to computing and engineering practices [3]. E-textiles include sewable microcontrollers that can be connected to sensors and actuators by stitching circuits with conductive thread to create wearable, interactive clothing, home furnishings, and soft toys [4]. By using e-textiles to help students learn about engineering and computing, Native arts and crafts can be connected with electronic computation. In this context, we can promote the 'design agency' of computer science learners in culturally responsive ways [8] by constructing software or

SIGCSE'14, March 05-08, 2014, Atlanta, GA, USA

10.1145/2538862.2538903

physical artifacts that facilitate the translation of their ideas into a technical realization—an idea very much in line with efforts to promote computational thinking [29]. As of yet, little attention has been paid to how cultural viewpoints situate engagement with computational thinking.

The focus of this paper is to examine, conceptually and empirically, how an ethnocomputing approach to learning with e-textiles can engage K-12 youth in formal and informal educational contexts in design agency, the processes through which individuals grapple with the constraints and possibilities of specific design tools to create artifacts and connect to cultural practices and concepts [8]. We present findings from two projects, a 10-week unit in a Native arts class and a 2-week intensive summer camp. Within these projects, 39 Native American youth created either individual or collective e-textile designs using the LilyPad Arduino e-textile construction kit. In the discussion we address how and in what ways e-textile activities provide a context for design agency and cultural connections, and how these findings can inform the design of introductory computational activities that broaden access for all.

2. BACKGROUND

Like the rest of US students, few American Indian/Alaska Natives ever venture into computer science [28]. While American Indians comprise 0.9% of the U.S. Population (2010 U.S. Census), they only received 0.4% of all bachelor's degrees, 0.2% of all master's degrees, and 0.1% of all doctorates awarded in computer science, computer engineering and information in 2012. In full numbers, this translates to American Indian/Alaska Natives having received 57 bachelor's degrees, 20 master's degrees, and 2 doctorates in computing-related fields in 2012 [30]. These statistics clearly indicate that current programs and efforts in schools are not meeting the needs of indigenous students and communities.

One key reason has been the lack of access [13]. While there are and have been efforts to increase the number of American Indians/Alaska Natives in STEM-related fields, most are targeted at undergraduate and graduate students. Several short-term summer experience programs, like the Native Explorers program (www.nativeexplorers.org) for high school students at Oklahoma State are the exception to the rule. These summer programs expose Indigenous students to STEM, some through culturally responsive pedagogies, but they are short-term and, therefore, unlikely to foster the kind of broad, systemic change that is needed. Moreover, the vast majority of these efforts target the few students who have both completed high school and maintained an interest in STEM. Thus they do not address the heart of the issue—the disconnections between indigenous conceptions of computing knowledge and approaches to teaching STEM content in schools.

Most ethnocomputing initiatives have employed approaches that are culturally responsive in nature, meaning that they value student knowledge, recognize differing knowledge systems, and prioritize community or local relationships [7, 26]. Culturally responsive computing is explicit about the complex computational and mathematical thinking present in local knowledge systems, so that students, through design activities, come to see computational thinking as part of their culture heritage. The virtual bead loom [7] and the game design curriculum [17] described in the introduction are illustrations of how these cultural connections to computing can be realized.

In our approach to ethnocomputing, we wanted to use culturally responsive computing not just as a context for situating computation (i.e., to make it relevant to existing cultural practices) but also as a context for challenging beliefs about computation (i.e., what is computing). By design, e-textiles integrate indigenous technologies of crafting and sewing with electronic technologies and computer programming [3] and thus provide a context for examining both connections and disconnects. On one side, practices such as basket weaving, beading, and pottery making have historically been a part of many American Indian cultures, with local (indigenous) knowledge about these practices being passed down from generation to generation [14]. Using electronic textiles thus links computational practices to traditional practices that were historically (and in many cases, remain) an integral part of community life, and can illustrate how people are connected to one another and their surrounding environment—relationships that are considered critical in Indigenous Knowledge Systems [1, 2, 16].

E-textiles are a relatively new addition to a long line of construction kits that merge the tangible with the virtual side of computing. There are few established academic canons to which students have to respond; instead, in the DIY tradition, most of the e-textiles community operates in informal settings, developing new applications and conventions. This feature makes e-textiles an especially promising context for broadening Indigenous communities' participation in computer science.

In making e-textiles, there is thus the opportunity for students to learn crafting physical artifacts, sewing circuits, and programming functionalities and, in the process, developing design fluency that facilitates the translation of their ideas and identities into a technical realization. This development of design agency is meant, "to encompass not only what we make but who is making it; at the same time we design things, they are designing us" [7, p.69]. Design agency thus connects to computational thinking [29] but adds a cultural dimension. Viewing computational thinking through the lens of design agency can take into account not only the constraints of digital tools but also the constraints imposed by a legacy of colonization. American Indian peoples, especially elders, often view electronic technology as yet another alienating vehicle of colonization—one that is responsible for making their youth English-language dominant and making them more interested in watching television than in listening to stories that have been passed down through the generations [5, 16]. In our two studies with American Indian youth and communities, we examined how students developed design agency in making e-textiles artifacts and how this was connected (or not) to community funds of knowledge and students' identities as American Indian youth.

3. E-TEXTILES IN CLASS AND CAMP

Our research on Ethno E-textiles (hereafter, e2textiles) takes place in an American Indian community outside of Phoenix, Arizona. The community is comprised of two tribes that have historically been allies and has roughly 10,000 enrolled members. One of the tribes is known for its pottery and the other for its basket making. When we initially developed our partnership with the community, we envisioned drawing upon these practices to engage students in computing activities. Since then, we have gone through an iterative process of co-designing with community partners and refining a series of e2textiles workshops focused on promoting design agency through the linkage of community funds of knowledge, including local indigenous knowledges (e.g., knowledge about beading, knowledge of plants), with computing and craft practices [11].

We began our research in March 2013 with 12 seventh and eighth grade students (3 males, 9 females) enrolled in a Native Arts class at a charter school located in the community. Working with an experienced American Indian art and mathematics teacher who we will call Ms. Kilgore, we co-designed a 10-week e2textiles unit to supplement the Native Arts curriculum. Based on findings from this workshop, we then designed a two-week e2textiles unit for a summer camp, this time with a more explicit focus on community funds of knowledge by designing a collaborative quilt project around local flora. 27 junior high students (9 male, 18 female), including 5 students from the Native Arts class, enrolled in the camp located at a community college on tribal lands. In both cases, students programmed their e-textile projects using the Modkit visual programming environment [21], which is designed as an overlay to the Arduino programming language. Through analysis of field notes and video logs of classroom sessions documenting students' emergent artistic and computational design processes, interview transcripts in which students reflected on their understandings of the relationships between e-textiles and community funds of knowledge, and artifacts themselves, we identified how students developed design agency in crafting and computing, and connected (or not) to their notions of their culture while making e-textile artifacts. We also examined the choices we, as instructors, made that promoted or hindered students' design agency.

E-Textile Class

The 10-week e-textile unit in the junior high Native Arts class was our first attempt at integrating community funds of knowledge and computing. Working together with Ms. Kilgore, we made a conscious decision to give students very few design constraints, since this was how Ms. Kilgore had approached all of the other projects students engaged in throughout the year. Students were told that they had to design and program an e-textile project with at least two LEDs (light emitting diodes) and a LilyPad Arduino. We showed examples of projects that we had made and that students had made in previous e-textiles workshops, but we did not give students any design constraints in terms of what they could or could not make. As a result, students mainly created felt patches with e-textile elements that could later be affixed to their hoodies or backpacks (see Figure 1).

Figure 1: Student-designed e-textiles from the Native Arts class with a Nyan Cat (left) and a flower (right).

The e-textile designs highlighted personal interests in youth media culture—favorite bands, anime characters, and YouTube videos. These designs were both similar and different from other items, mainly beaded bracelets and necklaces that students made in the Native Arts class. Ms. Kilgore told us that students' first attempt at creating something in a given medium often had a non-traditional design, such as a beaded Hello Kitty bracelet where the art form was a Native craft, but the design was from popular culture. Once students developed a sense of the medium, they often made second and third projects with more traditional designs, according to Ms. Kilgore.

In the case of the e-textiles unit, most students only made one e-textile project and even the small number of students who made two e-textile projects did not return to local cultural designs. Rather, they persisted with designs connected to personal interests in youth media culture and expanded their programming repertoire. For instance, seventh-grader Rachel made a heart and lightning bolt design for her first project. The lightning bolts flashed in a blinking pattern. For her second design, Rachel made a design inspired by her favorite anime show, whose logo she carried around inside the laminated cover of her binder. The e-textile project inspired by this design included two conductive fabric patches, which required more sophisticated programming skills to make the project work. Still, when we asked students to compare their experience with e-textiles to other things they had done in Native Arts, they stressed the similarity of using needle and thread and the difference of using electronic components.

While the e-textile artifacts students made were thematically similar to those made by other youth [15], the Native Arts students thoughtfully integrated craft and technology in ways not previously seen amongst novice designers. For instance, almost every single student chose to hide the LilyPad and even to cover the LEDs with felt to achieve particular types of "glowing" effects. Many students used stitches that were more advanced than the simple running stitch used by novice designers, opting instead to use blanket stitch for edging and satin stitch to cover LEDs. Students also had more extensive patterns within their programming loops, even at the simplistic level of making LEDs blink on and off. Rachel worked for several class periods to perfect the timing of the blinks for the LEDs behind her lightning bolts to make them look as if they were flashing. Some students also programmed their artifacts and then requested to change the programming several days later after showing the artifact off to peers at school and family at home. In these ways, we saw students exercising design agency. However, this sense of agency was not as connected to community funds of knowledge as we had hoped.

E-Textile Camp

Drawing upon our experiences with the Native Arts class, we worked closely with staff from the community's Cultural Resources Department and the American Indian Studies program at a local community college to design a second e2textiles workshop for an academically-oriented summer camp with 7th and 8th graders. Our goal for working with these partners was to respond to our observation that students often made e-textiles artifacts connected to popular youth culture rather than to their indigenous cultures because they had a working definition of technology, where technology was electronic technology and, therefore, located outside of community knowledges. Having shared our observations about students' views on technology with our community partners, we collectively arrived at the theme of agriculture and local plants because it allowed us to discuss how the community has used various kinds of technology throughout its history. We used a quilt in the shape of tribal lands to situate students' e-textile designs of local plants.

We began the e-textiles portion of the camp with a brief orientation to e-textiles and how to design circuits, and program sensors and actuators. Working with our community partners, we then provided students with different examples of community technologies while also drawing from local funds of knowledge. Examples were used to illustrate innovations of technology from inside the community and adaptations of technology appropriated from outside the community in order to show students that technology is an essential part of their heritage. Students were challenged to reflect upon ways to make computation useful and meaningful to their community, and reflective of their identities as local indigenous people. After having learned about local indigenous technologies and appropriations, students worked on designing e-textile squares for the community-quilt over the course of two weeks (see Figure 2).

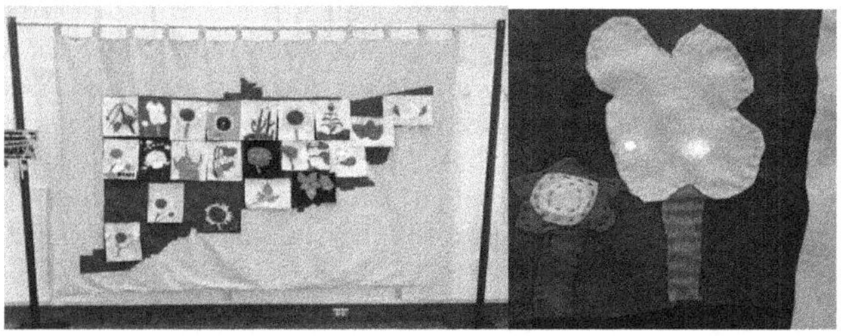

Figure 2: Student-designed quilt from the summer camp (left) and quilt square detail of Alex's design (right).

We asked each student to choose a plant to make into an e-textiles design from a binder containing pictures of about 20 local plants. When students chose the plant they wanted to represent, staff members from the Cultural Resources Department were present to answer students' questions about the plants and to provide them with the local indigenous names of the chosen plants. Students later designed quilt squares based on their chosen plants.

Based on prior experience, we encouraged design-agency through an iterative design process where students tested each electronic component and programmed it as they went along rather than waiting until the end to write a computer program. This kind of semi-structured design task (as opposed to the completely open-ended nature of the Native Arts class) facilitated the creation of designs that were more complex in terms of their circuitry and programming. Two students incorporated sensors, 2 students added sound, 1 student included an RGB light, and 1 student used 2 lilypads to support a system of 13 LED lights coded to blink in complex patterns. Several of the students transitioned from coding in Modkit (a graphical programming environment) to coding in Arduino (a syntactical programming environment) as the complexity of their coding developed. Another student, Alex, created a design that was the product of an iterative design process where he wrote multiple programs, incorporated sensors, a piezo speaker, and an RGB light. As he explored a broad range of hardware and software, Alex often worked additively to explore an idea and then subtractively to remove hardware in favor of previous ideas that he had already prototyped, or to simply try something new altogether. The result of this was a colorful design representing two stages of cotton growth augmented with colorful lights choreographed to a simple looping melody (see Figure 2). During the second week of production, we hung the quilt background, shaped to look like a map of tribal lands, in the classroom so that students could begin to envision their contributions as a part of their community quilt. On the final day of the workshop, students had the opportunity to temporarily affix their quilt square to the wall hanging (allowing them to take their work home after completing the workshop). Their quilt was displayed during a public reception where the students' families were invited to view their work.

4. DISCUSSION

In this paper, we proposed an approach to ethnocomputing that focused on culturally responsive open design and investigated how learning with electronic textiles about circuitry and computation in two different contexts, a class and a summer camp, situated students' understanding as members of an indigenous community. By culturally responsive open computing, we refer to practices that connect community funds of knowledge and computing in culturally relevant ways but with fewer design constraints than those imposed when students work with culturally situated design tools. We found that working with e-textiles was a productive context for students in the Native Arts class and the summer camp to develop design agency, though this occurred in different ways and with varying degrees of success depending on the context. Some examples of students exercising design agency might include: taking a photograph of a plant and abstracting it into a simpler more stylized design, designing novel solutions to connect hardware in ways that avoid short circuits, designing spatial solutions that enabled them to conceal the hardware within their designs, designing light and sound compositions that augment and animate their squares to reflect their imaginations and the nature of their subject matter, and thinking through logic to produce novel algorithms to mostly accomplish intentionality, as opposed to settling with accidental discoveries. Students also exhibited a high level of craft by executing straight and blanket stitches that were carefully sewn, as well as using applique shapes, which they carefully cut.

In the context of the Native Arts class where the design task was more open-ended, perhaps to a fault, students exercised their design agency by choosing to make projects connected to youth media culture and by focusing on honing their programming skills, such as when Rachel spent several class sessions thinking about whether or not how she had programmed her lights to blink really looked like lightning flashing. In the context of the more narrowly constructed design task in the summer camp, students pushed even further into the realms of circuitry and computation, adding sensors to their projects and learning how to program them. However, we noticed in informal debriefing interviews that students had forgotten the indigenous names for the plants they had represented in their quilt squares, suggesting that in the future we can improve our efforts to ensure that students retain local knowledges and computation.

In both of our workshops, we learned that students benefitted from an increased level of design constraint, at least insofar as their knowledge of computational concepts and practices was concerned. When their designs were constrained, students moved more quickly beyond the initial design phase and were able to devote more of their time to circuitry and programming. In addition, because there were a limited number of plant designs to choose from, one of the ways in which students could distinguish their design from others was through the use of additional sensors and actuators and through more complex programming. However, the more constrained design task did not necessarily lead to students to make more connections between community funds of knowledge and computing. This may have been because the workshop was still structured in such a way that about one-third of the time was focused on making cultural connections and the other two-thirds of the time was focused on crafting and programming the e-textiles artifacts themselves. One challenge going forward in working with more open-ended design tasks will be not only to find the right balance between local indigenous knowledge and computation in our workshops but also to integrate the kind of explicit connection between culture and computation made in Eglash and colleagues' CSDTs. One potentially productive avenue may be to explore the incorporation of some of the elements that have recently been identified as successful in introductory programming courses at the college level, such as having students program in pairs and having student-led instruction [24].

Our findings present an interesting conundrum that is a challenge at large for ethnocomputing. While culturally responsive design tools situate computation within an explicit, narrowly-defined cultural context, culturally responsive open design like the e2textiles workshops described in this paper situate computation within a broader cultural context. This has the potential to give the learner more agency about what he or she learns, but it also runs the risk that students will continue to view community funds of knowledge, such as local indigenous knowledges, and digital computation as distinct bodies of knowledge that do not and should not connect with one another. Ironically, the Cultural Resources Department, community college, and junior high staff members we worked with had far more expansive views of technology than the youth we worked with. This suggests that e-textiles and other more open-ended design tools without specific disciplinary connections in formal schooling are needed to develop a supportive space for youth to explore and work out their own identities and stances on technology. Further research and connections between researchers and community members are needed to determine the appropriate balance between community funds of knowledge and computation, as well as the appropriate level of constraints in these kinds of open-ended design tasks.

From Eglash and his colleagues' work, we learned that whether or not a computing task is culturally responsive matters more than whether or not the learner is situated within the culture of the design tool [8, 9]. In other words, a Latino student can learn as much about computation from engaging with a CSDT built around cornrows as an African American student can learn. However, we would argue that this approach fails to recognize that learning about culture in and of itself, particularly as it relates to students' identity development within their culture and place, is an equally important outcome—one where we suspect that context does matter.

There are some special considerations in the case of American Indians that need further exploration in future research, especially when we consider connecting craft knowledge to computing. Craft, like many other types of Indigenous knowledge, is rooted in particular places and connected to activities that extend beyond the space of a classroom and a computer screen. For instance, when we think about integrating community basket weaving practices with e-textiles materials, we know that there are certain times of the year during which reeds for making baskets can be collected. We also know that particular designs have cosmological significance, ties to origin stories, and are expressed within local aesthetic frameworks. Knowledges of these designs is not something that can be learned by anyone, but something that the learner must be prepared to know, coming to understand the responsibility that comes with such knowledge and the protocols for appropriate use. What might it look like to more fully engage cultural contexts in culturally responsive computing for Native American youth and communities? Would such an approach more fully engage participants and facilitate relationship building amongst participants and between participants and instructors [19, 22]? Would such an approach help students connect digital media to local indigenous technologies in ways that encouraged its appropriation and culturally responsive adaptive re-use? All these are questions for further research.

At the same time, we recognize that there are lessons from our research that contribute to the broader framework of culturally responsive computing and the goal of broadening participation in computing for all students. Echoing the work of other researchers interested in broadening participation in computing [19, 25], our implementation of two workshop models, one more open-ended and one more-constrained in terms of the design task and the cultural context, highlights the importance of providing a variety of different contexts in which youth can explore computing [19]. As such, it is important not only that we continue to develop culturally-specific models tied to heritage with a balance of design constraints and space for design agency to happen, but also that we create open-ended yet focused design tasks for those students with other interests, such as the students in our first workshop who primarily expressed interest in youth popular culture. We must remind ourselves that culture is not static; its dynamic nature allows that the integration of electronic technology and popular culture need not necessarily be at odds with the culture of one's ancestors. Indeed, culture isn't something that is fixed in the past; it is constantly in flux, the notion of culture is an approximation, and it is being made on a daily basis.

Through the work with our community partners, and American Indian youth, we learned that providing all students with design agency to imagine forms of computation responsive to their interests and identities has the potential to provide embodied learning experiences that allow students to see themselves as successful stakeholders of the digital age. Contextualizing computer science learning within local funds of knowledge and practices may provide students with the ability to tie what they are learning to the history and emergence of their respective communities in ways that can meaningfully broaden participation in computing. By broadening participation in computing we not are not only referring to the promotion of diversity in computing, but we also refer to the importance of cultivating learning scenarios designed to support diverse expressions of computing reflected by broader perspectives.

[i] Throughout this paper, we use American Indian, Alaska Native, American Indian/Alaska Native, Native or Native American, and Indigenous interchangeably. We are aware of the wide range and variation among the 500 tribal nation groups in United States.

[ii] By culture, we mean a shared way of thinking, engaging, and viewing the world by a group of people. Culture is often rooted in place, language, and ways of being, doing, learning, and thinking about things that are unique to a particular group. Our notion of culture is that it is fluid and not concrete, meaning that perceptions of culture, to certain degrees, vary among community members. Our understandings of culture in this project are driven by how our community partners define their own culture, and cultural pedagogy for their youth.

5. ACKNOWLEDGEMENTS

This work was supported by a collaborative grant (#1150150 and #1150604) from the National Science Foundation to Yasmin Kafai and Bryan Brayboy. Any opinions, findings, and conclusions or recommendations expressed in this paper are those of the authors and do not necessarily reflect the views of the National Science Foundation, the University of Pennsylvania or Arizona State University.

6. REFERENCES

[1] Basso, K.H. (1996). *Wisdom Sits in Places: Landscape and Language Among the Western Apache*. Albuquerque: University of New Mexico Press.

[2] Battiste, M. (2002). Indigenous knowledge and pedagogy in first nations education: A literature review with recommendations. Ottawa, Ontario, Canada: Indian and Northern Affairs Canada.

[3] Buechley, L. & Eisenberg, M. (2008). The LilyPad Arduino: Toward wearable engineering for everyone. *IEEE Pervasive Computing, 7*(2), 12-15.

[4] Buechley, L., Peppler, K., Eisenberg, M. & Kafai, Y. (Eds.) (2013). *Textile messages: Dispatches from the world of e-textiles and education.* New York: Peter Lang.

[5] Castagno, A.E. & Brayboy, B.M.J. (2008). Culturally responsive schooling for Indigenous youth: A review of the literature. *Review of Educational Research, 78*(4), 941-993.

[6] First Lego League (2008-9). *More than Robots: An Evaluation of the FIRST Robotics Competitions Participant and Institutional Impacts.* A Report by the First Lego League. Brandeis University, MA: Center for Youth and Communities Heller School for Social Policy and Management.

[7] Eglash, R. (2007). Ethnocomputing with Native American Design. In L.E. Dyson, M. Hendriks, & S. Grant (Eds.), *Information Technology and Indigenous People* (pp. 210-219). Hershey, PA: Information Science Publishing.

[8] Eglash, R. & Bennett, A. (2009). Teaching with hidden capital: Agency in children's explorations of cornrow hairstyles. *Children, Youth, and Environments, 19*(1), 58-73.

[9] Eglash, R., Gilbert, J., & Foster, E. Broadening participation: Toward culturally responsive computing education. *Communications of the ACM, 56*(7), 33-36.

[10] Eisenhart, M. & Edwards, L. (2004). Red-eared sliders and neighborhood dogs: Creating third spaces to support ethnic girls' interest in technological and scientific expertise. *Children, Youth, and Environments, 14*(2), 156-177.

[11] Gonzalez, N., Moll, L.C., & Amanti, C. (2005). *Funds of knowledge: Theorizing practices in households, communities, and classrooms.* New York: Routledge.

[12] Goode, J. (2007). If you build teachers, will students come? The role of teachers in broadening computer science learning for urban youth. *Journal of Educational Computing Research, 36*(1), 65-88.

[13] Gordon, A.C., Gordon, M., & Dorr, J. (2003). Native American technology access: The Gates Foundation in Four Corners. *The Electronic Library, 21*(5), 428-434.

[14] Hill, S.H. (1997). *Weaving new worlds: Southeastern Cherokee women and their basketry.* Chapel Hill: University of North Carolina Press.

[15] Kafai, Y., Searle, K., Kaplan, E., Fields, D., Lee, S., & Lui, D. (2013). Cupcake Cushions, Scooby Doo Shirts, and Soft Boomboxes: E-Textiles in High School to Promote Computational Concepts, Practices, and Perceptions. In, *Proceeding of the 44th ACM technical symposium on computer science education (SIGCSE '13)* (pp. 311-316). ACM: New York.

[16] Kawagley, O. (1995). *A Yupiaq Worldview.* Prospect Heights, IL: Waveland Press.

[17] Lameman, B.A., Lewis, J.E., & Fragnito, S. (2010). Skins 1.0: A curriculum for designing games with First Nations youth. In *Proceedings of FuturePlay 2010* (pp. 105-112). ACM: Vancouver BC, Canada.

[18] Margolis, J., Estella, R., Goode, J., Holme, J., & Nao, K. (2008). *Stuck in the shallow end: Education, race, and computing.* Cambridge, MA: MIT Press.

[19] Margolis, J., Ryoo, J.J., Sandoval, C.D.M., Lee, C., Goode, J., & Chapman, G. (2012). Beyond access: Broadening participation in high school computer science. *ACM Inroads, 3*(4), 72-78.

[20] Miller, C. (2011, June 10). Computer Studies Made Cool, on Film and Now on Campus. *The New York Times.* Retrieved on June 28, 2011, from http://www.nytimes.com/2011/06/11/technology/11computing.html?_r=1

[21] Millner, A. & Baafi, E. (2011). Modkit: Blending and extending approachable platforms for creating computer programs and interactive objects. In *Proceedings of the 10th International Conference on Interaction Design and Children (IDC '11)* (pp. 250-253). ACM: Ann Arbor, MI.

[22] Nasir, N.S. & Hand, V. (2008). From the court to the classroom: Opportunities for engagement, learning, and identity in basketball and classroom mathematics. *Journal of the Learning Sciences, 17*, 143-179.

[23] National Science Foundation (2009). Science and engineering degrees by race/ethnicity: 1997-2006. Retrieved on August 20, 2013 from http://www.nsf.gov/statistics/nsf10300/pdf/nsf10300.pdf.

[24] Porter, L., Guzdial, M., McDowell, C., & Simon, B. (2013). Success in introductory programming: what works? *Communications of the ACM, 56*(8), 34-36.

[25] Repenning, A. (2012). Programming goes back to school. *Communications of the ACM, 55*(5), 38-40.

[26] Scott, K. A., Aist, G., & Hood, D. (2009). COMPUGIRLS: Designing a culturally relevant technology program. *Educational Technology, 49*(6), 34-39.

[27] Tedre, M., Sutinen, E., Kahkonen, E., & Kommers, P. (2006). Ethnocomputing: ICT in cultural and social context. *Communications of the ACM, 49*(1), 126-130.

[28] Varma, R. (2009). Attracting Native Americans to computing. *Communications of the ACM, 52*(8), 137-140.

[29] Wing, J. M. (2006). Computational thinking. *Communications of the ACM, 49*, 33-35.

[30] Zweben, S. & Bizot, B. (2013). 2012 Taulbee Survey: Strong increases in undergraduate CS enrollment and degree production, Record degree production at doctoral level. *Computing Reserach News, 25*(5), 11-60.

Tracking @stemxcomet: Teaching Programming to Blind Students via 3D Printing, Crisis Management, and Twitter

Shaun K. Kane
Department of Information Systems
UMBC
Baltimore, MD 21201
skane@umbc.edu

Jeffrey P. Bigham
Human-Computer Interaction Institute
Carnegie Mellon University
Pittsburgh, PA 15217
jbigham@cs.cmu.edu

ABSTRACT
Introductory programming activities for students often include graphical user interfaces or other visual media that are inaccessible to students with visual impairments. Digital fabrication techniques such as 3D printing offer an opportunity for students to write programs that produce tactile objects, providing an accessible way of exploring program output. This paper describes the planning and execution of a four-day computer science education workshop in which blind and visually impaired students wrote Ruby programs to analyze data from Twitter regarding a fictional ecological crisis. Students then wrote code to produce accessible tactile visualizations of that data. This paper describes outcomes from our workshop and suggests future directions for integrating data analysis and 3D printing into programming instruction for blind students.

Categories and Subject Descriptors
K.3.2 [**Computers and Education**]: Computer and Information Science Education – *computer science education, curriculum.*

Keywords
Education, programming, accessibility, visual impairments, crisis informatics, 3D printing, fabrication.

1. INTRODUCTION
Advances in computer accessibility over the past few decades have resulted in many computing devices and applications that are accessible to blind and visually impaired individuals. However, computer programming tools still present significant accessibility challenges to blind people, and blind people are currently underrepresented in computer science [8]. This effect is likely due, at least in part, to a lack of compelling accessible instructional materials and tools for learning how to program [7].

Developing a supportive environment in which blind students can learn to program presents several challenges. First, the programming tools must be accessible to the student and must work with the assistive technology that he or she uses, *e.g.,* a screen reader, screen magnifier, or refreshable Braille display. Second, the student must be provided with programming tasks that hold their interest and provide encouraging feedback. Many common programming exercises that have been used to entice younger programmers, such as GUI programming or creating graphical games, are inaccessible to blind students. Thus, finding alternative introductory programming activities that are both interesting and accessible to blind students could encourage more blind students to learn to program.

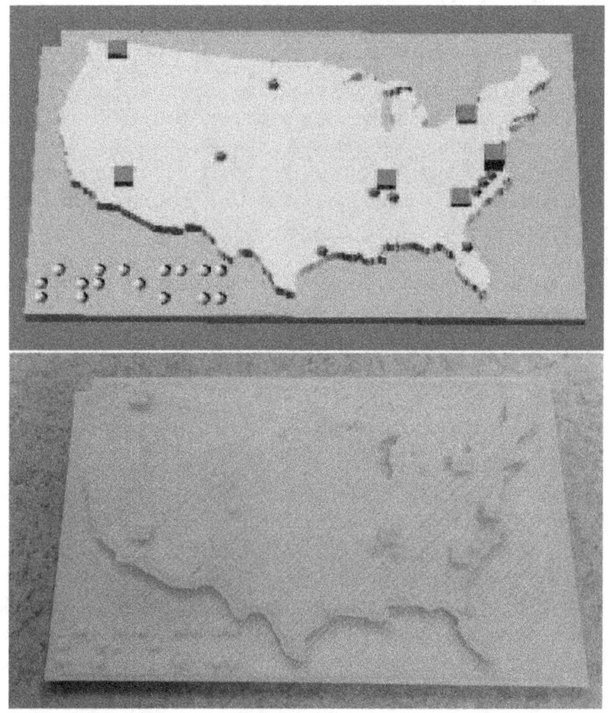

Figure 1. Blind high school students in our programming workshop analyzed Twitter data and visualized them using 3D printing. Top: 3D model generated from Twitter data, using our support libraries. Bottom: 3D-printed tactile graphic.

While prior attempts to improve programming accessibility for blind students have often focused on providing improved audio feedback (*e.g.,* [14,16]), there has been relatively little exploration of how tactile feedback could help blind students understand their programs or make programming more compelling. The increasing availability of digital fabrication or "making" technologies, such as 3D printers, presents an opportunity to connect student programming to the creation of physical, tactile objects that could be accessible to blind and visually impaired students.

In this paper, we describe the preparation and implementation of a four-day computer science workshop in which blind high school students explored Ruby programming by accessing social

SIGCSE '14, March 5-8 2014, Atlanta, GA, USA

ACM 978-1-4503-2605-6/14/03 $15.00.
http://dx.doi.org/10.1145/2538862.2538975

networking data via the Twitter API, manually explored that data via their code, and visualized that data via an interactive iPad application and 3D-printed tactile models (Figure 1). We then report the results of this activity and identify additional opportunities for integrating data analysis and 3D printing into accessible computer science programs.

2. RELATED WORK

A common problem with mainstream programming tools and integrated development environments (IDEs) is that they rely on visual information to convey structure and provide helpful hints [2]. This problem is not new, and researchers have explored various techniques for making programming tools more accessible to blind and visually impaired users.

One approach has been to create new programming languages that are easier to read and write using a screen reader. APL [12] is an audio programming language designed by and for blind programmers. Quorum (formerly Hop) is a programming language that was designed to be easy for both blind and sighted novice programmers [16]. Custom programming languages can help to overcome some of the accessibility challenges present in mainstream programming languages, but also have limitations: knowledge of a specialized programming language might not transfer to mainstream programming tasks, and specialized programming languages may restrict the programmer to specific functionality, libraries, or development tools. Other projects have produced accessible variations of existing programming tools, such as Visual Basic [14] and LEGO Mindstorms [5].

Researchers have also explored how mainstream languages and IDEs can be made more accessible. Emacspeak [10] is a screen reader for the Emacs text editor that was designed to support several text editing tasks, including programming tasks. Smith *et al.* [15] developed a plugin for the Eclipse IDE that provided sound feedback when blind programmers traversed code hierarchies. PLUMB EXTRA[3] [4] is a supplementary educational tool that allows blind programming students to explore data structures spatially using a talking graph exploration tool.

Finally, some researchers have explored curricula for introducing existing programming tools to blind students. Ludi and Reichlmayr [6] have used introductory robotics kits, such as Mindstorms, to teach computer science concepts to blind and visually impaired students in grades 7–12. Bigham *et al.* [2] conducted an introductory programming workshop in which blind high school students created instant messenger chat bots in C#. Our current approach is similar to this prior work, in that we have focused on teaching blind students using existing programming technologies (Ruby, the Twitter API, and OpenSCAD [9]), but provide supporting libraries to enable students to create working programs faster.

3. PROGRAMMING WORKSHOP

Over the past year, our research group has explored the use of 3D printers to create accessible technology such as tactile graphics [3]. As part of this ongoing work, we have explored how 3D design and printing can be used to help teach basic programming concepts to blind students. This section describes our preparation and implementation of a four-day introductory programming workshop for blind high school students.

3.1 Workshop Setup

The workshop took place over four days in July and August 2013, as part of the computer science track of the National Federation of the Blind's STEM-X program. STEM-X (formerly known as the NFB Youth Slam) is a week-long summer science camp for blind and visually impaired youth [7]. In 2013, STEM-X had fifty attendees from across the United States. STEM-X students chose one disciplinary track (computer science, chemistry, engineering, robotics, or aerospace science) to explore during the week. For four days, students spent half the day working with instructors in their track, and half the day participating in science enrichment and social activities. On the final day, students reconvened to show off their work to their peers.

Students in all subject tracks worked together to solve a shared problem: the (fictional) impact of Comet ISON. Students in the aerospace track built a working hovercraft, students in the chemistry track studied the science behind desalinization plants, and students in the robotics track built robots to help find people in trouble. Students in the computer science track monitored comet sightings using social media and wrote programs to produce tactile visualizations of the predicted impact zone. At the end of each day, students came together to share status updates about the impending comet impact, and to discuss next steps.

The computer science track featured 9 students (3 female) from grades 8 to 12. Students varied greatly in their prior computer and programming experience, and also varied in their visual abilities and preferred assistive technologies. The computer science track had 6 instructors: 2 faculty members, 2 graduate students, and 2 undergraduate students. The instructors were also assisted by 2 mentors, who helped students with any general issues that came up, including basic computer or screen reader problems. The high instructor-to-student ratio ensured that students did not have to wait for help for very long if they became stuck, which was especially beneficial as most students were programming novices. However, students were able to make independent progress even when instructors were unavailable, suggesting that this workshop could work well with fewer instructors.

3.2 Programming Tools

Choosing an environment for introducing students to computer programming can be challenging, especially for blind students, who might have difficulties working with standard programming tools. Thus, much of our preparation work focused on choosing appropriate programming tools and developing supporting library code for students to work with. Our primary goals in choosing programming tools were to create an environment that would be easy to start programming in, to use real programming languages if possible, and to enable students to try out several programming concepts over the course of the workshop.

We chose Ruby as the programming language for this workshop, as it had a number of advantages over competing languages. First, Ruby is a mainstream programming language that is available on many systems, and which offers many standard libraries. Second, Ruby syntax is comprised largely of text symbols (*e.g.*, "if", "then", "end"), and contains relatively few non-alphanumeric symbols that may be difficult to recognize via a screen reader. Third, Ruby provides an interactive interpreter, *irb*, that enables students to learn using a "read-eval-print loop" [13]. We considered using the Python programming language, which also satisfies these criteria, but Python uses whitespace to delimit code blocks, which could be confusing to navigate with a screen reader.

Since students only spent about 16 hours total in the workshop, they would be unable to make sophisticated programs completely on their own. To enable these novice students to interact with compelling applications, we created several library functions that students could call to interact with more advanced features. These functions were grouped into four major categories:

- **Twitter:** a wrapper for the Twitter API that enabled students to log in, search tweets, and post tweets;
- **Geocoding:** functions for reverse-geocoding tweets that contained location data;
- **Data visualization:** functions that added geocoded tweets to an accessible map visualization, which could be viewed interactively on an iOS-based device using VoiceOver;
- **3D printing:** functions that assembled geocoded tweets into a 3D model of a tactile map, which could be 3D printed.

Figure 2 shows example Ruby code that illustrates some of the functions made available in the support libraries.

```
require 'twit' # load an external library
startup() # load twitter credentials
point = getCoordinatesForTweet('#stemxcomet',0)
loc = reverseGeocode(point) # get location of tweet
tweets = searchByKeyword('#barelyseeit') # search
tweets.each { |tweet| puts tweet } # looping
interactiveMap('#onthehorizon') # generate map
print3D('#stemxcomet) # generate 3d model
post('Programming is fun!') # post to twitter
```

Figure 2. Sample code (written by the authors) using the APIs provided to students. By the end of the workshop, students had experience using the Twitter API, working with variables and functions, looping, and generating visualizations.

Students used Apple MacBook Pro laptops with the built-in VoiceOver screen reader [1] to read and write code during the workshop. Students wrote code using Apple's TextEdit text editor, and using the *irb* interpreter prompt running in Apple's Terminal program. The majority of students used screen reader software during the workshop, while some students used screen magnification software or refreshable Braille displays (Figure 3).

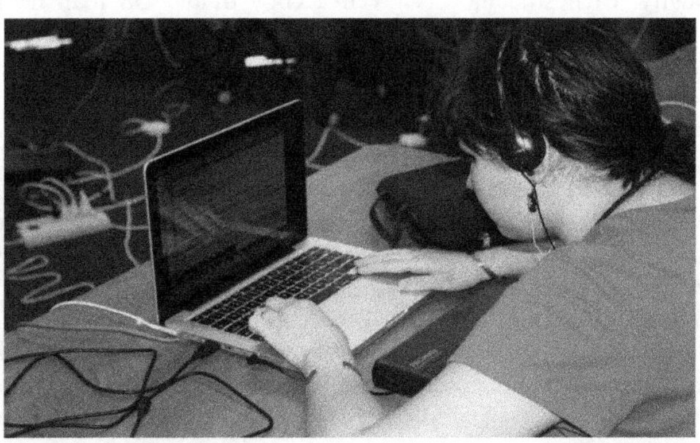

Figure 3. Students used a variety of assistive technologies to write code. This student used both a screen reader and a refreshable Braille display. Photo credit: National Federation of the Blind. Used with permission.

3.3 Dataset

Students participating in each of the STEM-X tracks worked together to solve a shared problem: tracking the trajectory of the Comet ISON, predicting its impact spot, and directing support resources where necessary. Students in the computer science track were tasked with monitoring sightings of Comet ISON via posts on Twitter and determining the comet's likely point of impact.

We chose this task because social networks are often used to monitor crisis events in the real world, and because tracking mentions of Comet ISON on Twitter would require students to gain understanding of Ruby, the Twitter API, and visualizing data. However, since Comet ISON was not actually at risk of striking Earth, there were no posts on Twitter discussing it. Thus, we recruited volunteers across the United States to post geotagged tweets describing their view of the comet. We created a custom web application that enabled volunteers to log in using their Twitter account, and to post a pre-written tweet describing their comet sighting. These pre-written tweets required little effort from volunteers, and used the volunteer's own geographic location and Twitter handle, thus creating a geographically diverse data set. Tweets generated by the application were addressed to the Twitter user @stemxcomet (to prevent followers unaware of the project from seeing them), and featured one of several hashtags determined by the volunteer's location: tweets near the expected impact site were tagged #rightonme, somewhat distant tweets were tagged #onthehorizon, tweets from further away were tagged #barelyseeit, and tweets from the furthest location were tagged #notvisible. In total, volunteers generated 19 geotagged tweets from locations over the United States, and from several international locations (Figure 4).

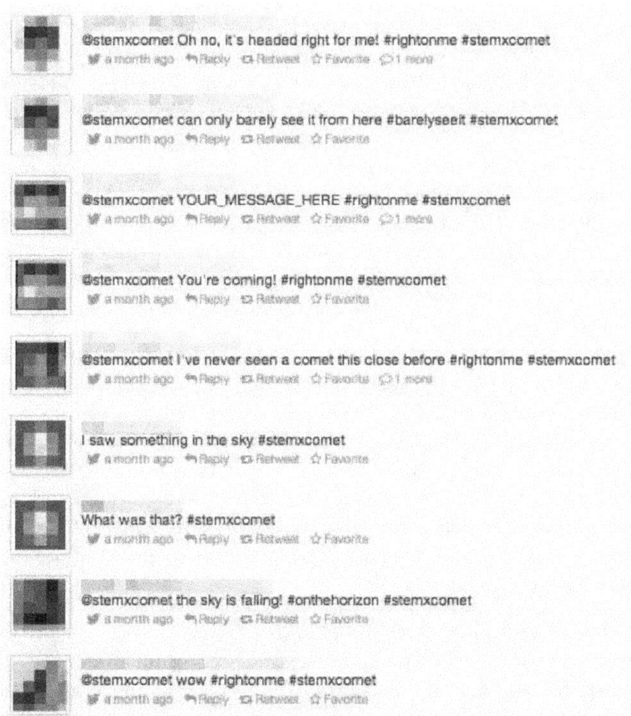

Figure 4. Twitter users posted sightings of Comet ISON as it approached the Earth in the fictional STEM-X narrative. Tweets posted close to the expected impact site were tagged differently than tweets posted from further away, enabling students to predict the impact site from Twitter data.

3.4 Workshop Curriculum

The programming workshop took place over four days, and met for four hours each day during this time. The majority of workshop time was spent working on programming activities. Each day also featured a guest speaker, who called in to discuss their work with the group. Guest speakers included a professor and crisis informatics researcher, a blind software engineer, and a blind computer science graduate student.

Because students began with different levels of background knowledge, we expected that they would proceed through the workshop activities at their own pace. Thus, students generally worked individually on the activities, and sought guidance from instructors or their peers if they became stuck. All workshop activities were written out as a step-by-step tutorial and posted on a single web page. The instructors set an approximate schedule for the workshop, as described below, and worked with students to help them complete each day's tasks. The major curriculum tasks are described below.

3.4.1 Introduction to Mac, VoiceOver, and Ruby

On the first day, students were introduced to the Macintosh computers and VoiceOver screen reader, opening the terminal, and running terminal commands. Students also created user accounts on Twitter and posted their first tweets from those accounts.

Once students became comfortable navigating with VoiceOver, they were directed to the tutorial web site, and began writing some basic Ruby code using the *irb* interpreter, including evaluating arithmetic operations and printing strings.

3.4.2 Interacting with the Twitter API

Once they had become comfortable using the Ruby interpreter, students downloaded the support libraries written by the instructors and loaded them as a module in Ruby. Because the Twitter API requires each user to be authenticated, students were required to locate their account's OAuth tokens and add them to the library file. Then, students used the libraries to log into Twitter and post a tweet via Ruby, and to begin to search tweets by hashtags. Students performed search queries on various Twitter hashtags using the *searchByKeyword* function, and inspected the returned post objects using *irb*.

3.4.3 Geocoding

Students were introduced to the @stemxcomet tweets generated by our volunteers. Students first used the *searchByKeyword* function to manually explore each of the hashtags from the generated dataset. Students were then introduced to the concept of geotagging and GPS data, and used the provided *getCoordinatesForTweet* and *reverseGeocode* functions to retrieve location data from geotagged tweets. Students were asked to explore the various tagged tweets to see if they could figure out where the comet might strike.

3.4.4 Exploring and Visualizing Data

Following the geocoding exercise, students were introduced to functions provided by the support libraries for visualizing aggregate tweet data. Two forms of visualization were provided. First, students could use the *interactiveMap* function and pass a list of tweets to a web service, designed by the authors, that plotted the tweet coordinates on a United States map (Figure 5). The function returned a URL to the generated map, which could be loaded in an iOS web browser and explored using VoiceOver: touching anywhere on the screen would speak out the number of tweets in that region of the map, while performing directional swipe gestures would read through each of the geotagged regions.

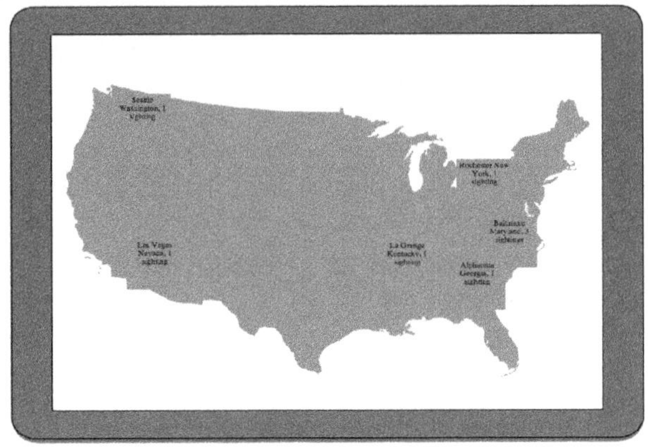

Figure 5. Tweets tagged #stemxcomet were generated and given location data across the United States. Geotagged tweets could be explored on a map using a screen reader.

Students could also call the *print3D* function from their Ruby code. This function passed tweet data to a second web service, which used OpenSCAD to generate a 3D tactile graphic based on the map. The tactile graphic is a credit-card-sized (85mm × 54mm × 5mm) version of a United States map. Geotagged tweets were shown on the map as bars: higher bars indicated more geotagged tweets in that region (Figure 1). During the workshop, the *print3D* function did not directly print the tactile graphic, but instead saved a printable stereolithography (*.stl*) file. Because each tactile graphic required approximately one hour to print, they were printed overnight and returned the next day. Tactile graphics were printed on a MakerBot Replicator 3D printer using ABS plastic.

3.4.5 3D Printing Demonstration

On the final day, the instructors brought one of the 3D printers to the workshop, and introduced it to the students. The instructors provided a verbal overview of the printer and its functions, and then began a demonstration print. While printing, students were able to examine the printer and to touch its non-moving parts. The instructors answered students' many questions about the printer, including how it worked and what could or could not be printed. Finally, each student was given a copy of the US map tactile graphic to take home. The tactile graphic was marked with the tweet locations from the volunteer dataset, the location of each student's hometown, and the word "STEMX" in 3D-printed Braille.

4. INSIGHTS FROM THE WORKSHOP

Overall, we considered the workshop to be successful. While not every student completed every activity, every student spent several days developing his or her programming skills. Spending four days teaching high school students to program in Ruby also provided valuable insights about the suitability of Ruby for blind programmers, about teaching beginning programmers to explore and visualize data, and about keeping students engaged through an intensive programming course.

4.1 Using Ruby for Blind Programming

Generally, students in our workshop were successful at writing Ruby programs, using the terminal to launch Ruby programs, and using *irb* to test code. There were, however, several usability issues relating to the interaction between Ruby and screen readers that created minor challenges.

Keeping track of scope: As found in prior explorations of blind programming (*e.g.*, [2]), our novice programmers sometimes had difficulty keeping track of their current program scope, and entered code in invalid locations. Ruby uses the keyword "end" to denote the end of a code block, such as a function, conditional statement, or loop. However, it is sometimes difficult to determine which block the "end" keyword is referring to without visual feedback. We thus encouraged students to add commends indicating the ends of blocks, and included such comments in our own example code, as shown in Figure 6.

```
def reverseGeocode(point)
    loc = Geocoder.search("#{point[0]},#{point[1]}")
    city = loc[0].city
    state = loc[0].state
    country = loc[0].country
    return "#{city},#{state},#{country}"
end
# end of function
```

Figure 6. In our sample code, we added comments to the end of function blocks to help students keep track of scope.

Conflicts between screen reader and console commands: The VoiceOver screen reader uses a combination of modifier keys (*Control* and *Option)* as a prefix for most commands. For example, *Control-Option-H* opens the VoiceOver help menu. However, VoiceOver also overrides the behavior of some keys, such as the arrow keys, which caused confusion when students attempted to use the arrow keys to browse the terminal or navigate through text files. VoiceOver provides alternative modes for accessing overridden keys, but students were not always familiar with these modes, and sometimes forgot to activate them.

Pronunciation: Ruby uses identifiable English words for many of its commands, and uses few unpronounceable symbols. However, some Ruby terms were consistently mispronounced. For example, the Ruby interpreter program, *irb,* is pronounced as "urb" by VoiceOver, and was frequently misspelled by students when using the terminal. Knowledgeable students knew to switch VoiceOver to read character-by-character, and could correctly copy the word, but not all VoiceOver users may know how to handle this type of error. Ruby also pronounced some characters in ways that could be confusing to a novice programmer. For example, the character "-" may be read and pronounced differently depending on its context: it may be "minus" in an arithmetic expression, "dash" when used as a command line parameter, and "negative" when used as a unary operator. By default, VoiceOver does not consider these distinctions, and universally refers to the "-" character as "minus", which could be confusing.

Typically, all of these problems were identified when the programming exercise was tested using a screen reader, but since the instructors were not everyday screen reader users, they sometimes missed these errors. Testing all programs and written content using a screen reader would help to identify and eliminate these types of errors before students encounter them. Fortunately, the specific problems mentioned above were all solved during the workshop, either by altering the written instructions or by advising students on how to change their screen reader settings.

4.2 3D Printing in Introductory CS

Students were clearly excited by the use of the 3D printer during the workshop. When the 3D printer was demonstrated, students paid careful attention and asked questions. Students were eager to touch the printer and observe its mechanics. We printed tactile graphics for each student, and most students were excited to take the tactile graphics home as a souvenir. When students had the opportunity to test both interactive touch screen graphics (presented on the iPad) and tactile graphics, students clearly seemed more interested in the tactile graphics. It is unclear whether students preferred the tactile graphics because they were unfamiliar, because they were accessible, or for some other reason, but even some students who were less enthusiastic about their programming activities were intrigued by the 3D printer hardware and its output.

We also found that students who did not read Braille were eager to explore the Braille printed on the tactile graphics. As Braille literacy has declined in recent decades, and because Braille literacy seems closely related to employment [11], using 3D-printed objects to motivate Braille learning presents an exciting opportunity for future work.

In general, it seemed clear that the 3D printer was a valuable addition to the computer programming workshop curriculum. However, there were some challenges in using the 3D printer in the classroom. First, the printer is quite slow: the tactile graphics, which were approximately the size of a credit card (85mm × 54mm × 5mm) each took approximately one hour to print on the MakerBot Replicator printer. Faster printing settings are available, but result in a more brittle object. As a result of the slow print time, we were not able to print each student's tactile graphics in class, but instead collected data at the second-to-last meeting, printed the tactile graphics overnight, and delivered them at the final meeting. Furthermore, even with the default settings used, the printed tactile graphics could be quite brittle. Some parts of the tactile graphics would easily wear or break off, including fine details such as the 3D-printed Braille. While the prints made with the current printer were usable, there remains room for improving the quality and durability of the 3D-printed tactile graphics, especially since tactile graphics are likely to be handled frequently.

4.3 Screen Readers as Musical Instruments

One of the most intriguing outcomes from this workshop was completely unplanned, and was instead the result of creative procrastination from the students. Throughout the week, several of the students took breaks from programming and decided to have fun with the VoiceOver screen reader. These students began adjusting the settings of VoiceOver's speech output (speech rate, voice, *etc.*) to make interesting noise, *e.g.*, clicks, beeps, and speech sounds. Over the course of the week, these sounds became more musical as students took longer breaks and invested more time in their music production.

Given the students' interest in experimenting with the screen reader, we set aside time on the second-to-last day to allow students to "perform" using their instruments. Nearly all of the students were engaged in this performance, and those who did not make music with their screen readers sometimes drummed on the table to contribute. The final performance was recorded, and was shared with students from the other STEM-X tracks on the final meeting day. In general, students seemed quite excited by their performance, and were eager to share the recording with their peers.

5. OPPORTUNITIES FOR FUTURE WORK

Our experiences in preparing and conducting this workshop suggest numerous possibilities for future work. First, the libraries that we created to support workshop participants could be extended into reusable tools to support both blind and sighted programmers. Although tools exist for programmatically generating tactile graphics (*e.g.,* VizTouch [3] and OpenSCAD [9]), these tools are not tightly integrated with standard programming languages. Universal tools for creating tactile visualizations of program output could benefit both blind and sighted programmers.

Second, although the progress made during the workshop was comparable to similar workshops with students at this ability level (*e.g.,* [2]), this workshop covered only a small subset of basic programming topics. Our approach could be extended to cover computing topics in more depth, using the provided libraries as scaffolding that is replaced with the student's own code over time. This approach may even be used as the foundation of a universally designed introductory programming course.

Third, while we did not conduct a formal evaluation of Ruby for blind programming, our informal testing during this workshop showed that Ruby was generally usable when programming with a screen reader. Ruby is an open source and mainstream programming language, and has significant potential as an introductory language for blind programmers. A more formal comparison between Ruby, other commercial programming languages, and specialized programming languages could identify opportunities and challenges to using Ruby as an introductory language for blind programmers.

Finally, while it was not part of our formal curriculum, all of our students were excited by the impromptu screen reader music session. A programming workshop in which blind students were trained to create interactive musical instruments might encourage musically inclined students to try programming. Our goal in including the tactile graphic production using 3D printing was to engage students by producing something "real." Unfortunately, this technology is still slow, whereas the product of music could be created in real time and therefore may be preferred.

6. CONCLUSION

Learning to program still presents many accessibility challenges for blind and visually impaired people. One major opportunity is to identify introductory programming experiences that are compelling to novice programmers, but that are also accessible to programmers with varied abilities. We argue that combining data analysis tools with visualization tools, and with the fabrication of tactile graphic-based visualizations, presents an ideal environment to teach programming to blind students.

Our results from a four-day workshop show that blind students were motivated to learn about 3D printing technologies, and to use their programming skills to create 3D-printed artifacts. We also found that Ruby and its interactive interpreter offer a sufficient, if not perfect, environment for teaching blind students to program. We hope that this work will motivate the development of software tools and curricula to support blind programming students in the process of exploring, analyzing, and visualizing data.

7. ACKNOWLEDGMENTS

We thank the National Federation of the Blind for organizing the STEM-X 2013 event. We also thank Patrick Carrington, Ben Gershowitz, Skye Horbrook, Karim Said, Md. Iftekhar Tanveer, and Clayonna Wheat for their help in running the workshop.

8. REFERENCES

[1] Apple. 2013. Accessibility: iOS: VoiceOver. Retrieved September 6, 2013 from http://www.apple.com/accessibility/ios/voiceover

[2] Bigham, J.P., Aller, M.B., Brudvik, J.T., Leung, J.O., Yazzolino, L.A. and Ladner, R.E. 2008. Inspiring blind high school students to pursue computer science with instant messaging chatbots. *ACM SIGCSE Bulletin*, 40, 1 (Feb. 2008), 449–453.

[3] Brown, C. and Hurst, A. 2012. VizTouch: automatically generated tactile visualizations of coordinate spaces. *Proceedings of TEI '12*, ACM Press, 131–138.

[4] Calder, M., Cohen, R.F., Lanzoni, J., Landry, N. and Skaff, J. 2007. Teaching data structures to students who are blind. *Proceedings of ITiCSE '07*, ACM Press, 87–90.

[5] Ludi, S., Abadi, M., Fujiki, Y., Sankaran, P. and Herzberg, S. 2010. JBrick: accessible Lego Mindstorm programming tool for users who are visually impaired. *Proceedings of ASSETS '10*, ACM Press, 271–272.

[6] Ludi, S. and Reichlmayr, T. 2011. The use of robotics to promote computing to pre-college students with visual impairments. *ACM Transactions on Computing Education*, 11, 3, 1–20.

[7] National Federation of the Blind. 2006. National Center for Blind Youth in Science. Retrieved September 6, 2013 from http://www.blindscience.org/ncybs-concept-paper

[8] National Science Foundation. 2013. Women, Minorities, and Persons with Disabilities in Science and Engineering: 2013. Special Report NSF 13-304. Retrieved December 3, 2013 from http://www.nsf.gov/statistics/wmpd/

[9] OpenSCAD. 2013. OpenSCAD–The Programmers Solid 3D CAD Modeller. Retrieved September 6, 2013 from http://www.openscad.org

[10] Raman, T.V. 1996. Emacspeak—a speech interface. *Proceedings of CHI '96*, ACM Press, 66–71.

[11] Ryles, R. 1996. The impact of Braille reading skills on employment, income, education, and reading habits. *Journal of Visual Impairment and Blindness*, 90, 219–226.

[12] Sánchez, J. and Aguayo, F. 2006. APL: Audio programming language for blind learners. *Computers Helping People with Special Needs*, Springer, 1334–1341.

[13] Sandewall, E. 1978. Programming in an interactive environment: the "Lisp" experience. *ACM Computing Surveys*, 10, 1, 35–71.

[14] Siegfried, R.M. 2006. Visual programming and the blind: the challenge and the opportunity. *ACM SIGCSE Bulletin*, 38, 1, 275–278.

[15] Smith, A.C., Cook, J.S., Francioni, J.M., Hossain, A., Anwar, M. and Rahman, M.F. 2004. Nonvisual tool for navigating hierarchical structures. *Proceedings of ASSETS '04,* ACM Press, 133–139.

[16] Stefik, A.M., Hundhausen, C. and Smith, D. 2011. On the design of an educational infrastructure for the blind and visually impaired in computer science. *Proceedings of SIGCSE '11*, ACM Press, 571–576.

An Assessment Model for Large Project Courses

Maria Vasilevskaya
Linköping University
Sweden
maria.vasilevskaya@liu.se

David Broman
UC Berkeley, USA and
Linköping University, Sweden
davbr@berkeley.edu

Kristian Sandahl
Linköping University
Sweden
kristian.sandahl@liu.se

ABSTRACT

Larger project courses, such as capstone projects, are essential in a modern computing curriculum. Assessing such projects is, however, extremely challenging. There are various aspects and trade-offs of assessments that can affect the quality of a project course. Individual assessments can give fair grading of individuals, but may loose focus of the project as a group activity. Extensive teacher involvement is necessary for objective assessment, but may affect the way students are working. Continuous feedback to students can enhance learning, but may be hard to combine with fair assessment. Most previous work is focusing on some specific assessment aspect, whereas we in this paper present an assessment model that consists of a collection of assessment activities, each covering different aspects. We have applied, developed, and improved these activities during a six-year period and evaluated their usefulness by performing a questionnaire-based survey.

Categories and Subject Descriptors

K.3.2 [**Computers and Education**]: Computer and Information Science Education—*computer science education, self-assessment*

Keywords

Project Courses; Assessment; Software Engineering

1. INTRODUCTION

Project-based courses are essential in a successful computing curriculum; capstone projects [16, 17] or large scale software engineering projects [2, 3, 12] make students learn how to apply technical skills in a simulated real-world scenario. Yet teaching such project courses is difficult. In particular, assessing student performance in terms of learning outcomes is a challenging, non-trivial task.

Project courses are typically organized by dividing students into groups, where each group develops their own software product. Assessing project results solely on a group's final product does not, however, recognize the difference between individual students' contributions [10]. Certain individuals may contribute significantly, whereas others fly under the radar, adding little to the project. Strictly individual assessment and grading may, on the other hand, result in too much individual focus, thus sacrificing the common group goal of producing a high quality product. As a consequence, good assessment techniques must balance between *individual* and *group assessment* aspects.

Teachers can only assess project parts that are observable. Students are usually working with little teacher involvement, making it very hard to assess what is really happening in a project. Getting teachers extensively involved in all project activities may not be possible within resource constraints. Teacher involvement can also change students' behavior: a group meeting with or without an observing teacher can be drastically different. An alternative is that the students perform the assessment themselves, using peer or self assessments [4, 18]. Clearly, assessment techniques need to involve both *teachers* and *students* and it is essential that such assessment techniques are both fair and accountable [5].

The primary purpose of assessment activities is usually to assess student performance, that is, to generate *feedout* for grading purposes. Such assessments are said to be *summative*. Alternatively, assessments may also be *formative*, meaning that the assessment activity gives *feedback* to students for improved learning [9]. Both summative and formative assessments are essential, but can be hard to combine.

Although tempting, it is very hard to find a single assessment activity that balances between individual and group assessment, involves both teachers and students, and is summative as well as formative. Previous work is focusing on specific aspects, such as self and peer assessments [4, 7, 18], formative vs. summative assessment [9], or grading of written projects [15]. Instead, we propose that a project course should include a collection of assessment activities, each covering certain aspects of the assessment landscape. In particular, we make the following contributions:

- We present an *assessment model* consisting of nine different activities. The key aspect of the model is that the assessment landscape is covered by categorizing the activities in three dimensions: (1) group/individual assessment, (2) teacher/student involvement, and (3) formative/summative assessment. We describe the essential parts of each activity and give rationales for the categorization (Section 2).
- The suggested assessment model is the result of applying and refining these activities in a larger software engineering project during a six-year period. We evaluate the model and its activities by performing a questionnaire-based survey with closed questions (Sections 3 and 4).

SIGCSE'14, March 5–8, 2014, Atlanta, GA, USA

http://dx.doi.org/10.1145/2538862.2538947.

2. ASSESSMENT MODEL

In this section, we first give an overview of the proposed assessment model and explain how it may be used. This is followed by a brief explanation of each assessment activity within the model.

2.1 Overview of the Model

Figure 1 depicts the proposed assessment model. Each activity is categorized within three dimensions: formative/summative assessment (x-axis), teacher/student involvement (y-axis), and group/individual assessment (represented with G, I, and G/I labels). For instance, *individual student interviews* is a summative assessment activity where both teachers and students are involved, but where the interviewees (the students) are in focus. This activity is only assessing an individual student (labeled I), whereas other activities may be group-based, meaning that the whole group is assessed as one entity (e.g., the *grading criteria* activity).

This assessment model may be seen as a *template* when designing assessment activities for a project bases course. For instance, when a teacher is designing a new capstone course, he/she can pick assessment activities that are relevant in the specific context[1]. One benefit of this model is that it emphasizes different aspects of the activities. For instance, if an activity should be used for grading purposes, an individual student report (partially summative) is more suitable than student coaching (only formative). It is important to select a wide range of activities, such that different aspects of assessments are covered. It is also essential that the assessment activities are aligned with the intended learning outcomes of the course [1]. For example, if oral communication skills are part of the learning outcome, oral feedback at student meetings may be more important than individual student reports.

The proposed model for assessing large student projects is general and may be applicable outside the field of software engineering. However, we find it particularly useful for handling the dynamics of this kind of projects that are characterized by changing requirements, flexible management needs, and multiplicity of roles.

We have applied and evaluated this model on a larger software engineering project course (see Section 3.1 and previous publication [3] for details of the course approach). The assessment activities have evolved and been refined over a six-year period. In particular, we have used student feedback in the form of course evaluations, emails, and informal interviews to continuously improve the activities[2].

We contend that this model is general and may be applied to other larger project-based courses. In the rest of this section, we describe the essence of each assessment activity of this model and motivates its categorization.

2.2 Grading Criteria

Description: The grading criteria activity is basically a list of requirements that a student group must fulfill to get a certain grade. This list should be available to all students before the course starts. Example of grading criteria are software engineering practices that shall be adapted (e.g., continuous integration and Scrum [13]) and artifacts that shall be produced (e.g., test plan and architecture). The grading criteria are formulated by teachers, but the student group decides on a target grade. Thus, students need to estimate and balance the workload and available resources (the number of members in a group, their skills, and available time).

Categorization: When grading students at the very end of a course, teachers should follow up the grading criteria to check if groups are meeting the requirements for a certain grade. Consequently, this activity is a tool for *summative* assessment where *teachers* are involved in the activity. On the other hand, grading criteria can also be used by students along the course as a checklist of things to do. Therefore, this activity also contributes to *formative* assessment that is characterized by *student* involvement. Finally, this activity is a *group* assessment; the requirements apply for the project group as a whole.

2.3 Oral Feedback at Student Meetings

Description: Oral feedback is a simple and efficient assessment activity. To implement it, teachers need to physically attend student meetings, such as status, project, or review meetings. At these meetings, a teacher monitors group progress and contributions of individuals. Teachers should give oral feedback to the whole group or directly to individuals.

Categorization: The main purpose of oral teacher feedback is to guide students towards learning goals. Based on this feedback, students have the opportunity to take appropriate actions. Thus, such oral feedback is mostly a tool for *formative* assessment. However, the information about how students address and identify problems may also be useful when grading students. Therefore, this activity is also partially *summative*. Finally, oral feedback contributes to both *group and individual* assessment; feedback may be given to the whole group or to separate individuals.

2.4 Student Coaching

Description: Student coaching accounts for all forms of peer assessment activities conducted by students within project groups. In particular, students are encouraged to assist each other by giving internal feedback. For example, students can give short tutorials, conduct hands-on sessions within their groups, or review produced artifacts.

Categorization: Peer assessment for grading is extensively explored for small group projects [6, 11]. Similarly to peer assessment, student coaching includes evaluation and monitoring by peers. However, student coaching included in our assessment model is a tool for pure *formative* assessment. Thus, the goal of student coaching is to give/receive feedback during the course rather than to grade work of others. Student coaching is conducted without teacher intervention and is, therefore, categorized as a *student* only activity. Both groups and individuals can be targets of student coaching. Therefore, we categorize it as a tool for both *group and individual* assessment.

2.5 On-Demand Artifact Feedback

Description: On-demand artifact feedback means that students may request, at any time during the course, feedback on their artifacts. Depending on the size of the artifact and timing in the course, the teacher may give oral feedback, written feedback, or both. The purpose of this activity is to give students early feedback, so that the quality of these artifacts can be improved during the course.

Categorization: As mentioned above, students are not obliged to request feedback on their artifacts. The final grade is neither affected by requesting feedback nor by the quality of intermediate versions of the artifact. Thus, this activity is a *formative* assessment. This activity requires both *teacher* and *student* involvement: it is the student who requests feedback, whereas the teacher gives

[1]Note that the collection of assessment activities that we present here is neither exhaustive nor complete. There are without doubt many more suitable assessment activities that may be categorized within this model.

[2]Some of the assessment activities were not present the first years that the course was given (e.g., individual student interviews and individual student reports), whereas some other activities have been gradually improved over the years.

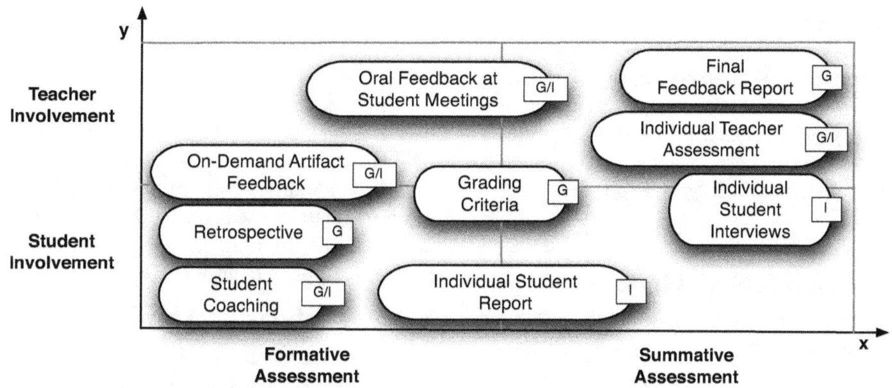

Figure 1: An assessment model of the relationship between formative/summative assessment and teacher/student involvement. Each oval defines an assessment activity. The different activities are marked as group-based (G), individual (I), or a combination (G/I).

the actual feedback. Reviews can be requested by both individual students and their groups. Therefore, this procedure contributes to both *group* and *individual* assessment.

2.6 Individual Student Report

Description: In this activity, each student prepares an individual report where he/she reflects on his/her own performance during the course. This report consists of the two parts: (a) what the student claims he/she has contributed to the group, and (b) what are the most important things that he/she learned.

Categorization: An individual report is meant to be used by students as a self-evaluation tool. As a consequence, students have the opportunity to improve their own learning. Hence, a student performs *formative* self-assessment through an individual report. Additionally, this document is used by teachers to analyze individual student contributions, which is also used for student grading. Therefore, individual student reports are also used for *summative* assessment. Naturally, only *students* are involved in this activity because each student writes the report individually.

2.7 Individual Teacher Assessment

Description: When a team of teachers is involved in the assessment of project groups, each teacher will have their own understanding of the different groups' performance and results. It is, therefore, important to take into account individual teachers' opinions when deciding on final grades. Therefore, we introduce an individual teacher assessment activity into the model, where each teacher first independently assesses groups and individual students. These individual assessments, including individual grading, are then discussed by all teachers together, so that a final grade can be agreed upon[3].

Categorization: Individual teacher assessment is carried out at the end of the course. Therefore, it contributes only to *summative* assessment where only *teachers* are involved. As previously mentioned, both *groups and individuals* are assessed in this activity.

2.8 Final Feedback Report

Description: Written teacher feedback is an efficient way of communicating student performance [15]. In our assessment model, this technique is represented as a final feedback report that is handed out at the last meeting. This report consists of two main components: a grading table and closing comments. The grading table consists of different grading areas, where each area is given a specific grade and a weight factor. This table is then used to calculate the final group grade. The closing comments include detailed feedback for each grading area. In particular, closing comments specify who performed the assessments (which teachers), what information was used (what documents and observations), positive and negative observations, pointers for further improvement, and rationale of the given grade with respect to other grades.

Categorization: The final feedback report is categorized as a tool for *summative assessment* because the received feedback (closing comments) cannot be used by students for improvements within the same course. Only teachers are involved in the assessment and the report concerns only the whole group, not individuals.

2.9 Individual Student Interviews

Description: It is always challenging to evaluate individual students when they work in large groups. Direct evidence of student work is often invisible for teachers. Therefore, we introduce an additional assessment activity where individuals are the main focus. At this event, each student is briefly interviewed at an informal meeting (10-15 minutes) with respect to their role in the group. Typically, only a subset of all students is interviewed. The selection can be based on the individual reports or information received during student meetings. The main purpose is to judge if individual students have contributed more or less than the average student in the group.

Categorization: All interviews are conducted at the end of a course. Therefore, this activity is only meant to contribute to *summative assessment*. Both *teachers* and *students* are involved in the interviews as interviewers and interviewees, respectively. The main goal of this activity is to gain better understanding of individual student contributions. Therefore, this activity contributes to assessment of *individuals*.

2.10 Retrospective

Description: If the project is organized into iterations (for instance by using an agile approach such as Scrum), an important assessment activity is to perform one or more retrospectives. In this activity, students discuss how they have been working during the last iteration. The main questions that should be discussed are: (1) what was good in the iteration? (2) what did not went well?, and (3) how can we improve? Retrospectives can also be used even if the project course is not based on iterations (for example by having the retrospective in the middle of the course).

[3]This activity has similarities to the Delphi method, which was originally designed for expert group judgments.

Categorization: A retrospective is meant to be *formative*. It is important for the students to acknowledge what is wrong early in the project so that they can improve. Retrospectives are pure student activities, although teachers may help the students to organize their first meeting. The activity may be seen as a self-assessment of a group. In particular, retrospectives are meant to improve the process (the way of working) for the whole group, not assessing specific individuals.

3. DESCRIPTION OF THE STUDY

In this section, we first describe the course that is studied, followed by methods used for collection and analysis of data for the survey.

3.1 Context

The assessment model presented in the previous section is the result of a six-year period of experimentation with a software engineering project course (see Broman *et al.* [3] for a detailed description of the course approach). The course is given as a master's level course. The students come from different curricula and countries. In 2012, when this study was performed, 88 students participated in the course and about 15% of the students were female.

The major goal of the course is for students to obtain fundamental understanding of a larger software engineering project and experience its challenges. Students should also learn organizational, process, and communication perspectives. Initially, students are divided by lottery into 3-4 groups of 20-30 students. One reason for having such large groups is that most functions and roles in a real company shall be present. All groups get the same task and the same customer representative. In 2012 the customer was an external product development company. The course runs during an entire semester and comprises two phases:

1. A prestudy phase where the students organize the group, assign roles, start education, interview the customer, and create a preliminary version of the architecture. The prestudy ends with a *tollgate* meeting where the continuation of the project is formally determined.

2. A series of 2-week iterations for implementation, prototype evaluation, testing, documentation, and configuration management. The project ends with a demonstration and experience seminar with all groups.

The students are free to organize themselves. However, we recommend them to organize into smaller, cross-functional teams after the prestudy and use a SCRUM-based process framework.

In total, four teachers/teaching assistants are involved in the course. During the course, each group meets one teacher for approximately one hour at least once a week. Depending on their needs, some individuals and small groups also arrange additional short meetings with the teachers (e.g., to ask questions about project planning and requirements documents). The summative assessment (grading and writing final feedback reports) is done in 2-3 consequent days where all teachers are involved. Performing all these activities may seem costly with a lot of communication overhead, but when all teachers know their role in the course our experience is that the course can be executed quite efficiently.

The course is, according to the official student evaluation, very popular and students are satisfied with their learning.

3.2 Data Collection

The evaluation is based on a questionnaire-based survey with closed questions. The students answered each statement by selecting one of the six options: strongly disagree, disagree, neutral, agree, strongly agree, and N/A. The blanks with questions were handed out during the first 15 minutes of the last mandatory meeting, just before the final grades were announced and the final feedback reports were given to the students. The answers from each group were collected in a closed envelope by an assistant not teaching the project and the group identities were randomly coded. No identification of the individual student was possible. The survey was conducted in December 2012. In total, 72 questionnaires were collected that corresponds to approximately 82% response rate.

3.3 Analysis Method

To process the obtained data, we used descriptive methods of SPSS (Statistical Package for the Social Sciences). The answers of students were analyzed as nominal scale measurements. There were seven independent variables (year of the course, age, sex, industrial experience, software development experience, curriculum, and result from theory exam) and 32 dependent variables (the questions). Among dependent variables, 21 were used for further analysis while the rest of variables were related to the general course evaluation. Out of these variables, 11 are detailed in this paper.

4. RESULTS AND DISCUSSIONS

In this section, we discuss the results of the study. We present the results in terms of the previously introduced dimensions.

4.1 Individual and Group Assessment

Although students work together in group-based courses, each student should be given an individual grade at the end of a course. As previously described, the assessment activities in our model (Figure 1) contribute to both group and individual assessment. A natural question then arises whether individual or group performance should be emphasized when deciding on the final grade.

According to the results of statement A1 in Figure 2(a), a strong majority believes that a mixture of individual and group-based performance gives fair grading. In particular, 69% of the students agrees or strongly agrees to statement A1, whereas only 6% of the students disagree or strongly disagree. Only 26% of students think that individual project grades should be based on their individual performance (A2), whereas 41% disagree. These two results show that most students do believe in mixed individual and group based assessments, although a minority still thinks that the assessment should be individual.

Collaboration among students is one of the primary learning goals in many group-based courses. Too strong focus on individual grading may, however, force students to focus solely on their individual performance, thus prevent fruitful collaboration. Fortunately, the results of this study do not point in this direction; 89% of the students confirm that such prevention of collaboration did not exist (statement A3).

4.2 Teacher and Student Involvement

To enable fair and valuable student feedback, teachers need to be present at certain occasions where they can observe the students' work. In the project course of this study, teachers are involved in student planning sessions and retrospective meetings, where students plan their work and discuss emerging problems.

A disadvantage of such an approach is that students may hesitate to express their opinions when a teacher is present. Consequently, this could prevent students from improving their way of working and learning. Statement B1 in Figure 2(b) shows, however, that this threat is quite mild; 91% of the students state that the teacher involvement does not restrain them from honest discussions.

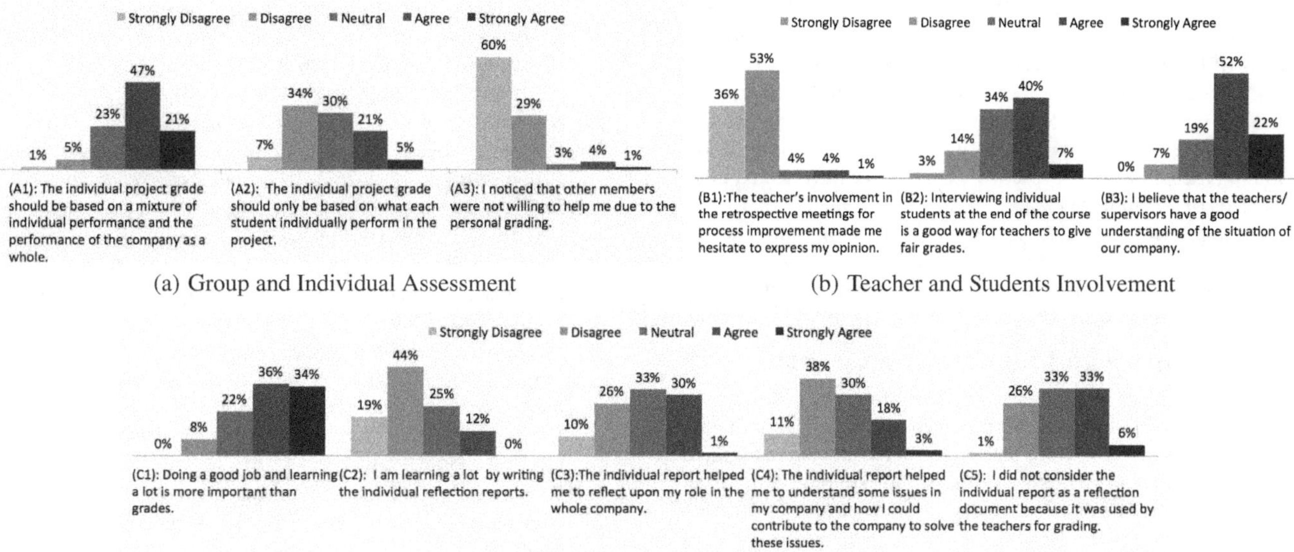

(a) Group and Individual Assessment

(b) Teacher and Students Involvement

(c) Formative and Summative Assessment

Figure 2: Results of the quantitative study. The diagrams are categorized according to the three dimensions of the assessment model. Missing and N/A answers are omitted for the sake of clarity.

When only teachers are involved in the assessment, it is extremely difficult to get a good understanding about individual students' contributions. This may lead to unfair summative assessment. To tackle this deficiency, our assessment model includes several activities with both student and teacher involvement (see Figure 1). In particular, we want to draw extra attention to the assessment activity of individual student interviews (see Section 2). The results of statement B2 clearly shows that individual interviews are appreciated; 47% of the students agree that this activity is a good way to assess and give fair grades (34% were neutral).

Finally, the result of statement B3 shows that 74% of the students believe that the teachers have a good understanding of the situations within the group. Although the students' belief of teachers' understanding does not express the teachers' actual understanding, we conclude that the teacher involvement in the course is vital and that the involvement suggested in this approach does not affect the team work negatively.

4.3 Formative and Summative Assessment

One possible consequence of too much focus on summative assessments is that students focus on obtaining good grades rather than effective learning. Our survey shows, however, that 70% of the students think that doing a good job and learning are more important for them than getting good grades (statement C1 in Figure 2(c)).

The individual student report (Section 2.6) is both a summative and formative assessment activity. Our experience (as teachers) confirms that an individual report is a useful tool for teachers to get better understanding of individual student performance. As a tool for formative assessment, an individual report is meant to be an instrument for self-reflection, helping students to obtain insights of the group and their individual role. Such self-reflection may also help students improve their way of working. The results of our survey show, however, that this goal is not completely achieved. Only 12% of the students confirm that writing an individual report helps them to learn (statement C2 in Figure 2(c)), whereas 63% of the students disagree with this statement.

Statements C3 and C4 show that an individual report is more successfully used by students to reflect upon their own way of working, compared to the whole group. Still, a large percentage (36% and 49% for statement C3 and C4, respectively) do not believe that individual reports are useful as a formative self-assessment activity.

Before we performed our survey, our hypothesis was that the use of an individual report for summative assessment may prevent students from honest reflection. This hypothesis is partly confirmed. In particular, 37% of the students did not consider the individual report as a reflection document because it was used for grading (statement C5 in Figure 2(c)), whereas 27% stated the opposite. However, to completely prove this hypothesis, further studies need to be performed. Moreover, additional education of students on self-reflection (e.g., as lectures or seminars) could also be used to better prepare students for self-assessment.

5. RELATED WORK

There is much research reported on capstone projects that are relevant to large project courses. In this section we compare our results.

5.1 Individual and Group Assessment

A student survey by Farell *et al.* [5] shows similar results as our study about student perception: 54% prefer a mix of individual and group marks and 30% want their mark only based on individual achievements. Teachers' means of getting individual results are written contributions statements (as suggested by Clark *et al.* [4]) and peer assessment [7]. A comprehensive introduction to several practically useful techniques is described by Wilkins and Lawhead [18] and Lejk *et al.* [11].

5.2 Teacher and Student Involvement

From Figure 1 we note that the right-bottom corner is empty. This is where peer assessment would go, an assessment method that is frequently researched. The reports point out both that students have confidence in peer assessment [5], and that the accuracy is acceptable [7, 10]. There seems to be no significant difference between students of different gender and nationality [7]. One of the challenges is to create smooth processes and tools that motivate the students to participate [4, 5]. Computer based tools such as SPARC have been well received by a majority of students [19] and tools combining assessment with assessor's confidence have scaled up to group sizes of 20 students [14].

In our approach, students are involved in a dialog with teachers and giving each other formative assessments. So far, we have not experimented with peer assessment, but we view it as interesting future work to evaluate and extend our model with peer assessment.

5.3 Formative and Summative Assessment

Providing formative assessment is challenging; the response on writing individual reflection reports shown in Figure 2(b) indicates an unexpectedly low degree of learning. Many students' submitted reports because it was required information for grading. Similar results have been reported by Hernandez [8] in a study of undergraduates in Hispanic studies. Both student and teacher perspectives were considered. When asked to rank the most frequent purpose of performing assessments students responded "grading students" in 24% of the cases, whereas teachers answered "grading student" in 13% of the cases. The study also investigated what students do with the assessment. Even though teachers gave feed-back by marking weak points and suggesting improvements, many students just took part of the summative information of the assessment. To make the students learn more from assessments, the assessments needs "feed-forward", that is, information about of what to do with the feed-back. This is probably most applicable to our course, especially since we expect students to make a self-assessment; we must teach them what to do with the results of their self-assessment. The inherent complexity of formative assessment is well described in the theoretical work of Yorke [20] who provides a multi-faceted tool for reasoning about course improvement.

6. CONCLUSIONS

In this paper, we present an assessment model for assessing large software engineering project courses. The model consists of nine assessment activities that have been evaluated by a questionnaire-based survey. We contend that this model can be useful when analyzing assessment activities in various software engineering courses.

Acknowledgement

The authors would like to thank all the students who participated in the software engineering course. This research was funded by the Department of Computer and Information Science, Linköping University, Sweden. The second author was funded by the Swedish Research Council #623-2011-955, with support from the Center for Hybrid and Embedded Software Systems (CHESS) at UC Berkeley.

7. REFERENCES

[1] J. Biggs. Enhancing teaching through constructive alignment. *Higher Education*, 1996.

[2] D. Broman. Should Software Engineering Projects be the Backbone or the Tail of Computing Curricula? In *Proceedings of the 23th IEEE Conference on Software Engineering Education and Training*, Pittsburgh, USA, 2010.

[3] D. Broman, K. Sandahl, and M. Abu Baker. The company approach to software engineering project courses. *IEEE Transactions on Education*, 55(4):445–452, 2012.

[4] N. Clark, P. Davies, and R. Skeers. Self and peer assessment in software engineering projects. In *Proceedings of the 7th Australasian conference on Computing education - Volume 42*, ACE '05, pages 91–100, Darlinghurst, Australia, Australia, 2005. Australian Computer Society, Inc.

[5] V. Farrell, G. Ravalli, G. Farrell, P. Kindler, and D. Hall. Capstone project: fair, just and accountable assessment. In *Proceedings of the 17th ACM annual conference on Innovation and technology in computer science education*, ITiCSE '12, New York, NY, USA, 2012. ACM.

[6] D. Hemer. Peer assessment of group-based software engineering projects. In *Australian Conference on Software Engineering*, 2008.

[7] N. Herbert. Quantitative peer assessment: can students be objective? In *Proceedings of the ninth Australasian conference on Computing education*, ACE '07, pages 63–71, Darlinghurst, Australia, Australia, 2007. Australian Computer Society, Inc.

[8] R. Hernández. Does continuous assessment in higher education support student learning? *Higher Education*, 64(4):489–502, 2012.

[9] P. T. Knight. Summative Assessment in Higher Education: Practices in disarray. *Studies in Higher Education*, 27(3):275–286, 2002.

[10] N. LeJeune. Assessment of individuals on CS group projects. *J. Comput. Sci. Coll.*, 22(1):231–237, Oct. 2006.

[11] M. Lejk, M. Wyvill, and S. Farrow. A survey of methods of deriving individual grades from group assessments. *Assessment & Evaluation in Higher Education*, 21(3):267–280, 1996.

[12] F. Meawad. The Virtual Agile Enterprise: Making the Most of a Software Engineering Course. In *Proceedings of the 24th IEEE Conference on Software Engineering Education and Training*, pages 324–332, 2011.

[13] K. Schwaber and M. Beedle. *Agile Software Development with Scrum.* Prentice Hall, 2001.

[14] L. Slivovsky, L. Jamieson, and W. Oakes. Evaluating Multidisciplinary Design Teams. In *Proceedings of the 2003 American Societey for Engineering Education Annual Conference & Exposition*, 2003.

[15] L. J. Smith. Grading written projects: what approaches do students find most helpful? *The Journal of Education for Business*, 83(6):325–330, 2008.

[16] R. H. Todd, S. P. Magleby, C. D. Sorensen, B. R. Swan, and D. K. Anthony. A survey of capstone engineering courses in north america. 84:165–174, 1995.

[17] D. A. Umphress, D. Hendrix, and J. H. Cross. Software process in the classroom: the capstone project experience. 19(5):78–85, 2002.

[18] D. E. Wilkins and P. B. Lawhead. Evaluating individuals in team projects. In *Proceedings of the thirty-first SIGCSE technical symposium on Computer science education*, SIGCSE, pages 172–175, New York, NY, USA, 2000. ACM.

[19] K. Willey and A. Gardner. Improving self- and peer assessment processes with technology. *Campus-Wide Information Systems*, 26(5):379–399, 2009.

[20] M. Yorke. Formative assessment in higher education: Moves towards theory and the enhancement of pedagogic practice. *Higher education*, 45(4):477–501, 2003.

Adding Unit Test Experience to a Usability Centered Project Course

Christopher Brown, Robert Pastel, Marika Seigel, Charles Wallace, Linda Ott
Michigan Technological University, Houghton, MI
cdbrown, rpastel, maseigel, wallace, linda @mtu.edu

ABSTRACT

This HCI course incorporated unit testing as a quality improvement initiative with an Experiential Learning Model. The focus of the research was on observation and conceptualization—students should be able to associate the benefits of usability and unit testing and apply them to more general situations. Based on our survey results and student interviews, the most difficult challenge incorporating unit testing in an experiential course was ensuring students overcome their negative bias to discover the benefits of functional testing. We recommend emphasizing the concrete benefits of unit tests and ensuring that all students fully participate in the testing experience.

Categories and Subject Descriptors

K.3.2 [**Computers and Education**]: Computer and Information Science Education - *computer science education, curriculum*;
D.2.9 [**Software Engineering**]: Management - *Software Quality Assurance*;
K.6.3 [**Management of Computing and Information Systems**]: Software Management - *Software development, Software process*

General Terms

Experimentation, Human Factors, Measurement, Verification

Keywords

HCI, Unit Testing, Experiential Learning

1. INTRODUCTION

This unit testing research is a step in the continual development of the combined graduate and undergraduate, multi-role Human Computer Interaction courses [10]. As the course grew, it became necessary for the projects to be more complete. To complement the usability testing in the course, we decided to add an emphasis on functionality through unit testing. We used Kolb's Experiential Learning Model (ELM) [8] to add functional testing to the course in order to improve the quality of the projects and provide a more complete testing experience.

The courses began as a combined graduate and undergraduate effort intended to provide a professional experience for both the graduate students as usability experts and the undergraduate students as developers [2]. As the original graduate and undergraduate courses grew, additional elements were added. The original courses' final product was a fictional hardware product with intentional restraints. With the advent of Google's Android Software Development Kit (Android SDK) [6], students in the course began to develop for a portable device. As part of a collaborative Citizen Science project, real customers were added to the course. These customers were scientists with a known desire pushing students to design to a specific need rather than their own fictional project [9].

It was the Citizen Science project that drove the need for software quality improvement. In the original iterations of the undergraduate course, the focus was on the usability of the project, and an incomplete project was still an appropriate learning scenario. With real customers, students had an obligation to have functioning code, and after the initial effort, it was decided that more emphasis on that functionality must be given. To accomplish this goal, unit testing was added as a new element to the course.

1.1 The Experiential Learning Model (ELM)

David Kolb combined three major experience based educational approaches to create the ELM [8]. In the ELM, he considers four mental activities taken by the learner and discusses the cycle of learning that develops from those stages. Kolb identifies the four stages as: Concrete Experience (CE), Reflective Observation (RO), Abstract Conceptualization (AC) and Active Experimentation (AE).

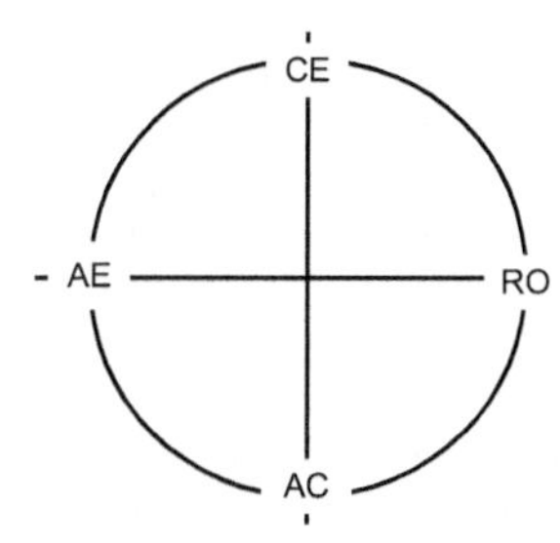

Figure 1: Experiential Learning Model.

See Figure 1 for the axial relationships and clockwise cycle of the four stages.

In addition, Kolb emphasizes the level of feedback as an

SIGCSE'14, March 5–8, 2014, Atlanta, GA, USA.

ACM 978-1-4503-2605-6/14/03 ...$15.00.
http://dx.doi.org/10.1145/2538862.2538964.

important component of the ELM. Without appropriate feedback, there is an imbalance along the observation/action axis (AE—RO). This means that the learner is either focused on taking actions and does not (or cannot) observe feedback or that they are focused on attempting to observe so refuse to take new actions.

One of Kolb's key points combines the Lewinian learning cycle with Dewey's idea of model development [8]. Each person has a model of an object or activity, which could be simplistic or incorrect. The ELM expects the cycle to begin with an experience that either supports, expands or replaces the learner's current model. Kolb emphasizes the necessity of the learner mentally participating in the experience. Without that participation, a learner will not update their mental model, and therefore, cannot learn. Kolb describes this as *model regression*. The learner's mental model will revert to their original, less complete model, and they will have gained nothing from the experience.

In our course, we provide the initial experience (CE) of Unit Testing through a tutorial activity and the project testing experience. Students are then given the opportunity to reflect on that experience (RO) as they prepare to begin their project. We provide a lecture as a framework for establishing the abstract concepts (AC) and benefits of unit testing. Finally, they are given assignments to create unit tests for their own project (AE), beginning the cycle anew.

1.2 Unit Testing in Education

One of the common testing methodologies is unit testing. Unit testing is a white-box testing approach with the following properties: Simplicity, Independence, and Documentation. Tests focus on elements of functionality within the program, ensuring that they work independently, for smoother integration. Unit testing is often automated, and a benefit of creating automated tests is that the purposeful thought of creating the tests causes students to avoid and discover errors quickly. JUnit is a tool for unit test development [1], and is supported by the Android SDK [6]; therefore, it is an appropriate choice for testing the Android projects in this course.

Introducing unit testing in an academic environment often involves introducing tools to improve student experience. The JUG tool allows students to see unit test results to provide feedback in their own code [3]. Saff introduced a tool to allow their IDE to perform testing continuously, much like current IDEs check for compilation errors while the program is being written [11]. These tools encourage experiences with unit testing, and demonstrate the benefit of testing to development. However, these two tools only assist with existing unit tests, they do not provide students assistance in writing unit tests.

When introducing the construction of unit tests, students need more guidance and encouragement. Kaner and Padmanabhan explored experiential learning of unit tests, emphasizing instructor enthusiasm and reporting on some areas where students become confused [7]. They identified the major confusion elements were "applying a standard procedure", "Figuring out (and explaining the choice of) boundary values" and "Identifying risks and associated error-revealing classes." Their solution to the confusion was to increase the models and example of testing.

Some other researchers introduced peer testing to provide enthusiasm for testing. Smith's introductory course used competitive peer-testing to encourage testing practices [12]. Students would get points for "breaking" their peers' code by writing unit tests for appropriately difficult cases. Smith's work was based on Clark, who introduced peer group testing in a project course [4]. Groups were assigned a few students from other groups to write their tests. Although this is a useful way of introducing unit testing to projects, we felt that students learning about another group's distinct project would introduce a much larger time requirement than we intended. We also wanted students to consider the difference between the functional and interface aspects of their project.

1.3 Research Questions

When introducing unit testing to the course, our primary research question was:

Can Unit Testing improve the quality of Human Computer Interaction projects?

However, after we discovered that students were not participating in the unit testing aspects of the course, we decided to expand the research to two other questions.

When introducing unit testing, what additional steps must be taken to ensure a positive learning experience?

What potential for regression of students' unit testing model is possible, and how can that potential be mitigated?

We decided to refocus our research on learning experiences and model regression because informal discussions during the course revealed prejudice against unit testing and its practicality. Our goal is to minimize the possibility of students regressing to those mindsets.

2. METHOD

The methodology for this research was similar to the methodology used for earlier additions to the course [2]. Students were given assignments that encouraged or required them to actively experience unit testing. The graduate students collected project data on effectiveness, and the undergraduate students participated in a survey and interview at the end of the course.

2.1 Initial Learning Activity

The ELM indicates that Reflective Observation occurs after feedback. To accomplish the first cycle, we required students to participate in an initial unit test activity. To help students get started Android programming, the course required building sample Android projects. The Android Software Development Kit also contains support for JUnit testing, including tutorials.

The first unit testing activity for students was to complete the Android JUnit test tutorials [6], followed by another sample project that extended the ideas of those tutorials. These sample projects were expected to take a few hours and ensure that students had their systems set up to handle processing unit tests. These assignments were given to each individual, not to the group, so that each person would be responsible for writing tests.

2.2 Unit Testing Lecture

The next step in the course was a lecture discussing unit testing and Test Driven Development (TDD). This lecture encouraged abstract conceptualization (AC) about the role unit testing plays in software development. The lecture built off the activities the students participated in, and offered some indirect feedback to the tutorials.

First, unit testing and TDD are defined and provided as an analogy. Second, a demonstration provided an example of some pitfalls to avoid when using Android's JUnit testing, building off the examples the students did. Next, the lecture reminded students of an indirect experience with unit testing most of them had earlier in the curriculum [3]. Finally, the lecture emphasized the role of the developers as testers and verifiers.

2.3 Assigned Testing

At the next stage of the course, students had a midterm interview with the instructor to narrow their focus to obtainable goals. After their initial experience into unit testing, but before they had begun major development into their project, students were assigned to build automated unit tests for one activity (screen) in their application. They were also asked to leave a different activity without automated testing as a point of comparison. Unit tests for other areas were left to their discretion.

The goal of dividing the project into tested and untested aspects was to demonstrate the benefit of unit tests. The activities in the programs had to be divided based on the individual project, but we took steps to find elements of similar difficulty. We did not require students to employ TDD since the techniques are usually developed after programmers are comfortable with test writing. We did encourage experienced testers to use TDD and asked all students questions about their experiences with TDD.

2.4 Usability Testing

Our previous work suggests that students have a certain satisfaction culminating the project with usability testing. From that idea, we decided to treat it as a functional release. The usability testing portion of the course provided a deadline for the project, which is the culmination of the project work. As with many software projects, during final testing, groups have technical problems with code working incorrectly or missing components. In previous semesters, the groups would fix the bugs for later usability tests and the graduate students may make a note distinguishing the "pre-fix" test subjects from the "post-fix" subjects.

To identify and document these functional problems, an additional assignment was added to the graduate students. They were to develop appropriate bug report forms for the different projects, and collect data concerning technical problems and functionality issues during usability testing. Both the graduate students and undergraduate students were responsible for filling out the bug reports.

2.5 Learning Evaluation

We used two methods of data collection to evaluate the learning objectives of the unit testing addition to the course. First, an interview was done with each group to get their perspective of the unit testing aspects of the course. The interview allowed students to provide free-form feedback and included discussion and questions related to their experiences. Students were quite frank in the discussion, and we discovered that some groups did not do the assigned unit testing.

Students also filled out an anonymous survey, including a self-reported inventory of their experience. The survey also included some knowledge verification questions, used to determine what aspects of unit testing students took away from the experience. Finally, the survey asked questions about their expected future use of unit testing, to ground their opinions of unit testing. This allowed us to compare groups and evaluate their answers to questions about usability testing with respect to their experience before and during the course.

3. RESULTS

The results for this research showed that the motivation for experiencing unit tests was insufficient for most of the groups. Unfortunately, that left very little data to evaluate the effectiveness of the experiential learning. The surveys and interview questions did provide some insight into the student's mental model, and we hope that this can be used for a more successful second attempt.

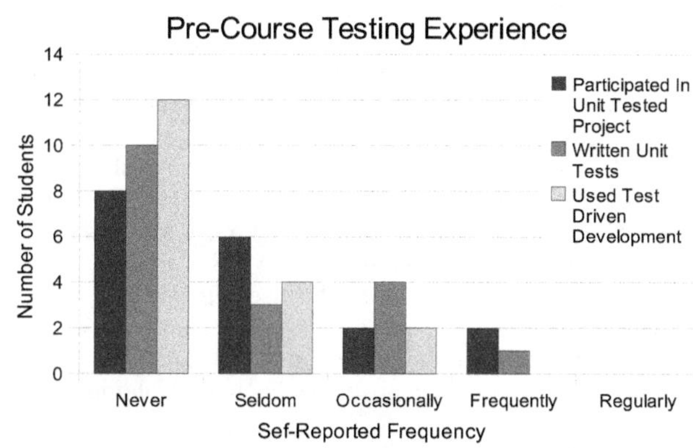

Figure 2: Prior Unit Testing Experience

3.1 Interviews

One of the groups, Stream Features, performed a significant amount of automated unit testing work. Two other groups also included unit tests, though their implementations were minimal. The final two groups did not include unit testing. One indicated that they could not unit test because they had too many abstract objects in their code. The other group did not create unit tests or participate in unit testing, since their project was incomplete.

The Stream Features project included strong database interaction, and they used unit tests to verify that their database connections worked properly. They employed TDD, writing their database tests and functions before they were used in the rest of the project. This was also the only group whose bug reports were purely cosmetic. The interview revealed that most of the group members were comfortable with unit testing from a previous course. They expressed the perspective "... sometimes JUnit testing [feels like] a lot of work that doesn't pay off." That perspective given by a successful group shed some light on the other groups' challenges with unit testing.

One member of the Lichen group created a single unit test, and later discussion indicated that they had difficulty creating tests for more complex actions. The student who wrote

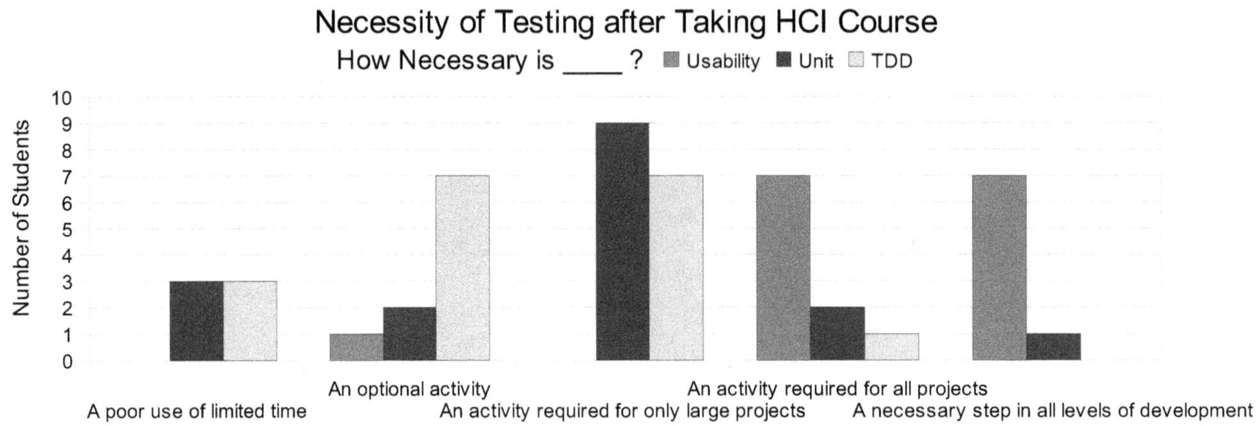

Figure 3: Views on the Necessity of Testing

the single unit test had positive feedback about the process and indicated regret at not writing the tests sooner. They also indicated that the unit test ran much faster than loading the emulator. These students did not have the same course experience as the Stream Features group and expressed a desire for more experience.

The Tracker Team wrote their unit tests after the usability tests were complete but before the interview. The primary reason they wrote the unit tests was to avoid a grade penalty.

Although the interviews seemed to indicate a positive experience with those students who used unit testing, we believe there is potential for stronger instructor interaction. The students who did not use unit testing struggled with time and had many more problems in their implementations.

3.2 Surveys

After the course and interviews were complete, students were requested to take an anonymous survey about their work in the course. Of the 21 students enrolled in the course, 18 responded to the survey. The survey included questions about their own history with unit testing, their views on testing, and the extent of their activity within their group. The survey included open-ended questions designed to expand on the multiple choice answers from other sections. There were also five questions which attempted to evaluate student understanding of the distinction between the purposes of unit tests and usability tests.

In terms of the ELM, most of the students have an immature mental model of unit testing. As shown in Figure 2, only 1 student reported writing unit tests frequently, and more than half the students who responded had never written unit tests for a project. Strangely, one student claimed to have used TDD, but indicated they had not participated in a project with unit testing or written unit tests. All students were required to take a Team Software Project course, however, as indicated by the interviews, not all iterations of that course introduced unit testing.

In Figure 3, we see that after the HCI course, students have a near unanimous positive view of the necessity of usability testing. In contrast, the common view of unit testing is that it is only useful in large projects. The phrasing "an activity required for only large projects" was used as a common answer when discussing automated testing casually with students. It was also a common perception among our students, as half the students responded with that answer. Students have a view of TDD that indicates it is less necessary than unit testing, with most students indicating that it is optional or a poor use of time.

The survey asked 6 questions about students anticipated use, indicating whether students would use or recommend different testing methodologies in the future. Overall, students support usability testing and favor unit testing in a professional environment. In Figure 4, this is represented by the Green and Light Blue bars. However, for personal use (the Dark Blue and Yellow bars), students are more neutral. Overall, students were neutral toward TDD in both personal and professional used (Light Blue and Maroon).

In each of the teams except Lichen, one of the team members claimed responsibility for writing tests. In the interview, only one of the members of the Lichen group reported writing unit tests, and based on the activity questions, we believe that student was one of the 3 that did not answer the survey. As discussed earlier, only three teams wrote unit tests, and of those, only one used TDD. One of the teams wrote their tests after usability testing, which means that they did not get the intended finalizing feedback of the usability tests as they pertained to the unit tests.

Responses to functionality problem questions indicated that bugs were discovered in program elements without unit tests. To avoid skew; however, we should only consider the two groups that wrote unit tests before usability testing. In the Stream Features group, the group that employed TDD, all four students responded that no functionality problems were found in unit tested code. Of the three students that responded in the Lichen group, two indicated that no problems were found in unit tested code, while the third indicated "a few" problems found in unit tested code, while "most" problems were found in untested code.

The free-form questions on the survey provided insight into the students roles and opinions of unit testing.

In the Stream Features group, one of the students indicated that they did not write a significant amount of code for any program element, and when asked about which elements were unit tested, they wrote "I have no idea." Within the Stream Features group, that student gave the only negative response to unit testing in the open-ended questions.

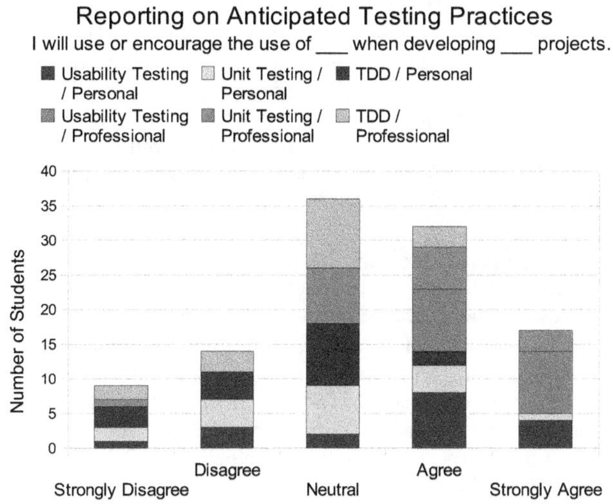

Figure 4: Responses to Future Testing Scenarios

The other three students wrote about positive experiences using unit testing to improve their code. In fact, one of the students from Stream Features indicated another element that they thought should have been unit tested.

In the Beach group (which did not include unit tests), students' free-form survey responses indicated that their choice to use anonymous classes prevented unit testing, but that they each had a desire to include unit testing. This group also had the only student who reported "frequently" using TDD before the course. This student also provided the only strongly positive experience of unit testing outside the Stream Features group.

The last question on the survey asked for additional comments, which provided a large number of negative comments toward unit testing. One student was concerned with writing tests for GUI elements when they did not have those elements complete until the last minute. A similar statement indicated that unit testing and TDD "have their place", but are "difficult to use... in projects that are largely GUI based." Another student said that unit testing "seemed like a very slow process and difficult to do", though their indications earlier in the survey indicated that they had not done unit testing before or during the course. A third student commented that they did not understand why unit testing was needed, because it only found a "couple minor bugs", and "we can do most of our debugging tests by hand." As described in the analysis, these comments unknowingly dismiss some major benefits of unit testing.

The questions which evaluated student understanding of the purpose for unit tests and usability tests were scenarios of a business website. The questions were ordered by increasing complexity. The premise was that students need to verify that they had completed the described work with appropriate testing. They were to select the type(s) of testing that would be most appropriate.

Most students answered the first two questions and the final question correctly, though some students answered "Both unit and usability tests" when one of the types of testing was inappropriate or excessive.

The third question was difficult for students, it concerned Autofill of street names. The idea behind this question is that students must identify functional aspect of determining a street name from a partial string, while also recognizing that the way an autofill presents information is a usability issue. Only 6 of the 18 students identified both the functional and usability aspects of this scenario.

The fourth question concerned verifying that the text of the website matched a brochure. In this case, unit testing is inappropriate because verifying the text within the unit test would be just as cumbersome as manually checking the site. Only 6 students identified the redundancy of a unit test in this scenario.

Although many of the students answered the easier questions correctly, the students who did not answer those correctly were also the students who offered the most negative comments in the open ended section of the survey.

4. ANALYSIS

We expected that adding a unit testing experience to a project based HCI course would flow naturally. Usability testing was already a focus of the course, and functionality had been a problem in the past. We speculated that adding functionality checks would improve the overall product. Instead, we discovered that students expected unit testing to be a negative experience and resisted.

The most difficult challenge for the course was ensuring that students experienced unit testing. Students resisted each stage of the process. During the lecture, an informal show of hands indicated that less than a third of the students had done the initial tutorial activity. After the lecture, a few students began arguing about the practicality of unit tests, eventually acknowledging that they had never participated in a project with unit testing. Near the end of the semester, during usability testing, only 2 of the 5 projects had used unit testing.

The successes of the groups that participated in unit testing and the opinions provided by all the students helped formulate answers to our research questions:

Can Unit Testing improve the quality of Human Computer Interaction projects?

Despite the limited data in regards to the effectiveness of unit testing, the group that did participate fully in the unit testing showed remarkable results, with no functional problems in their program. Their project also showed meaningful results in the usability tests, since they could function without problems, they were able to discover more subtle usability issues than could have been possible with a partially functioning program. In addition, their program was available for the Citizen Science project that it was intended, providing a positive experience for the students participating.

When introducing unit testing, what additional steps must be taken to ensure a positive learning experience?

A potential problem with the structure of the course may have been caused by adding additional experience to a high-intensity project course. Students treated the unit testing portion of the course as if it were a minimal part of the project, while completing the project was their primary focus. This perceptual divide implying that unit testing would delay project completion may be a result of de-emphasis at the curricular level. It may be the case that a curricular unit testing focus, as proposed by Goldwasser, could improve student attitudes [5]. In addition, many student's mental model of unit testing causes them to believe that test development would delay interface development.

One of the primary means of ensuring a positive learning experience is to emphasize the more concrete benefits of unit testing. For instance, the Lichen group discovered that unit tests would run more quickly than the emulator. It is also important to include warnings and suggestions, such as those provided by the Beach app to avoid anonymous classes. Finally, we must encourage the idea that TDD is not only possible, but straightforward for a GUI based application, so long as there is low coupling between the data and the GUI element (something the Android SDK strongly supports [6]). Emphasis on these three elements of testing Android programs could prepare and encourage students to have a positive experience.

What potential for regression of students' unit testing model is possible, and how can that potential be mitigated?

Based on the differences between responses of groups that experienced unit testing and those that did not, the biggest potential for model regression is students who choose not to fully participate in the experience. To mitigate this, the instructor could place a firmer emphasis on the requirement of unit testing as part of the course and request that students write tests for code other group members have produced. It is often easier to convince a programmer to test someone else's code rather than try to convince them that their code requires testing [4].

The other possible regression could be caused by confusion of the purpose of unit testing [7]. If a student's conviction is that unit testing is only being done for trivial or subjective aspects of a program, it can cause them to regress. The survey responses indicated that students had a belief that the only purpose of the unit test was to discover "minor bugs" and that "hand testing" works better. An emphasis on the scalability and practicality of automated testing (for instance, that it is faster than loading the emulator) could encourage more participation. In addition, students might relate to an analogy of unit test creation as a series of thought exercises about the code. Another area of confusion might be the tutorial example, its simplicity implies that unit tests must be done for trivial aspects of a program. To mitigate this, the instructor should demonstrate that the tutorial is a simplistic example, and follow with a more complex, yet concrete example.

5. CONCLUSIONS

Unit testing can improve the quality of projects in an HCI course, but the challenge lies in convincing the students that unit testing is valuable. We found students developed a positive attitude after experiencing usability testing. A stronger curricular and instructor emphasis on the benefits of unit testing could provide a similar attitude change. Within our course, the next step is to put structure and emphasis around the unit testing element of the course. Ultimately, the struggle of including unit testing into the programmer's knowledge base is that of participating fully in the experience.

6. ACKNOWLEDGMENTS

We would like to thank the students who participated in the unit testing experiences and for their participation in interviews and surveys. We would also like to thank the scientists and others working with us in the Citizen Science project. Partial funding for this research was provided by the National Science Foundation (Award Number OCI-1135523).

7. REFERENCES

[1] K. Beck. JUnit: Resources for test driven development. `http://www.junit.org/`, 1994.

[2] C. Brown and R. Pastel. Combining distinct graduate and undergraduate HCI courses: An experiential and interactive approach. In *Proceedings of the 40th ACM Technical Symposium on Computer Science Education*, SIGCSE '09, pages 392–396, New York, NY, USA, 2009. ACM.

[3] C. Brown, R. Pastel, B. Siever, and J. Earnest. JUG: A JUnit generation, time complexity analysis and reporting tool to streamline grading. In *Proceedings of the 17th ACM annual conference on Innovation and Technology in Computer Science Education*, ITiCSE '12, pages 99–104, New York, NY, USA, 2012. ACM.

[4] N. Clark. Peer testing in software engineering projects. In *Proceedings of the Sixth Australasian Conference on Computing Education - Volume 30*, ACE '04, pages 41–48, Darlinghurst, Australia, Australia, 2004. Australian Computer Society, Inc.

[5] M. H. Goldwasser. A gimmick to integrate software testing throughout the curriculum. *SIGCSE Bull.*, 34:271–275, Mar 2002.

[6] Google. Android software developer kit. http://developer.android.com/about, 2009.

[7] C. Kaner and S. Padmanabhan. Practice and transfer of learning in the teaching of software testing. In *Proceedings of the 20th Conference on Software Engineering Education & Training*, CSEET '07, pages 157–166, Washington, DC, USA, 2007. IEEE Computer Society.

[8] D. A. Kolb. *Experiential Learning: Experience as the Source of Learning and Development.* Prentice Hall, Englewood Cliffs, NJ, 1984.

[9] A. Mayer, R. Pastel, C. Wallace, S. Oppliger, and R. Donovan. Environmental cybercitizens: Engaging citizen scientists in global environmental change through crowdsensing and visualization. `http://www.nsf.gov/awardsearch/showAward?AWD_ID=1135523`, 2011.

[10] R. Pastel. CS4760 & CS5760: Human-computer interaction. `http://www.csl.mtu.edu/cs4760/www/`, May 2008.

[11] D. Saff and M. D. Ernst. An experimental evaluation of continuous testing during development. In *Proceedings of the 2004 ACM SIGSOFT International Symposium on Software Testing and Analysis*, ISSTA '04, pages 76–85, New York, NY, USA, 2004. ACM.

[12] J. Smith, J. Tessler, E. Kramer, and C. Lin. Using peer review to teach software testing. In *Proceedings of the Ninth Annual International Conference on International Computing Education Research*, ICER '12, pages 93–98, New York, NY, USA, 2012. ACM.

A Service Learning Practicum Capstone

Aaron Bloomfield
University of Virginia
aaron@virginia.edu

Mark Sherriff
University of Virginia
sherriff@virginia.edu

Kara Williams
Center for Nonprofit Excellence
kwilliams@thecne.org

ABSTRACT

We present the design and execution of a Service Learning Practicum (SLP) course sequence intended to be year-long capstone for computer science seniors. Students are teamed into groups of six, and develop software for local nonprofit organizations. In addition to the structure of the course, we describe the challenges faced (legal, organizational, etc.), student perceptions via survey results, and provide a number of suggestions for other institutions who are looking to create a similar course sequence. At the end of the capstone experience, the customers are provided with working software that meet their current needs.

Categories and Subject Descriptors

K.3.2 [**Computer and Information Science Education**]: Computer Science Education

General Terms

Management, Human Factors, Legal Factors

Keywords

Capstone courses, service learning, project based learning

1. INTRODUCTION

Keeping students involved and interested in long and complex projects can be challenging for even the most talented instructor. Toy projects created for pedagogical value can be useful, but students can often see beyond the assignment and know that what they are actually working on will not have any intrinsic value in the future. Layman and Williams might have put it best when they argued to just "make assignments meaningful" [3]. One way to make an assignment meaningful is to provide a focus for the assignment where the students are helping others.

We present this experience report describing a Service Learning Practicum (SLP) that was developed and implemented at the University of Virginia.

SIGCSE '14, March 5-8, 2014, Atlanta, Georgia, USA.
ACM 978-1-4503-2605-6/14/03.
http://dx.doi.org/10.1145/2538862.2538974.

The first of two goals of the SLP is to teach students about development of large software projects. These are concepts that are taught in many courses, but due to the nature of collegiate classes, few courses allow for the development of large projects in groups. In the SLP, students are teamed into groups of six students with one adviser or mentor. The students develop a year-long project in the same manner as a professional development company. The skills, knowledge, and concepts that they learned in their various classes can be put to use, while learning aspects of teamwork, customer interaction, and management skills.

Developing a project that is "not meaningful" can make the students feel that their time is not being respected as burgeoning professionals. This begets the second goal of the SLP: to write quality software for nonprofits in our community. Working with nonprofit organizations allows the students to interact with a real customer, developing real software with a real purpose. Furthermore, the software will have a measurable, positive impact on our community.

The result of the SLP is a capstone course that combines a significant software engineering project – including customer interaction – with a service learning experience.

We are certainly not the first to present a software engineering based capstone, nor the first to present a service learning course with a software engineering focus. However, we feel that we have synthesized the results of previous literature into the successful creation and implementation of our SLP, and we provide a number of structural suggestions and lessons learned that will be of use to a faculty member who is attempting to implement a similar practicum at his/her own institution.

2. RELATED WORK

One of the main aspects of service learning courses is in the idea that the project has intrinsic social value and meaning that the student can believe in. Layman and Williams examined assignments from CS1 and software engineering courses and found that computing instructors still need to look to meaningful assignments for their students [3]. They note that often the only change necessary for making an assignment social relevant is a wording or domain change for a particular computing problem. In our case, students worked mainly on database-driven web applications. These could have been for nearly any domain that the instructor could think of. However, by bringing in nonprofit organizations, the same assignment (creation of a database-driven web application) suddenly becomes something that the students can more easily get behind and be excited for. We contend that, while coordination is required to get nonprofits involved in the projects, the results are worthwhile.

There exist many different models for service learning courses in computer science. Many are single semester course offerings where a course project – or perhaps a semester-long project – is the service learning project itself. Some of these models were discussed at a recent SIGCSE panel [5].

Carnegie Mellon University has developed a model where students are consultants, and work with a nonprofit to help them solve their technical problems. Their approach is more systems engineering based rather than software based, and has achieved remarkable success – in the 14 years of the course's existence, it has had close to 400 partnerships [4].

Egan and Johnson report on incorporating service learning into an introductory CS course, as opposed to a capstone-type course as we implemented [2]. One major advantage that they saw from their course structure was an increase in retention rate of students from CS1 to CS2. This follows from the ideas of Layman and Williams that when assignments are meaningful, students are more engaged and are more likely to continue. However, other students had a less positive experience, as they reported additional homework and pressure on completing the project on time.

Traynor discusses two models for service learning [6]. The first is an early computing course where the students work to reduce the "digital divide" separating generations. Each student is grouped with a senior citizen and a 3rd grade student, and helps each of them with learning to use computers and the Internet. The second model is an upper-level HCI course where the project is to aid local nonprofits. Service examples of the latter include creating a website, and rewriting a computer manual into a format easier to understand by a non-technical person.

Many other institutions have used single semester courses where a project – either one of many projects or a semester-long project – is a service learning project. Since we are presenting the results of a two-semester service learning capstone sequence, and not a single semester course, we do not attempt to properly catalog such single semester offerings.

3. COURSE DESIGN

Our Service Learning Practicum was run last year (2012–2013) as a two semester, fall–spring academic year sequence (39 students, 7 projects). This year (2013–2014) is an ongoing iterative evolvement of last year (43 students, 7 projects). This article presents the results of the completed course (2012–2013), as well as describing some of how we modified it for the current (2013–2014) academic year.

The course is designed as a practicum-based course, and not a lecture-based course. Homework assignments for the course are made up of the multiple deliverables for the individual student projects. There were no exams, although there was an final project required of each student.

The course meets three times a week. On Mondays, we typically have a combined lecture for all the teams on a topic that we considered important for this course: requirements analysis, customer interaction, development methodologies, etc. Some Monday lectures are half-lecture, half group break-out session. Wednesdays are customer meeting days, where teams meet in person with their customer. These meetings often take place during the scheduled class period at other places around campus, but students can meet at another time during the day as well. Fridays are reserved for team work days. Student teams use the Friday class period for meetings with their teammates on particular aspects of the project or to get more in-depth help from the course instructor.

For the development of the projects themselves, we use features from a number of agile development methodologies. From the Rational Unified Process, we use the concept of inception and some of the documentation. From Extreme Programming we use the concept of the customer team member, collective ownership, short cycles, and continuous integration. From Scrum we use the ideas of regular scrum meetings, backlogs (both product and sprint), and burndown charts. We use Redmine, an online project management system, to help with project organization.

Our sprints or iterations are two weeks in length, and end on alternating Mondays. The customer meetings typically occurred on the second day of a sprint, which allowed the customer to view the results of the previous iteration and arrive with comments, questions, suggestions, and – all too often – requirement changes.

4. COMMUNITY PARTNERS

A practicum of this size is not feasible alone. In addition to the nonprofits that we developed the systems for, there were others in the community that we worked with.

4.1 Partner Nonprofit

While the course instructors have had some experience with local nonprofits (serving on boards, previous volunteer service, etc.), being as we are computer science faculty, nonprofit work is obviously not our primary job. Our contacts, knowledge, and experience with the local nonprofit community were not sufficient to allow us to generate the necessary response for the SLP. Thus, we needed to reach out to the nonprofit community.

We were fortunate to be able to partner with the Center for Nonprofit Excellence (CNE), a local nonprofit whose purpose is to strengthen other local nonprofits. CNE is "the area's primary resource for nonprofit management, leadership and collaboration" [1]. CNE has contacts with most of the local nonprofits, and thus has a feel for the type of projects that can best be of help – and who could most benefit. Indeed, when soliciting projects for the current year, a single email generated almost 50 nonprofit project requests. CNE performs a technology survey of nonprofits, and the results of this survey helped us to identify which nonprofits would benefit the most from a custom-developed system.

4.2 Mentors

Students working on these projects need advice and guidance, as they never have been involved on a software development project of this size. As the size of the course grows, it is not feasible for the course instructor to be at all the group meetings – for one reason, many of them are likely to happen at the same time but in different locations. This gave rise to the concept of a mentor: a professional software engineer with years of experience in software development. One mentor is assigned to each group of six students. A mentor attends the group meetings with the customer and generally keeps up with the development of the system. A mentor's job is to help advise the students, not to develop the software. Similarly, a mentor is not meant to be a replacement or a surrogate for the course instructor – s/he is somebody in an advisory role who has a lot of knowledge and experience in software development, and is interested in helping out with this type of project. Having a mentor act in an authoritative role could potentially introduce other problems – including a situation where a non-university individual has control over student work – as well as possibly negatively affect the student-mentor relationship.

The mentorship idea has a number of advantages. It allows the students to benefit from the years of experience from the mentor. It lets students get to know somebody in the software business, and helps the mentor get to know students who may soon be looking for employment. Lastly, it allows professional software developers to help out a local nonprofit while using their expertise.

We were concerned that we would not be able to find enough mentors, even though there are many local software development companies. However, one email announcement yielded enough mentors in only a few days, and then we had to start turning others away. At a meeting of the mentors and the course instructor, they were all very enthusiastic about being involved in such a project, and at being able to help their community while using their specialized training.

We feel that adding computing professionals in both the service and the educational aspects of the course makes our version of a service learning experience that much more compelling. Students get to work with a computing professional who has years of experience, and who can help the students learn to work effectively with customers. Computing professionals similarly get to have an outlet to use their skills in a socially relevant way. These partnerships can then lead to more community connections and even to more potential projects and mentors.

5. PROJECTS

The projects for our service learning course came from organizations of varied purpose, location, and outreach. In this section we discuss the challenges of finding the right mix of projects for students.

5.1 Requirements

Project selection was a challenge for this practicum. A project must be complex enough to serve as a year-long capstone for six computing seniors, yet be able to be completed within the context of a single academic year. Duplicating an existing piece of software did not seem like a viable use of our time. For example, one nonprofit wanted a system to manage collaborative document editing, and we referred them to Dropbox (which is fulfilling their needs quite well).

The course instructor met with various nonprofits during the summer prior to the academic year to help clarify the details of each project. This enabled a reasonable estimate for a properly complex and scoped project to emerge. The students are presented with a general requirements document for each project describing what is desired. Such a document is typically 3-5 pages, and is meant to get them started on understanding the technical details of the project.

Properly scoping a project can be a large concern for this type of course. Indeed, one of the biggest problems we encountered in the first instance of the course was trying for too large of a scope of features to include. To help mitigate this, each requirements document had three categories of requirements: minimum, desired, and optional. The minimum requirements are just that – the minimum requirements necessary to have a system that is of value to the nonprofit. The desired requirements are what we would like to have accomplished by the end of the academic year. The optional requirements include features to include if we choose too small of a scope. The selection was done so that our best estimate is that the desired requirements are feasible within a single year. We were highly accurate in this regard this past year. The students are told that they need to have a prototype of the system with all the minimum requirements at the end of the fall semester, and the full system (with all the desired features) deployed at the end of the academic year. We realize that the original set of minimum and desired requirements may not be feasible within the time allowed, and thus are flexible if those requirements categories need to change.

5.2 Project Restrictions

We specifically avoided certain organizations when we solicited projects. Religious organizations were acceptable, as long as the purpose of the charity – and thus the system to be developed – was for a secular charitable cause. Separation of church and state – as we are a state institution – dictates the necessity for this, as well as the fact that it may make some students uncomfortable otherwise. For example, one nonprofit organization we worked with, Appalachia Service Project, is such a religious organization with a secular charitable purpose.

We also decided that the nonprofit must have a charitable goal as its primary purpose. Many do not, such as athletic leagues, political organizations, fraternities and sororities, etc. Our definition of a political nonprofit here was one that contributed to one or more political candidates, either directly (through campaign donations) or indirectly (through activities such as lobbying).

5.3 Project Examples

In the two years that the SLP has existed, there have been 14 projects, 7 each year. We only describe two projects here; the full list can be found online[1].

Scheduling is a common area in which we found many projects. There are many organizations who have such specific scheduling constraints that there are no free or viable commercial software systems that are able to perform this scheduling. Since these are nonprofits with limited budgets, a system may not viable simply be because it is expensive.

The Virginia Institute for Autism works with autistic students. Teachers are assigned, generally one-on-one, to individual students for six periods throughout the day; teachers generally change students each period. There are numerous constraints on this scheduling: student and teacher absences change who is working with who, teachers can only work with students for which they are trained, lunch requires other teachers to cover their classes, etc. A daily schedule takes six people 30 minutes (i.e., 3 person-hours) to create. With the system in place, it took only one person about 30 minutes to create the schedule, as many pieces of data – such as who is absent that day – still needed to be entered.

Another common topic for projects was website-based or smartphone-based systems. There was sufficient complexity when such things as user accounts, data entry, and custom searches were features that were included in the system.

Habitat for Humanity of Greater Charlottesville builds residences for low-income individuals. Once a house is con-

[1] `http://www.cs.virginia.edu/~asb/slp/`

structed, Habitat generally hands off the management of the house to the new owner(s). However, there is interest in keeping track of the houses in a community that have been built. Habitat was keeping track of this data in many disparate places. The system that was developed allowed for a single place to enter the data, and was able to pull results from the data that was not possible in their previous setup. This has saved them significant time, especially with their reporting requirements, as the system can pull the necessary data from the common database very quickly.

5.4 Students and Projects

Students are allowed to specify their project choice preferences. Since the population size for this is relatively small (n = 39 students for the 2012-2013 academic year), the matching and project assignment is performed manually.

Once the student group is assigned, they have to choose a student to be the project lead. The lead performs much of the coordination for the team, such as scheduling, keeping the meetings moving along with their agenda, keeping the course instructor updated with the overall team progress, etc. It is an administrative position, not an authoritative one. We feel that this is a valuable experience for students, and that all of them should experience it at some point – so for that reason, the project lead rotates through each of the students throughout the year; this allows each student to be the lead for one or two months.

As much as possible, we prefer that team decisions are made by consensus. Ultimately the customer gets to choose what features should be implemented, what it should look like, etc. But the team can choose how it is to be developed in software. Recall that we did not want the mentors to act in an authoritative role, as described above.

We require the students to track their time spent on the project. This allows us to determine, at the end of the year, how many hours were devoted to nonprofit software development – a figure that is particularly useful when analyzing the impact of the SLP. To prevent hour inflation, we guarantee that a student's grade will *never* be evaluated based on the hours they submit. The reality is that if a student is not contributing sufficiently, there will be ample other ways to discern this fact.

6. LEGAL ISSUES

In consultation with our university's general counsel and the provost's office, we worked on developing an appropriate wording for a license with the nonprofit organizations. We wanted a nonprofit to be able to use the software forever, but university policy, consistent with US copyright law, dictates that students own the code that they develop. Most of the projects are developed using interpreted or scripting languages (PHP and Javascript being the most common), so the source code *was* the software. Regardless, one of the deliverables to the nonprofit would be the source code, even on a compiled platform; the other deliverables being the working system and appropriate documentation.

The result was a delicate balance between preserving the students' rights to the code they developed while also allowing the nonprofits to use it. The nonprofits would agree to a perpetual non-commercial, non-distributable, non-revocable license to the software. In addition, they can modify the source code. A summary of the license's terms follows:

- Perpetual: the nonprofit can use this software forever.
- Non-commercial: the nonprofit may not sell the software, nor make money off of charging individuals for using the software (i.e., it must be "free" to use). Some of the software may not be for public distribution – such as an internal scheduling system – but any public-facing part must be able to be used free of charge.
- Non-distributable: the nonprofit may not distribute the software. University policy (and US copyright law) dictates that undergraduate students own any code that they develop for a course (this is different than if a student is paid for the software development, such as a graduate student or a paid undergraduate research assistant). Because of this policy, the nonprofits do not own the code, and thus they cannot distribute it.
- Non-revocable: the license cannot be taken back from the nonprofit by the students or by the university.
- Modifiable software: the nonprofit would gain the actual source code; as mentioned above, it is often the case that the software *is* the source code, but even with a compiled system, the nonprofit would receive the source code. They are allowed to modify it, such as by hiring a developer to add features or remove bugs in the future; this modified version also cannot be distributed or sold.

Note that the agreement does not lessen students' rights at all; it only grants some (limited) rights to the nonprofit. While we could not require students to sign it, we did not encounter any significant opposition with the students signing the agreement. As the students owned the software, it was their decision as to what to do with it – release it under an open source license, attempt to sell it, etc.

As the course instructors, we developed some software for the projects, typically in the form of tutorials and source code examples. A conflict of interest situation arose here. We were developing software as part of our salaried job, giving it to students, and potentially claiming ownership of this code – which could imply partial ownership of the system, and thus could allow us to make a claim to some monetary gains if the students sold their code. For this reason, the course instructors relinquished any rights to the code that we provided to the students. Mentors do not develop any source code, and thus do not need to agree to this license.

The other legal concern that we encountered was the use of existing source code. There are many licenses that exist that both open source and free software are distributed under. Some licenses – specifically the GNU Public License (GPL) – require that any software developed that uses that GPL code be publicly distributed under a GPL-compatible license (which is usually just the GPL itself). This meant that students could not use any GPL software unless they were willing to publicly release their *entire system* under the GPL. Note that this does not apply to linking to a library compiled under the GPL – those libraries are generally covered under the LGPL license, which allows for linking without release of source code. While many people tend to ignore these licensing issues, because we were developing real software for other organizations, it was necessary to carefully adhere to the software license requirements.

There are many licenses that do not have the so-called "viral" licensing restrictions of the GPL. Such licenses – such as the Apache License, the MIT License, and the Mozilla Public License – allow for use of such code in a system without releasing the resultant source code to the public; however, one must typically include credit to the source code used (how this is to be done varies by the license).

7. LESSONS LEARNED

We felt the course was a success in most regards – students learned a lot, we delivered quality software, the nonprofits were happy with the results, and the community-student interaction was allowed to flourish. However, there are some important lessons learned that we share here.

Customer involvement. The customers were, generally, not familiar with software development. One of the aspects of Extreme Programming is the idea of the customer team member. We attempted this last year, but we did not sufficiently set the expectations of what is needed from the customer ahead of time. Some customers were very involved, and their projects flourished. Other customers put in the minimal amount of work necessary, and their projects did not fare so well. In the current year, we have created a customer agreement, which outlines what is expected of the customer. In particular, we mention three aspects: bi-weekly meetings, providing regular feedback, and early testing of the system. We feel that this agreement, and the associated sufficient buy-in from the customers, will solve the vast majority of the issues that arose last year.

Project start-up and transition. There is a large ramp-up at the beginning of the year, as the students acclimate to the project and the technologies used. In particular, learning the software framework will take them some time. In the second year of this course, we had them start on the projects two weeks into the semester. This year we are having them spend two more weeks (for a total of four) working on individual assignments meant to teach them the framework. This lessened the number of iterations by one, but allowed them to have a better understanding of how to design the system for when they start on their group project.

Towards the end of the project, there is the deployment, maintenance, testing, and documentation – all tasks that take non-zero time. We started planning for deployment as soon as the spring semester started, and it was still not enough time for two of the projects. This year, we worked with the customer to determine reasonable expectations before the deployment phase to hopefully alleviate this issue come this spring.

Maintenance Connected with the project transition lesson is the proper way to handle project maintenance post-release. At the end of the course, the nonprofits that we developed the projects for were quite happy with the results. We were generally able to complete the requirements specified. However, there is little means for maintenance, as the students will graduate and move on with their lives shortly after project delivery. We did ask the students at the end of the semester if they were willing to be contacted about helping to maintain the project in the future, and 79% of the class indicated they would (and at least 4 from each group).

Thus, it is critical that the nonprofits have some means to maintain the system. This could be through a volunteer in the community who is willing to take over this task; however, finding one skilled in the framework is a challenge. Local companies may be willing to take this over as well. On some projects, the students themselves were willing to be contacted again to help maintain the system, as they felt emotionally invested.

Requirement solicitation We quickly realized that the requirements needed to have some flexibility. Thus, we split the requirements into "minimum", "desired", and "optional", as described above. This allows us to focus on the core system first, the ideal system next, and then expand if they end up with extra time later.

8. RESULTS

At the end of the spring 2013 semester, we had the students fill out an extensive survey detailing their perception of the class and the various aspects therein. The survey consisted of both text fill-in answers as well as 5-point Likert questions. All the Likert questions were on a 1 to 5 scale. For the course-wide questions, $n = 38$. The results are shown in Table 1. For the results for a particular group (not shown in the table, but described below), $n = 6$.

All the projects had some requirement changes, and the number of changes was rated at 3.50. In one project, the customer changed her mind on the first day, and in another project the goal was to develop many of the requirements during the year. If you take these two projects out of consideration, then the overall rating of how many requirements changed was 3.10, which is very close to the "neutral" answer, meaning that it was a reasonable amount of changes for a project like this. The requirements changes were considered somewhat predictable by the students (3.13).

Satisfaction with the customers by the students was high (4.11), although one group was much less satisfied with their customer (3.00). We knew that this particular customer was a problem during the school year. If one does not consider that one group, then overall customer satisfaction increases to 4.35. Interestingly, this one group with low customer satisfaction was also the group that had the overall least project satisfaction (4.17), even though they were still mostly satisfied with their project. That project ran into many technical difficulties, so there were certainly other factors contributing to their lower project satisfaction.

Satisfaction of the mentors by the students was a bit lower, at 3.89. We attribute this to a number of factors. One was a lack of a clear set of mentor expectations. Another is that the mentors often were busy, and thus unable to attend the group meetings. However, the feedback that they provided was considered very helpful (4.18), and the students generally recommended the customers again (4.16), although there was much variation in the mentor survey results.

Overall project satisfaction was high (4.48), and students felt they would likely have chosen the project again, if they knew then what they know now (4.03). We were pleased to see that the groups worked together quite well (4.47).

We did not perform a formal survey of the customers. However, we do have some anecdotal evidence: each customer was contacted about their overall satisfaction, and all the responses were positive.

Question	Likert 1-5 scale (1 is a "bad" result, 3 is neutral, and 5 is a "good" result)	Avg	Stdev
Overall project satisfaction?	1 = very unsatisfied, 5 = very satisfied	4.45	0.76
How well did the group work together?	1 = terrible, 5 = wonderful	4.47	0.56
Amount of requirements that changed?	1 = everything, 5 = nothing	2.50	1.08
Predictability of requirements changes?	1 = very predictable, 5 = very unpredictable	2.87	0.70
Helpfulness of Redmine?	1 = very unhelpful, 5 = very helpful	3.97	0.94
Usefulness of group workdays in lecture?	1 = very useless, 5 = very useful	4.11	0.98
How burdensome were the reports?	1 = very burdensome, 5 = very unburdensome	3.50	0.98
Customer attentiveness?	1 = very inattentive, 5 = very attentive	3.79	1.19
Customer feedback usefulness?	1 = completely useless, 5 = very useful	3.71	1.23
Satisfied with the customer?	1 = very unsatisfied, 5 = very satisfied	4.11	0.89
Recommend customer again?	1 = never, 5 = completely	3.97	1.10
Mentor attentiveness?	1 = very inattentive, 5 = very attentive	3.34	1.02
Mentor feedback usefulness?	1 = completely useless, 5 = very useful	4.18	0.80
Satisfied with the mentor?	1 = very unsatisfied, 5 = very satisfied	3.89	0.92
Recommend mentor again?	1 = never, 5 = completely	4.16	0.95
Overall satisfaction with project?	1 = very unsatisfied, 5 = very satisfied	4.50	0.56
Choose project again?	1 = definitely not, 5 = definitely	4.03	1.13
Opinion of framework used?	1 = worst thing ever, 5 = greatest thing ever	4.18	0.87

Table 1: End of year survey questions and results ($n = 38$)

The students were required to report their hours. The projects had, on average, 703 hours spent throughout the entire year. The standard deviation was high (153), as might be expected from a group of such disparate projects. We believe the number of hours spent to be much higher, as we know many students did not report all of their hours.

9. CONCLUSIONS

We consider last year's SLP to have been a success. The students were very satisfied with their projects, and the nonprofits were happy with the results. The nonprofits were all presented with systems that fulfilled the agreed-upon requirements. For many of the nonprofits, this will save them a significant amount of time. We have addressed the reasons some projects did not fully succeed; many of those are inclued in the lessons learned section, above.

Based on the number of hours contributed to each project (we had students track their time) we generated an estimate for the monetary contribution of each project. If you assume a \$100 salary per hour for a software developer, then the average contribution per project was \$69,852 – and there were 7 projects. Thus, there was almost half a million dollars of free software development contributed to the community. Even if you assume a lower per-hour salary, it is still a significant contribution.

The nonprofits for the current year are quite excited about the projects that have been selected. Many of the projects will save the respective nonprofit staff members multiple hours of work per week. Others will save a significant amount of money from not having to hire a professional developer to create such a system for them. The projects will allow those nonprofits to focus their resources – both staff time and financial resources – on other areas to better help the community.

10. FUTURE WORK

This past summer a significant amount of time was spent approaching the nonprofits about potential projects, as well as trying to scope out these projects. As word of this program spreads, we hope to have an application process where the nonprofits will apply for such a project. The goal is to work with the nonprofits to ensure that their requested project meets the necessary requirements (viable within a one-year course, of sufficient complexity, etc.). A committee of faculty, professional software developers (likely the mentors of the projects), and individuals from the nonprofit community will then decide which projects are the best fit for the SLP and the community. We intend to implement this in the spring of 2014 for the 2014–2015 academic year.

11. REFERENCES

[1] CNE. *Center for Nonprofit Excellence*, 2012. `http://www.thecne.org`.

[2] M. A. L. Egan and M. Johnson. Service learning in introductory computer science. In *Proceedings of the fifteenth annual conference on Innovation and technology in computer science education*, ITiCSE '10, pages 8–12, New York, NY, USA, 2010. ACM.

[3] L. Layman, L. Williams, and K. Slaten. Note to self: make assignments meaningful. In *Proceedings of the 38th SIGCSE technical symposium on Computer science education*, SIGCSE '07, pages 459–463, New York, NY, USA, 2007. ACM.

[4] J. Mertz and S. McElfresh. Teaching communication, leadership, and the social context of computing via a consulting course. In *Proceedings of the 41st ACM technical symposium on Computer science education*, SIGCSE '10, pages 77–81, New York, NY, USA, 2010. ACM.

[5] J. A. Stone, B. MacKellar, E. M. Madigan, and J. L. Pearce. Community-based projects for computing majors: opportunities, challenges and best practices. In *Proceedings of the 43rd ACM technical symposium on Computer Science Education*, SIGCSE '12, pages 85–86, New York, NY, USA, 2012. ACM.

[6] C. Traynor and M. McKenna. Service learning models connecting computer science to the community. *SIGCSE Bull.*, 35(4):43–46, Dec. 2003.

Panel of Computing Students with Disabilities

Richard E. Ladner
Moderator
University of Washington
Seattle, WA 98195-2350
ladner@cs.washington.edu

Jillian Hall
Auburn University
Auburn, AL 36849

Samir Jain
Georgia Institute of Technology
Atlanta, GA 30332

CeAhna Lathon
Georgia College and State University
Milledgeville, GA 31061

Vincent Martin
Georgia Institute of Technology
Atlanta, GA 30332

ABSTRACT

A panel of college students with disabilities who are computing majors or have taken multiple computing courses will describe their experiences both in and out of the classroom. The goal of the panel is to provide the audience with an opportunity to hear first-hand how their educational needs were met as non-traditional computing students. In addition to the panelists' short presentations, the moderator will facilitate a dialog between the members of the audience and the panelists.

Categories and Subject Descriptors

K.3.2 [**Computer and Information Science Education**]

General Terms

Human Factors

Keywords

Education, Disability, Accessibility

1. INTRODUCTION

Because of the Individuals with Disabilities Education Act (IDEA) originally passed in 1975, the Rehabilitation Act of 1973, Section 504, and the Americans with Disabilities Act of 1990 more and more students with disabilities are attending college and becoming interested in computing fields. As a result we teachers of computer science are more likely now than in the past to have a blind, low-vision deaf, hard of hearing, mobility disabled, or cognitively disabled students in our classrooms or even as a graduate students. The purpose of this panel is for educators in computing fields to learn first-hand from students about their educational needs and how they can be met. No doubt there will be members of the panel audience who have experiences with students with disabilities which will enliven the discussion.

2. ACCESSCOMPUTING

AccessComputing (The Alliance for Access to Computing Careers) is a NSF-funded Broadening Participation Alliance with the goal of increasing the number and success of students with disabilities in computing fields. This panel is part of our effort to foster institutional change that will help make computing departments and organizations more welcoming and accessible to students with disabilities. In the past seven years we have held many capacity building workshops for educators and administrators to help empower them to improve the accessibility and welcoming atmosphere of their departments and organizations. We have found that one of the most effective ways to get the attention the workshop attendees is by having a panel of students with disabilities. Hearing the compelling stories from the students first-hand has had a huge impact on the attendees of these workshops.

In addition to institutional change the Alliance is involved in interventions that directly impact students with disabilities in building their capacity to succeed in the field. This is achieved through a large network of 90 partners and collaborators at institutions and organizations. We have had more than 325 students with disabilities in computing fields that form the AccessComputing Team. This group forms a peer mentoring group that we are in close contact with on a regular basis. Many have graduated and have moved on to their careers. We have chosen our panelists from the current members of our AccessComputing Team.

3. PANEL STRUCTURE

The panel will consist of four mature and thoughtful students with disabilities moderated by Richard Ladner. The students will have a variety of disabilities in order to address the kinds of needs that will arise. All the students will be majors or recent graduates in some computing field or related field. The students will be asked to make short 10 minute presentations that include the following:

- Demographic information: name, academic background, current school, year, disability.
- Description of accessibility needs in their computing classes and other academic activities, such as office hours and group projects.
- Description of how those needs were met at the university level, department level, and instructor level.
- Description of any physical or attitudinal barriers that needed to be overcome.
- Description of future goals.

After these introductory remarks the moderator will solicit questions from the audience and encourage a dialog between the students and members of the audience.

SIGCSE'14, March 5–8, 2014, Atlanta, Georgia, USA.
ACM 978-1-4503-2605-6/14/03.
http://dx.doi.org/10.1145/2538862.2538867

4. PANELISTS

Jillian Hall is a senior at Auburn University majoring in software engineering. She will be starting at IBM as a software consultant when she graduates in August 2014. Her ultimate goal is to attend graduate school. She will use her work experience to help find her passion for what she would like to specialize in for her graduate work.

Samir Jain is a sophomore at Georgia Tech majoring in biomedical engineering. He is interested in doing research on improving signal processing in cochlear implants. He also want to continue working on accessible technology and human-computer interaction.

CeAhna Lathon is a sophomore at Georgia College and State University majoring in physics. She is interested in robotics but is unsure yet if she will continue in electrical or mechanical engineering.

Vincent Martin is a graduate student at Georgia Tech in the Ph.D. program in human centered computing. He is based in Professor Bruce Walker's sonification lab where is works on both hardware and software for haptic and auditory interfaces for blind people. While working as a rehabilitation engineer for 20 years he consulted with many companies on usability and accessibility.

Richard E. Ladner, moderator, is a professor in computer science and engineering at the University of Washington. He is the Principal Investigator for AccessComputing. He has taught students with disabilities for the past 20 years in various enrichment programs. He has mentored numerous students with disabilities from high school through graduate school levels. He has an active research program in accessible technology.

5. RESOURCES

Those attending the panel will be provided informational packets including:

- AccessComputing Brochure
- Equal Access: Universal Design of Computing Departments
- Equal Access: Universal Design of Your Project
- Equal Access: Universal Design of Computer Labs
- Equal Access: Universal Design of Instruction

6. DISCUSSION

Panels at SIGCSE are quite varied, covering topics such as curriculum, diversity, policy, and opportunities. We are not aware of any panels in the recent past that were from the students' points of view. Educators hearing from other educators provides only a second-hand view of disabled students' needs and how they were met. A more powerful approach is to hear directly from the students.

Because of the novelty of having a student panel, we hope that the panel is more likely to attract a large audience. Attendees will want to meet students like those they are likely to encounter in the future. Attendees will expect to learn something new, not just boiler-plate from their university's office of disability resources for students.

7. ACKNOWLEDGMENT

AccessComputing is funded by the National Science Foundation (CISE BPC awards numbers CNS-0540615, CNS-0837508, and CNS-1042260.) Any questions, findings, and conclusions or recommendations expressed in this material are those of the authors and do not necessarily reflect the views of the federal government.

Rediscovering the Passion, Beauty, Joy, and Awe: Making Computing Fun Again, part 7

Daniel D. Garcia (moderator)
University of California, Berkeley
777 Soda Hall
Berkeley, CA 94720
+1 (510) 517-4041
ddgarcia@cs.berkeley.edu

Jennifer Campbell
University of Toronto
Department of Computer Science
Toronto, ON Canada M5S 2E4
+1 (416) 978-6320
campbell@cs.toronto.edu

Rebecca Dovi
Patrick Henry High School
12449 W. Patrick Henry Rd.
Ashland, VA 23005
+1 (804) 365-8000
dovimath@gmail.com

Cay Horstmann
San José State University
Department of Computer Science
San José, CA 95192-0249
+1 (408) 924-5060
Cay.Horstmann@sjsu.edu

Categories and Subject Descriptors

K.3.2 [**Computer and Information Science Education**]: Computer science education

Keywords

Computer science education, online learning, MOOC

1. SUMMARY

In his keynote at SIGCSE 2007, Grady Booch exhorted us to share the "passion, beauty, joy and awe" (PBJA) of computing [1]. This led to a series of room-packed sessions at the following six SIGCSE symposia to explore that idea from different angles [2-6]. They have provided a forum for sharing:

- **What we've done**: Highlighting successful PBJA initiatives the presenters have undertaken or seen and wish to trumpet.
- **What we should do (curriculum)**: Pointing out where our curriculum is lacking in PBJA, and how to fix it.
- **How we should do it (pedagogy)**: Sharing how a change in attitude / focus / etc. can make strides to improving PBJA.

While the initial PBJA sessions evolved from a need to understand and combat the enrollment crisis of eight years ago, we are now seeing an incredible resurgence in interest in our field, partially because "coders are hip and computer science is hot" [9]. There are colleges where the numbers have exceeded historic highs, and some rightfully claim the crisis is over [8]. This PBJA "movement" was born out of this enrollment crisis, but is not tied to it [7]. There is always value in sharing novel best practices and advocating techniques that make computing fun for beginners.

In the past, we either tried to gather educators who brought a wide variety of perspectives, who would focus on a particular issue, or who have instituted very creative and successful paths into the major. This year we have gathered three seasoned educators who have taken the leap and built online classes for introductory computing on three different platforms. What innovative ideas did they employ to support collaboration? Does the need to auto-grade mean students can no longer choose their own final projects, and how does that stifle PBJA? Do these auto-graded formative assessments feel like drill-and-kill? The hope with this panel is to explore how online offerings, in these crucial early years, extol (and perhaps suppress!) the PBJA of computing.

SIGCSE'14, March 5–8, 2014, Atlanta, Georgia, USA.
ACM 978-1-4503-2605-6/14/03.
http://dx.doi.org/10.1145/2538862.2538874

2. JENNIFER CAMPBELL

In Fall 2012 and Winter 2013, I co-developed and co-taught (with Paul Gries) two MOOCs on introductory programming in Python hosted on *Coursera*. We re-offered the first MOOC in Fall 2013. To date, there are over 270,000 registrants in our live and archived courses. Together, the video lectures for the two MOOCs correspond to our 12-week on-campus CS1 course.

For some learners, the MOOC experience is one of PBJA and we witness that on the discussion forums where "Aha!" moments are celebrated, mentor-mentee relationships are fostered, and gratitude is expressed. But it isn't all positive and some learners express confusion and frustration. Participants on the discussion forums represent only about 5-10% of those enrolled, so we don't know how the rest are experiencing the course.

For some, the opportunity for a PBJA experience seems to hinge largely on community and communication. Learners need the right support at the right times. A few practices that we view as key are: sending regular emails to support and encourage our learners, addressing problems promptly and communicating the outcome to learners, having a regular instructor presence on the discussion forums, structuring the discussion forums in a way that makes it simpler to navigate and minimizes duplication, and finally, for repeat offerings, inviting select former MOOC learners to serve as moderators.

3. REBECCA DOVI

In the summer of 2013, I developed the curriculum and recorded the lessons for the AP Computer Science MOOC to run through the 2013-14 school year. The goal was to provide a course geared toward high school students in preparation for the AP CS exam. To our knowledge, this was the first MOOC specifically designed for a K-12 audience. Currently, fewer than 10% of American high schools offer the AP CS course, so most students in the United States do not have access to the course in a traditional classroom setting.

Due to the age of the targeted group, several modifications to the traditional MOOC structure were made. The course was divided into two terms, beginning in early September and ending in early May. Course materials were also structured with this age group in mind, with each lesson containing a warm up, 2-5 video lectures, graded multiple choice and code questions, and independent practice problems. One of the biggest challenges has been adapting the AP style free response questions to the MOOC environment.

The MOOC itself was tiered into two groups. Anyone could enroll and follow the MOOC for free. The second option, *MOOC local*, trained a local adult to act as a coach for the students. The students met in person with this coach about once a week. There was a separate interface for these coaches that provided training and support materials, as well as a grade book interface to monitor student progress. We feel it was the human contact and 1-on-1 support the coach provided that really helped support the PBJA.

For the 2013-14 school year the MOOC was run as a free pilot. In future years the plan is to continue to run the public MOOC for free and charge a fee for the MOOC local access. This would allow students to get high school credit for the course. The fee system is similar to many of the Virtual School programs available in public schools throughout the country, with the primary difference being the support of the local coach.

4. CAY HORSTMANN

In Spring 2013, I designed and recorded a CS1/Java course with Udacity that was designed to be a complete equivalent to our brick-and-mortar class at San José State University. The course was offered for college credit in Summer 2013, taught by my colleague, Kathleen O'Brien, with about 800 registered students and over 15,000 MOOC participants who didn't take the course for credit. It will be revised and repeated in Spring 2014.

We struggled mightily to inject a measure of PBJA into what can be a rather dull environment. Here are some of the practices that I think worked out well. (1) Multiple lecturers with different personalities. A Udacity staff member, Sara Tansey, recorded about half of the material, focusing on worked examples, and we constantly switched back and forth. Several Stanford students made cameo experiences, telling students it was normal to be confused and frustrated, and how it all works out in the end. (2) Very short videos. The target for each video was 2 minutes, immediately followed by a question (mostly programming exercises and a few fill-in/mutliple choice), followed by an even shorter answer video. Repeat ad infinitum. (3) Engaging examples. I was given strict orders to avoid prime numbers and digits of π since, in Udacity's experience, one loses students quickly when the exercises don't interest them. We did a lot of work with image manipulation since it was visually interesting and worked well with the autograder. (4) A good autograder that allows quick authoring of hundreds of programming exercises. Instead of explaining students how to build up a complex example, we let them do the work, a programming problem at a time, changing a few lines of code here and there. I learned never to tell when I could ask.

But today's technology is still very primitive, and we just scratched the surface of what can be done. In particular, social aspects are almost entirely lacking. The discussion forum is a noisy mess. There is no way for students to showcase their own creative work. In my view, scaling from individual to collective PBJA is the next challenge of MOOC platforms.

5. REFERENCES

[1] Booch, G. 2007. Readn', writ'n, 'rithmetic… and code'n. *SIGCSE Bull.* 39, 1 (Mar. 2007), 197-197. **doi.acm.org/10.1145/1227504.1227380**

[2] Garcia, D. D., Cutler, R., Dodds, Z., Roberts, E., and Young, A. 2009. Rediscovering the passion, beauty, joy, and awe: making computing fun again, continued. In *Proceedings of the 40th ACM Technical Symposium on CS Education* (Chattanooga, TN, USA, March 04-07, 2009). SIGCSE '09. ACM, New York, NY, 65-66. **doi.acm.org/10.1145/1508865.1508889**

[3] Garcia, D. D., Chapman, G., Hazzan, O., Johnson, M., and Sudol, L. A. 2010. Rediscovering the passion, beauty, joy, and awe: making computing fun again, part 3. In *Proceedings of the 41st ACM Technical Symposium on CS Education* (Milwaukee, WI, USA, March 10 - 13, 2010). SIGCSE '10. ACM, New York, NY, 394-395. **doi.acm.org/10.1145/1734263.1734399**

[4] Garcia, D. D., Hutton, M. F., Lemon, E., and Paley, J. 2011. Rediscovering the passion, beauty, joy, and awe: making computing fun again, part 4. In *Proceedings of the 42nd ACM technical symposium on Computer science education* (SIGCSE '11). ACM, New York, NY, USA, 613-614. **doi.acm.org/10.1145/1953163.1953332**

[5] Garcia, D. D., Ericson, B., Goode, J. and Lewis, C. 2012. Rediscovering the passion, beauty, joy, and awe: making computing fun again, part 5. In *Proceedings of the 43rd ACM technical symposium on Computer Science Education* (SIGCSE '12). ACM, New York, NY, USA, 577-578. **doi.acm.org/10.1145/2157136.2157300**

[6] Garcia, D. D., Barr, V., Guzdial, M. and Malan, D.J. 2013. Rediscovering the passion, beauty, joy, and awe: making computing fun again, part 6. In *Proceeding of the 44th ACM technical symposium on Computer science education* (SIGCSE '13). ACM, New York, NY, USA, 379-380. **doi.acm.org/10.1145/2445196.2445308**

[7] McGettrick, A., Roberts, E., Garcia, D. D., and Stevenson, C. 2008. Rediscovering the passion, beauty, joy and awe: making computing fun again. In *Proceedings of the 39th SIGCSE Technical Symposium on Computer Science Education* (Portland, OR, USA, March 12 - 15, 2008). SIGCSE '08. ACM, New York, NY, 217-218. **doi.acm.org/10.1145/1352135.1352213**

[8] NY Times. *CS Programs Make a Comeback in Enrollment.* **www.nytimes.com/2009/03/17/science/17comp.html**

[9] NY Times. *Giving Women the Access Code.* **www.nytimes.com/2012/04/03/science/giving-women-the-access-code.html**

Alternatives to Lecture: Experience Peer Instruction and Pedagogical Code Reviews

Scott Grissom
Grand Valley State University
grissom@gvsu.edu

Christopher Hundhausen
Washington State University
hundhaus@wsu.edu

Phillip Conrad
University of California Santa Barbara
pconrad@cs.ucsb.edu

SUMMARY

This session will demonstrate best practices for introducing peer instruction and pedagogical code reviews into the computer science classroom. Presenters play the role of instructors on the first day of class. Audience members play the role of students as they collaborate on a variety of sample activities. By providing models of active learning in computing contexts, we seek to motivate instructors to adopt these pedagogies in their classrooms. Sufficient time will be reserved for questions and discussion.

Categories and Subject Descriptors

K.3.1 [**Computing Milieux**]: Computers and Education – *Collaborative learning*

General Terms

Design, Human Factors

Keywords

Active learning, student engagement pedagogies, student-centered learning, collaborative learning, peer instruction, evidence-based instructional practices, pedagogical code reviews

1. ENGAGEMENT PEDAGOGIES

There is significant evidence that student engagement pedagogies are more effective than traditional lecture and have benefits including improved student performance, increased attendance, and better retention in the major [9, 11]. These approaches are also referred to as evidence-based instructional practices, student-centered, active learning or cooperative learning. Calls for faculty to adopt these approaches have been widespread for many years but their impact remains limited.

For example, a majority of Physics faculty report awareness of these strategies but their students spend no more than a third of class time interacting with each other [6]. A survey of over 12,000 university professors suggests that well over half of class time in STEM fields is devoted to lecture [15]. Another survey revealed that only a third of 116 CS faculty use cooperative learning [1].

SIGCSE'14, March 5–8, 2014, Atlanta, Georgia, USA.
ACM 978-1-4503-2605-6/14/03.
http://dx.doi.org/10.1145/2538862.2538985

2. SESSION FORMAT

The session begins with a brief introduction to evidence-based instructional practices. Two twenty-five minute demonstrations are devoted to each of the practices: peer instruction and pedagogical code reviews. Attendees play the role of students and complete carefully selected exercises that demonstrate each approach. Session leaders play the role of instructors on the first day of class and present evidence why the approach is being used with respect to increased student learning, performance and motivation. The final fifteen minutes are reserved for questions and comments from the audience. Attendees will be invited to join a growing community of faculty who share resources and best practices.

2. PEER INSTRUCTION

Peer Instruction (PI) is am instructional practice often referred to by the physical object used during lecture – clickers [2]. However, recent innovations allow students to use their own devices including laptops, tablets, smart phones and even basic phones with SMS service. Students initially engage with the material, perhaps through assigned readings or watching videos of lectures, prior to class. Students are held accountable by completing an online quiz before class or at the start of class using clickers.

During class, students are posed a challenging multiple-choice question and vote on an answer using a clicker or similar device. They then discuss the question in small groups and are encouraged to explain their thinking to each other. After the discussion, everyone votes a second time. The instructor uses the responses to facilitate a class-wide discussion.

PI is based in constructivist learning theory, which tells us that information can't be dumped into the brain, but in fact that every person individually constructs their own understanding of new material. PI has been documented most thoroughly in physics but results can be found in biology, chemistry, computer science and math [3, 5, 12, 13].

3. PEDAGOGICAL CODE REVIEWS

Pedagogical Code Reviews (PCRs) [7] were developed for computing education as an adaptation of the studio-based learning process, which emphasizes collaborative critiquing as a central learning activity [8]. Modeled after the code inspection process used in the software industry [4], PCRs bring together small teams of 3-5 students to review each other's code. Led by a trained moderator (usually an upper-division computing student or graduate teaching assistant), student teams review each team member's code against an established checklist of coding best practices (see, e.g., [16]), augmented with a list of requirements for the specific programming solution being reviewed. Individual team members rotate through the following well-defined roles for each review:

- *Author*—the person whose code solution is being inspected; may be called upon to clarify his or her code as needed.
- *Reader*—reads the Author's code solution aloud.
- *Inspector*—takes a leading role in inspecting each line of code against the provided code review checklist.
- *Recorder*—documents issues that arise in the inspection in an inspection issue log that is provided.

Each code review is limited to thirty minutes, and follows a well-defined procedure in which the Reader reads each line of code aloud, summarizing or paraphrasing as necessary. As lines of code are read, other members of the team are invited to raise issues for discussion. The team classifies these issues by severity (minor, moderate, or major). They are then logged by the Recorder. At the conclusion of the inspection, the Author receives a copy of the inspection log, and is asked to resubmit his or her solution based on the results of the PCR.

It is important to note that, in contrast to traditional code inspections, which tend to focus on identifying flaws, the goal of the PCR process is to identify a solution's *strengths* and areas that could be improved. Moreover, whereas traditional code inspections tend to discourage lengthy discussion of solutions to coding issues [16], the PCR process aims to foster pedagogically-valuable discussions of common coding pitfalls and how to resolve them.

PCRs are rooted in social constructivist learning theory [10], which holds that the PCR process facilitates learning by providing students with opportunities to participate, in increasingly central ways, in the practices of a disciplinary community: as solution designers, code reviewers, discussants, and moderators. On this view, learning comes about through *changes in identity* facilitated by such participation, which, because it is mediated by learner-constructed artifacts (code solutions), is seen as especially valuable in bridging the gap between expert and novice perspectives. The effectiveness of PCRs in improving code quality, prompting students to consider and discuss coding practices at multiple levels, and facilitating positive attitudinal shifts, has been documented through a series of quasi-experimental studies [7].

4. REFERENCES

[1] Beck, Leland. 2011. personal communication.

[2] Carl Wieman Science Education Initiative, Clicker Resource Website. http://cwsei.ubc.ca/resources/clickers.htm

[3] Crouch, C. H., & Mazur, E. 2001. Peer instruction: Ten years of experience and results. *American Journal of Physics,* 69.

[4] Gilb, T. and Graham, D. *Software Inspection.* Addison-Wesley, Menlo Park, CA, 1993.

[5] Hake, R. R. 1998. Interactive-engagement vs. traditional methods: A six-thousand-student survey of mechanics test data for introductory physics courses. *American Journal of Physics.* 66 (1).

[6] Henderson, C., & Dancy, M.H. 2009. "The Impact of Physics Education Research on the Teaching of Introductory Quantitative Physics," Proceedings of the Physics Education Research Conference.

[7] Hundhausen, C.D., Agrawal, A. and Agarwal, P. 2013. Talking about code: Integrating pedagogical code reviews into early computing courses. *ACM Trans. Comput. Educ.* 13, 3 (Aug. 2013), 14:1–14:28.

[8] Hundhausen, C.D., Narayanan, N.H. and Crosby, M.E. 2008. Exploring studio-based instructional models for computing education. *Proc. 39th SIGCSE Technical Symposium on Computer Science Education.* ACM Press. 392–396.

[9] Johnson, D. W., Johnson, R. T., and Smith, K. A. 1991. *Active Learning: Cooperation in the College Classroom,* Interaction Book Company, Edina, MN.

[10] Lave, J. and Wenger, E. 1991. *Situated Learning: Legitimate Peripheral Participation.* Cambridge University Press, New York

[11] Michael, J. 2006. "Where's the Evidence that Active Learning Works?" *Advances in Physiology Education,* 30, pp. 159-167.

[12] Porter, L., Bailey-Lee, C., Simon, B, Zingaro, D. 2011. Peer Instruction: Do Students Really Learn from Peer Discussion in Computing? ICER 2011.

[13] Simon, B. Kohanfars, M., Lee, J., Tamayo, K. and Cutts, Q. 2010. "Experience report: peer instruction in introductory computing". *Proceedings of SIGCSE 2009.*

[14] Slavin, R. E. 1995. *Cooperative Learning: Theory, Research, and Practice* (2nd edition), Allyn & Bacon, Boston, MA.

[15] Trustees of Indiana University. 2011. Faculty Survey of Student Engagement,

[16] Wiegers, K. 1995. Improving quality with software inspections. *Software Development.* 3, 4 (1995), 55-64.

Injecting Parallel Computing into CS2

Joel C. Adams
Calvin College
Dept of Computer Science
Grand Rapids, MI 49546
(616) 526-8666
adams@calvin.edu

ABSTRACT

In today's multicore world, every CS student should learn about and gain experience with (at least) shared-memory parallelism. CS Curriculum 2013 acknowledges this by shifting parallel computing from elective status into the core. This paper argues that students should be introduced to parallelism early, that the CS2 (*Data Structures*) course is a natural place to do so, and reports our experience in doing this. The paper also argues that students should be taught to solve problems using *parallel patterns*, which are industry-standard best-practice strategies for parallel problem solving. To support such teaching, the paper presents *patternlets* – minimalist, scalable, executable programs, each illustrating the behavior of a parallel pattern – as a useful pedagogical tool for teaching parallel concepts. Several patternlets and their executions are given. The paper presents evidence that this injection of parallelism into CS2 has been successful.

Categories and Subject Descriptors

K.3.2 [**Computers and Education**]: Computer and Information Science Education – *Curriculum.*

General Terms

Algorithms, Design, Performance.

Keywords

CS2, multithreading, OpenMP, parallel, patterns, shared memory.

1. INTRODUCTION

In 2006, hardware manufacturers began producing dual-core CPUs in place of the single-core CPUs. Fast-forward to today and two-, four-, six-, eight-, ten-, and twelve-core CPUs are readily available [4]. Moreover, companies are manufacturing various *accelerators*, ranging from many-core *coprocessors* with dozens of cores [5] to *general purpose graphics processing units* (GPGPUs) with hundreds or thousands of cores [7].

Recognizing these seismic changes to today's hardware platforms, the ACM/IEEE CS Curriculum 2013 (CS2013) includes a new knowledge area *Parallel and Distributed Computing* (PDC) with 14 hours in the core (5 Tier 1; 9 Tier 2), plus additional PDC core topics in its *Systems Fundamentals* knowledge area [10]. This shift of parallel computing from elective to core topic creates a challenge for CS educators, since relatively few of us have been trained to design parallel algorithms or programs, especially ones that will scale when ported from a system with fewer cores to a system with more cores. Considering the ongoing changes in both the hardware and software levels, CS educators can be forgiven if this challenge seems more than a little daunting.

SIGCSE'14, March 5–8, 2014, Atlanta, Georgia, USA.
Copyright © 2014 ACM 978-1-4503-2605-6/14/03...$15.00.
http://dx.doi.org/10.1145/2538862.2538883.

1.1 The Parallel Hardware Landscape

There are three broad categories of parallel *hardware* systems:

1. *Shared-memory systems* are those in which multiple computational *cores* share the same main memory system, through which communication can occur. Today's smart phones, tablets, laptops, desktops, and so on, are all shared-memory parallel systems. Most systems with accelerators are a special case of shared-memory systems.
2. *Distributed-memory systems* are those in which multiple computational *nodes* each have their own local memories, but share no memory with one another. To support communication, the nodes are connected together using a network. Older Beowulf clusters and some supercomputers were distributed-memory systems.
3. *Hybrid systems* are distributed-memory systems in which the nodes are shared memory systems. Recent Beowulf clusters and supercomputers are generally hybrid systems.

The parallel topics included in the core of Curriculum 2013 focus primarily (but not exclusively) on shared-memory systems and multithreading. This is logical, as virtually all of today's CS majors will work with shared-memory systems after graduation; the same cannot be said for distributed-memory or hybrid systems. Shared-memory systems thus provide a good entry point for CS educators who are new to parallel computing.

1.2 Shared-Memory Software Options

Software for shared-memory systems can be written using either:

- *Multithreading*, in which the application consists of multiple *threads* that communicate with one another via the shared memory. These applications may be written in a language with built-in multithreading support (e.g., C++11, Java); or in a sequential language using an external library that provides multithreading (e.g., C/C++ with OpenMP or POSIX threads).
- *Multiprocessing*, in which an application consists of multiple *processes* that communicate with one another via message passing. These applications may be written in a language that supports message passing (e.g., Erlang, Scala); or in a sequential language using an external message passing library (e.g., C/C++ with MPI – the *message passing interface*).

Given the variety of available software options, different CS departments will undoubtedly make different choices in what to teach their students, based on their program outcomes, in-house expertise, faculty preferences, and other factors. This is a *Good Thing*, as it should yield a rich and diverse ecosystem of approaches to introducing students to parallelism.

1.3 Introducing Parallelism Early

We believe students should be introduced to parallelism early and often, throughout the CS curriculum. Before the multicore shift of 2006, we taught parallel computing as an advanced elective for over a decade, and most students found it quite difficult to make the transition from sequential to parallel thinking, because all of their previous training had conditioned them to think sequentially. If parallel thinking is to come naturally to our students, they need frequent and consistent exposure to it throughout the CS curriculum, rather than a crash-course in their final year.

This raises the question: Where in the CS curriculum should students *first* be introduced to parallelism?

In our department, our CS1 course covers GUI programming in Java to ground our introductory students in OOP. Our CS2 course has students build data structures in C++ so that they learn to manage dynamic memory. Our CS3 course is a semi-traditional algorithms course taught in C# to introduce students to the Microsoft platform. Since all of these languages support parallelism, we could first introduce students to parallelism in any of these courses. We have chosen to do so in CS2, because:

- CS2 students are no longer programming novices.
- CS2 data structures permit large quantities of data to be stored and processed; reducing the times to process such data collections provides a natural way to motivate parallelism.
- CS2 is the first course in which performance is a consideration (with the introduction of Big-Oh notation).

For these reasons, we have chosen to introduce our students to parallelism in CS2, though we limit their hands-on experience to problems whose solutions require no synchronization.

Since our CS2 course is taught in C++, we have several options for introducing parallelism, including:

- The POSIX thread library [2].
- C++11 [3], which has a standard thread library.
- OpenMP [1,8], an open, multi-language, platform-independent industry standard library for multithreading.
- MPI [9,11], an open, multi-language, platform-independent industry standard library for multiprocessing.

We strongly considered the MPI option because communicating via message passing between processes avoids the race conditions that plague multithreading in shared memory.

In the end, we chose the OpenMP option because of:

1. Its relative ease of use, and its support in multiple languages.
2. Its built-in support for commonly needed operations, such as reductions, mutual exclusion, etc.
3. Its non-proprietary status as an open industry standard.

In this paper, we report our experience using OpenMP to teach CS2 students about parallelism. Other institutions have made this same decision [1,8]. Our approach differs from theirs because of our use of *parallel patterns*. Section 2 provides an overview of our course; Section 3 explores our use of patterns; and Section 4 presents some assessment results.

2. PARALLELISM IN CS2

Since the focus of our CS2 course is the elementary data structures, we do not (yet) incorporate parallelism throughout the course, though we are considering this. To introduce our students to parallelism, we have added one week's worth of parallel material – three classroom sessions, one lab exercise, and one assignment – to an otherwise traditional CS2 course. We currently cover this material near the end of the course; it could go earlier. To make room for it, we shifted our coverage of graphs to CS3.

2.1 Lab Exercise

In our lab exercise, our students use OpenMP functions to time sequential addition and transpose operations on large matrices (e.g., 4096x4096). Students have seen matrices (2-D vectors) previously in the course, so this activity extends an already-familiar topic. (Image processing operations can also be parallelized instead of matrix operations [8].)

Given the size of the matrices, these operations take a relatively long time (about 10 secs) and the students become impatient. We have even had students kill their programs after not receiving an instantaneous response, assuming it had crashed. This impatience is exactly what we want, so that the students *experience* the benefits of parallelism.

After students have recorded the times for these sequential operations in a spreadsheet, they create parallel versions of those operations, run and time those parallel versions, and record those times in the spreadsheet. Creating multithreaded versions of these operations is simple using OpenMP's **`#pragma omp parallel for`** directive, which we describe in more detail below.

The students then further reduce the times of these operations by changing OpenMP's work-scheduling policy from *static* – in which thread work-loads are set at compile-time – to *dynamic* – in which thread work-loads are determined at run-time. This is also quite simple in OpenMP.

Students then use their spreadsheets to compute the speedup of each parallel version and create charts to help them visualize the performance improvement. In some ways, this is unnecessary because they have already *experienced* the improvement, but we want to give them the practice of creating such visualizations as part of quantifying their lab experiences.

2.2 Programming Assignment

The students' assignment is to use parallelization to speed up the other matrix operations. These include the default, explicit, and copy constructors; the assignment operation; the equality operation; the subtraction operation; and others.

Students who blindly parallelize the **`for`** loops in their **`Matrix`** class encounter problems if they do so with the file I/O operations. Text files are sequential structures, and normal file I/O is inherently sequential. Since threads share their process's open file table, a multithreaded input operation will interleave the threads' read operations, so the order of the values within the matrix will be different than their order in the input file. This provides a first exposure to the subtleties of multithreading and race conditions.

2.3 Classroom Sessions

During our weeklong introduction to parallelism, we have three 50-minute classroom sessions. The first session typically occurs before the lab exercise; the second and third sessions afterward.

In Fall 2012, we used these sessions as follows:

- Session 1: We explained the multicore hardware shift and introduced the concepts of threads and multithreading, to prepare students for the lab exercise.
- Session 2: We continued the exploration of multithreading concepts, in order to reinforce and help students understand what they had experienced in the lab exercise.
- Session 3: We introduced some basic ideas of parallel design, and used an active learning exercise in which the students explored parallel sorting, culminating in parallel merge sort.

In Spring 2013, we proceeded as in Fall 2012, except that (i) we added an OpenMP live-coding demo at the end of Session 1 to let the students see threads in action, and (ii) we replaced the purely conceptual coverage in Session 2 with an OpenMP live-coding session that demonstrated those same concepts in action. Everything else about our parallel week remained the same.

3. PATTERNS AND PATTERNLETS

In this section, we present some of the live-coding programs we presented in classroom Sessions 1 and 2 of our parallelism week during Spring 2013. Each of these programs illustrates a *parallel computing pattern* [6]: an industry-standard best-practice strategy that parallel computing practitioners have found to be frequently useful in solving problems over the past 20+ years.

If our goal is to produce students who are capable parallel problem-solvers, teaching our students about these patterns is a good investment of our limited classroom time. As the accrued computational wisdom of parallel practitioners, patterns are likely to remain useful in the future. Put differently, in the volatile domain of parallel computing hardware and software, parallel patterns represent a stable body of knowledge that seems likely to remain useful and applicable regardless of future changes. We thus use the body of patterns as a pedagogical framework for teaching parallel concepts that will have long-term relevance.

We have designed our live-coding programs to be:

- *Minimalist* in terms of eliminating non-essential features, so that students can easily grasp the pattern's essential concept.
- *Scalable* so that students can vary the number of threads and observe how the pattern's behavior changes.
- *Syntactically correct* so that students can use the pattern as a working model for their own coding.

Since these are "little programs" in the tradition of applets and servlets, we call these programs *patternlets*.

3.1 Fork-Join

OpenMP relies heavily on the *fork-join* pattern so we begin with a patternlet for it, as shown in Figure 1.

```
#include <stdio.h>      // printf()
#include <omp.h>        // OpenMP

int main(int argc, char** argv) {

    printf("\nBefore...\n");

//    #pragma omp parallel
    printf("\nDuring...");

    printf("\n\nAfter...\n\n");

    return 0;
}
```

Figure 1. ***forkJoin.c***

When run, this program produces the behavior shown in Figure 2.

```
Before...

During...

After...
```

Figure 2. ***forkJoin.c*****, Initial Behavior**

We then uncomment the `#pragma omp parallel` directive and recompile/rerun the program. On a quad-core computer, its behavior changes as shown in Figure 3.

```
Before...

During...
During...
During...
During...

After...
```

Figure 3. ***forkJoin.c*****, Modified Behavior**

When uncommenting one line of code produces such a marked change in program behavior, it gets a student's attention. We thus leverage a student's curiosity to understand what is happening; this motivates and helps them to understand the fork-join concept.

Students often ask questions, such as, *"Can you have more than one directive?"* or *"Can you control the number of threads?"* By live-coding, we can change *forkJoin.c* on the fly and let the students experience the answers to these questions, increasing their engagement in the classroom.

3.2 SPMD

Figure 4 shows our next program, which builds on fork-join to illustrate the *single program multiple data* (SPMD) pattern.

```
#include <stdio.h>
#include <omp.h>

int main(int argc, char** argv) {
  printf("\n");

//  #pragma omp parallel
  {
    int id = omp_get_thread_num();
    int numThreads = omp_get_num_threads();
    printf("Hello from thread %d of %d\n",
                         id, numThreads);
  }

  printf("\n");
  return 0;
}
```

Figure 4. ***spmd.c***

When run, this program produces the output shown in Figure 5.

```
Hello from thread 0 of 1
```

Figure 5. ***spmd.c*****, Initial Behavior**

We then uncomment the `#pragma omp parallel` directive, recompile and rerun the program. Again, on a quad core computer, this produces behavior like that in Figure 6.

```
Hello from thread 0 of 4
Hello from thread 2 of 4
Hello from thread 3 of 4
Hello from thread 1 of 4
```

Figure 6. ***spmd.c*****, Modified Behavior**

This provides a basis for exploring how the same variables in different threads of the same program can hold different values. It also provides a first look at non-deterministic behavior, and can be used to introduce the concept of data races, since the threads are "racing" to write their strings to the console.

We typically extend this example by adding a few lines of code that let us specify the number of threads on the command-line.

3.3 Parallel For Loop

Our lab exercise has the students parallelizing the **for** loops within matrix operations, so we use the program in Figure 7 to introduce the students to the *parallel for loop* pattern.

```
#include <stdio.h>     // printf()
#include <stdlib.h>    // atoi()
#include <omp.h>       // OpenMP

int main(int argc, char** argv) {
  const int REPS = 8;
  int id, i;

  printf("\n");
  if (argc > 1) {
    omp_set_num_threads( atoi(argv[1]) );
  }

  #pragma omp parallel for private(id, i)
  for (i = 0; i < REPS; i++) {
    id = omp_get_thread_num();
    printf("Thread %d performed iteration %d\n",
             id, i);
  }

  printf("\n");
  return 0;
}
```

Figure 7. ***parallelForBlocks.c***

When run with a single thread, that thread (0) performs all eight iterations of the loop. When run with two threads, the program produces behavior like that in Figure 8.

```
Thread 0 performed iteration 0
Thread 1 performed iteration 4
Thread 0 performed iteration 1
Thread 1 performed iteration 5
Thread 0 performed iteration 2
Thread 1 performed iteration 6
Thread 0 performed iteration 3
Thread 1 performed iteration 7
```

Figure 8. ***parallelForBlocks.c*, with 2 Threads**

This makes it easy to see that the iterations of the **for** loop are being divided into two halves or "blocks", with thread 0 doing iterations 0-3 and thread 1 doing iterations 4-7.

Using 4 threads, the program produces behavior like Figure 9.

```
Thread 0 performed iteration 0
Thread 2 performed iteration 4
Thread 3 performed iteration 6
Thread 1 performed iteration 2
Thread 0 performed iteration 1
Thread 2 performed iteration 5
Thread 3 performed iteration 7
Thread 1 performed iteration 3
```

Figure 9. ***parallelForBlocks.c*, with 4 Threads**

This lets students see that thread 0 is performing iterations 0 and 1, thread 1 is performing iterations 2 and 3, thread 2 is performing iterations 4 and 5, and thread 3 is performing iterations 6 and 7.

Since our students use this same pattern in our lab exercise to parallelize the matrix operations, exploring this patternlet helps them understand what the **#pragma omp parallel for** directive is actually doing, instead of it being a "black box".

Once students understand this grouping of the loop iterations into "blocks", its benefits for processing contiguous data structures can be discussed, in terms of memory accesses, cache hits, and so on. We are currently working on a graphical version of this patternlet, to let students more directly visualize the blocking behavior.

This same patternlet can also be used to introduce another parallel pattern known as *data decomposition*, a parallel form of divide and conquer that is frequently used in parallel algorithm design. This pattern divides a problem's data into blocks and gives each thread one or more blocks of the data to process. For example, when adding 4096x4096 matrices using 4 threads, each matrix can be divided into four 1024x4096 blocks. If each thread performs the addition operation on a different block, the problem is solved. This same pattern can be used to solve image-processing and similar problems.

3.4 Master-Worker

We do not want to leave our CS2 students with the impression that parallelism is merely parallel for loops, so we also show them the *master-worker* pattern using the patternlet in Figure 10.

```
#include <stdio.h>    // printf()
#include <omp.h>      // OpenMP

int main(int argc, char** argv) {
  int id = -1, numThreads = -1;
  printf("\n");

  #pragma omp parallel
  {
    id = omp_get_thread_num();
    numThreads = omp_get_num_threads();

    if ( id == 0 ) { // thread 0 is master
      printf("Greetings from the master, \
               #%d of %d threads\n",
                id, numThreads);
    } else {          // all others are workers
      printf("Greetings from a worker, \
               #%d of %d threads\n",
                id, numThreads);
    }
  }

  printf("\n");
  return 0;
}
```

Figure 10. ***masterWorker.c***

When run on a quad-core machine, this program produces output like that shown in Figure 11.

```
Greetings from a worker, #2 of 4 threads
Greetings from a worker, #3 of 4 threads
Greetings from the master, #0 of 4 threads
Greetings from a worker, #1 of 4 threads
```

Figure 11. ***masterWorker.c*, with 4 Threads**

To help the students see how this pattern can be useful, we typically add a shared, dynamically allocated array containing an entry for each thread; have each worker compute and store a value (e.g., the square root of its **id**) in its entry of the array; and then have the master/main thread output the values in the array.

3.5 Reductions

It does not take a very complicated example to show students some of the dangers of multithreading. One way to do so is by summing the values in a large array, as shown in Figure 12.

```
#include <stdio.h>    // printf()
#include <omp.h>      // OpenMP
#include <stdlib.h>   // rand()

void initialize(int* a, int n);
int sequentialSum(int* a, int n);
int parallelSum(int* a, int n);

#define SIZE 1000000

int main(int argc, char** argv) {
  int array[SIZE];

  initialize(array, SIZE);
  printf(
     "\nSequential:\t%d\nParallel: \t%d\n\n",
                sequentialSum(array, SIZE),
                parallelSum(array, SIZE) );

  return 0;
}

/* fill array with random values */
void initialize(int* a, int n) {
  int i;
  for (i = 0; i < n; i++) {
    a[i] = rand() % 1000;
  }
}

/* sum the array sequentially */
int sequentialSum(int* a, int n) {
  int sum = 0;
  int i;
  for (i = 0; i < n; i++) {
    sum += a[i];
  }
  return sum;
}

/* sum the array using multiple threads */
int parallelSum(int* a, int n) {
  int sum = 0;
  int i;
//  #pragma omp parallel for // reduction(+:sum)
  for (i = 0; i < n; i++) {
    sum += a[i];
  }
  return sum;
}
```

Figure 12. ***reduction.c***

With the **#pragma omp parallel for** directive commented out, the **parallelSum()** and **sequentialSum()** functions produce identical (correct) results, as shown in Figure 13.

```
Sequential:    499079147
Parallel:      499079147
```

Figure 13. *reduction.c*, Initial Behavior

However, when this directive is uncommented (but its **reduction** clause remains commented out), the functions no longer produce the same results, as shown in Figure 14.

```
Sequential:    499079147
Parallel:      128345408
```

Figure 14. *reduction.c*, Secondary Behavior

The problem is that the threads are all writing to the same (shared) **sum** variable, producing write-write conflicts that cause some of the writes to be lost. This problem can be avoided by using the *reduction pattern*, in which each thread computes the desired operation (e.g., addition) on its block of the array, storing the result in a local variable. When all threads are finished processing their array-blocks, the values in these locals are efficiently combined in parallel and the result stored in the shared variable.

OpenMP provides built-in support for this pattern via its **reduction** clause. When the entire directive in Figure 12 is uncommented and this clause is exposed, the two functions again produce identical results (the same as shown in Figure 13).

For t threads, the reduction pattern uses parallelism to combine the local temporary values in $O(lg(t))$ time, as shown in Figure 15.

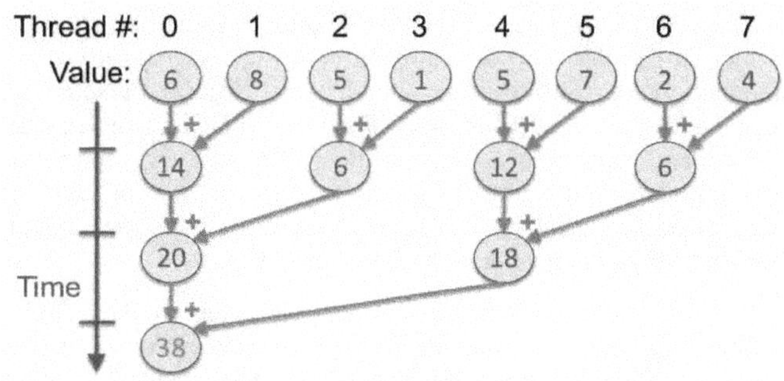

Figure 15. The Reduction Pattern in Action

The binary-tree structure used in this pattern provides a nice tie-in to the coverage of trees in a CS2 course, and provides students with a comparison of linear vs. logarithmic complexity in a practical context, helping them see the importance of these ideas.

3.6 Other Patterns and Uses

Patternlets provides a useful way to introduce students to the mental thought processes used by parallel program designers. Each patternlet's minimalist nature makes it a good tool for introducing students to the parallel thinking embodied in that particular program. By striving to eliminate all but the most essential details, a patternlet lets a student compare its source code against its output, allowing the student to more easily grasp the parallel behavior that is producing that output. Also, because many patternlets begin with a sequential behavior that the student alters to produce the parallel behavior (e.g., by uncommenting a line of code), the student can identify the precise lines of code that are generating the parallel behavior.

However, for students to truly appreciate the pattern, we believe it is important for them to also see the pattern in a more meaningful context, to see the pattern's utility in a "real-world" context. In our CS2 course, that context is operating on a large matrix, but other problems can be used, such as image processing [8].

While this paper details their use in CS2, the patternlets can be used in any course where it is desirable to introduce students to a particular pattern. We (and others) have found them to be useful in a variety of courses, including *Algorithms*, *Operating Systems*, *Computer Organization*, and *High Performance Computing*.

The patternlets are an evolving collection that at this time contains a total of 33 programs: 14 for OpenMP, 8 for POSIX threads, and 11 for MPI. The full collection is available for download at *CSinParallel.org*.

4. ASSESSMENT

One way that we assess student learning during this parallel week is through four questions on parallelism and OpenMP on our CS2 final exam. Since we *did not* use the patternlets in Fall 2012 but *did* use them in Spring 2013, we decided to see if their use produced any differences in student performance on these four exam questions. The group without patternlets scored an average of 2.95 out of 4 on these questions, while the group using patternlets scored 3.05 out of 4. This improvement was not statistically significant ($p = 0.293$), perhaps due to small sample size: we had 41 students in the Fall 2012 section and 38 in the Spring 2013 section.

However, the majority of the students in our Fall 2012 section were *3rd year electrical/computer engineering majors* who had demonstrated strong quantitative and analytical skills by successfully completed two years of our engineering program, which has a 50% attrition rate. By contrast, the majority of the students in our Spring 2013 section were *1st year students still considering computer science as a major*, with just one semester of college experience. Given this difference in experience, commitment, and maturity of the two groups, we believe the patternlets had a more significant effect in helping our students understand parallelism than the statistics indicate.

All courses at our institution are assessed using student course evaluations, in which students are free to comment on what they liked or disliked about the course. Several students in both semesters used this opportunity to comment that the week on multithreading was their favorite part of CS2. Space constraints prevent us from quoting them here, but the general sentiment of these comments was that the students enjoyed learning how to make their software run faster by taking full advantage of the hardware in their personal computers. None had been exposed to multithreading before, so this week brought a feeling of "freshness" and novelty to the CS2 course, where most of the concepts are decades old.

Based on our students' final exam results and comments, we think that our injection of parallelism into CS2 was successful, and that there is no good reason to avoid injecting parallelism into CS2.

5. CONCLUSIONS

With the advent of CS2013, CS departments must now face the question of how and where to integrate the CS2013 PDC knowledge units into their curricula. In this paper, we have argued that CS2 is a natural place to begin exposing students to parallelism, because (i) students are no longer novices, (ii) the data structures facilitate the solving of large problems, and (iii) performance/time-efficiency is already a key topic in CS2.

To introduce students to parallelism in CS2, we have used a hands-on lab session, a programming assignment, and 3 classroom sessions. For the classroom sessions, we have developed *patternlets*: minimalist, scalable, executable programs that allow a student to quickly grasp a pattern's essential concept. These are general enough to be useful in CS2 courses and beyond.

Lastly, we have argued that in the turbulent area of parallelism, the parallel patterns are a much-needed point of stability. Unlike ephemeral hardware platforms or programming languages, the patterns comprise an intellectual framework of parallel thought and knowledge that is likely to remain useful for our students throughout their professional futures.

6. ACKNOWLEDGMENTS

Our thanks to NSF DUE-1225739 that supported this work; and to Dick Brown, Libby Shoop, and several anonymous reviewers for their feedback on a preliminary version of this paper.

7. REFERENCES

[1] D. Ernst, D. Stevenson, and P. Wagner. 2009. Hybrid and Custom Data Structures: Evolution of the Data Structures Course. In *ACM SIGCSE Bulletin – ITiCSE'09* (41)3. 213-217. DOI= http://dx.doi.org/10.1145/1562877.1562945.

[2] J. Graham. 2007. Integrating parallel programming techniques into traditional computer science curricula. *ACM SIGCSE Bulletin* (39)4. 75-78 DOI= http://dx.doi.org/10.1145/1345375.1345419.

[3] J. Hummel. 2012. C++11 in Parallel. Workshop, *43rd ACM Technical Symposium on Computer Science Education* (Raleigh, NC) SIGCSE'12.

[4] Intel Corp. 2013, *Intel Xeon E7 Processor Family*. Retrieved August 24, 2013 from http://www.intel.com/content/www/us/en/processors/xeon/xeon-processor-e7-family.html.

[5] Intel Corp. 2013. *Intel Xeon Phi Product Family*. Retrieved August 24, 2013 from http://www.intel.com/content/www/us/en/processors/xeon/xeon-phi-detail.html.

[6] K. Keutzer, B. Massingill, T. Mattson, B. Sanders. 2010. A Design Pattern Language for Engineering (Parallel) Software: Merging the PLPP and OPL Projects. *Proceedings of the 2010 Workshop on Parallel Programming Patterns* (Carefree, AZ), ParaPLoP'10. DOI= http://dx.doi.org/10.1145/1953611.1953620.

[7] Nvidia. 2013. *CUDA Parallel Computing Platform*. Retrieved August 24, 2013 from http://www.nvidia.com/object/cuda_home_new.html.

[8] S. Massung and C. Heeren. 2013. Visualizing Parallelism in CS 2. *Proceedings of the 27th IEEE International Parallel and Distributed Processing Symposium* (Boston, MA), IPDPS'13. 1252-1256.

[9] A. Radenski. 2012. Integrating data-intensive cloud computing with multicores and clusters in an HPC course. In *Proceedings of the 17th ACM Annual Conference on Innovation and Technology in Computer Science Education* (Haifa, Israel), ITiCSE'12. 69-74. DOI= http://dx.doi.org/10.1145/2325296.2325316.

[10] M. Sahami, S. Roach, E. Cuadro-Vargas, and R. LeBlanc. 2013. ACM/IEEE-CS Computer Science Curriculum 2013: Reviewing the Ironman Report. *Proceedings of the 44th ACM Technical Symposium on Computer Science Education* (Denver, CO). SIGCSE'13. 13-14. DOI= http://dx.doi.org/10.1145/2445196.2445206.

[11] E. Shoop, R. Brown, E. Biggers, M. Kane, D. Lin, and M. Warner. 2012. Virtual Clusters for Parallel and Distributed Education. *Proceedings of the 43rd ACM Technical Symposium on Computer Science Education* (Raleigh, NC) SIGCSE'12, 517-522. DOI= http://dx.doi.org/10.1145/2157136.2157287.

On the Efficacy of Board Game Strategy Development as a First-Year CS Project

Ivona Bezáková James Heliotis Sean Strout

Rochester Institute of Technology
102 Lomb Memorial Drive
Rochester, NY 14623, U.S.A.
{ib,jeh,sps}@cs.rit.edu

ABSTRACT

We report on a study comparing an open-ended freshman-level CS2 project with a fully specified project of similar difficulty. We employed a randomized, controlled trial methodology. The students needed to use similar data structures and algorithms, presented during lectures, for both projects.

The first half of the milestones were almost identical for both groups, but the open-ended project asked students to develop a player strategy for a specific board game, while in the other project the students executed the game by communicating with the player modules and verifying the moves against the rules of the game. In the final stages of the project while one group of students worked on honing their own strategy, the other students implemented a pre-specified tie breaking mechanism used when two player strategies tie in a match. At the end of the term, both groups had a friendly tournament: the player strategies faced each other for the ultimate winner while the other group's submissions were ranked by a team of judges based on the implementation's correctness and style. The tournament was just for fun - it did not contribute to the final grade.

We hypothesized that the player group would enjoy the project more, would score higher, and would be better motivated and equipped to study computer science.

Our study confirmed higher enjoyment and interest of the study group participants. We did not observe statistically significant differences among other measured quantities, for example grade distribution, of the respective groups.

Categories and Subject Descriptors

K.3.2 [**Computers and Education**]: Computer and Information Science Education

Keywords

Introductory computer science, Learning in context, Basic data structures and algorithms, Open-ended project, Evaluation, Randomized controlled trial

SIGCSE'14, March 5–8, 2014, Atlanta, GA, USA.

ACM 978-1-4503-2605-6/14/03 ...$15.00.
http://dx.doi.org/10.1145/2538862.2538904.

1. INTRODUCTION

Because of all the basic material that must be covered in freshman computer science courses, students can easily see the work as a chore. Motivating students to carry on their studies in the computing disciplines can therefore be a challenge. To increase our chances of success, our school's courses have taken a problem-solving focus rather than employing a curriculum that runs in a language-construct-of-the-week style. One major problem we assign in CS2 is writing a strategy for a respected board game. Board games are discrete; the possible positions of playing pieces are finite and turn-taking prevents the issues of parallel actions that could make other games unsuitable in an early course. Instead, through these games, students get to choose and apply the algorithms and data structures they have been learning at this point in the curriculum.

Over the past four years we have effected a student focus on strategy issues through our providing of the "engine," the program that repeatedly informs each player module when it is their turn, gets the move from that player, checks it according to the game rules, and informs the other players of that move. This way all player modules can update their data structures to reflect the current state of the game.

The end of the term sees the running of a friendly competition dubbed the "Battle Royale." This allows the motivated student the opportunity to keep improving his or her strategy and have it tested against classmates' strategies. However, as far as a grade goes, to achieve full credit we simply ask our students to consistently beat a provided unsophisticated or random playing strategy. We choose games where this level of achievement is compatible with the difficulty of a CS2-level project. The competition has no influence on grades.

We conjectured that board games not only provide a suitable curricular context but that programming player strategies further increases student motivation by being open-ended and providing opportunities for experimentation.

In particular, we hypothesized that this project

- increases student enjoyment while working on the project,
- increases student motivation to go beyond what is required,
- results in higher project and course grades, and
- results in deeper understanding of computer science

when compared to traditional projects of similar difficulty.

To test our hypotheses, we employed a randomized, controlled trial. To minimize effects of individual instructors, time of the day, and other biasing attributes, we opted to randomly split each section of the course into two groups of equal size. The students in one section attended the same lecture but were split for their lab sessions where the study group designed and implemented player strategies while the control group implemented parts of the engine such as game rule verification. The rationale for the control group is to have them work with similar data structures and algorithms (indeed, about half of the work needed in the respective projects was identical), while essentially mimicking a traditional well-defined game-programming assignment (instead of an open-ended strategy-programming assignment).

2. RELATED WORK

Randomized controlled trials have long been considered the gold standard of medical research, where the study participants are randomly split into two groups subjected to two different treatments. The control group is given a placebo treatment while the study group receives the researched treatment. The outcomes from the two groups are then statistically compared. See, e. g., [14] for more details. Recently, randomized controlled trials found their way into education research, most typically studying proposed interventions for young (K-12) students with disabilities [1, 3]. In their influential paper in 2001, Torgerson and Torgerson [23] argue for the need for randomized controlled trials in education research in order to determine which instructional practices to adopt in order to avoid imposing "potentially harmful education initiatives upon the nation's children."

Nevertheless, most computer science education research we are aware of, at least at the introductory (CS1/2) level, does not follow the randomized controlled trial methodology. In preliminary research stages, authors typically report anecdotal evidence, see, e. g., [8]. In pilot studies evaluation is usually done by post-surveys and student interviews, grade assessments, or possibly by automatically collecting data about student behavior when using a specific software, see, e. g., [20, 12, 5, 4]. To better assess a proposed method's effectiveness, authors compare a study group with a control group [18, 21, 9, 19, 22]; yet these groups are typically not selected at random. For example, two sections of the same course might be compared where one section is subjected to a new education paradigm while the other section follows traditional instructional techniques. While more reliable than studies without a control group, these studies still suffer from a number of issues. For example, students in an advanced calculus course might have a conflict with the time of one of the sections, hence all advanced calculus students end up in the other section, biasing the study. The effects of different instructors, time of the day, etc., on student success have been well-documented. Some of these effects have been mitigated by, e. g., [18] where the same instructor taught both the study and the control group.

We are aware of few studies involving randomized controlled trials in computer science education [17, 16, 15]. In all these cases, the authors compare two different methods of delivery of the same material; e. g., computer visualization vs. pen-and-paper approach. Our study adds a new level of complexity as it necessitates the need to create an equivalent multiple-deliverable project for the control group, along with analogous (and as similar as possible) grading guides, project documentation, and skills required to complete each respective project part. We discuss this in detail in Section 4, demonstrating that a meaningful randomized controlled trial is possible even in such situations.

3. HYPOTHESES RATIONALE: BOARD GAME SELECTION

Before we dive into the details of the experiment setup, we describe the rationale behind our hypotheses. The board games on which the projects are based are carefully selected according to several criteria to motivate and interest a wide variety of students while targeting typical CS2 content.

We describe the most important criteria and briefly sketch the board games we selected over the past several years.

3.1 Criteria

Discrete: Since the assignment is given in a CS2 course, we need to relate it to concepts in a standard data structures curriculum. Therefore games with discrete states and transitions between them are important. This restriction also means we are dealing with turn-taking games.

Non-violent: It has been shown many times that not all students react positively to game metaphors that involve destruction, injury, and death. This is especially true of female populations in CS majors, which in most programs are small minorities. Therefore we have leaned toward games that instead involve activities like building, seeking, and obstacle avoidance.

Proven Popularity: We must take care to choose games that have already captured the attention of a sizeable audience. More obscure instructor-designed games may require exactly the software skills we seek, but if the game ends up being boring or annoying to our students, we are unable to test our hypothesis.

Multiple Strategy Opportunities: In order to produce an interesting tournament with uncertain outcomes, we cannot have games where the only reasonable thing an automated player could do is an exhaustive traversal of all possible next moves every time it is its turn. In that case the only unknown left would be the depth to which each player took its search. One way to maintain interest among the students is for them to ponder many solutions, some heuristic, some brute-force; some focused on specific situations and some more general.

3.2 Games Used So Far

Throughout the years we used a number of board games. We started with **The aMAZEing Labyrinth**, designed by Max J. Kobbert and published by Ravensburger [11]. In this game players try to collect a set of treasures in a labyrinth formed by a 7×7 tiled area that the players modify every turn by shifting a row or a column. Then, we used **Quoridor** by Mirko Marchesi, published by Gigamic [13]. This is also a maze-searching game where players in every turn either place a wall to expand a maze or move their pawn towards a target location. We followed with **San Francisco Cable Cars**, designed by Dirk Henn and published by Queen Games [10]. Players add tiles to an 8×8 initially empty board, forming cable car routes for both their own cars as well as their opponents'. The player with the overall longest routes wins. The most recent addition to our collection is **Gobblet**, designed by Thierry Denoual and sold by several game manufacturers [7]. It is an elaborate variation of a 4×4 tic-tac-toe where the pieces can "gobble" each other up (and hence, unlike tic-tac-toe, there is no clear winning strategy).

4. EXPERIMENT METHODOLOGY

In this section we describe the procedure we designed to test our hypothesis. The results are given in Section 5.

4.1 Randomized Controlled Trial

We split each section of the course between the study group and the control group through random selection. In particular, we generated a random permutation of students and assigned the first half to the study (player) group and the second half to the control (engine) group. The students attended a common lecture (2 hours per week), followed by a 2 hour lab session for the study group and another 2 hour lab session for the control group. Both labs were led by the lecture instructor. The split was done per section in order to eliminate the effect of different instructors. Both groups' projects were split into four, as analogous as possible, parts, accounting for three lab sessions. The rest of the labs were unrelated to the project and completely identical for both groups. All sections of the course used the same assignments, a common final exam, and identical grading schemes. Furthermore, in the middle of the quarter the two groups swapped the times of their labs.

We note that ideally in a randomized controlled trial, the study participants do not know which group they belong to – this is referred to as *blinding*. While we, obviously, could not guarantee full blinding, we made sure that the students were not told of the hypothesis of the experiment until after the course was over and all data was collected. They did know we were trying something experimental. (After all, they had to sign a release form and fill out surveys.)

4.2 The Project

As mentioned earlier, the experiment was done by comparing results from students doing the standard project and from students in a control group doing a similar project but where the option of trying out new designs to help their code win is eliminated.

In order to eliminate as many undesired variables as possible, we sought to create a project for the control group that exercised the same course skills as the standard one, had deliverables due on the same dates that were the same difficulty, and where we could still do some kind of competition in the end so that the teams with the "best" efforts could be recognized, the same as the standard project.

We chose to use the same project, the multiplayer board game, but instead insert a secondary student-written "engine" between the real game engine and the player modules. The student's engine would verify the player modules' game moves. This would force all students to design similar data structures and algorithms, as player modules would most likely have to check if a move they were considering was valid. In the final stages of the project, while the player groups were designing their own strategy, the other students implemented a pre-specified tie breaking mechanism used when two player strategies tie in a match.

4.3 Study Instruments

In addition to collecting project and course grades, we employed the Intrinsic Motivation Instruments (IMI) methodology [2, 6] to measure student motivation. The IMIs were a part of pre-project and post-project surveys designed by our evaluator.

There were seven questions in each survey on Interest and Enjoyment, seven on Perceived Competence, five on Effort and Importance, and five on Pressure and Tension. The questions sometimes refer specifically to the project, sometimes to the computer science field. The full surveys are available upon request.

4.4 Dry Run

We decided to do a practice run of the study in the spring of 2012. There were several reasons.

- While the engine assignment was designed to mimic a traditional game programming assignment (where the students implement the game logic but not player behavior or GUI), the actual assignment was brand new, so we wanted as many instructors as possible to be comfortable with it before the actual study began.
- We could use the surveys we initially designed and see if any changes would be warranted.
- Since this was the first time we were trying to integrate a student-written engine module into our game architecture, it was deemed preferable to "work the bugs out" on a smaller group of students. Our CS2 class normally ran in the winter quarter.

We used the Cable Car game for our first attempt to split the engine. We collected the survey data, but we did not have it formally evaluated due to a perceived bias in the student population (a significant percentage of students repeated the course as they did not achieve a passing grade in the winter quarter).

4.5 The Real Study

In the winter of 2012-2013 we ran the course with our large student population. The vast majority of the students taking this course are majors in Computer Science, Software Engineering, and Computer Engineering. There are also a few students from Bioinformatics, Applied Mathematics, and Computational Mathematics.

We opted to use Quoridor for the main study. We chose to return to a game that we understood well from a previous experience and where we could design equivalent player and engine project subparts. For the first part of the project, both groups searched for paths in the Quoridor maze. When we asked the player group to produce a valid move, the engine group needed to verify the validity of a given move. Due to the need to always be able to access a target location, both groups needed to search for paths in the maze, reusing their code from the first part.

Unlike Labyrinth and Cable Car, there is absolutely no randomness like a shuffled pile of items. So unless player modules are choosing randomly between moves, every game between a set of players will always end the same. This observation motivated the tie-breaking part of the project for the engine students. They randomly pre-populate the board with some walls in a symmetric fashion to change the course of the game.

While we used Quoridor in the past, our earlier version did not fully conform to the game rules, and we changed the API to support our new multi-language architecture. As such, from the students' perspective this was a brand new project for both the player and the engine groups.

No. of Q's	Category	Min Score	Max Max	Average	Std. Dev.
7	Interest and Enjoyment	7	49	31.66	8.97
7	Perceived Competence	7	49	35.69	9.05
5	Effort and Importance	5	35	25.56	6.86
5	Pressure Tension	5	35	15.68	8.57

Table 1: Pre-Data

No. of Q's	Category	Min Score	Max Max	Average	Std. Dev.
7	Interest and Enjoyment	7	49	31.36	9.80
7	Perceived Competence	7	49	35.35	9.98
5	Effort and Importance	5	35	28.70	5.76
5	Pressure and Tension	5	35	18.56	8.42

Table 2: Post-Data

5. STATISTICAL RESULTS FROM THE TERM OF THE OFFICIAL STUDY

A total of 377 students responded to the pre-course survey (pre data). However, some of these responders did not consent to participate, or were under age. Minus these students, 351 instances remained. The post-course survey generated 265 instances (post data).

The students were given incentive to fill out the surveys: each counted 1% towards their final grade. We suspect that one reason the post-course survey response was as low as it was was due to some students deciding the single extra point would not affect their grade enough to warrant the time to fill out the survey.

Joining the pre data, post data, and grade data provided by instructors of all the sections of the course, we ended up with complete records for 206 students. However, we chose not to include in the study students who had previously taken the course, so the final count was 193.

Of these, 172 were male and 21 were female; 95 students worked on the player module, and 98 made up the control group of students who worked on the engine module.

5.1 IMI Scores

Tables 1 and 2 show the scores from the questions on the surveys that dealt with IMI: Intrinsic Motivation Inventory and closely related factors.

We feel that the meanings of the IMI category names should be fairly clear, as long as one remembers that it is in the context of the student's perception of the course. One exception may be the "Effort and Importance" category. Here we asked questions about the amount of effort a student put in to the course or how hard it was, and if doing well was important.

For Interest/Enjoyment, Competence, and Effort/Importance, the higher the score, the more favorable the response. A favorable Pressure/Tension score should be low, indicating reduced stress on the student.

Note that each category contained several questions to ensure consistent responses by the students. Therefore, since all the questions were on a 7-point Likert scale, the minimum and maximum score totals for a category of questions is dependent on the number of questions in the category. These maxima and minima are included for clarity. Note that the tables include both the player and the control group and are shown to demonstrate the IMI methodology.

The overall results show that there was no significant difference before and after the course for Interest/Enjoyment or for Perceived Competence, these being the student perceptions we hope to improve. However the students' perception of the effort they needed for the course, and the importance of their work, did go up. There was also, as was expected from past anecdotal experience, a significant negative difference in Pressure/Tension.

Category	Engine Students	Player Students
Interest and Enjoyment	32.03 $\downarrow$ 28.74*	31.28 $\uparrow$ 34.06*
Perceived Competence	35.96 $\downarrow$ 34.6	35.42 $\uparrow$ 36.12
Effort and Importance	24.44 $\uparrow$ 28.85*	25.57 $\uparrow$ 28.54*
Pressure and Tension	15.48 $\uparrow$ 20.28*	15.87 $\uparrow$ 16.8

Table 3: Control Vs. Study Group. In each cell the first number indicates the corresponding pre-data IMI value and the second number indicates the post-data IMI value. The arrows indicate increase or decrease. For all but the last category, increase is a positive outcome. Stars mark statistical significance.

But when the engine and player groups are split, a different result is revealed, as shown in Table 3. Changes marked with an asterisk were found to be statistically significant through *t-score* calculation.

The most interesting result here is that there was a significant upswing in interest and enjoyment for Player students, coupled with an almost identical downswing for Engine students. And although all students perceived higher effort and importance of the material in the end, the Engine students experienced a quite significant increase in pressure and tension when all was said and done. We should admit that despite the dry run the previous spring, we were still redesigning the Engine students' assignments and the support software for them as winter term began. We cannot deny that we may have transferred some of our own pressure and tension to the students even though we all consciously tried not to. Section 7 addresses this and related issues.

One of our goals was to determine if what we were doing in the course would make it more agreeable and attractive to female students. Unfortunately our sample size of 21 female students (13 Player / 8 Engine) has made it impossible to come to any defendable conclusions. Nevertheless the numbers do seem encouraging:

The post Interest/Enjoyment scores for female Player students were 34.54 versus 21.0 for the female Engine students, despite the oft-cited aversion by females to competition.

Statement	Engine Students		Player Students	
	Agree	Disagree	Agree	Disagree
"The project helped me to better understand computer science."	81/142=57.04%	33/142=23.24%	79/122=64.75%	22/122=18.03%
"I enjoyed the experimentation with different problem solving strategies."	75/141=53.19%	33/141=23.40%	79/122=64.75%	18/122=14.75%
"Having to develop the algorithms helped me to see that the project was more than just programming."	81/141=57.45%	33/141=23.40%	81/123=65.85%	18/123=14.63%

Table 4: Additional Survey Results

The post Pressure/Tension scores for female Engine students were higher: 29.0 versus 21.54 for female Player students. These scores are nevertheless overall noticeably higher than the overall male-dominated course average.

Although perhaps anticipated, it was disappointing to see that Perceived Competency was lower for the female students, while Pressure/Tension was higher for them. But again, we cannot speak authoritatively due to the small sample size.

5.2 Additional survey results

We asked additional Likert-scale questions on the students' perception of computer science and problem solving. These questions were proposed by the authors and were accepted by the evaluation team. The answers are summarized in Table 4. We aggregated answers in the positive range (agreement: scores 5-7) and in the negative range (disagreement: scores 1-3). We report on the free-form questions in Section 6.

5.3 Effect on Grades

As stated earlier we joined the project grade data with the survey data to see if one of our two groups did better than the other. It turns out there was no impact on grades between the Player students and the Engine students. Although a difference may have been gratifying, the lack of a difference is not a failure. We should point out that we were looking at a bigger picture than performance in one course. Motivation and interest are things that can keep a student performing well in future courses.

As an aside, grades were not impacted by gender nor by pre-CS1 computing experience.

6. ANECDOTAL STUDENT FEEDBACK

We also included some free form questions on the surveys where we asked about the competitive aspect of the project. We are including some excerpts below. In short, the engine students were not happy about their contest but many stated that they enjoyed watching the players compete. The players overall enjoyed the contest. Some of the engine students commented on the project documentation which was, admittedly, less polished than the player part due to having less experience with engine projects, and due to our newly deployed client-server design, see Section 7.1, that influenced the engine students more than players.

For the engine group, these sentiments repeated frequently:

- *As an engine student, I didn't feel very connected to this aspect.*
- *I did enjoy the competition though it wasn't too elaborate on the engine side. I still found it interesting and worth putting extra effort in for.*
- *The engine students get shafted. Students who were assigned the player module had to create a whole AI on their own, while students who were assigned the engine module simply had to create a few pre-defined functions. It felt like the players got to build something that was actually theirs, while the engine students were just filling in the blanks on a pre-made form.*

For the players, typical answers included:

- *The competition of the project was by far my favorite part and really motivated me to do a lot better than I would have done otherwise. I also enjoyed doing a project that I could share with other people and that had easy to see uses.*
- *Yes, it was very interesting. Also, it helps me to learn more about better strategies from other teams so I can somewhat think about a better way to code the program.*
- *At first I did not because I'm not a very competitive person, but when we actually had the competition it was more fun than I expected.*

7. POSSIBLE CAVEATS

In this section we describe a couple of issues we encountered that have or might have influenced this study. First, compared to earlier years, we opted to redesign the engine architecture to allow for support of player strategies implemented in multiple languages without needing to rewrite the engine. While our new server-client design (described below) influences both player and engine students, the player code interacted only with the server while the engine code needed to interact with both player modules as well as the server. However, the same issue would be encountered without the client-server architecture: even if our provided engine (that takes care of the graphical interface) resided on the student's computer, they would still need to communicate with the provided engine as well as the player module code.

The second issue is a relative inexperience of the instructors with the engine-type project. Out of the seven instructors, three were directly involved with the project and familiar with its design. Nevertheless, except for one of them, they did not have previous experience helping students in the engine group. One additional instructor has taught the course previously and was familiar only with the player part. Two instructors were new to the course and they were not familiar with either part. The remaining instructor was involved in the dry run. To mitigate this issue and synchronize the course sections, the instructors held weekly meetings.

7.1 Architecture

Physically, the full game system usually sits in two locations. The actual game engine runs on a web server. It is capable of running a large number of games simultaneously.

The client computer hosts a program that is a combination of the code of the player modules and the run-time support software that interfaces the player modules to the server. The client computer also runs a web browser used by the remote engine to graphically display the state of the game.

We found this architecture useful for several reasons. First, a central server can record information about games played. Second, updates to the engine are much less likely to affect the students' software. Third, by having only a small amount of our software linked to the student's player module, we limit the amount of software we provide that must be written in the same programming language as the student's code. This makes porting the system to a new student programming language easier.

8. CONCLUSION

Our data supports the first part of our hypothesis: the player students are better motivated to work on the project and report having more fun doing so. The two groups fared similarly with respect to their grade assessment. Based on these findings, we plan to continue using the player strategy project in subsequent years. We created a website, `http://www.cs.rit.edu/~royale/games/`, where these projects are available for use at other institutions.

9. ACKNOWLEDGMENTS

We gratefully acknowledge support of the National Science Foundation (DUE award ID 1044721). We also thank Adam Oest, our student helper, who developed the engine used in the project. Additional thanks go to our main evaluator Trudy Howles, who developed the IMI-based surveys and did the corresponding analysis, and our external evaluation team consisting of Doug Baldwin and Sage Miller, who provided feedback on the evaluation throughout the project. Finally, we thank all the student participants in the study, their instructors, the student tutors, and the other faculty members who tried out our assignments at various workshops over the last few years.

10. REFERENCES

[1] Identifying and implementing educational practices supported by rigorous evidence: A user friendly guide. Institue for Education Sciences. http://ies.ed.gov/ncee/pubs/evidence_based/randomized.asp.

[2] Intrinsic Motivation Inventory. http://www.selfdeterminationtheory.org/questionnaires/10-questionnaires/50.

[3] Randomized controlled trial database. Institue for Education Sciences. http://ies.ed.gov/ncee/wwc/references/registries/RCTSearch/RCTSearch.aspx.

[4] A. Allevato and S. H. Edwards. RoboLIFT: engaging CS2 students with testable, automatically evaluated android applications. In *Proceedings of the ACM SIGCSE '12*, pages 547–552, 2012.

[5] S. Buchanan, B. Ochs, and J. J. LaViola Jr. CSTutor: a pen-based tutor for data structure visualization. In *Proc. of the ACM SIGCSE '12*, pages 565–570, 2012.

[6] E. L. Deci and R. Ryan. *The handbook of self-determination research.* University of Rochester Press, 2002.

[7] T. Denoual. *Gobblet.* Blue Orange Games, 2001. http://www.blueorangegames.com.

[8] P. Drake and K. Sung. Teaching introductory programming with popular board games. In *Proc. of the ACM SIGCSE '11*, pages 619–624, 2011.

[9] D. Ginat and R. Shmallo. Constructive use of errors in teaching CS1. In *Proceedings of the ACM SIGCSE '13*, pages 353–358, 2013.

[10] D. Henn. *San Francisco Cable Cars.* Queen Games, 2009. http://www.queen-games.de.

[11] M. J. Kobbert. *The aMAZEing Labyrinth Board Game.* Ravensburger, 1986. http://www.ravensburger.com.

[12] M. Luukkainen, A. Vihavainen, and T. Vikberg. A software craftsman's approach to data structures. In *Proc. of the ACM SIGCSE '12*, pages 439–444, 2012.

[13] M. Marchesi. *Quoridor.* Gigamic, 1997. http://www.gigamic.com.

[14] J. Matthews. *Introduction to randomized controlled clinical trials.* CRC Press, 2006.

[15] G. Nugent, K. Kupzyk, S. Riley, L. Miller, J. Hostetler, L.-K. Soh, and A. Samal. Empirical usage metadata in learning objects. In *Proceedings of the 39th IEEE international conference on Frontiers in education conference*, pages 1285–1290, 2009.

[16] M. C. Orsega, B. T. V. Zanden, and C. H. Skinner. Two experiments using learning rate to evaluate an experimenter developed tool for splay trees. In *Proc. of the ACM SIGCSE '11*, pages 135–140, 2011.

[17] M. C. Orsega, B. T. V. Zanden, and C. H. Skinner. Experiments with algorithm visualization tool development. In *Proceedings of the ACM SIGCSE '12*, pages 559–564, 2012.

[18] L. Porter and B. Simon. Retaining nearly one-third more majors with a trio of instructional best practices in CS1. In *Proceedings of the ACM SIGCSE '13*, 2013.

[19] S. Razak. A case for course capstone projects in CS1. In *Proceedings of the ACM SIGCSE '13*, pages 693–698, 2013.

[20] D. Riley. Using mobile phone programming to teach java and advanced programming to computer scientists. In *Proceedings of the ACM SIGCSE '12*, pages 541–546, 2012.

[21] B. Simon, J. Parris, and J. Spacco. How we teach impacts student learning: peer instruction vs. lecture in CS0. In *Proceedings of the ACM SIGCSE '13*, pages 41–46, 2013.

[22] R. Thies and J. Vahrenhold. On plugging "unplugged" into CS classes. In *Proceedings of the ACM SIGCSE '13*, pages 365–370, 2013.

[23] C. J. Torgerson and D. J. Torgerson. The need for randomised controlled trials in educational research. *British Journal of Educational Studies*, 49(3):316–328, 2001.

Transforming Introductory Computer Science Projects via Real-Time Web Data

Austin Cory Bart, Eli Tilevich, Simin Hall, Tony Allevato, Clifford A. Shaffer
{acbart,tilevich,thall57,allevato,shaffer}@vt.edu
Virginia Tech

ABSTRACT

While computing is becoming increasingly distributed, programming projects in introductory classes remain mostly divorced from the student's day-to-day computing experiences. These experiences entail interacting with real-time Web-based data from sources that include weather reports, news updates, and restaurant recommendations. The disconnect between student experiences and the content of their programming projects is known to drive some students away from computing. In addition, to adequately prepare students for the realities of modern software engineering, educators should introduce issues pertaining to distributed computing early in the curriculum. To address these problems, we have created RealTimeWeb—an architectural framework that makes real-time web data accessible for introductory programming projects. The framework effectively introduces important real-time distributed computing concepts without overwhelming students with the low-level details that working with such data typically requires. Preliminary results indicate that our approach can be effective in the context of a typical CS2 course, and that real-time data is relevant to students. RealTimeWeb libraries and associated resources are publicly available for use, with multiple language bindings to many real-time data sources. A rapid-prototyping tool available through the project's website facilitates the development of client libraries with easily accessible APIs for new real-time Web-based data sources.

Categories and Subject Descriptors

K.3.2 [**Computer and Information Science Education**]: Computer Science Education

General Terms

Design, Human Factors, Reliability, Experimentation

Keywords

distributed computing; projects; introductory courses

SIGCSE'14, March 5–8, 2014, Atlanta, GA, USA.

ACM 978-1-4503-2605-6/14/03 ...$15.00.
http://dx.doi.org/10.1145/2538862.2538941.

1. INTRODUCTION

Most people's experience with computing today involves distributed Web architectures and continuously updated, remote data sources. College students consume real-time Web-based data on their mobile devices. Examples abound. Weather information, traffic data, stock values, shopping deals—all of these real-time data sources are available as remote Web-based services that are then integrated into web-based applications available through browsers or mobile apps. Interacting with Web-based real-time data influences students' perception of what Computer Science is. This perception comes with them when they embark on studying the discipline.

Computing educators might do well to introduce issues related to real-time web data into the curriculum as early as possible for two reasons. First, meeting students' expectations that Computer Science studies exciting topics that are relevant to the students' experiences as computer users can help attract and retain good students [2, 1, 7]. Second, since distributed real-time data has entered the mainstream of computing, students should be introduced to the corresponding technical issues to prepare for the modern IT workforce. Indeed, the new ACM/IEEE Computer Science Curriculum 2013 advises 10 hours of material on a new dedicated *Networking and Communication* Knowledge Area [9].

Introducing real-time data is not only about increasing engagement. Perhaps more important, it is an avenue for exploring computing in a social context. The CS Curriculum 2013 emphasizes the importance of Social Issues [9], prescribing 16 hours on topics such as Social Context and Data Privacy. The ability to access real-world data streams enables introductory learners to deal with real-world problems. Consider assigning students to explore how geological data about earthquakes can be used to aid disaster relief. Another project might have students mine political data to find evidence of corruption. Yet another project, perhaps controversially, would involve analyzing social media data provided by services including Twitter or Facebook, to identify the cases of private data being left publicly available unintentionally. Tying actual class projects to such topics can powerfully convey computing's role in society to the introductory learner.

Alas, despite its ubiquity, incorporating distributed computing into the curriculum has proved difficult due to lack of educational resources. Even the seasoned software developer finds working with network protocols and parsing binary data streams conceptually complex, particularly in the presence of overwhelming technical issues that range from handling partial failure to dealing with distributed components evolving independently from each other. Not surprisingly, a common CS curricular design strategy is to leave the challenges of teaching distributed computing for later courses, when students will have accumulated sufficient technical expertise and tolerance for engineering non-trivial system designs.

The net effect of these curricular design choices is that the content of introductory courses remains isolated from issues pertaining to Web-based real-time data. Programming projects are particularly vulnerable to this omission. When working on programming projects, introductory students find themselves disconnected from familiar data from social media, news outlets, and local business. Instead, they find themselves given abstract, toy problems with limited context in their lives. Divorcing the content of programming projects from the students' experiences as computer users has a debilitating effect on motivation and engagement [2]. In fact, competent students are known to leave the major, having been discouraged by the lack of relevance for what they learn [1]. This problem is particularly acute for female students, for whom real-world application has been identified as the primary motivation for studying the discipline [7]. Our vision is that introductory courses can overcome the technical barriers inherent in working with real-time web data, enabling us to introduce novel, relevant projects to students.

2. PRIOR WORK

Insulating beginner programmers from complicated systems while still providing the ability to manipulate interesting data is not a novel concept. For example, most programming environments designed for novices feature convenient methods for manipulating images and sounds. Racket [6] treats images as a primitive data type, avoiding the complex, low-level programming that is typically required. While images and sounds have an obvious appeal, they lack the direct real-world connection afforded by real-time data. However, little work has focused on creating similar student-oriented interfaces for real-time data sources.

An example of a positive impact of working with real-time data on student learning is a project at Stanford in a Geological Sciences course. In this project, students worked with real-time data on earthquakes [5]. Although students did not program, scientific computational tools were used to analyze the data and reach conclusions. The instructor reported that students became significantly more engaged as they worked with data that had relevance to them. For instance, many students became excited when they discovered that there were earthquakes happening in their region all the time. The final assignment had students choose a city that they wanted eventually to live in and determine the geological risks of the area. The instructor reported that, even after the course had ended, students applied similar analysis to other geographical regions relevant to their lives. This assignment contextualized the learning experience for the student, and created "a personal connection and positive affect that motivates their future learning" [5]. Corresponding projects, perhaps even using the same data source, are ripe for a programming class.

Similar projects have been used in statistics courses [3] and data mining courses [10]. Although other domains seem ready and willing to bring real-world data into the classroom, the research literature on the topic is scarce. A project conducted by Dr. Marc Waldman introduces realistic open data into upper-level database courses [11]. In essence, this project challenges experienced learners by taking advantage of the complicated nature of real-world data. While our primary design objective is to accommodate novice users, we also strive to appropriately challenge more advanced users, enabling them to develop higher-level skills.

3. OUR APPROACH

We have created and distributed a software architecture framework (named "RealTimeWeb") that provides introductory programming students with an easy way to manipulate distributed real-time data. Our approach offers technical scaffolding for the students to gradually ease into (or completely circumvent if appropriate) some of the most vexing complexities of distributed computing. At the heart of our project are carefully engineered client libraries through which students can access the data provided by real-time web services. These libraries are readily available through an online curated gallery, designed to be quickly adapted to instructors' specific academic needs. This gallery also provides a tool for rapidly prototyping new libraries based on our framework.

3.1 Client Libraries

To connect students to real-time data sources, we have designed client libraries with features intended specifically for novice programmers. Each library offers a selection of method calls to request, parse, and return real-time data. Presently, we have created libraries to provide

- Business reviews from Yelp.
- Weather forecasts from the National Weather Service.
- Stock trading information from Yahoo Finance.
- Global earthquake reports from the US Geological Survey.
- Content from link-sharing site Reddit.com.

In theory, any publicly available online real-time data source can be targeted by our framework, and we intend to continuously offer new and improved client libraries.

3.1.1 Language

There are many different programming languages used in introductory CS courses [9]. To account for this, we implemented each library in a number of common beginner languages, including Python, Java, and Racket. We have also made an effort to provide compatibility on key platforms, including Android.

3.1.2 Scaffolding

The instructor can determine how data is returned, so as to provide varying levels of scaffolding. Choices include raw strings of data, semi-structured hashes and lists, or object-oriented classes. Some libraries are available in reduced variants that return atomic data (e.g., a derivative of the Weather Service client library returns only the current temperature, as opposed to a complete forecast including humidity, wind, etc.). In this way, how much work students must perform to manipulate the data can be altered to suit the class. This means that the libraries can be used in a wide variety of educational scenarios.

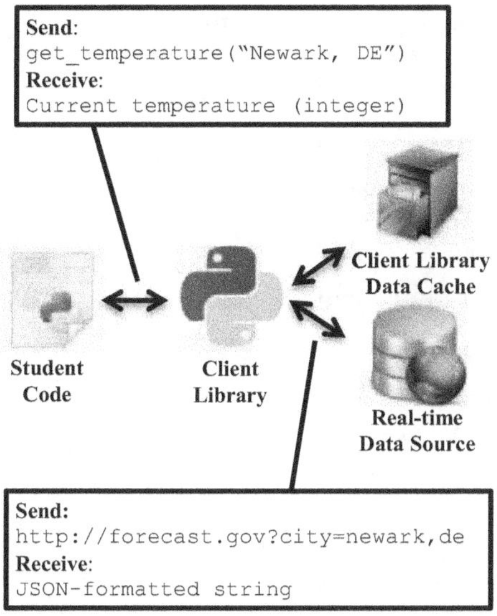

Figure 1: Client Library Architecture

3.1.3 *Internalized Data Cache*

Perhaps the single most useful feature of the libraries is the *internalized data cache*. The cache can be used to avoid making requests directly to the actual data source, instead accessing a local, static data store (a file). Figure 1 demonstrates the flow of data when using a client library. The cache option offers a number of advantages.

Idempotency By its nature, real-time data is subject to rapid temporal changes. Weather forecasts change on a daily basis, for example, and services like Reddit or Twitter change by the minute. Developing a program that uses such volatile data can be tricky, since it can change between runs of the program. To accommodate introductory students, the libraries make it possible to used cached local data, so consistency of input from run to run is guaranteed.

Consistency The content and structure of the web is highly dynamic, as are the web services composing it. Because service APIs commonly evolve at a dizzying pace, the libraries that depend on them must be updated accordingly. Even during a single semester, changes in the data source could be introduced that would result in an out-of-date library. However, this problem can be bypassed by keeping to the internal data cache until an updating fix is released, avoiding any serious delays in development.

Connectivity Although most campuses have gigabit internet connections, this is not universal. Additionally, many students live in off-campus settings with varying internet capabilities. Requiring students to develop an internet-based application with poor internet connections can be a tall order. However, the the cache allows client libraries to be used offline, if necessary.

Efficiency Even assuming a fast and stable connection, the performance of many web services is limited by the number of connections that the server can handle. Student developers can be polite consumers by developing with client-side data, greatly reducing the number of calls to the online service. This is especially important since many APIs throttle the number of requests (e.g., 100 API calls per day), sometimes penalizing abusers with time-outs and bans. To avoid this, web service clients typically use a polling architecture (with an artificial delay between requests); running with local-data negates the need for the delay, and makes large-scale testing practical.

Tests Instructors can use the cached data for testing, ensuring uniform coverage by all students. There is no need to worry about students missing out on edge cases not covered during a particular time interval, since they can be provided with the important cases in test files. Since the cache is stored in a convenient JSON-based data format, it can easily be modified by instructors to return specific results. The ability to ensure consistent tests is particularly useful for automated grading systems, such as Web-CAT [4].

3.1.4 *Threading*

To address the needs arising in an assortment of situations, the libraries offer the flexibility of returning the results of API calls either synchronously or asynchronously. Concurrent programming, although an important skill for students to develop, can be overwhelming for beginners. Even as work to integrate multiprogramming into lower-level courses moves forward, scaffolding is still required if we want intro students to develop applications with parallel processing capabilities. Using the asynchronous return mode, the hard problems of threading can be avoided.

3.1.5 *Open-source*

The libraries are meant to be good examples of API design. As students gain mastery, they can be encouraged to read the source code to learn how network communication and data parsing is implemented. They can then modify, extend, and even re-implement the API as they see fit. If students choose to create their own API based on our model, they can submit it to our gallery and gain wider recognition for their work.

3.1.6 *Examples*

Figure 2 demonstrates using the Java version of the Earthquake library. This sample program polls the online service for new earthquakes and then notifies the user. This polling architecture is a common pattern for web-service consumers, so it is useful to expose it to students. Note that if line 12 had been omitted, the library would have returned results from its internal cache instead of the online service. In turn, this would allow us to remove the `Thread.sleep` in line 32, and receive huge speed boosts. Also note the use of a `HashSet` - since data is returned from the past hour, but accessed every five minutes, there is a significant amount of redundant data that must be filtered out. The local cache replicates this redundancy for complete authenticity.

Figure 3 shows an example of using the reduced Racket WeatherService library, which only exposes a method to get the current temperature of a city.

3.2 Curated Gallery

Complete libraries and documentation are available at `http://research.cs.vt.edu/vtspaces/realtimeweb/`. Besides the various language bindings available for a service

Figure 2: A simple program demonstrating the Java Earthquake library

```
import java.util.List;
import java.util.HashSet;
import realtimeweb.earthquakeservice.main.EarthquakeService;
import realtimeweb.earthquakeservice.domain.Earthquake;

public class EarthquakeDemo {

    public static void main(String[] args) throws EarthquakeException {
        // Use the EarthquakeService library
        EarthquakeService es = EarthquakeService.getInstance();

        es.connect(); // Remove to use the local cache

        // 5 minute delay, but if we use the cache no delay is needed!
        int DELAY = 5 * 60 * 1000;

        HashSet<Earthquake> seenQuakes = new HashSet<Earthquake>();

        // Poll service regularly
        while ( true ) {
            // Get all earthquakes in the past hour
            List<Earthquake> latest = es.getEarthquakes(History.ALL);
            // Check if this is a new earthquake
            for (Earthquake e : latest) {
                if (!seenQuakes.contains(e)) {
                    // Report new earthquakes
                    System.out.println("New quake!");
                    seenQuakes.add(e);
                }
            }
            // Delay to avoid spamming the weather service
            Thread.sleep(DELAY);
        }
    }
}
```

Figure 3: A simple program demonstrating the Racket Weather library

```
(require "weather-offline.rkt")

; string -> string
; Consumes a city and returns whether its
; current temperature is "hot" or "cold"
(define (report-weather city)
    (cond [(< 70 (get-temperature city))
           "hot"]
          [else "cold"]))

; We use the offline version of the library
; for consistent check-expects
(check-expect (report-weather "Nome, AK")
              "cold")
(check-expect (report-weather "Miami, FL")
              "hot")
```

(e.g. Python, Racket, Java), there are a number of other useful pieces of information:

- API documentation and student-oriented user guides for each language and library.
- Alternative datasets for the internalized data cache (e.g., instead of business reviews from around "Blacksburg, VA", there might be another dataset for "Indianapolis, IN").
- Reduced variants of the libraries for targetted assignments.
- Example assignments that use the library.

All resources are open-source and fully supported. They are being continuously refined and extended.

3.3 Prototyping Tool

An important byproduct of our project is the creation of an online tool for rapidly prototyping new libraries. Most of the code used in our libraries follows the same pattern for any given language. First, requests are made to a web service and raw data is returned (typically as XML or JSON). Next, the data is parsed into some intermediary, semi-structured form using dictionary and list types that are native to the language. Finally, the data is encoded into a read-only class or struct, depending on the disposition of the language. For example, beginner students using Racket might deal with structs, instead of classes. This is not true in object-oriented languages such as Python and Java.

Because the data flow is consistent regardless of programming language or data source, we can leverage this similarity to fill out a template for the target languages based on a single, abstract meta-description (a "Client Library Specification"). The JSON-formatted Specificiation contains two parts: information about the methods exposed by the web service and the structure of the data returned. The system is compatible with several methods of sending arguments to web services, including Query Strings, POST Variables, and URL-Embedded data. Once a user has created a Specification, the tool generates valid and functionally-equivalent Racket, Python, and Java code to access the web services. These client libraries come ready-made with documentation provided through the Specification, and their source code is extremely straightforward to comprehend and extend.

The tool has already been successfully used to create five of the client libraries. The automatically-generated code usually requires only a few minor, manual tweaks before it is ready for public exposure. In fact, the most recently-created library (for connecting to a Magic: The Gathering card database) took less than an hour to specify, generate, and refine. The tool, documentation, and examples are available online as a component of the gallery.

4. TRANSFORMING COURSE PROJECTS

When integrated into a class project, our tools offer several features that positively impact student engagement. First, the availability of libraries for a multitude of services creates options for free-form projects, in which students enjoy greater *autonomy* in development. Second, the abundance of our library offerings also increases the chances of students finding data sources that are truly *relevant* to their interests. Third, the simple design of the libraries fosters a sense of *self-efficacy* and *competence* within the student; they can work with complicated real-world data without dealing with the frustrating real-world complications. These aspects are all recognized as increasing intrinsic motivation and engagement [8].

However, using real-world data does more than just engage students and increase their intrinsic motivation. Instructors can use the libraries to introduce real-world problems. Example project ideas include:

- Reddit Service: Social link-sharing website Reddit aggregates interesting content from around the web, including news and other real-time data sources. Students could be tasked with processing data from the site and finding interesting patterns in comments and posts. Even with only a rudimentary knowledge of string parsing, there are many interesting operations that can be performed, such as analyzing average comment length or finding a keyword.
- Weather Service: Planning a long-distance trip can be tricky, and preparing for weather is important. Students could investigate how to avoid bad weather between cities using different search algorithms to find best possible paths.
- Earthquake Service: Earthquakes happen around the world, all the time. Students could use a spatial data structure such as a Quadtree to record and analyze data about earthquakes and how they affect the world.

As a specific example of the potential educational benefits that RealTimeWeb can afford, consider two alternate sketches for a programming project that can be assigned to reinforce the topic of circular linked lists, a fixture of a typical data structures course. The first version uses abstract data, while the second one uses the data provided by the Business Service library that comes as part of the current RealTimeWeb catalog.

Original Version:

1. Create a circular list data structure capable of holding heterogeneous data.
2. Create a Data class that contains an integer ID and a String description.
3. Place Data objects whose ID fields represent consecutive integer values into each node of the list.
4. Remove all the nodes containing Data objects, whose ID fields are even numbers.

RealTimeWeb Version:

1. Create a circular list data structure capable of holding heterogeneous data.
2. Download a list of nearby restaurants and place them into the nodes of the list, sorted by their price levels.
3. Remove all the restaurants that do not offer vegetarian options.

Although both versions reinforce the same topic of circular linked lists and require a comparable amount of student effort, the RealTimeWeb version has students manipulate data they are likely to encounter in their day-to-day experiences, thus potentially increasing motivation and engagement.

It is important to recognize that integrating these services needs to be more than skin deep. Students should be given a situated perspective on how these data streams interact with the real world. Rather than just downloading an abstract list of data, assignments should lead to practical, interesting tools and results that the students can be proud of.

5. FORMATIVE EVALUATION

5.1 Usability Survey

We piloted our Business Service client library in a CS2-style course offered at Virginia Tech (CS 2114) during Spring 2013. This course covers topics typical to a second semester Computer Science course, including Object-Oriented concepts and the Java programming language. All students in the class are Computer Science majors and minors in their first or second year, with mostly limited prior programming experience. Every week, students use paired programming to complete a lab assignment. There are also three large projects meant to be completed over the course of the semester.

During one lab session, students were assigned a multi-part problem that required the use of the Business Service library. To personalize their experience with the library, the internal data cache was filled with data from the Blacksburg area. The description of the lab began with an overview of the problems and advantages inherent in using real-time data, and then described how the Business Service library could be used. In the first task, students used the library to create a list of highly rated businesses in the area. In the second, they expanded that list with more detailed information. The primary intent of this lab was to familiarize students with the client library.

Students had a second opportunity to work with the library in the third project of the course, where they built a more complicated "Restaurant Guide" Android application. Students again searched for a list of restaurants in a given region. This time, however, they were required to place the results in their implementation for a circular linked list data structure.

A voluntary survey was administered to the class after students had completed the project, and 17 responses were gathered. Overall, the results were positive. All but one student indicated that they found the API "applicable to day-to-day computing experiences", and all students thought that the API was "easy-to-use". Qualitative feedback from the students highlighted "clear, easy-to-figure-out methods" and that they "provided information that was easy to work with".

5.2 Relevancy Survey

In addition to this formative evaluation, a large-scale survey was conducted of 370 undergraduates at Virginia Tech in the Fall 2013. 68% of the respondents were Sophomores and Juniors, 87% were male, and 68% were Computer Science majors. Students were asked to gauge how much learning a given technology would benefit their future careers. Working with Real-time Data compared favorably with Mobile App Development and Website/Web Application Development (with most students feeling they would benefit or definitely benefit from these technologies), as opposed to Programming Robots, Game Development, and Raspberry Pi Development (with most students feeling somewhere between neutral and beneficial). This is extremely encouraging, especially since our RealTimeWeb framework is designed to be compatible with Mobile technologies and back-end web application development.

6. FUTURE WORK

Currently, there are five services available through our client libraries, each in three languages. Ultimately, we plan to have an extensive gallery that can cater to a wide range of student interests. We are particularly interested in soliciting feedback from the community on other services that would be of interest and languages that should be supported.

Although the results from our formative evaluation were positive, it is important not to overstate them. More surveys and careful evaluation will be required to determine the exact impact that real-time data assignments offer educators. We are using RealTimeWeb in programming projects during Fall 2013 at Virginia Tech in a sophomore/junior-level data structures course, and at University of Deleware in a freshman-level course.

7. CONCLUSION

Learning to handle real-time web data is an important skill for modern CS students to develop. This learning experience also makes introductory programming projects more relevant to the students' day-to-day computing experiences, thereby increasing engagement and motivation. In order to reduce the technical barriers inherent in interacting with distributed systems, we have created publicly available client libraries that make it possible to connect to popular web services in a student-friendly manner, enabling a gradual introduction to the complexities of distributed computing. Results from an early pilot indicate that our libraries are easy to use by introductory students. The RealTimeWeb framework provides a promising way to better engage students while preparing them for the realities of the modern IT workplace.

Acknowledgments

This research is supported by the National Science Foundation through the Grant TUES #1140318.

8. REFERENCES

[1] L. Carter. Why students with an apparent aptitude for computer science don't choose to major in computer science. In *Proceedings of the 37th SIGCSE technical symposium on Computer science education*, SIGCSE '06, pages 27–31, New York, NY, USA, 2006. ACM.

[2] D. I. Cordova and M. R. Lepper. Intrinsic motivation and the process of learning: Beneficial effects of contextualization, personalization, and choice. *Journal of educational psychology*, 88:715–730, 1996.

[3] A. B. Downey. *Think Stats*. O'Reilly Media, July 2011.

[4] S. Edwards. Using test-driven development in the classroom: Providing students with automatic, concrete feedback on performance. In *In Proceedings of the International Conference on Education and Information Systems: Technologies and Applications*, EISTA, 2003.

[5] A. E. Egger. Engaging students in earthquakes via real-time data and decisions. *Science*, 336(6089):1654–1655, 2012.

[6] M. Felleisen, R. B. Findler, M. Flatt, and S. Krishnamurthi. *How to Design Programs*. Second edition, 2012.

[7] A. Fisher, J. Margolis, and F. Miller. Undergraduate women in computer science: experience, motivation and culture. In *Proceedings of the twenty-eighth SIGCSE technical symposium on Computer science education*, SIGCSE '97, pages 106–110, New York, NY, USA, 1997. ACM.

[8] R. M. Ryan and E. L. Deci. Self-determination theory and the facilitation of intrinsic motivation, social development, and well-being. *The American psychologist*, 55(1):68–78, Jan. 2000.

[9] M. Sahami, S. Roach, E. Cuadros-Vargas, and D. Reed. Computer science curriculum 2013: reviewing the strawman report from the acm/ieee-cs task force. In *Proceedings of the 43rd ACM technical symposium on Computer Science Education*, SIGCSE '12, pages 3–4, New York, NY, USA, 2012. ACM.

[10] L. Torgo. *Data Mining with R, learning with case studies*. Chapman and Hall/CRC, 2010.

[11] M. Waldman. Keeping it real: utilizing nyc open data in an introduction to database systems course. *J. Comput. Sci. Coll.*, 28(6):156–161, June 2013.

Importance of Early Performance in CS1: Two Conflicting Assessment Stories

Leo Porter
Dept. of Mathematics and Computer Science
Skidmore College
Saratoga Springs, NY, USA
leo.porter@skidmore.edu

Daniel Zingaro
OISE
University of Toronto
Toronto, ON, Canada
daniel.zingaro@utoronto.ca

ABSTRACT

It is generally assumed that early success in CS1 is crucial for success on the exam and course as a whole. Particularities of students, densely-connected CS1 content, and recurring core topics each suggest that it is difficult to rebound from early misunderstandings. In this paper, we use Peer Instruction (PI) data, in addition to exam data, to explore relationships between in-class assessments and performance at the end of term and on the exam. We find that early course performance very quickly and strongly predicts performance on the final exam and that subsequent weeks provide no major increase in that predictive power. In contrast, early performance is similarly predictive of performance in the last weeks of PI questions, but subsequent weeks are increasingly more predictive. We speculate on what this means for the content of these assessments and potential future assessment practices.

Categories and Subject Descriptors

K.3.2 [**Computer Science Education**]: Computer and Information Science Education

Keywords

CS1, assessment, programming

1. INTRODUCTION

Why do some students succeed in CS1 and others fail? Are the reasons for success and failure unique to CS or do they apply generally across the post-secondary curriculum? Should we seek answers in the attributes of students or the features of our CS1 courses and discipline more generally?

Such questions pervade historical and contemporary CS education research. When researchers search for factors that predict success (e.g. [6, 4]), problematize the types of CS assessments in common usage [22], or offer accounts of the entwined substructure of CS1 concepts [15], they are at least implicitly interested in why some students succeed and others do not.

Understanding student success in CS1 has long been a disciplinary concern, highlighted particularly by the numerous studies of novice programmers (see [16] for a summary). More recently, reports of high failure rates [3] and substandard student performance on essential CS1 tasks [9] have led to renewed effort in understanding why such performance is observed. Many accounts suggest that early performance in CS1 is highly predictive of marks on the final exam. For example, those advocating "geek genes", Learning Edge Momentum [15], or stumbling blocks (see [2] for a review of these three) generally believe that early experience sets students on a particular path from which it becomes difficult to deviate. At the same time, the way that we assess our students on exams has come into question by those suggesting that our exams do not offer adequate opportunity for demonstrating learning [11].

Many relevant studies are conducted in CS1s that offer few assessment points, such as one or two midterms and a final exam. This makes it difficult to temporally discern the origins of difficulties observed on those assessments. We suggest that more fine-grained analyses of assessment data might yield new hypotheses and research directions regarding the relationship between early class performance and final exams.

In this paper, we use data generated from Peer Instruction (PI) to offer a picture of in-class data over the semester. This pedagogy engages students in discussing and answering multiple choice questions during class. As students respond with clickers, all data is captured automatically and can be used to chart performance through the semester. We use PI data to complement analysis of a typical CS1 final exam. On the exam, we see the expected pattern: early term performance (including PI data and midterm performance) correlates highly with final exam performance and subsequent weeks offer no additional predictive value. Yet, when we examine end-of-term PI data, we see a different pattern. Specifically, correlations between PI data and end-of-term data increase throughout the term, sharply contrasting the final exam findings. We offer our interpretations and speculate on what the data might mean for the ongoing assessment discussion.

SIGCSE'14, March 3–8, 2014, Atlanta, GA, USA.
Copyright 2014 ACM 978-1-4503-2605-6/14/03 ...$15.00.
http://dx.doi.org/10.1145/2538862.2538912.

2. BACKGROUND

2.1 CS1 Grade Distribution

It is commonly reported that CS1 course marks exhibit bimodal distributions. One mode represents those students who "get it", and the other represents those students who score very poorly [15, 7]. Whether the bimodal distribution exists in the first place is a point of contention [8], though many concede that an alarming number of students perform poorly and at least a small portion of students perform very strongly. Research suggests that 30% to 60% of students in general who take CS1 courses fail the course [3].

Recently, Robins [15] offered a Learning Edge Momentum (LEM) explanation for the supposed bimodal distribution of CS1 grades. The argument is that, compared to other disciplines, concepts in a CS1 are tightly integrated, so that understanding one concept leads to increased likelihood of understanding the following concepts. By contrast, failing to understand a concept leads to a diminished ability to understand further concepts. In both cases, students spiral: to the top or bottom of the grade distribution. In fact, the LEM effect may occur quite quickly: Robins notes that performance on Week 3 diagnostic tests are predictive of course performance. If there is indeed a LEM effect, then its detection may resist capture in those courses where the first assessment occurs after Weeks 3 or 4.

There are other hypotheses offered for understanding the prototypical CS1 distribution. For example, prior experience is a robust predictor of success in CS1 [6, 18, 10]. Students who studied programming in the past tend to do well compared to those with no programming experience. That is, any bimodal effects could be due to prior experience and be largely independent of what happens in the CS1 itself.

Such commentary on the nature of the discipline and the makeup of successful students accords well with those concerned with our assessments themselves. In general, researchers contend that our assessments test the same thing repeatedly [11] and in general do not accurately capture what our students know. Typical exams are largely composed of code-writing exercises and integrate many concepts [11]. If a student does not understand one of the core concepts required to answer such a code-writing question, they are unlikely to make much progress on the question, even when the misunderstood concept is not the conceptual focus of the question. This may lead to extreme high or low scores, depending on whether students can successfully orchestrate the use of multiple concepts.

2.2 Peer Instruction

Active classroom pedagogies have been gaining momentum in the CS education community over the past few years. One of the most-researched of such techniques is Peer Instruction (PI), where students use clickers to answer conceptual multiple choice questions in class. Recent research, for example, suggests that PI is advantageous for majors [17] and weak students [19], decreases failure rates [13] and contributes to increased retention [14]. That said, in this work, our primary interest is not in PI as a research-proven pedagogy, but in the trace of student data that PI affords. Specifically, for each question answered, students' responses are collected and categorized as correct or incorrect. As PI questions are used in every class, we use such data to chart student performance on such questions within small two-week intervals, rather than larger intervals associated with major term exams.

3. METHODOLOGY

3.1 Study Context

This study uses data from a CS1 taught in fall 2012 at a large campus of a Canadian research university. The instructor of the course had taught CS1 many times before, in both PI and non-PI offerings. This particular CS1 was taught using Python 3 using new materials developed especially for this course. Students participated in 34 PI class meetings and 8 practical labs, completed two assignments, and sat one midterm and one final exam.

Most of the class meetings centered around multiple choice questions. For each "PI cycle", the instructor posed a conceptual question on which students voted individually. Students then discussed the question with their seatmates for 2-3 minutes and voted again. Following the second vote, the instructor led a classwide discussion of relevant concepts and misconceptions. As students vote using clickers, the PI questions cannot directly ask for written code [21]. For that reason, the instructor also live-programmed during lecture. Students also had to prepare for lecture by reading sections of the textbook and playing with small pieces of code; reading quizzes are recommended as a PI best-practice [5, 20]. All materials for the course are available [1].

3.2 Data Analysis

Both midterm exam (occurring in week 7) and final exam scores are used in our analysis. Data was also collected from PI multiple choice questions throughout the term. On each PI question, students respond individually and then in groups; here, we use individual votes since post-group votes may not accurately capture student understanding [12]. There were typically 3-4 questions per class; given these small numbers, we combine questions across two-week boundaries (e.g. Weeks 1 and 2 were combined, Weeks 3 and 4 were combined, and so on) to reduce noise in the dataset. Student absences are also particularly problematic in producing noise and in potentially polluting the dataset. We have decided to consider missing a question (perhaps due to being absent) as equivalent to answering a question incorrectly. If a student did not answer any questions at all in a two-week period, then they were removed from that assessment but were retained for other two-week spans in which they did answer questions. To examine the relationship between student scores on different assessments, Pearson's correlation was used. We report r values for all tests performed.

4. RESULTS

In these sections we examine the predictive power of weekly in-class clicker performance and the midterm exam against two end-of-term metrics: final exam performance and in-class PI performance in the last two weeks.

4.1 Final Exam

Figure 1 provides a histogram of student scores on the final exam. Visually examining the figure shows that this distribution is unlike the bimodal distribution suggested in [8] as there appears to be a single mode around 60% with some additional features (possibly noise) around 30% and 90%.

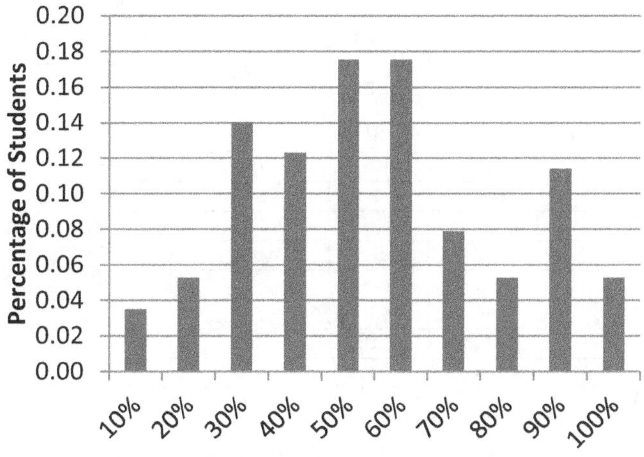

Figure 1: Histogram of student performance on the final exam.

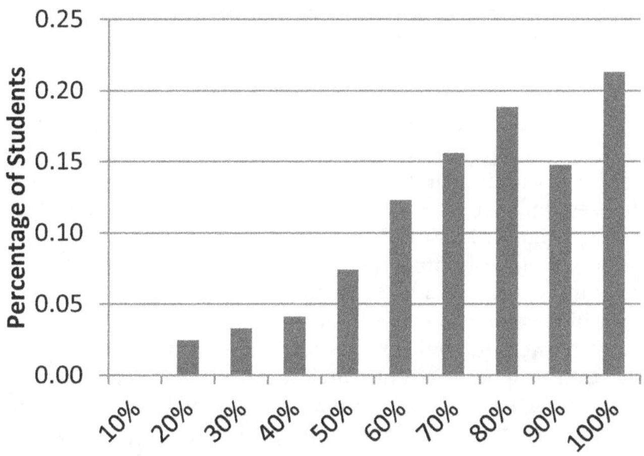

Figure 2: Histogram of student performance on the midterm exam.

Although the question of modality is important [2], the aim of this work is to identify what causes students to arrive at their respective scores on this exam.

The midterm, given in Week 7, shows slightly better performance (see Figure 2) and appears to be unimodal with a large percentage of students scoring 100% demonstrating a ceiling effect. (Researchers have noted that such ceiling effects are often confused as one mode in a possibly multimodal distribution [8].) Of importance to the current work is whether midterm performance predicts final exam performance. We find that the midterm scores are highly correlated with the final ($r = 0.69$). This implies that student performance as early as Week 7 is highly predictive of their outcome in the course.

To examine these results more closely, we look at student performance on clicker questions based on pairs of weeks of the term. These results appear in Figure 3 in the columns labelled Final Exam. In these results we find that performance in Weeks 3 and 4 predicts final exam performance well ($r = 0.38$). We would then expect that subsequent weeks might more closely predict the final exam as student performance on more material is gauged. What is surprising, however, is that subsequent weeks are very similarly

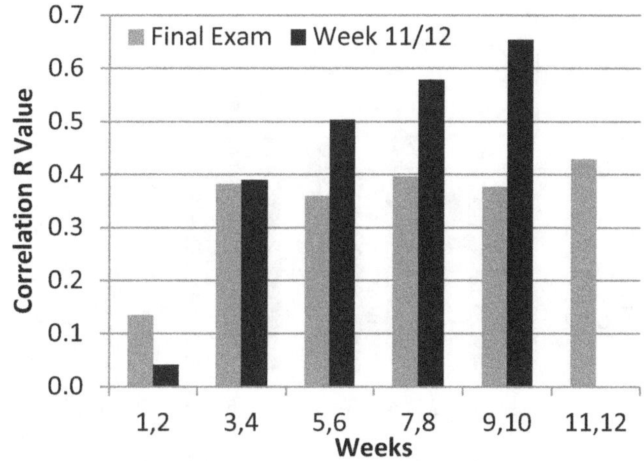

Figure 3: Correlation of student performance on clicker questions (in two-week intervals) with either the final exam or with clicker questions in the last two weeks of class.

predictive, with Weeks 11 and 12 only slightly more predictive ($r = 0.43$) than Weeks 3 and 4. At this point, one might wonder whether the concepts covered in Weeks 3 and 4 are particularly important. Weeks 3 and 4 cover conditionals and looping; we study this more closely in Section 4.3.

These results support a number of theories of student performance. Those who argue for innate talent ("geek gene") would say that such talent is represented in performance in Weeks 3 and 4 and students never change thereafter. However, Weeks 1 and 2 could be seen as detracting from that argument—if the talent is innate, why would Weeks 1 and 2 not be predictive ($r = 0.13$)?

Supporters of Learning Edge Momentum [15] would argue that these results confirm their predictions: that momentum is established quickly and dominates subsequent performance. Similarly, those who argue that there are early concepts that are "stumbling blocks" would point to Weeks 3 and 4 and say that the concepts covered in those weeks are candidate stumbling blocks.

Similar to the argument raised in [2], proponents of all three of these theories would take comfort in our finding that performance at the beginning of the term predicts final exam score. We revisit these issues later in this section, but first look for corroborating data from the clicker performance in the final weeks of the semester.

4.2 End-of-Term Clicker Performance

Figure 4 provides results from student performance in the last two weeks of class. Absent the two extremes, performance is nearly uniformly distributed.

Proceeding with analyses similar to those in the previous section, we now examine the predictive power of various assessments on end-of-term (Weeks 11 and 12) performance. Compared to its relationship with the final exam, the midterm is not as predictive of end-of-term clicker performance ($r = 0.29$). This leads us again to examine the predictive power of performance on clicker questions (groups in pairs of weeks).

We next examine the predictive power of term clicker performance on end-of-term clicker performance; these results appear in Figure 3 in the columns labelled Week11,12. We

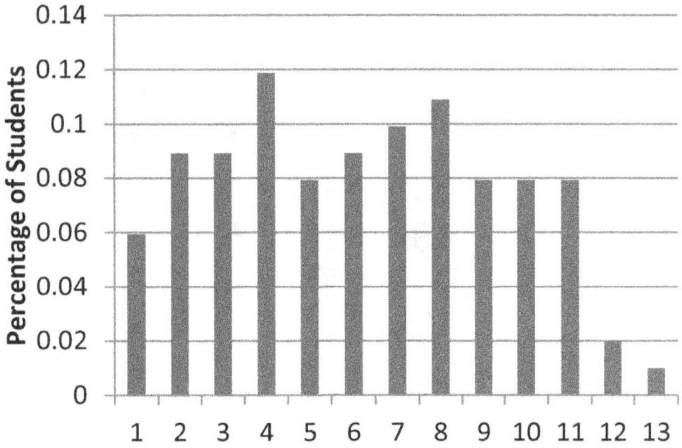

Figure 4: Histogram of student performance on 13 questions in Weeks 11 and 12.

find that the correlation rises steeply when examining Weeks 3 and 4. Unlike the results from the final exam, however, subsequent weeks are increasingly predictive. In fact, the two weeks directly before Weeks 11 and 12 (Weeks 9 and 10) are the most predictive ($r = 0.654$) of end-of-term in-class performance.

This finding is troubling for those who support student performance as primarily determined by innate talent ("geek gene") and are similarly troublesome for those who predict that student performance will be understood early in the term (Learning Edge Momentum and Stumbling Block). More critically, these theories are all designed to explain (and subsequently predict) a bimodal distribution in student performance—an effect not seen in Weeks 11 and 12.

In essense, Figure 3 tells two conflicting stories based on two forms of assessment. Performance on the final exam is generally understood as early as Weeks 3 and 4 and is strongly understood by the time of the midterm. In contrast, our understanding of performance on Week 11 and 12 clicker questions improves as the course progresses. To better understand the source of this apparent conflict, we examine the assessment mechanisms in more detail.

4.3 Class and Exam Content

To investigate the reason for these discordant trends, we examined the content of the course by week as well as the content of the final exam. Similar to exams deemed common in CS1 [11], the final exam consisted primarily of code-writing (60% of the points), conceptual questions (23% of the points), and code tracing (17% of the points).

Table 1 provides the concepts from the class, the weeks those concepts were taught, and the percentage of points on the final exam that depend on those concepts. This breakdown helps explain the phenomenon we saw with the final exam—that Weeks 3 and 4 predicts final exam performance—in that the bulk of the points on the exam depended on concepts from those weeks. Concepts from subsequent weeks are far less represented on the final and may help explain why student performance during those weeks was no more valuable in predicting student final exam performance.

The strong correlation between Weeks 3 and 4 and the final exam, and the concepts stressed on that exam, provides preliminary supporting evidence for the claim that student performance on exams suffers because we ask the same concept repeatedly [11]. We note that the instructor attempted to cover all course concepts on the exam but that the repetition of fundamental concepts in early weeks resulted in the seemingly uneven coverage. We revisit the issue of final exam design in Section 5.3.

Concept	Weeks	Final Exam	Week11,12
variables/types	1,2	80%	15%
functions	1,2	50%	0%
booleans	2	3%	0%
conditionals	3	38%	15%
loops	4,5	58%	15%
strings	4	44%	0%
lists/tuples	5,6	34%	15%
files	6	5%	15%
dictionaries	7,8	14%	0%
testing	8,9	8%	0%
classes	9,10	12%	0%
complexity	11	4%	35%
sorting	12	8%	40%

Table 1: Concepts from the CS1 course, the weeks they are taught, the percentage of points on the final that use the concept, and the percentage of questions in Weeks 11 and 12 that use the concept. (A single question can have multiple concepts, so the total marks in this table is more than the exam denominator.)

We also investigated the conceptual coverage of PI questions in Weeks 11 and 12. Relative to the final exam, a contrast in coverage is immediately apparent. Conceptual questions dominated the content (85%) with some code tracing questions appearing from a review day (15%). A fair portion of the questions (20%) dealt with abstract problem solving rather than any language- or programming-specific concept and hence did not fall under the tagging in Table 1. Lastly, a large majority (85%) of these questions dealt with a single concept, rather than combining multiple concepts into a single question. The remainder of the tagging of PI questions from Weeks 11 and 12 appears in Table 1.

4.4 Result Summary

The fact that correlations between PI questions and end-of-term questions improve with time is particularly encouraging. Unlike the final exam where performance is determined by Week 3 and 4 and latter weeks are no more predictive, student activities in weeks 5-10 can have a positive impact on their end-of-term performance. Hence, weeks 5-10 *matter* in terms of performance on end-of-term PI questions.

A potential criticism of this optimism would be to say that the improved correlation is merely an artifact of students being pushed to either extreme as Learning Edge Momentum takes hold. Recall, however, that the distribution of student performance on Weeks 11 and 12 is fairly uniform. Hence, student movement week to week is not being dominated by students being pushed to either extreme.

The correlation between Weeks 3 and 4 and the final exam ($r = 0.382$) is similar to the correlation between Weeks 3 and 4 and Weeks 11 and 12 ($r = 0.39$). For the final exam, this appears to be attributable to the large percentage of the exam that uses content from those weeks (conditionals and looping). For Weeks 11 and 12 (algorithmic complexity and sorting), there is considerably less overlapping of concepts.

Thus, Weeks 3 and 4 may be critical for success in CS1 in general. The story diverges after Weeks 3 and 4 as the predictive power of student performance in the remainder of the class improves considerably for Weeks 11 and 12, but does not do so for the final exam.

Hence, we see two contrasting stories. When assessed on multiple programming concepts in a predominately code-writing and code-tracing final exam, students' performance is largely governed by their performance early in the term. When assessed on high-level problem solving questions, performance throughout the term increasingly predicts success. We explore implications of these conflicting trends in the following section.

5. DISCUSSION

5.1 Threats to Validity

We acknowledge that data from student clicker performance can be extremely noisy. Students missing class, clicking for points without taking the question seriously, or guessing all lead to uncertainty in the data. To reduce this noise we excluded data corresponding to students being completely absent for a two-week period, excluded students who dropped or did not take the final, and measured student performance in pairs of weeks. Absent students are difficult to manage for this analysis and conclusions for those students may be limited.

Although the per-student data generated by PI was critical for this analysis, the pedagogy may limit the generalizability of the results. In particular, it is interesting to speculate on the effect of PI on the shape of the midterm and final exam distributions. As noted, we did not see bimodal distributions here, but perhaps this was caused by the frequent opportunities for success and feedback afforded by PI. Similar evaluation should be performed in a standard instruction class, perhaps through the use of frequent quizzes.

The fine-grained, week-by-week student performance data stem from responses to conceptual PI questions. Based on our analysis of Weeks 11 and 12 PI questions, such questions may differ substantially in content compared to a traditional midterm or final exam. To validate the hypothesis that student performance on a traditional, code-writing-heavy final is generally determined as early as Weeks 3 and 4, a more traditional assessment mechanism consisting of code-writing should be used in earlier weeks.

Although unlikely in the authors' opinion, the impact on student performance on conceptual (Weeks 11 and 12) questions could be attributable to practice effects with multiple choice questions, rather than increased problem-solving skill. Future work could pose open-ended high-level conceptual questions at the end of the term to further support or refute this claim.

5.2 Code Writing and Problem Solving

CS1 has been the subject of exhaustive study by this community in part because of the large demands placed on a single course. As computer scientists, we want our students to learn key concepts of problem solving and algorithm analysis. We also want our students to become capable programmers. The findings of this study have implications for both of these aims. Discouragingly, we find that student performance in early weeks of a term can have a strong effect on their performance on a traditional code-heavy CS1 exam. Encouragingly, we find that student performance week to week impacts their ability to solve high-level algorithmic questions.

Both Code-Writing and Problem Solving are critical components to being a successful computer scientist. This work shows that student activities throughout the term predict their in-class success at the end of term. Such efforts should be encouraged by communicating to students the importance of graduated practice and conceptual development. In contrast, the "traditional" code-writing final exam has previously been criticized for the consistent repetition of single concepts [11]. Problematically, code-writing problems almost always require multiple supporting concepts to test a target concept. For example, it is difficult to consider testing students' ability to write code that processes lists without also testing their ability to reason with loops and potentially conditionals and booleans. As such, we should either revisit how we assess code-writing ability or front-load course resources toward helping students over the hurtle of early fundamental concepts.

5.3 Implications for Instructors

The instructor put particular care into designing the final exam to arrive at an appropriate spread of points by topic. In fact, 46 of 100 points were questions from the latter half of the term. However, when we took into account the repetition of other concepts from earlier weeks, the concepts from the latter half of the term represented 46 of 278 (17%) points, even when one excludes the fact that nearly all questions (80 of 100 points) used variables/types. Given how natural it is to repeat concepts from early in the term, we caution instructors to keep this in mind when designing their exams.

This work, among others, clearly highlights the importance of understanding fundamental course concepts such as conditionals and looping. To think that student activities after the fourth week of the term do little to improve students' standing on a final exam should be disconcerting for any instructor. As such, we (again, among others) recommend that instructors pay extra attention to those concepts, perhaps performing early interventions with students who demonstrate relevant misconceptions. We also encourage instructors who perform interventionary techniques to conduct a similar evaluation to this study to determine the effectiveness of those interventions.

6. CONCLUSION

In this work, we find evidence that student performance on a code-writing-heavy final exam is predicted by performance on in-class Peer Instruction questions as early as Weeks 3 and 4. However, student performance following Weeks 3 and 4 is not substantially more predictive than early weeks, suggesting that in-class activities after Week 4 may have diminished relevance for the final exam. This story provides evidence for the predictive power of early performance suggested by learning edge momentum, stumbling-block theory, and perhaps even innate talent [2], but may be alarming to instructors concerned for those students who start slowly.

However, a disparate story is found when we examine our ability to predict performance on problem-solving PI questions in the last two weeks of the term (Weeks 11 and 12). Indeed, Weeks 3 and 4 are predictive of Weeks 11 and 12—as much so as they are predictive of the final exam—but predictive value increases over subsequent weeks. These results may conflict with conclusions drawn from the aforementioned theories for student performance, as each of those theories predicts that later performance is largely determined by performance in early weeks. In addition, these results are highly encouraging for CS educators as they suggest that student performance on activities throughout the term impacts students' ability to do well on end-of-term problem solving activities.

In summary, we find that theory-based predictions are accurate for final exam performance but not end-of-term problem-solving performance. We hypothesize that the poor student performance explained by these theories may be an artifact of the assessment mechanisms in common use. Further work is needed to explore the links between theories of performance, assessment practices, and student success in CS1.

7. REFERENCES

[1] Peer instruction for computer science. `peerinstruction4cs.org`, 2013.

[2] A. Ahadi and R. Lister. Geek genes, prior knowledge, stumbling points and learning edge momentum: parts of the one elephant? In *Proceedings of the ninth annual international ACM conference on International computing education research*, ICER '13, pages 123–128, New York, NY, USA, 2013. ACM.

[3] J. Bennedsen and M. E. Caspersen. Failure rates in introductory programming. *SIGCSE Bulletin*, 39:32–36, 2007.

[4] P. Byrne and G. Lyons. The effect of student attributes on success in programming. *SIGCSE Bulletin*, 33:49–52, 2001.

[5] C. H. Crouch, J. Watkins, A. P. Fagen, and E. Mazur. Peer instruction: Engaging students one-on-one, all at once. In E. F. Redish and P. J. Cooney, editors, *Research-Based Reform of University Physics*. American Association of Physics Teachers, College Park, MD, USA, 2007.

[6] D. Hagan and S. Markham. Does it help to have some programming experience before beginning a computing degree program? *SIGCSE Bulletin*, 32:25–28, 2000.

[7] M. A. Hudak and D. E. Anderson. Formal operations and learning style predict success in statistics and computer science courses. *Teaching of Psychology*, 17(4):231–234, 1990.

[8] R. Lister. Computing education research: geek genes and bimodal grades. *ACM Inroads*, 1(3):16–17, 2010.

[9] R. Lister, E. S. Adams, S. Fitzgerald, W. Fone, J. Hamer, M. Lindholm, R. McCartney, J. E. Moström, K. Sanders, O. Seppälä, B. Simon, and L. Thomas. A multi-national study of reading and tracing skills in novice programmers. In *ITiCSE-WGR '04: Working group reports from ITiCSE on Innovation and technology in computer science education*, pages 119–150, New York, NY, USA, 2004.

[10] M. Morrison and T. S. Newman. A study of the impact of student background and preparedness on outcomes in cs i. *SIGCSE Bulletin*, 33(1):179–183, 2001.

[11] A. Petersen, M. Craig, and D. Zingaro. Reviewing cs1 exam question content. In *Proceedings of the 42nd ACM technical symposium on Computer science education*, pages 631–636, New York, NY, USA, 2011.

[12] L. Porter, C. Bailey-Lee, B. Simon, and D. Zingaro. Peer instruction: Do students really learn from peer discussion in computing? In *Proceedings of the Seventh international Workshop on Computing Education Research*, New York, NY, USA, 2011.

[13] L. Porter, C. B. Lee, and B. Simon. Halving fail rates using peer instruction: A study of four computer science courses. In *Proceedings of the 44th ACM technical symposium on Computer science education*, pages 177–182. ACM, 2013.

[14] L. Porter and B. Simon. Retaining nearly one-third more majors with a trio of instructional best practices in cs1. In *Proceedings of the 44th ACM technical symposium on Computer science education*, pages 165–170. ACM, 2013.

[15] A. Robins. Learning edge momentum: A new account of outcomes. *Computer Science Education*, 20(1):37–71, 2010.

[16] A. Robins, J. Rountree, and N. Rountree. Learning and teaching programming: A review and discussion. *Computer Science Education*, 13:137–172, 2003.

[17] B. Simon, M. Kohanfars, J. Lee, K. Tamayo, and Q. Cutts. Experience report: Peer instruction in introductory computing. In *Proceedings of the 41st SIGCSE technical symposium on Computer science education*, pages 341–345, New York, NY, USA, 2010.

[18] B. C. Wilson and S. Shrock. Contributing to success in an introductory computer science course: a study of twelve factors. *SIGCSE Bulletin*, 33:184–188, 2001.

[19] D. Zingaro. Experience report: Peer instruction in remedial computer science. In *Proceedings of the 22nd World Conference on Educational Multimedia, Hypermedia & Telecommunications*, pages 5030–5035. AACE, 2010.

[20] D. Zingaro, C. Bailey-Lee, and L. Porter. Peer instruction in computing: the role of reading quizzes. In *Proceedings of the 44th ACM technical symposium on Computer Science Education*, pages 47–52. 2013.

[21] D. Zingaro, A. Petersen, Y. Cherenkova, and O. Karpova. Facilitating code-writing in pi classes. In *Proceedings of the 44th ACM technical symposium on Computer Science Education (SIGCSE)*, pages 585–590, New York, NY, USA, 2013.

[22] D. Zingaro, A. Petersen, and M. Craig. Stepping up to integrative questions on cs1 exams. In *Proceedings of the 43rd ACM technical symposium on Computer Science Education*, pages 253–258, New York, NY, USA, 2012.

Reinventing Homework as Cooperative, Formative Assessment

Don Blaheta
Department of Mathematics and Computer Science
Longwood University
Farmville, VA, USA
blahetadp@longwood.edu

ABSTRACT

Traditional processes for homework assignments are not always a good fit for the sorts of problems often seen in computer science classes. We present our experiences in implementing policies designed to encourage students to involve the instructor and fellow students in their learning process. By shifting to group assignments and permitting students a revision cycle, we improve student satisfaction and maintain or increase student outcomes while decreasing the instructor's grading load.

Categories and Subject Descriptors

K.3.2 [**Computers and Education**]: Computer and Information Science Education—*Computer science education*

Keywords

Formative assessment; Cooperative learning; Pedagogy

1. INTRODUCTION

Homework is a traditional, and often unexamined, tool in the educator's toolkit: guided practice to work on outside the classroom in order to develop skills and (hopefully) improve understanding. Though it may be graded work, we like to think of it as formative assessment, in the sense that it "helps students learn during the course of instruction."[5] The individual nature of homework, even among instructors who permit some degree of collaboration, is often seen as important precisely because of the opportunity it provides for individual practice and individual feedback.

The reality sometimes seems a little less rosy, however. We have observed that many students immediately file away graded work, spending little or no time reading instructor feedback; this greatly diminishes its value as formative assessment, of which feedback is a crucial component. D. Royce Sadler's earliest work on what he initially called "formative evaluation" was already enunciating an "iteration principle", that re-working an existing example seemed likely to be as important as, if not more important than, simply looking at an evaluation or trying to apply it to the next assignment.[4]

SIGCSE'14, March 3–8, 2014, Atlanta, GA, USA.

ACM 978-1-4503-2605-6/14/03 ...$15.00.
http://dx.doi.org/10.1145/2538862.2538915.

> Devise at least two interestingly-different tiebreakers for A* pathfinding on a 2D grid, and show a test case where they behave differently.
>
> Analyse which of your tiebreakers performs "best" on your test case, and discuss whether there is a tie-breaking strategy that will work well for all test cases or whether their relative performance depends on the problem.

Figure 1: A homework problem for an undergrad AI course (edited for length)

An additional problem with the more traditional homework model has to do with how it meshes with the idea of collaborative or cooperative learning among the students. To the extent that collaboration is permitted, any misconceptions held jointly by a group of students are not particularly well-addressed by separate, individual comments to each student. Individual students may believe they simply didn't quite understand what the group had talked about, or indeed that they might be the only one with the misunderstanding; this can hinder them from seeking out additional help or fixing the problem.

Although much of the work on formative assessment within computer science has focussed on developing new technology to support it (such as in [1, 2, 6]), we were interested to see how the existing tool—homework, using the classic "pencil and paper" technology—could be reimagined to better support the goal of formative assessment and cooperative learning. This idea seems similar in spirit to Tim S Roberts's work on adapting classically summative multiple-choice tests into a more formative assessment.[3]

In the spring of 2013, we taught an upper-level undergraduate elective on artificial intelligence. In that kind of course, typical homework questions (such as the one in Figure 1) often involve algorithm design and multiple points of subtlety, where the student will strongly benefit from interaction with the instructor and with fellow students. This paper reports on our experiences in that course, adapting our homework policy to provide a scaffold encouraging the use of student cooperation and instructor feedback to learn the course concepts.

2. REVISION CYCLES

As explained above, we had long observed that many students treat all assessment, including homework, as primarily summative rather than formative. Regardless of the type or quantity of comments written on their papers, many students would dutifully file away the graded homework, perhaps first looking at the overall grade, but spending little or no time on reading instructor feedback. Even many of the better students would read the feedback without really engaging with it. Furthermore, although students all had the ability to consult with the instructor during office hours or by email before the assignment was due, relatively few availed themselves of this opportunity. Students that got stuck early in a problem might never even begin to think about the more advanced material.

Our previous attempts to solve this problem involved simply letting students perform revisions after returning homework assignments. These efforts were largely unsuccessful. Many of the weaker students—who would most benefit from revisiting and revising their work—saw their original grade, deemed it acceptable, and ignored the revision opportunity entirely. Students who got good-but-not-perfect scores reacted similarly. The focus of many of the other students was on "recovering lost points" rather than really learning the material (which led to some frustrating teacher-student interactions). Moreover, the revision offer nearly doubled the amount of work for the instructor, since the original work was graded once, assigning partial credit as usual, and then the revision was graded again. The workload was not sustainable, especially in the face of negligible benefits.

The key insight that let us move forward on this problem was that we could use information asymmetry to shift the student's mindset away from points and grades: we can annotate the original submission with comments, but no scores. We developed this initial idea into a detailed plan surrounding revision-based homework:

1. Comments without grades
2. Revision cycle
3. Grades without comments
4. Limited scale

These four elements are each important to the plan, and work together in a few important ways.

Comments without grades. The professor hands back work with relatively detailed comments but no grades, while recording grades privately in case the original is lost or the student decides not to revise it. As noted, this is intended to take the focus away from their score, an extrinsic motivator and a source of stress, and to encourage a more internally-motivated, learning-oriented process.

Furthermore, from the perspective of the one writing the feedback, it is substantially easier to write helpful comments when not trying to simultaneously associate comments with individually gained/lost points from an analytic rubric. Rather than a defensive justification of lost points, the comments become constructive suggestions for improvement.

Revision cycle. Students have an opportunity to turn in a revised version of every homework problem. This element of the system is both central to the enterprise and also probably its least novel aspect. The "iteration principle" was part of Sadler's original description of formative assessment[4], and some form of revision or revisiting of assignments normally figures in any proposal for student-oriented formative assessment.

In the situation of homework with written comments, the particular advantage of the revision cycle is that it motivates all but the most detached of students to actually read and engage with the professor's feedback. It also addresses the classic weakness of one-shot graded homework, where two students who complete the course with full understanding may get different final grades: if one entered the course with some pre-existing understanding, under a traditional homework model that student "achieves a much higher points total... although their ultimate performances are equivalent."[4] If only the revision is graded, both students have the opportunity to achieve high final scores.

Grades without comments. Having received instructor comments on their original submission, on the revision the students will only receive a grade, without additional comments. This component has no direct advantage for the student, except inasmuch as it enables the rest of the system by not overloading the professor. The student has already received a full round of comments, though, so it is also not necessarily a disadvantage; and to some extent, this policy acknowledges the fact that many students would ignore them anyway, as many of them do in traditional single-round assignments. Students that wish to continue working on the material are, of course, encouraged to come to the professor's office hours.

Limited scale. The final component of the system is to simplify the rubric: scores would be assigned on a three-level scale as shown in Figure 2, rather than the more fine-grained per-problem analytic rubric scales we had used in previous courses. Rubrics with fewer distinct categories are a benefit to consistency and speed, with some cost to granularity. Such a pared-down rubric would probably be too harsh in an otherwise traditional system; but here, students whose *first* work demonstrated some understanding have a good opportunity to build on that and attain a 5 in the revision.

Furthermore, the limited scale contributes to the shift away from a grade-oriented mentality, as there is little opportunity to argue for small fractional points and no sense of "just missing" a particular score. It also contributes to the system as a sustainable teaching practice: assigning scores when only three levels are available is *much* easier. Together with the commenting/grading elements of the policy, which

---

5: The answer is correct, or may have very minor errors in areas not addressed by the problem (e.g. simple arithmetic mistakes)

3: The answer demonstrates substantial understanding but is incomplete or contains errors in areas relevant to the problem.

0: The answer may or may not have included relevant facts, formulas, or figures, but demonstrates little or no clear understanding of how to apply them or approach the problem.

Figure 2: Rubric for homework problems

ensure that the time-consuming full written feedback only occurs once, the more coarse-grained rubric ensures that the professor's workload is not nearly doubled. If anything, it may be somewhat lighter.

3. COOPERATIVE LEARNING

The other main thrust of our effort to improve students' engagement with homework assignments was to promote cooperative learning.

We had long been encouraging students to study together and discuss their assignments in order to improve their understanding and leverage their various strengths. However, their actual written work was expected to be done individually. This requirement had two somewhat negative effects. First, it discouraged the collaboration that we wished to promote, because students leery of cheating would prefer to avoid both the temptation and the appearance of working too closely with other students. Second, when students did collaborate, the requirement that they write up the work separately increased the grading load substantially, with limited benefit. Students working in a group would inevitably have similar problems with their answers, and so the grading would involve tediously writing out similar comments multiple times. While we believe that there was some benefit to requiring each student to compose their own answers, it's not entirely clear how large that benefit was, or whether it was worth the cost.

Thus, in conjunction with the policy changes discussed in the previous section, we decided to declare all homework assignments to officially be group work without restriction: students were permitted to work in groups of their own choosing, and all contributors would write their names at the top of the submission. In addition to solving or mitigating the problems described above, we hoped that this policy would work well in combination with the revision cycle to get students talking about the problems more than once and re-engaging with the concepts.

Such a policy is not without its potential problems, of course. Chief among them is the "free rider" problem: that without any rules or controls on the permissible level of collaboration, one or more students could receive credit for an assignment without having contributed to it substantially (or at all). In the extreme, one could imagine a single student doing the work for an entire group. A related worry was that the members of a group would split the work, each member separately doing one problem, but all receiving credit for all the problems. Before extending this policy to other courses, we very much wanted to see whether these problems would manifest in practice.

4. RESULTS

4.1 Early reactions

The early student reaction mostly focused on the group aspect and was fairly positive, although several students worried that there must be some sort of "catch". One asked if it would be within the rules for the entire section (about twenty students) to put their names on a single handin—which it was, although the logistical problems this would present for the students left us unconcerned that it would be a problem. In practice none of the groups that formed had more than five students.

Question	Response					Avg
	1	2	3	4	5	
Q1 Liked group work	0	0	2	3	8	4.46
Q2 Group work effective	0	0	5	2	6	4.08
Q3 Comment/revision effective	0	1	1	3	8	4.38

Table 1: Student responses to homework assignment format. (For text of survey questions and responses, see Appendix A.)

Anecdotal observation as the course progressed reassured us that our worst worries about the group work would not manifest. One group threatened to kick out a student unless that student began contributing, and in general it seemed that the students' attitude was to resent any freeloaders.

Another observation, also anecdotal, suggested that our willingness to *not* impose too much structure on the collaboration may have paid off in an unexpected way. One group developed a general workflow whereby they split up the problems and wrote them up separately for the initial handin; but then after receiving comments they met together to do the revision. They found it effective to have their "expert" on a problem explain it to the others as they read the instructor feedback and together worked out a revision. If we had imposed a structure on the cooperative aspect of the homework, this would not have been it; the students were able to make good use of their freedom to find a learning strategy that suited them.

4.2 Student response

At the end of the course, we asked the students to fill out a short survey about their experience. Out of 21 students who completed the course, $N = 13$ responded to the survey. Table 1 shows their responses to the homework policy: both changes met with overall student approval. The shift to group work was certainly popular (eight of the thirteen "really liked" this policy), but also seemed to them to improve their understanding: most respondents rated it as more effective at teaching the concepts in the course.

The effectiveness response was even stronger for the comment/revision policy: eleven of the thirteen responded that the revision opportunity made the homeworks more effective than a traditional homework format. In a free-response comment section of the survey, one student specifically observed that it "gave more motivation to actually read comments, and having the opportunity to address them definitely helped concepts sink in."

4.3 Outcomes

The size of the class ($N = 21$) was too small to draw any strong conclusions from the correlation of homework grades to exam grades, but we felt able to at least dispel the concerns about the "free rider" problem. Figure 3 on the next page shows a plot of the students' exam scores against their homework scores; the Pearson correlation coefficient of these scores is 0.66, a similar coefficient to those in this professor's other courses. More importantly, the distribution lacks any serious outliers, and the high-homework-low-exam quadrant is conspicuously empty. There appear not to have been any students who regularly attached their name to the group assignments without learning the material well enough to perform roughly as well on the exam as their group-mates.

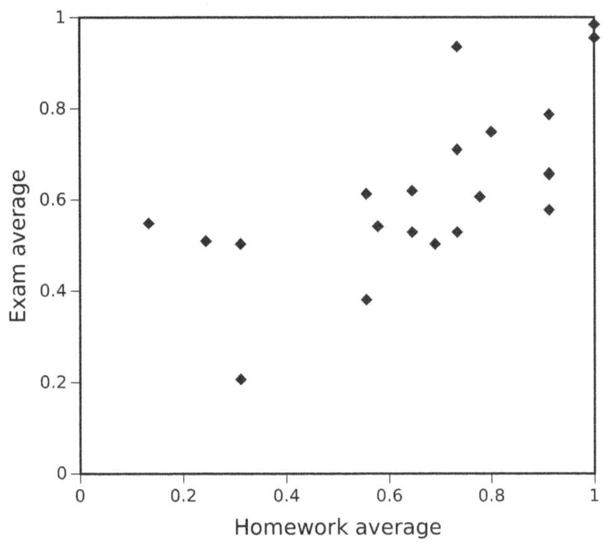

Figure 3: Comparison of homework and exam scores

The data shown here do not rule out the possibility that a student could join a group and passively absorb content without doing their fair share of work for the group, or that a student's pre-existing understanding coincidentally matches the products of the group they attach their name to. Neither possibility is a problem from a credentialing perspective, as long as the scores match, although they may be worth fixing for other reasons.

Another measure of the homeworks is particularly encouraging: Table 2 shows how the students responded to each revision opportunity. The table counts every problem that was handed in (once per group per problem), and tracks what that group subsequently did. Students were told that if they did not hand in a revision, their original grade (which was unknown to them) would stand. In just a few cases, a student or group decided not to revise their work, but in the vast majority of cases, at least minor revisions were made and handed in for the final grading.

About half of the 3s were improved to 5s, representing a substantial improvement. Most of the 0s were improved to 3s or even 5s as part of the revision. Students who did not hand in a problem are not counted here, so a zero in this table represents an actual attempt that was too incorrect to award even partial credit. Furthermore, this tactic engaged even the best students (those who were able to achieve a 5 on the first try); in general they performed minor revisions, but their second versions were more polished and often more thoughtful. At all levels, students made use of the revision cycle as an opportunity to pursue additional mastery of the topics.

5. CONCLUSIONS

Overall, the experience was definitely a success, and we are already using the new policies in other courses.

The students were nearly unanimous that this system is at least as good as a traditional homework model, with most finding it to be an improvement. The measurable outcomes do not contradict their assessment.

To the instructor (or grader) of a course, the policies decrease the overall grading load for a particular assignment. In addition, on a more subjective level, by decoupling the commenting from the grading, both aspects become somewhat easier. Knowing that the students are more likely to read the comments also helps.

The system did introduce a minor logistical weakness: with only one copy of a homework for multiple people, only one person can be the custodian of the handed-back work. This was a minor problem for studying at exam time, especially as the work groups were not the same on every assignment. Photocopies were an adequate if somewhat ham-handed solution to the problem, although in the future a move to electronic submission and feedback should solve the difficulty more completely.

The kinds of high-level algorithm and data structure problems used in a course on artificial intelligence seemed to be an especially good fit for an assignment structure that encouraged working with other students and making use of instructor feedback. We look forward to testing their effectiveness in a variety of other computer science courses, and to collecting more student response data in order to draw stronger conclusions about the policies.

Original score:	0	3	5
Count:	26	45	25

Original score	Revision score none	0	3	5
5	2			23
3	0		21	24
0	3	6	11	6

Final score:	0	3	5
Count:	9	32	55

Table 2: Frequency of scores on original submission and on revision

6. REFERENCES

[1] C. A. Higgins and B. Bligh. Formative computer based assessment in diagram based domains. In *Proceedings of the 11th Annual Conference on Innovation and Technology in Computer Science Education*, Bologna, 2006.

[2] A. Kyrilov and D. C. Noelle. Automatic formative assessment of exercises on knowledge representation in first-order logic. In *Proceedings of the 18th Annual Conference on Innovation and Technology in Computer Science Education*, Canterbury, 2013.

[3] T. S. Roberts. The use of multiple choice tests for formative and summative assessment. In *Proceedings of the Eighth Australasian Computing Education Conference (ACE2006)*, Hobart, 2006.

[4] D. R. Sadler. Evaluation and the improvement of academic learning. *The Journal of Higher Education*, 54(1):60–79, Jan–Feb 1983.

[5] L. A. Shepard. Formative assessment: caveat emptor. In *The future of assessment: shaping teaching and learning, ETS invitational conference 2005*, New York, 2005.

[6] A. Solomon. Linuxgym—software to automate

formative assessment of unix command-line and scripting skills. In *Proceedings of the 12th Annual Conference on Innovation and Technology in Computer Science Education*, Dundee, 2007.

APPENDIX

A. TEXT OF SURVEY QUESTIONS

Q1. Did you like or dislike having the ability to work with (and receive the same grade as) a group of people on the homeworks?

Choices for Q1: Really disliked / Somewhat disliked / Neither liked nor disliked / Somewhat liked / Really liked

Q2. Compared to a traditional do-it-on-your-own format, did you find that the group format for homeworks made them more effective or less effective at teaching you the concepts?

Q3. This term I introduced a homework format where I first wrote comments (but didn't tell you the grade), then permitted a revision, then assigned a grade (but didn't provide further comments). Compared to homeworks where comments and grade are both given at the same time (and no revisions allowed), was this course's homework format more effective or less effective at teaching you the concepts?

Choices for Q2 and Q3: Much less effective / Somewhat less effective / About the same / Somewhat more effective / Much more effective

Evaluating an Inverted CS1

Jennifer Campbell
Dept. of Computer Science
University of Toronto
campbell@cs.toronto.edu

Diane Horton
Dept. of Computer Science
University of Toronto
dianeh@cs.toronto.edu

Michelle Craig
Dept. of Computer Science
University of Toronto
mcraig@cs.toronto.edu

Paul Gries
Dept. of Computer Science
University of Toronto
pgries@cs.toronto.edu

ABSTRACT

This case study explores an inverted classroom offering of an introductory programming course (CS1). Students prepared for lecture by watching short lecture videos and completing required in-video quiz questions. During lecture, the students worked through exercises with the support of the instructor and teaching assistants. We describe the course implementation and its assessment, including pre- and post-course surveys. We also discuss lessons learned, modifications that we plan to make for the next offering, and recommendations for others teaching inverted courses.

Categories and Subject Descriptors

K.3.2 [**Computers and Education**]: Computer and Information Science Education—*Computer Science Education*

Keywords

inverted classroom; flipped classroom; CS1; novice programming; case study

1. INTRODUCTION

We report on our experience inverting a high-enrolment 12-week introductory programming course (CS1), where students prepared for lecture by watching videos developed by the course instructors, including in-video quizzes, which have been shown to improve both student focus and retention of course material [14].

The inverted classroom approach [8], also known as the flipped classroom, was created to reach students with diverse learning styles. Course material is delivered prior to class through a variety of resources such as online videos and textbooks. In the classroom, students do hands-on activities that have them apply the material.

The inverted classroom has been shown to be popular with students, as well as improve their learning [5, 4, 11, 10, 3].

SIGCSE'14, March 3–8, 2014, Atlanta, GA, USA.

http://dx.doi.org/10.1145/2538862.2538943.

In this case study, we explore student performance, enthusiasm for the course, interest in pursuing a computer science (CS) program, perceived difficulty of the course, time spent on the course, and enjoyment of the course. We investigated each of these outcomes within several subgroups of the student population, according to gender, prior programming experience, whether they were taking the course as part of a CS program, English language proficiency, commute time, course load, and time commitments outside of university.

Others have studied the use and production of online lectures [6, 13, 9, 12, 10]. We also report on our experience producing the materials for this course.

2. THE INVERTED COURSE

This CS1 course, offered at a research-intensive North American public university, uses the Python programming language and takes an objects-early classes-late approach. In winter 2013, the course was taught in an inverted style with three lecture sections and an initial enrolment of 570 students. The course was taught by two of the authors, experienced faculty who have each taught CS1 numerous times.

Traditionally, this course has three hours of lecture and a two-hour lab each week. For three quarters of the inverted semester, only two hours of lecture were held, along with the usual two-hour lab. This reduction in lecture hours was intended to free up students' time so that they could complete the required preparatory work before attending lecture.

Coursework also included four small auto-graded programming exercises, two larger programming assignments, a 50-minute midterm test, and a 3-hour final exam. Students were encouraged to work in pairs in the lab and on the assignments. Exercises were done alone.

2.1 Inverted Course Materials

The inverted course materials included seventy-five 5–15 minute videos, in-video quiz questions that popped up every few minutes and exercised the basic concepts introduced during the video, HTML lecture summaries (for student reference), and weekly practice exercises. The two course instructors each created roughly half of the videos. The videos were recorded in a recording studio and are screencast-style, where the instructor programs "live" during the video, demonstrating the result of executing code in the Python shell and running Python programs. The videos were also annotated with important terminology and concepts.

Name	Exact Question
Enthusiasm	How enthusiastic are you about CSC108?
Interest	How interested are you in pursuing a CS program (specialist, major or minor)?
Difficulty	How difficult is this course compared to other university courses you have taken?
Time	How much time did you spend on this course compared to other university courses you have taken?
Enjoyment	How much did you enjoy this course compared to other university courses you have taken?
More	Would you like the university to offer more of its courses in this format, with some material presented online and more active learning in lectures?

Table 1: Wording for each of the key outcome questions on the post-course survey.

The number of in-video quiz questions per week ranged from 5 to 24, with 14.5 questions on average. The weekly practice exercises each had about 15 multiple-choice and short-answer questions. Both the quiz questions and practice exercises were created by the instructors with help from a teaching assistant (TA). The lecture summary for each video gave an overview of important new concepts, such as definitions and the general form of Python statements, and a brief outline of the video content.

All of these materials were hosted on Coursera, a major Massive Open Online Course (MOOC) platform, and used as part of two MOOCs that each had tens of thousands of participants. Coursera also hosted a separate closed course with these materials that was accessible only to our CS1 students. Both the in-video quiz questions and the weekly practice exercises were auto-graded immediately upon submission. Students could submit as many times as they wished.

2.2 Course Delivery

The first week was taught in a traditional manner because the students could not be expected to prepare ahead of time for lecture. In weeks 2–12, students were assigned preparatory work to complete in advance of that week's lectures: they were asked to watch approximately 1 hour of lecture videos and complete the corresponding in-video quiz questions. A small fraction of the course grade (5.5%) was allocated for lecture preparation; students earned 0.5% each week for attempting all of the in-video quiz questions. The weekly practice exercises were not for course credit.

Because most of the content of the traditional lectures was shifted to the preparatory lecture videos, during lecture the students engaged in active learning activities that applied the concepts covered in the videos. At the start of lecture, the instructors distributed worksheets containing a set of exercises. Several different exercise formats were used during the course, including multiple choice, short answer, code tracing, memory model, and code writing questions. The majority of these exercises involved writing code. So that they would not program by trial and error, students were encouraged to work on paper, and most did.

Students first worked solo on each exercise and were frequently asked to discuss their answers with each other. In addition to the instructor, there were 1–2 TAs in attendance at each lecture. While the students worked on the exercises, the instructor and TAs circulated to observe students and to offer assistance. Once the majority of students had attempted the exercise, the instructor led the class through the problem solving steps and sample solutions, encouraging students to share their approaches with the class.

The instructors occasionally used the web-based Python Classroom Response System (PCRS) [15] to pose programming questions from the worksheets. Students who brought an internet-enabled device (typically a laptop or tablet) could submit their work electronically, and the system ran a set of test cases against their submissions to check for correctness. This allowed the instructors to view the set of student responses and show the class correct answers, as well as incorrect answers to demonstrate common errors.

Because the worksheets were not for credit, they were not collected, and students could keep them as part of their lecture notes. Students who missed lecture could visit their instructor to pick up the missed worksheets, but the worksheets were not posted online. No solutions were provided, although students were repeatedly encouraged to review the exercises with instructors during office hours.

3. EVALUATION OF THE COURSE

We were interested in the effectiveness of the inverted classroom offering in general, and also in the experience of students from different demographics. For instance, would students with long commutes enjoy it more because they could watch videos at home and attend class only when they felt it was necessary? We administered pre- and post-course surveys during the second and final weeks of the semester. The students whose data is reported here gave informed consent to the inclusion of their data in the study. 351 students completed the pre-course survey and 132 students completed the post-course survey, which is 62% and 30% of the students enrolled in the course at those times. 131 students completed both surveys. Surveys were done on paper during lecture and conducted by a faculty member who was not teaching the course.

The pre-course survey included questions about student enthusiasm for the course, interest in pursuing a CS program[1], gender, proficiency in English, commute time, course load, time commitments for activities and responsibilities outside of school, whether they had prior programming experience, and why they took the course.

The post-course survey re-asked the questions about students' enthusiasm for the course and interest in a CS program, and asked other questions comparing the course to others on several dimensions (see Table 1).

In addition to the surveys, lecture attendance was counted weekly, enrolment was tracked throughout the course, and the University's standard course evaluations were collected.

Anticipating the change we were about to make, we collected the same data during a traditional offering of this course in the previous semester. In this paper, we will occasionally use that traditional offering as a baseline for com-

[1]At our institution, a "program" refers to either a *minor* (which prescribes 20% of a 4-year degree), a *major* (40%), or a *specialist* (60%).

parison, however formal extensive comparison of the two offerings is problematic. The traditional offering was held in a fall semester while the inverted was in winter. Because the fall semester is the natural time to take the course for incoming students who intend to pursue a CS major, the two populations are likely to be very different. Indeed, we found statistically significant differences on several dimensions. To minimize such differences, we are conducting ongoing research that compares the traditional and inverted offerings of CS1 in two fall semesters.

3.1 Student Population

This CS1 course is taken by students pursuing a CS program, by students completing a requirement for a non-CS program, and by students taking an elective. The inverted offering took place during a semester in which 76% of the students were not planning to pursue a CS program.

Although no programming experience is required, many students do have some (not necessarily with Python). This semester, 62% reported having no prior experience. The remaining students reported having prior experience ranging from some self-guided learning to completion of one or more high school courses to previous attempts at this course.

Atypical of most CS courses [1], this offering included 53% females and 47% males. As mentioned earlier, we also collected data about students' course load, time commitments outside of school, commute time and fluency in English. This allows us to examine whether any subgroups fare better or report a different experience in the course.

4. RESULTS

4.1 Low Lecture Attendance

On average, only 57% of students in the inverted course attended lecture, as compared to 74% of the students taking CS1 as a traditional course in the previous semester. Not only did fewer students attend lecture in the inverted offering, they stopped attending earlier in the semester. Between weeks one and three, attendance in the inverted course dropped by 20%, but in the traditional course it dropped by only 8%. Figure 1 shows the percentage of enrolled students attending lecture each week. In each semester, the midterm exam took place during week seven, which accounts for the large increase in attendance that week.

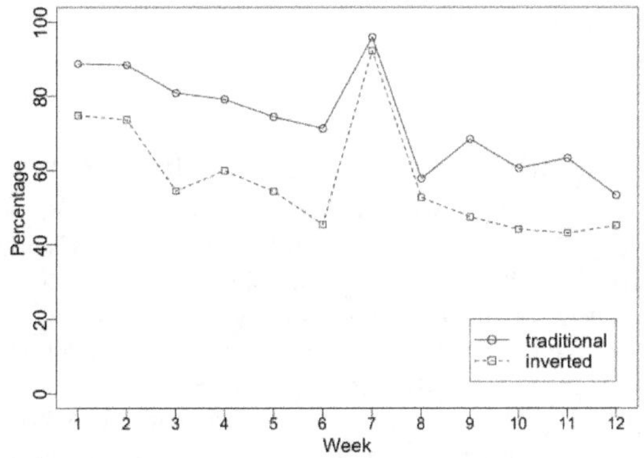

Figure 1: Weekly Lecture Attendance

Although low lecture attendance can be discouraging for the instructor, it is not necessarily bad for students. Ideally, the students who stop attending are those with prior programming experience or a strong grasp of the material, leaving only those who need the additional instruction. This would result in a classroom where students have a more similar level of understanding. In addition, with fewer students in lecture, the ones who do attend can get more help and feedback from the course staff.

We are concerned, though, that some students who choose not to attend really should. Although the concepts may seem clear from the videos, students may find that they struggle when the time comes to apply the concepts on their own. Section 5.3 discusses strategies to improve attendance.

4.2 High Completion of Lecture Preparation

Each week, credit was given for attempting all of the in-video quiz questions on time. For the students who completed the course, the average mark for all preparatory work was 81%. Interestingly, on average, far more students completed the preparatory work than attended lecture. The difference may be because credit was given for preparatory work but not for lecture attendance or in-class exercises.

4.3 Lecture and Online Material Helpfulness

Students in the inverted course found attending lectures to be helpful, but not as helpful as students in the comparable traditional course. As shown in Figure 2, only 74% of students in the inverted course found attending lectures to help either "quite a bit" or "a great deal", compared to 84% of those in the traditional course. A Wilcoxon rank-sum test confirms that these distributions are indeed significantly different ($p<.0001$).

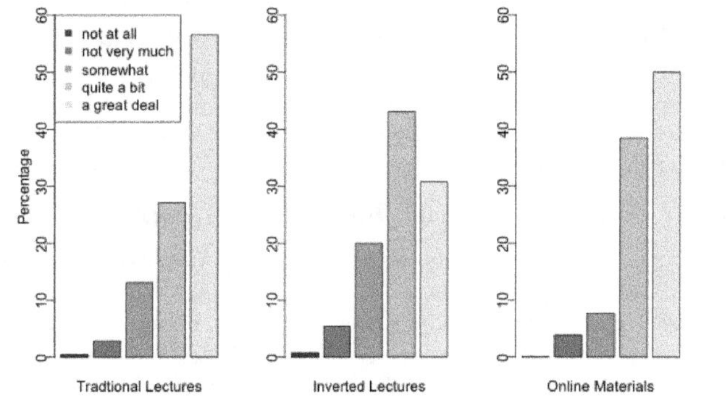

Figure 2: Helpfulness of Lectures

On the other hand, 88% of the students in the inverted section found the online course materials to help either "quite a bit" or "a great deal". There is no statistically significant difference between the helpfulness of the online course materials and the traditional lectures. The availability of online materials may have contributed to the decrease in the perceived helpfulness of lectures. This likely contributed to the decreased lecture attendance as well.

On the course evaluations for the inverted section, only one student made a negative comment about the value of attending lecture: "I attended almost every class until the midterm and then started skipping quite a few, however, I don't feel like that affected how much I learnt in the course!"

On the contrary, there were several positive comments about attending lectures, such as: "The lectures were well worth going to, and I attended every single one, which is more than I can say for any other class I've taken."

Interestingly, students reported using the online lectures for purposes beyond lecture preparation. For example, they used them either quite a bit (27%) or a great deal (40%) to prepare for the final exam, and even more reported that they used the online lectures to go over things they needed to know for the assignments.

4.4 Enthusiasm for CS1 Increased

We asked the *Enthusiasm* question from Table 1 in both the pre- and post-course surveys. Overall, students' enthusiasm for the course increased over the semester. Figure 3 shows the responses for those students who completed both surveys. A Wilcoxon rank-sum test indicates that the distributions are significantly different (p=.023).

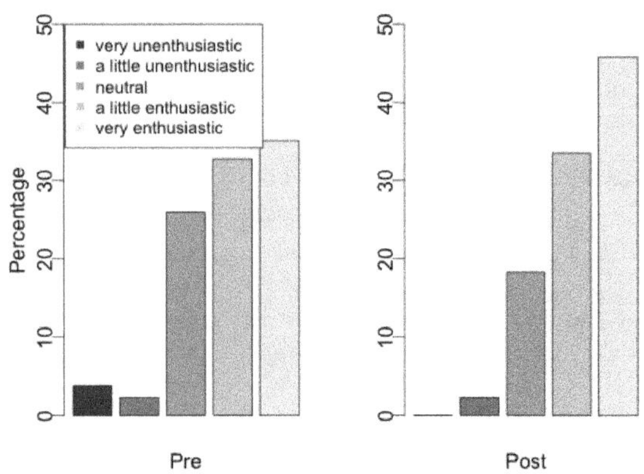

Figure 3: Pre- and Post-Course Enthusiasm

The *Interest* question was also included on both surveys. There was no significant change in interest in a CS program over the semester.

4.5 Enjoyed More Than Other Courses

Most students reported enjoying the course more than their other classes (Figure 4). To investigate whether some subgroups reported higher enjoyment than others, we examined the correlation between *Enjoyment* and each of the 9 explanatory variables (gender, commute time, etc.). We applied a Bonferroni correction to our original alpha of 0.05, and set our alpha to 0.0056. We found that only initial *Interest* (r=.29), initial *Enthusiasm* (r=.3) had significant correlations with *Enjoyment*. Whether or not the student was taking the course as a CS program requirement was mildly correlated (r=.21, p=.01) but below our corrected cut-off for significance. There was no practical correlation with the other explanatory variables.

4.6 Same Difficulty, More Time

On average, students found the inverted course about the same in difficulty as other courses, but 55% of the students reported spending more time on this course than their others. The full distribution of answers is shown in Figure 5.

We were surprised to discover that the only explanatory variable to correlate with *Difficulty* (r=.30) or with *Time* (r=0.25) was gender. Women found the course more difficult

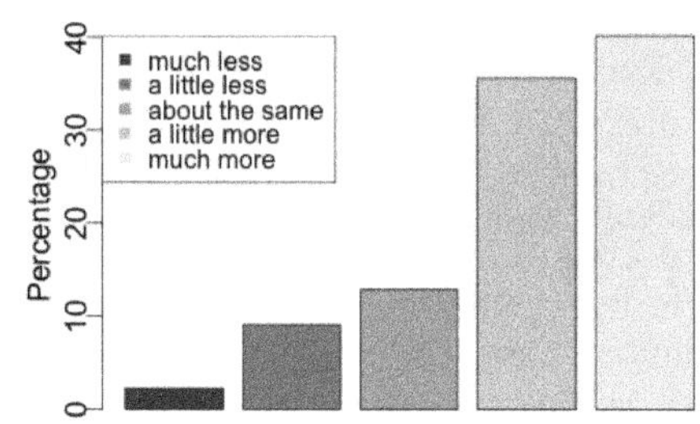

Figure 4: Enjoyment of This vs Other Courses

and spent more time on it than men. More surprising, prior experience was not correlated with difficulty or time spent on the course.

For the previous traditional offering, prior experience and difficulty were moderately but statistically significantly correlated (r=−.29, $p < 0.001$). The traditional offering also showed correlation between prior experience and time spent on the course (r=−0.28, $p < 0.001$). It might be tempting to conclude that this difference was due to the inverted nature of the course, but it is also possible that the nature of prior experience differs between the semesters. The traditional course was offered in the fall semester, when many more students are taking the course with the intention of pursuing a CS program. In our experience, their prior programming experience tends to be stronger than that of students in the winter semester.

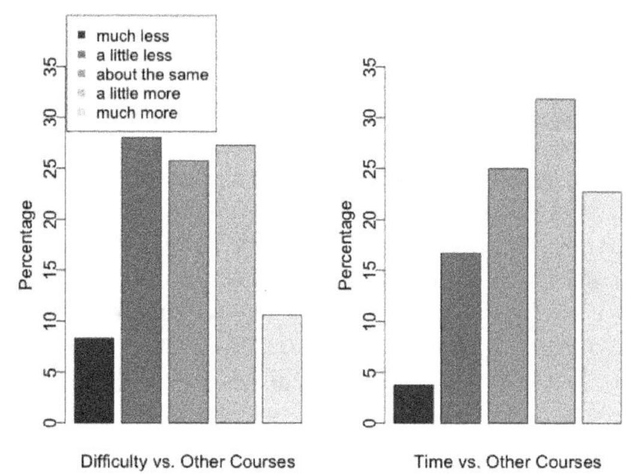

Figure 5: Relative Difficulty and Time Spent

4.7 Typical Drop, Pass and Failure Rates

Drop rates for CS1 are notoriously high [7] and this course is no exception. The drop rate for the inverted offering was approximately 25%. This is on par with recent offerings of the course during this particular semester of the year (a semester in which most students are non-CS), which had drop rates of 27% in 2012 and 28% in 2011.

For the inverted offering, 86% of the students who wrote the final exam passed the course. This pass rate is similar to those of the traditional offerings from the semester prior (89%) and from the same semester during the previous year (85%).

4.8 Comparable Performance

Did the students learn as well from the inverted offering as they would have in a traditional classroom? Acknowledging the threats to validity caused by the different student populations, we still attempted to do some performance evaluation by including extremely similar versions of three questions on the final exam in both offerings of the course. A t-test does not show a significant difference (p=0.103) in the mean grades of the two offerings.

We also wondered if the inverted delivery benefited some students more than others in terms of performance. To test for this we checked the correlation of final course grades and final exam grades with each explanatory variable. We found a small positive correlation in both cases with initial enthusiasm and a small negative correlation with external time commitments, but virtually no correlation with the other explanatory variables.

It is particularly noteworthy that performance did not correlate with prior experience or initial intention to pursue a CS program. In other words, students performed equally well in this inverted CS1 regardless of their prior experience and their interest in pursuing a CS program. We suspect that this at least partly explained by the low lecture attendance. Experienced students may have been overconfident and skipped lectures that they should have attended.

4.9 More Inverted

Perhaps the best summary of how our students received this inverted CS1 is whether they would like more inverted courses (see figure 6). 77% answered either "quite a bit" or "a great deal", and only 3% answered negatively. Since the survey was given in class, selection bias is a serious concern. We therefore looked to the university's course evaluations, done online and out of class, for corroboration. Roughly half of the comments on the course evaluations were about the inverted experience and the vast majority were positive.

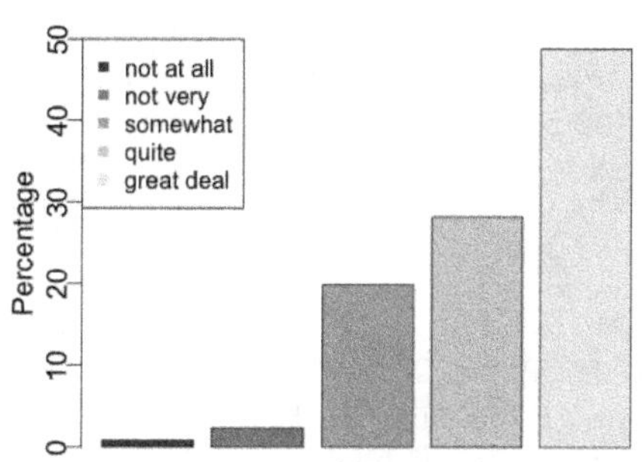

Figure 6: Would Like More Inverted

4.10 Threats to Validity

In addition to the challenges of comparing the very different populations of the fall (traditional) and winter (inverted) offerings of the course, another threat to validity stems from the fact that the surveys were delivered during lecture. In particular, many results reported here are for only students completing both surveys, and this includes only those who attended class on the final survey day in the last week of the semester. Questions regarding the helpfulness of lectures could be particularly influenced by this population bias.

5. LESSONS LEARNED

5.1 Resources

Development costs for the inverted materials are very high. Although the amount of time varied, the instructors estimate that it took approximately 8 hours to prepare a 10 minute video, including writing the script and the Python code, recording, and editing. The estimated total time spent preparing videos for this course is 600 hours. Videos for 7 of 12 weeks were created before the semester started. Recording all videos during the semester would have been infeasible and it would have been better to have them all prepared in advance. Development of 32 worksheets of in-class exercises took about 130 hours.

In addition, extra resources are required to run the course. To facilitate the in-class exercises, TAs attended lecture at a ratio of roughly 1:100 enrolled students. In practice, with low lecture attendance, the ratios were much better. The TA presence was valuable and we consider it be critical to the student experience and to the successful use of the inverted model in large classes.

In most weeks of the inverted course, the number of lecture hours was reduced from three to two. After the semester finished, we decided to revert to three for future offerings because it took longer than anticipated to work through the in-class exercises; the instructors often felt short on time.[2]

5.2 Lecture Delivery

Lectures involved solving in-class exercises without any formal review of the material covered in the video lectures. The first exercises were often multiple choice questions designed to address common misunderstandings and to provide an opportunity to quickly revisit several topics from the video lectures. Still, students sometimes had difficulty getting started on the in-class exercises. We feel that beginning each lecture with a worked example that recaps key concepts from the video lectures would be beneficial.

A major benefit of in-class exercises is that the instructors were able to observe common errors and misconceptions, and then address them immediately using just-in-time teaching to the entire class. For this process to work, there must be sufficient time for both the exercises and the resulting discussion. As previously mentioned, we will be increasing the number of lecture hours to facilitate this.

We variously encouraged students to work on the in-class exercises alone, in pairs, and in small groups. At times, we promoted a think-pair-share approach, but some students resisted working with others. We plan to continue encouraging both solo and group work, and we may incorporate Peer Instruction [2].

We plan to continue to use paper worksheets. Having the students complete the in-class exercises on paper helped prepare them to write the midterm and final exams, which are on paper, and also prevented programming by trial and error. One student commented that "... using pen and paper for [the worksheets] especially helped, as it meant I could

[2]In the fall 2013 offering, to save TA resources and to reduce the time commitments for students, the required 2-hour labs were replaced with online exercises. There were extensive TA office hours for students who wanted help with these exercises. This change freed up TA time for attending lectures and allowed the inverted course to be offered using the same number of TA hours as a traditional course.

step through the code in my head and get a better understanding of how it worked." The instructors noticed that, when they gave students the opportunity to submit their code to the PCRS, some students with laptops and tablets continued to work on paper. Only a small fraction of the class submitted their solutions to the PCRS.

5.3 Marking Scheme and Attendance

Completing the in-video quizzes was worth 5.5% of the course grade, but credit was not given for attending lecture or for the in-class exercises. There was a relatively high completion rate for the preparatory work but low lecture attendance. We may be able to boost attendance by giving credit for attendance, however, we are concerned that requiring attendance might lead to a negative lecture environment. Given our students' wide range of programming experience, novices might feel intimidated and more experienced students might resent being required to attend.

Giving credit for in-class exercises would also require more TA resources to evaluate that work, which is not possible within our current budget. One trade-off could be to evaluate the in-class exercises instead of the assignment on the same topic. This approach was used in the inverted portion of a third-year databases course at our institution and was considered unsuccessful. While 80% of the students did at least some work on the assignment, those who did none, on average, failed the corresponding exam question. The approach was also negatively received by some students.

To address the low attendance, the instructors of the next inverted offering assigned a weekly homework exercise (in place of the required labs). We hoped that the exercises, by providing timely feedback on their understanding of the material, would help students make a wise decision about attending class. Instructors should clearly indicate to struggling students (through email and online announcements) that lecture attendance is key for their understanding of the material.

6. CONCLUSION AND FUTURE PLANS

We felt that this inverted CS1 was successful enough that we offered it again in fall 2013, with the improvements noted above.

The initial development of the course consumed a huge amount of resources but much of this material can be reused with only minor changes. With the reduction of mandatory closed lab hours, we were able to offer the inverted course within our traditional TA budget. We expect that faculty can continue to update materials and deliver the course in roughly the same amount of time as required by the traditional delivery.

The biggest challenge to rigorously studying the effects of inverting the class was the substantial difference between the fall and winter student populations. As a result, we ran the same surveys in the inverted fall 2013 course, so we now can compare traditional and inverted instruction with similar populations. Among other questions, we will examine whether the routine of preparation and supported practise used in our inverted approach yields improved outcomes, in particular for inexperienced programmers. While we believe enough in our inverted approach to continue using it, we cannot yet recommend that others make the investment required to adopt it.

7. REFERENCES

[1] Computing Research Association Taulbee Survey. Retrieved September 3, 2013 from http://cra.org/resources/taulbee/.

[2] C. H. Crouch and E. Mazur. Peer instruction: Ten years of experience and results. *American Journal of Physics*, 69(9):970, 2001.

[3] J. A. Day and J. D. Foley. Evaluating a web lecture intervention in a human-computer interaction course. *IEEE Transactions on Education*, 49(4):420–431, 2006.

[4] G. C. Gannod, J. E. Burge, and M. T. Helmick. Using the inverted classroom to teach software engineering. In *Proceedings of the 30th international conference on Software engineering*, pages 777–786, 2008.

[5] M. J. Herold, T. D. Lynch, R. Ramnath, and J. Ramanathan. Student and instructor experiences in the inverted classroom. In *2012 Frontiers in Education Conference Proceedings*, pages 1–6, 2012.

[6] S. Kellogg. Developing online materials to facilitate an inverted classroom approach. In *Frontiers in Education Conference, 2009. FIE'09. 39th IEEE*, pages 1–6, 2009.

[7] P. Kinnunen and L. Malmi. Why students drop out CS1 course? In *Proceedings of the second international workshop on Computing education research*, pages 97–108, 2006.

[8] M. J. Lage, G. J. Platt, and M. Treglia. Inverting the classroom: A gateway to creating an inclusive learning environment. *The Journal of Economic Education*, 31(1):30–43, Jan. 2000.

[9] C. C. Lewis and H. Abdul-Hamid. Implementing effective online teaching practices: Voices of exemplary faculty. *Innovative Higher Education*, 31(2), May 2006.

[10] K. Lockwood and R. Esselstein. The inverted classroom and the CS curriculum. In *Proceeding of the 44th ACM technical symposium on Computer science education*, SIGCSE '13, pages 113–118, 2013.

[11] G. S. Mason, T. R. Shuman, and K. E. Cook. Comparing the effectiveness of an inverted classroom to a traditional classroom in an upper-division engineering course. *IEEE Transactions on Education*, pages 1–1, 2013.

[12] H. R. Sadaghiani. Online prelectures: An alternative to textbook reading assignments. *The Physics Teacher*, 50(5):301, 2012.

[13] T. Stelzer, G. Gladding, J. P. Mestre, and D. T. Brookes. Comparing the efficacy of multimedia modules with traditional textbooks for learning introductory physics content. *American Journal of Physics*, 77:184, 2009.

[14] K. K. Szpunar, N. Y. Khan, and D. L. Schacter. Interpolated memory tests reduce mind wandering and improve learning of online lectures. *Proceedings of the National Academy of Sciences*, 110(16):6313–6317, Apr. 2013.

[15] D. Zingaro, Y. Cherenkova, O. Karpova, and A. Petersen. Facilitating code-writing in PI classes. In *Proceeding of the 44th ACM Technical Symposium on Computer Science Education*, SIGCSE '13, pages 585–590, 2013.

Supporting CS Education via Virtualization and Packages

Tools for Successfully Accommodating "Bring-Your-Own-Device" at Scale

Andy Sayler, Dirk Grunwald, John Black, Elizabeth White, and Matthew Monaco
University of Colorado
Boulder, CO, USA
<first>.<last>@colorado.edu

ABSTRACT

Higher education is facing a paradigm shift in the ownership and use of computer hardware. The school computer lab is no longer the primary place of student computer use. Instead, students increasingly expect to use their own hardware to complete their school assignments. This creates a challenge for computer science educators: we must now support a wide range of heterogeneous hardware without the benefits of tight control over its use. To address this "Bring-Your-Own-Device" (BYOD) challenge, we leverage virtualization and software packaging systems to gracefully deploy and support a standardized development environment for all core CS courses across a range of both school-owned and student-owned computing devices. We have deployed and evaluated our system for the previous two years at scale and continue to actively use and develop it. It has effectively helped us support multiple classes comprising hundreds of students with very limited IT staffing. We describe the design and management of our system, present our experience using our system, and discuss the lessons we've learned. We also provide data reflecting current student user experience with our system. Our system has proven very effective in addressing the student BYOD challenge in a manageable, cost-efficient, and easy-to-use manner.

Categories and Subject Descriptors

K.3.2 [**Computers and Education**]: Computer and Information Science Education

General Terms

Management, Economics, Human Factors

Keywords

BYOD, Virtual Machines, Education, Development Environment, Package Management, Tools, Best Practices

SIGCSE'14, March 5–8, 2014, Atlanta, GA, USA.

ACM 978-1-4503-2605-6/14/03 ...$15.00.
http://dx.doi.org/10.1145/2538862.2538928.

1. INTRODUCTION

BYOD (Bring Your Own Device) has quickly become the buzzword du jour in many IT circles. The term refers to the increasing prevalence of employee-owned hardware in traditionally corporate-owned IT settings. Higher education is not immune to this trend. Increasingly, students show up to college with their own laptops and expect to complete all of their required assignments on these machines. We have observed many recent students graduating without ever having entered a school-owned computer lab or worked on a school-owned computer. This creates a challenge for educators and the IT departments that support them: how do we ensure that students can successfully complete assignments on their own machines? How can we guarantee a good experience doing so? And how can we achieve both of these objectives while adhering to budgetary limits, without prohibitive increases in support staff hours and overhead?

In computer science, the issue is exacerbated by the predominance of unfamiliar (at least to incoming students) applications and operating systems. Like many universities, our institution primarily uses a UNIX-derived development environment (GNU/Linux). While a Linux development environment has many advantages (discussed below), the fact that most students arrive without Linux installed on their computers poses a significant challenge. It is a non-trivial task to ensure students can run Linux, complete with a preconfigured suite of versioned compilers, debuggers, and editors to ensure uniform results across student, instructor, and grader machines, on their own hardware.

The problem could likely be solved with sufficient human resources: if we paired each student with an experienced CS practitioner to help them setup a dual-boot, properly-configured development environment on their machine, we could likely deploy and support a uniform environment across a range of hardware; this is in fact the method traditionally used in many educational computing environments. But in the age of shrinking budgets, growing teaching loads, and a push toward MOOC courses that can scale to thousands and tens of thousands of students, such a brute force approach is simply not feasible in most situations.

Instead, we have leveraged existing off-the-shelf virtualization and software management systems to create a common virtual machine that is used across all of our core computer science courses. This system allows us to provide students with an easily deployable solution that allows them to complete all of their CS work on their own machines without forcing them to significantly modify their existing setups. Our approach has allowed us to support over eight-hundred undergraduate students, many with little to no prior CS experience, for the cost of a single part-time graduate student appointment. The primary contributions of this paper are twofold: We demonstrate how VMs can be deployed *en masse* with minimal staffing to provide a single standardized department-wide development environment across both VM and lab machines. We also show how using centralized software management tools can simplify and streamline the distribution and maintenance of such a common development environment.

2. USING VIRTUAL MACHINES

Leveraging virtualization technology to provide a uniform development environment in an educational setting is not a new idea. At our institution, for example, individual faculty have used virtual machines (VMs) in classes for ≈ 7 years. For example, VMs have long proven useful in computer security courses, both for use as servers that students can practice attacking, as well as for use as clients that come pre-installed with the necessary security tools [15]. We have also used VMs since 2006 in a computer systems course to enable new pedagogic techniques. VMs have also proven useful in topics such as robotics [7] and SaaS [8]. These ad-hoc, per-course VM deployments have a several downsides: they require students to install a separate (and often large) VM image for each course, they require a separate VM support stack for each course, and they require students to learn simple tasks on multiple unfamiliar systems.

2.1 Our Requirements

To improve upon this situation, we have pursued the development a standard department-wide development environment. Our goal was simple: provide students with an easy to install and use development environment that they could use across all their CS courses. The development environment should be available both on department lab machines, and as a VM for use on student-owned machines (e.g. as a "lab in a box"). Underlying this goal were a number of expectations and requirements from various stakeholders in the education environment.

From the student perspective, our solution had to: a) Run on a range of host systems; b) Be easy to install; c) Be easy to use and maintain; d) Minimize side-effects on the host system; e) Provide a stable experience throughout the semester.

From the instructor perspective, our solution had to: a) Keep the students happy; b) Minimize instructor IT overhead; c) Provide consistent results across student, grader, and instructor machines; d) Provide all necessary software for the course; e) Provide the ability to update software as the course progresses.

From the IT and management perspective, our solution had to: a) Keep the students happy; b) Keep the instructors happy; c) Be easy to support and maintain; d) Minimize resource (personal, cost, etc) requirements.

2.2 Selecting Hypervisors and VMs

The first component of any virtualization system is the hypervisor: the software that allows the host machine to run virtual machines. There are a variety of hypervisors available addressing a range of applications from server to desktop environments. We chose to use Oracle's VirtualBox [10] hypervisor for several reasons.

First, VirtualBox is a true multi-platform hypervisor providing a single unified platform for Windows, OSX, and Linux. Unlike other products such as HyperV, Parallels, or VMWare, VirtualBox allows us to support a single piece of software across all common student platforms, reducing the burden of supporting a range of student hardware and operating systems. Second, VirtualBox is both Free and Open Source; students do not have to pay to use it, and they are able to analyze or modify the source code if they wish. This avoids requiring students or departments to purchase extra software and does not require students to install software on their personal machines that they have no means to vet or modify. Finally, VirtualBox has solid support for Linux guests. This made it easy for us to configure our guest OS to interact with VirtualBox in a manner that ensures an optimal experience, allowing us to support functions like copying between the VM and host system, sharing files between systems, automatically scaling display resolutions, etc.

Atop the hypervisor, we deploy a virtual machine based on the Ubuntu 12.04.3 Desktop OS [6] (the latest Long Term Support Ubuntu Linux release). We opted for a GNU/Linux-based development environment for its robust support for a variety of CS tools and software, its widespread industry appeal, and its free, open, and permissive licensing. We opted to use Ubuntu due to its large support base in the Linux community. Ubuntu also has a rich library of software packages, meaning that required software (i.e. ruby, scala, python, gcc, etc) would be available with little additional work. Ubuntu also provides a five-year supported product life-cycle and is designed to be fairly user-friendly for new Linux users.

Our VM image starts as a standard Ubuntu 12.04.3 install. We then configure it to work optimally on the average student system. We use disk images that provide up to 30GB of VM HD space using a disk format that expands on demand to minimize actual disk use on student host systems. We configure the system to use up to 2GB of RAM and up to 2 CPU cores by default. We make a few minor modifications to the system configuration directly (i.e. setting the desktop background to an image that includes information for using and getting help with the VM), but for the most part, the majority of the post-install VM config is handled automatically using a series of software meta-packages we have created (described below). We distribute our VM as a single Open Virtualization Format (`.ova`) image file which allows students to import/install it with a single click (assuming VirtualBox itself has already been installed).

2.3 Managing with Packages

One of the key challenges behind using a single VM across the entire department is how to manage the specific requirements of each individual class using the VM. This challenge is not unique to VMs: we also face the same issue when managing departmental computer labs. A multitude of instructors across a variety of courses all have specific requirements for what must be installed in a lab and how it must be configured. We decided to solve the general lab management issue and then apply the same solution to both the VM and our lab machines, leading to our ability to maintain a unified environment across both VM and lab images.

Fortunately, there already exist systems designed to make the management of software across a multitude of machines easy: package management utilities. In particular, given our use of Ubuntu, we looked to the Debian package management tools for building, serving, and managing `.deb` packages [2]. Debian packages traditionally contain several components: the executable code and auxiliary files for a specific program, a set of configuration scripts that guide the install/uninstall processes, and a list of other packages that must be installed as dependencies. We leverage the latter two components of a `.deb` package to control our lab software environment. To install all of the required software and configuration for a given course, we simply need to create a package that lists the required course-software as dependencies and contains any course-specific configuration in its install script. This type of dependency/script-only package is normally called a *meta-package* to differentiate it from a full-fledged program package. Installing such a course meta package via the normal tools (e.g. `apt-get`) will trigger the installation of all required software and configuration for the given course.

We set about creating meta-packages for each course in the department that required use of our lab machines or our common VM. Creating these packages in the standard Debian format is generally quite simple, requiring only a few basic text files that provide, among other things, a list of required software for a given course [5]. In cases where a course requires more in-depth configuration beyond simply ensuring all the required software is installed, we can also include configuration scripts to execute arbitrary operations within our development environment. Thus we can create a very powerful, per-course package that is capable of automatically deploying all required configuration and software for a given course. Our current course packages (and the scripts we use to build and maintain them) are open source and available on GitHub [13].

After creating packages for each course, we had to make our packages publicly available via a web-based package repository. Again, the standard Debian tools make it easy to deploy and manage such a repository in a manner no more complicated than creating and deploying a simple website [9]. Our `apt` repository is publicly available at [14]. We simply add our repository's web address to the repository list on the base VM and lab machines, install our package-signing key, and these machines have direct access to our packages alongside the standard Ubuntu packages. Configuring the lab or VM then becomes a simple matter of installing the package for each course. To simplify matters further, we actually created an additional meta package for both the lab and VM that simply lists all of the active courses in a given semester as dependencies. Thus, we must only install this single master package on the VM or lab machines to trigger the installation and configuration of the entire common development environment.

Packages have a number of additional benefits beyond a highly streamlined and simplified install process. For instance, they provide us with the ability to update lab and VM configurations during the semester without needing to redeploy the VM or lab images. If an instructor decides to use a different software library half way through the semester, we can simply update the package and push the update to the package server. All of the student VMs and lab machines will automatically pull down the new change and apply it seamlessly without requiring messy re-installs or manual intervention[1]. In addition, packages provide a simple centralized means to document all of the required software and settings for a given course. No longer do we have to tediously remember what configuration changes were applied in the lab or what software has been installed. It's all documented within the package configuration files themselves and can be easily managed and updated from semester to semester.

Finally, controlling all per-course configuration via packages is an efficient way to use a single VM that can be easily extended to support all courses. Students can download a "lean" version of the VM that has only the core course packages installed, and then they can install extra packages for any course they are currently enrolled beyond those included on the lean VM. This makes it easy for students to manage their own VMs from semester to semester and to grab all of the software for their current courses without having to waste hard drive space on courses they aren't taking. Students who have native Linux installs or otherwise prefer to set up their own machines without the use of the VM can also use our course packages to ensure their self-configured setups contain all of the same software as the VM or lab machines. VMs may provide the body of a lab machine on each student's personal computer, but per-course packages provide the brains that ensure everything stays manageable, uniform, and up-to-date across VM, lab, and self-installed environments.

3. SUPPORT INFRASTRUCTURE

In addition to providing the VM itself and packages for each course that uses it (or any other lab machines), we also provide the necessary support infrastructure for these systems. The goal of this support infrastructure is to shift the bulk of the burden of providing per-course IT support to a single individual or group in charge of the VM, course packages, and related lab environments. Currently, we employee a single grad student in a 20 hour/week appointment in charge of VM and course package support for ≈ 800 students spread across ≈ 5 core courses. We have found that when properly coordinated, such a position can easily support the scale we are operating at and beyond. We have found it far more efficient, both in terms of time and cost, to employ a single dedicated development environment support person over requiring each instructor to dedicate portions of their time to the support of their course IT. This arrangement allows instructors to focus on instruction while a small number of highly-trained environment support staff focus on environment support.

3.1 Supporting Students

Effectively supporting students proves to be particularly challenging: we need to have ≈ 800 students successfully using the virtual machine for their courses within about one week. To accomplish this, we provide a variety of support resources for students. First and foremost, we provide a central web-page [11] that provides information about the VM, download links, installation instructions, common troubleshooting steps, and related self-help information. We also

[1]In time sensitive situations, relying on the automatic update system is often undesirable due to its opportunistic nature. But even in this case, forcefully updating a VM or lab machine is a simple matter of manually running the system update program.

provide YouTube videos describing the installation and usage of the VM. We have found that about 80% of our user base [12] is capable of setting up the VM on their own using these resources.

For the remaining students who require or desire in-person help setting up the VM, we provide a series of "install sessions" at the beginning of each semester. We advertise these sessions to all courses using the VM and open them up to anyone who wishes to attend. During the sessions, we provide copies of the VM on USB flash drives (to avoid having to wait for students to download the image) and walk students through the install process step by step. We have one or more VM experts on hand during these sessions to assist with unforeseen issues and help students work through individual problems. Many students who attend these sessions do so after attempting to install the VM on their own and encountering some issue. They then attend the session as a fallback to installing the VM themselves.

After the initial install sessions, we provide two to four staffed hours of weekly VM support "office hours" through the remainder of the semester in a central department location open to all students. These weekly hours provide opportunities to assist students who encounter issues after the initial VM install or who require extra help getting up to speed with the usage of the development environments (Linux, editors, etc). These hours allow courses using the VM to focus their own office hours and contact time on course content and forward students with VM or environment issues to the dedicated VM office hours each week.

3.2 Supporting Instructors

Our support resources for instructors are focused primarily on communication, feedback, and training. Prior to the start of each semester, we meet with each instructor and gather a list of the required software and configuration for their courses. These are then used to build the per-course packages mentioned previously. We follow this up with a beta-release of the VM image that instructors and their TAs use to test their assignments in advance of the start of classes. Feedback from this beta release is then incorporated into the course packages (and thus the VM) prior to the student-facing VM release.

We also provide basic VM training to the instructors and their TAs in several group sessions at the start of each semester. This training focuses on the basics of what the VM does and how it works. The goal is not to make the TAs and instructors experts at supporting the VM directly, but to ensure that they are knowledgeable about its use during class demos and that they are capable of recognizing abnormal behavior when it occurs so that they can forward issues to the dedicated VM support staff. We continue meeting with instructors and TAs throughout the semester to elicit feedback on the VM, coordinate any mid-semester updates to the course packages, and monitor their ongoing experience with the VM. This culminates in a end-of-semester survey that we send to all VM users in an effort to gather feedback on the VM and to improve the system in subsequent semesters.

4. EVALUATION

We are currently in the second full year of using the common CS VM development environment. We have deployed the system for the previous three semesters, and are currently using it this semester with the largest user base yet. Over this time, we have had a thorough opportunity to evaluate the VM in both qualitative and quantitative measure across a range of users.

Each semester we deploy the VM, we have conduced an end-of-semester user survey. The survey is sent to all students, instructors, and TAs known to be using the VM as their primary development environment, which includes all of the core CS courses. The survey is web-based, anonymous, and optional. It takes about 5 minutes to complete. Figures 1 and 2 present data from our most recent survey: Fall 2013. The Fall 2013 survey had $\approx$ 300 responses from VM users, representing about 40% of the $\approx$ 800 student VM user base across our core courses. The full results of the survey, including user comments, are available in [12].

Figure 1a shows the basic demographic breakdown of the VM user base. Our current user base is primarily split between Engineering (BS) CS major, Arts and Sciences (BA) CS major, and non-major undergraduate students. Figure 1b shows the host Operating Systems that our VM users report using. This indicates the range of hardware that can be supported with a single common VM platform. At this time, we do not officially recommend a specific type of machine to incoming students, leaving them free to select any machine they like. The majority of our users run the VM on their personal laptops. A small portion use desktops, often at home or in their dorm rooms. About 57% of our VM user base uses Windows, primarily Windows 7 or Windows 8. About 38% of our users use OSX (Macs). The remaining 5% use Linux. Over three quarters of our users have machines with modern Intel Core i-series CPUs. With the benefit of multiple cores and hardware virtualization extensions, these processors are more than adequate to run the VM. About a quarter of our users tend to use slightly older CPUs, which may or may not run the VM optimally depending on their design.

Figure 2a shows our users' impressions related to using the VM. Two thirds of our users rated their experience using the VM as "Good" (4 out of 5) or "Excellent" (5 out of 5). Only 6% rates their experience as "Poor" (2 out of 5) or "Terrible" (1 out of 5). Thus, the vast majority of our users seem satisfied with their VM experience. Likewise, almost 80% of our users report using the VM for "All" or "Most" of their coursework, indicating that the system is in fact usable and preferable to the alternatives (working in the lab, installing Linux directly on their devises, etc). VM performance tends to be the most common complaint related to VM usage. Virtualization does impose an overhead on performance, especially in the absence of enabled processor virtualization extensions.

While Linux is a new experience for over half of our users, very few of them seem to struggle with the new OS. We provide both live and videotaped supplemental lectures covering the basics of the Linux OS and standard development tools for those that are interested in extra assistance or a more in-depth introduction, but only a fraction of the user base pursues this supplemental material. Modern Linux Desktop OSes like Ubuntu provide a very familiar experience for OSX and Windows users. Furthermore, in our introductory courses our users need only a small fraction of what Linux has to offer, reducing the scope of new OS functionality they must learn. We have observed more than one of our users

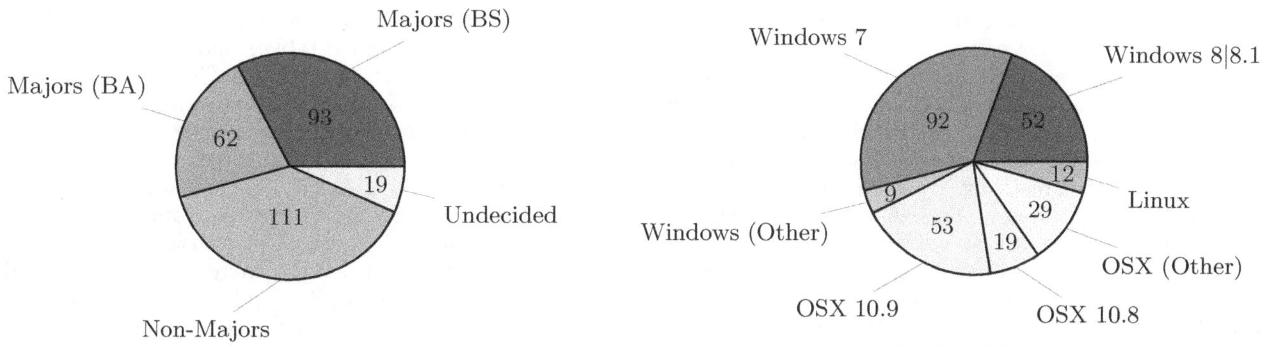

(a) User Major

(b) Host OS

Figure 1: VM Users

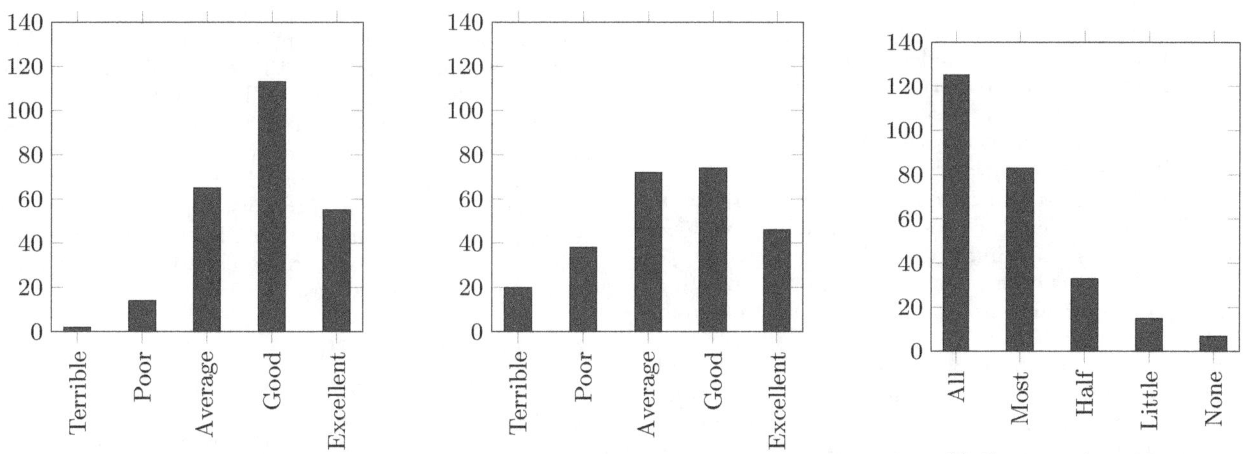

(a) Overall Experience

(b) Performance/Speed

(c) Coursework on VM

Figure 2: VM User Experience

struggle more with the switch from Windows 7 to Windows 8 than from Windows to Linux.

5. SOCIAL IMPACT

Before students owned their own machines, they were forced to sit in university-equipped labs, sometimes even queuing up to wait for an available machine. This often had a useful social benefit: students, in physical proximity, would form social bonds that enhanced their educational experience and transformed the lab into a social nexus. Our VM approach allows a student to "take the lab anywhere" and thereby removes the potentially-positive effect of required lab attendance.

While the lack of forced lab attendance is a potential concern, we have found the use of virtual-machines has actually promoted more effective pair and group-work by students. Students still work in the labs, but they use their laptops instead of the lab machines. In addition, they work together at many other locations on and off campus. The VM provides the flexibility to meet and work as a group anyware, without imposing the arbitrary limit of requiring access to a univerity compuer lab.

On a related note, the dedication and time-commitment required by a modern CS curriculum often has meant lab-bound students enter and leave the facility at all hours: it is not unusual to see students in our lab throughout the night. When informally surveyed, nine students (eight of them female) indicated discomfort at the idea of entering or leaving the lab after-hours due to safety concerns. Our approach alleviates this concern, and related concerns for others who are unable or uncomfortable gaining access to a university computer lab.

6. LESSONS LEARNED

Our experience with the VM has led us to develop a set of best practices, as well as to identify the continued sticking points that we hope to resolve in the future. In addition to the practices already discussed (per-course software packages, one-click installs, dedicated support staff, etc), we highlight a few additional best practices below. We recommend these guidelines, as well as the guidelines discussed in [12], to anyone looking to build a similar system.

Virtualization Extensions: Modern CPUs provide extensions that enable a fast, smooth and enjoyable VM experience (i.e. VT-x). Unfortunately, many non-Apple PC manufacturers ship their machines with these extension *disabled* in the BIOS. Getting students to enable these extensions can be a challenge, but makes a big difference in their overall impression of VM usability. One way to force students to enable these extensions is to use a 64-bit and/or multi-core VM, which VirtualBox will not start without virtualization extensions enabled. Such a VM will force students to either enable the extension themselves, or seek help at an install session, drastically improving their subsequent VM usage experience. Our experience has been that this approach requires an increase in start-of-semester help sessions, but the resulting boost in performance leads to higher overall satisfaction.

Multiple Distribution Methods: Each term starts with a rush of students trying to obtain the multi-GB VM image. Having a single direct download link is a sure way to overload your servers, overwhelm your network, and otherwise disrupt the initial VM roll out. We avoid these issues by distributing our VM images primarily via the BitTorrent peer-to-peer network [1]. We provide direct downloads to students who cannot use BitTorrent and also provide USB thumb drives with copies of the VM at all install sessions. This multi-pronged, distributed approach avoids a single bottleneck during the critical start-of-semester roll out.

Off-VM Backup System: Students are often unaware of the fact that virtual machines share the foibles of physical computers, including potential file system corruption if the VM is improperly "powered off". Thus, it's important to provide students with an easy-to-use off-VM backup mechanism. We settled on distributing the VM with the Dropbox [3] client pre-installed and encouraging students to use the free service to store their files on the VM, ensuring they are automatically synced to the cloud. We have also used GitHub [4] in a similar (although less transparent) manner. Using Dropbox or GitHub has the added benefit of providing an easy means for transferring files between the VM, the host machine, and/or other machines. Using such a system simplifies resolving VM issues by allowing our support staff to simply re-install a fresh copy of the VM when non-trivial issues arise. The student can then restore their work to their new VM install from Dropbox or GitHub.

Despite its continued success, there remain parts of our system we hope to improve. The main open issues are discussed below.

BIOS Access and Configuration: As mentioned above, getting virtualization to work smoothly often requires accessing the system BIOS and enabling virtualization extensions. This can be a challenge since the method for doing this differs by machine, and since many students have never had to access their system EFI/BIOS menus before.

Download Corruption: The majority of the VM install issues we see stem from corrupt VM image downloads. Even today, downloading multi-GB files over wifi networks tends to cause corruption in a notable number of cases. We publish md5 checksums for each VM image and encourage students to verify them before installing the VM.

No|Slow|ARM Computer: Some users can not use the VM do to their lack of machine or ownership of a low-spec machine (e.g. Intel Atom). In addition, the rise of ARM-based tablets and laptops and other non-traditional hybrid machines (ChromeBooks, iPads, etc) mean that some students are showing up with hardware incapable of supporting x86 virtualization at all. Such users must often fall back to using the actual computer lab. While our package system ensures that the lab is configured in the same manner as the VM, this still tends to put them at a disadvantage by limiting the spaces in which they may work. We are beginning to experiment with laptop loaner programs and virtual desktops to help mitigate these issues.

7. CONCLUSION

We believe our VM system has been very successful at allowing students to utilize their own hardware while also providing a common development environment that greatly simplifies instruction. We plan to continue expanding our system and improving upon the outstanding issues. We currently use the system across all core CS courses. We plan to expand the program to all CS courses, including electives and graduate classes, in the near future. We also plan to continue gathering feedback and data from users to drive the continued improvement of the system. Our system allows us to support a heterogeneous BYOD environment while still delivering an enjoyable learning experience to a wide range of students at minimal cost.

8. REFERENCES

[1] Bittorrent. `http://www.bittorrent.org/`.

[2] Debian policy manual. `http://www.debian.org/doc/debian-policy/`.

[3] Dropbox. `https://www.dropbox.com/`.

[4] Github. `https://www.github.com/`.

[5] M. Bialasinski. equivs. `http://packages.debian.org/wheezy/equivs`.

[6] Canonical. Ubuntu. `https://www.ubuntu.com/`.

[7] N. Correll, R. Wing, and D. Coleman. A one year introductory robotics curriculum for computer science upperclassmen. *IEEE Transactions on Education*, 56(1):54 – 60, 2012.

[8] A. Fox and D. Patterson. Engineering software as a service - bookware: Vm instructions. `http://beta.saasbook.info/bookware-vm-instructions`, 2013.

[9] B. R. Link. reprepro. `http://mirrorer.alioth.debian.org/`.

[10] Oracle. Virtualbox. `https://www.virtualbox.org/`.

[11] A. Sayler. Cu cs standard development environment. `http://foundation.cs.colorado.edu/sde/`.

[12] A. Sayler and D. Grunwald. Cu cs computign survey results - fall 2013. Technical report, Univerity of Colorado, Boulder, Decemeber 2013.

[13] A. Sayler and M. Monaco. Cu cs apt packages. `https://github.com/asayler/cu-cs-apt-packages`.

[14] A. Sayler and M. Monaco. Cu cs apt repository. `http://apt.cs.colorado.edu/`.

[15] G. Vigna. Teaching network security through live exercises. *Proceedings of the Third Annual World Conference on Information Security Education (WISE)*, June 2003.

Framing Classroom Climate for Student Learning and Retention in Computer Science

Lecia J. Barker
University of Texas
1616 Guadalupe Street
Austin, TX 78701-1213
+1-512-232-8364
lecia@ischool.utexas.edu

Melissa O'Neill
Harvey Mudd College
1250 North Dartmouth Avenue
Claremont, CA 91711-5980
+1-909-607-9661
oneill@cs.hmc.edu

Nida Kazim
University of Texas
1616 Guadalupe Street
Austin, TX 78701-1213
+1-512-471-3821
nida.kazim@gmail.com

ABSTRACT

Despite the best laid plans, counterproductive student behavior can interfere with faculty establishment of supportive classroom climates. This paper describes methods for framing the climate of the computer science classroom to minimize outspoken students' unwanted displays of intellectual prowess and engender co-learning behavior among students. Explicit framing of a supportive climate reduces student anxiety about their status among peers, leads them to expect to co-learn concepts, and reduces trepidations about speaking up in class. The framing is grounded by preemptively establishing expectations and addressing concerns through student discussion; asking students to go outside of their interaction style comfort zones for speaking in class; and explicitly describing teaching choices and classroom processes. The framing is reinforced by exposing wrong answers as useful rather than embarrassing, turn-taking techniques for equal student participation, and collaborative learning for assignments and in-class problem solving. Classroom-based retention techniques are important for retaining students who are less experienced with computer science and unsure how to interpret peers' public knowledge claims in relation to their own knowledge or faculty expectations.

Categories and Subject Descriptors

K.3.2 Computer and Information Science Education

General Terms

Human Factors

Keywords

Classroom climate; classroom management; student retention

1. INTRODUCTION

Most higher education faculty spend a great deal of time thinking about the contents of lectures, sequencing of material, examples to illustrate difficult concepts, what students should read, how they should exercise their newly-acquired skills, what counts as an appropriate demonstration of knowledge and knowledge gains, and much more. Rarely do faculty think about how they will manage the interactions among students and between themselves and students. We tend to think of college-aged students as adults who know how to behave. Yet like the rest of us adults, students are aware of themselves as part of the classroom social order. When students are overly concerned with establishing high status in relation to their peers, they can become outspoken, working hard to impress the teacher and each other. Others can also shut down, fearful that something they say may be evidence of their lack of knowledge compared to the rest of the class. Faculty may experience students as "engaged" v. withdrawn, not realizing that the classroom climate can shape students' behavior in negative ways. For students, social status concerns create an inexplicit cognitive load that keeps them from focusing on the task at hand: learning.

This paper presents a way of reframing student focus, a solution that has been effective at Harvey Mudd College. Below, we briefly review scholarship about classroom climate and management, then present a teaching approach that frames appropriate and expected classroom involvement. We conclude by discussing outcomes for student interaction and retention in computer science.

SIGCSE '14, March 05 - 08 2014, Atlanta, GA, USA

http://dx.doi.org/10.1145/2538862.2538959

2. CLASSROOM CLIMATE

Classroom climate is the social aspect of learning environment, which includes physical surroundings and the emotional and social conditions that can support or detract from learning in those surroundings [25]. Classroom climate is established through student-student and student-faculty interaction in classrooms [27]. Faculty engage in many communicative acts, such as asking and answering questions in class, delivering lectures, working out problems on the board, tutoring individuals and small groups, and more. Students interact with each other in problem solving groups and engage in before- and after-class chit chat. Students are fully aware of each other as actors, as they perform the role of student in the classroom and observe the performance of their peers. How students behave and how they interpret communicative behavior in classrooms is based on a lifetime of socialization about appropriate behaviors, roles, and activities in classrooms, relationships with other students and with teachers, tacit beliefs about the authority of teachers, and typical patterns of communication in classrooms [6]. Students also talk outside of class to each other, teaching assistants, lab assistants and tutors, professors, and others outside of the major or school. These conversations influence their own behavior and how they make sense of what goes on in class.

Each classroom takes on a social climate with its own norms, which emerge as a result of prior experience, social expectations, and the communication choices of the individual teacher and students in the class. Classroom climate can be placed on a continuum between supportive and defensive [10]. In a supportive climate, students feel socially safe making mistakes, giving wrong answers, or otherwise presenting themselves as unknowledgeable in front of their peers. Supportive climates enhance students' motivation, their ability to understand material, retention of knowledge, and opportunities to cooperate with their peers [4, 13, 18]. Defensive classroom climates lead students to feel socially threatened by and distrustful of others and to use coping mechanisms; as a result, they are less liked by students [6, 27].

In one study, "showoffs" who used class time to talk about knowledge or experiences that other students were unlikely to have had, and who received implicit praise or recognition by their teachers, caused inexperienced students to feel less valued in the classroom [22]. Early courses in undergraduate computer science can easily produce these conditions, because students enter with a wide range of programming experience. Co-author Barker and colleagues' observation of more than 300 hours of computer science classrooms and 150 interviews showed that when inexperienced students felt that their "showoff" peers knew more (often aligned with being "smarter" rather than more experienced) and struggled less with assignments, they became apprehensive and believed they did not belong in computer science [5]. Faculty understood showoffs to be showing off—not smarter or more knowledgeable—but did not recognize the intimidation it caused.

Other studies suggest that modes of communication among teachers and learners in classrooms contribute to motivating and demotivating learning experiences [33] and that effective classroom management using small group techniques and effective methods of encouraging questions benefit students [17]. Numerous studies in K-12 settings focus on creating learning environments to keep students on task and challenge them cognitively (e.g., [9]); however, few studies specifically discuss strategies in undergraduate or computer science education. In the next section, we present a method of framing classroom climate that reduces caustic behaviors and makes classrooms safe for making mistakes.

3. FRAMING CLASSROOM CLIMATE

In the early 1970s, sociologists Gregory Bateson and later Erving Goffman used the term frame to describe the set of tacit beliefs and rules that shape how people interpret words, behaviors, and experiences within particular types of situations [8, 11]. Bateson wrote, "[t]he playful nip denotes the bite, but it does not denote what would be denoted by the bite" ([8], 186). We differently understand the meaning of dogs snarling and using their teeth on each other if we frame the situation as "play" or as "dogfight." Because of our socialization and experience in cultures, we draw on implicit frames for interpreting "what's going on." For example, having deep experience of formal educational systems, most students observing a professor facing them and speaking loudly in the front of the room are likely to stop talking and begin taking notes on what the professor is saying. If the professor were not lecturing, he or she would have to explicitly point out that this discourse is not really part of "class" (e.g., "before we start class, let me tell you something funny about last weekend").

Framing how a set of actions in a situation should be interpreted is not usually made explicit, but can be made explicit. For example, if two persons viewing the biting, snarling dogs perceived the framework differently—one as dogs fighting and one as dogs playing—the two persons would likely give each other their good reasons for drawing one interpretation over the other. In a court of law, a judge usually instructs jurors to use certain laws for interpreting a defendant's behaviors and instructs the jurors as to what they are to use as evidence and what they cannot use as evidence. This kind of explicit framing is needed when the default frame will not lead to the desired outcomes.

Like a judge to the jury, faculty can explicitly frame to students how behavior in the classroom should and/or will be interpreted. Such explicit framing plays a crucial role in students' understanding of what they think is going on and can help faculty to maximize productive, learning-oriented classroom interaction. Co-author O'Neill developed the framing techniques described here and applies them in all the classes she teaches at Harvey Mudd College (HMC), including data structures and systems area topics such as programming languages and operating systems. She believes doing so helps improve the student experience in those classes and as student evaluations suggest, students agree. Below, we describe framing techniques applied to the HMC data structures class and students' perceptions of them. As a class that is seen as the gateway to the computer science major, it is vital that students experience data structures not as an entry barrier to a foreign land but as a welcoming entrance to their new occupational and intellectual home.

3.1. The Default Frame: Expectations and Behavior

HMC's Data Structures course uses C++ to teach:

> "Abstract data types including priority queues, dynamic dictionaries, and disjoint sets. Efficient data structures for these data types, including heaps, self-balancing trees, and hash tables. Analysis of data structures including worst-case, average-case, and amortized analysis. Storage allocation and reclamation. Secondary storage considerations. Extensive practice in implementing these data structures for a variety of applications." [14]

O'Neill uses a Socratic, dialogue-based approach to teaching. She usually comes to class with a problem and asks students "how do we get to a solution?" She tries to lay down "breadcrumbs" so that students will come upon the right answer themselves by asking questions and helping them explore. For example, she may ask students to evaluate an expression for getting to the ith element of an array pointed to by P. When they think it looks "ugly," she asks them what syntax they would prefer. Students propose ideas and she takes a vote on which they like the best. Of course, the favored syntax is an identity that already exists in C++. Through discussion and exploration, the logic underlying this identity is revealed, so students come to understand it as a choice of the language designer and explore its ramifications. Similarly, in discussing the value and key attributes of good programming style, rather than simply stating these attributes, students are given real-world code that exhibits poor style and asked to identify what is wrong with it and why the issue they have identified is a problem. After working in groups examining sample code (where not all groups see the same code), groups share their discoveries with the class, with O'Neill facilitating discussion and weaving student responses into a well-structured schema. The goal is to engender deep understanding rather than acceptance of arbitrary knowledge.

In the past, students have entered the class under the perception that it is a "weeder" course: a challenging, demanding class which, if passed, would indicate one belongs in the major and if not, would suggest one ought to switch out. O'Neill saw this attitude as setting negative expectations for the course and negatively shaping students' interpretations of course experiences.

When O'Neill first started teaching the course, she became frustrated because a minority of students would typically sit in the front of the classroom and shoot up their hands or blurt answers or comments at every opportunity. She intended her questions to be evocative and that answers would allow students to explore and demonstrate students' attempts to learn. Yet she felt that these students wanted to demonstrate to her what they had already learned, elsewhere. She was pleased that they already knew some answers and that they were engaged, but perceived their behavior as boasting, not engagement with learning. What is more, feedback from tests and office hours conversations with "quiet" students made her realize that oftentimes those who weren't speaking up in class actually knew at least as much, if not more, than the outspoken students. The more outspoken students may have been cherry-picking questions for which they already knew answers so that she and other students would consider them to be smart. The outspoken ones were framing the classroom environment as a competitive arena for demonstrating prowess rather than a laboratory for exploring ideas. The norms of classroom climate emerge through students' and faculty interactions; when it becomes normative that certain students speak and demonstrate their prowess, it becomes increasingly difficult to get the quiet ones to speak. Both quiet and outspoken students are conforming to the tacit norms that have developed: the outspoken students speak up and the quiet ones don't. But for O'Neill's Socratic teaching method, leaving some students out of the conversation is a failure.

O'Neill felt that the behavior by the outspoken students was creating a caustic atmosphere for other students. It was not only her perception, however. In evaluations, students wrote comments such as "I found myself not understanding and felt dumb asking questions," "A lot of distractions during class time, namely certain other students were very interruptive," and "The thing I hated about the class was the presence of loud, pedantic, distracting classmates who were far too concerned with demonstrating their 'knowledge' of the material. Class would have been vastly more enjoyable if they had been reined in. Seriously!" If this were perceived as the default standard for computer science classroom climate, many students would feel disengaged and leave the major. They would effectively be weeded out, not because of the difficulty of the course, but because of the behavior of peers.

This loss would be especially problematic given all the hard work the Harvey Mudd computer science faculty were doing to recruit women (often less experienced with computer science upon entering college) into the major. Research suggests that women leave the computer science major not because of their competence, but because they feel they do not belong or have lost confidence [16, 26, 30]. Students can lose confidence in their own ability in relation to their peers when they feel that others know so much more than they know, especially when the less knowledgeable student does not understand that these demonstrations of knowledge are often tangential, irrelevant, or acquired before the present course and that it is not expected that they would know it (yet).

3.2. Assigning a Frame

Seeing negative expectations and outspoken students as problems to be solved, O'Neill wanted to improve student experience in the course without reducing the course's level of challenge; instead, she wanted to change how students related to the challenges the course presented. O'Neill's first attempts to change student attitudes toward the course began in spring 2005 and she began to use more explicit framing on the first day of class in fall 2007. She has continued to add elements over time, using a trial and error approach to refine her framing so that the data structures course, while still thought of as a tough course to get through, greatly limits students' boastful behavior and changes students' expectations for who responds to questions and why. Her framing also changes students' interpretation of how learning occurs: from a relationship between teacher and each student (as teacher injects what she knows into the minds of her students) to a group relationship. She accomplishes this framework by presenting the ground rules for interpretation of classroom behavior, using a turn taking approach to calling on students, using occasional group problem solving in class, and requiring pair programming.

3.2.1. Preemptively Grounding the Frame

O'Neill begins the term by explicitly setting the ground rules for the class: what behaviors are expected and how they will be interpreted. She lets the students know that they will learn from each other and by asking and answering questions. They will also use in-class group discussion and pair programming for assignments. O'Neill explains in the first class that there are rules to follow with pairing and acknowledges that watching another person use a computer can be frustrating. In addition, she tells them that her greatest concern is what they learn in this class, announcing, "If you already know the answer to something and you knew it before you walked into class, then don't raise your hand. Leave the answer to someone who has learned it in this class." She explicitly asks them to go outside their comfort zone, saying that if they are the kind of person who is typically outspoken, they can try to reign themselves in a bit, and if they are the kind of person who normally is a bit shy, they can push themselves a bit. She tells them that every student can expect to be asked to respond to questions, as described in the next section.

Naturally, some students are fearful about the prospect of being called on and being wrong. On the first day of class, O'Neill explicitly sets the stage to reverse students' belief that a wrong answer is embarrassing by describing it as a positive pedagogical event for the class. Wrong answers allow the class to delve into the right answer and explore why it is right. Misconceptions are often shared by many other students. She urges students to see the value of learning through trial and error. She also points out that when a person gives a wrong answer, he or she may be concerned about the loss of face and status in the eyes of other students. But that is not what others are thinking at all: they are thinking that it could soon be their turn, and trying to make sure they can address the question well. She humorously tells them, "it's nice to think that you're the focus of everyone else's world, but you're not."

In the most recent iterations of the class, O'Neill has added student self-reflection as computer science learners. She grounds the first-day discussion with the results of a required, non-anonymous (to her) online questionnaire students complete a week before the first day of class. Students report previous CS courses taken as well as prior knowledge about programming languages and specific concepts; preferences for being in or away from the spotlight, feedback styles (blunt v. indirect), and attitude toward mistakes; and predictions for enjoyment and learning outcomes of the course. The questionnaire items for enjoyment and learning are all stated positively, an intentional choice intended to help frame a positive view of the course (e.g., "I'm expecting to learn a lot in this class" rather than "I know few of the concepts to be covered in this class"). Similarly, by asking, "what will you do to get the most out of this course?" O'Neill implies that students in fact want to get "the most" out of the course and that it is a shared responsibility between student and teacher.

O'Neill presents slides summarizing aggregated results of the questionnaire to the class. Although students are clearly interested in seeing where they stand relative to their peers, the presentation and discussion is most valuable for demonstrating the diversity of knowledge, attitudes, and preferences among students. The discussion allows O'Neill to suggest that although students may have certain default states, e.g., to dislike making errors, they have the capability to adjust themselves away from this default.

Because of students' varying personalities and experiences, one size doesn't fit all in classroom interactions. Some students need more gentleness and encouragement, and some can prefer a more direct approach. Using class discussion of the questionnaire, O'Neill lets the students themselves draw this conclusion. She then tells the students that she will try to meet them on a level that works for them and that they are in the driver's seat—if she's being too gentle or too quick with them, to let her know. These approaches diffuse the potential for problems with perceived unfairness of treatment of students.

Preparing advance strategies for managing students who are overzealous despite the framing is also important. O'Neill asks students to talk to her outside of class when they continue to dominate, try to answer every question, or blurt comments that do not help the class learn. Also, to take pressure off students who continue to worry about giving wrong answers, she lets the class know that at times she will divide them into small problem solving or discussion groups (e.g., Think-Pair-Share [32]). When a group has already talked and shared with each other before they are asked to share it with the class, students are more comfortable talking in front of the class and also gain confidence speaking up.

3.2.2. *Reinforcing the Frame: Trading Cards*

Early in her use of the question and answer approach, O'Neill would ask a question, then call on a student. Some students interpreted this as being picked on: that for some reason, the professor was asking an especially hard (or easy) question of them. Such a misunderstanding can increase fearfulness among students and lead to resentment. To avoid this misunderstanding, O'Neill reinforces the frame of the course using a turn-taking approach to answering questions. She prints "trading cards" of students with their pictures and names. The cards are shuffled before each class so that the order changes. Then, during each class period, she goes through the card deck and calls on students one at a time, though she may not get through all students in each class period or may go through it multiple times. This has the dual effect of keeping everyone engaged in the class and equalizing participation. When a student's turn comes up, they have three choices: they can answer the question, ask a clarification question of their own, or pass. Passing is not an attractive option, however. The student's card is inserted just a few cards down, not at the bottom.

Sometimes it is tempting to skip a student in the deck. For example, the card that comes up may belong to a student who is sitting at the back of the room with his head down. If this student hasn't been paying attention, it can be embarrassing for both him and the professor. O'Neill has found, however, that at least some of the time, the student's head will come up and a correct answer be produced. The student was on the same page with the class. This example is consistent with Barker's observation of computer science classrooms, where students would occasionally have no way of taking notes in front of them and be sprawled across the table or desk. Asked why they didn't take notes, they would respond that it was really important to concentrate on what they were hearing in class and note-taking interfered. O'Neill does not break her turn-taking rules with the cards, but also makes it explicit that when students are being called on, it is "just the rules," not the professor being vindictive or picking on anyone for any reason.

Although the groundwork has been laid for the value of wrong answers, it is also important to use non-threatening language in addressing them. If someone presents a wrong answer, it is important to make explicit statements that it is wrong, but use some sort of praise for stating the wrong answer because the class can explore it to see why it is wrong. For example, O'Neill might say "that is not the right answer, but I am so glad that you brought it up, because it is a common misconception and gives us the opportunity to come up with the right answer." Routine positive associations are needed to reinforce what has been said on the first day of class.

3.2.3. *Reinforcing the Frame: Pair Programming*

Research on college student persistence shows that students who become involved both academically and socially are more likely to be retained in their major [2, 3, 23]. Both student-faculty and student-peer interaction are shown to be predictors of retention in computer science [7]. Making sure that students are interacting in structured environments (i.e., classroom and lab) is especially important for women in undergraduate computing. They often have limited opportunities to naturally develop the important peer relationships more easily developed for their male peers, because they often are either the only woman or one of very few women in their individual classes. Women stand out as different, but are isolated and have limited personal interaction with their male peers, who, not knowing them, may unwittingly judge women on the basis of stereotypes. In an interview with a female undergraduate in computer science, Barker was told that when asked if she could join an all-male informal study group, one male replied, "why should we let you join? You're a girl. What do you know?" This honest young man was projecting a stereotype onto his female peer. Thus research on student retention in computer science supports creating an environment where students can truly get to know each other intellectually through discussions about and practice with computer science concepts and applications.

When students talk about what they are learning, they benefit from trying to articulate it as well as hearing their peers talk. The benefits of structured collaborative learning opportunities go beyond retention, however, to reinforce the framing that O'Neill hopes to accomplish: the role of students is to learn together and see each other as resources for learning. Requiring student collaboration sets the frame by making working together an unquestioned, expected condition. Co-author Barker observed a lab session for O'Neill's class in which about 26 students were working on an assignment. Two students whose regular partner were not there simply paired up informally. Students leaned inward to each other looking at their screens, and there was a constant buzz of talk. In that lab, it appeared that serious work was being done, but with no fear of speaking. The way that O'Neill implements pair programming also gives students many experiences talking with different students, reducing the anxiety of speaking up in class and reinforcing a belief that learning together is their role.

O'Neill uses a structured approach to pair programming, in which students take turns being driver and navigator, performing and switching roles according to best practices [15]. This structured approach implicitly reinforces the frame that students should take turns. Students are asked to self-organize into pairs three times a term and work with each partner on four lab assignments. As mentioned in Section 3.2.1, O'Neill preemptively addresses students' potential frustrations about working with a partner during the first class period. She tells them that it is always frustrating to watch another person using a mouse and working on a computer—but that it is equally frustrating for someone to watch them, so they should not be so quick to judge their programming partner.

4. EVALUATION FROM STUDENTS

End-of-semester questionnaires at HMC are similar to those at many other colleges and universities. They ask a range of questions about the course, the instructor, and the students' perceived outcomes. The graph in Figure 1 shows student responses to the item "The course stimulated my interest in the subject" in

O'Neill's data structures courses, during 16 terms in 11 years. Of the several questionnaire items, this is the best proxy for student engagement with the subject, a strong predictor of retention [23]. (Other items rate the instructor and the course.) The lines represent the standard error and the dot represents the mean, which has increased over time. Class size and related number of respondents have increased recently, with a mean of 21 (SD~5) responses per term through 2010, then doubling in 2011 and more than tripling to 75 in 2012. The variation in student responses have decreased over time while the mean scores have gone up.

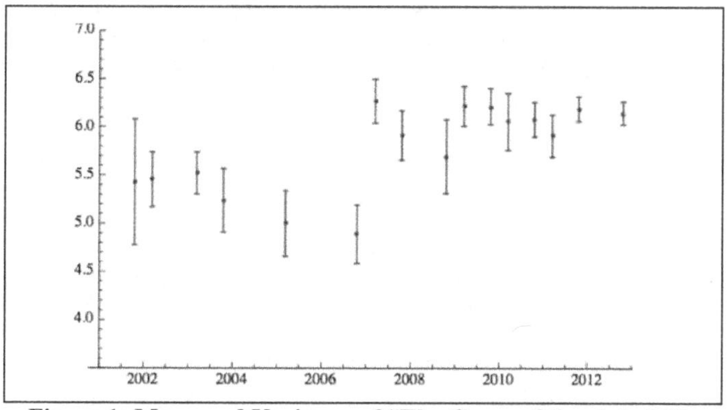

Figure 1: Mean and Variance of "The Course Stimulated My Interest in the Subject" for Data Structures, 16 Terms

Only a controlled experiment that rules out alternative explanations can suggest what caused the obvious upward trend in mean. For example, 11 more years experience teaching data structures is a reasonable explanation, although not everyone can improve their ratings over time. However, student comments related to outcomes of framing show that students appreciate the changes.

As reported in section 3.1, students had negative perceptions of outspoken students in class. O'Neill began experimenting with asking people to speak more if they were quiet and speak less if they were outspoken in 2005 to reduce domination by showoffs. Student comments showed appreciation that O'Neill had asked students who talked all the time to stop. Still, despite using the Socratic teaching style, about which students reported feeling as though they "were developing C++" and were "led to insight rather than lecturing," some students continued reporting annoyance at outspoken students in spring 2010. In fall 2010, O'Neill implemented the trading card system for turn taking. Students were aware that turn taking was the way class progressed and not only did comments about domineering students go away (despite a large increase in total number of comments), but students expressed appreciation at being pushed outside their comfort zone and to pay attention in class. For example, "[the trading card] system allowed me to speak (forced rather) and I am very appreciative of this fact. It also forces me to focus more in order not to screw up" and "it was guaranteed you weren't favoring students. Also, it actually got me to talk and be involved. I would still have enjoyed the class otherwise, but I would have been totally silent."

In 2003, O'Neill began requiring pair programming, making sure that students would have a partner to ask questions of. Responses have been mixed, with some students appreciative of and others disliking pairing. For example, one student wrote that having to pair was a time sink and not used in the "real world" while another wrote, "I liked pair programming because I had to explain my ideas before implementing them and had someone else to help when I got stuck." These responses are consistent with studies of pair programming [13,17, 24, 28]. O'Neill finds that because pair programming encourages students to work with each other to find answers, fewer students come to office hours to ask questions. Although it is not her goal to avoid students, she certainly wants to reduce student frustration caused by missing simple syntactical errors in solo programming. When they do have questions, the questions are more specific and faster to work through.

5. CONCLUSION

Explicitly framing the classroom climate and reinforcing that framing through daily turn-taking techniques and pair programming transformed the course from one where student showoffs shut down quieter students to one where students expected to speak and be spoken to routinely. Presenting wrong answers still made students nervous, but also became a routine event that did not make any individual student stand out as weak.

Harvey Mudd College is one of few colleges that require all students to take a computer science class, increasing all students' awareness of what computer science is and at least some understanding of computer science-based careers. This is often presented as a solution for increasing the participation of women and underrepresented minorities in computer science. Taking such a course, however, does not guarantee that students will declare the major. It is important also for students to be interested, feel that they can belong as a member of the community of practice, and feel confident that they will be successful [20]. In 2006, Harvey Mudd faculty made the introductory course sequence more attractive without dumbing it down, with the explicit goal to increase women's participation [1]. They also implemented other recruiting and retention tactics, such as sending letters of invitation from the president of the college and sending women to the Grace Hopper Celebration of Women in Computing. However, classroom practices are pivotal for sustaining interest, feelings of competence and confidence, and supporting the development of a sense of belonging and growing identity as a computer scientist. Word of mouth that follow-on courses will be interesting and supportive are drivers for getting recruits to declare the major.

The increase in percentage of women graduating at Harvey Mudd illustrates that the teaching method can aid with retention of an especially difficult group in computer science. Women often leave computer science with higher grades than the men who stay, suggesting it is not ability that pushes them away [16, 26, 30]. In both 2011 and 2012, 41 percent of Harvey Mudd computer science bachelor's degrees were awarded to women. Figure 2 shows how remarkable these figures are compared to prior years. Taking the data structures course is a step toward the major, but can still be counted as an elective if a student decides to leave. Using effective retention mechanisms is crucial.

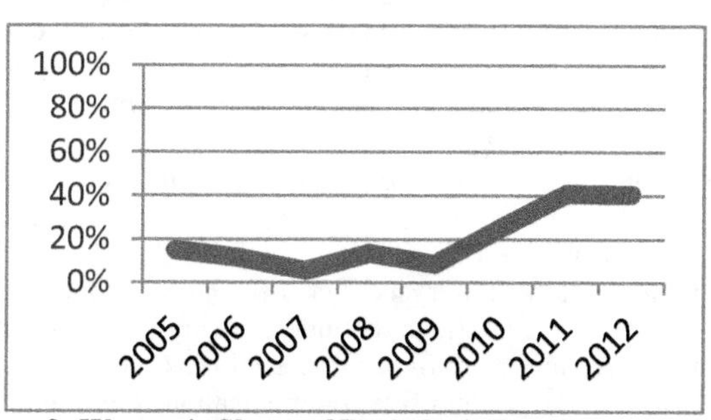

Figure 2: Women's Share of Bachelor's Degrees Awarded at Harvey Mudd College, 2005-2012 [31]

Framing the course and classroom environment as a challenging context in which it is okay to make and learn from mistakes, where all students will participate equally, and where co-learning is encouraged and even required is a valuable tool in the retention toolbox. In class and in lab, students recognize each other's contributions, participate equally, and learn with and from each other. The interpretive frame that makes this possible does not happen automatically, however. Faculty cannot change their students' personalities or background socialization, but they can set and reinforce rules that improve classroom climate.

6. RELATED WORK ON CLASSROOM MANAGEMENT

Several books and articles provide educators with practical tips and strategies for classroom management. Sterling [29] discusses the importance of setting up the physical environment of the class and setting expectations early on. Similarly, Lemov [19] and Good & Brophy [12] offer practical guidelines for classroom management. Powell & Powell [24] present strategies for communicating effectively and creating learning environments that address the many forms of diversity in classrooms. Thank you to an anonymous reviewer for pointing out some of these readings.

7. ACKNOWLEDGMENTS

This case study was funded by National Science Foundation Award #1123332. Thank you to transcriber Evan Hofmockel and data preparation consultant Richard Barker. Special thanks to our reviewers for suggesting improvements to the paper.

8. REFERENCES

[1] Alvarado, C. and Dodds, Z. 2010. Women in CS: an evaluation of three promising practices. *Proceedings of the 41st ACM technical symposium on Computer science education* (Milwaukee, Wisconsin, USA, 2010), 57–61.

[2] Astin, A.W. 1984. Student involvement: A developmental theory for higher education. *Journal of College Student Personnel*. 25, 4 (1984), 297–308.

[3] Astin, A.W. 1993. *What matters in college? Four critical years revisited.* Jossey-Bass.

[4] Baeten, M., Dochy, F. and Struyven, K. 2013. The effects of different learning environments on students' motivation for learning and their achievement. *British Journal of Educational Psychology*. 83, 3 (2013), 484–501.

[5] Barker, L.J. and Garvin-Doxas, K. 2004. Making visible the behaviors that influence learning environment: A qualitative exploration of computer science classrooms. *Computer Science Education*. 14, 2 (2004), 119–146.

[6] Barker, L.J., Garvin-Doxas, K. and Jackson, M. 2002. Defensive climate in the computer science classroom. *ACM SIGCSE Bulletin*. 34, 1 (2002), 43–47.

[7] Barker, L.J., McDowell, C. and Kalahar, K. 2009. Exploring factors that influence computer science introductory course students to persist in the major. *Proceedings of the 40th ACM technical symposium on Computer science education* (Chattanooga, TN, USA, 2009), 153–157.

[8] Bateson, G. 1972. *Steps to an ecology of mind; collected essays in anthropology, psychiatry, evolution, and epistemology*. Chandler Pub. Co.

[9] Blumenfeld, P.C., Mergendoller, J.R. and Swarthout, D.W. 1987. Task as a heuristic for understanding student learning and motivation. *Journal of Curricul*. 19, 2 (1987), 135–148.

[10] Gibb, J.R. 1961. Defensive communication. *Journal of Communication*. 2, 3 (1961), 141–148.

[11] Goffman, E. 1974. *Frame analysis: an essay on the organization of experience*. Harper & Row.

[12] Good, T.L. and Brophy, J.E. 2000. *Looking in classrooms*. Longman.

[13] Hanrahan, M. 1998. The effect of learning environment factors on students' motivation and learning. *International Journal of Science Education*. 20, 6 (1998), 737–753.

[14] Harvey Mudd College Computer Science Course Descriptions: *http://www.cs.hmc.edu/program/course-descriptions/*.

[15] Jacobson, N. and Schaefer, S.K. 2008. Pair programming in CS1: overcoming objections to its adoption. *SIGCSE Bull.* 40, 2 (2008), 93–96.

[16] Katz, S., Allbritton, D., Aronis, J., Wilson, C. and Soffa, M.L. 2006. Gender, achievement, and persistence in an undergraduate computer science program. *The DATA BASE for Advances in Information Systems*. 37, 4 (2006), 42–57.

[17] Knowles, M., Holton, E.F., III and Swanson, R.A. 2005. *The adult learner*. Elsevier.

[18] Lea, S.J., Stephenson, D. and Troy, J. 2003. Higher Education Students' Attitudes to Student-centred Learning: Beyond "educational bulimia"? *Studies in Higher Education*. 28, 3 (2003), 321–334.

[19] Lemov, D. 2010. *Teach like a champion*. Gildan Media.

[20] Lent, Brown and Hackett 2000. Contextual supports and barriers to career choice: A social cognitive analysis. *Journal of Counseling Psychology*. 47, 1 (2000), 36–49.

[21] McDowell, C., Werner, L., Bullock, H.E. and Fernald, J. 2003. The impact of pair programming on student performance, perception and persistence. *International Conference on Software Engineering* (Portland, Oregon, 2003), 602–607.

[22] Östberg, V. 2003. Children in classrooms: peer status, status distribution and mental well-being. *Social Science & Medicine*. 56, 1 (Jan. 2003), 17–29.

[23] Pascarella, E.T. and Terenzini, P.T. 1991. *How college affects students: Findings and insights from twenty years of research*. Jossey-Bass.

[24] Powell, R.G. and Powell, D. 2010. *Classroom communication and diversity: Enhancing instructional practice.* Routledge.

[25] R. D. Fulton 1991. A conceptual model for understanding the physical attributes of learning environments. *Creating environments for effective adult learning*. Hiemstra, R., ed. Jossey-Bass. 13–22.

[26] Roberts, M.R.H., McGill, T. and Koppi, T. 2011. What Students are Telling us about Why They Left Their ICT Course. *Innovation in Teaching and Learning in Information and Computer Sciences*. 10, 3 (Nov. 2011), 68–83.

[27] Schmuck, R.A. and Schmuck, P.A. 2001. *Group processes in the classroom*. McGraw Hill.

[28] Simon, B. and Hanks, B. 2008. First-year students' impressions of pair programming in CS1. *J. Educ. Resour. Comput.* 7, 4 (Jan. 2008), 5:1–5:28.

[29] Sterling, D.R. 2009. Classroom management: Setting up the classroom for learning. *Science Scope*. 32, 9 (2009), 29–33.

[30] Strenta, A.C., Elliott, R., Adair, R., Matier, M. and Scott, J. 1994. Choosing and Leaving Science in Highly Selective Institutions. *Res. High. Educ.* 35, 5 (1994), 513–547.

[31] The Integrated Postsecondary Education Data System: *http://nces.ed.gov/ipeds/*. Accessed: 2010-03-21.

[32] Think-Pair-Share: *http://serc.carleton.edu/introgeo/interactive/tpshare.html*. Accessed: 2013-09-06.

[33] Titsworth, B.S. 2001. Immediate and delayed effects of interest cues and engagement cues on students' affective learning. *Communication Studies*. 52, 3 (2001), 169–179.

[34] Williams, L.A. 2000. Strengthening the case for pair programming. *IEEE Software*. 17, 4 (2000), 17–25.

Multiple Case Study of Nerd Identity in a CS1 Class

Don Davis
University of Texas at San Antonio
Dept. of Interdisciplinary Learning and Teaching
Don.Davis@utsa.edu

Timothy T. Yuen
University of Texas at San Antonio
Dept. of Interdisciplinary Learning and Teaching
Timothy.Yuen@utsa.edu

Matthew Berland
University of Wisconsin at Madison
Dept. of Curriculum and Instruction
mberland@wisc.edu

ABSTRACT
This paper discusses two case studies of students observed in an introductory computer science (CS1) course. Observations reinforce notions of the potential benefits of culturally and personally relevant instruction in the computer science (CS) classroom and call into question the stigmatization of 'nerd' culture within the literature of CS education. As this study is qualitative and exploratory in nature, it does not provide definitive, statistically generalizable findings – however, it does unearth nuanced and potentially beneficial pathways of investigation for CS educators and researchers that many quantitative methods might miss. Specifically, observations highlight potential benefits of supporting students' perceptions of more diverse CS identities including broader understandings of the "CS nerd" identity.

Categories and Subject Descriptors
K.3.0 [**Computers and Education**]: K.3.0 General

General Terms
Human Factors.

Keywords
Nerd, CS identity, Case study, qualitative

1. INTRODUCTION
Even before diversity in CS matriculation began to seriously decline after 2000 [15, 48], there was substantial concern that the emergent "hacker" culture and similar cliques could alienate others from CS participation [24]. There have been frequent observations of CS classrooms highlighting that the visibility of "nerd" [4] culture might alienate and limit (nerd and non-nerd) participation in CS [5, 20, 29, 33]. The terms hacker, geek, and nerd are frequently used interchangeably [34]. Less frequently discussed is the notion that though such stigmatized perceptions may deter CS participation [cf. 34], there is also the possibility that such perceptions might (be adapted to) motivate people to enter the CS field. Although some extant literature examines benefits of diverse nerd identities [8, 17], there has been little documentation of such within more diverse CS classrooms. This paper will examine the observed role of identity in a CS1 course and potential relationships between nerd identity and engagement with CS course content.

SIGCSE'14, March 5–8, 2014, Atlanta, Georgia, USA.

ACM 978-1-4503-2605-6/14/03…$15.00.
http://dx.doi.org/10.1145/2538862.2538933

2. BACKGROUND
Researchers note certain elements concomitant with nerd persona such as a myopic focus on computers [33], obsession with video games [19, 29], and a love of science fiction [4]. Many researchers indicate that such nerd-related elements are counterproductive to CS participation [4, 19, 20, 29, 32, 33]. For example, previous research has highlighted that video games discussions can negatively influence the participation of non-videogame players as well as negatively impacting videogame players' CS success [19, 29]. Further, disproportionate amounts of bragging, which do not correlate with CS achievement, may unnecessarily impede participation by creating a hostile, negative CS classroom environment [1, 10, 29]. Moreover, perceptions of "nerdiness" may limit women's desire to participate in CS [19, 20, cf. 34]. Such findings reify perceptions of computer science as dominated by asocial, white, male nerds [4, 29, 33]. Consequently, in attempts to broaden participation, there has been a push to dissociate CS from maleness [23, 31] and from "nerdiness" [4].

2.1 Reducing CS stereotypes
Several studies highlight various ways in which countering prevalent CS stereotypes might support greater and more diverse CS participation. Townsend [31] found that by using video models of women CS role models, female students' affect towards CS could be longitudinally improved. Cheryan et al. [4] found that by removing "nerd" artifacts from a CS environment, a broader selection of students expressed interest in pursuing CS career pathways. Such findings seem to support the elimination of "nerd" associations from CS in order to promote greater diversity. However, in discussing problems of the "nerd" (or "geek") label, Varma [34] points out that such generalizations are highly problematic and are most applicable to "white women's experience in an elite university" in contrast to the struggles of racially/ethnically diverse women elsewhere (p. 373). Moreover, Betz and Sekaquaptewa's [2] findings indicate efforts to dissociate CS from "nerd" associations may have unanticipated consequences that may negatively impact students' participation in CS. Common to the studies critical of 'nerdiness' is the assumption that the path to broadening CS participation is to simply dissociate CS from any potentially 'nerdy' elements and remove all traces of nerd culture – in essence, the belief is that by removing 'nerds' from CS, diversity will increase. However, although a few studies have suggested potential benefits to reducing 'nerdiness' in the CS classroom, other studies highlight that there may be no or even adverse effects in trying to dissociate

CS from 'nerdiness'. This suggests that educators may want to reconsider simple nerd/no-nerd dichotomies.

2.2 The Need to (Re)consider "Nerd" Identity

Within the literature of CS, the impact of students' perceived possible selves is a recurrent theme, though perhaps not referred to as such. Many researchers note that underrepresented students may indicate they are not the types of students who do CS, often despite evidence to the contrary [20, 29, 33]. These student beliefs are significant because students' perceived possible selves [6, 7, 21] can and do significantly impact their career choices. These career choices, in turn, are especially important because they have a substantial impact on students' eventual careers, more so than test scores [28]. Underrepresented students' representation might especially suffer if lacking the necessary supports to promote CS careers as possible or relevant [6, 15, 33, 35]. Furthermore, for many students underrepresented in CS, class and program structures of CS represent greater obstacles than stereotypes, and such students may require additional supports [32–34]. In order to address such obstacles, we must first look at how current CS students face and/or overcome the challenges of stereotypes and underrepresentation. In particular, this paper examines how "nerd" identities facilitated students' engagement with computer science and bolstered their participation and persistence in an introductory CS course.

3. RESEARCH DESIGN

This study was a preliminary exploration into CS students' identities and their engagement in computer science. This study followed a multiple case study design in which more than one case was studied to draw generalizations regarding a phenomenon [27]. The findings presented are useful as they provide nuanced insight into phenomena and highlight potentially beneficial avenues of future research that other methods may miss [13, 26].

3.1 Setting

The study took place in a CS1 course at large university, an HSI (Hispanic Serving Institution), in south Texas during the summer of 2012. This CS1 course was an introductory programming course using Java, the first required course for the computer science major. Math and math education majors could also use this course as part of a computer science requirement for their degree. The course was held over a 10-week summer session. Classes were held in a computer lab twice a week for approximately 2 hours each meeting. The course format was a mix of lectures, interactive discussions, and hands-on activities. For example, the instructor would present a short lecture followed by some discussions in which students were asked to provide feedback. In most class meetings, the instructor gave time for students to work on practice programming activities or lab assignments while he walked around assisting the students. Students were encouraged to talk with each other and to seek help from one another.

3.2 Participants

Participants represented an opportunistic sample, recruited by the first author, from the CS course approximately four weeks into the summer session. The first author presented the study and described the terms of participation. Participants had to be registered in the CS course and over the age of 18. Participation was voluntary. There were two participants for this study. Other students volunteered but did not meet the minimum age requirement.

The two participants for this study were "David" and "Maria" (pseudonyms). Both David and Maria were eighteen-year-old undergraduate students enrolled in their first semester at the university. Students were not asked to list their ethnicities; however, observations of the class indicate that dichotomous groupings of students into "white" and "not-white" or similar would be a disservice to students and a gross oversimplification of the myriad facets of their identities.

Maria described herself as a "math nerd." She was not a CS major, but rather a math major fulfilling the university CS requirement. She seemed reserved, soft-spoken, and courteous. She interacted less often with classmates than David. Her courteous disposition was evident in frequent smiles and the regular use of phrases such as "nice to meet you", "hi, how are you?" and other such elements that might be described as polite.

David did not describe himself as a "nerd" to the researcher although many of his observable identity related behaviors such as those related to being an avid gamer and anime/manga fan (to be discussed later) strongly suggested such leanings. David was unsure whether he wanted to major in CS, though he did consider it a possibility, as both his parents were programmers. David was quite friendly and more extroverted. His amicable nature was evident in frequent smiles as well as humorous asides to classmates, the instructor, and the researcher.

3.3 Procedures

The first author observed and video recorded participants' during each class meeting of the last six weeks of the ten-week course except on test days (nine of eleven class days were filmed). The observer and field notes served as the primary instruments for data collection [20] supported by video recording of students' interactions with other students and the instructor. Video cameras were pointed at the participants as well as their computer screens in order to film their social interactions and their computer-based activities. The researcher filmed a total of nine meetings for about 27 hours (13.5 hours x two cameras) of video footage.

3.4 Researcher/Participant

The second author was the instructor of this course. The first author took the lead in designing and conducting the data collection. Thus, the second author did not know who consented to this study during the course. He was not in the room during recruitment. Additionally, multiple cameras were set up in a way that the second author was not aware of who was actually being recorded. The second author did not alter his teaching strategies. The methods described in a previous section are the methods he typically uses when teaching the course. The second author did not engage with this study until the course ended.

3.5 Analysis

As the purpose of this study was primarily exploratory, the first author relied on descriptive coding to develop themes throughout the ongoing analysis of data [25]. The two overarching themes (codes) identified were "reinforces (CS) nerd stereotype" and "contradicts (CS) nerd stereotype." It should be noted that quantifying qualitative observations is problematic and may be misleading as it may provide a false sense of generality [32]. Such figures are provided here as reference points rather than definitive measurements. As with other qualitative research, the findings presented here are intended to highlight possibilities and expose unexamined elements rather than provide concrete generalizations [13, 26].

Throughout the course of the study, the first author served as the primary instrument of data collection and analysis [13] keeping a detailed journal of in class observations. The first author then revisited the video recordings and transcribed student conversations [teacher talk was not transcribed]. Next, the first author used an open coding process [25] to highlight various types of discourse and potentially identify salient themes therein. Next, during the second cycle coding the first author was substantively guided by Carlone and Johnson's [3] Science Identity Model (developed to discuss women of color's science identities), Gee's figured worlds and big-D Discourse tools [11] (which examine participants' perceptions of their world and their perceived place in it) as well as the literature of CS and STEM underrepresentation, especially that of Goode [12], Kisselburgh et al. [18], and Varma [32]. Following Carlone and Johnson's model, the first author sought to identify discourse elements related to: competence, performance, and recognition (p. 1190) in relation to CS identities. In attempting to identify these elements and searching for an appropriate descriptor for the commonalities, researchers noted an underlying current of 'nerdiness' – the discourse was then revisited and re-examined to determine the potential role of 'nerdiness' in participants' discourse.

3.6 Strategies for Trustworthiness

The researchers sought to establish this study's trustworthiness primarily on the basis of credibility, transferability, authenticity, and coherence [13]. In order to establish the study's credibility, researchers documented the steps used and utilized a methodology aligned with the socio-cultural concerns identified in the literature. The researchers have attempted to provide detailed descriptions of the research process in order to bolster the study's transferability. Frequent use of participant language within research findings is intended to strengthen the study's authenticity. The study's methodology strongly aligns with the stated goals of the research, which reinforces the study's coherence.

4. RESULTS

Both David and Maria were among the top participators in class. Based on the first author's observations of the class, they and the other students in the front rows also seemed to be the most engaged and "happier" (as evidenced through their smiles, other facial expressions, and occasional "chuckles"). They both frequently asked questions of the teacher as well as provided answers (see Figures 1 and 2).

During class, Maria was most often engaged with taking notes or trying code examples in the (integrated development environment) IDE. When talking, Maria frequently asked genuine clarifying questions of the professor such as "How do you get it to change colors if it's a for-loop?" She would ask in her courteous, apologetic manner: "Sorry, I have a question. What if I want an array?" She also provided meaningful corrections to the professor's code examples as when she pointed out to the professor (after being prompted in the whole class format), "that one's not going to work because you don't have the second variable." She also provided frequent responses to the professor's queries for completions to code snippets and missing code elements.

Beginning with Maria's first observed conversation (beyond perfunctory "how do you do?") and continuing throughout the course, Maria's responses displayed a predilection for providing math related answers. Her first recorded response to the professor was "x times y." This was followed by an analysis of number patterns and calculations of string length. In subsequent classes, she provided procedures for identifying multiples of three, identified the need for finding a sum of two numbers, described procedures for identifying odd numbers (e.g. "if number mod 2 [equals] 1"), and replied to many questions requiring familiarity with integer variable types and the random number method. She even jested about how funny it would be if a die roll returned a decimal instead of an integer. She also displayed confidence with "logical or's" and Boolean logic more so than other classmates (including David).

David was a frequent contributor to classroom discussions. He seemed very comfortable within the class and with classmates. This was apparent in many of David's behaviors including his cheerful disposition (as noticeable through his smile and frequent banter) and friendly tone. He and his group of friends were typically the first to arrive in the classroom – they usually sat in the hall until class doors were opened thirty minutes before class began. Before class, David would sit and talk to his friends often while showing YouTube videos or other curiosities from the internet. Many of the videos observed were recordings of played videogames or Machinima.

David exuded a strong interest in games and other elements of what some might consider "nerd" culture. He consistently set his desktop background with the same image from the same videogame. He seemed particularly enthralled by this game and even described the game to the researcher. In talking with friends he mentioned video games, playing collectible trading card games, and similar pursuits. Before class, he watched anime and during class he could be seen looking at black and white manga on his iPad.

Although, he was occasionally observed engaging in off task behaviors during class, he provided frequent contributions to the class in addition to the occasional friendly aside to the professor. More frequently than the majority of other students (not including Maria), he answered many of the questions posed to the class by the professor.

His first observed responses involved explaining how to access a program from within the IDE, the pixel size of a screen to be drawn, and indicating a preference for graphics related assignments. He even found humor in the drawing of a circle intersecting the boundaries of a screen which he jested "could be quicksand." His responses seemed to gravitate towards 'for' loops and other conditional statements. He frequently displayed amusement with course content describing a project drawing flags as "cool," which is how he (alone) described Unicode and UTF-8 encoding (in response to the Asian characters) when it was presented to the class, as well as voicing enthusiasm ("whoo") for an explanation provided by the professor.

Despite off-task Manga reading or watching "the secret lives of cats," which provided a stark contrast to Maria's frequent note-taking, David engaged in many positive and supportive behaviors. He, in contrast to others in the room, would frequently photograph content on the white board. This frequently occurred when material was presented as an important new concept or during test reviews.

Moreover, David appeared very motivated to help others. He often provided assistance to others even asking the professor "is it OK if I help people?" On one occasion he went to the board to help another student. In fact, the professor found it necessary to occasionally redirect David's good-natured desire (apparent through a smile, tone of voice, and body language) to help others. This is not to indicate that David was convinced of his own infallibility; quite the contrary, he would admit struggles with the material indicating "it was really hard. I'll need some help."

David and Maria worked seemingly as equals. This relationship was apparent in that they would ask one another for help with approximately equal frequency. David could be seen looking over at Maria's screen for guidance with the same approximate frequency that Maria looked at David's screen. They also assisted one another with equivalent frequency stating "here do what I do", "just type…", or providing other direct instructions. Although they worked as equals, David helped Maria to smile (or even "chuckle") more so than vice-versa.

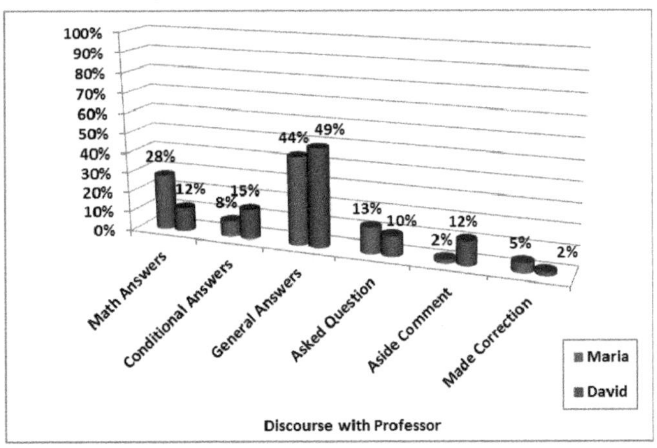

Figure 1. Percent of students' discourse with instructor

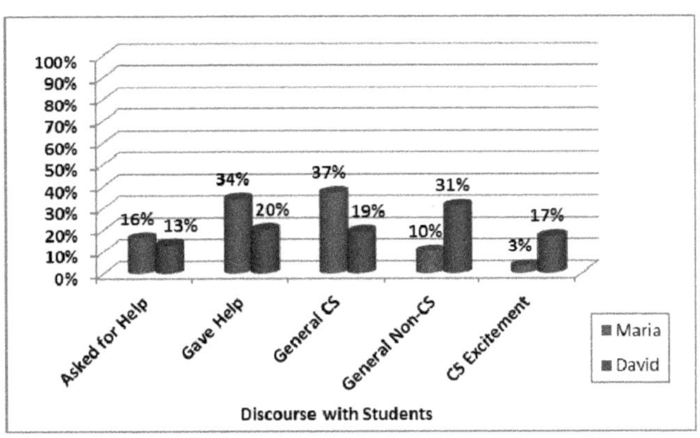

Figure 2. Percent of students' discourse with others

DISCUSSION

Contrasts to Previous Findings

David's behavior exhibited many of the "nerd" related attributes frequently identified in CS contexts. David displayed substantial interest in video (and other) games [cf. 19, 29]. His outside interests (e.g. manga, Scandinavian mythology, etc.) may have occasionally negatively impacted his focus in the class at times [cf. 29]. He also exhibited humor e.g. stating the instructor seemed "fancy" and asking if the instructor "partied," comments that may seem reflective of jocular CS classrooms described elsewhere [19, 20]. Additionally, comments such as "that's easy" or "haven't you finished yet?" to classmates could seem indicative of the negative, hierarchy building classrooms described by Garvin-Doxas and Barker [10]. Similarly, Maria's seeming interpersonal shyness could seem to reflect the alienated young women described in other CS literature [20, 29]. Her occasional corrections of the instructor could also be decontextualized and presented as exemplifying the hierarchy building discourse described by Barker and Garvin-Doxas [1]. However, this is not the case. As observed and interpreted within the classroom, Maria's and David's discourse was delivered with friendly tones and open body language that seemed to contribute to a positive, friendly, and supportive classroom environment.

4.1 Beneficial Nerd Engagement

Both David and Maria's interactions with one another, other students, and the instructor seemed to promote a positive supportive classroom environment. Their comments and behaviors revealed that they felt comfortable and engaged in the class. Interactions with the instructor and other students seemed to promote their learning and the learning of others rather than hinder it. As described within the observations section, their effusive comfort and engagement with the course seemed to be anchored in and interwoven with their nerd personae. It seemed that their nerd personae bolstered their engagement with and (apparent) concomitant success in the course.

Namely, the pattern and frequency of Maria's comments appeared substantively related to her math interests. This was evident (per Figure 1) in her frequent, seemingly "joyful" engagement with math related topics. For example, not only did she frequently respond to math related questions, but she utilized her understanding to support classmates, as when she explained to the class how to write a function to detect odd numbers using modulo. Her enthusiasm for math seemed to coincide with her ability to latch on to math related functions e.g. she quickly adopted and explained to others the use of random number functions in Java.

Similarly, as elements related to David's nerd identity presented themselves, David displayed marked enthusiasm. For example, David exclaiming "that's cool" in response to the use of Unicode for displaying "Asian" characters presented a stark contrast to the noticeably disinterested facial expressions of his classmates and may have related to his frequently observed interest in elements of Japanese pop-culture (an interest considered common among "nerds"). Such connected engagement also became apparent as he expressed interest in coding graphical elements (e.g. random functions for generating "fireworks") that related to his video game interests.

It is unclear to what extent David and Maria's nerd-related interests buoyed their overall increased participation in class. It was apparent, however, that such connections did bolster their enthusiasm and engagement and that many of their classmates may have benefitted from such connections.

4.2 Beyond Nerd Stigma

Varma [34] emphasizes that the estrangement caused by the "geek" label described elsewhere [19, 20] may not reflect the experiences of minorities (including minority women) at other institutions. Rather, she highlights that the "geek" (here "nerd") label might in fact be a welcome alternative to "working class" or "minority" labels [34]. She indicates that attributing the underrepresentation of women to "nerd" associations does a great disservice to the struggles of the greater majority of women (low-SES and minority) underrepresented in CS; rather, she emphasizes that there are many other, more significant, factors (finances, familial obligations) contributing the underrepresentation of women in CS [32–34].

Considering the significant difficulties faced by students attempting to study CS, it becomes apparent that measures must be taken to bolster students along their CS journey. There have been efforts to promote female participation in CS through role models that showed improved perceptions of CS [31] as well as substantive efforts with near-peer modeling that have bolstered Latina/o participation in CS [2, 15, 24]. This is necessary in order to meet the CS demands of the future including CS that provides software tailored to the needs of all demographics [9, 22, 30].

Though some research has attempted to remove the nerd stigma from CS in order to bolster participation [4], other research [2] highlights that attempts to remove all nerdiness may suffer unintended consequences. Significant research indicates the significance of students' perceived possible selves [6, 7, 15, 21] on their engagement and participation with academics. Such findings suggest that extending imaginations of who computer programmers are might broaden participation [16]. The identities performed and realized by David and Maria may reflect this to an extent.

4.3 Reimagining CS Nerds

As previously discussed, Maria and David exhibited strong components of "nerd" identities. Maria quite bluntly vocalized her identification stating she was a "math nerd." David's probable "nerd" persona was made apparent through his conversations and displayed behaviors. Both David and Maria contributed significantly to the class and were significantly engaged with the class content, seemingly bolstered by their "nerd" identities.

Maria and David (and others not included in the study) could be described as "nerds" but they diverged from the "asocial, white, male nerd" stereotype in many ways [4, 19]. Moreover, their nerd identities could be seen to bolster their participation. Rather than creating an asocial hostile environment, both David and Maria were quite amicable, courteous, and displayed strong helping behaviors rather than belittling or asserting superiority [cf. 10]. For both of them, their "nerd" identities seemed to bolster participation and engagement. For Maria, this was evidenced in her predilection for "math nerd" type questions. For David, it became apparent in his comfort and engagement with the classroom, his predilection for archetypal CS questions such as conditional statements [cf. 14] and his enthusiasm for the class and its assignments. Though they were both CS nerds, they confounded the stereotype while benefiting from its associations. So, rather than seeking to limit associations with the CS nerd, it may help to broaden conceptions of CS nerds.

5. IMPLICATIONS

Betz and Sekaquaptewa's [2] study shows that blatantly countering "nerd" stereotypes may cause more harm than help. Moreover, Varma [34] illustrates how "nerd" identities may be perceived as positive by some (especially, those most underrepresented in CS). Furthermore, in CS the focus should be on increasing perceived relevance (not limiting it) in order to encourage broader participation [6, 17]. The importance of identity to participation is replete throughout CSE literature and elsewhere. Hewner and Knobelsdorf [16] highlight the benefits of reimaging CS students to promote broader CS participation. Observations of David and Maria indicate that nerd identities may bolster success without reifying problematic aspects of the "white, male, asocial" nerd. Considering David and Maria through the lens of Varma [34] who indicates that a "geek" label is not really the problem, Hewner and Knobelsdof's [16] call to expand conceptions CS students, and significant literature detailing the importance of identity and perceived relevance to participation [8, 10, 26, 27, 31, 41, 49, 50], it may behoove researchers to examine potential benefits of broadening perceptions of CS nerd identity (e.g. to bolster Latina and other underrepresented nerds) rather than simply eschewing "nerds" out of hand.

5.1 Limitations

The main limitation to this study is the length of the engagement time with the participants. The 10-week summer schedule limited the number of weeks that the first author was able to conduct his observations. Future in-depth studies will follow participants beyond the first CS course and into other CS courses in order to examine the extent of the impact of identities and, perhaps, how those identities change throughout time.

6. CONCLUSIONS

Our analyses of David and Maria's discourse highlight how their nerd identities bolstered their participation and engagement within the CS1 classroom. More significantly, their nerd-grounded identities not only supported their interest in the content and its perceived relevance, but did so in such way that they were both jovial with and supportive of fellow classmates and the instructor. In contrast to many current perceptions of 'nerd' culture as solely the domain of white, asocial males, David and Maria built their CS engagement on the foundations of multi-faceted nerd identities at odds with common imaginings of 'nerdiness'. Owing to the benefits they and the class derived from their nerd identities, considering that many of the students substantively underrepresented in CS may be unfamiliar with (or unaffected by) the common CS nerd stereotypes, and noting that some attempts to dissociate STEM from nerdiness have had unintentional averse effects, perhaps approaches to nerd culture and its role and interpretation in the CS classroom should be reexamined. Rather than throw the baby out with the bath water, it may behoove CS educators and researchers to re-examine the potential role of 'nerd' identities – should they really be only relegated to asocial, white, males? Instead, researchers and educators might strive to identify how CS identities (including CS "nerd" identities) and students' concomitant perceived possible selves might be broadened (in the CS classroom and elsewhere) to support and engage greater numbers of CS students from diverse backgrounds without marginalizing those backgrounds. We recommend that, instead of simply seeking to remove nerds and nerd culture from CS in order to bolster and broaden CS participation, researchers and educators consider working to broaden students' perceptions of who can be a 'CS nerd' while seeking to foster and bolster a myriad of diverse CS nerd identities – whether they be CS math nerds, CS games nerds, CS sports nerds, CS (natural) language nerds, or some other nerd variation - through personally and culturally relevant code (and career) examples and class assignments.

7. REFERENCES

[1] Barker, L.J. and Garvin-Doxas, K. 2004. Making visible the behaviors that influence learning environment: A qualitative exploration of computer science classrooms. *Computer Science Education*. 14, (2004), 119–145.

[2] Betz, D.E. and Sekaquaptewa, D. 2012. My Fair Physicist? Feminine Math and Science Role Models Demotivate Young Girls. *Social Psychological and Personality Science*. (Mar. 2012).

[3] Carlone, H.B. and Johnson, A. 2007. Understanding the science experiences of successful women of color: Science identity as an analytic lens. *Journal of Research in Science Teaching*. 44, 8 (2007), 1187–1218.

[4] Cheryan, S. et al. 2009. Ambient belonging: How stereotypical cues impact gender participation in computer science. *Journal of Personality and Social Psychology*. 97, 6 (2009), 1045–1060.

[5] Cohoon, J.P. 2007. An introductory course format for promoting diversity and retention. *Proceedings of the 38th SIGCSE technical symposium on Computer science education* (New York, NY, USA, 2007), 395–399.

[6] Cuero, K. and Kaylor, M. 2010. Engaging in travesuras: A Latino fifth-grader's disassociation from the schoolboy label. *International Journal of Multicultural Education*. 12, 1 (2010), 1–15.

[7] Dunkel, C.S. and Anthis, K.S. 2001. The role of possible selves in identity formation: A short-term longitudinal study. *Journal of Adolescence*. 24, 6 (2001), 765–776.

[8] Eglash, R. 2002. Race, Sex, and Nerds. *Social Text*. 20, 2 (2002), 49.

[9] Everett, A. and Watkins, C. 2008. The power of play: The portrayal and performance of race in video games (pp. The ecology of games: Connecting youth. *Foundation Series on Digital Media and Learning*. The MIT Press. 141–166.

[10] Garvin-Doxas, K. and Barker, L.J. 2004. Communication in computer science classrooms: Understanding defensive climates as a means of creating supportive behaviors. *J.Educ.Resour.Comput.* 4, 1 (2004).

[11] Gee, J.P. 2011. *How to do discourse analysis: A toolkit*. Routledge.

[12] Goode, J. 2008. Increasing diversity in K-12 computer science: Strategies from the field. *SIGCSE Bulletin*. 40, 1 (2008), 362–366.

[13] Hays, D. and Singh, A. 2012. *Qualitative inquiry in clinical and educational settings*. The Guilford Press.

[14] Herman, G.L. et al. 2010. Creating the digital logic concept inventory. *Proceedings of the 41st ACM technical symposium on Computer science education* (New York, NY, USA, 2010), 102–106.

[15] Hertzberg, M. 1998. Having Arrived: Dimensions of Educational Success in a Transitional Newcomer School. *Anthropology & Education Quarterly*. 29, 4 (1998), pp. 391–418.

[16] Hewner, M. and Knobelsdorf, M. 2008. Understanding computing stereotypes with self-categorization theory. *In Proceedings of Koli Calling International* (2008).

[17] Kendall, L. 2008. "The Nerd Within": Mass Media and the Negotiation of Identity Among Computer-Using Men. *The Journal of Men's Studies*. 7, 3 (Sep. 2008), 353–369.

[18] Kisselburgh, L.G. et al. the meaning of work: Rearticulating science, technology, and engineering careers through communicative lenses. *Communication Yearbook*. 33, 259–299.

[19] Margolis, J. and Fisher, A. 2003. Geek Mythology. *Bulletin of Science, Technology & Society*. 23, 1 (2003), 17–20.

[20] Margolis, J. and Fisher, A. 2003. *Unlocking the clubhouse: Women in computing*. The MIT Press.

[21] Markus, H. and Nurius, P. 1986. Possible selves. *American Psychologist*. 41, 9 (1986), 954–969.

[22] Miliszewska, I. et al. 2006. The issue of gender equity in computer science - What students say. *Journal of Information Technology Education*. 5, (2006), 107–120.

[23] Moorman, P. and Johnson, E. 2003. Still a stranger here: Attitudes among secondary school students towards computer science. Paper presented at the. *Proceedings of the 8th Annual Conference on Innovation and Technology in Computer Science* (Education, Thessaloniki, Greece, 2003), 193–197.

[24] Rasmussen, B. and Håpnes, T. 1991. Excluding women from the technologies of the future?: A case study of the culture of computer science. *Futures*. 23, 10 (1991), 1107–1119.

[25] Saldaña, J. 2009. *The coding manual for qualitative researchers*. Sage Publications, Inc.

[26] Spector, B.S. 1984. Qualitative research: Data analysis framework generating grounded theory applicable to the crisis in science education. *Journal of Research in Science Teaching*. 21, 5 (1984), 459–467.

[27] Stake, R.E. 2006. *Multiple case study analysis*. Guilford Press.

[28] Tai, R.T. et al. 2006. Planning early for careers in science. *Science*. 312, (2006), 1143–1145.

[29] Teague, D.M. 2009. A people-first approach to programming. *Proceedings of the Eleventh Australasian Conference on Computing Education - Volume 95* (Darlinghurst, Australia, Australia, 2009), 171–180.

[30] Tornatzky, L.G. et al. 2002. *Latinos and information technology: The promise and the challenge*. The Tomás Rivera Policy Institute.

[31] Townsend, G.C. 1996. Viewing video-taped role models improves female attitudes toward computer science. *Proceedings of the twenty-seventh SIGCSE technical symposium on Computer science education* (New York, NY, USA, 1996), 42–46.

[32] Varma, R. 2006. Making computer science minority-friendly. *Commun.ACM*. 49, 2 (2006), 129–134.

[33] Varma, R. 2010. Why so few women enroll in computing? Gender and ethnic differences in students' perception. *Computers Science Education*. 20, (2010), 301–316.

[34] Varma, R. 2007. Women in computing: The role of geek culture. *Science as Culture*. 16, 4 (Dec. 2007), 359–376.

[35] Zambrana, R. and Zoppi, I.M. 2002. Latina students: Translating cultural wealth into social capital to improve academic success. *Journal of Ethnic & Cultural Diversity in Social Work*. 11, 1/2 (2002), 33–53.

Camp CyberGirls: Using a Virtual World to Introduce Computing Concepts to Middle School Girls

Caitlin Hulsey
School of Computing
Clemson University
Clemson, SC 29634-0974
cbhulse@clemson.edu

Toni B. Pence
School of Computing
Clemson University
Clemson, SC 29634-0974
tbloodw@clemson.edu

Larry F. Hodges
School of Computing
Clemson University
Clemson, SC 29634-0974
lfh@clemson.edu

ABSTRACT

In this paper we report on the design and results of a one-week, residential summer camp experience that introduced computing concepts to middle school girls in the context of an online, multiplayer, virtual world known as the Curiosity Grid. In contrast to programming environments designed specifically as teaching tools to introduce children to programming, virtual world programming exposes novice learners to a more representative computer science experience. Students write real code and get real syntax errors when their code is not correct. They also design objects in a three-dimensional world where knowledge of mathematical concepts such as 3-D global and local coordinate systems, and 3-D transformations are important to the creation of objects and behaviors. Programming artifacts from the camp and feedback from the camp participants provide a strong argument that middle school girls can handle the challenge of this approach and even be enthusiastic about it.

Categories and Subject Descriptors

K.3.2 [**Computers and Education**]: Computer and Information Science Education - *computer science education, literacy.*

General Terms

Design, Human Factors, Languages

Keywords

Outreach, Middle School Girls, Virtual Worlds, Educational Programming Environments

1. MOTIVATION

A recent report sponsored by the Association for Computing Machinery and the Computer Science Teachers Association makes it clear that we are failing to prepare students with the computing skills that are needed, not only for jobs in computer science and information technology, but for almost every career in the information age [24]. The number of high school students who take AP Computer Science is a tenth or less of those taking AP Calculus or AP Biology [16]. For women the statistics are even worse. In 2012 less than 19% of students taking AP Computer Science were female [6]. This pipeline continues to shrink in college. Data collected from 152 US computer science departments indicate that less than 13% of bachelor's degrees in computer science awarded in 2012 were to women [25]. One of the problems with increasing student interest in computing as a major or career is that they have almost no experience with computer science as a discipline while in middle school and high school. They are required to take courses in subjects such as mathematics, literature, history, and science. However, computer science is not considered to be a core discipline that high school students must take, and no US state requires a computer science course as a condition of a student's graduation [24].

In response to the need to provide middle and high school students with knowledge of and experience in computing, many colleges and universities offer weekend workshops or one-week summer camps in computer science with goals of both teaching computing concepts to students and motivating them to consider majoring in a computing discipline in college [2,4,5,7,11]. These experiences are usually designed around programming environments that have been created specifically as teaching tools. Popular examples include Alice and its successors such as Storytelling Alice and Looking Glass [7,8,9,11,13], Scratch [2,4], and Lego Robots [5,14]. Common characteristics of these environments are that they are designed to be visual environments that can be used for development of simple games or animated stories, they employ a drag-and-drop metaphor, and they require little mathematical sophistication. Recently there has also been a trend to build companion websites to encourage and support long-term engagement of students in programming [9].

In this paper we report on a one-week, residential summer camp experience that introduced computing concepts to middle school girls in the context of a virtual world. Virtual worlds are online, multiplayer, user customizable via geometric modeling and programming, three-dimensional, social spaces where players are represented by avatars. The largest and best known virtual world is Second Life [22], but many other choices are available that range from publicly accessible worlds such as those hosted on OSGrid [19] or Third Rock Grid [1] in addition to worlds that are privately run by business, the military, or educational initiatives [10]. Many are used for educational purposes for a varied list of subjects. Examples include programs in virtual worlds designed to inform students about geosciences [20], forensic science [17], diversity [15], and international culture and politics [23].

SIGCSE'14, March 5–8, 2014, Atlanta, Georgia, USA.

ACM 978-1-4503-2605-6/14/03…$15.00.
http://dx.doi.org/10.1145/2538862.2538881

However, we could find no reviewed literature on using virtual worlds to introduce middle school students to computing! This is surprising since virtual worlds already include many of the characteristics that are being designed into programming environments for young students. Virtual worlds are visual environments with highly developed scripting (programming) and modeling tools. Since all interactions take place within an online, multiplayer virtual space, they are also social environments by default. Issues that may have discouraged their use for teaching computing concepts could be related to the relative sophistication required for scripting and modeling objects in virtual worlds. Programming in a virtual world is not a drag-and-drop exercise. Students write real code and get real syntax errors when their code is not correct. They also design objects in a three-dimensional world where knowledge of mathematical concepts such as 3-D global and local coordinate systems, and 3-D transformations (rotations, translations, and scales) are important to the creation of objects and behaviors. There are also issues of online safety for younger students if the environment allows interaction with unknown or unauthorized players.

2. CAMP CYBERGIRLS DESIGN

Camp CyberGirls was a one-week residential camp for middle school girls with the objectives of introducing them to computing concepts and encouraging their interest in computing with respect to their future college and professional aspirations. Students arrived on a Sunday afternoon, and the program ended the following Friday morning with a presentation to family and friends. Lab-based, hands-on sessions were held for two hours each morning and for three hours each afternoon. Two instructors were present for each lab session. The camp was offered through funding support provided by the Charles H. Houston Center at Clemson University [3] and the Clemson School of Computing [21]. The students lived in college dorms for the week, ate in the student cafeteria, and took part in organized activities outside of the computing lab sessions that included a welcome cookout on Sunday night, bowling night, game night and movie night. Staff from the Charles H. Houston Center recruited the students, provided supervision of the students outside of class, and organized the social events during the week.

2.1 Participants

Sixteen girls took part in the camp. Five of the participants were rising eight graders, nine were rising ninth graders, one was a rising seventh grader, and one was entering tenth grade. Eight were Caucasian and eight were African-American. All but one student were from schools in the tri-county area around Clemson University. IRB approved consent letters asking permission to collect data from pre- and post-questionnaires were sent to parents before the camp and provided to students on the first day of the camp.

2.2 Curiosity Grid

All computing activities for Camp CyberGirls took place in the context of the Curiosity Grid (CG) online virtual world using the Imprudence viewer [12]. Curiosity Grid is owned and operated by 3rd Rock Grid [1] and was created to support education in the virtual world. CG differs from many similar platforms in that it is a limited access grid with strict procedures in place to make it a safe environment for minor students. Citizens (players under 18) were provided accounts only after being recommended through the Virtual Environments Group in the School of Computing at Clemson University. Mentors (18 and over) must go through a background check before interacting with Citizens on the Grid. Avatars representing citizens all have a common last name that differs from the last name of avatars that represent mentors so that players know whether they are interacting with another student or an adult.

A virtual piece of real estate in CG is called an island and visually appears as an island in a large ocean (Figure 1). Locations on an island are specified in (x,y,z) coordinates where z represents elevation, x is an East/West aligned axis, and y is a North/South aligned axis as measured in virtual meters from the southwest corner of square regions of size 256 by 256 meters. Camp CyberGirls was held on an island made up of four of these regions.

Figure 1. Virtual island on Curiosity Grid

CG's capabilities and interface are based on software originally developed by Linden Labs that is now distributed as an open source platform. Programming is done in the Linden Scripting Language (LSL). LSL has syntax similar to C/Java. LSL is event driven, and includes states, 3D variable types, and many built-in functions [18]. Modeling objects is done by modifying and connecting basic geometric shapes known as prims [18]. LSL programs are always connected to an object in the virtual world and control that object's behavior.

Figure 2 illustrates the menu-based modeling format that allows a user to select and modify a prim. The user can control position, size and rotation of the prim with respect to a three-dimensional coordinate space, texture and color of the prim, and modify the shape of the prim in a number of other ways with menu-based tools for hollowing, tapering, cutting, slicing, and twisting. Individual prims can be linked to other prims to create more complex models. Figure 3 shows a mailbox that was modeled by a student from seven prims. Associated with the mailbox is a script written in LSL that displays a message above the mailbox, allows a player to leave items in the mailbox, and allows the mailbox owner to open the mailbox and see items left for them (Figure 4).

2.3 Implementation

At the start of the Monday morning session of the camp, participants took a survey that addressed their interest in majoring in a computing discipline and their attitudes to computing. Next, participants received computer accounts to log into the lab computers and Curiosity Grid accounts that included being assigned one of three "standard" avatar designs.

During their first session, the instructors took the girls through all the options that were available to them to customize the avatar that would represent them in Curiosity Grid. CG offers a large set of menu-based controls that allow users to personalize their avatar's appearance and clothing. Each girl started with one of three "standard" avatar designs: *Ella*, *Bonnie* and *Maria.* The tools provided allowed the girls to end with a unique avatar to represent them in the virtual world and express their creativity. Figure 5 shows final avatars created by three students who started out as the standard *Ella* avatar. This exercise was followed by instruction on how to control their avatar and their environment in the virtual world via keyboard and menu commands. The day ended with a scavenger hunt to find and record the locations of ten objects on the island. This task allowed the girls to get used to controlling their avatars, further explore the virtual island, and become familiar with the coordinate system used to specify positions and elevations on the island.

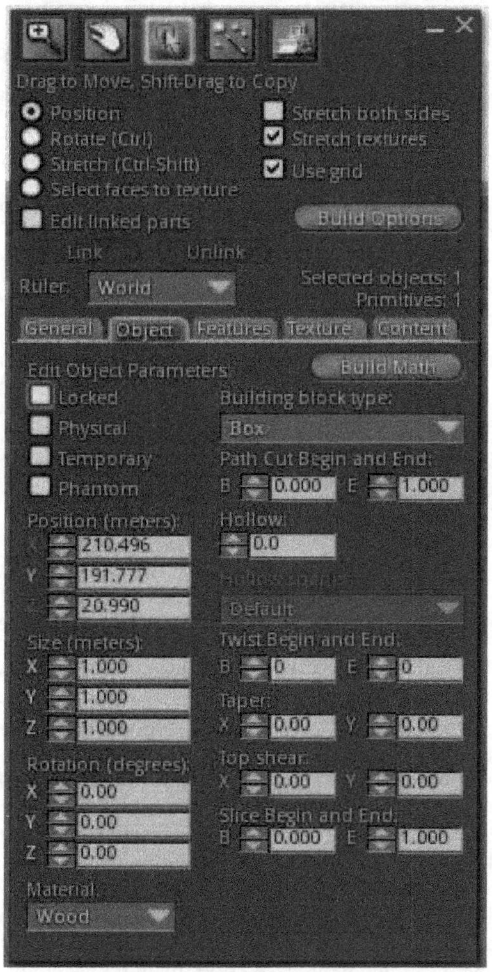

Figure 2. Modeling Interface

The remainder of the week's lab schedule was based around a series of programming and modeling challenges to be done in the virtual world. These challenges were used to teach concepts of computing including: 3D modeling, texturing, scripting structure and syntax, animation, events and event handlers, and coordinate systems, while also building up each girl's presence on the virtual island via adding new and interesting items to their claimed space. We also adopted the gaming idea of player expertise levels as an extra motivation to complete challenges. Students who completed the first ten challenges were promoted from the rank of *Novice* to the rank of *Apprentice* in our virtual world. At the end of the camp students were provided with instructions on how to access Curiosity Grid from their home computers and had the opportunity to continue with a second set of challenges in order to advance from the rank of *Apprentice* to *Journeyman.*

Figure 3. Mailbox modeled by a student.

```
default
{
   state_entry()
   {
      llAllowInventoryDrop(TRUE);
      llSetClickAction(CLICK_ACTION_OPEN);
      llSetText("Rylee Palmetto's Mailbox.",<1.0, 1.0, 1.0>, 1);
   }
}
```

Figure 4. LSL code to control mailbox.

In the first challenge, the girls used menu-based programming to create gestures. Gestures are short animations used for communication and entertainment on CG. The second challenge started off with each girl locating an "empty lot" on the virtual island to claim as their avatar's space and then building a sign to display that claim. The challenges became more difficult as the participants progressed and built upon the skills of previous challenges. The first day had a structured schedule for what tasks to do, but as the week progressed, the girls could complete challenges at their own pace. The goal was to complete ten challenges and be promoted from a *Novice* to an *Apprentice CyberGirl.* Each challenge consisted of a written set of instructions to create and/or program an object. The initial challenges had very detailed write-ups with step-by-step instructions for the tasks. Later challenges were less detailed and assumed that the previous challenges had been completed and understood. Instructors were always in the computer lab with the students going desk-to-desk answering questions.

Figure 5. The avatar on the top left is the original Ella avatar. The other three avatars are modifications of the Ella model created by three different girls.

The first ten challenges were:

1. Programming gestures and triggering them with a keyboard command.
2. Modeling and texturing a sign to mark out their area of the island.
3. Writing a script so that their sign displayed a message when an avatar approached it.
4. Modeling and texturing a mailbox.
5. Scripting their mailbox to receive messages.
6. Modeling a bench and scripting it so that that an avatar would sit on it correctly.
7. Building and scripting a fountain with a moving water texture.
8. Modeling and scripting a sliding door.
9. Modeling and scripting a complete house.
10. Modeling and scripting a working lamp for their house.

All the girls completed at least ten challenges by Friday morning, with several girls completing twelve challenges. Figure 6 shows the front of one of the houses that was created with working doors, a fountain with flowing water, furniture scripted so that an avatar could sit correctly on it, a scripted mailbox and working lamps.

3. FINDINGS AND DISCUSSION

Pre-camp and Post-camp surveys were given to camp participants to measure student intentions toward majoring in a computing discipline, attitudes toward computing, and overall satisfaction with the camp. All sixteen students participated in both the pre and post surveys. The results from the camp satisfaction survey (given on the last morning of the camp) contained eight questions that were scored on a Likert scale of 1 to 5 where 1 = highly dissatisfied, 2 = somewhat dissatisfied, 3 = neutral, 4 = somewhat satisfied, and 5 = highly satisfied (Figure 7). Mean scores on all questions indicated a high degree of satisfaction with all aspects of the camp.

Figure 6. House created and scripted by a student.

Survey questions that were asked both pre-camp and post-camp whose responses were rated as significantly different ($p < 0.05$) are shown in Table 1. These four questions were scored on a Likert scale of 1 to 5 where 1 = strongly disagree and 5 = strongly agree.

There was a significant positive increase in student attitudes toward computing, i.e., at the end of the camp they felt that applying to college in a computing discipline was more valuable and they were more confident that they could achieve good grades in computing courses. At the same time they were less confident that they coud learn to understand computing concepts and liking to use computer science to solve problems decreased.

How do we reconcile the mixed results in Table 1, particularly in light of the high overall scores the camp was given in Figure 7 indicating a high degree of satisfaction with the camp experience?

The modeling and scripting environment in a virtual world is more challenging than the typical tools used to introduce middle school students to computing. Most, such as Alice or Scratch, use a drag-and-drop metaphore for programming that isolates students from the need to pay attention to syntax. Indeed, avoiding syntax is often listed as a positive in programs desigend to motivate student interest in programming [8,13]. Alice and Scratch are also primarily 2-D environments that require little mathematical sophistication with respect to coordinate systems, rotations, translations or scales. Students can be successful in these environments, come away with a new interest in majoring in a computing discipline while also still remaining generally ignorant of many of the skills they must develop to be successful in a computing major. We could view this approach as equivalent to encouraging them to become a writer without exposing them to grammar.

Alternately, virtual world modeling and programming incorporate a wide variety of learning experiences that other approaches leave out. Curiosity Grid is a three-dimensional world. Modeling an object exposes students to both global and local 3D coordinate systems, scaling, translation, rotation, texture-mapping and RGB color coordinates.

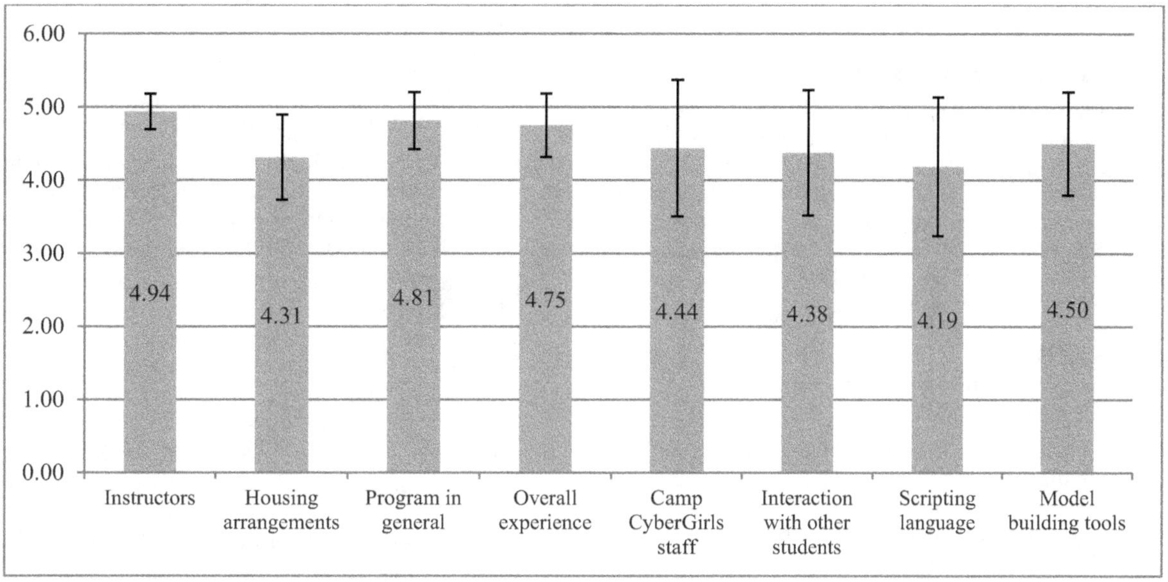

Figure 7. Camp Satisfaction Survey. Questions that were scored on a Likert scale of 1 to 5 where 1 = highly dissatisfied, 2 = somewhat dissatisfied, 3 = neutral, 4 = somewhat satisfied, and 5 = highly satisfied.

Table 1. Survey questions whose responses were rated significantly different ($p < 0.05$) post-camp as compared to pre-camp. Questions were scored on a 5-point Likert scale with 5 = strongly agree and 1 = strongly disgree.

Statement	Pre-Camp Mean/SD	Post-Camp Mean/SD
For me to apply to college in a computing discipline is (extremely valuable/ worthless)	3.812/0.8342	4.250/0.9309
I do think that I can learn to understand computing concepts.	4.813/0.4031	4.438/0.9639
I can achieve good grades (B or better) in computing courses.	4.375/0.7188	4.688/0.4787
I do like to use computer science to solve problems.	4.500/0.7303	3.938/1.123

With the Linden Scripting Language (LSL) students type in code and get syntax errors when the code is incorrect. Students experience that designing, building and scripting are challenging tasks that require sustained effort and attention. One student lost almost a full day's work when the girl sitting next to her tried to help her by pressing the wrong key on her neighbor's keyboard! The student who lost the work was very frustrated! However, she immediately began work on reproducing the models and scripts and ended up completing as many challenges as the other campers. She also learned a valuable lesson about saving her code!

Although challenging, learning programming in the context of a virtual world provides a great deal of motivation to make things work. The modeling and scripting languages are powerful. Every object can be coded so that it interacts with users and the world. Fountains can be modeled and then textured and programmed so that water flows. Lamps can be designed that actually light up. Objects (we had dogs, pandas, and sharks) can be modeled and then scripted to respond to basic questions from a user. The camp satisfaction means for both the programming language and the modeling tools indicate that our students were more than somewhat satisfied with the tools they learned to use. The fact that all sixteen students completed at least ten modeling and programming challenges indicates that, in the context of a week-long camp, middle school students can learn and use real computing and mathematical concepts that have not been watered down. Students who signed up for Camp CyberGirls were all confident or highly confident on the pre-camp survey that they could learn computing concepts. On the post-camp survey, 13 of the 16 remained confident or highly confident, even with a realistic introduction to what it takes to succeed.

In addition to our surveys we also asked for subjective feedback from the girls in a group feedback session held on the morning of the last day of the camp. When asked for suggestions on how we could improve the camp if it was offered next summer, there were no negative comments on the programming or modeling tools. They suggested that ending the lab sessions at 4:00 each day left them with an extra hour before dinner that they could have used to program. The class should have gone to 5:00. One girl commented that she would like to have had harder programming challenges. They also liked the events held outside of the lab times, particularly the welcome cookout that gave them the chance to get to know each other on the first night.

4. FUTURE WORK

Based on the success of our first summer camp using a virtual world to introduce students to computing, we are planning to expand our program to offer multiple camps next summer. For future camp sessions, we plan to gather more data from participants and monitor their participation after the camp by tracking if and when the participants log into the virtual world from home. We are also planning a weekend Camp CyberGirls reunion meeting this year for the participants. In conjunction with the Curiosity Grid, we will be posting our challenges and other materials online for other groups who might be interested in using them for their own programs.

5. ACKNOWLEDGMENTS

Our thanks to Ms. Starlett Craig and the Charles H. Houston Center for logistical and financial support for Camp CyberGirls. Thanks also to Jim Saint Clair (a.k.a. Laz) and the staff at Third Rock Grid who have worked closely with us since the beginning of this project to create Curiosity Grid and to support our activities. Partial support for this research was also provided by an NSF REU Site Grant CNS-0850695, the Palmetto Island Fund, and the C. Tycho Howle Endowment.

6. REFERENCES

[1] 3rd Rock Grid, Retrieved July 30, 2013 from http://www.3rdrockgrid.com/.

[2] Burke Q. and Kafai, Y.B., The writers' workshop for youth programmers: digital storytelling with scratch in middle school classrooms. In *Proceedings of the 43rd ACM technical symposium on Computer Science Education*, SIGCSE '12. ACM, 2012, 433-438.

[3] Charles H. Houston Center | Clemson University, South Carolina 2013. Retrieved July 31, 2013 from http://www.clemson.edu/centers-institutes/houston/.

[4] Craig, M. and Horton, D. Gr8 designs for gr8 girls: a middle-school program and its evaluation. In Proceedings of the 40th ACM technical symposium on Computer science education, SIGCSE '09, pages 221-225, New York, NY, USA, 2009. ACM, 221-225.

[5] Doerschuk, P., Jiangjiang, L., Mann, J., 2007. Pilot Summer Camps in Computing for Middle School Girls: From Organization Through Assessment, *ITiCSE'07*, June 23–27, 2007, Dundee, Scotland, United Kingdom, 4-8.

[6] ECS. Exploring Computer Science. CS Education Statistics, 2013, Retrieved July 31, 2013 from http://www.exploringcs.org/resources/cs-statistics.

[7] Gross, P. A., Herstand, M. S., Hodges, J. W., and Kelleher, C. L. 2010. A code reuse interface for non-programmer middle school students. In *Proceedings of the 15th international conference on Intelligent user interfaces* (IUI '10). ACM, New York, NY, USA, 219-228. DOI=10.1145/1719970.1720001 http://doi.acm.org/10.1145/1719970.1720001

[8] Hardnett, C., Gaming for Middle School Students: Building Virtual Worlds, GDCSE '08, Miami, FL, USA, February 2008, 21-25.

[9] Harms, K. J., Kerr, J. H., Ichinco, M., Santolucito, M., Chuck, A., Koscik, T., Chou, M., and Kelleher, C. L. 2012. Designing a community to support long-term interest in programming for middle school children. In *Proceedings of the 11th International Conference on Interaction Design and Children* (IDC '12). ACM, New York, NY, USA, 304-307. DOI=10.1145/2307096.2307152 http://doi.acm.org/10.1145/2307096.2307152

[10] Hill, V. and Meister, M. 2013. Virtual worlds and libraries: Gridhopping to new worlds. College & Research Libraries News 74, 43-47.

[11] Hu, H. H. 2008. A summer programming workshop for middle school girls. *J. Comput. Sci. Coll.* 23, 6 (June 2008), 194-202.

[12] Imprudence:Downloads - Kokua Wiki, Retrieved July 30, 2013 from http://wiki.kokuaviewer.org/wiki/Imprudence:Downloads.

[13] Kelleher, C., Pausch, R., and Kiesler, S. Storytelling alice motivates middle school girls to learn computer programming. In Proceedings of the SIGCHI conference on Human factors in computing systems, 2007, 1455-1464.

[14] Larkins, D. B., J. Moore, J. C., Rubbo, L. J., and Covington, L. R. 2013. Application of the cognitive apprenticeship framework to a middle school robotics camp. In *Proceeding of the 44th ACM technical symposium on Computer science education* (SIGCSE '13). ACM, New York, NY, USA, 89-94. DOI=10.1145/2445196.2445226 http://doi.acm.org/10.1145/2445196.2445226

[15] Lee, J. J., & Hoadley, C. M. Ugly in a world where you can choose to be beautiful: teaching and learning about diversity via virtual worlds. In Proceedings of ICLS 2006, 383-389.

[16] Libeskind-Hadas, R. The Computing Community Consortium Blog, A Service of the Computing Research Community. Towards a New AP Course in Computer Science, 2010, Retrieved July 31, 2013 from http://www.cccblog.org/2010/07/19/towards-a-new-ap-course-in-computer-science/.

[17] Monroy, C., Klisch, Y. and Miller, L. M. Emerging contexts for science education: embedding a forensic science game in a virtual world. In Proceedings of the 2011 iConference (Seattle, Washington, 2011), 622-629.

[18] Moore, D., Thome, M., and Haigh, K. Z. *Scripting your world, the official guide to second life scripting.* Wiley Publishing, Inc., Indianapolis, Indiana, 2008.

[19] OSgrid - OpenSimulator Metaverse, Retrieved July 30, 2013 from http://www.osgrid.org/.

[20] Russell, D., Davies, M., and Totten, I., "GEOWORLDS: Utilizing Second Life to Develop Advanced Geosciences Knowledge, *2008 Second IEEE International Conference on Digital Games and Intelligent Toys Based Education.* Nov. 2008, 93-97 doi: 10.1109/DIGITEL.2008.50

[21] School of Computing | Clemson University, SC 2013. Retrieved July 31, 2013 from http://www.cs.clemson.edu/.

[22] Second Life, Retrieved August 1, 2013 from http://www.secondlife.com/.

[23] Steinkuehler, C. and Alagoz, E. 2010. Out-of-school virtual worlds based programs: a cross-case analysis. In *Proceedings of the 9th International Conference of the Learning Sciences - Volume 2* (ICLS '10), Kimberly Gomez, Leilah Lyons, and Joshua Radinsky (Eds.), Vol. 2. International Society of the Learning Sciences, 304-305.

[24] Wilson, C., Sudol, L., Stephenson, C., and Stehlik, M., 2010. *Running on Empty: The Failure to Teach K-12 Computer Science in the Digital Age.* ACM Available as: http://www.acm.org/runningonempty/fullreport.pdf.

[25] Zweben, S. The Computing Research Association. *CRA Taulbee Survey* (2011-2012), 2013.

MyCS: CS for Middle-Years Students and their Teachers

Elizabeth Schofield
Harvey Mudd College
301 Platt Blvd.
Claremont, CA 91711
(909) 607 3850
eschofield@hmc.edu

Michael Erlinger
Harvey Mudd College
301 Platt Blvd.
Claremont, CA 91711
(909) 621-8912
mike@cs.hmc.edu

Zachary Dodds
Harvey Mudd College
301 Platt Blvd.
Claremont, CA 91711
(909) 607-1813
dodds@cs.hmc.edu

ABSTRACT

This paper describes the MyCS curriculum, which aims to encourage middle-years students, i.e., grades 4-10, to engage not only as consumers of CS, but as composers of computational artifacts. MyCS draws from many successful online tools and curricula, including Exploring Computer Science (ECS) and Scratch. MyCS's 18-week curriculum balances a broad treatment of the modern role of the computer with deepening students' hands-on skills through computational problem-solving, both *unplugged* and via programming. This paper summarizes assessments from several MyCS professional-development workshops, with an emphasis on eliciting teachers' needs and goals for their classrooms. In addition, we discuss the project's future in the format of a *teacher-mediated MOOC* that will enable a larger group of teachers to engage their students in CS.

Categories and Subject Descriptors

K.3.2 [**Computing Milieux**]: Computers and Education – *computer science education, curriculum.*

Keywords

Intro CS, Middle-years CS, online CS education, CS4FUN

1. INTRODUCTION

We enjoy, today, an embarrassment of introductory CS riches! Efforts such as Exploring Computer Science (ECS) [8], Computer Science Unplugged (CSU) [3], and Common Sense Media (CSM) [6] provide archives of beautiful, compelling lesson plans and activities, readily accessible for instructors to explore and share. Online courses, such as those from Codecademy and many MOOC providers, offer well-scaffolded settings for both skill building and big-picture insights. Undergirding these resources, Scratch 2.0 makes the language's syntax-free, user-friendly interface even more accessible.

From a "middle-years" teacher's perspective, roughly spanning ages 8-15 or U.S. grades 4-10, the merit of each of these individual resources is clear. All have seen great success in engaging students with CS [9,11,14,19]. However, while many have examined the success of these and other CS education resources [1,15,16,19], methods for combining them remain relatively unexplored. The challenge for these pre-college CS instructors, then, lies in selecting *which* tools to bring into the classroom and *how* to do so.

SIGCSE '14, March 05 - 08 2014, Atlanta, GA, USA

http://dx.doi.org/10.1145/2538862.2538901

This paper investigates one possible answer to this challenge. The *MyCS* curriculum [7], short for *Middle-years Computer Science*, synthesizes these resources into a comprehensive, engaging CS course targeted to middle-years students. Over the past four years, we have refined MyCS's combination of materials in order to better support middle-years teachers in meeting their classroom goals. Our research is unique in its emphasis on how these teachers can help us build and evaluate this curriculum to meet their needs directly. This paper outlines the MyCS curriculum and analyzes the feedback it has received from pre-college teachers who have taught MyCS and have participated in week-long professional development workshops. In addition, we summarize our efforts to reach a much larger group of future CS instructors via a teacher-mediated MOOC now under development.

1.1 The Middle-Years Audience

At the moment, relatively few pre-college students have access to CS courses. The numbers of AP CS exam-takers, for instance, is lower than the need for those skills [12]. We, along with the whole CS education community, are excited about the new AP CS Principles course [2] and its potential effects on high-school CS.

MyCS complements CS Principles's efforts by offering a *lead-in* curriculum to that AP course. We target middle-years students *and their teachers* in the design and deployment of MyCS, particularly focusing on school districts with substantial cohorts underrepresented in the field. MyCS's goal is simple: it seeks to guide younger students to an understanding that "CS is something that people like me do." To the extent that MyCS succeeds, it will support the much larger goals of AP and college-level CS study.

Thus, MyCS's curriculum focuses on developing a broad sense of what constitutes computer science rather than specific – and rapidly changing – facets of domain knowledge. It emphasizes the fun, interesting, and fulfilling aspects of working in the field. Whether cracking codes, making games, or solving problems, MyCS encourages its students and teachers to identify with *composing* computational interactions.

2. CURRICULUM

In adapting ECS's compelling model for a younger audience, MyCS's curriculum spans from hardware to software, from low-level data encodings to high-level programming and design, and from algorithmic logic to executable implementations. These disparate topics cohere in their goal of encouraging students toward developing a positive *computational identity*; that is, determining that CS is something they are both capable of and excited about doing.

In MyCS's six three-week units, topics alternate between the conceptual foundations of computer science and applications of those concepts via programming. Table 1 summarizes this structure:

Table 1. Outline of MyCS's six curricular units.

1: *What is CS?*	- What is computing? - What is a computer? - What are intelligence and AI?
2: *A-maze-ing Scratch*	- 100 graduated puzzles (mazes) that introduce much of Scratch - Do-it-yourself mazes designed by students for their peers
3: *Encoding and Decoding Data*	- Encoding and decoding puzzles - Data representation using binary - Lego computer architecture
4: *Interactive Scratch*	- Scaffolding interactive artifacts - Authoring games or challenges - Storytelling and choreography
5: *Problem Solving and Algorithms*	- Problem-solving strategies - Algorithmic thinking - Searching and sorting
6: *Algorithms in Scratch*	- Straight-line vs. looping sounds - Problem specification, decomposition, and implementation

Three of MyCS's units, 1,4, and 5, borrow heavily from the ECS curriculum; in particular, they select activities that become *more* compelling with re-exposure: constructing computational artifacts or considering the nature of computation. Despite how impacted high school schedules have become, our partnering districts are now considering ECS for older students; to facilitate this, we have been careful to ensure that ECS can smoothly follow MyCS.

2.1 Unit 1: *What is CS?*

Unit 1 asks students and teachers to grapple with the abstract questions "What is computation?" and "What is CS?" through the much more accessible question "What is a computer?"[1] The activities of this unit investigate intuitions (more than definitions) of computing, computer hardware, computer intelligence, and digital citizenship, with some more in-depth content on exploring and putting content on the Internet. Exercises include computer disassembly, an Internet scavenger hunt, and running a Turing test, to paint as broad as possible a landscape of CS's reach.

That this unit also focuses on Internet use – and effective use of Internet search tools in particular – may appear at odds with encouraging technology creators rather than consumers. For many, Internet search exemplifies a *consume-only* technology. In practice, however, that overlap with computer literacy is of enormous benefit to our efforts.

First, computer literacy, as well as the self-efficacy that derives from it, is crucial to building a positive computational identity. All of our partnering schools *already have a computer skills course*, which MyCS intentionally reiterates in order to ease its inclusion in – or replacement of – these existing traditions.

[1] Accessible, but not trivial. This summer we faced a significant challenge trying to tease out why a carnival mirror is ***not*** a computer, but a brain ***is***. Or, perhaps we were wrong… ?!

Further, the curriculum seeks to pull back the curtain of this ostensibly consume-only technology. For instance, choosing effective search keywords requires not only an understanding of what the user wishes to find, but also some intuition about how search engines function. It serves as a touchstone for many later topics, including the ways in which computers represent data (unit 2) and the algorithms they use to sort and search through huge datasets efficiently (units 5 and 6). The topic dovetails well not only with technology courses, but in many fields, making it easy for schools to adapt MyCS into other curricular streams.

2.2 Unit 2: Mazes in Scratch

MyCS's second unit introduces programming in Scratch, inspired by the many excellent introductions to this topic, e.g., [10,17]. Our curriculum begins not with exercises in creating entirely new programs, but instead with a series of 100 pre-made mazes organized via ten thematic "worlds" [13]. Each presents a Karel-like grid with a concrete challenge: *Create a program that leads the hero to the goal.* The puzzles are carefully graduated: each world introduces a large CS and Scratch skill/concept with a progression of challenges whose completion requires increasingly sophisticated applications of that skill/concept. For instance, world 1 introduces straight-line code and, later, *for* loops; world 2 introduces moving adversaries and the `wait` command to avoid them; world 3 requires conditionals; later worlds motivate more sophisticated sensing, indefinite iteration, and other fundamental building blocks of Scratch and structured programming.

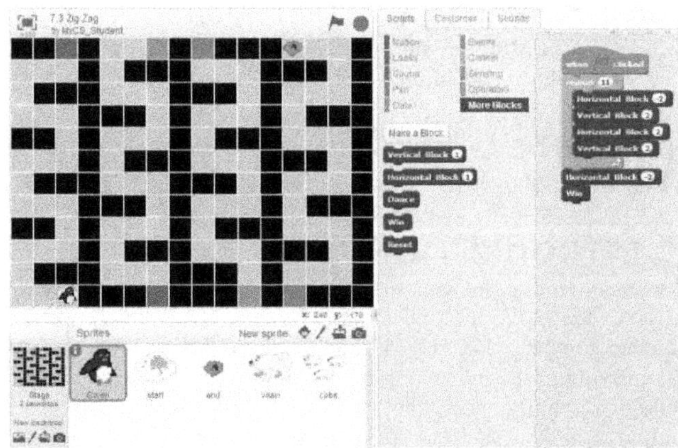

Figure 1. An example of one of the 100 Scratch mazes that guide students through many CS skills/concepts by solving a series of programming challenges with preexisting goals.

By the end of these mazes, or after completing a teacher-selected subset, students feel confident in their ability to create programs for moving or manipulating sprites on Scratch's stage. Additionally, template worlds allow students to create their own challenge mazes – including adversaries, portals, and other features – with which to challenge peers, friends, and classmates. This alternation between introducing skills and encouraging creative application of these skills in student-generated artifacts underlies MyCS's pedagogical approach throughout.

2.3 Unit 3: Encoding and Decoding Data

Unit 3 examines how computers and humans represent information differently. It motivates the many uses of encoded data, whether as a set of instructions for constructing an artifact, for arithmetic processes, or as a message intended for only a single recipient. Early versions of the curriculum focused on the binary representation of numeric data. Feedback from classroom practice, however, made it clear that more scaffolding would help clarify why binary is central to modern computation and would also build greater comfort with the multitude of different ways in which information can be stored.

Students begin unit 3 by deciphering coded messages of graduated difficulty. They follow by applying these insights to invent their own codes and messages to share with their peers; teachers have adapted these into assignments involving exchanges of coded emails. Only after seeing many examples of information encodings is binary introduced, building on the wonderful CSU and ECS materials available [3,8].

In the unit's capstone project, student pairs design and build their own Lego towers. As they do so, each pair first *encodes* all of their tower's features, brick-by-brick, to specify its construction using short English descriptions. Each pair then translates that English pseudocode into a binary representation. Lookup tables provide encodings for color, orientation, and the shape of each block; position is already numeric. Once finished, teams hide the towers and English descriptions, swapping only the binary descriptions with one another.

Decoding and reconstructing each original Lego tower has compelling results. Once each pair of teams performs a "reveal" in which the original and reconstituted towers are compared side-by-side, the teams must cooperate to find where, how, and why the towers differ. (They almost always do!)

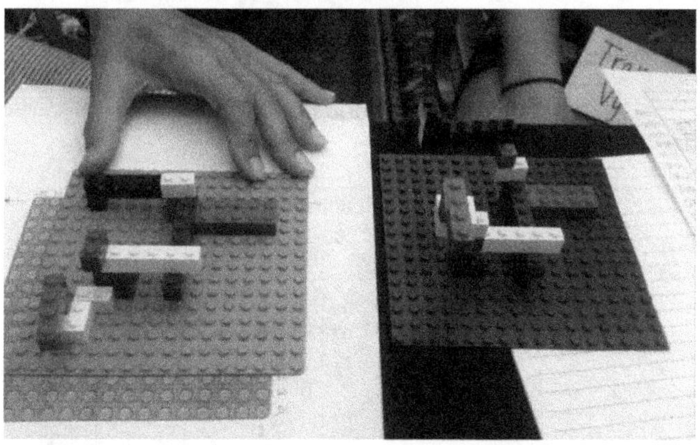

Figure 2. Comparison of two structures created by teams during the Lego-construction activity. A "typo" error is apparent at back; the *Tetris ambiguity* is in the left foreground.

The activity provides visceral insight into some of computation's deeper characteristics. While everything in a computer is fundamentally knowable, we humans don't always care to follow every bit to its logical conclusion. Our machines, however, do *exactly that* – and even one bit out of place can yield dramatically different results! For example, Figure 2 shows a subtlety that can arise beyond even the inevitable "typo" errors. We call this the *Tetris ambiguity*: when placing the next-specified block on a tower with overhanging pieces, does that block descend from on high (Tetris-like) or does it emerge from the baseplate?

Thus, in this series of interactive steps, students internalize the process of a human computer scientist designing an artifact, specifying its functionality, encoding it formally, and passing that code to a computer, in this case a pair of their peers, to attempt to execute the desired result! Student and teacher identification with the testing, analyzing, and debugging facets of computational interaction builds atop the personalized structures involved.

2.4 Unit 4: Interactive Scratch

Unit 4 continues MyCS's alternation between conceptual and programmatic skill-development. Here, we implement lessons from ECS, ScratchEd, and the Lewis curriculum to have students compose interactive artifacts, including games, original stories, and animations [8,10,17]. All of these projects can also serve goals external to CS *per se*. For example, one MyCS teacher used this unit to ask pairs of students to animate chapters from Farewell to Manzanar; at the end of the exercise, the class has created a Scatch interpretation of the entire book! Leveraging students' familiarity and confidence built from the scaffolded challenges of unit 2, this unit's flexibility made it the most widely adapted by teachers. A personalized adaptation shared by another teacher involved student teams creating individual sprites from their names or initials and then producing a custom animation that had to involve all of the different motion primitives Scratch provides.

2.5 Unit 5: Problem Solving and Algorithms

Having explored what computers are and how they interpret information, students focus on the algorithmic core of CS in the final two units. Through examples of algorithms everywhere – Google's image search, Netflix's recommendations, Shazam's music recognition – students develop intuition about what it means to think algorithmically[2]. The curriculum then focuses on searching and sorting, motivating their importance (web search) and showing how these problems can be solved in multiple ways. We adapt ECS's and CSU's cup-sorting activity into one easier to deploy at a moment's notice: sorting a list of words on sticky notes *where the ordering criterion is unknown to the students*. The result is a doubly-compelling challenge: as students record results for their pairwise comparisons, they both work through the ideas of sorting-by-comparison and try to discern that mystery criterion.

2.6 Unit 6: Algorithms in Scratch

Building from unit 5's conceptual foundations on problem-solving and algorithms, the final unit returns to Scratch to focus on algorithms' *implementation* and its concomitant skillset: careful specification, deliberate decomposition, and modular combination of the building blocks that Scratch quite literally provides. Students explore first how to generate melodies, truly making them *composers* for a time. They then explore Scratch's pen tool, systematically generating specified shapes and composing open-ended artwork. This content scaffolding is some of the CS education community's best-supported; MyCS builds upon [9,10].

2.7 Additional Content

The content described in these 6 units makes up the core of the 18-week MyCS curriculum. Because our priority is breadth of deployment, rather than purity of approach, we invite teachers from any background or specialty area to adapt the subset of materials they find compelling. To this end, an optional seventh three-week unit covers additional aspects of Internet safety and security, social responsibility, and web development. Digital citizenship content comes primarily from the Common Sense Media curriculum [6], while introductions to HTML, CSS, and Javascript are drawn in part from Codecademy [18].

---

[2] For years we resisted the venerable peanut-butter-and-jelly-making example, only to succumb to teachers' pressure in 2013. We were wrong all along; it was hugely popular.

3. ASSESSMENT

Pilot courses for both MyCS professional development and school-year MyCS began in the Pomona, CA and Lihue, HI unified school districts in 2011 and 2012. Twenty teachers of math, science, and technology joined those workshops, with over 400 students taking full MyCS courses as a result; an even larger number have taken hybrid technology skills/MyCS courses.

In the summer of 2013, we extended MyCS's reach through two week-long workshops for a total of 32 teachers of varied background. Pre- and post-assessments of students are happening throughout the 2013-2014 school year; this study sought to investigate how *teachers* previously unfamiliar with CS respond to the MyCS curriculum in affect and in action. Like many, we believe that pre-college teachers are *our community's most important resource* for broadening CS's reach [1,4,5,14,15,16]. Thus, this work sought to give much-needed attention to the perceptions and preferences of those teaching in the middle-years.

For the 2013 workshop, 84% of participants took pre- and post-workshop surveys on the impact of the curriculum in its current form, their workshop experiences, and their overall impressions of computer science education and their role within it. This data has highlighted which aspects of the MyCS curriculum are successful with teachers and which need attention and improvement.

3.1 Breadth, Depth, or Hybrid?

As MyCS's alternating structure suggests, the curriculum seeks a balance between breadth-based exploration of computational and algorithmic thinking and depth-based development of hands-on skills. We asked teachers participating in our workshop to express which of these approaches they prefer. Table 2 shows these post-workshop results. Recognizing that MyCS does not provide an unbiased basis from which to decide, we found a majority of respondents expressed a preference for a hybrid approach over pure skill-deepening or contextual scaffolding.

Table 2. Participants' post-workshop personal preferences for teaching computer science skills and concepts.

	Depth-based	Hybrid	Breadth-based
Post-wksh.	3.7%	92.6%	3.7%

In some ways, this is no surprise: striking a balance seems obvious. The voices of our middle-years instructors, however, did provide us new insights as to how/why they felt this stance was the right one for their students:

> "People need an overview of CS to learn about what they are most interested in… Topics are much more interesting as you learn more about them, so depth can be the engaging part."

Teachers rightly hope to provide sufficient breadth to interest their diverse cadres of students, along with sufficient depth to provide the students a chance to *build their own computational identity*:

> "Without depth it is hard to have meaning, but without an overview of CS it is hard for a student to find what they are passionate about."

Unfortunately, practicing this curricular philosophy is not as intuitive as explaining it. Depth-focused tools like Codecademy have gained increasing popularity among self-directed learners and instructors alike. The straightforward user interface, quick modular lessons, and immediate opportunity to apply and test coding concepts make it a successful environment for developing specific programming skills. Nonetheless, teachers agree that tools like Codecademy would ideally serve *as a part of a broader CS curriculum*, not as the central driver for the course. Instructors are eager to combine such tools with hands-on unplugged activities, theoretical discussions, and opportunities for students to examine where these ideas find application outside the classroom.

Table 3. Percentages for participants' agreement to a series of statements before and after completing the workshop, rated from 5 (Strongly Agree) to 1 (Strongly Disagree).

	Strongly Agree	4	3	2	Strongly Disagree
I feel confident about my ability to accomplish my goals in the MyCS program.					
Before	25.9%	51.9%	14.8%	3.7%	3.7%
After	53.8%	46.2%	0.0%	0.0%	0.0%
Middle school is a time in students' education where they should not have to work too hard.					
Before	3.6%	3.6%	10.7%	64.3%	17.9%
After	12.0%	12.0%	8.0%	40.0%	28.0%
Students learn best through project-based curricula that encourages them to be creative and self-expressive.					
Before	57.1%	28.6%	10.7%	0.0%	3.6%
After	88.5%	11.5%	0.0%	0.0%	0.0%
I have a personal interest in the field of computing.					
Before	42.9%	42.9%	7.1%	7.1%	0.0%
After	69.2%	23.1%	7.7%	0.0%	0.0%
I prefer to work on collaborative projects.					
Before	21.4%	25.0%	42.9%	3.6%	7.1%
After	42.3%	38.5%	11.5%	3.8%	3.8%
I can learn more from working on projects that are applied to real world problems/topics.					
Before	71.4%	17.9%	7.1%	0.0%	3.6%
After	88.5%	11.5%	0.0%	0.0%	0.0%
I think it's important to teach middle school students intellectually challenging curriculum.					
Before	64.3%	28.6%	3.6%	0.0%	3.6%
After	88.5%	11.5%	0.0%	0.0%	0.0%
I feel that hard work and effort is rewarded in teaching and learning.					
Before	53.6%	32.1%	10.7%	0.0%	3.6%
After	73.1%	19.2%	0.0%	7.7%	0.0%
The work of computer science and engineering benefits society.					
Before	75.0%	21.4%	0.0%	0.0%	3.6%
After	92.6%	7.4%	0.0%	0.0%	0.0%
I think that participating in the MyCS program will help me to better support my students.					
Before	67.9%	25.0%	3.6%	3.6%	0.0%
After	92.3%	7.7%	0.0%	0.0%	0.0%
I enjoy teaching others about scientific and technological topics.					
Before	64.3%	21.4%	10.7%	3.6%	0.0%
After	76.9%	11.5%	11.5%	0.0%	0.0%
There are sufficient opportunities to succeed in computing fields regardless of one's race/ethnicity.					
Before	50.0%	35.7%	7.1%	7.1%	0.0%
After	69.2%	7.7%	11.5%	7.7%	3.8%
There are sufficient opportunities to succeed in computing fields regardless of one's gender.					
Before	53.6%	32.1%	7.1%	3.6%	3.6%
After	61.5%	15.4%	7.7%	11.5%	3.8%

3.2 Self-Efficacy

Asked what they thought of the curriculum and their own CS attitudes and skills, the teachers expressed contentment, if not overwhelming enthusiasm. After viewing and participating in the curriculum, teachers had increased confidence in the MyCS program, support for engineering and CS education, and desire to work collaboratively and provide intellectually challenging curriculum. Table 3 summarizes those results.

Written feedback reflected this satisfaction. One teacher applauded the curricular reach, stating that the workshop "was complete as far as introducing and training us in providing CS to middle school students to ignite their interest and lure them to the study of CS... I see no stone unturned." Another celebrated the applications of CS that MyCS reveals: "I really had my eyes opened into how far reaching into the other disciplines CS really can go. Even if you do not have a robust infrastructure, just making students aware of the tools can spark their interest."

3.3 Assessing Computational Identity

Beyond finding satisfaction with the resources and presentation of MyCS, those who participated in the workshop saw changes in their identification with CS and computer science education. For instance, in evaluating the statement *I have a personal interest in the field of computing,* participants shifted from caution beforehand to universal, strong agreement afterward.

In their responses, teachers also shifted toward greater support for the overarching goals of CS curricula such as MyCS. When asked whether the workshop influenced their sense of the importance of *middle-years* introduction of CS, 89% responded with an enthusiastic "Yes." The other respondents, in fact, explained their choice was because they were "already convinced of the value."

Participants differed in *how* they planned to deploy the curriculum. Those who already taught technology courses planned to deploy it as-is; others foresaw adaptations to their fields. As an art teacher explained, "I think it is important for students to learn about the career options available to them as creative and technologically sophisticated students." A technology instructor echoed that "we need to have our kids more exposed to what computer science is and how this relate[s] to them being able to do all the things they do."

Finally, teachers expressed immediate desire to try out pieces of the MyCS curriculum with their students, e.g., a math teacher: "The mathematics and explanation on algorithms will be brought into my classroom within the first month of school." A prior MyCS instructor was as enthusiastic as the rest of the participants to see the curricular adjustments to make content "very user friendly" relative to the pilot offerings.

3.4 Challenges and Impact

Teachers' feedback has also established areas in which we can and should continue to improve both MyCS's content and its delivery in a professional-development workshop setting.

3.4.1 Another Look at Algorithms

When asked which was the most confusing or challenging element of the curriculum, 23% of our participants named the algorithm units, the most popular response. An additional 19% were most challenged by material relating to the optional web-development (HTML/CSS) and Python programming. In the words of one workshop attendee,

> I didn't know anything about programming [before attending the MyCS workshop]. I'm still confused, but I'm hoping that I can gain better understanding with practice.

Such concerns suggest an additional benefit of a middle-years layer to pre-college CS curriculum: building comfort with those patterns of thought that, in turn, can support the more technically demanding facets of high-school CS. As noted, web development and Python basics constitute an optional unit within the MyCS curriculum; these comments suggest that they should remain so.

3.4.2 A Slower Pace

Another sentiment shared by many teachers was a feeling that the curriculum was rushed at points (though more comfortable than in previous years). Several recommended extending the length of the workshop to two weeks, e.g., to "allow more time to experience lessons, programming, curriculum etc." While the current week-long workshop does press in order to build comfort with a full-semester curriculum, these requests also confirm that flexibility in deployment is crucial; some teachers reported only using one or two units (merged with other technology curriculum) in their first offering, with expanded offerings in the next semester (or year).

Even as these concerns show that MyCS's curriculum is not yet fully mature, we take heart in the positives reported by the teacher-participants. We look forward to continuing to gather feedback from these teachers and, in 2014, their students, as MyCS develops further.

4. MyCS ONLINE

One of the paramount goals for MyCS development has been making the materials "widely deployable". While all of MyCS is freely available [7], those materials cannot replicate one of the professional development workshops for the curriculum. As a result, we have begun implementing MyCS as a *teacher-mediated* Massive Open Online Course (MOOC) using the open-source platform provided by edX. Lesson plans and activity descriptions comprise a series of course days, tied together by the "progress ribbon" every MOOC host now uses.

The goal of teacher-mediated MOOCs is to provide all of the resources that a self-directed student might use, but tailored for use as curricular materials by teachers. The number of middle-years students reached by a self-directed MOOC is likely to be vanishingly small, while the number that can be reached by teacher-mediated MOOCs can be as large as the schools, and school districts, choose.

4.1 Video Content

Our approach to creating videos in our online course distinguishes our content from those of other CS MOOCs. We worked with a team of college students who, using simple filming equipment and editing software, developed a collection of 90 videos which, interleaved with other elements of the curriculum, create a comprehensive demonstration of the course's topics.

In contrast to many MOOCs, the videos are supplemental, not central, to the curriculum in this teacher-mediated MOOC. The classroom teacher may choose to use them, ignore them, or challenge students to create alternative video-explanations of the topic! A deliberate goal of the videos, neither too earnest nor too polished, is to create a course aesthetic that encourages students to compose and contribute their own content. This approach was suggested by the subset of teachers who specialize in media- and video-skills courses: they felt that the rough edges of the college students' efforts would invite their students to compose content for motivating a particular idea. As part of a teacher-mediated MOOC, a lack of polish may help create a *more personal* community of practice with the CS content and its presentation.

4.2 Response

Thus far, we have received positive responses from teachers for this effort, and not only because it affirms and supports, rather than replaces, their role. We envision that even teachers unable to attend a PD workshop could teach MyCS. The first offering would rely heavily on the teacher-mediated MOOC, though with the teacher still front-and-center of the human interactions that always supersede curricular concerns. In subsequent offerings, teachers could replace MOOC content with personalized lessons more carefully crafted to reach the specific needs of their charges.

5. PERSPECTIVE

The MyCS curriculum, in its current form, organizes many externally and internally developed curricular resources into one . This study has focused on the response of the *teachers* of middle-years students to the material and its deployment. We are excited that resources are now available for a full pre-/post-assessment of this academic year's MyCS students. Yet it has rightfully been *teachers* who have been MyCS's initial focus, as we seek to create resources that increase awareness, confidence, and identification with communicating computer science.

As sections 3 and 4 attest, MyCS is far from complete. However, this study has shown that middle-years teachers (a) support strong computer science education, (b) engage well with exceptional resources that are easy to introduce into their classes, and (c) thrive in both their teaching confidence and computer science knowledge when provided these resources.

Middle-years education suffers not from a lack but from an abundance of compelling computer-science resources. Its most vital contributors, middle-years teachers, tell us they benefit most from simultaneously fully-scaffolded and fully-flexible curricula that maximize the time and effort available to invest. Synthesizing our resources to meet the needs of these teachers – and through them, their students – will continue to challenge our community in the best possible way.

6. ACKNOWLEDGMENTS

We thank the teachers, students, and administrators who have helped develop and refine MyCS. We thank Google's CS4HS initiative for supporting the pilot years of MyCS, and the NSF, though project #1240939, for expanding our reach going forward.

7. REFERENCES

[1] Ahern, T. C. 2009. Bridging the gap: cognitive scaffolding to improve computer programming for middle school teachers. In Proceedings of the 39th IEEE Int. Conf. on Frontiers in Education (FIE'09). IEEE Press, 130-134.

[2] Astrachan, O., Briggs, J. C., Diaz, L., and Stephenson, C. 2012. Update on the CS principles project. In Proc. of the 43rd ACM Tech. Symp. on CS Education (SIGCSE '12). ACM, New York, NY, USA, 477-478. DOI=10.1145/2157136.2157276

[3] Bell, T., Witten, I., and Fellows, M. 2010. *Computer Science Unplugged.* URL = http://www.csunplugged.org

[4] Burns, R., Pollock, L., and Harvey, T. 2012. Integrating hard and soft skills: software engineers serving middle school teachers. In Proceedings of the 43rd ACM technical symposium on Computer Science Education (SIGCSE '12). ACM, New York, NY, USA, 209-214. DOI=10.1145/2157136.2157199

[5] Carter, E., Blank, G., Walz, J. 2012. Bringing the breadth of computer science to middle schools. In Proceedings of the 43rd ACM technical symposium on Computer Science Education (SIGCSE '12). ACM, New York, NY, USA, 203-208. DOI=10.1145/2157136.2157198

[6] Common Sense Media. 2012. *Scope and Sequence.* URL = www.commonsensemedia.org/educators/scope-and-sequence

[7] Dodds, Z., Erlinger, M., et al. *MyCS Homepage.* Harvey Mudd College. URL = http://www.cs.hmc.edu/MyCS

[8] Goode, J., Chapman, G., Margolis, J., Landa, J., Ullah, T., Watkins, D., and Stephenson, C. 2013. *Exploring Computer Science.* UCLA Graduate School of Education and Information Studies. URL = http://www.exploringcs.org

[9] Goode, J., Chapman, G., and Margolis, J. 2012. Beyond curriculum: the exploring computer science program. ACM Inroads 3, 2 (June 2012), 47-53. DOI=10.1145/2189835.2189851

[10] Lewis, C. 2013. *Scratch Curriculum.* URL = http://colleenmlewis.com/scratch/

[11] Lewis, C. and Shah, N. 2012. Building upon and enriching grade four mathematics standards with programming curriculum. In Proceedings of the 43rd ACM technical symposium on Computer Science Education (SIGCSE '12). ACM, New York, NY, USA, 57-62. DOI=10.1145/2157136.2157156

[12] *A National Talent Strategy: Ideas for Securing U.S. Competitiveness and Economic Growth.* URL = www.microsoft.com/en-us/news/download/presskits /citizenship/MSNTS.pdf.

[13] MyCS_Student. Scratch 2.0. URL = http://scratch.mit.edu/users/MyCS_Student/

[14] Ouyang, Y., Wolz, U., and Rodger, S. H. 2010. Effective delivery of computing curriculum in middle school: challenges and solutions. In Proceedings of the 41st ACM technical symposium on Computer science education (SIGCSE '10). ACM, New York, NY, USA, 327-328. DOI=10.1145/1734263.1734375.

[15] Rodger, S. H., Dalis, M., Gadwal, C., Hayes, J., Li, P., Wolfe, F., Zhang, W., and Liang, L. 2012. Integrating computing into middle school disciplines through projects. Proceedings of the 43rd ACM technical symposium on Computer Science Education (SIGCSE '12). ACM, New York, NY, USA, 421-426. DOI=10.1145/2157136.2157262

[16] Rodger, S. H., Hayes, J., Lezin, G., Qin, H., Nelson, D., Tucker, R., Lopez, M., Cooper, S., Dann, W., and Slater, D. 2009. Engaging middle school teachers and students with alice in a diverse set of subjects. SIGCSE Bull. 41, 1 (March 2009), 271-275. DOI=10.1145/1539024.1508967

[17] ScratchEd Team. 2009. *ScratchEd.* MIT. URL = http://scratched.media.mit.edu/

[18] Sims, Z. and Bubinski, C (founders). Codecademy. URL = http://www.codecademy.com

[19] Taub, R., Armoni, M., and Ben-Ari, M. 2012. CS unplugged and middle-school students' views, attitudes, and intentions regarding CS. ACM Trans. Comput. Educ. 12, 2, Article 8 (April 2012), 29 pages. DOI = 10.1145/2160547

Remedying Misperceptions of Computer Science among Middle School Students

Shuchi Grover
Graduate School of Education
Stanford University
Stanford, CA 94305
shuchig@stanford.edu

Roy Pea
Graduate School of Education/
H-STAR Institute
Stanford University
Stanford, CA 94305
roypea@stanford.edu

Stephen Cooper
Computer Science Department
Stanford University
Stanford, CA 94305
coopers@stanford.edu

ABSTRACT

Past research points to gross misperceptions of the discipline of computer science among students in middle and high school. As efforts to introduce computing education in K-12 gains traction in tandem with initiatives that address issues of interest and attitudes towards CS, misperceptions of computing as a discipline must also be addressed as early as middle school, since that is a key stage for identity building. This paper shares the results of a curricular intervention that aims to show CS to students in a new light- in real world contexts and as a creative and problem-solving discipline; as something bigger and broader than the "computer-centric" view that many students are known to harbor.

Categories and Subject Descriptors

K.3.2 [**Computers and Education**]: Computer and Information Science Education - *Computer Science Education, Curriculum, Literacy* K.7.1[**The Computing Profession**]: Occupations

Keywords

Middle School Computer Science Education, Perceptions of Computing, Identity, K-12 curriculum development, Definition of Computer Science.

1. INTRODUCTION

Recent years have seen a growing consensus around the view that all children must learn computational thinking [20] and be offered introductory exposure to computer science in K-12. Grover & Pea [7] provide a synthesis of several recent efforts among researchers and educators working in concert with organizations such as CSTA to define guidelines for and design K-12 (especially high school) curricula.

Although the numbers for students enrolling for CS courses in high schools across most of the nation is increasing [16] there is still a huge gap that must be bridged to meet the demands of a growing job market in CS (http://goo.gl/gxfmI). In addition to curricular efforts aimed at developing the required thinking skills, there are initiatives aimed at making CS a more attractive career choice especially for females and underrepresented minorities [17]. Prior research overwhelmingly reports a lack of awareness of the discipline coupled with negative attitudes towards Computer Science among students [2, 6, 13, 15, 21]. Martin [13] claimed that "CS has a fundamental image problem", and also asserted that students finishing high school have a difficult time seeing themselves as computer scientists since they do not have a clear understanding of what computer science is and what a computer scientist does. It therefore appears that misconceptions and a lack of awareness of computer science as a discipline potentially contribute to a lack of interest that in turn results in students not opting to enroll in a CS course in high school or beyond. Echoing past research that ties students' disinterest in CS to lack of familiarity with the subject [2], Hewner [9] supports the belief that "Students with an incomplete view of the field of CS might make poor educational decisions". To remedy the situation, therefore, student perceptions of the discipline of CS must develop early on in their school career and must also move beyond hardware, software, and programming to encompass a more realistic, broader, real-world context- as a discipline that equips students to build and use powerful tools to solve complex problems in service to society [13, 21].

When might be an appropriate time to do this? Middle school is a time for *identity building*, as children develop their affinity for and association with specific academic fields. This is supported by findings that eighth grade students who expected to enter a science-related career were much more likely to major in a science discipline than students who did not have science career aspirations at the end of eighth grade [18]. While elementary school children have ill-informed career aspirations, the middle school years, in contrast, represent a critical juncture in the K-12 educational journey to provide experiences that allow students to be open to diverse future opportunities as part of their "possible selves" [12]. Therefore any effort to broaden participation in a discipline must consider these years as critical.

This paper presents the results of research in the context of a middle school introductory computer science and programming curriculum that also consciously attempts to address issues of (mis)-perceptions of computing among 12 to 14 year olds. The goal was to answer the research question: *What is the change, if any, in middle school students' perceptions of computer science as a result of a 6-week introductory CS curriculum that is designed to include curricular materials aimed at increasing awareness of computer science as a discipline?*

2. RELATED WORK

There have been a number of studies on student perceptions of computer science that have been conducted at the middle and high school levels as well as at the undergraduate level. Regardless of school level, the results have overwhelmingly pointed to similar patterns in the narrow view of computer science held by students that is far off the mark, divorced from the reality of what computer scientists usually do. *It is worth noting however these*

SIGCSE'14, March 5–8, 2014, Atlanta, Georgia, USA.

http://dx.doi.org/10.1145/2538862.2538934

although earlier studies have extensively investigated perceptions of computer science, they don't appear to have studied the effects of consciously attempting to remedy them. The remainder of this section describes the studies that influenced our research.

Surveying over 800 high school students, Carter [2] found that students largely lacked formal classroom experience in computing, and the vast majority had no idea whatsoever of what it meant to study computer science in college. Among those that gave some response, many thought of CS as involving programming, repairing or building computers, knowing about how computers work and miscellaneous "computer stuff". The study concluded that lack of education was responsible for this ignorance and one of the recommendations was to "fix computer science's image" by *educating students on how computing is really used in the real world – "for special effects in movies, to improve the quality of life for people with missing limbs, and for allowing communication for people with speech impediments."*

Yardi and Bruckman's study [21] encompassed students aged 11 to 20, as well as graduate students for a comparative data set. Interviews with tech-savvy teenagers indicated a lack of interest in computer science and stereotypical views of the discipline as being difficult, boring, and asocial. In contrast, responses from graduate students led the authors to recommend *exposing children to the real-world relevance of computing and the diversity of career paths*, using students' interest in games as an entry point, the need for *underscoring computing as a creative discipline*, and the importance of role models. Martin [13] had incoming freshmen answer the question "What is computer science?" in addition to drawing a picture of a computer scientist. The majority of the students answered the question with a reference to programming and mentioned the study of hardware and software. In the drawing, none of the drawings by incoming freshmen showed attractive, appealing, or normal looking people. By contrast, more upper-level undergrads (including females and African Americans) drew people that looked like themselves and were patently able to view themselves as computer scientists suggesting that *learning about CS helped change the image of CS.*

Related findings for middle school students have been reported on two studies using surveys, drawings and interviews to examine sixth- and eighth grade students' perceptions of knowledgeable computer users and their self-perception as a 'computer-type person' [14]. Students were asked in one study to generate representations of computer users in pictures or words. In the second study, students were asked whether they believed that there was such a thing as a computer-type person and whether they perceived themselves to be one. Both studies suggest that while there is a male image of computer science in general, it is not overly negative and students' self-perception is not governed by their own gender as much as by other variables.

Questions similar to the ones in these studies were employed by Greening [6] in investigations of high school students who were asked to complete the sentence "Computer Science is mostly about…" and found most responses to be either null (no response), "trivial" or "computer-centric", and pointed to a weakness in the basis by which students choose to study (or not study) computing.

In terms of empirically testing how a curriculum shapes students' perceptions of computing, Taub, Armoni and Ben-Ari [19] surveyed and interviewed middle school students who were exposed to CS Unplugged activities [1] over the course of a semester. The research questions were aimed at ascertaining student perceptions of CS in addition to student attitudes towards computer science and their intent in studying and working in this field. The results of the mixed-methods study were mixed and showed some growth in students' perceptions of CS as a result of the curriculum.

More recently, Fidoten and Spacco [5] used quantitative surveys employing questions with Likert-scale responses to survey non-CS undergraduate faculty about what CS is. The title of their paper, "*What Do Computer Scientists Do?*" served as inspiration for the open response question used in this research. Additionally, as in [21], our research also included college students as a comparative data set.

3. METHODOLOGY

This section describes preliminary research (Study #0) and the first iteration (Study #1) of a design-based research study in the context of a 6-week middle school curriculum titled ***"Foundations for Advancing Computational Thinking" (FACT) designed to include elements aimed at consciously building awareness of computing as a discipline while promoting engagement with foundational computational concepts*** such as algorithmic flow of control comprising (a) sequence (b) looping constructs and (c) conditional logic through the use of the Scratch programming environment. A second iteration of this research with FACT (Study #2) has recently concluded, and we share preliminary results from that as well.

3.1 Preliminary Exploration of Student Perceptions of Computing

The preliminary phase of this research was an exploratory study (*Study #0*) that provided baseline insights into commonly held notions of computer science among middle school students. The sample comprised 23 students (20 male, 3 female; mean age ~12.7 years) in a San Francisco Bay Area public middle school enrolled in an elective class that involved making "computer creations" using Flash and a Scratch-like programming environment. (Note that this curriculum was unrelated to our FACT curriculum described below.) Participants were asked to answer the question: *"In your view, what does a computer scientist do?"*

A comparative data set was gathered by asking the same question of 168 college students in a major university in the same geographic area who had just completed a CS1 course that introduced students to Java and software engineering principles including object-oriented design, decomposition, encapsulation, abstraction, and testing.

All the responses were initially open coded and after the major categories depicting the responses emerged, a researcher unconnected to the research then coded all the responses. Figure 1 below depicts this coding as percentage values, where the numerator is the number of occurrences belonging to that coding category and the denominator is the sum total of responses across all categories. The difference in the response patterns between the two populations was stark. This despite the fact that the middle school students had engaged in a fair amount of programming at the time they were surveyed. The majority of middle school students' responses mostly spoke of "studying" and "building" new ***computers***, **programming** (apps or video games), or notions of research and '**experimentation**' (presumably inspired by the term 'science' in 'computer science'). As observed in earlier research, there were few references to problem solving or real world societal uses of computing that dominated responses from undergraduates. These responses from middle schoolers were very similar to those found in prior research to suggest that notions of CS for this middle school age population revolve around the machine, and are "computer-centric". Although one middle school student wrote that "[a computer scientist] sits at a computer and presses the buttons," such stereotypical views were not expressed more commonly.

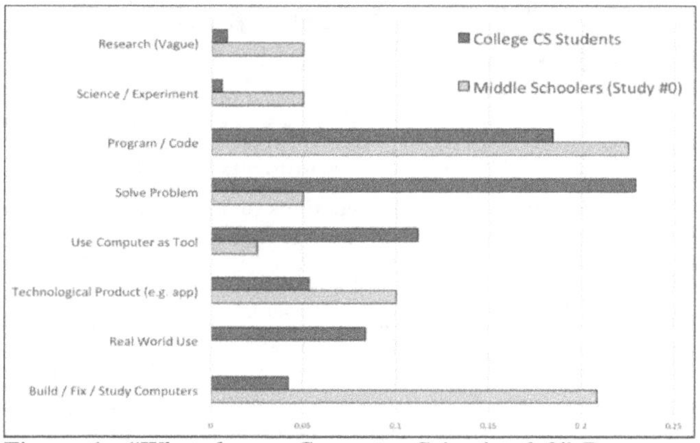

Figure 1: *"What does a Computer Scientist do?"* Responses from Middle School and College Students who had just completed a college-level CS1 course

The responses of the college students, in contrast, were closer to a mature view of computing as a problem solving discipline where computers were *used to solve a real world issue or improve lives*, rather than a discipline aimed at *studying about,* or *building,* computers. Also interesting among the college students' responses was the additional expressiveness that characterized their responses. Close to half the students either used some adverbs or notion of process to describe the act of programming or computation; words and phrases such as *creatively*, *logically*, *reliably*, *efficiently*, and *via computation*, *by decomposing*, *applying known skills*. Admittedly college students are not only older, but more importantly, their views were patently shaped by a college-level introductory CS course they had just completed.

We believe that introducing CS as a problem solving discipline that involves using computers to solve real world problems or improve lives, rather than simply understanding, studying, building or fixing computers, provides an importantly expansive framing [3] of computer science since it may foster an expectation that students will continue to use what they learn later in creative and productive activities rather than simply being focused on computers themselves. This preliminary investigation thus helped set the goals of this research, which was ***to examine whether an introductory CS/programming elective in middle school could be designed to help develop students' perceptions of computing so that it encompasses a more accurate problem-solving and real-world context.***

3.2 Curriculum Design to Address Perceptions of Computer Science

In keeping with the aforementioned goals, the FACT curriculum was designed to raise awareness among the students about computing as a discipline, what computer scientists do and the role CS plays in our world and daily lives today. The first weeklong unit titled '*Computing is Everywhere*' had two goals. The first was to remedy misconceptions and educate students about the real nature of computer science. The second goal was to get them motivated and excited about the remainder of the course that was devoted to introducing computational concepts through the use of the Scratch programming environment. Inspired by recommendations from earlier research to give students a sense for exemplary societal uses of CS such as *"for special effects in movies, to improve the quality of life for people"* [2], '*Computing is Everywhere'* was designed so that students would see examples of computing being used for varied purposes and in diverse fields. It was decided that there would be showing rather than telling during this time, so that students would develop a deeper sense of CS through watching and reflecting on real examples of the nature of computer scientists' work.

For this purpose, about 7 publicly available videos ranging between 1.5 and 6 minutes in length were identified on YouTube. For example, we chose videos like M.I.T. Computer Program Reveals Invisible Motion in Video and Untangling the hairy physics of Rapunzel that exemplified innovations in computing in ways that we believed kids would find interesting and also demonstrated computing being used in a context most children would not likely associate with computer science. The video of Sebastian Thrun's TED talk on Google's driverless car was an example of a CS project driven by a need to tackle the problem of fatalities in automobile accidents. Also included in this unit were a few videos created by CSEdWeek, such as http://y2u.be/t4nThJjI8yI. In addition to these, the lead researcher (and first author) recorded "vignettes of people and computing" - short 1-3 minute videos of diverse people in different fields describing how they used computing in their work. Some videos also included a brief demonstration of what they described. This video repository can be found at http://goo.gl/oatj4H.

3.3 Methods and Data Measures

3.3.1 Participants

For Study #1, the FACT curriculum was taught for six weeks in April-May, 2013 in a public middle school classroom in the San Francisco Bay Area (distinct from the Study #0 school site). The student sample comprised 26 children from 7th and 8th grade (21 boys and 5 girls, mean age: ~13 years) enrolled in a semester-long "Computers" elective class.

For Study #2, the FACT curriculum was taught in Sept-Oct, 2013 in the same middle school setting as Study #1 with a new cohort of students in the "Computers" elective class (19 boys, 9 girls, mean age: ~12.32 years). The data from this study is currently being analyzed, and only some preliminary results are shared in this paper. ***The sections below focus primarily on results from Study #1.***

3.3.2 Procedures

The class met for 55 minutes each day four times per week. The lead researcher on this effort was also the curriculum developer and teacher for the pilot 6-week FACT mini-course. The classroom teacher was present in the class at all times and in her own words, was "learning alongside the students" as she was relatively unfamiliar with programming and CS. She hopes to able to use the FACT curriculum in the future. Each 'Session' described in Table 1 below is equivalent to one 55-minute period.

For Study #2, largely the same curriculum was taught. Other more interesting videos based on student feedback replaced some of the ones used in Study #1. Additionally, we included one publicly

Table 1: Description of Week 1 Curriculum

Session 1	** Students watched 4 short videos from among the videos identified as described in Section 3.2 ** Students are asked to share their reactions to the videos on the discussion forums on Schoology, the course LMS used by the school. **Students shared their reactions to an image (from a publicly available Exploring CS curriculum - https://onramps.instructure.com/courses/723227) of a busy street intersection with people, vehicles, traffic signals and other everyday objects. They were asked to identify *all the things they saw where computing devices or computation were being used.*
Session 2	**Students watched a couple of videos (created by organizations such as NSF and CS EdWeek) that speak what CS is and its relevance in many fields of human endeavor.
	Additionally students watched some "vignettes of people and computing" as described above ** Students were asked to comment on the videos on Schoology after they watched each one, and comment on which video vignette they liked the best. ** They also participated in an online discussion (on Schoology) on how they use computers and ***computational devices* in their daily lives.
Session 3	Students watched a brief video of a CS professor describing briefly what computing is and the kinds of things that computer scientists do (along with a few examples). This was followed by a whole classroom discussion led by the facilitator-researcher on the nature of computer science that included talking about the distinction between programmers and computer scientists. Students answered some more questions and discussion prompts.

available video on YouTube (similar to those shown in week 1) and one "vignette of people & computing" every week in weeks 2 to 5 (in addition to those shown in week 1). This was done to reinforce ideas of real-world applicability of computing even as students proceeded to learn computational constructs and associated programming techniques.

3.3.3 Data Measures

The following data were gathered before, during and after the 6-week intervention.

a) A Pre-Survey that included the question: *"What do computer scientists do?"*
b) Pre-Post surveys on student interest in CS as in [4].
c) Student reactions to each of the videos they watched.
d) Post-survey responses to the question: *"What do computer scientists do?"* at the end of the 6-week FACT intervention.
e) As described in Section 3.1, the same question regarding computer scientists was asked of 168 college students at the end of their CS1 class (Study #0).

4. DATA ANALYSIS AND DISCUSSION

26 student responses to the discussion prompt at the end of Session 2 were open coded and the major categories depicting the responses that emerged were: (1) positive adjectives about CS (e.g. awesome, amazing, cool, exciting), (2) real-world and broad applicability of CS, (3) expression of intent to learn more about CS, (4) seeing CS in a new light (or a way they had not thought of before), and (5) commenting on the use of CS for creative expression. The following figure shows the frequency of occurrences of the responses in the various coding categories. Table 2 quotes sample reactions from students that were coded as seen in Figure 2.

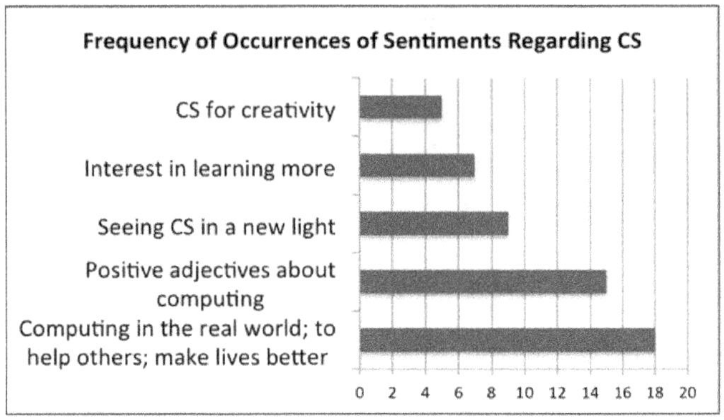

Figure 2: Post-Video Student Sentiments about CS (Day 2)

Table 2: Sample Student Reactions to Videos (Study #1)

I learned that Computer Science is not just programming, and coding. I found out that computing is part of everyday life. Computer science can be used everywhere.
For me, I really enjoyed Amit's video, not only because his invention was really cool, but because it was created by computer science and programming. Also, I think that the person in the third video created a creative program. It's one of the first times I've seen something like that.
I liked the second video with the music because that's something that I can relate to. I love music so I like things that have to do with music. When I thought of computer science before the video I think of computers and only about computers. But now I see that computer science goes so much further than that. Now I can't think of anything that doesn't use computer science. It's really cool.
I like the second video... It was a fun way to combine programming with music and art to create some music. I learned how much CS can be used to create something for fun, not just work-- for example, the Beat Table, and Evelyn's line program. The fun programs are what really changes the world immediately, as it affects more people than medical programs, for example
Some of the most interesting computer science videos I've seen I think, And I now really want to learn more about coding and what I can do with it.

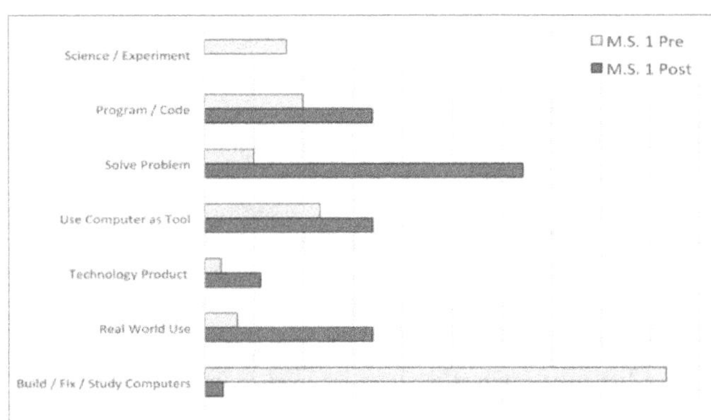

Figure 3: ***(Study #1) "What does a Computer Scientist do?"*** **Pre-Post intervention responses from middle school students**

The second set of data analyzed were the pre/post responses to the question, *What do computer scientists do?,* that were given before the start and after the end of the FACT course (Figure 3). The codes used to analyze these responses were the same as those used in Study#0- the preliminary study of middle school and undergraduate respondents. A researcher unconnected to the project coded the responses. Figure 4 below compares students' post-FACT responses with the responses of college students after their introductory course on software engineering (gathered in Study #0). Figures 3 and 4 represent a percentage value, where the numerator is the number of occurrences belonging to that coding category and the denominator is the sum total of responses across all categories. It is worth noting that some categories are not reflected on the chart (e.g. "process descriptions", "vague responses"), but their occurrences are counted towards the denominator. As before, responses of middle school students lacked the expressiveness of college students and were lacking in terms like 'logically', 'computationally', 'efficiently' and 'reliably', which characterized undergraduates' responses.

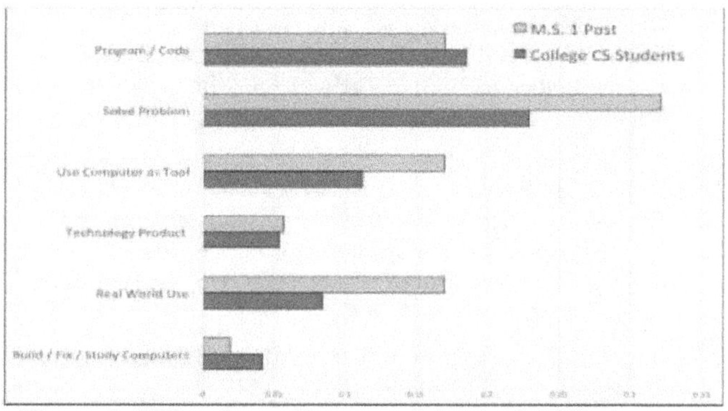

Figure 4: *"What does a Computer Scientist do?"* Post-survey responses from middle school students compared with those of college students (who had finished a college-level CS1 course)

Figure 5 below compares shows the frequency of occurrences of the responses in the various coding categories between Study #1 and Study #2. Responses in Study #2 also included more process descriptions and expressiveness. That and the increase in the overall count of the desired perceptions of computing suggest that the improvements to the FACT curriculum were successful.

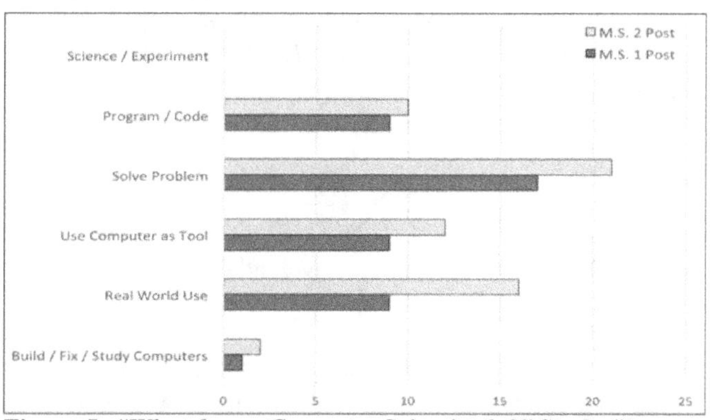

Figure 5: *"What does a Computer Scientist do?"* Study #1 vs. Study #2: Post-intervention responses from middle schoolers

Lastly, student responses to survey questions dealing with interest were analyzed. In response to the question "I like computing" on a 4-point likert scale (1=Strongly Agree; 4=Strongly Disagree), the net response from pre- to post-FACT was unchanged in Study #1, but registered a net gain of 5 points in Study #2. Huge swings in this were not expected as most students had self-selected into the elective class and were expected to have high interest- the average for the pre-FACT responses in Study #1 & #2 was 1.57 and 1.67, respectively. Further analysis of data and students' interest-related responses, especially in Study #2 is currently underway.

4.1 Discussion of Results

It is not surprising that the pre-course responses as to what computer scientists do focused heavily on notions of building, fixing, studying or improving computers with complete absence of the real world applications of computing to solve problems in various domains. This was in keeping with the results of the preliminary study, as well as with past research that shows students' inclination to describe CS in terms of hardware and software [13] and computer-centered and contrived answers [6] and lacking a real-world context [21]. Post-course responses, which were taken 6 weeks after the initial week that had the students watching videos about applications of computer science as part of the *'Computing is Everywhere'* unit, showed persistence of the idea of CS as a problem-solving discipline that helps make our lives easier.

The comparison of student responses before and after the curricular intervention indicates a marked positive shift in student perceptions of computer science toward the more mature perspectives of the college CS undergraduates in Study #0. The middle schoolers' responses post our intervention are comparable to those of college students in most categories; and our students outperformed the college students especially in the categories related to the problem-solving nature of CS, the use of computer as a tool and the real-world application of computer science to make people's lives easier. This despite that fact that in Study #1, after the first week the students did not watch any more videos and were immersed in learning about algorithms, programs, and ideas of sequence, loops and conditionals in programs.

5. CONCLUSIONS & FUTURE WORK

Although we are still in the process of analyzing additional data gathered during this research (especially from Study #2), the results of this iterative research are very encouraging. Several schools are taking the initiative to teach programming and introductory computing. However, as evidenced in preliminary investigations conducted (in Study #0), even as middle school students are increasingly engaging in programming and computational experiences, there is little attention given to consciously educating them about CS as a discipline. As a result, they have little idea of what computer science as a career entails or the broad applicability of computer science in many diverse fields of human endeavor, including creative fields and altruistic careers that may appeal to females, as indicated by research on the "technological imaginations" of boys and girls [10].

The research makes a significant contribution to the field in the form of a curriculum that aims to remedy student misperceptions and succeeds in achieving this goal. This study demonstrates that it does not take much instruction per se to make a difference in students' notions of computer science. ***Such a strategy and curriculum could therefore be easily adopted in schools including those that are lacking teacher capacity for a dedicated CS or programming class***. Inviting guest speakers from different CS careers to speak to students about their work has often been suggested as a strategy to get young teens interested in the field [11]. In the absence of access to such people, even short publicly available videos or the "vignettes of computing" suite of videos created for this curriculum can be re-used in any school setting. In fact, this was successfully attempted at a recent hour-long class titled "What do computer scientists (really) do?" taught to 55 students by the lead author and researcher through the Stanford Splash program (https://www.stanfordesp.org/). It included a version of this curriculum with the six top videos voted as favorites in student surveys at the end of Study #2.

The validity and generalizability of this research is somewhat limited by relatively small sample sizes, and small numbers of female students and minorities. Given that the ideas and curricular intervention (of using engaging and relevant videos) is relatively simple, it would be easy to try this in diverse settings with larger numbers of students, especially from underrepresented groups in computer science like female students and minorities.

How persistent will these views of computer science be in the long-term? It is essential that students' views of computing fostered in this research should be reinforced in subsequent engagement and experiences with computing in order for their perceptions to persist and for the maintenance of their evident interests in computer science. Past research has suggested that "belief centrality, the students' previous beliefs about computing may remain central while the things they learned in introductory computing change their peripheral beliefs in smaller ways" [8]. A follow-up study being contemplated is to follow the students in Study #1 and #2 to ask them to revisit the question about what computer scientists do after a period of six months since the curricular intervention.

As the move to introduce computing to K-12 schools gains momentum, several efforts are underway to change student attitudes towards—and increase interest in—computing. An important piece of this puzzle is remedying students' misconceptions of computing as a discipline centered on building and fixing computers, and studying about the internals of computers. Making children aware of exemplary societal uses of CS as a creative and engaging discipline with an impact in almost all other domains will certainly help the cause of broadening the CS pipeline and its associated learning trajectories.

6. REFERENCES

[1] Bell, T., Alexander, J., Freeman, I., and Grimley, M. 2009. Computer science unplugged: School students doing real computing without computers. *NZ J. Appl. Comput. Inf. Tech.* 13, 1, 20–29.

[2] Carter. L. 2006. Why students with an apparent aptitude for computer science don't choose to major in computer science. *In Proceedings of SIGCSE*, pages 27–31, Houston, Texas, USA. ACM

[3] Engle, R. A., Lam, D. P., Meyer, X. S., and Nix, S. E. 2012. How does expansive framing promote transfer? Several proposed explanations and a research agenda for investigating them. *Educational Psychologist*, 47(3).

[4] Ericson, B. and McKlin, T. 2012. Effective and sustainable computing summer camps. In *Proceedings of the 43rd ACM technical symposium on Computer Science Education* (pp. 289-294). ACM.

[5] Fidoten, H. and Spacco, J. 2012. What do computer scientists do?: a survey of CS and non-CS liberal arts faculty. In *Proceedings of the 17th ACM annual conference on Innovation and technology in computer science education* (pp. 279-284). ACM.

[6] Greening. T. 1998. Computer science: through the eyes of potential students. In *Proceedings of the 3rd Australasian conference on Computer science education*, pages 145–154, The University of Queensland, Australia, 1998. ACM.

[7] Grover, S. and Pea, R. 2013. Computational Thinking in K–12 A Review of the State of the Field. *Educational Researcher*, *42*(1), 38-43.

[8] Hewner,M. and Guzdial.M. 2008. Attitudes about computing in postsecondary graduates. In *Proceeding of ICER 2008*, pages 71–78, Sydney, Australia. ACM.

[9] Hewner, M. 2013. Undergraduate conceptions of the field of computer science. In *Proceedings of the ninth annual international ACM conference on International computing education research* (pp. 107-114). ACM.

[10] Honey, M., Moeller, B., Brunner, C., Bennett, D. T., Clements, P., and Hawkins, J. 1991. "Girls and Design: Exploring the Question of Technological Imagination." Tech Rep. No. 17. New York: Bank Street College of Education, Center for Technology in Education.

[11] Kim, K. A., Fann, A. J., & Misa-Escalante, K. O. (2011). Engaging women in computer science and engineering: Promising practices for promoting gender equity in undergraduate research experiences. *ACM Transactions on Computing Education (TOCE)*, *11*(2), 8.

[12] Markus, H., and Nurius, P. 1986. Possible selves. *American Psychologist, 41,* 954-969.

[13] Martin, C. D. 2004. Draw a computer scientist. In *Working Group Reports on Innovation and Technology in Computer Science Education (ITiCSE-WGR '04).* 11–12.

[14] Mercier, E. M., Barron, B., and O'Connor, K. M. 2006. Images of self and others as computer users: The role of gender and experience. *Journal of Computer Assisted Learning*, 22(5), 335-348.

[15] Mitchell, A., Purchase, H. C., and Hamer, J. 2009. Computing science: What do pupils think? In *Proceedings of the 14th Annual Conference on Innovation and Technology in Computer Science Education (ITiCSE '09).* 353–353.

[16] Roberts, E. S. 2011. Meeting the challenges of rising enrollments. *ACM Inroads*, *2*(3), 4-6.

[17] Simard, C. 2009. Obstacles and solutions for underrepresented minorities in technology. *Report for Anita Borg Institute for Women and Technology, Palo Alto, CA.*

[18] Tai, R., Qi Liu, C., Maltese, A.V., and Fan, X. 2006. Planning Early for Careers in Science. *Science.* 312(5777) 1143-1144

[19] Taub, R., Ben-Ari, M., and Armoni, M. 2009. The effect of CS unplugged on middle-school students' views of CS. In *SIGCSE Bulletin* (Vol. 41, No. 3, pp. 99-103). ACM.

[20] Wing, J. 2006. Computational Thinking. *Communications of the ACM.* 49(3), 33-36.

[21] Yardi, S. and Bruckman, A. 2007. "What is computing?: bridging the gap between teenagers' perceptions and graduate students' experiences," in *Proceedings of ICER 2007*, pp. 39–50

Workplace Scenarios to Integrate Communication Skills and Content: A Case Study

Mark E. Hoffman
Quinnipiac University
Hamden, CT 06518
mark.hoffman@quinnipiac.edu

Paul V. Anderson
Elon University
Elon, NC 27244
PaulAnderson@elon.edu

Magnus Gustafsson
Chalmers University of Technology
Gothenburg, Sweden
magusta@chalmers.se

ABSTRACT

A recent study of new software developers at Microsoft reveals the significance and integration of communication skills in their daily tasks. While the literature offers a variety of approaches to promote the integration of communication skills into the Computer Science curriculum, a discrepancy remains between what students get and what they need. In this paper, we propose using workplace scenarios that integrate communication skills with technical content situated in and mediating workplace activity. Workplace scenarios are based on an analysis of the workplace as an activity system. Guidelines for implementing workplace scenarios are provided. A case study analyzes the integration of communication skills with technical content using workplace scenarios in a software development course.

Categories and Subject Descriptors

K.3.2 [**Computer and Education**]: Computer and Information Science Education – *Computer Science education.*

General Terms

Documentation, Management, Theory.

Keywords

Workplace scenario, communication skills, situated learning, activity systems, genre

1. INTRODUCTION

There is general agreement in the literature that computer science (CS) graduates must be effective communicators to meet the needs of their employers and become successful professionals [4, 8, 9, 12, 14, 15, 18]. The literature also reveals that the profession finds most new CS graduates to be deficient in their communication skills [8, 9, 15]. A recent study of eight new software developers (i.e., ones with little or no experience beyond a limited internship) at Microsoft [1] provides new insight into the reasons that college CS programs have had difficulty equipping their students with them. As this study reveals, the communications that computer scientists prepare are integrated seamlessly with the highly specific technical functions they perform, and their communications are deeply influenced by the work processes and organizational structures in which they perform their tasks. Consequently, preparing students with what might be called "general" communication skills does not provide them with the ability to communicate effectively in the very specialized contexts of the CS workplace.

SIGCSE'14, March 5–8, 2014, Atlanta, Georgia, USA.

This insight into the situated nature of communication in the CS community of practitioners indicates the value of replacing the question, "How can we teach CS students to communicate effectively?" with this more refined definition of our goal: "How can college programs in computer science prepare graduates with the communication skills that are *significant* and *integral* components of the professional tasks in the CS workplace?"

Using evidence from the Microsoft study and theories about learning and communications in the workplace, we propose the creation of assignments involving workplace scenarios that reflect the integration of technical and communication tasks in the ways they are inextricably woven together in professional practice. In addition to providing guidelines for constructing and teaching with these scenarios, we present the case study of a course in which integrated workplace scenarios were used. We describe ways that scenarios can be scaffolded with increasing sophistication throughout a curriculum to progressively develop the high level of competence that will enable students to make rapid and successful transitions from school to work.

2. THE WORKPLACE LEARNING ENVIRONMENT

Begel and Simon's study of new software developers (NSDs) at Microsoft [1] provides important insights into what new CS graduates need to learn as they enter the professional workplace and—just as important—how they learn it. The authors portray software development as a social practice and characterize the process through which NSDs progress from novices to experts as socialization. Besides learning the functions of their particular jobs, NSDs learn the organizational hierarchy and how they fit in; they become familiar with organization's processes and the ways their work intersects with the work of others; and they build a network of colleagues from whom they can seek assistance and support. The social practice is mediated by soft (i.e., communication) skills (reading, writing, listening, speaking, and teaming).

In Begel and Simon's detailed description of NSDs' socialization into the CS workplace, we identify four features that suggest ways CS programs could teach communication skills more effectively.

First, in the workplace communication is fully integrated with technical work. For instance, of the fifteen steps Begel and Simon witnessed NSDs performing when fixing a bug, nine involve communication.

- Read a bug report [reading]
- Read the source code for the program [reading]
- Ask question of co-workers to understand the source code and the root cause of the bug [speaking, listening, and teaming]
- Convince co-workers that the fix is the right one under the circumstances [speaking and teaming]

- Get the fix reviewed by a manager or co-worker [teaming]
- Work with a tester to verify that the fix did not cause any regression [teaming]
- Attend a bug triage meeting to report the status of the bug [speaking and teaming]
- Meet with managers of other components that may be affected by the bug fix and persuade them to sign off on the fix [speaking, listening, and teaming]
- Write up the results of the investigation and bug fix in the bug report [writing]

Similarly, nine of the fourteen steps the NSDs performed when developing new program features involved communication. Communicating (including reading and writing documentation) is so integral to the work of CS professionals that it occupied more than 50% of the work time the researchers observed for five of the eight NSDs. For one NSD, it consumed more than 70%.

Second, in the CS workplace, communication activities derive their significance from the ways they advance *specific* technical work. To achieve their goals when reading bug reports, NSDs (and experts) must quickly and accurately extract the information on which they will act. To read in this way, they must use reading skills not required for reading a newspaper or novel. In addition to the communication skills needed in other speaking situations, CS professionals rely on specialized ones to persuade co-workers that the fix they are proposing is the most effective way to address a bug and that it is unlikely to create additional bugs.

Third, NSDs develop their technical and communication skills by participating in the professional practice where these two are woven together inextricably. At Microsoft, they can't fix a bug without reading the bug report and source code, without presenting the proposed fix to others for review, and without writing about their investigation and fix in a bug report. While the details of this and other processes vary in other organizations, the interdependence of technical and communication activities persists. By participating in the actual work of their employers' organizations, NSDs learn *specific* communication skills in the contexts that give these skills their significance.

Fourth, the NSDs learn through interactions with others, including their supervisors and mentors who provide feedback and guidance, as well as peers whom they ask for assistance.

For a variety of reasons, these four features of the workplace learning environment create an effective context for teaching new CS employees the technical and communication abilities they haven't learned in school. If we understand how these features of the workplace learning environment promote the development of NSDs' communication abilities, we can find ways to improve the teaching of communication skills in CS programs.

3. LEARNING IN THE WORKPLACE

Researchers who study learning in professional settings describe three concepts that explain why the distinctive features of the learning environment described by Begel and Simon [1] are so potent. The concepts are situated learning, activity-system learning, and genre learning.

Situated learning. Based on ethnographic studies of apprenticeship in a variety of fields, Lave and Wenger [16] describe the path by which someone becomes a practicing professional in any field, including CS. The researchers define a profession as a "community of practice," whose members have collaborative relationships, a joint enterprise or shared goals, and a shared repertoire of resources, such as concepts, methods, and experience. CS professionals are members of at least two overlapping communities of practice: the community of the particular organizations in which they work and the community of the discipline of CS professionals.

Within a community of practice, members have different levels of experience and expertise. Newcomers advance from their low levels of experience and expertise to become full members through a social process that Lave and Wenger [16] call situated learning or *legitimate peripheral participation*. That is, they learn by actually participating in selected professional activities with support from fuller members of the community. For example, the Microsoft NSDs were assigned genuine but peripheral tasks, such as fixing bugs or developing non-mission-critical new features of a program. By performing this work with guidance and feedback from supervisors, coworkers and mentors, they built their knowledge, advancing toward the next, less peripheral stage.

Activity system learning. When performing even peripheral tasks, newcomers and experts alike are immersed in complex sets of interactions with others. To fix bugs, the Microsoft NSDs interacted directly with co-workers to understand the source code and, later, to persuade co-workers that their fix is the right one. They interacted with managers to obtain approvals and with testers to verify the fix. They interacted indirectly with the person who wrote the bug report and with readers of their own report about the fix. These sets of actions and interactions are called activity systems [18, 19, 20]. In addition to bug fixing, every minor and major project in CS involves an activity system, whether creating a new feature, creating system requirements, or updating legacy code. While activity systems for different types of technical tasks often share steps or interactions, each is unique.

Newcomers must learn how to take the various actions and use the various tools that enable them to contribute effectively to the activity systems in which they perform their work. For instance, the Microsoft NSDs were given full responsibility—from start to finish—for completing specific projects, such as fixing a particular bug. Consequently, they learned simultaneously the relevant technical information and the communication skills required to interact effectively with the other actors in the associated activity system.

Genre learning. As CS professionals work within their activity systems, they read, write, speak, and listen to familiar forms of communication: the bug report, UML, system requirements report, test plan, test report, and so on. Each of these conventional forms is a genre, a type of communication that has developed in response to recurring situations [3, 20]. Many genres, including the kinds just named, have developed within specific professions—communities of practice—because of their effectiveness at enabling practitioners to collaborate effectively and efficiently within their activity systems.

To learn a genre is to learn a tool or common resource that is used by novices and experts alike in the community of practice. As they worked on their projects, the Microsoft NSDs learned the genres of those activity systems—as both creators of communications using them (e.g., writing a specification document for a new feature or making a status report) and as readers or listeners to communications presented in them (e.g., reading a bug report or program requirements document).

In sum, on the job, NSDs benefit from situated learning (legitimate peripheral practice) through which they develop the genre knowledge and the associated skills needed to communicate effectively in the activity systems of their technical work.

4. COMPARING WORKPLACE AND ACADEMIC LEARNING ENVIRONMENTS

While CS employers and academic programs share the goal of helping individuals become professionals, they function in very different learning environments, especially with respect to developing communication skills. Many CS programs focus so steadfastly on developing technical skills that little attention is given to developing students' communication abilities. Where communication instruction is provided, it often involves school genres, not workplace ones [6, 17, 18, 19], a situation that pervades higher education. In a national study of college writing, Melzer [17] found that the dominant forms of writing are short-answer exams with the teacher as the audience. Beaufort [2] and Dias et al. [6], among others, report on the difficulties college graduates encounter because they learn communication skills abstracted from situations in which they will communicate after graduation. Paretti [18, 19] analyzes the differences between the activity systems in engineering workplaces and classroom, concluding that differences in their goals have a significant impact on what students are asked to write, how their writing is used, and what they learn from the writing.

Various strategies have been proposed for introducing writing into CS courses where it is absent. Garvey [10] and Julia [12] describe strategies that CS instructors might use to create assignments for their courses. Dugan and Polanski [7] and Hoffman, Dansdill and Herscovici [11] provide taxonomies to help instructors identify the kinds of assignments (writing to learn, academic, and professional) they might incorporate. Cilliers [4] and Weikle [21] provide sample assignments for particular CS courses. Etlinger [8], Falkner and Falkner [9], and Karatsolis et al. [14] describe frameworks for designing communication components for any course. To bring communication instruction closer to the technical work in CS, some programs have replaced required technical communication courses taught by another department (often English) with similar courses designed specifically for their students [13, 15].

The Begel and Simon study [1] suggests the value of designing communication assignments that, to the extent possible, place students in situations, real or imagined, that mimic the workplace learning environment as a community of practice where students use domain-specific genres to contribute to specific activity systems. Potentially, this learning environment exists in senior design, software engineering, and other courses where students work on projects for clients, real or imagined. Often, however, these courses devote so much attention to technical issues that the opportunity for students to learn critical communication skills is lost. Paretti [18] suggests that "faculty can create and implement communications assignments that help students develop an analytical, metacognitive approach to reports and presentations that resembles, to a large degree, the engineering process." Dias et al. [6] suggest creating assignments that organize "the class as a working group with some degree of complexity, continuity, and interdependence of joint activity" of the workplace. Begel and Simon [1] cite several teaching strategies for software development courses as well as the practice of having younger students communicate with more advanced students as they work on their projects. Such arrangements provide instructors with opportunities to help students learn how to communicate effectively in the kinds of activity systems where they will work in their careers. Carter et al. [3] describe a procedure for creating workplace scenarios in which students perform integrated communication and technical tasks positioned in professional activity systems, a strategy that can be used with the activity systems relevant to any course in the CS curriculum. Students' progress from the periphery of professional practice can be achieved by using increasingly sophisticated scenarios in the later years of their study. Our approach to incorporating communication into the CS curriculum builds on and extends their strategy.

5. CREATING WORKPLACE SCENARIOS FOR INTEGRATING COMMUNICATION SKILLS INTO ANY CS COURSE

Our approach is simply storytelling. The instructor creates a story—or scenario—that embeds the students' technical task in a workplace activity system. Such a scenario has four elements: *professional role for the student* (e.g., new programmer; experienced software engineer), *technical task* (fix a bug; design a test plan), *communication task* (get the manager's approval for the fix; enable the tester to conduct the test), and *what the audience will use the communication to do* (determine whether to approve the fix; run the test). In many scenarios a fifth element is also needed: the *genre* the student is to use (bug report; test plan).

In the scenario, the person with whom the students communicate is not the instructor but rather another employee, client, or some other person borrowed from the workplace. The instructor's roles are to help students learn how to make their communications effective *from the point of view of the audience in the scenario* and to evaluate the students' work from that same perspective.

We suggest the following guidelines for making scenarios as effective as possible.

Embed workplace scenario activities within the broader context of a workplace activity system. Help students engage in their role by providing the general context for their work. What is the goal or objective of the work the employer (not you) has assigned? If the assignment is small, still let the students know how it fits into the broader context of the employer's goals and activities. If the assignment is large enough to have subparts, help the students understand how the parts fit together in the workplace.

Explicitly distinguish workplace scenario activities from purely academic activities. There is no need to connect every assignment to a workplace activity system. Purely academic assignments are useful for achieving various course and curricular objectives. It is important to be clear when an activity is academic and when it is embedded in a workplace activity system.

Present genres as conventional frames that can be executed with various levels of skills. When placing students in a workplace scenario, the goal is to help them learn how to create communications that are clear, useful, and persuasive to their audiences. Lessons to be learned include how to decide what to say (and what not say), how to sequence it, what to emphasize, what tone to use, and so on. The teaching opportunity is lost if students are given a checklist or a form to fill out with statements so short and so obvious that no communication skill is required.

Provide opportunities for practice and feedback. Situated learning takes place within a community of practice. Newcomers are effectively "apprentices" who learn by doing authentic activities (i.e., ones that have consequences) while receiving feedback they can act on in the next draft or iteration.

6. CASE STUDY: INTRODUCTION OF SOFTWARE DEVELOPMENT

This case study describes the use of a workplace scenario in Introduction to Software Development (CSC 225), a course that one of us (Hoffman) has taught since 2004. CSC 225 is the third in a three-course programming sequence whose objective is to guide students along a "ladder of competence" from beginner to advanced beginner to competent [5]. It is preceded by the equivalents of CS1 and CS2. Typically, CS majors take it in the first semester of their second year.

The CS department incorporated a workplace scenario into CSC 225 as a result of Hoffman's participation, beginning in summer 2010, in a three-year NSF-funded CPATH II project, "Incorporating Communication Outcomes into the Computer Science Curriculum."[1] The project brought together approximately 40 CS faculty and communication specialists to develop strategies to integrate content and communication skills into and across the CS curriculum.

In 2010, the course used an experiential pedagogy to develop students' basic software development knowledge and skills. Working in teams of 5 or 6, students created features for a two-dimensional, two-person Tank Wars game. Students participated in a limited form of Scrum. All student work was addressed to the instructor.

Workplace Scenario

In Fall 2011, the workplace scenario was added to reposition the students' technical work in a workplace activity system. In the scenario, the teams work for a software development company that has purchased another company that has several projects in various stages of completion. Each team is assigned to evaluate and then develop one of the partially complete projects. Writing assignments are reports to a supervisor who uses them to perform his or her own tasks. Table 1 provides the details for the Program Review Report assignment, which (like the other assignments) has its own context within the larger scenario: The supervisor cannot allocate resources needed to finish all of the partially completed projects. He or she will choose the project that is evaluated by the team that demonstrates in its report that it is the one most capable of identifying, prioritizing, and addressing the work required. (Of course, all student teams ultimately proceed to development.)

Table 1. Workplace Scenario for Program Review Report

Professional role	Member of a software development team
Technical task	Install, learn to operate, and evaluate a partially-completed project
Communication task	Report results of evaluation to project manager
How audience will use communication	Compare the team's ability to complete its project with the abilities of the other teams to complete their projects
Genre	Evaluation Report

Using workplace scenarios shifts the students' communication goal from persuading the instructor that they have mastered the technical content of the course to communicating the results of their technical work in a manner that helps their workplace readers perform their own work. The instructor can then teach students what information readers need in recurring situations and how to present the information in ways the readers will find easy to use and persuasive. The CS instructor still evaluates students' assignments, but does so from the perspective of their success at meeting the workplace readers' needs, a boon to instructors who previously had been uncertain how to evaluate "writing."

Course Assignments[2]

The scenario is used to link assignments within a realistic activity system in which students engage in frequent communication activities that are tied directly to the their ongoing technical work, as happens in the workplace.

Over the first five weeks of the semester, each team installs, learns to operate, and evaluates the partially complete project; works with potential customers to identify bugs and enhancements; develops a prioritized list of bugs and enhancements; selects project management tools; and develops a preliminary test plan. At the end of each week, student teams submit a report addressed to their supervisor and make a presentation of their findings. In the reports, students provide the supervisor with the information he or she needs in order to determine whether they are making good decisions and to provide needed guidance to them.

The assignments over the first five weeks are linked and cumulative.

- Program Review Report – Install, learn to operate, and evaluate the project
- Customer Requirements Report - Work with potential customers to identify bugs and enhancements
- Prioritized Bug/Enhancement Report - Develop a prioritized list of bugs and enhancements
- Project Management Tools Report - Select project and configuration management tools
- Preliminary Test Plan - Develop a preliminary test plan

The next eight weeks consists of four two-week Scrum cycles. In each cycle, teams select items from their backlog (prioritized list of bug and enhancements) and implement them. During the first class period of each cycle, student teams create a work plan. At subsequent classes, the teams meet together to give short (5-minute) status reports. At the end of each cycle, teams report (written and oral) progress and demonstrate their working project. They also conduct a post mortem to discuss lessons learned that they can act on in the next cycle. In this way, the assignments over the four two-week Scrum cycles are linked and cumulative.

At the end of the course, teams package their project, make a Final Report of their work, and demonstrate their project to a group of invited guests.

Instruction in communication

To develop students' communication abilities, instructors must not only make communication assignments but also provide instruction and feedback to the students. For both purposes, CSC 225 uses rubrics and example assignments, both of which are discussed with students.

[1] NSF CPATH-II Awards CCF-0939122 and CCF-0939081. http://cs-comm.lib.muohio.edu/about

[2] Examples of communication assignments for this course can be found at http://cs-comm.lib.muohio.edu/collections/show/4.

Each assignment includes a unique technical rubric. All share a common communication skills rubric that includes all the criteria that students will practice as they move toward mastery over the semester. Sets of criteria on the communication skills rubric and the accompanying instruction are introduced gradually. Each assignment focuses on a new set of criteria so students can focus on the new communication skills while practicing previous focal skills based on formative feedback. By the end of the semester, after several opportunities to practice these skills, students master them at a level appropriate for a first-semester second-year CS student. To help students understand the rubric, general criteria are supplemented by more detailed ones. For example, the general criterion "Report helps project manager make practical decisions efficiently" is supplemented by "Critical information is easily accessible to the reader."

While the rubric enables students to understand the criteria by which their workplace communications will be evaluated, the examples help them learn strategies they can use to achieve success. For instance, examples help students see how tables and bullet lists can make information "easily accessible to the reader." Instructor annotations in the examples draw students' attention to large and small features that contribute to or detract from their effectiveness. For instance, annotations highlight places where the tone is appropriately formal or the structure of a paragraph is especially effective at emphasizing a key point. For each writing assignment, the instructor provides two or more examples of annotated and graded student work from previous iterations of the course. On the day an assignment is distributed, the instructor and students discuss the examples and the section of the communication rubric that applies to the assignment. To avoid giving students the impression that there is one correct way to create each communication, the examples show various ways of organizing and presenting information to the reader.

Instructive feedback is also provided to students on work they have submitted. The instructor discusses evaluated student work with each team. Since assignments are cumulative with respect to communication skills, teams are able to use what they have learned through experience and evaluation to improve their performance on the next assignment as they move toward mastery

Results[3]

The development resulting from participation in the CPATH II project of assignments that use workplace scenarios has had a significant impact on student work. Examples help students understand what a particular report looks like as well as different ways the objective can been accomplished. It is interesting to note that teams do not tend to copy the form or format of the examples. They adapt the better ideas to their purpose with a desire to establish a unique identity.

Communications rubrics cumulatively implemented allow students to focus on a new set of communication skills and practice based on formative feedback from previous focal skills.

In addition to students' improved communication skills, we observed an associated improvement in their technical ability. The two, when integrated, amplify one another. Improved communication skills allow students to clearly communicate their technical knowledge, while their increased confidence in their ability to communicate facilitates their technical learning. Focusing on one while minimizing the other does not afford this amplifying effect.

At the end of the Fall 2011 semester students wrote a guided reflection on the course and course project. Here is one student's response to the question, "What was the *most important thing you learned* in this course this semester?"

"The most important thing I learned was that coding is not the only thing the role of a computer scientist involves. I learned that communication is just as, if not more, important as coding. In the first scrum cycle, we were not good at making meetings. Our terrible communication limited the amount of meetings we held, making it difficult to get our questions answered and our work done. As more cycles past it was crucial that we improved our communication skills, and we did. Going in to the class I thought it was all about coding, but just as in most other team related jobs, communication and cooperation are key components to success."

When asked "What Student Learning Outcome did you make the most progress toward achieving?" several students identified communications skills such as "To demonstrate the ability to work in a team and to communicate, orally and in writing, a software design to various audiences" or "Document a project plan, document progress, and communicate progress to users, peers, or the instructor." As one student commented, "all of these assignments forced us to work in teams, plan goals, work together, choose appropriate tools, make presentations, and compile well-written reports. I feel I made the most progress on these objectives because they are skills we had to practice throughout the entire semester."

Specifically asked to assess progress in developing communication skills, one student responded: "My reading skills have improved by being able to identify the key details and important information in a document and quickly access it to have a quick and thorough understanding of whatever I am reading. My writing skills have improved in similar ways that my reading skills have. I learned a new style of writing documents that is clear, easy to read, and straight to the point. Having to write documents that would make 'the managers' life easier was a great exercise to help us to fine-tune our writing into something that is very quickly and easily readable."

Finally, two students who took CSC 225 during the fall 2012 semester were on different internships over the summer of 2013. When asked how their internships were going, both volunteered that they attended stand-up meetings every morning. As one student reported, "We have daily standup meetings where everyone on the team or group relays what they have been working on and the progress that has been made." This is an important observation. During the four Scrum cycles in the course, students held a limited number of five-minute Scrum meetings to share progress toward prior objectives, obstacles to progress, and goals for the next meeting. While the exact form of the meetings (daily vs. a limited number of times in two weeks, sit down vs. stand-up) differed, students were able to recognize the genre, understand its purpose, and, most importantly, learn how to participate effectively.

The results of this case study suggest that workplace scenarios similar to those presented in this paper may be used across several courses or a curriculum with increasing sophistication to improve student learning of both technical and communication skills facilitating efficient and effective transition to any workplace on graduation.

[3]Examples of student work will be available at http://www.thinkingwriting.qmul.ac.uk/wishees/index.html.

7. CONCLUSION

We started with the question, "How can college CS programs provide graduates with the communication skills that will be a *significant* and *integral* component of their professional work?" Employing a theoretical framework that integrates situated learning, genre learning, and activity-system learning we explained why the answer is so elusive. We then offered guidelines for creating scenario assignments and the associated instruction that reflect the ways technical and communication tasks are integrated in the work of CS professionals. We also described a course that uses the scenarios, and we observed that employing increasing sophisticated scenarios can progressively develop students' mastery of meta-cognitive skills that better prepare them for the transition from school to work. One corollary question remains, "Will CS educators buy in?"

Many computer science educators protest that they are not prepared to teach writing and other communication skills, that the skills should be taught by communication experts in other departments, and that adding communication skills to CS courses would significantly increase their own already over-packed workloads. The message of this paper is that the communication skills CS graduates need are ones that many CS instructors already possess because of their own experience as CS professionals. In fact, colleagues in other departments are not as well prepared as they are to teach them to our students. CS instructors may need to devote significant time to learning how to develop scenarios and incorporate them into course schedules, but this effort is likely to diminish as the approach becomes familiar. Instructors without experience in the profession may also need to learn about the contexts in which most of their graduates will work. Positioning themselves as users of student work rather than judges changes the dynamics of evaluation—and simplifies it. As instructors, they shift dynamically between teacher and manager, taking on a role of a workplace manager who mentors new employees.

8. ACKNOWLEDGEMENTS

This work is supported by NSF CPATH II Awards CCF-0939122 and CCF-0939081 (Principle Investigators (Janet Burge, Jerry Gannod, Paul Anderson, Mladen Volk, and Michael Carter). This work is also supported by the College of Arts and Sciences at Quinnipiac University.

9. REFERENCES

[1] Begel A. and Simon B. 2008. Novice Software Developers, All Over Again. *ICER '08*, (Sydney, Australia, September 6-7, 2008)

[2] Beaufort A. 2007. *College Writing and Beyond A New Framework for University Writing*. Utah State University Press, Logan, UT.

[3] Carter M., Gannod G., Burge J., Anderson P., Vouk M, and Hoffman M. 2011. Communication Genres: Integrating Communication into the Software Engineering Curriculum. *CSEE&T-2011*. Honolulu, Hawaii, May 22024, 2001.

[4] Cilliers C. 2012 Student perception of academic writing skill activities in a traditional programming course. *Computers & Education*, 58 (2012), 1028-1041.

[5] Denning P. 2004. The Field of Programmers Myth. *CACM* 47,7 (July 2004), 15-20.

[6] Dias P., Freedman A., Medway P., and Pare A. 1999. *Worlds apart: Acting and writing in academic and workplace contexts*. Lawrence Erlbaum, Mahwah, NJ.

[7] Dugan R. and Polanski V. 2006. Writing for Computer Science: A Taxonomy of Writing Tasks and General Advice. *JCSC* 21, 6, (June 2006), 191-203.

[8] Etlinger H. 2006. A Framework In Which To Teach (Technical) Communications to Computer Science Majors. *SIGCSE '06*, (Houston, TX, March 1-5, 2006)

[9] Falkner K. and Falkner N. 2012. Integrating Communication Skills into the Computer Science Curriculum. *SIGCSE '12*, (Raleigh, NC, February 29-March 3, 2012).

[10] Garvey A. 2010. Writing in an Upper-Level CS Course. *SIGCSE '10*, (Milwaukee, Wisconsin, March 10-13, 2010).

[11] Hoffman M., Dansdill T. and Herscovici D. 2006. Bridging Writing to Learn to Writing in the Discipline in Computer Science Education. *SIGCSE'06*, (Houston, TX, March 1-5, 2006).

[12] Julia J. 2011. An Engineering Approach to Teaching Writing. *SIGCSE '11*, (Dallas, TX, March 9-12, 2011).

[13] Kaczmarczyk L. 2003. A Technical Writing Class for Computer Science Majors: Measuring Student Perceptions of Learning. *SIGCSE '03*, (Reno, NV, February 19-23, 2003).

[14] Karatsolis A., Cervesato I., Abu-Ghazaleh N., Cooper Y., Harras K., Oflazer K., and Sans T. 2011. Getting CS Undergraduates to Communicate Effectively. *ITiCSE '11*, (Darmstadt, Germany, June 27-29, 2011).

[15] Kayfetz J. and Almeroth K. 2008. Creating Innovative Writing Instruction for Computer Science Graduate Students. *ASEE/IEEE Foundations in Education Conference*, (Saratoga Springs, NY, October 22-25, 2008).

[16] Lave J. and Wenger E. 1991. *Situated learning: Legitimate peripheral participation*. Cambridge University Press, New York, NY.

[17] Melzer D. 2009. Writing Assignments Across the Curriculum: A National Study of College Writing. *CCC*, 61, 2 (December 2009), 240-261.

[18] Paretti M. 2012. Teaching Communication in Capstone Design: The Role of the Instructor in Situated Learning. *Journal of Engineering Education*, (October 2008), 491-503.

[19] Paretti M.,2013. Towards an Integrated Assessment Framework: Using Activity Theory to Understand, Evaluate, and Enhance Portfolio Assessment in Integrated Content and Language Learning. *Journal of Academic Writing 3* (1), 95-119. http://e-learning.coventry.ac.uk/ojs/index.php/joaw/article/view/100

[20] Russell D. 1997. Rethinking genre and society: an activity theory analysis. *Written Communication*. 14, 4 (October 1997), 504-554.

[21] Weikle D. 2013. Two Concrete Examples of Upper-Level Writing Assignments in an Algorithms Course. *JCSC*. 28, 3 (January 2013), 14-20.

Comparing Educational Experiences and On-the-Job Needs of Educational Software Designers

Marisa Exter
Learning Design and Technology, College of Education
Purdue University
West Lafayette, Indiana, USA
mexter@purdue.edu

ABSTRACT

This paper reports on part of the findings of a mixed-methods study which explored the educational experiences of Computing Professionals who design and develop educational software. A particular focus is given on the gaps professionals perceive between what was covered in their formal (university) education and the skills and knowledge that have been most important to them in their professional roles. Discrepancies were found particularly in areas related to practical skills (such as testing, maintaining code over time, use of source code control and development tools), communication, critical thinking and problem solving, and strategies used to continue learning on-the-job. Participant suggestions for improving university programs focused largely on the use of large scale, complex, authentic projects of significant duration. The author recommends further consideration be given to explicitly teaching the type of self-learning skills and strategies used by experienced professionals.

Categories and Subject Descriptors

K.3.2 [**Computing Milieux**]: computers and education – *computer and information science education.*, K.7.1 [**Computing Milieux**]: the computing profession – *occupations*

General Terms

Human Factors

Keywords

Computing Education, Computer Science Education, Non-formal Education, Informal Education, Curriculum, Pedagogy

1. INTRODUCTION

This study is part of a larger research agenda related to the formal (university) and non-formal educational experiences of Computing professionals. This paper, which reports on parts of a dissertation study [11], explores the experiences of software designers involved in one specific domain: educational software. This mixed-methods study uses both in-depth interviews and survey responses to address the following research questions:

SIGCSE'14, March 5–8, 2014, Atlanta, Georgia, USA.

http://dx.doi.org/10.1145/2538862.2538970

1. What elements of participants' formal educational experiences were most important in preparing them for their current role(s)?
2. What are the gaps in the competencies (e.g. skills, knowledge, and attitudes) acquired through participants' formal educational experience?
3. What are participants' recommendations for improving university programs?

2. LITERATURE REVIEW

As the ACM/IEEE-CS task force for the Computer Science 2013 curricular guidelines noted, compiling a realistic list of topics to be included in an undergraduate degree program is becoming increasingly difficult, given the number of topics considered part of the core of Computer Science along with the integration of topics from related disciplines [21]. A study in which in-practice software designers were asked to indicate how much they had learned in school, how much they currently knew, and how useful each of 75 topics identified in university curricula and Software Engineering Body of Knowledge (SWEBOK) standards, revealed that some topics covered extensively in college tended to be forgotten, while professionals augmented significantly with on-the-job learning on the job in other areas [16]. However, managers and practitioners believe that topics beyond those currently covered by most programs are needed, including additional knowledge and skills related to business strategy and applications, technology infrastructure and support, and organization and management [1]. A systematic review of literature showing gaps between industry expectations and abilities of graduates (including the perspectives of managers, experienced and new professionals, and senior level students) revealed a number of common "knowledge deficiencies" [20]. Topping the list were written and oral communication, followed by project management, software tools, and testing and teamwork, problem solving and critical thinking, programming, and requirements. Theory and practice must be balanced in order to address rapidly changing industry needs [3, 9, 12, 23]. Educators are further challenged to teach "soft" (social) skills within computing courses [2, 24].

Professionals typically take 10 years to gain expertise in their domain [7]. Self-directed learning accounts for the majority of continuing professional education [18, 22], and it may be particularly important for computing professionals because of the constantly changing nature of their work. If educators take the view that lifelong learning is a normal part of professional practice, they can create stronger and more useful preparation for professionals, and eliminate the need to "cover [all] the ground" in formal educational programs (p. 85) [14]. However, experts have a much better understanding of their own learning than novices do, and often use materials in a different way than intended by the designer [8] and take advantage of resources in a way that is relevant to the task they are currently working on [15]. Students may need guidance to develop the metacognitive skills necessary to monitor their own learning and maintain motivation to continue learning on their own [10].

In his "Eight principles of an undergraduate program", Walker [25] acknowledges that not every topic can be adequately covered in a degree program. Therefore, educators need to set priorities and provide a foundation for long-term study. This study will explore the question of how these priorities should be set by asking in-practice designers to reflect on their own formal and non-formal educational experiences, and by asking them directly for their recommendations for an "ideal" undergraduate program.

3. METHODS

3.1 Data Sources

Participants included in this study played one or more of the following roles: systems/software architecture, requirements/specification writing, high-level and low-level design or programming, and user experience design, *and* were or had recently been involved in the design of software used in k-12 or higher education.

Two data sources were used in this study. In-depth, semi-structured interviews were conducted with nine participants (all male). They included employees of small companies, large companies, and universities, and were currently involved in design and development of LMS components (3 participants), language education related applications (2 participants), and three individuals who worked on a lecture capture system, e-learning application, and a web-based interactive multimedia application, respectively. Most of the professionals interviewed had multiple degrees, with an eclectic mix of majors including Computer Science, Information Systems, Instructional Design, Education, Psychology, Classic languages, Physics, and English.

Interview data informed the development of an online survey instrument, which included both closed and open-ended items. Invitations to participate in the survey were sent in late 2010 via a snowball technique beginning with existing contacts, LinkedIn groups, listservs, and online forums. Seventy-four participants completed the survey, with 94 completing at least a portion.

Fifty-four percent (44 of 84) had one or more degrees in a Computing field (in areas such as Computer Science, Software Engineering, Information Systems, Human Computer Interaction, etc.)[1]. Twenty-nine percent (24 of 82) held at least one major in the areas of Instructional Design, Educational Technology, or another education-related field. Twelve percent (10 of 82) had at least one degree in both a computing-related and an education-related field. Only 16% (13 of 82) had not taken any formal coursework in Computing-, Instructional Design-, or Education-related areas. Participants also held degrees in physical and social sciences, Business, Philosophy, Law, and a variety of other areas.

Survey participants had a range of experience levels in Computing. Thirty-five percent had less than 5 years of experience, and 20% had 5-10 years of experience, 20% had between 11 and 15 years of experience, 11% had 16-20 years of experience, and 14% had 21 or more years of experience. Most were employed at educational software companies (40%) or universities (37%), with a few participants working in corporations that primarily produce other types of products (such as educational publishers) (12%), K-12 educators (3%), with a few who worked in multiple settings (3%) and miscellaneous others (7%). Organization sizes were fairly evenly spread between very small (single person, contractor, or company with <20 employees, 34%), medium (21—500 employees, 28%) and large (500 or more employees, 32%). Types of software developed by these organizations included LMS/CMS development, drill and practice applications, self-paced instruction, educational simulations and modeling tools, educational games, teacher tools, assessment tools, etc., with many companies developing multiple types of software.

Participants tended to play multiple roles, with 66% playing more than 3 roles and 45% playing more than 5 roles. In addition to those related to software design and development (software architecture, requirements gathering/writing, high-level design, programming, web development and database design), user experience design, and quality assurance, 47% of participants did some instructional design work, and 44% had management-related responsibilities. The majority of participants had played other roles across their career, and few had not played most of the roles listed at one time or another.

3.2 Data Analysis

A mixed methods approach was used to provide both breadth and depth of understanding [6]. Qualitative data was analyzed using the constant comparative method for naturalistic inquiry [17]. Descriptive statistics were used to examine demographic data. Mann-Whitney U test, Independent Sample Kruskal-Wallis, and Wilcoxon Signed Ranks tests were used to identify statistically significant differences between groups based on responses to paired questions using 3-point likert-like scales. Qualitative and quantitative data are reported together in this paper in order to give a rich picture of the experiences of the participants for each theme discussed.

4. FINDINGS

4.1 Impact of Coursework

4.1.1 Computing Courses

Figure 1 shows the level of importance survey participants gave to common Computing Education topics on the job, showing that for those working in this particular domain, interface design is the most important area after the computing "basics" and programming languages. When asked to describe the most important skills and knowledge acquired from Computing-related courses, interviewees indicated that "software design fundamentals" (such as Object-oriented design) were important. As will be discussed later, participants indicated that experience learning and interacting with one or more programming languages was important, but the specific language used was not.

4.1.2 "Unrelated" Coursework

Interviewees indicated that their non-computing and non-education-related coursework was very valuable. For example, one participant believed he "could not have taken a more valuable skill into the workplace" than his degree in English, explaining that "writing is at the center of almost every job". Figure 2 shows survey participants' responses to being asked how important various types of "unrelated" courses and topics are to them on the job. The degree of variation may have to do with the variety of roles played and types of organizations participants are employed by. Unsurprisingly based on interview findings and the literature, "Communications" is the most highly rated item in this set.

[1] Number of participants varies between items because of attrition in survey participation between sets of items.

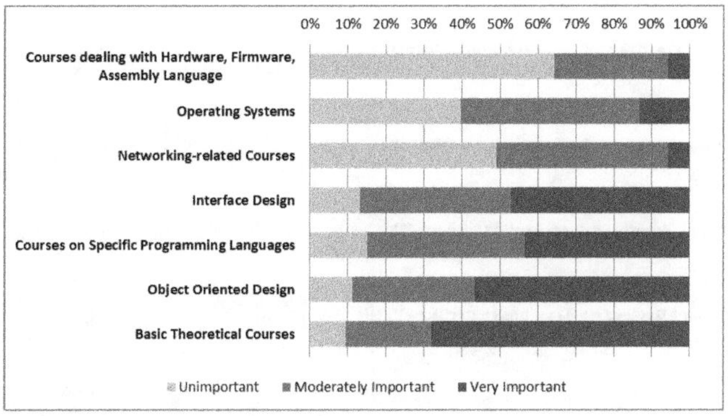

Figure 1. Importance of computing courses/concepts [2] *(N=53 who had taken Computing coursework)*

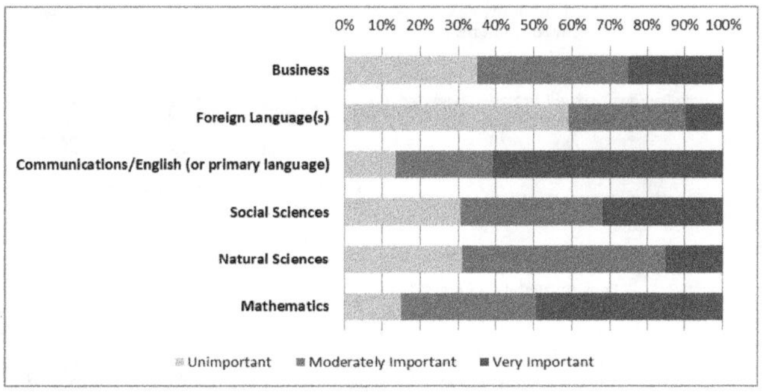

Figure 2. Importance of "unrelated" coursework [2] *(N=78)*

4.2 Gaps Between On-the-Job Needs and Formal Educational Preparation

4.2.1 Practical skills

Practical skills were high on the list of areas that interviewees felt unprepared for. As one explained, "more practically oriented courses might have... expedited my own development, as a designer. Otherwise, it seems I [had] to learn...just about all of the practical stuff on my own, or by the seat of my pants, as we used to say." Several indicated that topics such as software development methodologies were covered only at a high level, leaving them to learn detailed and practical skills on their own. As on interviewee explained, "software development methodologies [are] actually a huge part of the job... in a real, practical, low-level manner. [In university] they talk about it in general terms, but you can't apply that to everyday life. It's not useful." Survey participants were asked to rate the degree to which various practical technical skills and experiences were covered within their Computing coursework. As is shown in Figure 3, only a minority felt each of these areas was well covered.

Figure 5 compares participants' impressions of the degree of importance (red) and the degree covered in school (blue), for a number of practical skills. A 2-sided Related-Samples Wilcoxon Signed Ranks test was performed to determine whether participants' feelings about the importance of an item and the degree of coverage in degree programs attended were aligned. Statistically significant differences are noted with asterisks.

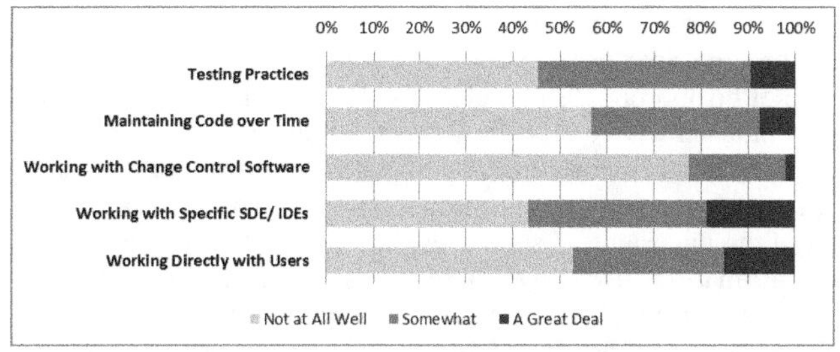

Figure 3. Degree of coverage of topics in Computing coursework [2] *(N=53 who had taken at Computing courses)*

Knowledge of specific programing languages and technologies was well covered in degree programs, but was seen as "highly important" by only about a third of the participants. As one survey participant explained, a program "should provide... strong foundational skills, not just a language. Then any language can be utilized".

An unexpected finding was the degree of importance given to interface design and user experience design principles were rated as more important overall, with less than 10% of participants indicating they were "unimportant". As one participant explained, students should ideally gain experience with "a lot of prototyping, and going through the process of user testing and user profiling - creating scenarios, and imagining users... people who might actually use the product and defining what those are specifically..."

Interviewees indicated that critical thinking and the ability to solve problems creatively were the most crucial skills to someone working in this field. As one participant explained, "[The most useful] courses show you to think in a certain structured way, to decompose problems into smaller bits." However, these skills were not equally well covered by all educational programs (see Figure 6) and were often developed in courses outside of the Computing or ID/Education major. For example, one interviewee explained that his English degree had provided him "the ability to do a thorough and clean and defensible analysis, and then to communicate it clearly, has benefitted me in every single aspect of my work." Another participant indicated that repeated use of the scientific method in Psychology courses prepared him to "[go] through the very deliberative process of coming up with a hypothesis and testing it". He explained that benefits included "understanding and appreciating research methods, but also understanding and appreciating a methodological approach to a given problem."

4.2.2 The ability to Teach Oneself & Use of Resources on the Job

The ability to teach oneself on the job was considered a very important aspect of the job in this field (See Figure 6). One interviewee explained, "I think software developers are one of the most susceptible professions to obsolescence unless you really take control of your own learning [sic]." Such on-the-job learning was not only in response to the development of new technologies. Participants indicated that in general, they would learn a specific skill or technique in response to a particular problem they were trying to solve in the moment. "I would learn things as needed. It was always from a standpoint of, 'I need this for a project, so I'm going to learn it.'"

Interviewees indicated that non-university training courses could be used to pick up new skills, or at least to help you to get to a certain point which you can build upon on your own. A good trainer can help provide a solid foundation for further learning.

[2] Adapted from [11]

However, several interviewees indicated they were not likely to take training courses, and some actively avoided them. Courses may not be appropriate for solving specific problems at hand, and may not teach what one really wants to know. Useful courses may not be available locally. Participants stressed that teaching themselves in a just-in-time fashion was an expected and natural part of the job. Figure 7 shows three of the most important sources of information used by these working professionals: peers (mentors and colleagues), examples (found in books or online), and the use of online communities for finding information on how others had dealt with similar problems in the past.

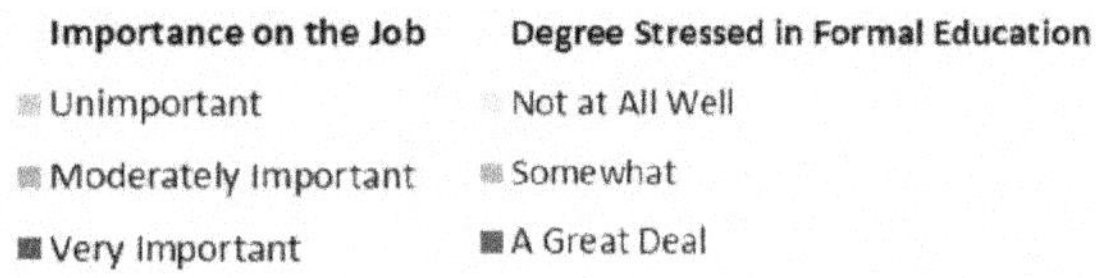

Figure 4. Captions for Figure 5 - Figure 9

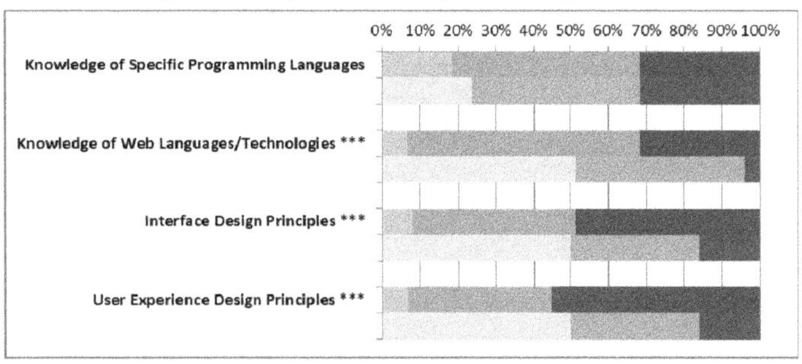

Figure 5. Specific technical skills and knowledge: importance on the job (red), and degree covered in formal education (blue)[2,3] *(N=76)*

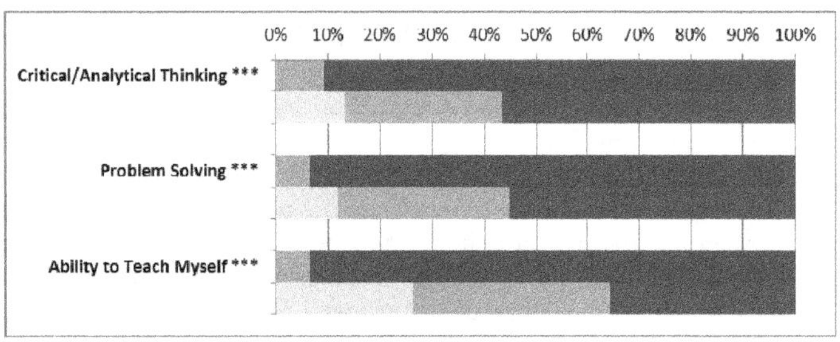

Figure 6. General Skills: importance on the job (red), and degree covered in formal education (blue)[2,3] *(N=76)*

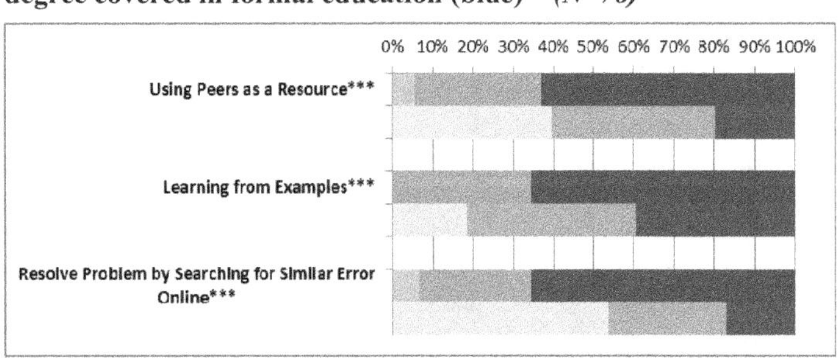

Figure 7. On-the-job learning resources: importance on-the-job (red); degree covered in formal education(blue)[2,3] *(N=76)*

[3] 2-sided Related-Samples Wilcoxon Signed Ranks test:

* statistically significant, p<0.05; ** statistically significant, p<0.01; *** statistically significant, p<0.001

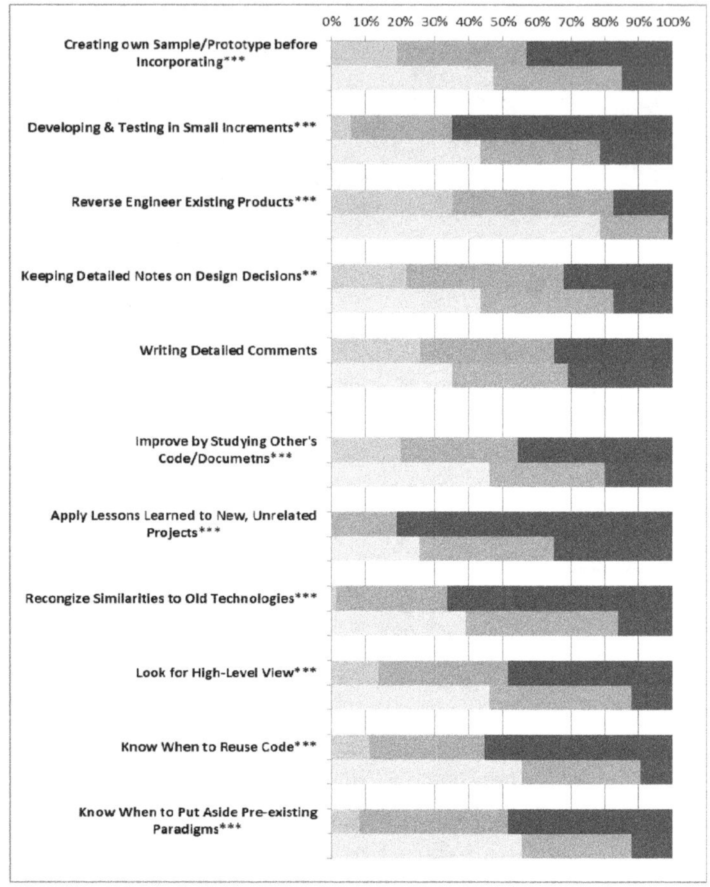

Figure 8. Thought strategies: importance on the job (red); degree covered in formal education (blue)[2,3] *(N=74)*

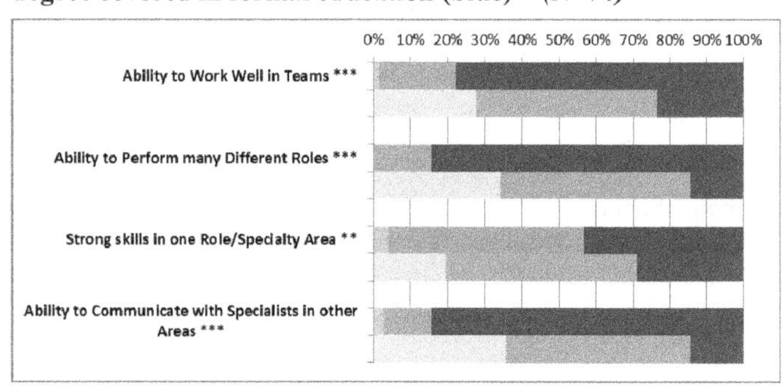

Figure 9. Collaboration & roles played: importance on the job (red), degree covered in formal education (blue)[2,3] *(N=76)*

Earlier studies revealed a number of strategies used by professionals to learn and adapt to the needs of new projects based on their own previous experiences and on their interactions with examples and other available resources [12; 13]. Very few survey participants found these areas "unimportant" (see Figure 8). However, based on participants' recollections, these areas do not appear to have been stressed within the degree programs they attended. Two-sided Related-Samples Wilcoxon Signed Ranks tests were performed on the items relating to resources (Figure 7) and strategies (Figure 8) used, to determine whether participants' feelings about the importance of an item and the degree of coverage in degree programs attended were aligned. Other than "writing detailed comments", the degree to which these strategies were focused on during formal educational experiences does not on average match with the degree of importance given by working professionals.

4.2.3 Collaboration skills & roles played

Participants placed high value on the ability to work well in teams, perform multiple roles, and communicate with specialists in other areas. More than 40% indicated that strong skills in a particular role or specialty area were "very important", with nearly all remaining participants indicating this was at least "moderately important". Formal education could play an important part in preparing individuals for this aspect of the job. As one participant explained, "Learning to ask the right questions to the right individuals is something that does not necessarily come easy to me. However, there were courses that provided a framework of what kinds of questions to ask." One interviewee mentioned that although she prefers to work on her own, she learned a lot from working on a class project with a remote team. "Identifying each other's strengths is vital to the success of any course and/or organization. This is where one learns who can be trusted, who will be able to meet the requirements and where things may have to be shifted."

Yet, only a minority of participants indicated that these areas were well-covered during their formal education, as seen in Figure 9. As one participant explained, "Working with people [is] critical and complex. [My] formal education never taught me how to work with a production team in an effective way, or to work with a staff in an effective way." Comments made during interviews further revealed concerns more senior participants have about recent graduates, especially in regards to written and verbal communication skills.

4.3 Recommendations for an Ideal Program

Both interviewees and survey participants were asked for their recommendations for an "ideal undergraduate program" to prepare graduates to work in this field. Participants stressed the importance of mixing theory and practice, which could include internships but also should include ongoing engagement with realistic, complex projects. As one survey participant expressed:

> An ideal program would bring existing large-scale real-world applications and infrastructures into the curriculum. Current traditional college degrees have a tendency to teach students how to ride a tricycle. This doesn't teach them how to work on a busted jalopy rigged with a car bomb.

Although theoretical foundations and experience with at least one programing language were important to such practical experiences, participants recommended that realistic projects begin as early as possible. These experiences could increase in complexity over time. As one participant suggested, "instruction and early labs may begin with simulated problems and clients but should eventually include both individual and group real-world projects with real clients." Several recommended that projects take place across multiple semesters or multiple years. This approach would foster a variety of practical technical skills which would not be required in smaller projects (such as the use of source control software, maintaining one's own or other's code over time, and the use of sophisticated testing techniques and related software packages). They also would provide experience in working on a team and in managing a sizable project, including budget and time constraints. Finally, projects as well as authentic examples used throughout courses would help students gain a realistic idea of what to expect once they graduate.

Interview and survey participants also indicated a number of personal traits that should be fostered, including communication and team skills, design judgment, creativity, the ability to see other perspectives, critical thinking, strategic, methodical thought process for problem solving, technical literacy for areas outside of one's own expertise, project management skills, the ability to teach oneself, and a passion for this type of work.

5. DISCUSSION

Comparing the participants' perceptions of what was covered during their formal education to the types of skills and knowledge they found most essential to their careers reveals that they did not get all of the skills and knowledge they need to succeed in their careers from their own university experiences – regardless of the degrees held. Clearly, not everything needed on the job was learned as part of a formal degree program, which could indicate troublesome gaps in degree program curricula. However, it is to be expected that educational software designers, like other professionals, continue to develop expertise once they are on the job [7]. Findings from this study indicate that non-formal, self-learning experiences are a normal part of software designers' lives, as would be expected based on Continued Professional Education literature [8; 10; 15]. As Walker [25] noted, not all topics can be covered in a university program, so the emphasis must be on providing graduates what they need to continue growing once on the job.

Based on the findings of this study and related literature, a strong foundation in theoretical underpinnings accompanied by many and varied practical experiences is more important than attempting to cover every potential topic. While balancing which topics to cover, it is important to ensure that students develop the ability to think critically and solve complex problems, good written and verbal communication skills, and habits of self-learning. Each of these areas can be fostered through carefully developed practical experiences. However, general education requirements, such as English and the sciences, will help in the development of these skills.

One of the more unique findings in this study was the stress participants placed on real-world experiences of significant duration beginning early in the program and continuing throughout it (larger than a typical one or two semester capstone). These authentic, large-scale project based experiences would ideally offer students the chance to engage with tools and techniques used in practice, interact with cross-disciplinary teams, and develop critical thinking and problem solving skills. Significant structural changes would be necessary to allow for this type of experience within most undergraduate programs. Although this may be a challenge within the institutional confines of many universities, a number of programs have found innovative ways to incorporate such experiences into their curricula, from a four-semester long "Software Studio" sequence [19] to a service-learning model which allows students to participate for up to 8 semesters in large, multi-year, interdisciplinary projects which are maintained throughout the product lifecycle [5]. Coleman & Lang [4] describe a complete curriculum beginning with small, highly scaffolded experiences in freshman courses and ending with a group capstone project in the final semester. These projects offer various approaches to support students' development of collaboration skills, as well as allowing them to tackle more realistic, complex large-scale problems and interact with clients, and, in several cases, with cross-disciplinary teams.

Another major theme discussed relates to the types of self-learning strategies and experimentation that participants indicated are a normal part of their work practice. Additional thought and research into the way that self-learning practices are taught or fostered would be warranted, since, as Driscoll notes, most novices do not have the necessary metacognitive strategies to direct their own self-learning that experts do [10]. One step in this direction may involve focusing more clearly on application rather than memorization (for example, by allowing students to bring in their own resources and requiring they use them in a novel problem during an exam.) However, the strategies described by participants go beyond simple use of reference materials (see Figure 8). They require complex thought and practice. Educational experiences that mimic and encourage expert practices might include having students: locate, "play with", and reverse engineer existing sample code; create small prototypes before proceeding to a larger project; collect sets of 'precedent materials' from similar projects before beginning to design or code a solution; explicitly consider reusing code before writing new code, and justify the decision made and keep detailed notes about design decisions made on an ongoing basis.

6. LIMITATIONS & FUTURE RESEARCH

This study focused specifically on educational software designers. These participants' experiences may differ from those working in other industries. This may be reflected by the fact that approximately one third of participants had taken no formal Computing coursework. Although invitations were sent to a variety of listserves and forums related to either Computer Science or Educational Technology, the highest number of respondents came from more academically-oriented groups such as the ACM SIGCSE and SIGITE listservs. This may explain the rather high number of participants with doctoral degrees (44%, 38 of 87). Therefore, findings of this study cannot be generalized to a larger population. However, the consistency with findings of earlier study involving individuals who worked in a range of industries [12] and other literature reviewed indicates that the gaps found represent trends that are worth continued investigation. As a next step, the researcher intends to refine the survey instrument used in this study and distribute it to Computing professionals working across industries.

7. ACKNOWLEDGMENTS

Professor Elizabeth Boling, Dr. Barbara Bichelmeyer, Dr. Kay Connelly, and Dr. Martin Siegel (dissertation committee) and Dr. Nilufer Korkmaz, Nichole Turnage, and Micah Modell.

8. REFERENCES

[1] S.J. Andriole and E. Roberts. 2008. Technology Curriculum for the Early 21st Century. *Communications of the ACM* 51, 7, 27-30.

[2] M.A. Arrdis, S.V. Chenoweth, and F.H. Young. 2008. The "soft" topics in Software Engineering education. In *38th ASEE/IEEE Frontiers in Education Conference*.

[3] D. Callahan and B. Pedigo. 2002. Educating experienced IT professionals by addressing industry's needs. *IEEE Software* 19, 5, 57- 62.

[4] B. Coleman and M. Lang. 2012. Collaboration across the curriculum: a disciplined approach todeveloping team skills. In *SIGCSE '12*. ACM, New York, NY, USA, 277-282. DOI=http://doi.acm.org/10.1145/2157136.2157220

[5] E.J. Coyle, L.H. Jamieson, and W.C. Oakes. 2005. EPICS: Engineering projects in community service. *International Journal of Enginering Educaiton* 21, 1, 1-12.

[6] J.W. Creswell and V.L.P. Clark. 2007. *Mixed Methods Reseach*. Sage, Thousand Oaks, CA.

[7] N. Cross. 2004. Expertise in design: An overview. *Design Studies* 25, 5, 427-441.

[8] B.J. Daley. 2000. Learning in professional practice. *New directions for adult and continued learning* 86, 33-42.

[9] R. Dawson. 2000. Twenty dirty tricks to train software engineers. In *Proceedings of the 2000 International Conference on Software Engineering* IEEE, Limerick, Ireland, 209-218.

[10] M.P. Driscoll. 2000. Motivation and Self-Regulation in Learning. In *Psychology of Learnign for Instruction* Allyn and Bacon, Needham Heights, MA.

[11] M. Exter. 2012. *The Educational Experiences of Software Designers working in Education/Instructional Technology Related Fields (Instructional Systems Technology)*. Ph.D. Dissertation. Indiana University, Bloomington, IN. UMI Order Number: 3491471.

[12] M. Exter and N. Turnage. 2012. Exploring Experienced Professionals' Reflections on Computing Education. *Trans. Comput. Educ.* 12, 3, Article 12 (July 2012), 23 pages. DOI=http://doi.acm.org/10.1145/2275597.2275601

[13] N.M. Harlin, M. Exter, and E. Boling. 2009. Software Designers' Use of Precedent. *The Annual meeting of the Association for Educational Communications and Technologies* (Lousville, KY, October, 2009).

[14] C.O. Houle. 1980. *Continued Learning in the Professions*. Jossey-Bass, San Fancisco, CA.

[15] A.B. Knox. 2000. The continuum of professional education and practice. *New Directions for Adult and Continuing Education* 86, 13-22.

[16] T.C. Lethbridge. 2000. What knowledge is important to a software professional. *Computer* 33, 5, 44-50.

[17] Y.S. Lincoln and E.G. Guba. 1984. Processing the Naturalistically Obtained Data. In *Naturalistic Inquiry* Sage, Beverly Hills, CA, 332-256.

[18] D. Livingstone. 2001. Adults' informal learning: definitions, findings, gaps and future research. In *T-Space at The University of Toronto Libraries: Centre for the Study of Education and Work (CSEW)*.

[19] T. Nurkkala and S. Brandle.2011. Software studio: teaching professional software engineering. In *SIGCSE '11*, New York, NY, USA, 153-158. DOI=http://doi.acm.org/10.1145/1953163.1953209

[20] A. Radermacher and G. Walia. 2013. Gaps between industry expectations and the abilities of graduates. In *SIGCSE '13* ACM, New York, NY, USA, 525-530. DOI=http://doi.acm.org/10.1145/2445196.2445351

[21] M. Sahmi, E. Cuadros-Vargas, S. Roach, and D. Reed. 2012. Computer Science curriculum 2013: Reviewing the strawman report from the ACM/IEEE Task Force. In *SIGCSE '12*, ACM, New York, NY, USA, 3-4. DOI=http://doi.acm.org/10.1145/2157136.2157140

[22] A.M. Tough. 1989. Self-directed learning: Concepts and practice. In *Lifelong education for adults: An international handbook* Pergamon, Oxford, 256-261.

[23] A. Tucker. 2002. On the balance between theory and practice. *IEEE Software* 19, 5, 94-97.

[24] H. Van Vliet. 2006. Reflections on Software Engineering Education. *IEEE Softwarwe* 23, 3, 55-61.

[25] H. Walker. 2010. Eight principles of an undergraduate program. *Inroads 1*, 1, 18-20.

Evaluating Industry-Inspired Pair Programming Communication Guidelines with Undergraduate Students

Mark Zarb
School of Computing
University of Dundee
Dundee, Scotland
+44 (0)1382 384 150

Janet Hughes
School of Computing
University of Dundee
Dundee, Scotland
+44 (0)1382 385 195

markzarb, jhughes @computing.dundee.ac.uk

John Richards
IBM T.J. Watson Research Center
Yorktown Heights
New York, USA
+1 914 945 2632
ajtr@us.ibm.com

ABSTRACT

A set of industry-inspired pair programming guidelines have been derived from qualitative examinations of expert pairs in order to aid novice programmers with their intra-pair communication. This research describes the evaluation of these guidelines with a set of student pairs, and demonstrates how novice pairs who were exposed to the guidelines were more comfortable communicating within their pairs.

Categories and Subject Descriptors

K.3.2 [**Computer and Information Science Education**]: Computer science education.

General Terms

Measurement, Performance, Experimentation, Human Factors, Standardization.

Keywords

Pair programming; communication skills; software engineering; collaboration; students.

1. INTRODUCTION

Pair programming is a method which describes two programmers working together on the same computer, sharing one keyboard. Typically, each member of the pair takes on a different role, swapping roles frequently: the driver creates the code while the navigator reviews it [16]. Pair programming requires its pairs to communicate frequently, which leads the pair to experience certain benefits over "solo" programming, such as a greater enjoyment, and an increased knowledge distribution [2].

Pair programming is one of the key aspects of Extreme Programming, which "favours both informal and immediate communication over the detailed and specific work products required by any number of traditional design methods" [14].

Novices find communication to be a barrier when they are pair programming, and industry-inspired guidelines have been presented as a possible solution [11, 16]. Initial student feedback with regards to their perceptions of the guidelines was positive. This research investigates an evaluation of the guidelines, in order to present evidence that they can be used to assist novice pairs in learning to communicate more effectively when working together.

SIGCSE'14, March 5–8, 2014, Atlanta, GA, USA.

http://dx.doi.org/10.1145/2538862.2538980

2. BACKGROUND

Due to the nature of pair programming, *communication*, both verbal and non-verbal, occurs constantly. Williams and Kessler [13] write that effective communication is "paramount", whereas Sharp and Robinson [10] describe pairing as a highly communication-intensive process.

Within the classroom, pair programming is seen as being generally valuable [1, 13], with research showing that its use in educational settings has rapidly increased within the last decade, with reported usage in the US, the UK, Germany, New Zealand, India and Thailand [4]. Furthermore, students working in pairs can be seen to be more satisfied with their work output, solve problems faster than non-paired students, and have improved team effectiveness, with pairing students being more likely to complete CS courses when compared to their solo counterparts, as well as gaining an improved comprehension of unfamiliar topics, as well as increased levels of confidence [5, 7, 11, 14, 15].

Many programmers approach their first pairing experience with scepticism, having doubts about their partner's working habits and programming style, and about the added communication aspects that this programming style entails [14]. In a pilot study, roughly 50% of first-time novice pair programmers reported that they perceived communication to be the main problem with the pairing process [9].

Freudenberg et al. write that "the cognitive aspects of pair programming are seldom investigated and little understood" [3]. Furthermore, many authors simply attribute theoretical importance to *communication* as an issue – as a result, few studies have investigated the aspect of communication within an agile team in detail [10, 12].

3. PAIR PROGRAMMING GUIDELINES

The industry-inspired pair programming guidelines [18] were created with the aim of delivering concise, industry-derived instructions to novice pairs to improve their understanding of successful pair communication.

An analytic coding schema was derived from the observation of the communication of expert pairs working in industry, with over 35 hours of communication being analysed across 11 different pairs was reported in [17]. This coding schema was further analysed, and led to the creation of industry-inspired pair programming guidelines, as reported in [18]. A preliminary qualitative examination suggested that the guidelines could be used by novice pairs to aid them in their intra-pair communication; this was evaluated in the present paper, and found to be true.

The guidelines are presented in three separate sections: restarting, planning and action [18]; they are summarised in the following section:

3.1 Restarting Guidelines

These guidelines should be used when the novice pair is stuck, and cannot seem to make good progress:

- If your pair is stuck in a thinking/silent loop and cannot seem to progress, actively break your focus by discussing something completely off-topic and unrelated to the issues at hand. This will allow you to tackle the problem with a fresh outlook. Following this stage, attempt to:
    - Look back on your last couple of steps and review your previous work;
    - Try to suggest next steps related to your end-goal in order to make progress;
    - Identify a fresh thought process.
- If your partner is attempting to break focus, don't dismiss this. Breaking one's focus using jokes, private conversations, etc. can lead to a fresh perspective, which your partner may need.

3.2 Planning Guidelines

These guidelines should be used when the novice pair needs to review legacy code, or start to plot future steps:

- Suggestions and reviews are optimal states that will allow you to drive your work forward. When in these states, feel free to alternate (e.g. review previous code, suggest an improvement, review methods to be changed, suggest potential impact).
- At each stage, do not hesitate to ask your partner for clarification as to what they are working on, or suggesting.
- Think about what your partner is saying and doing. Offering an explanation of the current state can help move the work forward.

3.3 Action Guidelines

These guidelines should be used when the novice pair needs to discuss code logistics, or start to write code:

- NAVIGATOR: While the driver is coding, actively look to make suggestions that contribute to the code.
- NAVIGATOR: If the driver is muttering, use this opportunity to make sure your suggestions have been properly understood.
- DRIVER: While you are programming, or thinking about your code, voice your thoughts (even if it is just mumbling and muttering while you're typing). This helps the navigator know that you are actively working, and will allow for them to make suggestions based on your current actions.

4. EVALUATION

A class of undergraduate third years was exposed to the guidelines during one of their taught modules ("Agile Software Engineering"). Exposure occurred during a 60-minute lecture where the guidelines were introduced by the lecturer and discussed within the class. A printed copy of these guidelines was given to the students for reference whilst they completed their lab work in the following weeks. Initial feedback was largely positive, as evidenced by the following quote:

> *"There's a definite benefit in introducing this. In pair programming, we're told to 'work in pairs: go!', and there weren't formal steps, apart from the fundamentals. There wasn't a lot of what to do if you became stuck."*

At this stage, it is imperative to understand whether there is any quantitative value to be gained by using these guidelines with novice pairs, and whether this exposure can improve novice intra-pair communication. For this purpose, a study was devised with the aim of producing quantitative data, with the following hypotheses:

- Exposure to the pair programming guidelines positively impacts the pair's success rate.
- Exposure to the pair programming guidelines leads to an improvement in the pair's ease of communication.
- Exposure to the pair programming guidelines positively affects the way partners contribute to the pairing session.

4.1 Methodology

In 2010, Murphy et al. researched conversations within pairs, focusing on transactive statements that were primarily about debugging. Their initial study was carried out with ten undergraduate Java students, and the authors note that "the pairs that talked more [...] attempted to solve more problems" [6]. Due to the study's focus on communication, the measurement of pair success, and a validated methodology, a similar process was proposed for this study, borrowing elements described in Murphy et al.'s research. The authors were contacted, and gave consent for permission to replicate the methodology, as well as providing a copy of the buggy code used in their original study.

Participants were recruited from the School of Computing at the University of Dundee, and a local college. An e-mail was circulated to all students, asking for their participation in exchange for a small compensation in the form of vouchers. Twelve students were recruited from Level 1, and eight students from Level 3, with six students studying at college-level.

All students were randomized into pairs – with each pair consisting of students who were matched to peers within the same level of study. A control group was set up, consisting of 12 students (6 pairs) from across all three levels of study, leaving an experimental group of 14 students (7 pairs). Informed consent was obtained from all participants.

The study was carried out during a 2-week period during the students' second semester of study. Pairs were invited to the test room separately, and on different days. The test room was equipped with one laptop, and consisted of a camera and a voice recorder. In line with the methodology used by Murphy et al. [6], all pairs were given a list of programs which consisted of buggy code. It was explained to all pairs that each program would compile – but consisted of one logical error. The pair was given 45 minutes to sequentially locate and fix as many errors as possible. During this time, the recording equipment was switched on, and the researcher left the room.

Both the control group and the test group followed the process described above; prior to the task, pairs within the test group were exposed to the pair programming guidelines by means of a verbal presentation, as well as a short 3-minute video showing an experienced pair applying the guidelines to try and overcome various situations.

Following the test period, the researcher would return, log the number of programs completed by the pair, and distribute post-test surveys, which were completed individually by the members of the pair. Each survey consisted of Likert-scale questions relating to their experience with communication and partner contribution during the test, as well as questions on the student's experience with programming, which were used to measure central tendencies and variance within the groups, in order to ascertain that there were no significant difference between the groups which would lead to threats to validity.

4.2 Results

Several measures were taken for each pair: *success* was measured by the number of programs completed successfully (when compared to the number of programs attempted); *ease of communication* and *perceived partner contribution* were measured using post-test Likert scales as discussed above.

4.2.1 Previous Pairing Experience

The post-test surveys consisted of questions relating to the individual's experience with solo programming, pair programming, and previous pair programming experience with the session's partner. These results were analysed to understand group tendencies and variance, as reported in Table 1 below:

Table 1: Student programming experience.

	Experimental Group		Control Group	
	M	SD	M	SD
Solo Programming Experience (weeks)	192.4	203.031	123.3	88.108
Pair Programming Experience (weeks)	10.8	11.359	326.9	631.992
Previous Pair Programming Experience with this Session's Partner (weeks)	1.9	4.721	0.0	0.000

The data shows that there was differing experience between the groups; on average, more individuals in the experimental group (exposed pairs) had solo programming experience, but more individuals in the control group (unexposed pairs) pairs had pair programming experience. Furthermore, two pairs within the experimental group had previous experience in pairing together.

Statistical tests were therefore carried out in order to establish whether the differences between the two groups were significant, and whether they would establish threats to validity of the data.

Mann-Whitney U tests were used for this analysis, as these tests are not affected by outliers to the same degree as independent-samples t-tests.

Differences in 'Solo' Programming Experience

A Mann-Whitney U test shows that there were no significant differences in 'solo' programming experience (in weeks) prior to the test between students who were exposed to the pair programming guidelines, and students who were not; $U = 69.5$, $z = -0.414$, $p = 0.687$ ($p > 0.05$).

Difference in Pair Programming Experience

A Mann-Whitney U test shows that there were no significant differences in pair programming experience (in weeks) prior to the test, between students who were exposed to the pair programming guidelines, and students who were not; $U = 91$, $z = 0.386$, $p = 0.742$ ($p > 0.05$).

Difference in Pair Programming Experience with this Session's Partner

A Mann-Whitney U test shows that there were no significant differences between students who were exposed to the pair programming guidelines, and students who were not when looking at the data for *previous pair experience with this session's partner*; $U = 72$, $z = -1.336$, $p = 0.560$ ($p > 0.05$).

From the analysis, it can be seen that any differences between the two groups (with respect to solo and pair programming experience) were not significant, suggesting that there would be no validity issues when analysing data between the two groups.

4.2.2 Success

Following the pair's 45-minute test, the number of tasks attempted was noted by the researcher, and scored at a later date. Each attempt was scored by the researcher, and also compiled, to see if the whether the code successfully compiled and produced the correct result. The total number of successfully completed tasks was then noted for each pair.

Independent-samples t-tests were used to analyse completion rates, which in turn were used to determine whether there were any differences in success levels between the exposed pairs and the control group.

There were no outliers in the data, as assessed by inspection of a boxplot (Figure 1). The exposed pairs have a marginally higher number of tasks completed (2.71 ± 3.04) than the unexposed pairs in the control group (2.17 ± 2.14) – however, this difference is not statistically significant: $t(11) = 0.369$, $p = 0.718$ ($p > 0.05$).

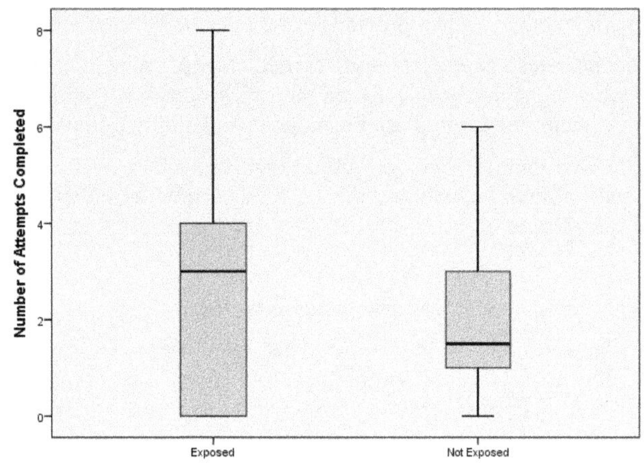

Figure 1: A boxplot showing the number of tasks completed between experimental group and the control group.

4.2.3 *Ease of Communication*

'Ease of Communication' was reported as a Likert scale on the post-test survey through the following statement: "*During this session, I found communicating with my partner to be easy*". The scale ranged from 1 (strongly disagree) to 5 (strongly agree).

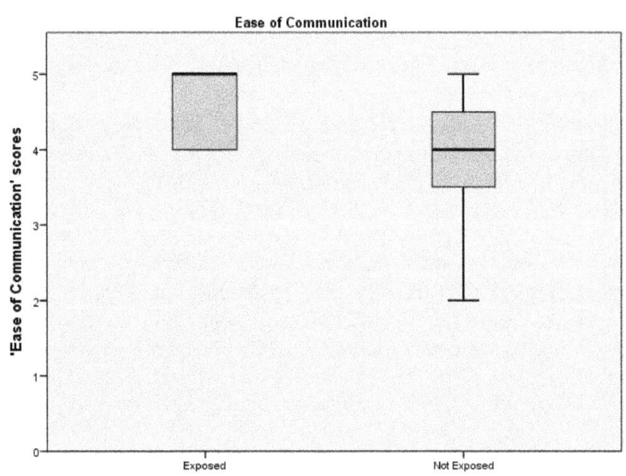

Figure 2: A boxplot showing the reported scores for ease of communication (ranging from 1 (strongly disagree) to 5 (strongly agree)) between the experimental group and the control group.

A boxplot (Figure 2) depicts the distribution of Likert scale scores reported by the individual students. It can be seen that students who were exposed to the guidelines generally reported a higher score (M=4.6; SD=0.514) than students who were not (M=3.9; SD=0.900).

As the data used is extracted from Likert scales, a Mann-Whitney U test was used for its analysis [8]. This test was run to determine any differences in *ease of communication* between the exposed group, and the control group.

There was a statistically significant difference in Ease of Communication scores between exposed students (Mdn = 5.00) and unexposed students (Mdn = 4.00), U = 48, z = -2.037, p = 0.042.

As $p < 0.05$, it can be seen that students who were exposed to the guidelines found their intra-pair communication to be easier than the students from the control group.

4.2.4 *Perceived Partner Contribution*

'Perceived Partner Contribution' was reported as a Likert scale on the post-test survey through the following statement: "*Rate your partner's contribution to today's session*". The scale ranged from 1 (no participation) to 5 (excellent).

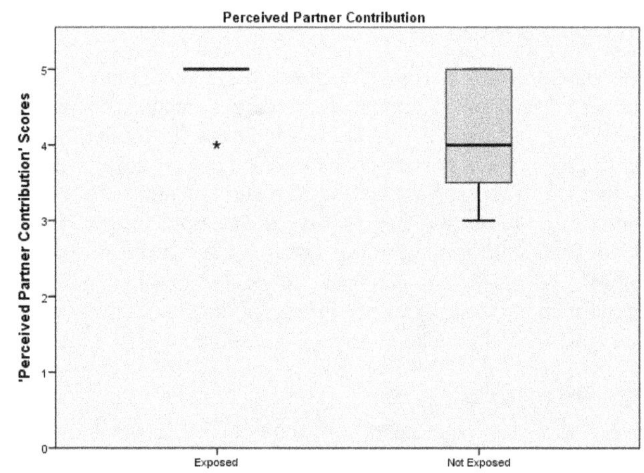

Figure 3: A boxplot showing the reported scores for the perceived partner contribution (ranging from 1 (no participation) to 5 (excellent) between the experimental group and the control group.

A boxplot (Figure 3) depicts the distribution of Likert scale scores reported by the individual students. It can be seen that students who were exposed to the guidelines generally rate their partner's contribution to be quite high, with low variance (M=4.8; SD=0.426) than students who were in the control group (M=4.1; SD=0.835).

The asterisk seen in the boxplot indicates outliers in SPSS, the statistics package used to carry out analyses for this study. The data in this case shows that 3 of the exposed students reported their perceived partner contribution to be '4' on the Likert scale, whereas the rest of the exposed group rated this as '5'.

A Mann-Whitney U test was run to determine if there were differences in Perceived Partner Contribution between the exposed and unexposed groups. There was a statistically significant difference in perceived partner contribution scores between exposed students (Mdn = 5.00) and unexposed students (Mdn = 4.00), U = 48.5, z = -2.113, p = 0.035.

As $p < 0.05$, it can be seen that students who were exposed to the guidelines were rated by their partners to have contributed more to the session, when compared to students from the control group.

4.3 Discussion

Following the analysis presented above, the following hypotheses are accepted:

1. The mean completion rate for pairs who were exposed to the guidelines and pairs who were not exposed is equal in the population.
2. The distribution of the pair's ease of communication scores differs by exposure to the guidelines.
3. The distribution of the pair's perceived partner contribution scores differs by exposure to the guidelines.

These results therefore suggest that exposure to the guidelines leads to the novice pair experiencing easier communication and improved perceived partner contribution – however, there are no changes to the task completion rates between the two groups.

Each pair had 45 minutes to debug as many programs as possible, following an ordered list of programs that had been presented to them. The fact that the exposed pairs did not perform significantly better than the pairs who were not exposed is perhaps to be expected: the students were exposed to the guidelines at the start of the 45 minute session, and whilst evidence shows that the guidelines were used to improve their intra-pair communication skills, one session might not have been enough time to completely take the guidelines on board and adopt them to improve their work output.

4.4 Feedback

All exposed students were invited to give detailed feedback on their experiences with using the guidelines by means of an online survey. A total of six students completed the survey. Their reported usage of the guidelines is reported in Figure 4 below.

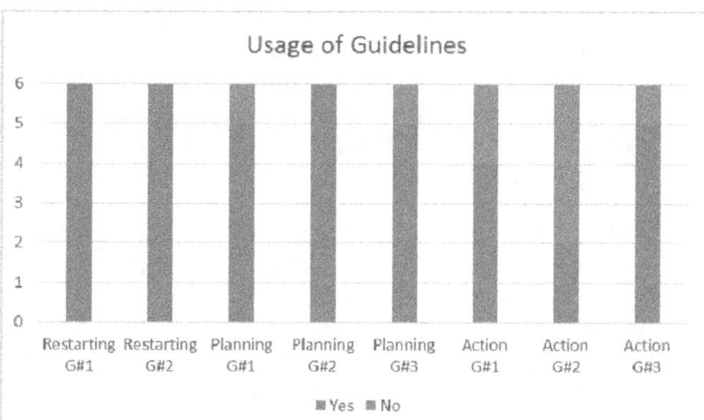

Figure 4: A bar chart plotting the answers to the question: "have you used this guideline?" from the online student survey.

It can be seen that most guidelines were used by most or all students who completed the survey. Two of the guidelines from the *Action* set were not as frequently used as the others (this is depictured as 'Action G#1' and 'Action G#2' in Figure 4 above, and correspond to the two *'Navigator'* guidelines from section 3.3 above).

As both these guidelines are only relevant to the navigator, it is possible that most of the respondents only contributed to the session as drivers, and therefore did not need to make use of these guidelines.

Furthermore, the second guideline actively points towards the driver muttering: if the respondents were navigating, it is also possible that their driver had not been muttering at the time, thus rendering the guideline ineffective.

4.4.1 Feedback regarding the Restarting Guidelines

All students who answered the survey indicated that they had made use of these guidelines whilst pair programming; "*When we were stuck, we lost focus and ended up going off-topic anyway before bringing it back to the task at hand*" / "*It was helpful to go for a walk, and then return less frustrated.*"

Students indicated that they found this to "*usually work quite well*", commenting that the "*use of jokes or venting frustrations were helpful towards giving us a break*".

Comments were positive – "*This was a useful technique*" / "*Quite happy with using it; worked well*", with some students suggesting that these guidelines tended to occur naturally to them, without much planning required – "*Tended to use this naturally*" / "*We both used it intuitively without thinking about it*".

Some comments focused on the possibilities of having problems when working with a new partner: "*I can imagine if you do not know your partner very well it would be more tempting to dismiss an attempt to break focus*" / "*If one of us lost focus, the other was generally losing focus at the same time*". Other comments, on the other hand, discuss possible solutions to this issue: "*Sometimes identifying when your partner wishes to break focus for this purpose can be difficult, particularly if you do not know your partner well or feel uncomfortable working with them. Having said this, it can be as simple as merely saying, 'let's take a quick break' – this can provide a clear indication of intentions.*"

4.4.2 Feedback regarding the Planning Guidelines

Feedback for these guidelines was positive – students felt that they had "*a natural flow*" and that "*group coding would be impossible without this*".

Students reported that "*[it was] helpful to know what [their] partner was thinking*", and explain that "*this can help to ensure that [both partners] understand the on-going work and are on the same page.*"

One student felt that "*asking what the partner is doing at every stage can be irritating and detrimental; sometimes it's best to sit back and watch*", suggesting that for some students, the constant offer or request for explanations might prove to be distracting. This shows that in some cases, it might be more beneficial for the pair to discuss the guidelines between themselves prior to adopting them, and develop a way for them both to be comfortable with their usage in terms of distractions and interruptions.

4.4.3 Feedback regarding the Action Guidelines

The reported feedback was quite positive; students expressed that their muttering "*helped keep the navigator involved and encouraged them to contribute*", meaning that at times, the problem is solved "*before you waste time getting neck-deep in useless code*". By looking at overall comments, it can be seen that this guideline was considered beneficial in helping the survey respondents understand the underlying logic behind their code.

Students felt that reading the code as it was being typed by the driver "*helped save time*", and agreed that following the code allowed them to be more proactive when helping, as they could make suggestions where the driver appeared to be struggling.

4.5 Further Work

As part of this study, it was not possible to determine a change in the pairs' success levels based on their limited exposure to the guidelines.

Further evaluations in the form of a longitudinal study are currently planned in order to determine whether repeated exposure to the guidelines can significantly affect the pair's measured success rate.

5. CONCLUSIONS

Research shows that novice pair programmers are sceptical about pair programming due to the added communication that will be required of them. This research has presented an evaluation of industry-inspired pair programming guidelines, to understand whether exposing novice pairs to the guidelines can have a positive impact on their success levels and communication.

Significant differences were identified between students who had been exposed to the guidelines and the control group when considering the individual members' perception of their experienced intra-pair communication, as well as their partner's contribution to the session. Furthermore, feedback obtained from the exposed students shows that the guidelines were found to be to be naturally-occurring, and complementary to the students' pairing approaches.

The results presented in this study show that the industry-inspired pair programming guidelines can be used to allow novices to communicate better within their pairs. This is of benefit to educators and students alike, as using these guidelines allows for a more structured introduction to pair programming, with clearer instructions on how to communicate with a new pairing partner.

6. ACKNOWLEDGMENTS

The authors would like to thank all the student pairs who have contributed time and effort towards giving feedback and evaluating these guidelines.

The research work disclosed in this publication is funded by the Strategic Educational Pathways Scholarship (Malta). The scholarship is part-financed by the European Union – European Social Fund (ESF) under Operational Programme II – Cohesion Policy 2007-2013, "Empowering People for More Jobs and a Better Quality of Life".

7. REFERENCES

[1] Begel, A. and N. Nagappan. *Pair programming: what's in it for me?* in *Proceedings of the Second ACM-IEEE international symposium on Empirical software engineering and measurement*. 2008: ACM.

[2] Bryant, S., P. Romero, and B. du Boulay, *The Collaborative Nature of Pair Programming*, in *Extreme Programming and Agile Processes in Software Engineering*, P. Abrahamsson, M. Marchesi, and G. Succi, Editors. 2006, Springer Berlin/Heidelberg. p. 53-64.

[3] Freudenberg, S., P. Romero, and B. Du Boulay. *"Talking the talk": Is intermediate-level conversation the key to the pair programming success story?* in *Agile Conference (AGILE), 2007*. 2007.

[4] Hanks, B., S. Fitzgerald, R. McCauley, L. Murphy, and C. Zander, *Pair programming in education: a literature review*. Computer Science Education, 2011. **21**(2): p. 135-173.

[5] McDowell, C., B. Hanks, and L. Werner, *Experimenting with pair programming in the classroom*. SIGCSE Bull., 2003. **35**(3): p. 60-64.

[6] Murphy, L., S. Fitzgerald, B. Hanks, and R. McCauley. *Pair debugging: a transactive discourse analysis*. in *Proceedings of the Sixth international workshop on Computing education research*. 2010: ACM.

[7] Nagappan, N., L. Williams, M. Ferzli, E. Wiebe, K. Yang, C. Miller, and S. Balik. *Improving the CS1 experience with pair programming*. in *ACM SIGCSE Bulletin*. 2003: ACM.

[8] Ryu, E. and A. Agresti, *Modeling and inference for an ordinal effect size measure*. Statistics in Medicine, 2008. **27**(10): p. 1703-1717.

[9] Sanders, D., *Student Perceptions of the Suitability of Extreme and Pair Programming*, in *Extreme Programming Perspectives*, M. Marchesi, et al., Editors. 2002, Addison-Wesley Professional. p. 168-174.

[10] Sharp, H. and H. Robinson, *Three 'C's of agile practice: collaboration, co-ordination and communication*, in *Agile Software Development*. 2010, Springer. p. 61-85.

[11] Srikanth, H., L. Williams, E. Wiebe, C. Miller, and S. Balik, *On Pair Rotation in the Computer Science Course*, in *Proceedings of the 17th Conference on Software Engineering Education and Training*. 2004, IEEE Computer Society. p. 144-149.

[12] Stapel, K., E. Knauss, K. Schneider, and M. Becker, *Towards Understanding Communication Structure in Pair Programming*, in *Agile Processes in Software Engineering and Extreme Programming*, A. Sillitti, et al., Editors. 2010, Springer Berlin Heidelberg. p. 117-131.

[13] Williams, L. and R.R. Kessler, *Pair Programming Illuminated*. 2002: Addison-Wesley Longman Publishing Co., Inc. 288.

[14] Williams, L., R.R. Kessler, W. Cunningham, and R. Jeffries, *Strengthening the Case for Pair Programming*. IEEE Software, 2000. **17**(4): p. 19-25.

[15] Williams, L., E. Wiebe, K. Yang, M. Ferzli, and C. Miller, *In Support of Pair Programming in the Introductory Computer Science Course*. Computer Science Education, 2002. **12**(3): p. 197-212.

[16] Williams, L.A. and R.R. Kessler, *All I really need to know about pair programming I learned in kindergarten*. Communications of the ACM, 2000. **43**(5): p. 108-114.

[17] Zarb, M., J. Hughes, and J. Richards, *Analysing Communication Trends in Pair Programming Using Grounded Theory*, in *Proceedings of the 26th BCS Conference on Human-Computer Interaction*. 2012, British Computer Society: Birmingham, United Kingdom.

[18] Zarb, M., J. Hughes, and J. Richards, *Industry-inspired guidelines improve students' pair programming communication*, in *Proceedings of the 18th ACM conference on Innovation and technology in computer science education*. 2013, ACM: Canterbury, England, UK. p. 135-140.

Experiences Mapping and Revising Curricula with CS2013

David Reed (Moderator)
Creighton University
Department of Journalism, Media & Computing
davereed@creighton.edu

Andrea Danyluk
Williams College
Department of Computer Science
andrea@cs.williams.edu

Elizabeth K. Hawthorne
Union County College
Department of Computer Science
hawthorne@ucc.edu

Mehran Sahami
Stanford University
Computer Science Department
sahami@cs.stanford.edu

Henry M. Walker
Grinnell College
Department of Computer Science
walker@cs.grinnell.edu

Categories and Subject Descriptors
K.3.2 [**Computers and Education**]: Computer Science Education; Curriculum.

General Terms
Documentation, Design, Standardization.

Keywords
Computing Curricula 2013: Computer Science, CS2013.

1. SUMMARY

Roughly once per decade, the ACM and IEEE-Computer Society form a joint task force to survey the discipline and produce curricular guidelines for undergraduate computer science programs. The latest guidelines document, Computer Science Curricula 2013 (CS2013), was released in the Fall of 2013 after multiple rounds of public review and feedback. A significant novel feature of CS2013 is the structuring of the Body of Knowledge core topics into two tiers. While Core-Tier1 topics are expected to be included in every undergraduate computer science program, individual programs may choose to cover only a subset of Core-Tier2 topics, depending upon institutional size, resources, and goals. CS2013 recommends at least 80% coverage of Core-Tier2, which provides flexibility for designing curricula that meet institutional constraints while still maintaining disciplinary standards.

In addition, CS2013 emphasizes institutional flexibility in the way that topics are packaged into courses. Topics in the Body of Knowledge are organized by Knowledge Areas (such as Software Development Fundamentals, Parallel and Distributed Computing, and Social Issues and Professional Practice), not by courses. Curricular designers are encouraged to package topics into courses in creative and innovative ways, and subsequently sequence those courses to form complete curricula. To support the design of innovative curricula, CS2013 includes an appendix with more than 80 course exemplars: syllabi of existing courses with mappings to Knowledge Area topics and learning outcomes. The appendix also includes four complete curricular exemplars from a variety of schools (a research university, two liberal arts colleges, and a community college). These curricular exemplars show four alternative ways that topics from the CS2013 Body of Knowledge can be packaged and sequenced to construct programs of study. More than just documenting current practices, these exemplars are also forward-looking, describing proposed revisions that would bring current models more in line with CS2013 recommendations.

This panel brings together the four authors (or co-authors) of the CS2013 curricular exemplars to discuss the process by which they developed these exemplars and how CS2013 recommendations are driving changes to their existing curricula. The authors will share insights and also provide guidance for educators who are considering reviewing their own curricula in light of CS2013.

SIGCSE '14, Mar 05-08 2014, Atlanta, GA, USA
ACM 978-1-4503-2605-6/14/03.
http://dx.doi.org/10.1145/2538862.2538864

2. ANDREA DANYLUK

Mapping the Williams College CS curriculum against the CS2013 core was an extremely interesting and helpful exercise at a time when the department was holding extensive curricular discussions in preparation for an external review. In order to ensure that students are free to explore a wide range of academic subjects in the liberal arts tradition, Williams places a limit on the number of courses that may be required for a major -- typically 9. While students are free to take many more courses in their majors, our challenge is to provide a curriculum that gives our students good breadth and depth, regardless of the trajectory they follow.

For our analysis, we mapped our required introductory and core sequence, as well as what a "typical" CS major might take. Specifically, we assumed the student would take the 6 intro and core courses, Discrete Math and three CS electives. (When computed over the last three graduating classes, we see that students take, on average, 3.6 electives.) The specific electives we used for the mapping were Digital Design and Modern Architecture, Artificial Intelligence, and Operating Systems.

We found that our common core provides fairly good coverage of the CS2013 core, and electives bring our curriculum even closer in line with the CS2013 recommendations. Doing the mapping reaffirmed our belief that we are especially strong in software development fundamentals, theory, and programming languages. While our electives provide very strong coverage of systems topics, it is possible for students to choose elective paths that steer clear of those. We were pleased to find that our curriculum provides better coverage of "new" areas (information assurance, parallelism and concurrency) than we predicted. It also confirmed that we are less good in formal software engineering processes. We are still in discussions about the shape of our major, but we have discussed several options that would give students additional formal exposure to software engineering and that would more explicitly steer them to a set of electives that together would ensure broad coverage of CS.

3. ELIZABETH K. HAWTHORNE

Mapping the CS2013 core curriculum against two different types of associate degrees was done collaboratively with Melanie Williamson and Cindy Tucker of Bluegrass Community and Technical College in Lexington, KY (www.bluegrass.kctcs.edu). According to the American Association of Community Colleges, the Associate in Science (A.S.) degree prepares student to transfer to upper division baccalaureate-degree programs, with half of the coursework in general education requirements. Bluegrass' A.S. degree mapped four core courses against CS2013: (1) Introduction to Computer Programming, (2) Introduction to Program Design, Abstraction and Problem Solving, (3) Introduction to Software Engineering and (4) Discrete Mathematics. The more discipline-focused Associate in Applied Science (A.A.S.) degree can similarly facilitate transfer or lead directly to employment, with only one-third of the requirements in general education. Bluegrass' A.A.S. degree mapped seven courses to the core of CS2013: (1) Computational Thinking, (2) Introduction to Computers, (3) Computer Hardware and Software, (4) Internet Technologies, (5) Introduction to Networking Concepts, (6) Database Design Fundamentals, and (7) Security Fundamentals.

While performing this detailed mapping exercise, Bluegrass discovered the A.S. degree covers the CS2013 core very well in the knowledge areas one would expect at a freshman-software level and completely satisfies all of the general education components required by Kentucky's four-year universities. The mapping exercise also confirmed the A.A.S degree, while it does not meet all general education requirements at the four-year level, covers the CS2013 core to a greater degree than the A.S. degree due to the additional seven core Computer and Information Technologies classes taken. Bluegrass was extremely pleased with the mapping exercise and continues to explore additional transfer options for their students.

4. MEHRAN SAHAMI

Mapping the CS curriculum at Stanford against the CS2013 guidelines led to insights not only with respect to CS2013, but also in regard to broader issues in our department's undergraduate program. Stanford has a track-based CS curriculum which requires all students to complete: (i) six "core" classes, (ii) four to five classes in one of nine depth areas (tracks) of a student's choosing, and (iii) two to four additional CS elective courses. While the multitude of options make it impossible to map all paths through our curriculum, solid insight was still gained by examining a single typical program that includes the six core courses, a standard path through the Systems track, and the minimal required selection of popular CS elective classes. This common program provided good coverage of the Core-Tier1 and Tier2 topics in CS2013. However, the mapping process also made us realize that other paths through the major might provide fairly different levels of Core coverage. For example, the coverage of many Core-Tier2 topics (e.g., in Architecture and Organization and Intelligent Systems) is quite dependent on students' choice of track and elective courses. This led us to the decision that trying to prevent outlier cases (students who craft very uncommon programs that still somehow manage to fit within our program requirements) was a lower priority than optimizing the common cases of what most students would be learning in our program.

At a more detailed level, the mapping helped to identify topical redundancies between courses and also rationalize coverage of some topics (and removal of others) as we considered course updates. We also discovered differences (sometimes significant) between the topical coverage provided by different instructors of the same course. We found that it was often possible to cover CS2013 learning outcomes not already in our curriculum by making modest modifications within existing courses. We also recognized that our quarter-based academic calendar affords a larger number of required courses in our curriculum and thus makes it easier to cover a broader range of topics from CS2013.

5. HENRY M. WALKER

Following a long-standing practice, Grinnell's CS faculty undertook a multi-pass approach to this curricular review. In the first pass, course syllabi from our multi-paradigm, three-course introductory sequence were examined, and hours estimated for each topic. Challenges in counting arose when one class session touched several CS2013 Knowledge Units (e.g., code development for an insertion sort might include loops, conditionals, arrays, functions and parameters, algorithm development, and sorting). After several passes, the allocation of time was judged an honest representation of hours spent, while also capturing appropriate themes and emphases in each course.

During and after a 3-day workshop in summer 2013, Grinnell's CS faculty next divided courses into groups (e.g., languages, systems, software development, etc.), and pairs of CS faculty collaborated to review each course in a group according to the both learning outcomes and level of mastery. After assembling results in a combined spreadsheet, we were surprised at how little of the Core-Tier1 topics was covered in our curriculum. We took it as a challenge to consider how to combine the new perspectives in CS2013 with our own focus on deep student understanding of algorithms, theory, and programming languages, a focus which our students and alumni tell us has long-standing value in their careers. Since a small liberal arts college like Grinnell limits a major to 32 credits (typically 8 4-credit courses), meeting CS 2013 recommendations required substantial creativity for both basic requirements and general advising. Once we had curricular mappings for learning outcomes, we used a formula to convert "learning-outcome hours" to in-class hours. With Grinnell's spiral approach to courses, hours spent meeting an objective in one course may not be allocated over several courses. Thus, Grinnell's CS faculty debated how best to report such hours.

Overall, utilization of CS2013 in the review of Grinnell's CS curriculum represented an extensive collaborative enterprise, including faculty members Janet Davis, Samuel A. Rebelsky, John David Stone, Henry M. Walker, and Jerod J. Weinman. Reporting of the final curricular mapping entailed extensive collaboration by Rebelsky and Walker.

CS Professional Development MOOCs

Erin Mindell (Moderator)
Google
76 9th Avenue
New York, NY 10011
mindell@google.com

Karen Brennan
Harvard University
13 Appian Way, Longfellow 324
Cambridge, MA 02138
karen_brennan@gse.harvard.edu

Gwendolyn Britton
Colorado State University-Global Campus
8000 East Maplewood Avenue
Greenwood Village, CO 80111
gwendolyn.britton@csuglobal.edu

Jennifer S. Kay
Rowan University
201 Mullica Hill Road
Glassboro, NJ 08028
kay@rowan.edu

Jennifer Rosato
College of St. Scholastica
1200 Kenwood Ave.
Duluth, MN 55811
jrosato@css.edu

ABSTRACT

CS4HS (Computer Science for High School) is an initiative sponsored by Google to promote Computer Science and Computational Thinking in high school and middle school curricula. In the past, workshops were offered in a face-to-face format; however, this left many K-12 computer science teachers unable to attend a workshop in their geographical region. During the 2013 round of funding, Google funded the creation of 4 workshops to be delivered in an online format, open to teachers across the United States and beyond. The panelists will share their experiences with development and deployment of large scale workshops that aim to fill the gap in professional development for K-12 computer science teachers.

Categories and Subject Descriptors

K.3.2 [**Computers and Education**]: Computer and Information Science Education.

General Terms

Design, Experimentation, Human Factors

Keywords

cs4hs, K-12 professional development, massive open online courses

1. ERIN MINDELL (Moderator)

Google's Computer Science for High School (http://www.cs4hs.com) is a program designed to give hands-on computer science professional development training to middle and high school teachers. For five years, these trainings had been offered in-person to an average of ~30 teachers per event. This past year, CS4HS launched an experiment to see what kind of reach the program could have if offered on a larger scale. Google awarded grants to four universities to design professional development Massive Open Online Courses (MOOCs) through four different approaches to computer science. Erin has been the Program Manager for CS4HS for the past three years. She has been with Google since 2008.

SIGCSE'14, March 5–8, 2014, Atlanta, Georgia, USA.
ACM 978-1-4503-2605-6/14/03.
http://dx.doi.org/10.1145/2538862.2538872

2. KAREN BRENNAN

Creative Computing (https://creative-computing.appspot.com/) is a semi-synchronous online workshop for educators who want to learn more about using the Scratch programming environment and supporting computational thinking in the classroom. Designed and facilitated by members of the ScratchEd Team at Harvard University, the objectives of the workshop are to support educators in creating (i.e., learning about Scratch in the classroom, both as a tool and as an approach to learning, through a series of hands-on activities and a self-directed project) and connecting (i.e., establishing relationships with other educators). More than 2,100 people enrolled in the initial offering of the six-week workshop, which was hosted from June 3 until July 12, 2013. As is typical of large-scale online learning environments, people participated in a variety of ways, from very actively (completing all activities and deeply contributing to the learning community) to much more peripherally (just exploring the workshop resources). Over the six weeks, participants created more than 4,700 Scratch projects, watched the collection of workshop videos more than 22,000 times, and posted more than 5,000 messages in the course forums, on Twitter, and via the Google+ Community. The panelist is an Assistant Professor of Education at Harvard University.

3. GWENDOLYN BRITTON

CSU Global's non-computer science workshop is organized into an eight week online course. The first half of the course focuses on introducing computer science teaching methods into regular education classrooms. The second half of the course focuses on integrating computer science concepts into the classrooms of non-computer science teachers. The workshop uses a problem based approach to help teachers integrate computer science concepts and activities into their specific subject matter lessons. The course is designed to support teachers with site-based, hybrid and fully online courses. A large component of the course requires students integrate their assignments into their own Google site.

The purpose of CSU Global's 8-week non-CS Teachers workshop is to:

- provide a fully online, self-directed, self-paced learning environment to encourage non-computer science teachers to integrate computer science concepts into their curriculum
- encourage non-computer science teachers to engage with computer science content and concepts within a regular k-12 classroom.

Integrating computer science concepts and project based learning into the regular education classroom helps students develop critical problem solving and computer science thinking skills necessary to succeed in the 21st century. Thinking like a computer scientist, approaching problems, and coming up with creative and logical ways of solving problems is very different than using technological tools to produce lesson artifacts. This course is NOT about how to create a website, a PowerPoint presentation, a cool spreadsheet or a nifty brochure. This course introduces teachers to best practices for creating projects and problem based lessons that integrate different computer science problem solving and thinking concepts into their respective curriculums. The course explores numerous programming environments including Scratch, Alice, Logo, Karel, Visual Studio Express and Python.

The panelist is an adjunct professor at Colorado State University Gobal, and the Executive Director of Online STEM Programs at Southern New Hampshire University.

4. JENNIFER S. KAY

The Rowan University Laboratory for Educational Robotics is offering a 5-week Introduction to Robot Programming for Absolute Beginners online workshop in the Fall of 2013 (http://cs4hsrobots.appspot.com/). This workshop is based on successful in-person workshops held at Rowan University in the summers of 2011 and 2012. The workshop uses the LEGO Mindstorms NXT robot both because of its wide popularity (many schools already own NXT robots) and the fact that the associated NXT-G software (which has a graphical, somewhat Scratch-like interface) is very approachable. While the workshop is open to everyone, our target audience is K-12 teachers. Programming and other aspects of computational thinking are not generally a part of the standard K-12 curriculum; we hope that teachers will be excited by robotics and will be motivated to find ways to introduce these subjects into their classroom and after-school activities. The workshop proceeds at a very slow pace in order to achieve as much teacher success as possible, with the goal of not only increasing their content knowledge but also their confidence in their own ability to learn and teach this material.

Incorporating hardware adds an additional twist to an online course for novices. We tried to anticipate the most common problems and offer "Help, Something Went Wrong," modules. In addition, our choice of the LEGO hardware enables workshop participants to make use of LEGO's free telephone technical support. While it's not clear how much help LEGO would offer in debugging a program, they can certainly help a student distinguish between a software bug and a hardware failure. Evaluation of students' work also presents a challenge, since the correctness of a solution to a project is dependent not only on the code itself, but also potentially on the robot design, hardware variations, and even environmental conditions such as ambient light levels. We have chosen to require participants to find a physically local peer to evaluate their work. This allows us to offer certificates of completion to teachers which are valid once certified by their school principal.

The panelist is a Professor of Computer Science at Rowan University and director of the Rowan University Laboratory for Educational Robotics.

5. JENNIFER ROSATO

The College of St. Scholastica (CSS) offered a 5-week workshop on integrating App Inventor activities into the classroom (http://cs4hs.css.edu). Participants indicating that they wished to earn a certificate of completion were assigned to professional learning community (PLC) groups with a mentor teacher for each PLC group. The mentor teacher assisted in establishing community among the PLC members, facilitated a weekly group hangout, and graded discussion board postings and curriculum projects. The workshop was divided into five units. The first unit served to introduce the workshop content and tools to the participants and did not include CS material. Each of the remaining four units consisted of a CS Unplugged activity, App Inventor tutorials, a guest speaker, a special topic related to CS education, a discussion topic and a unit assessment along with the PLC group hangout mentioned earlier. Special topics included computational thinking, the CSTA computer science standards, promising practices for supporting diverse students, and a curriculum project. Over 400 people registered for the workshop with 200 of them indicating a desire to earn a certificate of completion. Of those 200, 63 earned a certificate for a completion rate of just over 30%. Some of these participants are also completing a follow-up project for graduate education credit through CSS. While it is not feasible to have everyone in a MOOC participate in PLC groups at no cost, more MOOCs are starting to charge a fee for services such as these, including verification of learning. Jen Rosato is an Assistant Professor of Computer Science/Information Systems at the College of St. Scholastica.

Looking Outside: What Can Be Learnt from Computing Education Around The World?

Annemieke Craig (Moderator)
School of Information
and Business Analaytics
Deakin University
Australia
acraig@deakin.edu.au

Catherine Lang
Faculty of Education

La Trobe University
Australia
c.lang@latrobe.edu.au

Michail N. Giannakos
Department of Computer &
Information Science
Norwegian University of Science
and Technology
Norway
michailg@idi.ntnu.no

Carsten Kleiner
University of Applied Sciences & Arts

Hannover, Germany
carsten.kleiner@hs-hannover.de

Judith Gal-Ezer
Mathematics and Computer Science
The Open University of Israel
Israel
galezer@openu.ac.il

SUMMARY

There is a growing awareness of the importance of including computing education in the curriculum of secondary schools in countries like the United States of America, the United Kingdom, New Zealand, and South Korea. Consequently, we have seen serious efforts to introduce computing education to the core curriculum and/or to improve it. Recent reports (such as Wilson et al. 2010; Hubwieser et al. 2011) reveal that computing education faces problems regarding its lack of exposure as well as a lack of motivators for students to follow this line of study. Although students use computers for many tasks both at home and at school, many of them never quite understand what computer science is and how it relates to algorithmic thinking and problem solving. This panel will bring together leaders in computing education from Australia, Germany, Greece, Israel and Norway to describe the state of computing education in each of their countries. Issues raised will include how high school computer education is conducted in that country, how teachers are skilled /accredited, the challenges that are being faced today and how these challenges are being addressed. Panellists will suggest lessons other countries may find of value from their way of doing things. An important issue is how to recruit female students in to computer education at high school level and how to encourage them to continue in the discipline to university. The problem is exacerbated because computer education is still not included as a compulsory subject in the regular curriculum of high schools in all of these countries.

SIGCSE '14, March 5-8, 2014, Atlanta, Georgia, USA.
ACM 978-1-4503-2605-6/14/03.
http://dx.doi.org/10.1145/2538862.2538871

Categories and Subject Descriptors
K.3Computers and education; K.3.0 General

Keywords
International computer education

PANELISTS

The panellist are passionate about their involvement in improving computer education and see that as a result of exposing students (male and female) to computer science in high school it may dramatically change the way we all live through impacts on industry, economics, science and more

Prof Gal-Ezer's goal and mission as chair of the CS professional committee nominated by the Ministry of Education is to convince policy makers that computer science as a discipline is as important as the other sciences and even middle school students should be exposed to the basics of this scientific discipline. This is in line with the SCIENCE 2020 report (Emmott & Rison 2005), "...computer science is poised to become as fundamental to biology as mathematics has become to physics.....". Computer Science should be at least one of the electives students can take in high school.

Dr. Giannakos has been involved in several creative development workshops for primary/secondary school, and university students over the past 3 years in Greece and Norway. Dr Giannakos has conducted computing seminars and camps that expose female students and students with impairments to career opportunities in computing. He was one of the members of the ITiCSE WG about CS/Informatics in Secondary Education and co-guest editor of the special issue in Computer Science Education in Schools of ACM TOCE.

Prof Kleiner is a professor of secure information systems at the University of Applied Sciences & Arts in Germany. He teaches several different courses in the B. Sc. and M. Sc. programs in computer science such as theoretical computer science, data structures and algorithms as well as courses in database and information systems. Prof Kleiner holds a M. Sc. from both the Leibniz-University in Hannover, Germany, and Purdue University; a Dr. rer. nat. (Ph. D. equivalent) in Computer Science from the Leibniz-University Germany. He has been a member of ACM and GI for almost 20 years and is an ACM senior member. He has taken part in SIGCSE symposia on a regular basis and is a member of ACM SIGCSE for over 10 years now. He is currently co-developing a new program to increase female enrollment.

Prof Lang has been involved in outreach programs to improve student diversity in computing for many years. Her research found that a good teacher is often a motivator for students to select computing at university. She has recently moved from a Faculty of Computing to a Faculty of Education where the priority is improving teacher technical self-efficacy in all subject areas, not just computing education. Prof Lang will discuss the initiatives being undertaken in Australia to implement transformational pedagogies in classrooms through pre-service teacher education and the new digital technology curriculum proposed to be implemented Australia-wide. She is secretary of the Australian SIGCSE Chapter.

REFERENCES

[1] Australian Computer Society (2013) ACS submission to the ACARA Draft Curriculum. ACS Inc A.C.T.

[2] DEEWR: http://www.deewr.gov.au/HigherEducation/Publications/HEStatistics/Publications/Documents/2010/2010_Attachment_A.pdf

[3] Doukakis, S., Giannakos, M, N., Koilias, C., Vlamos, P. (2013). Measuring Students' Acceptance and Confidence on Algorithms and Programming: The Impact of the Engagement with CS on Secondary Education, Informatics in Education (forthcoming).

[4] Emmott, A & Rison S (2005) Towards 2020 SCIENCE, Microsoft Research, Available from http://research.microsoft.com/en-us/um/Cambridge/projects/towards 2020science

[5] Gal-Ezer & D. Harel (1999) Curriculum & Course Syllabi for High-School Computer Science Program, Computer Science Education,9,2,114-47.

[6] Gal-Ezer J. & D. Harel (1998) What (else) should CS educators know? Communications of the ACM, 41, 9, pp. 77-84.

[7] Gesellschaft für Informatik e. V. (ed.): Grundsätze und Standards für die Informatik in der Schule, 150/151, 2008, http://gi.informatikstandards.de/

[8] Giannakos, M, N., & Jaccheri, L. (2013a). What motivates children to become creators of digital enriched artifacts?. In 9th ACM Conference on Creativity & Cognition ACM Press, 104-113.

[9] Giannakos, M, N., & Jaccheri, L. (2013b). An Enriched Artifacts Activity for Supporting Creative Learning: Perspectives for Children with Impairments, In Proc. of Entertainment Computing – ICEC 2013, Springer, LNCS, 160-163.

[10] Giannakos, M. N., Jaccheri, L., & Proto, R. (2013). Teaching Computer Science to Young Children through Creativity: Lessons Learned from the Case of Norway. In CSERC '13, ACM.

[11] Hazzan, O., J. Gal-Ezer & Blum, L. (2008). A Model for High School Computer Science Education: The Four Key Elements that Make It! In *Proceedings of The 39th Technical Symposium on Computer Science Education*, 281-285.

[12] Hazzan,O., J. Gal-Ezer, & N. Ragonis (2010) How to establish a Computer Science Teacher Preparation Program at your University, The ECSTPP Workshop, *ACM Inroads*, 1, pp. 35-39.

[13] Hubwieser, P., Armoni, M., Brinda, T., Dagiene, V., Diethelm, I., Giannakos, M.N., Knobelsdorf, M., Magenheim, J., Mittermeir, R.T., & Schubert, S.E. (2011). Computer science/informatics in secondary education. In Proc.ITiCSE, 19-38.

[14] Israeli Central Bureau of Statistics Website: http://www.cbs.gov.il

[15] Lang C, (2012) "Sequential attrition of secondary school student interest in Information Technology courses and careers" *Information Technology and People* 25(3) pp. 281-299

[16] Statistisches Bundesamt: Bildung und Kultur Studierende an Hochschulen –Vorbericht Wintersemester 2012/2013, Destatis Fachserie 11 Reihe 4.1, Wiesbaden, 2013

[17] Wilson ,C. Sudol, L.A Stephenson C. & Stehlik, M. (2010), Running on Empty: The Failure to teach K-12 Computer Science in the Digital Age, ACM & CSTA www.acm.org/runningonempty/

[18] Zur Bargury. I., et al. (2012). Implementing a New Computer Science Curriculum for Middle School in Israel. *Proceedings of the FIE'12 Conference, Seattle, Washington, 886-891.*

[19] Zur-Bargury, I. (2012). A New Curriculum for Junior-High in Computer Science. *ITiCSE'12 Conference, July 3–5, Haifa, Israel.* ACM, New York, NY.

Peer Instruction Contributes to Self-Efficacy in CS1

Daniel Zingaro
OISE
University of Toronto
Toronto, ON, Canada
daniel.zingaro@utoronto.ca

ABSTRACT

Recent work in computing suggests that Peer Instruction (PI) is a valuable interactive learning pedagogy: it lowers fail rates, increases retention, and is enjoyed by students and instructors alike. While these findings are promising, they are somewhat incidental if our goal is to understand whether PI is "better" than lecture in terms of student outcomes. Only one recent study in computing has made such a comparison, finding that PI students outperform traditionally-taught students on a CS0 final exam. That work was conducted in a CS0, where the same instructor taught both courses, and where the only outcome measure was final exam grade. Here, I offer a study that complements their work in two ways. First, I argue for and measure self-efficacy as a valued outcome, in addition to that of final exam grade. Second, I offer an inter-instructor CS1 study, whose biases differ from those of intra-instructor studies. I find evidence that PI significantly increases self-efficacy and suggestively increases exam scores compared to a traditional lecture-based CS1 class. I note validity concerns of such an in-situ study and offer a synthesis of this work with the extant PI literature.

Categories and Subject Descriptors

K.3.2 [**Computer Science Education**]: Computer and Information Science Education

Keywords

CS1; peer instruction; clickers; classroom response; outcomes

1. INTRODUCTION

CS1 (Computer Science 1) is the first course taken by CS majors at the post-secondary degree level. As this course serves as entry into the CS curriculum, it has received significant attention by the CS education community. A recurring concern in the contemporary CS1 research is that students are not learning what we expect and that disproportionate numbers of students worldwide are failing CS1 [3]. Bimodal grade distributions [23] and assertions that programming skill cannot be taught [7] have quickened the pace with which student's grade-based outcomes have been measured and predicted. In general, this program of research seeks to predict students' CS1 grade or final exam grade through characteristics such as prior programming experience [10], math ability [4] and learning style [12], to name a few. The breadth of student predictors is both broad and creative, and serves as a testament to the effort put forth by the research community to thoroughly explore the hypothesized link between "what students have" and whether they succeed.

However, while the sheer number of studied predictors is comprehensive, two other areas of the research have gone largely unquestioned. First, the research narrowly defines success in CS1 as the student's score on an exam or the course as a whole. It rarely acknowledges the importance of self-efficacy as a valued outcome in and of itself. Second, it rarely acknowledges the potential importance of pedagogy in the link between student-based predictors and outcomes. This is a particularly important gap given the recent interest in Peer Instruction (PI) and other active learning pedagogies for teaching CS courses.

This paper contributes in two ways to the gaps mentioned here. I offer a comparison of two sections of a CS1, one taught using PI and the other taught traditionally. In this way, I can compare outcomes from courses that are otherwise held constant (subject to validity concerns as described later). Second, I take both final exam grade and post-course self-efficacy as independent, valued outcomes of CS1. This work complements a similar study of a CS0 that compared PI to a traditional section [26]. In that work, the PI section scored significantly higher on the final exam than the traditional section. In the present work, I find suggestive (but not statistically significant) evidence of the same finding. However, as I also measure self-efficacy, I document that students in the PI section show higher self-efficacy than the control section. The benefit of a broad conception of "success" is evident in that the self-efficacy increases would have been missed through a sole examination of final grade.

SIGCSE'14, March 3–8, 2014, Atlanta, GA, USA.

http://dx.doi.org/10.1145/2538862.2538878.

2. BACKGROUND AND LITERATURE REVIEW

2.1 Peer Instruction

Peer Instruction (PI) is a pedagogical technique developed in physics that has since been used with considerable success in CS. At the core of this pedagogy is the ConcepTest [6]: a multiple-choice question answered by students typically using clickers. Each ConcepTest sets off a well-defined pedagogical protocol: students first answer the question individually (solo vote), then discuss the same question for several minutes with their neighbors, and finally re-vote on the question in light of the group discussion (group vote). Following the group vote, the instructor facilitates a classwide discussion and explanation of the ConcepTest, before dynamically adjusting the class based on student performance. The instructor may lecture briefly before or after a ConcepTest, but the vast majority of lecture time engages students in discussions with peers. The role of the instructor is to help foster substantive discussions of core course concepts, and to focus students on each distractor rather than on answering the question correctly [25, 28]. This downplaying of lecture means that instructors cannot "cover" as much material, so students are typically required to read one or two textbook sections before class and complete a small preparatory reading quiz [6, 28].

In a taxonomy of observable learning activities, Chi [5] argues that "interactive" learning activities may be most powerful for engendering learning. Such activities are characterized by learners dialoguing and discussing concepts, where each peer makes substantive contributions to the discourse. Simply grouping students for PI does not guarantee that their discussions will be interactive as described here, but recent work suggests that students see PI as more interactive than traditional lecture [24]. We therefore expect PI students to exhibit strong gains, and for the most part this is borne out by the literature. For example, PI reduces failure rates [19], contributes to increased retention [20], and yields exam-inferred learning gains in CS0 courses [26]. Students learn from their discussions with peers [18] and students and teachers alike value the pedagogy for its effects on learning and argumentation [17]. See the recent reviews [29, 28] for further commentary on these and other benefits.

2.2 Self-Efficacy as Valued Outcome

The most observable measure of course success, and certainly one of the most important, is student grade. The vast majority of CS studies concerned with measuring outcomes have operationalized success as course grade or final exam grade. Further, these studies tend to study lecture-based offerings of CS1. The typical finding is that students with prior programming experience earn higher grades compared to inexperienced students. This finding is robust in the sense that even a small amount of prior programming experience is helpful [10]. Having taken a CS course [8], studied a programming language [10], or dabbled in programming as a hobby [11] all positively predict performance in a CS1. To be clear, there are isolated studies where this relationship is deemed not to hold, but the relevant features of those examples have resisted capture or replication. For example, in an objects-first CS1, no prior experience gap was evident [27]. Yet, in other "objects-first" courses, the gap is back [2]. I argue that a well-defined pedagogical shift — from traditional to PI — may yield more reliable results than particulars of the content being taught.

Most relevant to this discussion, Simon et al. [26] have recently reported a comparison of a PI section of a course to a traditional section. To determine whether PI students demonstrated enhanced learning, the sections' final exam grades were compared. They found that PI students scored almost 6% higher on the common final exam than traditional students.

While grade is an important outcome, it is not the only important outcome. Elsewhere, I have argued for the importance of measuring CS students' interest and enjoyment of CS to complement grade-based outcomes (Zingaro, in submission). Students take CS courses for a variety of reasons including job prospects, challenging themselves with difficult material, and understanding societal trends and changes [13, 9]. These are only peripherally-related to the grades students earn. There are other outcomes that may suggest that students are getting what they want from our courses, and we must measure these outcomes in order to broaden our understanding of student success.

One such outcome measure that may only partially overlap grades is self-efficacy. Self-efficacy is the most-studied sociocognitive attribute of CS1 students, but it is typically studied as a predictor of (grade) success, not as a legitimate outcome in itself. It is defined as the conviction that one can successfully orchestrate behavior to accomplish something [1]. Self-efficacy expectations are differentiated from outcome expectations, the latter of which refer to the instrumental relationship between a behavior and an outcome. Bandura [1] explains that efficacy judgments help determine whether coping behavior will be initiated, the amount of effort expended, and level of perseverance in the face of obstacles. It is for this reason that I take self-efficacy as an important measure of what students "get" from CS1. If students' self-efficacy is strengthened, then this is valuable whether or not it manifests immediately in heightened grades. For example, students with high self-efficacy following CS1 may be more likely to continue to a second CS course, where perhaps grade will catch-up to their belief in what they can do. Of course, self-efficacy expectations in and of themselves are not sufficient to produce successful behavior; but in the presence of sufficient skill and motivation, efficacy expectations are crucial in shaping consequent action. The most powerful mediator of self-efficacy is performance accomplishments, though vicarious experience, verbal persuasion, and associated physiological states also play a role.

The only widely-used self-efficacy scale for computer programming is that developed by Ramalingam and Wiedenbeck [22]. This scale contains 32 questions primed to object-oriented programming in C++. Students rate on a seven-point scale their confidence that they could carry out specific and relevant programming tasks. These authors administered the scale once prior to any instruction, and again after the final lecture. Factor analysis on the pre-self-efficacy administration suggests that this scale is composed of four factors: independence and persistence, complex programming tasks, self-regulation, and simple programming tasks. In the traditionally-taught CS1 courses, self-efficacy increases from pre-course to post-course [22, 21].

2.3 Hypotheses

PI courses give students considerable opportunities to experience small successes. Each class has students discuss and answer three or more important but small questions. If self-efficacy is tied largely to performance accomplishment, then it should be that PI increases self-efficacy beyond that of a traditional course offering. In addition, as PI has shown to improve grades over a traditional offering, I hypothesize that PI students' final exam scores will be higher than those of traditionally-taught students. My first two hypotheses are therefore:

- PI students leave CS1 with higher self-efficacy than traditionally-taught students.
- PI students will earn higher grades on a final exam than their traditionally-taught counterparts.

In addition, I suggest that links between previous programming experience and gender on the one hand and outcomes on the other might be moderated by pedagogy.

As noted earlier, the literature shows strong links between prior programming experience and grades, but that work was conducted solely in lecture sections. To the extent that PI gives students of lesser experience opportunities to learn from experienced peers, I hypothesize that the gap generated by prior experience might be smaller in the PI section.

In an ethnographic study of gendered experiences in CS, Margolis and Fisher [14] argue that contextualized learning is important for women's success. They describe the computing-related narratives of many male college students as approximating an in-born, magnetic attraction to computers. These males are attracted to the physical computer for its own sake, in contrast to females who often understand computers as serving larger societal goals. Women's stories run counter to the idea that CS majors "hack for hacking's sake". They are motivated by a desire to help others, an appreciation of the versatility of CS, and encouragement from family and friends. Large, impersonal and competitive lectures disadvantage women who are bolstered by social and academic support. Margolis and Fisher [14] give three suggestions for creating what they call a course in "contextualized computer science": situating technology in realistic settings, making connections to other disciplines, and using diverse problems and teaching methods. I contend that PI addresses, at least partially, the first and third of these guidelines, and therefore that the gender gap (if one exists in my setting) will be reduced in the PI section. My second set of hypotheses is therefore:

- PI will reduce the prior experience gap.
- PI will reduce the gender gap.

3. METHOD

I report on a CS1 taught in Fall 2012 at an undergraduate campus of a large Canadian research-intensive university. Two sections of the course, taught by different instructors, were offered: a PI offering and a traditional offering. The course covers traditional CS1 topics in imperative programming, and also spends one week each on sorting, complexity, and object-oriented programming. The course took place over 12 weeks, with three 50-minute lectures and one lab session per week. The course has been taught in Python 2 since 2008 and the two Fall 2012 instructors worked together to revamp the course for Python 3.

In the PI section, the instructor began the course by introducing the rationale for using PI, covering some of the research findings and goals for the peer discussions. Prior to each lecture, students completed a reading quiz; the instructor read the responses to help shape the following lecture. The reading quizzes were marked based on completion (not correctness) and were worth 4% of students' final grade; in-class clicker participation accounted for a further 5% of students' grade. Each lecture was focused on three to four ConcepTests, with mini-lectures interspersed when planned by the instructor or required based on question performance. The course instructor was a senior education graduate student with significant PI and CS teaching experience, and had taught CS1 using PI several times.

The traditional section was taught by an instructor with significant CS and Python teaching experience. This section used the same labs, assignments, midterm, and final exam as the PI section. The two sections of the course were synchronized both in the topics to be covered each class and the examples used to teach those topics. The PI instructor used multiple choice questions and the PI process, while the traditional instructor introduced and worked examples through a lecture format. Importantly, both instructors were teaching in their preferred modes (PI or traditional) and developed and followed agreed-upon plans for each lecture.

As the traditional offering did not have reading quizzes or class participation marks, those students were required to submit three small exercises throughout the semester that were each worth 3%. The PI instructor used some of the very same exercise questions in the students' reading quizzes so as to attempt to equalize exposure to these small programming questions.

Consenting students were asked to respond to two surveys: one at the start of term and one in the last two weeks of classes. On the first questionnaire, an initial measure of self-efficacy was collected, along with the number of prior CS courses taken. Prior programming experience was collected because of its reliable role in predicting student grade (e.g. [10, 15]). On the end-of-term questionnaire, a post-self-efficacy measure was obtained. The self-efficacy measure was adapted from [22] by replacing "Java" with "Python". Student final exam grades were obtained as the second outcome measure.

4. THREATS TO VALIDITY

As a quasi-experimental study, there are threats to the validity of the results here. I survey these threats, and in some cases describe how they were partially controlled:

Different Instructors. This is an inter-instructor study, where one instructor taught the PI section and the other taught the traditional section. This is to be contrasted with an intra-instructor study where the instructor teaches both sections [26]. These designs each have limitations that are only partially-overlapping. For example, an instructor may prefer one mode over the other, so intra-instructor studies force the instructor to teach in the mode they disprefer. In both designs, the quality of instruction in one section may be better than that in the other section. Inter-instructor studies, as the present one, successfully engage instructors in teaching in their preferred modes, but do so through a loss of control of general instructor effectiveness. For example, perhaps the PI instructor is globally "better" or overall works harder than the traditional instructor, or vice versa. In the present study, both instructors were teaching the Python 3 CS1 for the first time and developed their own lectures following the same teaching plan. Post-course student comments were positive in both cases, but of course such evaluations cannot disentangle instructor effects from pedagogy effects.

Different Students. The other obvious confound is that qualitatively different students enrolled in the two sections. However, the two sections were offered back-to-back, the two instructors were unknown to the students, and the students were unaware that the sections would use different pedagogies. Students could have switched sections early in the term, but anecdotally this was observed very infrequently. As an additional check, I found that pre-self-efficacy and prior experience measures did not statistically differ per section ($p > .05$ in both cases), giving credence to the suggestion that students were similar.

5. RESULTS

Across both sections, 221 students wrote the final exam. Data for the present study includes 109 (49%) of these students: these are the students that responded to both questionnaires and took at least 40 seconds to respond to the post-self-efficacy questionnaire. (The self-efficacy scale contains 32 questions; 40 seconds was used to remove submissions where students were unlikely to have read many of the questions at all.) The Cronbach's reliability of the self-efficacy questionnaire was 0.98.

Multiple regressions were used to test the predictors of post-self-efficacy and exam grade. Regressors were entered in two blocks. In the first block, main effects of gender, section, and prior experience were added. In the second block, interactions between section and gender and between section and prior experience were added. These models allow for the exploration of the four hypotheses of this study.

Post-Self-Efficacy.

The initial models failed to reject a test of non-constant variance; a square root transform on post-self-efficacy corrected the problem. Using a nested chi-square test, I compared the predictive power of the block-1 model (containing only the main effects) with the block-2 model (additionally containing the interactions). A non-significant result ($p = .65$) shows that the block-2 model is no better than the block-1 model. That is, there are no significant interactions between pedagogy and gender, or between pedagogy and prior experience.

The block-1 (main effects) model of self-efficacy is given in the left-hand column of Table 1. I find a significant effect of section ($p = .015$), such that PI students' self-efficacy (5.13) was higher than the self-efficacy of traditionally-taught students (4.65). A significant effect of gender ($p = 0$) shows that females have lower post-self-efficacy (4.12) than males (5.32). Finally, prior course-based programming experience was associated with higher post-self-efficacy ($p = .003$).

	self-efficacy	exam grade
(Intercept)	24.16 (1.06)*	57.08 (1.82)*
section	2.46 (1.00)*	2.43 (1.71)
gender	−4.34 (1.08)*	−3.52 (1.85)
prior_courses	3.00 (0.98)*	3.97 (1.68)*
R^2	0.27	0.12
Adj. R^2	0.25	0.09

$^*p < 0.05$

Table 1: Multiple regressions for post-self-efficacy and final exam grade.

Exam Grade.

Using a nested chi-square test, I compared the predictive power of the block-1 model (containing only the main effects) with the block-2 model (additionally containing the interactions). A non-significant result ($p = .74$) shows that the block-2 model is no better than the block-1 model. That is, there are no significant interactions between pedagogy and gender, or between pedagogy and prior experience. (This mirrors the finding for post-self-efficacy.)

The block-1 (main effects) model of final exam grade is given in the right-hand column of Table 1. Section is insignificant ($p = .16$), suggesting that PI and traditionally-taught students did not differ on final exam grade. PI students were predicted to score 2.4% higher on the exam, but this difference was not statistically significant (c.f. [26]). Using the full student roster (not just the subset of students that responded to the questionnaires), PI students scored 4.4% higher, but a t-test remained non-significant ($p = .10$). Moving on, I find a significant effect of prior experience ($p = .0198$), such that students who took prior programming courses performed better on the final exam. A near-significant effect of gender ($p = .06$) suggests that females performed more poorly than males when controlling for prior experience. On the final exam, males scored an average of 61% and females scored on average 52%.

6. DISCUSSION

I now return to the four hypotheses of the study.

As predicted, PI students' post-self-efficacy was higher than that of students in the traditional section. This is perhaps due to the numerous opportunities for quick, accurate feedback in the PI class, where students could experience small successes before tackling larger labs and assignments [22].

However, the second hypothesis — that PI students would also score higher on the final exam — was not supported. Considered together, this suggests an apparent contradiction: if PI students believe they can organize activity toward success, why were they no more successful on the final assessment? I suspect that this may have to do with the type of final exam that is typically administered in CS1s. Prior research shows that CS1 exams typically involve several large, integrative code-writing questions [16]. Students are required to synthesize several concepts in order to arrive at a coherent program to solve a problem, and this tends to limit opportunities for students to demonstrate what they know. (That is, there is a concern that these integrative questions measure all-or-nothing.) The instructors of the present CS1 intentionally designed such an exam to correspond to this CS1 practice. That is, the exam was mostly composed of integrative code-writing questions. This is to be contrasted with the earlier study by Simon et al. [26] where a PI section of a CS0 outperformed a traditional section. In that context, the final exam contained many multiple choice questions in addition to some short answer questions. What I am arguing is that the elevated self-efficacy of PI students did not present in terms of higher grades because the students may not yet have the required practice and experience to successfully orchestrate the mechanics required for integrative code-writing questions. Such self-efficacy, however, may prove useful for these students going forward.

The third and fourth hypotheses were not supported. I found overall evidence that males performed better than females, and that those with prior CS course experience performed better than those who hadn't taken a CS course. However, the use of PI did not moderate these relationships. That is, gender- and experienced-based gaps existed in this CS1, and they were not lessened by a change in pedagogy.

Overall, PI marginally (but insignificantly) led to increased final exam scores, and significantly contributed to post-self-efficacy. While these results are more equivocal than those previously reported for a CS0 [26], they do suggest the importance of multiple outcome measures to provide more nuanced understandings of pedagogical interventions. In future work, I seek to study a more balanced CS1 exam to determine (a) whether PI students outperform traditionally-taught students on some tasks and, if so, (b) precisely where the differences lie. That is, I do not argue here that PI did not help students conceptually, only that students may not have had the opportunity to demonstrate this understanding on the type of CS1 exam in common use. Of course, it may be that PI is more effective in a CS0 compared to a CS1, particularly when many questions on the final exam are multiple choice as in the Simon et al. study [26]. Questions of when and in what ways PI helps our students across different courses are exciting possibilities for future research.

7. CONCLUSION

When outcomes include more than final exam grade, our understanding of course success correspondingly broadens. In this CS1 study, I examine outcomes of final exam grade and self-efficacy for students taught using Peer Instruction (PI) and those taught in traditional lecture style. I find significant gains in self-efficacy for the PI students, but no significant evidence that final exam scores differed (though PI students did score marginally higher). I offer that the increased self-efficacy is a win in itself, and urge the community toward a multi-faceted conception of success in CS1. Students earn more than grades in our courses: they possibly become interested in CS, enjoy the lectures, gain self-efficacy, and so on. To truly understand the effect of a pedagogical shift requires an understanding of more than grade-based outcomes.

Acknowledgments.

I thank anonymous reviewer "Spino" for feedback on an early version of this work

8. REFERENCES

[1] A. Bandura. Self-efficacy: toward a unifying theory of behavioral change. *Psychological Review*, 84(2):191–215, 1977.

[2] J. Bennedsen and M. E. Caspersen. An investigation of potential success factors for an introductory model-driven programming course. In *Proceedings of the first international workshop on Computing education research*, pages 155–163. ACM, 2005.

[3] J. Bennedsen and M. E. Caspersen. Failure rates in introductory programming. *SIGCSE Bulletin*, 39:32–36, 2007.

[4] P. Byrne and G. Lyons. The effect of student attributes on success in programming. *SIGCSE Bulletin*, 33:49–52, 2001.

[5] M. T. H. Chi. Active-constructive-interactive: A conceptual framework for differentiating learning activities. *Topics in Cognitive Science*, 1(1):73–105, 2009.

[6] C. H. Crouch, J. Watkins, A. P. Fagen, and E. Mazur. Peer instruction: Engaging students one-on-one, all at once. In E. F. Redish and P. J. Cooney, editors, *Research-Based Reform of University Physics*. American Association of Physics Teachers, College Park, MD, USA, 2007.

[7] S. Dehnadi, R. Bornat, and R. Adams. Meta-analysis of the effect of consistency on success in early learning of programming. In *21st Annual Workshop of the Psychology of Programming Interest Group*, 2009.

[8] G. E. Evans and M. G. Simkin. What best predicts computer proficiency? *Communications of the ACM*, 32:1322–1327, 1989.

[9] A. Fisher, J. Margolis, and F. Miller. Undergraduate women in computer science: experience, motivation and culture. *SIGCSE Bulletin*, 29:106–110, 1997.

[10] D. Hagan and S. Markham. Does it help to have some programming experience before beginning a computing degree program? *SIGCSE Bulletin*, 32:25–28, 2000.

[11] E. Holden and E. Weeden. The impact of prior experience in an information technology programming course sequence. In *Proceedings of the 4th conference on Information technology curriculum*, pages 41–46. ACM, 2003.

[12] M. A. Hudak and D. E. Anderson. Formal operations and learning style predict success in statistics and computer science courses. *Teaching of Psychology*, 17(4):231–234, 1990.

[13] T. Jenkins. The motivation of students of programming. *SIGCSE Bulletin*, 33(3):53–56, 2001.

[14] J. Margolis and A. Fisher. *Unlocking the clubhouse: Women in computing*. The MIT Press, Cambridge, MA, USA, 2002.

[15] M. Morrison and T. S. Newman. A study of the impact of student background and preparedness on outcomes in CS I. *SIGCSE Bulletin*, 33(1):179–183, 2001.

[16] A. Petersen, M. Craig, and D. Zingaro. Reviewing CS1 exam question content. In *Proceedings of the 42nd ACM technical symposium on Computer science education*, pages 631–636. ACM, 2011.

[17] L. Porter, C. Bailey Lee, B. Simon, Q. Cutts, and D. Zingaro. Experience report: a multi-classroom report on the value of peer instruction. In *Proceedings of the 16th annual SIGCSE conference on Innovation and technology in computer science education*, pages 138–142. ACM, 2011.

[18] L. Porter, C. Bailey-Lee, B. Simon, and D. Zingaro. Peer instruction: Do students really learn from peer discussion in computing? In *Proceedings of the Seventh international Workshop on Computing Education Research*. ACM, 2011.

[19] L. Porter, C. B. Lee, and B. Simon. Halving fail rates using peer instruction: A study of four computer science courses. In *Proceedings of the 44th ACM technical symposium on Computer science education*, pages 177–182. ACM, 2013.

[20] L. Porter and B. Simon. Retaining nearly one-third more majors with a trio of instructional best practices in CS1. In *Proceedings of the 44th ACM technical symposium on Computer science education*, pages 165–170. ACM, 2013.

[21] V. Ramalingam, D. LaBelle, and S. Wiedenbeck. Self-efficacy and mental models in learning to program. *SIGCSE Bulletin*, 36:171–175, 2004.

[22] V. Ramalingam and S. Wiedenbeck. Development and validation of scores on a computer programming self-efficacy scale and group analyses of novice programmer self-efficacy. *Journal of Educational Computing Research*, 19:365–379, 1998.

[23] A. Robins. Learning edge momentum: A new account of outcomes. *Computer Science Education*, 20(1):37–71, 2010.

[24] B. Simon, S. Esper, L. Porter, and Q. Cutts. Student experience in a student-centered peer instruction classroom. In *Proceedings of the Ninth International Workshop on Computing Education Research*. ACM, 2013.

[25] B. Simon, M. Kohanfars, J. Lee, K. Tamayo, and Q. Cutts. Experience report: Peer instruction in introductory computing. In *Proceedings of the 41st SIGCSE technical symposium on Computer science education*, pages 341–345. ACM, 2010.

[26] B. Simon, J. Parris, and J. Spacco. How we teach impacts student learning: peer instruction vs. lecture in cs0. In *Proceedings of the 44th ACM technical symposium on Computer science education*, pages 41–46. ACM, 2013.

[27] P. Ventura. *On the origins of programmers: Identifying predictors of success for an objects first CS1*. PhD thesis, SUNY at Buffalo, 2003.

[28] D. Zingaro, C. Bailey-Lee, and L. Porter. Peer instruction in computing: the role of reading quizzes. In *Proceedings of the 44th ACM technical symposium on Computer Science Education*, pages 47–52. ACM, 2013.

[29] D. Zingaro, A. Petersen, and M. Craig. Stepping up to integrative questions on CS1 exams. In *Proceedings of the 43rd ACM technical symposium on Computer Science Education*, pages 253–258. ACM, 2012.

New CS1 Pedagogies and Curriculum, the Same Success Factors?

Christine Alvarado
University of California, San Diego
alvarado@cs.ucsd.edu

Cynthia Bailey Lee
Stanford University
cbl@standford.edu

Gary Gillespie
University of California, San Diego
ggillespie@ucsd.edu

ABSTRACT

New CS1 curricula and pedagogies have resulted in many positive outcomes over the last several years including lower fail rates and increased long-term retention. Given these positive outcomes, the question becomes how much do the traditional factors of prior experience and confidence still play a role in students' performance in and attitudes about these courses? Furthermore, given that increasingly recommended collaborative pedagogies (e.g. pair programming) force students to interact with their peers for a large percentage of their work in the class, how much does the confidence of their peers affect their own attitudes and performance? This paper presents a study investigating these questions. We find that prior experience and confidence still predict success, but only for some students. We also find that student confidence levels have little to no impact on the attitudes and performance of their peers.

Categories and Subject Descriptors

K.3.2 [**Computers and Education**]: Computer and Information Science Education—*Computer science education*

General Terms

Human Factors, Design, Measurement

Keywords

CS1, Peer Instruction, Pair Programming, Confidence, Gender, Prior Experience

1. INTRODUCTION

Over the last fifteen years, the computer science education community has focused much of its attention on developing new CS1 courses to attract a wide range of students and ensure their success. New curricula aim to make computer science accessible and relevant to students, while new pedagogies aim to give students support and increase their depth of learning as well as their comfort and sense of belonging. Fortunately, many of these efforts have been apparently quite successful, leading to reduced fail rates [15, 11], increased retention in the major [13], and better gender balance in the major [1].

Given these successes, our goal was to look deeper into students' experiences in these classes. Beyond high-level statistics such as pass/fail rates and retention, are there remaining issues that deserve continued attention in these state-of-the-art CS1 courses?

A large number of studies have examined a variety of CS1 courses for factors that influence student success (e.g., [18, 4, 2, 22], to name a few). Most of these studies find that prior experience and some variation on student confidence or comfort are significantly correlated with students' performance. To a lesser degree, gender sometimes has also been found to be a factor in students' performance [2]. Many of these previous studies focused on "traditional" CS1 courses (e.g. object-oriented programming in Java with lectures and outside of class programming assignments).

In this work, we examine two major factors that have been shown to influence student performance in a CS1 courses—prior experience and confidence—to determine how they affect a student's own performance in a CS1 course that incorporates many new best practices. We also look for the effect that a student's confidence has on *other* students in the class, given that many of these best practices (e.g., pair programming) force students to interact with each other much more than they would in a course that includes only lectures and individual programming assignments.

In particular, we investigate the following four primary research questions:

1. Does pre-course confidence or prior experience affect performance in the course?
2. Does pre-course confidence or prior experience affect student attitudes about working in peer groups?
3. Do students who are placed into similar pre-course confidence peer groups perform differently than students who are placed in mixed-confidence groups?
4. Do students who are placed into similar pre-course confidence peer groups feel differently about working in peer groups than students who are placed in mixed-confidence groups?

In pursuing answers to the above research questions, we also investigate the relationship between confidence and prior experience, and between these two factors and gender.

We find that both prior experience and confidence significantly predict student performance in the course, but only

SIGCSE'14, March 5–8, 2014, Atlanta, GA, USA.
Copyright 2014 ACM 978-1-4503-2605-6/14/03 ...$15.00.
http://dx.doi.org/10.1145/2538862.2538897.

for male students. These factors are also related to students' feelings about working in peer groups. Looking at the effect of peer-group composition, we find in most cases confidence level composition within peer groups has little to no effect on students' attitudes or performance, but that some effect may be present for students with high levels of experience. These results suggest that while new pedagogical designs have improved student outcomes, the playing field due to prior experience is not yet level, and that women and men still experience CS1 differently.

2. BACKGROUND AND RELATED WORK

2.1 Pedagogy Best Practices

The course that we studied uses three practices specifically designed to make CS more relevant and accessible, particularly to women and students of underrepresented groups: a context theme in its curriculum (Media Computation), pair programming during closed labs and out-of-class programming assignments, and peer instruction during class periods. This trio of practices in particular has been shown to significantly reduce fail rates and increase retention [13].

Media computation [15] (MediaComp) is an introduction to computer science and programming in Java that uses media manipulation (digital images and sounds) as a context in which to teach basic programming and CS topics. MediaComp has been shown to have long-term, wide-reaching positive effects, including equal success from men and women in the course, increased retention at several universities, and strong learning outcomes [5].

Pair programming (PP) is a technique in which two students program collaboratively at the same terminal, to produce a single computer program. Many studies have shown the positive effects of PP including increased performance [10], increased retention into subsequent courses and increased student confidence [9]. There are many studies and guidelines about how to best implement PP and how to form successful partnerships. Salleh et al. performed a meta-review on the literature and found that the most important factor in forming pairs is to match students' skill levels [17], a result recently confirmed by Tafliovich et al. [19]

Peer Instruction (PI) has emerged as an effective way to engage students in class [8, 12]. In a PI class, students are assigned preparatory work to do before class, and then held accountable for that work via a short quiz. In class, students answer questions and solve problems in a tightly scripted manner: students first think individually and respond via a classroom response system (typically "clickers," or a low-tech solution like colored index cards) with their individual answer. Next they discuss the question or problem with a pre-assigned peer group of between 2 and 4 students, attempting to come to a shared belief about the correct answer, which they again enter via the classroom response system. Finally, the instructor shows the response distribution from the second vote and leads a class-wide discussion to help dispel any remaining questions or misconceptions. Positive results of PI in CS1 courses include halving fail rates across four different computer science courses [11].

2.2 Experience and Confidence in CS1

In the extensive literature on factors that affect success in CS1, prior experience with CS, programming or math stands out as one of the most reliable factors [6, 22, 2]. Perhaps not surprisingly, Tafliovich et al. find that not only do students with prior experience perform better, but students also believe (correctly) that prior experience is beneficial in an introductory CS course [19].

On the other hand, courses that are designed to mitigate effects of prior experience are often successful. Ventura and Ramamurthy found prior experience did not have a significant effect on performance in a CS1 course that took a design-centric, objects-first approach [21]. Holden and Weeden report that prior experiences differences went away by the end of a specailly designed introductory sequence [7]. Here we investigate whether this effect also holds in a course that has such positive retention outcomes.

Factors related to confidence have also been found to impact students' performance in CS1 courses. Rountree et al. found that intention to get an A was the single biggest factor of success in the CS1 course of the factors they studied [16]. Bergin et al. found that comfort level was one of the three biggest factors (along with pre-university math experience and gender) in predicting success [2]. Other work shows a relationship between prior programming experience and self-efficacy, which in turn leads to higher performance [14].

While many studies have focused on the relationship between gender and success in CS1, a few have also looked at the confidence and prior experience in the context of gender, sometimes with seemingly contradictory results. Taylor and Mounfield found that prior experiences were more broadly beneficial for women students than for men in college CS courses [20]. Bergin and Reilly found that comfort level had a higher correlation with performance for male students than for female students [2]. Meanwhile Berstein found that while comfort was significantly correlated with test performance for female students, for male students other factors were more important [3].

3. METHODOLOGY

We designed a study to investigate the four research questions listed in Section 1. We chose to investigate the effect of confidence within peer groups instead of the effect of prior experience because there is already ample evidence that matching prior experience levels in PP partnerships can be beneficial. We wanted to know: Does the same result hold for confidence levels? And how do confidence levels affect students' experience in their in-class PI groups?

3.1 Study Context

The context for our study was three sections of a CS1 course (course number CSE 8A) in a single term at the University of California, San Diego (UCSD) in the 2012-2013 academic year. This course is an introduction to programming and computer science intended for CS majors with little or no experience with CS and programming; UCSD has a separate introductory stream for majors who enter with significant prior experience (e.g., AP CS).

Each section met for two 75-minute class periods per week and had an associated weekly 50-minute required closed-lab session. Each class section was taught by a different instructor (the authors of this paper), but all used the same curriculum and course materials. Assessments were identical across the sections. A total of 471 students, roughly evenly divided across the three sections, were enrolled after the final drop date and are included in our study.

This course used the MediaComp curriculum, peer instruction during the 75-minute class periods, and pair programming during the closed lab sessions and out of class programming assignments. Students were assigned to both their in class PI groups, and their closed lab PP dyads, but they were free to choose their own partners for the weekly out-of-class programming assignments.

3.2 Measuring Experience and Confidence

We gathered students' confidence levels and prior experience levels on the second day of class via the following two questions:

1. How confident are you about your ability to do well in this course?
   (A) Not at all confident (B) Sort of confident/sort of not (C) Totally confident
2. How much CS experience had you had before you started this course?
   (A) Absolutely none (B) A little (C) A fair amount

Students responded to these questions using clickers. These questions were asked among a series of background questions. Students register their clicker devices, so the clicker responses recorded on the instructor's laptop are associated with individual students.

We used such a light-weight instrument because we were most curious about how students' *perceptions* of their confidence and experience might affect their performance and attitudes. In addition, we felt that any recommendations we made would be easiest to implement elsewhere if the process for determining prior experience and confidence was as simple and quick as possible.

3.3 Peer-Group Composition Experiment

To investigate whether or not grouping by confidence would affect students' feelings about and performance in the class, we designed a between-subjects experiment where we controlled the composition their PI groups and PP dyads based on their self-assessed confidence.

Our experiment had two independent variables each with two values: group-work context (PI groups and PP dyads) and group confidence composition (same confidence level vs. mixed confidence level), creating four composition groups: SS (same confidence for both PI and PP), MS (mixed confidence for PI and same confidence for PP), SM, and MM. We evenly distributed the students from the different confidence levels among the groups, but otherwise randomly assigned students to groups.

Initial PI groups were formed at the start second week of the term, and we shuffled the PI groups once during the term. Pair programming dyads were changed weekly.

Although we asked students to rate their confidence in three levels, in our experiment and our analysis we collapsed low- and mid-confidence into one level due to too few students in the lowest level to form same-confidence groupings. In our data analysis we confirmed the validity of this approach; in no case did the low confidence (A) and mid confidence (B) groups ever significantly differ in their performance or attitudes.

Of the 428 students who reported their confidence (see Table 1), eight students were missing data at the time of the composition group assignment. Another 14 students from group MS and 10 students from group MM were inadvertently assigned to wrong-composition groups in the week

Group (PI PP)	Low Conf.	High Conf.	Total
SS	57	46	103
SM	55	48	103
MS	54	40	94
MM	50	46	96

Table 1: The number of students in each participant group, divided by confidence level. Abbreviations are described in Section 3.3.

6 reshuffling. These 32 students are excluded from analysis based on composition group, but included in analysis of confidence and prior experience.

Our analysis includes only students who completed the course, though not necessarily with a passing grade. We believe if anything this might reduce the performance differences we see based on confidence and experience, because it is more likely that low performing students dropped the class rather than high performing students.

Our dependent variables were student attitudes toward their PI and PP experiences and their grades in the class. We measured student attitudes via an end-of-term survey. The complete set of questions pertaining to PI and PP groups is given in Table 5. For the PI segment, we asked students to think only of their first PI group experience. For the PP segment we asked students to think about all of their partners over the term. We used a 7-point level of agreement Likert scale for the PI segment (Very Strongly Disagree through Very Strongly Agree) and a 5-point frequency scale for the PP segment (Almost Never through Almost Always). In total, 406 students responded to the survey, including 349 students who were included in the grouping study (i.e., those included in Table 1).

We measured students' grades on all major course assessment categories, including:

Participation (Par.) and reading quiz (RQ): The number of days a student participated in class using clickers, and the average score on daily short quizzes based on their assigned reading. Par. and RQ each drop three scores.

Programming assignment (PA): The average of the nine programming assignments in the course.

Lab (Lab): The average of their scores on short assessments given at the end of each closed-lab session.

Midterm exam (ME): The average of the students' three highest (out of four) midterm exam grades.

Final exam (FE): The score on the final exam.

Overall (OA): The score that determines the students' letter grade in the course, calculated using the following weighted average formula: $OA = 0.05 * Par + 0.05 * RQ + 0.25 * PA + 0.2 * Lab + 0.2 * ME + 0.25 * FE$.

4. RESULTS

We began by exploring the make up of our class and the relationship between students' confidence and experience. We also broke these categories down by gender. The three sections of the class did not statistically differ in terms of composition of gender, confidence or experience level, nor did they differ on any assessment scores. In our analysis, we aggregate all three sections. Table 2 shows the total number of students in each confidence and experience level. The number in parentheses in each cell indicates the number in each

Conf. \ Exper.	None	Some	A lot	N/R	Total
Low	121 (34)	94 (37)	8 (4)	8 (2)	231 (77)
High	63 (10)	83 (21)	49 (10)	2 (1)	197 (42)
N/R	2 (1)	3 (0)	0 (0)		5 (1)
Total	186 (45)	180 (58)	57 (14)	10 (3)	433 (120)

Table 2: The number of students who reported having each confidence and experience level. Numbers in parentheses give the number of women in each group. "N/R" indicates the number of students who did not respond to the question (but did respond to the other question).

Assess.	Low Conf.	High Conf.	p val.
Par.	0.92	0.93	0.25
RQ	0.99	0.99	0.81
Lab	0.92	0.92	0.75
PA	0.95	0.95	0.61
ME	0.85	0.88	**< 0.01**
FE	0.77	0.79	0.09
OA	0.88	0.89	0.06

Table 3: Scores (out of 1.0) on each assessment by confidence. See Section 3.3 for abbreviations.

Assess.	No Exp.	Some Exp.	A lot Exp.	p val.
Par.	0.93	0.92	0.95	0.16
RQ	0.99	0.99	0.99	0.47
Lab	0.91	0.92	0.95	**< 0.01**
PA	0.95	0.96	0.95	0.45
ME	0.85	0.87	0.92	**< 0.001**
FE	0.75	0.79	0.84	**< 0.001**
OA	0.87	0.89	0.92	**< 0.001**

Table 4: Scores (out of 1.0) on each assessment by prior experience. See Section 3.3 for abbreviations.

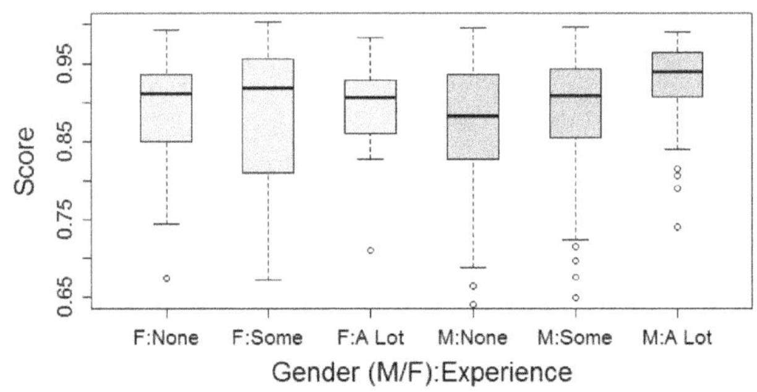

Figure 1: Overall score distribution for males (M) and females (F), with each gender grouped by experience level (None, Some, A Lot). All box graph shows medians, 1st and 3rd quartiles and 1.5*IQR.

category who were women. We found that confidence and experience are only weakly correlated ($r = 0.31, p < 0.001$). There is no significant difference between the prior experience of men and women ($p = 0.35$, Wilcoxon rank sum), but that men on average are significantly more confident than women coming in to the class ($p < 0.01$).

4.1 Confidence & Experience vs. Performance

We examined whether and how confidence and prior experience predict student performance in the course. We found that both confidence and prior experience correlate with higher performance, but only for some groups of students. Tables 3 and 4 show the scores for each assessment by confidence group and by experience level, respectively.

We ran t-tests and ANOVA tests on each grouping, respectively, and found statistically significant differences based on confidence level and prior experience for the midterm exams. We also found significant differences across experience levels for lab quiz scores, the final exam and the overall course average. Particularly for experience levels, the magnitude of these differences was non-trivial. For example, there is a 7 to 9 percentage point spread across experience levels for the exams, which translates to a 5 percentage point spread in the final course average (i.e. more than half a letter grade).

It appears that prior experience and confidence are still success factors even in a CS1 that incorporates many best-practices for retention. However, we find that these performance differences are not universal. Namely, when we split the students by gender, the women show no significant difference in performance by experience level or confidence. The men, on the other hand, show significant differences in performance by experience in their performance on lab quizzes, midterm exams, final exam and overall average (ANOVA, p < 0.01 in all cases). Figure 1 shows the overall course average of men and women, with each gender separated into groups by experience level. For example, in this figure the box labeled "F:Some" shows the distribution of overall average scores for females with some prior experience at the start of the class. A Tukey HSD post-hoc analysis reveals that there is a statistically significant six-point difference separating the overall average of the men with experience and the men with no experience, but no significant difference in performance between the groups of women. Distributions for the final exam and the midterm exam averages look similar, with an even larger spread between the men with a lot of experience and the men with no experience (11 percentage points on the final and 10 on the midterms).

Finally, we divided students by gender and found that for men confidence predicts their midterm exam performance, but for women it does not. A one-way ANOVA on the groups in Figure 2 reveals a significant effect ($p < 0.05$); a post-hoc analysis reveals that the only groups the differ significantly are high confidence men and low confidence men.

4.2 Confidence and Experience vs. Attitudes

. We also examined students' responses to our survey questions based on their confidence and experience. We found students' responses differed significantly by confidence, experience or gender for the statements labeled in Table 5, and the direction of the difference is as expected. For example, low confidence and low experience students felt more discouraged after talking to their group members than high confidence and very experienced students.

Finally we looked at the interaction between gender and experience in students' responses to these questions. As we found with students' grades, significant differences by experience given in Table 5 disappear or are greatly reduced

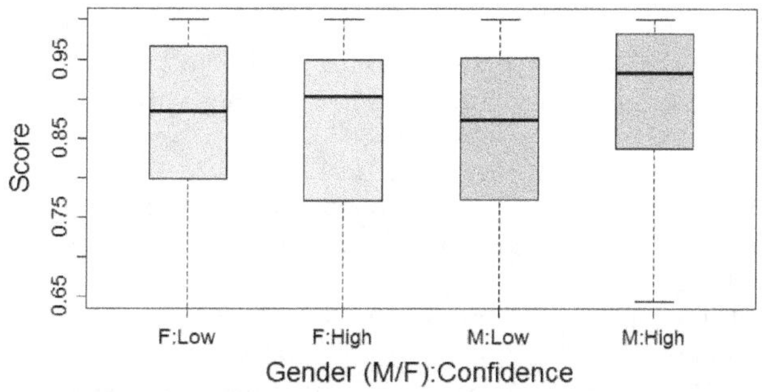

Figure 2: Midterm exam score distribution for men and women, by confidence level.

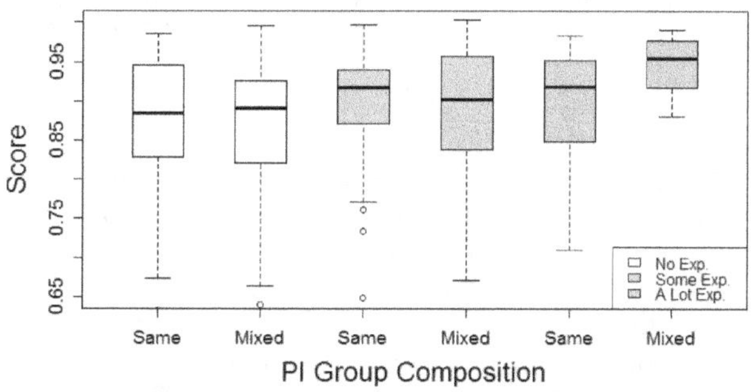

Figure 3: Overall performance by PI grouping (same or mixed) and Experience level.

when we focus only on women, while they are heightened when we focus on the male students.

4.3 Effects of Peer Group Composition

The results of our controlled grouping experiment help us address the third and fourth research questions from Section 1. In other words, how do students' own confidence levels affect others in a highly interactive class?

For the most part, we found that the different combinations of groupings predicted neither their performance in the class nor their attitudes about working with their peer groups. Using ANOVA, we found no significant difference in any of the assessments between the four treatment groups. We also found no significant differences between responses to any of the survey questions between the four treatment groups. Isolating students by gender and by confidence also revealed no significant differences between performance or survey response.

The only hint that peer group composition might affect students came when we divided students by prior experience level. Figure 3 shows the overall course scores for students in mixed confidence peer instruction groups (MS and MM, combined) vs. same confidence PI groups (SS and SM, combined), separated by experience level. Although we did not find significant post-hoc analysis differences between any of the pairs, the large (5 point) difference in median score between the high-experience mixed-confidence-group students and the high-experience same-confidence-group students suggests an area for future exploration.

Finally, we compared survey results across the PI groups. We found no significant differences for any combinations of the factors. It appears that the relative confidence of a student's peers does not affect the way that student feels about working closely with them in class or in the lab.

PI: Rate your level of agreement with the following:
I often felt that my group members knew more than me. (ce)
Talking to my group members often made me discouraged about my level of understanding. (ce)
My group members were respectful of everyone's ideas.
I felt comfortable voicing my thoughts within my group.
I felt I got along well with my fellow group members.
I generally felt that my fellow group members took my ideas and questions seriously.
I participated actively in my group during discussion.
I felt better about my level of understanding after talking to my group.
My group often came to a shared understanding at the end of the discussion.
I often felt that I knew more than my group members. (ceg)
In my group, everyone contributed to a joint discussion.
In general, I enjoyed interacting with my group.

PP: Rate how often each of the following was true:
My partner and I were balanced technically. (ce)
My partner was respectful to me. (g)
Working w/ my partner helped my learning. (cg)
I was stronger technically than my partner. (ce)
I felt comfortable expressing doubts or asking my partner questions.
My partner and I both contributed meaningfully to completing the lab.
I felt good about my understanding at the end of lab. (ce)
My partner was supportive of my learning.
My partner made me feel like I didn't know what I was doing.
I contributed to my partner's learning. (c)
My partner and I didn't really talk much during lab.
I felt lost at the end of lab. (c)
My partner was usually stronger technically than I am. (ce)
I enjoyed working with my partner.

Table 5: End-of-course survey questions. Bold statements were those where students' responses differed by (c)onfidence, (e)xperience, or (g)ender.

5. DISCUSSION AND FUTURE WORK

Overall, the peer-based pedagogical approaches used in this CS1 course appear to be working. The differences reported in Table 5 reflect differences that are not surprising given students' confidence levels and prior experiences. In fact, Table 5 is notable for the questions for which there is *not* a difference based on experience level or confidence. Low confidence and low-experience students feel equally respected and comfortable, and report participating just as actively and enjoying the group work just as much as their high-confidence, high-experience peers.

Differences in performance based on prior experience is consistent with previous findings, indicating that as much as these new pedagogies and curricula have helped with retention, they have not yet leveled the playing field based on prior experience. However, the fact that this difference is notable only for men raises some interesting questions. Is the fact that women report lower confidence levels despite equal levels of prior experience explained by the notion that women have lower confidence levels in general, or do women perhaps have lower-quality prior experiences that are not as beneficial to them in this CS1? Another hypothesis to test in future work is that being in a teacher role is exceptionally beneficial for learning, and perhaps experienced, high-confidence students are more likely to assert themselves in that role. If this is the case, inquiry is needed into how can we encourage experienced, able students with less confidence—in particular women, who are less likely to be confident—to assume that role.

A common anecdote in CS1 tells of a group of lower-confidence, less-experienced students being intimidated by a highly confident student who consistently shouts out irrelevant technical jargon. It seems that this dynamic could play out with dire consequences in student peer groups if low-confidence students were placed with high-confidence students. However, our findings show that this does not seem to be the case, or at least that the anecdote does not play out in a significant way. Our data does not support the use of confidence as a basis for group assignment, since students in any mixture of confidence level seem to have the same attitudes and performance. This is potentially encouraging for faculty who worry about the arduous and meticulous effort required to design group assignments based on demographic criteria, because it suggests that perhaps it is sufficient to allow students to group themselves. Further study is needed on use of other variables such as experience or pretest results, which may yield factors that are valuable for group assignments. In addition, further study is needed to investigate whether the effect of confidence may in fact be important, but only for students who come into the class believing they already have experience.

Finally, because prior experience confers benefits that are not entirely erased by even a pedagogically "state of the art" CS1 classroom, efforts to level the pre-college CS playing field become even more critical. Bridge programs and specially designed introductory sequences that help less experienced students catch up are important, but until access to K-12 CS eduction is equalized, students with no experience will continue to lag behind in college despite our best (and successful) efforts to retain them in a CS major.

6. CONCLUSION

CS1 education has come a long way. As a community we are retaining more students, and a more diverse group of students, than we were 10 years ago. But the work presented here shows that while some problems appear to be solved, some challenges and questions remain. Low-confidence students are more likely to feel frustrated by group work than those with high confidence, and these feelings do not seem to be affected by the confidence levels of those around them. Furthermore, experience is still a factor in (male) students' performance. MediaComp, pair programming and peer instruction are clearly beneficial to students overall; now we must work to refine these techniques (and potentially add others) to make them as beneficial as they can be for each individual student.

7. REFERENCES

[1] C. Alvarado and Z. Dodds. Women in CS: An evaluation of three promising practices. In *Proc. SIGCSE '10*, 2010.

[2] S. Bergin and R. Reilly. Programming: factors that influence success. *SIGCSE Bull.*, 37(1), Feb. 2005.

[3] D. R. Bernstein. Comfort and experience with computing: are they the same for women and men? *SIGCSE Bull.*, 23(3), Sept. 1991.

[4] P. Byrne and G. Lyons. The effect of student attributes on success in programming. *SIGCSE Bull.*, 33(3), June 2001.

[5] M. Guzdial. Exploring hypotheses about media computation. In *Proc. of ICER '13*. ACM, 2013.

[6] D. Hagan and S. Markham. Does it help to have some programming experience before beginning a computing degree program? *SIGCSE Bull.*, 32(3), July 2000.

[7] E. Holden and E. Weeden. The experience factor in early programming education. In *Proc. of CITC5 '04*. ACM, 2004.

[8] E. Mazur. *Peer Instruction: A User's Manual.* Addison-Wesley, 1996.

[9] C. McDowell and et al. Pair programming improves student retention, confidence, and program quality. *Commun. ACM*, 49(8), Aug. 2006.

[10] N. Nagappan and et al. Improving the CS1 experience with pair programming. *SIGCSE Bull.*, 35(1), 2003.

[11] L. Porter, C. Bailey Lee, and B. Simon. Halving fail rates using peer instruction: a study of four computer science courses. In *Proc. of SIGCSE '13*, 2013.

[12] L. Porter and et al. Experience report: a multi-classroom report on the value of peer instruction. In *Proc. of ITiCSE '11*, 2011.

[13] L. Porter and B. Simon. Retaining nearly one-third more majors with a trio of instructional best practices in CS1. In *Proc. of SIGCSE '13*, 2013.

[14] V. Ramalingam, D. LaBelle, and S. Wiedenbeck. Self-efficacy and mental models in learning to program. *SIGCSE Bull.*, 36(3), June 2004.

[15] L. Rich, H. Perry, and M. Guzdial. A CS1 course designed to address interests of women. *SIGCSE Bull.*, 36(1), 2004.

[16] N. Rountree, J. Rountree, and A. Robins. Predictors of success and failure in a CS1 course. *SIGCSE Bull.*, 34(4), Dec. 2002.

[17] N. Salleh, E. Mendes, and J. C. Grundy. Empirical studies of pair programming for CS/SE teaching in higher education: A systematic literature review. *IEEE Trans. on Software Engineering*, 37(4), 2011.

[18] Simon et al. Predictors of success in a first programming course. In *Proc. of ACE '06*. Australian Computer Society, Inc., 2006.

[19] A. Tafliovich, J. Campbell, and A. Petersen. A student perspective on prior experience in CS1. In *Proc. of SIGCSE '13*. ACM, 2013.

[20] H. G. Taylor and L. C. Mounfield. Exploration of the relationship between prior computing experience and gender on success in college computer science. *Journal of Educational Computing Research*, 11(4), 1994.

[21] P. Ventura and B. Ramamurthy. Wanted: CS1 students. no experience required. *SIGCSE Bull.*, 36(1), Mar. 2004.

[22] B. C. Wilson and S. Shrock. Contributing to success in an introductory computer science course: a study of twelve factors. *SIGCSE Bull.*, 33(1), Feb. 2001.

Social Effects of Pair Programming Mitigate Impact of Bounded Rationality

Zhen Li and Eileen Kraemer
Computer Science Department
The University of Georgia
Athens, GA 30606
1-706-542-5745
{janeli, eileen}@uga.edu

ABSTRACT

We conducted an observational case study of pair programmers and solo programmers in a challenging, time-limited programming exam in a split level course at the University of Georgia during the spring semester of 2013. Although we observed no significant difference in performance on the exam, we found that pair programming promoted the early application of critical thinking in the process of solving a challenging programming task. Specifically, the pair programmers were found to conduct more critical thinking and to ask important questions in the program design phase while solo programmers postponed the same required thinking activity and associated questions until the testing and debugging phase. We attribute the solo programmer's failure to delve into the difficult questions to the phenomenon of "bounded rationality" and propose that the social effects of pair programming serve to mitigate this phenomenon with the result that the pair programmers' behaviors better align with good software engineering practices and promote the acquisition of expertise.

Categories and Subject Descriptors

K.3.2 [**Computer and Information Science Education**] *Computer Science Education*

General Terms

Human Factors

Keywords

Pair programming, software engineering, case study

1. INTRODUCTION

Since pair programming was first identified and formally defined as "a practice in which two programmers work collaboratively at one computer on the same design, algorithm, code, or test" [27], its benefits and drawbacks in industrial settings have been widely discussed via both anecdotes [26] and controlled experiments [1] [8]. At the same time, the effectiveness of pair programming in academic settings has been widely reported. Pair programming has been found to

1) help improve the retention rate and course pass rates in introductory computer science courses [3] [6] [10] [11] [12] [15] [14] [16] [29]

2) contribute to greater persistence in computer science related majors [13] [29]

3) improve the quality of programs, programmers' confidence and enjoyment in their work [6] [11] [12] [28] [29]

4) help students with lower SAT scores to gain better individual programming abilities than similar students who do not engage in pair programming [2] [3]

5) be beneficial for women because it addresses factors that potentially limit their participation in CS [21].

However, few studies have revealed the reasons that pair programming is beneficial or have delineated the situations in which it is beneficial. A study by Arisholm, et al. [1] indicates that pair programming only helps in tasks that are complex relative to the programmers' expertise, which explains the consistently observed effectiveness of pair programming in academic settings, where the curriculum is purposefully designed so that students are exposed to progressively more complex programming tasks. However, this beneficial effect is not consistent in industrial settings, where the relationship between complexity of programming tasks and programmers' expertise is more variable. Bryant, et al. [4] explains the effectiveness of pair programming as stemming from the two programmers working at different levels of abstraction (the driver working at a highly detailed level while the navigator thinks at a more abstract level) and the communication of intermediate issues helps formulate effective design and programming. However, Chong, et al. [7] indicates that pair programmers collaboratively work through one facet of the problem a time at the same levels of abstraction. Yet another study [5] argues that the level of collaboration varies according to the task.

Our case study provides clues about how pair programming changes students' behavior and thought processes during a challenging programming task, and explains to some extent the effectiveness of pair programming in computer science education. Our study reinforces that pair programming is a collaborative process during which two programmers work on the same facet of a problem at the same level of abstraction, but that the two programmers contribute different information, according to their roles. Most importantly, our study indicates that this collaborative

SIGCSE'14, March 5–8, 2014, Atlanta, Georgia, USA.

http://dx.doi.org/10.1145/2538862.2538968

process of problem solving promotes early engagement in the software design phase of program development. The software design phase requires intensive cognitive activities to elicit requirements and organize components into an architecture that meets and balances design requirements of various dimensions. Such early engagement causes pair programmers to ask questions critical to the successful design of the final system much earlier than do solo programmers. We also observed that pair programmers ask "smarter" questions that are critical to the design of the system rather than ask questions about elements that are already clearly stated in the specification.

We believe the students in our study encountered a situation common in industrial and academic settings: somewhat unclear specification/requirements, multiple design considerations (efficiency and ease of implementation), and time pressures. Such vagueness inherently exists in the complex (ill-structured [23]) programming problems faced by computer science students. Overcoming the confusion and vagueness in the process of problem solving is not only critical to the quality of the final product but learning how to do this is also essential to the development of expertise and the success of pedagogy. Our study provides a new perspective on the use of pair programming in promoting the training of students as they engage in such cognitively intensive tasks.

2. BACKGROUND

Pair programming is an element of eXtreme programming that has been widely recognized in industry environments to improve productivity and programmer satisfaction [1]. Recognition of the benefits has also generated substantial interest in applying pair programming to computer science education. The advantages of adopting pair programming as a pedagogical approach have been widely researched in several empirical studies discussed below.

In 1999, Williams, et al. [11] carried out a study regarding the benefits of pair programming in an advanced undergraduate level course at the University of Utah.

Although pair programmers were required to finish more assignments in this study, the result of the study showed that they were more willing to work in pairs in the future. In addition, other findings regarding assignment quality, exam scores, overall pass rate and programmers' enjoyment were confirmed.

McDowell, et al. [6] at UCSC studied an introductory level CS1 course offered over four sections during the 2000-2001 academic year. In three of the four sections, students were required to complete all assignments using pair programming techniques.

Another study [8] at UCSC was conducted over three advanced computer science courses. Pairs were assigned and changed twice in the first two courses. In the third course, students had the option to work in pairs for each programming assignment and in most cases when students paired for more than one assignment they continued to work with the same partner.

The major findings of these two studies showed that pair programming improved course completion rates, persistence in computer science related majors, and the quality of students' products and students' programming abilities. This trend was particularly apparent in the retention of female computer science students who participated in pair programming.

Williams, et al. [9] at NCSU carried out studies on pair programming in a CS1 course over two semesters during the 2001-2002 academic year. In each semester, two nearly-identical sections of the course were offered, with the main difference being that one of the sections involved a paired closed lab session and the other section involved a solo closed lab session. The students were paired randomly and the pairs were re-assigned every two to three weeks. Besides the closed lab session, students also had the option to work in pairs on other programming projects assigned outside the lab session.

In contrast to previous studies, no significant differences were found between the pair and solo sections on exam scores but the benefits of pair programming on retention rates and the quality of students' products remained. Also, students in this study were found to have a more positive attitude toward working in collaborative environments, which is perceived as a long-term beneficial factor for their future professional life.

During 2004-2005, Mendes, et al. [2] [3] studied the effects of pair programming in a CS2 course in which software development and design are taught in the context of UML and Java OO.

One section of the course employed pair programming in the closed lab session while the other section did not. In the pair programming section, the students were randomly paired and the pair assignment changed about three times during the course.

This study showed that students in the pair programming section not only produced higher quality code, but also used less time and experienced more enjoyment during the procedure and were more confident about their work.

Braught, et al. [12] [4] studied pair programming in an introductory CS1 course during the academic years 2005-2007. In each year, one section adopted pair programming on open laboratory assignments while the other did not.

Students were initially randomly assigned into pairs. Later, students with similar assignment scores were paired. This re-assignment occurred approximately three times during the course.

This study explicitly evaluates students' acquisition of programming ability through pair versus solo programming. The authors found that students with lower SAT scores were able to achieve higher lab practica (individual programming tests in an examination environment) scores through the pair programming experience. Also, the benefit of pair programming in improving enjoyment level, confidence level and course completion rate was reinforced.

The wide array of findings--some which conflict--of prior work reinforces the notion that there is still much to be explored and learned about in incorporating pair programming principles in the classroom. Our study seeks to investigate the micro-level effects of pair programming, the effects on shifting programmer's behavior and cognitive procedures, in a semi-realistic environment, namely a time-limited programming-based exam.

3. CASE STUDY SETTINGS

We conducted our study in the context of a split-level course (a mix of upper-division undergraduates and graduate students) focused on the comprehension and implementation of concurrent programs. Students in this course learned to implement programs for a series of classical concurrency scenarios (bounded-buffer, dining philosophers, readers and writers, sleeping barbers) using three different approaches to concurrency: Java Threads, Scala Actors and Python Coroutines.

An observational study was performed during a programming-based final exam. In this exam, students were required to implement a single-lane bridge problem using their choice of implementation approach. The single-lane bridge problem simulates a bridge system in which cars from two directions use the single-lane of the bridge but may proceed from only one direction at a time. The main concern of the system was to guarantee that every car had a chance to use the bridge and that no cars crashed on the bridge (as a result of attempting to use both directions simultaneously). To simplify this problem, we defined and stated in the specification that the cars moving from left to right were red cars and those moving from right to left were blue cars. To avoid a safety violation, only one kind of car was allowed to be on the bridge at a time. Cars exit the bridge in the order in which they enter and the leading car may exit the bridge at any time. To guarantee fairness, the differences between the numbers of cars of each color that have used the bridge may not exceed a user input value, specified as *waitDiff* in the program requirement document. Students were given a code skeleton that included a full implementation of the utility and program entry codes as well as the declarations of some classes and key methods invoked by utility and program entry codes. Students were required to complete the code to guarantee the satisfaction of the above stated safety and fairness requirements and to program the system to export the status of the bridge (color and number of cars that have entered the bridge thus far and of cars currently on the bridge) according to a user input frequency, specified as *checkFreq* in the program requirement document.

The course had 11 students registered for letter-grade credit and 1 student auditing. These 12 students voluntarily formed 4 pairs (8 students) and 4 solos to work on the final exam. The groups were roughly equivalent based on prior performance in the class, with one solo and one pair classified as "strong", two solos and two pairs classified as "intermediate" and one solo and one pair classified as "novice". We think that after working closely with each other in such a small class that involved formal and informal discussions and permitted pair programming collaborations on various projects during the semester, all students were familiar with one another's strengths and weaknesses in programming expertise.

During the exam, students were allowed to access information online, from books and notes, and their previously written code. However, students were not allowed to phone, text or email for assistance. After students reported to the exam venue, we first distributed the program specifications and emphasized the exam regulations. Then we guided pair programmers to a separate working location to prevent their discussions from interrupting the concentration of the solo programmers. We rotated between the two exam locations frequently to answer questions and take notes on students' activities during the three-hour examination period.

4. RESULTS AND ANALYSIS

4.1 Comparison of Pair and Solo Behaviors

Students were observed and experimenter's notes were taken based on the activities students were engaged in and the timing of those activities during the 3-hour test period. Details of the observation notes may be seen in Table 1 and Table 2. For the convenience of discussion, we identify pair groups as P1 – P4 and the solos as S1 – S4. The exam ran from 12:00 pm to 3:00 pm. The first 20 minutes or so of the exam period were devoted to the distribution of materials, discussion of the 'ground rules', and getting students situated in the appropriate locations for their groups, with the actual work period beginning around 12:20. Table 1 contains experimenter's notes on the pair programming groups and Table 2 contains experimenter's notes on the solo programmers.

Table 1 Notes on Pair Programming Activity

Time	Pair's Activity
12:25	P2, P3, and P4 discuss specification P1 has one partner start coding and the other skim through specification
12:35	P1, P3, and P4 elicit specification P2 asks for clarification of *checkFreq* and *waitDiff*[1]
12:45	P1, P2, and P4 start coding P3 discusses program architecture
12:55	P1, P2, and P4 keep coding P3 starts writing code on paper P2 finds a typo[3] in the specification one partner of P4 checks online API document
1:15	P1-P4 all coding drivers perform simply as coders navigators perform as information providers (API, sample code), document finders, code checkers (for typo), "teddy bears", activity loggers and reminders as well as designers
1:25	P1 starts testing and code modification P2 asks for clarification of "using bridge"[4] P2 - P4 still coding
1:30	P1, P2 are in testing and code modification P3, P4 still coding
1:35	P1, P2 are in testing and code modification P2 asks about "tailing" issue of status check[5] (whether status check should always appear at the very end regardless of previous number of events) P4 asks for clarification of *waitDiff*[1] P3 starts coding but at the same time is still discussing other possible system organizations/patterns
1:45	P4 performs simulated execution for debugging P2 checks API calls on peek, push and pull P1 discusses and analyzes cause of a bug
1:55	P2 reaches a consistent version and checks boundary cases
2:00	P2 tests on different inputs and final check specification P4 tests on different inputs and encounters a bug P3 still coding
2:15	P2 asks whether printed car id should be in order of the sequence of arrival at bridge, then leaves P1, P4 debug and change code P3 is still coding
2:20	P4 checks fairness policy P1's navigator explains "*checkFreq*" to driver P3 is still coding
2:30	P3 is reasoning about the function and use of *checkFreq* P4 encounters stackOverFlow exception and searches on how to change maxPoolSize for Scala
2:45	P4 asks whether a random travel time on bridge is expected[2]

As seen from recorded activity notes shown in Table 1, three of the four pairs did not start actual coding until 25 minutes into the work period (45 minutes after the exam started). During this time, both partners of all pairs worked together to elicit specification requirements and sketch out the plan of implementation. In contrast, as seen in Table 2, all four solo programmers began to code just five minutes into the work period. In the next hour or so, the solo programmers worked back and forth between coding and reading the specifications and a reasonable interpretation of their activities is that the solo programmers did not have a full plan for the implementation of every requirement in the specification before starting to code. Rather, the solo programmers took the strategy of implementing an initial version and then augmenting the code by threading in new specifications as they continued to implement. On the other hand, the pair programmers had a more comprehensive discussion of each element of the requirements in the specification before starting to code.

Table 2 Notes on Solo Programming Activity

Time	Solo's Activity
12:25	4 solos all start coding
12:35	4 solos work back and forth between codes and specifications
12:45	S2 and S3 browse sample codes (available on course web page) for other concurrent system
12:55	S2, S3 ask whether a random travel time on bridge is expected[2] S4 asks for clarification of the method finish() in main
1:15	solos work with requirements, codes, outputs and online resources (API and sample codes)
1:25	S2-S4 are in testing and code modification S1 still coding
1:30	4 solos are in testing and code modification
1:35	
1:45	S2 stuck on a runtime issue S3 asks for clarification of information printed in status check[6] (which is clearly stated in specification) S1 searches previous code files (students are allowed to use any resource except phone and txt)
1:55	
2:00	S1 finishes and leaves
2:15	S2 asks whether waiting is counted as an event[7] (which is clearly stated in specification) S3, S4 are still debugging
2:20	S3 final check specification, asks for clarification of *checkFreq*[1]
2:30	S3 asks for clarification of "using a bridge"
2:45	S3 final checks specification, found the typo[3], ask about "tailing" issue of status check[5]

Table 3 contains a summary of the times at which questions were posed to the instructor. These questions are coded as "critical", "moderate" and "mild" based on their impact on the correct implementation of the program. As seen in Table 3, around 12:35, the partners of P2 asked for clarification of the *checkFreq* and *waitDiff* variables defined in the code skeleton, which was critical to the implementation of the simulation system. In contrast, questions regarding these two variables were not raised by solo programmers until 2:20. We suspect that all the programmers faced questions about these critical components in the code skeleton; however, having more comprehensive discussions before coding likely caused the pair programmers to think more carefully about implementation details of these components at a much earlier stage.

We postulate that during this design period, the social factors of pair programming were responsible for promoting early engagement in activities that require heavy cognition since the partners had to convince one another of both the general design and specific details to avoid the potential cost of later strategic changes. Therefore, fewer subjective assumptions were made and more deliberation was carried out.

Once the solo programmers started coding, it took slightly more time for them to enter the testing and debugging stages. We think that two factors made it easier for pair programmers to go through the coding period. One factor is that they had a better understanding and preparation of what and how to implement as a result of their comprehensive discussion before coding. The other factor is that, when two partners together work through various implementation issues, one (the "driver") may fully focus on the current implementation details while the other (the "navigator") takes on multiple other roles. The navigator not only searches and provides information from all sources (API, online guides, sample code, etc.), but also checks for typos and missing semicolons as a "human instant compiler". Moreover, the navigator serves as a "teddy bear" (someone for the driver to talk to) for the driver to clarify current micro-level algorithm details, keeps a to-do list and reminds the driver of previous design decisions if the driver deviates from the plan. Therefore, the "power of two minds" and the social pressure to keep things in order help to further reduce the effort in implementation.

After starting to test and debug, pair programmers seldom asked any more questions but followed their settled plan of checking different cases. In contrast, it was during the testing and debugging phase that the solo programmers most actively asked questions, including those identified as critical. We suspect that solo programmers only actively engaged in cognitively intensive procedures when they encountered bugs and exceptions during the later stages of development. It is only at this time that they started to consider and challenge the series of issues and design decisions they had earlier made swiftly as they started coding. It is also worth noting that although solo programmers asked more questions than pair programmers, 2 out of the 6 questions they asked were already clearly stated in the specification.

4.2 Implications to Engineering and Pedagogy

Our observation of both pair and solo students' activities and behaviors in completing the programming task of the final exam indicates that software programming is a complex problem solving process that requires significant mental operations at some point in the process. Pressman points out that Polya's description of the essence of problem solving [17] -- 1) understand the problem, 2) plan a solution, 3) carry out the plan, and 4) examine the result for accuracy – is also the "essence of software engineering practice" [18]. Good software engineering thus includes a series of actions such as iterative consideration of known/unknown conditions, frequent checks of implementation conformity with requirements, and active explorations into and applications of similar but solved problems and sub-problems.

In practice, software engineers are usually guided to fulfill these activities by asking themselves questions such as what data/functionality are available or does the solution satisfy the

Table 3 Comparison of the time questions being asked by pair and solo programmers

No.	Question	Comment	Pair	Solo
1	clarification of *checkFreq* and *waitDiff*	**critical**	**12:35**	**2:20**
2	random travel time	mild	2:45	12:55
3	typo in specification	**critical**	**12:55**	**2:45**
4	clarification of "using bridge"	**critical**	**1:25**	**2:30**
5	tailing issue of status check	moderate	1:35	2:45
6	information in status check	stated in specification		1:45
7	whether waiting is counted as an event	stated in specification		2:15

safety requirements or how can a sub-problem be defined. However, self-questioning and answering does not guarantee answers or their quality. According to the behavioral theory of bounded rationality [22], human beings usually lack the ability and resources to make optimal decisions but instead apply their rationality only after having greatly simplified the available choices. As we teach programming with concurrency in the course, we often see students make such simplifications in the design of concurrent systems by overlooking synchronization mechanisms or inter-thread communications and simply hoping to build a working system first and then make extensions later. Such simplification is also observed in the debugging of concurrent systems, where Fleming found that programmers are unwilling to explore all the possibilities but instead avoid the more complex possibilities (reasoning about concurrency in this case) and instead pursue a small number of hypotheses and fail to consider the more complex competitors [9].

The contrasting behaviors of the pair and solo programmers in our study indicate that pair programming may be a natural way for programmers to overcome the shortcomings induced by bounded rationality and therefore better fulfill good software engineering practices. This is achieved through two major characteristics of pair programming, a communication-based software development approach and the expanded cognitive ability and resources provided by two minds working on the same problem. The communication-based development approach assists the team to better question themselves by challenging one another's assumptions. When agreement cannot be reached among group members, external inputs are requested for resolving conflicts. We think this is the reason that pair programmers ask most of the critical design questions much earlier than do solo programmers and invest much more time in establishing a vision for the programming task rather than rushing to start coding. On the contrary, because their assumptions and decisions are not challenged, solo programmers swiftly commit simplifications without the necessary deliberation on design decisions. They pay for this in the later testing and debugging phase. Only when they encounter the challenges from compilation and test results do they begin to re-invest time and effort to explore the previously simplified and omitted design alternatives and turn to external resources (instructor) for further information. As a result, the critical questions were all raised by solo programmers at a much later time in the exam period, during testing and debugging.

We believe that pair programming provides a natural environment for the programmers involved to follow several of the general principles of software engineering [18], including 1) keep it simple, 2) maintain a vision, 3) produce for others to consume and 4) think hard, through its communication-based development process and expanded ability and resources integrating two programmers' experience.

From the pedagogical perspective, we think students better gain programming expertise after engaging in hard problem solving procedures in pairs. Most programming problems do not have only one correct solution. Instead, many design dimensions need to be considered and trade-offs must be made. When considering the variety of human beings involved in this procedure with their various formal experiences and differing familiarity with techniques that exist for programmers, the possible solution space is exponentially expanded. As a learner, the learning procedure is exactly the process of linking various elements of prior knowledge, transforming them and coming up with new patterns that solve the new challenge through a series of mental processes of recognition, recall, analysis, reflection, application, creation, comprehension and evaluation. We postulate that with an open-ended problem to solve, it is better for the learners to engage in active and social learning processes as the new knowledge (the final solution and an effective approach to the solution) is constructed through human agents rather than existing and awaiting discovery according to the constructivist perspective of education [24]. Thus, we suspect pair programming helps more naturally in developing students' abilities in solving open-ended problems of software design, development procedures and quality assurance approaches. In addition, success in their software engineering tasks elevates students' confidence and motivation to further learning, which in turn results in better pedagogical effects.

5. CONCLUSIONS AND FUTURE WORK

We report on an observational study of pair programmers and solo programmers engaged in a time-restricted programming task. The results of the study re-confirm the social effects of pair programming and further indicate that such social effects promote the occurrence of hard cognitive activities during an earlier stage of software development, which helps pair programmers to finish complex problem solving tasks more effectively and promotes student learning about programming. Also, our observational study reconfirms the "power of two minds", which conforms to the distributed cognition theory that knowledge is created through interaction among individuals. We further suspect the accumulation and development of expertise is better achieved through social interactions in the context of solving a complex problem.

Our work is an initial effort to investigate if and how pair programming changes students' programming behavior and advances them in acquiring expertise. More empirical evidence is needed and the investigation may also be extended to industrial settings.

Other work has revealed the power of pair programming in quantitative measurable success of students. Here, we have begun to probe an underlying change in the thinking and behavior patterns of pair programmers, which in turn likely affects their learning capabilities and outcomes, suggesting that educators and teaching practitioners may further benefit from pair programming in pedagogy and learning.

6. REFERENCES

[1] E Arisholm, H Gallis, T Dyba, and D I Sjoberg, "Evaluating Pair Programming with Respect to System Complexity and Programmer Expertise," *Software Engineering, IEEE Transactions on*, vol. 33, pp. 65-86, 2007.

[2] Grant Braught, L. M. Eby, and Tim Wahls, "The effects of pair-programming on individual programming skill," *SIGCSE Bull.*, vol. 40, pp. 200--204, mar 2008.

[3] Grant Braught, Tim Wahls, and L. M. Eby, "The Case for Pair Programming in the Computer Science Classroom," *Trans. Comput. Educ.*, vol. 11, pp. 2:1--2:21, feb 2011.

[4] Sallyann Bryant, Pablo Romero, and Benedict D. Boulay, "Pair programming and the mysterious role of the navigator," *International Journal of Human-Computer Studies*, vol. 66, pp. 519 - 529, 2008.

[5] Sallyann Bryant, Pablo Romero, and Benedict Boulay, "The Collaborative Nature of Pair Programming," vol. 4044, pp. 53-64, 2006.

[6] Jeffrey C. Carver, Lisa Henderson, Lulu He, Julia Hodges, and Donna Reese, "Increased Retention of Early Computer Science and Software Engineering Students Using Pair Programming," *Software Engineering Education and Training, Conference on*, vol. 0, pp. 115-122, 2007.

[7] Jan Chong and Tom Hurlbutt, "The Social Dynamics of Pair Programming," , 2007, pp. 354--363.

[8] Alistair Cockburn and Laurie Williams, "Extreme programming examined," pp. 223--243, 2001.

[9] Scott D Fleming, "Successful Strategies for Debugging Concurrent Software: An Empirical Investigation," phdthesis 2009.

[10] Brian Hanks, Charlie McDowell, David Draper, and Milovan Krnjajic, "Program quality with pair programming in CS1," *SIGCSE Bull.*, vol. 36, pp. 176--180, jun 2004.

[11] Charlie McDowell, Brian Hanks, and Linda Werner, "Experimenting with pair programming in the classroom," *SIGCSE Bull.*, vol. 35, pp. 60--64, jun 2003.

[12] Charlie McDowell, Linda Werner, Heather.E Bullock, and Julian Fernald, "Pair programming improves student retention, confidence, and program quality," *Commun. ACM*, vol. 49, pp. 90--95, aug 2006.

[13] Charlie McDowell, Linda Werner, Heather E Bullock, and Julian Fernald, "The impact of pair programming on student performance, perception and persistence," in *Proceedings of the 25th International Conference on Software Engineering*, Washington, DC, USA, 2003, pp. 602--607.

[14] Emilia Mendes, Lubna Al-Fakhri, and Andrew Luxton-Reilly, "A replicated experiment of pair-programming in a 2nd-year software development and design computer science course," *SIGCSE Bull.*, vol. 38, pp. 108--112, jun 2006.

[15] Emilia Mendes, Lubna B Al-Fakhri, and Andrew Luxton-Reilly, "Investigating pair-programming in a 2nd-year software development and design computer science course," *SIGCSE Bull.*, vol. 37, pp. 296--300, jun 2005.

[16] Nachiappan Nagappan et al., "Improving the CS1 experience with pair programming," *SIGCSE Bull.*, vol. 35, pp. 359--362, jan 2003.

[17] George Polya, *How to Solve It: A New Aspect of Mathematical Method*, Expanded Princeton Science Library Edition ed.: Princeton University Press, 2004.

[18] Roger S. Pressman, *Software Engineering: A Practitioner's Approach -- seventh edition.*: McGraw-Hill Companies, Inc, 2010.

[19] David Preston, "Using collaborative learning research to enhance pair programming pedagogy," *SIGITE Newsl.*, vol. 3, pp. 16--21, jan 2006.

[20] N. Salleh, E. Mendes, and John Grundy, "Empirical Studies of Pair Programming for CS/SE Teaching in Higher Education: A Systematic Literature Review," *IEEE Transactions on Software Engineering*, vol. 37, no. 4, pp. 509 -- 525, July-Aug 2011.

[21] Linda J. Sax, "Examining the Underrepresentation of Women in STEM Fields: Early Findings from the Field of Computer Science," *CSW Update Newsletter*, p. 6, Apr. 2012. http://www.escholarship.org/uc/item/84j9s1v1

[22] Herbert A Simon, "A Behavioral Model of Rational Choice," *The Quarterly Journal of Economics*, vol. 69, pp. 99-118, 1955.

[23] Herbert A. Simon, "The Structure of Ill Structured Problems," *Artif. Intell.*, pp. 181-201, 1973.

[24] L. S. Vygotskii and Michael Cole, *Mind in society : the development of higher psychological processes.*: Harvard University Press, 1978.

[25] Laurie Williams, "Integrating Pair Programming into a Software Development Process," in *CSEET '01 Proceedings of the 14th Conference on Software Engineering Education and Training*, Charlotte, NC, 2001, pp. 27--.

[26] Laurie A. Williams and Robert R. Kessler, "All I really need to know about pair programming I learned in kindergarten," *Commun. ACM*, vol. 43, pp. 108--114, may 2000.

[27] Laurie Williams and Robert R. Kessler, *Pair Programming Illuminated.*: Addison-Wesley Publishing Co., Inc., 2002.

[28] Laurie Williams, Robert R. Kessler, Ward Cunningham, and Ron Jeffries, "Strengthening the Case for Pair Programming," *IEEE Softw.*, vol. 17, pp. 19--25, jul 2000.

Improving Software Engineering Education through an Empirical Approach: Lessons Learned from Capstone Teaching Experiences

Andres Neyem
Computer Science Department
Pontificia Universidad Católica de Chile
Santiago, Chile
aneyem@ing.puc.cl

Jose I. Benedetto
Computer Science Department
Pontificia Universidad Católica de Chile
Santiago, Chile
jibenede@uc.cl

Andres F. Chacon
Computer Science Department
Pontificia Universidad Católica de Chile
Santiago, Chile
afchacon@uc.cl

ABSTRACT

Software Engineering is an important area within industry and academia. Empirical software engineering has grown in importance in the software engineering research and education community. This means that it has become very relevant to include empirical studies or practices into computer science and software engineering curricula. This paper shows the results of applying an empirical approach to teaching software engineering through real-life projects. The computer science capstone experience is designed to bridge the gap from university expectations to those of industry.

Categories and Subject Descriptors

K.3.2 [**Computer and Information Science Education**]: Computer and Information Science Education; D.2.9 [**Software Engineering**]: Management

General Terms

Management, Design, Human Factors

Keywords

Software Engineering, Requirements, Education, Experiential Learning, Capstone.

1. INTRODUCTION

Software Engineering is a very important area in academia and also within industry. Students who have completed their studies in Computer Science (CS), Software Engineering (SE) or Information Technology (IT) are currently in high demand, and studies reveal the availability of new job openings outpaces that of new professionals [4, 15].

The professional skills required for today´s software industry are highly sought after by software developers [1]. Software development is one of the scenarios where teamwork is mandatory. Team members have one or more roles (e.g. project manager, analyst, designer or programmer). Each role is in charge of particular activities, and their results are tightly correlated. Team members must co-ordinate their activities closely because time and budget constraints allow no room for misunderstandings. Capstone courses involving real-life experiences in software engineering have become commonplace in several universities [5, 9]. The reason for such a phenomenon is simple: no simulated assignment, despite its complexity, can capture the project dynamics involved in building real world applications [12]. Therefore, these experiences provide unparalleled opportunities for students to exercise the non-technical and technical skills they will need in their post-graduate careers.

SIGCSE '14, March 5-8, 2014, Atlanta, GA, USA

ACM 978-1-4503-2605-6/14/03 $15.00.
http://dx.doi.org/10.1145/2538862.2538920

Universities which are educating computer science professionals have an important responsibility in the provision of professional skills to their students [5, 6, 16]. The course at Pontificia Universidad Católica de Chile, named IIC2154: Proyecto de Especialidad, is a capstone course designed to transfer these skills to its students. This course is mostly taken in the last semester of an 11 semester CS curriculum. It involves groups of students working part-time for 13 weeks to solve a real-life problem through a software solution.

The projects undertaken in the course are pre-selected from proposal submissions made by different kinds of organizations - such as nonprofit organizations, university entities or startups - and are developed free of charge. Finally, at the end of the course, students will have acquired the necessary know-how required for pushing forward modern software projects. This is one of the most demanded professional skills by current software industries.

The next section outlines best practice in a general framework that should be implemented in the capstone course. Section 3 presents the implementation of the general framework using tools to support coordination, permanent coaching and evaluation of teamwork. Section 4 shows the application of scenarios for the course and illustrates two projects. Such scenarios are the instrument used to push the team to achieve coordinated team work. Finally, Section 5 presents conclusions and future work.

2. THE CAPSTONE COURSE FRAMEWORK

All software development projects follow some underlying development process that include stages such as the definition of requirements, functional design, features implementation, integration, and other steps according to the needs of the project. The way in which these stages are conducted, the tools that are used to support them, and the rationale for doing this varies widely in groups or organizations. Large companies tend to follow rigid practices entrenched over many years based on individual experience and tradition while smaller companies may prefer to depend on the hunches of single individuals. It would appear that, an industry standard on the development processes to be adopted for engaging a software project does not seem to exist. The main reason for this is that software engineering has failed to provide sufficient evidence to place a single model above all others [11].

This situation imposes a huge obstacle when researching optimal development processes for software engineering. There seems to be a lack of formal tools for measuring the efficiency of development practices rooted in any company, thus preventing us from identifying the rationale behind them. Without this information we cannot determine whether any decision made is based on faulty assumptions or if any improvement we propose will actually yield a positive result. Until we understand the specific factors driving these decisions, the development processes and the use of a particular technology may very well be considered a random act. Empirical studies are a key way to get this information and move towards more knowledge based decision making practices [19]. They are developed not only as formal experiments, but also as case studies, surveys, and prototyping exercises as well. No matter what its form is, the essence of an empirical study is the attempt to learn something useful by comparing theory to reality and to improve our theories as a result.

During more than four years of teaching software engineering through using results from empirical studies in a capstone course, we have learned some lessons after trying a number of different teaching methods. We learned about how to effectively teach software development. In order to describe a general reusable proposal, we have built a framework as a way of formalizing best practices that a professor should implement in the capstone course. Furthermore, our goals in this course are to familiarize students with best practices for developing high quality software to commercial standards in an environment not unlike the one found in today's top software industries.

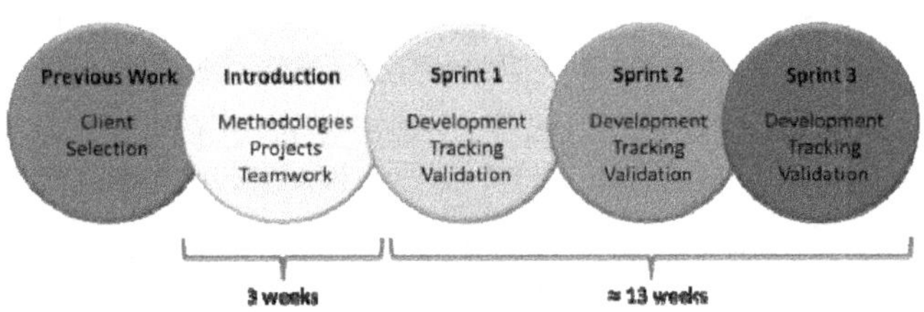

Figure 1. Course phases

Figure 1 shows a general outline for the course. We divide it into five different phases: previous work (course preparation), introduction and three distinct sprints focused on development purposes using agile practices, as is commonplace in industry [18]. *The Previous Work* phase focuses on an open 'Request for Proposal' (RFP) process to potential client organizations which must be prepared prior to the beginning of the academic term. Each organization must complete a project proposal document and submit it to participate in the selection process. Once the deadline for the RFP has been reached, we proceed to analyze the proposals received and select those that would most enrich the learning environment for students.

In the introduction phase, the course has two main goals. The first one introduces the students to best practices in commercial quality software application development that they will be expected to actively follow. Riffell et al. show that a hybrid methodology involving presentations and industry experts' testimonials, along with an active involvement of the students via e-learning material is particularly effective for transmitting new concepts [14]. The second goal focuses on establishing each of the teams as heterogeneously as possible. The professor creates the teams in order to guarantee not only gender ratio equality but also an even distribution of students with the necessary level of technical expertise. This allows us to improve the learning environment by sharing the experience of the most knowledgeable team members. Finally, given the complexity of the project, an experienced, full time coach dedicated to the project, is assigned to each team. Typically, the academic team (professor and coach) assume a supporting role in project planning and team organization. It is the student's responsibility to carry out all the activities involved in the project. Figure 2 shows the organizational structure of the different groups of people working on project development as part of the course.

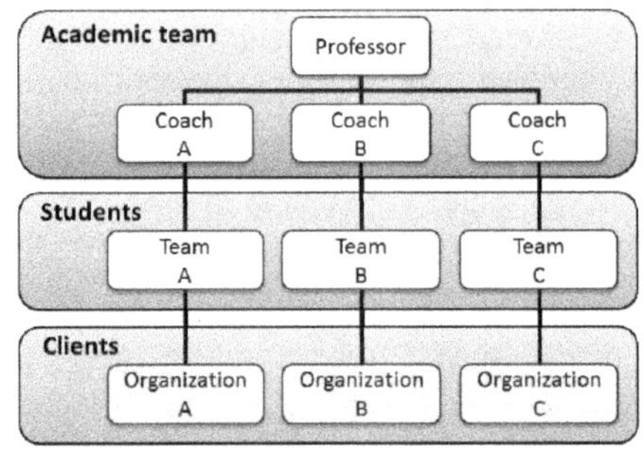

Figure 2. Structure of the working groups in the course

Between the introduction and development phases, there should be a small transition phase allowing students to develop a team identity, as it has been proven to improve team performance and effectiveness [10]. This phase involves carrying out activities for promoting bonding and trust building. Once the transition phase has been completed, the first sprint opens up with a client meeting in which the project is outlined. General requirements and the purpose of the expected solution are thus promptly defined.

Figure 3. 360-Degree team feedback

On the other hand, enhancing teamwork requires continuous feedback during the different software development sprints. Well-structured constructive feedback should be a key aspect in the learning environment. We propose applying the 360-Degree Team Feedback, which is an extension of what we have done so far based on the performance assessment model [17] adapted to team assessments. In this model (see Figure 3), feedback is required from the academic team, stakeholders, final presentation, deliverables, and team members themselves. Every week each team has a monitoring meeting with the assigned coach and the professor. This acts as a formal checkpoint. During the meeting the academic team provides insight and highlights any concerns about project evolution. Nevertheless, only broad directions are provided. The teams themselves are responsible for researching, selecting and negotiating with the stakeholders the best approaches to the problem in hand.

Stakeholders have an objective overview of the final solution focusing only on the product itself. They need to dedicate time, at least once a week, to the project, which may be used to attend and solve the student's doubts, review software prototypes or validate ideas.

At the end of each sprint, team progress must be evaluated through a presentation and a review of submitted deliverables. The presentation takes place in front of the whole class, as well as with the client, coaches and professor. All of the different parties should participate in this experience so that different teams may learn from each other. Deliverables include the source code, resources and documents used in the development of their project. Finally, team members may provide specific feedback on each and every one of their teammates, as they are the most familiar with the particulars of their involvement in every facet of the project.

Both process and product are graded separately and with varying weights according to the stage in the project (see Table 1). Process is given more importance in the beginning where project planning is critical. This emphasis gradually shifts towards the product as the project advances. For process grading, both the academic team and client's input are taken into consideration. Weekly meetings between these parties and the students ensure that they have a solid understanding of the team's planning efforts. Product grading on the other hand contemplates the solutions front-end (e.g. usability, responsiveness and stability); back-end (e.g. good design and programming practices); and lastly, documentation (e.g. requirements and design documents, and software installation and configuration guide). The final presentation is also taken into consideration.

Table 1. Course grading distribution

	Sprint 1	Sprint 2	Sprint 3
Process Evaluation	50%	45%	35%
Academic Team	40%	35%	20%
Client	10%	10%	15%
Product Evaluation	40%	45%	55%
Software Frontend	15%	20%	25%
Software Backend	5%	5%	10%
Documentation	20%	20%	20%
Final Presentation	10%	10%	10%

Finally, the project closure takes place at the end of the semester and clients may either accept or refuse the proposed solution. If the client does not accept the developed solution, the team automatically fails the course. Although this situation is unusual, some final adjustments may be suggested to facilitate a transition of the final software to meet the needs of the client. Thus, the client formally states their satisfaction with the product and they will take full responsibility for maintaining the solution. In case the client needs to add additional features, it is also possible to re-submit the project in the next semester.

The next section describes the implementation of the capstone course framework using tools to enhance coordination, coaching and evaluation of teamwork.

3. IMPLEMENTATION OF THE PROPOSED COURSE FRAMEWORK

The RFP phase follows a strict criterion for selecting the course projects. Because they are a valuable learning source for students, we prioritize those that constitute a technological challenge (e.g. use of mobile technologies or cloud computing) and tackle problems from different work contexts. Special care is taken to select projects whose difficulty requires a minimum dedication of 10 hours per week, per team member, for the duration of the semester. These estimates are based on personal experience.

In the second phase, the professor conducts a series of presentations explaining the course goals and how students are expected to meet them. Afterwards, the professor offers an introduction to areas vital in professional software development. Experience has shown that our students have significant weaknesses in the following areas: project tracking; testing; quality assurance; and lastly, large team management. Additionally, several industry experts are invited to share their testimonies about the key to leading a successful project. Special attention is taken to make contact beforehand with company CEO's and engineers at reputable companies such as Microsoft or Google for this purpose. In this phase, students are also required to take an active role in their learning experience. In order to accomplish this task, a large compendium of documents, tutorials, videos and e-learning material is made available for them on the courses official website.

The capstone nature of this course guarantees a high level of technical skills of the students taking it. While only software engineering and databases are prerequisites for taking this course, our experience has shown that at this point most students will have developed skills in a wide variety of different advanced topics (e.g. modern web and mobile frameworks, project management, cryptography, service-oriented solutions, etc.). Furthermore, several students often have previous professional experience in the industry as well. This wide array of skillsets requires the professor to take a key role in team building. He has to make sure that technical aspects of the project are covered by at least one of the team members to avoid having teams with unfair advantages. Thus, each student must submit their resume and fill out a rubric designed to measure different skillsets [1]. Since projects always have a web component interacting with a mobile one every team should have someone with previous experience in these areas.

All teams have one dedicated coach selected among the courses teaching assistants and one manager selected by the professor from the students. Eight to ten members will compose each of the teams, which is an appropriate number for agile software projects [18]. Most semesters, between 50 to 60 students take this course, leading to the establishment of 5 to 6 different teams. In order to promote group bonding, an agile game - e.g. the marshmallow challenge [20] - is carried out by students to learn about innovation, creativity, working as part of a team, collaboration, as well as the value of early prototyping and incremental delivery. After this group activity, a meeting is scheduled with the client in which the project is presented and the goals are defined. Students are required to go beyond the formal requirements and to improve on the proposed solution as well as suggesting additional features where appropriate.

This marks the beginning of the development phase. Empirical studies show that agile practices adapt well to the dynamic nature of software requirements and results in better developer and consumer satisfaction [8]. Thus, the official course methodology for the project follows agile practices in three sprints each around a month long [18]. Each sprint is like a mini-project with its own requirements, design, coding and testing (see Figure 4). The result of each sprint is a working software solution and it could be used as a Minimum Viable Product (MVP) [13]. No technical constraints are imposed on the students beforehand, they are free to choose whatever technology, framework or tool they deem appropriate to build their solutions. Nevertheless, every choice they make must be justified and approved by the client. Based on our records, most of our students develop a web application using Ruby on Rails deployed on Heroku, but we have had teams leaning towards ASP.NET MVC 3 with Azure, Symfony with AWS, and others.

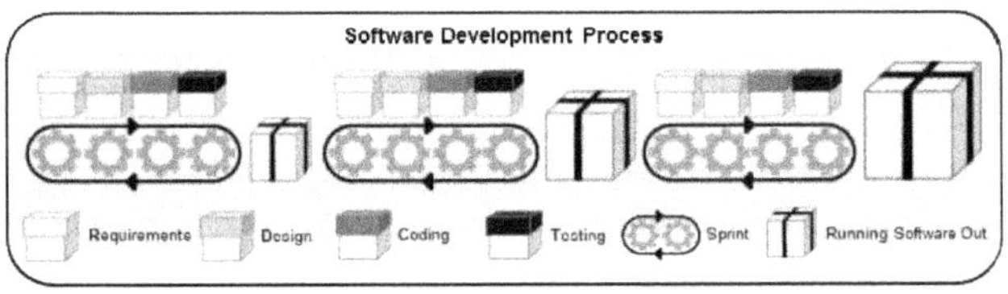

Figure 4. Structure of the software development process

During the development phase, in order to identify any pitfalls or areas to improve in the client's vision, students are requested to follow design-funneling principles. That is to start with information architecture with mockups and storyboarding (see Figure 5a), and then to conduct usability testing with the goal of gradually converging towards a functional prototype (see Figure 5b).

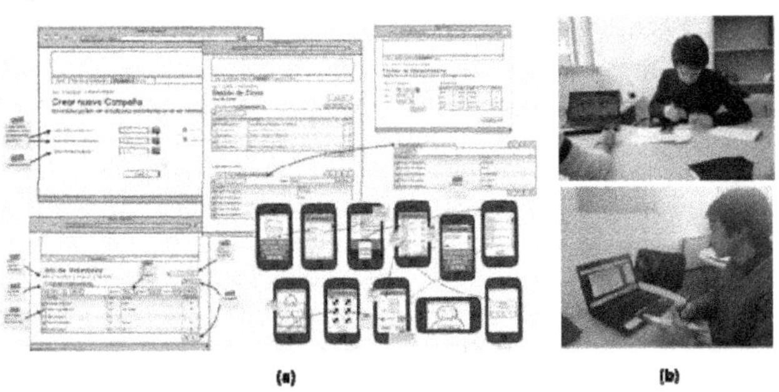

Figure 5. a) Mockups and storyboarding for web and mobile proposals; b) A stakeholder carrying out usability testing of the proposals.

Communication and coordination of the whole team are attained via coaching meetings (at least once a week), project tracking software tools and online communities. The official tool for this purpose is Kanbanery (see Figure 6), which allows the teams, coaches and professor to keep track of the work of every student and to be aware of the task they are working on at any given point in time. Successful coordination requires that each team member understands: first, who is responsible for which parts of the project; second, the relations between the tasks assigned to different members; and third, how the work is progressing with regard to the project timeline.

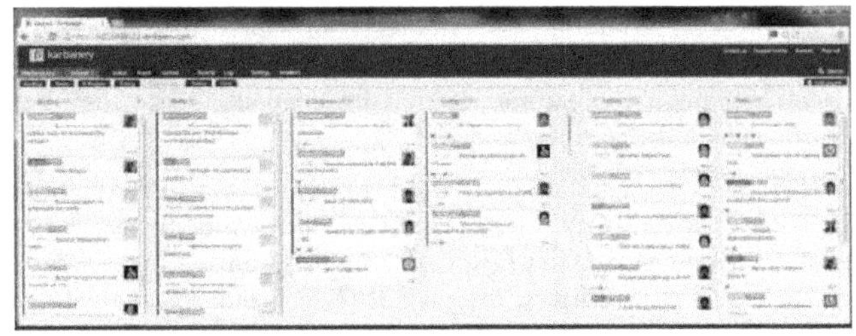

Figure 6. Kanbanery Project Tracking Tool

In addition, each team uses a Google Community tool to improve the visibility and feedback among stakeholders, teammates and the academic team (see Figure 7). The work and progress of the team should be visible to its members. This visibility is part of the feedback process and it ensures fair play. It also provides, by itself, communication and coordination throughout the team. Frequent communication between project stakeholders is core to agile software development, therefore the high availability, usability and infrastructure of the selected tool are all taken into account to ensure a fluid communication channel between all parties.

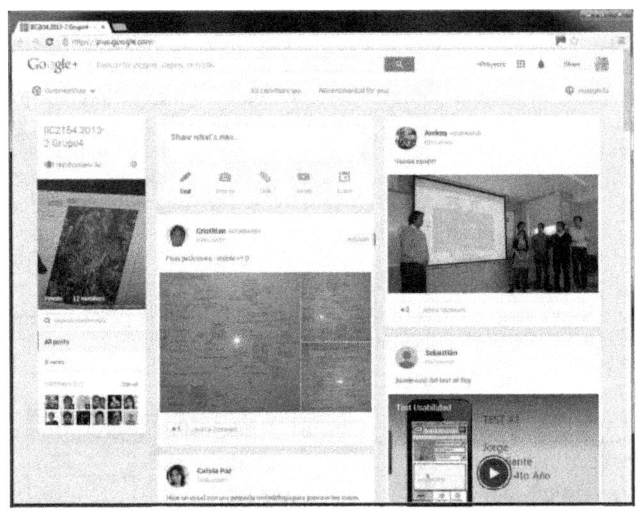

Figure 7. Google communities tool for communication media in software development.

Another aspect to be considered in the development of the project is the selection of the versioning control system. Distributed versioning control is preferred over subversion due to its significant advantages for collaborative projects [3]. Student groups use GIT to version the code and Github as a hosting platform. This not only plays a role in improving project management but also proves itself to be of great help when evaluating projects. This is because different tasks can be matched to specific team members in a user-friendly UI, therefore allowing the academic team to validate the contribution of each particular student (see Figure 8). Furthermore, experience has shown us the transparency of GitHub greatly enhances team-learning efforts. By being able to study how their peers coded, what others paid attention to, and how they solved problems, less experienced students are more able to efficiently integrate the knowledge of their peers.

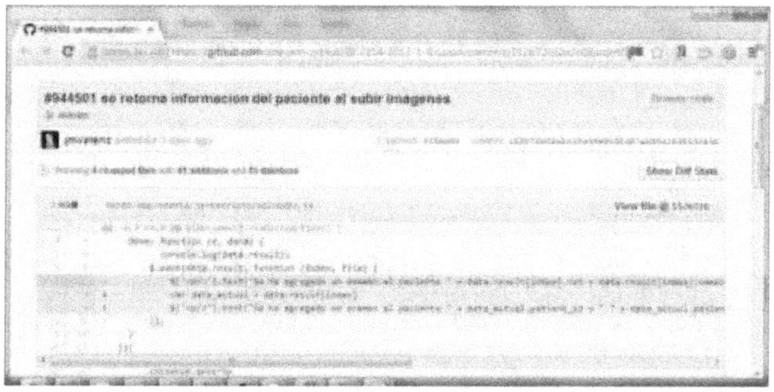

Figure 8. GitHub: Distributed versioning control system

Finally, by integrating Kanbanery with GitHub, we improve the traceability of each project by providing access to contextual information that can assist students in determining how a requirement was implemented and how it was tested. Figure 9 shows a task matched to its corresponding code blocks.

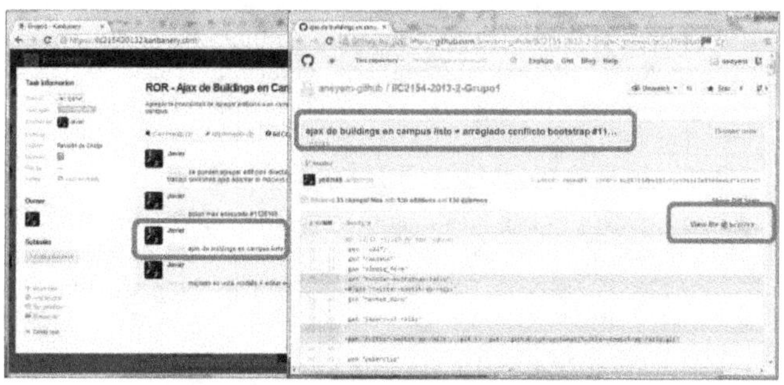

Figure 9. Kanbanery-Git integration via matching hashtags

4. EXPERIENCES DEVELOPING SOFTWARE PROJECTS

The following scenarios serve to demonstrate the positive results of our capstone course framework. These application scenarios represent empirical studies and they illustrate the feasibility of the proposed approach. Some examples of the projects developed in the capstone course are:

Nonprofit Organization: In Chile, the fire service is composed of a group of volunteers. This means they do not receive a salary and they have minimal support from governmental agencies. The firefighting community has an alarm center, in charge of raising the alarm, assigning resources to an emergency situation and coordinating the response efforts of the fire service. Each alarm center counts on two or three shared radio channels to coordinate all the emergency response efforts.

Although the radio-based communication has brought several benefits, it currently represents a limitation for the emergency response processes. Therefore, the Chilean Fire Department required a technology to coordinate logistics amongst their different branches. In the capstone course, students had to develop a platform which allows recording, representing and distributing information during urban emergency situations. The platform is designed to improve decision-making and coordination processes among firefighters.

Figure 10a shows the web solution as a virtual space where different fire companies can exchange opinions, share multimedia information, consume and create resources and visualize data in different ways. Figure 10b shows the mobile solution for Android devices to support the fieldwork under unstable connectivity conditions. It enhances the traditional report creation experience by taking advantage of all the integrated sensors in a modern smartphone/tablet.

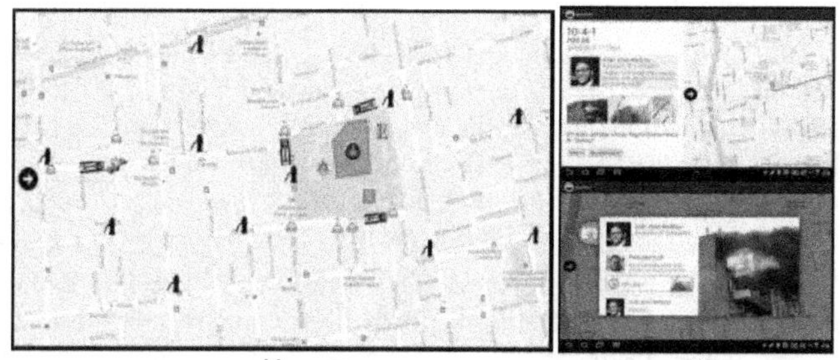

(a) (b)

Figure 10. Geo-referenced information shown in web and mobile applications during the emergency

University Centers: Wildlife conservation aims to save endangered species from extinction. Latin America has one of the richest and diverse ecosystems in the world. Many mammals, birds, reptiles and frogs are endangered and vast areas are barely known. In order to assess the risk of extinction, records or sightings are crucial to identifying unknown species and to understand their population status. Scientists and conservationists can greatly improve their understanding of key species by having incidental records from people about wildlife species around the region.

LiveANDES (Advanced Network for the Distribution of Endangered Species) is a project of the Fauna Australis Wildlife Laboratory at Pontificia Universidad Católica de Chile. LiveANDES is a novel way to contribute to biodiversity conservation. This project was selected by Microsoft Research Connection to be shown on Earth Day 2013 as a feature story regarding the preservation of Latin America's wildlife [2]. The aim of this project is to develop software to input, analyze, and share location data from wildlife sightings. The outcomes of geo-referenced data will be available to show on Bing maps to assist Governmental policies, promote data sharing between scientists and create a conservation community in the Andes region. Figure 11a shows the web solution where ecologists, scientists, park rangers, and even tourists can upload, share, and analyze geo-referenced data that is stored. Figure 11b shows the mobile solution for Windows Phone devices, that lets people take a picture of the species, locate the geographical point and upload the information to LiveANDES Web.

(a) (b)

Figure 11. The LiveANDES platform is designed to store and share information about Latin America's wildlife.

5. CONCLUSIONS AND FURTHER WORK

There is a growing demand for approaches to provide a greater learning environment to bridge the gap from university expectations to those of industry. This demand drives the need for effective methods of teaching Software Engineering to tomorrow's application developers. The implementation of this capstone courses methodology has shown a high degree of success amongst our client's organizations. Based on the results and the quality of projects delivered, user satisfaction is very high.

One of the greatest challenges to achieving the learning objectives and project goals of the course revolves around the need for long-term organization interaction and effective communication. We have established several long-term partnerships with organizations that have the human and resource capacity to ensure extensive and continuous involvement.

While overall results are very positive, we are still lacking some requirements for replicating modern professional environments. For instance, testing plays a pivotal role in assuring software quality and speeding up the development process. Therefore, our course requires students to perform constant unit testing and user studies. Nevertheless, further improvements may be achieved in this area by incorporating Test Driven Development and Continuous Integration practices which are very common in modern software industry environments [7, 18]. Time and technical constraints prevent us from implementing these practices. It remains an open question whether investing additional time and resources in this same class into teaching these concepts may improve the overall results or detract too much from the courses other objectives.

Finally, our approach is currently limited in scope to only CS students. Rarely does a real-life project encompass topics exclusive to the area of computer science. For instance, most software companies work hand in hand with designers for developing graphical user interfaces and consultants in different engineering branches. Most of our projects also include concepts from a broad array of fields, for which one may hypothesize inter-disciplinary groups should be more effective in delivering richer solutions.

6. ACKNOWLEDGMENTS

We acknowledge all the organizations that have contributed to the creation and continued operation of this course. In particular, we would like to acknowledge the Computer Science Department, Academic Development Center, Service Learning Direction and Undergraduate Direction of the Engineering School for continued support of this course. This work was partially supported by LACCIR Grant No. R1211LAC006 and VRI-PUC Interdisciplina No. 03/2013.

7. REFERENCES

[1] Ahmed, F., and Capretz, L. F. 2012. Evaluating the Demand for Soft Skills in Software Development. *IT Professional*, IEEE. 14,1, 44-49. DOI= http://dx.doi.org/10.1109/MITP.2012.7

[2] Bernard, R. 2013. Earth Day 2013 – Reflecting On Our Commitment to Sustainability. Retrieved June 19, 2013 from http://goo.gl/C73zq

[3] Bird, C., Rigby, P. C., Barr, E. T., Hamilton, D. J., German, D. M., and Devanbu, P.. 2009. The promises and perils of mining git. In *Mining Software Repositories, 6th IEEE International Working Conference.* DOI=http://dx.doi.org/10.1109/MSR.2009.5069475

[4] Brienza V.. 2012. Jobs Rated 2012: Ranking 200 Jobs From Best to Worst. Retrieved July 1, 2013 from http://goo.gl/ci3sS

[5] Chamillard, A. T., Braun, K. A. 2002. The software engineering capstone: structure and tradeoffs. In *Proceedings of the 33th SIGCSE Technical Symposium on Computer Science Education* (Cincinnati, NK, USA, 2002), 227-231. DOI= http://dx.doi.org/10.1145/563517.563428

[6] Criteria for Accrediting Computing Programs, 2012 – 2013. ABET. Retrieved June 19, 2013 from http://goo.gl/T5y3d

[7] Duvall, P., Steve M., and Andrew G. 2007. Continuous integration: improving software quality and reducing risk. *Addison-Wesley Professional.*

[8] Dybå, T., and Dingsøyr T. 2008. Empirical studies of agile software development: A systematic review. *Information and software technology*. 50, 9 (Aug. 2008), 833-859. DOI= http://dx.doi.org/10.1016/j.infsof.2008.01.006

[9] Goold, A. 2003. Providing process for projects in capstone courses. *ACM SIGCSE Bulletin*. 35, 3, 26-29. DOI= http://dx.doi.org/10.1145/961511.961522.

[10] Lembke, S., and Wilson, M. 1998. Putting the" team" into teamwork: Alternative theoretical contributions for contemporary management practice. *Human Relations*. 51, 7 (Jul. 1998), 927-944. DOI= http://dx.doi.org/10.1177/001872679805100704

[11] Perry, D. E., Porter A. A., and Votta L. G. 2000. Empirical studies of software engineering: a roadmap. In *Proceedings of the conference on The future of Software engineering.* ACM, 2000. 345-355. DOI= http://dx.doi.org/10.1145/336512.336586

[12] Reichlmay, T. 2006. Collaborating with industry: strategies for an undergraduate software engineering program. In *Proceedings of the 2006 international workshop on Summit on software engineering education*. 13-16. DOI= http://dx.doi.org/10.1145/1137842.1137848

[13] Ries, E.. 2011. The Lean Startup: How today's entrepreneurs use continuous innovation to create radically successful businesses. Crown Pub.

[14] Riffell, S. and Duncan S. 2003. Learning Online: Student Perceptions of a Hybrid Learning Format. *Journal of College Science Teaching*. 32, 6 (Mar. 2003), 394-399.

[15] Samson, T.. 2013. Software developers expected to see the highest IT job growth come 2020. InfoWorld. Retrieved July 1, 2013 from http://goo.gl/An5MB

[16] Shuman, L. J., Besterfield-Sacre, M., and McGourty, J. 2005. The ABET "Professional skills"—Can they be taught? Can they be assessed? *Journal of Engineering Education*. 94, 1 (Jan. 2005), 41-55. DOI= 10.1002/j.2168-9830.2005.tb00828.x

[17] Ward, P. 1997. 360-Degree Feedback. Chartered Institute of Personnel & Development.

[18] Williams, L. 2012. What agile teams think of agile principles. Communications, ACM. 55,4, 71-76. DOI= http://dx.doi.org/10.1145/2133806.2133823

[19] Wohlin, C., Runeson, P., Hst, M., Ohlsson, M. C., Regnell, B., and Wessln, A. 2012. Experimentation in software engineering. Springer Publishing Company, Incorporated.

[20] Wujec, T. 2010. The Marshmallow Challenge. Retrieved June 19, 2013 from http://goo.gl/jz9CH

Selecting Open Source Software Projects to Teach Software Engineering

Thérèse Smith, Robert McCartney, and Swapna S. Gokhale
Department of Computer Science and Engineering
University of Connecticut, Storrs, CT 06269
[tms08012, robert, ssg]@engr.uconn.edu

Lisa C. Kaczmarczyk
Consultant
San Diego, CA 92130
lisak@acm.org

ABSTRACT

Aspiring software engineers must be able to comprehend and evolve legacy code, which is challenging because the code may be poorly documented, ill structured, and lacking in human support. These challenges of understanding and evolving existing code can be illustrated in academic settings by leveraging the rich and varied volume of Open Source Software (OSS) code. To teach SE with OSS, however, it is necessary to select uniform projects of appropriate size and complexity. This paper reports on our search for suitable OSS projects to teach an introductory SE course with a focus on maintenance and evolution. The search turned out to be quite labor intensive and cumbersome, contrary to our expectations that it would be quick and simple. The chosen projects successfully demonstrated the maintenance challenges, highlighting the promise of using OSS. The burden of selecting projects, however, may impede widespread integration of OSS into SE and other computing courses.

Categories and Subject Descriptors

D.2.7 [**Software Engineering**]: Distribution, Maintenance, and Enhancement; K.3.2 [**Computers and Education**]: Computers and Information Science Education

General Terms

Documentation, Design, Experimentation

Keywords

Software Engineering, Maintenance, Program Comprehension, Open Source

1. INTRODUCTION AND MOTIVATION

The need for skilled software engineers has compelled nearly every computing curriculum to include Software Engineering (SE) as a mandatory course. The objective of this SE course is to train students in principles and practices of modern software engineering and to prepare them for careers in the software industry. An overwhelming number of software engineering activities involve understanding and evolving existing, legacy code. Comprehension of such legacy code may be difficult because it could: (i) have been subject to many fixes and enhancements, (ii) be poorly written, (iii) have little to no documentation, and/or (iv) lack support. Computing students must therefore be trained to "reverse engineer" design decisions and their rationale from such code, often under serious time and resource constraints.

A major difficulty in highlighting comprehension and evolution challenges to SE students is to find pre-existing code that has characteristics similar to that of industrial code but is commensurate with students' preparation and background. The rich and diverse Open Source Software (OSS) projects can readily supply such pre-existing code [6]. It can also provide a context to practice design, development, and testing skills. OSS-based SE projects will force students to comprehend sparsely documented and/or poorly written code. OSS can thus be leveraged to emulate industrial challenges in academic environments.

Our objective was to integrate OSS projects into our sophomore-level SE course. Because OSS projects exhibited large variability in terms of size, complexity, and quality, our greatest obstacle was to select suitable projects. The projects could not be too large or complex because students would not be able to understand them well enough to extend them. These projects also could not be too small or simple because the students would not find it necessary to use SE principles, rather they could fall back to the disorganized generate-and-test approaches that were sufficient in the introductory courses. Given these constraints, we sought to manually identify, evaluate, and prepare projects for integration. This paper describes how our selection effort was fraught with unexpected challenges and was labor intensive. The selected projects, however, provided opportunities for deep involvement with the code, meaningfully highlighting the maintenance difficulties. Our experience thus suggests that in order to use OSS for SE instruction, the burden of selecting and preparing projects must be alleviated.

This paper is organized as follows: Section 2 discusses the promise of OSS. Section 3 compares OSS repositories . Section 4 presents project selection process. Section 5 describes how the chosen projects met course objectives. Section 6 surveys related work. Section 7 concludes the paper.

SIGCSE'14, March 3–8, 2014, Atlanta, GA, USA.

ACM 978-1-4503-2605-6/14/03 ...$15.00.
http://dx.doi.org/10.1145/2538862.2538932.

2. OSS: PROMISE AND PERILS

The OSS revolution is having a lasting impact on the way software is developed, disseminated, and adapted. This is evident from the myriad of OSS projects already available, and the pace at which software engineers contribute to the development of these projects. This revolution has thus created easily accessible, exponentially growing [9] volume of code, some of which can be used as example code in SE education. Popular OSS repositories such as Sourceforge [29], Freecode [12], CodePlex [7], and W3C [33] host more than 200,000 projects. We use these repositories simply as code sources; students do not contribute back to them.

OSS projects span a variety of domains such as tools for software development, financial analysis, security and networking, data manipulation and visualization, audio and video engineering and text editing, operating and database systems, and games and entertainment [29]. These projects target common platforms including Windows and Linux and are written in languages such as C, C++, Perl, Fortran, Python, Java, Tcl, Objective-C, Ada, and Php. Although the OSS development process appears *ad hoc*, many projects are completed successfully with rich functionality and high reliability because their latent social structure allows the projects to grow in an organized manner [2, 31]. Moreover, because most engineers participate in OSS to build reputation, or for self-development [23] and altruistic reasons, they may be inherently committed to SE principles, which may lead to projects that are carefully designed, engineered, and maintained. OSS projects may thus exhibit varied characteristics and quality similar to industrial systems, even though their requirements processes may differ from that of traditional software systems [26]. These projects can thus provide a valuable resource for teaching SE.

The rich diversity of OSS systems, however, presents one of the greatest hurdles in teaching with these projects. All chosen projects must be of comparable difficulty and complexity. Independent selection by students from OSS repositories is not only unlikely to produce that result but it may also be inordinately time consuming. Therefore, teaching SE with OSS will require identification and evaluation of a collection of suitable projects. We seek a collection because it improves the chance that students will find an interesting project and also minimizes cross-group collaboration. Such collaboration is undesirable because it diminishes each student's contribution to critical analysis of the documentation and reflection on the architecture and data representation that is necessary for comprehensive understanding [27].

3. ANALYSIS OF OSS REPOSITORIES

Each OSS repository hosted a large number of projects and showed varying search and selection capabilities. Therefore, we explored many repositories, subject to a preliminary criteria, to identify those with potential for efficiently providing appropriate projects.

3.1 Preliminary Criteria

Our objective was to integrate OSS into an early, introductory SE course for sophomore and juniors. Our students had limited experience in Java programming and could write, test, and debug only small volumes of code after having taken a data structures course. They could also use Eclipse, create UML class diagrams, and produce documentation. Our SE course was "maintenance-centric" and the laboratory exercises performed on OSS projects challenged students to practice code comprehension, use appropriate tools (source code control systems, reverse engineering), and implement an enhancement of their choice. The students were expected to work methodically and document their activities systematically, especially, those undertaken to complete their enhancement. Given the background and skills of our students and the objectives of the course, we devised the following preliminary criteria:

- *Programming Language (PL):* The projects must be programmed completely in Java because it was the only language known by all of our students.
- *Code Size (CS):* Project size should be approximately 10,000 lines; smaller projects may not adequately emulate maintenance difficulties and larger ones may be beyond our students' capabilities [20].
- *Team Development (TD):* Projects with a team were desirable, for possibly quick resolution of issues.
- *Buildability (BD):* Projects should build within one to two days to preserve focus on understanding and enhancing the code.

3.2 Exploration of Repositories

We searched several OSS repositories subject to PL, CS, TD, and BD criteria to narrow a large pool of candidate projects. We believed that these preliminary criteria would be easy to assess; obviously it should be possible to determine code size, programming language and whether a team was involved with a project with minimal effort. Also, we expected most OSS projects to be close to building. Contrary to these expectations, however, we found that mostly large projects, which were beyond the code size criterion built easily and many smaller projects with acceptable code sizes failed to build. Therefore, we deferred examining for buildability and describe our findings in applying only the CS, PL and TD criteria to the OSS repositories.

- *Apache:* Apache hosted many projects with excellent quality, sizeable communities, noteworthy documentation, and passing the BD test. However, the smallest projects wildly exceeded the size.
- *CodePlex:* Projects at CodePlex could be rapidly filtered using "alpha or better," "beta or better," and "stable" only. There were over 9000 projects classified as "beta or better". Though Javascript is a tag, Java is not, and entering Java as a search term returned 389 projects, and restoring "beta or better" dropped the number to 195. Many of these 195 projects were Javascript. Even some in C# were returned, because these included Java in the tags or descriptive text. Thus, our initial impression was that the site was helpful and quick, but not many projects were suitable.
- *Code.google:* A relatively large percentage of projects at this repository were executables rather than source.
- *Freecode:* Freecode offered a very nice search experience, with a number of keywords. It, however, referred to many projects at various other repositories. The first dozen or so projects examined appeared to be executables unaccompanied by code. We inferred that Freecode was an improved search front end but not a repository and had many executable-only hits.

- *GNU:* GNU had many projects, including a subset for Windows, but those checked were not in Java.

- *Sourceforge:* Sourceforge had many projects, and useful search keywords beyond the general search area. Searching for Java projects, however, still yielded a small number of projects in other languages. It also permitted searches over several categories of activity and achievement such as "alpha", "beta", "stable", "mature", and "inactive". This was used to eliminate projects whose stages of development were too early or too late. Beyond these terms, users could create additional search qualifiers, which appeared to be matched against project text descriptions. The searches were not as selective and the results had to be pared manually. However, the popularity of the site combined with our experience indicated usable material.

- *Tigris:* This repository hosted several projects, but these exceeded the code size.

- *GitHub:* This repository offered search terms including language and most recent push date, which provided approximately 18,000 Java projects.

- *W3C:* W3C featured excellent quality software, some in Java, but the projects appeared too big.

Sourceforge appeared to be the most productive based on CS and PL, and hence, we explored it further against the TD criterion. However, limiting the code size to 10,000 lines while simultaneously requiring a team of developers virtually resulted in no projects. Many appealing projects with several developers but over 17,000 lines of code could be found easily. Several projects with fewer than 5,000 lines of code were by single individuals. It seemed that there were not many projects in the mature, stable or alpha, or even beta state with more than one developer that also had fewer than 12,000 lines of code. Thus, we revised the TD criterion because it conflicted with CS, and elected to accept single developer projects with approximately 10,000 lines, resulting in about 1000 projects for detailed evaluation.

3.3 Comparison of Capabilities

During our exploration, we found that the search and download capabilities of OSS repositories differed widely. All repositories could narrow projects with pre-defined key words and allowed users to create additional search terms. Matches to pre-defined key words, however, differed from matches to user-created search terms because projects may be manually classified according to pre-defined key words, while user-created key words may be matched against the text associated with the project. These conjectures arose because the search results were different with pre-defined key words *vs.* using them as user-defined search terms.

The repositories also differed in their specific pre-defined key words. The classification scheme "beta or better" seen at CodePlex was more closely aligned with users' thinking than the scheme at Sourceforge which has "beta" and "mature". Code.google and Freecode also supported pre-defined search criteria, but the labels at former were dramatically smaller than the number of search terms at the latter. GitHub provided a desirable ability to use recency as a search term, compared to obtaining that information after a search. The naming scheme may suggest content, source or "only" executables: src could be seen in the name.

The careful cataloging at Freecode greatly aided the search process, however, some projects found through Freecode were hosted at Sourceforge. The relative frequency of finding source code, as opposed to binaries, was higher via Sourceforge *vs.* Freecode. Thus, it appeared that Freecode placed relatively more emphasis upon searching and less emphasis on hosting than Sourceforge.

While each site appeared to be addressing a specific audience of software users and developers, the degree of coordination among the community of contributors could be different. Domains at Sourceforge could be imagined to have grown according to the contributions. Apache's emphasis on community process, and a seeming interrelatedness of the categories (e.g., Web server, mail, XSLT formatted output, XML parsing, etc.), suggested more coordination.

The repositories also exhibited varying support for searching based on project size. GitHub allowed searching based on repository size, which was only somewhat related to code size. At Code.google, the number of lines of code was reported only for some projects. Other repositories did not allow a search based on project size. Most of the sites offered reasonable support for downloading project artifacts. At Code.google, we found many projects made available as multiple individual files, unsuitable for download. Projects, if they were packaged to be downloaded as archives, could be imported directly into a prepared Java project in Eclipse as archive files. GitHub downloaded with a Git clone. Sourceforge downloaded with the originator's choice of CVS, SVN, Git and Mercurial.

Based on these lessons, we contemplated the characteristics of an ideal repository for project selection. Such a repository would host a large collection of projects, provide apt and usable search terms, and distinguish from unsuitable projects. For example, being able to separate "executable only" projects from those with source code could eliminate a large subset of the projects in one search query. The repository would also allow projects to be scoped and searched based on their size. Finally, it would facilitate downloading project artifacts. Being able to exercise one action, such as a repository clone, or a single download, would be preferred over manually downloading individual project files.

4. PROJECT SELECTION

A whole summer of 12 hour days was spent examining candidate software projects. Three computers were kept running, continuously downloading Java software that looked interesting based upon manual inspection of subject matter and age. Of the 1000 projects downloaded and (manually) examined, 200 passed the initial criteria. These 200 were further investigated. Several additional criteria were applied to ensure that the chosen projects were appropriate to meet the objectives of our maintenance-centric course.

- *Code Size (CS):* Initially, approximate sizes were estimated to lie between 5,000 and 10,000 lines. Accurate sizes were counted after eliminating duplicate files.

- *Programming Language (PL):* To be completely certain, PL was applied as a search qualifier rather than typing it in the search entry field because this could return projects with Java in their description, but were not necessarily programmed in Java. However, when Java was specified as a qualifier, the search produced projects written exclusively in Java.

- *Application Domain (AD):* We sought projects that were "cool" and appealing to the students. Our prior interactions with students suggested that projects with graphics such as 3D visualization, audio/video tools, and those with GUIs would satisfy this criteria. While the projects at Sourceforge were searchable according to domains, establishing correlation between domain and size was cumbersome. Although projects in most domains were too big, **some** in Home and Education, Audio and Video, and Games were of suitable size.

- *Modular Design (MD):* Projects should be modular and loosely coupled to effectively demonstrate best practices that aid maintenance. Modularity was assessed using metrics that characterized code organization including the number of files, number of directories, and the depth of the directory structure. Directory naming and structure such as the Model, View, Controller [13] was also used to provide clues about a project's modularity and organization.

- *Recent Activity (RA):* Projects with recent updates and commits were sought for ease of seeking help. We evaluated activity based on the date of the most recent commit, and the number of committers, if available.

- *Documentation Quality (DQ):* Projects should *not* be exceptionally well documented, because this would only trivialize the comprehension and evolution challenges. Moreover, all the projects should be documented more or less uniformly, so that the students would be challenged similarly. To assess quality, we considered multiple aspects such as readability, accuracy, degree of detail, availability, helpfulness, recency and correctness. If the documentation was not in English, we considered that in assessing its helpfulness, although strictly this aspect is different from quality. Despite our quest for uniformity, documentation differed widely and came in many forms including web sites, user guides, reuse from other sources, pictures and diagrams, and comments in the code.

- *Buildability (BD):* Initially, we immediately rejected projects that did not build. Upon realizing that only big projects built easily, we became lenient and invested reasonable time to build a project. Thus, we discarded a candidate project with ordinary appeal if it could not be compiled with an hour-long effort. A project, with highly desirable appeal was eliminated only if several hours of debugging failed to build it. Many projects did not build because of missing jar files, which could be obtained using jarfinder. Only a handful required elaborate and *ad hoc* search to obtain or substitute the missing files. We maintained a collection of the missing files that we found for future use. Thus, effort incurred in building projects could be categorized as "minimal", "moderate" or "extreme".

In summary, our process of evaluating Sourceforge projects revealed that: (i) It is difficult to find team projects with approximately 10,000 lines of code; (ii) Small, single developer projects do not build easily; (iii) Quality of documentation can vary widely; and (iv) Code organization may offer misleading clues into its modularity.

5. PROJECT SUITABILITY

Table 1 summarizes the characteristics of the 16 selected projects with respect to each criteria. Java projects spanned the domains of Games, Art, Skills, Indexing, Searching and Client/Server applications [25]. The projects were moderately modular and recent; being no more than two years old. Only a few projects had two developers. Sizes ranged from 5,500 to 10,500 lines, and most were lightly documented. After we spent hours, students could compile the projects quickly based on our guidance and readily available jar files.

Next, we discuss how these projects fared in meeting our maintenance-centric objectives. Table 2, which summarizes the range of enhancements, shows that most students engaged with both the architecture (A) and the data representation (DR) of their projects. Students were initially frustrated with the difficulties in understanding code that was not written by them, without much support. However, this initial frustration was later replaced with a healthy sense of pride, accomplishment, and self-achievement, as they navigated and completed their chosen extensions. End-of-the semester surveys [19, 14] indicated that the students appreciated that software maintenance and evolution was: (i) challenging, resource intensive, and time consuming; (ii) could be significantly aided by documentation and comments; and (iii) assisted by a good architecture but hindered by a brittle one. The chosen OSS projects thus successfully achieved our objectives of illustrating comprehension and evolution challenges and also provided a context to learn and practice the skills to meet these challenges.

Table 2: Project Enhancements and Engagement

Project	Enhancement	Engmnt
1. carDriving	GUI, Tutorial	A, DR
2. Coppit	GUI, Rules, Bug Fixes	A, DR
3. Domination	GUI	A, DR
4. Solitaire	GUI, Rules	A, DR
5. JigsawPuzzle	GUI	A, DR
6. JugglePat	GUI, Coordinate music	A, DR
7. Melosion	Entry of a new song	DR
8. Monopoli	GUI	A
9. Simulum	GUI, Coordinate music	A, DR
10. MusicCoach	Play, pause, rewind, GUI	A, DR
11. NocNorade	Rules	A, DR
12. Picofarm	GUI	A, DR
13. SlimeWarrior	GUI	A, DR
14. vgt-battleships	GUI	A, DR
15. Sudoku	Rules	DR
16. Puggle	Add doc types	A, DR

A = Architecture, DR = Data Representation

6. RELATED WORK

OSS projects have been used to teach SE activities such as design, testing, quality assurance, maintenance, and usability. They have also been used to teach basic and advanced programming and software development concepts. These works have adopted varied approaches for project selection; allowing students to choose with or without guidance [30,

Table 1: Characteristics of Selected OSS Projects

Project Name	Project characteristics	Project Name	Project Characteristics
1. carDriving	**AD:** Game, graphics, sound, physics **MD:** 25, 1, 1 **AL:** 2011/06/16, 2 committers **DQ:** Web site, some documentation **CS:** 8931 **BD:** Minimal	9. Simulum	**AD:** lovely, 3D effect **MD:** 42, 17, 2 **AL:** 2010/01/25 **DQ:** Web site **CS:** 7586 **BD:** Minimal
2. Coppit	**AD:** Board game with computer player **MD:** 17 files, 3 directories **AL:** 2010/10/05 **DQ:** Wikipedia page **CS:** 6461 **BD:** Minimal	10. MusicSkillsCoach	**AD:** Sound, useful for musicians **MD:** 33, 9, 4 **AL:** 2011/01/14 **DQ:** good naming **CS:** 5259 **BD:** Moderate
3. Domination	**AD:** Board game **MD:** 49, 6, 1 **AL:** 2010/10/08, 6 committers **DQ:** Web site, class explanations **CS:** 8006 **BD:** Moderate	11. NocNorade	**AD:** Partial game **MD:** 26, 8, 3 **AL:** 2007/01/08 **DQ:** Web site **CS:** 5586 **BD:** Moderate
4. FourRowSolitaire	**AD:** Card game **MD:** 16, 1, 1 **AL:** 2011/06/28 **DQ:** Comments at top and within files **CS:** 5633 **BD:** Moderate	12. Picofarm	**AD:** Client/Server, Soap, RMI **MD:** 33, 4, 1 **AL:** 2007/03/28 **DQ:** Website, extended comments **CS:** 7049 **BD:** Moderate
5. JigsawPuzzle	**AD:** Entertainment **MD:** 49, 11, 1 **AL:** 2010/07/10 **DQ:** comments every few lines of code **CS:** 7774 **BD:** Extreme	13. SlimeWarrior	**AD:** Animation **MD:** 20, 6, 3 **AL:** 2011/02/13 **DQ:** Included html pages, YouTube **CS:** 10401 **BD:** Moderate
6. JugglePat	**AD:** Patterns, animation **MD:** 20, 3, 3 **AL:** 2009/07/17 **DQ:** Comments, usage guide **CS:** 8411 **BD:** Moderate	14. vgt-battleships	GUI, computer opponent **MD:** 33, 6, 3 **AL:** 2010/01/25 **DQ:** Commands, variables in Polish **CS:** 5951 **BD:** Moderate
7. Melosion	**AD:** Music game, animation **MD:** 64, 13, 3 **AL:** 2011/08/02, at least 4 committers **DQ:** Dutch Web site, class diagram **CS:** 9229 **BD:** Extreme	15. Sudoku	**AD:** Puzzle generation **MD:** 102, 16, 5 **AL:** 2010/06/30 **DQ:** Readme, good naming **CS:** 10636 **BD:** Minimal
8. Monopoli	**AD:** Board game, nice animation **MD:** 33, 5, 2 **AL:** 2009/07/17, 2 committers **DQ:** Italian comments, every few lines **CS:** 5353 **BD:** Minimal	16. Puggle	**AD:** Search Indexing **MD:** 49, 8, 2 **AL:** 2011/04/07 **DQ:** HTML at Sourceforge **CS:** 10848 **BD:** Moderate

AD = Application Domain, MD = Modularity, AL = Activity Level, DQ = Documentation Quality, CS = Code Size, BD = Buildability

24, 18]; selection by faculty from familiar projects [16, 8, 21, 22], or popular ones such as Apache and Mozilla [4], JUnit [3], software studio [22], or pertaining to specific domains such as Web and Web 2.0 [34] or tools [5]; software written in graduate and upper division courses [17, 11, 10, 20], and soliciting projects from academia and industry [32]. Meneeley *et al.* [20] also faced disappointing results at Sourceforge when searching subject to similar criteria. In response, they decided to use a single project developed by their graduate students. We continued our search to find comparable projects, and hope that sharing our lessions would offer systematic guidance and tools for efficient project selection.

7. CONCLUSION AND FUTURE WORK

Open Source Software (OSS) can be used as example code in SE education to emulate the challenges faced by software engineers in comprehending and working with existing, legacy code. This paper reported on our experiences and lessons in selecting OSS projects for teaching SE. To enable project selection, despite the peculiarities of OSS repositories, we developed criteria that would result in suitable projects for a sophomore/junior-level SE course. Our search turned out to be far more time consuming and burdensome than anticipated, but it also led to interesting insights into the capabilities of OSS repositories. The selected projects were successful in demonstrating the comprehension and evolution challenges. Thus, the burden of selecting and preparing projects must be mitigated for OSS to be widely adopted in SE and computing education.

We propose to explore several avenues to reduce this selection burden. These include investigating repositories such as GitHub and social coding for good [28], slightly larger projects and those beneficial to users [15], and examining whether different code and community metrics can assess initial suitability before investing in preparing projects. Contributing the selected projects for use by other instructors [20, 1] is also a concern of the future.

8. ACKNOWLEDGEMENTS

This material is based on work supported by the National Science Foundation under grant DUE-1044061. Any opinions, findings, and conclusions or recommendations expressed in this material are those of the authors and do not necessarily reflect those of the National Science Foundation.

9. REFERENCES

[1] Computing Portal: Connecting Computing Educators. `http://www.computingportal.org/`.

[2] C. Bird, D. Pattison, R. D'Souza, V. Filkov, and P. Devanbu. Latent social structure in open source projects. In *Proc. of SIGSOFT Intl. Symp. on Foundations of Software Engineering*, pages 24–35, 2008.

[3] E. Brannock and N. Napier. "Real-World testing: Using FOSS for software development courses". In *Proc. of the Annual Conference on Information Technology Education*, pages 87–88, 2012.

[4] Y. Cai, J. Popyack, S. Mancoridis, and J. Salvage. Contemporary canonical software courses. NSF Proposal, 2009.

[5] D. Carrington and S. K. Kim. Teaching software design with open source software. In *Proc. of Annual Frontiers in Education Conference*, volume 3, pages S1C–9–14 vol.3, November 2003.

[6] T. Clear. Comprehending large code bases-the skills required for working in a brown fields environment. *ACM SIGCSE Bulletin*, 37(2):12–14, 2005.

[7] Codeplex. Codeplex - open source project hosting. `http://www.codeplex.com/`.

[8] D. Damian, C. Lassenius, M. Paasivaara, A. Borici, and A. Schroter. "Teaching a globally distributed project course using Scrum practices". In *Proc. of Collaborative Teaching of Globally Distributed Software Development Workshop*, pages 30–34, 2012.

[9] A. Deshpande and D. Riehle. The total growth of open source. *IFIP International Federation for Information Processing*, pages 197–209, July 2008.

[10] J. D. N. Dionisio and K. D. Dahlquist. Improving the computer science in bioinformatics through open source pedagogy. *SIGCSE Bull.*, 40:115–119, June 2008.

[11] J. D. N. Dionisio, C. L. Dickson, S. E. August, P. M. Dorin, and R. Toal. An open source software culture in the undergraduate computer science curriculum. *SIGCSE Bull.*, 39:70–74, June 2007.

[12] Freshmeat. Welcome to freshmeat.net. `http://freshmeat.net/`.

[13] E. Gamma, R. Helm, R. E. Johnson, and J. Vlissides. *Design Patterns. Elements of Reusable Object-Oriented Software.* Addison-Wesley, March 1995.

[14] S. Gokhale, R. McCartney, and T. Smith. "Teaching Software Engineering from a Maintenance-Centric View". *The Journal of Computing Sciences in Colleges*, page 42, 2013.

[15] M. Goldweber, J. Barr, T. Clear, R. Davoli, S. Mann, E. Patitsas, and S. Portnoff. A framework for enhancing the social good in computing education: A values approach. *ACM Inroads*, 4(1):58–79, 2013.

[16] D. Hepting, L. Peng, T. Maciag, D. Gerhard, and B. Maguire. Creating synergy between usability courses and open source software projects. *ACM SIGCSE Bulletin*, 40(2):120–123, 2008.

[17] C. Liu. Adopting open-source software engineering in computer science education. In *Proc. of ICSE Workshop on Open Source Software Engineering,*, pages 85–89, 2003.

[18] R. Marmorstein. "Open source contribution as an effective software engineering class project". In *Proc. of the Annual Joint Conference on Innovation and Technology in Computer Science Education*, pages 268–272, 2011.

[19] R. McCartney, S. Gokhale, and T. Smith. "Evaluating an early software engineering course with projects and tools from open source software". In *Proc. of the 9th Intl. Conf. on Computing Education Research*, pages 5–10. ACM, 2012.

[20] A. Meneely, L. Williams, and E. F. Gehringer. Rose: a repository of education-friendly open-source projects. *SIGCSE Bull.*, 40(3):7–11, June 2008.

[21] J. Nandigam and V. Gudivada. "Source Code Exploration as a Case Study Towards Application Comprehension". In *Proc. of the 9th Intl. Conference on Education and Information Systems, Technologies and Applications*, 2011.

[22] T. Nurkkala and S. Brandle. "Software Studio: Teaching Professional Software Engineering". In *Proc. of the Technical Symp. on Computer Science Education*, pages 153–158, 2011.

[23] S. Oreg and O. Nov. Exploring motivations for contributing to open source initiatives: The roles of contribution context and personal values. *Computers in Human Behavior*, 24(5):2055–2073, September 2008.

[24] M. Pedroni, T. Bay, M. Oriol, and A. Pedroni. Open source projects in programming courses. *SIGCSE Bull.*, 39(1):454–458, March 2007.

[25] E. Reynolds. "UConn Github". `https://github.com/`, 2011.

[26] W. Scacchi. Understanding the requirements for developing open source software systems. *IEE Proceedings Software*, 149(1):24–39, 2002.

[27] S. E. Sim and R. C. Holt. The ramp-up problem in software projects: A case study of how software immigrants naturalize. In *Proc. of the Intl. Conference on Software Engineering*, pages 361–370, 1998.

[28] `socialcoding4good.org` viewed 6/5/2013.

[29] Sourceforge. Sourceforge.net: Find and develop open source software. `http://sourceforge.net/`.

[30] S. Sowe and I. Stamelos. Involving software engineering students in open source projects: Experiences from a pilot study. *Journal of Information Systems Education*, 18(4), 2008.

[31] S. Sowe, I. Stamelos, and L. Angelis. Understanding knowledge sharing activities in free/open source projects: An empirical study. *Journal of Systems and Software*, 81(3):431–446, 2007.

[32] E. Stroulia, K. Bauer, M. Craig, K. Reid, and G. Wilson. "Teaching distributed software engineering with UCOSP: The undergraduate capstone open-source project". In *Proc. of the Community Building Workshop on Collaborative Teaching of Globally Distributed Software Development*, pages 20–25, 2011.

[33] w3c. World Wide Web Consortium. `http://www.w3.org/`.

[34] G. Xing. "Teaching software engineering using open source software". In *Proc. of the 48th Annual Southeast Regional Conference*, page 57, 2010.

Evaluating GameDevTycoon for Teaching Software Engineering

Claudia Szabo
School of Computer Science
The University of Adelaide
Adelaide, Australia
claudia.szabo@adelaide.edu.au

ABSTRACT

Academia and industry recognize the effectiveness of teaching Software Engineering through group-based project work supported by lectures discussing software engineering theory. However, while undertaking such project work, only a very small number of students in the team are exposed to team leadership and project management. This is because teams usually struggle with organization and timely task completion, and there is usually no time left to rotate leadership roles. To alleviate this problem, several gaming approaches have been proposed. In this paper, we analyze GameDevTycoon, the most recent addition to such games. We include a gameplay and reflection component in our group-based project course and perform a quantitative analysis of a team management and leadership aspects that the students encountered during their gameplay. We further compare and evaluate GameDevTycoon against five other software engineering-focused games. Our analysis shows the advantages and disadvantages of using GameDevTycoon for teaching project management and highlight further directions towards better inclusion in the curriculum.

Categories and Subject Descriptors

K.3.2 [**Computing Milieux**]: Computers and Education-Computer and Information Science Education

Keywords

Computer Science Education, Software Engineering

1. INTRODUCTION

Teaching Software Engineering through the practical applications of software engineering theory in the curriculum is recognized by both industry and academia [12]. This is usually achieved by constructing the software engineering course around a group-based student project that gives students the opportunity to develop a small to medium size project through all its lifecyle steps, from requirements gathering through to deployment [5]. The projects generally run over the entire duration of the teaching period and have students develop a software from scratch [9] or as an extension to an open source project [12]. Students produce documentation artefacts that accompany the codebase, and, by the end of the project, become versed in team-based software development and all that it entails. However, ensuring that all students in the experience team leadership remains a challenge [8, 10]. Experience shows that within the one semester lifespan of the projects, teams usually tend to have a single leader. While better organized teams might have leaders for various project aspects, e.g., testing leader, documentation leader, coding leader etc., it is rarely the case that all students experience a project-wide view of team leadership and management and its challenges [8]. Moreover, if the project is the first large project encountered by students, team leadership activities are usually focused around team organization and ensuring task completion on time. As such, issues such as turnover, training, research, and ethics are neglected or not considered [15].

Towards addressing these issues, the use of games has been proposed in recent years [3, 4, 10] as an enhancement to the traditional ways of teaching Software Engineering. By playing the games, students are exposed to various team management issues, from the idiosyncrasies of particular software process models to staff turnover and the quality (or lack thereof) of staff development skills. However, current games used for teaching are academic projects and students often report that the games become repetitive, do not have appealing interfaces, or require significant training before the start of play [10]. In 2013, GameDevTycoon [6], a tycoon-type game focussing on game development, was released and quickly became popular. It acquired Internet fame when it was revealed that the game developers had leaked a version of the game on torrent sites. Players that had pirated the leaked version soon found their own games being pirated by virtual users in the game, and flooded game forums searching for a solution for this issue, without realizing that the version they were using had been tampered with by the developers to include this behavior [2].

GameDevTycoon is a business simulation game in which players actively participate in gaming history, starting from the 1980s. Players initially develop simple games and, as these games sell, players can hire more staff, focus on research, training, and company development. Eventually the in-game software team grows and players are faced with other issues such as agreeing to sabotage offers or taking part in outreach activities. In this paper, we discuss the

SIGCSE'14, March 5–8, 2014, Atlanta, GA, USA.

http://dx.doi.org/10.1145/2538862.2538971.

suitability of using GameDevTycoon as a teaching tool in a Software Engineering Group Project (SEGP) course. The SEGP course, the first of three undergraduate group-based project courses part of our Software Engineering degree, has students build a medium to large-scale software from scratch in teams of up to five students. Software Engineering theory is taught through the use of lectures and two assignments, which had previously required the writing of a code review report and of an essay detailing the lessons learned during project development. The following two courses only consist of group-based project work taking up one and two semesters respectively. In the last course industry partners act as clients. We have observed that students who shy away from leadership roles in the first group-based project tend to do so for the entire duration of the degree. As such, we believe that there is a need to expose all students to team leadership and management roles as early in the degree as possible. Towards this, we replaced one of the SEGP assignments with a gameplay component in which we required students to play GameDevTycoon. To increase the effectiveness of this exercise, students participated in guided reflections once every three days[1]. We present a quantitative analysis of these reflections, with the aim of identifying the project development and team management and leadership issues that the game introduces, and how the students reflect upon them. We then compare GameDevTycoon with other Software Engineering games that are widely used in academia and present our conclusions.

2. RELATED WORK

Several approaches to employing games in the teaching of software engineering have been proposed, such as The Incredible Manager [3], SESAM [4], SimVBSE [7] and OSS [15] among others. In The Incredible Manager [3], the player acts as a team manager that has to complete a project within a given budget. The player manages a team of developers selected from a pool and controls the number of hours worked by each developer. The game focuses on the development of a project plan and on ensuring that the player follows the plan to completion. The player selects the developers who will be working (individually) on certain tasks and also decides the number of days that developers have to spend on a particular task. As the project is running, the player must be aware of the project behavior and take corrective actions when necessary, such as when developers become exhausted or tasks are late. The SESAM project [4] proposes to use a text-base interface to train software project managers. Players can hire or fire employees and ask them to perform a number of tasks such as reviewing the specification or testing the code. Employees report back with text statements that the player needs to analyze carefully as this is the only information received. Based on employee statements, the player takes additional actions.

SimVBSE [7] starts with a player's visit to the CEO's briefing room where the player is asked to assume the role of manager and is briefed on the game objective. The player then meets stakeholders who are important for the success of the project and is exposed to their values and their current level of satisfaction with the project. Based on the project, assigned team, and stakeholder values and requirements, the player is then asked to make a series of decisions about the next steps to be taken in the project, based on the scenario and several exogenous (no control by the player) and endogenous (controlled by the player) variables. The focus of the game seems to be on introducing students to stakeholder values and cost as the fundamental values behind software projects. When a player joins Open Software Solutions (OSS) [15] he is assigned to one of the four projects that the company is running. Each project has a project manager who also acts as the student's mentor. The project manager provides guidance, explains the tasks and how to achieve them, and offers task feedback, in the form of sample solutions generated offline by the lecturers. The player tasks range from preparing statecharts and specifying them in Z, to requirements gathering and specification writing, and finally to designing quality procedures to ensure the company's ISO9000 accreditation.

A popular game used in teaching project management is SimSE [10, 11], which proposes to reduce the gap between the theoretical software process model knowledge and its application. SimSE is a single-player game in which the player takes on the role of project manager of a team that must successfully complete a software engineering project. The team follows a pre-defined software process model that is specified by the lecturer from a number of available models such as waterfall, rapid prototyping and Rational Unified Process among others. The player manages the team using information about customers, tools, projects, and employees. At the end of the game, the player receives a score and an explanatory tool analyzes the gameplay. This offers a comprehensive and in-depth analysis about the consequences of particular software process models in real-life. However, issues such as repetitive gameplay and the need to adequately and properly instruct students into the use of SimSE still remain open [10]. Moreover, other aspects such as team leadership, paying attention to release dates and industry status, and becoming aware of other activities such as performing research and taking on implementation contracts are not addressed. In our degree, SimSE is used in an introductory software engineering course, complementary to other teaching methods, as suggested by SimSE authors [10]. In a similar manner, we employ GameDevTycoon in the first Software Engineering Group Project (SEGP) course in the Bachelor of Engineering (Software) at The University of Adelaide as discussed below. To the best of our knowledge, this is the first use of GameDevTycoon for this purpose and its recent release and attractive gameplay discussed in Section 3 make it an attractive complement to existing approaches.

3. GAME OVERVIEW

GameDevTycoon is a business simulation game released in early 2013 in which players actively participate in gaming history, starting from the 1980s [6]. Players start out developing simple games for various platforms, in a simulated garage, as shown in Figure 1. As the games become profitable, players move into an office, and can hire and train staff, as well as focus on research components, conduct industry-changing projects, and take on contracts. During game development, the players can control three main game characteristics, namely, gameplay, engines, and storyline. Games can be released with bugs or more time can be spent on fixing bugs before the release. The three main game characteristics together with the platform for which the game

[1]We note that students did not require any encouragement to play the game nor to write the reflections.

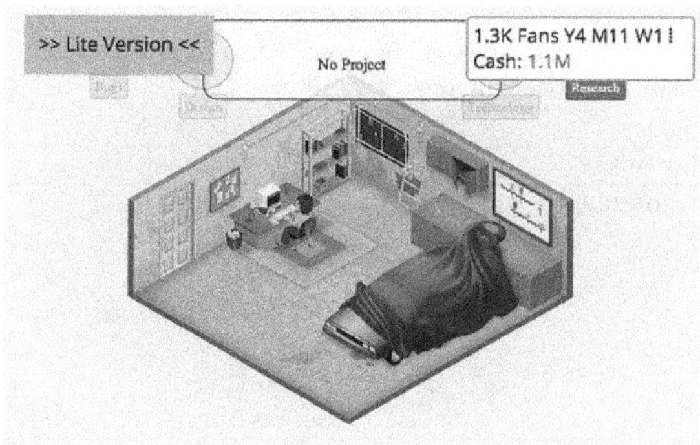

Figure 1: GameDevTycoon - Starting out in a garage

is developed influence the quality of the ratings the game obtains and how well the game sells. Throughout the gameplay, news reports describe various platform releases as well as crucial industry events that might influence game development, as shown in Figure 2 for the release of the new Ninvento gaming platform.

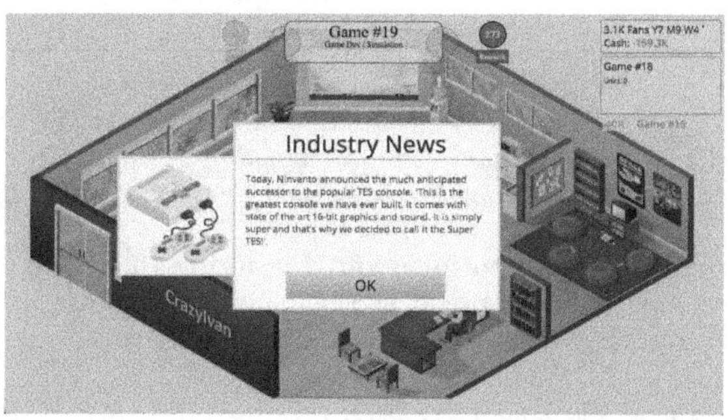

Figure 2: GameDevTycoon - New Platform Released

Once the company sells a number of successful games, it acquires enough funds to permit it to move into an office, hire new staff and develop larger, more exciting games. The player is faced with the challenges of managing a larger team of programmers, as well as creating and maintaining an active fan base, and dealing with piracy issues among others. Figure 3 shows an offer of sabotage that is proposed by Agent Blowfish. If the developed games are not successful, the company can obtain loans from in-game banks. If the company is unable to pay back the bank within a specified timeframe, then bankruptcy occurs and the game ends. GameDevTycoon does not focus on software process models as SimSE, but it is still an inherently complex game that seems to capture a large number of management and leaderships aspects. Moreover, its clean interface and ease of play makes it appealing and entertaining.

4. APPROACH

The research question that we aim to answer is whether GameDevTycoon is suitable as a complement to teaching Software Engineering in a group-based project course and how it compares with other software engineering-type games such as SimSE and SESAM among others. Towards this, we included a GameDevTycoon gameplay component in our Software Engineering Group Project course, valued at 10%

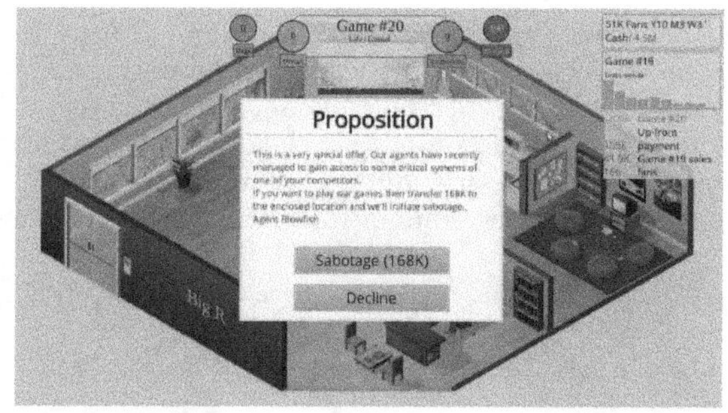

Figure 3: GameDevTycoon - Sabotage Offers

of the final course mark. Our vision for this gameplay was to complement the groupwork experience that the students were already obtaining from developing their group project and to give every student the chance to lead a team. In this component, students were required to play GameDevTycoon for four weeks and reflect on their gameplay every three days. Each student reflection was required to contain a description of the student's gameplay together with screenshots, as well as one or maximum two paragraph discussing how that gameplay session reflects on the perceived student's practice as a software engineer. Student reflections were uploaded using Piazza [13], on a private forum between each student and the lecturer. The lecturer commented on each reflection as it was posted.

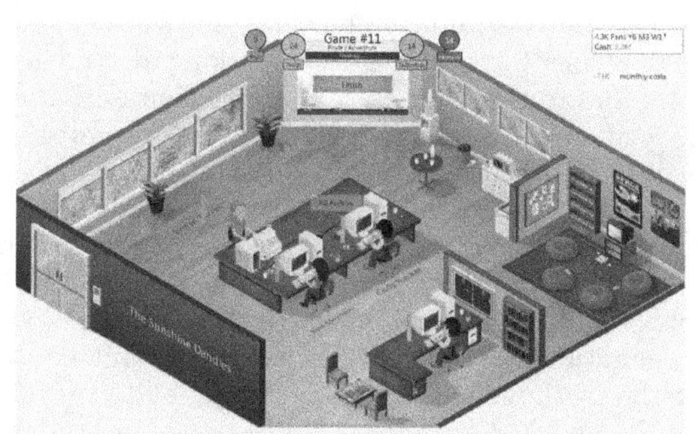

Figure 4: GameDevTycoon - A Large Team Incurs Costs

As the game progressed, we identified three main team leadership stages, namely, (i) the garage stage, (ii) the team management stage, and (iii) the world domination stage. The *garage stage* requires that the student focus on building high quality games for popular gaming platforms. The emphasis in this stage is on continuously producing high-quality, innovative games, requiring the students to spend more "gaming" time developing and fixing games, but also to pay attention to the latest industry news to observe recent trends. In the *team management stage*, players experience the cycle of hiring, training, firing, and managing a team of software developers. An increased awareness of the skillsets of all hired staff is required to optimize development time and the quality of the developed games. Lastly, the *world domination stage* requires timely and thoughtful management of all project aspects such as development, debugging, hiring, presence at gaming conferences, fanbase management and marketing among others. The challenges in this stage range from managing a large software team with its incurring cost to choosing the right avenue for promoting the company games, as shown in Figures 4 and 5. Marketing refers to any activity of either promoting the developed product or in analysis of the existing market before developing a software. A strong ethics component is also present: players

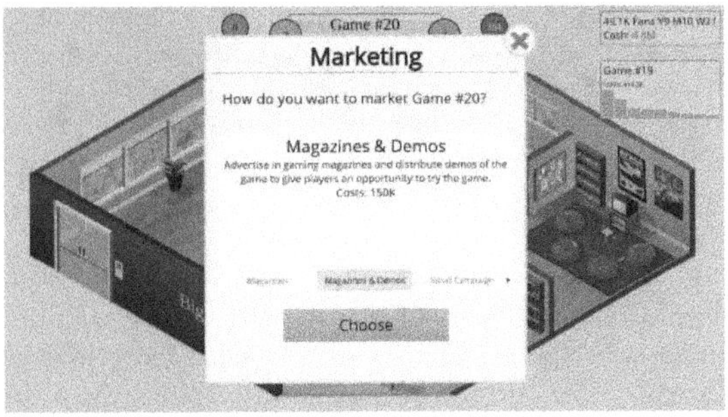

Figure 5: GameDevTycoon - Marketing Opportunities

are approached by questionable industry players who offer to perform sabotage or industrial espionage for the player's company. Students are specifically asked to reflect on the Kantian and utilitarian perspectives on their choices.

5. ANALYSIS

We propose to determine the suitability of GameDevTycoon as an additional medium for teaching software engineering team management and leadership. Looking at student comments, we aim to see what team management activities students identify and discuss with respect to three game stages: garage, intermediate, and world domination. We perform a quantitative analysis on gameplay reports collated from 14 students and show the results on NVivo matrix queries in Table 1. The reports totalled 110 pages excluding game screenshots and lecturer comments, and averaging at around 8 pages per student. The reflections were submitted every 3 days at the beginning of the assignment, and every 5 days towards the end, for a total of 6 reflections per student. As it can be seen, students wrote much more than the required one-two paragraphs. In total, 170 student reflections were relevant for our analysis. The *garage stage* does not appear many times in the student reflections as students tend to quickly move out of the garage and into team management, returning to a saved game if bankruptcy occurs in team management stages. Nevertheless, players quickly learn in the garage stage that in this game it is important to continuously innovate games in order to stay ahead of the market. The *team management stage* dominates reports: students hiried and trained staff, and invested in research. An important point was the need to assign development work to team members based on their skills:

> *I hired another staff member which has made allocating work in medium sized projects much easier as no one gets over-worked and I've been careful to allocate people to tasks considering their particular skills in tech/design.*

Another important observation is that all project areas need to be addressed by developer skills:

Table 1: Identified Software Quality Factors that Influence Maintenance (total = 170)

Category	Freq.	Sub-category	Freq.
Garage stage	18		
Team management stage	96	Hiring/firing staff	24
		Training	19
		Research	11
		Skill-based assignment	8
		Innovation	6
		Marketing	24
		Office upgrade	4
World domination stage	34	Hiring/firing	5
		Training	7
		Research	5
		Outreach	3
		Fanbase	14
Piracy		Kantian	13
		Protection against piracy	0
Overworked Employees			11
Bankruptcy	14	Contract work	5
		Too ambitious	8
		Fixing bugs	1

> *If an area of knowledge is neglected then it pulls the whole project down alot. I have found a couple of specialists (design and technology) and myself as an alrounder works quite well.*

Players also need to focus on is ensuring that their employees are not overworked as this causes a decrease in the quality of the games produced and the staffmorale:

> *Don't wear out your employees, they need time to rest, think and relax.*

Similarly, firing staff, while it might bring monetary benefits as a junior staff with less experience (and thus lower cost) might be hired, decreases the employee morale:

> *I did notice though, that firing staff has a negative impact on the other staff members. They lose motivation to work when staff is changed.*

In the *world domination stage* research focuses on building research and development labs rather than focussing on particular topics as in the team management stage. Outreach activities also appear as the player is invited to sponsor and contribute to "Women in Technology"-type events and give guest lectures at the local university:

> *One of my employees tell me his friend need sponsor to advertise that more women need into technology. It might lead to that more women developer want to work in my company which let me more easily find good staff.*

With respect to ethics and Kantian and utilitarian perspectives on piracy, 13 out of 14 students denied the sabotage and industry espionage offers from Agent Blowfish, in accordance with a Kantian perspective of universal right and wrong, and reflected on this as such. However, when fans reportedly pirated the games their company was developing, all students decided not to protect their games against

Table 2: Evaluation of Software Engineering Games

Criteria	GameDevTycoon	SimSE	OSS	Incredible Manager	SESAM	SimVBSE
Software Process Model	-	✓	-	-	-	-
Gameplay analysis	-	✓	✓	-	-	-
Hiring staff	✓	✓	-	✓	-	✓
Firing staff	✓	✓	-	-	-	-
Training	✓	-	-	-	-	-
Research	✓	-	-	-	-	✓
Skill-based assignment	✓	✓	-	✓	✓	✓
Overworked staff	✓	✓	-	✓	-	-
Innovation	✓	-	-	-	-	-
Marketing	✓	-	-	-	-	-
Fan base management	✓	-	-	-	-	-
Ethics issues	✓	-	-	-	-	-
Graphical User Interface	✓	✓	✓	✓	-	✓

piracy, to ensure fans thought positively about the company.

I get informed not long after the game is released that quite a few players have been using illegal copies of my game. I was asked whether to sue or warn them. [...] I feel it is better to accept it rather sue the offenders as it will keep my fans happier.

Fourteen bankruptcies were reported by students. Most bankruptcies occur because the team either fails to pay back the bank or to meet contract development agreements, because the company is living beyond its means:

[...] a very short time however to pay back the bank so I must act fast. I take on a contract hoping to quickly raise some money. In the middle of this contract however the bank comes knocking on my door asking for their money. I do not have enough money to pay them bank so I move to the corner of my basement and weep. Despite me having a great selling game on my hands, it was released too late.

One reported bankruptcy is caused by the player waiting to ensure that *all* issues with the code are fixed:

I should have released this game with a couple of bugs, but I got greedy waiting for the last bug to get fixed while 46K in the red. This resulted with me going bankrupt seconds before release.

5.1 Evaluation

In this section, we compare between GameDevTycoon and the five software engineering games discussed in Section 2 and present our results in Table 2. Where possible, such as in the case of SimSE and GameDevTycoon, the game itself was played. The information about the other games was collated from the respective publications. In our analysis, we employ a number of criteria as shown in Table 2. *Software process model* captures whether the game allows for the definition or the following of a software process model. This is crucial if the purpose of using the game is that of teaching the benefits or drawbacks of a particular software process model. As it can be seen, only SimSE allows both for the customization and the following of a software process model.

Next, *Gameplay analytics* assesses whether the game offers any post-play analysis of the decisions the students have made during the play and how these influence the outcomes. SimSE and OSS provide such analysis. However, the OSS analysis consists of sample, static solutions generated by lecturers for each of the four tasks that the player had to complete. During our analysis of using GameDevTycoon, we found that such analysis can be replaced with guided reflections. As the students were reporting on their gameplay every three days on the Piazza forum, conversations between the lecturer and the students helped fundament the observations that students had made or missed.

We observe that the *hiring of staff* is considered by most games, but that only GameDevTycoon and SimSE consider the reverse process as well. In SimSE, the firing of a good developer delays or cancels the project. Additionally, in GameDevTycoon, this has a negative effect on the morale of staff. Only GameDevTycoon considers the training of staff, whereas research is also considered by SimVBSE, although in a more limited capacity as an "investment" in new technology. None of the games with the exception of GameDevTycoon consider the development of specialized research and development labs and the benefits that specialized staff brings to the developed software. Almost all games consider the assignment of staff to tasks based on their skills. Lastly, GameDevTycoon, SimSE and SimVBSE model overworked employees. GameDevTycoon is the only game that rewards innovation either in research or in development, and considers marketing and fanbase management. GameDevTycoon achieves marketing through its news feeder, which keeps the player updated with any recent platform developments and corporate mergers, as well as through feedback about game quality that is continuously received either from gaming magazines or directly from fans. GameDevTycoon is also the only game in which ethics issues are considered.

Our evaluation and analysis presented above shows that GameDevTycoon is suitable as a complement to teaching project management in a software engineering group project. It immerses students into team leadership roles looking at hiring/firing staff, assigning staff to tasks based on their skills, and ensuring staff training and research into the latest technologies. It has an appealing user interface and boasts a non-repetitive gameplay. Its fundamental drawback when compared to SimSE is the lack of modelling of software process models. We have addressed this in two ways. Firstly, prior use of SimSE towards an introductory Software Engineering course that precedes SEGP, the group-based course in which we introduced GameDevTycoon, guaranteed that students had been exposed to teaching software process models in the SimSE manner before the use of GameDevTycoon. Secondly, the private forum on which students reported their gameplay ensured that lectures could emphasize any software engineering theoretical concept where it was appropriate. An example is discussing Brooks' law [1] as a reason why game development slowed down when the team size increases. However, this approach was somewhat ad-hoc as some of the nuances of the game were not immediately apparent. In the future, the inclusion of specific questions to be answered in each gameplay report will be investigated, e.g., reflection on what activities are most important (and why) for particular stages. Similarly, more scaffolding will be required to emphasize the importance of learning about team leadership rather than winning the game. In our sample, only one student seemed to be focused on winning, but this may not be the case in the future.

The perspective of GameDevTycoon is, from a player's point of view, less rooted in the Software Engineering theory, and focuses on innovation and advancement issues such as staff turnover, training, research, and marketing. Particularly appealing from a teaching perspective and industry perspective [14] is its treatment of ethical issues, with piracy the most prevalent one. The piracy and sabotage offers from Agent Blowfish can be used as starting points when discussing ethics in software engineering lectures.

6. CONCLUSION

Approaches to teaching software project management through games have recently seen the addition of GameDevTycoon, a business simulation game that focuses on a game development company. The game offers an appealing interface and an interactive and attractive gameplay. To determine its suitability for teaching project management and leadership in a software engineering course, we included a GameDevTycoon gameplay component as a complement to our group-based project course. The component required students to play the game and report on their play once every three to five days on a forum private between each student and the lecturer. We perform a quantitative analysis of the gameplay reports and distinguish among three stages of gameplay, namely, garage, team management and world domination. These three stages have the players focus on three areas of project and team management, namely, on developing bug-free, innovative games, on hiring, training, and managing a growing team, and on ensuring that proper marketing, outreach, and specialized innovation and research are performed respectively. Our analysis of student observations and reflections shows that GameDevTycoon is more complex than we had initially estimated, with subtle nuances and variations that make the gameplay appealing and realistic at the same time. Its only significant drawback when compared to SimSE is the lack of modeling of a software process model. In our approach, the lecturers were able to emphasize certain theoretical aspects as the students were reporting on their gameplay, but a more structured approach is required in the future.

7. ACKNOWLEDGMENTS

We would like to thank the students of SEGP1A at The University of Adelaide for bearing with us during this non-traditional assignment.

8. REFERENCES

[1] F. P. Brooks. *The Mythical Man-Month.* Wesley Publishing Company, 1995.

[2] CNET Australia. GameDevTycoon out-pirates the pirates. Technical report. http://www.cnet.com.au/game-dev-tycoon-out-pirates-the-pirates-339344132.htm, last accessed 26th August 2013.

[3] A. R. Dantas, M. de Oliveira Barros, and C. M. L. Werner. A Simulation-Based Game for Project Management Experiential Learning. In *Proceedings of the International Conference on Software Engineering and Knowledge Engineering*, pages 19–24, 2004.

[4] A. Drappa and J. Ludewig. Simulation in Software Engineering Training. In *Proceedings of the International Conference on Software Engineering*, pages 199–208, 2000.

[5] M. Gnatz, L. Kof, F. Prilmeier, and T. Seifert. A Practical Approach of Teaching Software Engineering. In *Proceedings of the Conference on Software Engineering Education and Training*, pages 120–127, 2003.

[6] Greenheart Games. GameDevTycoon. http://www.greenheartgames.com/. Last accessed 27th August 2013.

[7] A. Jain and B. Boehm. SimVBSE: Developing a Game for Value-based Software Engineering. In *Proceedings of the 19th Conference on Software Engineering Education and Training*, pages 103–114, 2006.

[8] L. Johns-Boast and S. Flint. Providing students with'real-world'experience through university group projects. In *Annual Conference of the Australasian Association for Engineering Education*, 2009.

[9] L. Johns-Boast and G. Patch. A Win-Win Situation: Benefits of industry-based group projects. In *Proceedings of Australasian Association for Engineering Education Conference (AaeE 2010)*, 2010.

[10] E. Navarro and A. Van Der Hoek. Multi-site Evaluation of SimSE. In *ACM SIGCSE Bulletin*, volume 41, pages 326–330, 2009.

[11] E. O. Navarro and A. van der Hoek. SimSE: an Educational Simulation Game for Teaching the Software Engineering Process. In *ACM SIGCSE Bulletin*, volume 36, pages 233–233, 2004.

[12] M. Petrenko, D. Poshyvattyk, V. Rajlich, and J. Buchta. Teaching Software Evolution in Open Source. *Computer*, 40(11):25–31, 2007.

[13] Piazza. Online collaborative learning. Technical report. http://piazza.com, last accessed 26th August 2013.

[14] A. Radermacher and G. Walia. Gaps between industry expectations and the abilities of graduates. In *Proceeding of the 44th ACM Technical Symposium on Computer Science Education*, pages 525–530, 2013.

[15] H. Sharp and P. Hall. An Interactive Multimedia Software House Simulation for Postgraduate Software Engineers. In *Proceedings of the International Conference on Software Engineering*, pages 688–691, 2000.

Online Discussions: Improving Education in CS?

Radu P. Mihail
University of Kentucky
329 Rose St.
Lexington, KY 40509
r.p.mihail@uky.edu

Beth Rubin
Miam iUniversity
307B Laws Hall
Oxford, OH 45056
rubinb@miamioh.edu

Judy Goldsmith
University of Kentucky
329 Rose St.
Lexington, KY 40509
goldsmit@cs.uky.edu

ABSTRACT

Asynchronous online discussions are considered the cornerstone of online education. Many instructors of face-to-face courses are "web-enabling" their classes to improve learning through critical inquiry using online discussions. In this exploratory study, we collected and analyzed online discussion data from two dissimilar computer science courses (one technical Graphics for Gaming (G4G) course and a writing intensive Science Fiction and Ethics (SF&E) course). Our findings suggest that, overall, making more posts, posting more questions and engaging in Devil's Advocacy have positive effects on learning, while making more informational posts, explaining to others and making longer posts do not. In the SF&E course, all students perceive that posting helped their learning, while in the G4G course students do not, but posting behavior differentiates those who perform well from those who perform poorly.

Categories and Subject Descriptors

K.3.2 [**Computer and Information Science Education**]: Concept Learning Knowledge Acquisition

General Terms

Experimentation, Measurement, Human Factors

Keywords

Web-enabled courses, online discussions, asynchronous discussions, student blogs

1. INTRODUCTION

We present a case study on the use of asynchronous online discussions in two web-enabled upper level computer science courses. The two courses were different in both content and student evaluation, but shared an online discussion component, introduced by the instructors to enhance the learning experience through collaboration and peer support. Collaborative learning can be loosely defined as any situation where two or more people work together to learn something. The addition of networked computers to connect people led to the computer-assisted collaborative learning paradigm, where intricacies of mixing technology with learning has been subject to multidisciplinary research for years [19]. As opposed to *cooperative* learning, where a task is solved by a divide and conquer approach, in *collaborative* learning the group works together on the same task (e.g., problem solving, concepts, project, etc.) Our intended use of online discussions fell into the later category; posts were visible to the entire class and students collaborated to learn a common concept or helped one another to solve a problem.

Computer assisted collaborative learning implies some form of communication (usually verbal), and can be synchronous (e.g., chat or IM) or asynchronous, thanks to data persistence (e.g., discussion boards). This study is based on data collected from online discussions, in the form of posts on Blackboard® discussion boards and blogs during one semester and a research survey from students who opted to participate in the study.

One of the web-enabled courses was technical, designed to develop students' knowledge of graphics programming in video games; the other was a CS ethics course with a strong emphasis on writing. In both, online discussions were required and students were given credit for participation. It is almost universally accepted that higher education benefits from web enabled tools [3]. Online discussions, specifically asynchronous discussions, are considered imperative to online courses [21] and researchers agree that collaborations foster learning and facilitate student-content interactions.

The scope of this study is to compare and contrast the characteristics of online posting in two dissimilar CS classes and their effect on learning outcomes. When students are allowed to pick discussion topics of interest to them (related to class materials), we are interested in determining the relationship between learning outcomes and posting habits. *More specifically, we ask what type of posts are associated with actual and perceived increased learning.*

SIGCSE'14, March 5–8, 2014, Atlanta, GA, USA.
ACM 978-1-4503-2605-6/14/03.
http://dx.doi.org/10.1145/2538862.2538898.

1.1 Course Descriptions

Science Fiction and Ethics (SF&E).

At present, our university has no regular CS ethics course. This was offered on a trial basis as a special topics course, open to all students. The syllabus [citation suppressed] was built on specific ethical topics, supplemented by readings in the ethics textbook, as well as short stories, movies, and two novels. Grades were based on online blog posts and responses (30%), in-class participation (10%), occasional short essay responses to prompts (25%), and midterm and final papers/projects/creative writing exercises (15% and 20%, respectively).

The semester was divided into weeks; students received 1 point (out of 100) per week for a blog post, and 1 point for a response. Some students wrote more than that, and one student was asked to limit their postings at the beginning, before others had begun to use the blogs.

Students used the posts to discuss ethical issues in the readings, viewings, and occasionally the news. They also shared critical opinions about the sf, and used the posts to explore their own ambivalence about societal responsibilities.

Teaching Graphics for Games using XNA (G4G).

This course was offered to create a bridge from graphics courses with a traditional focus on algorithms, to game development courses where both technical concepts and higher level game programming is taught. We designed this course with a focus on graphics programming for games using a library with low level algorithm implementations (Microsoft XNA) and designed the assignments so that visual feedback would help students assimilate the course material. We refer our most interested readers to [12] for a detailed description of the course and pedagogical methods used. The required mathematical skills were taught and assessed in a traditional face-to-face context.

Grades were based on 5 programming assignments (35%), quizzes (10%), midterm examination (15%), final project (30%) and online discussions (10%). Asynchronous online discussions were introduced in the class mainly as a peer-support tool, but also to strengthen student-content interactions. As opposed to traditional online or web-enhanced discussions with clear directives/topics for posts, the choice of topics were mostly left up to the student, constrained to remain within the topics covered in the respective week.

2. RELATED WORK

Asynchronous discussions are currently considered the foundation of most online and web-enhanced courses [4]. Discussions through a learning management system (e.g., Blackboard) allow students to discover different perspectives and to recognize personal knowledge gaps [4]. Students gain cognitive benefits by extending classroom discussions, posing questions to other students, answering questions and playing "Devil's Advocate". In other words, by communicating outside the physical classroom, students build a community. Synchronous online discussions (e.g., chat or private messaging) have been found to complement asynchronous discussions by Oztok et al. [13], who showed that the active forum posters are also active in private messaging.

A meta-analysis performed by Department of Education [11] compared online, blended and face-to-face instruction; one key conclusion was that face-to-face elements combined with online instruction result in better student learning outcomes, particularly for collaborative environments (i.e., students working together and/or with instructor presence). Wu et al. [21] indicated that students' perceived learning also improve when using asynchronous online discussions. Ginns et al. [9] found that student perceptions of online discussions have a significant association with grades by clustering students in blended courses into groups based on their perceptions and interactions.

The Community of Inquiry framework, proposed by Garrison, Anderson & Archer [6, 5, 7] offers one way to conceptualize deep learning in the concept of "cognitive presence." It presents critical inquiry as a key goal of online learning using asynchronous discussion. This process of critical inquiry occurs through asking and answering questions, exploring different perspectives and considering and integrating alternative viewpoints. However, it is difficult for students to achieve the higher levels of critical discourse, where they integrate and differentiate concepts, through online discussion [8, 16, 17]. Instructional techniques that have clearly defined roles and explicitly require students to confront other perspectives support higher order critical analysis [10]. Two of the activities students engage in during online discussion comprise lower level thinking processes of understanding and application: the processes of asking questions about the course ideas and applications, and answering those questions and providing information from the course. A third activity, exploring alternative perspectives through processes such as playing Devil's Advocate, produces deep learning [16].

Another key task that is accomplished in course discussion is the development of personal relationships, trust and a sense of connection with class members, which is accomplished in part through personal comments and recognition [15, 18, 20]. Another is class administration, including clarifying course requirements and deadlines [1, 2]. Last, when posting is required, some posts are made only to meet course requirements and have little substance to add to the learning.

The instructor plays an important role in the effectiveness of online discourse. Richardson et al. [14] investigated the effects of various instructional strategies as described in the Community of Inquiry framework. They found that the majority of students prefer open-ended discussions, but that doesn't necessarily help critical thinking. In our study, discussion topics were chosen by the students, mostly limited to material covered in the respective week. Threads were visible to everyone in the class.

3. DATA COLLECTION AND ANALYSIS

Data were collected from Blackboard posts throughout the semester, and a survey delivered at the end of the semester.

Subjects.

Subjects were students enrolled in the two computer science courses described above. 22 students in the SF&E class participated, as did 21 in the G4G course. The SF&E class had a more diverse set of respondents. Four out of 43 students were graduate students, all of whom took the SF&E course. Twelve students were female, most (nine) in the SF&E class where they comprised 40% of respondents versus 14% of the G4G respondents. In the G4G class, students ranged in age from 18 through 35 with a mean of 22.88 and Standard Deviation of 2.94, without significant differences between the classes in age.

Coding.

We downloaded and coded the student posts from Blackboard in 2 categories of initial post and response, each with one of 6 possible sub-categories:

1. asking for information or ideas
2. answering one or more questions or providing information
3. exploring alternatives (i.e., Devil's Advocate)
4. administrative issues
5. supportive or personal comments
6. off-topic or distracting

We applied the coding scheme to an initial set of 20 posts and calibrated their evaluation. The same process was followed after the next 50 posts, and we continued to verify coding practices thereafter to ensure consistency. We used the end of semester survey to gather information on students' opinions of the online discussion. We collected student demographic information: age, gender, class (e.g., undergraduate or graduate student) and which course they took.

The survey asked for Likert-type scale responses to questions about students' opinions of the online learning discussion (see Appendix). Questions ask about the usefulness of the online discussion to class learning, the helpfulness of other classmates' questions and responses to learning class concepts, and whether the survey responder helped other students by answering questions or providing information. The survey also collected information about the amount of time students spent on the online discussion, and if the online discussion led the student to think about class concepts outside of class time, and for how long.

Analysis.

Class grades were calculated for all work except posting. Because there was a restriction of range in class grades (Mean = 92.97, SD = 8.46), a dummy code was created to distinguish the top one-third of students from the bottom one-third.

The survey questions with a 5-point Likert-type scale were factor analyzed using Principle Components extraction and varimax rotation. Three factors were identified with eigenvalues greater than 1.0. Rotated factor loadings are shown in Table 1. Items were identified that had factor loadings $> .70$ on their factor, and $< .40$ on other factors. Eight items met this criterion for the first factor, three for the second and only one for the third. The questions were combined into scales for the first two factors. Cronbach's alpha scores were then calculated to assess the internal consistency reliability of the first two scales, and found alpha coefficients of .96 for the first (eight-item) scale and .76 for the second (three-item) scale. Both of these are high for the number of items, and indicate that students responded to the items similarly, and therefore they can be combined into scales. The first scale contains items describing how useful the online posting was, while the second scale included items describing the professor's support for online posting. The third single-item factor described how much students explained concepts to their classmates in the online discussion.

Very few students posted administrative, Devil's Advocate or personal posts. Therefore, the number of posts of each type (asking questions, providing information, Devil's Advocacy, administrative, personally supportive or off-topic/null) were combined across initial and responding posts, producing 6 categories.

Table 1: Rotated Factor Loadings

	1	2	3
Q1 Ask help	.43	-.24	.67
Q2 Ansr Qs	.51	-.09	.72
Q3 Learnd Lt	.87	-.32	.19
Q4 Helped Und	.85	-.14	.35
Q5 Helped Aply	.88	-.17	.23
Q6 Helped Hrd	.81	-.13	.44
Q7 I Explained	.14	-.14	.92
Q8 Enjoyable	.77	-.25	.27
Q9 Expl Hlpd Ln	.79	-.23	.21
Q10 Useful Lrn	.86	-.22	.26
Q11 Thnk Outsd	.81	-.39	.11
Q12 ClearExp	-.16	.78	-.15
Q13 Pts Appr	-.52	.58	-.08
Q14 Prof Rec	-.38	.71	-.01
Q15 Prof Resp mr	-.08	.82	-.20

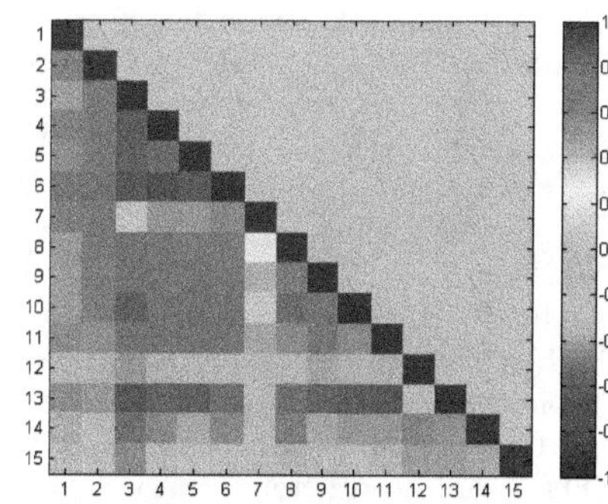

Figure 1: Correlation coefficient matrix of survey questions for both classes. $N = 36$.

4. RESULTS

Overall, students posted many more questions ($M = 21.48$, $SD = 9.31$) than they provided information ($M = 8.12$, $SD = 6.17$). On average, they perceived that posting helped them ($M = 3.67$, $SD = 1.15$), and they explained things to others ($M = 3.44$, $SD = 1.14$), but had lower perceptions of professors' support for their posting ($M = 2.26$, $SD = 0.71$).

As expected, there were many differences between the classes, as shown in the Analysis of Variance (Table 2). Students in the SF&E course posted more frequently and much longer (word count), and reported spending more time posting online. The students in the SF&E course posted more in nearly every category, including initiating posts, asking questions and sharing information. This likely reflected both the content of the courses and the greater emphasis on posting in the grade (30% vs. 10%). The only exceptions, where students in the G4G course posted more, were administrative and personal posts. The students in the SF&E course perceived that the posting was quite useful, while overall the students in the G4G course did not. On the other hand, students in the G4G course felt that the instructor support/response was higher than did those in the SF&E course. Grades were similar in both courses, as was the length of time the spent thinking about the course.

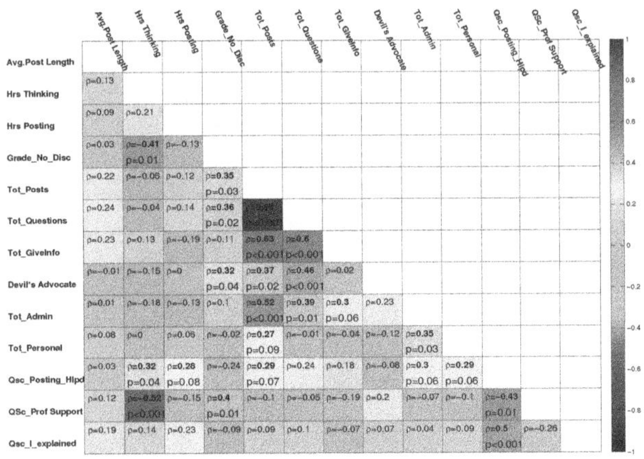

Figure 2: Partial correlation matrix with class as control variable. Color codes as in Fig. 1.

To examine whether posting behavior affected learning, Analysis of Variance compared the behavior of those students who scored in the top third of the classes with those who scored in the bottom third, exclusive of grades for posting; this is presented in Table 3. Students who scored better posted more than those who scored worse. They also responded more to others than did low-scorers. There was a strong trend that did not quite reach statistical significance for them to ask more questions and engage in more Devil's Advocacy.

On the other hand, there were no significant differences between the high-scoring and low-scoring students on how much information they provided to others, the number of hours they reported spending online, nor on how long their posts were. There were no differences in the posting about administrative or personal topics. In addition, there were no differences between the students' perceptions of how much posting helped them, how much the professor supported their posting, how much they explained to others, nor how much time they reported spending posting.

Table 3 also presents Analysis of Variance results within each class. Within the G4G course, students who scored higher posted more overall, including slightly more initial posts and many more responding posts. They also asked many more questions and made more Devil's Advocate posts. However, within the SF&E course, none of these factors differentiated students by their class performance. The only difference between the top versus the bottom third was that the better-scoring students perceived more support from their professor for posting.

Relationships between posting behaviors, perceptions and outcomes were examined by means of partial correlations to statistically remove the effect of the course taken; these are shown in Figure 2. With the course constant, the grade *is* related to the number of posts and, in particular, the number of questions and Devil's Advocate posts, and also students' perceptions of professor's support for posting. The grade is negatively related to self-described hours spent thinking about the course. However, the grade is not related to the average length of the posts, or to students' perception that posting was useful to their learning, or to how much they report explaining to others. This indicates that students' perceptions of how much posting helped was not reflected in their grades. Providing information was not correlated to grade, nor was writing more. But asking questions and

Table 2: Analysis of Variance by Class.

Variable	Course[1,2]	Mean	SD	F	Sig.
Gender^a	GP	1.86	(0.36)	3.96	#
	SFE	1.59	(0.50)		
Age^a	GP	23.1	(2.10)	0.21	
	SFE	22.68	(3.58)		
Class (G or UG)^a	GP	1	(0.00)	4.45	*
	SFE	1.18	(0.39)		
Q're Posting Helped^a	GP	2.76	(1.24)	15.25	***
	SFE	3.94	(0.68)		
Q're Prof Support^a	GP	2.52	(0.69)	6.1	*
	SFE	2.02	(0.66)		
Q're I Explained^a	GP	3.38	(1.16)	0.11	
	SFE	3.5	(1.14)		
Hrs Thinking^a	GP	6.41	(4.80)	2.16	
	SFE	4.39	(4.22)		
Hrs Posting^a	GP	1.31	(0.65)	5.07	*
	SFE	1.89	(0.98)		
Total Number of Posts^b	GP	21	(9.87)	7.86	**
	SFE	28.36	(7.03)		
Avg. Post Length^b	GP	125.27	(60.74)	295.35	***
	SFE	1222.16	(279.20)		
Total Initial Posts^b	GP	7.7	(3.05)	38.15	***
	SFE	12.91	(2.41)		
Total Response Posts^b	GP	13.3	(7.15)	1.27	
	SFE	15.45	(5.16)		
Total Question Posts^b	GP	15.35	(8.16)	26.99	***
	SFE	27.05	(6.40)		
Total Informational Posts^b	GP	3.65	(3.87)	38.14	***
	SFE	12.18	(4.95)		
Total Admin Posts^b	GP	1.25	(0.72)	48.67	***
	SFE	0.09	(0.29)		
Total Pers'l posts^b	GP	2.75	(2.65)	20.69	***
	SFE	0.14	(0.47)		
Total Devil's Advoc. Posts^b	GP	0.15	(0.37)	3.7	#
	SFE	0	(0.00)		
Total Other/ Off-Toipic Posts^b	GP	0.6	(0.94)	0.23	
	SFE	0.45	(1.01)		
Grade 1/3 Dummy^c	GP	0.53	(0.51)	0.006	
	SFE	0.55	(0.52)		

Notes: Sig=significance, df = degrees of freedom

F = F-test of the equality of variances

$*** p < .001$; $** p < .01$; $* p < .05$; $\# p < .10$;
[1]GP: Graphics in G4G; [2]SFE: SF&E
$^aN = 20$ and 22, with df(1, 41); $^bN = 21$ and 22, with df(2, 40)
$^cN = 17$ and 11, with df(1, 26)

exploring by playing Devil's Advocate, directly challenging ideas — those posts led to greater mastery. This provides evidence that in web-enhanced courses, online discussion involving critical inquiry supports more learning in CS courses, while simply providing information does not.

It seems that "hours thinking" about the class served as a measure of how difficult the courses were, subjectively. That would explain why it had a negative correlation with grade (-.41) and perceived professor support for posting (-.52), and positive with how much posting helped (.32). One possible interpretation for this finding is that students found the work to be difficult, and the professor did not answer all questions or give them the correct answers, so they perceived that they spend a lot of time on it — although that time was not necessarily productive.

5. CONCLUSIONS AND FUTURE WORK

In this exploratory study, the authors examined student posting behaviors in two dissimilar courses (writing intensive and technical). The results of this experiment provide

Table 3: Analysis of Variance by Grade

		Both Classes				G4G				SF&E			
Variable	**Grade**	**Mean^{a,b}**	**SD^{a,b}**	**F**	**Sig**	**Mean^{c,d}**	**SD^{c,d}**	**F**	**Sig**	**Mean**	**SD^{e}**	**F**	**Sig.**
Gender	Bottom 1/3	1.77	(0.44)	0.04		1.88	(0.35)	0.01		1.6	(0.55)	0.09	
	Top 1/3	1.73	(0.46)			1.89	(0.33)			1.5	(0.55)		
Age	Bottom 1/3	23	(2.48)	0.01		23.75	(2.82)	1.12		21.8	(1.30)	0.87	
	Top 1/3	22.93	(2.30)			22.63	(1.06)			23.33	(3.44)		
Class (G or UG)	Bottom 1/3	1.08	(0.28)	0.01		1	(0.00)	0		1.2	(0.45)	0.02	
	Top 1/3	1.07	(0.26)			1	(0.00)			1.17	(0.41)		
Class	Bottom 1/3	1.38	(0.51)	0.01									
	Top 1/3	1.4	(0.51)										
Q're Posting Helped	Bottom 1/3	3.38	(1.33)	0.01		2.83	(1.43)	0		4.25	(0.45)	0.01	
	Top 1/3	3.42	(1.35)			2.83	(1.41)			4.29	(0.66)		
Q're Prof Support	Bottom 1/3	2.13	(1.02)	1.11		2.54	(1.02)	0		1.47	(0.65)	4.84	#
	Top 1/3	2.44	(0.51)			2.56	(0.47)			2.28	(0.57)		
Q're I Explained	Bottom 1/3	3.31	(1.38)	0.55		3	(1.41)	1.78		3.8	(1.30)	0.12	
	Top 1/3	3.67	(1.18)			3.78	(0.97)			3.5	(1.52)		
Hrs Thinking	Bottom 1/3	7.58	(6.85)	2.32		8.08	(6.88)	1.5		6.8	(7.53)	0.67	
	Top 1/3	4.63	(2.89)			5	(2.96)			4.08	(2.97)		
Hrs Posting	Bottom 1/3	1.62	(0.92)	0.01		1.14	(0.62)	0.81		2.4	(0.82)	0.37	
	Top 1/3	1.67	(0.99)			1.44	(0.77)			2	(1.26)		
Total Number of Posts	Bottom 1/3	19.77	(9.79)	4.96	*	14.13	(6.53)	8.98	**	28.8	(6.87)	0.1	
	Top 1/3	28.13	(10.01)			26.56	(9.96)			30.5	(10.50)		
Avg. Post Length	Bottom 1/3	546	(551.20)	0.02		148.86	(77.62)	0.93		1181.43	(284.20)	0.2	
	Top 1/3	574.95	(602.91)			119.64	(44.53)			1257.92	(285.90)		
Total Initial Posts	Bottom 1/3	8.92	(4.37)	1.34		6.13	(1.96)	3.95	#	13.4	(3.13)	0	
	Top 1/3	10.73	(3.90)			9	(3.64)			13.33	(2.80)		
Total Response Posts	Bottom 1/3	10.85	(5.73)	7.04	*	8	(4.78)	10.98	**	15.4	(4.04)	0.19	
	Top 1/3	17.4	(7.13)			17.56	(6.78)			17.17	(8.28)		
Total Question Posts	Bottom 1/3	16.31	(10.86)	3.98	#	9.25	(5.01)	11.07	**	27.6	(7.13)	0.13	
	Top 1/3	23.87	(9.20)			20.22	(8.03)			29.33	(8.62)		
Total Informational Posts	Bottom 1/3	6.69	(6.69)	0.24		2.38	(3.93)	1.37		13.6	(3.21)	0.02	
	Top 1/3	7.93	(6.61)			4.44	(3.36)			13.17	(7.03)		
Total Admin Posts	Bottom 1/3	0.77	(0.60)	0.25		1.13	(0.35)	0.71		0.2	(0.45)	0.02	
	Top 1/3	0.93	(1.03)			1.44	(1.01)			0.17	(0.41)		
Total Pers'l Posts	Bottom 1/3	1.77	(2.31)	0.01		2.88	(2.36)	0.03		0	(0.00)	0.82	
	Top 1/3	1.67	(2.32)			2.67	(2.55)			0.17	(0.41)		
Total Devil's Advoc. Posts	Bottom 1/3	0	(0.00)	3.02	#	0	(0.00)	3.53	#	0	(0.00)	0	
	Top 1/3	0.2	(0.41)			0.33	(0.50)			0	(0.00)		
Total Other/Off-Topic posts	Bottom 1/3	0.38	(0.65)	1		0.38	(0.52)	1.14		0.4	(0.89)	0.04	
	Top 1/3	0.73	(1.10)			0.89	(1.27)			0.5	(0.84)		

Notes: Sig=significance, df = degrees of freedom , F = F-test of the equality of variances
*** $p < .001$; ** $p < .01$; * $p < .05$; # $p < .10$;
$^{a}N = 13$ and 15, with df(1, 26) for all variables except age $^{b}N = 13$ and 14, with df(1, 25) for age
$^{c}N = 8$ and 9, with df(1, 15) for all variables except age $^{d}N = 8$ and 8, with df(1, 14) for age
$^{e}N = 5$ and 6, with df(1, 9)

insights about posting behavior and initial evidence which supports that certain posts lead to increased learning. The online student interactions, particular information-seeking and devil's advocacy challenges, correlate with good grades. We conjecture that giving students assignments which require questioning and challenging other ideas leads to increased learning. We relate this to Kanuka and Rourke's findings [16] that some types of activities (e.g., debates) lead to more higher order learning than others (e.g., case analysis). We believe that the act of formulating questions suitable for sharing with peers was a significant part of the learning process.

We also noticed, in both classes, that students who were unwilling or unable to speak up in class were able to post. The SF&E class discussed this, prompted by a self-identified introvert, and some students reported that they appreciated the time they took to formulate their posts and responses.

It may be that the association between asking questions and achievement reflected different kinds of questions. Some questions support basic understanding of concepts and applications, while others reflect higher-order critical inquiry by seeking alternative explanations or viewpoints. We differentiated this "higher order" category in providing information, but not in asking questions. In future work, we will revise the coding scheme to differentiate questions that support basic learning from higher-order analysis. We will also revise the coding scheme to differentiate answering questions from providing information without answering others. It may be that stronger students did help others by answering their questions, but the effect was washed out by the many posts that provided basic ideas or information.

6. REFERENCES

[1] T. Anderson, L. Rourke, D. R. Garrison, and W. Archer. Assessing teaching presence in a computer conferencing context. *Journal of Asynchronous Learning Networks*, 5(2):1–17, 2001.

[2] J. B. Arbaugh, M. Cleveland-Innes, S. R. Diaz, D. R. Garrison, P. Ice, J. C. Richardson, and K. P. Swan. Developing a community of inquiry instrument: Testing a measure of the Community of Inquiry framework using a multi-institutional sample. *Internet and Higher Education*, 11:133–136, 2008.

[3] W. G. Bowen and S. Ithaka. *Interactive learning online at public universities: Evidence from randomized trials.* Ithaka S+ R, 2012.

[4] P. A. Ertmer, A. Sadaf, and D. J. Ertmer. Student-content interactions in online courses: The role of question prompts in facilitating higher-level engagement with course content. *Journal of Computing in Higher Education*, 23(2-3):157–186, 2011.

[5] D. R. Garrison, T. Anderson, and W. Archer. Critical inquiry in a text-based environment: Computer conferencing in higher education. *The internet and higher education*, 2(2):87–105, 1999.

[6] D. R. Garrison, T. Anderson, and W. Archer. Critical thinking, cognitive presence, and computer conferencing in distance education. *American Journal of Distance Education*, 15(1):7–23, 2001.

[7] D. R. Garrison, T. Anderson, and W. Archer. The first decade of the community of inquiry framework: A retrospective. *The Internet and Higher Education*, 13(1):5–9, 2010.

[8] D. R. Garrison and M. Cleveland-Innes. Facilitating Cognitive Presence in Online Learning: Interaction Is Not Enough. *The American Journal of Distance Education*, 19:133–148, 2005.

[9] P. Ginns and R. Ellis. Quality in blended learning: Exploring the relationships between on-line and face-to-face teaching and learning. *The Internet and Higher Education*, 10(1):53–64, 2007.

[10] H. Kanuka. Interaction and the online distance classroom: Do instructional methods effect the quality of interaction? *Journal of Computing in Higher Education*, 23(2-3):143–156, June 2011.

[11] B. Means, Y. Toyama, R. Murphy, M. Bakia, and K. Jones. Evaluation of evidence-based practices in online learning: A meta-analysis and review of online learning studies. Technical report, US Department of Education, 2010.

[12] R. P. Mihail, J. Goldsmith, N. Jacobs, and J. Jaromczyk. Teaching Graphics for Games using Microsoft XNA. In *International Conference on Computer Games*, 2013.

[13] M. Oztok, D. Zingaro, C. Brett, and J. Hewitt. Exploring asynchronous and synchronous tool use in online courses. *Computers & Education*, 2012.

[14] J. C. Richardson and P. Ice. Investigating students' level of critical thinking across instructional strategies in online discussions. *The Internet and Higher Education*, 13(1):52–59, 2010.

[15] L. Rourke, T. Anderson, D. R. Garrison, and W. Archer. Assessing social presence in asynchronous text-based computer conferencing. *Journal of Distance Education*, 14:50–71, 1999.

[16] L. Rourke and H. Kanuka. Barriers to online critical discourse. *The International Journal of Computer-Supported Collaborative Learning*, 2:105–126, 2007.

[17] L. Rourke and H. Kanuka. Learning in Communities of Inquiry: A Review of the Literature . *The Journal of Distance Education/Revue de l'Éducation à Distance*, 23(1):19–48, 2009.

[18] A. P. Rovai. Facilitating online discussions effectively. *The Internet and Higher Education*, 10(1):77–88, Jan. 2007.

[19] G. Stahl, T. Koschmann, and D. Suthers. Computer-supported collaborative learning: An historical perspective. *Cambridge Handbook of the Learning Sciences*, 2006, 2006.

[20] K. Swan. Building Learning Communities in Online Courses: the importance of interaction. *Education, Communication & Information*, 2(1):23–49, 2002.

[21] D. Wu and S. R. Hiltz. Predicting learning from asynchronous online discussions. *Journal of Asynchronous Learning Networks*, 8(2):139–152, 2004.

APPENDIX

Survey Questions.

5 point Likert scale (Strongly Agree, Agree, Neither Agree nor Disagree, Disagree, Strongly Agree):

1. I regularly asked for help understanding concepts in the online discussion/blog.
2. I regularly answered classmates' questions in the online discussion/blog.
3. I learned a lot from my classmates in the online discussion/blog.
4. My classmates' responses to questions in the online discussion/blog helped me understand the topics in this course.
5. My classmates' online posts helped me accurately apply the concepts in this course.
6. My classmates' online posts helped me figure out hard concepts in this course.
7. I explained concepts to my classmates in the online discussion/blog.
8. Responding to my classmates in the online discussion/blog was enjoyable.
9. Explaining something to my classmates in the online discussion/blog helped me learn.
10. The online discussion/blog was very useful to my learning in this course.
11. Posting in the online blog/discussion led me to think about course concepts outside of class time.
12. The professor's expectations about how to post in the online discussion/blog were clear.
13. The points assigned for online posting were appropriate.
14. The professor recognized how much I posted in the online discussion/blog.
15. I received more response from the professor during class because of my online posting.

CrowdGrader: A Tool For Crowdsourcing the Evaluation of Homework Assignments*

Luca de Alfaro
Computer Science Dept.
University of California
Santa Cruz, CA 95064, USA
luca@ucsc.edu

Michael Shavlovsky
Computer Science Dept.
University of California
Santa Cruz, CA 95064, USA
mshavlov@ucsc.edu

ABSTRACT

CrowdGrader is a system that lets students submit and collaboratively review and grade homework. We describe the techniques and ideas used in CrowdGrader, and report on the experience of using CrowdGrader in disciplines ranging from Computer Science to Economics, Writing, and Technology. In CrowdGrader, students receive an overall *crowd-grade* that reflects both the quality of their homework, and the quality of their work as reviewers. This creates an incentive for students to provide accurate grades and helpful reviews of other students' work. Instructors can use the crowd-grades as final grades, or fine-tune the grades according to their wishes. Our results on seven classes show that students actively participate in the grading and write reviews that are generally helpful to the submissions' authors. The results also show that grades computed by CrowdGrader are sufficiently precise to be used as the homework component of class grades. Students report that the main benefits in using CrowdGrader are the quality of the reviews they receive, and the ability to learn from reviewing their peers' work. Instructors can leverage peer learning in their classes, and easily handle homework evaluation in large classes.

Categories and Subject Descriptors

K.3.2 [**Computer and Information Science**]: Education

Keywords

Crowdsourcing, Grading, Peer evaluation

1. INTRODUCTION

Grading complex assignments, such as essays or computer-science submissions that require compilation or build steps, can be a cumbersome and time-consuming process. Especially for large classes, the grading burden on the instructor and teaching assistants may limit the amount of in-depth feedback that the students receive for their submissions. At the same time, students are often receptive in learning from their peers, and they can benefit from being able to compare and discuss their solutions with other students (see, e.g., [2, 4]).

To explore the use of peer feedback in grading homework, we developed CrowdGrader, a web-based tool for the collaborative grading and evaluation of homework assignments. Students submit their solutions to homework problems to CrowdGrader, and they are then asked to review and grade a small number (usually, 4 to 6) of submissions by other students. The overall grade they receive in a homework assignment depends both on the (aggregate) grade they receive for their submission, and on their effort and precision in reviewing their peer's submissions. Thus, students have an incentive to provide accurate evaluations. CrowdGrader is publicly available at `http://www.crowdgrader.org`. So far, it has been used for assignments ranging in topic from Computer Science, to Economics, Biology, Literature, Technology, and Writing; the class size ranged from a dozen students to many hundreds.

In building CrowdGrader, we hoped students would benefit from being able to examine the solutions submitted by other students: accomplished students would be able to look at alternative ways of solving the same problem, and students who encountered difficulties would be able to study several working solutions to the problem while grading. We also hoped that students would benefit from their peer's feedback, which can be more varied and more detailed than what can be provided by a single instructor, or a few teaching assistants, in charge of a large class.

We describe the ideas and techniques used in CrowdGrader, and we report on the experience and quantitative results in using CrowdGrader in seven classes: four Computer Science classes focused on Android and Web development, algorithms and C++, and Java; one Economics class, and two Engineering classes in which homework consisted in essay-writing.

The lifecycle of an assignment in CrowdGrader consists of three phases: a submission phase, a review phase, and a grading phase.

The submission phase is standard: students can submit their solutions either individually or, if the homework assignment allows it, as groups of collaborating students.

In the review phase, each student must review a given number of submissions. In our experiments, asking that each submission was reviewed by 5 or more students yielded sufficient accuracy, while resulting in acceptable workload for the students. The problem of assigning reviews to students turned out to be more complex than expected. In every assignment, there are students who do not do their reviews, and naive approaches to assigning reviews led to some submissions receiving too few reviews. We eventually resorted to an on-line algorithm, in which students are assigned a review task only upon completing the previous one; the algorithm

*CrowdGrader is a trademark of CrowdGrader LLC. This work was supported in part by the Google Research Award "Crowdsourced Ranking". The authors are listed in alphabetical order.

SIGCSE'14, March 5–8, 2014, Atlanta, GA, USA.

ACM 978-1-4503-2605-6/14/03 ...$15.00.
http://dx.doi.org/10.1145/2538862.2538900.

dynamically estimates the probability that each will be completed, on the basis of previous history, and assigns review tasks to try to achieve uniform coverage.

When students are assigned a submission to evaluate, they must review it, and evaluate its quality. We experimented with two approaches to quantitative evaluation: one based on ranking, the other based on grades. We initially asked students to rank the submissions they reviewed in quality order. We thought that, while students might not always be able to assign absolute grades with precision, they are likely to have a correct opinion of the relative merits of the submissions. This approach did not work well in practice: students instinctively disliked the process, often omitting the ranking step, and they expressed doubts about the accuracy of the final result. Consequently, we switched to grades, asking students to assign grades to the submissions they review. We experimented with several algorithms for aggregating the grades received by each submission into a single *consensus grade* for each submission; some initial results are reported in [6]. For the results given in this paper, we used the algorithm used in Olympic competitions: the lowest and highest grades received are discarded, to help eliminate outliers, and the remaining grades are averaged.

To provide an incentive for students to be accurate in their grades and helpful in their reviews, CrowdGrader assigns to each student an overall *crowd-grade* that combines three grades:

- the *consensus grade* computed for the student's submission;
- an *accuracy grade* that measures the precision of the student in grading submissions;
- a *helpfulness grade* that measures how helpful were the reviews written by the student.

Making the review accuracy and helpfulness part of the overall grade received by the student generates an incentive to provide good quality reviews and evaluations that worked well in practice: the results show both a high participation in the review process, and a high average helpfulness of the resulting reviews. Instructors can either directly use the crowd-grades as grades for the assignment, or they can fine-tune them before assigning them: the instructor is thus always in control of the final assigned grades.

The students perceived the richness of feedback, and the ability to inspect several working solutions of the homework assignments, as the main benefits of CrowdGrader compared to evaluations by a teaching assistant. Instructors can easily grade assignments in large classes, and by having access to all reviews, they can quickly identify how well the students are learning the subject matter.

In the remainder of the paper, we describe in more detail the various phases of the review and grading process, and we describe the experimental results we obtained in using CrowdGrader in several classes.

2. PREVIOUS WORK

The work most closely related in goals to ours is the proposal to crowdsource the review of proposals for use of telescope time by [12], as well as the recent NSF pilot project for reviewing funding proposals [14]. As in those approaches, we also distribute the task of reviewing the submissions to the same set of people who submitted the items to be reviewed. Both for proposals submitted to a specific panel, and for solutions submitted to the same homework assignment, the submissions are on sufficiently related topics that the problem of matching submission topic with reviewer expertise can be disregarded. For proposals, of course, care must be taken to avoid conflicts of interest; our situation for homeworks is relatively simpler. Where the problems differ is that proposal reviewing is essentially a top-k problem: the best k proposals must be selected for funding. Homework grading, on the other hand, is an evaluation problem: each item needs to be graded on a scale. In top-k problems, the most important consideration is precision at the top; mis-ranking items that are far from the top k carries no real consequence. In our evaluation problem, each evaluation carries approximately the same importance, and we do not need to precisely rank students whose submissions have approximately the same quality. While there are techniques that can be applied to both problems, this difference in goals justifies the reliance of [12, 14] on comparisons, and ours on grades.

The works of [12] and [14] discuss incentive mechanisms for reviewers, consisting in awarding a better placement in the final ranking to proposals whose authors did a better job of reviewing. We follow the same approach, but we have the additional constraint that students must find the reviewing work appropriately rewarded with respect to the time it takes. For this reason, we let instructors choose the relative weights of the consensus grade of the submission, versus the accuracy and helpfulness grades of the reviews, so that the grades can properly account for the fraction of time spent in the various activities.

The effect of review incentive on the quality of the ranking is examined in depth in [13]. The main problem, also raised in [12], is that the incentive mechanism makes the grading a "Keynesian beauty contest", where reviewers are rewarded for thinking like other reviewers; in turn, this may encourage a "race to mediocrity", in which non-controversial, blander proposals may fare better than more audacious and original ones. We agree with the authors of [13] that this may be a true problem for proposal review. However, we believe that in the context of homework assignments, the problem may be minor. The helpfulness and accuracy grades do not overly punish students who mis-evaluate a single submission; this gives more leeway to students presented with a homework submission that does not follow the beaten path. We also believe that the less competitive evaluation setting, as compared to a top-k setting, may lessen the problem.

The topic of crowdsourced grading has been discussed also in an influential blog post [5]. The blog post advances the idea that one of the main benefits of crowdsourced grading consists in teaching the skill to analyze and evaluate the work of others, a view we share.

3. THE REVIEW PHASE

The review phase is of primary importance for the accuracy of the generated ranking, and we experimented with several designs.

3.1 Review assignment

CrowdGrader implements an anonymous review process. Since students cannot choose which submissions they review, and they do not know the identity of the submissions' authors, they have limited ability to collude and cause their friends to receive higher grades.

In conferences, it is customary to assign papers to program-committee members in a single batch; each member then has a period of time to read the papers and enter all reviews. CrowdGrader instead assigns submissions for review one at a time: students are assigned a new review task only upon completion of the previous ones. Unlike conference papers, solutions submitted to assignments can be quite similar one to the other: by having students work on one review at a time, we hoped to reduce the likelyhood of students mixing up the submissions and their reviews. Indeed, we received no valid reports of mis-directed reviews. Furthermore, by delaying the assignment of new reviews until students have finished previous ones, CrowdGrader can better ensure that all submissions receive roughly the same number of reviews, even if some students fail to do any reviewing work. For each submission, CrowdGrader computes the number of *likely reviews,* consisting of the completed reviews, along with the review tasks that had been assigned only a short time before. When assigning reviews, CrowdGrader chooses from submissions having least number of likely reviews.

3.2 Ranking vs. grades

For the first two homework assignment conducted using CrowdGrader, we decided to ask students to rank homework submissions, rather than grade them. Ranking is a simpler problem than grading, since it involves only a relative, rather than absolute, judgement. Consequently, we thought that asking students to rank the submissions they reviewed would lead to more precise results than grading; an extensive body of literature attests to the fact that precise global rankings can be obtained by merging partial rankings [7, 1, 3, 11, 9, 10, 8].

Unfortunately, many students skipped the ranking step, leaving the submission they just reviewed in the default position where it was placed: at the bottom of the rank. To confirm this, we measured the fraction of times that students would rank the just-reviewed submission higher than a previously-reviewed submission. This fraction should have been close to 50%, since submissions are assigned in an order that does not depend on their quality. Instead, in the first assignment this fraction was only 36%. Even after strongly reminding students to provide a ranking, the fraction rose only to 41% in the second assignment that relied on ranking.

Talking to students, we understood that they were skipping the ranking step because of a combination of forgetfulness, and unwillingness. Several students mentioned that they felt uncomfortable with providing a ranking of their peers. They complained about having to rank arbitrarily submissions they considered roughly equivalent, and they considered ranking a blunt instrument, unable to differentiate between the cases of submissions of similar, and widely different, quality. After the second assignment, we decided to base CrowdGrader on grades: this led to markely increased student satifaction.

3.3 Declining evaluations

We discovered early on that it was important to allow students to decline some review tasks, without incurring negative consequences. In our programming assignments, there were many cases in which students were unable to review submissions due to factors beyond their control. In the CS/Android class, their installation of Eclipse and Android SDK occasionally misbehaved in a way that left students unable to load and review the code submitted by other students. In the CS/C++ class, glitches or differences in the build environment occasionally prevented students from compiling and executing the submissions under review. Initially, when students were required to enter a grade to receive credit for their review effort, they entered very low grades for the submissions they could not evaluate. This caused upset among the recipients of the low grades, and it was the largest source of discrepancy among the grades assigned to the same submission. The solution was to let students flag a review task as "declined", omitting the grade, and providing as review an explanation of why they were declining it.

4. GRADE ASSIGNMENT

Once the review phase is over, CrowdGrader computes for each student a *crowd-grade* that is the result of combining three grades: the *consensus grade* received by the submission, and the *accuracy* and *helpfulness grades* reflecting the quality of the student's review work.

4.1 Consensus grade

We experimented with several techniques for aggregating the grades each submission received into a single *consensus grade.* Currently, CrowdGrader computes the consensus grades by relying on a reputation system, which gives more weight to the grades assigned by the students who have a high measured grading accuracy; the details can be found in [6]. For the sake of simplicity, the results presented in this paper are obtained using the well-known technique used in Olympic competitions: for each submission, we discard the highest and lowest grades, and we average the remaining grades. We nickname this technique *maverage,* as it is a mix of median and average methods; compared to average, maverage is more resistant to outliers. In general, if n grades are available, maverage discards the $\lfloor n/4 \rfloor$ lowest and the $\lfloor n/4 \rfloor$ highest grades before averaging.

4.2 Accuracy grade

To quantify the accuracy of each student in assigning grades, we compare the grading accuracy of the student to the grading accuracy of a fully random grader. Precisely, consider a set S of submissions, and U of users (students). Let $R \subseteq S \times U$ be the set of reviews performed, and let $R \circ j = \{i \mid (i,j) \in R\}$ be the set of submissions reviewed by student j, and $i \circ R = \{j \mid (i,j) \in R\}$ be the set of reviewers of submission i.

For $(i,j) \in R$, denote by g_{ij} the grade assigned by j to i, and let $\hat{g}_i$ be the consensus grade of submission i, computed using the maverage method described above. The average square error $\tilde{v}_j$ of a student $j \in U$ with respect to the consensus grades is:

$$v_j = \mathrm{E}\{(g_{ij} - \hat{g}_i)^2\}_{i \in R \circ j} \ .$$

A hypothetical "fully random" grader, who assigns to each submission a grade picked at random from the complete set of assigned grades, would have average square error given by:

$$\tilde{v} = \mathrm{E}\{(g_{ij} - \hat{g}_l)^2\}_{(i,j) \in R, l \in S} \ .$$

We assign to each student j an *accuracy grade* that measures how much better the student is than such a fully random grader using:

$$a_j = 1 - \sqrt{\frac{\min(v_j, \tilde{v})}{\tilde{v}}} \ .$$

4.3 Helpfulness grade

To provide an incentive for students to write helpful reviews, CrowdGrader allows students to rate and leave feedback on each review they receive. The feedback provided on reviews goes some of the way towards providing an incentive to write helpful reviews: all students naturally like to receive praise for their work, rather than having sloppiness or imprecisions pointed out to them. Furthermore, students can rate the reviews they receive, assigning them integer ratings ranging from -2 (incorrect, completely unhelpful) to $+2$ (very helpful), with 0 being the neutral rating. These review ratings are used to compute the *helpfulness grade* $h_j \in [0,1]$ of each reviewer $j \in U$, as follows. Let L_j be the list of review feedbacks received by j (this list may be shorter than the number of reviews performed by j, as some reviews might not have received any feedback). We drop from L_j one of the lowest feedbacks f with $f = \min L$, obtaining L'. For a feedback $f \in \{-2, \ldots, +2\}$, we let the weight of feedback f be $w(f) = 2$ if $f < 0$, and $w(f) = 1$ if $f \geq 0$, so that negative feedback weighs twice as much as positive feedback. We then compute the helpfulness grade of student $j \in U$ via:

$$h_j = \max\left[0, \min\left[c\left(1 + \frac{\sum_{f \in L'} f\, w(f)}{2 \sum_{f \in L'} w(f)}\right)\right]\right] ,$$

Class	N students	N assign.	N req revs	α
CS/Android	68	5	6	25%
CS/Web	78	2	5	25%
CS/C++	102	5	5	25%
CS/Java	22	1	4	25%
Eng/Essay1	55	2	5	2%
Eng/Essay2	232	1	6	15%
Econ	61	6	5	25%

Table 1: Number of students, number of assignments for the class, number of required reviews, and relative weight α of reviews (expressed as percentage), for the various classes considered.

where $0.5 \leq c \leq 1$ is the default helpfulness for reviewers who receive no feedback for their reviews. This equation has been hand-tuned based on experience; we currently use $c = 0.7$. We discard the lowest rating from L in order to prevent tit-for-tat behaviors, in which students who receive a low grade react by labeling the associated review as unhelpful. Students receive a low helpfulness grade only if multiple of their reviews are labeled as unhelpful, with insufficient helpful reviews to mitigate such negative ratings.

4.4 Crowd-grade and final grade

Once the consensus, accuracy, and helpfulness grades have been computed, they are merged into the *crowd-grade* γ_j of student $j \in U$ by giving a weight $\alpha \in [0, 1]$ to the review work of the student. Indicating by M the maximum grade for the assignment, by n_j the number of reviews performed by j, and by N the number of reviews that every student was supposed to complete, we let:

$$\gamma_j = (1 - \alpha)\hat{g}_j + \alpha M \frac{(a_j + h_j)\ \min\{n_j, N\}}{2N} .$$

In CrowdGrader, instructors can choose the percentage α for which the review activity of a student enters in the crowd-grade. Many instructors leave α unchanged from its default value of 25%; as we will see in the next section, this value generates a sufficient incentive to perform the reviews, leading to most of them being completed. Once the crowd-grades are computed, the instructor can either assign them directly as final grades, or the instructor can fine-tune them, changing individual grades to correct mistakes occurred during the review phase, as well as re-scaling them to modify the overall grade distribution to better reflect the level of accomplishment of students in the class. This leaves the instructor always in full control of the grades that are assigned to the students.

5. RESULTS

We provide results on the student participation in the review phase, and on the accuracy of the grades computed by CrowdGrader. Our results are drawn from seven classes that have been taught using CrowdGrader as the primary means of grading assignments: four are Computer Science classes on Android, web, C++, and Java; one is an Economics class, and two are Engineering classes which involved essay writing. The assignments in Computer Science classes consisted in programming assignments in which students had to turn in bundles of files that consituted the applications. The assignments in the Economics class involved answering questions in English. The classes in Engineering involved writing summaries and essays on specific topics. For each of these classes, we include in our statistics all the assignments that used CrowdGrader. Table 1 summarizes some basic data about the classes.

Class	N	Perc rev	Min rev	Avg rev	Avg len
CS/Android	5	106%	50%	90%	203
CS/Web	2	95%	70%	96%	463
CS/C++	5	95%	56%	90%	406
CS/Java	1	100%	75%	105%	79
Eng/Essay1	2	78%	40%	77%	130
Eng/Essay2	1	92%	50%	89%	329
Econ	6	98%	82%	101%	163

Table 2: Participation in the CrowdGrader review phase. *N* is the number of assignments for the class. *Perc rev* is the percentage of students who did at least one review, expressed as percentage of students who submitted a solution; this percentage can be greater than 100% since some students may have only reviewed. *Min rev* and *Avg rev* are respectively the minimum and average number of reviews received by submissions, expressed as percentages of the number of reviews required in the assignments. *Avg rev len* is the average length of an individual review, in number of characters.

Assignment	$\lvert S\rvert$	RevsDue	MinRevs	AvgRevs
CS/Android hw 1	60	6	2	5.4
hw 2	61	6	2	5.3
hw 3	68	6	0	4.8
hw 4	62	6	6	6.1
hw 5	57	6	5	5.3
CS/C++ hw 1	102	5	0	4.6
hw 2	97	5	3	4.6
hw 3	91	5	4	5.1
hw 4	97	5	3	4.6
hw 5	90	5	4	5.1

Table 3: Number of reviews assigned and performed for the homework assignments that are part of the dataset. $|S|$ is the number of submissions, RevsDue is the number of reviews that each student ought to have done, MinRevs is the minimum number of reviews received by a submission, and AvgRevs is the average number of reviews per submission.

5.1 Quality of review phase

The participation in the review process in these classes is summarized in Table 2. Participation in the review phase was high, and most submissions received a number of reviews that was close to the desired value. The average review length was also reasonably high.

Table 3 provides more detailed data on the CS/Android and CS/C++ classes, giving the minumum and average number of reviews received by submissions in each of their assignments. These were the first two classes conducted using CrowdGrader. In the first three assignments of the CS/Android class and in the first assignment of the CS/C++ class, CrowdGrader used a simple approach that assigned submissions to review uniformly at random among the submissions in need of review. Since not all students did the required review work, this simple review assignment method led to some submissions receiving an inadequate number of reviews. Once the predictive algorithm described in Section 3.1 was adopted in later assignments, CrowdGrader was able to guarantee a sufficient number of reviews for all submissions.

Figure 1 gives the histogram of the review feedback provided by the students in the class Eng/Essay2; the data indicates that students generally found the reviews to be helpful. Eng/Essay2 was

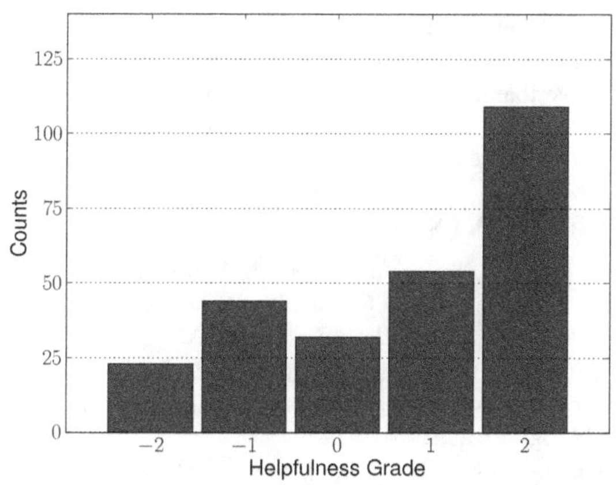

Figure 1: Histogram of review helpfulness grades for the Eng/Essay2 class.

Class	Average grade stdev
CS/Android	15.2%
CS/Web	10.4%
CS/C++	11.8%
CS/Java	14.5%
Eng/Essay1	8.0%
Eng/Essay2	8.2%
Econ	9.6%

Table 4: The average standard deviation of the grades received by individual submissions in a class, expressed as a percentage of the maximum grade M.

the only class in which review feedback and ratings were solicited uniformly: in the other classes, we had only a handful of ratings, compared to hundreds of reviews. As there is currently no incentive for students to rate and provide feedback on reviews, few students do so unless reminded by the instructor.

5.2 Quality of consensus grades

5.2.1 *Consistency of student grades*

Table 4 gives the average standard deviation of the grades received by individual submissions in a class. Precisely, for each submission i we compute $s_i = \text{std}_{j \in i \circ R}\{g_{ij}/M\}$, where $[0, M]$ is the grading range used for the assignment, and where std$\{\cdot\}$ is the standard deviation operator; we then report the average of s_i over all submissions i of a class.

In four CS/C++ assignments, we were also able to measure the difference between the consensus grades of submissions we knew were identical; this gives direct information on the "noise" present in CrowdGrader consensus grades. In these CS/C++ assignments, students were able to work in groups. Since at the time CrowdGrader did not support group submissions (the feature has since been added), the students were asked to each submit a solution: the student submissions would be graded independently, and the TA, who had a list of groups and their members, would later average the grades received by the students in the same group. This meant that we had available several pairs of identical submissions, coming from members of the same group, and graded by CrowdGrader independently one from the other. In Table 5, we report the square root of the mean square difference $(\hat{g}_i - \hat{g}_l)^2$, computed over all pairs (i, l) of identical submissions, expressed as percentage of the grade range M. Except for CS/C++ Homework 2, where the number of identical submission pairs is only 6, we see that the difference is about 10%. As we will discuss in the conclusions, in this class there were some grading problems due differences in the development and testing environments used for the C++ code, and perhaps these problems contributed to the grade noise reported in Table 5.

Assignment	D	N. pairs
CS/C++ hw 2	18.0%	6
CS/C++ hw 3	11.8%	12
CS/C++ hw 4	10.3%	20
CS/C++ hw 5	10.9%	20

Table 5: Grade variation between independently graded identical submissions. D is the square root of the mean square difference of the grades received by identical submissions, expressed as a percentage of the maximum grade M.

5.2.2 *Evaluation using control grades*

For some assignments, we had available control grades given by the instructor, or other domain experts, for a randomly selected subset of submissions that numbered at least 20. We note that this evaluation is inherently approximate: while instructor and TAs are typically more knowledgeable than students in the subject matter, they can nevertheless make mistakes when grading homeworks, failing to spot problems, or not giving credit to great aspects of the work that go undetected.

For the Android assignments, the control grades were assigned by a teaching assistant who was a fairly accomplished Android developer. For the Java assignment, the control grades were provided by the instructor. For the CS/C++ assignments, the authors graded 20 or more randomly selected submissions for each assignment. We compared the control grades with the consensus grades according to the following metrics:

- ρ: the coefficient of statistical correlation (also known as Pearson's correlation) between the control grades $\{\tilde{g}_i\}$ and the consensus grades $\{\hat{g}_i\}$.
- norm-2: the norm-2 distance $(\sum_i(\tilde{g}_i - \hat{g}_i)^2)^{1/2}$ between the control grades $\{\tilde{g}_i\}$ and the consensus grades $\{\hat{g}_i\}$, expressed as percentage over the grading range M.
- s-score: we first normalize the control grades $\{\tilde{g}_i\}$ and the consensus grades $\{\hat{g}_i\}$, so that they both have zero mean and unit variance, obtaining $\{\tilde{g}'_i\}$, $\{\hat{g}'_i\}$ Then, we compute the standard deviation s of $\{\tilde{g}'_i - \hat{g}'_i\}$, and we report the s-score $1 - s/\sqrt{2}$.

The results for the various assignments are reported in Table 6. We see that, except for the Android Homework 3, the statistical correlation between consensus grades and control grades is about 0.8. For all of these homeworks, the difference between consensus and control grades averaged about 15%. The low correlation (and low s-score) for the Android Homework 3 can be explained by the fact that this was a particularly easy homework, in which many students received similar high grades. In other words, grades were concentrated in the high range of the scale $[0, M]$. So, even if the norm-2 distance of Android Homework 3 is similar to that of the other assignments, the correlation and norm-2 results are worse, owing to the more tightly clustered grades.

Assignment	ρ	norm-2	s-score
CS/C++ hw 2	0.75	14.0%	0.50
CS/C++ hw 3	0.84	14.9%	0.60
CS/Android hw 3	0.39	16.3%	0.22
CS/Java hw 2	0.85	17.5%	0.61

Table 6: Grading accuracy: consensus vs. control grades.

6. CONCLUSIONS

The main benefit students report from CrowdGrader consists in the quality of the feedback they receive, and in their ability to learn from studying the submissions of their classmates. From the point of view of the instructor, the benefit lies in facilitating student learning, and in the ability to handle the grading and evaluation of large classes. In this latter respect, the grading precision provided by CrowdGrader was sufficient for assigning, at the end of each class, the portion of the grade due to homework. If we assume that the control error has similar error to the consensus grade, and the errors are uncorrelated, the control error of about 15% reported in Table 6 corresponds to an error with respect to a "true" grade of $15\%/\sqrt{2} \approx 10\%$, which is roughly the noise in consensus grades measured in Tables 4 and 5. In our experience, such an imprecision is not uncommon in grading complex homeworks that require judgement on the part of the grader. Indeed, the number of students who complained about mis-gradings was about the same as the one we typically experience using TAs. When a mis-grading was reported, the instructor was able to read the reviews and the grades provided by the students, in addition to accessing the submission. Resolving the mis-gradings, when indeed they were mis-gradings, was simple; as usual, many of the reported mis-gradings were really mis-perceptions of the quality of one's own submission.

One of the authors taught the CS/Web and CS/Android classes. In these classes, we noted that students were generally more ready to reward originality than teaching assistants. The main goal of a teaching assistant is often to avoid controversy, in order to avoid confrontations with students. Thus, teaching assistants generally felt a stronger obligation to follow a rigid grading scheme, for the sake of consistency, and subtract a fixed number of points for each type of error encountered. Students felt less constrained by the need for full consistency, as the authors of the submissions they graded could not easily identify or compare the grades they received from the same grader.

In the computer-science assignments we considered, the greatest source of errors was the non-uniformity between the coding environments of the authors of homework submissions, and of the students who graded the submissions. In the C++ assignments, students would develop under linux, and their code was build under Mac OS X for grading, or vice versa: build instructions and Makefiles often did not work, or libraries were missing. In the Android assignments, students had to cope with the somewhat temperamental nature of the Android SDK in Eclipse, which occasionally malfunctioned, or with libraries that due to complex build settings were occasionally omitted. The fact that some students tested assignments on Android emulators, while others relied on actual phones or tablets, along with the different formats and screen sizes of the various Android devices, also contributed to evaluation variability. The clarity and precision of homework assignments is likely the major factor in the precision of any tool, or any TA, in evaluating submitted solutions.

Acknowledgements

We thank Ira Pohl at UC Santa Cruz for being an early adopter of CrowdGrader, and for providing insight and encouragement for this work. We thank Marco Faella at the University of Naples for agreeing to use Crowdgrader in his class when the tool was still in an early, very much experimental, version.

7. REFERENCES

[1] J. Bartholdi, C. Tovey, and M. Trick. Voting schemes for which it can be difficult to tell who won the election. *Social Choice and Welfare*, 6(2):157–165, 1989.

[2] D. J. Boud, R. Cohen, and J. Sampson. *Peer learning in higher education: learning from & with each other.* Psychology Press, 2001.

[3] R. Bradley and M. Terry. Rank analysis of incomplete block designs: I. the method of paired comparisons. *Biometrika*, 39(3/4):pp. 324–345, 1952.

[4] K. Cho, T. Chung, W. King, and C. Schunn. Peer-based computer-supported knowledge refinement: An empirical investigation. *Communications of the ACM*, 51(3):83–88, 2008.

[5] C. Davidson. How to crowdsource grading, 2009. `http://www.hastac.org/blogs/cathy-davidson/how-crowdsource-grading`.

[6] L. de Alfaro and M. Shavlovsky. Crowdgrader: Crowdsourcing the evaluation of homework assignments. Technical Report UCSC-SOE-13-11, UC Santa Cruz, 2013. arXiv:1308.5273.

[7] J.-C. de Borda. *Memoire sur les Elections au Scrutin.* 1781.

[8] C. Dwork, R. Kumar, M. Naor, and D. Sivakumar. Rank aggregation methods for the web. In *Proceedings of the 10th international conference on World Wide Web*, pages 613–622. ACM, 2001.

[9] A. Elo. *The Rating of Chess Players Past and Present.* New York, Arco, 1978.

[10] M. Glickman. *Paired Comparison Models with Time-varying Parameters.* Harvard University, 1993.

[11] R. Luce. *Individual choice behavior : a theoretical analysis.* Wiley N.Y, 1959.

[12] M. Merrifield and D. Saari. Telescope time without tears: A distributed approach to peer review. *Astronomy & Geophysics*, 50(4):4–16, 2009.

[13] P. Naghizadeh and M. Liu. Incentives, quality, and risk: A look into the NSF proposal review pilot. *Arxiv*, 1307.6528v1, 2013.

[14] National Science Foundation. Dear colleague letter: Information to principal investigators (PIs) planning to submit proposals to the sensors and sensing systems (sss) program October 1 , 2013 deadline, 2013.

Teaching Composition Quality at Scale

Human Judgment in the Age of Autograders

John DeNero
Computer Science Division
University of California, Berkeley
Berkeley, CA
denero@cs.berkeley.edu

Stephen Martinis
Computer Science Division
University of California, Berkeley
Berkeley, CA
stephenmartinis@gmail.com

ABSTRACT

We describe an effort to improve the *composition quality* of student programs: the property that a program can be understood effectively by another person. As a semester-long component of UC Berkeley's first course for majors, CS 61A, we gave students composition guidelines, scores, and qualitative feedback—all generated manually by a course staff of 10 graders for over 700 students.

To facilitate this effort, we created a new online tool that allows instructors to provide feedback efficiently at scale. Our system differs from recently developed alternatives in that it is a branch of an industrial tool originally developed for internal code reviews at Google and used extensively by the open-source community. We found that many of the features designed for industrial applications are well-suited for instructional use as well. We extended the system with permissions controls and comment memories tailored for giving educational feedback.

Using this tool improved the consistency of the feedback we gave to students, the efficiency of generating that feedback, and our ability to communicate that feedback to students. Emphasizing composition throughout the course improved the composition of our students' code. The quality of student programs improved by a statistically significant margin ($p < 0.01$) over those from a previous semester, measured by a blind comparison of student submissions.

Categories and Subject Descriptors

K.3.2 [**Computer Science Education**]

General Terms

Human Factors

Keywords

Introductory Programming, Web-Based Feedback

SIGCSE'14, March 5–8, 2014, Atlanta, GA, USA.

ACM 978-1-4503-2605-6/14/03 $15.00.
http://dx.doi.org/10.1145/2538862.2538976.

1. INTRODUCTION

For the programs used most widely in the world, their source code is read by many developers. By contrast, student assignments are typically read at most once by an instructor. In large courses, evaluations of correctness are performed most efficiently by scripts, rather than instructors, as the effort of autograder development is amortized across a large number of students [4]. Although autograding has tremendous benefits [11, 7, 6], it can potentially deemphasize the importance of writing programs that other people can understand. This paper describes a software tool and associated policies that mitigate this effect by explicitly promoting *composition quality*—that entirely subjective property of a program that it can be understood easily by a person.

Efforts to encourage students to write comprehensible programs can be traced back through decades of computer science education (e.g., [1]). Teaching composition quality necessarily involves manual feedback—a fellow human is the best judge of whether a program can be understood by people. In CS 61A, UC Berkeley's first course for majors, we have always provided some manual feedback. In Fall 2012, we improved this component of the course by developing a software tool that manages the feedback work flow in tandem with autograding scripts that perform correctness evaluation. The tool was designed to scale to large courses. In CS 61A, more than 3000 project submissions from more than 700 students were evaluated by 10 student graders.

Our web-based tool is designed to promote consistent evaluation, an efficient process, and smooth communication with students. It is a branch of an existing industrial tool and therefore includes many features originally designed for a professional setting, such as integration with multiple version control systems. We extended the open-source Rietveld[1] project, which was originally developed for code reviews at Google and is used widely in the open-source developer community. We found many features of this system to be useful for providing feedback at scale, such as difference visualization, threaded conversations, file navigation, versioning, the ability to save drafts, and email generation. Our branch of the tool also includes a permissions model and comment sharing mechanism designed for giving composition feedback to students. Our code review tool[2] and its source code[3] are publicly available for general use.

Our purpose in using this tool was to improve the composition quality of student programs. To measure this effect,

[1]`http://code.google.com/p/rietveld`
[2]`http://composingprograms.com/codereview.html`
[3]`http://github.com/moowiz/ucb-codereview`

we asked a group of advanced undergraduate judges to compare student submissions across semesters, before and after introducing this new tool. Results of a blind and randomized survey show that quality improved by a statistically significant margin for submissions from students who received online composition feedback, compared to those from a year before when students instead received comments on printouts of their submissions.

2. RELATED WORK

Web-based feedback mechanisms have provided substantial benefit to many CS courses. Our tool shares key features of successful previous systems, such as the ability to give comments inline with the source code [5] and also allowing summary comments [10]. Because it extends the existing open-source tool Rietveld that is maintained by a large team of 16 committers, our tool also contains a breadth of additional features. For example, it integrates with Mercurial, Subversion, Git, Perforce, and CVS. Its user interface automatically collapses long stretches of matched lines. Keyboard shortcuts are implemented for file and comment navigation. Submissions are indexed and searchable through both a web form and a JSON-based REST API. Perhaps most importantly, common tasks such as deployment and uploading are fully documented on the Rietveld Wiki[4] pages.

Evaluations of past systems have shown improvements in course staff experience with the use of a web-based feedback tool. For example, MacWilliam and Malan [10] found that the total time required to provide feedback was substantially reduced with a web-based system over a PDF-based process. Likewise, Jones and Jamieson [8] report faster grading times with a web-based system. Bridge and Appleyard [2] report giving faster feedback to students.

Student experience has also been shown to improve with online submission and feedback. For instance, Bridge and Appleyard [2] report that students prefer to submit assignments online. Online feedback has also correlated with higher exam scores [5].

3. COURSE POLICIES

CS 61A has always espoused the idea that programs are a medium of communication among people; that "programs must be written for people to read, and only incidentally for machines to execute," [1]. At the same time, we believe that forcing students to adhere to a rigid and prescriptive low-level style guide would draw their attention away from the central aspects of program composition: concise implementations, clear naming, modular decomposition, and effective functional abstraction. We give our students the following guidelines to promote composition quality without suppressing their personal stylistic judgment.

3.1 Composition Guidelines

Our general composition guidelines emphasize the following aspects of program design:

Names Choosing names that evoke the purpose or meaning of the values to which they refer.

Functions Defining functions with a clear role in the program that abstract the implementation of a behavior.

Purpose Removing all unused and unnecessary code and comments, leaving behind only code with a purpose.

Brevity Preferring concise implementations to convoluted ones, without explicitly minimizing the line count.

Students were instructed that these elements together determined a program's overall composition quality. The original guidelines[5] given to students during the Fall 2012 semester in which this paper's experiments were conducted also include examples and links to further reading.

3.2 Scoring and Feedback

To provide a direct incentive for students to write comprehensible programs, we assigned a small composition score for every assignment, in addition to the correctness score assigned by our autograding scripts. A composition score indicated a coarse-grained classification of the overall quality of the submission. 12 of 94 total project points (13%) were assigned for composition across 4 programming projects.

This composition score was assigned by 10 members of the course staff, who selected those scores after writing composition feedback for each submitted project. Consistent scoring proved to be a major challenge. At the outset, we agreed on a feedback rubric for each project and discussed sample submissions in a group meeting, in order to calibrate responses. However, questions still arose among the course staff about what feedback to give for individual student responses. The features of the online tool described in the next section facilitated those discussions effectively.

4. INSTRUCTIONAL CODE REVIEW

All composition feedback was given through a web-based interface that managed the work flow of the course staff and all communication with students. A screenshot of the tool appears in Figure 1.

This section highlights the features of the tool that proved important to giving consistent, efficient, and effective feedback in a large course. These features were either available already as part of Rietveld or straightforward to add to its extensible code base, indicating a strong overlap between the use case of industrial code review and instructional feedback.

4.1 System Overview

Rietveld is a web application that manages the process of code reviews for software projects with large developer communities. Originally authored by Guido Van Rossum, Rietveld is used today by developers of the standard distribution of the Python programming language[6], the Chromium browser[7], and the Go programming language[8].

The data model groups all submissions by a student into a sequence that begins with the starter code distributed by the course staff. Students can revise their projects in response to feedback, and changes are tracked across revisions. Feedback comments and responses are each associated with a line of code in a particular submission of a project. The interface allows a user to browse the different submissions by a student and shows the feedback comments inline.

[4]`https://code.google.com/p/rietveld/w/list`

[5]`http://inst.eecs.berkeley.edu/~cs61a/fa12/composition.html`

[6]`http://www.python.org`

[7]`http://www.chromium.org`

[8]`http://golang.org`

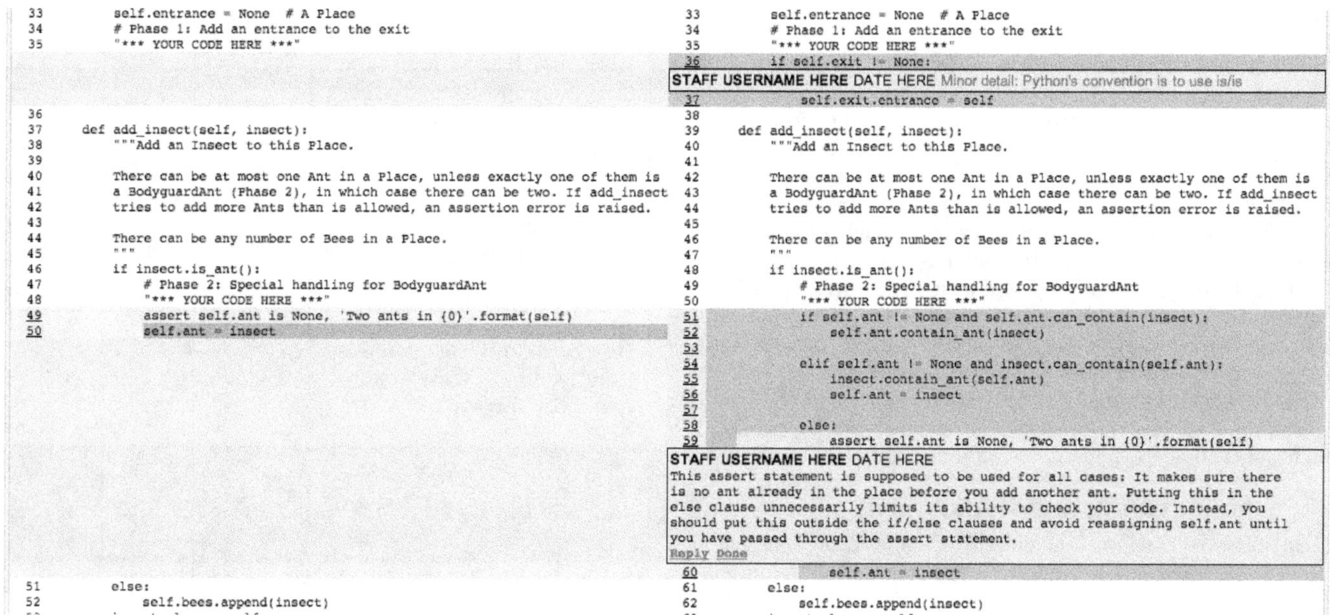

Figure 1: A screenshot of the code review tool used to give composition feedback. This view is presented to a course staff member when writing feedback for a student. Red text was removed from the starter code. Green text was added by the student. Inline comments can be expanded or collapsed to a single line.

4.2 Difference Visualization

The standard view of a submission is a highlighted difference visualization between the submitted code and the starter code distributed to students. As our projects include a substantial amount of scaffolding, having a clear visualization of what was changed by the student is a boon for grader efficiency.

Difference visualizations can also be displayed for multiple submissions by the same student, so that revisions made in response to feedback can be easily tracked.

4.3 Conversation Threading

Each feedback comment begins a threaded conversation. Students are able to respond to individual comments, asking for clarification or justifying their original choices.

We did not require that students respond to comments, but we encouraged them to do so if they did not agree or wanted clarification.

4.4 Workflow Management

The tool provides instructors with a list of unfinished tasks, including ungraded assignments and responses from students that need to be addressed.

The tool tracks both students and instructors as users of the system. It assigns each student submission to a particular instructor, who is responsible for providing feedback. We chose to assign each student to the same grader for every project, so that graders could track their students' progress. In the future, we plan to experiment with a rotation of graders so that students are exposed to multiple opinions.

4.5 Permissions Control

All instructors are given permission to view all student submissions, and submissions are given unique URLs. Hence, one instructor may ask another to help review a tricky case by emailing a link. In our experience, shared access to submissions facilitated useful discussions among the course staff.

Students are only able to see their own submissions, along with any comments made by the course staff. They view the same interface as the instructors, and therefore can make comments on any line of code. In this way, they can use the tool to ask direct questions about their submissions. Shared access among the course staff facilitates auditing in the case that a student complains about the feedback that she or he received.

This permissions model is customized for instructional use. In Rietveld, all issues are public.

Extending the permissions model has proven to be straightforward. For instance, we were also able to adapt the tool to support an anonymous peer reviewing experiment wherein students commented on each other's submissions. While the details of that experiment are beyond the scope of this paper, it is worth noting here that the modular design of Rietveld allowed for substantial changes with minimal fuss.

4.6 Communication

Students receive emails from the tool when they have submitted and when they are given feedback from an instructor. The feedback is included directly in the email, along with corresponding line numbers. Thus, students do not need to log into a separate system to read their feedback.

We believe that students read a much larger portion of the feedback given to them via this email-based tool, compared to our old system of writing comments on paper and returning that paper to students. In previous years, vast stacks of unclaimed printed assignments would accumulate. As a result, the course staff was not motivated to provide helpful feedback. With this tool, all students receive their feedback and some even respond.

4.7 Repeated Feedback

Snippets are another feature we added to tailor the system to instructional use.[9] The interface for writing comments includes access to previously authored comments from the current instructor and a pool of comments shared among all instructors. Any comment can be added to this cache of snippets. In this way, members of the course staff can share their most frequent responses with each other, and consistent messages are sent to students.

This feature is particularly helpful in suggesting alternate implementations to students. One instructor can generate a good example solution to a question, and all others can suggest it to their students when appropriate.

The shared snippet memory also alerts each member of the grading staff to the types of issues encountered by others, which helps to keep the entire staff synchronized.

4.8 Configuration and Deployment

The software runs on Google App Engine, a hosting service that manages all server configuration and distributed data storage. User authentication and email addresses are managed via Google accounts. The system administration effort required is minimal.

In our institution, all student email addresses are associated with Google accounts, and so no sign-up or registration is required. Free Gmail accounts would also suffice. Extending the system to use additional forms of authentication should be feasible, although we have not tried to do so.

4.9 Version Control Integration

The tool accepts changes by reading the commit diff formats of various version control systems. Thus, students can submit their projects simply by tagging a commit to version control, then running a script to upload their submission. This upload script is maintained and distributed as part of Rietveld.

Our course does not require students to use version control. They submit via a command-line script, and we execute the necessary version control commit and upload calls to push their submissions to the online system.

4.10 Usage

The software scaled effectively to a course with more than 700 students enrolled. In the semester that we introduced the tool, a total of 8505 comments were made for 3325 project submissions. All of these comments and their responses are tracked in a database to support analysis.

5. EVALUATIONS

We developed our tool and associated course policies in order to improve the composition quality of project submissions. We evaluated our students' experience through an end-of-course survey, and we evaluated their composition quality by comparing their submissions to those of a previous semester, Fall 2011, in a blind survey.

5.1 Student Survey Results

At the end of the course, we asked students three questions related to the composition component of the course. Table 1 lists the questions and mean responses. Students answered each question using a sliding scale from 1 to 5.

Question	Female	Male	Total
How much did you read of the composition feedback that you received on your project submissions?	4.30	4.13	4.17
How helpful was the composition feedback you received?	3.60	3.37	3.42
How well did the composition feedback software system work for you?	3.92	3.71	3.75
Number of responses	134	485	626

Table 1: Mean student response to three end-of-semenster questions about the composition feedback effort. Possible responses to each question were 1 through 5 on a sliding scale (5 is better). Mean responses by gender are given for students who willingly reported their gender identity.

The majority of students report reading the feedback, with 74% responding a 4 or 5 out of 5. Those who reported their gender as *female* gave higher responses overall by a statistically significant margin ($p < 0.05$) by a Pearson's chi-squared test with four degrees of freedom.

About half of students reported that the feedback was helpful, with 49% responding 4 or 5 out of 5. Again, those students identifying as *female* gave higher responses overall, but the difference was not statistically significant.

Three fifths of students reported that the software tool was helful, with 60% responding 4 or 5 out of 5. Those students identifying as *female* gave higher responses overall, but the difference was not statistically significant.

Overall, students regarded our composition quality effort positively. In a free response survey question, some students indicated that scores for composition quality seemed arbitrary and too harsh. In the future, we intend to calibrate scores across graders, as suggested by MacWilliam and Malan [10].

5.2 Blind Survey Design

To evaluate whether composition feedback led to higher quality submissions, we performed a comparison of responses to a single question that was unchanged between Fall 2011, before our composition feedback effort, and Fall 2012, when this effort was implemented using our web-based tool. We chose this targeted setting to minimize other sources of variance across semesters.

The problem we evaluated was to implement a function to compute the centroid of a polygon, represented as a sequence of adjacent vertices. This problem appeared in their second project [3], after they had received composition feed-

[9]Snippet memories were implemented by Chenyang Yuan.

Question	Fall 2011	Fall 2012
To what extent do names introduced in the implementation convey the meaning and purpose of their values?	2.14	2.25
To what extent is their implementation concise?	1.81	2.21
Overall, to what extent has the implementation fulfilled the composition guidelines?	1.86	2.07

Table 2: Mean grader response to a blind survey comparing student submissions from semesters before (Fall 2011) and after (Fall 2012) the implementation of our composition feedback effort. Possible responses to each question were "Somewhat" (a score of 1), "Mostly" (a score of 2), or "Completely" (a score of 3).

back from their first project [12]. Students were directed to the Wikipedia page on Centroids[10] to complete their implementation. Correctness tests were provided in the project.

Submissions are mostly comparable across semesters. The course content and assignments remained largely the same. The problem wording was unchanged between years. However, the Wikipedia page describing how to compute a centroid was edited during the Fall 2012 semester: one of the students was dissatisfied with the original notation and improved it during the course of the semester. However, we don't believe that this change substantially affected student submissions, as the course forums in both semesters contained several descriptions of the computation that clarified any issues with the Wikipedia description.

We sampled uniformly without replacement 16 submissions from each year, filtering out any submissions that failed to implement the centroid function. We isolated the student code for finding a polygon centroid and removed any personally identifying information and cues about the semester from which the submission came. These submissions were then shuffled randomly into a 32-sample test set.

Each submission was evaluated by six graders from the Fall 2013 course offering. Graders have all completed the full course and received excellent overall scores and participation scores, so we consider them to be expert raters for this task. None of these graders were involved in the original composition quality effort as course staff. One of them did report that he believed his submission from the course in Fall 2012 was included in the random test set.

5.3 Blind Survey Results

These expert graders were asked to rate each submission on several dimensions, responding either "Somewhat" (score of 1), "Mostly" (score of 2), or "Completely" (score of 3). Table 2 shows their mean responses. Graders were also given a "Not at all" option, but it was never used.

[10]`http://en.wikipedia.org/wiki/Centroid`

Effective use of names in their implementation improved slightly in Fall 2012, but the margin of increase is not significant. A centroid computation does have intermediate values, but they don't have natural names. Hence, a wide range of arbitrary naming strategies were used by students. We cannot draw a meaningful conclusion about whether students improved their use of names based on this single problem.

On the other hand, Fall 2012 submissions were more concise by a significant margin ($p < 0.001$). A strong emphasis was placed on concise implementations in the feedback from the first project, and students appear to have responded by submitting more direct implementations rather than convoluted ones.

Overall, submissions in Fall 2012—the semester that included composition feedback—were judged to have better fulfilled the composition guidelines described in Section 3.1. This difference is statistically significant ($p < 0.01$) by a Pearson's chi-squared test with two degrees of freedom.

6. CONCLUSION

We introduced a new tool to facilitate feedback at scale, based on an existing open-source project. We used the tool to place renewed emphasis on the composition quality of student submissions. In the semester that we began providing feedback with this tool, the composition quality of student submissions improved.

We have confirmed many of the observations of previous similar efforts in other courses, as well as outlined some of the features of our tool that proved particularly effective in a large course. We look forward to improving the tool based on the feedback of other users in the computer science community.

7. REFERENCES

[1] H. Abelson and G. Sussman. *Structure and Interpretation of Computer Programs.* MIT Press McGraw-Hill, Cambridge, Mass. New York, 1985.

[2] P. Bridge and R. Appleyard. A comparison of electronic and paper-based assignment submission and feedback. *British Journal of Educational Technology,* 39(4):644–650, 2008.

[3] J. DeNero and A. Muralidharan. The twitter trends project. In *Nifty Assignments Track of SIGCSE,* New York, NY, USA, 2013. ACM.

[4] S. H. Edwards and M. A. Perez-Quinones. Web-CAT: automatically grading programming assignments. In *Proceedings of the 13th annual conference on Innovation and technology in computer science education,* ITiCSE '08, pages 328–328, New York, NY, USA, 2008. ACM.

[5] D. Heaney and C. Daly. Mass production of individual feedback. In *Proceedings of the 9th annual SIGCSE conference on Innovation and technology in computer science education,* ITiCSE '04, pages 117–121, New York, NY, USA, 2004. ACM.

[6] J. Hollingsworth. Automatic graders for programming classes. *Communications of the ACM,* 3(10):528–529, Oct. 1960.

[7] D. Jackson and M. Usher. Grading student programs using assyst. In *Proceedings of the twenty-eighth SIGCSE technical symposium on Computer science education*, SIGCSE '97, pages 335–339, New York, NY, USA, 1997. ACM.

[8] D. Jones and B. Jamieson. Three generations of online assignment management. *What works and why : reflections on learning with technology : ASCILITE*, 1997.

[9] D. Knuth. *Literate Programming.* Center for the Study of Language and Information, Stanford, Calif, 1992.

[10] T. MacWilliam and D. J. Malan. Streamlining grading toward better feedback. In *Proceedings of the 18th ACM conference on Innovation and technology in computer science education*, ITiCSE '13, pages 147–152, New York, NY, USA, 2013. ACM.

[11] D. Morris. Automatic grading of student's programming assignments: an interactive process and suite of programs. In *Frontiers in Education, 2003. FIE 2003 33rd Annual*, volume 3, pages S3F–1–6 vol.3, 2003.

[12] T. Neller. Pig. In *Nifty Assignments Track of SIGCSE*, New York, NY, USA, 2010. ACM.

A Journey toward Obtaining Our First NSF S-STEM (Scholarship) Grant

An-I Andy Wang, Gary Tyson, David Whalley, Robert van Engelen, Zhenghao Zhang
Florida State University
Department of Computer Science
253 Love Building
Tallahassee, FL 32312
1 (850) 644-0058
{awang, tyson, whalley, engelen, zzhang}@cs.fsu.edu

ABSTRACT

Computer science Ph.D. training provides numerous opportunities to prepare doctoral graduates to write research grant proposals. However, writing scholarship grant proposals is a very different process, and a newcomer might go through many attempts before obtaining their first awarded grant.

This paper documents our four proposal submissions prior to acquiring our first NSF S-STEM grant for the Department of Computer Science at Florida State University. This paper also highlights major issues to consider when writing such proposals. We hope that future newcomers will be able to avoid some of the pitfalls we encountered in obtaining scholarship grants of a similar nature.

Categories and Subject Descriptors

K.3.2 [**Computer and Education**]: Computer and Information Science Education—computer science education

Keywords

Computer science, scholarship grant, underrepresented and minority groups.

1. INTRODUCTION

The process of obtaining a doctoral degree in computer science is strongly oriented toward steering one to become a research professor. Major milestones such as the area survey and the prospectus prepare a doctoral candidate for becoming a good researcher and writing successful research grant proposals later on down the road. However, writing successful scholarship proposals is an entirely different story, since the essence of these types of proposals is administrative planning.

As a first-time applicant for any grant, we tried to gain access to examples of prior successful proposals. Since our institution has no prior examples, we had to obtain examples from other institutions through personal contacts. However, even with these examples, mapping university functions and special circumstances and needs is not always clear. In addition, it is difficult to identify the pitfalls to avoid, which are often documented in reviewers' comments, especially on prior failed proposals, which people are less willing to share.

SIGCSE'14, March 5–8, 2014, Atlanta, Georgia, USA.

http://dx.doi.org/10.1145/2538862.2538884

This paper documents our four submissions prior to obtaining our first NSF S-STEM (Scholarships in Science Technology Engineering and Math) grant [2013] for the Department of Computer Science at FSU (the Florida State University). The purpose is to highlight various issues raised by proposal reviewers, so that future newcomers can avoid some of the pitfalls we encountered in obtaining scholarship grants of similar nature.

2. The NSF S-STEM Grant

The NSF S-STEM grant creates the scholarships to promote participants in the areas of science, technology, engineering, and mathematics, to mentor and support students through degree completion, and to partner with employers to facilitate student career placement in the STEM workforce. A scholarship recipient must be a U.S. citizen/permanent resident, a U.S. national, or an otherwise qualified alien and must demonstrate academic ability and potential as well as financial need (as defined by the Free Application for Federal Student Aid (FAFSA)). The total proposed scholarship amount can be up to $600,000 for 5 years, and each full-time student can receive up to $10,000 per year, depending on financial need.

The proposal instructions are straightforward. However, we have gone through four iterations prior to obtaining this grant.

2.1 Why Single Out Computer Science?

The percentage of computer science students enrolled in STEM has remained low (Figure 2.1.1) [NSF 2012]. In addition, the growth rate of the computer science major needs to be at least 20% in order to meet the 760,000 job openings by 2020 in computer and information technology as projected by the U.S. Bureau of Labor Statistics [Lockard and Wolf 2010].

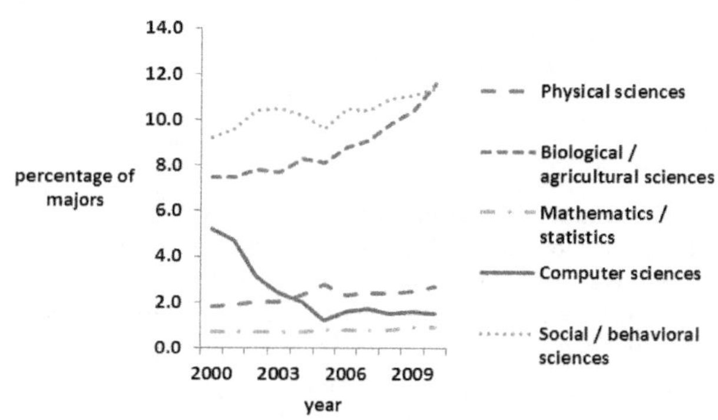

Figure 2.1.1. Percentage of students enrolled in STEM majors [NSF 2012].

3. First Attempt (Failed)

For our first attempt, we gathered examples of successful proposals from a top research university (with more than 6,000 STEM undergraduate students) and a top teaching university (with more than 700 STEM undergraduate students). For research universities like FSU, the scale of operation can allow scholarship grants to be targeted toward only computer science students. Teaching universities have to target more general STEM students because of the small size of their computer science departments. Also, the level of coordination within school units and operation can vary widely. For example, one university allows a cohort to live in the same residential hall, which we cannot easily provide. In addition, since we had no prior similar scholarship grants, we cannot build our proposal on the success of previously proven support infrastructure.

We learned about the existing student support infrastructure on campus and included it in the proposal, along with the many opportunities for leadership and K-12 outreach within our department. We included the ideas for collaborating with the biology department to increase the number of women and underrepresented students, and we aimed to sponsor two fully funded cohorts of entering freshmen for four years. The cohorts are co-registered in courses to promote opportunities for collaboration and retention.

3.1 Reviews

The review came back with G (good), G, G, and VG (very good), and here are the major comments: (1) Our *selection process and contents of application packet are not defined*, (2) *What happens if a student does not qualify for renewal of the scholarship?* (3) One reviewer observed our *good outreach plan*, while the others thought that we have *too much emphasis on engaging students in outreach activities*. (4) *More faculty involvement is needed.* (5) In terms of our collaboration with the biology department, we need *validation of institutional support (letters)*.

3.2 Response to the Comments

Prior to updating the proposal for the next round, we should first address comments from the reviewers.

3.2.1 How to Select Students?

Three components of our selection criteria include academic qualification, personal qualities, and recommendation letters.

Academic qualifications: One concern is that scholarships are awarded to talented students who will complete the degree regardless of the availability of the scholarships [Baker and Finn 2008, Whalen and Shelley 2010]. To address this concern, we will extend our application considerations to the top 25% of applicants. We will also give special consideration to women and underrepresented groups.

Personal qualities: During our interviews, we will examine the candidate's motivation, leadership, maturity, persistence, and dedication to achieving a degree in computer science. Active involvement in extracurricular activities, community service, and work experience are strong indicators of such personal qualities.

Recommendation letters: Recommendation letters for applicants will complement our interview results when we consider the final scholarship recipients.

3.2.2 How to Design the Application?

To ease application processing, we can ask an applicant to fill out and upload all pieces of information that we seek such as forms and reference letters. However, the application process can be tedious and can duplicate the university application process in many ways. Additionally, the application may contain many pieces of information that are difficult to verify independently at the departmental level (e.g., citizenship status, high school GPA). For these reasons, we resort to using a one-page application with short essay questions that ask a student about his or her career goals and personal qualities. We will retrieve any associated records from the admission and financial aid offices. Depending on the extent of system integration, this approach may be cumbersome for the student coordinator, who will need to track down all related information for each applicant.

3.2.3 Scholarship Renewal

When a student fails to maintain the GPA necessary to remain in the major, we must put the student on probation for one semester to regain his/her status. It may become problematic as the remaining cohort moves on to other set of co-registered courses. The student left behind may become out of sync with the cohort even if the student remains in the program. However, since the cohort is an effective support structure, we will consider managing all undergraduate students with this cohort co-registration approach. Thus, if a student becomes out of sync with one cohort, the student can easily join another.

If a student fails to renew the scholarship for two semesters, the student will lose the scholarship. The available cohort slot will be open to other students with similar standing in the degree program.

3.2.4 Conflicting Comments on Outreach Activities

We followed the recommendation by the majority of reviewers to reduce the number of outreach activities. Our next submission also included a section at the beginning that summarized our responses to prior comments, so that the reviewers would not contradict the reviews of this round.

3.2.5 More Faculty Involvement

We added weekly gender-informed team mentoring sessions [Chesler and Chesler 2002]. We also leverage our faculty members' participation in the NSF Research Experience for Undergraduate Program to sponsor undergraduates, either in the form of an honors thesis or independent research. Most students involved in the undergraduate independent research have decided to pursue graduate degrees, and the retention rate within the mentored pool is nearly 100%. Thus, we will encourage S-STEM scholars to partake in undergraduate research opportunities. Having graduate-school-like experience will also help them in making informed decisions when choosing between going to graduate school and getting a job in industry.

3.2.6 Support Letters

Based on our experience serving on NSF panels, letters may or may not carry weight. However, in this case, we added the support letters.

4. Second Attempt (Failed)

We addressed various concerns raised by reviewers, and we made some changes to our awards. Since the scholarship award amount then was between $5,000 and $10,000, we decided to maximize the number of recipients by awarding a fixed minimum amount for students with financial needs greater than $5,000. Since we wanted students to focus on their studying, we required students to ask us for approval for side jobs (including work study).

4.1 Reviews

The second set of reviews came back with G, G, G, VG, and E (excellent). Although our proposal was declined, our rating had improved, and having one excellent was very encouraging, since someone on the panel might have been championing our proposal.

The reviewers provided the following major comments: (1) The reviewers would like to see our *current enrollments along with a desired level of achievement.* (2) The reviewers would like to have a *justification of the determination of the amount* to be awarded. Our requirement that a student should not be employed elsewhere for financial motives *appears harsh.* (3) Another concern is we only advertise to students who are already admitted to FSU, ignoring *potential students that would have applied to FSU had they known about the potential awards.* (4) Our proposal *relies too much on existing services and offers no new support system.* In particular, first-year students *need support in adjusting to college life.*

4.2 Response to the Comments

Responding to this round of comments requires much more thoughtful planning based on the data and knowledge of our department and campus.

4.2.1 Quantified Enrollment Goals

We had to coordinate with our Institutional Research and Financial Aid units to compile enrollment, graduation, demographic, and financial-need statistics within the past three years and to compare these numbers with national and state averages. Our overall enrollment trends are reflective of the national trend. However, in terms of genders, our department is 5% below the national average for female computer science student enrollments. In terms of ethnicity, we are 10% below the state average for Hispanic students and 6% below the state average for African American students. These numbers also helped us focus on how to target the scholarships to achieve realistic quantifiable improvements in those numbers.

4.2.2 What Award Amount and Duration?

Two major parameters for administering a scholarship program are the amount and duration. One option is to provide maximum support for 4 years, so that students can focus on academic pursuit. However, this minimizes the number of students we can support. Depending on the size of the target student population in the department, this may or may not lead to significant results. Another option is to reduce the support to, say, the first two years, but we need to justify the choice of time frame (e.g., based on year-to-year persistence rates). There are other possibilities.

The option we chose was partial support for 4 years, so that we could support two cohorts of 15+ students. Our target goal is to promote female and underrepresented students among our undergraduate students. We also decided to use scholarships to replace student loans, since studies have shown that underrepresented students are more debt-averse, more likely to work full-time, and more likely to leave college without a degree [Cunningham and Santiago 2008]. Additionally, the acceptance of our scholarship must not preclude other financial aid possibilities such as work study, which is crucial for students with financial need beyond what our scholarships can provide.

4.2.3 How to Reach Students?

Clearly, the simplest way to attract applicants is to advertise to students who have already been admitted to the computer science major. However, other than achieving better retention, this approach is less likely to noticeably shift the demographics within the student body.

Going beyond the department includes advertising to all students admitted to the university through various forms of welcome packages. This advertising channel precludes students who may have come to FSU if they had known about this scholarship.

To broaden the reach, in the past we have attempted to hold field trips for local high schools. However, we found that even if they are feeder schools for the university, the conversion ratio for students to major in computer science is low. Thus, we have budgeted participant support funds for student ambassadors, who can go back to their high schools (with our targeted demographic characteristics) during breaks to advertise this scholarship opportunity. We also explored the use of social networks, so that scholarship recipients can advertise to their contacts in their high schools.

4.2.4 Retention Support

We have budgeted participant support for numerous one-to-one or shared tutoring hours. Those tutoring hours will be used for diverse purposes. For example, to ease the first-year transition from high school to college, the tutors will host a one-week workshop. The program will cover topics from the perspectives of computer science students, ranging from adapting to college life and time management to study skills and campus resources. Before each semester begins, these tutors will host a workshop on the cohort registered courses, so that S-STEM scholars can start their first homework assignments early. Throughout each semester, S-STEM scholars can request either one-on-one tutoring or group tutoring based on common needs.

5. Third Attempt (Failed)

This round of the update was quite time-consuming, due to the need to interact with different campus units to gather financial and demographic information for computer science students. As we were compiling and comparing the year-to-year persistence rates of women and underrepresented groups to the rest of the student body, we found that this number can be tricky to process. Many students might skip a year before continuing due to special circumstances. In addition, a significant number of students declare their major late, which skews the persistence rate for juniors and seniors.

To reflect the mission of the STEM program, S-STEM students who change their majors to other STEM disciplines will still be supported, provided (1) they are able to retain good standing (e.g., full-time, GPA requirements, etc.), and (2) they can locate a mentor in another STEM discipline to fulfill reporting requirements.

5.1 Reviews

The reviews came back with G, VG, VG, VG, and VG ratings. The overall average rating was improving. However, the lack of an excellent rating shows that we failed to get someone excited on the panel to champion for us. This could be simply due to the randomness of the panel selection process.

The reviewers raised the following major concerns: (1) Our proposal *should include the specific selection criteria* beyond what we had. (2) The reviewers worried that *students could 'shop' the scholarship, then take the scholarship with them if they transfer to another department.* (3) Reviewers share general *concerns about the employment and career roles for a Computational Biologist. Is growing programs in the spirit of this scholarship program?* (4) Reviewers concern about our *ability to manage, train, and supervise* the tutors. (5) The proposal should include *an external evaluator not involved with the project.* (6) Finally, *a more detailed concise project timeline should be developed.*

5.2 Response to the Comments

Based on the comments, it seems that evaluation and dedicating scholarships to grow the computational biology program are the central concerns. The remaining concerns are more easily addressable.

5.2.1 Additional Details on Selection Criteria

In addition to the criteria we mentioned in Section 3.2.1, we added that the top 25% of students are determined by equal weightings of high school GPA, SAT/ACT scores, and the number of leadership positions held in various extracurricular activities. For example, the high school GPA for our top 25% female minority students is 3.9; SAT, 1,250 (verbal + math); and ACT, 28 (composite score).

We are aware that some high schools may not offer AP courses, and we hope that using GPA as only a part of the qualification equation can compensate somewhat for this difference.

5.2.2 Major Switching

One concern is how to handle students who switch to non-computer science majors. If a student switches to a non-STEM major, we can simply terminate the support. The trickier case is when the new major is within the STEM area; the continued support still adheres to the mission of the NSF S-STEM program. However, it becomes problematic when evaluating our outcome. It also creates an opportunity for students to "shop" for the computer science scholarship and then switch to another STEM disciplines. Thus, we decided to terminate the support if a student decides to switch out of the computer science major.

5.2.3 Scholarship Focus

We deemphasized building the computational biology program and focused on mitigating the low percentage of female enrollment in computer science [Zweben 2013]. While the causes of this situation are debatable, studies suggest that the social aspect is an important element. The nerd stereotype [Beyer et al. 2003] and long hours of socially isolated programming sessions [Declue 1997; Amelink and Creamer 2010] are possible causes for female attrition in computer science enrollment. As the world becomes entwined with computing, having a wealth of female computer science expertise is essential to avoid gender biases in areas as software application design, authoring educational software, sustaining the number of female computer scientists, and shaping the societal norm for future generations.

We further highlight the trend beyond the area of computer science that underrepresented students are less receptive to taking out student loans [Cunningham and Santiago 2008]. For example, Hispanic students are less likely to borrow student loans (20%) compared to Caucasian and African American students (35% and 43%). Debt-averse African American and Hispanic students who do not take out student loans are more likely to work full-time, and 9% to 11% are more likely to leave college without a degree. While the overall impact is felt for all disciplines, the throttling of production of computer science majors will further exacerbate the projected labor shortage.

For us to build a critical mass of underrepresented students, each cohort will enroll in the same set of classes. This enrollment scheme will create opportunities for the students to form study groups and experience a collaborative learning environment to promote retention [Cohoon 2005]. We collaborated with the computer science department at Florida Agricultural and Mechanical University, a historically black university, to provide a dual-enrollment program. Dual enrollment helps FSU recruit and retain more African American students with a small critical mass. We have developed interdisciplinary programs (e.g., computational biology and computer criminology) to work with majors with large pools of women and underrepresented students.

5.2.4 Quality of Tutors

To ensure quality, we specify that our tutors will be required to go through the same training process required by FSU for all teaching assistants and will be required to attend on-campus teaching conferences.

5.2.5 How to Evaluate Our Project?

The evaluation has two components. The external evaluation is conducted annually by a non-FSU reviewer with a research background in education. The internal evaluation is conducted more frequently by S-STEM faculty members.

Internally, we will monitor our S-STEM scholars in terms of their academic progress, professional development, and interactions with various student support infrastructures. S-STEM faculty members will communicate weekly and meet formally once a semester to evaluate the progress of the project, cohorts, and each student, and make recommendations on the renewal of scholarships. Each undergraduate course will gather surveys that identify gender and culture biases in terms of course examples, assignments, and examinations.

The evaluation component of this project will be used for both formative and summative purposes. Throughout the project, information will be gathered in order to contribute to (a) decisions about the project development, implementation and modification, and (b) strategies to improve the areas of project focus. The evaluation will culminate with analyses designed to determine if the project objectives have been met.

Ongoing formative evaluation measures will be used to identify effective components of the project and to monitor the progress of project implementation. The formative portion of the evaluation will address the following key areas: (1) progress on each of the project objectives, (2) outcome completion in relation to the project timeline, (3) incremental project impact on students related to the expected outcomes, and (4) arising issues affecting the successful implementation of the project.

The external reviewer will conduct an annual data collection and analyses in the following areas:

1. Enrollment in various computer science undergraduate degree programs
2. Enrollment of female and minority students
3. Relative performance of S-STEM scholars and non-scholarship students
4. Internships with local or national companies
5. Rate of progress toward graduation and retention of majors
6. Semesters taken to earn a degree
7. Separations for reasons other than graduation
8. Job and graduate school placements

The reviewer will follow up on each student supported by this project who leaves the program. For those who complete a degree, we will seek to identify their placement. If any student changes to a different degree program, we will seek to identify the new program and the reason for switching majors. If any S-STEM scholars leave the university without completing a degree, we will seek to identify the reason.

In addition to participating in the S-STEM data collection activities by NSF, we will also examine and compare the interactions within each of the two S-STEM cohorts with the interactions within naturally formed student groups. We aim to understand the factors that influence the enrollment of women and underrepresented groups in computer science. For example, we can examine the correlation of the performance of S-STEM scholars with the amount of scholarship awarded, the type of support services used, student activities attended, and the extent S-STEM scholars work together. We will also analyze the surveys gathered from the gender- and culture-neutral curriculum initiative to better understand the subtle factors that can promote diversity in computer science. Resulting quantitative data will be disaggregated by important categorical variables and analyzed using descriptive and inferential statistical methods.

6. Fourth Attempt (Successful)

We deemphasized building the computational biology program and focused on mitigating the low percentage of female enrollment in computer science. We terminated the scholarship support for students who switched out from the computer science major. We recruited an external evaluator who specializes in evaluating educational programs. We added a detailed administrative timeline. Finally, in the section that summarizes our responses to prior comments, we added our appreciation for the reviewers' time to help us strengthen the proposal.

Our final review ratings for our award were G, VG, VG, VG, and E. The main concern from the reviewers was that we could not reserve the scholarship to a particular group of people; thus, when administering our grant, our decisions must be based on applicants' holistic views. Finally, the reviewers appreciated *the PIs persistence in pursuing the S-STEM grant.*

7. Lessons Learned

This paper has highlighted the major issues when writing a scholarship proposal and documented our four attempts to obtain the first NSF S-STEM grant for FSU. Overall, we present the following general lessons for future new scholarship grant proposal writers.

- ***Leverage institutional strengths.*** Every educational institution is different (e.g., has access to detailed student statistics, close ties with industry). The proposal should be tailored to leverage an institution's unique strengths.
- ***Set focused and quantifiable goals.*** The proposal needs to show the extent of how the limited resources provided by the scholarship can make a difference for students from certain demographics.
- ***Be inclusive.*** The scholarship selection criteria should include students who might not have been able to demonstrate their potential due to financial hardship.
- ***Be specific.*** Program proposals need to be specific enough for grant administrators to implement them swiftly.
- ***Address important corner cases.*** The proposed program needs to address situations such as students who change majors and students who still need to work while receiving the scholarship.
- ***Streamline the application process.*** The student grant application process should leverage existing university and departmental admission procedures.
- ***Address earlier reviewers cumulatively.*** To avoid reviewers giving conflicting reviews in different submission rounds, state how the proposal addresses concerns from the previous round of reviews.

Finally, perhaps the most important aspect of getting any proposal funded was summarized by a reviewer in one word —persistence.

8. ACKNOWLEDGMENTS

We would like to thank the anonymous SIGCSE reviewers for their invaluable comments. We would also like to thank 19 anonymous NSF S-STEM program reviewers and program managers for providing us with encouragement and invaluable feedback to strengthen our proposal. We further thank Peter Reiher and Geoff Kuenning for commenting on early versions of this draft. Finally, we thank Esther Diaguila, Betty Stanton, Stephen Nettles, Edward Jones, Don Levitan, Jim Clamons, and Carl Owenby for supporting and contributing to our proposal. This work is sponsored by NSF DUE-1259462. Opinions, findings, and conclusions or recommendations expressed in this document do not necessarily reflect the views of the NSF, FSU, or the U.S. Government.

9. REFERENCES

[Amelink and Creamer 2010] Amelink CT, Creamer EG. Gender Differences in Elements of the Undergraduate Experience that Influence Satisfaction with the Engineering Major and the Intent to Pursue Engineering as a Career, *Journal of Engineering Education*, 99(1):81-92, 2010.

[Baker and Finn 2008] Baker JG, Finn MG. Can a Merit-Based Scholarship Program Increase Science and Engineering Baccalaureates, *Journal for the Education of the Gifted*, 31(3), pp. 322-337, 2008.

[Beyer et al. 2003] Beyer S, Rynes K, Perrault J, Hay K, Haller S. Gender Differences in Computer Science Students. *Proceedings of the 34thTechnical Symposium on Computer Science Education*, 2003.

[Cheryan et al. 2009] Cheryan S, Plaut VC, Davies PG, Steele CM. Ambient Belonging: How Stereotypical Cues Impact Gender Participation in Computer Science, *Journal of Personality and Social Psychology*, 97(6):1045-1060, 2009.

[Chesler and Chesler 2002] Chesler NC, Chesler MA. Gener-Informed Mentoring Strategies for Women Engineering Scholars: On Establishing a Caring Community. *Journal of Engineering Education*, 2002.

[Cohoon 2005] Cohoon JM. Just Get Over It or Just Get On with It. *Women and Information Technology: Research on Under-Representation*, MIT Press, 2005.

[Cunningham and Santiago 2008] Cunningham AF, Santiago DA. Student Aversion to Borrowing: Who Borrows and Who Doesn't, *The Institute for Higher Education Policy and Excelencia in Education*, 2008.

[DARPA 2010] DARPA, DARPA-RA-10-03 Computer Science, Technology, Engineering, and Mathematics (CS-STEM) Education Research Announcement (RA) for Information Processing Techniques Office (IPTO) Defense Advanced Research Projects Agency (DARPA), 2010.

[Declue 1997] Declue T, Academic Computer Science and Gender: A Naturalistic Study Investigating the Causes of Attrition. Dissertation, Southern Illinois University, 1997.

[Kiplinger 2012] Kiplinger's Best Values in Public Colleges. http://www.kiplinger.com/tools/colleges/index.php?state_code%5B%5D=ALL&id%5B%5D=6354&table=public#colleges, 2012.

[Lockard and Wolf 2010] Lockard CB, Wolf M. Occupational Employment Projection to 2020, *Monthly Labor Review*, 2010.

[NSF 2012] NSF, Science and Engineering Indicators 2012, http://www.nsf.gov/statistics/seind12/c2/c2s2.htm#s2, 2012.

[NSF 2013] NSF Scholarships in Science, Technology, Engineering, and Mathematics (S-STEM), https://www.nsf.gov/funding/pgm_summ.jsp?pims_id=5257, 2013.

[U.S. News and World Report 2013] Top Public Schools National Universities, *U.S. News and World Report*, http://colleges.usnews.rankingsandreviews.com/best-colleges/rankings/national-universities/top-public/page+2, 2013.

[Whallen and Shelley 2010] Whallen DF, Shelley MC, Academic Success for STEM and non-STEM Majors, *Journal of STEM Education*, 11(1,2):45-60, 2010.

[Zweben 2013] Zweben S. Computing Degree and Enrollment Trends. *CRA Taulbee Survey*, 2013.

A Support Program for Introductory CS Courses that Improves Student Performance and Retains Students from Underrepresented Groups

Tia Newhall, Lisa Meeden, Andrew Danner
Ameet Soni, Frances Ruiz, Richard Wicentowski
Computer Science Department
Swarthmore College
Swarthmore, PA 19081

ABSTRACT

In line with institutions across the United States, the Computer Science Department at Swarthmore College has faced the challenge of maintaining a demographic composition of students that matches the student body as a whole. To combat this trend, our department has made a concerted effort to revamp our introductory course sequence to both attract and retain more women and minority students.

The focus of this paper is the changes instituted in our *Introduction to Computer Science* course (i.e., CS1) intended for both majors and non-majors. In addition to changing the content of the course, we introduced a new student mentoring program that is managed by a full-time coordinator and consists of undergraduate students who have recently completed the course.

This paper describes these efforts in detail, including the extension of these changes to our CS2 course and the associated costs required to maintain these efforts. We measure the impact of these changes by tracking student enrollment and performance over 13 academic years. We show that, unlike national trends, enrollment from underrepresented groups has increased dramatically over this time period. Additionally, we show that the student mentoring program has increased both performance and retention of students, particularly from underrepresented groups, at statistically significant levels.

Categories and Subject Descriptors

K.3.2 [**Computer and Information Science Education**]: Computer Science Education

General Terms

Human Factors

SIGCSE'14, March 5–8, 2014, Atlanta, GA, USA.

ACM 978-1-4503-2605-6/14/03 ...$15.00.
http://dx.doi.org/10.1145/2538862.2538923.

Keywords

Mentoring, Diversity, CS1, CS2

1. INTRODUCTION

In *Unlocking the Clubhouse*, Margolis and Fisher provide a number of recommendations for making computing curricula more widely accessible [5]:

1. Pay close attention to the quality of the student experience.
2. Accommodate a wide range of computing experience among incoming students.
3. Create a curriculum that reflects the many facets and impacts of computing.
4. Establish structures for under-represented students to come together for support.

Given these broad recommendations there are a number of possible implementations. In revamping our curriculum we focused on addressing the first two recommendations: attending to the quality of student experience and accommodating a wide range of backgrounds. We wanted to create a welcoming and helpful environment for students who might be intimidated by CS culture. Our approach was twofold: first, to improve the structure and content of the course and second, to create a new staff position with the title *Student Mentor Coordinator* to develop and manage a student mentoring program. For this program, we recruit a diverse set of mentors from the pool of students who have successfully completed CS1. The Coordinator trains the mentors to assist current students during in-class lab exercises and evening and weekend study sessions. The Coordinator also monitors the progress of all students taking CS1 and proactively seeks out students at the first sign of trouble to get them assistance immediately.

We first piloted these changes in CS1, and as they proved to be successful we carried them over into CS2. This paper describes the changes we made in detail, and then demonstrates their success at attracting and retaining a more diverse set of students through a longitudinal evaluation of the student population taking our introductory courses. We show that the number of women and underrepresented minorities (URMs) taking CS1 has significantly increased post changes. The demographics of the students taking CS1 now more closely track the demographics of the College as a whole. One result of our changes is an overall increase in student enrollment in CS: over 55% of the students at the college will take at least one CS course. Moreover, the numbers of women and URMs taking CS2 is increasing as well, but there is still more work to be done here. Furthermore, we have surveyed the student mentors, and the results show that being a part of this support program played an important role in making them feel more confident in their abilities and in their place within the department.

1.1 Related Work

A number of recent studies have looked specifically at how to better attract and retain women students in computer science. Harvey Mudd College instituted three new practices that had a significant impact on creating more gender balance: making CS1 a breadth-first view of the discipline, offering trips to first-year women to attend the Grace Hopper Celebration of Women in Computing conference, and providing research opportunities for women after their freshman year[1]. Other successful initiatives at the college level include requiring students to do pair programming in their introductory courses, offering several themed CS1 options, redesigning CS1 to emphasize applications in areas of interest to women, and creating majors that combine CS with other areas [2, 4, 6].

One promising study done at a collection of eight diverse colleges and universities demonstrated that peer-led team learning (PLTL) increased the participation and success of underrepresented groups in introductory CS classes [3]. This program involved actively recruiting women and minority students to register for computing classes. Then once enrolled, all students were assigned to small groups (4-8 students) that met weekly for several hours to do additional problem-solving sessions with a trained peer leader. Our mentoring program shares some similarities with this one, but is more voluntary in nature. The mentors are available during class and/or lab times to assist students one-on-one or in small groups. The mentors also run weekend and night help sessions to which the entire class is invited, but not required to attend. Despite these differences, the two programs were both successful at recruiting and retaining underrepresented groups.

Student mentoring programs are now becoming more commonplace in Computer Science, however our program incorporates some unique features that we feel have been instrumental to its success. First, the mentors are very integrated into the course; they meet weekly with the faculty member and coordinator to discuss how the class is going, what concepts students are struggling with, and how best to assist students. Feedback from the mentors is taken seriously and modifications are made as a result of their observations. Second we select mentors not based solely on how they performed in the course, but often on other factors such as their friendliness and ability to relate to students who may be struggling. Third we choose mentors in part to retain them in the department; by selecting them, we are demonstrating our confidence in their abilities.

1.2 Institution Background

Swarthmore is a small, highly selective, coed liberal arts college situated in the suburbs of Philadelphia, Pennsylvania. Swarthmore College created a provisional computer science program in 1984, with a single full-time faculty member. The program was converted to a permanent department in 2001 and now has six full-time faculty members. Over the past 30 years the department has grown significantly from enrollments of 30 students per semester in 1984 to 400 students per semester today. We offer both a major and a minor in Computer Science, and currently have 54 majors in the class of 2014, the second largest major at the College behind Economics.

The computer science major at Swarthmore College consists of nine CS courses, and two math courses (discrete and linear algebra are recommended). Majors are required to take three introductory courses: CS1, CS2, and Introduction to Systems. Once these three courses are completed, students are prepared to take any upper-level course. Upper-level courses are divided into three groups: Theory & Algorithms, Systems, and Applications. Majors must take one course from each group. To complete the major, they must complete two elective upper-level courses and a senior project-based seminar.

CS1 serves two important roles in our curriculum. First, it is typically the initial course for potential majors. Second, it serves as a general science course for students who need to fulfill a distribution requirement. Given that it serves these two roles it must be welcoming to students who have never programmed before while also showing students the breadth of the discipline.

Perhaps surprisingly, most of the students who ultimately become CS majors at the College did not try CS while in high school. Instead, they try CS1 as a freshman or sophomore, find that they really enjoy it, and then decide to pursue CS further. Since the pool of potential majors is primarily being drawn from the students enrolled in CS1, it is essential that CS1 attracts and retains a diverse set of students in order to increase the diversity of CS majors.

1.3 Goals and Overview of Changes

We had a number of goals in the re-design of the introductory curriculum. First, and foremost, we wanted to make CS1 accessible to a wider range of students, including students who might not have a strong level of math preparedness. Secondly, we wanted to increase the diversity in CS1 to ultimately match the college-wide demographics. To accomplish this goal, we decided that our program needed to provide more direct support. To do so, we created a new staff position to manage our new support program, which would consist of student mentors. In choosing student mentors, we sought out students from diverse backgrounds to serve as role models. We also hoped that being selected as a mentor in the program would demonstrate our confidence in the students and encourage them to continue on in the major. Lastly, we wanted to ensure that the new students we drew into CS1 would not fall through the cracks, but would experience a warm and helpful environment. By providing more frequent opportunities for feedback (e.g., direct contact, frequent quizzes, lab hours), we could proactively seek out and assist struggling students as early as possible.

2. INTRODUCTORY COURSE CHANGES

We present details of the changes we made to our CS1 and CS2 courses. These include changes to course content and to pedagogical approaches as well as changes to how we evaluate and support students in these classes. Our changes to CS1 began in Fall 2006. Because of their success, we incorporated similar changes into CS2 starting in Fall 2008.

2.1 CS1 Content Changes

In Fall of 2006, we switched to Python as the primary programming language, after a one year experiment of Java, and several previous years of C. Switching to Python immediately allowed instructors to focus more on problem solving and less on syntax. To detect potential problems early, and provide students feedback quickly, we introduced bi-weekly quizzes throughout the semester, replacing a longer midterm examination from previous semesters. In Fall of 2007, we changed the course title from *Algorithmic Problem Solving* to *Introduction to Computer Science*. While no change in course content accompanied this name change, we wanted to emphasize that any Swarthmore student could take this course, and it was not limited to those with prior CS experience. CS1 meets in a closed lab with 34 computers for interactive, hands-on lectures (2.5 hours per week) and also meets for open lab time each week with the professor to work on weekly assignments (1.5 hours per week).

2.2 Support Program

2.2.1 Role of Student Mentors

A core component of our support framework is the introduction of a new student mentoring program. Our student mentors are assigned to our introductory courses, contributing in two ways; first, student mentors attend class sessions for the course. Second, the student mentors are responsible for running weekly evening help sessions.

In their capacity as student mentors, they serve several roles. During class sessions, the student mentors' main responsibility is to provide assistance to students during in-class exercises. This includes aiding students having difficulty with the exercise/assignment as well as adding context or extra challenges to students who have completed the assignment early. One evening session per week is oriented around the week's lab assignment, allowing students to get one-on-one direct assistance. For CS1, a second session each week focuses on emphasizing course material and preparing for the bi-weekly quizzes.

Student mentors are trained with the primary goal of providing a supportive and friendly environment to introductory students. Student mentors are in place to be helpful, but to also ensure that the students are learning as opposed to simply getting answers. Lastly, mentors provide an important feedback mechanism for faculty, reporting how students are doing overall with the weekly lab assignment and the major sticking points in course material.

2.2.2 Student Mentor Selection

When choosing student mentors, we seek out students who are patient and encouraging when working with their peers. We also look for students who are dependable and prompt. We require that student mentors take a CS class during every semester they mentor, and that they have completed the class they will student mentor for in good standing. Our policy is also generally not to accept seniors as student mentors, due to the goal of the student mentor program to encourage the mentors to considering pursuing a CS major.

We feel it is very important for students to see and interact with role models who are similar to them in the role of mentors. We therefore make sure to balance the student mentors by gender (one male and one female student mentor for each section/shift/lab). We also make efforts to select a diverse range of students from different backgrounds. We tend to prefer students who actually started out in CS1 without much (if any) CS experience prior to Swarthmore. These student mentors often are less intimidating to the students, and they are able to relate to the struggles faced by students coming into the program with no CS background. That is not to say we never hire very experienced students, but those are the minority of our student mentors.

2.2.3 Student Mentor Training

Ongoing training is provided through weekly student mentor meetings, of which thirty minutes are for student mentor training with the Student Mentor Coordinator, and fifteen to thirty minutes are to go over the week's lab assignment with the professor. Weekly topics include general tutoring advice such as "How not to give away answers", and "What to do if a student gets frustrated." We also delve into specific CS topics that are necessary for the student mentors to understand such as "How to draw the function call stack". The student mentor meetings also provide an opportunity for open discussion, in which the student mentors can ask questions and learn from sharing anecdotes about challenging situations they have encountered that week and how they handled them. These anecdotes serve as a starting point for the student mentors to come up with additional tactics that could also be drawn upon in similar situations.

2.2.4 Role of Student Mentor Coordinator

The mentoring program is supported in part by the Student Mentor Coordinator, a 10-month full-time staff member. The coordinator attends introductory course and lab sections, as well as a few evening sessions, in order to observe the student mentors and students. These observations serve two purposes. First, the coordinator draws from these observations in preparing each week's training topics and in giving individualized feedback to the student mentors. Second, during these class observations the coordinator also interacts closely with the students enrolled in the class, providing the coordinator with unique insights into the strengths, weaknesses, and personality traits of all the students in our introductory courses. These insights enable the coordinator to effectively assist the faculty in selecting new student mentors each semester.

The coordinator also holds office hours during which time students enrolled in the introductory classes can come for help. Some students, particularly freshmen, are intimidated about visiting a faculty member during their office hours. However, because the coordinator is not a faculty member, does not teach any courses, and has no role in assigning grades for the class, many students choose to visit the coordinator during office hours. The coordinator performs triage for most of the basic questions. For more complex questions and situations, the coordinator encourages students to visit with the faculty while also informing the faculty member about the student's situation.

The support coordinator also is responsible for scheduling and staffing the evening help sessions, helping to choose student mentors, producing training resources, and running the weekly mentor group meetings. The coordinator is an important liaison between the faculty and the mentors and between the faculty and the students in the class.

2.3 CS2

Following the observed initial success of the student mentor program in CS1, we have since added mentor support to our intermediate course CS2. Mentors in CS2 started in Fall 2008. Mentors and quizzes both take a reduced role in CS2, as part of our goal is to prepare students for independent learning in upper-level courses without the need for such active student mentor support. Mentors do not attend the lecture part of the course and instead attend lab sections to provide direct assistance on exercises. In addition, student mentors run a single four-hour long help session once per week. In the first few weeks of the semester, CS2 mentors are typically assisting with syntax and basic debugging, as we migrate from Python in CS1 to C++ in CS2. In later weeks, the mentors help students with more advanced debugging, including using a debugger and/or memory leak checkers, unit testing, and improving top-down design. Mentors hold extra sessions during quiz and exam weeks to provide additional support for the theoretical concepts covered in class.

2.4 Costs

The development of a student mentoring program takes on various costs, requiring both institutional and departmental financial support as well as an increase in faculty time.

Financial costs arise from the addition of support staff, i.e., the Student Mentor Coordinator and student mentors. Mentors are paid for attending class and/or lab sessions, evening help sessions, and weekly meetings with faculty and the coordinator. In addition, students receive one hour's wages for time to familiarize themselves with lab assignments. The Student Mentor Coordinator position is a full-time staff member. Lastly, the department provides juice and snacks for evening help sessions.

Faculty incur costs in the form of additional time commitments. These commitments include lab contact hours (90 minutes per lab per week), designing and grading more frequent quizzes, and attending weekly mentor meetings.

3. EVALUATION

We present results from two studies evaluating our project. The first is a longitudinal study evaluating student success, recruitment, and retention in CS1 and CS2. The second is a survey of current and former student mentors. Overall, our studies show many improvements in the representation and retention of students from underrepresented groups since our changes went into effect. They also show that the support program is doing well in meeting its goals both for the students receiving the support and for the students acting as mentors.

Historically women and some US minorities have been very underrepresented in computer science. For example, since 2007 the numbers of students pursuing bachelor degrees in computer science in the US has grown by around 50% [9]. However, the percentage of CS bachelors degrees awarded to woman has not improved, and in fact has stayed near 12% over the last decade, after dropping from a high of about 18% in 2001. Similarly, the percentages of CS bachelors degrees awarded to US underrepresented minority (URM) students has remained very low.

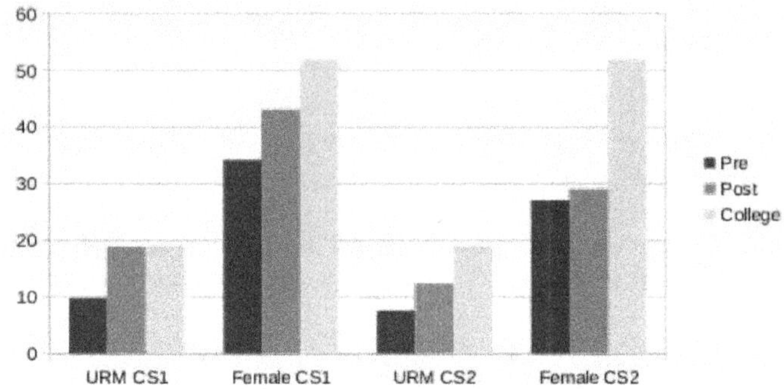

Figure 1: Average Enrollments of URM and Female students in CS1 and CS2 before and after our changes. ***The data are presented as average enrollment percentages over two academic year ranges representing Pre and Post change periods. College-wide average for URM and female students are also shown.***

3.1 Longitudinal Study

We performed statistical analyses of 13 years of data from our CS1 and CS2 courses. The data are from the academic years starting in 1999-2000 and continuing through 2012-2013. We collected final grade data, demographic information (URM status, gender, first generation status), math preparedness measured by Math SAT scores, and help session attendance starting in 2006 for CS1 and starting in 2011 for CS2. In analyzing these data, we asked the following questions about our program:

1. Are there improvements in recruiting and retaining students from underrepresented groups?
2. Is there a correlation between attending help sessions and success in CS1 and CS2?
3. Are there any other predictors of success in CS1 and CS2?

We use enrollment data to illustrate the effects of our program on recruitment and retention of different demographic groups. Figure 1 shows average enrollment data for URM and female students in CS1 and CS2 over two ranges of academic years. The first range (first bar in each group) reflects enrollments prior to our changes (from F99-S07), the second range represents the effects of our changes (from F07-S13) [1]. The last range shows the college-wide demographic information for each group. The graph shows increases in women and URM students in both CS1 and CS2. The increases are statistically significant for both groups in CS1, and for URM students in CS2.

There has also been a significant increase in total enrollments in both courses between the two time ranges: a 96% increase in CS1 enrollments (an average of 75 vs. 147 students per year); and a 64% increase in CS2 enrollments (average of 36 vs. 59 students per year). These data show that as our enrollments have increased so have the percentages of students from underrepresented groups; this differs from national trends where there has been little to no increase in the

[1]We expect to start seeing the effects a semester or two after we first introduced the changes, thus the second range begins in Fall 2007 rather than Fall 2006.

percentage of students from underrepresented groups during this recent period of rapidly increasing CS enrollments.

To evaluate the effects of help session attendance on success as measured by course final grade, we performed an Ordinary Least Squares Regression of the data. The results show that when controlling for math preparedness, there is a a 0.48 improvement in final grade for students who attended CS1 help sessions vs. those who did not. This represents an improvement of one half a letter grade due to help session attendance. We also found that female students attended help sessions more frequently than male students, possibly contributing to their increased representation in the class.

Taking a closer look at how help session attendance affects students within different math backgrounds, we grouped students into three "math preparedness" sets based on Math SAT scores (<= 700, 710 − 750, > 750). The data show that help session attendance improved final grade within each math grouping. The largest positive effect is on the middle group. However, there is a statistically significant positive correlation between CS1 help session attendance and final grade within each group.

The results for CS2 similarly show that help session attendance is positively correlated with improved final grade. We also found that students' prior CS1 help session attendance was positively correlated with improvements in their CS2 final grade, indicating lasting effects of the support in CS1 on our students' success in CS2. We suspect that the peer support and structured practice provided by these sessions has a positive longterm effect on our students' learning and confidence in future CS courses. Unlike the CS1 results, the CS2 results are are not statistically significant, in large part due to only having two years of attendance data. However, both show stable increasing trends in success in CS2 corresponding to help session attendance.

Finally, our results show that math preparedness is the strongest predictor of success in CS2. This follows results from other studies showing math preparedness as being one of the biggest predictors of success in introductory CS courses [7, 8, 10]. This result indicates that requiring a certain level of math pre-requisite for CS2 may better prepare students for success in the course. Based on this result, we have recently added a recommendation that students take Discrete Math before taking CS2. We are also encouraging student advisees to start in mathematics their first year to better ensure their success in CS.

Overall the analyses yield several statistically significant improvements since implementing our changes. These include an increase in the recruitment and retention of students from underrepresented groups, and a positive correlation between course grade and help session attendance. We have additionally increased the percentages of URM and female students in CS2, although this increase is currently only statistically significant for URM students.

Increasing the numbers of female students taking CS1 and continuing on into CS2 is a crucial first step to increasing the numbers of female students graduating with CS degrees. As can be seen in Figure 2, the percentage of female CS majors at Swarthmore has dramatically increased in the last three years, by far exceeding the national average of 12% [9].

3.2 Student Mentor Survey Results

We conducted a survey of our current and former student mentors, asking them questions about the program and

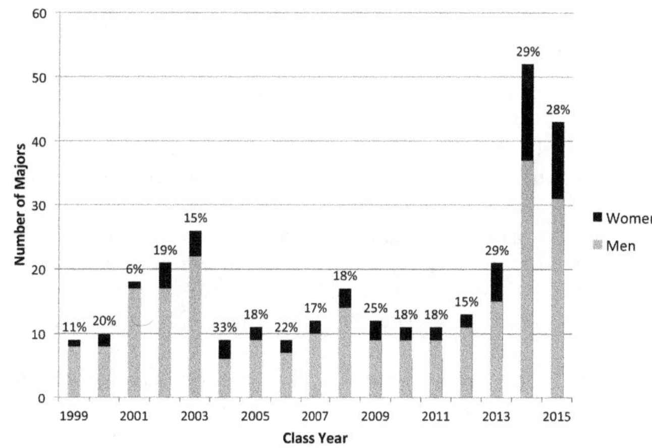

Figure 2: Total number of CS majors at Swarthmore College since 1999 and the percentage of Women vs Men.

about their participation in the program. The survey included a few quantitative questions asking them to rate their overall experience and several open-ended questions asking them what they thought were strengths and weaknesses of the program and what they felt they got out of participating. We had 27 responses, and the results are discussed below.

Quantitative Results

We asked only a few quantitative questions, most were to evaluate the usefulness of some aspects of their training. A couple, however, asked them to give overall rankings to their experiences. These questions and results are:

1. How would you rate your overall experience as a student mentor?
   Results: On a scale of 1-5, with 5 being best,
   Average: 4.5.
2. Did your experience as a student mentor help you feel more connected, less connected, or no change, to the department?
   Results: **100% said more connected**

These results indicate that the mentoring experience is very positive for the students. Anecdotally, the fact that we have more students express an interest in becoming a mentor than we could ever hire, also speaks to how well our students enjoy being mentors.

Qualitative Results

We asked several open-ended questions about being student mentors, including:

1. Which parts of your experience being a student mentor were most satisfying to you?
2. Why were you initially interested in becoming a student mentor?
3. Did you feel that being a student mentor had any effect on your own abilities as a computer science student?

Again, the results were overwhelmingly positive. In addition to enjoying the process of helping their peers learn, students commented that serving as a mentor helped them to solidify their knowledge in CS:

- "It gave me a better understanding of the different ways to look at a problem, so now, when I encounter something new, I have more tools available for learning the material and different ways of explaining it to myself."
- "Mentoring has allowed me to see various topics for a second time, giving me a much better understanding of material covered within each course and allowing me to make connections that I missed when I took the class."
- "My understanding of the CS2 material is deeper after spending time teaching it and thinking of multiple ways to explain it, particularly more abstract concepts."
- "It definitely helped my ability to explain difficult concepts and my teaching abilities. As a TA in grad school, my office hours are always the most highly attended and students come see me instead of their assigned TA."

One of the most prominent features of the survey responses was that students who had served as student mentors felt that this program had boosted their confidence and made them feel like more integral members of the department:

- "When I was asked to be a student mentor, it made me feel like an important part of the department which increased my confidence in CS overall."
- "I felt like a staff member and that I had a vested interest in the department. I also felt closer to the profs and more comfortable going to their office hours or asking them to let me do research with them."
- "I felt like a more valuable *asset* to the department, rather than just a student. It definitely upped my involvement and interest inside the department."
- "It felt like affirmation that I was doing well in the department and belonged there."
- "Being a student mentor made me feel I was more deeply a part of the department than I had been before. I ended up getting to know more people, and feeling more connected to the department."
- "I decided to major in CS partially as a result of student mentoring. The confidence shown in me by recommending me as a student mentor made me think that I was smart enough to do computer science, and that kept me going when the course work got difficult."
- "I didn't feel very confident of my place in the CS Department initially. I didn't think of myself as particularly good at science and was concerned that I wouldn't excel in the department. Being a mentor has improved my confidence in myself as a student."

It is clear that the act of being a mentor provided many key benefits to the students. The process of sitting in on classes and labs gave them a better understanding of the introductory curriculum. Running help sessions and interacting with their peers provided them with extra practice at problem solving and explaining abstract ideas. Perhaps most importantly, being chosen to serve in this role validated students and invested them in the department, helping them to persevere and be successful.

4. CONCLUSIONS

Over the seven years that we've been utilizing this mentoring program we've seen dramatic improvements in numbers of students taking our introductory sequence, in overall student success in our courses, and in increased representation and retention of women and underrepresented minorities in CS, beyond national trends. The addition of the student mentoring program has also had a noticeable effect on our departmental culture: students have created their own support groups, including a very active *Women in CS* group; students are more cooperative and helpful in class and lab; students feel more connected to the department; and students are the biggest promoters of our courses, encouraging other students across the College to try CS. Based on the success of this approach, we are now implementing it in our new course *Introduction to Computer Systems.* We continue to evaluate and adjust our program to better meet student needs. We are very pleased with the success of our program, and feel that it could be easily adopted at other institutions.

Acknowledgements

We would like to thank Robin Shores and Jason Martin in the Office of Institutional Research for their invaluable help with the longitudinal study. We also thank Betsy Horner for her help in developing the first student mentor program in our department.

5. REFERENCES

[1] Alvarado, C., and Dodds, Z. Women in CS: An evaluation of three promising practices. In *SIGCSE: Technical Symposium on Computer Science Education* (2001).

[2] Barr, V. Create two, three, many courses: An experiment in contextualized introductory computer science. In *Proceedings of CCSCNE* (2012).

[3] Horwitz, S., Rodger, S. H., Biggers, M., Binkley, D., Frantz, C. K., Gundermann, D., Hambrusch, S., Huss-Lederman, S., Munson, E., Ryder, B., and Sweat, M. Using peer-led team learning to increase participation and success of under-represented groups in introductory computer science. In *SIGCSE: Technical Symposium on Computer Science Education* (2009), pp. 163–167.

[4] Klawe, M., Whitney, T., and Simard, C. Women in computing—Take 2. *Communications of the ACM 52*, 2 (2009).

[5] Margolis, and Fisher. *Unlocking the Clubhouse: Women in Computing.* MIT Press, 2002.

[6] McDowell, C., Werner, L., Bullock, H. E., and Fernald, J. The impact of pair programming on student performance, perception and persistence. In *ICSE Proceedings of the 25th International Conference on Software Engineering* (2003).

[7] Morrison, M., and Newman, T. S. A study of the impact of student background and preparedness on outcomes in CS I. In *SIGCSE: Technical Symposium on Computer Science Education* (2010).

[8] Stein, M. V. Mathematical preparation as a basis for success in CS-II. *Computing Sciences in Colleges 17* (2002).

[9] The Computer Research Association (CRA). The 2012 Taulbee Survey. http://cra.org/resources/taulbee/, 2012.

[10] Wilson, B. C., and Shrock, S. Contributing to success in an introductory computer science course: A study of twelve factors. In *SIGCSE: Technical Symposium on Computer Science Education* (2001).

Project Rise Up 4 CS: Increasing the Number of Black Students who Pass Advanced Placement CS A

Barbara Ericson
Georgia Institute of Technology
801 Atlantic Drive
Atlanta, GA, 30332
+1-404.385.2107
ericson@cc.gatech.edu

Shelly Engelman, Tom McKlin
The Findings Group
1201 Clairmont Road
Decatur, GA, 30030
+1-404.633.9005
{shelly,tom}@thefindingsgroup.com

Ja'Quan Taylor
Georgia Institute of Technology
801 Atlantic Drive
Atlanta, GA, 30332
jtaylor306@gatech.edu

ABSTRACT

This paper describes *Project Rise Up 4 CS,* an attempt to increase the number of Black students in Georgia that pass the Advanced Placement (AP) Computer Science (CS) A exam. In 2012 Black students had the lowest pass rates on the AP CS A exam both in Georgia and nationally. Project Rise Up 4 CS provided Black students with role models, hands-on learning, competitions, a financial incentive, and webinars on AP CS A content. The first cohort started in January of 2013 and finished in May 2013. Of the 27 students who enrolled in the first cohort, 14 met all of the completion requirements, and 9 (69%) of the 13 who took the exam passed. For comparison, in 2012 only 22 (16%) of 137 Black students passed the exam in Georgia. In 2013, 28 (22%) of 129 Black students passed the exam in Georgia. This was the highest number of Black students to pass the AP CS A exam ever in Georgia and a 27% increase from 2012. In addition, students who met the completion requirements for Project Rise Up 4 CS exhibited statistically significant changes in attitudes towards computing and also demonstrated significant learning gains. This paper discusses the motivation for the project, provides project details, presents the evaluation results, and future plans.

Categories and Subject Descriptors

K.3.2 [**Computers and Education**]: Computer and Information Science Education–computer science education.

Keywords

AP CS A, Financial Incentives, Underrepresented Minorities

1. INTRODUCTION

The Institute for Computing Education (ICE) was created in 2004 to increase the quantity and quality of secondary computing teachers in Georgia and the quantity and diversity of secondary computing students [7,8]. ICE offers professional development for teachers, computing summer camps for 4th – 12th grade students [9], weekend workshops with youth serving organizations, a lending library of equipment, and competitions.

ICE is particularly focused on increasing the number of students who take the Advanced Placement (AP) Computer Science (CS) A exam. Research has shown that students who take the AP CS A exam take more computing courses in college than students who haven't had AP CS A in high school, and that they are more likely to major or minor in the discipline [17]. ICE worked with the state Department of Education to allow AP CS A to count as a 4th science for high school graduation in Georgia for students who graduated in 2012 and beyond. To broaden participation, ICE has also sent letters to the parents of female and underrepresented students who do well on the PSAT to explain why their children should take the AP CS A course.

SIGCSE'14, March 5–8, 2014, Atlanta, Georgia, USA.

http://dx.doi.org/10.1145/2538862.2538937

One measure of the success of ICE is that the number of students who took the AP CS A exam in Georgia increased from 389 in 2004 to 1,261 in 2013 [2]. AP exams are graded on a scale from 1 to 5. A score of 3 or higher qualifies as a passing score. The number of students passing the AP CS A exam has risen since 2006 in Georgia as shown in Table 1. However, the results were not as positive for some racial groups.

The number of Black students who took the exam in Georgia has varied from a low of 40 students in 2007 to a high of 137 in 2012. The pass rate for Black students has been consistently lower than the overall pass rate as seen in Table 1.

Table 1. AP CS A Data for Georgia 2004-2013

Year	Total	Pass	% Pass	Black	Black Pass	% Black Pass
2004	389	187	48%	66	5	8%
2005	388	182	47%	58	7	12%
2006	427	166	39%	67	2	3%
2007	422	213	50%	***40***	9	23%
2008	585	267	46%	84	9	11%
2009	583	304	52%	69	7	10%
2010	692	388	56%	68	16	24%
2011	884	448	50%	79	17	22%
2012	1037	481	46%	***137***	22	16%
2013	1261	644	51%	128	28	22%

Black students in Georgia had the lowest pass rates on the AP CS A exam from 2006 to 2013 as shown in Table 2. In this table the Hispanic category includes the College Board reported categories of Mexican American, Other Hispanic, and Puerto Rican. The

College Board does not report the scores for categories that have less than 5 students so the Hispanic pass rates are actually a minimum. Black students also have lower pass rates than other races at the national level for AP CS A as shown in Table 3.

Table 2. AP CS A Pass Rates in Georgia 2006-2013

	White	Asian	Hispanic	Black
2006	45%	54%	21%*	3%
2007	51%	63%	23%*	23%
2008	54%	51%	32%*	11%
2009	61%	56%	41%*	10%
2010	63%	55%	30%*	24%
2011	56%	54%	39%*	22%
2012	54%	50%	38%*	16%
2013	57%	52%	41%*	22%

Table 3. AP CS A Pass Rates Nationally 2006-2013

	White	Asian	Hispanic	Black
2006	63%	61%	36%	23%
2007	61%	60%	35%	20%
2008	61%	61%	35%	25%
2009	67%	66%	37%	23%
2010	69%	71%	42%	27%
2011	68%	69%	37%	32%
2012	66%	70%	40%	27%
2013	69%	73%	45%	36%

It is interesting to contrast the AP CS A data with data from other AP exams in Georgia for 2012. As Table 4 shows Black students had the lowest pass rate in Biology, Calculus AB, Computer Science A, English Language and Composition, and US History. This problem of Black students having a lower pass rate on AP exams is pervasive, as the national data for the 2012 exam show in Table 5.

Table 4. AP Pass Rates in Georgia in 2012

	White	Asian	Hispanic	Black
Biology	52%	64%	30%	18%
Calculus AB	60%	63%	42%	22%
CS A	54%	50%	38%	16%
English Lang	69%	72%	48%	29%
US History	60%	66%	47%	30%

Table 5. AP Pass Rates Nationally in 2012

	White	Asian	Hispanic	Black
Biology	55%	63%	27%	22%
Calculus AB	64%	67%	38%	29%
CS A	66%	70%	36%	27%
English Lang	70%	70%	37%	31%
US History	61%	66%	32%	29%

ICE created Project Rise Up 4 CS to increase the number of Black students who pass the AP CS A exam in Georgia. ICE has had some success increasing the number of Black students that take the AP CS A exam the last 3 years as shown in Table 1, but failing the exam could certainly have a chilling affect on interest in computing. Research has shown that believing that one can succeed in an occupation is a critical factor in choosing that occupational field [6].

2. Related Research

A WGBH-ACM study of college-bound teens found that the majority (74%) of college-bound males thought that computing careers were a good or very good choice for someone like them. Surprisingly, college-bound Black and Hispanic teens were even more likely than white students to be interested in computing careers; even through they are underrepresented in computing [21].

One factor preventing more underrepresented minority students from majoring in computing is a lack of access. In the 2011-2012 school year just 2,103 schools offered AP CS A. During the same year 11,694 schools offered AP Calculus AB [1]. In Georgia during that same year just 72 schools (15%) offered AP CS A out of over 460 high schools. As highlighted in the book *Stuck in the Shallow End,* underrepresented minorities often don't have access to rigorous computer science courses [16]. In Georgia, Black students are 37% of all the public school students, but in 2012 they made up only 13% of AP CS A exam takers.

Another problem is that traditional computing curriculum may not engage underrepresented minorities. EarSketch is a Computing Education for the 21st century project that is attempting to broaden participation in computing by introducing students to computing concepts by having them write Python programs to remix music [15]. While the EarSketch evaluation has been promising, the EarSketch curriculum has been developed for the new Computer Science Principles course, and not the AP CS A course.

The Glitch Project was a joint project between Morehouse College and Georgia Tech to increase Black male high school students' interest in studying computer science by paying them to be game testers and also teaching them computing concepts [5]. The project did result in an increase in the percentage of students in the project who were interested in a career in computing from an initial 20% to 65%. In the students' first year they were taught computing concepts using Media Computation [11] and Alice [19]. In the students' second year they were taught the material for AP CS A, in the hope that they would take the AP CS A exam, but only one student took the exam [4]. The Glitch students weren't taking the AP CS A course at their schools and would have had to travel to another school early in the morning to take the exam. The researchers attribute some of the Glitch Project's success to the fact that the program provided role models, financial incentives, competitions, and exposure to a college campus. We included these elements in the design of Project Rise Up 4 CS. However, we decided to focus on Black students that were already enrolled in AP CS A courses.

Other groups have used financial incentives to increase the number of underprivileged students that take and pass Advanced Placement exams. The Advanced Placement Incentive Program (APIP) started in 10 Dallas schools in 1996 and has expanded to over 66 schools in Texas [12]. The program is run by AP Strategies. It offers financial incentives for both students and teachers. Teachers and students both earn between $100 and $500 for each AP score of 3 or higher. The program also offers professional development for teachers and test preparation sessions for students at local high schools. Most of the funds for the program come from private donors, and the rest comes from school districts. The private donors get to pick which school districts they want to fund. The program has resulted in more students taking AP exams at the participating schools, more students passing the exams, and more students going on to college. The program has especially increased the number of Black and Hispanic students taking AP exams in participating schools. Since 2008 the National Math and Science Initiative (NMSI) has awarded grants to replicate this program in over 460 schools in 18 states [18].

While the AP Strategies Advanced Placement Incentive Program has had great results, it is expensive. It costs about $100,000 to $200,000 per school per year. There are more school districts that want to join the program than private donors who are willing to fund the program [12]. The AP Strategies program is also only in Texas. The National Math and Science Initiative (NMSI) AP program is also promising, but it is only in 1.5% of the high schools in America [18].

3. PROJECT DETAILS

ICE started Project Rise Up 4 CS in January 2013 to increase the number of Black students who pass the AP CS A exam in Georgia. The project uses aspects from the Glitch project and from the AP Strategies Program in Texas. Unlike the AP Strategies Program, we did not have a private donor. With our limited funds we decided to offer a financial incentive of $100 to Black students who attended at least 4 help sessions and passed the exam.

We adopted the following elements from the successful Glitch Project: exposure to a college campus, undergraduate students as role models, competitions, and financial incentives. The in-person help sessions were held at Georgia Tech in the College of Computing Building. Undergraduate students led the help sessions and were role models for the participants. We had one competition using Greenfoot and one with practice multiple-choice questions. We differed from Glitch in that the students were enrolled in an AP CS A course and we only paid them if they attended 4 or more help session and passed the exam.

In May we added one more reward for Project Rise Up 4 CS participants. We held two advanced app development summer camps; one for Android devices and one for iOS devices. The fee for these one-week non-residential camps was $500, but Project Rise Up 4 CS participants only had to pay $75. Four of the male participants from Project Rise Up 4 CS attended an advanced app camp. Two of the participants had passed the AP CS A exam and two had not.

3.1 Recruitment

ICE maintains a mailing list of AP CS A teachers. We added additional AP CS A teachers by gathering school information from the AP course audit webpage [1] and then contacted schools to get an e-mail address for the AP CS A teacher. For the 2012-2013 school year 83 schools in Georgia passed the audit for AP CS A. We asked teachers on the ICE AP CS A mailing list to notify their students about the project. Barbara Ericson also visited two schools to try to recruit students directly.

Interested students had to fill out a pre survey, which recorded their race, grade, school, teacher, experience in computing, intended major, and intended college or university. A total of 40 students filled out the pre survey from 15 different schools and 1 student was homeschooled. Two students were disqualified since they did not self-report as Black. Students had to self identify their race and could pick multiple racial categories. Of the 40 applicants 7 were female (18%) and 33 were male (82%).

3.2 Enrollment in the Project

The student and a parent or guardian for each student had to complete consent forms to be eligible to enroll in the project. In addition, each student had to take a pre attitude survey and a pre content knowledge assessment of 30 multiple-choice questions. Of the 40 students who completed the pre survey, 27 completed all of the enrollment requirements. Of the 27 students, 4 were female (15%) and 23 male (85%). Most of the students, 13, were in 12th grade (48%), 8 were in 11th grade (30%), and 6 were in 10th grade (22%). The students were from 11 different schools and 1 was homeschooled. All of the schools were within 40 miles of Georgia Tech, except for one school, which was 78 miles away. Two students came from this school. Of the 26 students who enrolled and answered the question about their most likely major, 15 (58%) were interested in a computing career (computer science, software engineering, computer technician, web development, computer graphics and game design), 8 were interested in engineering (31%), 2 in law (8%), and 1 (4%) in science or nursing.

3.3 Help sessions

Enrolled students were offered a series of help sessions from January to May 2013 and had to attend at least four help sessions to be eligible for the $100 financial incentive if they passed the exam. The four help sessions could be any combination of in-person sessions or webinars. The webinars only required access to the Internet and a web browser via Blackboard Collaborate.

The in-person help sessions were offered once a month at Georgia Tech on Sunday afternoons from 1pm to 4pm. There was one extra session in May to help students prepare for the AP CS A exam. These in person sessions introduced the students to creating games and simulations using Greenfoot [13], programming Finch robots in Java [14], understanding sorting algorithms, answering free response questions, and practicing multiple-choice questions. Undergraduate students usually ran the in-person sessions, but Barbara Ericson led the first session and last session.

Four undergraduate students assisted with the first cohort of Project Rise Up 4 CS. The undergraduate students were selected to present a diverse range of potential role models. One of the undergraduates was a freshman and the rest were seniors. One of the seniors was also a teaching assistant. Two of the students were male and two were female. Two of the students were Black and two were Asian with ancestry from the Indian subcontinent.

One-hour webinars were held on Wednesdays at 7:00pm and Saturdays at 11:00am. The webinars were recorded and all participants had access to the recordings. Undergraduate students led the webinars and used a drawing tablet to help illustrate computing concepts. Topics covered included: for loops, one and two dimensional arrays, lists, searching, sorting, recursion, number conversion, creating classes, overriding methods, visibility modifiers, polymorphism, inheritance, old free response questions, practice multiple choice questions, and the Grid World case study.

3.4 Results

Of the 27 students in the first cohort, 14 met all of the requirements, and 9 (69%) of the 13 who took the AP CS A exam passed. Recall that in Georgia in 2012, only 22 Black students passed out of 137 who took the exam for a pass rate of 16%. In 2013, 129 Black students took the exam and 28 passed for a pass rate of 22%. That was a 27% increase over 2012 and the highest number of Black students to ever pass the exam. However, only 1 of the 4 females in the group of 27 participating students passed the exam. One female dropped out of the project in February and one female didn't take the exam.

3.5 Project Cost

The cost for the undergraduates to lead help sessions was approximately $3,000. The total for the payment of the $100 for the 9 students who met the requirements and passed the exam was $900. In addition, we gave about $600 in prizes for the competitions. The total project cost was $3,000 + $900 + $600 = $4,500.

4. EVALUATION

A pre and retrospective post attitudinal survey was administered to gauge students' growth across 8 psychosocial constructs as shown in table 6. Participants were also asked to take pre and post content knowledge multiple-choice exam. Additional feedback was elicited via an in-person focus group with six participants and through e-mail.

4.1 Changes in Attitudes

In June 2013, 12 of the 14 retained students, who attended at least 4 help sessions, completed the 16-item retrospective attitudinal survey. Table 6 summarizes these students' pre and post responses across 8 psychosocial constructs. In general, Table 6 suggests that the program was effective in statistically significantly increasing students' confidence in computing, enjoyment, perceptions of computing's usefulness and importance, motivation to succeed, feelings of belongingness, intention to persist, and creative expression in computing. Importantly, statistically significantly more students report seeing themselves working in a computing field in the future after participating in the program.

4.2 Changes in Content Knowledge

A 30-item content knowledge assessment was administered to retained students at pre and post. Among students who attended at least 4 sessions, the average percent correct statistically significantly improved from 36% at pretest to 61% at posttest. Students who attained at least 67% correct on the post content knowledge assessment were likely to pass the exam.

4.3 Retention

Despite the positive attitudinal gains reported by students, the number of first cohort students who completed was approximately

Table 6. Retrospective Pre/Post Attitudinal Results

Construct	Sample Item	Pre (n=12)	Post (n=12)	Paired Samples t-test
Computing Confidence	*I can get good grades in computing.*	4.00	4.79	0.007**
Computing Enjoyment	*Computers are fun.*	3.63	4.29	0.025*
Importance & Perceived Usefulness	*I will use computing in many ways throughout my life.*	3.83	4.79	0.002**
Motivation to Succeed	*When a computing problem arises that I can't immediately solve, I stick with it until I have the solution.*	3.75	4.71	0.003**
Identity and Belonging	*I feel like I "belong" in computing.*	3.73	4.55	0.011*
Gender Equality	*Girls can do just as well as boys in computing.*	4.17	4.54	0.121
Creativity in Computing	*I can be creative with computing.*	3.72	4.51	0.005**
Intent to Persist	*I see myself working in a computing field.*	4.17	4.67	0.039*

Note. Scale= 1, Strongly Disagree to 5, Strongly Agree. **p<.01; *p<.05; n=12.

52%. Specifically, of the 27 students who initially enrolled, only 14 students fulfilled the requirements of attending at least 4 help sessions. Table 7 compares retained and non-retained students' baseline (pre) attitudinal responses. The data for the retained students is different in this table compared to table 6 because not all retained students completed the post attitude survey. Comparing averages per psychosocial construct, it is evident that the retained students scored well above non-retained students across all psychosocial constructs. In particular, the data suggests a wide gap between retained and non-retained students' enjoyment of computing and motivation to succeed in computing. We may, thus, tentatively conclude that the retained students entered the program with more motivation to persist in computing, more positive attitudes towards the field in general, and, arguably, more determination to "pass" the AP CS exam.

Table 7. Baseline (Pre) Attitudinal Differences

Construct	Non-Retained (n=13)	Retained (n=14)	Independent Samples t-test
Computing Confidence	4.23	4.57	0.250
Computing Enjoyment	3.46	4.00	0.033*
Motivation to Succeed	3.77	4.36	0.063†
Identity and Belonging	3.54	3.93	0.336
Gender Equality	4.62	4.79	0.356
Creativity in Computing	3.92	4.18	0.398
Intent to Persist	4.08	4.39	0.328

Note. Scale= 1, Strongly Disagree to 5, Strongly Agree. **p<.01; *p<.05; †p<.10 (*approaching significance*). Items related to Importance and Perceived Usefulness in Computing were not administered at baseline.

Students who didn't attend at least 4 help sessions attributed it to being too busy, or "senioritis". A student who was a senior reported, "The project really couldn't have done much more to encourage my attendance. I think it was very well run and should be applauded for such. The one thing I would say is that I would have liked for it to start in the fall, as soon as school started. After getting into the colleges of my choice, my motivation wavered." One female student dropped out of the program early saying, "I felt that [the program] isn't for me. I wanted to learn other things and wasn't passionate about the program." Even though 18 of the 27 students attended a school that was more than 30 miles from Georgia Tech, students didn't report the distance as a problem.

Examining differences in baseline (pre) content knowledge scores, Table 8 indicates that retained students scored significantly higher than non-retained students. At baseline, non-retained students scored 31% correct while retained students scored 39% correct. Combining this information with the attitudinal data displayed in Table 7, it is evident that in addition to holding more positive attitudes towards computing, retained students also demonstrated significantly greater computing knowledge than non-retained students at the beginning of the program.

Table 8. Baseline (Pre) Content Knowledge Differences

	Non-Retained (n=9)	Retained (n=14)	Independent Samples t-test
Content Knowledge Baseline Test: % Correct	31%	39%	0.050*

Note. 30-item Content Knowledge Test; **p<.01; *p<.05; †p<.10 (*approaching significance*).

4.4 Financial Incentives

Interestingly, the students in the program did not mention the financial incentive for passing the exam as a motivation. Research shows that monetary incentives can yield mixed success. Brock and Richburg-Hayes, for instance found that performance based awards significantly increased community college students' GPAs and graduation rates [3]. A series of randomized experiments found that short-term monetary incentives do not improve student performance [10,20]. Given these mixed findings, researchers conclude that financial incentives may have the potential to address the achievement gap between underrepresented (e.g. African-American) and non-underrepresented (White; Asian) students. However, such efforts must also address psychosocial obstacles (e.g. Stereotype Threat) that can harm academic performance for underrepresented students. Evidence from the retrospective attitudinal survey (see Table 6) indicates that Rise UP 4 CS was effective in increasing retained students' confidence and feelings of identity and belongingness in computing. This provides some evidence for the effectiveness of the program in providing students with psychosocial support. However, additional research is needed to assess the impact of the monetary incentive on students' decisions to persist in the program.

4.5 Student Feedback

In open-ended responses, a number of retained students praised the program for providing them with helpful webinars and hands-on instructional support. For example, a student said that the webinars "allowed us to ask any questions…and get professional help…on how to do things and apply them to real life." Importantly, the "various real life situations" presented by the instructors received high marks by the students; this pedagogical approach helped make the material relatable. For example, when discussing sorting algorithms our undergraduate students told the participants to imagine that an airplane company had offered them a job, and that the company needed to sort the passenger id numbers. Students were also encouraged to come up with their own scenarios. One student who was really into shoes mentioned owning his own shoe company and having to sort the inventory for his company.

One student indicated that socializing and working with other Black students were the best aspects of the program. The program may, thus, have cultivated a strong social network for participants; this may have provided them with the communal support and the necessary social encouragement to persist in a field where they are underrepresented.

Four students attended the advanced app development camps during the summer of 2013. One student wrote, "I wanted to thank you for [the] discount for the Android App camp. I really enjoyed the camp and learned a lot from it. " Of the four Project Rise Up 4 CS participants who attended the advanced app camps, three have asked if they could work future computing camps.

For future improvements, students overwhelmingly stated that the program should have started earlier in the year. For example a student wrote "the program [should start] early so that [they] can go over the basics the first semester and practice free responses the second semester." Students also suggested offering more competitions and more practice on free response questions.

4.6 Reasons for Failing the Exam

The four students who attended at least 4 of the help sessions and yet failed the exam were asked what the project could have done to help them pass the exam. One student reported, "I got a 1 on the exam because I didn't fully commit to the program and didn't put enough effort into studying. I needed help with a little bit of everything. " One student who failed was homeschooled. He said, "I had gotten sick at the beginning of the school year which caused me to miss several weeks of class during the core concept learning. That was a big thing I think that contributed to my low score because I had to go quicker through the course to get caught up. The program itself was great though! "

5. DISCUSSION

While the Black pass rate increased in Georgia in 2013, we can't be sure that Project Rise Up 4 CS caused the increase. It may be that the students in Project Rise Up 4 CS would have passed the exam anyway. After all in 2013, 28 Black students passed the AP CS A exam in Georgia which is more than the 9 that passed from Project Rise Up 4 CS. However, students indicate that the program significantly improved their ability to pass the AP CS exam. Specifically, 85% of retained students report that they have a "very good" or "excellent" chance of passing the exam after participating in the program, compared to only 25% before the program. Comments from the students also support the idea that Project Rise Up increased their chances of passing the AP CS A exam. "Before [the program] started, I was completely lost. And our teacher…can't really sit down with each of us and go through any of the problems individually. But since I got the extra help from Project Rise Up…I can understand it more." Another student reported, "without this program, [I] doubt a 3 would be in [my] future."

6. 2013-2014 COHORT

As recommend by the past participants, we started the 2013-2014 cohort for Project Rise Up 4 CS in October of 2013. We had 45 students fill out the pre survey and 33 students completed the enrollment requirements. There are 14 females (42%) and 19 males (58%). We are offering in-person sessions on Alice 3, Media Computation, Finch robots, and Greenfoot. Since we started earlier, we increased the required number of help sessions to 6. We have applied for a Google Rise grant, which would allow us to pay the participants $100 for attending the help sessions as well as $100 for passing the exam, give prizes for more competitions, and replicate the project in Maryland and South Carolina. By paying students $100 to attend the required number of help sessions we hope to increase the number who complete that requirement.

7. CONCLUSION

Project Rise Up 4 CS was a fairly low-cost intervention that resulted in statistically significant improvements in attitudes towards computing, interest in computing careers, and gains in content knowledge. There was a 27% increase in the number of Black students who passed the AP CS A exam in Georgia in 2013. Other colleges and universities could offer similar projects. Many undergraduates know Java well enough to be able to help local Black students prepare for the AP CS A exam, and can be role models for the project participants. Exposure to the college environment can increase feelings of belongingness. Financial incentives didn't appear to be a huge factor in the success of Project Rise Up 4 CS, so they may not be necessary.

8. ACKNOWLEDGMENTS

Thank you to Elizabeth DiSalvo for her input on the design for Project Rise Up 4 CS. The funding for Project Rise Up 4 CS came from National Science Foundation grants CNS-0940394 and CNS-1228352 as well as a grant from the Toyota Foundation.

9. REFERENCES

[1] Advanced Placement Course Audit webpage: https://apcourseaudit.epiconline.org/ledger/

[2] Advanced Placement Data from the College Board http://research.collegeboard.org/programs/ap/data

[3] Brock, T., & Richburg-Hayes, L. 2006. Paying for persistence: Early results of a Louisiana scholarship program for low-income parents attending community college. New York: MDRC.

[4] DiSalvo, B. and Bruckman, A. 2011. From interests to values. *Commun. ACM* 54, 8 (August 2011), 27-29. DOI=http://doi.acm.org/10.1145/1978542.1978552

[5] DiSalvo, B., Guzdial, M., Meadows, C., Perry, K., McKlin T., and Bruckman, A. 2013. Workifying Games: Successfully Engaging African American Gamers with Computer Science. In *Proceeding of the 44th ACM technical symposium on Computer science education* (Denver, Colorado, USA 2013). ACM, New York, NY, USA, 317-322. DOI=http://doi.acm.org/10.1145/2445196.2445292

[6] Eccles, J. S. Who Am I and What Am I Going to Do With My Life? Personal and Collective Identities as Motivators of Action. *Educational Psychologist*, 44, 2 2009, 78-89.

[7] Ericson, B., Guzdial, M., and Biggers, M. 2005. A model for improving secondary CS education. In *Proceedings of the 36th SIGCSE technical symposium on Computer science education* (St. Louis, Missouri, USA, 2005). ACM, New York, NY, USA, 332-336.

[8] Ericson, B., Guzdial, M. and Biggers, M. 2007. Improving secondary CS education: progress and problems. In *Proceedings of the 38th SIGCSE technical symposium on Computer science education* (Covington, Kentucky, USA, 2007). ACM, New York, NY, 298-301. DOI=http://doi.acm.org/10.1145/1227310.1227416

[9] Ericson, B. and McKlin, T. Effective and sustainable computing summer camps. In *Proceedings of the Proceedings of the 43rd ACM technical symposium on Computer Science Education* (Raleigh, North Carolina, USA, 2012). ACM, New York, NY, 289-294. DOI= http://doi.acm.org/10.1145/2157136.2157223

[10] Fryer, R. G. 2011. Financial incentives and student achievement: Evidence from randomized trials. The Quarterly Journal of Economics, 126, 1755-1798.

[11] Guzdial, M. 2013. Exploring hypotheses about media computation. In *Proceedings of the ninth annual international ACM conference on International computing education research* (ICER '13). ACM, New York, NY, USA, 19-26. DOI=http://doi.acm.org/10.1145/2493394.2493397

[12] Jackson, C. K. 2010. A Little Now for a Lot Later A Look at a Texas Advanced Placement Incentive Program. Journal of Human Resources, 45, 591-639.

[13] Kölling, M. 2010. The Greenfoot Programming Environment. *Trans. Comput. Educ.* 10, 4, Article 14 (November 2010), 21 pages. DOI=http://doi.acm.org/10.1145/1868358.1868361

[14] Lauwers, T. 2013. The Finch, a robot for the CS classroom. *J. Comput. Sci. Coll.* 28, 3 (January 2013), 104-104

[15] Magerko, B., Freeman, J., McKlin, T., McCoid, S., Jenkins, T., and Livingston, E.. 2013. Tackling engagement in computing with computational music remixing. In *Proceeding of the 44th ACM technical symposium on Computer science education* (Denver, Colorado, USA, 2013). ACM, New York, NY, USA, 657-662. DOI=http://doi.acm.org/10.1145/2445196.2445390

[16] Margolis, J., Estrella, R., Goode, J. and Holme, J. J. *Stuck in the Shallow End: Education, Race, and Computing*. The MIT Press Cambridge, MA, 2008.

[17] Morgan, R. & Maneckshana, B. 2000. AP students in college: an investigation of their course-taking patterns and college majors. ETS Statistical Report 2000-09. Princeton, NJ: Educational Testing Service.

[18] National Math and Science Initiative AP Program http://nms.org/Programs/APProgram.aspx

[19] Pausch, P. 2008. Alice: a dying man's passion. In *Proceedings of the 39th SIGCSE technical symposium on Computer science education* (SIGCSE '08). ACM, New York, NY, USA, 1-1. DOI=http://doi.acm.org/10.1145/1352135.1352137

[20] Scott-Clayton, J. (2011). On Money and Motivation A Quasi-Experimental Analysis of Financial Incentives for College Achievement. Journal of Human Resources, 46, 614-646.

[21] ACM-WGBH Interim report 2009. http://www.acm.org/press-room/news-releases/2009/nic-interim-report.

Interdisciplinary Computing Classes: Worth the Effort

Lori Carter
Point Loma Nazarene University
Department of Mathematical, Information, and Computer Sciences
San Diego, CA 92106
LoriCarter@pointloma.edu

ABSTRACT

The benefits of interdisciplinary computing classes have been widely discussed. For the computing students, they provide a context in which to apply their skills, and appear to aid in recruitment and retention. For non-computing students, they provide additional skills to enhance their own crafts. For both, interdisciplinary programs open up new career possibilities and hone soft skills. In consideration of these and other benefits, the Point Loma Nazarene University Mathematical, Information, and Computer Sciences department have teamed up with the Biology, Chemistry, and Physics departments to offer several opportunities for interdisciplinary experiences to their students. In addition to the benefits, however, these programs produce significant challenges. This paper reviews the benefits of interdisciplinarity and discusses three different models of interdisciplinary experiences used at PLNU. It reports on the challenges that arose in each, and ways these difficulties were resolved. Finally, it discusses the hurdle of recruiting for such courses.

Categories and Subject Descriptors

J.2 [**Computer Applications**]: Physical Sciences J.3 [**Computer Applications**]:Life and Medical Sciences. K.4.3 [**Computing Mileux**]: Computers and Society - *Computer-supported collaborative work*

General Terms

Design, Human Factors

Keywords

Computational Science, Computational Biology, Computational Chemistry, Computational Physics, Interdisciplinary Computing, Multidisciplinary Computing, Team Teaching

1. INTRODUCTION

Over the course of the last three years, the Mathematical, Information, and Computer Sciences department and the natural science (Biology, Chemistry, Physics) departments at Point Loma Nazarene University (PLNU) have worked at creating multiple interdisciplinary experiences for its majors. In the fall of 2012, after two years of research and planning, we launched a Computational Science minor. The goal of the minor is to allow the computational (computer science and mathematics) students to gain limited knowledge in one of biology, chemistry or physics, preparing them to help scientists with the computational needs in their research. In a similar way the minor is also designed to expose science (biology, chemistry and physics) majors to enough computational techniques to help them identify when a mathematician or computer scientist could help with research.

SIGCSE '14, March 05 - 08 2014, Atlanta, GA, USA
Copyright 2014 ACM 978-1-4503-2605-6/14/03…$15.00.
http://dx.doi.org/10.1145/2538862.2538882

In addition to creating the minor, the science and computational faculty are committed to eventually providing an interdisciplinary experience for all freshmen in their departments. To that end, in the summer of 2013, we piloted an interdisciplinary freshman seminar that included soon-to-be-sophomores with majors in computer science, mathematics, physics, chemistry, and biology and was taught by a team of professors with a team member from the each of those disciplines.

The benefits of interdisciplinary teaching and research have been touted by many. In 1997 sociologist Nissani published a paper entitled Ten Cheers for Interdisciplinarity [13]. In it, he listed ten reasons that people should pursue interdisciplinary studies. These included:

- Creativity often requires interdisciplinary knowledge.
- Immigrants often make important contributions to their new field.
- Disciplinarians often commit errors which can be best detected by people familiar with two or more disciplines.
- Some worthwhile topics of research fall in the interstices between the traditional disciplines.
- Many intellectual, social and practical problems require interdisciplinary approaches.
- Interdisciplinarians enjoy greater flexibility in their research.

More recently and specifically related to interdisciplinary computing, other benefits have been added to the list.

- Research has shown that employers in software engineering are increasingly looking for soft skills in addition to the hard, academic skills [4]. Experience reveals that working and learning in interdisciplinary teams requires exceptional attention to clear communication, forcing participants to learn good communication skills if anything is to be accomplished [1, 2]. By the very nature of interdisciplinary coursework, teamwork (another highly valued soft skill) is essential [2, 6].

- Computing in a context aids retention and attracts students to computational majors and minors and research experiences that would not otherwise pursue computing education [1, 10, 14]. The inaugural class of the PLNU Computational Science minor had seven natural science students. In the fall of 2013, 19 biology, chemistry, and physics students are enrolled in Introduction to Computer Programming, the first class of the sequence for the minor.

- Computing in a context appears to be more attractive to women [3, 9], a typically underrepresented group in computing. Women also express a desire to do something that makes a difference in the world. Science applications are rife with opportunities to make a difference. One female computer science student, after completing a project supporting drug resistance research exclaimed "I learned that I could help save lives!" In addition, the science students that have enrolled in our minor courses have been predominantly female, increasing the female population in general for these courses. Our female computer science students have enjoyed the unexpected camaraderie.
- Interdisciplinary courses can draw on the expertise of faculty from different, but related disciplines, to enable classes that cross those disciplines [11].
- Interdisciplinary efforts including computer science, mathematics, physics, biology, and chemistry students and professors provide more opportunities for efficient, realistic research experiences than would be possible for researchers in any of these disciplines alone. Raicu and Furst report on an interdisciplinary REU model that was attractive to science and CS students, providing early experiences in real world settings [14].
- We have observed that our interdisciplinary classes exhibit increased interaction between students and professor during lectures. One possibility is that students in a core major class resist asking questions for fear of appearing ignorant in front of faculty or peers in a field that is supposed to be their growing expertise. Students from other disciplines taking the same class (but outside of their major) don't seem to experience that same pressure, and are willing to ask questions that add clarification for major students as well.
- In the first 2 years of these programs, we have observed that the interdisciplinary courses are attracting top students from other disciplines. It appears that students who are likely to pursue additional coursework outside of their major really enjoy learning, and eagerly embrace the challenge.
- The students from the science disciplines are enthusiastic and appreciative. After completing her second computing course, one biology student announced, "It was so great to find out that I don't have to do all of my research manually – I wasted so much time!"

Certainly interdisciplinary collaboration has many significant benefits, but it is not to be entered into casually. While it is the opinion of our PLNU collaborators that the benefits far outweigh the challenges, there are hurdles that must be intentionally addressed. These challenges range from administrative, to financial, to curricular, to different learning and research styles and are expanded upon in [2]. This paper focuses on addressing the challenges related to various forms of interdisciplinary collaboration in the classroom, and particularly involving students and faculty from the computational and natural sciences. It also addresses the hurdle of recruiting science majors and faculty - a requirement to make the programs truly interdisciplinary.

2. THREE MODELS OF INTERDISCIPLINARITY

Cassel suggests that "for computing, interdisciplinarity means collaborative efforts, involving at least two fields, with at least one of them being computing" [5]. She further explains that "real interdisciplinarity requires that each participant has some level of understanding of the whole problem domain, while each brings depth in one of the required areas." Still, "real interdisciplinarity" can manifest itself at different levels, each with its own set of obstacles. At PLNU we have implemented courses at three different levels.

The curriculum, (discussed in depth in [2]), for the PLNU Computational Science minor consists of a choice of science sequences along with a fixed set of computational courses. These computational courses are a mix of previously existing courses and courses created specifically for the minor. The previously existing courses (Calculus, Statistics, and Intro to Computer Programming) are taught by a single mathematics or computer science professor who has intentionally re-tooled the course to include science-related examples and labs. Students pursuing the minor as well as students taking the courses for major requirements are included in the course populations. The level of interdisciplinarity in these courses is the most modest of the three models. Students come from different academic areas; the professor's depth is computational, but augmented with knowledge gained from books, interdisciplinary research experience, and lab ideas submitted from colleagues in the natural sciences.

The newly-created courses are MATLAB for Computational Science, Python and UNIX Scripting for Computational Science and Data Management for Computational Science. These courses have a more significant science content and each is taught by a professor in a computational field who has been involved in research working alongside biologists, chemists, and/or physicists at some level. The students in the class are either Computational Science minors, or computational students taking the class for elective credit, fully aware of the interdisciplinary focus.

The freshman seminar, on the other hand, is taught by a team of professors with members from each of the disciplines in the natural and computational sciences at PLNU. While professors from different disciplines are in the classroom simultaneously and there is interaction, each is presenting primarily from his or her expertise.

2.1 A Re-tooled Course: Introduction to Computer Programming

The first course in the minor sequence is Introduction to Computer Programming using Java. This course is also the first course in the computer science core, and a requirement for all mathematics students. The format for this course is one hour of lecture followed by one hour of lab two days each week. An existing class, it was initially retooled to include lab assignments that had, almost exclusively, a scientific context. Part of the lecture time was used to provide enough science information for the labs to be completed by all students. Examples of lab assignments were: 1) using DNA sequences to teach string functions (search, substring etc), and 2) building an animation of the trajectory of a ball thrown at different angles and speeds when learning graphics and timer functions. The computational students tended to be freshman in their first semester of college, while the science students were sophomores or juniors.

The challenges in this context centered on completely new subject matter for almost all students, seasoned science students that were used to a different type of learning and testing style, and the requirement that the professor find interesting and appropriate science-related material for labs. A correlated challenge was that the professor be aware of the different learning styles, and be somewhat conversant in the scientific concepts and vocabulary.

2.1.1 Learning completely unfamiliar material

Not surprisingly, almost all of the students in the Introduction to Computer Programming class were new to programming. It was surprising, however, that the science students entered the class believing that they would be behind in their programming knowledge. Consequently, it was important to administer and to divulge the results of a first week survey regarding previous programming experience amongst members of the class. In addition, it was important to intentionally create interdisciplinary discussion groups during the lecture portion of the class to show science students that they were, indeed, at the same level of expertise as their computational peers.

While we believed that it was essential to include science-related labs in the course so that the science students could immediately see the utility of programming to their disciplines, these labs were not universally appreciated. All students were interested in the context in the beginning, but as the computing material became more complex, this changed. The science students found comfort in the science-related labs, but the computational students started getting overwhelmed. They felt that in addition to learning the new language of Java, they were also learning a new science vocabulary and concepts. Since many of the students in the class were not Computational Science minors, a compromise had to be reached. Towards the end of the semester the professor started offering choices on some of the labs – one science-related, and one in a more generally-familiar context. This was appreciated by the students. It became apparent that context is helpful only until it becomes a barrier to learning the basic content.

2.1.2 Different learning and testing styles

Labs in the sciences can be very different from labs in computing. In biology, physics, and chemistry labs tend to consist of a set of steps that the students are given to complete during the lab period. In computer programming labs, the students are often expected to create the steps (algorithm) to solve the problem themselves, and may have to finish the labs on their own time. One way that this difference was addressed was to allow time for algorithm development during the end of the lecture. Students were then armed with a set of steps going into the lab. Secondarily, the lab assistants hosted office hours in the evening to help with unfinished labs.

The Weizmann Institute of Science looked at interdisciplinary research groups and noted difficulties between team members because of the ways that the computational and natural scientists approached data. The more computational members felt that the biological data was "full of details and that it was hard for them to locate the central details to find the guiding logic" [16]. We noticed this problem with exams. Biologists wanted to memorize details in studying for exams, but computational exams tend to be about understanding and applying central concepts. The professor found that it was helpful to provide practice quizzes in between major exams to help the science students understand and get practice with the kinds of questions that they would be asked. Happily, computational students appreciated these practice exams as well.

2.1.3 Extra burden on professor

It is probably apparent by now that the professor teaching a cross disciplinary course shoulders the burden of learning concepts from another academic area and of creating labs related to those concepts. We found no quick fix for this. It is true that the professors involved must appreciate the benefits of this type of class enough to want to put in the work. One of the professors teaching this and other interdisciplinary classes was given sabbatical time for development. Another had gotten his PhD in applied math where the application was biology. Beck and colleagues suggest committing the time to attend introductory courses in the complementary disciplines [1]. Fortunately, there are an increasing number of books teaching computing in context, and even computing texts written by science professionals for science students. In addition, asking science colleagues for lab ideas has the benefit of getting them interested in the coursework.

2.1.4 Scheduling challenges

A challenge that might not be so apparent, but exists particularly in a small university with only one section of required classes is potential schedule conflicts between core computational and natural science classes. Once schedules are roughly built for the various disciplines, we found it helpful to send emails to students enrolled in the interdisciplinary programs asking if they can build a schedule for the next semester. If it is early enough in the process, it may be possible to reschedule or negotiate a compromise with the professor of the conflicting class. Still, it may not be possible to meet everyone's needs.

2.2 A New Minor-Specific Course: Python and UNIX Scripting

A two unit semester class, this scripting course consists of two 75 minute meetings a week divided between lecture and lab as needed. During the first 12 weeks of the semester, the students are presented with science-related problems and computational tools based in Python and UNIX that might be used to solve them. In our first offering, some of the computational background, and much of the required science was disseminated by the students themselves. A key component of the course was the "3 minute presentation." During the first week of class, students chose from a list of topics in their area of expertise and prepared a 3-5 minute presentation about that topic for the rest of the class. Presentations were made throughout the semester, the timing of which was determined by the point at which the information was needed for completing the labs. The goal was to provide enough information that the related lab could be understood, but not so much that a student unfamiliar with the topic would be overwhelmed. Furthermore, the student had to avoid using discipline-specific terminology without first defining the term. Students in the audience had to listen carefully enough, and ask enough clarifying questions, to write a summary of the topic after the presentation. Three examples follow:

- The first topic we tackled in the class was UNIX. Most science students were completely unfamiliar with what operating systems were in general. A computer science student gave a presentation on operating systems.
- An early lab that we completed called for transforming longitude and latitude data from the web into a more usable form using regular expressions in a UNIX-based text editor. A physics student talked about what the degrees, minutes, and seconds of a longitude or latitude value meant.
- One of the very first labs written in Python calculated the melting point required for denaturation of a DNA sequence. A biology student explained the denaturation (breaking apart of the base pairs comprising the DNA double helix) process and why it was important to the biologist.

The students performed peer evaluations and wrote summaries for each presentation. The presenter's grade was based on the peer and professor evaluations, and the grades of the students in the audience were based on their summaries. A sample evaluation is shown in Figure 1. Students received three points for a rank of "definitely" down to zero points for "not at all."

	Definitely	Almost	Somewhat	Not at all
The presenter presented just enough, but not too much				
I understood the concept presented by the end of the presentation				
The presenter used terms that I was familiar with or that he/she adequately defined.				
The presenter was able to answer questions.				
The presenter was well prepared				

Figure 1: Three minute presentation peer assessment

The final three weeks of the semester were spent working in groups of combined computational and science students. It was the job of the science student to find a real project from the natural sciences and then to explain and manage that project. These projects were presented in an end-of-the-semester poster session with 75% of all computational and science professors at PLNU in attendance.

Challenges addressed in this class resembled those seen in the real world of interdisciplinary teams.

2.2.1 Developing appropriate soft skills

Certainly communication is an issue in any workplace, but especially in an interdisciplinary environment. Not only must presentations be clear and organized, they must be given with the knowledge that not everyone in attendance shares the same vocabulary. The presenter must have the ability to present the material in a way that all participants can understand [15, 16].

Communication was intentionally addressed via the "3 minute presentations". Both science and computational students experienced trying to explain personally familiar topics to a less knowledgeable audience – so both understood the challenge and were sympathetic to their counterparts. An added benefit was that over the course of the semester all students became better at asking clarifying questions due to the fact that they were responsible for writing a graded post-presentation summary.

Another soft skill that is often overlooked is the ability to appreciate what team members bring to the table. Towards the end of the course, science students admitted initially being afraid that their computational peers would see them as inferior or "dumb". The fear was real in that this was primarily a course focusing on computational tools and the computational students in the class had more experience than the science students did in this area.

The 3 minute presentations were helpful here too. The opportunity for the science students to explain complex natural science concepts to others in the class allowed them to, in their own words, "show that they were smart." The rapport and respect that developed between the students was remarkable.

2.2.2 Effectively utilizing the unique skill sets of the team members

In performing preliminary research on the Computational Science minor, it became very clear that experience working in interdisciplinary teams was essential to future employers. However, finding appropriate projects can be a challenge for the computational faculty members.

As noted, our solution was to leave the determination of the science projects to the scientists. Science students knew from the beginning of the class that they were expected to come up with a potential team project. Armed with recently-acquired knowledge of computational tools, they suggested projects from their own undergraduate research experiences, or from the research of science professors with whom they had relationships. One project included the creation of an interactive plasmid (circular DNA molecule) map given the set of genes that should combine to make that plasmid. Another project used Python-driven image processing to search through thousands of pictures taken via a movement and heat triggered mechanism in search of animals in remote locations.

In addition to finding interesting projects, the science students presented the projects to the class, managed the projects, and if the project was completed for a science professor, the science student was the interface between the researcher and the computing students. The computational students, on the other hand were responsible for the majority of the technical aspects of completing the project.

2.2.3 Evaluating team members based on their expected contributions

As mentioned, the goal of the Computational Science minor is different for science students than for computational students. The focus of computational students is to learn the tools, and enough science vocabulary to communicate with the science-based client. The job of the science students is to learn to describe the science-related tasks in ways that the computing personnel can understand and to be familiar with what the computational tools can accomplish for them. With these goals in mind, science students were given more opportunities to present, manage, and act as liaisons as discussed in the previous section. For the project, their grades were largely dependent on their presentation and communication skills, rather than on the technical accomplishments. Conversely, while soft skills were factored in, the technical outcome of the project had the largest influence on the project grade of the computational students. Throughout the class, in exchange for additional "3 minute presentation" work, science students were given the option of working with a computational student on the more complex labs.

Equitable exams turned out to be a consideration as well. Even though all students were tested on both the science content and the computational tools learned in the class, the exams were more heavily weighted towards the computational tools since that was the emphasis of the course. While the science students didn't complain (and did quite well), when asked, one science student suggested that exams contain a set of questions that everyone answered, and a set of questions where students could choose which to answer. This suggestion will likely be implemented in future offerings of the course.

2.3 Freshman Interdisciplinary Seminar Pilot

The Mathematical, Information, and Computer Sciences department along with the Biology, Chemistry, and Physics departments at Point Loma Nazarene University are committed to helping our students understand, as early as possible, how their disciplines connect with others and how that informs the career options open to them. To that end, we are working on creating a freshman seminar that includes all of these majors. The first pilot of that freshman program occurred during the summer of 2013. It was taught by a team of six professors with at least one representative from each of the disciplines. During the five week pilot, students tackled two real-life problems in interdisciplinary groups using computational tools presented during the seminar. The first problem dealt with the possibility of life on other planets, and the second with the spread of the HIV virus. The teaching approach to this class was a combination of interactive and rotational models of team teaching [12]. During the first half of the class, the physics and computer science professors taught and both were present modeling real-time interaction between the disciplines. The team of biology, mathematics, and chemistry professors then rotated in for the second half to present the concepts and tools associated with the HIV problem. In addition, a sixth faculty member attended every class handling logistics and providing continuity.

While some of the difficulties in this course were similar to those in the previous examples, this section will focus only on the challenges related to team-teaching.

2.3.1 Discovering interesting problems whose solutions where interdisciplinary

Since our goal for this seminar was to show interactions between disciplines, scientific problems that require interdisciplinarity had to be carefully chosen. We found that it was essential to meet as a group of six for the initial planning of the seminar. Typically, science faculty suggested topics in which they were interested, and the group brainstormed together how technology might be used to help address an issue related to that topic. This was definitely a learning experience for all. Through the process we learned a lot more about each other's disciplines and methodologies. We discovered, as did Duesing and Hodgins with their animation and technology collaboration, that "like the students, we depend on the expertise from the other side of the 'cultural divide.'[7]"

2.3.2 Not only describing, but demonstrating interdisciplinary collaboration

There are multiple styles of team teaching, the choice of which must be tied to the intended goal. When Pittsburg State University wanted to add a class on computer security and information assurance, faculty members created a class taught by a team of computer science and information systems faculty. Their rationale: "The team teaching approach with four faculty members reduced the learning curve for departmental faculty and it allowed faculty to focus on the security topics most closely related to their area of expertise"[11]. However, in our case, the goal was different. We wanted our students to see that coming at a problem with tools and knowledge from multiple disciplines working together could create new knowledge that wouldn't be possible with a single discipline alone.

We chose a hybrid interactive model of teaching in an effort to demonstrate this integration. At least two professors actively presented during a single seminar session. In their presentation on team teaching, Stanford professors Anderson and Landy suggest "the ten commandments of team teaching." We found four to be particularly relevant and took care to follow them: 1) Thou shalt plan everything together. 2) Thou shalt attend they neighbor's lectures. 3) Thou shalt refer to thy neighbor's ideas. 4) Thou shalt have something to say, even when thou art not in charge [12]. Knowing what a teammate has presented and will present, allows the other to refer to this material in the process of his or her own presentation. As to the fourth commandment listed, this is an opportunity for the non-presenting professor to model the kinds of questions that can be asked, and inferences that can be made.

2.3.3 Combining different styles of presentation and planning

Teaching styles differ, as do the application of those styles. Furthermore, professors may have different thresholds regarding the degree of advanced planning that is comfortable. Another advantage of the group-of-six meetings in the planning stages is that they allowed us to become more familiar with other's styles. This helped us to determine who could best be paired together. In addition, these meetings established respect and rapport that could be drawn upon when compromises had to be made.

3. THE RECRUITMENT CHALLENGE

If you build it, will they come? No matter how great the program, no matter how carefully considered are the challenges, no interdisciplinary program will succeed without the student participants and faculty collaborators. This section deals with recruitment tips discovered via trial and error and finally success.

3.1 Recruiting students

- Keep an eye out for students in your service courses that are good candidates, and approach them individually. For example, most science majors are required to take calculus and/or statistics. Some of our best students in the minor were recruited from these classes
- Ask science professors if you can make a quick presentation to freshman level core courses. Even better, let current

students in the interdisciplinary programs do the talking. We've found that they are the best ambassadors. Visiting the freshman classes engages potential students early enough that they still have flexibility in scheduling. Visiting classes at any level serves to educate not only the students, but the professors on the programs offered.

3.2 Recruiting faculty collaborators

- Meet with potential collaborators to hear about their research. Listen especially for information storage and manipulation issues, or tasks that they do manually but repeatedly. Everyone is looking for ways to make their work more efficient. Once you have gained their confidence by helping them with tedious tasks, you can explore more interesting collaboration in the future.
- The poster session following the Python and UNIX class created a lot of "ah hah" moments for once skeptical faculty members as they saw how the interaction between the disciplines could actually occur.
- Organizations such as NSF and Howard Hughes Medical Institute are currently funding interdisciplinary research. Find a grant opportunity that works for you and a colleague, and make the suggestion.
- We've found that once student researchers learn the benefit of computational assistance, they are its advocates with their professors.

4. CONCLUDING REMARKS

Despite numerous challenges, at PLNU we believe that wading into the waters of interdisciplinary computing has definitely been worth the effort. Enrollment has risen dramatically in several computing classes and the changes made in these classes to make them more accessible to science majors have pleased the computational students as well. We've seen excitement for the interdisciplinary classes from both computational and natural science students. Interdisciplinary research has increased amongst science and computational faculty. The creation of these programs has required research, intentionality, and expanded comfort zones. But, we have seen success build on success, and what was once a little known idea is now an accepted trajectory amongst the computational and natural science faculty at PLNU.

5. ACKNOWLEDGMENTS

Many thanks to the students and professors in the computational and natural science departments at PLNU who have provided valuable ideas and feedback for the curriculum and this paper.

6. REFERENCES

[1] Beck, J., Buckner B., and Nikolova,O. 2007. Using interdisciplinary bioinformatics undergraduate research to recruit and retain computer science students. *SIGCSE Bull.* 39, 1 (March 2007), 358-361. DOI=http://doi.acm.org/10.1145/1227504.1227436

[2] Carter,L., Botts, R., and Crockett,C. 2012. Computational science programs: The background research. In *Proceedings of the 2012 IEEE Frontiers in Education Conference (FIE)* (FIE '12). IEEE Computer Society, Washington, DC, USA, 1-6. DOI=http://dx.doi.org/10.1109/FIE.2012.6462218

[3] Carter,L. 2011. Ideas for adding soft skills education to service learning and capstone courses for computer science students. In *Proceedings of the 42nd ACM technical symposium on Computer science education* (SIGCSE '11). ACM, New York, NY, USA, 517-522. DOI=http://doi.acm.org/10.1145/1953163.1953312

[4] Carter,L. 2006. Why students with an apparent aptitude for computer science don't choose to major in computer science. *SIGCSE Bull.* 38, 1 (March 2006), 27-31. DOI=http://doi.acm.org/10.1145/1124706.1121352

[5] Cassel,L. 2011. Interdisciplinary computing is the answer: now, what was the question?. *ACM Inroads* 2, 1 (Feb 2011), 4-6. DOI=http://doi.acm.org/10.1145/1929887.1929888

[6] Domik,G. 2009. Who is on my team: building strong teams in interdisciplinary visualization courses. In *ACM SIGGRAPH ASIA 2009 Educators Program* (SIGGRAPH ASIA '09). ACM, New York, NY, USA, , Article 9 , 7 pages. DOI=http://doi.acm.org/10.1145/1666611.1666620

[7] Duesing,J. and Hodgins,J.,K.. 2004. Team teaching animation art and technology. In *ACM SIGGRAPH 2004 Educators program* (SIGGRAPH '04), Tony Longson (Ed.). ACM, New York, NY, USA, 4-. DOI=http://doi.acm.org/10.1145/1186107.1186112

[8] Fetrow, J.,S. and John, D.J. 2006. Bioinformatics and computing curriculum: a new model for interdisciplinary courses. *SIGCSE Bull.* 38, 1 (March 2006), 185-189. DOI=http://doi.acm.org/10.1145/1124706.1121399

[9] Fisher, A. and Margolis,J. 2002. Unlocking the clubhouse: the Carnegie Mellon experience. *SIGCSE Bull.* 34, 2 (June 2002), 79-83. DOI=http://doi.acm.org/10.1145/543812.543836

[10] Guzdial, M. Does contextualized computing education help? Inroads (Dec 2010), 4-6. DOI=http://doi.acm.org/10.1145/1869746.1869747

[11] Harris,J., Cummings,M., Dreher,F., and Chandra,K. 2004. A team teaching approach to inclusion of a security component in IS and CS curricula. *J. Comput. Sci. Coll.* 19, 4 (April 2004), 16-27.

[12] Landy,J. and Anderson,L.*Ten Commandments of Team Teaching*,http://www.stanford.edu/dept/CTL/Newsletter/teamteaching.pdf

[13] Nissani, M. 1997. Ten cheers for interdisciplinarity: the case for interdisciplinary knowledge and research. The social Science Journal, Volume 34, 201-216.

[14] Raicu, D.,S. and Furst,J.,D. 2009. Enhancing undergraduate education: a REU model for interdisciplinary research. *SIGCSE Bull.* 41, 1 (March 2009), 468-472. DOI=http://doi.acm.org/10.1145/1539024.1509027

[15] Tymann,P, Computer Science and Bioinformatics, IN: Math and Bio 2010: linking undergraduate disciplines (L.A. Steen, ed.) The Mathematical Association of America, Washington. DC 2005.

[16] Yarden,A. and Esterman,N. 2008. The effect of disciplinary identity on interdisciplinary learning during scientific group meetings. In *Proceedings of the 8th international conference on International conference for the learning sciences - Volume 2* (ICLS'08), Vol. 2. International Society of the Learning Sciences 475-482

Computing in the Arts: A Model Curriculum

Bill Manaris, Renée McCauley, Marian Mazzone, William Bares
College of Charleston
Computer Science and Arts Departments
Charleston, SC USA
{manarisb | mccauleyr | mazzonem | bareswh}@cofc.edu

ABSTRACT

In this paper, we describe Computing in the Arts (CITA), an innovative interdisciplinary major, which combines computer science with artistic theory and practice. CITA is relatively easy to implement across a variety of higher education institutions, because it repurposes existing courses and resources in computer science and the arts. CITA is relatively easy to implement across a variety of higher education institutions, because it repurposes existing courses and resources in computer science and the arts. At our institution, this involves three tracks (music, visual art, and theatre). CITA incorporates four synthesis courses, one per academic year, which help students interweave the two distinct curricular experiences into a cohesive whole in preparation for their capstone project. CITA has been fully implemented at the authors' institution. In the three years of its existence, it has increased participation in computer science by 23% mainly from an underserved population (students interested in the arts). Approximately 40% of these students are women. While these students are not necessarily strong in mathematics, they tend to be strong in design and creativity, thus enriching the pool of computing professionals with people able to envision new technologies and surprising innovations. Such people are fully versed in computer science so they can easily collaborate with more traditional computing professionals such as software engineers and scientific programmers. We discuss our successes, and provide pointers for others to establish similar degree programs, including potential challenges and lessons learned.

Categories and Subject Descriptors

K.3.2 [**Computing Milieux**]: Computers and Education - Computer and Information Science Education

General Terms

Human Factors

Keywords

Computing, art, music, theatre, game programming, creativity, design, degree, major, curriculum, education

SIGCSE'14, March 5–8, 2014, Atlanta, Georgia, USA.

http://dx.doi.org/10.1145/2538862.2538942

1. INTRODUCTION

Computing in the Arts (CITA) is an innovative, interdisciplinary Bachelor of Arts degree program, which integrates computer science and information technology with art theory and practice.[1] The CITA curriculum incorporates tested pedagogy in Computer Science (CS) and the Arts. It is based on proven curricula and structured synthesis approaches [1-5, 13, 14], and previous curricular experiences by the authors [1, 6-10, 15]. The CITA program provides a liberal arts and sciences experience because the students acquire the knowledge and skills to combine creativity in the arts with the tools and conceptual modeling systems of computing.

The CITA major consists of 50 credit hours of required coursework in computer science, mathematics, an art area (music, visual art or theatre) and CITA synthesis courses. The major is structured around several synthesis experiences, at the freshman, sophomore, junior, and senior levels, each involving computing and one or more arts areas. The sequence of synthesis courses is designed to vertically integrate computational thinking in the arts throughout the undergraduate experience.

2. MOTIVATION

The goal was to create an innovative interdisciplinary degree that combined computing and arts, and allowed students to pursue coursework usually sequestered into separate schools or divisions. For several years, we had offered courses such as Computing in the Arts, Computer Music, and Game Programming. These courses attracted students from across campus and the courses always filled up. Students often asked if there was a follow-up course that they might take.

Some faculty expertise existed in the Computer Science (CSCI) Department, and faculty in both CSCI and the Arts disciplines were interested in collaborating. Our beliefs were that:

- Artists and musicians increasingly need to understand the conceptual framework and possibilities of computing, but most did not have the necessary computational thinking skills. Twenty-first century artists want to understand computational tools and techniques so that they may incorporate them comprehensively and effectively into the creative process to achieve their artistic vision.
- Computer scientists increasingly need to incorporate creativity, aesthetics and design into their work. Art enriches computational thinking with creative and aesthetic

[1] This effort has been supported in part by an NSF TUES grant (DUE #1044861).

expression, resulting in new techniques, innovative products, improved problem solving, and original inquiry.

At the time this degree was conceptualized (discussion began in 2008), the computing community was discussing new models for undergraduate education in computing. Through this degree we realized that we could also:

- Address the computational thinking needs of the educated individual in the 21st century (on our campus and beyond); and
- Broaden participation in computing by attracting students who were not attracted to the traditional computer science degree program.

2.1 Gauging Student Interest

Prior to moving forward with implementing the CITA major, we conducted a survey of students in first-year seminar classes at our institution in fall 2009. These classes spanned various disciplines including Biology, Philosophy, Physics, Political Science, Psychology, and Teacher Education. We also surveyed students in a few classes in Music, Art History and Computer Science (for non-majors).

The survey asked:

> *If you were in high school, how likely would Computing in the Arts have been your choice of college major?*
>
> *Scale: 1 (low) – 7 (high)*

Three hundred fifty-four (354) surveys were returned providing the following data:

Totals for each choice (1 low, 7 high)							**Total**
1	**2**	**3**	**4**	**5**	**6**	**7**	
93	70	52	52	51	24	12	354
26%	*20%*	*15%*	*15%*	*14%*	*7%*	*3%*	*100%*

We interpreted these results as supporting our plan to move forward with the new major. In particular, we decided to view choices 6 and 7 (above) as indicative of true student interest. In other words, 36 of 354 students (or 10%) would have considered CITA as their major. Assuming an incoming freshman population of 2,500 students (average at our institution), this would translate to 250 students who would seriously consider CITA as their major. Even more conservatively, focusing only on choice 7 (i.e., 12 of 354 or 3.39%), then 85 incoming students would consider CITA as their major.

2.2 CITA Advisory Committee

A committee of faculty from CSCI and Arts disciplines formed to develop the curriculum. The committee worked collaboratively to plan and implement the curriculum, modeling some of the integrative activity we hoped to encourage in our students. Faculty from each discipline determined what content from their discipline was essential. While the program is clearly interdisciplinary in scope, a decision was made to house the degree in the Computer Science Department in the School of Sciences and Mathematics. (The Arts departments are in the School of the Arts.) Three years later, the committee continues to meet, and collaborate across social media.

3. CURRICULUM

CITA incorporates existing computer science courses from an ABET-accredited B.S. degree program. It also includes 7 synthesis courses that are interspersed throughout the curriculum to integrate the different bodies of knowledge – computer science and the students' chosen art disciplines.

As it builds upon existing courses, CITA is an easy-to-implement curriculum model for infusing undergraduate computing education across the liberal arts and humanities.

3.1 Foundations

In developing CITA, we explored various curricular models for integrating computing and the arts. These included Cornell University's *Computing in the Arts* (CitA) concentration (offered by the CIS department) [3], UC San Diego *Interdisciplinary Computing and the Arts* major (offered by the Music and Visual Arts Departments) [13], and Yale University's *Computing and the Arts* curriculum (offered by the CSCI department) [14], among others. Of these, we selected Yale's curriculum (Yale model) as the most flexible curriculum that could be adapted and extended. Like the Yale model, CITA reuses available resources (e.g., faculty and courses) as much as possible. This minimizes implementation costs, making it easier to adopt. We modified the Yale model to fit the constraints of a mainstream undergraduate institution. Specifically, the CITA curriculum

- incorporates CSCI courses from an ABET-accredited B.S. degree program; and
- introduces several synthesis courses throughout the curriculum to help mainstream university students integrate the two separate bodies of knowledge (CSCI and an art discipline).

Implementation of the CITA model can be accomplished minimally with the addition of four new synthesis courses. These courses are discussed in detail in sections 3.3.2.1 and 3.3.2.2.

3.2 Learning Outcomes

The CITA program is designed to provide a liberal arts and sciences experience – students will acquire the knowledge and skills to combine creativity in the arts with the techniques and conceptual modeling systems of computer science and information technology.

CITA is designed to prepare graduates to:

- model processes, particularly those in arts applications;
- investigate, visualize, speculate, and invent using computing and computational thinking;
- synthesize innovative software applications and media combining music, images, sounds, lighting and stage design, and other digital artifacts; and
- explore the potential of computational thinking and its influence on society.

The characteristics of CITA graduates overlap with those expected of Computer Science graduates, thus many of the learning objectives in our existing courses for CSCI majors were applicable. Specifically, select learning outcomes/objectives, specified in CC2008 & now in CC2013, for Algorithms and Complexity, Computational Science, Graphics and Visualization,

Programming Fundamentals (subsumed by Software Development Fundamentals in CC2013), Discrete Structures, Human-Computer Interaction, Information Management, Platform-Based Development were found to be relevant [1, 2].

Moreover, the learning outcomes specified for several of our existing courses, which also conform to learning objectives in CC2008 and CC2013 and the requirements for ABET-accreditation, were appropriate to CITA. This enabled us to reuse existing courses in Math and Computer Science.

Table 1. Credit hour requirements by discipline

Credit Hours Required	Discipline
10	Computing in the Arts (CITA)
16	Computer Science (CSCI)
6	Mathematics (MATH)
18	Arts concentration (ARTS/H, MUSC, or THTR)
50	**TOTAL**

3.3 Curriculum details

The 50 credit hour program is an interdisciplinary Bachelor of Arts degree program with a blend of existing courses offered by Computer Science, Mathematics, Music (MUSC), Art/Art History (ARTS/H), and Theatre (THTR). (See Table 1.) The major is structured around several synthesis experiences (CITA courses), at the freshman, sophomore, junior, and senior levels, each involving computing and one or more arts areas. (See Figure 1.) Majors select an Arts concentration area from Visual Art (ARTS/H), Music (MUSC) or Theatre (THTR).

3.3.1 Computer Science and Math Requirements

CITA majors complete 16 credit hours of CSCI and 6 credit hours of math courses. Table 2 lists the existing CSCI and math courses that were folded into the CITA curriculum. The CSCI courses taken by CITA majors are the same ones taken by CSCI and other majors offered through the CSCI department. No new math or CSCI courses need to be developed to implement the CITA degree program.

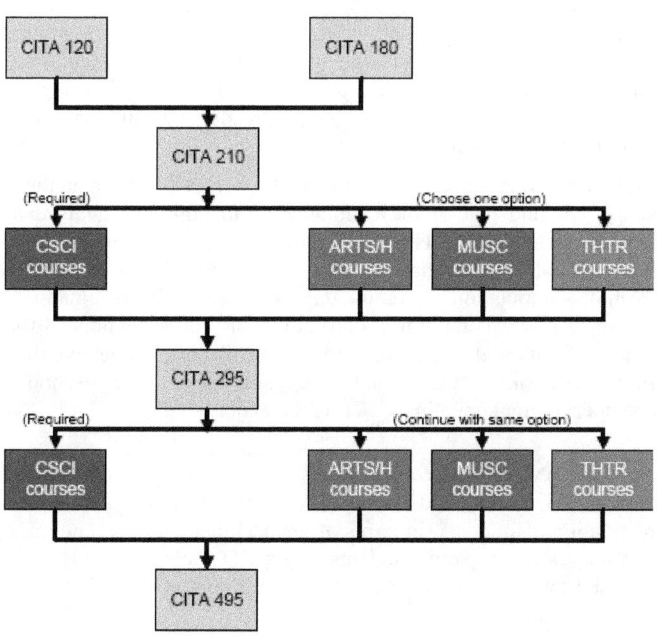

Figure 1: Curriculum overview by course type

3.3.2 CITA Requirements

The CITA synthesis courses are strategically placed throughout the curriculum to ensure a cohesive degree program for mainstream undergraduate students. As shown in Figure 1, students start with a sequence of two introductory synthesis courses. This ensures that they get an integrated foundation upon which to base their subsequent learning. A synthesis seminar is taken again in the middle of study, after students have taken several freshman and sophomore courses. Finally, a capstone experience is used to finalize the integration of the two bodies of knowledge (computing and their chosen art discipline).

Table 2. Computer science and math requirements

Computer Science
Computer Programming I & lab (4 credits)
Computer Programming II (3 credits)
Three courses (9 credit hours) from:
Data structures and algorithms
Computer organization
Imperative programming languages
Declarative programming languages
User-interface development
Artificial intelligence
Computer graphics
Software architecture and design
Special topics courses, with permission
Mathematics
One course from:
Pre-calculus
Business calculus
Discrete mathematics

3.3.2.1 Introductory synthesis courses

Three CSCI courses that synthesize computing and the arts existed prior to the implementation of the CITA degree: CSCI 120, 180, 210 (descriptions below). These courses were originally created due to faculty interest and in an attempt to create CSCI courses that would attract majors, from across campus, into computing. Enrollments in these courses were healthy. When the CITA program was implemented, we cross-listed them as both CSCI and CITA courses: CITA 120, 180, 210. They are still cross-listed and continue to attract CS, CITA and other majors.

CITA 120: Building Virtual Worlds: This course synthesizes computational thinking with animation, storytelling, set design, movement through 3D space, lighting, etc. This course routinely includes guest lectures from Theatre faculty on topics such as costume design, lighting, choreography, and set design. (Students in the THTR concentration are encouraged to take this course.)

CITA 180: Computers, Music and Art: This course synthesizes computational thinking with creating music, sounds, images and other digital artifacts. The environments currently being used are MIT's Scratch, MIT's Processing, and jMusic with Jython, among others. This course routinely includes guest lectures from Art

History, Studio Art, and/or Music faculty on related topics. (Students in the MUSC and ARTS/H concentration are encouraged to take this course.)

CITA 210: Game Programming: This course introduces principles of game programming, including computer modeling, data visualization and animations, media transformations, and video game ethics. Students are exposed to several game engines, a scripting language, and develop at least one game. This course, in the guise of computer game development, exposes students to the synthesis of computational thinking with graphic design, sound design, animation, storyboards, programming, etc.

CITA majors choose one of CITA 120 & 180; all majors take CITA 210. Students completing the two-course sequence have the necessary computing background and motivation to place subsequent area concentration courses (Visual Art, Music, and Theatre) in a CITA context.

Since implementation of the CITA degree program, several new introductory synthesis courses have been developed (through funding from NSF). These new courses are described in Section 6. These courses were developed to make CITA into a national model curriculum; for this reason, they are listed separately. Some of these new courses are appropriate substitutes for CITA 120 or 180 in our own curriculum.

3.3.2.2 Upper-level synthesis courses

The following courses were developed to provide synthesis experiences at the junior and senior levels. These courses have been offered concurrently, once a year; a student cannot enroll in 295 at the same time as 495.

CITA 295: Seminar: Junior-level CITA majors participate in the seminar through readings, discussion, and individual library research to apply and expand their understanding of how to integrate computing and the arts. Students develop a prospectus on their future capstone project and identify a faculty advisor. This gives them a year to work on synthesis towards designing and implementing their capstone project. This course spans Bloom's Taxonomy levels 1-3 (Recall, Comprehension, Application).

CITA 495: Capstone: Senior-level CITA majors participate in the capstone through readings, discussion, preparation, and presentation of individual capstone projects under the guidance of the CITA advisor(s). This course spans Bloom's Taxonomy levels 4-6 (Analysis, Synthesis, Evaluation).

Successful completion of CITA 495 requires the development and presentation of a capstone project, and submission of a final report concerning the project. Projects must be approved by an arts advisor and the director of the CITA program. The project must synthesize arts and computing and must include software development (possibly incorporating open-source software, with permission of the instructor).

3.3.3 Concentration Requirements

There are three arts concentration areas in the curriculum: Art/Art History (ARTS/H in Figure 1), Music (MUSC), and Theatre (THTR).

The ARTS/H concentration requires 18 hours. This includes 6 hours of Studio Art and Art History courses, namely Drawing I, and New Media in Contemporary Art. It also includes 12 hours of electives from a list of major arts courses relevant to CITA, such as Themes in the History of Art, Introduction to Film Art, Drawing (II, III, and IV), Photography (I, II, III, and IV), Painting (I, II, III, and IV), Printmaking (I and II), Sculpture (I, II, III, and IV), The Cinema: History and Criticism, Studies in Modern, Contemporary & Film Arts, Contemporary Art, and Advanced Studio Practice. Prerequisite chains exist and must be satisfied.

The MUSC concentration requires 6 hours, namely Music Fundamentals, and Music Theory I. Additionally, it requires 12 hours of Music courses, from a list of major Music courses relevant to CITA, such as Music Theory (II, III, and IV), Composition (I and II), Music History (I and II), and Jazz Theory. Prerequisite chains exist and must be satisfied.

The THTR concentration requires 9 hours, namely Script Analysis, Acting I, and Playwriting I. It also includes 9 hours of electives from a list of major Theatre courses relevant to CITA, such as Costume (I and II), Stagecraft, Theatre History and Literature (I and II), Drafting and Rendering for Theatre, Creative Drama, Screenwriting, and Playwriting. Prerequisite chains exist and must be satisfied.

4. ASSESSMENT

After the three years of implementation, 56 students have declared CITA as their major. Of these, 8 have already graduated (by transferring earlier courses to satisfy the 4-year degree requirements). The remaining 48 students currently in CITA represent a 22% increase in students studying computing on our campus. This is significant because the majority of these students would not have chosen a computing major otherwise.

Of the CITA students currently enrolled, 40% (19 of 48) are female. In particular, the junior CITA honors synthesis class has 53% (7 of 13) female students; and the senior CITA capstone experience has 80% (4 of 5) female students. In other words, CITA, as implemented at the authors' institution, clearly attracts and retains female students. This should be compared to the recent 22% ratio of female students earning CS degrees nationally [11].

Enrollments have not yet stabilized, so it is unclear how these statistics will change in the future. We believe that, as our advertising efforts increase (we have done minimal marketing thus far, other than our web presence and one brochure), and word-of-mouth from our graduates spreads, our numbers will continue to grow, before they stabilize.

Comparing our current enrollments to our pre-implementation study, we find that of the estimated 85 incoming students that would consider the CITA major, about 22% of them actually matriculated. This translates roughly to 1% of our incoming freshman population. (Again, this is mostly a fresh, untapped population for computing, consisting of approximately 40% females.) Although rough (and not yet stabilized), we believe this first-three-years statistic may be useful to other schools considering implementing a CITA-like major.

5. LESSONS LEARNED

The CITA major and the CITA courses attract a broader population of students (in terms of gender) than our CSCI courses and majors have. Some students trying CITA courses, and being exposed to computer programming, have gone on to change their major to CSCI or CITA.

In the first three years of our CITA major, after various discussions among the CITA faculty constituents and through observations of student experiences and behaviors, we are considering the following improvements to our implementation of the CITA degree program.

Of most importance, we have concluded that all synthesis experiences (courses) should be three credit hour courses. Since inception, CITA 295 (the junior seminar) has been a 1 credit hour course. That gives the impression to some students that the course content and requirements, which includes deciding on a project topic and identifying faculty advisors, is not as important as their other classes. A change from 1 to 3 credit hours has already been approved by the faculty.

We want to recruit more arts faculty to work with CITA students as advisors. Several of our CS faculty are themselves artists, and can assist CITA majors as they creatively develop their project ideas. However, the combined talents from both CS and arts faculty acting as advisors will only strengthen a student's project. While being an art advisor does not require a major commitment of time, and in many cases will benefit the faculty member as much as the student, we have found that many art faculty prefer to remain within their traditional non-computing art constraints. A few notable exceptions (1 or 2 faculty per art area) have contributed to the forming of the CITA major, and are committed to advising and evaluating CITA students. However, we hope to gradually engage more (if not all) of the arts faculty, in one way or another, since there is much untapped talent in that pool of faculty. And as computing continues to spread through all arts disciplines, engaging with CITA is likely to become increasingly beneficial to arts faculty in terms of professional development.

The teaching of the capstone course can be taxing on the CS faculty involved, especially if some of the students are not as committed, or need a lot of support. Thanks to the web, in general, and YouTube and Vimeo, in particular, it is easy to have students find and present inspiring projects related to their interests. Requiring that they find research papers that have appeared in computing-related conferences helps identify projects that exist in the intersection of computing and the arts, and also have substance and promise to generate a capstone project. Many students have difficulty making the transition from YouTube (level 2 of Bloom's Taxonomy - understanding), to reading and discussing research papers (levels 3 and 4 of Bloom's Taxonomy - applying and analyzing), to coming up with a new, innovative idea that builds on earlier projects without replicating them (levels 4 and 5 of Bloom's Taxonomy - analyzing and synthesizing). Of course that is also a challenge in other situations where a thesis is expected (e.g., graduate school).

Evaluation of student capstone projects is another challenge, as the projects are often quite different in terms of content and the level of development can vary quite a bit. In particular, submitted work requires **analysis**, **evaluation**, and **creation** of CITA ideas, concepts, and materials into various deliverables, such as annotated bibliographies, project reports, and software (e.g., see [10, 12]). CITA graduates need to demonstrate their ability to model and apply process (i.e., to use programming skills) to achieve an artistic vision or project. We have found the following general guidelines to be useful in guiding the grading of projects:

- The grade of A is for work that involves high-quality achievement in all three Bloom areas.
- The grade of B is for work that involves high-quality achievement in at least two Bloom areas, and medium-level achievement in the other.
- The grade of C is for work that involves high-quality achievement in at least one Bloom area, and medium-level achievement in the others.
- The grade of F is for work that does not meet above criteria.

Advising/mentoring is time-consuming, but does not count as a class. So it adds to faculty workload without much recognition.

Finally, we have had some weaker CSCI majors switch to the CITA major, because they perceived it to be an easier degree (at least in terms of Math and CSCI requirements). However, these students may find creativity expectations of the capstone experience to be as equally challenging as the CSCI degree requirements. This is exacerbated by that fact that these students often switch into the curriculum late and attempt to compress all arts and synthesis courses into one or two years, which does not give them the time needed to synthesize the fields.

6. ADDITIONAL CITA COURSES

The CITA program allows us to explore possibilities for additional growth, and for strengthening ties between computing and the arts. For instance, through collaboration between CS and Arts faculty funded by NSF, we have developed the following new CITA synthesis courses:

CITA 101: #creativity (3 credit hours) This introductory course is an exploration of creativity and its applications for contemporary technology, business, art, and sciences. Students will gain understanding of the principles of creativity, participate in creativity exercises, and expand upon their creative skill-set. Small group projects, reviews of notable creative figures, examination of real world scenarios, and practical applications of creativity will foster the engagement and inquiry of creativity.

CITA 140: Drawing with Code (6 credit hours) This course seeks to provide the student with a historical, theoretical, aesthetic, conceptual, and technical introduction to the challenges presented by the relatively recent collision of art, culture, and computing power. Students will explore thinking algorithmically by deconstructing large ideas into programmable steps alongside lessons on how an artist thinks creatively through drawing.

CITA 160: Mobile Computing and Musical Theatre Fusion (3 credit hours) This course introduces musical theatre and computer science students to the fundamental principles of computer programming, playwriting, and song writing. Students will explore the intersection of technology and live theatre leading to ways that those ideas can be harnessed within the creation of a "mini-musical".

CITA 381: Computer Music on a Laptop: Composing, Performing, Interacting (3 credit hours) Principles of music composition and computer programming for developing interactive computer music environments. Team-based, project-driven exploration of Python programming, time-based structures, algorithmic processes, soundscapes, graphical user interfaces, musical language and style.

Syllabi and materials for all developed CITA courses are publicly available at http://www.cs.cofc.edu/~manaris/cita/

The following courses, which explore aspects of visual arts including animation or film, are in development:

Digital Sculpting and Modeling – This course starts with traditional modeling in clay or stone and moves to digital 3D modeling. Students create physical models then use a 3D scanner to digitize their work. They next learn to modify the shape and color properties of the scanned digital model. By the end of the course students will create digital models directly in the modeling software. Potentially, utilizing a 3D printer, they could print physical renditions of their artifacts.

Virtual Production – Previsualize and plan productions for television, film, and theatre through storyboards and modeling 3D digital stand-ins for scenery, props, and performers. Covers artistic conventions of visual storytelling and cinematography. Analysis and hands-on practice using emerging tools including performance capture, virtual

Compositing and Special Effects – Students learn how to use digital compositing software to blend live footage with digital backgrounds as well as to write their own algorithms to implement composites and special effects.

Once developed, course materials, including syllabi and exercises, for these courses will also be available through http://www.cs.cofc.edu/~manaris/cita/

7. CONCLUSION

We have presented Computing in the Arts (CITA), an innovative, interdisciplinary BA major, which introduces computing around a theme of creative expression. This major integrates computer science with art theory and practice. This CITA model is relatively easy to implement across mainstream institutions, as it reuses existing courses and resources in computer science and the arts. Only two new courses had to be developed to implement the curriculum. CITA incorporates four synthesis courses, one per academic year, which help students interweave the two distinct curricular experiences into a cohesive whole in preparation for their capstone project.

CITA attracts creative students who might otherwise have studied arts or the humanities. Finally, it attracts and retains about 40% female students compared to about 20% in traditional computing degrees [11].

8. ACKNOWLEDGMENTS

Development of the CITA curriculum model has been supported in part by NSF under a TUES (Transforming Undergraduate Education in Science, Technology, Engineering and Mathematics) grant, DUE #1044861). The authors acknowledge the significant support of the following on-campus collaborators: Chris Starr (Computer Science), Yiorgos Vassilandonakis (Music), Blake Stevens (Music), Charlie Calvert (Theatre), Jarod Charzewski (Studio Art), and Susan Kattwinkel (Theatre). Also, the following off-campus collaborators are acknowledged for various conversations on enhancing and disseminating the CITA model: Jennifer Burg (Wake Forest University), Susan Reiser (Univ. of North Carolina, Asheville), and Rebecca Bruce (Univ. of North Carolina, Asheville).

9. REFERENCES

[1] Computer Science Curriculum 2008: An Interim Revision of CS2001". ACM Interim Review Task Force. Retrieved Sep. 5, 2013 from http://www.acm.org/education/curricula/ComputerScience2008.pdf.

[2] Computer Science Curricula 2013, Ironman draft, http://ai.stanford.edu/users/sahami/CS2013/ironman-draft/cs2013-ironman-v1.0.pdf

[3] Cornell University, Computing in the Arts, Retrieved Sep. 5, 2013 from http://www.cis.cornell.edu/ComputingArts/

[4] Georgia Tech University College of Computing. 2013. "Welcome to 'Georgia Computes!' — Georgia Computes!" Retrieved Sep. 5, 2013 from http://gacomputes.cc.gatech.edu

[5] Guzdial, M. 2010. "Does Contextualized Computing Education Help?" *ACM Inroads*, 1 (4), pp. 4–6.

[6] Hanks, B., Murphy, L. Fitzgerald, S., McCauley, R., Thomas, L., and Zander, C. 2009. "CS1 Students Speak: Advice for Students by Students." *Proceedings of the 40th SIGCSE Technical Symposium on Computer Science Education*, Chattanooga, TN, pp. 19–23.

[7] Manaris, B. 2007. Invited Editorial, "Dropping CS Enrollments: Or The Emperor's New Clothes?" *ACM Inroads* (December), pp. 6–10.

[8] Manaris, B., Wainer, M., Kirkpatrick, A.E., Stalvey, R.H., Shannon, C., Leventhal, L., Barnes, J., Wright, J., Schafer, J.B., and Sanders, D. 2007. "Implementations of the CC'01 Human-Computer Interaction Guidelines Using Bloom's Taxonomy." *Computer Science Education Journal* 17 (1), pp. 21–57.

[9] Simon, B., McCauley, R., Morrison, B., Murphy, L. and Zander, C. 2009. "For Me Programming Is ..." *Proceedings of the 5th International Computing Education Workshop*, Berkley, CA, pp. 106–116.

[10] Starr, C.W., Manaris, B., and Stalvey, R.H. Bloom's Taxonomy Revisited: Specifying Assessable Learning Objectives in Computer Science, *Proceedings of the 39th ACM Technical Symposium on Computer Science Education* (SIGCSE '08), Portland, OR, pp. 261-265, Feb. 2008.

[11] Stross, R. What Has Driven Women Out of Computer Science? *The New York Times*, Nov. 15, 2008 (accessed online).

[12] Thompson, E., Luxton-Reilly, A., Whalley, J.L, Hu, M., and Robbins, P. *Bloom's taxonomy for CS Assessment, Proceedings of the 10th Conference on Australasian Computing Education*, vol. 78 (ACE '08), Wollongong, Australia, pp. 155-161.

[13] UC San Diego. ICAM: Interdisciplinary Computing and the Arts Major. Retrieved Sep. 5, 2013 from http://visarts.ucsd.edu/icam-interdisciplinary-computing-and-arts-major

[14] Yale University, Computing and the Arts. Retrieved Sep. 5, 2013 from http://www.yale.edu/yalecollege/publications/ycps/chapter_ii/computing_arts.html

[15] Zander, C., Thomas, L., Simon, B., Murphy, L., McCauley, R., Hanks, B., and Fitzgerald, S. 2009. "Learning Styles: Novices Decide." Proceedings of the 2009 ACM Conference on Innovation and Technology in Computer Science Education (ITiCSE 2009), Paris, France, pp. 223–227.

E pluribus, plurima: The Synergy of Interdisciplinary Class Groups

Debra S. Goldberg
University of Colorado Boulder
430 UCB
Boulder, CO 80309, USA
+1-303-492-7514
debra@colorado.edu

Elizabeth K. White
University of Colorado Boulder
430 UCB
Boulder, CO 80309, USA
+1-303-492-7514
Elizabeth.white@colorado.edu

ABSTRACT

Computer science is increasingly becoming interdisciplinary, with applications not only in scientific disciplines, but also in the arts, humanities, and social sciences. Training computer scientists to work in diverse application disciplines is imperative for modern departments. We have had success using interdisciplinary groups for this purpose in a computational biology class, *Algorithms for Molecular Biology*. In this class, carefully-balanced interdisciplinary groups learn to take advantage of each other's abilities, and to communicate effectively with students with a much different background.

From this diversity, we get much more (*e pluribus, plurima*) than would be possible if we tried to train all students to have a more homogeneous blend of multiple disciplinary knowledge. Within a single semester, students go from virtually no understanding of one discipline to completing research projects on a relevant problem that they have defined themselves.

Categories and Subject Descriptors

K.3.2 [**Computers and Education**]: Computer and Information Science Education – [*computer science education]*.

General Terms: Algorithms, Design, Human Factors.

Keywords: Experience report, active learning, cooperative learning, project-based learning, communication skills, interdisciplinary education, computational biology.

1. INTRODUCTION

As the field of computer science becomes more interdisciplinary, we must consider how best to educate computer science students for this new reality. There is no single pedagogical method that will work best for all students, so we must have a variety of approaches available to them.

One way to train interdisciplinary computer scientists is to educate them with strong disciplinary knowledge in multiple domains. However, this not only takes more years, which many students are unwilling to invest, but distinct disciplines often require different ways to address problems, which is difficult to master for many students with specific learning strengths.

Rather than trying to cram the equivalent of two degrees-worth of knowledge and experience into a single degree program, an alternative is to train students strongly in one discipline, and give them sufficient knowledge of another discipline as well as the communication skills to allow them to effectively work together with similarly-trained scholars in the other discipline. This is the premise for our *Algorithms for Molecular Biology* course.

There are many reasons to introduce group work into coursework. Employers complain that engineering graduates lack the communication and social skills to function in a team environment, even though this skill is essential to the workplace [1]. Closer to home, a 2004 survey by Waite et al. [19] showed that companies who hire CU graduates perceived significant gaps in these students' preparation for the work force. Specifically, they reported that students had sufficient technical knowledge but lacked the social skills to apply it in groups.

Collaborative learning and active learning models have been proposed to alleviate these problems [15][16], but are no panacea. Waite et al. [19] found high resistance to incorporating teamwork into lower-division coursework. Students accustomed to a passive learning model are understandably unhappy about learning to navigate a different system, and many are intimidated by the open-ended questions posed by actual research. Group work also presents students with logistical problems, like arranging meeting times [8] and new social dilemmas, like bullying or freeloading [6][14]. Team projects tend to lead to productive behaviors, like brainstorming, but students often have trouble sifting through the wealth of ideas they generate to find the most promising ones [8]. More generally, teams entail reliance on the other group members; student surveys indicate that engineering students in particular find this proposition to be onerous [4][5][19].

We believe that grouping together students with very different disciplinary backgrounds, but who are compatible in other respects, may alleviate many of these problems. We have had success with this approach in a computational biology class, *Algorithms for Molecular Biology*. Students may better appreciate the knowledge that others bring to the group when they themselves are not familiar with the area. Freeloading also seems to be less of a problem than in most group work, perhaps because there is no one else in the group who has the knowledge needed to complete a task.

SIGCSE'14, March 5–8, 2014, Atlanta, Georgia, USA.

ACM 978-1-4503-2605-6/14/03…$15.00.
http://dx.doi.org/10.1145/2538862.2538979

In this class, students are assigned to carefully-balanced interdisciplinary groups. These groups work together on in-class exercises and homework designed to require the expertise of a biologist, a computer scientist, and a mathematician. In this way, students learn how to take advantage of each other's abilities, and more difficult material can be covered than most students could handle alone. Each interdisciplinary group develops an algorithm for a real biological problem, often based on data from the lab one of the group members works in.

2. THE COURSE

Since 2008, University of Colorado Boulder has offered a course in *Algorithms for Molecular Biology*. This course, cross-listed in the Department of Computer Science (CS) and the Department of Molecular, Cellular, and Developmental Biology (MCDB) has drawn students from over ten departments (CS, MCDB, Biochemistry, Chemical Engineering, and Applied Mathematics, among others). Both undergraduate and graduate students enroll in this course, giving an additional dimension to the diversity in this class that, when managed appropriately, adds to the learning experience. Few students come into this class with all of the necessary knowledge to understand the algorithms at work. Such courses offer an ideal laboratory for cooperative learning, and we have successfully integrated group projects as a central part of the coursework. This paper describes the techniques we have found to be most helpful and summarizes the results of cooperative learning in this interdisciplinary context.

Prerequisites for the course are comfort with mathematics and/or some programming experience, as well as more advanced understanding (upper undergraduate) of any relevant discipline, e.g., computer science, math, molecular biology, or chemistry. We have defined learning objectives in accordance with the Accreditation Board for Engineering and Technology (ABET) criteria [7]. Two objectives of this class for which the group projects are particularly useful:

- Students acquire the skills required to collaborate with biologists, mathematicians, and computer scientists.
- Students improve communication and presentation skills.

2.1 Course Logistics

The course is taught by a single instructor whose background in computer science is distinctly stronger than her background in molecular biology. Her weakness in biology becomes a strength of the course, as it is used to entice (initially) the biologists taking the course to answer questions from other students and to clarify or rephrase any content. This soon provides a climate in which most students feel comfortable speaking in class. In this way, she models the course philosophy that everyone in the class has valuable knowledge and insights to contribute, and that an interdisciplinary researcher need not be expert in all involved disciplines but can rely on others, provided she has a sufficient foundation in the other areas and is able to communicate effectively with scientists with complementary understanding.

This class has generally had 10-20 students each time it has been offered. This year, enrollment jumped to over 40 students, with an excellent balance of computer scientists, biologists, and other quantitative scientists. Instructor workload is relatively high, especially during the periods of group assignments and defining group projects, and also in the weeks leading up to major project milestones, since every group is required to meet with the instructor outside of class one or more times for each milestone. An advanced doctoral student or postdoctoral researcher has served as an assistant instructor on two occasions: the first year the course was offered (to help with course development) and this year (to help with the larger class). Assistant instructors have been

2.2 The Introductory Weeks

The first two weeks of the class are largely introductory material, to bring all students up to a minimum baseline of knowledge in both biology and computer science. We tell students that research shows that they learn better when they talk in class than when the instructor talks, and that they all have valuable perspectives to share with the class, and gradually through the first weeks the level of discussion within the classroom grows. This sets up the value of communication amongst students for their group projects.

Over the next few weeks, some of the most commonly used algorithms in molecular biology are covered. These are the most likely algorithms that will be adapted in group projects, but more importantly, they give concrete examples of abstractions that can be used for biological data, and show that an understanding of both the computer science and the molecular biology contributes towards useful algorithms. Biologists who are not interested in doing any programming of their own learn that an understanding of the underlying algorithms is essential for determining the correct parameter settings for different data and to know when computational results can be trusted. By week six, the students are required to come up with a research topic, as described below.

2.3 Group Assignment

The first challenge in this course model is to create balanced and diverse groups. Groups are comprised of 3 or 4 students, and the groups persist throughout the semester, provided that no pathological group interactions surface. It is critical that each member of the group has an opportunity to contribute uniquely to the work. In forming groups, the instructor takes into account the different backgrounds of the students, as well as their maturity. For example, a sophomore in computer science will have some of the required knowledge of code writing, but may need more mentoring to estimate and meet deadlines; such a student may be placed in a group with a graduate student in chemistry, under the assumption that the more experienced member can assist with this process. Similarly, an older student who has already had a successful career in industry can provide the group with valuable grounding in staying on task. On the other hand, students like this can inadvertently dominate the group and intimidate younger or less experienced members; thus, we might counterbalance her group with another graduate student, to help ensure that group work is the result of dialogue between all the members.

Students fill out a student information sheet in the second week, after the add/drop deadline. This sheet includes a number of questions that are used to create balanced groups. Factors that strongly determine group placement include the educational level (undergraduate vs graduate students), extent of computer science background, knowledge of molecular biology, current affiliation with an experimental biology lab, and general areas of primary interest. Each group must have at least one member with a strong CS background and one member with a strong molecular biology background. Each group generally includes at least one undergraduate and one graduate student. To the extent possible, exactly one student is placed in each group who can provide molecular biology data from their research lab.

Based on feedback from students in the first iterations of this class, we have found that a critical component of group composition is that work habits should be relatively homogeneous. A student who starts early, works steadily, and can't tolerate being in a group with last-minute participants should not be in a group with a student who, due to other commitments, cannot commit to completing group work early and steadily. Students are asked to rate their work habits on a scale with four options from one of these extremes to the other, and students within a group will differ by no more than one category.

Although gifted students are not generally considered at-risk, studies have shown they have special needs that are often not met in the classroom [2][18]. Many high-ability students get little challenge in their schools [3] and some are quite discouraged about the prospect of continued academics [12]. Many of these students approach collaborative work with dread, as they've done the lion's share of a group's work all too often. Such students need to be grouped together with other high-ability students so that they can truly be allowed to exercise their minds, a privilege for them that most students take for granted [11][13]. Although requiring differentiated assignments, this minority of students must also be taught the value of hard work and to push the limits of their abilities [3][9]. With this research in mind, we added a question that we termed "learning styles." Four choices are given for the question "Which best describes your learning style?":

- I often breeze through classes, and appreciate greater challenge (but not longer tasks).
- I often don't get good grades because I won't jump through unnecessary hoops, but often understand concepts more quickly than others.
- I generally earn good grades by working hard.
- Getting good grades is challenging (e.g., professors/books don't teach to my learning style).

The first two answers, although seemingly very different, are both used to identify high-ability students in combination with other student information. In fact, many students who indicate one also indicate the other. Although we don't indicate the commonality, these students are likely to be grouped together. When these groups meet with the instructor, they are guided towards more complex projects than other groups.

We also ask an open-ended question about what students have liked and/or disliked about previous group work. This can inform us further on each student's work habits, learning styles, and other attributes (e.g., leadership style) that will impact group dynamics. For example, students who feel another group member often takes over their work are not grouped with students who feel other group members leave all the work for them.

We have found that the schedule constraints that students report is generally not a useful factor for forming groups. Students' schedules often change after the first week, and students often have more flexibility than they report. When students in a group share a common interest, have complementary knowledge, and have compatible working and learning styles, they usually manage to find times that they can meet together outside of class. Exceptions to this are students who commute and those who work full time and can only get to campus certain times.

Groups are formed initially after the first two weeks of the course. These groups initially work together on in-class activities, and discuss schedules and common interests for possible group projects. Students are given the opportunity to privately inform the instructor of any perceived conflicts (without need to indicate if it is a schedule, personality, or other type of conflict), and a week later groups are reassigned. Some groups need to be rebalanced after other changes are made, so students who have not requested a change do not know why their group composition has changed. After this, groups rarely change.

2.4 Defining a Research Problem

Many pedagogical studies have shown that students at the college level are adequately exposed to theoretical knowledge, but are unable to connect what they have learned to practical problems in an intuitive way (Hurst 1995). *Algorithms for Molecular Biology* differs from most other classes students have taken in that they get to work on open problems, and not problems with known solutions that can be perceived as toy assignments.

Defining an original problem, without a list of possible choices, is often a daunting task for students. Most have never been expected to do this before. Most groups will include a member who has some type of data that can be used for a group project, and this provides a good focal point to initiate discussion. Groups without a source of data must begin by brainstorming what questions or what type of publicly available data might be of interest. Typically 15-30 minutes of each 75-minute class session are devoted to group exercises, during which time the instructor circulates and helps direct some brainstorming with each group.

After student groups have had a week or two to brainstorm amongst themselves, each group meets individually with the instructor. Most groups have not yet sketched out a specific problem to tackle, and the instructor directs a brainstorming session in which each student mentions some interests, and group members start building on the ideas of others in the group. These sessions usually end with each group member taking on something specific to research: a literature search to see what is already known about a particular topic; to learn what has already been done for a particular problem; to find existing software that can be modified; or contacting another researcher about gaining access to their data. Then a second meeting with the instructor is scheduled to complete the identification of a group problem. Generally, a suitable problem can be agreed on quickly by the beginning of the second meeting.

Some groups have sketched out a suitable problem before their first meeting with the instructor, and proceed immediately to the agenda for the second meeting. At these, students discuss the project's viability and potential pitfalls. Often students are too optimistic about what they can accomplish in the approximately ten weeks remaining in the semester, and the instructor guides them towards reducing the scope of the project. It is important to give groups a high probability of success, and open-ended problems often take more time than planned as unexpected pitfalls are encountered, so we try to err on the side of smaller scope. However, we define possible extensions that can be worked on if the originally defined project is on track for early completion.

We require that each member have a clearly defined set of independent subtasks to complete, and that these jobs are tailored to the expertise of each student. Fong [8] argues that this approach reduces both freeloading and fear of making mistakes, which can otherwise paralyze a group. Suggestions are made to each group if it struggles with this. If a division of labor can't be found for which each group member feels they can contribute their expertise and the division seems fair to all, another project must be found. This rarely happens, as by the time the group has agreed upon a project, all group members have considered the project and what their contribution might be.

2.5 From Groups to Teams

Given the diversity of backgrounds in the groups, when the students have to prioritize project goals or weigh tradeoffs between them, they must learn to pitch their case in language free of jargon, and to respect and engage with collaborators from other areas. The instructor scaffolds these new collaborative skills in class and with individual groups, e.g., by pointing out jargon that needs explaining. When students in a group navigate the process of choosing a project, proposing a way to solve it, dividing tasks up between the members, planning deadlines with each other, integrating code from each member into the project, and writing tests to verify the results, not only do they gain a firsthand understanding of the software engineering process, but they also learn how to negotiate with stakeholders from completely different backgrounds to produce a working product.

Through this process, students learn collective responsibility—that others depend on them, and that they can depend on others. No one likes to be perceived as a shirker by their peers, and if they are helped to find a way they can contribute, most students will rise to the challenge. Our challenge is to help them find their way, despite other demands on them. Being the expert on one aspect of an interdisciplinary project, and being able to help others understand concepts that are second nature to you (even while struggling with concepts that others are helping you understand) can be a powerful motivator.

Groups meet with the instructor periodically throughout the remainder of the semester. Problems encountered are discussed, as well as changes to the original plan that result from these problems and/or a better understanding of the problem. These meetings help ensure that problems are dealt with early on, and group directions can be modified before the problems compound.

2.6 Scientific communication

Communication is one of the 4Cs (communication, collaboration, critical thinking, and creativity) of 21st Century Skills [17] that are increasingly embraced by educators, and communication skills are frequently cited by employers as essential skills for success that young employees often need to learn [1]. When groups are first formed, students are given information about working in a group and group project planning. In addition to the informal communication that occurs within groups and during class discussions, students get feedback from six different forms of scientific communication: a project proposal, problem presentation, project update, class presentation, poster session, and scientific paper. Required elements are discussed during the group's meetings with the instructor before each milestone.

The project proposal, due in week six (of a 15 week semester), includes the following elements:

- A motivating introduction with enough background to explain why something new is needed
- Problem description
- What is new about the proposed algorithm—examples are provided for how an algorithm can be new to some extent but still feasible within the semester timeframe
- A description of the input and output data
- An overview of the proposed approach, and a description of each step or task in the approach
- A list of group members and responsibilities—possible individual contributions provided to students include:
  - Biological domain expert to ensure biological meaning
  - Review the literature to find related work, software, etc.
  - Acquire data online and/or from a lab on campus
  - Format data so it can be used in group's programs
  - Lead development of any mathematical formulae
  - Code main algorithms and/or specific routines
  - Develop test software
  - Determine test data
- A preliminary literature survey

Shortly after the project proposals are submitted, groups give a brief (5-10 minute) presentation of the problem they are addressing (but not the proposed methods) to the class. Each student in the group must participate. In doing this, they learn that most jargon is not understood by the entire class, and learn how to phrase things so that everyone can understand.

Around week ten, groups submit a written project update. This document includes an abstract with an overview of the information from the project proposal, assessment plans, changes to the original proposal, accomplishments and plans for each group member, optional or alternative tasks if there is time or if planned tasks cannot be completed, what the group needs from others (e.g., the instructor), and a complete list of references.

Students also present their final results in two venues; this is done first in class (every group member gives part of the 30 minute presentation), and later at a poster session, to which science and engineering faculty are invited. This provides the students with a rare opportunity to practice communicating scientific ideas to other experts in their field.

Finally, students must submit a paper in a format accepted by a scientific journal. Students are encouraged to publish their results (when reasonable). Formats accepted by PLoS ONE are encouraged, but not required. PLoS ONE is a journal that will publish any paper that is scientifically sound, without the authors needing to convince reviewers of the significance of the results. This format has many advantages, and many significant results have been published therein, but it is also a plausible publishing venue for many group projects. Although we consider at least half of the group projects to have produced results that would be publishable with little or no additional research, and have offered assistance to any group members that want to pursue this, none have yet taken that final step to get the work published. This may be due to the extreme time limitations of a one-semester research project – most groups obtain results in the final weeks of the semester, leaving little time to write a manuscript worthy of publication. We are beginning to discuss the possibility of expanding the class to two semesters.

2.7 Grading

At the end of the course, the students in a group each evaluate the contributions of each member, including themselves. Studies have shown that students in teams resent being given one grade for the entire team, because they perceive it as giving freeloaders an unfair advantage [10]. Each student's grade for the group's products are modified by the feedback from these evaluations. To further validate these evaluations, each group is required to use a shared workspace (e.g., a wiki, blog, or google doc) that tracks modification history by author, and allow access to the instructor. The instructor looks through these periodically to ensure that all group members are contributing appropriately to the project.

It is important to note that students are not graded on the quality of their results. Although most groups do get positive results within the time constraints of a term project, some get negative results, and more rarely projects do not fulfill the plan, and group members are not penalized for this if they have brought real effort to the task. Students are graded on how well they have learned and participated in the process of defining and implementing a research project, and how effectively they have collaborated with students from different disciplines.

2.8 Feedback

The course is now in its seventh iteration, and we have solicited student feedback via an anonymous survey and made changes each year. While space constraints preclude detailed tables, here we give a brief overview of some of the key results. For instance, we have made homework assignments smaller and more frequent, to provide a more consistent workload. Group forming proceeds by a more sophisticated algorithm that takes student maturity into account as well as student background. The instructor now meets with each group more often to assess how the project is going, which provides more timely resolution of problems than waiting for students to recognize group issues on their own. We have also put more effort into reaching out to other faculty at our college to improve lecture content and assignments, present guest lectures, and supply groups with raw data for analysis. Two years ago we had a consultation by an associate for our campus teaching excellence program interview students in the absence of the instructor and provide valuable feedback on course strengths and weaknesses.

While formal evaluations were initially relatively low, as expected in project-based learning classes [4][5][19], they have recently improved. Furthermore, many students have gone out of their way (even long after grades are due) to remark on the value of the class. The consultant's evaluation report indicated that the greatest strength of the class was "good group composition (mixed bio & cs students, undergrad and graduate students)." Clearly the group portion of this course is working.

2.9 Exceptional Results

Many of the group projects have yielded exceptional results within a single semester. Some of the more remarkable:

- When different strains of a virus infect an individual, new viral particles may have elements of each. One group developed an algorithm to identify these reassortment events in Influenza A, predicting the "parental" strains as those that co-existed and jointly explain a new strain. While simple, we believe this was the first computational method for this.
- When distinguishing between DNA variants in a diploid cell and sequencing errors, existing software assumes that the expected frequency of one variant could be 0, 0.5, or 1. Some organisms have more than two copies of each chromosome, and one group modified open source software to allow for this.
- A group of three undergraduates developed a scoring scheme to combine gene expression and sequence data to improve identification of the targets of a microRNA, a small RNA molecule which regulates the expression of its target genes.

3. CONCLUSION/DISCUSSION

It is always difficult to develop a new course from scratch, particularly one that draws on as many disciplines as these classes do. Teaching these courses with a focus on collaboration presents additional risks: closer supervision of student groups is required to prevent students from dominating groups or hitchhiking with more active group members. Most importantly, student resistance to depending on their peers must be overcome. Even with these caveats, however, we see great promise in this approach. Over the past seven years, the course has generated ongoing research collaborations between students from biology and computer science, and we have received many positive comments from students about the value of these courses over courses taught according to more traditional models. For example, the following unsolicited note of thanks was sent to the instructor well over a year after the student took the class:

> "...of all the classes I took as an undergraduate at [X], yours has proven to be among the most useful. While I was taking the class, I didn't really have much perspective on how useful it would be. .... As you well know, though, all of molecular biology today is inseparable from computer science and having delved deeper into the discipline, it amazes me when those of my colleagues who have only extensive biological background take the output of a computer program at face value—taking for granted that it is correct and relevant without much awareness of what the computer science means biologically. ... I'm a long ways off in understanding much or any of the programming from the perspective of a computer scientist, but I can tell already that the perspective I garnered from your class has helped me as a biologist."

The rules we use to form groups, which include both experienced and less experienced members, yield unexpectedly productive collaborations. We offer several reasons as possible explanations for why these groups work better than traditional groups:

- Students who are allowed to be experts in specific areas have more respect for the expertise of their collaborators.
- There is less freeloading because there is no one else who can do a student's tasks.
- Students are better engaged because they define the project themselves.
- Projects are meaningful and engaging (akin to service learning), and give an introduction to real research.
- Scaffolding is provided for defining projects, dividing work, communicating without jargon, and managing conflicts.
- The course attracts strong, motivated students.

While this last explanation does not reflect as strongly on our specific methods as do others, we believe that no one reason fully explains the success of these interdisciplinary group projects, and that the reputation of the course is responsible at least in part for attracting such strong students. We foster a classroom culture in which all members contribute, and we advise (but do not manage) groups to help them circumvent problems. This model for interdisciplinary work allows our students to experience the pleasure of being local experts, and it brings out the best in them over the semester. Compared to cross-training students to expertise in two or more fields, this approach is nimble. We argue that this method is ideal for modeling genuine scientific collaboration at both undergraduate and graduate levels. As collaborations involving computer scientists are becoming prominent in a wide variety of fields, we see interdisciplinary classes that focus on communication and collaborative skills with projects of significance as a great way to prepare students to work happily and productively in this kind of future.

4. ACKNOWLEDGMENTS

Our thanks to our college and department for providing funding for initial course implementation, to Tim Dunn for his assistance with the class in recent years, to our colleagues for many fruitful discussions, and to anonymous reviewers for helpful comments. We thank Peter White for help composing the Latin phrase in the title. Finally, we thank all the students who have taken this course and thereby helped others learn and make the course a success.

5. REFERENCES

[1] Adams, S. G. and Laksumange, B. Building successful student teams in the engineering classroom. *Journal of Science, Mathematics, Engineering, and Technology*. 4 (3/4), 2003.

[2] Colangelo, N., S. Assouline, et al. *A Nation Deceived: How Schools Hold Back America's Brightest Students*, The Connie Belin & Jacqueline N. Blank International Center for Gifted Education and Talent Development, University of Iowa. 2004.

[3] Davidson, J., B. Davidson, et al. *Genius Denied: How to Stop Wasting Our Brightest Young Minds*, Simon & Schuster, New York, NY. 2005.

[4] Diwan, A., Waite, W. M. et al. An infrastructure for teaching skills for group decision making and problem solving in programming projects. *Proceedings of the 33rd ACM SIGCSE Technical Symposium for Computer Science Education*. Covington, Kentucky: 276-280. 2002.

[5] Drury, H., Kay, J., et al. Student satisfaction with groupwork in undergraduate computer science: do things get better? *Fifth Australasian Computing Education Conference (ACE2003)*, Adelaide, Australia. CRPIT, 20. Greening, T. and Lister, R., Eds. ACS. 77-85. 2003.

[6] Felder, R. M. and Brent, R. Navigating the bumpy road to student-centered instruction. *College Teaching* 44 (2): 43-47. 1996.

[7] Felder, R. M. and Brent, R. Designing and teaching courses to satisfy the ABET engineering criteria. *Journal of Engineering Education* 92 (1): 7-25. 2003.

[8] Fong, P. Building Teams that Learn: A Study of Learning Effects in Engineering Student Teams. *Journal of Professional Issues in Education and Practice*. 121-127. 2010.

[9] Gilman, B. *Challenging Highly Gifted Learners*. Prufrock Press, Waco, TX. 2008.

[10] Lejk, M. and Wyvill, M. Group learning and group assessment on undergraduate computing courses in higher education in the UK: Results of a survey. *Assess. Eval. High. Educ.* 22(1) 81-93. 1997.

[11] National Association for Gifted Children. Grouping [Position Paper]. Washington, DC. Retrieved: www.nagc.org. 2009.

[12] Rimm, S.B. *Why bright kids get poor grades and what you can do about it*. Great Potential Press, Scottsdale, AZ. 2008.

[13] Rogers, K. B. Using current research to make "good" decisions about grouping. *NASSP Bulletin*, 82(595), 38-46. 1998.

[14] Rosser, Sue V. Group work in science, engineering, and mathematics. *College Teaching* 46(3): 82-88. 1998.

[15] Springer, L., Stanne, M. E., et al. Effects of small-group learning on undergraduates in science, mathematics, engineering, and technology: A meta-analysis. *Review of Educational Research* 69 (1): 21-51. 1999.

[16] Terenzini, P. T., Cabrera, A. F., et al. Collaborative learning vs. lecture/discussion: Students' reported learning gains. *Journal of Engineering Education* 90(1): 123-130. 2001.

[17] Trilling, B. and Fadel, C. *21st Century Skills: Learning for Life in Our Times*. Jossey-Bass, San Francisco, CA. 2009.

[18] U.S. Department of Education. *National excellence: A case for developing America's talent*. Office of Educational Research and Improvement: Washington, DC. 1993.

[19] Waite, W. M., Jackson, M. H., et al. Student culture vs. group work in computer science. *Proceedings of the 35th ACM SIGCSE Technical Symposium for Computer Science Education*. New York, NY: 12-16. 2004.

Teaching Tips We Wish They'd Told Us Before We Started, High School Edition

Daniel D. Garcia (moderator)
University of California, Berkeley
777 Soda Hall
Berkeley, CA 94720-1776
+1 510-642-9595
ddgarcia@cs.berkeley.edu

Baker Franke
The University of Chicago Laboratory Schools
1362 E. 59th Street
Chicago, IL 60637
+1 773-702-9450
bfranke@ucls.uchicago.edu

Stephanie Hoeppner
Clermont Northeastern Schools
5327 Hutchinson Rd.
Batavia, OH 45176
+1 513-685-1413
smhoeppner@gmail.com

Josh Paley
Henry M. Gunn High School
780 Arastradero Road
Palo Alto, CA 94306
+1 650-354-8200
josh.paley@gmail.com

SUMMARY

"Seldom was any knowledge given to keep, but to impart; the grace of this rich jewel is lost in concealment." – Bishop Hall

At the SIGCSE Symposiums in 2007 and 2011, we presented panels in which seasoned teachers shared the teaching tips we wished we'd known before starting our careers [1,5]. The difference from earlier "Teaching Tips" panels [6] was that our suggestions were meant to be hidden gems less often highlighted by our colleagues or by some of the best-known teaching resources [2,3,4,7,8,9]. We clustered these tips into categories: **Grading, Lecturing**, **Office** (hours), **Staff** (mentoring), **Exams** (authoring & administering), **Labs** (authoring & running), **Section** (TA-led discussion), **Projects** (and homework; authoring & supporting), **Classroom** (organization, interactions, and incentives), **Personal** (fostering relationships), and **Meta** (advice spanning categories). The sessions were received quite well, and the audience contributed many of their own teaching tips throughout the presentations.

This year, we're presenting a "High School edition", and have invited inspirational teachers from a broad variety of schools. The position statements that follow offer a random sampling of two of these "hidden" pearls; presenters will share many more during the session, and time will be provided for audience participation. We'll endeavor to capture all the tips for the online collection.

Categories and Subject Descriptors

K.3.2 [**Computer and Information Science Education**]: Computer Science Education

SIGCSE'14, March 5–8, 2014, Atlanta, Georgia, USA.
ACM 978-1-4503-2605-6/14/03.
http://dx.doi.org/10.1145/2538862.2538870

General Terms

Documentation, Experimentation, Human Factors, Management

Keywords

Computer science education, teaching tips, high school

1. BAKER FRANKE

Inspire from bottom up, not top down. (Projects) Students are much more inspired when they learned about some new, cool, socially relevant thing *after* they had just completed a project that was some facsimile of it. They are much more inclined to say, "Hey, I could do that!", or "Oh, I see how that works now" when they understood that they were on the path toward it. Going the other way doesn't work as well. I tried, for example, to inspire students by starting with an inspiring reading like Luis Von Ahn's *Games With A Purpose* article [10] to motivate students to invent their own GWAP. The students were inspired, but quickly discouraged as they realized they were not experienced or skilled enough to actually produce something that they were intellectually capable of conceiving. The result was the cringe-inducing refrain: "Ugh, programming is hard. Only people smarter than me could do this. I'll just get someone else to do it." NOOOOOOO! So, instead, decide on a project that you think is achievable that relates to the inspirational goal. Figure out how to build up to that project as you normally would. THEN show them the great, inspirational, high-level thing and show how it relates to what they just did. This builds students' confidence and sense of empowerment, rather than leaving them disappointed/discouraged that they couldn't do what they wanted.

Reverse Quizzes (Classroom, Exams) High school students are often less-than-good at having a sense of what they don't know, and even worse at admitting it in public. In my AP Java class my lectures are usually some version of live coding, which is great except some kids do slip through the cracks if they don't participate, and moreover, a student can be a passive observer. So to fix this, in a way that (a) gave the students instant feedback and

(b) didn't cause me to have to grade anything, I've started doing "reverse quizzes." Here's how it works: I keep a stack of several hundred half-sheets of paper at the front of the room. Each sheet has printed on the top-right corner the name of some animal - aardvark, cat, mouse, shark, etc. During live coding, we'll arrive at some method that needs to be written, say writing the *indexOf* method for a Linked List, and instead of doing it with typical Q&A, I'll give them a few minutes to write it down on one of the half-sheets of "animal paper" and turn it in anonymously. I collect them and in about 4 minutes I can go through the entire stack and say, "Cobra, correct. Canary, correct. Bear...not quite, you returned the node, not the index" and so on. Students can easily remember which animal they had – numbered sheets are too easily confused – and I can single them out without publicly embarrassing or attaching a grade to it. Also, if there are major misconceptions in the group (e.g., everyone is doing the same wrong thing), I can address it right-away, and answer students' questions before they even know they have them.

2. STEPHANIE HOEPPNER

Relatable examples: (Meta) Most students show up in a programming or CS course for one of three reasons: (1) Have been coding secretly at home and are thrilled to finally show someone and talk to someone about it. (2) Thought it might be a fun class because there are computers. (3) Guidance counselor made me do it (various reasons as to why....). If I had known this, my first few years may have gone smoother. Students in groups 2 and 3 need someone to bring them into computer science carefully and safely, while the students in group 1 need a better understanding of why they are doing what they are doing. My solution is what I call *relatable examples*. They need examples on their terms, in their words, and in their environment.

Pedagogy trumps content knowledge: (Meta) We all have this grand feeling of accomplishment when we have achieved our college degree and have come from the realm where abstract thought and the creation of new ideas is exciting and motivating. Then we step into a classroom full of students who again are in one of the three groups mentioned above. I wish I had known earlier that pedagogy is more important than content knowledge. Don't misunderstand; you certainly need to know your content, but *how* you teach it relates directly to the students' success. You have to be able to impart your knowledge to the students or create an environment where the students attain it themselves but through avenues you provide. Using different strategies to present material, using pair programming, integrating multiple facets of computing into one course, allowing students to choose assignments, and even allowing students to teach content are some easy ways to reach your students effectively.

3. JOSH PALEY

The best projects are ones students choose themselves! (Projects) The whole idea of CS is to figure out how computers can be used to make great things! Many students can create their own great things and are inspired to do so … give them credit for this work! Make it extra credit or do something else that makes them feel really good about what they have done. (I've given As for projects that are inspired and awesome even if other parts of a student's work are less awesome. I don't regret it.) Help your students to be creative! If that means they don't do all of your assigned work, they'll live and you'll live if give them credit for stuff that is at least as good as your assigned work!

Don't grade the homework! (Grading, Projects) This sounds crazy at first, but consider a typical math class. Who determines if a problem has been done correctly? Whether it is a student, peers, or a teacher, typically the referee is a human. This means that the turnaround time for the learner to verify whether or not they have solved a problem is not instantaneous and can vary in quality. Now consider a closed lab, a typical setup for a CS class at a high school. The teacher can be in the position of observing the student and the computer referee without having to do most of the work of the referee. If the referee says something is wrong, then the teacher can intervene, but often, students can sort things out on their own. Most students need far less feedback on homework from the teacher; some need none. When I deal with homework, I take a look at those students who are genuinely struggling to see if there are patterns in the kinds of mistakes they make. I can often give holistic feedback targeted only at students who need it. This is much better than spending hours preparing feedback for every student, including those who do not need it. (But it is nice to tell those students they are doing great in class!)

4. REFERENCES

[1] Astrachan, O., Parlante, N., Garcia, D. D., and Reges, S. 2007. Teaching tips we wish they'd told us before we started. In *Proceedings of the 38th SIGCSE Technical Symposium on Computer Science Education* (Covington, Kentucky, USA, March 07 - 11, 2007). SIGCSE '07. ACM, New York, NY, 2-3. http://doi.acm.org/10.1145/1227310.1227314

[2] Bain, K. *What the Best College Teachers Do*. Harvard University Press, Cambridge, MA, 2004.

[3] Boice, R. *Advice for New Faculty Members*. Allyn & Bacon, Needham Heights, MA, 2000.

[4] Davis, B. *Tools for Teaching,2/e*. Jossey-Bass, SF, CA, 2009.

[5] Garcia, D. D., Dodds, Z., Huang, T., and Rebelsky, S. A.. 2011. Teaching tips we wish they'd told us before we started, small college class edition. In *Proceedings of the 42nd ACM technical symposium on Computer science education* (SIGCSE '11). ACM, New York, NY, USA, 317-318. http://doi.acm.org/10.1145/1953163.1953257

[6] Grissom, S., Naps, T., Parlante, N., and Lawhead, P. 2001. Practical teaching tips from around the world. In *Proceedings of the Thirty-Second SIGCSE Technical Symposium on Computer Science Education* (Charlotte, North Carolina, United States). SIGCSE '01. ACM, New York, NY, 419. http://doi.acm.org/10.1145/364447.364807

[7] McKeachie, W. J. Mckeachie's *Teaching Tips: Strategies, Research And Theory for College And University Teachers*. Houghton Mifflin, Boston, MA, 2005.

[8] Reis, R. M. *Tomorrow's Professor: Preparing for Careers in Science and Engineering*. IEEE Press, New York, NY, 1997.

[9] Royce, D. *Teaching Tips for College and University Instructors: A Practical Guide*. Allyn & Bacon, Needham Heights, MA, 2000.

[10] von Ahn, L. and Dabbish, L. 2008. Designing games with a purpose. Commun. ACM 51, 8 (August 2008), 58-67. DOI=10.1145/1378704.1378719

Introductory Programming Meets the Real World: Using Real Problems and Data in CS1

Ruth Anderson[1] Michael D. Ernst[1] Robert Ordóñez[2] Paul Pham[3] Steven A. Wolfman[4]
[1]University of Washington [2]Southern Adventist University [3]The Evergreen State College [4]U. of British Columbia
{rea,mernst}@cs.uw.edu rordonez@southern.edu phamp@evergreen.edu wolf@cs.ubc.ca

1. Summary

Too many students in introductory programming classes fail to understand the significance and utility of the concepts being taught. Their low motivation impacts their learning. One contributing factor is pedagogy that emphasizes computing for its own sake and assignments that are abstract, such as computing the factorial function.

Many educators have improved on such traditional approaches by teaching concepts in contexts that students find more relevant, such as games, robots, and media. Now, it is time to take the next step.

In this special session, participants will develop and discuss ways to teach introductory programming by means of real-world data analysis problems from science, engineering, business, and the humanities. Students can be motivated to learn programming in order to analyze DNA, predict the outcome of elections, detect fraudulent data, suggest friends in a social network, determine the authorship of texts, and more (see Section 3.4 for more examples). The approach is more than just a collection of "nifty assignments": rather, it affects the choice of topics and pedagogy, all of which together lead to greater student satisfaction.

The approach has been successfully used at 4 colleges and universities. The classes were effective for both CS and non-CS majors. Neither the computing material nor the problems need to be "dumbed down". At the end of the term students were amazed and delighted at the real data analysis that they could perform. They were excited about applying computation in their work and about learning more.

The special session contains a mix of activities, including comparative analysis of introductory classes; group discussion of curriculum design; a mini-panel discussing how the approach has worked in practice; and brainstorming about example assignments and curriculum revision.

Categories and Subject Descriptors: K.3.2 [**Computers and Education**]: Computer and Information Science Education—*Computer science education*; J.0 [**Computer Applications**]: General

General Terms: design, documentation, languages, measurement

Keywords: CS1, introductory computing, data programming, data processing

2. Audience and objective

This session is intended for instructors who teach introductory computing (CS1) to CS majors, non-CS majors, or a mix. It is also relevant to those responsible for curriculum design.

In this SIGCSE Special Session, participants will learn:

SIGCSE'14, March 5–8, 2014, Atlanta, Georgia, USA.
ACM 978-1-4503-2605-6/14/03.
http://dx.doi.org/10.1145/2538862.2538994.

- The benefits of an approach grounded in real-world problems and data.
- How the real-world approach is more than a collection of "nifty assignments"; rather, it affects the choice of topics and pedagogy.
- The challenges and successes of applying this approach at multiple colleges, including pitfalls to avoid.
- Principles of creating an assignment or adapting an existing one to support and reinforce the computing concepts.

Participants will be given a packet of materials to take home, as well as online links to web resources including assignments, syllabi, handouts, and more.

Participants will leave the session prepared to make positive curricular change at their own institutions, whether creating a new class, adapting one from another institution to your curriculum, or revising your current offerings.

3. Outline

A brief outline of the session follows.

- Description of, and motivation for, the overall approach including example end-of-term student projects (15 mins)
- Group discussion of pros and cons of this and other approaches to CS1 including appropriateness for different students, place in the curriculum, etc. (15 mins)
- Project idea brainstorming. (20 mins)
- Experience reports and Q and A. Instructors who have applied the approach will report on its successes and failures and will offer advice to those who wish to adopt it. (20 mins)
- Creation of support groups for followup after SIGCSE is over, to help instructors put their ideas into practice. Also, all discussions and ideas during the session will be collected, summarized, and shared on a publicly-accessible wiki. (5 mins)

3.1 A real-world approach to CS education

The key idea of our approach is that *every assignment uses an existing real-world dataset to answer a question that is relevant to science, engineering, or business.* Neither the questions nor the datasets are artificial.

This approach serves the following goals:

- motivate and excite students about computation
- enable students to process data to solve real problems
- teach computer programming
- teach computer science concepts
- serve both CS and non-CS majors

3.2 Comparison to other teaching approaches

Traditional introductory programming classes take their examples and assignments from the domains of puzzles, games, and abstract mathematics. For instance, students might be shown how to reverse a list or assigned to compute the Fibonacci sequence. This puzzles-and-games approach works well to motivate some students, but it alienates others. Students find it difficult to appreciate the practical importance of the skills they are learning.

Recognizing the deficiencies of the puzzles-and-games approach, other classes have incorporated realistic demonstrations and assignments. We acknowledge our debt to these pioneering classes, which provide inspiration and examples. At the same time, we aspire to take the next step.

Media Computation [7, 9, 13] introduces students to images, sounds, and HTML pages, then shows students how to manipulate these data. The problem domain is more connected to entertainment and computers than to real-world problems. Other classes share this theme. Stevenson's real-world programming assignments [10, 11] are a web crawler, spam evaluator, and steganography. DePasquale [2] presents three data sources: stock quotes, and the APIs from Google and Slashdot.

The ITiCSE working group [4] offers 14 projects related to "social good" that motivate students and provide them with skills to solve complex problems; Erkan et al. [3] do the same for a data structures class. We weave the themes throughout the class. Similarly, Isbell et al. [5] combine mathematics, computation, and experiments to solve engineering problems.

Some classes that address realistic problems and data focus on visualization [8], statistics [1], or databases [12]. By contrast, we focus on computation and programming.

3.3 Effect on pedagogy

In order to support students' experience with realistic datasets, it is desirable to make a few changes to the topics, order, and presentation of traditional introductory material. Here are a few examples.

We introduce the foreach loop but not the for loop with an explicit index. Students use data structures, but they do not re-implement basic data structures [6]. We use GUIs solely for plotting, but never for pictures or animation. We do not create GUIs nor any other user interface. We use file I/O but not console I/O. We introduce recursion at the end of the term, as an enrichment topic, but it is not used in the assignments.

We use the Python language, because it is easy to use and is widely adopted in the sciences. Because Python has a significant and usable procedural subset, we do not discuss object orientation. We discuss the notion of a type extensively, but not static typing nor compilation.

We introduce a few concepts that are often missing from CS1 classes but are desirable for data analysis, such as basic statistics and how to plot a graph.

Overall, students learn the same concepts as in any other CS1 class, but a slightly different toolset that enables them to do better-motivated tasks. Our choice of topics is motivated by viewing our class not just as CS1 but also as CSΩ: it should give a solid foundation for subsequent practical and theoretical work, but should also be useful even if the student never takes another computer science class.

3.4 Example assignments and projects

The presenters and audience will discuss some of the assignments that we have used and will give away handouts for others. The assignments illustrate the class philosophy of using real datasets and problems. This runs deeper than using some nifty assignment, but the assignments could be repurposed for an existing CS class.

Given files of DNA data, categorize organisms according to their GC count. Along the way, the students discover the need for data cleaning and perform that step.

Determine which environmental factors affect Archaea population biodiversity. Archaea are single-celled microorganisms, and the environmental factors include ocean salinity, temperatures, and chemical concentrations. Students learn to process tabular data.

Given polling data leading up to U.S. presidential elections, replicate the election prediction performed by Nate Silver of the FiveThirtyEight blog. This requires ranking, weighting, and averaging, and it illustrates the difference between sampling error and pollster bias.

Given Facebook social network data, create multiple algorithms for recommending friends. Evaluating them on the real data via Monte Carlo methods shows the utility of randomization.

Statistically analyze the least significant digits of election results from the U.S. and Iran to detect fraud that is revealed as anomalies against the expected uniform distribution.

Statistically analyze the most significant digits geographical data from the real world and from literary fiction to detect anomalies from the expected Benford's-Law distribution. The two statistics assignments illustrate statistical methodology via a modeling and sampling approach, without a long detour into mathematics. It also shows the importance of considering sample size when determining whether a given sample is anomalous. They also show how abstraction permits problems that seem different to share most of their code.

Linguistically analyze texts to determine their authenticity: clean noisy transcriptions and compare the vocabulary and phrases with known-authentic texts. This shows how to use data structures and control flow constructs to write concise, powerful, understandable code.

Analyze the mood, or sentiment, of Twitter posts to determine correlations with geography. Other known correlations include with biological rhythms and economic indicators.

In some of our offerings, we have given students the opportunity to define a scientific question about a real-world dataset of their own. The final projects from one offering (`http://courses.cs.washington.edu/courses/cse140/13wi/projects/`) include:

- Examining decay mechanisms of the Higgs Boson
- What makes H5N1 avian influenza "Avian"? (Why not "H5N1 tiger influenza"?)
- Spatial variability in the Antarctic circumpolar current in a global climate model
- Evaluating the effectiveness of the European Union Emissions Trading System
- Local causes, public amenities, and poverty level
- Urban growth and unemployment
- Correlation between statistics and wins in major league baseball
- Payroll and success in Major League Baseball
- An iterative strength-based model for the prediction of NCAA basketball games

References

[1] R. Catrambone and M. Guzdial. Computational freakonomics. `http://swiki.cc.gatech.edu/compfreak`, 2012.

[2] P. DePasquale. Exploiting on-line data sources as the basis of programming projects. In *SIGCSE*, pages 283–287, 2006.

[3] A. Erkan, T. Pfaff, J. Hamilton, and M. Rogers. Sustainability themed problem solving in data structures and algorithms. In *SIGCSE*, pages 9–14, 2012.

[4] M. Goldweber, J. Barr, T. Clear, R. Davoli, S. Mann, E. Patitsas, and S. Portnoff. A framework for enhancing the social good in computing education: a values approach. *ACM Inroads*, 4(1):58–79, Mar. 2013.

[5] C. L. Isbell, L. A. Stein, R. Cutler, J. Forbes, L. Fraser, J. Impagliazzo, V. Proulx, S. Russ, R. Thomas, and Y. Xu. (Re)defining computing curricula by (re)defining computing. *SIGCSE Bull.*, 41(4):195–207, Jan. 2010.

[6] H. P. Langtangen. *A Primer on Scientific Programming with Python*. Springer, 3rd edition, 2012.

[7] L. Rich, H. Perry, and M. Guzdial. A CS1 course designed to address interests of women. In *SIGCSE*, pages 190–194, 2004.

[8] K. A. Robbins, D. M. Senseman, and P. E. Pate. Teaching biologists to compute using data visualization. In *SIGCSE*, pages 335–340, 2011.

[9] B. Simon, P. Kinnunen, L. Porter, and D. Zazkis. Experience report: CS1 for majors with media computation. In *ITiCSE*, pages 214–218, 2010.

[10] D. E. Stevenson and P. J. Wagner. Developing real-world programming assignments for CS1. In *ITICSE*, pages 158–162, 2006.

[11] D. E. Stevenson, M. R. Wick, and S. J. Ratering. Steganography and cartography: interesting assignments that reinforce machine representation, bit manipulation, and discrete structures concepts. *SIGCSE Bull.*, 37(1):277–281, Feb. 2005.

[12] D. G. Sullivan. A data-centric introduction to computer science for non-majors. In *SIGCSE*, pages 71–76, 2013.

[13] S. L. Tanimoto. *An Interdisciplinary Introduction to Image Processing: Pixels, Numbers, and Programs*. MIT Press, 2012.

Guided Inquiry Learning in Context: Perspectives on POGIL in CS

Helen H. Hu
Westminster College
hhu@westminstercollege.edu

Matthew Lang
(Moderator)
Moravian College
lang@moravian.edu

Clif Kussmaul
Muhlenberg College
kussmaul@muhlenberg.edu

Chris Mayfield
James Madison University
mayfiecs@jmu.edu

Tammy Pirmann
Springfield Township School District
tpirmann@gmail.com

Categories and Subject Descriptors: K.3.2 [Computers and Education]: Computer and Information Science Education

General Terms: Human Factors

Keywords: POGIL, active learning, communication, inquiry learning, teamwork, high school

1. SUMMARY

Process oriented guided inquiry learning (POGIL) is an active, student-centered approach to teaching/learning [6]. In a POGIL classroom, students work in small teams on inquiry-based activities that guide students to discover concepts. These activities are designed to align with the learning cycle [8] and include elements that are designed to additionally develop process skills (*e.g.*, team work, conflict resolution, written and oral communication, *etc.*). The role of the instructor in a POGIL classroom is to facilitate student discovery, rather than to deliver lecture.

The POGIL approach was developed and refined within the physical sciences and its success in general and organic chemistry courses has been documented in a variety of university contexts. In particular, POGIL classes contain fewer failing grades and withdrawals [9] and result in a high degree of mastery [5] than traditional classes. Because of its success, the approach has begun to be adopted by the computer science community and has generated increasing interest and activity at SIGCSE ([4], [3], [7], [2]).

Though the POGIL approach is well-documented, there is no single way to implement a POGIL classroom. The purpose of this panel is to examine the varying challenges to adopting POGIL in different institutional contexts and to explore how POGIL has been implemented in a wide variety of computer science classrooms. In addition to giving a brief overview of the POGIL approach, panel members will discuss the following:

- As classroom sizes scale, how does effective facilitation of student learning and assessment in POGIL change?
- How does the implementation of POGIL change across different courses (*e.g.*, what is the difference between a POGIL CS1 course and a POGIL advanced-level course)?
- What challenges are unique to high school computer science classrooms vs. university classrooms?
- Does broader educational culture affect POGIL's success and adoption?
- What elements of the POGIL approach are emphasized or deemphasized in different contexts/course levels?

Panel members include both university faculty and high school teachers from both large universities and small liberal arts colleges and have experience using POGIL in both introductory and advanced courses. In addition, panel members also have experience encouraging and assisting other computer science faculty to adopt the POGIL approach.

Attendees will have the opportunity to interact with panel members at institutions similar to their own gain insight into how the POGIL approach might be adopted in their courses.

2. HELEN H. HU

At Westminster College, computer science and chemistry faculty co-teach an upper-division Scientific Computing course for science majors. Class sizes have ranged from six students in the first course offering (Fall 2005) to 26 students in Spring 2013. We have developed 24 POGIL activities for the class, approximately half of which help students learn how to program in Python, while the other half focuses on building computational models of scientific applications. During class, students primarily work in POGIL teams of four students, but break up into pair-programming pairs for each programming exercise and longer programming problems, as described fully in [3]. At the end of each POGIL activity, teams are required to reflect on their learning and their group process skills.

POGIL activities were first incorporated in Westminster's CS 1 course in Fall 2012. Multiple sections of CS 1 are taught each year, and each section is capped at 20 students. CS 1 students are grouped in the same hybrid of POGIL and pair

SIGCSE '14, March 5-8, 2014, Atlanta, Georgia, USA.
ACM 978-1-4503-2605-6/14/03.
http://dx.doi.org/10.1145/2538862.2539019.

programming teams as the Scientific Computing course, but seem to require more motivation, structure and facilitation to work well in a team. While CS 1 students seem to understand the importance of learning how to collaborate, they needed to be reminded to discuss issues and build consensus. I now provide each group with POGIL role cards (available online [1]) and require one member to report on strengths and weaknesses of the group's learning process.

3. CLIFTON KUSSMAUL

My first experiences with POGIL were in a graduate course with 15 students at the University of Kerala, in south India. I wrote activities in the days (sometimes hours or minutes) before class. The students were accustomed to a traditional lecture format, but came to realize that they were learning more with POGIL, and learning *how* to learn. In many POGIL classrooms, each student gets a paper copy of the activity, but this wasn't feasible, so instead I used PowerPoint slides. I also noticed that teams often chose to work in Hindi or Malayalam, not English, enabling them to focus on concepts rather than struggling to follow (my American) English.

When I returned to my small liberal arts college in the US, I wrote a successful NSF TUES proposal to develop POGIL activities for CS, and for the last 3 years I continued to write and use POGIL activities, particularly in CS2 and Software Engineering, usually with classes of 5-15 students. I have also facilitated a variety of POGIL workshops in the US.

During the summers of 2011, 2012, and 2013 I returned to south India (Kerala and Andhra Pradesh) to give a variety of talks and workshops on POGIL for K-12 and college teachers across a range of disciplines. Some of my former students had become teachers themselves, and invited me to give presentations or workshops at their institutions. Although there are certainly differences in culture and institutional setting, I have been pleasantly surprised by the similarities—both concerns and excitement.

4. MATTHEW LANG

I was introduced to POGIL three years ago and quickly adopted the model as a framework for developing and assessing the inquiry-based learning I was already doing at a small liberal arts college. In addition to using POGIL in introductory courses (*viz.*, CS1 and CS2), I also use POGIL practices and have developed activities for upper-level courses, including Operating Systems and Theory of Computation, where class sizes range from 10–15 students.

In my experience, both introductory students as well as advanced students benefit from the POGIL model. However, the implementation of POGIL varies between novice and advanced students along with their process skill ability.

5. CHRIS MAYFIELD

At James Madison University, we have enjoyed great success teaching with POGIL over the past five years. POGIL is our pedagogy of choice in our introductory courses, and several of our faculty have developed a variety of activities for nearly every topic of CS1. Consequently, that course is moving in the direction of becoming entirely based on POGIL. We are currently in the process of refining and disseminating our activities via the repository on cspogil.org. Since we started using POGIL, we have observed many educational benefits ranging from increased student performance and engagement to improved retention rates. We have achieved similar results using POGIL in upper level courses like Programming Languages and Software Engineering.

More recently we have begun collaborating with high school computer science teachers to develop and evaluate POGIL activities in AP and pre-AP courses. This summer we organized a week-long CS4HS workshop that included sessions on POGIL. More than a dozen participants enrolled in a follow-up course that met asynchronously during the month after the workshop. The purpose of this course (in addition to helping participants earn graduate credit towards certification) was for teachers to design and review each other's lessons based on techniques presented at workshop. Several teachers created new POGIL activities particularly geared for high school students. We look forward to learning and sharing results from their experiences this year.

6. TAMMY PIRMANN

I was introduced to POGIL several years ago. At almost the same time, I received an NSF Research Experience for Teachers for which I needed to produce a lesson in Big Data that could be disseminated to other high schools. In the lession, I used POGIL to introduce the main concepts of data analysis. Since then, I have used other educators' POGIL activities with adaptations as needed for my high school computer science classes. My classes are currently about 10% POGIL, and I hope to increase that as more POGIL resources become available for high school computer science and I develop my own resources.

7. REFERENCES

[1] High School POGIL Initiative implementation guide. website, 2012.

[2] H. H. Hu, C. Kussmaul, and M. Lang. Using POGIL activities in computer science classes. In *Proceeding of the 44th ACM technical symposium on Computer science education*, pages 753–753. ACM, 2013.

[3] H. H. Hu and T. D. Shepherd. Using POGIL to help students learn to program. *Trans. Comput. Educ.*, 13(3):13:1–13:23, Aug. 2013.

[4] C. Kussmaul. Process oriented guided inquiry learning (POGIL) for computer science. In *Proceedings of the 43rd ACM technical symposium on Computer Science Education*, pages 373–378. ACM, 2012.

[5] G. McKnight. Effectiveness of POGIL. `http://www.pogil.org/about/effectiveness`, 2004. [Online; accessed 2-September-2013].

[6] R. S. Moog and J. N. Spencer. *Process oriented guided inquiry learning (POGIL)*. Oxford University Press, USA, 2008.

[7] L. M. Olivieri. Piloting POGIL in an introductory Python programming course. *J. Comput. Sci. Coll.*, 28(6):194–195, June 2013.

[8] J. E. Stice. Using kolb's learning cycle to improve student learning. *Engineering education*, 77(5):291–96, 1987.

[9] A. Straumanis and E. A. Simons. A multi-institutional assessment of the use of POGIL in organic chemistry. *RS Moog, J. N. Spencer, Eds., Process Oriented Guided Inquiry Learning, Oxford University Press, New York*, pages 226–239, 2008.

No Tests Required: Comparing Traditional and Dynamic Predictors of Programming Success

Christopher Watson
School of Engineering and Computing Sciences
University of Durham
United Kingdom
christopher.watson@dur.ac.uk

Frederick W.B. Li
School of Engineering and Computing Sciences
University of Durham
United Kingdom
frederick.li@dur.ac.uk

Jamie L. Godwin
School of Engineering and Computing Sciences
University of Durham
United Kingdom
j.l.godwin@dur.ac.uk

ABSTRACT

Research over the past fifty years into predictors of programming performance has yielded little improvement in the identification of at-risk students. This is possibly because research to date is based upon using static tests, which fail to reflect changes in a student's learning progress over time. In this paper, the effectiveness of 38 traditional predictors of programming performance are compared to 12 new data-driven predictors, that are based upon analyzing directly logged data, describing the programming behavior of students. Whilst few strong correlations were found between the traditional predictors and performance, an abundance of strong significant correlations based upon programming behavior were found. A model based upon two of these metrics (Watwin score and percentage of lab time spent resolving errors) could explain 56.3% of the variance in coursework results. The implication of this study is that a student's programming behavior is one of the strongest indicators of their performance, and future work should continue to explore such predictors in different teaching contexts.

Categories and Subject Descriptors

K3.2 [**Computer and Information Sciences Education**]: Computer science education.

General Terms

Measurement, Experimentation, Human Factors, Verification.

Keywords

CS1; predictors of success; programming behavior; learning strategies; learning styles; prediction; watwin; error quotient;

1. INTRODUCTION

Programming courses have a reputation for high difficulty and failure rates [1], and as a result, predicting a student's performance in a first programming course is a well studied problem. Although early work focused upon using standardized aptitude testing [5] over the past fifty years, various predictors have been proposed. These include a range of demographic, psychological, academic, and cognitive factors, such as: previous programming experience [2,18,25], math background [17,24], science background [2,6], behavioral traits [2], self-esteem [4], learning styles [7,9,10], learning strategies [3], and attributions of success [8,11,18].

However studies to date are limited by a lack of verification, and a tendency to yield inconsistent results [23]. Additionally the previously researched predictors require the use of lengthy tests to gather predictive data. The learning strategies assessed by [15] for instance requires students to complete over 80 questions. Given potentially high enrollment numbers, the use of such tests to collect predictive data can take a considerable amount of time for an instructor to process. Even if a test was indicative of performance, by the time it was processed, it may be too late for students to withdraw, or for instructors to intervene to prevent students from failing [3]. The criteria used for prediction is a further limitation of these studies. Whilst psychological or background traits may be indicative of performance, they are not directly related to the regular programming behavior of a student, or the programming tasks which they are required to perform. The previously researched predictors therefore cannot reflect changes in the learning behavior and progress of a student over time.

Possibly due to these shortcomings, recent research [12,16,23] has moved towards exploring more data-driven approaches where aspects of the programming behavior of students (such as number of errors made) is directly logged by augmenting an IDE, and the resulting datasets analyzed to identify relations with performance. Compared to traditional tests, the main advantage of this approach is convenience. As predictions are made using directly logged data, neither an instructor, nor student has to process a batch of lengthy tests. Predictions are formed based upon aspects of a student's programming behavior, therefore can reflect changes in their learning progress over time. Also, as well as being able to dynamically identify struggling students, such predictors can be applied to drive an expert system, so that students can be provided with appropriate interventions when required. However to date, no paper has compared the performance of these data-driven predictors against test-based predictors. Contributions include:

1. The verification of 38 traditional test-based predictors of performance where previous research yielded inconsistent results, or a small number of studies had been conducted.
2. An exploration of 10 new data-driven dynamic predictors.
3. The first paper to perform a comparative evaluation of the performance of both data-driven and test-based predictors.

SIGCSE '14, March 5–8, 2014, Atlanta, GA, USA.

http://dx.doi.org/10.1145/2538862.2538930

2. RESEARCH DESIGN

There were two main purposes for this study. The first, was to address the need to verify findings of previous research on predictors of programming performance where either a limited number of studies had been performed, or research findings were inconsistent. The second was to compare the performance of these traditional test-based predictors, against predictors that did not require tests and were based upon aspects of a student's ordinary programming behavior.

2.1 Participants

The introductory programming module at our university was designed to teach Java to students of varying abilities. Students were supported by two weekly lectures and a lab session where they would practice solving programming problems using the BlueJ IDE. The sample of students used in this study consisted of volunteers from both the 2011/12 and 2012/13 cohorts. The structure of the course was similar for both years, with the only difference being the removal of the final exam in 2012/13. The teaching approach and learning materials were identical each year.

2.2 Instruments

Seven instruments were used to collect data from subjects: a questionnaire on the academic background of students and prior programming experience; attributions of success; Rosenberg's self-esteem scale; Kolb's learning style instrument; Gregorc style delineator; the motivated strategies for learning questionnaire (MSLQ); and a logging extension was added to the BlueJ IDE to collect data describing the programming behavior of students.

The background questionnaire was designed in-house, and gathered data on a student's: (1) gender, (2) GPA: high school, college, (3) lectures attended per week, (4) math and science background: courses taken and grades, (5) prior programming: for each language: years of experience, longest program written.

Measuring attributions of success in this study was based upon repeating the method used by [8], where students were asked to rank order four possible reasons for their success in the course. They were attribution to ability, task difficulty, luck, and effort.

Rosenberg's self-esteem scale (RSE) is perhaps the most widely used self-esteem measure in social science research. It consists of 10 questions and has been shown to in general to have a high reliability [15]. The RSE uses 4 point scales, ranging from strongly agree to strongly disagree. The only study to date [4] was replicated by using the reworded questions provided that modified the scale to relate self-esteem with a programming context.

Kolb's Learning Style Inventory (LSI) measures an individual's intrinsic learning style, or predisposition in any given learning situation. Kolb describes learning as a cycle of involvement, starting with concrete experiences and followed by a period of reflection, observation, and application of those experiences to solve problems. The LSI consists of a set of 12 sentences where individuals rank order four completions on a scale of 1 to 4. The LSI provides scores (range 12 to 48) for an individual's predisposition toward concrete experience, reflective observation, abstract conceptualization, and active experimentation.

The Gregorc style delineator describes an individual's learning style based on four dimensions: concrete random, concrete sequential, abstract random, and abstract sequential. The instrument consists of a set of 10 sentences where individuals rank order four completions on a scale of 1 to 4. The highest score among the four channels determines the dominant learning style.

The motivated strategies for learning questionnaire was co-designed by Pintrich [15] and is used to measure the motivations and learning strategies (cognitive, meta-cognitive, and resource management strategies) or students. It measures 17 different scales: 6 motivational and 9 learning strategies. The scales can be used together, but given their modular design, they can also be administered individually. The MSLQ uses a 7 point scale, ranging from 1 (not at all true of me), to 7 (very true of me).

A logging extension was used to gather data describing aspects of a student's ordinary programming behavior as they completed programming exercises using the BlueJ IDE. Each time a student compiled code on a university PC, the extension would log a snapshot of the code being compiled, along with the student's username, a timestamp, event type (compilation success or failure), and the error message reported with line number (if applicable). To explore aspects of a student's programming behavior and how it may relate to performance, we applied the data cleaning and processing procedure presented in [23] to each of our datasets. The procedure takes as an input directly logged compilation and invocation data, and produces a set of successive compilation pairings, for each file that a student attempted to compile during a session. These pairings describes how a student's programming behavior in terms of how their source code evolved between two consecutive compilations. For example, if a student compiled a file and encountered an error, in the next compilation of that file, were they able to resolve it? The procedure we selected has been shown to be more robust [23] than related approaches [12] which simply construct compilation pairings on a per-session basis, and instead constructs parings on per-session, per-file basis. The procedure also uses invocation information to refine estimates of the time a student spent between compilations – allowing their error resolve time for different types of error to be more accurately profiled.

In total 37 students (32 male) from the 2011/12 cohort and 45 students (42 male) from the 2012/13 cohort consented to us logging data describing their programming behavior over a period of 19 weeks. From the 2012/13 cohort 39 students (36 male) completed the six questionnaires. A one-way ANOVA showed no significant differences in the performance of the three samples of students on the reference criterion, $F(2, 118) = .18, p = .83$.

2.3 Predictor Variables

The relationships between 50 predictors and student performance in the introductory programming course at our university were examined. These predictors fall into 8 categories, including:

1. previous programming experience: has prior experience, number of languages previously studied, longest program written, years of experience.
2. previous academic experience: college grades: physics, chemistry, maths; university grades: discrete, calculus, GPA: college, high school.
3. attributions of success: scores for 4 scales outlined.
4. behavioral traits: lectures attended, hours part time job.
5. self esteem: overall score on Rosenberg.
6. learning styles: 8 scales taken from ILS and Gregorc.
7. learning strategies and motivations: 12 MSLQ scales.
8. programming behavior: 5 measures based on error frequency, 5 measures based on time, 2 measures based on an overall scoring of programming behavior.

2.4 Criterion Variable

To maintain an identical criterion variable for all students, we used overall coursework mark as the measure of programming ability in this study. This mark consisted of a weighting of a student's marks on a mid-term exam (25%), project (25%), a practical exam (40%), and weekly programming exercises (10%).

3. RESULTS

A priori analysis was carried out to verify that no significant differences existed between the mean overall scores of the class on the reference criterion, and those who agreed to participate in the studies conducted. Test assumptions of normality (Shapiro-Wilks test) and equality of variance (Levene test) were satisfied, and a set of *t*-tests showed no significant differences between the performance of those who participated in the: 2011/12 logged data sample ($t(78) = .28$, $p = .77$), 2012/13 logged data sample ($t(97) = 1.08$, $p = .29$), or the 2012/13 questionnaire sample ($t(91) = .56$, $p = .57$) and the remainder of their respective cohorts. In the remainder of this section, the findings on the relationships among each of the predictors examined and performance are presented.

3.1 Previous Programming Experience

All 39 students completed the background questionnaire section on prior programming experience. A *t*-test revealed significant differences in the performance those students who had prior programming experience prior to enrolling on the course ($n = 15$, $M = 71.76$, $SD = 10.47$) and those students who did not ($n = 24$, $M = 64.34$, $SD = 10.70$), ($t(37) = 2.12$, $p < .05$). These findings are consistent with previous research such as [25], but contradict research such as [2, 18]. Further analysis showed more interesting relations between prior experience and performance; however none of the following measures were significant, ($p > .05$). The number of languages that a student had previously studied weakly correlated with performance, $r = .24$, the longest program that a student had written prior to enrolment on the course also weakly correlated, $r = .15$, and surprisingly years of programming experience negatively correlated with performance, $r = -.20$. 5 students had prior Java experience, but no relation was found between the longest Java program they had previously written and performance, $r = .01$. In general, these results suggest that whilst prior programming experience may be useful to students, specific aspects such as years of experience, or the number of languages a student has studied, has little impact on performance.

3.2 Previous Academic Experience

To establish the relationship between previous academic experience in mathematics and science, the achievable grades for each subject were ranked, with the highest rank given to the highest possible grade, and the lowest rank given to the lowest possible grade. No significant correlations were found ($p < .05$) between either: grades in college physics ($n = 26$, $r = .31$), chemistry ($n = 15$, $r = .27$), math ($n = 28$, $r = .20$), university discrete math grade ($n = 15$, $r = .06$), or college GPA ($n = 35$, $r = .21$). But, marginally significant correlations were identified between performance and university calculus grade ($n = 26$, $r = .37$, $p = .06$), and high school GPA ($n = 38$, $r = .27$, $p = .10$). These findings are consistent with previous research that suggest generally academic background factors are weakly correlated with programming performance [2, 6], and that grades obtained in calculus courses are more strongly related to programming performance, than grades obtained in discrete courses [17]. But a total lack of correlation between discrete math and programming performance was contradictory to previous research [24].

3.3 Attributions of Success

All 39 students completed the background questionnaire section on their attributions of success. To date only 3 studies [8, 11, 18] have explored relationships between attributions and performance. Significant ($p < .05$), but weak, correlations were found between performance and attributions of success to task difficulty ($r = -.10$), and attributions to effort ($r = .07$). A moderate and marginally significant correlation was found for attribution of success to luck ($r = -.31$, $p = .05$) and a moderate, significant correlation was found for attribution of success to ability ($r = .40$, $p < .05$). The correlations reported by this study are consistent with, and within the range of correlations reported by the previous three studies on attributions to: task difficulty ($r = -.20$ to $.20$), and effort ($r = .07$ to $.16$). However much stronger relations for both attributions to ability ($r = .07$ to $.16$) and attributions to luck ($r = -.22$ to $.05$) were found. These conflicting results suggest that further research on how attributions of success relate to performance is required.

3.4 Behavioral Traits

All 39 students reported their lecture attendance. No relationship was found between lectures attended and performance, ($r = .02$, $p > .10$). 7 students reported the weekly hours that they worked in a part time job whilst studying. A strong negative correlation between the hours a student worked in a part time job and programming performance was found ($r = -.64$, $p < .01$). But this result should be interpreted with caution due to the small sample.

3.5 Self-Esteem

All 39 students completed Rosenberg's self-esteem scale. A weak, not significant, relation between score obtained on the instrument and programming performance was found ($n = 39$, $r = .13$, $p = .42$). Only one other study to date [4] used Rosenberg's instrument to examine the relationship between self-esteem and programming performance. However a moderate correlation between these two variables ($n = 54$, $r = .36$) was reported. The differing results between this study and prior research suggests that further research on the relations between programming self-esteem and programming performance would be beneficial.

3.6 Learning Styles

38 students completed both learning style instruments. Only 3 studies to date [7, 9, 10] have reported correlations between scores on the 4 dimensions of Kolb's ILS and performance. In this study no significant relations between learning style and performance were found for any of the 4 dimensions: concrete experience (CE) ($r = -.18$, $p = .29$), reflective observation (RO) ($r = -.07$, $p = .69$), abstract experimentation (AE) ($r = .14$, $p = .39$), abstract conceptualization (AC) ($r = .10$, $p = .53$). These correlations are consistent with, and within the range of the correlations reported by the previous three studies, (CE: $r = -.16$ to $-.23$; RO: $r = -.36$ to $.06$; AE: $r = .02$ to $.16$; AC: $r = .15$ to $.26$). These results suggest that in general that there is little to no relation between Kolb's ILS and the performance of students. Results for the Gregorc learning style were more encouraging. No significant correlation for the concrete/random dimension and performance was found ($r = -.14$, $p = .39$); But moderate and marginally significant correlations were found for each of remaining dimensions: abstract/random ($r = -.33$, $p = .05$), concrete/sequential ($r = .27$, $p = .10$) and abstract/sequential ($r = .29$, $p = .08$). Only 2 studies to date [13, 14] have explored the use of Gregorc's instrument as a predictor. Our findings are consistent with these studies.

Table 1. Pearson correlations (r) of this study compared to previous research MSLQ. (* $p < .10$, ** $p < .05$, *** $p < .01$)

MSLQ Dimension	This Study	[3]	[4]
Critical thinking	.28 *	.57	
Total metacognitive	.14	.54	
Resource strategy; Effort	.28 *	.62	
Resource strategy: Peer	-.06	.37	
Total resource strategy	.04	.56	
Task value	.06	.54	.44
MSLQ total	.22 *		.49
Intrinsic goal orientation	.33 *		.51
Total self-efficacy	.54 ***		.54

Compared to previous research, a similar moderate correlation for the concrete/sequential dimension ($n = 218$, $r = .35$) was reported by [13]. [14] found an identical moderate correlation ($n = 131$, $r = .30$) for abstract/sequential dimension, compared to this study. This suggests that the Gregorc learning style delineator may perform as a reasonable indicator of programming performance.

3.7 Learning Strategies and Motivations

All 39 students completed the MSLQ. Results are presented in Table 1. Only 2 studies to date [3, 4] have explored the relations between programming performance and scores on the various motivational and learning strategies scales on the MSLQ. Compared to prior research, an identical strong correlation for the self-efficacy for learning and performance dimension ($r = .54$, $p < .01$) was found. Marginally significant ($p < .10$) correlations were found for: intrinsic goal orientation ($r = .33$, $p = .04$), critical thinking ($r = .28$, $p = .08$), resource strategies: effort ($r = .29$, $p = .08$), and MSLQ total score ($r = .22$, $p = .09$). These findings confirm the research by [3, 4] who suggested that students who perform well in programming courses have high levels of intrinsic motivation and self-efficacy. However the findings of this study differed with previous researchers on a number of dimensions. No significant correlations were found between the total scores on the resource strategies scale ($r = .05$, $p = .76$), task value ($r = .06$, $p = .70$) scale, and the metacognitive strategies scale ($r = .15$, $p = .37$) was found to have a significantly lower correlation than previous researchers reported. These findings suggest that whilst certain dimensions of the learning strategies employed by students are related to their programming performance, further research is required to identify the dimensions that are the most significant.

3.8 Programming Behavior

10 metrics based upon the programming behavior of students were examined. Each metric was based upon the specific types of event pairings that students produced, measured as a percentage of their total number of pairings. Percentages were chosen as a means of standardizing the number of event pairings against all pairings each student produced, and as prior research has shown that metrics based upon event counts alone are poor indicators of performance [23]. 5 metrics were based upon the frequency of specific types of pairings a student produced. 5 metrics were based upon the percentage of lab time a student spent working on specific types of pairing. Results are shown in Table 2.

Unlike the traditional test-based predictors that we have examined throughout this section, an abundance of strong and significant relations were found between metrics of programming behavior and the performance of students. In terms of the percentage of specific types of pairings logged for each student, a strong significant correlation was found for the percentage of pairings where an error persisted for two successive compilations ($n = 82$, $r = -.51$, $p < .01$). Moderate correlations were also identified for the percentage of pairings where any errors existed in two successive compilations ($n = 82$, $r = -.46$, $p < .01$), and for the percentage of pairings where two successive compilations were successful ($n = 82$, $r = .38$, $p < .01$). Consistent with [12, 23], these results suggest weaker students are characterized by a high percentage of successive errors during lab sessions, whilst stronger students are characterized by having a high percentage of successive successful compilations.

Examining the relations between the time students spent on different types of event pairings, further significant correlations were found. A strong significant correlation was found for the percentage of lab time that students spent working on pairings where any errors existed in two successive compilations ($n = 82$, $r = -.50$, $p < .01$). An inverse relation was found for the percentage of lab time that students spent working on pairings where two successive compilations were successful ($n = 82$, $r = .39$, $p < .01$). A further moderate correlation was found for the percentage of lab time that students spent working on pairings where an error persisted for two successive compilations ($n = 82$, $r = -.42$, $p < .01$). These results suggest that not only are weaker students characterized by producing a high percentage of successive errors during lab sessions, but also, weaker students will generally spend a greater percentage of their lab time interacting with uncompilable code, than stronger students.

Table 2. Pearson correlations (r) between programming behaviors and performance (* $p < .10$, ** $p < .05$, *** $p < .01$)

Programming Behavior	2011/12	2012/13	Total
	$n = 37$	$n = 45$	$n = 82$
Based on Frequency of Events. Percentage of pairings:			
Error to Same Error	-.50 ***	-.54 ***	-.51 ***
Error to Different Error	-.32 *	-.43 ***	-.37 ***
Error to Any Error	-.48 ***	-.48 ***	-.46 ***
Error to Success	.18	.54 ***	.38 ***
Success to Success	.44 **	.37 **	.38 ***
Based on Time. Percentage of Lab Time Spent On:			
Error to Same Error	-.35 **	-.51 **	-.42 ***
Error to Different Error	-.44 ***	-.43 ***	-.41 ***
Error to Any Error	-.54 ***	-.51 ***	-.50 ***
Error to Success	.07	-.09	-.01
Success to Success	.41 **	.38 **	.39 ***
Overall Quantification Measures:			
Error Quotient [12]	-.42 **	-.47 ***	-.44 ***
Watwin Score [23]	-.60 ***	-.65 ***	-.60 ***

The use of programming behavior as a predictor of performance was further explored by applying two overall quantification algorithms to our datasets: Error Quotient (EQ) [12] and Watwin Score [23]. Both algorithms work by applying a scoring algorithm to the different types of compilation pairings that a student produces during a lab session. The major difference between the two algorithms is that Watwin [23] relatively penalizes a student based upon how their resolve time for different types of error, compares to the resolve times of their peers on the same error. The EQ moderately correlated with performance (n = 82, r = -.44, p < .01). However Watwin score showed a significantly stronger correlation (n = 82, r = -.60, p < .01). These findings suggest that aspects of a student's programming behavior are strongly related to their performance in programming courses and that hybrid algorithms may be one of the best data-driven predictors.

3.9 Regression Analysis

To investigate whether the various factors examined were predictive of performance in the module, three regression analyses were performed. As 5 of the students who completed the questionnaires did not provide consent for us to log their programming behavior, our sample size is reduced to 34 students.

The first model was designed to determine the predictive potential of the six written questionnaires. Consideration was given for all the traits examined in this study, with the exception of: previous programming experience, academic background (apart from GPA), hours worked in a part time job, due to a small number of students in each of these categories. Using a stepwise regression, a significant model was found with $F(3, 24) = 8.56$, $p < .01$, and an adjusted R-square of 45.6%. Significant values were found for MSLQ test anxiety (β = -.33, p = .04), MSLQ total metacognitive self regulation (β = .34, p = .03), and score on the Gregorc abstract/random dimension (β = -.40, p = .01).

The second model was designed to determine the predictive potential of the 12 programming behavior traits. Using a stepwise regression, a significant model was found with $F(2, 33) = 22.21$, $p < .01$, and an adjusted R-square of 56.3%. Significant values were found for Watwin score (β = -.56, p < .00) percentage of lab time spent working on error to success pairings (β = .41, p < .01).

A third model was designed to determine whether a hybrid of both traditional predictors and those based on programming behavior could explain more variance than the previous two models. All characteristics used to construct the previous two models were entered into the regression. A significant model was found with $F(3, 27) = 17.92$, $p < .01$, and an adjusted R-square of 60.6%. Significant values were Watwin score (β = -.77, p < .01), MSLQ total resource management strategies (β = .29, p < .01), and MSLQ total control of learning beliefs (β = .29, p < .01).

4. DISCUSSION

For almost 50 years, researchers have examined how prior academic experience, attributions of success, behavioral traits, self-esteem, learning styles, and learning strategies relate to the programming performance of students. But, with the exception of self-efficacy measured by the MSLQ (r = .54, p < .01) this study found no predictor within any of these traditional categories that strongly correlated with the performance of our students. Figure 1 shows the top 20 predictors found by this study. As can be seen, whilst 9 of the traditional test-based predictors are in the top 20, the strength of their correlations with programming performance are concentrated around the weak-moderate range. The remaining 29 traditional predictors outside the top 20 performed similarly.

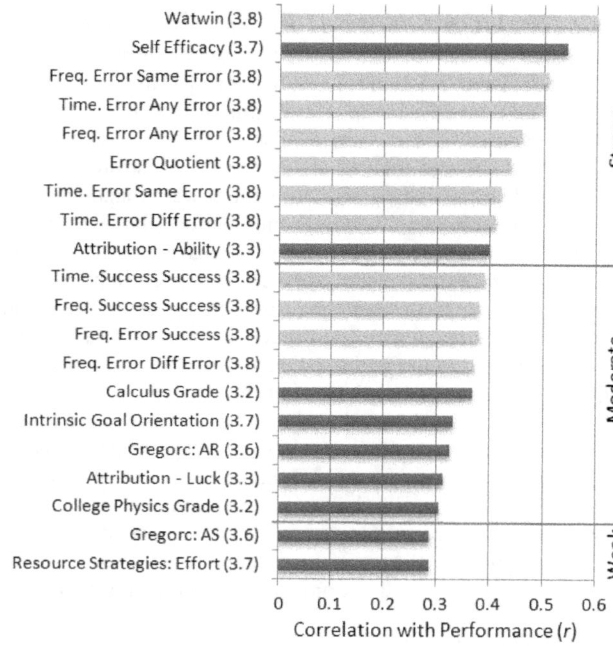

Figure 1. Bar chart showing the top 25 predictors of programming performance identified by this study. Correlations shown are absolute values and references to corresponding sections are shown in brackets. Programming behavior predictors are yellow, test-based predictors are blue.

In contrast, 11 of the 12 predictors based upon programming behavior were within the top 20, and were found to significantly relate to the programming performance of students. As can be seen from Figure 1, a total of 7 predictors based on programming behavior were found to strongly correlate with performance, and the remaining 4 moderately correlated. The implication of this research is that traditional test-based predictors are substantially less effective at reflecting the programming ability of students, and that data-driven approaches offer a more accurate method of prediction. In this study the results for test-based predictors were mostly inconsistent. The results for the programming behavior metrics (Table 2) were mostly consistent. It is worth stressing the further advantages of using predictors based on programming behavior. Traditional test-based approaches mainly examine traits that are static in nature and fail to reflect changes in the students learning progress over time. Although such approaches may have a chance of identifying weaker students, their one-shot, static nature, means that they cannot be dynamically used to support such students, e.g., by providing automatic interventions to assist weaker students when they are struggling. The programming behavior metrics however could be used in such circumstances, without the requiring any additional workload for either instructors or students.

Finally we acknowledge the limitations of this study. There are numerous difficulties associated with identifying predictors of programming performance. Our data was consistent with previous researchers in terms of the frequency and distribution of different types of error [12,16,23]. However conditions, such as the language taught or tools used to program vary considerably across different teaching contexts. Whilst this study has shown that several aspects of programming behavior can significantly correlate with a student's performance, further verification is required to determine the general applicability of these metrics across a variety of different teaching contexts and situations.

5. CONCLUSION AND FUTURE WORK

In this paper, 38 traditional test-based predictors of programming performance were reexamined, and compared to 12 dynamic predictors that were based upon analyzing aspects of a student's regular programming behavior. Whilst only one strong relation was identified between traditional predictors and performance, an abundance of strong and significant relations were found between aspects of programming behavior and performance. A model based upon two aspects of programming behavior could account for 56.3% of the variance in coursework marks, an improvement of approximately 25% when compared to a model based on traditional predictors alone. The results are encouraging, and the implication of this study is that predictors based upon aspects of programming behavior may be one of the strongest predictors of performance. Researchers should continue to explore their potential further, and work is essential to verify the performance and applicability of such predictors across a variety of teaching contexts. Future work will aim to develop techniques of applying the metrics within practical contexts, such as visualizations of learning progress [19], game-based tools [21,22], or tools to improve the compiler feedback provided to novice students [20].

6. REFERENCES

[1] Bennedsen, J. and Caspersen, M.E. 2007. Failure rates in introductory programming. *SIGCSE Bull.* 39(2), 32-36.

[2] Bergin, S. and Reilly, R. 2005. Programming: factors that influence success. *SIGCSE Bull.* 37(1), 411-415.

[3] Bergin, S., Reilly, R. and Traynor, D. 2005. Examining the role of self-regulated learning on introductory programming performance. In *Proc. of the 1st Int. Workshop on Computing Education Research (ICER)*, 81-86.

[4] Bergin, S. and Reilly, R. 2005. The influence of motivation and comfort-level on learning to program. In *Proc. of the 17th PPIG Workshop*, 293-304.

[5] Biamonte, A.J. 1964. Predicting success in programmer training. In *Proc. of the 2nd SIGCPR Conference on Computer Personnel Research*, 9-12.

[6] Byrne, P. and Lyons, G. 2001. The effect of student attributes on success in programming. *SIGCSE Bull.* 33(3), 49-52.

[7] Campbell, V. and Johnstone, M. 2010. The Significance of Learning Style with Respect to Achievement in First Year Programming Students. In *Proc. of the 21st Australian Software Engineering Conference (ASWEC)*, 165-170.

[8] Cantwell-Wilson, B. and Shrock, S. 2001. Contributing to success in an introductory computer science course: a study of twelve factors. *SIGCSE Bull.* 33(1), 184-188.

[9] Chamillard A.T. and Karolick, D. 1999. Using learning style data in an introductory computer science course. *SIGCSE Bull.* 31(1), 291-295.

[10] Corman, L.S. 1986. Cognitive style, personality type, and learning ability as factors in predicting the success of the beginning programming student. *SIGCSE Bull.* 18(4), 80-89.

[11] Henry, J.W., Martinko, M.J., and Pierce, M.A. 1994. Attributional style as a predictor of success in a first computer science course. *Computers in Human Behavior*, 9(4), 341-352.

[12] Jadud, M.C. 2006. Methods and tools for exploring novice compilation behaviour. *Proc. of the 2nd Int. Workshop on Computing Education Research (ICER)*, 73-84.

[13] Lau, W.W., and Yuen, A.H. 2009. Exploring the effects of gender and learning styles on computer programming performance implications for programming pedagogy. *British Journal of Educational Technology*, 40(4), 696-712.

[14] Lau, W.W., and Yuen, A.H. 2011. Modelling programming performance: Beyond the influence of learner characteristics. *Computers & Education*, 57(1), 1202-1213.

[15] Pintrich, P. R., Smith, D. A., García, T., & McKeachie, W. J. 1993. Reliability and predictive validity of the Motivated Strategies for Learning Questionnaire (MSLQ). *Educational and psychological measurement*, 53(3), 801-813.

[16] Rodrigo, M.M.T., Baker, R.S., Jadud, M.C., Amarra, A.C.M., Dy, T., Espejo-Lahoz, M.B.V, Lim, S.A.L., Pascua, S.A.M.S., Sugay, J.O., and Tabanao, E.S. 2009. Affective and behavioral predictors of novice programmer achievement. *SIGCSE Bull.* 41(3), 156-160.

[17] Stein, M.V. 2002. Mathematical preparation as a basis for success in CS-II. *Computing Sciences in Colleges*, *17*(4), 28-38.

[18] Ventura, P. 2005. Identifying predictors of success for an objects-first CS1. *Computer Science Education,* 15(3), 223-243.

[19] Watson, C., Li, F.W.B., and Lau, R.W.H. 2010. A pedagogical interface for authoring adaptive e-learning courses. In *Proc. of the 2nd Int. Workshop on Multimedia Technologies for Distance Learning,* 13-18.

[20] Watson, C., Li, F.W.B., and Godwin, J.L. 2012. BlueFix: using crowd sourced feedback to support programming students in error diagnosis and repair. In *Proc. of 11th Int. Conference on Advances in Web-Based Learning*, 228-239.

[21] Li, F.W.B., and Watson, C. 2011. Game-based concept visualization for learning programming. In *Proc. of the 3rd Int. Workshop on Multimedia Technologies for Distance Learning (MTDL)*, 37-42.

[22] Watson, C., Li, F.W.B., and Lau, R.W.H. 2011. Learning programming languages through corrective feedback and concept visualisation. In *Proc. of 10th Int. Conference on Advances in Web-Based Learning (ICWL)*, 11-20.

[23] Watson, C., Li, F.W.B., and Godwin, J.L. 2013. Predicting Performance in an Introductory Programming Course by Logging and Analyzing Student Programming Behavior. In *Proc. of the 13th IEEE International Conference on Advanced Learning Technologies (ICALT)*, 319-323.

[24] White, G., and Sivitanides, M. 2003. An empirical investigation of the relationship between success in mathematics and visual programming courses. *Information Systems Education*, 14(4), 409-416.

[25] Wiedenbeck, S. 2005. Factors affecting the success of non-majors in learning to program. In *Proc. of the 1st Int. Workshop on Computing Education Research (ICER)*, 13-24.

Integrating Computational and Creative Thinking to Improve Learning and Performance in CS1

L.D. Miller, Leen-Kiat Soh, Vlad Chiriacescu
Department of Computer Science and Engineering
University of Nebraska, Lincoln
{lmille, lksoh, vchiriac}@cse.unl.edu

Elizabeth Ingraham
Department of Art and Art History
University of Nebraska, Lincoln
eingraham2@unl.edu

Duane F. Shell
Melissa Patterson Hazley
Department of Educational Psychology
University of Nebraska, Lincoln
dshell2@unl.edu, mpatterson.hazley@gmail.com

ABSTRACT
Our research is based on an innovative approach that integrates computational thinking and creative thinking in CS1 to improve student learning performance. Referencing Epstein's Generativity Theory, we designed and deployed a suite of creative thinking exercises with linkages to concepts in computer science and computational thinking, with the premise that *students can leverage their creative thinking skills to "unlock" their understanding of computational thinking.* In this paper, we focus on our study on differential impacts of the exercises on different student populations. For all students there was a linear "dosage effect" where completion of each additional exercise increased retention of course content. The impacts on course grades, however, were more nuanced. CS majors had a consistent increase for each exercise, while non-majors benefited more from completing at least three exercises. It was also important for freshmen to complete all four exercises. We did find differences between women and men but cannot draw conclusions.

Categories and Subject Descriptors
K.3.2. [**Computer and Education**]: Computer and Information Science Education

General Terms
Measurement, Performance, Design, Experimentation, Human Factors.

Keywords
Computational thinking, creative thinking, CS1.

1. INTRODUCTION
The increased demand for computational thinking (e.g., [23][24]) has led to numerous articles in educational research venues. These articles demonstrate the increasing momentum of research addressing the need for effective education in computational thinking, both for CS and across the broader spectrum of STEM and non-STEM disciplines. This research is diverse, ranging from course specifications to course development, from community building to setting policies, and from teaching and learning to assessment [3][4][9][12][14][24].

SIGCSE'14, March 5–8, 2014, Atlanta, Georgia, USA.

http://dx.doi.org/10.1145/2538862.2538940

Adding to the above body of research, we proposed an innovative approach [16] by which we aim to improve the learning of computational thinking by blending it with creative thinking. Creative thinking is thinking patterned in a way that tends to lead to creative results [17]. It is not limited to the arts but is an integral component of human intelligence that can be practiced, encouraged and developed within any context [13][15][22]. Epstein's Generativity Theory breaks creative thinking down to four core competencies: *capturing* novelty, *challenging* established thinking and behavior patterns, *broadening* one's knowledge beyond one's discipline, and *surrounding* oneself with new social and environmental stimuli [8]. Our premise is that by blending computational and creative thinking *students can leverage their creative thinking skills to "unlock" their understanding of computational thinking* [20]. In this way, we should be able to make computational thinking more generally applicable to STEM and non-STEM disciplines where students may have creative thinking skills but lack understanding of computing concepts.

Towards ascertaining the feasibility and understanding the impact of our approach, we designed and deployed four creative thinking exercises during the Fall 2012 semester at the University of Nebraska, Lincoln. Over 200 students in four different introductory CS1 courses took the exercises and the exercises counted as part of their final course grades. Each course was tailored to a different target group (CS majors, engineering majors, combined CS/physical sciences majors, and humanities majors) and so these courses contained a mix of students with differing levels of both computational and creative thinking skills. In a previously reported study, Miller *et al.* [16] found that *exercise completion produced a linear increase in course grades and retention of core computational thinking principles in the four CS1 courses.*

Questions remain, however, about whether there are differential impacts on different student populations that might influence decisions about exercise adoption. First, while we can educate students from non-CS disciplines about using computational thinking to support their own disciplinary creative problem solving, there is a potentially serious problem for expanding computational thinking from CS into other non-CS disciplines. The students in non-CS disciplines come from diverse backgrounds and most are likely to have limited understanding of computing concepts that are used as the basis for computational thinking. Without a basic level of understanding, these students may have a very difficult time developing computational thinking fluency. We need to know whether the creative thinking exercises are benefiting these non-CS majors in the same way that they are CS majors.

Second, the CS1 courses involved have students of different experience, including years in school. Implementing and delivering integrated computational thinking and creative thinking requires understanding of what level of experience is needed to best benefit. While all students in CS1 classes are novices in computer science and computational thinking, freshmen students might benefit less from the addition of creative competencies as they have less general knowledge and less experience in college coursework. Also, the creative competencies involved in the exercises, such as broadening and surrounding, draw on larger interdisciplinary bodies of knowledge and more extensive academic and social experiences. Students having more experience to bring to the exercises may be more able to utilize them effectively. To address this, we need to know if freshmen students who are less widely experienced derive fewer benefits from the exercises than more advanced, upper class students, regardless of their majors.

Finally, we incorporate activities into the exercises that are livelier, more contextual, and more hands-on in their "sensory" aspects. This can potentially help broaden participation in CS by engaging more underrepresented female students, and motivating them to study computer science; however, we need to determine how female students may differentially benefit from the exercises.

Hence, we report in this paper the results of an extended study to examine our central contentions about the benefits of merging computational and creative thinking by determining if there were differential impacts on different student populations. Our research questions were: (1) *Is the effect of creative thinking exercises the same for CS majors and non-CS majors?* (2) *Is the effect of creative thinking exercises different for beginning students (freshmen) than for students with more expertise (non-freshmen)?* (3) *Is the effect of creative thinking exercises different for women and men students?*

2. DESIGN PRINCIPLES

Creative thinking is flexible, imaginative, innovative thinking which draws on all of one's skills and experience [1], involves all of one's senses [22], draws on multiple intelligences [11] and uses a variety of primary thinking tools (such as visualizing, imaging, abstracting, scaling, modeling and analogizing [19]) to produce new outcomes (things or processes) of value [18]. Creative thinking is not an innate talent but instead a process that is an integral component of human intelligence which can be practiced, encouraged and developed within any context [13][15][22].

Based on Generativity Theory, Epstein [6][7][8] has identified the following four core cognitive competencies involved in creative thinking: (1) *Broadening*. The more diverse one's knowledge and skills are the more varied and interesting the possible novel new patterns and combinations that might emerge. To be creative one must broaden one's knowledge by acquiring information and skills outside one's current domains of study and expertise. (2) *Challenging*. Novelty emerges from situations where existing strategies and behaviors are ineffective. The more difficult the challenge the more likely a creative, novel solution will emerge. (3) *Surrounding*. Exposure to multiple, ambiguous situations and stimuli create environments where novel strategies and behaviors may emerge—e.g., looking at things in new ways, interacting with new people, and considering multiple sensory representations. (4) *Capturing*. Novelty is occurring all the time, but most of it passes without recognition. Creativity requires attention to and recording of novelty as it occurs.

As made clear in Robinson [18] and Friedman [10], *creative thinking skills are vital not only to be creative designers or artists but to also to work and compete effectively in our complex, interconnected, rapidly changing global society*, we thus see Epstein's core creative thinking competencies are a universally applicable skill set that everyone would be eager to learn and use, just as the case for the universality of computational thinking articulated by Wing [23].

Therefore, in our framework, both computational thinking and creative thinking are viewed as cognitive tools that expand the knowledge and skills that one can apply to a problem. The blending of computational thinking with creative thinking is not conceived as a set of dichotomies, but rather as complementary or symbiotic abilities and approaches. Computational tools expand the knowledge and skills that one has available thereby broadening the array of knowledge that one may bring to a problem. For example, *Challenging* forces computational tools to be used in unanticipated and unusual ways leading to the development of new computational approaches to both old and new problems, *Surrounding* creates new ways of looking at problems and attention to different stimuli and perspectives that may be relevant to how a problem is approached computationally, and *Capturing* forces consideration of new ways to represent and save data and solution procedures.

The principles underlying the design of our creative thinking exercises are (1) balancing of attributes between computational and creative thinking and (2) mapping between computational and creative concepts and skills as they manifest in different disciplines. Table 1 below shows the differing attributes, concepts, and skills that need to be balanced and mapped.

3. EXERCISE DESIGN

All our exercises combine hands-on collaborative problem solving with written analysis and reflection—with sufficient scope and depth such that that each requires creative thinking and teamwork. Each exercise has four common components.

First, the *Objectives* component, at the beginning of the exercise handout, lists the computational and creative thinking objectives for the exercise to help the student understand why they are doing these exercises by showing how an exercise lacking any programming code is related to CS concepts and how students can use relevant creative thinking skills (described in terms of Epstein's core competencies of Surrounding, Capturing, Challenging and Broadening) to solve the exercises.

Second, the majority of the content of an exercise handout is the *Tasks* component which lists all the tasks the group of students must complete during the two weeks of the exercise. These tasks require students to work collaboratively (and may require individual contributions as well.

Third, the *CS Light Bulbs* are additional text snippets highlighting linkages between the exercise tasks and a set of CS topics to help students recognize the associated or practiced computational thinking skills while performing the creative thinking tasks.

Fourth, the *Questions* component uses open-ended questions that require collaboration among students as they engage in both analysis and reflection. To answer these questions, students must apply *creative thinking* to CS problems and revise the results of their original tasks using *computational thinking*. Questions thus build upon the CS Light Bulbs and reinforce the connections between the creative thinking fostered by the tasks and the computational thinking in the CS topics.

Table 1. Balancing attributes and mapping concepts and skills between computational and creative thinking.

BALANCING OF ATTRIBUTES	
Computational Thinking	**Creative Thinking**
Convergent thinking.	Surrounding with new social and environmental stimuli.
Linear and sequential "flow"	Challenging established solutions and algorithms.
Rational & logical processes	Broadening possible solutions through additional paradigms
Methodical	Capturing novelty and spontaneous outputs
MAPPING CONCEPTS & SKILLS	
Computational Thinking	**Creative Thinking**
Algorithmic Thinking – algorithms as models of computational processes*	Challenging accepted solutions and procedures; fostering novel solutions
Programming Fundamentals: (i.e. data models, encapsulation, testing and debugging)*	Broadening applications through new ways of framing and applying fundamental computational knowledge.
Computing Environments – languages & paradigms, tools, applications*	Surrounding with new social and physical environments to broaden perspectives
Data representation: (i.e. data types, variables)*	Capturing new ways of representing/storing data & algorithms.

*CC2001: IEEE/ACM Computing Curriculum, 2001

Although developed separately, our creative thinking exercises are most conceptually similar to the creative thinking activities in the CS4HS project [2]. The two main differences are that our exercises are designed for students, rather than instructors, and cover CS content suitable for college rather than high school.

4. EXERCISE EXAMPLES

Here we describe one of the creative thinking exercises in more detail. We developed four different exercises for the Fall 2012 deployment: (1) Everyday Object where students identified an everyday object (e.g., a hammer, a nail clipper) and described its functionality and I/O as if the object has not been invented, (2) Storytelling where students work on different pieces of a story separately and then come together to resolve all inconsistencies to produce a coherent story, (3) Cipher where student teams developed mapping rules to encode messages and then decode those messages from other teams, and (4) Exploring where students visited a particular location on campus and documented what they sensed. Due to space considerations we only highlight Everyday Object in the following exercise description.

4.1 Objectives

There are two sets of objectives: computational and creative. ***Computational***: (1) Learning about the description and design process for modular programming by describing an everyday object in detail including why the object is needed and how the object functions; (2) Learning about abstraction and function characterization by identifying properties of an everyday object. ***Creative***: (1) Surrounding: looking at an everyday object in new ways, using all of your senses to understand how it's made and how it functions; (2) Capturing: using written language to describe all the different details and characteristics of this everyday object so you can work with it in new ways; (3) Challenging: describing the operations of an everyday object with words and also as a computer program; (4) Broadening: imagining that this object doesn't exist and acting like its inventor who is trying to fulfill a need by creating something new and useful.

4.2 Tasks

The tasks are divided into two weeks, during which the students will be using language to try to clearly and thoroughly describe the functions of an ordinary object that they might use every day. The students are prompted to act like the inventor of that object, imagining that it does not yet exist and trying to describe what need would be fulfilled by their chosen (new) object and how (specifically) it will function.

Each group will choose a common, everyday object from the list—e.g., zipper, mechanical pencil, binder clip, Ziploc bag, nail clipper, umbrella, can opener, sticky notes, etc. Their challenge is to imagine that this object does not exist and to describe in written language (1) the mechanical function of your object, (2) what need is fulfilled by this object, and (3) the physical attributes and characteristics of their chosen object.

During week 1, each team must describe the object's function, the need it will fulfill and its attributes in clear, non-technical language which any user could understand. Their description must be specific enough so that someone who had never seen the object could recognize it and understand how it works and understand what benefits it provides. Week 2 activities involve analysis and reflection on week 1 activities.

Figures 1 shows an example screenshot of student work where the chosen object to be described was a nail clipper.

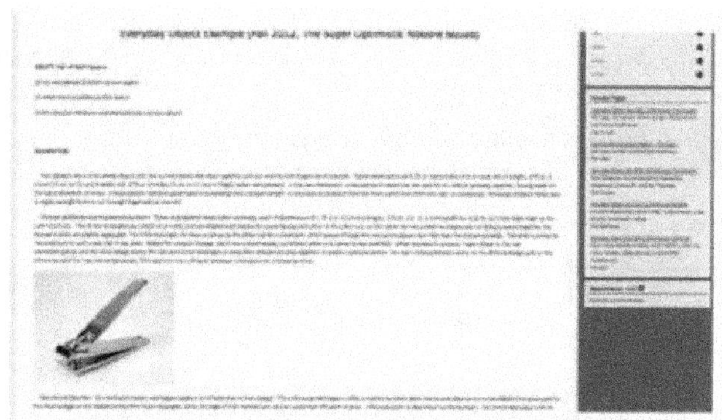

Figure 1. Screenshot example of student work on the Everyday Object exercise: Object Description.

4.3 CS Light Bulbs

CS Light Bulbs are text snippets highlighting the linkages between the exercise and some CS concepts. Here we provide one example lightbulb. "This description process is very important for developing algorithms in computer science. An algorithm consists of the series of steps necessary to solve a given problem. By using algorithms, we can solve problems without having to constantly "reinvent the wheel" and spend the time, money, etc. to figure out each step ourselves. However, if one or more of these steps are unclear, we can have difficulty following the algorithm which can lead to serious repercussions as described in the following two examples. First, if the formulation algorithm used to mix the concrete for a road or bridge is unclear, workers may make a mistake during pouring leading to reduced service life. Second, if the business plan algorithm for a new company is confusing, venture capitalists may be reluctant to invest leading to failure of the business. To avoid these repercussions, the developer should make every effort to make the algorithm's description as clear as possible for all steps. In other words, characterization of processes is key; it allows us to abstract a process and then convert it into a formal problem or solution."

Note: The handout also includes three other Light Bulbs on writing functions in CS, the diagramming process, and abstraction in programming languages.

4.4 Questions

For each exercise, there are two sets of questions: Analysis and Reflection. Analysis questions are designed to help them relate to CS concepts as well as to re-examine or revisit the details of the activities. Reflection questions are designed to prompt students to think about the activities at a more abstracted level, and how the lessons learned relate to problem solving in general.

Analysis: (1) Consider your object as a computer program. Draw a diagram that shows all its functions as boxes (name them), and for each function, its inputs and outputs. Are there shared inputs and outputs among the functions? (2) Consider the list of physical attributes and characteristics. Organize these such that each is declared as a variable with its proper type. Can some of these attributes/characteristics be arranged into a hierarchy of related attributes/characteristics?

Reflection: (1) Consider your response to Analysis 1, are there functions that can be combined so that the object can be represented with a more concise program? Are there new functions that should be introduced to better describe your object such that the functions are more modular? (2) Have you heard of abstraction? How does abstraction in computer science relate to the process of identifying the functions and characteristics as you have done in this exercise.

Figures 2 shows another example screenshot of student work in addressing one of the analysis questions.

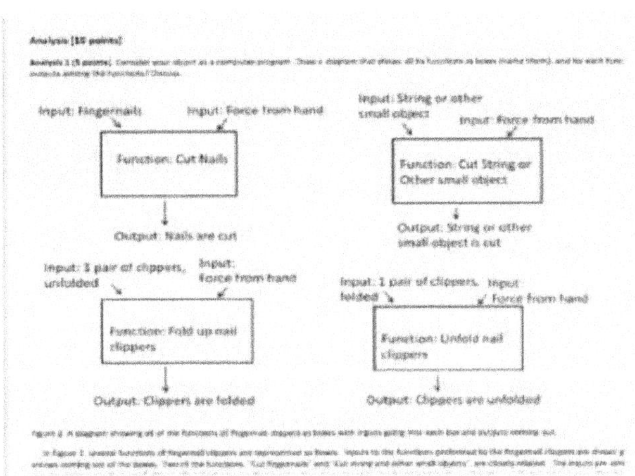

Figure 2. Screenshot example of student work on the Everyday Object exercise: Analysis Question.

5. DEPLOYMENT AND PLATFORM

The exercises were deployed using the Written Agora system [5]. This is a wiki system designed to facilitate online collaboration between groups of students. The wiki system includes a content page where students can work together on completing the tasks and an online forum where students can discuss, with group members, the responses to the analysis and reflection questions. As the wiki was always online, students could log in and work on the exercises whenever it was convenient. The wiki also kept track of all the revisions so that we could determine which students were contributing to the group.

The exercises represented 3-5% of the final grades depending on the course. After completing the tasks and answering the questions, students in each group were assigned individual grades based on their contributions to the group's wiki page.

6. METHODS

Students voluntarily participated in evaluation data collection which was approved by the University of Nebraska, Lincoln Institutional Review Board. The CS1 courses had 241 students initially enrolled and 196 students who completed the courses. Of those who completed the courses, 150 students (133 male, 17 female; 59 freshmen, 49 sophomore, 32 junior, 13 senior; 3 other) consented to participation in the evaluation and 129 students (114 male; 15 female) consented to the use of their course grades and university grade point average. Samples for specific analyses vary due to missing data and are shown in Tables.

Course grades were used to determine impact on student achievement in the course. To standardize grades across courses, grades were converted to Z-scores within each course. Retention of core computational thinking knowledge and skills was assessed by a test developed by CSCE faculty [21]. The computational thinking knowledge test contained 13 conceptual and problem-solving questions for the core computational thinking content common to all CS1 classes. The coefficient alpha reliability estimate was .76. The computational thinking test was administered on a Web platform (Survey Monkey®) during the last week of classes as part of broader evaluation data collection. Students' cumulative Grade Point Averages (GPA) were obtained from university records adjusted to remove the CS1 course grade.

We used Analysis of Covariance (ANCOVA) to test whether the number of exercises completed was associated with higher course grades and computational thinking test scores. Because of low numbers of participants in some cells, we collapsed 0, 1, and 2 exercises completed into a single group.

7. RESULTS AND DISCUSSIONS

7.1 Results

We included students' cumulative GPA as a covariate in all analyses to statistically control for differences that might be attributable to students' general level of academic ability. Students' cumulative GPA was a significant covariate for course grades in all analyses. Students with higher GPAs earned higher grades indicating that that their achievement in the class generally reflected their overall academic achievement. Students' cumulative GPA, however, was not a significant covariate for the knowledge test in all analyses, indicating that general academic achievement was not related to retention of core computational thinking knowledge and skill.

CS Majors and Non-Majors. For course grades (Table 1), cumulative GPA was a significant covariate ($F(1, 107) = 104.64$, $p < .0001$, partial $Eta^2 = .494$). With GPA controlled, the number of exercises completed was significantly associated with course grade ($F(2, 107) = 11.27$, $p < .0001$, partial $Eta^2 = .174$). There was a significant linear trend in planned comparisons ($p < .0001$) from 0-2 to 4 exercises completed. Majoring or intent to major was significantly associated with grades ($F(1, 107) = 3.55$, $p =$

.002, partial $Eta^2 = .089$). Students considering or already a CSCE major or minor had higher grades ($M = .088$) than those not considering a CSCE major or minor ($M = .014$). The major or minor by exercise interaction also was significant ($F(2, 107) = 7.50$, $p = .001$, partial $Eta^2 = .123$). The interaction can be seen in Table 1. Students who were or were considering a CSCE major or minor followed the general overall linear trend. Students who were not considering a CSCE major or minor had a considerable jump from 0-2 exercises to 3 exercises completed and a much smaller increase from 3 exercises to 4 exercises.

Table 2. Course Grades by Exercises and CS Major

Exercises Completed	Major or Considering			Not Considering		
	M	*SD*	*N*	*M*	*SD*	*N*
0-2	-.462	1.11	18	-.788	.894	22
3	.043	.861	18	.393	.858	14
4	.624	.424	20	.575	.684	22

For the computational thinking knowledge test (Table 2), cumulative GPA was not a significant covariate ($F(1, 96) = 0.84$, $p = .361$, partial $Eta^2 = .013$). With GPA controlled, the number of exercises completed was significantly associated with knowledge test scores ($F(2, 96) = 4.01$, $p = .021$, partial $Eta^2 = .077$). Planned comparisons indicated a significant linear trend ($p = .006$) from 0-2 to 4 exercises completed. Majoring or intent to major in CSCE was not significant ($F(1, 96) = 0.20$, $p = .652$, partial $Eta^2 = .002$). The intent to major or minor by exercise interaction also was not significant ($F(2, 96) = 0.85$, $p = .430$, partial $Eta^2 = .017$).

Table 3. Knowledge Retention by Exercises and CS Major

Exercises Completed	Major or Considering			Not Considering		
	M	*SD*	*N*	*M*	*SD*	*N*
0-2	5.50	3.29	16	6.35	3.47	20
3	7.44	3.42	16	7.38	3.10	13
4	8.82	1.59	17	7.71	2.61	21

Class Standing. For course grades (Table 3), cumulative GPA was a significant covariate ($F(1, 107) = 57.70$, $p <.0001$, partial $Eta^2 = .350$). With GPA controlled, the number of exercises completed was significantly associated with course grade ($F(2, 107) = 13.09$, $p < .0001$, partial $Eta^2 = .197$). There was a significant linear trend in planned comparisons ($p < .0001$) from 0-2 to 4 exercises completed. Class standing was significantly associated with grades ($F(1, 107) = 4.67$, $p = .033$, partial $Eta^2 = .042$). Upper class students had higher grades ($M = .238$) than freshmen ($M = -.237$). The class standing by exercise interaction also was significant ($F(2, 107) = 3.80$, $p = .026$, partial $Eta^2 = .066$). The interaction can be seen in Table 5. Although there is an overall linear trend, freshmen students do not differ for 0-2 exercises and 3 exercises but increase for 4 exercises and upper class students increase dramatically from 0-2 exercises to 3 exercises, then increase a much smaller amount from 3 exercises to 4 exercises. It appears that freshmen students only showed gains when all exercises were completed; whereas, upper class students gained from completing either three or four exercises.

Table 4. Course Grades by Exercises and Class Standing

Exercises Completed	Freshmen			Upper Classman		
	M	*SD*	*N*	*M*	*SD*	*N*
0-2	-.474	1.043	20	-.808	.951	20
3	.-468	1.026	11	.544	.511	21
4	.282	.696	14	.757	.365	28

For the computational thinking knowledge test (Table 4), cumulative GPA was a not a significant covariate ($F(1, 96) = 0.68$, $p = .411$, partial $Eta^2 = .007$). With GPA controlled, the number of exercises completed was significantly associated with knowledge test scores ($F(2, 96) = 3.77$, $p = .026$, partial $Eta^2 = .073$). Planned comparisons indicated a significant linear trend ($p = .007$) from 0-2 to 4 exercises completed. Class standing was not significant ($F(1, 96) = 2.42$, $p = .123$, partial $Eta^2 = .025$). The class standing by exercise interaction also was not significant ($F(2, 96) = 0.28$, $p = .750$, partial $Eta^2 = .006$).

Table 5. Knowledge Retention by Exercises & Class Standing

Exercises Completed	Freshmen			Upper Classman		
	M	*SD*	*N*	*M*	*SD*	*N*
0-2	5.24	3.56	17	6.63	3.13	19
3	6.56	3.94	9	7.80	2.87	20
4	7.93	1.59	14	8.38	2.58	24

Gender. For course grades (Table 5), cumulative GPA was a significant covariate ($F(1, 107) = 71.49$, $p <.0001$, partial $Eta^2 = .401$). With GPA controlled, the number of exercises completed was significantly associated with course grade ($F(2, 107) = 11.29$, $p < .0001$, partial $Eta^2 = .174$). There was a significant linear trend in planned comparisons ($p < .0001$) from 0-2 to 4 exercises completed. Gender was not significant ($F(1, 107) = 0.12$, $p = .721$, partial $Eta^2 = .001$). The gender by exercise interaction also was not significant ($F(2, 107) = 2.26$, $p = .109$, $Eta^2 = .041$).

Table 6. Course Grades by Exercises and Gender

Exercises Completed	Men			Women		
	M	*SD*	*N*	*M*	*SD*	*N*
0-2	-.618	.967	37	-.927	1.583	3
3	.112	.805	25	.497	1.063	7
4	.570	.558	38	.868	.234	4

For the computational thinking knowledge test (Table 6), cumulative GPA was a not a significant covariate ($F(1, 96) = 1.28$, $p = .261$, partial $Eta^2 = .013$). With GPA controlled, the number of exercises completed was not significantly associated with knowledge test scores in the overall model ($F(2, 96) = 2.34$, $p = .102$, partial $Eta^2 = .047$). Planned comparisons, however, indicated a significant linear trend ($p = .034$) from 0-2 to 4 exercises completed. Gender was not significant ($F(1, 96) = 0.84$, $p = .361$, partial $Eta^2 = .009$). The gender by exercise interaction also was not significant ($F(2, 96) = 0.61$, $p = .548$, $Eta^2 = .012$).

Table 7. Knowledge Retention by Exercises and Gender

	Men			Women		
Exercises Completed	*M*	*SD*	*N*	*M*	*SD*	*N*
0-2	6.06	3.28	33	5.00	5.00	3
3	7.78	3.30	23	6.00	2.68	6
4	8.17	2.29	35	8.67	2.08	3

7.2 Discussions and Implications

Research Question 1. *The creative thinking exercises appeared to affect the achievement of non-CS majors more than CS majors.* Non-CS majors who completed two or fewer exercises received grades well below those of CS majors who completed a similar number of exercises and well below the average for non-CS majors. However, non-CS majors completing three or four exercises received grades well above the average for even CS majors and grades equivalent to or even above CS majors completing a similar number of exercises. *The exercises appeared to affect the retention of core course content equally for both CS majors and non-majors.* These findings support our contention that *the creative thinking exercises can bring CS* *computational concepts to non-CS disciplines and improve non-CS students' understanding of computational thinking.*

Research Question 2. *The creative thinking exercises appeared to affect freshmen and upper class students differently.* Upper class students doing either three or four exercises had higher grades. Freshmen students, however, only had higher grades when doing all four exercises. Although upper class students had higher grades overall, freshmen doing four exercises had grades above the average for all upper class students. *The exercises appeared to affect the retention of core course content in similar ways for both freshmen and upper class students, although upper class students scored higher at all exercise completion levels.* These findings suggest that *while more advanced students may perform better overall and may derive somewhat more benefit from the creative thinking exercises, beginning freshmen students also see improvements in their course achievement and knowledge retention.* Nevertheless, it appears to be important for freshmen students to complete all exercises.

Research Question 3. *There were no differential effects for women and men.* Our analysis of gender was limited by the low number of women students. This makes any findings very tentative. In relation to our contention that the addition of creativity may be especially appealing and beneficial to women, there is some indication in Table 5 that the exercises *may* have been associated with higher course achievement for women. This, however, was not statistically significant.

8. CONCLUSIONS

The findings support our central contention that the incorporation of creative thinking exercises based on Epstein's [8] creative competencies can improve learning of computational thinking. Results expand on the Miller *et al.* [16] findings of a linear "dosage effect" for exercise completion by examining whether there were differences in this effect for CS majors and non-majors and freshmen and upper class students. In relation to retention of core computational thinking knowledge from the courses, there were no differential effects of the exercises. For all students the linear "dosage effect" was present with student completion of each additional exercise increasing retention. For grades, the effects were more nuanced. CS majors had a consistent linear increase for each exercise completed, while non-majors had grade increases only for completing at least three exercises. Upper class students had increases for completing at least three exercises, while freshmen students needed to complete all four exercises before there were grade increases. These results suggest that the "dosage effect" is less strong for grades among some sub-populations. We did not find differences between women and men but cannot draw conclusions because of sample size.

We believe that the exercises impact student achievement and learning because they make students deal with computational principles and skills abstracted from coding. This enhances their ability to connect the computational thinking knowledge to more diverse applications consistent with the Unified Learning Model (ULM) [20]. Also consistent with the ULM, completing exercises provides more retrieval and repetition of course creative thinking content, which will strengthen knowledge connections as indicated in the "dosage effect".

Findings are limited by the implementation in only one semester and four courses. Sample sizes in all analyses preclude broad generalization without follow-up studies, which we currently have in progress. However, our results are encouraging. The merger of computational and creative thinking can be realized in exercises that can be successfully implemented in introductory CS1 courses. Furthermore, these exercises can help students improve their course achievement and learning of computational thinking.

9. ACKNOWLEDGMENTS

This material is based upon work supported by the National Science Foundation under grant no. 1122956. Additional support was provided by a UNL Phase II Pathways to Interdisciplinary Research Centers grant.

10. REFERENCES

[1] Andreasen, N. C. 2005. *The Creating Brain: The Neuroscience of Genius.* Dana Press.

[2] Blum, L. and Cortina, T. 2007. CS4HS: An Outreach Program for High School CS Teachers. *SIGCSE* 39, 19-23.

[3] Denning, P. J. 2007. Computing is a Natural Science. *CACM* 49, 33-35.

[4] Denning, P. J. 2009. The Profession of IT beyond Computational Thinking. *CACM* 52, 28-30.

[5] Eck, A. Soh, L-K., and Brassil, C. 2013. Supporting active wiki-based collaboration. In *Proc. of CSCL*, 176-183.

[6] Epstein, R. 1996. Cognition, creativity, and behavior: Selected essays. *Praeger.*

[7] Epstein, R. 2005. Generativity theory and creativity. *Theories of creativity.* Hampton Press.

[8] Epstein, R., Schmidt, S., Warfel, R. 2008. Measuring and Training Creativity Comptencies: Validation of a New Test. *Creativity Research Journal* 20, 7-12.

[9] Fletcher, G. H. L. 2009. Human Computing Skills: Rethinking the K-12 Experience. *CACM* 52, 23-25.

[10] Friedman, T. L. 2006. *The World is Flat: A Brief History of the Twenty-First Century.* Farrar, Straus and Giroux.

[11] Gardner, H. 2007. *Five Minds for the Future.* Harvard Business School Press.

[12] Guzdial, M. 2008. Paving the Way for Computational Thinking. *CACM* 51, 25-27.

[13] Kraft, U. 2005. Unleashing Creativitity. *Scientific American Mind* 16, 19-12.

[14] Lewis, C., Jackson M. H., and Waite, W. M. 2010. Student and Faculty Attitudes and Beliefs about Computer Science. *CACM* 53, 78-85.

[15] Michalko, M. 2001. Cracking Creativity. *Ten Speed Press.*

[16] Miller et al. 2013. Improving Learning of Computational Thinking using Creative Thinking Exercises in CS-1 Computer Science Courses. *Frontiers in Education* 43, 1426-1432.

[17] Perkins, D. N. 1984. Creativity by Design. *Educational Leadership* 42, 18-25.

[18] Robinson, K. 2001. *Out of Our Minds: Learning to be Creative.* Capstone.

[19] Root-Bernstein, R. S. and Root-Bernstein, M. M. 2001. *Sparks of Genius: The Thirteen Thinking Tools of the World's Most Creative People.* Mariner Books.

[20] Shell, D. F., Brooks, D. W., Trainin, G., Wilson, K., Kauffman, D. F., and Herr, L. 2010. *The Unified Learning Model: How Motivational, Cognitive, And Neurobiological Sciences Inform Best Teaching Practices.* Springer.

[21] Shell, D. F., Soh, L-K. 2013. Profiles of motivated self-regulation in college computer science courses: Differences in major versus required non-major courses. *J. Sci. Edu. Tech. Technology.* DOI 10.1007/s10956-013-9437-9.

[22] Tharp, T. 2005. *The Creative Habit: Learn it and Use it for Life.* Simon & Schuster.

[23] Wing, J. 2006. Computational Thinking. *CACM* 49, 33-35.

[24] Wing, J. 2010. Computational Thinking: What and Why. *Link Magazine*

Perspectives on Co-linking Design and Development Courses in CS

Yolanda J. Reimer
Computer Science Department
University of Montana
Missoula, MT
yolanda.reimer@umontana.edu

Michael Cassens
Computer Science Department
University of Montana
Missoula, MT
michael.cassens@umontana.edu

ABSTRACT
An on-going problem with many courses across the CS curriculum is finding time to incorporate programming activities that are necessary for other critical aspects of the course. For example, in UI design the practice and evaluation of good design principles typically depends on the creation of at-least a semi-functional software prototype. However, having to include software implementation in courses whose main focus lies elsewhere can distract from core concepts, and oftentimes there are pedagogical reasons to separate out implementation. By co-linking upper-division courses in our CS program, we attempted to solve this problem by leveraging concepts of software design and implementation across two courses. In this experience report, we describe how the co-linked courses were structured, what we encountered, what worked well and what still needs improvement. Other CS educators might capitalize on our successes, and learn from our mistakes, in similar set-ups within their own curriculums.

Categories and Subject Descriptors
K.3.2 [**Computer and Information Science Education**]: *Computer science education, Curriculum.*

Keywords
Computer science education research, user interface design, mobile application development, co-linking courses.

1. INTRODUCTION
Computer Science (CS) programs around the country experience particular strains associated with the demand that their curriculums remain current, an undeniable challenge given the rapid growth of technology. There is also increasing pressure for CS programs to be adaptive to numerous other disciplines that they frequently work in concert with, such as math, business, and the sciences. The ACM and IEEE computing societies remain active in discussing, drafting, disseminating and evaluating new CS curriculum recommendations [e.g., 1, 10]. Rising expectations and the ever-changing landscape in computer science demands that educators continue to find new ways to deliver an already difficult curriculum while remaining current and effective.

The first author has been heavily involved in prior research focusing on user interface (UI) design taught using a studio-based learning (SBL) approach [6]. One of the results of this earlier work showed a need for more clear separation between design and implementation, something hard to accomplish during a typical 15-week semester [9]. In UI design courses, a significant part of the material focuses on principles of good design along with interface evaluation methods. For students to learn these concepts most effectively, they need to create a somewhat functional interactive prototype that they can practice on and use for testing. However, instructors and students alike express frustration at the ways in which design and implementation are often integrated in the classroom environment, especially given the relatively short period of time in which they are expected to accomplish both. Instructors want students to focus solely on creating the best designs without having their ideas limited by impending implementation factors (i.e, students tend to design only what they know they can program); they need ample time to model the process of design with and for the students; and they need ample time to incorporate iterative critiques (or crits) into the process of design. Students, on the other hand, resent having to create prototypes that are not entirely functional and thus essentially "throw-away"; they bemoan only having 4 or 5 weeks to devote to prototype implementation; and they regret having to control so many aspects of user testing because of the often static nature of their final systems.

A potential solution identified at the end of that earlier study was to co-link UI design courses with courses in system development. Doing so would separate design from implementation, which in turn would theoretically allow for more time and focus on each. This report describes our experience co-linking a UI design course with a course in Game and Mobile Application Development. The broader impact of our work to the computer science education community includes a model around which other co-linked courses might be based, along with a description of what worked well and what did not. After considering our experiences, other educators will be better positioned to propose and create similar arrangements that benefit their own programs and student population.

SIGCSE'14, March 5–8, 2014, Atlanta, Georgia, USA.

http://dx.doi.org/10.1145/2538862.2538953

2. RESEARCH METHOD

The primary impetus for co-linking two courses together in our curriculum was to alleviate frustrations associated with our user-interface (UI) design class as described earlier. Since it was not feasible for us to offer a year-long UI sequence of classes (i.e., a semester of design followed by a semester of implementation and evaluation), we opted instead to co-link our regular UI design class with a Game & Mobile App Development class. These two courses made good partners because the topic areas of each complemented one another. Students learn programming techniques associated with mobile apps in the one course, and how to apply and evaluate good principles of design in the other. These two courses were also well suited for our experiment because they are both taught at the same upper division/graduate level, during the same semester, and the instructors of both classes were flexible about potential curriculum modifications. It is important to note that although these courses were co-linked, each met separately throughout the semester, and each operated under its own schedule, set requirements, and grading scales.

Although not a main reason why we settled on the mobile app development course as a partner in this experiment, we note that integrating mobile computing into the CS curriculum has become an increasingly popular pedagogical movement [10]. In our case, we believed that by working on the same project across both courses, but pushing system programming and implementation entirely to the development course, we could better focus on principles of design and interface evaluation in UI design. We hoped that this arrangement would ease the frustrations of both UI instructors and students, and that the new structure would prove beneficial to both groups in ways not always anticipated.

Once we had selected the right course to co-link UI design with, a few initial decisions had to be made prior to the start of the semester. First and foremost, we had to decide whether or not we would require students to take both courses at the same time, which was the ideal, or if we would allow them to enroll in one without the other. Because we wanted to remain as inclusive as we could, we opted to let students enroll in one of the two courses only, but we strongly encouraged them to take both. With the preliminary registration list in hand, we carefully composed the student groups that would work together in both classes for the entire semester.

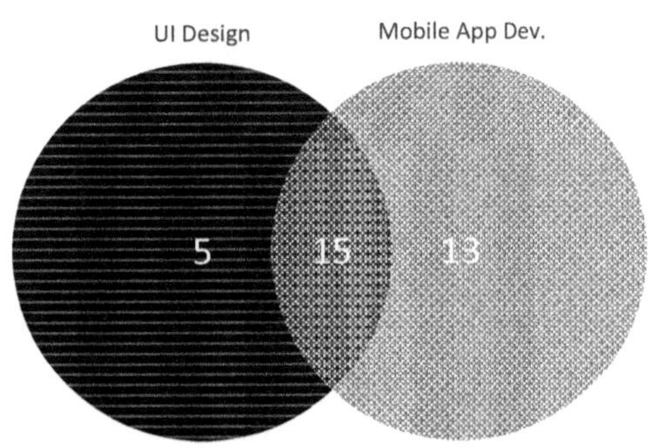

Figure 1. Student numbers for each course, Spring 2012.

Eleven undergraduates and 9 graduate students enrolled in the UI design class during the spring 2012 semester. In the mobile app development course, there were 18 undergraduates, 8 graduate students, and 2 post-baccalaureate students. Figure 1 shows the overlap of 15 students who enrolled in both courses at the same time. In terms of group composition, all but one had at least one student enrolled in the UI design class, or the mobile app development class, or both. A single group was comprised exclusively of students from the mobile application class; this was deemed acceptable because they had an established foundation for their class project and their design had already been evaluated. We also intended to keep the graduate students together, but ended up having to make exceptions to balance group sizes and to accommodate specific student interests.

2.1 Game & Mobile App Development

This class met three times a week, 50 minutes at a time, for roughly 15 weeks. There were 9 individually based assignments (totaling 50% of the final grade), plus 5 group-based projects (milestones) (15%), a mid-term presentation (15%) and a final presentation at the conclusion of the semester (20%). All projects included a written report from each team member discussing his or her contribution and an analysis of team members. During this particular course offering, final projects revolved around the following software engineering tasks:

- *Milestone 1* – Discussion of project ideas.
- *Milestone 2* – Outline of functional and non-functional specifications.
- *Milestone 3* – Delivery of design, including UML class design, database design, use-case scenarios, state transition diagrams, etc.
- *Milestone 4* – Discussion of current progress including any notable challenges and successes.
- *Mid-term presentation* – Presentation of current progress; discussion of all design documentation.
- *Milestone 5* – Discussion of current progress, including incorporation of mid-term feedback.
- *Final Presentation* – Discussion of final project status (what was completed, what was removed, why, etc); discussion of user testing results.

2.2 User-Interface Design

The UI design course met two times a week during the semester of this experimental study, 80 minutes at a time, for roughly 15 weeks. Student grades were based on five projects (totaling 65% of the final grade for undergrads, 60% for grad students), one exam (15%), and miscellaneous assignments and class participation (20%). Graduate students in the class also had an extra assignment to complete that was worth 5% of their final grade. All regular projects included a written report and an in-class design critique (this was a final presentation for project 5). Students were expected to present the state of their current work during crits, open the discussion up to questions and review, and incorporate feedback into subsequent projects as applicable. Design crits are an essential part of the UI design course, and a substantial amount of in-class time is devoted to them. All projects built upon one another and revolved around the mobile app also being developed in the other course. The general goals of each project in the UI design course were as follows:

- *Project 1* (Individually based): Preliminary design of system, including user descriptions, usability requirements, functional requirements, and low-fidelity prototype sketches.
- *Project 2* (Combination of individual and group based components): Iterative design, including combining individual designs into one comprehensive design, and generation of medium-fidelity prototype.

- *Project 3* (Mostly individually based, but some group consultation): Evaluating design in the absence of users, including cognitive walkthrough and heuristic evaluations [4,5,7,8].
- *Project 4* (Group based): Usability testing with real users.
- *Project 5* (Group based): Reflections on design, including a visual narrative of design process from start to end.

2.3 Schedule

Because our two courses were so reliant on one another, it was critical that we closely integrate topic schedules and project due dates. The following diagram shows how the course lecture topics and assignments were interwoven on a week-by-week basis throughout the semester. Week 11 is not included since it was spring break week and no classes were held.

Table 1. Schedules of co-linked courses

Wk	UI design topic	UI design crits & projects due	Mobil App topic	Mobil App assignments due
1	Overview; Human behavior		Introduction to game development	
2	Principles of good design		Team roles	Milestone 1 (IDEATION)
3	Functional reqs; habits of studio	Proj 1 (PRELIMINARY DESIGN)	Effective communication	
4	Functional reqs; design for mobile devices		Game production	Milestone 2 (SPECIFICATIONS)
5	User-centered design [3]: Reqs analysis		Game concept and characters	
6	Preliminary design		Game requirements	Milestone 3 (DESIGN)
7		Proj 2 (ITERATIVE DESIGN) – design crits with Michael's class	Game plan	
8	Cognitive walkthrough, heuristic eval; GOMS/KLM		Production cycle	Milestone 4 (PROGRESS REPORT)
9	Usability test plan		Voice and music	
10		Proj 3 (EVALUATION, NO USERS)		Midterm presentations (PROGRESS RPT)
12	IRB; Usability test materials		Testing	Milestone 5 (ITERATION)
13	Exam; Game day (prototype showcase)		Marketing	
14	Grad projects		Deployment	
15		Proj 4 (USER TESTING)		Final presentations (STATUS UPDATE)
16	Final exam week	Final project (REFLECTIONS)	Final exam week	Final presentations (STATUS UPDATE)

3. (RESULTS) WHAT WORKED

Throughout the semester, we heard anecdotally from students about how the co-linking between the two classes was going. At the end of the semester, a more thorough questionnaire was posted on SurveyMonkey, which all 20 students in the UI design class completed. This survey contained both closed and open-ended questions. After gathering and reviewing the students' responses, we were able to get a good idea of what worked well in the co-linking experience, and what did not. We report these results in this section and the next.

To begin with an overview, Table 2 shows student responses to a variety of general statements about the classes. Statements were presented using both positive and negative language to ensure that overall results were as unbiased as possible. Some of the reactions seen in this table are supported further by open-ended questions discussed later in the section. What is most noticeable about the student responses shown in Table 2 is their overall concurrence that communication within groups and across the two classes went well, and that overall it was a positive experience that allowed them to leverage their skill sets and create high quality finished projects. What also stands out is that we need to do a better job synchronizing the schedules between the two classes, a point that we elaborate on further in the next section.

Table 2. UI student reactions post-semester

	Strongly agree	Some what agree	Neutral	Some what disagree	Strongly disagree	N/A
Communication with my teammates in the other class went well throughout the semester; there were no problems	**45.0% (9)**	25.0% (5)	0.0% (0)	0.0% (0)	15.0% (3)	15.0% (3)
My teammates in the other class did not seem open or willing to accept our input on the system design.	5.0% (1)	5.0% (1)	15.0% (3)	20.0% (4)	**40.0% (8)**	15.0% (3)
It's been nice having this other group to work with	**40.0% (8)**	15.0% (3)	5.0% (1)	5.0% (1)	20.0% (4)	15.0% (3)
This arrangement between the two classes allows us to leverage ideas between the two classes	**35.0% (7)**	15.0% (3)	15.0% (3)	10.0% (2)	15.0% (3)	10.0% (2)
I would prefer to work on a design project that is separate from this other class	15.0% (3)	10.0% (2)	25.0% (5)	15.0% (3)	**30.0% (6)**	5.0% (1)
Being co-linked to this other class detracted from my learning this semester	20.0% (4)	15.0% (3)	15.0% (3)	5.0% (1)	**35.0% (7)**	10.0% (2)
It was difficult to keep our work synchronized with the other team/class throughout the semester	15.0% (3)	**25.0% (5)**	10.0% (2)	15.0% (3)	**25.0% (5)**	10.0% (2)
We were able to accomplish work of a higher quality because of the co-linking between the courses	**35.0% (7)**	10.0% (2)	25.0% (5)	20.0% (4)	5.0% (1)	5.0% (1)
The instructors of the two classes need to make the work schedules of the two classes more synchronized	**40.0% (8)**	30.0% (6)	15.0% (3)	5.0% (1)	0.0% (0)	10.0% (2)
The teaching styles and expectations of the two classes were more or less consistent	10.5% (2)	21.1% (4)	5.3% (1)	**26.3% (5)**	10.5% (2)	**26.3% (5)**
Taking both classes at the same time solidified in my mind how many computer science topics overlap and build on one another	**35.0% (7)**	15.0% (3)	10.0% (2)	15.0% (3)	0.0% (0)	25.0% (5)

3.1 Leveraging Content & Workload

For students who took both courses simultaneously, when asked what the best aspects of co-linking were, many seemed to appreciate the way the courses worked together, and how the format gave them a more complete view and some experience with the coupling of design and implementation. Some noted being able to use the knowledge they were gaining in one course and applying it directly to the work they were doing in the other. Examples of student reactions to this question include:

"The best aspect was separating the design from the implementation. It was great to see the big picture of working on a fairly extensive project!"

"Being enrolled in both courses seemed to simulate the real world environment. ... game and mobile course kind of played the role of the stake holders when paired with UI Design ... without taking both I don't believe I would have seen the benefit in either one separately."

"The usability testing was very nice to have in terms of making our game more usable and a more polished final product."

"It was great to see how our designs applied to the actual implementation of our game. Lessons learned in the User Interface Design class allowed us to make sure the game felt and looked consistent."

Many students also said that they liked being able to share the workload across two courses. Their comments to this effect are consistent with another closed-ended question we had on the survey where 68% of respondents said the workload was "About right" for both classes combined considering the total of 6 credits they were worth together. In at least one case, being able to work on the same project across two different classes led to a student enrolling in the UI design course when he or she previously would not have. *"If UI hadn't have been co-linked with Game Development, I wouldn't have considered taking it. Because it was though, I learned that the topic is actually quite interesting and useful."*

3.2 Expanded Functionality

As alluded to previously, a major frustration of students in the UI design class during previous offerings (i.e., before this co-linking experience) concerned prototype implementation. Students frequently lamented on their inability to develop more fully functional and complete systems due to the severe time limitations of the prototype implementation phase (typically allotted only 4 of 15 weeks to accommodate the rest of the curriculum). Many groups used non-programming software environments like PowerPoint to create systems that only had to appear as though they were functional for user testing, but were in fact often fairly static with data hardcoded throughout. One of the side-effects of the non-functional prototypes was that users had to be tightly controlled during testing. In other words, users had to be given specific tasks to complete that the developers knew were stubbed in rather than allowing them free rein to explore and use the system as they would have liked. Some of these frustrations are further detailed in [9].

In our co-linking experiment, however, system implementation was pushed entirely onto the Game & Mobile App Development class, where students learned how to develop a wide range of mobile applications for various platforms. This separation of design and implementation automatically resolved some of the previous frustrations since students had more time to create the fully functional systems they envisioned. With more complete prototypes, students were able to create more realistic testing environments. They were able to allow their users more range in using the prototype without having to restrict them to particular functionality as before. As evidence of this positive result, when asked what the best aspects of co-linking the two courses were, one student said:

"I liked that because we were able to work on the same project in two courses the breadth of the project could be expanded. In other words, I liked being able to work on a more substantial and complete project than what I've done in other classes. We ended up with a product that could almost be submitted to an app store rather than just a small part of an application."

Others commented that,

"More time and made the overall project feel more like a full project instead of just a 'do this for the class' sort of thing."

"It was great actually implementing a product instead of a prototype."

"I am happy that I could apply HCI techniques to a fully functioning project."

To illustrate the completeness and scope of functionality that many students achieved with the programs they developed between these two classes, Figure 2 (next page) shows a few screen shots of an app that one team created. GrizSpace was designed for the Apple iOS platform to aid students as they seek out classrooms and other locations around campus. Figure 3 also shows how this app was tested using a GoPro camera mounted on the user's head. This format allowed developers to record a birds-eye view of what users saw as they interacted with and used the product, including problems they may have encountered.

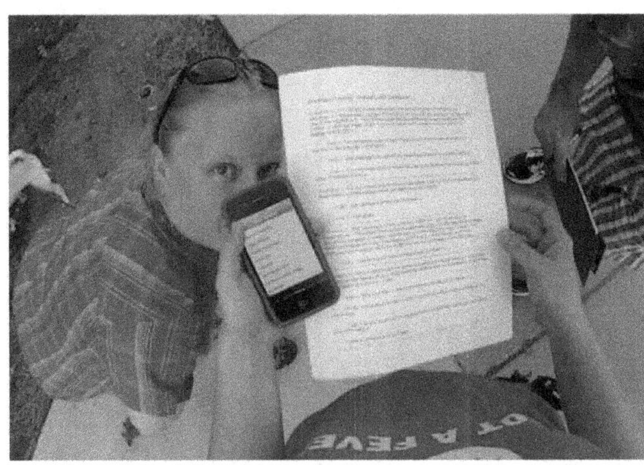

Figure 3. User testing, checking camera, ©Jon-Michael Deldin, William Lyon, Jaylene Naylor, Kevin Scott

3.3 Team Management Skills

Another result of our co-linking experiment was that students had to practice group management skills more than normal. This was particularly challenging because groups spanned two classes, both of which had their own timelines and set of expectations, and some groups were mixed in the sense that they might be comprised of peers taking both or only one of the classes. An added difficulty was that not all students had the same existing

Figure 2. GrizSpace, ©Jon-Michael Deldin, William Lyon, Jaylene Naylor, Kevin Scott

knowledge base, forcing teams to leverage their individual skill sets in the most effective way. We know experiences like these can sometimes be frustrating to students, as expressed in the following quote: "*I realized early on that I would be unable to teach my team mates about software development, especially since they were unwilling to listen to me or produce items on schedule.*" In one case during this experiment, communication proved ultimately unsuccessful as a group was unable to resolve their differences and disbanded. However, we maintain that despite the frustrations and sometime failures, encounters like these provide critical learning moments for students and, once again, they help simulate real world working environments many students will soon face.

On the other hand, many other students seemed to genuinely enjoy and appreciate their teammates and the group interaction overall, making comments like "*I got lucky and got a great group*", "*These courses were hard, but I had fun and I enjoyed working with a team of focused, hard-working coders and artists. Thanks!*", and "*We gained experience working in multiple groups and forcing communication between them.*" In the end, providing new and sometimes complex group situations that students have to work through in order to be successful, which was the case in our experiment, proved to be a sometimes difficult but always important learning experience.

4. (RESULTS) NEEDS IMPROVEMENT

On the final survey, students who took both courses simultaneously were asked an open-ended question about the main issues or problems they experienced throughout the semester.

4.1 Syncing of Schedules

Perhaps the most frequent criticism we heard had to do with the syncing of topic and assignment schedules between the two courses. Some students felt that the design and implementation assignments did not dovetail seamlessly between the two classes, causing either a slowdown in one class, or a crazy rush to finish in the other. Despite class discussions and lectures describing the iterative nature of design, whereby design and implementation are often revisited throughout the software development lifecycle, this was often impractical for students to apply. They felt that the product design had to be complete before implementation could begin in earnest, but because design spanned a large portion of the UI design class, implementation still got pushed back too late in the semester for the comfort of many. Students commented on these issues as:

> "*Timing. In the end it all worked out, but initially I was somewhat frustrated that I felt stalled with the implementation.*

Several design projects had to be completed before beginning implementation."

"The main problem was a lack of coordination between the assignments due in the two classes. Often one class would have an assignment due that required a certain level of completeness in the gam/app while the other class was still in a design phase, resulting in a disconnect between the two classes."

"One class was all design and it sort of kept pushing back the implementation because we felt like we needed to finish designing before we could implement."

In retrospect, we understand that the design activities in the UI design course are more drawn out than those in the mobile app class, where programming took earlier precedent. Even co-linking the courses and thus providing more time for implementation did not alleviate this issue since many students wanted to wait until the design was solid before progressing too far in implementation. In some ways, co-linking the courses may have even exacerbated this issue because students were so clearly being held accountable for producing higher quality working systems in mobile app development than when they take UI design in isolation. In the end, students still seem to feel as though the implementation phase of their project was rushed, a recurring issue in the UI design class as mentioned previously. A couple of students suggested offering these two courses as a sequence rather than simultaneously. One potential problem with this approach, though, is that implementation comes right in-between design and evaluation, making it difficult to sequence these activities.

4.2 Benchmark Measurements

We also discovered during this experiment that using a broad stroke approach to usability measurements does not always work. In other words, certain benchmark measurements for usability that can be applied to task-based software, like a scheduling system for example, do not translate well to the gaming genre. Since students worked on prototypes of their own choice across these two classes, some chose productivity software while other groups chose games, making it difficult to discuss a one-size fits all set of usability benchmark measurements. As a simple example of this, with productivity software, time to complete tasks is a commonly used measure of effectiveness (i.e., the quicker a user can complete a task with the software, the better). However, in games this is clearly not the case. In fact, the longer a user spends with a game program the better, as it typically indicates enjoyment using the system, a key measure of success for that genre.

We also know that varying device platforms can impact usability measurements. For example, software designed and built for small devices, like a phone, have different limitations and constraints than those built for full-scale computer monitors. Because of our flexibility in allowing students to choose their projects, platforms, and devices, we had significant variability in these aspects as well, once again making generalizations difficult. To resolve this issue in future instances where these two classes are co-linked, the usability benchmarks will have to be defined and taught differently based on the genre, device and purpose of the software being developed. Particular attention will have to be given for usability measures in games [e.g., 2] if this user interface genre continues to be a common choice for student projects, as we suspect it will.

5. SUMMARY AND FUTURE WORK

The co-linking experiment presented in this report represents a good first step at alleviating a number of challenges many CS programs face. In particular, we were successful in providing a learning environment for students that that helped them leverage knowledge across the curriculum while mitigating workload somewhat; that allowed students to experience more of a real-world development environment, also resulting in higher-quality and more complete final projects; and that created situations whereby students had to practice and further develop their communication and group management skills in order to be successful. While it is a goal of most CS curriculums to have courses overlap and build upon one another, often culminating in a capstone project or sequence of sorts, our co-linking experiment provides another tangible example of how this might be done and the benefits gained by an integrative approach.

We hope to repeat this experiment again in the future, although we realize that before we do, we need to more closely synchronize course schedules and the interplay between system design, implementation, and evaluation. We will also either more tightly control the type of systems students develop, or work to integrate a wider variety of usability measurements that span multiple genres, platforms and devices.

6. REFERENCES

[1] ACM/IEEE-CS Joint Task Force on Computing Curricula. (2013). Computer Science Curricula 2013 Ironman draft v1.0. Retrieved September 6, 2013 from http://ai.stanford.edu/users/sahami/CS2013//ironman-draft/cs2013-ironman-v1.0.pdf

[2] Bernhaupt, R. (Ed.) (2010) *Evaluating User Experience in Games: Concepts and Methods*. London: Springer.

[3] Gould, J.D. (1988). How to design usable systems (excerpt). In R. Baecker, J. Grudin, W. Buxton, & S. Greenberg (Eds.), *Readings in human-computer interaction, toward the year 2000*, 93–121. New York, NY: Morgan-Kaufman.

[4] Lewis, C., and Rieman, J. (1993). *Task-centered user interface design: A practical introduction*. Retrieved September 6, 2013 from http://hcibib.org/tcuid/

[5] Lewis, C., Polson, P., Wharton, C., and Rieman, J. (1990). Testing a walkthrough methodology for theory-based design of walk-up-and-use interfaces. *Proc. CHI '90*, 235-242.

[6] Narayanan, N.H., Hundhausen, C., Hendrix, D., and Crosby, M. (2012). Transforming the CS classroom with studio-based learning. *Proc. SIGCSE 2012*, 165-166.

[7] Nielsen, J. (1994). Heuristic evaluation. In Nielsen, J., and Mack, R.L. (Eds.), *Usability Inspection Methods*. John Wiley & Sons, NY.

[8] Nielsen, J., and Molich, R. (1990). Heuristic evaluation of user interfaces, *Proc. CHI '90*, 249-256.

[9] Reimer, Y.J., Cennamo, K., & Douglas, S. (2012). Emergent themes in a UI design hybrid-studio course. *Proc. SIGCSE 2012*, 625-630.

[10] Rowan, M., and Dehlinger, J. (2013). A Systematic Literature Review on using Mobile Computing as a Learning Intervention. *Proc. ITiCSE '13*, 339.

[11] Sahami, M., Roach, S., Cuadros-Vargas, E., and LeBlanc, R. (2013). ACM/IEEE-CS Computer Science Curriculum 2013: Reviewing the Ironman Report. *Proc. SIGCSE '13*, 13-44.

They Can't Find Us: The Search for Informal CS Education

Betsy DiSalvo, Cecili Reid and Parisa Khanipour Roshan
Georgia Institute of Technology
Atlanta, GA
bdisalvo@cc.gatech.edu | creid31@gatech.edu | khanipour@gatech.edu

ABSTRACT

In this study we found that search terms that would likely be used by parents to find out-of-school computer science (CS) learning opportunities for their children yielded remarkably unproductive results. This is important to the field of CS education because, to date, there is no empirical evidence that demonstrates how a lack of CS vocabulary is a barrier to accessing informal CS learning opportunities. This study focuses on the experience of parents who do not have the privilege of education and technical experience when searching for learning opportunities for their children. The findings presented will demonstrate that issues of access to CS education go beyond technical means, and include ability to conduct suitable searches and identify appropriate computational learning tools. Out-of-school learning is an important factor in who is motivated and prepared to study computer science in college. It is likely that without early access to informal CS learning, fewer students are motivated to explore CS in formal classrooms.

Categories and Subject Descriptors:

K.3.2 Computer and Information Science Education.

General Terms

Human Factors

Keywords

Search, Informal learning, Online education

1. INTRODUCTION

The great number of free software and classes that are offered online for CS learning suggest that young people with technical means should be able to access tools for learning computer science (CS) at anytime. Informal learning tools are important in increasing motivation, community and belonging around a given topic [12]. Experience with informal learning in CS - often introduced by parents - is associated with those who choose to pursue computer science as a career [14; 15; 20]. Research suggests that parents are choosing many of the informal learning experiences for their children [6] and parents heavily influence the establishment of an ecology of technology learning [2].

SIGCSE'14, March 5–8, 2014, Atlanta, Georgia, USA.

http://dx.doi.org/10.1145/2538862.2538933

We sought to understand how a parent with little experience in computing, technology or education would help facilitate the informal learning experience of a child who has an interest in computing. This study looked at common Internet search term low-income parents would likely use for accessing informal CS learning opportunities in different geographic setting across the United States. Each term was used in the Google [8] search engine to compare access to information about online and offline informal learning opportunities including cost, accessibility, and location to determine if informal CS learning opportunities are accessible to parents in the United States (US). We anticipated that the results from the search would not be as productive. However, the complete absence of the rich and free tools for informal CS Learning that are frequently presented at SIGCSE was surprising and troubling.

2. BACKGROUND

Recently, there has been an explosion of educational courses offered online. Khan Academy launched a set of CS lessons [9], Coursera recently announced partnership to offer a range of courses including computer science courses and Udacity.com, offers a number of university level CS courses [7]. Virtual instruction is not the only type of online resource for CS learning. Sandbox computing activities, educational games, and the broad expanse of news, blogs and other media provide access to online play and discovery that is an important part in shaping learners for the 21st century. There are many free informal learning tools online that provide resources for learning content and content creation with computing. For example, one can download free drag and drop programming tools, such as Alice [5] and Scratch [13], which encourage sandbox play with computation.

While the above learning resources are frequently free, some question if these resources increase educational inequalities [17; 18]. It is suggested that unequal awareness of online informal learning, coupled with the way they are marketed, cultural values of audiences, and access makes these resources more available to the well-educated and the wealthy, which broadens the gap between the rich and poor in terms of education and income.

Issues of inequality in technology access can be addressed through research on access and use, and design of systems that specifically speak to marginalize communities. In other domains, such as health, targeting parents as users of online resources has proven to be effective in improving information delivery among marginalized communities. Research with mothers has begun to explore how their use of online resources for health information may lead to positive outcomes such as seeking appropriate health care [21]. Beyond health applications, access to online resources has been shown to improve general parenting skills. Na and Chia [16] found that access to online resources increased parents' confidence in their parenting skills, the amount of time they spent with their children, and perceived level of knowledge of their children's development.

To date there has been little research to understand how parents access information about informal learning opportunities. We see a need to address accessing online learning because, while some audiences are able to navigate and critically evaluate online resources, the groups that may be in the greatest need, low-income and low-educational families, have not been addressed. The field of CS education may have particular issues in that the field itself cannot agree on what is "computer science" and what is not. The study presented in this paper is a first step in understanding how a lack of common vocabulary around CS education may be impacting parents' (particularly low-income parents) access to CS education tools.

3. DATA COLLECTION METHODS

Internet queries were conducted to find informal CS learning opportunities. We selected three main search terms: *kids computer camp, kids computer classes*, and *kids computer learning*, based upon popularity in Google Analytics. These three terms were paired with the names of twelve cities from four different US regions. These cities were also chosen to represent different populations, including large cities, mid-sized cities, and small cities. To better understand how computing as a subject compared with other discipline specific searches we also conducted searches for *kids math learning, kids physics learning and kids animal learning* (seeking natural sciences learning resources)

3.1 Selection of Search Engine & Terms

We used two methods in the selection of search terms. First we looked at an analytical tool provided by Google to find the most popular terms associated with computers, learning, and children. Second, we validated these terms in a study with a search task given to parents in a financially depressed neighborhood.

3.1.1 Google Search Terms Selection

Google search was selected as the search engine of choice due to its popularity in the US across regions and socio-economic status [11]. First, we brainstormed a list of possible search terms for finding informal CS learning opportunities for children. This list included:

- Topic search terms such as, *computation, computer, computer science, computing, programming*
- Environment search terms, such as *after school, camp, classes, education, informal, learning, out of school, learning*
- Audience search terms, such as *children, K-12, kids, middle school, teens*

We then used *Google Insights for Search [1]* to determine the most popular terms among this list. For example, we found that *kids* was used twice as frequently as *children* in searches. We included the term *learning* to be a catch all for other types of informal learning. We recognized that some search terms that were less popular (such as computer science or informal learning), might produce more accurate results for finding informal computer science learning opportunities. However, we determined that it would be more appropriate for this study to select terms that were more popular and more likely to be chosen by parents who are not in a technology field or involved in educational research. We selected our search terms, not to compare terms, but to get the best representation of what we suspected, and *Google Insights for Search* indicated, as terms parents would use in searching for informal computer science learning opportunities.

To compare with other science, technology, engineering and mathematics (STEM) disciplines we conducted searches using the terms *kids learning* paired with *physics, math* and *animal*. We chose the terms *math* and *physics* to find results for similar disciplines to CS. We chose the term *animal* to help us understand searches in other disciples that might occur when parents seek learning opportunities based upon their child's interest rather than seeking learning for a specific discipline. We relate parents searching for learning around a child's interest in animals to a parent seeking learning around a child's interest in computing. They may not know the academic name for the STEM fields related to those interests, such as computer science or biology, but they see an opportunity for leveraging that interest into learning.

Two researchers conducted the searches between March and October 2012. All data for each search was collected on one day to limit variations for the search terms. Seasonal variance may have affected search results and is a limitation of the study. For each search, the researchers emptied their cache and cleared their browser history. Based upon prior research that showed 94% of users click only on a first page result, and less than 6% click to the second page we limited our search to the first twenty results as they appeared on the first two pages of default Google results [4].

3.1.2 Parents' Search Terms Selection

Two researchers recruited parents or legal guardians of school age children at a back to school event in a financially depressed neighborhood in Atlanta. Researchers held an information booth at the event providing information about the educational resources available for teens at Georgia Institute of Technology and at the same time asked parents if they were interested in participating in our study. Those who were interested in participating were then asked to search for educational resources for their children on a laptop. Sixteen participants were recruited, however one of them did not complete the study. Out of the sixteen participants, 15 were female while one was male and all identified as African-American. While we did not ask participants age, the range included young mothers in their early 20's to grandmothers in their 50's. Participants were given T-shirts and water bottles at the completion of their participation.

Parents were given a laptop with an open Google Chrome browser and asked to show how they would look for an educational tool or an online resource, if their child expressed interest in computing, via any website or search engine of their choosing. The participants were asked to continue their search until they found a source they identified as related and useful, and recorded their screen as well as their search history and the keywords they used. To avoid affecting the search result, the search history was cleared after each use. Parents were asked about their experience, how they chose which link to open in the search results, and how they identified their final choice as a useful resource for their child.

The analysis of search terms provided some insight into preferences of parents within this demographic. Of the 16 participants only one explicitly expressed preference for use of Bing search engine rather than Google's. Amongst the participants were one illiterate parent, one that did not understand how to go about the task, and one deaf parent. Of all of the parents, only one found a site deemed relevant according to the specifications used for the searches in this overall study (see section 4.1). The site was *Simple Code Works* (simplecodeworks.com). Another important observation is that none of the parents went past the second page of results justifying our resolution to only evaluate the first two pages we received.

3.2 Selection of Cities

Our objective was to consider residents across a broad spectrum of the US both by the size of the city they live in and the region they live in. Given these objectives we selected the four largest cities in the US, four mid-size cities, (non-suburban areas with a population between 125,000 and 115,000) and four small cities, (non-suburban areas with a population between 15,000 and 5,000). Cities were also chosen to represent four regions of the US, the Northeast, Midwest, South and West.

Table 1. Cities Paired with Search Terms

Region	Large Cities /Population (in millions)	Mid Cities /Population	Small Cities /Population
Northeast	*New York, NY* /8.2449	*Allen Town, PA* /119,141	*Olean, NY* /14,363
Midwest	*Chicago, IL* /2.7071	*Springfield, IL* /117,076	*Thief River Falls, MN* /8,660
South	*Houston, TX* /2.1451*	*Gainesville, FL* 125326	*Crowley, LA* 13,309
West	*Los Angeles, CA* /3.8197	*Visalia, CA* 126,432	*Susanville, CA* 17,685
Other	No additional text used with search terms	*Online* used with search terms	

4. ANALYSIS AND RESULTS

After conducting the 42 computer related searches (the 3 search terms independently, then each paired with the term *online*, then each paired with the 12 cities) we had 840 results and classified the results in a number of ways to better understand our data and the implications for access to informal learning. The first step was to combine the duplicate results within each set of search results and then to determine which terms were relevant to CS learning.

4.1 Relevance to Children's CS Learning

Search results were considered relevant to children's CS learning if they meet the following criteria:

- *Relevant to computer science* - We only included results that had relevance to learning computer science. In many cases this was easy to determine because the search result was related to something unrelated to computers all together, such as horseback riding, or obviously related to computer science, such as a game programming summer camp. In other cases this was more difficult. For example, the educational goal of some programs was to teach Microsoft Word. We limited the criteria to searches that provide more than teaching Microsoft Office suite, such as those that focused on software applications were more likely to serve as an entry point to more advanced computing skills, such a Photoshop or Illustrator. When in doubt we included the entry as relevant.

- *Relevant to children* – We only included results that had relevance to children, meaning those under the age of 18. In cases such as community colleges, where a child could possibly attend but it was not a welcoming environment for children without special accommodations we did not include the results. In a few cases, it was unclear if a course that was designed for adults was also appropriate for children (For example a library offered classes on HTML for 17 years of age an up). In these cases we included the results as relevant to children.

4.2 Duplicate result

A number of relevant results came up multiple times for each search that was conducted... After eliminating the duplicate results from each set of search results, (but not across searches) we had 191 out of 840 sites that were relevant to children's CS learning.

4.3 Type of Site / Service

We coded each site by the type of site it was or the service it provided or sold. There were 8 codes that we identified ranging from intensive summer camps to links to books for self-directed learning. Table 2 outlines the criteria used to assign categories.

Table 2. Codes for Types of Educational Services Offered

Code	Name	Description
A	Camp	Web sites for location-based camps only with informal CS learning.
B	Afterschool program	Web sites for location-based afterschool programs only that offered informal CS learning.
C	Camp / afterschool	Web sites for location-based programs like camps and afterschool programs.
D	Higher Education	Web sites for colleges & technical schools that offer classes for children.
E	Online activities	Web sites that offered online tutorials, games or activities to be downloaded in print form or interacted with online.
F	Online classes / learning	Web sites that offer CS online courses, distance learning classes for children, or home schooling curriculum
G	Directory	Web sites that list children's learning resources for CS
H	News, videos, or social networks	Web sites that feature news articles, blogs, videos or Facebook profiles that suggest other resources for encouraging interest in CS.

4.4 Cost

It was difficult to measure cost. Summer camps and after school programs were not comparable in terms of intensity or time. To address this we found the lowest cost option for any camp, after school program, or course and then determine what the daily rate would be. In some cases there were only overnight camp options and in other cases the course only covered two or three hours. We did not reduce this down to an hourly rate because the amount of material coved in a three-hour course may be more equal to the amount of instruction offered at an overnight camp than the hourly rate would reflect. However, we recognize this lack of equable ways to compare cost is a limitation of the study and try to address this in reporting our results.

4.5 Camps and Afterschool Programs

The category of camps resulted in the most unique sites. The camp results were dominated by a handful of for-profit nationally run summer camps including Digital Media Academy (appeared for 17 different search terms), Emagination Computer Camps (appeared for 5 different search terms), ID Tech Camp (appeared for 15 different search terms) and Institute for Mathematics and Computer Science (IMACS) (appeared for 5 different search terms). The average lowest daily cost of most of these camps is between \$100 - \$200. An exception is IMACS, which accredits other learning centers who have a greater range of prices including some lower cost options.

In addition to these national chains there were a handful of camps and after school programs that catered to local populations at much lower cost, such as Camp Katy in Houston, TX, the College of the Sequaoias in Visalia, CA, and Planet Bravo in Los Angeles, CA. These lower cost camps and after school programs were more available in the larger cities and none were found for the four smaller cities (see Table 3).

Table 3. Unique Search Results by Category & City Size

	Big 4 cities	Mid 4 cities	Small 4 cities	Online / no term	Total
A – Camp	29	13	0	20	62
B – After-school	3	0	0	2	5
C – Camp / afterschool	6	0	0	5	11
D - HigherEd	3	3	0	1	7
E - Online activities	1	0	0	5	6
F – Online classes	0	0	0	7	7
G –Directory	23	14	1	10	48
H – Article/ blog	29	4	1	11	45
Total	94	34	2	61	191

4.6 Articles, blogs and videos

Of the 45 search results that were article, blogs, or videos, most were lists of summer camps or classes one could enroll their child in to learn more about computer science. Several were news articles about a local resource for computer science education; a few were articles, blogs or videos that emphasized the importance of computer learning.

4.7 Online Activities and Courses

To better understand searches for informal learning resources for online or at home we paired the three terms (*kids computer camp, kids computer classes*, and *kids computer learning*) with the word *online* or with no additional term. Among these searches there were seven unique resources for remote CS learning. Three were online or distance learning courses. Four were tutorials or lessons to purchase, print out or view for use at home including: *Kids, Computers and Learning, Computer Connections: Inside & Out, Kids-Online Click-N-Learn, Homeschool Programming Inc.*

In the review of the first page of all of the 191 search result we looked for online educational computer programming tools[1]. There was only one case where one of these tools was mentioned. In this case, the program *Scratch* appeared on the first page of a site in response to a 2011 question posted on a site called Quora.com asking if there are good classes in Los Angeles for kids to learn programming.

[1] CS Learning tools we looked for include Agent Sheets, Alice, BlueJ, CodingBat, E-Slate, Greenfoot, Hackety Hack, JES, Kodu, Logo, Mama, Phrogram, Problets, and Scratch.

4.8 Higher Education & Outreach

Among the search terms there were seven search results for colleges, technical schools or adult community programs that offer classes appropriate for children. These classes were free or lower in price than the camps, around $50 per day. Most of these classes targeted students in junior high through high school.

4.9 Location

The most successful searches were those with no location paired with the search terms (*kids computer camp, kids computer classes*, and *kids computer learning)* or with *online* paired with the search terms. These averaged 10.2 unique search results for each of the three terms. In the dispersion of these terms camps were among the leading search results (see Table 3). This may be due to including camp in our search. However, these camps appeared on all searches.

To understand the variations in between the different sized cities and cities in different regions we conducted one-way analysis of variance (ANOVA) for the types of educational services offered (Table 2) among the search results produced for each set of cities by size and by region. To better analyze these findings, we collapsed related types of educational resources into three groups. These three groups consisted of:

1. *Onsite* resources: A. Camps, B. Afterschool programs, C. Camp and afterschool, & D. Higher education classes.
2. *Online* tools: E. Activities, tutorials and games, F. online classes and distance learning
3. *Pointers* to CS learning: G. Directories, H. Articles & blogs

4.9.1 City Size

The one-way between subjects ANOVA was conducted to compare the types of educational services (*Onsite, Online, and Pointer*) among the search results produced for cities with Large, Mid, and Small population sizes (see Figure 1).

Figure 1. Mean Number of Related *Onsite*, *Online*, and *Pointers* Search Results by City Population Size.

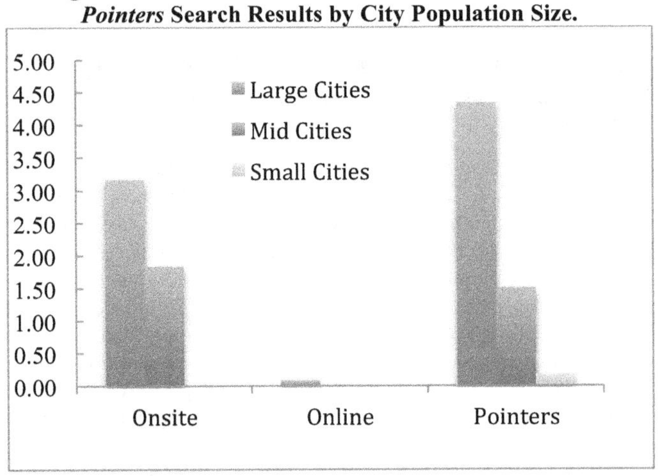

There was a significant effect of population size on relevant *Onsite* search results at the p<.001 level for the three conditions [F(2, 33) = 37.66, p = 0.000] (Table 4). Post hoc comparisons using the Tukey HSD test indicated that the mean score for the larger population cities (M = 3.17, SD = 1.34) was significantly different than the midrange population cities (M = 1.83, SD = 0.79). Similarly, the small population cities (M = 0, SD = 0) which had no relevant results, was significantly different than both the large and mid sized cities.

Table 4. ANOVA of *Onsite* Search Results by City Size.

	SS	df	MS	F	p
Between:	60.677	2	30.339	37.666	<0.001
Within:	26.581	33	0.805		
Total:	87.258	35			

As illustrated in Figure 1, there was only one *online* resources listed. These were insufficient result to have significant differences.

The *Pointer* results were the most frequent occurrences for larger and small city searches. Again we found there was a significant effect of population size on relevant *Pointer* resources search results at the p<.001 level for the three conditions [F(2, 33) = 24.496, p = 0.000]. (Table 5)

Table 5. ANOVA of *Pointer* Search Results by City Size.

	SS	df	MS	F	p
Between:	108.633	2	54.317	24.496	<0.001
Within:	73.175	33	2.217		
Total:	181.808	35			

Post hoc comparisons using the Tukey HSD test indicated that the mean score for the large cities *Pointer* results (M = 4.333 SD = 2.100) was significantly different than the searches in mid (M = 1.500, SD = 1.446) and small cities (M = 0.167, SD = 0.389). However there was no significant difference between the mid sized and small cities.

4.9.2 Regional Differences

A one-way between subjects ANOVA was conducted to compare the effect of region on the number of relevant Onsite, Online and Pointer search results. Onsite and Pointer results for US cities in the Northeast, Midwest, South and in West showed no statistical differences. The Online results did demonstrate statistical difference between regions. However, because there was only one result among the four regions, this significance is not reliable.

4.10 Non-CS Terms

The first two pages from Google engine searches for the three non-CS terms, *kids math learning*, *kids physics learning* and *kids animal learning* resulted in 48 unique results out of the 60 total results. Thirty-one of these results were in the form of online activities, such as games or interactive learning tools. There were also a number searches results that had opportunities for children to take classes at higher education institutions (10 unique search results) or through online classes or distance learning (5 unique search results). This high number of unique resources (an average of 16 per term) can be contrasted to our results from the *kids computer learning* and *kids computer learning online* search terms, which resulted in only 7 unique results (an average of 3.5 per term). Another striking difference is that 46 of these non-CS terms results linked to free learning resources in contrast to 2 free resources provided by the *kids computer learning (online)* searches.

These results may indicate that many more learning resources exist for math, physics and biology. However, the lack of the many pointer sites and irrelevant search results that we found with the CS terms, indicates that the problem, at least in part, is related to the search terms used and how searchers are parsed by the Google search engine.

DISCUSSION

Not surprisingly the larger, more densely populated cities had more resources for informal CS learning and the type of resources were more varied. Some of this may be a flaw in the search method because residents in mid size or smaller cities may overcome the lack of relevant search results by pairing with better regional terms, such as the county or a near by city. We found no evidence of regional differences in the search results, suggesting this is a national pattern. Across all of the searches the number of unique search results was less than we expected. The amount of repetition, the number of directory sites, articles and blog post (which tended to be less useful as pointers to learning resources than our Google searches) meant that most searches resulted in less than 2 useful results.

While we anticipated that the search results would not be very productive. But the complete absence of the most powerful and free informal learning tools shocked us. The absences of tools such as *Scratch*, *Alice*, or *Greenfoot* in the 840 searches result suggest that if one has little experience with these learning tools or with CS it is unlikely one could find robust CS learning tools.

We were again surprised that free classes and tutorials such as Khan Academy and Udacity never appeared in our searches. There were a few fee based distance-learning programs that target home school audiences as formal classroom equivalents for CS learning. But the fees and formalized structure of these would not appeal to most informal learners. The high percentage of camps that appeared among the small number of useful results was also of concern. The camps were generally over $100 a day, with additional cost of funding students' lunch and aftercare in many cases. For students coming from lower income households this may be too expensive for them to participate in.

The results from our non-CS searches produced a much greater number of unique results that were leading to more free online tools and resources than the computing searches. This could be because there are more relevant learning opportunities to be found for math, physics, and biology than for CS. Yet we know there are a number of useful informal learning tools that are free and easy to access once found and that most of the MOOCs have CS offerings. The findings suggest that in general, informal CS, programing or computational literacy is not accessible to parents with little technical background or financial resources in the same way that other STEM fields are.

5. CONCLUSION

Looking through the proceedings of SIGCSE we see a rich array of tools to teach computer science. Some are free tools or programs that one can access online [5; 10; 13]. Others are community outreach programs that target lower income students [13]. And others are tool kits for play [3]. These computational construction kits and others have been available for some time [19]. And the recent influx of free classes and courses would seem to be new opportunities to engage with CS learning at home. Yet none of these opportunities appeared in our search engine results and only one reference among the 840 searches suggested one of them.

Without a background in CS or education one might not be aware that these types of CS education tools exist. This is a lost opportunity for those that cannot afford expensive camps or do not live near to one of the few less expensive informal learning opportunities. It also demonstrated the pattern of open educational resources increasing educational inequalities rather than closing the metaphorical *digital divide* [18].

The solution to these inequity issues lie in the hands of CS educators, researchers, and educational tool developers. Simple steps may make a difference, such as improving search engine optimization by creating metadata that includes more common terms such *kids*, *computers*, and *classes* rather than terms like *educational programming tools* (which turned up a rich list of free CS learning tools). Another opportunity could be found in partnering with camps that appeared repetitively in (and at the top of) our searches. Many of these camps use tools like Scratch or Alice. By encouraging the camps to have links to these free tools on their home page, it could provide new avenues for informal learning among those who cannot afford or who are not yet sure if they want to commit $500 to $1,000 for a camp experience. Finally, these issues are additional motivation for the field of CS education to develop a shared vocabulary, and a vocabulary that parents and non-technical members of the public can use to access CS education.

This study provides baseline data and motivation for future work in CS education that directly address issues of access and equity. This is empirical evidence that our efforts to create free CS learning tools are not reaching marginalized groups who are so often left out of CS education. For future work, we seek to apply our findings in better understanding the role that parents play in selecting and encouraging their children's CS learning experiences. From these further studies we hope to develop community resources of educational technology tools that reach underrepresented and marginalized groups.

For example, we are developing a community based social network for parents in a low-income neighborhood in Atlanta. Using a strong narrative blog structure we hope that parents will communicate about educational issues and interest of their children. Research staff and community members will then create links to informal technology and CS learning opportunities that might be good fits for the families. We anticipate this work will serve as a model for other neighborhoods and seed a database of keywords that are more intuitive for parents and less intuitive for educators and researchers.

6. REFERENCES

[1] 2012. Google Insights for Search Google.

[2] Barron, B., 2004. Learning Ecologies for Technologiecal Fluency: Gender and Experience Differences *Journal of Educational Computing Research 31*, 1, 1-36.

[3] Buechley, L., Eisenberg, M., Catchen, J., and Crockett, A., 2008. The LilyPad Arduino: using computational textiles to investigate engagement, aesthetics, and diversity in computer science education. In *SIGCHI Conference on Human Factors in Computing Systems* ACM, Florence, Italy, 423-432.

[4] Chitika, 2010. The Value of Google Results Positioning.

[5] Cooper, S., Dann, W., and Pausch, R., 2000. Alice: a 3-D tool for introductory programming concepts. In *Consortium for Computing Sciences in Colleges*, 107-116.

[6] Crowley, K. and Jacobs, M., 2002. Building islands of expertise in everyday family activity. In *Learning conversations in museums* Citeseer 333-356.

[7] Gee, S., 2012. Sebastian Thrun Resigns from Stanford to Launch Udacity.

[8] Ghemawat, S., Gobioff, H., and Leung, S.T., 2003. The Google file system ACM, 29-43.

[9] Khan Acadamy, 2013. KhanAcademy 226,116,151 lessons delivered. In *Learn almost anything for free*.

[10] Kölling, M., Utting, I., Mccall, D., Brown, N., Stevens, P., and Berry, M., 2011. Greenfoot Programming Education Tools Group, Computing Education Research Group at the School of Computing, University of Kent, Canterbury, UK.

[11] Langville, A.N. and Meyer, C.D., 2006. *Google page rank and beyond*. Princeton Univ Pr.

[12] Lave, J. and Wenger, E., 1991. *Situated learning: Legitimate peripheral participation*. Cambridge Univ Pr.

[13] Maloney, J.H., Peppler, K., Kafai, Y., Resnick, M., and Rusk, N., 2008. Programming by choice: urban youth learning programming with scratch. *SIGCSE Bull. 40*, 1, 367-371.

[14] Margolis, J., 2008. *Stuck in the shallow end: Education, race, and computing*. The MIT Press, Cambridge, MA

[15] Margolis, J. and Fisher, A., 2002. *Unlocking the clubhouse: Women in computing*. MIT Press, Cambridge, MA

[16] Na, J.C. and Chia, S.W., 2008. Impact of online resources on informal learners: Parents' perception of their parenting skills. *Computers & Education 51*, 1, 173-186.

[17] Reardon, S.F., 2011. The widening academic achievement gap between the rich and the poor: New evidence and possible explanations. *Whither opportunity*, 91-116.

[18] Reich, J., 2011. Open Eductional Resources Expand Educational Inequalities. In *Educational Technology Debate*.

[19] Resnick, M., Bruckman, A., and Martin, F., 1996. Pianos not stereos: Creating computational construction kits. *interactions 3*, 5, 40-50.

[20] Schulte, C. and Knobelsdorf, M., 2007. Attitudes towards computer science-computing experiences as a starting point and barrier to computer science. In *Third international workshop on Computing education research* ACM, New York, NY, USA, Atlanta, Georgia, USA.

[21] Ybarra, M.L. and Suman, M., 2006. Help seeking behavior & the Internet: a national survey. *International Journal of Medical Informatics 75*, 1, 29-41.

Curriculum is Not Enough: The Educational Theory and Research Foundation of the Exploring Computer Science Professional Development Model

Joanna Goode
University of Oregon
Education Studies
Eugene, OR 97403-5277
541-346-2826
goodej@uoregon.edu

Jane Margolis
UCLA
Graduate School of Education & Information Studies
Los Angeles, CA 90095-1521
310-794-4481
margolis@ucla.edu

Gail Chapman
UCLA
Graduate School of Education & Information Studies
Los Angeles, CA 90095-1521
310-794-4481
chapgail@gmail.com

ABSTRACT
In recent years, the computer science education community has shown strong commitment to broadening participation in computing in K-12 classrooms. Educational research highlights the critical role of professional development in supporting teachers to attract and effectively teach underrepresented students in computing. In this paper we present the Exploring Computer Science (ECS) professional development model and the research on which it is based. We also present findings about the impact of ECS professional development on teachers' practice. As computing education initiatives become increasingly concerned with scaling up from a regional to a nationwide presence, it is important to consider how the essential components of effective professional development can drive this reform.

Categories and Subject Descriptors
K.3.2 [**Computers and Education**]: Computer and Information Science Education – *computer science education, curriculum.*

General Terms
Human Factors

Keywords
Professional Development, Inquiry, Pedagogy, Learning Theory, CS Reform, Gender and Ethnicity, Broadening Participation in Computing

1. INTRODUCTION
As the computer science (CS) education community commits to broadening participation in computing, we must remember that access to courses and curriculum is not enough. While the courses, curriculum content, lessons, and activities are the critical framework, it is the teacher practice, pedagogy, and classroom norms that bring purpose and engagement to student learning. For this reason, CS teacher professional development (PD) is critically important, and its components must be understood.

In this paper, we will focus on the major activities enacted in the Exploring Computer Science (ECS) PD program, as well as the learning theory and research behind this PD model. We will also present current findings about the impact of the ECS PD experience on teachers' practice.

2. EXPLORING COMPUTER SCIENCE PROGRAM
Exploring Computer Science is an educational reform program built to address the lack of computer science curriculum, engaging pedagogy, and institutional support available for schools serving high numbers of students of color. It was designed in direct response to the issues surfaced through the research presented in *Stuck in the Shallow End* [16]. ECS is a yearlong high school computer science curriculum, and has now been adopted in several major urban districts nationwide. The ECS curriculum includes lessons for six units over the course of a year: 1) Human Computer Interaction; 2) Problem Solving; 3) Web Design; 4) Introduction to Programming; 5) Computing and Data Analysis; and 6) Robotics [12].

The core of the Exploring Computer Science curriculum highlights the problem solving, computational practices, and modes of inquiry associated with doing computer science, rather than just a narrow focus on coding, navigating particular syntax or tools.

Very importantly, ECS is a *program* that includes the ECS curriculum *in combination* with ECS teacher professional development. Our experiences with observations in classrooms and interviews with teachers show the complexities of teaching for broadening participation in computing, and that simply adopting the curriculum without sustained professional preparation is insufficient to develop the particular pedagogical strategies and classroom norms that must accompany the ECS curriculum.

3. ECS PROFESSIONAL DEVELOPMENT: CENTRAL FEATURES
The ECS PD is designed around five key activities, each of which is summarized in this following section. Though the PD is designed to support learning in ECS classrooms, the instructional features described are not curriculum or content specific. These same instructional experiences can be used to support the

SIGCSE '14, March 05 - 08 2014, Atlanta, GA, USA

ACM 978-1-4503-2605-6/14/03…$15.00.
http://dx.doi.org/10.1145/2538862.2538948

development of inquiry-based teaching practices across courses, including the forthcoming AP Computer Science Principles course.

What tie all of these activities together are the three pillars of the ECS program: CS content, inquiry and equity. The activities and teaching philosophy emanate from a body of research on successful teaching and learning [4,7,9,18]. ECS PDs are spaces of *active, participatory, creative, and engaged learning,* modeling what should occur in the classroom. Participating teachers are committed to teach the ECS curriculum.

3.1 Immersion into Inquiry

Exploring Computer Science PDs are filled with activity, collaboration, and reflection. There is often a lot of noise, as small groups of teachers and then the whole group are engaging in lesson planning, collaborating about how to solve the challenges they just encountered, and then reflecting on their own experiences teaching a lesson. From the very first hour teachers realize that this is not a passive, and unfortunately more typical, PD; instead ECS PDs are purposefully structured so that every teacher is participating, actively learning, and engaged.

This last point is very important. Too often PDs –across many subject areas---are passive events with teachers being *talked at*. And in computer science learning environments, too often a small group of participants who feel they know the most dominate all the discussions. The purposeful intention of the ECS PD, in contrast, is to create an equitable learning environment, where everyone is participating actively, establishing a community learning norm in which process and thinking is much more important than specific outcome or "correct" answers, and everyone recognizes that they have something to contribute.

ECS PDs open with a brief icebreaker to allow teachers to introduce themselves and the schools they represent. Immediately following, participants are immersed in the first inquiry activity. Professional development leaders model an introductory lesson from the ECS curriculum. This modeling typically includes: placing teachers in cooperative groups that offer diverse experience and knowledge in each group; a short journal prompt asking each participant to write about their understandings of a particular computing topic and how it relates to their lives along with a short debrief; as groups are engaged in a task facilitators roam the room, distributing necessary resources to each group and asking guiding questions to help groups move forward with their inquiry.

Beginning with a lesson that everyone can participate in is very important. For example, exploring the question "What is a computer?" teachers begin by counting the computers in the room. Teachers then share ideas in their small groups: Is an iPhone a computer? A digital watch? A thermostat? A light switch?

Following, the facilitators then bring the groups together to discuss their findings and reflections on their process. Then, as a whole group, the professional developers facilitate the dialogue as it moves from teachers reflecting on the particular activity as a learner, to the instructional implications about teaching this activity to urban high school students.

Therefore, within the first hour of the ECS PD, participants not only engage with computer science content, but they have an immersive inquiry experience that allows them to view computer science learning from the role of a student. An essential part of this activity, however, is the final whole-group debrief where the facilitators make the inquiry-based instruction explicit – including activity preparation, resources, journal prompts, scaffolding, guiding questions, drawing from student experience, cooperative group setup, facilitator interaction, etc. – and highlight inquiry strategies teachers need to use in their classrooms. Further, this debrief focuses on teaching practices appropriate for *all* students. In addition, asking participants to reflect on group dynamics and their overall experiences as learners in this activity typically then makes visible how gender, preparatory privilege, and other equity considerations materialize in computer science classrooms.

3.2 Teacher-Learner-Observer Model

Following this immersive modeling of an ECS lesson, the participants are then introduced to the primary set of activities for the duration of the PD week: *Teacher-Learner-Observer lessons*. Each small group is assigned one lesson from the introductory units of ECS that they will plan together and co-teach to the rest of the PD participants. Though the curriculum instructional guide already contains the framework of the lesson, it is up to the teachers together to "make music" with the notes on the page.

For the remainder of the weeklong PD, each group takes turns teaching key assigned lessons, chosen because they offer central CS concepts or have historically been challenging for ECS teachers. The content addressed in these lessons includes binary numbers, algorithms, searching and sorting algorithms, networked graphs, and data visualization and analysis.

The PD is structured so one group of teachers teach the lesson, most of the other participants engage in the activity as students, and the PD facilitators act as silent observers, noting the engaging and learning of participants during the lesson. After the activity, the debrief begins with the group of co-teachers reflecting on the effectiveness of the lesson, then the learners reflecting on their experience with the lesson, and finally, the observers noting what they saw during the sample lesson. Then the conversation is opened up, once again, to talk about the implications for teaching this lesson through inquiry for diverse high school students. After each lesson, groups that have not yet presented have short periods of time to meet and modify their lesson as necessary, to draw on the now prior knowledge of the participants. Thus, the cycle of the activity is (re)planning->teaching->reflecting.

This signifying ECS activity is based on the premise that teachers learn best about a common curriculum by teaching it and reflecting on it. As Loucks-Horsley and colleagues [15] note, "demonstration lessons can provide opportunities for teachers to enhance their content knowledge, practice their instructional approaches, and collaborate with other teachers as they implement the curriculum over time" (p. 248).

3.3 Professional Learning Community

The extensive and ongoing face-to-face interaction of the ECS PD model fosters a powerful professional learning community in which teachers learn from one another, support and share strategies for strengthening their teaching. Research by McLaughlin and Talbert shows how strong professional cultures are essential to changing norms of practice and pedagogy [17]. In the ECS Teacher-Learner-Observer model, each teacher recognizes the challenges associated with teaching a lesson to peers with the knowledge that the lesson will be analyzed and debriefed. Creating this space for reflection and observation presents an opportunity for teachers to work in a space of professional vulnerability and honesty. One ECS teacher reflected this way on the support of the ECS community:

> [ECS] *PD's have been extremely helpful to keep up to date and share and learn from other colleagues. The ECS PD's has helped me be part of a network of teachers that share similar concepts and practices. It is nice to talk to people that can share the same teaching area and understand each other.*

This space also serves to distribute wisdom of practice as well as a forum for developing teacher leadership in future PD or curricular endeavors.

3.4 Equitable Practices

Equity serves as a central guiding theme and component to the ECS PD. Equitable practices are both woven throughout and modeled during the PD institute. Research-based practices are specifically identified at each debrief: from structuring activities so that all students are actively learning, collaborating, and engaged: validating student ideas; drawing on students' cultural knowledge; using visuals to aid English language learners, modifications for students with special needs; and very importantly, deliberate scaffolding of the curriculum so that all students, from novices to more experienced students, are able to participate and feel that they belong in the class [5,6,13].

Beyond learning about instructional practices that address equity concerns, the ECS PD directly addresses teacher belief systems about who can (or cannot) excel in computer science classrooms. Drawing from central themes presented in *Stuck in the Shallow End* [16], teachers jigsaw the reading about computer science education in three ethnically diverse high schools in Los Angeles. After discussing the structural and psychological issues of access and equity presented in the book, particularly along lines of race and socioeconomics, participants discuss the notions of *deficit thinking* and *preparatory privilege* to deconstruct the relationship between opportunity and ability. When this conversation is revisited several days later after teachers have time to reflect on the readings and discussion and connect those with the ECS lessons that are taught during the week, often the equity issues become deeper, more concrete, and more personal. As one teacher reflected on his teaching practice after these discussions:

> *I must not take current level of interest and current level of knowledge [of students] as the only (or even a very good) indicator of future success in computer science. I have had experiences teaching Algebra 1 that I can think back to--kids who came in hating it, learning to love it, and then even choosing to study math. I will have to be very open to the possibility of the same kinds of stories in my computer science classes.*

Allowing for this period of time for teachers to absorb and process computer science equity issues elevates both the lesson debriefing discussions and more formalized discussions around *Stuck in the Shallow End* as it is reexamined later in the week.

3.5 Professional Development Into the Classroom and Throughout the Year

Acknowledging that teacher learning is dynamic and takes place over time, a central premise of the ECS PD model is the establishment of a long-term relationship between the teachers themselves and with PD providers. Rather than presenting PD as a one-stop drive-by event, a culture of ongoing community learning and reflection is established amongst the participants. The ECS PD activities mentioned above are first implemented in a one-week summer institute, then reinforced and built upon in subsequent gatherings. Quarterly follow-up PD sessions, followed by a second summer's institute, provides space to reflect and acknowledge the notion that much of teacher learning takes place in their own classrooms. The on-going PDs provide opportunities for teachers to continue working with the content, pedagogy, reflection about student work and learning assessment. Recognizing the research that finds how teacher learning as a process, rather than a discrete event in an off-campus location, is an essential element of the ECS PD design [15].

4. RESEARCH FOUNDATION OF ECS PD: WHAT WE KNOW ABOUT TEACHING

These above activities of an ECS PD are designed in response to educational research on effective teaching and learning. In her review of research on teaching and learning, educational scholar Darling-Hammond [9] notes that studies across disciplinary domains find that highly effective teachers support the process of meaningful learning by:

- Creating *ambitious and meaningful tasks* that reflect how knowledge is used in the field;
- Engaging students in *active learning*, so that they apply and test what they know;
- Drawing *connections to students' prior knowledge* and experiences;
- Diagnosing student understanding in order to *scaffold the learning process* step by step;
- *Assessing student learning continuously* and adapting teaching to student needs;
- Providing *clear standards*, *constant feedback*, and opportunities for work;
- Encouraging *strategic and metacognitive thinking*, so that students can learn to evaluate and guide their own teaching (p. 5).

It is these tenets of effective teaching that get folded into and modeled in our ECS PD activities. Darling-Hammond and colleagues point out that connecting these principles with particular teaching strategies differs depending on a sophisticated understanding of the content, the learner, and the goals of instruction [10]. *Pedagogical content knowledge* is a term offered to capture the particular pedagogical techniques that are appropriate for designing meaningful tasks, addressing common misconceptions, and engaging in ongoing, formative assessment of student learning within a particular discipline [3]. For our ECS PD model, we have taken these educational research findings and apply them for CS pedagogical content knowledge.

5. INQUIRY-BASED TEACHING AND LEARNING

5.1. Defining Inquiry-Based Approaches

Exploring Computer Science is based on an inquiry-instruction approach to learning. The family of approaches that can be considered inquiry-based includes project-based learning, problem-based learning, and design-based learning [4]. Though each approach has its own unique characteristics, they all share a common premise that students should be actively engaged in building their own learning through meaningful long-term learning experiences. Learning scientists and educational researchers point to a set of studies that conclude students learn more deeply and perform better on complex tasks if they have the opportunity to engage in more authentic learning [9]. Rather than learn within a constrained and disconnected context, this authentic learning approach encourages students to connect real world problems to the subject matter at hand. Research has shown that students who learn subject matter through an inquiry-based approach demonstrate increased performance on intellectually challenging performance tasks when compared to their direct-instruction peers. Inquiry-based learning also leads to significant gains in problem-solving abilities, curiosity, creativity, independence, and positive feelings about school [4].

Further, educators note that engaging students in the context of complex, meaningful projects that require sustained engagement, critical thinking, collaboration, management, communication, and management of resources to develop final products or presentations builds the types of 21st century skills advocated by new sets of national standards.

5.2 Inquiry-based Learning Requires Structure

Successfully enacting an inquiry-based approach to teaching requires extensive pedagogical content knowledge and understanding of student culture to create, facilitate, and assess the opportunities that activate learning for students. Inquiry requires well-designed and carefully planned classroom practices in order for students to have the necessary opportunities to make connections between key concepts across a discipline. Otherwise, the activity can fall into unstructured chaos with no purpose or clear understanding of curricular meaning of the activity at hand.

The same caution is true about cooperative small group learning, a key strategy of inquiry-based instruction. Though initially conceived of by social psychologists to help seed interpersonal friendships across races following desegregation [2], small groups of students working together showed instructional benefits, too. Cohen defines cooperative grouping as "students working together in a group small enough that everyone can participate on a collective task that has been clearly assigned" [8]. Studies overwhelmingly show that there are significant learning benefits for students working on activities in small groups as opposed to activities when students work individually [4,14]. Even on later individual assessments, students working in cooperative groups outperform students who learned the same material individually. But as with any element of inquiry, providing explicit structure to the cooperative learning activity is necessary to avoid devolving into lost instructional time. The teacher's role in facilitating the assignment of group roles, collaboration-worthy tasks, modes of communication, facilitating discussions through critical thinking and questioning, and individual accountability in group settings are essential elements for thriving cooperative groups.

Many domain experts may take exception to an inquiry-based model and note that they themselves learn effectively with direct instruction. This view is not necessarily at odds with inquiry-based learning. Studies show that lectures can be effective for people who have previously engaged in an activity and have an established understanding of the conceptual connections within a domain. But, sole direct instruction does not seem to bolster student learning as does the incorporation of inquiry [9].

6. RESEARCH ON STEM PROFESSIONAL DEVELOPMENT

As noted earlier in the article, settings of PD are sites of learning and teaching, highlighting the need for well-designed PD experiences that model and build the types of inquiry-based instruction encouraged for the classroom. PD is most effective when it is not in isolation, but rather, rooted in the realities of what teachers can implement in their classrooms. Disparities between PD and what teachers can do in their classroom decrease the effectiveness of the PD. In a nationwide survey, teachers reported that their knowledge and skills grew and their practice changed when they received PD that was coherent, *aligned with curriculum, focused on content knowledge, and involved active learning* [11].

This type of PD requires sustained periods of time. Two studies demonstrated that teachers who attended 80 or more hours of PD in inquiry-based science during the previous year were more likely to use this instructional method than teachers who attended fewer hours [11]. Another study examining the correlation between sustained PD and student achievement found that the largest positive effects were for programs offering between 30-100 hours and spread out over 6-12 months. This large-scale study also found that PDs that are based on active learning, include content knowledge, and have a strong coherence to broader teaching context develops teacher knowledge and skills, which in turn leads to substantial changes in teaching practice. Clearly, this research demonstrates that the "drive-by workshop" approach to transformative PD is not sufficient for transforming teaching practices.

In *Designing Professional Development for Teachers of Science and Mathematics* [15], Loucks-Horsley and colleagues suggest that it is fruitful to examine PD as a dynamic decision-making process, rather than as a static set of models. They propose that first articulating a common vision for the PD, then understanding the unique resources and conditions facing the local site, and finally identifying critical issues to be aware of should be done before designing particular strategies or experiences to enhance teacher learning and practice. This is an iterative process that acknowledges evolving needs, so each design cycle is followed by reflection and revision by the professional developers.

In their review of effective teaching, learning, and PD in STEM disciplines, Loucks-Horsley and colleagues identify the following features of effective PD:

- PD must have students and student learning at the core of the PD, where all students are considered so that issues of equity and access are addressed from the beginning.
- PD should include the active involvement of those with experience in teaching the subject-area successfully in high school: those who understand teaching, pedagogy, and pedagogical content knowledge.
- PD must be focused on pedagogical content knowledge, but reinforce and leverage knowledge that teachers already have; it should be designed so that teachers with different backgrounds and abilities can succeed and flourish.
- PD takes time. Because of the focus on pedagogy and teaching, face-to-face meetings with PD participants are essential, and should not be devoted solely to disseminating content.
- PD should be designed to nurture leaders so that participants see a path to professional growth as well as development.
- PD should help build communities of learners and build them locally when possible. This requires an understanding of local issues, constraints, and opportunities.

These are part of the guiding principles of our ECS PD model.

7. RESEARCH ON ECS PD IMPACT

Below we present a research analysis of teacher reflections about their ECS PD experience and the connections they see between their PD experiences and changes in their teaching practice. These reflections were gathered through end-of-year teacher surveys, teacher interviews, and PD evaluations. We also have conducted a full year of extensive classroom observations. These teacher reflections have been "triangulated" with our analysis of classroom observations and interviews that we are currently finalizing.

7.1 Research Process

During the 2012-13 school year, 31 LAUSD ECS teachers actively participated in the ECS program across 25 schools in Los Angeles County. They taught between one to four ECS classes each for a total of approximately 57 classes, over 2000 students. The majority of students qualify for "free and reduced lunch," (an indicator of low-income poverty levels) and the 2012-13 ECS student enrollment demographics are 45% females, 81% Latino, and 6% African American. These percentages closely mirror the District population demographics.

Of these, 23 teachers completed at least some portion of an end-of year survey. Participants range from first year ECS teachers to those with four years of experience teaching ECS. All of the participants are LAUSD teachers, except for one who is now working in another school district within the county.

7.2 Perceived Utility of ECS PD

As shown in Table 1, 91% of the teacher respondents categorized the ECS PD sessions as very useful (74%) or useful (17%). Teachers also rated the value of the ECS community, specifically networking with colleagues, as very useful (65%) and useful (26%).

Table 1. Teachers' perceived utility of ECS activities (n=22)

	Not useful at all # (%)	Somewhat useful	Useful	Very useful
ECS PD sessions	0	1 (4%)	4 (17%)	17 (74%)
Networking with colleagues	0	1 (4%)	6 (26%)	15 (65%)

7.3 Teacher Changes in Practice

On the end-of-year survey, teachers were asked to share what first came to mind when asked how they have changed, if at all, in their practice after participating in ECS. Almost all respondents agreed or agreed strongly with the statement – *I have become more skilled in using inquiry-based strategies by participating in ECS.* An example of a teachers' elaboration of this is:

> *Having faith in my students ability, not volunteering the answer, and empowering my students to trust their reasoning and unique way of solving problems is the major change in my teaching.*

Teachers also shared their new understanding of the connection between the curriculum, pedagogy, and equitable teaching practices. One teacher wrote:

> *This [ECS PD] also made me reexamine how I teach my classes. The course begins with activities that are accessible to all yet build the necessary CS concepts. The activities gave students a way to learn and at the same time get over crippling ideas that they cannot be successful in studying CS.*

Another teacher reflected further on the ties between equity and inquiry teaching practices:

> *My thinking has changed tremendously towards "equity in CS." I used to think by just providing the proper equipment, classroom, textbooks, lesson material, lecturing, available at off hours and having students work independently I was providing plenty of equity. After this workshop, I realized I really never provided equity to ALL students. Today my thinking has changed, I saw collaboration in action and it can really work, my outlook has changed towards the concept and I will be actively participating, planning and promoting. I have a lot of work to do by learning to be a good facilitator and begin practicing on my inquiry techniques.*

All except two agreed or agreed strongly with the statement – *I know more about computer science concepts as a result of participating in ECS.* This is very important finding as we recognize the challenge teachers face in teaching a new curriculum and particularly new content. In ECS PD's, CS content is happening all the time, in the context of learning and working with inquiry and equitable teaching practices.

Teachers also wrote about gaining confidence in their teaching, gaining knowledge and skill in particular aspects of the CS curriculum and getting a better sense of the "big picture." Accompanying their own gain in confidence was a gain in confidence in their students' ability to tackle problems. As shown in Table 2, all but one teacher felt that the ECS PD had a large and/or some impact on their teaching of the three pillars of ECS (CS content, inquiry and equity).

Table 2. Perceived impact of ECS program on practice

	Not sure	No impact	Some impact	Large impact
Inquiry-based instruction	0	1 (4%)	9 (39%)	11 (48%)
CS content knowledge	0	1(4%)	8 (35%)	13 (57%)
Equity-based instruction	0	1 (4%)	11 (48%)	9 (39%)

ECS teacher Leslie Aaronson, in her personal blog describes her own change of practice that was prompted by working in the ECS program [1]. Beginning with the opening line " I have a secret" Aronson reveals that she is "no longer the most knowledgeable person in her classroom." She then explains:

> *My confidence in inquiry grew this past year when I started teaching Exploring Computer Science which stresses inquiry as one of the three major components of teaching the curriculum. It is also stressed when I go to professional developments about developing critical thinking and using project based learning. I have found that now that I don't*

easily have the answers I am much stronger at asking questions in order to get the students to think and begin to ask more questions on their own.

Maybe that is my secret.

Now, instead of feeling insecure when I don't know something, I celebrate the thinking and inquiry coming from the students. "Yes, that is a good question," I respond. "How can you find out the answer? Where would you look? What keywords would you use to research it? Have you asked other people in the room if they have found a solution?" Now they are learning to trust themselves to find the answers. They know that questions are great and solutions are there for them to figure out on their own. And that is what I call successful learning.

In fact, it is the teaching of CS content through these inquiry and equity practices that engage students with the real learning of computer science.

8. CONCLUSION

Because our ECS curriculum is more than "notes on a page," and is integrally linked to inquiry instruction and commitment to equitable practices, we have committed to partnering with and supporting projects that have adopted the ECS program---*both* curriculum and PD model. The traditional curriculum and methods of teaching computer science have left too many students feeling that computer science is "not for me." As a community we must learn from the extensive body of educational research about teaching, learning, and PD planning. Broadening participation in computing will require CS teacher professional learning communities, and teachers who focus intensely on new forms of pedagogy and classroom norms.

By developing this ECS computer science teacher PD and learning community model, we are working to deepen and strengthen the national high school college preparatory infrastructure for computer science education and broadening participation in computing. But, we believe that the importance of our work extends beyond computer science. In line with this year's SIGCSE theme, "Leveraging Computing to Change Education", the issues we address are at the center of our country's educational crisis: what is effective teaching, how to deepen students' critical thinking, what is the importance of PD, what is the research behind effective models, and very importantly, how do we broaden participation and engagement in computing and in all of education.

9. ACKNOWLEDGEMENTS

We acknowledge the contributions of our evaluation team from UCLA CRESST, specifically Christine Ong and Kevin Binning. We also gratefully acknowledge the "Broadening Participation in Computing" program of the National Science Foundation for funding this research.

10. REFERENCES

[1] Aaronson, L. 2013. *You don't need to be an expert.* Weblog. Retrieved September 1, 2013 from http://leslieaaronson.weebly.com/1/category/all/1.html

[2] Aronson, E. and Bridgeman, D. 1979. Jigsaw groups and the desegregated classroom: In pursuit of common goals. *Personality and Social Psychology Bulletin*, 5, 4, 438-466.

[3] Ball, D. L. 1993. With an Eye on the Mathematical Horizon: Dilemmas of Teaching Elementary School Mathematics. *The Elementary School Journal*, 93, 4, 373-397.

[4] Barron, B. and Darling-Hammond, L. 2008. *Teaching for meaningful learning.* Jossey Bass, San Francisco, CA.

[5] Barton, A. C. and Tan, E. 2010. We be burnin'! Agency, identity, and science learning. *The Journal of the Learning Sciences*, 19, 2, 187-229.

[6] Boaler, J. 2008. Creating mathematical futures through an equitable teaching approach. *Teachers College Press*, 33, 4, 239-258.

[7] Bransford, J., Brown, A. L. and Cocking, R. R. 1999. *How people learn: Brain, mind, experience, and school.* National Academy Press, Washington, D.C.

[8] Cohen, E. G. Restructuring the classroom: Conditions for productive small groups. 1994. *Review of Educational Research*, 64, 1-35.

[9] Darling-Hammond, L. 2008. *Powerful learning: What we know about teaching for understanding.* Jossey-Bass, San Francisco, CA.

[10] Darling-Hammond, L. and Bransford, J. 2007. *Preparing teachers for a changing world: What teachers should learn and be able to do.* Jossey-Bass, San Francisco, CA.

[11] Darling-Hammond, L. and Richardson, N. 2009. Teacher learning: What matters. *Educational Leadership*, 66, 5, 46-53.

[12] Goode, J. and Chapman, G. 2008. *Exploring computer science.* Computer Science Equity Alliance, Los Angeles, CA.

[13] Howard, T. 2010. *Why race and culture matter in schools.* Teachers College Press, NY.

[14] Johnson, D. W. and Johnson, R. T. 1989. *Cooperation and competition: Theory and research.* Interaction Book Company, Edina, MN.

[15] Loucks-Horsley, S., Stiles, K. E., Mundry, S., Love, N. and Hewson, P. W. 2010. *Designing professional development for teachers of science and mathematics.* Corwin Pr, Thousand Oaks, CA.

[16] Margolis, J., Estrella, R., Goode, J., Holme, J. J. and Nao, K. 2008. *Stuck in the shallow end: Education, race, and computing.* MIT Press, Cambridge, MA.

[17] McLaughlin, M. W. and Talbert, J. E. 2001. *Professional communities and the work of high school teaching.* University of Chicago Press, Chicago, IL.

[18] National Research Council. 2000. *Inquiry and the National Science Education Standards: A guide for teaching and learning.* National Academies Press, Washington, DC.

[19] Stein, M. K., Smith, M. S. and Silver, E. A. 1999. The development of professional developers: Learning to assist teachers in new settings in new ways. *Harvard Educational Review*, 69, 3, 237-270.

[20] Yoon, K. S., Duncan, T., Lee, S. W. Y., Scarloss, B. and Shapley, K. L. 2007. *Reviewing the evidence on how teacher professional development affects student achievement.* Institution of Education Sciences, Washington, DC.

Sneaking In Through The Back Door: Introducing K-12 Teachers to Robot Programming

Jennifer S. Kay
Computer Science Department
Rowan University
Glassboro, NJ 08028
+1 (856) 256-4593
kay@rowan.edu

Janet G. Moss
Teacher Education Department
Rowan University
Glassboro, NJ 08028
+1 (856) 256-4500 x3806
moss@rowan.edu

Shelly Engelman
The Findings Group
1201 Clairmont Road
Decatur, GA 30030
+1 (404) 633-9091
shelly@thefindingsgroup.com

Tom McKlin
The Findings Group
1201 Clairmont Road
Decatur, GA 30030
+1 (404) 633-9091
tom@thefindingsgroup.com

ABSTRACT

Few question the need to offer excellent programs in computer science at the Bachelors and Graduate Levels. But computer science is not just for computer scientists! An understanding of key computer science concepts is essential to comprehending the underpinnings of what drives much of the culture and environment that students will encounter upon graduation. Unfortunately, in the United States most state, regional, and national K-12 standards do not include computer science among the core competencies required of all students.

However, careful study reveals many opportunities to satisfy mandatory non-computer-science standards while simultaneously teaching important concepts in computer science. This paper begins with an overview of these standards and suggests that educational robotics could be incorporated into K-12 curricula to satisfy these standards.

But even if robots truly are a magic panacea, most K-12 teachers have never used them. The remainder of this paper discusses a pair of 3 day workshops we offered in the summers of 2011 and 2012 which were designed to introduce K-12 teachers with no prior programming experience to LEGO robot programming. We discuss the content of the workshops, how teachers' skills and attitudes changed as a result of these workshops, and how teachers used the material they learned in their schools.

SIGCSE'14, March 5–8, 2014, Atlanta, Georgia, USA.

ACM 978-1-4503-2605-6/14/03…$15.00.
http://dx.doi.org/10.1145/2538862.2538972

Categories and Subject Descriptors

K.3.2 [**Computers and Education**]: Computer and Information Science Education – *accreditation, computer science education, curriculum, literacy.*

General Terms

Experimentation, Standardization, Languages.

Keywords

Computer Science Education, K-12 Education, Non-majors, Education Standards, Educational Robotics.

1. INTRODUCTION

There is a clear need in the United States for well-trained computer scientists. Official reports from bodies such as the U.S. Bureau of Labor Statistics project that many new computer science related jobs will be created at a much faster than average rate in the next decade,[6] and few question the need to offer excellent computer science programs at the Bachelors and Graduate levels.

But computer science is not just for computer scientists! An understanding of key computer science concepts is essential to comprehending the underpinnings of what drives much of the culture and environment that students will encounter upon graduation. Many prominent educators argue that computer science skills should be considered a core competency for today's students. For example, Wing [27] asserts that "computational thinking is a fundamental skill for everyone, not just for computer scientists. To reading, writing, and arithmetic, we should add computational thinking to every child's analytical ability." Forte and Guzdial [11] go even further, arguing that a basic understanding of programming is an important part of all students' computational literacy. Thus, it is critical that we bring computer science concepts into K-12 classrooms.

Unfortunately, there are many barriers to doing so. Very few teacher education programs have the capacity or curriculum to adequately train pre-service teachers to teach computer science at the K-12 level. [26] There is also a need for more professional development opportunities for in-service computer science teachers. [26] Furthermore, the education standards for subjects like computer science are not as mature as those for the more traditional STEM areas such as mathematics, biology, chemistry, and physics. [13] Indeed, only 9 states allow computer science courses to count as a required math or science high school graduation credit and not one state requires any computer science credits for high school graduation. [26] While there is a major movement in computer science to highlight this deficiency [26] and create computer science standards, [8] there remains a lot of work to be done.

Even if it were possible to sidestep all of these barriers, an almost insurmountable hurdle remains: this material is not a required part of most curricula. Those K-12 standards mandated by a state's department of education are a key part of the everyday operation of schools. Such standards often leave teachers struggling to cover all of the required material with little freedom to introduce anything beyond the explicit requirements. [19] Of course there is always the option of offering extra-curricular programs that teach computer science concepts, but many of those students who choose to participate may very well be the same ones who would choose to take computer science electives during the school day.

Clearly our goal should be to make computer science a part of <u>every</u> student's education. In the absence of standards mandating that computer science is part of K-12 and undergraduate education, we need to find ways to "sneak" computer science into other subjects.

There is no indication that this will happen without a serious push from the CS Education community. We must recognize the importance of national and state education standards and begin to understand them. As we study the standards, we can identify specific areas which seem ripe for integrating computer science concepts and for which we may be able to offer engaging contexts to support learning. At the same time, we need to provide a means to introduce the CS content to K-12 educators and work with them to find ways to incorporate the material into their lesson plans and instructional practice. Finally, we need to demonstrate to others that these new lesson plans that incorporate computer science are at least as good at teaching the standards as the original ones were.

This paper begins with an introduction to state, regional, and federal K-12 education requirements to make the case that there are opportunities to introduce computer science concepts within core curricular areas. We then discuss a pair of 3-day workshops we offered in the summers of 2011 and 2012 which were designed to introduce K-12 teachers with no prior programming experience to LEGO robot programming. We discuss the content of the workshops, how teachers' skills and attitudes changed as a result of the workshops, and look at how those teachers who participated in our workshops subsequently used the material they learned in and outside of their classrooms.

2. SATISFYING K-12 REQUIREMENTS WITH COMPUTER SCIENCE

2.1 The Lack of Computer Science Standards

At the K-12 level, state departments of education are responsible for establishing standards for what students should learn throughout their school years. Two-thirds of states in the U.S. have few computer science standards at the secondary school level, and the majority of states do not treat computer science as part of high school students' core education, but rather simply as electives. [26]

2.2 The Common Core Mathematics Standard

2.2.1 Overview

The fact that states are responsible for establishing their own standards can, of course, result in significant differences in what students learn between states. While attempts to establish national standards in some subjects have been quite controversial [20] [25], the vast majority of states [4] have joined the "Common Core State Standards Initiative" [2] which has developed national standards for English Language Arts and Mathematics. If Computer Science is to have any hope of becoming relevant in K-12, then it is essential that the CS community begin to understand and pay attention to these standards.

While the Common Core Mathematics Standards are available in printed form [1], the best way for a novice to become familiar with them is by browsing through them on the web site. [3]

The Common Core describes standards that specify both concepts students are expected to understand as well as specific skills students should achieve. Related standards are grouped together to form *clusters*, and related clusters form *domains*. Domains, clusters, and standards are described year-by-year for students from K-8. At the high school level the domains, clusters, and standards are divided by subject area, including standards that all students should know to be prepared to enter college and the workforce, as well as additional advanced topics that some students may study.

As soon as one begins to examine the Common Core Math Standard with an eye towards introducing computer science topics into the curriculum, a myriad of possibilities emerge. Here we offer one example from the seventh grade standard to provide those unfamiliar with this standard an introduction to their form.

The seventh grade Common Core Math Standard specifies five domains: "ratios & proportional relationships," "the number system," "expressions & equations," "geometry," and "statistics & probability." The geometry domain includes two clusters: "draw, construct, and describe geometrical figures and describe the relationships between them," and "solve real-life and mathematical problems involving angle measure, area, surface area, and volume." The latter cluster consists of three standards, including 7.G.5, "Use facts about supplementary, complementary, vertical, and adjacent angles in a multi-step problem to write and solve simple equations for an unknown angle in a figure."

2.2.2 Satisfying the Common Core Math Standard with Computer Science Topics

We imagine that upon reading standard 7.G.5 above you may have come up with your own way to meet that standard while simultaneously integrating computer science topics. We have found the area of educational robotics to be both popular and valuable in both our work with K-12 teachers and non-computer science-major undergraduates and so our first thoughts focused on this domain. For example, seventh grade teachers familiar with educational robotics could work with their students to compute the unknown angles in a complex figure. Students could then write simple programs to have a robot trace out the figure to demonstrate that their computation was accurate.

2.3 State Standards

Of course, beyond the Common Core each state establishes its own standards in other disciplines. Again, a careful analysis of these standards can provide a wealth of potential avenues that might be used to introduce computer science to students. For example, the authors' home state of New Jersey includes Core Curriculum Content Standards in both Science and Technology that provide additional opportunities for creative curricula.

2.4 Looking to the Future: Additional Standards with the Potential for Significant National Impact

Four additional groups of standards are worth noting.

An attempt to establish national science standards is currently underway: the final version of the Next Generation Science Standards (NGSS) [22] was released in April 2013 [12]. As of September 2013 seven states had adopted these standards [9] The NGSS standards include standards for Physical Sciences (PS), Life Sciences (LS), Earth & Space Sciences (ESS), and Engineering, Technology, & Applications of Science (ETS). [10] Unfortunately, Computer Science is noticeably absent, even from the ETS standards, students are only expected to be able to "Use a computer simulation to model the impact of proposed solutions…" rather than incorporate any Computer Science skills [14]

The Partnership for 21st Century Skills [24] encourages states to receive the P21 Leadership designation by showing their commitment to incorporate the "three Rs and four Cs (critical thinking & problem solving, communication, collaboration, and creativity & innovation)" into their own standards. Sixteen states are currently affiliated with the partnership. [23]

Another widely recognized advocacy group is the International Society for Technology in Education (ISTE) [15] which has established sets of National Education Technology Standards for both students and educators. [16] While ISTE now has a set of standards for Computer Science *Educators* [17] and has begun to acknowledge the importance of computational thinking [5], the ISTE standards for students still focus on the use of technology rather than an understanding of underlying computer science concepts. [21]

Finally, the Computer Science Teachers Association [7] actively works to develop standards for K-12 Computer Science. [8] Hopefully over time their standards will be adopted at both the state and national levels.

3. INTRODUCING CURRENT K-12 TEACHERS TO ROBOT PROGRAMMING

As mentioned above, we believe that there are many opportunities to make use of robots within the K-12 classroom to teach core requirements while simultaneously introducing students to fundamental computer science topics. Teachers routinely make use of manipulatives in their classrooms to support hands-on learning, from household objects like toothpicks and coins to specialized tools such as molecular model sets and springs. In this context, the robot can be seen as simply a digital manipulative.

But most K-12 teachers have little or no experience with computer science and programming, let alone robotics. It is our belief that anyone qualified to teach STEM (Science, Technology, Engineering, and Math) subjects at the middle and secondary school level is highly capable of learning the basics of programming. However we are also very cognizant of the fact that many skilled math and science teachers have a fear of all things computer science – unfortunately we've heard statements like "computers just don't like me" all too often.

Thus, we decided to investigate whether a short workshop on robot programming for current middle school teachers might be sufficient to achieve two equally essential goals: first, to provide them with sufficient content knowledge in robot programming to be able to solve problems and design activities, and second, to ensure that they had sufficient confidence in their own ability to be comfortable with the idea of introducing robotics to their students. The remainder of this paper presents a brief overview of a 3-day workshop we ran first in June 2011 and then again (with minimal modifications) in June 2012 and the impact of these workshops on the teachers involved and their students.

4. WORKSHOP OVERVIEW

Our target audience was middle school teachers with no prior programming experience. We chose to introduce these teachers to the LEGO Mindstorms NXT robot for a number of very practical reasons:

- LEGO robots are fairly robust, and thus appropriate for a school environment.
- The standard kits include several interesting (and surprisingly good) sensors.
- The NXT-G programming language is a simple graphical blocks-based language that virtually eliminates the potential for syntax errors. It also seems less "intimidating" than more traditional text-based languages.

We took great care from the very beginning to emphasize to teachers that they would not be overwhelmed by our workshop. All of our literature emphasized that teachers would be learning a visual programming language and that no prior programming experience was required.

Because we anticipated that the majority of our teachers would not necessarily see a specific need for computer science in their curricula, we wanted to give them a clear vision of how they might use this material beyond the classroom. Thus we titled the program "Start Your Own Robotics Club: Robot Programming for Absolute Beginners" and included material on the FIRST LEGO League (FLL) Robotics program for 9 to 14-year-olds. Our hope was that our workshop would provide them with the confidence and skills to start FLL clubs at their schools, and that success with extra-curricular activities might motivate them to find ways to incorporate the robots into their regular math curriculum.

The workshop introduced teachers to each of the five sensors included with the NXT (sound, touch, light, and ultrasonic), and included lessons on simple outputs (displaying pictures and text on the NXT's small LCD screen and controlling motors). Key programming concepts introduced included loops, event handling, conditionals, functions, and variables.

Each workshop included roughly 20 participants and thanks to a generous grant from Google's CS4HS program each participant was given a full LEGO NXT robot kit to bring back with them to their school at the conclusion of the program. A more detailed description of the workshops can be found in [18].

5. EVALUATING THE WORKSHOPS

We advertised our workshops as appropriate for teachers of grades 4-8, though both workshops actually attracted teachers of grades 4-12.

5.1 The 2011 Workshop Survey

The 2011 workshop included 20 teachers, 19 of whom completed our exit survey. 89% of these teachers had little or no programming experience before attending the workshop. Our evaluation of the 2011 workshop was quite informal and very limited, but we were very encouraged by the teachers' change in confidence over the course of the workshop:

"Prior to taking this class how confident were you that YOU would be able to learn to program a robot?" Result: 2.68 on a scale of 1 ("Not at all confident") to 5 ("Very confident")

"Now that the workshop is over, how has your confidence changed?" Result: 4.21 on a scale of 1 ("Much less confident") to 5 ("Much more confident").

5.2 The 2012 Workshop Survey

The 2012 workshop included 24 participants: 22 teachers and 2 individuals with Bachelor degrees in a field other than teaching who were in the process of getting teaching certification. 22 of the participants filled out both a pre- and post-workshop questionnaire. 95% reported that they had little or no programming experience prior to our workshop. A more thorough evaluation plan and analysis of the survey data from this workshop enabled us to demonstrate the dramatic impact that such a workshop can have on teachers' confidence and instructional practice:

- As a result of the workshop, participants showed a statistically significant (p<.01) increase in their reported confidence in both learning and teaching programming. After the workshop, 100% of participants indicated that they were more confident in the abovementioned areas (see Table 1).
- Participants also reported that their teaching efficacy – beliefs in their ability to facilitate learning in STEM – had statistically significantly (p<.05) increased from before to after the workshop. Specifically, as a result of the workshop, significantly more participants indicated that they have the necessary skills to teach STEM, would invite a principal to evaluate their STEM teaching, feel comfortable explaining why STEM experiments work, and feel that they have the skills to teach STEM effectively.
- Statistically significant (p<.01) increases in knowledge and skills in LEGO robot programming were reported by teachers from before to after the workshop. Before the workshop, over 70% of teachers considered themselves as "novices" in programming; after the workshop, over 90% of teachers reported that they perceived themselves as being competent or skilled in programming.
- Results from the content knowledge assessment administered to participants before and after the workshop suggest that programming knowledge was enhanced as a result of the workshop. Overall, this provides measurable evidence that participants' knowledge objectively increased from pre to post (see Figure 1.

Table 1. Confidence, Pre/Post Analysis

	Pre/ Post	n	Mean	Paired Samples t-test	Not at all Confident/ Much less confident (1)	Somewhat confident/ Somewhat less confident (2)	Neutral/ Remained the same (3)	Quite confident/ Somewhat more confident (4)	Extremely confident/ Much more confident (5)
1. At the beginning of the workshop, we asked you about your confidence in your own ability to **LEARN** robot programming. Now that the workshop is over, how has your confidence changed?	Pre	22	3.73	.008**	5%	14%	9%	50%	23%
	Post	21	4.48		0%	0%	5%	43%	52%
2. At the beginning of the workshop, we asked you about your confidence in your ability to **TEACH YOUR STUDENTS** robot programming. Now that the workshop is over, how has your confidence changed?	Pre	22	3.41	.000**	0%	32%	18%	27%	23%
	Post	21	4.52		0%	0%	0%	48%	52%

Note. **p<.01, *p<.05, †<.10 (approaching significance)

Figure 1. Content Knowledge Pre/Post Analysis by Question

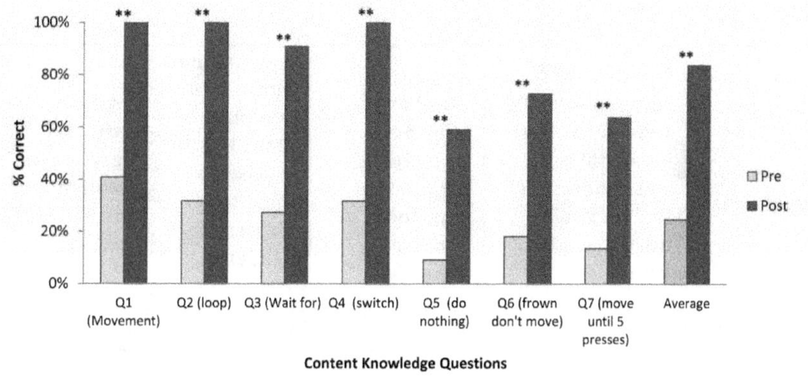

Note. **p<.01, *p<.05, †<.10 (approaching significance); Teachers, n=22

5.3 Follow-up Surveys: Impact in Schools

In March 2012 (approximately 9 months after our first workshop) and then again in January 2013 (approximately 19 months after our first workshop and 7 months after our second) we sent email to *all* of our workshop participants asking them to complete an online survey. We asked teachers to let us know if they had used (or planned to use) the materials in their schools that academic year and if so:

- How many students had been exposed to the material so far in and outside of the classroom that academic year
- How many additional students they anticipated exposing during the remainder of the academic year
- How many non-students they had exposed to the material.[1]

The results of these surveys are summarized in Table 2.

6. CONCLUSION

While it may be several years before state, regional, and national education standards mandate computer science for all students, careful study of existing standards reveals many opportunities to use educational robotics to introduce computer science concepts to K-12 students. Furthermore our workshop data indicates that current teachers with no prior programming experience are able to learn the basics of robot programming and share their knowledge with their students. While we are certainly not trying to argue that our workshop participants are now fully qualified to bring the full wealth of computer science concepts into their classrooms, our results suggest that it is possible to improve teachers' computer science confidence and skills in a way that can benefit students. Our post-workshop surveys indicate that many of these teachers are sharing material not only with their own students but with other teachers and administrators. As teachers begin to integrate computer science into their own curricula, hopefully their approaches will be adopted by other teachers in their schools. Perhaps we can work from the bottom up to create a groundswell of support for computer science education in K-12 which will encourage large-scale adoption of computer science K-12 standards.

Our own work continues; in the fall of 2013 we are offering a free online version of our workshop which has attracted hundreds of participants from around the globe. We eagerly await data from this course to try and begin to understand who might be attracted to this massively open online course (MOOC) format, the effectiveness of the course (particularly unique in light of the fact that it has a significant hardware component), and how participants plan to use what they have learned.

7. ACKNOWLEDGEMENTS

This work was made possible thanks to generous grants from Google's CS4HS program.

8. REFERENCES

[1] "Common Core State Standards for Mathematics," http://www.corestandards.org/assets/CCSSI_Math%20Standards.pdf, accessed May 2012.

[2] "Common Core State Standards Initiative | Home," http://www.corestandards.org/, accessed May 2012.

[3] "Common Core State Standards Initiative | The Standards | Mathematics," http://www.corestandards.org/the-standards/mathematics, accessed May 2012.

[4] "Common Core State Standards Initiative | In the States," http://www.corestandards.org/in-the-states, accessed May 2012.

[5] "Computational Thinking," http://www.iste.org/learn/computational-thinking, accessed November 2013.

[6] "Computer and Information Technology Occupations: Occupational Outlook Handbook: U.S. Bureau of Labor Statistics," http://www.bls.gov/ooh/computer-and-information-technology/home, accessed May 2012.

[7] "Computer Science Teachers Association," http://csta.acm.org, accessed May 2012.

[1] We asked respondents to describe the non-students who had been exposed to the material. In most cases participants reported exposing the material to other teachers and school administrators, but in the 2013 survey one participant reported exposing the material to a group of 75 people consisting of parents and board of education members, and another reported exposing the material to a group of 10 people including assistant coaches, mentors, and professional engineers.

Table 2. Follow-up Surveys (March 2012 & January 2013)

Workshop Attended	Academic Year Studied	Total number of respondents	Number of respondents who reported using or planning to use material in their schools during academic year	Approximate number of students already exposed in classroom in academic year	Approximate number of students already exposed outside of classroom in academic year	Additional student exposures anticipated in academic year	Approximate number of non-student exposures in academic year
2011	2011/2012	11	8	215	67	72	14
2011	2012/2013	10	7	320	59	120	134[1]
2012	2012/2013	12	11	340	73	459	19

[8] "Computer Science Teachers Association – CSTA K-12 Standards," http://csta.acm.org/Curriculum/sub/K12Standards.html, accessed April 2012.

[9] Delaware 7th State to Adopt NGSS | Next Generation Science Standards, "http://www.nextgenscience.org/delaware-7th-state-adopt-ngss," accessed November 2013.

[10] "DCI Arrangements of Standards | Next Generation Science Standards," http://www.nextgenscience.org/search-standards-dci, accessed November 2013.

[11] Forte, A., and Guzdial, M., "Motivation and Nonmajors in Computer Science: Identifying Discrete Audiences for Introductory Courses," *IEEE Transactions on Education*, 48(2), 2005, pp. 248-253.

[12] "Frequently Asked Questions | Next Generation Science Standards," http://www.nextgenscience.org/frequently-asked-questions#3.5, accessed November 2013.

[13] Holdren, John P., Lander, Eric, Varmus, Harold, et. al., *Prepare and Inspire: K-12 Education in Science, Technology, Engineering, and Math (STEM) for America's Future*, Presidents Council of Advisors on Science and Technology, September 2010.

[14] "HS-ETS1 Engineering Design | Next Generation Science Standards," http://www.nextgenscience.org/hsets1-engineering-design, accessed November 2013.

[15] "ISTE | Membership, NETS Standards, Books, Journals and Professional Development for Teachers," http://www.iste.org/, accessed May 2012.

[16] "ISTE | NETS Standards," http://www.iste.org/standards.aspx, accessed November 2013.

[17] "ISTE Standards for Computer Science Educators," http://www.iste.org/standards/standards-for-computer-science-educators, accessed November 2013.

[18] Kay, Jennifer S., and Moss, Janet G., "Using Robots to Teach Programming to K-12 Teachers," *Proceedings of ASEE/IEEE Frontiers in Education Conference,* October 2012.

[19] Meier, Deborah, Kohn, Alfie, Darling-Hammond, Linda, Sizer, Theodore R., Wood, George, et al, *Many Children Left Behind: How the No Child Left Behind Act is Damaging Our Children and Our Schools*, Beacon Press, 2004.

[20] Nash, Gary B., and Dunn, Ross E., "National History Standards: Controversy and Commentary," *Social Studies Review* 34(2) 1995, pp. 4-12.

[21] "nets-s-standards-6.pdf," http://www.iste.org/docs/pdfs/nets-s-standards.pdf?sfvrsn=2, accessed November 2013.

[22] "Next Generation Science Standards," http://www.nextgenscience.org/, accessed November 2013.

[23] "Overview of State Leadership Initiative – The Partnership for 21st Century Skills," http://www.p21.org/state-initiatives/overview-of-state-work, accessed May 2012.

[24] "The Partnership for 21st Century Skills," http://www.p21.org/, accessed May 2012.

[25] Wilgoren, Jodi, "Politicized Scholars Put Evolution on the Defensive," *The New York Times,* August 21, 2005.

[26] Wilson, Cameron, Sudol, Leigh Ann, Stephenson, Chris, and Stehlik, Mark, *Running on Empty*, Association for Computing Machinery & Computer Science Teachers Association, 2010.

[27] Wing, Janet, "Viewpoint: Computational Thinking," *Communications of the ACM* Vol 49 (3) 2006, pp. 33-35.

Quantitative Correlation between Ability to Compute and Student Performance in a Primary School

Osvaldo Luiz de Oliveira
Faculty Campo Limpo Pta
R. Guatemala, 167, Jardim América
Campo Limpo Paulista, SP, Brazil
55 11 4812-9407
osvaldo@cc.faccamp.br

Maria do Carmo Nicoletti
Faculty Campo Limpo Pta & UFSCar
R. Guatemala, 167, Jardim América
Campo Limpo Paulista, SP, Brazil
55 11 4812-9400
carmo@cc.faccamp.br

Luis Mariano del Val Cura
Faculty Campo Limpo Pta
R. Guatemala, 167, Jardim América
Campo Limpo Paulista, SP, Brazil
55 11 4812-9400
delval@cc.faccamp.br

ABSTRACT
Many studies have provided qualitative arguments for the premise that the ability to compute is fundamental and therefore should be treated at all levels of education. This work presents a quantitative indication of the validity of this premise for primary school students. In order to precisely define what ability a student should have to use a model of computation to compute, this work reports an experimental study that shows a significant correlation between the student's ability to compute and his/her academic performance in a primary school.

Categories and Subject Descriptors
K.3.2 [**Computers and Education**]: Computer and Information Science Education - *Computer Science Education.*

Keywords
Computational Thinking, Computing Education, Reasoning, Model of Computation, Empirical Research.

1. INTRODUCTION
Recent studies suggest that the ability to compute is fundamental and is necessary for the development of many human activities [7, 8, 9, 11, 20]. For example, having observed a set of symptoms, a physician computes a diagnosis; having as basis the needs and different ways to occupy a space, an architect computes an architectural design; having evidence, facts, circumstances and laws, a lawyer computes a discourse for the defense or prosecution [11]. Even fundamental knowledge, such as reading, writing and performing arithmetic operations, may be described as computational processes. For instance, reading can be understood as computation with set of words, meanings, sentences and paragraphs to establish an interpretation for a discourse; writing can be understood as computation with set of facts, concepts, data, information, news, etc. to develop a text; and performing arithmetic operations can be understood as computation with set of numbers, operators and numerical theories to calculate quantities. In all these examples an intuitive notion of computation is present, even if people are not aware of it.

Assuming qualitative arguments as the premise that the ability to compute is basic and ubiquitous, researchers have considered how to revamp primary, middle and undergraduate courses by placing a major emphasis on computational concepts [7, 13, 15, 19]. This work investigates quantitatively the hypothesis that there is a correlation between the student's ability to compute and his/her academic performance in primary school. The empirical evidence that supports the proof of this hypothesis can be considered a quantitative indication of the validity of the above mentioned premise.

Since computing is associated with many activities and contexts, the term computation needs to be defined to avoid possible misunderstandings regarding the sense in which we use it in this study. As quoted below, Alfred Aho suggests to use the term computation along with a model of computation that has a clear and well defined semantics. *"Since computation refers to a process that is defined in terms of some underlying model of computation, we would achieve clearer communication if we made clear what the underlying model is. ... Computer Science already has a number of useful clearly defined models of computation whose behaviors and capabilities are well understood. We should use such models as part of any definition of the term computation."* [1, p. 2].

To gather empirical evidence to support the established hypothesis, this work proposes and develops a model of computation based on the Turing Machine model [16], which has been named DMM (Drawing Machine Model). To make DMM comprehensible to primary school students, the computation mechanism of the machine is graphically described rather than by traditional means i.e., using mathematical relations. Also, the DMM operates on a set of drawings on a grid paper instead of a binary alphabet on a tape, for example. The model has been used in an experiment to test and evaluate the student's ability to use it to compute. Statistical tools were employed to calculate the correlation between the test results and the students' academic performance in school. The remainder of this paper is organized as follows. Section 2 describes the basics of the DMM and defines precisely what ability students should have to use the model to compute. The conducted experiment to test the student's ability to use the model to compute is detailed in Section 3. Section 4 presents the results and Section 5 describes related work. Section 6 highlights the main conclusions, summarizes a few of our views on the work done and points out directions for further research.

SIGCSE'14, March 5–8, 2014, Atlanta, Georgia, USA.

http://dx.doi.org/10.1145/2538862.2538890

2. MODEL OF COMPUTATION AND STUDENT'S ABILITY TO COMPUTE

This section addresses the necessary ability a student should have to use a model of computation to compute. Section 2.1 proposes a model of computation appropriate for primary school students using the Turing Machine model as base. The ability that a student should have to use the model to compute is described in detail in Section 2.2.

2.1 DMM Model of Computation

The proposed model is based on the Turing Machine, a classic model of computation [16]. The Turing Machine model is simple and powerful enough to simulate any computational process and is very suitable for our purposes. However, the Turing Machine is a model of computation that operates on binary alphabets, states and a set of mathematical relations defined on these elements, and is not appropriate for primary school students. Therefore, we developed our own model of computation based on the Turing Machine concept. We use grid paper instead of a tape, drawings instead of a binary alphabet, a robot that can walk, read and draw in cells of grid paper instead of a recording and reading head, and programs described by graphical symbols instead of mathematical relations. The proposed model is equivalent to the Turing Machine in terms of the sets of accepted languages (computational power of expression) and is more suitable for our research subjects. Proof of equivalence between the models is beyond the scope of this work.

The machine of the DMM operates on a grid paper by interpreting a drawing-based language and producing a result. The machine receives as input a grid paper with drawings, transforms the drawings, and delivers as output a grid paper showing the changes made. Figure 1 shows a machine M that reverses the color (black or white) of the drawing it receives as input.

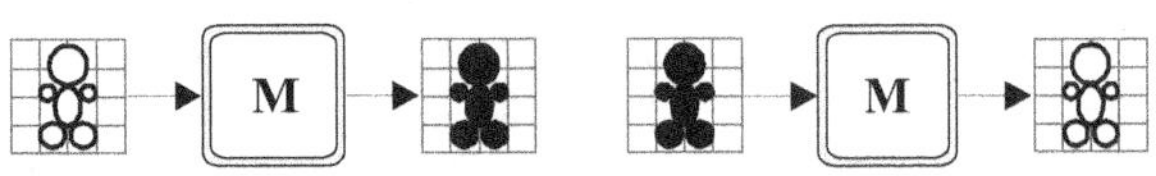

Figure 1. Computation by machine M, which reverses the color (black or white) of the drawing it receives as input.

The computation mechanism of a machine is defined by a procedure that uses and interprets a pictorial language defined by the symbols shown in Figure 2.

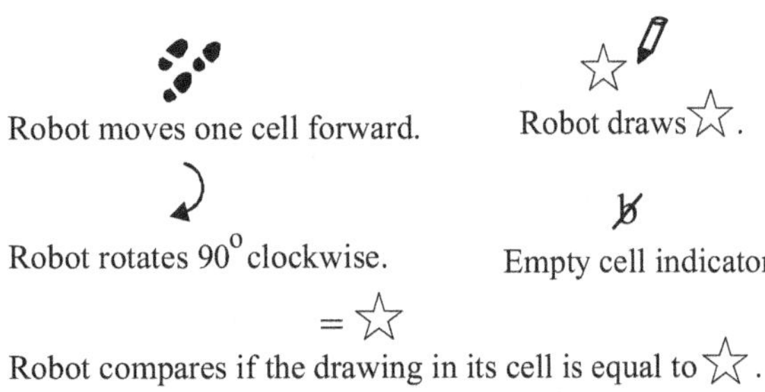

Figure 2. Symbols used to describe a machine computation mechanism.

As an example, Figure 3(a) shows the computation mechanism used by a machine to draw cupcakes. Figures 3(b)–(i) show the computation sequence for a grid paper divided into four cells; cupcakes are already drawn in the two lower cells. The final configuration shown in Figure 3(i) is the machine output.

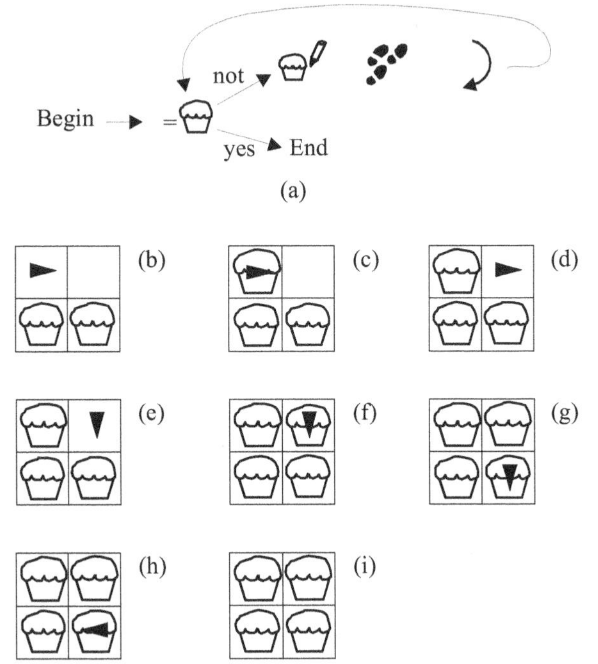

Figure 3. (a) Computation mechanism (program) used by a machine. (b) The robot always starts on the top left cell, pointing to the right. (c) The robot checks if it is on an empty cell and, if that is the case, draws a cupcake. (d) It moves forward one cell. (e) It rotates 90° clockwise. (f) A new cycle starts. The robot checks if it is on an empty cell and then draws a cupcake. (g) It moves forward one cell. (h) It rotates 90° clockwise. (i) It checks if it is on an empty cell; since it is not, the computation terminates. The configuration shown in (i) is the output of the machine.

2.2 Ability that a student should have to use the DMM

Algebraically, the computation performed by a machine that implements the DMM can be viewed as a function $f : D \rightarrow D$, where D is the plane drawing set. In this section, the concept of function will be used to detail the student's ability to use the DMM. The student's ability for using the DMM for solving a task can be approached as a conjoint of four main skills, namely:

- *Abstraction:* knowing elements of the domain of a function and their corresponding images, the student has to abstract what the function does. For example, using information about machine M inputs and outputs (Figure 1), the student has to abstract that M reverses the fill color (black or white) of the drawing given as input.
- *Calculation:* knowing what a function does, the student has to calculate the image for a given domain element. For example, knowing that the machine M reverses the fill color (black or white) of a drawing, the student has to calculate the output of the machine when it receives as input a drawing of a flower as the one presented in question 1 of the Appendix I.

- *Reading and Understanding*: knowing a function description presented in some language, the student has to read and understand what the function does. For example, knowing the computation mechanism used by the machine presented in the Figure 3(a), the student has to read and understand what the machine does.

- *Designing and Writing*: knowing what a function does, the student has to design and write a function description using some language. For example, knowing what the machine in Figure 3 draws cupcakes in empty cells of a grid paper divided into four cells, the student has to design and write the computation mechanism of such machine.

3. MATERIALS AND METHODS

3.1 Test for Student's Ability to Compute

Using the model of computation described in Section 2.1, we designed a test to measure the student's ability to use the model to compute. The test was previously validated in a pilot experiment applied to eight students who did not participate in the final experiment. The test was then refined and small problems fixed; its final version is presented in Appendix I.

The test consists of seven objective questions, each containing five alternatives. The test is divided into two parts. Part 1 (questions 1–5) evaluates the student's ability to abstract and calculate. Each question in this part has one or more input–output pairs for one or more machines. Using information about the input–output pairs, the student has to abstract what each machine does. Considering what has been abstracted and also, the other input (when that is the case), the student has to calculate the output produced by one or more machines. For example, for question 1 in Appendix I, from two input–output pairs for machine M, the student has to abstract that the machine reverses the color of the drawing received as input. Considering this abstraction and knowing that the machine gets as input the drawing of a flower, the student has to calculate what drawing the machine will deliver as output.

Part 2 (questions 6 and 7) assesses the student's ability to read, understand, design and write. Each question in this part offers a single input–output pair for a machine, so to abstract what the machine does is trivial. Knowing what the machine does and an incomplete computation mechanism, the student has to read and understand the incomplete computation mechanism, then design and write instructions to complete it. For example, for question 6 in Appendix I, knowing that the machine draws a face on an empty grid paper, the student has to design and write two instructions to complete the computation mechanism.

3.2 Subjects

A total of 81 students attending a primary school in Brazil participated in the survey (Table 1). The school offers primary education and participants were from grades 6, 7, 8 and 9. The number of participants represented 95% of the school population attending these grades.

3.3 Experimental Setup

At the beginning of an academic day, students individually answered the test questions in their classrooms. The evaluators did not interact with the students during the test. The test form described all instructions to be followed. The maximum time allowed for answering the test was 20 minutes. A score from 0 to 7, corresponding to the number of questions correctly answered, was assigned to each student.

Academic student's performance was measured as the overall mean obtained in three quarters of a year for Mathematics, Language, History, Geography and Science.

For each grade (class), a table containing both results per student, i.e., the test and the academic scores, was produced. Appendix II presents the table showing results of the sixth-grader students.

Table 1. Profile of the experiment participants.

Class (grade)	Gender, n (%)		Age, years		
	Female	Male	Range	Mean	Median
6	11 (52)	10 (48)	11–12	11	11
7	8 (42)	11 (58)	11–13	12	12
8	6 (27)	16 (73)	13–14	13	13
9	10 (53)	9 (47)	13–15	14	14

4. RESULTS AND DISCUSSION

For each class, the correlation between students test scores and student academic scores was analyzed. As a statistical measure for correlation, we use the Pearson product-moment correlation coefficient, also known as Pearson's r [10]. This coefficient is a measure of the linear correlation between two variables and is a real value between 0 (no systematic concordance) and 1 (perfect agreement).

To check the statistical significance of Pearson's r we used Student's t-test [10], for which a p-value ≤ 0.01 has been considered statistically significant. Table 2 lists values of Pearson's r for correlations between the test scores and the academic scores. Figure 4 shows the scatter plots of the obtained correlations.

Table 2. Pearson's r coefficient for correlation between test scores and academic scores.

Class	Pairs	Pearson's r	t	p-value
6	21	0.62 (strong)	3.41	0.002
7	19	0.55 (moderate)	2.71	0.01
8	22	0.62 (strong)	3.57	0.002
9	19	0.60 (strong)	3.12	0.006

The results show that there was significant ($p \leq 0.01$) correlation between the test scores and academic scores for all classes. There were strong (classes 6, 8, and 9) and moderate (class 7) correlations between the ability to compute, as measured by the proposed experiment, and student performance in the school surveyed. Next we discuss the meaning of these results taking into account the hypothesis of an existing correlation.

First, statistical evidence indicates that the hypothesis is true for the classes studied. The results motivate new experiments to verify the hypothesis considering other groups of students.

Second, correlations are a measure of the strength and direction of relation between two variables, but are not cause and effect relations. Our results suggest the existence of common elements between the ability to compute and the ability to understand subjects taught in school. It is possible that these common elements are specific to computing activity or then are based on the mental processes that support the activity of computing and learning in the school. Again, there is room for further investigations.

Third, the results also motivate to investigate whether activities designed to improve the ability of computing can positively affect students' performance at school.

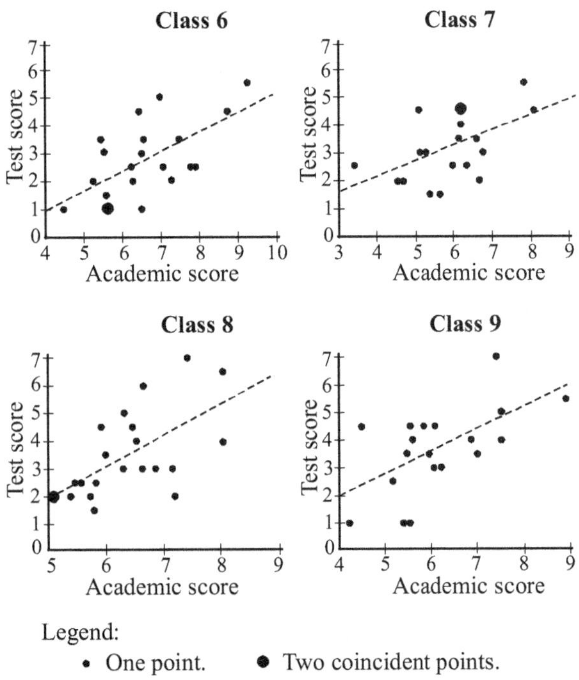

Figure 4. Scatter plots of the correlation between test and academic scores.

5. RELATED WORK

In the 1960s Papert pioneered the idea that children could use computers as a tool for thinking and learning [12]. The programming activity is at the center of the learning process conceived by Papert. In a seminal paper, Wing refers to various Computer Science artifacts, not only programming, and uses the term "computational thinking" stating that "*it represents a universally applicable attitude and skill set everyone, not just computer scientists, would be eager to learn and use*" [20, p. 33].

However Wing does not define the term "computational thinking", and this notion remains speculative. Subsequent studies investigated what computational thinking is [5] and what we can do with it [8, 9, 14]. Other works describe the introduction and enhancement of computational thinking activities and assessments in primary, middle and high schools [3, 7, 13, 15, 17, 19]. How to integrate computational thinking across disciplines is discussed in [2, 4, 18]. A Review of the State of discourse on computational thinking in K–12 education is presented in [6].

Oliveira's work [11] is more closely related to this study. Using a precise statement of what it is to compute, Oliveira found statistical evidence of a correlation between mental ability to compute and student performance in four undergraduate courses at a university. In common with Oliveira, we found a significant correlation between the ability to compute and student performance in a primary school. Our study differs from that by Oliveira as follows. (1) We worked with primary school students as research subjects. (2) We used a model of computation based on drawings on grid paper which, we believe, is closer to the universe of primary school students. (3) We measured academic performance as the average of scores obtained in three quarters of an year, while Oliveira used the mean of the scores obtained in the subjects already taken.

6. CONCLUSION

The main contribution of this work is an experimental verification of the existence of significant correlation between the ability to compute and the performance of primary school students. This contribution has value on its own and provides quantitative evidence that reinforces the validity of the premise that the ability to compute is fundamental.

The study also offers other contributions. The understanding that computation refers to a process that is defined in terms of some model of computation, and the positioning of the research subject as one who has the ability of use a model to compute, is sufficiently general to be employed in many other studies.

Based on a classical Turing Machine formalism, the proposed DMM uses drawings on grid paper, which makes it suitable for our research subjects and for other purposes.

The proposed test is small, since it has only seven questions, which can be answered in approximately 20 minutes. It is therefore easy to apply with a minimum disruption of the school daily routine. We also suspect that a longer test might introduce an undesirable greater interference in the routine of the school.

In relation to the DMM we intend next to enlarge its symbolic language by extending its set of basic actions (and corresponding symbols) to allow the representation of more complex procedural tasks.

Finally, the study reveals future directions for research, as described in Section 4.

7. ACKNOWLEDGMENTS

We would like to thank all subjects who volunteered for the experiment for their invaluable contribution to this work.

8. REFERENCES

[1] Aho, A. V. 2011. Computation and Computational Thinking. *Ubiquity* 2011, January (Jan. 2011), article no. 1. DOI=10.1145/1922681.1922682.

[2] Basawapatna, A., Repenning, L. and Lewis, C. 2013. The Simulation Creation Toolkit: An Initial Exploration Into Making Programming Accessible While Preserving Computational Thinking. In *Proceeding of the 44th ACM Technical Symposium on Computer Science Education* (Denver, Colorado, USA, March 06 - 09, 2013). SIGCSE'13.

ACM, New York, NY, 501-506. DOI=10.1145/2445196.2445346.

[3] Basawapatna, A, Repenning, A., Koh, K. H. and Nickerson, H. 2013. The Zones of Proximal Flow: Guiding Students Through a Space of Computational Thinking Skills and Challenges. In *Proceedings of the Ninth Annual International ACM Conference on International Computing Education Research* (San Diego, California, USA, August 12 - 14, 2013). ICER'13. ACM, New York, NY, 67-74. DOI= 10.1145/2493394.2493404.

[4] Bort, H. and Brylow, D. 2013. CS4 Impact: Measuring Computational Thinking Concepts Present in CS4HS Participant Lesson Plans. In *Proceeding of the 44th ACM Technical Symposium on Computer Science Education* (Denver, Colorado, USA, March 06 - 09, 2013). SIGCSE'13. ACM, New York, NY, 427-432. DOI=10.1145/2445196.2445323.

[5] Gouws, L., Bradshaw, K. and Wentworth, P. 2013. Computational Thinking in Educational Activities. In *Proceedings of the 18th Annual Joint Conference on Innovation and Technology in Computer Science Education* (Canterbury, England, UK, July 01 - 03, 2013). ITiCSE'13. ACM, New York, NY, 10-15. DOI=10.1145/2462476.2466518.

[6] Grover, S. and Pea, R. 2013. Computational Thinking in K–12: A Review of the State of the Field. *Educational Researcher* 42, 1, 38-43. DOI=10.3102/0013189X12463051.

[7] Guzdial, M. 2009. Teaching Computing to Everyone. *Communications of the ACM* 52, 5 (May 2009), 31-33. DOI=10.1145/1506409.1506420.

[8] Hu, C. 2011. Computational Thinking: what it might mean and what we might do about it. In *Proceedings of the 16th Annual Joint Conference on Innovation and Technology in Computer Science Education* (Darmstadt, Germany, June 27 - 29, 2011). ITiCSE'11. ACM, New York, NY, 223-227. DOI=10.1145/1999747.1999811.

[9] Lu, J. J. and Fletcher, G. H. L. 2009. Thinking about Computational Thinking. In *Proceedings of the 40th ACM Technical Symposium on Computer Science Education* (Chattannoga, Tennesse, USA, March 03 - 07, 2009). SIGCSE'09. ACM, New York, NY, 260-264. DOI=10.1145/1508865.1508959.

[10] Miles, J. and Shevlin, M. 2004. *Applying Regression and Correlation: A Guide for Students and Researchers*. Sage Publications, London, UK.

[11] Oliveira, O. L. 2012. Statistical Evidence of the Correlation between Mental Ability to Compute and Student Performance in Undergraduate Courses. In *Proceedings of the 17th Annual Joint Conference on Innovation and Technology in Computer Science Education* (Haifa, Israel, July 03 - 05, 2012). ITiCSE'12. ACM, New York, NY, 111-115. DOI=10.1145/2325296.2325326.

[12] Papert. S. 1993. *Mindstorms: children, computers, and powerful ideas*. 2nd ed. Basic Books, New York, USA.

[13] Qualls, J. A. and Sherrell, L. B. 2010. Why Computational Thinking Should be Integrated into the Curriculum. *Journal of Computing Sciences in Colleges*, 25, 5 (May 2010), 66-71.

[14] Settle, A. 2011. The Computational Thinking across the Curriculum Workshop. In *Proceedings of the 2011 Conference on Information Technology Education* (West Point, New York, USA, October 20-22, 2011). SIGITE'11, ACM, New York, NY, 311-312. DOI=10.1145/2047594.2047678.

[15] Settle, A., Franke, B., Hansen, R., Spaltro, F., Jurisson, C., Rennert-May, C. and Wildeman, B. 2012. Infusing Computational Thinking into the Middle- and High-School Curriculum. In *Proceedings of the 17th Annual Joint Conference on Innovation and Technology in Computer Science Education* (Haifa, Israel, July 03 - 05, 2012). ITiCSE'12. ACM, New York, NY, 22-27. DOI=10.1145/2325296.2325306.

[16] Turing, A. M. 1936. On Computable Numbers, with an Application to the Entscheidungsproblem. In *Proceedings of the London Mathematical Society* (London, UK, 1936), Ser. 2, vol. 42, 230-265. [Also available on-line at http://www.cs.ox.ac.uk/activities/ieg/e-library/sources/tp2-ie.pdf (August 29th, 2013)].

[17] Walden, J., Doyle, M., Garns, R and Hart, Z. 2013. An Informatics Perspective on Computational Thinking. In *Proceedings of the 18th Annual Joint Conference on Innovation and Technology in Computer Science Education* (Canterbury, England, UK, July 01 - 03, 2013). ITiCSE'13. ACM, New York, NY, 4-9. DOI=10.1145/2462476.2483797.

[18] Webb, H. C. and Rosson, M. B. 2013 Using Scaffolded Examples to Teach Computational Thinking Concepts. In *Proceeding of the 44th ACM Technical Symposium on Computer Science Education* (Denver, Colorado, USA, March 06 - 09, 2013). SIGCSE'13. ACM, New York, NY, 95-100. DOI=10.1145/2445196.2445227.

[19] Werner, L., Denner, J., Campe, S. and Kawamoto, D. C. 2012. The Fairy Performance Assessment: Measuring Computational Thinking in Middle School. In *Proceedings of the 43rd ACM technical symposium on Computer Science Education* (Raleigh, North Carolina, USA, February29–March 3, 2012). SIGCSE'12. ACM, New York, NY, 215-220. DOI=10.1145/2157136.2157200.

[20] Wing, J. 2006. Computational Thinking. *Communications of the ACM* 49, 3 (Mar. 2006), 33-35. DOI=10.1145/1118178.1118215.

Appendix I - Testing Student´s ability to Use the DMM

1) 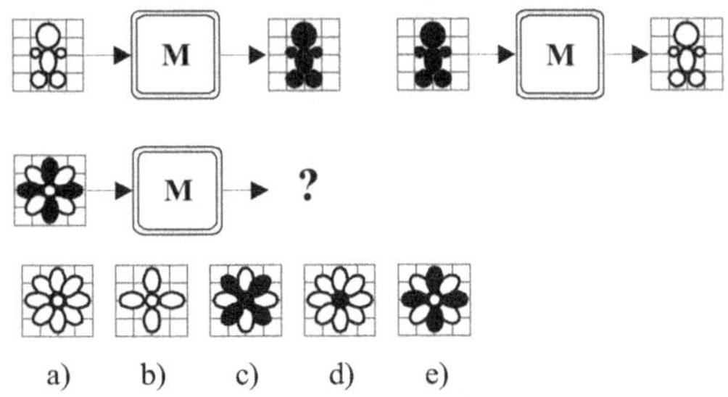

2) 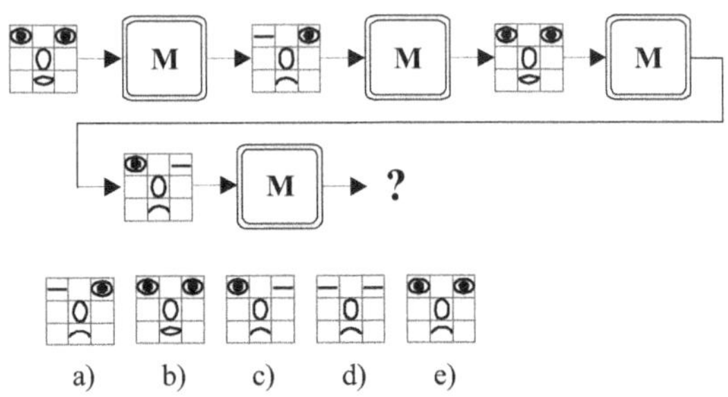

3) 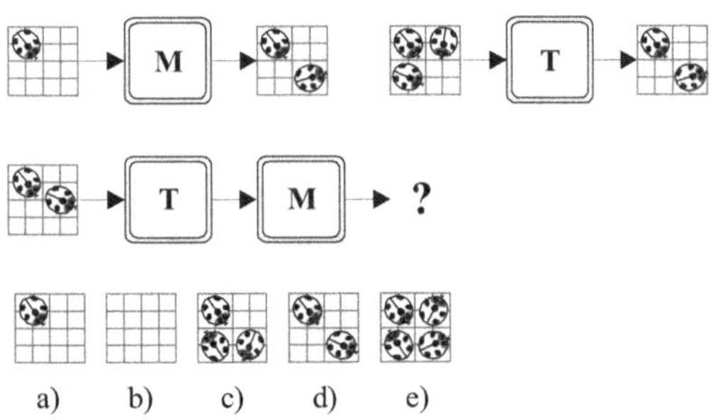

4) 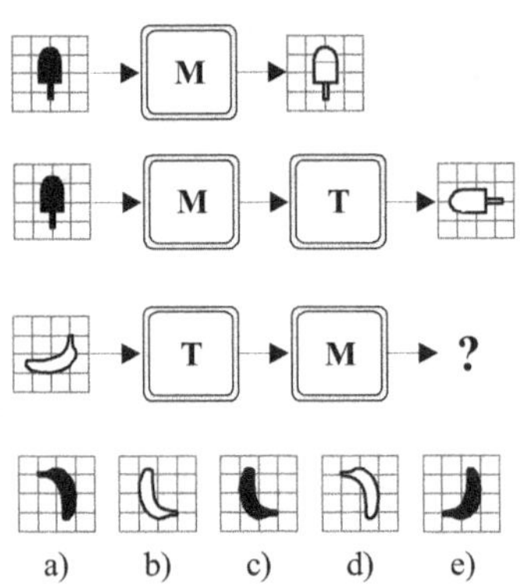

5) 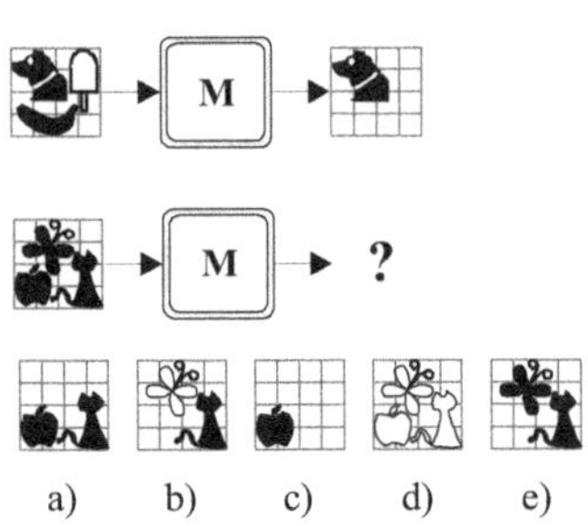

6) 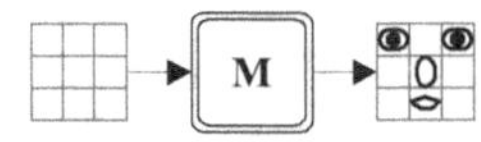

What symbols should replace the questions marks?

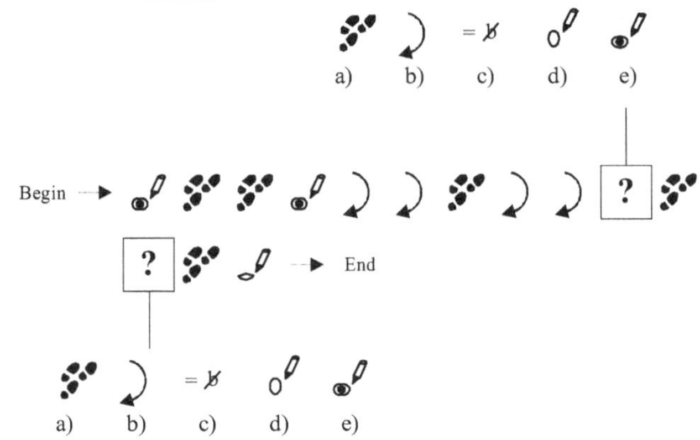

7) 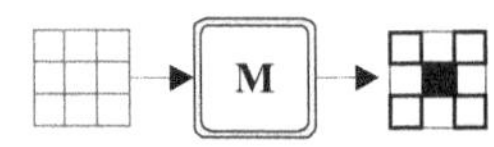

What symbols should replace the questions marks?

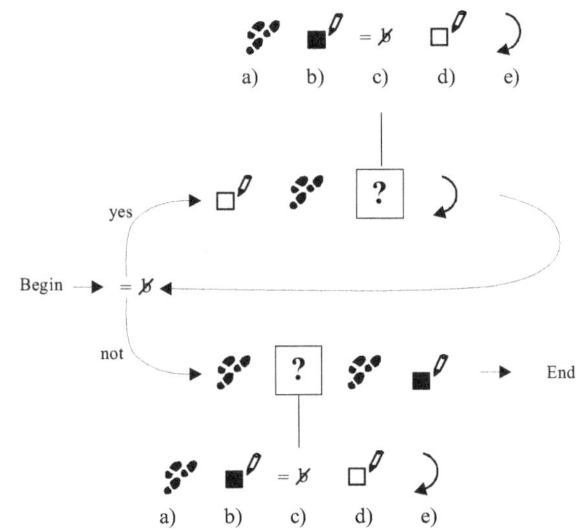

Answers: 1- c, 2 - b, 3 - d, 4 - a, 5 - e,
6 top - b, 6 bottom - d, 7 top - a, 7 bottom - e.

Appendix II - Test and Academic Scores of the 21 Sixth-grader Students

Student	Test (0 .. 7)	Academic (0 .. 10)		Student	Test (0 .. 7)	Academic (0 .. 10)
A	2	5.27		L	2	6.27
B	2.5	7.80		M	1	4.47
C	3.5	5.43		N	3	5.53
D	3.5	6.57		O	1	5.63
E	4.5	8.77		P	2.5	7.07
F	1	6.50		Q	3	6.50
G	2.5	7.87		R	2	7.30
H	1.5	5.60		S	4.5	6.43
I	3.5	7.50		T	5	7.00
J	1	5.64		U	2.5	6.23
K	5.5	9.27				

Identifying Elementary Students' Pre-Instructional Ability to Develop Algorithms and Step-By-Step Instructions

Hilary Dwyer‡, Charlotte Hill†, Stacey Carpenter‡, Danielle Harlow‡, and Diana Franklin†
† Department of Computer Science ‡ Gevirtz Graduate School of Education
UC Santa Barbara

ABSTRACT

The desire to expose more students to computer science has led to the development of a plethora of educational activities[16, 7, 15, 4] and outreach programs to broaden participation in computer science. Despite extensive resources (time and money), they have made little impact on the diversity of students pursuing computer science. To realize large gains, computational thinking must be integrated into K-12 systems, starting with elementary school. In order to do so, existing resources need to be adapted for a school setting.

In order to make a curriculum with lessons that build on each other over several years, and accountability for student learning, we need standards, an understanding of how students learn, and identification of what students know before exposure to the curriculum.

In this paper, we present our detailed findings of what fourth graders know before encountering a computational thinking curriculum. Groups of students participated in activities modified from CS Unplugged[4] in order to discover their knowledge (rather than provide instruction). We identify aspects of the activities students were able to complete successfully, and where they will need further instruction. We then explain how we used these results to modify our pilot curriculum.

Categories and Subject Descriptors

K.3.2 [**Computers and Education**]: Computer and Information Science Education; K.4.m [**Computers and Society**]: Miscellaneous—*Diversity and Outreach*

General Terms

Design, Human Factors

Keywords

diversity, K-12 education, outreach, assessment

1. INTRODUCTION

For decades, computer scientists have been developing computer science activities for young students in an effort to engage them early. Responding to a national need for computer scientists, the National Science Foundation has funded the Broadening Participation in Computing program, and later the CE21 program, to increase the diversity, and thus absolute numbers, of students pursuing computer science.

SIGCSE'14, March 5–8, 2014, Atlanta, GA, USA.

ACM 978-1-4503-2605-6/14/03 ...$15.00.
http://dx.doi.org/10.1145/2538862.2538905.

This and other efforts have led to many educational platforms, activities [16, 7, 15, 4] and outreach programs [3, 2, 12]. Unfortunately, very little progress has been made in broadening computer science participation. In fact, the percentage of females has been dropping almost monotonically since the early 1980's[1], and underrepresented ethnic minorities continue to make up a very small percentage of students[20, 24].

Outreach programs reach a small percentage of the population, and they require enormous portions of facilitators' time. To diversify and increase the computer science population, as well as those equipped to innovate existing software, computer science must find a place in K-12 schools. That requires developing standards, curricula, and assessments.

In 2011, the CSTA released a set of K-12 standards [10] and scaffolded charts to illustrate intermediate points. While an important step, much work remains before computer science catches up to its STEM counterparts in developing research-based curricula. At a high level, two large gaps remain - empirical evidence to confirm and/or refine the information presented in the scaffolding charts, and lower anchor points to determine the proper starting points for the curriculum.

In this paper, we analyzed groups of fourth grade students participating in two activities modified from CS Unplugged - creating step-by-step instructions to draw a picture and sorting a small set of canisters. Our purpose was to identify what students were able to complete successfully without our help, and with what concepts students required assistance. We present these findings, as well as how we have used these to modify our initial curriculum.

The rest of the paper is organized as follows. We provide a background on theories of learning that guide our work in Section 2 with a brief summary of related work in Section 3. Sections 4 and 5 present our curriculum from a high level and the methodologies derived from educational research used in our study. We present our results - what we found in our focus groups and how that informed our learning progressions and curriculum - in Section 6. Finally, Section 7 contains our conclusions and future work.

2. BACKGROUND

Our work is informed by both constructivist theories of learning and constructionist perspectives on instruction. Constructivism is a theory of learning that explains learning as a process of making sense of new information through the lens of what one already knows [11]. This implies that curriculum developers must be cognizant of learners' prior knowledge and design experiences that allow them to build on and challenge their existing ideas. Further, it places the instructor in the role of guide and designer of educational experiences rather than someone who simply imparts knowledge.

Constructionism is a theory of learning and teaching proposed by Papert who, building on constructivist ideas, posited that people learn best "in a context where the learner is consciously engaged in constructing a public entity"[18]. That is, people learn by making something. Constructionism has been embraced by many educational scholars[14] who argue that a "design mentality" can support students' development of ideas.

A constructivist perspective on learning requires us to first identify the pre-instructional ideas that students develop about computational thinking. These ideas will inform how we develop instruction. Our ultimate goal is to construct a *learning progression* for computational thinking at the upper elementary school level. A learning progression [9] is an empirically-determined model of how students learn a particular set of ideas and skills. Learning progressions are bounded by lower anchor points which describe ideas that students are expected to have prior to instruction, and upper anchor points which describe the expected goals or standards students should meet by the end of instruction. Between the upper and lower points are multiple intermediate levels. Initial hypothetical learning progressions proposed by researchers serve as models for student learning and are repeatedly tested against evidence and revised.

3. RELATED WORK

The development and refinement of outreach programs using curricula based on CS Unplugged, Scratch, and Alice have matured in their goals and assessments through time. These assessments have had various time / information-yielded trade-offs. Early assessments used surveys to gauge student attitudes, and later assessments inspected final projects or tests to determine what students knew at the end. These have been very helpful in giving a glimpse of what students are capable of at different ages. The next step is to create a picture of how students learn in order to inform future curricula. We want to be able to design the curriculum, demonstrate that it worked and explain how and why it worked.

Researchers have mined the wealth of completed Scratch projects to determine what concepts were displayed in completed projects. Over 500 Scratch projects created by urban youth during an afterschool program showed that youth learned key programming concepts without specific instructional interventions or experienced mentors[17]. Wilson et al[22] adapted a prior coding scheme[8] to find the most common programming concepts used by children who created games with Scratch.

Another effort [19] used existing projects across different grade levels to identify how computational thinking concepts varied by level in their Progression of Early Computational Thinking (PECT) Model. Finally, Franklin et al[13] used a combination of field notes, hand analysis and automated analysis[5] of Scratch projects to determine which concepts students learned initially and were able to transfer to a culminating project from a 2-week summer camp for middle school students.

There have also been attempts to seek deeper information through more detailed assessments, but they still focus on what students understand at the conclusion of instruction. As part of the effort to understand variation in computational thinking across students, Werner et al[21] developed a performance assessment tool to assess algorithmic thinking and effective use of abstraction and modeling among middle school students. Finally, Brennan et al [6] used portfolio analysis, artifact-based interviews, and design scenarios

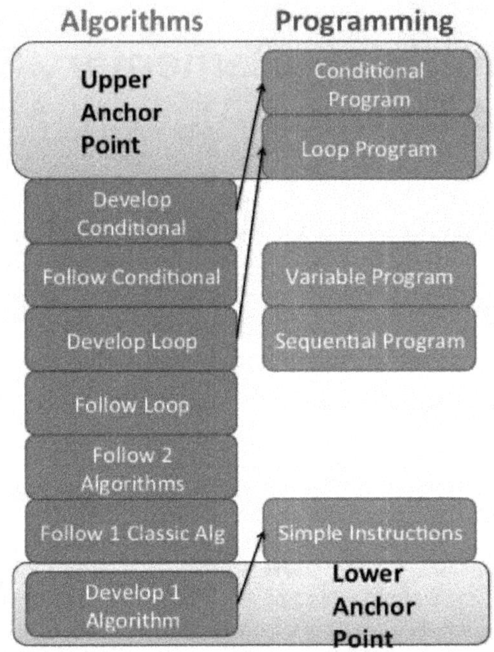

Figure 1: The two strands of our hypothetical learning progression that are the subject of this study. We focus on the lower anchor points.

to assess children's computational thinking based on a framework comprised of computational concepts, practices, and perspectives.

Our work is distinct because it focuses on what students know before they encounter a formal computational thinking curriculum. This is just a first step towards the larger goal of understanding how students learn computational thinking. Once a more detailed model is developed for students progressing through the curricula, we will better target and provide appropriate instruction.

4. CURRICULUM

Research on how children learn often depends on the curriculum that supports that learning. This is true of our work on learning progressions. We began with a pilot curriculum which we will iteratively revise as we adjust our hypothetical learning progression. Figure 1 shows our hypothetical learning progressions for two aspects of computational thinking: algorithms and programming. Because this study focuses on identifying lower anchor points, we focus on those elements in Figure 2.

Our curriculum helps students develop ideas about computational thinking with two types of activities: activities done off the computer and programming activities done on the computer. The first, which we call FiredUp, are loosely modeled after CS Unplugged activities[4]. During these activities, students encounter computational thinking concepts in the context of their everyday lives. FiredUp activities are followed by WiredUp activities - projects programmed in the Scratch programming language[23]. These relate to content included in 3rd or 4th grade, such as planets, geography, and erosion both to increase the chances that the curriculum will be adopted by elementary schools, and to show students how computational thinking can be integrated into multiple subjects. We also include bonus projects for students who finish early and would like to explore more creatively.

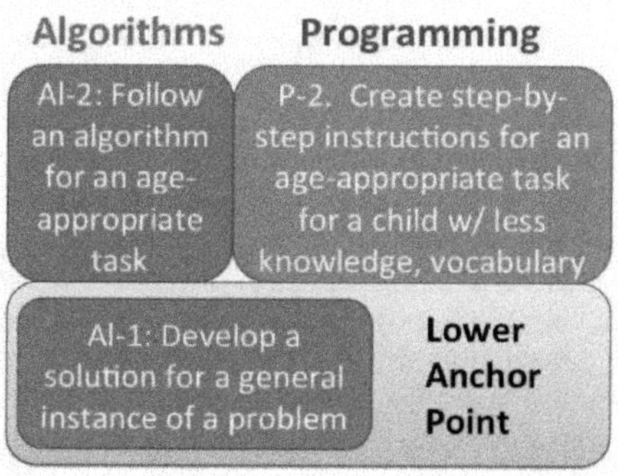

Figure 2: The expanded description for the items within and directly above the lower anchor points.

In this paper, we describe activities conducted in focus interviews that were related to FiredUp activities. We focused on fourth graders who had not been formally taught computational thinking or computer science. Thus, our results informed our *lower anchor points*. From our interviews, we identified what students were already able to do as well as what they were not able to do. This helped to better define our lower anchor points and inform our curriculum development.

5. METHODOLOGY

There are several steps to the iterative process of testing and modifying hypothetical learning progressions. We first present the methodology that we plan to use for the entire process. We then describe the methodology used for the particular findings we present in this paper.

We began by studying the CSTA K-12 Computational Thinking Standards, attending closely to the K-6 standards. This was done in two parts - first, reviewing the standards (an end-point or *upper anchor point*) and second, examining the scaffolding charts (not dissimilar to learning progressions, but as yet untested). We chose a subset of standards to target and designed a detailed learning progression for those subjects. Figure 1 shows the hypothetical learning progression relevant to the subjects we address in this paper.

Educational researchers use a combination of methods to discover details on how students learn. These methods include focus group discussions, observations of individual and group activities, talk-alouds in which students describe their thought process as they work, and analysis of student projects. Typically, pre- and post- assessments are used to evaluate the curriculum itself, whereas more detailed and frequent methods are used to discover how students learn - the paths students take in their journey from the lower anchor point to the upper anchor point.

In this study, we are identifying *lower anchor points*, or the starting point, for fourth graders before instruction. We conducted fifteen focus group interviews with fourth grade students at four different elementary schools in Southern California during May 2013. A total of 55 fourth graders participated in these interviews. The schools were selected to represent a broad range of demographics. The percentage of English Language Learners (ELL) ranged from 22% at Vista Grande[1] to 81% at Cabrillo, and students receiving free or reduced lunch ranged from 29% at Vista Grande to 100% at Cabrillo.

[1]All school and student names changed for confidentiality

Each focus group interview lasted approximately 30 minutes and was moderated and filmed by two graduate students. The interviews focused on three themes (knowledge about computers, complex decisions, and sequential procedures), and ended with one of four activities that were designed to elicit ideas related to aspects of computational thinking.

The discussions from the activities were transcribed and analyzed for discourse that supported or challenged our proposed model. Text was coded by its connection to the hypothesized learning progressions in our model of computational thinking. All results were independently coded by a computer science graduate student and education graduate student.

6. RESULTS

In our initial focus groups, we identified some aspects of what students were able to do and what they were not able to do related to two strands of our learning progression: step-by-step instructions and algorithmic development. These were used to refine our initial activities.

For each of the topic areas, we first present the activity, then what we discovered from the students, and finally how we used that information to make changes to our initial curriculum.

6.1 Step-by-Step Instructions

Giving step-by-step instructions is a base-line skill that contributes to two areas of computational thinking: algorithms and programming. The activity we used to elicit this was based on the CS Unplugged activity Marching Orders[4], in which students are given a picture and asked to give instructions to another student, who draws the picture based on the directions. The purpose of the activity is to show students the importance of providing precise instructions to others, and the challenging nature of such a task when one has been restricted to only written instructions. We adapted this exercise to discover how well students could a) initially create directions, b) analyze the strengths and weaknesses of a set of instructions and c) improve upon the original attempt.

We adapted the activity in the following ways. First, we did the activity in three rounds, each progressively more difficult than the former. In the first round, the picture was simple: a circle, square, and triangle vertically arranged and touching. In the second, the picture was a square with lines bisecting different sections. In the final round, the picture included multiple shapes and lines, haphazardly organized. We also adapted the activity so that students participated in different ways during each round. In the first two rounds, one student gave directions to the other students. In the third round, students worked together and created directions for the interviewer, who would draw a picture based on their description. Six focus groups (17 students) participated in the drawing activity. As this was a semi-structured interview, if a student wanted to try giving alternate directions for the same picture, we allowed it and considered these included in the same round.

Findings Related to Step-by-step Instructions.

Four distinct ideas related to step-by-step instructions emerged from our data. The first two describe things that the students were able to do prior to any instruction and the third is related to what they could not do. Below we list all four findings for this topic and then discuss the data that led to these findings.

- Finding 1a: Fourth graders recognized the need for specific instructions.
- Finding 1b: Fourth graders were able to identify what was lacking in instructions.

- Finding 1c: Fourth graders described more attributes following critique and discussion.
- Finding 1d: Fourth graders struggled to employ precision and cover all attributes consistently.

From our data, students' initial attempts lacked many attributes of specific instructions. In particular, during the drawing activity, many students identified included shapes to be drawn and explained roughly their position; however, they did not consistently include sufficient details (such as absolute position, size, or orientation) needed so that other students (or the interviewer) could draw the object.

The subsequent discussion illustrated that students seemed to recognize the need for specific instructions, identified when others' instructions were vague and provided suggestions about how to amend the instructions. Our first two findings emerged when the fourth graders were asked to compare the drawings they created when following someone else's directions to the original drawing. They recognized that the drawings did not match and identified aspects of the directions that should have been clarified. For example, one student provided the instructions, "There's a circle on the top." followed by "There's a triangle - there's a square in the middle. There's a triangle at the bottom." Other students recognized that knowing whether the shapes were organized in such a way that the shapes were "touching" was a key piece of information that would have improved their drawings.

This left a gap between what students can identify about others' instructions and what students produce themselves. We then attempted to narrow down this gap by allowing the students to produce instructions for a final drawing, with the only new information being their own discussion about what should have been clarified about the first attempt. We found that they still struggled to produce specific instructions themselves even after discussing how to improve their peers' instructions. After the discussion, students improved their instructions in one regard - they described additional attributes (Finding 1c). Table 1 shows how many groups mentioned an attribute at least once during a round (this was per round, not per shape). We see that during initial rounds, several groups failed to mention certain attributes such as orientation and absolute position. After the discussion, almost every group remembered to mention all attributes except for orientation.

What the table does not express is how consistently students remembered to mention every attribute (once per round vs for every shape) or to describe precisely each attribute (the line is short vs the width of my thumb). We found that students struggled on both accounts. So while there was improvement, their final instructions were far from complete (Finding 1d).

Implications for Curriculum.

Since students demonstrated difficulty improving their instructions after analyzing their and others' first attempt, we greatly expanded the "discussion" portion of the activity. We now have a complete lesson on procedural writing, including the importance of sequencing, the concepts that need to be expressed, and vocabulary words one can use.

6.2 Algorithm Development

Our second set of findings relates to algorithm development. We consider an algorithm to be broader than what can be solved by a computer; it refers to the ability to develop a sequence of steps or other problem-solving operations. As such, we were interested in identifying how well students could develop a sequence of steps to most efficiently solve a problem. To elicit this, we used an activity that was based on the CS Unplugged activity Lightest and Heaviest[4], in which students were given eight canisters and a scale. They were asked to perform a series of order-based tasks, starting with finding the lightest and ending with sorting all eight canisters. The initial tasks of the original CS Unplugged activity were intended to build the knowledge students will need to solve the sorting problem efficiently. We adapted this activity to discover how well students could a) create an algorithm for a small problem without initial instruction, b) extrapolate how their algorithm would work on a larger number of canisters, and c) analyze how their algorithm could be sped up. Below we describe how we adapted the activity for our purposes and the findings we inferred from the data.

In our modified version of this activity, we asked fourth graders to sort 6 film canisters from lightest to heaviest (each film canister contained different weights). The students worked as a group, and could only lift two canisters off the table at a time. Students were not provided a scale - instead, they compared the weights with their hands.

When they finished, the interviewer led a discussion about how to make the sorting faster, especially if they had more canisters to sort. Four focus groups (20 students) participated in this activity.

Findings Related to Algorithm Development.

From the focus group interviews, we identified five ideas that helped refine our learning progression for algorithm development. These findings describe what students can do as well as limitations in what they cannot do. Below we list the five findings. Following this, we discuss each one in more detail.

- Finding 2a. Fourth graders developed an algorithm that would successfully sort 6 canisters.
- Finding 2b. Fourth graders suggested many ways for speeding up the implementation of their algorithm.
- Finding 2c. Some fourth graders identified the limitations of their algorithms when scaled to a larger number of items.
- Finding 2d. Some fourth graders recognized that breaking a large problem into parts made solving it easier.
- Finding 2e. Fourth graders often bypassed necessary comparisons because they remembered canister weights from earlier trials.

In our first finding, fourth graders developed an algorithm to solve the task. Across several schools, all focus groups developed the same general algorithm. They first paired the canisters and performed an independent comparison of each pair of canisters, splitting them into two groups of three canisters. They then performed sorts within each group of three to sort them locally. They had two lines of three canisters, each sorted from left to right, lightest to heaviest. In order to merge the two groups, they placed the "light" line on the left and the "heavy" line on the right. They then performed local bubbling left and right to adjust the middle canisters.

While all students correctly sorted their set of 6 canisters, the initial algorithm chosen was not scalable (Finding 2c). Moreover, the merges were inefficient. Students assumed that placing the groups next to each other was close to the sorted order, because they had performed the initial splits into groups of heaviest and lightest. They then "cleaned up" the ordering with some final check passes. When scaling the problem, they would need to resolve this merge issue because the number of steps to fix the merge would increase substantially.

We inferred our other findings in this area from discussions following the initial sort about how to scale their algorithm. When we

Attribute	Example	Round 1	Round 2	Discussion	Round 3
Shape	circle, square	6	5	4	6
Orientation	facing upwards, horizontal, up and down	1	3	2	2
Relative Position	Touching, on top of	5	4	4	5
Absolute Position	middle of paper	3	3	0	5
Size	units, big/small	1	5	1	5

Table 1: The attributes necessary to give precise drawing directions, and the number of groups that used that attribute at least once in their directions. The groups improved after the discussion.

Type	Name	Description	Groups
Algorithmic	Split	Split into smaller piles to sort	2
	Split and Merge	Both split and proper merge suggested	1
	Insert Sort	Compare next one to existing sorted line of them until you find place	1
	Organization	Put them into a line	1
Implementation	Shake	Shake canisters by listening and feeling	2
	Scale	A scale would be faster than using their hands	2
	2+	If you can touch more than two, weighing is faster	1
	Fast Pick-up	Pick them up really fast	1
	Practice	It will be faster second time around due to familiarity	1
	Less Repetition	Only one person compares, not all	1

Table 2: Student suggestion, the type (Algorithmic or Implementation) and how many groups had this suggestion

asked students to suggest improvements if they were given many canisters, we did not specify what kind of improvements. Students provided two kinds of suggestions - implementation and algorithmic.

When asked how they could speed up their sorting, students easily provided suggestions to improve the implementation of the algorithm (Finding 2b). Table 2 shows the suggestions. We define an implementation suggestion as one that would involve speeding up the execution of the algorithm, but without changes to the order or number of comparisons. Implementation suggestions included picking up the canisters very quickly, using a scale, shaking canisters, and practicing the process. Students were much less likely to think of algorithmic suggestions.

Related to this is finding 2c. Two groups figured out that their original algorithm would not scale well. One group observed that it was wasteful to compare two new canisters each time, rather than a new canister and a previously sorted canister. They adjusted their algorithm to be a form of insertion sort. The second group noted the inefficiency in making two piles initially, and thus placed them in a line, also performing an insertion sort.

Also, students suggested ways to simplify a larger problem. Two different groups suggested that if they received more canisters, they would break them up into more than 2 groups (Finding 2d). One group even suggested a better merge algorithm - taking the lightest ones from each group and comparing those.

Our final finding is not directly related to items in our existing learning progression for algorithm development but is important nonetheless. In finding 2e, children remembered weights of the original canisters and thus bypassed steps that a computer would be required to complete to solve the algorithm. In this exercise, it is useful for students to sort the canisters multiple times. We found that, while they still "weighed" the canisters, they were not "comparing" them directly the second time. Instead, they remembered approximate weights. While this is a valid algorithm if you know you will get the same weights each time, and is somewhat analogous to having some hash table with the weight mapped to the final location, this is not what we were hoping for.

Implications for Curriculum.

Our findings have led us to modify this activity for our curriculum in three ways, and we will consider more major changes depending on whether the first two are sufficient during field testing.

First, we need to explicitly distinguish between the speed of the algorithm and the speed of implementing the algorithm. Like the original CS Unplugged activity, we will focus on counting the number of comparisons.

Second, developing and describing algorithms takes more time and depth, and this is perhaps why students would either only describe a way to speed up execution, would develop incomplete algorithms, or would start describing an algorithm but then get sidetracked by more execution speed suggestions. We need to give the students more time to develop algorithms and encourage they test new algorithms as they arise. In addition, we need to give the students new canisters each time with different weights so they cannot use their prior knowledge. Finally, when asking about solving with more canisters, we should be ready with a large number of canisters so the exercise can be less theoretical.

Third, we need to provide students with techniques for analyzing algorithms, including examples and vocabulary. This is similar to the expanded lesson we will provide for the Marching Orders activity to teach students how to give precise instructions.

6.3 Changes to Learning Progression

Figure 3 reflects the changes, additions, and confirmations to the lower items in the learning progression, including the lower anchor points. For Algorithms, we split "Develop a solution for a general instance of a problem" into two parts - develop a solution for a specific instance of a problem and develop a solution for a general instance of the problem (i.e. N canisters rather than 6). In addition, we identified an important concept - distinguishing between efficiency of the implementation and the algorithm. In Program-

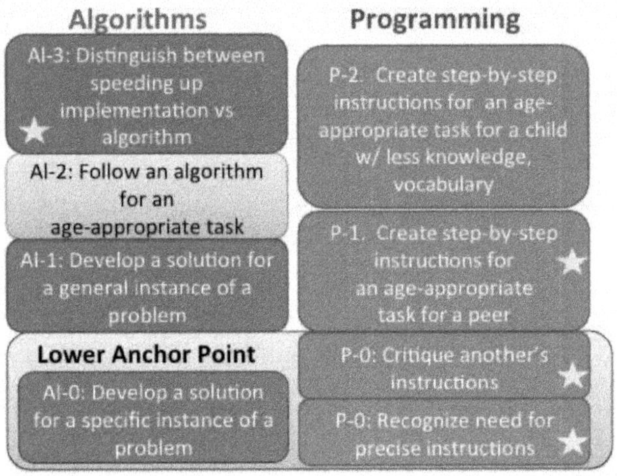

Figure 3: Final learning progression. Al-1 was split into Al-0 and Al-1. New items are starred. Al-2 was not tested in this study, so its position is still hypothetical.

ming, we identified several precursors to creating step-by-step instructions for someone with limited knowledge and/or vocabulary. Students were not yet able to create precise step-by-step instructions for a peer, but they did recognize the need for precise instructions and were able to critique another's instructions.

7. CONCLUSIONS AND FUTURE WORK

We have shown initial results from in-depth focus groups. These focus groups informed three lower anchor points for the learning progressions of two CSTA K-12 strands and how that knowledge informed our pilot curriculum. We found that students could analyze existing directions for deficiencies, and their analysis led to incrementally better directions, but they were unable to produce thorough, precise instructions themselves. Finally, students were able to solve a small instance of a problem, but they had difficulty describing a working algorithm when the problem was scaled. In addition, they often focused on accelerating the mechanics of the operation rather than the algorithm itself.

In the future, we will study multiple classrooms and their progress through our pilot curriculum. Our goal is to produce more complete learning progressions and refine our curriculum with the information we gather through interviews, videos, and assessments. Our end goal is a three-year curriculum for computational thinking.

8. ACKNOWLEDGMENTS

This work is supported by the National Science Foundation BPC Award CNS-0940491 and and CE21 Award CNS-1240985.

9. REFERENCES

[1] Percent female bachelor's degrees.

[2] S. Alliance. The stars alliance: A southeastern partnership for diverse participation in computing. NSF STARS Alliance Proposal. http://www.itstars.org/.

[3] I. Arroyo et al. Effects of web-based tutoring software on students' math achievement. In *AERA*, 2004.

[4] T. Bell, I. H. Witten, and M. Fellows. *Computer Science Unplugged*. 2006.

[5] B. Boe, C. Hill, M. Len, G. Dreschler, P. Conrad, and D. Franklin. Hairball: Lint-inspired static analysis of scratch projects. In *SIGCSE '13*, March 2013.

[6] K. Brennan and M. Resnick. New frameworks for studying and assessing the development of computational thinking. In *AERA*, 2012.

[7] W. Dann, S. Cooper, and R. Pausch. Making the connection: programming with animated small world. *ITiCSE*, 2000.

[8] J. Denner, L. Werner, and E. Ortiz. Computer games created by middle school girls: Can they be used to measure understanding of computer science concepts? *Computers and Education*, 58:240–249, January 2011.

[9] R. A. Duschl, H. A. Schweingruber, and A. W. Shouse. *Taking science to school: Learning and teaching science in grades K-8*. 2007.

[10] C. S. T. Force. *CSTA K-12 Computer Science Standards*. Association for Computing Machinery, 2011.

[11] C. Fosnot. *Constructivism: A psychological theory of learning*. Teachers College Press, 1997.

[12] D. Franklin, P. Conrad, G. Aldana, and S. Hough. Animal tlatoque: attracting middle school students to computing through culturally-relevant themes. In *SIGCSE '11*, 2011.

[13] D. Franklin, P. Conrad, B. Boe, K. Nilsen, and C. H. et al. Assessment of computer science learning in a scratch-based outreach program. In *SIGCSE '13*.

[14] J. Gee. What video games have to teach us about learning and literacy. *Computers in Entertainment (CIE)*, 1(1):20–20, 2003.

[15] C. S. Hood and D. J. Hood. Teaching programming and language concepts using legos. In *ITiCSE*, June 2005.

[16] J. Maloney et al. The scratch programming language and environment. *Trans. Comput. Educ.*, 10(4):16:1–16:15, Nov. 2010.

[17] J. Maloney, K. Peppler, Y. B. Kafai, M. Resnick, and N. Rusk. Programming by choice: Urban youth learning programming with scratch. In *SIGCSE '08*. ACM Press, 2008.

[18] S. Papert. *Constructionism: research reports and essays 1985-1990*. Ablex Publishing Corporation, 1991.

[19] Seiter and Forman. Modeling the learning progressions of computational thinking of primary grade students. In *International Computing Education Research (ICER)*. ACM, 2013.

[20] J. Vegso. Cra taulbee trends: Ph.d. programs and ethnicity. *Computing Research News*, 2007.

[21] L. Werner, J. Denner, S. Campe, and D. C. Kawamoto. The fairy performance assessment: Measuring computational thinking in middle school. In *SIGCSE12*. ACMPress, 2012.

[22] A. Wilson, T. Hainey, and T. M. Connolly. Evaluation of computer games developed by primary school children to gauge understanding of programming concepts. In *6th European Conference on Games-based Learning (ECGBL)*, 2012.

[23] G. C. Y B Kafai, K A Peppler. High tech programmers in low income communities: Creating a computer culture in a community technology center. *Proceedings of the Third International Conference on Communities and Technology*, pages 545–562, 2007.

[24] S. Zweben. Computing degree and enrollment trends. *Computing Research News*, 2011.

Code Club: Bringing Programming to UK Primary Schools through Scratch

Neil Smith
Centre for Research in Computing
The Open University
Milton Keynes, UK
n.smith@open.ac.uk

Clare Sutcliffe
Code Club
London, UK
clare@codeclub.org.uk

Linda Sandvik
Code Club
London, UK
linda@codeclub.org.uk

ABSTRACT

Code Club is a network of after-school programming clubs for primary (US: elementary) schoolchildren, run by technically-competent volunteers in conjunction with (generally technically-unskilled) teachers. The main motivation of Code Club is to inspire children with a sense of fun and achievement for programming and digital creativity. This paper reports on the first year of Code Club in 1000 UK schools. The results were extremely positive, but some children had difficulty understanding the concepts behind the projects.

Categories and Subject Descriptors

K.3.2 [**Computers and Education**]: Computer and Information Science Education; K.3.1 [**Computers and Education**]: Computer Uses in Education; D.1.7 [**Programming Techniques**]: Visual Programming

General Terms

Active Learning, K-12 Instruction

Keywords

introductory programming, elementary school, primary school, K-12

1. INTRODUCTION

Eric Schmidt's 2011 MacTaggart speech [17] galvanised an overhaul of the UK's K-12 Computing education provision. He pointed out that a generation of UK schoolchildren was not receiving a substantive Computing education. Prior to 2011, ICT (Information and Communication Technologies) education in UK schools consisted mainly of lessons in how to drive office automation software with little, if any, programming or other technical expertise being developed. However, experience with tools such as Scratch [15] and Storytelling Alice [14] show that primary (age 5–11) schoolchildren can engage profoundly with computing concepts.

SIGCSE '14, March 05 - 08 2014, Atlanta, GA, USA

http://dx.doi.org/10.1145/2538862.2538919

Seeing that primary schoolchildren were being abandoned by the current ICT education provision, two of the current authors decided to do something about it. In 2012, they founded Code Club, a network of after-school clubs in primary schools. Code Club is intended to provide an easy and *fun* introduction to digital creation that will motivate children to pursue Computing throughout their school careers and beyond. In the process, the children will learn the basics of programming and fundamental CS concepts.

Meanwhile, the proposed new Computing curriculum [9] is following Code Club's direction. The new government-mandated national curriculum includes major changes, such as the introduction of algorithms to children under 7 years old. However, it will not be in place before September 2014, and there remain significant challenges with its deployment, including the lack of expert teachers [10].

2. CODE CLUB'S APPROACH

The idea of Code Club formed after a hack day in early 2012. Hack days are events where designers and developers come together to produce a new technology product. One key characteristic of these events is that they are *fun* for the participants. Anecdotal questioning of various industrial IT practitioners indicates that *fun* was a fundamental reason for them progressing in the industry: the fun of meeting a challenge, of inventing a new product, of understanding a difficult concept. For many current IT practitioners, their passion was ignited at school, often during after-school clubs. These impressions are borne out by Schulte & Knobelsdorf [18], who indicate that prior experiences of design activities (including programming) encourage people to engage more fully in Computing at university, as well as fostering a more positive view of CS. Many practitioners are keen to contribute to bringing their passion to a new generation, but lack the pedagogic skills, child-protection accreditation, and access to children to do so effectively.

This desire must be seen in the changing context of Computing in UK schools. Since Schmidt's speech, the UK government and other organisations have started a process of major changes in how Computing is taught in school. This involves both updating the curriculum and training the teachers; many years of neglect of Computing in schools had left little Computing expertise among the teaching staff with many non-specialists now teaching the subject [10]. Much of this effort is directed at secondary (age 11–18) schools. However, primary schoolchildren are capable of productive engagement with Computing concepts [16, 15, 14, 2, 6] but the problem of teacher expertise is even more acute: few primary school staff have a technical background and therefore lack both the skills and confidence to bring programming to their pupils.

Therefore, the obvious solution was to provide a vehicle by which IT professionals could productively engage primary schoolchildren in fun digital design and implementation activities. If we could excite children's interest in Computing, they would absorb the basics of CS by engaging with the material. However, there was no way that a pair of outsiders to education could usefully influence the ongoing governmental plans for the revision of CS education, especially in the short term. Code Club was the solution to this quandary.

The Code Club model is an after-school club, run by an technically-adept volunteer in tandem with a teacher in the school. The volunteer brings the necessary technical expertise to the club, while the teacher provides additional pedagogic support and "crowd control" expertise. Code Club provides a set of materials for the children to work through, guiding them to create a rich multimedia project, generally a game (games are recognised as strongly motivating children to engage with programming concepts [8, 22, 1]). Code Club also provides volunteers with an easy route to child-protection vetting via the UK government's existing STEM Ambassador programme. Code Club does not technically vet the volunteers or provide any technical training. This does not seem to cause any issues, especially as the programming is straightforward for anyone with programming experience.

Code Club's approach has limitations, mainly due to Code Club's self-selecting nature. Initially only the more forward-thinking and technically-aware schools signed up for Code Club, though this is becoming less of an issue as more clubs sign up. Code Club can only run if the school already has sufficient PCs available and if there is a committed volunteer nearby. As an after-school club, attendance by children is both voluntary and limited, meaning that only a few of the most interested children will attend. However, we consider that Code Club is the best we can do in the short term.

In April 2012, Code Club was announced and the news quickly spread. Within weeks, over a thousand volunteers and two hundred schools had expressed an interest in setting up a Code Club. A steering committee of nine (including all of this paper's authors) was assembled to produce and oversee the Code Club materials. Twenty-two schools, with enthusiastic and technically-skilled teachers, were selected to pilot Code Clubs at the end of the 2012 summer term. Code Club opened to all schools in September 2012. 250 clubs were active by the end of 2012; by October 2013, over 1300 clubs were registered. The international branch of Code Club, Code Club World, launched in June 2013 with 60 clubs registered outside the UK by October 2013. News of Code Club continues to spread mostly by word of mouth, with additional exposure from articles in widely-read publications (e.g. *Wired UK* [12, 21], national newpapers *The Guardian* [7] and *The Indepenent* [11]) and highly public awards [20].

3. SCRATCH

We chose Scratch [15] as the first programming environment. This was due to its known ease of use by primary schoolchildren, the range of media resources easily available, and support for saving and sharing projects via the Scratch website. Scratch can be used for a variety of projects, often animations, simple games, and interactive stories.

Figure 1: The Scratch environment.

Scratch is a visual programming environment (see Figure 1). It features a set of *sprites* that move around a world (called the *stage*). Sprites have one or more costumes and the stage has one or more backgrounds, which define their appearance. Both sprites and the stage can have their own behaviours, defined by *scripts*. Sprites and the stage can have multiple scripts which run concurrently and asynchronously. Scripts are formed by clicking together pre-defined code *blocks*, selected from a number of themed palettes. Some blocks perform operations such as moving sprites, changing their appearance, changing costumes, playing sounds, detecting collisions, and so on. Other blocks expose much information about sprites, such as position and direction. More blocks implement standard control structures, including a variety of loops, if-then-else selections, and pauses. Scripts are triggered by either user input (mouse clicks and keyboard presses), broadcast messages sent from other scripts, or the "green flag" button on the Scratch UI; the latter is often used to start a project. Programmers can create variables with with scope either global or local to a sprite. Sprites can communicate either through global variables or broadcast messages.

We have created further projects using HTML5 and Python, though these projects have not yet received sufficient use to form reliable conclusions on their reception.

4. PEDAGOGY

There are several existing programmes of study for teaching children the basics of computing and programming (e.g. [6, 2]) but none was suitable for Code Club. The published curricula generally assume that the teaching will be delivered during a formal, class-based, teacher-led programme of study, lasting from a term to a year or more. Code Club runs as a ten-week after-school club with one hour sessions (including allocating time for children to arrive and pack up). Existing programmes of study assume that children will attend virtually all the sessions. Attendance at after-schools clubs is more erratic. The emphasis in the existing programmes is on the skills and behaviours that the children should acquire. The intent of Code Club was to create a sense of fun and excitement in its child participants and inculcate a desire to engage with Computing, with skill de-

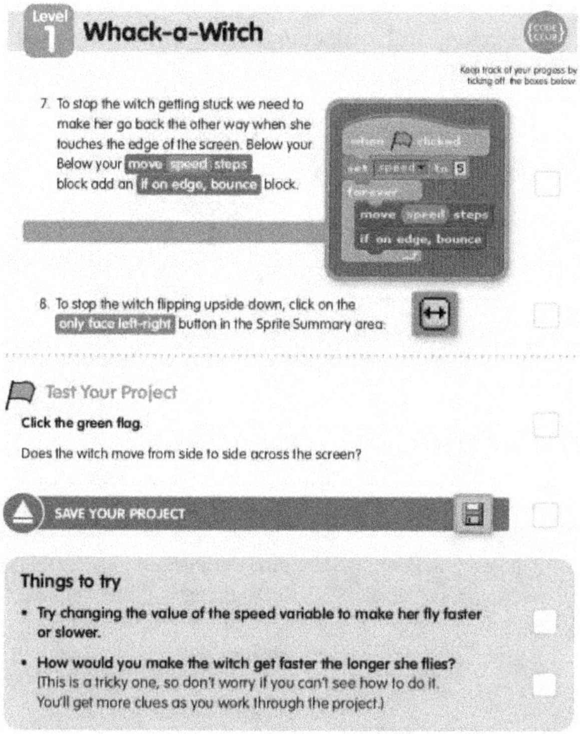

Figure 2: A sample project step.

velopment a secondary concern.

We adopted a project-based pedagogy [5]. Each project creates a specific Scratch application, such as a game or a drawing package. The projects are broadly similar to others designed for a similar age group (e.g. [13]), though earlier projects are smaller to allow them to be completed in a single club session.

The first term's activity consists of nine projects, with each project expected to take one or two sessions. Each project is divided into a series of steps (see Figure 2 for an example). The first few steps are directed with a restricted scope and aim to give the child a basic, working application within around twenty minutes. Subsequent steps extend the basic project. Some steps are directed and add specific pieces of additional functionality. Some steps describe an extension for the project but leave its implementation to the pupil. Others are more open ended, inviting pupils to explore how they can customise or extend the application. As the projects progress throughout the term, the level of direction decreases and pupils are increasingly asked to design and implement their own ideas and extensions. The first term concludes with a "capstone" project where pupils design and build their own game, drawing together what they have learnt from previous projects.

All project steps include specific prompts for pupils to test their projects and to save their work. The projects make extensive use of Scratch Cards [19], quick summaries of often-used functionality, to emphasise skill and knowledge transfer across projects.

The second term of Scratch projects is organised as three larger projects (an animated monster, a suite of musical instruments with recording and playback, and a platform game), each intended to be completed over three to four weeks. These projects contain a substantial design component, with at least one session dedicated to the students designing their projects. These projects contain little sample code for the children to copy. Instead, they are expected to create their own scripts, prompted by what they have achieved already or suggested samples in the projects.

The project-based approach has several advantages for Code Club. First, it emphasises work on authentic problems. This motivates the children to engage with the material and hence learn the programming skills they need, almost as a by-product. Second, pupils produce a discrete artefact, which gives the children a sense of achievement as well as the ability to show off the products of their labours to friends and family (assisted by Scratch's ability easily to share projects via its website). Third, it allows for much more flexibility in attendance; the material allows for children to miss sessions at different times and still be a full participant on their return. Fourth, it gracefully allows for differentiation across pupils of different ability, with pupils able to progress through projects at the speed most appropriate to them.

5. THE FIRST YEAR

We evaluated the adoption and progress of Code Club with two surveys, performed by club leaders completing online questionnaires. We received 150 responses (of approximately 280 clubs) to the first survey in December 2012, and 130 responses (of approximately 800 clubs) to the second survey in June 2013. We also examined a sample of 22 completed capstone projects, where clubs made them available to us.

5.1 Survey Results

The first survey concentrated on the demographics of the club members; the second on the results of up to a year of Code Club.

The first survey revealed 2233 children enrolled in 150 clubs, giving an average of 14.9 children per club (Figure 3). 40% of club members were girls. Club sizes ranged from one to eighty children; we assume the latter were where Code Club was used in lessons in schools across year groups. Extrapolating this across all clubs meant that in December 2012 there were over 5800 children in Code Clubs and over twelve thousand children in Code Clubs by July 2013. 77% of club members had no prior programming experience; 20% had used Scratch before.

By the end of the year, children had completed an average of six projects each (Figure 4), though some clubs have completed ten or more projects. This low number is expected as many clubs started at various points throughout the year.

We also asked the club organisers to rate the children's confidence with different programming concepts (Figure 5). "Confidence" was reported on a ten-point Likert scale and respondents were asked to give a rating for the club overall. Several respondents commented that children in their club had a range of confidence in these concepts. Despite this, the ratings are encouraging, with most clubs showing that most people are at least reasonably confident using a variety of programming concepts. Children are reported as being less confident with debugging than with any of the programming concepts. These confidence levels are borne out in the analysis of the projects, below.

We asked respondents to rate how many of their club

Figure 3: Code Club sizes.

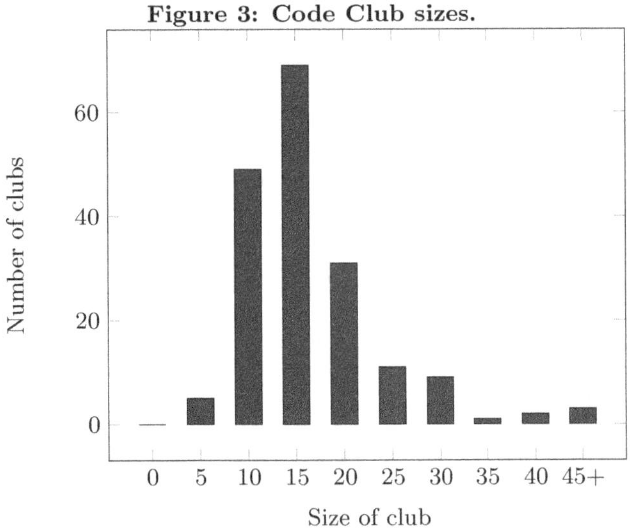

Figure 4: Number of completed projects.

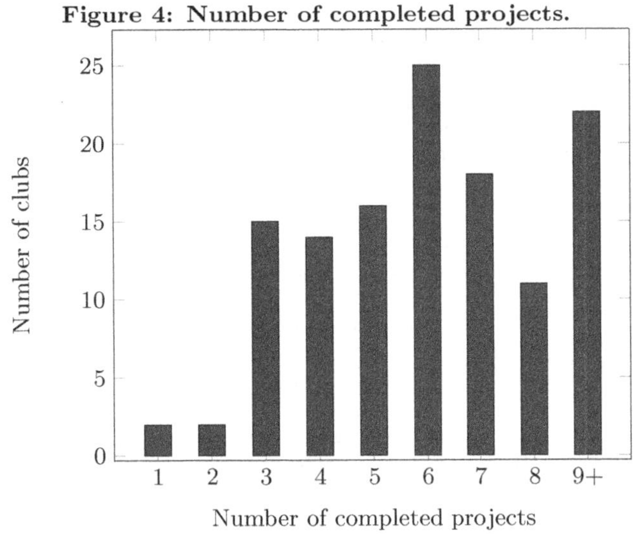

Figure 5: Confidence with concepts.

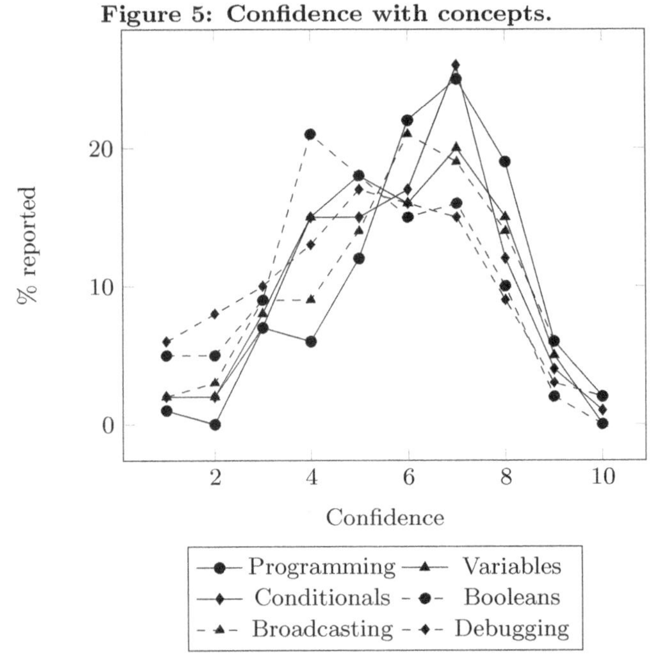

members engaged in programming or some other form of digital making outside Code Club. The results were surprisingly evenly split, with one third saying that less than one third of their club members engaged in such activities, one third said about half did, and one third saying that more than two thirds did some form of digital making outside Code Club.

Finally, we asked respondents an open-ended question for further comments. Most were positive, with many mentioning minor errors in the project sheets. The most common substantive comment was about the transition from following instructions to open-ended tasks. Many respondents commented that children were able to follow the early, guided instructions but were unable to apply any knowledge to unguided challenges. This will require a revision of our pedagogy to give more structure to these challenges, such as Bagge's Scratch projects [3] which show the blocks to be used in a challenge step without showing how they should be assembled.

5.2 Project Analysis

We analysed a sample of 22 of the final 'build your own game' projects to see what programming concepts were contained within them. These projects were designed and built by the children themselves, rather than following any instructions from a Code Club sheet. We analysed the programming concepts used in these projects (see Table 1), noting whether the concepts were properly used or just attempted. We made no judgements about the presence of bugs or the quality of the gameplay! Many of the final projects were based on earlier Code Club projects, but all contained their own variations in program code. Some projects were completely novel, including a two-player game of tennis and a wizardly duel. As can be seen in this table, most of the projects appropriately used user input (often as a game control), control statements, parallel execution (both multiple sprites and multiple, simultaneous execution of scripts

Table 1: Concepts used in 'build your own' projects.

Concept	Correctly used	Incorrectly used
Variables	13	0
User input	21	1
Broadcast within a sprite	1	0
Broadcasting between sprites	13	2
Control statements	20	1
Boolean connectives	7	0
Parallel execution	22	0
Detecting state	20	0

within the same sprite), and detecting and acting on states in the project (normally collision detection).

The more tricky concepts of variables and message passing were used in over half the projects, mostly appropriately. Where variables were used, they were always used appropriately, normally as score counters or game timers. Where variables were not used in the project, they were generally not needed. Message passing was often used to allow sprites to communicate game events, such as losing a life.

The distributed nature of Code Club, and the flexibility of timetabling individual projects, made it impractical for us to observe a representative sample of children developing their own projects in a club. Observation of children in our own clubs and at other events indicates that children are generally comfortable with most of the concepts listed in Table 1. Children seemed to start the design of their projects from considering the end result and bringing in programming concepts as appropriate to that end. We rarely saw children wanting to achieve some functionality and not knowing how to approach it. We did not perform more in-depth exercises to gauge children's design processes, such as "think aloud" design sessions.

6. CONCLUSIONS AND FUTURE WORK

Code Club is a new network of after-school clubs aimed at introducing primary schoolchildren to the joy of programming. Surveys of Code Clubs show that Code Club is achieving its objectives. The children have fun. They successfully engaged with a range of digital design and implementation tasks, creating several artefacts along the way. The children coped remarkably easily with some difficult programming concepts. Children were able to show off their creativity within the projects and many children were eager to continue developing projects outside Code Club. Code Clubs continue to spring up across the UK and internationally.

Code Club continues the work of other projects that bring programming experience to schoolchildren [14, 15, 8]. Code Club is distinct because it is addressed exclusively at primary schoolchildren, and it has a national, and increasinly international, scope. It is an initiative that answers the call to arms of how to update the Computing curriculum [4].

Code Club continues to expand. We are still aiming to have Code Club in 25% of UK primary schools by the end of 2014. Additional project types are being developed, using HTML5 and Python. After a period of rapid expansion and development, we intend to consolidate our progress with the project materials, revising them as necessary to improve their ease of use and to smooth the transition from following instructions to designing your own code. We will continue to monitor and evaluate Code Club across these changes.

7. REFERENCES

[1] J. C. Adams and A. R. Webster. What do students learn about programming from game, music video, and storytelling projects? In *Proceedings of the 43rd ACM technical symposium on Computer Science Education*, pages 643–648, 2012.

[2] C. at School Working Group. *Computer Science: A Curriculum for Schools.* Computing at School, 2012.

[3] P. Bagge. Junior Computer Science Scratch Projects, 2013. Available from http://code-it.co.uk/year4/scratchprojects.html

[4] V. Barr and C. Stephenson. Bringing computational thinking to K-12: what is involved and what is the role of the computer science education community? *ACM Inroads*, 2:48–54, 2011.

[5] P. C. Blumenfeld, E. Soloway, R. W. Marx, J. S. Krajcik, M. Guzdial, and A. Palincsar. Motivating project-based learning: Sustaining the doing, supporting the learning. *Educational Psychologist*, 26(3/4):369–398, 1991.

[6] K. Brennan, M. Chung, and J. Hawson. Scratch curriculum guide draft, 2011.

[7] J. Butterworth. Primary Code. In *The Guardian*, 15 July 2013. Available from http://www.theguardian.com/science/life-and-physics/2013/jul/15/programming-schools-children

[8] M. Carbonaroa, D. Szafronb, M. Cutumisub, and J. Schaefferb. Computer-game construction: A gender-neutral attractor to computing science. *Computers & Education*, 55(3):1098–1111, 2010.

[9] Department for Education. National curriculum review: new programmes of study and attainment targets from September 2014, 2013. Available from https://www.gov.uk/government/consultations/national-curriculum-review-new-programmes-of-study-and-attainment-targets-from-september-2014

[10] S. Furber. *Shut Down or Restart? The Way Forward for Computing in UK Schools.* The Royal Society, 2012.

[11] R. Garner. Welcome to Code Club: UK programme that teaches children computer coding goes global. In *The Indepenent*, 24 July 2013. Available from http://www.independent.co.uk/news/education/schools/welcome-to-code-club-uk-programme-that-teaches-children-computer-coding-goes-global-8730806.html

[12] D. Geere. Afterschool 'Code Clubs' planned to teach kids programming. In *Wired.co.uk*, 17 April 2012. Available from http://www.wired.co.uk/news/archive/2012-04/17/code-club

[13] LEAD Project. *Super Scratch Programming Adventure!* No Starch Press

[14] C. Kelleher, R. Pausch, and S. Keisler. Storytelling Alice motivates middle school girls to learn computer programming. In *Proceedings of the SIGCHI Concerence on Human Factors in Computing Systems*, pages 1455–1464. ACM, 2007.

[15] J. Maloney, K. Peppler, Y. Kafai, M. Resnick, and N. Rusk. Programming by choice: Urban youth

learning programming with scratch. In *Proceedings of the 39th SIGCSE Technical Symposium on Computer Science Education*, pages 367–371. ACM, 2008.

[16] M. Petre and B. Price. Using robotics to motivate 'back door' learning. *Education and Information Technologies*, 9:147–158, 2004. (Draft available from http://mcs.open.ac.uk/bp5/papers/2004-eit/2004-EIT-Robotics-Backdoor.pdf)

[17] E. Schmidt. *MacTaggart Lecture*. Edinburgh Television Festival, 2011.

[18] C. Schulte and M. Knobelsdorf. Attitudes towards computer science-computing experiences as a starting point and barrier to computer science. In *Proceedings of the third international workshop on Computing education research*, pages 27–38, 2007.

[19] Scratch. Scratch cards, 2012. Available from http://info.scratch.mit.edu/Support/Scratch_Cards.

[20] Talk Talk. Digital Heroes Award, 2012. Information available from http://www.talktalk.co.uk/digitalheroes/winners.php

[21] N. Tufnell. Code Club Robo-Boogie competition asks kids to invent a robot dance. In *Wired.co.uk*, 15 November 2013. Available from http://www.wired.co.uk/news/archive/2013-11/15/kids-get-coding-with-robo-boogie

[22] L. Werner, S. Campe, and J. Denner. Children learning computer science concepts via Alice game-programming. In *Proceedings of the 43rd ACM technical symposium on Computer Science Education*, pages 427–432, 2012.

Teaching the Security Mindset with Reference Monitors*

Justin Cappos
NYU Poly
Brooklyn, NY 11201, U.S.A.
jcappos@poly.edu

Richard Weiss
The Evergreen State College
Olympia, WA 98505 U.S.A.
weissr@evergreen.edu

ABSTRACT

One of the central skills in computer security is reasoning about how programs fail. As a result, computer security necessarily involves thinking about the corner cases that arise when software executes. An unfortunate side effect of this is that computer security assignments typically necessitate deep understanding of a topic, such as how the stack is laid out in memory or how web applications interact with databases.

This work presents a series of assignments that require very little background knowledge from students, yet provide them with the ability to reason about failures in programs. In this set of assignments, students implement two very simple programs in a high-level language (Python). Students first implement a reference monitor that tries to uphold a security property within a sandbox. For the second portion, the students are provided each others' reference monitors and then write attack code to try to bypass the reference monitors. By leveraging a Python-based sandbox, student code is isolated cleanly, which simplifies development and grading.

These assignments have been used in about a dozen classes in a range of environments, including a research university, online classes, and a four year liberal arts school. Student and instructor feedback has been overwhelmingly positive. Furthermore, survey results demonstrate that after a 2-3 week module, 76% of the students who did not understand reference monitors and access control learned these key security concepts.

Categories and Subject Descriptors

K.3.2 [**Computer and Information Science Education**]: Computer science education; D.4.6 [**Security and Protection**]: Access controls; K.6.5 [**Security and Protection**]: Unauthorized access (e.g., hacking, phreaking)

*This work was partially supported by the NWDCSD and NSF grants 1141341, 0834243, 1223588, 1205415, and 1241568.

SIGCSE'14, March 5–8, 2014, Atlanta, Georgia, USA.

http://dx.doi.org/10.1145/2538862.2538939

General Terms

Computer Security Education

Keywords

Security, Python, Access Control, Reference Monitor

1. INTRODUCTION

One of the central concepts in security is to understand how systems can fail, and be made to fail, in different ways. The ability to think about failures and how to trigger them is often termed having a security mindset. It also extends to questioning assumptions and think analytically about their implications. This could be something simple such as, "What can I assume about this web page that is asking for my password?" to "What is the set of invalid strings that an attacker could send to this application that would make it fail?" The analysis of the implications often leads to an exploration of the subtleties of failure cases and requires detailed knowledge of the underlying concept. For example, to understand buffer overflows, a student must understand memory layout and how the stack functions. To understand DNS cache poisoning, one must understand how name resolution functions on the Internet. To understand SQL injection and XSS, one must understand the basics of web applications and databases. To understand these specific applications of the security mindset, one needs some advanced domain knowledge. For this reason, security is typically only emphasized very late in the computer science curriculum which causes some students to miss it. However, the security mindset can be understood independently of the application, and it should be possible to give experiential training in lower division classes.

In this work, we describe a set of programming assignments that require very little background, but provide students with an experience in understanding failure modes (i.e. a security mindset) in the context of a reference monitor. A reference monitor is a method or function that implements an access control policy for a set of resources and is usually specified in terms of what capabilities are allowed. Our goal is to effectively teach this topic in a way that requires minimal background for the students.

In the first part of the assignment, students construct a defensive program that functions as a reference monitor and attempts to meet a specific security goal. This gives the students the experience of thinking as a defender and reinforces the concepts of how to build a secure system. The second part of the assignment involves the students attacking each others' defensive programs created in the first part of the assignment. This allows students to see security from the attackers standpoint and think about how to trigger failures. The third part of the assignment provides the students with a working attack that bypassed their defense written by another student. The students are then asked to categorize the faults that led to the failure in their defensive program and to provide a patch that fixes these problems.

These assignments have been used in about a dozen classes in a range of environments, including both in class and online classes at NYU Poly as well as classes at The Evergreen State College, a four-year liberal arts school. The student feedback has been overwhelmingly positive, with students repeatedly remarking on the effectiveness of the assignments during course evaluations. Furthermore, a pre- and post-assessment of the learning objectives from this portion of the class shows significant improvement in student understanding. In the case of one content question that was directly about the exercise, and required some higher-level understanding, 76% of the students who got the question wrong on the pre-survey were able to answer it correctly on the post-survey.

2. BACKGROUND

The assignment described in this work uses the sandbox used in the Seattle testbed [2, 24, 12, 19]. Seattle's sandbox consists of a programming language virtual machine where students write code in a subset of Python and it executes locally on their computer. Seattle's sandbox is write-once, run anywhere, so the assignment works for students that have Linux, Mac, Windows, BSD, or other operating systems.

In addition to its use in this context, Seattle is a peer-to-peer platform upon which students and researchers can run their own code on end-user devices distributed across the world [2]. One of the main goals of Seattle was to be able to observe real Internet behavior by running software on the everyday devices that are used by the community. However, the security assignments described in this work do not utilize the distributed nature of Seattle.

Seattle has seen broad educational use in 45 classes (primarily on the topics of networking, distributed systems, and security) at over a dozen universities [24, 2]. Students have repeatedly lauded Seattle as easy to use and easy to learn. There exists a wide array of instructional modules that leverage Seattle which are available through different sources [7, 14]. As of August 2013, Seattle is the top rated educational resource on the ACM SIGCOMM Educational Resources Site [1]. Assignments using Seattle are being included into the next edition of the most widely used networking textbook [10].

Interestingly, the Seattle sandbox provides a good environment for the students to explore security because it isolates what both the defensive and attack programs can do. This is achieved with Seattle's multilayer security design, as is shown in Figure 1. User programs must access kernel operations through reference monitors that are isolated using the security layers technique [3]. Seattle itself has been designed to handle the insertion of security functionality and ensures that even if a student writes effective attack code, they can do no harm to other students' systems or the host system [3]. The student's security module sits on top of the security monitors that are built into Seattle.

A reference monitor enforces an access control policy on

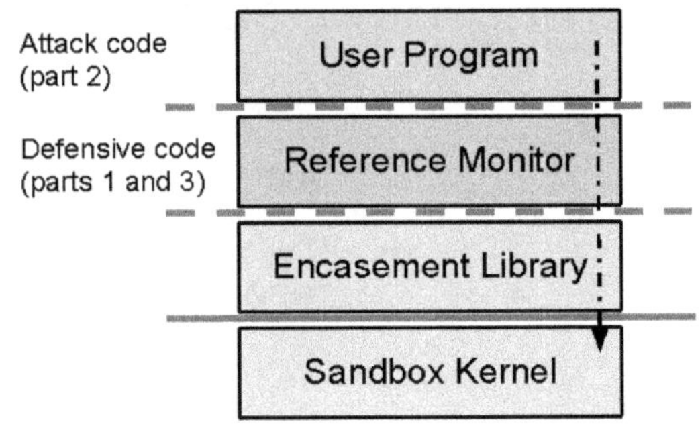

Figure 1: A reference monitor intercepts requests provided by the user program and decides how to process them. The encasement library provides memory isolation between the reference monitor and the user program. There is a clearly defined boundary between the reference monitor and user program, which are implemented in different files. The vertical arrow indicates the only possible call-path from user code passes through the reference monitor before going into the sandbox TCB.

untrusted code. Seattle provides a mechanism for the user to create new reference monitors that sit between untrusted application code and methods in system libraries and the kernel that are to be protected. As an example of how this might be used, some files might have permissions set so that the operating system would allow all users to modify them arbitrarily. A reference monitor can programmatically decide what to do in response to file operations, and so can can do fine-grained operations such as block file writes that would write known malware signatures.

3. THE ASSIGNMENT

The access control reference monitor exercise provides a good opportunity for students to get a feeling of what it means to have a security mindset and to own one's code. The assignment itself is general and can be customized when used, perhaps to prevent cheating or allow the assignment to be reused in multiple classes. For concreteness this section describes one instance of the assignment (the "MZ" version) before discussing other variations. A complete module writeup for each part with detailed instructions (and instructor-only solutions) is available online [17, 15]. There are three main parts to the exercise.

Part One. In the first part, students write a defensive program that enforces an access control policy [17]. For example, the first time the assignment was given, students implemented a reference monitor to prevent a malicious application from writing the characters "MZ" to the first two bytes of a file. (Historically, this is an indicator for an old executable format.) The exercise is to do this by adding security rules to the functions available for reading from a file and writing to a file. The exercise tests the student's ability to write secure code. The students are assessed on their successful use of three design paradigms: accuracy, efficiency, and security. An example of what the vulnerable code that

```
def writeat(self,data,offset):
if data.startswith("MZ") and (offset == 0):
     raise ValueError("Cannot start file with MZ!")
else:
     return self.file.writeat(data,offset)
```

Figure 2: An excerpt from the example (inadequate) defensive code students are provided.

attempts to enforce this looks like is shown in Figure 2.

- Accuracy: The reference monitor should only stop certain actions from being blocked. All other actions should be allowed. For example, If a user tries to write "MX" as the first two bytes of a file, this should be allowed. As a second example "ZM" should be allowed as well. In fact, "MZ" can be written in the file as well, so long as this is not at the first two characters. Accuracy ensures all valid operations are permitted.
- Efficiency: The reference monitor should use a minimum number of resources, so performance is not impacted. This means the defensive code must not do things like re-read the file before each write. Efficiency ensures the reference monitor is not overly costly in terms of unnecessary I/O.
- Security: The attacker should not be able to circumvent the reference monitor. Hence if the attacker can first write "Z" as the second character and later writes "M" as the first character, the action must be blocked. Security ensures the reference monitor does not allow an attacker to circumvent the goal of the reference monitor.

Part Two. For the second part of the exercise [15], each student's code from the first part is made available to every other student in the class. A student will create a series of one or more test cases that attempt to cause security problems or impact the accuracy of the system. To find these flaws, we have observed students employing a variety of techniques. Essentially all students look at each others code to find ways to compromise the reference monitor. This provides students with some experience in bug-finding through reading code. Many students also chose to write routines to fuzz input to the reference monitors to further uncover problems that they could exploit. A few students also wrote tests that attempt to trigger time-of-check-to-time-of-use (TOCTTOU) bugs by causing race conditions in the code.

Part Three. In the third part of the assignment (which has not been used at all of the schools), the students are given the attack code that bypassed their reference monitor. They are asked to fix the reference monitor so that the security it provides cannot be bypassed in the same way. The student also must write a document that classifies the bugs in their code according to type (such as TOCTTOU, error handling logic, or similar issues). This helps to reinforce to the student why these issues occurred and what they might do to avoid them in the future.

Types of Errors Students Make. Writing effective defensive code for this assignment is a deceptively hard task. In prior classes, about 80% of the students wrote a reference monitor that other students could find a flaw in. (In fact, most instructors who have attempted the assignment also have errors in their reference monitor.) While in a few cases, students simply do not adequately test their code and have obvious programming errors, this is not the common cause of issues. Students tend to write insecure code due to overlooking a few common issues (listed from most to least commonly exploited).

- The reference monitor needs to track the state of the information on disk, but cannot re-read it for every access (due to efficiency concerns). A common mistake is when the attacker can cause the reference monitor's state to diverge from the underlying system's state, especially in error conditions. For example, if the program attempts to write past the end of a file (or before the beginning of a file), the reference monitor may incorrectly update its state. As a result, the reference monitor will improperly block or allow writes since the disk contents differ. This can cause both security and accuracy issues.
- Time-of-check-to-time-of-use (TOCTTOU) bugs and other types of race conditions are a fairly common oversight for students. Some students write test cases that attempt to trigger a race condition to exploit these problems. This can result in essentially any sort of attack, even infinite loops in the reference monitor in some cases.
- Some reference monitors inappropriately share state for different files. For example, there may be a global set of state that is used to store the first two bytes. By opening multiple files, an attacker may be able to overwrite this state and cause security and accuracy issues.
- In rare cases, a student's reference monitor may inappropriately retain state for a file. For example, an attacker may create a file, write some data, then close and delete the file. If the attacker recreates a file with the same name, the state should be cleared.

One of the important features of this exercise is that students can get experience in both offensive and defensive roles. When defending a system, the more attacks one knows, the better. Getting students to own their code is a significant challenge. In order for students to write secure code, they must be able to see both sides. One unexpected benefit of the assignment is that students seemed to enjoy seeing each others' solutions to assignments. Many students said that being able to learn from (and exploit) these pieces of code was much more rewarding than submitting exercises and having them graded by the instructor or TA. From the instructor's standpoint, it has the additional benefit that student feedback can be used in grading. The defensive parts of the assignments can be graded based upon how well they hold up to the offensive portion. (We provide scripts that automate the grading process.) Simply by validating each student's attacks against the other students' defenses, makes an easy way to provide meaningful feedback and scoring.

3.1 Variations

The assignment can also be easily customized or modified to allow reuse. The ease of doing this is an important feature because most faculty have limited time to develop

ASSIGNMENT:

```
In this assignment you will create a reference moni-
tor which stops the attacker from reading data securely
written in a file.  You will create a function called
privatewrite which allows the user to write data into a
file which cannot be read back from the file.  The data
can be overwritten but isn't readable under any circum-
stance.  You will do this by adding security rules to
the functions available for reading from and writing to
a file.  Think of this as a method to write some data
securely into a file.  The future of the system depends
on your ability to write secure code!
```

Figure 3: An excerpt from the assignment description for the privatewrite variation.

new curriculum. One such variation that we have tried is the Private Write assignment. Instead of simply interposing on an existing file system API call, as the 'MZ' assignment does, the Private Write assignment adds a new call as is specified in Figure 3. The complete module writeup with detailed instructions for both the defense and attack code are also available [18, 16].

As with the original assignment, we provided the students an example reference monitor so they could see how to integrate and run their code. By examining the attack and defense scores, this variation was of about the same difficulty as the original assignment. This demonstrates that it is easy to adapt the assignment to the preferences of the individual instructor. As a result, the assignments can be reused or customized to better fit different portions of the curriculum.

4. METHODOLOGY FOR ASSESSMENT

This group of reference monitor exercises has been used in about a dozen classes at multiple schools (NYU Poly and The Evergreen State College). The assignment is very straightforward to modify in minor ways to fit the class, and this has been done by several instructors who used it. The ease of modifying the exercise makes it easy for faculty to adapt it to their classes and resist students posting and copying answers.

When this assignment has been given in regular classes, the students are usually given one week to complete each part. In order to make the assignments easier to complete, especially for students with no experience with Python, we gave the students a template consisting of a simple reference monitor which inadequately checks the desired security property. For example, this may check to see that the first two characters in a single call to write are not "MZ". A snippet of this code is shown in Figure 2. Students are also given an example of an attack program that tries to write "MZ" in the first two characters. This provides students with a starting point and demonstrates to them how to run the program and see how an ineffective attack can be blocked.

Description of the courses we taught and how the exercises were used: One of the faculty used this exercise in an upper-division class on network security at The Evergreen State College, a liberal arts college. Many of the students did not know Python, and they were still able to do the exercise. However, they made some mistakes due to the fact that they were not thinking about concurrency and thread safety which are covered in other classes such as operating systems.

	Q1	Q2	Q3	Q4
Pre-survey: number of correct answers out of 57	29 (51%)	27 (47%)	21 (37%)	42 (74%)
Post-survey: number of correct answers out of 38	32 (84%)	23 (61%)	20 (53%)	29 (76%)
For paired responses: number of incorrect answers on pre-survey	21	17	21	10
For paired responses: number of correct answers on post-survey, given incorrect answer on the pre-survey	16	11	12	5

Table 1: Survey results from classroom use of the exercise.

This exercise was also given to a faculty attending the CSAW Summer Research and Training for College Faculty, a summer workshop on security [4]. These faculty were not necessarily experts in security and they were only given one evening to work on the assignment. Several of the faculty did not know Python before starting the assignment. All of the faculty completed both the defensive and offensive assignments. While there were a few whose programs passed all of the tests, the majority made mistakes. We think that this shows that the exercise requires analysis skills and questioning assumptions (security mindset), and not just knowledge.

We were interested to know whether students fully engaged in the exercises and learned the main concept. We asked students a brief set of knowledge questions (listed in Figure 4) before and after they were assigned the reference monitor module. These questions were intended to obtain a baseline of student understanding with respect to the concepts that lie at the core of the module as well as related concepts. Our survey asked questions on how a reference monitor is used, how it relates to access control matrices and how it relates to capability systems. It also asked a general question about access control. The first question was a core one, and that showed a direct relationship to the exercise. The others potentially indicated higher cognitive levels at which the student could make connections to related concepts at the level of 'synthesis' in Bloom's taxonomy. With laboratory exercises it is often possible for students to go through the motions of doing the exercise without reflecting deeply on it or even understanding what they are doing. The four questions we asked were designed to measure understanding at a range of cognitive levels on a relative scale. The first question was a knowledge question about how a reference monitor is used. The other three questions were about access control and required different levels of understanding. The levels of difficulty can be inferred from the larger sample of students who took the post-survey and it agreed with the *a priori* ranking of difficulty and cognitive level. The four content questions were multiple choice, each with four possible answers except the first, which had three.

5. RESULTS

We analyzed the survey results from the introductory security class at NYU Poly in the Fall of 2012. Our results demonstrate that a significant number of students learned the main concept of reference monitor and how it relates to other concepts in access control. All of the students in the

Q1. Suppose that an application is running in an environment with a reference monitor. The application gains access to the operating system:

- Directly
- Through the reference monitor
- Either through the reference monitor or not at the application programmer's discretion

Q2. Which of the following is easy to do with an access matrix system:

- Trust revocation of "open" resources
- Listing all users with access to a resource
- Authentication of users
- Building a reference monitor

Q3. Which of the following is easy to do in a capability system:

- Trust revocation of "open" resources
- Listing all users with access to a resource
- Authentication of users
- Building a reference monitor

Q4. Which of the following is crucial to every access control system:

- Correct authentication of users
- Confidentiality
- Strong passwords
- Long cryptographic keys

Figure 4: Survey questions to measure learning in the exercise.

class turned all three portions of the assignment. The average number of lines of code for each part of the assignment was under 100. Although there were about 70 students in the class, the number students who completed both pre- and post-surveys using matching names was 34. The results are summarized in Table 1.

The most significant result from the surveys was for the first question (Q1) which was directly about the exercise. For this question, of the 34 students with paired surveys, 21 students answered the question incorrectly on the pre-survey. Of the 21, the number who answered it correctly on the post-survey was 16. This demonstrates a significant learning outcome. If none of those 21 students had learned the concept and had guessed on the post-survey, we would expect only 7 of them to have gotten the right answer. The probability that 16 or more would have guessed the right answer is less than 0.01. This result suggests that 76% of the students who did not know the concept before, were able to learn it by completing the exercise. Of the 13 who answered it correctly on the pre-survey, one got it wrong on the post-survey, suggesting that only one or two students in that group were guessing. Note that the answer to the question on the survey did not appear in the description of the exercise. As we know from experience, it is possible for students to do an exercise mechanically without grasping the meaning, and that does not seem to be the case here.

Question 4 (Q4) was a general question about access control and was not addressed by the assignment. Of the 10 students who got it wrong on the pre-survey, 5 got it right on the post-survey, which allows us to reject the null hypothesis ($p = .035$) that no one learned the concept in the the time frame of the assignments. Our explanation is that in the process of attending lectures and reading for the assignment, students also learned related material not directly covered. This is important to track because a good assignment will engage students in the subject and prime them for learning related information. Questions 2 and 3 were related to the assignment, and in this context required a higher level of cognitive understanding than question 1 because they were not specifically addressed in the assignments. For question 2, of the 17 students who got it wrong on the pre-survey, 11 got it correct on the post-, giving statistical significant positive outcome with a $p = .04$ and an estimated learning rate of 65%.

Question 3 is problematic for a couple of reasons. First, depending on the way that the capability system is implemeneted, there can be more than one correct answer. As a result, we consider two answers as being potentially correct. This greatly reduces the statistical guarantees that students are not guessing and that the improvements in scores are not due to chance. Thus, although the percentage of students who got it right increased whether it was scored with one or two correct answers, the results were not statistically significant in either case.

6. RELATED WORK

Security Injections [20] presents a compelling set of exercises for CS0, CS1 and CS2 that address the problem of adding security-related exercises to an existing curriculum at an introductory to intermediate level. However, their examples (such as buffer overflows and integer overflow) do not give students the opportunity to engage in both defensive and offensive roles. They focus on safe coding practices without giving them an opportunity to think actively about how to attack vulnerable code. The SEED project [6] presents a set of more advanced exercises and projects, but they also do not involve both defensive and offensive roles.

There are a number of hands-on exercises in the form of games. The competitive exercise firesim [23] does give students an opportunity to assume both roles in a competitive exercise about firewalls, although the attack role is limited to a small set of options. CyberSIEGE is an interactive video game with a number of high-level scenarios that emphasize defense and risk management [21]. Players decide how to allocate resources to defend a network. It includes scenarios about component configuration (e.g., ACLs; filters; VPNs; etc.), policies/training, patch management, network topology, use of cryptography, use of background checks, and physical security. In spirit it seems to address the security mindset, although it does not model vulnerability analysis at a high level of detail and does not put players in the role of attacker. EDURange [8] is an (as of yet unreleased) environment for developing competitive games with both offensive and defensive roles. However, EDURange requires deeper technical knowledge of networking, port scanning, and similar tasks than the assignments described here. The Control-Alt-Hack [5] card game teaches security awareness, but does not involve analysis or the security mindset.

There are at least two platforms that provide an environment for running cybersecurity exercises. They are DETER [11] and RAVE [13]. They provide a virtual private network which is flexible isolated from the Internet, so they can be used for offensive and defensive exercises. These are more suitable for advanced tasks like network exploitation and penetration testing, while our assignments require much less background and expertise.

The Google Gruyere [9] and OWASP Webgoat [22] projects provide students with an opportunity to play the role of attacker of vulnerable web applications. Gruyere also includes tutorial material which helps students with a wide range of backgrounds. Neither one provides an opportunity to harden an application against attacks.

7. CONCLUSIONS AND FUTURE WORK

In order to be meaningful, practical, and engaging for students, we believe that the computer security curriculum must include hands-on exercises that develop both defensive and offensive skills. This is integrally related to the security mindset, which is about not trusting input and interfaces, examining failure modes and questioning assumptions. This topic is particularly important in the knowledge domain of access control, which is one of the fundamental concepts in computer security and arises with firewalls, file protections and information processing in general. We believe that the assignments we used challenged students to reassess failures and think through assumptions in this key domain.

We applied pre- and post-surveys to assess whether students learned the fundamental concept of a reference monitor in the context of access control. The results showed that there was a significant improvement at the knowledge level and at higher levels, as well. While we did not show causation, we did show correlation over a short period of time. We plan to collect additional survey data from other classes.

In the future, we would like to test more directly whether students can learn the security mindset from doing exercises that require them to take on both attacker and defender roles. We believe that this can be done with exercises similar to the one that we described in this paper. Although we do not have any data for CS1 or CS2, we believe that there is an opportunity to teach and assess the security mindset and the concepts of access control using the defender and attacker roles even in lower division classes. We intend to explore these assignments in lower division classes to determine their effectiveness early in the curriculum.

8. REFERENCES

[1] ACM SIGCOMM Educational Resources. `http://edusigcomm.info.ucl.ac.be/`.

[2] J. Cappos, I. Beschastnikh, A. Krishnamurthy, and T. Anderson. Seattle: a platform for educational cloud computing. *SIGCSE Bull.*, 41(1):111–115, 2009.

[3] J. Cappos, A. Dadgar, J. Rasley, J. Samuel, I. Beschastnikh, C. Barsan, A. Krishnamurthy, and T. Anderson. Retaining Sandbox Containment Despite Bugs in Privileged Memory-Safe Code. In *The 17th ACM Conference on Computer and Communications Security (CCS '10)*. ACM, 2010.

[4] Csaw summer research and training for college faculty. `http://www.poly.edu/events/2013/07/08/csaw-summer-research-and-training-college-faculty`.

[5] T. Denning, T. Kohno, and A. Shostack. Control-alt-hack: a card game for computer security outreach and education (abstract only). In *Proceeding of the 44th ACM technical symposium on Computer science education*, SIGCSE '13, pages 729–729, New York, NY, USA, 2013. ACM.

[6] W. Du and R. Wang. Seed: A suite of instructional laboratories for computer security education. *Journal on Educational Resources in Computing (JERIC)*, 8(1):3, 2008.

[7] Educational Portal –Seattle – Trac. `https://seattle.poly.edu/wiki/EducationalPortal`.

[8] EDURange Description. `http://blogs.evergreen.edu/edurange`.

[9] Google Gruyere Home. `http://google-gruyere.appspot.com/`.

[10] J. F. Kurose and K. W. Ross. *Computer Networking: A Top-Down Approach Featuring the Internet*. Pearson/Addison-Wesley, 2005.

[11] J. Mirkovic, T. Benzel, T. Faber, R. Braden, J. Wroclawski, and S. Schwab. The deter project: Advancing the science of cyber security experimentation and test. In *Technologies for Homeland Security (HST), 2010 IEEE International Conference on*, pages 1–7, 2010.

[12] Monzur Muhammad and Justin Cappos. Towards a Representive Testbed: Harnessing Volunteers for Networks Research. In *The First GENI Research and Educational Workshop*, GENI'12, 2012.

[13] K. Nance, B. Taylor, R. Dodge, and B. Hay. Creating shareable security modules. In *Information Assurance and Security Education and Training*, pages 156–163. Springer, 2013.

[14] Main Page – NW-DCSD. `http://ai.vancouver.wsu.edu/~nwdcsd/wiki/index.php/Main_Page`.

[15] Attacking a reference monitor that implements access control. `https://seattle.poly.edu/wiki/EducationalAssignments/SecurityLayerPartTwo`.

[16] Attacking private write. `https://seattle.poly.edu/wiki/EducationalAssignments/PrivateWritePartOne`.

[17] Building a reference monitor that implements access control. `https://seattle.poly.edu/wiki/EducationalAssignments/SecurityLayerPartOne`.

[18] Building a reference monitor that implements private write. `https://seattle.poly.edu/wiki/EducationalAssignments/PrivateWritePartOne`.

[19] Seattle. `https://seattle.poly.edu/`.

[20] B. Taylor and S. Kaza. Security injections: modules to help students remember, understand, and apply secure coding techniques. In *Proceedings of the 16th annual joint conference on Innovation and technology in computer science education*, pages 3–7. ACM, 2011.

[21] M. Thompson and C. Irvine. Active learning with the cyberciege video game. In *Proceedings of the 4th conference on Cyber security experimentation and test*, pages 10–10. USENIX Association, 2011.

[22] OWASP Webgoat Project. `http://www.owasp.org/index.php/Category:OWASP_WebGoat_Project`.

[23] K. Williams. Firesim Project. `http://williams.comp.ncat.edu/firesim`.

[24] Yanyan Zhuang and Albert Rafetseder and Justin Cappos. Experience with Seattle: A Community Platform for Research and Education. In *The Second GENI Research and Educational Workshop*, GREE'13, 2013.

Harnessing the Cloud for Teaching Cybersecurity

Khaled Salah
Electrical and Computer Engineering Department
Khalifa University of Science, Technology and Research (KUSTAR), UAE
khaled.salah@kustar.ac.ae

ABSTRACT

Cloud computing has become an attractive paradigm for many organizations in government, industry as well as academia. In academia, the cloud can offer instructors and students (whether local or at a distance) on-demand, dedicated, isolated, unlimited, and easily configurable machines. Such an approach has clear advantages over access to machines in a classic lab setting. In this paper, we show how cloud services and infrastructure could be harnessed to facilitate practical experience and training for cybersecurity. We used the popular Amazon Web Services (AWS) cloud; however, the use cases and approaches laid out in this paper are also applicable to other cloud providers.

Categories and Subject Descriptors

K.3.2 [**Computer and Information Science Education**]: Computer Science Education, curriculum, Information systems education.

Keywords

Cybersecurity; Network Security; Computer Security; Education; Cloud; Amazon AWS.

1. INTRODUCTION

Cybersecurity has become one of the emerging areas of paramount importance to industry, government, and society. US and UK governments have been investing heavily on IT and cybersecurity education and training [1,2]. The demand for highly trained and skillful cybersecurity professionals is skyrocketing; and it seems evident that such a demand will remain to be a key recruitment area for many years to come. In addition, the market for long-distance teaching of cybersecurity is huge as many of the IT professionals, who wish to study cybersecurity, are already employed.

Effective pedagogy and delivery of cybersecurity material requires not only knowledge-based outcomes but more importantly practical and skill-based outcomes. This way, mastery of the topic is achieved with theoretical competence as well as practical experience. Students (whether local or at a distance) are expected to apply theory and principles to a realistic environment by means of labs and hands-on exercises, particularly in employing popular security tools, packages, and software commonly used for cyber attacks and defenses.

Facilitating practical cybersecurity work and training for both local and remote students can pose a major challenge. In a classic lab setting, for local students, a cybersecurity lab is established with a number of machines equipped with relevant security tools and software packages. These machines are typically interconnected via a network which is isolated from the production network either physically or by means of a firewall. For remote students taking the course and living at another campus, a similar lab has to be established at the remote campus. For individual remote students spread at different locations, such an option becomes not viable.

In a classic lab setting, configuration, installation, scheduling and management of lab equipment and workstations become costly for a lab technician or an instructor. Other than the cost associated with the operation and maintenance of lab machines, it may become formidable for an instructor in which a good percentage of the instructor's time is consumed by troubleshooting issues related to configuration and installation of software and tools which get misconfigured and tampered with by numerous students. More importantly, students may get frustrated by being distracted spending most of their time dealing with configuration and installation errors or competing for machines and lab time. Unfortunately, under such classic lab setting, the lab exercises often turn into setup and installation exercises for the instructor and the students, rather than focused, meaningful, and enjoyable exercises with clear objectives of gaining practical skills and knowledge that solidify the theoretical aspects delivered in the lectures. Moreover, under a classic lab setting, scheduling of lab usage for large classes and with a lab of limited resources becomes another formidable issue, especially prior to assignment deadlines as students rush to compete for lab time and resources. Obviously, these management and scheduling problems get exacerbated with long-distance education.

Cloud computing paradigm remedies most, if not all, of the classic lab problems associated with cost, operation, scheduling, and management. The cloud provides on-demand, dedicated, isolated, scalable, unlimited, easily configurable and accessible machines for both the instructor and students whether they are local or at a distance. In this paper, we share our experience in harnessing the power of the cloud to facilitate practical and hands-on cybersecurity experience and training. We used Amazon AWS cloud, but the use cases and approaches laid out in this paper are also applicable to other cloud providers such as Rackspace, Google Compute Engine, GoGrid, HP Cloud, Salesforce, etc. The one-semester US-system course was taught in Spring-2013 for

SIGCSE'14, March 5–8, 2014, Atlanta, Georgia, USA.
Copyright © 2014 ACM 978-1-4503-2605-6/14/03…$15.00.
http://dx.doi.org/10.1145/2538862.2538880

senior undergraduate students from two campuses via a virtual classroom setup with live audio and video. The course, including lecture and lab components, was taught by a single instructor with no extra help from a lab or teaching assistant.

The remainder of the paper is organized as follows: Section 2 gives a brief overview of Amazon AWS cloud environment and the concept of base images and virtualized instances. Section 3 highlights key advantages of using the cloud for teaching cybersecurity. Section 4 describes briefly a list of cybersecurity hands-on exercises that are suitable to be carried out by students on the cloud. Section 5 describes some of the limitations for cloud-based cybersecruity training and discusses ways to overcome these limitations. Section 6 gives an overview of related work found in the literature. Finally, Section 7 concludes the study.

2. AMAZON AWS CLOUD

Amazon AWS is the most popular cloud provider these days. Basically, it is an infrastructure as a service (IaaS) in which compute resources are offered to cloud users in terms of virtual machines or instances called EC2 (Elastic Compute Cloud). EC2 instances come in different sizes from "t1.micro" instances of one core and small RAM of 613MB to "h1.4xlarge" instances of 16 cores and 60 GB of RAM [3]. In the cloud, an instance is a virtual machine, and depending on the instance size, a physical machine can host one or multiple instances. Instances are launched from Amazon Machine Image (AMI). An AMI is a template that contains a pre-configured operating system with applications, tools and other software packages. As shown in Figure 1, from an AMI, a single or multiple instances can be launched. Amazon provides different types of AMIs which could be Windows or Linux based. These AMIs are provided by Amazon, the public, or can be purchased from the AWS Marketplace. It is also possible that a user could create his own AMI and import it to Amazon AWS cloud. Users can connect to Linux instances via a secure shell and to Windows instances via a remote desktop utility.

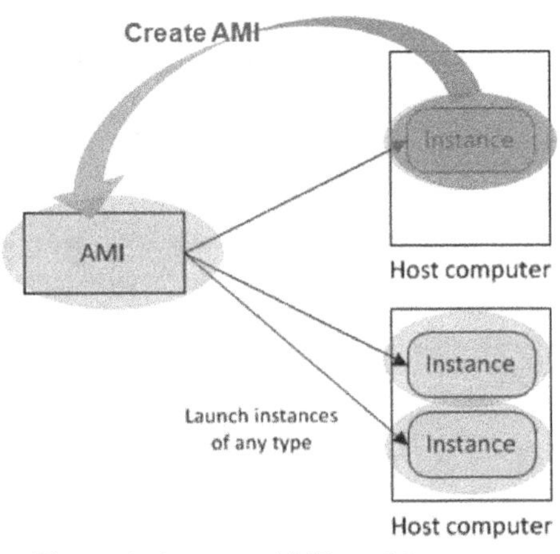

Figure 1. Amazon AMIs and instances

One key feature of Amazon AMIs and instances is that Amazon instances can create AMIs, as shown in Figure 1. This is indeed a great feature for instructors and students, which can tremendously save time in troubleshooting problems related to installation and configuration. For a particular lab exercise that requires certain operating system and software packages, the instructor can start with a base AMI with a bare operating system like Windows or Linux, launch an instance and then install the needed software packages and tools. The instructor can test and ensure the installed tools and software packages whether they are working properly. After that, the instructor can create a new AMI off this instance, and this AMI can be made available for students to use. When the student launches this AMI, there would be no need for him/her to perform any type of installation or configuration. It is almost guaranteed that the software tools will work properly and as expected. Therefore, the instructor and students are not distracted by setup and installation activities, and can primarily focus on carrying out the lab exercises to satisfy the exercise objectives.

To illustrate further the concept of AMIs and instances, Figure 2 shows a snapshot of the web-based AWS management dashboard showing two AMIs: one is named "DionaeaSqlite" which runs on Linux and the other is named "NWSec_lab5" which runs on Windows. The former AMI contains Linux with installed Dionaea honeypot. Students can use this AMI to launch Dionaea instances (e.g. "SalahDionaea" as shown in Figure 3). From the "NWSec_Lab5" AMI, students can launch Windows instances with preconfigured security tools that will be used to carry out some set of activities, as part of Lab 5 assignment. Figure 3 shows different types and sizes of instances running on Amazon datacenter located in "Ireland". The figure shows three Linux-based instances (Snort, Nessus, and Dionaea) and two Windows-based instances (for Lab 4 and Lab 5), with two running instances and three stopped instances.

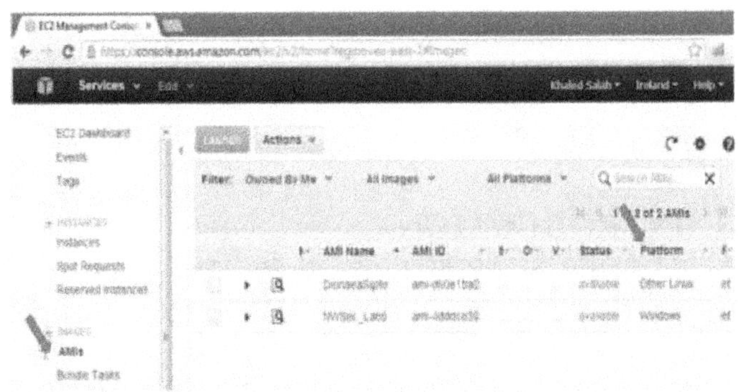

Figure 2. A snapshot of AWS dashboard showing two AMIs of Linux and Windows

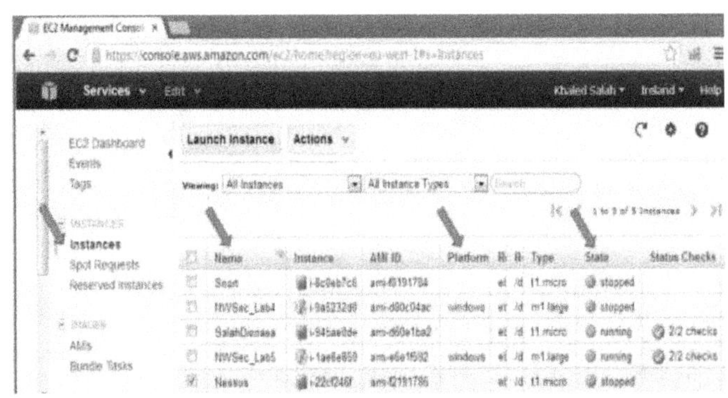

Figure 3. A snapshot of AWS dashboard showing stopped and running instances

To connect to running Linux instances, a JAVA SSH client or "putty" can be used. Figure 4 shows a snapshot of SSH client connected to a running Dionaea instance. The snapshot verifies that Dioanae is running using the "ps" Linux command. The snapshot also shows the network connections collected by Dionaea. These connections are stored in Sqlite database and could be displayed using Sqlite commands, as shown in Figure 4. On the other hand, connecting to running Windows instances is performed using the remote desktop Windows utility. Figure 5 shows a Windows instance with preconfigured applications and security tools. The figure lists three security applications being launched; namely XeNmap, Cain&Abel, and Wireshark.

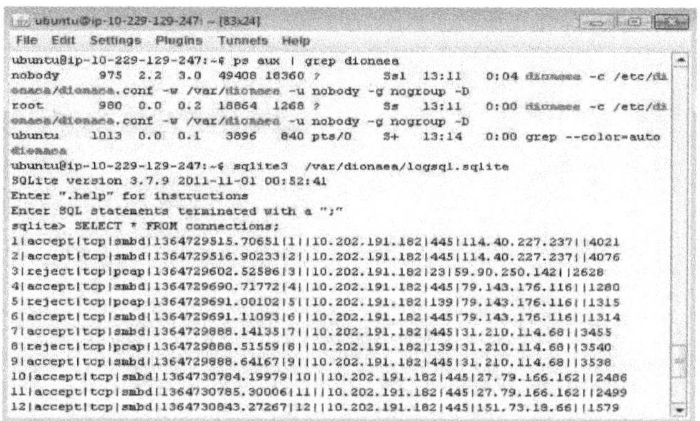

Figure 4. SSH client screen connected to a Linux instance running Dionaea and Sqlite

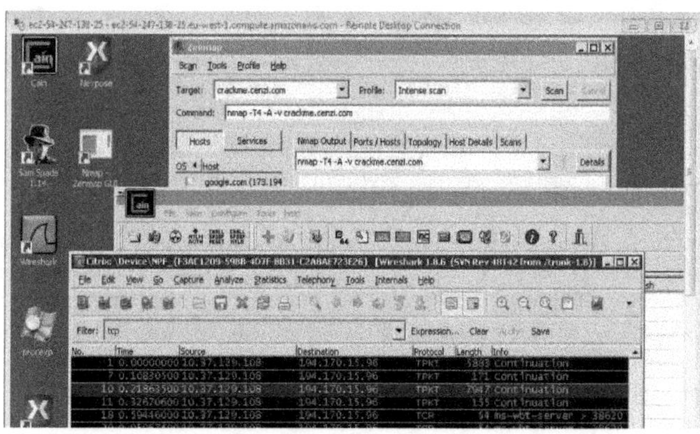

Figure 5. Remote desktop screen connected to a Windows instance with preconfigured security tools

3. CLOUD ADVANTAGES

In this section, we briefly discuss and summarize key advantages of using the cloud for teaching cybersecurity. A key advantage is the use of preconfigured AMIs with required security tools and software packages. Some cybersecurity tools, such as Wireshark, Cain&Abel, NetCat, Openssl, XeNmap, JohntheRipper, etc, are easy to install and configure. However, many other the tools, such as Snort, Nessus, Nexpose, NetWitness, MetaSploit, etc, are known to be cumbersome to install and configure. For less-skillful students and for those students less familiar with Linux, installing Snort can be an overwhelming task. However, using the cloud, the instructor needs only to develop a single AMI that has Snort properly installed only once, and then make this AMI available to students. Then students need only to launch an instance from this AMI and thereafter dive into carrying out Snort activities.

There are other key benefits in using the cloud infrastructure for running cybersecurity exercises. First, students can rapidly allocate resources and launch instances. If an instance fails, the student can rapidly launch or restart a new instance. This is a desirable feature especially when running security tools and software which often crash and cause crashes to the operating system. Second, as a byproduct, instances running on the cloud are not affecting production networks, whatsoever. Therefore, cybersecurity exercises are conducted by the students in a safe and contained environment away from campus production network. Third, some foreign governments, ISP, and universities often block unwanted web sites that are identified to contain malicious content. Examples of these sites are www.oxid.it and www.milw0rm.com. In teaching a cybersecurity course, students need access to these sites to either download tools or be familiar with their content as a way to broaden their scope of knowledge.

Finally, in the cloud and for an instructor, troubleshooting and grading of students' work and assignments is a major key advantage. With Amazon AWS cloud, the instructor is granted the main account in which she/he uses to manage and create student accounts with unique username and passwords. The instructor, acting as a system administrator for these accounts, can restrict and control their access policy by adding them to a particular security group. The instructor can also have access to running student instances. This means in the cases when a student has a problem, the instructor can remotely log into the student instance and troubleshoot it. This is indeed a great and convenient feature that would save the student and the instructor a considerable amount of time spent on debugging. More importantly, at the time of grading the assignment, the instructor can verify the student work by launching and logging into the student instances.

4. CLOUD-ENABLED EXERCISES

We briefly describe a list of cloud-based cybersecurity hands-on exercises that were assigned to our senior students as part of the coursework for an introductory course on network security. These exercises complement in-class theoretical material and aim to spark student interest and enhance their learning experience. In most of these exercises, students were asked to submit a report with adequate snapshots of their work. In several occasions, the instructor had to login into student instances to troubleshoot configuration and also to verify their work after submission for grading.

- Packet Sniffing. Wireshark and TCPDump tools were used to sniff packets and analyze network traffic generated by the web browser and utilities like FTP, ICMP Ping, and Traceroute. The commands to generate this traffic were executed from a Windows and Linux EC2 instances targeting remote sites such as catless.ncl.ac.uk, hack.me, www.crackmes.de and crackme.cenzic.com. For the site crackme.cenzic.com, students were asked to capture packets containing username and passwords. Students also used Cain&Abel tool to filter and capture easily without examining packets usernames and passwords sent via HTTP protocol.
- Network Footprinting and Port Scanning. Tools like XeNmap, Whois, Hping, Traceroute, and Maltego were installed on an AMI and launched by students to footprint

and gather information about email and IP addresses. Also sites like geektools.com, geopiptool.com, shodanhq.com and dnsstruff.com were used to gather more accurate information.

- Vulnerability Assessment and Penetration Testing. A Windows-based AMI with Nexpose and Nessus were made available to students to perform vulnerability assessment against another instance running Dionaea honeypot containing simulated vulnerabilities. Then Metasploit framework, which was also installed in the same AMI, was used to perform penetration and remote exploitation of some of these vulnerabilities.
- Backdoor Establishment. Netcat was used to establish a backdoor shell via DNS port 53 to bypass firewall rules. The backdoor was created between an EC2 instance and the student's local machine.
- Firewalls. Students experimented first with configuring an Amazon EC2 firewall by setting and testing simple firewall rules for inbound and outbound traffic to a group of EC2 instances. Then, students experimented with Windows firewall utility via "$netsh advfirewall" and with Linux IPTables to set and test simple firewall rules. Simple rules were set for passing and denying FTP and HTTP traffic. In addition students were asked to examine the impact of changing the order of the rules.
- Snort NIDS. A Linux-based AMI of Snort intrusion detection system was made available for students to experiment with. After launching the AMI, students used Nessus, Nmap and ping reconnaissance utilities to trigger alerting and logging of malicious activities involving different types of network scanning.
- Dionaea Honeypot. An AMI with Dioneae honeypot was launched by students. Ping and Nmap utilities were used to target Dionaea instance to force it to log events. Students were then asked to analyze and examine the collected logs and data stored in Dionaea's Sqlite database.
- OpenSSL. To complement the cryptography theoretical component in the lectures, students launched an AMI with installed OpenSSL. Students were then asked to perform variety of tasks using OpenSSL, such as creating symmetric and asymmetric keys, X.509 certificates, encrypting, decrypting, and hashing files with different modes and options.

In addition, many other hands-on cybersecurity exercises and experiments are of key interest to cybersecurity training. Some of these exercises are discussed in [4-7]. The majority of these cybersecurity exercises can be easily augmented to be carried out in the cloud. Those exercises include OS hardening, password cracking, dictionary and rainbow attacks, denial of service attacks, detecting spoofing, buffer overflow vulnerabilities, SQL injection, cross-site scripting, fuzzying, web security and vulnerabilities, Rootkit detection, malware analysis and software cracking, and forensics of captured disk images.

5. LIMITATIONS

In this section, we note some obvious challenges and limitations for using the cloud for teaching cybersecurity. We also suggest, whenever possible, alternatives to these limitations. Clearly, cloud-based teaching requires a learning curve for both instructors and students. From our experience, the learning curve is reasonable and not that steep as Amazon AWS provides ample videos and webinars for simply creating a Linux or Windows instance and for more advanced features of building elastic applications [8]. Another limitation to note is that not all of the cybersecurity lab exercises are amenable to be carried out using the cloud. For example, certain exercises involving disk and smart phone forensics require hardware write-blockers and smart phone devices. Another example of lab exercises that are impractical to perform in the cloud are those relevant to cracking wireless security protocols; namely, WEP and WPA. For these wireless security exercises and as an alternative to the cloud, students can be asked to perform cracking exercises by setting an AP (Access Point) using their home wireless router or smart phone and then perform the experiment using a bootable Backtrack CD from their laptop or home desktop.

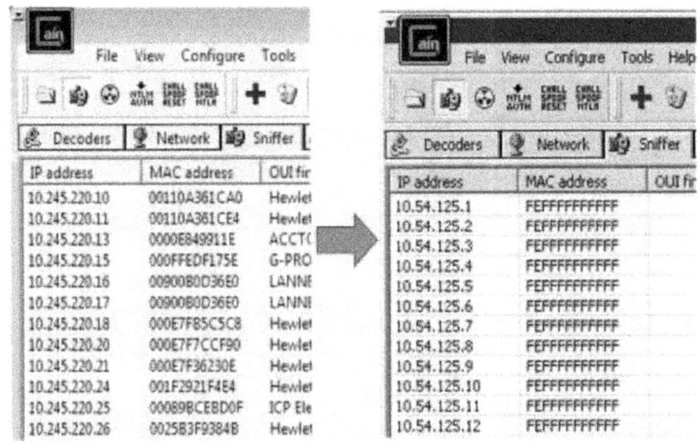

Figure 6. A snapshot of Cain&Abel sniffer output from a local physical machine (Left) and from Amazon EC2 instance (Right)

Network security exercises involving eavesdropping and MITM (Man-In-The-Middle) attacks are not feasible in the cloud. The main reason has to do with virtualization of network resources in which the hypervisor masks out the MAC addresses of running instances. Figure 6 shows two snapshots when running Cain&Abel sniffer to scan and reveal the MAC addresses of hosts within the local network. We ran the sniffer on a local physical machine and on the cloud. As shown in Figure 6(Right), the MAC addresses of running EC2 instances are meaningless. These MAC addresses are needed to perform ARP poisoning to carry out a successful MITM attack. As an alternative to this limitation, the instructor can ask the students to run Cain&Abel from their laptop on their home network.

Using AWS, user account management for students is not straightforward. In AWS, the instructor is granted an admin account to create and manage accounts for students [9]. Such a setup allows for centralized management, monitoring, and control of all students' instances. However, under such setup, it was noted that students have unauthorized access to other students' instances with ability of stopping and terminating theirs. This concern has been communicated to AWS team to resolve. However, a way to circumvent this limitation in the future, if not resolved by AWS team, is to allow each student to have his/her account with full access given by the student to the instructor for grading and troubleshooting. The issue with this approach is that the instructor has to make the course AMIs *publically* available.

6. RELATED WORK

In the literature, virtual laboratories for cybersecurity training exist in different forms. Among the popular virtual security lab projects are VITAL (Virtual Information Assurance Laboratory) [10], DeterLab, [11,12] and Tele-Lab [13]. These virtual labs can provide experiments where students can configure a number of networked virtual machines to carry out security offense and defense exercises. The use of virtual machine technologies in constructing virtual security laboratories are described in adequate detail in [14-19]. Unlike the cloud-based platform, in almost all of these projects, the virtual lab environment and platform do not have open access, and are not scalable or reusable. Moreover, these platforms offer limited centralized access by the instructor for management, monitoring, and control.

NETinVM is yet another form that is used for cybersecurity training. NETinVM is a standalone virtualized environment that can be used for security training [20]. NETinVM runs multiple virtual machines on a single Linux host utilizing the concept of UML (User-Mode Linux). Running experiments with reasonable performance when having many virtual machines launched within NETinVM requires the student to own a high-speed laptop or a desktop with large RAM. Unlike the cloud, NETinVM does not offer remote control access to the instructor to troubleshoot, check, and grade student hands-on coursework. Consequently, this makes NETinVM not a good fit for students taking the course remotely.

7. CONCLUSION

This paper has highlighted our experience in using today's Amazon AWS cloud for teaching a one-semester course on cybersecurity. The paper showed how the cloud infrastructure and resources can be harnessed for facilitating lab and practical experience in cybersecurity. It has been noted that except for a few exercises, which require local physical hardware, the majority of hands-on exercises in cybersecurity can be carried out in the cloud. At the end of the one-semester course, the overall reaction from the students and instructor was very positive. The feedback received from local and remote students was very encouraging. Students expressed that the cloud-based hands-on exercises were highly educational and motivational, and more importantly enjoyable to carry out conveniently from their home and dormitory. Moreover, the instructor, who ran the course by himself, found that such a cloud-based teaching experience is rewarding, convenient and time saving for him and his students. Throughout the course, configuration and setup problems were rarely reported by the students to the instructor. The instructor had indeed noticed that students invested the majority of their time on carrying out the actual assignment tasks with little time wasted in resolving installation and setup problems.

8. ACKNOWLEDGEMENTS

This work has been supported by a research grant provided by Amazon AWS in Education [9].

9. REFERENCES

[1] US NSC. 2013. The Comprehensive National Cybersecurity Initiative. Available at http://www.whitehouse.gov/cybersecurity/ comprehensive-national-cybersecurity-initiative

[2] HM UK Government. 2013. A strong Britain in an age of uncertainty: the national security strategy, Available at http://www.direct.gov.uk/ prod_consum_dg/groups/dg_digitalassets/ @dg/@en/documents/digitalasset/dg_191639.pdf

[3] Amazon Web Services. 2013. Amazon Elastic Compute Cloud (EC2) User Guide, March 19, 2013, Available at http://aws.amazon. com/documentation/ec2/

[4] Abler, R., Contis, D., Grizzard, J. and Owen, H. 2006. Georgia Tech Information Security Center Hands-On Security Laboratory, *IEEE Transactions on Education*, Vol. 49, No. 1, February 2006, pp. 82-87.

[5] Owen, H. 2013. Archive of Network Security and Information Assurance Hands on Laboratory Assignment, Available at http://users. ece.gatech.edu/~owen/

[6] Carlos Brustoloni, J. 2006. Laboratory Experiments for Network Security Instruction, *ACM Journal on Education Resources in Computing*, Vol. 6, No. 4, Dec. 2006.

[7] McClure, S., Scambray, J. and Kurtz, G. 2012. *Hacking Exposed 7: Network Security Secrets and Solutions*,7th Edition, McGraw-Hill Publisher, July 2012.

[8] Amazon AWS Videos and Webinrars. 2013. Available at http://aws. amazon.com/resources/webinars/

[9] Education Grants, Amazon AWS. 2013. Available at http://aws.amazon. com/education

[10] VITAL, "Virtual Lab", Available at https://vital.poly.edu/

[11] Mirkovic, J. and Benzel, T. 2012. Teaching cybersecurity with DeterLab, *IEEE Security & Privacy*, January 2012, pp. 73–76.

[12] DeterLab: http://deter-project.org and http://education.deter-lab.net

[13] Willems, C., Klingbeil, T., Radvilavicius, L., Cenys, A. and Meinel, C. 2011. A distributed virtual laboratory architecture for cybersecurity training, *In Proc. of the 6th International Conference on Internet Technology and Secured Transactions*, 2011, pp. 408–415.

[14] Nance, K., Hay, B., Dodge, R., Seazzu, A. and Burd, S. 2009. Virtual Laboratory Environments: Methodologies for Education Cybersecurity Researchers, *Journal of Methodological Innovations Online*, Vol. 4, No. 3, 2009, pp. 3-14

[15] Willenms, C. and Meinel, C. 2012. Online Assessment for Hands-On Cybersecurity Training in a Virtual Lab, *In Proc. of IEEE Global Engineering Education Conference (EDUCON)*, Morocco, April 2012.

[16] Border, C. 2007. The development and deployment of a multi-user, remote access virtualization system for networking, security, and system administration classes, *SIGCSE Bulletin*, 39(1): pp. 576–580, 2007.

[17] Bullers, W. I., Burd, S., and Seazzu, A. 2006. Virtual machines – an idea whose time has returned: application to network, security, and database courses, *In Proc. 37th SIGCSE technical symposium on Computer science education*, Houston, Texas, USA, 2006.

[18] Keller, J. and Naues, R. 2006. A Collaborative Virtual Computer Security Lab*, In Proc. 2nd IEEE International Conference on e-Sciece and Grid Computing (e-Science '06)*, IEEE Computer Society, Amsterdam, Netherlands, 2006.

[19] Lahoud, H. A. and Tang, X. 2006. Information Security Labs in IDS/IPS for Distance Education, *In Proc. 7th Conference on Information Technology Education (SIGITE '06)*, ACM Press, pp. 47–52, 2006.

[20] Perez, D. and Perez, C. 2013. NETinVM: A Tool for Teaching and Learning about Systems, Networks and Security, June 2013, Available at http://informatica.uv.es/~carlos/docencia/netinvm/netinvm.html

Taking a Walk on the Wild Side: Teaching Cloud Computing on Distributed Research Testbeds

Yanyan Zhuang[†‡], Chris Matthews[*], Stephen Tredger[*], Steven Ness[*]
Jesse Short-Gershman[*], Li Ji[*], Niko Rebenich[*], Andrew French[*]
Josh Erickson[*], Kyliah Clarkson[*], Yvonne Coady[*], Rick McGeer[◁]
[*]Department of Computer Science, University of Victoria
[†]Department of Computer Science and Engineering, NYU Poly
[‡]Department of Computer Science, University of British Columbia
[◁]HP Labs

ABSTRACT

Distributed platforms are now a de facto standard in modern software and application development. Although the ACM/IEEE Curriculum 2013 introduces Parallel and Distributed Computing as a first class knowledge area for the first time, the right level of abstraction to teach these concepts is still an important question that needs to be explored. This work presents our findings in teaching cloud computing by exposing upper-level students to testbeds in use by the distributed systems research community. The possibility of giving students practical and relevant experience was explored in the context of new course assignment objectives. Furthermore, students were able to significantly contribute to a pilot class project with medium-scale computation based on satellite data. However, the software engineering challenges in these environments proved to be daunting. In particular, these challenges were exacerbated by a lack of debugging support relative to the environments students were more familiar with—requiring development practices that out-stripped typical course experiences. Our proposed set of experiments and project provide a basis for an evaluation of the trade-offs of teaching cloud and distributed systems *on the wild side*. We hope that these findings provide insight into some of the possibilities to consider when preparing the next generation of computer scientists to engage with software practices and paradigms that are already fundamental in today's highly distributed systems.

Keywords

Distributed systems, experimental facilities, course design

1. INTRODUCTION

Traditional simple client-server architecture supports many conveniences affordable to popular applications. New peer-to-peer style infrastructures not only lie at the heart of content distribution networks, but also within all devices housing multiple processing elements. Over the past decade, computer systems have been dominated by large-scale, highly parallel, and loosely-coupled systems. Common examples include parallel computation frameworks such as MapReduce [16] and Hadoop [21], Distributed Hash Tables [19], key-value stores [20], to take a few examples among many.

A key challenge for computer science educators is teaching students how to construct and use distributed systems. As an example, today's generation of students should be able to launch many types of MapReduce jobs, and help design services such as web search engine, which processes a vast quantity of information to service queries in milliseconds. There is tremendous commercial interest in these systems. Social-networking and Internet information provider firms such as Google, Facebook, Amazon, Yahoo!, Twitter, Ebay, Steam, and Zynga are highly dependent on the distributed computation technologies, and therefore require new employees to either know them or be able to learn them. But teaching students about distributed systems typically requires resources far beyond the scale available to an individual course or department. For example, a *clique* of servers at Yahoo! – the management unit for that ISP – is *20,000 servers*.

In order to cope with this requirement for resources at very large scale, computer science researchers have constructed a number of medium-scale testbeds over the past decade, with different capabilities and usage models. Emulab [17] is designed for short-duration, small-to-medium scale cluster and network experiments in laboratory conditions. PlanetLab [15] is designed for long-running services and network measurements in the wide area. Seattle [14] is designed as a very large, very lightweight services and experiment deployment platform at the network edge, with particular emphasis on mobile devices. GENICloud [5], as part of US National Science Foundation's Global Environment for Network Innovations (GENI) project, is a classic infrastructure-as-a-service (IaaS) cloud computing platform designed for multi-site federated deployment.

We designed a senior undergraduate/beginning graduate systems course which explores the properties of each of these testbeds and platforms, to give students experience with the foundational technologies of large-scale distributed systems. In this course, we chose assignments which were tailored to give students a sense of designing wide-area measurement systems; parallel back-end computation; scalable network-

SIGCSE'14 March 05 - 08 2014, Atlanta, GA, USA

http://dx.doi.org/10.1145/2538862.2538931.

ing systems; and issues of latency and bandwidth in the wide area. We used Emulab as our primary development platform; PlanetLab and Seattle as the deployment platform for wide-area systems and measurement; and GENICloud was also used as the deployment platform for cluster-based systems in a pilot project.

The contributions in this paper are twofold. First, we introduce a pedagogical approach that would be easy to adopt at any institution by taking the advantage of the above existing distributed testbeds, via the design of a series of assignment tasks. Second, by incorporating students' contribution in a challenging pilot course project, our experience uncovered some of the possibilities for educating the next generation of computer scientists, and evaluated trade-offs of teaching cloud and distributed systems *on the wild side.*

2. RELATED WORK

Parallel and cloud computing is an emerging computing paradigm for delivering computing services. In recent years, both industry and academia are starting to adopt the new parallel and cloud computing techniques. In 2007, Google and IBM announced a cloud computing university initiative [6]. There are also a number of universities and colleges offering computer science courses on the topic of networking, distributed systems and cloud computing. St. Olaf College implemented *Hadoop at Home* [13], based on the observation that today's leading technology depends on programming models to deliver services based on data-intensive scalable computing (DISC). Tufts offered an introductory course on cloud computing [1] that taught students a broad view from how to program a cloud application, to the business cases for using the cloud for common tasks.

University of Washington implemented Seattle [14], a surprisingly flexible platform that supports a variety of pedagogical uses for cloud computing, grid computing, peer-to-peer networking, and distributed systems. It makes programming assignments much easier, such as implementing a reliable protocol over UDP, building application-level services like a webserver, and building a chat server over HTTP, etc. UC Berkeley successfully taught MapReduce in a large undergraduate lecture course using public cloud services [18]. Using the cloud, every student could carry out scalability benchmarking assignments on realistic hardware. This is a large-scale demonstration that it is feasible to use pay-as-you-go billing in the cloud for a large undergraduate course. The course was designed intentionally to draw students' attention to the economic aspects of cloud computing, or cost management. Their course also demonstrated that students could see parallel speed up by using the cloud provided services, which have consistent performance.

3. ASSIGNMENT & TESTBED FACILITIES

Motivated by these previous success stories, we decided to redesign our course in distributed systems, which had previously focused on writing applications using Java Remote Method Invocation (RMI).

Course Objectives and Design Criteria. Objectives for a distributed systems course typically fall into either theory or practice. Theory encompasses topics spanning core principles of locking, concurrency, scheduling, etc. Practice includes actual experience in designing, implementing and debugging real distributed systems. We believe it is also important to introduce an understanding of the popular mechanisms, practices, techniques and paradigms that have emerged to support distributed applications. These include virtualization, concurrent programming, cloud computing, and MapReduce-like techniques. The course is designed to provide students with continuous training. Students bring up services first on Emulab, do small-scale experiments, then deploy their projects to PlanetLab. This way, experience gained from small scale experiments can benefit the students in their follow-up implementation.

3.1 Testbed Overview

We designed the course assignments around the practical usage of the following four large-scale testbeds. Each assignment comes with conceptual questions and programming.

Emulab [3] is essentially a Hardware-as-a-Service platform, though users can now get "Containers" as services. Emulab is designed for testing distributed systems under controlled network conditions. To some extent, it can also be used as a development platform. Our students were instructed to design an experiment by hooking up nodes with a GUI, configuring the nodes by specifying an OS image (e.g., "FEDORA15-STD" for FedoraCore 15) for each node, then swapping the experiment in. Next they log in to each node, load any software they need, perform their experiment by running any scripts they need on the various nodes, then swap the experiment out. Emulab can also be used as a staging platform for PlanetLab.

PlanetLab [11] is a distributed Containers-as-a-Service platform. A container is largely indistinguishable from a virtual machine (VM); the principal difference is users don't have a choice in OS. In this case, we get a stripped Linux distribution. Stripped because PlanetLab is a deployment, not development platform, so the goal is that users bring up the environment needed in each container. There are various tools to help, including the one on Emulab. PlanetLab has about 1,000 nodes at 300 sites worldwide. It is designed for both short-duration experiments and long-running services. Two services (Coral and CoDeeN) have been running on PlanetLab since 2002.

Seattle [14] gives the programmer a high-level programming environment on many devices of various sorts: everything from smartphones to servers. We primarily use it to test the infrastructure services students will be writing. It was used as a test environment because heavy weight computing is not permitted on the platform, due to the concerns of using community based and donated resources, such as people's home computers and smartphones. Programming in Seattle is done in Restricted Python (RePy); a form of Python with strongly constrained I/O and metered use of system resources, so that students can play safe on other people's systems. We used this chance to introduce Python to our students, and assigned several entry level programming tasks using RePy.

GENICloud [5] is a centralized infrastructure-as-a-service system based on containers. Up till today, GENICloud is considered a work in progress, as part of the larger GENI project [4]. It will build a GENI federation interface for compute clusters based on PlanetLab and running Openstack [10], a popular, open-source software for building a cloud computing infrastructure. This interface will allow Openstack clusters to federate via the Slice-based Federation Architecture (SFA) [12], and will enable experimenters

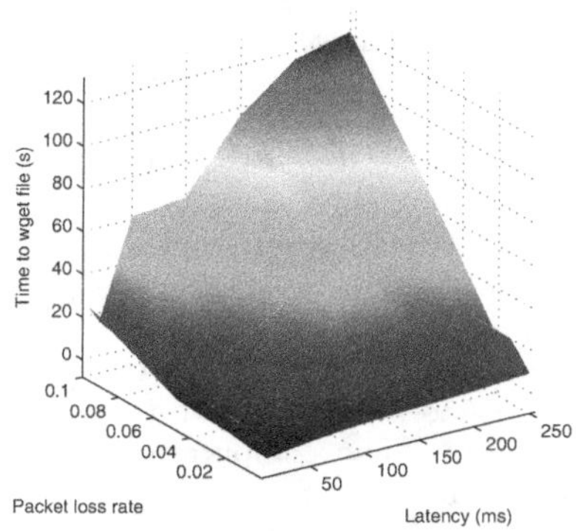

Figure 1: Download time vs. packet loss rate and client-server latency for an Emulab experiment.

to seamlessly deploy and configure slices spanning PlanetLab and multiple Openstack installations. Ultimately, we want to use GENICloud for centralized cloud services, such as MapReduce/Hadoop.

3.2 Assignment

This section presents the assignment results by students on different testbeds. We also present the insights we obtained, and the potential pitfalls of the current course design.

3.2.1 *Emulab*

In the Emulab experiment, students instantiate a small experiment with two nodes, a server and a client, and one link between them. Both the server and client run on the FEDORA15-STD operating system image. By modifying the link delay and loss rate between two nodes, both the available bandwidth and data transmission time will vary.

Emulab's ability to assume different network topologies motivates this assignment. Emulab uses the "NS" ("Network Simulator") [9] format to describe network topologies. This is similar to the Tcl-based format used by ns-2. Although students can use a GUI interface on Emulab to specify the topology, it is highly recommended they use Tcl. Familiarity with the language allows for fine grained control over the Emulab experiment, and facilitates debugging.

After uploading the topology script to Emulab, two physical nodes will be allocated to this experiment, i.e., *swapped in*. Then students install Apache on the server via remote login, and download files on the client node through the HTTP service provided by Apache. The link bandwidth is initialized to 2,000 Kbps and packet loss rate to 0, as defined in the Tcl script. To emulate a realistic network, students can dynamically create node and modify link properties with `tevc` command to set different latency, and packet loss rate of the link between nodes.

In each experiment, the client node uses `wget` to download a 1 MB text file hosted on the server, and measures the time it takes to get this file as well as the average bandwidth. The results are plotted in Figure 1 by students in this course. The figure shows that the download time increases with the increasing link latency and packet loss rate. It is quite intuitive to observe such results, and students are expected to hand in their results shown in similar graphics.

Skill set: Students need to have the knowledge of SSH, Tcl and shell script (GNU core utilities such as `sed`, `awk`, and pipes). Also, plotting techniques such as Matlab, Gnuplot or any other preferred visualization tool are required. After this experiment, students will see how certain network parameters affect the systems performance quantitatively.

Pitfalls: As mentioned before, Emulab is designed for short-duration, small-scale testing of distributed systems under controlled network conditions. Therefore, all Emulab experiments will be *swapped out* once they have been idle for a certain period of time (2 hours by default). Once the experiment has been swapped out, students need to swap it in again and re-deploy the experiment. The difficulty is that the default Emulab images are stateless. Once an experiment gets swapped out, all previous configurations are lost, except the content in the home directory. Although students learned this in a hard way, they came up with writing shell scripts to automate the configuration process.

3.2.2 *Seattle*

In this experiment, students instantiate a Seattle slice and add 10 nodes to the slice. These Seattle nodes are geographically distributed. Students are asked to write a short RePy program to access the 1 MB file they created from their Apache server at Emulab in the previous experiment, and record the download times from each slice, then use Google Maps API [7] to plot their Seattle nodes and download times.

Acquiring resources in Seattle is straight-forward. VMs in Seattle are called vessels, which can be obtained on the Seattle Clearinghouse website. By a script `seash.py` students can launch their command line shell for Seattle, i.e., `seash`. `seash` allows students to easily run their RePy programs on a single vessel, or across multiple vessels simultaneously.

Skill set: Students need to have the knowledge of Python and RePy, socket programming and HTTP protocol, etc. After this experiment, students will experience the excitement of deploying programs in the wild, and see how location affects the systems performance. Students also get a chance to work with Google Map API and review knowledge on JavaScript and related topics.

Pitfalls: However, the downside of Seattle becomes obvious also in a world-wide setting. Seattle is very careful about using private resources such as home computers and smartphones, thus it limits the resources usage such as the bandwidth of each node. As a result, students can only modify the bandwidth on their local machine, but not remote vessels. This can be seen from Figure 2, where the download times of the 1 MB file from all Seattle nodes at different locations (from the Apache server on Emulab deployed in the previous task) are very similar, varying between 102 to 105 seconds. These results are also plotted by students in this course. PlanetLab platform in Figure 2 will be introduced in the next section.

3.2.3 *PlanetLab*

In this experiment, students join the PlanetLab slice we created on the site at our institution, and add 10 nodes (slivers) that are geographically distributed to the slice. Then they start an Apache server on each PlanetLab node. Students need to modify their Seattle clients as they previously set up, so that each Seattle client pulls the 1 MB file from the PlanetLab node closest to them. Finally, they are asked to use Google Map to plot the Seattle clients, PlanetLab servers, and download times.

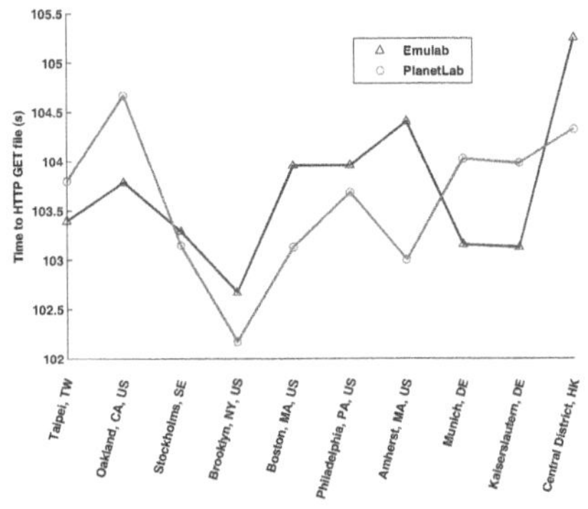

Figure 2: Seattle clients vs. download times for Emulab server and closest PlanetLab server.

There are a number of ways students can accomplish this task. Examples include analyzing physical locations of nodes via latitude and longitude provided by a geolocation service, or by using network tools such as `ping` and `traceroute` to compare the round trip time and hop number. Figure 2 also shows the results of the above PlanetLab experiment generated by students.

Skill set: Students need to have basic grounding in networks and systems knowledge in order to accomplish this task. Based on previous two experiments, they experience a gradual process of applying their knowledge to solve a real problem.

Pitfalls: While PlanetLab is a highly flexible testbed, the pitfalls of this experiment set still comes from Seattle. The download times from different clients still do not vary much given their different geographic locations, due to the bandwidth limit.

4. PROJECT IMPLEMENTATION & STUDENT CONTRIBUTION

In this course we design a medium-scale, computation-intensive project in the form of a simple geographic information system (GIS). This GIS system uses images captured by Landsat series of satellites [8] as the data set, and cloud computing services as its storage and computation platform. Given the large amount of data, the computations must be distributed. This project is of enough size that the students must deal with many of the problems they would experience in a real-world application. The computing platform we chose is GENICloud [5]. The project had a hard deadline, and was demonstrated at a conference demo session.

4.1 Project Design & Software Deployment

The task of the project system is calculating the amount of *greenspace* contained within a city using satellite imagery, doing so for all cities on earth, and finding out the *greenest* cities in the world. The greenspace calculation itself is simple. Given a set of satellite images, the algorithm generates a pseudo-color landscape image, and count what percentage of pixels are *green* inside a defined city area. The dataset for images which cover most of the world in 3 bands of light (one visible bands, two non-visible bands) is about 2 TB of zipped tiff files. The largest VMs on GENICloud only have 500 GB of disk space, so the dataset has to be distributed across machines. Each greenspace calculation requires between 3 and 12 images, which are about 100 MB each when unzipped. Those images have to be combined into a single large image before the calculation starts. On a small VM, each city takes between 2 and 10 minutes to process, resulting in a calculation that would take in the ballpark of 50 days to complete if left single threaded.

The students were given an existing single threaded, single machine example of how to do the greenspace calculation written in Python. The students were instructed to make it distributed and parallel. We broke the class up equally into two teams, a storage team and a computation team, 12 students in total. The computation team was tasked with building the computation part of the calculation using a MapReduce based technology. The storage team was instructed to split the data across the sites and store it using the OpenStack Swift object storage technology, a open source alternative to Amazon's S3 service.

4.2 Storage

Multi-Site Swift Storage. Our first version of image storage was in a single Swift cluster at one site: one proxy and several storage nodes. To parallelize the data storage, as well as the computation, the storage team decided to transfer data from the main Swift cluster to the distributed Swift servers at multiple locations.

The storage team first divided the entire land area of the world into four groups of continents, which were then input into the database as a table *continents*, with multi-polygons delineating each of the groups. The strategy was to run a different continent group on each of the Swift clusters in a distributed network. To transfer the data to different clusters, the students wrote a PostGIS database query that joined the data in *continents* table with the data in the *tiff* table to find which images corresponded to each cluster. To transfer data, students divided the process in two steps: temporarily store a list of the images to be transferred from the main Swift cluster, and then transfer the images. With such a process, whenever the transfer process encountered errors, the program could simply checkpoint the process where there was an error in transfer and continue from that point, reducing the amount of redundant data to be transferred to the distributed nodes.

4.3 Computation

Image Crawler. The image crawler is a Python script that extracts the geographic information from a Landsat Geotiff image, and then inserts the information into the *tiff* table of the PostGIS database. The most important geographic information extracted from the image is a polygon representing the area covered by the Landsat image, represented by a bounding box.

The crawler works by downloading representative files (one band for each Landsat image) from Swift and using `gdalinfo` to extract the geographic information. `gdalinfo` is part of the open source Geospatial Data Abstraction Library (GDAL) which performs various functions on raster geospatial data. From the output of gdalinfo we then construct a polygon using well known text (WKT), which is then inserted into the *tiff* table if the image has not yet been processed by the crawler. Multiple instances of the crawler can be run concurrently, as all they need to function is a connection to the Swift proxy and the PostGIS/PostgreSQL database.

Greenspace Calculation. The greenspace calculation is a Python script which assigns a value to a city to represent how much greenspace the city contains. The calculation script first gets a city that does not have a calculated greenspace value, then pulls that city's bounding box from the *map* table in the PostGIS database. From the city boundary we then query the *tiff* table of the database to find all the images that intersect the city, which are then downloaded from Swift.

The script crops each band to contain only what lies inside the city using the `ogr2ogr` tool included in the GDAL library, then merges the cropped images into a single pseudocolor image with `gdal_merge`. To calculate the greenspace we iterate over each pixel checking if it is within the city boundary. If so, it is counted as a *greenspace pixel* if the value from band 4 (green) is greater than the other two bands. Finally the greenspace value is returned as the number of greenspace pixels over all pixels within the city. Multiple instances of the greenspace calculator can also run simultaneously as the computation for each image is independent.

Web Interface. The demo was presented through a web interface. The database tables were exposed through a Web Mapping System (WMS) interface, and a OpenLayers web frontend was provided to the students. The webmap showed each of the cities and color coded them based on their green value. If a city is clicked on by the user of this web interface, a pop-up with the imagery used for that calculation is shown. The map also shows the footprints of all the images, and how work was partitioned between sites.

Disco. The computation team elected to use a MapReduce framework for Python called Disco [2]. Disco has many of the features of other common MapReduce frameworks like Hadoop: features for defining custom input streams, multistage computations, and its own distributed file system. Disco suited the team's familiarity with Python, and made porting the old code easier since it was written in Python.

Disco was installed on several machines in each cluster, and the students found the installation process difficult. Disco is a relatively young project, and its error handling is a little weak. Although the course TAs helped the students get through the installation issues, it consumed a lot of time in lab sessions. Almost two of the 3 hour labs were spent dealing with Disco related issues. The MapReduce job used is very simple. There is no reduce phase, and the map phase is passed a city, which triggers the normal calculation to take place and store the result in the database. After properly installed, Disco allowed us to run 256 jobs in parallel on one cluster—a rewarding result for the students.

5. STUDENT FEEDBACK

In this section we introduce student evaluation on this course, from their expectation, experience to their feedback on different platforms we used.

5.1 Student Experience

We are glad to see that students' feedback on their experience in class is aligned with our expectations. In an anonymous class survey, students stated that they have improved their skills in: Linux basic knowledge, scripting languages (such as perl, python, etc.), knowledge about networking, distributed storage and concurrency. This class survey was based on a total of 12 students, two of which are undergraduates from Computer Science, and the rest are graduate students from Computer Science and Electrical Engineering.

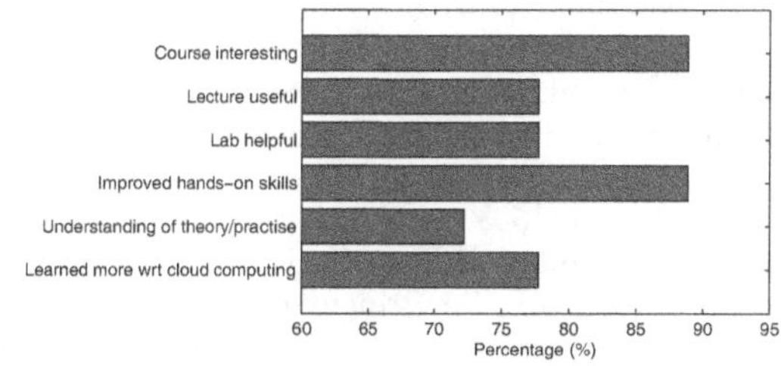

Figure 3: Student experience.

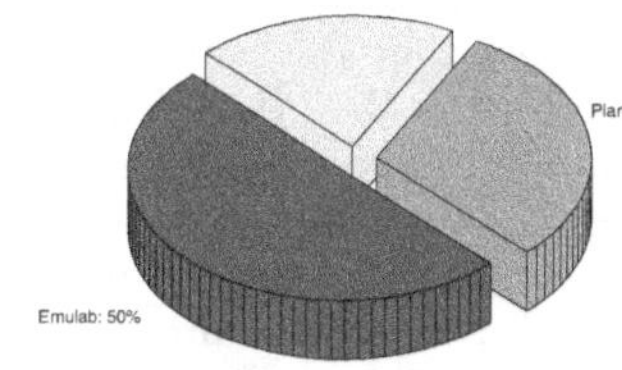

Figure 4: Student feedback on testbed facilities.

5.1.1 Expectation & Overall Impression

Students had expectations on us just as we have expectations on them. They came to the class not only hoping for gaining knowledge in parallel and distributed computing, but also applying the theoretical foundations to systems *on the wild side*. In the same survey, students stated that they feel closer to the real world by doing assignments and projects that are hands-on and system based. The course is more enjoyable especially it is more "learning what you want" and less "memorizing information for your final". Close to 90% of students think the course is interesting, and helped them improved their hands-on and programming skills. Almost 80% of them stated they have learned more about cloud computing. Other survey data and student opinions are plotted in Figure 3.

However, students also expressed certain level of frustration because of the various testbeds and software involved. One student wrote his course experience in the anonymous survey: *"Swift installation instructions provided by the developers were certainly adequate, but tedious when installing on a large number of nodes. By scripting the installation steps, deployment was able to be done rapidly and accurately across multiple nodes, which freed up human capital."*

The observation from students revealed that current Computer Science curriculum lacks the much needed development practices for students to prepare for the real world. The testbed environments and software tools also lack debugging support for the installation and configuration. On the other hand, we believe that the experiences in this course on software development and automation practices are beneficial to the students. Despite various levels of difficulties, taking a walk *on the wild side* and teaching cloud computing on distributed research testbeds prepare the next generation of computer scientists to engage with real world development practices.

5.2 Testbed Facilities

In the same survey, we also asked students' opinions about

the different cloud computing platforms used in this course. Figure 4 shows the percentage breakdown of the platform that each student liked the most. Since GENICloud was only used in the pilot project for experimental purpose, we did not include it in Figure 4. As the most stable testbed, Emulab was voted by 50% of all the students in the course. The next highest ranked is PlanetLab, which is both stable and flexible. However, only Principal Investigator (PI) has the privilege to create PlanetLab slices. Such management of PlanetLab makes it difficult for students to fully control the testing facilities.

Last but not least, Figure 4 also reveals that the students had unrealistic expectations for Seattle, thus this is not a fair comparison in terms of the result reported. Though they knew that security is the primary goal of Seattle, the ramifications of running experiments on donated machines and devices did not become clear until after they had tried to surpass the constraints of their permissions. Students often become frustrated when encountering scenarios where operations are not supported or permitted. However, in our case, these students are starting to write their own libraries, such as Trigonometric functions, which can be integrated in the Seattle base.

6. DISCUSSION AND CONCLUSIONS

Over the past decade, practical considerations for building distributed systems have changed dramatically. Today's students have opportunities to genuinely create computations that span the globe. In this paper we introduced the research testbeds used in our exploratory course, details of the assignment and project used, along with initial student feedback about their perspectives on this experience. We have demonstrated that using distributed research test facilities could give students the opportunity to experience distributed systems in a realistic way.

While getting first-hand experience with distributed application deployment in the cloud is an important step in career preparation, we found the raw exposure to research infrastructure is challenging. When students were stripped of the luxury of higher level debugging facilities, they found the experience to be daunting. In some cases, the battles with the infrastructure actually prevented students from focusing on the underlying technologies. We do, however, believe this kind of exposure is necessary and ultimately sharpens problem solving abilities once the students survive the initial shock. We hope our findings provide insight into software practices and paradigms that are fundamental to modern Computer Science education.

Acknowledgements

This research was partially supported by Mitacs Accelerate Cluster IT01858 with Biosphere's Management, and the GENI Project Office under contract 1779.

7. REFERENCES

[1] Clouds and power-aware computing, `http://www.cs.tufts.edu/comp/150CPA/`.

[2] The disco project, `http://discoproject.org/`.

[3] Emulab—network emulation testbed home, `https://www.emulab.net/`.

[4] GENI: Exploring networks of the future, `http://www.geni.net/`.

[5] GENICloud, `http://groups.geni.net/geni/wiki/GENICloud`.

[6] Google and IBM announce university initiative to address internet-scale computing challenges, `http://www-03.ibm.com/press/us/en/pressrelease/22414.wss`.

[7] Google map API, `https://developers.google.com/maps/`.

[8] Landsat then and now, `http://landsat.gsfc.nasa.gov/about/`.

[9] The network simulator - ns-2, `http://www.isi.edu/nsnam/ns/`.

[10] Openstack: Open source software for building private and public clouds, `http://www.openstack.org/`.

[11] PlanetLab, `http://www.planet-lab.org/`.

[12] SFA overview, `http://svn.planet-lab.org/wiki/SFAGuide`.

[13] R. Brown. Hadoop at home: large-scale computing at a small college. In *ACM SIGCSE Bulletin*, volume 41, pages 106–110. ACM, 2009.

[14] J. Cappos, I. Beschastnikh, A. Krishnamurthy, and T. Anderson. Seattle: a platform for educational cloud computing. In *ACM SIGCSE Bulletin*, volume 41, pages 111–115. ACM, 2009.

[15] B. Chun, D. Culler, T. Roscoe, A. Bavier, L. Peterson, M. Wawrzoniak, and M. Bowman. Planetlab: An overlay testbed for broad-coverage services. *ACM SIGCOMM Computer Communication Review*, pages 3–12, 2003.

[16] J. Dean and S. Ghemawat. Mapreduce: simplified data processing on large clusters. *Commun. ACM*, 51(1):107–113, Jan. 2008.

[17] M. Hibler, R. Ricci, L. Stoller, J. Duerig, S. Guruprasad, T. Stack, K. Webb, and J. Lepreau. Large-scale virtualization in the Emulab network testbed. In *ATC'08: USENIX 2008 Annual Technical Conference on Annual Technical Conference*, pages 113–128, Berkeley, CA, USA, 2008. USENIX Association.

[18] A. Rabkin, C. Reiss, R. Katz, and D. Patterson. Experiences teaching mapreduce in the cloud. In *Proceedings of the 43rd ACM technical symposium on Computer Science Education*, pages 601–606. ACM, 2012.

[19] A. I. T. Rowstron and P. Druschel. Pastry: Scalable, Decentralized Object Location, and Routing for Large-Scale Peer-to-Peer Systems. In *Middleware '01: Proceedings of the IFIP/ACM International Conference on Distributed Systems Platforms Heidelberg*, pages 329–350, London, UK, 2001. Springer-Verlag.

[20] T. Schütt, F. Schintke, and A. Reinefeld. Scalaris: reliable transactional p2p key/value store. In *ERLANG '08: Proceedings of the 7th ACM SIGPLAN workshop on ERLANG*, pages 41–48, New York, NY, USA, 2008. ACM.

[21] T. White. *Hadoop: The Definitive Guide*. O'Reilly Media, Inc., 1st edition, 2009.

Recruit and Retain Women in Undergraduate Computing: Success Stories using Research-Based Practices

Leisa D. Thompson
(Moderator)
National Center for Women & IT (NCWIT)
University of Virginia
1-210-883-6204
leisadthompson@gmail.com

Crystal Eney
University of Washington
Computer Science & Engineering
1-206-685-7571
ceney@cs.washington.edu

Ruth Davis
Santa Clara University
Computer Engineering
1-408-554-4358
rdavis@scu.edu

Tiffany Grady
University of Texas - Austin
Computer Science
1-512-471-9523
tgrady@cs.utexas.edu

SUMMARY

Many undergraduate computing departments seek to increase recruitment and retention of women in their programs. Increasing participation and graduation of women in computing requires a systemic approach that includes [1, 2]:

- Recruiting strategically
- Retaining with pedagogy
- Retaining with curriculum
- Retaining with student support
- Institutional support of your initiatives
- Evaluating your efforts

This panel will share research-based recruitment and retention practices implemented by three U.S. universities that have led to high enrollments and high graduation rates of women in their computer science and computer engineering programs. Each institution is an Academic Alliance member of the National Center for Women & Information Technology (NCWIT), a previous client institution with the NCWIT Extension Services for Undergraduate Programs (ES-UP), and is an NCWIT Pacesetter school.

Categories and Subject Descriptors

K.3.2 Computer and Information Science Education

Keywords

Recruitment, Retention, Gender, Women, Diversity, Research-based practices

1. Leisa D. Thompson

Director of Research and Consulting for the NCWIT Extension Services for Undergraduate Programs (ES-UP). As the moderator, she will describe the NCWIT ES-UP and Pacesetter programs that have contributed to the success of these institutions. In addition, she will discuss some of the recruitment and retention resources developed by NCWIT (www.ncwit.org/resources) that can be implemented by faculty and introduce the other panelists.

SIGCSE '14, Mar 5-8 2014, Atlanta, Georgia, USA.
ACM 978-1-4503-2605-6/14/03
http://dx.doi.org/10.1145/2538862.2538865

2. Crystal Eney

The University of Washington-Seattle (UW) Computer Science & Engineering Department is very involved in several key efforts to recruit and retain women and underrepresented students in our field. In our computer science major, 28% of the students are women and we have had success in retaining both male and female students. Our attrition rate is roughly 7-10% among declared majors. For the 2009-10, 2010-11, 2011-12, and 2012-13 academic years, our graduation rates for women were 21%, 26%, 27%, and 26% respectively. We have implemented several research-based practices that have contributed to our success:

- Targeted recruitment: Approximately 60 women per year take a one-credit seminar along with Programming I and II, which provides an opportunity to visit local companies, attend research presentations, and meet current student CSE majors and alumnae working in industry.
- Faculty and Peer Interaction [3]: We invite high-performing women from our introductory courses to share tea and cookies with an Intro Programming instructor to hear more about CSE from current students, advisors, and young alumnae in industry.
- Student Support: The CSE department sends 10-15 female students to the Grace Hopper Celebration each year, plus an undergraduate advisor.
- Encourage Persistence [4]: Our dedicated advising staff is trained to pay attention to the students' experience in the major and proactively contact students who are struggling and encourage them to seek help. We have retained several women who have considered leaving the major by having conversations about their goals, concerns, and options to stay. We often match women with more-advanced women in industry to help them consider longer-term opportunities.
- Mentoring: Our department has a mentor program where all new students are paired with a "veteran" CSE major mentor.
- Student-Teacher Assistant Interaction: Teaching assistants (TAs) contribute to retention by helping carry out professors' pedagogical intentions in the classroom and lab. We train our undergraduate TAs to be accessible and encouraging for their students. This outstanding group of students is typically 40% women.

3. Ruth Davis

At Santa Clara University (SCU) Computer Engineering department (COEN), we are committed to engaging and retaining young women in our computing programs. We track our female computing majors as they enter their junior year to help us measure success in both recruitment and retention. For the 2010-

11, 2011-12, and 2012-13 academic years, our graduation rates for women were 25%, 29%, and 25% respectively. In the spring of 2013, women comprised about 33% of the junior class so we expect 33% of the graduates in 2014 to be female. SCU has implemented the following strategies:

- Over 50% of the full-time faculty in the COEN department are women.
- Summer Engineering Seminar (SES): We offer a residential camp for high school juniors that introduces them to several fields of engineering, including computing. Enrollment is always 50% women and at least 50% minority students. From our 2011 program, 21 of 79 (26.6%) participants enrolled in engineering at SCU.
- Multiple pathways to the major: The COEN department created a Web Design and Engineering degree that has attracted a large percentage of women (currently 58%) to the major.
- Faculty-Student Interaction: Our department sponsors an informal luncheon for women computing majors on the first day of finals every term and celebrates all of our female engineering students at our "Women in Engineering" dinner every year.
- Student Support: We raise funds to sponsor student attendance at the Grace Hopper Conference each year along with coordinating transportation to the Anita Borg Institute's Women of Vision banquet.
- One female faculty member has implemented a volunteer tutoring program in her programming classes that have helped retention of both tutors and those requiring help.
- Collaborative learning: Most of our programming classes require students to work in pairs or small teams. This strategy promotes improved learning, greater retention, and the development of a sense of identity and belonging as a computing student [5].

4. Tiffany Grady

The Computer Science (CS) Department at the University of Texas at Austin (UT) graduation rate for women in CS was 20% for the spring 2013 semester. The UTCS department set a goal to increase the number of women entering our programs through carefully targeted steps [6, 7] and we have doubled the number of new female students in one year. For the fall 2013 semester, we have 415 new students, including freshmen and transfer students, which 73 of these students are women (17.6%). Our success has included the following practices:

- Targeted recruiting: We focused efforts to recruit high school girls from our First Bytes residential summer camp. For the fall 2013 semester, 19 former First Bytes campers were admitted to the CS department and 12 of these young women enrolled as freshmen. In addition, many faculty members encourage students taking our Elements program, which is a set of CS courses targeted toward non-majors, to consider a CS major.
- Financial support: Our department offers scholarships to many of our incoming female freshmen, as well as scholarships for winners of the NCWIT Aspirations in Computing Award.
- UTCS Ambassadors: Current undergraduate students meet with prospective students and their families to give tours and talk about life at UTCS. The students visit a classroom, have lunch with an ambassador, and meet with a faculty member. We try to pair prospective women with current female students.
- Mentoring: We provide faculty and student mentoring for first-year women, which has helped tremendously with retention.
- Women in Computer Science (WICS) support: We have always had a very active WICS group and in the past two years more and more women and men have become involved in the organization. We are housed in a new CS complex that offers incredible opportunity for collaboration, building community, and a sense of belonging.

5. ACKNOWLEDGMENTS

This material is based upon work supported by the National Center for Women and Information Technology with funding from the National Science Foundation awards HRD-0533565/0533580/0813956. Any opinions, findings, and conclusions or recommendations expressed in this material are those of the authors and do not necessarily reflect the views of the National Science Foundation or other supporting organizations.

6. REFERENCES

[1] National Center for Women & Information Technology. 2008. Gearing Up for Change: Institutional Reform in Undergraduate Computing Programs. http://www.ncwit.org/orgchange

[2] National Center for Women & Information Technology. 2013. Resources For Change Agents. http://www.ncwit.org/changeagentresources

[3] Barker, L.J.,McDowell, C. & Kalahar, K. Exploring factors that influence computer science introductory course students to persist in the major. In *SIGCSE '09 Proceedings of the 40th ACM Technical Symposium on Computer Science Education* (Chattanooga, TN USA, March 4-7,2009) ACM, New York, NY, 153-157. DOI= http://dl.acm.org/citation.cfm?doid=1508865.1508923

[4] Cohoon, J.M. and Aspray, W. 2008. Retaining women in undergraduate computing. In *Women and information technology: Research on underrepresentation*. MIT Press, Cambridge, MA, 2006, 137-180.

[5] Barker, L., Cohoon, J.M. 2007. How Do You Retain Women through Collaborative Learning? Pair Programming. http://www.ncwit.org/pairpractice

[6] National Center for Women & Information Technology. 2010. Strategic Planning for Recruiting Women into Undergraduate Computing: High Yield in the Short Term. http://www.ncwit.org/recruitingworkbook

[7] National Center for Women & Information Technology. 2009. Strategic Planning for Retaining Women in Undergraduate Computing. http://www.ncwit.org/retainingworkbook

CS Principles Professional Development: Only 9,500 to go! Lessons Learned from our CS10K Summer 2013 PD

Jan Cuny (moderator)
National Science Foundation
4201 Wilson Boulevard
Arlington, VA 22230
+1 (703) 292-8900
jcuny@nsf.gov

Diane A. Baxter
UC San Diego
9500 Gilman Dr.. UCSD-0505
La Jolla, CA 92093-0505
+1 (858) 822-5482
dbaxter@ucsd.edu

Daniel D. Garcia
UC Berkeley
387 Soda Hall
Berkeley, CA 94720-1776
+1 510-642-1042
ddgarcia@cs.berkeley.edu

Jeff Gray
University of Alabama
Dept. of Computer Science
Tuscaloosa, AL 35487
+1 (205) 348-2847
gray@cs.ua.edu

Ralph Morelli
Trinity College
Dept. of Computer Science
Hartford, CT 06106
+1 (860) 297-2220
ralph.morelli@trincoll.edu

Categories and Subject Descriptors
K.3.2 [**Computer and Information Science Education**]: Computer science education

Keywords
Computer science education, professional development, CS10K, AP CS Principles

1. SUMMARY
Our grand challenge is to scale high-quality computer science curriculum and instruction to reach all high school students. **CS10K** – an NSF and ACM-sponsored project – is working to do just that by supporting curriculum development, computer education research and professional development through the Computing Education for the 21st Century (CE21) program at NSF [2]. Professional Development (PD) is a key piece of the project, as we need to train 10,000 teachers to teach rigorous computing courses in 10,000 high schools by 2016 – the school year that a new Advanced Placement Course will be rolled out. This panel will provide an overview of the PD landscape and then each panelist will discuss the unique aspects of their PD project for high school teachers.

2. DIANE BAXTER
Computing Principles for All Students' Success (*ComPASS*) introduces secondary and lower-division college students to computing principles and computational thinking skills through an Alice-based curriculum and a compelling pedagogy that demands active student engagement through clicker questions, peer learning approaches, and facilitated, directed discussion. Developed initially as a non-majors course, CSE3 at UC San Diego demonstrated early success at attracting and engaging women and minorities in computing [6]. Comprehensive evaluation showed its effectiveness in teaching students deeper level computational thinking skills and imbuing in them enthusiasm for subsequent programming classes. Project co-PIs Baxter and Simon cultivated partnerships with high school teachers who agreed (or were asked by their administration) to help us translate what worked for UCSD freshmen into a high school-level curriculum. The high school-level curriculum (both the students' "CS Principles - Explorations through Alice" and "CS Principles - Guide through Alice" for teachers) is now available online (with author and publisher permission) to teachers and students without charge [3, 4]. Two cohorts into the project of introducing the new high school ComPASS curriculum into San Diego area schools, we can share many lessons learned at the same time as we celebrate unanticipated success at district-wide adoption.

Professional development for ComPASS teachers requires a series of 8 weekly, 2-hours classes, introducing teachers to Alice, the curriculum, the online community of practice, and additional topics on CS in Society. The course is taught using the pedagogical methods that we ask the teachers to use themselves. Reflection is peppered throughout the course, demanding that teachers recognize and appreciate the role of the pedagogy at the same time as they gain comfort with the content. Class videos from the college-level course are available as podcasts for teachers who need additional time to feel ready to teach. An intensive, 3-day summer Pedagogy Boot Camp demands that the teachers begin using the methods, tools, and curriculum to teach to one another. Each effort is an opportunity for additional discussion and hands-on learning. Teachers develop a course outline for themselves and meet mentors – teachers from UCSD and from the previous year's cohort – who continue to support them through once-a-week conference calls, Piazza, and the CS10K Community of Practice portal throughout the year.

SIGCSE'14, March 5–8, 2014, Atlanta, Georgia, USA.
ACM 978-1-4503-2605-6/14/03.
http://dx.doi.org/10.1145/2538862.2538876

3. DAN GARCIA

The *Beauty and Joy of Computing* (BJC) is a non-majors CS0 course designed independently, and later aligned fully with the CS Principles framework [5, 9]. However, it does not stop there; it introduces the powerful ideas of recursion and functions-as-data through the graphical language of *SNAP!* (Build Your Own Blocks, based on Scratch) [10]. Our students read chapters from the excellent *Blown to Bits* book [1], as well as other relevant articles and videos, and have discussions of the positive and negative impacts of computing, driven by news articles of current events every lecture. The course has had tremendous success in broadening participation at UC Berkeley, highlighted by the spring 2013 offering, the first-ever computing course on campus to have more female than male students (106 to 104)! The course was adapted by co-PI Tiffany Barnes (then at UNC Charlotte) and augmented with *App Inventor* and *GameMaker*.

Our PD requires 6 full-time weeks of commitment from teachers. We follow a "1-4-1" model: one face-to-face setup week, four weeks of an online course (an abbreviated version of our 15-week college course), and one face-to-face concluding week. We spend the time in the face-to-face sessions covering the CS Principles framework and performance-based tasks, giving brief workshop-style tutorials on Snap! and the more difficult programming constructs students will learn. We also spend time with the teachers mapping the course to their situation, talk about techniques to engage women and under-represented minorities, and have veteran teachers share best practices and pedagogical content knowledge. We follow up with all teachers through monthly webinars and daily via the *BJC TEACHERS* Piazza group embedded within the CS10K community of practice.

4. JEFF GRAY

The *CS4Alabama* project is a collaboration between the University of Alabama (UA), A+ College Ready (A+CR), and the Alabama State Department of Education (ALSDE). The goal of CS4Alabama is to train 50 teachers over the next three years to introduce the CS Principles course across a geographically and demographically diverse group of Alabama high schools. The PD model is adopted from the National Mathematics and Science Initiative (NMSI), of which A+CR is a member. The NMSI concept of a *Teacher Leader* is being followed whereby a cohort of 10 teachers who already offer rigorous CS courses at their schools assist in training future peer cohorts (with 20 new teachers invited to the project in years two and three) who come from other STEM and CTE backgrounds.

CS4Alabama is currently in its first year and the initial cohort of teachers have participated in a week-long face-to-face PD session, two face-to-face weekend sessions with assignments and bi-weekly meetings occurring over the summer and academic year. Over a dozen new lesson plans have already been created by this first cohort of Teacher Leaders. Additionally, more than 400 students are enrolled during the first year, with some high schools receiving such high demand that multiple sections of CS Principles are being offered by the same teacher. The project has multiple measurements of evaluation through collaboration with Haynie Research and Evaluation. On this panel, I will share some of the early observations made from our PD efforts, and describe our plans for engaging existing STEM teachers in our future cohorts.

5. RALPH MORELLI

Mobile Computer Science Principles (*MobileCSP*) is a CS Principles curriculum [8] based on the blocks-based graphical programming language, *App Inventor for Android* [7]. While originally developed and hosted at Google, App Inventor is now based at the Center for Mobile Learning at MIT. It is currently supporting almost 1 million individuals who have created more than 2 million projects. The MIT server currently hosts more than 5000 active users per day. A growing number of teachers at all levels, from grade school to university, are using App Inventor in their computing courses.

Our PD effort is aimed primarily at getting MobileCSP taught in Connecticut schools. It consists of a full-time 6-week in person course. The teachers in this year's cohort ranged from technology teachers to social studies and graphic arts teachers. Only one of the 10 teachers had any formal training in computer science. Prior to enrolling in the PD, teachers and their principals are required to sign an agreement to teach the MobileCSP course to 11th graders in their schools. During summer 2013 we trained 10 Hartford-area teachers. In addition, a small group of CSTA members from the Boston area participated in the PD by using the online resources. The Hartford-area teachers are supported in their classrooms by our project's itinerant *Teacher's Consultant*, who has extensive teaching experience in App Inventor and CS Principles. By the end of this academic year we expect to have data on student attitudes and performance with the MobileCSP curriculum from ~300 students.

6. REFERENCES

[1] Abelson, H., Ledeen, K., Lewis, H. *Blown to Bits: Your Life, Liberty, and Happiness After the Digital Explosion*. Addison-Wesley Professional, Cambridge, MA, 2008.

[2] Briggs, A. and Snyder, L. 2012. Computer science principles and the CS 10K initiative. ACM Inroads 3, 2 (June 2012), 29-31. `doi.acm.org/10.1145/2189835.2189847`

[3] CS Principles Alice Curriculum - Student Guide: https://sites.google.com/a/eng.ucsd.edu/expeditions-through-alice/home, Beth Simon, Sarah Esper, Quintin Cutts.

[4] CS Principles Alice Curriculum - Teacher Guide: https://sites.google.com/a/eng.ucsd.edu/guides-through-alice-2/home, Beth Simon, Sarah Esper, Quintin Cutts, and Tasha Frankie

[5] Garcia, D., Harvey, B. and Segars, L. 2012. CS principles pilot at University of California, Berkeley. *ACM Inroads* 3, 2 (June 2012), 58-60. DOI=10.1145/2189835.2189853

[6] Simon, B. and Cutts, Q. 2012. Bits and Bytes: How to Implement a Peer Instruction-Designed CS Principles Course. ACM Inroads 3, 2 (June 2012), 72-74.

[7] MIT. 2013. *App Inventor for Android.* Website. `http://appinventor.mit.edu/`

[8] MobileCSP. 2013. Website. `https://sites.google.com/site/mobilecsp/`

[9] UC Berkeley. 2013. *The Beauty and Joy of Computing*. Website. `http://bjc.berkeley.edu/`

[10] UC Berkeley. 2013. *SNAP!*. Website. `http://snap.berkeley.edu/`

Blocks-based Programming Languages: Simplifying Programming for Different Audiences with Different Goals

Paul Medlock-Walton
Massachusetts Institute of Technology
paulmw@mit.edu

Kyle J. Harms
Washington University in St. Louis
harmsk@seas.wustl.edu

Eileen T. Kraemer
(Moderator)
University of Georgia
eileen@uga.edu

Karen Brennan
Harvard University
karen_brennan@gse.harvard.edu

Daniel Wendel
Massachusetts Institute of Technology
djwendel@mit.edu

Summary

In this panel, the moderator, who has expertise in computer science education and HCI, but with no ties to any particular blocks-based programming environment in particular, will provide a brief overview of the state of the field of visual programming for education generally, and blocks-based visual programming environments and the languages that go with them more specifically. As early as in 1986, blocks-based visual programming environments were conceived of and built as research studies (Glinert & Smith, 1986)). However, the last five to ten years have seen a proliferation of these kinds of programming languages. Scratch and Alice are probably the most widely known of these programming interfaces, but there are many. Among these, many share common traits: the goal of simplifying the syntax of programming, a related goal of making what were once difficult tasks relegated to arcane languages simpler, and often another related goal of opening computer programming up to a wider audience than has recently traditionally engaged in programming activities. The moderator will be followed by four panelists, representing four blocks-based programming environments that share these affordances, but which more interestingly, are distinct in a number of ways. These panelists, experts in MIT App Inventor, Scratch, Looking Glass, and ToolBlox, respectively, will each have ten minutes to discuss their respective language and the possibility-space it aims to simplify. Specifically, each language will be examined from three perspectives: the reason the tool was created, the target audience for the tool, and how the tool engages those users in computational thinking and learning to program. The moderator will then lead a substantive discussion with the audience and panel members on the material presented.

Categories and Subject Descriptors

K.3.2 [**Computers and Education**]: Computer and Information Science Education – *Computer science education.*

SIGCSE'14, March 5–8, 2014, Atlanta, Georgia, USA.
ACM 978-1-4503-2605-6/14/03.
http://dx.doi.org/10.1145/2538862.2538873

General Terms

Design, Human Factors, Languages.

Keywords

blocks-based programming, visual programming

1. Paul Medlock-Walton

MIT App Inventor seeks to democratize personal mobile computing by allowing relative novices to create apps which can run on Android devices. The intended audience is made up of newcomers to programming, who are excited by the possibility of expressing themselves through creation of applications for this relatively new class of mobile computers. The creators of App Inventor sought to engage these novices with programming, something they might otherwise not choose to pursue.

2. Karen Brennan

Scratch (scratch.mit.edu) is an authoring environment that makes it easy for kids to create their own interactive media and then to share their creations with other young programmers via an online community. One of the main goals of Scratch is to engage a diverse range of kids in computational self-expression using computer code as a creative medium. Since Scratch's launch in 2007, hundreds of thousands of kids (mostly between the ages of 8 and 16) have created more than 3 million projects (Resnick et al, 2009; Brennan, 2013). As kids work with Scratch, they develop as computational thinkers – learning particular computational concepts, negotiating those concepts through computational practices, and developing new computational perspectives about themselves and the world around them (Brennan & Resnick, 2012).

3. Kyle J. Harms

Looking Glass is a novice programming environment designed for kids ages ten and up that is designed to support learning computer programming from examples. Kids program their own 3D animated stories and share them to an online community accessible directly from Looking Glass. These shared programs then serve as examples for others through remixing. Remixing in Looking Glass enables kids to reuse code snippets from programs created by others and easily adapt them for use in their own programs. New tools for exploring program execution help kids to connect interesting output in a program with the lines of code that caused it. This can introduce kids to new programming elements and inspire them to try using these elements in their own programs (Gross, 2010).

4. Daniel Wendel

ToolBlox allows users to see inside the "black box" of agent-based simulations, enabling them to query underlying assumptions and tinker with rules and parameters. Its agent-centric language and 3D graphics engine also make ToolBlox an ideal tool for beginners to program their own games and simulations from the ground up. The target audience for the tool includes a wide range of users from middle school students learning to program to college students and beyond who need an easily programmable, powerful simulation-building environment. ToolBlox is intentionally designed to increase interest and ability in programming among its target audiences.

5. ACKNOWLEDGMENTS

The material presented by Karen Brennan is based on work supported by the National Science Foundation under grant #1019396.

The work presented by Kyle Harms on Looking Glass was funded by NSF grant #1054587.

The material presented by Daniel Wendel on ToolBlox is based on work supported by the NSF under grant #0822241.

Any opinions, findings, and conclusions or recommendations expressed are those of the author and do not necessarily reflect the views of the NSF.

6. REFERENCES

[1] Brennan, K. (2013). Learning computing through creating and connecting. IEEE Computer, Special Issue: Computing in Education. doi:10.1109/MC.2013.229

[2] Brennan, K., & Resnick, M. (2012). New frameworks for studying and assessing the development of computational thinking. American Educational Research Association meeting, Vancouver, BC, Canada

[3] Glinert, E. P. and Smith, C. D.. PC-TILES: A Visual Programming Environment for Personal Computers Based on the BLOX Methodology. Technical Report 86- 21, Dept. of Computer Science, Rensselaer Polytechnic institute, 1986..

[4] Gross, P.A. et al. 2010. A code reuse interface for non-programmer middle school students. *Proc. IUI*, 219–228.

[5] Resnick, M. et al. 2009. Scratch: Programming for All. *Communications of the ACM.* 52, 11 (Nov. 2009), 60-67

7. AUTHORS' ADDRESS INFORMATION

Paul Medlock-Walton
Massachusetts Institute of Technology
77 Massachusetts Avenue
Building E15-301
Cambridge, MA 02139

Kyle J. Harms
Washington University in St. Louis
1 Brookings Drive
Saint Louis, MO, 63130

Eileen Kraemer
University of Georgia
415 Boyd Grad Studies Building
Athens, GA 30602

Karen Brennan
Harvard University
13 Appian Way
Longfellow 324
Cambridge, MA 02138

Daniel Wendel
Massachusetts Institute of Technology
77 Massachusetts Avenue
Building E15-301
Cambridge, MA 0213

Teaching Parallel Design Patterns to Undergraduates in Computer Science

Richard A. Brown (Moderator)
St. Olaf College
rab@stolaf.edu

Joel C. Adams
Calvin College
adams@calvin.edu

Clayton Ferner
UNC Wilmington
cferner@uncw.edu

Elizabeth Shoop
Macalester College
shoop@macalester.edu

Barry Wilkinson
UNC Charlotte
abw@uncc.edu

SUMMARY

The industry shift emerging forms of parallel and distributed computing (PDC), including multi-core CPUs, cloud computing, and general-purpose use of GPUs, have naturally led to increased presence of PDC elements undergraduate Computer Science curriculum recommendations, such as the new and substantial "PD" knowledge area in the joint ACM/IEEE CS2013 recommendations[1]. How can undergraduate students grasp the extensive and complex range of PDC principles and practices, and apply that knowledge in problem solving, while PDC technologies continue to evolve rapidly?

Parallel design patterns are descriptions of effective solutions to recurring parallel programming problems in particular contexts and have emerged from long-standing industry practice. Parallel patterns occur at all computational levels, ranging from low-level concurrent execution patterns (such as *message passing* or *thread pool* patterns) to high-level software design patterns suitable for organizing entire systems or their components (such as *model-view-control* or *pipe and filter* patterns). The sheer number of parallel patterns, which reflect the full breadth and complexity of PDC, can be quite daunting for a newcomer. However, the ubiquity of parallel patterns in all forms of parallel and distributed computation makes these patterns relevant and illuminating at all undergraduate levels. Knowledge of parallel patterns, being reusable elements of parallel design, guides problem-solving during the creation of parallel programs; and those enduring design patterns remain relevant and useful as new PDC infrastructure emerges in this rapidly evolving field.

This panel presents four viewpoints representing various approaches for teaching parallel patterns to CS undergraduates at multiple academic levels. Moderator Dick Brown co-directs (with Adams and Shoop) the CSinParallel project (csinparallel.org), which produces and shares modular materials for incrementally adding parallelism to existing undergraduate computer science courses [2]. A former director of CS at St. Olaf, he serves as an officer and executive board member of EAPF (eapf.org). Brown will briefly review the goals of the session (3-4 min), introduce each panelist (10 min each), and moderate discussion.

SIGCSE'14, March 5–8, 2014, Atlanta, Georgia, USA.
ACM 978-1-4503-2605-6/14/03.
http://dx.doi.org/10.1145/2538862.2538875

Categories and Subject Descriptors

K.3.2 [**Computers and Education**]: Computer and Information Science Education – *Curriculum.*

D.1.3 [**Programming Techniques**]: Concurrent Programming – *Distributed programming, Parallel programming.*

D.2.11 [**Software Engineering**]: Software Architectures – *Patterns.*

D.1.3 [**Programming Languages**]: Language Constructs and Features – *Patterns.*

General Terms: Algorithms, Design, Performance.

Keywords

Parallel computing, parallelism, distributed computing, education, parallel design patterns, curriculum, design patterns, Seeds, Paraguin, patternlets, exemplars.

1. JOEL ADAMS

Joel Adams is Professor and Chair of the Department of Computer Science at Calvin College, and has been teaching his students about concurrency and parallelism for more than 20 years. He has been the principle architect of four Beowulf clusters, is a two-time Fulbright scholar, and is an ACM Distinguished Educator.

Statement: A *patternlet* is an executable program that shows the behavior of a parallel pattern, that is:

- *Minimalist* in terms of eliminating non-essential features, so that students can easily grasp the program's essential concept.
- *Scalable* so that students can vary the number of threads and observe how the program's behavior changes.
- *Syntactically correct* so that students can use the program as a working model for their own coding.

Each patternlet provides a simple way to introduce students to a particular pattern. Patternlets are designed to be a flexible pedagogical tool to help students master a particular parallel concept in any appropriate course, whether as a hands-on activity by students or as a live-coding demonstration by instructors.

Patternlets are an evolving collection; there are at this time 25 of them – 14 in OpenMP and 11 in MPI – illustrating the *single program multiple data (*SPMD), *fork-join*, *master-worker*, *parallel for loop*, *barrier*, *message passing*, *mutual exclusion*, *scatter*, *gather*, *broadcast*, *reduction*, *data decomposition*, and other parallel patterns. Adams will present several patternlets and discuss different ways they can be used to introduce parallelism into the CS curriculum.

2. ELIZABETH SHOOP

Libby Shoop co-directs (with moderator Brown and co-panelist Adams) the CSinParallel project (csinparallel.org) [2]. She teaches several courses in the CS curriculum, ranging from the introductory level to computer systems organization, software development, and parallel and distributed systems.

Statement: The parallel and distributed computing (PDC) curricular recommendations a decade from now may differ as radically from today's curricular recommendations as the PDC aspects of CS2013 differ from those of CS2001. However, PDC in some form is here to stay in the CS curriculum. As educators we must ask ourselves two key questions: 1) Apart from parallel algorithms, *are there principles that we can teach our students in the context of today's PDC hardware and software milieu that will remain relevant and abiding for the unforeseeable technologies of the next decade?* 2) Since all computing students must now learn about PDC and some may not be interested in PDC, *how can we motivate today's computing students to engage with this rapidly evolving field*?

We propose a two-pronged approach to addressing these issues. Our first "prong" is *parallel programming patterns*, which emerge directly from the experience of professional practitioners. These offer a practical and relevant collection of problem-solving strategies that transcend particular technologies, enabling students to acquire enduring intellectual and useful skills in PDC. Our second "prong" is *exemplar applications* that apply PDC topics and techniques in solving some (more or less) realistic problem. Such exemplars provide convenient and useful resources for presenting and comparing parallel and distributed computing technologies. They also motivate students to learn PDC principles and practices by helping them see how PDC makes an impact in other fields. The combination of patterns and exemplars provides a unified approach for motivating undergraduates to develop parallel thinking, often with modest or even negligible added costs to existing course syllabi.

3. BARRY WILKINSON

Barry Wilkinson is Professor of Department of Computer Science at University of North Carolina, Charlotte and has been involved in parallel computing since the 1970's. He was a *Supercomputing 2011* Undergraduate Engineering and Sciences award finalist in 2011. He has published six textbooks, four with second editions, including *Programming: Techniques and Application Using Networked Workstations and Parallel Computers*, with M. Allen, 1999, 2nd ed. 2005, Prentice Hall.

Statement: A pattern programming framework called Seeds has been developed at UNC-Charlotte that enables programmers to select a parallel pattern such as *workpool* and create parallel executable code without writing any low-level message passing code (MPI) [3]. The framework self-deploys on any parallel or distributed computing platform including a single multicore computer. This framework is currently being used in a senior undergraduate parallel programming class taught to six universities across North Carolina on the NCREN televideo network. We believe pattern programming offers a very promising approach to teaching parallel programming. We are strong advocates for using patterns as they provide a guide to best practices and provide scalable design structures. Parallel programming is much easier for students, less likely to be flawed, more scalable, and it allows others to understand the code better. One can concentrate upon issues such as data partitioning and performance. Wilkinson will present the Seeds framework and its use in the undergraduate CS curriculum.

4. CLAYTON FERNER

Clayton Ferner is a professor of Computer Science at the University of North Carolina Wilmington (UNCW). He has been a faculty member at UNCW for 14 years and taught courses on parallel computing, grid computing, programming languages, compiler construction, operating systems, and data structures. He has developed a parallelizing compiler that generates MPI code suitable to run on a distributed-memory parallel system.

Statement: The *Paraguin* compiler, being developed at UNC-Wilmington, is a source-to-source compiler that will translate programs written in a style similar to OpenMP to a program that runs in parallel on a distributed-memory system using MPI to handle communication. Like OpenMP, the programmer directs the parallelization through the use of `pragma` statements to create the MPI code. The level of abstraction is much higher using the Paraguin compiler than with MPI. Because it is a source-to-source compiler, the user is free to inspect the result to see how their algorithm was implemented as well as modify it.

Since OpenMP uses `pragmas` to create parallel code for execution on shared-memory systems, our compiler can easily create a hybrid program by passing the OpenMP `pragmas` through to the MPI output code. The resulting output code is a hybrid parallel program that uses MPI to create parallelization for distributed-memory systems while simultaneously using OpenMP to create parallelization between cores of processors.

The compiler also supports a few patterns through the use of `pragmas`. The *scatter/gather* and *stencil* patterns have been implemented with more patterns planned in the next year. Students can create correct parallel programs implemented in MPI using these patterns while avoiding issues such as deadlocks and race conditions.

ACKNOWLEDGMENTS

Adams, Brown, and Shoop are supported by NSF DUE-1225739/1225796/1226172. Ferner and Wilkinson are supported by NSF DUE-1141005/1141006.

REFERENCES

[1] ACM/IEEE-CS Joint Task Force, "Computer Science Curricula 2013." [Online]. [Accessed: 07-Sep-2013]: http://ai.stanford.edu/users/sahami/CS2013/.

[2] R. Brown and E. Shoop, "Modules in community: injecting more parallelism into computer science curricula," in *Proceedings of the 42nd ACM technical symposium on Computer science education*, New York, NY, USA, 2011, pp. 447–452.

[3] B. Wilkinson, J. Villalobos, and C. Ferner, "Pattern programming approach for teaching parallel and distributed computing," in *Proceeding of the 44th ACM technical symposium on Computer science education*, New York, NY, USA, 2013, pp. 409–414.

Teaching Operating Systems Using Code Review

Christoffer Dall
Dept of Computer Science
Columbia University
New York, NY
cdall@cs.columbia.edu

Jason Nieh
Dept of Computer Science
Columbia University
New York, NY
nieh@cs.columbia.edu

ABSTRACT

Learning about operating systems often involves modifying a large and complex code base. Grading student projects can be difficult and time consuming, yet students often do not learn from their programming errors and struggle to understand core operating system concepts. We present GradeBoard, a code review system designed to simplify grading for instructors and enable students to understand and learn from their errors. GradeBoard provides an easy-to-use Web interface that allows instructors to annotate student code submissions with grading comments and scores, and students to discuss the comments and scores with instructors. GradeBoard presents student code changes with syntax highlighting and lets users collapse or expand code sections to provide a desired level of context, making it easier to read and understand student programming project submissions. Comments and scores are easily identifiable by visual cues, improving interaction between instructors and students. We have deployed and used GradeBoard in a large operating systems course involving Linux kernel programming projects. GradeBoard provided robust, easy-to-use functionality for reviewing Linux kernel code changes, improved the instructional staff grading experience, and over 90% of students surveyed indicated that GradeBoard improved their understanding of the kernel programming projects better than other alternatives.

Categories and Subject Descriptors: D.4.0 [Operating Systems]: General; K.3.1 [Computers and Education]: Computer Uses in Education–distance learning; K.3.2 [Computers and Education]: Computer and Information Science Education–computer science education

Keywords: Operating Systems, Code Review, Instructional Tools

1. INTRODUCTION

Programming projects are an important aspect of learning about operating systems (OSes) [8, 10]. Many approaches have been developed for providing such hands-on programming experience, including OS simulation environments, pedagogical OSes, and kernel development in commercial OSes. However, students often struggle with writing OS code and a disproportionate amount of time is spent by instructors evaluating student code without contributing to the actual learning process.

OS hands-on programming assignments typically provide students with some common software code base as a starting point for their programming projects, whether it be a small pedagogical OS in which students add substantial components or a large commercial OS that students modify to provide new features. Grading these projects can be especially hard because the projects involve not just writing an assignment from scratch in isolation, but modifying code throughout a potentially large and complex existing code base. To provide useful feedback to students to help them learn from their mistakes, students can be asked to give live demonstrations of their work, but this carries the risk of missing errors in handling important corner cases such as concurrency and synchronization, which are especially important and at the same time difficult to get right. Another approach is to run automated tests on student implementations, but test cases treat an implementation largely as a black box and do not cover subtle error cases or code design and readability.

To properly evaluate student work and give students useful feedback, it is crucial to review the code itself. This can be difficult to do for a variety of reasons. For example, many approaches simply provide feedback in terms of a grade sheet that summarizes the points deducted for various mistakes. This provides no direct correlation with the actual submitted code, leaving students with little choice but to try to hunt through numerous lines of code to identify the mistakes they made. Even if instructors refer to code using file names and line numbers, finding and following these references is tedious and error prone for both instructors and students, making it unlikely for students to learn from the process.

An alternative approach is to manually inline instructor comments directly in submitted code and make the commented code available to students to review. Unfortunately, this is at best a time consuming grading process for both instructors and students. Instructors are provided little help in grading numerous lines of code that may be embedded in large complex pieces of software, making the grading process difficult. Students must then use command line tools to find instructor comments with no visual structure or road map for figuring out where those comments might be and which ones might be of greatest importance for learning. The end result is that such grading is often a one-way process in which students see their grades but do not gain a complete understanding of their programming errors.

To address these problems, we present GradeBoard, a Web-based code submission and review system for providing grading feedback to students to help them learn more efficiently. GradeBoard provides a rich and flexible Web interface to make code more accessible, which helps instructors grade and comment on code and

SIGCSE'14, March 5–8, 2014, Atlanta, GA, USA.

ACM 978-1-4503-2605-6/14/03 ...$15.00.
http://dx.doi.org/10.1145/2538862.2538894.

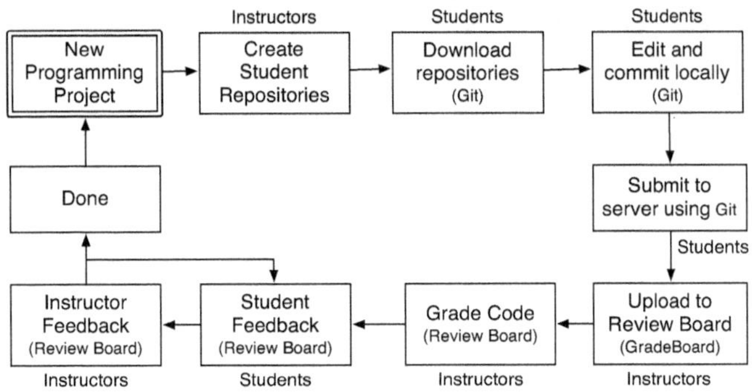

Figure 1: GradeBoard workflow

helps students read and understand code comments. Code changes are shown in a side-by-side *diff view* with code syntax highlighting, making it much easier to read and understand changes to a large existing code base than reading code diffs using command line tools. GradeBoard collapses large chunks of unmodified code, letting instructors focus on grading changed or new code, a feature especially useful when instructors need to consider small changes to large files. Students receive summaries of grading comments and see instructor comments as visual overlays in the code, which they can click on to ask questions about grading comments. Instructors can reply in one or several rounds to provide additional feedback. GradeBoard's Web-based interface is easily accessible from any computer with a Web browser without any further configuration or installation.

GradeBoard is based on standard widely used software development tools, the Git version control system [13] and the Review Board code review system [3]. This provides several benefits. First, because these tools are commercially supported, we can focus limited resources on teaching rather than spending time on in-house tool development. Second, because these tools are widely used in industry, students gain experience with real-world software development. Third, because these tools are open-source and widely-used in commercial settings, they continue to be developed and improved, which naturally evolves the tools and enables students to learn in a modern context.

We successfully deployed and used GradeBoard in a large introductory OS course at Columbia University. Our experience shows that GradeBoard proved very useful for both instructors and students. Over 90% of students participating in a survey found that using GradeBoard improved their understanding of programming projects. Many students even said that using GradeBoard encouraged them to submit well-formatted code. The instructional staff found that GradeBoard significantly reduced time spent on grading kernel source code and reduced the number of grading mistakes by conveniently showing instructors the necessary context to code changes. Instructors were also very pleased with the ease of use and convenient overview of graded and ungraded projects. GradeBoard also facilitated more consistent grading by allowing instructors to inspect and discuss each other's grading.

2. USAGE MODEL

Figure 1 shows the GradeBoard workflow. It leverages a code distribution and submission system based on Git and a Web-based code review system based on Review Board. GradeBoard runs on an instructor-controlled server. Students can access GradeBoard from any computer and work on their programming projects on any computer on or outside the University network.

To assign a new programming project, an instructor creates a Git repository on the GradeBoard server containing the common code base used as a starting point for the student projects. For example, projects using Linux will typically use the Linux kernel as the common code base. Once the base repository is set, an instructor issues a single `create-hmwk` command and the repository is automatically duplicated, or *cloned*, for each student so that each student has a copy of the common code base. Student repositories can be cloned for individual students or teams of students, based on instructor preference.

To work on an assigned programming project, students download their repositories to their own computers using standard Git commands. Students can only access repositories assigned to them by the instructor. Students work on the code using their own computers and make incremental commits to their Git repositories using standard Git commands. Students are allowed to make commits and push those commits to the GradeBoard server up until a specified project deadline, at which point any further attempts to submit are blocked. The last pushed commit is considered the student's final submission to be graded.

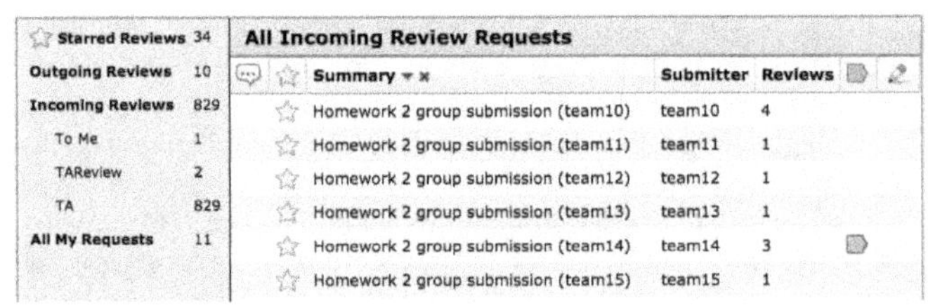

Figure 2: GradeBoard dashboard

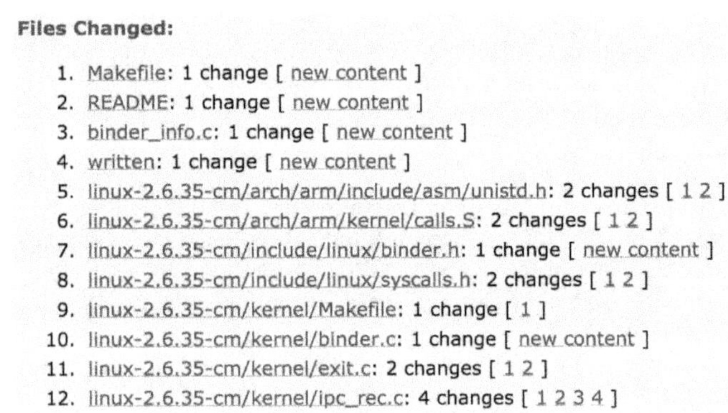

Figure 3: GradeBoard diff file overview

To upload the submissions to the GradeBoard review system for grading, an instructor simply executes a single `create-review` command, which causes GradeBoard to go through each student submission and upload and make it available for review through the Web-based Review Board system. As shown in Figure 2, a dashboard lists all the uploaded student submissions, along with information about each submission such as a summary description, the submitter, how many times the submission has been reviewed by instructional staff, and if there are any comments created by the specific instructional staff member currently logged in. Multiple instructional staff members is supported, which can include, for example, an instructor and multiple teaching assistants or graders. Instructors can add additional columns of information and can sort, filter, and search on all columns.

To grade a student submission, instructors select an ungraded submission from the dashboard and see a side-by-side diff view

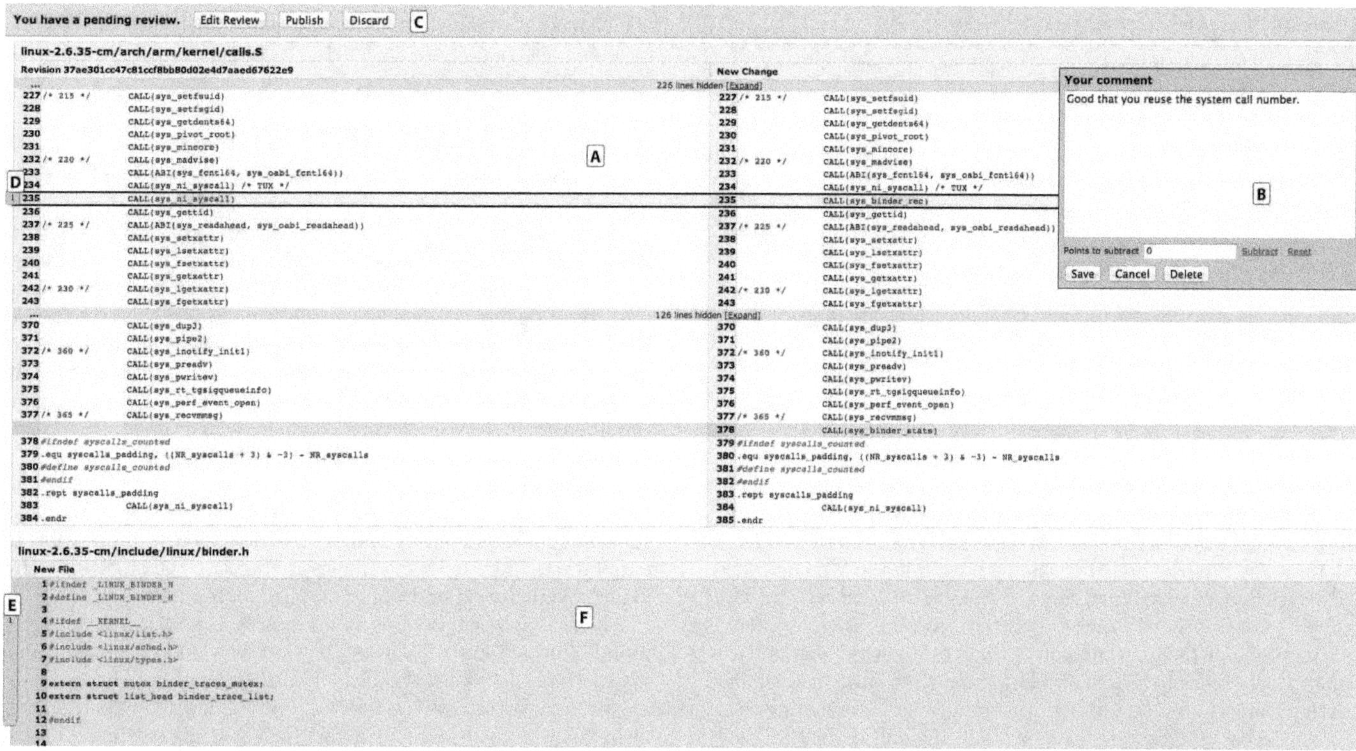

Figure 4: GradeBoard instructor view of submitted homework assignment. Part (A) shows changes to an existing file. When clicking a line, the comment dialog for that line appears (B). When writing the first comment, the review status bar (C) appears at the top of the screen. Existing comments are shown as overlays on the line numbers for either single lines (D) or multiple lines (E). New files are shown as a single column (F). Numbers in comment overlays indicate number of comments on the line.

of the submitted code. As can be seen in Figure 3, the top of the diff view shows an overview of modified and added files. The overview shows the full path and file name and the number of changed code blocks for each file and reviewers can click on a file to scroll to changes in that file.

Figure 4 shows the main part of the instructor diff view. Each new file is clearly marked with a separate box with the full path and file name in the header of each box. The side-by-side diff view (A) shows the new version of a file on the right and the old version of a file on the left. New files are annotated as such and show only a single column (F). Source code is syntax highlighted to ease reading code. Green lines are new lines, yellow lines are modified lines, and red lines are deleted lines. Large chunks of unmodified lines are collapsed to a single gray line, and users can click to expand these lines. The ability to expand lines and see the full context of a modified file is especially useful for reviewing kernel code, where contextual information can be crucial to understand added code. Changes on a particular line are also highlighted so users easily can pinpoint the exact changes. Line numbers are shown on both the original and changed file. Instructors comment on a single line or a block of lines by simply clicking anywhere on these lines, causing a dialog window to appear (B) where instructors can easily enter comments. GradeBoard supports a live Web 2.0-style interface with ad-hoc commenting by continuously saving comments whenever a user edits them. GradeBoard stores a collection of comments to a code submission as a *review*. When the first comment is added, a review is automatically created and a review status bar (C) is added to the top of the screen. Reviews are initially created as *drafts* not accessible by other instructors until they are *published*, and not

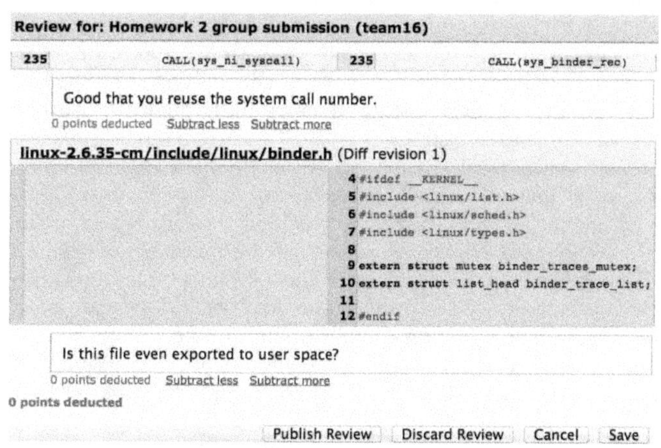

Figure 5: GradeBoard summary of review

accessible by students until they are *released*. Overlays (D) and (E) on the line numbers indicate instructor comments for those lines.

Instructors grade submissions by commenting on source code lines as described above and choose a number of points to deduct in the comment dialog for each grading comment. Instructors can also edit a draft review by clicking the Edit Review button in the review status tool bar, which presents a summary view allowing instructors to edit comments and subtracted points. Figure 5 shows the summary view, which displays the total number of deducted points and is useful to check the grading of a project before publishing the review. Publishing a review does not make the grading available to students, but lets other instructors access the

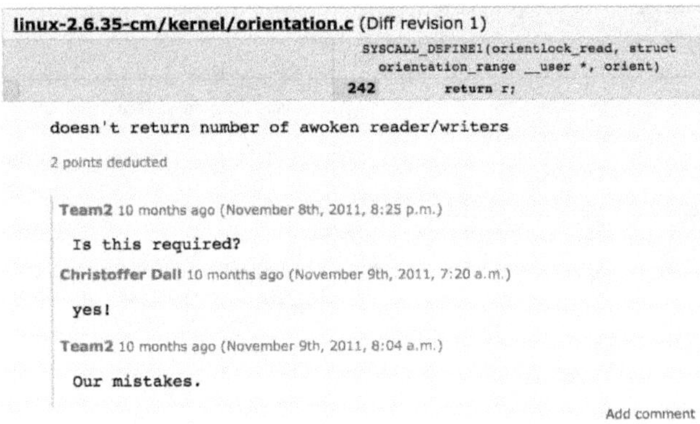

Figure 6: GradeBoard inline grading comment discussion

review so they can discuss the grading style and points deducted internally before releasing grades to students. When all submissions have been graded, instructors can release all grades to the students at the same time by simply clicking a button in the Web interface.

Students review their grading by logging into GradeBoard where they can only see their own submitted projects. When students click on one of their submissions they are presented with a summary view similar to that shown in Figure 5 and a diff view similar to that shown in Figure 4, except that students cannot modify their grading score. Students see comments in the diff view as overlays on the line numbers and simply moving the mouse cursor over the overlays shows the comment. Students reply to comments directly in the summary view or by clicking comment overlays in the diff view. Students can prepare a *draft response* similar to how instructors create draft reviews. A *response* is a collection of questions on grading comments and students publish a response by clicking the Publish button on the response status bar analogous to the review status bar. There is no release step for students since there is no need for all student comments to be sent to instructors at the same time. GradeBoard shows the questions and answers as a threaded discussion under each grading comment in the summary view as shown in Figure 6. Instructors reply to student questions similarly to how students ask questions and this feedback loop can be repeated as many times as required to explain concepts to students.

Students and instructors are notified through e-mail when grades are released, when students ask questions about grading comments, and when instructors answer student questions. The e-mails contain a link to the submission being discussed and a summary of the grading comments and related discussions for that review. The e-mail summary additionally provides a link on each comment directing users to a response form for that comment on the Web interface.

Using GradeBoard to discuss grading comments improves the learning experience for students for a number of reasons. First, replying to a grading comment is faster and more convenient than sending an e-mail or attending office hours to ask for clarification, making it more likely that students ask questions about areas in which they struggle. An increase in the number of student questions on grading comments is a good thing, since answering these questions directly ensures that students understand the core concepts they struggle with. Second, GradeBoard's user interface provides a discussion type layout of the questions and answers to grading comments making it easy to track the conversation. The discussion thread is shown inline in the code so instructors and students can easily inspect the code being discussed and refer to it in questions and answers. Third, the entire instructional staff has access to the grading comments and discussions, which allows one instructor to answer a question when another instructor is not available and allows one instructor to further clarify the answer from another instructor.

3. SYSTEM ARCHITECTURE

GradeBoard consists of three major components: The first component is a source code revision system, Git, used to distribute a common code base to students, to collaborate on projects within student teams, and to submit final solutions to programming projects. The second component is a Web-based code review system based on the commercially maintained open-source software Review Board. The third component is a management tool used to integrate Git and Review Board for a teaching environment. Git is used completely unmodified and GradeBoard is only slightly modified from Review Board making it easy to leverage new features from new releases of both systems.

GradeBoard is easy to install and configure on any Linux server. We install the Git management system Gitosis [15] to manage repository access control and the Review Board application is easily installed by following the instructions on the official Review Board Web site [4] and applying our small patch.

The management tool provides instructors with a set of commands that are executed from the instructor's local machine and interact remotely with the GradeBoard server. GradeBoard management tools abstract low-level Git and Review Board commands from instructors and let instructors issue a single command on behalf of all students and their teams. For example, instructors issue a single `create-hmwk` command and all student template repositories for that programming project are automatically created. The management tool accomplishes this by maintaining a central list of enrolled students and their teams. When student enrollment changes during the course of the semester, instructors need only to change the central list of enrolled students, and the system adjusts authentication settings and group memberships accordingly to prevent, for example, that a student who dropped the course receives future e-mails from the system. Similarly, if a student joins the class late, an instructor simply adds that student and her team assignment to the list of enrolled students and GradeBoard automatically sends out a welcome e-mail with instructions on how to get started with the system to the new student.

Instructors create template repositories for each student or student team from a single shared code base by first creating a base repository on the server, for example containing a copy of the Linux kernel. Instructors then use the management tool to clone the base repository for each registered student or student team. GradeBoard leverages existing Git features to use hard links for every shared file, inducing minimal disk space overhead. A standard version 2.6.35 Linux kernel repository consumes 492MB of disk space, which would amount to 50GB of disk space for 100 students if the repositories were to be simply copied or created from scratch for each student. Using hard links only consumes 128KB per extra unmodified clone, resulting in less than 500MB of total used disk space for all unmodified student repositories. In addition to imposing only modest hardware requirements, the low disk space usage also simplifies backup procedures.

The management tool command `create-review` utility collects all student changes to the base project source code repository and uploads these changes to the code review system. Review Board accesses the base repository to generate a combined diff of the changes and uses the original source code to show context when, for example, users expand a collapsed section in the diff view.

Review Board's authentication system supports creating user groups, which allows us to configure access permissions such that

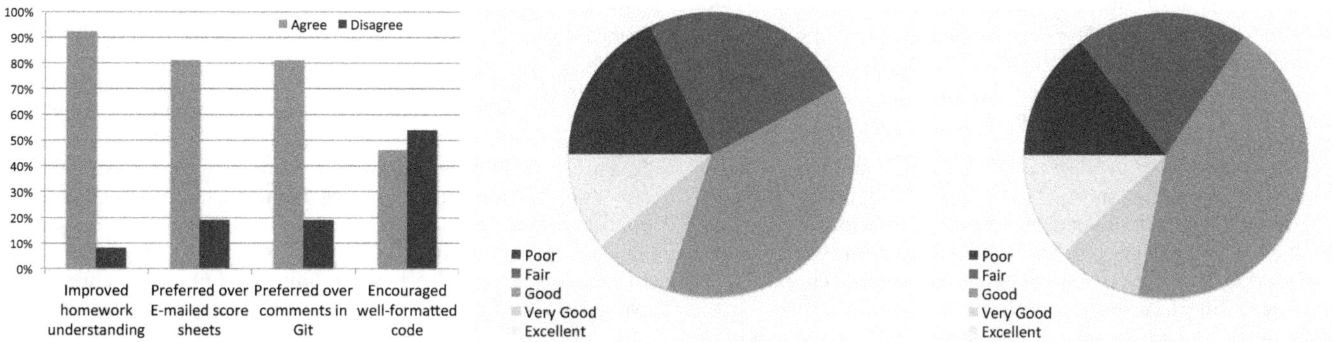

(a) Overall student experiences (b) Usefulness of discussion features (c) Improved experience reading diffs

Figure 7: Survey Results

students can only access their own submissions and instructors can access all submissions. Review Board's default configuration lets submitters modify their own submissions without any restrictions, which does not work in a teaching environment where students cannot be allowed to modify a submission after a project deadline. To address this limitation we changed Review Board's default behavior to not allow users to upload or edit submissions. We also added a custom authentication setting that allows specific users to upload and edit all submissions, and we configure Review Board to only apply this setting to the instructor authentication group.

A modest number of simple changes are required to the standard Review Board lines of code in Review Board v1.6.1, less than 100 lines of Python code and about 200 lines of HTML/JavaScript have been added to support the authentication mechanism and calculating grading scores. These changes are non-intrusive to Review Board's standard functionality as a code review tool and do not modify existing features. They only add new optional features and can therefore easily be integrated in the standard Review Board code base without compromising other functionality. For example, we applied the same patch to two different versions of Review Board without any complications.

4. EXPERIENCES

We implemented and evaluated the use of GradeBoard in the Fall 2011 introductory OS class at Columbia University. During the course, six two-week programming projects were assigned [1]. Each project involved modifying the Linux kernel relating to a core OS subject and included a written non-programming part as well as the programming project. To run GradeBoard, we used a single central server with two Intel Xeon 3.06GHz CPUs, 2GB RAM, and 16GB RAID-1 storage, though more modest hardware could have been used. 2GB RAM was useful to keep the Linux kernel repository and Web server state in memory.

The GradeBoard commenting feature was heavily used. Students commented on over 80% of the graded programming projects, often asking for further clarification of a programming error. For example, a number of students did not fully understand problems in their programming project relating to synchronization and race conditions, a topic which students typically struggle to fully comprehend. GradeBoard's commenting feature allowed instructors to easily tailor the level of explanation detail for each student.

At the end of the course, we asked students to evaluate their experiences using GradeBoard. Out of more than 100 students enrolled at the end of the semester, 57% of the students, completed the evaluation survey. Figures 7a, 7b, and 7c show the results of the survey. More than 90% of the students who completed the survey said that the use of GradeBoard improved their understanding of the programming projects by being able to see comments from instructors directly in context with the submitted source code lines. More than 80% of the students preferred GradeBoard to e-mailed score sheets or viewing instructor comments committed to source code repositories. Almost half the students who completed the survey, said that using GradeBoard encouraged them to submit easier-to-read, more well-formatted code. Finally, the majority of the students found GradeBoard useful for discussing grading with the instructional staff, and improved the experience of reading code diffs compared to reading flat diff files. However, a few students also felt that the GradeBoard Web interface was difficult to learn.

In addition to being well received by students, GradeBoard was tremendously beneficial for the instructional staff. TAs were very pleased with the interface and felt that it significantly improved the experience of grading and strongly preferred using GradeBoard compared to manually have to write up grade sheets or clone repositories and add comments to student code. This was confirmed by TAs from previous years, who told us they would have strongly preferred using GradeBoard compared to other alternatives.

GradeBoard also turned out to be helpful when interacting in person with students, for example during office hours, where students would often ask questions about grading comments or would ask for help to understand design flaws or other errors in their submission. In this situation, instructors and students benefited from accessing GradeBoard on a shared computer to inspect and discuss the code and comments together. This avoided the need to search for previous e-mail discussions, look up grade sheets, or spend time waiting to download the student source code, improving the efficiency and experience of office hours for both instructional staff and students alike.

5. RELATED WORK

Some structured grading systems have been developed. Version control systems have been proposed [7, 11] for grading feedback by allowing instructors to directly edit student assignments and commit grading comments in student source code repositories. This command line based approach is inconvenient and does not provide an easy-to-use graphical or Web interface for browsing through graded programming assignments. This is problematic as the students who need the most feedback are those who are also most likely to have less developed skills at reading patches directly and using version control tools to be able to find and review grading feedback. In contrast, GradeBoard does not require students to use any command line utilities to read and understand grading comments. GradeBoard's Web interface is easy-to-use and provides syntax highlighting and the ability to view the full context of code changes combined with visual cues to instructor comments and student feedback.

Praktromat [16] provides basic automatic testing of submissions and allows students to review each other's programming projects. However, Praktomat only provides a text dump of the entire programming project submission. Unlike GradeBoard, it does not provide any way to view only the changes made to a common code base, and lacks a convenient easy-to-use dynamic and graphical Web-based interface for code review.

Caesar [12] focuses on social reviewing where code submissions are broken up into chunks and each chunk is reviewed by different reviewers, who can be other students or members of the instructional staff. Caesar is not suitable for OS kernel programming projects where the amount of code may be small, but extremely dense, and solutions must be read as a whole to verify correctness. Caesar lacks GradeBoard's ability to easily switch back and forth among different views of a code submission, seeing parts of files, whole files or only code changes, all valuable features especially for reviewing OS programming projects.

CodeWave [14] provides an Integrated Development Environment (IDE) with shared real-time editing and record/replay functionality focusing on evaluating the development process in addition to final submissions. However, its IDE may not be suitable for OS programming and is not designed for viewing changes to a large common code base. CodeWave also lacks GradeBoard's ability to easily switch between different views of a code submission.

MarkUs [9] is an open-source Web-based tool for grading student submissions. However, it is designed to only show complete submitted files and not changes to an existing large code base. MarkUs's inability to view diffs limits its utility for reviewing any programming projects involving large common code bases, such as OS kernel programming projects. OSBLE [6] is another Web-based code review tool that does not support reviewing code changes to a common code base and lacks GradeBoard's ability to easily switch back and forth among different views of a code submission. These pedagogical code review systems have to be separately maintained by a limited community of volunteer open-source developers or students, resulting in maintenance overhead and limited functionality. In contrast, GradeBoard builds on open-source tools that are already widely used in commercial software development with strong commercial community support, ensuring robust functionality that can scale to support large code bases and programming projects, such as those used in many Linux-based OS courses.

While GradeBoard builds on Review Board, other commercial code review systems are also available. Our experience with those systems indicates that they may be less well-suited for providing grading feedback. For example, Gerrit [5], used for the Android Open Source Project (AOSP), does not provide a convenient summary view of a code review, requiring students to click through all submitted files to look for annotations that could be used for instructor comments. It is built around a vastly more complicated authentication model and has a more complicated and less intuitive user interface. As another example, Atlassian Crucible [2] is proprietary, cannot be easily modified to work in a teaching environment, and may incur licensing fees.

6. CONCLUSIONS

We have developed GradeBoard, a Web-based code review system that saves time for both teachers and students by simplifying the process of reading, grading, and commenting on student code submissions. GradeBoard makes it easy to identify student code changes to an existing code base with syntax highlighting and lets users collapse or expand code sections to provide the desired level of context. These features make GradeBoard especially useful for teaching operating systems, since students may modify code throughout a large and complex code base. Students learn more from hands-on programming projects when using GradeBoard for two reasons. First, grading comments are much easier to understand as they are shown as annotations directly on student code. Second, students and instructors can easily engage in dialog directly in context with the grading comments, ensuring that students fully understand and learn from their mistakes. Because GradeBoard builds on widely used commercial tools, it is easy to maintain and keep up with commercial practice, and introduces students to standard code review procedures and tools, enhancing their educational experience. Our experiences teaching operating systems using GradeBoard show that GradeBoard is preferred by students over other alternatives, improved students' understanding of their homework code, and significantly improved the instructors' experience of grading compared to other alternatives.

7. ACKNOWLEDGEMENTS

This work was supported in part by NSF grants CNS-1162447, CCF-1162021, and CNS-1018355.

8. REFERENCES

[1] J. Andrus and J. Nieh. Teaching Operating Systems Using Android. In *Proceedings of the 43rd ACM Technical Symposium on Computer Science Education (SIGCSE 2012)*, pages 613–618, Mar. 2012.

[2] Atlassian. Crucible. http://www.atlassian.com/software/crucible/.

[3] Beanbag Inc. Review Board. http://www.reviewboard.org.

[4] Beanbag Inc. Review Board Installation Guide. http://www.reviewboard.org/docs/manual/dev/admin/installation/linux.

[5] Google. Gerrit Code Review. http://code.google.com/p/gerrit.

[6] C. Hundhausen, A. Agrawal, and K. Ryan. The Design of an Online Environment to Support Pedagogical Code Reviews. In *Proceedings of the 41st ACM Technical Symposium on Computer Science Education (SIGCSE 2010)*, pages 182–186, Mar. 2010.

[7] O. Laadan, J. Nieh, and N. Viennot. Teaching Operating Systems Using Virtual Appliances and Distributed Version Control. In *Proceedings of the 41st ACM Technical Symposium on Computer Science Education (SIGCSE 2010)*, pages 480–484, Mar. 2010.

[8] O. Laadan, J. Nieh, and N. Viennot. A Structured Approach to Linux Kernel Projects for Teaching Operating Systems. In *Proceedings of the 42nd ACM Technical Symposium on Computer Science Education (SIGCSE 2011)*, pages 287–292, Mar. 2011.

[9] MarkUs Project. MarkUs. http://www.markusproject.org.

[10] J. Nieh and C. Vaill. Experiences Teaching Operating Systems Using Virtual Platforms and Linux. In *Proceedings of the 36th ACM Technical Symposium on Computer Science Education (SIGCSE 2005)*, pages 520–524, Feb. 2005.

[11] K. L. Reid and G. V. Wilson. Learning by Doing: Introducing Version Control as a Way to Manage Student Assignments. In *Proceedings of the 36th ACM Technical Symposium on Computer Science Education (SIGCSE 2005)*, pages 272–276, Feb. 2005.

[12] M. Tang. Caesar: A Social Code Review Tool for Programming Education. Master's thesis, Massachusetts Institute of Technology, Sept. 2011.

[13] L. Torvalds. Git. http://git-scm.com.

[14] J. Vandeventer and B. Barbour. CodeWave: A Real-Time, Collaborative IDE for Enhanced Learning in Computer Science. In *Proceedings of the 43rd ACM Technical Symposium on Computer Science Education (SIGCSE 2012)*, pages 75–80, Feb. 2012.

[15] T. Virtanen. Gitosis: Software for Hosting Git Repositories. https://github.com/res0nat0r/gitosis.

[16] A. Zeller. Making students read and review code. In *Proceedings of the 5th Annual Conference on Innovation and Technology in Computer Science Education (ITiCSE 2000)*, pages 89–92, Sept. 2000.

A Virtual Graphics Card for Teaching Device Driver Design

Christopher Corsi
School of Computing
Clemson University
Clemson, South Carolina
ccorsi@clemson.edu

Robert Geist
School of Computing
Clemson University
Clemson, South Carolina
geist@clemson.edu

Dennis Lingerfelt
School of Computing
Clemson University
Clemson, South Carolina
dlinger@clemson.edu

ABSTRACT

Open source Linux has become increasingly popular as a vehicle for incorporating hands-on experience with a real system into both undergraduate and graduate operating systems courses. System virtualization tools, such as VMWare, Xen, VirtualBox, and KVM, allow students to freely experiment with kernel modifications without requiring dedicated hardware and without generating significant concern for the ill-effects of system crashes. Nevertheless, certain kernel projects that are highly desirable from an educational standpoint remain unavailable under standard approaches to virtualization. One such project that is known to carry substantial instructional value is the design and implementation of an SMP-safe driver for a high-performance graphics card. Standard virtualization tools export only a minimally-capable, SVGA graphics adapter, which is an inadequate architecture for such a project. This paper describes an extremely simple, kernel-independent, software tool for use by instructors of operating systems courses. The tool provides a virtual, high-performance graphics card that is suitable for Linux device driver design and implementation. The code for the virtual card, which is relatively short, is easily modified by instructors to present different interfaces each semester. The code for both the virtual card and a sample Linux 3.2.36 driver for it may be freely downloaded from *http://people.cs.clemson.edu/~ccorsi/kyouko/*.

Categories and Subject Descriptors

D.4.7 [**Operating Systems**]: Organization and Design;
D.4.0 [**Operation Systems**]: General—*Linux*;
K.3.2 [**Computers and Education**]: Computer and Information Science Education

Keywords

Operating Systems, Virtualization, Graduate Education

1. INTRODUCTION

The classical undergraduate course in operating systems, which focuses on operating systems principles, imparts some valuable information on operating systems theory, but it leaves students woefully unprepared for careers in modern systems software design. The complexity of any real operating system is comparatively enormous, and the simplicity suggested by a study of principles alone belies this complexity. As a result, many educators have begun to take advantage of open source Linux in order to include significant hands-on experience with a real system in their operating systems courses [5, 7, 9]. This has been the approach taken in the graduate-level course, CPSC 822, at Clemson University for many years. This course is a structured walk-through of the current Linux kernel, and it includes several student projects that require significant modifications to the kernel, most often to improve performance on targeted workloads.

Until recent years, in spite of high demand, the course has had severely limited enrollment. Students writing system-level code frequently crash their systems, often with disk-corrupting failures. Thus the course has required both dedicated hardware, one machine per student team, and the laboratory space in which to house it, which has collectively represented a large expense for a single course. The advent of x86 system virtualization, through *VMWare* [12], *Xen* [1], *VirtualBox* [4], or Linux *KVM* [8], coupled with the Intel's VT-x and AMD's AMD-V hardware extensions, opened the door to the possibility of using virtual machines for the course, which would reduce costs and increase course availability.

Nevertheless, a significant obstacle remained. The most important course project, both in terms of class time allocated and subsequent evaluation by course graduates and employers thereof, has always been the design and implementation of an SMP-safe device driver for a modern, high-performance graphics card. The importance of the project derives from the fact that an effective device driver for such a card is a microcosm of the operating system itself. To deliver high performance at the user level, the driver requires memory management, DMA transfers, resource allocation, security, process scheduling, process communication, and interrupt handling. The obstacle to complete course virtualization is then clear: available system virtualization tools (VMWare, Xen, VirtualBox, KVM) have traditionally exported only a minimally-capable, SVGA graphics adapter, which is an inadequate architecture for such a project. In recent years, there has been a push to provide 3D graphics acceleration to guests in both VMWare and VirtualBox. Nevertheless, their virtual devices are targeted solely at graphics acceleration. The VMWare device is proprietary, and the VirtualBox device does not provide an interface suitable for driver design.

Starting in 2009, we solved this problem using the technique proposed by Geist et al. [6]. They constructed a functional emulator of a 3DLabs Permedia II card [11] that was structured as a pair of communicating kernel modules together with a user-space background daemon. The background daemon handled screen up-

SIGCSE'14, March 5–8, 2014, Atlanta, Georgia, USA.

http://dx.doi.org/10.1145/2538862.2538895.

dates after reading a page of virtual device register values that had been memory-mapped from one of the kernel modules. In order to present the students who were writing drivers with a completely unmodified kernel source tree, numerous kernel functions were dynamically intercepted and replaced using a modified version of the Linux *kprobes* facility. The fact that the card was virtual remained essentially invisible to the students.

This approach was quite effective. The students became adept at driver design, and they particularly enjoyed the visual feedback afforded by a successful driver implementation. Nevertheless, the module-daemon communication code and the *kprobes*-based code were both elaborate and delicate. Linux kernel authors apparently have little regard for backward compatibility of internal structures. Each kernel version change broke the virtual graphics card, and this required extensive revision of the enabling code. Such changes occurred every semester. Thus we have sought a new solution, one that is, to the largest extent possible, independent of particular Linux kernel versions, is easily modified by course instructors to present a new architecture each semester, and is capable of emulating sophisticated card architectures with on-board memory, multiple modes of execution, DMA transfer, interrupt handling, and memory mapping of on-board registers. We present here the design of such a solution.

The remainder of the paper is organized as follows. In the next section we briefly review related work in using Linux as an instructional tool in operating systems courses. The design of our virtual graphics card, called *Kyouko*, follows, after which we describe the design of key components of a Linux driver for this card. A performance comparison of rendering speed using the new virtual card, the *kprobes*-based virtual card, and the underlying, real hardware is presented in Section 5. Student outcomes from the first use of the new virtual card in CPSC 822 are presented in Section 6, and conclusions follow in Section 7.

2. RELATED WORK

Clearly the idea for creating a virtual graphics card that is suitable for teaching device driver design was taken from the work of Geist et al. [6]. Our goal here is simply to provide an alternative virtual graphics card design (and sample driver) that is smaller, faster, portable across a broad range of Linux kernel versions, and whose code is easily modified by instructors to provide fresh card designs each semester.

We were also motivated by the work of Laadan et al. [9], whose course of instruction now includes a wide range of interesting Linux projects on system calls, synchronization, scheduling, virtual memory, and file systems. We would characterize their projects as kernel-inward facing and our own projects as kernel-outward facing. The two sets are quite complementary in nature.

In earlier work using Linux kernel projects in an undergraduate operating systems course, Hess and Paulson [7] observed that example problems from standard principles courses, "skirt the issue of operating systems practice," and "really only reinforce operating systems theory". They further argue that protecting senior undergraduates from the details of a production operating system is neither necessary nor beneficial. Although our own course is graduate level, it is frequently taken by our stronger undergraduates, and we completely concur with Hess and Paulson's conclusions.

Finally, Gaspar and Goodwin [5] argue for including hands-on Linux experience in an operating systems course by focusing on the use of loadable kernel modules. This mechanism allows the students to quickly develop new kernel code from scratch without first having to master an enormous code base. Our device driver design project fits nicely within this argument.

3. THE KYOUKO DEVICE

The key to building a virtual graphics card that is essentially independent of the Linux kernel, and so largely immune to the transient nature of its internal structures, was to build the virtual card outside the kernel and inside the emulator. QEMU (Quick Emulator) [2] is a dynamic translator that is often used in conjunction with KVM to run unmodified target operating systems inside virtual machines. QEMU itself is supported on several host operating systems, and, most importantly, QEMU has a relatively stable, slowly changing code base.

The available virtual graphics cards in QEMU include a Cirrus CLGD 5446 PCI VGA card, a standard VGA graphics card with Bochs VBE, a VMWare SVGA II compatible adapter, and a QXL paravirtual card designed for the SPICE protocol. Although none of these was suitable for our purposes, QEMU is open-source and distributed with an appropriate build tree that makes rebuilding from source very easy. Thus we could build a new virtual card of our own design. Our design was based on the VMWare SVGA adapter, found in ~/hw/vmware_vga.c and ~/hw/vmware_vga.h. Nevertheless, our virtual card provides very different capabilities, and it is much smaller, 556 lines of code rather than 1,070 lines.

We wanted the virtual card to provide two modes of operation, FIFO and DMA. Under FIFO, the driver can write values to our on-board device registers, but these writes are indirect. The bank of virtual device registers, which contains both state registers and command registers, is protected. Register writes by the driver are captured and stored as register-value pairs in an on-board FIFO queue. An internal *Kyouko* call, *vgpu_fifo_process( )*, removes entries from the queue and either updates state or executes the command. Since FIFO queue space is finite, the driver could attempt to overload it. In this case the commands are lost. So that the driver may avoid this, a readable register, *InfFIFO*, always contains the number of available slots in the queue.

Under DMA, the *Kyouko* virtual card will download a driver's DMA buffer to an on-board buffer of size 128KB and then execute the commands therein through the internal *Kyouko* call, *vgpu_dma_process( )*. The driver initiates this action by writing (under FIFO) the physical address of its current DMA buffer to the *CmdDMABuffer* register and a count of the number of commands in the buffer to the *CmdDMACount* register.

The internal operation of the virtual card is relatively simple. Initialization is encapsulated in a single function, *pci_kyouko_initfn( )*. The first important task of initialization is allocation of memory for the virtual device registers. This is done with a QEMU call, *memory_region_init_rom_device()*, which allocates the physical space for the virtual registers and then sets the write callback function that will load the FIFO queue on each attempted write to the register bank by the driver. We somewhat arbitrarily use one page (4KB) for the size of this register bank. The virtual framebuffer (8MB) is allocated by calling the QEMU function *vga_common_init( )* and is used for VESA device emulation. The second important task is to register both the virtual framebuffer and the memory region containing the virtual device registers with the PCI bus so that the driver may locate them during its bus probe. This is done with the QEMU command *pci_register_bar( )*. The framebuffer is assigned to PCI resource 0, and the register bank is assigned to PCI resource 1. The third essential task is initializing the MSI (Message Signaled Interrupt) system with a call to QEMU function *msi_init( )*. MSI interrupts are rapidly replacing the standard, PCIe INTx interrupts because the latter requires requires interrupt sharing and MSI does not. We want the *Kyouko* card to generate an interrupt on each DMA buffer completion, so that the driver may specify the next buffer of commands, if there is one waiting, and wake any user process that may have suspended awaiting an empty driver buffer, that is, available driver DMA memory space. Finally, we register our basic update function, *kyouko_update_display( )*, with QEMU using the QEMU function *graphic_console_init( )*.

After initialization, control is completely in the hands of this basic update function, which is repeatedly called by QEMU. This function first examines virtual card state to determine whether a mode switch (VGA compatibility mode to graphics mode or vice versa) has been called for, and, if so, it effects the switch. If the switch was into VGA compatibility mode, *vgpu_fifo_process( )* is called, and then the update returns. If the switch was into graphics mode, *vgpu_fifo_process( )* is called, then *vgpu_dma_process( )* is called, and then the update returns.

The design of the *Kyouko* command set and supporting registers is completely flexible. The current layout (available sample) is designed to emulate the basic structure of modern devices such as the Intel HD 3000 [3], although it is greatly simplified to make it suitable for a class project. We anticipate that instructors will change it frequently to keep the device driver project fresh each semester. QEMU runs in user address space, and so *Kyouko* command execution can employ standard, user-level libraries. We use OpenGL. QEMU by default utilizes the Simple DirectMedia Layer (SDL) for graphical output, and this is supported by a display driver located in the QEMU source, in ~/ui/sdl.c. We added an OpenGL display driver, whose source may be downloaded, along with that of the *Kyouko* card and the sample card driver, from the authors' website. This display driver creates the necessary OpenGL rendering context, and it must be paired with *Kyouko* card.

Having OpenGL available offers a practically limitless set of choices for the *Kyouko* primitive command set and state registers. Basic commands can range from very low level, in which only a handful of primitive graphic elements are available, to very high level, in which register state includes lighting, shading, texturing, and view transformation values. As an example, code for the *Kyouko* command *CmdVertex* is shown in Figure 1, where s→vtx contains vertex state upon entry.

```
case CmdVertex:
// Save time if there's been no state change.
if(s→vtx.vtx_dirty){
      glColor4fv(s→vtx.color);
      glNormal3fv(s→vtx.normal);
      glTexCoord2fv(s→vtx.texcoord);
      s->vtx.vtx_dirty = false;
      }
// Emit a vertex.
glVertex4fv(s→vtx.position);
break;
```

Figure 1: Sample Kyouko Command Implementation

The complete *Kyouko* command and state register space is shown in Table 1. This is, in effect, a 1-page hardware reference manual.

4. DRIVER DESIGN

We describe a Linux 3.2.36 driver for the *Kyouko* card. In principle, writing a device driver for a PCI card is entirely straightforward. After the card is inserted into an available motherboard slot, its command registers appear at fixed offsets from a physical base address. The driver then merely loads these registers with bit strings that comprise commands understood by the device hardware. In practice, it is more difficult. Linux, like most operating systems, uses paged memory management with both kernel mode and user mode address translations. Devices have no knowledge of these address translations, and yet they often operate independently of the CPU to transfer data under DMA control and then act upon it. Devices also issue interrupts, which are usually legitimate requests for service from the CPU, but they can be spurious. Even in a single-user environment, interrupt handlers may execute concurrently with service initiation requests, and they may attempt to access the same registers. Finally, ensuring good device performance demands effective management of on-board device memory, which is usually a scarce resource.

Our *Kyouko* device is treated as a standard Linux character device, and the driver is structured as a dynamically loadable kernel module. Linux character devices are created with the *mknod* command, and they support a collection of functions with fixed signatures, defined in the kernel structure *struct file_operations*. Our sample driver implements only four of these functions: *open, release, mmap,* and *ioctl*.

Linux kernel modules are collections of C functions that extend the kernel. They may be dynamically loaded with the command */sbin/insmod* and unloaded with */sbin/rmmod*. There is no "main", but two of the functions are special. An initialization function, identified by the macro *module_init*, is executed upon load, and an exit function, identified by *module_exit*, is executed upon removal.

Our initialization function loads a kernel structure of type *struct cdev* with major and minor *Kyouko* device numbers (# defines) and pointers to the four implemented file operations. It then calls *pci_register_device* which will launch a bus search for the matching (major, minor) pair. When the device is found, a driver-defined probe function is called to recover the physical base addresses of the frame buffer (resource 0) and the register bank (resource 1). The probe function will also enable bus-mastering on the device.

The driver's *open* function, which is invoked by a user-level call to open the file */dev/kyouko*, is nearly trivial. Its only real function is to call the kernel's *ioremap* to translate the physical base address of the register bank, recovered by the probe, into a kernel virtual address. We need the kernel virtual address to initialize the card (write to the card registers) from within the driver. All recovered and translated addresses are stored in an internal driver structure.

The driver's *release* function, which is invoked by a user-level call to close the device, is only slightly more involved. Its principal task is to release allocated resources (memory and interrupt lines) and ensure that the card has been left in VGA text mode.

The *mmap* function is not used in the final version of our driver, but, during early driver development, students are encouraged to use this function to memory map the card device registers back to user space for direct loading. This helps them quickly reach a point where they are comfortable with card settings under FIFO operation. Memory mapping the device registers is a 1-line call to the kernel function *io_remap_pfn_range*, where one argument is the physical base address of the device registers, right shifted by 12 bits (PAGE_SHIFT).

Most of our driver is devoted to the *ioctl* function, which is often termed the "Swiss Army Knife" of system calls, in that one of its arguments is a command string that may be used inside a driver switch statement to effectively implement many commands in one. We have three such command strings, *BIND_DMA*, to initialize driver DMA operation, *START_DMA*, to launch a filled buffer of *Kyouko* commands, and *VMODE* to switch video modes between VGA text and graphics modes of various resolutions.

The *BIND_DMA* command initializes the MSI system and uses *request_irq* to attach the driver's interrupt handler function to the interrupt that will be generated by the *Kyouko* card upon each buffer

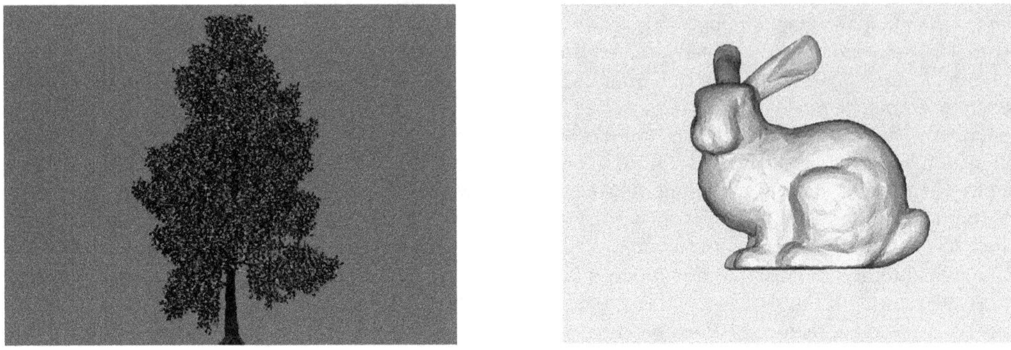

Figure 2: Sample Renders from the *Kyouko* device

completion. It allocates driver-resident DMA buffers and organizes them as a circular pool. It memory maps these buffers to the calling user's address space and returns, as a function value, the user virtual base address of the first available buffer. The user then simply loads the buffer with *Kyouko* commands and calls *START_DMA*, which will cause the driver to invoke the card's DMA operation by loading the *CmdDMABuffer* and *CmdDMACount* registers. In response to the call to *START_DMA*, the driver will return, as a function value, the user virtual base address of the next available buffer.

Of course, the user may fill buffers faster than the card can download and execute them. If the call to *START_DMA* fills the last available buffer in the circular pool, the driver must suspend the calling user process. Thus the driver side of the *START_DMA* call and the interrupt handler together function as a classical producer-consumer pair with respect to the driver's pool of DMA buffers.

We maintain two indices into the pool, *fill* and *drain*, indicating which buffer is in play, if any, by the producer and by the consumer. The condition *fill* = *drain* does not, by itself, determine whether the buffer pool is empty or full, but such can be determined from context. When the pool fills, the driver suspends the user on a kernel wait queue with a call to *wait_event_interruptible*.

Access to the buffer pool is guarded by a spinlock, and this introduces a complication that many students find challenging during their driver design. Upon discovering the need to suspend the caller, the driver's *START_DMA* code must first release the spinlock. If the condition supplied to *wait_event_interruptible* were simply *fill* != *drain*, a rapid fire of completion interrupts after the lock release and prior to the conditional suspension could move the buffer pool from full to empty before the condition is tested. At this point, the condition would be false, and the user process would suspend forever. Thus we suggest an additional boolean, *queuefull*, which is set prior to the lock release and reset only by the interrupt handler. The wait condition is then *!queuefull*. When the interrupt handler discovers *fill* = *drain* upon initiation, it does the reset and sends the wakeup to the wait queue.

5. PERFORMANCE

We ran benchmarks to compare the relative performance of the two virtualized graphics cards, the *kprobes*-based card and the *Kyouko* card. We included baseline tests with native OpenGL using an NVIDIA Quadro FX 5600 as a reference.

All tests were conducted using an Intel i7-980X CPU with 6 physical cores, 12 threads, and 12 GB of RAM. The hypervisor OS was Linux Fedora 16. The *kprobes*-based card was run using VMware's VMplayer 5.0, and the *Kyouko* card used QEMU 1.0.50. Three million smooth-shaded triangles were rendered at randomized positions on each system, and timing information was gathered. The slowdown factor, the ratio of virtual card performance to native OpenGL performance, is shown in Table 2.

	Execution Time (s)	Slowdown Factor
Native OpenGL	2.043	1.00
Kprobes-based	22.07	10.8
Kyouko	11.83	5.79

Table 2: Comparison of Device Performance

Although there is still overhead with a virtual hardware layer, the performance obtained by integrating directly with the hypervisor shows a significant improvement over the *kprobes*-based approach. This allows for more interesting scenes to be rendered or, equivalently, allows a greater number of virtual machines on shared hardware. Two sample renders using the *Kyouko* virtual card are shown in Figure 2. The first scene consists of a paper birch tree model with 307,336 faces. The second scene is of the well-known Stanford Bunny model and contains 4,804 faces. The two scenes, including initialization of their graphics context in the driver, took 3.31s and 1.00s to render, respectively.

6. STUDENT OUTCOMES

The *Kyouko* card was used for the first time as the target architecture for the device driver design project in CPSC 822 during the Spring semester of 2013. We compare here the drivers produced by the student teams with those produced in the same course during the Spring semester of 2012, when the *kprobes*-based card was used. The same instructor (author Geist) taught both courses.

The assignment, which was identical in both semesters, except for the virtual card name, is shown in Figure 3.

In each semester there were 6 student teams. All teams in both semesters were able to produce a driver and attendant user-level code that would put smooth-shaded triangles on the screen. Nevertheless, there were marked differences, particularly in SMP safety. There were no SMP safe drivers produced in Spring of 2012 for the *kprobes*-based card, although some of the drivers were quite robust and would require highly improbable sequences of events to violate safety. In contrast, 4 of the 6 teams in the Spring of 2013 produced SMP safe drivers for the *Kyouko* card.

We used the C and C++ Code Counter [10] to measure lines of code, number of modules, and McCabe's cyclomatic number for each group, and then we conducted a t-test for differences in means. The results are shown in Table 3.

We see that the *Kyouko* drivers were almost certainly smaller, probably more modular, and probably not different from the *kprobes*-based drivers in overall complexity.

CPSC 822 Project 1   A Device Driver   January 24, 2013

Write a device driver for the Kyouko PCI graphics card that resides in each of the virtual Linux machines of the IBM "blue" bladeserver. The device driver should be built as a kernel module and should be structured so that the card appears as a character device (major 500, minor 127) accessible through system calls open(), close(), mmap() and ioctl().

The driver must deliver sufficient capability to the user level to enable the user to draw smooth-shaded triangles. Further, the driver must provide this capability in two ways:

1. directly, through the FIFO facility, using memory-mapped control registers, where the memory-mapping is invoked by a user-level system call to mmap()
2. indirectly, through the DMA facility, using driver-allocated DMA buffers that have been memory-mapped to user space

For the latter, DMA completion interrupt handling must be included (no polling), and the driver must be SMP safe. Complete card specifications are available on the class web page. Solutions, which must include both device driver code and user-level code that demonstrates driver capability, are due February 28.

Figure 3: Device Driver Assignment

(means)	*Kyouko*	*kprobes*-based	p-value
Lines of Code	230	413	0.0012
Module Count	3.2	2.2	0.1248
Cyclomatic Number	39.6	45.8	0.4687

Table 3: Comparison of Code Metrics

The difference in SMP safety was certainly the most important factor reflected in the course grade differences. The average team grade on this project in the Spring of 2012 was 77.72 (B), and the average team grade in the Spring of 2013 was 82.45 (B+/A-).

Although the empirical evidence is limited, we believe that all of these differences may be attributed to the differences in virtual card architectures. Integrating the *Kyouko* device directly into the emulated hardware allowed that card to have a smaller collection of virtual device registers and a more powerful set of primitive instructions than those available in the *kprobes*-based card. As a result, the students spent less time exploring the effects of the various register settings that were required to draw triangles and more time designing the driver's internal structures and operation.

7. CONCLUSIONS

We have described a new software tool for use by instructors of operating systems courses. The tool provides a fast, portable, kernel-independent, virtual graphics card of reasonably sophisticated design that is suitable for teaching device driver design to senior undergraduates and beginning graduate students. The virtual card architecture is easily modified by instructors to present alternative interfaces, so that a different functionality may be presented to students each semester. Since the virtual card executes in user space, debugging a new design requires little more than a few *printf* statements.

We used the *Kyouko* virtual card as the target architecture for the device driver design project in CPSC 822 at Clemson University for the first time in the Spring semester of 2013. We compared the results with data from the Spring semester of 2012, where a kernel-dependent virtual card based on the Linux *kprobes* facility [6] was used. A striking difference was in the SMP safety of the drivers. No drivers for the *kprobes*-based card were SMP safe, but two-thirds of the drivers for the *Kyouko* card were SMP safe.

We are investigating the construction of a meta-system that would automatically generate new virtual devices of this type from very high-level specifications. The meta-system would apply to devices of many classes including graphics cards, sound cards, and network interface cards. The meta-system would produce, as its output, source code suitable for input to the QEMU build tree. This would extend the range of our efforts beyond educational tools and into the realm of device prototyping. Driver design, development, and testing could then proceed in parallel with new hardware prototyping, which could reduce time to market for new devices.

8. REFERENCES

[1] P. Barham, B. Dragovic, K. Fraser, S. Hand, T. Harris, A. Ho, R. Neugebauery, I. Pratt, and A. Warfield. Xen and the art of virtualization. In *Proc. 19th ACM Symp. on Operating System Principles*, pages 164–177, Bolton Landing, New York, October 2003.

[2] F. Bellard. Qemu, a fast and portable dynamic translator. In *ATEC '05: Proceedings of the USENIX Annual Technical Conference*, pages 41–46, Anaheim, CA, 2005.

[3] Intel Corp. 2010. Intel Hd Graphics Opensource PRM: Vol. 1 part 1: Graphics core. Retrieved Oct. 22, 2013 from http://www.x.org/docs/intel/HD/IHD_OS_Vol_1_Part1_BJS.pdf.

[4] Oracle Corp. 2013. Oracle VM VirtualBox User Manual. Retrieved Oct. 22, 2013 from https://www.virtualbox.org/manual/UserManual.html.

[5] A. Gaspar and C. Godwin. Root-kits & loadable kernel modules: exploiting the linux kernel for fun and (educational) profit. *J. Comput. Sci. Coll.*, 22(2):244–250, December 2006.

[6] R. Geist, Z. Jones, and J. Westall. Virtualizing high-performance graphics cards for driver design and development. In *Proc. 19th Annual Int. Conf. of the IBM Centers for Advanced Studies (CASCON 2009)*, Toronto, Ontario, Canada, November 2009.

[7] R. Hess and P. Paulson. Linux kernel projects for an undergraduate operating systems course. In *Proceedings of the 41st ACM technical symposium on Computer science education*, SIGCSE '10, pages 485–489, New York, NY, USA, 2010. ACM.

[8] A. Kivity, Y. Kamay, D. Laor, U. Lublin, and A. Liguori. *kvm*: the Linux virtual machine monitor. In *Proceedings of the Linux Symposium*, pages 225–230, Ottawa, Ontario, Canada, July 2007.

[9] O. Laadan, J. Nieh, and N. Viennot. Structured linux kernel projects for teaching operating systems concepts. In *SIGCSE '11*, pages 287–292, 2011.

[10] T. Littlefair. 2013. C and C++ Code Counter. Retrieved Oct. 22, 2013 from http://sourceforge.net/projects/cccc/.

[11] Texas Instruments. 1997. TVP4020 Permedia 2. Retrieved Oct. 22, 2013 from http://ftp.netbsd.org/pub/NetBSD/misc/cegger/hw_manuals/3dlabs.

[12] VMWare, Inc. 2007. Understanding Full Virtualization, Paravirtualization, and Hardware Assist. Retrieved Oct. 22, 2013 from http://www.vmware.com/files/pdf/VMware_-paravirtualization.pdf.

Offset	Register	Access	Type	Description
Immediate Register Space				
Configuration Registers				
0x0000	CfgSupported	RO	Boolean	1: Supported, 0: Not supported
0x0004	CfgMode	R/W	Bitfield	Bit 0: Graphics, Bit 1: Transform, Bit 2: Lighting, Bit 3: Texturing
0x0008	CfgAccel	R/W	Bitfield	Bit 0: 2d-Accel, Bit 1: 3d-Accel
0x000C	CfgWidth	R/W	Unsigned 10-bit	Width in pixels of requested mode
0x0010	CfgHeight	R/W	Unsigned 10-bit	Height in pixels of requested mode
0x0018	CfgFrame	R/W	Bitfield	Bits 0-3: Red bits, Bits 4-7: Green bits, Bits 8-11: Blue bits, Bits 12-15: Alpha bits, Bits 16-23: Depth bits, Bit 24: Double buffered
0x001C	CfgFlags	R/W	Bitfield	Flags indicating current state of card. Bit 0 indicates whether a DMA transfer is pending acknowledgment (write 0 back to this bit to indicate it has been acknowledged). Bit 1 indicates whether the card has encountered an error. If the error bit is set, the card will not respond to FIFO commands until the bit is reset. The card may be in an undefined state depending on the type of error.
0x0020	CfgFeatures	RO	Bitfield	Bits 0-7: Card revision number, Bits 8-15: Card Vendor, Bit 16: Texturing support, Bit 17: Lighting support, Bit 18: Extended DMA features
FIFO Register Space				
Command Registers				
0x0800	CmdReboot	WO	N/A	Any write reboots card. If & CfgSupported == 0& in current configuration, result is undefined
0x0804	CmdPrimitive	WO	Enum	0 -> None, 4 -> Triangle, 5 -> Triangle Strip, 6 -> Triangle Fan, 8 -> Quads, 9 -> Quad Strip
0x0808	CmdVertex	WO	N/A	Any write emits a vertex with state of current state registers
0x080C	CmdSync	WO	N/A	Any write will suspend FIFO processing until the next vertical sync period
0x0814	CmdActiveBuffer	WO	Bitfield	Bit 0: Active Screen Buffer, Bit 1: Active Draw Buffer
0x0818	CmdClear	WO	Bitfield	Bit 0: Clear color buffer to current VtxColor, Bit 1: Clear depth buffer
0x0820	CmdDMABuffer	WO	Address	Address from which to perform DMA operation. The lower 12 bits are assumed to be 0.
0x0824	CmdDMACount	WO	Bitfield	Writes to this initiate a DMA transfer. Bit 0: Type (Must be 0 for command buffers), Bits 1-16: Number of bytes to transfer
State Registers				
0x0900	VtxPosition	WO	Float4	XYZW of current vertex
0x0910	VtxColor	WO	Float4	RGBA of current vertex
0x0930	VtxTexCoord	WO	Float2	Pixel-Space UV coordinates
0x0A00	VtxTransform	WO	Float16	Column-Major transformation matrix
0x0F00	InfFIFO	RO	Integer	Current depth of the FIFO queue. The FIFO queue is guaranteed to be of length at least 32, but implementations may differ.

Notes: All writes to the configuration registers happen instantaneously, and the results may be read back without delay. Writes to any region in the FIFO space will be placed on the card's internal queue for processing. Care must be taken to ensure that the driver does not cause an overflow in the queue. The InfFIFO register may be used to synchronize access. It is expected that drivers will use the FIFO only for debugging and initialization. Most communication will occur indirectly via DMA buffers. Under DMA, the formatting of commands is as follows: All values are stored in 4 bytes, and they are read in sequential order from the buffer. For each command, the address of the command to execute is first, followed by any arguments. The same applies to the state registers, but these may only be accessed from their base register addresses. For example, to set the current vertex color to red, the value 0x910 in little endian would be written, followed by the proper RGBA values (1.0,0.0,0.0,0.0) in the binary32 IEEE-754 (float) format. It is not possible to issue changes to only a particular channel of a state register when issuing commands through DMA. When a DMA transfer is initiated by placing its physical address and buffer content size onto the FIFO queue, the card will begin execution of its commands as quickly as possible. Once the card has completed executing all commands from the buffer, or an error condition has occurred, an interrupt will be sent to the system via the PCI-Express' MSI system. The card will not continue execution until the interrupt (or error) has been acknowledged.

Table 1: The Current *Kyouko* Hardware Reference Manual

PLCC: A Programming Language Compiler Compiler

Timothy Fossum
Computer Science Department
SUNY College at Potsdam
Potsdam, NY 13676
fossumtv@potsdam.edu

ABSTRACT

This paper describes PLCC, a compiler-compiler tool to support courses in programming languages, compilers, and computational theory. This tool has proven to be useful for implementing interpreters, building compilers, and creating parsers for context-free languages.

PLCC is a Perl program that takes an input file that specifies the tokens, syntax, and semantics of a language and that generates a complete set of Java files that implement the semantics of the language. PLCC stands for "Programming Language Compiler-Compiler".

PLCC is not intended to be a production-quality tool. Rather, it supports understanding and implementing the essential elements of lexical analysis, parsing, and semantics without having to wrestle with the complexities of dealing with "industrial-strength" compiler-compiler tools. Students quickly learn how to write PLCC "grammar" files for small languages that have straightforward syntax and semantics and use PLCC to build Java-based parsers, interpreters, or compilers for these languages that run out-of-the-box.

Input to PLCC is a text file with a token definition section that defines language tokens as simple regular expressions, a syntax section that specifies the grammar rules of an LL(1) language as simple Backus-Naur Form (BNF) productions, and a semantics section that defines the language semantics as Java methods.

PLCC generates a set of Java source files that are entirely self-contained and that import only standard elements of `java.util` in JDK5 and above. For testing purposes, PLCC generates a read-eval-print loop that (1) reads standard input, (2) scans, parses, and evaluates the input, and (3) prints the evaluation to standard output.

Categories and Subject Descriptors

D.3.4 [**Software**]: Programming Languages—*processors*

SIGCSE'14, March 3–8, 2014, Atlanta, GA, USA.
Copyright 2014 ACM 978-1-4503-2605-6/14/03 ...$15.00.
http://dx.doi.org/10.1145/2538862.2538922.

General Terms

Languages

Keywords

Compiler-compiler, parser, interpreter, syntax, semantics

1. INTRODUCTION

My decision to write PLCC was inspired by the book *Essentials of Programming Languages* (EOPL) by Friedman, Wand, and Haynes[4]. I had used EOPL for more than ten years to teach an upper-level course in Programming Languages. Since Java is the principal language our students take in introductory courses, I found the time required for them to learn Scheme, the implementation language used in EPOL, ate into the time I wanted to cover other topics in my Programming Languages class.

What I liked about EOPL was the emphasis on writing simple interpreters for languages that grow incrementally in complexity as the course progresses. Many of these languages are purely functional, giving students much-needed exposure to a different programming paradigm. My *ITiCSE* paper[2] describes how I use the EOPL approach to define a language with classes as first class objects, which is based on material in Chapter 5 (Objects and Classes) of EOPL.

EOPL comes with a Scheme tool set called `sllgen`, a parser-generator written in Scheme. Input to `sllgen` consists of specifications (represented as Scheme lists) of a language's lexical structure and grammar. `Sllgen` uses the lexical specification to generate a scanner for the language and uses the grammar specification (which must be LL(1)[1, Chapter 5]) to generate a set of Scheme "datatypes" that implement the elements of a parse tree for a program in the language. The `sllgen`-generated recursive descent parser returns an instance of the datatype for the start symbol of the grammar; this instance is the root of the parse tree for the input program in the language. An `sllgen`-generated `read-eval-print` loop reads a program in the language, tokenizes and parses it, evaluates the resulting parse tree based on semantics provided by the implementer in an `eval` procedure, and prints the result.

The "datatypes" generated by `sllgen` are akin to Pascal's *variant records*[6]. When two or more grammar rules have the same left-hand-side nonterminal, the `sllgen` parser chooses the correct grammar rule to apply based on the current token (using the LL(1) properties of the language) and returns an instance of the nonterminal's datatype that identifies what grammar rule was used in the parse. Scheme procedures like `eval` that perform semantic actions on these datatypes must use a `cases` construct – like a `switch` in Java or C – to identify the particular instance of the datatype and to carry out an appropriate semantic action on that instance. Writing `eval` code using a `cases` construct can be messy. Each of the grammar rules having the same left-hand-side nonterminal requires a `cases` entry to code the `eval` behavior of a particular variant of the datatype. This makes coding cumbersome, and it doesn't facilitate a clean physical or conceptual separation of responsibilities to handle the `eval` semantics that the different right-hand-sides represent.

I observed that processing the variants of a datatype could be accomplished through dynamic dispatch in an object-oriented language. Instead of using a `cases` construct to `eval` a Scheme datatype representing a node in a parse tree, I could use inheritance to dispatch an `eval` method call on the Java object that represents the particular node in the parse tree. Dynamic dispatch has the advantage that the `eval` code for the object representing a node in the parse tree node is unique to the object.

I also wanted to represent the lexical and grammar specifications of a language in a way that is more straightforward than using Scheme lists. In particular, I wanted to use *regular expressions*[3] to define the tokens in the language and to use conventional Backus-Naur Form (BNF) style for specifying the grammar rules. Finally, I wanted the entire language specification to be monolithic, with the lexical, grammar, and semantic specifications all in one file.

I liked being able to implement the increasingly complex sequence of languages as given in the EOPL book. I wanted to ensure that the PLCC project would allow me to process these languages as I had done using Scheme and `sllgen`.

My goals in this project were thus to:

- Target Java as the implementation language
- Use a single file to specify the language's lexical, grammar, and semantic structure
- Use regular expressions to specify the lexical structure of a language
- Use BNF to define the grammar rules of a language
- Generate recursive-descent parsing code that is easy to read and understand
- Make a clear separation of semantics from the syntax
- Make use of dynamic dispatch to implement semantic actions corresponding to different grammar rules having the same left-hand-side nonterminal
- Be capable of handling language examples in EOPL
- Use standard Perl and Java to implement the project

After building PLCC and using it in my Programming Languages course based on EOPL, I found that PLCC would also serve as a framework for teaching a course on compilers. For my Compilers course, I replace the simple PLCC token scanner based on regular expressions with a separately built token scanner based on a finite-state machine (also using an object-oriented approach) that can handle, for example, comments that cross line boundaries. When used to generate a compiler, PLCC handles target code generation in the same way it handles evaluation semantics for an interpreter, except that the "value" of a program in the source language is a generated program in the target language (I use assembly language), and the read-eval-print loop is replaced by a read-parse-generate method.

A bare-bones PLCC specification without any evaluation semantics (other than returning "pass" or "fail") can be used to generate parsers for many context-free languages encountered in a Computational Theory class. It's easy to construct a simple specification file for a language with a small number of tokens and grammar rules that PLCC can turn into a read-eval-print loop to check for membership in the language.

2. THE PLCC TOOL

2.1 Lexical specifications

The EOPL `sllgen` toolkit defines the lexical specification of a language in terms of a Scheme list. The following is a lexical specification in `sllgen` that skips whitespace and comments (beginning with the '%' character) and that identifies patterns for variables (`var`) and numeric literals (`lit`):

```
(define the-lexical-spec
  '((whitespace
      (whitespace) skip)
    (comment
      ("%" (arbno (not #\newline))) skip)
    (var
      (letter (arbno (or letter digit))) var)
    (lit
      (digit (arbno digit)) lit)))))
```

In PLCC, I represent these patterns as regular expressions. Here is the the same lexical specification written in PLCC, which I regard as more straightforward. This approach also gives students the opportunity to learn about regular expressions, which can prove to be useful to them as they pursue a computing-related career.

```
skip WHITESPACE '\s+'
skip COMMENT '%.*'
LIT '\d+'
VAR '[a-zA-Z]\w*'
```

PLCC assumes that tokens do not cross line boundaries. This means that a pattern such as '`%.*`' will terminate at the end of the current line. This assumption makes token processing simpler, but it does mean that the PLCC-generated scanner cannot handle multi-line skips or tokens. To allow for more general lexical analysis behavior, PLCC can be directed to skip generating the scanner-related classes, allowing the user to provide an externally written scanner. As noted above, I use this in my compiler class, where we spend time implementing a stand-alone scanner.

`Sllgen` gathers reserved words from the grammar rules, so the following `sllgen` grammar rule would result in defining tokens corresponding to '`if`', '`then`', and '`else`':

```
(exp
  ("if" exp "then" exp "else" exp)
  if-exp)
```

In PLCC, these tokens need to be defined explicitly in the lexical specification section:

```
IF 'if'
THEN 'then'
ELSE 'else'
```

The PLCC-generated scanner skips input that matches the lexical `skip` definitions. It then returns the next input token by examining all of the token definitions, in the order given in the specification file, and determining which ones match one or more characters of the current input. The scanner returns the token with the longest match: among matches of the same length, it returns the token corresponding to the first definition it encounters. This means that the lexeme '`if`' would be returned as an IF token, not a VAR token, with the following token specifications:

```
skip WHITESPACE '\s+'
skip COMMENT '%.*'
IF 'if'
THEN 'then'
ELSE 'else'
LIT '\d+'
VAR '[a-zA-Z]\w*'
```

When I ask students to add a new reserved word such as '`while`' to the token specifications, some will add it *after* the VAR specification, so '`while`' would be regarded as a `VAR` instead of a `WHILE`: both patterns match the string '`while`', and both matches have have the same length, but `VAR` comes first. This provides a good learning opportunity: a test program that should work with a `while` will not parse properly if `while` is treated as a `VAR`. Some students who make this error ask why their solutions don't work, and they have an "aha" experience when they discover – often with my help – why not, and how to fix it by simply moving a line in the token specifications. Others who submit incorrect solutions without even writing test programs are greeted with a pointed query asking if they tested their solutions.

2.2 Grammar Rules

`Sllgen` grammar rules are given as a Scheme list. Here is an example subset of grammar rules for expressions in one of the EOPL languages:

```
(exp (lit) lit-exp)
(exp (var) var-exp)
(exp
  ("if" exp "then" exp "else" exp)
  if-exp)
(exp
  ("let" (arbno var "=" exp) "in" exp)
  let-exp)
(exp
  ("proc" "(" (separated-list var ",") ")" exp)
  proc-exp)
```

The first two grammar rules above can be written in PLCC as follows:

```
<exp>:LitExp ::= <LIT>
<exp>:VarExp ::= <VAR>
```

The `arbno` construct in `sllgen` corresponds to a "Kleene star" repetition construct in Extended BNF. PLCC does not allow a Kleene star operator to be used in the middle of the right-hand-side of a grammar rule. Instead, a separate grammar rule construct, introduced by '`**=`', must be used to identify a rule where the entire right-hand-side can appear zero or more times. For example, the `(arbno var "=" exp)` construct can be written as a separate rule in PLCC as follows:

```
<letDecls> **= <VAR> EQUALS <exp>
```

Armed with this, the `sllgen` grammar `let-exp` rule can be written in PLCC as shown here:

```
<exp>:LetExp ::= LET <letDecls> IN <exp>
<letDecls>   **= <VAR> EQUALS <exp>
```

The `separated-list` construct in `sllgen` identifies a rule where items can appear zero or more times – similar to `arbno` – but the items must be separated by a specified token if there are more than one of them. This is used, in `proc-exp` for example, when specifying function parameters as a comma-separated list:

```
(separated-list var ",")
```

PLCC uses '`**=`' to introduce such a construct, with the separator token appearing at the end preceded by a `+` sign:

```
<formals> **= <VAR> +COMMA
```

A `proc-exp` in PLCC will then become

```
<exp>:ProcExp ::= PROC
    LPAREN <formals> RPAREN <exp>
<formals>      **= <VAR> +COMMA
```

(Note that the first two lines above appear folded to fit the column width. In the PLCC file, these would appear on one line.)

2.3 Classes generated from grammar rules

PLCC generates a Java class for each left-hand-side nonterminal given in the grammar rules. Nonterminals in the grammar rules section must begin with a lower-case letter and can be followed by any number of additional letters, digits, or underscores. The name of the Java class generated by PLCC is the same as the name of the nonterminal, except with its first letter converted to uppercase. From the nonterminals `<exp>`, `<letDecls>` and `<formals>` PLCC generates the classes `Exp`, `LetDecls` and `Formals`.

When a language has two or more grammar rules with the same left-hand-side nonterminal, the left-hand-side nonterminal class is declared as `abstract`, and subclasses are created for each of these grammar rules. The name of a particular subclass is specified in the grammar rule by the class name that follows a colon '`:`' after the nonterminal. For example, the following grammar rules

```
<exp>:LitExp ::= <LIT>
<exp>:VarExp ::= <VAR>
```

define classes named `LitExp` and `VarExp` that extend the abstract class `Exp`. PLCC ensures that there is a one-to-one correspondence between the generated non-abstract class names and the grammar rules.

2.4 Class fields

As described above, every grammar rule line defines a unique non-abstract Java class. Each such class has a number of `public` fields corresponding to the items on the right-hand-side of the rule. Only those right-hand side items that appear in angle brackets '`<...>`' have fields defined in the class. If the item is a nonterminal such as `<exp>`, the corresponding field is named `exp` and has type `Exp`. If the item is a terminal such as `<VAR>`, the corresponding field is named `var` and has type `Token`. The class has a single constructor that assigns its arguments to these fields.

For example, from the grammar rule

```
<exp>:LetExp ::= LET <letDecls> IN <exp>
```

PLCC generates a `LetExp` class having two fields, a constructor, and a static `parse` method:

```
// <exp>:LetExp ::= LET <letDecls> IN <exp>
public class LetExp extends Exp {

    public LetDecls letDecls;
    public Exp exp;

    public LetExp (LetDecls letDecls,
                   Exp exp) {
       this.letDecls = letDecls;
       this.exp = exp;
    }

    public static LetExp parse(Scan scn) {
        scn.match(Token.Val.LET);
        LetDecls letDecls = LetDecls.parse(scn);
        scn.match(Token.Val.IN);
        Exp exp = Exp.parse(scn);
        return new LetExp(letDecls, exp);
    }
...

}
```

The static `LetExp.parse` method returns an instance of this class by processing, in order, the items in the right-hand-side of the grammar rule: matching the terminal `LET`, calling the `LetDecls.parse` method, matching the terminal `IN`, and calling the `Exp.parse` method. The resulting `letDecls` and `exp` values are used to construct and return a `LetExp` object.

PLCC declares its generated class fields to be `public`. While this practice can be considered unsafe, it makes coding semantic methods more straightforward.

A Java class generated by a grammar rule with repetitions – one that uses the `**=` repetition construct – can have zero or more field instances corresponding to items on its right-hand-side. For such a class, the values are collected into `ArrayList` fields whose names are the same as for a non-repeating rule, with the string '`List`' appended. For example, the following grammar rule

```
<letDecls> **= <VAR> EQUALS <exp>
```

generates a Java class named `LetDecls` having a field named `varList` of type `ArrayList<Token>` and a field named `expList` of type `ArrayList<Exp>`. A successful call to the `parse` method on this class returns an instance of a `LetDecls` object: the `varList` will be populated with a number of `Token` objects, and the `expList` will be populated with the same number of `Exp` objects. Similar remarks apply to repeating rules with a separator.

Both of the repeating rules can be replaced with suitably chosen recursive grammar rules: PLCC makes such replacements internally, but only to check for LL(1). However, there are significant advantages to using repeating rules:

- The resulting parse trees for grammars using repeating rules are shallower than those using recursive grammar rules, since the `ArrayLists` flatten out the parse tree.
- The `parse` methods for a class defined by a repeating rule can employ a loop instead of recursive calls, resulting in run-time improvements in space and time. The same remark applies to methods that implement repeating rule semantics.
- Repeating rules are easier to read and understand than their recursive counterparts: there are fewer productions, and it's easy to spot the repeating parts.
- The `ArrayList` fields in a repeating rule conveniently package the repeating elements of a parse in a way that is more direct and compact than spreading them out in the parse tree. Processing these `ArrayLists` to carry out semantic actions is straightforward using iterators.

2.5 Parsing

Parsing a program that conforms to a PLCC grammar specification is easy: call the `parse` method on the class generated by the start symbol of the language, which is always the first left-hand-side nonterminal appearing in the grammar rules. The `parse` method is static in all of the PLCC-generated classes. Each `parse` method is passed a `Scan` object (see Section 3 below) that delivers tokens for parsing. For an abstract class such as `Exp`, the `parse` method returns a parsed instance of one of its subclasses: the current input token determines the appropriate grammar rule to apply (based on the LL(1) property of the grammar) which in turn determines the appropriate subclass to instantiate. For a non-abstract class such as `LetDecls`, the `parse` method returns an instance of the class itself.

When the top-level parse completes successfully (exceptions can occur when there is a syntax error or when the `Scan` class is unable to deliver a token) the result is an instance of the Java class corresponding to the start symbol. In many EOPL languages, this is an instance of the `Program` class.

The following Java code represents the essence of PLCC-generated scanning and parsing, returning an instance of the `Program` class, the class associated with the start symbol `<program>`:

```
Program.parse(new Scan(System.in));
```

2.6 Semantics

The PLCC-generated read-eval-print loop parses a program in the language by calling the static `parse` method on the Java class generated by the start symbol of the language. This is done *before* any semantics are applied to the resulting parse. Thus the entire program is scanned and parsed prior to carrying out any semantic actions.

The default PLCC semantics of a program is to print the Java `String` value of the parse. In other words, the entirety of the default PLCC lexical analysis, parsing, and semantics is embodied in the following one-liner (folded for your viewing pleasure):

```
System.out.println(
  Program.parse(
    new Scan(System.in)
  )
);
```

In the absence of overriding the `toString` method of a `Program` object, the above statement will produce something like

```
Program@768965fb
```

which simply says that the default semantics of this program is a `Program` object.

In its simplest form, implementing the non-default semantics of a PLCC language consists of overriding the default `toString` method in the start symbol class. Here is a grammar fragment (the tokens specifications are similar to those given above) for a simple language:

```
<program>     ::= <exp>
<exp>:LitExp ::= <LIT>
<exp>:VarExp ::= <VAR>
```

To override the default `toString` behavior in the `Program` class, we create a code fragment that defines a `toString` method and associate it with the `Program` class as follows:

```
Program
%%{
    public String toString() {
        return exp.eval();
    }
%%}
```

The first line, beginning with `Program`, identifies the Java class whose source code will be modified, and the items between the lines `%%{` and `%%}` will be added to the code already in the `Program.java` source file. (In the above example, recall that `exp` is a field in the `Program` class that is populated by its `parse` method. The `eval` method will be defined in the subclasses of the `Exp` class.) This code, and all other code that defines the language semantics of the grammar rules, appears in the PLCC language specification file following the grammar rules for the language, after a line with a single '%'.

An entire Java class source file can be created in the semantics section by naming the class (as long as it is different from the PLCC-generated classes) and including the code to be inserted into the class between `%%{` and `%%}` lines. This is useful when Java classes other than those automatically generated by PLCC are needed to implement language semantics.

Continuing the example above, the `eval` semantics for a `LitExp` might be given as follows:

```
LitExp
%%{
    public String eval() {
        return lit.toString();
    }
%%}
```

In this example, `lit` is the only field in the `LitExp` class: it has type `Token`, and evaluating `lit.toString()` returns the string value of the token as it appears in the program source.

2.7 Putting it all together

The three sections of a PLCC specification – lexical, grammar, and semantics – appear in one file, with the sections separated by a line with a single '%' sign. Comments can appear in the PLCC lexical and grammar specifications starting with a # and continuing to the end of the line.

Here is a complete specification example. The evaluation semantics of a numeric literal is the literal itself, and the evaluation semantics of a variable symbol is the uppercase version of the symbol.

```
# a simple language with numeric literals
#   and variable symbols
# lexical specification
skip WHITESPACE '\s+'
skip COMMENT '%.*'
LIT '\d+'
VAR '[a-zA-Z]\w*'
%
# grammar rules
<program>     ::= <exp>
<exp>:LitExp ::= <LIT>
<exp>:VarExp ::= <VAR>
%
# semantics
Program
%%{
    public String toString() {
        return exp.eval();
    }
%%}

Exp
%%{
    public abstract String eval();
%%}

LitExp
%%{
    // return the literal string
    public String eval() {
        return lit.toString();
    }
%%}

VarExp
%%{
    // return the symbol in uppercase
    public String eval() {
        return var.toString().toUpperCase();
    }
%%}
```

2.8 Read-eval-print

PLCC automatically generates a read-eval-print `Rep` class whose `main` method repeatedly prints a prompt, creates an instance of the `Scan` class from `System.in`, and parses and prints the grammar start symbol class. A sample interaction running the Java `Rep` program using the above language specification looks as follows:

```
--> 42
42
--> xyZzY % should print XYZZY
XYZZY
```

3. PLCC ARCHITECTURE

I chose Perl to write PLCC because Perl has good string handling and pattern matching capabilities. The output of PLCC is a set of Java programs, all of which are text files and are generated in a subdirectory of the current directory named `Java`.

PLCC reads the token specifications and creates a file named `Token.java` that contains `enum` entries for both skip tokens and normal tokens. PLCC generates these entries from the regular expressions given in the token specifications, turning them into Java `String`s with appropriate escaping. PLCC uses a template file called `Token.pattern` as the basis for filling in the appropriate token definitions drawn from the specification file to create the `Token.java` file. The end of the token specification is a line with a single `%`.

PLCC then reads the grammar rules and creates entries for each class, noting which classes must be abstract (because the nonterminal appears more than once on the left-hand-side of the grammar rules), and keeping track of the corresponding right-hand-sides. It checks the grammar for being LL(1) and reports an error if not. Each repetition grammar rule (with `**=`) is turned into multiple rules that use recursion instead of repetition, but only for the purpose of checking for LL(1).

Once the grammar is determined to be LL(1), PLCC generates class stubs for each of the grammar rules, as well as a `Rep.java` file to implement the read-eval-print loop. The class stubs include generated code for the `parse` methods specific to the grammar rules.

The `Rep.java` file is built from a template that only needs to have the name of the start symbol class filled in. The end of the grammar section is a line with a single `%`.

PLCC then reads the semantics specification entries, each of which starts with a class name followed by lines sandwiched between lines containing `%%{` and `%%}`. If the class name is one of the stubbed classes, the given lines are inserted into the stub class verbatim. If the class name is not one of the stub classes, PLCC creates a new class containing the given lines.

The `Scan.java` program is part of the PLCC standard code library and is automatically included in the generated code directory. Using the generated `Token` class, the `Scan` class does all of the dirty work of reading lines of the input stream (a `BufferedReader`), skipping over input that matches the `skip` specifications, and returning the next token.

All of the Java source files created by PLCC are deposited into a subdirectory named `Java`. Once these Java files are generated and compiled (errors in creating the semantic routines can be uncovered here), the `Rep` program can be run to test the resulting language implementation.

In order to make it easier to deal with the separate parts of the semantics of a PLCC specification, an `include` directive can be used in the semantics specification section, giving the name of the file to include in the specification. The contents of this file then become part of the PLCC specification input. This is useful, for example, to separate code that implements semantics specific to grammar classes from code that is used to implement auxiliary classes used in semantic actions. For particularly complex languages, it may be useful to have several of these files.

4. COMPARISON WITH OTHER PARSER GENERATORS

A Wikipedia comparison of parser generators[7] for deterministic context-free languages lists about 90 entries. Parsers for non-LL(1) languages are typically table-driven or backtracking, and the code generation for such languages is much more difficult for students to read and understand than the code for simple LL(1) predictive parsers (as generated by PLCC) based on recursive descent. Of the entries in this list, 12 of them clearly target languages that are LL(1) or that generate recursive descent parsers. Of these, only Coco/R[5] targets Java (the latest version also targets C# and C++).

However, Coco/R mixes syntax and semantics: semantic actions are specified in-line with the grammar rules, so Coco/R does not satisfy my goal of clearly separating syntax and semantics. Furthermore, the format of specifying Coco/R grammar rules is more complex than the simple BNF-style used in PLCC. Getting started using Coco/R is more difficult and time-consuming than learning how to use PLCC. I conclude that PLCC meets my course-related goals in a way that no other parser-generator does.

5. COURSE CONSIDERATIONS

I have used PLCC in two offerings of a Programming Languages course at my institution, and I plan to continue its use when I offer this course in the future. I have also used PLCC as the compiler-compiler for an offering of a Compilers class.

I have observed that my students learn how to use PLCC quickly, more so than when I was using `sllgen` and needed to cover the elements of `Scheme` from scratch. I have been able to cover more and richer language examples once I started using PLCC. Students coming into my Programming Languages class have experience with Java, but they generally do not have a good understanding of abstract classes: using PLCC gives them the opportunity to become familiar with abstract classes and how to use them.

6. PLCC AVAILABILITY

The entire PLCC toolkit consists of the `plcc` Perl program (1320 lines) and a set of template files used to to generate the scanner and read-eval-print loop (a total of 371 lines). These can all be downloaded from `http://cs.potsdam.edu/PLCC`.

7. REFERENCES

[1] C. Fischer and R. LeBlanc Jr. *Crafting a Compiler with C.* Benjamin/Cummings, Redwood City, CA, 1991.

[2] T. Fossum. Classes as first-class objects in an environment-passing interpreter. In *Proceedings of the Tenth Annual Conference on Innovation and Technology in Computer Science Education* (Lisbon,Portugal), pages 261-265. ACM, 2005.

[3] J. Friedl. *Mastering Regular Expressions.* O'Reilly Media, Sebastapol, CA, 2006.

[4] D. Friedman, M. Wand, and C. Haynes. *Essentials of Programming Languages (2nd ed).* The MIT Press, Cambridge, Massachusetts, 2001.

[5] H. Mössenböck. A generator for production quality compilers. In *Springer Verlag Lecture Notes in Computer Science*, 477:42-55, 1990.

[6] Pascal: ISO Standard 7185. 1990. Retrieved December 2, 2013 from http://pascal-central.com/docs/iso7185.pdf.

[7] Wikipedia.Org. 2013. Comparison of Parser Generators. Retrieved September 5, 2013 from http://en.wikipedia.org/wiki/.

Teaching and Learning Computer Science Soft Skills Using Soft Skills: The Students' Perspective

Orit Hazzan
Department of Education in Science and Technology
Technion – Israel Institute of Technology
Haifa, 32000
Israel
oritha@technion.ac.il

Gadi Har-Shai
Department of Education in Science and Technology
Technion – Israel Institute of Technology
Haifa, 32000
Israel
gadi.harshai@gmail.com

ABSTRACT

This paper continues a previous paper [1] in which we described students' gradual understanding of computer science (CS) and software engineering (SE) soft skills. Our study focused on a course we taught on soft skills in CS and SE, offered by the Department of Computer Science at the Technion – Israel Institute of Technology. The course was developed in response to a call by the Israeli hi-tech industry to equip Technion CS graduates with such skills. In [1] we presented the nature of CS soft skills, described the course schedule, including the teaching principles applied in the course, and showed how, in the course of the course, students gradually constructed a mental perception of CS soft skills in a 4-stage process. In this paper, we refine the comprehension process into a 6-rung ladder, based on further data analysis and additional experience gained when teaching the course for a second time. We elaborate on the additional rungs and further illuminate the results of two evaluation surveys on the course that were distributed to the students (in addition to the formal course evaluation administrated by the Technion's Center for the Promotion of Teaching). One of our main conclusions is that the course provides students with the opportunity to express their desire to be more involved in the teaching process of the course and to discuss and analyze their own soft skills. In other words, students realize the importance and significance of learning soft skills by actually implementing these skills in the learning process. In the Summary part of the paper, we present several pedagogical conclusions that are based on this observation and that we intend to implement in the future when teaching this course.

Categories and Subject Descriptors

K.3.0 [**Computing Milieux**]: Computers and Education – *General.*

General Terms

Management, Economics, Human Factors, Legal Aspects.

Keywords

Software engineering education, soft skills, undergraduate students, social, managerial and cognitive aspects

1. INTRODUCTION

This paper describes a course offered by the Technion's Department of Computer Science (CS) to undergraduate CS and software engineering (SE) students. According to a report by an international review committee, which reviewed the Department in May 2008, "The Technion's Computer Science Faculty is an excellent department of computer science, comparable to the top ten in the United States"[1]. In 2011, it was ranked 15th in the Academic Ranking of World Universities in CS (Shanghai ranking)[2].

The department is the second largest academic unit in the Technion, with about 1,300 undergraduate students (about one-eighth of the total number of Technion students) and over 200 graduate students. Its 50 or so faculty members are of international repute and have expertise in a wide variety of fields. The faculty's main areas of research are theory, systems, artificial intelligence, intelligent systems, and scientific computation.

The department is also the largest CS department in Israel, supplying the Israeli hi-tech industry with its most talented graduates. Thus, it can be argued that the department played a central role in Israel's becoming *The Startup Nation* [2]. The department's unique standing with the Israeli hi-tech industry enables structured interaction between the department and the Israeli and international hi-tech industries. As part of this interaction, calls have been received from several hi-tech companies for the department to equip its graduates not only with excellent scientific and engineering skills, but also with soft skills, such as teamwork, interpersonal communication skills, and presentation skills. Such skills are, according to Sukhoo *et al.* (2005) "concerned with managing and working with people, ensuring customer satisfaction with the intention of retaining them and creating a conducive environment for the project team to deliver high quality products within budget and on time and exceeding stakeholders expectations" ([3], p. 693-694).

A quick Google search suffices to reveal that almost all problems associated with software development processes are connected to people (mainly customers and team members) and that their origin is rooted not in technological aspects but rather in cognitive, social and managerial aspects – i.e., the expression of soft skills. In practice, however, not many courses on soft skills are offered. Examples of courses on soft skills that are offered by other institutions and universities are listed in [1].

The course described in this paper was designed for both CS and SE students, first, to expose them to a variety of soft skills, and second, to enable them to acquire these skills gradually by experiencing them and reflecting upon them. In addition, the close acquaintance of the course instructor and TA[3] with the software

SIGCSE'14, March 5–8, 2014, Atlanta, Georgia, USA.

http://dx.doi.org/10.1145/2538862.2538885

[1] See: https://www.cs.technion.ac.il/about/

[2] See: http://www.shanghairanking.com/SubjectCS2011.html

[3] The Department of CS approached the first author of the paper, a faculty member at the Technion's Department of Education in Technology and Science, who is a researcher of human aspects of SE with a long and deep acquaintance with the Israeli hi-tech industry, to teach the course. The

industry enabled them to teach the course within various practical contexts and to share real-life situations with the students.

In this paper we describe the course (taught in the 2012 and 2013 Spring semesters), elaborate on the additional rungs of the comprehension ladder presented in [1], and illustrate different ways in which students express their desire to be more involved in the course so as to foster their soft skills. In other words, we illustrate how the students realized that in order to understand the course ideas, they must actually experience and practice the said soft skills. Based on this observation, we plan to implement several modifications in the course structure.

2. COURSE DESCRIPTION

The contents of the course described in this paper comply with the recommendations of the ACM/IEEE-CS Computer Science Curricula 2013 - Strawman draft[4]:

> The education that undergraduates in Computer Science receive must adequately prepare them for the workforce in a more holistic way than simply conveying technical facts. Indeed, "soft skills" (such as teamwork and communication) and personal attributes (such as identification of opportunity and risk) play a critical role in the workplace. Successfully applying technical knowledge in practice often requires an ability to tolerate ambiguity and work well with others from different backgrounds and disciplines. These overarching considerations are important for promoting successful professional practice in a variety of career paths. (p. 11)

The course was designed based on two main working assumptions:

First, we took into the consideration that the work skills required in CS and in SE are different in essence. While the work of a computer scientist consists mainly of theoretical investigation, a software engineer works with people: customers and teammates. At the same time, however, we are witnessing a situation in which, in many cases (a) software engineers and computer scientists receive almost identical education, which in most cases is provided by CS departments and, therefore, emphasizes primarily scientific aspects, and (b) many computer scientists eventually work as software engineers.

Second, soft CS and SE skills cannot be formally defined or instructed. This stems from the fact that the expression of soft skills depends, among other factors, on the individual's personality and on the specific human interaction in which that individual is involved.

Specific teaching principles derived from the above working assumptions, such as active learning and diversity, are presented in [1].

Course Structure

So far, the course was taught twice (during the 2012 and 2013 Spring semesters) and lasted 14 weeks each time. Each weekly session consisted of 3 academic hours (150 minutes). The course was held at the Department of Education in Technology and Science, which is approximately a 10-minute in-campus walk from the Department of CS. Twenty-four students were enrolled in each of the two courses. Table I presents an outline of the course schedule in 2012; the 2013 schedule was similar but with small changes in the order of topics learned.

As can be seen, each session highlighted one soft skill; other soft skills were, however, addressed as well. For example, principles of effective presentations processes were addressed in most sessions, but they were the "official" topic of Session 11, in which other soft skills were naturally applied as well (such as openness to diversity and time management skills).

Grading

Homework assignments were given on a weekly basis on alternating weeks during the semester and had to be submitted within two weeks. In addition, a final assignment was submitted one month after the end of the semester.

Attendance in class was compulsory and the final grade was composed as follows: 75% - average grade of top 5 homework assignments (out of 7 in the Spring 2012 semester or 9 in the Spring 2013 semester) and 25% - final assignment.

Table 1. Course schedule

Session	Topic
1	Introduction – Soft concepts in CS and SE
2	Feedback skills
3	Diversity
4	Simulation of an international software company
5	Reflection in teams
6	Change management and time management.
7	Time management (cont.) The reflective practitioner's perspective: Reflection on the individual level
8	Business writing – Email and more
9	Business writing – Email and more (cont.) Midterm summary – Part I: Elicitation of students' questions
10	Midterm summary – Part II: Answering of students' questions Conflicts in teamwork Characteristics of soft skills Collaboration and reward in teamwork
11	Collaboration and reward in teamwork (cont.) Guest lecturer Basic principles of effective presentations
12	Knowledge transfer in global companies Ethics of SE
13	Guest lecturer Ethics of SE (cont.)
14	Summary: Students' suggestions for topics to be included in a consecutive course on soft skills

3. STUDENTS' GRADUAL CONSTRUCTION OF SOFT CS SKILLS

In this section we illustrate the gradual mental construction of the concept of soft CS skills by the students. We base our description on class observations, homework assignments, and short interviews with the students.

In [1] we presented a 4-rung ladder that described the students' gradual mental construction of soft skills (presented again in Table 2).

Based on further data analysis as well as on additional experienced gained teaching the course for the second time, we have refined the ladder and its updated version now includes six rungs. Since the original four rungs are described at length in [1], we briefly present all six rungs and focus more extensively on the two new rungs (#4 and #6). As is illustrated in this section, students repeatedly expressed the idea that soft skills should be learned by expressing and experiencing them and conveyed their desire to be more involved in the course design and learning processes.

second author of the paper, who was the course TA, has over 20 years of managerial experience in international hi-tech companies in product development, business development, and global customer support roles.

[4] See: http://cs2013.org/strawman-draft/cs2013-strawman.pdf

Table 2. Stages in students' mental construction of soft skills

Stage	Description	New (yes/no)
1	Students distinguish between soft skills and skills acquired during their other studies at the Department of CS	No
2	Students characterize soft skills	No
3	Students rank soft skills	No
4	Students identify soft skills they want to learn in the course	Yes
5	Students define the concept of a soft skill	No
6	Students formulate the final assignment of the course	Yes

Stage 1 (see [1] for more details): Students' perceptions of soft skills at this stage of the course reflect differences they have observed between what they learn elsewhere in the Department of CS and the topics they expect to learn in the course.

Stage 2(see [1] for more details): Students characterize a soft skill as follows:

- cannot be measured (or defined by a formula);
- depends on the individual's personality;
- can be implemented in different ways;
- should be implemented differently in different situations according to the specific circumstances;
- is developed gradually.

Stage 3 (see [1] for more details): The following skills were mentioned by at least 25% of students as being important for teamwork: listening skills, different aspects of teamwork, interpersonal communication, giving feedback, flexibility, time and pressure management, knowledge transfer, and patience.

Stage 4 (new): Students identify soft skills they want to learn in the course

Around mid-semester of the second course (2013), the students were asked (as one of their homework assignments) to specify which soft skills they wish to learn during the second half of the semester. All soft skills that were suggested by at least one student were then presented to the students in another homework assignment two weeks later. This time they were asked to indicate their level of interest in learning each soft skill on the list (using the 4-point scale: not at all interested, not interested, interested, highly interested).

Only a handful of soft skills (e.g. persuasiveness) were identified as soft skills that all (or most) of the students wish to learn in the course. The fact that only a few skills were ranked by most of the students as skills they were "highly interested" in learning can be explained from the perspective of diversity: students naturally vary in their personality, personal objectives, skills and priorities, and therefore have different perception of their own needs.

Table 3 illustrates this idea by presenting a random sample of soft skills that were each suggested by at least one student as a skill he or she wants to learn in the course (first assignment) alongside the students' ranking of the interest they have in learning them (second assignment).

The observation we wish to highlight here is the wide variety of soft skills that students mentioned as soft skills they wish to learn in the course (see Table 4). This collection is inspiring, first, because most of the suggested soft skills were never even mentioned during the course by the teaching staff and, second, because they reflect the students' ability to identify the soft skills they need to improve.

Table 3. Sample of soft skills suggested by students as skills they wish to learn in the course and students' ranking of their interest in learning them

Ranking Soft Skills	Highly interested	Interested	Not interested	Not at all interested
Persuasiveness	87%	13%	0%	0
Public speaking	33%	27%	27%	13%
Feedback	7%	60%	20%	13%
Decision making	53%	33%	7%	7%
Time management	40%	33%	13%	13%

Table 4. Comprehensive list of soft skills suggested by students as skills they wish to learn in the course

Flexibility and ability to compromise	Inter-personal communication skills	Ability to ask for and receive assistance
Identification and location of relevant information	Ability to connect with a wide variety of people	Openness towards and understanding of organizational changes
Ability to express oneself in a concise and matter-of-fact manner	Ability to analyze data, drawing conclusions, and acting upon them	Ability to formulate and understand requirements
Openness	Patience	Teamwork
Learning abilities	Decision making	Listening skills
Respect for diversity	Risk assessment	Working with clients
Time planning and scheduling	Teaching and instructing skills	Knowledge management
Teaching and instructing colleagues	Remedying unpleasant situations	Budget planning and staying within budget
Coping with uncertain situations	Ability to learn from mistakes	Ability to adapt to changing situations
Fundraising	Receiving feedback	Public speaking
Solving and managing conflicts	Ability to learn from mistakes	Interpersonal communication skills
Self-awareness	Interviewing skills	Ability to initiate
Team management	Identification and exploitation of professional opportunities	Creativity

Stage 5: Students define the concept of soft skills

The first year we taught the course, the concept of soft skills was left undefined up until the 11th session of the course. Yet, as illustrated above, the students had already gained some sense of the meaning of the concept. The second time we taught the course, a year later, the concept of soft skills was presented at the onset of the course, as part of a presentation on the course objectives, as follows:

"To improve soft skills that are involved in software projects management and development processes that relate to teamwork and interpersonal communications."

Nevertheless, when students were asked to define the concept in their last homework assignment, they did so, highlighting its multifaceted nature, as illustrated by the following examples:

- A soft skill is a personality trait, an interpersonal attribute or skill that, together with hard skills, enhances work and is manifested during interactions with people.
- A soft skill is a personality trait or skill that may be developed during interaction with various people. It is usually related to sensitivity towards other people.
- A skill that is manifested in the way we execute everyday actions that involve communication between people.
- Soft skills are the collection of a person's traits, his communication and language capabilities, aspects of his

character, friendships, etc. that characterize the person's relations with other people.

- A soft skill is a personality trait that enhances the individual's reciprocal relations and work performance. As opposed to hard skills, which are a person's set of skills and the ability to perform a certain kind of activity, soft skills refer to the person's ability to communicate effectively with colleagues and clients. Soft skills also apply extensively both in and outside the work place.
- Soft skills characterize the person's character, traits, emotions, creativity, etc. They are perceived as being inherited, but it turns out that they can be learned over time and with practice.
- A soft skill is a personal trait that can improve the individual's personal reactions and increase efficiency and work performance, and enhance any other situation that involves teamwork.

Stage 6 (new): Students formulate the final assignment of the course

Towards the end of the semester, the students were asked to suggest their preferred topics for the final assignment. The first year the course was taught, we presented six options for the final assignment based on the ten options offered by the students, and each student had to choose one task to work on. The six tasks were:

1. Apply at least five of the topics you learned in the course to a team project that you have completed. The project can be either from your job, your studies, or a personal project.
   a. Describe the project and the topics that you applied. Present examples to demonstrate how the topics were applied.
   b. Analyze mutual relationships among the different topics.
   c. Describe how ideas learned in the course will influence your behavior in future projects.
   d. Reflect on the execution of the final assignment. Indicate at least five new things you learned while working on it.
2. Choose a project that you worked on in the past that was not completed successfully and whose failure can be attributed to the lack of one or more soft skills.
   a. Describe the project.
   b. Explain why, in your opinion, the project failed.
   c. Refer to five soft skills that you believe could lead to the successful completion of the project. For each skill, demonstrate and explain how it could improve the project outcomes.
   d. Analyze mutual relationships among the different skills.
   e. Reflect on the execution of the final assignment. Indicate at least five new things you learned while working on it.
3. Construct a concept map of the topics learned in the course.
   a. Those who are not familiar with concept maps should first familiarize themselves with the concept.
   b. Reflect on the execution of the final assignment. Indicate at least five new things you learned while working on it.
4. Choose five soft skills that in your opinion you are good at and five soft skills that in your opinion you should improve at.
   a. For each soft skill that you are good at, describe a case that illustrates this.
   b. For each soft skill that you should improve at, suggest how you can improve and how you will document the improvement process.
   c. Reflect on the execution of the final assignment. Indicate at least five new things you learned while working on it.
5. Choose one stage in the life cycle of a company (establishment, building the development team, selling the company, etc.) or a specific department in the company (marketing, service, selling, etc.).
   a. Describe the company and the stage or department you chose.
   b. Describe five soft skills that are required at the chosen stage of the company or by the chosen department and explain their special importance at that stage or in that department.
   c. Reflect on the execution of the final assignment. Indicate at least five new ideas that you learned while working on it.
6. Prepare a 4-session lesson plan on the use of presentations.
   a. Describe the lesson, including guidelines for the person teaching the lesson.
   b. Construct a presentation to accompany the lesson.
   c. Describe at least five soft skills that, in your opinion, are important to implement in the preparation and teaching of this lesson.
   d. Reflect on the execution of the final assignment. Indicate at least five new things you learned while working on it.

As Table 5 indicates, most of the students chose to work on their own soft skills[5] rather than on a task that requires the analysis of a situation, a company, or the course. We interpret this as indication of (a) the importance they attribute to improving their own soft skills; (b) their personal engagement in the course contents; (c) their desire to work on a task that they find directly relevant for them; and (d) their wish to learn soft skills by actual implementing soft skills, in this case, the skill of analyzing their own soft skills.

Table 5. Distribution of the students' choices of final assignment

Task	Description	Number of students
1	Application of soft skills in a project	0
2	Analysis of a failed past project	2
3	Concept maps	1
4	Evaluation of personal soft skills	13
5	Analysis of a company or a department	6
6	Lesson plan for using presentations	2

Table 6 lists skills that different students mentioned in their work, either as soft skills that they have already acquired or as soft skills that they wish to improve. For example, five students stated that they had already acquired the soft skills of receiving and giving feedback, while six students admitted that they need to improve on this skill (i.e. these skills appeared in both categories - already acquired and need improvement). Table 7 lists soft skills mentioned only either as skills that students have already acquired or as skills that warrant improvement (i.e. these skills appeared in only one of the two categories). For example, sense of humor was mentioned only as a skill that has already been acquired; self-confidence was mentioned only as a skill that should be improved.

As can be seen, most of the skills were mentioned both as skills that the students already have acquired and as skills that should be improved.

Table 6. Soft skills that students mentioned both as already acquired and as skills that should be improved

Soft skills students mentioned both as having and as requiring improvement	No. of students who mentioned having the skill	No. of students who mentioned a need to improve the skill
Teamwork	8	2
Creativity	5	3
Presentation skills	6	6
Reflective skills	2	2
Knowledge management	4	3
Organization skills	2	2
Time management	4	9

[5] The total grade (100 points) for this task was allocated as follows: 8 points for each soft skill (2×5×8) and 4 points for each topic mentioned in the reflection (4×5).

Listening	6	1
Receiving and giving feedback	5	6
Decision-making skills	2	3
Working under pressure	3	2
Flexibility and ability to adjust to changes	3	2
Perseverance	1	2
Patience and tolerance	3	5
Leadership	1	1

Table 7. Soft skills students mentioned as either having them or as requiring improvement

Soft kills mentioned as skills that students have	No. of students who mentioned having the skill	Soft kills mentioned as skills that need improvement	No. of students who mentioned a need to improve the skill
Motivation to learn and develop new skills and ability to identify opportunities for growth	3	Ability to cope with uncertain situations	1
Interpersonal relations and communication	4	Ability to solve/mange conflicts	3
Strong work ethic	1	Self confidence	2
Sense of humor	1	Group learning	1
Ability to assimilate new material	1	Business writing	1
		Positive attitude	1
		Self-criticism	1
		Financial negotiation	1
		Sharing [personal things]	1
		Self-composedness	3
		Ability to promote oneself	1

Among other insights that can be gained from Tables 6 and 7, we note that Table 6 reflects the importance of diversity in software teams. Since soft skills are implemented differently by different people (according to the individual's personality) and should be implemented differently according to the specific circumstances, no one person can successfully implement them all in the myriad of possible situations encountered in the changing world. Thus, the fact that not all students admitted to having the same soft skills reflects the assumption that team diversity can compensate for the individual's limitations in successfully expressing all soft skills in all possible situations.

The second time we taught the course, this task (evaluation of personal soft skills) was not suggested by the students as an option for the final assignment but due to its popularity the first time around, we added it to the other options the students suggested. This time 14 students (out of 22) chose it. This reveals that, indeed, students are interested in pursuing their *personal* involvement in the learning process of the course rather than analyzing situations that are beyond their current environments. We propose that this phenomenon results from the fact that the students are in their very preliminary learning stage of the topic of soft skills, in which they associate soft skills with themselves, rather than with an external entity such as a situation or an organization.

4. COURSE EVALUATION

In this section we present results of two surveys conducted among the course students in addition to the tradition teaching evaluation conducted by the Technion's Center for the Promotion of Teaching. The first was conducted by the Faculty of CS and the second was conducted by the authors one year after the end of the course.

4.1 Evaluation by the Faculty of CS

Towards the end of the first course, in order to decide whether or not to offer the course to CS students as an elective course, the Faculty of CS decided to conduct an additional survey to that conducted for all Technion courses each semester by the Technion's Center for the Promotion of Teaching. Based on this evaluation, the course was added as an elective course offered to CS students.

The course evaluation was summarized by the faculty itself (i.e. not by the authors), as follows.

Seventy-four percent of students stated that the course enriched them professionally and all of them said that they learned skills that they had not acquired in any other course at the Technion. Eighty-seven percent gave the course format a positive evaluation, saying that it enabled them to experience and practice the skills they learned. Ninety-one percent stated that they enjoyed the course and that the course enriched their learning experience at the Technion.

Seventy-eight percent said that they improved their knowledge about communicating with stakeholders, ethical dilemmas, and teamwork. Two topics were mentioned as being covered only in part: (1) knowledge management and transfer in hi-tech companies, and (2) communication management in international companies. Fifty-two percent of students indicated that more attention should be given to the topic of preparing and presenting presentations.

Following is a selection of comments that students were invited to add if they so wished:

- An interesting and enriching course that imparted applied tools that have practical value for work in the industry.
- Should be in every student's toolbox.
- The course opens the mind; I wholeheartedly recommend it to every CS student and to every Technion student in general.
- The course was a "departure from routine" and it opened up a rich world of content and new learning methods.
- Studying outside of the faculty, at the Department of Education in Science and Technology, is an advantage (more relaxed).

Students were also asked to offer their suggestions for improving the course:

- Focus more on presenting presentations and maybe even include an individual assignment of building a presentation and presenting it (*this comment was given repeatedly*), as well as marketing and communicating with clients and investors.
- Include meetings with industry stakeholders and offer more "real-life" examples.
- Focus should be placed on applied aspects and on solutions rather than on theory. More relevant and less artificial examples from the world of software should be presented.
- Some of the content lacked conclusions ("a bottom line").
- Reduce the breadth and increase the depth (Consideration should be given to the fact that many students work in the industry and have gain certain experience in teamwork, etc. so that superficial addressing of these topics contributes nothing).

4.2 Evaluation after one year

In order to assess the actual contribution of the course not just immediately after it was completed, we distributed a questionnaire to the attending students one year after its completion (in parallel to the second time it was taught).

Ten students responded to the questionnaire. Table 8 presents students' assessment of specific aspects of the course. Though in general it is evident that the course improved the students' soft skills, we note the low ranking of the statement "The course improved my presentation skills". Indeed, in the first course (2012), the students were offered fewer opportunities to present. Therefore, in the course's second year, a greater deal of attention was given to presentations, also in response to the aforementioned call of the hi-tech industry to equip graduates with better presentation skills. We note, however, that in all cases, presentations were discussed in the context of CS and SE topics and not in general terms, so as to enable the students to practice their presentation skills in the same context in which they will likely use them in the future.

Table 8. Students' evaluation after one year

To what degree did the course:	To a very great degree	To a great degree	Slightly	Not at all
Help me in my further studies	50%	20%	10%	20%
Improve my soft skills in general	50%	30%	10%	10%
Improve my teamwork skills	40%	40%	10%	10%
Increase my awareness to the way in which I compose email messages	60%	0%	30%	10%
Improve my presentation skills	20%	10%	60%	10%
Increase my awareness to differences among people	60%	20%	10%	10%
Increase my awareness of soft skills	50%	40%	0%	10%
Increase my awareness of my colleagues' soft skills	50%	30%	10%	10%
Improve my ability to offer feedback	60%	20%	0%	20%
Improve my ethical norms	10%	30%	30%	30%
Improve my time management skills	10%	10%	60%	20%

In addition, 90% of students said they would be interested in attending another course on soft skills and 80% said they would recommend it to their friends.

The students were also asked to describe the course in three sentences. Following are several such descriptions that highlight the course from different perspectives:

The first description addresses the course contents:

- Topics and skills required to work efficiently and pleasantly in various work settings are discussed in the course. The skills covered in the course complement the technical skills taught in other studies towards the degree.

The second description highlights the contribution of the course to students' understanding of the environment in which they are likely to function in the future:

- The course is fascinating and it enables the students to understand that they are ultimately part of a system and a company and so they must know how to communicate with it. I think that a person who goes to work, besides being a genius, must also know how to work with the other people in the company and so it is important to know how to impart and present your knowledge and ideas, to be receptive to others' ideas, to learn from mistakes that others have found in your work, because this is the only way to develop.

The following quotes reflect the course uniqueness in a spirit similar to that of the course characterization performed on the first rung of the comprehension ladder (see Table 2):

- A change from the study routine - imparts tools that contribute and will contribute significantly in the industry [...].
- Experiential, enriching, essential, recommended, a routine breaker, applicable in everyday life.

In interviews conducted with three students one year after they completed the course in the Spring 2012 semester, we heard once again about the students' desire to be involved in the course and their understanding that in order to acquire soft skills they must be actively involved and actively practice using them. One student, for example, suggested integrating more practical experience into the course in the form of simulations of dealing with communication problems with customers and other stakeholders. He emphasized the importance of focusing on the daily interaction with people, with whom one has close contact (for example, getting people to cooperate and to answer emails, or soliciting help from people who are busy and for whom providing assistance is not part of their job description). Another student suggested increasing students' participation in the course and providing them with more opportunities to present (not just after class work but after homework as well, so as to give them more time to practice).

5. SUMMARY

The uniqueness of the course described in this paper is in the wide range of soft CS and SE skills that it addresses, both theoretically and practically, in the context of the hi-tech industry.

We conclude by highlighting the students' desire to be more involved in the course in different ways. By assuming this attitude students actually reflect their understanding that learning of soft skills should be based on experiential activities in a setting that enables the manifestation of soft skills and promotes listening, openness to diversity, presentation skills, expressing feelings, overcoming emotional obstacles, giving and receiving feedback, etc. We explain this by the students' realization of the significant and broad changes, both conceptual and behavioral, that are required from them in the course, which are not required in regular CS courses.

The course will now be offered once a year during the Spring semester. We plan to continue to address students' requests in general, and increase their involvement in particular, in several ways:

- By enabling the students themselves to teach part (or all) of the course contents thus providing them with a true stage for presenting and teaching. Naturally, we will work with them prior to such lessons according to need.
- By creating a database of real-life cases experienced by students at their places of work, and by discussing them. All cases that will be examined in the classroom will be real cases recounted by students.
- By requiring that homework assignments be submitted as professional email messages and/or video clips so that students will have to delve deeper into those contents.

In our talk we add details and present additional evidence to support all of our claims.

6. REFERENCES

[1] Hazzan, O. and Har-shai, G. (2013). Teaching computer science soft skills as soft concepts, SIGCSE 2013 - The 44th ACM Technical Symposium on Computer Science Education, Denver, CO, USA, pp. 59-64.

[2] Senor, D. and Singer, S. (2008). *Start-up Nation: The Story of Israel's Economic Miracle*, Twelve.

[3] Sukhoo, A., Barnard, A., Eloff, M. M and Van der Poll J. A. (2005). Accommodating soft skills in software project management, *Issues in Informing Science and Information Technology*, Vol. 2, pp. 691-704

Promoting Ecoliteracy in an Introductory Database Systems Course

Activities for the First Week

Daniela Inclezan
Miami University
501 E High Street
Oxford, Ohio 45056
inclezd@MiamiOH.edu

Luis Pradanos
Miami University
501 E High Street
Oxford, Ohio 45056
pradanli@MiamiOH.edu

ABSTRACT

Promoting *sustainability*, *critical thinking*, and *ethical awareness* are goals that appear in the vision statements of the majority of universities in the United States nowadays. One way of achieving these goals is by increasing the ecological literacy (i.e., ecoliteracy) of our students. In order to be effective, ecoliteracy should be taught not only in environmental studies classes, but rather across the institutional curriculum. In this paper we present three activities designed to be used in the first week of class in an introductory Database Systems course. Our activities promote critical thinking, systemic thinking, ethical behavior, and an increased awareness of ecological problems – building blocks that set up the stage for teaching ecoliteracy.

Categories and Subject Descriptors

K.3.2 [**Computers and Education**]: Computer and Information Science Education

General Terms

Experimentation; Human Factors

Keywords

Sustainability; critical thinking; ethical responsibility; ecoliteracy; database systems; first week activities

1. INTRODUCTION

The debate about the role of higher education in teaching ecological literacy (i.e., ecoliteracy) [12, 13] is very alive today, as more and more publications appear every year targeting this issue from different and interdisciplinary perspectives [2, 15, 8]. Thus, a number of universities are now incorporating into their institutional visions, goals, and statements words like *sustainability*, *global consciousness*, and *critical thinking*. In the last few years, many colleges have created sustainability task force to help achieve institutional environmental goals and advance toward campus sustainable management. There is also a current proliferation of interdisciplinary Faculty Learning Communities trying to incorporate knowledge of environmental and sustainability perspectives into their fields of teaching and scholarship. Many professors teaching in disciplines other than environmental studies are connecting their various research interests with environmental issues and are fostering ecological literacy inside their classrooms [9]. This synergy is responsible for the development and popularity of new scholarship at the intersection of the traditional disciplines, such as ecological economics, environmental engineering, political ecology, industrial ecology, eco-design, biomimicry, and so forth. In most cases, the mentioned scholarship is a result of incorporating the scientific knowledge and advances of the twentieth century (ecology, thermodynamics, systems theory, etc.) into much older fields. We should do the same in our younger discipline of Computer Science, in order to prepare our students for dealing with the pressing issues of our time. Some studies indicate that, in the near future, more jobs related to ecotechnology will emerge as the global energetic and environmental crisis aggravates [14]. Thus, students of Computer Science will be required to have ecological literacy to successfully assist other engineers and scientists mitigate these issues.

This is a challenging endeavor as it requires instructors to redefine dominant notions taken for granted for some time in our academic culture. First, that the goal of education is to primarily prepare students to compete successfully in a global economy, as opposed to thinking critically about whether or not that competitive socioeconomic model is really sustainable and desirable in a context of global ecological restrictions and biophysical limitations. Second, that humans are somehow separated from the rest of the biotic community, which grants us permission to control or abuse it. However, if we acknowledged that humans' survival depends on the well-being of the planetary ecosystems, we would not be able to ignore the alterations that our technologies cause to these ecosystems. An example is that our society is celebrating the information age while the real information of the planet (the genetic information) is disappearing at an unprecedented pace due to an ongoing mass extinction of species [5].

Therefore, an education that fosters ecoliteracy and critical thinking needs to emphasize the ethical responsibility of

SIGCSE'14, March 3–8, 2014, Atlanta, GA, USA.

ACM 978-1-4503-2605-6/14/03 ...$15.00.
http://dx.doi.org/10.1145/2538862.2538909.

our actions and, in order to do so, it has to train students to make visible the broad and complex consequences of what we do, beyond the mere marketable product. In sum, it is important for the students not just to know *how* to develop or manage a tool such as a database system, but to ask *why* and in what cases it is better to use it that not to; what are the ethical implications of its usage; or in which new and creative ways could it be used to improve simultaneously the health of ecosystems and the well-being of human communities. The students need to be taught that the proper use of high tech tools requires a high level of responsibility and integrity, not just certain usage skills.

This paper is intended as a contribution to the emergent teaching approach that focuses on computing for the social good [6, 7], and especially to the much smaller ecologically-oriented approach. Thus, the paper explores some effective ways to teach ecoliteracy in an introductory Database Systems class. Our goal is to include the ecological component in a natural way, so that students do not perceive it as tangential, but rather intrinsically connected, to the topic of study. We will focus on the first week of class because it is an especially relevant period for the professor to establish course expectations and unveil hidden and relevant connections between the discipline of Computer Science and ecological issues, which are not obvious to the average student. To effectively teach ecoliteracy, it is also crucial to pay attention not just to the selected content but as well to the way in which it is taught. Specifically, focusing on collaboration and social cohesion rather than competition is one way of achieving this goal.

With all this in mind we conceived a number of activities for the lesson plan of the first week of class. Each activity is designed to engage students in conversations related to the introduction to Database Systems, while covering one or more of the following building blocks for ecoliteracy:

(a) critical thinking (i.e., *why* instead of *how*);

(b) systemic thinking (i.e., paying attention to context and a larger scale);

(c) increased awareness of ecological problems (e.g., e-waste);

(d) ethical implications of our actions (e.g., how our e-waste may affect other communities).

The activities ought to be performed together and in the order provided here, in order to progress student thinking and transmit the importance of ecoliteracy in relation to the field of database systems. In what follows, we start by describing the activities in detail. Afterwards, we present some preliminary findings related to our effectiveness of promoting ecoliteracy, and we end with conclusions.

2. THE ACTIVITIES

In order to promote cohesion and collaboration, the progression of activities presented in this section are conducted with the students working in groups. This is an opportunity to expose the class to other ways of thinking by mentioning other societies (both human or non-human) in which collaboration is valued more than competition. One good example is the traditional Andean communities, in which members of the group take turns in helping each other [10].

2.1 Activity 1: Ethical Implications of Database Applications

A question that is typically addressed in the first class session of a Database Systems course is *"Why is it important to study database systems?"*. Frequently, students are not expected to seriously contemplate this question, but rather to take for granted the answer provided by the instructor. Instead, we suggest an activity that requires students to come up with their own answers to this question, and to look with a critical eye at what our society considers to be useful or important.

The activity starts by asking students to get into groups of four or five, and discuss the following basic questions:

(1) *Why are you taking this class?*

(2) *Why is it important to study database systems?*

(3) *What applications do you know that use database systems?*

(4) *What database application would you like to or expect to create after graduation?*

In answering question (3) above, students convince each other (or themselves) that database systems must be important because they are used in nearly every web application today, or because database systems are capable of storing and managing large amounts of data, etc. By using this active learning approach, students not only come to the answers that the instructor would have provided, but they also get the chance to find something meaningful *to them* in the subject of study (see question (4)). As a result, their motivation to actively engage in the course increases, as seems to be the case according to our findings reported in Section 3.

While questions (1)-(4) do not target ecoliteracy directly, the students' answers open up the floor for questions that promote critical thinking. For instance, common answers to question (3) include social media or e-commerce applications. This is a good opportunity to ask:

(5) *Can applications that use database systems be unequivocally deemed as useful, beneficial, or ethical?*

(6) *Is the ability of storing and managing large amounts of data necessarily a good thing?*

These questions allow students to be critical with the common views in our society, and challenge the discourse that uncritically celebrates technology. Instead, students learn to view technology as a tool that should be used responsibly.

Students' answers to questions (5)-(6) tend to reflect their awareness of issues related to the lack of privacy of their data, which may be accessed by governmental or commercial entities, or of negative effects of social media usage on the users' social life. However, students are normally not aware of the ecological ramifications of these two questions. This is a good opportunity to increase the students' awareness of certain ecological problems. For instance, the instructor can mention that e-commerce applications use marketing strategies to coerce customers into buying more things than they initially intended. The effect is that more resources are consumed to produce the goods that are bought, and more waste is generated, thus leading to a global ecological problem.

A summary of the learning outcomes addressed by this activity, both traditional and ecoliteracy-oriented, can be seen in Table 1.

Table 1: Learning Outcomes Targeted by Activity 1

Traditional learning outcomes:
• Students can enumerate aspects that make the study of database systems important.
Ecoliteracy learning outcomes:
Students can • recognize multiple perspectives on a topic; • generate new, non-mainstream perspectives on a topic; • identify indirect consequences of their actions; • perceive their own blind spots with respect to global ecological problems; • raise questions about the ethical implications of their own actions.

2.2 Activity 2: Non-Western Record-Keeping Traditions

Another typical point of discussion for the first week of class in a Database Systems course is the comparison between the database approach and the traditional file-processing approach. We transformed this exercise into an activity that promotes ecoliteracy by focusing on the comparison between database systems and non-Western record-keeping traditions.

We started by presenting two systems of record-keeping with which the students were not likely to be familiar. We first introduced the Mesoamerican Codices – accordion-like books made out of bark and written by pre-Colombian and colonial-era Mixtecs and Aztecs. The earliest known codices are Mixtec and date from the eleventh or twelfth century AD. The Mesoamerican codices represent information in pictorial form mostly, but they may include writings as well. They generally describe mythological or historical events, but some of them, for example Codex Vergara and Códice de Santa María Asunción [18], collect census data for taxation purposes. The census data records family relations and the number of dependents in each family (represented pictorially in a way similar to a family tree), as well as the land properties of each family. Note that this information is also recorded and taken into account by the IRS when calculating due taxes.

The second example we presented were the *quipus / khipus* (or *talking knots*) used in the Andean region of South America. A *quipu* is a collection of colored threads or cords from llama or alpaca hair, attached to a base rope. Information is encoded in a *quipu* by knots placed on strings at specific positions; the color of the cords is also important. *Quipus* are known to have been in use in 3000 BC, and are still used for ritual purposes in Peru. Archaeologists believe that one of the uses of *quipus* in the past was to record census and taxation information [17].

This presentation alone achieves an important goal. Most students are only familiar with one specific tradition of recording information – the Western tradition that led to the development of databases – in which written information was recorded for centuries in tabular form on a piece of paper. By exposing the class to the solutions invented by other societies for the storage and manipulation of data, students learn to think on a larger scale that comprises other cultures outside of their own culture. We also hope that this activity stimulates creativity, as it shows that there are many ways to solve a problem such as record-keeping, ways that may be different from the conventional approach in our society.

In the next step of this activity, the students were asked to discuss in groups how present-day database systems differ from the two ancient record-keeping examples. They were specifically asked to address the question:

(7) *Have our data management systems* evolved *since the times of the Aztec codices and the* quipus*?*

Normally, such questions are not asked, as technology is always assumed to be a factor of development and progress. However, students should be encouraged to ask and answer such questions in order to develop their critical thought.

Our students were able to pinpoint the advantages of current database systems in relation to the two given examples. In doing so, they reflected on the important features of a database system (which the two traditional systems lacked): the ability to store large amounts of data, the ease of adding new data or updating existing data, etc. They had problems, however, in coming up with possible disadvantages of database systems with respect to traditional record-keeping systems.

To give them some guidance, we encouraged the class to think about the material aspects of a database system (or of any computational system in general) by asking the following question:

(8) *How do current database systems compare to traditional record-keeping systems in terms of their impact on the environment?*

At this point, students were able to see disadvantages of our database systems and mentioned the dependence of such systems on electricity, which is often obtained by burning coal and thus increasing CO_2 emissions. We pushed students to think not just in terms of the *useful lifetime* of a database server (or any other computing device used by database systems), but rather to its *whole life-cycle* from extraction of the necessary prime matter to disposal. Specifically, we asked students whether they were aware of the toxicity of some of the metals used in building electronics, the negative environmental impact of the extractive industry related to these metals, and the societal, health, and environmental costs of the electronic waste resulting at the end of the useful lifetime of such products [3, 11]. To make the discussion more concrete, we presented images that illustrated the problems generated by e-waste in Ghana. This issue has received some visibility in the international media. According to the media,[1] e-waste is sent to Ghana by companies that abuse existing laws concerning obsolete electronics. At the destination, the e-waste gets sent to the slums where it accumulates in piles. From there, the toxic metals on the circuit boards leach into the water supply and thus affect all life forms in the area. People living in the slums recycle useful pieces of metal by hand and burn the remaining plastic, unaware of the negative consequences of this practice on their health.

Alternatively, instead of photos, the instructor may choose to discuss the following excerpts by Campbell, MacKinnon, and Stevens [1]:

[1]http://www.pbs.org/frontlineworld/stories/ghana804/

(i) "Roughly 500–1000 different toxic chemicals, including arsenic, mercury, lead, and cadmium, go into computer production, making it one of the more toxic industries. According to the UNEP, roughly 50 million tons of waste from electronic goods is generated each year. Burning is a common way to dispose of e-waste, but it is a practice that releases toxins into the air and into the soil. Rather than dealing with it themselves, many developed countries ship their waste to developing countries. A study conducted by the Basel Action Network reports that 'a minimum of 100,000 computers a month are entering the Nigerian port of Lagos alone,' most of which are useless." (p. 144)

(ii) "One fairly recent development has been the use of coltan. While coltan is mined in Australia, the world's biggest reserves are in the Democratic Republic of Congo. Mining here has helped fuel a civil war where various militias use the sale of coltan to finance their military activities. The illegal mining has led to massive environmental damage, as hillsides have been denuded of trees, and gorilla, elephant, and other species' habitats have been destroyed." (p. 144–145)

Notice that the activity addresses various ecoliteracy learning outcomes, while not forgetting to cover outcomes that are associated to traditional Database Systems courses as well, as shown in Table 2.

Table 2: Learning Outcomes Targeted by Activity 2

Traditional learning outcomes:
Students can • define the terms: database, DBMS (database management system), and database system; • compare current database systems with previous approaches.
Ecoliteracy learning outcomes:
Students can • recognize multiple solutions to a problem; • appreciate new, non-mainstream solutions to problems; • identify the multiple causes of a problem; • identify indirect consequences of their actions; • perceive their own blind spots with respect to global ecological problems; • raise questions about the ethical implications of their own actions.

2.3 Activity 3: Gross Domestic Product and the Relational Model

Most introductory database courses discuss the *relational model* – a database model based on first-order predicate logic, proposed by Edgar F. Codd [4]. Some instructors, as was our case, introduce this model (at least intuitively) during the first week of class. The activity we present here intends to familiarize students with the basic concepts of the relational model by giving them the opportunity to actively use the associated terms in communication with their peers. At the same time, the exercise promotes systemic thinking and encourages students to ponder *why* instead of *how*.

The activity begins by introducing the main concepts of the relational model (e.g., relation, relation name, domain, attribute, tuple) via a graphical example that considers some common relation such as Employee. After students acknowledge that they have grasped the intuitive meanings of the basic concepts, they are asked to get into groups for the next part of the activity in which they will apply these concepts to a real-life problem. In this exercise, the students assume the role of a database designer that is asked to capture, via one or more relations, an aspect of their choice that is relevant to the calculation of the Gross Domestic Product (GDP).

Before the class starts working on the exercise, the instructor shortly describes what the Gross Domestic Product is supposed to calculate (roughly speaking, all monetary transactions officially recorded in a specific territory during a specific period of time), and some of the important factors that go into its calculation (e.g., imports and exports, services, exchanged goods, etc.). The instructor emphasizes the fact that the GDP is considered an important measurement in our economic system, often associated by the media, politicians, and common belief with the well-being of our society.

While developing their relations, students are allowed to look for more information about the GDP on the Internet. Once they are satisfied with their solutions, each group of students is asked to sketch their relation(s) on the board, and to explain their solution using the recently learned technical vocabulary. From our experience, students are able to produce reasonable relations, and different groups address different factors relevant to the GDP calculation.

The part of the exercise presented so far should make the students realize that they have (or will learn in this course) the tools necessary to answer the *how* question:

(9) *"How would you represent the data relevant to the calculation of the GDP?"*

They must be made aware that there is also a *why* question that should be made explicit:

(10) *"Why is the GDP commonly considered an indicator of the well-being of a society?"*

The instructor should illustrate the importance of this question via a story like the following one, adapted from [16].

Imagine a population living by a river and consuming the water in this river, after filtering it through a simple and natural filtration system. If a company builds a factory up the river and dumps its waste into the river, the GDP goes up multiple times. First of all, the government may fine the company. This is a monetary transaction and thus the GDP will increase. The company will have to pay to have the water cleaned, and hence the GDP will go up. For the time being at least, the local population will have to buy bottled water to secure their health. In case they have already drank the water, they will have to pay for a visit to the doctor and possibly buy medicine to cure their ailments. All this increases the GDP. On the other hand, the environment (including the local population) will suffer multiple times: the initial pollution will destroy the living ecosystems in the river, including some of the food resources of the local population; filtration operations and the pharmaceutical industry have a high environmental impact; the empty plastic bottles will remain in the environment for centuries to come, etc.

A more impacting example at the personal level may be:

Think of a couple with toddlers that live in close proximity to the children's grandparents. The parents ask the grandparents to babysit the babies from time to time when they go to work. The grandparents do this for free as they enjoy spending time with their grandchildren and they feel useful in helping their children. Imagine that, for some reason, the parents decide to put the grandparents in a retirement home. Now, the parents will have to take their children to the day-care when they go to work. This increases the GDP, as the parents will have to pay for the day-care and also for the gas that allows them to take their children to the day-care or to visit the grandparents. On the other hand, the parents may feel more miserable because they spend more time driving, the children may miss their grandparents, and the grandparents may now feel lonely and useless.

These examples show why we should question the appropriateness of using the GDP as an indicator of the well-being or happiness of a society. Students should be asked to provide other measures that may be more suitable for this purpose. In our class, students have suggested looking for instance at divorce rates, criminality rates, and alcohol consumption. The activity may continue by asking students to repeat the design process, but this time create relations that capture the data relevant to the newly suggested measures. As an anecdote, the instructor may tell the class about measures proposed by other countries, such as the Gross National Happiness in Bhutan. This is also an opportunity to emphasize the difficulty of capturing non-quantifiable data, and possible limitations of databases.

Table 3 summarizes the learning outcomes targeted by this activity.

Table 3: Learning Outcomes Targeted by Activity 3

Traditional learning outcomes:
Students can • define the relational model and its basic concepts; • use technical vocabulary in communication.
Ecoliteracy learning outcomes:
Students can • recognize assumptions in the Western way of thinking; • identify and appreciate other ways of thinking; • identify multiple causes and consequences of actions; • perceive their own blind spots with respect to global ecological problems; • raise questions about the ethical implications of their own actions.

3. ASSESSMENT

The above activities were tested in a third-year introductory course in Database Systems at a public university. Activities 1 and 2 were conducted during the first class session of the semester; activity 3 was put into practice during the second session. To assess the effectiveness of these exercises, we conducted two surveys – one after each of the two class sessions. The surveys contained open-ended questions that elicited the students' feed-back on the three activities, or generally on the class conducted that day (see Table 4). All 27 students enrolled in the class responded to each of the questions in the surveys. The vast majority of responses showed a highly positive reaction to our activities. Students found them engaging and did not perceive them as tangential to the subject of the course.

A large percentage of the students' comments demonstrate that our activities made them think more critically and on a larger scale, while also increasing their awareness of current socio-environmental problems. We select here a few of these comments:

Table 4: Survey Questions

Day 1:
Q_1 What makes the study of database systems meaningful or relevant to you? Q_2 Has this class changed your perspective on database systems and their applications? If so, how? Q_3 Is there something interesting/unexpected that you have learned in this class today? If so, what?
Day 2:
Q_4 What did you like and dislike about today's class? Q_5 What did you think of the Gross Domestic Product (GDP) activity?

- *Learning about ethical and environmental concerns was particularly important in changing my perspective, because I had never thought about these issues in relation to databases.*
- *I never considered the deeper ethical implications of databases.*
- *I had already known that electronic recycling programs caused a lot of harm to those countries that participate in it, but I am hopeful about learning to think more critically of such practices and think more carefully about the consequences of using newer technologies.*
- *I never considered the waste factor of computer equipment/server equipment previously. Discussing this opened my eyes to the issue.*
- *They're more destructive to the environment than I considered. That was a fascinating discussion to me.*
- *I knew that toxic materials and electronic waste were being discarded in third-world countries, but I didn't expect the huge piles of old electronics I saw in the pictures from Ghana.*
- *I also learned about all of the hazardous wasted* [sic] *in Ghana, and started thinking of ways to possibly eliminate those hazards in the future.*
- *I didn't know that disposing all these electronics could be so hazardous. Obviously all the trash is not good for the planet but I didn't know how toxic the materials themselves were.*
- *I know very little about computer recycling processes, but now I will go learn more.*
- *I also enjoyed [...] thinking critically about what measurements (such as GDP) are supposed to measure and whether or not these are accurate/ appropriate ways to measure what is intended.*
- *I thought it was interesting how you pointed out how GDP may not actually be a good measure of how happy or well a country is doing. A lot of times I hear a country is doing well when their GDP is high but now I know to look at that with a more critical eye.*

We would like to remark that many of these responses, and others not included here, contain words like "ethical," "ethics," "critical," or "critically," which did not appear in the formulation of the survey questions. Ten out of the 27 answers to question Q_2 from Table 2, and nine out of the answers to question Q_3 contained words or expressions derived from the words "ethics," "environment," "concern," "negative," and "good." Fifteen responses to Q_2 and ten responses to Q_3 contained expressions referring to starting to think more critically or having an increased awareness of ecological problems (e.g., "I have never thought/ considered," "I now realize/ see," "this made me more aware," "it has changed my perspective," "I had my eyes opened, " "I will go learn more" etc.). Moreover, ten of the 27 answers to Q_3 mention electronic waste as something interesting or unexpected learned that day (five of these responses actually contain the word "Ghana"), while nine mention the Mesoamerican Codices.

Some of the students' responses seem to indicate that our activities have achieved additional goals, besides of our objective to promote ecoliteracy. We have reasons to believe that Activity 1 increased the students' *motivation* and *interest* in studying the subject of database systems, as indicated by comments like:

- *I wasn't quite aware of how important database systems are. I'll be honest I thought this class was not going to be very interesting but now I see how this knowledge can apply to so many things in this world. I'm excited!*
- *Listening to classmates' perspectives on the usefulness of databases and the way they want to utilize these in the future was particularly interesting and informative.*
- *I found it interesting that so many students are taking this class, not because it is a requirement, but because they just want to!*

A couple of comments also suggest that Activity 2 may be useful in stimulating *creativity*:

- *The knot "database" system from hundreds of years ago was interesting just because of how creative of an idea it is.*
- *It really surprised me how old records were taken with things like pictures and knots on a bunch of strings. I thought it was very interesting how, even hundreds of years ago, people were trying to keep track of the same information we keep track of now in databases with much less sophisticated technology.*

We did not conduct a formal assessment of our activities because (1) we did not have a control group for comparison given the size of our university; and (2) we are not aware of any other activities designed to promote ecoliteracy in a Database Systems or any other Computer Science course.

4. CONCLUSIONS

In this paper, we have presented three activities for teaching ecoliteracy in a third-year course on Database Systems. Our activities focus on the building blocks of ecoliteracy (critical thinking, systemic thinking, increased awareness of ecological problems, and ethical behavior) and are meant to be conducted in the first week of class. We have argued that it is important to teach ecoliteracy in Computer Science courses in order to better prepare our students for the increasing number of engineering jobs that target current environmental problems. Moreover, by integrating ecoliteracy in our courses we would actively foster *sustainability, critical thinking,* and *ethical awareness* – goals that are frequently mentioned in the vision statements of our academic institutions. Although designed for a specific course, our activities can be easily adapted to other areas in Computer Science.

5. REFERENCES

[1] P. J. Campbell, A. MacKinnon, and C. R. Stevens. *An Introduction to Global Studies.* Wiley-Blackwell, 2010.

[2] F. Capra. The new facts of life, 2008. Available at http://www.ecoliteracy.org/essays/new-facts-life.

[3] F. Ciambrone. *Environmental Life Cycle Analysis.* Lewis Publishers, 1997.

[4] E. F. Codd. A relational model of data for large shared data banks. *Communications of the ACM,* 13(8):377–387, 1970.

[5] R. Fernández Durán. *El Antropoceno: La expansión del capitalismo global choca con la biosfera.* Virus Editorial, 2011.

[6] M. Goldweber. A day one computing for the social good activity. *ACM Inroads,* 3(3):46–49, 2012.

[7] M. Goldweber, J. Barr, T. Clear, R. Davoli, S. Mann, E. Patitsas, and S. Portnoff. A framework for enhancing the social good in computing education: a values approach. *ACM Inroads,* 4(1):58–79, 2013.

[8] D. Goleman, L. Bennett, and Z. Barlow. *Ecoliterate: How Educators Are Cultivating Emotional, Social, and Ecological Intelligence.* Jossey-Bass, 2012.

[9] J. Hoeg, W. Homestead, R. Català, J. D. Anderson, and K. S. Larsen, editors. *Ometeca,* volume 14–15, 2010.

[10] F. Huanacuni Mamani. *Buen Vivir / Vivir Bien: Filosofía, políticas, estrategias y experiencias regionales andinas.* Coordinadora Andina de Organizaciones Indígenas - CAOI, 2010.

[11] R. Nixon. *Slow Violence and the Environmentalism of the Poor.* Harvard University Press, 2011.

[12] D. W. Orr. *Earth in Mind: On Education, Environment, and the Human Prospect.* Island Press, 10th edition, 2004.

[13] D. W. Orr. What is higher education for now? In Worldwatch Insitute, editor, *State of the World,* pages 75–82. W. W. Norton & Company, 2010.

[14] A. Ramey. Going "green": Environmental jobs for scientists and engineers. *Occupational Outlook Quarterly,* 53(2):2–11, 2009.

[15] M. K. Stone. *Smart by Nature: Schooling for Sustainability.* Watershed Media, 2009.

[16] C. Taibo, editor. *Decrecimientos: Sobre lo que hay que cambiar en la vida cotidiana.* Catarata, 2010.

[17] G. Urton and C. J. Brezine. Khipu accounting in ancient Peru. *Science,* 309:1065–1067, 2005.

[18] B. J. Williams and H. R. Harvey. Content, provenience, and significance of the Codex Vergara and the Códice de Santa María Asunción. *American Antiquity,* 53(2):337–351, 1988.

Developing CS/SE Students' Communication Abilities through a Program-Wide Framework

Janet E. Burge
Gerald C. Gannod
Miami University
205 Benton Hall
Oxford, OH 45056
+1 513-529-0347
{burgeje, gannodg}@muohio.edu

Michael Carter
Alanna Howard
Brian Schultz, Mladen Vouk
David Wright
North Carolina State University
890 Oval Drive, Raleigh, NC 27695
+1 919-513-7234
{mpc, avhoward, bschult, vouk, drwrigh3}@ncsu.edu

Paul Anderson
Elon University
Center for Writing Excellence
Elon, NC 27244
+1 336-278-6646
PaulAnderson@Elon.edu

ABSTRACT
Communication skills, including reading, writing, speaking, and teaming, are among the most sought after by employers of recent Computer Science/Software Engineering (CS/SE) graduates. We have been conducting a project that has developed a general framework for program-level integration of communication into CS/SE education. Our framework has been developed through workshops and field evaluation of training materials (and other resources) by faculty from a wide variety of institutions under the guidance of experts in writing and communication across the curriculum. This paper discusses the current state of communication teaching in the CS/SE domain, and presents our framework and experiences for program-wide implementation of communication skills.

Categories and Subject Descriptors
K.3.2 [**Computing Milieux**]: Computer and Information Science Education – *accreditation, Computer science education, Curriculum*

Keywords
Communication, Learning Outcomes, Reading, Writing, Speaking, Teamwork

1. INTRODUCTION
Communication skills, including reading, writing, speaking, and teaming, are among the most sought after by employers of recent Computer Science/Software Engineering (CS/SE) graduates. While technical skills are certainly important, a lack of strong communication skills can often result in miscommunication in a project. This can ultimately lead to an increased number of software faults, lower reliability of the product in the field, increased development costs, and even complete project failure [1][2]. We developed a framework for defining CS/SE-specific communication program outcomes and then designing curricular pathways and teaching strategies for progressively developing students' communication expertise toward these outcomes throughout their undergraduate studies [3]. Our approach focuses on the integrated use of two pedagogical practices: the constructive alignment of the instruction to intentionally and deliberately build students' communication skills as they progress from their introductory to their capstone courses [4], and the creation of learning objects that focus on workplace scenarios [5]. Our work provides a general framework for program-level integration of communications into CS/SE education. The framework was developed through workshops and field evaluation of training materials (and other resources) by faculty from a wide variety of institutions, and under the guidance of experts from the field of writing and communication across the curriculum.

We have found a number of different strategies for supporting communication within technical fields that, we believe, ultimately lead to an increased set of professional communication skills for CS/SE graduates. We contrast our approach with other approaches, for example those that involve one or more writing-intensive but unrelated courses to the CS/SE major, or that relegate communication instruction to departments outside the technical field of interest. Although these other approaches could be components of a program-wide constructive alignment, by themselves they miss significant opportunities for preparing students for the communications they will be expected to do in their careers.

Section 2 reviews current practices within computing programs. Section 3 presents the taxonomy of approaches to program-wide constructive alignment and suggests strategies for undertaking integration efforts. Section 4 identifies issues related to implementing these strategies. Finally, Section 5 concludes and discusses future work.

2. CURRENT PRACTICES
Current practices typically fall into two broad categories: the use of stand-alone technical communication courses, and the use of writing-intensive courses which, in the latter case, may or may not be taught by CS/SE domain experts. Some programs use both in different combinations, so the two are not mutually exclusive. Both practices have long histories dating back to the end of the nineteenth century [6][7].

Reave's [8] survey of 73 top colleges of engineering in North America (50 U. S., 23 Canada) provides a good starting point for describing the extent to which stand-alone courses are incorporated into engineering curricula and the strategies used to staff these courses. She found that 44 of these required a stand-alone technical writing course, 28 of which were given "in house." Eighteen programs required technical communication courses taught by the English department or a writing program. No matter the home of the course, teachers were typically trained in technical communication rather than engineering.

SIGCSE'14, March 5–8, 2014, Atlanta, Georgia, USA.

http://dx.doi.org/10.1145/2538862.2538986

To determine the current practices in CS/SE curricula, we searched the program websites of the 277 CS/SE programs accredited by ABET (http://www.abet.org). We also sent surveys to all these programs and received 40 responses back. We chose to study ABET accredited programs because ABET requires that communication be taught to CS/SE students.

In the website search we examined undergraduate degree requirements, and used catalogs/bulletins to identify the home of the stand-alone communication courses beyond any first-year requirements. One hundred and four of the programs required such courses, 93 of which were located outside the CS/SE department and 11 located within. The 93 courses had prefixes indicating that they were taught in English, communication, speech, or writing departments. One hundred seventy-three programs had no course specifically designated as having a focus on communication. Whereas Reave found that 60% of the programs in her analysis required a stand-alone communication course, only 37% of the CS/SE programs in our analysis did so.

The data collected through the survey included: Carnegie classification; degrees offered; number of undergraduate students in the program; required and optional communication-specific courses and whether those courses were offered by the program or by another program/unit at the institution; and levels of reading, writing, speaking, and teaming emphasis in eight common core courses (CS1, CS2, Data Structures, Operating Systems/Computer Architecture, Databases, Algorithms/Computational Theory, Software Engineering, and Senior Design/Capstone). Analysis of the 40 surveys received back indicates no statistically significant correlation between Carnegie Classification, degrees offered, or the number of students and the level of emphasis placed on communication skills in any of the core courses. Table 1 lists the percentages of responses indicating a strong or very strong emphasis on the four communication skills in each of the eight core courses. In the interest of space, comments from respondents about communication skills in their programs, required courses (other than core courses), and about what they would like to change in their programs to place a greater emphasis on communication skills development are discussed elsewhere.

Table 1 Strong emphasis on communication skills

Course	Writing	Reading	Speaking	Teaming
CS1	6%	6%	0%	12%
CS2	9%	9%	0%	12%
Data Structures	12%	18%	3%	9%
Operating Systems	9%	23%	11%	14%
Databases	9%	21%	6%	27%
Algorithms	9%	26%	6%	6%
Software Engineering	54%	37%	40%	74%
Capstone	73%	33%	87%	90%

Reave's study also provides a basis for understanding courses within the engineering discipline that include a significant amount of writing. At many schools, these courses are designated as "writing intensive" and students are required by their institution or department to take one or more (we know of no requirement for more than three) in order to complete their degrees [9]. Of the 73 programs she studied, Reave found that twenty-eight offered approaches that integrated instruction in communication and engineering, either in addition to or as a substitute for the stand-alone course. These approaches included partnerships of communication and engineering/computer science teachers, collaborations of teams of communication and engineering teachers in a single course, instructional modules in communication added to an engineering course, responses to student communication products by experts in communication, and communication systematically applied across multiple courses in a curriculum.

Though our study was limited to an analysis of stand-alone courses, we suspect that some of these 173 programs incorporate integrated courses such as those described by Reave. However, with relatively few programs requiring stand-alone courses, it may be that CS/SE programs would benefit from a program-wide approach to preparing their students to be effective communicators in the field. Our survey (Table 1) does seem to indicate that currently most of the emphasis appears to be happening in Junior/Senior level core courses.

We have found no programs outside of those involved in our study that have used constructive alignment to organize the communication instruction provided in multiple courses into an intentional sequence for the development of more advanced writing abilities. Even in programs that require more than one writing-intensive course or that require both a stand-alone technical writing course and a writing-intensive one, we have not found an intentional developmental link between the two. Without diminishing the value of learning some writing skills in courses, whether technical communication or writing-intensive, one cannot deny the significance of the observation that "Writing skill learned to pass a course but unused thereafter is learning that is not developmental" [10].

The challenge of developing writing abilities beyond students' first introduction to them is especially imposing in CS/SE programs where students may encounter instruction in many types of writing, each requiring a different set of skills, only once. Unfortunately, for many, the effect of years of practice is simply to produce, for example, increasingly fluent bad writing [11].

3. PROGRAM-WIDE ALIGNMENT

A goal of our project has been to identify an approach that would enable CS/SE programs to develop their students' communication abilities to a higher level than is generally the case. The literature on the development of writing abilities during the undergraduate college years provides a pattern for understanding the development of other communication abilities as well. Research confirms what common sense tells us: acquiring expertise—even writing competence—requires consistent instruction, practice, and feedback (e.g.,[12][13] No single course, no small number of courses can turn any of us into master communicators. In fact, North Carolina State University tracks development of student reading and writing skills, and for CS students there is a steady growth during their undergraduate years [3]. We all continued (and continue) to develop our writing after receiving our bachelor's degrees, whether in our graduate studies or careers or both. We must focus on students' writing throughout their studies with us. This project focused on six courses spanning from the introductory class to senior design.

Another significant line of research establishes the importance of having each individual department define the communication outcomes and pathways for its students, rather than leaving these responsibilities to another department, such as English, or a general studies program. What researchers have found is that what constitutes effective writing differs from one discipline or profession to another [14][15]. These findings reflect deep differences in the underlying intellectual work that distinguishes expertise in, for example, software engineering, biochemistry, and medicine—to say nothing of political science, accountancy, and anthropology. We see this every time a CS/SE student writes poorly according to our definition because he or she has applied to one of our assignments the good writing practices of another field, such as literary studies. This understanding of the context-specific nature of effective writing does not diminish that value of composition or technical communication courses that teach skills that transcend boundaries of domain-specific genres [5], but it does suggest their limitations. If CS/SE programs are to succeed in developing the domain-specific communication abilities students will need in their careers, CS/SE programs need to define the specific communication abilities their graduates should develop (because they are the ones who understand what these abilities are) and they need to find ways to include instruction, practice, and feedback—constructively aligned—into their own courses (because they are the ones prepared to assign, explain, and provide feedback from the authentic perspective of their field).

Actualizing the full benefit of persistent attention to domain-specific communication abilities requires planning the ways in which the experiences in various courses will fit together to create progressive pathways for continuous development of students' abilities [4]. Achieving this requires a curriculum-wide approach.

3.1 Program-Wide Communication Goals

The first step towards implementing a program-wide approach is to identify specific goals and outcomes—what communication skills are desired in CS/SE graduates. Accreditation bodies such as ABET and curriculum guidelines such as SE2004 (http://sites.computer.org/ccse/) state that it is important that students develop effective communication skills, but they do not provide specific guidance as to how that can be achieved. There are several methods that can be used by a department to define what skills are needed: working with faculty to identify what communication skills they value in their field, a capstone-driven approach that identifies what skills students need coming into their capstone or senior design course (which is typically where the students need these skills the most), and asking industry contacts (alumni or collaborating partners) what skills graduates should possess.

The first approach focuses on what communication goals should exist based on the values of the faculty. At NC State we used this approach. It began with asking faculty to identify the technical skills every CS/SE student is expected to be able to master upon graduation. Then, for each of those skills, the faculty designated the kinds of communication students should be able to do in order both to master the skills and demonstrate that mastery. The result was a complementary list of technical and communication outcomes. For example, one of the technical skills outcomes was "by the time a student graduates, he or she should be able to plan and execute appropriate tests in order to identify ways in which the software does not meet the requirements and, where it does not, to redesign, implement and retest until it meets the requirements." The complementary communication abilities included creating a test plan and a test report but also reading requirements to establish criteria for software that meets user needs and revising the design so that the software better meets those needs.

Most CS/SE programs involve some form of senior capstone or design course in which students implement a team development project over the course of one or two semesters. This is where their communication abilities, particularly the ability to work in teams, becomes critical. Miami University implemented a curricular investigation called "Communication Coming into the Capstone" because of concerns that not all students would have experience in teamwork, speaking, and technical writing prior to starting the two-semester course their senior year. The course that addressed those skills was the sophomore-level software engineering course which was taken early by SE majors but sometimes postponed until the senior year by CS majors. The investigation used course outcomes and instructor experience to identify what skills needed to be taught in the curriculum in courses taken prior to the capstone.

A final approach for generating program-wide communication goals is to gather information from professionals in the field about what kinds of communication abilities recent CS/SE graduates should possess in order to be successful in the workplace. This approach has the advantage of a direct link to the workplaces that most students will enter upon graduation. The expectations of managers and other CS/SE professionals can be translated into program goals and outcomes. Many CS/SE programs have advisory boards or alumni who could provide this information. There are also some articles that have used interviews and focus groups to determine expectations of professionals. For example, [16] identified 39 communication outcomes from "Evaluate communication situations and design communication appropriately for different purposes and audiences" to "Inform managers and team members of potential problems before the problems become serious." Our project also invited professionals in the field from companies ranging from fewer than 5 to thousands of employees to describe their expectations for effective communication [17].

3.2 Auditing Current Program Practice

In addition to defining program goals, it is also important to assess current program practices for incorporating communication. One method for doing this is to analyze existing course descriptions and outcomes to see where communication is addressed either explicitly or implicitly. Some courses, such as software engineering, involve explicit communication outcomes by requiring team projects and presentations. Many more courses have implicit communication involved by having course outcomes that state that students will be able to define or describe something taught in the class (such description is often done through writing). This could be done for the entire curriculum or for a targeted set of courses. In our project, courses were chosen that all students were required to take for both the CS and SE degrees. This involved CS1, CS2, data structures, databases (Miami only), software engineering, and capstone/senior design.

A variation of this method was applied at NC State using outcomes created by faculty for ABET. In some cases, communication was explicitly stated in some outcomes. For instance, the outcome "a student will be able to create a software requirements document, including security and privacy requirements" spelled out the kind of communication the student was expected to produce. In other instances, the communication was implicit in an outcome: "a student will be able to describe basic design modeling techniques, including UML class diagrams and simple design patterns (e.g. model/view/controller), and indicate how and when to use them." The teachers expected students to be able to describe modeling techniques and indicate how and when to use them. This task required some form of communication. Finally, there were outcomes that seemed to have no communication involved, such as "a student will be able to correct syntax errors and distinguish between them and runtime errors or errors in logic." Asking a teacher how he or she knows students are able to achieve this outcome elicited a description of communication the students were producing to demonstrate the ability.

Another method is to enlist the help of students entering their capstone course. We designed a survey that listed communication activities students would be expected to perform in the capstone and are expected to master before they graduate. For example, this list included "Have you reviewed requirements to verify whether or not they meet users' needs?" (reading), "Have you written software requirements specifications?" (writing), and "Have you worked on a team that created meeting agendas and minutes?" (teaming). For each of these activities, students were to identify the course in which they performed the activity, the level of importance of it in the course, and their level of confidence in performing the activity in the capstone course. This student perspective on the curriculum is valuable not only in determining current instruction and practice in communication in the curriculum but also in ascertaining the level of preparation of students for the capstone experience.

Finally, we also conducted student focus group studies and analyzed student work to gain an understanding of students' awareness of employers' expectations of workforce skills, students' methods for learning about employers' expectations of workforce skills (CS/SE and Communications), students' expectations for experiences in CS/SE courses, and similar. This is discussed further in [25].

It is also important to remember that some of the communication skills may come to students laterally not only through external courses focused on communications (e.g., those given by English departments), but also through their internships, co-ops, and industry related fellowships which tend raise student awareness of the importance of inter-human communications and provide the students with practical training in that domain [3].

3.3 Constructive Alignment among Courses

By using an audit to obtain a comprehensive understanding of communication instruction currently provided in its courses, a program gains invaluable information it can use as it seeks to create or refine the communication instruction in various courses to create an intentional pathway for development of students' abilities. Miami's "Communication Coming into the Capstone" project focused on five already existing courses as candidates for improved instruction in reading, writing, speaking and teaming. Each course was examined independently by someone who had taught the course before to determine the level of proficiency students were expected to have in reading, writing, speaking, and teaming coming into each course and where they should be after completing each course. The results were then used to identify gaps between courses (such as expecting students to have teamwork experience in lower-level courses) and to compare student experience at the end of the sequence with what was needed for them to have a successful capstone/senior design experience. The instructors then met to discuss the differences and to negotiate where material and outcomes needed to be inserted to address proficiency gaps. One challenge in doing this analysis is that not all the courses had to be taken in a prescribed order.

Rather than identifying gaps and filling them, an alternative approach that has been used in MIS and other non-CS/SE programs involves what might be thought of as designing the developmental pathway from scratch. It is suited to programs that have not thought previously about the ways in which the communication abilities taught in one course prepare students for the more advanced communication instruction they will receive in subsequent courses. After defining the desired graduation-level communication abilities, the program identifies a specific sequence of courses required for all of its majors that can used to create a pathway from the beginning course to completion of the capstone. For each of these courses, specific communication outcomes are defined and appropriate instruction, assignments, and feedback are created so that the course can fulfill its role in the students' overall development. Often, the new assignments and instruction are created by modifying existing course elements, but the result is a much more intentional approach to enabling students to develop high levels of communication expertise.

A hallmark of both of these approaches to aligning practice with program goals is the integration of communication instruction and practice with the students' technical work.

4. IMPLEMENTATION

Assuming we've identified outcomes and how they fit into the program and the courses that comprise it, the next step is implementation. It is not sufficient to simply design assignments that force students to communicate; rather, it is necessary to provide instruction and other modes of guidance to help students learn to communicate. This involves designing assignments that incorporate communication, providing students the instruction they need to successfully complete those assignments, and responding to student work in a way that provides meaningful assessment and feedback.

4.1 Transferable Knowledge and Skills

For students to build on the communication knowledge and abilities they develop in one course, they must be able to transfer significant portions what they learned in the first course to the different context of the second [18]. Various writing researchers have theorized the conceptual frameworks and practical abilities this involves [15][19][20].

Our approach, based in the theory of genres (types) of communication, has been pragmatic. It involves the creation of scenarios. Students are given a workplace narrative in which they must solve a technical problem and also communicate the results to someone else who must use these results to perform his or her own work [5]. In most cases, the scenarios require students to use a specific genre, such as a bug report, requirement specification, design specification, UML, or developer guide. According to genre theory, genres are typified communication types that address the needs of both writer and reader in recurring situations [21]. By using scenarios to concretize the ways that genres transact practical action in the CS/SE profession, we transform what might be for students the more or less rudimentary act of filling in the outline of a genre. By using scenarios, our approach asks students to learn how to *use* genres to meet the specific needs of specific persons. Thus, for instance, they learn not only what kind of information goes into a particular part of a design specification but also exactly how much detail is required to satisfy a particular designer's need, what kind of information should be omitted because it would be distracting, and how the information could be organized and formatted to make it as easy as possible for the designer to use. The transferable content of this kind of learning includes understanding the nature of genres, the ways genres need to be adapted to specific situations, the techniques used in the CS/SE profession to make these adaptations, and (above all) the importance of designing communications to serve their readers. Even if students don't create a certain genre again in their studies, they have gained transferable knowledge and skills from their one encounter with it.

This approach provides for development along several lines. First, as students advance through their studies, the complexity of the information they need to communicate increases—and increased complexity requires enhanced communication skill. Similarly, as students advance through their studies, they learn more about the overall process and workflows in which they will work. Students also learn more about the intricacies of the communication challenges they will face in their careers. Courses that introduce these higher levels of communication challenge can also introduce more sophisticated communication strategies to students. Also, the projects students work on for real clients, whether in the senior design course or other classes, present them with opportunities for faculty to teach them even more sophisticated communication abilities.

4.2 Alternatives

There are different ways to approach student instruction. One is to have communication instruction provided by CS/SE faculty. This was the approach proposed and demonstrated by our project. It has two main advantages. One is that CS/SE faculty members are (or should be) the experts in the types of communication used in their domain and are best equipped to situate communication in a CS/SE context. The second advantage is that having CS/SE faculty provide the instruction reinforces the fact that communicating is a critical skill for computer scientists and is central to their career success.

An alternative approach is to create partnerships between CS/SE faculty and communication specialists in which they work jointly to create assignments but the communication instruction is provided by the communication faculty. Large-scale efforts that encompass many departments exist, for example, at MIT [22] and Chalmers [23] Institutes of Technology. Perelman [24] discusses the substantial expense of maintaining a large enough staff to provide sufficient support for such arrangements—and, using data from MIT, argues that the money is well spent.

NC State uses a hybrid model in which CS/SE faculty provide the communication instruction in all courses except senior design, in which a communication specialist is fully integrated into the course. For instance, this specialist meets regularly with design teams throughout their projects. At Chalmers, project teams have back-to-back meetings with their technical and communication mentors.

4.3 Training Faculty

Including assignments that require communication is not sufficient to improve student skills. It is necessary to provide instruction and useful feedback to the students.

Faculty training can be done by people on our campuses who specialize in communication across the curriculum (CAC). These specialists study the different kinds of communication appropriate to different fields. They can help CS/SE faculty provide instruction and guidance in teaching their students to become more effective communicators. For example, they provide advice in creating assignments, assignment sheets, and evaluation rubrics. They can present effective strategies for responding to student work and improving student performance and writing, speaking, and teamwork. They can also provide guidance on using rubrics for faculty and TA training in assessing communication.

Not all institutions will have access to CAC specialists or other dedicated personnel to assist with communication instruction. Plus, as described earlier, there are advantages in having the CS faculty provide the training. While CS faculty are familiar with the types of communication used in their domain, they may not be comfortable teaching communication in the classroom or in assessing the results and providing meaningful feedback. One approach to assisting faculty is to provide workshops on teaching and assessing communication. Our project involved several summer workshops in which faculty were given instruction on creating assignments that integrated communication in with the technical material and on writing rubrics for assessing communication skills. These workshops also included the opportunity to do peer evaluation to compare strategies and receive feedback. An abbreviated version of these workshops was conducted at SIGCSE in 2012, where sessions were held on teaching, writing, speaking and teaming; situating communication in a real-world context; and writing rubrics to evaluate and provide feedback on communication assignments.

In order to support faculty (both currently involved in the project and future faculty that may want to use our resources), we configured and deployed two online software packages meant to facilitate collaboration and sharing of resources. First, we provided access to a social networking system, based on Elgg (http://elgg.org), where participants could post and comment on assignments according to disciplinary teams created for the project. Second, we created a digital archive where instructors could post final version of their assignments, rubrics, and other support materials. While the first system was meant for facilitating collaboration, this second system, implemented using Omeka (http://omeka.org), was meant for distribution to a wider audience and supports many of the features found in digital archiving systems including content and metadata-based search, and social tagging. To date, the repository (located at http://cs-comm.lib.muohio.edu) has over 100 assignments and instructional guides related to the integration of communication into CS/SE curricula.

5. SUMMARY AND CONCLUSIONS

General and domain-specific reading, writing, speaking, and teaming, are essential abilities for a good computer scientist or software engineer. Today such skills are transferred to graduates either through stand-alone technical communication courses, or through writing-intensive courses, or a mixture of both. In the case of courses resident in domain-specific colleges and departments, communication skills may or may not be taught by CS/SE domain experts. While the CS/SE education community is conscious of the need to teach communication skills and a considerable amount of communication takes place in more human-interaction focused courses (such as software engineering, and hands-on capstone courses), it appears to be far less common to have a conscious and explicit program-wide integration of teaching such skills by CS/SE domain-specialists.

We discussed the current state of communication teaching in the CS/SE domain, and a framework we developed for program-wide implementation of communication skills starting in the freshmen year and culminating with capstone projects. Data, examples and lessons learned were derived from 12 USA CS/SE departments. Program-wide teaching of communications skills to CS/SE students involves not only (relatively unobtrusive) interventions at the individual course level throughout the curriculum, but also nurturing of the cumulative effect of such efforts; course-level and program-level assessment, such as conscious and explicit tracking of the growing communications skills of the students throughout the curriculum (including those that may come in laterally through internships and co-ops); and explicit training of the domain-specific faculty to both raise their awareness and provide them with approaches and methods that work but which they can customize to their specific courses and comfort. In fact, appropriate sensitization of the faculty to the issue may be one of the most important components of success. However, institutional, or at least program department-level, support and involvement is essential in order to replace heroic efforts of enthusiastic individual instructors with a sustainable institutional implementation. This higher-level support is necessary to overcome faculty concerns about the effort required to teach and assess communication. The work on this project continues with an evaluation of the student work collected during the project. At project completion, a collection of resources (intervention content, tools, approaches, assessment tools, training materials) will be made available to the broader community. Current results are available at http://cs-comm.lib.muohio.edu.

6. ACKNOWLEDGMENTS

This work was funded by NSF CPATH-II Awards CCF-0939122 and CCF-0939081. Opinions, findings, and conclusions or recommendations expressed in this material are those of the authors and do not necessarily reflect the views of the National Science Foundation (NSF). We would also like to acknowledge the invaluable contributions of our project participants.

7. REFERENCES

[1] Walia, G., and Carver, J. 2007. "Development of Requirement Error Taxonomy as a Quality Improvement Approach: A Systematic Literature Review." Technical Report, Department of Computer Science and Engineering, Mississippi State University, April 4, 2007. MSU-07040.

[2] Naphas, J. 2010. "PREDICTING SOFTWARE FAULTS" an FAA publication, Federal Aviation Administration/AST-300, 800 Independence Avenue SW, Washington, DC 20591, USA; 2010,

[3] Burge, J., Gannod, G., Anderson, P., Rosine, K., Vouk, M., Carter, M. 2012. Characterizing Communication Instruction in Computer Science and Engineering Programs, to appear in Frontiers in Education

[4] Biggs, J. 1999 Teaching for Quality Learning at University, Buckingham, UK: SRHE and Open UP.

[5] Carter, M., Gannod, G., Burge, J., Anderson, P., Vouk, M., Hoffman, M. 2011 Communication Genres: Integrating Communication into the Software Engineering Curriculum, Proc. Of CSEE&T 2011

[6] Russell, D. R. 2002. Writing in the Academic Disciplines: A Curricular History. Carbondale: Southern Illinois UP.

[7] Connors, R. J. 1982. The rise of technical writing instruction in America. Journal of Technical Writing and Communication, 12.4: 329-353.

[8] Reave, L. 2004. Technical communication instruction in engineering schools: A survey of top-ranked U.S. and Canadian programs. Journal of Business and Technical Communication, 18(4), pp. 452-490.

[9] Townsend, M. 2001. "Writing Intensive Courses and WAC." WAC for the New Millennium: Strategies for Continuing WAC Programs, eds. Susan H. McLeod, Eric Miraglia, Margot Soven, and Christopher Thaiss. Urbana: NCTE (2001), 223-258.

[10] Haswell, R.H., 1991. Gaining Ground in College Writing: Tales of Development and Interpretation. Southern Methodist University Press.

[11] Bereiter, C., Scardamalia, M.. 1993 Surpassing Ourselves: An Inquiry into the Nature and Implications of Expertise. Chicago: Open Court.

[12] Walvoord, B. E., McCarthy, L.P., 1991 Thinking and Writing in College: A Naturalistic Study of Students in Four Disciplines. Urbana, IL: National Council of Teachers of English.

[13] Dias, P., Freedman, Medway, P., and A. Pare, A. 1999, Worlds apart: Acting and writing in academic and workplace contexts. Mahwah, NJ: Erlbaum.

[14] Bazerman, C. 1982. Scientific writing as a social act. In New Essays in Technical and Scientific Communication, ed. P. V. Anderson, R.J. Brockmann, and C. R. Miller. Farmingdale, NY: Baywood.

[15] Beaufort, A. 2007. College Writing and Beyond: A New Framework for University Writing Instruction Logan, UT: Utah State UP.

[16] Ruff, S., Carter, M. 2009. Communication learning outcomes from software engineering professionals: A basis for teaching communication in the engineering curriculum. *2009 Frontiers in Education Conference*, (W1E) 1-6.

[17] Burge, J., Anderson, P., Gannod, G., Carter, M., Vouk, M. 2012. First Steps Toward Integrating Communication Instruction Throughout Computer Science and Software Engineering Curricula, Computers in Education Journal, April-June 2012

[18] Moore, J. 2012. Mapping the Question: The state of writing-related transfer research. Composition Forum. http://compositionforum.com/issue/26/. Accessed September 6, 2012.

[19] Flower, L. Hayes, J.R., 1981 A cognitive process theory of writing. College Composition and Communication. 32.4: 365-387.

[20] Carter, M. 1990. The idea of expertise: An exploration of the cognitive and social dimensions of writing. College Composition and Communication. 41.3: 265-286.

[21] Miller, C. R. 1984. Genres as social action. Quarterly Journal of Speech. 70: 151-167.

[22] MIT. 2012. "Why a WAC Lecturer?" http://writing.mit.edu/wac/CIM/whyaWAClecturer. Accessed September 5, 2012.

[23] Chalmers University of Technology. 2012 "Language and Communication." http://www.ait.gu.se/english/language-and-communication/. Accessed September 5, 2012.

[24] Perelman, L. 2011 "WAC Revisited: You Get What You Pay For." The Writing Instructor. http://www.writinginstructor.com/30wac. Accessed September 5, 2012.

Metaphors We Teach By

Joseph P. Sanford
Dept. of Computer Science
Tufts University
Medford, MA, USA
joe@cs.tufts.edu

Aaron Tietz
Dept. of Computer Science
Tufts University
Medford, MA, USA
aaron.tietz@tufts.edu

Saad Farooq
Dept. of Computer Science
Tufts University
Medford, MA, USA
sfarooq@cs.tufts.edu

Samuel Guyer
Dept. of Computer Science
Tufts University
Medford, MA, USA
sguyer@cs.tufts.edu

R. Benjamin Shapiro
Dept. of Computer Science
Dept. of Education
Tufts University
Medford, MA, USA
ben@cs.tufts.edu

ABSTRACT

In this paper we present an initial study of how metaphors are used by university-level Computer Science instructors. The goal of this research is to gain a better understanding of the role that metaphors play in Computer Science education, to catalog the kinds of metaphors that are used, and to assess their effectiveness in supporting learning. We interviewed 10 educators in Computer Science about the metaphors they have used in the classroom, with a focus on introductory "CS1" programming courses. We analyze these interviews with an existing theory of metaphors, which provides a framework for describing their structure and features. The theory predicts that most metaphors have limitations, and eventually fall apart. Therefore, we also asked educators to assess how far they could push their metaphors with and to describe what happens at the breaking point. Our preliminary findings provide a foundation to inform and guide more in-depth analyses in the future.

Categories and Subject Descriptors

K.3.2 [**Computer and Information Science Education**]: Computer Science Education

General Terms

Human Factors, Theory

Keywords

metaphors, CS1, pedagogical content knowledge, teaching

SIGCSE'14, March 5–8, 2014, Atlanta, GA, USA.

ACM 978-1-4503-2605-6/14/03 ...$15.00.
http://dx.doi.org/10.1145/2538862.2538945.

> "[...] unless you are at home in the metaphor, unless you have had your proper poetical education in the metaphor, you are not safe anywhere. Because you are not at ease with figurative values: you don't know the metaphor in its strength and its weakness. You don't know how far you may expect to ride it and when it may break down with you. You are not safe with science; you are not safe in history."
> – Robert Frost[2]

1. INTRODUCTION

Research on teaching increasingly points to the importance of teachers' knowledge about how to teach in ways that are not only responsive to the general needs of learners, but to particularities of learning in different disciplinary areas [15, 3, 14, 5]. Knowledge that is particular to the intersection of content knowledge and teaching has been called Pedagogical Content Knowledge (PCK)[16]. A common way in which teachers adapt pedagogical knowledge for the particular content of Computer Science (i.e., generate PCK) is by utilizing metaphors that explain computing concepts with the aid of ideas that are already familiar to students.

Many fields of teaching use metaphor to explain disciplinary ideas. They do so because metaphors offer a mapping from a concept familiar to students (the source domain) to a new concept (the target domain). Investigations of metaphors in teaching have been conducted for other STEM fields of study such as Biology[12], Chemistry[17], and Mathematics[1]. While the use of metaphors is commonplace in Computer Science classrooms, there is a paucity of research on this practice. While metaphorical language in teaching Computer Science has been previously touched on[13], including discussions of particular metaphors[4, 10], metaphorical language has not been examined in detail, such as through investigation of the various metaphors used by teachers to explain different CS topics, or through examination of the cognitive consequences for students of different metaphorical explanations of the same topics.

One facet of metaphors that should be of interest to researchers and teachers is the limitations of metaphors, both in general and in particular instances. A feature of many metaphors is that when their mappings are pushed beyond their user's intended limits, they eventually break down[9]. Those intended limits may be unknown to learners, and thus opportunities for spurious inferences arise. It may be helpful to instructors to be able to anticipate common misunderstandings caused by learners' overstretching of metaphors into mismatches between metaphorical source domains and their explanatory targets, leading to explanatory breakdown. As yet, Computer Science educators have no published literature about commonly used metaphors, which metaphors are most helpful to students' learning, what the common breakdown points of those metaphors are, and how those breakdowns are manifested in student activity. As Computer Science education continues to grow as a field of study, investigating metaphor use, particularly with an eye toward discovering how to use metaphors more productively in the classroom, may enable the development of pedagogies to support the retention and success of more students in computing.

This paper reports on a study of the use of metaphors for teaching Computer Science concepts through interviews of CS1 instructors. The goal of this preliminary study is to identify CS1 topics where metaphors are used, what metaphors are used to explain those topics, to search for any common themes that are present across these metaphors, and to gather data about how instructors think about breakdowns of the metaphors that they use.

2. BACKGROUND

Metaphorical language is employed in everyday life, both in thought and action, and is now considered to be a crucial component of thinking[7]. In particular, conceptual metaphors (i.e., cognitive mechanisms which project from a source domain to a target domain in order to facilitate understanding of a concept[11] in the target domain) are of interest in educational environments.

To fully comprehend the cognitive effects of combining metaphor and pedagogy, a general framework of the correlation between metaphor and understanding must be defined. The theories behind metaphors and their use has been recently redefined, thus leading to a "contemporary theory of metaphor" [6]. This theory, proposed by Lakoff, introduces the nature, structure, and aspects of metaphors, and provides a framework in which metaphors can be defined, explained, and evaluated.

Lakoff's theory explains that metaphors are the primary means in which we comprehend abstract concepts, while also expanding on the Aristotelian definition of metaphors. The differences between these two theories lies primarily in several assumptions, particularly that everyday language is rich with metaphor, and therefore widely used (including pedagogically), and that information can be understood without the use of metaphor.[7]. In both Lakoff and Aristotle's definitions, metaphors are defined as mappings across different conceptual domains that allow for understanding of relatively abstract or unstructured subject matter in the terms of a more defined subject matter. These mappings are from a source domain to a target domain, with the source domain defined as the familiar, real-world concept that maps to the target domain, defined as the concept that is being taught. For instance, the metaphor "pointers are like file folders" has a source domain of file folders and a target domain of pointers. At their core, these mappings are:

Partial in that no source domains can map to every aspect of a target domain.

Fixed in mappings, with a static set of correspondences between entities in a source domain and those in a target domain.

Based upon everyday knowledge in order to create mappings from source domains that are already understood.

These aspects of metaphor are important to consider when analyzing metaphors, as they not only demonstrate the importance of source domains used in metaphors, but also explain that no metaphor contains a full, one-to-one mapping across domains, which may lead to limitations. Using this structure and theory of metaphor provides a foundation upon which metaphors can be broken down and examined. Lakoff himself used this theory when discussing understanding mathematical concepts[8].

Thornbury used Lakoff's theory to investigate and evaluate metaphors used for teaching and training[18]. This provided a framework of the nature, structure, and aspects of metaphors for reviewing awareness of metaphor use, evaluation of metaphors, and arguments for using metaphors in training within the scope of teaching English as a second language. In a similar vein, this paper will analyze and compare metaphors using the same definitions laid out by Lakoff.

3. THE STUDY

One-on-one, semi-structured interviews of approximately 15 minutes were conducted with each participant via telephone, VOIP, or face-to-face. Each audio-recorded interview consisted of 7 questions, along with any follow-up questions for clarification.

3.1 Participants

Participants were 10 instructors that teach or have taught CS1 at a university level in the United States. The participants were found through recommendations by the researchers' colleagues and a posting on the SIGCSE mailing list, and volunteered to participate. Participants' mean number of years of Computer Science teaching experience was 12.9 years, with a minimum of 2 years and a maximum of 40 years.

3.2 Study Protocol

Interviewers asked all participants the following questions:

1. At what levels have you taught Computer Science?
2. How long have you been teaching Computer Science?
3. Please tell me about a metaphor you have used in your teaching to help explain some idea or technique from Computer Science.
4. Can you describe how the metaphor explains the CS topic?
5. What are common questions that students have?
6. Where does the metaphor start to break down?
7. How do you handle that when you're teaching?

Follow-up questions were asked as appropriate; in some cases, multiple metaphors were discussed. Upon request by participants, the questions and motivation for the interview were provided in advance, allowing them time to contemplate their responses.

4. FINDINGS

All but two participants offered at least one metaphor. Each interview was analyzed utilizing the previously discussed theory of conceptual metaphors. Given the defining factors and features of metaphors under Lakoff's definition, we were able to investigate the metaphorical mappings, how these mappings hold, target domains of the metaphors, and therefore make conjectures on how effective the metaphors used can be. Table 1 details the mappings of target and source domains of the metaphors discussed by participants.

The components of metaphors used by instructors can be categorized by what they ask students to focus on. Categories include a process (e.g., a recipe mapping to a program), a whole action (e.g., a verb mapping to a function), a collection of spatial relationship between two locations (e.g., consecutive street addresses mapping to an array), a physical relationship between two objects (e.g., a box and its contents mapping to a variable and its contents), and a relationship between a value and a location (e.g., a card in a card catalog and the book it describes mapping to a pointer and its target). Many metaphors contain components in multiple categories. For example, a portkey was offered as a metaphor for a return statement in response to a large proportion of students incorrectly responding to exam questions on the topic. Many students believed that multiple return statements in one function enumerated a set of values that are returned, rather than a single value that is returned once the return statement is executed. This shows that some metaphors are selected due to particular student misunderstandings. This metaphor also contains one component that describes a relationship between two physical locations, one that describes an action (immediately leaving one context for another), and one that describes a value standing for something else (some knowledge in an item representing another location).

4.1 Atomic vs. Complex Metaphors

Another feature found was the difference in scope of the metaphors. Some metaphors mapped a single feature between the source and target domains rather than a complex, algorithmic process. These algorithmic processes have multiple mappings between the source and target domains, some of which are explicitly elaborated in the intended usage. The most striking example was one participant's use of the portkey from *Harry Potter*. In *Harry Potter*, a portkey is a magical object that when touched, returns a person to a specific location. This was employed as a metaphor for return statements. The participant stated that the usage of the metaphor arose from confusion among the students regarding the number of values returned by a function that had multiple return statements, as in the following pseudocode:

```
def foo():
    if bar == 1:
        return 1
    else if bar == 2:
        return 2
    return False
```

Source Domain	Target Domain
Harry Potter portkeys	Return statements
Cookbooks and recipes	Functions, subroutines, looping, etc.
Cooking	Functions, encapsulation, storing data, etc.
Driving a car	Sequence of execution in code
Verbs	Functions
The Grim Reaper	Garbage collector
Learning a human language	Learning to program
Inception	Recursion
Street addresses	Recursive array indexing
Boxes	Variables and arrays
Containers	
Bookmarks	Return addresses
Telling a story	Algorithms
Card catalogs	Pointers
File folders	
Zombies	
Splitting students into two groups	Relationship of memory and CPU
Prioritizing customers for car repairs	Heaps
Campus dining hall dishes	Stacks and heaps
Cookie cutters and cookies	Classes and objects

Table 1: Source and target domains for metaphors reported by participants.

The portkey metaphor itself only deals with one specific action and is rooted in the fact that the source domain has additional, minor components, that are related to one predominant property, that it transfers context. It does not explain sequential control flow in programming in general but only one atomic action, as opposed to the aforementioned metaphors that deal with an entire process and are therefore more complex in their mappings with the source domain.

Boxes and containers were also atomic metaphor source domains that were noted on three separate occasions by different participants. The domains were all mapped to the same target domain, variables, in the same manner. Containers were presented as being able to hold an object (or value) in a simple one-to-one mapping. The only extension of this metaphor was the target domain of an array. This is arguably still the same metaphor repeated, and still maintains its atomicity.

Another atomic metaphor very similar to the portkey metaphor was the use of the source target of a physical bookmark mapped to a target domain of a return statement. The participant who discussed this metaphor stated that it only had one simple use, and the source and domain mappings could no longer be expanded. It was noted that adding another feature, such as a value to a return statement, invalidated the metaphor. Despite this, the participant still noted that this atomic metaphor was useful as a subset of the cookbook source domain.

While many atomic metaphors may be seen as simple, they have been reported to still be of value – whether considered individually or as a subset of a larger metaphor. It was reported that these metaphors never elicited any questions from students. This may indicate that atomic metaphors are much easier for students to grasp.

4.2 Usage of Same Source Domain Mappings

We also found that the same source domains were mapped to more than one target domain. One participant with over 10 years of experience explained that a cookbook provided an excellent way to teach new students about the techniques of programming during their first two weeks of class. These mappings include a recipe's steps being mapped to imperative commands, acting differently based on a food property being mapped to selection, stirring until smooth being mapped to looping, sub-recipes (e.g., a sauce for a dish) being mapped to subroutines, a book mark being mapped to a return address, and referencing a recipe written in full only once mapping to abstraction, easily updated code, and code reuse. This participant admitted that after the first two weeks the metaphor wasn't of much use, but expressed that students had few problems with it and that it helped them get used to a new set of ideas.

Another participant, also with greater than 10 years of experience, felt that the recipe metaphor fell so short as to not be very useful. The participant explained that while students have a familiarity with cooking, they do not have one with programming language primitives. While this line of thinking led the first participant to use the cooking metaphor, the second expressed the need to identify with the discomfort students were feeling about learning a new language. This participant compared learning to program to learning a human language.

The use of the same source domains with mappings to different target domains is notable as elements can represent various aspects of different target domains. This may indicate that some source domains may be more useful than others, and may even be used repeatedly throughout an instructor's pedagogy. They may also be richer and more complex, allowing for more mappings between source and target domains.

4.3 Usage of Same Target Domain Mappings

During the study, it was also found that the same target domain was mapped to more than one source domain. Several participants described how they used metaphors to explain pointers, though the source domains that they drew from – and therefore the mappings to the target domain as well – were different. One participant used the source domain of a card catalog, mapping the cards to the pointers themselves and shelves to memory, with the data residing on the shelves. Another participant used a somewhat similar source domain of the organization of file folders, with indices of both which drawer the paper (i.e., data) was stored, and which folder within that drawer. Both of these metaphors mapped to a physical source domain with similar features, such as objects containing other objects and a referent to where the "data" could be found. However, the file folders source domain is slightly more extensible, as it can refer to double indirection. While the target domain was the same as the previous two metaphors, a third participant described pointers with the source domain of zombies. This was described as zombies containing nothing in their head, and can just point to "real" data, or humans. Unlike the first two source domains for pointers, this domain does not use inanimate objects that students could physically interact with, but instead actual agents that the students themselves could represent.

The first source domain of a card catalog was cited as a poor source domain, due to being a concept that students may be less familiar with. However, the second source domain of file folders was perceived to be easily understood by the students, and it was cited that the physical aspect and extensible nature of this domain led to this understanding. The third source domain followed in the same pattern, as it was described as extensible as well. It was reported that as students had certain questions, they were easily answered within the domain (e.g., "What does a zombie initially point to?" which was answered as zombies are useless until they are assigned a victim). However, the zombie and file folder source domains may promote different levels of understanding, as one contains actual agents instead of inanimate objects. Though the source domains varied, there seemed to be similar features present across all domains.

The use of the same target domains with mappings to different source domains is notable as it shows that some target domains can be mapped to more than one source domain. While this may be simply a difference in pedagogical strategies between respondents, it may also show insight into these metaphors. The difficulty in understanding target domains might lead to a variety of source domains being used for a single target, as instructors attempt to find a useful tool to mitigate student confusion, but this is yet to be studied. It may also serve as a means of comparison between source domains.

4.4 Limitations of Metaphors

While limitations of any pedagogical strategy may be seen as a negative aspect, understanding the limitations of metaphors in Computer Science can aid in making them more effective. When asked questions 6 and 7 of the protocol, many instructors responded by stating that once a metaphor has reached its limit, they no longer use it in the classroom. Others, however, reported that sometimes these limitations in what a metaphor can explain can sometimes lead to more confusion. For example, one respondent noted that they believed students attempted to extend a metaphor to a point where they believed false, additional mappings between domains. Limitations were found across many different facets of the metaphors discussed. Limitations were found regarding the source domain, target domain, and/or mappings of these domains. For example, source domains were reported to sometimes be obscure (e.g., certain films that students may have not seen), and mappings between domains were reported to sometimes be limited (e.g., the variables are containers metaphor is limited in extensibility). Other limitations were aspects of metaphor defined under Lakoff's definition of metaphor. Table 2 lists some of the main limitations both reported by participants, and others of note.

Out of date or obscure source domains can be a large limitation of using metaphors in the classroom. For example, the source domain of a card catalog may be foreign to many students as many students may have not used a card catalog previously. If students are not familiar enough with the source domain of a metaphor, their understanding of the

Out of date/obscure source domains	Cultural differences
Mapping to low-level details often fails	Increases in target domain complexity
Limited mappings	None reported

Table 2: Common limitations found across responses.

concept may not be increased. Instructors reported that the most effective metaphors were those that had source domains that students were very familiar with. One respondent in particular noted that their source domains for their metaphors often changed once the domains were no longer part of popular culture. The participant stated that certain metaphors, such as the source domain *Inception* mapping to the target domain of recursion may not be used much longer by the participant. This is due to the participant recognizing the limitations of the metaphor, as the source domain will eventually be less familiar to students, and a new source domain would be used in its place. It was reported that this has occurred in the past, and changing to more modern source domains has always been the participant's response to out-of-date source domains. Cultural differences are also a limitation of metaphors as their source domains, as students from different cultures may not have any familiarity with the source domain.

Another reported limitation of metaphors is that, at a certain point, they begin to break down and can no longer be expanded to further explain a concept (or related concepts). Three participant instructors stated that while metaphors can offer a high-level framework for a concept, they cannot be extended to low-level features of the target domain (such as the implementation of a data structure). This is an inherent feature of metaphors, as source and target domains are not identical. Because metaphors are only partial mappings between source and target domains, they may break down as learners explore a concept in more detail, or examine a concept as part of a larger system.

4.5 Students' Understanding of Metaphors

Three participants stated that there were no limitations of their metaphors. No participants were able to give examples of students' misunderstandings caused by confusion about metaphorical mappings, aside from some of them mentioning the places they tend to break down. It has been previously reported that all metaphors do in fact break down[9], leading us to hypothesize that either *a*) there is something special about metaphors in CS that enable them to withstand breakdown or *b*) instructors have poor understandings of their students' thinking about the metaphors that are used in their courses, including how metaphorical breakdown leads to misunderstandings of CS1 concepts. Given that *b* seems far more likely, there is a need for research into what these misunderstandings are and how teachers can better reason about student thinking around them in the classroom. If limitations are known, certain metaphors may be abandoned or limitations disclaimed to students in order to reduce confusion. Further research involving teaching assistants and students will help to illuminate where gaps in teachers' knowledge exist, and how they might be closed.

5. CONCLUSIONS

This preliminary study provides initial insights into the use of conceptual metaphors in Computer Science education. While metaphor may be a very useful pedagogical tool, it is also one that must be used with knowledge of its limitations. What those limitations are for different Computer Science topics, and for mappings between particular source and target domains, would, thus, seem to be vital Pedagogical Content Knowledge. Given our findings that CS1 teachers use a wide variety of metaphors but that those same instructors were generally unable to explain common questions and misunderstandings students had when using those metaphors, further research is needed into student thinking about CS1 topics when scaffolded by metaphors. This may aid in broader understanding of the range of metaphors that are currently used, and deeper understandings of which are more effective in presenting new concepts, and why.

6. FUTURE WORK

One direction for future research is to analyze how metaphors break down. Further insight into why, when, and how some metaphors break down is needed. Three participants noted that metaphors they used never ceased to explain the target domain, however attempting to extend these metaphors past their limits will likely show that, in fact, all metaphors do break down. Additionally, determining exactly when certain metaphors fall apart may show common features of the metaphors themselves, and may help identify when other metaphors lose their effectiveness, ultimately supporting a theory of breakdown which might predict student misunderstandings. Such a theory might encompass different dimensions which affect metaphor breakdown. The mapping between source and target domains may not be strong initially, or the similarities between domains may be shallow.

Despite the limited size of this preliminary study, we found shared target and source domains in instructor metaphor use. Examining the use of the same source domains may offer insight into how effective these domains may be for students, as they map to the same target domain. Also of note is the use of the same target domain, as the overlap in mappings may also have an effect on students' understanding. Another similar observation was that the complexity of mappings can affect the implementation of metaphors in instruction. Atomic metaphors may have less potential for future confusion due to their simplicity of mappings. However, these mappings may be limited and less extensible. Future studies may show if these features of source and target domains continues to be a dominate feature of metaphor use in CS1.

Another area of interest would be examining the views of students with regards to certain metaphors used in the classroom. As students' understanding is a facet of Pedagogical Content Knowledge, it may offer further insight regarding how useful metaphors can be in Computer Science. While three participants responded that no students had any follow up questions, that does not necessarily rule out any confusion or misunderstanding that the students may have. Instructors may also hold false assumptions of some metaphors used, and may overestimate students' understanding. Additionally, metaphors may break down to students much earlier than some participants believed. Students may also attempt to extend metaphors on their own, not knowing the limitations of these metaphors. Gauging student understanding may be accomplished through the use of clickers for instant feedback for instructors, or student interviews. Studying the classroom as a whole may be most beneficial, as both sides of understanding and pedagogy of the use of metaphors could be examined simultaneously through the viewpoints of instructors, teaching assistants, and students.

Not only would this further research be of academic interest (supporting our understandings of how learning happens in Computer Science courses), but it is also of crucial practical importance. Research on metaphor and other pedagogical techniques in CS1 could produce a useful, empirically grounded knowledge base[3] for teachers illuminating the most productive ways to support students' learning of different computational ideas. At minimum, it should offer a guide to what the most effective metaphors are to explain particular ideas, and ideally should go well beyond this to include guidance on how to construct in-class activities for students that push them to explicate, refine, and build upon their emerging computational ideas. Such a knowledge base could be a nexus of strong partnership between researchers of Computer Science education and teachers that could not only advance research on learning, but improve outcomes for a large number of students.

7. ACKNOWLEDGMENTS

We would like to thank all of the participants for offering their time to this study.

8. REFERENCES

[1] P. Boero, L. Bazzini, and R. Garuti. Metaphors in teaching and learning mathematics: a case study concerning inequalities. In *PME Conference*, volume 2, pages 2–185, 2001.

[2] R. Frost. Education by poetry. *Selected Prose of Robert Frost*, pages 33–46, 1966.

[3] J. Hiebert, R. Gallimore, and J. W. Stigler. A knowledge base for the teaching profession: What would it look like and how can we get one? *Educational researcher*, 31(5):3–15, 2002.

[4] R. Jiménez-Peris, C. Pareja-Flores, M. Patiño-Martínez, and J. Á. Velázquez-Iturbide. The locker metaphor to teach dynamic memory. In *ACM SIGCSE Bulletin*, volume 29, pages 169–173. ACM, 1997.

[5] V. Kind. Pedagogical content knowledge in science education: perspectives and potential for progress. *Studies in science education*, 45(2):169–204, 2009.

[6] G. Lakoff et al. The contemporary theory of metaphor. *Metaphor and thought*, 2:202–251, 1993.

[7] G. Lakoff and M. Johnson. *Metaphors we live by.* University of Chicago press, 2008.

[8] G. Lakoff and R. E. Núñez. *Where mathematics comes from: How the embodied mind brings mathematics into being.* Basic books, 2000.

[9] S. J. McCarthey and E. B. Moje. Identity matters. *Reading Research Quarterly*, 37(2):228–238, 2002.

[10] W. W. Milner. A broken metaphor in java. *ACM SIGCSE Bulletin*, 41(4):76–77, 2010.

[11] R. E. Núñez. Mathematical idea analysis: What embodied cognitive science can say about the human nature of mathematics. 2000.

[12] N. A. Paris and S. M. Glynn. Elaborate analogies in science text: Tools for enhancing preservice teachers' knowledge and attitudes. *Contemporary Educational Psychology*, 29(3):230–247, 2004.

[13] R. T. Putnam, D. Sleeman, J. A. Baxter, and L. K. Kuspa. A summary of misconceptions of high school basic programmers. *Journal of Educational Computing Research*, 2(4):459–472, 1986.

[14] E. Seung, L. A. Bryan, and M. P. Haugan. Examining physics graduate teaching assistants' pedagogical content knowledge for teaching a new physics curriculum. *Journal of Science Teacher Education*, 23(5):451–479, 2012.

[15] L. S. Shulman. Those who understand: Knowledge growth in teaching. *Educational researcher*, 15(2):4–14, 1986.

[16] L. S. Shulman. Knowledge and teaching: Foundations of the new reform. *Harvard educational review*, 57(1):1–23, 1987.

[17] G. P. Thomas and C. J. McRobbie. Using a metaphor for learning to improve students' metacognition in the chemistry classroom. *Journal of Research in Science Teaching*, 38(2):222–259, 2001.

[18] S. Thornbury. Metaphors we work by: Efl and its metaphors. *ELT Journal*, 45(3):193–200, 1991.

'Explain in Plain English' Questions Revisited: Data Structures Problems

Malcolm Corney
Queensland University of Technology
Brisbane, QLD, Australia
m.corney@qut.edu.au

Sue Fitzgerald
Metropolitan State University
St. Paul, MN USA
sue.fitzgerald@metrostate.edu

Brian Hanks
BFH Educational Consulting
Seattle, WA USA
brianhanks@acm.org

Raymond Lister
University of Technology, Sydney
Sydney, Australia
Raymond.Lister@uts.edu.au

Renée McCauley
College of Charleston
Charleston, South Carolina USA
mccauleyr@cofc.edu

Laurie Murphy
Pacific Lutheran University
Tacoma, WA USA
lmurphy@plu.edu

ABSTRACT

Recent studies have linked the ability of novice (CS1) programmers to read and explain code with their ability to write code. This study extends earlier work by asking CS2 students to explain object-oriented data structures problems that involve recursion. Results show a strong correlation between ability to explain code at an abstract level and performance on code writing and code reading test problems for these object-oriented data structures problems. The authors postulate that there is a common set of skills concerned with reasoning about programs that explains the correlation between writing code and explaining code. The authors suggest that an overly exclusive emphasis on code writing may be detrimental to learning to program. Non-code writing learning activities (e.g., reading and explaining code) are likely to improve student ability to reason about code and, by extension, improve student ability to write code. A judicious mix of code-writing and code-reading activities is recommended.

Categories and Subject Descriptors

K.3.2 [**Computing Milieux**]: Computers and Education - Computer and Information Science Education

General Terms

Human Factors

Keywords

Explain in plain English, CS2, computer science education research, data structures, qualitative research methods, mixed methods, SOLO taxonomy, neo-Piaget.

SIGCSE'14, March 5–8, 2014, Atlanta, Georgia, USA.

http://dx.doi.org/10.1145/2538862.2538911

1. INTRODUCTION

Several recent studies have explored the relationship between the ability of novice programmers to read and explain code and their ability to write code [3, 7, 9, 10, 16, 17]. Whalley et al. (2006) [17] reported on a study in which first-semester students in an end-of-semester exam were given a question that began "In plain English, explain what the following segment of Java code does". They analyzed student responses to these "explain in plain English" (EiPE) problems using the Structure of the Observed Learning Outcome (SOLO) taxonomy [2]. The five SOLO reasoning categories describe how students understand problems in increasingly abstract ways. Table 1, adapted from Whalley et al., and copied from Murphy et al. [9], provides definitions for the first four SOLO categories for describing code. The highest level of reasoning shown in Table 1, *relational* reasoning, occurs when a student can describe the purpose of a code segment, with minimal or no reference to specific details of the code.

The fifth and highest SOLO level, *extended abstract*, is the stage at which an individual generalizes and applies his/her abstractions to new domains. Neither subjects in Whalley's study nor in this study were given problems which explored their ability to extend knowledge and therefore the extended abstract stage is not discussed further.

Table 1. SOLO Categories for Student Responses to "Explain in Plain English" (EiPE) problems

Category	Description
Relational	Provides a summary of what the code does in terms of the code's purpose.
Multistructural	A line-by-line description is provided of all the code.
Unistructural	Provides a description for only one portion of the code.
Prestructural	Substantially lacks knowledge of constructs or is unrelated to the question.

Whalley et al. found that the better a student performed on other programming-related tasks in that same exam, including code writing tasks, the more likely the student was to provide a relational response to an EiPE question. As a result, they hypothesized that "a vital step toward being able to write programs is the capacity to read a piece of code and describe [its function]."

Lopez et al. [7] built upon the work of Whalley et al., using stepwise regression to analyze first-semester student responses to an end-of-semester exam. They found that, when combined with student performance on code tracing problems, the ability to provide a correct relational response to an EiPE question accounted for almost half the variance in student performance on a code writing question in that same paper-based exam. That is, although student code writing performance varied considerably, on average code writing and code explaining combined were a good predictor of student ability to write code.

Venables, Tan and Lister [16] also found a strong correlation between first-semester student performance on tracing problems, EiPE problems, and code writing problems in a paper-based exam. Murphy et al. [9] also studied the relationship between introductory students' ability to explain code and to write code at the end of their first programming course. However, unlike the earlier studies in which students wrote code on paper, Murphy et al. [9] required students to write and implement code on a computer. Murphy et al. found results similar to those in the paper-based coding studies.

The success of some newer pedagogies in CS 1 [11] may be partly attributable to their support for the development of code explaining skills. For example, partners request and provide explanations of their code when pair programming [6] and students taught using peer instruction gain a deeper understanding of course material by explaining concepts to each other and by hearing others' explanations [14].

While previous studies have demonstrated a relationship between writing and explaining code in CS0 and CS1 courses, there have been no studies using "explain in plain English" problems beyond those introductory courses. While there appears to be benefit for students in introductory courses in explaining code to themselves and each other, the benefits of doing so as students progress have not previously been shown. This study investigates the relationship between students' ability to explain code and to write code in a data structures course. Our null hypothesis is:

H_0: There is no correlation between code writing and explaining code for students in a course on data structures.

This paper is organized as follows: Section 2 describes the study methodology. The results are presented in Section 3 and discussed in Section 4. Section 5 presents pedagogical implications and Section 6 gives ideas for future work.

2. METHODOLOGY

2.1 Participants

Participants were 120 out of 137 undergraduate students (14 female, 123 male) enrolled in their third programming related course titled "Data Structures and Algorithms", which was taught at a large publicly funded university. The semester-long course was taught using C++. In prior courses students programmed in Python and C#, and some participants were also concurrently enrolled in a software development course that used Java. Most participants were traditional college students (around 20 years of age) and most spoke English as their first language.

2.2 Data Collection

All data were collected during a written final exam that was scored out of 50 points and made up 50% of the final grade for the course. Problems on the exam required students to trace code, compare implementations and write code involving C++ pointers and standard template library classes, and compare and identify the runtimes of common data structure algorithms. The exam was preceded by two programming assignments. Assignment 1 was about poker hand evaluation (worth 20% of the final grade). Assignment 2 was an implementation of an algorithm for finding approximate solutions to the travelling salesman problem, using a minimum spanning tree and depth first search (worth 30% of the final grade).

2.3 Test Instrument

The problems of interest for this study were worth one point each (4 points total) out of 50 points for the written final exam. They were part of a larger question, which was worth 10 points. The problems asked students to trace and explain recursive methods that operated on a linked list. The tracing problems (3a and 3c below) were multiple choice and required students to trace code for a specific list made up of only two nodes. The explanation problems (3b and 3d below) required students to reason about the code generally and describe what it would do for any linked list.

Prolog to problems 3a & 3b

The questions that follow refer to the class `Node`. Below is the code that commences the definition of this class. This class is used to form a linked list. Each instance of class `Node` contains an integer `data`.

```
#include <cstddef>
using namespace std;
class Node {
   private:
     int data;
     Node *next;
   public:
     Node(int num, Node *nextNode) {
       data = num;
       next = nextNode;
     }
     int GetData() { return data; }
   // rest of class Node not shown here
};
```

The following code builds a linked list of two nodes, where `head` points to the first **Node** in the linked list:

```
Node *x = new Node(1, NULL);
Node *head = new Node(2, x);
```

That linked list is represented by the following diagram:

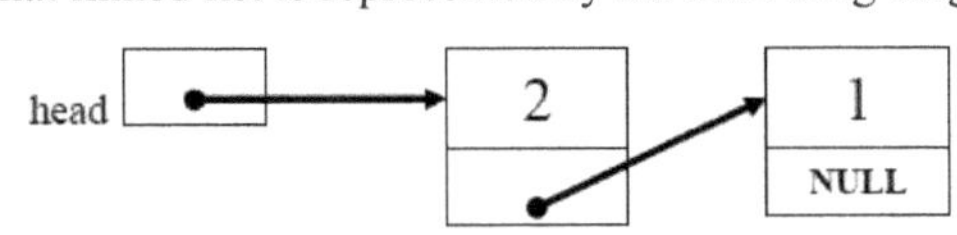

The function **Puzzle** is shown below and is a public function in the **Node** class.

```
bool Puzzle() {
   if (next == NULL)
      return true;
   else
      if (data < next->GetData())
        return false;
      else
        return next->Puzzle();
}
```

3a. If the function **Puzzle** was executed on the linked list shown [above] by executing the expression **head->Puzzle()** which one of the following statements is correct:

(i) The **Puzzle** functions in both objects would execute and both would return **false**.

(ii) The **Puzzle** functions in both objects would execute and both would return **true**.

(iii) Only the **Puzzle** function in the object containing **data = 2** would execute and it would return **false**

(iv) Only the **Puzzle** function in the object containing **data = 2** would execute and it would return **true**

(v) The **Puzzle** function in the object containing **data = 1** would return **true** and the **Puzzle** function in the object containing **data = 2** would return **false**.

(vi) The **Puzzle** function in the object containing **data = 1** would return **false** and the **Puzzle** function in the object containing **data = 2** would return **true**.

3b. Complete the following sentence: If the function call **head->Puzzle()** is invoked on **any** linked list of two or more nodes, then **head->Puzzle()** will return **true** if and only if ________________.

Prolog to problems 3c & 3d

The functions **Conundrum** and **Teaser** are shown below and are public functions in the **Node** class:

```
Node* Conundrum() {
        if (next == NULL)
                return this;
        else
                return next->Teaser(this);
}
Node* Teaser(Node *p) {
        Node *temp;
        if (data < p->GetData())
                temp = this;
        else
                temp = p;
        if (next == NULL)
                return temp;
        else
                return next->Teaser(temp);
}
```

3c. If the function **Conundrum** was executed on the linked list shown in (a), by executing the expression **head->Conundrum()**, which of the following statements is correct:

(i) The **Conundrum** function would return a pointer to the object containing **data = 1**.

(ii) The **Conundrum** function would return a pointer to the object containing **data = 2**.

3d. Complete the following sentence: If the function call **head->Conundrum()** was executed on **any** linked list of two or more objects of class **Node**, that expression would return a pointer to ________________.

2.4 Data Coding

Five of the six authors (henceforth the five "analysts") independently categorized the students' responses to the explanation problems (3b and 3d above) according to the SOLO taxonomy, as shown in Table 1. The analysts did not teach the course in which the data was collected (it was taught by the first author) although they were involved in the design of the test problems. All are experienced teachers and researchers. The researchers comprise a multi-national group.

Initially, each analyst coded independently. Then analysts met to discuss ratings, and tried to come to consensus on responses where there were differences. Details of these discussions are covered in section 3.1. Inter-rater agreement, from a statistical view, is discussed in section 3.2.

3. RESULTS

The code in 3a & b verifies that a list is in descending order. The correct answer for 3a is ii. The code in 3c & d returns a pointer to the node with the lowest data value. The correct answer for 3c is i.

Table 2 shows examples of typical responses to problems 3b and 3d which fall into each SOLO category.

Table 2. Examples for Each SOLO Reasoning Category

Category	Example Responses
Relational (R)	data in each node is in descending order (3b) pointer to the node with the lowest value (3d)
Multistructural (M)	following items in the list had a greater data value and second last element pointed to a list item with a greater data value and null for the next item (3b) first node that is smaller than its previous node or last node in list if all nodes are larger than previous (3d)
Unistructural (U)	next is not equal to null (3b) the last value in the list (3d)
Prestructural (P)	all values = null (3b) pointer to first object contains data = 1 and next = null (3d)

Through discussion among analysts, it became apparent that there were several responses that some analysts considered relational while others considered them to be multistructural. Similarly, there were a number of responses that received a mix of prestructural and unistructural ratings. After some consideration, it became clear the responses were largely divisible into two groups: those where the reasoning was at least multistructural, and those where the reasoning was unistructural at most. Given the nuances of these understandings, relational and multistructural answers were combined and unistructural and prestructural answers were combined for the purposes of statistical analysis.

3.1 Reliability of Data Coding

Analysts agreed on the ratings for a majority of participant responses. When answers were clean, concise and correct as shown in the first row in Table 2, all raters categorized them as relational. Answers which erred only in direction ("nodes sorted by data value in ascending order" rather than the correct "descending order") were also marked as relational. Similarly, nonsensical answers such as those in the last row of Table 2 were rated as prestructural by all analysts.

However, they disagreed on a fair number of responses and their discussions led to further consideration of how to apply the SOLO taxonomy to programming tasks. In the interests of explaining the use of the SOLO taxonomy as a tool for evaluating the quality of student explanations, a detailed discussion of the analysts' interpretations is given below.

Analysts disagreed on answers such as "all linked values are smaller than previous." Three of five analysts considered this correct answer to be relational because it demonstrated that the participant understood that the code verified that the nodes were in descending order. These analysts opined that a student can have a correct answer even if that answer is not expressed in the clearest possible way. The other two analysts rated this correct answer as multistructural since it provided a detailed explanation, rather than the succinct clarity indicating a deep understanding of the problem. These analysts argued that a correct answer is not necessarily relational; any answer explained in a detailed, line-by-line way is multistructural.

Other considerations were debated. During discussion, it became clear that some analysts took a strict interpretation of the SOLO categorization as described in Table 1. They focused on the student's description of the code. However, others considered a node by node discussion of the data structure to be multistructural. That is, they did not interpret multistructural as referring only to code but intuitively extended the definition to include descriptions of the data structure. This suggests a different interpretation than that used by Whalley et al. [17] in earlier studies of array-based problems for CS 1 students.

There were also some unresolved differences between ratings of unistructural and prestructural. This was perhaps a reflection of the individual analyst's willingness to read meaning into an answer. All analysts agreed that for many problems, there was little difference between incorrect unistructural and nonsensical prestructural answers. Unistructural and prestructural answers were combined for the purposes of statistical analysis.

A few answers triggered a wider range of classifications and sparked considerable discussion, for example, this answer to question 3b:

> "deeper values are less than predecessor" (1U, 2M, 2R)

Some analysts interpreted "deeper" as "nodes further along in the list", a relational answer, while other raters were not willing to add meaning to the written answer and judged the answer as multistructural or even unistructural.

Similarly, there was no consensus on the SOLO ranking for this answer to question 3b:

> "if next node returns true, the only way for the second node to return true is if the third node returns true as well" (1P, 1U, 3M)

Three raters noted that the student mentioned multiple nodes and interpreted this answer as multistructural. Others were unable to find meaning and interpreted it as prestructural or unistructural.

This response to question 3d also generated a mixed rating:

> "first node that has a smaller data value than the previous node" (3U, 2M)

Clearly this answer is not correct; the correct answer is "the code returns a reference to the smallest node". However, the subject refers to more than one node, leading to a multistructural categorization by 2 analysts. Yet, only two nodes are referenced which does not imply that the condition holds for the entire list. As a consequence three analysts categorized the answer as unistructural.

3.2 Quantitative Results

As mentioned previously, the final exam was worth 50 points, and the two EiPE problems studied were part of question 3, which was worth a total of 10 points. For the quantitative analysis in this section, the scores on question 3 were excluded from the final exam score, as the goal was to see how student performance on the EiPE problems was related to scores on other types of problems. Including question 3 would have artificially increased the correlation between the SOLO ratings and student performance. Thus, the final exam, for purposes of this study, was worth 40 points.

The SOLO ratings of P, U, M, and R were converted to integer equivalents (P -> 1, U -> 2, M -> 3, and R -> 4) for quantitative analysis. An average SOLO rating was computed for each participant's response on each problem. Indecisive ratings (e.g., a rating of "R/M") by individual analysts were scaled down (in this case, to "M"). Prior to the consensus meeting, there were 16 such indecisive ratings for responses to problem 3b and 20 for problem 3c (out of 600 ratings per problem); after the meeting, there were no indecisive ratings on either problem.

Participants were divided into two groups for each problem, based on average SOLO rating. One group (labeled the "R/M" group) had an average SOLO ranking of at least 3.0 (which means that their response was at least multi-structural). The other group (labeled "U/P") had an average SOLO ranking of at most 2.0, indicating that their response was unistructural at best.

Because the exam score and SOLO ratings were not uniformly distributed, nonparametric statistical tests were used for analysis. Specifically, the R statistical package [12], with a p value of .05 for significance was used.

Inter-rater Agreement

Inter-rater agreement was computed using Spearman's rank correlation coefficient rho, which is appropriate when there are more than two raters and the data is on an ordered scale. First, rho was computed for each pair of raters, and then the average of these values was computed. The level of inter-rater agreement before and after the meeting to discuss ranks and attempt to come to consensus was also computed.

On problem 3b Spearman's rho ranged from 0.669 to 0.938 with an average of 0.817 before the raters compared their results. After negotiation, rho ranged from 0.875 to 0.967, with an average of 0.921. On problem 3d, inter-rater agreement ranged from 0.827 to 0.930 with an average of 0.885 before rater negotiation. After rater negotiation, the correlation values ranged from 0.911 to 0.971, with an average of 0.936. All correlation values were significant at the $p < .001$ level. These are all high levels of agreement, and indicate that the analysts were consistent in their interpretation of the SOLO scale.

Problem 3b

There was a high correlation (Spearman's rho = 0.508, $p < .001$) between the average SOLO ranking on problem 3b and the students' total exam scores (with problem 3 excluded).

On this problem, there were 74 students with responses in the R/M group (that is, the response was seen as at least multistructural), and 43 students in the U/P group (that is, these responses were regarded as unistructural or preoperational). Only 3 responses had average rankings between 2 and 3.

Looking at students' exam scores by SOLO category (summarized in Table 3), the average exam score for the students in the R/M group was 23.2 (out of a possible 40), while the average score for the students in the U/P group was 15.1. This difference was highly significant (Wilcoxon rank sum test W=13689, $p < .001$).

Table 3. SOLO Categorizations for Problem 3b

	Combined categories - # (%)	Average Exam Score (%)
Relational	74 (61.7)	23.2 (58.0)
Multistructural		
Unistructural	43 (35.8)	15.1 (38.8)
Prestructural		

Problem 3d

There was also a highly significant correlation between the average SOLO ranking on problem 3d and a student's performance on the exam, with Spearman's rho = 0.451, $p < .001$.

On problem 3d (summarized in Table 4 below), 55 students were in the R/M group, and 64 students were in the U/P group. There was only one response that received an average SOLO rank between 2 and 3. The mean final exam score for the R/M group was 24.5; for the U/P group it was 16.8. Again, this difference was highly significant (W = 14161, $p < .001$).

Table 4. SOLO Categorizations for Problem 3d

	Combined categories - # (%)	Average Exam Score (%)
Relational	55 (45.8)	24.5 (61.2)
Multistructural		
Unistructural	64 (53.3)	16.8 (42.0)
Prestructural		

For both problems 3b and 3d, the students in the "R/M" group received an approximately 50% higher score on the remainder of their exam than the students in the "U/P" group.

At the university where this exam was conducted, a 50% score is the pass/fail boundary. For both "explain in plain English" problems used in the exam, students in the "R/M" group earned more than 50% of the possible points on the remainder of the exam. The average exam score for students in the problem 3b "R/M" group was 58%, and the problem 3d "R/M" group students had an average test score of 61%. Students in the "U/P" group received less than 50% on the remainder of the exam, with an average of 39% for the problem 3b group and 42% for the 3d group. Thus, students who were able to explain what code does (at least at a multistructural level) were more likely to pass the course.

4. DISCUSSION

On the basis of these results, the null hypothesis is rejected – there is a correlation between code writing and explaining code for students in (at least) this particular course on data structures. The results for this CS2 class are therefore consistent with earlier studies of CS1 students.

However, no claim is made that the ability to write code is dependent upon the ability to explain code, or vice versa. To do so would be to make a well-known fallacy of statistical reasoning commonly identified as "correlation does not imply causation". We believe that the more likely explanation for a correlation between writing code and explaining code is that both writing and explaining depend upon a common set of skills concerned with reasoning about programs. Research on the psychology of programming has demonstrated that, as expertise develops, a programmer's knowledge is organized into more abstract, flexible forms, which would benefit both code writing and code explaining [1, 4, 5, 8, 13, 15].

5. IMPLICATIONS FOR TEACHING

If reasoning about code is the underlying skill that is common to both code writing and code explaining, then the crucial pedagogical question is how to most efficiently develop that underlying skill.

Clearly, there are lessons about code writing that can only be learned by writing code. However, traditional pedagogical practices emphasize code writing to such an extent that almost all the active learning exercises (i.e., laboratory exercises and assignments) require novices to write code. For example, prior to the final exam analyzed in this paper, the students had completed two program writing assignments, worth half of their final grade. Many students who submitted those assignments, especially the students around the pass/fail boundary, probably expended significant amounts of time in relatively unproductive activities, such as a "scatter gun" approach to debugging, in which students essentially guess at what might be the cause of an error, because those students lack the reasoning skills to deduce the error. Such students might write code more productively if they first improved their ability to reason about code, through non-writing learning activities such as reading and explaining code. We believe that a judicious mix of code-writing and code-reading is the most effective way for students to ultimately develop good programming skills.

A pragmatic difficulty with using EiPE problems as summative assessment (e.g., in final exams) is that there are only a relatively small number of algorithms covered in an introductory data structures course. A student might rote learn appropriate EiPE answers for all code studied during the semester, and then in the final exam choose the appropriate answer to give based upon superficial features of a piece of code. The value of EiPE problems may therefore be more as formative assessment rather than summative assessment. For example, rather than have the instructor explain a piece of code, these empirical results and the recent successes of peer instruction [14] suggest that students gain a deeper understanding of course material by explaining the code to each other and by hearing the explanations of other students. The format of the problems used in this study, those that require students to first trace code for a specific case and then explain the code in the general case, may be useful for peer instruction during programming courses. Since peer instruction typically utilizes multiple choice "clicker" questions [14], students' incorrect open-ended responses on written assessments could serve as reasonable multiple-choice distractors during peer instruction.

The ability to explain code clearly and concisely is a valued and necessary skill in industry and one CS educators strive to develop in their students, particularly at the upper-level undergraduate level. For example, software engineering students are required to explain their code when they write detailed documentation, give technical presentations, or participate in peer code reviews. EiPE problems give novice and intermediate level students opportunities to practice these valuable skills on a smaller scale. Other such opportunities might include asking students to explicitly explain code to their partners in plain English during pair programming, or to instruct them to use EiPE as a guide when documenting their code.

In some educational institutions, there is an increasing emphasis on establishing that graduates, regardless of their degree, have acquired certain generic attributes, such as communication skills. If it is necessary to develop communication skills as part of a course on data structures, then code explanation tasks provide one possible avenue of doing so.

Educators should also keep in mind that many of the students in this study had difficulty articulating a clear and concise explanation of the code. It is also likely some students may be similarly confused when shown code during lecture and that instructors may overestimate how quickly or how well they understand it. Asking students to explain code they have just seen may be a useful means of self-assessment and prompt them to ask questions to further their understanding.

6. FURTHER WORK

While it was revealed in this study that many students could not explain code, no effort was made to determine why those students struggled. To establish this will require more direct means of studying students. The next phase of this work we will involve one-on-one interaction with students, having them "think out loud" as they attempt to explain the purpose of pieces of code in an attempt to determine how they reason as they read code. If "why students struggle" can be precisely identified, we will be better positioned to develop educational materials and approaches designed to help those students.

7. REFERENCES

[1] Adelson, B. 1984. When novices surpass experts: The difficulty of a task may increase with expertise. *Journal of Experimental Psychology: Learning, Memory, and Cognition* 10, 3 (July 1984), 483-495.

[2] Biggs, J. and Collis, K. 1982. *Evaluating the quality of learning: Structure of the Observed Learning Outcome Taxonomy*. Academic Press, New York, NY.

[3] Corney, M., Lister, R., and Teague, D. 2011. Early Relational Reasoning and the Novice Programmer: Swapping as the "Hello World" of Relational Reasoning. In *Proceedings of the Thirteenth Australasian Computing Education Conference* (Perth, Australia, January 17-20, 2011). ACE 2011. 95-104.

[4] Corritore, C. and Wiedenbeck, S. 1991. What Do Novices Learn During Program Comprehension? *Int. J. of Human-Computer Interaction* 3, 2, 199-222.

[5] Fix, V., Wiedenbeck, S. and Scholtz, J. 1993. Mental representations of programs by novices and experts. In *Proceedings of the International Conference on Human-Computer Interaction - jointly organised with ACM Conference on Human Aspects in Computing Systems* (Amsterdam, The Netherlands, April 24-29, 1993). INTERACT '93 and CHI '93. ACM, New York, NY, 74-79.

[6] Hanks, B., Fitzgerald, S., McCauley, R., Murphy, L. and Zander, C. 2011. Pair Programming in Education: A Literature Review. *Computer Science Education* 21, 2 (June 2011), 135-173.

[7] Lopez, M., Whalley, J., Robbins, P. and Lister, R. 2008. Relationships between reading, tracing and writing skills in introductory programming, In *Proceedings of the 4th International Computing Education Research Workshop* (Sydney, Australia, Sept 6-7, 2008). ICER '08. ACM, New York, NY, 101-112.

[8] Mayer, R. 1981. The Psychology of How Novices Learn Computer Programming. *ACM Computing Surveys* 13, 1 (March 1981), 121-141. http://doi.acm.org/10.1145/356835.356841

[9] Murphy, L., Fitzgerald, S., Lister, R. and McCauley, R. 2012. Ability to 'Explain in Plain English' Linked to Proficiency in Computer-based Programming. In *Proceedings of the International Computing Education Research Conference* (Auckland, New Zealand, Sept. 10-12, 2012). ICER '12. ACM, New York, NY, 111-118.

[10] Murphy, L., McCauley, R. and Fitzgerald, S. 2012. 'Explain in plain English' questions: Implications for teaching. In *Proceedings of the ACM Technical Symposium on Computer Science Education* (Raleigh, North Carolina, USA, Feb. 29-March 3, 2012). SIGCSE '12. 385-390.

[11] Porter, L., Guzdial, M., McDowell, C., and Simon, B. 2013. Success in introductory programming: What works?. *Commun. ACM* 56, 8 (August 2013), 34-36. DOI=10.1145/2492007.2492020 http://doi.acm.org/10.1145/2492007.2492020

[12] R Core Team. 2012. R: A language and environment for statistical computing. R Foundation for Statistical Computing, Vienna, Austria. ISBN 3-900051-07-0. http://www.R-project.org/(last accessed Sept 2, 2013).

[13] Schneiderman, B. and Mayer, R. 1979. Syntactic/semantic interactions in programmer behavior: A model and experimental results. *International Journal of Computer and Information* 8, 3, 219-238.

[14] Simon, B. and Cutts, Q. 2012. Peer instruction: A teaching method to foster deep understanding. *Communications of the ACM* 55, 2 (Feb. 2012), 27-29.

[15] Soloway, E. 1986. Learning to program = learning to construct mechanisms and explanations. *Communications of the ACM* 29, 9 (Sept 1986), 850-858. http://doi.acm.org/10.1145/6592.6594

[16] Venables, A., Tan, G., and Lister, R. 2009. A closer look at tracing, explaining and code writing skills in the novice programmer. In *Proceedings of the International Computing Education Research Workshop* (Berkeley, CA, USA, Aug. 10-11, 2009). ICER '09. 117-128.

[17] Whalley, J., Lister, R., Thompson, E., Clear, T., Robbins, P., Kumar, P. and Prasard, C. 2006. An Australasian study of reading and comprehension skills in novice programmers, using the Bloom and SOLO taxonomies. In *Proceedings of the 8th Australasian Computing Education Conference* (Hobart, Australia, Jan. 16-19, 2006). ACE '06. 243-252.

A Formative Study of Influences on Student Testing Behaviors

Kevin Buffardi
Virginia Tech
2202 Kraft Drive
Blacksburg, VA 24060
+1 540-231-5723
kbuffardi@vt.edu

Stephen H. Edwards
Virginia Tech
2202 Kraft Drive
Blacksburg, VA 24060
+1 540-231-5723
edwards@cs.vt.edu

ABSTRACT

While Computer Science curricula teach students strategic software development processes, assessment is often product- instead of process-oriented. Test-Driven Development (TDD) has gained popularity in computing education, but evaluating students' adherence to TDD requires analyzing their development processes instead of only their final product. Consequently, we designed an adaptive feedback system for reinforcing incremental testing behaviors.

In this paper, we compare the results of the system with different reinforcement schedules and with- or without- visually salient testing goals. We analyzed snapshots of students' programming projects gathered during development and interviewed students at the end of the academic term. From our findings, we identify potential for influencing student development behaviors and suggest future direction for designing adaptive reinforcement.

Categories and Subject Descriptors

K.3.2 [**Computers and Education**]: Computer and Information Science Education; D.1.5 [**Programming Techniques**]: Object oriented Programming; D.2.5 [**Software Engineering**]: Testing and Debugging.

Keywords

Software development process, Test-Driven Development (TDD), Test-first, Unit testing, Automated testing, Web-CAT, Instructional Technology.

1. INTRODUCTION

Computer science curricula commonly include software engineering methods and techniques such as Test-Driven Development (TDD) that prescribe specific software development procedures. Likewise, the Accreditation Board for Engineering and Technology (ABET) requires computing departments to prepare students with "An ability to use current techniques, skills, and tools necessary for computing practice" [1]. However, computer science courses typically only evaluate the product students deliver while disregarding the processes students follow during development. Since students often work on programming assignments outside of instructors' direct oversight, instructors cannot evaluate their development process with only a single deliverable.

With the emergence of automated grading systems that allow students to submit their work throughout development, instructors gain improved granularity of students' work patterns. While exams may evaluate how well students *understand* a development technique, snapshots of students' development over time may reveal how they *apply* the technique. Furthermore, when students receive automated feedback while they are still working, there are opportunities to influence their behavior.

At our university, we teach Test-Driven Development (TDD) in introductory CS1 and CS2 courses. TDD involves an incremental "test a little, code a little" process meant to encourage confidence and improve maintainability [2]. However, students may find the test-first approach unnatural or intimidating. Consequently, they may benefit from repeated reinforcement during programming assignments.

In this paper, we describe a system we designed to encourage students' adherence to TDD. We compare the results of implementing different schedules of reinforcement and the presence or absence of specific goals in automated, adaptive feedback. In addition, we explore influences on students' testing behaviors through interviewing them about their experiences developing programming assignments and interacting with the adaptive feedback system.

2. BACKGROUND

Integrating Test-Driven Development (TDD) in computer science education incorporates real-world applicability since TDD is popular in the software industry as an element of eXtreme Programming (XP) and Agile Methods [2][7]. Additionally, TDD may also aid students' confidence and improve the quality of their code. Moreover, by practicing TDD on programming assignments, students may engage higher-order thinking skills by leveraging "reflection-in-action" rather than inferior "trial-and-error" problem-solving skills [6].

However, student programmers routinely demonstrate reluctance to adopt TDD. Melnik and Maurer observed that students particularly struggle with TDD because its test-first approach is "almost like working backwards". Correspondingly, Buffardi and Edwards surveyed students' attitudes and opinions after experience with TDD and found that while they generally appreciate the benefits of incremental testing, students neither perceived value or desire to test-first [3]. Spacco and Pugh recommend that incentives may motivate students to change from their tendencies to adopt a

SIGCSE'14, March 5-8, 2014, Atlanta, Georgia, USA.

ACM 978-1-4503-2605-6/14/03...$15.00.
http://dx.doi.org/10.1145/2538862.2544317

"test-late mentality of writing their implementation and then testing it at the very end" [11].

Operant conditioning is a long-established psychological technique for promoting desired behaviors by applying reinforcement or punishment following respective wanted and unwanted behaviors. By similarly applying Applied Behavior Analysis, Linehan, et al. propose empirically validated guidelines for leveraging reinforcement techniques in educational games. They emphasize that when designing educational systems, *"we must carefully consider not only what to use as a reward, but also how and when learners should gain access to those rewards."*

Accordingly, incentives can reward target behaviors at different schedules of reinforcement. For example, *fixed ratio and fixed interval* schedules offer rewards after target behaviors are demonstrated, but not on every occasion. Instead, fixed interval schedules steadily reinforce behaviors only after a fixed amount of time. Alternatively, fixed ratio offers rewards only after a fixed number of behavioral observations. In addition, Linehan, et al. suggest that clearly defined goals help learners strive toward *"achievable goals and [...] not present any challenge without providing [...] the skills required to pass it."* While most programming assignments are quite distinct from educational games, "gamification" is an approach to applying effective motivational and engaging gaming techniques to non-gaming contexts [4].

3. AN ADAPTIVE FEEDBACK SYSTEM

Hoping to encourage students to adhere to Test-Driven Development (TDD), we recognized an opportunity to reinforce incremental testing behaviors on programming assignments. However, it is first necessary to be able to *identify* the behaviors before attempting to *reinforce* them. Consequently, we leveraged an automated grading system to provide students with feedback while they worked.

Web-CAT is an automated grading system that provides students with unlimited opportunities to submit their work and view evaluation of their code [5]. With each submission, students receive feedback including analysis of code style, correctness, and testing quality. The *correctness* is calculated by the percent of instructor-written tests (obscured from the student) that pass when run against the students' code. Testing quality is represented by code *coverage*, or the percent of statements, conditionals, and branches executed by the student's own unit tests. Additionally, Web-CAT highlights the student's code to reveal where coverage is lacking. After receiving feedback, students may correct their code and resubmit to Web-CAT without punishment.

With each student submission, Web-CAT collects and analyzes a snapshot of their code during development. As students resubmit their evolving work, changes in their code reveal development patterns. From these patterns, inferences can be made about the process a student follows. Specifically, a student following TDD should consistently add corresponding solution and test code, maintaining high *coverage* while her project *correctness* improves.

To reward students, the adaptive feedback system tracks changes in coverage and gives incentives for high coverage scores. Every instructor-written test has a corresponding hint so that when a test fails, the hint provided caters to the student's specific problem. Students may accumulate access to more hints by consistently achieving at least 85% coverage while improving their solution and tests. While students have less than full (100%) coverage, they are required to improve their coverage by at least 10% of the remaining disparity.

We explored the impact of the visibility of this steadily increasing coverage goal by implementing two treatments of the adaptive system: with- and without- the goal clearly stated in Web-CAT's feedback. **Figure 1** illustrates the adaptive feedback with an earned hint and a target coverage goal to achieve additional hints. On one hand, salient goals may provide students with attainable objectives in improving test coverage. However, on the other hand, broad encouragement to improve coverage—in the absence of a specific goal—may instead motivate students to achieve full coverage.

In addition, we investigated how three different reinforcement schedules could influence students' testing behaviors. The *constant* treatment rewarded students with hints every time they met the coverage goal. With this treatment, matching target test behaviors always activates reinforcement. On the contrary, the *delayed* treatment only rewards a student once within a fixed interval (60 minutes), even if he meets successive goals several times within that duration. This way, the student receives steady reinforcement for good behavior, but may become less dependent on constant, external motivations.

Lastly, the *random* treatment used a pseudo-random number generator to set 50% chance of receiving a reward each time a goal is met. This variable ratio schedule prevents the student from being able to predict when she will receive an award for sufficient testing. Consequently, rewards should be more surprising which may increase students' emotional valence, thereby increasing their motivation in response.

4. METHOD

By introducing our adaptive feedback system to students, we aimed to observe common testing behaviors and investigate how the feedback influences those behaviors. Using students' submissions to Web-CAT provides insight into the changes in their code over time. However, this approach has two principal limitations in discerning test behaviors. Firstly, the data only

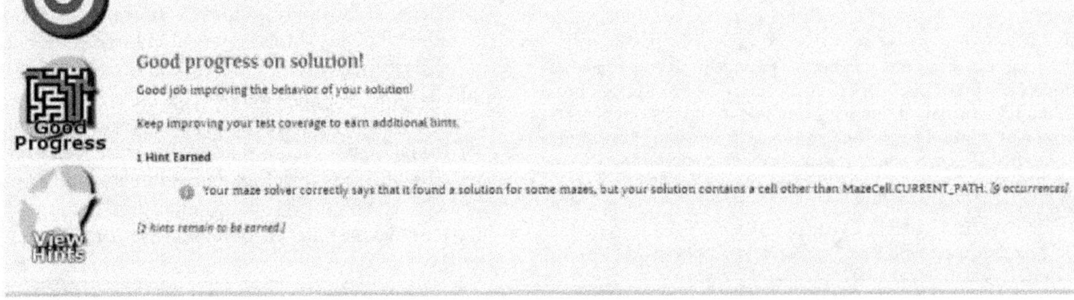

Figure 1. Adaptive feedback displays a hint and target coverage goal to achieve more hints.

reflects changes in students' code after they first submit to the automated grading system. We found that the average first submission already had 71% (sd=25%) of non-comment lines of code (NCLOC) when compared to their respective final submission NCLOC. Consequently, the data is blind to the beginning stages of development.

Secondly, there is no benefit for students to submit tests before writing the corresponding solution code (as encouraged by TDD) since without the solution, correctness will not improve. Likewise, Web-CAT cannot evaluate test coverage in the absence of solution code. Therefore, we cannot differentiate the incremental patterns "test a little, code a little" and "code a little, test a little" since students will only submit test code along with solution code. Continuous data collection would be necessary to determine the fine-grain order of testing versus coding the solution.

Consequently, we conducted interviews with students so they could explain their development processes and testing behaviors. This mixed-method approach benefits from quantitative, empirical analysis from code collection supplemented by explanations and clarifications from the students themselves.

4.1 Qualitative Investigation

While quantitative assessment can offer empirical data demonstrating testing behaviors, it lacks insight into explaining why students adopt particular processes and strategies. Previous studies have speculated into reasons for students' attitudes and behaviors from anecdotes and surveys [3][9]. However, we recognized a need to speak directly to the students in depth. Consequently, at the conclusion of the Spring 2013 academic term, we recruited students to participate in group interviews to explain their personal strategies, procedures, and motivations behind their behavior.

Twelve students volunteered to participate in the interviews, of whom seven showed and consented to participate (5.5% of 128 who sat the final exam). Volunteers were provided a meal (valued approximately $10 USD/person) to participate in group interviews for about one hour.

While this sample size may sound small, one should remember that the intent of the interviews is to elicit formative feedback rather than to empirically test hypotheses. By comparison, user experience studies often report that the majority of findings are discovered within the first five participants [10]. Likewise, in the interviews, we concentrated on eliciting feedback on students' experience with the adaptive feedback system and generating broad motivations and testing strategies.

Interviews were scheduled in two groups (n=4 and n=3) so that students could compare and contrast their experiences and strategies to generate discussion. Unlike focus groups, *each* participant was specifically prompted to respond to *every one* of the interviewer's questions and while there was discussion between participants, there was no attempt to collaborate on- or agree to a consensus opinion.

After providing written consent and doing quick introductions, the group interviews began with an opportunity for each participant to explain their top priorities and objectives when a programming project is first assigned. Then, the participants were asked to each share and discuss their personal testing strategies—including when they began testing, testing incrementally or periodically in large portions, and testing first or after corresponding solution code.

Next, participants were shown an example screen capture of Web-CAT feedback and they discussed the different parts of the feedback. Without leading them to specific parts of the page, participants were asked to explain what they paid attention to and what was most important to them after their first submission to Web-CAT. They were also asked to explain what then influenced their next step in development. This series of discussions was repeated for screens representing resubmissions where they first earned hints and then again, once they achieved high (but not quite perfect) correctness and coverage scores.

Lastly, they were specifically probed on parts of Web-CAT's feedback to discuss what is or is not helpful and how different elements of feedback may play a part in development going forward. The screen elements discussed include (visually from top to bottom): grade summary, individual file details, adaptive feedback, results from running student's tests, code coverage from student's tests, estimation problem correctness, and interpreting correctness/testing scores. The interviewer particularly encouraged explanations about the adaptive feedback's goals and hints.

Next, each participant was asked if (and how) their individual testing strategies evolved over the duration of the academic term. The group discussions concluded with each participant completing a brief questionnaire on paper to reflect on and summarize their testing habits. each individual's reflection over their personal testing habits. The questionnaire asked participants to rate how often (from 1, rarely, to 5, often) they did the following:

- Started writing tests early in development
- Started writing tests late in development
- Wrote one test at a time to test a small part of the solution code
- Wrote many tests at a time to test large portions of the solution code
- Wrote tests before writing its corresponding solution code
- Wrote tests after writing its corresponding solution code

Likewise, the questionnaire asked to rate the same six behaviors by *"how likely you are to do the following in the future, from: (1 Very Unlikely) to (5 Very Likely)."* At the bottom of the questionnaire, participants had empty space to *"Please describe how your testing and development strategies may change or stay the same, depending on the size of the program you are working on."* Comparing differences between current behavior and projected future behavior could reveal influences on long-term testing strategies.

Finally, each participant was given a blank sheet of paper and a pencil and were asked to draw a timeline that depicted their typical project development from when it is assigned to the participant's last submission to Web-CAT. They were given freedom to express their development as best they could, but were asked to also identify when they worked on the solution, when they tested, and when they submitted to Web-CAT.

4.2 Quantitative Evaluation

While Web-CAT provides students with feedback upon each submission, it also collects a snapshot of their work that we can later analyze. Since we are particularly interested in students' testing behaviors, we analyzed each submission for both quantity and quality of test code as well as that of solution code. Web-CAT allows for part of students' grades to be manually entered by instructional staff by considering aspects such as design and documentation. However, to eliminate subjective judgments and potential inconsistency between graders, we only included Web-CAT's automated measurements in our quantitative assessment.

4.2.1 *Code and Test Metrics*

As previously mentioned, *correctness* describes how well students' solution code performs, as measured against the instructors' obscured tests. On the other hand, the test coverage describes the thoroughness of testing. *Coverage* represents the percent of statements, conditionals, and branches in the student's code exercised when run against her own tests. Influences of feedback on students' testing will be illustrated in *Δ coverage*, or how coverage on the final submission compares to that of the first submission. Positive values represent improvements in coverage while negative values suggest complacency or neglecting testing.

In addition to these measurements of code quality, we examined the quantity of code written. Non-comment lines of code (*NCLOC*) is the self-explanatory amount of semantic code. We maintained records of test and solution NCLOC separately to compare the relationship between amount of test and solution code. Similarly to coverage, we concentrated on how test NCLOC might change in response to adaptive feedback. *Δ test NCLOC* reveals increases or decreases in the amount of test code from the first to last submission within an assignment.

To check for normality of their distributions, we performed the Shapiro-Wilk test on measurements used for these metrics. All of the following measurements (with significantly small p-values) rejected the null hypothesis of normal distribution: correctness (M=0.91, sd=0.16, $p<0.0001$), first submission test NCLOC (M=129.83, sd=125.63, $p<0.0001$) and coverage (M=0.69, sd=0.32, $p<0.0001$), and final submission test NCLOC (M=247.15, sd=162.20, $p<0.0001$) and coverage (M=0.98, sd=0.08, $p<0.0001$). Consequently, all comparisons between treatments used Wilcoxon tests for non-parametric data.

4.2.2 *Experimental Design*

In Spring 2012, students in a CS2 (Software Design and Data Structures) course received feedback for their programming assignments using our adaptive feedback system with its initial design with *constant* (C) reinforcement schedule and *hidden* (H) coverage goals. Students received feedback according to this treatment for the entire term, encompassing four independent programming assignments. Of the 129 students who sat the final exam, 78 (60%) provided written consent to include their data in our analysis.

Following the preliminary semester, we implemented additional treatments of the adaptive feedback system, including *delayed* (D) and *random* (R) reinforcement schedules, each with separate *shown* (S) and *hidden* (H) goal combinations. Of the 128 students who sat the final exam in 2013, 84 (66%) consented to include their work in the data analysis. We planned a 3x2 factorial design of the treatments, treatments would be assigned to the five different course sections for each assignment to enable both within- and between-group comparisons.

However, constraints prevented us from implementing our planned experimental design. Firstly, the CS2 instructor developed new projects so that the Spring 2013 offering would not replicate the assignments completed in Spring 2012. In good faith, we could not ask the instructor and his students to forgo innovative course material for the sake of experimental validity. Secondly, we recognized a technical flaw in the adaptive feedback when applied to Spring 2013's first assignment. As a result, we had to exclude Project 1's data and use the semester's three remaining assignments to make comparisons between the five alternate treatments.

Consequently, we resolved to randomly assign each of the five course sections a unique experimental group. While this design excludes the possibility of within-subject comparisons, it controls for potential ordering effects of being exposed to different treatments on subsequent projects.

To see if the assignments between the two terms were of comparable size and difficulty, we compared the size and outcome of assignments between the two terms. Using the Mann-Whitney-Wilcoxon test, we found assignments from 2012 (M=325.79, sd=134.33) required significantly more solution NCLOC ($p<0.0001$) code than those assignments given in 2013 (M=290.20, sd=194.85). Moreover, the students performed better ($p<0.05$) on correctness for assignments in 2013 (M=0.91, sd=0.16) than for assignments in 2012 (M=0.84, sd=0.27).

Our previous study also found that the CH adaptive feedback treatment in Spring 2012 failed to improve either testing quality or quantity when compared to the same assignments in Fall 2011 (without the adaptive feedback system) [Anon]. Consequently, with too many confounding variables in comparing students with different outcomes on different assignments with different scopes and difficulties in different years, we decided to compare only the remaining five treatments in this study: CS, DH, DS, RH, and RS.

Although the consequential design excludes the 2012 experimental treatment combination (CH), CS, RH, and DH provide insight into the individual dimensions of CH. While a balanced, full 3x2 factorial design would be ideal for within-group comparisons, it was impractical to execute such a controlled design within the constraints of the academic term. Since the study's investigation of influences on student testing behaviors is for formative design purposes, between-treatment comparisons should still offer valuable insights.

5. RESULTS

5.1 Qualitative Investigation

When describing their initial motivations and objectives once a project is assigned, the participants concentrated mostly on reviewing the assignment's specifications and devising broad outlines and plans for completing the solution. However, their opinions diverged once discussion lead to testing strategies.

Four of the seven participants explained their habits of waiting to test until a substantial amount of the solution is complete. Three explicitly stated with confident tone that while they understood that the instructor encourages testing early, it only makes sense to them to test at the very end of their development process.

The remaining participants explained that their testing strategy varied between assignments. Meanwhile, one participant explained that she felt overwhelmed and dissatisfied with her work early in the term until she adopted an incremental testing strategy. She reported that she consequently grew more confident in her work and improved her grades considerably.

The responses on the participants' questionnaires reflected similar behaviors and attitudes. All participants reported that they more often start testing late than early in development and test after writing solution rather than before. However, reports on incremental testing were split. Four participants usually tested in large portions while two usually tested in smaller increments and one remaining participant does both equally often.

Nevertheless, on average, participants reported that in the future they expect to increasingly test early, test in small increments, and test before coding the solution. Correspondingly, they also expect to decrease testing late and testing after coding the solution.

Table 1. Summary of Questionnaire Responses

	Current Rare 1 - Often 5		Future V.Unlikely 1 - V.Likely 5	
	M	sd	M	sd
Test Early	1.86	0.63	2.43	0.90
Test Late	4.29	1.03	3.71	1.16
Small Increments	2.57	1.29	3.29	1.28
Large Portions	3.86	0.64	4.14	0.64
Test First	1.43	0.49	1.71	0.45
Test After	4.86	0.35	4.14	0.64

In other words, participants predicted that in the future, they will draw closer to being equally likely to exhibit TDD practices as demonstrating its antithesis. **Table 1** summarizes the average ratings for all of the ratings.

The participants who were confident in testing last suggested that their testing strategies were not likely to change regardless of the size of the project. One such participant wrote: *"While we've been encouraged to 'test as we go', I still feel like it makes the most sense to test a method only AFTER it's completely written."* Others anticipated that larger or more challenging projects will require more thought and effort to devote to testing and consequently they will need to begin testing earlier.

Participants provided more granularity into their development process by drawing timelines. None of the participants illustrated any test-first behavior. Two participants represented strictly test-last strategies where the only testing took place as the last activity on the timeline. The left timeline in **Figure 2** provides an example of this test-last approach. However, the other five participants all demonstrated some degree of incremental testing with at least two iterations of "code a little, test a little." Notably, three of the seven participants illustrated at least one event on their timeline where testing and either "debugging" or "fixing" problems or issues were combined as a single marker. The timeline on the right of **Figure 2** shows a common "write tests / fix issues" activity near the end of the development process.

In addition to discussing development and testing strategies, participants also provided their opinions and experiences with Web-CAT and particularly with the adaptive feedback system. Although students expressed appreciation for Web-CAT, there were general notions that the feedback page could be more concise. When asked about what was most important, what first caught their attention, and what influenced their future behavior, participants nearly always identified the red bars that indicate incomplete correctness and coverage as focal points.

When asked specifically about the adaptive feedback, participants explained that they understood the intent to encourage more testing. However, as one participant explained when talking about the target and coverage goal: *"I know why it's there. But I know I'm supposed to get 100% coverage because that is part of the grade. I don't need this to tell me to improve my coverage because I already know that."* Likewise, the participants described that the hints were usually important but that they did not usually purposely add tests to earn more hints; instead, when they added more tests, they did so to improve their coverage score.

5.2 Quantitative Evaluation

Since each of the five treatments includes a combination of two dimensions for each research question, we adjusted the significance level using Bonferonni correction to counteract testing multiple hypotheses. A Wilcoxon each-pairs test compared each of the ten combinations of experimental groups ($\alpha=0.008$). Likewise, a Wilcoxon each-pairs test compared each of the three different treatments (C, D, R) of the reinforcement schedule dimension ($\alpha=0.0333$) independently. Finally, a Wilcoxon-Mann-Whitney test compared the two treatments (S, H) of the goal dimension ($\alpha=0.10$) independently.

Since each project required a different amount of work but we want to consider each with equal weight, Δ test NCLOC was adjusted to account for difference in project sizes. Its values were divided by the mean solution NCLOC for each respective project: project 2 (M=215.67, sd=39.66), project 3 (M=159.18, sd=21.16), and project 4 (M=495.75, sd=216.87). Larger projects would typically require a greater amount of test code and time spent developing. However, when making comparisons across all projects, we are concerned with the amount of code and amount of time spent relative to the size of the project. Otherwise, large projects (such as project 4) would unduly influence the results due to their considerably larger absolute measurements, before adjustment.

First, we compared the Δ test NCLOC between all experimental groups and found no significant differences, as shown by insignificant p-values in **Table 2**.

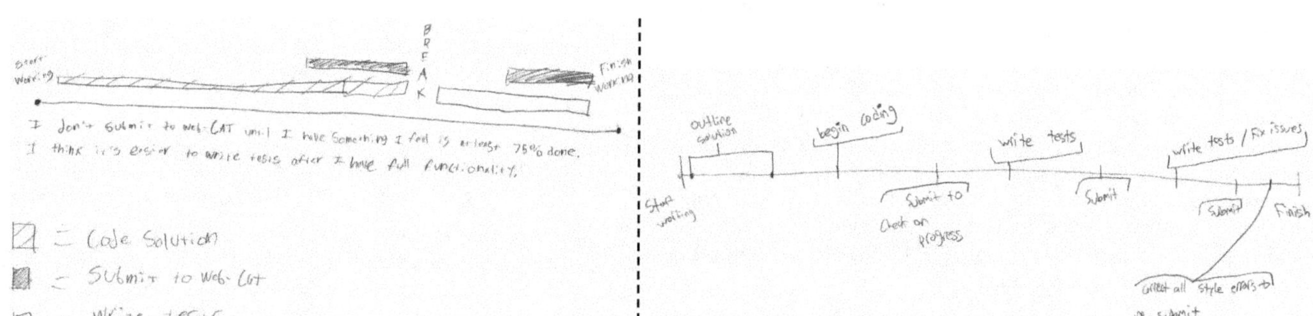

Figure 2. Development timelines contrasting test-last approach (left) and periodic testing (right)

Table 2. Wilcoxon each-pairs comparison of Δ test NCLOC

(M,sd)	CS	DH	DS	RH	RS
CS(.25,.25)		p=.73	p=.49	p=.73	p=.85
DH(.21,.22)			p=.13	p=.17	p=.40
DS(.27,.33)				p=.56	p=.41
RH(.23,.16)					p=.67
RS(.22,.18)					

Likewise, similar *constant* (M=0.25, sd=0.25), *delayed* (M=0.24, sd=0.27), and *random* (M=0.23, sd=0.17) **Δ test NCLOC** demonstrated no significant difference between *constant* and *delayed* (p=0.86), *constant* and *random* (p=0.89), and *delayed* and *random* (p=0.68) pairwise comparisons. In addition, the *shown* (M=0.25, sd=0.27) and *hidden* (M=0.22, sd=0.19) goal treatments yielded no significant difference (p=0.39).

After finding no differences in quantity of test code, we compared the test code quality. **Table 3** shows the pairwise comparisons between each experimental group.

Table 3. Wilcoxon each-pairs comparison of Δ coverage

(M,sd)	CS	DH	DS	RH	RS
CS(.35,.36)		p=.02	p=.96	p=.64	p=.22
DH(.20,.26)			p=.01	p=.03	p=.21
DS(.35,.35)				p=.66	p=.20
RH(.31,.32)					p=.34
RS(.24,.29)					

While no pairwise comparisons were significantly different at the α=0.008 level, DS (M=0.35, sd=0.35), CS (M=0.35, sd=0.36), and RH (M=0.31, sd=0.32) approached significantly greater improvement in coverage (p=0.01, 0.02, and 0.03, respectively) than DH (M=0.20, sd=0.26). When comparing the Δ coverage for the reinforcement schedules, there was no difference (p=0.16) between *constant* (M=0.35, sd=0.36) and *delayed* (M=0.27, sd=0.31) reinforcement. There was also no significant difference between *constant* and *random* (M=0.28, sd=0.31; p=0.37) or between *delayed* and *random* (p=0.42). However, *shown* goals (M=0.32, sd=0.34) nears significantly greater (p=0.10) Δ coverage than *hidden* goals treatment (M=0.26, sd=0.30).

6. DISCUSSION

Our investigations verify suggestions from previous studies that students are reticent to adhere to test-first procedures. However, the interviews revealed unique insight into students' reasons for their behaviors. The students who expressed particularly strong reticence to follow Test-Driven Development (TDD) also happened to be students who were especially confident in their programming skills. The assignments' difficulty and scope may not be demanding enough to warrant confident students from changing behaviors that have worked for them. While another participant found her confidence by using TDD, trends in students' development timelines are revealing.

The proximity of testing and its frequent association with debugging suggest that within students' mental models, testing is a process for fixing problems rather than proactively avoiding them. In order for students to adopt different behaviors, this mental model would have to change. A test-first approach represents a considerable departure from conventional engineering and problem solving processes. We found no significant effect of different reinforcement schedules using the conservative Bonferonni correction and constricted to only between-group comparisons. Consequently, we need not abandon adaptive reinforcement, but successfully invoking change in complex behavior—like adopting new strategies for software development and problem solving—will most likely require novel combinations of persuasive and pedagogical techniques.

More immediate and persistent feedback for self-monitoring adherence to a formal method has potential for scaffolding complex behavioral change. While it is unlikely that any rewards or gamification techniques will ever influence students' behaviors as much as the expectations set by graded requirements, we observed a strong impression that simple red-to-green status bars have on students' attention.

Dissonant visual cues such as error icons, incomplete progress bars, or unattended notifications may implicitly change student behaviors as they are compelled to resolve the dissonance. Correspondingly, introducing similar visual cues of incomplete testing coverage within students' integrated development environment may motivate change. Future work needs to explore such implicit interventions where visual cues may enable students to self-monitor and reflect over their behavior. Moreover, delivering persistent feedback within students' development environment will offer immediate reinforcement to their behaviors instead of passively waiting until students overtly seek feedback.

7. REFERENCES

[1] ABET (2013). "Criteria for Accrediting Computing Programs, 2013-2014." Retrieved May, 2014, from http://www.abet.org/

[2] Beck, K. (1999). "Embracing change with extreme programming." Computer 32(10): 70-77.

[3] Buffardi, K. and S. H. Edwards (2013). Impacts of adaptive feedback on teaching test-driven development. Proc. of SIGCSE. Denver, Colorado, USA, ACM.

[4] Buffardi, K. and S. H. Edwards (2012). Exploring influences on student adherence to test-driven development. Proc. of ITiCSE. Haifa, Israel, ACM: 105-110.

[5] Deterding, S., M. Sicart, et al. (2011). Gamification. using game-design elements in non-gaming contexts. SIGCHI Extended Abstracts. Vancouver, BC, Canada, ACM.

[6] Edwards, S. H. "Web-CAT." from https://web-cat.cs.vt.edu.

[7] Edwards, S. H. (2004). "Using software testing to move students from trial-and-error to reflection-in-action." SIGCSE Bull. 36(1): 26-30.

[8] Fraser, S., D. Astels, et al. (2003). Discipline and practices of TDD: (test driven development). ACM SIGPLAN OOPSLA. Anaheim, CA, USA, ACM: 268-270.

[9] Linehan, C., B. Kirman, et al. (2011). Practical, appropriate, empirically-validated guidelines for designing educational games. Proc. of SIGCHI. Vancouver, BC, Canada, ACM.

[10] Melnik, G. and F. Maurer (2005). A cross-program investigation of students' perceptions of agile methods. Proc. of ICSE. St. Louis, MO, USA, ACM: 481-488.

[11] Nielsen, J. and T. K. Landauer (1993). A mathematical model of the finding of usability problems. Proc. of CHI '93. Amsterdam, The Netherlands, ACM.

[12] Spacco, J. and W. Pugh (2006). Helping students appreciate test-driven development (TDD). SIGPLAN OOPSLA. Portland, Oregon, USA, ACM: 907-913.

Using a Software Framework to Enhance Online Teaching of Shader-Based OpenGL

James R. Miller
Electrical Engineering and Computer Science
1520 W. 15 Street; 2001 Eaton Hall
University of Kansas; Lawrence, KS 66045
1-785-864-7384
jrmiller@ku.edu

ABSTRACT

Shader-based OpenGL is a powerful and exciting tool for individuals with data visualization needs, interests in gaming, a need to create and manipulate synthetic environments, and a variety of other high-performance tasks. It is well-known that shader-based OpenGL is difficult to learn for programmers with no prior graphics API experience – some have even claimed it's impossible to teach to individuals without such prior exposure. In this paper, we report on our experiences developing an educational approach that we believe has contributed to the base of evidence that it is not only possible, but also desirable to do so. Our overriding goal has been to learn and exploit the extent to which mastering a complex graphics API like modern shader-based OpenGL can be enhanced by using a software design framework into which relevant concepts can be placed, thus facilitating more rapid assimilation and mastery of the concepts. We have been using this technique in our Introduction to Computer Graphics course in which we have two primary goals: teach shader-based OpenGL to students who have no prior experience using a graphics API, and present a framework to students that will scale up to medium and large scale applications, both in terms of code size as well as data size. We do not in any way suggest that our architecture is the "best" for all advanced graphics applications, or even for teaching. Instead we simply claim that use of such a framework helps students master complex OpenGL concepts and develop nontrivial interactive 3D applications. Once students fully understand the basics, they should find it easy to migrate to other perhaps quite different architectures.

Categories and Subject Descriptors

K.3.1 [**Computers and Education**]: Computer Uses in Education – *distance learning*

K.3.2 [**Computers and Education**]: Computer and Information Science and Education – *computer science education; self-assessment*

SIGCSE'14, March 5–8, 2014, Atlanta, Georgia, USA.

http://dx.doi.org/10.1145/2538862.2538892

General Terms

Design, Experimentation, Languages.

Keywords

Computer-aided Learning; Educational Technology; Computer-Graphics; Self-paced learning; Mastering Shader-Based OpenGL.

1. INTRODUCTION

OpenGL [4] has regained its status as the preeminent interactive 3D modeling and rendering API for scientific, engineering, and gaming applications. It has done so in part by changing the nature of how graphics data are specified, processed, and rendered, explicitly exposing an intimate cooperation between the CPU and the GPU. In so doing, the learning curve for so-called shader-based OpenGL has become a little steeper. So much so, in fact, that many have opined that it is not practical to teach to introductory students at the undergraduate level without at least some exposure to the older, simpler version of the API. See, for example, [1] in which this prevailing opinion is cited, but rebutted. We agree with the rebuttal, and the purpose of this paper is to present the approach we have adopted to make it work.

We have been teaching shader-based OpenGL in our introductory computer graphics course since the Fall of 2011 when [1] first appeared. This course is targeted towards senior undergraduate computer science and computer engineering majors, although we frequently attract several graduate students as well since the material serves as a prerequisite to several graduate courses in visualization and modeling. Moreover, graduate students are allowed to apply this course towards their graduate degree.

While the Fall 2011 semester was a bit rocky, we have developed an approach based on the use of a consistent software architectural framework that allows students to progressively learn increasingly sophisticated aspects of OpenGL, in part by relating them to the framework. The bulk of the material is online and is embodied in an increasingly sophisticated set of examples that share the framework. Packaged with each example is a detailed description of the new features introduced in the example along with complete source code so that students can run, modify, and experiment with the example programs.

The framework we use serves a dual purpose. Obviously the main purpose is that it helps students organize their growing understanding of how portions of the OpenGL system operate and cooperate. Secondarily, it is a C++ object-oriented framework that serves as a realistic example of several advanced C++/OO design patterns that students have typically only seen previously in unrealistically small abstract contexts, if they have even seen them at all.

A major goal is to present a framework that will scale up to medium and large scale applications, both in terms of code size as well as data size. However we also recognize and emphasize to students that this framework is not intended to represent the "best" architecture for all advanced graphics applications. Indeed, very different architectural styles and organizational methods may well be needed in different application contexts. Our philosophy is instead that this is a useful framework with which to master OpenGL concepts and develop nontrivial interactive 3D applications. Once students fully understand the basics, they will be well-prepared to migrate their expertise into other architectures.

2. RELATED WORK

There are online tools developed to aid students in mastering complex concepts related to interactive 3D modeling and rendering. The Exploratories project [2], for example, offers a wealth of free software and tools for teaching fundamental concepts including color theory, viewing in 3D, illumination models, and others. Standalone applications illustrating such concepts are available as well as component tools to help developers with basic tasks like drawing axes and 3D shapes (boxes, cylinders, etc.). These are high-quality tools that serve an important purpose, but one that is somewhat different from what we are trying to accomplish here.

Most existing standard graphics textbooks focus on teaching the theoretical concepts of computer graphics modeling and rendering and then relating them to a concrete API like OpenGL (e.g., [1]). This is unquestionably an important and valuable function, and we definitely exploit that fact in our course by using such a textbook for readings on those underlying graphics concepts. Again, we believe our contribution is best seen as serving a companion, but orthogonal purpose: namely the development of a software architectural framework that both helps students organize their new knowledge and lets them develop skills that will help them design and implement large scale applications that make effective use of the graphics functionality they are learning to solve real-world problems in data visualization and other areas.

Talton and Fitzpatrick describe their rationale and approach to teaching GLSL in the introductory computer graphics course [6]. They argue that exposing introductory students to GLSL is ultimately an advantage, in part because it forces them to come to grips with the internal mathematics, algorithms, and data structures required while removing the "black box" aspect of the process. They go on to state their belief that students getting this exposure are "more likely to produce visually and technologically impressive course projects than those who are taught to use only the fixed-function OpenGL API." Since their paper appeared, the entire fixed-function pipeline to which they allude has been deprecated as has a large portion of the basic geometry definition API. These developments appeared in OpenGL 3.3 released in March 2010, and they have reinforced the steep learning curve, making the issue much more critical.

3. MODEL-VIEW-CONTROLLER

Our basic framework is based on a simplified version of the well-known Model-View-Controller (MVC) design pattern. We begin by briefly explaining the motivation for and use of the MVC pattern in general, and especially its popularity for interactive modeling and rendering applications. We then observe that in introductory graphics applications such as the ones they will develop in this course, it is frequently the case that the "model" will not really have a use outside the context of the graphics program itself. Indeed, there may not even be a standalone representation of the model aside from its implicit representation in code and data declarations. Hence we introduce a simplification of the MVC pattern by proposing two generic classes: a combined "ModelView" and a "Controller". Since there really is no separable "Model", our merged ModelView makes sense because we only access the model in the context of generating a view of it. This simplified pair of classes then forms the core of the framework we develop for the course.

An OpenGL program can produce and interact with images in multiple windows, and each window is managed by a single Controller. Multiple models (i.e., ModelView instances) can be created; each can be added to one or more Controllers and hence rendered in the corresponding windows.

4. MAIN CONTRIBUTIONS OF THIS EFFORT

We believe the approach to teaching the introductory computer graphics course described here accomplishes several useful goals:

- Students get significant experience with the common MVC design pattern (albeit a somewhat simplified version of it). They get the big picture while using our simplified ModelView – Controller architecture for projects.
- Of course the primary goal is to master the somewhat complex art of shader-based OpenGL, including getting significant experience with cooperative CPU-GPU software design, development, and debugging issues. Students see how to exploit the massively parallel GPU for their rendering code, and we now very briefly introduce them to general-purpose GPU-based computation between frame refreshes via OpenGL's Compute Shaders. Included is an introduction to the idea that large numbers of GPU program instances simultaneously receive and process "work assignments", the common paradigm for data parallel computational models.
- Students gain practical experience with several intermediate-level object-oriented concepts, such as class hierarchy design, and the need to understand, embrace, and exploit the differences between instance and class methods as well as between instance and class variables. Students typically have been minimally exposed to these ideas to various extents, but they typically have not yet seen realistic examples of where and how they can be effectively used. We are exploiting a synergy here: learning graphics in the context of a useful software architecture helps students master the graphics concepts; conversely, employing useful software design patterns in a realistic setting helps them become more comfortable with sophisticated design patterns, and hence better software engineers.
- Students find it both a blessing and a curse that they gain experience studying and understanding an established design and code infrastructure inside of which they will build their own projects. Some have expressed a lack of enthusiasm for reading and studying existing code bases, but the counterargument is that that is more representative of what they will be doing in industry than is starting a program from scratch

every few weeks. Moreover, the established code base they must understand in order to do the course projects is small.

- Once they have mastered the framework itself, students can focus more attention on "normal" graphics issues such as how to build, manipulate, illuminate, render, and interact with large 2D and 3D models.
- All the examples, code, and explanatory information are on the web site (http://people.eecs.ku.edu/~miller/Courses/OpenGL/OpenGL.html), hence students can – to a certain extent – proceed through the material at their own pace. Specifically, if a student is eager and wants to move faster than our in-class discussions are proceeding, they are certainly able to do that.

5. PROGRESSION THROUGH THE ONLINE PORTION OF THE COURSE

The primary online web site for the shader-based material just cited above is structured generally as follows. There are initial pages that describe the relevant background and history of OpenGL as well as the general architecture of an OpenGL program. Following a review of the overall course goals, an initial "Hello, OpenGL" application is presented which simply defines and renders a triangle. In spite of the simplicity of this example, students see the bulk of the control and communication patterns that are used throughout the course. Following this simple example, we briefly summarize review the primary OpenGL "draw modes", relating them to the order in which points are placed in buffers sent to the GPU.

Following this overview, the primary online materials that develop the software framework are presented as a succession of increasingly sophisticated example programs organized into "Sample Program Sets". Each introduces two or three new concepts, the first by extending "Hello, OpenGL" so that students do not have to start from scratch understanding a new model.

5.1 Hello, OpenGL

We begin by explaining the high-level execution model employed by our ModelView–Controller architecture (Fig. 1). The main program is very small, basically just creating a Controller (and hence its window on the screen) and a ModelView. It then adds the ModelView to the Controller's list of managed models and hands off to the event handling loop of OpenGL's window system interface GLUT [4]. The following briefly summarizes the key concepts introduced in each step.

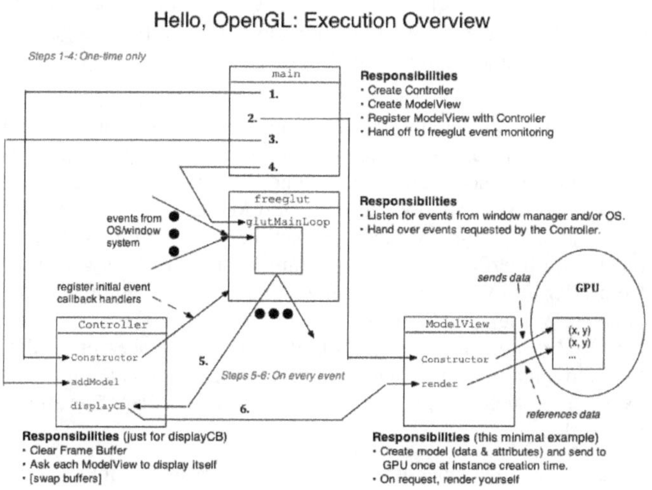

Figure 1: Basic Communication and Control Flow.

Step 1 creates the Controller along with its Rendering Context (RC – an encapsulation of OpenGL state in a window). Event handling in OpenGL is based on event callback registration. Client code registers a function in the OpenGL RC that is to be invoked when a given event occurs. OpenGL is not object-oriented, hence only external functions (as opposed to, say, class instance methods) can be registered. C++ class methods can be registered as callback functions since they are called in a manner identical to that for regular C functions. This observation allows us to illustrate a common pattern to students for translating non-object-oriented API callbacks to object-oriented instance methods. In the simplest case, for example, a Controller class method is registered as the callback function, and a Controller class variable is used to remember the last Controller instance created. When the class method is called in response to a registered event, it uses the saved Controller class variable pointer to hand off responsibility for processing the event to the appropriate Controller instance method.

The following captures the essence of the idea as presented to the students:

```
Controller* Controller::theController = NULL;
Controller::Controller()
{
    ...
    theController = this;
}
// A class method registered with GLUT:
void Controller::anEventCallback(…)
{
    if (theController != NULL)
        theController->handleEvent(…);
}
// The instance method to handle the event:
void Controller::handleEvent(…)
{
    ...
}
```

While this simple scheme of translating class methods registered as callback functions to instance methods works in single-window (and hence single Controller) applications, alternative designs are discussed with students that are capable of handling multiple Controller situations. The typical solution is to use a mapping from GLUT window IDs retrievable during event processing to the corresponding Controller pointer.

The second step in this generic execution model creates one or more ModelView instances. From the perspective of teaching core shader-based OpenGL concepts, we need to reinforce the distinction between what happens at model creation and/or modification time as opposed to rendering time. Model data is copied to buffer objects on the GPU; storage for these objects must be managed in much the same way normal dynamically allocated storage is on the CPU. The ModelView constructor is responsible for dynamically allocating GPU buffer storage and initializing it with the required model data. The destructor is then responsible for releasing this buffer storage. If model modifications are performed (typically in response to events), other ModelView methods are used to rewrite all or part of the data in the buffers stored on the GPU. It is clear to students that these creation and modification operations are performed infrequently as compared to the much simpler operations performed to support dynamic updates such as animation, which we shall revisit below in steps 5 and 6.

Core rendering is performed using shader programs written in OpenGL's GLSL GPU shader language. These programs must be explicitly compiled, linked, stored on the GPU, and executed on demand by the host CPU program. Typically several instances of a ModelView class will share the same shader program(s), so we use this as an opportunity to illustrate how class variables can be used to manage the storage and variable location data for the shader programs, allowing a single compiled and linked shader program to be shared among all the instances. We illustrate how a reference counting scheme can also be used so that – when the last ModelView instance has been deleted – the storage associated with the common compiled and linked program can be released.

Step 3 simply registers the ModelView(s) with the Controller so that each instance can be located for rendering during display callbacks. Step 4 then transfers control to the main GLUT event monitoring loop.

When the GLUT recognizes the need to recreate the display in a window, it calls the registered display callback (a class method in Controller). That callback delegates to an instance method as discussed above which in turn invokes a render method of each ModelView instance registered with the Controller. Here students observe that very little CPU-GPU communication is required – typically just simple directives involving minimal CPU-GPU data transfer that establish values for certain attributes and trigger the rendering of data stored in buffers already on the GPU.

This simple framework and mode of operation will require only minor extensions to get through the bulk of the introductory online material that needs to be conveyed to students during the first half of the course. Following this basic introductory example students progress through a series of sample program sets, a brief summary of which follows.

5.2 Sample Program Set Structure

Once we have completed discussion of "Hello, OpenGL", we move on to the portion of the web site that contains a series of increasingly sophisticated example applications. Each sample program has the same MVC structure, of course, and this allows us to focus on just the new features being considered in each example. Each set is presented in a web page in which each example of the set is introduced using the common general format, a portion of which is illustrated in Fig. 2.

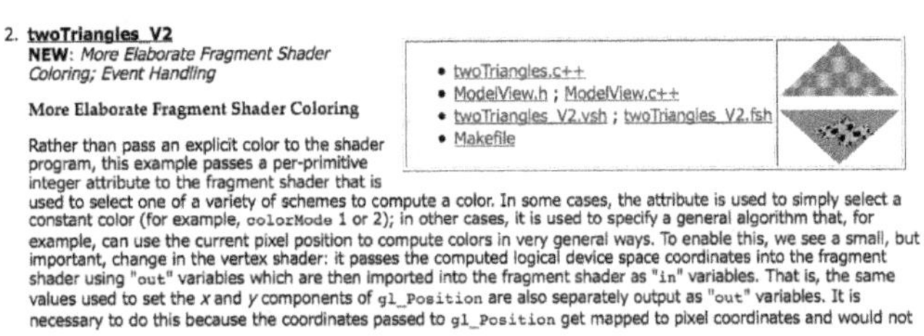

2. **twoTriangles_V2**
NEW: *More Elaborate Fragment Shader Coloring; Event Handling*

- twoTriangles.c++
- ModelView.h ; ModelView.c++
- twoTriangles_V2.vsh ; twoTriangles_V2.fsh
- Makefile

More Elaborate Fragment Shader Coloring

Rather than pass an explicit color to the shader program, this example passes a per-primitive integer attribute to the fragment shader that is used to select one of a variety of schemes to compute a color. In some cases, the attribute is used to simply select a constant color (for example, `colorMode` 1 or 2); in other cases, it is used to specify a general algorithm that, for example, can use the current pixel position to compute colors in very general ways. To enable this, we see a small, but important, change in the vertex shader: it passes the computed logical device space coordinates into the fragment shader using "`out`" variables which are then imported into the fragment shader as "`in`" variables. That is, the same values used to set the *x* and *y* components of `gl_Position` are also separately output as "`out`" variables. It is necessary to do this because the coordinates passed to `gl_Position` get mapped to pixel coordinates and would not

Figure 2: Introducing Example 2 of Sample Program Set 1

The description contains a textual overview of the example, beginning with a short list of new features presented followed by a brief narrative of each new feature. Links to all source files for the examples are given, and a thumbnail of the generated output is presented. Each sample program set also contains a link to a master tar file that contains the source code for all examples in that program set.

5.3 Sample Program Set 1

Using programs that continue to generate only small numbers of triangles, this set introduces, in turn, the following important concepts:

- Coordinate system issues including generalized communication between the Controller and its several managed ModelView instances in which each ModelView instance reports its spatial extent to the Controller; the Controller uses this information to maintain a master spatial extent that can then be used to map from world coordinate data to logical (and later physical) coordinates on the device.
- Aspect ratio preservation, including when it is and is not appropriate.
- Attributes – both "per-primitive" and "per-vertex" attributes.
- General event handling schemes including inverse coordinate mapping that allows pixel coordinates to be mapped back to world coordinates.
- Program design patterns illustrating different common approaches to how responsibility for geometry and appearance generation can be divided between the CPU program and the GLSL shader program running on the GPU. Included is a glimpse into how procedural modeling in GLSL can be used to completely determine the appearance of geometry stored in buffers on the GPU. For example, Fig. 3 is a screen shot from a demonstration program showing how two simple triangles can be rendered in a half dozen very different ways based strictly on choices made in the GLSL fragment shader program.

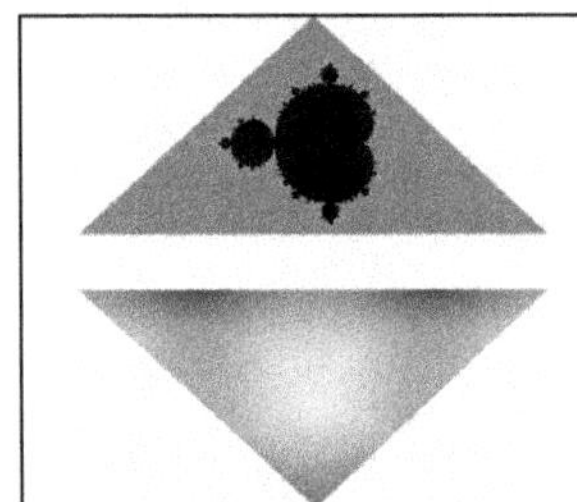

Figure 3: Two Triangles

5.4 Other Sample Program Sets

The remaining online sample sets continue to add to the students' repertoires by introducing concepts involving fonts, general color space and color modeling issues, simple animation using timer callbacks, and modeling techniques. We use a font library based on utilities developed by George Sealy [5], slightly modified to work in the context of our execution environment. It is the general modeling techniques introduced at this stage that merit the most attention here.

While certain variations can be reasonably introduced in different ModelView instances, students quickly run into limitations as they attempt more elaborate scenes. Our first approach to overcome these limitations is to convert ModelView to an abstract base class. Keeping ModelView simple – basically preserving only those interfaces needed to communicate effectively with the Controller and factoring out a few common tools required by all concrete ModelView subclass instances – we quickly arrive at a modified design that allows multiple unique instances of models to be maintained and rendered in this environment. Our first example of such a scene results in a "mountain village" as shown in Fig. 4.

Three concrete subclasses of ModelView are used: House, Tree, and Mountain. Each can be parameterized on creation with different relative and absolute sizes, labels, etc. Students see how different subclasses can have their own GLSL shader programs for rendering their instances. For example, the House subclass render method sends to its GLSL program information describing the part of the house being rendered, and the GLSL program is then responsible for creating an appropriate rendered appearance.

Figure 4: A Mountain Village.

5.5 Moving to 3D

Making the transition from 2D to 3D is always difficult. Of course 3D coordinate data is required; 3D normal vector descriptions and material reflectance properties are required as well to support lighting models. Students must cope with a more complex viewing model involving line of sight, field of view, etc. The good news is that neither a new nor an expanded set of APIs is required with shader-based OpenGL. It is of course necessary to explain the mathematical aspects and discuss what computations must be performed and where (e.g., on the CPU or on the GPU using GLSL). But no new APIs are required in order to render a 3D scene with a given lighting environment. Once students know what needs to be done and what data needs to be sent to the GPU, they simply use interfaces they have been using all along to make that happen. Even implementation of dynamic 3D viewing operations like rotations, panning, and zooming can all be accomplished using APIs they are now well on the path towards mastering.

This base familiarity with the core API means we can also begin to back away from presenting complete running examples, focusing instead on conceptual material and code snippets that introduce new modeling and rendering techniques. We include focused code samples where needed, but expect the students to exercise their understanding of the overall structure so as to be able to incorporate these into shader programs and/or CPU code as needed.

Subsequent online and in-class materials continue to develop more advanced 3D modeling techniques. Some new APIs are required along the way for certain advanced techniques, most notably texture mapping. Given their overall familiarity with the architecture and the OpenGL API, we find that students are able to simply focus on mastering the concepts while plugging implementations of the new functionality they are learning into the architecture as needed.

Figures 5 and 6 below show examples of student-generated projects from the last time the course was offered. In addition to the 3D scenes, it was a requirement to support walking through or otherwise exploring the 3D environments, and students generally had few problems doing so.

6. DISCUSSION

As mentioned in the Introduction, a very common perception is that it is impractical to teach pure shader-based OpenGL programming without first exposing students to required introductory concepts using the older, simpler, and now deprecated interface. There are a number of problems with this approach that makes seeking ways to avoid that initial experience worth pursuing. One obvious problem is that students must learn two different APIs. Somewhat worse is the fact that two overlap considerably, so when "making the move" to the pure non-deprecated shader-based OpenGL API, they must pay careful attention to what they can (and in fact must) still use as opposed to functionality they must eschew. It was the goal of the online material briefly introduced here to help fast-track students into an adequate comfort level with shader-based OpenGL so that they could demonstrate solid skills by the end of a single semester.

It should come as no surprise that the first time through the course was a bit rough. Students struggled as I tried to identify the best order in which to cover the various required concepts. Exam scores were noticeably lower than usual. Submitted student projects were much less sophisticated and more quirky and buggy than those in previous semesters.

Typical comments from the first offering of the course included:

- "Don't know if he realizes how difficult some of the stuff is for beginners."
- "More frequent smaller projects would help build a better understanding."

These comments along with my general observations and experiences from the first offering led to several modifications including a significant restructuring and reordering of the online topics covered, better up-front explanations of high-level concepts, and more and smaller projects.

By the second – and especially the third – offering of the course in this new format, significant improvements were noticed as evidenced by all measures noted above. Submitted student projects were less buggy and much more sophisticated (see Fig. 5 and 6 below), many including elaborate indoor or outdoor scenes. Performance on exams was markedly better, and end-of-semester course evaluations reflected a higher level of satisfaction. For example:

- "This is the most challenging and one of the most rewarding classes I have taken."

To be sure, many students still commented that the material was quite difficult and that they struggled. But the overall sense was much more positive than that from the first offering.

7. FUTURE DIRECTIONS

The jump to 3D has always been a difficult one – even when teaching the older deprecated API. It continues to be a significant hurdle for students when using pure shader-based OpenGL. It is my sense, however, that we have reached the point where the primary difficulties have reverted to those that are intrinsic to 2D versus 3D rather than being unique to the use of pure shader-based OpenGL. Primary difficulties encountered by students in this class include conceptual issues surrounding (i) 3D modeling and (ii) generating appropriate views of 3D scenes. Problems surrounding the latter are heavily related to visualizing the relationships among the various coordinate systems that APIs like OpenGL use. Specifically, coordinates are mapped in turn across a series of 3D coordinate systems: modeling coordinates to world coordinates to viewing ("eye") coordinates to logical device space coordinates and ultimately to pixel coordinates. Students must fully understand these different coordinate systems and know which they are dealing with at various points in time when creating and manipulating data on either the CPU or in GLSL on the GPU. We continue to use our *metaview* to help students master these concepts [3].

Figure 5: Student project: Garden with thatched roof hut.

Our future plans to address the other ongoing concerns are multifaceted. We plan to incorporate specific "Modeling 101" materials to both the online web site as well as in-class discussions. While especially needed for 3D modeling, such materials will also be helpful in 2D, and the 2D materials can be constructed in such a way as to feed into the 3D version of "Modeling 101".

We would also like to find a way to incorporate at least introductory material on some of the other programmable stages. For example, geometry and tessellation shaders could be introduced, and possibly even the new compute shaders. The course is fairly tightly packed, however, so some of these advanced topics might be relegated to "optional extensions" status of some sort and/or used by follow-on advanced graphics courses.

8. SUMMARY

We have discussed our approach to the teaching of pure shader-based OpenGL, an approach that has evolved over the past couple of years. We have found that teaching the concepts in the context of a useful software architecture – specifically, a simplified version of the well-known Model-View-Controller architecture – has allowed us to present material typically found by undergraduate students to be quite complex in an incremental style that most find to be manageable, albeit still challenging.

This approach has also been found to have several additional benefits, for example:

- exposure to certain intermediate and advanced object-oriented concepts in a realistic setting.
- experience with the common and useful Model-View-Controller design pattern. They use our simplified version, but also learn enough of the complete pattern so that they should be able to recognize and comfortably move to this pattern if and when appropriate.
- experience with data-parallel GPU programming, GPU work assignments, and CPU-GPU coordination and communication.

Figure 6: Student project: Castle basement with trunk.

9. ACKNOWLEDGMENTS

I am most indebted to the students who enrolled in the first couple of offerings of this new shader-based version of the graphics course. In spite of my warnings at the start of the class, their willingness to be a part of this grand adventure was truly appreciated, and their comments were taken to heart.

REFERENCES

[1] Angel, E. and Shreiner, D., 2012. *Interactive Computer Graphics: A Top-Down Approach With Shader-Based OpenGL*. Addison-Wesley, Boston, MA. (6th edition).

[2] Brown. 2013. *Exploratories*. Retrieved August 8, 2013 from http://www.cs.brown.edu/exploratories.

[3] Miller, J. R. metaview: A Tool for Learning About Viewing in 3D, *SIGCSE '12: Proceedings of the ACM Conference on Computer Science Education*, Feb-March 2012, pp. 135-140.

[4] Schreiner, D., Sellers, G., Kessenich, J. and Licea-Kane, B., 2013. *OpenGL Programming Guide*. Addison-Wesley, Boston, MA. (8th ed.).

[5] Sealy, G., 2013. *Adding Font Support in OpenGL*, Retrieved August 20, 2013 from http://acornheroes.com/2009/04/adding-font-support-in-opengl/.

[6] Talton, J. O. and Fitzpatrick, D., Teaching Graphics with the OpenGL Shading Language, *SIGCSE '07: Proceedings of the ACM Conference on Computer Science Education*, March 2007, pp. 259-263.

Dynamic Program Visualizations – An Experience Report

James H. Cross II
Auburn University
Auburn, AL 36849-5347
334-844-6315
crossjh@auburn.edu

T. Dean Hendrix
Auburn University
Auburn, AL 36849-5347
334-844-6305
hendrtd@auburn.edu

Larry A. Barowski
Auburn University
Auburn, AL 36849-5347
334-844-4330
barowla@auburn.edu

David A. Umphress
Auburn University
Auburn, AL 36849-5347
334-844-6305
umphrda@auburn.edu

ABSTRACT
In this paper, we describe our experiences using dynamic program visualizations in our Java-based CS1 and CS2 courses during the spring semester 2013. The visualizations were constructed by both faculty and students using the new viewer canvas in jGRASP. A public beta version was downloaded and installed in our computer labs and on student and faculty machines. Program visualizations were used in the classroom as well as in lab activities and programming projects. Since the viewers had already been evaluated in controlled experiments, our focus was on ease of use of the viewer canvas by the students and the utility of the program visualizations in helping students understand their programs. Direct observations in the lab and individual meetings with students to discuss their work indicated that students could indeed build dynamic visualizations that, in conjunction with the debugger, helped them understand and correct bugs in their programs much more effectively than using the debugger alone.

Categories and Subject Descriptors
D.2.6 [**Software Engineering**]: Programming Environments—*Graphical environments, Integrated environments, Interactive environments, Programmer workbench*; H.5.2 [**Information Systems**]: User Interfaces – *Interaction Styles*; K.3.2 [**Computing Milieux**]: Computers and Information Science Education – *Computer Science Education*

General Terms
Design, Experimentation, Human Factors, Verification.

Keywords
Program visualization, algorithm animation, data structures.

1. INTRODUCTION
Consider the scenario where a student has downloaded an example program and is studying it by reading through the code and by running the program. The adventurous student may even set a breakpoint and step through the program in a debugger to see the variables coming in and out of scope and changing values in an effort to understand the program's behavior. For many insightful example programs, the key to understanding may lie in observing a few specific variables that range from primitives to simple objects to traditional data structures. Unfortunately, examining the values of these in the debugger may require more effort than the student deems reasonable. This is especially true when the items of interest are complex and require unfolding (e.g., a linked structure) or when variables are in separate scopes and not viewable at the same time (i.e., student must switch the debugger context via the call stack in order to see the variables).

SIGCSE'14, March 5–8, 2014, Atlanta, Georgia, USA.

http://dx.doi.org/10.1145/2538862.2538958

Now consider a second scenario where the student builds his/her own program visualization for the example program. Note that this scenario is also applicable when students are writing and debugging their own programs. Instead of running the program in the traditional way, the student clicks *run in canvas* which launches the debugger and opens an empty viewer canvas window. Now as the student steps through the program, any variable dragged from the debug tab onto the viewer canvas opens an associated dynamic viewer. After all items of interest have been dragged onto the canvas and arranged, the canvas is saved. Now when the student clicks *run in canvas*, the canvas file is opened and the canvas window displays the names and outlines of the viewers that were saved. When the student clicks *play*, the program begins auto-stepping and as the variables on the canvas come into scope, their respective viewers are opened. The canvas can be paused, single-stepped, sped up, slowed down, etc. as the student observes the program's behavior in his/her own dynamic program visualization.

In the third scenario, instead of having the student create the program visualization, the instructor provides a canvas file along with the example program. In this case, the student simply opens the program and then clicks *run in canvas* and *play* in order to see the program visualization. This allows the instructor to create a canvas that displays the elements essential for understanding the example and thus to focus the student's attention appropriately. This might be the same canvas the instructor would use in class to explain the example. However, now the student can *play* the program and watch the visualization repeatedly, pausing, single-stepping, etc. as needed, until a useful level of understanding is achieved.

In this paper, we describe our experience in CS1 and CS2 with all three of the scenarios described above. We begin in section 2 with a brief overview of jGRASP and program visualizations. In section 3, we use numerous examples to describe how the canvas was used in our courses. These examples are representative of the many program visualizations that were used in class to explain programs, in lab for graded activities, and in programming assignments for debugging. Section 4 describes the supporting evaluation results for the viewers and canvas. Related work is described in section 5, and the paper concludes in Section 6 with a look at future directions for program visualizations in jGRASP.

2. OVERVIEW OF jGRASP AND DYNAMIC PROGRAM VISUALIZATIONS

jGRASP is a lightweight IDE that provides both static and dynamic visualizations of the user's program (see jgrasp.org for a complete description). In this section, we provide the rationale for the new viewer canvas in version 2.0 which facilitates the drag-and-drop creation of dynamic program visualizations that can be saved and replayed as needed.

Previous versions of jGRASP allowed the user to open viewers on variables during a debug or workbench session by simply dragging them from the Debug or Workbench tab. The particular viewer for a variable could be selected from a list based on the variable's type. For example, the viewers available for a String variable include Presentation Char Array, Basic, Formatted, etc., and each viewer had settings that could be configured. If the user had several viewers open, these could be arranged and sized in a useful way to show the behavior of the running program. The caveat was that when the debug or workbench session ended and the variables disappeared, so did the viewers. To get the viewers back, the user would have to drag the variables out again during the next debug or workbench session. Although individual viewer settings were maintained for the duration of the jGRASP session, the arrangement of the viewers was not. For a single variable that references an object such as a linked list, this was fine. In fact, our structure identifier viewer does a nice job of determining if an object is one of the traditional data structures (stack, queue, linked, list, binary tree, etc.) and then rendering it accordingly as the user steps through the code. However, when creating visualizations from multiple variables from different scopes, users found that losing the arrangement and individual viewer settings each time the program ended was a major inhibitor for using the dynamic viewers. In other words, using the viewers was just not convenient.

The new viewer canvas solves all of these issues and makes creating and sharing dynamic visualizations quite convenient. The user simply drags the variables from the Debug tab or Workbench tab into a canvas window, arranges, resizes, and adjusts the settings of the viewers as needed, and then saves the canvas. To replay the visualization, the user just clicks *run in canvas* and *play*. To share the visualization, the user provides the source code and canvas file(s) to others.

3. VISUALIZATIONS IN CS1 AND CS2

Perhaps the most obvious use for program visualizations is in the classroom when example programs are presented and discussed. This can be during a traditional lecture or a "flipped" classroom – essentially any setting where the goal is for the students to understand a program. For example, if the goal is to introduce arrays, the instructor might use a textbook-like rendering of an array showing its state at some step in an example program. Multiple renderings could be used to illustrate how the array is being updated as the program progresses. In place of the static visualizations found in a textbook or PowerPoint slides, we used dynamic visualizations in our CS1 and CS2 courses. The viewer canvas was used in conjunction with example programs that are normally presented in the classroom to introduce new concepts. One of our goals was to ensure that students could create their own visualizations when needed to understand an example or to debug their own programs. We found that the best way to accomplish this was to have students create a canvas during their graded activities in lab and then demo it for their TA.

3.1 The Scanner Presentation Viewer

Early in CS1, we introduce the Scanner class for reading input from the keyboard. Figure 1 shows part of a program that calculates and prints the total costs for a dinner group. The program is running in the debugger and is about to print the result after reading in *name*, *numOfPersons*, and *costPerPerson* using *scan*, a Scanner object on System.in. These variables are shown in the Debug tab on the left. The canvas in Figure 2 was created by dragging these variables from the Debug tab to an empty canvas window. By default, primitives are shown with the Basic viewer. The Scanner Presentation viewer in the canvas shows the character stream coming in from the keyboard. Note that the small green arrowhead indicates that the 22.95 has been read, but the carriage return and newline characters that follow 22.95 have not. Later in the course the Scanner viewer is used to see data being read from files. Being able to see a visualization of a Scanner object as an input steam is consumed provides students with an opportunity to have a better understanding of the object.

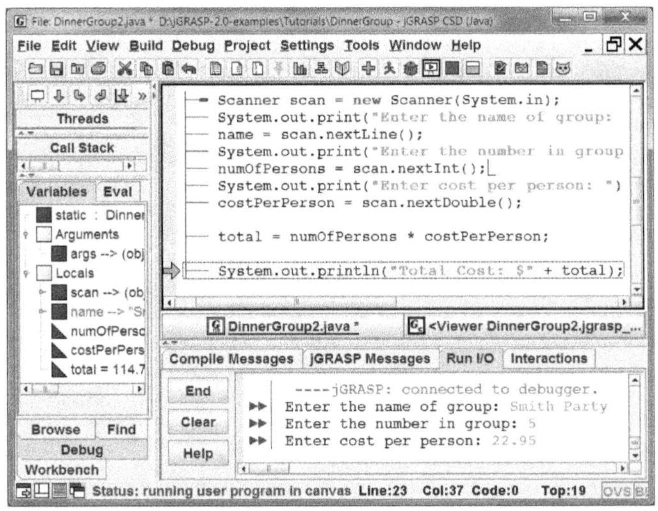

Figure 1. Using the Scanner to read in values

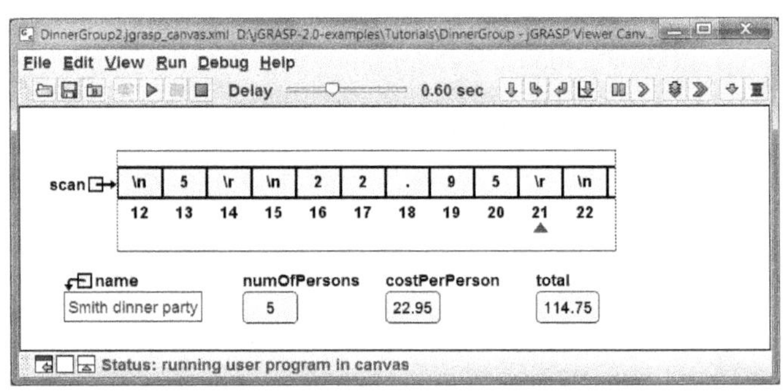

Figure 2. Canvas showing progress of Scanner *scan*

3.2 The Basic Viewer for Objects

In our next example, we show how we used the canvas to help students understand the concept of creating objects from their own classes. Figure 3 shows a simple program that creates three Book objects and prints them out. The program is being *run in a canvas* that was created on a previous run by dragging each of the Book variables onto the canvas.

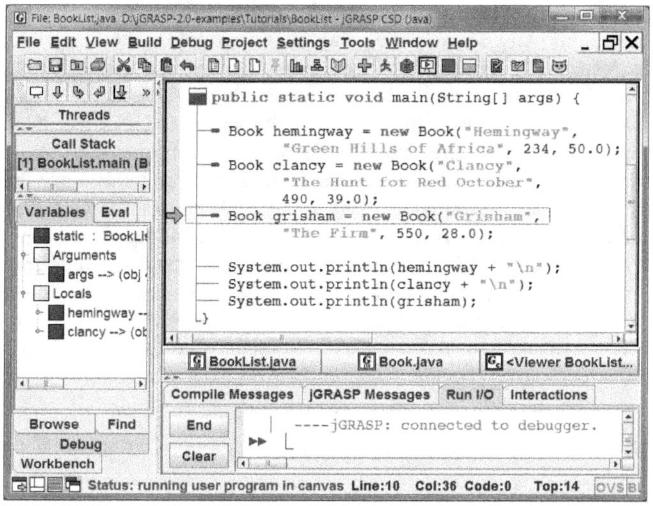

Figure 3. BookList after Hemingway and Clancy have been created

When the user *plays* the canvas, the program auto-steps-in at each statement, requiring no user control. When the program steps into the Book constructor to create the object for *grisham*, the user can see each of the fields set to its respective value from the corresponding parameters in the local *this* Book object. Figure 4 shows the program stepping in the constructor after *author* and *title* have been assigned and before *pages* has been assigned.

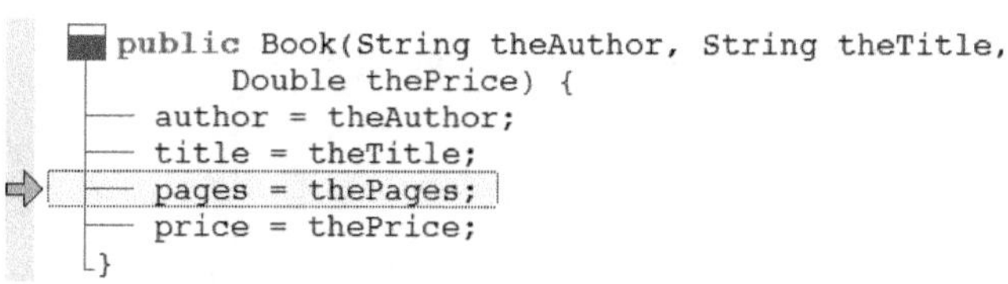

Figure 4. Stepping in the Book constructor

In order to see the construction of a Book object in the canvas, the Book object *this* was also dragged onto the canvas while paused inside the constructor. Figure 5 shows the canvas after two Book objects, *hemingway* and *clancy*, have been created. The outline for grisham will be replaced with the Book object for *grisham* when the constructor completes. In Figure 5, we can also see that the Book object *this* is being updated per Figure 4. When the constructor completes, the value of *this* is assigned to *grisham* in the main program. Note that in Figure 5, the variables *hemingway*, *clancy*, and *grisham* are grayed out to indicate that they are out of scope. As soon as scope returns to main, only the variable *this* will be grayed out.

As students begin to develop their own classes, we provide lab activities where they work through examples that include the creation of a canvas for each program. At the end of these activities, the students demo their work by running their programs in the canvas. Students then use the canvas with their weekly programming projects. For example, after implementing a class, they may create instances by entering code in the Interactions tab. The objects can then be dragged from the Workbench tab to the canvas window. When methods are invoked on an object (via interactions or the Invoke Method dialog), the results are indicated in the canvas.

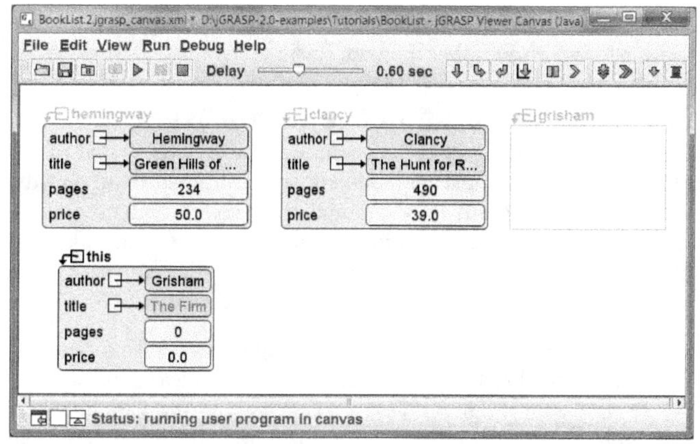

Figure 5. Book object *this* being updated in the constructor

3.3 The Basic Viewer for Arrays

Figure 6 shows a simple program being *run in canvas* after *double* values have been stored in an array named *sides* and a Polygon object called *shape* has been created using *sides* as a parameter.

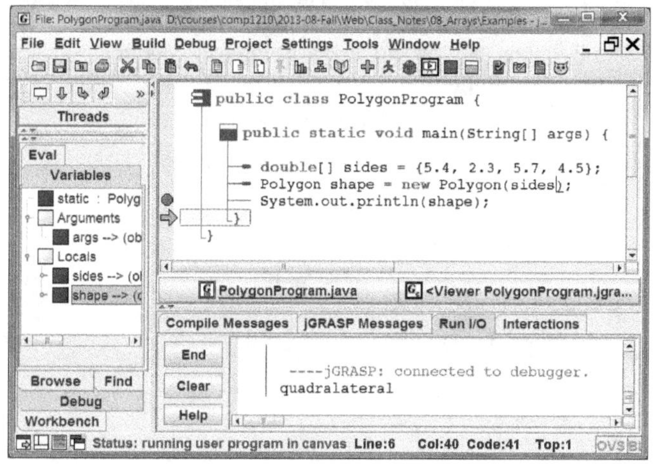

Figure 6. PolygonProgram after *sides* and *shape* are created

Figure 7 shows the canvas after the *sides* array and *shape* have been dragged onto the canvas and then *shape* was dragged onto the canvas a second time. The *sides* array and the first viewer for *shape* are shown using the Basic viewer. Note that Polygon *shape* has a single field of type *double* [] called *sideLengths*. The second copy of *shape* has been set to the toString() viewer which, as its name implies, displays the result of invoking the Polygon toString() method on *shape*.

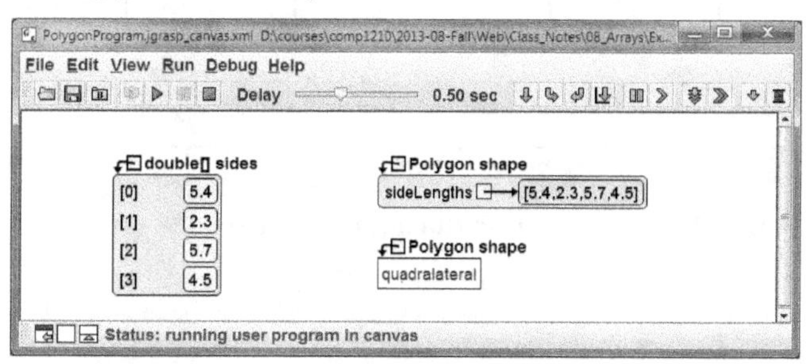

Figure 7. Canvas showing *sides* and two *views* of shape

Most variable types have multiple viewers associated with them to provide flexibility in creating the desired program visualization. In the next section, we will use the Presentation viewer for an array rather than the Basic viewer.

3.4 The Presentation Viewer for Arrays

One the most important concepts introduced in CS1 is that of the algorithm. While most methods are straightforward early in the course, at some point they become complex enough to require more than a cursory explanation. In this section, we take a look at a simple binary search method and see how the canvas can be used to visualize the algorithm in an animated way.

Consider the binarySearch method in Figure 8 which takes an int *key* and an int[]*intArray* as parameters and returns the index of *key* in *intArray*. Figure 9 shows a canvas with the variables *key*, *low*, *mid*, *high*, and *intArray*. The Presentation viewer has been selected for each of these variables. In addition to showing *low*, *mid*, and *high* in separate viewers, the array Presentation viewer for *intArray* has been set to show these variables as indices. When the student *plays* the program that invokes the binarySearch method, each viewer on the canvas is updated at each step in the method. More importantly, the user can see the indices move toward the array element containing the value of *key*. The *play*, *pause*, and *stop* buttons along with the delay slider and debug controls, allow the student to have complete control over the program visualization.

```
public static int binarySearch(int key, int[] intArray) {
   int low = 0;
   int high = intArray.length - 1;
   while (low <= high) {
      int mid = (low + high) / 2;
      if (key < intArray[mid]) {
         high = mid - 1;
      }
      else if (key > intArray[mid]) {
         low = mid + 1;
      }
      else {
         return mid;
      }
   }
   return -1;
}
```

Figure 8. A binarySearch method for int arrays

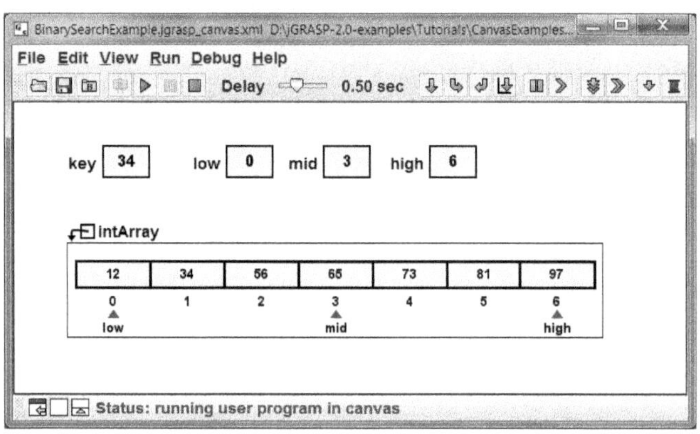

Figure 9. Canvas showing BinarySearch method in progress

As students transition from CS1 to CS2, the viewer canvas can play an even more important role in program understanding. Now we consider the selection sort method shown in Figure 10.

Figure 11 shows the canvas as the method progresses. Note that *ia* was passed in as the formal parameter *list* and that, even though *ia* is out of scope, its viewer is continually updated because *ia* and *list* are referencing the same object. Two viewers in the canvas are open on ia: (1) the Bar Graph viewer for arrays and (2) the Presentation array viewer with the *index*, *min*, and *scan* set as indices. When the canvas is played, the student can see the indices moving beneath the array as the program auto-steps. As each iteration of the outer loop completes, the next smallest item will moved to its final place in *ia* and both viewers for *ia* are updated accordingly. In Figure 11, the value 0.61 has just been placed in *ia*[4] so the first five elements have been sorted. Note that *scan* is out of scope and not shown as an array index since the inner loop has terminated. The Bar Graph viewer for *ia* makes the animation easy to follow as the values are moved in the array during the run. When the method ends, the values in the array will be in ascending order. While this is similar to many "canned" animations of selection sort algorithms, the major difference is that the student can quickly create a program visualization of his/her own program. This is especially useful when the students need to debug their programs.

```
static void selectionSort(double[] list) {
   int min;
   double temp;

   for (int index = 0; index < list.length - 1; index++) {
      min = index;
      for (int scan = index + 1; scan < list.length; scan++) {
         if (list[scan] < list[min]) {
            min = scan;
         }
      }

      // Swap the values.
      temp = list[min];
      list[min] = list[index];
      list[index] = temp;
   }
}
```

Figure 10. A selectionSort method for int arrays

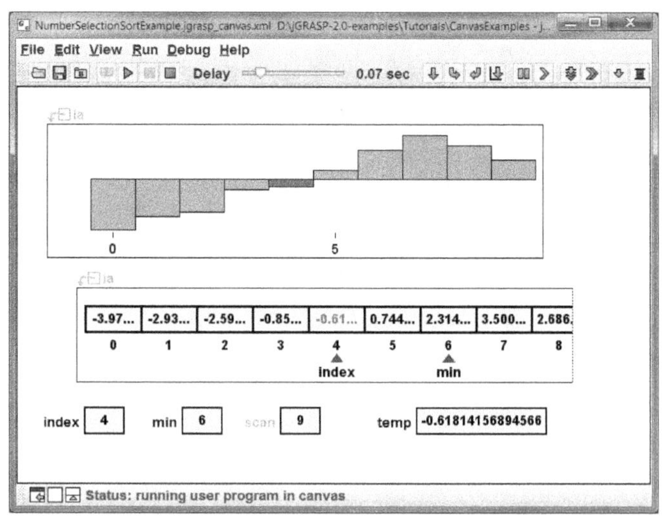

Figure 11. Canvas as the selectionSort method progresses

3.5 The Viewers for Data Structures

Since the focus of CS2 is data structures, the viewer canvas can play an important role in helping faculty present the material and helping students understand it. When students implement their own data structures, the program visualizations created by the students can go a long way toward lowering the frustration level that many students suffer in their first venture into data structures and their associated algorithms.

When any object is dragged onto the canvas, the object is always examined by the Structure Identifier viewer (SI) to determine if it is a traditional data structure (stack, queue, linked list, binary tree, etc.). If it is, the SI viewer is opened with a conceptual rendering of the structure. The SI viewer has over a 95% recognition rate for stack, queue, linked list, and binary tree examples found in most data structure textbooks. Examples are also included with the jGRASP distribution. Since space is short, we show an example of a binary search tree in Figure 13. The canvas shows that the value 1 is about to be inserted in the BinaryTree *bt*.

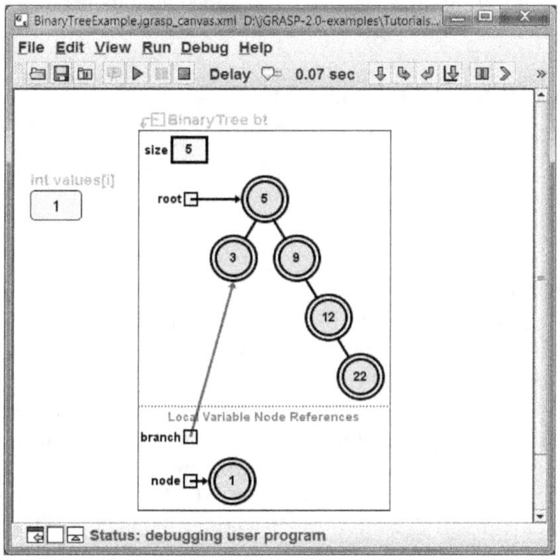

Figure 12. Canvas with conceptual rendering of a BinaryTree as an element is inserted

We now routinely provide canvas files with many of our example programs that are intended to illustrate important concepts such as searching and sorting. With the source file and canvas file in hand, the student can see the animation with literally two clicks: *run in canvas* and *play*.

4. SUPPORTING EVALUATION

The development of the viewer canvas was informed by the results of a comprehensive evaluation of their primary component, the dynamic viewers. The efficacy of the viewers was evaluated using both controlled experiments and user questionnaires.

Four experiments were conducted to investigate the effect, if any, that the viewers had on student performance on common programming tasks, including both development and debugging [2]. Two experiments were based on singly linked lists, and were performed near the beginning of a CS2 course just after linked structures had been introduced. The other two experiments were based on binary search trees and were performed near the end of the same CS2 course, after the students had experience working with more complex data structures and algorithms. All four experiments were designed to test the hypotheses that (1) students would be able to develop code with fewer logic errors when using the viewers, and (2) students would be able to identify and correct logic errors in existing code when using the viewers.

The results of the experiments were uniformly supportive of the positive effect of the viewers on student performance. Specifically, students using the viewers developed code faster, made fewer errors during development, found errors in existing code faster, found a larger number of errors in existing code, and injected fewer errors when repairing the existing errors, as compared to students not using the viewers. Furthermore, each of these performance differences was statistically significant.

Based on these strongly positive results, we continued to refine the viewers for widespread use in computing curricula. In the summer of 2011, we surveyed 21 veteran CS1, CS2, and Algorithms faculty members who participated in an NSF-funded workshop on visualization in CS1 and CS2, held at Auburn University. The faculty members were from 20 different institutions across the country (not Auburn) and represented four-year, two-year, and high school levels. Each respondent had experience in using jGRASP for instructional purposes. The survey instrument consisted of sixteen items grouped into four evaluation categories (EC). EC1 – Successful integration of visualization and IDE; EC2 – Usability; EC3 – Suitability for use in courses; EC4 – Aid in student learning. The 21 faculty members were asked to respond to each item on a scale of 1 to 5, where 1 indicated that the respondent strongly disagreed with the statement and 5 indicated that the respondent strongly agreed with the statement.

While it is significant that the results are extremely positive across all evaluation question categories, it is particularly important to examine the responses that correspond to the effect on student learning (EC4). Item 12: *jGRASP can positively affect the students' knowledge, skills, and behavior.* **Mean = 4.62**; Item 13: *Students can acquire additional programming knowledge by using jGRASP (e.g., inheritance, data structure implementation).* **Mean = 4.43**; Item 14: *Students can acquire additional programming skills by using jGRASP (e.g., debugging, code reading).* **Mean = 4.48**; Item 15: *When appropriate, students will use visualizations in their approach to solving problems.* **Mean = 4.05**; Item 16: *When students use visualizations in their approach to solving problems, they can inherently gain a deeper understanding of the problem.* **Mean = 4.57**. The faculty responding to the survey clearly believed that the visualizations in jGRASP could positively affect student learning.

After a year of further refining the viewers, we administered a similar survey to CS2 students at Auburn University. The viewers and a beta version of the canvas were used during this offering of the CS2 course. The survey instrument consisted of 14 items grouped into the same evaluation categories as above. The students were asked to respond to each item on a scale of 1 to 5, where 1 indicated that the respondent strongly disagreed with the statement and 5 indicated that the respondent strongly agreed with the statement. Again, the results are extremely positive across all evaluation question categories and the students' opinions of the affect on learning mirror those of the faculty above. Item 10: *The use of jGRASP can positively affect my programming knowledge, skills, and behavior.* **Mean = 4.29**; Item 11: *I can acquire additional programming knowledge by using jGRASP (e.g., inheritance, data structure implementation).* **Mean = 3.82**; Item 12: *I can acquire additional programming skills by using jGRASP (e.g., debugging, code reading).* **Mean = 4.35**; Item 13: *When appropriate, I use visualizations in my approach to solving problems.* **Mean = 4.06**; Item 14: *When I use visualizations in solving problems, I inherently gain a deeper understanding of the problem.* **Mean = 4.12**.

Five questions that specifically addressed the efficacy of the canvas were added to the student survey. Item 15: *The Viewer Canvas makes the current data structure visualizations in jGRASP (viewers) even more useful.* **Mean = 4.47**; Item 16: *The Viewer Canvas is particularly helpful when debugging.* **Mean = 4.47**; Item 17: *The Viewer Canvas is particularly helpful when trying to understand a program that someone else wrote.* **Mean = 4.29**; Item 18: *The Viewer Canvas is particularly helpful when trying to understand a new algorithm.* **Mean = 4.06**; Item 19: *The Viewer Canvas is particularly helpful when trying to understand a new data structure.* **Mean = 4.47**. Again, these results were extremely positive and clearly showed that the students responding to the survey believed that the canvas was a useful aid to learning.

In the spring semester of 2013, sections of our CS1 course were required to complete an in-lab activity using the viewer canvas. The activity was focused on linear search and binary search on arrays in Java. A canvas file configured by the course instructor was provided for each algorithm (as implemented in a Java method). The activity required each student to interact with the canvas as the underlying program executed.

There were 50 students completing the activity with the canvas. At the end of the activity, each student was asked to respond to the following statements on a scale from 1 to 5, where 1 was strongly disagree and 5 was strongly agree. Item 1: *The canvas was helpful in understanding linear search.* **Mean = 4.04**; Item 2: *The canvas was helpful in understanding binary search.* **Mean = 4.01**. After using the canvas for these specific learning tasks, the students clearly felt that the canvas positively affected their learning. The utility of the canvas was also confirmed by direct observation in the lab as students worked through activities and by unsolicited comments during individual meetings with students to discuss their work.

5. RELATED WORK

Software visualization research has been directed toward two main areas of interest: (1) program visualization, in which source code, data structures, or runtime behavior is represented, and (2) algorithm animation, in which views are provided of conceptual behavior at the algorithmic rather than the implementation level [3, 5, 9]. Algorithm animation offers a dynamic perspective, often at a higher level of abstraction than the source code [9]. Whether the animation is produced from source code or independently of any implementation, its primary purpose is to increase the comprehensibility of the underlying algorithm and the associated program behavior. Extensive research has been carried out in an effort to understand the effects that algorithm animations have on learning and comprehension. Although some results were negative, it has generally been shown that appropriate animations can be effective aids to student learning, given the right circumstances [6, 7, 8]. There are various tools that provide visualizations similar to those described in this paper. For example, both Jeliot [1] and MatrixPro [4, 5] provide animations comparable to those provided by jGRASP, but they are not IDEs nor do they have the functionality that jGRASP offers.

6. FUTURE DIRECTIONS

Although our focus in this paper has been the use of visualizations in CS1 and CS2, the viewer canvas is, in fact, suitable for viewing Java programs of any level of complexity. And while we are pleased with our results thus far, there is much left to be done. Future directions for dynamic program visualization must include support for C/C++ programs since they are arguably more difficult to understand than Java programs. During this next phase, we would also refine the current viewers and canvas to include a viewer API for customized viewers and advanced features such as global scaling and automatic layout. In addition, custom structure identifiers could be built for families of user structures in specific application domains. After GNU-based support is in place, we would like to pursue a plug-in for Eclipse that would bring all of the visualization functionality in jGRASP to the Eclipse framework.

7. ACKNOWLEDGMENTS

The research reported in this paper was funded by NSF Award 0920632. We thank all of the students and faculty who provided valuable feedback during the implementation of the viewer canvas in jGRASP.

8. REFERENCES

[1] Ben-Bassat Levy, R., Ben-Ari, M., & Uronen, P. A. (2003). The Jeliot 2000 program animation system. Computers & Education, 40(1), 1-15.

[2] Cross, J. H., Hendrix, T. D., Umphress, D. A., Barowski, L.A., Jain, J., and Montgomery, L. N. (2009). Robust Generation of Dynamic Data Structure Visualizations with Multiple Interaction Approaches, ACM Transactions on Computing Education, Vol. 9, Issue 2 (June 2009), 13:1–13:32.

[3] Ihantola, P., Karavirta, V., Korhonen, A., and Nikander, J. (2005). Taxonomy of Effortless Creation of Algorithm Visualizations. Proceedings of the First International Workshop on Computing Education Research (ICER '05), October 1-2, 2005, Seattle, Washington, pp. 123-133.

[4] Karavirta, V., Korhonen, A., Malmi, L., and Stalnacke, K. (2004). MatrixPro – A tool for on-the-fly demonstration of data structures and algorithms. Proceedings of the Third Program Visualization Workshop, University of Warwick, UK, pp. 26-33.

[5] Karavirta, V. (2007). Integrating algorithm animation systems. Proceedings of the Fourth Program Visualization Workshop, Amsterdam, The Netherlands, pp. 79-87.

[6] McNally, M., Naps, T., Furcy, D.,Grissom, S., and Trefftz, C. (2007). Supporting Rapid Development of Pedagogically Effective Algorithm Visualizations. Journal of Computing Sciences in Colleges, Vol. 23, Issue 1, pp. 80-90.

[7] Parker, B. and Mitchell, I. (2006). Effective Methods for Learning: A Study in Visualization. Journal of Computing Sciences in Colleges, Vol. 22, Issue 2, pp. 176-182.

[8] Rößling , G., Naps, T., Hall, M.S., Karavirta, V., Kerren, A., Leska, C., Moreno, A., Oechsle, R., Rodger, S.H., Urquiza-Fuentes, J., and Velazquez-Iturbide, J.A. (2006). Merging Interactive Visualizations with Hypertextbooks and Course Management. ACM SIGCSE Bulletin, Working Group Reports on Innovation and Technology in Computer Science Education (ITiCSE-WGR '06), Vol. 38, Issue 4, pp. 166-181.

[9] Shaffer, C.A., Cooper, M., Edwards, S.H. (2007). Algorithm Visualization: A Report on the State of the Field. Proceedings of the 38th SIGCSE Technical Symposium on Computer Science Education (SIGCSE '07), Vol. 39, Issue 1, pp. 150-154.

Opportunities for Android Projects in a CS1 Course

Ivaylo Ilinkin
Gettysburg College
Gettysburg, PA
iilinkin@gettysburg.edu

ABSTRACT

Mobile devices have become ubiquitous in our daily lives and are replacing the desktop for email, social networking, daily planner, and so on. A typical mobile device now integrates a wide range of accessories, such as camera, GPS receiver, accelerometer, and offers a touch-screen with gesture-based interaction. This makes mobile devices an exciting platform for software development and programming projects for mobile devices have great potential to provide engaging experiences for computer science majors.

This paper describes a pedagogical tool for introducing Android in a traditional CS1 course. The goal is not to teach Android programming, but to create a framework that integrates seamlessly with the CS1 course structure and supports the introduction of the fundamental computer science concepts by creating an engaging learning environment. The framework enables the students to port their CS1 projects to an Android device with minimal effort.

Categories and Subject Descriptors

K.3.2 [**Computers and Education**]: Computers and Information Science Education—*Curriculum*

General Terms

Design, Experimentation, Human Factors

Keywords

Mobile devices, Java, Android, CS1

1. INTRODUCTION

The capabilities of modern mobile phones have opened a rich area for creative applications. This has great potential to enrich the computer science curriculum and will continue to increase in relevance with each generation of new students. A typical mobile phone now integrates a camera, GPS receiver, accelerometer, and provides a convenient way of interaction via a touch-screen interface. This allows for greater range of exploration and could lead to programming projects that have built-in motivation and the capacity to maintain student engagement. Furthermore, experience with developing applications for mobile devices could open new career opportunities for graduating CS majors. In fact, software development for mobile devices has received enormous recognition in recent years, particularly since the introduction of the iOS and Android operating systems, with Windows CE, Java ME, and Blackberry bringing the first wave of mobile technology in the curriculum [10, 12, 13, 14]. Of the modern platforms, Android, which is based on the Java programming language, has the potential for wide adoption due to the popularity of Java in the computer science curriculum.

Since these technologies have a fairly steep learning curve a lot of the effort has naturally focused on adopting them in the upper-level courses and in senior capstone projects [3, 7, 11, 15, 16]. There have also been successful efforts to integrate Android programming in CS2 [2, 8, 9], and in fact, it is easy to see the potential for using Android in a CS2 course without significant disruption to the course structure, particularly for introducing event-driven GUI programming and the Model-View-Controller pattern. Finally, creative ideas have been reported for introducing mobile programming at the CS0 and high-school level [1, 19, 20, 21]. The latter approaches rely on the *App Inventor* framework which brings the strengths of the visual programming environments of *Scratch* and *Alice* to mobile application development.

While Android has been integrated to some extent at most levels of the curriculum, little has been reported of its adoption at the CS1 level. In a sense this is understandable — approaches that work at the CS0 level (e.g. *App Inventor*) aim for a gentler high-level introduction to programing with a focus on application design, and are therefore, less likely to enhance instruction in CS1. The fact that Android is based on Java makes it tempting to introduce it in CS1 directly, but the programming model is quite different and even a *Hello World* application is fairly involved, which is likely to detract from the main goals of CS1. Direct introduction of Android is feasible in CS2, where programming maturity is expected and the possibilities for creative projects that fit neatly with material are likely to enhance instruction. A promising approach targeting the CS1/CS2 level is described in recent work on the *Sofia* framework [6] using a *micro-world* library designed to fit within an *objects-early* CS1 curriculum. Positive results are reported with using

SIGCSE'14, March 5–8, 2014, Atlanta, GA, USA.

ACM 978-1-4503-2605-6/14/03 ...$15.00.
http://dx.doi.org/10.1145/2538862.2538983.

the *ALE* game development platform for Android for a final project at the end of a CS1 course [4].

The contribution of this paper is to suggest opportunities for introducing Android in CS1 through a pedagogical tool that is compatible with an *objects-late* approach and can be introduced very early in the CS1 curriculum. The paper introduces a framework, called *CS1App*, that fits seamlessly with the CS1 course structure and hides away all of the complexity of setting up an Android application. The students can deploy their projects on an Android device with straightforward modifications to their desktop applications.

The main difficulty in integrating Android in CS1 is that the event-driven model and activity life-cycle in an Android application require fairly sophisticated programming background. The Android requirement that applications should not block the main UI thread makes it difficult to obtain touch and keypad input and leads to a flow of control that is quite different from the straightforward sequential nature of early examples in a typical CS1 course. The advantage of the proposed framework is that it works around this limitation and provides blocking input, for both touch and keypad, so that from the student's perspective input works similar to the `Scanner` and the flow of control has the familiar nature. This makes it possible to port easily desktop applications to Android without knowledge of object-oriented programming. By contrast, the *Sophia* framework, for example, still retains the event-driven model (disguised to some extent) and requires some familiarity with classes and objects. While both *Sophia* and *ALE* offer a wide range of capabilities, that brings a higher level of complexity. The proposed framework has a very low requirements threshold, yet it still affords opportunities for creative projects.

The design of the proposed framework was guided by the following objectives:

- require no knowledge of Android development
- require no knowledge of object-oriented concepts (inheritance, polymorphism, classes, objects, etc.)
- have minimal impact on the planned course schedule

The need for the first goal is obvious if the framework is to be used in CS1. The second goal is motivated by the fact that we use the *objects-late* approach and cannot expect familiarity with object-oriented concepts. We only expect knowledge, introduced as needed, at the level of using `Scanner`, `Random`, or `String` — i.e. an intuitive understanding that a *dot* followed by a fairly obvious phrase, accomplishes what the phrase indicates, such as `scanner.nextInt()` or `myName.length()`. The fact that we target the *objects-late* level means that students exposed to the *objects-early* approach will have no difficulty using the framework. Finally, our last goal acknowledges the fact that Android should be introduced only if it does not disrupt the instructor's plan.

We remark that our goal is not to teach Android programming. In fact, students who use the framework will not learn anything about Android. Yet, they will be able to create with little effort applications that run on Android devices.

Source code for several examples of popular programming projects (*Tic-Tac-Toe*, *Memory Tiles*, *Hangman*, etc.), documentation, and a compiled version of the library are available at `http://www.cs.gettysburg.edu/~ilinkin/cs1app` .

Our approach is inspired by the numerous graphics libraries that have been developed to support teaching in CS1. A graphics library provides an intuitive interface to the students and helps the instructors create engaging assignments to achieve the learning goals. The concepts of drawing primitive shapes are so familiar to the students that a graphics library does not get in the way of learning, and instead, provides a fun and rewarding experience.

The proposed framework is essentially a graphics library for Android. It grew out of a Java graphics library for desktop applications written to support our CS1 and since the Android version retained the same interface, the student projects that worked successfully in the past can now be deployed on an Android device. The framework requires little on the part of the instructor in terms of updating the assignment write-ups and it requires little work from the students to modify their projects, especially compared to the excitement factor of running a non-trivial CS1 application on an Android device and sharing it with friends.

In the rest of the paper Section 2 presents the framework and illustrates the differences between a desktop and an Android application (in particular, subsections 2.2, 2.3, and 2.5 show how to handle touch and keypad input); Section 3 offers ideas for programming projects; Section 4 discusses how to integrate the framework with *DrJava*; and Section 5 closes with concluding remarks.

2. PROPOSED FRAMEWORK

The proposed framework grew out of a graphics library that we have used for teaching CS1 in Java for a number of years. The graphics library offers the standard capabilities for drawing primitive 2D shapes, text, and images on a canvas, and provides an interface to read input from the user. The design and API is similar to that of the graphics library created by John Zelle [23] for introducing computer science through Python.

The graphics library provides an object-oriented interface and a procedural-style interface. Since our course is designed as *objects-late* we use the procedural-style interface, but objects are supported as well. For example, here is how one might draw a red circle of radius 10 centered at $(30, 20)$:

```
(a) canvas.drawCircle(30, 20, 10, "red");

(b) Circle c = new Circle(new Point(30, 20), 10);
    c.setColor("red");
    c.draw();
```

We use the first style and the students quickly guess how to draw other shapes, text, and images.

This simple interface is sufficient to design a number of engaging projects that enhance CS1 instruction, a notion that has been recognized for some time in the computer science education community [5, 17, 18, 22].

2.1 Android App Structure

One of the very first desktop applications that we typically develop in class is to draw a smiley face given its center and radius based on pre-defined face proportions. This has been an effective example for introducing *methods*, *parameters*, and *variables* in a context that is fun and easy to set up.

Figure 1 shows a comparison between a desktop and an Android application for drawing a smiley face. There are only two differences:

- the Android version does not have a **main** method
- the Android version must include **extends AndroidApp**

The base class **AndroidApp** is the one that sets up the view and activity of the application and the process is completely transparent to the students – they don't need to be familiar with the concept of inheritance to appreciate the need for the **extends** clause, since they are building an *Android app*.

No change is needed to the student code to build and run the application on an Android device:

```
class Smiley
{
    // draw a color smiley face of size r at (x, y)
    void drawSmiley(int x, int y, int r, String color)
    {
        // code to draw the smiley face
    }

    // run/test the application
    void run()
    {
        drawSmiley(30, 20, 10, "yellow");
    }

    // we ignore the main method and use run() instead
    public static void main(String[] args)
    {
        new Smiley().run();
    }
}

class SmileyApp extends AndroidApp
{
    // draw a color smiley face of size r at (x, y)
    void drawSmiley(int x, int y, int r, String color)
    {
        // code to draw the smiley face
    }

    // run/test the application
    void run()
    {
        drawSmiley(30, 20, 10, "yellow");
    }
}
```

Figure 1: Comparison between a desktop and an Android application for drawing a smiley face.

2.2 Handling Keypad Input

The framework offers functionality for obtaining user input through an API that is similar to the **Scanner** (Figure 2 (*a*)). For example,

```
float gpa = canvas.readFloat("Enter your GPA");
```

Unlike the **Scanner** the framework also includes functionality for user input via selection lists (Figure 2 (*b*)):

```
String color = canvas.readSelection("Pick a color",
                            "red", "green", "blue");
```

It is important to note that the **canvas.readXXXX** calls are blocking, i.e. execution is suspended until the user has entered the data in the dialog box. One of the difficulties in using Android in CS1 is that the event-driven model of a standard Android application requires non-trivial understanding of object-oriented concepts. The framework removes this obstacle by providing blocking calls that behave exactly as the **Scanner nextXXXX** calls, so the flow of control remains the same as in a desktop application.

(*a*) (*b*)

Figure 2: Screenshots of input dialogs.

2.3 Handling Touch Input

Touch input has greatly enhanced the richness of user experience on mobile devices. The framework makes it possible to detect and handle touch events by providing information about the location of the event, the number of taps (either 1 or 2), and the shape on which the event occurred (for students familiar with objects):

```
Touch touch = canvas.waitForTouch();
int x = touch.getX();
int y = touch.getY();
int taps = touch.getTaps();
```

Again, note that this is a blocking call, so the flow of control remains the same as in a desktop application. We can now combine keypad and touch input to enhance the example from Figure 1 by rewriting the **run()** method:

```
void run()
{
    // could wrap in a while (true) { ... } loop
    int radius = 40;
    String color = canvas.readSelection("Pick a color",
                                "red", "green", "blue");
    Touch touch = canvas.waitForTouch();
    if (touch.getTaps() == 2)
        radius = 2*radius;
    drawSmiley(touch.getX(), touch.getY(), radius, color);
}
```

2.4 Hangman App

In this section we discuss the conversion between a desktop and an Android application in a more complicated example. We use the *Hangman* game to illustrate how little is required to port a non-trivial assignment to an Android device.

The *Hangman* game is one of the popular CS1 assignments. It requires no lengthy introduction and provides an opportunity to exercise in a fun and engaging way a number of fundamental computer science concepts (e.g. *methods*, *control structures*, *for loops*, and *linear structures (strings)*). Creating a desktop *Hangman* application provides a sense of accomplishment for the students, who are just starting to learn about programming; it is all the more rewarding to be able to run it on a personal device and share it with friends.

This is a fairly substantial assignment (a typical submission is about 200 lines of code), and yet it requires little modification to convert it to an Android application. In fact, since the Android framework shares the same interface as the desktop graphics library, other than the changes illustrated in Figure 1 (removing the `main()` method and adding the `extends` clause), the only other modification is to replace:

```
System.out.print("Guess a character:");
char guess = (char) System.in.read();
```

with:

```
char guess = canvas.readChar("Guess a character:");
```

A more interesting variation is to enhance the user experience via touch input. Tapping one of the letters in the alphabet row (see Figure 3) can provide the user's next guess.

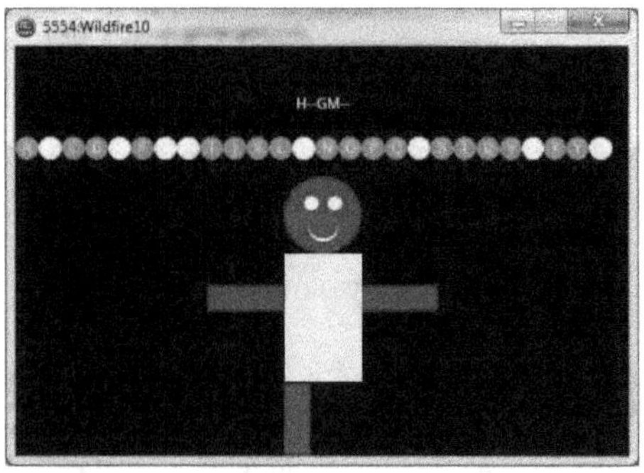

Figure 3: Student submission for *Hangman* project.

Students familiar with objects could use `touch.getShape()` to find which letter was selected and can then interact with the shape object directly. Students who come from *objects-late* background can use the following strategy — in the *Hangman* app the alphabet spans the whole width of the canvas, and therefore, the index of the selected letter can be found with a simple divison. Thus, the keypad input can be replaced with:

```
Touch touch = canvas.waitForTouch();
int index = touch.getX() / letterDiam;
char guess = alphabet.charAt(index);
```

(A careful student might also consider checking if the y coordinate of the touch is close to the alphabet baseline.)

While this may seem a contrived example, it actually generalizes to a wide range of applications. In particular, it can be applied to many board games (e.g. *Tic-Tac-Toe*, *Memory Tiles*, *Minesweeper*, etc.) which have a natural reference point from which one can derive the *row* and *column* of a selected object in a grid:

```
Touch touch = canvas.waitForTouch();
int row = (touch.getY() - BOARD_ULY) / CELL_SIZE;
int col = (touch.getX() - BOARD_ULX) / CELL_SIZE;
```

2.5 Handling Fling Input

The framework supports a variation of the touch input that is recognized as a *fling* across the device screen. For fling events the framework provides information about the start and end points of the gesture, and its direction and velocity. The following example illustrates a possible application of this gesture — the goal is to fling the image in the top-left corner, so that it floats on top of the image in the bottom-right corner (see Figure 4):

```
void run()
{
    int birdX = 60, birdY = 60;
    int pigX = 420, pigY = 260;

    // draw "background.png", "pig.png", "bird.png"

    Fling fling = canvas.waitForFling();
    int dx = fling.getDx();
    int dy = fling.getDy();

    int speedX = 3, speedY = 6;
    while (distance(birdX, birdY, pigX, pigY) > 15 &&
           isVisible(birdX, birdY)) {
        birdX = birdX + speedX*dx;
        birdY = birdY + speedY*dy;

        canvas.sleep(.01);

        // clear canvas, redraw scene
    }
}
```

The two missing methods are straightforward to implement, so this is essentially the complete code for the app. A simple modification can make this even more compelling by choosing a random starting x position for the target image.

Figure 4: Example app for handling fling events.

3. PROGRAMMING PROJECTS

This section introduces examples of programming projects that we have used for several years. With the introduction of the framework we created Android versions as well.

3.1 NimGame and MineSweeper

The *NimGame* is an assignment that we use early in the semester to introduce *methods*, *control structures*, *boolean expressions*, and *while loops*. The students build a variation of a *Nim* game in which two players take turns removing coins from two piles with the restriction that a player must remove at least one, but no more than five, coins per turn from one of the rows (or the same number from both rows). Converting this project to an Android app is straightforward and follows the same pattern as outlined in *Hangman*, Section 2.4. An interesting user-interface challenge posed in *NimGame* is how to distinguish whether to remove coins from a single row or from both rows. We find which coin has been selected (using the strategy as in *Hangman* to select a letter) and remove from a single row on *single tap* and from both rows on *double tap*.

MineSweeper was assigned as a final project just prior to the development of the framework. A student submission was converted to an Android application as proof-of-concept. In fact, despite its greater complexity compared to the other projects it only required the inclusion of the code portion at the end of Section 2.4 for finding the *row* and *column* of the selected cell. Had the framework been available at the time, it would have certainly been a nice way for the students to end the course with their own version of *MineSweeper* on their phones.

Representative images of the applications are shown in Figures 5 and 6.

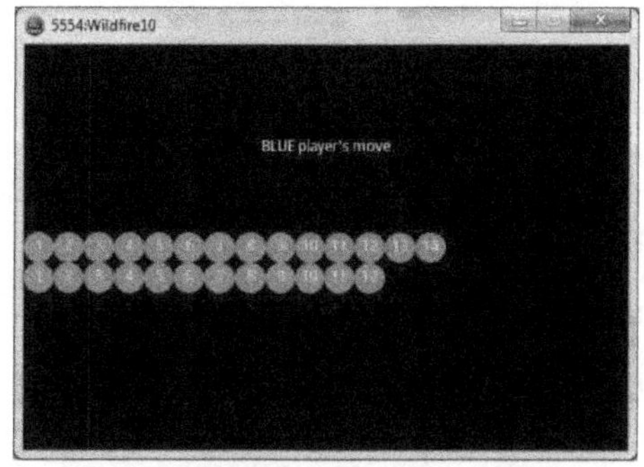

Figure 5: Student submission for *NimGame* project.

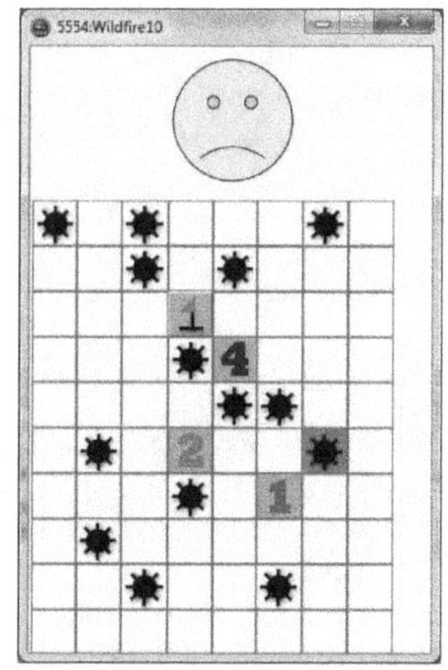

Figure 6: Student desktop submission for *MineSweeper* project converted to Android application as proof-of-concept.

4. INTEGRATION WITH DRJAVA

In this section we discuss our experience with using the proposed framework with *DrJava*. The simple and intuitive interface of *DrJava* has made it our choice of teaching environment in CS1. In CS2 we transition to the significantly more complex, but also more powerful, Eclipse.

Integrating Android and the proposed framework with Eclipse is straightforward. Eclipse manages the required Android plug-ins and the framework only needs to be included as an external `.jar` file to the project. Courses using Eclipse in CS1 will have no difficulty editing, building, and running the examples from the previous sections.

DrJava provides no integration Android, but the setup is quite manageable. The students can still edit and compile their Android applications, provided that they add to the class path the `.jar` file from the Android distribution and the `.jar` file of the framework via the *Edit→Preferences→ Resource Locations* menu. This step is done only once and detailed instructions are provided.

Running the application and setting up a project is currently done outside of *DrJava* via a simple tool, which lets the students set up a new project, load an existing project, and run a loaded project. Since an Android application needs to have a particular directory structure, creating a project cannot be done in *DrJava*. Thus, before starting a new project the students need to run the setup tool and choose a location for the project. The tool automatically builds the required directory structure and creates a `.java` skeleton application file for the project. This file can then be opened and the *Edit→Compile* cycle can be carried out in *DrJava*. Running the project is done again via the external tool which loads the app on the emulator (the emulator is started automatically when the tool is started).

Using the external tool does not hinder development, since it is only used once to setup the project structure. Editing and compiling is still done in *DrJava* and only after the compilation errors have been fixed and the project is ready to run the students need to hit the *Run* button in the external tool instead of the *Run* button in *DrJava*. We are exploring ways to integrate the setup tool functionality with *DrJava* via the *Language* menu with Android as an option.

5. CONCLUSION

This paper described a framework for Android application development and offered examples of programming projects that are feasible at the CS1 level. The goal is not to teach the intricacies of Android programming, but to provide a framework that seamlessly integrates with the course structure and offers another vehicle of introducing the fundamental concepts in a fun and engaging way. Just as graphical desktop application are a great source of motivation, so are applications that the students have built on their own that they can share with their peers through their own phones.

Testing and debugging can be a source of frustration, if the students attempt to build the Android version directly. Uploading to the emulator has a noticeable delay and the idle time may sap some of the energy that could be devoted to the project. (This can be mitigated by plugging in an Android device, so that the application is run on the device instead of the emulator, which is significantly faster.) Alternatively, the students can first build the desktop version and then work on the minor changes that are required to convert it to an Android app. Thus, they can build on the excitement of having a finished product and invest the extra effort to gain an even greater sense of accomplishment.

6. REFERENCES

[1] K. Ahmad and P. Gestwicki. Studio-based learning and App Inventor for Android in an introductory CS course for non-majors. In *Proc. 44th SIGCSE*, pages 287–292, New York, NY, USA, 2013. ACM.

[2] A. Allevato and S. Edwards. Robolift: Engaging CS2 students with testable, automatically evaluated Android applications. In *Proc. 43rd SIGCSE*, pages 547–552, New York, NY, USA, 2012. ACM.

[3] J. Andrus and J. Nieh. Teaching operating systems using Android. In *Proc. 43rd SIGCSE*, pages 613–618, New York, NY, USA, 2012. ACM.

[4] J. Bayzick, B. Askins, S. Kalafut, and M. Spear. Reading mobile games throughout the curriculum. In *Proc. 44th SIGCSE*, pages 209–214, New York, NY, USA, 2013. ACM.

[5] K. Bruce, A. Danyluk, and T. Murtagh. A library to support a graphics-based object-first approach to CS1. In *Proc. 32nd SIGCSE*, pages 6–10, New York, NY, USA, 2001. ACM.

[6] S. Edwards. Re-imagining CS1/CS2 with Android using the Sofia framework. In *Proc. 44th SIGCSE*, pages 759–759, New York, NY, USA, 2013. ACM.

[7] J. Fenwick, Jr., B. Kurtz, and J. Hollingsworth. Teaching mobile computing and developing software to support computer science education. In *Proc. 42nd SIGCSE*, pages 589–594, New York, NY, USA, 2011. ACM.

[8] M. Goadrich, M. Jadud, and J. Jennings. Exploring the use of Android in CS2. In *Proc. 24th CSEE&T (SMACK '11)*, Honolulu, HI, USA, 2011.

[9] S. Heckman, T. Horton, and M. Sherriff. Teaching second-level Java and software engineering with Android. In *Proc. 24th CSEE&T*, pages 540–542, Washington, DC, USA, 2011. IEEE Computer Society.

[10] S. Kurkovsky. Engaging students through mobile game development. In *Proc. 40th SIGCSE*, pages 44–48, New York, NY, USA, 2009. ACM.

[11] S. Loveland. Human-computer interaction that reaches beyond desktop applications. In *Proc. 42nd SIGCSE*, pages 595–600, New York, NY, USA, 2011. ACM.

[12] Q. Mahmoud and A. Dyer. Integrating BlackBerry wireless devices into computer programming and literacy courses. In *Proc. 45th SE*, pages 495–500, New York, NY, USA, 2007. ACM.

[13] Q. Mahmoud and A. Dyer. Mobile devices in an introductory programming course. *Computer*, 41(6):108–107, June 2008.

[14] Q. Mahmoud, T. Ngo, R. Niazi, P. Popowicz, R. Sydoryshyn, M. Wilks, and D. Dietz. An academic kit for integrating mobile devices into the CS curriculum. In *Proc. 14th SIGCSE*, pages 40–44, New York, NY, USA, 2009. ACM.

[15] J. Muppala. Teaching embedded software concepts using Android. In *Proc. 6th WESE*, pages 32–37, New York, NY, USA, 2011. ACM.

[16] D. Riley. Using mobile phone programming to teach Java and advanced programming to computer scientists. In *Proc. 43rd SIGCSE*, pages 541–546, New York, NY, USA, 2012. ACM.

[17] E. Roberts. A C-based graphics library for CS1. In *Proc. 26th SIGCSE*, pages 163–167, New York, NY, USA, 1995. ACM.

[18] E. Roberts and A. Picard. Designing a Java graphics library for CS1. In *Proc. 6th CTC and 3rd ITiCSE*, pages 213–218, New York, NY, USA, 1998. ACM.

[19] K. Roy. App Inventor for Android: report from a summer camp. In *Proc. 43rd SIGCSE*, pages 283–288, New York, NY, USA, 2012. ACM.

[20] E. Spertus, M. Chang, P. Gestwicki, and D. Wolber. Novel approaches to CS0 with App Inventor for Android. In *Proc. 41st SIGCSE*, pages 325–326, New York, NY, USA, 2010. ACM.

[21] D. Wolber. App Inventor and real-world motivation. In *Proc. 42nd SIGCSE*, pages 601–606, New York, NY, USA, 2011. ACM.

[22] U. Wolz and E. Koffman. simpleIO: A Java package for novice interactive and graphics programming. In *Proc. 4th ITiCSE*, pages 139–142, New York, NY, USA, 1999. ACM.

[23] J. Zelle. *Python Programming: An Introduction to Computer Science 2nd Edition.* Franklin, Beedle & Associates Inc., Wilsonville, OR, USA, 2010.

Nifty Assignments

Nick Parlante, Julie Zelenski
(moderators)
Stanford University
nick.parlante@cs.stanford.edu
zelenski@cs.stanford.edu

John DeNero
University of California, Berkeley
denero@cs.berkeley.edu

Josh Hug
Princeton University
jhug@cs.princeton.edu

Antti Laaksonen
University of Helsinki
ahslaaks@cs.helsinki.fi

Frank McCown
Harding University
fmccown@harding.edu

John Nicholson
Austin Peay State University
nicholsonja@apsu.edu

Arto Vihavainen
University of Helsinki
avihavai@cs.helsinki.fi

Kevin Wayne
Princeton University
wayne@cs.princeton.edu

Categories and Subject Descriptors
K.3.0 [**Computers and Education**]: General.

General Terms
Algorithms, Design, Languages

Keywords
Education; assignments; homeworks; examples; repository; library; nifty; pedagogy

Abstract
A great CS assignment is a delight to all, but the path to one can be most roundabout. Many CS students have had their characters built up on assignments that worked better as an idea than as an actual assignment. Assignments are hard to come up with, yet they are the key to student learning. The Nifty Assignments special session is all about promoting and sharing the ideas and ready-to-use materials of successful assignments.

Each presenter will introduce their assignment, give a quick demo, and describe its niche in the curriculum and its strengths and weaknesses. The presentations (and the descriptions below) merely introduce each assignment. A key part of Nifty Assignments is the mundane but vital role of distributing the materials – handouts, data files, starter code – that make each assignment ready to adopt. The Nifty Assignments home page, **http://nifty.stanford.edu**, gathers all the assignments and makes them and their support materials freely available.

If you have an assignment that works well and would be of interest to the CSE community, please consider applying to present at Nifty Assignments. See the nifty.stanford.edu home page for more information.

SIGCSE '14, March 5-8, 2014, Atlanta, Georgia, USA.
ACM 978-1-4503-2605-6/14/03.
http://dx.doi.org/10.1145/2538862.2538995

Analyzing the Google Books Dataset (CS1) - Josh Hug
The Google books Ngram dataset provides, among other things, a tabulation of the number of times that any particular English word appeared in any known volume in any particular year since the 1500s. For example, "thou" appeared 23,166 times in 1805.

In the first part of this assignment, students create something like the Google Ngram Viewer, allowing them to visualize the relative popularity of a specified set of words over a specified time interval, e.g. "God" is dead (as of the 1850s), but he's seemingly staging a comeback. To this end, students read an input .csv file and build a simple associative array per word and use these mappings to draw basic plots.

In the second part of this assignment, students explore aggregate properties of an entire dataset, including the frequencies of English letters, the distribution of word frequencies (revealing the surprising Zipf's law), and the average length of words in books, allowing us to crudely probe the hypothesis that we're all getting a little bit dumber. This necessitates a more sophisticated associative array that stores the entire input file.

This assignment is intended to be a two week assignment, and was originally built as a highly scaffolded introduction to associative arrays, string processing, high level (CSV) file I/O, and visualization for novice programmers. The difficulty can be tweaked by varying the degree of scaffolding, and there are ample opportunities for exploring additional properties of the dataset.

Game of Sticks (CS1) - Antti Laaksonen, Arto Vihavainen
For this nifty assignment, we approach a traditional game in a very novel way. Game of Sticks is a turn-based game that starts with a heap of sticks on a board. On each turn, the player has to take one, two or three sticks from the heap, and the player who clears the board loses the game.

In this assignment the students first implement game of sticks as a two-player game and then craft a simple AI that is able to learn from its mistakes. Once the AI has been implemented, the students study the learning process of the AI and derive an optimal strategy. In addition, the students can be asked to give a mathematical proof on why the strategy works.

The main strength of this assignment is that it acts as an introduction to AI that can learn from its mistakes, and also shows that often there is little magic behind learning algorithms — one just has to start small. In our context the assignment has been a hit; many are awed by the fact that, in their first semester of studies, they can produce an AI that is able to learn how to beat them (and their friends) at a game.

Purple America (CS1) - Kevin Wayne

Write a program to visualize U.S. national or statewide election results, coloring each region in a combination of red, green, and blue to illustrate the fraction of votes won by the Republican, Indepenent, and Democratic political party candidates. The visualization is a mashup of geometric data of state and county boundaries (from the U.S. Census Bureau) and election results (from David Leip's Atlas of U.S. Presidential Elections). The results reveal that the U.S. is not as polarized as some political pundits would have us believe.

In this assignment, students build several simple data structures to model the geometric and election return data (e.g., polygons, counties, states, and elections). We provide the data in easily-parsable text files. By combining about 100 lines of good code with the prepared data, students produce striking election-map visualizations.

This assignment also features numerous opportunties for embellishment, extension, and exploration:

- Design a different color palette.
- Visualize the change in votes from one election to the next.
- Apply a different map projection, such as Albers, Mercator, or Gall-Peters.
- Find, parse, screen scrape, scrub, and incorporate data from elections in other countries.
- Create an interactive GUI that reports election results for a region, as the user hovers over it.

Object-Oriented Tower Defense (CS1) - John DeNero, Tom Magrino, and Eric Tzeng

Students build a game called Ants Versus SomeBees, a Python clone of the popular Plants Versus Zombies mobile puzzle game. The game logic is chosen to illustrate a breadth of object-oriented programming concepts such as inheritance, method overloading, and class attributes. An extra credit question probes the interaction of the Python object system and higher-order functions.

The niftiest aspect of the project is that students start developing the game logic as a command-line tool, testing specific interactions interactively, one turn at a time. Then, they can play the same game with a graphical interface provided to them. Playing the game graphically prints out method invocations used, so that students can trace issues with their implementation back to specific method definitions without using a visual debugger or blanketing their source code with print statements.

Graphics are themed by university logos. By default, the Cal ants defend their colony from the Stanford bees. Instructors can customize the graphics to any pair of NCAA Division 1 teams or other uploaded images using our project generator.

Among four projects in Berkeley's introductory programming course, CS 61A, 56% of students listed this project as their favorite. The project has an exhaustive suite of test cases that we distribute to our students. There is ample room for extension beyond the required questions.

Segregation Simulation (CS1) - Frank McCown

Racial segregation has always been a pernicious social problem in the United States, extending into our schools, churches, and neighborhoods. Why is it such a difficult problem to eradicate? This nifty assignment has students implement the economist Thomas Schelling's segregation model which gives some insight as to why people often choose to self-segregate even when they do not have an explicit desire to do so. This fascinating program models how individuals move about from location to location until they settle in a place where they are surrounded by similar individuals.

CS1 students can write this program knowing only 2D arrays and console I/O although more visually appealing programs might take advantage of a programming language's graphics capabilities. This assignment has also been given to upperclassmen who used HTML5 and jQuery to create visually appealing interfaces. The project parameters can be altered easily to increase or decrease the level of implementation difficulty for students.

Schelling's model of segregation gives instructors an opportunity to discuss a real societal problem that students are naturally interested in. The assignment gives students the chance to implement a program which is visually compelling and one that produces an often unintuitive result.

Image Stacking and the Pesky Tourist (CS2) - John Nicholson

Image Stacking and the Pesky Tourist are two related assignments used to introduce basic image-processing techniques. They rely on the text-based PPM image format, and help students learn to manage multiple files inside one program. These assignments are targeted towards students who have been introduced to reading and writing files and are ready to be introduced to basic file formats such as the PPM format. Students are able to create programs that solve real-world problems and have strong visual feedback.

The Image Stacking assignment introduces image averaging in which multiple noise-filled images of the same object are averaged together to create a new noise-free image. An image from the Hubble telescope is processed by the instructor to create a set of noisy images, which mimic the noise that occurs when photographing long-range objects. Students then create a noise-free image of the celestial object by averaging the noisy images together. That the student's code can transform a bunch of bad images into one great image has the feeling of magic.

The Pesky Tourist assignment demonstrates a related noise removal technique, the median filter, in which the median value for each pixel from multiple images is used to create a noise-free image. The noise in this case is a tourist who keeps blocking a statue. Students are given a series of photos of a statue, with the tourist in a different position in each image. When students apply the median filter to these images, the final image only shows the statue with the tourist being completely removed.

Interdisciplinary Computing in Many Forms

Lillian (Boots) Cassel
Villanova University,
Lillian.Cassel@villanova.edu
(Moderator)

Bonnie MacKellar
St. John's University
mackellb@stjohns.edu

Joan Peckham
University of Rhode Island
joan@cs.uri.edu

Carol Spradling
Northwest Missouri St Univ.
c_sprad@nwmissouri.edu

Han Reichgelt
Southern Polytechnic State
hreichge@spsu.edu

Suzanne Westbrook
University of Arizona
suzanne.westbrook@arizona.edu

Ursula Wolz
William Paterson Univ.
wolzu@wpunj.edu

SUMMARY – Cassel (Moderator)

At SIGCSE 2010, program officers from the National Science Foundation presented a panel on "Interdisciplinary Computing Education for the Challenges of the Future."[1]. An outcome was a funded project "Toward a Climate for Interdisciplinary Computing" (OCI-1058623); PIs Lillian Cassel and Ursula Wolz led four national meetings with a mix of computing and non-computing professionals. Over the ensuing three years an amazing diversity of people described successful experiences and brainstormed methods to overcome roadblocks. The overall conclusion is that Interdisciplinary Computing is alive and well and looking to broaden its impact. This intentionally large panel represents the diversity of the meetings. Very short presentations allow for over half the session to be spirited interaction with the audience, thus illustrating the high energy dynamic of this exciting and inspiring project.

Categories and Subject Descriptors

K.3.2 Computer and Information Science Education

General Terms

Documentation, Design, Experimentation

Keywords

Multidisciplinary, Interdisciplinary, Computing, Education

1. New Discipline, New Startup – Wolz

Over a decade ago faculty in Art, English and Computer Science at The College of New Jersey (TCNJ) founded the program in Interactive Multimedia (IMM). Students develop proficiency as both designers (artists) and developers (programmers) of digital media. Within the last year it finally became a department within the School of Arts and Communication. All but one of the full time faculty members hold joint appointments in related programs and represent three distinct schools within the college. Through this program, Microsoft funded curriculum development in Game Design [2] that won recognition from Princeton Review as one of the 50 best video game programs in 2010. This led to NSF funding for Interactive Storytelling. The process of founding IMM provided the intellectual exhilaration of "extreme interdisciplinary collaboration" and the frustration of solving the "bean counting" of silo-based professional advancement, course scheduling, accreditation constraints, and simple politics. I learned that any setback in creating interdisciplinary computing can be solved with creativity and patience It inspired me to found a small interdisciplinary company where artists get equal pay with programmers. Fostering interdisciplinary computing requires both strong visionary leadership (at TCNJ this was a Vice President) and profound mutual respect among collaborators.

SIGCSE'14, March 5–8, 2014, Atlanta, Georgia, USA.
ACM 978-1-4503-2605-6/14/03.
http://dx.doi.org/10.1145/2538862.2538866

2. Curricula and Extra-curricular – Reichgelt

There are many reasons for promoting interdisciplinary computing, not least among which is the fact that potential employers of computing graduates put a premium on candidates who combine knowledge of and skills in computing with knowledge of and skills in a particular application domain, whether this is business, criminal justice, education, public administration, and so on. There have been a number of attempts to build undergraduate programs that try to enable their students to acquire both. Such programs have met with limited success, primarily because such programs often relied on existing courses and did not give students sufficient opportunity to integrate the knowledge they had acquired of an application domain with their knowledge of computing. Based on an aborted attempt to achieve this at another institution for programs in Information Technology, we are attempting to overcome this hurdle in a program that we are currently designing. However, a promising alternative is to look at extra-curricular activities to ensure that students develop the importance of interdisciplinary collaboration, and we will briefly discuss the success we have had, and the lessons we have learned, from one such effort, namely game jams.

3. New School Growing Fast - Westbrook

The School of Information: Science, Technology, and Arts (SISTA) at the University of Arizona emerged in August 2008 from an idea for a home of interdisciplinary education and research where computing is a necessary foundation to solve big data problems. SISTA was approved in spring 2009. Curriculum development began in spring 2010 with support of an NSF CPATH award and two undergraduate majors were in place by fall 2010; a BS in Information Science and Technology and a BA in Information Science and Arts. Fall 2013 is our seventh semester offering undergraduate and graduate courses with 780 students enrolled. We now have 150 undergraduate SISTA majors; up 56% from last year, the biggest growth in the College of Science. We teach 31 classes with a core group of 9.5 faculty and a number of affiliate faculty from other units (Philosophy,

Music, Library, Statistics, iPlant Collaborative). Our faculty's research interests include: artificial intelligence and modeling human cognitive development, computer vision, information visualization, HCI, natural language processing, education informatics, computational music and arts, gaming, and computing education. Our major challenges are in supporting the increasing numbers of undergraduates, getting a graduate program in place, improving research funding, hiring additional faculty, and negotiating our relationship with the Computer Science department from which we started.

4. Faculty Driven Initiatives – MacKellar

I have been involved in interdisciplinary research and educational efforts in both industry and higher education. I currently teach both in a traditional computer science program and an inherently interdisciplinary program, healthcare informatics. I collaborated with faculty in biology and English on an NSF TUES proposal that would have set up a faculty-driven initiative to integrate computational thinking and advanced computing into a wide range of disciplines. Although the proposal was not successful, the aftereffects of developing this proposal have lived on, including a university wide email list on interdisciplinary computing that involves faculty from many disciplines, a new digital humanities working group and new collaborations between biology and computer science. In addition, my institution sponsors the Teaching and Technology Fellows program that provides financial support for faculty projects that bring technology and computing into courses, and involves them in a monthly meeting in which computing and technology issues are discussed. I was involved in this, which led to a collaborative project with a pharmacy professor in which pharmacy students meet with students in my healthcare informatics course to design and build mobile apps for pharmacists [3]. We plan to continue and significantly expand this project in the coming year. My experiences led me to believe that, while support from administrators is crucial, the process itself must be faculty-driven and even student-driven in order to really take hold.

5. Big Team Teaching – Spradling

My interdisciplinary experiences date back to 2001 when three departments (Art, Computer Science, and Mass Communication) developed an interdisciplinary major, Interactive Digital Media, at Northwest Missouri State University. My recent interdisciplinary experience involves a one-semester course that combines 32 highly select undergraduate students from six disciplines (computer science, English, graphic design, marketing, mass communications, and public relations) into one interactive and collaborative course, entitled Knacktive, which is supervised by five faculty from five academic backgrounds. The course replicates the intense teamwork atmosphere of a technology-oriented, professional marketing communication agency in which student-led teams conduct market research, analyze data, write creative strategies, and ultimately develop an integrated, digital, marketing communication campaign and promotional materials for an actual client. Each team makes a formal presentation at the end of the course, or client pitch, in an attempt to convince the client that their campaign plan provides the best promotional solutions. Our interdisciplinary course is successful because of the support from students, faculty, administrators and industry.

6. Multi-major Experiences – Peckham

At the University of Rhode Island, there have been several efforts to promote interdisciplinary computing. These include: (1) Student projects with industry in which interdisciplinary teams of undergraduate computer science, art, and computer engineering students, led by MBA students and supported by experts in the company design and develop prototype software products (2) with funds from NIH INBRE, interdisciplinary bioinformatics and programming (for scientists) classes were developed, (3) "tracks" were developed through our degree programs in which students complement their computing studies with expertise in another discipline, and complete interdisciplinary capstone projects/classes, (4) support for graduate students in computing who wish to secure a major advisor (or co-major advisor) from another discipline, X, to supervise their computational X thesis or dissertation, (5) Success hiring several interdisciplinary scholars through novel partnerships among different departments and colleges. We have formed a collaborative of faculty, staff and deans to compete for a "data exploration" cluster hire.

The classes are a big success in preparing students for interdisciplinary research projects. There are some glitches when science students try to work with computer science students that we have repaired with the programming classes where students work on their own projects based on their own majors/interests. Interdisciplinary graduate degrees are tough on the students because of the rigidity of the degree programs, but this is made easier by programs like those funded by NSF IGERT. Other barriers include reluctance of departments to put energy into classes for other majors. Overall these efforts have yielded robust results and this generation of students seems to hunger for interdisciplinary engagement.

7. REFERENCES

[1] Amoussou G., Boylan, M. and Peckham J. 2010. *Interdisciplinary Computing Education for the Challenges of the Future.* In *Proceedings of SIGCSE '2010,* DOI=978-1-60558-885-8/10/03

[2] Wolz, U., C. Ault and T. M. Nakra, "Teaching Game Design through Cross-Disciplinary Content and Individualized Student Deliverables", *The Journal of Game Development*, adapted based on invitation from presentation at the 2nd Annual Microsoft Academic Days Conference on Game Development , February 22 - 25, 2007

[3] MacKellar, B. and Liebfried, M, Designing and Building Mobile Pharmacy Apps in a Healthcare IT Course, The 14th Annual Conference on Information Technology Education, October 2013, to appear.

Special Session: "Hands-On" Tutorial: Teaching Software Correctness with RESOLVE

Murali Sitaraman
Clemson University
School of Computing
Clemson, SC 29634
1-864-656-3444
murali@clemson.edu

Bruce W. Weide
The Ohio State University
Computer Science and Engineering
Columbus, OH 43210
1-614-292-1517
weide.1@osu.edu

SUMMARY

Program correctness is central to computing, with instructors striving to convey the importance of "getting it right" starting in CS1. Teaching this material carefully demands a uniform framework to specify, implement, and reason about software correctness. To make these ideas accessible to educators and students, the tutorial will use RESOLVE, an integrated specification and programming language with a toolset especially designed for building verified components. The tutorial will also discuss how to get students involved through hands-on activities with software construction and modular verification using a web-integrated environment that requires no software installation and that features a prototype "push-button" verifying compiler. The proposers have taught the ideas contained here using engaging pedagogical methods in introductory and advanced CS courses to thousands of students and dozens of educators over the past 20 years, and this SIGCSE tutorial will leverage that experience.

Categories and Subject Descriptors

D.2.4 [**Software/Program Verification**]: Including but not limited to the following – *programming by contract, class invariants, correctness proofs, formal methods.*

F.3.1 [**Specifying and Verifying and Reasoning about Programs**]: Including but not limited to – *assertions, invariants, pre- and post-conditions, specification techniques.*

F.4.1 [**Mathematical Logic**]: Including but not limited to – *proof theory, set theory, temporal logic.*

Keywords

Components, correctness proofs, programming by contract, specification, and verification.

1. OVERALL OBJECTIVE

Internalizing the close connections between mathematics and software engineering requires an understanding of the nature and use of mathematical modeling in software development. Students learn the connections between mathematics and physics because they practice making those connections. Do they learn similar connections for software engineering? Experience shows that students *can* reason rigorously and mathematically about software behavior—*when* they understand a few key principles and have the right tools.

SIGCSE'14, March 5–8, 2014, Atlanta, Georgia, USA.
ACM 978-1-4503-2605-6/14/03.
http://dx.doi.org/10.1145/2538862.2538987

In the process, they realize the importance of the mathematics they learn for software development. Educators need compelling examples and assignments to make such connections, and often they are difficult to come up with, because the environments and backgrounds of students at different institutions vary widely. This session aims to provide a forum at SIGCSE where educators can share the joys of teaching mathematical reasoning principles throughout the computing curriculum using a framework especially designed for the purpose. The contents of the tutorial are suitable for teaching basic principles in introductory computer science, data structures, and discrete structures courses as well as more advanced topics in programming language and software engineering courses.

2. OUTLINE

Whatever doubts one might have had about the potential for automated verification a quarter-century and more ago [1, 2], automatically verified software can hardly be dismissed today. Empirical evidence now shows that verification conditions (VCs) implying software correctness are generally rather simple mathematically. In most situations, verification is "just" an enormous bookkeeping task involving VCs that modern theorem-provers often—yet still not always—can prove mechanically [3].

The tutorial will be of broad interest because it addresses how formal behavioral specifications, imperative programs, and supporting mathematics should be engineered for verification to be fully automated. The ideas apply in any language and under any verified software paradigm. Examples will deal with problems and solutions that illustrate how verified software can become closer to reality.

The tutorial will raise and address several issues, including the following. It will discuss the technical elements necessary for modular verification of software, i.e., proof of correctness one component at a time. It will illustrate the impact of macro-level and micro-level engineering of component specifications so that subsequent verification based on those specifications is amenable to automation. It will address how reusable mathematical developments can simplify specifications (e.g., by avoiding quantifiers) and ease automated verification. It will discuss necessary and sufficient annotations to be provided by engineers of object-based implementations to justify their correctness. It will consider verification in the presence of higher-order specifications, generic components, and components built by reusing yet other components. Verification of code involving computational and memory bounds will be among the topics of discussion.

A significant component of the tutorial will be "hands-on" activities with developing verified software [4, 5, 6, 7]. This will allow the attendees to explore several "what if" scenarios, and among other ideas, understand how building software for verification naturally eases debugging and integration of component-based systems. The activities will be done through a web interface with no software installation, so attendees will be strongly encouraged to bring their laptops and participate directly in real-time on their own solutions to exercise problems.

The session will be organized as follows. The proposers will take the first 30 minutes to motivate and demonstrate how one might approach teaching rigorous reasoning about software correctness to undergraduate students. Following the introduction, about 15 minutes will be devoted to the attendees engaging in a simple exercise to reinforce their understanding using the RESOLVE web IDE. This will be followed by another 10 minutes of tutorial and a second exercise lasting about 10 minutes. Throughout the tutorial, the presenters will take clarification questions from the audience, while leaving more detailed questions to the end. The last few minutes will be devoted to seeking feedback from session participants on the format of the session, the choice of exercises, and other ways the tutorial could be improved for the future.

3. EXPECTATIONS

The intended audience is SIGCSE educators who teach courses ranging from an introductory sequence to ones that cover more advanced topics. The attendees will learn principles for developing verified software components, including the required close connections to mathematics, and understand how to engage students in exploring those principles for specification and verification through a web-integrated environment.

4. SUITABILITY FOR SPECIAL SESSION

Learning how to build correct software—software that behaves according to its specification—is an implicit or explicit learning outcome of most computing courses. There are no educational systems available today that support professors in communicating the necessary principles for developing correct software components. This tutorial will address the missing pieces. The presentation is intended as a tutorial supported with online materials and a web-integrated environment, and it fits the special session requirements. The proposers have been involved with SIGCSE for many years and have the qualifications necessary to make this an engaging and informative special session.

SIGCSE has routinely had a sizeable audience with interests in mathematical reasoning (and its use in related areas, such as programming languages and software engineering) as evidenced by panels (e.g., [8, 9]) and a continuing series of BoF sessions on mathematical thinking [10]. This tutorial will be of direct interest to that audience. It will also be of interest to attendees looking for innovative language alternatives to teach core CS principles.

Murali Sitaraman is Professor of Computer Science in the School of Computing at Clemson University. He directs the RESOLVE/Reusable Software Research Group (RSRG) at Clemson. His research spans a spectrum of foundational, practical, and educational topics in software engineering, and it has been supported by US NSF grants continuously for over 20 years. He has co-edited a book on *Foundations of Component-Based Systems* with Gary Leavens for Cambridge University Press. Together with members of his group, he has published over 100 papers in various forums. He has offered tutorials and workshops to educators on teaching mathematical reasoning at the ACM SIGCSE conference several times, including each of the last four years. Sitaraman has taught these ideas to graduate and undergraduate students for over 20 years.

Bruce W. Weide is Professor Emeritus of Computer Science and Engineering at Ohio State University. He and his colleagues in the RSRG at Ohio State have studied and taught design, specification, and verification of component-based software for over 30 years. Weide and his colleague, Tim Long, were awarded the IEEE Computer Society Computer Science and Engineering Undergraduate Teaching Award in 2000 "for innovative work in the content and pedagogy of introductory computer science education, linking research advances in software engineering with educational delivery of the material taught in the introductory courses."

5. ACKNOWLEDGMENTS

The members of our research groups contributed significantly to the ideas contained in this proposal. We also acknowledge NSF grants CCF-0811748, CCF-1161916, CCF-1162331, CNS-0745846, DUE-0942542, DUE-1022191, and DUE-1022941. Any opinions, findings, conclusions, or recommendations expressed here are those of the authors and do not necessarily reflect the views of the National Science Foundation.

6. REFERENCES

[1] DeMillo, R.A., Lipton, R.J., and Perlis, A.J. "Social Processes and Proofs of Theorems and Programs", *CACM 22*, 1979, 271-280.

[2] Fetzer, J.H., "Program Verification: The Very Idea", *CACM 31*, 1988, 1048-1063.

[3] Sitaraman, M., Adcock, B., Avigad, J., Bronish, D., Bucci, P., Frazier, D., Friedman, H.M., Harton, H., Heym, W., Kirschenbaum, J., Krone, J., Smith, H., and Weide, B.W., "Building a Push-Button RESOLVE Verifier: Progress and Challenges," *Formal Aspects of Computing 23*, 2011, 607-626.

[4] Cook, C.T., Harton, H.K., Smith, H., and Sitaraman, M., "Specification Engineering and Modular Verification Using a Web-Integrated Verifying Compiler," *Proc. 34th International Conference on Software Engineering*, IEEE/ACM, 2012, 1379-1382.

[5] Cook, C.T., Drachova, S. V., Sun, Y-S., Sitaraman, M., Carver, J., and Hollingsworth, K. E., "Specification and Reasoning in SE Projects Using a Web-IDE," *Proc. 26th Conference on Software Engineering Education and Training*, IEEE, 2013.

[6] Welch, D., Cook, C. T., Sun, Y-S., and Sitaraman, M., "A Web-Integrated Verifying Compiler for RESOLVE: A Research Perspective," *Proc. 7th India Software Engineering Conference*, ACM, February 2014.

[7] http://www.cs.clemson.edu/group/resolve (3 Sept 2013).

[8] Krone, J., Baldwin, D., Carver, J.C., Hollingsworth, J.E., Kumar, A., and Sitaraman, M., "Teaching Mathematical Reasoning Across the Curriculum", *Proc. 43rd ACM Technical Symposium on Computer Science Education*, ACM, 2012, 241-242.

[9] Gries, D., Marion, B., Henderson, P., Schwartz, D., "How Mathematical Thinking Enhances Computer Science Problem Solving", *Proc. 32nd ACM Technical Symposium on Computer Science Education*, ACM, 2001, 390-391.

[10] Baldwin, D., "Math-thinking-l – Mathematical reasoning in CS curricula", at: http://mail.geneseo.edu/mailman/listinfo/math-thinking-l/ (3 Sept 2013).

Tutorial: Team Projects with Alice 3

Wanda Dann
Department of Computer Science
Carnegie Mellon University
Pittsburgh, PA 15213
1-412-268-9959
wpdann@cs.cmu.edu

Dennis Cosgrove
Department of Computer Science
Carnegie Mellon University
Pittsburgh, PA 15213
1-412-268-9959
dennisc@cs.cmu.edu

Don Slater
Department of Computer Science
Carnegie Mellon University
Pittsburgh, PA 15213
1- 412-268-9959
dslater@cs.cmu.edu

Dave Culyba
Department of Computer Science
Carnegie Mellon University
Pittsburgh, PA 15213
1- 412-268-9959
culyba@cs.cmu.edu

SUMMARY

In this special session, attendees will learn about techniques of teaching with team projects with Alice 3's new Save Type, Import Type, and Merge capabilities. Using this technique, students in introductory level programming courses can participate in team projects where students work as a team in various stages of design, development, and testing. As part of this process students may work independently to code one or more classes and then merge their work with that of other members of the team to create the final project.

Categories and Subject Descriptors

K.3.2 [**Computer and Information Science Education**]: Computer science education.

General Terms

Human Factors.

Keywords

Team Project, Programming, Alice.

1. OBJECTIVE

Team projects have long been a major activity in undergraduate computing courses. In today's world, we have noted that the Common Core standards [3] for K-12 education have benchmarks that emphasize creativity, collaboration, critical thinking, presentation and demonstration, and problem solving skills.

The primary objective of this special session is to provide a tutorial that will enable teachers and students to engage in team projects that provide an activity and environment for creative collaboration and teamwork, using the latest innovative features of Alice 3, as publically released in December, 2013.

SIGCSE'14, March 5–8, 2014, Atlanta, Georgia, USA.
ACM 978-1-4503-2605-6/14/03.
http://dx.doi.org/10.1145/2532333.2532340

2. OUTLINE OF SESSION

Dann and Slater will be presenters of the pedagogy and team project framework. Cosgrove and Culyba (the software engineers who developed the features to support Team Projects) will engage in an interactive session with attendees to answer any questions with regard to feature capability and functionality.

The following list outlines the time allocated to the topic/activities proposed for the special session:

- Introduction the special session [5 minutes]
- Presentation of the Team Project framework [10 minutes]
- Demonstration of Implementation features
    - Save Type [5 minutes]
    - Import Type [5 minutes]
    - Merge [10 minutes]
- Sample Team Project and Team management [20 minutes]
- Question and Answer. [15 minutes]

  Attendees will have an opportunity to interact with presenters and developers to discuss adaptations of the presented project framework and the features of Alice 3 that support team projects.

3. EXPECTATIONS

This special session is intended for high school and college-level instructors who want to integrate a team project that gives students an opportunity to experience working collaboratively to create and present a 3D animation project, which may be a short film, a game, a simulation or a tutorial.

This special session will cover a commonly used team project framework, but the goal of the session is not to promote a special team framework. We expect to provide ideas and stimulate interaction between the attendees, presenters, and software developers to enable communication and facilitate sharing of ideas.

The software system that will be presented is Alice3, in its 2013 release. [1] Alice 3 is one of two versions (Alice 2 and Alice 3) available in a suite of Alice tools. The pedagogy and effectiveness of the use of Alice has been reported in formal studies supported by grants from the National Science Foundation and published in SIGCSE proceedings, e.g. [2, 5] and CACM. [4]

Feedback from the attendees will take the form of a Question and Answer session.

4. ACKNOWLEDGMENTS

Our thanks to the sponsors of the Alice Project, who include and have included Oracle, Sun Microsystems, Electronic Arts, Google, Disney, the Hearst Foundations, the Heinz Endowments, and Hyperion.

.

5. REFERENCES

[1] Alice 3. Available online at www.alice.org. Referenced on 9/3/2013.

[2] B. Moskal, D. Lurie, and S. Cooper. Evaluating the Effectiveness of a New Instructional Approach in Proceedings of the ACM SIGCSE 2004 Conference, 2004, pp. 75-79.

[3] Common Core State Standards Initiative. Online at http://www.corestandards.org/resources/myths-vs-facts. Referenced on 9/3/2013.

[4] Dann, W. and Cooper, S. (2009). Alice3: Concrete to abstract. *Communications of the ACM*, 52(8), 27-29.

[5] Dann, W., Cosgrove, D., Slater, D., Culyba, D., and Cooper, S. 2012. Mediated transfer: Alice 3 to Java. In *Proceedings of the 43rd ACM technical symposium on Computer Science Education (SIGCSE '12)*. ACM, New York, NY, USA, 141-146.

Defining and Evaluating Conflictive Animations for Programming Education: The Case of Jeliot ConAn

Andrés Moreno
School of Computing
University of Eastern Finland, Finland
amoreno@cs.uef.fi

Erkki Sutinen
School of Computing
University of Eastern Finland, Finland
sutinen@cs.uef.fi

Mike Joy
Department of Computer Science
University of Warwick, UK
m.s.joy@warwick.ac.uk

ABSTRACT

A review of the practical uses of errors in education reveals three contexts where errors have been shown to help: teaching conceptual knowledge, changing students' attitudes and promoting learning skills. Conflictive animations form a novel approach to teaching programming that follows a long tradition on research and development on program animation tools. Conflictive animations link the benefits of errors with program animation tools and programming education. This approach involves presenting to the students conflictive animations that do not animate faithfully the programs or concepts taught. Conflictive animations are versatile enough to cover the fundamental building blocks of programs such as operators, expressions and statements. With conflictive animations a novel set of learning activities can be introduced to computer science classes. This conflictive dimension of activities augments an engagement taxonomy for animation tools at all levels. They are an example of activities that promote critical thinking. A particular implementation of conflictive animations has been empirically evaluated aiming for ecological validity rather than statistical significance. Results indicate that students using conflictive animations improve their metacognitive skills, and, when compared to a control group, their conceptual knowledge improves at a better rate.

Categories and Subject Descriptors

K.3.2 [**Computers and Education**]: Computer and Information Science Education—*Computer Science Education*

Keywords

CS1; animation; programming; conflictive animation; constructivism

1. INTRODUCTION

While constructivism has a place in computer science education, it is still accepted that students should reliably acquire the foundational knowledge of computers and programming, and put aside their misunderstandings and misconceptions [1]. As a consequence, computer science educators and researchers have been trying to improve students' learning by creating new ways to interact and engage with the material they produce. In an effort to make the material more relevant, researchers have explored and developed the possibilities of using visualizations as learning material to present the dynamic aspects of programs and algorithms. With these tools educators can propose different activities to the students in order to engage with the material. As with books, animation tools show the execution of programs and algorithms following the experts' understanding of the underlying concepts [9, 2], which we assume to be correct.

Unfortunately, and despite the efforts of computer science educators, visualization tools do not appear to significantly improve the programming knowledge of first year students [7]. A meta-study of algorithm animation evaluations pointed out that the content of the visualizations are not as decisive for learning as the intended use of the visualizations [7]. In other words, "what" they see is second in learning to "how" they interact with what they see.

If we take the idea that what students see is not the key factor for the students to learn with animations, we can propose that students could just see an erroneous animation: now, the animation does not match the expert's representation. Errors, or errata, appear in learning material or information sources, and have been explicitly used before to foster learning. In this article, the roles of errors for learning are explored. Moreover, the use of errors may address problems previously identified in programming education and program visualization in particular.

2. ROLES OF ERRORS IN EDUCATION

Postman [18] proposed using errors as the basis for a new teaching and learning practice. He argued that making students aware of human limits, and hence the occurrence of errors, could raise a generation of critical learners and thinkers. Students' awareness of frequent scientific errors and historical misrepresentations would prevent them from making assumptions about the truth of information presented to them, and force them to check the facts and theories built upon that information.

In a similar manner, Borasi [5] used errors as *springboards for inquiry*. In her exploratory research, students took part in activities that centered around errors, including those made by the students themselves and by teachers and mathematicians. Students were asked to reflect on those errors

SIGCSE'14, March 3–8, 2014, Atlanta, GA, USA.

ACM 978-1-4503-2605-6/14/03 ...$15.00.
http://dx.doi.org/10.1145/2538862.2538888 .

and discuss possible corrections, and as a result of the experiment she determined that working with errors empowered students to think mathematically.

Constructivism follows a similar principle, its focus is on students constructing their own knowledge, and the teacher's mission is to guide students' learning. Researchers in constructivism have promoted cognitive conflict as a way to correct students' misconceptions, and this has been successfully used in physics education [10]. Students are asked to explain an empirical observation, and their incorrect explanations are challenged with further empirical observations that they cannot explain or refute. This should cause a cognitive conflict that allows for conceptual change, as students are ready for alternative explanations after their own have been shown to be wrong.

Große and Renkl [6] proposed and studied the use of worked examples — detailed descriptions about how a particular problem is solved — which contained errors, in order to improve understanding and problem solving skills. In their experiments, groups had to find errors in worked examples and correct them, and they concluded that correct and incorrect worked examples allowed for a more comprehensive understanding (*far transfer*), but only to students with prior knowledge. Students with little prior knowledge performed better only by using correct examples.

To summarize, errors have been used in education for improving three key aspects of learning: *conceptual knowledge* [19, 10, 6], *student skills* [6] and *student attitudes* [18, 5].

Roles of errors in learning programming.

Coping with uncertainty, errors and unexpected results is an important competence of all IT professionals throughout their careers: programmers correct their own errors while debugging, security researchers look for errors in other people's programs. When it comes to learning, studies have listed errors students make while programming, debugging or understanding programs [8]. However, the active use of errors in lectures and programming exercises has rarely been applied or researched in depth.

Cognitive conflict is one of the exceptions, as it has been applied to programming education. Ma *et al.* [11] proposed and evaluated an instructional design where cognitive conflict and animation take a central role in explaining value assignment and reference assignment. Their results indicated that cognitive conflict combined with correct animations leads to conceptual change. This effect was more evident with easier concepts, like simple assignment, than harder ones such as reference assignment.

Regarding programming skills, it is acknowledged that the practice of programming is non-linear. A programming solution requires substantial and frequent error correcting before reaching an acceptable state. Bennedsen and Caspersen [4] argue for the need to expose the programming process to students, highlighting how errors occur in the process and showing the way experts deal with them.

Finally, debugging is a fundamental skill that students are expected to acquire, and in which errors have a prominent role. Specific activities and tools have been designed to help them start debugging, but in most cases students develop the skill while working on other tasks. According to Perkins *et al.*et al. [16], tracing is a demanding task, and students often fail to follow the correct execution of the program and consequently do not diagnose the error.

3. PROGRAM VISUALIZATION AND ITS LIMITATIONS

Program visualization tools depict the steps taken by programs during execution. They illustrate and animate programming concepts, from basic programming constructs to object oriented design issues [2]. It is postulated that the use of multimodal presentation of information increases the level of comprehension by students [12]. In program visualization, animations present the abstract source code or algorithm in a graphical way, providing an alternative representation to a standard text document, and this presentation should help students to construct their own knowledge [1].

However, when working in new or complex fields such as programming, understanding the graphical clues provided by the visualizations requires a level of expertise not always found in learners [17]. To fully benefit from the animations or visualizations, students should make the effort to understand the graphical notation used. Thus, rather than easing the student's learning process, visualizations and animations can initially impose a new extraneous cognitive load. Vainio and Sajaniemi [21] even recommend programming teachers not to present diagrams to students, or ask them to draw their own, before they understand the concepts and the mapping between concepts and diagrams, lest the diagrams introduce more confusion to the students. Both Petre [17] and Vainio and Sajaniemi [21] seem to indicate that the use of graphical representations, animated or not, are not recommended in the case of novice programmers. This results in a vicious circle: educators would like to use graphical representations to help student understand programming concepts, but educators cannot because students do not understand yet those concepts.

However, empirical studies of algorithm animation and program visualization conclude that the educational tools can be beneficial for learning *under certain conditions* [7]. For example, in order to be beneficial, visualizations and animations should be used consistently during a course, and animations should increase in complexity as the students progress[3].

4. CONFLICTIVE ANIMATIONS

Moreno et al. [14] defined conflictive animations as those that deliberately may not reproduce what the animated code or algorithm is programmed to perform. An extreme example would be an animation of a different algorithm than the one presented; for example, a bubblesort algorithm that animates a heapsort algorithm instead. In contrast to the usage of animations proposed by Ma *et al.* [11] – solving a cognitive conflict – conflictive animations continually *create* a cognitive conflict, and it is the student's task to resolve it by consulting lecture materials, watching correct animations, or asking teachers and peers. The learning is now centered on the student.

Theoretically, conflictive animations serve the three key aspects of errors in learning identified in Section 2. The next subsections illustrate the possibilities that conflictive animations offer to conceptual knowledge of programming (Sec. 4.1), higher order thinking skills (Sec. 4.2), and attitudinal and motivational factors promoted by the use of animations (Sec. 4.3).

4.1 Programming Concepts in Conflictive Animations

A program is the largest construct that compilers and interpreters deal with, and can be the source for a conflict in an animation. However, smaller program components provide more opportunities to create conflictive animations that should help the student focus on fundamental programming concepts. Moreno *et al.* described the categories of concepts which can generate conflictive animations [13]. The categories were deduced from the main production rules of the Python grammar[1]. The chosen categories were: literal, operator, function call, expression, statement and module. For example, in the *statement* category, which determines the execution path and data flow, a conflictive animation of an *if-statement* can, for example, animate the *then-block* when the condition of the *if-statement* is *false*.

4.2 Promoting Programming Skills with Conflictive Animations

Programming skills cover a range of skills that are useful when practicing with the conceptual knowledge acquired. Conflictive animations may increase the student's metacognition, and reveal the student's lack of knowledge. The possibility of an error changes the way the student processes the graphical information, and forces the student to concentrate and to *decipher* the animation. This active attempt at deciphering the animation may increase the student's metacognition, and reveal the student's lack of knowledge.

Other programming skills which potentially benefit from conflictive animations are debugging and quality awareness. As the animation executes the program step by step, the student can learn how to trace the execution better than with normal program animation, in which the student can visualize the animation without stopping at each step.

4.3 Attitude Change with Conflictive Animations

Identifying an error can serve as a means for assessment, and a good one, as it requires proper understanding, but — as in Postman's vision [18] — it is important that students change their attitude towards the animation and their learning. They cannot be passive when they are told that the tool is cheating them, and they need to become in control of the animation. In turn, the barrier between the tool that produces the animation and the student is lowered. Now the tool can fail, and the student is in position to make a contribution.

This change of attitude may push students to make the effort to understand the animation and the concepts represented. This way we can break the vicious circle hinted by Petre [17] and elicited by Vainio and Sajaniemi [21]. Ironically, it would be the wrong information displayed that would make graphical representations and animations useful.

5. PEDAGOGICAL USES OF CONFLICTIVE ANIMATIONS

Naps *et al.* [15] introduced a taxonomy of engagement or interaction with algorithm animations. This taxonomy lists six levels of increasing engagement, 1)*no viewing*, 2)*viewing*, 3)*responding*, 4) *changing*, 5) *constructing*, and 6)*presenting*. However, the increasing engagement of the student does not always lead to increased grades [20]. This result may indicate that classical grading does not evaluate all the benefits of engaging educational tools. Moreno *et al.*[14] explained how conflictive animations add a new dimension to the engagement taxonomy as they trigger different activities not considered in the original taxonomy. For example, in the *responding* category students are asked to spot the error or errors in the animation. Identifying the error does not necessarily mean that the student has wholly grasped the concept, but at least that they have a functional mental model of the program execution or algorithm.

6. CREATING CONFLICTIVE ANIMATIONS

With the previous description of levels and pedagogical issues, specific applications of conflictive animations can be imagined or prepared in practical settings. Teachers can manually create animations with existing tools (e.g. [9]) or modify existing ones from publicly available repositories[2] to introduce errors in them and use them in their lectures.

Using conflictive animations at the responding and changing levels can especially improve students' attitudes. Activities at those levels are similar to puzzles where students have to find all the pieces or correct the errors. The construction and presenting levels can be extended further to allow for other gaming activities, either collaborative or competitive.

As described by Moreno *et al.*, automatic animation tools like Jeliot 3 [2] produce conflictive animations when new rules are introduced that modify the interpretation of programming constructs, i.e., creating a *conflictive interpreter* [13].

7. EVALUATION

To compare the effectiveness of conflictive animations with the normal animations in learning, a new version of Jeliot 3, called Jeliot ConAn, has been modified to produce them automatically [13]. The Jeliot family of animation tools is a successful lineage that has resulted in a wide range of solutions [2] to support learners in different contexts, e.g., at high schools, and universities, in e-learning. The evaluations carried out in those contexts have led the further development of the Jeliot family.

Jeliot 3 animates in its right-hand pane the execution of the code entered by the student. This way students can observe the steps taken by their programs, as illustrated in Figure 1. Jeliot ConAn shares the same user interface and animation graphics. It has been modified to misinterpret certain statements that result in conflictive animations pertaining to object-oriented concepts. As well, students can indicate the moment they think a conflict has happened by pressing a button. Thus, Jeliot ConAn engages students at the *responding* level with conflictive animations of *statements* and *function calls*.

To evaluate Jeliot ConAn and the impact of conflictive animations in programming, an empirical study within a programming course was performed. In the study, a subset of the conflictive animation characteristics was evaluated: the conflictive animations related to the *function call* conceptual level (see Section 4.1) and the *responding level* (Section 5) of the engagement taxonomy. Eighteen students (11 male,

[1] http://docs.python.org/2/reference/grammar.html

[2] http://www.animal.ahrgr.de/Anims/animations.php3

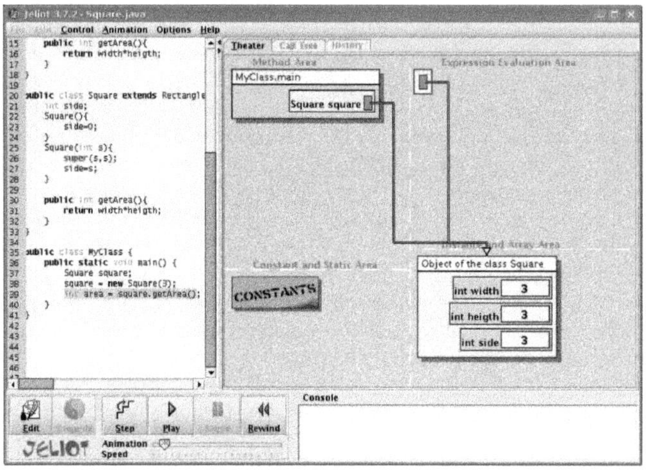

Figure 1: Screenshot of Jeliot. Showing one step in the object allocation process.

7 female) from an introductory programming course in Java volunteered to take part in the study. The students were taking part in an international Master's program in information technology and had very different backgrounds and programming knowledge. To ensure the ecological validity of the experiment, the experiment was performed during one of the practical sessions of the course, and after the lecture and practical session on the topic of object-oriented inheritance. Thus, the experiment would measure the knowledge, skills, and attitude of actual programming students in a realistic setting.

Students were randomly assigned to the control group (9 subjects) and to the experimental group (9 subjects), and the procedure was similar for both of them except for the visualization task. In the visualization task, the control group used Jeliot 3 to debug two programs, and the experimental group used Jeliot ConAn to find the conflict in two different animations. The programs dealt with the concept of inheritance and shared most of the code apart from the error students had to debug: thus, they were of similar difficulty. The visualization task duration was limited to 40 min.

Before the visualization task, students completed a questionnaire about their previous programming experience, and a pre-test with multiple-choice questions about inheritance. Afterwards, they completed several evaluation forms: 1) a post-test identical to the pre-test, 2) a graphical questionnaire with screenshots of the animations they had seen to assess their understanding of the animations and the concepts represented by them, and 3) a feedback form about the animation tool to assess their attitude regarding the tool. As well, the first author, who facilitated the experiment, took notes during the sessions regarding students' activities and interactions with the computer.

7.1 Results

Students were divided into five categories according to their reported experience with programming languages. The self-reported Java programming experience previous to the Java course was similar in both groups, with a majority having none or low previous experience in Java (8 out of 9 in both groups). For other programming languages the Jeliot 3 control group had a majority of students with medium to high experience (6 out of 9), while in the Jeliot ConAn experiment group a majority had low experience (7 out of 9) in other programming languages.

In the following results, non-parametric statistical tests for significance were run. However, due to the small size of the groups (N=18) and small differences, the results were not statistically significant.

Knowledge tests. The pre-test and post-test consisted of 10 multiple-choice questions. The test grade was obtained by giving one point per right answer and deducting half a point per wrong answer, in order to discourage students to randomly answer. Table 1 shows the average results for these tests in both groups.

The Jeliot ConAn group did improve the grade in the post-test (Wilcoxon Signed-rank test, p-value= 0.1). The Jeliot 3 group did not improve at all.

The grading test, the same for pre-test and post-test, contained questions related to the concepts that were the cause of the conflictive animations in the group using Jeliot ConAn: method overloading (2 questions) and constructors (3), and general object-oriented questions (5). To find out if Jeliot ConAn had any effect in the learning of those concepts for the experimental group, the pre-test and post-test were divided according to those three categories (method overloading, constructor, and general object-oriented knowledge). Results of this division are presented in Table 4.1. In the table, the third column, *maximum gained points possible*, is calculated by subtracting the total of points that all students can get for a given concept. The fourth column adds the increase in points for each student in the Jeliot ConAn group. The fifth column shows the p-value of the Wilcoxon Signed-rank test.

For the method overloading concept, there was no change in score after the intervention. Two out of nine students found the conflict present in the animation. For the constructor concept, three students increased their score, and three students found the conflict. Only one student increased their score and found the conflict for the constructor concept. In the general object-oriented knowledge group two students improved their score and one worsened.

Graphical questionnaires. The graphical questionnaire consisted of 11 questions related to the animation of an object allocation. Two points were awarded for each right answer, one for each answer that had some truth in it, and 0 if the answer was empty. One point was deducted for each wrong answer. The first five questions asked the students to describe the screenshots depicting the five main steps in the execution, and the other six questions focused on components of the animation. The average score result for this questionnaire was higher in the control group, 6.82 points, than in the experimental group, 4.82.

Previous programming experience shows a correlation with the graphical questionnaire results in both groups (Spearman's test: Jeliot 3 group p-value= 0.03; Jeliot ConAn group p-value=0.12). Expert students described better the animation than non-expert students. There is no correlation between the gain and the experience in any of the groups.

Feedback. The feedback form consisted of nine questions, five questions used a Likert scale to record the answers and

Table 1: Average and standard deviation of previous programming experience, pre-test, post-test, and the difference between those two (gain).

Group	Prog. experience	Pre-test	Post-test	Gain
Jeliot 3 (N=9)	2.73 (σ 1.56)	3.00 (σ 2.52)	2.89 (σ 2.31)	-0.11 (σ 1.34)
Jeliot ConAn (N=9)	3.11 (σ 1.36)	1.38 (σ 2.91)	2.16 (σ 2.54)	0.78 (σ 1.28)

Table 2: Results from the Jeliot ConAn group are analyzed regarding their improvement in the concepts demonstrated with conflictive animations.

Concept	Number of questions	Maximum gained points possible	Accumulated gained points	Number of students finding the conflict	p-value
Method Overloading	2	18	0	2	NA
Constructor	3	22	4	3	0.25
General object-oriented	5	20	1	NA	1

four were open questions. According to the responses, many more students from the control group felt that the animation tool had helped them to understand Java and inheritance, 89% from the control group and 44% from the experimental group. However, students from both groups disagreed with the fact that the tool had not had an influence in their Java knowledge (67% both groups), i.e., students thought the tool had a positive influence in their knowledge. Both groups of students from the experimental group felt that the animation tool was not hard to use (56% and 67%), but only 55% would like to have had more exercises using the tool. On the contrary, 89% of the students from the control group would have liked more debugging exercises with the tool.

When answering the open questions, students from both groups emphasized the need for textual information to complement the animation, and the need to simplify certain aspects of the visualization like the multiple references to the objects.

From the notes taken during the sessions, it was observed that two students did refer to the online resources that were available for them in case of need. Both students belonged to the experimental group.

7.2 Discussion

Conceptual knowledge. The results regarding the improvement of students' conceptual knowledge of the topics presented in the experiment point to a higher impact of the conflictive animations, even if not statistically significant. Students from the experimental group had improved their knowledge, if only by half a point, after interacting with the conflictive animations for 40 minutes.

When the results obtained by the experiment group were scrutinized more closely, the conflictive animations, which were at the conceptual level of "function call" (Sec 4.1), did not significantly improve students' post-test grades on the topics that were addressed, namely method overloading and inheritance. The slight improvement in inheritance understanding may be due to the fact that both conflictive animations tasks dealt with inheritance, although only one had one error related specifically to it, and students' exposure was double.

It is worth mentioning that the experiment tried to shed light on students' understanding of very subtle and complex execution steps of object-oriented programs. Future research should evaluate the impact of conflictive animations on different conceptual levels that are also prone to misconceptions, e.g., "statements" level concepts such as assignments. Even though Úrquiza-Fuentes and Velázquez-Iturbide [20] found that the impact of animations is higher in complex topics, this has not been the case, and there may be a barrier for *very* complex topics.

Surprisingly, the slight improvement in inheritance understanding from the experimental group did not correlate with a good understanding of the graphical metaphor that was evaluated by the graphical questionnaire: the control group understood better the static depictions of the animation according to their descriptions. The ability to describe in their own words the animation is correlated to the previous programming experience of the participants, no matter the intervention. This finding is consistent with Petre's research [17], in which novices have more problems understanding graphical notations. Also, the students that found the conflict did not automatically improve their grades.

Programming skills. On one hand, the de-learning effect of the control group after debugging, negative learning gain, contrasts with their high confidence in the beneficial effects of the tool in their learning. It highlights the problems with traditional program animation where learners do not assess their knowledge, and we can say that their meta-cognition is poor.

On the other hand, two students from the experimental group checked the lecture notes while doing the task. This indicates that the conflictive animations improved their metacognitive skills. They had been aware of something they did not understand and decided that they needed to correct that. No one from the control group stopped to check the learning material.

Attitude change. This short intervention cannot capture all the potential of conflictive animations for attitudinal change. In any case, the students showed a negative attitude towards the conflictive animation tool and the activities it promotes, 63% of experimental group versus 89% of thecontrol group asking for more activities with their version of the tool. This possibly reflects the discomfort produced by the new conflictive task, and it is an unexpected result, as we had imagined the engagement and motivation would have been larger with the conflictive activities. A way to solve this would be to advance through the conflictive engagement taxonomy, and have students *viewing* some conflictive animations during the lectures before attempting to work on the *responding* level. As well, the Jeliot ConAn focuses too much on finding the error, i.e., being critical. A more constructive approach could benefit the attitude change towards conflictive animations and thus balance the critical thinking. Future research will evaluate the impact of working at the *constructive* level with conflictive animations.

8. CONCLUSION

The paper is a first step to understanding the consequences of using errors in computer science education. Conflictive animations form a flexible resource that can change the way computer science is taught. The conflictive animations in the *responding* category evaluated here have had a small impact in the students using them. However, results point to students improving their meta-cognitive skills and knowledge when compared to using normal animations for debugging. In any case, more research is needed to confirm those suggested effects. As well, more activities should be designed and evaluated to fully address the impact of conflictive animations in education.

Conflictive animations do not solve all the factors that partially explain the low retention rate and problematic mental models of students. Conflictive animations try to put within a computer science context ideas already used in other disciplines. Indirectly, conflictive animations can address the problems that current visualization systems and practices have by providing a different reason for students to look at the visualizations.

9. REFERENCES

[1] M. Ben-Ari. Constructivism in computer science education. *Journal of Computers in Mathematics and Science Teaching*, 20(1):45–73, 2001.

[2] M. Ben-Ari, R. Bednarik, R. Ben-Bassat Levy, G. Ebel, A. Moreno, N. Myller, and E. Sutinen. A decade of research and development on program animation: The jeliot experience. *Journal of Visual Languages & Computing*, 22(5):375 – 384, 2011.

[3] R. Ben-Bassat Levy, M. Ben-Ari, and P. A. Uronen. The Jeliot 2000 program animation system. *Computers & Education*, 40(1):1 – 15, 2003.

[4] J. Bennedsen and M. E. Caspersen. Exposing the programming process. In J. Bennedsen, M. E. Caspersen, and M. Kölling, editors, *Reflection on the Teaching of Programming*. Springer, 2008.

[5] R. Borasi. Capitalizing on errors as "springboards for inquiry": A teaching experiment. *Journal for Research in Mathematics Education*, 25(2):166–208, 1994.

[6] C. S. Große and A. Renkl. Finding and fixing errors in worked examples: Can this foster learning outcomes? *Learning and Instruction*, 17(6):612–634, 2007.

[7] C. D. Hundhausen, S. A. Douglas, and J. T. Stasko. A meta-study of algorithm visualization effectiveness. *Journal of Visual Languages and Computing*, 13(3):259–290, 2002.

[8] J. Jackson, M. Cobb, and C. Carver. Identifying top java errors for novice programmers. In *Proceedings of the 35th ASEE/IEEE Frontiers in Education Conference*, 2005.

[9] V. Karavirta, A. Korhonen, L. Malmi, and K. Stalnacke. Matrixpro - a tool for demonstrating data structures and algorithms ex tempore. In *Proceedings of ICALT 2004*, pages 892–893, 2004.

[10] M. Limón. On the cognitive conflict as an instructional strategy for conceptual change: a critical appraisal. *Learning and Instruction*, 11(4–5):357–380, 2001.

[11] L. Ma, J. D. Ferguson, M. Roper, I. Ross, and M. Wood. Using cognitive conflict and visualisation to improve mental models held by novice programmers. In *SIGCSE '08: Proceedings of the 39th SIGCSE technical symposium on Computer science education*, pages 342–346, New York, NY, USA, 2008. ACM.

[12] R. E. Mayer. *Multimedia Learning*. Cambridge University Press, 2001.

[13] A. Moreno, M. Joy, N. Myller, and E. Sutinen. Layered architecture for automatic generation of conflictive animations in programming education. *Learning Technologies, IEEE Transactions on*, 3(2):139–151, 2010.

[14] A. Moreno, E. Sutinen, R. Bednarik, and N. Myller. Conflictive animations as engaging learning tools. In R. Lister and Simon, editors, *Seventh Baltic Sea Conference on Computing Education Research (Koli Calling 2007)*, volume 88 of *CRPIT*, pages 203–206, Koli National Park, Finland, 2007. ACS.

[15] T. L. Naps, G. Rößling, V. Almstrum, W. Dann, R. Fleischer, C. Hundhausen, A. Korhonen, L. Malmi, M. McNally, S. Rodger, and J. Á. Velázquez-Iturbide. Exploring the role of visualization and engagement in computer science education. In *ITiCSE-WGR '02: Working group reports from ITiCSE on Innovation and technology in computer science education*, pages 131–152, New York, NY, USA, 2002. ACM Press.

[16] D. N. Perkins, C. Hancock, R. Hobbs, F. Martin, and R. Simmons. Conditions of learning in novice programmers. In J. C. Spohrer and E. I. Soloway, editors, *Studying the Novice Programmer*, pages 261–279. Ablex Publishing Company, 1989.

[17] M. Petre. Why looking isn't always seeing: readership skills and graphical programming. *Communications of the ACM*, 38(6):33–44, 1995.

[18] N. Postman. *The End of Education*, chapter The Fallen Angel. Vintage, 1996.

[19] J. P. Smith, III, A. A. diSessa, and J. Roschelle. Misconceptions reconceived: A constructivist analysis of knowledge in transition. *The Journal of the Learning Sciences*, 3(2):115–163, 1993-1994.

[20] J. Urquiza-Fuentes and J. Velázquez-Iturbide. Toward the effective use of educational program animations: The roles of student's engagement and topic complexity. *Computers & Education*, 67(0):178 – 192, 2013.

[21] V. Vainio and J. Sajaniemi. Factors in novice programmers' poor tracing skills. *SIGCSE Bulletin (Association for Computing Machinery, Special Interest Group on Computer Science Education)*, 39(3):236–240, 2007.

RSAvisual: A Visualization Tool for the RSA Cipher

Jun Tao, Jun Ma
Department of Computer Science
Michigan Technological University
Houghton, MI
{junt,junm}@mtu.edu

Melissa Keranen
Department of Mathematical Sciences
Michigan Technological University
Houghton, MI
msjukuri@mtu.edu

Jean Mayo, Ching-Kuang Shene, Chaoli Wang
Department of Computer Science
Michigan Technological University
Houghton, MI
{jmayo,shene,chaoliw}@mtu.edu

ABSTRACT

This paper describes a visualization tool RSAvisual that helps students learn and instructors teach the RSA cipher. This tool permits the user to visualize the steps of the RSA cipher, do encryption and decryption, learn simple factorization algorithms, and perform some elementary attacks. The demo mode of RSAvisual can be used for classroom presentation and self-study. With the practice mode, the user may go through steps in encryption, decryption, the Extended Euclidean algorithm, two simple factorization algorithms and three elementary attacks. The user may compute the output of each operation and check for correctness. This helps students learn the primitive operations and how they are used in the RSA cipher. The opportunity for self-study provides an instructor with greater flexibility in selecting a lecture pace for the detailed materials. Classroom evaluation was positive and very encouraging.

Categories and Subject Descriptors

K.3.2 [**Computers and Education**]: Computer and Information Science Education—*Computer science education, information systems education*

General Terms

Algorithms, Security

Keywords

Cryptography, visualization

1. INTRODUCTION

Information security is fundamental to many computer applications and cryptography is the cornerstone on which security solutions are constructed. Landmark textbooks and handbooks have appeared [3, 6, 8, 9] and universities and colleges routinely offer courses in cryptography. The demographics of the students taking these courses can be a challenge for educators. Computer Science students commonly have difficulty dealing with the sophisticated mathematics that cryptosystems are built upon, while Mathematics majors often get lost in the details of the complicated algorithms. Pedagogical research on cryptography is at its very beginning and is scarce. Most studies are about security with minimal focus on cryptography. Visualization did play a role in cryptography. Most of these tools focus on security, rather than the algorithm operation, or have a limited scope. Some of them are Java applets or have simple visual aids while a few offer a visualization framework [2, 5].

This paper describes a tool, RSAvisual, that leverages visualization in order to meet this challenge for the RSA algorithm. RSAvisual is designed to help students understand how the RSA algorithm operates, including encryption, decryption, use of the Extended Euclidean algorithm to calculate the private key, and Fermat and Pollard $p-1$ factorization. RSAvisual is flexible in that it can be used for in-class demonstrations or it can be made available to students for self-study. RSAvisual is one component of a visualization system designed for teaching cryptography to undergraduates [10, 11]. RSAvisual was used in a junior-level introductory cryptography course. The evaluation showed that RSAvisual was effective as a tool for self-study and learning the concepts. Students used it for doing homework, checking details and preparing for the final.

In the following, Section 2 provides the background of our cryptography course, Section 3 presents our visualization tool, Section 4 has a detailed study of our findings from a survey, and Section 5 is our conclusions.

2. COURSE INFORMATION

RSAvisual was used in a cryptography course, MA3203 Introduction to Cryptography, that is offered out of the Department of Mathematical Sciences at Michigan Technological University. It is a junior level course that gives a basic introduction to the field of cryptography. This course covers classical cryptography, the Data Encryption Standard (DES), the Advanced Encryption Standard (AES), the RSA algorithm, discrete logarithms, hash functions, and elliptic curve cryptography. For each cryptosystem, we study how it was designed, why it works, how one may attack the system, and how it has been used in practice.

SIGCSE'14, March 3–8, 2014, Atlanta, GA, USA.
Copyright 2014 ACM 978-1-4503-2605-6/14/03 ...$15.00.
http://dx.doi.org/10.1145/2538862.2538891.

Public key cryptography was a major breakthrough in the field of cryptography. It allows two parties to communicate secretly with each other without first meeting to agree upon a key. Because this advancement in the field was so critical in the history of cryptography, a significant portion of the course is dedicated to the RSA algorithm and discrete logarithms. Although there is a good amount of number theory that is involved in RSA and discrete logarithms, it is all taught within the course. Thus, the course is accessible to all students who are mathematically mature but do not necessarily have a strong background in number theory.

Because the course is offered out of the Department of Mathematical Sciences, there is a heavy focus on the mathematical theory behind each of the algorithms studied. However, it is typically the case that the majority of students taking the course are not Math majors, and many of them come from Computer Science.

Due to some development delay, RSAvisual was introduced near the end of the semester after the RSA algorithm was discussed. It was used as the students were preparing for the final exam. The demonstration mode allowed the instructor to go through examples of the algorithm quickly so that the students were able to see an overview of the algorithm, rather than focusing on details. The instructor also discussed the module that demonstrates the Extended Euclidean algorithm for finding inverses, as well as the module which describes a few simple factoring techniques.

RSAvisual has a practice mode which allows students to test themselves on how well they understand the RSA algorithm. In this mode, students are led through the algorithm while being asked to complete the main components on their own. The next section has all the details of the system.

RSAvisual was made available to students to download on their own computer. After the students had access to the software for a week, the instructor distributed a survey to the class. Extra credit was offered to anyone who used the software and completed the survey.

3. SOFTWARE DESCRIPTION

RSAvisual is designed to help students learn the RSA algorithm. It supports Linux, Windows and MacOS. RSAvisual has four components: `RSA`, `E. Euclidean` (Extended Euclidean algorithm), `Factorization` and `Attacks`, each of which corresponds to a page in the system. The `RSA` component has a demo mode and a practice mode. The demo mode shows the details of the computations step by step and is useful in classroom demonstration. The practice mode allows the user to step through the computations, fill in the answers for each step and check for correctness. The two prime numbers p and q are restricted to 5-digit numbers in the demo mode for the user to easily follow the computation steps. Moreover, p and q are restricted to three digits in the practice mode so that the user can perform the computations by hand. RSAvisual always starts from the `RSA` page and the user can switch to other pages freely. The `E. Euclidean` page illustrates the use of the Extended Euclidean algorithm to calculate the inverse of a number. The `Factorization` page demonstrates how to factorize a number with Fermat's algorithm and Pollard's $p-1$ algorithm, respectively. The `Attacks` page has three elementary attacks on the RSA cryptosystem.

3.1 The RSA algorithm

The demo mode of the `RSA` component provides the user with an overall procedure of the RSA algorithm. Given two prime numbers p and q, a public key e, and the plaintext M, it shows how n, $\phi(n)$ and the private key d are computed. Two equations are displayed to show how a sender encrypts the plaintext with public key e and the receiver decrypts that ciphertext with private key d (Figure 1). The user can change the two prime numbers p and q, the public key e and the plaintext M, and the computation will be updated automatically. The user can also click the `New Instance` button to randomly generate a new set of p, q, e and M.

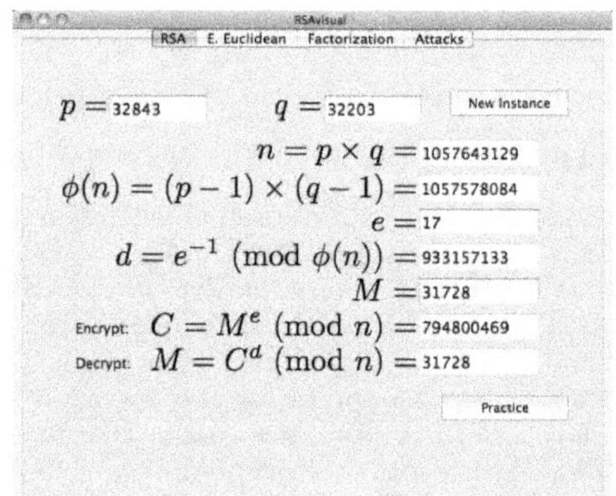

Figure 1: Demo mode of the RSA page

In the practice mode, the user can step through the computation (Figure 2); however, all equations are hidden. In each step, a correct result is required to advance to the next step. RSAvisual verifies the input and displays a green tick if the answer is correct. Otherwise, a red cross is shown so that the user can either enter a new value or skip a step by clicking the corresponding `show` button for the system to fill in the correct answer.

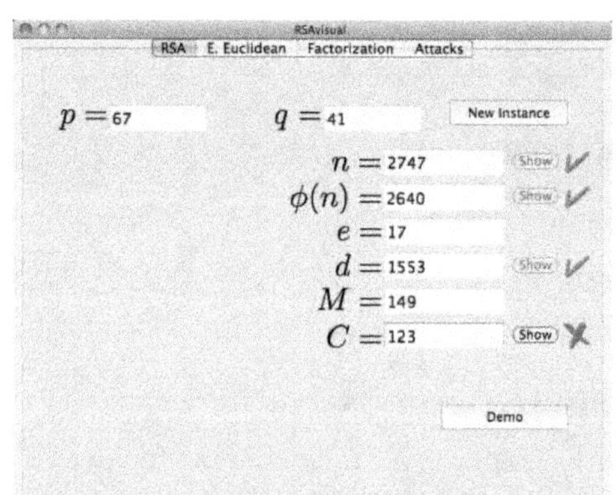

Figure 2: Practice mode of the RSA page

3.2 The Extended Euclidean algorithm

The `E. Euclidean` page demonstrates how to compute the inverse of a number using the Extended Euclidean algorithm. Given two integers a and b, it illustrates the computation of x, y and $\texttt{gcd}(a, b)$ in $ax + by = \texttt{gcd}(a, b)$, where $\texttt{gcd}(a, b)$ is the greatest common divisor of a and b. The values of a and b are set to the public key e and $\phi(n)$, respectively, so that x gives the value of private key d. The computation is shown as a table in which each row represents the intermediate results for each step (Figure 3). Two cells of the same color in adjacent rows indicate that the lower one inherits the value from the upper one. The user follows the color of cells to trace the numbers across steps to learn how the values of a and b are exchanged between steps. The values of x and y are not filled bottom-up from where $\texttt{gcd}(a, b)$ is calculated. Instead, they are filled top-down so that it is easier for the user to follow.

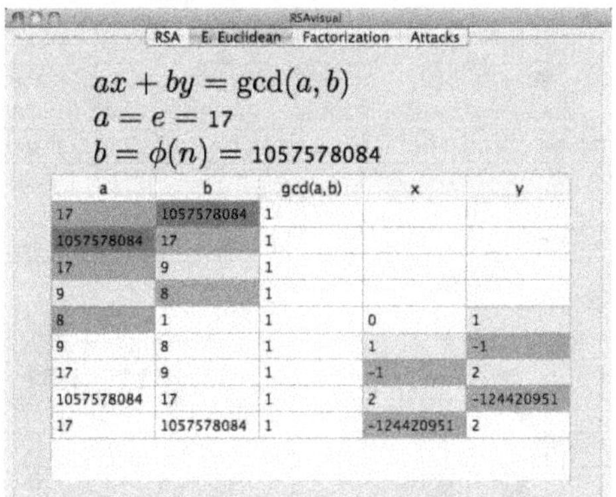

Figure 3: Computing the Inverse of e Using the Extended Euclidean Algorithm

3.3 Factorization

The `Factorization` component consists of the visualization of two factorization algorithms: Fermat's algorithm and Pollard's $p-1$ algorithm. They are on two different sub-pages. Fermat's algorithm starts with $k = \lceil\sqrt{n}\rceil$. At each step, it calculates $h = \sqrt{k^2 - n}$. The values of k and h are recorded and displayed in a table for each step until h is an integer. Finally, the values of p and q are given by $p = k + h$ and $q = k - h$, respectively (Figure 4).

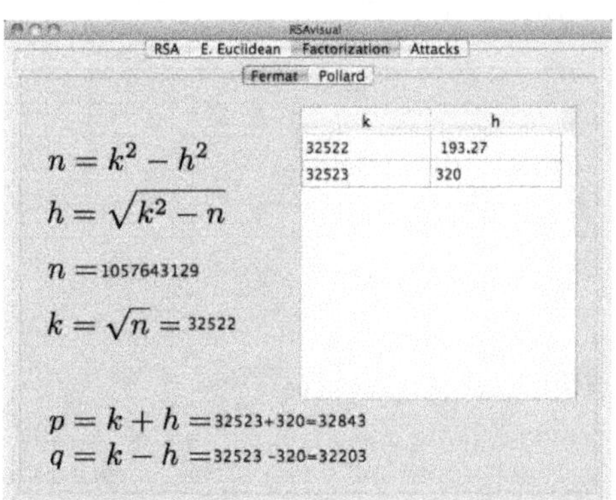

Figure 4: Factorizing n Using Fermat's Algorithm

The Pollard algorithm page illustrates how to factorize n by computing $\texttt{gcd}(b-1, n)$, where $b = a^{B!}$ $(\texttt{mod}\ n)$. When B is large enough, $\texttt{gcd}(b-1, n)$ yields a non-trivial factor of n. The value of B is initialized to be the smallest B with such a property. The value of B can be edited by the user, and RSAvisual will update the value of $\texttt{gcd}(b-1, n)$. In this way, the user will be able to discover that if B is small we have $\texttt{gcd}(b-1, n) = 1$, and that only if B is large enough $\texttt{gcd}(b-1, n)$ is a non-trivial factor. The values of B and b are listed in a table, so that the user can verify this property easily (Figure 5). Note that $\texttt{gcd}(b-1, n)$ is a button for the system to show the computation details.

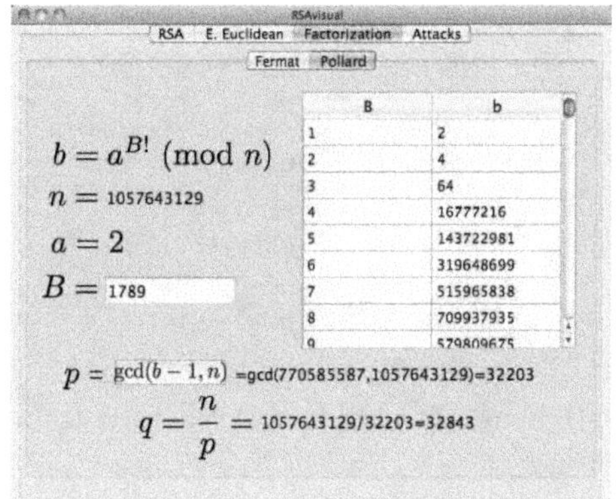

Figure 5: Factorizing n Using Pollard's Algorithm

3.4 Attacks

The `Attacks` component has three elementary attacks on the RSA cryptosystem: chosen plaintext attack, chosen ciphertext attack and common modulus attack [7, 12]. Each of these attacks occupies a sub-page on the `Attacks` page. The same values of e, d, n and M are used and interfaces are similar. For each attack, RSAvisual gives the initial conditions and then displays the attack operations in chronological order. The role of each operation (*i.e.*, sender, receiver and eavesdropper) is specified explicitly (Figure 6, 7 and 8).

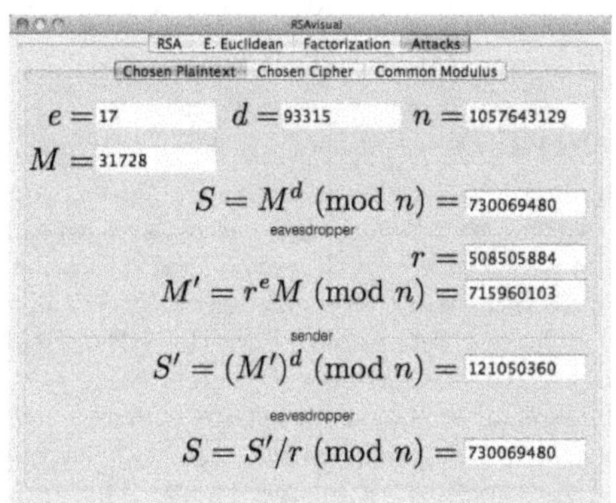

Figure 6: Chosen Plaintext Attack to Forge the Signature of the Sender

4. EVALUATION

The RSAvisual survey consists of two components, a set of 10 questions (Table 1) and 11 write-in comments. The three elementary attacks on RSA were not evaluated because this component was added after the survey was done. Choices available are 5:strongly agree, 4:agree, 3:neutral, 2:disagree, and 1:strongly disagree. Because we intend to study the impact of RSAvisual on multiple disciplines, students were asked to fill in their disciplines. We collected 27 survey forms. The distribution of majors was as follows: 3 in computer network and system administration (CNSA), 10 in electrical and computer engineering (EE/CpE), 9 in computer science (CS and Computer Systems), 3 in mathematics (Math), 1 in Service System Engineering, and 1 undeclared.

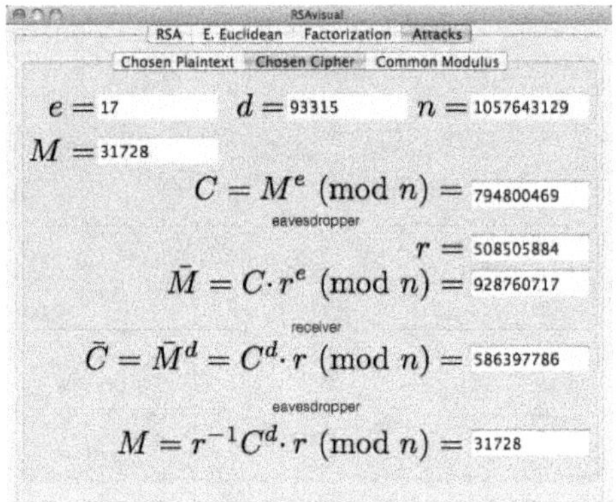

Figure 7: Chosen Ciphertext Attack to Recover the Plaintext

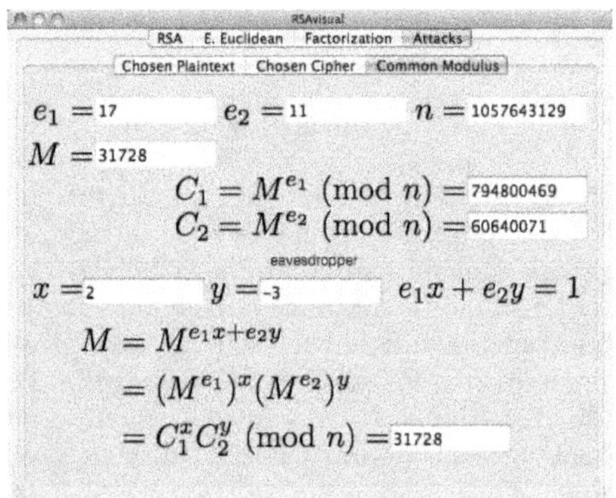

Figure 8: Common Modulus Attack to Recover the Plaintext

4.1 General Discussion

Table 2 shows the mean and standard deviation of each question. In general, reactions to RSAvisual were positive. The highest score of 4.1 with a standard deviation 0.7 was given to Q1, indicating that students agreed highly that RSAvisual helped them understand the RSA cipher. Q2, Q5, Q6 and Q10 received scores no less than 3.9, suggesting that RSAvisual enhanced self-study and the course. The two factorization related questions, Q3 and Q4, were rated at 3.4, the lowest score of all questions. This may be due to the use of variable names (Section 4.3). Thus, while Q3 and Q4 received lower rating, the general trend of student reactions was still on the positive side.

The ratings of each question are loosely positive related with the highest correlation being 0.65 for the (Q1,Q10) pair and 0.63 for the (Q1,Q2) pair although both are not very high (Table 3). This suggests that those who believed the demo mode was helpful tended to rate the demo mode higher and considered that RSAvisual enhanced the course. Students who understood the RSA algorithm more after using the tool (Q8) also believed the demo mode helped them understand the RSA algorithm (Q1), the Extended Euclidean algorithm (Q2) and the Fermat Factorization algorithm (Q3), although the correlation coefficients are between 0.52 and 0.57. Pairs (Q2,Q6), (Q3,Q6), (Q4,Q6), (Q4,Q8) and (Q4,Q9) have very low but negative correlation coefficients. The Q6 pairs are understandable because Q6 is about encryption and decryption that are irrelevant to the Extended Euclidean and factorization algorithms (Q2, Q3 and Q4). The (Q4,Q8) and (Q4,Q9) pairs share the same reasoning. However, the (Q4,Q7) pair with a correlation of -0.31 is somewhat puzzling, suggesting that even though students believed RSAvisual helped them understand the RSA algorithm better, they tended to rate the Pollard's $p-1$ factorization algorithm visualization in a slightly negative way.

Table 1: Survey Questions

No.	Question
Q1	RSAvisual 's demo mode helped me understand
Q2	RSAvisual 's demo mode helped me better understand the Extended Euclidean algorithm
Q3	RSAvisual 's demo mode helped me better understand the Fermat Factorization algorithm
Q4	RSAvisual 's demo mode helped me better understand the Pollard $p-1$ Factorization algorithm
Q5	RSAvisual 's demo mode was helpful for my self-study
Q6	RSAvisual 's practice mode helped me remember how to encrypt and decrypt with the RSA algorithm
Q7	RSAvisual 's practice mode helped me understand how to find inverses using the Extended Euclidean algorithm
Q8	I understand the RSA algorithm more after using RSAvisual
Q9	By using RSAvisual I was able to identify the parts of the RSA algorithm that I did not understand
Q10	RSAvisual enhanced the course.

Table 2: Mean μ and Standard Deviation σ

	Q1	Q2	Q3	Q4	Q5	Q6	Q7	Q8	Q9	Q10
μ	4.1	3.9	3.4	3.4	4.0	3.9	3.7	3.8	3.6	3.9
σ	0.7	0.9	0.9	0.8	0.7	0.8	0.8	0.7	0.7	0.7

Table 3: Correlation Matrix of Questions

	Q2	Q3	Q4	Q5	Q6	Q7	Q8	Q9	Q10
Q1	0.63	0.49	0.35	0.44	0.30	0.07	0.57	0.32	0.65
Q2		0.57	0.28	0.23	-0.07	0.44	0.52	0.32	0.40
Q3			0.56	0.28	-0.07	0.12	0.54	0.10	0.42
Q4				0.19	-0.13	-0.31	-0.06	-0.02	0.40
Q5					0.47	0.06	0.45	0.35	0.26
Q6						0.08	0.20	0.42	0.06
Q7							0.46	0.29	0.13
Q8								0.36	0.37
Q9									0.44

4.2 Statistical Analysis

The differences among student groups were studied using ANOVA for each question. Since the questions may correlate with each other, we also applied MANOVA (Multivariate ANOVA) to investigate the overall differences. For MANOVA, Wilk's Lambda test was used and all questions were considered at the same time. The students were grouped by their majors: CS, EE, CpE, Csys (Computer Systems), CNSA, Math and Other. The group Other contained a student who did not provide his discipline information and a student who majored in Service System Engineering. Although the MANOVA result suggested significant differences among student groups with p-value of 0.032, we did not find differences at significance level of 0.05 for any question using ANOVA. The smallest p-value in ANOVA results was 0.077 for Q7. The p-values for the other questions were all larger than 0.231. This suggests that the rating of students from different disciplines did not vary significantly.

To better understand the possible differences among students, we applied cluster analysis to group the students. The Ward's method with the Mahalanobis distance was used for a hierarchical agglomerative clustering and two groups were formed as shown in Figure 9. MANOVA showed that the two groups of students rated very differently (p-value = 0.00006). ANOVA for each individual question also found significant differences for Q4 and Q5 with p-values of 0.014 and 0.005, respectively. The mean values of rating from these two groups revealed that the students in Group 1 usually offered higher ratings than those in Group 2, except for Q6 (3.875 against 4) and for Q10 (3.875 against 3.909), which were still close. Students in Group 1 rated the first five questions 0.4 higher than Group 2. However, no clear and significant evidence, such as disciplines, can be found to explain these differences. It was more likely that the higher rates of Group 1 were just a personal preference rather than discipline-related. This was also consistent with our findings from the results where the students were grouped by majors.

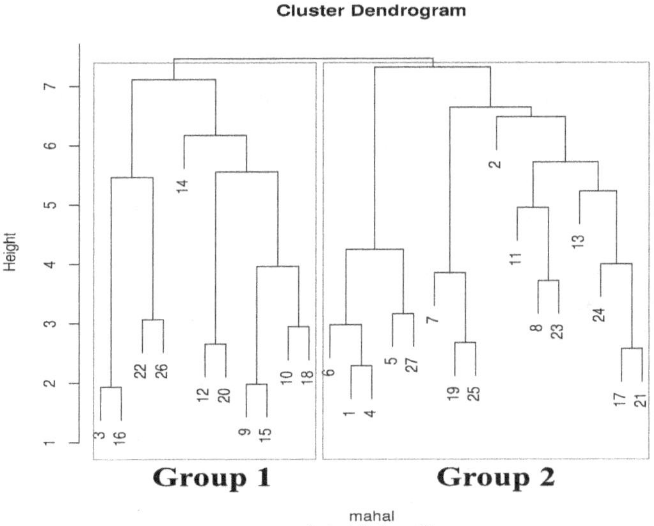

Figure 9: Cluster Analysis Result

4.3 Student Comments

The set of 11 write-in questions is designed to allow students to make suggestions which can be used for future development. We focus on the following issues: the restriction of using 5-digit numbers, whether the Extended Euclidean algorithm needs improvement, whether the display/use of Fermat Factorization is good enough, whether the display/use of Pollard Factorization is good enough, the evaluation of the demo and practice modes, the evaluation of the practice mode, frequency of using RSAvisual for self-study, and software installation issues.

Most of the student comments did not consider the use of 5-digit numbers a limitation. Typical comments were "*I think only 5 digits was helpful because the smaller numbers were easier to try by hand*", "*For the purpose of example problems, this was not a significant limitation*" and "*No, the concept is what is important here*". One student said "*It was okay, but didn't let me try all the examples I worked*". On the other hand, another student indicated "*I find it easier to use 2 digits when playing with the visualization software*". Therefore, we believe that the use of 5-digit numbers is a very reasonable restriction.

Students were positive about the Extended Euclidean module, the Fermat Factorization module and the Pollard module. Typical comments on the Extended Euclidean module were "*This module provided me with a simplified way to perform the Extended Euclidean algorithm*", "*I thought it was easy enough as it seemed to be useful for understanding/grasping the concept*" and "*Helpful for reviewing the Extended Euclidean algorithm. It showed a faster way to find inverses*". Due to the many ways of performing a typical Euclidean algorithm (*i.e.*, recursive, tabular and formula substitution), some students were initially confused about the tabular presentation. However, students also noted that after a classroom presentation, they were able to understand the content of the table and felt it was easy to follow. The Fermat and Pollard modules followed the same trend. Most students felt that both modules were "*straightforward*", "*easy enough to use and understand*" and "*illustrative of concept*". A handful of students were not used to the tabular presentation even though the simple formulas were shown next to the table. Some students complained about the use of variable names being different from those in the textbook. We do not think this is a significant issue because different textbooks may use different variable names.

The practice mode was well received with comments like "*The practice mode is great! I like that it is step by step and I can try any instance I want*", "*The program is of most use as a way to check your work on RSA problems*", "*Simple and straight-forward*", "*When you input an incorrect answer the program does not automatically display the correct answer and lets you re-enter another answer without starting over. This helps me to really work out the solutions multiple times if needed*" and "*Good, easy tool for determining ability level of using the algorithm*". Students also offered suggestions to improve the practice mode. In addition to font size and spacing adjustments, a few students wished to see hints and/or explanations of each step so that their understanding can be reinforced.

The demo mode was not universally welcome because some students considered that the demo mode would replace blackboard work. Along this line of thinking, they would prefer blackboard work because the pace was slower allowing the instructor to show the detailed work step by step. This may be due to the fact that the RSA algorithm was presented in class as a lecture, but RSAvisual was demonstrated weeks later during the final exam review. Therefore, when the students saw the demo mode in action, it was presented quickly because it had already been covered in detail. Students may have had a different reaction if RSAvisual had been introduced along with the backboard presentation of the algorithm. On the other hand, the majority of students indicated that the demo mode was helpful and correctly pointed out that "*The two parts together were definitely necessary*", "*Wouldn't want one without the other*" and "*I would not say that the program should replace the blackboard but it is a good supplement*". Typical comments were "*The most effective part was that you could clearly see all of the steps and calculations at the same time*" and "*I really liked how you could enter your own values and that it went through the steps*". Major improvement suggestions include adding hints and explanations when needed and providing an option so that the computation would be shown step by step under the control of the user. We have taken all of these suggestions into consideration and are working on an update.

Students indicated that "*I really appreciate the simplicity of the layout*" and "*Layout was simple*". The most needed improvements include font size and space issues, a mechanism to activate hints, formulas and descriptions, variable speed and step-by-step execution in the demo mode and some way to tell the user what went wrong about the input and intermediate values in the practice mode.

Students only had a week to play with RSAvisual before taking this survey and the frequency of using this tool is not very high. Most of them used the tool a few times, and a few played with the tool "often". They used RSAvisual for solving problems, checking for details, and preparing for the final. Students reported some installation issues such as missing shared libraries, mostly from MacOS users as they perhaps did not install the needed libraries properly. Windows 7 and Vista users did not report major installation issues.

In summary, we believe RSAvisual has helped students learn and the instructor teach the RSA cipher effectively. With the comments and suggestions, we should be able to improve RSAvisual significantly in the near future.

5. CONCLUSIONS

This paper presented a visualization tool RSAvisual for teaching and learning the RSA algorithm, the Extended Euclidean algorithm for finding inverses, Fermat's and Pollard's factorization algorithms, and some elementary attacks. With RSAvisual, instructors are able to present all the details and inner working of these algorithms. It also helps students see the "flow" of each algorithm, learn the concepts and practice the computation steps using the practice mode. Evaluation results showed that RSAvisual was effective in classroom presentation and for student self-study. While students in this class were from more than five disciplines, our analysis did not find clear and significant evidence of discipline-specific rating differences. Thus, although a cluster analysis grouped the student ratings into two clusters, we concluded that the rating differences may be due to a pure personal preference.

RSAvisual only uses five digits in the demo mode and three digits in the practice mode, and implements the "textbook" version of the RSA algorithm. While nearly all students indicated these restrictions worked fine, we are looking at ways to extend RSAvisual and alleviate these limits. In addition to font size and spacing issues, we plan to **(1)** increase the number of digits, which is user selectable, so that the system can still be easy to use, **(2)** include a padding module, **(3)** consider better or more visualization styles for the Extended Euclidean and factorization algorithms, and **(4)** add a few more elementary attacks on RSA.

We are also investigating some recent advances in prime number related research results and hope to determine if they are worthwhile to be mentioned for our course. It has been known for decades that determining if a positive integer is a prime (*i.e.*, **PRIMES**) is in $\mathcal{NP} \cap$ co-$\mathcal{NP}$. However, Manindra Agrawal, Neeraj Kayal and Nitin Saxena (AKS) proved in 2004 that **PRIMES** is actually in $\mathcal{P}$ [1, 4]. A more recent and surprising result was proved by Yitang Zhang in 2013, indicating the gap between two consecutive prime numbers is less than 7×10^7 [13]. Whether these results can contribute to or be used to the development of fast factorization algorithms is under investigation.

RSAvisual is a part of larger development of cryptography visualization tools supported by the National Science Foundation. In addition to RSAvisual, DESvisual for the DES cipher and ECvisual for the elliptic curve based ciphers are available online and new tools SHAvisual and AESvisual for SHA and AES will become available soon. Tools, evaluation forms, and installation and user guides for Linux, MacOS and Windows can be found at the following URL:

`www.cs.mtu.edu/~shene/NSF-4.`

6. REFERENCES

[1] M. Agrawal, N. Kayal, and N. Saxena. PRIMES is in P. *Annual of Mathematics*, 160:781–793, 2004.

[2] G. Cattaneo, A. D. Santis, and U. F. Petrillo. Visualization of Cryptographic Protocols with GRACE. *Journal of Visual Languages and Computing*, 19:258–290, April 2008.

[3] D. E. R. Denning. *Cryptography and Data Security*. Addison-Wesley, 1982.

[4] M. Dietzfelbinger. *Primality Testing in Polynomial Time: from Randomized Algorithms to "PRIMES is in P"*. Springer-Verlag, 2004.

[5] D. Ebeling and R. Santos. Public Key Infrastructure Visualization. *Journal of Computing in Small Colleges*, 23:247–254, October 2007.

[6] A. J. Menezes, P. C. V. Oorschot, and S. A. Vanstone. *Handbook of Applied Cryptography*. CRC Press, 1996.

[7] R. A. Mollin. *RSA and Public-Key Cryptography*. Chapman & Hall/CRC, 2003.

[8] A. Salomaa. *Public-Key Cryptography*. Springer-Verlag, 1992.

[9] B. Schneier. *Applied Cryptography: Protocols, Algorithms, and Source Code in C*. Wiley, second edition, 1995.

[10] J. Tao, J. Ma, M. Keranen, J. Mayo, and C.-K. Shene. DESvisual: A Visualization Tool for the DES Cipher. *Journal of Computing Science in Colleges*, 27:81–89, October 2011.

[11] J. Tao, J. Ma, M. Keranen, J. Mayo, and C.-K. Shene. ECvisual: A Visualization Tool for the Finite Field Elliptic Curve Cipher. In *Proceedings of the ACM Technical Symposium on Computer Science Education*, pages 571–576, 2012.

[12] S. Y. Yan. *Cryptanalytic Attacks on RSA*. Springer-Verlag, 2008.

[13] Yitang Zhang. Bounded Gaps between Primes. *Annual of Mathematics*. (to appear).

Acknowledgment

The authors are supported by the National Science Foundation under grants DUE-1140512, DUE-1245310 and IIS-1319363.

Pythy: Improving the Introductory Python Programming Experience

Stephen H. Edwards, Daniel S. Tilden, and Anthony Allevato
Department of Computer Science, Virginia Tech
2202 Kraft Drive
Blacksburg, VA 24060 USA

edwards@cs.vt.edu, tilden@vt.edu, allevato@vt.edu

ABSTRACT
Pythy is a web-based programming environment for Python that eliminates software-related barriers to entry for novice programmers, such as installing an IDE or the Python runtime. Using only a web browser, within minutes students can begin writing code, watch it run, and access support materials and tutorials. While there are a number of web-based Python teaching tools, Pythy differs in several respects: it manages student assignment work, including deadlines, turn-in, and grading; it supports live, interactive code examples that instructors can write and students can explore; it provides auto-saving of student work "in the cloud", with full, transparent version control; and it supports media-computation-style projects that manipulate images and sounds. Pythy provides a complete ecosystem for student learning, with a user interface that follows a more familiar web browsing model, rather than a developer-focused IDE interface. An evaluation compares student perceptions of Pythy in relation to JES, another student-friendly beginner Python environment. Classroom experiences indicate that Pythy does reduce the novice obstacles that it aims to address.

Categories and Subject Descriptors
D.2.6 [**Software Engineering**]: Programming Environments—*Integrated environments*; D.3.2 [**Programming Languages**]: Language Classifications—*Python;* K.3.2 [**Computers and Education**]: Computer and Information Science Education—*Computer science education.*

General Terms
Languages, Human Factors.

Keywords
Python, interactive, web-based, browser, Skulpt, on-line, media computation.

1. INTRODUCTION
Learning to program for the first time can be challenging, not only due to the programming language itself or the thought processes required to describe a problem so that a computer can understand, but also because of the tools that students must use for development. More often than not, suitable beginner tools do not exist, forcing instructors to use professional-level programming environments that are intimidating to novices and require a significant amount of effort to install and configure properly.

SIGCSE'14, March 5–8, 2014, Atlanta, Georgia, USA.

http://dx.doi.org/10.1145/2538862.2538977

Pythy is a new web-based programming environment for Python that eliminates these steep barriers to entry for novice programmers. Using Pythy, students need not install any development environment or even have a Python runtime. The only software they will need is a web browser and within seconds they can write code, watch it run, and access support materials and tutorials. Student work is stored "in the cloud," giving them access to their code from anywhere and reducing the need to worry about file structure and organization at the outset.

Some online IDEs already exist, but often adhere closely to the traditional user interface style of a standalone IDE. While this might ease a students' "graduation" to a professional IDE later, it does not serve them well at the beginning when they should be focusing on problem solving and learning to write code, rather than wrestling with the tools. Pythy takes a more drastic departure from the traditional IDE to be more approachable for novices—in the spirit of BlueJ, but modernized for Python and the Web 2.0 generation.

While there are a number of browser-friendly Python implementations, Pythy is notably different because it:

- Manages student assignment work, including deadlines, turn-in, and automated grading for correctness.
- Supports live, interactive code examples that instructors can write and students can explore.
- Provides auto-saving and implicit version control of all student assignment work.
- Supports media-computation-style Python exercises and assignments that manipulate images and sounds.
- Provides a complete ecosystem for students learning python, rather than just providing access to a Python interpreter.

This experience report describes the design goals behind Pythy, early experiences using it to teach an introductory Python course for non-majors, and how students reacted to using the environment. Classroom experiences indicate that Pythy is popular with students and does reduce many of the novice obstacles that it was designed to address. As Pythy evolves, we plan to enhance it further based on feedback received from students.

2. RELATED WORK
Some online IDEs have already been developed for educational audiences. JavaWIDE [1] is one of the most popular, used to teach Java at over 120 institutions. One issue with systems like JavaWIDE is that they adhere closely to the traditional user

interface style of a standalone IDE: a plethora of menus, toolbar buttons, tabs, and docked views for project management and program I/O. Such an interface requires the student to develop a mental model of software projects, how they relate to the file system, and how they are managed. For beginners, especially students who are not computer science majors, learning the model behind a traditional IDE interface can be distracting at the start of a course when they should be focusing on developing an understanding of core algorithmic concepts instead. In contrast to the traditional IDE interface model, the Light Table project [2] contains an innovative alternative interface that is inspired by direct manipulation and web-based interaction styles. IDE-oriented approaches only address project management, code execution, and (in some cases) debugging needs, however, without addressing any of the other learning needs of the student.

The Online Python Tutor [3][4] is a web-based Python code visualization tool that allows students to step through the execution of Python code and visualize the changes to program state that occur. Code visualizations can even be embedded in web pages, and the Online Python Tutor is used for embedded interactive examples in some on-line books, such as *How to Think Like a Computer Scientist: Interactive Edition* [5]. The Online Python Tutor addresses an important need, allowing students to visualize the execution of and debug their own code. Nevertheless, it does not address the broader set of concerns that Pythy aims to resolve.

Skulpt [6] and Brython [7] are two entirely in-browser implementations of Python that allow code to be executed client-side. Skulpt is used in a number of embeddable Python tools, including a number of live examples in *How to Think Like a Computer Scientist: Interactive Edition* [5]. Python implementations such as these provide a unique approach to giving students access to a "run anywhere" Python runtime, but do not solve the other problems that beginning students face.

3. DESIGN GOALS

Pythy is targeted at introductory programming courses that use Python. Pythy's overarching goal is to provide a simple, clean path for non-CS students in such a course to begin learning to program through assignments and examples: to write, run, debug, and turn in code. Pythy's name is a portmanteau of Python and pithy, meaning "concise and forcefully expressive." To address the needs of introductory students simply and cleanly, Pythy's design is based on a series of mutually supporting objectives.

Web-based: Installing programming languages and development tools can be a challenge—often the first obstacle that students face in their first computer science course. Pythy eliminates this obstacle entirely by being completely web-based. Students need not install any development environment or even have a Python runtime. The only software they need to use Pythy is a web browser.

Web-inspired user interface: In their first computing course, most students have no concept of a "software project" or how it might be organized in their computer's file system, and tools that model their interface on such concepts can be difficult for beginners. However, nearly all students have significant exposure to a wide variety of web sites, including sophisticated AJAX-based sites such as Gmail and Facebook. Instead of using a traditional IDE-oriented interface, Pythy leverages the multi-tabbed web browser interface that students are already familiar with, using browser-based navigation instead of a "file tree" model. Source code is edited "in place" on the page with full

Figure 1: A Pythy code edit window.

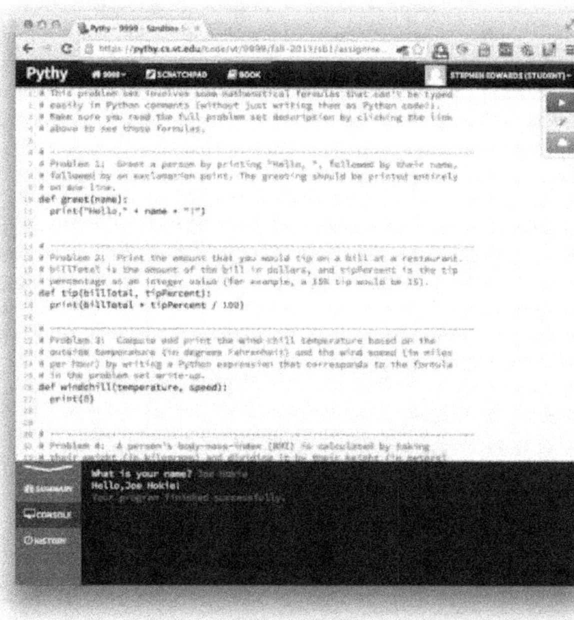

Figure 2: Pythy's console appears when code is running, showing input and output.

syntax highlighting support, and both program output and test results are cleanly integrated into the source code's web page instead of appearing as separate windows or views. Pythy uses Bootstrap for visual styling to achieve a clean, modern look.

Supporting assignments: Pythy also supports students by providing a "one-stop shop" for programming assignments, from homework exercises through larger programming projects. Instructors can post assignment write-ups on Pythy (using markdown notation, or embedded HTML), set due dates, provide "starter" file contents so that students do not have to start with a blank page, and even provide executable reference tests to automatically check the correctness of student work. Students can

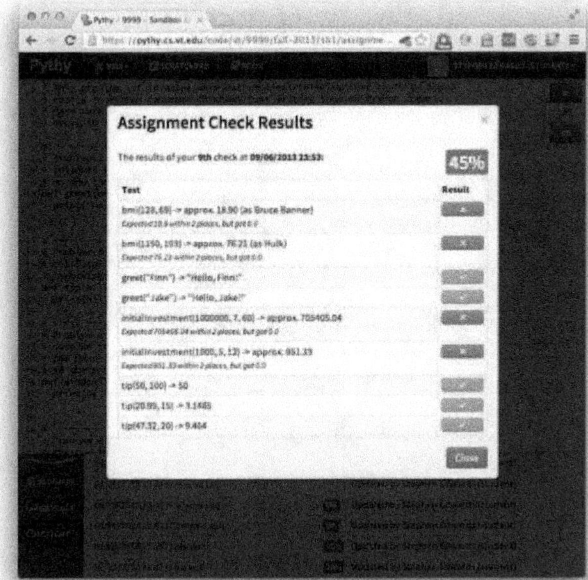

Figure 3: Results from checking work-in-progress for correctness.

view assignments and their deadlines, start or resume working on an assignment, view multiple present or past assignments or code files in different browser tabs, submit work for automated checking, and electronically turn in their work.

Supporting examples: Instructors can use Pythy live in class to present examples, and students can explore and interact with those examples. Further, as an instructor writes or edits an example live in class, students viewing the same example in their web browser see real-time updates that keep their content in sync with the modifications. Students can even modify and explore the behavior of such examples live, changing and running the code, or work with examples out of class later or when they need to review. Real-time updates to the student's view of the example are temporarily shut off while the student is changing or running the code, and can be resumed any time the student is ready. Pythy even supports a "scratchpad" where students can play around with arbitrary Python code they want to write and run, outside the context of any assignment or example.

Cloud storage: Pythy stores student work "in the cloud," giving them access to their code from anywhere and reducing the need to worry about file structure and organization at the outset. Student work in Pythy is automatically saved whenever the student pauses editing, so work is never lost. Even the scratchpad works this way. Every time a student returns to a code page they have written, it appears the same way they last left it.

Version control: Unlike most alternative environments, however, Pythy stores student work in a server-side Git repository, giving full change history support to students. While the underlying Git organization is completely transparent to students, they can easily roll back changes in their work or switch to an earlier version with a one-click action in a simple "history tab" in the web interface. Novice programmers very frequently end up in situations where attempts at fixing bugs cause them to delve further "down the rabbit hole" as they write patches and new code, only to find that they are no closer to the correct solution (or even further away) and wishing that they could revert easily to a previous version. They can also see the score results for any past version they submitted for automated checking.

Media computation: Many introductory Python courses use media computation to provide context to computing tasks, a strategy first adopted by Georgia Tech [8]. Unfortunately, many Python implementations—including all of those developed for the web—do not support media computation well. In contrast, Pythy provides support for media manipulation using a port of the Jython-based media library developed at Georgia Tech. Pythy provides for in-browser presentation of images being manipulated by the student's code, supporting activities often used in media-computation-style courses. Allowing students to see image transformations applied to images live within the browser improves interactivity and engagement.

Pythy is implemented as a Ruby-on-Rails (v.4) application. It uses a modified version of Skulpt [6] for its Python implementation, so that when students run their code, it happens client-side right in their browser. Skulpt modifications include support for media computation, and an internal redesign so that Skulpt is properly reentrant, allowing execution of Python code to be interrupted and resumed to better support debugging and to avoid blocking the browser's user interface thread when long-running Python programs are encountered. Pythy is open-source, hosted on Github.

4. EVALUATION

Pythy was first deployed in the classroom in January 2013 in a new service course at Virginia Tech for non-CS majors needing to take a programming course: Computational Problem Solving in Python. This course was designed as an updated alternative to an existing C++ class commonly taken by non-CS majors. The new Python course used Miller et al.'s book [5] as the primary text. 53 students took the course. Pythy was used for all programming assignments and homework exercises in the course.

As a basis for comparison, Virginia Tech also offers a CS1 course based on Georgia Tech's media computation course, where students learn Python using JES, the Jython Environment for Students. JES is the official IDE prescribed for use with media computation classes. While it is reasonably easy it install, it suffers from a number of issues, including unfamiliar button and menu placement, an inability to open more than a single file at a time, lack of assignment support, limited debugging facilities, and so on. Nevertheless, it is targeted at a similar audience and aims to be easy to use for novices.

While the two courses are not completely analogous—using different textbooks and teaching approaches, and serving somewhat different student populations—the media computation course was the best available choice to use as a basis for comparison.

4.1 Student Experiences

To assess student experiences with the two environments, we designed a survey instrument focused on the primary obstacles Pythy was intended to resolve. The survey questions were worded generically without referring to a specific tool, so that students in both classes could be given identical surveys. The survey was administered near the end of the semester after students had used their respective tools for months. The survey included a series of Likert-scale questions on common issues and habits students experience, and also included free-response questions to elicit more detail about what features students used most often or found the most frustrating.

Table 1: Survey average responses from students who used Pythy and students who used JES (statistically significant differences marked with *).

Question	Pythy	JES	p
When I first started using the software, I had no trouble figuring out how to run my programs.	4.05	2.88	0.0053*
The software made it easy for me to find out how well my programs' behavior fulfilled assignment goals.	3.84	3.06	0.0447*
I frequently encountered errors in my programs.	3.47	4.06	0.0794
When my program wouldn't even run because of an error, the error messages helped me to find and fix the problem.	3.11	3.07	0.9287
When my program ran, but got an error later on, the error messages helped me to find and fix the problem.	3.26	3.27	0.9930
When my program didn't have errors, but also didn't do what it was supposed to, the software helped me to figure out why.	2.74	1.81	0.0013*
When my programs had errors, the software helped me to understand what part of my program was the problem.	3.47	3.00	0.1838
Error messages provided by the program were unclear.	3.00	3.44	0.2247
The software made it easy keep track of assignments in the class.	4.68	2.94	<0.0001 *
I often wanted to look at past programs when writing new ones.	4.53	4.56	0.8789
The software made it easy for me to look at my past programs when writing new ones.	4.00	2.88	0.0168*
The software made finding and opening my past programs easy.	4.26	3.38	0.0223*
I frequently looked at programming examples from class while working on my programs.	4.53	4.12	0.2221
The software made looking at programming examples from class easy.	4.42	3.00	0.0005*
When I wanted to consult an in-class example, the software helped me to do so.	4.16	2.75	0.0008*

A total of 35 survey responses were received, 19 from the course using Pythy (out of 53 students, 36%), and 16 from the course using JES (out of 42 students, 38%). Table 1 summarizes the main results from the survey. Students rated answers on a scale from Strongly Disagree to Strongly Agree, which were converted to an ordinal scale from 1-5. A more detailed analysis of the survey results appears in [10].

The survey results indicate that students who used Pythy agreed more strongly that it was easier to begin using, that it provided more support for assignments, that it made it easier to consult examples, and that it helped them figure out when their programs did not behave as required by the assignment. Of course, these results are not surprising, since JES was not designed to provide these capabilities. It does not have features to help students manage or work with assignments, to check the correctness of student work, or to help navigate and work with classroom examples. Nevertheless, the evaluation does help support the idea that Pythy's features in this regard were useful to students.

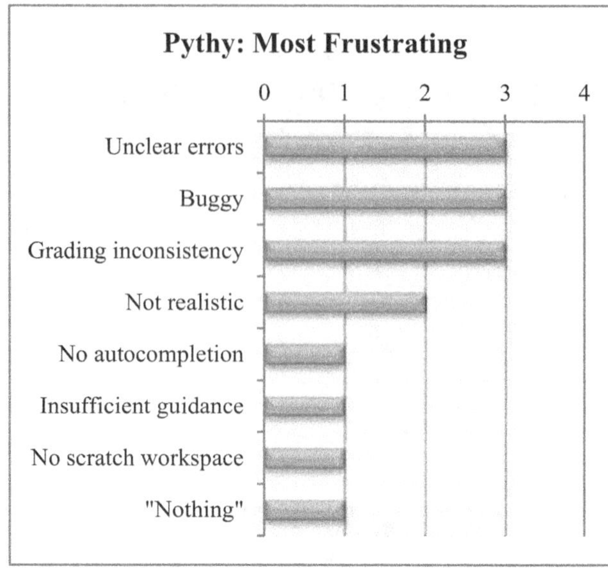

Figure 4: Pythy Responses to the question: What was the single most frustrating thing about the software?

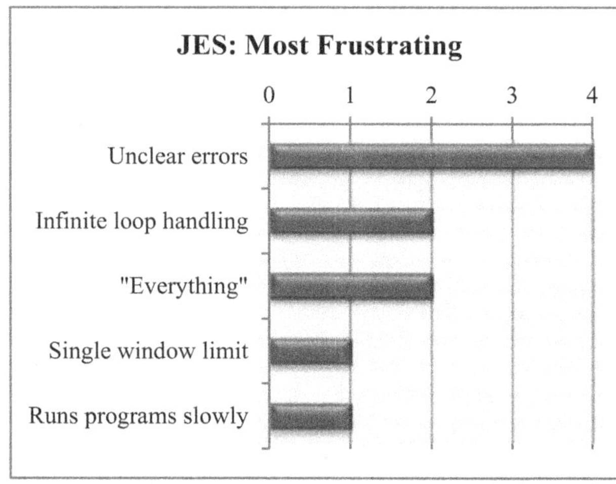

Figure 5: JES Responses to the question: What was the single most frustrating thing about the software?

Also, two of the questions on the survey showed strong agreement between both groups of students. Both groups of students indicated that they often wanted to look at past programs when writing new ones (all respondents but one chose Agree or Strongly Agree). Both groups of students also indicated that they frequently looked at classroom examples when working on programs (all but 4 respondents chose Agree or Strongly Agree). This suggests that looking at exemplars is an important task for novices, and one that should be supported by introductory tools. Similarly, the midrange scores for program error messages and whether the tool helps find problems suggest there is more room for improvement.

In a free response question, students were asked to identify the single most frustrating thing about the software they used. Responses are summarized in Figures 4 and 5. Interestingly,

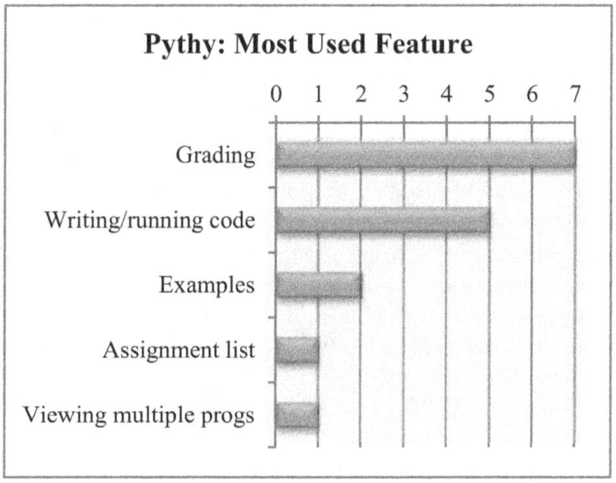

Figure 6: Pythy Responses to the question: What feature of the software did you use the most?

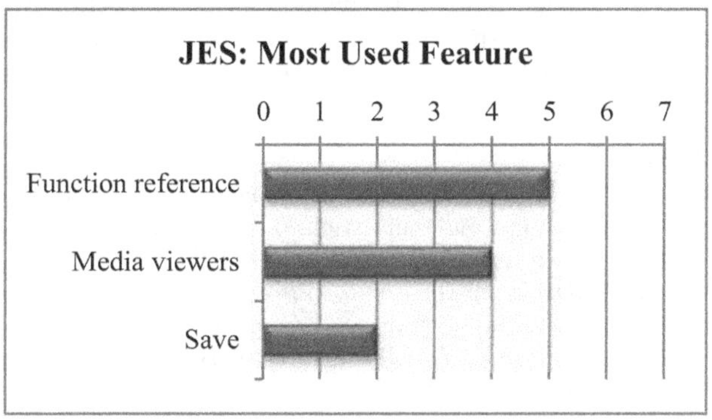

Figure 7: JES Responses to the question: What feature of the software did you use the most?

unclear error messages were the most frequent complaint for both tools. Many other frustrations with Pythy stemmed from the fact that it was new and this was the first course that had used it on a realistic scale. As Pythy has matured, some of the issues (lack of a scratchpad, for example) have been addressed.

Students were also asked to identify what feature of the software they used the most. Responses are summarized in Figures 6 and 7. For Pythy, students heavily used the grading feature, as well as running their code interactively and interacting with examples. JES users most heavily used the built-in function reference and media viewers. When asked to identify what aspect of the software students found most helpful, these same choices appeared most frequently among responses in the respective groups.

Similar trends emerged when students were asked which aspect of the software saved them the most time, as shown in Figures 8 and 9. Students were also asked: "What aspect of the software caused you to waste the most time?" In both groups, unclear error messages were the most frequently cited issue. Minor syntax errors were also cited as a time waster in both groups. As with the results in Table 1, this indicates that improvements to error messages and diagnostics would be welcome for beginners.

By examining the log data from Pythy, we can also see roughly how much students used different features. For example, students spent 31.8 hours working on code writing assignments in Pythy over the course of the 15-week semester. In comparison, they spent 38.9 hours working with classroom examples, a significant

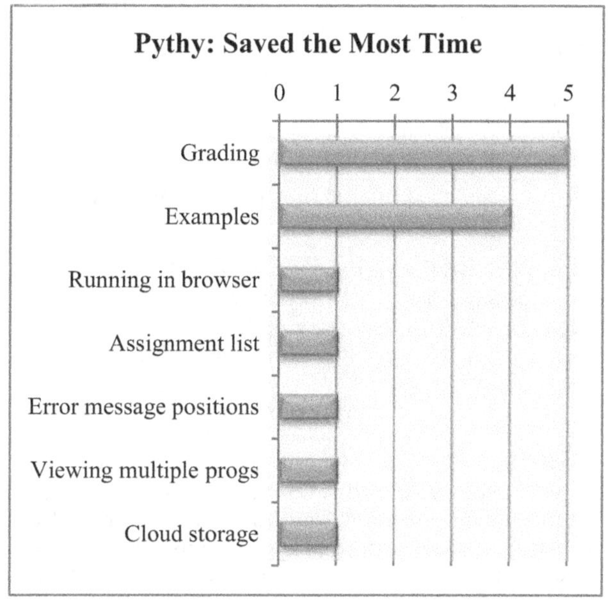

Figure 8: Pythy Responses to the question: What aspect of the software saved you the most time?

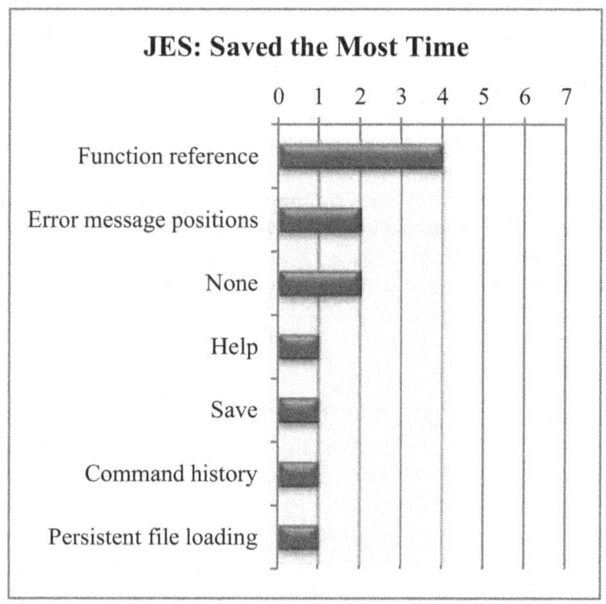

Figure 9: JES Responses to the question: What aspect of the software saved you the most time?

difference (Welch's two-sample t-test, $t = -2.27$, $p < 0.03$). This can be explained by the fact that most students who attended class did open examples in their browser to follow along with live coding demonstrations by the instructor in class, and this in-class time spent with examples contributes a significant portion to the total time spent.

When checking work on an assignment, students submitted their work for automated correctness checking a mean of 14.5 times per assignment. Assignments were split into homework-style problem sets that consisted of a number of functions the student needed to write, and programming projects that required completing larger tasks, such as implementing a game of hangman. It appeared that students submitted their work for checking more frequently for problem sets than for larger programming projects. One plausible reason for this is that students working on problem sets were checking their work incrementally, resubmitting as they completed each required function in the assignment. When working on a project, on the other hand, students did not submit their work for checking until the project had reached a state of reasonable completion.

A full analysis of the entire survey and all free response questions appears in [10].

5. CLASSROOM EXPERIENCES

From a teaching point of view, Pythy was quite successful in the classroom. Students had very little trouble getting started. Pythy's features also made it ideal for live coding demonstrations in the classroom, and using it in this way also repeatedly illustrated by example how Pythy's navigation structure and features were used. Most importantly, the combination of familiar web-style navigation with a directly editable, in-browser view of the source code made Pythy very approachable for beginners. Students heavily used both in-class examples and also the assignment checking/submission features provided by Pythy, and reported positively on them in the survey and in course evaluations.

At the same time, however, this was the first semester that Pythy was used on a realistic scale, with a full class of non-majors. This pointed out a number of its shortcomings, such as lack of Online Python Tutor-style step-by-step code visualization and program state rendering. Pythy was inspired in part by the Online Python Tutor, and we fully intend to add support for program state visualization and associated debugging features, but these items remain for future work. Similarly, while Pythy provides support for media computation-style image manipulation, the audio manipulation features were not completed in time for use in the Spring 2013 semester, although we hope to use them more fully in the coming academic year. Also, while Pythy was always intended to support multi-file projects for students, the initial implementation does not offer visible navigation controls for managing student assignments with more than one Python file. While this is similar is spirit to the way the Online Python Tutor and JES work, some students were interested in learning more about modularization and this limitation does significantly affect the way students organize their work. Fortunately, Pythy's internal design fully supports such projects, so this extension can be added in the coming year.

The most critical limitation of the current version of Pythy is that assignment checking consists purely of functional correctness tests. There was insufficient time before the Spring 2013 semester to provide any interface for supporting manual code grading and markup. Fortunately, many automated grading systems also support manual markup, and lessons learned from such systems can be incorporated into Pythy. Further, there are no technical barriers to adding this feature within Pythy's infrastructure.

Overall, in spite of these limitations, Pythy's first use in the classroom was successful for both students and instructors. As a result, Pythy is currently being used by a new team of teaching staff for the Python service course this semester.

6. CONCLUSION

Pythy was developed to provide a simple, clean path for non-CS students in such a course to begin learning to program through assignments and examples: to write, run, debug, and turn in code. It achieves this goal by adopting a completely web-based deployment strategy, using a web-inspired user interface instead of one modeled on a traditional IDE model, supporting all aspects of classroom assignments, supporting instructor-provided classroom examples with real-time updates pushed to all clients viewing the example, providing cloud storage with automatic saving of all changes, using transparent version control to preserve student work histories, and supporting media computation activities.

Initial experiences with Pythy in the classroom suggest that students value its features and find it helpful in referring to previous programs or examples when students have to write new code. There are many areas of future work where Pythy can be improved, but it already shows promise as an alternative to more traditional natively-installed development tools. Pythy is open-source, and is available at http://github.com/web-cat/pythy.

ACKNOWLEDGEMENTS

This work is supported in part by a SIGCSE Special Projects grant, and by an equipment grant from the Student Engineers' Council at Virginia Tech. Any opinions, findings, conclusions, or recommendations expressed in this material are those of the authors and do not necessarily reflect the views of SIGCSE or the Student Engineers' Council.

REFERENCES

[1] Jam Jenkins, Evelyn Brannock, Thomas Cooper, Sonal Dekhane, Mark Hall, and Michael Nguyen. 2012. Perspectives on active learning and collaboration: JavaWIDE in the classroom. In *Proceedings of the 43rd ACM Technical Symposium on Computer Science Education (SIGCSE '12)*. ACM, New York, NY, USA, 185-190. DOI=10.1145/2157136.2157194.

[2] Light Table—a new IDE concept. http://www.lighttable.com/.

[3] Online Python Tutor. http://www.pythontutor.com/.

[4] Philip J. Guo. 2013. Online Python Tutor: Embeddable web-based program visualization for CS education. In *Proceeding of the 44th ACM Technical symposium on Computer science education (SIGCSE '13)*. ACM, New York, NY, USA, 579-584. DOI=10.1145/2445196.2445368.

[5] Brad Miller et al. 2013. *How to Think Like a Computer Scientist: Learning with Python: Interactive Edition 2.0.* http://interactivepython.org/courselib/static/thinkcspy/.

[6] Skulpt. http://www.skulpt.org/.

[7] Brython. http://www.brython.info/.

[8] Mark Guzdial. 2003. A media computation course for non-majors. In *Proceedings of the 8th Annual Conference on Innovation and Technology in Computer Science Education (ITiCSE '03)*, David Finkel (Ed.). ACM, New York, NY, USA, 104-108. DOI=10.1145/961511.961542.

[9] Mark Guzdial. 2011. Why is computing with media so rarely supported in programming languages? http://computinged.wordpress.com/2011/06/17/why-is-computing-with-media-so-rarely-supported-in-programming-languages/.

[10] Dan Tilden. 2013. *Design and Evaluation of a Web-Based Programming Tool to Improve the Introductory Computer Science Experience.* M.S. Thesis, Virginia Tech.

Five Years of Game Programming Outreach: Understanding Student Differences

Antti-Jussi Lakanen, Ville Isomöttönen, Vesa Lappalainen
Department of Mathematical Information Technology
University of Jyväskylä, Finland
{antti-jussi.lakanen, ville.isomottonen, vesal}@jyu.fi

ABSTRACT

This paper presents lessons learned from five years of teaching a five-day game design and programming outreach course. The course was offered in summer time and targeted at middle and high school students. In total, 462 youngsters have taken part in 21 course instances. We describe our course concept, and discuss our successes and challenges. In particular, we focus on understanding our student populations by presenting descriptives and statistics of the events, and performing a statistical cluster analysis based on pre- and post-surveys. The cluster analysis was complemented with an analysis of the qualitative data, also originating from the surveys. Taken together, students could be classified into five groups with substantial differences: *Enthusiasts*, *Newbies*, *Uncertains*, *Experimenters*, and *Unsatisfieds*. Awareness of the clusters helps instructors of similar courses in developing course content, designing differentiated instruction, and planning follow-up or advanced courses.

Categories and Subject Descriptors

K.3.2. [**Computers and education**]: Computers and Information Science Education—*Computer Science Education*

General Terms

Experimentation, Human Factors

Keywords

K-12; outreach; game programming; recruitment

1. INTRODUCTION

Computer games are a fruitful contextualization for computing education. They incorporate many disciplines such as mathematics, artificial intelligence, and physics as well as art and design, serving as a catalyst for arousing motivation for learning computer science (CS) [3]. Our faculty started an outreach program in 2009 to expose middle and high school students to the concepts of computer science and computational thinking, and to enthuse youngsters about computer science through game programming. The program has included week-long programming courses in the summertime, a coding club during the school year, and collaboration courses with local area high schools. In this study we focus on the summer courses. The first author has been involved in teaching the course since its inception in 2009.

The restricted time frame of the course (25 hours, 5 days), as well as the variation in students' age, prior knowledge, background, and motivation towards computer science studies, have provided a challenging experience for the instructors. In this paper, we aim to develop an understanding of the student populations by classifying students into groups using statistical clustering analysis, which we then complement with qualitative data. We will also look at the background of the project, and describe our teaching methods and rationale for choosing the tool set. Furthermore, we will discuss the challenges we have faced along the way, and go through the descriptives and statistics from the five years. We have changed the course concept only slightly over the years, which improves the reliability of the results.

SIGCSE'14, March 3–8, 2014, Atlanta, GA, USA.

ACM 978-1-4503-2605-6/14/03 ...$15.00.
http://dx.doi.org/10.1145/2538862.2538914.

2. BACKGROUND AND RELATED WORK

Our project can be classified as what Black et al. [1] call "extra-curricular engagement". The aim within these (typically summer) events is to acquaint young students, ranging from 8 to 18 years, with computers and computing [2, 10, 11]. These events can be based, for example, on game programming (as in this study), electronics [8] and contests involving a wide range of computing activities [10]. Students often work in an explorative manner, and social and collaborative aspects of computing are deliberately included.

Projects such as these, as well as our own, not only aim to enthuse students about CS more generally, and increase their awareness of the topic, but also, as educational institutions, hope to increase enrollment in further CS studies. In this connection, according to Myers and Fouts [12], a high level of involvement and personal support are highly interconnected with a positive attitude towards science studies. Singh et al. [14] called for the provision of more information to students about science subjects and their future use in order to stimulate their interest in science. They urged the engendering of more positive attitudes (including interest) toward science by promoting more positive experiences in science learning. Including the above aspects, Xu et al. [17] summarize the literature on student interest, highlighting factors such as that students can be encouraged to develop an interest in science and want to work for it, even when initially they show little or no interest. These findings are relevant to this study as our aim is to reach students with no prior programming experience or interest in CS.

In this study, we examine what groups can be identified from the student cohort who take the outreach course, and distinguish possible differences between the groups. Use of cluster analysis in a classroom context is supported by, e.g., Myers and Fouts [12], who found differences in how classroom environment and attitudes towards science interrelate.

3. COURSE DESCRIPTION AND LEADING IDEAS

The course is a 5-day, 5-hours-a-day study module targeted at middle and high school students (aged between 12–18 years in Finland). Earlier programming experience is not assumed. The course is given several times per summer and participants are divided so that on one course week there is a maximum of 25–30 students. We want these events not only to give a positive image of the field and industry, but also to emphasize the connection between creating computer games and real-world problems in computer science. Obviously, another goal is to also give the students a fast-paced course in basic programming skills needed for making simple 2D games and a toolkit to continue programming independently after the course. The design of the course can be condensed into three main points.

1. **The use of textual programming**. Gives students a realistic experience of programming and professional environments, avoids challenges in transitition to other languages [13] but still gives equal learning results [9].
2. **The very first game comes about easily**. Even though we find no intrinsic value in writing short programs, we think that students should be able to concentrate on game mechanics and content rather than inessential routines.
3. **Have fun and get inspired with programming**. Even the students without prior programming knowledge can create a functioning game, and many indeed continue developing games in their spare time [7].

3.1 Class structure and Pong project

Each course day starts with a short lecture, where a new programming concept is introduced. The lectures are carried out in a dialogic manner, and the students are encouraged to ask questions. Apart from the lecturing hours the course is practically *learning by doing*. We will cover this next.

During the first day of the course, all students are required to complete a *Pong game* project, which takes about 6 hours of work. The students follow our Pong tutorial, which is divided into seven phases, each addressing a particular programming concept (e.g. variables, procedures, function return value, etc.). Each student has to write the game code him/herself, since copying large chunks of example code from the website is deliberately made practically impossible. Even though the material is written to be as self-explanatory as possible, writing code for the first time and learning a whole new language can be tricky. For this reason we encourage the students to ask the instructors anytime they feel that they are not on the right track. Typical issues at this point relate to syntax; for example, writing brackets and semicolons.

The purpose of the mandatory project is to practice the syntax of C# language and to get familiar with the common programming structure. The code written in the tutorial and the exercises can be utilized later on when students start writing their own game.

Another purpose of this "one-size-fits-all" project is that while the instructors observe the students performing the project they get a good sense of the students' skill level. This way they can rapidly adapt their teaching approach for each student and differentiate the instructions accordingly. For example, we have created a collection of extra exercises for those who assimilate the content of the tutorial rapidly. Students can go through the excercises at their own pace.

3.2 Game project

On the second day students start making a design for their own game. Each student has a named page in our wiki, where he/she describes the background story, mechanics and the goal of the game along with a rough execution plan for the next three–four days. Students also sketch the game and the game characters, which are then scanned and attached onto their webpage. After making the design the students start working on the game project. A typical game is a platformer with self-made graphics, level design and tally mechanics.

Using the broad learning material in our wiki and a comprehensive tutorial for making the Pong game we aim to support the students to work independently and encourage them to solve issues with their game projects by checking the material first, searching the web, and only then asking the instructors. However, the students often have difficulties understanding where to start with making their games. To address the problem, we have created a project template for a platformer game which a student can choose when creating a new project in IDE. The template includes a ready-made elephant character which the player can control with arrow keys. There are also collectable items and a text file containing a level design example, which can be modified with a text editor.

Even with all the material available, making a game project from scratch (or from a template) can be a challenging task for novice programmers. On the other hand, game concepts can be very unique or students' questions very specific in some other way, and the learning material cannot give a direct answer to their question. Therefore, students very much need the help of the instructors to be able to complete the project on time. On average, we have had 4–6 teaching assistants in a 25–30 student classroom, and they all are more or less fully engaged with the students' questions for the whole five days.

On the final day of the course each attendee demonstrates the game to the rest of the class. Students vote for the best game, which is rewarded with a small prize. Based on our observations, waiting for the demonstration keeps the students motivated and inclined to fine-tune the game mechanics and its appearance. The demonstration is also a nice social experience where students can show what they have focused on. Games can offer an environment to integrate fact and fiction, foster creativity and imagination [4]. One way this is represented in the demonstration is that both presenter and audience react to the possible bugs or flaws with humour as if they were a part of the creative and imaginatory process. Furthermore, the showcase is often the only chance for the students to see what kind of games others have made since during the week everyone is busy developing their own projects.

3.3 Tool set

We introduced the *Jypeli* library in 2009 and have continued using and developing it ever since. Jypeli is built on top of Microsoft XNA and is written in C#. Jypeli is an API that encapsulates low-level details of XNA and C#. For example, while XNA – as well as many other game programming frameworks for beginners – necessitates the programmer to take care of target devices and routines for initializing, loading, unloading, updating, and drawing the game content, Jypeli hides the device handling and encapsulates the basic routines into a single method. We have also a built-in physics engine. This enables the student to reach the "fun part" very fast with his first game. For example, making a ball bounce and change its color while colliding with the borders of the level requires 22 lines of code and two methods, see `http://bit.ly/pelikurssi`.

Even though there exists a number of novice programming environments (see, e.g. [5]), we have found several advantages in creating and using our own tool. The first, and probably the most important aspect, is that developing our own library has allowed us to give students detailed technical support and to add features to the library "on-the-fly" based on students' requests. This means that it is possible to achieve more of the student's wishes for his or her game. Based on our observations this makes the experience fun for the students, enhances ownership of their work and even highlights the notion of software development as being teamwork.

We also wanted to give students an experience similar to what they will have when they enter advanced courses or the university. For example, in our faculty we use traditional programming languages in introductory programming courses, and therefore concepts and practices learned on the summer course can be utilized efficiently. It is also interesting that students often ask if these are tools that are also used in the industry, "in real life". Telling them that the programming language and IDE used in the course are amongst the most popular in the industry gives them a motivational boost.

We should point out that even though it is very easy to write the first lines of code with Jypeli to make, for instance, a ball bounce on the screen, a typical platformer or space shooter game would be about 200–300 lines at the end of the week, maybe even more. In that sense it is not our sole intention to write games with the minimum amount of characters, but rather to let students canalize their efforts into developing game mechanics and content of their choice and free them from excessive worry about standard game routines, such as collision detection or graphics and control device handling.

4. DESCRIPTIVES AND STATISTICS

4.1 Questionnaires

Two surveys were conducted during each course instance, one at the beginning and one at the end. Data were collected using questionnaires. The 2013 version of the questionnaire included a total of 27 quantitative and 11 open-ended questions[1]. The quantitative questions were designed using a five-point Likert scale with the following options: "strongly disagree" (1), "somewhat disagree", "not agree nor disagree", "somewhat agree", "strongly agree" (5). A few questions have been added or removed during the years, and some questions have been rephrased.

4.2 Student background

Demographic data is given in Table 1. There are a few things to be noted. The proportion of girls has declined to nearly zero in the last couple of years. We have discussed how to improve the situation in terms of gender distribution, but the fact is that girls do not attend our course. Our hypothesis is that there are at least two possible explanations for this. Firstly, in marketing and publicity we tend to emphasize *programming* and *games* over *game design*, which may lead to the idea of narrowly and technically focused programming classes or tight bonding into a "gamer culture". Giving greater weight to game design, creativity or narrativity could perhaps change the ratio (see, for example [15, 6]). Secondly, we have had the misfortune not to find a single female teaching assistant, which in part feeds the image of computer science as being a masculine field and – in our speculations – has prevented the few girls who attend from coming to the course again. In contrast, the proportion of freshmen women in computer science and ICT in Finland is around 20 %.

Table 1: Demographics from the years 2009–2013.

Year	09	10	11	12	13	Total
N	45	105	83	114	115	**462**
Girls	7	6	9	6	3	**31**
Repeaters	-	4	23	23	44	**94**
Av. age	13.8	14.2	14.7	14.7	14.3	**14.4**

The share of students taking the course a second or third time has increased every year. Some have participated up to five times and a few students have attended more than one course in a summer. In 2013 the number of repeaters nearly doubled from 2012. As yet, we do not have large enough numbers on how taking the course multiple times correlates with the student's career choices. However, repeated course attendance (during middle school) seems to increase the likelihood of attending our other outreach programs, including coding clubs and high school collaboration courses, e.g. CS1. Participants coming with zero programming experience have declined from 47 % to 32 % (see Figure 1). On the other hand, students with at least some experience reached its all-time high in 2013, nearly 50 % – this is at least partly because of the repeaters.

4.3 Feedback

Overall satisfaction has remained at a high level throughout the years: the mean was 4.66 and peaked in 2013 at 4.78.

As mentioned in Section 3.3, one object of the course was to give a realistic image of programming, but also affect the possibly distorted conceptions about programming. One of

[1]All the questions are visible at `http://bit.ly/pelikurssi`

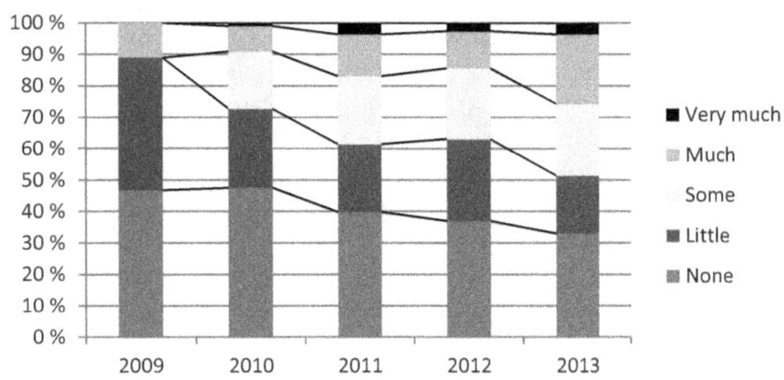

Figure 1: Students with zero programming experience (the lowest part of each bar) have declined.

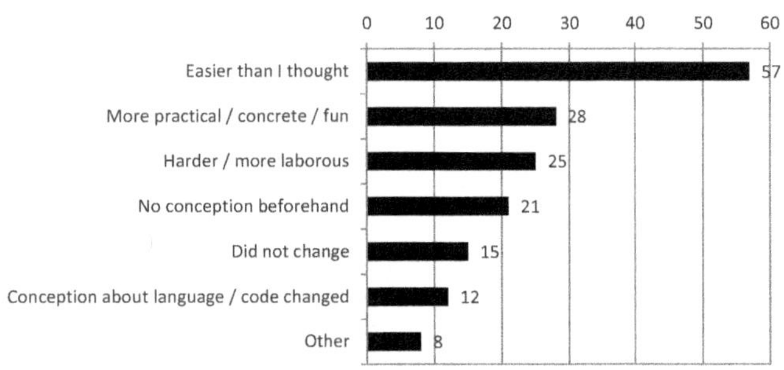

Figure 2: After the course students typically find programming to be easier, more practical, concrete or fun than they had thought.

the questions in the post-survey was phrased "My conception of programming changed during this course". Of all students 41 % agreed, 35 % disagreed and 24 % neither agreed nor disagreed. The students could comment on their answers (open-ended question). We obtained 166 answers and classified them according to the occurring themes and the similarities between the answers, and discovered that the answers can be divided into seven categories. The categories and the distribution according to our classification are presented in Figure 2.

The question "I'm interested in applying for studying science/computing" was included in the pre- and post-questionnaires. When compared, we notice a small rise in the total mean figure (pre 3.4 → post 3.6, scale 1–5). Another interesting finding is that the course seemed to have had an even stronger effect on those students who were initially *not interested* in studying computer science (see Table 2).

We have to remember that these are numbers given after an experience which the participants clearly found fun. The above-mentioned change is somewhat expected; however, change in *actions* is a sum of multiple affecting factors, which were not measured in this study.

5. CLUSTER ANALYSIS

To investigate what kind of groups students form we made a deeper dive into the research data. To be able to use many different numerical variables in the analysis we ended up forming clusters of students using a statistical cluster analysis. Before introducing the clusters, we want to note that we did not use any instruments for measuring learning during the course. Thus, the cluster analysis does not produce information about, for example, whether the students learn a little or a lot. Rather, by using multiple factors (pre- and post-questionnaire questions), the analysis expresses students' views on themselves as programmers, conceptions about programming, attitudes and possible changes in these. We ran a hierarchical cluster analysis several times using different parameters. Through exploring different number of clusters we found the five cluster solution to be the most appropriate and informative. A total of 286 valid cases were included. The final solution included one additive cluster with one case, but after examining the data the cluster was discarded due to invalid data or peculiar answers that may have been caused by misunderstood questions.

Table 2: Interest in applying for CS studies changes during the course. Scale 1=disagree. . . 5=agree.

Answer in pre	1	2	3	4	5
Avg change in post	+1.45	+.92	+.23	+.03	-.25

The Table 3 presents the mean values of each variable per cluster, which give a general view on the differences among the student groups. After determining the appropriate number of clusters and getting a general view based on the mean values, cluster by cluster and variable by variable, we looked at the students' open-ended answers to identify common patterns. Examining the qualitative data in addition to the quantitative data enabled a deeper and more fundamental analysis of the clusters found. The clusters were then named according to this information. The integration of quantitative and qualitative analyses is indicative of mixed methods research approach [16, p. 8].

5.1 Cluster 1: Enthusiasts (n=83)

The students in this cluster may well stand out the most. They have a good deal of prior knowledge of programming, they consider themselves experienced computer users, do not think programming is hard and are willing to apply for computer science studies in the future. *Enthusiasts* have tried several programming languages and have done many things beforehand, for example, web and mobile development, games and scripts. Examining the data reveals that they are the most inclined to work in the computer science field, when compared to the other groups. Participating in the course does not affect their conceptions too much, since they already have built a view of programming. However, they are very pleased with the course, and many in this group have come to the course a second or third time.

Enthusiasts have gathered some earlier programming experience so their views on the hard things in programming drill down to things like "optimization", "compatibility issues multi-platform software", "algorithms" and "reading undocumented code". They do not worry too much about "little bugs" or "remembering unessential details" like, for example, students in the *Unsatisfieds* group (see Section 5.5).

It is worth noting that the students in this group are from the older end of the scale, 15.2 years on average. This was also the largest cluster of all.

5.2 Cluster 2: Newbies (n=63)

The students in this group have the second lowest average value in earlier programming experience, 1.6, only the *Experimenters* having a lower number. This group also contains

Table 3: Clusters' mean variable values. All questions were on a scale of 1=disagree... 5=agree, except for age. (Pgm = programming)

Cluster	1	2	3	4	5
Students in cluster	83	63	76	13	48
Age	15.2	14.1	14.5	14.5	14.6
I play computer games often	4.8	4.6	4.5	3.1	4.6
Earlier pgm experience	3.1	1.6	2.4	1.3	1.7
I am a skilled computer user	4.3	3.4	3.9	2.8	3.0
Pgm is hard	2.3	3.3	2.9	3.1	3.2
I'm going to apply for CS...	4.5	3.4	2.8	3.5	3.3
Overall satisfaction	4.8	4.9	4.8	4.4	4.1
Assignments were hard	2.2	2.7	2.2	2.9	2.8
Course met my expectations	4.4	4.2	4.2	3.1	4.0
My view on pgm changed	2.3	4.0	2.8	3.7	3.1
pgm is harder than I thought	2.1	3.0	1.9	2.8	3.3
I would recommend the course	4.6	4.7	4.6	4.4	4.0
I'm going to apply for CS...	4.7	3.7	3.1	3.6	3.3

the youngest students with an average age of 14.1 years. The *Newbies* tend to think programming is difficult. One student said he had programmed a calculator a bit at school and said "it was awful". Unlike the students in other clusters, the *Newbies* rather freely reveal their conceptions, or even misconceptions, about what they find hard in programming. These included, for example, "writing complex and nuts equations", "having to handle many different software" and even "viruses" (which might be a joke). In addition, a significant number of students stressed memorizing and the need to know an enormous number of "code words". On the other hand, several students mentioned "imagination" and "creativity" as valuable skills that a programmer needs. This implies that despite the rather restricted perspective on programming the students were ready to abandon that impression and try out something that they have never tried before.

The course had a mixed effect on the way students in this cluster viewed programming: 32 % of the *Newbies* agreed with the question about programming being harder than they thought. On the other hand, roughly the same proportion said quite the opposite, and the rest could not say. Either way, the change in their conception of programming was drastic: the average number was 4.0, the highest of all clusters. The *Newbies* also experienced the course assignments as a tad harder than other groups.

5.3 Cluster 3: Uncertains (n=76)

This group was the most difficult to name, since the group does not stand out in any particular way. They have a little programming experience, are somewhat interested in computer science but were not going to apply for CS studies at the time of the pre-questionnaire. As with the *Newbies*, some of the *Uncertains* think "remembering" and "learning commands" are rank among the hardest things in programming. However, quite a few highlight certain concepts inside the programming domain, such as "classes", "structs" and "functions". Their interest towards CS studies increases by the end of the course, but not much, leaving them uncertain as to future studies. As with other groups, they are very pleased with the summer course. An interesting detail about the *Uncertains* is that they almost completely disagree with the claim "Programming is harder than I thought". In the open-ended answers only one respondent directly said "It was harder [than I thought]." This suggests that these students actually have a decent programming background, they might have taken another similar course, or have attended this course before.

5.4 Cluster 4: Experimenters (n=13)

This was a very small cluster, and dominated by girls – nine out of 13 were girls. We named this group the *Experimenters* since the students in this cluster have no prior programming experience, feel that the assignments were hard, and the data reveal that they know little about what to expect from the course. They also spend significantly less time playing computer games than other students. In that regard, both programming *and* games are less familiar to them than to the students in other clusters. The course has only a subtle effect on their interest towards CS studies, but it does however change their view on programming. Even though this group consists almost completely of non-programmers, they were inclined to think that their future career could be in CS.

5.5 Cluster 5: Unsatisfieds (n=48)

Even though the cluster's name is rather harsh, not all in this group were completely unsatisfied with the experience. However, several students point out small details about the tools, the teaching or the atmosphere that they were not completely satisfied with. For example, some were expecting (that they would have seen) "better games" or "fancier physics". A few commented that the lessons started too early in the morning, and another one said he did not expect that he "had to independently study the [Pong] tutorial".

Even though many students in this group did not have earlier programming experience, the course had a mixed effect on their view of programming. Examining the open-ended supplements in part reconfirms the unfavorable connotation of this group's name: not all were happy discovering that it takes quite a lot of work to program a working computer game. On the other hand, in the post-survey, many enjoyed learning new things, and a few students highlighted that the most important offering of the course was that "now I know that making good computer games is challenging". One could speculate about the motive for a cluster 5 student's participation: was he on the course to *learn to program* (games), or maybe something else? As an interesting sidenote, it seems that parents in fact urged *Unsatisfieds* to participate more often than, for example, *Enthusiasts* (asked in pre-questionnaire).

The course does not seem to have an effect on the students' thoughts about computer science studies; the cluster average remains at 3.3 in both pre- and post-questionnaires.

The research data did not reveal a reason for this discontent. One possible explanation is that this group needed instruction and support more than other groups. In the post-questionnaire's "challenges" part many students mentioned that the number of teaching assistants was too small, the course advanced too rapidly, or that they would have expected more instruction and support. The size of this cluster's was 17 % of all the valid cases. This implies that the focus of the instruction and support needs to be carefully mapped out to prevent students from feeling that they are left alone with their programming challenges.

6. DISCUSSION AND CONCLUSIONS

In this paper, we described lessons learned from game programming outreach courses and examined what groups can be found in the student cohort using a statistical cluster analysis. A five-cluster solution divided the students into groups that we named *Enthusiasts*, *Newbies*, *Uncertains*, *Experimenters* and *Unsatisfieds*.

As members of the organization running outreach events, we would like to see every student get enthusiastic about computer science, game programming, and all the topics that one might go through on a five-day summer course. However, this study reveals that there are substantial differences among the students. Even though our course is an extra-curricular activity and the students participate voluntarily, not all of them are necessarily fully orientated to studying, ready to think about their future choices too much or decide whether they would be interested in computer science as a career choice. This challenge, showing up here especially in the *Experimenters* and *Unsatisfieds* groups, calls for more attention in our future courses.

From a teacher's perspective, the analysis based on pre- and post-questionnaires, however, may come too late if the teacher wants to fine-tune his course or target his instruction based on the cluster division. Would it be possible to end up with the same grouping, with acceptable reliability, using only the pre-questionnaire? This is left for future study.

7. ACKNOWLEDGEMENTS

This study and the programming course presented in this paper were partly funded by the Technology Industries of Finland Centennial Foundation.

8. REFERENCES

[1] J. Black, J. Brodie, P. Curzon, C. Myketiak, P. W. McOwan, and L. R. Meagher. Making computing interesting to school students: teachers' perspectives. In *Proceedings of the 18th ACM conference on Innovation and technology in computer science education*, ITiCSE '13, pages 255–260, New York, NY, USA, 2013. ACM.

[2] M. A. L. Egan and T. Lederman. The impact of IMPACT: Assessing students' perceptions after a day of computer exploration. In *Proceedings of the 16th annual joint conference on Innovation and technology in computer science education*, ITiCSE '11, pages 318–322, New York, NY, 2011. ACM.

[3] M. Guzdial and E. Soloway. Teaching the nintendo generation to program. *Commun. ACM*, 45(4):17–21, Apr. 2002.

[4] M. Kangas. Creative and playful learning: Learning through game co-creation and games in a playful learning environment. *Thinking Skills and Creativity*, 5(1):1 – 15, 2010.

[5] C. Kelleher and R. Pausch. Lowering the barriers to programming: A taxonomy of programming environments and languages for novice programmers. *ACM Comput. Surv.*, 37(2):83–137, 2005.

[6] C. Kelleher and R. Pausch. Using storytelling to motivate programming. *Commun. ACM*, 50(7):58–64, 2007.

[7] A.-J. Lakanen, V. Isomöttönen, and V. Lappalainen. Life two years after a game programming course: longitudinal viewpoints on K-12 outreach. In *Proceedings of the 43rd ACM technical symposium on Computer Science Education*, SIGCSE '12, pages 481–486, New York, NY, 2012. ACM.

[8] W. W. Lau, G. Ngai, S. C. Chan, and J. C. Cheung. Learning programming through fashion and design: a pilot summer course in wearable computing for middle school students. *SIGCSE Bull.*, 41(1):504–508, Mar. 2009.

[9] C. M. Lewis. How programming environment shapes perception, learning and goals: Logo vs. Scratch. In *SIGCSE '10: Proceedings of the 41st ACM technical symposium on Computer science education*, pages 346–350, New York, NY, USA, 2010. ACM.

[10] B. R. Maxim and B. S. Elenbogen. Attracting K-12 students to study computing. In *ASEE/IEEE Frontiers in Education Conference, 39th Annual*, pages M1H–1. IEEE, 2009.

[11] B. R. Maxim, W. I. Grosky, and J. P. Baugh. Work in progress - introducing information technology through game design. In *ASEE/IEEE Frontiers in Education Conference, 37th Annual*, pages T1B–1. IEEE, 2007.

[12] R. E. Myers and J. T. Fouts. A cluster analysis of high school science classroom environments and attitude toward science. *Journal of Research in Science Teaching*, 29(9):929–937, 1992.

[13] K. Powers, S. Ecott, and L. M. Hirshfield. Through the looking glass: teaching cs0 with alice. *SIGCSE Bull.*, 39(1):213–217, 2007.

[14] K. Singh, M. Granville, and S. Dika. Mathematics and science achievement: Effects of motivation, interest, and academic engagement. *The Journal of Educational Research*, 95(6):323–332, 2002.

[15] G. Smith and A. Sullivan. The five year evolution of a game programming course. In *Proceedings of the 43rd ACM technical symposium on Computer Science Education*, SIGCSE '12, pages 87–92, New York, NY, USA, 2012. ACM.

[16] C. Teddlie and A. Tashakkori. *Foundations of mixed methods research : integrating quantitative and qualitative approaches in the social and behavioral sciences.* SAGE, Los Angeles, 2009.

[17] J. Xu, L. T. Coats, and M. L. Davidson. Promoting student interest in science: The perspectives of exemplary african american teachers. *American Educational Research Journal*, 49(1):124–154, 2012.

Challenging Stereotypes and Changing Attitudes: The Effect of a Brief Programming Encounter on Adults' Attitudes toward Programming

Polina Charters, Michael J. Lee, Andrew J. Ko, Dastyni Loksa
Information School
University of Washington
{polinac, mjslee, ajko, dloksa}@uw.edu

ABSTRACT

Computer programming is now used broadly across many industries, with a diversity of working adults writing programs and interacting with code as part of their jobs. However, negative attitudes toward programming continue to deter many from studying computer science and pursuing careers in technology. To begin understanding adults' attitudes toward computer programming and how we can improve them, we used an educational video game to give 200 adult participants a concrete programming experience via the web, and then collected their self-reported opinions about programming. We found that adults initially had poor attitudes toward programming, believing that it was difficult, boring, and something they generally could not learn. After the online learning experience, their attitudes improved significantly, regardless of gender, population density, or level of education. These results demonstrate that adult attitudes toward programming, while initially negative, can be quickly changed with a brief, positive exposure to programming.

Categories and Subject Descriptors

K.3.2 Computer Science Education: Introductory Programming

General Terms

Human Factors, Experimentation

Keywords

Programming attitudes; adult programming; novice programming.

1. INTRODUCTION

Programming in the workplace is becoming more commonplace for many of today's careers. In fact, research based on U.S. Bureau of Census and Bureau of Labor data shows that while there are about 3 million professional programmers in the United States, over 13 million more people say they do programming at work, and over 90 million use spreadsheets and databases [5,26]. American workers program using spreadsheet systems, web authoring tools, business processing tools such as Visual Basic, graphical languages, and even professional languages such as Java [18]. These workers, or end-user programmers, are primarily adults who write code in order to complete other tasks, like designing a web page, doing office work such as accounting, and conducting scientific research [18]. Recent surveys have found that the computer literacy requirements have skyrocketed in almost every end-user category with one showing that over 70 percent of the surveyed companies now require computer competency in their middle and senior management positions [6]. As more adults continue or switch their careers, they will likely need to become end-user programmers to sustain gainful employment in many fields.

Even though computer programming has become a technical skill of millions, workers sometimes may not recognize what they do as "programming" [19]. For example, despite their considerable programming skills, many system administrators [2] and research scientists [5] view their programs as only a means to facilitate their other work, such as keeping a network or other services online. Sadly, many Americans even hold negative perceptions of computer science and people who work with code [23]. Some believe that programming is too difficult to learn, associating the ability to do so with intelligence, logical thinking, and genius they do not possess [3]. Moreover, many believe that programmers lack interpersonal skills [1], are socially awkward [23], and are so obsessed with technology that they have no other interests [23]. These views are especially more pronounced in younger girls and women [7]. These stereotypes can create negative attitudes toward programming, discouraging individuals from learning and accepting programming as a skill necessary for their professional development. Attitudes are important because they, in combination with perceptions of expected behavior, determine how one is likely to act towards specific activities [14] such as learning computer programming. For example, positive attitudes toward computers have been shown to increase computer use and understanding of subsequent computer-related skills in youth and older adults [11,26,32].

In an effort to reduce negative stereotyping and improve attitudes toward programming, educators and researchers have targeted elementary, middle school, and high school students with interventions such as computing camps and educational games [32] that facilitate exposure to basic programming concepts. While these efforts are necessary for helping students and other young adults to view computer science and programming as something within reach, little research has investigated adult attitudes towards programming [29]. In his mainstream 2012 magazine article, Wisniewski urges adults who are interested in programming to "... swallow [their] pride and seek out resources aimed at kids," which demonstrates the lack of content designed for consumption by adults [33]. Unfortunately, we know little about the adults who would find programming appealing and how they react to initial programming experiences.

SIGCSE '14, March 05 - 08 2014, Atlanta, GA, USA
Copyright 2014 ACM 978-1-4503-2605-6/14/03□$15.00
http://dx.doi.org/10.1145/2538862.2538938

To begin exploring adult behavior and attitudes towards programming, we exposed 200 adult participants to a simple online educational programming environment that asked them to complete a series of basic programming tasks [20,21,22]. We then asked them to describe their views toward programming. We also explored how these views vary by individual demographic factors – such as age, gender, population density, and education – and how these demographic factors may influence adults' attitudes. In the rest of this paper, we discuss prior work on efforts to improve computer-related attitudes in youths, elderly adults, and end-user programmers; we then describe our methodology, present our results, and conclude with a discussion of our results' implications on computing education.

2. RELATED WORK

Besides working adults, researchers have identified many other groups of end-user programmers, including young children [25] and middle-school students [17]. Although contemporary youth sometimes engage with environments such as video game design where they unwittingly learn end-user programming skills, they still hold negative views toward programming [25]. Some think that code is too difficult to learn [17], that it is boring [16], "geeky" [1], and is ultimately a solitary occupation that does not generalize to other fields of interest [23]. Fun and engaging learning environments, such as Scratch, Alice, and Greenfoot seek to improve kids' perceptions of programming [32].

Working adults have been mostly studied in the fields of Information Systems and Education in the context of end-user computer training; there is little research focusing on working adults' attitudes towards or experiences with programming. The goal of end-user training is to produce a motivated user who has the skills needed to perform a job-related task [30]. Studies show that positive attitudes play a critical role in learning outcomes and successful progress in end-user training [12]. For example, Szajna and Mackay concluded that attitudes toward computing and achievement were related to adults' performance with basic Information Technology skills [30]. Another study showed that providing more training to database users led to more positive attitudes, which led to better understanding of the material [28]. These studies indicate the importance of positive attitudes in the context of training, but do not offer insights about adults' views toward programming specifically.

A large amount of literature is dedicated to improving elderly adults' attitudes toward computers and increasing their basic computer use, such as Internet navigation [6]. This research has reliably shown that exposure to and experience with computing tasks lead to improved computer attitudes. An intervention to learn how to use the computer and the Internet for one year resulted in elderly adults demonstrating increased participation in social activities and hobbies and an improvement in self-reported feelings of being more in control of their lives [30]. Similarly, Czaja and Sharit demonstrated that even brief exposure to a limited set of computer tasks resulted in more positive attitudes [8]. Jay and Willis found that elderly adults' attitudes toward computers are modifiable through direct computer experience emphasizing comfort and efficacy [14].

3. METHOD

Previous research has established the potential for adults to make positive changes in their attitudes and self-perceptions related to basic computer use. Fewer works have investigated if this can also apply to computer programming. The purpose of our study is to investigate how a concrete learning experience, in the form of an educational programming game, affects adults' attitudes of computer programming. Our hypotheses were:

1. Adults will initially have negative attitudes toward programming.
2. Adults' views on computer programming will positively change after a basic educational programming experience.
3. Adults' demographic characteristics of age, gender, population density, and level of education will influence their attitudes towards computer programming.

Table 1. Demographic Factors of the Sample.

Gender	N	*Percent*
Male	113	56.5%
Female	87	43.5%
Population Density		
Urban	28	14.0%
Suburban	103	51.5%
Rural	40	20.0%
Education		
No High School Degree	2	1.0%
High School Degree	25	12.5%
Some College	85	42.5%
College Degree or Higher	88	44.0%

3.1 Participants

We targeted self-reported non-programmers, defined as individuals who said that they had never written computer code. To recruit participants, we used Amazon's Mechanical Turk (MTurk), an online marketplace where individuals can receive micro-payments for doing small Human Intelligence Tasks (HITs). The task we posted explained that participants would be asked to play a game and then complete a survey, that they could quit at any time after the first level, and that they would receive \$0.30 USD for starting the HIT, and an additional \$0.10 for each level completed. We used an initial pricing and validation model from studies involving the same educational programming game [20,21], setting the base reward high enough to attract workers, and the bonus low enough so participants would not feel obligated to play the game.

A total of 200 respondents, including 113 men and 87 women ranging in age from 18-64 years participated in the study, as detailed in Table 1. The median self-reported age was 27.

3.2 Procedure

Although traditional survey measures are commonly used to understand views toward computing [19], they often ask about attitudes abstractly, or without exposing participants to actual programming. In our study, adults played an educational programming game called Gidget (described in detail in [20,21,22]), which asked participants to complete a series of debugging puzzles, finding and fixing errors in a virtual robot's programs in order to proceed. The game taught basic programming concepts including conditionals, variables, loops, and functions. Participants completed a median of 8 levels (*min* = 2, *max* = 37). Median playing time was 34 minutes, with a minimum of 6.88 minutes and a maximum of 142.29 minutes.

After the game, participants completed a short survey that included demographic questions and the five following free-response questions related to attitudes toward programming:

1. What motivated you to play the game?
2. What was the *most* motivating part of playing the game?
3. What was the *least* motivating part of playing the game?
4. Describe your attitude/view towards programming *before* playing the game.
5. Describe your attitude/view towards programming now, *after* playing the game.

Although it would have been valid to ask participants about their attitudes toward programming before they played the game, it was critical that the participants were not told that the game involved programming before they were asked to play. Thus, we attempted to mitigate the effects of negative stereotypes that influence the outcome of the experience, and the participants' decision to participate in the learning activity.

4. RESULTS

We provide both quantitative and qualitative evidence to support our hypotheses. We used the SPSS statistical package to analyze our data. Throughout the analyses, we used nonparametric tests as our data was ordinal and not normally distributed. Because we first coded the attitude responses on an ordinal scale, we used chi-square tests of independence to see potential relationships between nominal demographic factors (gender, population density, and levels of education) and ordinal categories of motivations and attitudes. To determine potential correlations between the continuous variable of age and attitudes labeled on ordinal scales, we used the Spearman R test. We then sorted participants' text-based responses into emerging themes, and used a multinomial regression model to observe the relationships between adults' motivations and attitudes with age.

4.1 Changes in Programming Attitudes

The overall programming attitudes score was computed by coding the sentiment of participants' text-based responses on an ordinal Likert scale from -2 to 2, where -2 = very negative ("scary," "intimidating, "difficult"), -1 = moderately negative ("don't care about it), 0 = neutral or no opinion, 1 = moderately positive ("interested in learning") and 2 = very positive attitude ("I love it"). This score was calculated so the results of this study could be discussed relative to other studies that used Likert scales.

In order to assess the validity of the scale, we selected a random, 12.5% subset of the data and independently coded participants' *before* and *after* attitudes across three researchers according. For attitudes toward programming before the game, researchers reached 81% agreement; for attitudes after the game, researchers reached 83% agreement. To account for some agreement by chance, researchers further analyzed their agreement via the Cohen Kappa statistic. A value above .60 is conventionally considered to be adequate [24]. For attitudes *before* the game, the obtained result of 0.89 indicates that inter-coder agreement was high. For attitudes *after* the game, obtained results of 0.64 indicate that inter-coder agreement for this variable was adequate.

In support of our first hypothesis, adults reported having an initial overall negative attitude toward programming (Mdn = -2.00, min = -2, max = 2). However, as shown in Figure 1, participants reported having significantly better attitudes toward programming after the game (X^2 (16, N = 197) = 83.542, $p < .001$).

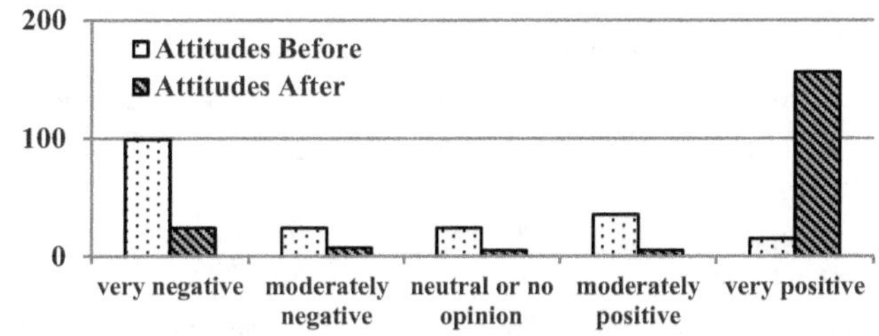

Figure 1. Number of participants exhibiting a particular sentiment toward programming before and after the game.

To better understand the reasons underlying these changes in attitudes, the first author categorized participants' *before* and *after* attitudes further into their emerging themes. As seen in Tables 2 and 3 (N = 188), most participants reported that prior to playing the game, they thought of programming as boring and unfamiliar, or something they wanted to learn but did not know how to approach. After playing the game, there was a distinct shift toward positive sentiments and a belief that learning to program was possible, even if difficult.

4.2 Categorized Attitudes and Demographics

To better understand how these improvements in attitudes might be affected by individual differences, we considered how demographic factors might influence participants' views. Chi-square tests of independence were performed to examine the relationships between all demographic factors and adults' attitudes. As shown in Table 4, differences in gender, population density, and level of education were generally not related, although adults from suburban neighborhoods (n = 35) were marginally more likely to report that the difficulty of programming concepts discouraged them from continuing to play the game, (X^2 (16, N = 196) = 25.57, p = 0.06). There was also a significant relationship between Level of Education and Ordinal Attitudes *after* the game: those with some college education (n = 66) and those with a bachelor's degree (n = 47) were significantly more likely to report positive perceptions of programming, (X^2 (24, N = 197) = 43.68, $p < .05$). However, these results may not be widely generalizable due to the fairly large number of tests, since at the 5% level it's likely that 1 out of 20 results will be significant by chance. A correlational analysis also revealed that as age increased, initial attitudes towards programming worsened, (r (200) = -0.181, $p < .05$).

4.3 Motivations and Demographics

To better understand participants' reasons for continuing to learn and their reasons for eventually quitting, the first author categorized all text-based responses from the three motivation questions in the survey. In response to the question of *"What motivated you to play the game?"*, participants reported that they thought the game might be *fun* (27.5%, n = 55), because they wanted to *learn* (25.5%, n = 51), out of *curiosity* (16.0%, n = 32), because they wanted a *challenge* (9.5%, n = 19), to play a *game* (8.5%, n = 17), due to *novelty* (5.0%, n = 10), *boredom* (3.0%, n = 6), and because they liked *solving puzzles* (1.5%, n = 3). A few participants played the game just for monetary compensation (2.5%, n = 5). As seen in Table 4, there was no relationship between these categories and any of the demographic variables.

Table 2. Positive and negative categories of attitudes toward programming *before* the learning experience.

Programming is...	Frequency	Example Quotation
too difficult to understand	**31%,** *n* = 62	*"Difficult to learn, hard to understand how it works."*
something I've wanted to learn	**16%,** *n* = 32	*"I've always wanted to learn how to program, I just haven't found a good resource that I can focus on to do so."*
boring	**12%,** *n* = 24	*"I always thought it was very complicated and somewhat boring."*
something I did not know about	**8.5%,** *n* = 17	*"Didn't know much about it. You occasionally see it in various places online and in popular culture. I was pretty neutral on it before...just didn't really understand all the intricacies of it."*
something I did not want to learn	**7%,** *n* = 14	*"I thought it was too complex to learn."*
a foreign concept	**5.5%,** *n* = 11	*"I think my view towards programming was very negative. I didn't think it was something that I could learn. It's like a foreign language to me."*
enjoyable	**5.5%,** *n* = 11	*"I thought programming might be enjoyable."*
important to know	**4%,** *n* = 8	*"It is a useful but boring tool that I'd like to know more about."*
an innate ability	**2.5%,** *n* = 5	*"I felt that it was something that was difficult for individuals who had a different mind than myself."*
too time consuming	**1%,** *n* = 2	*"I thought it was complicated and not something I had time to learn."*
nerdy	**1%,** *n* = 2	*"I thought the people who did it were super nerdy geniuses. And I thought that programming was probably extremely complicated."*

Table 3. Categories of self-reported attitudes toward computing *after* the learning experience.

Programming is...	Frequency	Example Quotation
something I can or want to learn	**32%,** *n* = 64	*"I'm definitely more interested in taking a course in programming or trying to learn more about it on my own."*
fun	**25%,** *n* = 50	*"I now know that programming can be fun and easy, also anyone can do it."*
easy to start	**20.5%,** *n* = 41	*"It's not as difficult to learn the basics as I thought."*
difficult	**11.5%,** *n* = 23	*"I think some programming might be manageable for me to do although the more complicated stuff I will be leaving to experts."*
an innate ability	**3%,** *n* = 6	*"I'll leave it to the pro's. I'll stick to my field and let them people good at this do their jobs."*
takes practice	**2%,** *n* = 4	*"The basics are fun and easy. Its still like a language I don't understand but at least now I can understand a little bit of what is going on in the code. I also feel like with practice I could grasp the more complicated concepts."*
something I don't want to learn	**1%,** *n* = 2	*"Something I could never learn."*

In response to the question *"What was the most motivating part of playing the game?"*, participants primarily mentioned *accomplishing goals/finishing levels* (35%, *n* = 70) and *learning* (23%, *n* = 46). Some were motivated by the *challenge* (9%, *n* = 18), *gameplay* (7%, *n* = 14), *puzzle solving* (6%, *n* = 12), *fun* (5%, *n* = 10) and *curiosity* (1%, *n* = 2). Some participants were only motivated by the monetary compensation (12.5%, *n* = 25). Quotes such as this one were representative of participants' responses:

> *"The most motivating part of the game was knowing that the levels got harder as the game went on and I felt like I was accomplishing a goal." (female, 29 years old, 19 levels completed)*

As seen in Table 4, these motivations did not vary by the demographic variables that we measured.

In response to the question *"What was the least motivating part of playing the game?"*, participants mentioned many experiences that give insight into why they quit learning, including that the programming itself was *too difficult* (29.9%, *n* = 59) and too *tedious* (16%, *n* = 32). Participants also did not like making *mistakes* (13.5%, *n* = 27), did not like the *gameplay* (11%, *n* = 22) and could not commit more *time* (10%, *n* = 20). Some had problems with *instructions* (8%, *n* = 16) and *system failure* (2%, *n* = 4). A respectable number of participants (8.5%, *n* = 17) did not find anything demotivating about the game. The following is a representative response for those who got discouraged by programming:

> *"I just got stuck...wanted to play more but knowing nothing about programming I guess I needed more guidance." (male, 30 years old, 9 levels completed)*

As with the other motivations, none of the demographic factors that we measured were statistically related to these categories of demotivating aspects of the learning experience.

4.4 Threats to Validity

Our study has several limitations that may restrict its generalizability. First, we solicited attitudes from adults who self-reported they did not have any prior programming experience, which may explain many participants' initial negative or apathetic attitudes toward programming. Next, rather than simply surveying participants, we gave them a specific learning experience in which

Table 4. Demographic Factors and Participants' Attitudes and Motivations.

	Gender				Population Density				Level of Education			
	df	*N*	X^2	*p*	*df*	*N*	X^2	*p*	*df*	*N*	X^2	*p*
Ordinal attitudes *after* the game	4	196	0.77	*n.s.*	8	196	5.33	*n.s.*	**24**	**197**	**43.68**	**<.05***
Ordinal attitudes *before* the game	8	196	0.99	*n.s.*	8	196	4.51	*n.s.*	24	197	17.08	*n.s.*
Categorized attitudes *before* the game	10	188	16.69	*n.s.*	20	187	22.20	*n.s.*	60	188	63.93	*n.s.*
Categorized attitudes *after* the game	6	196	0.98	*n.s.*	12	189	7.32	*n.s.*	36	197	29.31	*n.s.*
What motivated you to play the game?	8	198	11.23	*n.s.*	16	200	12.45	*n.s.*	48	198	36.61	*n.s.*
What was the *most* motivating part of playing the game?	7	197	4.75	*n.s.*	14	198	19.54	*n.s.*	42	197	39.88	*n.s.*
What was the *least* motivating part of playing the game?	8	200	9.04	*n.s.*	**16**	**188**	**25.57**	*n.s.*	48	197	31.24	*n.s.*

***Note: Starred p-value is significant, with 28 cells (80.0%) of expected count less than 5.** *"n.s" p-value stands for "not significant."*

to ground their attitudes before asking them about their initial attitudes toward programming. Participants may have misremembered their attitudes prior to playing, or at least reported them differently than if asked beforehand.

Additionally, MTurk allows participants to self-select into HIT's, given that they meet certain qualifications. Our HIT only required that participants were living in the USA and had no programming experience. Additionally, filtering HITs for certain payouts could have affected participant recruitment. These limitations introduce a sampling bias, which may limit the generalizability of our results to the particular population found on MTurk. MTurk workers generally make up a diverse group, including a range of ages, education levels, and socio-economic status, although the workers are primarily from highly industrialized countries [13].

Our results are also grounded in the reactions of participants to Gidget, which is a particular learning technology designed for explicit instruction via the web [20,21,22]. Had participants been asked to learn by using other popular environments, such as Scratch or Alice, the changes in attitudes might have been different in magnitude and direction.

5. DISCUSSION AND CONCLUSION

This study investigated adults' attitudes and opinions toward computer programming and how demographic characteristics might affect these opinions. In line with literature on programming stereotypes among youth [1], we found that adults initially had poor attitudes toward programming, believing that it was difficult, boring, and something they generally could not learn. However, we found that even a brief, concrete learning experience can have a significant positive impact on many adults and their attitudes towards programming. After playing the game, adults viewed programming as fun, easier to begin learning than they had initially thought, and something they could potentially learn. These effects did not significantly vary by gender, population density, or level of education, although college-educated adults reported being more likely to want to continue learning. These results complement a growing literature about the effect of programming experiences such as camps on youth attitudes toward programming [32]; adults' attitudes can also be improved even with a brief exposure to programming.

These results, and the body of literature on which they build, have important implications for future work in online learning resources for computing education. For example, because we used an educational game, our results suggest the need for a much wider variety of learning experiences for adults that do not assume an existing motivation to learn and instead embed programming in compelling learning experiences that create and sustain motivation to learn. If the motivation to learn can be sustained, adults' positive attitudes toward programming may also influence their children's motivation to learn programming. Our results also show that with careful design, these learning opportunities can also be gender and age inclusive. Websites like Codecademy, Coursera, Kahn Academy, and Udacity, which currently market to those already interested in learning programming, might reach a much broader audience if their learning materials were designed to not just teach, but also to engage. Our findings also suggest that more traditional education settings, job training programs, and even ad hoc efforts to learn programming at work may just need a careful and controlled introduction to programming to have a positive, reinforcing learning experience

These results, of course, also raise many questions for future research. For example, what are the essential characteristics of learning technologies for computer programming that engender positive changes in attitudes? How sustainable are positive changes in adult attitudes through longer learning experiences? What else is necessary beyond positive attitudes to compel adults to engage in further learning? Do the positive changes in attitudes we observed occur in more formal learning settings, where learning might be compulsory? What else is necessary beyond positive attitudes to compel adults to engage in further learning? How can we motivate students or adults to learn programming languages without fearing them? With the rising interest in learning to code and the proliferation of resources to do so, answers to these questions will be a key part of developing effective pedagogy and learning technologies for making programming accessible to the growing millions who will program as part of their everyday lives at work and at home.

6. ACKNOWLEDGEMENTS

This material is based upon work supported by Microsoft and the National Science Foundation (NSF) under Grants CNS 1240786, CCF 0952733, CCF 1339131, and OISE 1210205. Any opinions, findings, and conclusions or recommendations expressed in this material are those of the authors and do not necessarily reflect the views of the NSF.

7. REFERENCES

[1] Anderson, N., Lankshear, C., Timms, C., & Coutney, L. (2008). 'Because it's boring, irrelevant and I don't like computers': Why high school girls avoid professionally oriented ICT subjects. *Computers and Education,* 50, 1304–1318.

[2] Barrett, R., Kandogan, E., Maglio, P.P., Haber, E.M., Takayama, L.A., & Prabaker, M. (2004). Field studies of computer system administrators: Analysis of system management tools and practices. *ACM CSCW,* 388–395.

[3] Beckwith, L., Inman, D., Rector, K., & Burnett, M. (2007). On to the real world: Gender and self-efficacy in Excel. *IEEE VL/HCC.* 119–126.

[4] Burnett, M. (2009). What is end-user software engineering and why does it matter? In *End-User Development*, 15-28. Springer Berlin Heidelberg.

[5] Carver, J., Kendall, R., Squires, S. & Post, D. (2007). Software engineering environments for scientific and engineering software: a series of case studies. *ACM/IEEE ICSE,* 550–559.

[6] Chu, A., Huber, J., Mastel-Smith, B., Cesario, S. (2009). Partnering with seniors for better health: Computer use and internet health information retrieval among older adults in a low socioeconomic community. *J. of the Medical Library Association, 97,* 12–20.

[7] Creamer, E. G., Lee, S., & Meszaros, P.S. (2006). Factors associated with women's interest in computing fields. *Association for the Study of Engineering Education.*

[8] Czaja, S.J., & Lee, C.C. (2001). The Internet and older adults: Designs challenges and opportunities. In N. Charness & D. C. Parks (Eds.), *Communication, and aging: Opportunities and challenges for the future*, 60–78.

[9] Downey, G.L., Lucena, J. C., Moskal, B. M., Parkhurst, R., Bigley, T., Hays, C., Nichols-Belo, A. (2006). The globally competent engineer: Working effectively with people who define problems differently. *J. of Engineering Education, 95*(2), 107-122.

[10] Gupta, S., Bostrom, R.P., & Anson, R. (2010). Do I matter? The impact of individual differences on training process. *ACM SIGCPR*, 112-120.

[11] Hewner, M., & Guzdial, M. (2008). Attitudes about computing in postsecondary graduates. *ACM ICER*, 71-78.

[12] Huang, H. M. & Liaw, S.S. (2005). Exploring user's attitudes and intentions toward the web as a survey tool. *Computers in Human Behavior*, 21(5), 729-743.

[13] Ipeirotis, P. (2010). Demographics of Mechanical Turk, *CeDER-10–01 working paper*, New York University.

[14] Jay, G. M., Willis, S. L., Gerontol, J.B. (1992). Influence of direct computer experience on older adults' attitudes toward computers. *The J. of Gerontology Series B: Psychological Sciences and Social Sciences, 47,* 250-7.

[15] Jenkins, T. (2002). On the difficulty of learning to program. *Conf. of the LTSN Centre for Information and Computer Sciences*, *4*, 53-58.

[16] Kelleher, C., & Pausch, R. (2005). Lowering the barriers to programming: A taxonomy of programming environments and languages for novice programmers. *ACM CSUR, 37*(2), 83-137.

[17] Kelleher, C., Pausch, R., and Kiesler, S. (2007). Storytelling alice motivates middle school girls to learn computer programming. *ACM CHI,* 1455-1464.

[18] Ko, A.J., Abraham, R., Beckwith, L., Blackwell, A., Burnett, M., Erwig, M., et al. (2011). The state of the art in end-user software engineering. *ACM CSUR, 43*(3), 21.

[19] Kölling, M., & Utting, I. (2012). Building an open, large-scale research data repository of initial programming student behaviour. *ACM SIGCSE*, 323-324.

[20] Lee, M.J., & Ko, A.J. (2012). Investigating the role of purposeful goals on novices' engagement in a programming game. *IEEE VL/HCC*, 163-166

[21] Lee, M.J., & Ko, A.J. (2011). Personifying programming tool feedback improves novice programmers' learning. *ACM ICER*, 109-116.

[22] Lee, M. J., Ko, A. J., & Kwan, I. (2013). In-game assessments increase novice programmers' engagement and level completion speed. *ACM ICER*, 153-160.

[23] Margolis, J., & Fisher, A. (2002). *Unlocking the clubhouse: Women in computing.* Cambridge, MA: *MIT Press.*

[24] McHugh, M. L. (2012). Interrater reliability: The kappa statistic. *BiochemiaMedica, 22*(3), 276-282.

[25] Petre, M., & Blackwell, A.F. (2007). Children as unwitting end-user programmers. *VL/HCC,* 239-242.

[26] Scaffidi, C., Brandt, J., Burnett, M., Dove, A., & Myers, B. (2012). SIG: end-user programming. *ACM CHI, Extended Abstracts,* 1193-1996.

[27] Shayo, C., & Olfman, L. (2000). The role of training in preparing end users to learn related software. *J. of Organizational and End User Computing*, 12(1), 3-13.

[28] Slegers, K., van Boxtel, M.P., & Jolles, J. (2008). Effects of computer training and Internet usage on the well-being and quality of life of older adults: A randomized, controlled study. *The J. of Gerontology Series B: Psychological Sciences and Social* Sciences, 63(3), 176-184.

[29] Sung, K., & Shirley, P. (2004). Algorithm analysis for returning adult students. *J. of Computing Sciences in Colleges*, 20(2), 62-69.

[30] Szajna, B., & Mackay, J. M. (1995). Predictors of learning performance in a computer user training environment: A path analytic study. *Int'l. J. of Human Computer Interaction*, 7(2), 167-185.

[31] U.S. Department of Labor, Bureau of Labor Statistics. (2012). Occupational outlook handbook, 2012-13: Accountants and auditors. *Retrieved from http://www.bls.gov/cps/lfcharacteristics.htm#emp*

[32] Utting, I., Cooper, S., Kölling, M., Maloney, J., & Resnick, M. (2010). Alice, greenfoot, and scratch – a discussion. *ACM TOCE, 10*(4), 17.

[33] Wisniewski, J. (2012). Parlez-Vous Code? *Online*, 36(6), 57-60.

[34] Wong, J., & Hong, J. (2007). Making mashups with Marmite: Towards end-user programming for the web. *ACM* CHI, 1435-144

The Consume - Create Spectrum : Balancing Convenience and Computational Thinking in STEM Learning

Ashok Basawapatna
University of Colorado Boulder
Department of Computer Science
Boulder, CO. 80303 USA
basawapa@colorado.edu

Alexander Repenning
University of Colorado Boulder
Department of Computer Science
Boulder, CO. 80303 USA
ralex@cs.colorado.edu

Kyu Han Koh
University of Colorado Boulder
Department of Computer Science
Boulder, CO. 80303 USA
kohkh@colorado.edu

Mark Savignano
University of Northern Colorado, Dept. of Education
1868 Ute Creek Dr
Longmont, Colorado
Savi6521@bears.unco.edu

ABSTRACT

Future school science standards, such as the Next Generation Science Standards (NGSS), emphasize the integration of simulation and modeling activities in the classroom environment. The extremes of these activities have two vastly different implementations. On one hand, a teacher can have students experiment on a pre-made simulation associated with the material. On the other hand, students can use, for example, an end-user programming tool to create the simulation from scratch. This allows students to not only experiment on, but also, to model the real world phenomenon being studied– a key component of computational thinking. However, the greater amount of time necessary for student authoring of simulations can make such an approach infeasible in the classroom environment. This paper presents a spectrum of strategies for integrating simulations into classrooms emphasizing our research at the Scalable Game Design Lab, University of Colorado Boulder as well as research from other entities. Starting at consuming simulations and adding more user interaction and authoring elements begins to provide a gentle slope from consumption towards simulation creation. Results indicate that many of these strategies are quite effective.

Categories and Subject Descriptors

K.3.2 [**Computing Milieux**]: Computers and Education—*Computer Uses in Education*

General Terms

Algorithms, Design, Experimentation, Human Factors

SIGCSE'14, March 3–8, 2014, Atlanta, GA, USA.

http://dx.doi.org/10.1145/2538862.2538950 .

Keywords

High School Computer Education, Middle School Computer Education, Simulation and Modeling, Computational Thinking, Next Generation Science Standards

1. INTRODUCTION

Classrooms across the United States are looking for ways to integrate aspects of computational thinking into their curriculum [15]. As of now, computational thinking is defined as a problem solving process that includes the following: *Formulating Problems* such that they can be solved by a computer, *Logically Organizing and Analyzing Data*, *Representing Data Through Abstractions* such as models and simulations, *Automating Solutions* through algorithmic thinking, *Identifying Analyzing and Implementing Solutions Efficiently*, and *Generalizing and Transferring This Process* to solve a wide variety of problems [3].

Activities related to simulation authoring offer a unique opportunity to integrate computational thinking into the classroom environment. Future standards, such as the Next Generation Science Standards (NGSS) and the Common Core Curriculum Standards (CCC) emphasize the use of simulations. For example, the NGSS states in its *Structure, Function, and Information Processing* section that, in grades 9-12, "*students who demonstrate understanding can use modeling to explain the function of positive and negative feedback mechanisms in maintaining homeostasis that is essential for organisms* [2]."

Simulation authoring enables classrooms, such as Life Science and Biology classes for example, to meet upcoming science standards and effectively integrate computational thinking. However, at present time, very few teachers across the United States are employing simulation or modeling activities [10]. One major barrier to integrating simulations authoring activities is finding the class time as well as appropriate activities [6].

In our experiences, at the University of Colorado Scalable Game Design Lab, we have students successfully author simulations employing the end-user agent-based programming tool AgentSheets and its subsequent 3D version

AgentCubes. AgentSheets and AgentCubes is meant for students with little or no prior programming experience enabling them to make their first visual game or simulation within five hours [18]. Though it may seem like a relatively small amount of time, five hours equals a 1 week project which can be prohibitive in classrooms.

There are alternatives to authoring simulations from scratch that are time efficient, and begin to integrate computational thinking concepts. For a particular classroom's constraints, one might wonder if one of these alternatives yields a "sweet spot" between convenience and computational thinking efficacy. In this paper we attempt to outline a variety of options that create a gentle-slope path, from consuming pre-made simulations to authoring simulations, taken from both our research experiences and others. It is our aim to give teachers, curriculum designers, and researchers insight into the spectrum of simulation related classroom activities.

The remainder of this paper will outline and discuss this space in-depth along with data and observations from novel approaches, contained within this spectrum.

2. GENTLE SLOPE APPROACH TOWARDS SIMULATION AUTHORING

Figure 1 is a depiction of how computational thinking relates to simulation creation; the basic problem solving process outlined involves model development, computational expression of ideas, running the simulation code, visualizing the consequences of this implementation, and possibly revising the model based on this visualization. The subtext of this figure is that the student develops a strategy to gain insight into a real world problem through the use of simulations in the representational domain. The ability of a student to create a simulation enables the investigation depicted in Figure 1. Furthermore, Figure 1 begins to give us a criteria to evaluate the extent a simulation related activity contains computational thinking concepts.

Figure 2 depicts the Consume-Create spectrum of simulation activities that range from convenient activities to those that heavily integrate computational thinking. These include animations, interactive simulations, collective simulations, construction set simulations, pattern based authoring, end-user programming, and traditional programming languages.

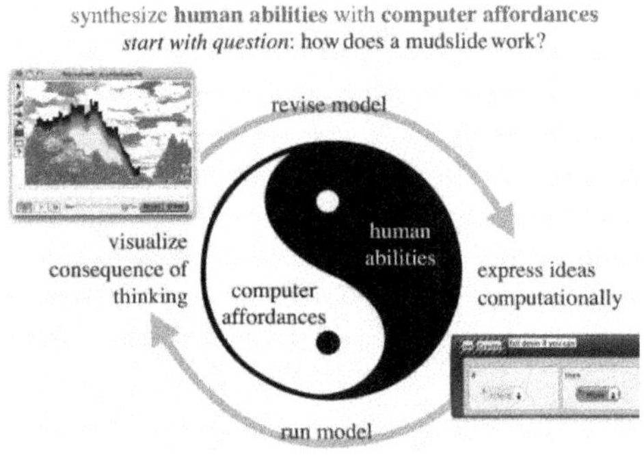

Figure 1: How creating simulations relates to computational thinking. Users start with a question, develop a model, express the model computationally, run the model, visualize the consequence of their thinking and possibly revise the model

It should be noted that Figure 2 is by no means an exhaustive list but serves as a good beginning point for a discussion of simulation use in the classroom environment. Starting from the left and going to the right of Figure 2, we see activities that begin to offer the user greater control over the simulation mechanics itself by enabling higher degree of expressive freedom. Furthermore, with each item there exists limitations that are overcome by traveling to the right. For example, one way an animation, located on the far left, is limited is that the animation does not enable changing a parameter associated with the animated phenomenon. By giving the user an interactive simulation instead, located to the right of animations, eliminates this limitation providing a more open-ended exploration of the phenomenon. Conversely, for any activity in Figure 2, we see that this activity contains the option of doing all the activities to the left of it. For example, by using a programming language, like C++ or Java, the user hypothetically has the ability to do everything offered through end-user programming all the way to creating a simulation animation that can be displayed to enhance student understanding (though such a tact might be infeasible for students with little programming experience). What follows is an analysis of each of the activities listed in Figure 2 emphasizing their benefits as an in-class activity, including supporting science learning goals, and a focused appraisal of their relationship to computational thinking.

2.1 Animations

Scientific animations are not simulations per se, but similar to simulations in that they create a representation of a scientific phenomena. Animation activities entail a student watching a movie depicting a representation of a given scientific system, often times accompanied by a narrative. Examples of these activities include the suite of animations on the BrainPop[1] website and The Institute for Chemistry Literacy through Computational Science (ICLCS) [2]. Figure 3 depicts screenshots of example animation activities.

In the left activity depicted in Figure 3, students watch an animated model of ice melting on a molecular level. These activities typically take minutes to complete (depending on the length of the animation) and are often accompanied by text that describes the phenomenon being depicted. This activity is usually accompanied by a worksheet for students to help synthesize the academically one way lesson. This pedagogy of learning regards to Bloom's Taxonomy revised of learning ranks on the pyramid– Factual knowledge/Remember [14]. However useful for efficiency when navigating the curriculum, the students do not get a chance to interact and synthesize learning.

By running an animation, students are not using any computational thinking skills– students do not have to create an algorithm or abstract the real world into the representational domain. However, there is good evidence that these visual representations do yield better student understanding. One large scale study, for example, claims that students in classes that used BrainPOP increased their science scores on the SAT 10 test by one to two grade levels, when compared to control classrooms [1].

2.2 Interactive Simulations

[1]www.brainpop.com

[2]iclcs.illinois.edu/

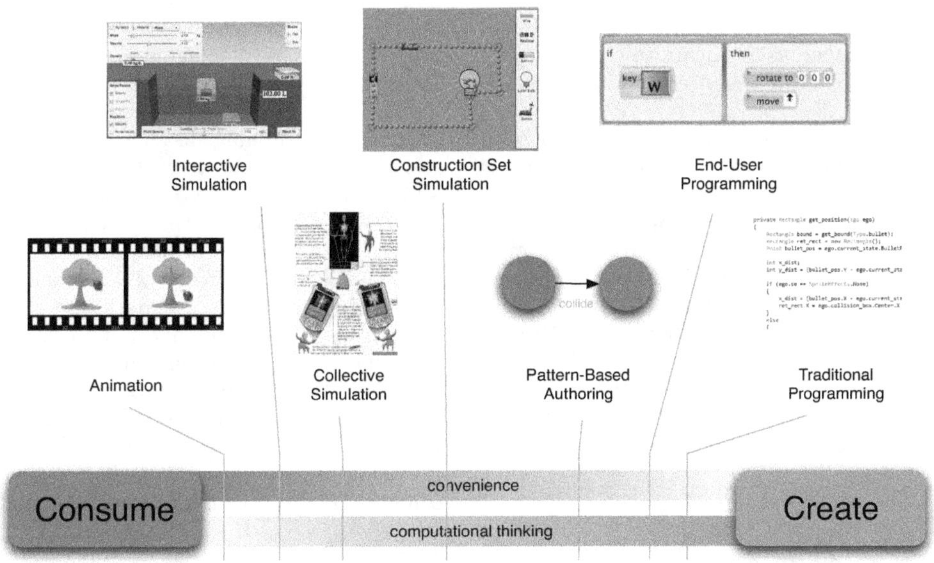

Figure 2: Gentle slope spectrum of options from using (convenient) to authoring (computational thinking) simulations.

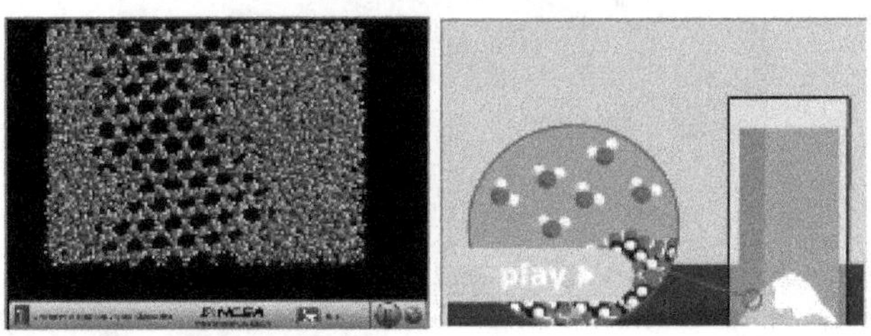

Figure 3: Two animation examples. The left image depicts an ICLCS simulation animation of ice melting and the right image depicts a BrainPOP animation on diffusion

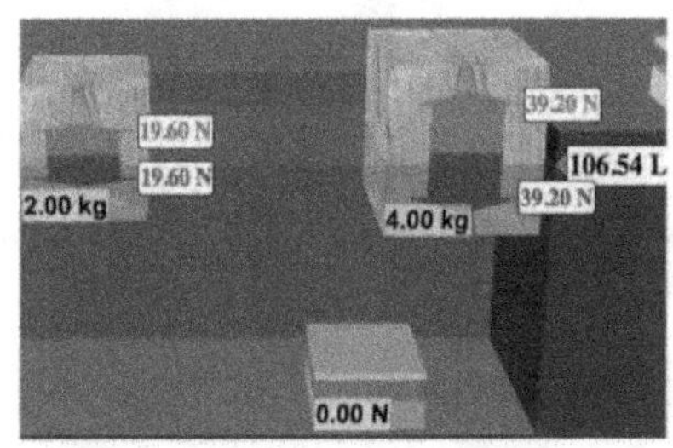

Figure 4: The image depicts PhET simulation that enables students to explore buoyancy

Interactive simulations allow users to alter parameters and run the simulation to see the effect of these modifications; unlike animations, students can run multiple experiments to better understand the effect of various parameter changes. Interactive simulations are usually centered around a specific concept, in a limited domain, and can take very little class time [16] . Examples of Interactive simulations are the Physics Education Technology (PhET)[3] Buoyancy simulation and the suite of simulations offered at National Taiwan Normal University's (NTNU) Virtual Physics Laboratory[4]. Figure 4 depicts a screenshot of the Phet simulation.

The NTNU wave simulation allows users to vary the direction and period of a plotted electromagnetic wave. The PhET buoyancy simulation in Figure 4, allows user to put two different blocks in water or oil and displays the buoyancy forces on the blocks. The blocks can be either the same mass, the same volume, or the same density.

PhET reports that students play with simulations for hours, find the activities engaging, and show a greater degree of conceptual learning as compared to control groups [19]. However, other research points to the idea that these simulations might give students an oversimplified view of scientific inquiry actually hindering their scientific literacy and ability to do science outside of the pre-made simulation environment; for example, many of these simulations assume ideal simulation environments with no experimentation flaws [7]. If students were to author these simulations, they could at least be aware of these ideal conditions.

Compared to animations, interactive simulations allow for a deeper inquiry of a given concept. However, students are exposed to little, if any, computational thinking concepts. In fact, much of the computational thinking, such as the abstraction necessary in creating this representational system and what parameters to include and ignore in this representational system, is done for the students by the simulation author.

2.3 Collective Simulations

Collective simulations (also called "participatory simulations") are similar to interactive simulations with the addition of a collaborative social element. In collective simulations, instead of controlling every parameter value, each student takes on a specific role and adjusts parameters associated with that role in real time. Often these simulations rely on students communicating with each other to develop

[3]phet.colorado.edu
[4]www.phy.ntnu.edu.tw/ntnujava/

an overarching strategy to achieve a specific goal. These interactions also begin to introduce students to the idea of local decisions yielding global consequences through peer-student feedback.

In Mr. Vetro, a National Institute of Health sponsored project that focused on how the body reacts to various activity, students played the role of lungs, heart, and dictated the amount of physical activity (exercise) applied to a virtual human named Mr. Vetro [11]. Each role has a set of parameters students can control. Students playing the role of the heart , for example, could define things like Mr. Vetro's heart rate and stroke volume. In Gridlock, written in HubNet, a collective simulation environment based off of NetLogo, students each control the state of a traffic light and and attempt to optimize traffic flow through a city [20]. Figure 5 depicts Mr. Vetro collective simulation.

Figure 5: Students working on Mr. Vetro.

In terms of computational thinking, collective simulations enable students to embody the representation of the system. In this respect, students are the abstraction between the real world and the representational domain. Furthermore, students interact with classmates who represent other aspects of the real world. This necessitates peer organization and real-time integration of data among students to arrive at a collective algorithm through each moment in time. Like interactive simulations, students are varying parameters, but students are modifying these parameters constantly in response to peer feedback in order to achieve the collective group goals.

The results of Mr. Vetro show a strong indication of enhanced student understanding. For example, using Mr. Vetro for 1-2 periods in highschool classrooms indicated strong learning gains, as compared to control instruction covering the same material without the use of a collective simulation, over a diverse group of students [11]. Evidence also suggests strong student engagement during the activity with some students referring to it as one of the most intense classroom experiences [11].

The limitations of collective simulations mirror those of interactive simulations in that students can only change the parameters provided to them. Collective simulations begin to incorporate elements of computational thinking; however, students still do not get to set up the simulation or participate in simulation parameter selection deciding which aspects of the real world to emphasize and ignore.

2.4 Construction Set Simulations

Construction set simulations give users the freedom to set up the physical placement of pre-programmed simulation objects in addition to varying simulation parameters. Examples include construction kits, that enable users to solve a focused problem in a limited domain. For example, the Pinball Construction Kit allows users to prototype their own pinball game by placing flippers, bumpers, and other elements of a pinball game on a level [9]. Similarly, the PhET Circuit Construction Kit, depicted as an example of construction set simulations in Figure 2, allows users to place resistors, bulbs, and other electrical components in a circuit and run it [19]. The CyberMOD project, funded by the National Institute of Health, involves classroom integration of construction set simulations meant for the high school biology classroom. One CyberMOD construction set simulation allows students to investigate blood glucose homeostasis by placing liver cell agents and pancreas cell agents in different sections of the simulation world to achieve homeostatic regulation of blood sugar. In doing this, users not only see and interact with a simulation of how the human body works, but also, can experiment with different formations of cells investigating things such as type 2 diabetes. Figure 6 is a screenshot of the CyberMOD blood sugar regulation activity.

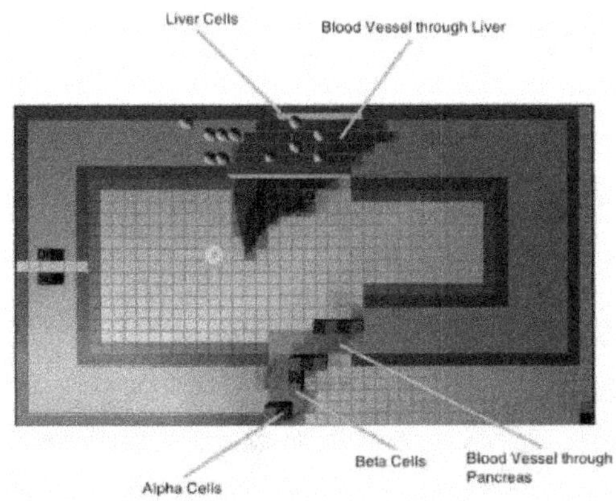

Figure 6: The Blood Sugar Homeostasis CyberMOD simulation.

Construction set simulations enable a measure of computational thinking in that students have to build the representational system world to solve or gain insight into a particular problem. Data from CyberMOD indicates students not only enjoyed the construction set simulation exercise, but after the exercise, the students were significantly more likely to answer questions related to the human blood sugar regulation system correctly. Furthermore, the effect sizes for 71 students between two pre and post test sections relating to blood sugar regulation, were 0.881 and 1.242, which is quite large for such a small (1 hour) in-class intervention [17].

Construction set simulations give students an opportunity to be exposed to computational thinking and have the potential to greatly increase understanding. The inability to program simulation behaviors present a big limitation. Investigating how different behaviors of agents effect the simulation, beyond parameter changes, necessitates a move towards simulation authoring.

2.5 Pattern Based Authoring

In pattern based authoring, users begin to author the behaviors of simulation actors present in the simulation. Instead of using low level behavior rules of end-user programming tools, pattern based authoring allows users to create interactions between simulation agents at a higher level. Examples of pattern based authoring approaches include Magic Paper and the Simulation Creation Toolkit.

The Simulation Creation Toolkit, built on top of AgentCubes, allows users to apply high level Computational Thinking Patterns, such as one agent absorbing another agent or one agent tracking another agent, in order to create agent interactions [4, 5]. To accomplish this, users pick the interaction they want present in their simulation from a palette of generic objects acting out different behaviors– for example, one generic agent tracking another generic agent for the tracking pattern. Finally the user specifies how the pattern should work, i.e. how quickly the tracking should occur and the background agents that the tracking agent can move on etc. Figure 7 is a screenshot of the Simulation Creation Toolkit.

In Magic Paper, users can author physics simulations from scratch by drawing high level physical formations and defining things like where objects are anchored, the forces involved, and add wheels and friction to various objects [8]. The force that one object exerts on another object can be defined by outlining how one agent behaves in respect to another agent. Magic paper assumes sketching in a limited domain wherein a rich graphical lexicon has already been established– these symbols within the context of the sketching environment make up the "high level" patterns. Other domains in Magic Paper include a circuit construction environment and a molecular chemical configuration environment.

Figure 7: The Simulation Creation Toolkit

Both of these pattern based authoring examples rely on the user's ability to preserve interactions while abstracting out the specific agents involved in the interactions. In this sense, these approaches both force the user to think computationally to create these interactions. Research on the Simulation Creation Toolkit begins to show that this does indeed occur as users not only transfer the use of Computational Thinking Patterns to various contexts, but are also able to program simulations via analogy using these patterns [5, 4]. Pattern based authoring of simulations includes every mechanism outlined in Figure 1. Additionally, programming at the pattern level enables users to quickly create simulations without having to implement time-consuming lower level code. For example, seventh grade students with no prior experience using the Simulation Creation Toolkit, completed and experimented on a predator/prey simulation in four days or less of class time; this simulation, in previous experiences, would take high school students over a week to create including the time it takes to learn the AgentCubes end-user programming tool [6].

Pattern based authoring empowers users with the ability to quickly add interactions to simulations without using lower level code. However, a major limitation of pattern based authoring is that students are reliant upon the high level patterns offered; therefore, if a simulation creation exercise does not lend itself to one of the patterns offered, creating that simulation may be impossible or may lead students to make faulty representational systems [5]. Overcoming this limitation requires students to master lower level simulation programming.

2.6 End User Programming and Programming Languages

Tools such as AgentCubes, Scratch, and Alice allow students, with little prior programming experience, to create simulations using drag and drop rules instead of tedious syntax[12]. For example, in AgentCubes, agent behavior is dictated by dragging conditions and actions from a pre-made palette to construct if/then conditionality statements. This strategy has proven effective in enabling students to make visual games more quickly and easily than in traditional programming languages like C++ or Java.

In creating their first game students begin to learn the tools necessary to create simulations. Students actually implement Computational Thinking Patterns by combining if/then conditionality statements. Students begin to think computationally when they apply these learned Computational Thinking Pattern implementations to create and experiment on simulations giving them insight into a real world phenomenon [18]. In terms of Figure 1, end-user programming gives students much more expressive ability to model the real world than adding agent interactions at the pattern level.

The major barrier to integrating simulation end-user programming into the science classroom is finding the necessary time. As mentioned above, high school students can take over a week to learn an end-user programming tool and subsequently, create a simulation. Given enough time and resources, however, end-user programming of simulations allows students to accomplish everything outlined Figure 1.

2.7 Traditional Programming

Traditional Programming gives users the most expressive power out of all the choices in Figure 2. For example, since AgentCubes is agent-based, it is hard to create a physically accurate projectile motion simulation. However, in a traditional language like C++ or Java, such a simulation is possible, and in fact, has been done by authors of the PhET environment (which is written in Java)[19]. Other environments such as Greenfoot and Starlogo are educational tools that enable students to begin learning programming constructs and employ syntax akin to traditional programming as opposed to graphical drag and drop rules employed by end-user programming tools. Greenfoot, for example, gives students and introduction to Java programming and Starlogo, based on Logo programming, enables agent based simulation modeling [13, 12] .

Traditional programming languages have been used to create games and simulations in CS1 undergraduate classes [13]. Like end-user programming, students apply every step in

Figure 1. However, the time necessary to make students proficient at traditional programming is much greater than end-user programming; therefore, outside of actual programming classes, this strategy is unrealistic.

3. DISCUSSION AND CONCLUSION

Looking at the options outlined Figure 2, we see tradeoffs involved with every strategy presented that a teacher might employ to integrate simulation creation activities into their classroom environment. To the far left we see choices, such as pre-made simulations, that are convenient, in terms of preparation and class time, but do not necessarily require students to think computationally. Conversely, to the far right are choices, such as employing end-user and traditional programming to create simulations, that do require students to think computationally but are extremely time consuming. In between these two extremes are choices teachers can make that begin to introduce aspects of simulation authoring and computational thinking while preserving convenience. For example, teachers might substitute a construction set simulation or a collective simulation in place of a unit that currently integrates an interactive simulation without adding a significant amount of class time.

Figure 2 is an initial attempt to describe the space of simulation related activities that teachers can do in the classroom. As mentioned above, this figure is by no means exhaustive but is an interesting space to place any activities currently being researched and developed for in-class use. Using this spectrum, we can begin to populate this space with more activities and this can be an important tool helping teachers meet upcoming science standards while equipping students with the computational and problem solving skills necessary to be competitive in the 21st century.

4. ACKNOWLEDGMENTS

Part of this work is supported by the National Science Foundation under Grant Numbers 0833612, 0848962, 1138526 and the National Institute of Health under Grant Numbers 1R43 OD012081-01, 1R43 RR022008-0, and 1R43 RR022008-02 . Any opinions, findings, and conclusions or recommendations expressed in this material are those of the authors and do not necessarily reflect the views of the National Science Foundation or the National Institute of Health. Alexander Repenning is the founder of AgentSheets Inc.

5. REFERENCES

[1] *A Study Of The Effectiveness Of BrainPOP*. SEG Research, New Hope, PA, 2010.

[2] *Next Generation Science Standards*. Achieve, Inc. on behalf of the twenty-six states and partners that collaborated on the NGSS, Washington, DC, 2013.

[3] D. Barr, J. Harrison, and L. Conery. Computational thinking: A digital age skill for everyone. *Learning & Leading with Technology*, 38(6):20–23, 2011.

[4] A. Basawapatna, K. H. Koh, A. Repenning, D. C. Webb, and K. S. Marshall. Recognizing computational thinking patterns. In *Proceedings of the 42nd ACM technical symposium on Computer science education*, pages 245–250. ACM, 2011.

[5] A. R. Basawapatna. *Creating science simulations through Computational Thinking Patterns*. PhD thesis, University of Colorado, Boulder, 2012. 3549158.

[6] A. R. Basawapatna, A. Repenning, and C. H. Lewis. The simulation creation toolkit: an initial exploration into making programming accessible while preserving computational thinking. In *Proceeding of the 44th ACM technical symposium on Computer science education*, pages 501–506. ACM, 2013.

[7] S. Chen. The view of scientific inquiry conveyed by simulation-based virtual laboratories. *Computers & education*, 55(3):1123–1130, 2010.

[8] R. Davis. Magic paper: Sketch-understanding research. *Computer*, 40(9):34–41, 2007.

[9] G. Fischer and A. C. Lemke. Construction kits and design environments: Steps toward human problem-domain communication. *HumanâĂŞComputer Interaction*, 3(3):179–222, 1987.

[10] L. Gray, N. Thomas, and L. Lewis. Teachers' use of educational technology in u.s. public schools: 2009. first look. nces 2010-040. *National Center for Education Statistics*, May 2010.

[11] A. Ioannidou, A. Repenning, D. Webb, D. Keyser, L. Luhn, and C. Daetwyler. Mr. vetro: A collective simulation for teaching health science. *International Journal of Computer-Supported Collaborative Learning*, 5(2):141–166, 2010.

[12] C. Kelleher and R. Pausch. Lowering the barriers to programming: A taxonomy of programming environments and languages for novice programmers. *ACM Comput. Surv.*, 37(2):83–137, June 2005.

[13] M. Kölling and P. Henriksen. Game programming in introductory courses with direct state manipulation. In *Proceedings of the 10th annual SIGCSE conference on Innovation and technology in computer science education*, ITiCSE '05, pages 59–63, New York, NY, USA, 2005. ACM.

[14] D. R. Krathwohl. A revision of bloom's taxonomy: An overview. *Theory into practice*, 41(4):212–218, 2002.

[15] I. Lee, F. Martin, and J. e. a. Denner. Computational thinking for youth in practice. *ACM Inroads*, 2(1):32–37, February 2011.

[16] N. R. C. C. on Science Learning. *Learning Science Through Computer Games And Simulations*. The National Academies Press, Washington, DC, 2011.

[17] A. Repenning, A. Basawapatna, and M. Klymkowsky. Making educational games that work in the classroom: A new approach for integrating stem simulations. In *Games Innovation Conference (IGIC), 2013 IEEE International*, pages 228–235. IEEE, 2013.

[18] A. Repenning, D. Webb, and A. Ioannidou. Scalable game design and the development of a checklist for getting computational thinking into public schools. In *Proceedings of the 41st ACM technical symposium on Computer science education*, pages 265–269. ACM, 2010.

[19] C. E. Wieman, W. K. Adams, and K. K. Perkins. Phet: Simulations that enhance learnings. *Science*, 322(5902):682–683, November 2008.

[20] U. Wilensky and W. Stroup. Networked gridlock: Students enacting complex dynamic phenomena with the hubnet architecture. In *Fourth international conference of the learning Sciences*, pages 282–289, 2000.

Facilitating Human Interaction in an Online Programming Course

Joe Warren, Scott Rixner, John Greiner, Stephen Wong
Department of Computer Science
Rice University
Houston, Texas
jwarren@, rixner@, greiner@, swong@rice.edu

ABSTRACT

Human/human interaction is a critical component of learning in many domains including introductory computer programming. For on-campus courses, lectures and problem sessions provide opportunities for students to interact with the instructor(s) and their peers. For online courses, opportunities for human/human interaction are more limited and usually correspond to activities like forum postings and online study groups. For online programming courses, the situation is potentially even worse since many of the computational tools designed to facilitate learning to program, such as unit testing, emphasize human/machine interaction and can be frustrating for beginning students.

In this paper, the authors describe their experience in teaching an introductory programming MOOC. The guiding philosophy for this course is that learning to program should be a social experience that emphasizes human/human interaction, not human/machine interaction. Both the tools and assessment methods deployed in this course were chosen to help achieve this goal. In particular, this paper discusses a key tool that supports human/human interaction and several aspects of the course that contributed to its success.

Categories and Subject Descriptors

K.3.1 [**Computers and Education**]: Computer Uses in Education—*Collaborative learning*
; K.3.2 [**Computers and Education**]: Computer and Information Science Education—*Computer science education*

Keywords

CS1, Python, MOOC

1. INTRODUCTION

The price of a higher education has outpaced the means of the vast majority of students to afford such an education. Massive open online courses (MOOCs), offered by providers such as Coursera, edX and Udacity, are one attempt to remedy this situation. These courses provide a mechanism for students, many with no access to traditional higher education, to learn advanced material from experts in the field. While MOOCs have been promoted as a solution to many of the ills of higher education, they face some key educational challenges if they are to deliver an educational experience that is on par with the typical classroom experience.

Perhaps the most common criticism of MOOCs is that, with their size and reliance on technology, they are unable to replicate the social experience (*i.e.*, human/human interaction) that is the linchpin of classroom education. (Of course, large on-campus classes are also often impersonal.) We set out to teach an introductory programming MOOC that would allow people to learn to program despite the challenges of online education at scale. We identified the following key issues that we felt needed to be addressed in order to be successful:

1. **Ease of use and consistency of the programming platform.** With tens of thousands of students, it is impossible to troubleshoot individual problems arising from multiple versions of a language and libraries, as well as different editors, all running under different operating systems. For beginning students, these issues can be a significant barrier to success when there is no one to help them get their system setup, let alone actually start programming.

2. **Instructor accessibility.** This is likely one of the greatest criticisms of large scale education. How can a student be successful if he/she can never interact with the instructor?

3. **Availability of timely and relevant feedback.** While a machine grader can instantly tell a student whether their code works or not, it cannot easily give advice on coding style or how to fix problems in the same way that human graders could. At scale, the staff can't possibly provide such individual feedback in a timely fashion (or at all).

4. **Peer interaction.** A significant element of an introductory programming class is the shared experience among the students. Seeing others struggle along with you, helping each other solve problems and sharing each others' successes are powerful motivators.

We went to significant effort to address each of these potential weaknesses of MOOCs. We have found that the mas-

SIGCSE'14, March 5–8, 2014, Atlanta, GA, USA.

http://dx.doi.org/10.1145/2538862.2538908.

sive number of students in a MOOC combined with well-chosen technology makes the creation of a highly social online learning space possible. We have found that it is possible to provide human assistance to MOOC students in a number of innovative ways in such a space. At the core of our approach are tools that support easy creation and sharing of course material (generated by both student and instructor) with minimal effort.

Related work: Our social approach to teaching programming is grounded in previous work. [1] describes a community-based approach to the general problem of learning, while [6] observes that computer science and mathematics are social disciplines. A meta-analysis of studies on game-based learning [10] suggests that collaborative learning and instructional support positively influence learning outcomes.

One specific topic related to our work is the design of programming environments to enhance the social aspects of learning to program. [2] describes an environment that supports the computer language Logo and shows that (on a small scale) this environment facilitates peer interaction for social problem solving. Both Alice [5] and Scratchpad [8] are highly collaborative, social environment that are designed to engage students learning to program.

Contributions: In this paper, we relate our experience in teaching an online introductory programming class, in both on-campus and MOOC form. In particular, we describe a programming environment developed for these classes that was designed to promote human/human interaction. As our main contribution, we discuss the ways in which we leveraged this tool to create a social learning space for the MOOC students that did not exist for the on-campus students. This space, formed by students in the MOOC, compensated (at least partially) for the lack of an in-person component that benefitted on-campus students.

2. A TOOL FOR SHARING CODE

Our particular online course "An Introduction to Interactive Programming in Python"[1] (IIPP) focuses on teaching beginning students how to program in Python with the motivation of learning to build simple games. This course was designed to be offered both on-campus (supplemented by in-person lab work) and online as a MOOC. This class has been offered on-campus in Fall 2012 and Fall 2013 to 25 and 40 students, respectively. IIPP has also been offered online in MOOC form three times. Between the Fall 2012, Spring 2013 and Fall 2013 sessions, nearly 19,000 students have completed IIPP and received a Statement of Accomplishment.

In designing a class suitable for both on-campus and online delivery, one key issue is how students create and assess their work. In popular introductory programming courses such as Udacity's CS101[2] or MIT's 6.00x[3], students create their code in a stand-alone programming environment and submit this code to a server for automated assessment via a collection of unit tests. This arrangement has several advantages. Machine tests are typically very precise and provide students with fairly prompt feedback.

[1] `https://www.coursera.org/course/interactivepython`
[2] `https://www.udacity.com/course/cs101`
[3] `https://www.edx.org/course/mit/6-00x/introduction-computer-science/586`

However, this approach also has weaknesses. The very precision of machine tests can lead to student frustration in that code that is very close to working may be scored the same as code that is not even close to correct. The error message provided by a failed unit test may be cryptic and not provide a sufficient hint on how to correct the program.

This issue has prompted research into automated hint systems for MOOCs [9]. In that work, the authors report that their system can provide meaningful feedback on approximately 2/3 of all incorrect submissions for their class. However, for some types of programs such as interactive ones with visual output (the main type of programs created in our class), machine grading and automated hint-generation systems are beyond the scope of current technology.

Since many of the weaknesses with the human/machine approach to teaching introductory programming can be improved or eliminated via interaction with a human instead of a machine, we focused on creating a programming environment that is optimized to support human/human interaction and foster a social space for learning to program. To this end, we made a number of critical design decisions when creating this environment.

- The programming environment should be web-based, so that students do not need to download and install a stand-alone development environment. This choice allows us to deploy and update the environment for all students quickly and easily. This choice also ensures that all students work in an identical programming environment, making sharing of code much more reliable.
- Student code should run entirely in the web-browser, avoiding the need to upload and execute code on a remote server. This choice enables interactivity and avoids the possibility of server-lag during high demand periods before assignment submission.
- Student code should be stored anonymously in a cloud-based file storage system. This choice avoids the need for accounts or authentication and removes another impediment to easy sharing of code.
- Finally, the environment should support download and execution of student or instructor code via a single URL. Any auxiliary assets such as custom Python modules, images and sound would load inside the program via specified auxiliary URLs.

Starting from the browser-based Python runtime system Skulpt[4],we developed a web-based programming environment for IIPP. This system, CodeSkulptor[5], allows students to create visual, interactive Python programs in their web browser, save these programs in the cloud with a single click, and share these programs via a single URL.

Figure 1 shows an image of a simple stopwatch program available for sharing via CodeSkulptor. The left code pane shows part of the body of the stopwatch program. The frame on the lower right shows a collection of buttons and a canvas displaying the stopwatch created by the program. This program can accessed and shared via the CodeSkulptor URL: `http://www.codeskulptor.org/#user18_3aa8ykZlInMlVWd_0.py`

[4] `http://www.skulpt.org`
[5] `http://www.codeskulptor.org`

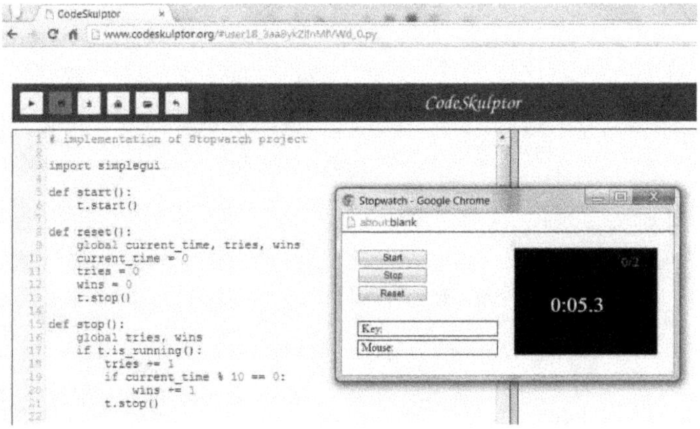

Figure 1: A stopwatch program in CodeSkulptor

which is displayed in the address bar. A new random hash ("3aa8ykZlInMlVWd" in this example) is generated automatically by CodeSkulptor for each save.

With this design, the flow of saving, sharing and running a program requires at most seconds of work and entails four simple steps. A user saves the program generating a new CodeSkulptor URL (first step). This user can then transmit this link to a second user via email, a forum post or link submission (second step). This second user then clicks the received URL to open CodeSkulptor with the saved file preloaded (third step). Finally, the second user can run the program via a single click (fourth step). In our opinion, this ultra-streamlined work flow for sharing code is the key enabler for our social approach to teaching programming.

The design of CodeSkulptor was influenced by other web-based programming environments that employ web-based editing and cloud-based saving such as `jsfiddle.org`, `repl.it`, and `cloud9.io`. However, one key issue that distinguishes CodeSkulptor from these environments is its ability to run modestly complex, interactive Python programs entirely in the web-browser. These related environments either lacked the efficiency to run interactive programs with even moderate computational requirements in the web-browser (making them unsuitable for use in IIPP) or required the computational support of a back-end server (raising the issue of server cost and loading).

3. SOCIAL ASPECTS OF A CS MOOC

CodeSkulptor enabled the creation of a MOOC in which learning to program was a highly social endeavor. CodeSkulptor enables and facilitates human/human interaction in IIPP in ways that never manifested in the on-campus version of the class. In this section, we discuss the various social components of our introductory programming class and discuss how CodeSkulptor facilitated the success of some of these components.

3.1 The Code Clinic

One well-taken criticism of MOOCs is that they provide limited opportunities for personal interaction with a subject expert, compared to an on-campus class. Thus, one of our primary focuses when designing our online class was to provide mechanisms for students to receive timely, informative answers to their questions.

For massive online classes, the discussion forums are the standard mechanism for students to post questions and receive answers about class material. As we shall see in section 3.3, these forums were a tremendous resource for our class. However, the efficacy of the forums was clearly limited in certain situations.

For example, students often had bugs in their implementations of the weekly mini-projects. Posting a link to their erroneous code in the class forums when seeking help from their peers or course staff often represents an irresistible opportunity for other students to copy the posted code. Thus, posting partial or even incorrect solutions before the assignment due date violates the class Honor Code. As a result, forum posts requesting help in debugging code are often vague to avoid revealing potential solutions.

In IIPP, we have developed an additional social mechanism to allow students to receive knowledgeable assistance on coding questions. The *Code Clinic* is a class service that allows students to email a link to their code to the course staff and receive answers to specific questions related to their code. For example, a student might ask for help in debugging a part of their program that has a hard-to-locate error. The course staff member would then respond by explaining the error and even, perhaps, sending back a link to a corrected program. As opposed to the class forums, the student is able to share their code directly with a knowledgeable member of the course staff.

In the on-campus setting, standard email (or in-person office hours) are sufficient to support this type of service. However, in the MOOC setting, this type of service would most likely overwhelm a simple email account. To avoid this situation, we retained a professional help desk service (`helpscout.net`) to host the Code Clinic. This help desk service routes student email to a central web-site where course staff could then respond to these requests. This help desk service includes a number of helpful features that facilitate our handling of these requests: an auto-response on submission of a help request, a set of customizable stock responses to common questions, assignment and tracking of help requests, and automatic detection of simultaneous responses.

One potential objection to this private help desk approach is that feedback generated by answering student questions goes only to the questioner. As part of maintaining the Code Clinic, the staff noted common questions and problems and then posted sanitized examples back to the main class forums to alert the remainder of the class to these issues.

The Code Clinic has proven to be a very popular feature of IIPP. Figure 2 shows a plot of the number of help requests handled by the Code Clinic and the average response times for these requests for the Spring 2013 session. Overall, 1201 students (around 1/6 of the total finishers) made 2503 help requests. Each help request (and possible follow up questions) generated on average 1.87 replies from the course staff. The average response time for a help request was approximately 45 minutes with an average handle time (the time between viewing and responding to a request) of approximately 6 minutes. Note that this remarkably low handle time was due almost entirely to CodeSkulptor's ability to facilitate code sharing.

While this number of student help requests may seem daunting, the total amount of time dedicated to running the Code Clinic is sizeable, but tractable. The course staff sent

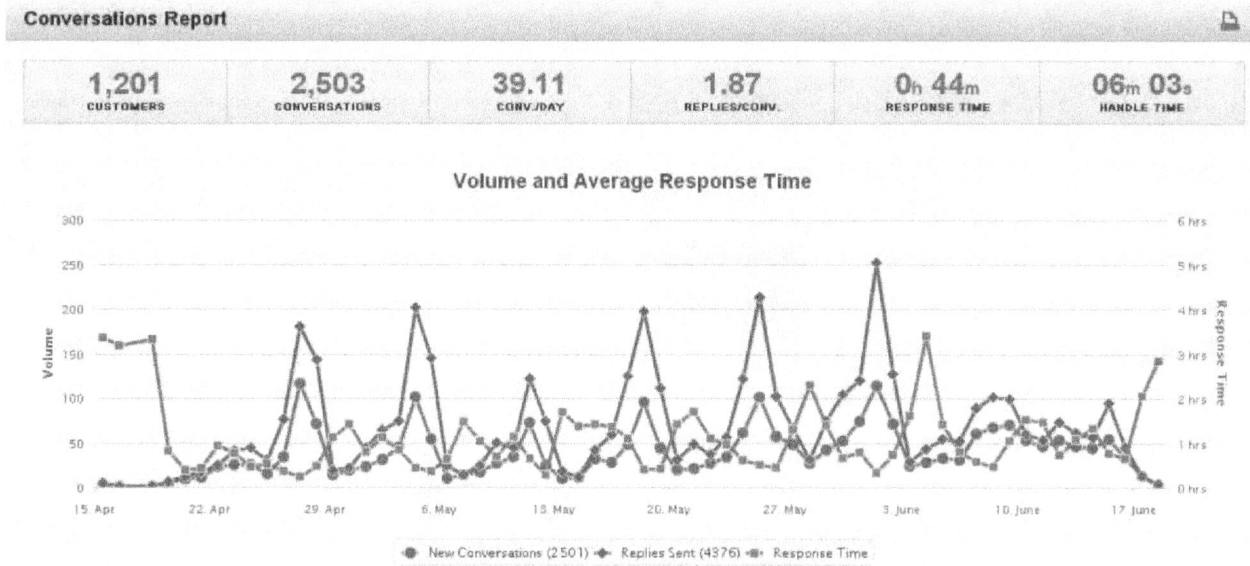

Figure 2: Help request statistics from Spring 2013

approximately 4800 replies to help requests and follow up questions. The key to replying to this number of requests is the 6 minute handle time per student email. In practice, 2/3 of the replies were generated by 3 course staff members (including one instructor) representing approximately 15 hours of work per week for each of these three people during the nine week course.

Figure 3 shows a typical weekly cycle of help requests for the Code Clinic. Help requests typically peaked on the weekend when mini-projects were due. On these days, the class would usually submit between 75–100 help requests. While this is a substantial number of requests, the peak demand (4–12 hours before the deadline) was easily handled by 3 staff members. As an interesting note, observe that the average response time on due days was approximately 15 minutes, much faster than the average response time overall. This phenomenon was due to the higher volume of help requests on due dates. On those days, at least one member of the course was staff was usually actively engaged in responding to help requests throughout the day. This engagement led to response times that are much faster than most on-campus classes could achieve.

These statistics lead us to the most important conclusion in this paper: **providing individual expert help to the students in a MOOC is absolutely possible**. In both the Fall 2012 and the Spring 2013 sessions, every email help request from our students was answered. Most of these requests (83%) were answered within an hour (or even more quickly on due days). In the Fall 2012 session, all the 1000+ help requests (sent to a custom Google Group) were personally answered by an instructor. In the Spring 2013, the help desk was used to prioritize help requests so that all "difficult" help requests were routed to an instructor while teaching assistants processed routine requests.

3.2 Assessments

The on-campus and MOOC versions of our class rely on two types of assessments: mini-projects (due weekly, 50–250 lines of Python) and quizzes (two per week with 8–10 questions). We next discuss some of the social aspects of each type of assessment.

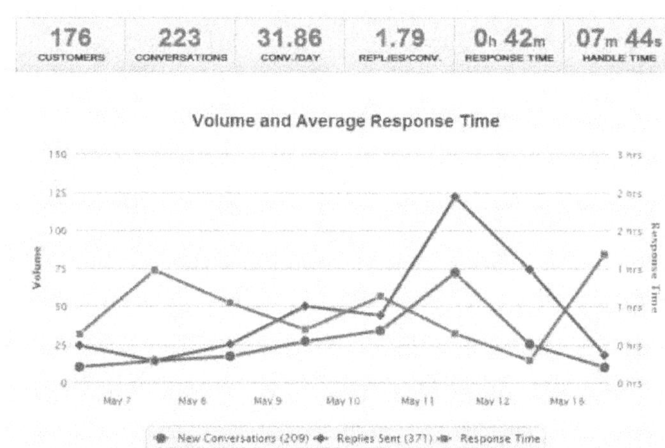

Figure 3: A typical week of help requests

Mini-projects: One of our motivational tools in teaching programming is the fact that many students love games. Our class focuses on building simple interactive games based on games such as Pong, Memory, Blackjack and Asteroids. Since machine-grading these types of programs is currently beyond the state of the art due to the interactive and visual nature of the programs, we choose a social method, peer assessment, to grade class mini-projects.

For smaller in-person classes, peer assessment has been used and studied extensively. [3] provides a meta-analysis of the effectiveness of peer assessment in higher education and concludes that peer assessment can be effective when grading rubrics are well designed. While [4] notes that peer assessment has been observed to enhance student perfor-

- 1 pt - The program successfully opens a frame with the stopwatch stopped.
- 1 pt - The program has a working "Start" button that starts the timer.
- 1 pt - The program has a working "Stop" button that stops the timer.
- 1 pt - The program has a working "Reset" button that stops the timer (if running) and resets the timer to 0.
- 4 pts - The time is formatted according to the description in step 4 above. Award partial credit corresponding to 1 pt per correct digit.
- 2 pts - The program correctly draws the number of successful stops at a whole second versus the total number of stops. Give one point for each number displayed.
- 2 pts - The "Stop" button correctly updates these success and attempts numbers. Give only one point if hitting the "Stop" button changes these numbers when the timer is already stopped.
- 1 pt - The "Reset" button clears the success and attempts numbers.

Figure 4: Grading rubric for stopwatch mini-project

mance, the study also raises questions about the accuracy of the resulting peer grades. In the last year, peer grading has been used in humanities MOOCs as well as more technically-oriented MOOCs [7] with similar questions.

With this issue in mind, we took special care in designing both the programming environment and the peer assessment component of the class. To facilitate consistent assessment of submitted programs, CodeSkulptor simplifies the process of sharing and running a peer's code and ensures a common shared environment for everyone executing this code. Second, we spent a large amount of time carefully designing the rubrics for class mini-projects. One factor in our favor compared to other MOOCs was that the work being graded, instead of being an essay, was an interactive computer program with a fairly precise behavior.

Figure 4 shows a rubric associated with an early mini-project. Note that the items in the rubric have a small point range and are very specific (*i.e.*, "The program has a working Stop button that stops the timer."). In essence, our approach was to design a rubric that mimicked the specificity of machine-based unit tests and restricted the scope of judgment for the human assessor. Rubrics for later, more complex projects consisted of 15–20 specific evaluation items, each valued discretely at 1 or 2 points.

Students were asked to assess five of their peer's mini-projects. To reduce the impact of outliers on the student's grade, the median score for the peers' assessment for each item in the rubric was used in computing the student's grade. Student were also required to provide written comments on items that did not receive full scores.

With this approach, we found that the vast majority of the students in both the on-campus version and the MOOC version of our class were very positive about the use of peer assessment. Students appreciated the flexibility of human evaluation versus machine evaluation and particularly appreciated the helpful written comments that many students included with their peer assessment. (These comments were mandatory if an assessor deducted points.)

In the Spring 2013 session of IIPP, the exit survey for the session asked the following question, "How helpful have you found your peers' evaluations and comments on your mini-project?" Out of 4429 responses, 71% found their peers' evaluations and comments helpful, 28% found them neither helpful nor unhelpful while 1% found them unhelpful.

In our class, most students also found the process of examining a peer's solution to a problem to be beneficial. In particular, they like the fact that peer assessment exposed them to the solutions, coding practices and errors of other students. On the exit survey for the Spring 2013 session, we asked "How helpful have you found examining your peers' code during peer assessment?" Out of 4429 responses, 81% found examining their peer's code to be helpful, 17% found this activity neither helpful nor unhelpful while 2% found this activity unhelpful.

Quizzes: Peer assessment is an inherently social mechanism. Our second assessment mechanism, the quiz, was machine-graded. As noted previously, this choice has the important advantage that student feedback on their performance is immediate. However, we observed instances of student frustration with the form or formatting of quiz answers that is common with the use of machine grading. In the on-campus version of our class, questions concerning this issue were resolved during in-person meetings. For the MOOC version, we augmented machine-grading with a social approach involving the class forums.

Our social approach to these quizzes was to allow multiple attempts at the quiz to encourage mastery of the material as well as to give students the opportunity to discuss the quiz problems in the class forums. In particular, we created a single sub-forum for each individual quiz. IIPP students were instructed to attempt the quiz at least once before visiting the specific quiz sub-forum. Inside the sub-forums, the rules for discussing quiz questions were very relaxed. Students were allowed to discuss the problems in substantial detail with the only restriction being that explicit answers should not be posted. This decision encourage substantial and detailed forum discussion (10–20 threads per quiz with 5–20 responses) of questions that were either difficult or perceived as ambiguous. As instructors, we rarely entered into these threads to avoid stifling discussion.

3.3 Class forums

Perhaps the most well-known social component of online classes are the discussion forums. For the on-campus version of our class (with 25 students), the class forums were essentially unused. On-campus students typically resolved questions concerning class material during either during in-person class meetings or via email exchanges with the instructor. Note that neither of these mechanisms provide particularly fast feedback for on-campus students.

However, in IIPP, the class forums were incredibly active, especially around class deadlines. For example, the forums for the Spring 2013 session included 8244 threads that generated more 65000 posts and comments. During peak forum times (4–12 hours before deadlines), new threads would be created at a rate of 10–20 per hour with each thread typically generating 3–5 responses within 20 minutes.

This highly active forum was a tremendous educational resource available to participants of the MOOC seeking timely answers to their questions. However, this social opportunity is not particularly unique to IIPP. Such forum activity should exist in any massive online class in which the level of activity reaches a critical threshold where it continually engages student attention and encourages active monitoring of forums. However, we leveraged CodeSkulptor and the forums in two ways that we believe are novel.

Peer feedback threads: While peer assessment was a popular component of IIPP, our students embraced the social nature of the class in a way that we did not fully anticipate. In the Fall 2012 session, approximately 13500 students submitted the first mini-project by the required deadline. After the deadline, we were besieged by requests from hundreds of students to extend the deadline and allow late submission. Due to the logistics of peer assessment, we could not allow extensions. As a way to provide these students with a feedback mechanism for their work, we created a "Peer feedback" thread in the sub-forum for the mini-project and encouraged students to anonymously post the URL for their mini-project in this thread. The directions for the thread asked that, if you posted in the feedback thread, you should review and comment on three of your peer's posted programs.

This idea proved to be highly popular with class participants. More than 700 students posted links to their mini-projects in this thread generating more than 2200 peer comments. Most of the posted code received comments that were helpful to the submitter. As was the case for traditional peer assessment, the open anonymous nature of these reviews also provided a valuable educational opportunity for students, allowing them to view a wide range of possible solutions as well as their peers' comments on these solutions.

The Hall of Fame: The knowledge level of the participants in IIPP was very diverse. Most of the students were either complete novices or had a very limited programming background. However, a significant minority of the class was relatively advanced and participating in the class to learn more about building games. As instructors, we viewed the participation of these students in the class as being beneficial since many of them actively participated in the class forums and answered novice questions.

To challenge and nurture this segment of the class, we create a special class forum known as "The Hall of Fame". This forum included two sub-forums, one for enhancements to existing class mini-projects and one for original game design ideas. The Hall of Fame allowed advanced students to challenge themselves beyond the basic mini-projects required in the class while motivating less advanced students to work hard at honing their skills so they could create a game for their peers. During the Spring 2013 session, approximately 250 enhanced versions of class mini-projects and 125 original games were developed by class participants.

Again, this activity was made possible due to the web- and cloud-based nature of CodeSkulptor. Students could share a project via a single URL with all assets (such as art and sound) hosted on the web. Several of the games were the results of collaborative development between multiple students in which one student would post an initial version and other students would then post enhanced versions with new features.

4. CONCLUSIONS

Our students' views of our class were extremely positive. Out of 4442 exit survey respondents for the Spring 2013 session, 66% rated the class as "Excellent", 28% "Very good", 5% "Good", 0.5% "Fair" and 0.0005% (2 responders) "Poor".

In our opinion, much of this popularity is due to the social environment that we created and helped foster in the class. Students actively engaged with each other to learn and teach themselves. The tools and format we provided, including CodeSkulptor, the Code Clinic, peer assessment, and the structure of the class forums made this possible.

In summary, we believe that a critical key to the success of massive online courses in the future will be the development of web-based environments that allow for fast, simple creation, saving and sharing of student assignments. In our case, the development of CodeSkulptor has also paid dividends for Rice's on-campus introductory CS classes by allowing students and instructors to create, share and assess code in a very streamlined manner. More generally, we see the advent of MOOCs as an opportunity to develop and test technology that will enhance the learning experience for both on-campus and online students.

Thanks: This research was supported in part by NSF Award CCF-1320860: "Computer-Aided Grading, Feedback, and Assignment Creation in Massive Online Programming Courses".

5. REFERENCES

[1] A. Bruckman. Community support for constructionist learning. *Computer Supported Cooperative Work (CSCW)*, 7(1–2):47–86, 1998.

[2] D. H. Clements and B. K. Nastasi. Social and cognitive interactions in educational computer environments. *American Educational Research Journal*, 25(1):87–106, 1988.

[3] N. Falchikov and J. Goldfinch. Student peer assessment in higher education: A meta-analysis comparing peer and teacher marks. *Review of Educational Research*, 70(3):287–322, 2000.

[4] S. Freeman and J. W. Parks. How accurate is peer grading? *CBE-Life Sciences Education*, 9(4):482–488, 2010.

[5] C. Kelleher, R. Pausch, and S. Kiesler. Storytelling Alice motivates middle school girls to learn computer programming. In *Proceedings of the SIGCHI conference on Human factors in Computing Systems*, pages 1455–1464. ACM, 2007.

[6] R. D. Pea. Cognitive technologies for Mathematics Education. *Cognitive science and Mathematics Education*, pages 89–122, 1987.

[7] C. Piech, J. Huang, Z. Chen, C. Do, A. Ng, and D. Koller. Tuned models of peer assessment in MOOCs.

[8] M. Resnick, J. Maloney, A. Monroy-Hernández, N. Rusk, E. Eastmond, K. Brennan, A. Millner, E. Rosenbaum, J. Silver, B. Silverman, et al. Scratch: programming for all. *Communications of the ACM*, 52(11):60–67, 2009.

[9] R. Singh, S. Gulwani, and A. Solar-Lezama. Automated feedback generation for introductory programming assignments. *arXiv preprint arXiv:1204.1751*, 2012.

[10] P. Wouters, C. van Nimwegen, H. van Oostendorp, and E. D. van der Spek. A meta-analysis of the cognitive and motivational effects of serious games. *Journal of Educational Psychology*, 105(2):249, 2013.

An Environment for Learning Interactive Programming

Terry Tang
Department of Computer Science
Rice University
Houston, Texas
terry.tang@rice.edu

Scott Rixner
Department of Computer Science
Rice University
Houston, Texas
rixner@rice.edu

Joe Warren
Department of Computer Science
Rice University
Houston, Texas
jwarren@rice.edu

ABSTRACT

We describe a web-based programming environment designed to support teaching introductory programming for a massive open online class. We discuss some of the thought processes behind the design of this environment and then focus on two key innovations incorporated in our environment: a simplified GUI library for interactive Python programming and a browser-based tool for visualizing the execution of event-driven Python programs.

Categories and Subject Descriptors

K.3.1 [**Computers and Education**]: Computer Uses in Education—*Computer-assisted instruction (CAI)*
; K.3.2 [**Computers and Education**]: Computer and Information Science Education—*Computer science education*

General Terms

Languages, Human Factors, Experimentation

Keywords

CS1, interactive, Python, visualization

1. INTRODUCTION

Learning introductory programming is a critical part of the education of any student interested in Computer Science. While introductory programming has long been a staple of on-campus instruction, the last decade has seen online delivery substantially extend the availability of introductory programming to a wider range of students. In the summer of 2012, the authors committed to designing and teaching a massive open online class (MOOC) on introductory programming for tens of thousands of students. As part of this class, the authors developed a programming environment designed to support novice students learning to code.

The design of the class and its programming environment embodied several important choices that we believe significantly influenced the success of the MOOC.

SIGCSE'14, March 5–8, 2014, Atlanta, GA, USA.

http://dx.doi.org/10.1145/2538862.2538908.

- Due to its popularity and simplicity, Python was chosen as the programming language for this class.
- To engage and motivate students, the class focused primarily on creating simple interactive games in Python.
- For ease of deployment and uniformity, the class environment for coding and running interactive Python programs was entirely web-based.

In early Fall 2012, the authors implemented a web-based environment for creating and running interactive Python programs known as CodeSkulptor[1]. Figure 1 shows CodeSkulptor running a simple interactive program that spawns a separate frame that displays the message "Welcome!". For this program, clicking the button labeled "click me" will change the displayed message to "Good job!". The Python code for this program is displayed in the code pane on the left while the frame overlays a console on the right where textual output is displayed.

In Fall 2012, Spring 2013 and Fall 2013 sessions, CodeSkulptor was used as the primary coding environment for the authors' MOOC, "An Introduction to Interactive Programming in Python"[2]. This class (IIPP) was a substantial success, awarding Statements of Accomplishment to almost 19,000 students and receiving several thousand positive reviews at multiple external MOOC review sites. In our view, the design of CodeSkulptor contributed to much of this success.

Contributions While the design of CodeSkulptor leverages many existing ideas, CodeSkulptor also incorporates several novel features.

- To harness the motivational power of building games, CodeSkulptor needed to support an interactive GUI library. After reviewing the existing GUI libraries for Python, we decided to create a simplified GUI library for interactive Python with a pedagogical focus.
- To assist students in understanding the behavior of their interactive, event-driven programs, we created a browser-based tool that records a trace of the execution of an event-driven program. The tool allows the student to manually fire events such as draws and timers that are normally triggered automatically during program execution. Further, the tool allows the students to step through the resulting trace at either a statement level or an event level while visualizing the associated program state.

[1] `http://www.codeskulptor.org/viz/`
[2] `https://www.coursera.org/course/interactivepython`

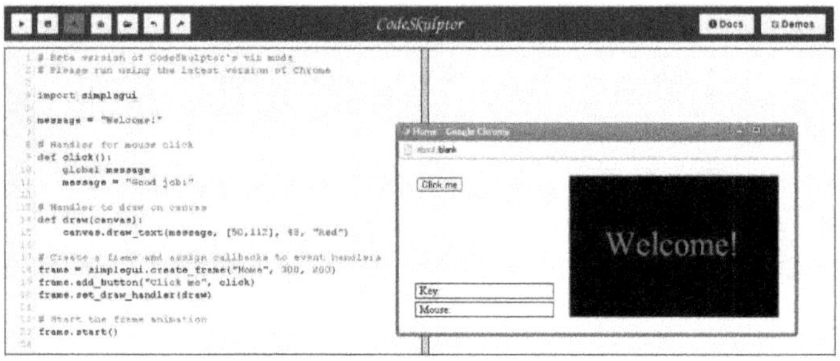

Figure 1: CodeSkulptor

2. RELATED WORK

Our synthesis of CodeSkulptor took place in the context of a large body of related work. We review this work and and discuss our rationale behind the design of CodeSkulptor in the context of this work.

Web-based programming tools In the summer of 2012, a number of web-based environments for programming already existed. Examples of these environments include repl.it, jsfiddle.org, and Cloud9 [1]. All of these environments include two features that we believe are critical for use in MOOCs. The environments offer web-based creation and cloud-based saving and sharing of programs.

Out of these environments, only repl.it offers support for Python that is completely browser-based. Unfortunately, our preliminary tests with repl.it indicated that its performance in running Python programs in a browser was insufficient to support building even games of modest complexity. This situation led us to create CodeSkulptor, which is a fusion of Code Mirror[3] and Skulpt[4], a tool for running Python programs in a web browser. Like the other environments listed above, CodeSkulptor supports cloud-based saving and sharing of programs.

Game-based introductory programming In designing a MOOC to teach introductory programming, one of our first priorities was to create a class that engaged the interest and imagination of our students. One well-established approach is to focus introductory programming classes on building games [11, 8]. This approach has been shown to be effective in maintaining and increasing the motivation of students [2, 10]. Programming environments geared towards games such Alice [3] and Scratch [13] are very popular and have attracted large communities. However, as was the case for an environment like Greenfoot [7] (focused on Java), we decided to teach a language that is more commonly used like Python to retain a wider appeal.

GUI libraries for Python Given our decision to focus on building games in Python, our next task was to decide on a GUI library for use with Python. A number of full-featured GUI libraries such as Tkinter [4] and wxPython [12] are available for Python. Another Python GUI that is specifically game-focused is Pygame [9]. Ultimately, we decided against using an existing GUI library for Python for the reasons discussed in section 3.

Tools for visualizing programs To help novice programmers understand the behavior of their programs, some environments for learning programming include tools to visualize the execution of programs. [14] surveys some of the existing techniques for visualizing program execution with Greenfoot, Jype (Python) [6], and Online Python Tutor [5] being particularly relevant.

Since none of these tools are fully-browser based or provided the capability to visualize the execution of event-driven programs, we decide to create an extension to CodeSkulptor that incorporates the frame/object visualization capabilities of Online Python Tutor while allowing both statement level and event level stepping through a program trace.

[3]`http://codemirror.net`

[4]`http://skulpt.org`

3. A GUI LIBRARY FOR PYTHON

Python has a number of GUI libraries (Tkinter, wxPython, Pygame, etc.) available for creating interactive programs. Two issues swayed us against using one of these libraries in our course. First, none of these libraries are designed to support browser-based Python. So we would need to port any existing library that we chose to the browser. Second, these libraries are moderately complex to use since they are designed to create full-featured user interfaces. As a result, the GUIs have a level of complexity in their design that might be overwhelming for novice programmers. These observations led us to choose to design and implement a web-based GUI for Python called SimpleGUI.

3.1 Pedagogical design of SimpleGUI

The SimpleGUI library supports the standard event-driven programming model in which the behavior of an interactive Python program is modeled as a sequence of events triggered either manually via controls such as buttons, input fields, key presses or mouse clicks or automatically via timers or drawing. In this model, the user creates a frame and then associates an event handler with this frame for each of these types of events. To generate visual output on the canvas associated with the frame, the user has a small set of drawing commands for entities such as text, simple geometric shapes, and rotated images. To generate audio output, the user can play start, pause and rewind a sound.

In designing SimpleGUI, our objective was to balance the complexity of the GUI library versus its expressiveness. In particular, we were interested in having the ability to create moderately complex games (on the level of 1980/1990s arcade games) using a relatively easy-to-learn GUI library. For example, full-featured GUIs allow precise control over the button layout, but at the expense of numerous parameters and options. However, for the class of games that we envisioned students building, precise control of button placement was not particularly important. Thus, we provided only limited options for button placement and reduced the complexity of SimpleGUI in that instance.

In general, we added features to SimpleGUI only when these capabilities significantly extended the expressiveness of the library. With this approach, students were able to create a range of games in SimpleGUI using relatively small Python programs. Weekly class projects included Rock-paper-scissors-lizard-Spock (50 lines), Pong (100 lines), Blackjack (200 lines), and Asteroids (350 lines in 2 weeks).

We found that one bonus from taking an event-driven approach was that students could create surprisingly interesting interactive programs using only a small set of programming constructs. For example, weekly projects in the first half of the class like "Guess the number", Stopwatch, and

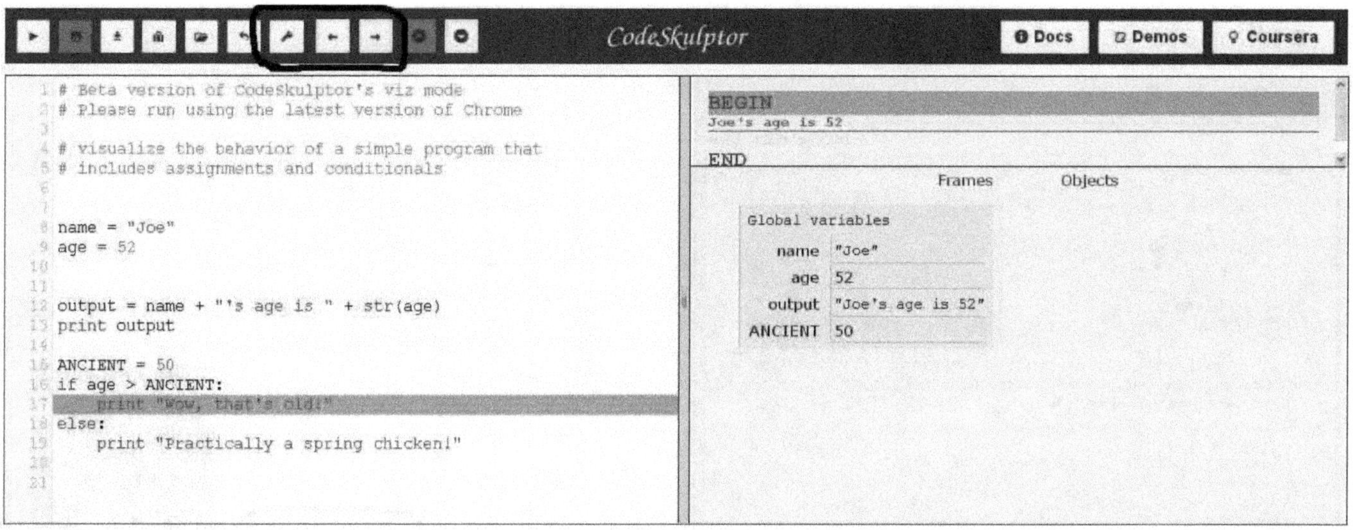

Figure 2: Visualizing the state of a simple test program in CodeSkulptor. Circled buttons activate Viz mode (wrench icon) and step through the program trace at a statement level (left/right arrow icons).

Pong require no knowledge of loops or mutation. As a result, we were able to delay introduction of these more advanced concepts until the second half of the class.

3.2 Technical structure of SimpleGUI

Internally, CodeSkulptor utilizes Skulpt[5] as a Python engine. Specifically, Skulpt translates Python code into Javascript and then executes the resulting Javascript in the browser. This approach provides sufficient performance for modest interactive games, unlike other web-based Python programming environments which either incur too much overhead or execute code on the server-side.

In a similar manner, our implementation of SimpleGUI supports event-driven programming by translating event-driven Python code into its Javascript equivalent. SimpleGUI supports creation of an interactive frame with a control area and drawing canvas as well as audio using a combination of Javascript and HTML5. Specifically, SimpleGUI allows Python programs to:

- Create a frame (`simplegui.create_frame`),
- Create timers (`simplegui.create_timer`),
- Load images (`simplegui.load_image`),
- Load sounds (`simplegui.load_sound`).

The SimpleGUI module can be imported into CodeSkulptor programs using `import simplegui` and provides an easy to use GUI library that runs across web browsers such as Chrome, Firefox and Safari. SimpleGUI is not meant to be a full-featured GUI library. However, it provides a consistent and easy to use environment for building modestly complex games.

4. BROWSER-BASED VISUALIZATION

Many programming environments, especially those designed for pedagogical purposes, incorporate tools that allow users to visualize the execution of their programs. Our visualization tool for CodeSkulptor follows a philosophy similar to that of Online Python Tutor[6], allowing statement level visualization of program state via a frame/object diagram. Here, the frame portion of the diagram displays pending function calls and their associated variables while the object portion displays reference diagrams for mutable objects.

In evaluating Python Tutor for use in IIPP, we hesitated in using Python Tutor as is for two reasons. First, Python Tutor uses a back-end server to construct the execution trace used during visualization. We worried that this design might prove problematic during periods of high demand around due dates for IIPP. Second, Python Tutor lacks the capability to visualize the execution of event-driven programs.

4.1 Visualizing sequential programs

In light of these issues, we decide to integrate Python Tutor's capabilities directly into CodeSkulptor. The key technical obstacle to this integration was avoiding the need for a back-end server to generate the execution trace of the program. Our approach was to add an option to CodeSkulptor that, when enabled, would instrument the Javascript code created during compilation of a Python program by Skulpt. Executing this instrumented Javascript code would then not only evaluate the corresponding Python program, but also generate an execution trace for the Python program. We could then use Python Tutor's frame/object diagram visualization capabilities (available in open source form as Javascript) to display a selected state in this trace.

To activate Viz mode in CodeSkulptor, the user clicks the activation button (the leftmost circled button with the wrench icon) on the upper left row of buttons. This action enables instrumentation of the compiled Python code and updates the UI for CodeSkulptor in two ways.

- A pair of yellow previous/next buttons is placed to the right of the wrench. These buttons allow the user to navigate the execution trace at a statement level.

[5] `http://www.skulpt.org`

[6] `http://pythontutor.com`

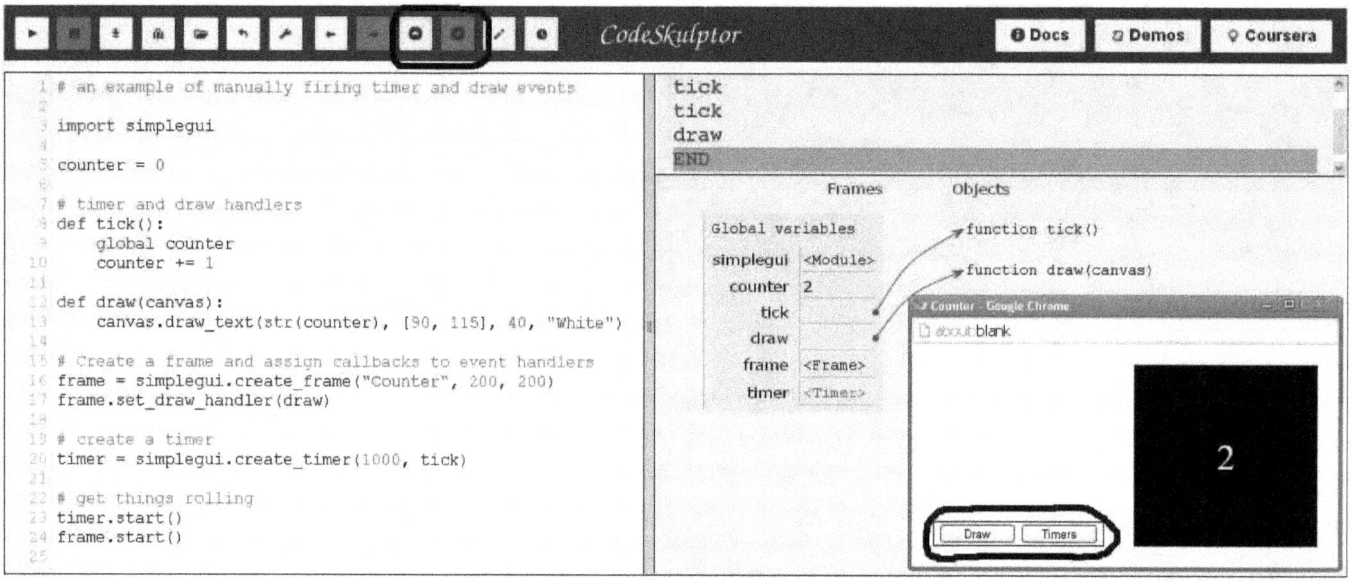

Figure 3: Visualizing the state of a counter program that spawns a frame and displays a counter on the canvas (lower right). The two circled buttons on the frame allow manual firing of draw and timer events. The upper two circled buttons allow event level navigation of the associated program trace.

- The console is restricted to the upper portion of the righthand pane while the lower portion is used to display the frame/object diagram corresponding to the program state for the selected statement.

Figure 2 shows an example of visualizing one particular state during the execution trace of a simple sequential Python program[7]. This program involves no user interaction and simply prints computed output to the console.

After running the program, the user has navigated through the resulting execution trace using the circled buttons and selected the `print` statement highlighted on the left. The output and state of this program **prior** to the execution of the selected statement are highlighted in the console (upper right) and the frame/object diagram (lower right), respectively. Note that the output `"Joe's age is 52"` from a previously executed `print` statement is displayed in the console. On the other hand, the output `"Wow, that's old!"` from the currently highlighted `print` statement is only faintly displayed to indicate that it has not yet been executed.

Viz mode may also be used to debug programs that throw an error. Executing such a program in Viz mode generates a program trace up to the point at which the error is thrown and is very helpful in debugging.

4.2 Visualizing event-driven programs

During normal execution of event-driven programs, timers and draws may automatically generate hundreds of events in a very short period. Attempting to visualize the behavior of such programs by adding `print` statements to the handlers for these events often results in a blizzard of textual output to the console. In Viz mode, CodeSkulptor requires that all events including draws and timer ticks be triggered manually to avoid this issue. When a program including draw or timer events is run in Viz mode, CodeSkulptor automatically adds buttons to the user interface allowing manually firing of these events when desired.

Figure 3 shows the state of a program that creates a frame, updates the value of a counter via a timer and displays the value of that counter on the canvas associated with the frame[8]. The console shows a log of the events that have been manually fired by the user using the circled "draw" and "timer" button on the frame. Specifically, the user has fired two timer `tick()` events, updating the value of `counter` to 2, as shown in the state diagram. Finally, the user has fired draw event that draws the value of the counter on the canvas using a SimpleGUI canvas operation. Note that the label "END" in the console is highlighted to alert the user that the displayed state corresponds to the end of the current trace.

At this point, the user may navigate between existing events using the circled prev/next event buttons to visualize the program state prior to the execution of each event. Inside a particular event, the user can navigate at a statement level using the next/prev statement buttons. While stepping through a draw event, the canvas is updated after each SimpleGUI canvas operation allowing the user to visualize the composition of the canvas dynamically.

The user may also fire new events by clicking the "draw" and "tick" buttons. These new events are appended to the event log displayed in the console and the execution traces associated with these event are appended to the current program trace. This functionality allows the user to visualize the state of the program interactively via the frame/object diagram. Note that the updated program trace is generated entirely in the browser. This design is essential in enabling the interactivity of this process. Otherwise the browser would need to send the code for the event and the current program state to a remote server to generate a trace for each new event that is fired.

[7] `http://www.codeskulptor.org/viz/#viz_tutorial_state.py`

[8] `http://www.codeskulptor.org/viz/#viz_tutorial_drawing.py`

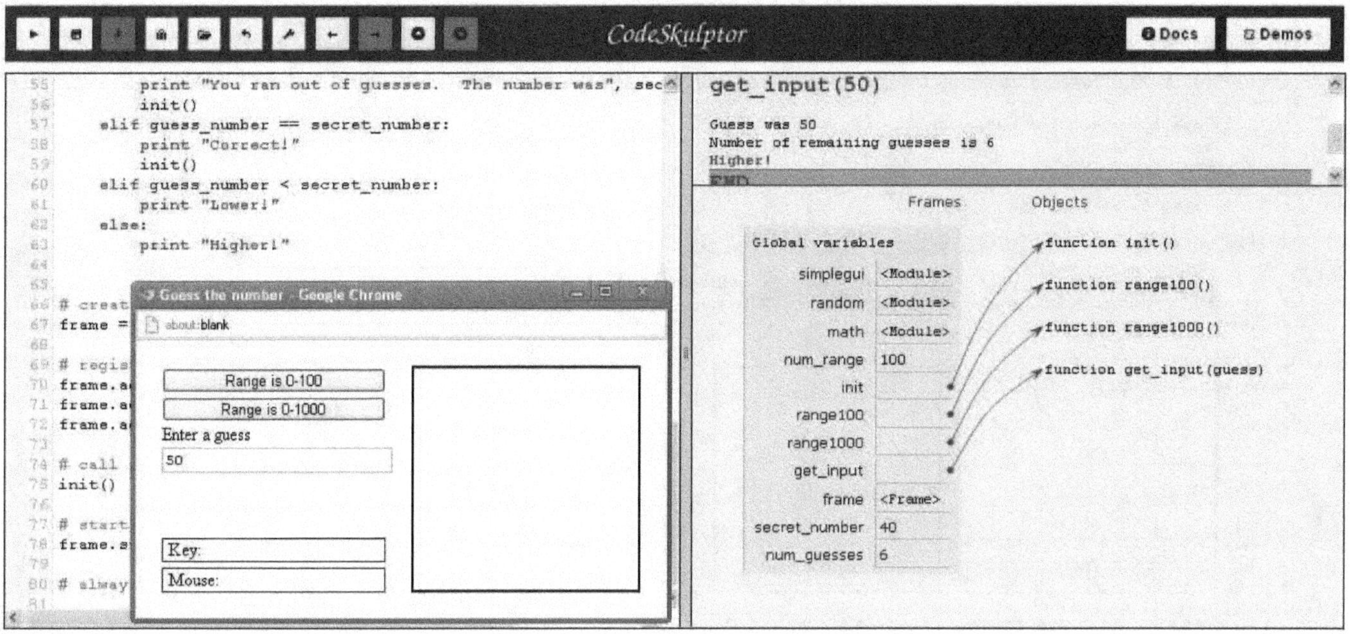

Figure 4: Final state of "Guess the number" after an "input" event

4.3 A pedagogical example

In this subsection, we consider a simple illustrative example of using CodeSkulptor's Viz mode to understand the behavior of an incorrectly-coded interactive program. "Guess the number" is a simple game in which the computer generates a secret number between 0 and 100. The player then inputs numbers in that range and the computer responds `Higher!` or `Lower!` based on the value of the guess and the secret number.

Figure 4 shows the state of an implementation of the game "Guess the number"[9] after the player has entered an initial guess of `"50"`. The value of the secret number, 40, is displayed in the frame/object diagram while the value 50 for the input event is specified in the event log in the console. At this point, the user notes that text message in the console incorrectly displays `Higher!` instead of `Lower!`.

Based on this observation, the user navigates the trace of the execution of this event. Figure 5 shows the state of the program prior to the execution of the incorrect `print` statement. At this point, the user has all of the information in the frame/object diagram necessary to resolve the error. In particular, the `secret_number` is 40 while `guess_number` is 50 yet the execution ended up in the "Higher!" clause of the conditional statement. These clues point to the error: the comparison used in the `elif` clause is reversed causing the `Higher!` and `Lower!` messages to be switched.

The example illustrates the basic approach that we suggest in using CodeSkulptor's Viz mode to understand the behavior of an interactive program.

- CodeSkulptor executes the body of the program and records a trace of the execution. The frame/object diagram and the console display the program state and output.
- The user then manually fires events using either timer/draw buttons or by interacting with the frame. The output of the program is then visualized via the console and canvas while the state is visualized via the frame/object diagram.
- When the user observes an event whose effect on the output or state is unexpected, they then explore execution of the particular event using the statement navigation buttons.

In practice, we have found the ability to manually fire events and immediately visualize program state after each event to be valuable in understanding the behavior of interactive programs.

5. FUTURE WORK

Viz mode records a log of the events associated with a specific execution. In future work, we plan to incorporate the ability to load and save these event logs to facilitate easier testing and debugging of event-driven programs. In particular, we intend to investigate the possibility of creating a unit testing scheme for event-driven programs.

One key task would be to specify the state of the canvas formally after each draw event as a sequence of canvas draw operations. Verifying the correctness of submitted program would boil down to checking the equivalence of this sequence with the sequence produced by the submitted program algorithmically. We believe that this capability is easily within the capability of modern program verification and would enhance our ability to specify the behavior of interactive programs as well as the student's ability to verify that their programs work correctly.

In summary, we have described a web-based environment for creating and running interactive Python programs. The GUI portion of the environment (SimpleGUI) has been successfully used by tens of thousands of students in three sessions of IIPP. Viz mode was released for informal use in Fall

[9] `http://www.codeskulptor.org/viz/#viz_pedogogicalExample.py`

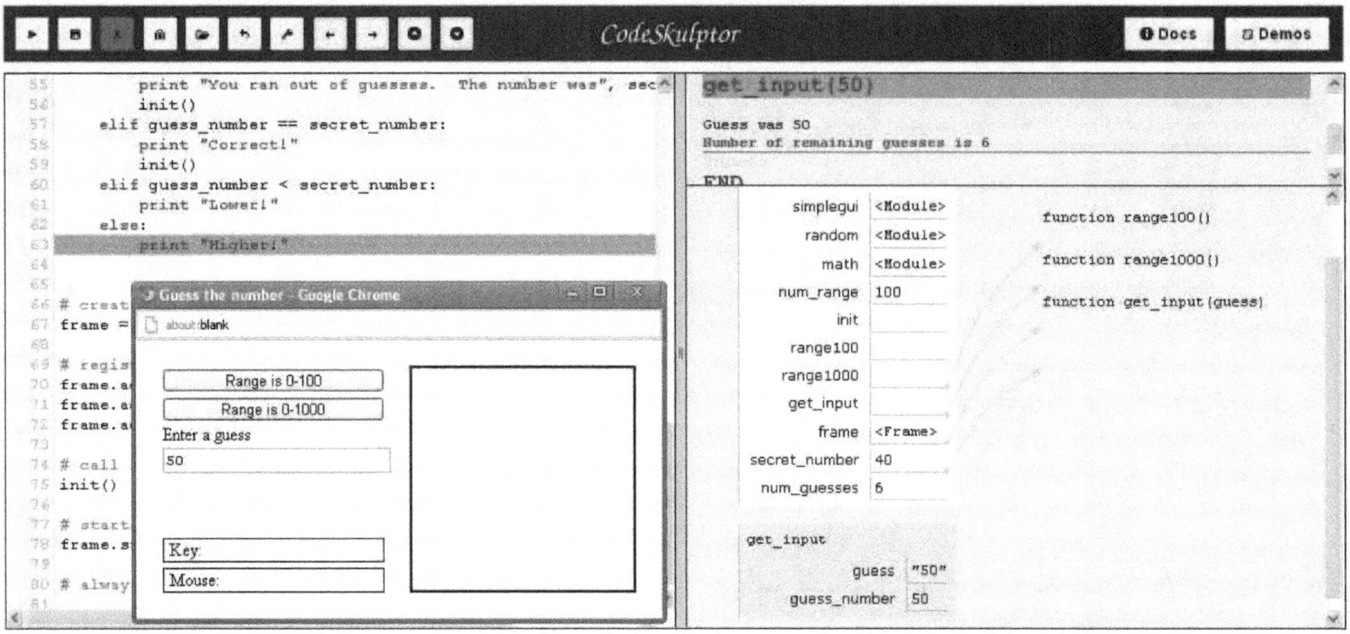

Figure 5: An earlier state during the execution of the "input" event

2013 session of IIPP. In future sessions, we plan to integrate Viz mode into the pedagogy of the class and engage in a user study to assess the effectiveness and usability of Viz mode.

Acknowledgements This research was supported by NSF Award CCF-1320860: "Computer-Aided Grading, Feedback, and Assignment Creation in Massive Online Programming Courses". We would like to extend our thanks to the Online Python Tutor project for making their state visualization code available for use in CodeSkulptor. Finally, we would like to thank John Greiner and Stephen Wong for their assistance in creating and teaching IIPP.

6. REFERENCES

[1] L. Ciortea, C. Zamfir, S. Bucur, V. Chipounov, and G. Candea. Cloud9: a software testing service. *ACM SIGOPS Operating Systems Review*, 43(4):5–10, 2010.

[2] D. C. Cliburn. The effectiveness of games as assignments in an introductory programming course. In *Frontiers in Education Conference, 36th Annual*, pages 6–10. IEEE, 2006.

[3] S. Cooper, W. Dann, and R. Pausch. Alice: a 3-d tool for introductory programming concepts. In *Journal of Computing Sciences in Colleges*, volume 15, pages 107–116. Consortium for Computing Sciences in Colleges, 2000.

[4] J. E. Grayson. *Python and Tkinter programming.* Manning Publications Co., 2000.

[5] P. J. Guo. Online python tutor: Embeddable web-based program visualization for cs education. In *Proceeding of the 44th ACM Technical Symposium on Computer science education*, pages 579–584. ACM, 2013.

[6] J. Helminen and L. Malmi. Jype-a program visualization and programming exercise tool for python. In *Proceedings of the 5th International Symposium on Software Visualization*, pages 153–162. ACM, 2010.

[7] M. Kölling and P. Henriksen. Game programming in introductory courses with direct state manipulation. *ACM SIGCSE Bulletin*, 37(3):59–63, 2005.

[8] S. Leutenegger and J. Edgington. A games first approach to teaching introductory programming. In *ACM SIGCSE Bulletin*, volume 39, pages 115–118. ACM, 2007.

[9] W. McGugan. *Beginning Game Development with Python and Pygame.* Will McGugan, 2007.

[10] A. M. Phelps, C. A. Egert, and J. D. Bayliss. Media impact: Games in the classroom: Using games as a motivator for studying computing: Part 1. *Multimedia, IEEE*, 16(2):4–8, 2009.

[11] R. Rajaravivarma. A games-based approach for teaching the introductory programming course. *ACM SIGCSE Bulletin*, 37(4):98–102, 2005.

[12] N. Rappin and R. Dunn. *wxPython in Action.* Manning, 2006.

[13] M. Resnick, J. Maloney, A. Monroy-Hernández, N. Rusk, E. Eastmond, K. Brennan, A. Millner, E. Rosenbaum, J. Silver, B. Silverman, et al. Scratch: programming for all. *Communications of the ACM*, 52(11):60–67, 2009.

[14] J. Urquiza-Fuentes and J. Á. Velázquez-Iturbide. A survey of successful evaluations of program visualization and algorithm animation systems. *ACM Transactions on Computing Education (TOCE)*, 9(2):9, 2009.

Teaching Creative Problem Solving in a MOOC

Pascal Van Hentenryck
NICTA and The University of Melbourne
Lvl 2 / Bldg 193, The University of Melbourne
Melbourne, VIC, Australia, 3010
pvh@nicta.com.au

Carleton Coffrin
NICTA
Lvl 2 / Bldg 193, The University of Melbourne
Melbourne, VIC, Australia, 3010
carleton.coffrin@nicta.com.au

ABSTRACT

The practice of discrete optimization involves modeling and solving complex combinatorial problems which have never been encountered before and for which no universal computational paradigm exists. Teaching such skills is challenging: Students must learn, not only the core technical skills, but also an ability to think creatively in order to select and adapt a paradigm to solve the problem at hand. This paper explores the question of whether the teaching of such creative skills translates to massive open online courses (MOOCs). It first describes a methodology for teaching discrete optimization that has been successful on campus over fifteen years. It then discusses how to adapt the campus format to a MOOC version. The success of the approach is evaluated through extensive data analytics enabled by the wealth of information produced by MOOCs.

Categories and Subject Descriptors

K.3.2 [**Computer and Information Science Education**]: Computer science education—*MOOC*

Keywords

Problem Solving; MOOC; Artificial Intelligence; Inquiry-Based Learning; Experience Report

1. INTRODUCTION

Discrete optimization is a subfield of artificial intelligence and operations research focusing on the task of solving NP-hard optimization problems, such as the knapsack and the traveling salesman problems. Due to the computational complexity of these applications, the practice of discrete optimization has remained more an art than a science: practitioners are constantly confronted with novel problems and must determine which computational paradigm, modeling, and searching techniques to apply to the problem at hand. As a consequence, the teaching of discrete optimization must not only convey the core concepts of the field but also develop the intuition and creative thinking necessary to apply these skills in novel situations. Teaching such skills is a challenge for instructors who must present students with complex problem-solving tasks and keep them motivated over a long period of time.

These challenges are further exacerbated in Massively Open Online Classes (MOOCs), which have generated substantial interest since the success of Stanford's computer science MOOCs [3, 4, 8, 5]. There are now several start-up companies (e.g., Coursera, Udasity, and edX) offering MOOC platforms and numerous leading universities have partnered with these providers. MOOCs present unique teaching challenges, from the material presentation to the design of assignments and student motivation without traditional interaction patterns. It is thus important to determine whether successful frameworks for teaching problem-solving skills in traditional university settings translate, or can be adapted, to teaching and learning within a MOOC. This question is largely unaddressed in the literature. Existing publications and technical reports on MOOCs [6, 7] focus primarily on what happened in a course: They report various cohort statistics [7] and aim at understanding key performance indicators such as completion rates [6]. Few papers discuss the design and effectiveness of MOOC assessments [9] and how to motivate students to succeed in MOOCs.

This paper is an attempt to shed some light on how to teach problem-solving skills in a MOOC. Section 2 documents the design of a discrete optimization class that has been honed for over fifteen years at a leading U.S. institution and was highly popular among senior undergraduate and graduate students, Section 3 then presents how the teaching philosophy behind this class was adapted to a MOOC setting. This is followed in Section 4 by extensive data analytics, enabled by the wealth of information collected in a MOOC, to validate the design decisions in both the traditional and MOOC versions of the class. In particular, the data analytics results indicate how gamification, community development, and an open course structure were key ingredients to the success of the MOOC. Finally, Section 5 concludes the paper.

2. THE DISCRETE OPTIMIZATION CLASS

Discrete Optimization is an introductory course designed to teach students how to solve NP-Hard problems in practice. The prerequisites are strong programming skills and familiarity with classic computer science algorithms (e.g. sorting, depth first search, minimum spanning tree) and basic

SIGCSE'14, March 3–8, 2014, Atlanta, GA, USA.

ACM 978-1-4503-2605-6/14/03 ...$15.00.
http://dx.doi.org/10.1145/2538862.2538913.

linear algebra. It covers an introduction to three core topics in the discrete optimization field, Constraint Programming, Local Search, and Mixed Integer Programming. Each of the topic areas is relatively independent and any presentation order is admissible. The pedagogical philosophy of the course is that inquiry-based learning is effective in teaching creative problem solving skills.

The class assignments consist of designing algorithms to solve five NP-Hard problems of increasing complexity, knapsack, graph coloring, traveling salesman (TSP), warehouse location, and capacitated vehicle routing (CVRP). The approach to solving these problems attempts to emulate a real-world discrete optimization experience, which is, your boss tells you *"solve this problem, I don't care how"*. This situation is simulated by providing the students with a problem specification and their task is to produce high quality solutions to the problem by any means necessary. The lectures contain the necessary ideas to solve the problems, but the best technique to apply is left for the students to discover [2]. This assignment design not only prepares students for how optimization is conducted in the real-world but is also pedagogically well-founded under the guise of guided inquiry-based learning [1].

Like many design tasks in STEM subjects, NP-Hard problems are open ended since there is no known "ideal" solution. This makes the algorithm design task a very creative process. This is the *art* of discrete optimization. The class fosters this creativity in several ways: all paths to high quality solutions are rewarded equally; students are encouraged to work in pair programming teams; all students are encouraged to collaborate and share ideas outside of class to complete the assignments, although the implementation details should be their own work.

2.1 Assignment Structure

Discrete optimization tasks have a general declarative specification in the form of an objective function f and a system of constraints g_i $(i \in C)$. This allows the instructor to specify the task at hand rigorously. Let $\mathbf{x}$ be a vector of decision variables and $\mathbf{w}$ a vector of input data, an optimization problem seeks to minimize $f(\mathbf{w}, \mathbf{x})$ subject to $g_i(\mathbf{w}, \mathbf{x})$ $(\forall i \in C)$. Due to the nature of NP-Hard problems, the assignments can be incredibly difficult to solve well, but verifying the quality of a solution is very easy. Furthermore, the objective function provides a simple quantitative measure for marking and comparing student solutions. To make the assignments more concrete, we discus the first assignment in detail.

$$\begin{aligned} \max \quad & \sum_{i \in I} v_i x_i \\ \text{s.t.} \quad & \sum_{i \in I} w_i x_i \leq K \\ & x_i \in \{0,1\} \ (i \in I) \end{aligned} \tag{KS}$$

The knapsack problem (KS) is the most common NP-Hard problem covered in undergraduate computer science curriculum and hence it makes an excellent warm-up assignment in a discrete optimization class. The problem is defined as a container with capacity K and a set of items I. Each item $i \in I$ has a value v_i and a weight w_i. The goal is to find a subset of the items $I^* \subseteq I$ that has the highest value and does not exceed the capacity K. By introducing a decision variable $x_i \in \{0,1\}$ $(\forall i \in I)$ to indicate whether an item is placed in the container or not, this problem can be modeled as the system of linear equations in (KS). The student's task is to design an algorithm that can find a high-quality assignment of the decision variables $\mathbf{x} = \{x_1, x_2, \ldots, x_{|I|}\}$ given any problem input $\mathbf{w} = \{K, v_1, w_1, v_2, w_2, \ldots, v_{|I|}, w_{|I|}\}$.

2.2 Assignment Grading

There are many possibilities for the grading of algorithm design tasks. In the spirit of the "by any means necessary" theme of the assignments, we focus on a very quantitative metric: the solution quality on six to eight problem inputs for each assignment, T. Each input data $i \in T$ is graded on a 10 point scale using four basic categories: 0 points, 3 points, 7 points, and 10 points. Two thresholds (h_i^1, h_i^2) are defined. These thresholds correspond to the objective value of a good and a great solution respectively, where "good" is qualitatively defined as a solution that can be achieved by using the material provided in the lectures and "great" requires the student to go beyond the lecture material. With these values defined, the grading is done by the following algorithm: (1) submissions not conforming to the output specification or infeasible are given 0 points; (2) any feasible solution receives at least 3 points; (3) feasible solutions exceeding the "good" threshold (i.e., $f(\mathbf{w}_i, \mathbf{x}) \leq h_i^1$) receive at least 7 points; and (4) feasible solutions exceeding the "great" threshold (i.e., $f(\mathbf{w}_i, \mathbf{x}) \leq h_i^2$) receive a full 10 points. This point based system is carefully designed to reward two general approaches to the material equally: (1) a high quality approach that does not scale to the largest input values; and (2) a medium quality approach that solves all of the inputs similarly. Notice that $10\frac{|T|}{2} + 3\frac{|T|}{2} \approx 7|T|$. This allows students two viable meta-strategies for approaching the assignments and rewards both similarly.

Student performance on the assignments is evaluated weekly and delivered in class. However, due to the open ended nature of these algorithm design tasks and the independence of the course topics, students are often inspired later in the course to revise their solutions to earlier assignments. Pursuing these inspirations is encouraged by allowing students to return to all previous assignments at any point and improve their grades. The final grade is based on the solution quality on the last day of class.

2.3 Motivation and Gamification

Given the challenging nature of the assignments in discrete optimization, the ability of students to maintain a high level of motivation is critical to their successful completion of the course. Employing a liberal collaboration policy in discrete optimization has the effect of creating a *buzz* about the assignments. Outside the classroom, students are constantly sharing information about the best solutions they have found and how they found them. This informal feedback has an effect of keeping the students engaged and motivated to complete the assignments. However, two additional class activities were used to amplify the effects of this feedback: (1) a friendly class competition was created via a *leader board*, which directly compares student performances at the start of each week; (2) students had to prepare *show-and-tell*-style presentations discussing how they approached the assignments. The most successful algorithms were disseminated through these peer education sessions, bridging the gap between the lecture material and the assignments. The leader board is an essential and fairly unique part of

Student	Input 1	Input 2	Input 3
A	$f(\mathbf{w}_1, \mathbf{x}_1^a)$	$f(\mathbf{w}_2, \mathbf{x}_2^a)$	$f(\mathbf{w}_3, \mathbf{x}_3^a)$
B	$f(\mathbf{w}_1, \mathbf{x}_1^b)$	$f(\mathbf{w}_2, \mathbf{x}_2^b)$	$f(\mathbf{w}_3, \mathbf{x}_3^b)$
C	$f(\mathbf{w}_1, \mathbf{x}_1^c)$	$f(\mathbf{w}_2, \mathbf{x}_2^c)$	$f(\mathbf{w}_3, \mathbf{x}_3^c)$
...	...	...	...

Table 1: A Leader Board for Sharing Solution Quality.

the discrete optimization class and warrants a detailed explanation.

It is interesting to notice that the objective function (f) allows students to share information about the quality of their algorithm without revealing the details. This unique way of sharing information can be used to build a table comparing students performance. Table 1 illustrates how a *leader board* can be constructed. In the table, the leader board indicates the solution quality of three students $\{A, B, C\}$ on three problem inputs $\{1, 2, 3\}$, where $\mathbf{w}_1$ is the input data for problem 1 and $\mathbf{x}_1^a$ is student A's solution to problem 1. The class competition generated by the leader board, not only increases discussion among the students, but also has an additional benefit of pushing the best students to go beyond full credit (i.e., 10 points) and improve their solution to be the best in the class.

2.4 Success on Campus

Discrete optimization is traditionally offered as an advanced undergraduate and introductory graduate level class. The typical enrollment is between twenty and thirty students annually. Based on classroom critical review surveys, the students indicated that: they worked around 15 hours per week on average; the course material was challenging; they learned a lot; and the overall experience was very positive. Common statements captured via students open ended comments include: *"[praise for] the professor's consistent encouragement of student participation"* — *"[the] rigorous assignments were found to be most instrumental to success in this class"* — *"the majority of learning occurred when students worked on the projects."* — *"[the projects] were crazy hard, but crazy fun!"*. As we will see in the next Section, many of these aspects were successfully recreated in the MOOC version.

3. THE MOOC

Adaptation of discrete optimization from the classroom to a MOOC poses three core challenges: (1) how to scale assessments to a huge number of students; (2) how to accommodate the heterogeneity of the student body; (3) how to recreate the community dimension, which fueled the students' motivation to complete the course, and naturally developed through co-location of students on a campus. This section discusses how these three challenges were addressed in the adaption of discrete optimization to the MOOC setting.

Assessment Scaleability.

Based on the assignment specification, it is relatively simple to make the grading process fully automated. This makes these assignments ideal for a MOOC setting, where scalability is paramount. Furthermore, the leader board also scales to MOOC delivery. Hence, the assignments and leader board in the MOOC were identical to the classroom version.

Accommodating Heterogeneity.

The student body in a MOOC is much less homogenous than in a typical classroom. Many of the students are seeking continuing education. These students have many unpredictable scheduling requirements such as, work, family, and vacation. The age of the students is very broad and the skills of the student body can vary widely. Some may have a degree in the subject area, while others have no exposure at all (including high-school students) [7]. One major advantage of the MOOC format is that this heterogeneity can be at least partially accommodated by making the content always available. Discrete optimization provides the entire course material on the first day of class. This allows students to design a study plan around their life constraints and to go at their own pace, accommodating their varying degrees of proficiency in the subject area.

Community Development.

The greatest challenge in the MOOC version of discrete optimization is to replace the community aspect of the class. We hypothesize that the buzz and community, which motivates students in the classroom version, is fostered by a combination of challenging problems, encouragement of teamwork, and iterative, continuos assignment feedback. In an attempt to build a similar sense of community in the MOOC, several feedback mechanism were employed.

Grading is the first feedback provided to the students. In the campus version, grading feedback was provided every two weeks. However, students would implicitly discuss solution quality between these weekly reports. To compensate for this lack of social interactions, we allow the assignments to have an unlimited number of submissions. The students can then seek feedback as often as they wish.

The leader board is the second feedback mechanism. In the classroom version, the leader board was updated weekly and reviewed during the lecture period. To improve feedback in the MOOC, the leader board is continuously updated. This encourages students to stay engaged with their peer's solutions regularly, rather than once a week. Once again, this replaces an activity that happened in the classroom by face-to-face contact and word of mouth.

A very liberal collaboration policy for sharing information on the forums is the third feedback mechanism. Students are encouraged to share their experience on the forums and can provide very detailed accounts (e.g., even pseudo code) of how they achieved good solutions to the assignments. This was complemented with very active participation by the teaching staff in the forum, allowing the staff to guide the class discussion and providing a replacement for campus-based informal instructor feedback, such as office hours.

A weekly *mailbag* video is the final feedback mechanism. These videos include weekly announcements, an official response to popular discussion threads in the forums, and weekly statistics on the class's progress and demographics. Once again, revealing aggregate class statistics to the students provides a feeling for the boarder community they are a part of. Some of the most important weekly statistics, such as the class points plot (see Figure 1), were presented live on the course page so that students could actively engage with the status of the class in real time. Table 2 summarizes the differences between the classroom and MOOC versions of discrete optimization.

Topic	Classroom	MOOC
Content Presentation	linear	open
Lectures	live in class	recorded video
Assignments Feedback	weekly	real-time
Leader Board	weekly	real-time
Student Discussion	face-to-face	forum
Team Work	pair programming	pseudo code
Professor Feedback	class discussion	weekly mailbag

Table 2: Classroom versus MOOC Course.

4. UNDERSTANDING THE MOOC

Section 2 introduced the pedagogical philosophy of discrete optimization and Section 3 discussed the adaptation to a MOOC including a hypothesis about community development and student motivation. Both sections postulate how the design of discrete optimization affects the student learning experience. This section leverages the huge amount of data produced by a MOOC to provide some evidence of the claims in previous sections. This data does not include rigorous experiments to make these claims irrefutable. However, we believe the evidence provided here is immensely informative for the design of such rigorous experiments and is valuable to the community in its current form. Before discussing the details of the student experience in the discrete optimization MOOC, we will provide some perspective by reviewing the basic class statistics.

4.1 Inaugural Session Overview

The inaugural session of the discrete optimization MOOC ran over a period of nine weeks. During the nine months between the first announcement of discrete optimization and the course launch, 50,000 individuals showed an interest in the class. As is typical of a MOOC, less than 50% (17,000) of interested students went on to attend class and view at least one video lecture [6, 7]. Around 6,500 students experimented with the assignments and around 4,000 of those students made a non-trivial attempt at solving one of the algorithm design tasks.

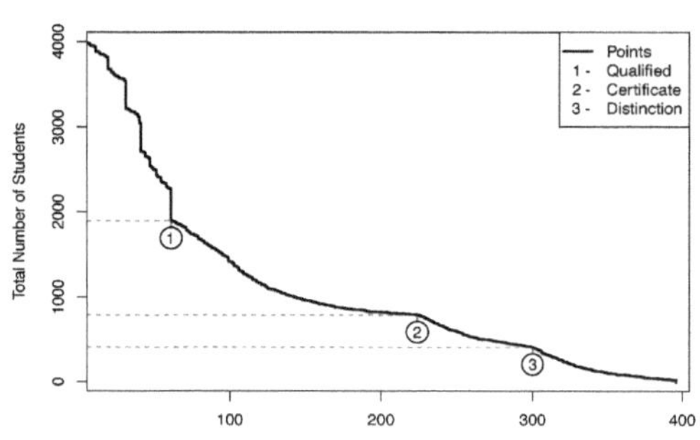

Figure 1: The Cumulative Distribution of Grades.

By the end of discrete optimization, 795 students earned a certificate of completion. This was truly remarkable: less than 500 students graduated from the classroom version in fifteen years of teaching. The typical completion rate calculation of 795/17000 = 4.68% could be discouraging. However, a detailed inspection of the number of points earned by the students is very revealing. Figure 1 presents the total number of students achieving a particular point threshold (i.e., a cumulative distribution of student points). Within the range of 0 and 60 points, there are several sheer cliffs in this distribution. These correspond to students abandoning the assignments as they get stuck on parts of the warm-up knapsack assignment (students meeting the prerequisites should find this assignment easy). At the 60 point mark (*1* in Figure 1), 47% of the students (i.e., 1884) remain. We consider these students to be *qualified* to complete the course material, as they have successfully completed the first assignment. The remainder of the point curve is a smooth distribution indicating that the assignments are challenging and well calibrated. Two small humps occur at locations indicated by *2* and *3*: These correspond to the certificate threshold values. The shape indicates that students who are near a threshold put in some extra effort to pass it. However, the most important result from this figure is that if we only consider the population of active students who attempted the assignments and were qualified, the completion rate is 795/1884 = 42.2%.

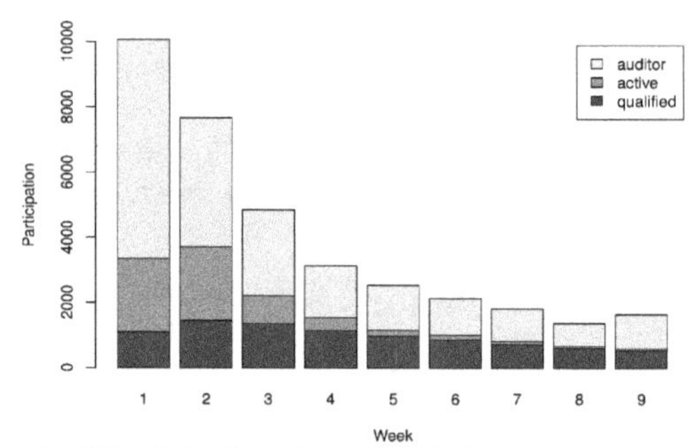

Figure 2: Weekly Student Activity by Auditors, Active Students, and Qualified Students.

Due to the open nature of MOOCs, it is interesting to understand the student body over time. Figure 2 indicates the number of students who were active in the class over the nine-week period. The active students are broken into three categories: *"auditors"* those who only watch videos; *"active"* students who worked on the assignments; and *"qualified"* active students who passed the qualification mark in Figure 1. The steady decline in total participation is consistent with other MOOCs [7], but the breakdown of students into the active and qualified subpopulations is uncommon and revealing. In fact, the retention rate of the qualified students is very good and differs from other student groups.

4.2 Gamification

This section presents results suggesting the positive effect of the leader board in motivating students to push their solutions beyond a grade of 100%. Indeed, there is, in general, a significant gap between a grade of 100% and the best-known solutions on some of the hardest assignments. To illustrate the changes in the leader board over time, Figure 3 provides a detailed example of the submission behavior of a few of the best students on a representative assignment. Each line in the figure represents the submission quality over time of a single student and the solid dots indicate new solution submissions. The horizontal dashed line indicates the quality threshold the student must achieve to get a perfect grade (i.e., h^2). The plot indicates that some students choose to stop working on the problem after achieving 10 points (e.g., the single dot at the center of the figure), while others continue to work on the problem after achieving full credit (e.g., the concentration of points in the bottom right). Although

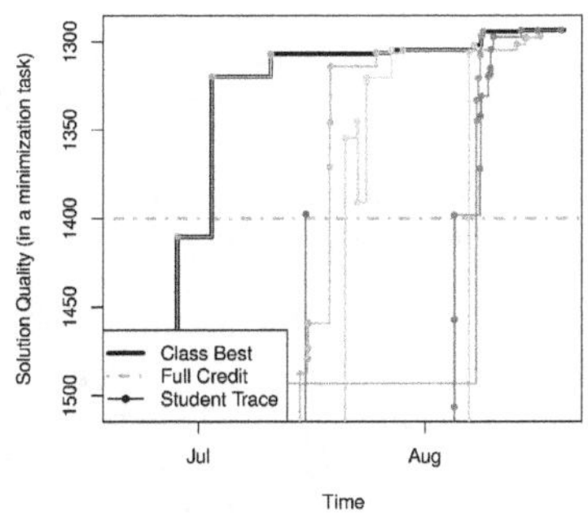

Figure 3: The Submission Behavior of the Best Students on a Particular Assignment over Time.

the true motivations of these student is unknown, the submission behaviors are consistent with a competition for the best position on the leader board.

Figure 3 is somewhat anecdotal and it is important to consider the class as a whole. Of the 4,000 students who participated seriously in the assignments, 89.4% received at least one full-credit score and 61.6% went on to make additional submissions beyond the 10 point mark. Focusing on the 61.6% of students that made additional submissions, the majority of those students submitted twice, but over 500 students submitted 3, 4, or 5 times after achieving a perfect score. The most active students submitted over 20 times after getting full credit. These aggregate results indicate that many students are submitting after receiving full credit and beg a more formal study of the leader board to precisely understand student motivations.

4.3 Open Course Structure

Section 3 suggested that the open course structure helped accommodate the heterogeneous student body. This section analyzes the assignment submission behavior of the students to better understand how the open course structure affected assignments. Figure 4 shows the submissions of the assignments on each day, over the 9 weeks (63 days) the course was open. Observe that the number of submissions on a given day greatly exceeds the number of students active in the assignments. This indicates that students are submitting their results for feedback often. The submissions are broken down by assignment to indicate which assignment students are working on. In a classic rolling assignment deadline design, one would expect a series of peeks as students focused on finishing the assignments before the deadline. In this figure, we see only two peaks: on the knapsack assignment in the first two weeks of class and on the last CVRP assignment at the end of class when students put in extra effort just before the final deadline. The lack of peaks in the assignment submissions between the start and end of the course could be explained by two student behaviors: (1) students are taking advantage of new insights and bouncing between assignments to improve their solutions; (2) the students are working at very different rates on the assignments. The next analysis supports these two points and focuses on the 800 students who attempted every assignment at least once.

To understand how students switch between assignments we can model their submission behavior as a state transition diagram, as in Figure 5. States in the diagram are assignments and edges represent the average number of transitions

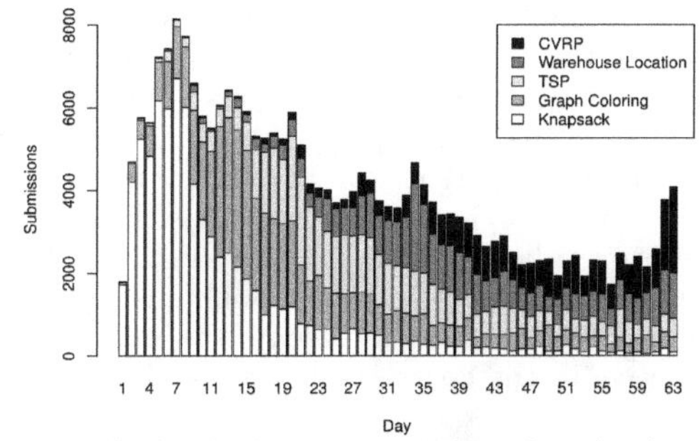

Figure 4: Submissions over Time by Assignment.

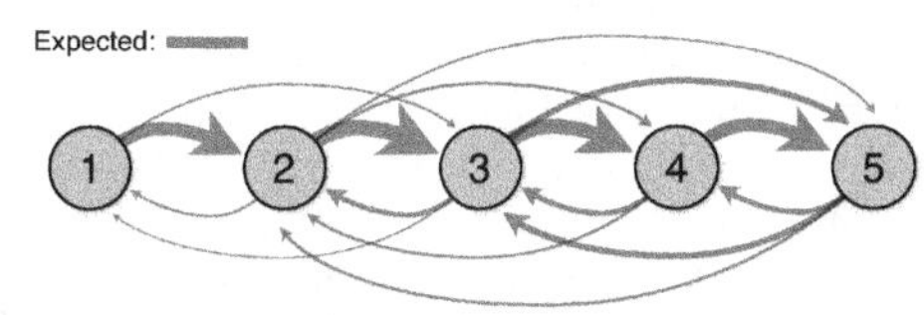

Figure 5: Transition Activity (without self-loops and edges below 10%).

between assignments for the student body. In a classic design of rolling assignment deadlines, this transition diagram would have strong self-loops (i.e., from assignment x to assignment x) where students repeatedly work on the same assignment and strong transitions to the next assignments (i.e., from assignment x to assignment x+1). All other transitions are only possible in an open assignment design. Figure 5 presents the assignment transition behavior in the discrete optimization MOOC. On average, we would expect each student to make one transition between each assignment. This is indicated by an expected line thickness in the diagram. The figure reveals that there is a strong trend for students to move in a serial manner between the assignments. However, a significant number of students move between the assignments. The strongest trend is between assignments 3 (TSP) and 5 (CVRP), which is particularly revealing as there is a strong mathematical connection between those two problems.

The transitions between assignments alone cannot explain the submission distribution in Figure 4. The other explanation is that students are working in a serial manner but the rate at which they complete the assignments is very different. To understand the rate that students complete the assignments, we can look at the total number of days between their first and last submissions. The median value reveals that half of the students took more than 50 days while the other half took less then 50 days to complete the assignments. Several students even completed the course in just two weeks. This wide variety of completion rates helps to explain Figure 4 and indicates the variety of skill levels and time investments of the student body.

4.4 Community Development

The success of the community development goals are the most challenging to demonstrate, but some insight is provided by behavioral statistics. The students took great advantage of the unlimited assignment feedback. Among the 800 students who attempted all five assignments, each student submitted a solution 5.9 times on average. Students viewed the leader board often, leading to a total of 61,000 views over the class duration. In a survey where students were asked if they enjoyed the leader board, 66% responded "yes", 3% responded "no" and 31% were indifferent. It was observed that the leader board inspired some students to ask direct questions to the best students of the class in the forums. This led to excellent threads where the best students shared their experience on the assignments. Students enjoyed the live analytics of Figure 1, which accumulated 13,000 views over the seven weeks it was available. The mailbags were very popular with number of unique views ranging from 9,000 to 2,000, which represents the vast majority of students active in the course on the week the mailbag was delivered.

The most telling evidence for the successful community development appears in the thousands of free form text that student produced via the class forums and surveys, which are difficult to summarize in this paper. Hundreds of students shared similar sentiments to this representative comment *"the continuous TAs presence in the forums and the mailbags make [the course] feel alive, instead of being simply a pre-recorded set of information pills fed to us."* Despite the apparent benefits discussed here, this topic could be expanded significantly with further study and analysis.

4.5 Success as a MOOC

Although awarding 795 certificates of completion was a great success in itself, there are many other ways to measure a class's success. The goal of discrete optimization was to provide a challenging course where dedicated students would learn a lot. The following statistics from a post-course survey of the students ($n = 622$) indicate those goals were achieved. 94.5% of students said they had a positive overall experience in the course with 40.7% of students marking their experience as excellent. 71.9% of students found the course to be challenging while only 6.11% thought that it was too difficult. The students were very dedicated to the challenging material with 56.6% working more than 10 hours per week. Despite the significant time investment, the vast majority, 93.7%, of students, felt that the assignment grading was fair. 94.5% of students said that they learned a significant amount from the course and 74.9% feel confident in their ability to apply the course material to real-world applications. It is also interesting to compare the MOOC post-course survey data to those collected in the classroom critical review. Table 3 compares four of the key survey questions across both version of the class. Despite the vastly different delivery system, the results are remarkably similar.

Topic	Scale	Classroom $n = 22$	MOOC $n = 622$
Hours per Week	1 to 20	14.5	12.2
Overall Experience	1-pos., 5-neg.	1.50	1.85
Difficulty	1-hard, 5-easy	1.64	1.14
Learned	1-lot, 5-little	1.41	2.04

Table 3: Classroom vs MOOC Experience.

When the students were asked the open ended question, *"My favorite part of this this course is ..."*, many aspects of the course were discussed. However, looking at the top five most common words in their responses, $\langle assignment, 222\rangle$, $\langle programming, 196\rangle$, $\langle lectures, 141\rangle$, $\langle time, 124\rangle$, $\langle search, 84\rangle$, it is clear that the programming assignments were one of the most popular parts of the class. Which is also consistent with the critical review of the classroom version of discrete optimization (see quotes from Section 2.4).

5. CONCLUSIONS

Teaching the creative problem skills required by discrete optimization practitioners is a challenging task. This paper has reviewed our experience in teaching such skills in the classroom and in a MOOC. Both course designs were motivated by discovery-based learning, continuous feedback, and gamification. Surprisingly, the students from both classes reported similar learning experiences in terms of time commitment, overall experience, difficulty, and overall learning, which suggests that the learning experience of the classroom was effectively replicated in the MOOC version. A first look at the data provided by the MOOC suggests that the course design choices, had a positive effect on student motivation and online learning. However, these findings are still anecdotal and we hope this work will support and inspire new, rigorous studies on how these course design choices can create effective online learning experiences at the MOOC scale.

6. ACKNOWLEDGMENTS

The authors would like to thank Victor Pillac and Gregor Kennedy for their criticism and insight in the preparation of this paper, the Learning and Teaching initiative at the University of Melbourne for supporting this work, and the students and teaching assistants of the classroom version. This work was conducted in part at NICTA and is funded by the Australian Government as represented by the Department of Broadband, Communications and the Digital Economy and the Australian Research Council through the ICT Centre of Excellence program.

7. REFERENCES

[1] H. Banchi and R. Bell. The many levels of inquiry. *Science and Children*, 46(2):26–29, 2008.

[2] J. S. Bruner. The act of discovery. *Harvard Educational Review*, 31:21–32, 1961.

[3] S. Cooper and M. Sahami. Reflections on stanford's moocs. *Commun. ACM*, 56(2):28–30, Feb. 2013.

[4] P. Hyman. In the year of disruptive education. *Commun. ACM*, 55(12):20–22, Dec. 2012.

[5] J. Kay, P. Reimann, E. Diebold, and B. Kummerfeld. Moocs: So many learners, so much potential ... *Intelligent Systems, IEEE*, 28(3):70–77, 2013.

[6] R. F. Kizilcec, C. Piech, and E. Schneider. Deconstructing disengagement: analyzing learner subpopulations in massive open online courses. In *Proceedings of the Third International Conference on Learning Analytics and Knowledge*, LAK '13, pages 170–179, New York, NY, USA, 2013. ACM.

[7] MOOCs@Edinburgh Group. Moocs @ edinburgh 2013: Report #1, may 2013.

[8] C. Severance. Teaching the world: Daphne koller and coursera. *Computer*, 45(8):8–9, 2012.

[9] A. Vihavainen, M. Luukkainen, and J. Kurhila. Multi-faceted support for mooc in programming. In *Proceedings of the 13th annual conference on Information technology education*, SIGITE '12, pages 171–176, New York, NY, USA, 2012. ACM.

Introducing Undergraduate Database Students to K-12 Education Research

Chris Mayfield
James Madison University
Harrisonburg, Virginia, USA
mayfiecs@jmu.edu

Carole Ottenheimer
Center for Innovative Technology
Herndon, Virginia, USA
carole.ottenheimer@cit.org

Bethann Canada
Virginia Department of Education
Richmond, Virginia, USA
bethann.canada@doe.virginia.gov

Brooke Bell
Center for Innovative Technology
Herndon, Virginia, USA
brooke.bell@cit.org

ABSTRACT

Apps4VA is a bold initiative to improve K-12 education by leveraging data on Virginia public school students' progress toward college and career readiness. The goal of the project is for students, professionals, and the general public to create "apps" that explore new ways of using K-12 education data to aid in better data-driven decisions and intervention strategies. In Spring 2013, sixty students in a database systems course participated in a semester-long project based on Apps4VA. This paper describes our teaching experiences, reports our lessons learned working with education data, and documents improvements in student outcomes. We also describe how instructors of database and data analytics courses may partner with local governments to adopt similar projects in their communities.

Categories and Subject Descriptors

K.3.2 [**Computer and Information Science Education**]: Computer Science Education

General Terms

Management, Verification

Keywords

Project-based learning, peer assessment, longitudinal data

1. INTRODUCTION

Since the advent of No Child Left Behind (NCLB) in 2001, the role of performance-based standards in K-12 education in the United States has greatly increased. Departments of Education—and ultimately individual teachers—are under increasing pressure to demonstrate student success via measurable outcomes, including standardized test scores and graduation rates [1]. A recent study of rural school systems details the challenges and pressures that principals experience in fulfilling NCLB. Recruiting highly qualified, committed teachers as well as "ensuring that all students achieve at levels mandated by NCLB" is overwhelming [10].

SIGCSE'14, March 5–8, 2014, Atlanta, GA, USA.

ACM 978-1-4503-2605-6/14/03 ...$15.00.
http://dx.doi.org/10.1145/2538862.2538957.

The US Congress passed additional legislation in 2009 under The American Recovery and Reinvestment Act (ARRA) that allocated billions of dollars of funding for states to make improvements to their education systems. One of the selection criteria was "Data Systems to Support Instruction," which resulted in a number of states creating or enhancing systems to track the performance of individual students over the course of their entire K-12 education [6]. The intent was that by using selected sets from the wide array of publicly available data, educators and policy makers will be better able to make informed decisions to improve the efficiency and effectiveness of their schools.

Notwithstanding the controversies fomented by these requirements and systems [8], they are creating new opportunities for leveraging computing to make a positive impact on education at all levels [11]. State departments of education are collecting and releasing an ever increasing amount of data. As computer science educators, we can take advantage of these new sources of data to engage and motivate our students through projects that are relevant to them. After all, today's university students are among the first generation of K-12 students that modern "Data Systems to Support Instruction" were designed to assess.

This paper describes our experiences integrating education research into an undergraduate database systems course. Over the course of a semester, sixty students participated in a coordinated effort to create new applications featuring publicly available data for education researchers. For many of the students, the data was about them, their schools, and their state. We observed a substantial increase in student engagement and performance as a result of this work. In addition, the students gained valuable insight into how large amounts of data may be used to help improve the K-12 education system.

1.1 Apps4VA Initiative

In 2009, the Virginia Department of Education (VDOE) developed a data system that would include linking teachers to their students (while protecting student privacy and confidentiality) known as the Virginia Longitudinal Data System (VLDS).[1] This system, supported through a federal grant funded through the ARRA program, was created to provide educators and policy makers aggregate data on Virginia school students' progress toward college and career readiness. In order to raise awareness of the existence of VLDS and to highlight its power and potential, VDOE, in collaboration with the Center for Innovative Technology's (CIT) CIT Connect,[2] launched a software application development program known as Apps4VA. This program was the first apps competition sponsored by a state education department. It challenged the public to review K-12 data and use it to design software solutions ("apps") that would be new and innovative tools to aid in better data-driven decisions and intervention strategies.

A successful apps challenge engages a wide demographic of participants, many of whom might not normally be engaged in the education arena. To that end, in addition to employing traditional methods of outreach, Apps4VA undertook a number of unconventional events and programs to promote community engagement and to reach targeted audiences[3] including: a weekend-long startup challenge, four simultaneous hackathons,[4] a competition for Virginia public high school students, and an open competition for the general public. Participants in all events were encouraged to identify educational needs and to develop software applications to address these needs.

The only development limitation placed on participants was a requirement that these applications would be based on at least one of the published data sets from the VLDS catalog. Simply incorporating a small piece of the data in an application (i.e., as an afterthought) was insufficient. To be competitive, developers must have created new ways for stakeholders and/or the public at large to analyze, understand, and make informed decisions based on the data. Mashups with other data sources were not only allowed, but encouraged. Cash prizes were offered for the winners of the various competitions as incentives to participate.

1.2 VLDS Data Sets

The following nine data sets are available online for researchers and developers. Each data set is a collection of CSV files, with one file for each year. In January 2013, the files comprised about 4.5 GB of data. The data sets are well documented, and a dictionary of each attribute is available on the VDOE website.[5] Each row of data is uniquely identified using the following values: school year, division number, school number, grade level, and demographic group (which includes race, gender, disabled status, English proficiency, and disadvantaged status).

- **Fall Membership:** Number of students enrolled in Virginia public schools on Sep 30th.
- **Dec 1st Count:** Number of students with disabilities receiving special education.
- **Test Data:** Average scores and pass/fail rates for English, History, Math, and Science.
- **CTE Completers:** How many students completed Career and Technical Education course sequences.
- **HS Graduates:** Number of high school graduates and completers of similar diplomas.
- **Annual Dropouts:** Summer and term dropouts in grades 7–12 (who did not return by Oct 1st).
- **Cohort Rates:** On-time graduation rates for students entering 9th grade together.
- **Postsecondary Enrollment:** High school graduates enrolled in postsecondary institutions nationwide.
- **Postsecondary Achievement:** High school graduates enrolled in public higher education in Virginia who earned one year of college credit within two years.

What makes these data sets particularly interesting for use in a university-level database course is that the underlying information is both *aggregated* and *suppressed*. As stated on the download site, "The datasets are compiled using all the possible combinations of all the demographics about students, so each row within the dataset contains a rate or count in addition to the demographics used to arrive at the rate or count." And further, "Within each dataset, rows were withheld if deemed that the number of students in the group could lead to the identification of a single student. In most cases, student groups of nine or fewer are suppressed."

1.3 About the Course

Given the richness of the VLDS data and the availability of materials from prior competitions, we decided to adopt Apps4VA as a semester-long project. Our course is an introduction to database systems that uses the textbook from Ullman and Widom [12]. One expected learning outcome of the course is that students will design and implement a substantial three-tier application. At this point in our CS department's curriculum, students have completed the introductory programming sequence and courses in data structures and software engineering. The database course is an ideal opportunity for students to synthesize what they have learned in these prerequisites.

A major benefit of this project-based learning approach is that students have a meaningful running example throughout the course. When we first looked at how data can be represented (e.g., entity-relationship model, relational model, semi-structured model), we illustrated the pros and cons of each model using VLDS data. Later in the course, students learned how to write relational algebra and SQL statements using VLDS data. In addition, we were able to motivate

[1]For more information on the Virginia Longitudinal Data System, visit `http://www.doe.virginia.gov/info_management/longitudinal_data_system` and `vlds.virginia.gov`.

[2]CIT is a state-chartered non-profit organization with a mission to accelerate technology development in the Commonwealth of Virginia. Recognizing a need in the marketplace, CIT Connect was established to help federal, state, and corporate consumers of technology to identify and assimilate innovation.

[3]In addition to the general public, some of the communities targeted were computer programmers, software developers and designers, Web designers, researchers, entrepreneurs, and educators.

[4]The hackathons were 24-hour events in which computer programmers, software designers, graphic designers and others formed teams to develop usable software applications.

[5]See `http://www.doe.virginia.gov/statistics_reports/research_data/`

functional dependency theory using VLDS, especially since the data had been joined and aggregated prior to release. As a result, students not only learned the content of the course, they also became familiar with nuances in the data that, ultimately, would direct their semester projects.

2. PROJECT DELIVERABLES

Students worked on their Apps4VA projects throughout the semester, submitting work about every two weeks. In this section, we briefly describe the nature of the assigned deliverables and how they were assessed, with the intent that readers will be able to adopt similar projects in their own courses. Additional information about each project is available on our website: `http://apps4va.cs.jmu.edu/`

In order to stimulate creativity and to help students to imagine the types of applications that could be developed, we discussed the submission of a finalist of the Apps4VA Open Competition.[6] This developer generated a KML file suitable for Google Earth that enabled users to navigate the VLDS data set in new and interesting ways. In general, students could be allowed to develop a wide variety of solutions ranging from traditional desktop software to mobile apps and web services. But to level the playing field and to simplify the administration of the projects, we required our students to develop a web application using Servlets and JSPs. (Java is the primary language of our introductory course sequence.)

The specific language and database technology being used are not as important as being consistent within the course. In previous years (before we adopted Apps4VA), we allowed students to make their own technology choices with the understanding that the instructor would not be able to provide support beyond examples shown in class. But doing so led to problems with one or two students being enthusiastic about their chosen framework (e.g., Ruby on Rails) while the rest of their team became frustrated and unable to contribute to the project.

2.1 Written Proposal

As with many semester-long projects, we began by having students write a short proposal (750 to 1000 words). We require this assignment as early as possible, typically at the beginning of the second week. The early assignment, in turn, requires the students to select their teammates during the first week of class. To help students understand the project as a whole and to help them to decide on the type of applications they would build, we directed them to review the Apps4VA website. This website has several resources[7] that we found to be useful.

- *Educational Data Primer*: Describes what data is collected, why it is important, and how it can be used to make improvements to the K-12 educational system.
- *Idea Bank and Blog*: Highlights the needs, requests, and suggestions from teachers, administrators, and policy makers, as well as the community at large.
- *Data Sets*: Provides detailed instructions on accessing the required data from VLDS, as well as optional data from other governmental agencies (e.g., census records, health statistics).

[6]See `http://www.starsman.com/VEGAS.html`

[7]See `http://www.apps4va.org/resources.html`

Students were instructed to spend at least two hours reviewing the website's resource information before starting their actual write-ups. We found that the most important aspect of this assignment was for students to identify a "specific K-12 education research problem" to be addressed through their projects. Having students focus on education research not only made the project more focused, it also prevented students from adding unnecessary features for the sake of turning in copious amounts of code at the end of the semester.

We spent nearly an entire class period for students to review proposal submissions from other teams. Each team received a folder containing three proposals and three copies of a rubric that was available to them when the assignment was posted. They were to spend ten minutes reading and marking up each proposal as a team, and then filling out the rubric to determine its grade. We then collected the rubrics and set up a rotation for each team to meet with the authors they reviewed and give to constructive feedback for improving the proposal.

This peer assessment encourages collaboration, facilitates the exchange of ideas, communicates expectations, and provides an active learning environment [5]. Students were encouraged to revise and resubmit their work by the next class period. As a result, the research questions and project ideas were clearly specified, and the writing quality was much better when the instructor reviewed the proposals in detail.

2.2 Schema Design

The next phase of the project required students (1) to create an initial set of tables to support their applications and (2) to write scripts designed to extract, transform, and load VLDS data into their database. Most of our students have little, if any, prior experience designing databases. At this point of the semester, they are familiar with relational algebra and SQL, but have not yet studied functional dependencies and normalization. We found that having students work though the design process early motivates theoretical topics later in the course.

We also introduced students to Subversion and required them to maintain all project-related files in a repository. This practice not only helped them to develop a useful skill, it made it easier for them to make changes to the database design throughout the semester [9]. During their subsequent projects and homework assignments, students learned how to improve their work, identify what was missing, and/or develop new ideas. Since their entire databases were created using scripts, they were free to experiment with incremental changes without the risk of losing their work.

To assist the instructor in assessing their designs, we required students to create a relational database diagram that indicated the number of rows imported into each table. Most of the major mistakes that students made in writing the queries that transformed the VLDS data became apparent by looking at the row counts. The tasks of designing and importing real data reinforced one other and, in turn, helped students to understand the nature of the relational model.

2.3 Example Queries

For this project, students had complete flexibility in the direction they took. The basic requirements were (1) to revise their schema based on instructor feedback and (2) to design and implement ten queries their application would use. As in the previous assignment, the two steps reinforced one other. As students began to design queries, they discovered false assumptions they made about the underlying data sets. They also identified aspects of their designs that made writing some queries more difficult than necessary. Once they completed this assignment, they were ready to begin analyzing the data and answering the educational research problems they originally proposed.

For those interested in adopting this type of semester project, some deliverables should, ideally, include a formative community-based assessment. So that students might have the benefit of a real-world perspective, we invited three representatives from industry and government to meet with each group of students during class time. These visitors were experts in the field of data analytics for K-12 education, and their involvement generated a high level of engagement among the students. Each group had the opportunity to explain their research problems and demonstrate results from some of their queries. The feedback students received greatly influenced the direction of their projects by identifying additional resources and refining their educational research questions.

2.4 Detailed Design

Now that students had proposed, designed, and "sold" their projects, they were ready to develop their final applications. The deliverable for this assignment was a detailed list of functional requirements and a table that outlines which JSPs will implement which features. In addition, students were to fully implement at least one web form. Since most students had little or no experience in web development, the goal of this assignment was to give them a big picture of three-tier architecture and to clarify the technical steps of setting up and deploying their projects. In addition, students spent time learning any third party tools or APIs they planned to use, such as Google Charts and Google Maps.

The feedback that students received from this project was primarily summative. Most, if not all, student groups were able to get something up and running by this point. Some feedback about their choices of requirements was necessary in order for all to agree on a final deliverable, but that often happened during class time while we discussed each group's progress on their design.

2.5 Initial Prototype

We deliberately made this deliverable the most important deadline of the semester. Rather than giving students until the last week of class to complete their projects, we evaluated their prototype systems two weeks before their final presentations. The only instruction they were given was that they had to complete the requirements they submitted in the previous assignment. Students were provided a rubric that specified the review criteria for three aspects of their projects: functionality, performance, and code quality. The instructor evaluated each project during class time so that students could conduct an interactive demonstration of their work. Specific follow-up requirements were given for students to complete by the end of the semester.

2.6 Final Presentation

Finally, students presented their work to the class and to the industry and government mentors described previously. Their presentations focused on the educational research problems addressed by their applications, their applications' main features, the primary users and beneficiaries of their work, what improvements to education they might expect to result from their applications, and any future work they have identified. As with the third deliverable, we incorporated a community-based assessment into this final presentation. The industry and government collaborators participated as review panelists. They congratulated students on their hard work and offered real-world critiques and insights on their applications and the results they generated.

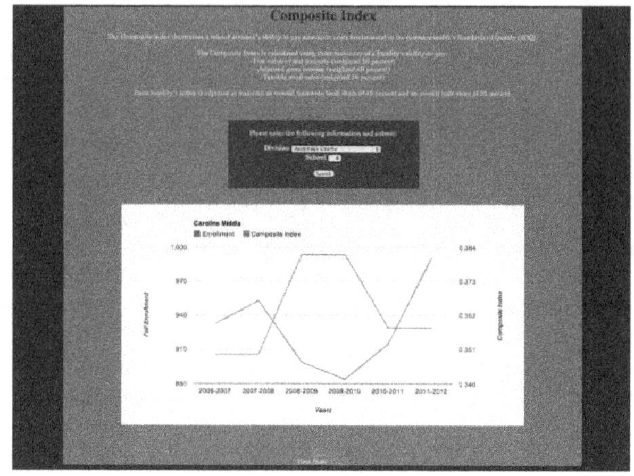

Figure 1: Screenshot of Graduation Rates vs Funding Levels

3. EXAMPLE APPLICATIONS

We now present three web-based applications that students developed during the course. These concrete examples illustrate the types of projects students can pursue using the VLDS data. The particular applications we have selected are representative of those developed by all student teams and provide context for the outcomes described in the next section of the paper.

3.1 Graduation Rates vs Funding Levels

One team of students was particularly interested in helping educators and administrators prepare more effectively for future student enrollment. They also were concerned about how tax dollars would be spent: "Our application enables policy makers and educators to view information on different student groups by referencing divisions, schools, test scores, and graduation rates in Virginia in order to distribute funding to the areas that are most in need." Figure 1 shows how the application compares a school division's enrollment count (lower line) with the community's ability to pay education costs (upper line). This "composite index" is based on property values, adjusted gross income, and taxable retail sales. In this example, enrollment suddenly increased while the composite index decreased.

3.2 Education Programs vs Workforce Needs

Another team asked two questions that often resonate with parents of high school students: "(1) Are students being prepared for real-world jobs? (2) What jobs are in demand in their area of the state?" The students explained, "Our application allows policy makers and superintendents of school

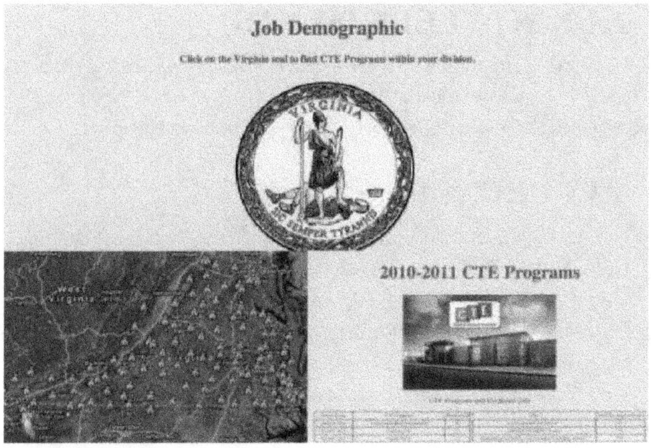

Figure 2: Screenshot of Education Programs vs Workforce Needs

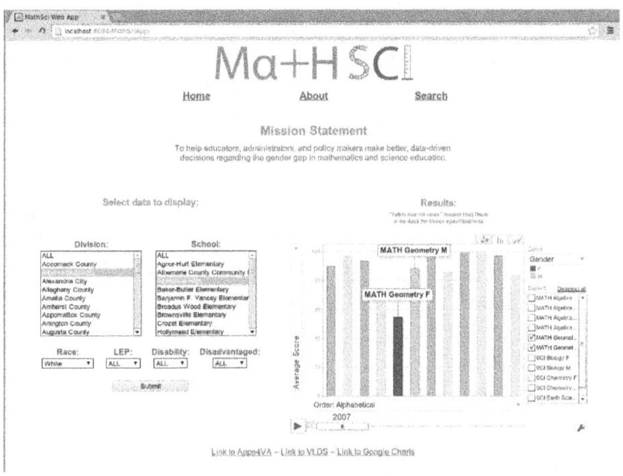

Figure 3: Screenshot of Gender in Math and Science Education

divisions to look at the industry projections for different careers and match them to the programs they offer at their career and technical education schools. The app is based on the CTE Program Graduates and Completers VLDS 2010–2011 data, as well as Labor Force and Industry Projections from the Virginia Workforce Connection. These individuals will utilize our app to determine which CTE programs they need to offer based on the top industry projections."

As illustrated in this example, most student groups developed applications for administrators, policy makers, and teachers. However, these types of users already have access to sophisticated tools and reports tied directly to VLDS. One lesson we learned during the mid-semester and final presentations is there is a substantial need (and an emerging market) for tools that focus on local communities. If parents, students, and local leaders understand what the data is saying about their schools, they will be in a better position to ask for meaningful changes in curricula and programs.

3.3 Gender in Math and Science Education

Our final example project examines the gender gap in mathematics and science test performance across grade levels. These students leveraged motion charts to "enable policy makers and administrators to view data regarding mathematics and science education among different genders and identifying factors." Figure 3 shows the relative test scores between males and females at a specific school (selected on the left). Each pair of bars represents the math and science exams offered in each grade level. By clicking the play button or dragging the slider, the user can see how scores increase and decrease over time. This visualization makes it relatively easy for someone unfamiliar with VLDS to understand the types of data available and to use it in a meaningful way.

4. STUDENT OUTCOMES

In comparison to previous offerings of the course, students involved with Apps4VA were particularly engaged in their semester-long projects. Although we did not conduct a rigorous study to measure student attitudes quantitatively, we do have some data points that indicate our adoption of Apps4VA was successful. For one, the number of students who withdrew or failed the course greatly decreased as shown in Table 1. (Note: Students who withdraw from the course before the mid-semester deadline receive a W grade on their transcript. Since W grades are not counted in GPA calculations, this action is recommended to students who are likely to receive an F grade at the end of the semester.)

Year	D	W	F	Rate
2012	4	6	4	23%
2013	7	1	1	15%

Table 1: Comparison of D, W, and F grades (same course, same instructor, 60 students each year)

The course project in 2012 introduced students to computer science research literature by requiring them to build a web application featuring citation data from DBLP.[8] We required the same deliverables as those described in this paper, and we used DBLP as a running example throughout the course. However, we did not have a community-based assessment (i.e., external collaborators reviewing the students' work) and the resulting projects simply were not intended to impact society at large. These factors may have contributed to a higher level of cohesion and commitment among this year's group members.

We did not see a significant difference in overall student performance in the course, in terms of their final exams or individual project scores. However, the overall rigor and expectations of the course were much higher in 2013. Both the quality of the final presentations and student feedback on course evaluations showed vast improvement from the previous offerings. Based on these assessments, students appeared to learn more content and learn it more efficiently than in prior years.

After the course concluded, one of the organizers of the Apps4VA competitions who helped to evaluate this year's final presentations observed the following: "While one of the goals of the program was to discover creative uses for the data, it turned out that discovering creative stakeholders and participants was a surprisingly welcome outcome. The apps developed by these student developers rivaled and, in some cases, eclipsed those designed by professional developers." A number of students indicated via email and in

[8]See `http://dblp.uni-trier.de/`

private conversations that Apps4VA gave them something concrete to discuss in their job interviews.

5. RELATED WORK

This work documents effective practices for the teaching of database systems and data analytics. In recent years, a number of experience papers have proposed complementary techniques for enhancing database courses. [4] demonstrated promising results by incorporating a "Contributing Student Pedagogy" where groups of students become responsible for the delivery of course content. The paper reports on two iterations using this teaching method and shows that having multiple deliverables helps students to produce higher quality presentations. [7] explored the use of "Just-in-Time Teaching" in a database course, where students completed online warm-up assignments prior to each class. Warm-ups make it possible to address students' specific needs, and the paper shows how this practice improves exam scores and final grades. [3] introduced a suite of exercises using "Language INtegrated Query" (LINQ) in the database curriculum. The paper showed how LINQ not only can meet learning objectives of typical database assignments, but also support program outcomes by exposing students to functional programming.

Two important aspects of our work include community-based assessments and collaborative student projects. As shown in [2], these "developmental interaction experiences" lead to more career development, business knowledge, and psychosocial support among students. Our work is also related to the growing body of literature that studies No Child Left Behind and other recent legislation. The references in the Introduction of this paper provide a good starting point. As computer science students begin to wrestle with these complex social issues within the context of their major courses, they make connections to the human dimension that results in significant learning [5].

6. CONCLUSION

We have described our experiences in integrating K-12 education research into an introductory database course. Our hope is that other instructors will achieve similar results and benefits by implementing these projects in their courses. The data sets provided by Apps4VA and VLDS are rich and meaningful, well documented, and freely available. We encourage readers of this paper to form partnerships with departments of education and local governments to make similar data sets available from their respective states and countries. This type of application development has the potential to impact students and local communities in many positive ways. In our experience, students were motivated to develop successful, high-quality projects because the data was about them and the future of their educational system.

7. ACKNOWLEDGMENTS

We thank the students of teams *Infinity*, *JobDemo*, and *MathSci* for allowing us to write about their projects, use their screenshots, and quote their presentations.

8. REFERENCES

[1] K. Anthes. *School and District Leadership.* No Child Left Behind Policy Brief. Education Commission of the States, Denver, CO, USA, 2002.

[2] C. D'Abate. Developmental Interactions for Business Students: Do They Make a Difference? *Journal of Leadership and Organizational Studies*, 17(2):143–155, 2010.

[3] S. W. Dietrich and M. Chaudhari. LINQ ROX!: Integrating LINQ into the Database Curriculum. In *Proceedings of the 42nd ACM Technical Symposium on Computer Science Education*, SIGCSE '11, pages 293–298, 2011.

[4] H. A. Etlinger. Adding a Contributing Student Pedagogy Component to an Introductory Database Course. In *Proceedings of the 44th ACM Technical Symposium on Computer Science Education*, SIGCSE '13, pages 299–304, 2013.

[5] L. D. Fink. *Creating Significant Learning Experiences: An Integrated Approach to Designing College Courses.* Jossey-Bass, San Francisco, CA, USA, 2003.

[6] J. C. Kabaker. 20 States Receive State Longitudinal Data Systems Grants. New America Foundation, Washington, DC, USA, May 2010.

[7] A. Martinez. Using JITT in a Database Course. In *Proceedings of the 43rd ACM Technical Cymposium on Computer Science Education*, SIGCSE '12, pages 367–372, 2012.

[8] R. Reback, J. Rockoff, and H. L. Schwartz. *Under Pressure: Job Security, Resource Allocation, and Productivity in Schools Under NCLB.* NBER Working Paper 16745. National Bureau of Economic Research, Cambridge, MA, USA, 2011.

[9] D. Rocco and W. Lloyd. Distributed Version Control in the Classroom. In *Proceedings of the 42nd ACM Technical Symposium on Computer Science Education*, SIGCSE '11, pages 637–642, 2011.

[10] A. P. Scandrett. *Principals' Perspectives of the No Child Left Behind Act of 2001 as They Relate to Personnel in a Rural School System.* PhD thesis, Mercer University, 2010.

[11] J. Supovitz, E. Foley, and J. Mishook. In Search of Leading Indicators in Education. *Education Policy Analysis Archives*, 20(19), 2012.

[12] J. D. Ullman and J. Widom. *A First Course in Database Systems.* Prentice-Hall, Inc., Upper Saddle River, NJ, USA, 2007.

Remediation and Student Success in CIS Programs

Douglas A. Kranch
North Central State College
2441 Kenwood Circle
Mansfield, OH 44901
419-755-4788
dkranch@ncstatecollege.edu

ABSTRACT
This retrospective study of the performance of Computer Information Systems (CIS) students from between 1987 and 2010 found evidence that remedial math, reading, and writing courses can significantly increase student mean GPA, persistence, and completion in a CIS program. Remediation was most effective when verbal as well as mathematical deficiencies were addressed, and the performance of fully remediated students was indistinguishable as a group from students not requiring remediation.

Categories and Subject Descriptors
K.3.2 [Computers and Education]: Computer and Information Science Education

General Terms
Measurement, Human Factors.

Keywords
Remediation, novice learner, computer science readiness.

1. INTRODUCTION
Teaching computer studies courses has had notoriously low success for decades. Programming, for example, has been a problem "for almost 40 years" [Bennedsen and Caspersen, 2008, p. 2] that is significant enough to make the effective teaching of programming one of the seven grand challenges of computing [McGettrick, et al., 2005]. Students regard programming courses as difficult and many drop out before completing them [Robins, Rountree, & Rountree, 2003]. One approach to discovering the reason for this is to focus on the way the material is presented; however, to the knowledge of this researcher, no published study has compared student success in remediation courses with success in computer studies programs.

Previous studies have pointed to mathematic readiness and, to a lesser extent, reading readiness as reliable predictors of success in a computer studies program. This study explored the readiness of students in these two areas as they began their postsecondary studies and the relationship between remediating critical knowledge and skill gaps in these areas and program success. The goal of this study was to evaluate the impact remedial courses had on student success in computer studies.

SIGCSE'14, March 5–8, 2014, Atlanta, Georgia, USA.

2. LITERATURE REVIEW
The literature review focuses on studies that looked for relationships between mathematics, reading, or writing and performance in CS1 or other programming courses. Since the nature of programming has remained essentially the same over the past 40 years, any relevant study from this period is included. The studies reviewed here assessed performance as measured by the score received on an assessment instrument or instruments within a single course (generally the first programming course) or course module. While such studies cannot predict the long-term success in an entire computer studies program, they provide a starting point for exploring what knowledge and skill gaps there are in students who did not perform well in the courses.

2.1 Mathematics
Research studies have consistently shown that indirect indicators of mathematics proficiency are positively correlated with successful post-secondary course performance. An oft-studied indicator is the number of high school mathematics courses taken. Werth [1986] found that the letter grade for a CS1 course correlated moderately with the number of high school mathematics courses completed ($r=0.252$, $p<.05$). Evans and Simkin [1989] also found the number of high school mathematics courses completed was the most significant factor in a stepwise linear regression on homework assignments; however, R^2 was only .23. Leeper and Silver [1982] found a similar result for the number of high school mathematics courses taken ($R^2 = .25$, $p <$ 001). They also used the SAT mathematics score as a second surrogate for mathematical achievement and found a lower but still significant coefficient of determination ($R^2 = .18$, $p < .001$). Konvalina, Wileman, and Stephens [1983] determined that students in their group who took significantly more high school and college math courses beforehand persisted longer in a CS1 course. Wilson and Shrock [2001] found mathematics background to be second in importance in their general linear model in predicting the score on the midterm grade.

Several reasons can be put forward why the number of courses taken in high school would increase performance and persistence. People tend to continue in areas in which they find success. Also, persistence breeds persistence; students who tenaciously complete courses that they start will carry that tenacity into post-secondary education. While the significance is high, number of courses explained only between 6 and 25 percent of the variance in these studies. Ventura [2005], in fact, found *no* correlation between the number of high school mathematics courses taken and success in an objects-first CS1 course. This would hint strongly that the manner in which the CS1 material is presented to students is a significant determinant of the relevance of previous math learning to CS1.

A second set of indirect math proficiency indicators that have been studied are achievement exams. Byrne and Lyons [2001] found a significant correlation between the examination score in a CS1 course and both a student's Irish Leaving Certificate mathematics result ($r = 0.35$, $p < .01$) and science result ($r = 0.57$, $p < .01$). For the 123 students in Bergin and Reilly's [2006] study, a higher Irish Leaving Certificate mathematics grade and programming self-esteem scores correlated with better CS1 course performance in four Irish postsecondary institutions. They used these two factors together with the number of hours playing computer games to correctly classify 82% of the students as weak or strong performers. Leeper and Silver [1982] used the SAT mathematics score as a surrogate for mathematical achievement and found a significant coefficient of determination ($R^2 = .18$, $p < .001$).

The importance of secondary school achievement exam scores to predicting performance in post-secondary courses centers on the validity of the exams. Mattern and Patterson [2009] show that the SAT score foreshadows second-year retention in that 95.5 percent of those in the highest score band (2100 to 2400) returning compared with 63.8 percent of those in the lowest score band (600 to 890). The SAT also discriminates within high school GPA bands. Students who have a high school GPA of A+, A, or A- and score 2100 or higher on the SAT have a mean retention rate of 96.0 percent while those who score between 900 and 1190 on the SAT have a mean retention rate of 76.8 percent. Studies such as these demonstrate that high school achievement exams have face validity. The Leaving Certificate math score explained 12 percent of the variance while the science score explained 32 percent. Science's emphasis on applying math to solve problems may help account for its greater role in the variance.

In a stepwise multiple regression analysis, Hostetler [1983] found a combination of factors to be effective in predicting success in a CS1 course as measured by the final score: two tests from the Computer Programmer Aptitude Battery (CPAB) (measuring the ability to convert a word problem into mathematical statements and the ability to convert a problem into a logical sequence of steps); a math scale indicating by an integer the most advanced mathematics course a student had passed, the higher the integer the more advanced the course; and the student's GPA at the beginning of the semester. Interestingly, Hostetler found that the math scale by itself had a correlation with course success of only .030.

Hostetler's results lead one to infer that the ability to see problems in terms of math statements and then to arrange those statements into a working algorithm are skills needed to perform well in CS1. Also, the quantity of high school courses rather how advanced they were seems to hold sway on future CS1 success. It seems the hours spent in math courses working word problems with interrelated demands develops necessary math skills to succeed in CS1.

2.2 Verbal Skill

Verbal skills have a lesser but still significant relationship with CS1 performance. Leeper and Silver [1982] found that the Verbal SAT score exhibited a moderate correlation with the CS1 grade students received ($r=.38$, $p<.001$). The correlation was even stronger for the units high school English completed ($r=.47$, $p<.001$) and foreign language completed ($r=.49$, $p<.001$).

Austin [1987] sought predictors of successful completion of a CS1 course, and included measures for program reading, program writing, and lab exercises. A composite measure was calculated from these component measures. He found verbal ability and the absence of negative computer attitudes to be the strongest predictors of program writing success.

Irons [1982] noted a "relatively strong relationship" [p. 222] between composing FORTRAN program code and induction and syllogistic reasoning ability. He also found the Delta Vocabulary test to be a reliable predictor of the CS1 total score, demonstrating a possible crossover between verbal and programming grammar skills. Wong, Cheung, and Chen [1998], however, found no correlation between expertise in a programming language and skill in using English and concluded that each may require a qualitatively different knowledge base. This seems to contradict the finding of Leeper and Silver [1982] above relating CS1 performance to units high school English completed. An important difference in these two studies is that Leeper and Silver used native English speakers while Wong, et al. did not. Wong et al. were comparing English as a language to English as a source for programming constructs while Leeper and Silver's units of high school English measured whether students took higher level English courses that used methods of analysis on genres of English literature.

In all of these studies, students are evaluated based on their performance on programming assignments, quizzes, and major examinations in a single CS1 course or module. Programming assignments require students to apply concepts from lecture material to solve stated problems. Exam material ranges from objective questions on theory and facts to the actual writing of programs. Performance on one or more of these measures is then compared with certain independent variables. What has not been done is (a) track student performance throughout the entire career to final outcomes at the post-secondary institution, (b) compare incoming levels of math, reading, and writing to outcomes, and (c) compare levels of these incoming variables *after remediation* to outcomes. This study addresses this gap.

3. HYPOTHESES AND DEFINITIONS

Definition 3.1 (GP). GP refers to the grade points assigned to an individual course. Grade points are assigned to a course according to letter grade where A = 4.00, A- = 3.67, B+ = 3.33, B = 3.0, B- = 2.67, C+ = 2.33, C = 2.00, C- = 1.67, D+ = 1.33, D = 1.00, D- = 0.67, and F = 0.00.

Definition 3.2 *(GPA).* GPA refers to the average of all grade points of all courses taken by a student and weighted by credit hours. If a discipline precedes GPA (e.g., CIS GPA), then it represents the weighted average of all grade points of all courses in that discipline alone.

Definition 3.3 (First CIS course). First CIS course is the first course taken in the CIS program by a student. The exact course varied depending on what quarter the student started and the interest of the student. For the majority of students this course was either an introductory programming or introductory networking course.

Definition 3.4 (Mean CIS GPA). Mean CIS GPA is the average of all grade points of all CIS courses taken by the student, weighted by credit hour. This was used as the measure of student success in the CIS program following the lead of the studies reviewed above. Specifically, Werth [1986] and Hostetler [1983] used the letter grade for a CS1 course; Evans and Simkin [1989] used homework assignment scores; Konvalina, Wileman, and Stephens [1983] used CS1 persistence; Wilson and Shrock [2001] used the score on the midterm exam; Byrne and Lyons [2001] used the final examination score in a CS1 course; and Bergin and Reilly's [2006] used a general measure of CS1 course performance.

Three hypotheses were tested in this study, all stated in null form. The first focused on whether a good grounding in mathematics, reading, and writing was significantly correlated with mastering CIS program knowledge and skills as measured by program completion rate.

HYPOTHESIS I. There is no significant correlation between the program completion rate of students and their entry course placement in mathematics, reading, or writing.

The next hypothesis compares the mean CIS GPA of students who entered the college needing remediation in mathematics, reading, or writing and passed all their remediation courses with students who needed no remediation.

HYPOTHESIS II. There is no significant difference in the mean CIS GPA between students who enter the college requiring and passing all required remedial mathematics, reading, and writing courses and students who enter requiring no remedial courses.

The last hypothesis tests the program completion rate of students needing no remediation and students who are fully remediated as indicated by having passed all required remediation courses.

HYPOTHESIS III. There is no significant difference in the program completion rate between students who enter the college requiring and passing all required remedial mathematics, reading, and writing courses and students who enter requiring no remedial courses.

4. STUDY BACKGROUND

The current study is a retrospective analysis of student academic records approved by the Institutional Review Board of the college whose records were used. Academic records were obtained for 1,304 students who had enrolled in a total of 6, 932 CIS courses at a Midwestern community college. After removing students who took only the Computer Literacy service course or only audited courses, 1,173 students remained. The dates of enrollment ranged from 1987 to 2011, with 91% of the enrollments being between 2000 and 2011. The records were anonymous, identified only by an ID number that was generated for this study. The data included gender; birth year; scores for the Compass Pre-Algebra, Compass Algebra, Compass Reading, Compass Writing, ACT Math, ACT Reading, and ACT English exams; and the grade, quarter, and year for the first English course and all Computer Information Systems, math, remedial reading, and remedial writing courses taken. All grades were reported on a letter scale and converted to a number scale as follows: A = 4.00, A- = 3.67, B+ = 3.33, B = 3.0, B- = 2.67, C+ = 2.33, C = 2.00, C- = 1.67, D+ = 1.33, D = 1.00, D- = 0.67, and F = 0.00.

Entry mathematical competence was determined by the mathematics course into which the student was placed after entrance testing. The math placement levels in Roth [2009] were used to establish the math placement courses for entering students and are shown in Table 1.

Incoming students were tested for reading and writing skills and then assigned either to take remedial reading or writing courses or the first course in the English series. Students who entered at math, reading, or writing levels 1 or 2 by the scale used in this study were assigned to remedial mathematics, reading, or writing courses, respectively. Table 1 shows that there are two remedial courses each for reading (RDG115 and RDG116) and writing (WRT115 and WRT116) and these are listed as Entry Reading Levels 1 and 2 and Entry Writing Levels 1 and 2, respectively. RDG110 is listed in Table 1, but as only one instance of RDG110 appeared in the data, it was equated with RDG115. Students who were placed directly into the first English course were ranked at level 3 for both reading and writing. The outcomes of these level 1 and 2 courses can be obtained by emailing the author.

Up until the 2007-2008 academic year, students had two program tracks available: programming and networking. Each track contained courses unique to it, allowing the identification of students in each track. Beginning with the 2008 – 2009 academic year, only one combined programming/networking track was available to students. All students were required to pass a capstone course to graduate, and the prerequisites for the course were set so that nearly all coursework was completed before entry into it was permitted. For this reason, it is assumed that a student who successfully completed the capstone course ultimately completed the associate's degree program.

Table 1. Remedial Mathematics, Reading, and Writing Courses and Their Equivalent Entry Levels

Entry Level	Mathematics Course	Reading Course	Writing Course
1	MTH100 Introductory Mathematics	RDG110 Reading Lab RDG115 College Reading I	WRT115 Introduction To College Writing I
2	MTH101, MTH102 Pre-Algebra	RDG116 College Reading II	WRT116 Introduction To College Writing II

4.1 Demographics

The study population was drawn from students taking CIS courses at a medium-sized Midwestern 2-year public college as classified by Goan, Cunningham, and Carroll [2007]. According to statistics provided by the college, the student cohort entering in the fall 2004 quarter had an average age of 24.7 years. The percentage of entering students was 59% female in fall 2006. About 90% of the entering student population was white and 41% received Pell grants. Goan et al. [2007] report that public 2-year institutions of all sizes enrolled a student population of between 58.1 and 61.9 percent female, between 36.2 and 47.1 percent in their twenties, between 56.4 and 82.9 percent white, and between 28.1 and 41.6 percent receiving Pell grants. In all but ethnicity the student population of the college matched the general population of students attending public two-year postsecondary institutions. About 50 percent of students in the college arrived with mathematics skills below the college level, while nationally 60.7 percent of two-year college students in the same years were in the lowest admissions test (ACT/SAT) score range of between 400 to 840 [National Center for Educational Statistics, 2010]. Roth [2009] showed that students in such a range will be highly likely to require remedial mathematical courses. The general student population of this college was thus representative of the general population of two-year public college students in the United States at that time. The population in this study came from students who took CIS courses at the college between 1987 and 2011.

5. DATA ANALYSIS

Hypothesis I posited no significant correlation between the program completion rate of students and their entry course placement in mathematics, reading, or writing. Not all of the 1,173 students whose grades were available for the study had scores for every course and assessment instruments; hence, the total N for these measures is below 1,173 and the N for different courses and instruments varies widely. An analysis of variance on capstone grades was performed by program track and no significant main effect was found, $F(3, 138) = 1.11$, $p = .348$. Thus, the program track of the student can be discounted as a significant contributor to differences in program success.

Tables 2 and 3 show that there were significant differences in mean CIS GPA and persistence between students needing specific types of remediation. In every case except reading, students having no deficiency earned significantly higher mean GPAs (approximately .5) and persisted on average significantly longer (something over 1 course) than those with a deficiency.

Table 2. Descriptive Statistics for Mean CIS GPA and Course Persistence of Students Needing and Not Needing Remediation

Needing Remed-iation	Mean CIS GPA			Number of CIS Courses Attempted	
	N	Mean CIS GPA	S.D.	Mean No. Courses	S.D.
Developmental Math Course					
Yes	380	2.32	1.14	5.00	5.02
No	568	2.78	1.01	6.18	5.62
Developmental Reading					
Yes	137	2.22	1.13	5.07	5.09
No	765	2.62	1.13	5.56	5.37
Developmental Writing					
Yes	277	2.21	1.09	4.43	4.43
No	623	2.71	1.15	5.97	5.61

Table 3. T-test Results Comparing Mean CIS GPA and Persistence for Students Who Did and Did Not Need Remedial Courses

Area	Measure	t	df	Sig. (2-tailed)
Math	Mean CIS GPA	6.13	946	< .001
	No. Courses	3.51	951	<.001
Reading	Mean CIS GPA	6.18	898	< .001
	No. Courses	1.03	968	.304
Writing	Mean CIS GPA	3.71	900	< .001
	No. Courses	4.58	711	< .001

Tables 4 and 5 show that there was a sizeable and significant difference between the mean CIS GPA of students needing no remediation and those needing any remediation. Those who were not assigned to remedial courses had a significantly higher mean CIS GPA than those who were and, with the exception of reading, persisted longer. Hypothesis I is therefore shown to be false.

Table 4. Descriptive Statistics for Mean CIS GPA of Students Needing and Not Needing Remediation

Category	CIS GPA		
	N	Mean	S.D.
Students Needing No Remediation (Benchmark)	406	2.82	1.11
Students Needing Remediation, Remediated or Not	477	2.33	1.15
Students Needing Remediation and Failing Remedial Courses	388	2.22	1.18
Students Needing Remediation and Passing Only Math Remedial Courses	123	2.70	.95
Students Needing Remediation and Passing All Remedial Courses	90	2.80	.87

Table 5. T-test Results Comparing Mean CIS GPA of Students Not Needing Remediation and Students Completing Various Remediation Courses

Students Not Needing Remediation vs.	t	df	Sig.
Students Needing Remediation and Passing All Remedial Courses	.171	160	.865
Students Needing Remediation and Passing Only Math Remedial Courses	1.39	516	.166
All Students Needing Remediation, both Passing and Not Passing Remedial Courses	6.49	882	< .001

Hypothesis II examines the difference in mean CIS GPA between students who enter the college requiring and passing all required remedial courses and students who enter requiring no remedial courses. The first line in Table 4 lists the descriptive data for students who did not need remediation upon entry. They had the highest mean CIS GPA of any group (2.82) and so serve as the benchmark for all other groups of CIS students. The second line in Table 4 shows the descriptive data for students who by their math, reading, or writing placement were shown to need remediation. It includes both students who passed and who failed the remediation courses. Their mean CIS GPA of 2.33 is significantly lower than the mean CIS GPA of students not needing remediation. The third line in Table 4 shows the data for students who needed remediation but failed one or more of the remediation courses. At 2.22, this group had the lowest mean CIS GPA, 0.60 points lower than the benchmark mean CIS GPA.

The fourth line in Table 4 shows that if students needing math remediation passed the math remedial course, their mean CIS GPA rose to 2.70 regardless of how they fared in the reading and writing courses. The second line in Table 5 shows that the difference in mean CIS GPA between these students and those not needing remediation was not significant. Thus the difficulties addressed in the math remediation courses are the primary, but not only, barrier to best performance in the CIS courses.

The last line in Table 4 shows that students who passed all the remediation courses assigned to them, including reading and writing, earned as a group a mean CIS GPA of 2.80. This essentially matches the mean CIS GPA benchmark of students entering with no remediation needed, and Hypothesis II is shown to be true.

Table 6. Descriptive Statistics for Mean CIS GPA and Course Persistence of Students Passing and Not Passing Remedial Courses

Grade	Mean CIS GPA			No. Courses Completed		
	N	Mean	S.D.	N	Mean	S.D.
Developmental Math Course						
Passed	215	2.59	1.00	229	6.16	5.49
Not Passed	55	1.81	1.07	61	4.62	5.16
Developmental Reading						
Passed	59	1.76	1.00	65	3.78	4.35
Not Passed	11	1.13	1.02	12	4.17	4.84
Developmental Writing						
Passed	142	2.11	1.06	151	4.26	4.26
Not Passed	45	1.56	1.12	48	4.27	4.26

Hypothesis III tests the ultimate measure of academic success: persistence through to completion. Table 7 shows that 21.4 percent of benchmark group of students who entered needing no remediation persisted to completion of the capstone course. This compares with 18.8 percent of students who needed remediation and passed all remediation courses. This completion rate was the closest any group needing remediation came to the benchmark rate. The next highest completion rate (17.8 percent) was seen in the students who passed the needed remedial math course(s), once again showing the importance of math skills to computer training. The worst completion rate was had by students who failed their remedial courses. Only 2 out of 126 passed the capstone course.

Table 7. Descriptive Statistics of Capstone Course Passing by Students in Various Remediation Groups

Passed Capstone	Mean CIS GPA	N	S.D.	%
Students Needing No Remediation Courses				
N	2.47	330	1.34	78.6
Y	3.36	90	0.46	21.4
Students Needing Any Remediation Courses				
N	2.22	664	1.33	88.2
Y	3.23	89	0.49	11.8
Students Needing but Failing Some Remediation Courses				
N	1.56	126	1.29	98.4
Y	3.43	2	0.65	1.6
Students Needing Any Remediation and Passed Math				
N	2.37	97	1.14	82.2
Y	3.23	21	0.56	17.8
Students Needing and Passing All Remediation Courses				
N	2.47	78	1.12	81.2
Y	3.30	18	0.52	18.8

6. DISCUSSION

Hypothesis I focused on the effect that the lack of the required college entrance mathematics, reading, and writing skills had on the performance of students entering the CIS program. The entry math level had a significant effect on the mean CIS GPA. If a deficiency in reading, writing, or especially in math were observed, student performance was on average lower than students who had no deficiencies.

It is important to note that deficiencies may not be only in the measured knowledge and skills; they may also be in the methods the students use to obtain that knowledge and those skills. One interpretation of these findings would be that good students perform well in nearly all of their subjects. Factors in their favor could include study methods, interest, work ethic, no need to hold down a job, and an ability to block out distractions. All that is known when a deficiency is discovered is that there is a knowledge or skill gap. We do not know the cause.

Since a math deficiency had the greatest effect on success, having students in a computer curriculum take math courses, especially remedial ones, before they take the first computer course may pay dividends as they progress through the program. The significant correlation between the mean CIS GPA and both entry math level and prior math coursework shows that strong math preparation before entering the program brings a better likelihood of success. It may also help the student discover other causes for not mastering material such as those listed above.

Reading and writing deficiencies also had significant effects on CIS GPA. A link between verbal skills and CIS courses has face validity. Both human and computer languages follow syntax rules. In addition, programmers must accurately understand verbal descriptions of users' needs. Novices depend on surface features to recognize the syntax elements of a new computer language. Since they have learned only the most basic perceptual chunks, their approach to computer problem solving is to match surface features and cobble together sometimes inappropriate language segments in a bottom-up approach [Adelson, 1981; Spohrer & Soloway, 1988; Rist, 1989; Corritore & Wiedenbeck, 1991]. However, as error prone as novices are, it is reasonable to conclude that students who achieve high marks in language courses by carefully following the syntax rules of human language will carry that same attention to detail over to reading and writing computer language statements.

Hypothesis II focused on performance differences between entering students who required remediation and those who did not. Tables 4 and 5 indicate that students who were assigned to remedial math, reading, or writing courses and passed them earned a significantly higher mean CIS GPA than those who did not pass the remedial courses. The data also show that students who passed only the math remedial course increased their mean CIS GPA to 2.70 and persisted through significantly more CIS courses than those who did not. If those students also passed the remedial reading and writing courses, the mean CIS GPA rose to 2.80, essentially identical to the mean CIS GPA of 2.82 of students who entered needing no remediation. Passing the additional remedial reading or writing courses did not significantly alter persistence.

The student group who passed all their remediation courses had as high a mean CIS GPA as those who did not need remediation, while those who did not pass the remediation courses did significantly worse. This is evidence that (a) if students could pass the remediation course at this institution, they had the knowledge and skills (in the broad academic sense) needed to succeed in the CIS program as students who entered not needing remediation, (b) mathematics, reading, and writing courses teach knowledge and skills that can make a significant difference in CIS course success, and (c) the remediation courses these students took provided the knowledge and skills that they needed to succeed at a level on par with students deemed not needing remediation.

This result suggests that passing the assigned remedial courses closed an essential knowledge and skill gap. What lies in that gap? From the study results, remediation is something that is difficult for the majority of students assigned to the courses to achieve. Only 96 of the 753 students assigned to remedial courses in the file of records used in the study passed them all. The nature and source of this difficulty would be an important topic for future research. For example, Edwards and Zhang [2010] developed an online remedial program for programming that they believe has the strengths of being voluntary, has faculty feedback and encouragement, stimulates peer instruction and small group collaboration, and addresses individual student weaknesses. An early study remediated self-selected trainees with a ninth-grade equivalent education and trained them to be mainframe computer operators (Gilbert and Mayer [1969]). They focused on short range concentrated efforts to fill gaps to understanding the technical books and material. Only the aspects of the equipment and the work for the job that was awaiting them was taught. It was crucial in their program that once a learning design was agreed to, that it be strictly adhered to or much student anxiety resulted. Those who remediate computer studies students should consider assessing for and remediating reading and writing deficits as being equal in importance to remediating math deficits.

There are several threats to the validity of this study. The first is change that occurred to both the faculty and the curriculum during the time the students in the study attended the college. The curricular changes that occurred up until 2008 were small and did not affect students taking either the programming or networking tracks. Only one faculty position changed during the time between 2000 and 2009 when over 90% of the students in the study attended; however, this change affected networking courses and could have had an effect on student success in those courses.

7. CONCLUSION

This study demonstrated that remediation did have a significant effect on the CIS GPA, persistence, and completion of students who successfully completed at least the math remedial courses. Students who also completed any reading and writing remediation courses performed as a group at the same level as students not needing remediation, as measured by mean CIS GPA in an entire CIS program taken over a period of years. The linkage to verbal skills was small but significant, making a difference in mean CIS GPA in this study of perhaps one-tenth of a point, and supports earlier studies finding such a link. The study results show the importance of assessing beginning computer studies students for deficiencies in mathematics, reading, and writing and remediating those deficits early in their academic career, preferably before the first CIS course is taken. When the students received the knowledge and skills that the remedial courses in the study imparted to them, their performance, persistence, and completion rates improved to the level of students entering the CIS program with all the prerequisite knowledge and skills. It was also found that completing remedial courses seemed difficult for students as only a small percentage of them did so. This study showed that remediation can be effective for those who complete it. Increasing the numbers of students who complete needed remedial courses should help increase computer program student retention.

8. REFERENCES

[1] Austin, H. S. (1987). Predictors of Pascal programming achievement for community college students. *SIGCSE Bulletin*, 19(1), 161-164. DOI=10.1145/31726.31752

[2] Bennedsen J. and Caspersen, M. E.. 2008. Optimists have more fun, but do they learn better? On the influence of emotional and social factors on learning introductory computer science, *Computer Science Education, 18,* 1, 1–16.

[3] Bergin, S. and Reilly, R. 2006. Predicting introductory programming performance: A multi-institutional multivariate study. *Computer Science Education, 16,* 4, 303-323.

[4] Byrne, P. and Lyons, G. 2001. The effect of student attributes on success in programming. In *Proceedings of the 6th annual conference on Innovation and technology in computer science education, Canterbury, United Kingdom, 2001.* ACM, New York, 49-52.

[5] Corritore, C. L. and Wiedenbeck, S. 1991. What do novices learn during program comprehension? *International Journal of Human-Computer Interaction, 3,* 2, 199-222.

[6] Edwards, A., and Zhang, K. 2010. A programming remediation plan. *J. Comput. Sci. Coll. 25*, 5, 41-47.

[7] Evans, G. E. and Simkin, M. G. 1989. What best predicts computer proficiency? *Commun. ACM, 32,* 11, 1322-1327.

[8] Gilbert, J. P., and Mayer, D. B. 1969. Experiences in self-selection of disadvantaged people into a computer operator training program. In *Proceedings of the seventh annual conference on SIGCPR* (SIGCPR '69), Monroe Fein (Ed.). ACM, New York, NY, USA, 79-90. DOI=10.1145/800163.805183

[9] Goan, S. K., Cunningham, A. F., and Carroll, C. D. 2007. *Differential Characteristics of 2-year Postsecondary Institutions: Postsecondary Education Descriptive Analysis Report.* National Center for Education Statistics, Washington, D.C.

[10] Hostetler, T. R. 1983. Predicting student success in an introductory programming course. *SIGCSE Bulletin, 15,* 3, 40-43.

[11] Irons, D. M. 1982. Cognitive correlates of programming tasks in novice programmers. In *Proceedings of the 1982 Conference on Human Factors in Computing Systems.* Gaithersburg, MD, 1982. ACM, New York, 219-222.

[12] Konvalina, J., Wileman, S. A., and Stephens, L. J. 1983. Math proficiency: a key to success for computer science students. *Commun. ACM, 26*, 5, 377-382.

[13] Leeper, R. R. and Silver, J. L. 1982. Predicting success in a first programming course. *SIGCSE Bulletin, 14*, 1, 147-150.

[14] Mattern, K. D., and Patterson, B. F. (2009). Is performance on the SAT® related to college retention? *College Board Research Report No. 2009-7.* The College Board, New York. Retrieved August 31, 2013, from http://research.collegeboard.org/publications/content/2012/05/performance-sat-related-college-retention

[15] McGettrick, A., Boyle, R., Ibbett, R., Lloyd, J., Lovegrove, G., and Mander, K. 2005. Grand challenges in computing: Education – A summary. *The Computer Journal, 48,* 1, 42-48.

[16] National Center for Educational Statistics. 2010. *QuickStats: Beginning college students in 2003-04, followed through 2006.* http://nces.ed.gov/datalab/quickstats/createtable.aspx

[17] Rist, R. R. 1989. Schema creation in programming. *Cognitive Science, 13*, 389-414.

[18] Robins, A., Rountree, J., and Rountree, N. 2003. Learning and teaching programming: A review and discussion. *Computer Science Education, 13,* 2, 137-172.

[19] Roth, J. 2009. Examples of Possible ASSET, ACT, and COMPASS "Stage 1" *Cut Off Scores for Consideration in Student Placement Advising.* ACT, Iowa City, Iowa.

[20] Spohrer, J. C. and Soloway, E. 1988. Novice mistakes: Are the folk wisdoms correct? *Commun. ACM, 297*, 624-632.

[21] Ventura, P. R. 2005. Identifying predictors of success for an objects-first CS1. *Computer Science Education, 15,* 3, 223-243.

[22] Werth, L. H. 1986. Predicting student performance in a beginning computer science class. In *Proceedings of the Seventeenth SIGCSE Technical Symposium on Computer Science Education,* Cincinnati, Ohio, 1986. J. C. Little and L. N. Cassel, Eds. ACM, New York, 138-143.

[23] Wilson, B. C. and Shrock, S. 2001. Contributing to success in an introductory computer science course: a study of twelve factors. *SIGCSE Bulletin, 33,* 1, 184-188.

[24] Wong, S. Y., Cheung, H., and Chen, H. C. 1998. The advanced programmer's reliance on program semantics: Evidence from some cognitive tasks. *International Journal of Psychology, 33,* 4, 259-268.

Identifying Challenging CS1 Concepts in a Large Problem Dataset

Yuliya Cherenkova, Daniel Zingaro, and Andrew Petersen
University of Toronto Mississauga
{yuliya.cherenkova, daniel.zingaro, andrew.petersen}@utoronto.ca

ABSTRACT

We examine student difficulties with CS1 concepts by analyzing a dataset containing 266,852 student responses to weekly code-writing problems. We find that conditionals and loops prove particularly problematic, even when considering "second chance" data; and that, while we observe some evidence of improvement, certain straightforward applications of loops continue to be problematic at the end of the term. Our contribution is the corroboration of earlier findings, and a call to use online repositories of student submissions as rich sources of data on the student learning experience.

Categories and Subject Descriptors

K.3.2 [**Computer Science Education**]: Computer and Information Science Education

Keywords

CS1

1. INTRODUCTION

CS1 is a difficult course for many students. Research suggests that 30% or above is not an uncommon failure rate [1], and many CS1 distributions contain a large mode of students who perform poorly [6]. To understand why students struggle with this material, we must develop an appreciation of the difficulty of core concepts and how that difficulty might change over the course.

Several online platforms that allow students to solve programming problems are currently available for use in CS1 courses. These services generate a tremendous amount of data due to the large class sizes common in today's CS1 courses and the number of exercises that students are typically asked to complete. This data can be a powerful tool for understanding broad trends in student performance across a CS1. However, filtering through the large amount of data generated is a challenge and requires automated approaches.

SIGCSE'14, March 5–8, 2014, Atlanta, GA, USA.

http://dx.doi.org/10.1145/2538862.2538966.

In this paper, we offer an investigation into student difficulties that arise during students' use of CodeLab, a web-based interactive programming problem system for introductory programming classes. We mine the submissions from a single course offering to identify the conceptual difficulties encountered by students in the course. We report on the analysis of that data and attempt to corroborate previous literature in the area of concept difficulty. However, our primary contribution is insight into the process of mining large problem datasets, and we discuss the decisions we made while defining "difficulty" and attempting to categorize the sources of student errors.

2. RELATED WORK

The CS education community has examined the importance and difficulty of CS1 topics in a number of ways. Several groups directly consulted experts to help them identify key and challenging topics in computing [8, 2], while others have examined exams [5, 9, 10].

Several researchers have indicated that conditionals and loops present particular challenges to novice programmers. In 1983, Soloway et al. identified particular strategies that students employed while writing loops [12]. More recently, Simon et al. found that students prefer post-test loops [11], and VanDeGrift et al. [13] reported that students understand conditionals better if both branches are made explicit. Kaczmarczyk discussed misconceptions about programming and noted that "while" loops were especially challenging [3].

Our study is most like the work of Robins et al. [7]. These researchers asked laboratory teaching assistants to record every question that students asked to identify where students had concerns. They found that while the frequency of some topics decreased (such as loops, conditionals, and arrays), the frequency of others remained constant (such as reference types, visibility and scope), suggesting that some topics became easier with experience and some did not.

We are similarly interested in whether some topics are particularly challenging and whether students improve over the term. However, we have taken a different approach. Instead of monitoring student questions, we mine a collection of over 250,000 coding problem submissions that were collected over an entire semester.

3. DATA

The present research uses data collected from CodeLab. For each submission, students are shown which test cases pass and fail, as well as expected results for each failed test. The system keeps track of the problems that have been correctly solved by each student. Students can retry as many times as they like (subject to timeout constraints instituted by course instructors), and instructors can obtain aggregated attempt and completion information for the problems that they have released.

The data we examined consists of Codelab submissions from students at a large North American research-intensive university. The students belonged to two different sections of a CS1 that were taught in 2011 at two separate campuses by different instructors. The instructors collaborated to offer equivalent courses that spent roughly the same amount of time on each topic and that were evaluated by the same assignments. The CS1 courses were taught in Python 2. The first section of the course had 253 students and the second had 605 students. We examined a total of 266,852 problem submissions in both sections over the entire term.

Week	Number of Problems	Students Submitting	Concepts
1	11	605	Expressions, Syntax
2	8	576	Typecasting, Function Calls, Function Structure
3	16	577	Booleans, Conditionals, Function Structure
4	8	548	Strings
5	12	520	Lists
6	9	499	Lists
7	8	461	Loops
8	9	393	Tuples, Dictionaries
9	6	405	Dictionaries
10	11	380	Review Problems
11	5	370	Review Problems
12	22	210	Optional Problems
13	22	79	Optional Problems

Figure 1: Course Structure and Submission Counts

Figure 1 displays the number of problems and the number of students submitting each week in the larger course section. It also provides a summary of the main concepts covered by problems in each week. Each section did, occasionally, use a Codelab problem not used in the other section. A total of 175 problems were used in both sections. We compared these problems and found that student submission behavior was consistent across the sections, so we include all problems (not just those used in both sections) in later analysis.

	Section 1		Section 2	
	Conditionals	Other	Conditionals	Other
Correct	31.97%	41.19%	32.91%	44.79%
Split	19%	81%	19%	81%

Figure 2: Concept Breakdown for Week 3

4. IDENTIFYING DIFFICULT CONCEPTS

The Codelab dataset allows us to identify problems (or sets of problems) that are particularly difficult for students. We identified difficult problems by calculating the rate at which students solved a problem correctly and also identified the concepts involved in each problem. Our definition of "correctness" is described in the next section.

To classify the problems, we selected relevant codes from schemes used in two studies of student work [5, 9] and then tagged each problem using the selected codes. Each question was examined and tagged by two researchers.

4.1 Defining Correctness

Initially, we classified a student as answering a problem correctly if they provided a correct answer at any point. However, Codelab allows students to submit as many times as desired, and we therefore found that most students eventually answered most problems correctly (except, of course, when a student did not approach a problem at all). Therefore, to identify difficult concepts, we consider the first (and, later in the paper, the second) submission by each student. We examined larger numbers of submissions to verify that the features we observed continue to exist, but that data is not presented in this paper.

As the number of attempts a student makes is important, we initially planned to use the fraction of students submitting to refine our understanding of correctness. However, we did not have access to the actual student population over the semester, so we cannot ask why some students chose to submit many times while others submitted fewer responses. Therefore, we base the rate of correct submissions on the number of students who submitted at least one problem in any given week. While some students may have been registered for the course but not submitting Codelab problems, we deem this an acceptable loss of data as completing the Codelab problems was worth course credit.

4.2 Concept Difficulty

Figure 3 lists the submission data collected for both course sections. In addition to the rate at which correct solutions were submitted, the table lists the median number of submissions made on problems in the problem set for that week.

The elevated performance of Section 1 over the first three weeks was likely caused by the fact that those students had to solve more problems during this period and many of those problems were quite similar. Later, we examine whether increased opportunities to solve similar problems leads to corresponding increases in correctness.

Many weeks contain a mix of problem types; to identify difficult concepts, we considered the set of problems tagged with that concept (rather than looking at weekly aggregates). However, we observe that students have particular difficulty in weeks 3 and 7, and in each of these two weeks, a significant, new concept is introduced.

4.2.1 Conditionals and Booleans

Problems in week 3 contained pure boolean questions and questions that required conditional statements. Figure 2 describes performance on these two kinds of questions, with the "split" row indicating the share of total questions belonging to a particular concept. As shown in the figure, correctness for conditional statements is significantly lower than for problems that focus only on boolean expressions. The problem set also contained problems about function structure, and students were generally able to complete those problems on the first attempt.

Week	Number of Problems		Rate of Correctness		Median Attempts		Concepts
	Section 1	Section 2	Section 1	Section 2	Section 1	Section 2	
1	18	11	70.27%	59.96%	1.28	1.45	Expressions, Syntax
2	10	8	56.32%	52.53%	1.7	1.75	Typecasting, Function Calls, Function Structure
3	21	16	42.89%	39.64%	5.6	2.56	Booleans, Conditionals, Function Structure
4	16	8	49.02%	54.30%	1.88	1.5	Strings
5	17	12	59.11%	66.86%	1.53	1.25	Lists
6	12	9	53.83%	58.94%	1.75	1.56	Lists
7	8	8	28.34%	24.54%	3.88	3.63	Loops
8	13	9	39.92%	48.10%	2.33	1.56	Tuples, Dictionaries
9	7	6	42.71%	45.11%	2	1.67	Dictionaries
10	11	11	43.56%	44.94%	2.09	1.91	Review
11	9	5	43.26%	49.92%	2.11	1.6	Review
12 & 13	44	44	35.72%	38.54%	2.71	2.18	Optional Problems

Figure 3: Problem Submission Statistics

4.2.2 *Loops*

The problems in week 7 all contained loops, and all of the problems exhibited low rates of correctness. However, week 8 also contained some loop questions, so those questions were analyzed in more detail. Figure 4 displays data from week 8. It presents correctness for both sections, as well as the proportion of questions that did and did not contain loops.

	Section 1		Section 2	
	Loops	Other	Loops	Other
Correct	27.80%	58.26%	24.45%	55.39%
Split	33%	67%	50%	50%

Figure 4: Concept Breakdown for Week 8

Though one of the course sections required students to answer more loops questions than the other (17 vs. 13), correctness was similar across sections. Providing additional, similar problems does not appear, in this case, to have provided students with an immediate benefit. We believe that, by design, more difficult loops questions were selected for week 8 (the second week), so next, we examine similar problems provided later in the term to determine if there is evidence of improvement.

4.2.3 *(Lack of) Improvement?*

	Section 1		Section 2	
	#	Correct	#	Correct
Conditionals	1	38.34%	2	33.74%
Loops	3	26.22%	3	26.22%
Loops with Conditionals	3	32.54%	5	36.44%

Figure 5: Difficult Concepts in Weeks 10–11

Our next step was to check whether correctness rates improve on the difficult concepts by the end of the semester. We have focused on weeks 10 and 11, since they contained mandatory (marked) review questions. Figure 5 contains the results of analyzing these weeks. Some of the loop questions in these weeks involved conditional statements, so the final row in the figure provides data on these questions separately.

The # column indicates how many problems of each type were analyzed. The number of problems is small, so the risk of external factors skewing the result is high. Nevertheless, we do not see significant evidence of improvement in either concept. However, questions that combined the two concepts appear to have higher rates of correctness than problems with just loops; we believe this is because specific "recipes" were discussed in class for cases very similar to the problems presented.

4.2.4 *Problem Complexity*

Before proceeding under our hypothesis that conditionals and loops are particularly problematic, we consider whether students might have difficulty reading or understanding problems of this type. According to Landauer and Way [4], the complexity of text students encounter during their high school years is significantly lower than the complexity of text they encounter during their secondary education. The level of difficulty of problem text could influence correctness and consequently introduce noise in the data.

First, we used the Pearson reading complexity metric to examine relationships between text complexity and correctness but found that questions varied little on this metric. Second, we looked at text length but found no significant differences between these problems and others in the set. Finally, we considered vocabulary and cultural references by counting word occurrences and filtering out python keywords, articles, and prepositions. However, none of the problems contained challenging vocabulary or cultural references outside of computer science.

One other factor that plays a key role in influencing correctness is length of solution. Many questions in the data sample required expressions as an answer or could be answered with one line of code. However, as the course curriculum progressed, solutions tended to get longer, introducing more room for typos – or providing more opportunities for misconceptions to appear in the code. Average length of solution definitely had an impact on correctness, and this pattern was expected. This factor cannot be disregarded while analyzing the performance, so we need to examine the types of errors that are encountered (in particular, the rates at which syntax errors and other similar "trivial" errors are introduced).

4.3 Common Errors

We would like to identify the common errors associated with failures to solve problems related to conditional statements and loops. We would also like to explore whether difficulties with loops, in particular, are simply an artifact of solution length. To do so, we selected three problems that minimize use of other concepts that are not of interest. Then, we wrote test cases for each problem that each indicate a particular common error when the code fails that test. In addition to the carefully constructed test cases, we also collected data on other common results: exceptions and timeouts.

In the tables that follow, we report the percentage of students who attempted the question that triggered each error at least once. If a student submits multiple attempts that trigger the same error, they are only counted once. This data does not consider the number of attempts the students made; it is very possible that a single student with many submissions may be represented in many rows in the table. The results obtained from each section were comparable, so we report the results in aggregate.

4.3.1 Conditionals

The conditional statement question that was selected was answered by 782 students. The question text is as follows:

> Write a conditional that decreases the value associated with shelf_life by 4 if the value associated with outside_temperature is greater than 90.

Error	Students (%)
1. Reversed comparison operator	28.52
2. Not checked border value	26.73
3. Assigning 4 instead of decreasing by 4	1.15
4. Increasing instead of decreasing	2.30
Modified original values	0.26
Timeout	0.39
IndentationError	11.00
NameError	7.54
SyntaxError	30.82

Figure 6: Test Case Results for Conditionals

The question was eventually solved by 99.36% of students, and 42.33% solved the question on the first attempt. Figure 6 contains the results of our test cases.

A significant fraction of the students do have trouble with basic structural issues of syntax and indentation. A smaller but still significant number either have a typo in a variable name or reference a variable that is only created when the conditional is true (NameError). However, a significant number (more than 25%) exhibit the common errors of failing to check the border condition or reversing the conditional.

4.3.2 Loops

The question on loops was answered by 602 students. The question text is as follows:

> Associate the average of the numbers from 1 to n (where n is a positive integer value) with the variable avg.

Error	Students (%)
1. Omitted last number in sum	8.64
2. Sum not calculated correctly	56.64
3. Reported sum, not average	0.66
4. Used integer division	54.65
Modified original values	4.32
Timeout	12.12
AttributeError	0.50
IndentationError	6.15
IndexError	0.33
NameError	19.27
SyntaxError	22.92
TypeError	15.12
ZeroDivisionError	3.32

Figure 7: Test Case Results for Loops

This question was eventually solved by 95.51% of students, but only 20.60% solved the question on the first attempt. In order to protect testrun results from additional noise, we prepared an additional, very basic testcase (n = 3) that the submission had to pass before being run against other testcases. 47.67% of students failed the basic testcase at least once, which implies that their code was syntactically correct but did not loop correctly on any input. Figure 7 displays the remaining results associated with this problem.

Test case 4 is a Python-specific issue. By default, dividing an integer by an integer resulted in an integer in Python 2, and the problem failed to mention that a floating point number was expected.

Syntax and indentation errors continue to be significant, but they have decreased in comparison to the conditionals problem. TypeErrors, however, are probably caused by similar misunderstandings. They are caused by a method being invoked on an object of the wrong type; for example, a student may have decided to put all of the items into a list and to sum the list. The TypeError would have been triggered when adding an integer type to a list type.

Other errors, like test cases 1 and 2, are more directly tied to loops. In addition, NameError likely indicates an uninitialized variable that is used to accumulate a sum in the loop.

4.3.3 Loops with Conditionals

We selected one problem that used both loops and conditionals. This question was answered by 594 students. The question text is as follows:

> Given: a variable named incompletes that refers to a list of student ids, and a variable student_id. Write some code that counts the number of times the value associated with student_id appears in the list associated with incompletes and assigns this value to number_of_incompletes. You may use, if you wish, an additional variable, k. You may use only k, incompletes, student_id, and number_of_incompletes.

Figure 8 displays the results associated with this problem. Similar to our process for the loops question, we designed a basic testcase to filter submissions that could not run on a basic input. The basic testcase involved a list that contained only one element, and that element matched student_id. Of

Error	Students (%)
1. Indexing into empty list	9.76
2. Reversed boolean operator	4.71
3. Sum not calculated correctly	0.34
4. Stop incrementing sum	5.39
5. Off by 1	5.56
Modified original values	0.84
Timeout	2.53
IndentationError	8.42
IndexError	3.37
NameError	11.78
SyntaxError	20.37
TypeError	8.25

Figure 8: Test Case Results for the Loops and Conditionals Question

the complete target population, 22.73% submitted solutions that failed the basic testcase at least once. We also included a testcase that checked if the students used a built-in method rather than a loop to solve the problem. 21.89% of students failed this test, which indicates that they completed the problem without a loop.

The question was eventually solved by 96.97% of students, and 46.46% solved the question on the first attempt. These numbers are significantly higher than the basic loop question. This, as well as the significant decrease in the number of timeouts, is evidence of improvement, since the number of students attempting the problem is roughly the same as the loop problem.

Syntax and indentation errors remain lower than for the conditionals problem and on par with the loops problem. Since the solution length is significantly higher, this suggests that the length of the solution is not the main contributor to the large number of incorrect submissions.

We see only a small number of failures in test case 2, which exposes an error with the conditional. The basic testcase used to filter results potentially conceals some conditional statement related misconceptions, since there could have been submissions that successfully looped but which did not compare the student IDs appropriately. Therefore, we are unable to determine what fraction of the basic test failures are caused by misunderstandings related to conditional statements.

The solutions also exhibit a different pattern of errors when compared to the pure loops question. A significant fraction of students commit a boundary error (testcases 1 and 5), but there is an additional opportunity to commit that error (on an empty list) that did not exist in the loops question. As compared to the loop question, a small fraction failed to compute the sum properly, which is additional evidence of improvement.

4.4 Revisiting (Lack of) Improvement

Earlier, in Sections 4.2.2 and 4.2.3, we saw that students failed to exhibit improvement in pure loop questions but that they tended to do better on questions that mixed loops and conditionals. In some cases, this improvement can be attributed to students using methods that allow them to avoid using loops. However, the previous section suggested that students do exhibit a different pattern of errors in the combined loop-conditional problem. This may be taken as evidence of improvement, as the errors their code generates exhibit differences from the errors generated in the loops question. These two pieces of evidence are contradictory, so we revisited the problems themselves.

The main difference that we can identify is one of context. The pure loop questions that were assigned ask the students to work in purely mathematical areas (computing sums or sequences), while the combined questions ask students to apply loops to solve problems in the context of data structures. These data structures are examined in more detail (several weeks are associated with lists and dictionaries), so it may be that the students are receiving additional examples of loops with data structures but that they are having trouble translating that knowledge back to problems that force them to deal purely with loops. This phenomenon requires additional investigation.

5. PROBLEMS: SECOND ATTEMPT

In Section 4.1, we define correctness on the basis of the first submission. However, in our dataset, the students often submitted multiple solutions to a single problem. By only considering the first attempt, we are not fully capturing how students interact with and learn from problems.

In this section, we investigate the sequences of submissions generated by students as they attempted to solve the three questions in the previous section. The sample population consisted of the 393 students who attempted all three questions. In addition to tracking the number of submissions, we also estimated how similar solutions are to one another. Code similarity is measured by translating each submission into an abstract syntax tree and measuring the difference between subsequent submissions using the Zhang-Shasha algorithm [14]. This method ignores small but potentially important changes like changes to constants or variable names, but it does provide a measure of structural change that allows us to differentiate between minor and major changes.

Based on the time between submissions, most students tend to attempt problems in one sitting until either they solve the problem or give up. Many of the sequences we saw included a rapid change in solutions' similarity scores, which suggests that a student has switched to a completely new solution, perhaps after consulting an external source. We are unable to query students about how they decided to make the switch and where they obtained assistance.

Difficulty of Selected Concepts			Percentage of Students	
Conditional Statements	Loops	Mixed Concepts	First Attempt (%)	Second Attempt (%)
ok	ok	ok	5.85	18.07
difficult	ok	ok	5.34	6.36
ok	difficult	ok	15.78	27.48
ok	ok	difficult	2.04	8.14
difficult	difficult	ok	17.05	11.45
difficult	ok	difficult	4.83	2.80
ok	difficult	difficult	19.59	17.81
difficult	difficult	difficult	29.52	7.89

Figure 9: Sequences of Concept Difficulty

Earlier, we defined correctness by examining the first submission. Figure 9 examines what would happen if our definition of correctness were based on the second submission. The second submission is interesting because students were able to correct minor syntax errors and to incorporate feedback from failed test cases. The figure lists what fraction of students found a particular combination of concepts difficult after both the first and second submission. For example, the first line (ok/ok/ok) represents students who were able to correctly solve problems from all three categories in one attempt (5.85%) and within two attempts (18.07%).

The number of students who correctly answer all problems increases significantly (from 5.85% to 18.07%), and there is a similar decrease in the number of students who struggle with all three problems (from 29.52% to 7.89%). However, most students continue to struggle on at least one concept even after the second attempt. The most notable results are increases in the number of students who found only loops to be difficult (from 15.78% to 27.48%) and those who find loops problematic but are able to solve problems that use loops within the context of a data structure (38.93%). This suggests that loops are the more challenging concept.

6. CONCLUSION

Our investigation of a large number of coding problems corroborates previous work that suggests that students have significant trouble with conditionals and loops, with loops being particularly challenging. These concepts continued to be troublesome for the students through the end of the course, though we also see evidence of improvement over the term (as in Robins et al. [7]). The situation is complex, as students appear to become comfortable with looping based on data structures but, in some cases, remain unable to complete problems that contain loops over ranges of integers.

This work suggests several avenues for future investigation. First, access to data from multiple institutions could be used to broaden the study and consider factors such as programming language and student demographics. In addition, we encountered multiple situations, in particular when examining sequences of submissions, where insight from the students would have helped us interpret observed behavior. A future study that takes place in parallel with a course would help us better understand how students typically interact with problems.

7. ACKNOWLEDGEMENTS

Our thanks to David Arnow and Gerald Weiss, who provided us with the CodeLab data. Thanks also to Anqi Lu who contributed to the brainstorming of ideas regarding correctness representation.

8. REFERENCES

[1] J. Bennedsen and M. E. Caspersen. Failure rates in introductory programming. *SIGCSE Bulletin*, 39(2):32–36, 2007.

[2] K. Goldman, P. Gross, C. Heeren, G. L. Herman, L. Kaczmarczyk, M. C. Loui, and C. Zilles. Setting the scope of concept inventories for introductory computing subjects. *Trans. Comput. Educ.*, 10(2):5:1–5:29, June 2010.

[3] L. C. Kaczmarczyk, E. R. Petrick, J. P. East, and G. L. Herman. Identifying student misconceptions of programming. In *Proc. 41st Technical Symposium on Computer Science Education*, pages 107–111, 2010.

[4] T. Landauer and D. Way. Improving text complexity measurement through the reading maturity metric. Presented at the *Annual Meeting of the National Council on Measurement in Education*, Apr. 2012.

[5] A. Petersen, M. Craig, and D. Zingaro. Reviewing CS1 exam question content. In *Proc. 42nd ACM Technical Symposium on Computer Science Education*, pages 631–636, 2011.

[6] A. Robins. Learning edge momentum: A new account of outcomes. *Computer Science Education*, 20(1):37–71, 2010.

[7] A. Robins, P. Haden, and S. Garner. Problem distributions in a CS1 course. In *Proc. 8th Australian Conference on Computing Education*, pages 165–173, 2006.

[8] C. Schulte and J. Bennedsen. What do teachers teach in introductory programming? In *Proc. Second International Workshop on Computing Education Research*, pages 17–28, 2006.

[9] J. Sheard, Simon, A. Carbone, D. Chinn, M.-J. Laakso, T. Clear, M. de Raadt, D. D'Souza, J. Harland, R. Lister, A. Philpott, and G. Warburton. Exploring programming assessment instruments: a classification scheme for examination questions. In *Proc. Seventh International Workshop on Computing Education Research*, pages 33–38, 2011.

[10] Simon, D. D'Souza, J. Sheard, J. Harland, A. Carbone, and M.-J. Laakso. Can computing academics assess the difficulty of programming examination questions? In *Proc. 12th Koli Calling International Conference on Computing Education Research*, pages 160–163, 2012.

[11] B. Simon, T.-Y. Chen, G. Lewandowski, R. McCartney, and K. Sanders. Commonsense computing: what students know before we teach (episode 1: sorting). In *Proc. 2nd International Workshop on Computing Education Research*, pages 29–40, 2006.

[12] E. Soloway, J. Bonar, and K. Ehrlich. Cognitive strategies and looping constructs: an empirical study. *Comm. of the ACM*, 26:853–860, November 1983.

[13] T. VanDeGrift, D. Bouvier, T.-Y. Chen, G. Lewandowski, R. McCartney, and B. Simon. Commonsense computing (episode 6): logic is harder than pie. In *Proc. 10th Koli Calling International Conference on Computing Education Research*, pages 76–85, 2010.

[14] K. Zhang and D. Shasha. Simple fast algorithms for the editing distance between trees and related problems. *SIAM J. Comput.*, 18(6):1245–1262, Dec. 1989.

Advanced Placement Computer Science: AP Computer Science A and AP Computer Science Principles

Paul T. Tymann
Rochester Institute of Technology
Rochester, NY 14623
+1 585-475-7908
paul.tymann@rit.edu

Frances P. Trees
Rutgers, the State University of New Jersey
Piscataway, NJ 08854
+1 848-445-7299
fran.trees@cs.rutgers.edu

Robert Glen Martin
School for the Talented and Gifted
Dallas, TX
+1 972-925-6311
gmart039@dallasisd.org

Richard Kick
Conejo Valley Unified School District
Thousand Oaks, CA 91362
+1 805.498.3676
kickrg@gmail.com

Lien Diaz
College Board, AP Program
Duluth, GA
770-225-4012
ldiaz@collegeboard.org

Categories and Subject Descriptors
K.3.2 [**Computer and Information Science Education**]: computer science education, curriculum

General Terms
Algorithms, Design, Experimentation

Keywords
CS0, CS1, case studies, active learning. computing applications.

1.SUMMARY

College Board has joined national efforts to improve the state of STEM education, in particular to address the challenge of increasing participation with a diverse population of computer scientists to meet the growing demands of the field of computing. The Advanced Placement (AP) Program is pleased to endeavor in enhancing AP Computer Science offerings by maintaining college level integrity and addressing issues of equity and access for students and teachers. In addition to the established AP Computer Science A course, the AP Program is engaged in the development of a forthcoming AP Computer Science Principles course. The additional option for high school students to study college level computing will provide more students with an opportunity to be introduced to important computer science concepts, gain a broader perspective of the field of study, and have access to a larger pathway into computing.

This session will review information regarding the AP Computer Science A course and will discuss updated course content and exam development. It will then discuss the new Computer Science Principles course and plans for the development and launch of the course. The session will conclude with a Q&A session addressing questions regarding both courses. The session will be moderated by members of the Computer Science A and Principles Development Committees.

SIGCSE'14, March 5–8, 2014, Atlanta, Georgia, USA.
ACM 978-1-4503-2605-6/14/03.
http://dx.doi.org/10.1145/2538862.2538986

2.SESSION OBJECTIVES
In recent years, the AP CS A course and examination has been the subject of substantial discussion and debate. How should computer science be introduced? What topics should be included? What pedagogy is appropriate? To what extent should programming be involved? This session seeks to clarify the role of the AP CS A course and examine how the new AP CS Principles course will complement the exam offerings of the College Board. This motivation leads to the following session objectives.

- Review information regarding the AP Computer Science A course and learn about updated course and exam development.
- Examine and discuss similarities and differences between the AP Computer Science A and the AP Computer Science Principles course.

- Learn how an enhanced AP Computer Science program will help to address national challenges in computer science education.

3.OUTLINE OF THE SESSION

The following outline envisions questions and discussion during the last 40 minutes of the session. Realistically, some questions may arise during the initial presentations, so the question-answer time may be revised as the session progresses.

- The AP CS A course and examination --- 10 minutes, Tymann
  - Purpose: college credit and/or placement
  - Content overview
  - The AP CS Principles course and examination --- 10 minutes, Kick
    - Purpose/motivation for the Course
    - Assessment
  - Development and launch of CS Principles --- 10 minutes, Trees
- AP Computer Science Program – Evolution and Prospect (e.g., two CS course offerings, new course descriptions, college involvement) --- 5 minutes, Martin/Diaz (*What do you think of this?)*

- Questions, audience feedback, discussion --- 40 minutes

4.EXPECTATIONS

This proposed session will serve several audiences:

- Teachers of introductory computer science (at HS and College levels) who are interested in nation-wide trends and practices regarding their courses.
- Educators and administrators who want to better understand the role and goals of AP CS A and CS Principles.
- Guidance counselors and student advisors who want to guide students in the transition from high school CS courses to college courses.
- Department chairs and deans who are monitoring placement and credit policies regarding AP courses.
- AP CS teachers who are interested in having their students receive college credit

With the diversity of practices regarding introductory CS at the college level, the results reported in this session will likely generate considerable discussion and debate. Thus, the session will conclude with a 40-minute question-answer-feedback session involving attendees.

5.SUITABILITY FOR A SPECIAL SESSION

This special session responds to many inquiries over the years regarding the extent to which the AP CS A course and examination relate to introductory CS courses at the college level. Thus, this special session serves as something of a report by the AP CS A Development Committee.

- *The session does not represent a traditional SIGCSE paper:* The material presented discusses the direction the AP CS program is taking. The session is not a presentation of educational research or pedagogy, following the form for usual SIGSE papers.
- *The session does not bring together multiple viewpoints as would be found in a typical SIGCSE panel:* The session leaders represent the AP CS Development Committees, and the session will discuss practices used by the College Board and the AP CS Development Committees over the next few years.

Altogether, the material for this session continues an on-going dialog between the AP CS program and the broad computing community, The nature of the session does not seem to fit well with either a paper or panel format, but the content seems of general interest to the overall community. The special session framework seems best suited for this type of discussion.

6.ACKNOWLEDGMENTS

The Advanced Placement Computer Science A Development Committee thanks the College Board for its efforts in obtaining feedback from community college, college, and university faculty throughout the United States regarding introductory courses at the college level.

7.REFERENCES

[1] College Board, *Advanced Placement Computer Science College Curriculum Study,* June 2011.

[2] College Board, *The Computer Science A Course Description*, 2010. http://apcentral.collegeboard.com/apc/public/repository/ap-computer-science-course-description.pdf

[3] College Board, *The Computer Science A Course Description*, 2014. (forthcoming)

[4] College Board, *Computer Science College Comparability Study*, 2012.

[5] College Board, *AP Computer Science Faculty Colloquium Results*, December 10, 2008.

A Public/Private Partnership for Expanding Computer Science in Schools

Owen Astrachan
Duke University
ola@cs.duke.edu

Amy Briggs
Middlebury College
briggs@middlebury.edu

Gail Chapman
UCLA / ECS
chapgail@gmail.com

Joanna Goode
U Oregon / ECS
goodej@uoregon.edu

Brook Osborne
Code.org
brook@code.org

Pat Yongpradit
Code.org
pat@code.org

Categories and Subject Descriptors

K.3.2 [**Computers and Education**]: Computer and Information Science Education – *computer science education*

Keywords

Computer Science Education, K-12 Curriculum, CS Principles, Exploring Computer Science, Code.org, Outreach, Professional Development.

1. SUMMARY

Changing the landscape of computer science education for both K-12 and higher education is now facilitated by collaboration between industrial and publicly funded initiatives; by curricula, professional development, and outreach designed to reach every student; and by a community working together to achieve this at scale.

This special session brings together leaders from three groups: code.org, Exploring Computer Science [1-3](ECS) and Computer Science Principles [4, 5] (CSP) who have formed a public/private partnership to generate resources for introductory computer science students at many levels. These leaders report on work completed as well as ongoing and future work to help the community broaden participation in computer science while scaling and facilitating communities of students and teachers in high school and college.

In the past, several special sessions, panels, and papers have presented the work of ECS and CSP [6, 7]. This session highlights how the collaboration of an agile, non-profit (code.org) is working with the ECS and CSP communities to help reach the goals of the CS10K initiative.

Code.org is helping teachers, schools, districts, and communities by developing curricular and professional development resources based on both the ECS and CSP projects, working to ensure that the individualized needs of different schools and districts are addressed. We will discuss the synergies and benefits enabled by this public/private partnership, the challenges of ensuring that the partnership is done equitably and with full consideration of the educational community, and how the community can actively contribute to the partnership.

SIGCSE'14, March 5–8, 2014, Atlanta, Georgia, USA.
ACM 978-1-4503-2605-6/14/03.
http://dx.doi.org/10.1145/2538862.2538991

2. The big picture of Code.org (Pat Yongpradit)

CSP and ECS are the two successful cornerstones of the CS10K initiative, working to scale nationwide in the US and beyond. Both projects were built on community input and provide integrated curriculum and professional development. As an educational non-profit dedicated to growing computer science education, code.org is in a unique position to help bring such cohesive well-designed CS programs to more districts, and support long-term efforts for their success. During the special session we will discuss the role of code.org in the ongoing efforts to scale the adoption of ECS, CSP, and other programs that seek to broaden participation in computer science teaching and learning.

Pat Yongpradit is Director of Education at Code.org.

3. Expanding CS Principles at scale (Owen Astrachan)

CS Principles (CSP) is a new Advanced Placement course designed and constructed by a community of educators. It is far more than an a traditional introduction to programming and the fundamental concepts of computing — it is a rigorous, engaging, and approachable course designed so that each student will understand how these concepts are transforming the world we live in and how each student can use the concepts in their own lives, studies, and in collaborating to participate in that transformation [6]. This course is intended to broaden participation with the goal of a massive increase in both the number and diversity of students taking computer science courses at many levels. Reaching this goal requires an expansion in the type, number, and reach of schools and teachers involved in teaching computer science.

Owen Astrachan is the PI of the CS Principles project, he now works to help the community of educators working on this and related projects achieve their goals.

4. ECS: A foundational high school course (Joanna Goode)

Exploring Computer Science (ECS) is an NSF-sponsored educational reform program built to address the historical lack of computer science curriculum, engaging pedagogy, and institutional support available for schools serving high numbers of students of color [refs]. ECS lessons are designed to promote an inquiry-based approach to teaching and learning foundational concepts in computer science. The core of the ECS curriculum highlights the computational practices and problem solving associated with doing computer science, rather than narrowly focusing only on particular syntax or tools.

A key component of the *Exploring Computer Science* program is the extensive and ongoing professional development support, which helps foster a teacher learning community that focuses on issues of effective pedagogy and inclusive practices.

Joanna Goode is a co-PI on the Exploring Computer Science project and a computer science education researcher..

5. Expanding ECS (Gail Chapman)

In the five years since this course was first offered in LAUSD, enrollment statistics point to a marked success in reaching a highly diverse student population. The success of this course and the instructional design of the program for broadening participation in computing can serve as a model for other districts and local regions looking to expand computer science education. Since 2011, the Exploring Computer Science program has been implemented in multiple areas of the US. Current partners include the Chicago Public Schools, San Jose California area, Oregon, Utah, and DC Public Schools. Several other sites are on the near horizon, with many others having expressed interest for future adoption. With expansion come challenges. In this special session we will discuss how programs can scale effectively while maintaining program integrity and building a foundation in current sites that can sustain into the future.

Gail Chapman is one of the designers of the ECS curriculum and leads the ECS Professional Development.

6. Broadening participation in CS Principles (Amy Briggs)

The CS Principles course has been designed to broaden participation in computer science education with an accessible, engaging curriculum and an assessment designed to encourage and facilitate an equitable and student-centered approach. We will engage in a dialog relevant to how performance-based tasks that constitute a portfolio can be part of a course designed to succeed in many diverse schools and districts as well as for diverse students. Just as the CSP framework was designed and built collaboratively, the partnership represented in this special session continues this community-driven collaboration to support adoption by many different groups at scale.

Amy Briggs is co-PI of the CS Principles she has overseen the development of the curriculum framework and worked to ensure that the framework broadens participation.

7. Code.org's first year of scaling CSP and ECS (Brook Osborne)

Code.org is working to support the needs of teachers working with ECS and CSP through a comprehensive curriculum and PD model that supports diverse sets of learners. As of Spring 2014, Code.org will have 100 high schools and 200 K-8 schools in the first of a four phase of a professional development experience. During the special session we will discuss the supports code.org has developed and deployed to scale up the adoption of ECS and CSP.

Brook Osborne is 9-12 Program Manager at code.org. Previously she was the Outreach and Pilot Coordinator for CS Principles and the National Director of Outreach in Computer Science at Duke University.

8. Intended Audience

This special session is designed for all educators interested in broadening participation in computer science teaching. Best practices in educational research, in using established pedagogical approaches designed to change how students learn, and in providing professional development opportunities for teachers will be discussion topics that transcend their particulars in the case of Computer Science Principles and Exploring Computer Science.

9. REFERENCES

[1] J. Goode and G. Chapman. (2013). *Exploring Computer Science.*

[2] J. Margolis, R. Estrella, J. Goode, J. J. Holme, and K. Nao, *Stuck in the shallow end: Education, race, and computing*: MIT Press, 2008.

[3] J. Goode and J. Margolis, "Exploring Computer Science: A Case Study of School Reform," *ACM Transactions on Computing Education,* vol. 11, 2011.

[4] O. Astrachan and R. B. Osborne. (2012) Computer Science Principles: portfolio-based assessment. *ACM SIGCSE Bulletin.* 4.

[5] A. Arpaci-Dusseau, O. Astrachan, D. Barnette, M. Bauer, M. Carrell, R. Dovi, B. Franke, C. Gardner, J. Gray, J. Griffin, R. Kick, A. Kuemmel, R. Morelli, D. Muralidhar, R. B. Osborne, and C. Uche, "Computer Science Principles: Analysis of a Propsed Advanced Placement Course," in *SIGCSE Technical Symposium on Computer Science Education*, Denver, CO, 2013.

[6] B. Franke, J. Century, M. Lach, C. Wilson, M. Guzdial, G. Chapman, and O. Astrachan, "Expanding Access to K-12 Computer Science Education: Research on the Landscape of Computer Science Professional Development," in *SIGCSE Technical Symposium on Computer Science Education*, Denver, CO, 2013.

Data Science as an Undergraduate Degree

Paul Anderson
College of Charleston
66 George Street
Charleston, SC 29424
1-843-953-8151
andersonpe2@cofc.edu

James McGuffee (moderator)
Northern Kentucky University
Nunn Drive
Highland Heights KY 41099
1-859-572-7931
mcguffeej1@nku.edu

David Uminsky
University of San Francisco
2130 Fulton Street
San Francisco, CA 94117
1-415-422-6637
duminsky@usfca.edu

Categories and Subject Descriptors

K.3.2 [**Computers and Education**]: Curriculum

General Terms

Management, Design

Keywords

Curriculum Design, Data Analytics, Data Science, Interdisciplinary, Transdisciplinary

1. SUMMARY

The purpose of this panel is to discuss the creation and implementation of a data science degree program at the undergraduate level. The panel includes representatives from three different universities that each offers an undergraduate degree in Data Science as of fall 2013. We plan to share information on the logistics of how the data science programs came to exist at each of our schools as well as encourage a robust interactive discussion about the future of data science education at the undergraduate level.

The Data Science Program at the College of Charleston is supported by the joint efforts of the Department of Computer Science and the Department of Mathematics. Paul Anderson is an assistant professor of Computer Science and director of the Data Science Program at the College of Charleston. [4]

The Bachelor of Science in Data Science at Northern Kentucky University (NKU) is a transdisciplinary degree program administratively housed in the Computer Science Department which is part of the College of Informatics. There are tenure track faculty positions for this degree plan from at least three separate departments: Computer Science, Business Informatics, and Statistics. James McGuffee is an associate professor and chair of the Department of Computer Science. [2]

The Bachelor of Science degree in Data Science at the University of San Francisco (USF) is an interdisciplinary major with core courses from Computer Science, Mathematics, and Economics. David Uminsky is an assistant professor of Mathematics and the director of the Bachelor of Science degree in Data Science at USF. [3]

SIGCSE '14, March 5-8, 2014, Atlanta, GA, USA.
ACM 978-1-4503-2605-6/14/03.
http://dx.doi.org/10.1145/2538862.2538868

2. PAUL ANDERSON

We describe Data Science, a four-year undergraduate program in predictive analytics, machine learning and data mining implemented at the College of Charleston, Charleston, SC, USA in 2005. We present a ten-year status report detailing the program's origins, successes, and challenges. Our experience demonstrates that education and training for big data concepts and tooling is both possible and practical at the undergraduate level. The development of this program parallels the growing demand for finding utility in data sets and streaming data. The curriculum is a seventy-seven credit-hour program that has been successfully implemented in a liberal arts setting by the faculties of computer science and mathematics.

In May of 2003, after studying the graduate offerings of Knowledge, Discovery, and Data Mining (KDD) programs in the United States [1], a group of faculty members in Math, Statistics, Computer Science and Biology at the College of Charleston (Charleston, SC) believed that it would be possible to create a four-year undergraduate program based on KDD as an emerging discipline. The primary challenge was finding a way to implement it within a liberal arts environment. This panel will discuss the program development effort, the results of implementing the program, and a review of data collected during the last eight years of deployment.

3. JAMES MCGUFFEE

The question facing every organization today is how to use data effectively: not just their own data, but all data that is relevant and available. The data science practitioner must holistically approach massive and varied data sources. This requires many activities, including finding, conditioning, exploring, warehousing, and modeling of data, as well as the final step of making sense of the data, using visualization, machine learning, and statistics, and explaining it to others. The Data Science degree at Northern Kentucky University emphasizes the critical arc that runs from data to information, information to knowledge, and knowledge to decision making.

While the field of data science is known by a variety of names, including data analytics, business analytics, and business intelligence, there is no question that there is a huge demand for data science professionals. Starting in Fall 2013, Northern Kentucky University began offering the Midwest's first Bachelor of Science in Data Science degree. Building on a core of computer science, information systems, statistics and mathematics, the curriculum focuses on foundations of data science, statistical modeling, data mining, business analytics, and scientific visualization. A capstone experience, in which students will obtain, condition, explore, model, and interpret a big data set, is central to the degree. Students can focus their studies in one of the two tracks (business analytics or computation intensive) or maintain flexibility by not choosing a track.

Our expectation is that graduates of the Data Science program will be able to understand the mathematical and statistical foundations of data science and understand the business context in which data science functions. We also expect students to be able to implement algorithms for data aggregation, cleaning, and analysis, select and apply appropriate data analysis techniques to a variety of tasks, and communicate data analysis findings with appropriate visualizations.

I would like to thank and acknowledge the assistance of Dr. James Walden, associate professor of Computer Science at Northern Kentucky University for his leadership in developing this degree program and for his assistance in writing the description for this panel.

4. DAVID UMINSKY

In recognition of the emerging and immensely important field of "big data," the University of San Francisco has established a Bachelor of Science degree in Data Science (BSDS). This major is a challenging and interdisciplinary program that engages the student in rigorous academic training in the rapidly developing field of data science. The student will gain significant mathematical and quantitative skills, strong programming experience and flexible training to attack problems in burgeoning data-intensive fields such as economics, biology, computer science to name just a few.

The core of the BSDS major is focused around training in Mathematics and Computer Science with 52 units distributed among these two departments. This core represents the backbone of the training which will uniquely prepare a student with an impressive array of mathematical, statistical and computational skills to confidently enter the new field of "big data" careers. There are an additional three optional concentrations which would allow for a student to dive further into a specific subject and would be strongly encouraged for students considering graduate studies. These concentrations include Mathematical Data Science, Computational Data Science, and an Economic Data Science focus for a total of 64 units.

In addition to being career-ready upon graduation the student will be ready to continue into graduate training in analytics, financial engineering, computer science, economics and applied mathematics. The most successful students in this program will have the option to enroll in a 4+1 program with USF's own Masters in Analytics, where the student can complete her professional training with further course work and an industrial practicum where the student will gain hands on experience working with companies around the Bay Area on real world, big data problems.

REFERENCES

[1] ACM's Special Interest Group on Knowledge, Discovery, and Data Mining, http://www.sigkdd.org

[2] Bachelor of Science in Data Science, Computer Science Department, College of Informatics, Northern Kentucky University, http://datascience.nku.edu

[3] Bachelor of Science in Data Science, The Department of Mathematics, College of Arts and Sciences, University of San Francisco, http://usfca.edu/artsci/bsds/

[4] Data Science Program, College of Charleston, http://datascience.cofc.edu/

Poster Session 1

Application of a Blended Active Learning Model in Teaching Computer Programming to Non-majors

Chunming Gao, *Michigan Technological University*
Noriyuki Iwane, *Hiroshima City University*
Contact: chgao@mtu.edu

Introducing computer programming to non-computer science students has been a challenge. Concerns deal mainly with various backgrounds and expectations of students, planning of course components, and the adoption of effective teaching methods. This poster presents a guided active learning model with blended approach to help teaching computer programming to non-majors. The model starts with an outline of course objectives and the selection of textbooks, online tools, classrooms, and lab rooms. Under the blended approach, the model consists of classroom modules, lab room face-to-face modules, and online modules. It considers active learning in: online modules before and after classes or labs, in-class module, and in-lab module. The model concludes with the course evaluation which feeds back to the start for future improvement. By using this blended active learning model for five years, it has proven to be effective in engaging students in the course study and flexible to integrate various educational techniques. In the future, we plan to further study its flexibility by integrating innovative e-text learning techniques into the model.

ACM Categories & Descriptors: K.3.2 [Computer and Information Science Education]: Computer Science Education

Keywords: Active learning model; Blended learning; Learning models; College teaching

An Analysis of Difficulties Encountered by Novice Alice Programmers

Kuan-Yu Lin, *Taipei Municipal Jianguo High School*
Janet Mei-Chuen Lin, *Natioanl Taiwan Normal University*
Hue-Ching Kao, *Taipei Municipal Nan Gang High School*
Contact: mjlin@ntnu.edu.tw

This study investigated the difficulties encountered by novice Alice programmers. The researchers conducted one-on-one clinical interviews with 22 10th-grade students at a senior high school in Taipei, Taiwan. The participants were offered nine Alice programming tasks, each requiring the use of a different set of programming constructs, which included objects, primitive methods, expressions, built-in functions, variables, conditional execution, repetition control, arrays, user-defined methods, and parameter passing. Each participant was observed closely as s/he worked through the given tasks. Whenever an impasse occurred while a student was trying to solve a problem, the observer would intervene by asking a sequence of questions with increasing specificity, ranging from *strategic prompts* to *hints* to *provides*, in order to determine the cause of the impasse. This study summarized the common difficulties for each of the Alice programming constructs used by the participants in the programming tasks, and students' difficulties were categorized into four types: *connection*, *location*, *usage*, and *math-and-other* difficulties. Students having *connection* difficulties were unable to apply appropriate programming constructs to implement the actions required; *location* difficulties indicated students' inability to locating, in the Alice interface, the programming constructs they needed; *usage* difficulties referred in general to semantic errors in a student's programs; whereas *math-and-other* difficulties were caused mainly by students' inadequate math knowledge. It is hoped that the findings of this research will help Alice instructors to improve their students' performance by familiarizing themselves with the existence of the identified difficulties, and by addressing the missing conceptions or misconceptions underlying those difficulties.

SIGCSE'14, March 5–8, 2014, Atlanta, Georgia, USA.
ACM 978-1-4503-2605-6/14/03.

ACM Categories & Descriptors: D.1.5 Object-Oriented Programming

Keywords: Alice Programming; Programming Instruction; Programming Difficulties; Object-oriented Programming

Exploring Cognitive Processes in Program Comprehension Based on Eye-movement Analysis

Ting-Yun Hou, *National Taiwan Normal University*
Yu-Tzu Lin, *National Taiwan Normal University*
Yu-Chih Lin, *Yuanpei University*
Cheng-Chih Wu, *National Taiwan Normal University*
Contact: linyt@ntnu.edu.tw

This study investigates the cognitive processes involved in program comprehension based on eye gaze tracking. Thirty-eight participants were asked to comprehend the test programs. Eye-movement analysis was employed to track the students' gaze paths while they traced the programs for comprehension. Cognitive processes were then obtained by sequential analysis of the gaze data to investigate the significant sequences of attention areas. The mined cognitive processes were compared between high and low comprehenders. The experiment results show that most subjects focused on major part of the program to comprehend the program. However, high comprehenders traced the program in a more logical manner. In addition, low comprehenders needed more manual calculation and also needed to trace back to prior statements for recalling required information, which might be because they had limited working memory capacities for computing and memorizing. Subjects performed better on cognitive processes involved in the working memory (short-term memory, mental arithmetic, and logical thinking) also performed better on program comprehension. Working memory seems to play an important role in program comprehension. These results can provide suggestions for researchers/instructors to develop adaptive instructional strategies for students of different characteristics.

ACM Categories & Descriptors: K.3.2 [Computer and Information Science Education]: Computer Science Education

Keywords: Program comprehension; cognition process; eye tracking

ACCE: Automatic Coding Composition Evaluator

Stephanie Rogers, *University of California, Berkeley*
Steven Tang, *University of California, Berkeley*
Julia Oh, *University of California, Berkeley*
Dan Garcia, *University of California, Berkeley*
Contact: srogers11@berkeley.edu

Coding style is important to teach to beginning programmers, so that bad habits don't become permanent. This is often done manually at the University level because automated Python static analyzers cannot accurately grade based on a given rubric. However, even manual analysis of coding style encounters problems, as we have seen quite a bit of inconsistency among our graders. We introduce ACCE--Automated Coding Composition Evaluator--a module that automates grading for the composition of programs. ACCE, given certain constraints, assesses the composition of a program through static analysis, feature extraction, supervised learning and clustering (unsupervised learning), automating the subjective process of grading based on style and identifying common mistakes. Further, we create visual representations of the clusters to allow readers and students understand where a submission falls, and the overall trends. We have applied this tool to CS61A--a CS1 level course at UC, Berkeley experiencing rapid growth in student enrollment--in an attempt to help expedite the involved process as well as reduce human grader inconsistencies.

ACM Categories & Descriptors: K.3.1 Computer Uses in Education; I.5.3 Clustering

Keywords: Composition; Clustering; Unsupervised Learning; Autograding; Assessment; Gephi; Visualization; Grading; Style; CS1; Evaluation

Guidelines for Group Work in CS1

Cecily Heiner, *Southern Utah University*
Contact: cecilyheiner@suu.edu

In CS1, students have a limited set of programming skills and they often represent a wide range of experience levels; this combination can make group work especially challenging. I describe guidelines for selecting group work projects and problems, suggestions for forming groups and assigning roles, and four projects appropriate for group work in CS1.

ACM Categories & Descriptors: K.3.2 Computer and Information Science Education

Keywords: Group Work; CS1

SIGCSE'14, March 5–8, 2014, Atlanta, Georgia, USA.
ACM 978-1-4503-2605-6/14/03.

Technique for Retaining Low Performing Students: High-Need Student Mentoring Program

Shearon Brown, *North Carolina A&T State University*
Xiaohong Yuan, *North Carolina A&T State University*
Contact: sab@ncat.edu

It has been a challenge to retain computer science students, especially underrepresented students such as woman and minority. This poster describes our experiences in implementing a mentoring program to improve computer science retention and graduate rates at North Carolina A&T State University (NCATSU). NCATSU is among the United States' Historically Black Colleges and Universities (HBCU) serving more than 10,000 students. The Department of Computer Science on the average enrolls 195 undergraduate students, among them approximately 90% are African American and 30% are African American woman. The Computer Science Department at NCATSU in an attempt to increase retention and graduate rates of minority and women students developed the High-Need Student Mentoring Program supported by the Department of Education Minority Science and Engineering Improvement Program (MSEIP). This poster describes the High-Need Student Mentoring Program (HNSMP). HNSMP is designed to provide special attention to undergraduate students who show signs of having academic difficulty. The goal of this Program is to increase retention by increasing the academic performance of these students. HNSMP's strategy is to assist these students before they reach the point of academic probation or suspension. We will describes data we collected, our findings and challenges we encountered in implementing this program, and our proposed strategies to overcome these challenges. Our experiences and the effective techniques found may be beneficial for other colleges and universities in retaining computer science students, especially African American students.

ACM Categories & Descriptors: A.0 General Literature

Keywords: Retention; Underrepresented Students; Low Performing Students

Intelligence and Security Informatics: Developing Curricular Modules in Context

Wingyan Chung, *Stetson University*
Albert Chan, *Fayetteville State University*
Daniel Plante, *Stetson University*
Ray Villalobos, *Seminole State College*
Joseph Woodside, *Stetson University*
Contact: wchung@stetson.edu

Intelligence and Security Informatics (ISI) is a cross-disciplinary field that connects advanced information technologies, systems, algorithms, and databases with international, national and homeland security related applications. Our NSF-funded project, titled Computing in Context, has a focus of developing new teaching modules and pedagogies for the ISI discipline at the undergraduate level. In this poster, we present five exemplar modules that we developed for the ISI discipline: database design for cybercrime investigation, securing private data on the Internet, data visualization for understanding privacy sentiment, security intelligence for healthcare mobility, and program design for digital forensics. Our materials are designed for inquiry-based learning and for active engagement of students through discussion, hands-on practices, and various exercises.

ACM Categories & Descriptors: K.3.2 Computer and Information Science Education; H.2.8 Database Applications; K.4.1 Public Policy Issues; K.3.1 Computer Uses in Education

Keywords: Curricular Module Development; Active Learning; Inquiry-based Learning; Computing in Context; Intelligence and Security Informatics; Business Intelligence and Analytics; Data Privacy; Database Development

Teaching Artificial Intelligence as a Lab Science: Basic and Informed Search

Stephanie E. August, *Loyola Marymount University*
Michael A. Fraser, *Loyola Marymount University*
Miguel A. Vazquez, *Loyola Marymount University*
Contact: saugust@lmu.edu

The Teaching Artificial Intelligence as a Laboratory Science (TAILS) project is designed to develop a new paradigm for teaching introductory artificial intelligence (AI) concepts by implementing an experimental approach modeled after the lab sciences. In the Basic and Informed Search module of TAILS students learn about various search algorithms by first observing how each algorithm searches a map, watching the construction of the corresponding search tree as the path planning proceeds. Once students understand the differences between algorithms, they proceed to exercises. Students are provided a version of the program with the search algorithm replaced by a comment that guides the students through the process of implementing each algorithm and testing it with the existing application. This enables the students to focus on the AI aspect of the coding without requiring them to also develop the user interface. This poster describes the search module and assessments and presents preliminary results.

ACM Categories & Descriptors: K.3 Computers and Education; I.2.8 Problem Solving, Control Methods, and Search

Keywords: Artificial Intelligence; Heuristic Search; Basic Search; CS Education Research

Analysis of Interaction Logs for Online Tutorials

Daniel A. Breakiron, *Virginia Tech*
Eric Fouh, *Virginia Tech*
Sally Hamouda, *Virginia Tech*
Clifford A. Shaffer, *Virginia Tech*
Contact: shaffer@vt.edu

As the use of online interactive tutorials becomes more widespread, there will be more opportunities to use fine-grained interaction log data to deduce student behavior. Log data can help debug usability or pedagogical problems with the tutorials, or guide redesign to discourage pedagogically poor student behavior. OpenDSA is a collection of open source interactive materials for teaching data structures and algorithms. We present a case study analysis of the activity logs from use of OpenDSA tutorials by roughly 150 students over several weeks. We identified clusters of student use based on when they completed exercises, verified the reliability of estimated time requirements for exercises, provided evidence that a majority of students do not read the text, and found evidence that students complete additional exercises after obtaining credit. Furthermore, we determined that slideshow use was fairly high, but that skipping to the end of slideshows was common.

ACM Categories & Descriptors: E.1.3 Data Structures; K.3.2 Computers and Education - Computer and Information Science Education

Keywords: Electronic Textbook; Algorithm Visualization; Automated Assessment; Event Log Analysis

ACM Associate-Degree IT Curricular Guidance

Elizabeth K. Hawthorne, *Union County College*
Cara Tang, *Portland Community College*
Jim Nichols, *Estrella Mountain Community College*
Cindy Tucker, *Bluegrass Community and Technical College*
Contact: cara.tang@pcc.edu

Directed by the ACM Education Board, the ACM CCECC (Committee for Computing Education in Community Colleges) has produced curricular guidance for associate-degree IT programs consisting of core IT learning outcomes with associated assessment rubrics. The learning outcomes express core IT competencies which should be common to all IT-related associate-degree programs. The three-tiered assessment rubrics provide further clarity and meaningful evaluation metrics for each outcome, as well as facilitate integration into assessment-based curricula. The outcomes have been influenced by current and future needs of business and industry, certifications, related curricula, and government and standards bodies, along with the intent of being adaptable, not overly technology specific, and having reasonable staying power. These results are being made available during the poster session, in the exhibit hall at the committee booth, and online at www.capspace.org.

ACM Categories & Descriptors: K.3.2 Computer and Information Science Education

Keywords: Information Technology;Two-Year College; Associate-Degree Programs; Curriculum Guidance

Supporting Computational Algorithmic Thinking (SCAT): Development of a Complex Cognitive Capability in African-American Middle-School Girls

Jakita O. Thomas, *Spelman College*
Contact: jakita.owensby@gmail.com

Computational algorithmic thinking (CAT) is the ability to design, implement, and assess the implementation of algorithms to solve a range of problems. It involves identifying and understanding a problem, articulating an algorithm or set of algorithms in the form of a solution to the problem, implementing that solution in such a way that it solves the problem, and evaluating the solution based on some set of criteria. Supporting Computational Algorithmic

SIGCSE'14, March 5–8, 2014, Atlanta, Georgia, USA.
ACM 978-1-4503-2605-6/14/03.

Thinking (SCAT) is a research project that explores how African-American middle-school girls develop CAT capabilities over time in the context of game design. SCAT is also a free enrichment program designed to expose middle school girls to game design. Spanning three years, participants, also called SCAT Scholars, develop CAT capabilities as they design more and more complex games. This poster presents the Supporting Computational Algorithmic Thinking (SCAT) project, which is an on-going longitudinal between-subjects research project whose goals are: 1) to guide African-American middle school girls through the iterative game design cycle over three years resulting in a set of complex games around broad themes, and 2) to expose them to the broad range of opportunities that exist for them in all types of industries and areas if they develop their CAT capabilities.

ACM Categories & Descriptors: K.3.1 Computer Uses in Education: Collaborative Learning

Keywords: Computational algorithmic thinking; game design; game design cycle; SCAT; African-American; Middle-school; Girls; Complex Cognitive Capability

Towards Engaging Big Data for CS1/2

Nadeem Abdul Hamid, *Berry College*
Steven Benzel, *Georgia Highlands College*
Contact: nadeem@acm.org

A number of contextualized approaches to teaching introductory Computer Science (CS) courses have been developed in the past few years, catering to students with different interests and learning styles. For instance, entire courses have been developed around media computation or robots (real and virtual). There is however one context which, to our knowledge, has not been exploited in a systematic fashion - that of "big data," by which we mean massive, openly accessible online datasets from a wide variety of sources. We present progress on a code framework and methodology to facilitate the incorporation of large, online data sets into traditional CS1 and CS2 courses. The goal of our project is to develop a way to provide students a library that relieves them from low-level issues of reading and parsing raw data from web-based data sources and that interfaces with data structures and representations defined by students themselves. In addition, the library requires minimal syntactic overhead to use its functionality and allows students and instructors to focus on algorithmic exercises involving processing live and large data obtained from the Internet. At a minimum, the library should serve to create drop-in replacements for traditional programming exercises in introductory courses - raising the engagement level by having students deal with "real" data rather than artificial data provided through standard input.

ACM Categories & Descriptors: K.3.2 Computer science education; H.3.5 Online Information Services

Keywords: Big data; CS1

Integrating Computer Science and Mathematics in Middle School with Alice

Susan H. Rodger, *Duke University*
Daniel MacDonald, *Duke University*
Elizabeth Onstwedder, *Duke University*
Bella Onwumbiko, *Duke University*
Edwin Ward, *Duke University*
Contact: rodger@cs.duke.edu

The Adventures in Alice Programming project at Duke University has created a variety of Alice curriculum materials for integrating computer science into other disciplines at the K-12 level, focusing on both computer science topics and animation topics. For example, one of our new animation tutorials shows how to attach multiple camera views to an object to move with the object through a virtual Alice world. Our newest curriculum materials focus on integrating computer science into middle school mathematics. Our math related tutorials guide users on programming math projects from scratch, and our math challenges are partially built programs for students to complete. We use topics that are attractive to middle school students. For example, we have created a wizard world math and programming challenge that is an eight-level game. Each level in the game is titled similarly to courses one might take in the school Hogwarts in the Harry Potter book series by J.K. Rowling. Students must add code related to either a math or computer science concept in order to complete a level and move to the next level. Since 2008, we have taught extensive multi-week Alice beginner workshops every summer to K-12 teachers, teaching over 200 teachers. Our new curriculum materials are mapped to both the CSTA and the Common Core Math standards, and are available for free at www.cs.duke.edu/csed/alice/aliceInSchools along with teacher lesson plans.

ACM Categories & Descriptors: K.3.2 Computer and Information Science Education

Keywords: Alice; virtual worlds; K-12 education; middle school; introductory computer science; mathematics

Use of Problem-Solving Approach to Teach Scratch Programming for Adult Novice Programmers

Chiung-Fang Chiu, *National Chi Nan University*
Contact: cfchiu@ncnu.edu.tw

Novice programmers usually fail to combine abstract concepts and knowledge into program design, even though they know the syntax and semantics of individual statement. Adult novice programmers with little computer background knowledge might face more difficulties than young ones do. Therefore, it's important to choose feasible teaching approach and proper programming language to teach adult novice programmers basic programming concepts. This study aims to investigate the use of problem-solving approach to teach Scratch programming for adult novice programmers. A total of 10 graduate students aged from 24 to 45 participated in this study. In additional to the lectures of Scratch programming concepts, students solved programming problems by the scaffoldings of worksheets, which is a problem-solving approach. The worksheets contained a sequence of questions which guide the principles of problem-solving approach – problem analysis, solution design, coding, testing and debugging. Students were then asked to design and implement their projects by following this approach after learning fundamental programming concepts. The experiment lasted for one semester. The findings of the questionnaire survey and results of interviews with students revealed that most students had positive attitudes toward learning Scratch programming by the problem-solving approach. They considered this approach useful in enhancing their comprehension of the program design process and helping them to implement the programming project more effectively.

ACM Categories & Descriptors: K.3.2 [Computers and Education]: Computer and Information Science Education – *Computer science education*
Keywords: Problem-Solving; Programming; Scratch; Computer Science Education

Motivational Active Learning for Computer Science Education

Johanna Pirker, *Graz University of Technology*
Christian Gütl, *Graz University of Technology*
Contact: jpirker@iicm.edu

Motivational Active Learning (MAL) is an innovative pedagogical approach based on MIT's teaching format TEAL (Technology-Enabled Active Learning) combined with advanced motivational strategies based on gamification design aspects. The main idea of MAL is to enhance learning outcomes using motivational and social learning experiences. The lecture format is designed for courses, which combine theory in computer science with hands-on programming challenges and collaborative in-course problem solving. The main features of MAL include collaborative learning, constant activities to stimulate interactions between instructor and students, immediate feedback for self-assessment, and motivational feedback such as badges or leaderboard information. The course is structured in the form of mini lectures with constant interactive challenges and interactions such as small arithmetic problems, programming challenges, or research and discussion assignments, which are available using a learning management system as supportive in-course technology to provide the interactive course content and according immediate feedback. First outcomes show positive impact on student motivation and attention during the lessons. Also, more students are willing to complete bonus tasks volunaryly do gain extra points.

ACM Categories & Descriptors: K.3.1. Computer Uses in Education; K.3.2. Computer and Information Science Education

Keywords: Interactive Learning; Motivational Learning; Computer Science Education; Teachnology Enabled Active Learning

The Impact of Math Preparedness on Introductory Programming (CS1) Success

Emmett Tomai, *University of Texas – Pan American*
Christine Reilly, *University of Texas – Pan American*
Contact: reillycf@utpa.edu

SIGCSE'14, March 5–8, 2014, Atlanta, Georgia, USA.
ACM 978-1-4503-2605-6/14/03.

At our university, like at many other institutions, the pass rate in the introductory programming (CS1) course is relatively low, in the approximate range of 50% to 75%. We would like to discover factors that have an impact on student success in introductory programming in order to better advise and place our students into the course at the appropriate point in their academic careers. Our main motivation for increasing the CS1 pass rate is to help our students graduate on time. It has long been thought that mathematics background is a factor in determining a student's success in introductory computer science courses. Currently, our students must be concurrently enrolled in college algebra or placed into a higher mathematics course. However, given our current low pass rate, we wonder whether this is the proper prerequisite. In order to gather information about mathematics background, we administered a questionnaire to the students enrolled in the class during Spring 2013. We then analyzed the pass rate of our introductory programming students in relation to their mathematics background. Our findings indicate that students who are prepared to take calculus I in the same semester as they take introductory programming were more likely to pass introductory programming. These findings suggest that changing our math prerequisite to pre-calculus may increase the pass rate in our introductory programming course.

ACM Categories & Descriptors: D.3.3 Language Constructs and Features; K.3.2 Computer and Information Science Education;

Keywords: Introduction to Programming; Computer Science 1; Student Success

How Do We Measure Success? A New Instrument for Evaluating Girls' Progress in Middle and High School Computing Programs

Catherine Ashcraft, *University of Colorado*
Wendy Dubow, *University of Colorado*
Zhen Wu, *University of Colorado*
Contact: catherine.ashcraft@colorado.edu

Girls and women continue to be underrepresented in technology. This persistent underrepresentation inhibits innovation by ignoring the diverse perspectives and life experiences women bring to invention and problem solving. Furthermore, disregard for girls and women's participation exacerbates existing economic disparities for women. To reverse these trends, a number of programs designed to engage girls in computing have emerged in recent years. Often these programs are not evaluated, or if they are, informal surveys are used. These instruments are usually unable to adequately assess change in interest, confidence and future plans for computing. In addition, sample sizes tend to be small and, because different programs use different surveys, results cannot be aggregated or compared across programs. To address this gap, NCWIT has been piloting a new evaluation instrument informed by Social Cognitive Career Theory (Lent et al., 2008). The instrument was piloted with two groups of girls: 312 Globaloria middle and high school students and 1500 girls who applied to NCWIT's Aspirations program from 2007 to 2013. Reliability analysis and confirmatory factor analysis were conducted for both datasets, showing high internal consistency. This poster session will provide more detail on the instrument, how it has been used and tested, and next steps in scaling its use. In making this tool widely available, we hope to increase consistency in the evaluation of girls' participation in computing education programs, enabling us to increase sample sizes; compare results across programs; and accelerate contributions to the gender and computing knowledge base.

ACM Categories & Descriptors: K.3.2 Computer and Information Science Education

Keywords: Gender and Computing; Broadening Participation in Computing; Diversity; K-12 Education

Developing a Game-Based Learning Curriculum for "Big Data" in Middle School

Allison G. Martínez-Arocho, *Meredith College*
Philip Sheridan Buffum, *North Carolina State University*
Kristy Elizabeth Boyer, *North Carolina State University*
Contact: amartine@email.meredith.edu

Exposing students early to computer science may influence their choice of career, and there is increasing recognition that even for students who do not pursue computer science careers, computational literacy is important. This poster reports on a project targeting the development of a new middle school computer science curriculum. This research aims to highlight the role of computation in Big Data in the context of middle school computer science education, which serves as a catalyst to keep students engaged in computer science through middle school via the ENGAGE narrative game-based learning environment. This poster discusses steps taken to validate one activity meant to highlight the role of computation in the context of Big Data: skip list manipulation. While we found that most of the middle school students performed poorly in assessments after the skip list activities, several students showed they were capable of completing the activity successfully, implying that a repetition of the revised skip list study and additional pilot studies for other Big Data activities are needed to pave the way for the development of this Big Data curriculum. This activity will be just one part of a broader curriculum designed to showcase the social relevance and power of Big Data.

ACM Categories & Descriptors: K.3.2 **[Computers and Education]**: Computers and Education – *Computer science education, Literacy, Curriculum.*

Keywords: Game-Based Learning; Big Data; Middle School; ENGAGE

SIGCSE'14, March 5–8, 2014, Atlanta, Georgia, USA.
ACM 978-1-4503-2605-6/14/03.

Kodu, Alice and Computer Science Unplugged: A Model of Effective Introducing Middle School Students to Computer Science and Computational Thinking

Daniela Marghitu, *Auburn University*
Lavaris Thomas, *Auburn University*
Yasmeen Rawajfih, *Auburn University*
Jillian Hall, *Auburn University*
Andrew Marshall, *Auburn University*
Contact: marghda@auburn.edu

This poster describes the "Computer Science for All Bulldogs" (CS4ALL-B) pilot, a 7-week long course taught in Fall 2013 at Opelika Middle School, located in the Auburn- Opelika, Alabama Metropolitan Area (https://cs4allb.eng.auburn.edu). The program marks the first time a formal Computer Science (CS) course has been taught in an Alabama middle school. The CS4ALL-B curriculum builds upon the Auburn University innovative "three-step" model of K-12 computing and robotics instruction that introduces CS and Computational Thinking (CT) concepts for K-12 students. This model uses programming frameworks such as Kodu, Alice, App Inventor, Lego NXT-G and Tetrix, and Computer Science Unplugged (CSU) activities. While moving between the three steps, students explore the fundamentals of CS/CT concepts.

The CS4ALL-B curriculum is structured in four main sections: First, introduction to Kodu for 7th graders and Alice for 8th graders; Second, introduction to CS/CT Concepts; Third, participation in selected CSU activities, then students develop their programs to demonstrate their abilities to design and create Kodu or Alice worlds that implement the concepts learned while participating in CSU activities; Fourth, students build their own course project that includes all concepts and skills grasped throughout their training. This model helps maintain high levels of motivation, concentration, and engagement during the entire course.

The results of the pilot assessment, including tools such as traditional written assessments (e.g. quizzes, tests) as well as alternative assessments tools (e.g. projects and blog posts), will be presented. We have found that our methods foster the learners' nascent development in CS.

ACM Categories & Descriptors: G.4 Alice; D.2.2 Microsoft Windows; D.3.2 Language Classifications

Keywords: Computer Science; Computational Thinking; Middle School Formal Computer Science class

Who Drops CS1?

Diane Horton, *University of Toronto*
Michelle Craig, *University of Toronto*
Contact: mcraig@cs.toronto.edu

In the interest of better understanding why many students fail to complete CS1 successfully, we analyze a class of 555 CS1 students, 127 of whom either failed or dropped the course. We find that students with previous experience are more likely to pass even if the experience is not a formal programming course. Contrary to intuition, students who drop have enrolled in fewer courses and have fewer hours of non-school commitments than those who stay. We present a classification scheme to categorize student outcomes based on their performance at a course midpoint.

ACM Categories & Descriptors: K.3.2 [Computers and Education]: Computer and Information Science Education—Computer Science Education

Keywords: CS1; drop rate; failure rate

Revitalizing the Computer Science Undergraduate Curriculum Inside and Outside of the Classroom Using Mobile Computing Platforms

Shiva Azadegan, *Towson University*
Josh Dehlinger, *Towson University*
Siddharth Kaza, *Towson University*
Contact: jdehlinger@towson.edu

Computer Science educators are constantly reinventing introductory CS0, CS1 and CS2 courses to retain students and increase their learning and motivation. While the focus on drawing students into Computer Science is vital to maintain enrollment, it is also paramount to sustain student motivation by using new pedagogical approaches, contextualized to how students learn, throughout the curriculum to develop technical and interpersonal skills. Many educators have developed one-off courses employing new technology or a project-driven approach to engage students and transfer ready industry skills. Yet, too few have woven a combination of pedagogical approaches sensitive to how students learn with in-demand technology and skills contiguously throughout the upper-level curriculum and tied it to opportunities outside of the classroom. In this poster, we present the initial results of a project with two aims to: (1) design, pilot, and offer new curriculum materials for three upper-level Computer Science courses using a mobile computing platform paired with pedagogical approaches sensitive to the learning styles of today's student; and, (2) develop out-of-classroom learning opportunities including mobile computing student seminars, externship opportunities and service-learning projects reinforcing in-classroom technical skills. We believe that these two components synergistically, can be leveraged to revitalize the undergraduate Computer Science curriculum, better motivate student learning and provide in-demand technical skills to students without losing the fundamental Computer Science concepts. This project is partially supported by NSF DUE#1140781.

ACM Categories & Descriptors: K.3.2 Computer and Information Science Education

Keywords: Computer Science education; mobile computing

A First Year Common Course on Computational Problem Solving and Programming

Bruce W. Char, *Drexel University*
Thomas T. Hewett, *Drexel University (emeritus)*
Contact: bchar@cs.drexel.edu

This is work-in-progress on an entry-level course on computational problem-solving and programming for engineering students. It has been run since 2006 at our institution at a scale of 800 students/term, as a hybrid in-person lab and out-of-class on-line autograded exercises using Maple TA. The course is in the process of changing languages (from Maple to Matlab), with upgraded resources: a lecture period, some manually graded assignments, projects, and automatic code testing.

To date the assessment of the impact of the course has been through conventional means: assigning grades and indications as to whether student grades are consistent with those obtained in other courses taken. During the transition from Maple to Matlab more detailed and individualized performance assessment plans are being developed which are intended to enable the staff and students to better judge weaknesses in program knowledge and who would benefit from additional personal contact.

ACM Categories & Descriptors: K.3.2 Computer Science Education

Keywords: Autograding; active learning; non-major courses

Altruism among Programmers: The Availability and Effectiveness of On-line, Spontaneous Peer Mentoring in Competitive Problem Solving

David Sturgill, *North Carolina State University*
Contact: dbsturgi@ncsu.edu

This poster presents preliminary investigation of the content and quality of on-line peer mentoring in competitive problem solving. Discussion board postings from the Queue-ICPC Challenge were analyzed with respect to content, including type of communication, topic, intended audience and accuracy, as well as attempts at relationship building. Responses outnumbered questions more than 2 to 1, suggesting that even in a competition, people are willing to assist others. Interestingly, some of the most successful competitors were also the most willing to offer help to others.

As part of a voluntary competition, this kind of peer mentoring is useful resource for attracting and supporting new participants. In the academic context, peer mentoring may be an essential aspect of learner support for large, traditional classes. In very large scale efforts such as MOOCs, it may provide a scalable resource for helping participants to succeed and remain engaged.

ACM Categories & Descriptors: K.3.0 Computers and Education, General

Keywords: Tools; Libraries; Learning Environments

Observations of First Learners with Different Capabilities

Amber Wagner, *University of Alabama*
Jeff Gray, *University of Alabama*
Contact: ankrug@bama.ua.edu

During the Summer of 2013, we participated in a United Cerebral Palsy supported summer camp for children with disabilities. While our initial motivation for attending the camp was to conduct a user study of a Vocal User Interface, we worked with the camp attendees outside of testing and beyond computer activities, and during these activities, we were able to ask the attendees about their computer experience and interest. The attendees' experience and interest was noted along with the results of the study. The study demonstrated that voice was a useful modality for this audience; however, we were more surprised to learn that the majority of the attendees were not enthusiastic about using the computer and preferred more social activities. Three different types of computer science education activities were offered during the six week camp. The first activity was a group activity in which roughly ten students participated. The next activity was completed with smaller groups consisting of 2-3 attendees in which five students participated throughout the camp. The final activity was a one-on-one activity, and only three students chose to participate in the one-on-one activity. This poster presents the details of these activities, results of the user study, and thoughts as to why few attendees chose to participate in the smaller group activities based on observations during the summer camp.

ACM Categories & Descriptors: K.4.2 Social Issues; K.3.1 Computer Uses in Education

Keywords: Human Factors; Computer Science Education; First Learners

"Come Code with Codester": An Educational App that Teaches Computer Science

Gili Rusak, *Siena College*
Darren Lim, *Siena College*
Contact: rusakgili@gmail.com

Despite dramatic changes in technology over the past several years, educating young students in computer science at the elementary school level remains a challenge. Tackling this issue, we created "Codester," a novel Android application, as a tool to engage learners in the basics of computer science and to teach them computational thinking. Unlike other educational coding programs such as Scratch and Lego Mindstorms, our app is unique because it is mobile and allows users to learn a variety of concepts at a rapid rate. By running user studies for participants in grades 1-3 and 4-6, we quantified the effectiveness of Codester. Students were challenged and developed logic skills throughout the sessions. Using surveys, pretests, and posttests, we found an improvement in the five main computational thinking concepts that Codester teaches: sequencing, iteration, code reuse, decision-making, and logic. The participants especially showed an increased understanding of the code reuse concept: grade 1-3 students improved by 32% at the end of the program; grade 4-6 users improved by 43%. Additionally, the software and the tablet platform were attractive to the participants. Eighty percent of students stated that they enjoyed using the tablets to learn new material, and 72% said that they would like to continue learning with Codester. These figures show a promising increase of interest in coding and thus match the goal of our app: teach youngsters programming in a fun and challenging way. Please see www.codesterapp.com.

ACM Categories & Descriptors: K.3.2 [Computers and Education]: Computer and Information Science Education – *computer science education*

Keywords: Computer Science Education; Computational thinking; Problem solving

Implementing a Living Lab Approach to Foster Innovation in an Advanced Software Engineering Course

Jean H. French, *Coastal Carolina University*
Contact: jennis@coastal.edu

The living lab concept promotes innovation by solving problems in an open, user-centric environment. A living lab approach was implemented in an undergraduate, advanced software engineering course to develop applications for the Leap Motion. The Leap Motion is a novel device that provides touch-less interaction with computer systems. Sixteen students worked toward the common goal of developing applications for the Leap Motion. All aspects of the project were supported in the student-led, open environment, from initial research to implementation. Because the Leap Motion device was not available until shortly before the semester, students had no prior experience in application development for the technology, adding to the difficulty and uniqueness of the task. This poster provides the details of the living lab implementation as the project progressed through the semester.

ACM Categories & Descriptors: K.1.3 Computer Uses in Education

Keywords: Living laboratory

MyCS: Building a Middle-years CS Curriculum

Thomas Ashmore, *Harvey Mudd College*
Sorathan Chaturapruek, *Harvey Mudd College*
Zachary Dodds, *Harvey Mudd College*
Corinne Druhan, *Harvey Mudd College*
Bridgette Eichelberger, *Harvey Mudd College*
Michael Erlinger, *Harvey Mudd College*
Elizabeth Schofield, *Harvey Mudd College*
Contact: tum_chaturapruek@hmc.edu

In this poster we present a CS curriculum aimed at "middle-years" students. In the U.S., this corresponds roughly to students aged 11-15. This MyCS curriculum provides a hands-on introduction to computer science through six distinct modules. Three programming modules use the Scratch environment to build computational sophistication and procedural intuition within an inviting development environment. Alternating with Scratch are three

SIGCSE'14, March 5–8, 2014, Atlanta, Georgia, USA.
ACM 978-1-4503-2605-6/14/03.

problem-solving modules whose activities deepen awareness and facility with computation through novel exercises. More than 25 classrooms and 900 students have participated in MyCS's pilot years within the Pomona, CA and Lihue, HI school districts. 2013-15 will see an expansion of its workshops, academic-year classes, and program evaluation. Course materials will be served by the OpenEdX platform both at HMC and on Amazon EC2. This poster shares our development and deployment of MyCS to date, and invites feedback from other institutions in their efforts to foster adolescents' computational identities. A laptop is recommended.

ACM Categories & Descriptors: K.3.2 [Computers and Education]: Computer Science Education Subjects: Curriculum

Keywords: Middle-school computer science; Online computer science education

OCTAL: Online Course Tool for Adaptive Learning

Daniel Armendariz, *University of California, Berkeley*
Zachary MacHardy, *University of California, Berkeley*
Daniel D. Garcia, *University of California, Berkeley*
Contact: danallan@cs.berkeley.edu

The Online Course Tool for Adaptive Learning (OCTAL) is an adaptive exercise system that customizes the progression of question topics to each student. By creating a concept dependency graph of topics in a course and modeling a student's knowledge state, the tool will present questions that test knowledge within a student's zone of proximal development. We intend OCTAL to be a formative assessment tool that is not tied to any specific course by providing language-agnostic questions on computer science concepts. While the tool will be generalizable for many courses, our first prototype will include a concept map and question set from an introductory CS1 course, UC Berkeley's CS10: The Beauty and Joy of Computing. Using the tool, we are investigating metacognitive improvements in the identification of knowledge gaps by presenting online course material in a nonlinear fashion.

ACM Categories & Descriptors: K.3.1 Computer-assisted instruction (CAI); K.3.2 Computer science education

Keywords: Adaptive assessment; Non-linear courses; Concept map; Student modeling

SIGCSE'14, March 5–8, 2014, Atlanta, Georgia, USA.
ACM 978-1-4503-2605-6/14/03.

Poster Session 2

Use of Mobile Application to Improve Active Learning and Student Participation in the Computer Science Classroom

Debzani Deb, *Winston-Salem State University*
Mohammad Muztaba Fuad, *Winston-Salem State University*
Contact: fuadmo@wssu.edu

This poster addresses a significant learning barrier experienced at many CS departments, especially at predominantly minority institutions, which is the problem of students' inability to keep engaged and interested in classroom. In this research, we investigate the applicability of using mobile devices in the classroom and incorporation of interactive problem solving using those devices to increase class engagement and active learning for students. By allowing the students to solve problems in their preferred devices, the research expects to create a friendly learning environment where the students want to retain, be active and skillful. The poster will present the design aspects of Mobile Response System (MRS) software that will be utilized to communicate, collaborate and evaluate interactive problems using mobile devices. The poster will also showcase several interactive problem-solving activities utilizing mobile devices and MRS software, which have been developed and are being adopted in CS and IT courses at Winston-Salem State University (WSSU). It is expected that this research will invigorate interest in Computer Science among minority and underrepresented students through exposure to the technology-rich learning environment. By enhancing student learning and problem solving abilities, it is also expected that this research work will improve the quality and quantity of underrepresented minority students in STEM workforce or graduate study. The successful execution of this project will advance research and the knowledge of mobile device usage in CS classrooms and more importantly the way it impact teaching strategy and student learning at WSSU and other institutions.

ACM Categories & Descriptors: K.3.1 Computer Uses in Education; K.3.2 Computer and Information Science Education

Keywords: Mobile apps; Technology-rich learning; Active learning

New Hands-on Labs on Browser Security

Wenliang (Kevin) Du, Syracuse University
Li Yang, Joseph Kizza, *University of Tennessee at Chattanooga*
Xiaohong Yuan, *North Carolina A&T State University*
Contact: Li-Yang@utc.edu

SIGCSE'14, March 5–8, 2014, Atlanta, Georgia, USA.
ACM 978-1-4503-2605-6/14/03.

Browser security as an important and relatively new area is yet not part of existing IA curriculum or National Security Agency (NSA) knowledge units. Browser security incorporate threats, vulnerabilities, risks, and countermeasures faced by browsers and browser-based applications ranging from design principles, security architecture to applications. Our effort contributes to courseware development and IA education in terms of browser security. Hands-on labs are effective to improve student learning in IA and sharpen their skills in real-world settings. We develop hands-on labs to help students to build necessary skills on developing secure browser and browser-based applications. Our developed hands-on labs can be adopted in various levels of undergraduate Computer Science (CS) and Information Assurance (IA) courses. The developed hands-on exercises tied with each browser security topic teach students exploitation and defense for web browsers or browser-based applications. These labs can be "plugged" into courses at different levels from junior to senior courses such as network security, security management, etc. Our approach enriches experiential learning materials in IA.

ACM Categories & Descriptors: J.1 Education

Keywords: browser security

An Integrated Approach to Teaching of Abstract Query Languages and their Implementations

Rajshekhar Sunderraman, *Georgia State University*
Contact: raj@cs.gsu.edu

The treatment of abstract query languages such as Relational Algebra, Relational Calculus, and Datalog in introductory database courses varies considerably across the various computer science departments around the world. We propose an integrated approach in which students learn how to express a natural language query in Domain Relational Calculus (DRC), apply a query-transforming algorithm to the DRC expression tree to produce Datalog Rules (DLG), and finally apply another query-transforming algorithm to the DLG rules to produce an equivalent Relational Algebra (RA) expression. This systematic approach works very well for "forall-queries" in which the forall-quantifier is necessary in the DRC expression. To make this approach even more effective, the students are required to use DRC, DLG, and RA interpreters that allow them to execute query expressions as well as produce equivalent expressions. The students are also involved in implementing these interpreters to get a deeper understanding of querying in relational systems.

ACM Categories & Descriptors: H.2.3 Languages, Relational Query Languages.

Keywords: Domain Relational Calculus, Datalog, Relational Algebra, Interpreters, Translators

The Rising Renaissance Engineer Spectrum Awards

Martha J. Kosa, *Tennessee Technological University*
Ambareen Siraj, *Tennessee Technological University*
Contact: mjkosa@tntech.edu

We describe a new annual awards program, the *Rising Renaissance Engineer Spectrum Awards*, which recognizes a diverse body of students across all engineering departments at our institution for their initiatives and achievements in educational, research, and professional development activities. This award is unique at our institution because it is inclusively for students from all six engineering departments and specifically promotes underrepresented groups. This awards program complements existing engineering awards honoring faculty, staff, and alumni for their research, teaching, and service. It is modeled after the NCWIT (National Center for Women in Information Technology) Aspirations in Computing Award, which has successfully encouraged many female high school students to persist in computing careers. With the Computer Science Department spearheading the effort, this project is a collaborative partnership among representatives from all engineering departments.

ACM Categories & Descriptors: K.3.2 Computer Science Education

Keywords: gender; diversity; lifelong learning; professionalism; outreach; recognition; encouragement; persistence; community building

Developing and Using an In-house Plugin for Easy Social Network Programming

Anna Koufakou, *Florida Gulf Coast University*
Dahai Guo, *Florida Gulf Coast University*
Contact: akoufakou@fgcu.edu

Incorporating social networks in the curriculum to better engage students has gained a lot of attention as a result of the popularity of social networks with college students. We introduce EasySocial, a social network plugin for Eclipse, written by a CS educator, the second author of this poster. The goal of the plugin is for students to be able to easily write code using their own personal data, e.g. on their Facebook or Twitter account, with minimal knowledge of the specific social network API. The EasySocial plugin has several features which makes it useful in our CS classes: it seamlessly embeds the process for authenticating with Facebook; it abstracts the process for making HTTP requests and parsing various data formats, such as JavaScript Object Notation (JSON); it integrates Gephi functionality, so that students can access Gephi's powerful functions for network analysis and visualization in their Java programs. We used the plugin in our Fall 2013 Data Mining course for CS undergraduate students in order to quickly introduce them to social data visualization and social network analysis concepts such as community detection. The students easily wrote Java code to visualize their network graph and detect communities. We received a very positive response, and several students expressed enthusiasm about the programming aspect as well as the application topic. Future plans include further employing EasySocial in other courses, for example to help students in entry-level courses understand programming concepts, such as arrays and loops.

ACM Categories & Descriptors: K.3.2 Computer and Information Science Education

Keywords: social networks; social data; student engagement; computer science education

Utilizing Gamification with Social Network to aid students in programming languages lessons in Higher Education IT Courses

Marcell Almeida Mesquita, *Centro Universitário do Estado do Pará (CESUPA)*
Armando Maciel Toda, *Universidade Estadual de Londrina*
Jacques Duílio Brancher, *Universidade Estadual de Londrina*
Ricardo Casseb do Carmo, *Centro Universitário do Estado do Pará (CESUPA)*
Contact: almeidamarcell@gmail.com

Programming Languages and its uses play a vital role in IT higher education courses, because it is necessary that students have a good understanding in order to become full-fledged developers. We made a study to verify the initial reception of this method regarding the students satisfaction and so, this meta-paper proposes the continuation of this research. It involves the utilization of a Social Network and gamification concepts, like badges, points, levels and leader boards to improve students participation.

ACM Categories & Descriptors: K.3.2 [Computer and Information Science Education]

Keywords: Gamification, Game-based learning, Higher Education, Social Networks

A Comparison of Two Approaches for Hint Generation in Programming Tutors

Andrew Hicks, *North Carolina State University*
Barry Peddycord III, *North Carolina State University*
Irena Rindos, *North Carolina State University*
Christopher Simmons, *North Carolina State University*
Contact: aghicks3@ncsu.edu

Intelligent tutoring systems have been shown to significantly aid in student learning without requiring extensive instructor intervention. One feature of intelligent tutors is their ability to provide hints to students who get stuck, but the production of hints by hand is prohibitively expensive. Hint Factory (Stamper et al., 2008) is a domain-independent technique for generating hints from interaction graphs. In this work, we explore approaches for creating graphs that represent interactions in an educational programming game called BOTS. We use data from seven programming puzzles that contain a total of 1100 interactions with the game. We believe that we can begin by seeing what works in the small language of a programming

SIGCSE'14, March 5–8, 2014, Atlanta, Georgia, USA.
ACM 978-1-4503-2605-6/14/03.

game to inform how we can scale the techniques for "real" languages in "real" tutors.

ACM Categories & Descriptors: K.3.1 Computer Uses in Education; K.3.2 Computer and Information Science Education

Keywords: Intelligent tutoring; hint factory; educational data mining; programming tutor; educational games

Collaborative Programming Exercises in Virtual Worlds

Johanna Pirker, *Graz University of Technology*
Christian Gütl, *Graz University of Technology*
Frank Kappe, *Graz University of Technology*
Contact: jpirker@iicm.edu

Organizing a Programming 101 course for a thousand computer science freshmen poses a challenge. One major problem is the high dropout-rate due to insufficient social interactions and the missing feeling of presence. Collaborative home assignments can help to overcome such issues. However, due to scheduling conflicts not all students are able to meet in person to work together. Many tools support collaborative online programming, but have several disadvantages in comparison to face-to-face meetings. This work presents a virtual world environment, where student groups can meet online, but experience the advantages of face-to-face interactions. They can commonly use different tools for collaborative problem solving at one shared virtual location. They experience the feeling of presence, which increases the individual contribution, even from distant sites. Furthermore, the environment provides facilitated possibilities for tutor meetings, where students can discuss and present their solutions. In this work a first prototype of the environment is described. In addition advantages as well as potential issues or difficulties are discussed

ACM Categories & Descriptors: D.2.6 Programming Environment; H.5.1 Multimedia Information Systems; H.5.3 Group and Organization Interfaces; K.3.1 Computer Uses in Education; K.3.2 Computer and Information Science Education

Keywords: Virtual World; Collaborative Programmig; Interactive Learning

Impact of Programming Language on Success in High School Programming Contests

Stoney Jackson, *Western New England University*
Heidi Ellis, *Western New England University*
Robert Crouse, *Western New England University*
Contact: hjackson@wne.edu

Programming contests have been used at the high school level to motivate students to study computing and generate excitement about computing topics. However, little investigation has been done into whether the selection of programming language impacts success in such contests. This poster presents the results of an analysis of five years of high school contest results held at Western New England University. The analysis looks at the languages used by winning teams and number of submissions. Results appear to indicate that winning teams use Java and Python for programming languages while less successful teams use BASIC, VisualBasic and C++. Interestingly, the majority of teams used BASIC as their programming language. Another interesting result was that low performing teams tend to have a disproportionately large number of submissions.

SIGCSE'14, March 5–8, 2014, Atlanta, Georgia, USA.
ACM 978-1-4503-2605-6/14/03.

ACM Categories & Descriptors: K.3.2 [Computers and Education]: Computer and Information Science Education

Keywords: Programming Contests

Mission Critical: Building Community to Engage Women in Computer Science

Amanda Ochsner, *University of Wisconsin-Madison*
Rane Johnson-Stempson, *Microsoft Research*
Matthew Berland, *University of Wisconsin-Madison*
Contact: aochsner@wisc.edu

This project consists of a collaborative effort between the Games+Learning+Society Center at the University of Wisconsin-Madison and Microsoft Research to create an online community to engage girls in computer programming and game design. The goals of this community are threefold: 1) to support initial interest in computer science among young women and then build on that interest through increasingly involved participation within the community; 2) to foster the learning of programming specifically, and computational and design thinking more broadly; and 3) to provide support to the young women within the community at the critical engagement and learning points. At SIGCSE 2014 we will present the first major phase of the project—an updated version of our team's *Studio K* curriculum for teaching game design and computational thinking to middle and high school students. We will also report on early research findings from the first all-girl cohorts to complete the curriculum.

ACM Categories & Descriptors: K.3.2 Computer and Information Science Education

Keywords: diversity; gender; education; community; access

Interactive E-Learning Modules for Teaching Secure: A Pilot Study

Sagar Raina, *Towson University*
Blair Taylor, *Towson University*
Siddharth Kaza, *Towson University*
Contact: sraina1@students.towson.edu

Addressing the crucial need for cybersecurity learning materials, the Security Injections @ Towson project (towson.edu/securityinjections) has developed modules for CS0, CS1, CS2 and Computer Literacy courses that target key secure coding concepts including integer overflow, buffer overflow, and input validation. Assessment results indicate that these modules have led to an increase in students' security-awareness and their ability to apply secure coding principles. Each security injection module includes four sections - background, code responsibly (includes methods to avoid security issues), laboratory assignment with a security checklist, and discussion questions. In this study, we are proposing to enhance these modules by incorporating e-learning strategies including lesson segmentation, instant feedback, and self-paced lessons to increase student learning. In addition, we are designing a system with auto-grading functionality and dashboards to encourage adoption by instructors. Segmenting modules into smaller sections and including 'gatekeeper' questions will facilitate learning and reduce cognitive overload. Providing feedback on incorrect answers encourages students to revisit relevant sections. The goal of this feedback based approach is to improve student learning and content retention. The nature of the enhanced modules allows for self-paced learning which is applicable for online learning environments. We conducted a pilot study using a module in CS0 undergraduate computer science class that included 60 in-class and 9 online students. The results of the pilot study indicated increased attention towards the content and possible improvement in retention of concepts. This project is partially supported by NSF under grant DUE-1241738

ACM Categories & Descriptors: K.3.2 Computers and Education

Keywords: CS0; CS1; CS2; Secure Coding; Security Injections; e-Learning; Feedback-based Learning

A Comparison of Two Hands-On Laboratory Experiences in Computers, Networks and Cyber Security for 10th-12th Graders

Lisa M. Marvel, *US Army Research Laboratory*
Stephen Raio, *US Army Communications-Electronics Research, Development and Engineering Center*
Lori Pollock, *University of Delaware*
David Arty, *US Army Communications-Electronics Research, Development and Engineering Center*
Gerard Chaney, *US Army Research Laboratory*
Giorgio Bertoli, *US Army Communications-Electronics Research, Development and Engineering Center*
Christopher Paprcka, *US Army Communications-Electronics Research, Development and Engineering Center*
Wendy Choi, *US Army Communications-Electronics Research, Development and Engineering Center*
Erica Bertoli, *US Army Communications-Electronics Research, Development and Engineering Center*
Sandra K. Young, US Army Research Laboratory
Contact: lisa.m.marvel.civ@mail.mil

In this poster, we describe our experience of designing and executing two different weeklong programs for 10th – 12th grade students. The goal of our program is to attract students to the field of computing, increase their computing confidence and familiarize them with ways that computing impacts our community. Student groups consist of 32 students for each week with a 1:0.8 male-to-female ratio. No prerequisite knowledge is required to attend. We compare the different facets of the curriculums by evaluating the impact of each week both quantitatively and qualitatively. Our evaluation implies the attraction of cyber security topics to this age group, particularly male students, and presents a curriculum that may help increase confidence in computing concepts, particularly for female students. We solicit feedback and welcome input on our curriculum and evaluation method.

SIGCSE'14, March 5–8, 2014, Atlanta, Georgia, USA.
ACM 978-1-4503-2605-6/14/03.

ACM Categories & Descriptors: K.3.2 Computer and Information Science Education and Literacy

Keywords: K-12 STEM Education,; Cyber Security Education

Scare and Prepare: Increasing Awareness, Safety, and Passion for Cyber-Security

Prem Uppuluri, *Radford University*
Jeff Pittges, *Radford University*
Joseph Chase, *Radford University*
Contact: puppuluri@radford.edu

Radford University's Scare and Prepare (SP) program is being developed to enable high-school teachers to cultivate security conscious cyber-citizens and, in the process, spark a passion for computer science. We are accomplishing this in two ways: (a) incentivize high school teachers to incorporate security into their curriculum with little investment in resources (hardware, software and personnel), and (b) introduce computer science concepts such as programming (e.g., Javascript) and basic operating system functionality (e.g., file organization and memory management). Our experience shows that success of high school CS programs depends on the teacher's motivation. SP will reduce preparation times for teachers by providing all the necessary learning materials in the form of screencast lectures and portable and remote hands-on labs. Ultimately, we propose to develop a dual enrollment college credit course. SP's learning materials are intended to spark interest among students by both scaring and preparing them. The first strategy is to scare students with the potential implications of cyber-attacks on aspects that matter to them: social networking sites and smart phones. Next, students are prepared to defend against such attacks. Finally, to sustain interest prepared high schools students will compete in cyber-defense exercises.

ACM Categories & Descriptors: K.3.2 Computer Science Education; K.3.m Computer literacy;

Keywords: Security Education; Privacy Education; K-12

An Extensible Scene Graph Library for Teaching Computer Graphics along the Programmable Pipeline

Volker Ahlers, *University of Applied Sciences and Arts Hannover*
Contact: volker.ahlers@hs-hannover.de

Computer graphics is a subject which is typically enjoyed by students and which has the potential to attract pupils to consider studying computer science. Although the programming methods used by computer graphics have significantly changed in recent years due to the integration of programmable shaders into the graphics rendering pipeline, a lot of computer graphics courses still start with the fixed-function pipeline. In view of future applicability, however, it is desirable to teach students modern concepts of computer graphics from the beginning. One problem with teaching shader-based computer graphics is that a lot of technical tasks lie in the hand of the programmer: loading and compiling shader programs, managing buffer objects, defining transformations by means of matrices, etc. This poster presents a scene graph library which is fully based on the programmable rendering pipeline. It uses the OpenGL 3.2 core profile, which does not allow deprecated fixed-function functionality. The teaching approach combines the high-level abstraction of a scene graph with the low-level programming of shader cores, which are attributed to scene graph nodes. The presented scene graph library has a simple and clear structure and is extensible in order to let students implement advanced concepts taught in the lecture, like shadows or particle systems. Finally, the poster presents code samples, results of student projects, and student evaluation results.

ACM Categories & Descriptors: I.3.4 Graphics Utilities; K.3.2 Computer and Information Science Education

Keywords: Computer Graphics; Scene Graph; Rendering Pipeline; Programmable Shaders; Software Library; Laboratory

Teaching Mobile App Software Development is a Challenge!

Roy P. Pargas, *Clemson University*
Punit Kulkarni, *Clemson University*
Greg Edison, *Clemson University*
Barbara J. Speziale, *Clemson University*
Contact: pargas@clemson.edu

Teaching a mobile device software development course is very different from teaching a CS1, CS2, or advanced programming class. In a traditional software development class the target computer (on which the software being developed is to run) is a laptop or desktop computer. In a mobile device software development course, the target computer is a smartphone or tablet that has a large number of features (web access, a camera, GPS, a gyroscope, media display, etc.) that can be controlled by software. The material that must be covered in such as course is so broad that new approaches to delivering course content must be used. This poster describes the overall method by which we have taught such a course. We describe four challenges: (1) The content is new and constantly changing. (2) The material to be covered is very broad and includes diverse components. (3) The course requires that the students understand databases design and implementation, topics often taken in the final year of the curriculum and too late for this course. (4) Finally, finding meaningful course projects is difficult and we benefit greatly from a program such as Clemson's Creative Inquiry Undergraduate Research Program. We explain how we address each of these challenges and describe the structure of the course in detail. We conclude with the results we have produced over the past five years, evaluation by students, and successes students have achieved. We also demonstrate both iOS and Android apps that have been developed through this course.

ACM Categories & Descriptors: D.2.6 Programming Environments, J.m Computer Applications Miscellaneous

Keywords: App development, iOS, Android, Capstone, Mobile, Smartphone, Tablet

The Relationship Between Task Difficulty and Emotion in Online Computer Programming Tutoring

Joseph B. Wiggins, *North Carolina State University*
Joseph F. Grafsgaard, *North Carolina State University*
Kristy Elizabeth Boyer, *North Carolina State University*
Eric N. Wiebe, *North Carolina State University*
James C. Lester, *North Carolina State University*
Contact: jbwiggi3@ncsu.edu

Emotion, or affect, plays a central role in learning. In particular, promoting positive emotions throughout the learning process is important for students' motivation to pursue computer science and for retaining computer science students. Positive emotions, such as engagement or enjoyment, may be fostered by timely individualized help. Especially promising are interventions if the student is having difficulty completing a task. Recognizing when a student is facing a complex task may better inform teachers or adaptive learning environments about the students' affective states, which in turn can inform instructional adaptations. We approach this research goal by analyzing a data set of student facial videos from computer-mediated human tutorial sessions in Java programming. Students and tutors interacted with a synchronized web-based development environment. The tutorial sessions were divided into six lessons each with subtasks, and featured corresponding learning objectives for the students. In post-hoc analysis, we identified "difficult" tasks by comparing the frequencies of student-tutor interaction and task behaviors such as running the program and the time to complete tasks. Nonverbal behaviors, such as gesturing or postural shifting, were then compared with task difficulty. Understanding such nonverbal behavior can inform individualized interventions, which may keep students engaged and foster greater learning gains.

ACM Categories & Descriptors: I.4.9 Applications

Keywords: Affective modeling; Facial detection; Postural detection

Looking Glass: A C++ Library for Testing Student Programs through Reflection

Scott Turner, *University of North Carolina at Pembroke*
Contact: scott.turner@uncp.edu

Looking Glass is a library designed to support the testing of students' C++ code through reflection. Instructors can design tests that compile even if there are mismatches between the instructor's and student's code (like misspelled function names or parameters that do not have the expected types). Using the autogenerated metadata, instructors can search for and call functions or methods in the student code, including the main

SIGCSE'14, March 5–8, 2014, Atlanta, Georgia, USA.
ACM 978-1-4503-2605-6/14/03.

function, while providing feedback (rather than a compile error) if the required code is not found. Although not suitable for all C++ programs, Looking Glass was designed to support instructors in introductory and intermediate classes and to be transparent to the students.

This poster describes the setup and use of Looking Glass with examples of the functionality it currently supports.

ACM Categories & Descriptors: D.2.5 Testing and Debugging; K.3.2 Computer and Information Science Education

Keywords: C++; reflection; unit testing; instructor tests

Parallel Programming Paradigms Illustrated

David P. Bunde, *Knox College*
Michael Graf, *Knox College*
Deyu Han, *Knox College*
Jens Mache, *Lewis & Clark College*
Contact: dbunde@knox.edu

There are many different ways to write parallel programs. We illustrate a variety of relevant language paradigms by presenting implementations of the Game of Life, a simple simulation motivated by living organisms. Featured paradigms include shared memory, GPU acceleration, message passing, and Partitioned Global Address Space (PGAS).

ACM Categories & Descriptors: D.1.3 Concurrent Programming; D.3.2 Language Classifications

Keywords: Parallel programming; Parallel programming languages; Game of Life; Shared memory; GPGPU; Message passing; PGAS

RIT's New Minor in Free and Open Source Software and Free Culture

Stephen Jacobs, *Rochester Institute of Technology*
Amit Ray, *Rochester Institute of Technology*
Jonathan Schull, *Rochester Institute of Technology*
Contact: sj@mail.rit.edu

This poster will briefly show and describe the five year history of FOSS course offerings and projects in the School of Interactive Games and Media that led to the development of the minor and then diagram and describe the Minor's design and content. It will show how the Humanitarian focus of the student work, beginning with the development of educational games for the One Laptop per Child and Sugar communities built a foundation for the minor. It will then discuss the design of the minor, how the required courses leading to advanced electives also prepare students to become contributors and, potentially, project leaders within Free and Open Source Software and Free Culture communities within the students' own academic specializations. It will diagram the paths that both technical and non-technical students can take to succeed in completing the minor.

ACM Categories & Descriptors: K.3.2 Computer and Information Science Education

Keywords: Open Source

Making Use of the Cognitive Apprenticeship Framework in an Undergraduate Robotics Course

D. Brian Larkins, Coastal Carolina University
Contact: blarkins@coastal.edu

Modern robotics are at the locus of several related disciplines including computer science, mechanical engineering, electrical engineering, and others. The interleaving of these disciplines within a single robotic system can make teaching the fundamentals of robotics to undergraduate students within a traditional computer science curriculum a challenging task. One way to address this challenge is with an immersive, experiential approach that exposes students to these different facets of robot design in context. This poster describes the application of the Cognitive Apprenticeship (CA) framework to an undergraduate robotics course comprising of projects that touch on several different engineering disciplines. CA techniques are used to help students gain insight and understand how contributions from a variety of domains are interwoven to build a functioning robotic system. Throughout the class, students work on teams to complete projects at different levels of abstraction using two different robot platforms. Students learn about software design and implementation by constructing reactive paradigm behaviors on a Khepera III robot in the first part of the course. Later, students construct a quadcopter UAV from a kit, handling all aspects of construction, calibration, and configuration. This work focuses on two perspectives of this course: the use of the CA framework as a structure for experiential learning and also to describe a set of projects that emphasize the interdisciplinary nature of robotics.

ACM Categories & Descriptors: K.3.2 Computer and Information Science Education

Keywords: Cognitive Apprenticeship; Education; Robotics

Copper Country Programmers: A Novel Curriculum for Beginning Programmers in Middle and High School

Leo C. Ureel II, *Michigan Technological University*
John Earnest, *Michigan Technological University*
Charles Wallace, *Michigan Technological University*
Contact: ureel@mtu.edu

With the continued and alarming lack of involvement in computing among college students, attention has recently focused on engaging students at the middle and high school levels. Our "Copper Country Programmers" club began as a community outreach program to fill a gap left by the elimination of the computing curriculum in the local school district. In our club, university faculty and students provide curriculum, tools, and classroom tutoring for young novice programmers across the school district. Our curriculum teaches programming through a series of exercises involving HTML, BASIC, LOGO, and Processing (a graphics-oriented Java variant.) Contrary to

SIGCSE'14, March 5–8, 2014, Atlanta, Georgia, USA.
ACM 978-1-4503-2605-6/14/03.

some other approaches, we present students initially with a low level, bare bones programming model and development environment, then gradually increase the functionality and complexity. We find that students readily grasp the simple, transparent initial model, then experience first-hand the motivations for adding functionality (and complexity). Our cross-curricular programming topics include graphic design, interactive fiction, computer generated poetry, mathematical simulation, computational geometry, game physics, computer art, artificial intelligence, video game development, and critical thinking. We provide examples of our curriculum, student work, problems encountered, and how they were resolved.

ACM Categories & Descriptors: K.3 Computers and Education; K.3.2 Computer and Information Science Education - Computer Science Education; K.3.2 Computer and Information Science Education - Curriculum

Keywords: K-12 Instruction; K-12 Computer Science Curriculum; Outreach

Studio K: A Game Development Environment Designed for Gains in Computational Thinking

Gabriella Anton, *University of Wisconsin-Madison*
Matthew Berland, *University of Wisconsin-Madison*
Contact: gabby.anton@gmail.com

Studio K is a game design curriculum constructed to provide middle school students an engaging entry into computer science and programming. Developed at the University of Wisconsin-Madison, the program employs Microsoft's 3D programming environment, Kodu, in tandem with support and analytic tools for facilitators, and an online community that provides players with a support system. These key features are bolstered with incorporation of telemetry data gathered through design sessions that are used to improve site functioning, curriculum relevancy, and administrative tools. This program is applied across contexts, with applications in formal classrooms, informal extracurricular clubs or camps, and alternative learning environments such as library systems or home schools. *Studio K* provides a well-supported, unique entry into computer science in which programming knowledge becomes a tool that supports learners' goals in designing and developing games.

ACM Categories & Descriptors: D.1.3 Concurrent K.3.2[Computers and Education]: Computers and Information Science Education – *computer science education*

Keywords: Computer science education; game design

SIGCSE'14, March 5–8, 2014, Atlanta, Georgia, USA.
ACM 978-1-4503-2605-6/14/03.

PVA (Privacy through Visual Anonymity) Lab for Enhancing CS Education and Outreach

Ankur Chattopadhyay, *Adams State University*
Thomas Nehring, *Adams State University*
Contact: achattop@adams.edu

Given that many modern computing technologies have led to privacy issues in today's digital world, the latest CS curriculum (CS2013 - Ironman Version 1.0) has recommended a strong need for inclusion of privacy topics within the present body of knowledge. According to the above curriculum, there is a requirement for global awareness of today's growing privacy concerns with technology. Our proposed lab caters to the above curricular recommendation. We present a physical security focused lab, which is based on the technology of PVA (Privacy through Visual Anonymity). Through this hands-on PVA lab, we teach pre-university and university students the notion of privacy in images/videos and educate them in the technique of VA (Visual Anonymity), which can help safeguard one's privacy by obscuring the individual identity in pictures/videos captured by cameras. Using this lab, we intend to enhance CS education and outreach by making students aware of the global issue of privacy invasion in today's surveillance and by demonstrating how the issue can be addressed via VA. The lab exercises are based on two open-source applications, namely 'ObscuraCam' and 'YouTube-FaceBlur'. These applications are used as tools for enabling students to learn the concept of PVA. In this process, we show students an innovative aspect of balancing security and privacy in technology, thereby drawing their focus to the humanitarian side of CS applications. Our topic of PVA also enhances the IAS knowledge area in the latest CS curriculum.

ACM Categories & Descriptors: K.4.1 Public Policy Issues, Subjects: Privacy; Ethics; Human safety; K.3.2 Computer and Information Science Education, Subjects: Computer science education; Curriculum; Information systems education, Nouns: PASLAB; K.6.5 Security and Protection (D.4.6, K.4.2), Subjects: Physical security; Image Processing and Computer Vision: Applications (I.4.9), Object Recognition (I.4.8)

Keywords: Privacy; Visual Anonymity; Education; Outreach; Curriculum; Global Awareness; Physical Security; Humanitarian Cameras; Video Surveillance; Identity Obscure; Face Blur; IAS

Adventures in Hackademia: Leveraging Humanitarian Free/Open Source Software Development in the Class Room

Remy DeCausemaker, Rochester Institute of Technology
Stephen Jacobs, Rochester Institute of Technology
Contact: remydcsi@rit.edu

This poster will briefly describe the components of the Humanitarian Free/Open Source Software Development (HFOSS) course offered by the Department of Interactive Games and Media at Rochester Institute of Technology in Upstate NY. It will depict this model of an "Open" Course (i.e. Open Courseware, Open Curriculum, Open Classroom, and Open Code) informed both by academic theory, and industry best practice. It will show the results of designers, developers, and project leaders, working in tandem with professors, staffers, and administrators to offer students a chance to apply research, and put theory into practice. It will discuss strategies of engagement, metrics of success and failure, and what resources are available for others to do the same.

ACM Categories & Descriptors: K.3.2 Computer and Information Science Education

Keywords: Open Source

Data-Driven Broadened Participation

Michele S. Roberts, *IUPUI*
Contact: mroberts@cs.iupui.edu

While programming has long been utilized as a recruitment path into computer science, data analysis as a recruitment path is relatively under-explored. Through a series of modular curriculum units developed in computational thinking, the potential impact of explorations in data analysis to impact teacher and student affect toward and interest in computer science is being investigated. Developed units include exercises such as statistically determining the author of selected text passages, modeling roller coaster simulations, solving crime mysteries and controlling zombie contagions. Computational thinking modules have been delivered in a CS Pilot course, as well as in K-12 outreach programs in non-computing courses (STEM and non-STEM), including classes in English literature, sociology, biology, physics and math). Initial results show significant and promising opportunities to utilize data analysis to create computing interest in a broadened population of students and teachers, extending the impact of computational thinking into a variety of subject domains.

ACM Categories & Descriptors: A.1 Introductory and Survey

Keywords: Data; Broadening Participation; Computational Thinking

Introducing CodeWorkout: An Adaptive and Social Learning Environment

Kevin Buffardi, *Virginia Tech*
Stephen H. Edwards, *Virginia Tech*
Contact: kbuffardi@vt.edu

Rudimentary programming skills are essential to developing fundamental proficiency in computer science. However, learning programming techniques can be challenging and frustrating for many students. CodeWorkout is an online learning environment that offers drill-and-practice exercises with novel social and adaptive scaffolding. Learners can track their progress on an assortment of computer science areas and skills while taking advantage of social features to discuss questions and help teach each other. Meanwhile, objective measurements of questions and teaching hints help promote the best, most effective content for learning. Our poster demonstrates how both computer science students and teachers benefit from joining the CodeWorkout community and taking advantage of its unique features.

SIGCSE'14, March 5–8, 2014, Atlanta, Georgia, USA.
ACM 978-1-4503-2605-6/14/03.

ACM Categories & Descriptors: K.3.1 Computer-assisted instruction (CAI); K.3.2 Computer science education

Keywords: Drill and Practice; Programming Exercises; Adaptive Feedback; Collaborative Learning; eLearning Systems

A First-Year Experience Report on a Model for Statewide Deployment of CS Principles Courses

Jeff Gray, *University of Alabama*
Mokter Hossain, *University of Alabama*
Jonathan Corley, *University of Alabama*
Amber Wagner, *University of Alabama*
Cassidy Lamm, *University of Alabama*
Mary Boehm, *A+ College Ready*
Carol Crawford, *A+ College Ready*
Kathleen Haynie, *Haynie Research and Evaluation*
Sheryl Packman, *Haynie Research and Evaluation*
Deepa Muralidhar, *North Gwinnett High School*
Jeff Baker, *Huntsville High School*
Roy Black, *Loveless Academic Magnet Program*
Sandy Falgout, *Baker High School*
Leella Holt, *Muscle Shoals High School*
Albert Lilly, *Alabama School of Math and Science*
Gina McCarley, *Lawrence County High School*
Jim Morse, *New Century Technology High School*
Jennie Rountree, *Bob Jones High School*
Jill Westerlund, *Hoover High School*
Carol Yarbrough, *Alabama School of Fine Arts*
Contact: gray@cs.ua.edu

This poster describes our first-year experience in developing and evaluating a CS Principles professional development model for training a cohort of teachers across an entire state geography. The scalable deployment and sustainable persistence of the new CS Principles course adopts the successful practices of a national AP training program developed by the National Math and Science Initiative (NMSI). It applies those practices in a professional development program based on year-long in-person training and distance learning collaboration. A statewide "Teacher Leader" model is being explored where those already teaching more rigorous CS courses will assist in training new peer cohorts as they establish CS Principles in their schools. Teachers in these cohorts collaborate together on content and pedagogical learning experiences, fostered by peer leaders. The assessment is uncovering the facets of our model that are most suitable for building a sustainable network of CS Principles teachers. This poster is focused on a description of our first-year experiences and extensive evaluation results. The poster will describe the curriculum that is being developed by our teachers, a set of lessons learned from our PD experiences, and the details of our evaluation. The Teacher Leaders will be available near the poster to discuss their experience with anyone who has an interest in our professional development model for CS Principles.

ACM Categories & Descriptors: K.3.2 Curriculum; K.3.2 Computer science education

Keywords: CS Principles, Professional Development

Remote Pair Programming (RPP) in Massively Open Online Courses (MOOCs)

Jonathan McKinsey, *University of California, Berkeley*
Samuel Joseph, *Hawaii Pacific University*
Armando Fox, *University of California, Berkeley*
Daniel D. Garcia, *University of California, Berkeley*
Contact: mckinsey@berkeley.edu

Pair programming, a form of collaborative learning where two programmers work on the same computer, enhances learning in novice programmers and improves code quality in experienced programmers. Remote pair programming (RPP) brings the pedagogical technique of pair programming to the distributed online environment of Massively Open Online Courses (MOOCs). UC BerkeleyX's CS169 Software as a Service MOOC successfully uses a Google+ community for students to generate their own RPP events or join events created by their peers. We will examine survey results summarizing the RPP experiences and RPP technologies of student pairings in the Fall 2013 offering of CS169, as well as analyze RPP sessions. In the future, the aim is to generalize RPP methodology, expand its applications to other MOOCs and traditional classrooms, and compare its effectiveness to in-person pair programming.

ACM Categories & Descriptors: K.3.1 Computer Uses in Education; K.3.2 Computer and Information Science Education

Keywords: Remote Pair Programming; Massively Open Online Course; Online Education; CS Education; RPP; MOOC

Resources for Teaching Web Science to Computer Science Undergraduates

Frank McCown, *Harding University*
Michael L. Nelson, *Old Dominion University*
Contact: fmccown@harding.edu

This poster reports on course materials that have been developed for teaching an Introduction to Web Science course to computing majors at the undergraduate level. This is the first comprehensive collection of resources that we are aware of that targets undergraduates in the exciting new field of Web Science. The course materials include slides, reading assignments, homework assignments, programming projects, and exams. We hope these materials will make adopting a Web Science course easier for a computing department or for creating an interdisciplinary course which could expose computing to a more diverse and broader group of students. Course materials may be obtained from the authors and from the following URLs:

http://www.harding.edu/fmccown/classes/comp475-s13/
http://www.cs.odu.edu/~mln/teaching/cs595-f13/

This work was supported by the National Science Foundation (IIS 1008492).

ACM Categories & Descriptors: K.3.2 Computer and Information Science Education - Curriculum

Keywords: Web Science; Network Science; Big Data; Social Networks; Web Search Engines; Collective Intelligence;Teaching Resources

SIGCSE'14, March 5–8, 2014, Atlanta, Georgia, USA.
ACM 978-1-4503-2605-6/14/03.

Birds of a Feather: Flock 1

Promoting Professional Responsibility and Ethics: The Pledge of the Computing Professional

John K. Estell, *Ohio Northern University*
Ken Christensen, *University of South Florida*
Contact: j-estell@onu.edu

The Pledge of the Computing Professional (http://computing-professional.org), endorsed by SIGCAS and the ACM Committee on Professional Ethics, was developed to both support professional responsibility in computing and to raise awareness of one's ethical responsibilities. To date, 25 institutions across the US have conducted Pledge Ceremonies to welcome their graduates into the computing profession. In a recent *Inroads* article, Don Gotterbarn asserts that, if one's ethics is influenced by those around us, then "just being aware of the existence of this Pledge helps to refocus us all on our own responsibility and the profession's responsibility." So in what ways can this Pledge be used both inside and outside of the classroom to better promote such traits? This session is for those interested in computing ethics and professional responsibility to get together and collaborate on new initiatives featuring The Pledge of the Computing Professional as a means to this end.

ACM Categories & Descriptors: K.7.4 [**Professional Ethics**]: Codes of ethics, Codes of good practice. K.4.2 [**Computers and Society**]: Social issues. K.7.2 [**Organizations**]

Keywords: Computer ethics; rite of passage ceremony; professional responsibility

An Exploration of Mentor-Protégé Relationships and How to Train Future Mentors

Elissa Redmiles, *University of Maryland*
Jandelyn Plane, *University of Maryland*
Contact: eredmiles@cs.umd.edu

Mentors-protégé relationships have been shown to improve retention of women and under-represented students in computing (Cohoon, 2011). Mentorship relationships are also the driving factor in female students' selection and completion of a computing career (Ashcraft, Eger, & Friend, 2012). More generally, mentor-protégé relationships are a significant factor in retaining and encouraging under-represented students in many academic fields. Beginning with a brief discussion of our experience facilitating mentorship between female undergraduate and middle school computing students, this Birds of a Feather Session will provide a platform for the exploration of mentor training techniques and mentor-protégé relationships. We will discuss and share different strategies (e.g. readings, hands-on workshops) for training mentors and facilitating strong mentor-protégé relationships. We will also explore how mentorship relationships affect student performance in all school subjects and how to best create a broad mentorship experience that extends beyond computing. Using a summary of recent literature as a springboard, we will consider optimal mentor-protégé age gaps, experience levels and interaction frequencies. Finally, we will explore session participant's personal experiences as mentors/protégés and compile a list of "do's and don'ts" for those facilitating or participating in mentorship programs.

ACM Categories & Descriptors: K.3.1 Collaborative learning; K.3.2 Computer science education

Keywords: Mentorship; retention; underrepresented students

Privacy between Technological Capabilities and Society's Expectations

Ernest Leiss, *University of Houston*
Lila Ghemri, *Texas Southern University*
Contact: ghemri_lx@tsu.edu

The unprecedented use of social networking, the Web and other related technologies by all fringes of population, has not been accompanied by an adequate awareness of its potential for abuse, privacy violation and cybercrimes. Furthermore, technology nowadays provides extensive capabilities which often times clash with society's laws and ethics. In particular, modern societies have certain expectations of privacy; that may be contradicted by the capabilities of new technology. It seems then incumbent upon computer science instructors to raise awareness of these risks and threats among the students they teach. The purpose of this session is to provide a forum for discussing technologies that are widely used by CS and non CS professionals alike, and that may well be at variance with society's privacy expectations. A second purpose of this session is to introduce instructional modules currently under development that may assist instructors in addressing some of the relevant themes in courses, in particular privacy in social networks, on the internet, in mobile apps and also privacy in electronic voting and law enforcement. We expect that attendees will provide varying opinions and insight that will help shape the course offering. In addition, attendees will be invited to share their experience teaching or talking about privacy issues and the approaches, resources and techniques they have used in presenting the topic to students.

ACM Categories & Descriptors: K.4.1 COMPUTERS AND SOCIETY, Public Policy Issues; Privacy

Keywords: Computers and Society; Non-Majors; Privacy; Security; Social Networks

CSTA Chapters: Building a CS Community

Frances P. Trees, *Rutgers University*
Lissa Clayborn, *CSTA*
Contact: fran.trees@cs.rutgers.edu

As part of its commitment to developing a strong community of computer science educators, the Computer Science Teachers Association (CSTA) supports the development of regional CSTA chapters. A CSTA chapter is a local branch of CSTA designed to facilitate discussion of local issues, to provide member services at

SIGCSE'14, March 5–8, 2014, Atlanta, Georgia, USA.
ACM 978-1-4503-2605-6/14/03.

the local level, and to promote CSTA membership on the national level (http://www.csta.acm.org/About/sub/CSTAChapters.html). With the recently announced AP® Computer Science Principles Course to Launch in Academic Year 2016–17, local CS communities are vital. This BOF will provide a platform for the discussion of CSTA chapter formation, CS education community building, and tools and techniques used to successfully host professional development for K-12 CS teachers.

ACM Categories & Descriptors: K.3.2 Computer and Information Science Education

Keywords: K-12 CS Ed, Professional Development, Outreach, Community, CSTA, chapters

What Analogies/Metaphors/Similes Do You Use When Teaching CS Concepts?

William (Bill) Pulling, *Fanshawe College*
Contact: wpulling@fanshawec.ca

Teaching by analogy or simile is a strategy many of us employ when we try to explain fundamental CS concepts. One popular analogy for explaining the difference between a class and an object is that the class is the "blueprint" and the object is the "house" that gets built from the blueprint. Others describe the class as the "cookie cutter" and the object is the "cookie". Another example is that an indeterminate loop is like a person hammering a nail into a board. We know that the loop will end when the nail is flush with the board. However, we are not sure how many strokes or iterations the loop will take, as it depends on who is doing the hammering, the length of the nail, etc. This BOF will encourage attendees to describe analogies, metaphors, and similes they use in the classroom to help illustrate different concepts in programming, or in other areas such as database or networking fundamentals. Discussion will also include "analogies that seemed like a good idea at the time" but did not work out as well as had been hoped.

ACM Categories & Descriptors: K.3.2 Computer Science Education.

Keywords: analogy, analogies, metaphor, metaphors, simile, similes, teaching, teaching strategies, CS0, CS1

Teaching Track Faculty in CS

Mark Sherriff, *University of Virginia*
Daniel Garcia, *University of California, Berkeley*
Jody Paul, *Metropolitan State College at Denver*
Contact: sherriff@virginia.edu

Many computer science departments have chosen to hire faculty to teach in a teaching-track position that parallels the standard tenure-track position. These teaching-track positions include the possibility for promotion, longer-term contracts and greater pay as demonstrated by excellence in teaching, educational material development, and service. Since this type of position is relatively new in CS departments, the expectations and responsibilities for such faculty varies from one university to another, but they certainly differ from the traditional tenure-track positions. This birds-of-a-feather is designed to gather educators who are currently in such a position to share their experiences as members of the faculty of their departments and schools, and to provide opportunities for schools considering such positions to gather information. In past sessions, we have laid the groundwork for keeping this community together through online discussions and consolidating information about teaching-track positions at various universities together into an online database.

ACM Categories & Descriptors: K.3.2 Computer and Information Science Education: Computer Science Education

Keywords: Non-tenure track faculty, teaching faculty

Fighting Impostor Syndrome

Aidan Feldman, *GitHub*
Matthew McCullough, *GitHub*
Contact: aidan.feldman@gmail.com

When working in the constantly challenging field of Computer Science, all but the most brazen individuals will inevitably feel "in over their heads", which is the simplest incarnation of impostor syndrome. This issue affects members of this field at all levels: students, teachers, researchers, etc. For students, impostor syndrome is a great barrier to success, because they don't have full context of the skills necessary to be successful in CS.

Computer Science attrition rates are extremely high relative to other areas of study, particularly among first and second-year college students. What can be done by educators and the industry to retain talent, that would otherwise be lost by those individuals not feeling like they belong? How can we instill confidence and encourage growth? How can these strategies applied personally, or to other experienced members of the field?

ACM Categories & Descriptors: K.3.0 General Computers and Education; K.7.1 Occupations

Keywords: Imposter Syndrome;Impostor Syndrome

No News in Database Education by All Accounts – Seriously?

Carsten Kleiner, *University of Applied Sciences & Arts Hannover, Germany*
Contact: carsten.kleiner@hs-hannover.de

The number of papers on database system education has been close to zero at recent conferences. As database systems are a fundamental part of computer science curricula this comes as a surprise. The apparent draught in new ideas in database system education is even more surprising given the fact that this area of computer science has arguably undergone its most significant changes for more than 30 years within the last 5 years. Many new database system paradigms (most of them appearing under the NoSQL label) have been introduced for various reasons. Some of these massively distributed database systems facilitate unprecedented data processing capabilities often labeled as BigData. In order to offer a sustainable and practical CS education, at least some of those new paradigms and methodologies should probably be included into database education. This BoF can be a starting point for a discussion about which of those deserve inclusion into a typical CS curriculum and (even more interestingly) at what time in

SIGCSE'14, March 5–8, 2014, Atlanta, Georgia, USA.
ACM 978-1-4503-2605-6/14/03.

the curriculum and by replacing what other topics. Depending on interest of the audience a decision could be made as to what is the correct technology support for continuing the discussion beyond the conference. The BoF will also offer participants a forum to share their opinions, ideas and experiences on recent and future changes in database system education in general. ***Laptop optional.***

ACM Categories & Descriptors: H.2.4 Systems; K.3.2 Computer and Information Science Education

Keywords: database systems; Big Data; NoSQL; database paradigms; curriculum; database courses

A Town Meeting: SIGCSE Committee on Expanding the Women-in-Computing Community

Gloria Childress Townsend, *DePauw University*
Contact: gct@depauw.edu

In January 2004, we organized the second SIGCSE Committee ("Expanding the Women-in-Computing Community"). Our annual Town Meeting provides dissemination of information concerning successful gender issues projects, along with group discussion and brainstorming, in order to create committee goals for the coming year. We select projects to highlight through listserv communication and through our connections with NCWIT, ABI, ACM-W, CRA-W, etc. This year we will highlight ACM-W Chapters and ACM-W Celebrations of Women in Computing.

ACM Categories & Descriptors: K.4 Computers and Society; K.4.2 Social Issues

Keywords: Gender Issues

Using the Cloud to Replace Traditional Physical Networking Laboratories

Magdy Ellabidy, *Wentworth Institute of Technology*
John Russo, *Wentworth Institute of Technology*
Contact: russoj@wit.edu

The cloud has become prevalent today and is used both in academia as well as industry. Many services, such as Amazon Web Services, provide an inexpensive way to provision servers in many different platforms. These cloud providers also have prebuilt instances which have many different popular configurations, such as LAMP and many popular databases. This bird of a feather session will discuss experiences with utilizing the cloud both as a temporary fix for times when hardware is unavailable for laboratories (such as during renovations) as well as using the cloud as a permanent replacement for physical labs.

ACM Categories & Descriptors: C.5 Computer System Implementation

Keywords: Virtual Labs; Cloud Computing; Virtual Servers; Academic Computing

SIGCSE'14, March 5–8, 2014, Atlanta, Georgia, USA.
ACM 978-1-4503-2605-6/14/03.

Toolmaker or Scientist?

Brian Patterson, *Oglethorpe University*
William E J Doane, *IDA Science & Technology Policy Institute*
Contact: bpatterson@oglethorpe.edu

Often underlying discussions with those who are not professional computer scientists is the idea that computer scientists are programmers and programmers make tools. Yet many computer science professionals view themselves primarily as scientists, with programs being used to create and express a deeper understanding of computation. This Birds of a Feather session discusses how participants can effectively bridge the gap between toolmaker and scientist views, either through modifying their own view or changing the viewpoint of others.

Topics include: participants' personal balance between how they view themselves as scientists and toolmakers; how to encourage students to see themselves as scientists and toolmakers in balance; how to effectively conduct group work with a variety of viewpoints present; how student motivation interacts with how they see themselves as computer scientists; and other viewpoints that exist about what it means to be a computer scientist.

Computer scientists and non-computer scientists welcome. Laptop not recommended.

ACM Categories & Descriptors: K.3 Computers and Education; K.7 The Computing Profession

Keywords: Diverse Perspectives; Collaboration; Interdisciplinary; Epistemology; Identity; Broadening Participation

Inspiring a Love of Computer Science through the Education of our Youth

Paige H. Meeker, *Presbyterian College*
Contact: mpmeeker@presby.edu

There is a tremendous need for computer science in every discipline; however, our K-12 institutions seem reluctant to alter traditional teaching methods and curriculum in order to include computing concepts at an early age. Therefore, most students are not exposed to computer science until they reach college. In this BOF, I'd like to explore what can be done to help introduce more young people to this exciting discipline, as well as encourage educators and administrators to incorporate computer science curriculum in their schools. As a leader in my children's school for the "Hour of Code" initiative, I was able to witness firsthand how children as youg as four and as old as high school seniors are hungry for more when it comes to programming. During this talk, we will explore what can be done from this point to encourage schools, teachers, and administration to continue (or begin) our youth's knowledge and experience with programming.

As a nation, the United States is failing in the proper instruction of our children in the field of computer science. While employment for computer related fields is rising, and knowledge of the discipline is necessary no matter what the ultimate field of study or occupation of the student, only about two thirds of the states within the United States have computing education standards for grade levels K-12 (http://www.acm.org/runningonempty/roemap.html). As an educator (and a mother) I find this disturbing. A good work was begun by "Code.org" this past December, with more than 15 million students logging in to the site and working through the tutorials there. How can we promote and continue this initiative in our local schools and encourage up to date requirements for our students.

ACM Categories & Descriptors: K.3 Computers and Education; K.4 Computers and Society

Keywords: K-12 Education Policies

Debugging Teacher Certification

Jian Zhang, *Texas Woman's University*
Philip Sweany, *University of North Texas*
Contact: jzhang@twu.edu

The need for workers in the information technology and computing industry is on the rise. Code.org estimates that by 2020, there will be more that 1 million more computer jobs available than there will be computer science graduates to fill them. Efforts, by organizations such as the Computer Science Teachers Association (CSTA) and code.org, to attract students to information technology and computing appear to be working. While it appears that there will be students to teach, will there be qualified teachers to teach them? The CSTA report "Bugs in the System: Computer Science Teacher Certification in the U.S." asserts that the "certification/licensure processes for Computer Science in the U.S. are deeply flawed."

The goal of this session is to bring together educators from the high school and college level to discuss what the CS Education community needs to do to address this problem.

ACM Categories & Descriptors: K.3.2 Computer and Information Science Education; K.7.3 Testing, Certification, and Licensing

Keywords: Computer Science Education;Teacher Certification

Introduction to Programming for Scientists and Engineers

Peter H. Fröhlich, *Johns Hopkins University*
Joanne Selinski, *Johns Hopkins University*
Contact: phf@cs.jhu.edu

At many universities, computer science departments traditionally offer introductory programming as a "service course"' to other departments. In recent years, however, more and more outside departments—apparently dissatisfied with the CS courses—have begun to offer their own versions of introductory programming. Our BOF will provide a forum to discuss this development and to exchange ideas for addressing it.

ACM Categories & Descriptors: D.1 Programming Techniques

Keywords: programming education; discipline-specific

SIGCSE'14, March 5–8, 2014, Atlanta, Georgia, USA.
ACM 978-1-4503-2605-6/14/03.

China's Perspective from the Viewpoint of Computational Thinking on CS1 for Non-majors

Ming Zhang, *Peking University*
Bo Li, *Xian Jiaotong University*
Ginnie Lo, *University of Oregon*
Contact: mzhang@net.pku.edu.cn

A key challenge for the Chinese educational system is the development of a CS1 course for non-major college students that can meet the unique environment in our country. In mainland China, CS1 is required of all freshmen at their first semester, approximately 7 million freshmen per year. We have named this CS1 course "Fundamentals of University Computer Science" to reflect our ambitions to bring our students to the cutting edge of information technology and society. Over the past few years, many Chinese universities have advanced and experimented with their ideas for introducing computational thinking into CS1, the important core course. In this BOF session, we want share our ideas and concrete solutions and to engage in dialogue with our international colleagues in order to enrich and improve our approach.

This BOF Session is sponsored by the ACM China Subcommittee on Education.

ACM Categories & Descriptors: A.1 Introductory and Survey; D.1 Programming Techniques; D.1.3 Concurrent Programming; D.3.2 Language Classifications

Keywords: Computational Thinking; Problem Solving; CS1 Course; K.3 Computer and Education

IT Curricular Guidance for Associate-Degree Granting Institutions

Elizabeth K. Hawthorne, *Union County College*
Robert D. Campbell, *CUNY Graduate Center*
Jim Nichols, *Estrella Mountain Community College*
Cara Tang, *Portland Community College*
Cindy Tucker, *Bluegrass Community and Technical College*
Contact: jim.nichols@estrellamountain.edu

At the direction of the Association for Computing Machinery (ACM) Education Board, the ACM Committee for Computing Education in Community Colleges (CCECC), has undertaken a project to produce IT curricular guidance which defines core IT competencies accompanied by well-designed assessment measures. To that end, the ACM CCECC convened a task force of subject matter experts from both academe and industry to define core IT learning outcomes which should be common to all associate-degree IT programs. Assessment consultants worked alongside these subject matter experts to create easy-to-use evaluation rubrics. The session will include an overview of the findings from this project including mappings to other curriculum models, as well as a discussion concerning curriculum, assessment and pedagogy of IT courses and programs at associate-degree granting institutions.

ACM Categories & Descriptors: K.3.2 Computer and Information Science Education

Keywords: Information Technology;Two-Year College; Associate-Degree Programs;Curriculum Guidance

Preparing Computer Science Students for a Sustainable Future

Daniela Inclezan, *Miami University*
Contact: inclezd@miamioh.edu

Computer science students graduating in the next decade will face the big energy and environmental challenges of the 21st century. According to current trends, an increasing number of them will be employed in "green jobs" and will contribute to promoting biodiversity, minimizing the consumption of energy and materials, or restoring environmental quality. It is our job to prepare them for the task ahead. While the vast majority of textbooks and materials used in different areas of CS are oblivious to these problems, many resources can be found at the boundaries with other disciplines (e.g., environmental science, architecture, agriculture, etc.). Moreover, new computer applications are created every day for the analysis of current environmental problems and the evaluation of their possible solutions, but these applications are normally not mentioned in CS classes. This is a lost opportunity for engaging our students in the real world challenges we are facing today. Environmental problems can be addressed in the CS classroom in a way that does not impede the learning of the technical content, but rather increases students' ability to think critically about complex systems. This BoF intends to brainstorm innovative resources, examples, activities, and assignments that can be incorporated into the CS classes, in order to raise students' awareness to current ecological problems and, at the same time, illustrate the role computer scientists can play in solving them. *For this BoF session, a laptop is optional.*

ACM Categories & Descriptors: K.3.2 Computer and Information Science Education

Keywords: Sustainability; Critical Thinking; Systemic Thinking; Ecological Literacy; Ethical Responsibility

SIGCSE'14, March 5–8, 2014, Atlanta, Georgia, USA.
ACM 978-1-4503-2605-6/14/03.

Birds of a Feather: Flock 2

State-Level Advocacy for Computing Education Reform

William Richards Adrion, *University of Massachusetts, Amherst*
Contact: adrion@cs.umass.edu

While it is exciting to see an increasing number of national efforts to reform computing education, such as those led by CSTA, Computing in the Core, ACM, NCWIT, code.org and many others, real change at the state, district and school level requires the active participation of individuals and local organizations to engage policy makers, superintendents and communities. The U.S. education system is highly distributed, with critical decisions pushed more to the community level and less at the national (or even state) level – with large differences between neighboring states. The system is organized along pathways of elementary schools, middle and high schools, community colleges, four-year colleges, and universities. A reform process for improving computing education pathways will take place at multiple levels and state by state. This birds-of-a-feather session will bring together emerging leaders at the state level with representatives from national initiatives to share best practices for implementing change.

ACM Categories & Descriptors: K.3.2 Computer and Information Science Education; K.4.1 Public Policy Issues; K.7.1 Occupations; K.7.2 Organizations

Keywords: Computing Education Pathways; Computing Education Reform; Policy Advocacy

How to Decode Student Bottlenecks to Learning in Computer Science

Adrian German, *Indiana University Bloomington*
Suzanne Menzel, *Indiana University Bloomington*
Joan Middendorf, *Indiana University Bloomington*
John F. Duncan, *Indiana University Bloomington*
Contact: dgerman@indiana.edu

After thirty years or more of the scholarship of teaching and learning (SoTL) many students still struggle to learn at the university level, while ever more techniques are being developed to help students learn and measure their success. In practice, however, efforts to reshape classes begin with questions such as: "How can I make use of this new technique?" Or, "How can I increase my students' critical thinking?" Such questions are often too broad to provide a clear focal point for designing efficient strategies. They sometimes draw attention to parts of the course not in great need of reform, and generally focus the process on the means (teaching) rather than the end (student learning). A shift is taking place in higher education so that teaching is approached not from content or from the teaching methods, but from the mental processes that are crucial to functioning in a discipline. Decoding the Disciplines (Middendorf & Pace, 2004) is an evidence-based, learner-centered methodology that can conclusively improve teaching by prioritizing what really matters in making meaning in a discipline and boosting learning outcomes in the classroom. It offers a meta-strategy, providing both a framework to define the task at hand and a means to determine which tools would be most useful in accomplishing it. Starting from the bottlenecks, the places where students get stuck, and connecting them with what experts do so they won't get stuck, the crucial mental processes drive the teaching and learning so students can be successful.

ACM Categories & Descriptors: K.3.2 Computer and Information Science Education

Keywords: Evidence-Based Teaching; Reflective Teaching; Learner-Centered Methodologies

Engaging College Students in Service Learning to Grow the K-12 Computing Pipeline and Prepare the 21st Century Workforce

Jamie Payton, *University of North Carolina at Charlotte*
Tiffany Barnes, *North Carolina State University*
Jason Black, *Florida A&M University*
Cheryl Seals, *Auburn University*
Contact: payton@uncc.edu

The demand for computing professionals in the U.S. workforce is expected to increase over the next several years, while the number of students intending to major in computing has declined. In this BOF session, we focus on the use of service learning to address the growing concern of creating a sustainable pipeline for computing professionals, with an emphasis on broadening participation in computing. We center the discussion around our experiences with the STARS Computing Corps, which engages college students in service-learning to address the national computing talent shortage. The model has been shown to be effective in retaining college students in computing, and STARS alumni credit participation in STARS with helping to develop professional skills.

This session will include interactive small group discussions on goals, obstacles, and strategies for applying service learning to broaden participation in computing, grow the K-12 pipeline, and prepare college students with skills demanded in the 21st century workforce.

ACM Categories & Descriptors: K.3.2 computer and Information Science Education; K.4 Computers and Society; K.7 The Computing Profession

Keywords: service learning; broadening participation in computing; T-shaped professional

Data Fluency: Curricular Issues for All Majors

Suzanne W. Dietrich, *Arizona State University*
Don Goelman, *Villanova University*
Contact: dietrich@asu.edu

Given the ever-growing importance of data across all disciplines, there is a need to enhance the fluency and comfort with data

SIGCSE'14, March 5–8, 2014, Atlanta, Georgia, USA.
ACM 978-1-4503-2605-6/14/03.

technology for a diversity of majors, not just technical ones. Which topics should be included in a data fluency course for all majors? A non-exhaustive list of possible topics includes spreadsheets, relations and relational databases, querying, conceptual design, bar graphs, charts, other data visualization, XML, and "Big Data." Join the discussion to brainstorm a data experience for students with diverse majors.

ACM Categories & Descriptors: K.3.2 Computer and Information Science Education; H.2.m Database Management - Miscellaneous

Keywords: Data; Information; Non-majors

Teaching Open Source (Software)

Karl Wurst, *Worcester State University*
Lori Postner, *Nassau Community College*
Stoney Jackson, *Western New England University*
Contact: hjackson@wne.edu

Integrating Free and Open Source Software (FOSS) into our curricula can provide students with a rich, motivating learning experience that helps them develop technical as well as soft skills. However, integrating FOSS into curricula does have its challenges. This birds-of-a-feather (BoF) seeks to bring together faculty to discuss challenges, share resources, share solutions, and make connections. So, whether you are considering integrating FOSS into a class for the first time, or you are looking for ways to improve what you are already doing, this BoF is for you. Members of the Teaching Open Source (http://teachingopensource.org) and the foss2serve (http://foss2serve.org/) communities will help guide the discussion and be on hand for questions.

ACM Categories & Descriptors: K.3.2 [Computers and Education]: Computer and Information Science Education

Keywords: Teaching Open Source Software

Including HCI and User Experience (UX) Methodologies in Computing Curricula

Debra Lee Davis, *Florida International University*
Dave Berque, *DePauw University*
Janet Davis, *Grinnell College*
Matt Jadud, *Berea College*
Paul Resnick, *University of Michigan*
Contact: dledavis@fiu.edu

With a growing awareness of the importance of Human Computer Interaction (HCI) and User Experience (UX) Design and Research in industry, many departments are examining ways to integrate this topic into their curriculum. What are the best ways to do this? Should HCI and UX be integrated into existing courses such as event-driven programming or mobile computing? Or should it be a separate course that integrates visual design, psychology and ergonomics? How important is this topic to students looking for internships and entry-level jobs? At what levels should these topics be taught in the curriculum? This is important as there is a growing demand in industry for User Experience specialists due to an increased focus on software quality and product success. A major complaint of employers is that this skill is lacking in many college graduates. Teaching computing students how to incorporate UX into the design and development process helps to address this critical need. This BOF will let participants share their ideas and learn from their peers. Some of the discussion leaders led a similar lively and enthusiastic discussion at SIGCSE 2013. Discussion spanned the role of HCI in the participants' various curricula; modules versus dedicated courses; projects versus standalone assignments; and textbooks, tools, and other pedagogical materials. Bringing together new and previous participants will bring new insights and expansion of these, including discussions of our recent experiences and lessons learned, as well as the broaching of new topics such as the roles of non-computing courses in HCI education.

ACM Categories & Descriptors: K.3.2 Computer and Information Science Education; H.1.2 User/Machine Systems; H.5.2 User Interfaces; D.2.2 Design Tools and Techniques; D.2.10 Design

Keywords: Computing Curriculum; Human-Computer Interaction; User Experience; HCI; UX; Computing Instruction; Curriculum Issues

Ensemble: The Sharing Community

Lillian N Cassel, *Villanova University*
Lois Delcambre, *Portland State University*
Greg Hislop, *Drexel University*
Contact: cassel@acm.org

The Ensemble computing portal originated under the NSF NSDL program and enjoys the respect and continued interest of the computing education community. The project has reached a maturity level at which it is time to focus on the long-term viability of the activity. The original proposal included a commitment from the Villanova University library to adopt the system and keep in running in perpetuity. However, merely keeping the system running will not preserve nor extend the true promise of the project. That requires an active, engaged community. The leaders of the Ensemble project invite our partner projects and the SIGCSE community to join us in an initial meeting of an organization devoted to the continued development and support of the Ensemble vision: that of a community of educators sharing their best efforts, showcasing the best resources, and archiving materials that deserve long term preservation. Until now, the ownership and development has rested with a small group – the original PIs of the grant. It is time for that group to be extended, for the wider community to have a larger say in the directions taken and the choices made. This is a critical phase for the Ensemble project and we cannot imagine a better venue than SiGCSE.

ACM Categories & Descriptors: K.3.1 Computer Uses in Education

Keywords: Computing Education, Education Repository, Community, Computing Educator Resources

SIGCSE'14, March 5–8, 2014, Atlanta, Georgia, USA.
ACM 978-1-4503-2605-6/14/03.

Survey Courses and AP CS Principles

Chris Mayfield, *James Madison University*
Dennis Brylow, *Marquette University*
Contact: mayfiecs@jmu.edu

With initiatives like CS Ed Week, Code.org, and the AP CS Principles course, many educators are designing new and engaging ways to introduce students to computer science. But are we doing a good enough job presenting computer science as a field? Is it sufficient for prospective students to understand that CS is about creativity, abstraction, data, algorithms, programming, the Internet, and impact? Or should they also learn something about computer architecture, operating systems, networking and security, programming languages, software engineering, database systems, and so forth? This BOF will discuss how survey courses can meet the learning objectives of AP CS Principles, while providing a wealth of content knowledge that maps directly to undergraduate computer science programs.

ACM Categories & Descriptors: K.3.2 Computer and Information Science Education

Keywords: AP CS Principles; Survey Course

Incorporating Mobile Computing into the CS Curriculum

Shiva Azadegan, *Towson University*
Josh Dehlinger, *Towson University*
Siddharth Kaza, *Towson University*
Contact: jdehlinger@towson.edu

Computer Science (CS) educators are constantly reinventing introductory and advanced courses contextualized with new technology to better engage, retain students and increase their learning and motivation. Mobile and wearable computing are the most recent examples. However, while it is important to attract students into CS, it is equally vital to sustain student motivation by using pedagogical approaches contextualized to how students learn throughout the curriculum without losing fundamental, core concepts. Many educators have developed one-off courses employing new technology or a project-driven approach to engage students and transfer ready industry skills. Yet, too few have woven a combination of pedagogical approaches sensitive to how students learn with in-demand technology and skills contiguously throughout the upper-level curriculum and tied it to opportunities outside of the classroom. To ensure that CS educators are not simply adopting the newest technological fad at the expense of students learning and fundamental, core CS concepts, the CS education community must understand how mobile computing technology can be successfully leveraged to change education through measured, contextualized pedagogical approaches. To start facilitating this dialog, this Birds of a Feather session will provide a platform for the discussion of how mobile computing has been successfully (and unsuccessfully) incorporated into CS courses; the mobile platforms and tools used; and, the pedagogical utility of using mobile computing as a learning intervention. This project is partially supported by NSF DUE#1140781.

ACM Categories & Descriptors: K.3.2 Computer and Information Science Education

Keywords: Computer Science education; mobile computing

NSF/IEEE-TCPP Curriculum Initiative on Parallel and Distributed Computing - Core Topics for Undergraduates

Sushil K. Prasad, *Georgia State University*
Almadena Chtchelkanova, *National Science Foundation*
Anshul Gupta, *IBM T.J. Watson Research*
Arnold Rosenberg, *Northeastern University*
Alan Sussman, *University of Maryland*
Charles Weems, *University of Massachusetts*
Contact: sprasad@gsu.edu

Parallelism pervades all aspects of modern computing, from in-home devices such as cell phones to large-scale supercomputers. Recognizing this - and motivated by the premise that *every* undergraduate student in a computer-related field should be prepared to cope with parallel computing - a working group sponsored by NSF and IEEE/TCPP, and interacting with the ACM CS2013 initiative, has developed guidelines for assimilating parallel and distributed computing (PDC) into the core undergraduate curriculum. Over 100 Early-Adopter institutions worldwide are currently modifying their computer-related curricula in response to the guidelines. Additionally, the CDER Center for Curriculum Development and Educational Resources, which grew out of the working group, is currently assembling a book of contributed essays on how to teach PDC topics in lower-level CS/CE courses, to fill the serious lack of textual material for students and instructors.

This session is intended: (i) to report on the current state of this initiative; (ii) to bring together authors of book chapters and Early Adopters and other interested parties for discussions on ongoing activities and needs; (iii) to discuss the initiative and collect direct feedback from the community.

ACM Categories & Descriptors: K.3.2 [Computing Milieu]: Computers and Education- Computer and Information System Education [Curriculum, Computer science education]

Keywords: Education; Undergraduate Curriculum; Parallel and Distributed Computing; Bloom's Classification; Learning Outcomes; Early Adopters; Educational Resources

Integrating Active Learning Techniques into Systems Courses

Michael S. Kirkpatrick, *James Madison University*
Leo Porter, *Skidmore College*
Contact: kirkpams@jmu.edu

There is a growing body of evidence showing active learning pedagogies are effective for ensuring long-term student learning, reducing course failure rates, and retaining majors. While active learning pedagogies are more often employed in lower divisional CS courses, systems classes—such as OS, architecture, and networks—are just beginning to see a shift from standard lecture to

SIGCSE'14, March 5–8, 2014, Atlanta, Georgia, USA.
ACM 978-1-4503-2605-6/14/03.

active learning. This BOF will provide a forum for sharing ideas of how to integrate active learning techniques into systems courses, using the following questions as starting points:

- What are active learning techniques, and how are they used?
- What impact does active learning have on coverage?
- Must adoption of active learning techniques entail abandoning lectures entirely? If not, how can I use active learning to augment, rather than replace, my lectures?
- What transitional steps can I take toward active learning methodologies?
- If you've tried active learning techniques, what results have you seen?

ACM Categories & Descriptors: K.3.2 Computer and Information Science Education

Keywords: Active learning; Peer Instruction; Team-based Learning; Computer Science Education; Pedagogy; Computer Systems

Teaching Security Using Hands-on Exercises

Richard Weiss, *The Evergreen State College*
Michael E. Locasto, *The University of Calgary*
Jens Mache, *Lewis & Clark College*
Elizabeth Hawthorne, *Union County College*
Justin Cappos, *NYU-Polytechnic University*
Contact: weissr@evergreen.edu

We see teaching information security through hands-on, interactive exercises as a way to engage students. Some of the exercises that we have seen require significant preparation on the part of the instructor. Having a community makes it easier to share exercises, knowing what works and what problems students and instructors have encountered. The purpose of this BOF is to bring together instructors who have used hands-on exercises and those who would like to. We recognize that few CS programs can afford new required courses, so we would be discussing ways to integrate security-related exercises into existing ones. This could include networking, OS, computer architecture, programming languages, software engineering and algorithms. The questions we will ask are, "What exercises have you tried? What are your experiences? What are you looking for?"

ACM Categories & Descriptors: C.2.0 Computer-Communication Networks; K.4.4 Electronic Commerce

Keywords: Your own keywords;Separated with Semi-Colons; Security; Information Assurance; Cybersecurity; Laboratory Exercises

SIGCSE'14, March 5–8, 2014, Atlanta, Georgia, USA.
ACM 978-1-4503-2605-6/14/03.

Community Engagement and Service Learning Opportunities in Computer Science

Douglas E. Harms, *DePauw University*
Contact: dharms@depauw.edu

Many computer science students and faculty want to participate in service projects; these projects might include service learning in the classroom, service experiences in the local community, or service projects at a domestic or international site. Developing service projects that incorporate computer science and/or technology skills that are both interesting and meaningful often presents a challenge. During this BOF participants will discuss and answer questions about service projects in which they have participated, their successes and failures, techniques for finding appropriate partners, logistical issues, etc. This session will be helpful to faculty having no prior service experience, as well as veteran faculty who have organized multiple service trips.

ACM Categories & Descriptors: K.3.2 [Computers and Education]: Computer and Information Science Education - *Computer Science Education, Curriculum*

Keywords: Service Learning; Community Engagement

Technology that Educators of Computing Hail (TECH): Come, share your favorites!

Daniel D. Garcia, *University of California, Berkeley*
Dan Armendariz, *University of California, Berkeley*
Contact: ddgarcia@cs.berkeley.edu

The pace of technology for use in computing education is staggering. In the last five years, the following tools / websites have completely transformed our teaching: *Piazza*, *Google Docs*, *PandaGrader*, *YouTube*, *Doodle* and *whenisgood.net*, *Skype* and *Google Hangout*, and *Khan Academy* among others. Hardware has also played a part – we love our *Zoom H2 digital voice recorder* (for recording CD-quality lecture audio), *Blue Yeti USB mike* (for audio/videoconferences), and *iClickers* (for engaging students in class).

Do you wish you could easily share your favorites? Want to find out what the others know that you don't? Have a tool you've built and want to get some users? Come to this BOF! We'll also show the TECH website we've built that attempts to collect all of these tools in one place.

ACM Categories & Descriptors: K.3.2 [**Computer and Information Science Education**]: Computer Science Education

Keywords: ensemble Computing Portal; TECH; Technology and Tools; Educational Technology for Teaching Computing; Drupal

Using Science Fiction in CS Courses

Rebecca Bates, *Minnesota State University, Mankato*
Judy Goldsmith, *University of Kentucky*
Valerie Summet, *Emory University*
Nanette Veilleux, *Simmons College*
Contact: bates@mnsu.edu

Are you interested in incorporating some of your favorite science fiction in your classes? Did you know it can help improve student interest in the technical topic? Come join us as we talk about ways to connect SciFi to artificial intelligence, robotics, networking, intellectual property, and other topics. We'll start with overviews of how we've used SciFi and have plenty of time for discussion of new works and old that connect to the material we need to cover, while drawing students into the content and the field.

ACM Categories & Descriptors: K.3.2 Computer science education

Keywords: Science Fiction; Student Engagement

Using and Sharing Programming Exercises to Improve Introductory Courses

David Hovemeyer, *York College of Pennsylvania*
Jaime Spacco, *Knox College*
Robert Duvall, *Duke University*
Stephen Edwards, *Virginia Tech*
Amruth Kumar, *Ramapo College of New Jersey*
Andrew Petersen, *University of Toronto Mississauga*
Daniel Zingaro, *University of Toronto*
Contact: jspacco@knox.edu

Short, automatically-assessed programming exercises, and other types of short practice problems, are a useful way to introduce and reinforce concepts and techniques in introductory programming courses. When delivered over the web, they allow students to learn and practice, with immediate feedback, at any time and place where they have access to a web browser. However, such exercises do not seem to be as widely used as they could be. Similarly, there is not a lot of literature on the effectiveness of these types of problems. The purpose of this BOF is to bring together users (and potential users) of programming exercises with developers of programming exercise systems to discuss how exercises could be used more widely and effectively. Possible discussion topics include: What features are absolutely essential for faculty to consider adoption? What are the major obstacles preventing more widespread adoption? Are faculty willing to share their exercises under an open/non-commercial license? Should exercises best used for extra practice, as graded assignments, or both?

ACM Categories & Descriptors: K.3.2 Computer and Information Science Education.

Keywords: computer science education; online exercises

Making Induction Meaningful, Recursively

Peter-Michael Osera, *University of Pennsylvania*
Brent Yorgey, *University of Pennsylvania*
Contact: posera@cis.upenn.edu

Induction is a notoriously difficult topic for beginning computer science students to understand. Even if they can produce an inductive proof of some mathematical fact, many students never see the relevance of inductive reasoning outside of the classroom for anything beyond the natural numbers. This is unfortunate because inductive reasoning is closely intertwined with algorithm design and one of the cornerstones of reasoning about (recursive) programs. With the adoption of functional programming into the CS curricula core, it is a good time to revisit how we teach induction and try to make more explicit this fundamental connection between inductive reasoning and recursive programming. In this BoF session, we will discuss curriculum, strategies, and fun examples for teaching induction with an eye towards giving induction tangible and practical relevance for the computer science undergraduate.

SIGCSE'14, March 5–8, 2014, Atlanta, Georgia, USA.
ACM 978-1-4503-2605-6/14/03.

ACM Categories & Descriptors: K.3.2 [Computers and Education]: Computer and Information Science Education --- computer science education; G.2.0 [Mathematics of Computing]: Discrete Mathematics --- general

Keywords: Computer Science Education; Discrete Mathematics; Induction; Functional Programming

Web Programming

Marty Stepp, *Stanford University*
Jessica Miller, *Microsoft Research*
Contact: stepp@cs.stanford.edu

Several times in the past few years we have held BoF sessions about teaching web programming at the college level. Our feedback indicates that the most valuable aspect of the past sessions was simply to get everyone together for an exchange of ideas and information, so this will be the focus of the session again. We'd like to bring together two groups of web programming instructors: Newcomers who have not yet taught this material before (or are just starting) and want to soak up information, and veterans who have now taught it and have insights to share with the group. Newcomers can ask questions about materials, languages and technologies to use, what works and what doesn't, and so on. Veterans can share tips from the classroom and helpful resources. We can also discuss the latest technologies such as HTML, ECMAScript/JavaScript, iPhone/iPad, Android, and web application frameworks such as Node.js, Rails, AngularJS, and more.

ACM Categories & Descriptors: D.m Miscellaneous

Keywords: CSS; html; javascript; web development; web programming

Can 3D Virtual World Environments and Game-based Learning Effectively Teach Computer Science Concepts?

Stephanie E. August, *Loyola Marymount University*
Jungwoo Ryoo, *Pennsylvania State University-Altoona*
Contact: saugust@lmu.edu

MOOCs, 3D virtual world environments, game-based learning, simulations, digital story-telling, and other learning-focused digital interactions hold tremendous potential for presenting information science concepts and problem-solving strategies to the generations of the 21st century. We use them to present both theoretical and practical concepts in an engaging manner, tailored to specific age groups and at many levels of abstraction. An abundance of recent projects have examined these individually and brought to light many common concerns. This session explores several interrelated questions: How can these varied activities can be integrated to effectively teach programming concepts, problem solving strategies, and programming skills at age- and discipline-appropriate levels? Do interactive digital simulations and visualizations facilitate construction of the mental models underlying computing concepts? What assessments will be effective in determining whether we are achieving our knowledge- and skill-related goals? How are these tools related to student learning styles and learning objectives? How can these artifacts be disseminated and sustained in the context of dynamic delivery platforms? This brainstorming session is an opportunity to share ideas and explore future collaborations.

ACM Categories & Descriptors: H.5.1 Multimedia Information Systems; H.5.2 User Interfaces; K.3.1 Computer Uses in Education; K.3.2 Computer and Information Science Education

Keywords: Game-based Learning; 3D Virtual World Environments; Digital Story Telling; Second Life; OpenSim; Digital Learning Aids

SIGCSE'14, March 5–8, 2014, Atlanta, Georgia, USA.
ACM 978-1-4503-2605-6/14/03.

Wednesday Workshops

ITSEED: Hands-on Labs for IT Security Education

Yan Bai, *University of Washington Tacoma*
Xinli Wang, *Michigan Technological University*
Contact: yanb@uw.edu

With NSF funding, we have developed a collection of instructional laboratories to enhance the security component in IT education. The labs are developed with a layered and modular design that can be tailored for different courses, accommodating new tools and being conducted in various environments with minimum modifications. This workshop introduces to participants these labs and the environment to conduct them. The workshop proceeds in four sessions in which we: 1) introduce the labs, techniques and environment; 2) demonstrate a lab; 3) guide participants to practice with a lab, 4) debrief. The intended audience is educators who teach IT security courses or other courses with security components at colleges or universities. Experience is not required.

Each participant receives an electronic version of 1) the lab assignments that we have developed and used in our teaching practice, and 2) preconfigured virtual machines and tools used to conduct the labs. Laptop required.

ACM Categories and Subject Descriptors: K.3.2 [**Computing Milieux**]: Computer and Information Science Education – Information systems education

Keywords: Hands-on Laboratory; IT Security; Education

Making Games and Apps in Introductory Computer Science

Tiffany Barnes, Ph.D., *North Carolina State University*
Veronica Catete, *North Carolina State University*
Drew Hicks, *North Carolina State University*
Barry Peddycord III, *North Carolina State University*
Contact: tmbarnes@ncsu.edu

The new CS Principles curriculum, a pilot Advanced Placement course, offers novice students an exciting opportunity to learn computing in a hands-on, fun way. High school and college teachers of introductory computer science course are invited to this workshop to learn basic game and mobile phone development. Participants will learn GameMaker, AppInventor, and Touch Develop. These tools allow students to create and have fun with computing while teaching object-oriented and event-driven programming and game architectures. Participants should bring their own laptops (ideally with AppInventor installed). Windows 7 phones will be provided during the workshop. We will provide links to curricular modules for the CS Principles: Beauty and Joy of Computing course.

SIGCSE'14, March 5–8, 2014, Atlanta, Georgia, USA.
ACM 978-1-4503-2605-6/14/03.

ACM Categories & Descriptors: K.3.2 Computer science education, curriculum;

Keywords: BJC; Curriculum; Games; Mobile Apps

Reviewing NSF Proposals: Learn about Effective Proposal Writing via the Review Process

Valerie Barr, *National Science Foundation*
Paul Tymann, *National Science Foundation*
Contact: ptymann@nsf.gov

This workshop focuses on the NSF proposal review process. Via close examination of the review process, participants gain an understanding of how to write good reviews and how to improve their own proposal writing. The workshop covers the following topic areas: the proposal review process from submission of a proposal to award or decline; elements of a good review; NSF merit criteria (intellectual merit and broader impacts); elements of a good proposal; and how to volunteer to review proposals.

The workshop uses a structured guided-interactive methodology to lead participants through each topic by introducing related issues, engaging participants in group exercises designed to explore and share their understanding of the issues, and then providing some "expert" opinion on these issues. Good and bad examples and a Top Ten List of Do's and Don'ts will be provided.

ACM Categories & Descriptors: K.0 General

Keywords: Grant Writing, NSF Review Process

Integrating Software Testing into Programming Courses (WISTPC 2014)

Peter J. Clarke, *Florida International Univeristy*
Yujian Fu, *Alabama A&M University*
James Kiper, *Miami University*
Gursimran Walia, *North Dakota State University*
Contact: clarkep@cis.fiu.edu

The WISTPC workshop introduces participants to a minimally intrusive approach to integrating software testing into software engineering and advance programming courses using a cyberlearning environment. The focus of the workshop will be to introduce participants to (1) software testing techniques, and (2) the features of WReSTT – Web-Based Repository of Software Testing Tutorials, that supports testing in the classroom. WReSTT integrates aspects of collaborative learning and social networking to improve students' ability to learn software testing techniques and testing tools. We expect participants to know Java and we assume they have little or no formal training in software testing. At the end of the workshop participants should: (1) have a basic understanding of software testing and testing tools, (2) be able to use WReSTT in their classes, and (3) be able to use learning objects to support software testing instruction. URL: http://wrestt.cis.fiu.edu/cen/wistpc-14 Laptop Required – a web browser and wifi enabled

ACM Categories & Descriptors: D.2.5 Testing and Debugging; K.3.1 Computer Uses in Education

Keywords: Software Testing; Testing Tools; Collaborative Learning; Learning Objects

Teaching Computing with the IPython Notebook

Greg Wilson, *Mozilla Foundation*
Fernando Pérez, *University of California, Berkeley*
Peter Norvig, *Google Inc.*
Contact: greg@mozillafoundation.org

The IPython Notebook is an interactive browser-based environment where you can combine code execution, text, mathematics, plots, and rich media into a single document. Originally designed for use as an electronic lab notebook for computational science, it is increasingly being used in teaching as well, and a rich ecosystem of open source plugins and extensions for teaching is growing around it. The first half of this hands-on workshop will introduce the Notebook and present examples of lessons and instructional materials built around it. In the second half, attendees will explore future directions for the Notebook as a teaching platform. For more information, please view materials in our GitHub repository at https://github.com/gvwilson/sigcse2014-ipython-workshop. Please note that participants are expected to bring a laptop.

ACM Categories & Descriptors: K.3.2 Computer and Information Science Education

Keywords: Python; electronic lab notebook

Teaching Service-Oriented Programming to CS and SE Undergraduate Students

Xumin Liu, *Rochester Institute of Technology*
Rajendra K. Raj, *Rochester Institute of Technology*
Thomas J. Reichlmayr, *Rochester Institute of Technology*
Alex Pantaleev, SUNY Oswego
Chunmei Liu, Howard University
Contact: xl@cs.rit.edu

Service-Oriented Programming (SOP) is a relatively new programming paradigm that supports the development of new software applications using existing web services as building blocks. SOP has gained significant popularity in industry as it increases software reuse and productivity. As the SOP paradigm can improve modern software development, the presenters have created a course-module based approach for incorporating SOP into Computer Science (CS) and Software Engineering (SE) curricula; a course module is a distinct, self-contained curricular unit such as a lab or teaching component that an instructor may incorporate into an existing course, typically without requiring formal curricular approval. The workshop presenters have developed SOP course modules for inclusion in standard CS and SE courses. There is an introductory SOP module for a course such as Computer Science 2, a mid-level SOP module for a course such as Programming Language Concepts, and a more advanced module for a course such as Software Engineering or Web Services. These developed course modules have been used in courses at three universities, and have been improved based on these teaching experiences. This workshop will present basic concepts and techniques of SOP and the three course modules, and describe how the course-module approach toward SOP can be adapted for the participants' own teaching.

ACM Categories & Descriptors: D.1.0 Programming Techniques: General D.2.13 Resuable Software H.3.5 Online Information Service

Keywords: Service-Oriented Programming; Web Services; CS2, PLC, Software Engineering; Computer Science; Course Modules

GENI as a Virtual Laboratory for Networking and Distributed Systems Classes

Vicraj Thomas, *BBN Technologies*
Niky Riga, *BBN Technologies*
Sarah Edwards, *BBN Technologies*
Contact: vthomas@bbn.com

This hands-on workshop will introduce GENI to instructors of computer networking and distributed systems classes. Instructors can use GENI [http://groups.geni.net/geni/wiki], an easy-to-use virtual laboratory, to improve the educational experiences of their students by having them experiment with new concepts without requiring expensive laboratory facilities. It has been used by over twenty graduate and undergraduate classes.

GENI is being used by over 1200 researchers and educators. It enables them to run large-scale, well-instrumented, end-to-end experiments engaging real users. These experiments may be fully compatible with today's Internet, variations or improvements on today's Internet protocols, or indeed radically novel "clean slate" designs. GENI includes compute and communications resources distributed across the United States. GENI is "deeply programmable" i.e. experimenters can install their custom software or operating systems on the compute nodes and can program the behavior of the switches that connect these nodes.

GENI is funded by the National Science Foundation and is free to use for research and education.

Workshop participants will have the opportunity to set up and run experiments using GENI. They will also learn about class logistics when using GENI and support resources such as ready-to-use exercises. Those doing the hands-on activity will need a laptop running relatively a recent version of Mac OS, Windows or Linux; at least 4GB of memory; a modern processor (at least dual core and faster than 1.5 GHz) and a WiFi interface.

ACM Categories & Descriptors: C.2 Computer-Communications Networks; K.3.2. Computer and Information Science Education

Keywords: Networking and Distributed Systems Instruction; Virtual Laboratory; Programmable Infrastructure

SIGCSE'14, March 5–8, 2014, Atlanta, Georgia, USA.
ACM 978-1-4503-2605-6/14/03.

CABECT: Collaborating Across Boundaries to Engage Undergraduates in Computational Thinking

S. Monisha Pulimood, *The College of New Jersey*
Kim Pearson, *The College of New Jersey*
Diane C. Bates, *The College of New Jersey*
Contact: pulimood@tcnj.edu

Innovative solutions for complex problems entail diversity of perspectives, and students must learn to integrate concepts from multiple disciplinary areas. Yet, to provide collaborative experiences that cross disciplinary boundaries, educators must navigate numerous administrative and pedagogical challenges. In this hands-on workshop participants will learn how to leverage existing courses for students and faculty to collaborate across disciplines and with a community partner, to develop socially-relevant computational solutions for real-world problems. Participants will also brainstorm ideas on addressing specific challenges at their own institutions. The intended audience is educators interested in engaging their students in deep computational thinking through immersive multidisciplinary collaborative experiences. Registered participants will be reimbursed the workshop registration fee through NSF Award# 1141170. We will additionally offer a stipend to participants who adopt our model, administer assessments and provide us with their results for analysis and inclusion in reports. More information will be available at http://tardis.tcnj.edu/cabect/. Laptop Recommended.

ACM Categories & Descriptors: K.3.2 Computer and Information Science Education - Computer science education

Keywords: Collaboration; Community Engaged Learning; Computational Thinking

Enhancing Computer Science Education (CSE) with the Use of 3D Printer Technology

Robert Lutz, *Georgia Gwinnett College*
Evelyn Brannock, *Georgia Gwinnett College*
Contact: rlutz@ggc.edu

This workshop provides an introduction to three-dimensional (3D) printing. This tutorial will: cover the general background of 3D printing, summarize popular software tools, describe associated challenges and offer suggestions for application within computer science (CS) coursework. Participating CSE educators will get hands-on experience with 3D printing tools and will be able to print a limited number of items during the workshop. Attendees will perform a full lifecycle exercise in the printing workflow, progressing from a concept, to a digital model, to a physical implementation. The workshop will also describe the authors' experience integrating this authentic learning into several IT and CS courses. Experience gained will be useful after the session in both printer and printer-less environments. See http://tinyurl.com/k65jxsm for more information. ***Laptop required***.

SIGCSE'14, March 5–8, 2014, Atlanta, Georgia, USA.
ACM 978-1-4503-2605-6/14/03.

ACM Categories & Descriptors: K.3.2 Computers and Information Science Education: Computer science education

Keywords: 3D Printing

Scala for Introductory CS and Parallelism

Mark Lewis, *Trinity University*
Konstantin Läufer, *Loyola University Chicago*
George K. Thiruvathukal, *Loyola University Chicago*
Contact: mlewis@trinity.edu

Scala is one of a new breed of hybrid languages with both object-oriented and functional aspects. It happens to be the most successful of these languages coming in at #12 on the Red Monk language ranking and leading all languages in their 2nd tier. This workshop will introduce participants to the Scala programming language, how it can be used effectively in introductory CS courses, and the parallel tools that are available for it. We begin with simple examples in the REPL and scripting environment, then look at doing larger, object-oriented projects. We finish off with an exploration of composable futures and the Akka actor library. Participants are strongly recommended to bring a laptop.

ACM Categories & Descriptors: D.1.0 General; D.1.1 Applicative (Functional) Programming; D.1.3 Concurrent Programming; D.3.3 Language Constructs and Features; K.3.2 Computer and Information Science Education

Keywords: CS1; CS2; Scala; Parallelism

Teach Algorithm Design and Intractability with a Project-Based Curriculum Centered on a Single Intractable Problem: Three Domains to Choose From

Andrea F. Lobo, *Rowan University*
Ganesh R. Baliga, *Rowan University*
Contact: lobo@rowan.edu

This workshop presents an award-winning, NSF-funded, project-based curriculum for algorithm design that includes algorithmic strategies for intractable problems. This curriculum is a sequence of laboratory projects comprising increasingly sophisticated solvers for a single intractable problem, designed to integrate into existing, one-term, undergraduate courses that teach algorithm design and/or intractability without sacrificing traditional course content. The presenters have used the curriculum in the Design and Analysis of Algorithms course at their institution to help students tackle and appreciate intractability. This workshop presents versions of the curriculum centered on TSP, SAT and Sudoku. Attendees will receive adoption materials and access to an adopters' forum. NSF is funding the development, evaluation, dissemination and adoption of the curriculum. Potential adopters are encouraged to apply for funding to attend this workshop and SIGCSE 2014 at http://www.rowan.edu/~lobo/AlgosCurriculum. This material is based upon work supported by the National Science Foundation under Grant No. 1140753. Laptop optional.

ACM Categories & Descriptors: F.2 Analysis of Algorithms and Problem Complexity; K.3.2 Computer and Information Science Education

Keywords: Algorithms; Intractability; Project-Based Curriculum; Algorithmic Strategies; Design Techniques; TSP; SAT; Sudoku; Traveling Salesperson; Satisfiability

Friday Workshops

Exploring Computer Science: Computational Practices in Action

Gail Chapman, *University of California, Los Angeles*
Joanna Goode, *University of Oregon*
Contact: chapgail@gmail.com

The ECS program includes an inquiry-based college-preparatory curriculum that introduces students to the creative nature of computing, technology as a tool for solving problems, and the relevance and impact of CS. This workshop will provide participants the opportunity to engage in activities from the ECS curriculum that highlight the six computational practices common to ECS and CS Principles. We will explicitly model the inquiry-based design of the activities and facilitate discussions that highlight how inquiry manifests itself in the computational practices. This workshop is appropriate for K-12 educators and college/university faculty who are interested in deepening their understanding of how teacher pedagogy is critical to broadening participation in computing. Laptop Optional.

ACM Categories and Descriptors: I.0 General

Keywords: K-12; teaching; equity

Teaching Shared Memory Parallel Concepts with OpenMP

Joel Adams, *Calvin College*
Richard Brown, *St Olaf College*
Elizabeth Shoop, *Macalester College*
Contact: adams@calvin.edu

Curriculum 2013 brings parallelism into the CS curricular mainstream. This hands-on workshop is intended for faculty with little or no background in parallel computing. OpenMP is a platform independent, industry-standard library for shared-memory parallel programming supported by all modern C and C++ compilers. The workshop introduces the basics of OpenMP multithreading using parallel patterns, including single program multiple data (SPMD) execution, fork-join threading, and pragmas for parallel loops, parallel blocks, mutual exclusion, etc. The workshop includes: (i) an overview of OpenMP, (ii) self-paced hands-on experimentation with the OpenMP programs, and (iii) a discussion of how these may be used to achieve the goals of Curriculum 2013. Workshop materials will be distributed from csinparallel.org. Participants will receive and explore 15 short programs designed to help students understand multithreading concepts, plus longer programs that use OpenMP to solve significant problems. A participant may explore these programs on their own laptop, provided it has installed a C/C++ compiler that supports OpenMP (e.g., gcc 4.2 or later; Visual Studio 2008 or later). Those comfortable with the command-line may explore the programs on our remote servers using a laptop or tablet with a suitable SSH client. Laptop recommended.

ACM Categories & Descriptors: D.1.3 Concurrent Programming, *Parallel programming*; D.2.11 Software Architectures, *Patterns*; K.3.2 Computer and Information Science Education, *Computer science education*

Keywords: C/C++; Education; Multicore; Multithreading; OpenMP; Parallel; Patterns; Programming; Shared-Memory; Threads

Creating Stimulating, Relevant, and Manageable Introductory Computer Science Projects that Utilize Real-Time Web-Based Data

Eli Tilevich, *Virginia Tech*
Clifford A. Shaffer, *Virginia Tech*
Austin Cory Bart, *Virginia Tech*
Contact: tilevich@cs.vt.edu

This workshop introduces participants to RealTimeWeb, a technology developed under the auspices of an NSF-funded project at Virginia Tech. RealTimeWeb is a software architecture framework that makes real-time web data, such as weather reports, news updates, and restaurant recommendations, accessible for introductory programming projects. The presented technology offers technical scaffolding for the students to gradually ease into some of the most vexing complexities of distributed computing. At the heart of RealTimeWeb are carefully engineered client libraries through which students can access the data provided by real-time web services. To support computing educators teaching introductory CS classes in a variety of programming languages, each library is available in Python, Java, and Racket, with compatibility on key platforms, including Android. These libraries are readily available through an online curated gallery, designed to be quickly adapted to instructors' specific academic needs. This gallery also provides a tool for rapidly prototyping new libraries based on our framework. RealTimeWeb enables computing educators to introduce important real-time distributed computing concepts without overwhelming students with the low-level details that working with such data typically requires. This workshop introduces RealTimeWeb via a hands-on approach by introducing participants to the core functionality of our architectural framework and client libraries. The participants will work through a case study of creating a programming project in a typical CS 2 course; rapidly prototype a new library of their choice; and critically discuss the technology in small and large groups. Further information is at: http://research.cs.vt.edu/vtspaces/realtimeweb/.
A laptop is mandatory.

ACM Categories & Descriptors: K.3.2 [Computer and Information Science Education]: Computer Science Education; D.1.3 [Programming Techniques]: |Distributed Programming

Keywords: Distributed Computing; Programming Projects; Introductory Courses

SIGCSE'14, March 5–8, 2014, Atlanta, Georgia, USA.
ACM 978-1-4503-2605-6/14/03.

Computational Remixing with EarSketch

Brian Magerko, *Georgia Tech*
Jason Freeman, *Georgia Tech*
Christopher Michaud, *Marist School*
Mike Reilly, *Lanier High School*
Contact: magerko@gatech.edu

Our work has focused on how to create a learning experience that is highly personally motivating for students, has a low barrier of entry for creation an artistic computational artifact, and is scalable for use in formal and informal education settings at the national level. We have created a learning environment called EarSketch that addresses student engagement through a STEAM learning experience that provides authentic learning in both the technical (i.e. computing) and artistic domains (i.e. music remixing). EarSketch is an integrated curriculum, software toolset, audio loop library, and social sharing site that teaches computing principles through digital music composition and remixing. Attendees will use Python to place audio clips, create rhythms, and add and control effects to a multi-track digital audio workstation (DAW) while learning computing concepts such as variables, iteration, conditionals, strings, lists, and functions. Participants write code to make music, with a focus on popular genres such as hip hop. The agenda outlines the pedagogy of connecting musical expression to computation. EarSketch has been used in introductory computing summer camps, secondary school classes, and is currently working towards integration with CS Principles pilot programs.

All participants will need a laptop for running the EarSketch software. EarSketch will run on OSX and Windows laptops. Participants will also need headphones for listening to projects created using EarSketch. It is highly suggested that participants download the EarSketch installer at http://earsketch.gatech.edu/downloads and install the software prior to the workshop.

ACM Categories & Descriptors: J.5 [**Arts and Humanities**], K.3.2 [**Computer Education**]: Computers and Information Science Education – *computer science education, curriculum*

Keywords: music remixing; computer music; K-12 education; media computation; Python; CS Principles

Scratch + Xbox Kinect: A Magical Combination for Outreach

Victor Norman, *Calvin College*
Contact: vtn2@calvin.edu

Participants will learn how to install Scratch, the Xbox Kinect libraries, and the software that integrates the two. The participant will then practice basic Scratch programming, and then learn how to program Scratch when connected to an Xbox Kinect. Five programming challenges will be given to participants, ranging from easy to difficult. During these activities, the participants will experience the excitement of using their bodies (instead of a mouse and keyboard) as the program controller. Discussions will be held to think about human-computer interactions, standard interaction models, etc., as well as how to help students engage more deeply with computer programming activities. Participants will work in teams of 3 or 4 using participant-supplied laptops running Windows 7.

ACM Categories & Descriptors: K.3.1 [Computing Milieux]: Computers and Education - *computer uses in education*

Keywords: Scratch; Xbox; Kinect; Outreach; Education

The Absolute Beginner's Guide to JUnit in the Classroom

Stephen H. Edwards, *Virginia Tech*
Manuel A. Pérez-Quiñones, *Virginia Tech*
Contact: edwards@cs.vt.edu

Software testing has become popular in introductory courses, but many educators are unfamiliar with how to write software tests or how they might be used in the classroom. This workshop provides a practical introduction to JUnit for educators. JUnit is the Java testing framework that is most commonly used in the classroom. Participants will learn how to write and run JUnit test cases; how-to's for common classroom uses (as a behavioral addition to an assignment specification, as part of manual grading, as part of automated grading, as a student-written activity, etc.); and common solutions to tricky classroom problems (testing standard input/output, randomness, main programs, assignments with lots of design freedom, assertions, and code that calls `exit()`).

ACM Categories & Descriptors: D.2.5 [**Software Engineering**]: Testing and Debugging—testing tools; D.1.5 [**Programming Techniques**]: Object oriented Programming; K.3.2 [**Computers and Education**]: Computer and Information Science Education

Keywords: Software testing; test-driven development; test-first coding; Java; programming assignments; automated assessment

Teaching with HFOSS to Provide Students with Real World Experience: An Introduction

Darci Burdge, *Nassau Community College*
Lori Postner, *Nassau Community College*
Becka Morgan, *Western Oregon University*
Heidi J. C. Ellis, *Western New England University*
Stoney Jackson, *Western New England University*
Gregory W. Hislop, *Drexel University*
Michelle Purcell, *Drexel University*
Contact: ellis@wne.edu

Have you ever wanted your students to contribute to or learn from a real-world software project that benefits society? Want some help getting started? Many students find involvement in Humanitarian Free and Open Source Software (HFOSS) projects engaging and motivating. As a first step, this workshop will introduce faculty to FOSS tools and culture. Through a virtual field trip into the world of HFOSS you will learn how to find a project, discern characteristics of a good project for student participation and understand how to use IRC, a communication

SIGCSE'14, March 5–8, 2014, Atlanta, Georgia, USA.
ACM 978-1-4503-2605-6/14/03.

tool used by FOSS developers. The use of version control to support project development will also be discussed. Along the way, you will learn how to support student learning in such projects. All topics will be covered at an introductory level. Participants will take away exercises that can be used in the classroom. Additionally, participants will have access to support in the creation of assignments or curriculum and their implementation from teachers experienced in supporting students in HFOSS participation. Additional information at: http://www.foss2serve.org/index.php/SIGCSE_2014_Workshop Laptop required.

ACM Categories & Descriptors: K.3.1 Computer Use in Education; K.3.2 Computer and Information Science Education

Keywords: Teaching Open Source; Free and Open Source Software; Instructor Preparation

Guiding Students to Discover CS Concepts and Develop Process Skills using POGIL

Clifton Kussmaul, *Muhlenberg College*
Helen H. Hu, *Westminster College*
Matthew Lang, *Google*
Contact: kussmaul@muhlenberg.edu

This workshop is for anyone who teaches CS, and introduces process-oriented guided inquiry learning (POGIL) in computer science. POGIL is based on learning science, and shares characteristics with other forms of active, discovery, and inquiry learning. In a POGIL classroom, teams of 3-5 learners work on instructor-facilitated activities. Through scripted inquiry and investigation, learners discover concepts and construct their own knowledge. Using assigned team roles and meta-cognition, learners develop process skills and individual responsibility. Studies show that POGIL can significantly improve student performance. POGIL has particular potential for CS education. Software development is largely a team-based problem-solving activity, and POGIL helps students to learn from each other and develop problem-solving abilities as well as important team process skills. POGIL has been developed and validated over the last 15 years in a range of STEM disciplines.

The workshop consists primarily of hands-on team activities. Workshop participants will experience POGIL activities, learn core practices, and draft activity pieces. POGIL materials for a variety of CS concepts will be shared. More information and materials are available at http://cspogil.org and http://pogil.org, including sample activities for CS1, CS2, and other courses. Laptops optional. This material is based upon work supported by the National Science Foundation under grant DUE-1044679.

ACM Categories & Descriptors: K.3.1 Computer Uses in Education; K.3.2 Computer and Information Science Education

Keywords: Active Learning; Communication; Guided Inquiry; POGIL; Process Skills; Teams

SIGCSE'14, March 5–8, 2014, Atlanta, Georgia, USA.
ACM 978-1-4503-2605-6/14/03.

Mobile Computational Thinking with App Inventor 2

Franklyn Turbak, *Wellesley College*
Fred Martin, *University of Massachusetts Lowell*
Shaileen Crawford Pokress, *Massachusetts Institute of Technology*
Ralph Morelli, *Trinity College*
Mark Sherman, *University of Massachusetts Lowell*
David Wolber, *University of San Francisco*
Contact: fturbak@wellesley.edu

Computational Thinking through Mobile Computing is an NSF-funded project for introducing students to computational thinking through creating mobile apps. In this hands-on workshop, which is targeted at undergraduate and secondary school computer science teachers, participants will develop Android apps using MIT App Inventor 2. This is a new version of the visual blocks-based programming environment with additional language features (e.g., local variables) and browser-based blocks editing. The workshop will also present pedagogical materials (lessons, tutorials, assignments), evaluation materials (blocks-based quizzes, surveys, project rubrics), and student projects. All of the pedagogical materials presented in the workshop, as well as all of the materials used by the workshop presenters in their individual courses, are posted on the Web and are available to everyone under a Creative Commons license. A laptop is required for this workshop. Each participant will be provided with an Android mobile device to use during the workshop. Participants who have their own Android phones or tablets can use them if they choose. This workshop is based upon work supported by the National Science Foundation under Grant Numbers 1225680, 1225719, 1225745, 1225976, and 1226216.

ACM Categories & Descriptors: K.3.2 Computer Science Education; D.2.6 Graphical environments

Keywords: Blocks Programming; Computational Thinking; CS0; Event-based Programming; Mobile Computing

Using the New Lego MindStorms EV3 Robotics Platform in CS Courses

Frank Klassner, *Villanova University*
Ben Schafer, *University of Northern Iowa*
Contact: Frank.Klassner@villanova.edu

This workshop will conduct an exploration of the newly released Lego MindStorms EV3 robot platform and its applicability to the college computer science curriculum. Participants will learn about the EV3 through handouts and hands-on programming exercises. The first part of the workshop will focus on demonstrating EV3 robots as well as the STEM concepts and computing concepts they illustrate. The second part of the workshop will focus in on the new capabilities of the EV3. This workshop will be more detailed than the vendor led workshop. It will be of benefit to participants new to MindStorms robotics as well as those with NXT/RCX experience who want to see the evolution of the platform and new components featured in the EV3. These include a revision of the controller brick hardware and software, new color and gyroscopic sensors, and increased processing and memory capabilities. The organizers have a combined 20 years of experience using MindStorms in CS courses (including courses in introductory programming, systems, and artificial intelligence) with Lego and third party programming environments. Participants must bring a Bluetooth-capable laptop (Mac or Windows), and will have a robot, software, and kit to use for the workshop. Participants will receive a promotion code to purchase a 10% discounted MindStorms kit. ***Laptop Mandatory***

ACM Categories & Descriptors: B.m Miscellaneous; D.1.m Miscellaneous

Keywords: Lego; Mindstorms; EV3; Educational Robotics

AP CS Principles and The Beauty and Joy of Computing Curriculum

Daniel D. Garcia, *University of California, Berkeley*
Brian Harvey, *University of California, Berkeley*
Tiffany Barnes, *North Carolina State University*
Nathaniel Titterton, *University of California, Berkeley*
Dan Armendariz, *University of California, Berkeley*
Jon McKinsey, *University of California, Berkeley*
Zachary MacHardy, *University of California, Berkeley*
Omoju Miller, *University of California, Berkeley*
Barry Peddycord, *North Carolina State University*
Eugene Lemon, *Ralph J Bunche High School*
Sean Morris, *Albany High School*
Josh Paley, *Henry M. Gunn High School*
Contact: ddgarcia@cs.berkeley.edu

The Beauty and Joy of Computing (BJC) is an introductory computer science curriculum developed at UC Berkeley (and adapted at the University of North Carolina, Charlotte), intended for high school juniors through university non-majors. It was used in two of the five initial pilot programs for the *AP CS Principles* course being developed by the College Board and the National Science Foundation. Our overall goal is to support the CS10K project by preparing instructors to teach the AP CS Principles course through the BJC curriculum. In this workshop, we will share our experiences as instructors of the course at the university and high school level, provide a glimpse into a typical week of the course, and share details of NSF-funded summer professional development opportunities. *Laptops with a modern browser (we recommend Chrome) will be required.*

ACM Categories & Descriptors: K.3.2 [**Computer and Information Science Education**]: Computer Science Education

Keywords: AP CS Principles; BJC; Beauty and Joy of Computing; Computational Thinking; professional development

Hands-on Cybersecurity Exercises with EDURange Framework

Richard Weiss, *The Evergreen State College*
Jens Mache, *Lewis & Clark College*
Michael E. Locasto, *The University of Calgary*
Vincent Nestler, *Capitol College*
Contact: weissr@evergreen.edu

Cybersecurity is a topic of growing interest for CS educators. The goal of this workshop is to provide faculty with tools and interactive exercises that would facilitate adding this topic to their curriculum. We will introduce the EDURange framework for developing interactive cybersecurity exercises. We have several exercises for participants to try, including network scanning and firewall configuration. We will give an introduction to some tools such as nmap, as well as the basic concepts. We have tested our framework several times in classrooms and workshops for students and faculty. One of its advantages is that faculty can use it in their classes with very little set-up. It uses Amazon's EC2/AWS to make the exercises readily available, so instructors will be able to access them with an account. We will also discuss other security exercises, including ones in the RAVE. It also provides each user with a number of VMs with tools and vulnerabilities. We will discuss using exercises as assessment tools. No previous experience in security is necessary. ***Laptop required***. http://blogs.evergreen.edu/edurange

ACM Categories & Descriptors: C.2.0 Computer-Communication Networks; K.4.4 Electronic Commerce

Keywords: Your own keywords;Separated with Semi-Colons; Security; Information Assurance; Cybersecurity; Laboratory Exercises

SIGCSE'14, March 5–8, 2014, Atlanta, Georgia, USA.
ACM 978-1-4503-2605-6/14/03.

Saturday Workshops

Server-side Web Development with JavaScript and Node.js

Ariel Ortiz, *Tecnológico de Monterrey, Campus Estado de México*
Contact: ariel.ortiz@itesm.mx

Node.js is one of the hottest open source web platforms currently available. It's built on Google Chrome's V8 JavaScript runtime engine and it allows you to write all kinds of network applications and servers in just a few lines of code. Node.js uses an asynchronous programming model built on non-blocking I/O and a single-threaded event loop. What this means, basically, is that you don't need to be concerned with awful race conditions or synchronization issues that arise when programming for a concurrent multi-user environment. This workshop is aimed mainly at web development instructors that would like to consider teaching a single programming language, JavaScript, for both client-side and server-side coding. Participants will learn how to employ Node.js on Windows, Mac OS or Linux in order to write scalable web servers and applications. Additionally, the Express web framework will be introduced in order to demonstrate how to quickly program traditional webapps and single-page applications (SPA) with the aid of jQuery, AJAX and RESTful web services. The resulting programs will be usable from any modern web browser, including those found in desktop and laptop computers, and mobile devices such as tablets and smart-phones. Participants should have prior working knowledge of client-side (running on a browser) JavaScript and HTML. More information: http://node.arielortiz.info/ Laptop Required.

ACM Categories & Descriptors: K.3.2 Computer and Information Science Education; C.2.4 Distributed Systems

Keywords: JavaScript; Node.js; Server-side programming

Artbotics with Lego Mindstorms

Adam Norton, *University of Massachusetts, Lowell*
Holly Yanco, *University of Massachusetts, Lowell*
Contact: anorton@cs.uml.edu

This workshop introduces participants to the Artbotics program, which combines art and robotics to teach students about computer science while creating kinetic, interactive sculptures. The material covered will be provided in introductory fashion, requiring no prior experience with computer science, art, or robotics. The Lego Mindstorms NXT platform will be used to create two projects during the workshop: a spirograph-like drawing produced by programming a car holding a marker to drive using a sequence of motor movements (teaching the need for looping in programming) and an interactive, kinetic sculpture that reacts to sensor input (teaching the need for decisions in programming and building simple mechanisms). Examples of both projects can be seen at youtube.com/artbotics. The workshop will end with a short discussion of lessons learned and best practices, using examples from previous Artbotics programs for a variety of ages. Topics will include appropriate time frames, how to best use limited resources, and appropriate levels of depth for each age group. The workshop administrators will be providing laptops with the proper Lego Mindstorms NXT software, Lego Mindstorms NXT kits, and all needed building materials. ***For additional information see artbotics.org/lego. Bringing your own laptop is optional.***

ACM Categories & Descriptors: J.2 Physical Sciences and Engineering

Keywords: computer science; art; robotics; Artbotics; education; interactive; kinetic sculpture; drawing

Using the AP CS Labs in the Classroom

Robert Glen Martin, *School for the Talented & Gifted*
Paul Tymann, *Rochester Institute of Technology*
Lester Wainwright, *Charlottesville High School*
Contact: paul.tymann@rit.edu

The Advanced Placement (AP) Computer Science (CS) A Development Committee is replacing the large case study (GridWorld) with a hands-on structured lab component with the following characteristics:

- At least three labs explore computing in context at a significant level, building upon supplied code that provides examples of good style and appropriate use of programming language constructs
- Each lab contains a significant problem-solving component in which students study alternative approaches for solving a problem, solve new problems, or modify existing code to solve altered problem.
- At least one lab provides students with experience working with programs involving multiple interactive classes and may involve decomposing a program into classes and using inheritance, interfaces, and other object-oriented concepts as identified in the AP Computer Science A topic outline.
- Collectively, lab experiences will cover at least 80% of the topics listed in the course description and will involve at least 20 hours of class time.

In investigating the use of labs, the AP CS A program developed three labs that cover many introductory topics and may be used at various times throughout a course. Since these labs cover many basic concepts and perspectives, the labs are appropriate for both AP CS A courses and many college CS1 courses. This workshop will introduce teachers to the AP CS A lab materials and provide practical experience in using these materials within introductory courses.

ACM Categories & Descriptors: K.3.0 General

Keywords: AP Courses and Curriculum; K-12 Instruction

SIGCSE'14, March 5–8, 2014, Atlanta, Georgia, USA.
ACM 978-1-4503-2605-6/14/03.

Learn Java in *N* Games

Peter Drake, *Lewis & Clark College*
Mark Goadrich, Centenary College of Louisiana
Contact: drake@lclark.edu

The Learn Java in N Games project (LJING) aims to teach topics in CS1, CS2, and other courses by having students implement a variety of games. Each game is presented as a stand-alone module, easily incorporated into an existing course without committing to major curricular changes. Modules include unusually clear solution code, skeleton code for students to complete, JUnit tests for quick feedback to students and automated grading, and clear assignment statements with learning objectives. Program code strictly separates game logic from graphic user interfaces (GUIs), allowing the same code to be used in both conventional and mobile Android environments. In this three-hour tutorial, participants will complete two assignments. These assignments are ready to be used in classes the next day. Participants are strongly encouraged to bring laptops.

ACM Categories & Descriptors: K.3.2 [**Computer and Information Science Education**]: Computer Science Education

Keywords: Education; Java; games

Chapel: A Versatile Tool for Teaching Undergraduates Parallel Programming

David P. Bunde, *Knox College*
Kyle Burke, *Colby College*
Contact: dbunde@knox.edu

Chapel is a programming language being developed for high-performance applications. It is well suited for teaching parallelism in a wide variety of undergrad courses. Chapel is easy to learn since it supports a low-overhead style like a scripting language as well as a full OO style. It is concise, needing a single keyword to launch an asynchronous task, run a parallel loop, or perform a reduction. This helps undergrads focus on the main point of examples and lets them quickly try different parallel algorithms. It is also versatile, usable on both multicore systems and clusters. In this workshop, attendees will learn basics of Chapel, complete hands-on exercises, and see possible uses in algorithms, programming languages, and parallel programming courses. **Laptop with SSH client required.**

ACM Categories & Descriptors: K.3.2 Computer and Information Science Education; D.1.3 Concurrent Programming

Keywords: Paralell programming; Chapel

Introduction to Analysing the BlueJ Blackbox Data

Neil C. C. Brown, *University of Kent*
Contact: nccb@kent.ac.uk

The Blackbox project, launched in 2013, collects large amounts of data about beginner student behaviour in the BlueJ IDE. In this workshop, we will introduce researchers to the Blackbox data and show them how to get started with analyzing it to answer their own research question(s). The workshop provides an ideal opportunity to find out what can be done with the Blackbox data, and will be run by the system's architect and maintainer. The data set includes Java source code as well as information about compilations, debugger usage and other compiler interactions. The Blackbox project has over 150,000 users, over 10,000,000 compilations and tens of gigabytes of source code. (For more detailed information, see the paper "Blackbox: A Large Scale Repository of Novice Programmers' Activity" by Brown et al. in the SIGCSE 2014 proceedings.) Computing education researchers may apply for free, permanent access to the data, but is not necessary to do so before this workshop. The session will be hands-on, and participants should bring a laptop that is capable of running an SSH terminal (e.g. Mac OS X, Linux, or PuTTY on Windows) over a wireless connection.

ACM Categories & Descriptors: K.3.2 Computer and Information Science Education

Keywords: Blackbox; BlueJ; Data analysis

Introducing Secure Coding in CS0, CS1, and CS2

Blair Taylor, *Towson University*
Siddharth Kaza, *Towson University*
Elizabeth Hawthorne, *Union County College*
Contact: skaza@towson.edu

The CS 2013 curriculum includes Information Assurance and Security as a pervasive knowledge area. However, introducing security in lower level courses is challenging because of lack of appropriate teaching resources and training. This workshop will provide a well-tested strategy for introducing secure coding concepts in CS0, CS1, and CS2. We will introduce attendees to secure coding through hands-on exercises, and provide self-contained, lab-based modules designed to be injected into CS0-CS2 with minimal impact on the course (www.towson.edu/securityinjections). Participants will be encouraged to bring in their own syllabus and labs to modify to include secure coding concepts. The first 15 participants will be reimbursed for the workshop cost on attendance through NSF DUE-1241738. Laptop recommended.

ACM Categories & Descriptors: K.3.2 Computers and Education

Keywords: CS0; CS1; CS2; Secure Coding; Security Injections

Projects for Computing Summer Camps for 4th-12th Grade Students

Barbara J. Ericson, *Georgia Institute of Technology*
Christopher Michaud, *Marist School*
Xin Xu, *Georgia Gwinnett College*
Krishnendu Roy, *Valdosta State University*
Contact: ericson@cc.gatech.edu

This workshop will provide details on the projects that we recommend for non-residential computing summer camps for 4th – 12th grade students. Georgia Tech has been offering computing summer camps since 2004. These camps are financially self-sustaining and effective at improving attitudes towards

SIGCSE'14, March 5–8, 2014, Atlanta, Georgia, USA.
ACM 978-1-4503-2605-6/14/03.

computing, especially for females and African-American students. Items used in the camps include: CS Unplugged, LightBot, Scratch, Alice, LEGO robots (WeDo, NXT, and Tetrix), EarSketch, and App Inventor. Georgia Tech has also helped eleven other colleges and universities in Georgia start or expand computing summer camps. Some of these other institutions also offer camps on GameSalad, GameMaker, and web development. These other camps have also improved attitudes towards computing.

The workshop will include an overview of the projects that we have found to be successful and include hands-on work with App Inventor, GameSalad, LEGO NXT robots, and LEGO EV3 robots. ***laptop optional***

ACM Categories & Descriptors: K.3.2 Computer and Information Science Education

Keywords: Robotics; App Developmemt; Summer Camps; Student Workshops; Scratch, Alice; CS Unplugged; App Inventor; LEGO robots; GameSalad

Snap*!* (Build Your Own Blocks)

Brian Harvey, *University of California, Berkeley*
Daniel D. Garcia, *University of California, Berkeley*
Tiffany Barnes, *North Carolina State University*
Nathaniel Titterton, *University of California, Berkeley*
Omoju Miller, *University of California, Berkeley*
Dan Armendariz, *University of California, Berkeley*
Jon McKinsey, *University of California, Berkeley*
Zachary Machardy, *University of California, Berkeley*
Eugene Lemon, *Ralph J Bunche High School*
Sean Morris, *Albany High School*
Josh Paley, *Henry M. Gunn High School*
Contact: bh@cs.berkeley.edu

This workshop is for high school and college teachers of general-interest ("CS 0") computer science courses, especially the AP CS: Principles course.

SNAP! (Build Your Own Blocks) is a free, browser-based, graphical, drag-and-drop language inspired by Scratch. The beauty of the Scratch programming environment, designed for 8-14 year olds, is that it makes abstract concepts more concrete and understandable to a broader audience. SNAP! extends Scratch to support older learners (14-20) with built-in named procedures (thus recursion), procedures as data (thus higher order functions), structured lists, and sprites as first class objects with inheritance.

Participants will learn SNAP! hands-on. See http://snap.berkeley.edu for details. Network connected laptop required.

ACM Categories & Descriptors: D.3.3 Language Constructs and Features. Subjects: Procedures, functions, and subroutines; Recursion; Inheritance

Keywords: higher order functions; graphical programming; CS education; outreach; visual programming language; AP CS Principles

SIGCSE'14, March 5–8, 2014, Atlanta, Georgia, USA.
ACM 978-1-4503-2605-6/14/03.

Puzzle-Based Learning: Introducing Creative Thinking and Problem Solving for Computer Science and Engineering

Raja Sooriamurthi, *Carnegie Mellon University*
Nickolas Falkner, *The University of Adelaide*
Ed Meyer, *Baldwin Wallace University*
Zbigniew Michalewicz, *The University of Adelaide*
Contact: raja@cmu.edu

Puzzle-based learning (PBL) is a new and emerging model of teaching critical thinking and problem solving. Today's market place needs skilled graduates capable of solving real problems of innovation in a changing environment. A learning goal of PBL is to distill domain independent transferable heuristics for tackling problems. While solving puzzles is innately fun, companies such as Google and Yahoo also use puzzles to assess the creative problem solving skills of potential employees. In this interactive workshop we will examine a range of puzzles and games. What general problem solving strategies can we learn from the way we solve these examples? Participants will emerge with the needed pedagogical foundation to offer a full course on PBL or to include it as part of another course.

ACM Categories & Descriptors: K.3.2 Computer and Information Science Education

Keywords: Problem Solving; Critical Thinking; Computational Thinking; Puzzles

Dynamic Program Visualizations for Java

James Cross, *Auburn University*
Dean Hendrix, *Auburn University*
David Umphress, *Auburn University*
Contact: crossjh@auburn.edu

This workshop will focus on using the new jGRASP viewer canvas which provides an exciting new dimension to dynamic program visualization. The *canvas* allows students and instructors to organize dynamic viewers of multiple objects and primitives to quickly form coherent program visualizations. Students can quickly build and save visualizations of their own programs, and faculty can create visualizations and provide them to students with example programs. "Playing" a program in canvas mode brings the visualization to life as objects come into scope and the canvas is updated automatically. All educators who teach Java will benefit from this workshop. It will be especially suitable for instructors who teach CS1 (introduction to programming), CS2 (introduction to data structures), and CS3 (introduction to algorithms), as well as for instructors of AP courses in high schools. jGRASP is a freely available educational IDE (http://www.jgrasp.org/); no prior experience with jGRASP is expected. **Laptop required**.

ACM Categories / Descriptors: D.2.6 [**Software Engineering**]: Programming Environments – *Graphical environments, Integrated environments, Interactive environments, Programmer workbench*; H.5.2 [**Information Systems**]: User Interfaces – *Interaction Styles*; K.3.2 [**Computing Milieux**]: Computers and Information Science Education – *Computer Science Education*

Keywords: Program visualization; algorithm animation; data structures

Mobile Computer Science Principles: A Professional Development Sampler for Teachers

Ralph Morelli, *Trinity College*
David Wolber, *University of San Francisco*
Jennifer Rosato, *College of St. Scholastica*
Chinma Uche, *Greater Hartford Academy of Math and Science*
Pauline Lake, *Trinity College*
Contact: ralph.morelli@trincoll.edu

The College Board's CS Principles (CSP) Project is an effort to develop a language-neutral, breadth-first advanced placement (AP) course in computer science. *MobileCSP* is an NSF-funded effort to train high school teachers to teach a CSP course that engages students in building mobile apps with App Inventor. The workshop will provide an overview of MobileCSP training including a hands-on introduction to App Inventor and a representative sample of CSP-based lesson plans, assessment materials, and other resources. MobileCSP training will be available for free to all high school teachers in summer 2014 through an online course. Attendees will be provided information about getting involved in the summer 2014 training. Target audience: high school teachers. Laptop required.

ACM Categories & Descriptors: K.3.2 Computer and Information Science Education

Keywords: Mobile Computer Science Principles; App Inventor

SIGCSE'14, March 5–8, 2014, Atlanta, Georgia, USA.
ACM 978-1-4503-2605-6/14/03.

SIGCSE 2014 SRC Undergraduate Student Research Abstracts

CABECTPortal: An Investigation of Social Computational Systems

Joseph Canero and Conor Kelton, *The College of New Jersey*

We are investigating a way to disseminate ideas, models, projects and resources related to collaborations between computer science and diverse disciplines, and to track how these are being propagated. To do this we are designing a self-sustaining portal that leverages concepts from social computational systems. Such systems interleave human computation with social media, or any other medium that leverages natural human behavior, by providing motivation and mechanisms for quality control and task routing. We are accomplishing our task by developing a system that motivates its community to sustain it and to ensure that projects are kept up-to-date with reliable data, even past the funding period for the project.

Building a Collision Free Environment Using Reciprocal Velocity Obstacles Methods

David Cherry, *Morehouse College*

Reciprocal Velocity Obstacles (RVO) method was used to produce collision avoidance for crowd simulations generated using the game engine Unity 3D. There are three methods for generating crowd simulation using RVO collision avoidance in this experiment. The first method consists of taking user input on the starting position, goal position, and speed of each agent to simulate a virtual environment and the information will be exported to a file. The second method is loading a pre-existing file into Unity for the information to input for the simulation. The third method was to start with only one agent that continuously moves to random goal positions and can be duplicated to produce more agents. This experiment was combined with predictive forces collision avoidance to compare both methods.

BookNav: A System for Accessible Indoor Navigation on Mobile Android Devices

Patrick D'Errico, *The College of New Jersey*

BookNav is an indoor navigation system designed to direct patrons of the TCNJ library to specific books via WiFi. Navigation occurs through fingerprinting to approximate signal strengths at various points in the library, which are compared to the strengths at the user's location. Dijkstra's shortest path algorithm is used to develop turn-by-turn directions. BookNav was designed to provide accessible support to a broad range of end users through the use of the Android platform, which is easily available compared to other hardware used to support navigation systems for the visually impaired. BookNav requests the user to input the call number of the book they wish to find. After signal fingerprinting, BookNav provides a map and optional voiced directions to the desired book's bookcase.

A Novel Approach to Analyze Adult Users' Learning of Technology by Utilizing Usability Study

Shannon Fallon, Nik Gardipee, Lindsay Vogt, Joshua Werner, and Mohsen Doroodchi, *Cardinal Stritch University*

The research project entitled A Novel Approach to Analyze Adult Users' Learning of Technology by Utilizing Usability Study utilizes the QUEM model of quantitative usability evaluation to analyze the usability of websites for a target group of adults between the ages of 40 and 60. By performing a usability analysis on members of the target group using a control group and an experimental group which will receive training in the use of the websites being analyzed, this research project also examines the effects of education on usability.

Network Analysis of Nuclear Databases

John A. Hirdt, *St. Joseph's College*

Looking at a non-network data set as a network may be a puzzling idea. But when you think about how a network is simply a series of data points connected in various ways, then we may think of anything as a network. Looking at an International Nuclear Reaction Database that dates back to the Manhattan Project as a network in order to try to determine what data is most central and utilized is an innovative approach to data analysis. We utilized network theory to analyze clusters of data not connected in any way to other clusters or to the standard data entries. By doing so we were able to see the larger picture and what data users are classifying as most important. Our analysis will radically alter the data sets thought to be most important, ultimately standardizing the data that truly is most important, utilized and necessary. This research could lead to the discovery of a new type of network that could have a large impact on the world of computer science.

Comparative Review of the ECA and SMS Recycling Tools

Jassiem Ifill and Joshua Posey, *Morehouse College*

Relational Agents are computational artifacts designed to build long-term, social-emotional, relationships with their users. They are able to build relationships with their users that increases the user's enjoyment of the application. The disadvantage of this technology is that when the relational agent appears unrealistic, some users will find it challenging to build a relationship with the agent. Short Message Service, or SMS, is a method through which six billion messages are sent from person-to-person through mobile phones every day making SMS an alternative interface to which many individuals will have mobile access. Using the Twilio API, an interface was developed with the same conversational functionality as Relational Agents. This paper investigates the potential of SMS interfaces as an alternative to interfaces using an Embodied Conversational Agent in specific scenarios.

Strengthening Computer Science Education with Scribbler Robots

Connor Kerns and Kyle Wong, *University of Southern California*

We created a free online course using Google's Course Builder that introduces programming in Python with the Scribbler robot. The course contains setup guides, demo programs, videos, and challenge problems to target both independent learners and teachers who want to incorporate robotics in their classrooms, with the goal of inspiring middle school students to pursue STEM fields. Two middle school STEM teachers with no prior programming experience worked with us over the summer to test the course, learn programming, and design a curriculum for their students. We tested their computational thinking skills and evaluated how the robot affected their learning by giving them challenge programming problems that they had never seen before.

A Modern CS2: Implementing Social Good and Mobile Technologies into CS2

Spencer B. Liberto, Lea M. Sonnenschein, and Daniel Torres, *Grinnell College*

This paper describes our redesign of CS2. We introduce the Android mobile development platform, so that students can write Java code in a motivating environment. We introduce the Ushahidi platform, from which students can access large data sets that detail socially good incidents. We introduce Git, a version-control system. At the end of the course, students will complete a client-based project. The curriculum has been implemented in the classroom as of August 2013. The latest version of the curriculum can be found online. We hope to enhance the students' learning experience and convince them to pursue computing more in depth.

A Real-Time Visualization of Topic Popularity on Twitter

Elise Richards, *Moravian College*

Every day, social networks and microblogging sites generate massive amounts of publicly available data (some even allow real-time capture). Mining this data allows us to discover trends, learn of news and events, and help to understand the world. In recent years, many methods have been developed for sifting through this data: some quantitative, some qualitative, and some more abstract. This project aims to add to this body of work by providing a method for the real-time visualization of the relative popularity of topics on Twitter in a visually interesting, yet succinct and understandable manner. The merit of this project is both artistic and technical: a software program to visualize in real-time the relative popularity of term sets on Twitter that is currently on public display.

Properties of Twitter Network Communications among Teenagers

Gili Rusak, *Siena College*

We study, quantitatively, for the first time, the traits of Twitter teenager networks. The results are compared with general population users, and show that teenagers behave uniquely. Teens tend to follow more users, and increase friendships over time. They tend to friend individuals online who they already know offline. Teenagers also use Twitter as a news media and form supportive communities. These networks are dense and have two degrees of separation: within a tweet and retweet, the entire community can see a message. These results shed new light on the traits of teenager communities and can be channeled to find solutions to emerging problems involving the massive use of social media. For example, Twitter can be used as a positive tool for prevention bad habits among teens.

Linac Early Symptoms Detection

Kevin Sanders, *St. Joseph's College*

The Linac Early Symptoms Detection project is a software program that monitors data that is collected from a 200MeV particle accelerator, the Linac, at Brookhaven National Laboratory. The data used a simple algorithm that compared measurements collected to set point values, and the user accessed this program by using a graphic user interface that was written and designed from scratch. The software is successfully able to monitor the data using synchronous data collection, and if implemented, could help the staff of the Linac Group during operation of the Linac.

Collision Sensing with Sphero's Accelerometer

Daniel Tobin and Melissa Mulcahy, *Central Connecticut State University*

Sphero is a small, ball-shaped robot designed to be used as a physical bluetooth gaming device for iOS and Android systems. It is equipped with two hardware sensors: a gyroscope and an accelerometer. The objective of this project was to collect, process, and analyze the real-time data streamed from Sphero's accelerometer as it interacted with its surroundings. From this information, it was possible to detect a collision with an obstacle occurred solely from the accelerometer data and determine the collision parameters, such as the angle of collision.

SIGCSE 2014 SRC Graduate Student Research Abstracts

Using Interactive Storytelling Agents to Broaden Participation in Computing

David Brickler, *Clemson University*

It has been extensively documented the need for increased participation from under-represented minorities in Science, Technology, Engineering and Mathematics (STEM) fields. This research aims to address this problem by using interactive storytellers. Interactive Storytelling (IS) is a form of digital entertainment in which users create or influence a dramatic storyline through actions, either by issuing commands to the story's primary character, or acting as a general director of events in the narrative. Interactive storytelling is a medium where the story can be influenced in real-time by the user of the system. An interactive storyteller was created to teach users strategies when pursuing a doctoral degree in computing. A pilot study was conducted with five undergraduate computer science majors to collect initial feedback about the tool and their experience. Overall, students enjoyed working with the agent and were more motivated to attend graduate school.

Computational Thinking Pattern Analysis

Kyu Han Koh, *University of Colorado at Boulder*

End-user game design affords teachers a unique opportunity to integrate computational thinking concepts into their classrooms. However, in game and simulation projects, it is not always apparent what computational thinking related skills students have acquired. Computational Thinking Pattern Analysis (CTPA) enables teachers to visualize which patterns students have mastered in game design that can then be used to create simulations. CTPA has the potential to automatically recognize and calculate student computational thinking skills as well as to map students' computational thinking skill progression as they proceed through the curriculum. Thus, CTPA can be used to determine when and how teachers can expand students' learning capability.

Evaluating Quality of Student-Written Tests

Zalia Shams, *Virginia Tech*

Automated systems use code-coverage to measure quality of students' tests. Code-coverage has a number of limitations. All-pairs and mutation testing are two alternative approaches where a student's tests are evaluated by all other students' errors and artificially injected detects. These measures have technical challenges to use which have been overcome recently. However, which one of them is the best indicator of bugs, is still unknown. We design a study to compare defect-revealing capability of the three measures with a CS2 assignment having more than 200,000 test runs. Our results show that all-pairs testing is the best test quality measure.

Myna: A VUI for Programming by Voice

Amber Wagner, *University of Alabama*

Graphical User Interfaces often require the use of a mouse and keyboard, which motorically challenged users might be unable to adopt due to the dexterity required. As an alternative, a Vocal User Interface (VUI) allows users to describe their intentions to an application via vocal commands. This research uses Programming by Voice (PBV) as a paradigm for writing a program using a VUI rather than using the mouse/keyboard. Specifically, Myna is a VUI created for Scratch, a graphical block language used to make teaching computer programming concepts to children easier and more fun. Myna has been tested with both CS students and students from the target population. Results illustrate that Myna is a viable alternative to the mouse/keyboard and provides an enjoyable experience for the user.

Secure Coding Integrative Touchpoint Model

Michael Whitney, *University of North Carolina Charlotte*

The Integrative Touchpoint Model enhances the secure coding instructional process by turning the student's IDE into a real-time secure programming instructional resource. This model capitalizes on the out of class, in the IDE time by providing layered educational opportunities whenever the student writes specific code patterns (i.e., vulnerable code) in a fashion similar to Microsoft's Grammar Checker. In this manner, the Integrated Touchpoint Model provides students with the opportunity to learn secure coding principles and practices concurrently with the lessons they are learning in their respective courses.

Author Index

www.ingramcontent.com/pod-product-compliance
Lightning Source LLC
LaVergne TN
LVHW080105011026
849160LV00013B/1032
* 9 7 8 1 4 5 0 3 3 1 0 4 3 *